# LIST OF OFFICERS

OF THE

# Army of the United States

FROM

1779 to 1900

# LIST OF OFFICERS

OF THE

# Army of the United States

FROM

1779 to 1900

EMBRACING A REGISTER OF ALL APPOINTMENTS BY THE PRESIDENT OF THE UNITED STATES IN THE VOLUNTEER SERVICE DURING THE CIVIL WAR AND OF VOLUNTEER OFFICERS IN THE SERVICE OF THE UNITED STATES JUNE 1, 1900.

COMPILED BY


## Colonel Wm. H. Powell



GYAN

*Published by*

Gyan Publishing House
5, Ansari Road
Daryaganj, New Delhi-110002
Phone: 011-47034999, 9811692060
E-mail: books@gyanbooks.com

*Distribution Network*
gyanbooks.com
India, USA, Canada, UK, Australia



ISBN: 978-93-6208-170-4 (PB)
First Published, 1900

2nd Impression 2024

*Printed at:* Gyan Press, Delhi.



**LIST OF OFFICERS OF THE ARMY OF THE UNITED STATES FROM 1779 TO 1900**

Compiler: WM. H. POWELL

# LIST OF OFFICERS

OF THE

# Army of the United States

FROM

## 1779 to 1900

EMBRACING A REGISTER OF ALL APPOINTMENTS BY THE PRESIDENT OF THE UNITED STATES IN THE VOLUNTEER SERVICE DURING THE CIVIL WAR AND OF VOLUNTEER OFFICERS IN THE SERVICE OF THE UNITED STATES JUNE 1, 1900.

---

Compiled from the Official Records

...BY...

Colonel Wm. H. Powell, U. S. Army

---

NEW YORK
L. R. HAMERSLY & CO.
1900

# PREFACE.

In the preparation of the following work the editor has consulted Gardner's "Dictionary of the Army," Cullum's "Biographical Register of the Graduates of the Military Academy," Powell's "Records of Living Officers U. S. Army," Hamersly's "Register of the Army 1779 to 1879," Heitman's "Historical Register of the U. S. Army," and the Official Registers issued by the War Department.

No pains have been spared to render this work thoroughly correct in its details, and any errors or omissions that may be discovered are occasioned only by lack of opportunity to obtain proper information.

A list of the Volunteer Officers in the service of the Government, June, 1900, has been added to the work, which will be found to add importance to its general character.

W. H. Powell.

# PREFACE

[illegible]

# Table of Contents.

# Abbreviations Used in the Work.

A. A. G.—Assistant Adjutant General
Acad.—Academy
A. C. G. S.—Ass't Commissary General of Subsistence
A. C. S.—Acting Commissary of Subsistence
Addl.—Additional
A. de C.—Aide-de-Camp
Adj.—Adjutant
A. I. G.—Assistant Inspector General
A. G.—Adjutant General
A. Q. M.—Assistant Quartermaster
Art.—Artillery
Asst.—Assistant
Ass'd—Assigned
Batt.—Battalion
Batty—Battery
Brig.—Brigadier
Bvt.—Brevet
Capt.—Captain
Cav.—Cavalry
C. G.—Commissary General
Col.—Colonel
Corpl.—Corporal
C. S.—Commissary of Subsistence
Dep.—Deputy
Dept.—Department
Drag.—Dragoons
Eng.—Engineers
Gen.—General
Hosp.—Hospital
I. G.—Inspector General
Inf.—Infantry
J. A.—Judge Advocate
Lieut.—Lieutenant
Maj.—Major
Mil.—Military
Ord.—Ordnance
P. M.—Paymaster
Priv.—Private
Prof.—Professor
Q. M.—Quartermaster
Q. M. D.—Quartermaster Department
Q. M. G.—Quartermaster General
R. Q. M.—Regimental Quartermaster
Reg.—Regiment
R. C. S.—Regimental Commissary of Substance
Sergt.—Sergeant
Surg.—Surgeon
Trans.—Transferred
Vol.—Volunteer
Vols.—Volunteers
Names of States and names of months are abbreviated as in general use

# LIST

OF THE

# OFFICERS OF THE ARMY

# 1779—1780.

---

NOTE.—The method by which Officers were first promoted in the American Army being irregular, particularly in cases where officers were prisoners, several alterations were afterwards made, and commissions antedated, even to the vacancies they were to fill up, in order to do justice to the injured, which has occasioned some apparent inconsistencies.

The following lists were made from a variety of documents, viz: Resolves of Congress, Returns and Registeries of Commissions in the War Office.

## A General Register of the Officers in the American Army for 1779.

### GENERAL OFFICERS.

*Commander-in-Chief.*

George Washington, 15 June, 1775.

*Major-Generals.*

Charles Lee, 17 June, 1775.
Philip Schuyler, 19 June, 1775. Resigned 1 April, 1779.
Israel Putnum, 19 June, 1779.
Horatio Gates, 16 March, 1776.
Will. Heath, 9 Aug., 1776.
John Sullevan, 9 Aug., 1776. Resigned 30 Nov., 1779.
Nathan Green, 9 Aug., 1776.
Earl of Sterling, 19 Feb., 1777.
Thomas Mifflin, 19 Feb., 1777. Resigned 25 Feb., 1779.
Arthur St. Clair, 19 Feb., 1777.
Benj. Lincoln, 19 Feb., 1777.
Bened. Arnold, 19 Feb., 1777.
Marq. de la Fayette, 31 July, 1777.
Baron de Kalb, 15 Sept., 1777.
Robert How, 20 Oct., 1777.
Alex. McDougal, 20 Oct., 1777.
Baron Steuben, 5 May, 1778.

*Brigadiers.*

Will. Thompson, 1 March, 1776.
John Nixon, 9 Aug., 1776.
James Clinton, 9 Aug., 1776.
Sam. Holden Parsons, 9 Aug., 1776.
Will. Moultrie, 16 Sept., 1776.
Laughlin McIntosh, 16 Sept., 1776.
Will. Maxwell, 23 Oct., 1776.
Will. Smallwood, 23 Oct., 1776.
Henry Knox, 27 Dec., 1776.
Enoch Poor, 21 Feb., 1777.
John Glover, 21 Feb., 1777.
John Patterson, 21 Feb., 1777.
Anth. Wayne, 21 Feb., 1777.
Will. Woodford, 21 Feb., 1777.
P. Meuhlenberg, 21 Feb., 1777.
Jams. M. Varnum, 27 Feb., 1777. Resigned 5 March, 1779.
George Clinton, 25 March, 1777.
Charles Scott, 1 April, 1777.
George Wheedon, 1 April, 1777.
Edwd. Hand, 1 April, 1777.
Ebenezer Learnerd, 2 April, 1777.
Jedediah Huntington, 12 May, 1777.
Count Pulaski, 15 Sept., 1777. Killed at Savannah, 1779.
John Stark, 4 Oct., 1777.
Chev. du Portail, 17 Nov., 1777.
Jethro Summer, 9 Jan., 1779.
James Hogan, 9 Jan., 1779.
——— Hugar, 9 Jan., 1779.
Mordecai Gist, 9 Jan., 1779.
Will. Irwine, 12 May, 1779.

---

CORPS OF ENGINEERS formed agreeable to a resolve of Congress, 11 March, 1779, with 3 Companies of Sappers and Miners directed to be raised by resolve of 27 May, 1778, and to be under the direction of the Chief Engineer.

*Chief Engineer.*

*Brig. General.*

Chev. du Portail.

*Colonels.*

Thadeus Kosciuzko, 18 Oct., 1776.
——— de la Raddiere, 8 July, 1777. Died.
——— Laumoy.

*Lieut. Colonel.*

Cheval. de Cambray.

*Majors.*

——— du Gouvion, 8 July, 1777. Promoted Lieut. Col.
Cheval. de Villefranche, 1 Jan., 1778.
John Bern. Murmand, 1 March, 1778.

*Captains.*

——— l'Enfant, 18 Feb., 1778.
Joseph Detzon, 18 Oct., 1779.
——— Nevin, 25 April, 1779.

*Colonel.*

Jedathun Baldwin, 14 Aug., 1776.

*Major.*

Ferdin. de Brahm, 11 Feb., 1778.

---

SAPPERS AND MINERS.

*Captains.*

——— Nevin, 25 April, 1779.
——— Bebee, 2 Aug., 1779.
——— Murray, 2 Aug., 1779.
——— de Veil, 2 Aug., 1779.

*Capt. Lieutenants.*

——— Gilleland, 2 Aug., 1779.
——— Bushnell, 2 Aug., 1779.
——— Cleveland, 2 Aug., 1779.

*Lieutenant.*

——— Welsh, 2 Aug., 1779.

---

ARTILLERY. IV Battalion. Raised by the State of Pennsylvania and taken into Continental service 20 June, 1777.

*Colonel.*

Thomas Proctor, 5 Feb., 1777.

*Lieut. Colonel.*

Thomas Forrest, 2 Dec., 1778.

*Major.*

Benjamin Eustice, 2 Dec., 1778.

*Captains.*

Isaac Craig, 3 March, 1777.
Amos Wilkinson, 3 March, 1777. Resigned 1 June, 1779.
Joseph Rice, 4 March, 1777.
Francis Proctor, 16 July, 1777.
Charles Turnbull, 16 July, 1777.
Patrick Duffy, 3 March, 1778.
Will. Ferguson, 14 April, 1778.
John Brice, 1 June, 1778.

*Capt. Lieutenants.*

Robert Coltman, 14 March, 1777. Promoted Captain, 3 March, 1779.
Worsley Emes, 16 July, 1777.
Lawrence Allman.
Thomas Douglass, 14 April, 1778.
Will. Ritter, 1 April, 1777. Resigned 11 March, 1779.
Will. Martin, 1 June, 1778.
Jonathan Brewer. Resigned 10 Feb., 1779.
John Landenberger, 27 April, 1777. Resigned 3 Feb., 1779.

*1st Lieutenants.*

James Loyd, 14 March, 1777. Promoted Capt. Lieut., 9 Feb., 1779.
Robert McConnel, 14 March, 1777. Promoted Capt. Lieut., 3 June, 1779.
James Smith, 14 March, 1777. Promoted Capt. Lieut., 3 June, 1779.
John Shute, 1 April, 1777.
Jesse Crosley, 1 April, 1777.
John Stricker, 1 April, 1777.
Matth. McGuire, 18 Dec., 1778.
James Norris, 1 April, 1777.
John B. Webster, 11 May, 1779.
Samuel Story, 11 May, 1779.

ARTILLERY. An Independent Company raised in Pennsylvania, agreeable to a resolve of Congress of December, 1776.

*Captain.*

Gibb Jones, 1 Jan., 1777.

*Capt. Lieutenant.*

Jerem. Freeman, 1 Jan., 1777.

*1st Lieutenant.*

David Fick, 1 Jan., 1777.

---

An Independent Company raised by the State of North Carolina, and taken into Continental service 19 July, 1777.

*Captain.*

John Kingsbury, 19 July, 1777.

*Capt. Lieutenant.*

Philip Jones, 19 July, 1777.

*1st Lieutenant.*

John Carlow Vance, 8 July, 1779.

---

A Company raised in Pennsylvania to work in Laboratory agreeable to a resolve of Congress.

*Captain.*

Isaac Coran, 1 Feb., 1777.

*Capt. Lieutenant.*

Will. Godfrey, 1 July, 1777.

*1st Lieutenant.*

Anthony Wright, 1 March, 1777.

*2nd Lieutenant.*

Andrew Caldwell, 1 April, 1777. Resigned 23 July, 1779.

---

Three Companies raised in Maryland agreeable to a resolve of Congress. These by an Act of the Council were reduced to one Company, the 3rd of September, 1779.

*Captains.*

Will. Brown, 22 Nov., 1777.
Rich. Dorsey, 24 Nov., 1777.
Edward Gale, 3 Sept., 1779. Died Oct., 1779.

*Capt. Lieutenants.*

James Smith, 22 Nov., 1777.
Ebenezer Finley, 24 Nov., 1777.
Sam'l Sadler, 3 Sept., 1779.

*1st Lieutenants.*

James McFaddon, 22 Nov., 1777.
Robert Willmot, 24 Nov., 1777.
Jaquies Baequies, 3 Sept., 1779.

*2nd Lieutenants.*

Clemont Sherret, 1 Oct., 1778.
Nich. Ricket, 25 Aug., 1778.
John Carson, 1 May, 1779.
Isaac Rawlings, 3 Sept., 1779.
Young Wilkinson, 3 Sept., 1779.
John Chiver, 8 Sept., 1779.
John White, 13 Sept., 1779.

---

An Independent Company.

*Captain.*

James Lee.

*Capt. Lieutenant.*

Will. Powers.

*1st Lieutenant.*

Samuel Doty.

---

CAVALRY. I Regiment of Light Dragoons raised in Virginia, and taken into Continental service.

*Colonel.*

Theoderick Bland. Resigned 10 Dec., 1779.

*Lieut. Colonel Commanding.*

Ant. Walton White, 15 Feb., 1777. Removed from 4th to the command of this, 10 Dec., 1779.

*Captain.*

Andrew Nixon.

---

CAVALRY. II Regiment raised agreeable to a resolve of Congress of 12 Dec., 1776, but by another resolve of 14 June, 1777, takes rank from 25 Nov., 1776.

*Colonel.*

Elisha Sheldon, 12 Dec., 1776.

*Lieut. Colonels.*

Samuel Blackdon, 7 April, 1777. Resigned 1 Aug., 1779.
John Jameson, 1 Aug., 1779.

*Major.*

Benj. Talmage, 7 April, 1777.

*Captains.*

Josiah Stoddard, 31 Dec., 1776. Died 24 Aug., 1779.
Epaphras Bull, 10 June, 1777.
Ezek. Port. Beldon, 7 April, 1777.
John Shethar, 11 Oct., 1777.
John Webb, 1 Jan., 1778.
David Edgar, 23 Nov., 1778.

*Lieutenants.*

Jeronym Hogland, 7 Oct., 1777. Promoted Capt. 18 Dec., 1779.
John Brown, 11 Oct., 1777.
Thomas Burkman, 20 Oct., 1777.
George Hurlbert, 25 Dec., 1777.
Elijah Wadsworth, 1 Jan., 1778.
John Simonet, 1 Jan., 1778.
Will. Stanton, 1 April, 1778.
James Paton, 2 June, 1778.
James Willis, 2 June, 1778.
Jedediah Rogers, 2 June, 1778.
Horace Seymour, 2 June, 1778.
Samuel Mills, 2 June, 1778.
Aaron Bull, 5 Nov., 1778.
Silvanus Dickinson, 1 Dec., 1778.

*Cornets.*

David Mumford. Promoted Lieut., 14 Nov., 1779.
Thom. Fred. Jackson. Promoted Lieut., 15 Nov., 1779.
Elijah King, 16 Nov., 1779.
Joshua Jones, 16 Nov., 1779.

*Adjutant.*

Jeron. Hogland, 7 Oct., 1777.

*Paymaster.*

Will. Stanton, 1 March, 1777.

*Surgeon.*

John Homans, 18 Dec., 1776.

CAVALRY. III Regiment of Light Dragoons raised in Virginia, agreeable to a resolve of Congress, 5 Jan., 1777.

*Colonel.*

George Baylor, 8 Jan., 1777.

*Lieut. Colonel.*

Will. Washington, 20 Nov., 1778.

*Major.*

Richard Call, 2 Oct., 1778.

*Captains.*

George Lewis, 1 Jan., 1777.
Robert Smith, 9 Jan., 1777.
Cadwell Jones, 6 Feb., 1777.
John Swan, 26 April, 1777.
Churchil Jones, 1 June, 1777.
Carter Page, 10 April, 1778.

*Lieutenants.*

John Steth, 6 Feb., 1777. Promoted.
John Baylor, 15 Feb., 1777.
Charles Randolph, 14 June, 1777.
Walker Baylor, 1 July, 1777. Promoted.
Hill Carter.
Will. Barrett, 10 April, 1778.

*Cornets.*

Will. Parsons. Promoted 1 Jan., 1779.
Criswell Barrett. Promoted 2 Jan., 1779.
Robert Morrow. Promoted 3 Jan., 1779.
Presley Thornton, 20 Feb., 1777. Promoted.
Francis Dade, 1 May, 1778. Promoted.
Peregrine Fitzhugh, 16 June, 1778.
Benj. Hart, 26 July, 1778.
Edwd. Connor, 27 July, 1778.

*Adjutant.*

Robert Morrow, 1 June, 1778.

*Quartermaster.*

Will. Woolfolk.

*Paymasters.*

Criswell Barrett. Resigned 1 Nov., 1779.
Ambrose Gordon, 1 Nov., 1779.

*Surgeons.*

George Evans. Resigned 1 Aug., 1779.
Michael Barry, 1 Nov., 1779.

*Mate.*

Thomas Evans. Resigned 1 June, 1779.

---

CAVALRY. IV Regiment of Light Dragoons raised in Pennsylvania in 1777.

*Colonel.*

Stephen Moylan, 8 Jan., 1777. By brevet 5 June, 1776.

*Lieut. Colonel.*

Ant. Walton White, 15 Feb., 1777. Removed to 1st Regt., 10 Dec., 1779.

*Captains.*

Moore Fontleroy, 21 Jan., 1777. Promoted Major 1 Aug., 1779.
David Hopkins, 21 Jan., 1777.
John Heard, 8 Feb., 1778.
George Grey, 1 March, 1778. Resigned 1 May, 1779.
John Craig, 22 Dec., 1778.
Zebulon Pike, 25 Dec., 1778.

*Lieutenants.*

Peter Manifold, 1 May, 1778. Promoted Capt. 15 April, 1779.
Larkin Smith, 4 Sept., 1778. Promoted Capt. 1 Aug., 1779.
Henry Willis, 22 Dec., 1778.
Erasmus Gill, 25 Dec., 1778.

*Cornets.*

Thomas Overton. Promoted Lieut. 1 July, 1779.
Larkin Smith, 1 Aug., 1778. Promoted Lieut. 1 Jan., 1779.
Laur. Trent. Promoted Lieut. 1 Oct., 1779.
Dade Payton, 1 Jan., 1779. Promoted Lieut. 2 June, 1779.
John Sullivan, Promoted Lieut. 1 Oct., 1779.
Jonah Hallet. Promoted Lieut. 2 Oct., 1779.

*Adjutants.*

Zebulon Pike, 20 Nov., 1777. Resigned.
Thomas Overton, 1 July, 1779.

*Quartermaster.*

Laur. Trent.

*Paymaster.*

Will. Henderson.

*Surgeons.*

Will. Cathcart, 1 April, 1777. Resigned.
Thos. Hax McCauly, 1 May, 1778.

---

Three troops of Light Dragoons raised in North Carolina.

*Captains.*

Martin Phiser.
Casmo de Medici.
Samuel Ash.

*Paymaster.*

Will Hardy.

---

Marechause Light Dragoons. One troop raised agreeable to a resolve of Congress of 27 May, 1778, to attend the Provost Martial.

*Captain.*

Barthol. Van Hear, 1 June, 1778.

*Lieutenants.*

Christ. Manaeké, 1 July, 1778.
Jacob Maitinger, 1 Aug., 1778.
Philip Strubing.

---

Cavalry. I Legion of Cavalry and Infantry raised agreeable to a resolve of Congress, 1778.

*Brigadier General.*

Count Pulaski. Killed at Savannah, 1779.

*Colonel.*

——— Cowatch. Killed before Charlestown, 11 May, 1779.

*Lieut. Colonel.*

——— Bedeau.

*Majors.*

Count de Monfort. Resigned 23 Jan., 1779
Pet. Jos. Franch Vernier, 23 Feb., 1779. Killed 9 Oct., 1779.

*Captains.*

Paul Bentalou, 12 April, 1778.
Joseph Baldesqui, 10 May, 1778. Resigned 23 Dec., 1779.

——— Oneuil, 1 March, 1779.
Baron de Frey.
Charles de Frey. Died Dec., 1779.

*Lieutenants.*

——— Girard. Promoted Brevet Lieutenant Colonel, 13 Feb., 1779.
Baptiste Verdier, 1 March, 1777.
——— Beaulieu, 1 March, 1779.
——— Kavleman, 1 March, 1779. Resigned 1 Sept., 1779.
——— la Close, 1 March, 1779.

*Cornet.*

——— Conture, 1 July, 1779.

---

Cavalry. II Legion. The 13 July, 1779, Captain McLane's company was detached from the Delaware Regiment and united to this corps.

*Major.*

Henry Lee.

*Captains.*

Allan McLane.
Henry Payton, 2 July, 1778.
Joseph Eggleston.
John Rudulph, 1 Oct., 1778.
Mich. Rudulph.
Robert Forsyth, 1 July, 1778.

*Lieutenants.*

Joseph Eggleston, 21 April, 1778.
Patrick Carns, 22 April, 1778.
Ferdinand Neal.
George Haney.
Matthew Irwin.
James Armstrong, 1 Jan., 1779.

*Cornets.*

Ferdinand Neal, 22 April, 1778.
William Winston.
George Guthry.
James Heard.
Henry Archer, 1 Jan., 1779.

*Adjutant.*

John Gordon.

*Quartermaster.*

Stephen Lewis.

*Mate.*

Charles Adams.

---

Cavalry. III Legion.

*Colonel.*

——— Armand, 10 May, 1777.

*Captains.*

Charles Markle, 8 Feb., 1778.
George Schaffner, 8 Feb., 1778.
——— Sigounier, 9 Feb., 1778.
Viscount Lomange, 11 Feb., 1778.
——— Le Brun, April, 1778.
——— Berth, 7 June, 1778.

*Lieutenants.*

John Sharp, 10 Feb., 1778.
Henry Seibert, 6 June, 1778.
——— Vegnera, July, 1778.
Augustus Brissault, 13 Jan., 1779.
——— Verdis, April, 1779.
——— Ludeman, 1 June, 1779.
Bern'd de Cicaty, 6 June, 1779.
——— Suber. Resigned 1 June, 1779.

*2nd Lieutenant.*

Freder. Segern, 1 May, 1778. Promoted Lieutenant 1 June, 1779.

*Cornet.*

——— des Conture, 31 July, 1779.

*Ensign.*

Henry Riedel, 1 June, 1778.

INFANTRY. General Washington's Guards.

*Major.*

Caleb Gibbs, 29 July, 1778.

*Lieutenant.*

Will. Colfax.

INFANTRY. I New Hampshire Regiment.

*Colonel.*

Joseph Cilly, 22 Feb., 1777.

*Lieut. Colonel.*

Jerem. Gilman, 20 Sept., 1777.

*Major.*

Will. Scott, 20 Sept., 1777.

*Captains.*

Amos Morrill, 8 Nov., 1776.
Jason Wait, 8 Nov., 1776.
Amos Emerson, 8 Nov., 1776.
Ebenezer Fry, 8 Nov., 1776.
Isaac Farwell, 8 Nov., 1776.
Nat. Hutchings, 2 April, 1777.

*Capt. Lieutenant.*

Simeon Satwell, 20 Sept., 1777. Ranks as Captain.

*Lieutenants.*

Moody Dustin, 5 March, 1778. Ranks as Captain.
Benj. Kimble, 8 Nov., 1776.
Matthew McCawley, 8 Nov., 1776.
Josiah Monroe, 20 Sept., 1777.
Daniel Clapp, 5 March, 1778.
Will. Hutchins, 5 March, 1778.
Asah Senter, 5 March, 1778.
Jeremiah Pritchard, 5 March, 1778.

*2nd Lieutenants.*

Bazaleel Howe, 1 Jan., 1777.
Simeon Morrill, 20 Sept., 1777.
Jonath. Willard, 10 Jan., 1778.
Joshua Thompson, 5 March, 1778.
Thomas Blake, 12 May, 1778.

*Ensigns.*

Jonath. Perkins, 29 July, 1777.
Joseph Mills, 20 Sept., 1777.
Hubbart Carter, 28 Sept., 1777.
Samuel Thompson, 10 Jan., 1778.

INFANTRY. II New Hampshire Regiment.

*Lieut. Colonel Commandant.*

George Reed, 5 March, 1778.

*Major.*

Benj. Titcomb, 2 April, 1777.

*Captains.*

Caleb Robinson, 8 Nov., 1776.
James Carr, 8 Nov., 1776.
Elijah Clays, 8 Nov., 1776.
Will. Rowel, 2 April, 1777.
Moses Dustin, 30 Sept., 1777.
Jerem. Fogg, 9 Oct., 1777.
Enoch Chace, 22 Dec., 1777.

*Capt. Lieutenant.*

Samuel Cheny, 22 Dec., 1777.

*Lieutenants.*

Michael Holt, 22 Dec., 1777.
Ebenezer Light, 22 Dec., 1777.
Noah Robinson, 22 Dec., 1777.
Joseph Potter, 22 Dec., 1777.
Pelatiah Whittimore, 22 Dec., 1777.
James Nichols, 22 Dec., 1777.
Will. Mord. Bell, 22 Dec., 1777.
George Bep. Frost, 22 Dec., 1777.

*2nd Lieutenants.*

Luke Woodbury, 20 Sept., 1777.
Samuel Adams, 9 Oct., 1777.
Will. Taggard, 22 Dec., 1777.

*Ensigns.*

Joshua Merrow, 2 April, 1777.
Daniel Gookin, 6 May, 1777.
Caleb Blodget, 16 Sept., 1777.
Georg Bunham, 20 Sept., ——.
Will. Twombley, 9 Oct., 1777.
Thomas Chalis, 22 Dec., 1777.

INFANTRY. III New Hampshire Regiment.

*Colonel.*

Alexan. Scammel, 1 Jan., 1777.

*Lieut. Colonel.*

Henry Dearborn, 19 Sept., 1777.

*Major.*

James Norris, 20 Dec., 1777.

*Captains.*

Daniel Livermore, 8 Nov., 1776.
Isaac Fry, 1 Jan., 1777.
Will. Ellis, 4 April, 1777.
David McGregore, 4 Aug., 1777.
Nicholas Gilman, 12 Sept., 1778.

*Capt. Lieutenant.*

Will. Adr. Hawkins. Promoted Captain 22 May, 1779.

*Lieutenants.*

Thomas Simpson. Promoted Capt. Lieutenant 22 May, 1779.
John Dennet, 1 May, 1778.
Benj. Ellis, 1 May, 1778.
Adna Penniman, 1 May, 1778.
Jonath. Cass, 1 May, 1778.
Joseph Boynton, 1 May, 1778.
Dudley Leavit Chase, 1 May, 1778.
Nath. Holt, 28 Oct., 1778.
Nath. Leavit, 12 Sept., 1778.

*2nd Lieutenant.*

James Blanchard, 22 May, 1779.

*Ensigns.*

Jonath. Cilley, 4 Aug., 1777.
Arch. Stark, 20 Sept., 1777.
Nathan Ware, 8 Oct., 1777.
Neal McGaffey, 14 Nov., 1777.
Bradbury Richards, 1 May, 1778.
John Harvey, 1 May, 1778.

An Independent Company.

*Captain.*

Simon Spalding, 26 Sept., 1776.

*Lieutenant.*

Tom Jenkins, 6 July, 1778.

NEW HAMPSHIRE RANGERS.

*Major.*

William Whitcomb.

*Captain.*

George Aldrich.

*Lieutenants.*

Thomas Lyford.
Jonas Butterfield.
Nath. Taylor.

---

INFANTRY. I Massachusetts Bay Regiment.

*Colonel.*

Joseph Vasse, 21 Jan., 1777.

*Lieut. Colonel.*

Elijah Vasse, 21 Jan., 1777.

*Major.*

Thomas Cogswell, 21 Jan., 1777.

*Captains.*

Moses Ashley, 5 Nov., 1775.
Nathan Cushing, 1 Jan., 1777.
Orringle Stoddard, 1 Jan., 1777.
Abraham Hunt, 1 Jan., 1777.
Jeremiah Miller, 1 Jan., 1777.

*Capt. Lieutenant.*

John Mills. Promoted Captain 16 April, 1779.

*Lieutenants.*

Belcher Handcock. Promoted Capt. Lieutenant 16 April, 1779.
Francis Green, 1 Jan., 1777.
Alexander Orr, 1 Jan., 1777.
Jesse Hollister, 1 Jan., 1777.
Ebenezer Williams, 1 Jan., 1777.
Thomas Cushing, 1 Jan., 1777.
Oliver Hunt.
John Grace.

*2nd Lieutenants.*

Ralph H. Bowles. Promoted Lieutenant 16 April, 1779.
Nathan Nason, 1 Jan., 1777.
Nathan Stone, 1 Jan., 1777.

*Ensigns.*

Benj. Wills.
Azariah Egleston.
James Webb.
Elisha Gilbert.
Jonath. Rawson.
Ebenezer Wild.
John Starbird.

---

INFANTRY. II Massachusetts Bay Regiment.

*Colonel.*

John Bailey, 1 July, 1775.

*Lieut. Colonel.*

Ezra Badlam, 7 July, 1777.

*Major.*

Andrew Peters, 1 Jan., 1777.

*Captains.*

Seth Drew, 1 Jan., 1777.
Judah Alden, 1 Jan., 1777.
Luther Bailey, 11 Aug., 1777.
Abner Hayward, 19 Sept., 1777.
Adam Bailey, 1 Nov., 1778.
——— Dunham. Resigned.

*Capt. Lieutenant.*

Robert Bradford. Promoted Captain 21 June, 1779.

*Lieutenants.*

Simeon Lord. Promoted Capt. Lieutenant 21 June, 1779.
Will. Taylor, 1 Jan., 1777.
Robert Muzzy, 1 Jan., 1777.
Will. Torrey, 1 Jan., 1777.
Hezek. Ripley, 1 Jan., 1777.
Jotham Emmes, 1 Jan., 1777.
Silas Morton, 1 Jan., 1778.
Samuel Eldred, 1 Nov., 1778.

*Ensigns.*

Marlbury Turner. Promoted Lieut. 21 June, 1779.
Joshua Farnold, 1 June, 1777.
Ebenezer Brown, 28 Sept., 1777.
Ratheureus Mitchel, 1 Nov., 1777.
Sturgeon Slone, 1 Nov., 1777.
Henry Nelson, 1 March, 1778.

---

INFANTRY. III Massachusetts Bay Regiment.

*Colonel.*

John Greaton, 1 July, 1775.

*Lieut. Colonel.*

Jotham Loring, 1 Jan., 1777. Broke 12 Aug., 1779.

*Major.*

Robert Oliver, 1 Nov., 1777.

*Captains.*

Samuel Flowers.
Job Sumner, 1 July, 1777.
Joseph Williams, 1 July, 1777.
Abraham Watson, 1 July, 1777.
Edward Crumpton, 11 Nov., 1777.
James Fisdale, 3 Nov., 1778.

*Capt. Lieutenant.*

Thomas Pritchard, 1 Jan., 1777.

*Lieutenants.*

Samuel Burnham, 1 Jan., 1777.
Jabez Snow, 1 Jan., 1777.
Dan. Lee, 1 Jan., 1777.
John Maynard, 11 Nov., 1777.
James Davis, 1 Jan., 1778.
James Chiney, 1 Jan., 1778.
Samuel Mellick, 16 Sept., 1778.
Joseph Croker, 16 Sept., 1778.

*2nd Lieutenants.*

Henry Savage, 1 Jan., 1777.
John Smith, 1 Jan., 1777.
Ebenezer Stocker, 1 Jan., 1777.

*Ensign.*

John Meacham, 1 Jan., 1777.

---

INFANTRY. IV Massachusetts Bay Regiment.

*Colonel.*

Will. Sheppard, 4 May, 1776.

*Lieut. Colonel.*

Will. Stacey, 1 Jan., 1777.

*Major.*

Libbeus Ball, 1 Nov., 1777.

*Captains.*

Isaac Pope, 1 Jan., 1777.
George Webb., 1 Jan., 1777.
John Bannister, 1 April, 1778.
Simeon Larned, 5 Nov., 1778.

*Capt. Lieutenant.*

James Wright. Promoted Capt. 20 May, 1779.

*Lieutenants.*

Will. Moore. Promoted Capt 15 June, 1779.
Ebenezer Field. Promoted Capt. Lieut. 15 June, 1779.
E. Drew, 1 Jan., 1777.
David Halbrook, 1 Jan., 1777.
Jonathan Felt, 1 Jan., 1777.
Lemuel Snow, 1 Jan., 1777.
Edward Walker, 1 Jan., 1777.
Samuel Chapler, 1 Nov., 1777.
Simeon Spring, 3 Jan., 1778.
Eleazer Beamis, 5 Nov., 1778. Resigned 18 Aug., 1779.

*Ensigns.*

Haskall Freeman, 1 Nov., 1777. Promoted Lieut. 18 Aug., 1779.
Jabez Bull, 1 Nov., 1777.
John Davis, 3 Jan., 1778. Lt. and Adjt. 14 April, 1780.
John Yeoman, 10 Feb., 1778. Lieut. 15 April, 1780.
Benj. Ray, 26 Feb., 1778.
Thomas Cole, 5 Nov., 1778.
Thomas Covill, 30 March, 1779. Resigned 18 Aug., 1779.
Levi Bradi, 30 March, 1779.
Jacob Town, 18 Aug., 1779. Lieut. 27 May, 1782.
Spencer Wood, 18 Aug., 1779.
Samuel Day, 18 Aug., 1779.

---

INFANTRY. V Massachusetts Bay Regiment.

*Colonel.*

Rufus Putnam, 5 Aug., 1776.

*Lieut. Colonel.*

Ezra Newhall, 17 May, 1777.

*Major.*

Jonathan Allen, 17 May, 1777.

*Captains.*

John Whipple, 1 Jan., 1777.
Jonath. Goodall, 1 Jan., 1777.
Hiffield White, 1 Jan., 1777.
Daniel Shays, 1 Jan., 1777.
Joshua Benson, 1 Jan., 1777.
Benjamin Gardner, 1 Nov., 1778.

*Capt. Lieutenant.*

Joseph Killam, 1 Nov., 1778.

*Lieutenants.*

John Trotter, 1 Jan., 1777.
Jonath. Stone, 1 Jan., 1777.
Ezekiel Cooper, 1 Jan., 1777.
Oliver Rouse, 1 Jan., 1777.
Peter Welsh, 1 Jan., 1777.
John Cotton, 1 Jan., 1777.
Ivory Holland, 11 Nov., 1778.
——— Tucker. Resigned 11 July, 1779.

*Ensigns.*

Joseph Smith, 7 Nov., 1777. Promoted Lieut. 10 July, 1779.
Theoph. Clark. Promoted Lieut. 10 July, 1779.
Gibeon Hooker, 1 Jan., 1777.
John Blake, 1 Jan., 1777.
John Soule, 1 Jan., 1777.
Elisha Hammond, 1 Jan., 1777.
Peletah Everett, 1 Jan., 1777.
Park Holland, 7 Nov., 1777.
Zibeon Cooper, 7 Nov., 1777.
Edward Challoner, 7 Nov., 1777.
Theophilus Clarke, 7 Nov., 1777.

INFANTRY. VI Massachusetts Bay Regiment.

*Colonel.*

Thomas Nixon, 9 Aug., 1776.

*Lieut. Colonel.*

Daniel Whiting, 29 Sept., 1778.

*Major.*

Peter Harwood, 29 Sept., 1778.

*Captains.*

John Spurr, 1 Jan., 1776.
Japheth Daniels, 1 Jan., 1776.
Abel Holden, 1 Jan., 1776.

*Capt. Lieutenant.*

John Holden. Promoted Capt. 6 March, 1779.

*Lieutenants.*

Benj. Haywood. Promoted Capt. 10 April, 1779.
Rich'd Buckmaster. Promoted Capt. 10 June, 1779.
Matthew Chambers. Promoted Capt. Lieut. 10 June, 1779.
Dudley Tyler, 1 Jan., 1777. Promoted Capt. 11 Nov., 1779.
Benj. Pike, 1 Jan., 1777.
Sam. Frost, 1 Jan., 1777.
Peter Clays, 1 Jan., 1777. Promoted Capt. Lieut. 11 Nov., 1779.
Mason Wattles, 1 Jan., 1779.
Nath. Halbrook, 1 March, 1777.

*2nd Lieutenants.*

Samuel Fairbanks. Promoted Lieut. 10 June, 1779.
John Crane. Promoted Lieut. 10 June, 1779.
Levi Holden, 22 Dec., 1777. Promoted Lieut. 6 March, 1779.
John Lilley, 23 March, 1778. Promoted Lieut. 10 April, 1779.
John Holden, 27 April, 1778.
Benj. Lynds, 9 May, 1778.

*Ensigns.*

Stephen Fowler, 1 Jan., 1777.
Joseph Balcome, 12 Nov., 1777.
Nath. Wheeler, 6 March, 1779.
James Weston, 10 April, 1779.
Nath. Miller, 10 June, 1779.
Solomon White, 4 Sept., 1779.
John Thompson, 11 Nov., 1779.
Benj. Gilbert.
Moses Cotton.

---

INFANTRY. VII Massachusetts Bay Regiment.

*Lieut. Colonel Commanding.*

John Brooks, 11 Nov., 1778.

*Major.*

Samuel Darby, 1 Nov., 1778.

*Captains.*

Will. Henry Ballard, 1 July, 1775.
Asa Coburn.
Luke Day, 1 Jan., 1777.
Benjam. Warren, 1 Jan., 1777.
John Reed, 1 Jan., 1777.
Dan. Lane, 1 Jan., 1777.

*Capt. Lieutenant.*

James Parker. Promoted Capt. 5 July, 1779.

*Lieutenants.*

Will. White. Promoted Capt. Lieut. 5 July, 1779.
Will Curtis.
Eliphalet Thorp.
Jonath. Maynard.
Ebenez. Peabody.
Sam. Buffington.
James Lunt.
Aaron Holden.

*2nd Lieutenants.*

Luther Trowbridge. Promoted 5 July, 1779.
Stephen Carter.
Robert Givins.
Elijah Day.

*Ensigns.*

Rich'd Bagnall.
Joseph Tucker.
Will McKindrey.
Andrew Garrett.
Levi Parker.

---

INFANTRY. VIII Massachusetts Bay Regiment.

*Colonel.*

Mich. Jackson, 1 Jan., 1777.

*Lieut. Colonel.*

Tobias Fernald, 6 March, 1779.

*Major.*

Will. Hull, 1 Jan., 1777.

*Captains.*

James Keith, 1 July, 1775.
John Wiley, 16 Aug., 1775.
James Varnum, 10 Aug., 1776.
James Brancroft, 16 July, 1776.
John Burnham, 1 July, 1777.
Thomas Hartshorn, 30 Oct., 1778.

*Capt. Lieutenant.*

Ebenezer Fish. Dead.

*Lieutenants.*

Will. Story, 1 Jan., 1777. Promoted Capt. Lieut. 23 July, 1779.
Silas Pierce. 1 Jan., 1777.
Abner Wade, 1 Jan., 1777.
Ebenezer Smith, 1 Jan., 1777.
Simon Jackson, 1 Jan., 1777.
Obadiah Wither, 5 Jan., 1777.
Will. Green, 5 Jan., 1777.
Samuel Armstrong, 7 Oct., 1777.
John Sawyer. Resigned.

*Ensigns.*

Samuel Benjamin. Promoted Lieut. 28 March, 1779.
John Green. Promoted Lieut. 1 April, 1779.
Simeon Jackson, 22 Sept., 1777.
Mich. Jackson, 2 Oct., 1777.
Francis Tufts, 3 Oct., 1777.
James Bancroft.
Will. Haldreth.
Sam'l Blaizdell.
Thomas Foster.
Benjamin Pierce.
Dan'l Parker.
Joel Jenkins.

---

INFANTRY. IX Massachusetts Bay Regiment.

*Colonel.*

James Wesson, 1 Jan., 1777.

*Lieut. Colonel.*

James Miller, 1 Jan., 1777.

*Major.*

Joseph Pettingill, 26 July, 1779.

*Captains.*

Samuel Carr, 1 July, 1777.
Amos Cayswell, 1 July, 1777.
Abrah. Child, Feb., 1777. Resigned 6 Sept., 1779.
Nathan Dix, March, 1777.
John Blanchard, March, 1777.

*Capt. Lieutenant.*

Will. Watson. Promoted Capt. 26 July, 1779.

*Lieutenants.*

Mich. Furley. Promoted Capt. Lieut. 26 July, 1779.
Joseph Edes, 1 Jan., 1777.
Rich'd Welsh, 1 Jan., 1777.
Caleb Clap, 1 Jan., 1777.
Joseph Noyes, 1 Jan., 1777.
——— Woodward. Resigned.
——— Claffen. Resigned.

*Ensigns.*

Benj. Parker. Promoted Lieut. 10 July, 1779.
Joseph Leland. Promoted Lieut. 12 July, 1779.
Henry White. Promoted Lieut. 26 July, 1779.
Edw'd White, 1 Jan., 1777.
Nathan Fry, 1 Jan., 1777.
Oliver Rice, 2 June, 1778.
Caleb King, 2 June, 1778.
Ebenezer Davis, 2 March, 1779.

---

INFANTRY. X Massachusetts Bay Regiment.

*Colonel.*

Thomas Marshall, 1 Jan., 1777.

*Lieut. Colonel.*

Joseph Thompson, 19 Dec., 1777.

*Major.*

Nath. Winslow, 19 Dec., 1777.

*Captains.*

Samuel King, 8 March, 1776.
Amasa Soper, 8 March, 1776.
Will. Warner, 8 March, 1776.
Christopher Marshall, 1 Jan., 1777.
Jacob Wales, 1 Nov., 1777.

*Capt. Lieutenant.*

Will. Park, 15 Dec., 1778.

*Lieutenants.*

Thomas White, 1 Jan., 1777.
Barlet Hynde, 1 Jan., 1777.
Samuel Bass, 1 Jan., 1777.
Jonathan Turner, 1 Jan., 1777.
Othniel Taylor, 1 Jan., 1777.
John Currey, 10 Aug., 1777.
Natth. C. Allen, 21 Oct., 1778.
Levi Dodge, 15 Sept., 1778.

*Ensigns.*

Daniel Brown, 1 Nov., 1777.
Reuben Dodge, 1 Nov., 1777.
Peleg Turner, 1 Nov., 1777.
Josiah Smith, 2 April, 1779.
Richard Miller, 4 April, 1779.
Barthol. Thayer, 6 April, 1779

INFANTRY. XI Massachusetts Bay Regiment.

*Colonel.*

Benjamin Tupper, 7 July, 1777.

*Lieut. Colonel.*

Noah M. Littlefield, 1 Jan., 1777.

*Major.*

Moses Knap, 5 Nov., 1778.

*Captains.*

Will. Porter. 1 Jan., 1777.
Moses Greenleaf, 1 Jan., 1777.
Samuel Page, 1 Jan., 1777.
Stephen Abbot, 28 May, 1778.

*Capt. Lieutenant.*

Silas Clarke. Pro. Capt. 28 March, 1779.

*Lieutenants.*

John Francis, Pro. Capt. 25 June, 1779.
Thomas Francis. Pro. Capt. Lieut. 25 June, 1779.
Willm. Burley, 1 Jan., 1777.
Silas Chadburn, 1 Jan., 1777.

*2nd Lieutenants.*

Willm. Histey. Pro. Lieut. 28 Mar., 1779.
Nehem. Emmerson. Pro. Lieut. 28 Mar., 1779.
Jonathan Libbey. Pro. Lieut. 25 June, 1779.
Hugh Mulloy, 1 Jan., 1777.
James Buxton, 1 Jan., 1777.

*Ensigns.*

Aaron Francis, 1 Jan., 1777.
John Littlefield, 1 Jan., 1777.
Will. McKenney, 3 April, 1778.
Benj. Shaw, 2 October, 1778.

INFANTRY. XII Massachusetts Bay Regiment.

*Lieut. Colonel Commanding.*

Ebenezer Sprout, 29 Sept., 1778.

*Major.*

Thomas Barnes, 6 March, 1779.

*Captains.*

Silas Burbank, 1 July, 1777.
John Williams, 7 July, 1777.

*Capt. Lieutenant.*

Abrah. Williams. Pro. Capt. 6 March, 1779.

*Lieutenants.*

Henry Sewall. Pro. Capt. 25 June, 1779.
John Pray. Pro. Capt. 5 July, 1779.
John Manes. Pro. Capt. 5 July, 1779.
Luke Hitchcock. Pro. Capt. 5 July, 1779.
Timothy Remick. Pro. Capt. 5 July, 1779.
Samuel Miller, 1 Jan., 1777.
Andrew English, 1 Jan., 1777.

*Ensigns.*

Joseph Foot. Pro. Lieut. 6 March, 1779.
Andrew Warner. Pro. Lieut. 1 July, 1779.
Eleazar Storer. Pro. Lieut. 5 July, 1779.
John Whiting. Pro. Lieut. 5 July, 1779.
Asah Ballord. Pro. Lieut. 5 July, 1779.
John Hubbel. Pro. Lieut. 5 July, 1779.
Joshua Mason, 13 June, 1777.
Joshua Danforth, 26 Nov., 1779.
Samuel Jenkins, 26 Nov., 1779.
Samuel Myrick, 26 Nov., 1779.
Darius Howe, 26 Nov., 1779.
Benj. Tucker, 26 Nov., 1779.

INFANTRY. XIII Massachusetts Bay Regiment.

*Lieut. Colonel Commanding.*

Calvin Smith, 10 March, 1779.

*Major.*

John Porter, 30 May, 1777.

*Captains.*

Noah Alden, 2 Oct., 1776.
Daniel Pilsbury, 1 Jan., 1777.
John Kilby Smith, 12 Feb., 1778.

*Capt. Lieutenant.*

Peter Page. Pro. Capt. 30 March, 1779.

*Lieutenants.*

Ebenezer Smith. Pro. Capt. 30 March, 1779.
Christian Woodbridge. Pro. Capt. 30 March, 1779.
Thomas Smart. Pro. Capt. 15 June, 1779.
John Fowles. Pro. Capt. 30 June, 1779.
Walter Dean, 20 Oct., 1777.
John Philan, 1 Jan., 1778.
Will. Wigglesworth, 1 Jan., 1778.
Leonard Miller, 5 Jan., 1778.
Benjam. Dana, 7 Feb., 1778.
Will. Greenleaf, 13 Feb., 1778.

*Ensigns.*

Ephr. Emmery. Pro. Lieut. 10 April, 1778.
Joshua Fenton. Pro. Lieut. 15 June, 1779.
Jacob Brown, 1 Jan., 1778.
James Green, 30 March, 1778.
Will. Baker, 7 March, 1779.
Joseph Miller, 30 March, 1779.
Edward Annable, 30 March, 1779.
Nehem. Bettis, 10th April, 1779.

INFANTRY. XIV Massachusetts Bay Regiment.

*Colonel.*

Gamaliel Bradford, 1 Jan., 1777.

*Lieut. Colonel.*

Barakiah Basset. 1 Jan., 1777.

*Major.*

Joseph Morse, 11 Nov., 1778.

*Captains.*

Thomas Turner, 8 May, 1776. Res'd 9 Oct., 1779.
Zebedee Redding, 8 May, 1776.
James Cooper, 1 Jan., 1777.
Joseph Wadsworth, 1 Jan., 1777. Res'd 8 Oct., 1779.
Joseph Stetson, 1 Jan., 1777.
Elnath. Haskell, 1 April, 1778.

*Capt. Lieutenant.*

Adam Fish, 1 April, 1778. Pro. Capt. 8 Oct., 1779.

*Lieutenants.*

Joseph Bates, 1 Jan., 1777. Pro. Capt. 8 October, 1779.
Rufus Lincoln, 1 Jan., 1777. Pro. Capt. Lieut. 8 Oct., 1779.
John Fuller, 1 Jan., 1777.
Zebedee King, 1 Jan., 1777.
David Patterson, 1 Jan., 1777.
Will. Mills, 1 Jan., 1777.
Thomas Freeman, 1 April, 1778.

*Ensigns.*

Joshua Brumhall. Pro. Lieut. 1 Feb., 1779.
Andrew Bradford, 1 Jan., 1777. Pro. Lieut. 8 Oct., 1779.

Crocker Sampson, 1 Jan., 1777.
Gamal. Bradford, 8 Oct., 1779.
George Reek, 8 Oct., 1779.
Elish. Faxon, 8 Oct., 1779.
Obadiah Lovejoy, 8 Oct., 1779.
Hudson Bailey, 8 Oct., 1779.

---

INFANTRY. XV. Massachusetts Bay Regiment.

*Colonel.*

Timothy Bigelow, 8 Feb., 1777.

*Lieut. Colonel.*

Henry Haskell, 8 Feb., 1777.

*Major.*

Hugh Maxwell, 7 July, 1777.

*Captain.*

Sylvanus Smith, 1 Jan., 1777.

*Capt. Lieutenant.*

Joshua Pierce. Pro. Capt. 1 March, 1779.

*Lieutenants.*

Moses Roberts. Pro. Capt. 1 March, 1779.
Phineas Boisman. Pro. Capt. 19 Ap., 1779.
Will. Crossman. Pro. Capt. 20 June, 1779. Broke 7 Nov., 1779.
Gabriel Fondrie. Pro. Capt. 28 June, 1779.
Abner Dow. Pro. Capt. 9 Nov., 1779.
Joseph Brown. Pro. Capt. Lieut. 28 June, 1779.
Samuel Henley, 1 April, 1777.

*Ensigns.*

Joel Pratt. Pro. Lieut. 1 March, 1779.
Joseph Washburn. Pro. Lieut. 2 April, 1779.
Will. Eysandean. Pro. Lieut. 2 April, 1779.
John Kennedy. Pro. Lieut. 19 April, 1779.
John Stower. Pro. Lieut. 20 June, 1779.
Henry Marble. Pro. Lieut. 28 June, 1779.
Jonathan Porter. Pro. Lieut. 28 June, 1779.
Daniel Simmonds, 1 March, 1779.
Will. Bancroft, 1 March, 1779.

---

INFANTRY. I Rhode Island Regiment.

*Colonel.*

Christopher Green, 1 Jan., 1777.

*Lieut. Colonel.*

Samuel Ward, 26 May, 1778.

*Major.*

Ebenezer Flag, 26 May, 1778.

*Captains.*

Elijah Lewis, 1 Jan., 1777.
Thomas Cole, 1 Jan., 1777.
John S. Dexter, 1 Jan., 1777.
Thomas Arnold, 21 March, 1777. Trans. to Invalid Regt. 1 Nov., 1779.
John Holden, 10 Oct., 1777.
Edward Slocum, 26 May, 1778.

*Capt. Lieutenant.*

Joseph Arnold, 1 June, 1778.

*Lieutenants.*

Daniel Pierce, 11 Feb., 1777.
Zephaniah Brown, 11 Feb., 1777.
Robert Rogers, 19 Feb., 1777.
David Johnson, 19 Feb., 1777.
Elias Thompson, 19 Feb., 1777.
Enoch Stanton, 19 Feb., 1777.
Charles Pierce, 1 June, 1778.
John Cooke, 1 June, 1778.

INFANTRY. II Rhode Island Regiment.

*Colonel.*

Israel Angel, 13 Jan., 1777.

*Lieut. Colonel.*

Jeremiah Olney, 13 Jan., 1777.

*Major.*

Simeon Theyer, 13 Jan., 1777.

*Captains.*

Will. Tew, 13 Jan., 1777.
Coggeshall Olney, 13 Jan., 1777.
William Allen, 13 Jan., 1777.
Thomas Hughs, 23 June, 1777.
Will. Humphreys, 22 Oct., 1777.

*Capt. Lieutenant.*

Will. Littlefield, 1 Jan., 1777. Resigned.

*Lieutenants.*

Dutee Jerauld, 11 Feb., 1777. Promoted.
Thos. Waterman, 11 Feb., 1777. Dismissed.
Ebenezer Macumber, 12 June, 1777.
David Sayles, 12 June, 1777.
Eliver Jenches, 25 June, 1777.
Benedict Tew, 22 Oct., 1777. Resigned.
Abel Carpenter, 1 Jan., 1778. Resigned.
Thomas Waterman, Jun., 1 Jan., 1778.

*Ensigns.*

Benj. L. Peckham, 11 Feb., 1777.
John Hubbart, 12 Feb., 1777. Pro. Lieut. 18 May, 1779.
Joseph Wheaton, 1 March, 1779. Pro. Lieut. 1 Sept., 1779.
John Mosely Green, 1 March, 1779.
John Rogers, 1 May, 1779.
Will. Pratt, 1 May, 1779.
Joseph Mashury, 1 May, 1779.
Jerem. Grinman, 1 May, 1779.

---

INFANTRY I Connecticut Regiment

*Colonel.*

Josiah Start, 27 May, 1777. Formerly Col. Jed. Huntington's.

*Lieut. Colonel.*

David T. Sill, 5 March, 1778.

*Major.*

Christ. Darrow, 15 April, 1778.

*Captains.*

Eliphalet Holmes, 1 Jan., 1777.
John Shumway, 1 Jan., 1777.
Will. Richards, 1 Jan., 1777.
Ithamar Harvey, 1 Jan., 1778. Resd. 20 June, 1779.
Ebenezer Perkins, 1 Jan., 1778.
Ezra Selden, 1 Jan., 1778.

*Capt. Lieutenant.*

Enoch Reed, 1 June, 1778.

*Lieutenants.*

Henry Hill, 1 Jan., 1777. Resd. 20 June, 1779.
David Dorrance, 1 Jan., 1778.
Richard Douglass, 1 Jan., 1778.
John Tiffany, 6 Feb., 1778.
Will. Colfax, 18 March, 1778.
James Lord, 1 June, 1778.
Simeon Avery, 1 June, 1778.
Ezra Lee, 1 June, 1778.

*2nd Lieutenants.*

Darius Peek, 16 Feb., 1778. Resd. 1 May, 1779.
Ichabod Spencer, 29 May, 1778.
Rufus B. Abel, 1 June, 1778.
Thomas Anderson, 1 June, 1778.

*Ensigns.*

Will. Tracey, 30 July, 1777.
Robert Allen, 1 Nov., 1777.
Reuben Saunderson, 29 Dec., 1777.
Josiah Tiffany, 1 Jan., 1778.
Joseph Fellows, 1 June, 1778.

---

INFANTRY. II Connecticut Regiment.

*Colonel.*

Zebulon Butler, 13 March, 1778.

*Lieut. Colonel.*

Isaac Shannon, 1 Jan., 1777.

*Major.*

Amos Walbridge, 27 May, 1777.

*Captains.*

Ichabod Hinkley, 1 Jan., 1777.
David Parsons, 1 Jan., 1777.
Stephen Betts, 1 Jan., 1777.
Erastus Walcott, 27 May, 1777.
James Bebee, 25 Dec., 1777.
Henry Ten Eyck, 13 May, 1777.

*Capt. Lieutenant.*

Roger Alden, 1 June, 1778.

*Lieutenants.*

Benoni Shipman, 27 May, 1777.
Timothy Taylor, 1 Sept., 1777.
Moses Cleveland, 7 Dec., 1777.
Peter Robinson, 25 Dec., 1777.
Nath. Chipman, 29 Dec., 1777.
James Andrews, 29 Dec., 1777. Resigned 1 Aug., 1779.
Solomon Fenton, 1 May, 1778.
Joseph Austin, 1 June, 1778. Resigned 1 Aug., 1779.
John Mix, 16 June, 1778.

*2nd Lieutenants.*

Isaac Keeler. 27 May, 1777.
Jabes Pearsons, 1 Sept., 1777.
Eli Barnum, 7 Dec., 1777.
Samuel Shiock, 1 Sept., 1777.
Israel Strong, 7 Dec., 1777.
Josiah Buck, 25 Dec., 1777.
Will. Lynn, 29 Dec., 1777.

---

INFANTRY. III Connecticut Regiment.

*Colonel.*

Samuel Willys, 1 Jan., 1777.

*Lieut. Colonel.*

Thomas Grosvenor, 3 March, 1778.

*Major.*

William Clift, 15 Oct., 1778.

*Captains.*

Daniel Allen, 1 Jan., 1777. Resigned 31 June, 1779.
Henry Champion, 1 Jan., 1777.
Robert Warner, 1 Jan., 1777.
Will. Judd, 1 Jan., 1777.
John Barnard, 1 Jan., 1777.
Edward Ellis, 1 Jan., 1777.

*Capt. Lieutenant.*

Elias Stilwell, 1 June, 1778.

*Lieutenants.*

Jonathan Hart, 1 Jan., 1777.
Samuel Richards, 1 Jan., 1777.
Sylvanus Perry, 1 Jan., 1777.
Peleg Heath, 1 Jan., 1777.
Obadiah Gore, 1 Jan., 1777.
Charles Miller, 14 April, 1778.
Silas Goodale, 25 April, 1778.
Ralph Pomeroy, 1 June, 1778.

*2nd Lieutenants.*

Hezekiah Hubbard, 1 Jan., 1777.
Samuel Gibbs, 1 Jan., 1777.
Theoph. Woodbridge, 1 Jan., 1777.
Elijah Ranform, 1 Jan., 1777.
Reuben Pride, 11 Nov., 1777.
Heziah Bailey, 14 April, 1778. Resigned 29 April, 1779.
Prentis Hosmer, 25 April, 1778.

*Ensigns.*

Alex'r McDowell, 1 Jan., 1777. Resigned 25 June, 1779.
Will. Higgins, 23 July, 1777.

---

INFANTRY. IV Connecticut Regiment.

*Colonel.*

John Durkee, 1 Jan., 1777.

*Lieut. Colonel.*

John Sumner, 27 May, 1777.

*Major.*

Benj. Troop, 25 May, 1778.

*Captains.*

John Harman, 1 Jan., 1777.
John McGreigier, 1 Jan., 1777.
Nathan Webb, 1 Jan., 1777.
Andrew Fitch, 1 Jan., 1777.
Robert Halham, 31 July, 1777.
Seth Philips, 25 May, 1778.

*Capt. Lieutenant.*

Samuel Clift, 1 June, 1778.

*Lieutenants.*

Daniel Wait, 1 Jan., 1777.
John Buel, 24 July, 1777.
John Durkee, Jr., 31 July, 1777.
Joseph Chapman, 31 July, 1777.
Simeon Belding, 25 May, 1778.
Downal Deming, 15 Nov., 1778.
Charles Fanning, 15 Nov., 1778.
Ed. Slaxter Coleman, 15 Nov., 1778.

*2nd Lieutenants.*

Will. Adams, 24 July, 1777.
Ezra Smith, 31 July, 1777.
Ebenezer Wales, 31 July, 1777.
Andrew Griswold, 15 Nov., 1777.
Silas Holt, 13 Jan., 1778.
Libbens Loomis, 1 March, 1778.

*Ensigns.*

Diah Hartshorn, 31 July, 1777.
James Hyde, 27 Dec., 1777.
Elias Robinson, 27 Dec., 1777.

---

INFANTRY. V Connecticut Regiment.

*Colonel.*

Philip Bur. Bradley, 1 Jan., 1777.

*Lieut. Colonel.*

Jonath. Johnson, 15 April, 1778.

*Major.*

Albert Chapman, 5 March, 1778.

*Captains.*

Abner Prior, 1 Jan., 1777.
Jos. Alleyn Wright, 1 Jan., 1777.
Josiah Lacy, 1 Jan., 1777.
Samuel Hait, 1 Jan., 1777.
Will. Green, 17 March, 1778.
John St. John, 25 May, 1778.

*Capt. Lieutenant.*

Thaddeus Weed, 1 June, 1778.

*Lieutenants.*

Elijah Chapman, 1 Jan., 1777.
James Morris, 1 Jan., 1777.
David Strong, 1 Jan., 1777.
Roger Wadsworth, 1 Jan., 1777.
Edward Palmer, 1 Jan., 1777.
Hezekiah Rogers, 12 July, 1777.
Cornelius Higgins, 17 March, 1778. Resigned 16 Aug., 1779.
Thaddeus Keeler, 25 March, 1778.

*2nd Lieutenants.*

Cornelius Russel, 12 Dec., 1777.
Nehemiah Gorham, 15 Dec., 1777.
Othniel Clark, 1 Jan., 1778.
Will. Henshaw, 4 Jan., 1778.
Daniel Bradley, 13 Jan., 1778. Appointed Ensign 28 April, 1777.
Jobe Smith, 9 May, 1778.
Jasper Mead, 1 June, 1778.

*Ensigns.*

Samuel Deforest, 15 Dec., 1777.
David Beach, 4 Jan., 1778.

---

INFANTRY. VI Connecticut Regiment.

*Colonel.*

Return Jonath. Meigs, 12 May, 1777.

*Lieut. Colonel.*

Ebenezer Grey, 15 Oct., 1778.

*Major.*

Eli Leavenworth, 18 Sept., 1777.

*Captains.*

Jonas Prentice, 11 Oct., 1777. Resigned 31 March, 1779.
Charles Pond, 1 Jan., 1777. Dismissed 19 April, 1779.
Joseph Mansfield, 1 Jan., 1777.
Elijah Humphries, 1 Jan., 1777.
David Humphries, 1 Jan., 1777.
Elijah Eli, 1 Jan., 1777.

*Capt. Lieutenant.*

Eleazar Claghorn, 1 Jan., 1778. Promoted Capt. 19 April, 1779.

*Lieutenants.*

David Hall, 1 Jan., 1777. Promoted Capt. Lieut. 19 April, 1779.
Peter Starr, 1 Jan., 1777.
Stephen Potter, 1 Jan., 1777.
Sam. Still. Aug. Parker, 1 Jan., 1777.
Asa Lay, 1 Jan., 1777.
Will. Smith, 1 Jan., 1777.
John Ball, 15 Nov., 1778.
Joseph Shaler, 15 Nov., 1778.

*2nd Lieutenants.*

John Mansfield, 1 Jan., 1777. Promoted Lieut. 19 April, 1779.
Charles Burrel, 1 Jan., 1777. Resigned 29 April, 1779.
Levi Monson, 1 Jan., 1777.
Joseph Shayler, 1 Jan., 1777.
John Trowbridge, 1 Jan., 1777.
Gideon Bailey, 1 Jan., 1777. Resigned 1 July, 1779.
John Sharman, 7 Oct., 1777.
Giles Curtis, 15 Nov., 1777.
Elias Mather, 15 Nov., 1778.

---

INFANTRY. VII Connecticut Regiment.

*Colonel.*

Herman Swift, 1 Jan., 1777.

*Lieut. Colonel.*

Hezekiah Holdridge, 25 May, 1778.

*Major.*

Theodore Woodbridge, 10 Feb., 1778.

*Captains.*

Titus Watson, 1 Jan., 1777.
Stephen Hall, 1 Jan., 1777.
Aaron Stephens, 1 Jan., 1777.
Ebenezer Hills, 1 Sept., 1777.
Thomas Converse, 3 Nov., 1777.
Ephraim Chamberlain, 15 Nov., 1778.

*Capt. Lieutenant.*

Caleb Baldwin, 1 June, 1778.

*Lieutenants.*

John Holomback, 1 Jan., 1777.
Charles Mell, 1 Jan., 1777.
Samuel Barnum, 1 Jan., 1777.
Tryal Tanner, 1 Sept., 1777.
James Chapman, 25 Oct., 1777.
Stephen Billings, 3 Nov., 1777.
Phineas Grover, 2 Dec., 1777.
James Barnes, 15 Nov., 1778. Resigned 20 June, 1779.

*2nd Lieutenants.*

Augustine Taylor, 1 Jan., 1777.
Joseph Wilcox, 1 Sept., 1777.
Israel Jones, 25 Oct., 1777. Resigned 19 April, 1779.
Thomas Starr, 2 Nov., 1777. Ensign 28 April, 1777.
Will. Starr, 3 Nov., 1777. Ensign 28 April, 1777.
Philemon Hall, 10 March, 1778. Ensign 28 April, 1777.
Henry Duggett, 24 April, 1778.

*Ensigns.*

James Bennet, 1 Sept., 1777.
Talmadge Hall, 25 Sept., 1777.

---

INFANTRY. VIII Connecticut Regiment.

*Colonel.*

Giles Russel, 5 March, 1778.

*Lieut. Colonel.*

Joseph Hait, 18 Sept., 1777.

*Major.*

David Smith, 13 March, 1778.

*Captains.*

Samuel Mattocks, 1 Jan., 1777. Resigned 20 April, 1779.
Paul Bringham, 1 Jan., 1777.
Samuel Cumstock, 1 Jan., 1777.

Theophilus Manson, 1 Jan., 1777.
Nehemiah Rice, 15 Nov., 1777.
Samuel Sandford, 15 Dec., 1777.

*Capt. Lieutenant.*

Daniel Barns, 1 June, 1778.

*Lieutenants.*

Selah Benton, 1 Jan., 1777.
Asakel Hodge, 1 Jan., 1777.
Rich'd Sill, 15 Dec., 1777.
Ephraim Kimberly, 14 Feb., 1778.
David Judson, 10 March, 1778.
Samuel Hotchkock, 19 March, 1778. Resigned 19 May, 1779.
Nathan Jackson, 21 March, 1778.
Aaron Benjamin, 7 May, 1778.

*2nd Lieutenants.*

Salmon Hubbel, 10 March, 1778. Promoted Lieut. 19 May, 1779.
John Strong, 10 March, 1778.
Levi Hotchkiss, 21 March, 1778.
John Hobarts, 21 March, 1778.
Eli Curtis, 21 April, 1778. Resigned 14 Dec., 1779.
Will. Beaumont, 15 Dec., 1777.
James Olmstead, 24 Dec., 1777.
Johna Whitney, 31 Dec., 1777.
Timothy Tuthill, 16 June, 1778. Resigned 11 May, 1779.

---

INFANTRY. I New York Regiment.

*Colonel.*

Goose Van Schaick, 28 June, 1775.

*Lieut. Colonel.*

Cornel Vandyck, 21 Nov., 1776.

*Majors.*

——— Lydiard. Resigned 26 March, 1779.
John Graham, 26 March, 1779.

*Captains.*

John Wendell, 1 March, 1776.
John Copp, 15 April, 1776. Resigned 14 July, 1779.
Andrew Finch, 16 July, 1776.
Benj. Hicks, 16 July, 1776.
Nich. Van. Ranselair, 1 Sept. 1778.

*Capt. Lieutenant.*

Charles Parsons. Promoted Capt. 26 March, 1779.

*Lieutenants.*

Guy Young. Promoted Capt. Lieut. 26 March, 1779.
Banent S. Salisbury, 1 March, 1776.
John C. Ten Brock, 1 March, 1776.
Adiel Herwood, 1 March, 1776.
Peter B. Tearse, 1 March, 1776.
Nathan Henry, 21 Nov., 1776.
Will. Scudder, 21 Nov., 1776.
Abrah. Hardenbergh, 21 Nov., 1776.

*Ensigns.*

Ephraim Snow. Promoted Lieut. 26 March, 1779.
Barth. Van Valkenburg, 21 Nov., 1776.
Christ. Muller, 21 Nov., 1776.
Henry Van Woert, 21 Nov., 1776.
Abr. Ten Eyck, 21 Nov., 1776.
Jacob Hy. Wendell, 21 Nov., 1776.
Jacob Illock, 21 Nov., 1776.
Wilkelmur Rickman, 21 Nov., 1776.
Benjamin Gilbert, 21 Nov., 1776.

INFANTRY. II New York Regiment.

*Colonel.*

Philip Courtland, 21 Nov., 1776.

*Lieut. Colonel.*

Pierre Regnier, 21 Nov., 1776.

*Major.*

Nicholas Fish, 21 Nov., 1776.

*Captains.*

Charles Graham, 21 Nov., 1776.
Samuel I. Pell, 21 Nov., 1776.
Jacob Wright, 21 Nov., 1776.
Jonath. Hallet, 21 Nov. 1776.
Abner French, 1 June, 1778.
Isaac Van Wert, 15 Oct., 1778.

*Capt. Lieutenant.*

Charles Mukirk, 21 Nov., 1776.

*Lieutenants.*

Elihu Marshall, 21 Nov., 1776.
Christ. Codwise, 21 Nov., 1776.
James Fairley, 21 Nov., 1776.
John L. Hardenbergh, 21 June, 1777.
Will. Munday, 10 Oct., 1777.
Gilb. I. Levingston, 7 April, 1778.
Charl. T. Weisenfels, 1 Sept., 1778.
Ijirch Buckman, 1 Sept., 1778.

*2nd Lieutenants.*

Andrew White, 21 Nov., 1776.
Will. Glenny, 21 June, 1777.
Tunis Van Wagenen, 10 Oct., 1777.

*Ensigns.*

Robert Provost, 1 Sept., 1778.
Bernard Swartswout, 1 Sept., 1778.
John Brown, 1 Sept., 1778.

---

INFANTRY. III New York Regiment.

*Colonel.*

Peter Gansevoort, 27 Nov., 1776.

*Lieut. Colonel.*

Marinus Willet, 21 Nov., 1776.

*Major.*

Robert Cockran, 21 Nov., 1776.

*Captains.*

Aaron Corson, 21 Nov., 1776.
Thomas de Witt, 21 Nov., 1776.
Cornelius J. Jansen, 21 Nov., 1776.
Leonard Bleachen, 21 Nov., 1776.
James Gregg, 21 Nov., 1776.
Henry Tiebout, 21 Nov., 1776.

*Capt. Lieutenant.*

George Sytez, 28 May, 1778.

*Lieutenants.*

Philip Conine, 21 Nov., 1776.
Will. Japp, 21 Nov., 1776.
Thomas McClelan, 21 Nov., 1776.
Prentice Bowen, 21 Nov., 1776.
Grant Staats, 21 Nov., 1776.
Benj. Bogardus, 21 Nov., 1776.
Will. Colbreath, 20 Nov., 1777.

*Ensigns.*

Christ. Hutton, 6 Nov., 1777. Promoted Lieutenant 6 Feb., 1779.
Peter Magee, 21 Nov., 1776.
John Spoor, 21 Nov., 1776.
Josiah Bagley, 21 Nov., 1776. Promoted Lieutenant 31 March, 1780.
Samuel Lewis, 21 Nov., 1776.
George T. Deniston, 21 Nov., 1776.
Jerem. Van Ranselair, 28 May, 1778.

Benj. Herring, 28 May, 1778.
Garret G. Lansing, 6 Feb., 1779.
John Burhance, 6 Feb., 1779.

---

INFANTRY. IV New York Regiment.

*Colonel.*

Henry B. Levingston. Resigned 13 Jan., 1779.

*Lieut. Colonel Commanding.*

Frederick Weisenfels, 13 Jan., 1779.

*Major.*

Joseph McCraken, 29 May, 1778.

*Captains.*

Samuel Sachett, 15 Nov., 1775.
John Davis, 6 Feb., 1776.
Benj. Walker, 26 Nov., 1776.
Irael Smith, 26 Nov., 1776.
Jonathan Titus, 26 Nov., 1776.
Nath. Horton, 23 April, 1778.
Theodosius Fowler, 23 April, 1778.

*Capt. Lieutenant.*

Edward Dunscomb, 23 April, 1778.

*Lieutenants.*

Silas Gray, 13 March, 1777.
Peter Elsworth, 2 Sept., 1777.
Peter Benstooten, 9 Nov., 1777.
Thomas Hunt, 9 Nov., 1777.
Abrah. Hyatt, 9 Nov., 1777.
Rand. Van Hovenburgh, 9 Nov., 1777.
Joseph Feylick, 9 Nov., 1777.
James Barritt, 9 Nov., 1777.

*Ensigns.*

Daniel Denison, 9 Nov., 1777.
Azariah Tuthell, 9 Nov., 1777.
Samuel Talmage, 9 Nov., 1777.
Ephraim Woodroffer, 9 Nov., 1777.

---

INFANTRY. V New York Regiment.

*Colonel.*

Lewis Dubois, 21 Nov., 1776. Resigned 22 Dec., 1779.

*Lieut. Colonel.*

Jacob Bruyer, 21 Nov., 1776.

*Major.*

Samuel Logan, 21 Nov., 1776.

*Captains.*

Jacobus Rosekrans, 3 Aug., 1775.
James Stewart, 20 Nov., 1776.
Phil. Dubois Bevoir, 20 Nov., 1776.
Henry Godevin, 20 Nov., 1776.
John F. Hamtrank, 20 Nov., 1776.
John Johnston, 20 Nov., 1776.

*Capt. Lieutenant.*

Henry Dubois, 1 Sept., 1778.

*Lieutenants.*

Henry Vandenburgh, 21 Nov., 1776.
Henry Dodge, 21 Nov., 1776.
Henry Pawling, 21 Nov., 1776.
Mich. Connely, 21 Nov., 1776.
Samuel Dodge, 1 Oct., 1777.
John Furman, 1 Sept., 1778.
Samuel English, 1 Sept., 1778.
James Bettes, 1 Sept., 1778.

*2nd Lieutenants.*

Ebenezer Mott, 21 Nov., 1776.
Dan. Birdsall, 21 Nov., 1776.

*Ensigns.*

Henry Swartswout, 21 Nov., 1776.
John McCloughry, 21 Nov., 1776.
Henry J. Vandenburgh, 21 Nov., 1776.
Abrah. Legget, 21 Nov., 1776.
Francis Hanmer, 21 Nov., 1776.
James Johnston, 25 June, 1777.
Barthol. Vandenburgh, 1 May, 1778.

---

INFANTRY. I New Jersey Regiment. Raised for one year, agreeable to a resolve of Congress of 9 October, 1775, which time being near expired, the Government of New Jersey, in consequence of a requisition of Congress, resolved to raise four regiments.
The officers of the three first to be taken from the regiment then in being, and of the fourth from the Militia in actual service, only three of these regiments existed at the beginning of this year.

*Colonel.*

Matthias Ogden, 1 Jan., 1777.

*Lieut. Colonel.*

David Brearly, 1 Jan., 1777. Resigned 4 Aug., 1779.

*Major.*

Daniel Piatt, 4 Jan., 1778.

*Captains.*

John Foreman, 23 Nov., 1776.
Giles Meades, 29 Oct., 1777.
Alex. Mitchell, 1 Nov., 1777.
Peter Van Voorhees, 4 Jan., 1778.
Thos. Buchanan. Resigned 15 Oct., 1779.

*Capt. Lieutenant.*

John Holmes. Promoted Capt. 4 Jan., 1779.

*Lieutenants.*

Aaron Ogden.| Promoted Capt. 2 Feb., 1779.
Jacob Piatt, 10 Jan., 1777. Promoted Capt. Lieut.
Will. Piatt, 15 Jan., 1777.
Cyrus Dehart, 4 Oct., 1777.
John Howell, 29 Oct., 1777.
Will. Barton, 1 Nov., 1777.
Absalom Martin, 2 Nov., 1777.
Ephraim Whitlock, 23 Nov., 1777.
Eden Burrowes, 4 Jan., 1778.

*2nd Lieutenants.*

Peter Lott. Promoted Lieut. 22 Jan., 1779.
Jonath. Snowden, 13 April, 1778. Promoted Lieut. 26 Oct., 1779.
Samuel Seely, 29 Oct., 1778.
Silas Perrott, 29 Oct., 1778.
Absalom Bonham, 1 Nov., 1778.

*Ensigns.*

Aaron Rhea, 12 Sept., 1778.
Asher Levi, 12 Sept., 1778. Resigned 14 June, 1779.
John Geary, 1 Feb., 1779.
John Bishop, 1 Feb., 1779.

---

INFANTRY. II New Jersey Regiment. Raised agreeable to a resolve of Congress of 9 October, 1775.

*Colonel.*

Israel Shreeve, 1 Jan., 1777.

*Lieut. Colonel.*

Will. Dehart, 1 Jan., 1777.

*Majors.*

Rich'd Howell, 1 Jan., 1777. Resigned 7 April, 1779.
John Ross, 7 April, 1779.

*Captains.*

John Hollingshead, 30 Nov., 1776. Promoted Major to 3rd, 5 July, 1779.
John Nob. Cumings, 30 Nov. ,1776.
Samuel Readings, 1 Jan., 1777.
Nath. Bowman, 11 April, 1777.
Jonath. Phillips, 1 Dec., 1777.
Will. Holmes, 1 Dec., 1777.

*Capt. Lieutenant.*

Samuel Hendry, 30 Nov., 1776. Promoted Capt. 5 July, 1779.

*Lieutenants.*

Samuel Nagles, 30 Nov., 1776.
Jonath. Holmes, 1 Jan., 1777.
Abel Weyman, 1 Nov., 1777.
Derrick Lane, 8 Nov., 1777.
Luther Halsay, 9 Nov., 1777.
John Peck, 10 Nov., 1777.
Sam'l Conn, 12 Nov., 1777.
Abrah. Stout, 1 Jan., 1778.
Abrah. Appleton, 1 Jan., 1778.

*2nd Lieutenants.*

Nath. Jenkins, 1 Jan., 1778.
John Shreeve, 11 July, 1777.
Sam'l Shute, 11 Sept., 1777.
Samuel Paul, 1 Dec., 1777.
Jonath. Rhea, 1 April, 1778.
Benj. Osmun, 12 Sept., 1778.
George Walker, 12 Sept., 1778.
Joseph Buck, 1 Feb., 1779.

---

INFANTRY. III New Jersey Regiment. Raised agreeable to a resolve of Congress of 9th October, 1775.

*Colonel.*

Elias Dayton, 9 Feb., 1776.

*Lieut. Colonel.*

Francis Barber, 1 Jan., 1777.

*Major.*

John Conway, 29 Oct., 1777. Promoted Lieut. Col. to 1st, 5th July, 1779.

*Captains.*

John Ross, 13 March, 1776.
Will. Gilford, 1 Jan., 1777.
Rich'd Cox, 1 Jan., 1777.
Jerem. Ballard, 26 Oct., 1777.
Joseph J. Anderson, 26 Oct., 1777.
Bateman Loyd, 12 Nov., 1777.

*Capt. Lieutenant.*

Seth Johnson, 2 Dec., 1777. Promoted Capt. 7 April, 1779.

*Lieutenants.*

Jonathan Dayton, 1 Jan., 1777. Promoted Capt. Lieut. 7 April, 1779.
Nath. Learnard, 1 Jan., 1777.
Edw'd D. Thomas, 11 Nov., 1777.
Sam'l Sheppard, 12 Nov., 1777.
Ephraim Darby, 12 Nov., 1777.

*2nd Lieutenants.*

John Blair. Promoted Lieut. 1 Nov., 1779.
Benj. Horn. Promoted Lieut. 1 Nov., 1779.
John Reed. Promoted Lieut. 1 Nov., 1779.
John Rencastle, 1 Nov., 1777. Promoted Lieut. 7 April, 1779.
Nath. Wilkinson, 1 Nov., 1777.
Will. Kersey, 1 Nov., 1777.
Jervis Bloomfield, 1 Nov., 1777.
Wessel T. Stout, 1 Nov., 1777.

*Ensigns.*

James Rogers, 1 Feb., 1779.
James Decamp, 1 Feb., 1779.
John Burhance. Resigned 8 Dec., 1779.

---

INFANTRY. I Pennsylvania Regiment, formed of eight companies of a rifle regiment raised by the State in 1775, and taken into Continental service, July, 1776, but retaining its rank from the time it was raised.

*Colonel.*

James Chambers, 28 Sept., 1776.

*Lieut. Colonel.*

Thomas Robinson, 7 June, 1777.

*Major.*

James Moor, 20 Sept., 1777.

*Captains.*

James Hamilton, 10 March, 1776.
Samuel Craig, 1 Oct., 1776.
Mich. Simpson, 1 Dec., 1776.
James Willson, 6 Jan., 1777.
Will. Willson, 2 March, 1777.
Aaron Norcross, 14 Sept., 1777. Resigned 12 May, 1779.

*Capt. Lieutenant.*

Thomas Buchanan, 1 Oct., 1777. Resigned 15 May, 1779.

*Lieutenants.*

David Zeigler, 16 Jan., 1777. Promoted Capt. 8 Dec., 1778.
Benj. Lyon, 16 July, 1777. Promoted Capt. Lieut. 8 Dec., 1778. Resigned 18 May, 1779.
John McClallan, 11 Sept., 1777. Promoted Capt. Lieut. and Capt. 1 Oct., 1779.
Thomas Boyd, 14 Jan., 1778. Killed.
John Hughs, 20 March, 1778. Promoted Capt. Lieut. 1 Oct., 1779.
James McFarland, 21 March, 1778.
Will. McDowell, 22 March, 1778.
Edwd. Crawford, 23 March, 1778
Andrew Johnson, 24 March, 1778. Promoted Lieut. 12 May, 1778.

*2nd Lieutenants.*

David Hammond, 14 Sept., 1777. Promoted Lieut. 12 May, 1779.
Joseph Collier, 18 April, 1777. Promoted Lieut. 17 May, 1779.
Benj. Chambers, 2 June, 1778. Promoted Lieut. 13 Sept., 1779.
Henry McCormick, 1 March, 1779.
Sam. Claypole, 2 March, 1779.
Mich. Hoffman, 28 May, 1779. Promoted Lieut. 1 Oct., 1779.
George Stevenson, 28 May, 1779.
James Campbel, 28 May, 1779.
Isaac Davis, 28 May, 1779.

---

INFANTRY. II Pennsylvania Regiment, raised agreeable to a resolve of Congress of 12 October, 1775, and called the 1st till July, 1776.

*Colonel.*

Walter Stewart, 17 June, 1777.

*Lieut. Colonel.*

John Murray, 10 Dec., 1778.

*Major.*

James Hamilton, 10 Dec., 1778.

*Captains.*

Jacob Ashmed, 6 Sept., 1776. Resigned.
John Bankson, 25 Sept., 1776.
Sam. Talber, 2 Oct., 1776.
John Patterson, 1 Jan., 1777.
Peter Gosner, 1 Jan., 1778.
John Cobea, 11 March, 1779.

*Capt. Lieutenant.*

John Irwin, 1 Jan., 1777. Promoted Capt. 16 May, 1779.

*Lieutenants.*

John Stoy, 1 Jan., 1777. Promoted Capt. 16 May, 1779.
Henry Piercy, 12 March, 1777.
James Whitehead, 12 March, 1777.
James Morris Jones, 12 March, 1777.
Will. Moor, 18 April, 1777.

*2nd Lieutenants.*

Philip Waggoner. Promoted Lieut. 11 March, 1779. Resigned 3 May, 1779.
John Gregg. Promoted Lieut. 12 March, 1779. Resigned.
Thos. Norton. Promoted Lieut. 12 March, 1779. Resigned.
John Park, 1 Aug., 1777. Promoted Lieut. 15 April, 1779.
John Stricker, 1 Oct., 1777. Promoted Lieut. 1 May, 1779.
Henry Purcell, 4 Oct., 1777. Promoted 3 Sept., 1779.

*Ensigns.*

Jacobus de Hart, 2 June, 1778. Promoted 16 May, 1779.
Will. Murran, 19 May, 1779.
John Tildon, 28 May, 1779.
Autrim de Marcellin, 28 July, 1779.
George le Roy, 28 July, 1779.

---

INFANTRY. III Pennsylvania Regiment, raised agreeable to a resolve of Congress of 9 December, 1775, and called 2nd till July, 1776.

*Colonel.*

Thomas Craig, 1 Aug., 1777.

*Lieut. Colonel.*

Will. Williams, 5 June, 1777.

*Major.*

Thomas L. Boyles, 8 June, 1777.

*Captains.*

Thomas L. Moore, 21 May, 1776. Promoted Major to 9th, 12 May, 1779.
James Cristie, 9 Aug., 1776.
Thomas Butler, 4 Oct., 1776.
John Riely, 20 May, 1777.
Isaac Bud Dunn, 1 June, 1777.
Will. Creig, 4 July, 1777. Resigned 1 June, 1779.
George McCally, 20 Oct., 1777.

*Capt. Lieutenant.*

George Henderson. Promoted Capt. 12 May, 1779.

*Lieutenants.*

John Marshall, 10 June, 1777. Promoted Capt. 18 June, 1779.
Dan'l St. Clair, 1 April, 1777.
Robert King, 20 May, 1777. Left out of the arrangement 23 June, 1779.
John Boyd, 20 May, 1777. Promoted 18 June, 1779.
Percival Butler, 1 Sept., 1777.
Blackwell Will. Ball, 11 Sept., 1778.
Andrew Engle, 20 Dec., 1778.

*2nd Lieutenant.*

John Armstrong, 11 Dec., 1777. Promoted Lieut. 12 May, 1779.

*Ensigns.*

Rich'd Fullerton, 19 June, 1778. Promoted Lieut. 18 June, 1779.
John Wigdon, 19 June, 1778. Promoted 18 June, 1779.
Peter Smith, 19 June, 1778. Promoted 18 June, 1779.
Thos. Huling, 19 June, 1778.
Robert Hamilton, 23 May, 1779.
Abrah. Kinney, 24 May, 1779.
Peter Cunningham, 1 July, 1779.
Henry Brower, 4 July, 1779.

---

INFANTRY. IV Pennsylvania Regiment, raised agreeable to a resolve of Congress of 9 December, 1775, and reckoned the 3rd till July, 1776.

*Colonel.*

Lambert Cadwallader. Resigned 22 Jan., 1779.

*Lieut. Colonel.*

Will. Butler, 30 Sept., 1776. Lieut. Col. Com. 22 Jan., 1779.

*Major.*

Thomas Church, 11 March, 1779.

*Captains.*

George Tudor, 13 May, 1776.
Adam Betting, 4 Oct., 1776.
Will. Grey, 3 Jan., 1777.
Benj. Fisbourne, 3 Jan., 1777.
John McGowen, 3 Jan., 1777.
George Steddiford, 12 Oct., 1777.
Will. Bicker, 15 May, 1778.
Will. Henderson, 16 May, 1778.
Benj. Bird. Resigned 11 May, 1779.
Edward Scull. Resigned 11 May, 1779.

*Capt. Lieutenant.*

David Brown. Promoted Captain 11 May, 1779.

*Lieutenants.*

Will. Sproat. Promoted Capt. Lieutenant 11 May, 1779.
Garret Steddiford, 12 Oct., 1777.
Thomas Campble, 3 Jan., 1778.
George Blewer, 3 Jan., 1778.
Arcurius Beatly, 2 June, 1778.
Peter Summers, 2 June, 1778.
Alexander Ramsey, 3 June, 1778.
George Boss, 4 June, 1778.

*2nd Lieutenants.*

Edward Fitz Randolph. Resigned 10 May, 1779.
Wilder Bevins. Promoted Lieutenant 11 May, 1779.
Matthew Petan. Promoted Lieutenant 11 May, 1779.

*Ensigns.*

John Pratt, 1 July, 1779.
Henry Henly, 2 July, 1779.
Andrew Henderson, 4 July, 1779.
Nathan Smith, 5 July, 1779.

INFANTRY. V Pennsylvania Regiment, raised agreeable to a resolve of Congress of 9 December, 1779, and reckoned the 4th till July, 1776.

*Colonel.*

Francis Johnson, 27 Sept., 1776.

*Lieut. Colonel.*

Francis Mentges, 9 Oct., 1778.

*Major.*

Christ. Steward, 28 Feb., 1777.

*Captains.*

Benj. Bartholmew, 2 Oct., 1776.
John Christie, 23 Oct., 1776.
Sam. Smith, 1 March, 1777.
Isaac Suly, 20 Sept., 1777.
Thomas Boude, 23 Sept., 1777.
Mich. Ryan, 23 Jan., 1778. Resigned 13 June, 1779.

*Capt. Lieutenant.*

John Vernon, 23 Jan., 1778. Promoted Captain 13 June, 1779.

*Lieutenants.*

John Barclay, 23 Oct., 1776. Promoted Capt. Lieutenant 13 June, 1779.
Levi Griffith, 1 June, 1777.
John Harper, 1 June, 1777.
George North, 1 June, 1777.
James McCulloch, 1 June, 1777.
Andrew Lytle, 20 June, 1777.

*Ensigns.*

David Marshall, 5 Nov., 1778. Promoted Lieut. 13 June, 1779.
John Bigham. Promoted Lieutenant 1 Feb., 1779.
Henry Hockley. Never joined.
Benj. Marshall, 21 April, 1779. Promoted Lieutenant 13 June, 1779.
James Gilchrist, 1 July, 1779.

---

INFANTRY. VI Pennsylvania Regiment, raised agreeable to a resolve of Congress of 9 December, 1775, reckoned the 5th till July, 1776.

*Colonel.*

Robert McGaw, 3 Jan., 1776.

*Lieut. Colonel.*

Josiah Harmer, 6 June, 1777.

*Major.*

Jeremiah Talbot, 25 Sept., 1777.

*Captains.*

John Nice, 13 June 1776.
John Doyle, 6 July, 1776.
Walter Finney, 10 Aug., 1776.
Robert Wilkie, 10 Oct., 1776.
Jacob Humphrie, 15 Feb., 1777.
Jacob Bower, 15 Feb., 1777.

*Capt. Lieutenant.*

Will. McElhaiton, 1 Oct., 1776. Transferred to Invalids 1 July, 1779.

*Lieutenants.*

Isaac Van Horn, 15 Feb., 1777. Promoted Capt. 1 July, 1779.
Edward Hovenden, 15 Feb., 1777.
James Gibbon, 15 Feb., 1777.
James Glentworth, 15 Feb., 1777.
Benj. Lodge, 11 Oct., 1777.
Stewart Herbert, 9 Jan., 1778.



*2nd Lieutenants.*

Francis McPherson. Promoted Lieutenant 15 Jan., 1779.
Thomas Doyle. Promoted Lieutenant 1 March, 1779.
Philip Gibbons, 17 Oct., 1777.
John Markland, 19 Oct., 1777. Promoted Lieutenant 1 July, 1779.
Edward Spear, 7 Feb., 1778.

*Ensigns.*

Thomas Dungan, 2 June, 1778.
Sanky Dixon, 2 Aug., 1779.
John Humphrey, 2 Aug., 1779.

---

INFANTRY. VII Pennsylvania Regiment.

*Colonel.*

Will. Irwine, 9 Jan., 1776. Promoted 12 May, 1779.

*Lieut. Colonel.*

Morgan Connor. Promoted Lieut. Colonel Commanding 12 May, 1779.

*Major.*

James Parr, 9 Oct., 1778.

*Captains.*

Will. Alexander, 1 June, 1776.
Will. Bratton, 12 Jan., 1777. Resigned 17 April, 1779.
Alex. Parker, 20 March, 1777.
John Alexander, 20 March, 1777.
Samuel Montgomery, 20 March, 1777.
Andrew Irwin, 25 Sept., 1777.

*Capt. Lieutenant.*

Will. Miller, 2 Feb., 1778. Promoted Captain 17 April, 1779.

*Lieutenants.*

Will. Lusk, 20 March, 1777. Promoted Capt. Lieutenant 17 April, 1779, and Captain 12 May, 1779.
Samuel Kennedy, 20 March, 1777. Promoted Capt. Lieutenant 12 May, 1779.
John Bush, 20 March, 1777.
Sam. Bryson, 20 March, 1777.
James McMichael, 20 June, 1777.
——— Williams. Resigned 16 April, 1779.
Robert McPherson, 1 Sept., 1777. Resigned 16 April, 1779.
Alex. Russel, 1 Sept., 1777. Resigned 16 April, 1779.
Joseph Torrence, 2 Feb., 1778. Resigned 15 April, 1779.

*2nd Lieutenants.*

Will. Blair, 20 Jan., 1777. Resigned.
James Williamson, 19 March, 1777. Resigned 6 April, 1779.
Robert Pebbles, 24 April, 1777. Promoted Lieutenant 16 April, 1779.
James Millegan, 1 Sept., 1777. Promoted Lieutenant 16 April, 1779.
John McCullom, 25 Sept., 1777. Promoted Lieutenant 16 April, 1779.
John Hughes, 25 Sept., 1777.

*Ensign.*

John Raniston, 24 July, 1779.

---

INFANTRY. VIII Pennsylvania Regiment, raised in consequence of a resolve of Congress of 15 July, 1776, for the defence of the frontier, seven companies in Westmoreland County and one in Bedford County. Capt. Moorhead's independent company was joined to this regiment this year.

*Colonel.*

Dan. Brodhead, 29 Sept., 1776.

*Lieut. Colonel.*

Stephen Bayard, 23 Sept., 1777.

*Major.*

Frederick Vernon, 7 June, 1777.

*Captains.*

——— Van Swerlngen, 9 Aug., 1776. Resigned 10 Aug., 1779.
Samuel Dawson, 16 July, 1776. Died 3 Sept., 1779.
James Fr. Moore, 24 Oct., 1776. Resigned 2 Aug., 1779.
John Clark, 28 Feb., 1777.
James Carnaghan, 18 April, 1777.
Joseph Finley, 20 Oct., 1777.
John Finley, 22 Oct., 1777.

*Capt. Lieutenant.*

Samuel Brady, 17 July, 1776. Promoted Capt. 25 Sept., 1779

*Lieutenants.*

Brasil Prather. Resigned 31 March, 1779.
John Crawford, 18 April, 1777.
John Harding, 13 July, 1777.
Gabriel Patterson, 26 July, 1776.
John Stotsbury, 9 April, 1777.
Benj. Neilley, 4 Oct., 1777.
Arch. Reed, 13 Dec., 1778

*2nd Lieutenants.*

Alex. Graham. Promoted 1 April, 1779. Resigned.
John Ward.

*Ensigns.*

John Guthrie, 21 Dec., 1778.
John Morrison, 21 Dec., 1778.
Thomas Wyatt, 21 Dec., 1778.
Will. Copper, 19 April, 1779.
Joshua Davidson, 19 April, 1779

---

INFANTRY. IX Pennsylvania Regiment, raised agreeable to a resolve of Congress of 16 September, 1775.

*Colonel.*

Richard Butler, 7 June, 1777.

*Lieut. Colonel.*

Caleb North, 22 Oct., 1777.

*Majors.*

Francis Nichols, 7 Feb., 1777. Resigned 12 May, 1779.
Thomas L. Moore, 12 May, 1779.

*Captains.*

Joseph McClelan, 15 July, 1776.
Thomas B. Bowen, 2 Sept., 1776.
John Davis, 15 Nov., 1776.
George Grant, 3 May, 1777. Died 10 Oct., 1779.
John Pearson, 7 Sept., 1777.
Will McKey, 30 Oct., 1777.

*Capt. Lieutenant.*

Will. Vanlear, 27 Jan., 1779. Promoted Capt. 10 Oct., 1779.

*Lieutenants.*

Stephen Stevenson, 16 March, 1778. Promoted Capt. Lieut. 10 Oct., 1779.
John McKinney, 18 March, 1778.
Will. Thompson, 16 June, 1778.

*Ensigns.*

Ephra. Douglass. Promoted Lieut. 27 Jan., 1779.
Edward Butler. Promoted Lieut. 28 Jan., 1779.
George Knox. Promoted Lieut. 9 Feb., 1779.
Abner Dunn, 31 March, 1779. Promoted Lieut. 31 May, 1779.
John Markland, 31 March, 1779. Promoted Lieut. 31 May, 1779.
Llewellin Davids, 31 March, 1779. Promoted Lieut. 10 Oct., 1779.
Robert Fortner, 31 March, 1779.
James Ennis, 31 March, 1779.

---

INFANTRY. X Pennsylvania Regiment, raised agreeable to resolve of Congress of 16 September, 1776.

*Colonel.*

Richard Hampton, 1 Oct., 1776.

*Lieut. Colonels.*

Adam Hubley, 4 Oct., 1776. Promoted Lieut. Col. Com. of 11th the 13 Feb., 1779.
Samuel Hay, 2 Feb., 1778.

*Major.*

James Grier, 23 Oct., 1777.

*Captains.*

George Calhoon, 13 Nov., 1776. Died 21 March, 1779.
James Long, 4 Dec., 1776. Resigned.
Robert Sample, 4 Dec., 1776.
Harman Stout, 4 Dec., 1776.
Jacob Weaver, 13 Jan., 1777.
Jacob Stake, 12 Nov., 1777.

*Capt. Lieutenant.*

John Steel, 27 May, 1778. Promoted Capt. 21 March, 1779.

*Lieutenants.*

Ebenezar Carson, 18 April, 1777. Promoted Capt. 1 April, 1779.
Robert Patton, 17 Oct., 1777. Promoted Capt. Lieut. 1 April, 1779.
Giles Hicks, 30 Oct., 1777.
Will. Feltman, 2 Nov., 1777.
Peter Drummond, 12 Nov., 1777.
Enos Reaves, 31 March, 1778.
Will. McMurry, 2 June, 1778. Promoted Capt. 1 April, 1779.
James Banks, 3 June, 1778.

*Ensigns.*

James McLean, 2 June, 1778. Promoted Lieut. 21 March, 1779.
Nicholas White, 2 June, 1778. Promoted Lieut. 2 Aug., 1779.
Robert Rice, 2 June, 1778. Broke.
John Hambright, 2 June, 1778. Resigned.
Robert Martin, 19 July, 1779.
Michael Everly, 1 Oct., 1779.

---

INFANTRY. XI Pennsylvania Regiment, formed the 13 January of this year by the junction of Col. Hartley's and Patten's regiments (except Capt. McClean's Company of the latter, annexed to the Delaware line), and some independent Companies raised in this State, but joined to Col. Malcolm's regiment, from which they were removed, and the 30 July Capt. Wilkins' independent Company was likewise joined to this regiment.

*Colonel.*

——— Hartley. Resigned 13 Jan., 1779.

*Lieut. Colonel.*
Adam Hubley, 13 Feb., 1779.

*Major.*
Evan Edwards, 10 Dec., 1778.

*Captains.*
George Bush, 13 Jan., 1777.
Laurance Keen, 13 Jan., 1777.
James Forrester, 12 Nov., 1777.
Andrew Walker, 23 Jan., 1778.
Abrah. Geor. Claypole, 10 June, 1778.
Isaac Sweeny, 23 July, 1778.
Henry Carbury, 30 Nov., 1778.
——— Davis. Killed 23 April, 1779.

*Lieutenants.*
Jerem. Jackson. Promoted Capt. Lieut. 13 April, 1779.
Septimus Davis, 7 July, 1777. Promoted Capt. Lieut. 13 April, 1779.
Edward Burk, 4 Oct., 1777.
Will. McCurdey, 12 Nov., 1777.
John Mahon, 1 June, 1778.
Will. Lemmon, 23 July, 1778.
Benj. Street, 30 Nov., 1778.

*2nd Lieutenants.*
Samuel Morrison. Promoted Lieut. 13 Feb., 1779.
James Pettigrew. Promoted Lieutenant 13 Feb., 1779.
Will. Huston, 2 June, 1778.
Jacob Wetzell, 2 April, 1779.

*Ensigns.*
Robert Allison, 1 Feb., 1778.
——— Thornburg, 2 Feb., 1778.
Sam. Reed, 5 Aug., 1779.
Henry Burley, 19 July, 1779.

---

Companies of RANGERS authorized under resolve of Congress of 25 Feb., 1779.

*Captains.*
Joseph Erwin, 7 April, 1779.
Thomas Camble, 7 April, 1779.
Thomas Clullage.

*1st Lieutenants.*
Alex. Parker, 7 April, 1779.
George Calhoon, 8 June, 1779.
John Jemison, 14 Aug., 1779.
George Groom.
Alex. Armstrong.

*2nd Lieutenants.*
Thomas Glass, 8 June, 1779.
Moses Danley, 26 June, 1779.
Henry Armstrong, 14 Aug., 1779.
Moses Donaldson.

---

INFANTRY. Delaware Regiment, raised agreeable to a resolve of Congress of 9 December, 1775.

*Colonel.*
David Hall, 4 Jan., 1777.

*Lieut. Colonels.*
Charles Pope. Resigned 13 Dec., 1779.
Joseph Vaughan, 14 Dec., 1779.

*Major.*
John Patten, 14 Dec., 1779.

*Captains.*
Robert Kirkwood, 1 Dec., 1776.
James Moore, 2 Dec., 1776.
James Larmonth, 4 Jan., 1777.
Peter Jaquet, 4 Jan., 1777.
John Willson, 15 Oct., 1777.
John Corse, 26 Jan., 1778.

*Lieutenants.*
John Rhodes. Promoted Capt. Lieutenant 1 March, 1779.
Will. McKannon, 4 Jan., 1777.
Dan. Powel Cox, 4 Jan., 1777.
George Purvis, 15 Oct., 1777.
Paul Quenoualt, 26 Jan., 1778.
Henry Duff, 7 Sept., 1778.
Caleb Brown, 7 Sept., 1778.
John Hyat, 7 Sept., 1778.

*2nd Lieutenants.*
James Campble. Promoted Lieutenant 1 March, 1779.
Caleb P. Bennet.
Joseph Horseman, 14 Aug., 1778.
Elijah Skillington, 7 Sept., 1778.
Charles Kidd, 7 Sept., 1778.
Edward Roche, 10 Sept., 1778.
Thomas Anderson, 10 Sept., 1778.
Steph. McWilliam, 27 Aug., 1779.

---

INFANTRY. I Maryland Regiment, raised by the State, and taken into Continental service 6 July, 1776.

*Colonel.*
John Hoskin Stone, 10 April, 1777. Resigned 1 Aug., 1779.

*Lieut. Colonel.*
Uriah Stone, 17 April, 1777. Removed to 7th, 1 Aug., 1779.

*Major.*
Levin Winder, 17 April, 1777.

*Captains.*
Alex. Roxburgh, 1 Jan., 1777.
Henry Geither, 17 April, 1777.
Edward Prawl, 10 June, 1777.
Walker Muse, 10 June, 1777.
John Jordan, 20 Dec., 1777.
James Peal, 1 March, 1778. Resigned 2 June, 1779.

*Capt. Lieutenant.*
James Fernandes, 1 March, 1778. Resigned 15 July, 1779.

*Lieutenants.*
John Mitchel, 10 June, 1777. Promoted Captain 15 July, 1779.
Will. Bruce, 10 June, 1777. Promoted Captain 1 Aug., 1779.
Charles Smith, 20 Feb., 1778. Promoted Capt. Lieutenant 1 Aug., 1779.
Richard Waters, 27 May, 1778.
John McPherson, 27 May, 1778.
James Simms, 27 May, 1778.
Arch. McCallster, 27 May, 1778.
Christ. Richmond, 27 May, 1778.

*2nd Lieutenants.*
Bignal Hillery, 10 April, 1777. Promoted 1st Lieutenant 1 Aug., 1779.
Will. Layman, 10 June, 1777.
Elihu Hall. Promoted 1st Lieutenant 15 July, 1779.
Vachel Burgess, 20 Feb., 1778. Resigned 22 Aug., 1779.

*Ensigns.*
Sam. Hanson, 24 July, 1777. Promoted 1st Lieutenant 15 July, 1779.
Edmond Compton, 27 May, 1779.
Arthur Harris, 27 Aug., 1779.
Edward Simms, 11 Sept., 1779.

INFANTRY. II Maryland Regiment, formed of seven independent companies of 100 men each, regimented and taken into Continental service 6 July, 1776.

*Colonel.*

Thomas Price, 1 Jan., 1777.

*Lieut. Colonel.*

Thomas Woolford, 17 April, 1777. Promoted Lieut. Col. Commandant to 5th, 22 Oct., 1779.

*Major.*

John Steward, 17 April, 1777.

*Captains.*

Sam. Turbot Wright, 1 Jan., 1777. Resigned 1 July, 1779.
John Davidson, 1 Jan., 1777.
Lilbern Williams, 17 April, 1777.
Richard Grace, 17 April, 1777.
Robert Chesley, 10 June, 1777.
John Gale, 10 Dec., 1777.

*Capt. Lieutenant.*

Ben. Price, 27 May, 1778. Promoted Capt. 1 July, 1779.

*Lieutenants.*

John Gassaway, 17 April, 1777. Promoted Capt. Lieutenant 1 July, 1779.
John Hardman, 17 April, 1777.
Edward Duvall, 17 April, 1777.
Edward Edgarly, 27 May, 1778.
Edward Dyer, 27 May, 1778.
James Erwine, 27 May, 1778.
James Winchester, 27 May, 1778.
John Road, 27 May, 1778. Resigned 11 April, 1779.

*2nd Lieutenants.*

Will. Woolford, 17 April, 1777. Promoted Lieutenant 11 April, 1779.
Philip Hill, 17 April, 1777.
Levasha de Vanbonne, 17 April, 1777.
Thomas Rouse, 17 April, 1777.
Hezek. Ford, 1 Sept., 1777.
Zedekiah Moore, 27 May, 1779.
Thomas Boyd, 27 Oct., 1779.

---

INFANTRY. III Maryland Regiment.

*Colonel.*

Mordecai Gist, 20 Jan., 1777. Promoted Brig. 9 Jan., 1779.

*Lieut. Colonel.*

Nathan Ramsey, 1 Jan., 1777.

*Major.*

Arch. Anderson, 10 June, 1777.

*Captains.*

Benj. Brooks, 1 Jan., 1777.
Joseph Marbury, 1 Jan., 1777.
Jacob Brice, 1 Jan., 1777.
John Smith, 1 Jan., 1777.
Sam'l Jones, 6 Aug., 1777.
Horatio Clagget, 10 Oct., 1777.
Will. Wilmot, 15 Oct., 1777.

*Capt. Lieutenant.*

George Armstrong, 12 Oct., 1778.

*Lieutenants.*

Henry Lyles, 20 Feb., 1777.
John Bailey, 20 Feb., 1777. Resigned 13 Nov., 1779.
Francis Revelly, 15 April, 1777.
Peter Clarke, 15 April, 1777. Resigned 13 July, 1779.
Nich. Manger, 15 Oct., 1777.

*2nd Lieutenants.*

Sam'l Farmer. Promoted Lt. 12 April, 1779.
Osburne Williams. Promoted Lt. 12 April, 1779.
Isaac Duval. Promoted Lt. 12 April, 1779.
John James, 10 April, 1777. Promoted Lt. 13 July, 1779.
John Carr, 10 April, 1777. Promoted Lt. 13 Nov., 1779.
Nicholas Gassaway, 10 April, 1777.

*Ensigns.*

Thomas Rice, 27 May, 1778.
Henry Baldwin, 27 May, 1778.
John McGuire, 27 May, 1778.

---

INFANTRY. IV Maryland Regiment.

*Colonel.*

Josias Carvill Hall, 1 Jan., 1777.

*Lieut. Colonel.*

Sam'l Smith, 20 Feb., 1777. Resigned 22 May, 1779.
Edward Tillard, 22 May, 1779.

*Major.*

John Dean, 11 March, 1778.

*Captains.*

Thomas Lansdale, 1 Jan., 1777.
Jonath. Selman, 1 Jan., 1777.
Edward Oldham, 20 May, 1777.
Will. Reiley, 15 Oct., 1777.
John Sprig Belt, 15 Dec., 1777.

*Capt. Lieutenant.*

Edw'd Spurrier. Promoted Capt. 21 May, 1779.

*Lieutenants.*

James Smith. Promoted Capt. Lieut. 21 May, 1779. Resigned 20 June, 1779.
Thomas Cromwell, 20 May, 1777. Promoted Capt. 20 July, 1779. Resigned 15 Dec., 1779.
Adam Hoops, 15 Oct., 1777. Promoted Capt. 15 Oct., 1779.
Stephen Shelmerdine, 19 Nov., 1777. Resigned 15 Dec., 1779.
Matth. Twining, 20 Nov., 1779. Resigned 1 Jan., 1779.
John Hamilton, 1 Feb., 1778.
John Colgate, 4 Aug., 1778.
Parker Hall Lee, 16 Oct., 1778.

*Ensigns.*

John Harshorn, 27 May, 1778. Promoted Lieut. 21 May, 1779.
John Hamilton, 27 May, 1778. Promoted Lieut. 1 June, 1779.
George Winchester. Promoted Lieut. 15 Sept., 1779.
Isaac Hamson, 8 Nov., 1779. Promoted Lieut. 15 Dec., 1779.
Nathan Smith, 18 Nov., 1779. Promoted Lieut. 15 Dec., 1779.

---

INFANTRY. V Maryland Regiment.

*Colonel.*

Will. Richardson, 1 Jan., 1777. Resigned 22 Oct., 1779.

*Lieut. Colonel.*

John Eager Howard, 11 March, 1778. Removed to 2nd, 22 Oct., 1779.

*Major.*

John Eccleston, 10 Dec., 1777.

*Captains.*

John Lynch, 1 Jan., 1777.
Levi Handy, 1 Jan., 1777.
John Hawkins, 20 Feb., 1777.
John Woolford Grey, 26 Dec., 1777.
George Hamilton, 25 Jan., 1778.
Perry Benson, 11 May, 1778.

*Lieutenants.*

Mark Benton. Promoted Capt. Lieut. 21 May, 1779. Resigned 1 June, 1779.
Rich'd Bird, 10 May, 1777. Promoted Capt. Lieut. 1 June, 1779, and Capt. 23 Oct., 1779.
Jonath. Gibson, 26 Jan., 1778. Promoted Capt. Lieut. 23 Oct., 1779.
Thos. Bogdon Hugo, 26 Jan., 1778.
James Gould, 11 March, 1778.
——— Coleman, 15 June, 1778.
Philip Read, 13 Oct., 1778.
Benj. Garrel, 13 Oct., 1778.

*Ensigns.*

Will. Freem'n Stoddart. Promoted Lieut. 21 May, 1779.
Arthur Harris. Promoted Lieut. 20 Sept., 1779.
James Wanlids, 27 May, 1778. Promoted Lieut. 20 Sept., 1779.

---

INFANTRY. VI Maryland Regiment.

*Colonel.*

Otho Hall Williams, 1 Jan., 1777.

*Lieut. Colonel.*

Benj. Ford, 17 April, 1777.

*Majors.*

Edward Tillard, 20 Feb., 1777. Promoted Lieut. Col. to 4th, 22 May, 1779.
Henry Hardman, 22 May, 1779.

*Captains.*

Harry Dobson, 1 Jan., 1777.
Will. Dent Beal, 1 Jan., 1777.
Alex. Freeman, 1 Jan., 1777.
John Ghiselin, 4 July, 1777. Resigned 1 June, 1779.
John Smith, 9 Nov., 1777.
Christ. Orendorff, 1 April, 1778.

*Capt. Lieutenant.*

James Somervil. Promoted Capt. 1 June, 1779.

*Lieutenants.*

Nathan Williams, 1 April, 1777. Promoted Capt. Lieut. 1 June, 1779.
John Jerem. Jacobs, 7 Oct., 1777.
James Bruff, 7 Oct., 1777.
Rich'd Donovan, 1 April, 1778.
George Jacobs, 14 Sept., 1778.
Jacob Norris, 26 Nov., 1778.

*Ensigns.*

Charles Bevin. Promoted Lieut. 18 May, 1779.
Edmond Moran. Promoted Lieut. 21 May, 1779.
John Lynn, 26 May, 1779. Promoted Lieut. 1 June, 1779.
Will. Murdoch, 11 Sept., 1779.
Sam'l Hamilton, 27 May, 1779.

INFANTRY. VII Maryland Regiment.

*Colonel.*

John Gunby, 17 April, 1777.

*Lieut. Colonel.*

Peter Adams, 20 Feb., 1777. Promoted Lieut. Col. Command't to 1st, 1 Aug., 1779.

*Major.*

Dan. Jenifer Adams, 10 April, 1777. Resigned 8 June, 1779.

*Captains.*

Henry Hardman, 1 Jan., 1777. Promoted Major to 6th, 22 May, 1779.
Adam Grosh, 1 Jan., 1777. Promoted to 7th, 8 June, 1779.
Jonath. Morris, 14 April, 1777.
In's Courts Jones, 20 Sept., 1777.
Rich'd Anderson, 15 Nov., 1777.
Will. Beaty, 14 Sept., 1778.

*Lieutenants.*

David Lynn. Promoted Capt. Lieut. 18 May and Capt. 22 May, 1779.
Thomas Meason. Promoted Capt. Lieut. 22 May and Capt. 8 June, 1779.
Lloyd Beal. Promoted Lieut. 8 June, 1779.
Will. Lamar, 15 Nov., 1777.
Peter Hardcastle, 14 Sept., 1778.
Edward Wright, 14 Sept., 1778.
Gassaway Watkins, 14 Sept., 1778.
Jas. John Skinner, 14 Sept., 1778.
James Bracco, 14 Sept., 1778.

*2nd Lieutenants.*

Thomas Mason, 1 July, 1777. Promoted Lieut. 17 April, 1779.
Charles Porter, 7 July, 1777. Promoted Lieut. 22 May, 1779.
Will. Adams, 14 April, 1778. Promoted Lieut. 8 June, 1779.

*Ensigns.*

Patrick Donnely, 27 May, 1778. Promoted Lieut. 7 Oct., 1779.
Robert Denny, 27 May, 1778.
Edward Wright. Resigned 8 Oct., 1779.

---

INFANTRY. I Virginia Regiment.

*Colonel.*

Richd. Parker, 10 Feb., 1778.

*Lieut. Colonel.*

Burgess Ball, 17 Dec., 1777.

*Major.*

Richd. C. Anderson, 10 Feb., 1778.

*Captains.*

Will. Lewis, 6 Aug., 1776.
Charles Pelham, 11 Nov., 1776.
Clayburn N. Lawson, 18 Oct., 1777.
Callohil L. Minnis, 18 Nov., 1777.
Tarlton Payne, 4 Feb., 1778.
Curtis Kendall, 26 May, 1778.

*Capt. Lieutenant.*

James Cuthbertson, 7 Nov., 1776. Promoted Capt. 12 May, 1779.

*Lieutenants.*

Holman Mines, 2 Jan., 1777. Promoted Capt. 25 June, 1779.
Arch. Denholm, 9 Aug., 1777. Promoted Capt. Lieut. 25 June, 1779.
Francis Minnis, 9 Aug., 1777.

Philip Sansum, 15 Sept., 1777.
Joseph Scott, 4 Oct., 1777.
Thomas Brown, 18 Oct., 1777.
Samuel Hoggs, 18 Dec., 1777.
Marks Vanduvall, 4 Feb., 1778.
Thomas Overton, 9 March, 1778.

*2nd Lieutenants.*

Matthew Clay, 16 March, 1777. Promoted Lieut. 25 June, 1779.
Ballard Smith, 9 Aug., 1777. Promoted Lieut. 22 July, 1779.
James Soldon, 15 Sept., 1777.
Thomas Holt, 4 Oct., 1777.
John Steel, 26 May, 1778.

*Ensigns.*

Jacob Brown, 15 Sept., 1779.
Philip Coastney, 4 July, 1779.

---

INFANTRY. II Virginia Regiment.

*Colonel.*

Christ. Fibiger, 26 Sept., 1777.

*Lieut. Colonel.*

Charles Simms, 12 July, 1777. Resigned 7 Dec., 1779.

*Majors.*

Thomas Massey, 20 Feb., 1778. Resigned 25 June, 1779.
Charles Pelham, 25 June, 1779.

*Captains.*

John Willis, 15 June, 1776.
Will. Taylor, 21 Nov., 1776. Promoted Major to 9th, 7 Dec., 1779.
John P. Harrison, 4 May, 1777.
Alex. Parker, 1 June, 1777.
Benj. Talliaferro, 23 Sept., 1777.
John Stokes, 20 Feb., 1778.

*Capt. Lieutenant.*

Thomas Callet, 26 Nov., 1776. Promoted Capt. 8 March, 1779.

*Lieutenants.*

John Worsham, 13 Jan., 1777. Promoted Capt. Lieut. 8 March, 1779. Died.
Colin Cache, 2 Feb., 1777. Promoted Capt. 9 Dec., 1779.
Francis Coward. Promoted Capt. Lieut. 9 Dec., 1779.
Valentine Harndan, 13 June, 1777.
Henry Moss, 11 July, 1777.
Beverly Stubblefield, 7 Aug., 1777.
John Jordan, 3 Sept., 1777.
Francis Parker, 13 Oct., 1777.
James Mahoon, 23 Dec., 1777.

*2nd Lieutenants.*

John Crawford, 4 May, 1777. Promoted Lieut.
Will. Eskridge, 15 June, 1777. Promoted Lieut.
Will. Porter, 15 June, 1777.
John Cannon, 9 Sept., 1778. Superseded.
Rodham Moxley, 9 Sept., 1778.

*Ensigns.*

Peter Field Archer, May, 1778.
John Coleman, 4 July, 1779.
Payton Powel, 4 July, 1779. Returned to 7th.
George Blackmore, 4 July, 1779.
Will. Brodace, 25 Sept., 1779.
George Washington.

INFANTRY. III Virginia Regiment.

*Colonel.*

Will. Heath, 30 April, 1778.

*Lieut. Colonel.*

Thomas Gaskins, 16 May, 1778.

*Major.*

James Lucas, 23 April, 1778.

*Captains.*

Robert Powhl, 26 Dec., 1776. Resigned.
Will. Fowler, 1 April, 1777. Resigned.
John Fr. Mercer, 27 June, 1777. Resigned.
John Anderson, 12 Aug., 1777.
John Blackwell, 15 Sept., 1777.
Valentine Payton, 4 Oct., 1777.

*Capt. Lieutenant.*

Will. Bentley, 26 Dec., 1776. Promoted Capt. 1779.

*Lieutenants.*

Robert Beale, 11 Feb., 1777. Promoted Capt. 19 June, 1779.
Leroy Edwards, 21 Feb., 1777. Promoted Capt. 19 June, 1779.
John Fitzgerald, 1 April, 1777.
John Hawkins, 11 Sept., 1777.
Will. Moore, 28 Oct., 1777.
Arthur Lynd, 8 Nov., 1777.
Beverly Roy, 28 Nov., 1777.
Nath. Anderson, 21 Dec., 1777.
Obadiah Smith, 12 Feb., 1778. Resigned.

*2nd Lieutenants.*

Robert Levingston, 1 April, 1777.
David Miller, 21 Dec., 1777. Promoted Lieut. 1779.
Will. Stephens, 21 Dec., 1777. Promoted Lieut. 19 June, 1779.
David Allen, 10 May, 1778. Promoted Lieut. 19 June, 1779.
John Roney, 9 Sept., 1778.
Lipscomb Norvill, 9 Sept., 1778.

*Ensigns.*

Phil. Clayton, 4 July, 1779.
James Delaplane, 4 July, 1779.

---

INFANTRY. IV Virginia Regiment.

*Colonel.*

John Nevill, 11 Dec., 1777.

*Lieut. Colonels.*

Robert Ballard, 4 Oct., 1777. Resigned 4 July, 1779.
Samuel Jordan Cable, 15 Dec., 1778.

*Major.*

Will. Croghan, 16 May, 1778.

*Captains.*

George Wallis, 27 Sept., 1776. Resigned.
John Stitch, 12 March, 1777.
Jason Riddick, 10 June, 1777.
Abrah. Kerkpatrick, 10 Aug., 1777.
Isaac Israel, 23 Nov., 1777. Dismissed for non attendance.
John Steed, 30 March, 1778.

*Capt. Lieutenant.*

Leond. Cooper, 10 May, 1777. Promoted Capt., 1779.

*Lieutenants.*

James Curry, 24 Sept., 1777. Promoted Capt. 23 Sept., 1779.

Will. Lovely, 25 Sept., 1777. Promoted Capt. Lieut. 23 Sept., 1779.
Edwd. Allen, 4 Oct., 1777.
John Willson, 1 April, 1778.
James Morton, 1 April, 1778.
Robt. Brackenridge, 4 April, 1778.

*2nd Lieutenants.*

Peter Higgins, 4 Oct., 1777. Promoted Lieut.
Philip Hoffman, 2 Nov., 1777. Promoted Lieut. 9 March, 1779.
Benj. Lawson, 3 March, 1778. Promoted Lieut.
Philip Easton. Promoted Lieut. 10 Aug., 1779.
Thos. Miller, 4 April, 1778. Promoted Lieut. 23 Sept., 1779.
Will. Dennis Kelly, 9 Sept., 1778.

*Ensigns.*

Martin Carney, 9 Sept., 1778.
Javan Miller, 4 July, 1779.
Robert Keys, 4 July, 1779.
Will. Scott, 4 July, 1779.

---

INFANTRY. V Virginia Regiment.

*Colonel.*

Will. Russell, 19 Dec., 1776.

*Lieut. Colonel.*

Holt Richardson, 18 Oct., 1777. Resigned 10 May, 1779.

*Major.*

John Webb, 26 Jan., 1778. Promoted Lieut. Col. to 5th, 4 July, 1779.

*Captains.*

Thomas Hill, 13 Nov., 1776. Promoted Maj. to 5th, 4 July, 1779.
Will. Mosely, 13 Dec., 1776.
Henry Young, 20 Dec., 1776.
James Baytop, 11 Dec., 1777. Resigned.
Adam Wallace, 29 June, 1778.
Thomas Buckner, 3 Oct., 1778.

*Capt. Lieutenant.*

Mayo Carrington, 3 Oct., 1778. Promoted Capt. 12 May, 1779.

*Lieutenants.*

Will. White, 28 September, 1777. Promoted Capt. 4 July, 1779.
Henry Warring, 10 Oct., 1777. Resigned 29 Aug., 1779.
Tarpley White. Promoted Capt. Lieut. 29 Aug., 1779.
John Lapsley, 3 April, 1778. Resigned 7 May, 1779.
Rich'd Coleman, 20 May, 1778.
John Nelson, 20 May, 1777.
Thomas Quirk.
Isaac Webb, 30 Oct., 1778.

*2nd Lieutenants.*

Rich'd Stark, 1 Feb., 1777. Promoted Lieut. 7 May, 1779.
Robert Jowel, 28 Sept., 1777. Promoted Lieut. 12 May, 1779.
John White, 30 April, 1778. Promoted Lieut. 4 July, 1779.
Henry Vowels, 9 Sept., 1778. Resigned 10 May, 1779.
Matth. Ray, 9 Sept., 1778. Promoted Lieut. 4 July, 1779.
Benj. Mosely, 10 Sept., 1778. Promoted 29 Aug., 1779.

*Ensign.*

Isaac Jefferies, 25 May, 1779.

INFANTRY. VI Virginia Regiment.

*Colonel.*

John Greene, 26 Jan., 1778.

*Lieut. Colonel.*

Sam'l Hewes, 1 March, 1777.

*Major.*

Thomas Ridley, 1 March, 1777.

*Captains.*

John Gillison, 17 Feb., 1777.
Richd. Stevens, 18 Feb., 1777.
Pugh Woodson, 2 Sept., 1777.
Clough Skelton, 13 Jan., 1778.
Nath. Lamme, 18 Sept., 1778.

*Capt. Lieutenant.*

James Williams, 1 March, 1777. Promoted Capt. 10 Sept., 1778.

*Lieutenants.*

Thomas Hord, 1 March, 1777. Promoted Capt. Lieut. 10 Sept., 1778.
Thomas Barbee, 22 Sept., 1778.
Thomas Fox, 30 Oct., 1777.
Joseph Blackwell, 30 Nov., 1777.
James Hamilton, 13 Jan., 1778.
Will. Evins, 10 Sept., 1778.
Sam'l Basherville, 14 Sept., 1778.
Thomas Pearson, 14 Sept., 1778.

*2nd Lieutenants.*

John Hackley, 10 July, 1777. Promoted Lieut. 14 Sept., 1779.
Nicholas Talliaferro, 20 Oct., 1777.
John Robinson, 9 Sept., 1778.
Charles Jones, 9 Sept., 1778.
Will. Smith, 9 Sept., 1778.

---

INFANTRY. VII Virginia Regiment.

*Colonel.*

Dan. Morgan, 12 Nov., 1776.

*Lieut. Colonel.*

John Cropper, 26 Oct., 1777.

*Major.*

Thomas Pasey, 30 April, 1778.

*Captains.*

Gabriel Long, 23 July, 1776. Resigned 13 May, 1779.
Peter Bruin, 13 Dec., 1776.
Charles Porterfield, 3 Feb., 1777. Resigned 2 July 1779.
Will. Johnson, 19 Feb., 1777.
John Marshall, 1 July, 1777.

*Capt. Lieutenant.*

Philip Slaughter, 1 Nov., 1778. Promoted Capt. 13 May, 1779.

*Lieutenants.*

Josiah Marks, 15 March, 1777. Promoted Capt. 13 May, 1779.
James Wright, 25 March, 1777. Promoted Capt. 2 July, 1779.
Robert Porterfield, 1 June, 1777. Promoted Capt. Lieut. 2 July, 1779.
Thomas Ransdell, 1 July, 1777.
John Towns, 1 July, 1777.
Timothy Feeby, 6 Nov., 1778.

*2nd Lieutenants.*

Benj. Ashbey, 1 June, 1777. Promoted Lieut. 13 March, 1779.

John Hughs. Promoted Lieut. 25 April, 1779.
Reuben Long, 1 June, 1777. Promoted Capt. 10 May, 1779.
John Barns, 7 Nov., 1778. Promoted Lieut. 13 May, 1779.

*Ensigns.*

David Williams, 1 July, 1777. Promoted Lieut. 2 July, 1779.
Robert Rankins, 4 July, 1777.
Samuel Phillips, 4 July, 1777.
Spencer Morgan, 4 July, 1777.
John Lee, 4 July, 1777.
Payton Powel, 4 July, 1779.

---

INFANTRY. VIII Virginia Regiment.

*Colonel.*

James Wood, 12 Nov., 1776.

*Lieut. Colonel.*

Jonath. Clark, 10 May, 1779.

*Major.*

Andrew Waggoner, 15 Dec., 1778.

*Captains.*

William Voss, 9 Feb., 1777.
Andr. Wallace, 13 March, 1777.
Thomas Boyer, 5 April, 1777.
Benj. Casey, 1 Sept., 1777. Resigned.
Robert Gamble, 7 March, 1778.

*Capt. Lieutenant.*

Prasley Neville, 9 Nov., 1776. Promoted Capt. 10 May, 1779.

*Lieutenants.*

Abraham Hite, 12 Feb., 1777. Promoted Capt. 14 April, 1779.
Joseph Swaringer, 1 March, 1777. Promoted Capt. Lieut. 14 April, 1779.
Conway Oldham, 20 April, 1777.
Sigismond Stribling, 19 May, 1777.
Hezekiah Morton, 30 Aug., 1777.
Robert White, 1 Sept., 1777.
David Williams, 7 March, 1778.
John McDowel, 7 Sept., 1778.

*2nd Lieutenants.*

Will. Foster, 20 May, 1777. Promoted Lieut. 14 April, 1779.
Will. Porter, 30 Aug., 1777. Promoted Lieut. 14 April, 1779.
Albert Russel. Promoted Lieut. 15 Dec., 1779.

*Ensigns.*

John Bowen, 10 Sept., 1777.
Henry Bowyer, 15 Nov., 1777.
Will. Bayles, 9 Sept., 1778.
Jos. Hite, 10 Sept., 1778.
Thos. Wallace, 2 June, 1779.
Edwd. Williams, 4 July, 1779. Resigned 30 Dec., 1779.
Joseph Vanmetre, 4 July, 1779.
Will. Spencer, 25 Sept., 1779.
Lovet Harrison, 25 Sept., 1779.

---

INFANTRY. IX Virginia Regiment.

*Colonel.*

John Gibson, 25 Oct., 1777.

*Lieut. Colonel.*

Richard Campbell, 20 Feb., 1778.

*Major.*

Richd. Taylor, 4 Feb., 1778. Promoted Lieut. Col. to 2nd, 7 Dec., 1779.

*Captains.*

Robert Bell, 15 Dec., 1776.
Benj. Harrison, 16 Dec., 1776.
Thos. Moore, 23 Jan., 1778.
Simon Morgan, 15 March, 1778.
Robert Vance, 19 Aug., 1778.
Uriah Springer, 25 Aug., 1778.

*Capt. Lieutenant.*

Benj. Beggs, 7 Nov., 1778.

*Lieutenants.*

George Berry, 16 Dec., 1776.
Arthur Gorden, 19 Dec., 1776.
Lewis Thomas, 19 Dec., 1776.
John Harrison, 1 Oct., 1778.
Andrew Lewis, 2 Oct., 1778.
Laurence Harrison, 3 Oct., 1777.

*2nd Lieutenants.*

Ephraim Ralph. Promoted Lieut. 5 April, 1779.
John Dent. Promoted Lieut. 6 April, 1779.

*Ensigns.*

Jacob Springer, 31 Oct., 1778.
Henry Dawson, 31 Oct., 1778.
John Beck, 31 Oct., 1778.
Jacob Coleman, 5 April, 1779.
Will. Conner, 6 April, 1779.
Joseph Wenlock, 6 April, 1779.
John Mills, 6 April, 1779.
Josiah Tannehill, 6 April, 1779.

---

INFANTRY. X Virginia Regiment.

*Colonel.*

Will. Davis, 20 March, 1778.

*Lieut. Colonel.*

Samuel Hopkins, 19 June, 1778.

*Major.*

Will. Lewis, 12 May, 1779.

*Captains.*

Nathan Reed, 28 Jan., 1777.
Drury Oliver, 10 March, 1777. Resigned 7 May, 1779.
John Marks, 15 March, 1777.
John Winstone, 17 March, 1777.
Peter Jones, 10 April, 1777.
John Overton, 4 Oct., 1777.

*Capt. Lieutenant.*

Thomas Holt, 10 March, 1777. Promoted Capt. 12 March, 1779.

*Lieutenants.*

Nathan Terry. Promoted Capt. Lieut. 12 March, 1779.
Will. Epps, 30 Aug., 1777.
George Holland, 4 Oct., 1777.
Abrah. Maury, 8 Oct., 1777.
John B. Johnston, 1 Feb., 1778.
David Walker, 2 March, 1778.

*2nd Lieutenants.*

Alex. Ewing. Promoted Lieut. 14 Feb., 1779.
Richd. Worsham, 13 Nov., 1777. Promoted Lieut. 12 March., 1779.
David Merewether, 8 Dec., 1777. Promoted Lieut. 7 May, 1779.
Will. Pointer, 8 Dec., 1777.
Joseph Conway, 22 Dec., 1777.
Thomas Burfoot, 9 Sept., 1778.

*Ensigns.*

Simpson Foster, 4 July, 1779.
Elisha King, 4 July, 1779.

INFANTRY. XI Virginia Regiment.

*Colonel.*

Abrah. Buford, 16 May, 1778.

*Lieut. Colonel.*

Gustav. B. Wallace, 20 March, 1778.

*Major.*

David Stephenson, 4 May, 1778.

*Captains.*

John Gregory, 23 Feb., 1777.
James Grey, 16 March, 1777.
Thomas Edmonds.
Thomas Willis, 21 July, 1777.
Sam. Booker, 1 Aug., 1777.
David Mason, 20 April, 1778. Resigned 14 May, 1779.

*Capt. Lieutenant.*

Laurence Butler, 18 March, 1777. Promoted Capt. 14 May, 1779.

*Lieutenants.*

Robert Maibries, 19 March, 1777. Promoted Capt. Lieut. 14 May, 1779.
Thomas Lewis, 20 March, 1777.
Richd. Muse, 20 March, 1777. Resigned 14 May, 1779.
Will. Smith, 20 March, 1777.
Philip Mallary, 1 April, 1778.
Samuel Jones, 1 April, 1778.
James Craine, 1 April, 1778.
Binns Jones, 1 April, 1778.

*2nd Lieutenants.*

John Chrittendon, 21 July, 1777. Promoted Lieut. 14 May, 1779.
John Eppes Scott, 21 July, 1777. Promoted Lieut. 14 May, 1779.
Charles Stewart, 24 July, 1777.
Thos. Davis, 1 Aug., 1777.
James Holt, 1 April, 1778.
Luke Cannon, 1 April, 1778.
Albridgston Jones, 9 Sept., 1778.

*Ensign.*

Robert Craddock, 25 Sept., 1779.

---

INFANTRY. I North Carolina Regiment, raised by the State, and taken into Continental service 28 Nov., 1775.

*Colonel.*

Thomas Clark, 5 Feb., 1777.

*Lieut. Colonel.*

Robert Mebane, 26 Nov., 1776. Promoted Lieut. Colonel Command't to 3rd Reg., 9 June, 1779.

*Major.*

John Baptist Ash, 26 Jan., 1777.

*Captains.*

Jno. Griffith McRee, 16 April, 1776.
Joseph Bowman, 18 Sept., 1776.
Tilman Dixon, 5 Feb., 1777.
Howel Tatum, 3 April, 1777.
James Read, 8 July, 1777.
John Summers, 10 July, 1778.
John Gambier Scull, 26 April, 1777.

*Capt. Lieutenant.*

James Verner, 8 May, 1777.

*Lieutenants.*

James King, 3 April, 1777.
Robert Nicholson, 19 April, 1777. Resigned.
Thomas Callender, 8 July, 1777.
Will. Walton, 15 Aug., 1777.
James Craven, 29 Aug., 1777. Broke 20 Nov., 1779.
Peter Bacot, 4 Oct., 1777.
George Cook, 10 July, 1778.

*Ensigns.*

Dixon Marshall, 26 April, 1777.
Will. Slade, 26 April, 1777.
Dan. Shaw, 11 April, 1777.
Rich'd Dickenson, 12 April, 1777. Broke 20 Nov., 1779.
Thomas Pasteur, 29 Dec., 1777.
Robert Hays, 1 Jan., 1778.
David Right, 15 Feb., 1778.
Will. Hargrave, 16 Feb., 1778.

---

INFANTRY. II North Carolina Regiment, raised by the State, and taken into Continental service 28 Nov., 1775.

*Colonel.*

John Pàtten, 22 Nov., 1777.

*Lieut. Colonel.*

Selby Harney, 22 Nov., 1777.

*Major.*

Hardy Murphrie, 1 Jan., 1777.

*Captains.*

Benj. Williams, 19 July, 1776.
Clement Hall, 19 April, 1777.
Benj. Coleman, 30 April, 1777.
Robert Fenner, 20 May, 1777.
John Ingles, 24 Oct., 1777.
Thomas Armstrong, 25 Oct., 1777.

*Capt. Lieutenant.*

John Craddock, 21 Dec., 1777.

*Lieutenants.*

Nicholas Steward, 30 April, 1777.
Thomas Evans, 15 May, 1777.
John Davis, 4 Oct., 1777.
Jesse Reed, 25 Oct., 1777.
Saml. Budd, 11 Nov., 1777.
James Campen, 21 Dec., 1777.
Anth. Cotgrave, 26 March, 1778.
Charles Gerrard, 1 June, 1778.

*Ensigns.*

Will. Terrill, 8 Sept., 1777.
Rich'd Andrews, 1 Nov., 1777.
Thomas Finney, 12 Nov., 1777.
Nath. Lawrence, 4 Sept., 1778.
Rich'd Masson, 4 Sept., 1778.
Stephen Slade, 5 Sept., 1778.

---

INFANTRY. III North Carolina Regiment, raised agreeable to a resolve of Congress of 16 Jan., 1776.

*Colonel.*

James Hogun, 26 Nov., 1776. Promoted Brig. 9 Jan., 1779.

*Lieut. Colonel.*

Will. Lee Davidson, 4 Oct., 1777. Removed to 1st Regt. 9 June, 1779.

*Majors.*

Thomas Hogg, 19 Oct., 1777.

*Captains.*

Francis Child, 26 Jan., 1777.
Reading Blount, 16 April, 1776.
John Baker, 6 July, 1777.

Michael Quinn, 1 Aug., 1777.
Keder Ballard, 4 Oct., 1777.
George Boadley, 19 Sept., 1778.

*Capt. Lieutenant.*

Joseph Montfoot. Promoted Capt. 9 Jan., 1779.

*Lieutenants.*

Edward Yarborough. Promoted Capt. Lieut. 9 Jan., 1779.
James Campbell, 19 April, 1777.
James Powers, 20 April, 1777.
Will. Turbee, 6 July, 1777.
Will. Fawn, 4 Oct., 1777.
John McNas, 20 Nov., 1777.
Anth. Hart, 22 Nov., 1777.
John Clandenin, 23 Dec., 1777.
Thos. Allen, 17 March, 1778.

*Ensigns.*

Reubin Wilkinson, 1 May, 1777.
Robert Connill, 20 Aug., 1777.
Francis Graves, 26 Oct., 1777.
Curtis Ivory, 19 Dec., 1777.
James Tetum, 1 Jan., 1778.
James Verrier, 17 March, 1778.
James Wallis, 30 Nov., 1778.
John Ford, 30 Nov. 1778.

---

INFANTRY. I South Carolina Regiment, raised by the State, and taken into Continental service 4 Dec., 1775.

*Capt. Lieutenant.*

Levaliet de St. Marie. Promoted Capt. 9 Oct., 1779.

*Lieutenant.*

Will. Jackson. Promoted Capt. 9 Oct., 1779.

---

INFANTRY. A Regiment first raised in Canada, in consequence of a resolve of Congress, of 8 January, 1776, and for some time called 1st Canada Regiment.

*Colonel.*

James Levingston.

*Lieut. Colonel.*

Rich'd Levingston.

*Major.*

George C. Nicholson.

*Captains.*

Abran. Levingston.
Robert Wright.
Peter Van Ranselear.
Dirk Hanson.
John Robickhearse.
John Bap. Allen. Broke.
Augustin Loiseau. Broke Jan., 1779.

*Lieutenants.*

Anthony Welp.
Francis Monte.
Peter F. Vosburgh.
Will. Wallace.
Isaac Nichols.

*2nd Lieutenant.*

Peter Rutan.

*Ensigns.*

Will. Belknap.
John Gates.
Ezekiel Cooke.

*Chaplain.*

Louis Lotbiniere, 26 Jan., 1775.

INFANTRY. A regiment intended to be raised in Canada, agreeable to a resolve of Congress, of 20 January, 1776, and for some time called the 2nd Canada Regiment; another resolve 24 September, 1776, directed it should be recruited in the United States.

*Colonel.*

Moses Hazen, 22 Jan. 1776.

*Lieut. Colonel.*

Edw'd Antil. 22 Jan., 1776.

*Majors.*

John Torrey.
Tarlton Woodson.
James R. Reid. Appointed Capt. 8 April, 1777.

*Captains.*

Will. Satterlee.
Matth. McConnell, 8 April, 1777.
Will. Popham, 8 April, 1777.
James Heron, 8 April, 1777.
Robert Burns, 8 April, 1777.
Laur. Olivia.
Philip Liebart.
John Carlisle, 8 April, 1777.
Moses White.
Will. Monson.
Mich. Gilbert. Appointed 1st Lieut. 8 April, 1777.
Rich'd Loyde.
Thol. Pry. Appointed 1st Lieut. 8 April, 1777.
Reuben Taylor. Appointed 1st Lieut. 8 April, 1777.
James Duncan. Appointed 1st Lieut. 8 April, 1777.
John Hughes. Appointed 1st Lieut. 8 April, 1777.
Anthony Pauland.
Clement Goslain.

*Lieutenants.*

Thomas Bell.
Palmer Cadey.
Joseph Lewis.
Murdoch McPherson.
James Anderson. Appointed Ensign 8 April, 1777.
Germaine Dionne.
Mich. Montgomery.
Noah Lee.

*Ensigns.*

Alex. Feriole.
Laur. Marming.
Benj. Moers.
Francis Gilmand.
Samuel Sanford.
Lewis Goslain.
Pierre Boileau.
Andrew Lee.
David Fellows.
Foelix Victor.

---

INFANTRY. German Battalion raised agreeable to a resolve of Congress of 25 May, 1776. Four companies in Pennsylvania, and four in Maryland, to which was added a ninth company, by a resolve of 9 July, 1777.

*Lieut. Colonel.*

Ludwick Weltener.

*Major.*

Dan'l Burchart, 9 April, 1777. Resigned 2 July, 1779.

*Captains.*

Jacob Bunner, 8 July, 1776.
Peter Boyer, 9 May. 1777.

Charles Baltzel.
Will. Rice, 4 Jan., 1778.
Bernard Hubley. 24 Feb., 1778.
Christian Myers, 12 March, 1778.
Michael Bayer, 25 May, 1778.

*Capt. Lieutenant.*

Philip Schrauder, 8 Feb., 1778.

*Lieutenants.*

John Weidman, 14 May, 1777.
Martin Sugart, 15 Nov., 1777.
Jacob Gremeth, 4 Jan., 1778.
Jacob Cramer. 24 Feb., 1778.
Godfrey Swartz 1 March, 1778.
Marcus Young, 12 March, 1778.
David Morgan, 8 April, 1778.

*Ensigns.*

John Weidman, 14 May, 1777. Promoted Lieut. 8 Feb., 1779.
Henry Shrupp. Resigned 3 July, 1779.
David Desenderfer, 24 July, 1778.
Henry Speck, 24 July, 1778.
Jacob Raboldt, 24 July, 1778.
Christoph. Glickner, 24 July, 1778.
Will. Prux, 24 July, 1778.
Henry Hehn, 24 July, 1779.

---

INFANTRY. An Independent Corps of 150 men, raised agreeable to a resolve of Congress of 5 December.

*Captains.*

John Paul Schott.
Anthony Selim, 1776.

*1st Lieutenants.*

Lawrence ———, April 1777.
Baron ———, April, 1777.

---

INFANTRY. A regiment raised agreeable to a resolve of Congress of 5 July, 1776.

*Colonel.*

Seth Warner, 5 July, 1776.

*Lieut. Colonel.*

Samuel Safford, 5 July, 1776.

*Captains.*

Simeon Smith, 1 Jan., 1776.
Gideon Brownson, 5 July, 1776. Promoted Maj. 16 July, 1779.
Weight Hopkins, 5 July, 1776.
Giles Woolcott, 3 Jan., 1777.
John Chipman, 1 Aug., 1777.
Will. Moulton, 1 March, 1778.
Thomas Sill, 4 Nov., 1778.

*Capt. Lieutenant.*

David Baits, 13 Feb., 1777. Promoted Capt. 16 July, 1779.

*Lieutenants.*

Mich. Dunning, 1 October, 1776. Promoted Capt. Lieut. 16 July, 1779.
James Coon, 16 Sept., 1776.
Joseph Safford, 16 Sept., 1776.
John Chapman, 16 Sept., 1776.
David Valiance, 27 Oct., 1776. Resigned 12 May, 1779.
Benj. Hopkins, 2 May, 1778.
George Sexton, 28 Sept., 1778.
Benj. Butterfield, 28 Sept., 1778.
Samuel Beach, 14 Sept., 1778.

*2nd Lieutenants.*

Francis Payne. Promoted Lieut. 2 May, 1779.
Thomas Lyon, 27 Oct., 1776.
Walter Sevitts, 15 Nov., 1776.
Will. Moulton, 16 Sept., 1776.

*Ensigns.*

Jacob Safford, 18 Aug., 1778. Resigned 18 Dec., 1779.
Alex. Bush, 18 Aug., 1778. Resigned 12 May, 1779.
Thomas Talman, 14 Aug., 1778.
Bonane Grand, 14 Aug., 1778.
Will. Lighthall, 14 Aug., 1778.
Oliver Barrett, 14 Aug., 1778.
Alex. McLowry, 2 May, 1779.
Martin Eno, 7 Aug., 1779.
Reuben Church, 7 Aug., 1779.
Ebenezer Stevens, 7 Aug., 1779.

---

INFANTRY. A regiment formed in April, this year, by the junction of three of the additional regiments raised 27 December, 1776, viz: Henly's, Lee's and Jackson's.

*Colonel.*

Henry Jackson, Jan., 1777.

*Lieut. Colonel.*

David Cobb, Jan., 1777.

*Major.*

Samuel ———, May, 1778.

*Captains.*

Peter ———.
Will. Scott, 1 Jan., 1777.
James Jones, 1 Feb., 1777.
Will. North, 10 May, 1777.
John Hastings, 20 May, 1777.
Joseph Fox, 23 June, 1777.

*Capt. Lieutenant.*

Thomas Hunt, 1 Feb., 1777. Promoted Capt. 24 April, 1779.

*Lieutenants.*

Thomas Turner. Promoted Capt. 24 April, 1779.
John Hobby, 1 Feb., 1777. Promoted Capt. Lieut. 24 April, 1779.
Thomas Lamb, 1 Feb., 1777.
Thomas Edwards, 31 May, 1777.
Patrick Phelan, 20 June, 1777.
Sam. Rogers, 26 June, 1777.
Samuel Cogg, 1 July, 1777.
John Nesmith, 16 July, 1777.

*2nd Lieutenants.*

Charles Sheldon. Promoted Lieut. 5 March, 1779.
John Hollis Condy, 1 Feb., 1777. Promoted Lieut. 24 April, 1779.
Peter Castaing. Promoted Lieut. 24 April, 1779.
Jeremiah Hill, 23 June, 1777.
John Barker, 1 July, 1777.
Ephraim Hunt, 1 May, 1778.

*Ensigns.*

Nath. Thacher, 1 Feb., 1777.
James Sewell, 25 May, 1777.
Sam'l Phelan, 1 July, 1777.
Robert Williams, 24 April, 1777.
Ebenezer Leland, 7 June, 1779.

---

INFANTRY. One of the additional sixteen regiments raised agreeable to the resolve of Congress of 26 Dec., 1776. It was this year united to Col. Webb's.

*Colonel.*

Henry Sherburn, 1 March, 1777.

*Captains.*

James Webb, 1 March, 1777.
Abijah Savage.
Benj. Burton, 5 March, 1777.
Amos Stanton.
——— Blackman.
John Thraston, 1 June, 1777.

*Lieutenants.*

Seth Chapin, 9 July, 1777.
Zadock How.
Samuel Winn, 12 Jan., 1777.
Henry Williams.
John Smith, 8 April, 1777.
Ephraim Carey, 12 Jan., 1777.

*2nd Lieutenants.*

Ephraim Sherburn, 1 Sept., 1777.
Jesse Peek.
Ebenezer Stanton.
Josiah Brown, 28 Feb., 1777.

*Ensigns.*

Henry Shearman, 1 Sept., 1777.
Amos Galpin.
Thomas Russel, 4 Oct., 1777.

---

INFANTRY. A regiment composed of two of the sixteen additional regiments raised agreeable to the resolve of Congress of 26 Dec. 1776, viz: Webb's and Sherburn's.

*Colonel.*

——— Webb.

*Lieut. Colonel.*

Ebenezer Huntington, 10 Oct., 1778.

*Majors.*

John P. Willis, 10 Oct., 1778.
Will. Bradford.

*Captains.*

Edw'd Buckley, Jan., 1777.
John Hart, Jan., 1777.
Charles Whiting, 14 Feb., 1777.
Abijah Savage, 25 Feb., 1777.
Elija Blackman, 28 Feb., 1777.
Joseph Walker, 22 Aug., 1777.
Elija Hopkins, 10 Oct., 1778.

*Capt. Lieutenant.*

Benj. Burton, 1 March, 1777.

*Lieutenants.*

John Reily, 1 Feb., 1777. Promoted Capt. 10 July, 1779.
John Smith, 8 April, 1777.
Zadock Howe, 16 April, 1777.
Seth Galpin, 9 July, 1777.
Henery Williams, 9 Nov., 1777.
John Meigs, 15 Feb., 1778.
Wyllard Wright, 16 May, 1778.
Roger Wells, 16 May, 1778.

*2nd Lieutenants.*

Sam. Mears. Promoted Lieut. 13 March.
Ebenezer Frothington. Promoted Lieut. 26 May, 1779.
Ebenezer Stanton, 9 Nov., 1777.
Asa Lyon, 19 Nov., 1777.
Giles Mumford, 10 May, 1778.
Sam. Wadworth, 16 May, 1778.
Will. Verstile, 16 May, 1778.
Solomon Mears, 16 May, 1778.

*Ensigns.*

Amos Galpin, 3 March, 1777.
Thomas Russel, 1 Oct., 1777.

INFANTRY. A regiment composed of two of the additional regiments raised agreeable to a resolve of Congress of 26 Dec., 1776, viz: Col. Malcolm's and Spencer's. Towards the end of this year it was joined to the New Jersey line as the 4th.

*Colonel.*

Oliver Spencer, 15 Jan., 1777.

*Lieut. Colonel.*

Will. S. Smith, 1 Jan., 1777.

*Major.*

——— Pawling, 27 Jan., 1777. Resigned 5 March, 1779.

*Captains.*

John Burrow, 1 Jan., 1777.
Jonath. Pearson, 3 Feb., 1777.
James Broderick, 18 Feb., 1777.
Benj. Weatherby, 23 Feb., 1777.
John Santford, 11 March, 1777.
Nathan Tom, 17 March, 1777.
——— Black, 11 March, 1777.
Abrah. Neely, 10 Oct., 1778.

*Capt. Lieutenant.*

Richd. Esdel, 6 Sept., 1777.

*Lieutenants.*

James Bonnel. Promoted Capt. 24 April, 1779.
Will. Beach, 6 Sept., 1777. Promoted Capt. Lieut. 12 April, 1779.
Will. Bull, 16 Sept., 1777.
——— Robert, 6 Feb., 1777.
John Hammond, 7 Feb., 1777.
——— Monnel, 20 March, 1777.
——— Nealy, 25 March, 1777.
——— Oliver, 12 Oct., 1777.
Robert Pemberton, 1 Jan., 1778.
John Orr, 10 Oct., 1778.

*Ensigns.*

Uzal Meeker. Promoted Lieut. 10 Feb., 1779.
Peter Tallman. Promoted Lieut. 1 April, 1779.
Finch Gildersleeve. Promoted Lieut. 12 April, 1779.
David Kirkpatrick. Promoted Lieut. 24 April, 1779.
Anth. Maxwell. Promoted Lieut. 24 April, 1779.
John Stagg. Promoted Lieut. 24 April, 1779.
Andrew Simpson.
John Reed, 12 May, 1779.
Benj. Esdel, 12 May, 1779.
Moses Ogden, 12 May, 1779.
John McEwen, 12 May, 1779.

---

INFANTRY. A regiment formed in April this year by the junction of Col. Grayson's and Gist's additional regiments raised agreeable to a resolve of Congress of 26 December, 1776.

*Colonel.*

Nathan Gist.

*Major.*

Nath. Mitchel, 23 Dec., 1777.
John Gist, 9 March, 1777.
Sam. Lapsley, 10 March, 1777.
Strother Jones, 14 May, 1777.
Joseph Smith, 31 Aug., 1777.
Thomas Bell, 19 April, 1778.

*Capt. Lieutenant.*

Alex. Brackeridge. Promoted Capt. 23 April, 1779.

*Lieutenants.*

Francis Muire. Promoted Capt. Lieut. 23 April, 1779.
Thomas Drew, 1 Feb., 1778.
Will. B. Wallace, 3 Feb., 1778.
Sam. Bell, 3 Feb., 1778.
Will. Brownloe, 19 April, 1778.
Robert Kirk, 19 April, 1778.
John Linton, 29 Dec., 1778.
Will. Triplet, 10 May, 1778.

*2nd Lieutenants.*

Joseph Britton. Promoted Lieut. 23 April, 1779.
George Winchester. Promoted Lieut. 1 May, 1779.
David Lucket. 4 July, 1779.
John Nelson, 4 July, 1779.

---

INFANTRY. An additional regiment raised agreeable to a resolve of Congress of 26 December, 1776. It appears by the resolve of 23 Jan., 1779, that only three companies were to be continued.

*Colonel.*

——— Rawlin.

*Captains.*

Admison Tannahill, 1 April, 1778.
Alex. Lawson Smith.

INFANTRY. An Invalid regiment formed agreeable to a resolve of Congress of 20 June, 1777.

*Colonel.*

Lewis Nicola, 20 June, 1777.

*Captains.*

David Woelpper, 17 July, 1776. Transf. 11 June, 1778.
Will. Williams, 1 April, 1778. Transf. 1 July, 1778.
Robert Campble, 1 Jan., 1778. Transf. 5 Aug., 1778. Killed 4 Oct., 1779.
Moses McFarland, 16 March, 1779. Transf. 16 March, 1779.
Will. McElhalton, 1 Oct., 1776. Transf. 6 July, 1779.
Thomas Arnold, 21 March, 1777. Transf. 1 Nov., 1779.

*Lieutenants.*

Osgood Carleton, 1 Jan., 1777. Transf. 1 Dec., 1778.
Ephraim Minot, 1 Jan., 1777. Transf. 18 Feb., 1778.
Will. Honeyman, 15 Jan., 1777. Transf. 1 July, 1778.
Abrah. Wood, 24 March, 1777. Transf. 6 Oct., 1778.
Jonath. Pughter, 1 June, 1777. Transf. 6 Oct., 1778.
Will. Lamont, 18 March, 1779. Transf. 18 March, 1779.
Will Maynard, 1 June, 1779. Transf. 1 June, 1779.

---

## A General List of the Officers in the American Army for 1780.

GENERAL OFFICERS.

*Commander-in Chief.*

George Washington, 15 June, 1775.

*Major-Generals.*

Charles Lee, 17 June, 1775.
Israel Putnam, 19 June, 1775.
Horatio Gates, 16 Nov., 1776.
Will. Heath, 9 Aug., 1777.
Nathan Green, 9 Aug., 1777.
Earl of Sterling, 19 Feb., 1777.
Arthur St. Clair, 19 Feb., 1777.
Benj. Lincoln, 19 Feb., 1777.
Benedict Arnold, 19 Feb., 1777. Deserted to the Enemy.
Marquis de la Fayette, 31 July, 1777.
Baron de Kalb, 15 Sept., 1777. Killed at the battle of Camden, 16 Aug., 1780.
Robert How, 20 Oct., 1777.
Alex. McDougal 20 Oct., 1777.
Baron Steuben, 5 May, 1778.

*Brigadiers.*

Will. Thompson, 1 March, 1776.
John Nixon, 9 Aug., 1776. Resigned 12 Sept.
James Clinton, 9 Aug., 1776.
Sam. Holden Parsons, 9 Aug., 1776. Promoted 23 Oct.
Will. Moultrie, 16 Sept., 1776.
Laughlin McIntosh, 16 Sept. 1776.
Will. Maxwell, 23 Oct., 1776.
Will. Smallwood, 23 Oct., 1776. Promoted Maj. Gen. 15 Sept.
Henry Knox, 27 Dec., 1776.
Enoch Poor, 21 Feb., 1777. Died Sept.
John Glover, 21 Feb., 1777.
John Patterson, 21 Feb., 1777.
Anthony Wayne, 21 Feb., 1777.
Will. Woodford, 21 Feb., 1777. Died Nov.
P. Muhlenberg, 21 Feb., 1777.
George Clinton, 25 Nov., 1777.
Charles Scott, 1 April, 1777.
George Weedon, 1 April, 1777.
Edwd. Hand, 1 April, 1777.
Ebenezer Learnerd, 2 April, 1777.
Jedediah Huntington, 12 May, 1777.
Count Pulaski, 15 Sept., 17.. Killed at the attack of Savannah.
John Stark, 4 Oct., 1777.
Chev. du Portail, 17 Nov., 1777.
Jethro Sumner, 9 Jan., 1779.
James Hogun, 9 Jan., 1779.
——— Hugar, 9 Jan., 1779.
Mordecai Gist, 9 Jan., 1779.
Will. Irwine, 12 May, 1779.
Danl. Morgan, 13 Oct., 1780.

---

CORPS OF ENGINEERS formed agreeable to the resolve of Congress of 11 March, 1780.

CHIEF ENGINEER.

*Brigadier.*

Chev. du Portail.

*Colonels.*

Thadeus Kosciuszko, 18 Oct., 1776.
——— De la Radierre, 8 July, 1777. Died.
——— Laumoy.

Three companies of SAPPERS AND MINERS ordered to be raised by resolve of 27 May, 1778, and to be under the command of the Chief Engineer.

*Captains.*

——— Nevin, 25 April, 1779.
——— Bebee, 2 Aug., 1779.
——— Murray, 2 Aug., 1779.
——— Du Veil, 2 Aug., 1779.

*Capt. Lieutenant.*

——— Gilleland, 2 Aug., 1779.
——— Rushnell, 2 Aug., 1779.
——— Cleveland, 2 Aug., 1779.

*Lieutenants.*

——— Welsh, 2 Aug., 1779.

---

## List of General Officers in Continental Service, January 1st, 1782.

*General and Commander-in-Chief.*

George Washington, Esq.

*Major Generals.*

Israel Putnam, Conn, 15 June, 1775. Superannuated.
Horatio Gates, Va. App. Brig. 18 June, 1775. Promoted 16 May, 1776.
Wm. Heath, Mass. App. Brig. 22 June, 1775. Promoted 9 Aug., 1776.
Nath. Green, R. I. App. Brig. 22 June, 1775. Promoted 9 Aug., 1776.
Wm. Earl Stirling, Jersey. App. Brig. 1 March, 1776. Promoted 19 Feb., 1777.
Ar. St. Clair, Penn. App. Brig. 9 Aug., 1776. Promoted 19 Feb., 1777.
Lincoln, Mass. 19 Feb., 1777. Secretary of War.
Mar's De Lafayette, France. 12 May, 1777. France.
Robt. Howe, N. C. App. Brig. 1 March, 1776. Promoted 20 Oct., 1777.
Alex. McDougal, N. Y. App. Brig. 9 Aug., 1776. Promoted 20 Oct., 1777.
Baron Steuben, Germany. 5 May, 1778. Inspect. General.
Wm. Smallwood, Md. App. Brig. 23 Oct., 1776. Promoted 15 Sept., 1780.
Sam'l H. Parsons, Conn. App. Brig. 9 Aug, 1776.
Chev'r du Portail, France. App. Brig. 15 Nov., 1777. Eng. Gen., France.

*Brigadier Generals.*

James Clinton, N. Y., 9 Aug., 1776.
Wm. Moultrie, S. C., 16 Sept., 1776.
Sach. McIntosh, Georgia, 1* Sept., 1776.
Henry Knox, Art., Mass., 27 Dec., 1776, Artillery.
J. Glover, Mass., 21 Feb., 1777.
J. Patterson, Mass., 21 Feb., 1777.
Anto. Wayne, Penn., 21 Feb., 1777.
Geo. Wedon, Va., 21 Feb., 1777.
Peter Muhlenberg, Va, 21 Feb., 1777.
Geo. Clinton, Gov., N. Y., 5 March, 1777. Gov. N. Y.
Edw. Hand, Penn. 1 April, 1777. A. G.
Chas. Scott, Va., 1 April, 1777. Prisoner of War.
Jedediah Huntington, Conn., 12 May, 1777.
Jethro Sumner, N. C., 9 Jan., 1779.
Isaac Huger, S. C., 9 Jan., 1779.
Mordecai Gist, Md., 9 Jan., 1779.
——— Irving, Penn. St. Corps.
——— Morgan, Va.
——— Hazen, Canada. Brevet.
——— Stark, N. H.

---

## General Officers, Resigned, Dismissed, Etc.

*Major Generals.* 11.

Artimas Ward, Mass., 18 Jan., 1775. Resigned 23 April, 1776.
Chas. Lee, Va., 18 Jan., 1775. Dismissed 1880.
Philip Schuyler, N. Y ,.19 June, 1775. Resigned.
Jos. Spencer, Mass. App. Brig. 22 June, 1775. Promoted 9 Aug., 1776. Resigned.
John Sullivan, N. H. App. Brig. 22 June. 1775. Promoted 9 Aug., 1776. Resigned.
Tho. Mifflin, Penn. App. Brig. 17 May, 1776. Promoted 19 Feb., 1777. Resigned.
Ad. Stephens, Va. App. Brig. 4 Sept., 1776. Promoted 19 Feb., 1777. Dismissed.
Bened. Arnold, Conn. App. Brig. 10 Jan., 1776. Promoted 2 May, 1777. Deserted to the Enemy.
Baron De Kalb, France. Promoted 1777. Killed 16 Aug., 1780.
Chr. Thos. Conway, France. App. Brig. 13 May, 1777. Promoted 1778. Resigned.
Richard Montgomery, N. Y. App. Brig. 22 June, 1775. Promoted 9 Dec., 1775. Killed 1 Jan., 1776.

*Brigadier Generals.* 29.

Seth Pomeroy, Mass., 22 June, 1775. Never acted.
Dew. Wooster, Conn., 22 June, 1775. Killed.
John Thomas, Mass., 22 June, 1775. Died.
Joseph Frey, Mass., 10 Jan., 1776. Resigned 23 April, 1776.
John Armstrong, Penn., 1 March, 1776. Resigned 4 April, 1777.
And. Lewis, Va., 1 March, 1776. Resigned 15 April, 1777.
James Moore, N. C., 1 March, 1776. Died 9 April, 1777.
Baron De Woodthe, 16 March, 1776.
John Whitecomb, Mass., 5 June, 1776.
Hugh Mercer.
James Reed.
Chr. Gadsden.
Chev. De Tormoy.
Fra. Nash.
Jam. M. Varnum.
J. O. De Haas.
J. Cadwallader.
Ben. Learned.
James Hogan.
Jo. Reed.
Count Pulaski.
Ja. Wilkinson.
——— De Bhore.
——— De Coudre.
Wm. Thomson.
John Nixon.
Wm. Maxwell.
Enoch Poor.
Wm. Woodford.

| | | |
|---|---|---|
| 14 Generals, 150 dollars per month, or $1800 per year | $25,200 | |
| 15 Rations each per day, at 9d per Ration | 7,665 | |
| | | $32,865 |
| 20 Brigadiers, 125 dollars per month, or $1500 per year | 30,000 | |
| 12 Rations each per day, at 9d per ration, is | 8,760 | |
| | | 38,760 |
| 34 Generals, besides Wagons, Horses and Forage ]]] | | 71,625 |
| | | Stg. £16,115 12s 6d |

| | *Major Gen.* | *Brig. Gen.* | *Quota.* |
|---|---|---|---|
| Hampshire has had | 1 | 1 | 2 Regs. Infantry. |
| Massachusetts | 5 | 10 | 11 Infantry and Art. |
| Rhode Island | 1 | 1 | 1 |
| Connecticut | 3 | 2 | 6 Infantry and Cav. |
| New York | 3 | 2 | 3 Infantry and Art. |
| Jersey | 1 | 1 | 2 |
| Pennsylvania | 2 | 8 | 9 Inf., Art., Cav., Art. |
| Delaware | .. | .. | 1 |
| Maryland | 1 | 1 | 5 |
| Virginia | 3 | 7 | 11 Inf., Cav. and Art. |
| North Carolina | 1 | 4 | 4 |
| South Carolina | .. | 2 | 2 |
| Georgia | .. | 1 | 1 |
| Foreigners | 5 | 6 | .. |

# A LIST OF THE OFFICERS

OF THE

# ARMY OF THE UNITED STATES,

From 1st January, 1784, to 1st January, 1785,

*As arranged by General Washington, and under Resolutions of Congress, from Original Muster Rolls and other Official Sources.*

*NOTE.—Honorably discharged and disbanded, 20 June, 1784, pursuant to Resolution of Congress, of 2 June, 1784.

## GENFRAL STAFF.

### Commander-in-Chief.

*Major General.*

*KNOX, HENRY. 15 Nov., 1781. [Born in Mass. Appointed from Mass.] Col. Continental Art., 7 Nov., 1775. Brig. Gen. Art., 27 Dec., 1776. Commanding U. S. Army from 23 Dec., 1783.

### Inspector-General.

*Major General.*

DE STEUBEN, BARON. 5 May, 1778. [Born in Prussia. Appointed at Large.] Vol. I. G., 18 Feb., 1778. Resigned 15 April, 1784.

### Inspector.

*Major.*

NORTH, WILLIAM. 15 April, 1784. [Born in Maine. Appointed from Mass.] Bvt. Maj., 11 Sept., 1783. 2nd Lieut. Mass. Art., 9 May, 1776. Capt. 16th Mass. Continental Inf., 10 May, 1777. A. De C. to Maj. Gen. Baron de Steuben. Appointed by Congress on resignation of, and recommendation by Baron de Steuben. [Adj. Gen. U. S. A., 19 July, 1798.

### Quartermaster General.

*Colonel.*

PICKERING, TIMOTHY. 5 Aug., 1780. [Born in Mass. Appointed from Mass.] Col. 1st Reg. Essex Co. Mass. Militia, 13 Feb., 1775. Col. and Adj. Gen. U. S. A., 25 April, 1777. Member Board of War, 13 Jan., 1778.

*Paymaster General.*

PIERCE, JOHN. 19 Jan., 1781. [Born in Conn. Appointed from Conn.]
1st Lieut. (Col. Israel Hutchinson's Conn. Reg. Inf.) 27th Foot Continental Army, 1775. Asst. P. M. Gen. U. S. A., 10 Feb., 1776. Dep. P. M. Gen. "Main Army," 1 June, 1779.

*Commissary of Military Stores.*

HODGDEN, SAMUEL. 1 Feb., 1777. [Born in Mass. Appointed from Mass.]
Dep. C. G. Mil. Stores for Northern Dept., 11 Feb., 1778.

---

## CORPS OF ARTILLERY.

Composed of the 1st Co., 2nd Reg. Continental Corps of Art., organized 6th Jan., 1776, as the "New York Provincial Artillery Co.;" of detachments* from the 3rd Reg. Continental Corps of Art., organized 1st Jan., 1777 (G. O. Army Headquarters, West Point, N. Y., 23rd Dec., 1783); and of the Art. Co. raised by Pennsylvania, pursuant to resolution of Congress of 3rd June, 1784.

New York, 12 July, 1776.
Long Island, 27 August, 1776.
Harlem Heights, 16 September, 1776.
Pelham Manor, 18 October, 1776.
White Plains, 28 October, 1776.
New Brunswick, 1 December, 1776.
Trenton, 26 December, 1776.
Assunpink, 2 January, 1777.
Princeton, 3 January, 1777.
Brandywine, 11 September, 1777.
Stillwater, 19 September, 1777.
Germantown, 4 October, 1777.
Saratoga, 7 October, 1777.
Monmouth, 28 June 1778.
Springfield, 23 June, 1780.
Yorktown, 28. Sept.,—19 Oct., 1781.

*Major Commandant.*

*BAUMAN, SEBASTIAN. 12 Sept., 1778. [B. Frankfort-on-the-Main. App. N. Y.]
Capt., 30 March, 1776, of the N. Y. Continental Art. Co., which was attached to Col. H. Knox's Reg. Art., 19 April, 1776, and transferred to 2nd Reg. Continental Corps Art., 1 Jan., 1777, as the 2nd Co. Bvt. Lieut. Col. U. S. A., 14 April, 1787.

*Captains.*

DOUGHTY, JOHN. 1 March, 1777. [Born in N. J. Appointed from N. Y.]
Bvt. Maj., 11 Sept., 1783. Capt. Lieut. N. J. "Eastern Art. Co.," 1776. Promoted to Capt. "N. Y. Provincial Co. of Art" (subsequently 1st Co. 2nd Reg. Continental Corps Art.), *vice* Capt. Alexander Hamilton, appointed Lieut. Col. and A. de C. to Gen. Washington. Commanding Co., organized 6 Jan., 1776.

DOUGLAS, THOMAS. 12 Aug., 1784. [Born in Penn. Appointed from Penn.]
Late Capt. 4th Reg. Continental Corps Art., 12 Oct., 1781. Commanding Co. organized Aug., 1784.

*Capt. Lieutenants.*

JOHNSTON, WILLIAM. 9 Nov., 1776. [Born in Mass. Appointed from Mass.]
Col. H. Knox's Continental Reg. Art., subsequently re-organized as the 3rd Reg. Continental Corps Art., 1776.

FENNO, EPHRAIM. 1 Jan., 1777. [Born in N. Y. Appointed from N. Y.]

*Lieutenants.*

PRICE, WILLIAM. 12 Sept., 1778. [Born in Mass. Appointed from Mass.]
3rd Reg. Continental Corps Art. Appointed Dep. C. of Mil. Stores, 1 Jan., 1784, and dropped from Corps Art.

JEFFERDS, SAMUEL. 1 Oct., 1778. [Born in Mass. Appointed from the Army.]
Sergt. in Capt. Edward Burbeck's Co. (Col. Knox's Reg.), Continental Art. 2nd Lieut. 3rd Reg. Continental Corps Art., 1 Jan., 1777.

*BLISS, JOSEPH. 1 Oct., 1778. [Born in N. Y. Appointed from N .Y.]
2nd Reg. Continental Corps Art. Appointed Corps P. M., 29 Jan., 1784.

BRADFORD, JAMES. 12 Sept., 1779. [Born in Penn. Appointed from N. Y.]
Vol. and Acting Lieut. 2nd Reg. Continental Corps Art., 12 Sept., 1778. Captured near King's Ferry, Jan., 1779. Adj. 2nd Reg. Continental Corps Art., 2 Oct., 1782.

*CUNNINGHAM, HENRY. 12 Sept., 1779. [Born in N. Y. Appointed from N. Y.]
2nd Reg. Continental Corps Art.

*REED, JOHN. 17 Dec., 1780. [Born in N. Y. Appointed from N. Y.]
2nd Reg. Continental Corps Art.

ASHTON, JOSEPH. 12 Aug., 1784. [Born in Penn. Appointed from Penn.]
Late Capt. Lieut. 4th Reg. Continental Corps Art., 19 April, 1781. (1st Sergt. Capt. John Lamb's N. Y. Independent Co. Continental Art., 16 July, 1775, and captured in assault on Quebec, 31 Dec., 1775. Lieut. 2nd Reg. Continental Corps Art., 1 Jan., 1777. Adj. 2nd Reg. Continental Corps Art., 21 June, 1777—16 Jan., 1781.)

*Surgeon's Mate.*

COGSWELL, WILLIAM. 19 Jan., 1781. [Born in Mass. Appointed from Mass.]
Late Priv. (Jan., 1776, to Jan., 1777) in his brother's (Capt. Thos. C.'s) Co., Col. L. Baldwin's Reg. Mass. Continental Inf. and at Siege of Boston. Chief Medical Officer U. S. A., 20 June, 1784, to 12 Aug., 1785.

## FIRST AMERICAN REGIMENT OF INFANTRY

### OF THE CONTINENTAL LINE.

*Organized from Companies of the Massachusetts Brigade and two Companies of the 1st New Hampshire Continental Infantry.*

Bunker Hill, 17 June, 1775.
Long Island, 27 August, 1776.
Harlem Heights, 16 Sept., 1776.
White Plains, 28 Oct., 1776.
Trenton, 26 Dec., 1776.
Princeton, 3 Jan., 1777.
Brandywine, 11 Sept., 1777.
Stillwater, 19 Sept., 1777.
Germantown, 4 Oct., 1777.
Saratoga, 7 Oct., 1777.
Monmouth, 28 June, 1778.
Quaker Hill, 29 Aug., 1778.
Springfield, 23 June, 1780.
Yorktown, 28 Sept.—19 Oct., 1781.

*Colonel.*

*JACKSON, HENRY. 12 Jan., 1777. [Born in Mass. Appointed from Mass.] Bvt. Brig. Gen., 30 Sept., 1783. 4th Reg. Mass Continental Inf.

*Lieut. Colonel.*

HULL, WILLIAM. 12 Aug., 1779. [Born in Conn. Appointed from Mass.] 3rd Reg. Mass. Continental Inf. [At Siege of Boston as Capt., 6 July, 1775. Col. Webb's 19th Reg. Conn. Inf.) Graduated at Yale College, 1772. [Brig. Gen. U. S. A., April, 1812.]

*Major.*

*GIBBS, CALEB. 29 July, 1778. [Born in R. I. Appointed from Mass.] 2nd Reg. Mass. Continental Inf. (Wounded at Yorktown.)

*Captains.*

*SUMNER, JOB. 1 Jan., 1777. [Born in Mass. Appointed from Mass.] Bvt. Maj., 30 Sept., 1783. 3rd Reg. Mass. Continental Inf. (Lieut. in Capt. Moses Draper's Co. of Gardner's Reg. at Bunker Hill.] Commanding Light Inf. Co., West Point.

*WILLIAMS, JOSEPH. 1 Jan., 1777. [Born in Mass. Appointed from Mass.] Bvt. Maj., 30 Sept., 1783. 3rd Reg. Mass. Continental Inf. [Ensign in Col. Asa Whitcomb's [6th] Reg. Mass. Inf., in 1776.) Commanding 1st Co., Springfield Arsenal.

*FRYE, ISAAC. 1 Jan., 1777. [Born in N. H. Appointed from N. H.] Bvt. Maj., 30 Sept., 1783. 1st Reg. N. H. Continental Inf. (Q. M. in Col. James Reed's N. H. Reg. Inf., 26 April, 1775, and at Bunker Hill.) Commanding 2nd Co., West Point.

*HASKELL, ELNATHAN. 1 April, 1778. [Born in Mass . Appointed from Mass.] Bvt. Maj., 30 Sept., 1783. 4th Reg. Mass. Continental Inf. (Lieut. in Col. Thomas Marshall's [10th] Reg. Mass. Inf., 5 July, 1776.) Commanding 3rd Co., West Point.

*HUNT, THOMAS. 1 March, 1779. [Born in Mass. Appointed from Mass.] 4th Reg. Mass. Continental Inf. (Ensign in Col. William Bond's [25th] Reg. Mass. Inf., 1775. At battles of Lexington and Bunker Hill, and wounded at Stony Point.) Commanding 4th Co., West Point. [Appointed Capt. 2nd U. S. Inf., 4 March, 1791.]

*MILLS, JOHN. 3 May, 1779. [Born in Mass. Appointed from Mass.] 1st Reg. Mass. Continental Inf. (Ensign in Col. Asa Whitcomb's [6th] Reg. Mass. Ing., 1776, and at Siege of Boston.) Commanding 5th Co., West Point. Ass'd to command it *vice* Capt. Wm. Mills, 4th Mass. Reg. Continental Inf., who relinquished Co.—(G. O. Hd. Qrs., West Point, 20 Jan., 1784.) [Adj.] Gen. U. S. A., 13 May, 1794.]

*HOBBY, JOHN. 24 July, 1781. [Born in Mass. Appointed from Mass.] 3rd Reg. Mass. Continental Inf. (1st Lieut. in 16th Mass. Continental Inf., 1 Feb., 1777.) Commanding 6th Co., West Point.

*POTTER, JOSEPH. 1 March, 1782. [Born in N. H. Appointed from N. H.] 1st Reg. N. H. Continental Inf. (Lieut. in 2nd N. H. Continental Inf., 8 Nov., 1776.) Commanding 7th Co., West Point.

*JACKSON, SIMON. 1 April, 1782. [Born in Mass. Appointed from Mass.] 4th Reg. Mass. Continental Inf. (Lieut. in 8th Mass. Continental Inf., 1 Jan., 1777.) Commanding 8th Co., West Point.

*Lieutenants.*

*PHELON, PATRICK. 20 June, 1777. [Born in Mass. Appointed from Mass.] Bvt. Capt., 30 Sept., 1783. 3rd Reg. Mass. Continental Inf. [Capt. 2nd U. S. Inf., 4 March, 1791.]

*CUSHING, THOMAS HUMPHREY. 12 Jan., 1778. [Born in Mass. App. from Army.] Bvt. Capt., 30 Sept., 1783. 1st Reg. Mass. Continental Inf. (Sergt. in his brother Lieut. Nathaniel Cushing's Co., 1776. Capt. Lemuel Trescott's Co. of Col. Asa Whitcomb's [6th] Reg. Mass Inf. In Arnold's Naval Battle on Lake Champlain, 13 Oct., 1776. 2nd Lieut. 1st Mass. Continental Inf., 1 Jan., 1777. Taken prisoner by the British, 14 May, 1781.) [Capt. 2nd U. S. Inf., 4 March, 1791; Maj. 1st U. S. Inf., 3 March, 1793. Inspector U. S. A., 24 Feb., 1797. Adj. and Inspector of the Army, 1 April, 1802. Lieut. Col. 2nd U. S. Inf., 1 April, 1802. Col. 2nd U. S. Inf., 7 Sept., 1805. Adj. Gen. U. S. A., 6 July, 1812. Brig. Gen. U. S. A., 2 July, 1812.]

*HASKELL, JONATHAN. 5 Feb., 1779. [Born in Mass. Appointed from Mass.] Bvt. Capt., 30 Sept., 1783. 4th Reg. Mass. Continental Inf. (Ensign 14th Mass. Continental Inf., 13 Jan., 1777.) [Capt. 2nd U. S. Inf., 4 March, 1791.]

*CONDY, THOMAS HOLLIS. 1 March, 1779. [Born in Mass. Appointed from Mass.]
Bvt. Capt., 30 Sept., 1783. 4th Reg. Mass. Continental Inf. 2nd Lieut., 16 Mass. Inf., 31 Jan., 1777. Regimental P. M., 1 May, 1783.
*BOWLES, RALPH HART. 16 April, 1779. [Born in Mass. Appointed from Mass.]
Bvt. Capt., 30 Sept., 1783. 2nd Lieut., 1st Mass. Inf., 1 Jan., 1777.
*STONE, NATHANIEL. 16 Jan., 1780. [Born in Mass. Appointed from Mass.]
Bvt. Capt., 30 Sept., 1783. 2nd Lieut., 1st Mass. Inf., 28 March, 1777.
*MERROW, JOSHUA. 12 July, 1780. [Born in N. H. Appointed from N. H.]
Ensign 2nd N. H. Reg. Continental Inf., 2 April, 1777.
*BRADFORD, GAMALIEL, Jr. 3 Sept., 1780. [Born in Mass. Appointed from Mass.]
4th Reg. Mass. Continental Inf. Ensign 14th Mass. Continental Inf., 8 Oct., 1779.
*ADAMS, JOHN. 6 Oct., 1781. [Born in N. H. Appointed from N. H.]
Ensign, 1st N. H. Reg. Continental Inf., 8 March, 1781.
*RICKARD, WILLIAM. 14 April, 1782. [Born in Mass. Appointed from Army.]
4th Reg. Mass Continental Inf. Ensign 16th Mass. Continental Inf., from Sergt. 24 April, 1779. Appointed Lieut. 2nd U. S. Inf., 4 May, 1792.

*Ensigns.*

*SWAN, CALEB. 26 Nov., 1779. [Born in Me. Appointed from Army.]
4th Reg. Mass. Continental Inf. Ensign 8th Mass. Continental Inf. P. M. Gen. U. S. A., 8 May, 1792.
*SEVER, JAMES. 1 Feb., 1781. [Born in Mass. Appointed from Mass.]
4th Reg. Mass. Continental Inf. Ensign, 7th Mass. Continental Inf. Graduated Harvard College, 1781. Appointed Post Capt. U. S. Navy, 11 May, 1798.
*SAWYER, JAMES. 22 Feb., 1781. [Born in Vt. Appointed from Mass.]
Ensign, 4th Mass. Continental Inf.
*HORTON, ELISHA. 2 April, 1781. [Born in Mass. Appointed from Mass.]
Ensign, 1st Mass. Continental Inf.
*LORD, JEREMIAH. 15 June, 1781. [Born in Mass. Appointed from Mass.]
4th Reg. Mass. Continental Inf. Ensign, 6th Mass. Continental Inf.
*ROWE, JOHN, Jr. 15 June, 1781. 4th Reg. Mass. Continental Inf. Priv. Capt. Jno. Rowe's Co., 1775, at Bunker Hill. Ensign, 8th Mass. Continental Inf.
*GREATON, JOHN WHEELWRIGHT. 16 July, 1782. [Born in Mass. Appointed from Mass.]
Ensign, 3rd Mass. Continental Inf.
*JACKSON, AMASA, 13 Oct., 1782. [Born in Mass. Appointed from Mass.]
4th Reg. Mass. Continental Inf. Ensign 8th Mass. Continental Inf.
*JACKSON, CHARLES. 4 Feb., 1783. [Born in Mass. Appointed from Mass.]
4th Reg. Mass. Continental Inf. Ensign, 8th Mass. Continental Inf.

REGIMENTAL STAFF.

*1st Lieutenant and Adjutant.*

*SELDEN, CHARLES. 4th March, 1778. [Born in Conn. Appointed from Army.]
Bvt. Capt., 30 Sept., 1783. Lieut., 4th Reg. Mass. Continental Inf. 2nd Lieut., 16th Mass. Continental Inf., 16th July, 1777. Wounded in assault and capture of Stony Point. Adj., 16 June, 1783. Graduated at Yale College, 1777.

*1st Lieutenant and Quartermaster.*

*NELSON, HENRY. 15 March, 1782. [Born in Mass. Appointed from Mass.]
Ensign 2nd Mass. Continental Inf., 1 March, 1778.

*Surgeon.*

*HART, JOHN. 1 Jan., 1777. [Born in Mass. Appointed from Mass.]
2nd Reg. Mass. Continental Inf. Surgeon in Col. William Prescott's Reg. Mass. Inf., 1775.

*Surgeon's Mate.*

*LEAVENWORTH, NATHANIEL. 1 Feb., 1780. [Born in Mass. Appointed from Mass.]
4th Reg. Mass. Continental Inf. Surg. Mate, 8th Mass. Continental Inf.

---

## FIRST REGIMENT OF U. S. INFANTRY.

(NOW 3RD U. S. INFANTRY.)

(*Organized by Resolution of Congress of 3rd June,* 1784.)

*Lieut. Colonel Commandant.*

HARMER, JOSIAH. 12 Aug., 1784. [Born in Penn. Appointed from Penn.]
Late Lieut. Col. 1st Penn. Reg. Continental Inf., 6 June, 1777, and Brevet Col. U. S. A., 30 Sept., 1783. Commanding U. S. Army since 12 Aug., 1784.

*Captains.*

FINNEY, WALTER. 12 Aug., 1784. [Born in Penn. Appointed from Penn.]
Late Capt. 3rd Penn. Reg. Continental Inf., 10 Aug., 1776, and Bvt. Maj. U. S. A., 30 Sept., 1783. Taken prisoner at Battle of Long Island, 27 Aug., 1776.
ZIEGLER, DAVID. 12 Aug., 1784. [Born in Saxony. Appointed from Penn.]
Late Capt. 1st Penn. Reg. Continental Inf., 8 Dec., 1778, and Brigade Inspector, Penn. Brigade, Dept. of the South.
McCURDY, WILLIAM. 12 Aug., 1784. [Born in Penn. Appointed from Penn.]
Late Capt. 1st Penn. Reg. Continental Inf., 18 May, 1781.
LANE, DERRICK. 18 Aug., 1784. [Born in N. J. Appointed from N. J.]
Late Capt. 2nd N. J. Reg. Continental Inf., 11 Feb., 1783. 2nd Lieut. 4th N. J. Reg. Continental Inf., 28 Nov., 1776.

*Lieutenants.*

MERCER, JOHN. 18 Aug., 1784. [Born in N. J. Appointed from N. J.]
Late Capt. 1st N. J. Reg. Continental Inf., 15 Feb., 1777. Ensign 1st N. J. Reg. Continental Inf., 7 Nov., 1775. Prisoner of war. Exchanged 6 Nov., 1780.

HERBERT, STEWART. 12 Aug., 1784. [Born in Penn. Appointed from Penn.]
Late Lieut. 1st Penn. Reg. Continental Inf., 9 Jan., 1778. Wounded at Springfield, 23 June, 1780. Appointed Adj., 12 Aug., 1784.

BEATTY, ERCURIES. 12 Aug., 1784. [Born in Penn. Appointed from Penn.]
Late Lieut. 3rd Penn. Reg. Continental Inf., 2nd June, 1778, and Regimental P. M., 22 May, 1783. Bvt. Capt., U. S. A., 30 Sept., 1783.

DOYLE, THOMAS. 12 Aug., 1784. [Born in Penn. Appointed from Penn.]
Late Lieut. 3rd Penn. Reg. Continental Inf., 15 March, 1779. Bvt. Capt. U. S. A., 30 Sept., 1783.

PENNINGTON, WILLIAM. 18 Aug., 1784. [Born in N. J. Appointed from N. J.]
2nd Lieut. 2nd Reg. Continental Corps Art., 12 Sept., 1778. Bvt. Capt. U. S. A., 30 Sept., 1783. Sergt. 2nd Reg. Continental Corps Art., 7 March, 1777.

*Ensigns.*

ARMSTRONG, JOHN. 12 Aug., 1784. [Born in Penn. Appointed from Penn.]
Late Lieut. 3rd Penn. Reg. Continental Inf., 12 May, 1779. Bvt. Capt. U. S. A., 30 Sept., 1783.

HENDERSON, ANDREW. 12 Aug., 1784. Born in Penn. Appointed from Penn.]
Late Lieut. 3rd Penn. Reg. Continental Inf., 31 Dec., 1779. Resigned 21 Oct., 1784.

KERSEY, WILLIAM. 18 Aug., 1784. [Born in N. J. Appointed from N. J.]
Late Lieut. 1st N. J. Reg. Continental Inf., 30 March, 1780. Bvt. Capt. U. S. A., 30 Sept., 1783. Priv. 3rd N. J. Reg. Continental Inf., March, 1776. Ensign 3rd N. J. Reg. Continental Inf., 1 Nov., 1777.

FORD, MAHLON. 18 Aug., 1784. [Born in N. J. Appointed from N. J.]
Late Lieut. 3rd N. J. Reg. Continental Inf., 30 March, 1780. Bvt. Capt. U. S. A., 30 Sept., 1783. Ensign 3rd N. J. Reg. Continental Inf., 28 Nov., 1777.

DENNY, EBENEZER. 12 Aug., 1784. [Born in Penn. Appointed from Penn.]
Late Lieut. 3rd Penn. Reg. Continental Inf., 23 May, 1781.

McDOWELL, NATHAN. 21 Oct., 1784. [Born in Penn. Appointed from Penn.]
Cadet, 12 Aug., 1784 (*vice* Henderson, resigned).

*Surgeon.*

McDOWELL, JOHN. 12 Aug., 1784. [Born in Penn. Appointed from Penn.]
Late Surg. 2nd Penn. Reg. Continental Inf., 5 Feb., 1778.

*Surgeon's Mate.*

ALLISON, RICHARD. 12 Aug., 1784. [Born in Penn. Appointed from Penn.]
Late Surg. Mate 3rd Penn. Reg. Continental Inf., 30 March, 1778.

# REGISTER

OF THE

# ARMY OF THE UNITED STATES,

*As recognized and adopted by the first Congress under the Constitution, 29 September, 1789; from Original Muster Rolls and other Official Sources.*

---

*NOTE.—The anomalous position of these Officers is due to the fact that some States did not fill their quotas as soon as others, and under decision of the War Department of 17th January, 1787, the original vacancies took rank with each other according to their late Revolutionary rank.

## GENERAL STAFF.

*General-in-Chief.*

HARMON, JOSHUA. 31 July, 1787. [Born in Penn. Appointed from Penn.]
Bvt. Brig. Gen., late Lieut. Col. and Bvt. Col. 1st Penn. Reg. Continental Inf. Lieut. Col. Commandant 1st U. S. Inf.

*Paymaster General.*

HOWELL, JOSEPH, Jr. 28 Aug., 1788. [Born in Penn. Appointed from Penn.]
Late Capt. 1st Penn. Musketry Batt. (Col. Samuel J. Atlee), and captured at Battle of Long Island, 27 Aug., 1776. Subsequently Auditor Army Accounts.

*Acting Adjutant General.*

DENNY, EBENEZER. 28 Oct., 1788. [Born in Penn. Appointed from Penn.]
Late Lieut. 3rd Penn. Continental Inf. Adj. 1st U. S. Inf.

*Acting Quartermaster General.*

PRATT, JOHN. 28 July, 1786. [Born in Conn. Appointed from Conn.]
Late Lieut. and Q. M. 3rd Penn. Continental Inf. Q. M. 1st U. S. Inf.

---

## U. S. BATTALION OF ARTILLERY.

*(Organized as a Battalion by Resolution of Congress,* 20 *October,* 1786.)

New York, 12 July, 1776.
Long Island, 27 Aug., 1776.
Harlem Heights, 16 Sept., 1776.
Pelham Manor, 18 Oct., 1776.
White Plains, 28 Oct., 1776.
New Brunswick, 1 Dec., 1776.
Trenton, 26 Dec., 1776.
Assunpink, 2 Jan., 1777.
Princeton, 3 Jan., 1777.
Brandywine, 11 Sept., 1777.
Germantown, 4 Oct., 1777.
Monmouth, 28 June, 1778.
Springfield, 23 June, 1780.
Yorktown, 28 Sept.—19 Oct., 1781.

*Major Commandant.*

DOUGHTY, JOHN. 7 Aug., 1786. [Born in N. J. Appointed from N. J.]
Bvt. Maj., 11 Sept., 1782. Capt. Lieut. Eastern Co. N. J. Art. (4th Continental Reg. Corps Artillery), 1 March, 1776. Promoted Capt. N. Y. Provincial Co. Art. (2nd Continental Reg. Corps Art.), 1 March, 1777. Continuously in service from 1776 (graduated at Columbia College, 1770.)

*Captains.*

FERGUSON, WILLIAM. 20 Oct., 1785. [Born in Penn. Appointed from Penn.]
Late Capt. 4th Reg. Continental Corps Art. Commanding 2nd Co. Art., organized in Pennsylvania by resolution Continental Congress, 3 June, 1784.

BRADFORD, JAMES. 7 Aug., 1786. [Born in Penn. Appointed from N. Y.]
1st Lieut. 2nd Reg. Continental Corps Art., 12 Sept., 1779. Commanding 1st Co. Art., which was organized 6 Jan., 1776, as the N. Y. Provincial Co. Art., subsequently ass'd as a Co. to the 2nd Reg. Continental Corps Art. (Col. John Lamb), and since continuously in service. (Now Batty "F," 4th Art.)

BURBECK, HENRY. 20 Oct., 1786. [Born in Mass. Appointed from Mass.]
Late Capt. and Bvt. Maj. 3rd Reg. Continental Corps Art. Commanding 3rd Co. Art., organized in Massachusetts by resolution of Continental Congress, 20 Oct., 1786.

SAVAGE, JOSEPH. 20 Oct., 1786. [Born in Mass. Appointed from Mass.]
Late Capt. 2nd Reg. Continental Corps Art. Commanding 4th Co. Art., organized in Massachusetts by resolution of Continental Congress, 20 Oct., 1786.

*Lieutenants.*

FOYD, MAHLON. 17 March, 1786. [Born in N. J. Appointed from N. J.]
Late 1st Lieut. Bvt. Capt. 3rd N. J. Continental Inf. In 2nd Co. Art.

SCHUYLER, DIRCK. 7 Aug., 1786. [Born in N. Y. Appointed from N. Y.]
Late Lieut. 2nd N. Y. Continental Reg. Inf. In 1st Co. Art.

PEIRCE, JOHN. 20 Oct., 1786. [Born in Mass. Appointed from Mass.]
Late Capt. Lieut. 3rd Reg. Continental Corps Art. In 3rd Co. Art.

MOOR, WILLIAM. 20 Oct., 1786. [Born in Mass. Appointed from Mass.]
Late 1st Lieut. and Bvt. Capt. 3rd Reg. Continental Corps Art. In 3rd Co. Art.

PORTER, MOSES. 20 Oct., 1786. [Born in Mass. Appointed from Mass.]
Late 2nd Lieut. 3rd Reg. Continental Corps Art. In 4th Co. Art.

FOWLE, EBENEZER SMITH. 20 Oct., 1786. [Born in Mass. Appointed from Mass.]
Late 2nd Lieut. 16th Mass. Continental Reg. Inf. In 4th Co. Art.

ERNEST, MATTHEW. 21 Oct., 1786. [Born in N. Y. Appointed from N. Y.]
Late Priv. in Capt. Cornelius Wynkoop's Co. (Col. J. DeWitt's N. Y. Reg.) Inf. In 1st Co. Art.

SPEAR, EDWARD. 10 Sept., 1787. [Born in Penn. Appointed from Penn.]
Late Lieut. 1st Penn. Continental Reg. Inf. In 2nd Co. Art.

*Surgeon's Mate.*

HAYWARD, NATHAN. 20 Oct., 1786. [Born in Mass. Appointed from Mass.]
Late Priv. in Capt. Staple's Co. (Col. Abner Perry's Mass. Reg. Inf.)

---

## FIRST REGIMENT OF INFANTRY.

(NOW 3RD U. S. INFANTRY.)

*(Organized by Resolution of Congress, 3rdJune,* 1784.)

GENERAL-IN-CHIEF.

*Lieut. Colonel Commandant.*

HARMAR, JOSIAH. 12 Aug., 1784. [Born in Penn. Appointed from Penn.]
Bvt. Brig. Gen. 31 July, 1787. Late Lieut. Col. and Bvt. Col. 1st Penn. Continental Inf.

*Majors.*

WYLLYS, JOHN PALSGRAVE. 9 June, 1785. [Born in Conn. Appointed from Conn.] Late Maj. 1st Conn. Continental Inf. Graduated at Yale College, 1773.
HAMTRAMCK, JOHN FRANCIS. 20 Oct., 1786. [Born Canada. Appointed from N. Y.] Served as commissioned officer from 1775, and at Quebec. Appointed Capt. 1st U. S. Inf., 12th April, 1785.

*Captains.*

ZIEGLER, DAVID. 12 Aug., 1784. [Born in Saxony. Appointed from Penn.] Late Capt. 1st Penn. Continental Inf., and Inspector.
HEART, JONATHAN. 9 June, 1785. [Born in Conn. Appointed from Conn.] Late Capt. 1st Conn. Continental Inf. Graduated at Yale College, 1768.
STRONG, DAVID. 15 July, 1785. [Born in Conn. Appointed from Conn.] Late Capt. 2nd Conn. Continental Infantry.
*McCURDY, WILLIAM. 12 Aug., 1784. [Born in Penn. Appointed from Penn.] Late Capt. 1st Penn. Continental Inf.
MERCER, JOHN. 24 Nov., 1785. [Born in N. J. Appointed from N. J.] Late Capt. 1st N. J. Continental Inf.
SMITH, JOHN. 21 Oct., 1786. [Born in Mass. Appointed from N. Y.] Late Lieut. 2nd Reg. Continental Corps Art.
ASHTON, JOSEPH. 1 Sept., 1787. [Born in Penn. Appointed from Penn.] Late Capt. Lieut. 4th Reg. Continental Corps Art. Captured at Quebec, 25th Dec., 1775, as 1st Sergt. in Lamb's N. Y. Co. Art.
BEATTY, ERKURIES. 29 Sept., 1789. [Born in Penn. Appointed from Penn.] Late 1st Lieut. and Bvt. Capt. 3rd Penn. Continental Inf. Appointed P. M. 3rd Penn. Continental Inf., 22 May, 1783.

*Lieutenants.*

DOYLE, THOMAS. 12 Aug., 1784. [Born in Penn. Appointed from Penn.] Late 1st Lieut. and Bvt. Capt. 3rd Penn. Continental Inf.
ARMSTRONG, JOHN. 8 Sept., 1785. [Born in Penn. Appointed from Penn.] Late 1st Lieut. and Bvt. Capt. 3rd Penn. Continental Inf.
*FROTHINGHAM, EBENEZER. 15 July, 1785. [Born in Conn. Appointed from Conn.] Late 1st Lieut. 3rd Conn. Continental Inf.
*PRATT, JOHN. 15 July, 1785. [Born in Conn. Appointed from Conn.] Late 1st Lieut. 3rd Penn. Continental Inf. Appointed Q. M. 3rd Penn. Continental Inf., 22 May, 1783. Appointed Q. M. 1st U. S. Inf., 3 Oct., 1786.
KERSEY, WILLIAM. 24 Nov., 1785. [Born in N. J. Appointed N. J.] Late 1st Lieut. and Bvt. Capt. 1st N. J. Continental Inf.
PETERS, WILLIAM. 27 June, 1786. [Born in N. Y. Appointed from N. Y.] Late Ens. 2nd N. Y. Continental Inf.
KINGSBURY, JACOB. 15 Oct., 1787. [Born in Conn. Appointed from Conn.] Late Ensign 3rd Conn. Continental Inf.
DENNY, EBENEZER. 10 Nov., 1787. [Born in Penn. Appointed from Penn.] Late Lieut. 3rd Penn. Continental Inf. Appointed Adj. 1st U .S. Inf., 8 Sept., 1785.

*Ensigns.*

LUSE, FRANCIS. 17 March, 1786. [Born in N. J. Appointed from N. J.] Late Ensign 2nd Reg. N. J. Continental Inf.
SEYDAM, CORNELIUS RYKER. 17 March, 1786. [Born in N. J. Appointed from N. J.] Late Ensign 1st Reg. N. J. Continental Inf.
*McDOWELL, NATHAN. 21 Oct., 1784. [Born in Penn. Appointed from Penn.] Cadet 1st U. S. Inf., 12 Aug., 1784.
JEFFERS, JOHN. 20 Oct., 1786. [Born in Conn. Appointed from Conn.] Late Priv. 4th Co. 2nd N. Y. Continental Inf. Served throughout Revolutionary War.
PRIOR, ABNER. 21 Oct., 1786. [Born in N. Y. Appointed from N. Y.] Late Surg. Mate, 2nd N. Y. Continental Inf.
HARTSHORNE, ASA. 15 Oct., 1787. [Born in Conn. Appointed from Conn.]
THOMSON, ROBERT. 26 Nov., 1787. [Born in Penn. Appointed from Penn.] Late 1st Lieut. 2nd Batt. Chester Co. Mil. Son of late Brig. Gen. William Thomson.
MELCHER, JACOB. 29 Sept., 1789. [Born in Penn. Appointed from Penn.] Cadet 1st U. S. Inf., 12 Dec., 1787.

## MEDICAL DEPARTMENT.

*Surgeon.*

ALLISON, RICHARD. 24 July, 1788. [Born in Penn. Appointed from Penn.] Late Surg. Mate 3rd Penn. Continental Reg. Inf. Appointed Surg. Mate 1st U. S. Inf., 12 Aug., 1784.

*Surgeon's Mates*

ELLIOTT, JOHN. 12 April, 1785. [Born in N. Y. Appointed from N. Y.] Late Surg. Mate 1st N. Y. Continental Reg. Inf.
SUMNER, JOSHUA. 9 June, 1785. [Born in Conn. Appointed from Conn.]
SCOTT, JOHN M. 17 March, 1786. [Born in N. J. Appointed from N. J.]
CARMICHAEL, JOHN F. 24 July, 1788. [Born in N. J. Appointed from Penn.]

# LIST OF THE

# Officers of the Army of the United States, 1797.

*Brig. General.*

James Wilkinson.

*Quartermaster General.*

John Wilkins, Jr.

*Paymaster General.*

Caleb Swan.

---

DRAGOONS.

*Captains.*

Solomon Van Rensselaer, 17 July, 1793.
James Taylor, 20 Feb., 1794.

*Lieutenants.*

William K. Blue, 14 July, 1794.
Matthias Slough, Jr., 20 Aug., 1794.
James V. Ball, 19 Oct., 1795.
Paul M'Dermot, 1 Oct., 1796.

---

ARTILLERISTS AND ENGINEERS.

*Lieut. Colonel Commandant.*

Stephen Rochefontaine, 26 Feb., 1795.

*Major.*

Henry Burbeck, 4 Nov., 1791.
Louis Tousard, 26 Feb., 1795.
John Jacob Ulrich Rivardi, 26 Feb., 1795.
Constant Freeman, Jr., 28 Feb., 1795.

*Captains.*

Mahlon Ford, 4 March, 1791.
John Pierce, 15 Oct., 1791.
Moses Porter, 4 Nov., 1791.
George Ingersoll, 2 April, 1793.
Griffith J. McRee, 2 June, 1794.
Richard Scott Blackburn, 2 June, 1794.
James Bruff, 2 June, 1794.
Alexander Thomson, 2 June, 1794.
William Littlefield, 2 June, 1794.
Frederick Frye, 2 June, 1794.
Michael Kaltlesen, 18 July, 1794.
Donald Grant Mitchell, 8 Aug., 1794.
Abimael Youngs Nicoll, 29 Nov., 1794.
Staats Morris, 26 Feb., 1795.
George Demler, 20 Aug., 1795.
Joseph Elliott, 19 July, 1796.

*Lieutenants.*

Piercy S. Pope, 5 March, 1792.
Ebenezer Massay, 5 March, 1792.
John M'Clellan, 2 June, 1794.
Nehemiah Freeman, 2 June, 1794.
James Sterrett, 2 June, 1794.
George Izard, 2 June, 1794.
Robert Rowan, 2 June, 1794.
Jonathan Robeson, 2 June, 1794.
Henry Muhlenburg, 2 June, 1794.
David Hale, 17 July, 1794.
Theophilus Elmer, 17 July, 1794.
William Wilson, 17 July, 1794.
Horiatio R. Dayton, 17 July, 1794.
William Morris, 29 July, 1794.
John M. Lovell, 26 Feb., 1795.
Peter Tallman, 26 Feb., 1795.
Joseph Guimpe, 26 Feb., 1795.
John Saunders, 26 Feb., 1795.
Thomas Underwood, 26 Feb., 1795.
Peter A. Dransey, 12 April, 1795.
Alexander Marscholk, 1 Nov., 1796.
Howell Cobb, 1 Nov., 1796.
Joseph Campbell, 1 Nov., 1796.
Richard Whiley, 19 Dec., 1796.
Philip Landais, 19 Dec., 1796.
Philip Rodrigue, 19 Dec., 1796.
James Triplett, 19 Dec., 1796.
Thomas J. Vandyke, 19 Dec., 1796.
Samuel T. Dyson, 19 Dec., 1796.
George Ross, 19 Dec., 1796.
James Rand, 19 Dec., 1796.
Robert Parkison, 19 Dec., 1796.

*Surgeon.*

Charles Brown.

*Surgeon's Mates.*

John Gorham Coffin.
John Lynch.
Samuel Osburn.
William Steele.

---

I REGIMENT OF INFANTRY.

*Lieut. Colonel Commandant.*

John F. Hamtramck, 18 Feb., 1793.

*Majors.*

Thomas Hunt, 18 Feb., 1793.
Thomas H. Cushing, 3 March, 1793.

*Captains.*

Jacob Kingsbury, 28 Dec., 1791.
Thomas Martin, 5 March, 1792.
Thomas Pasteur, 5 March, 1792.
Abner Prior, 2 June, 1792.
Daniel Britt, 13 Dec., 1793.
Samuel Tinsley, 9 Feb., 1794.
Hamilton Armstrong, 20 Feb., 1794.
Bernard Gaines, 1 April, 1794.

*Lieutenants.*

William H. Harrison, 2 June, 1792.
John Whistler, 27 Nov., 1792.
Jacob Kreemer, 13 Dec., 1792.
Daniel Bissell, 3 Jan., 1794.
Charles Hyde, 20 Feb., 1794.
John Michael, 1 April, 1794.
Ferdinand L. Claiborne, 30 June, 1794.
Elijah Strong, 1 July, 1794.

*Ensigns.*

Nicholas Rosencrantz, 12 May, 1794.
Robert Semple, 12 May, 1794.
Daniel M'Intosh, 12 May, 1794.
Robert Torrans, 2 June, 1794.
Yelverton Peyton, 17 July, 1794.
Jonn W. Thompson, 17 July, 1794.
Meriwether Lewis, 1 May, 1795.

*Surgeon.*

John Elliott.

*Surgeon's Mates.*

Elijah Tisdale.
Charles Watrous.

II REGIMENT OF INFANTRY.

*Lieut. Colonel Commandant.*

David Strong, 19 Feb., 1793.

*Majors.*

John H. Buell, 20 Feb., 1793.
Joseph Shaylor, 1 Oct., 1793.

*Captains.*

Cornelius Lyman, 30 July, 1792.
Richard H. Greaton, 18 Feb., 1793.
Russell Bissell, 19 Feb., 1793.
Edward Miller, 21 Feb., 1793.
Edward D. Turner, 11 Nov., 1793.
Theodore Sedgwick, 29 Dec., 1793.
Bartholomew Shaumburg, 30 June, 1794.
Andrew M'Clary, 19 Jan., 1797.

*Lieutenants.*

Peter Shoemaker, 3 March, 1793.
Jesse Lukens, 1 Oct., 1793.
Nanning J. Visscher, 1 May, 1794.
Archibald Grey, 1 May, 1794.
Robert Lee, 1 May, 1794.
Rezin Webster, 6 July, 1794.
Richard Butler, 20 Aug., 1794.
Charles Martin, 19 Jan., 1797.

*Ensigns.*

Benjamin Rand, 12 May, 1794.
James Richmond, 12 May, 1794.
David Thompson, 12 May, 1794.
John M'Clary, 12 May, 1794.
Samuel Allison, 2 June, 1794.
George Callender, 1 May, 1795.

*Surgeon.*

George Gillaspie.

*Surgeon's Mates.*

William McCoskry.
Thomas Farley.

---

### III Regiment of Infantry.

*Lieut. Colonel Commandant.*

Henry Gaither, 1 Oct., 1793.

*Majors.*

Jonathan Cass, 21 Feb., 1793.
William Kersey, 30 June, 1794.

*Captains.*

Zebulon Pike, 5 March, 1792.
Isaac Guion, 5 March, 1792.
John Heth, 5 March, 1792.
Richard Sparks, 5 March, 1792.
Howell Lewis, 5 March, 1792.
Thomas Lewis, 5 March, 1792.
William Rickard, 30 Jan., 1794.
John Wade, 30 June, 1794.

*Lieutenants.*

Samuel Vance, 5 March, 1792.
John Bowyer, 7 March, 1792.
Aaron Gregg, 30 June, 1792.
John Steele, 21 Feb., 1793.
Peter Marks, 10 Sept., 1793.
Charles Wright, 12 Nov., 1793.
Andrew Shanklin, 30 Jan., 1794.
Samuel Davidson, 9 Feb., 1794.

*Ensigns.*

William P. Smith, 12 May, 1794.
Hugh M'Call, 12 May, 1794.
David Fero, 12 May, 1794.
George Strother, 12 May, 1794.
Henry P. Sterling, 12 May, 1794.
Samuel Speak, 12 May, 1794.
William Scott, 1 May, 1795.

*Surgeon.*

Joseph Phillips.

*Surgeon's Mates.*

George Balfour.
John C. Wallace.

---

### IV Regiment of Infantry.

*Lieut. Colonel Commandant.*

Thomas Butler, 1 July, 1794.

*Majors.*

William Peters, 1 July, 1794.
Daniel Bradley, 19 Jan., 1797.

*Captains.*

Edward Butler, 5 March, 1792.
Joseph Brook, 5 March, 1792.
Alexander Gibson, 5 March, 1792.
William Preston, 5 March, 1792.
William Eaton, 5 March, 1792.
Henry De Butts, 28 Dec., 1792.
Robert Thomson, 16 April, 1794.
Ross Bird, 1 July, 1794.

*Lieutenants.*

Benjamin Lockwood, 5 March, 1792.
Benjamin Strother, 5 March, 1792.
William Diven, 9 June, 1792.
Peter Grayson, 28 Dec., 1792.
Jonathan Taylor, 26 March, 1793.
Robert Purdy, 19 April, 1793.
Campbell Smith, 10 Sept., 1793.
Hartman Leitheiser, 23 Feb., 1794.

*Ensigns.*

John Wallington, 23 Feb., 1793.
Francis Johnston, 23 Feb., 1793.
Thomas Swaine, 12 May, 1794.
Henry Bowyer, 12 May, 1794.
Samuel Dold, 12 May, 1794.
Richard Chandler, 12 May, 1794.
George Salmon, 1 May, 1795.
Larkin J. Dickinson, 16 Sept., 1796.

*Surgeon.*

John F. Carmichael.

*Surgeon's Mates.*

John Hamill.
David Davis.

---

### Additional Surgeon's Mates.

Cyrus Dart.
Frederic Dalcho.
George Pheiffer.
William A. M'Crea.
Thomas Augustine Claiborne.
David Patteson.

# Organization of the Army, June 1, 1802, under Act of March 16, 1802.

GENERAL STAFF.

*Brigadier General.*

James Wilkinson, Md., 5 March, 1792. Revolutionary Army.

ADJUTANT AND INSPECTOR.

*Lieut. Colonel.*

Thomas H. Cushing, Mass., 1 April, 1802. Revolutionary Army.

*Paymaster.*

Caleb Swan, Mass., 8 May, 1792. Revolutionary Army.

---

CORPS OF ENGINEERS.

*Major.*

Jonathan Williams, Pa., 16 Feb., 1801.

*Captain.*

William A. Barron, Mass., 6 May, 1800.

*1st Lieutenant.*

James Wilson, 26 May, 1800.

---

REGIMENT OF ARTILLERY.

*Colonel.*

Henry Burbeck, Mass., 1 April, 1802. Revolutionary Army.

*Lieut. Colonel.*

Constant Freeman, Mass., 1 April, 1802. Revolutionary Army.

*Majors.*

Daniel Jackson, Mass., 4 June, 1798. Revolutionary Army.
Decius Wadsworth, Conn., 9 Jan., 1800.
Moses Porter, Mass., 26 May, 1800. Revolutionary Army.
William MacRea, Va., 31 July, 1800.

*Captains.*

George Ingersoll, Mass., 2 April, 1793. Revolutionary Army.
Richard S. Blackburn, Va., 2 June( 1794, Revolutionary Army.
James Bruff, Md., 2 June, 1794. Revolutionary Army.
Michael Kaltieson, S. C., 18 July, 1794. Revolutionary Army.
Abimael Y. Nicoll, N. Y., 29 Nov., 1794.
Amos Stoddard, Mass., 4 June, 1798.
Lemuel Gates, Mass., 4 June, 1798.
James Read, Pa., 4 June, 1798.
James Stille, N. J., 4 June, 1798.
John McClallan, N. Y., 24 July, 1798.
Nehemiah Freeman, Mass., 6 Aug., 1798.
James Sterrett, Pa., 11 March, 1799.
George Izard, S. C., 12 July, 1799.
Jonathan Robeson, N. C., 3 March, 1800.
Henry M. Muhlenburgh, Pa., 26 May, 1800.
John W. Livingston, N. Y., 12 Nov., 1800.
Lloyd Beall, Md., 16 Feb., 1801. Revolutionary Army.
Josiah Dunham, N. H., 16 Feb., 1801.
George W. Carmichael, Pa., 20 May, 1801.
William L. Cooper, N. Y., 15 Aug., 1801.

*Lieutenants.*

Peter Tallman, N. J., 26 Feb., 1795. Revolutionary Army.
John Saunders, Va., 26 Feb., 1795.
Howell Cobb, Ga., 1 Nov., 1796.
Richard Whiley, N. Y., 19 Dec., 1796.
Philip Roderique, France, 19 Dec., 1796.
Samuel T. Dyson, Md., 19 Dec., 1796.
James B. Many, Del., 4 June, 1798.
John Fergus, Jr., N. C., 4 June, 1798.
Nathaniel Leonard, Vt., 4 June, 1798. Revolutionary Army.
Charles Wolstonecraft, Pa., 4 June, 1798.
Robert W. Osborn, Pa., 4 June, 1798.
George Waterhouse, R. I., 22 Feb., 1799.
Leonard Williams, Vt., 22 Feb., 1799.
Samuel Fowle, Mass., 22 Feb., 1799.
James House, Pa., 22 Feb., 1799.
Ebenezer Beebe, Conn., 22 Feb., 1799.
William Yates, N. Y., 22 Feb., 1799.
John De B. Walbach, France, 16 Feb., 1801.
John B. Barnes, Md., 16 Feb., 1801.
Addison B. Armistead, Va., 16 Feb., 1801.
Geofge Armistead, Va., 16 Feb., 1801.
Charles Hunt, Mass., 16 Feb., 1801.
Lewis Howard, N. J., 16 Feb., 1801.
William Cocks, N. Y., 16 Feb., 1801.
Moses Swett, N. H., 16 Feb., 1801.
John F. Powell, Va., 16 Feb., 1801.
Peter Lumpkin, Va., 16 Feb., 1801.
George Peter, Md., 16 Feb., 1801.
Clarence Mulford, N. J., 16 Feb., 1801.
Hezekiah W. Bissell, Conn., 16 Feb., 1801.
Joseph Cross, Md., 16 Feb., 1801.
Pierson Titcomb, N. H., 16 Feb., 1801.
William Wilson, Md., 16 Feb., 1801.
Samuel Welsh, Mass., 16 Feb., 1801.
Augustus Strong, Conn., 16 Feb., 1801.
Lewis Landais, France, 16 Feb., 1801.
William A. Murray, N. Y., 16 Feb., 1801.
Killian P. Van Renselaer, N. Y., 16 Feb., 1801.
Enoch Humphreys, Conn., 16 Feb., 1801.
Stephen Worrell, Pa., 8 June, 1801.

---

I REGIMENT OF INFANTRY.

*Colonel.*

John F. Hamtramck, N. Y., 1 April, 1802, Revolutionary Army.

*Lieut. Colonel.*

T omas Hunt, Mass., 1 April, 1802. Revolutionary Army.

*Major.*

Zebulon Pike, N. J., 21 March, 1800. Revolutionary Army.

*Captains.*

Thomas Pasteur, N. C., 5 March, 1792. Revolutionary Army.
Cornelius Lyman, Mass., 30 July, 1792. Revolutionary Army.
Russell Bissell, Conn., 19 Feb., 1793.
Edward D. Turner, Mass., 21 Nov., 1793.
John Whistler, Md., 1 July, 1797.
Daniel Bissell, Conn., 1 Jan., 1799.
Elijah Strong, Conn., 23 Oct., 1799.
Meriwether Lewis, Va., 5 Dec., 1800.
James Richmond, Jr., N. J., 21 May, 1801.
John McClary, N. H., 1 July, 1801.

*1st Lieutenants.*

John Whipple, 2 March, 1799.
George W. Stall, Pa., 2 March, 1799.

Moses Hooke, Mass., 23 Oct., 1799.
Zebulon M. Pike, N. J., 1 Nov., 1799.
Nathan Heald, Mass., 1 Nov., 1799.
Eli B. Clemson, Pa., 30 April, 1800.
James Rhea, N. J., 15 June, 1800.
William Swan, Mass., 16 Feb., 1801.
Ninian Pinkney, Md., 16 Feb., 1801.
William Carson, Pa., 16 Feb., 1801.
Horatio Stark, Va., 16 Feb., 1801.

*2nd Lieutenants.*

Simon Owens, Va., 16 Feb., 1801.
John W. Brownson, Vt., 16 Feb., 1801.
Daniel Hughes, Md., 16 Feb., 1801.
Alexander Macomb, Jr., N. Y., 16 Feb., 1801.
Daniel Baker, Vt., 16 Feb., 1801.
Ambrose Whitlock, N. W. T., 16 Feb., 1801.
Joseph Miller, Pa., 16 Feb., 1801.
Henry Hopkins, Md., 16 Feb., 1801.
William Whistler, N. W. T., 8 June, 1801.

*Ensigns.*

William Richardson, N. Y., 2 April, 1802.
Anthony Campbell, Pa., 2 April, 1802.
Thomas B. Steele, Md., 2 April, 1802.
James Porter, Pa., 2 April, 1802.
John C. Symmes, N. W. T., 2 April, 1802.
Joseph Dorr, Vt., 3 May, 1802.
Simeon Knight, Vt., 3 May, 1802.

---

II REGIMENT OF INFANTRY.

*Colonel.*

Thomas Butler, Pa., 1 April, 1802. Revolutionary Army.

*Lieut. Colonel.*

Thomas H. Cushing, Mass., 1 April, 1802. Revolutionary Army.

*Major.*

Jacob Kingsbury, Conn., 15 May, 1797. Revolutionary Army.

*Captains.*

Edward Butler, Pa., 5 March, 1792. Revolutionary Army.
Richard Sparks, Pa., 5 March, 1792.
Benjamin Lockwood, Va., 10 July, 1797.
Samuel C. Vance, Pa., 25 July, 1797.
John Bowyer, Va., 14 Jan., 1799.
Aaron Gregg, Va., 2 March, 1799.
Robert Purdy, Pa., 2 March, 1799.
Hugh McCall, S. C., 19 Aug., 1800.
Francis Johnston, N. Y., 15 Nov., 1800.
William R. Boote, 15 Nov., 1800.

*1st Lieutenants.*

Thomas Swaine, 1 Dec., 1797.
George Salmon, 2 March, 1799.
John Campbell, Va., 2 March, 1799.
Peter P. Schuyler, N. Y., 2 March, 1799.
James Bomer, Tenn., 2 March, 1799.
John Haines, Tenn., 2 March, 1799.
Samuel Lane, Md., 12 May, 1799.
Mathew Arbuckle, Va., 24 Oct., 1799.
Samuel Erwine, Pa., 16 Feb., 1801.
John Braham, Va., 16 Feb., 1801.

*2nd Lieutenants.*

Edmund P. Gaines, Tenn., 16 Feb., 1801.
Robert G. Barde, S. C., 16 Feb., 1801.
Bartholomew D. Armistead, Va., 16 Feb., 1801.
Benjamin Wilkinson, Md., 16 Feb., 1801.
William H. Woolridge, Ky., 16 Feb., 1801.
James Biddle Wilkinson, Md., 16 Feb., 1801.
Richard Buck, Pa., 16 Feb., 1801.
Henry R. Graham, 16 Feb., 1801.
William Piatt, N. J., 21 March, 1801.
William Lawrence, Md., 8 June, 1801.

*Ensigns.*

George T. Ross, Pa., 3 May, 1802.
Henry B. Brevoort, N. Y., 7 May, 1802.

---

MILITARY AGENTS.

*Agent for Northern Department.*

Peter Gansevoort, N. Y., 3 May, 1802. Revolutionary Army.

*Agent for Middle Department.*

William Linnard, Pa., 3 May, 1802.

*Agent for Southern Department.*

Abraham D. Abrahams, Ga., 3 May, 1802.

---

MEDICAL DEPARTMENT.

*Surgeons.*

John F. Carmichael, N. J., 5 March, 1792. Fort Adams, Miss.
David Davis, Pa., 1 April, 1802. Detroit.

*Surgeon's Mates.*

Samuel M. Griffith, Va., 24 July, 1800. Fort Johnston, N. C.
George Dill, R. I., 3 Aug., 1800. Fort Wolcott, R. I.
Charles Blake, Mass., 3 March, 1801. Fort Independence.
Prescott Barron, R. I., 3 March, 1801. Fort McHenry.
Edward Reynold, Md., 3 March, 1801. Mouth of the Ohio.
Philip Turner, Conn., 1 April, 1802. Fort Niagara.
John P. Fisher, N. Y., 1 April, 1802. Fort Mifflin.
Francis Le Barron, Mass., 1 April, 1802. Michilimackinac.
Alexander A. Peters, N. C., 1 April, 1802. Fort Johnston, N. C.
Southworth Harlow, Mass., 1 April, 1802. Fort Wilkinson, Ga.
John Rippey, Pa., 1 April, 1802. Chickasaw Bluffs.
Thomas R. Jack, Ga., 1 April, 1802. Mobile.
Robert Stark, Va., 1 April, 1802. Norfolk.
Trueman Tuttle, Pa., 1 April, 1802. Kaskakia.
Lyman Spaulding, N. Y., 1 April, 1802. Fort Jay, N. Y.
Henry Jackson, Ga., 1 April, 1802. For. Artillery in Ga.
James Lee, Conn., 1 April, 1802. Fort Trumbull, Conn.
Nathaniel Bedford, Pa., 1 April, 1802. Fort Wayne, N. W. T.
Samuel McKee, Jr., Inda. T., 1 April, 1802. Vincennes, Inda. T.
Thomas J. Van Dyke, Del., 1 April, 1802. S. W. Point, Tenn.

## A List of Officers in the Regiment of Artillerists, as arranged to Companies and Stations, 1 January, 1805.

FIELD OFFICERS.

*Colonel.*

Henry Burbeck, Washington City.

*Lieut. Colonel.*

Constant Freeman, New Orleans.

*Majors.*

Moses Porter, Territory of Louisiana.
William MacRea, South West Point.
James Bruff, St. Louis.
Abimael Y. Nicoll, New Orleans.

*Captains.*

Michael Kalterson, Fort Johnson.
Amos Stoddard, Saint Louis.
Lemuel Gates, Fort Constitution.
James Read, Fort Mifflin.
James Stile, New Orleans.
John McClellan, St. Louis.
Nehemiah Freeman, Fort Independence.
James Sterrett, Natchitoches.
Jonathan Robeson, New Orleans.
Lloyd Beall, Fort Wolcott.
Josiah Dunham, Michilimackinac.
George W. Carmichael, Chickasaw Bluffs.
William L. Cooper, New Orleans.
John Saunders, Fort Nelson.
Howell Cobb., S. W. Point.
Richard Wiley, Fort Jay.
Samuel T. Dyson, Detroit.
James B. Many, New Orleans.
John Fergus, New Orleans.
Nathaniel Leonard, Niagara.

*1st Lieutenants.*

John B. Barnes, Fort Johnson.
Clarence Mulford, St. Louis.
Moses Swett, Fort Constitution.
James House, Fort Miflin.
William Wilson, New Orleans.
George Peter, St. Louis.
Leonard William, Fort Independence.
Enoch Humphrey, Natchitoches.
Joseph Kimbole, New Orleans.
Charles Wollstoncraft, Fort Wolcott.
Lewis Howard, Fort Wolcott.
Joseph Cross, Michilimackinac.
Robert W. Osborn, Chickasaw Bluffs.
George Waterhouse, New Orleans.
Adn. B. Armistead, Fort Nelson.
William Yates, S. W. Point.
John B. Walback, Fort Jay.
William Cocks, Detroit.
William A. Murray, New Orleans.
Stephen Worrell, New Orleans.
George Armistead, Niagara.

*2nd Lieutenants.*

Robert Robert, Fort Johnson.
James Reed, St. Louis.
Robert Ritchie, Fort Constitution.
Joseph Hanham, Fort Mifflin.
Michael Welch, New Orleans.
Samuel Gates, St. Louis.
James McKellar, Fort Independence.
Thomas A. Smith, Natchitoches.
Thomas Murry, New Orleans.
William Clark, Michilimackinac.
James S. Swearingen, Chickasaw Bluffs.
Francis Newman, New Orleans.
John Livingston, Fort Nelson.
Reuben Smith, S. W. Point.
Jonathan Eastman, Fort Jay.
Porter Hanks, Detroit.
Joseph R. Henderson, New Orleans.
James S. Smith, New Orleans.
Hannibal M. Allen, Niagara.

## A List of Officers in the Regiments of Infantry, as arranged to Companies and Stations, 1 January, 1805.

I REGIMENT OF INFANTRY.

FIELD OFFICERS.

*Colonel.*

Thomas Hunt, Detroit.

*Lieut. Colonel.*

Jacob Kingsbury, Territory of Louisiana.

*Major.*

Zebulon Pike. On Furlough without limit.

*Captains.*

Cornelius Lyman, Fort Massac.
Russell Bissell, St. Louis.
John Whistler, Fort Dearborn, Mich.
Benjamin Lockwood, St. Louis.
Daniel Bissell, Fort Adams.
Elijah Strong, St. Louis.
Merriwether Lewis, St. Louis.
James Richmond, St. Louis.
John McClary, St. Louis.
John Whipple, Fort Wayne.

*1st Lieutenants.*

Nathan Heald, Fort Massac.
Zebulon M. Pike, St. Louis.
Moses Hooke, Fort Dearborn, Mich.
William Carson, St. Louis.
William Swan, Fort Adams.
Ninian Pinkney, St. Louis.
James Rhea, St. Louis.
Horatio Stark, St. Louis.
Eli B. Clemson, St. Louis.
Simon Owens, Fort Wayne.

*2nd Lieutenants.*

Ambrose Whitlock, Fort Massac.
Thomas B. Steele, St. Louis.
William Whistler, Fort Dearborn, Mich
William Richardson, St. Louis.
Daniel Hughes, Fort Adams.
Joseph Miller, St. Louis.
Henry Hopkins, St. Louis.
John C. Symmes, St. Louis.
Daniel Baker, St. Louis.

*Ensigns.*

Neal Duffee, Fort Massac.
Alpha Kingsley, St. Louis.
Jonathan Eastman, St. Louis.
Hezekiah Johnson, Fort Adams.
Simeon Knight, St. Louis.
Joseph Dorr, St. Louis.
John Roney, St. Louis.
John Brownson, Fort Wayne.

II Regiment of Infantry.

Field Officers.

*Colonel.*

Thomas Butler, New Orleans.

*Lieut. Colonel.*

T. H. Cushing, St. Louis.

*Major.*

Thomas Pasteur, Territory of Orleans.

*Captains.*

Richard Sparks, Fort Adams.
Edward D. Turner, Natchitoches.
John Bowyer, Attakapas.
Hugh McCall, Fort Wilkinson.
Francis Johnston, Natchitoches.
William R. Boote, Fort Wilkinson.
Thomas Swaine, Fort Stoddert.
John Campbell, Fort Adams.
Peter B. Schuyler, Fort Stoddert.
Joseph Bowmar, Natchitoches.

*1st Lieutenants.*

Richard Buck, Fort Adams.
William Piatt, Natchitoches.
William Lawrence, Attakapas.
Barthol. D. Armistead, Fort Wilkinson.
Mathew Arbuckle, Natchitoches.
Henry R. Graham, Fort Wilkinson.
John Hanes, Fort Stoddert.
John Brahan, Fort Adams.
Edward P. Gaines, Fort Stoddert.
James Wilkinson, Natchitoches.

*2nd Lieutenants.*

James Logan, Fort Adams.
Josiah Taylor, Natchitoches.
Henry B. Brevort, Attakapas.
Samuel Williamson, Fort Wilkinson.
Williams Simmons, Natchitoches.
John Miller, Fort Wilkinson.
Alfred Sebastian, Fort Stoddert.
William P. Clyma, Fort Adams.
Reuben Chamberlin, Fort Stoddert.
Gilbert C. Russell, Natchitoches.

*Ensigns.*

George W. Sevier, Fort Adams.
James Bludsworth, Natchitoches.
Robert Peyton, Attakapas.
Charles Magnan, Fort Wilkinson.
John Hackett, Natchitoches.
Anthony Foster, Fort Wilkinson.
John R. N. Luckett, Fort Stoddert.
William Mead, Fort Adams.
Benjamin S. Smoot, Fort Stoddert.
John Joseph Duforest, Natchitoches.

---

## Rank of the Captains and Subalterns in the United States Regiment of Artillery, 1806.

Field Officers.

*Colonel.*

Henry Burbeck, 1 April, 1802.

*Lieut. Colonel.*

Constant Freeman, 1 April, 1802.

*Majors.*

Moses Porter, 26 May, 1800.
William MacRae, 31 July, 1800.
James Bruff, 15 Nov., 1803.
Abimael Y. Nicoll, 1 Dec., 1804.

*Captains.*

Michael Kaltiesen, 18 July, 1794.
Amos Stoddard, 4 June, 1798.
James Read, 4 June, 1798.
Nehemiah Freeman, 6 Aug., 1798.
Lloyd Beall, 16 Feb., 1801.
Josiah Dunham, 16 Feb., 1801.
William Cooper, 15 Aug., 1801.
John Saunders, 30 April, 1803.
Richard Whiley, 15 Nov., 1803.
Samuel T. Dyson, 15 Sept., 1804.
James B. Many, 1 Oct., 1804.
John Fergus, 1 Dec., 1804.
Nathaniel Leonard, 1 Dec., 1804.
Charles Wollstoncraft, 13 March, 1805.
George Waterhouse, 20 Sept., 1805.
James House, 1 Nov., 1805.
William Yates, 31 Dec., 1805.
John B. Walback, 31 Jan., 1806.
Addison Armistead, 30 Sept., 1806.
George Armistead, 31 Oct., 1806.

*1st Lieutenants.*

Lewis Howard, 16 Feb., 1801.
William Cocks, 16 Feb., 1801.
Moses Swett, 16 Feb., 1801.
George Peter, 16 Feb., 1801.
Clarence Mulford 16 Feb., 1801.
Joseph Cross, 16 Feb., 1801.
William Wilson, 16 Feb., 1801.
William A. Murray, 16 Feb., 1801.
Enoch Humphrey, 16 Feb., 1801.
Stephen Worrell, 8 June, 1801.
Francis Newman, 13 March, 1805.
James S. Swearingen, 16 May, 1805.
Thomas A. Smith, 31 Dec., 1805.
William Clark, 31 Jan., 1806.
Hannibal M. Allen, 31 Jan., 1806.
James S. Smith, 31 April, 1806.
Joseph Kimble, 18 Sept., 1806.
Robert Roberts, 30 Oct., 1806.
James Hannam, 31 Oct., 1806.
Robert W. Osborn.

*2nd Lieutenants.*

Michael Walsh, 17 Jan., 1805.
James Reed, 17 Jan., 1805.
Porter Hanks, 17 Jan., 1805.
Thomas Murray, 17 Jan., 1805.
Jonathan Eastman, 31 March, 1805.
William Gates, 6 March, 1806.
Julius Heileman, 6 March, 1806.
Pascal V. Bouis, 6 March, 1806.
John Gansevort, 6 March, 1806.
Alexander Laneuville, 6 March, 1806.
Elias Prible, 6 March, 1806.
Hopeley Yeaton, 6 March, 1806.
Jacob Jackson, 6 March, 1806.
Thomas N. Vaughn, 21 April, 1806.
Samuel Maclay, 21 April, 1806.
Joseph Provaux, 14 Nov., 1806.
Thomas Bennett, 14 Nov., 1806.
Ethan Allen, 14 Nov., 1806.
Robert Lucas, 14 Nov., 1806.
John D. Wyndham, 14 Nov., 1806.

## Rank of the Captains and Subalterns in the 1st United States Regiment of Infantry, 1806.

FIELD OFFICERS.

*Colonel.*

Thomas Hunt, 11 April, 1803.

*Lieut. Colonel.*

Jacob Kingsbury, 11 April, 1803.

*Major.*

Zebulon Pike, 21 March, 1800.

*Captains.*

Russell Bissell, 19 Feb., 1793.
John Whistler, 1 July, 1797.
Benjamin Lockwood, 10 July, 1797.
Daniel Bissell, 1 Jan., 1799.
Elijah Strong, 23 Oct., 1799.
Meriwether Lewis, 5 Dec., 1800.
John McClary, 1 July, 1801.
John Whipple, 11 April, 1803.
Moses Hooke, 13 March, 1805.
Zebulon M. Pike.

*1st Lieutenants.*

Nathan Heald, 1 Nov., 1799.
Eli B. Clemson, 30 April, 1800.
James Rhea, 15 June, 1800.
William Swan, 16 Feb., 1801.
Ninian Pinkney, 16 Feb., 1801.
William Carson, 16 Feb., 1801.
Horatio Stark, 11 April, 1803.
Simon Owens, 15 Dec., 1803.
Daniel Hughes.
Daniel Baker.

*2nd Lieutenants.*

Ambrose Whitlock, 16 Feb., 1801.
William Whistler, 18 June, 1801.
William Richardson, 12 Oct., 1802.
John C. Symmes, 1 May, 1804.
Joseph Dorr, 23 March, 1805.
Simeon Knight, 1 April, 1805.
Alpha Kingsley, 25 June, 1805.
John Roney, 24 Aug., 1806.
Hezekiah Johnson, 20 June, 1806.
Benjamin Marshall.

*Ensigns.*

John Brownson, 27 June, 1804.
John Magouen, 27 June, 1804.
John F. Bouel, 6 March, 1806.
Thomas Hambleton, 6 March, 1806.
Joseph McKean, 6 March, 1806.
James R. Peyton, 6 March, 1806.
Jacob Albright, 6 March, 1806.
John Read, 21 April, 1806.
Louis Laranice, 14 Nov., 1806.
Philip Ostrander, 14 Nov., 1806.

---

## Rank of the Captains and Subalterns in the 2nd United States Regiment of Infantry, 1806.

FIELD OFFICERS.

*Colonel.*

Thomas H. Cushing, 7 Sept., 1805.

*Major.*

Richard Sparks, 29 July, 1806.

*Captains.*

John Bowyer, 14 Jan., 1799.
Hugh McCall, 19 Aug., 1800.
Francis Johnston, 15 Nov., 1800.
William R. Boote, 15 Nov., 1800.
Thomas Swaine, 1 July, 1802.
John Campbell, 30 Sept., 1803.
Peter P. Schuyler, 20 Dec., 1803.
John Hanes, 30 Nov., 1805.
Mathew Arbuckle, 20 June, 1806.
John Brahan, 29 July, 1806.

*1st Lieutenants.*

Edmund P. Gaines, 27 April, 1802.
Bartholomew D. Armistead, 12 Aug., 1802.
James Wilkinson, 30 Sept., 1803.
Richard Buck, 30 Nov., 1803.
Henry R. Graham, 20 Dec., 1803.
William Platt, 16 June, 1804.
William Lawrence, 12 Oct., 1804.
Henry B. Brevort, 30 Nov., 1805.
John Miller, 20 June, 1806.
William P. Clyma ,29 July, 1806.

*2nd Lieutenants.*

Reuben Chamberlin, 20 Dec., 1803.
Samuel Williamson, 16 June, 1804.
Gilbert C. Russell, 3 Sept., 1804.
Alfred Sebastian, 12 Oct., 1804.
George W. Sevier, 22 Aug., 1805.
John R. N. Luckett, 30 Nov., 1805.
Robert Peyton, 20 June, 1806.
Benjamin S. Smoot, 3 July, 1806.
Charles Magnan, 29 July, 1806.
John J. Duforest.

*Ensigns.*

John Hackett, 17 Jan., 1805.
William C. Mead, 17 Jan., 1805.
John Pemberton, 6 March, 1806.
Thomas Clements, 6 March, 1806.
Thomas W. Small, 6 March, 1806.
Auguste Chouteau, 20 June, 1806.
David C. Dean, 14 Nov., 1806.
James H. Mitchell, 14 Nov., 1806.
William F. Ware.

## The Army of the United States, April, 1809.

### GENERAL STAFF.

*Brig Generals.*

James Wilkinson, 5 March, 1792.
Wade Hampton, 15 Feb., 1809.
Peter Gansevoort, 15 Feb., 1809.

### ADJUTANT AND INSPECTOR.

*Major.*

Abimael Y. Nicoll, 2 April, 1807.

*Paymaster.*

Robert Brent, 1 July, 1808.

### CORPS OF ENGINEERS.

*Colonel.*

Jonathan Williams, 23 Feb., 1808.

*Lieut. Colonel.*

Jared Mansfield, 25 Feb., 1808.

*Majors.*

Alexander Macomb, 23 Feb., 1808.
Joseph G. Swift, 23 Feb., 1808.

*Captains.*

Walker K. Armistead, 30 Oct., 1806.
George Bomford, 23 Feb., 1808.
Wm. McRee, 23 Feb., 1808.
Charles Gratiot, 23 Feb., 1808.

*1st Lieutenants.*

Alden Partridge, 30 Oct., 1806.
Eleazer D. Wood, 23 Feb., 1808.
William Partridge, 23 Feb., 1808.
Prentiss Willard, 23 Feb., 1808.

*2nd Lieutenants.*

Joseph G. Totten, 23 Feb., 1808.
Samuel Babcock, 23 Feb., 1808.
Daniel A. A. Buck, 23 Feb., 1808.
Sylvanus Thayer, 23 Feb., 1808.

---

### REGIMENT OF ARTILLERISTS.

*Colonel.*

Henry Burbeck, 1 April, 1802.

*Lieut. Colonel.*

Constant Freeman, 1 April, 1802.

*Majors.*

Moses Porter, 26 May, 1800.
William MacRea, 31 July, 1800.
Abimael Y. Nicoll, 1 Dec., 1804.
Amos Stoddard, 30 June, 1807.

*Captains.*

James Read, 4 June, 1798.
Nehemiah Freeman, 6 Aug., 1798.
Llo"d Beall, 16 Feb., 1801.
Richard Wiley, 15 Nov., 1803.
Samuel T. Dyson, 15 Sept., 1804.
James B. Many, 1 Oct., 1804.
Nathaniel Leonard, 1 Dec., 1804.
Charles Wollstonecraft, 13 March, 1805.
James House, 1 Nov., 1805.
John De B. Walbach, 31 Jan., 1806.
Addison B. Armistead, 30 Sept., 1806.
George Armistead, 31 Oct., 1806.
Lewis Howard, 1 Nov., 1806.
William Cocks, 11 April, 1807.
Moses Swett, 30 June, 1807.
Clarence Mulford, 30 April, 1808.
William Wilson, May, 1808.
William A. Murray, 21 May, 1808.
Joseph Cross, 7 Nov., 1808.
Enoch Humphrey, 9 Jan., 1809.

*1st Lieutenants.*

Francis Newman, 13 March, 1805.
James S. Swearingen, 15 May, 1805.
Hannibal M. Allen, 31 Jan., 1806.
Joseph Kimball, 18 Sept., 1806.
Robert Roberts, 31 Oct., 1806.
James R. Hannam, 1 Nov., 1806.
Michael Walsh, 1 Nov., 1806.
James Reed, Dec., 1806.
Porter Hands, 31 Dec., 1806.
Thomas Murray, 11 April, 1807.
Jonathan Eastman, 30 June, 1807.
William Gates, 3 Nov., 1807.
Julius F. Heileman, 30 April, 1808.
John Gansevoort, May, 1808.
Alexander Laneuville, 21 May, 1808.
Esaias Preble May, 1808.
Hopley Yeaton, 31 July, 1808.
Thomas N. Vaughan, Sept., 1808.
Samuel Maclay, Nov., 1808.

*2nd Lieutenants.*

Joseph Proveaux, 14 Nov., 1806.
Thomas Bennett, 14 Nov., 1806.
Ethan A. Allen, 14 Nov., 1806.
Robert Lucas, 14 Nov., 1806.
John D. Wyndham, 14 Nov., 1806.
Archibald Darragh, 27 Feb., 1807.
Mann P. Lomax, 10 June, 1807.
Justus Post, 9 Dec., 1807.
Satterlee Clark, 9 Dec., 1807.
Samuel Champlin, 9 Dec., 1807.
John Anderson, 9 Dec., 1807.
Samuel B. Bathbone, 13 June, 1808.
Heman A. Fay, 13 June, 1808.
Milo Mason, 9 Jan., 1809.
Christopher Van DeVenter, 9 Jan., 1809.
John Fitzgerald, 9 Jan., 1809.
John Erving, Jr., 9 Jan., 1809.
Solomon G. Conklin, 24 Jan., 1809.
Augustus W. Magee, 24 Jan., 1809.
Abraham L. Sands, 18 Feb., 1809.

---

### REGIMENT OF LIGHT ARTILLERY.

*Major.*

John Saunders, 9 Jan., 1809.

*Captains.*

George Peter, 3 Nov., 1807.
Winfield Scott, 3 May, 1808.
Abraham Eustis, 3 May, 1808.
William N. Irvine, 3 May, 1808.
Joseph Chandler, 3 May, 1808.
Josiah G. Telfair, 3 May, 1808.
Daniel Gano, 3 May, 1808.
Solomon N. Townsend, 3 May, 1808.
Nathan Esterbrook, 3 May, 1808.
John R. Spann, 1 July, 1808.

*1st Lieutenants.*

Thomas Pitts, 3 May, 1808.
Alexander S. Brooks, 3 May, 1808.
Samuel Watson, 18 June, 1808.
John H. T. Estes, 1 July, 1808.
James S. McKelvey, 1 July, 1808.
James Gibson, 12 Dec., 1808.
William Campbell, 12 Dec., 1808.
Robert H. Macpherson, 12 Dec., 1808.
John N. McIntosh, 12 Dec., 1808.
Samuel Price, 12 Dec., 1808.

*2nd Lieutenants.*

Killian N. Van Rensselaer, 3 May, 1808.
Andrew McDowell, 18 June, 1808.
Samuel H. Holley, 12 Dec., 1808.
Samuel Newman, 12 Dec., 1808.
Alpheus Roberts, 12 Dec., 1808.
Luther Leonard, 12 Dec., 1808.
Henry Le Nud, 12 Dec., 1808.
Benjamjin Branch, 12 Dec., 1808.
George W. Melvin, 12 Dec., 1808.

*Surgeon.*

Dennis Claude, 12 Dec., 1808.

*Surgeon's Mate.*

Peter Turner, 12 Dec., 1808.

---

REGIMENT OF LIGHT DRAGOONS.

*Lieut. Colonel.*

Leonard Covington, 9 Jan., 1809.

*Major.*

Electus Backus, 7 Oct., 1808.

*Captains.*

Alexander F. Rose, 3 May, 1808.
Clement C. Biddle, 3 May, 1808.
Jacint Laval, 3 May, 1808.
David Brearly, 3 May, 1808.
Noah Lester, 13 June, 1808.
James Thomas, 1 July, 1808.
Isaac A. Coles, 16 Jan., 1809.
Nelson Luckett, 23 Feb., 1809.

*1st Lieutenants.*

Alexander S. Lyle, 3 May, 1808.
Bille. Williams, 3 May, 1808.
Thomas A. Helms, 3 May, 1808.
James J. Bowie, 3 May, 1808.
Arthur P. Hayne, 3 May, 1808.
Asa Morgan, 13 June, 1808.
John M. Barclay, 18 June, 1808.
Seleck Osborn, 8 July, 1808.

*2nd Lieutenants.*

Silas Halsey, 3 May, 1808.
Samuel M. Lee, 3 May, 1808.
Alexander Cummings, 3 May, 1808.
George Nicols, 13 June, 1808.
William M. Littlejohn, 1 July, 1808.
Jonas Munroe, 8 July, 1808.
Ferdinand Ludlow, 12 Dec., 1808.
George Haig, 12 Dec., 1808.

*Cornets.*

Levi Hukill, 3 May, 1808.
Elijah Boardman, 13 June, 1808.
John Hollingshead, 18 June, 1808.
Joseph Kean, 1 July, 1808.
Henry Whiting, 20 Oct., 1808.
Robert P. McKelvay, 12 Dec., 1808.
George Birch, 12 Dec., 1808.
Milton Haxtun, 25 Jan., 1809.

*Surgeon.*

Lewis Dunham, 12 Dec., 1808.

---

FIRST REGIMENT OF INFANTRY.

*Colonel.*

Jacob Kingsbury, 18 Aug., 1808.

*Lieut. Colonel.*

Daniel Bissell, 18 Aug., 1808.

*Major.*

Zebulon Pike, 21 March, 1800.

*Captains.*

John Whistler, 1 July, 1797.
Elijah Strong, 23 Oct., 1799. Promoted Major 7th, 15 Dec., 1808.
Nathan Heald, 31 Jan., 1807.
Eli B. Clemson, 4 March, 1807.
James Rhea, 29 July, 1807.
William Swan, 15 Nov., 1807.
Ninian Pinkney, 9 Dec., 1807.
William Carson, 20 Jan., 1808.
Horatio Stark, 3 May, 1808.
Simon Owens, 18 Aug., 1808.

*1st Lieutenants.*

Daniel Hughes, 23 March, 1805. Promoted Capt. 15 Dec., 1808.
Daniel Baker, Aug., 1806.
Ambrose Whitlock, 31 Jan., 1807.
William Whistler, 4 March, 1807.
John C. Symmes, 29 July, 1807.
Simeon Knight, 9 Dec., 1807.
Alpha Kingsley, 20 Jan., 1808.
Hezekiah Johnson, 18 Aug., 1808.
Benjamin Marshall, 14 Oct., 1808.

*2nd Lieutenants.*

John Brownson, Jan., 1807.
Thomas Hamilton, June, 1807.
James R. Peyton, July, 1807.
Jacob W. Albright, Nov., 1807.
John Read.
Louis Loramier, 20 Jan., 1808.
Philip Ostrander, May, 1808.
Nathaniel Pryor, May, 1808.
Seth Thompson, 18 Aug., 1808.
Michael Immell, 14 Oct., 1808.

*Ensigns.*

Samuel Perkins, 9 Dec., 1807.
Linai T. Helm, 9 Dec., 1807.
William H. Lithgow, 9 Dec., 1807.
James W. Bryson, 23 April, 1808.
Robert C. Page, 23 April, 1808.
John Campbell, 13 June, 1808.
Dixon Stansbury, 13 June, 1808.
Parker Greenough, 12 Dec., 1808.
Lewis Bissell, 12 Dec., 1808.

---

II REGIMENT OF INFANTRY.

*Colonel.*

Thomas H. Cushing, 7 Sept., 1805.

*Lieut. Colonel.*

Richard Sparks, 29 July, 1806.

*Major.*

John Bowyer, 18 Aug., 1808.

*Captains.*

Hugh McCall., 19 Aug., 1800.
Francis Johnston, 15 Nov., 1800.
William R. Boote, 15 Nov., 1800.
John Campbell, 30 Sept., 1803.
Peter P. Schuyler, 20 Dec., 1803.
Mathew Arbuckle, 20 June, 1806.
John Brahan, 29 July, 1806.
Edmund P. Gaines, 28 Feb., 1807.
Bartholomew D. Armistead, 18 Aug., 1808.
James B. Wilkinson, 8 Oct., 1808.

*1st Lieutenants.*

William Platt, 16 June, 1804.
William Lawrence, 12 Oct., 1804.
Henry B. Brevoort, 30 Nov., 1805.
John Miller, 20 June, 1806.
Reuben Chamberlin, Oct., 1806.

John R. N. Luckett, Aug., 1807.
Robert Peyton, Jan., 1808.
Benjamin S. Smoot, 3 May, 1808.
John V. Duforest, Aug., 1808.
John Hackett, Dec., 1808.

*2nd Lieutenants.*

William C. Mead, Feb., 1807.
John T. Pemberton, 27 Feb., 1807.
William F. Ware, Jan., 1808.
John C. Carter, Jan., 1808.
John M. Davis, May, 1808.
John Wetzel, July, 1808.
Alexander Brownlow, Sept., 1808.
Jesse White, Oct., 1808.
Samuel Noah, 18 Aug., 1808.

*Ensigns.*

Robert G. Seeley, 9 Dec., 1807.
John Stanard, 9 Dec., 1807.
John Mathers, 13 June, 1808.
Benedict Stewart, 13 June, 1808.
Robert Cherry, 13 June, 1808.
John T. Wirt, 12 Dec., 1808.
John H. Robinson, 12 Dec., 1808.
Evert Bogardus, 12 Dec., 1808.
Hezekiah Bradley, 12 Dec., 1808.
Barony Vasquez, 12 Dec., 1808.

---

## III Regiment of Infantry.

*Colonel.*

Edward Pasteur, 3 May, 1808.

*Lieut. Colonel.*

John Smith, 9 Jan., 1809.

*Major.*

Homer V. Milton, 3 May, 1808.

*Captains.*

John Darrington, 3 May, 1808.
Mossman Houston, 3 May, 1808.
Abner Pasteur, 3 May, 1808.
Ross Bird, 1 July, 1808.
John Nicks, 1 July, 1808.
Henry Atkinson, 1 July, 1808.
Jacob J. Faust, 1 July, 1808.
Prentiss Law, 1 July, 1808.
John McClelland, 1 July, 1808.
James Woodruff, 12 Dec., 1808.

*1st Lieutenants.*

William Butler, 3 May, 1808.
Cadwalader Jones, 3 May, 1808.
Robert McDougall, 3 May, 1808.
Robert B. Moore, 3 May, 1808.
Duncan L. Clinch, 1 July, 1808.
James E. Dinkins, Jr., 1 July, 1808.
Lays G. White, 1 July, 1808.
William S. Hamilton, 1 July, 1808.
James Moore, 12 Dec., 1808.
William R. Davis, 27 Jan., 1809.

*2nd Lieutenants.*

Samuel W. Butler, 3 May, 1808.
Henry Chotard, 3 May, 1808.
William Johnson, 3 May, 1808.
Timothy Spann, 1 July, 1808.
Benajmin D. Herriott, 1 July, 1808.
Benjamin M. Jackson, 1 July, 1808.
Charles C. McKenzie, 1 July, 1808.
Holloway James, 12 Dec., 1808.
Edward Mason, 12 Dec., 1808.

*Ensigns.*

Stephen Rose, 3 May, 1808.
Samuel C. Mabson, 1 July, 1808.
Robert Watson, 1 July, 1808.
John Burnett, 1 July, 1808.
Joel Lyon, 1 July, 1808.
Sterling Anderson, 1 July, 1808.
William Laval, 12 Dec., 1808.
Benjamin Harvey, Jr., 12 Dec., 1808.

---

## IV Regiment of Infantry.

*Colonel.*

John P. Boyd, 7 Oct., 1808.

*Lieut. Colonel.*

John Whiting, 8 July, 1808.

*Major.*

James Miller, 8 July, 1808.

*Captains.*

William C. Baen, 3 May, 1808.
Paul Wentworth, 3 May, 1808.
David Byers, 3 May, 1808.
Stephen Ranney, 13 June, 1808.
Joel Cook, 13 June, 1808.
Isaiah Doane, 13 June, 1808.
George W. Prescott, 18 June, 1808.
John Binney, 12 Dec., 1808.

*1st Lieutenants.*

Alden G. Cushman, 3 May, 1808.
Josiah Snelling, 3 May, 1808.
Robert C. Barton, 3 May, 1808.
William Welsh, 13 June, 1808.
Nicoll Fosdic, 13 June, 1808.
Oliver G. Burton, 18 June, 1808.
Samuel Haines, 18 June, 1808.
Nathaniel F. Adams, 18 June, 1808.
Samuel Page, 18 June, 1808.
Charles Fuller, 1 July, 1808.

*2nd Lieutenants.*

Charles Larrabee, 13 June, 1808.
Ebenezer Way, 18 June, 1808.
Minor Huntington, 18 June, 1808.
Jackson Durant, 18 June, 1808.
Lewis Harrington, 1 July, 1808.
Samuel Borden, 1 July, 1808.
John L. Eastman, 12 Dec., 1808.
Benjamin Hill, 12 Dec., 1808.

*Ensigns.*

Timothy Gerrish, 3 May, 1808.
Frederick Conklin, 18 June, 1808.
Abraham Hawkins, 18 June, 1808.
George P. Peters, 18 June, 1808.
Jonathan Simonds, 13 June, 1808.
John Smith, 18 June, 1808.
Lewis Peckham, 12 Dec., 1808.
George Gooding, 12 Dec., 1808.
Anson Hall, 27 Jan., 1809.
Josiah Bacon, Jr., 27 Jan., 1809.

*Surgeon.*

Josiah D. Foster, 12 Dec., 1808.

---

## V. Regiment of Infantry.

*Colonel.*

Alexander Parker, 3 May, 1808.

*Lieut. Colonel.*

William D. Beall, 12 Dec., 1808.

*Major.*

Tully Robinson, 16 Jan., 1809.

*Captains.*

Nimrod Long, 3 May, 1808.
George Gibson, 3 May, 1808.

Richard C. Dale, 3 May, 1808.
Edward Dillard, 3 May, 1808.
Benjamin Wallace, 18 June, 1808.
James Bankhead, 18 June, 1808.
Colin Buckner, 1 July, 1808.
William E. Williams, 16 Jan., 1809.
John Johnson, 25 Jan., 1809.
Fayette Roane, 25 Jan., 1809.

*1st Lieutenants.*

George M. Brooke, 3 May, 1808.
Richard Whartenby, 3 May, 1808.
Townsend Stith, 3 May, 1808.
Roger A. Jones, 3 May, 1808.
James Fonerdon, 3 May, 1808.
Mordecai Griffith, 3 May, 1808.
Henry Saunders 3 May, 1808.
Alexander McIlhenny, 18 June, 1808.
Talbot Chambers, 18 June, 1808.
James Dorman, 1 July, 1808.

*2nd Lieutenants.*

William S. Henshaw, 3 May, 1808.
Leroy Opie, 3 May, 1808.
Richard H. Bell, 3 May, 1808.
Jacob Hindman, 3 May, 1808.
Washington Lee, 3 May, 1808.
William King, 3 May, 1808.
George Washington, 24 Oct., 1808.
Elias Edmunds, Nov., 1808.

*Ensigns.*

Robert Carson, 3 May, 1808.
John Jamison, Jr., 1 July, 1808.
James Saunders, 1 July, 1808.
Daniel Ward, 12 Dec., 1808.
Jeremiah Yancey, 12 Dec., 1808.
Joseph Owens, 12 Dec., 1808.
John Suter.
Edward L. Lomax, 25 Jan., 1809.

*Surgeon.*

William Upshaw, 12 Dec., 1808.

---

## VI Regiment of Infantry.

*Colonel.*

Jonas Simonds, 8 July, 1808.

*Lieut. Colonel.*

Joseph Constant, 7 Oct., 1808.

*Major.*

Zebulon M. Pike, 3 May, 1808.

*Captains.*

William P. Bennett, 3 May, 1808.
Ebenezer Cross, 3 May, 1808.
Samuel Cherry, 3 May, 1808.
John T. Bentley, 3 May, 1808.
Thomas Davis, 3 May, 1808.
Jonathan Brooks, 18 June, 1808.
William Cock, 18 June, 1808.
William Pennell, 12 Dec., 1808.

*1st Lieutenants.*

Ebenezer Bebee, 3 May, 1808.
John Christie, 3 May, 1808.
James Chambers, 3 May, 1808.
John Machesney, 3 May, 1808.
George Nelson, 3 May, 1808.
John T. Arrowsmith, 3 May, 1808.
Gad Humphreys, 3 May, 1808.
John Walworth, 12 Dec., 1808.
Peter Muhlenberg, Jr., 12 Dec., 1808.
John Stewart, 25 Jan., 1809.

*2nd Lieutenants.*

Clement Sadlier, 3 May, 1808.
William Nicholas, 3 May, 1808.
Abel Morse, 3 May, 1808.
Robert Sterry, 3 May 1808.
James E. A. Masters, 3 May, 1808.
Chauncey Pettibone, 3 May, 1808.
Henry Philips, 3 May, 1808.
John J. Plume, 18 June, 1808.
James J. Voorhees, 18 June, 1808.
John Gilland, 25 Jan., 1809.

*Ensigns.*

Neil Shaw, 3 May, 1808.
William Gamble, 3 May, 1808.
Edward Webb, 3 May, 1808.
Charles K. Gardner, 3 May, 1808.
Henry Shell, 3 May, 1808.
Jacob Sinn, 3 May, 1808.
Jacob Heet, 3 May, 1808.
Asa Grimes, 18 June, 1808.
John Reigart, 25 Jan., 1809.

*Surgeon.*

Isaac Davis, 12 Dec., 1808.

*Surgeon's Mate.*

William E. Lee, 12 Dec., 1808.

---

## VII Regiment of Infantry.

*Colonel.*

William Russell, 3 May, 1808.

*Lieut. Colonel.*

Robert Purdy, 9 Jan., 1809.

*Major.*

Elijah Strong, 15 Dec., 1808.

*Captains.*

Gilbert C. Russell, 3 May, 1808.
Robert C. Nicholas, 3 May, 1808.
George R. C. Floyd, 3 May, 1808.
Thomas J. Vandyke, 3 May, 1808.
Thornton Posey, 3 May, 1808.
Edward Hord, 3 May, 1808.
Arthur Morgan, 3 May, 1808.
James Desha, 12 Dec., 1808.
Thomas Beall.

*1st Lieutenants.*

Uriah Blue, 3 May, 1808.
Martin Duralde, 3 May, 1808.
Richard Oldham, 3 May, 1808.
James Doherty, 3 May, 1808.
Enos Cutler, 3 May, 1808.
Zachariah Taylor, 3 May, 1808.
Walter H. Overton, 3 May, 1808.
Cary Nicholas, 3 May, 1808.
William McClellan, 3 May, 1808.
Alexander Calvit.

*2nd Lieutenants.*

Alexander A. White, 3 May, 1808.
Thomas S. Jesup, 3 May, 1808.
Elisha Edwards, 3 May, 1808.
Narcissus Broutin, 12 Dec., 1808.
Jesse Jennings, 12 Dec., 1808.
Archibald Greer, 12 Dec., 1808.
Jeoffrey Robertson, 12 Dec., 1808.
Duff Green, 12 Dec., 1808.
Alexander Smith, 12 Dec., 1808.
Isaac Dunbar.

*Ensigns.*

John Hughes, 3 May, 1808.
William S. Allen, 3 May, 1808.
James S. Waide, 3 May, 1808.
Samuel Vail, 3 May, 1808.
Samuel McCormick, 3 May, 1808.
Lewis P. Ducros, 12 Dec., 1808.
George C. Allen, 12 Dec., 1808.

Elijah Montgomery, 12 Dec., 1808.
Joseph Philips, 12 Dec., 1808.
David McClellan, 12 Dec., 1808.

*Surgeon.*

Alfred Thurston, 12 Dec., 1808.

---

REGIMENT OF RIFLEMEN.

*Colonel.*

Alexander Smyth, 8 July, 1808.

*Lieut. Colonel.*

William Duane, 8 July, 1808.

*Major.*

John Fuller, 12 Dec., 1808.

*Captains.*

Thomas A. Smith, 3 May, 1808.
George W. Sevier, 3 May, 1808.
James McDonald, 3 May, 1808.
John Ragan, 3 May, 1808.
Moses Whitney, 18 June, 1808.
David Findley, 18 June, 1808.
Alexander S. Walker, 1 July, 1808.
Benjamin Forsythe, 1 July, 1808.

*1st Lieutenants.*

Abraham A. Massias, 3 May, 1808.
Thomas Spencer, 3 May, 1808.
Fielder Ridgeway, 3 May, 1808.
Charles Porterfield, 3 May, 1808.
Michael C. Hays, 3 May, 1808.
Dill. Armor, 18 June, 1808.
Benjamin Champney, 27 Oct., 1808.
George Morrison, 12 Dec., 1808.
David Moss.

*2nd Lieutenants.*

Elzey L. James, 3 May, 1808.
Lodowick Morgan, 3 May, 1808.
Matthew Cannon, 3 May, 1808.
Daniel Appling, 3 May, 1808.
Joshua Hamilton, 18 May, 1808.
Horace S. White, 12 Dec., 1808.
Lewis Weir, 12 Dec., 1808.
Thomas A. Patterson, 12 Dec., 1808.
Thomas Ramsey, 27 Jan., 1809.
William Smith.

*Ensigns.*

Joseph S. Pepper, 3 May, 1808.
Elias Stallings, 3 May, 1808.
Arthur W. Thornton, 3 May, 1808.
Francis Stribling, 3 May, 1808.
Augustus L. Langham, 3 May, 1808.
John Logan, 1 July, 1808.
William D. Jones, 12 Dec., 1808.
Edmund Foster, 12 Dec., 1808.
James Johnson, 12 Dec., 1808.

*Surgeon.*

Smith Cutler, 12 Dec., 1808.

*Surgeon's Mate.*

Enos Lewis, 12 Dec., 1808.

SURGEONS AND SURGEON'S MATES.

*Surgeons.*

Oliver H. Spencer, 9 Oct., 1804.
Francis Le Barron, Dec., 1808.

*Surgeons' Mates.*

Samuel McKee, 26 March, 1802.
William C. Smith, 2 July, 1802.
John F. Hellman, 2 July, 1802.
George W. Maupin, 5 Nov., 1802.
Joseph Goodhue, 8 Feb., 1803.
John Watson, 22 Nov., 1803.
Abraham Edwards, 8 June, 1804.
Antony Saugrain, 17 Jan., 1805.
Reuben Everitt, 6 March, 1806.
Abraham Stewart, 6 March, 1806.
James H. Sargent, 6 March, 1806.
Alexander Macauley, 11 June, 1806.
James V. Stewart, 27 Feb., 1807.
Alexander H. Morrison, 27 Feb., 1807.
Robert Huston, 27 Feb., 1807.
Charles Slocum, 25 March, 1807.
Henry Skinner, 30 July, 1807.
William H. Emery, 9 Dec., 1807.
Sylvester Day, 9 Dec., 1807.
John Biglow, 9 Dec., 1807.
Lemuel B. Clarke, 4 Jan., 1808.
Robert Simpson, 13 June, 1808.
John L. Murray, 13 June, 1808.
William T. Davidson, 13 June, 1808.
John Cooper, 13 June, 1808.
William A. Dandridge, 12 Dec., 1808.
Thomas A. Holland, 2 Feb., 1809.
Joseph West, 10 June, 1809.

---

## Casualties, U. S. Army, since January 1, 1809.

RESIGNATION OF OFFICERS.

William A. Murray, Capt. Artillerists, 1 Oct., 1809.
Joseph Kimball, 1st Lieut Artillerists, 1 Aug., 1809.
George Peter, Capt. Light Artillery, 11 June, 1809.
Joseph Chandler, Capt. Light Artillery, 1 Sept., 1809.
Daniel Gano, Capt. Light Artillery, 20 April, 1809.
Samuel Watson, 1st Lieut. Light Artillery, 11 Sept., 1809.
Samuel H. Holley, 2nd Lieut. Light Artillery, 1 Jan., 1810.
Alexander F. Rose, Capt. Light Dragoons, 10 Nov., 1809.
Clement Biddle, Capt. Light Dragoons, 30 Sept., 1809.
Isaac A. Coles, Capt. Light Dragoons, 18 Jan., 1810.
John M. Barclay, 1st Lieut. Light Dragoons, 1 Sept., 1809.



George Nichols, 2nd Lieut. Light Dragoons, 4 July, 1809.
Jonas Munroe, 2nd Lieut. Light Dragoons, 15 Sept., 1809.
Ferdinand Ludlow, 2nd Lieut. Light Dragoons, 15 Dec., 1809.
John Read, 2nd Lieut. 1st Infantry, 31 Jan., 1809.
John Brahan, Capt. 2nd Infantry, 1 Jan., 1810.
Benjamin S. Smoot, 1st Lieut. 2nd Infantry, 1 April, 1809.
John Hacket, 1st Lieut. 2nd Infantry, 31 Jan., 1809.
Abner Pasteur, Capt. 3rd Infantry, 1 Jan., 1810.
Charles C. McKenzie, 2nd Lieut. 3rd Infantry, 15 Oct., 1809.
Nicoll Fosdic, 1st Lieut. 4th Infantry, 1 Dec., 1809.
Samuel Haines, 1st Lieut. 4th Infantry, 15 June, 1809.
Lewis Harrington, 2nd Lieut. 4th Infantry, 15 Oct., 1809.

Timothy Gerrish, Ensign 4th Infantry, 1 Sept., 1809.
Alexander Parker, Col. 5th Infantry, 31 Dec., 1809.
Tully Robinson, Major 5th Infantry, 9 May, 1809.
Roger A. Jones, 1st Lieut. 5th Infantry, 1 Sept., 1809.
James Fonerdon, 1st Lieut. 5th Infantry, 16 April, 1809.
Mordecai Griffith, 1st Lieut. 5th Infantry, 10 July, 1809.
Jeremiah Yancey, Ensign 5th Infantry, 20 Oct., 1809.
Ebenezer Cross, Capt. 6th Infantry, 10 June, 1809.
Thomas Davis, Capt. 6th Infantry, 1 Jan., 1810.
William Cock, Capt. 6th Infantry, 31 Dec., 1809.
William Pennell, Capt. 6th Infantry, 1 Sept., 1809.
Abel Morse, 2nd Lieut. 6th Infantry, 10 Nov., 1809.
John Gailland, 2nd Lieut. 6th Infantry, 11 Nov., 1809.
William Gamble, Ensign 6th Infantry, 30 April, 1809.
Asa Grimes, Ensign 6th Infantry, 31 May, 1809.
Edward Hord, Capt. 7th Infantry, 1 Jan., 1810.
James Desha, Capt. 7th Infantry, 1 Dec., 1809.
Duff Green, 2nd Lieut. 7th Infantry, 6 Oct., 1809.
Alexander Smith, 2nd Lieut. 7th Infantry, 1 Nov., 1809.
John Hughes, Ensign 7th Infantry, 2 May, 1809.
William S. Allen, Ensign 7th Infantry, 20 Oct., 1809.
Horace S. White, 2nd Lieut. Riflemen, 1 July, 1808.
Joseph S. Pepper, Ensign Riflemen, May, 1809.
Angus Langham, Ensign Riflemen, 15 April, 1809.
John Logan, Ensign, Riflemen, 1 Oct., 1809.
Edmund Foster, Ensign Riflemen, 1 July, 1809.
Enos Lewis, Surgeon's Mate Riflemen, 1 Sept., 1809.
Thomas H. Holland, Surgeon's Mate, Peace Establishment, 1 Sept., 1809.

### Dismissal of Officers, by Sentences of General Courts Martial.

Robert McDougal, 1st Lieut. 3rd Infantry, 7 Aug., 1809.
Isaiah Doane, Capt. 4th Infantry, 12 June, 1809.
David Byers, Capt. 4th Infantry, 31 Oct., 1809.
Alden G. Cushman, 1st Lieut. 4th Infantry, 3 July, 1809.
Alexander S. Walker, Capt. Riflemen, 1 Jan., 1810.
Matthew Cannon, 2nd Lieut. Riflemen, 1 Jan., 1810.

---

### Deaths of Officers.

Alpheus Roberts, 2nd Lieut., Light Artillery, 27 Aug., 1809, New Orleans.
James I. Bowie, 1st Lieut. Light Dragoons, 27 May, 1809, New Orleans.
Milton Haxton, Cornet Light Dragoons, 29 Dec., 1809, Carlisle, Pa.
William Lithgow, Ensign 1st Infantry, 19 June, 1809, New Orleans.
Francis Johnson, Capt. 2nd Infantry, 17 Feb., 1809, Columbian Springs.
John C. Carter, 2nd Lieut. 2nd Infantry, 2 April, 1809.
Edward Mason, 2nd Lieut., 3rd Infantry, 19 June, 1809, New Orleans.
Robert Watson, Ensign 3rd Infantry, Oct., 1809, Point Coupee.
John T. Bentley, Capt. 6th Infantry, 20 Oct., 1809, New Orleans.
James Chambers, 1st Lieut. 6th Infantry, 10 Oct., 1809, New York.
Lewis P. Ducros, Ensign 7th Infantry, 20 June, 1809, New Orleans.
David Finley, Capt. Riflemen, 1 July, 1809, Fort Adams, M. T.
George Morrison, 1st Lieut. Riflemen, 21 May, 1809.
William D. Jones, Ensign Riflemen, 22 Aug., 1809, New Orleans.
Samuel McKee, Surgeon's Mate, Peace Establishment, 5 Nov., 1809, Vincennes.
John Biglow, Surgeon's Mate, Peace Establishment, 1808.

# LIST

OF THE

# OFFICERS OF THE ARMY

# 1812—13.

---

WAR DEPARTMENT.

*Secretary of War.*

John Armstrong.
Colonel David Henly, clerk, employed at his lodgings in recording proceedings of court martials.

*Adjutant General.*

Thomas H. Cushing.

*Assistant Adjutant Generals.*

Abimael Y. Nicoll.
Washington Lee.
Enos Cutler.

*Paymaster of the Army.*

Robert Brent.

*Commissary General of Ordnance.*

Decius Wadsworth.

*Deputy Commissary.*

Capt. John Morton.

---

GENERAL OFFICERS.

*Major Generals.*

Henry Dearborn, Mass., 27 Jan., 1812.
Thomas Pinckney, S. C., 27 March, 1812.

*Brig. Generals.*

James Wilkinson, Md., 5 March, 1792. Major General by Brevet.
Wade Hampton, S. C., 15 Feb., 1809.
Joseph Bloomfield, N. J., 27 March, 1812.
James Winchester, Tenn., 27 March, 1812.
William Hull, Mass., 8 April, 1812.
Thomas Flouroy, Ga., 18 June, 1812.
John Chandler, Mass., 8 July, 1812.
William H. Harrison, Indiana Ter., 22 Aug., 1812.
John P. Boyd, Mass., 26 Aug., 1812.

---

GENERAL STAFF OFFICERS.

*Adjutant General.*

Thomas H. Cushing, Mass., 6 July, 1812. Rank of Brigadier.

*Inspector General.*

Alexander Smyth, Va., 6 July, 1812. Rank of Brigadier.

*Quartermaster General.*

Morgan Lewis, N. Y., 3 April, 1812. Rank of Brigadier.

*Adjutant and Inspector.*

A. Y. Nicoll, N. Y., 2 April, 1807. Major of Artillerists.

*Paymaster of the Army.*

Robert Brent, Dist. of Col., 1 July, 1808.

---

QUARTERMASTER'S DEPARTMENT.

*Deputy Quartermasters*

Anthony Lamb, N. Y., 3 April, 1812.
William Linnard, Penn., 3 April, 1812.
William Swann, Mass., 3 April, 1812.
Jacob Eustis, Mass., 8 April, 1812.
Bart. Shaumburgh, La., 15 May, 1812.
James Thomas, Mass., 1 Sept., 1812.

---

ORDNANCE DEPARTMENT.

*Commissary General.*

Decius Wadsworth, Conn., 2 July, 1812. Rank of Colonel.

*Assistant Commissary General.*

George Bumford, N. Y., 18 June, 1812. Major of Engineers.

*Deputy Commissaries.*

Sylvanus Thayer, Mass., 11 Sept., 1812. Rank of Captain.
John Morton, N. Y., 11 Sept., 1812. Rank of Captain.
Abraham R. Woolley, N. J., 4 Dec., 1812. Rank of Captain.
John H. Magart, S. C., 31 Dec., 1812. Rank of Captain.

---

PURCHASING DEPARTMENT.

*Commissary General.*

Callender Irvine, Penn., 8 Aug., 1812.

*Deputy Commissaries.*

John M'Kinney, Dist. of Col., 25 April, 1812.
Benjamin Morgan, La., 18 May, 1812.
J. H. Plummer, Tenn., 4 June, 1812.
Thomas Buford, Ky., 4 June, 1812.
John Langdon, Jun., N. H., 4 June, 1812.
John Cumings, Ga., 18 June, 1812.
Amasa Stetson, Mass., 22 June, 1812.
Benjamin Cudworth, S. C., 6 July, 1812.
John Stith, Va., 6 July, 1812.
Hanson Kelly, N. C., 6 July, 1812.
Elisha Tracy, Conn., 6 July, 1812.
William Jarvis, Vt., 18 Aug., 1812.
Samuel Russell, N. Y., 18 Sept., 1812.

---

HOSPITAL AND GARRISON SURGEONS AND MATES.

*Hospital Surgeons.*

John M'Daniel, Va., 7 July, 1809.
James Mann, Mass., 9 April, 1812.
Garrett E. Pendergrast, Penn., 25 April, 1812.
David C. Kerr., Va., 30 April, 1812.
Samuel Akerly, N. Y., 6 July, 1812.
John Parker Gouch, S. C., 6 July, 1812.

*Garrison Surgeons.*

Oliver H. Spencer, Ohio, 9 Oct., 1804.
Francis Le Barron, Mass., 14 Dec., 1808.

*Hospital Surgeon's Mates.*

William Thomas, N. Y., 7 July, 1809.
Rogers Smith, N. H., 14 May, 1812.
James Stephenson, Va., 27 May, 1812.
Stephen Sutton, Va., 27 May, 1812.
Hosea Blood, Ky., 6 July, 1812.
Samuel Schofield, N. Y., 15 Sept., 1812.

*Garrison Surgeon's Mates.*

Joseph West, 10 June, 1802.
John F. Hirlman, Mass., 2 July, 1802.
George W. Mauphin, Va., 5 Nov., 1802.
Joseph Goodhue, N. H., 8 Feb., 1803.
Abraham Stewart, 6 March, 1806.
James H. Sargent, 6 March, 1806.
Robert Huston, Penn., 27 Feb., 1807.
Charles Slocum, Conn., 25 March, 1807.
Henry Skinner, 30 July, 1807.
Sylvester Day, 9 Dec., 1807.
Lemuel B. Clark, 4 Jan., 1808.
William T. Davidson, Penn., 13 June, 1808.
Thomas Pinkerton, Md., 1 May, 1809.
John H. Turner, 1 May, 1810.
William Turner, 9 July, 1810.
Cornelius Cunningham, 15 Oct., 1810.
Thomas Lawson, 8 Feb., 1811.
Jonathan T. Cool, 8 Feb., 1811.
William Ballard, 24 March, 1812.
John H. Sackett, 25 March, 1812.
Samuel Duremberg, 25 March, 1812.
Alexander Wolcott, 25 March, 1812.
Anthony Benezet, 25 March, 1812.
John T. Priestly, 25 April, 1812.
William Turner, R. I., 23 Sept., 1812.
Daniel Nielson, Penn., 3 Dec., 1812.

---

CORPS OF ENGINEERS, OLD ARMY.

*Colonel.*

Joseph G. Swift, Mass., 31 July, 1812.

*Lieut. Colonel.*

Walker R. Armistead, Va., 31 July, 1812.

*Major.*

George Bumford, N. Y., 6 July, 1812.
William McRee, N. C., 31 July, 1812.

*Captains.*

Charles Gratiot, Louisiana Ter., 23 Feb., 1808.
Alden Patridge, Vt., 23 July, 1810.
Eleazer D. Wood, Vt., 1 July, 1812.
Prentis Willard, Vt., 6 July, 1812.
Joseph G. Totten, Conn., 31 July, 1812.
Samuel Babcock, 20 Sept., 1812.

*1st Lieutenants.*

Sylvanus Thayer, Mass., 1 July, 1812.
Alexander J. Williams, Penn., 1 July, 1812.
William Cutbush, Penn., 1 July, 1812.
Edward De Russey La., 6 July, 1812.
Thomas P. Finley, Conn., 31 July, 1812. Paymaster.
Frederick Lewis, N. Y., 20 Sept., 1812.

*2nd Lieutenant.*

James Gadspen, S. C., 2 Dec., 1812.

*Professor of Natural and Experimental Philosophy.*

Jared Mansfield, Ohio.

*Teacher of French.*

Floromond de Masson, N. J.

*Teacher of Drawing.*

Christian E. Zoeller.

---

FIRST REGIMENT OF LIGHT DRAGOONS.

*Colonel.*

Leonard Covington, Md., 15 Feb., 1809.

*Lieut. Colonel.*

Electus Bachus, N. Y., 15 Feb., 1809.

*Major.*

Jacint Laval, S. C., 15 Feb., 1809.

*Captains.*

Nelson Luckett, Md., 23 Feb., 1809.
Thomas A. Helmes, N. J., 30 Sept., 1809.
Arthur P. Hayne, S. C., 10 Nov., 1809.
Asa Morgan, Conn., 18 Jan., 1810.
Seleck Osborne, Mass., 20 Feb., 1811.
Silas Halley, N. J., 31 May, 1811.
Alex. Cummings, Penn., 1 Nov., 1811.

*1st Lieutenants.*

Wm. Littlejohn, Va., 1 Oct., 1809.
George Haig, Ga., 10 Nov., 1809.
Levi Hukill, Md., 18 Jan., 1810.
Elijah Boardman, Conn., 3 May, 1810.
John Hollinshead, N. J., 20 Feb., 1811. Assistant Deputy Quartermaster.
Joseph Kean, Va., 31 May, 1811.
Henry Whiting, Mass., 20 Aug., 1811.
George Birch, Penn., 1 Nov., 1811.

*2nd Lieutenants.*

Dillon Thomas, Dist. of Maine, 27 March, 1812.
Francis S. Belton, Md., 27 March, 1812.
William Nelson, Md., 1 May, 1812.
Louis Laval, S. C., 1 May, 1812.
James Barton, S. C., 27 May, 1812.
Loring Austin, Mass., 28 Sept., 1812.
Valent. P. Luckett, Md., 12 Oct., 1812.
Edward Carrington, Va., 9 Oct., 1812.

*Cornets.*

Owen Ransom, Conn., 14 Sept., 1812.
Thomas Heriot, S. C., 30 Oct., 1812.

*Surgeon.*

Lewis Dunham, N. J., 12 Dec., 1808.

REGIMENT OF ARTILLERISTS.

*Colonel.*

Henry Burbeck, Mass., 1 April, 1802. Brigadier by Brevet.

*Lieut. Colonel.*

Constant Freeman, Mass., 1 April, 1802. Colonel by Brevet.

*Majors.*

William MacRea, Va., 31 July, 1800. Lieut. Colonel by Brevet.
A. Y. Nicoll, N. Y., 1 Dec., 1804. Adjutant and Inspector.
Amos Stoddard, Mass., 30 June, 1807.
James Read, Penn., 12 March, 1812.

*Captains.*

Nehemiah Freeman, Mass., 6 Aug., 1798. Major by Brevet and Dist. Paymaster.
Lloyd Beall, Md., 16 Feb., 1801. Major by Brevet.
Samuel T. Dyson, Md., 15 Sept., 1804. Prisoner of War.
James B. Many, Del., 1 Oct., 1804.
Nathaniel Leonard, Vt., 1 Dec., 1804. Assistant Deputy Quartermaster.
Chas. Woolstoncroft, Penn., 13 March, 1805.
James House, Penn., 1 Nov., 1805. Assistant Deputy Quartermaster.
John B. Walback, Penn., 31 Jan., 1806. Assistant Deputy Quartermaster.
Add. B. Armistead, Va., 1 Oct., 1806.
George Armistead, Va., 1 Nov., 1806.
Moses Swett, Vt., 30 June, 1807.
William Wilson, Md., 3 May, 1808.
Joseph Cross, Mass., 7 Nov., 1808.
Enock Humphrey, Conn., 9 Jan., 1809.
Francis Newman, Md., 1 Oct., 1809.
Js. S. Swaringen, Va., 13 Jan., 1811.
Hannibal M. Allen, Vt., 29 Jan., 1811.
James Hanham, Md., 10 July, 1811.
Michael Walsh, N. O., 31 Oct., 1811.
James Reed, Penn., 12 March, 1812.

*1st Lieutenants.*

Thomas Murray, Md., 11 April, 1807.
Jonathan Eastman, 30 June, 1807. District Paymaster.
William Gates, Mass., 3 Nov., 1807.
Julius Hielman, Mass., 30 April, 1808.
John Gansevoort, N. Y., 3 May, 1808.
Hopley Yeaton, 31 July, 1808. Assistant Deputy Quartermaster.
Samuel Maclay, Penn., 7 Nov., 1808.
Joseph Proveaux, S. C., 9 Jan., 1809.
Thomas Bennet, 1 Aug., 1809.
Ethen A. Allen, Vt., 1 Oct., 1809.
Archibald Darrak, Penn., 29 Jan., 1811.
Mann Page Lomax, Va., 30 June, 1811.
Jotham Post, Vt., 1 July, 1811.
Satterlee Clarke, Vt., 10 July, 1811.
Samuel Champlain, Vt., 31 Oct., 1811. District Paymaster.
Heman A. Fay, Vt., 23 Dec., 1811. District Paymaster.
Milo Mason, Vt., 29 Feb., 1812.
Christ. Vandeventer, Vt., 12 March, 1812. Assistant Deputy Quartermaster General.
John Fitzgerald, Va., 14 March, 1812.
John Erving, Jun., Mass., 16 Aug., 1812. Assistant Deputy Quartermaster.

*2nd Lieutenants.*

Sam. B. Rathburn, N. Y., 3 June, 1808. Deceased.
Abraham L. Sands, N. Y., 18 Feb., 1809.
Thomas J. Beall, Md., 1 March, 1811.
James Dalliba, N. Y., 1 March, 1811.
Gustavus Loomis, Vt., 18 Feb., 1811.
Ezra Smith, Vt., 1 March, 1811.
Richard H. Ashley, Conn., 1 March, 1811.
John S. Brush, N. Y., 3 Jan., 1812.
Nathan W. Osgood, Vt., 3 Jan., 1812.
Fabius Whiting, Mass., 10 Feb., 1812.
Samuel Spotts, Del., 10 Feb., 1812.
William Parker, Penn., 10 Feb., 1812.
Levi Whiting, Dist. of Maine, 10 Feb., 1812.
James W. Rouse, S. C., 27 March, 1812.
Burgis B. White, Md., 14 April, 1812.
Peter St. Medard, Mass., 30 April, 1812.
Abel B. Chase, 30 April, 1812.
James Baker, N. Y., 1 May, 1812.
William H. Nicoll, Ga., 6 July, 1812.
Guy Duplantier, N. O., 13 Nov., 1812.

---

REGIMENT OF LIGHT ARTILLERY.

*Colonel.*

Moses Porter, Mass., 12 March, 1812.

*Lieut. Colonel.*

John R. Fenwick, S. C., 2 Dec., 1811.

*Major.*

Abraham Eustis, Mass., 15 March, 1810.

*Captains.*

Thomas Pitts, Dist. of Maine, 20 April, 1809.
James Gibson, Del., 2 May, 1810.
William Campbell, Vt., 30 May, 1810.
Rt. H. M'Pherson, Penn., 15 July, 1810.
John N. M'Intosh, Ga., 1 May, 1811.
Samuel Price, Ky., 15 Aug., 1811.
Andrew M'Dowell, Dist. of Maine, 1 April, 1812.
Luther Leonard, Vt., 6 July, 1812.
Benjamin Branch, Va., 24 Aug., 1812.
George W. Melvin, Ga., 24 Aug., 1812.

*1st Lieutenants.*

Arth. W. Thornton, Va., 1 March, 1811.
Francis Stribling, S. C., 1 March, 1811.
Marie V. Boisaubin, N. J., 1 March, 1811.
Adam Larrabee, Conn., 1 May, 1811.
Henry A. Hobert, Dist. of Maine, 15 Aug., 1811.
Thomas Ketcham, N. Y., 1 Sept., 1811.
James D. Cobb, Vt., 1 April, 1812.
Armstrong Irvine, Penn., 6 July, 1812.
John R. Beall, N. Y., 24 Aug., 1812.
Francis B. Murdock, Conn., 24 Aug., 1812.

*2nd Lieutenants.*

Thomas B. Randolph, Va., 3 Jan., 1812.
Wm. F. Hobart, Dist. of Maine, 3 Jan., 1812.
William Sumpter, S. C., 3 Jan., 1812.
George W. Hight, Vt., 3 Jan., 1812.
Wm. W. Smith, N. J., 1 June, 1812.
Jonas Dickson, N. C., 31 Dec., 1812.

---

FIRST REGIMENT OF INFANTRY.

*Colonel.*

Jacob Kingsbury, Conn., 18 Aug., 1808.

*Lieut. Colonel.*

Robert C. Nichola, Ky., 15 Aug., 1812.

*Major.*

Zebulon Pike, N. J., 20 March, 1800. Lieut. Colonel by Brevet.

*Captains.*

John Whestler, Md., 1 July, 1797. Major by Brevet.
Eli B. Clemson, Pa., 4 March, 1807.
William Swan, Mass., 15 Nov., 1807. Dep. Quarter Master.
Ninian Pinkney, Md., 9 Dec., 1807.

Horatio Stark, Va., 3 May, 1808.
Simon Owens, Va., 18 Aug., 1808.
Daniel Hughes, Md., 15 Dec., 1808.
Daniel Baker, Vt., 12 March, 1812.
Ambrose Whitlock, Va., 26 Aug., 1812. District Paymaster.

*1st Lieutenants.*

William Whistler, Mich. Ter., 4 March, 1807.
John C. Symmes, Ohio, 29 July, 1807. Assistant Deputy Quartermaster.
Simeon Knight, Vt., 9 Dec., 1807. District Paymaster.
Alpha Kingsley, Conn., 20 Jan., 1808. District Paymaster.
Hezekiah Johnson, Md., 18 Aug., 1808. Assistant Deputy Quartermaster.
Benjamin Marshall, Dist. of Maine, 14 Oct., 1808.
John Brownson, 8 Dec., 1808.
Thomas Hamilton, 15 Dec., 1808.
Jacob W. Albright, Pa., 26 Aug., 1808. Assistant Deputy Quartermaster.

*2nd Lieutenants.*

Philip Ostander, 1 May, 1808.
Samuel Perkins, 30 Nov., 1808. Assistant Deputy Quartermaster.
Lina Helm, N. Y., 8 Dec., 1808.
James W. Bryson, Pa., 31 Jan., 1809. Assistant Deputy Quartermaster.
John Campbell, Va., 31 Dec., 1809.
Dixon Stansbury, Md., 1 April, 1810.
Barony Vesquez, Missouri Ter., 4 March, 1811.
Lewis Bissell, Conn., 12 March, 1812.
William Anderson, Pa., 6 Aug., 1812.
John A. Shaw, 6 Aug., 1812.

*Ensigns.*

Ormond Marsh, 1 March, 1811.
Daniel Cartis, Michigan Ter., 3 Jan., 1812.
Robert McCabe, Indiana Ter., 3 Jan., 1812.
Newton E. Westfall, Indiana Ter., 3 Jan., 1812.
John O. Fallon, Ky., 28 Sept., 1812.

---

SECOND REGIMENT OF INFANTRY.

*Colonel.*

Richard Sparks, Pa., 6 July, 1812.

*Lieut. Colonel.*

John Bowyer, Va., 6 July, 1812.

*Major.*

William R. Boote, Ga., 6 July, 1812.

*Captains.*

Hugh McCall, Ga., 19 Aug., 1800. Major by Brevet.
William Carson, Pa., 20 Jan., 1808.
James Wilkinson, Md., 8 Oct., 1808.
William Piatt, N. J., 17 Feb., 1809. Dep. Quartermaster General.
William Lawrence, Md., 1 Jan., 1810.
Henry B. Brevort, N. Y., 1 May, 1811.
John Miller, Md., 12 March, 1812.
Reuben Chamberlin, N. H., 6 July, 1812.
John R. N. Luckett, Md., 6 July, 1812.
Robert Peyton, Va., 15 Aug., 1812.

*1st Lieutenants.*

John T. Pemberton, Ky., 17 Feb., 1809. District Paymaster.
William F. Ware, Ga., 1 April, 1809.
John Davis, Pa., 1 Jan., 1810. Regimental Paymaster.
Alex. Brownlow, Va., 1 Jan., 1810.
John Mathers, Dist. of Col. 1 May, 1810.
John T. Wirt, Del., 6 July, 1812. Assistant Deputy Quartermaster.
Evert Bogardus, N. Y., 6 July, 1812.
Hezekiah Bradley, Indiana Ter., 15 Aug., 1812.

*2nd Lieutenants.*

Perrin Willis, Va., 13 Feb., 1810.
Hippolite H. Villard, Dist. of Col., 1 March, 1811.
John Bliss, 1 March, 1811.
Hen. A. Burchsted, 13 March, 1811.
Jonathan Bell, 14 April, 1811.
Isaac L. Baker, Ky., 6 July, 1811.
Thomas Dagget, Va., 28 Sept., 1811.
William O. Butler, Ky., 28 Sept., 1811.

*Ensigns.*

Nathaniel Clark, Ga., 14 Sept., 1812.
Robert Sturgus, Ky., 28 Sept., 1812.
James Stewart, Tenn., 28 Sept., 1812.
Henry Conway, Jr., Tenn., 28 Sept., 1812.
William M. Smith, Va., 29 Oct., 1812.

---

THIRD REGIMENT OF INFANTRY.

*Colonel.*

Joseph Constant, N. Y., 3 Sept., 1810.

*Lieut. Colonel.*

Gilbert C. Russell, Tenn., 6 June, 1811.

*Major.*

Matthew Arbuckle, Va., 15 Aug., 1812.

*Captains.*

Ross Bird, S. C., 1 July, 1808.
John Nicks, N. C., 1 July, 1808.
Henry Atkinson, N. C., 1 July, 1808.
John McClelland, N. C., 1 July, 1808.
James Woodruff, Ga., 12 Dec., 1808.
William Butler, Ga., 31 Dec., 1809.
Robert B. Moore, Ga., 1 Sept., 1810.
Duncan L. Clinch, N. C., 31 Dec., 1810.
James Denking, S. C., 6 Feb., 1811.
Hays G. White, N. C., 11 May, 1811.

*1st Lieutenants.*

Wm. R. Davis, S. C., 1 July, 1808.
Samuel W. Butler, 7 Aug., 1809. Regimental Paymaster.
Henry Cholard, Mississippi Ter., Dec. 31, 1809.
Ben. D. Herriot, S. C., 1 Dec., 1810.
Samuel C. Mabson, N. C., 31 Dec., 1810.
John Burnett, N. C., 1 March, 1811.
Wm. Laval, S. C., 11 May, 1811.
Joseph M. Wilcox, Ohio, 4 Jan., 1812.
Joseph M. Wilcox, Ohio, 3 Jan., 1812.
John L. Carey, Ga., 1 Nov., 1812.

*2nd Lieutenants.*

John F. Everitt, Ga., 3 Jan., 1812.
Wm. Triplett, Ga., 3 Jan., 1812.
John W. Hansell, Ga., 3 Jan., 1812.
Thomas Hunter, S. C., 3 Jan., 1812.
Ben. Harvey, Jun., S. C., 3 Jan., 1812.
Wm. Christian, Orleans, 3 Jan., 1812.
Walter Bourke, Orleans, 12 March, 1812.
John Tarrant, S. C., 12 March, 1812.
Archim. Donoho, N. C., 1 Nov., 1812.

*Ensigns.*

James Smith, S. C., 27 March, 1812.
Tilman Turner, Ga., 27 March, 1812.
Robert Goodwin, Md., 14 April, 1812.
John Martin, 27 May, 1812.
Wm. L. Robeson, N. C., 31 Oct., 1812.
John A. Watson, N. C., 31 Oct., 1812.
Richard Cocke, N. C., 23 Nov., 1812.

James Hart, S. C., 2 Dec., 1812.
Wm. T. Caldwell, S. C., 2 Dec., 1812.

*Surgeon.*

Richard Shubrick, S. C., 8 Aug., 1809.

---

FOURTH REGIMENT OF INFANTRY.

*Colonel.*

Robert Purdy, Tenn., 26 Aug., 1812.

*Lieut. Colonel.*

John Darrington, S. C., 6 July, 1812.

*Major.*

Nathan Heald, Mass., 26 Aug., 1812.

*Captains.*

Stephen Ranney, Conn., 13 June, 1808.
Joel Cook, Conn., 13 June, 1808.
George W. Prescott, N. H., 18 June, 1808.
John Binney, Mass., 12 Dec., 1808.
Return B. Brown, Conn., 18 March, 1809.
Josiah Snelling, Mass., 12 June, 1809.
Oliver G. Burton, Vt., 25 Aug., 1811.
Nathan F. Adams, N. H., 29 Oct., 1811.
Charles Fuller, Mass., 9 Nov., 1811.
Charles Larrabee, Conn., 15 Sept., 1812.

*1st Lieutenants.*

Ebenezer Way, Conn., 15 June, 1809.
Jackson Durant, Dist. of Maine, 31 Oct., 1809.
John L. Eastman, N. H., 9 June, 1810.
Frederick Conklin, Conn., 1 June, 1811.
Abraham Hawkins, Conn., 25 Aug., 1811.
George P. Peters, Vt., 29 Oct., 1811. Regimental Paymaster.
John Smith, N. H., 31 Oct., 1811.
Lewis Peckham, R. I., 9 Nov., 1811.
George Gooding, Dist. of Maine, 15 Feb., 1812.

*2nd Lieutenants.*

Josiah Bacon, Mass., 1 Dec., 1810.
Parker Greenough, 20 Feb., 1811.
Michael Bulley, Mass., 3 Jan., 1812.
Joseph Plymton, Mass., 3 Jan., 1812.
George W. Hovey, Mass., 3 Jan., 1812.
Robert Clark, N. H., 3 Jan., 1812.
Phineas Wheelock, Mass,, 3 Jan., 1812.
Winthrop D. Ager, Mass., 3 Jan., 1812.
Shubael Butterfield, N. H., 3 Jan., 1812.
Rufus Preble, Dist. of Maine, 25 Feb., 1812.

*Ensigns.*

Samuel Armstrong, Mass., 14 April, 1812.
Samuel Legate, Mass., 14 May, 1812.
Paul Peckham, R. I., 15 May, 1812.
Johnson Ranney, Conn., 19 May, 1812.
Edmund Kirby, Conn., 6 July, 1812.
Charles Munroe, Mass., 16 Sept., 1812.
Jac. Porter Norton, Mass., 28 Sept., 1812.
Abial Wilson, Jun., N. H., 31 Dec., 1812.

*Surgeon's Mates*

Amos Farnsworth, Mass., 14 April, 1812.
Joseph M. Harper, N. H., 19 Jan., 1813.

---

FIFTH REGIMENT OF INFANTRY.

*Colonel.*

Daniel Bissell, Conn., 15 Aug., 1812.

*Lieut. Colonel.*

Homer V. Milton, Ga., 3 Sept., 1810.

*Captains.*

Benjamin Wallace, Penn., 18 June, 1808.
James Bankhead, Va., 18 June, 1808.
Colin Buckner, Va., 1 July, 1808.
John Johnson, Penn., 25 Jan., 1809.
George M. Brooke ,Va., 1 May, 1810.
Richard Whartenby, Penn., 3 May, 1810.
Townsend Stith, Va., 30 Sept., 1810.
Alex. M'Ilhenny, Penn., 1 Sept., 1811.
Talbert Chambers, Penn., 31 Oct., 1811.
James Dorman, Va., 9 Nov., 1811.

*1st Lieutenants.*

Wm. Henshaw, Va., 16 April, 1809..
Leroy Opie, Va., 10 July, 1809.
Richard H. Beall, Va., 1 Sept., 1809.
John Jamieson, Va., 31 Oct., 1811.
James Saunders, Va., 9 Nov., 1811.
Joseph Owens, Va., 3 Jan., 1812. Regimental Paymaster.
Richard W. Chick, Va., 12 March, 1812.
John S. Allison, Md., 6 July, 1812.
John R. Corbaly, Md., 6 July, 1812.
Wm. C. Bird, Md., 1 Sept., 1812.

*2nd Lieutenants.*

Phil. P. Greenwell, Md., 3 Jan., 1812.
John G. Blarke, Penn., 3 Jan., 1812.
John Gassaway, Md., 3 Jan., 1812.
Henry O. Hill, Md., 3 Jan., 1812.
John W. Smoot, Md., 3 Jan., 1812.
James M'Gunegle, Penn., 12 March, 1812.
James Cummings, Penn., 6 July, 1812.
Wilson Prestman, Md., 6 July, 1812.
James H. Hook, Md., 1 Sept., 1812.

*Ensigns.*

George D. Snyder, Md., 30 April, 1812.
John Fendall, Md., 27 May, 1812.
John B. Taylor, Va., 6 July, 1812.
John Darnell, Jun., Md., 13 Nov., 1812.
Matthew Galt, Jun., Dist. of Col., 4 Dec., 1812.
James M'Cahan, Penn., 31 Dec., 1812.

*Surgeon*

Adam Hays, Penn., 10 Feb., 1812.

*Surgeon's Mate.*

Alexander Blair, Penn., 6 July, 1812.

---

SIXTH REGIMENT OF INFANTRY.

*Colonel.*

Jonas Simonds, Penn., 8 July, 1808.

*Lieut. Colonel.*

James Miller, Mass., 30 Nov., 1810.

*Major.*

John Campbell, Tenn., 6 July, 1812.

*Captains.*

Ebenezer Beebe, N. Y., 19 Jan., 1809. Deputy Adjutant General.
John Machesney, N. J., 10 June, 1809.
John T. Arrowsmith, N. J., 20 Oct., 1809.
Goa. Humphreys, N. Y., 31 Dec., 1809.
John Walworth, Vt., 1 Jan., 1810.
Peter Mulenberg, Penn., 1 Oct., 1810.
Clement Sadlier, N. Y., 15 Nov., 1811.
Robert Sterry, N. Y., 3 Jan., 1812.
Js. E. A. Masters, N. Y., 4 June, 1812.

*1st Lieutenants.*

Henry Philips, Penn., 20 Oct., 1809. District Paymaster.
John J. Plume, N. J., 31 Dec., 1809.
Edward Webb, N. Y., 1 Oct, 1810.
Henry Shell, Penn., 9 March, 1811.
James Bailey, N. Y., 3 Jan., 1812.
Londus L. Buck, 3 Jan., 1812.

Alexander R. Thompson, N. Y., 3 Jan., 1812.
Thomas T. Blauvelt, N. J., 4 June, 1812.
John Chapman, N. J., 6 July, 1812.

*2nd Lieutenants.*

Wm. Hazard, N. Y., 3 Jan., 1812.
Gerard D. Smith, N. Y., 3 Jan., 1812.
George W. Tenbroocke, N. Y., 3 Jan., 1812.
S. Burton Cuyler, N. Y., 3 Jan., 1812.
David Vander Heyden, N. Y., 3 Jan., 1812.
George W. Runk, N. J., 3 Jan., 1812.
Henry R. Windle, N. Y., 3 Jan., 1812.
Henry Cooke, N. Y., 12 March, 1812.

*Ensigns.*

Nathaniel Sherman, N. Y., 3 Jan., 1812.
Robert M'Clellan, Jun., N. Y., 3 Jan., 1812. Regimental Paymaster.
Isaac L. Dubois, N. Y., 1 May, 1812.
William B. Staats, N. Y., 31 Dec., 1812.
Isaac Tucker, Penn., 4 Jan., 1813.
Abraham Quackinbush, N. Y., 13 Jan., 1813.
James Young, Penn., 13 Jan., 1813.
John Sisk, Penn, 13 Jan., 1813.
Aloy. Van Horn, Penn., 19 an., 1812.
Wm. Bezean, Penn., 19 Jan., 1812.
Henry Myers, Penn., 22 Jan., 1812.

*Surgeon.*

Isaac Davis, 12 Dec., 1808.

*Surgeon's Mate.*

Wm. Beaumont, 3 Dec., 1812.

---

SEVENTH REGIMENT OF INFANTRY.

*Colonel.*

William Russell, Ky., 3 May, 1808.

*Lieut. Colonel.*

George R. C. Floyd, Ky., 26 Aug., 1812.

*Major.*

George Gibson, Penn., 9 Nov., 1811.

*Captains.*

Thornton Posey, Ky., 3 May, 1808.
Arthur Morgan, Orleans, 3 May, 1808.
Uriah Blue, Ky., 9 May, 1809.
Richard Oldham, Ky., 1 Dec., 1809.
James Doherty, Tenn., 1 Jan., 1810.
Enos Cutler, Ohio, 3 Sept., 1810. Assistant Adjutant General.
Zachariah Taylor, Ky., 30 Nov., 1810. Major by Brevet.
Walter H. Overton, Tenn., 3 Dec., 1810.
Carey Nicholas, Ky., 1 March, 1811.
Wm. M'Clelland, Tenn., 1 March, 1811.

*1st Lieutenants.*

Alexander White, Tenn., 9 May, 1809.
Thomas S. Jessup, Ohio, 21 Dec., 1809.
Narcissus Broutin, Orleans, 1 Jan., 1810.
Jeoffrey Robertson, Tenn., 30 Nov., 1810.
James S. Wade, Mississippi Ter., 3 Dec., 1810.
Samuel Vail, Ky., 1 March, 1811.
George C. Allen, Tenn., 1 March, 1811.
Elijah Montgomery, Ky., 24 June, 1811.
David M'Clelland, Tenn., 10 Feb., 1812.
Thos. R. Richardson, Ohio, 10 Feb., 1812.

*2nd Lieutenants.*

Jacob Miller, Ky., 10 Feb., 1812.
Michael M'Clelland, Ohio, 10 Feb., 1812.
Samuel Kerchival, Ohio, 10 Feb., 1812.
Robert Todd, R. S., Ky., 10 Feb., 1812.
Isaac Bickley, Ky., 10 Feb., 1812.
Etheldred Taylor, Tenn., 10 Feb., 1812.
Wm. Snodgrass, Tenn., 10 Feb., 1812.
Henry Pope Helm, Ky., 10 Feb., 1812.
Wm. Prosser, Ohio, 10 Feb., 1812.
James Forsythe, Ky., 10 Feb., 1812.

*Ensigns.*

John Hays, Tenn., 10 Feb., 1812.
John Meak, Ohio, 10 Feb., 1812.
John N. Carrick, Tenn., 10 Feb., 1812.
Elisha T. Hall, Mississippi Ter., 10 Feb., 1812.
Thomas Blackstone, Tenn., 10 Feb., 1812.
John Weaver, Ky., 10 Feb., 1812.
Isaac M. Riley, 8 May, 1812.
Wm. K. Beall, 6 July, 1812.
Levi Wells, Ky., 28 Sept., 1812.

*Surgeon.*

Adam Goodlet, 10 Feb., 1812.

---

RIFLE REGIMENT.

*Colonel.*

Thomas A. Smith, Ga., 6 July, 1812.

*Lieut. Colonel.*

George W. Sevier, Tenn., 6 July, 1812.

*Major.*

James M'Donald, Ohio, 1 Aug., 1812.

*Captains.*

Benjamin Forsythe, N. C., 1 July, 1808.
Henry A. Graham, Ky., 8 March, 1809.
Abraham A. Massias, N. Y., 1 July, 1809.
Fielder Ridgeway, Md., 31 July, 1810.
Michael C. Hays, Ohio, 1 June, 1811.
Lodowick Morgan, Md., 1 July, 1811.
Daniel Appling, Ga., 1 July, 1812.
Joshua Hamilton, Penn., 6 July, 1812.
Thomas A. Patterson, 1 Aug., 1812.

*1st Lieutenants.*

Thomas Ramsey, Ohio, 31 July, 1810.
Wm. Smith, 31 Oct., 1810.
Elias Stallings, Ga., 16 March, 1811.
Lewis G. A. Armistead, Va., 10 Feb., 1812.
Wm. E. Morris, S. C., 30 April, 1812.
John Findley.
Henry Swearingen, Va., 6 July, 1812.
Edward Wadsworth, Ohio, 1 Aug., 1812.
Wm. Townley, 1 Aug., 1812.
Wm. C. Beard, Md., 27 Sept., 1812.

*2nd Lieutenants.*

James Reyan, Ga., 24 April, 1812. Regimental Paymaster.
George Gray, Jun., Ky., 4 June, 1812.
Harvey Murray, 17 Oct., 1812.
James M'Intosh, Ga., 13 Nov., 1812.
Joseph Calhoun, S. C., 2 Dec., 1812.
Hyem Cohen, S. C., 2 Dec., 1812.
Wm. Arnold, Ky., 3 Dec., 1812.
John M'Intire, Ky., 3 Dec., 1812.
John Shortridge, Ky., 3 Dec., 1812.

*Ensigns.*

John Hanson, Mass., 13 Nov., 1812.
John Harley, S. C., 2 Dec., 1812.
Josiah Hill, Ga., 2 Dec., 1812.
Samuel V. Hamilton, Va., 4 Dec., 1812.
Robert M'Farland, Tenn., 31 Dec., 1812.
Jacob Tipton, Tenn., 31 Dec., 1812.
Joseph P. Bunting, Penn., 4 Jan., 1813.
Wm. Armstrong, Ohio, 19 Jan., 1813.
Bennet Riley, Md., 19 Jan., 1813.
Lambert Norton, N. Y., 22 Jan., 1813.

*Surgeon.*

Wm. Wilmot Hall, Md., 24 March, 1812.

SECOND REGIMENT OF LIGHT DRAGOONS. ADDITIONAL MILITARY FORCE.

*Colonel.*

James Burn, Penn., 25 April 1812.

*Lieut. Colonel.*

Arch. T. Macniell, N. C., 6 July, 1812.

*Majors.*

John T. Woodford, Va., 27 March, 1812.
James V. Ball, Va., 16 Sept., 1812.

*Captains.*

John Butler, N. H., 12 March, 1812.
Samuel D. Harris, Mass., 12 March, 1812.
Henry Hall, Md., 12 March, 1812.
Joseph Selden, Va., 12 March, 1812.
Stephen R. Proctor, S. C., 12 March, 1812.
Samuel G. Hopkins, Ky., 19 March, 1812.
John A. Bird, Penn., 12 March, 1812.
Charles Smith, Penn., 1 May, 1812.
Jonas Holland, N. Y., 1 May, 1812.

*1st Lieutenants.*

Abel Wheelock, Mass., 12 March, 1812.
Arch. H. Sneed, N. C., 12 March, 1812. Regimental Paymaster.
Walter German, N. Y., 12 March, 1812.
Benjamin Pratt, Vt., 12 March, 1812.
Beverly Turpin, Ga., 12 March, 1812.
James Hedges, Ohio, 12 March, 1812.
John Nicholas, Jun., Va., 12 March, 1812.
Gabriel Barbour, Va., 14 April, 1812.
John D. Hart, Penn., 15 May, 1812.
Charles J. Nourse, Dist. of Col., 7 May, 1812.

*2nd Lieutenants.*

Ira Williams, Vt., 12 March, 1812.
Edward Conway, Tenn., 12 March, 1812.
Walter Coles, Va., 12 March, 1812.
Benjamin Smith, Penn., 12 March, 1812.
Thomas S. Johnson, N. Y., 12 March, 1812.
Fayette Roane, Va., 12 March, 1812.
John C. Tillotson, N. Y., 10 Aug., 1812.

*Cornets.*

Andrew M'Farland, Vt., 12 March, 1812.
James Martin, S. C., 12 March, 1812.
James Trippe, Ga., 12 March, 1812.
Harman A. Hayes, Tenn., 12 March, 1812.
Armstr. M'Kinney, Va., 12 March, 1812.
Benjamin Wilds, Penn., 17 March, 1812.
Benjamin Burd, Penn., 21 Sept., 1812.
Clinton Wright, Md., 19 Jan., 1813.

*Surgeon.*

Wm. Hor. Buckner, Va., 6 July, 1812.

*Surgeon's Mate.*

Lewis M. Bailey, Va., 7 May, 1812.

---

SECOND REGIMENT OF ARTILLERY.

*Colonel.*

George Izard, Penn., 12 March, 1812.

*Lieut. Colonel.*

Winfield Scott, Va., 6 July, 1812.

*Majors.*

Wm. Lindsay, Va., 14 May, 1812.
Daniel M. Forney, N. C., 12 March, 1812.

*Captains.*

Jesse Robertson, Ga., 12 March, 1812.
Jacob Bond, Jon., S. C., 12 March, 1812.
Robert M. Gill, S. C., 12 March, 1812.
Philemond Hawkins, Jun., N. C., 12 March, 1812.
Samuel B. Archer, Va., 12 March, 1812.
John Ritchie, Va., 12 March, 1812.
John Goodall, Va., 8 April, 1812.
George W. Russell, Va., 25 April, 1812.
Spotwood Henry, Va., 8 May, 1812.
Nathan Towson, Md., 12 March, 1812.
Joseph Philips, Tenn., 12 March, 1812.
James N. Barker, Penn., 27 May, 1812.
Wm. Nichols Penn., 12 March, 1812.
Thos. Riddle, Jun., Penn., 9 April, 1812.
Saunders Donoho, N. C., 2 July, 1812.
Wm. A. Whitted, N. C., 2 July, 1812.
Jacob Hindman, Md., 2 July, 1812.
Daniel Cushing, Ohio, 2 July, 1812.
Stanton Shoales, Penn., 2 July, 1812.
Frederick Evans, Penn., 6 July, 1812.

*1st Lieutenants.*

Henry Slaughter, Ga., 12 March, 1812.

Lowndes Brown, S. C., 12 March, 1812.
Adrian Niel, S. C., 12 March, 1812.
Wm. Js. Cowan, N. C., 12 March, 1812.
Robert R. Ruffin, N. C., 12 March, 1812. Regimental Paymaster.
James H. Dearing, N. C., 15 May, 1812.
John Smith, Peyton, Va., 12 March, 1812.
John Fontaine, Va., 24 March, 1812.
Thos. M. Randolph, Jun., Va., 14 May, 1812.
Jonathan Kearsley, Penn., 12 March, 1812.
Henry K. Craig, Penn., 17 March, 1812.
Joseph H. Larwell, Ohio, 12 March, 1812.
Joseph Nevill, Jun., Va., 15 May, 1812.
Pat. M'Donough, Penn., 12 March, 1812.
August G. Munroe, Va., 2 July, 1812.
Luther Scott, Penn., 24 March, 1812.
Wm. M. Read, Penn., 6 July, 1812.

*2nd Lieutenants.*

Thomas Winn, S. C., 12 March, 1812.
Jacob Warley, S. C., 12 March, 1812.
Edwin Sharpe, N. C., 12 March, 1812.
John Ruffin, Va., 12 March, 1812.
Wm. Tyler, Va., 1 May, 1812.
John W. Kincaid, Va., 15 May, 1812.
Robert Stewart, Del., 7 May, 1812.
Lewis Morgan, Penn, 12 March, 1812.
Isaac Davis, Tenn., 15 May, 1812.
James H. Gamble, Ohio, 12 March, 1812.
Alexander A. Meek, Penn., 8 May, 1812.
Rich. A. Zantzinger, Penn., 12 March, 1812.
Fran. Otway Byrd, Va., 2 July, 1812.
Robert Goode, Va., 2 July, 1812.
Thomas D. Ridley, N. C., 2 July, 1812.
Isaac Roach, Penn., 2 July, 1812.
Wm. Smith, Va., 6 July, 1812.

*Surgeon.*

Jacob de la Motta, S. C., 1 May, 1812.

*Surgeon's Mates.*

James Trimble, Penn., 6 July, 1812.
Louis L. Near, Del., 6 July, 1812.

---

THIRD REGIMENT OF ARTILLERY.

*Colonel.*

Alexander Macomb, N. Y., 6 July, 1812.

*Majors.*

Samuel Nye, Mass., 6 July, 1812.
George E. Mitchell, Md., 1 May, 1812.

*Captains.*

James M'Keon, N. Y., 12 March, 1812.
John W. Gookin, N. H., 12 March, 1812.
Alexander S. Brookes, Mass., 12 March, 1812.
Wm. Van Duerson, Jr., Conn., 12 March, 1812.
Benjamin S. Ogden, N. J., 12 March, 1812.
Horace H. Watson, Mass., 9 April, 1812.

Ichabod B. Crane, N. Y., 23 April, 1812.
David Fleming, N. Y., 2 July, 1812.
James S. B. Romayne, N. Y., 2 July, 1812.
Charles K. Gardiner, N. Y., 2 July, 1812.
Roger Jones, Va., 2 July, 1812.
James H. Boyle, Penn., 6 July, 1812.
Rufus M'Intire, Mass., 6 July, 1812.
Eben. S. Morse, Mass., 6 July, 1812.
Thomas Stockton, Del., 10 Sept., 1812.
Jonathan Brookes, N. Y., 24 Sept, 1812.
Stephen Collins, Conn., 13 Jan., 1813.

*1st Lieutenants.*

John M. O'Conner, N. Y., 12 March, 1812.
Benjamin K. Pierce, N. H., 12 March, 1812.
Moses J. Chase, Mass., 12 March, 1812.
James Green, Jun., Mass., 12 March, 1812.
John Farley, Mass., 12 March, 1812.
Samuel Weston, Mass., 12 March, 1812.
Al. C. W. Fanning, Mass., 12 March, 1812.
Sylvester Churchill, Vt., 12 March, 1812.
Benjamin Brearly, N. J., 12 March, 1812.
John W. Green, Conn., 12 March, 1812.
George H. Richards, Conn., 12 March, 1812.
Richard M. Bailey, N. Y., 12 March, 1812.
Peter Pifer, N. Y., 12 March, 1812.
Jeremiah L. Tracy, Mass., 8 April, 1812.
Samuel M. Dewey, Mass., 25 April, 1812.
Wm. De Peyster, N. Y., 1 May, 1812.
Harold Smith, Va., 14 April, 1812.

*2nd Lieutenants.*

Wm. Shannon, N. H., 12 March, 1812.
Greenleaf Dearbon, Mass., 12 March, 1812.
Wm. King, Mass., 12 March, 1812.
John P. Bartlett, Mass., 12 March, 1812.
Daniel Smalley, N. J., 12 March, 1812.
Joseph H. Rees, N. Y., 12 March, 1812
Adam A. Gray, N. Y., 12 March, 1812.
Wm. A. Henry, N. Y., 12 March, 1812.
Wm. R. Duncan, Penn., 9 April, 1812.
Chester Root, N. Y., 25 April, 1812. Regimental Paymaster.
Thomas C. Legate, Mass., 30 April, 1812.
John Mountford, Mass. 24 March 1812.
Matthew Jenkins, N. Y. 15 May, 1812.
Philip D. Spencer, N. Y. 22 May, 1812.
Felix Ansart, Mass., 2 July, 1812.
John Biddle, Penn., 6 July, 1812.
Chas. M. Macomb, N. Y., 6 July, 1812.
Charles Martins, Conn., 6 July, 1812.
John J. Cromwell, N. Y., 23 Nov., 1812.

*Surgeon.*

John Watts, Jun., N. Y., 6 July, 1812.

*Surgeon's Mates.*

Joseph Eeaton, Mass., 14 April, 1812.
German Senter, Mass., 14 April, 1812.

---

EIGHTH REGIMENT OF INFANTRY.

*Colonel.*

Patrick Jack, Ga., 6 July, 1812.

*Lieut. Colonel.*

Moffman Houston, Ga., 6 July, 1812.

*Major.*

Lawrence Manning, Ga., 12 March, 1812.

*Captains.*

Ch. Crawford, Jun., Ga., 12 March, 1812.
Philip Cook, Ga., 12 March, 1812.
Wm. Jones, Ga., 12 March, 1812.
David E. Twiggs, Ga., 12 March, 1812.
Wm. Chisolm, Ga., 12 March, 1812.
Felix B. Warley, S. C., 12 March, 1812.
Wm. M. Queen, Ga., 2 July, 1812.
Robt. Cunningham, S. C., 12 March, 1812.
Matthew I. Keith, S. C., 12 March, 1812.
Thomas W. Farrar, S. C., 12 March, 1812.

*1st Lieutenants.*

Thomas C. Hunter, S. C., 12 March, 1812.
Stephen Ford, S. C., 12 March, 1812.
Otis Dyer, Ga., 12 March, 1812.
Hamlin Cook, Ga., 12 March, 1812. Regimental Paymaster.
Hughes Walton, Ga., 12 March, 1812.
Roswell P. Johnson, S. C., 12 March, 1812.
Thomas S. Bailey, Ga., 6 July, 1812.

*2nd Lieutenants.*

Beverly Martin, Ga., 12 March, 1812.
James Wilde, Ga., 12 March, 1812.
John Mallory, Ga., 12 March, 1812.
Moses A. Robberts, Ga., 27 April, 1812.
Robert Lamar, Ga., 12 March, 1812.
James A. Black, S. C., 12 March, 1812.
Edward Holloway, S. C., 12 March, 1812.
Wm. Bee, Jun., S. C., 15 May, 1812.

*Ensigns.*

Samuel Coleman, Ga., 12 March, 1812.
Peter Lequeux, Ga., 12 March, 1812.
James Colson, Ga., 8 May, 1812.
Thomas Lane, S. C., 12 March, 1812.
James Ferguson, S. C., 28 Sept., 1812.
Thomas F. Wells, Ga., 2 Dec., 1812.
John J Contrurier, S. C., 22 Jan., 1813.
Charles Stephens, S. C., 22 Jan., 1813.

*Surgeon.*

Southwalk Harlow, Ga., 31 Dec., 1812.

*Surgeon's Mates.*

Wm. Merriwether, Ga.
Joseph W. Caldwell, Ga., 6 July, 1812.

---

NINTH REGIMENT OF INFANTRY.

*Colonel.*

Simeon Larned, Mass., 12 March, 1812.

*Lieut. Colonel.*

John L. Tuttle, Mass., 12 March, 1812

*Major.*

Thomas Aspinwall, Mass., 12 March, 1812.

*Captains.*

Seth Banister, Mass., 12 March, 1812.
Joseph Bucklin, Mass., 12 March, 1812.
Chester Lyman, Mass., 12 March, 1812.
John Nye, Mass., 12 March, 1812.
Philip White, Mass., 9 April, 1812.
Ebene. Thompson, Mass., 30 April, 1812.
Turner Crooker, Mass., 14 May, 1812.
Moses Holt, Mass., 15 May, 1812.
Elihu Jones, Mass., 12 March, 1812.

*1st Lieutenants.*

Edmund Foster, Mass., 12 March, 1812.
James F. Norris, Mass., 12 March, 1812.
Jared Ingersoll, Jun., Mass., 12 March, 1812.
Wm. Warren, Mass., 12 March, 1812.
John Reed, Jun., Mass., 30 April, 1812.
Joseph Fuller, Mass., 14 May, 1812.
George Bender, Jun., Mass., 15 May, 1812.
David Townshend, Jun., Mass., 6 July, 1812.

*2nd Lieutenants.*

Ebenezer Childs, Mass., 12 March, 1812.
Skelton Felton, Mass., 12 March, 1812.
Stephen Turner, Mass., 12 March, 1812.
Wm. L. Foster, Mass., 12 March, 1812.
Loring Palmer, Mass., 12 March, 1812.
David Perry, Mass., 12 March, 1812.
John Powle, Jun., Mass., 9 April, 1812. Regimental Paymaster.

Aaron Lewis, Mass., 30 April, 1812.
Samuel L. Allen, Mass., 30 April, 1812.
John H. Cranson, Mass., 2 Dec., 1812.

*Ensigns.*

Elliot Claflin, Mass., 12 March, 1812.
Wm. Browning, Mass., 12 March, 1812.
Daniel Chandler, Mass., 12 March, 1812.
Edward Norton, Mass., 12 March, 1812.
Otis Fisher, Mass., 12 March, 1812.
Charles Foster, Mass., 12 March, 1812.
Henry Wellington, Mass., 12 March, 1812.
Lewis Norris, Mass., 12 March, 1812.
Wm. Lyman, Mass., 25 April, 1812.
Joseph Gleason, Mass., 22 Jan., 1813.

*Surgeon.*

Joseph Lovell, Mass., 15 May, 1813.

*Surgeon's Mates.*

James H. Bradford, Mass., 24 April, 1813.
Thomas G. Mower, Mass., 2 Dec., 1813.

---

### TENTH REGIMENT OF INFANTRY.

*Colonel.*

James Welborn, N. C., 12 March, 1812.

*Lieut. Colonel.*

Andr. Pickens, Jun., S. C., 12 March, 1812.

*Major.*

Thomas Taylor, N. C., 12 March, 1812.

*Captains.*

George Cloud, N. C., 12 March, 1812.
Jesse Copeland, N. C., 12 March, 1812.
Jacob Bryant, N. C., 12 March, 1812.
Philip Brittain, N. C., 12 March, 1812.
Robert Mitchell, N. C., 14 April, 1812.
Josiah Woods, Va., 14 April, 1812.
Emanuel J. Leigh, Va., 12 March, 1812.
Mark Harden, N. C., 12 March, 1812.
Joseph Clay Va., 12 March, 1812.
Thomas M. Nelson, Va., 12 March, 1812.

*1st Lieutenants.*

William Bailey, Va., 12 March, 1812.
George Vashon, Va., 12 March, 1812.
Abner Lewis, N. C., 12 March, 1812.
George Strother, N. C., 12 March, 1812.
Charles Lutterloh N. C., 12 March, 1812.
Hugh H. Carson, N. C., 30 April, 1812.
Wm. Ward, N. C, 30 April, 1812
William S. Rhodes, N. C., 12 March, 1812.
Spencer Hinton, Va., 25 April, 1812.

*2nd Lieutenants.*

Joseph J. Clinch, N. C., 12 March, 1812.
Thomas Barker, N. C., 25 April, 1812.
Thomas D. Kelly, N. C., 12 March, 1812.
Arthur Fox, N. C., 2 July, 1812.
Wm. L. Dusphey, N. C., 15 May, 1812.
William Irvine, Va., 5 June, 1812.
Joseph G. Wall, Va., 12 March, 1812.
George Wyche, Va., 15 April, 1812.
Richard Plummer N. C., 12 March, 1812.

*Ensigns.*

Burwell Goodwin, Va., 12 March, 1812.
John Garrett, Va., 12 March, 1812.
Anthony G. Glynne, N. C., 12 March, 1812. Regimental Paymaster.
James Roane, N. C., 12 March, 1812.
Robert Logan, N. C., 12 March, 1812.
Jehu Bird, N. C., 8 April, 1812.
Joseph Merrick, Penn, 19 May, 1812.
Wm. Lancaster, N. C., 19 Jan., 1813.
James Hill, N. C., 22 Jan., 1813.

*Surgeon's Mate.*

Egbert H. Bell, N. C., 12 March, 1812.

### ELEVENTH REGIMENT OF INFANTRY.

*Colonel.*

Isaac Clark, Vt., 12 March, 1812.

*Lieut. Colonel.*

Moody Bedel, N. H., 9 April, 1812.

*Major.*

Timothy Upham, N. H., 12 March, 1812.

*Captains.*

John M'Neal, Jun., N. H., 12 March, 1812.
Jonathan Stark, N. H., 12 March, 1812.
John W. Weeks, N. H., 12 March, 1812.
Samuel Gordon, Vt., 12 March, 1812.
Phinehas Williams, Vt., 12 March, 1812.
Samuel H. Holley, Vt., 12 March, 1812.
Benjamin S. Egerton, Vt., 12 March, 1812.
Charles Follett, Vt., 12 March, 1812.

*1st Lieutenants.*

John Bliss, N. H., 12 March, 1812.
Richard Bean, N. H., 12 March, 1812.
William S. Foster, N. H., 12 March, 1812.
Malachi Corning, N. H., 12 March, 1812.
Valentine R. Goodrich, Vt., March 12, 1812.
Horace Hall, Vt., 12 March, 1812.
Benjamin Smead, Vt., 12 March, 1812.
Rufus Hatch, Vt., 12 March, 1812. Acting Deputy Quartermaster.

*2nd Lieutenants.*

James Greene, N. H., 12 March, 1812.
James Wells, N. H., 12 March, 1812.
Edw. Gerald, Jun., N. H., 12 March 1812.
Abel Farewell, Vt., 12 March, 1812.
Rufus Bucklie, Jun., Vt., 12 March 1812.
Wm. S. Heaton, Vt., 12 March, 1812.
Walter Sheldon, Vt., 12 March, 1812. Regimental Paymaster.
David Crawfor, Vt., 7 May, 1812.
Henry J. Blake, Vt., 1 May, 1812.

*Ensigns.*

Thomas Levake, Vt., 12 March, 1812.
Fred. A. Sawyer, Vt., 12 March, 1812.
Newman S. Clark, Vt., 12 March, 1812.
Timothy Aldrich N. H., 9 April, 1812.
Wm. F. Hall, Vt., 27 May, 1812.
John V. Barron, N. H., 15 May, 1812.
Ezekiel Jewett, N. H., 30 April, 1812.
Thomas Staniford, Vt., 12 Oct., 1812.
Horace Morris, 2 Dec., 1812.
Isaac Clark, Jun., Vt., 31 Dec., 1812.

*Surgeon.*

Jonathan Shaw, Vt., 29 Sept., 1812.

*Surgeon's Mates.*

Jacob B. Moore, N. H., 9 April, 1812.
James Stark, N. H., 9 April, 1812.

---

### TWELFTH REGIMENT OF INFANTRY.

*Colonel.*

Thomas Parker, Va., 12 March, 1812.

*Lieut. Colonel.*

James P. Preston, Va., 19 March, 1812.

*Major.*

David Campbell, Va., 6 July, 1812.

*Captains.*

James Gibson, Va., 12 March, 1812.
Archibald C. Randolph, Va., 14 May, 1812.
James Charlton, Va., 12 March 1812.
Thomas P. Moor, Va., 12 March, 1812.
Charles Page, Va., 12 March, 1812.

Andr. L. Madison, Va., 14 April, 1812.
Willoughby Morgan, Va., 25 April, 1812.
Thomas Sangster, Dist. of Col., 30 April, 1812.
James Paxton, Va., 12 March, 1812.

*1st Lieutenants.*

Lewis B. Willis, Va., 12 March, 1812. Regimental Paymaster.
John G. Camp, Va., 12 March, 1812.
Lackville Morgan, Va., 12 March, 1812.
Angus M'Donald, Va., 12 March, 1812.
Richard P. Fletcher, Va., 15 April, 1812.
Robert G. Hite, Va., 30 April, 1812.
Thomas Gist, Md., 12 March, 1812.
Thomas Post, Md., 25 April, 1812.
Archibald Kerr, Penn., 9 April, 1812.
John Johnson, Penn., 12 March, 1812.

*2nd Lieutenants.*

Peter Magruder, Md., 12 March, 1812.
Russel Harrison, Va., 12 March, 1812.
Wm. Stone, Jun., Va., 1 May, 1812.
John Key, Jun., Va. 12 March, 1812.
John Kenney, Va., 12 March, 1812.
Matthew Hughes, Va., 14 April, 1812.
John Towles, Va., 15 April, 1812.
Otho W. Callis, Va., 14 May, 1812.
Robert Houston, Va., 12 March, 1812.

*Ensigns.*

J. W. Gevock, Jun., Va., 12 March, 1812.
Isaac Keyes, Va., 12 March, 1812.
Joseph Shommo, Va., 12 March, 1812.
Bailey Bruce, Va., 12 March, 1812.
Philip Wager, Va., 12 March, 1812.
Wm. C. Parker, Va., 25 April, 1812.
David P. Polk, Dist. of Col., 22 June, 1812.
Thomas B. Barton, Va., 31 Dec., 1812.
Mathew M. Claiborne, Va, 13 Jan., 1813.

*Surgeon.*

James C. Bronaugh, Va., 28 April, 1812.

*Surgeon's Mate.*

Joseph Berry, Va., 25 April, 1812.

---

THIRTEENTH REGIMENT OF INFANTRY.

*Colonel.*

Peter P. Schuyler, N. Y., 12 March, 1812.

*Lieut. Colonel.*

John Christie, N. Y., 12 March, 1812.

*Major.*

John V. Huyck, N. Y., 25 April, 1812.

*Captains.*

Hugh R. Martin, N. Y., 12 March, 1812.
Myndert M. Dox, N. Y., 12 March, 1812.
John E. Wool, N. Y., 14 April, 1812.
Rich. M. Malcom, N. Y., 8 April, 1812.
John Sproull, N. Y., 12 March, 1812.
Mordecai Myers, N. Y., 12 March, 1812.
Peter Ogilvie, Jun., N. Y., 12 March, 1812.
Robert H. Morris, N. Y., 25 April, 1812.
Hen. B. Armstrong, N. Y., 9 April, 1812.
Wm. D. Lawrence, N. Y., 12 March, 1812.

*1st Lieutenants.*

Samuel Haring, N. Y., 12 March, 1812.
John L. Fink, N. Y., 12 March, 1812.
Israel Turner, N. Y., 14 April, 1812.
Rt. Smith Gardiner, N. Y., 12 March, 1812. Regimental Paymaster.
John Keyes Paige, N. Y., 17 March, 1812.
John Campbell, N. Y., 15 May, 1812.
Wessell Gansevoort, N. Y., 1 May, 1812.
Steph. W. Kearney, N. Y., 12 March, 1812.
Wm. B. Adams, N. Y., 12 March, 1812.

*2nd Lieutenants.*

Daniel Huganin, N. Y., 12 March, 1812.
Wm. W. Carr, N. Y., 1 May 1812
Daniel B. Willcox, N. Y., 1 May, 1812.
Richard H. Root, N. Y., 1 May, 1812.
Alfred Philips, N. Y., 25 April, 1812.
Jacob Sammons, N. Y., 1 May, 1812
Hugh Robeson, N. Y., 25 April, 1812.
Joseph C. Eldridge, N. Y., 12 March, 1812.

*Ensigns.*

John Kirby, N. Y., 12 March, 1812.
George Reab, Jun., N. Y., 1 May, 1812.
Henry Devo, N. Y., 1 May, 1812.
Thomas W. Denton, N. Y., 1 June, 1812.
George Keese, N. Y., 1 May, 1812.
Joseph H. Dwight, N. Y., 25 April, 1812.
John Gates, Jun., N. Y., 1 May, 1812.
Jas. W. Lent, Jun., N. Y., 1 May, 1812.
John Williams, N. Y., 14 April, 1812.

*Surgeon.*

John Y. Lansing, N. Y., 1 Oct., 1812.

*Surgeon's Mates.*

John M'Call, N. Y., 15 April, 1812.
H. Y. Hoevenburgh, N. Y., 6 July, 1812.

---

FOURTEENTH REGIMENT OF INFANTRY.

*Colonel.*

Wm. H. Winder, Md., 6 July, 1812.

*Lieut. Colonel.*

Charles G. Bœrstler, Md., 12 March, 1812.

*Major.*

Timothy D'x, Jun., N. H., 12 March, 1812.

*Captains.*

James Britton, Md., 12 March, 1812.
Thos. Montgomery, Md., 12 March, 1812.
Robert W. Kent, Md., 12 March, 1812.
Kenneth M'Kenzie, Md., 12 March, 1812.
Samuel Lane, Md., 12 March, 1812.
Henry Grindage, Del., 12 March, 1812.
Isaac D. Barnard, Penn., 12 March, 1812.
Wm. M'Ilvain, Penn., 12 March, 1812.
Henry Fleming, Penn., 8 April, 1812.

*1st Lieutenants.*

Benjamin Nicholson, Md., 12 March, 1812.
Richard Arett, Del., 12 March, 1812.
Thomas Kearney, Md., 12 March, 1812.
David Cummings, Md., 12 March, 1812.
Peter Rich, Md., 12 March, 1812.
Joseph Marshall Md., 12 March, 1812.
Reuben Gilder, Md., 12 March, 1812.
Joseph S. Nelson, Md., 12 March, 1812.
James M'Donald, Md., 12 March, 1812.

*2nd Lieutenants.*

Benjamin Nicholson, Md., 12 March, 1812.
Amos Woodward, Md., 4 June, 1812.
Edward Wilson, Md., 12 March, 1812.
John Beckett Md., 12 March, 1812.
John Waring, Md., 12 March, 1812.
Jn. W. Thompson, Md., 12 March, 1812.
George Murdock, Md., 15 April, 1812.
Thomas Randall, Md., 12 March, 1812.
John B. Sparks, Md., 12 March, 1812.

*Ensigns.*

James H. Gale, Md., 12 March, 1812.
Wm. G. Sanders, Md., 12 March, 1812.
Abraham Clark, Md., 12 March, 1812.
Kimmel Godwin, Md., 12 March, 1812.
Robert W. Long, Md., 12 March, 1812.
St. F. Donaldson, Md., 12 March, 1812. Regimental Paymaster.

Richard Bennett, Md., 12 March, 1812.
Wm. G. Mills, Md., 30 April, 1812.
Nich. N. Robinson, Del., 2 July, 1812.
John Linch, Md., 9 Oct., 1812.

*Surgeon.*

John Young, Md., 4 June, 1812.

*Surgeon's Mates.*

Samuel B. Hugo, Md., 12 March, 1812.
George Nicholas, Md., 14 Oct., 1812.

---

### Fifteenth Regiment of Infantry.

*Colonel.*

Zebulon Montgomery Pike, N. J., 6 July, 1812.

*Lieut. Colonel.*

David Brearly, N. J., 12 March, 1812.

*Major.*

Ephraim L. Whitlock N. J., 1 May, 1812.

*Captains.*

William King, Md., 2 July, 1812.
Charles W. Hunter, N. J., 12 March, 1812.
Charles Carson, N. J., 12 March, 1812.
John Scott, N. J., 12 March, 1812.
Zachariah Rossell, N. J., 12 March, 1812.
Henry H. Van Dalsem, N. J., 12 March, 1812.
John L. Hoppoch, N. J., 12 March, 1812.
Abraham Reynolds, N. J., 12 March, 1812.
White Youngs, N. Y., 12 March, 1812.
Joseph L. Barton, N. J., 30 Sept., 1812.

*1st Lieutenants.*

Jeremiah D. Hayden, N. J., 12 March, 1812.
George M'Glassen, Penn., 12 March, 1812.
Abraham Peter Lee, N. Y., 17 March, 1812.
Aaron Sutphir, N. J., 12 March, 1812.
James Platt, N. J., 12 March, 1812.
William Barnett, N. J., 12 March, 1812.
Jacob D. Howell, N. J. 12 March, 1812.
Joseph Schofield, N. Y., 14 April, 1812.
Richard L. Howell, N. J., 15 Sept., 1812.
Samuel M'Dougall, N. J., 30 Sept., 1812.

*2nd Lieutenants.*

Moses O. Bloomfield, N. J., 15 May, 1812.
David Curtis, N. Y., 12 March, 1812.
David Biddle, Penn., 9 April, 1812.
Richard Edsall, Jun., N. J., 12 March, 1812.
Abraham Godwin, N. J., 12 March, 1812.
George Henry, N. J., 12 March, 1812.
Charles Stewart, N. Y., 14 April, 1812.
William G. Scott, N. Y., 15 Sept., 1812.
John Scott, N. Y., 30 Sept., 1812.

*Ensigns.*

Christopher Noyes, N. J., 12 March, 1812.
William Coffie, N. J., 12 March, 1812.
Jacob Dickerson, N. J., 12 March, 1812.
Donald Fraser, Penn., 12 March, 1812.
Joseph Moore, N. J., 15 May, 1812.
Henry K. Mullen, N. J., 2 July, 1812.
John Collins, N. J., 2 July, 1812.
John T. David, Penn., 7 May, 1812. Regimental Paymaster.
Daniel E. Burch, N. Y., 7 Oct., 1812.
John Rose, N. J., 7 Oct., 1812.
Chas. H. Roberts, N. J., 7 Oct., 1812.

*Surgeon.*

Fenn Danning, N. Y., 14 April, 1812.

*Surgeon's Mates.*

Reuben T. Baker, N. J., 12 March, 1812.
Burton W. Halsey, N. Y., 23 Sept., 1812.

### Sixteenth Regiment of Infantry.

*Colonel.*

Cromwell Pearce, Penn., 25 April, 1812.

*Lieut. Colonel.*

Richard Dennis, Penn., 25 April, 1812.

*Major.*

Robert Carr, Penn., 12 March, 1812.

*Captains.*

Washington Lee, Penn., 12 March, 1812. Assistant Adjutant General.
Jacob Schener, Penn., 12 March, 1812.
James F. M'Elroy, Penn., 9 April, 1812.
Robert Gray, Penn., 14 April, 1812.
Alexander M'Ewen, Penn., 12 March, 1812.
Thomas Lyon, N. Y., 12 March, 1812.
George G. Steele, Penn., 12 March, 1812.
William Davenport, N. C., 28 Sept., 1812.

*1st Lieutenants.*

Terah Jones, Penn., 12 March, 1812.
Miles Greenwood, N. Y., 12 March, 1812.
George G. Phinney, N. Y., 1 May, 1812.
Pet. Donnelly, Jun., N. Y., 27 May, 1812.
John Caldwell Jun., Penn., 12 March, 1812.
Jonath. W. Aitkin, Penn., 12 March, 1812. Regimental Paymaster.
John Machesney, Penn., 17 March, 1812.
John Baldy, Penn., 12 March, 1812.

*2nd Lieutenants.*

John D. Coon, N. Y., 4 June, 1812.
Nath. M'Laughlin, Penn., 17 March, 1812.
Isaac Finch, N. Y., 14 April, 1812.
Fras. D. Cummings, N. Y., 8 May, 1812.
John Martin, Penn., 9 April, 1812.
Thomas Horrell, Penn., 12 March, 1812.
Samuel Weighs, Penn., 9 April, 1812.
Thos. M. Powers, Penn., 30 April, 1812

*Ensigns.*

John Rohm, Penn., 8 May, 1812.
Isaac Myers, Penn., 1 June, 1812.
Jacob Whistler, Penn., 9 April, 1812.
Henry Hale, N. Y., 1 May, 1812.
Wm. C. Enos, N. Y., 1 May, 1812.
Thomas Mahon, Penn., 12 Oct., 1812.
Thomas Evans, Penn., 17 Oct., 1812.
Thomas J. Martin, Penn., 13 Nov., 1812.

*Surgeon.*

Samuel Gilliland, Penn., 15 May, 1812.

*Surgeon's Mate.*

Gustavus Baylies, R. I., 2 Dec., 1812.

---

### Seventeenth Regiment of Infantry.

*Colonel.*

Samuel Wells, Ky., 12 March, 1812.

*Lieut. Colonel.*

William M'Millan, Ky., 12 March, 1812.

*Captains.*

George Crogham, Ky., 12 March, 1812.
Wm. Bradford, Ky., 12 March, 1812.
David Holt, Ky., 12 March, 1812.
Robert Edwards, Ky., 12 March, 1812.
James Duncan, Jun., Ky., 12 March, 1812.
Richard Hightower, Ky., 12 March, 1812.
Wm. J. Adair, Ky., 12 March, 1812.
James Mead, Ky., 12 March, 1812.
James Hunter, Ky., 12 March, 1812.
Charles Querry, Ky., 8 May, 1812.

*1st Lieutenants.*

Benjamin Johnson, Ky., 12 March, 1812.
Benjam. W. Sanders, 12 March, 1812.
Alex. Robertson, Ky., 12 March, 1812.
Thomas G. Graves, Ky., 12 March, 1812.
Mer. W. Fisher, Ky., 12 March, 1812.
Martin L. Hawkins, Ky., 12 March, 1812.
Henry Crittenden, Ky., 15 May, 1812.
Caleb H. Holder, Ky., 12 March, 1812.
Thomas J. Overton, Ky., 12 March, 1812.
Robert Logan, Ky., 12 March, 1812.

*2nd Lieutenants.*

Philip King, Ky., 12 March, 1812.
Thomas Mountjoy, Ky., 12 March, 1812.
John T. Redding, Ky., 12 March, 1812.
Parry Hawkins, Ky., 12 March, 1812.
Ashton Garret, Ky., 12 March, 1812.
James Hackley, Ky., Jr., 12 March, 1812.
Nimrod H. Moore, Ky. 12 March, 1812. Regimental Paymaster.
Cyrus A. Baylor, Ky., 15 May, 1812.

*Ensigns.*

Thomas Hawkins, Ky., 15 May, 1812.
Edmund Shipp, Jr., Ky., 8 May, 1812.
Samuel H. Craig, Ky., 12 March, 1812.
Thos. S. Morgan, Ky., 12 March, 1812.
Reuben Taylor, Ky., 12 March, 1812.
James Mundy, Ky., 12 March, 1812.
Joseph Duncan, Ky., 12 March, 1812.
James Gray, Ky., 12 March, 1812.
Philip S. Sharer, Ky., 12 March, 1812.

*Surgeon.*

Alex. Montgomery, Ky., 12 March, 1812.

*Surgeon's Mate.*

Wm. S. Madison, Ky., 2 Dec., 1812.

---

EIGHTEENTH REGIMENT OF INFANTRY.

*Colonel.*

Wm. Drayton, S. C., 6 July, 1812.

*Lieut. Colonel.*

Benajah White, N. C., 12 March, 1812.

*Major.*

Wm. Strother, S. C., 12 March, 1812.

*Captains.*

Arthur Simkins, Jr., S. C., 12 March, 1812.
Henry P. Taylor, S. C., 12 March, 1812.
Wm. Taylor, S. C., 12 March, 1812.
Owen Clinton, N. C., 12 March, 1812.
Thos. J. Robeson, N. C., 12 March, 1812.
Edward King, S. C., 12 March, 1812.
Michael J. Kenan, N. C., 25 April, 1812.
John G. Blount, Jr., N. C., 27 May, 1812.
George Butler, S. C., 2 July, 1812.

*1st Lieutenants.*

Wm. Winn, S. C., 12 March, 1812.
John W. Farrow, S. C., 12 March, 1812. Regimental Paymaster.
Ben. T. Elmore, S. C., 12 March, 1812.
Wm. Tisdall, N. C., 12 March, 1812.
Alex. King, N. C., 12 March, 1812.
Elias D. Diek, S. C., 12 March, 1812.
Montag. G. Waage, N. C., 25 April, 1812.
Wm. A. Blount, N. C., 8 May, 1812.
James Hamilton, S C., 15 April, 1812.

*2nd Lieutenants.*

Thos. Reynolds, S. C., 12 March, 1812.
Jeho. Watkins, S. C., 12 March, 1812.
Richard Thruston, S. C., 12 March, 1812.
Samuel M. Cantey, S. C., 12 March, 1812.
Wm. N. Miller, S. C., 12 March, 1812.
Hamilton Brown, N. C., 12 March, 1812.
Eman. S. Hawkins, N. C., 12 March, 1812.
John Street, N. C., 12 March, 1812.
Rt. Mebane, Jun., N. C., 12 March, 1812.
Thos. C. Wilhight, N. C., 12 March, 1812.

*Ensigns.*

Alexander Pagan, S. C., 12 March, 1812.
John Peebles, S. C., 12 March, 1812.
John Mickle, Jun., S. C., 12 March, 1812.
Wm. Tyler, S. C., 12 March, 1812.
John Pritchard, N. C., 12 March, 1812.
Abner P. Neale, N. C., 8 May, 1812.
Horatio Dade, N. C., 13 Jan., 1813.
Fred. Kinlock, S. C., 22 Jan., 1813.

*Surgeon.*

Joseph F. Lee, S. C., 6 July, 1812.

*Surgeon's Mates.*

Wm. M'Caw, S. C., 1 May, 1812.
James B. Hill, N. C., 6 July, 1812.

---

NINETEENTH REGIMENT OF INFANTRY.

*Colonel.*

John Miller, Ohio, 6 July, 1812.

*Lieut. Colonel.*

John B. Campbell, Ky., 12 March, 1812.

*Major.*

George Tod, Ohio, 12 March, 1812.

*Captains.*

Angus L. Lanham, Ohio, 12 March, 1812.
Wilson Elliott, Ohio, 12 March, 1812.
James Herron, Ohio, 12 March, 1812.
Abraham Edwards, Ohio, 12 March, 1812.
Hugh Moore, Ohio, 12 March, 1812.
Harris H. Hickman, Ohio, 12 March, 1812.
Richard Graham, Ky., 4 June, 1812.
John T. Chunn, Indiana Ter., 14 April, 1812.
Asahil Nearing, Conn., 6 July, 1812.

*1st Lieutenants.*

John D. Fleming, Ky., 12 March, 1812.
Stephen Lee, Ky., 12 March, 1812.
Samuel Booker, Ohio, 12 March, 1812.
David Gwinnie, Ohio, 12 March, 1812. Regimental Paymaster.
James Campbell, Ohio, 12 March, 1812.
George W. Jackson, Ohio, 12 March, 1812.
Lewis Howell, Ohio, 12 March, 1812.
John Anderson, Michigan Ter., 12 March, 1812.
John Hezelton, Penn., 12 March, 1812.
James Morrow, Penn., 12 March, 1812.

*2nd Lieutenants.*

Benjamin Byerly, Penn., 25 April, 1812.
Henry B Turner, Penn., 14 April, 1812.
Jonathan Rees, Ohio, 12 March, 1812.
Henry Frederick, Ohio, 12 March, 1812.
Philip P. Price, Penn., 12 March, 1812.
Joseph Watson, Michigan Ter., 12 March, 1812.
John D. Reeves, Ohio, 1 May, 1812.

*Ensigns.*

John Whistler, Jr., Michigan Ter., 12 March, 1812.
John Miligan, Ohio, 12 March, 1812.
Battle Harrison, Ohio, 12 March, 1812.
Asher Phillips, Ohio, 12 March, 1812.
Charles Mitchell, Ky., 15 May, 1812.
Edward B. Basherville, Ohio, 4 June, 1812.

Hugh May, Penn., 14 May, 1812.
John Cochran, Penn., 25 April, 1812.
John Stockton, Ohio, 31 Dec., 1812.

*Surgeon's Mates.*

Charles Marvin, Ohio.
Daniel Turney, Ohio, 31 Dec., 1812.

---

TWENTIETH REGIMENT OF INFANTRY.

*Lieut. Colonel.*

Isaac A. Coles, Va., 6 July, 1812.

*Captains.*

Lewis L. Taylor, Va., 12 March, 1812.
Hodijah Meade, Va., 14 May, 1812.
Robert C. Nicholas, Va., 12 March, 1812.
John A. Thornton, Va., 6 July, 1812.
John Macrae, Jun., Va., 19 March, 1812.
John Stannard, Va., 12 March, 1812.
Byrd C. Willis, Va., 14 May, 1812.
Ww. S. Jett, Jun., Va., 25 April, 1812.
Richard Pollard, Va., 14 April, 1812.

*1st Lieutenants.*

Charles Gee, Va., 12 March, 1812.
Thomas Harris, Va., 12 March, 1812.
Matthew M. Payne, Va., 12 March, 1812.
Clement White, Va., 12 March, 1812.
John P. Duvall, Va., 9 April, 1812.
Reuben Crawford, Va., 5 June, 1812.
Bernard Peyton, Va., 12 March, 1812.
Walter G. Hayes, Va., 19 March, 1812.
Wm. A. Shelton, Va., 12 March, 1812.
Micajah Lynch, Va., 2 July, 1812.

*2nd Lieutenants.*

Thomas Howson, Va., 12 March, 1812.
George Hatchett, Va., 12 March, 1812.
William Ligon, Va., 12 March, 1812.
John H. Howard, Va., 12 March, 1812.
Thomas Munroe, Va., 12 March, 1812.
John Archer, Va., 8 April, 1812. Regimental Paymaster.
George Evans, Jun., Va., 14 May, 1812.
Thomas Blackwell, Va., 12 March, 1812.
Benjamin Smith, Va., 12 March, 1812.
Sam. Hairston, Jun., Va., 12 March, 1812.

*Ensigns.*

Joseph Pettipool, Va., 12 March, 1812.
Thomas Grady, Va., 12 March, 1812.
Samuel Harris, Va., 12 March, 1812.
Edw. B. Randolph, Va., 15 May, 1812.
George M'Laughlin, Va., 19 May, 1812.
Wm. F. Pendleton, Va., 5 June, 1812.
Thos. H. Saunders, Va., 19 March, 1812.
John B. Hogan, Va., 12 March, 1812.
Wm. H. Godwin, Va., 12 March, 1812.
James M. Glassell, Va., 1 May, 1812.

*Surgeon.*

Wm. H. Brown, Va., 15 May, 1812.

*Surgeon's Mates.*

Horace Wellford, Va., 15 May, 1812.
Hugh W. Houston, Va., 5 July, 1812.

---

TWENTY-FIRST REGIMENT OF INFANTRY.

*Lieut. Colonel.*

Eleazer W. Ripley, Mass., 12 March, 1812.

*Major.*

Samuel S. Conner, Mass., 12 March, 1812.

*Captains.*

Daniel Libby, Jun., Mass., 12 March, 1812.
Jeremiah Chapman, Mass., 12 March, 1812.
Lemuel Bradford, Mass., 12 March, 1812.
Charles E. Tobey, Mass., 12 March, 1812.
Charles Proctor, Mass., 12 March, 1812.
Joseph Grafton, Mass., 24 March, 1812.
Joseph Treat, Mass., 12 March, 1812.
Benjamin Ropes, Mass., 12 March, 1812.
Josiah H. Vose, Mass., 9 April, 1812.

*1st Lieutenants.*

Morrill Marston, Mass., 12 March, 1812.
Wm. S. Moore, Mass., 12 March, 1812.
Ebenezer White, Mass., 12 March, 1812.
Lawson Kingsbury, Mass., 12 March, 1812.
Sullivan Burbank, Mass., 12 March, 1812.
Samuel Harper, N. H., 12 March, 1812.
Jon. Eastman, Jun., N. H., 12 March, 1812.
Daniel Henderson, N. H., 12 March, 1812.
Leonard Ross, Mass., 6 Oct., 1812.

*2nd Lieutenants.*

Ira Aldrich, N. H., 12 March, 1812.
Josiah Bartlett, N. H., 12 March, 1812.
Ira Drew, Mass., 12 March, 1812.
Azor Orne, Mass., 12 March, 1812.
John Dawner, Mass., 12 March, 1812.
Peter Pelliam, Mass., 12 March, 1812.
William Bowman, Mass., 12 March, 1812.
Perez Loring, Mass., 9 April, 1812.
Henry Bender, Mass., 30 April, 1812.
Thomas Harrison, Mass., 15 April, 1812.

*Ensigns.*

Ebenezer Knox, Mass., 12 March, 1812.
Aaron Bigelow, Mass., 12 March, 1812.
Francis Carr, Jun., Mass., 12 March, 1812.
Nathaniel N. Hall, Mass., 12 March, 1812.
James Pratt, Mass., 12 March, 1812.
Joseph Cilley, N. H., 12 March, 1812.
John Duncan, N. H., 9 April, 1812.
William Ross, N. H., 2 Dec., 1812.
David J. Hopkins, N. H., 4 Dec., 1812.

*Surgeon's Mates.*

William Thorndike, Mass., 6 July, 1812.
Ira Wright, Mass., 6 July, 1812.

---

TWENTY-SECOND REGIMENT OF INFANTRY.

*Colonel.*

Hugh Brady, Penn., 6 July, 1812.

*Lieut. Colonel.*

George M'Feely, Penn., 12 March, 1812.

*Major.*

John M'Cluney, Penn., 17 March, 1812.

*Captains.*

Silas Amberson, Penn., 12 March, 1812.
Daniel M'Farland, Penn., 12 March, 1812.
David Millikin, Penn., 12 March, 1812.
Sampson S. King, Penn., 12 March, 1812.
Jacob Carmack, Penn., 12 March, 1812.
John Foster, Penn., 2 July, 1812.
John Pentland, Penn., 30 April, 1812.
George W. Barker, Penn., 19 Jan., 1813.

*1st Lieutenants.*

David Espy, Penn., 12 March, 1812.
Joseph Henderson, Penn., 12 March, 1812.
James M. Stewart, Penn., 12 March, 1812.
John Larken, Penn., 12 March, 1812.
Willis Foulk, Penn., 12 March, 1812.
Thomes Y. Sprogell, N. J., 17 March, 1812.
William Morrow, Penn., 17 March, 1812.
James Huston, Penn., 9 April, 1812.
Fred. A. Wise, Penn., 25 April, 1812.
Thomas Lawrence, Penn., 19 May, 1812.

*2nd Lieutenants.*

Eli Thomas, Penn., 12 March, 1812.
William Sturgus, Penn., 12 March, 1812.
James M'Ghee, Penn., 9 April, 1812.
Dominick Cornyn, Penn., 9 April, 1812.
Jacob Fetter, Penn., 8 May, 1812.
Geo. W. Ferguson, Penn., 9 April, 1812.
Samuel A. Reppey, Penn., 8 May, 1812.
John H. Wise, Penn., 8 May, 1812.
John Greene, Penn., 12 March, 1812.

*Ensigns.*

John D. Kehr, Penn., 12 March, 1812.
Thomas Wright, Penn., 9 April, 1812. Regimental Paymaster.
George Mytinger, Penn., 8 May, 1812.
John Armstrong, Penn., 14 May, 1812.
John R. Guy, Penn., 15 May, 1812.
Michael Sturgeson, Penn., 27 May, 1812.
William Gillispie, Penn., 27 May, 1812.
Gideon Law, Penn., 1 June, 1812.
James M'Kenney, Penn., 1 June, 1812.
John Culbertson, Penn., 17 March, 1812.
John C. Farrell, Penn., 13 Nov., 1812

*Surgeon.*

Julius R. Shumate, Penn., 31 Dec., 1812.

*Surgeon's Mates.*

Prestly H. Craig, Penn., 6 July, 1812.
Jesse Magaw, Penn., 6 July, 1812.

---

TWENTY-THIRD REGIMENT OF INFANTRY.

*Colonel.*

Daniel Brown, N. Y., 25 April, 1812.

*Major.*

James R. Mullany, N. Y., 13 March, 1812.

*Captains.*

Willard Troll, N. Y., 12 March, 1812.
Thomas Delano, N. Y., 14 April, 1812.
Herman Finney, N. Y., 14 April, 1812.
Joshua Wilday, N. Y., 14 April, 1812.
Peter Mills, N. Y., 14 April, 1812.
Abraham F. Hull, N. Y., 14 April, 1812.
David Scott, N. Y., 15 April, 1812.
Derick VanVechten, N. Y., 27 April, 1812.
Horace G. Armstrong, N. Y., 25 Sept., 1812.
Lezier B. Canfield, N. Y., 25 Sept., 1812.

*1st Lieutenants.*

Simon D. Wattles, N. Y., 14 April, 1812.
Ephraim F. Gilbert, N. Y., 8 April, 1812.
John M'Cartey, N. Y., 25 April, 1812.
Samuel Coldwell, N. Y., 25 April, 1812.
Azariah W. Odell, N. Y., 25 April, 1812.
Richard Goodell, N. Y., 1 May, 1812.
Samuel Chipman, N. Y., 15 April, 1812.
Benj. H. Mooers, N. Y., 15 May, 1812.
William Clark, N. Y., 12 March, 1812.

*2nd Lieutenants.*

Chandler W. Drake, N. Y., 12 March, 1812.
Rodolphus Simons, N. Y., 1 May, 1812.
Peter L. Hogeboom, N. Y., 1 May, 1812. Regimental Paymaster.
Henry Whiting, N. Y., 1 May, 1812.
Frederick Brown, N. Y., 14 April, 1812.
Richard M. Harrison, N. Y., 1 May, 1812.
Abijah Bennett, N. Y., 1 May, 1812.
John P. Livingston, N. Y., 25 Sept., 1812.

*Ensigns.*

Justus Ingersoll, N. Y., 12 March, 1812.
Samuel R. Hill, N. Y., 1 May, 1812.
Alphonso Wetmore, N. Y., 14 April, 1812.
John Jones, N. Y., 25 April, 1812.
Ezra Post, Jun., N. Y., 1 May, 1812.
Samuel Tappan, N. Y., 1 May, 1812.
Ezra King, N. Y., 1 May, 1812.
Richard Phillips, N. Y., 1 May, 1812.
Levi S. Burr, N. Y., 1 May, 1812.
Zadock P. Morse, N. Y., 14 April, 1812.

*Surgeon.*

Silas Fuller, Conn., 6 July, 1812.

*Surgeon's Mates.*

William M. Ross, N. Y., 6 July, 1812.
John Gale, N. H., 6 July, 1812.

---

TWENTY-FOURTH REGIMENT OF INFANTRY.

*Colonel.*

Wm. P. Anderson, Tenn., 6 July, 1812.

*Lieut. Colonel.*

Edmund P. Gaines, Tenn., 6 July, 1812.

*Captains.*

James M. Anderson, Ky., 12 March, 1812.
James H. Campbell, Ky., 12 March, 1812.
John A. Rogers, Ky., 12 March, 1812.
Robert Desha, Ky., 12 March, 1812.
Robert Butler, Ky., 12 March, 1812.
Alexander Gray, Ky., 12 March, 1812.
Francis Armstrong, Ky., 12 March, 1812.
John Ballinger, Orleans Ter., 12 March, 1812.
Andrew H. Holmes, Mississippi Ter., 12 March, 1812.
William O. Allen, La., 14 April, 1812.

*1st Lieutenants.*

William Scott, Tenn., 12 March, 1812.
Don Carolus Dixon, Tenn., 12 March, 1812, Regimental Paymaster.
Isaac Walton, Tenn., 12 March, 1812.
Michael W. Toomy, Tenn., 12 March, 1812.
Wm. O. Winston, Mississippi Ter., 13 March, 1812.
Minor Sturgus, Mississippi Ter., 8 April, 1812.
Walter Wilkinson, La., 2 July, 1812.
Silas Stephens, Tenn., 8 May, 1812.
Frank Hampton, S. C., 2 July, 1812.
James Stewart, Tenn., 31 Dec., 1812.

*2nd Lieutenants.*

Samuel Scott, Tenn., 12 March, 1812.
Uriah Allison, Tenn., 12 March, 1812.
Avery Clarke, Tenn., 12 March, 1812.
Joseph D. Smith, Tenn., 12 March, 1812.
Joseph Anthony, Tenn., 12 March, 1812.
Taliaferro Richards, Tenn., 12 March, 1812.
Robert Buntin, Jun., Indiana Ter., 14 April, 1812.
Caleb G. Fobes, Ohio, 12 Sept., 1812.
Tim. E. Danielson, Ohio, 12 March, 1812.
Beverly Roy, Ky., 12 March, 1812.
Joseph Perkins, Mississippi Ter., 22 Jan., 1813.

*Ensigns.*

T. P. Favrot, Orleans Ter., 12 March, 1812.
Adam Peck, Jun., Tenn., 12 March, 1812.
Littleton Johnson, Tenn., 12 March, 1812.
Anth. W. Putney, Tenn., 12 March, 1812.
John Butler, Tenn., 28 Sept., 1812.
Joseph A. Martin, Tenn., 19 Jan., 1813.
Francis Valle, Missouri Ter., 22 Jan., 1813.

*Surgeon's Mates.*

Anthony Foster, Tenn., 31 Dec., 1812.
Carlisle Humphries, Tenn., 25 April, 1812.

TWENTY-FIFTH REGIMENT OF INFANTRY.

*Lieut. Colonel.*

Jonas Cutting, Vt., 12 March, 1812.

*Major.*

Joseph Lee Smith, Conn., 12 March, 1812.

*Captains.*

Seth Phelps, Conn., 12 March, 1812.
George Howard, Conn., 12 March, 1812.
Peter Bradley, Conn., 12 March, 1812.
Festus Cone, Conn., 21 May, 1812.
Henry Leavenworth, Conn., 25 April, 1812.
William Battey, R. I., 12 March, 1812.
David Bartlett, R. I., 12 March, 1812.

*1st Lieutenants.*

Thomas M. Read, R. I., 12 March, 1812.
John Bates Murdock, Conn., 12 March, 1812.
Henry Dyer, Conn., 12 March, 1812.
Joseph Kinney, Conn., 6 July, 1812.
Charles M'Lean, Conn. 6 July, 1812.
John A. Thomas, Conn., 6 July, 1812.
Minor Robbins, Conn., 6 July, 1812.

*2nd Lieutenants.*

Benjamin Watson, R. I., 12 March, 1812.
Edward White, Mass., 12 March, 1812.
Archibald C. Crary, R. I., 12 March, 1812.
Thomas S. Seymour, Conn., 6 July, 1812.
Daniel Forwood, Conn., 6 July, 1812.
Joseph S. Staring, N. Y., 6 July, 1812.
James Burbidge, Conn., 6 July, 1812.
Jesse Beach, Conn., 6 July, 1812.
Daniel Ketchum, Conn., 6 July, 1812.

*Ensigns*

John G. Munz, Conn., 12 March, 1812.
Ephraim Shaylor, Conn., 12 March, 1812.
Joseph Hutchinson, Conn., 12 March, 1812.
Eli Terry, Conn., 6 July, 1812.
Alexander T. F. Bill, Conn., 6 July, 1812.
Clark Robbins, Conn., 6 July, 1812.
Russell Eday, N. Y., 1 May, 1812. Regimental Paymaster.
George M'Chain, N. Y., 14 April, 1812.
John Gifford, N. Y., 22 Jan., 1813.
James D. Brown, Conn., 22 Jan., 1813.

*Surgeon.*

Giles Gridley, Mass., 9 April, 1812.

*Surgeon's Mates.*

Phinehas Woodbury, Vt., 6 July, 1812.
John L. Comstock, R. I., 2 Dec., 1812.

---

# OFFICERS OF THE ARMY,

## 1813.

GENERAL STAFF.

WAR DEPARTMENT, *Washington.*

---

*Adjutant and Inspector General.*
*Inspector General.*

Abimael Y. Nicoll, 18 March, 1813. Maj. 1st Art. Washington.

*Assistant Adjutant General.*

Charles K. Gardner, 18 March, 1813. Maj. 25th Inf.

*Commissary General Ordnance.*

Decius Wadsworth, 2 July, 1812. Washington.

*Deputy Commissaries Ordnance.*

John Morton, 11 Sept., 1812. Washington
Edwin Tyler, 5 Aug., 1813. Washington.

*Assistant Commissar Ordnance.*

Nehemiah Baden, 6 Aug., 1813. Washington.

*Paymaster of the Army.*

Robert Brent, 1 July, 1808. Washington.

*Assistant Topographical Engineer.*

James Kearney, 12 April, 1813. Lieut. 5th Inf. Washington.

MILITARY DISTRICT, NO. 1.

*Massachusetts and New Hampshire.*

*Brig. General.*

T. H. Cushing, commanding.

*Adjutant General.*

Peter P. Schuyler, 28 April, 1813. Col. 13th Inf.

*Assistant Inspector General.*

Enos Cutler, 18 March, 1813. Capt. 7th Inf.

*Assistant Deput Quartermaster General.*

Jonathan Allen, 20 April, 1813.

*Hospital Surgeon.*

Benjamin Waterhouse, 29 June, 1813.

*Garrison Surgeon's Mates.*

Joseph Goodhue, 8 Feb., 1803.
James H. Sargent, 8 March, 1806.

*District Paymasters.*

Nehemiah Freeman. Boston.
Jos. C. Boyd. For Militia, Etc. Maine.

*Deputy Commissaries of Purchases.*

Amasa Stetson. Boston.
John Langdon, Jr. Portsmouth.

*Military Storekeepers.*

Samuel Devans. Charlestown.
John Rice. Portsmouth.
John Chaffee. Springfield.

---

MILITARY DISTRICT, NO. 2.

*Rhode Island and Connecticut*

*Brig. General.*

H. Burbeck, Brevet, commanding.

*Inspector General.*

Jacob Kingsbury, 28 April, 1813. Col. 1st Inf.

*Assistan Deputy Quartermaster General.*

Rich. H. Ashley, 11 April, 1813. Lieut. 1st Art.

*Garrison Surgeon's Mate.*

William Turner, 28 Sept,, 1813.

*District Paymaster.*

George L. Perkins. New London.

*Deputy Commissary of Purchases.*

Elisha Tracy. Norwich.

*Military Storekeeper.*

Giles L'Hommedieu. Norwich.

---

MILITARY DISTRICT, NO. 3.

*New York from the Sea to the Highlands, and East Jersey.*

*Major General.*

Henry Dearborn, commanding. New York.

*Adjutant General.*

John R. Fenwick, 18 March, 1813. Lieut. Col. Light Art. New York

*Assistant Adjutant General.*

Thos. Chrystie, 18 March, 1813. Lieut. 3rd Art. New York.

*Inspector General.*

Nicholas Gray, 18 March, 1813. New York.

*Assistant Inspector General.*

J. C. Tillotson, 18 March, 1813. Lieut. 2nd Light Dragoons. New York.

*Deputy Quartermaster General.*

Theophilus W. Smith, 2 April, 1813. New York.

*Assistant Deputy Quartermaster General.*

William A. Barron, 2 April, 1813.

*Engineer.*

William Cutbush. 1st Lieut. Fort Columbus.

*Deputy Commissary Ordnance.*

George Talcott, Jr., 5 Aug., 1813. Lieut. 25th Inf. New York.

*Assistant Deputy Commissary Ordnance.*

Aeneas M'Kay, 12 March, 1813. New York.

*Judge Advocate.*

Evart A. Bancker, 18 March, 1813. New York.

*Hospital Surgeon.*

Samuel Akerly, 6 July, 1812. Fort Columbus.

*Garrison Surgeon's Mate.*

Alexander Wolcott, 25 March, 1812. Fort Columbus.

*Chaplain.*

Peter I. Vanpelt, 2 April, 1813.

*District Paymaster.*

Samuel H. Eakin. New York.

*Deputy Commissary of Purchases.*

Samuel Russell. New York.

*Military Storekeepers.*

John Fellows. New York.
Jonathan Snowden. West Point.
H. P. Deering. Sagg Harbor.

---

MILITARY DISTRICT, NO. 4.

*West Jersey, Pennsylvania and Delaware.*

*Brig. General.*

Joseph Bloomfield. Philadelphia.

*Adjutant General.*

William Duane, 22 March, 1813. Philadelphia.

*Assistant Inspector General.*

Robert Sterry, 10 May, 1813. Capt. 6th Inf. Philadelphia.

*Quartermaster General.*

William Linnard 12 April, 1813. Philadelphia.

*Deputy Quartermaster General.*

J. S. Swearingen, 17 March, 1813. Capt. 1st Art. Pittsburg.

*Assistant Deputy Quartermaster Generals.*

Robert Patterson, 24 June, 1813. Lieut. 32nd Inf. Province Island.
Samuel Duncan, 6 Aug., 1813. Carlisle.

*Deputy Commissary Ordnance.*

Abraham R. Wooley, 4 Dec., 1812. Pittsburg.

*Assistant Deputy Commissaries Ordnance.*

William Wade, 12 March, 1813. Pittsburg
William C. Lyman, 19 April, 1813. Pittsburg.

*Assistant Topographical Engineer.*

Thomas Clark, 1 April, 1813. Lieut. 2nd Art. Philadelphia.

*Apothecary General.*

Francis Le Barron, 11 June, 1813.

*Garrison Surgeon's Mate.*

John F. Heileman, 2 July, 1802. Province Island.

*District Paymasters.*

Henry Phillips. Capt. 6th Inf. Philadelphia.
Jacob W Albright. Lieut. 1st Inf. Pittsburg.

*Commissary General of Purchases.*

Callender Irvine. Philadelphia.

*Military Storekeepers.*

Richard Parker. Carlisle.
William C. Bennett. Wilmington.
D. Kirkpatrick. Newcastle.
John M. Taylor. Philadelphia.

---

MILITARY DISTRICT, NO. 5.

*Maryland and Virginia.*

*Adjutant General.*

James Bankhead, 9 Sept., 1813. Maj. 7th Inft.

*Quartermaster General.*

William Swan, 7 Aug., 1813. Maj. 2nd Inf.

*Deputy Quartermaster General.*

Paul Bentalou, 29 June, 1813.

*Assistant Deputy Quartermaster General.*

Ferdinand Marsteller, 17 July, 1813.

*Engineer.*

Walker K. Armistead. Lieut. Col.

*Assistant Engineer.*

Samuel Babcock. Captain.

*Topographical Engineer.*

Paul H. Perrault, 12 April, 1813.

*Hospital Surgeon's Mate.*

William Jones, 2 July, 1813.

*Garrison Surgeon's Mates.*

George W. Maupin, 5 Nov., 1802.
Lemuel B. Clark, 4 Jan., 1808.

*District Paymasters.*

Saterlee Clark. Lieut. 1st Art. Annapolis.
Samuel Turner. Petersburg.

*Deputy Commissaries of Purchases.*

John M'Kinney. Washington.
James Calhoun, Jr. Baltimore.
Robert C. Jennings. Norfolk.

*Military Storekeepers.*

Edwin Starke. Norfolk.
Samuel Annin. Harper's Ferry.
Thomas B. Rutter. Baltimore

---

MILITARY DISTRICT, NO. 6.

*North Carolina, South Carolina and Georgia.*

*Major General.*

Thomas Pinckney. Commanding.

*Adjutant General.*

Francis K. Huger, 6 April, 1813. Lieut. Col. 2nd Art.

*Assistant Adjutant General.*

John Erving, 6 April, 1813. Lieut. 1st Art.

*Inspector General.*

William R. Boote, 6 April, 1813. Maj. 2nd Inf.

*Deputy Quartermaster Generals.*

Samuel Chaplain, 18 March, 1813. Lieut. 1st Art.
Thomas Bourke, 19 April, 1813.

*Assistant Deputy Quartermaster Generals.*

Peter Lequex, 31 Aug., 1813. Lieut. 8th Inf.
William Cox, 31 Aug., 1813.
Joseph B. Paine, 31 Aug., 1813.
James Ward, 31 Aug., 1813.

*Engineer.*

Prentiss Willard. Captain.

*Deputy Commissary Ordnance.*

John H. Margart, 31 Dec., 1812.

*Assistant Deputy Commissaries Ordnance,*

Daniel Bruckner, 6 Aug., 1813.
Christopher Keyser, 6 Aug., 1813.

*Judge Advocate.*

Thomas T. Dent, 19 July, 1813.

*Hospital Surgeons.*

William M'Caw, 20 May, 1813.
George V. Proctor, 11 June, 1813.
Thomas Akin, 29 June, 1813.

*Hospital Surgeon's Mates.*

John H. Sackett, 22 March, 1813.
Joseph L. Stephens, 29 June, 1813.
William Merriwether, 19 July, 1813.

*Garrison Surgeon's Mates.*

William Ballard, 24 March, 1812.
Samuel Dusenbury, 25 March, 1812.

*District Paymaster.*

Hamlin Cook. Lieut. 8th Inf.

*Military Storekeeper.*

Henry Simmons. Charleston.

---

MILITARY DISTRICT, NO. 7.

*Louisiana, the Mississippi Territory, and Tennessee.*

*Brigadier Generals.*

Thomas Flournoy, commanding.
David R. Williams.

*Assistant Adjutant General*

Carey Nicholas, 25 April, 1813. Capt. 7th Inf.

*Assistant Inspector General.*

Daniel Hughes, 7 Aug., 1813. Capt. 1st Inf.

*Quartermaster General.*

William Piatt, 23 June, 1813. Capt. 2nd Inf.

*Assistant Deputy Quartermaster General.*

John T. Wirt, 25 April, 1813 Lieut. 2nd Inf.

*Hospital Surgeon.*

David C. Kerr, 30 April 1812.

*Garrison Surgeon.*

Oliver H. Spencer, 9 Oct., 1804.

*Hospital Surgeon's Mates.*

James Stephenson, 27 May, 1812.
Stephen Sutton, 27 May, 1812.

*Garrison Surgeon's Mates.*

Robert Huston, 27 Feb., 1807.
Charles Slocum, 25 March, 1807.
William T. Davidson, 13 June, 1808.

*District Paymasters.*

S. Knight. For Volunteers. Capt. 1st Inf'y.
John T. Pemberton. Capt. 2nd Inf'y. New Orleans.
Alpha Kingsley. Capt. 1st Inf'y. Tennessee.

---

MILITARY DISTRICT, NO. 8.

*Kentucky, Ohio, and the Territories of Indiana, Michigan, Illinois and Missouri.*

*Major General.*

William H. Harrison. Upper Canada.

*Brigadier Generals.*

Duncan M'Arthur. Detroit.
Lewis Cass.

*Adjutant General.*

Edm'nd P. Gaines, 1 Sept., 1813. Col. 25th Inf'y. Upper Canada.

*Assistant Adjutant General.*

Robert Dunn, 22 March, 1813. Lieut. 22nd Inf'y.

*Assistant Inspector General.*

Levi Hukill, 6 April, 1813. Capt. 1st Light Dragoons. Upper Canada.

*Quartermaster General.*

John C. Bartlett, 12 April, 1812.

*Deputy Quartermaster General.*

Taylor Berry, 31 March, 1813. Lieut. 17th Inf'y.

*Assistant Deputy Quartermaster Generals.*

James W. Bryson, 25 April, 1813. Lieut. 1st Inf'y. Newport.
Joseph Wheaton, 28 April, 1813.

*Engineers.*

Charles Gratiot. Captain.
El. D. Wood. Capt. and Maj. Brevet.

*Topographical Engineer.*

Simon Z. Watson, 20 Aug., 1813.

*Deputy Commissary Ordnance.*

Robert D. Richardson, 5 Aug., 1813.

*Assistant Deputy Commissary Ordnance.*

Thomas L. Hawkins, 6 Aug., 1813.

*Judge Advocate.*

John S. Wills, 7 May, 1813.

*Hospital Surgeon.*

John R. Martin, 2 July, 1813.

*Hospital Surgeon's Mate.*

Hugh Stanard, 20 May, 1813.

*Garrison Surgeon's Mates.*

William Turner, 9 July, 1810.
Cornelius Cunningham, 15 Oct., 1810.
Anthony Benezet, 25 March, 1812.
Samuel Meriwether, 1 Aug., 1813.

*Regimental Surgeon.*

S. M'Keehan, 29 July, 1813.

*Regimental Surgeon's Mate.*

John M'Culloch, 29 July, 1813.

*Chaplains.*

Stephen Lindsley, 29 July, 1813.
Thomas Hersey, 20 Aug., 1813.

*District Paymasters.*

A. Whitlock. Capt. 1st Inf'y. Vincennes.
James Taylor. Kentucky.
Samuel Huntington. Head Quarters.
Jesse Hunt. Ohio.

*Deputy Commissary of Purchases.*

John H. Piatt. Ohio.

*Assistant Deputy Commissary of Purchases.*

Robert Irvine. Detroit.

*Military Storekeeper.*

Thomas Martin. Newport.

*Brigadier General.*

Benjamin Howard. St. Louis.

*Assistant Deputy Quartermaster General.*

William Christy.

*Garrison Surgeon's Mates.*

Abraham Stewart, 19 April, 1813.
Jonathan S. Cool, 6 March, 1806.

*District Paymaster.*

Thompson Douglass, 8 Feb., 1811.

---

MILITARY DISTRICT, NO. 9.

*New York, North of the Highlands, and Vermont.*

*Major Generals.*

James Wilkinson. Commanding.
Morgan Lewis.

*Brigadier Generals.*

John P. Boyd.
Jacob Brown.
Leonard Covington. Dead.

*Quartermaster General.*

Robt. Swartout, 21 March 1813. Dead. Dept.

*Adjutant General.*

John B. Walbach, 6 Aug., 1813. Capt. 1st Art'y.

*Assistant Adjutant Generals.*

John Johnson, 2 April, 1813. Maj. 21st Inf'y.
Ebenezer Beebe, 2 April, 1813. Capt. 6th Inf'y.
Talbot Chambers, 2 April, 1813. Capt. 5th Inf'y.

*Inspector General.*

James Gibson, 13 July, 1813. Capt. Light Inf'y.

*Assistant Inspector General.*

John R. Bell, 29 Sept., 1813. Lieut. Light Dragoons.

*Quartermaster General.*

Elisha Jenkins, 22 April, 1813. Of the District.

*Deputy Quartermaster Generals.*

Chris. Van de Venter, 26 March, 1813. Lieut. 1st Art'y. Prisoner in Canada.
Samuel Brown, 26 March, 1813.

*Assistant Deputy Quartermaster Generals.*

Gustavus Loomis, 19 April, 1813. Lieut. 1st Art'y.
Ezra Smith, 19 April, 1813. Lieut. 1st Art'y.
John Bliss, 28 April, 1813. Lieut. 2nd Inf'y.
Thomas B. Baldwin, 3 May, 1813.
John G. Camp, 20 May, 1813. Lieut. 12th Inf'y.
Marshal Jenkins, 20 May, 1813.
Abraham Ten Eyck, 20 May, 1813.
Thomas Campbell, 29 July, 1813.
Timothy Burr, 31 July, 1813.
James Rees, 1 Aug. 1813.

*Chief Engineer.*

Joseph G. Swift. Colonel.

*Engineer.*

George Bomford. Major.

*Assistant Engineer.*

J. G. Totten. Capt. and Maj. Brev.

*Topographical Engineers.*

John Anderson, 12 April, 1813. Capt. 19th Inf'y. Prisoner on Parole.
Isaac Roberdeau, 29 April, 1813.

*Assistant Topographical Engineer.*

Benjamin Connor, 3 Aug., 1813. Lieut. 1st Art'y.

*Deputy Commissary General's Ordnance.*

James Daliba, 5 Aug., 1813. Lieut. 1st Art'y.
Thomas L. Campbell, 5 Aug., 1813.

*Asst. Dep. Com. Generals Ordnance.*

Rufus L. Baker, 12 March, 1813.
George Larned, 19 April, 1813.
James Baker, 6 Aug., 1813.

*Judge Advocates.*

Philip S. Parker, 2 April, 1813.
Stephen Lush, Jr., 5 Oct., 1813.

*Physician and Surgeon General.*

James Tilton, 11 June, 1812.

*Hospital Surgeons.*

James Mann, 9 April, 1812.
Garret E. Prendergast, 25 April, 1812.
William M. Ross, 18 March, 1813.
Hosea Blood, 5 May, 1813.
Ezekiel W. Bull, 8 Aug., 1813.

*Hospital Surgeon's Mates.*

William Thomas, 7 July, 1809.
Rogers Smith, 14 May, 1812.
Samuel Scofield, 15 Sept., 1812.
Joshua B. Whitridge, 30 March, 1813.
Henry Van Hoevenburg, 31 March, 1813.
Edward Purcell, 2 May, 1813.
William W. Hazzard, 14 May, 1813.
Henry Brundige, 16 May, 1813.
William E. Horner, 2 July, 1813.
John Rodgers, 13 July, 1813.
Joseph Wallace, 13 July, 1813.
Abraham Vanhoy, 13 July, 1813.
Eleazer Aspinwall, 15 July, 1813.

*Garrison Surgeon's Mates.*

Joseph West, 10 June, 1802.
John H. Turner, 1 May, 1810.
David Neilson, 3 Dec., 1812.
Charles Taylor, 3 April, 1813.

*Chaplains.*

David Jones, 2 April, 1813.
Robert Elliott, 20 May, 1813.
Aaron J. Booge, 16 June, 1813.

*Deputy Paymaster General.*

Washington Lee. Maj. 16th Inf'y. Utica.

*Assistant Deputy Paymaster Generals.*

Joseph H. Rees, Lieut. 3rd Art'y.
Donald Fraser, Lieut. 15th Inf'y.

*District Paymaster.*

George Merchant. Albany.

*Deputy Commissary of Purchases.*

John H. Plummer. Albany.

*Assistant Deputy Commissaries Purchases.*

Mathew Irwin. Champlain.
George Wadsworth. Burlington.
James E. Herron. Niagara.

*Military Storekeeper.*

John Shaw. Albany.

*Right Wing—Lake Champlain.*

*Major General.*

Wade Hampton.

*Brigadier Generals.*

Thomas Parker.
George Izard.

*Adjutant General.*

William King, 18 July, 1813. Maj. 15th Inf'y.

*Inspector General.*

Henry Atkinson, 25 April, 1813. Capt. 3rd Inf'y.

*Quartermaster General.*

James Thomas, 28 April, 1813.

*Assistant Deputy Quartermaster General.*

Henry Stanton, 12 July, 1813. Lieut. Light Art'y.

*Engineer.*

William M'Ree. Major.

*Assistant Engineer.*

Sylvanus Thayer. 1st Lieut.

*Assistant Topographical Engineer.*

Daniel Rose, 20 July, 1813. Lieut. 21st Inf'y.

*Hospital Surgeons.*

Samuel Shaw, 6 April, 1813.
Walter V. Wheaton, 28 March, 1813.

*Hospital Surgeon's Mate.*

Thomas C. Walker, 2 July, 1813.

*Garrison Surgeon's Mate.*

Israel Stoddard, 18 Feb., 1813.

*District Paymaster.*

Walter Sheldon. Lieut. 11th Inf'y.

GENERAL OFFICERS, RANK, DISTRICTS, STATIONS, &C.

*Major Generals.*

Henry Dearborn, 27 Jan., 1812. 3rd dist.
Thomas Pinckney, 27 March, 1812. 6th dist.
James Wilkinson, 2 March, 1813. 9th dist.
Wade Hampton, 2 March, 1813. 9th dist.
Morgan Lewis, 2 March, 1813. 9th dist.
William H. Harrison, 2 March, 1813. 8th dist.

*Brig. Generals.*

Joseph Bloomfield, 27 March, 1812. 4th dist.
James Winchester, 27 March, 1812. Prisoner of war.
William Hull, 8 April 1812. Prisoner of war on parole.
Thomas Flournoy, 18 June, 1812. 7th dist.
Thomas H. Cushing, 2 July, 1812. 1st dist.
John Chandler, 8 July, 1812. Prisoner of war.
John P. Boyd, 26 Aug., 1812. 9th dist.
Thomas Parker, 12 March, 1813. 9th dist.
George Izard 12 March, 1813. 9th dist.
William H. Winder, 12 March, 1813. Prisoner of war.
Duncan McArthur, 12 March, 1813. 8th dist.
Lewis Cass, 12 March, 1813. 8th dist.
Benjamin Howard, 12 March, 1813. 8th dist.
David R. Williams, 9 July, 1813. 7th dist.
Jacob Brown, 19 July, 1813. 9th dist.
Leonard Covington, 1 Aug., 1813. 9th dist. Dead.

*Brig. Generals, Brevet.*

Henry Burbeck, 10 July, 1812. 2nd dist.
Moses Porter, 10 Sept., 1813. 9th dist.

---

QUARTERMASTER'S DEPARTMENT.

*Chief of Department.*

*Brig. General.*

Robert Swartwout, 21 March, 1813.

*Quartermaster Generals.*

*Colonels.*

William Linnard, 12 April, 1813. 4th dist. Philadelphia.
John C. Bartlett, 12 April, 1813. 8th dist.
Elisha Jenkins, 22 April, 1813. 9th dist. Albany.
James Thomas, 28 April, 1813. 9th dist.
William Platt, 23 June, 1813. 7th dist. New Orleans.
William Swan, 7 Aug., 1813. 5th dist. Norfolk.

*Deputy Quartermaster Generals.*

*Majors.*

James S. Swearingen, 17 March, 1813. 4th dist. Pittsburg.
Samuel Champlain, 18 March, 1813. 6th dist. Charleston.
C. Van De Venter, 26 March, 1813.
Samuel Brown, 26 March, 1813. 9th dist.
Taylor Berry, 31 March, 1813. 8th dist. St. Louis.
Theoph. W. Smith, 2 April, 1813. 3rd dist. New York.
Thomas Bourke, 19 April, 1813. 6th dist. Savannah.
Paul Bentalou, 29 June, 1813. 5th dist. Baltimore.

*Assistant Deputy Quartermaster Generals.*

*Captains.*

William A. Barron, 2 April, 1813. 3rd dist. New York.
Richard H. Ashley, 11 April, 1813. 2nd dist. Newport.
Gustavus Loomis, 19 April, 1813. 9th dist.
Ezra Smith, 19 April, 1813. 9th dist.
William Chrystie, 19 April, 1813. 8th dist. St. Louis.
Jonathan Allen, 20 April, 1813. 1st dist. Pittsfield.
John T. Wirt, 25 April, 1813. 7th dist. Mobile.
James W. Bryson, 25 April, 1813. 8th dist. Newport.
John Bliss, 28 April, 1813. 9th dist.
Joseph Wheaton, 28 April, 1813. 8th dist.
John G. Camp, 20 May, 1813. 9th dist.
Abraham Ten Eyck, 20 May, 1813. 9th dist.
Robert Patterson, 24 June, 1813. 4th dist.
Henry Stanton, 12 July, 1813. 9th dist.
Ferdinand Marsteller, 17 July, 1813. 5th dist. Washington.
Thomas Campbell, 29 July, 1813. 9th dist.
Timothy Burr, 31 July, 1813. 9th dist.
James Rees, 1 Aug., 1813. 9th dist.
Samuel Duncan, 6 Aug., 1813. 4th dist. Carlisle.
Peter Lequex, 31 Aug., 1813. 6th dist.
William Cox, 31 Aug., 1813. 6th dist.
Joseph B. Paine, 31 Aug., 1813. 6th dist.
James Ward, 31 Aug., 1813. 6th dist.
Joseph Miller, 1 Sept., 1813. 9th dist.

---

TOPOGRAPHICAL DEPARTMENT.

*Topographical Engineers.*

*Majors.*

John Anderson, 12 April, 1813. 4th dist. Prisoner of War.
Paul H. Perrault, 12 April, 1813. 5th dist.
Isaac Roberdeau, 29 April, 1813. 4th dist.
Simon Z. Watson, 20 Aug., 1813. 8th dist.

*Assistant Topographical Engineers.*

*Captains.*

Thomas Clark, 1 April, 1813. 4th dist.
James Kearney, 12 April, 1813. 9th dist. War Office.
Daniel Rose, 20 July, 1813. 9th dist.
Benjamin Connor, 3 Aug., 1813. 9th dist.

---

ADJUTANT GENERAL'S DEPARTMENT.

*Adjutant Generals.*

*Colonels.*

John R. Fenwick, 18 March, 1813. 3rd dist. New York.
William Duane, 18 March, 1813. 4th dist. Philadelphia.
Francis K. Huger, 6 April, 1813. 6th dist. Charleston.
Peter P. Schuyler, 28 April, 1813. 1st dist. Boston.
William King, 18 July, 1813. 9th dist.
John B. Walbach, 6 Aug., 1813. 9th dist.
Edmund P. Gaines, 1 Sept., 1813. 8th dist.
James Bankhead, 9 Sept., 1813. 5th dist. Norfolk.

*Assistant Adjutant Generals.*

*Majors.*

Charles K. Gardner, 18 March, 1813.
Thomas Chrystie, 18 March, 1813. 3rd dist.

Robert Dunn, 28 March, 1813. 8th dist.
John Johnson, 2 April, 1813. 9th dist.
Ebenezer Beebe, 2 April, 1813. 9th dist.
Talbot Chambers, 2 April, 1813. 9th dist.
John Erving, 6 April, 1813. 6th dist.
Cary Nicholas, 25 April, 1813. 9th dist.

---

INSPECTOR GENERAL'S DEPARTMENT.

*Inspector Generals.*

*Colonels.*

A. Y. Nicoll, 18 March, 1813.
Nicholas Gray, 18 March, 1813. 3rd dist.
William Boote, 6 April, 1813. 6th dist.
Henry Atkinson, 25 April, 1813. 9th dist.
Jacob Kingsbury, 28 April, 1813. 2nd dist.
James Gibson, 13 July, 1813. 9th dist.

*Assistant Inspector Generals.*

*Majors.*

Enos Cutler, 18 March, 1813. 1st dist.
John C. Tillotson, 18 March, 1813. 3rd dist.
Levi Hukill, 6 April, 1813. 8th dist.
J. Snelling, 25 April, 1813. 9th dist.
Robert Sterry, 10 May, 1813. 4th dist.
Daniel Hughes, 7 Aug., 1813. 7th dist.

---

ORDNANCE DEPARTMENT.

*Commissary General.*

*Colonel.*

Decius Wadsworth, 2 July, 1812. Washington.

*Assistant Commissary General.*

*Major.*

George Bomford, 18 June, 1812. 9th dist. Albany.

*Deputy Commissaries.*

*Captains.*

John Morton, 11 Sept., 1812. Washington.
Abraham R. Woolley, 4 Dec., 1812. 4th dist. Pittsburg.
John H. Margart, 31 Dec., 1812. 6th dist. Charleston.
James Daliba, 5 Aug., 1813. 9th dist. Albany.
Thomas L. Campbell, 5 Aug., 1813. 9th dist.
Edwin Tylor, 5 Aug., 1813. 5th dist.
R. D. Richardson, 5 Aug., 1813. 8th dist. N. W. Army.
George Talcott, Jr., 5 Aug., 1813. 3rd dist. New York.

*Assistant Deputy Commissaries.*

*Lieutenants.*

Æneas McKay, 12 March, 1813. 3rd dist. New York.
William Wade, 12 March, 1813. 4th dist. Pittsburg.
Rufus L. Baker, 12 March, 1813. 9th dist. Albany.
William C. Lyman, 19 April, 1813. 4th dist. Pittsburg.
George Larned, 19 April, 1813. 9th dist. Albany.
Nehemiah Baden, 6 Aug., 1813. 5th dist. Washington.
Daniel Bruckner, 6 Aug., 1813. 6th dist.
Christopher Keiser, 6 Aug., 1813. 6th dist. Charleston.

Thomas L. Hawkins, 6 Aug., 1813. N. W. Army.
James Baker, 6 Aug., 1813. 9th dist. Albany.

---

JUDGE ADVOCATES.

E. A. Bancker, Esq., 18 March, 1813. 3rd dist.
Philip S. Parker, Esq., 2 April, 1813. 9th dist.
John S. Willis, Esq., 7 May, 1813. 5th dist.
T. T. Dent, Esq., 19 July, 1813. 6th dist.
Stephen Lush, Jr., Esq., 5 Oct., 1813. 9th dist.

---

HOSPITAL DEPARTMENT.

*Physician and Surgeon General.*

James Tilton, 11 June, 1813. 9th dist.

*Apothecary General.*

Francis Le Baron, 11 June, 1813. 9th dist.

*Hospital Surgeons.*

James Mann, 9 April, 1812. 9th dist.
G. E. Prendergast, 25 April, 1812. 9th dist.
David C. Kerr, 30 April, 1812. 7th dist.
Samuel Akerly, 6 July, 1812. 3d dist.
William M. Ross, 18 March, 1813. 9th dist.
W. V. Wheaton, 28 March, 1813. 9th dist.
Samuel Shaw, 6 April, 1812. 9th dist.
Hosea Blood, 5 May, 1813. 9th dist.
William McCaw, 20 May, 1813. 6th dist.
George D. Proctor, 11 June, 1813. 6th dist.
B. Waterhouse, 29 June, 1813. 1st dist.
Thomas Akin, 29 June, 1813. 6th dist.
John R. Martin, 2 July, 1813. 8th dist.
E. W. Bull, 8 Aug., 1813. 9th dist.

*Hospital Surgeon's Mates.*

William Thomas, 7 July, 1809. 9th dist.
Roger Smith, 14 May, 1812. 9th dist.
James Stephenson, 27 May, 1812. 7th dist.
Stephen Sutton, 27 May, 1812. 7th dist.
Samuel Schofield, 15 Sept., 1812. 9th dist.
John H. Sackett, 22 March, 1813. 5th dist.
J. B. Whitredge, 30 March, 1813. 9th dist.
H. Van Hoevenberg, 31 March, 1813. 9th dist.
Edward Purcell, 2 May, 1813. 9th dist.
William W. Hazard, 14 May, 1813. 9th dist.
Henry Brundidge, 16 May, 1813. 9th dist.
Joseph L. Stevens, 29 July, 1813. 6th dist.
Thomas C. Walker, 2 July, 1813. 9th dist.
William Jones, 2 July, 1813. 5th dist.
William E. Horner, 2 July, 1813. 9th dist.
John Rogers, 15 July, 1813. 9th dist.
Joseph Wallace, 15 July, 1813. 9th dist.
E. Aspinwall, 15 July, 1813. 9th dist.
Abraham Vanhoy, 15 July, 1813. 9th dist.
William Meriwether, 19 July, 1813. 6th dist.
A. Torbling, 4 Oct., 1813. 9th dist.

*Garrison Surgeon.*

Oliver H. Spencer, 9 July, 1804. 7th dist. New Orleans.

*Garrison Surgeon's Mates.*

Joseph West, 10 June, 1802. 9th dist. Niagara.
John F. Heileman, 2 June, 1802. 4th dist. Fort Mifflin.
George W. Maupin, 5 Nov., 1802. 5th dist. Fort Nelson.
Joseph Goodhue, 8 Feb., 1803. 1st dist. Fort Constitution.
Abraham Stewart, 6 March, 1806. 8th dist. St. Louis.

James A. Sergent, 6 March, 1806. 1st dist. Fort Independence.
Robert Huston, 27 Feb., 1807. 7th dist. Fort Stoddart.
Charles Slocum, 25 March, 1807. 7th dist. Natchitoches.
Lemuel B. Clark, 4 Jan., 1808. 5th dist. Norfolk.
William T. Davidson, 13 June, 1808. 7th dist. Fort Stoddart.
John H. Turner, 1 May, 1810. 7th dist.
C. Cunningham, 15 Oct., 1810. 8th dist. Detroit.
Jonathan S. Cool, 8 Feb., 1811. 8th dist. Fort Osage.
William Ballard, 24 March, 1812. 6th dist. Fort Hawkins.
Samuel Dusenbury, 25 March, 1812. 6th dist. St. Mary's.
Alexander Wollcott, 25 March, 1812. 3rd dist. New York.
Anthony Benezet, 25 March, 1813. 8th dist. Fort Wayne.
William Turner, 29 Sept., 1812. 2nd dist. Newport, Rhode Island.
David Neilson, 3 Dec., 1812. 9th dist.
Israel Stoddard, 18 Feb., 1813. 9th dist. Burlington.
Charles Taylor, 3 April, 1813. 9th dist.
Samuel Meriwether, 1 Aug., 1813. 8th dist. St. Louis.

### Chaplains.

David Jones, 2 April, 1813. 9th dist.
Peter J. Van Pelt, 2 April, 1813. 3rd dist.
James I. Wilmer 20 May, 1813. 8th dist.
Robert Elliott, 20 May, 1813. 9th dist.
Aaron J. Booge, 16 June, 1813. 9th dist.
Stephen Lindsley, 29 July, 1813. 8th dist.
Thomas Hersey, 20 Aug., 1813. 8th dist.

### Military Academy.

Senior Officer of Engineers, *Superintendent.*
Jared Mansfield, *Professor Natural and Experimental Philosophy.*
Andrew Elliott, *Professor of Mathematics.*
Alden Partridge, *Professor Art of Engineering.*
F. De Masson, *Teacher of French.*
C. E. Zoeller, *Teacher of Drawing.*
Samuel Walsh *Surgeon.*
Adam Emple, *Chaplain.*

### Purchasing Department.

*Commissary General.*

C. Irvine, Esq., 8 Aug., 1812. Philadelphia.

*Deputy Commissaries.*

John McKinney, 25 April, 1812. 5th dist. Washington.
John H. Plummer, 4 June, 1812. 9th dist. Albany.
John Langdon, 4 June, 1812. 1st dist. Portsmouth.
Amasa Stetson, 22 June, 1812. 1st dist. Boston.
Elisha Tracy, 6 July, 1812. 2nd dist. Norwich.
Samuel Russell, 18 Sept., 1812. 3rd dist. New York.
John H. Piatt, 18 Sept., 1812. 8th dist. Cincinnati.
James Calhoun, Jr., 29 June, 1813. 5th dist. Baltimore.
Robert C. Jennings, 19 July, 1813. 5th dist. Norfolk.

*Assistant Commissaries.*

Matthew Irwin, May, 1813. 9th dist. Champlain, New York.
George Wadsworth Sept., 1813. 9th dist. Burlington, Vermont.
Robert Irvine. 8th dist. Detroit.
James E. Herron. 9th dist. Niagara.

*Military Storekeepers.*

John M. Taylor, 1813. 4th dist. Philadelphia.
Samuel Devens, 1813. 1st dist. Charlestown.
John Shaw, 1813. 9th dist. Albany.
John Fellows, 1813. 3rd dist. New York.
Jonathan Snowden. 3rd dist. West Point.
H. P. Deering, 22 March, 1813. 3rd dist. Sagg Harbor.
Richard Parker. 4th dist. Carlisle.
D. Kirkpatrick, 1813. 4th dist. Newcastle.
William C. Bennett, 1813. 4th dist. Wilmington.
Henry Simons, June, 1813. 6th dist. Charleston.
Thomas Martin, 1813. 8th dist. Newport.
Giles L'Hommedieu, 1813. 2nd dist. Norwich.
Edwin Starke, 1813. 5th dist. Norfolk.
John Rice, 1813. 1st dist. Portsmouth.
John Chaffee, 1813. 1st dist. Springfield.
Samuel Annin, 1813. 5th dist. Harper's Ferry.
Thomas B. Rutter, 1813. 5th dist. Baltimore.

### Pay Department.

*Paymaster of Army.*

Robert Brent, Esq., 1 July, 1808.

*Deputy Paymaster General.*

*Major.*

Washington Lee, 13 April, 1813. Northern Army.

*Assistant Deputy Paymaster Generals.*

*2nd Lieutenant.*

D. Fraser, 4 Aug., 1813. Frontiers New York.

*1st Lieutenant.*

J. H. Rees, 24 Sept., 1813. Frontiers New York.

*District Paymasters.*

*Major.*

Nehemiah Freeman, 16 March, 1802. 1st dist. Boston.

*Captains.*

Ambrose Whitlock, 13 June, 1805. 8th dist. Vincennes.
Simeon Knight, 24 March, 1808. 7th dist. Natchez.
Alpha Kingsley, 9 Feb., 1810. 7th dist. Nashville.
John T. Pemberton, 4 June, 1812. 7th dist. New Orleans.
Henry Phillips, 12 June, 1812. 4th dist. Philadelphia.

*1st Lieutenants.*

Jonathan Eastman, 4 March, 1806. Prisoner of war, parole.
Satterlee Clark, 15 Aug., 1810. 5th dist. Washington.
Hamlin Cook, 26 July, 1813. 6th dist. Charleston.
Walter Sheldon, 4 Aug., 1813. 9th dist. Burlington, Vt.
Jacob W. Albright, 4 Sept., 1813. 4th dist. W. Pennsylvania.

*Citizens.*

Samuel H. Eakin, 3 June, 1812. 3rd dist. New York City.
James Taylor, 4 June, 1812. 8th dist. Newport. Prisoner of war.
Joseph Watson.
Thompson Douglass, 12 June, 1812. 8th dist. St. Louis.
Samuel Turner, 12 June, 1812. 5th dist. Petersburg.
Jesse Hunt, 22 Sept., 1812. 8th dist. Cincinnati.
George Merchant, 29 Sept., 1812. 9th dist. Albany.
Samuel Huntington, 3 Oct., 1812. 8th dist. N. W. Army.
Joseph C. Boyd, 14 Jan., 1813. 1st dist. Portland.
Robert Gardner, 3 Aug., 1813. Quebec, Pay Pr.
George L. Perkins, 7 Sept., 1813. 2nd dist. New London.

## Corps of Engineers.

*Colonel.*

Jos. G. Swift, 31 July, 1812.

*Lieut. Colonel.*

Walker K. Armistead, 31 July, 1812.

*Majors.*

G. Bomford, 6 July, 1812.
Wm. McRee, 31 July, 1812.

*Captains.*

Charles Gratiot, 23 Feb., 1808.
A. Partridge, 23 July, 1810.
Eleazer D. Wood, 1 July, 1813. Major brevet, 6 May, 1812.
J. G. Totten, 31 July, 1813. Major brevet, 6 June, 1812.
Sam. Babcock, 20 Sept., 1812.

*1st Lieutenants.*

Sylvester Thayer, 1 July, 1812.
Wm. Cutbush, 1 July, 1812.
Ed. De Russy, 6 July, 1812.
Thos. P. Finley, 31 July, 1812. Paymaster.
Fred. Lewis, 20 Sept., 1812. Aid of Maj. General Dearborn.
James Gadsden, 17 March, 1813.

*2nd Lieutenants.*

T. W. Maurice, 1 Aug., 1813.
Hipolite Dumas, 3 Aug., 1813.
D. B. Douglass, 1 Oct., 1813.
George Trescott, 16 Oct., 1813.
J. L. Smith, 16 Oct., 1813.

---

## Regiment of Light Artillery.

*Colonel.*

Moses Porter, 12 March, 1812. Brig. Gen. brevet, 10 Sept., 1813.

*Lieut. Colonel.*

J. R. Fenwick, 2 Dec., 1811. Adjutant General.

*Majors.*

Abm. Eustis, 15 March, 1810. Lieut. Col. brevet, 10 Sept., 1813.
Thos. Pitts, 20 Jan., 1813.

*Captains.*

James Gibson, 2 May, 1810. Inspector General.
Wm. Campbell, 30 May, 1810.
R. H. McPherson, 15 July, 1810.
J. N. McIntosh, 1 May, 1811.
Samuel Price, 15 Aug., 1811.
And. McDowell, 1 April, 1812.
Luth. Leonard, 6 July, 1812.
Benj. Branch, 24 Aug., 1812.
G. W. Melvin, 24 Aug., 1812.
A. W. Thornton, 20 Jan., 1813.

*1st Lieutenants.*

Fras. Stribling, 1 March, 1811.
Thos. Ketchum, 1 Sept., 1811.
John R. Bell, 24 Aug., 1812. Assistant Inspector General.
F. B. Murdoch, 24 Aug., 1812.
W. F. Hobart, 5 April, 1813.
W. Sumpter, 27 May, 1813.
G. W. Hight, 10 Aug., 1813.
Wm. W. Smith, 1 Oct., 1813.
Wm. K. Beall, 23 Oct., 1813.
G. N. Morris, 23 Oct., 1813.

*2nd Lieutenants.*

J. H. Wilkins, 30 March, 1813.
John Gates, Jr., 1 April, 1813. Adjutant.
Nelson Freeland, 4 April, 1813.
J. T. McKinney, 5 April, 1813.
S. M. Mackay, 27 May, 1813.
B. F. Robb, 30 June, 1813.
Wm. Bazeau, 10 Aug., 1813.
G. E. Wells, 1 Oct., 1813.
Elijah Lyon, 23 Oct., 1813.
S. Washburn, 23 Oct., 1813.

*3rd Lieutenants.*

Henry Stanton, 29 June, 1813. Assistant Deputy Quartermaster General.
Joseph Scott, 2 July, 1813.
Lloyd Hilleary, 1 Aug., 1813.
Edm. M. Giles, 1 Aug., 1813.
Rich. W. Fields, 1 Aug., 1813.

*Surgeon.*

A. Tombling, 4 Oct., 1813.

---

## First Light Dragoons.

*Colonel.*

Jacint Laval, 1 Aug., 1813.

*Lieut. Colonel.*

Nelson Luckett, 1 Aug., 1813.

*Majors.*

T. A. Helms, 7 June, 1813.
A. P. Hayne, 1 Aug., 1813.

*Captains.*

Asa Morgan, 18 Jan, 1810.
Seleck Osborne, 20 Feb., 1811.
Silas Halsey, 31 May, 1811.
A. Cummings, 1 Nov., 1811.
W. M. Littlejohn, 1 Dec., 1812.
George Haig, 20 Jan., 1813.
Levi Hukill, 7 June, 1813. Assistant Inspector General.
E. Boardman, 1 Aug., 1813.

*1st Lieutenants.*

Joseph Kean, 31 May, 1811. Adjutant.
H. Whiting, 20 Aug., 1811. Aid to Brig. General Boyd.
George Birch, 1 Nov., 1811.
F. S. Belton, 20 Jan., 1813. Paymaster.
Wm. Neilson, 7 June, 1813.
Louis Laval, 28 July, 1813.
James Barton, 1 Aug., 1813.
Loring Austin, 3 Sept., 1813.

*2nd Lieutenants.*

V. P. Luckett, 9 Oct., 1812.
Ed. Carrington, 12 Oct., 1812.

Owen Ransom, 1 Dec., 1812.
Thomas Heriot, 20 Jan., 1813.
W. Hampton, Jr., 17 March, 1813.
T. B. Barton, 27 July, 1813.
F. H. Lissenhoff, 1 Aug., 1813.
John A. Binns, 3 Sept., 1813.

*3rd Lieutenants.*

Thomas F. Hunt, 2 July, 1813.
Benj. Desha, 1 Aug., 1813.
T. J. Harrison, 15 Aug., 1813.
L. P. Gustine, 29 July, 1813.

*Cornets.*

Thomas Hogan, 9 Sept., 1813.
Philip Anspach, 25 Sept., 1813.

*Surgeon.*

Lewis Dunham, 12 Dec., 1808.

*Surgeon's Mate.*

S. H. Littlejohn, 3 April, 1813.

---

SECOND LIGHT DRAGOONS.

*Colonel.*

James Burn, 6 July, 1812.

*Lieut. Colonel.*

A. T. Macneil, 6 July, 1812.

*Majors.*

J. T. Woodford, 6 July, 1812.
James V. Ball, 16 Sept., 1812. Lieut. Col. Bvt., 18 Dec., 1812.

*Captains.*

S. R. Proctor, 6 July, 1812.
S. G. Hopkins, 6 July, 1812.
Henry Hall, 6 July, 1812.
Sam. D. Harris, 6 July, 1812.
John A. Burd, 6 July, 1812.
Jos. Selden, 6 July, 1812.
Jonas Holland, 6 July, 1812.
John Butler, 6 July, 1812.
Chas. J. Nourse, 15 Aug., 1813.

*1st Lieutenants.*

Abel Wheelock, 6 July, 1812.
Beverly Turpin, 6 July, 1812.
Walter German, 6 July, 1812.
J. Nicholas, Jr., 6 July, 1812.
James Hedges, 6 July, 1812.
A. H. Sneed, 6 July, 1812. Paymaster.
Gabriel Barbour, 6 July, 1812.
Fayette Roane, 16 April, 1813.
T. S. Johnson, 16 May, 1813.
Edw. Conway, 31 Oct., 1813.

*2nd Lieutenants.*

Walter Coles, 6 July, 1812.
Ira Williams, 6 July, 1812.
Benj. Smith, 6 July, 1812.
J. C. Tillotson, 10 Aug., 1812. Assistant Inspector General.
Robt. H. Craig, 18 March, 1813. Adjutant
P. Callan, 18 March, 1813.
Isaac Griffith, 18 March, 1813.
Dan. Bartling, 22 April, 1813.
James Martin, 30 April, 1813.
Benj. Burd, 16 May, 1813.

*3rd Lieutenants.*

Geo. Watts, 18 March, 1813.
Jas. Trippe, 29 April, 1813.
H. A. Hays, 29 April, 1813.
A. M'Farland, 29 April, 1813.
C. Wright, 29 April, 1813.
Hugh Sterling, 29 April, 1813.
John Hoomes, 20 May, 1813. Aid to Maj. Gen. Hampton.
John L. Elbert, 20 June, 1813.

*Cornets.*

T. Bracken, 16 May, 1813.
Sylv. Booth, 19 July, 1813.
Chas. Clarkson, 29 July, 1813.
R. Northington, 29 July, 1813.
Claiborne Cain, 1 Oct., 1813.
Wm. Johnson, 11 Oct., 1813.

*Surgeon.*

W. H. Buckner, 6 July, 1812.

*Surgeon's Mate.*

L. M. Bailey, 7 May, 1812.

---

FIRST ARTILLERY.

*Colonel.*

Henry Burbeck, 1 April, 1802. Brig. Gen. Bvt., 10 July, 1812.

*Lieut. Colonel*

Const. Freeman, 1 April, 1802. Col. Bvt., 10 July, 1812.

*Major.*

Wm. Mac Rea, 31 July, 1800. Lieut. Col. Bvt., 10 July, 1812.
A. Y. Nicoll, 1 Dec., 1804. Inspector General.
Jas. B. Many, 5 May, 1813.

*Captains.*

Lloyd Beall, 16 Feb., 1801. Maj. Bvt., 10 July, 1812.
S. T. Dyson, 15 Sept., 1804.
Nat. Leonard, 1 Dec., 1804.
C. Wollstonecraft, 13 March, 1805.
J. B. Walbach, 31 Jan., 1806. Adjutant General.
Moses Swett, 30 June, 1807.
Wm. Wilson, 3 May, 1808.
E. Humphreys, 9 Jan., 1809.
Frs. Newman, 1 Oct., 1809.
J. S. Swearingen, 13 Jan., 1811. Deputy Quartermaster General.
Jas. Hanham, 10 July, 1811.
Michael Walsh, 31 Oct., 1811.
James Reed, 12 March, 1812.
Thos. Murray, 10 Feb., 1813.
Wm. Gates, 3 March, 1813.
J. F. Heileman, 5 May, 1813.
J. Gansevoort, 11 May, 1813.
Hopley Yeaton, 20 May, 1813.
Sam. Maclay, 20 June, 1813.

*1st Lieutenants.*

Jona. Eastman, 30 June, 1807. District Paymaster.
Josh. Proveaux, 9 Jan., 1809.
Thos. Bennett, 1 Aug., 1809.
Ethan A. Allen, 1 Oct., 1809.
Arch. Darrah, 29 Jan., 1811.
M. P. Lomax, 30 June, 1811.
Justus Post, 1 July, 1811. Agent Fortifications.
S. Clarke, 10 July, 1811. District Paymaster.
S. Champlain, 31 Oct., 1811. Deputy Quartermaster General.
Heman A. Fay, 23 Dec., 1811.
Milo Mason, 29 Feb., 1812.
C. Van de Venter, 12 March, 1812. Deputy Quartermaster General.
J. Fitzgerald, 14 March, 1812.
J. Erving, Jr., 16 Aug., 1812. Assistant Adjutant General.
A. L. Sands, 10 Feb., 1813.
Thos. J. Beall, 3 March, 1813.
James Dalliba, 3 March, 1813. Deputy Commissary Ordnance.
Gus. Loomis, 5 May, 1813. Assistant Deputy Quartermaster General.

Ezra Smith, 11 May, 1813. Assistant Deputy Quartermaster General.
R. H. Ashley, 20 May, 1813. Assistant Deputy Quartermaster General.
J. S. Brush, 20 June, 1813.
F. Whiting, 10 Feb., 1812.
Samuel Spotts, 10 Feb., 1812.
Wm. Parker, 10 Feb., 1812.
Levi Whiting, 10 Feb., 1812.
J. W. Rouse, 27 March, 1812.
B. B. White, 14 April, 1812.
P. St. Medard, 30 April, 1812.
Abel B. Chase, 30 April, 1812.
James Baker, 1 May, 1812.
W. H. Nicoll, 6 July, 1812.
J. W. Lent, Jr., 12 March, 1813. Aid to Brig. Gen. Burbeck.
Charles Clark, 12 March, 1813
Thomas Elfe, Jr., 17 March, 1813.
S. Rockwell, 20 March, 1813.
Josh. Bosque, 12 April, 1813.
A. W. Forbush, 5 May, 1813.
Peter Melendy, 29 June, 1813.
B. C. Bartlett, 29 June, 1813.

*3rd Lieutenants.*

M. M. Russell, 10 July, 1813.
Hugh Orr, 19 July, 1813.
J. Bennett, 1 Aug., 1813.
W. J. Sever, 1 Aug., 1813.
Edmd. Hopkins, 1 Aug., 1813.
Benj. Conner, 3 Aug., 1813. Assistant Topographical Engineer.
John Ellison, 29 Sept., 1813.

---

SECOND ARTILLERY.

*Colonel.*

Winfield Scott, 12 March, 1813.

*Lieut. Colonel*

F. K Huger, 3 March, 1813: Adjutant General.
Wm. Lindsay, 12 March, 1813.

*Majors.*

D. M. Forney, 6 July, 1812.
J. Hindman, 26 June, 1813.

*Captains.*

Nathan Towson, 6 July, 1812.
S. B. Archer, 6 July, 1812.
Wm Nicholas, 6 July, 1812.
J. N. Barker, 6 July, 1812.
J. B. I'on, 6 July, 1812.
Sanders Donoho, 6 July, 1812.
Thos. Biddle, Jr., 6 July, 1812. Brigade Major.
Jos. Philips, 6 July, 1812.
John Ritchie, 6 July, 1812.
John Goodall, 6 July, 1812.
Jesse Robinson 6, July, 1812.
Robert M. Gill, 6 July, 1812.
P. Hawkins, Jr., 6 July, 1812.
Dan. Cushing, 6 July, 1812.
Stanton Sholes, 6 July, 1812.
G. W. Russell, 6 July, 1812.
Spots. Henry, 6 July, 1812.
Fred'k Evans, 6 July, 1812.
A. J. Williams, 12 March, 1813.
T. M. Randolph, 26 June 1813.

*1st Lieutenants.*

John S. Peyton, 6 July, 1812.
Hy. K. Craig, 6 July, 1812.
Adrian Neil, 6 July, 1812.
P. M'Donough, 6 July, 1812.
Wm. M. Read, 6 July, 1812.
Jonan. Kearsley, 6 July, 1812. Adjutant.
Wm. J. Cowan, 6 July, 1812.
John Fontaine, 6 July, 1812.
J. H. Larwill, 6 July, 1812.
Lowndes Brown, 6 July, 1812
Luther Scott, 6 July, 1812.
Robert R. Ruffin, 6 July, 1812. Paymaster.
Hy. Slaughter, 6 July, 1812.
J. H. Dearing, 6 July, 1812.
Isaac Davis, 13 March, 1813.
R. A. Zantzinger, 13 March, 1813.
Robt. Stewart, 13 March, 1813.
J. L. Edwards, 28 March, 1813.
Edwin Sharpe, 26 June 1813.
Wm. Tyler, 14 Aug., 1813.

*2nd Lieutenants.*

Jacob Warley, 6 July, 1812.
Wm. Smith, 6 July, 1812.
Lewis Morgan, 6 July, 1812.
John Ruffin, 6 July, 1812.
J. H. Gamble, 6 July, 1812.
John W. Kincaid, 6 July, 1812.
Robert Goode, 6 July, 1812.
Francis O. Byrd, 6 July, 1812.
Thomas Winn, 6 July, 1812.
Thomas Clark, 16 April, 1813. Assistant Topographical Engineer.
Cld. D. Cooper, 16 April, 1813. Aid to Brig. Gen. Izard.
Jos. P. Prince, 16 April, 1813.
G. Doneghey, 16 April, 1813.
P J. Nevill, 20 April, 1813.
M. S. Massey, 13 May, 1813.
J. P. Bunting, 26 June, 1813.
J. Henderson, 26 June, 1813.
T. Shubrick, 26 June, 1813.

*3rd Lieutenants.*

W. E. Broadwater, 2 July, 1813.
Benj. Lawson, 9 July, 1813.
H. M. Campbell, 19 July, 1813.
John Mitchell, 19 July, 1813.
Hy. L. Duffell, 1 Aug., 1813.
W. Berryman, 1 Aug., 1813.
Jas. C. Pickett, 4 Aug., 1813.
Britton Evans, 15 Aug., 1813.
J. Watmough, 22 Sept., 1813.
Wm. Kenny, 23 Sept., 1813.
N. Henderson, 12 Oct., 1813.

*Surgeon.*

J. De La Motta, 1 May, 1812.

*Surgeon's Mates.*

James Trimble, 6 July, 1812.
Louis L. Near, 6 July, 1812.

---

THIRD ARTILLERY.

*Colonel.*

A. Macomb, 6 July, 1812.

*Lieut. Colonels.*

G. E. Mitchell, 3 March, 1813.
James House, 3 March, 1813.

*Majors.*

Samuel Nye, 6 July, 1812.
G. Armistead, 3 March, 1813.

*Captains.*

Ich. B. Crane, 6 July, 1812.
Roger Jones, 6 July, 1812. Brigade Major.
J. H. Boyle, 6 July, 1812.
A. S. Brooks, 6 July, 1812.
J. W. Gookin, 6 July, 1812.
W. VanDeursen, Jr., 6 July, 1812.
J. S. B. Romayne, 6 July, 1812.
Hor. H. Watson, 6 July, 1812.
Evan B. Morse, 6 July, 1812.
James M'Keon, 6 July, 1812.
Rufus M'Intire, 6 July, 1812.
Benj. S. Ogden, 6 July, 1812.
Jonan. Brooks, 24 Sept., 1812.

Steph. Collins, 13 Jan., 1813.
A. C. W. Fanning, 13 March, 1813.
S. M. O'Conner, 13 March, 1813. Late Quartermaster.
G. H. Richards, 13 March, 1813.
S. M. Dewey, 20 May, 1813.
S. Churchill, 15 Aug., 1813.
B. K. Pierce, 1 Oct., 1813.

*1st Lieutenants.*

Jas. Green, Jr., 6 July, 1812.
J. L. Tracy, 6 July, 1812.
Moses J. Chase, 6 July, 1812.
W. DePeyster, 6 July, 1812.
John Farley, 6 July, 1812.
Harold Smith, 6 July, 1812.
Peter Pifer, 6 July, 1812.
Benj. Brearley, 6 July, 1812.
John W. Green, 6 July, 1812.
Samuel Weston, 6 July, 1812.
C. M. Macomb, 13 March, 1812. Adjutant.
Jos. H. Rees, 13 March, 1812. Assistant Deputy Paymaster General.
W. R. Duncan, 13 March, 1812.
Chester Root, 13 March, 1812. Paymaster.
Matth. Jenkins, 13 March, 1812.
P. D. Spencer, 13 May, 1812.
Jno. Mountfort, 20 May, 1812.
G. Dearborn, 1 Oct., 1812.
Felix Ansart, 1 Oct., 1812.
Wm. King, 1 Oct., 1812.

*2nd Lieutenants.*

T. C. Legate, 6 July, 1812.
John P. Bartlett, 6 July, 1812.
Adam A. Gray, 6 July, 1812.
J. I. Cromwell, 23 Nov., 1812.
Thos. Chrystie, 18 March 1813. Assistant Adjutant General.
F. P. Woolsey, 20 May, 1813.
W. M'Clintock, 20 June, 1813.
L. H. Osgood, 20 June, 1813.
R. M. Kirby, 9 July, 1813.
G. B. Sheldon, 9 July, 1813.
Wm. B. Read, 29 July, 1813.
T. B. Chickering, 1 Aug., 1813.
Ed. Baynton, 1 Oct., 1813.
D. Blaney, Jr., 1 Oct., 1813.
Libbeus Custis, 1 Oct., 1813.
Wm. Lyon, 1 Oct., 1813.

*3rd Lieutenants.*

C. Newkirk, 1 Oct., 1813.
Oliver Bangs, 11 Oct., 1813.

*Surgeon.*

J. H. Bradford, 3 Oct., 1813.

*Surgeon's Mates.*

Joseph Eaton, 14 April, 1812.
German Senter, 14 April, 1812.

---

First Infantry.

*Colonel.*

J. Kingsbury, 18 Aug., 1808. Inspector General.

*Lieut. Colonel*

R. C. Nicholas, 15 Aug., 1812.

*Majors.*

Z. Pike, 20 March, 1800. Lieut. Col. Bvt., 10 July, 1812.
E. B. Clemson, 20 Jan., 1813.

*Captains.*

John Whistler, 1 July, 1797. Major Bvt., 10 July, 1812.
Simon Owens, 18 Aug., 1808.
D. Hughes, 15 Dec., 1808. Assistant Inspector General.
Daniel Baker, 12 Mar., 1812. Aid to Maj. Gen. Lewis.
A. Whitlock, 26 Aug., 1812. District Paymaster.
W. Whistler, 31 Dec., 1812.
J. C. Symmes, 20 Jan., 1813.
Simeon Knight, 20 Jan., 1813. District Paymaster.
A. Kingsley 20 Jan., 1813. District Paymaster.
H. Johnson, 20 Jan., 1813.

*1st Lieutenants.*

Benj. Marshall, 14 Oct., 1808.
J. Brownson, 8 Dec., 1808.
T. Hamilton, 15 Dec., 1808.
J. W. Albright, 26 Aug., 1812. District Paymaster.
S. Perkins, 31 Dec., 1812.
L. T. Helm, 20 Jan., 1813.
J. W. Bryson, 20 Jan., 1813. Assistant Deputy Quartermaster General.
J. Campbell, 20 Jan., 1813.
D. Stansbury, 20 Jan., 1813.
B. Vasquez, 30 July, 1813.

*2nd Lieutenants.*

Lewis Bissell, 12 March, 1812.
J. A. Shaw, 26 Aug., 1812.
Ormond Marsh, 30 Oct., 1812.
Danl. Curtis, 31 Dec., 1812.
R. A. M'Cabe, 31 Dec., 1812.
N. E. Westfall, 20 Jan., 1813.
W. Anderson, 20 Jan., 1813. Assistant Deputy Quartermaster General.
John O. Fallan, 20 Jan., 1813. Aid to Maj. Gen. Harrison.

*Ensigns.*

J. C. Wooding, 1 Aug., 1813.
H. Carrington, 1 Aug., 1813.

*Surgeon.*

H. Catlett, 18 Feb., 1813.

*Surgeon's Mate.*

S. C. Muir, 7 April, 1813.

---

Second Infantry.

*Colonel.*

Richard Sparks, 6 July, 1812.

*Lieut. Colonel.*

John Bowyer, 6 July, 1812.

*Majors.*

Wm. R. Boote, 6 July, 1812. Inspector General.
Wm. Swan, 20 Jan., 1813. Quartermaster General.

*Captains.*

Hugh M'Call, 19 Aug., 1800. Major Bvt., 10 July, 1812.
Wm. Piatt, 17 Feb., 1809. Quartermaster General.
W. Lawrence, 1 Jan., 1810.
H. B. Brevoort, 1 May, 1811.
John Miller, 12 March, 1812.
R. Chamberlain, 6 July, 1812.
J. T. Pemberton, 20 Jan., 1813. District Paymaster.
Wm. F. Ware, 5 May, 1813.
John M. Davis, 30 May, 1813. Late Paymaster.

*1st Lieutenants.*

A. Brownlow, 1 Jan., 1810. Adjutant.
John Mathers, 1 May, 1811.
John T. Wirt, 6 July, 1812. Assistant Deputy Quartermaster General.

E. Bogardus, 6 July, 1812.
H. Bradley, 15 Aug., 1812. Quartermaster.
B. Willis, 1 Nov., 1812.
H. H. Villard, 10 Jan., 1813.
John Bliss, 20 Jan., 1813. Assistant Deputy Quartermaster General.
H. A. Burchsted, 5 May, 1813.
J. Bell, 30 May, 1813. Aid to Maj. Gen. Wilkinson.

*2nd Lieutenants.*

T. Doggett, 28 Sept., 1812.
H. Sturges, 1 Nov., 1812.
James Stuart, 27 Dec., 1812.
H. Conway, Jr., 10 Jan., 1813.
N. Clarke, 20 Jan., 1813.
W. M. Smith, 20 Jan., 1813.

---

THIRD INFANTRY.

*Colonel.*

H. V. Milton, 15 Aug., 1813.

*Lieut. Colonel.*

G. C. Russell, 6 June, 1811.

*Majors.*

M. Arbuckle, 15 Aug., 1812.
Wm. Carson, 20 Jan., 1813.

*Captains.*

John Nicks, 1 July, 1808.
H. Atkinson, 1 July, 1808. Inspector General.
J. M'Clelland, 1 July, 1808.
Jas. Woodruff, 12 Dec., 1808.
Wm. Butler, 31 Dec., 1809.
R. B. Moore, 1 Sept., 1810.
J. Denking, 6 Feb., 1811.
H. G. White, 11 May, 1811.
W. R. Davis, 4 Aug., 1813.
S. W. Butler, 15 Aug., 1813.

*1st Lieutenants.*

H. Chotard, 31 Dec., 1809. Adjutant.
B. D. Herriott, 1 Dec., 1810.
S. C. Mabson, 31 Dec., 1810.
John Burnett, 1 March, 1811. Quartermaster.
Wm. Laval, 11 May, 1811.
J. M. Wilcox, 3 Jan., 1812.
Geo. Morley, 24 April, 1812.
J. L. Carey, 1 Nov., 1812.
J. F. Everitt, 4 Aug., 1813.
Wm. Triplett, 15 Aug., 1813.

*2nd Lieutenants.*

J. W. Hansell, 3 Jan., 1812.
T. Hunter, 3 Jan., 1812.
Wm. Christian, 3 Jan., 1812.
W. Bourke, 12 Mar., 1812.
John Tarrant, 12 Mar., 1812.
A. Donoho, 1 Nov., 1812.
James Smith, 19 Nov., 1812.
T. Turner, 4 Aug., 1813.
R. Goodwin, 15 Aug., 1813.

*3rd Lieutenants.*

John Martin, 12 March, 1813.
W. L. Robeson, 12 March, 1813.
J. A. Watson, 12 March, 1813.
James A. Hart, 12 March, 1813.
Jack F. Ross, 20 May, 1813.
T. W. Barton, 1 Aug., 1813.

*Ensigns.*

C. Stephens, 29 June, 1813.
Thos. Rogers, 29 June, 1813.
W. V. Cobbs, 4 Aug., 1813.

*Surgeon.*

R. Shubrick, 8 Aug., 1809.

FOURTH INFANTRY.

*Colonel.*

R. Purdy, 26 Aug., 1812.

*Lieut. Colonel.*

J. Darrington, 6 July, 1812.

*Majors.*

N. Heald, 26 Aug., 1812.
S. Ranney, 20 Jan., 1813.

*Captains.*

J. Binney, 12 Dec., 1808.
R. B. Brown, 18 March, 1809.
J. Snelling, 12 June, 1809. Maj. Bvt., 9 Aug., 1812.
O. G. Burton, 25 Aug., 1811.
C Fuller, 9 Nov., 1811.
C Larrabee, 15 Sept., 1812.
E. Way, 20 Jan., 1813.
J. L. Eastman, 15 Aug., 1813.
F. Conkling, 2 Sept., 1813.

*1st Lieutenants.*

A. Hawkins, 25 Aug., 1811.
G. P. Peters, 29 Oct., 1811. Paymaster.
John Smith, 31 Oct., 1811.
L. Peckham, 9 Nov., 1811.
G. Gooding, 15 Feb. 1812.
Josiah Bacon, 15 Sept., 1812. Quartermaster.
P. Greenough, 20 Jan., 1813.
M. Bulley, 31 July, 1813.
J. Plympton, 15 Aug., 1813.
G. W. Hosey, 2 Sept., 1813.

*2nd Lieutenants.*

P. Wheelock, 3 Jan., 1812.
S. Butterfield, 3 Jan., 1812.
Rufus Preble, 15 Feb., 1812.
S. Armstrong, 15 Sept., 1812.
S. Legate, 20 Jan., 1813.
Paul Peckham, 19 May, 1813.
J Ranney, 30 May, 1813.
E. Kirby, 31 July, 1813.
C. Munroe, 2 Sept., 1813.

*3rd Lieutenants.*

J. P. Norton, 12 March, 1813.
A. Wilson, Jr., 12 March, 1813.
N. Wadhams, 27 March, 1813.
G. W. Boyd, 16 April, 1813.
Thomas Hunt, 6 May, 1813.
J. L. Gardner, 20 May, 1813.
T. Green, Jr., 20 May, 1813.

*Ensigns.*

John Drake, 20 May, 1813.
James Dean, 19 July, 1813.

*Surgeon.*

Sylvester Day, 13 March, 1813.

*Surgeon's Mates.*

A. Farnsworth, 14 April, 1812.
J. M. Harper, 19 Jan., 1813.

---

FIFTH INFANTRY.

*Colonel.*

Daniel Bissell, 15 Aug. 1812.

*Lieut. Colonel.*

George Gibson, 15 Aug., 1813.

*Majors.*

N. Pinkney, 20 Jan., 1813. Aid to Maj. Gen. Wilkinson.
Benj. Wallace, 30 April, 1813.

*Captains.*

Colin Buckner, 1 July, 1808.
G. M. Brooke, 1 May, 1810.
R. Whartenby, 3 May, 1810.
Townsend Stith, 30 Sept., 1810.
A. M'Ilhenny, 1 Sept., 1811.
T. Chambers, 31 Oct., 1811. Assistant Adjutant General.
James Dorman, 9 Nov., 1811.
W. S. Henshaw, 30 April, 1813.
Leroy Ople, 26 June, 1813.
Richd. H. Bell, 15 Aug., 1813.

*1st Lieutenants.*

John Jamieson, 31 Oct., 1811. Adjutant.
J. Saunders, 9 Nov., 1811. Aid to Brig. Gen. Parker.
Josh. Owens, 3 Jan., 1812. Paymaster.
R. W. Chick, 12 March, 1812.
J. S. Allison, 6 July, 1812.
J. R. Corbaly, 6 July, 1812.
Wm. C. Bird, 1 Sept., 1812.
P. B. Greenwell, 30 April, 1812.
J. G. Clark, 26 June, 1812.
John Gassaway, 15 Aug., 1812.

*2nd Lieutenants.*

Henry O. Hill, 3 Jan., 1812.
John W. Smoot, 3 Jan., 1812.
J. M'Gunegle, 12 March, 1812. Quartermaster.
J. Cummings, 6 July, 1812.
S. W. Priestman, 6 July, 1812.
G. D. Snyder, 1 Sept., 1812.
John Fendall, 30 April, 1813.
J. B. Taylor, 26 June, 1813.
J. Darnall, 14 Aug., 1813.
George Murray, 15 Aug., 1813.

*3rd Lieutenants.*

Matth. Galt, Jr., 12 March, 1813.
James Kearney, 11 April, 1813. Assistant Topographical Engineer.
Jas. Smith, Jr., 16 April, 1813.
J. A. B. Harding, 25 April, 1813.
George Rea, 14 Aug., 1813.
Jacob Swoyer, 14 August, 1813.
Wm. C. Yates, 14 Aug., 1813.
T. Murphey, 14 Aug., 1813.
M. Fishback, 15 Aug., 1813.
George Brent, 1 Oct., 1813.

*Ensigns.*

Baily Buckner, 2 July, 1813.
Albert Vincent, 19 July, 1813.
G. Liftwich, 19 July, 1813.
T. W. Morgan, 19 July, 1813.
John Maul, 29 July, 1813.
Robert Means, 29 July, 1813.
John Wells, 29 July, 1813.
W. R. Richardson, 31 July, 1813.
A. Whitehead, 15 Sept., 1813.
Azel Gates, 15 Sept., 1813.

*Surgeon.*

Adam Hays, 10 Feb., 1812.

*Surgeon's Mates.*

Alexander Blair, 6 July, 1812.
Clajou Reily, 22 March, 1813.

---

## SIXTH INFANTRY.

*Colonel.*

Jonas Simonds, 8 July, 1808.

*Lieut. Colonel.*

James Miller, 30 Nov., 1810. Col. Bvt., 9 Aug., 1812.

*Majors.*

J. Campbell, 6 July, 1812.
Horatio Stark, 20 Jan., 1813.

*Captains.*

Ebenez. Beebe, 19 Jan., 1809. Assistant Adjutant General.
J. Machesney, 10 June, 1809.
J. T. Arrowsmith, 20 Oct., 1809.
G. Humphreys, 31 Dec., 1809.
J. Walworth, 1 Jan., 1810.
P. Muhlenburg, 1 Oct., 1810.
Clem. Sadller, 15 Nov., 1811.
Robert Sterry, 3 Jan., 1812. Assistant Inspector General.
J. E. A. Masters, 4 June, 1812.
Henry Phillips, 13 Oct., 1812. District Paymaster.

*1st Lieutenants.*

Edward Webb, 1 Oct., 1810.
Henry Shell, 9 March, 1811.
James Bailey, 3 Jan., 1812.
Londus L. Buck, 3 Jan., 1812.
A. R. Thompson, 3 Jan., 1812.
J. Chapman, 6 July, 1812.
Wm. Hazard, 13 Oct., 1812. Quartermaster.
G. D. Smith, 31 Oct., 1812. Adjutant.
G. W. Ten Broeck, 20 March, 1813.
R. B. Cuyler, 1 April, 1813.

*2nd Lieutenants.*

D. Vander Heyden, 3 Jan., 1812.
G. W. Runk, 3 Jan., 1812.
H. R. Windle, 3 Jan., 1812.
Henry Cooke, 12 March, 1812.
N. Sherman, 4 Oct., 1812.
R. McClellan, 4 Oct., 1812. Paymaster
I. L. Dubois, 13 Oct., 1812.
George Keese, 1 Feb., 1813.
W. B. Staats, 20 March, 1813.
A. Quackinbush, 1 April, 1813.

*3rd Lieutenants.*

James Young, 12 March, 1813.
John Sisk, 12 March, 1813.
Henry Meyer, 12 March, 1813.
Patrick Ford, 20 May, 1813.
John Harris, 19 July, 1813.
Charles Rowan, 19 July, 1813.

*Ensigns.*

W. Bicker, Jr., 29 July, 1813.
John Wood, 29 July, 1813.

*Surgeon.*

T. Lawson, 21 May, 1813.

*Surgeon's Mate.*

W. Beaumont, 2 Dec., 1812.

---

## SEVENTH INFANTRY.

*Colonel.*

Wm. Russell, 3 May, 1808.

*Lieut. Colonel.*

Thorn. Posey, 30 April, 1813.

*Majors.*

J. Bankhead, 15 Aug., 1813. Adjutant General.
Ross Bird, 15 Aug., 1813.

*Captains.*

Uriah Blue, 9 May, 1809.
Richd. Oldham, 1 Dec., 1809.
James Doherty, 1 Jan., 1810.

Enos Cutler, 3 Sept., 1810. Assistant Inspector General.
Zach. Taylor, 30 Nov. 1810. Major Bvt., 5 Sept, ,1812.
W. H. Overton, 3 Dec., 1810.
Carey Nicholas, 1 March, 1811. Assistant Adjutant General.
W. McClellan, 1 March, 1811 .
Alex. A. White, 6 June, 1811.
Narcis. Broutin, 6 April, 1813.

*1st Lieutenants*

J. Robertson, 30 Nov., 1810. Adjutant.
J. S. Wade, 3 Dec., 1810.
Samuel Vail, 1 March, 1811.
George C. Allen, 1 March, 1811.
E. Montgomery, 24 June, 1811.
D. McClellan, 10 Feb., 1812. Quartermaster.
T. R. Richardson, 10 Feb., 1812.
Jacob Miller, 10 Feb., 1812.
M. McClelland, 20 Jan., 1813.
S. Kercheval, 6 April, 1813.

*2nd Lieutenants.*

E. Taylor, 10 Feb., 1812.
W. Snodgrass, 10 Feb., 1812.
H. P. Helm, 10 Feb., 1812.
Wm. Prosser, 10 Feb., 1812.
J. Forsythe, 10 Feb., 1812.
John Hays, 10 Feb., 1812.
John Meek, 20 Jan., 1813.
J. N. Carrick, 20 March, 1813.
T. F. Thomas, 9 July, 1813.

*3rd Lieutenants.*

E. T. Hall, 12 March, 1813.
T. Blackstone, 12 March, 1813. Paymaster.
John Weaver, 12 March, 1813.
I. M. Rieley, 12 March, 1813.
A. Ross, 2 May, 1813.
John Noble, 2 May, 1813.
T. B. Rice, 9 Aug., 1813.
D. Burford, 9 Aug., 1813.
Noble Johnson, 9 Aug., 1813.

*Ensigns.*

William Query, 2 July, 1813.
A. Neilson, 19 July, 1813.
Wilson Creed, 19 July, 1813.
F. S. Gray, 6 Aug., 1813.
R. B. DeWitt, 6 Aug., 1813.
W. S. Doherty, 9 Aug., 1813.

*Surgeon.*

A. G. Goodlet, 10 Feb., 1812.

---

EIGHTH INFANTRY.

*Colonel.*

Patrick Jack, 6 July, 1812.

*Lieut. Colonel.*

L. Manning, 15 Aug., 1813.

*Majors.*

W. Cumming, 25 March, 1813.
Philip Cook, 15 Aug., 1813.

*Captains.*

D. E. Twiggs, 6 July, 1812.
R. Cunningham, 6 July, 1812.
W. Chisolm, 6 July, 1812.
F. B. Warley, 6 July, 1812.
W. Jones, 6 July, 1812.
T. W. Farrar, 6 July, 1812. Aid to Brig. Gen. Flournoy.
W. McQueen, 6 July, 1812. Brigade Major.
M. I. Keith, 6 July, 1812.
C. Crawford, 6 July, 1812.
H. Walton, 15 Aug., 1813.

*1st Lieutenants*

Hamlin Cook, 6 July, 1812. District Paymaster.
R. P. Johnson, 6 July, 1812.
T. S. Bailey, 6 July, 1812.
T. C. Hunter, 6 July, 1812.
Otis Dyer, 6 July, 1812.
J. H. Mallory, 5 May, 1813.
M. A. Roberts, 5 May, 1813.
James Wilde, 5 May, 1813. Paymaster.
William Bee, Jr., 14 Aug., 1813.
E. Halloway, 15 Aug., 1813.

*2nd Lieutenants.*

J. A. Black, 6 July, 1812.
B. Martin, 6 July, 1812.
R. Lamer, 6 July, 1812.
Henry Bill, 25 March, 1813.
R. V. Marye, 25 March, 1813.
P. Lequex, 5 May, 1813. Assistant Deputy Quartermaster General.
J. Ferguson, 5 May, 1813. Aid to Maj. Gen. Pinckney.
T. F. Wells, 5 May, 1813.
L. Gresham, 14 Aug., 1813.
W. W. Davis, 15 Aug., 1813.

*3rd Lieutenants.*

S. Coleman, 5 May, 1813.
James Colson, 5 May, 1813.
J. G. Bostwick, 5 May, 1813.
William Wayne, 5 May, 1813.
A. Dousset, 5 May, 1813.
R. J. Easter, 5 May, 1813.
J. A. Beaulard, 15 Aug., 1813.

*Ensigns.*

H. L. O'Neal, 20 May, 1813.
Jas. Gignilliat, 20 May, 1813.
J. G. Stallings, 2 July, 1813.

*Surgeon.*

W. R. Waring, 11 April, 1813.

*Surgeon's Mates.*

J. W. Caldwell, 6 July, 1812.
Charles Lewis, 19 July, 1813.

---

NINTH INFANTRY.

*Colonel.*

Simon Learned, 6 July, 1812.

*Lieut. Colonel.*

T. Aspinwall, 12 March, 1813.

*Majors.*

C. Lyman, 26 June, 1813.
H. Leavenworth, 15 Aug., 1813.

*Captains.*

T. Crooker, 6 July, 1812.
A. F. Hull, 6 July, 1812.
E. Foster, 13 March, 1813.
J. Ingersoll, Jr., 16 April, 1813.
D. S. Townsend, 13 May, 1813.
G. Bender, Jr., 13 May, 1813.

J. F. Norris, 26 June, 1813.
T. Harrison, 15 Aug., 1813.

*1st Lieutenants.*

S. L. Allen, 23 March, 1813.
W. L. Foster, 23 March, 1813.
B. F. Greene, 30 March, 1813.
J. Fowle, Jr., 16 April, 1813. Paymaster.
S. Turner, 13 May, 1813.
E. Childs, 13 May, 1813.
Loring Palmer, 26 June, 1813.

David Perry, 30 June, 1813.
Aaron Lewis, 15 Aug., 1813.
J. H. Cranson, 15 Aug., 1813.

*2nd Lieutenants.*

W. Browning, 13 March, 1813.
D. Chandler, 13 March, 1813.
H. Wellington, 13 May, 1813.
Charles Foster, 13 May, 1813.
W. Lyman, 26 June, 1813.
Otis Fisher, 30 June, 1813.
E. Norton, 15 July, 1813.
J. Gleason, 14 Aug., 1813. Adjutant.

*3rd Lieutenants.*

J. Howard, 17 March, 1813.
J. Christie, 15 Aug., 1813.
David Foot, 15 Aug., 1813.
A. Burghardt, 15 Aug., 1813.
T. Childs, Jr., 15 Aug., 1813.

*Ensigns.*

E. Badger, 30 Aug., 1813.
J. W. Colburn, 29 Sept., 1813.

*Surgeon.*

J. Lovell, 15 May, 1812.

*Surgeon's Mate.*

T. G. Mower, 2 Dec., 1812.

---

TENTH INFANTRY.

*Colonel.*

James Welborn, 6 July, 1812.

*Lieut. Colonel.*

A. Pickens, Jr., 6 July, 1812.

*Majors.*

W. S. Hamilton, 3 March, 1813.
A. L. Langham, 15 Aug., 1813.

*Captains.*

G. Cloud, 6 July, 1812.
T. M. Nelson, 6 July, 1812.
Philip Brittain, 6 July, 1812.
Robert Mitchell, 6 July, 1812.
Eman. I. Leigh, 6 July, 1812.
Mark Harden, 6 July, 1812.
Joseph Bryant, 6 July, 1812.
Josiah Woods, 6 July, 1812.
Joseph Clay, 6 July, 1812.
Jesse Copeland, 6 July, 1812.

*1st Lieutenants.*

George Vashon, 6 July, 1812. Adjutant.
George Strother, 6 July, 1812.
Wm. Bailey, 6 July, 1812.
H. H. Carson, 6 July, 1812.
Abner S. Lewis, 6 July, 1812.
Charles Lutterloh, 6 July, 1812.
W. L. Dufphey, 15 April, 1813.
William Irvine, 14 Aug., 1813.
Joseph J. Clinch, 15 August, 1813.

*2nd Lieutenants.*

Thomas D. Kelly, 6 July, 1812.
Jos. G. Wall, 6 July, 1812.
Arthur Fox, 6 July, 1812.
R. Plummer, 6 July, 1812.
S. A. Miller, 23 March, 1813.
Lewis Yancey, 23 March, 1813. Paymaster.
Jehu Bird, 15 April, 1813.
A. G. Glynn, 14 Aug., 1813.
James Roane, 15 Aug., 1813.
B. T. Goodwyn, 15 Aug., 1813.

*3rd Lieutenants.*

John Garrett, 24 March, 1813.
W. J. Gordon, 24 March, 1813.
James Norris, 24 March, 1813.
Isaac Craton, 24 March, 1813.
F. McRae, 24 March, 1813.
G. R. Bridges, 24 March, 1813.
W. Lancaster, Jr., 14 Aug., 1813.
James K. Hill, 14 Aug., 1813.
S. Thomas, 14 Aug., 1813.
W. Alexander, 15 Aug., 1813.

*Ensigns.*

R. Wood, 24 March, 1813.
N. S. Wade, 24 March, 1813.
R. H. Goodwyn, 24 March, 1813.
M. Parkes, 2 July, 1813.
W. Pannill, 2 July, 1813.
John Carney, 19 July, 1813.
T. H. Ferguson, 31 July, 1813.
S. H. Bryant, 1 Aug., 1813.
John Rice, 9 Sept., 1813.

*Surgeon.*

I. Foster, 10 July, 1813.

*Surgeon's Mates.*

E. H. Bell, 12 March, 1812.
R. Everitt, 24 March, 1813.

---

ELEVENTH INFANTRY.

*Colonel.*

Isaac Clark, 6 July, 1812.

*Lieut. Colonel.*

Moody Bedel, 6 July, 1812.

*Majors.*

O. C. Merrill, 3 March 1813.
J. McNeal, Jr., 15 Aug., 1813.

*Captains.*

J. W. Weeks, 6 July, 1812.
B. S. Egerton, 6 July, 1812.
Samuel Gordon, 6 July, 1812.
W. S. Foster, 13 March, 1813.
John Bliss, 13 March, 1813.
Richard Baen, 26 June, 1813. Late Quartermaster.
V. R. Goodrich, 26 June, 1813.
Horace Hale, 15 Aug., 1813.
Benj. Smead, 15 Aug., 1813.

*1st Lieutenants.*

M. Corning, 6 July, 1812.
W. Sheldon, 13 March, 1813. District Paymaster.
W. S. Heaton, 13 March, 1813.
James Wells, 13 March, 1813.
James Greene, 13 May, 1813.
H. J. Blake, 26 June, 1813.
D. Crawford, 26 June, 1813.
R. Bucklin, Jr., 15 Aug., 1813.
N. S. Clarke, 15 Aug., 1813. Adjutant.
Thomas Levake, 15 Aug., 1813.

*2nd Lieutenants.*

W. F. Hall, 13 March, 1813.
Ezek. Jewett, 13 May 1813.
F. A. Sawyer, 26 June, 1813.
T. Aldrich, 26 June, 1813.
J. V. Barron, 26 June, 1813.
T. Staniford, 26 June, 1813.
Isaac Clark, Jr., 14 Aug., 1813.
Wm. Risley, 15 Aug., 1813.
J. E. Merritt, 15 Aug., 1813.
Enoch Cooper, 15 Aug., 1813.

*Ensigns.*

S. C. Cotton, 19 July, 1813.
J. C. Walker, 19 July, 1813.
John Levake, 29 July, 1813.
Joseph Hopkins, 4 Aug., 1813.
Thomas Tupper, 23 Aug., 1813.
P. S. Sanford, 23 Aug., 1813.
Hazen Bedel 21 Sept., 1813.
B. Stephenson, 21 Sept., 1813.
H. Webster, 22 Sept., 1813.

*Surgeon.*

G. P. Spencer, 7 April, 1813.

*Surgeon's Mates.*

T. Woodward, 9 Aug., 1813.
John Sackett, 9 Aug., 1813.

---

TWELFTH INFANTRY.

*Colonel.*

Isaac A. Coles, 12 March, 1813.

*Lieut. Colonel.*

Thos. Taylor, 15 Aug., 1813.

*Majors.*

R. C. Nicholas, 3 March, 1813.
W. Morgan, 26 June, 1813.

*Captains.*

T. P. Moore, 6 July, 1812.
James Gibson, 6 July, 1812.
James Paxton, 6 July, 1812.
Thos. Sangster, 6 July, 1812.
A. C. Randolph, 6 July, 1812.
James Charlton, 6 July, 1812.
Charles Page, 6 July, 1812.
A. L. Madison, 6 July, 1812.
Thomas Post, 29 March, 1813.
Robert G. Hite, 26 June, 1813. Late Adjutant.

*1st Lieutenants.*

Z. Morgan, 6 July, 1812.
J. G. Camp, 6 July, 1812.
L. B. Willis, 6 July, 1812.
A. McDonald, 6 July, 1812.
John Key, Jr., 29 March, 1813.
Robert Houston, 29 March, 1813.
John Kenney, 29 March, 1813.
Oth. W. Callis, 26 June, 1813. Quartermaster.
Wm. Stone, Jr., 26 June, 1813.
R. Harrison, 30 Sept., 1813.

*2nd Lieutenants.*

P. Magruder, 6 July, 1812.
M. Hughes, 6 July, 1812.
John Towles, 6 July, 1812.
W. C. Parker, 29 March, 1813.
Bailey Bruce, 29 March, 1813.
A. Eggleston, 30 March, 1813.
R. Booker, 30 March, 1813.
Isaac Keyes, 26 June, 1813.
Jos. McGavock, 26 June, 1813.
David P. Pope, 30 Sept., 1813.

*3rd Lieutenants.*

C. Randolph, 29 March, 1813.
P. C. Johnson, 29 March, 1813.
John Strother, 29 March, 1813.
David Hunter, 29 March, 1813.
John Macky, 29 March, 1813.
F. L. Dade, 29 March, 1813.
Philip Wager, 29 March, 1813.
Joseph Shommo, 29 March, 1813.
Joseph Thomas, 29 March, 1813.
M. W. Claiborne, 14 Aug., 1813.



*Ensigns.*

George Eskridge, 29 March, 1813.
Michael Crupper, 29 March, 1813.
Thomas Blair, 19 April, 1813.
John Robinson, 18 May, 1813.
S. Grantland, Jr., 20 May, 1813.
N. C. Kindey, 2 July, 1813.
DeLaf. Johnson, 9 July, 1813.
Robert Call, 1 Aug., 1813.
R. Randolph, 1 Aug., 1813.
S. Bartlett, 1 Aug., 1813.

*Surgeon.*

J. C. Bronaugh ,28 April, 1812.

---

THIRTEENTH INFANTRY.

*Colonel.*

P. P. Schuyler, 6 July, 1812. Adjutant General.

*Lieut. Colonel.*

S. S. Conner, 12 March, 1813.

*Majors.*

J. V. H. Huyck, 6 July, 1812.
R. M. Malcolm, 3 March, 1813.

*Captains.*

John Sproull, 6 July, 1812.
Hugh R. Martin, 6 July, 1812.
Mordecai Myers, 6 July, 1812.
Myndert M. Dox, 6 July, 1812.
W. D. Lawrence 6 July, 1812.
S. W. Kearney, 1 April, 1813.
Samuel Haring, 1 April, 1813.
John K. Paige, 13 May, 1813.
W. B. Adams, 13 May, 1813.
John Campbell, 15 Aug., 1813.

*1st Lieutenants.*

R. S. Gardiner, 6 July, 1812. Paymaster.
W. Gansevoort, 6 July, 1812.
John L. Fink, 6 July, 1812.
Israel Turner, 6 July, 1812.
Daniel Hugunin, 1 April, 1813.
Alfred Phelps, 13 May, 1813.
Hugh Robinson, 13 May, 1813.
Wm. W. Carr, 13 May, 1813.
D. B. Wilcox, 15 Aug., 1813.

*2nd Lieutenants.*

Jacob Sammons, 6 July, 1812.
Jos. H. Dwight, 1 April, 1813. Quartermaster.
John Williams, 1 April, 1813.
John Kirby, 1 April, 1813.
George Reab, Jr., 20 April, 1813.
T. W. Denton, 13 May, 1813.
John Graham, 20 June, 1813.
Mason Ronalds, 20 June, 1813.
John Haight, 15 Aug., 1813.
W. Anderson, Jr., 15 Aug., 1813.

*3rd Lieutenants.*

F. J. Wheeler, 2 May, 1813.
C. Harrison, 16 May, 1813.
M. C. Cantine, 1 Aug., 1813.
G. Helmbold, 15 Aug., 1813.
R. Humphreys, 30 Sept., 1813.
R. M. Harrison, 30 Sept., 1813.
A. Schuyler, 17 Oct., 1813.

*Surgeon.*

J. Y. Lancing, 15 Oct., 1812.

*Surgeon's Mates.*

John McCall, 15 April, 1812.
David March, 1 April, 1813.

### FOURTEENTH INFANTRY.

*Colonel.*

C. G. Boerstler, 20 June, 1813.

*Lieut. Colonel.*

Timothy Dix, 20 June, 1813.

*Majors.*

Samuel Lane, 3 March, 1813.
I. D. Barnard, 26 June, 1813.

*Captains.*

H. Grindage, 6 July, 1812.
T. Montgomery, 6 July, 1812.
Henry Fleming, 6 July, 1812.
Wm. McIlvain, 6 July, 1812.
K. McKenzie, 6 July, 1812.
D. Cummings, 13 March, 1813.
Thomas Karney, 13 May, 1813.
Reuben Glider, 26 June, 1813.
Jos. Marshall, 15 Aug., 1813.

*1st Lieutenants.*

J. McDonald, 6 July, 1812.
Richard Arell, 6 July, 1812.
Peter Rich, 6 July, 1812.
John Waring, 13 March, 1813.
Thomas Randall, 13 March, 1813.
John Beckett, 13 March, 1813.
Edward Wilson, 12 May, 1813.
A. Woodward, 13 May, 1813.
J. W. Thompson, 26 June, 1813.
J. B. Sparks, 15 Aug., 1813.
James Christie, 6 July, 1812.
George Murdoch, 6 July, 1812.
Wm. G. Mills, 13 March, 1813. Aid to Brig. General Winder.
James H. Gale, 13 March, 1813.
Kimmel Godwin, 13 March, 1813.

*2nd Lieutenants.*

S. F. Donalson, 13 March, 1813. Paymaster.
R. Bennett, 12 May, 1813.
N. N. Robinson, 12 May, 1813.
W. G. Sanders, 13 May, 1813.
John Lynch, 15 Aug., 1813. Adjutant.

*3rd Lieutenants.*

Abraham Clark, 13 March, 1813.
Thomas Barton, 13 March, 1813.
Robert Beall, 30 April, 1813.
J. H. Falconar, 4 May, 1813.
C. Comegys, Jr., 10 May, 1813.
B. Ricketts, 12 May, 1813.
Masson Mudd, 12 May 1813.
W. Thompson, 12 May, 1813.
D. McCrimmin, 13 May, 1813.

*Ensigns.*

W. G. Shade, 18 March, 1813.
John A. Dix, 10 May, 1813.
Henry Parker, 12 May, 1813. Quartermaster.
T. Davidge, 12 May, 1813.
Jesse Keen, 19 July, 1813.
Asa Partridge, 24 Sept., 1813.

*Surgeon.*

John Young, 4 June, 1812.

*Surgeon's Mates.*

S. W. Magruder, 28 March, 1813.
R. C. Downes, 12 May, 1813.

---

### FIFTEENTH INFANTRY.

*Colonel.*

D. Brearley, 12 March, 1813.

*Lieut. Colonel.*

Robert Carr, 15 Aug., 1813.

*Majors.*

E. L. Whitlock, 6 July, 1812.
William King, 3 March, 1813. Adjutant General.

*Captains.*

Z. Rossell, 6 July, 1812.
C. W. Hunter, 6 July, 1812. Brigade Major.
White Youngs, 6 July, 1812.
H. H. VanDalsem, 6 July, 1812.
S. L. Barton, 30 July, 1812.
J. D. Hayden, 13 March, 1813.
Aaron Sutphen, 13 May, 1813.
Abm. Per Lee, 13 May, 1813.
Jacob D. Howell, 15 Aug., 1813.
G. McGlassin, 15 Aug., 1813.

*1st Lieutenants.*

Wm. Barnett, 6 July, 1812.
James Piatt, 6 July, 1812.
J. Schofield, 6 July, 1812.
S. L. Howell, 15 Sept., 1813. Brigade Major.
S. McDougall, 30 Sept., 1813.
David Riddle, 13 March, 1813.
A. Godwin, Jr., 13 May, 1813.
David Curtis, 13 May, 1813.
C. Stewart, 15 Aug., 1813.
John Scott, 15 Aug., 1813.

*2nd Lieutenants.*

D. Fraser, 13 March, 1813. Assistant Deputy Paymaster General.
J. Dickerson, 13 March, 1813.
William Coffie, 13 March, 1813. Quartermaster.
C. Noyes, 13 May, 1813.
H. K. Mullin, 13 May, 1813. Adjutant.
J. T. David, 12 May, 1813. Paymaster.
C. H. Roberts, 13 May, 1813.
D. E. Burch, 15 Aug., 1813.
John Rose, 15 Aug., 1813.

*3rd Lieutenants.*

Levi Heath, 1 Aug., 1813.
Wm. B. Howell, 1 Aug., 1813.
Floreat Meline, 1 Oct., 1813.

*Ensigns.*

J. C. Dehart, 9 Sept., 1813.
Ch. W. Lee, 30 Sept., 1813.

*Surgeon.*

Fenn Deming, 14 April, 1812.

*Surgeon's Mate.*

R. T. Baker, 12 March, 1812.

---

### SIXTEENTH INFANTRY.

*Colonel.*

C. Pearce, 6 July, 1812.

*Lieut. Colonel.*

R. Dennis, 6 July, 1812.

*Majors.*

W. Lee, 3 March, 1813. Deputy Paymaster General.
Robert Gray, 15 Aug., 1813.

*Captains.*

G. G. Steele, 6 July, 1812.
A. McEwen, 6 July, 1812.
J. F. McElroy, 6 July, 1812.
W. Davenport, 28 Sept., 1812.
J. Machesney, 13 March, 1813.

M. Greenwood, 16 April, 1813.
John Baldy, 16 April, 1813.
J. W. Aitken, 15 Aug., 1813. Late Paymaster.
F. D. Cummins, 15 Aug., 1813. Late Adjutant.
J. D. Coon, 15 Aug., 1813.

*1st Lieutenants.*

N. McLaughlin, 16 April, 1813.
Thomas Horrell, 16 April, 1813.
T. M. Powers, 16 April, 1813.
Isaac Finch, 15 Aug., 1813.
John Rahm, 15 Aug., 1813. Quartermaster.
Jacob Whisler, 15 Aug., 1813.
Thomas Mahon, 15 Aug., 1813.
Samuel Weigly, 15 Aug., 1813.
Thomas Evans, 15 Aug., 1813.
E. Olmstead, 30 Sept., 1813.

*2nd Lieutenants.*

Charles Fisler, 16 May, 1813.
T. P. McMahon, 19 May, 1813.
Wm. Downey, 15 Aug., 1813.
S. Nicholson, 15 Aug., 1813.
S. Roberts, 15 Aug., 1813.
Thomas Lyon, 15 Aug., 1813.

*3rd Lieutenants.*

Thos. Findley, 15 Aug., 1813.
John Williams, 15 Aug., 1813.

*Ensigns.*

George Bryan, 1 Aug., 1813.
Samuel Ladd, 1 Aug., 1813.
Hector Burns, 1 Aug., 1813.
Thos. Martin, 1 Aug., 1813.
L. Diffenbuch, 14 Aug., 1813.
Nathan Young, 19 Aug., 1813.

*Surgeon.*

S. Gilliland, 15 May, 1812.

*Surgeon's Mate.*

G. Baylies, 2 Dec., 1812.

---

SEVENTEENTH INFANTRY.

*Colonel.*

Samuel Wells, 6 July, 1812.

*Lieut. Colonel.*

Wm. M'Millan, 6 July, 1812.

*Majors.*

George Croghan, 30 March, 1813. Lieut. Colonel brevet, 2 Aug., 1813.
Richard Graham, 30 March, 1813.

*Captains.*

Wm. Bradford, 6 July, 1812.
Charles Quiray, 6 July, 1812.
R. Hightower, 6 July, 1812.
David Holt, 6 July, 1812.
James Hunter, 6 July, 1812.
Wm. J. Adair, 6 July, 1812.
James Duncan, Jr., 6 July, 1812.
C. H. Holder, 29 March, 1813.
B. W. Sanders, 16 April, 1813.
M. L. Hawkins, 16 April, 1813.

*1st Lieutenants.*

Benj. Johnson, 6 July, 1812.
Alex. Robertson, 6 July, 1812.
H. Crittenden, 6 July, 1812.
M. W. Fisher, 6 July, 1812.
J. Hackley, Jr., 13 March, 1813.
A. Garrett, 13 March, 1813. Paymaster.
T. Mountjoy, 13 March, 1813.
C. A. Baylar, 16 April, 1813.
Parry Hawkins, 16 April, 1813.
Philip King, 15 Aug., 1813.

*2nd Lieutenants.*

Ed. Ship, Jr., 13 March, 1813.
James Munday, 13 March, 1813.
Joseph Duncan, 13 March, 1813.
Chesteen Scott, 30 March, 1813.
Taylor Berry, 30 March, 1813. Deputy Quartermaster General.
Thos. Hawkins, 16 April, 1813.
James Gray, 16 April, 1813.
Wm. Baylor, 15 Aug., 1813.
T. Buckley, 15 Aug., 1813.
Sam. S. Berry, 15 Aug., 1813.

*3rd Lieutenants.*

John Hamilton, 6 April, 1813.
G. J. Floyd, 6 April, 1813.
S. H. Craig, 12 April, 1813.
Reuben Taylor, 12 April, 1813.
T. S. Morgan, 12 April, 1813.
Wm. Hughes, 13 May, 1813.
Wm. Eubank, 15 Aug., 1813.
John Taylor, 15 Aug., 1813.

*Ensigns.*

G. M. Beall, 6 April, 1813.
Jas. Maxwell, 11 June, 1813.
R. W. Ewing, 16 June, 1813.
J. Mershon, 18 June, 1813.
Richard Doyle, 2 July, 1813.
Ander. Evans, 1 Aug., 1813.

*Surgeon.*

Wm. Turner, 7 April, 1813.

*Surgeon's Mate.*

W. S. Madison, 2 Dec., 1812.
J. M. Talbot, 13 March, 1813.

---

EIGHTEENTH INFANTRY.

*Colonel.*

Wm. Drayton, 6 July, 1812.

*Lieut. Colonel.*

Benajah White, 6 July, 1812.

*Majors.*

Wm. Strother, 6 July, 1812.
M. J. Kenan, 26 June, 1813.

*Captains.*

J. G. Blount, Jr., 6 July, 1812.
George Butler, 6 July, 1812.
Wm. Taylor, 6 July, 1812.
Edward King, 6 July, 1812.
H. P. Taylor, 6 July, 1812.
Owen Clinton, 6 July, 1812.
T. I. Robison, 6 July, 1812.
Jas. Hamilton, 13 March, 1813.
M. G. Waage, 26 June, 1813.

*1st Lieutenants.*

W. A. Blount, 6 July, 1812.
B. T Elmore, 6 July, 1812.
Elias D. Dick, 6 July, 1812.
J. W. Farrow, 6 July, 1812. Paymaster
Alexander King, 6 July, 1812.
Wm. Tisdale, 6 July, 1812.
Thos. Reynolds, 13 March, 1813. Quartermaster.
T. C. Wilhight, 26 June, 1813.
E. S. Hawkins, 30 June, 1813.

*2nd Lieutenants.*

W. N. Miller, 6 July, 1812.
R. Mebane, Jr., 6 July, 1812.
John Watkins, 6 July, 1812.

H. Brown, 6 July, 1812.
R. Thurston, 6 July, 1812.
John Street, 6 July, 1812.
Alex. Pagan, 13 March, 1813.
John Peebles, 13 March, 1813.
W. D. Freeman, 30 June, 1813.

*3rd Lieutenants.*

Horatio Dade, 13 March, 1813.
Fred'k Kinloch, 13 March, 1813.
S. W. Smith, 16 June, 1813.
John S. Todd, 22 July, 1813.

*Ensigns.*

W. Whattey, 29 June, 1813.
George Bruton, 29 June, 1813.
J. W. Allston, 29 June, 1813.
George Taylor, 6 Aug., 1813.
A. B. Addison, 11 Oct., 1813.

*Surgeon's Mates.*

Wm. M'Caw, 1 May, 1812.
James B. Hill, 6 July, 1812.

---

NINETEENTH INFANTRY.

*Colonel.*

John Miller, 6 July, 1812.

*Lieut. Colonel.*

J. B. Campbell, 6 July, 1812. Colonel brevet, 18 Dec., 1812.

*Majors.*

George Todd, 6 July, 1812.
Thos. S. Jessop, 6 April, 1813.

*Captains.*

A. Edwards, 6 July, 1812.
H. H. Hickman, 6 July, 1812.
Wilson Elliott, 6 July, 1812.
James Herron, 6 July, 1812.
John T. Chunn, 6 July, 1812.
Hugh Moore, 6 July, 1812.
Asahel Nearing, 6 July, 1812.
John Anderson, 16 March, 1813. Topographical Engineer.
David Gwyne, 30 March, 1813.
G. W. Jackson, 15 Aug., 1813.

*1st Lieutenants.*

Samuel Booker, 6 July, 1812.
Stephen Lee, 6 July, 1812.
John Hazelton, 6 July, 1812.
James Campbell, 6 July, 1812.
James Morrow, 6 July, 1812.
J. D. Fleming, 6 July, 1812.
Philip P. Price, 30 March, 1813.
Jonathan Rees, 30 March, 1813.
H. Frederick, 15 Aug., 1813.
Battle Harrison, 15 Aug., 1813.

*2nd Lieutenants.*

C. Mitchell, 30 March, 1813.
J. Whistler, Jr., 30 March, 1813.
E. T. Langham, 6 April, 1813.
Geo. Atchison, 6 April, 1813.
A. E. Hoffman, 6 April, 1813.
W. Blanchard, 6 April, 1813.
George W. Stall, 6 April, 1813.
Asher Phillips, 20 May, 1813.
John Milligan, 15 Aug., 1813.
John Stockton, 15 Aug., 1813.

*3rd Lieutenants.*

Jacob Anderson, 6 April, 1813.
Mason Seward, 6 April, 1813.
Robert Carr, 6 April, 1813.
D. L. Carney, 6 April, 1813.
Wm. Leavitt, 6 April, 1813.
A. C. Looker, 15 Aug., 1813.

*Ensigns.*

John Cochran, 6 July, 1812.
E. B. Baskerville, 6 July, 1812.
Hugh May, 6 July, 1812.
John Simmons, 19 July, 1813.
C. Niswanger, 19 July, 1813.
T. R. M'Night, 19 July, 1813.
John Jolly, 19 July, 1813.
D. E. Jackson, 29 July, 1813.

*Surgeon.*

Levi Rogers, 28 Jan., 1813.

*Surgeon's Mates.*

Charles Marvin, 12 March, 1812.
Daniel Turney, 31 Dec., 1812.

---

TWENTIETH INFANTRY.

*Colonel.*

T. M. Randolph, 3 March, 1813.

*Lieut. Colonel.*

D. Campbell, 12 March, 1813.

*Majors.*

John Stanard, 3 March, 1813.
Lewis L. Taylor, 3 March, 1813.

*Captains.*

Richard Pollard, 6 July, 1812.
W. S. Jett, Jr., 6 July, 1812.
J. A. Thornton, 6 July, 1812.
J. Macrae, Jr., 6 July, 1812.
Byrd C. Willis, 6 July, 1812.
W. A. Shelton, 5 April, 1813.
T. B. Randolph, 5 April, 1813.
Charles Gee, 16 April, 1813.
Bernard Peyton, 16 April, 1813.

*1st Lieutenants.*

Micajah Lynch, 6 July, 1812.
John P. Duval, 6 July, 1812.
M. M. Payne, 6 July, 1812.
W. G. Hayes, 6 July, 1812.
R. Crawford, 6 July, 1812.
Clement White, 6 July, 1812.
Thomas Harris, 6 July, 1812.
Benjamin Smith, 5 April, 1813.
Thomas Howson, 16 April, 1813.
Thos Munroe, 16 April, 1813.

*2nd Lieutenants.*

Thomas Blackwell, 6 July, 1812.
John Archer, 6 July, 1812. Paymaster.
J. H. Howard, 6 July, 1812.
George Evans, Jr., 6 July, 1812.
William Ligon, 6 July, 1812.
John B. Hogan, 16 April, 1813.
W. F. Pendleton, 16 April, 1813.
J. M. Glassell, 16 April, 1813.
E. B. Randolph, 14 Aug., 1813.
Daniel Booker, 15 Aug., 1813.

*3rd Lieutenants.*

John Wiley, Jr., 30 March, 1813.
John Hill, 30 March, 1813.
H. Saunders, Jr., 4 April, 1813.
Jacob Koontz, 12 April, 1813.
Thomas Rawlins, 16 April, 1813.
Frs. Callaway, 16 April, 1813.
Jos. Barnett, 16 April, 1813.
Samuel Harris, 14 Aug., 1813.
W. H. Godwin, 14 Aug., 1813.
G. M'Laughlin, 15 Aug., 1813. Quartermaster.

*Ensigns.*

J. Pettipool, 6 July, 1812.
Dabney Morris, 3 May, 1813.
H. Lewis, 2 July, 1813.

James Fuller, 2 July, 1813.
John Baker, 29 July, 1813.
Robert Carter, 1 Aug., 1813.
Joseph B. Scott, 1 Aug., 1813.

*Surgeon.*

M. C. Buck, 2 July, 1813.

---

TWENTY-FIRST INFANTRY.

*Colonel.*

El. W. Ripley, 12 March, 1813.

*Lieut. Colonel.*

Timothy Upham, 12 March, 1813.

*Majors.*

John Johnson, 26 June, 1813. Assistant Adjutant General.
Joseph Grafton, 26 June, 1813.

*Captains.*

Josiah H. Vose, 6 July, 1812.
Chas. E. Tobey, 6 July, 1812.
Joseph Treat, 6 July, 1812.
Charles Proctor, 6 July, 1812.
Jer. Chapman, 6 July, 1812.
Benjamin Ropes, 6 July, 1812.
Lem. Bradford, 6 July, 1812.
S. Burbank, 13 March, 1813.
M. Marston. 26 June, 1813.
J. Eastman, Jr., 30 June, 1813.

*1st Lieutenants.*

Dan. Henderson, 6 July, 1812.
Perez Loring, 13 March, 1813.
Azor Orne, 13 March, 1813. Adjutant.
Peter Pelham, 16 April, 1813.
Henry Bender, 13 May, 1813.
J. Bartlett, 26 June, 1813.
Ira Drew, 14 Aug., 1813.

*2nd Lieutenants.*

Wm. Bowman, 6 July, 1812.
John Downer, 6 July, 1812.
James Pratt. 13 March, 1813.
Nathl. N. Hall, 13 March, 1813.
A. Bigelow, 16 April, 1813. Quartermaster.
Joseph Cilley, 13 May, 1813.
N. Blassdell, 15 Aug., 1813.
Edward Hall, 15 Aug., 1813.

*3rd Lieutenants.*

Brackett Paine, 15 Aug., 1813.
Daniel Rose, 15 Aug., 1813. Assistant Topographical Engineer.

*Ensigns.*

H. C. Babcock, 1 Aug., 1813.
J. W. Holding, 5 Aug., 1813.
Benj. Jackson, 5 Aug., 1813.
Francis Larned, 1 Oct., 1813.
Nich. Tilman, 1 Oct., 1813.
Brad. Farnum, 17 Oct., 1813.

*Surgeon.*

A. Trowbridge, 1 Aug., 1813.

*Surgeon's Mates.*

Josiah Everett, 21 July, 1813.
Elisha Allen, 21 July, 1813.

---

TWENTY-SECOND INFANTRY.

*Colonel.*

Hugh Brady, 6 July, 1812.

*Lieut. Colonel.*

George M'Feely, 6 July, 1812.

*Majors.*

Robert Lucas, 3 March, 1813.
Ralph Marlin, 3 March, 1813.

*Captains.*

Sampson S. King, 6 July, 1812.
Jacob Carmack, 6 July, 1812.
John Pentland, 6 July, 1812.
John Foster, 6 July, 1812.
Silas Amberson, 6 July, 1812.
David Espy, 16 April, 1813.
Jos. Henderson, 16 April, 1813.
Th. Lawrence, 20 June, 1813.
Willis Foulk, 20 June, 1813.

*1st Lieutenants.*

John Larken, 6 July, 1812.
Thos. Y. Sprogell, 6 July, 1812.
James Huston, 6 July, 1812.
Wm. Morrow, 6 July, 1812.
John Greene, 13 March, 1813. Adjutant.
S. A. Rippey, 16 April, 1813.
G. W. Ferguson, 16 April, 1813.
Wm. Sturgis, 20 June, 1813.
D. Coryn, 20 June, 1813.
James M'Ghee, 20 June, 1813.

*2nd Lieutenants.*

Jacob Fetter, 6 July, 1812.
J. Culbertson, 13 March, 1813.
John D. Kehr, 13 March, 1813. Quartermaster.
Robert Dunn, 16 April, 1813. Assistant Adjutant General.
Gideon Low, 16 April, 1813.
Thos. Wright, 16 April, 1813. Paymaster.
Robert R. Hall, 20 June, 1813.
John R. Guy, 20 June, 1813.
John Armstrong, 20 June, 1813.
John Fee, 26 June, 1813.

*3rd Lieutenants.*

James M'Kenney, 13 March, 1813.
Wm. Gillaspie, 13 March, 1813.
Peleg Slocum, 16 June, 1813.
O. Martine, 26 June, 1813.
R. M. Davidson, 26 June, 1813.
Samuel Brady, 26 June, 1813.
John Arrison, 26 June, 1813.
J. H. Vanderslice, 19 July, 1813.
G. S. Wilkins, 29 July, 1813.

*Ensigns.*

James Stewart, 19 July, 1813.
Joseph Stahle, 29 July, 1813.
John Clark, 29 July, 1813.
Geo. F. Semple, 1 Aug., 1813.
John Semple, 4 Aug., 1813.
Robert Beans, 14 Aug., 1813.
Fred. Hennings, 1 Oct., 1813.

*Surgeon.*

Wm. N. Mercer, 7 Aug., 1813.

*Surgeon's Mates.*

P. H. Craig, 6 July, 1812.
Jesse Magaw, 6 July, 1812.

---

TWENTY-THIRD INFANTRY.

*Colonel.*

Jas. P. Preston, 15 Aug., 1813.

*Lieut. Colonel.*

Jas. R. Mullany, 3 March, 1813.

*Majors.*

H. B. Armstrong, 12 April, 1813.
D. M'Farland, 15 Aug., 1813.

*Captains.*

Peter Mills, 6 July, 1812.
Derick VanVeghten, 6 July, 1812.
David Scott, 6 July, 1812.
Thomas Delano, 6 July, 1812.
H. G. Armstrong, 25 Sept., 1812.
L. B. Canfield, 25 Sept., 1812.
Isaac Roach, Jr., 13 April, 1813.
S. D. Wattles, 20 June, 1813.
A. W. Odell, 20 June, 1813.
E. F. Gilbert, 20 June, 1813.

*1st Lieutenants.*

John M'Cartey, 6 July, 1812.
R. Goodell, 6 July, 1812.
Wm. Clarke, 6 July, 1812.
R. H Mooers, 6 July, 1812.
John M. Lowe, 17 March, 1813.
W. J. Worth, 19 March, 1813. Aid to Maj. General Lewis.
H. Whiting, 20 June, 1813.
P. L. Hogeboom, 20 June, 1813. Paymaster.
Fred. Brown, 20 June, 1813.
Abijah. Bennet, 20 June, 1813.

*2nd Lieutenants.*

Rod. Simons, 6 July, 1812.
J. P. Livingston, 25 Sept., 1812.
Levi. S. Burr, 18 March, 1813.
J. M'Aulay, Jr., 16 April, 1813.
Jus. Ingersoll, 20 June, 1813. Quartermaster.
Samuel Tappan, 20 June, 1813.
Alph. Wetmore, 26 June, 1813.

*3rd Lieutenants.*

W. G. Belknap, 5 April, 1813.
S. B. Griswold, 5 April, 1813.
Zadoc P. Morse, 16 April, 1813.
John Jones, 16 April, 1813.
Rd. C. Smyth, 3 May, 1813.
James S. Abeel, 3 May, 1813.
Abm. Cantine, 10 May, 1813.
J. P. Dieterich, 10 May, 1813.
Rd. Phillips, 13 May, 1813.
Samuel R. Hill, 21 June, 1813.

*Ensigns.*

Ezra King, 6 July, 1812.
J. Cauldwell, Jr., 7 April, 1813.
John B. Truax, 4 May, 1813.
Francis Blaize, 12 May, 1813.
Dudley Lamb, 4 Oct., 1813.

*Surgeon.*

Silas Fuller, 6 July, 1812.

*Surgeon's Mates.*

John Gale, 9 July, 1812.
Henry White, 28 July, 1813.

---

TWENTY-FOURTH INFANTRY.

*Colonel.*

W. P. Anderson, 6 July, 1812.

*Lieut. Colonel.*

Joseph L. Smith, 12 March, 1813.

*Majors.*

F. Armstrong, 26 June, 1813.
Robert Butler, 15 Aug., 1813.

*Captains.*

Aw. H. Holmes, 6 July, 1812.
Alexander Gray, 6 July, 1812.
John A. Rodgers, 6 July, 1812.
Wm. O. Allen, 6 July, 1812.
Robert Desha, 6 July, 1812.
J. H. Campbell, 6 July, 1812.
Minor Sturges, 13 May, 1813.
Frank Hompton, 26 June, 1813.
W. O. Winston, 15 Aug., 1813.
W. Wilkinson, 15 Aug., 1813.

*1st Lieutenants.*

Silas Stevens, 6 July, 1812.
James Stuart, 6 July, 1812.
Samuel Scott, 13 March, 1813. Paymaster.
Joseph Anthony, 26 June, 1813.
Rt. Buntin, Jr., 26 June, 1813.
Tal. Richards, 15 Aug., 1813.
Uriah Allison, 15 Aug., 1813.
Caleb G. Fobes, 15 Aug., 1813.
John O. Fallon, 15 Aug., 1813. Aid to Major General Harrison.
Joseph Perkins, 15 Aug., 1813.

*2nd Lieutenants.*

Abner Hynes, 20 April, 1813.
T. P. Favrot, 26 June, 1813.
Adam Peck, Jr., 26 June, 1813.
Litt. Johnston, 26 June, 1813.
Sam'l T. Balch, 14 Aug., 1813.
John Butler, 14 Aug., 1813.
Jos. A. Martin, 14 Aug., 1813.
W. M. Crawford, 15 Aug., 1813.
Daniel Green, 15 Aug., 1813.
J. S. Williamson, 15 Aug., 1813.

*3rd Lieutenants.*

Francis Valle, 13 May, 1813.
John Gilbreath, 13 May, 1813.
Rd. M. Woods, 13 May, 1813.
F. Bairidge, 13 May, 1813.
Wm. Martin, 9 Aug., 1813.
W. G. Childress, 15 Aug., 1813.
Lewis M. Ayer, 15 Aug., 1813.
Hezk. Jackson, 15 Aug., 1813.

*Ensigns.*

Robert Renfroe, 9 Aug., 1813.
Alex. Hamilton, 9 Aug., 1813.
H. M'Combs, 9 Aug., 1813.
W. K. Pauling, 9 Aug., 1813.
Wm. Johnson, 9 Aug., 1813.
Abm. Fine, 1 Oct., 1813.

*Surgeon.*

Henry Skinner, 5 April, 1813.

*Surgeon's Mates.*

C. Humphries, 25 April, 1812.
Harry Bradford, 9 Aug., 1813.

---

TWENTY-FIFTH INFANTRY.

*Colonel.*

E. P. Gaines, 12 March, 1813. Adjutant General.

*Lieut. Colonel.*

Jonas Cutting, 6 July, 1812.

*Majors.*

C. K. Gardner, 26 June, 1813. Assistant Adjutant General.
William Battey, 15 Aug., 1813.

*Captains.*

George Howard, 6 July, 1812.
Peter Bradley, 6 July, 1812.
Joseph Kinney, 13 March, 1813.
T. M. Read, 16 April, 1813. Late Quartermaster.
J. B. Murdoch, 16 April, 1813.
Henry Dyer, 20 June, 1813.
Minor Robbins, 26 June, 1813.
J. A. Thomas, 15 Aug., 1813.
Benj. Watson, 15 Aug., 1813.
D. Ketchum, 30 Sept., 1813.

*1st Lieutenants.*

J. Burbidge, 13 March, 1813.
Edward White, 16 April, 1813.
Daniel Forward, 16 April, 1813.
Arch. C. Crary, 16 April, 1813.
T. S. Seymour, 20 June. 1813.
Jesse Beach. 26 June, 1813.
E. Shaylor, 15 Aug., 1813.
Alex. T. F. Bill, 15 Aug., 1813.
John G. Munn, 15 Aug., 1813.
George M'Chain, 30 Sept., 1813. Quartermaster.

*2nd Lieutenants.*

J. Hutchinson, 13 May, 1813.
G. Talcott, Jr., 10 July, 1813. Deputy Commissary Ordnance.
Russell Eddy, 13 July, 1813. Paymaster.
Clark Robbins, 13 July, 1813.
John Gifford, 13 July, 1813.
J. D. Brown, 15 Aug., 1813.
S. H. Devotion, 28 Sept., 1813.

*3rd Lieutenant.*

Henry De Witt, 17 Oct., 1813.

*Surgeon.*

Giles Gridley, 9 April, 1812.

*Surgeon's Mates.*

P. Woodbury, 6 July, 1812.
J. L. Comstock, 2 Dec., 1812.

---

RIFLE REGIMENT.

*Colonel.*

T. A. Smith, 6 July, 1812.

*Lieut. Colonel.*

G. W. Sevier, 6 July, 1812.

*Majors.*

J. M'Donald, 1 Aug., 1812.
Benj. Forsyth, 20 Jan., 1813.

*Captains.*

H. R. Graham, 8 March, 1809.
A. A. Massias, 1 July, 1809.
F. Ridgeway, 31 July, 1810.
Michael C. Hays, 1 June, 1811.
L. Morgan, 1 July, 1811.
Daniel Appling, 1 April, 1812.
Josh. Hamilton. 6 July, 1812.
T. A. Patterson, 1 Aug., 1812.
T. Ramsay, 30 Nov., 1812.
Wm. Smith, 20 Jan., 1813.

*1st Lieutenants.*

Elias Stallings, 16 March, 1811.
L. G. A. Armistead, 10 Feb., 1812.
W. E. Morris, 30 April, 1812. Aid to Major General Pinckney.
John Findley, 30 April, 1812.
H. V. Swearingen, 6 July, 1812.
E. Wadsworth, 1 Aug., 1812.
Wm. Townly, 1 Aug., 1812.
W. C. Beard, 27 Sept., 1812.
James Ryan, 30 Nov., 1812.
George Gray, 20 Jan., 1813. Quartermaster.

*2nd Lieutenants.*

Harvey Murray, 17 Oct., 1812.
J. S. M'Intosh, 13 Nov., 1812.
J. Calhoun, Jr., 2 Dec., 1812.
Hyem Cohen, 2 Dec., 1812.
Wm. Arnold, 3 Dec., 1812.
John M'Intire, 3 Dec., 1812.
J. Shortridge, 3 Dec., 1812.
John Hanson, 4 Dec., 1812.
John Harlee, 20 Jan., 1813.
Josiah Hill, 20 Jan., 1813.

*3rd Lieutenants.*

S. V. Hamilton, 12 March, 1813.
R. M'Farland, 12 March, 1813.
Jacob Tipton, 12 March, 1813.
W. Armstrong, 12 March, 1813.
Bennet Riley, 12 March, 1813.
L. Norton, 12 March, 1813.
J. S. Gray, 20 May, 1813.
Andrew Lindsay, 29 June, 1813.

*Ensigns.*

T. F. Smith, 2 July, 1813.
Samuel Cobbs, 2 July, 1813.
G. Davidson, 2 July, 1813.
F. Howard, 19 July, 1813.
J. H. Stannon, 29 July, 1813.
Peter Albright, 1 Aug., 1813.
Edward Drake, 7 Aug., 1813.

*Surgeon.*

W. W. Hall, 24 March, 1812.

*Surgeon's Mates.*

S. Gantt, 2 July, 1813.

---

LINEAL RANK.

MAJOR GENERALS.

Henry Dearborn, 27 Jan., 1812.
Thomas Pinckney, 27 March, 1812.
James Wilkinson, 2 March, 1813.
Wade Hampton, 2 March, 1813.
Morgan Lewis, 2 March, 1813.
Wm. H. Harrison, 2 March, 1813.

BRIGADIER GENERALS.

Joseph Bloomfield, 27 March, 1812.
James Winchester, 27 March, 1812.
William Hull, 8 April, 1812.
Thomas Flournoy, 18 June, 1812.
T. H. Cushing, 2 July, 1812.
John Chandler, 8 July, 1812.
John P. Boyd, 26 Aug., 1812.
Thomas Parker, 12 March. 1813.
George Izard, 12 March, 1813.
W. H. Winder. 12 March. 1813.
D. M'Arthur, 12 March, 1813.
Lewis Cass. 12 March, 1813.
Benjamin Howard, 12 March, 1813.
D. R. Williams. 9 July, 1813.
Jacob Brown, 19 July, 1813.
L. Covington, 1 Aug., 1813.

COLONELS.

1 *April,* 1802.

H. Burbeck, 1st Artillery. Brig. Gen. Bvt.

3 *May,* 1808.

Wm. Russell, 7th Infantry.

8 *July,* 1808.

Jonas Simonds, 6th Infantry.

18 *August,* 1808.

J. Kingsbury, 1st Infantry. In staff.

12 *March,* 1812.

M. Porter, Light Artillery. Brig. Gen. Bvt.

6 *July,* 1812.

Richard Sparks, 2nd Infantry.
Alexander Macomb, 3rd Artillery.
Thomas A. Smith, Rifle.
P. P. Schuyler, 13th Infantry. Staff.
Simon Larned, 9th Infantry.
James Burn, 2nd Light Dragoons.
Isaac Clark, 11th Infantry.
Hugh Brady, 22nd Infantry.
Wm. P. Anderson, 24th Infantry.

Cromwell Pearce, 16th Infantry.
Patrick Jack, 8th Infantry.
Samuel Wells, 17th Infantry.
John Miller, 19th Infantry.
William Drayton, 18th Infantry.
James Welbourn, 10th Infantry.

31 *July*, 1812.

Joseph G. Swift, Engineer.

15 *August*, 1812.

Daniel Bissell, 5th Infantry.

26 *August*, 1812.

Robert Purdy, 4th Infantry.

3 *March*, 1813.

T. M. Randolph, 20th Infantry.

12 *March*, 1813.

Edmund P Gaines, 25th Infantry. Adjutant General.
Winfield Scott, 2nd Artillery.
David Brearly, 15th Infantry.
Isaac A. Coles, 12th Infantry.
Elea. W. Ripley, 21st Infantry.
L. Laval, 1st Light Dragoons.

20 *June*, 1813.

Charles G. Boerstler, 14th Infantry.

15 *August*, 1813.

Homer V. Milton, 3rd Infantry.
James P. Preston, 23rd Infantry.

LIEUTENANT COLONELS.

1 *April*, 1802.

C. Freeman, 1st Artillery. Colonel Bvt.

30 *November*, 1810.

J. Miller, 6th Infantry. Colonel Bvt.

6 *June*, 1811.

Gilbert C. Russell, 3rd Infantry.

2 *December*, 1811.

J. R. Fenwick, Light Artillery. Colonel, staff.

6 *July*, 1812.

John Bowyer, 2nd Infantry.
John Darrington, 4th Infantry.
George W. Sevier, Rifle.
A. T. Macneill, 2nd Light Dragoons.
William M'Millan, 17th Infantry.
J. B. Campbell, 19th Infantry. Colonel Bvt.
Benaja White, 18th Infantry.
Jonas Cutting, 25th Infantry.
George M'Feely, 22nd Infantry.
Richard Dennis, 16th Infantry.
Moody Bedel, 11th Infantry.
Andrew Pickens, 10th Infantry.

31 *July*, 1812.

W. K. Armistead. Engineer.

15 *August*, 1812.

Robert C. Nicholas, 1st Infantry.

3 *March*, 1813.

Geo. E. Mitchell, 3rd Artillery.
James R. Mullany, 23rd Infantry.
James House, 3rd Artillery.
F. K. Huger, 2nd Artillery. Colonel, staff.

12 *March*, 1813.

Samuel S. Conner, 13th Infantry.
Timothy Upham, 21st Infantry.
Thomas Aspinwall, 9th Infantry.
Joseph L. Smith, 24th Infantry.
David Campbell, 20th Infantry.
William Lindsay, 2nd Artillery.

30 *April*, 1813.

Thornton Posey, 7th Infantry.

20 *June*, 1813.

Timothy Dix, 14th Infantry.
N. Luckett, 1st Light Dragoons.

15 *August*, 1813.

George Gibson, 5th Infantry.
Robert Carr, 15th Infantry.
Thomas Taylor, 12th Infantry.
Lawrence Manning, 8th Infantry.

MAJORS.

21 *March*, 1800.

Z. Pike, 1st Infantry. Lieut. Col. Bvt.

31 *July*, 1800.

W. M'Rea, 1st Artillery. Lieut. Col. Bvt.

1 *December*, 1804.

A. Y. Nicoll, 1st Artillery. Colonel, staff.

15 *March*, 1810.

A. Eustis, Light Artillery. Lieut. Col. Bvt.

6 *July*, 1812.

W. R. Boote, 2nd Infantry. Colonel, staff.
John Campbell, 6th Infantry.
George Bomford, Engineer.
Eph. L. Whitlock, 15th Infantry.
John T. Woodford, 2nd Light Dragoons.
Samuel Nye, 3rd Artillery.
William Strother, 18th Infantry.
Daniel M. Forney, 2nd Artillery.
John V. H. Huyck, 13th Infantry.
George Todd, 19th Infantry.

31 *July*, 1812.

William M'Ree, Engineer.

1 *August*, 1812.

James M'Donald, Rifle.

15 *August*, 1812.

Matthew Arbuckle, 3rd Infantry.

26 *August*, 1812.

Nathan Heald, 4th Infantry.

16 *September*, 1812.

J. V. Ball, 2nd Light Dragoons. Lieut. Col. Bvt.

20 *January*, 1813.

Eli B. Clemson, 1st Infantry.
W. Swan, 2nd Infantry. Colonel, staff.
Ninian Pinkney, 5th Infantry.
William Carson, 3rd Infantry.
Horatio Stark, 6th Infantry.
Arthur Morgan, 7th Infantry.
Stephen Ranney, 4th Infantry.
Benjamin Forsyth, Rifle.
Thomas Pitts, Light Artillery.

3 *March*, 1813.

George Armistead, 3rd Artillery.
Washington Lee, 16th Infantry.
W. King, 15th Infantry. Colonel, staff.
Samuel Lane, 14th Infantry.
John Stanard, 20th Infantry.
Richard M. Malcolm, 13th Infantry.
Lewis L. Taylor, 20th Infantry.
Robert C. Nicholas, 12th Infantry.
Robert Lucas, 22nd Infantry.

Wm. S. Hamilton, 10th Infantry.
Ralph Marlin, 22nd Infantry.
Orsa C. Merrill, 11th Infantry.

25 *March*, 1813.

William Cumming, 8th Infantry.

30 *March*, 1813.

G. Croghan, 17th Infantry. Lieut. Col. Bvt.
Richard Graham, 17th Infantry.

6 *April*, 1813.

Thomas S. Jessop, 19th Infantry.

12 *April*, 1813.

H. B. Armstrong, 23rd Infantry.

30 *April*, 1813.

Benjamin Wallace, 5th Infantry.

5 *May*, 1813.

James B. Many, 1st Artillery.

7 *June*, 1813.

Thomas A. Helms, 1st Light Dragoons.

26 *June*, 1813.

J. Johnson, 21st Infantry. In staff.
Jacob Hindman, 2nd Artillery.
Charles K. Gardner, 25th Infantry.
Willo. Morgan, 12th Infantry.
Francis Armstrong, 24th Infantry.
Joseph Grafton, 21st Infantry.
Isaac D. Bernard, 14th Infantry.
Michael J. Kenan, 18th Infantry.
Chester Lyman, 9th Infantry.
A. P. Hayne, 1st Light Dragoons.

15 *August*, 1813.

J. Bankhead, 7th Infantry. Colonel, staff.
Ross Bird, 7th Infantry.
Ang. L. Langham, 10th Infantry.
Henry Leavenworth, 9th Infantry.
Daniel M'Farland, 23rd Infantry.
Robert Butler, 24th Infantry.
John M'Neal, 11th Infantry.
William Battey, 25th Infantry.
Robert Gray, 16th Infantry.
Philip Cook, 8th Infantry.

CAPTAINS.

1797.

J. Whistler, 1st Infantry. Major Bvt.

1800.

H. M'Call, 1st Infantry. Major Bvt.

1801.

L. Beall, 1st Artillery. Major Bvt.

1804.

Samuel T. Dyson, 1st Artillery.
Nathaniel Leonard, 1st Artillery.

1805.

Charles Wollstonecraft, 1st Artillery.

1806.

J. B. Walbach, 1st Artillery. Colonel, staff.

1807.

Moses Swett, 1st Artillery.

1808.

Charles Gratiot, Engineer.
William Wilson, 1st Artillery.
John Nicks, 3rd Infantry.
H. Atkinson, 3rd Infantry. Colonel, staff.
John M'Clelland, 3rd Infantry.
Colin Buckner, 5th Infantry.
Simon Owens, 1st Infantry.
John Binney, 4th Infantry.
James Woodruff, 3rd Infantry.
D. Hughes, 1st Infantry. Major, staff.

1809.

Enoch Humphreys, 1st Artillery.
E. Beebe, 6th Infantry. Major, staff.
W. Platt, 2nd Infantry. Colonel, staff.
Henry R. Graham, Rifle.
Return B. Brown, 4th Infantry.
Uriah Blue, 7th Infantry.
John Machesney, 7th Infantry.
J. Snelling, 4th Infantry. Major Bvt.
Abraham A. Massias, Rifle.
Francis Newman, 1st Artillery.
J. T. Arrowsmith, 6th Infantry.
Richard Oldham, 7th Infantry.
William Butler, 3rd Infantry.
Gad. Humphreys, 6th Infantry.

1810.

William Lawrence, 2nd Infantry.
James Doherty, 7th Infantry.
John Walworth, 6th Infantry.
Asa Morgan, 1st Light Dragoons.
George M. Brooke, 5th Infantry.
J. Gibson, Light Artillery. Colonel, staff.
Richard Whartenby, 5th Infantry.
William Campbell, Light Artillery.
Robt. H. M'Pherson, Light Artillery.
Alden Partridge, Engineer.
Fielder Ridgeway, Rifle.
Robert B. Moore, 3rd Infantry.
E. Cutler, 7th Infantry. Major, staff.
Townsend Stith, 5th Infantry.
Peter Muhlenberg, 6th Infantry.
Z. Taylor, 7th Infantry. Major Bvt.
Walter H. Overton, 7th Infantry.

1811.

J. S. Swearingen, 1st Artillery. Major, staff.
James Denking, 3rd Infantry.
Seleck Osborne, 1st Light Dragoons.
C. Nicholas, 1st Infantry. Major, staff.
William M'Clelland, 7th Infantry.
Henry B. Brevoort, 2nd Infantry.
John N. M'Intosh, Light Artillery.
Hays G. White, 3rd Infantry.
Silas Hasley, 1st Light Dragoons.
Michael C. Hays, Rifle.
Alexander A. White, 7th Infantry.
Lodowick Moragn, Rifle.
James Hanhan, 1st Artillery.
Samuel Price, Light Artillery.
Oliver G. Burton, 4th Infantry.
Alex. M'Ilhenny, 5th Infantry.
Michael Walsh, 1st Artillery.
T. Chambers, 5th Infantry. Major, staff.
Alex. Cummings, 1st Light Dragoons.
Charles Fuller, 4th Infantry.
James Dorman, 5th Infantry.
Clement Sadler, 6th Infantry.

3 *January*, 1812.

R. Sterry, 6th Infantry. Major staff.

12 *March*, 1812.

John Miller, 2nd Infantry.
Daniel Baker, 1st Infantry.
James Reed, 1st Artillery.

1 *April*, 1812.

Andrew M'Dowell, Light Artillery.
Daniel Appling, Rifle.

4 *June*, 1812.

J. E. A. Masters, 6th Infantry.

1 *July*, 1812.

E. D. Wood, Engineer. Major Bvt.

6 *July*, 1812.

Reuben Chamberlain, 2nd Infantry.
Luther Leonard, Light Artillery.
Joshua Hamilton, Rifle.
Ichabod B. Crane, 3rd Artillery.
Roger Jones, 3rd Artillery.
James N. Boyle, 3rd Artillery.
Alexander S. Brooks, 3rd Artillery.
Nathan Towson, 2nd Artillery.
Samuel B. Archer, 2nd Artillery.
William Nicholas, 2nd Artillery.
James N. Barker, 2nd Artillery.
Stephen R. Proctor, 2nd Light Dragoons.
Jacob B. I'on, 2nd Artillery.
Sanders Donoho, 2nd Artillery.
Samuel G. Hopkins, 2nd Light Dragoons.
Henry Hall, 2nd Light Dragoons.
Thomas Biddle, Sr., 2nd Artillery.
Thomas P. Moore, 12th Infantry.
Henry Grindage, 14th Infantry.
John W. Gookin, 3rd Artillery.
Richard Pollard, 20th Infantry.
Zachariah Rossell, 15th Infantry.
George Cloud, 10th Infantry.
Joseph Philips, 2nd Artillery.
Thomas M. Nelson, 10th Infantry.
Andrew H. Holmes, 24th Infantry.
John Sproull, 13th Infantry.
Josiah H. Vose, 21st Infantry.
William Bradford, 17th Infantry.
Peter Mills, 23rd Infantry.
James Gibson, 12th Infantry.
Wm. Van Deursen, 3rd Artillery.
Samuel D. Harris, 2nd Light Dragoons.
John A. Byrd, 2nd Light Dragoons.
Abraham Edwards, 19th Infantry.
Joseph Selden, 2nd Light Dragoons.
Turner Crooker, 9th Infantry.
John G. Blount, 18th Infantry.
Charles Quiray, 17th Infantry.
Jas. I. B. Romayne, 3rd Artillery.
George G. Steele, 16th Infantry.
Hugh R. Martin, 13th Infantry.
David E. Twiggs, 8th Infantry.
Richard Hightower, 17th Infantry.
Charles W. Hunter, 15th Infantry.
Sampson S. King, 22nd Infantry.
George Howard, 25th Infantry.
John W. Weeks, 11th Infantry.
George Butler, 18th Infantry.
Dk. Van Veghten, 23rd Infantry.
Charles E. Tobey, 21st Infantry.
Thos. Montgomery, 14th Infantry.
James Paxton, 12th Infantry.
Har. H. Hickman, 19th Infantry.
Hor. H. Watson, 3rd Artillery.
Joseph Treat, 21st Infantry.
Alexander Gray, 24th Infantry.
Robert Cunningham, 8th Infantry.
Philip Brittain, 10th Infantry.
Mordecai Myers, 13th Infantry.
John Ritchie, 2nd Artillery.
Hodijah Meade, 20th Infantry.
Ebenezer B. Morse, 3rd Artillery.
Jonas Holland, 2nd Light Dragoons.
Thomas Sangster, 12th Infantry.
Ar. C. Randolph, 12th Infantry.
John Goodall, 2nd Artillery.
Jacob Carmack, 22nd Infantry.
Myndert M. Dox, 13th Infantry.
William Chisholm, 8th Infantry.
Charles Proctor, 21st Infantry.
William S. Jett, Jr., 20th Infantry.
Wilson Elliott, 19th Infantry.
James M'Keon, 3rd Artillery.
White Youngs, 15th Infantry.
William M'Ilvain, 14th Infantry.
John A. Thornton, 20th Infantry.
Rufus M'Intire, 3rd Artillery.
David Holt, 17th Infantry.
John A. Rodgers, 24th Infantry.
John Butler, 2nd Light Dragoons.
John Pentland, 22nd Infantry.
Felix W. Warley, 8th Infantry.
Robert Mitchell, 10th Infantry.
Jesse Robinson, 2nd Artillery.
William Taylor, 18th Infantry.
Alexander M'Ewen, 16th Infantry.
James Herron, 19th Infantry.
Robert M. Gill, 2nd Artillery.
William Jones, 8th Infantry.
William O. Allen, 24th Infantry.
John Macrae, Jr., 20th Infantry.
Philemon Hawkins, 2nd Artillery.
Edward King, 18th Infantry.
H. H. Van Dalsem, 15th Infantry.
W. D. Lawrence, 13th Infantry.
Emanuel I. Leigh, 10th Infantry.
Jeremiah Chapman, 21st Infantry.
Daniel Cushing, 2nd Artillery.
James Hunter, 17th Infantry.
James Charlton, 12th Infantry.
John Foster, 22nd Infantry.
Benjamin S. Ogden, 3rd Artillery.
James F. M'Elroy, 16th Infantry.
Robert Desha, 24th Infantry.
John T. Chunn, 19th Infantry.
Byrd C. Willis, 20th Infantry.
Stanton Sholes, 2nd Artillery.
Henry P. Taylor, 18th Infantry.
William J. Adair, 17th Infantry.
Mark Harden, 10th Infantry.
George W. Russell, 2nd Artillery.
Charles Page, 12th Infantry.
Andrew L. Madison 12th Infantry.
Joseph Bryant, 10th Infantry.
Benj. S. Egerton, 11th Infantry.
Thomas W. Farrar, 8th Infantry.
Spotswood Henry, 2nd Artillery.
Samuel Gordon, 11th Infantry.
Hugh Moore, 19th Infantry.
Frederick Evans, 2nd Artillery.
Benjamin Ropes, 21st Infantry.
Peter Bradley, 25th Infantry.
James H. Campbell, 24th Infantry.
William M'Queen, 8th Infantry.
Josiah Woods, 10th Infantry.
Samuel Bradford, 21st Infantry.
Joseph Clay, 10th Infantry.
Asahel Nearing, 19th Infantry.
Owen Clinton, 18th Infantry.
James Duncan, 17th Infantry.
Silas Amberson, 22nd Infantry.
Matthew I. Keith, 8th Infantry.
Thomas I. Robeson, 18th Infantry.
Jesse Copeland, 10th Infantry.
Charles Crawford, 8th Infantry.
David Scott, 23rd Infantry.
Henry Fleming, 14th Infantry.
Ken. M'Kenzie, 14th Infantry.
Thomas Delano, 23rd Infantry.
Abraham F. Hull, 9th Infantry.

31 *July*, 1812.

J. G. Totten, Engineer. Major Bvt.

*August*, 1812.

Thos. A. Patterson, Rifle.
Benjamin Branch, Light Artillery.
George W. Melvin, Light Artillery.
Ambrose Whitlock, 1st Infantry.

*September*, 1812.

Charles Larrabee, 4th Infantry.
Samuel Babcock, Engineer.
Jonathan Brooks, 3rd Artillery.
H. G. Armstrong, 23rd Infantry.
Lizur B. Canfield, 23rd Infantry.
William Davenport, 16th Infantry.
Joseph L. Barton, 15th Infantry.

*October*, 1812.

Henry Philips, 6th Infantry.

*November*, 1812.

Thomas Ramsay, Rifle.

*December,* 1812.

W. M. Littlejohn, 1st Light Dragoons.
William Whistler, 1st Infantry.

*January,* 1813.

Stephen Collins, 3rd Artillery.
John C. Symmes, 1st Infantry.
Simeon Knight, 1st Infantry.
Alpha Kingsley, 1st Infantry.
Hezekiah Johnson, 1st Infantry.
John T. Pemberton, 2nd Infantry.
Ebenezer Way, 4th Infantry.
George Haig, 1st Light Dragoons.
William Smith, Rifle.
Arch. W. Thornton, Light Artillery.

*February,* 1813.

Thomas Murray, 1st Artillery.

*March,* 1813.

William Gates, 1st Artillery.
Alex. J. Williams, 2nd Artillery.
John Machesney, 16th Infantry.
James Hamilton, 18th Infantry.
David Cummings, 14th Infantry.
A. C. W. Fanning, 3rd Artillery.
John M. O'Connor, 3rd Artillery.
George H. Richards, 3rd Artillery.
Edmund Foster, 9th Infantry.
Jeremiah D. Hayden, 15th Infantry.
William S. Foster, 11th Infantry.
Joseph Kinney, 25th Infantry.
Sullivan Burbank, 21st Infantry.
J. Anderson, 19th Infantry. Major staff.
Caleb H. Holder, 17th Infantry.
Thomas Post, 12th Infantry.
David Gwynne, 19th Infantry.

*April,* 1813.

Stephen W. Kearney, 13th Infantry.
Samuel Haring, 13th Infantry.
William A. Shelton, 20th Infantry.
Thos. B. Randolph, 20th Infantry.
Narcissus Broutin, 7th Infantry.
Isaac Roach, Jr., 23rd Infantry.
David Espy, 22nd Infantry.
Jared Ingersoll, Jr., 9th Infantry.
Thomas M. Read, 25th Infantry.
Miles Greenwood, 16th Infantry.
Charles Gee, 20th Infantry.
Bernard Peyton, 20th Infantry.
Benj. W. Sanders, 17th Infantry.
John B. Murdoch, 25th Infantry.
Joseph Henderson, 22nd Infantry.
Mar. L. Hawkins, 17th Infantry.
John Baldy, 16th Infantry.
William S. Henshaw, 5th Infantry.

*May,* 1813.

Julius F. Heileman, 1st Artillery.
William F. Ware, 2nd Infantry.
John Gansevoort, 1st Artillery.
David S. Townsend, 9th Infantry.
Thomas Karney, 14th Infantry.
Minor Sturges, 24th Infantry.
Aaron Sutphen, 15th Infantry.
Abraham Per Lee, 15th Infantry.
John K. Paige, 13th Infantry.
William B. Adams, 13th Infantry.
George Bender, Jr., 9th Infantry.
John Bliss, 11th Infantry.
Hopley Yeaton, 1st Artillery.
Samuel M. Dewey, 3rd Artillery.
John M. Davis, 2nd Infantry.

*June,* 1813.

L. Hukill, 1st Light Dragoons. Major staff.
Samuel Maclay, 1st Artillery.
Simon D. Wattles, 23rd Infantry.
Azariah W. Odell 23rd Infantry.
Henry Dyer, 25th Infantry.
Thomas Lawrence, 22nd Infantry.
Leroy Opie, 2nd Artillery.
Willis Foulke, 22nd Infantry.
T. M. Randolph, Jr., 2nd Artillery.
Robert G. Hite, 12th Infantry.
Montgom. G. Waage, 18th Infantry.
Frank Hampton, 24th Infantry.
Ephraim F. Gilbert, 23rd Infantry.
Richard Baen, 11th Infantry.
Morrell Marston, 21st Infantry.
Reuben Gilder, 14th Infantry.
Minor Robins, 25h Infantry.
Val. R. Goodrich, 11th Infantry.
James F. Norris, 9th Infantry.

*July,* 1813.

Jonathan Eastman, 21st Infantry.
Jackson Durant, 4th Infantry

*August,* 1813.

Elijah Boardman, 1st Light Dragoons.
William R. Davis, 3rd Infantry.
Samuel W. Butler, 3rd Infantry.
Richard H. Bell, 5th Infantry.
John L. Eastman, 4th Infantry.
Jacob D. Howell, 15th Infantry.
Charles J. Nourse, 2nd Light Dragoons.
Sylvester Churchill, 3rd Artillery.
Benjamin Watson, 25th Infantry.
J. D. Coon, 16th Infantry.
William O. Winston, 24th Infantry.
Hughes Watson, 8th Infantry.
John Campbell, 13th Infantry.
Jonathan W. Aitkin, 16th Infantry.
George W. Jackson, 19th Infantry.
John A. Thomas, 25th Infantry.
George M'Glassin, 15th Infantry.
Walter Wilkinson, 24th Infantry.
Horace Hall, 11th Infantry.
Benjamin Sneed, 11th Infantry.
Joseph Marshall, 14th Infantry.
Thomas Harrison, 9th Infantry.
F. D. Cummins, 16th Infantry.
F. Conkling, 4th Infantry.
Daniel Ketchum, 25th Infantry.
Benjamin R. Pierce, 3rd Artillery.

---

*The following Fourteen Regiments were raised for One Year.*

TWENTY-SIXTH INFANTRY.

*Lieut. Colonel.*

T. B. Van Horn, 9 April, 1813.

*Majors.*

Jos. Jenkins, 19 Feb., 1813.
W. A. Trimble, 18 March, 1813.

*Captains.*

W. H. Puthuff, 20 May, 1813.
J. Lockhart, 20 Mai, 1813.
John Lucas, 20 May, 1813.
S. Swearingen, 20 May, 1813.
George Kisling, 20 May, 1813.
John Moore, 20 May, 1813.
Chris. Wood, 20 May, 1813.
Joel Collins, 20 May 1813.
R. C. Talbott, 20 May, 1813

*1st Lieutenants.*

Wm. Baird, 20 May, 1813.
George Will, 20 May, 1813.
C. A. Trimble, 20 May, 1813.
Chas. A. Norton, 20 May, 1813 Aid to Brig. Gen. Cass.
Wm. M'Donald, 20 May, 1813.
D. M'Farland, 20 May, 1813.
A. Delerae, 20 May, 1813.
R. Anderson, 20 May, 1813.
B. Maltbrie, 7 Aug., 1813.

*2nd Lieutenants.*

Wm. Huston, 20 May, 1813.
A. Spencer, 20 May, 1813.
John Brown, Jr., 20 May, 1813.
Clarkson Price, 20 May, 1813.
Jacob C. Leslie, 20 May, 1813.
Robt. Stockton, 20 May, 1813.
Joseph M'Lean, 20 May, 1813.
Collin M'Cloud, 20 May, 1813.
Geo. S. Bryan, 1 June, 1813.

*3rd Lieutenants.*

Robt. Nevill, 20 May, 1813.
James Abbott, 20 May, 1813.
J. Swearingen, 20 May, 1813.
John Goode, 20 May, 1813.
John C. Avery, 20 May, 1813.
John Hall, 20 May, 1813.
J. G. Talbott, 20 May, 1813.
John Elvain, 20 May, 1813.
W. M'Donald, Jr., 1 June, 1813.
John Meldrum, 7 Aug., 1813.

*Ensigns.*

Charles Cissna, 20 May, 1813.
John Noel, 20 May, 1813.
Abijah Johns, 20 May, 1813.
Robt. Young, 20 May, 1813.
Robt. Smith, 20 May, 1813.
Wm. Watson, 20 May, 1813.
Wm. Catrige, 20 May, 1813.
Leonard Cole, 7 Aug., 1813.
Thomas Shanks, 7 Aug., 1813.

*Surgeon's Mate.*

P. Sperrick, Jr., 26 April, 1813.

---

TWENTY-SEVENTH INFANTRY.

*Colonel.*

George Paull, 29 June, 1813.

*Lieut. Colonel.*

Robt. Morrison, 29 June, 1813.

*Majors.*

J. R. Munson, 18 March, 1813.
Thos. Roland, 29 June 1813.

*Captains.*

Henry Northup, 20 May, 1813.
Alex. Hill, 20 May, 1813.
Joseph Cairns, 20 May, 1813.
G. Saunderson, 20 May, 1813.
William Gill, 20 May, 1813.
John Spencer, 20 May, 1813.
Absalom Martin, 20 May, 1813.
Jas. Applegate, 20 May, 1813.
Jas. A. Harper, 20 May, 1813.
I. Van Horne, Jr., 20 May, 1813.

*1st Lieutenants.*

A. P. Pinney, 20 May, 1813.
Saml. Shannon, 20 May, 1813.
W. Warner, 20 May, 1813.
Elias Gilman, 20 May, 1813. Paymaster.
Abraham Shane, 20 May, 1813.
N. Gregory, 20 May, 1813.
E. Benedict, 20 May, 1813.
Chas. L. Cass, 20 May, 1813.
Samuel Drennan, 20 May, 1813.

*2nd Lieutenants.*

James Blair, 20 May, 1813.
J. Collins, 20 May, 1813.
John Eagan, 20 May, 1813.
Sam. Coleman, 20 May, 1813.
John Carroll, 20 May 1813.
Avory Buttles, 20 May, 1813.
John Mifford, 20 May, 1813.
T. C. Shields, 20 May, 1813.
Q. F. Atkins, 7 Aug., 1813.

*3rd Lieutenants.*

Michael Halm, 20 May, 1813.
A. Bushnell, 20 May, 1813.
James Nixon, 20 May, 1813.
O. Granger, 20 May, 1813.
A. Strethers, 20 May, 1813.
A. Patterson, 20 May, 1813.
Philip Houtz, 20 May, 1813.
John Booten, 7 Aug., 1813.

*Ensigns.*

J. G. Pigman, 20 May, 1813.
James Shannon, 20 May, 1813.
John H. Simons, 20 May, 1813.
William Hall, 20 May, 1813.
N. L. Reeves, 20 May, 1813.
John Willby, 20 May, 1813.
John Patterson, 20 May, 1813.
N. M'Fadden, 20 May, 1813.
Thomas Riddle, 20 May, 1813.
J. J. Tullass, 7 Aug., 1813.

*Surgeon.*

John Hamm, 16 April, 1813.

*Surgeon's Mate.*

Ed. B. Jackson, 28 April, 1813.

---

TWENTY-EIGHTH INFANTRY.

*Colonel.*

T. Deye Owings, 11 March, 1813.

*Lieut. Colonel.*

Anthony Butler, 11 March, 1813.

*Majors.*

William Trig, 11 March, 1813.
James Smiley, 11 March, 1813

*Captains.*

Benj. Moseby, 20 May, 1813.
Geo. Stockton, 20 May, 1813.
Henry C. Gist, 20 May, 1813.
John Lowrey, 20 May, 1813.
J. Megowan, 20 May, 1813.
N. H. Moore, 20 May, 1813.
Henry Daniel, 20 May, 1813.
Jep. Dudley, 20 May, 1813.
T. L. Butler, 30 June, 1813.

*1st Lieutenants.*

Joseph Clark, 20 May, 1813.
Joseph C. Bell 20 May, 1813.
David M'Nair, 20 May, 1813.
Hugh Inis, 20 May, 1813.
Mat. H. Jouitt, 20 May, 1813. Paymaster.
James Hickman, 20 May, 1813.
Robert Stockton, 20 May, 1813.
John Mason, 20 May, 1813.
Thos. Edmonson, 20 May, 1813.
Reasin H. Gist, 30 June, 1813.

*2nd Lieutenants.*

Charles Larned, 20 May, 1813.
David G. Cowan, 20 May, 1813.
James F. Moore, 20 May, 1813.
W. D. Hayden, 20 May, 1813.
John C. Kouns, 20 May, 1813.
Williams Henry, 20 May, 1813.
W. Greenup, 20 May, 1813.
W. Stewart, 20 May, 1813.
Richard Price, 30 June, 1813.
John Trumbs, 30 June, 1813.

*3rd Lieutenants.*

J. G. Reynolds, 20 May, 1813.
J. Heddleston, 20 May, 1813.

Thomas Griffith, 20 May, 1813.
Joseph Taylor, 20 May, 1813.
John Wyatt, 20 May, 1813.
Robert Clark, 20 May, 1813.
Daniel Conner, 20 May, 1813.
Jonas Jordan, 20 May, 1813.
James Howerton, 20 May, 1813.
C. Harrison, 30 June, 1813.

*Ensigns.*

Ch. L. Harrison, 20 May, 1813.
John B. Clark, 20 May, 1813.
John M'Nair, 20 May, 1813.
Peter Davis, 20 May, 1813.
W. P. S. Blair, 20 May, 1813.
Joseph Dawson, 20 May, 1813.
W. N. Bryan, 20 May, 1813.
O. W. Crockett, 30 June, 1813.
Jonas Roads, 30 June, 1813.
Daniel Brown, 30 June, 1813.

---

TWENTY-NINTH INFANTRY.

*Colonel.*

M. Smith, 12 April, 1813.

*Lieut. Colonel.*

G. D. Young, 12 April, 1813.

*Majors.*

John E. Wool, 13 April, 1813.
Asa B. Sizer, 13 April, 1813.

*Captains.*

Chas. G. Jones, 24 March, 1813.
F. Y. Waterman, 25 March, 1813.
P. B. VanBeuren, 30 April, 1813.
B. Schuyler, 30 April, 1813.
M. D. Danvers, 30 April, 1813.
Elam Lynds, 30 April, 1813.
J. C. Rochester, 30 April, 1813.
Jas. B. Spencer, 30 April, 1813.
T. Machin, Jr., 30 April, 1813.

*1st Lieutenants.*

A. B. Conant, 30 April, 1813.
A. Spencer, Jr., 30 April, 1813.
A. C. Spencer, 30 April, 1813.
Aaron Ward, 30 April, 1813.
H. B. Stebbins, 30 April, 1813.
G. Dumbleton, 30 April, 1813.
Aaron Walters, 30 April, 1813.
Joel Peebles, 30 April, 1813.
J. B. Stewart, 30 April, 1813. Paymaster.
Tennis Hanson, 30 April, 1813.

*2nd Lieutenants.*

B. A. Boynton, 30 April, 1813. Adjutant.
R. A. Barrett, 30 April, 1813.
T. Brownson, 30 April, 1813.
Daniel Adams, 30 April, 1813.
Thos. Dunham, 30 April, 1813.
H. Van Antwerp, 30 April, 1813.
Thos. Sutton, 30 April, 1813.
J. Rosecrantz, 30 April, 1813.
Sylvanus Mott, 30 April, 1813.

*3rd Lieutenants.*

S. B. Hickcock, 30 April, 1813.
Alex. M'Knight, 30 April, 1813.
S. D. Kellogg, 30 April, 1813.
James Palmer, 30 April, 1813.
J. I. Wynkoop, 30 April, 1813.
John Frasher, 30 April, 1813.
Daniel Smith, Jr., 30 April, 1813.
J. W. Edwards, 30 April, 1813.
Alton Nelson, 30 April, 1813.
P. R. Halstead, 30 April, 1813.

*Ensigns.*

Thomas Vail, 30 April, 1813.
S. Newcomb, 30 April, 1813.
T. Turner, Jr., 30 April, 1813.
J. R. Townsend, 30 April, 1813.
L. H. Mitchell, 30 April, 1813.
Walter Smith, 30 April, 1813.
John Sing, 30 April, 1813.
John Wynkoop, 30 April, 1813.
J. W. Lansing, 7 Aug., 1813.

*Surgeon.*

Martin Jennison, 1 July, 1813.

*Surgeon's Mate.*

R. G Walmsley, 1 July, 1813.

---

THIRTIETH INFANTRY.

*Colonel.*

Elias Fasset, 23 Feb., 1813.

*Lieut. Colonel.*

Martin Norton, 23 Feb., 1813.

*Majors.*

Hains French, 23 Feb., 1813.
John Bayley, 23 Feb., 1813.

*Captains.*

S. Wright, 30 April, 1813.
Salmon Clark, 30 April, 1813.
David Sanford, 30 April, 1813.
Peabody Utley, 30 April, 1813.
John Wires, 30 April, 1813.
A. J. Brown, 30 April, 1813.
D. Farrington, 30 April, 1813.
G. Spencer, Jr., 30 April, 1813.
S. Danforth, 30 April, 1813.
James Taylor, 30 April, 1813.

*1st Lieutenants.*

Wm. Miller, 30 April, 1813.
S. Robinson, 30 April, 1813.
Wm. Barney, 30 April, 1813.
Wm. Myrick, 30 April, 1813.
J. M. Young, 30 April, 1813.
G. W. Kendall, 30 April, 1813.
Shev. Weeks, 30 April, 1813.
Israel Smith, 30 April, 1813. Paymaster
R. Salsbury, 30 April, 1813.
G. Brownson, 15 Aug., 1813.

*2nd Lieutenants.*

J. H. Burton, 30 April, 1813. Adjutant.
Stephen Rumsey, 30 April, 1813.
A. Bostwick, 30 April, 1813. Quartermaster.
Gideon Hawley, 30 April, 1813.
Thos. Stephens, 30 April, 1813.
Andrew Rublee, 30 April, 1813.
Abel Gibbs, 30 April, 1813.
Elisha Smith, 30 April, 1813.
James Johnson, 30 April, 1813.
M. L. Selden, 15 Aug., 1813.

*3rd Lieutenants.*

Benj. Darby, 30 April, 1813.
Benj. Fasset, 30 April, 1813.
Nath. Spalding, 30 April, 1813.
R. B. Hyde, 30 April, 1813.
Phelps Smith, 30 April, 1813.
Almerin Smith, 30 April, 1813.
Return Strong, 30 April, 1813.
H. Wadams, 30 April, 1813.
James Smith, 30 April, 1813.
Th. Chittenden, 15 Aug., 1813.

*Ensigns.*

Henry Hendrix, 30 April, 1813.
S. Hatheway, 30 April, 1813.

A. B. Dake, 30 April, 1813.
J. R. Pettibone, 30 April, 1813.
R. R. Childs, 30 April, 1813.
Daniel Griswold, 30 April, 1813.
W. B. Ferris, 30 April, 1813.
Stephen Webb, 30 April, 1813.
T. Matthews, 30 April, 1813.

*Surgeon.*

P. S. Mason, 29 June, 1813.

*Surgeon's Mates.*

Wm. Paddock, 29 June, 1813.
W. A. Needham, 19 July, 1813.

---

### THIRTY-FIRST INFANTRY.

*Colonel.*

Danel Dana, 23 Feb., 1813.

*Lieut. Colonel.*

Huckens Storrs, 23 Feb., 1813.

*Major.*

M. Ormsbee, 23 Feb., 1813.

*Captains.*

D. A. A. Buck, 30 April, 1813.
Asa Aikens, 30 April, 1813.
L. Egerton, 30 April, 1813.
Rufus Stewart, 30 April, 1813.
N. Noble, 30 April, 1813.
Ethan Burnap, 30 April, 1813.
Cyrus Johnson, 30 April, 1813.
Joseph Morril, 30 April, 1813.
Silas Dickinson, 30 April, 1813.

*1st Lieutenants.*

C. L. Rockwood, 30 April, 1813.
Andrew Arnold, 30 April, 1813.
J. S. Bicknell, 30 April, 1813.
Presbury West, 30 April, 1813.
Wm. Bingham, 30 April, 1813.
Levi Powers, 30 April, 1813.
Enos Walker, 30 April, 1813.
D. C. Bryant, 30 April, 1813.
John Merrill, 30 April, 1813.

*2nd Lieutenants.*

Levi Cox, 30 April, 1813.
A. W. Brown, 30 April, 1813.
Chas. Livermore, 30 April, 1813.
Simon Brown, 30 April, 1813.
Asa Baker, 30 April, 1813.
Fifield. Lifford, 30 April, 1813.
John Putnam, 30 April, 1813.
John Farwell, 30 April, 1813.
John Hatch, 30 April, 1813.

*3rd Lieutenants.*

Luther Bugbee, 30 April, 1813. Adjutant.
E. Emmons, 30 April, 1813.
Eleazar Davis, 30 April, 1813. Quartermaster.
John Pratt, Jr., 30 April, 1813.
Jonathan Eddy, 30 April, 1813.
S. Wetherbee, Jr., 30 April, 1813.
John Atwood, 30 April, 1813.
Jonas Gates, 30 April, 1813.
F. Nickinson, 30 April, 1813.
James Adams, 30 April, 1813.

*Ensigns.*

Harvy Gilman, 30 April, 1813.
Jeremiah York, 30 April, 1813.
S. M. Perkins, 30 April, 1813.
Asa Peabody, 30 April, 1813.
J. Y. Sawyer, 30 April, 1813.
S. Stephens, Jr., 30 April, 1813.
Isaac Briggs, 30 April, 1813.
J. Greenleaf, 30 April, 1813.
Aaron Matson, 30 April, 1813.

*Surgeon.*

Truman Powell, 19 July, 1813.

*Surgeon's Mate.*

E. Littlefield, 19 July, 1813.

---

### THIRTY-SECOND INFANTRY.

*Colonel.*

S. E. Fotterall, 6 May, 1813.

*Lieut. Colonel.*

S. B. Davis, 6 May, 1813.

*Major.*

Geo. H. Hunter, 6 May, 1813.

*Captains.*

G. F. Goodman, 18 March, 1813.
Wm. Smith, 18 March, 1813.
Samuel Borden, 17 May, 1813.
Thomas Town, 17 May, 1813.
John Steele, Jr., 17 May 1813.
J. J. Robinson, 17 May, 1813.
Jona. B. Smith, 17 May, 1813.
Horatio Davis, 17 May, 1813.

*1st Lieutenants.*

Robt. Patterson, 5 April, 1813. Acting Deputy Quartermaster General.
Peter P. Walter, 17 April, 1813. Adjutant.
Claud. F. LeGrand, 17 April, 1813.
Richard Bache, 17 April, 1813. Aid to Brig. Gen. Bloomfield.
Maskline Clark, 17 April, 1813.
R. G. Rawlins, 17 April, 1813.
John Suter, 17 April, 1813.

*2nd Lieutenants.*

John Wilson, 17 May, 1813.
Jas. M'Karahar, 17 May, 1813.
C. B. Hopkins, 17 May, 1813.
Joseph Baldwin, 17 May, 1813.
William Crosier, 17 May, 1813. Paymaster.
Anthony Bonnaffon, 17 May, 1813.
Thos. F. Hargis, 17 May, 1813.
Charles Kean, 17 May, 1813.

*3rd Lieutenants.*

De. E. Sweeny, 17 May, 1813.
A. L. Gamble, 17 May, 1813.
H. M'Clelland, 17 May, 1813.
Geo. Dannaker, 17 May, 1813.
Thos. M'Elwe, 17 May, 1813.
Geo. K. Hall, 17 May, 1813.

*Ensigns.*

John Stewart, 17 May, 1813.
Henry Wilson, 17 May, 1813.
G. W. Hunter, 17 May, 1813.
Michael E. Israel, 17 May, 1813.
Henry Gulick, 17 May, 1813.
James Irvine, 17 May, 1813.
Jas. M'Ilvaine, 17 May, 1813.
G. F. H. Crocket, 17 May, 1813.

*Surgeon's Mates.*

Frank. Bache, 17 May, 1813.
Henry Hall, 17 May, 1813.

---

### THIRTY-THIRD INFANTRY.

*Colonel.*

Isaac Lane, 23 Feb., 1813.

*Lieut. Colonel.*

John A. Harper, 19 July, 1813.

*Major.*

Daniel Lane, 23 Feb., 1813.

*Captains.*

Benjamin Adams, 30 April, 1813.
Benjamin Dunn, 30 April, 1813.
Elias Foss, 30 April, 1813.
Noah Haley, Jr., 30 April, 1813.
Francis Drew, 30 April, 1813.
R. K. Goodenow, 30 April, 1813.
Isaac Hodsdon, 30 April, 1813.
Charles Lothrop, 30 April, 1813.
Thos. Dinsmore, 30 April, 1813.
James Currey, 30 April, 1813.

*1st Lieutenants.*

Joel Milliken, 30 April, 1813.
G. Newbegin, 30 April, 1813.
Josiah Moulton, 30 April, 1813.
Steph. Bean, 30 April, 1813.
Jere. Goodwin, 30 April, 1813. Paymaster.
Geo. Scammon, 30 April, 1813. Adjutant.
Ebenezer Seavey, 30 April, 1813.
Alex. McColley, 30 April, 1813.
James Weeks, 30 April, 1813.
Jos. Morrison, 30 April, 1813.

*2nd Lieutenants.*

D. M'Glaughlin, 30 April, 1813.
Isaac F. Snow, 30 April, 1813. Quartermaster.
Henry Cole, 30 April, 1813.
Solomon Strout, 30 April, 1813.
Alex. Worster, 30 April, 1813.
T. Buckminster, 30 April, 1813.
James Willey, 30 April, 1813.
Mija M. Lane, 30 April, 1813.
Wm. Morris, Jr., 30 April, 1813.
S. Woodman, Jr., 30 April, 1813.

*3rd Lieutenants.*

N. Edgecomb, 30 April, 1813.
S. Hopkinson, 30 April, 1813.
Wm. Cutts, 30 April, 1813.
Joseph Bryant, 30 April, 1813.
B. Palmer, Jr., 30 April, 1813.
Hanson Hayes, 30 April, 1813.
John Dunn, 30 April, 1813.
Rufus K. Lane, 30 April, 1813.
Jona. Goodwin, 30 April, 1813.

*Ensigns.*

James Warren, 30 April, 1812.
James Walker, 30 April, 1813.
Nath. Webster, 30 April, 1813.
James Banks, 30 April, 1813.
George Dunham, 30 April, 1813.
J. B. Hartford, 30 April, 1813.
Joseph Snow, 30 April, 1813.
Samuel Powell, 30 April, 1813.
B. D. Gardner, 30 April, 1813.
William Marr, 30 April, 1813.

*Surgeon.*

Perl. F. Groves, 10 April, 1813.

*Surgeon's Mates.*

Ward Bassett, 10 April, 1813.
John P. Briggs, 10 April, 1813.

---

THIRTY-FOURTH INFANTRY.

*Colonel.*

J. B. Larned, 23 Feb., 1813.

*Lieut. Colonel.*

Eben. Smith, 23 Feb., 1813.

*Major.*

T. M. Vinson, 23 Feb., 1813.

*Captains.*

Robert Douglass, 30 April, 1813.
Sherm. Leland, 30 April, 1813.
Robt. R. Kendall, 30 April, 1813.
Peter Chadwick, 30 April, 1813.
Benj. Poland, 30 April, 1813.
Benj. Bailey, 30 April, 1813.
Wm. Sweet, 30 April, 1813.
Isaac Carter, 30 April, 1813.
Danl. Crossman, 30 April, 1813.
Jos. C. Adams, 30 April, 1813. Paymaster.

*1st Lieutenants.*

John Merrill, 30 April, 1813. Quartermaster.
Thomas Bailey, 30 April, 1813.
Wm. Stevens, 30 April, 1813.
John Lee, 30 April, 1813.
Jeremiah Edes, 30 April, 1813.
Ed. Barneville, 30 April, 1813.
Elihu Norton, 30 April, 1813.
Thomas Clarke, 30 April, 1813.
Ben. Woodman, 30 April, 1813.
Nat. Gookin, 16 May, 1813.

*2nd Lieutenants.*

N. S. Benton, 30 April, 1813.
W. A. Springer, 30 April, 1813.
Joseph Sumner, 30 April, 1813.
Wm. Nash, 30 April, 1813.
Nath. Wilson, 30 April, 1813.
David Sherman, 30 April, 1813.
Wm. Nevers, 30 April, 1813.
S. Dearborn, 30 April, 1813.
Timothy Bacon, 30 April, 1813.
Calvin Crocker, 30 April, 1813.

*3rd Lieutenants.*

Otis Robbins, 30 April, 1813.
Royal D. Simons, 30 April, 1813.
Thos. Johnson, 30 April, 1813.
Robert Gibson, 30 April, 1813.
Moses Clough, 30 April, 1813.
Jos. McClure, 30 April, 1813.
Edw'd Springer, 30 April, 1813.
Isaac Townsend, 30 April, 1813.
Sup. B. Gookin, 1 July, 1813.
Flavil Sabin, 15 Aug., 1813.

*Ensigns.*

Henry Taylor, 30 April, 1813.
Elias Morse, 30 April, 1813.
Oliver Blake, 30 April, 1813.
Steph. Morrell, 30 April, 1813.
John Nash, 30 April, 1813.
D. Farnsworth, 30 April, 1813.
Josiah Parlin, 30 April, 1813.
G. W. Thomas, 30 April, 1813.
Cotton Ward, 1 July, 1813.

*Surgeon.*

Jotham Forbes, 30 April, 1813.

*Surgeon's Mates.*

Charles Loring, 20 May, 1813.
Thad. Hubbard, 20 May, 1813.

---

THIRTY-FIFTH INFANTRY.

*Colonel.*

Jos. Goodwyn, 3 March, 1813.

*Lieut. Colonel.*

Robert Pegram, 3 March, 1813.

*Majors.*

Aug. C. Smith, 3 March, 1813.
A. I. M'Connico, 22 March, 1813.

*Captains.*

Danl. C. Butts, 31 March, 1813.
Saml. M'Guire, 31 March, 1813.
M. Taliaferro, 31 March, 1813.
John Thorp, 31 March, 1813.
B. Hardaway, 31 March, 1813.
Benj. B. Jones, 31 March, 1813.
F. E. Walker, 31 March, 1813.
W. T. Cocke, 31 March, 1813.
Isaac T. Preston, 31 March, 1813.

*1st Lieutenants.*

John W. Stith, 31 March, 1813.
Christn. Miller, 31 March, 1813.
Jas. H. Belcher, 31 March, 1813.
Th. J. Parker, 31 March, 1813.
Francis H. Hooe, 31 March, 1813.
John G. Crump, 31 March, 1813.
Blair Bolling, 31 March, 1813.
Edw. L. Pegram, 31 March, 1813.
John Garland, 31 March, 1813.

*2nd Liutenants.*

L. Dangerfield, 31 March, 1813.
Wm. Rivers, 31 March, 1813.
Henry Cook, 31 March, 1813.
Wm. Loyall, 31 March, 1813.
S. C. Williams, 31 March, 1813.
James Minor, 31 March, 1813.
David B. Stith, 31 March, 1813.
John B. Hall, 31 March, 1813.
Robert Eskridge, 31 March, 1813.

*3rd Lieutenants.*

Chas. R. Rose, 31 March, 1813.
David Shelton, 31 March, 1813.
Chas. Hutchings, 31 March, 1813.
Edwin Jones, 31 March, 1813.
Thomas K. Ball, 31 March, 1813.
William Dunn, 31 March, 1813.
F. D. Charlton, 31 March, 1813. Paymaster.
R. Crockwell, 31 March, 1813.
Winfield Jones, 31 March, 1813.

*Ensigns.*

Samuel Kirby, 31 March, 1813.
John Thompson, 31 March, 1813.
R. W. Scott, 31 March, 1813.
P. R. Burwell, 31 March, 1813.
John Huson, 31 March, 1813.
Robt. R. Conrad, 31 March, 1813.
Law. M. Gale, 31 March, 1813.

*Surgeon.*

Wright Tucker, 19 July, 1813.

*Surgeon's Mate.*

W. W. Southall, 20 July, 1813.

---

THIRTY-SIXTH INFANTRY.

*Colonel.*

Henry Carbery, 22 March, 1813.

*Lieut. Colonel.*

Wm. Scott, 25 March, 1813.

*Majors.*

Alex. Stuart, 25 March, 1813.
Henry Lee, Jr., 8 April, 1813.

*Captains.*

Joseph Hook, 30 April, 1813.
Henry C. Neale, 30 April, 1813.
Jos. S. Nelson, 30 April, 1813.
C. C. Randolph, 30 April, 1813.
Thos Carbery, 30 April, 1813.
Samuel Rasin, 30 April, 1813.
J. J. Merrick, 30 April, 1813.
Mort. D. Hall, 30 April, 1813.
H. W. Deneale, 30 April, 1813.
Thos. Corcoran, 30 April, 1813.

*1st Lieutenants.*

Wm. C. Hobbs, 30 April, 1813.
James Neale, 30 April, 1813.
John Ricaud, 30 April, 1813. Paymaster.
James Ord, 30 April, 1813.
Francis J. Neale, 30 April, 1813. Quartermaster.
John Chauncey, 30 April, 1813.
Wm. N. Earle, 15 Aug., 1813.

*2nd Liutenants.*

Jas. H. Ballard, 30 April, 1813. Adjutant.
Wm. L. Rogers, 30 April, 1813.
Richard K. Watts, 30 April, 1813.
Clement Sewell, 30 April, 1813.
Charles Queen, 30 April, 1813.
W. Hindman, Jr., 15 Aug., 1813.
Wm. Merrick, 15 Aug., 1813.
Wm. A. Rind, 15 Aug., 1813.

*3rd Lieutenants.*

George Slye, 30 April, 1813.
Wright Hall, 30 April, 1813.
Henry Redman, 30 April, 1813.
F. J. Wheeler, 30 April, 1813.
J. M. Burgess, 30 April, 1813.
Philip Fisher, 15 Aug., 1813.
John Clark, 15 Aug., 1813.
Edward Scott, 15 Aug., 1813.

*Ensigns.*

Julius Germane, 30 April, 1813.
Edwd. Hopkins, 30 April, 1813.
Richd. H. Lee, 30 April, 1813.
W. T. S. Beall, 30 April, 1813.
Wm. Gallop, 30 April, 1813.
Geo. Johnson, 30 April, 1813.
John Mansfield, 30 April, 1813.

*Surgeon.*

Thos. P. Hall, 10 July, 1813.

*Surgeon's Mate.*

John H. Beall, 31 July, 1813.

---

THIRTY-SEVENTH INFANTRY.

*Lieut. Colonel.*

A. Benjamin, 11 March, 1813.

*Majors.*

Roswell Lee, 3 March, 1813.
Saml. Hoadley, 11 March, 1813.

*Captains.*

Elizur Warner, 30 April, 1813.
Christ. Ripley, 30 April, 1813.
Chauncey Ives, 30 April, 1813.
S. B. Northrop, 30 April, 1813.
Riley Sweet, 30 April, 1813.
Noah T. Ferry, 30 April, 1813.
D Waterbury, 30 April, 1813.
Stepn. D. Tilden, 30 April, 1813.
S. B. Dickinson, 30 April, 1813.
Guy Gaylord, 31 May, 1813.

*1st Lieutenants.*

John Brown, 30 April, 1813.
H. W. Huntington, 30 April, 1813. Adjutant.
David C. Welsh, 30 April, 1813. Paymaster.
William Morgan, 30 April, 1813.
Stepn. Drummer, 30 April, 1813.
Elipha. Ripley, 30 April, 1813.
Demas Deming, 30 April, 1813.
Chaun. Hosford, 30 April, 1813.
David Gibbs, 30 April, 1813.
Solomon Dewey, 31 May, 1813.

*2nd Lieutenants.*

Henry Starr, 30 April, 1813.
Dan'l Bicknell, 30 April, 1813.
Eldad Ruggles, 30 April, 1813.
Jas. L. Raynolds, 30 April, 1813.
Eli Bradley, 30 April, 1813.
David Tracey, 30 April, 1813.
W. Wakeman, 30 April, 1813.
Nathan Clark, 19 May, 1813.

*3rd Lieutenants.*

Saml. Keeler, 30 April, 1813.
Ralph Steele, 30 April, 1813.
Thomas Weller, 30 April, 1813.
J. R. Warren, 30 April, 1813.
G. H. Parmele, 30 April, 1813.
Saml. Robinson, 30 April, 1813.
Andw. Andrews, 30 April, 1813.
Irad. Storrs, 30 April, 1813.
John Phelps, Jr., 3 June, 1813.

*Ensigns.*

Saml. Keeler, 30 April, 1813.
Oren Hatch, 30 April, 1813.
Lyman Mallory, 30 April, 1813.
Henry Lord, 30 April, 1813.
Thomas Hewit, 30 April, 1813.
John Fellows, 30 April, 1813.
Wm. Kellogg, 30 April, 1813.
Ebenezer Fisk, 3 June, 1813.
James Smith, Jr., 22 June, 1813.

*Surgeon.*

Elijah Butts, 20 May, 1813.

*Surgeon's Mate.*

Asahel Hall, 19 Sept., 1813.

---

THIRTY-EIGHTH INFANTRY.

*Colonel.*

Peter Little, 19 May, 1813.

*Lieut. Colonel.*

Wm. Steuart, 19 May, 1813.

*Majors.*

Leon. Fralley, 19 May, 1813.
George Keyser, 19 May, 1813.

*Captains.*

James H. Hook, 20 May, 1813.
James Haslett, 20 May, 1813.
Isaac Aldridge, 20 May, 1813.
John Rothrock, 20 May, 1813.
John Brookes, 20 May, 1813.
John Buck, 20 May, 1813.
A. Miltenberger, 20 May, 1813.
Henry O'Neil, 20 May, 1813.
Chas. Stansbury, 20 May, 1813.
S. C. Leakin, 20 May, 1813.

*1st Lieutenants.*

John Mowton, 20 May, 1813. Adjutant.
James Smith, 20 May, 1813.
William Ford, 20 May, 1813.
Henry S. Geyer, 20 May, 1813.
G. S. Eichelberger, 20 May, 1813. Quartermaster.
Wm. R. Gwinn, 20 May, 1813. Paymaster.
William Hall, 20 May, 1813.
Joshua Medtart, 15 Aug., 1813.

*2nd Liuetenants.*

James Holmes, 20 May, 1813.
B. B. Sweeting, 20 May, 1813.
Jerem. Green, 20 May, 1813.
J. M Barrett, 20 May, 1813.
William Jones, 20 May, 1813.



James S. Griffin, 20 May, 1813.
George Fletcher, 20 May, 1813.
John Sticher, 20 May, 1813.
Wm. H. Bates, 15 May, 1813.

*3rd Lieutenants.*

D. W. Duncan, 20 May, 1813.
Peter Keyser, 20 May, 1813.
Saml. Barkley, 20 May, 1813.
Wm. Hardwood, 20 May, 1813.
Hynson Crabbin, 20 May, 1813.
F. W. Hoffman, 20 May, 1813.
Henry Huber, 20 May, 1813.
Benj P. Head, 15 Aug., 1813.
Geo. W. Lee, 15 Aug., 1813.

*Ensigns.*

Cassa. Watkins, 20 May, 1813.
John Savery, 20 May, 1813.
Rich. M. Sands, 20 May, 1813.
Wm. Camp, Jr., 20 May, 1813.
John B. Martin, 20 May, 1813.
John Spicknall, 20 May, 1813.
W. H. Addison, 20 May, 1813.

*Surgeon.*

Tobias Watkins, 20 May, 1813.

---

THIRTY-NINTH INFANTRY.

*Colonel.*

John Williams, 18 June, 1813.

*Lieut. Colonel.*

Th. H. Benton, 18 June, 1813.

*Majors.*

L. P. Montgomery, 29 July, 1813.
Wm. Peacock, 29 July, 1813.

*Captains.*

John Phagan, 29 July, 1813.
Wm. Walker, 29 July, 1813.
Benj. Reynolds, 29 July, 1813.
George Hallam, 29 July, 1813.
John B. Long, 29 July, 1813.
A. H. Douglass, 29 July, 1813.
Hen. Henninger, 29 July, 1813.
John Jones, 29 July, 1813.
James Davis, 29 July, 1813.
Thomas Stuart, 29 July, 1813.

*1st Lieutenants.*

Willie Martin, 29 July, 1813.
James Gray, 29 July, 1813.
R M. Somerville, 29 July, 1813.
Benj. Wright, 29 July, 1813.
D. Lauderdale, 29 July, 1813.
James Sharp, 29 July, 1813.
Samuel Wilson, 29 July, 1813.
James M'Donald, 29 July, 1813.
Nath. Smith, 29 July, 1813.
Joel Denton, 29 July, 1813.

*2nd Lieutenants.*

B. M. Patterson, 29 July, 1813.
M. C. Molton, 29 July, 1813.
James Leith, 29 July, 1813.
Ashley Stanfield, 29 July, 1813.
Jesse C. Tate, 29 July, 1813.
J. R. Henderson, 29 July, 1813.
Guy Smith, 29 July, 1813.
David M'Millen, 29 July, 1813.

*3rd Lieutenants.*

Jos. S. Jackson, 29 July, 1813.
Ellis Thomas, 29 July, 1813.
Benj. Duncan, 29 July, 1813.
H. W. M'Clellan, 29 July, 1813.
Isaac Pangle, 29 July, 1813.

Simpson Payne, 29 July, 1813.
J. M Armstrong, 29 July, 1813.
Rand. Quarles, 29 July, 1813.

*Ensigns.*

Saml. Houston, 29 July, 1813.
T. C. Hindman, 29 July, 1813.
Joel Parrish, 29 July, 1813.
Andrew Greer, 29 July, 1813.
Jacob K. Snap, 29 July, 1813.
John M'Henry, 29 July, 1813.
Thomas Easten, 29 July, 1813.
J. H. Anderson, 29 July, 1813.

*Surgeon's Mate.*

John H. Read, 2 July, 1813.

---

*The following Five Regiments were raised for the War by Act of July 5, 1813.*

FORTIETH INFANTRY.

*Colonel.*

Jos. Loring, Jr., 31 July, 1813.

*Lieut. Colonel.*

John Breck, 19 July, 1813.

*Majors.*

Perley Putnam, 19 July, 1813.
Hen. C. Brown, 19 July, 1813.

*Captains.*

J. B. Varnum, 19 July, 1813.
Seth W. Nye, 19 July, 1813.
James Perry, 29 July, 1813.
Leonard Ross, 1 Aug., 1813.
M. N. Sanborn, 1 Aug., 1813.
Robert Neale, Jr., 1 Aug., 1813.
John Leonard, 6 Aug., 1813.
John Bailey, 1 Sept., 1813.
Elisha Field, 1 Sept., 1813.
John Fillebrown, 1 Sept., 1813.

*1st Lieutenants.*

Robert Carter, 29 July, 1813.
Danl. P. Brown, 1 Aug., 1813.
Chas. Durant, 1 Sept., 1813.
J. Orne Bowden, 1 Sept., 1813.
Joseph M'Comb, 1 Sept., 1813.
Sam. Hodges, Jr., 1 Sept., 1813.

*2nd Liuetenants.*

James Harris, 1 Sept., 1813.
Samuel C. Pope, 1 Sept., 1813.
John Spalter, 1 Sept., 1813.
Elias Goodspeed, 1 Sept., 1813.
R. H. Blanchard, 1 Sept., 1813.

*3rd Lieutenants.*

John Parrott, 29 July, 1813.
Saml. H. Russell, 1 Sept., 1813.
Enoch Manning, 1 Sept., 1813.
Andrew Lewis, 1 Sept., 1813.
Moses Aldrich, 1 Sept., 1813.

*Ensigns.*

Jas. Perry, Jr., 29 July, 1813.
Nich. B. Proctor, 1 Sept., 1813.
Perez Alexander, 1 Sept., 1813.
Isaac Carpenter, 1 Sept., 1813.

---

FORTY-FIRST INFANTRY.

*Colonel.*

Robt. Bogardus, 29 July, 1813.

*Lieut. Colonel.*

J. W. Livingston, 29 July, 1813.

*Majors.*

Darby Noon, 1 Aug., 1813.
Jas. D. Wallace, 1 Aug., 1813.

*Captains.*

Gilbert Seaman, 1 Aug., 1813.
Alex. Hamilton, 1 Aug., 1813.
Alph. Sherman, 1 Aug., 1813.
S. B. Romaine, 1 Aug., 1813.
Saml. Berrian, 1 Aug., 1813.
James Campbell, 1 Aug., 1813.
Wm. S. Radcliff, 3 Aug., 1813.
Chas. Humphrey, 7 Aug., 1813.
John B. Scott, 30 Sept., 1813.
Francis Allyn, 30 Sept., 1813.

*1st Lieutenants.*

Thomas Barker, 1 Aug., 1813.
M. M. Quackenbos 1 Aug., 1813.
John Ingersoll, 7 Aug., 1813.
James M'Cullen, 7 Aug., 1813.
Wm. Loudon, 9 Aug., 1813.
John L. Clark, 30 Sept., 1813.
J. L. Bogardus, 30 Sept., 1813.
J. M. Schermerhorn, 30 Sept., 1813.

*2nd Liuetenants.*

Jud. Hammond, 30 Sept., 1813.
T. E. Beekman, 30 Sept., 1813.
Alex. Clinton, 30 Sept., 1813.
Daniel Wisbart, 30 Sept., 1813.
Wm. Seaman, 30 Sept., 1813.
John Tabalee, 30 Sept., 1813.
Geo. Hamilton, 30 Sept., 1813.
John H. Sims, 30 Sept., 1813.
Henry Brown, 30 Sept., 1813.
Luther Hand, 30 Sept., 1813.

*3rd Lieutenant.*

Sol. Sutherland, 1 Aug., 1813.

*Ensigns.*

George West, 6 Aug., 1813.
Jeremiah Smith, 30 Sept., 1813.
John Webb, Jr., 30 Sept., 1813.
Lawr. Rigail, 30 Sept., 1813.
Wm. Hammet, 30 Sept., 1813.
Isaac Miller, 30 Sept., 1813.
Asher Corles, 30 Sept., 1813.
George Maxwell, 30 Sept., 1813.
John C. Hart, 30 Sept., 1813.

*Surgeon.*

John Neilson, 30 Sept., 1813.

*Surgeon's Mates.*

Fayette Cooper, 30 Sept., 1813.
Henry White, 30 Sept., 1813.

---

FORTY-SECOND INFANTRY.

*Colonel.*

Wm. N. Irvine, 4 Aug., 1813.

*Lieut. Colonel.*

Jas. G. Forbes, 1 Aug., 1813.

*Major.*

Tunis Riker, 1 Aug., 1813.

*Captains.*

Thos. Stockton, 20 Sept., 1813.
George W. Barker, 10 Jan., 1813.
E. S. Mendenhall, 1 Aug., 1813.
Wm. G. Oliver, 1 Aug., 1813.
Thos. Hanson, 4 Aug., 1813.

Edm. B. Duvall, 4 Aug., 1813.
John Junkin, 7 Aug., 1813.
Arms. Irvine, 1 Oct., 1813.
John Biddle, 1 Oct., 1813.

*1st Lieutenants.*

Josiah S. Carty, 3 Aug., 1813.
James Laken, 3 Aug., 1813.
Thomas Traquir, 4 Aug., 1813.

*2nd Lieutenants.*

Robert Shaw, Jr., 1 Aug., 1813.
Joseph Hall, 1 Aug., 1813.
P. Mendenhall, 4 Aug., 1813.
Howerton Cross, 7 Aug., 1813.
Alex. Trotter, 9 Sept., 1813.

*3rd Lieutenants.*

J. B. Welhenson, 1 Aug., 1813.
Daniel Saint, 3 Aug., 1813.
Fredk. Lazarus, 25 Sept., 1813.
Martin Grant, 25 Sept., 1813.
J. Armstrong, 30 Sept., 1813.

*Surgeon's Mate.*

James M. Kelly, 1 Aug., 1813.

---

FORTY-THIRD INFANTRY.

*Colonel.*

Nicholas Long, 4 Aug., 1813.

*Lieut. Colonel.*

Dunc. L. Clinch, 4 Aug., 1813.

*Majors.*

James Campbell, 1 Aug., 1813.
Thos. D. King, 4 Aug., 1813.

*Captains.*

Jno. J. Goodwyn, 1 Aug., 1813.
Theo. L. Gurdin, 1 Aug., 1813.
G. H. Manigault, 1 Aug., 1813. Aid to Brig. Gen. Izard.
Joel E. Grace, 1 Aug., 1813.
Edward F. Tattnall, 4 Aug., 1813.
Thomas Hyde, 4 Aug., 1813.
Henry Garrett, 4 Aug., 1813.
Robt. Love, Jr., 4 Aug., 1813.
George Dabney, 4 Aug., 1813.

*1st Lieutenants.*

Abner H. Hicks, 1 Aug., 1813.
Saml. A. Taylor, 1 Aug., 1813.
W. Edmonson, 1 Aug., 1813.
Sam. Farrow, Jr., 1 Aug., 1813.
Charles Cantey, 3 Aug., 1813.
John Smallwood, 4 Aug., 1813.
James Smith, 4 Aug., 1813.
Geo. R. Gilman, 4 Aug., 1813.
Wm. W. Holt, 4 Aug., 1813.

*2nd Lieutenants.*

Robert Stark, 1 Aug., 1813.
Joshua Irby, 1 Aug., 1813.
Robt. H. Briggs, 1 Aug., 1813.
W. Timberlake, 4 Aug., 1813.
Edward Hare, 4 Aug., 1813.
John M. Neel, 4 Aug., 1813.
Robt. L. Coombs, 4 Aug., 1813.
Archibald Bigby, 4 Aug., 1813.
James Moss, 4 Aug., 1813.
R. Campbell, Jr., 16 Oct., 1813. Aid to Brig. Gen. Williams.

*3rd Lieutenants.*

Wm. Miles, 1 Aug., 1813.
Marshall Ayres, 1 Aug., 1813.
Holomon Battle, 4 Aug., 1813.
Wm. H. Norman, 4 Aug., 1813.
Wm. Welsh, 4 Aug., 1813.
Elisha Gates, 4 Aug., 1813.
Levin V. Greer, 4 Aug., 1813.

*Ensigns.*

James B. Moore, 1 Aug., 1813.
John Vereen, 3 Aug., 1813.
Daniel Wall, 3 Aug., 1813.
John H. Lawson, 4 Aug., 1813.
Joseph Oliver, 4 Aug., 1813.
Lar. L. Baldwin, 4 Aug., 1813.
W. H. Fairchild, 4 Aug., 1813.

---

FORTY-FOURTH INFANTRY.

*Colonel.*

Geo. T. Ross, 1 Aug., 1813.

*Lieut. Colonel.*

René Trudeau, 1 Aug., 1813.

*Majors.*

Henry D. Piere, 1 Aug., 1813.
Waters Clark, 1 Aug., 1813.

*Captains.*

Isaac L. Baker, 5 April, 1813.
Wm. O. Butler, 5 April, 1813.

*1st Lieutenant.*

Nathl. Pryor, 30 Aug., 1813.

*2nd Lieutenant.*

Elzr. B. Billings, 9 Aug., 1813.

*Surgeon.*

Squire Lea, 1 Aug., 1813.

---

RANGERS.

*Captains.*

Wm. Dunn, 12 April, 1813.
Pierre Andér, 12 April, 1813.
James Bigger, 30 April, 1813.
Fred. Shoultz, 20 May, 1813.
Andrew Ramsey, 19 July, 1813.
David Musick, 19 July, 1813.
Daniel M. Boone, 19 July, 1813.
James B. Moore, 1 Aug., 1813.
William B. Whiteside, 1 Aug., 1813.
Jacob Short, 1 Aug., 1813.
Jas. Manary, Sr., 5 Aug., 1813.
Sam. McCormick, 7 Aug., 1813.

*1st Lieutenants.*

Henry Brinton, 12 April, 1813.
Hyacin. Lassell, 12 April, 1813.
John Carr, 30 April, 1813.
James Morrison, 19 July, 1813.
P. K. Robbins, 19 July, 1813.
Wm. Massey, 19 July, 1813.
Jos. Borough, 1 Aug., 1813.
David Robinson, 1 Aug., 1813.
Nathl. Journey, 1 Aug., 1813.
John Hopkins, 5 Aug., 1813.
James Flinn, 1 Oct., 1813.

*2nd Lieutenants.*

Henry Ristine, 12 April, 1813.
Homer Johnson, 12 April, 1813.
James Curray, 30 April, 1813.
Sylvester Pattie, 19 July, 1813.
James Calloway, 19 July, 1813.
Peter Craig, 19 July, 1813.
Sam. Gilham, 1 Aug., 1813.
Arthur Morgan, 1 Aug., 1813.
And. Bankston, 1 Aug., 1813.
Brat. Crawford, 5 Aug., 1813.
John Knox, 1 Oct., 1813.

*3rd Lieutenants.*

David Hillis, 12 April, 1813.
John Hadden, Jr., 12 April, 1813.
W. P. Meredith, 30 April, 1813.
Wm. McHenry, 1 Aug., 1813.
Steph. Rector, 1 Aug., 1813.
William Boon, 1 Aug., 1813.
David Steal, 5 Aug., 1813.
Wm. G. Sems, 1 Oct., 1813.

*Ensigns.*

Green B. Fields, 12 April, 1813.
David L. Gregg, 12 April, 1813.
John Owens, Jr., 30 April, 1813.
David Bailey, 19 July, 1813.
John McNair, 19 July, 1813.
Drakeford Gray, 19 July, 1813.
John Journey, 1 Aug., 1813.
Aaron Armstrong, 1 Aug., 1813.
Ebn. F. Seaman, 5 Aug., 1813.
Wm. Patterson, 1 Oct., 1813.

---

UNITED STATES VOLUNTEERS.

*From Maine and New Hampshire.*

*Colonel.*

Denny McCobb, 23 Dec., 1812.

*Lieut. Colonel.*

Aquila Davis, 13 Jan., 1813.

*Captains.*

Elijah Hall, 1 Oct., 1812.
Benj. Bradford, 18 Nov., 1812.
Josh Danforth, 20 Nov., 1812.
Daniel Holden, 15 Dec., 1812.
Nathan Stanley, 15 Dec., 1812.
Smith Elkins, 1 Jan., 1813.
Joseph Flanders, 24 Jan., 1813.

*1st Lieutenants.*

Th. B. Sylvester, 1 Nov., 1812. Adjutant.
John Butterfield, 18 Nov., 1812.
Daniel M. Gregg, 18 Nov., 1812.
David Doane, 20 Nov., 1812.
A. P. Cochran, 2 Dec., 1812.
Henry Snow, 15 Dec., 1812.
Daniel George, 12 Jan., 1813.

*2nd Lieutenants.*

Benj. White, Jr., 1 Oct., 1812.
Joseph Low, 18 Nov., 1812.
Marshall Baker, 2 Dec., 1812.
David Denison, 2 Dec., 1812.
Daniel Patch, 15 Dec., 1812. Quartermaster.
Daniel Page, 15 Dec., 1812.
Sam. Sylvester, 1 Jan., 1813.
James Bean, 12 Jan., 1813.

*Ensigns.*

John Neal, Jr., 1 Oct., 1812.
Wm. Kendall, 16 Nov., 1812.
Wm. Reed, 16 Nov., 1812.
Jonas G. Brooks, 1 Dec., 1812.
Joseph Berry, 1 Jan., 1813.
Enoch Page, 24 Jan., 1813.
Parker Chase, 26 March, 1813.

*Surgeon's Mates.*

John Trivett, 1 March, 1813.
James Bates, 12 March, 1813.

---

UNITED STATES VOLUNTEERS.

*From New York. Second Regiment.*

*Colonel.*

Saml. Hawkins, 15 Feb., 1813.

*Lieut. Colonel.*

Gilbert Ketcham, 15 Feb., 1813.

*Major.*

W. S. Tallmadge, 15 Feb., 1813.

*Captains.*

Edm. G. Perlee, 5 Nov., 1812.
J. D. Wadsworth, 5 Nov., 1812.
Thomas Bruyn, 5 Nov., 1812.
John S. Suffern, 5 Nov., 1812.
David Crawford, 5 Nov., 1812.
John McCamley, 5 Nov., 1812.
John Miller, 1 Dec., 1812.
Joseph Delafield, 1 Dec., 1812.
Gabrl. Y. Denton, 21 Jan., 1813.
Robt. Gourlay, Jr., 1 Feb., 1813.

*1st Lieutenants.*

Sanford Allyn, 5 Nov., 1812.
Moses Burnet, 5 Nov., 1812.
Richard Eldred, 5 Nov., 1812.
Z. Schoonmaker, 9 Dec., 1812. Paymaster.
J. A. Rapalje, 21 Dec., 1812.
Job Wright, 21 Dec., 1812.
Jos. De La Montanya, 1 Jan., 1813. Quartermaster.
R. W. Nelson, 16 Jan., 1813.
James Darrow, 1 Feb., 1813.
E. B. Baldwin, 9 Feb., 1813.
J. L. Bleecker, 10 Feb., 1813.
Aw. D. Willson, 16 April, 1813.

*2nd Lieutenants.*

John Bailey, 5 Nov., 1812.
Platt Ketcham, 17 Nov., 1812. Adjutant.
Jacob Montross, 25 Dec., 1812.
G. S. Caldwell, 4 Jan., 1813.
John Peters, 10 Jan., 1813.
Morris Janson, 11 Jan., 1813.
Epens. Wheeler, 1 Feb., 1813.
Geo. S. Allison, 10 Feb., 1813.
Jesse Barlow, 16 Feb., 1813.
John Wilson, 16 April, 1813.

*3rd Lieutenant.*

James Archer, 1 July, 1813.

*Surgeon.*

Steph. Rapalje, 14 Nov., 1812.

*Surgeon's Mate.*

Josiah Torrey, 30 Dec., 1812.

---

UNITED STATES VOLUNTEERS.

*From New York. Third Regiment.*

*Lieut. Colonel.*

Alex. Denniston, 1 Feb., 1813.

*Captains.*

Gouvr. S. Bibby, 8 Dec., 1812.
Christn. Hartell, 28 Dec., 1812.
Geo. K. McKay, 9 Jan., 1813.
Chas. Hughes, 16 Jan., 1813.
Jonan. Gidney, 18 Jan., 1813.
John Hatfield, 23 Jan., 1813.
Benjamin Wood, 30 Jan., 1813.
Ths. Shearwood, 31 Jan., 1813.
Isaac Little, 1 Feb., 1813.

*1st Lieutenants.*

Thos. Earle, 20 Aug., 1812.
Thos. Darling, 31 Dec., 1812.
Wm. Perron, 1 Jan., 1813.
Edwin Baldwin, 2 Jan., 1813.
Stephen Baxter, 9 Jan., 1813. Paymaster
James Kerr, 25 Jan., 1813.
Wm. Walsh, 28 Jan., 1813.
Robert P. Ross, 31 Jan., 1813.
Ephraim Clark, 1 March, 1813.

*2nd Lieutenants.*

Ebenezer Cole, 23 Dec., 1812.
Peter Holmes, 1 Jan., 1813.
Allen Reynolds, 20 Jan., 1813. Adjutant.
Isaac Percy, 25 Jan., 1813.
Eras. H. Weed, 28 Jan., 1813.
Caleb Crane, 30 Jan., 1813.
Matthew D. Coe, 31 Jan., 1813.
Chas. T. Butler, 1 March, 1813.

*3rd Lieutenants.*

Wm. Buttre, 1 Feb., 1813.
Danl. L. Scott, 28 Feb., 1813.
N. G. Carmer, 15 Aug., 1813.

*Surgeon.*

Robt. C. Hunter, 31 Jan., 1813.

*Surgeon's Mate.*

Elias C. Badeau, 9 Feb., 1813.

---

UNITED STATES VOLUNTEERS.

*From Richmond, Virginia.*

*Captain.*

Richd. Booker, 1 Dec., 1812.

*1st Lieutenant.*

John W. Ellis, 1 Dec., 1812.

*2nd Lieutenant.*

B. Hazlegrove, 1 Dec., 1812.

*Ensign.*

Robt. Kennedy, 1 Dec., 1812.

---

UNITED STATES VOLUNTEERS.

*From the Mississippi Territory.*

*Brigadier General.*

F. L. Claiborne, 1 March, 1813. Commanding the Two following Regiments.

*Colonel.*

Joseph Carson, 30 April, 1813.

*Major.*

Daniel Beasley, 15 Feb., 1813.

*Captains.*

Philip A. Engle, 9 Jan., 1813.
Archilaus Wells, 15 Jan., 1813.
Randall Jones, 27 Jan., 1813.
William Jack, 28 Jan., 1813.
Wm. C. Mead, 29 Jan., 1813.
Benjamin Dent, 31 Jan., 1813.
Hath. Middleton, 31 Jan., 1813.
Abm. M. Scott, 31 Jan., 1813.
James Foster, 31 Jan., 1813.
D. V. Foelkill, 1 Feb., 1813.
C. G. Johnson, 1 March, 1813.
Hans Morrison, 8 March, 1813.

*1st Lieutenants.*

James Baily, 12 Oct., 1812.
Richn. Bowman, 18 Dec., 1812.
A. L. Osborn, 15 Jan., 1813.
Wm. Morgan, 15 Jan., 1813.
J. D. Rodgers, 20 Jan., 1813.
W. R. Deloach, 1 Feb., 1813. Adjutant.
Theron Kellog, 6 Feb., 1813.
A. Montgomery, 9 Feb., 1813.
John Camp, 10 Feb., 1813.
Alex. Calvit, 24 Feb., 1813.
John Allen, 25 Feb., 1813.
Robt. Layson, 4 March, 1813.
Benj. F. Salvage, 12 March, 1813. Quartermaster.

*2nd Lieutenants.*

Kean Caldwell, 12 Oct., 1812.
Charles Moore, 1 Dec., 1812.
Charles Baron, 15 Jan., 1813.
S. M. Osborn, 8 Feb., 1813.
N. Lockridge, 5 March, 1813.
R. C. Anderson, 6 March, 1813.
Geo. Dougherty, 15 March, 1813.
Robert Swan, 15 March, 1813.
James Luckett, 15 March, 1813.
George H. Gibbs, 15 March, 1813.
Robt. Burton, 15 March, 1813.
D. M. Callihan, 15 March, 1813.

*Ensigns.*

Stephen Mays, 28 Feb., 1813.
Y. R. McDonald, 6 March, 1813.
Benj. Blanton, 6 March, 1813.
Benj. Stowell, 6 March, 1813.
Wm. S. Britt, 12 March, 1813.
Isaac W. Davis, 15 March, 1813.
Robert Davis, 23 May, 1813.
Charles West, 12 Aug., 1813.
Samuel Guest, 15 Aug., 1813.
Richard Smith, 15 Aug., 1813.

*Surgeon's Mate.*

Wm. R. Cox, 17 Feb., 1813.

---

UNITED STATES VOLUNTEERS.

*From Louisiana.*

*Major.*

Wm. Henry, 30 April, 1813.

*Captains.*

P. A. Rivery, 20 Nov., 1812.
John Mowry, 24 Nov., 1812.
A. Perychaud, 16 Dec., 1812.
E. de Mirepoix, 19 Dec., 1812.
Ferd. Amelung, 28 Dec., 1812.
L. de Marans, 13 Jan., 1813..
Abram. Miller.

*1st Lieutenants.*

Hugh Davis, 22 Oct., 1812.
George Russel, 25 Nov., 1812.
Noel G. Dupuy, 27 Nov., 1812.
Joseph Bige, 28 Dec., 1812.
J. P. Thebault, 28 Dec., 1812.
Francis Hewit, 25 Jan., 1813.
Benj. Bridges, 15 Aug., 1813.

*2nd Lieutenants.*

D. Hutchings, 5 Dec., 1812.
Adrian F. Duval, 9 Jan., 1813.
John Koen, 15 Aug., 1813.
James M'Arthur, 15 Aug., 1813.
John Files, 15 Aug., 1813.
W. R. Chambles, 15 Aug., 1813.
T. C. Vaughn, 15 Aug., 1813.

*Ensigns.*

Curtis Lewis, 5 Dec., 1812.
Patk. M'Clasky, 6 Feb., 1813.
Robert Steele, 15 Aug., 1813.
Lewis W. Brant, 15 Aug., 1813.
John Booth, 15 Aug., 1813.

*Surgeon.*

Peter Lambert, 26 Dec., 1812.

SEA FENCIBLES.

*Captains.*

Thos. M. Newell, 1 Aug., 1813.
John Nicholson, 1 Aug., 1813.
Lemuel Morris, 4 Aug., 1813.
John Du Bose, 4 Aug., 1813.
Fredk. Brooks, 7 Aug., 1813.

*1st Lieutenants.*

Abraham Nicols, 1 Aug., 1813.
Jas. J. Cumming, 1 Aug., 1813.
John J. Couturier, 4 Aug., 1813.
Richd. Baynor, 7 Aug., 1813.

*2nd Lieutenants.*

Ferd. A. O'Neal, 1 Aug., 1813.
William Lytle, 1 Aug., 1813.
Byrd B. Mitchel, 1 Aug., 1813.

*3rd Lieutenants.*

Henry B. Jones, 1 Aug., 1813.
John Hardwick, 4 Aug., 1813.
John Boner, 7 Aug., 1813.

---

# List of the Officers of the Army

## 1814.

---

ADJUTANT AND INSPECTOR GENERAL'S OFFICE,
*Washington, May 12th*, 1814.

GENERAL ORDERS.

The 1st and 2nd Regiments of Dragoons are consolidated, and will form one Regiment of light Troops.

The 1st, 2nd and 3rd Regiments of Artillery will compose one Corps of Twelve Battalions, each Battalion to consist of Four Companies.

The 17th, 19th, 26th and 27th Regiments of Infantry are also consolidated, and will form Two Regiments, to be numbered the 17th and 19th Regiments of Infantry.

The Officers attached to these Corps and Regiments will be as follows, viz:

REGIMENT LIGHT DRAGOONS.

*Colonel.*

James Burns, 6 July, 1812.

*Lieut. Colonel.*

Jacint Laval, 7 June, 1813.

*Majors.*

James V. Ball, 16 Sept., 1812.
Thos. A. Helms, 7 June, 1813.

*Captains.*

Arthur P. Hayne, 10 Nov., 1809.
Alex. Cummings, 1 Nov., 1811.
Sam. G. Hopkins, 6 July, 1812.
Henry Hall, 6 July, 1812.
Saml. D. Harris, 6 July, 1812.
John A. Burd, 6 July, 1812.
W. M. Littlejohn, 1 Dec., 1812.
George Haig, 20 Jan., 1813.

*1st Lieutenants.*

Henry Whiting, 20 Aug., 1811.
George Birch, 1 Nov., 1811.
Chas. J. Nourse, 7 May, 1812.
Beverly Turpin, 6 July, 1812.
A. H. Sneed, 6 July, 1812.
F. S. Belton, 20 Jan., 1813.
Wm. Nielson, 7 June, 1813.
Louis Laval, 28 July, 1813.

*2nd Lieutenants.*

R. H. Craig, 18 March, 1813.
Isaac Griffiths, 18 March, 1813.
James Martin, 30 April, 1813.
F. H. Lissenhoff, 1 Aug., 1813.
George Watts, 19 April, 1814.
James Trippe, 19 April, 1814.
H. A. Hays, 19 April, 1814.
C. Wright, 19 April, 1814.

*3rd Lieutenants.*

Hugh Sterling, 29 April, 1813.
John Hoomes, 20 May, 1813.
J. L. Elbert, 20 June, 1813.
L. P. Gustine, 29 July, 1813.
T. S. Bracken, 19 April, 1814.
R. Northington, 19 April, 1814.
Thos. Hogan, 19 April, 1814.
Philip Anspach, 19 April, 1814.

*Cornets.*

Claiborn Cain, 1 Oct., 1813.
Wm. Johnson, 11 Oct., 1813.
Wm. Gale, 11 Oct., 1813.
Th. Robinson, 11 March, 1814.
S. H. Cummings, 11 March, 1814.
J. Caldwell, 11 March, 1814.
Arth Chambers, 11 March, 1814.
Henry Stone, 11 March, 1814.

*Surgeon.*

W. H. Buckner, 6 July, 1812.

*Surgeon's Mates.*

L. M. Bailey, 7 May, 1812.
S. H. Littlejohn, 3 April, 1813.

---

CORPS OF ARTILLERY.

*Lieut. Colonels.*

Cons. Freeman, 1 April, 1802.
Geo. E. Mitchell, 3 March, 1813.
James House, 3 March, 1813.
F. K. Huger, 3 March, 1813.
Wm. Lindsay, 12 March, 1813.
Wm. McRea, 19 April, 1814.

*Majors.*

D. M. Forney, 6 July, 1812.
Samuel Nye, 6 July, 1812.
Geo. Armistead, 3 March, 1813.
James B. Many, 5 May, 1813.
James Hindman, 26 June, 1813.
Lloyd Beall, 21 April, 1814.

*Captains.*

Sam. T. Dyson, 15 Sept., 1804.
C. Wollstonecraft, 15 March, 1805.
John B. Walbach, 31 Jan., 1806.
Moses Sweet, 30 June, 1807.
Wm. Wilson, 3 May, 1808.
E. Humphreys, 9 Jan., 1809.
Fran. Newman, 1 Oct., 1809.
James Hanham, 10 July, 1811.
Michael Walsh, 31 Oct., 1811.
James Reed, 12 March, 1812.
I. B. Crane, 6 July, 1812.
Roger Jones, 6 July, 1812.
J. H. Boyle, 6 July, 1812.
A. S. Brooks, 6 July, 1812.
Nath. Towson, 6 July, 1812.
Sam. B. Archer, 6 July, 1812.
Wm. Nicholas, 6 July, 1812.
Jas. N. Barker, 6 July, 1812.
Jacob B. Pon, 6 July, 1812.
S. Donoho, 6 July, 1812.
Th. Biddle, Jr., 6 July, 1812.
John W. Gookin, 6 July, 1812.
Joseph Phillips, 6 July, 1812.
J. T. B. Romayne, 6 July, 1812.
H. H. Watson, 6 July, 1812.
Jas. McKeon, 6 July, 1812.
John Ritchie, 6 July, 1812.
John Goodall, 6 July, 1812.
Rufus McIntire, 6 July, 1812.
Par. Hawkins, Jr., 6 July, 1812.
Danl. Cushing, 6 July, 1812.
Stanton Sholes, 6 July, 1812.
G. W. Russell, 6 July, 1812.
Fred. Evans, 6 July, 1812.
Th. Murray, 10 Feb., 1813.
Wm. Gates, 3 March, 1813.
A. J. Williams, 12 March, 1813.
A. C. W. Fanning, 13 March, 1813.
J. M. O'Connor, 13 March, 1813.
G. H. Richards, 13 March, 1813.
J. F. Helleman, 5 May, 1813.
Hopley Yeaton, 20 May, 1813.
Thos. Bennett, 20 June, 1813.
S. Churchill, 15 Aug., 1813.
B. K. Pierce, 1 Oct., 1813.
James Green, Jr., 29 Oct., 1813.
J. S. Peyton, 15 Dec., 1813.
H. R. Craig, 23 Dec., 1813.

*1st Lieutenants.*

Ethan A. Allen, 1 Oct., 1809.
A. Darrah, 29 Jan., 1811.
M. P. Lomax, 30 June, 1811.
Justus Post, 1 July, 1811.
S. Champlain, 31 Oct., 1811.
Heman A. Fay, 23 Dec., 1811.
Milo Mason, 29 Feb., 1812.
C. Van de Venter, 12 March, 1812.
J. Fitzgerald, 14 March, 1812.
J. L. Tracy, 6 July, 1812.
Adrian Neil, 6 July, 1812.
John Farley, 6 July, 1812.
P. McDonogh, 6 July, 1812.
W. M. Read, 6 July, 1812.
H. Smyth, 6 July, 1812.
W. J. Cowan, 6 July, 1812.
J. Fontaine, 6 July, 1812.
J. H. Larwill, 6 July, 1812.
Lowndes Brown, 6 July, 1812.
L. Scott, 6 July, 1812.
R. R. Ruffin, 6 July, 1812.
H. Slaughter, 6 July, 1812.
J. H. Dearing, 6 July, 1812.
John Erving, 16 Aug., 1812.
A. L. Sands, 10 Feb., 1813.
James Daliba, 3 March, 1813.
R. A. Zantzinger, 13 March, 1813.
C. M. Macomb, 13 March, 1813.
J. H. Rees, 13 March, 1813.
R. Stewart, 13 March, 1813.
W. R. Duncan, 13 March, 1813.
Chester Root, 13 March, 1813.
Mat. Jenkins, 13 March, 1813.
J. L. Edwards, 28 March, 1813.
Gustav. Loomis, 5 May, 1813.
Ezra Smith, 11 May, 1813.
Philip D. Spencer, 13 May, 1813.
R. H. Ashley, 20 May, 1813.
John Mountfort, 20 May, 1813.
John S. Brush, 20 June, 1813.
Fabius Whiting, 20 June, 1813.
Edwin Sharpe, 26 June, 1813.
G. Dearborn, 1 Oct., 1813.
Felix Ansart, 1 Oct., 1813.
Wm. King, 1 Oct., 1813.
Thos. C. Legate, 29 Oct., 1813.
J Warley, 15 Dec., 1813.
Wm. Smith, 23 Dec., 1813.

*2nd Lieutenants.*

Saml. Spotts, 10 Feb., 1812.
Wm. Parker, 10 Feb., 1812.
Levi Whiting, 10 Feb., 1812.
J. W. Rouse, 27 March, 1812.
Benj. B. White, 14 April, 1812.
A. B. Chase, 30 April, 1812.
James Baker, 1 May, 1812.
J. P. Bartlett, 6 July, 1812.
Lewis Morgan, 6 July, 1812.
Wm. H. Nicoll, 6 July, 1812.
John Ruffin, 6 July, 1812.
J. H. Gamble, 6 July, 1812.
J. W. Kincaid, 6 July, 1812.
R. Goode, 6 July, 1812.
Francis O'Byrd, 6 July, 1812.
J. I. Cromwell, 23 Nov., 1812.
J. W. Lent, Jr., 12 March, 1813.
Chas Clarke, 12 March, 1813.
Thos. Elfe, Jr., 17 March, 1813.
Thos. Christie, 18 March, 1813.
Saml. Rockwell, 20 March, 1813.
James Bosque, 12 April, 1813.
Thos. Clark, 16 April, 1813.
C. D. Cooper, 16 April, 1813.
J. P. Prince, 16 April, 1813.
G. Doneghey, 16 April, 1813.
P. J. Neville, 20 April, 1813.
A. W. Forbush, 5 May, 1813.
M. S. Massey, 13 May, 1813.
F. P. Woolsey, 20 May, 1813.
Wm. McClintock, 20 June, 1813.
L. H. Osgood, 20 June, 1813.
J. P. Bunting, 26 June, 1813.
J. Anderson, 26 June, 1813.
Peter Melendy, 29 June, 1813.
Ben. C. Bartlett, 29 June, 1813.
Benj. Lawson, 30 Sept., 1813.
R. M. Kirby, 1 Oct., 1813.
Geo. B. Sheldon, 1 Oct., 1813.
W. B. Read, 1 Oct., 1813.
T. B. Chickering, 1 Oct., 1813.
Edwd. Baynton, 1 Oct., 1813.
Daniel Blaney, 1 Oct., 1813.
William Lyon, 1 Oct., 1813.
H. M. Campbell, 12 Oct., 1813.
M. M. Russell, 20 Oct., 1813.
John Mitchell, 16 Nov., 1813.
H. L. Duffell, 15 Dec., 1813.
Walter Berryman, 23 Dec., 1813.
J. Bennett, 24 Dec., 1813.
W. J. Sever, 31 Dec., 1813.
E. Hopkins, 31 Dec., 1813.
James C. Pickett, 19 April, 1814.
Britton Evans, 19 April, 1814.
James Bailey, 19 April, 1814.
T. J. Harrison, 19 April, 1814.
John Watmaugh, 19 April, 1814.
W. Kenny, 19 April, 1814
Chas. Newkirk, 19 April, 1814.

Oliver Bangs, 19 April, 1814.
Nat. Henderson, 19 April, 1814.
G. W. Gardiner, 1 May, 1814.
C. S. Merchant, 1 May, 1814.
Nath. G. Dana, 1 May, 1814.
John Monroe, 1 May, 1814.
J. S. Allanson, 1 May, 1814.
Steph. Birdsall, 1 May, 1814.
L. G. De Russy, 1 May, 1814.
Thos. Childs, 1 May, 1814.
Saml. L. Dana, 1 May, 1814.
John S. Shoemick, 1 May, 1814.
S. G. Bloomfield, 1 May, 1814.
T. W. Freeman, 1 May, 1814.
Cassius Carter, 1 May, 1814.
Thos. V. Earle, 1 May, 1814.
Jonathan Pell, 1 May, 1814.
Chas. Mellon, 1 May, 1814.
Geo. H. Britt, 1 May, 1814.
James Hall, 1 May, 1814.
Aug. Aisquith, 1 May, 1814.
John S. Pierce, 1 May, 1814.
Elijah Brown, 1 May, 1814.
Joseph Gilbert, 1 May, 1814.
E. L. Davis, 1 May, 1814.
Allen Lowd, 1 May, 1814.

*3rd Lieutenants.*

D. S. Andrews, 19 April, 1814.
Wm. Jones, 20 April, 1814.
Geo. Watson, 20 April, 1814.
Nat. Wilkinson, 20 April, 1814.
D. C. Nicholls, 26 April, 1814.
Wm. Elgin, 12 May, 1814.

---

SEVENTEENTH REGIMENT OF INFANTRY.

*Colonel.*

John Miller, 6 July, 1812.

*Lieut. Colonel.*

J. B. Campbell, 6 July, 1812.

*Majors.*

George Todd, 6 July, 1812.
Richd. Graham, 30 March, 1813.

*Captains.*

H. H. Hickman, 6 July, 1812.
David Holt, 6 July, 1812.
John T. Chunn, 6 July, 1812.
James Herron, 6 July, 1812.
Wm. J. Adair, 6 July, 1812.
John Anderson, 16 March, 1813.
Caleb H. Holder, 29 March, 1813.
B. W. Saunders, 16 April, 1813.
M. L. Hawkins, 16 April, 1813.
G. W. Jackson, 15 Aug., 1813.

*1st Lieutenants.*

H. Crittenden, 6 July, 1812.
Stephen Lee, 6 July, 1812.
James Campbell, 6 July, 1812.
J. Morrow, 6 July, 1812.
J. Hackley, Jr., 13 March, 1813.
A. Garrett, 13 March, 1813.
T. Mountjoy, 13 March, 1813.
P. P. Price, 30 March, 1813.
Jona. Rees, 30 March, 1813.
Philip King, 15 Aug., 1813.

*2nd Lieutenants.*

Chesteen Scott, 30 March, 1813.
Geo. Atchison, 6 April, 1813.
A. E. Hoffman, 6 April, 1813.
Geo. W. Stall, 6 April, 1813.
Thos. Hawkins, 16 April, 1813.
James Gray, 16 April, 1813.
Asher Phillips, 20 May, 1813.
Wm. Baylor, 15 Aug., 1813.
T. Buckley, 15 Aug., 1813.
J. Anderson, 20 Sept., 1813.

*3rd Lieutenants.*

D. L. Carney, 6 April, 1813.
John Hamilton, 6 April, 1813.
G. J. Floyd, 6 April, 1813.
Reuben Taylor, 12 April, 1813.
Wm. Eubank, 15 Aug., 1813.
John Taylor, 20 Sept., 1813.
John Cochran, 20 Sept., 1813.
George M. Beall, 19 Jan., 1814.
John Simmons, 7 March, 1814.
T. R. McKnight, 7 March, 1814.

*Ensigns.*

John Mershon, 18 June, 1813.
Richd. Doyle, 9 July, 1813.
Anderson Evans, 1 Aug., 1813.
Saml. McGuire, 10 Aug., 1813.
C. B. Campbell, 24 Oct., 1813.
Wm. Featherston, 11 March, 1814.
Rice L. Stewart, 17 March, 1814.
Wm. Griffith, 26 March, 1814.
Wm. H. Shang, 30 March, 1814.
Owen Evans, 20 April, 1814.

*Surgeon.*

Wm. Turner, 7 April, 1813.

*Surgeon's Mates.*

W. S. Madison, 12 Dec., 1812.
Clayton Tiffin, 11 March, 1814.

---

NINETEENTH REGIMENT OF INFANTRY.

*Colonel.*

Geo. Paull, 29 June, 1813.

*Lieut. Colonel.*

T. B. Van Horne, 9 April, 1813.

*Majors.*

W. A. Trimble, 18 March, 1813.
Th. Rowland, 29 June, 1813.

*Captains.*

Wm. Bradford, 6 July, 1812.
Rich. Hightower, 6 July, 1812.
Hugh Moore, 6 July, 1812.
Geo Kisling, 20 May, 1813.
Hen. Northup, 20 May, 1813.
Joel Collins, 20 May, 1813.
Alex. Hill, 20 May, 1813.
William Gill, 20 May, 1813.
R. C. Talbott, 20 May, 1813.
I. Van Horn, Jr., 20 May, 1813.

*1st Lieutenants.*

A. P. Pinney, 20 May, 1813.
W. Baird, 20 May, 1813.
George Will, 20 May, 1813.
Saml. Shannon, 20 May, 1813.
C. A. Trimble, 20 May, 1813.
W. Warner, 20 May, 1813.
Ch. A. Norton, 20 May, 1813.
N. Gregory, 20 May, 1813.
W. McDonald, 20 May, 1813.
C. L. Cass, 20 May, 1813.

*2nd Lieutenants.*

James Blair, 20 May, 1813.
Jacob C. Leslie, 20 May, 1813.
Robt. Stockton, 20 May, 1813.
Saml. Coleman, 20 May, 1813.
J. Carroll, 20 May, 1813.
Collin McCloud, 20 May, 1813.
T. C. Shields, 20 May, 1813.
Geo S. Bryan, 1 June, 1813.
Q. F. Atkins, 7 Aug., 1813.
James Fisk, 10 Aug., 1813.

*3rd Lieutenants.*

A. Bushnel, 20 May, 1813.
R. Neville, 20 May, 1813.
J. Swearingen, 20 May, 1813.
James Nixon, 20 May, 1813.
O. Granger, 20 May, 1813.
Joseph Goode, 20 May, 1813.
A. Patterson, 20 May, 1813.
John Hall, 20 May, 1813.
John Elvain, 20 May, 1813.
J. Booten, 20 May, 1813.
James Shannon, 20 May, 1813.
Chas. Cissna, 20 May, 1813.
Abijah Johns, 20 May, 1813.
John H. Simons, 20 May, 1813.
N. L. Reeves, 20 May, 1813.
Robert Young, 20 May, 1813.
John Patterson, 20 May, 1813.
Robert Smith, 20 May, 1813.
N. M. Fadden, 20 May, 1813.
Thos. Riddle, 20 May, 1813.

*Surgeon.*

John Hamm, 16 April, 1813.

*Surgeon's Mates.*

P. Spench, Jr., 26 April, 1813.
E. B. Jackson, 26 April, 1813.

---

# ORGANIZATION OF THE ARMY

## 1814.

Ensigns Benjamin S. Rue, Elisha Walker, Benjamin Davis, Thomas B. Young, William S. Wills, and William Nelson, appointed in the 17th Regiment, are transferred to the 24th Regiment of Infantry, and will report to Col. W. P. Anderson, at Nashville, Tennessee.

Ensigns Granville N. Love and Richard Mitchell, oppointed in the 17th Regiment, and Ensigns James Findlay, Peter Bryan, Philip S. Richardson and Biram Williams, appointed in the 19th Regiment, are transferred to the 28th Regiment of Infantry, and will report to Col. Thomas Deye Owings, at Olimpian Springs, Kentucky.

All the Officers of the 1st and 2nd Regiments of Light Dragoons, 1st, 2nd and 3rd Regiments of Artillery, 17th, 19th, 26th and 27th Regiments of Infantry, whose names are not retained in the foregoing order of consolidation, or transferred to other Regiments, or whose resignation have not been accepted previously to the date of this order, will consider themselves disbanded from and after the first day of June next, from which date they will be entitled to receive three months' pay according to law, in such case made and provided.

The 47th Regiment, commanded by Lieutenant Colonel Alexander Dennison, is numbered the 27th Regiment of Infantry; the 48th Regiment, commanded by Colonel Isaac Clark, is numbered the 26th Regiment of Infantry.

By order of the Secretary of War:
(Signed,) J. B. Walbach, *Adjutant General.*

### General Officers.

*Major Generals.*

Henry Dearborn, 27 Jan., 1812. 1st dist.
Thomas Pinckney, 27 March, 1812. 6th dist. Charleston.
James Wilkinson, 2 March, 1813.
Morgan Lewis, 2 March, 1813. 3rd dist.
George Izard, 24 Jan., 1814. 9th dist. 1st Division.
Jacob Brown, 24 Jan., 1814. 9th dist. 2nd Division.
Andrew Jackson, 1 May, 1814. 7th dist. New Orleans.

*Brigadier Generals.*

Joseph Bloomfield, 27 March, 1812. 4th dist. Philadelphia.
James Winchester, 27 March, 1812.
Thomas Flournoy, 18 June, 1812. 6th dist.
Thos. H. Cushing, 2 July, 1812. 2nd dist. New London.
John Chandler, 8 July, 1812.
John P. Boyd, 26 Aug., 1812. 7th dist. New Orleans.
Wm. H. Winder, 12 March, 1813. 9th dist. Chief Staff, N. Army.
Duncan M'Arthur, 12 March, 1813. 8th dist.
Benjamin Howard, 12 March, 1813. 8th dist. St. Louis.
Alexander Macomb, 24 Jan., 1814. 9th dist. 1st Division.
Thos. A. Smith, 24 Jan., 1814. 9th dist. 1st Division.
Daniel Bissell, 9 March, 1814. 9th dist. 1st Division.
Edmond P. Gaines, 9 March, 1814. 9th dist. 2nd Division.
Winfield Scott, 9 March, 1814. 9th dist. 2nd Division.
Elea. W. Ripley, 15 April, 1814. 9th dist. 2nd Division.

*Brigadier Generals by Brevet.*

Henry Burbeck, 10 July, 1812. 9th dist. Green Bush.
Moses Porter, 10 Sept., 1813. 5th dist. Com. Art., Norfolk.
Joseph G. Swift, 19 Feb., 1814. Chief of Corps of Engineers.

---

### Quartermaster's Department.

*Quartermaster Generals.*

*Colonels.*

William Linnard, 12 April, 1813. 4th dist. Philadelphia.
Elisha Jenkins, 22 April, 1813. 9th dist. Albany.
James Thomas, 28 April, 1813.
William Swan, 7 Aug., 1813. 5th dist. Norfolk.
Jas. S. Swearingen, 21 March, 1814. 8th dist.

*Deputy Quartermaster Generals.*

*Majors.*

Samuel Champlain, 18 March, 1813. 6th dist. Charleston.
C. Van de Venter, 26 March, 1813.
Samuel Brown, 26 March, 1813. 9th dist.
Taylor Berry, 31 March, 1813. 8th dist. St. Louis.
Theos. W. Smith, 2 April, 1813. 3rd dist. New York.
Paul Bentalou, 29 June, 1813. 5th dist. Baltimore.
Benjamin Romaine, 28 Feb., 1814. 3rd dist. New York.
Abraham Edwards, 15 March, 1814. 4th dist. Pittsburg.
John Bleeker, 17 March, 1814. 9th dist.
James Rees, 25 April, 1814. 9th dist.
Augustus Porter, 18 May, 1814. 9th dist.
Abram B. Fannin, 23 May, 1814. 6th dist. Savannah.
John Jammison, 28 May, 1814. 7th dist. New Orleans.

*Assistant Deputy Quartermaster Generals.*

*Captains.*

William A. Barron, 2 April, 1813. 3rd dist. New York.
Gustavus Loomis, 19 April, 1813. 9th dist.
Ezra Smith, 19 April, 1813. 9th dist.
William Chrystie, 19 April, 1813. 8th dist. St. Louis.
Jonathan Allen, 20 April, 1813. 1st dist. Pittsfield.
John T. Wirt, 25 April, 1813. 7th dist. Mobile.
James W. Bryson, 25 April, 1813. 8th dist. Newport.
John Bliss, 28 April, 1813. 9th dist.
Joseph Wheaton, 28 April, 1813. 5th dist.
John C. Payne, 19 May, 1813. 8th dist.
Benjamin Gardner, 19 May, 1813.
John G. Camp, 20 May, 1813. 9th dist. Promoted to Department.
Abr. Ten Eyck, 20 May, 1813. 9th dist.
John B. Hogan, 1 June, 1813. 9th dist. Promoted to Department.
James M'Claskey, 24 June, 1813.
Ferd. Marsteller, 17 June, 1813. 5th dist. Washington.
Thomas Campbell, 29 June, 1813. 9th dist.
Peter Lequeux, 31 Aug., 1813. 6th dist.
William Cox, 31 Aug., 1813. 6th dist.
Joseph B. Paine, 31 Aug., 1813. 6th dist.
James Ward, 31 Aug., 1813. 6th dist.
Thos. P. Townsley, 11 Jan., 1814. 6th dist.
Charles Smith, 11 Jan., 1814. 6th dist.
Josiah Dillon, 3 March, 1814. 6th dist.
John A. Rodgers, 21 March, 1814. 6th dist.
Thomas Porter, 24 March, 1814. 4th dist. Carlisle.
Caleb Benjamin, 28 May, 1814. 9th dist.
B. S. Ogden, 5 June, 1814. 4th dist.

---

TOPOGRAPHICAL DEPARTMENT.

*Topographical Engineers.*

*Majors.*

John Anderson, 12 April, 1813. 4th dist.
Paul H. Perrault, 12 April, 1813. 5th dist. Norfolk.
Isaac Roberdeau, 29 April, 1813. 4th dist.
J. C. Warren, 30 March, 1814. 6th dist.

*Assistant Topographical Engineers.*

*Captains.*

Thomas Clark, 1 April, 1813. 4th dist.
James Kearney, 12 April, 1813. War Office.
Daniel Rose, 20 July, 1813. 9th dist.

ADJUTANT GENERAL'S DEPARTMENT.

*Adjutant Generals.*

*Colonels.*

William Duane, 18 March, 1813. 4th dist. Philadelphia.
Francis K. Huger, 6 April, 1813 6th dist. Charleston.
Peter P. Schuyler, 28 April, 1813. 1st dist. Boston.
John B. Walbach, 6 Aug., 1813.
James Bankhead, 9 Sept., 1813. 5th dist. Norfolk.
William Cumming, 16 Feb., 1814. 9th dist. 1st Division.
Robert Butler, 5 March, 1814. 8th dist. Detroit.
Charles K. Gardner, 12 April, 1814. 9th dist. 2nd Division.

*Assistant Adjutant Generals.*

*Majors.*

Thomas Chrystie, 18 March, 1813. 3rd dist. New York.
Ebenezer Beebee, 2 April, 1813. 9th dist. 1st Division.
John Erving, Jr., 6 April, 1813. 6th dist.
Cary Nicholas, 25 April, 1813. 7th dist.
Roger Jones, 3 Aug., 1813. 9th dist. 2nd Division.
Robert G. Hite, 6 Aug., 1813. 9th dist. 1st Division.
Mann P. Lomax, 3 March, 1814. 9th dist. 1st Division.
James N. Barker, 8 April, 1814. 4th dist. Philadelphia.

---

INSPECTOR GENERAL'S DEPARTMENT.

*Inspector Generals.*

*Colonels.*

Nicholas Gray, 18 March, 1813. 3rd dist. New York.
William R. Boote, 6 April, 1813. 6th dist. Charleston.
Jacob Kingsbury, 28 April, 1813. 2nd dist. New London.
Ninian Pinkney, 1 Dec., 1813. 9th dist. 1st Division.
Josiah Snelling, 12 April, 1814. 9th dist. 2nd Division.
Arthur P. Hayne, 12 April, 1814. 7th dist. New Orleans.

*Assistant Inspector Generals.*

*Majors.*

Robert Sterry, 10 May, 1813. 4th dist. Philadelphia.
John R. Bell, 29 July, 1813. War Office.
Daniel Hughes, 7 Aug., 1813. 7th dist. New Orleans.
Sylvester Churchill, 29 Aug., 1813. 9th dist. 1st Division.
George P. Peters, 29 Aug., 1813. 1st dist. Boston.
Azor Orne, 1 Sept., 1813. 9th dist. 2nd Division.
Charles S. Todd, 1 Nov., 1813. 8th dist.
James Saunders, 2 Feb., 1814. 5th dist. Norfolk.
M. C. Waage, 16 March, 1814. 6th dist.
Nathaniel N. Hall, 25 April, 1814. 9th dist. 2nd Division.
H. G. Armstrong, 1 June, 1814. 9th dist. Sackett's Harbor.

## ORDNANCE DEPARTMENT.

*Commissary General.*

*Colonel.*

Decius Wadsworth, 2 July, 1812. War Office.

*Assistant Commissary General.*

*Major.*

George Bomford, 18 June, 1812. 9th dist. Albany.

*Deputy Commissaries.*

*Captains.*

John Morton, 11 Sept., 1812. Washington.
Abrm. R. Woolley, 4 Dec., 1812. 4th dist. Pittsburg.
John H. Margart, 31 Dec., 1812. 6th dist. Charleston.
James Daliba, 5 Aug., 1813. 9th dist. 2nd Division.
Thos. L. Campbell, 5 Aug., 1813. 9th dist. Albany.
Edwin Tyler, 5 Aug., 1813. 5th dist.
R. D. Richardson, 5 Aug., 1813. 8th dist.
George Talcott, Jr., 5 Aug., 1813. 3rd dist. New York.

*Assistant Deputy Commissaries.*

*Lieutenants.*

Æneas M'Kay, 12 March, 1813. 3rd dist. New York.
William Wade, 12 March, 1813. 4th dist. Pittsburg.
Rufus L. Baker, 12 March, 1813. 9th dist. Albany.
William C. Lyman, 19 April, 1813. 4th dist. Pittsburg.
George Larned, 19 April, 1813. 9th dist. Rome.
Nehemiah Baden, 6 Aug., 1813. 5th dist. Washington.
Daniel Brucknor, 6 Aug., 1813. 6th dist.
Christopher Keiser, 6 Aug., 1813. 6th dist. Charleston.
Thos. L. Hawkins, 6 Aug., 1813.
James Baker, 6 Aug., 1813. 9th dist. Albany.

*Conductor Artillery.*

John H. Peters, 14 April, 1813.

---

## JUDGE ADVOCATES.

E. A. Bancker, Esq., 18 March, 1813. 3rd dist.
Philip S. Parker, Esq., 2 April, 1813. 9th dist.
John S. Wills, Esq., 7 May, 1813. 8th dist.
J. T. Dent, Esq., 19 July, 1813. 6th dist.
Steph. Lush, Jr., Esq., 5 Oct., 1813. 9th dist.

---

## HOSPITAL DEPARTMENT.

*Physician and Surgeon General.*

James Tilton, 11 June, 1813. 9th dist.

*Apothecary General.*

Francis Le Baron, 11 June, 1813. 9th dist. Albany.

*Hospital Surgeons.*

James Mann, 9 April, 1812. 9th dist. Plattsburg.
David C. Kerr, 30 April, 1812. 7th dist. New Orleans.
Samuel Akerly, 6 July, 1812. 3rd dist. New York.
W. V. Wheaton, 28 March, 1813. 9th dist. 2nd Division.
Samuel Shaw, 6 April, 1813. 9th dist. Green Bush.
Hosea Blood, 5 May, 1813. 9th dist. Sackett's Harbor.
William M'Caw, 20 May, 1813. 6th dist.
George D. Proctor, 11 June, 1813. 6th dist.
B. Waterhouse, 29 June, 1813. 1st dist. Boston.
Thomas Akin, 29 June, 1813. 6th dist.
John R. Martin, 2 July, 1813. 9th dist. 2nd Division.
E. W. Bull, 9 Aug., 1813. 9th dist. 2nd Division.
William Thomas, 18 Feb., 1814. 9th dist. Sackett's Harbor.
Henry Huntt, 17 March, 1814. 9th dist. Burlington.
Adam Hays, 30 March, 1814. 8th dist. 2nd Division.
Tobias Watkins, 30 March, 1814. 5th dist. Norfolk, Va.
J. C. Bronaugh, 15 March, 1814. 9th dist. 1st Division.

*Hospital Surgeon's Mates.*

James Stephenson, 27 May, 1812. 7th dist.
Stephen Sutton, 27 May, 1812. 7th dist.
Samuel Schofield, 15 Sept., 1812. 9th dist.
David March, 1 March, 1813. 9th dist. Sackett's Harbor.
John H. Sackett, 22 March, 1813. 3rd dist.
J. B. Whitredge, 30 March, 1813. 9th dist.
Edward Purcell, 2 May, 1813. 4th dist. Fort Mifflin.
Wm. W. Hazard, 14 May, 1813. 9th dist.
Joseph L. Stephens, 29 June, 1813. 6th dist.
Thomas C. Walker, 2 July, 1813. 9th dist.
William Jones, 2 July, 1813. Washington City.
William E. Horner, 2 July, 1813. 9th dist.
Joseph Wallace, 15 July, 1813. 9th dist.
E. Aspinwall, 15 July, 1813. 9th dist.
Abraham Vanhoy, 15 July, 1813. 9th dist.
Gustavus Baylies, 20 Oct., 1813. 9th dist. Sackett's Harbor.
William Stewart, 30 March, 1814. 5th dist. Baltimore.
William Marshall, 30 March, 1814. 5th dist. Norfolk.
Joseph Eaton, 15 April, 1814. 1st dist. Salem.
C. Gigniliiat, 15 April, 1814. 6th dist. Hampton.
Alfred Porter, 15 April, 1814. 4th dist. Carlisle.
Elisha C. Downes, 15 April, 1814. 9th dist. Niagara.
Edward Brux, 15 April, 1814. 9th dist. Niagara.
Samuel Pennington, 13 May, 1814. 9th dist. Niagara.
Lewis M. Baily, 13 May, 1814. 5th dist.
David M. Wharry, 13 May, 1814.
Robert Archer, 13 May, 1814. 5th dist. Norfolk.
John O'Conner, 13 May, 1814. 5th dist. Fort Washington.
Josiah L. Ford, 21 May, 1814. 9th dist.
Hugh F. Rose, 21 May, 1814. 9th dist.

*Garrison Surgeon's.*

Oliver H. Spencer, 9 July, 1804. 7th dist. New Orleans.
Foster Swift, 18 Feb., 1814. 2nd dist. Newport, R. I.

*Garrison Surgeon's Mates.*

Joseph West, 10 June, 1802. 9th dist. Niagara.
John F. Heileman, 2 June, 1802. 4th dist. Fort Mifflin.
George W. Maupin, 5 Nov., 1802. 5th dist. Fort Nelson.
Joseph Goodhue, 8 Feb., 1803. 1st dist. Fort Constitution.
Abraham Stewart, 6 March, 1806. 8th dist. St. Louis, M. T.
James H. Sargent, 6 March, 1806. 1st dist. Ft. Independence.
Charles Slocum, 25 March, 1807. 7th dist. Natchitoches.
Lemuel B. Clark, 4 Jan., 1808. 5th dist. Norfolk.
Wm. T. Davidson, 13 June, 1808. 7th dist. Fort Stoddard.
C. Cunningham, 15 Oct., 1810. 2nd dist.
Jonathan S. Cool, 8 Feb., 1811. 8th dist. Fort Osage.
William Ballard, 24 March, 1812. 1st dist. Boston.
Alexander Wolcott, 25 March, 1812. 3rd dist. New York.
Anthony Benezet, 25 March, 1813. 8th dist. Fort Wayne.
William Turner, 29 Sept., 1812. 2nd dist. New London.
David Neilson, 3 Dec., 1812. 9th dist.
Charles Taylor, 3 April, 1813. 9th dist.
Sam. Merriweather, 1 Aug., 1813. 8th dist. St. Louis.
William M. Scott, 2 April, 1814. 8th dist. Detroit.
Elias C. Badeau, 8 April, 1814. 3rd dist.
John Trevett, 8 April, 1814.
P. Macauley, 8 April, 1814. 4th dist.
Solomon Wolcott, 8 April, 1814. 6th dist.
Arnold Elzy, 15 April, 1814. 5th dist. Washington City.

---

CHAPLAINS.

David Jones, 2 April, 1812. 9th dist.
Peter J. Van Pelt, 2 April, 1813. 3rd dist.
James I. Wilmer, 20 May, 1813. 8th dist.
Robert Elliott, 20 May, 1813. 9th dist.
Aaron J. Booge, 16 June, 1813. 9th dist.
Stephen Lindsley, 29 July, 1813. 8th dist.
Thomas Hersey, 20 Aug., 1813. 8th dist.

---

MILITARY ACADEMY.

*Senior Officer of Engineers, Superintendent.*
Jared Mansfield, *Professor Natural and Experimental Philosophy.*
Andrew Ellicott, *Professor of Mathematics.*
Alden Partridge, *Professor Art of Engineering.*
F. De Masson, *Teacher French Language.*
C. E. Zoeller, *Teacher of Drawing.*
Samuel Walsh, *Surgeon*, 9 Aug., 1813. 3rd dist.
Adam Empie, *Chaplain and Professor of Ethics.*

---

PURCHASING DEPARTMENT.

*Commissary General.*

C. Irvine, Esq. Philadelphia.

*Deputy Commissaries.*

John M'Kenny. 5th dist. Washington.
John H. Plummer, 9th dist. Albany.
John Langdon. 1st dist. Portsmouth.
Amasa Stetson. 1st dist. Boston.
Elisha Tracy. 2nd dist. Norwich.
Samuel Russell. 3rd dist. New York.
James Calhoun, Jr. 5th dist. Baltimore.
Robert C. Jennings. 5th dist. Norfolk.
Peter Revery. 7th dist. New Orleans.
William B. Foster. 4th dist. Pittsburg.

*Assistant Commissaries.*

Matthew Irwin. 9th dist. Champlain, N. Y.
Robert Irvine. 8th dist. Detroit.
James E. Herron. 9th dist. Sackett's Harbor.
Joseph W. Pinder.
Maurice Prevost.
Robinson R. Moore. 9th dist.

*Military Storekeepers.*

John M. Taylor. 4th dist. Philadelphia.
Samuel Devins. 1st dist. Charleston.
— Bloodgood. 9th dist. Albany.
John Fellows. 3rd dist. New York.
Jonathan Snowden. 3rd dist. West Point.
H. P. Deering. 3rd dist. Sagg Harbor.
D. Kirkpatrick. 4th dist. Newcastle.
William C. Bennett. 4th dist. Wilmington.
Thomas Martin. 8th dist. Newport.
Robert Wilson. 6th dist. Charleston.
Morgan Tompkin. 5th dist. Richmond.
G. L'Hommedieu. 2nd dist. Norwich.
Edwin Starkie. 5th dist. Norfolk.
John Rice. 1st dist. Portsmouth.
John Chaffee. 1st dist. Springfield.
Samuel Annin. 5th dist. Harper's Ferry.
Thomas B. Rutter. 5th dist. Baltimore.

---

PAY DEPARTMENT.

*Paymaster of the Army.*

Robert Brent, Esq. War Office.

*Deputy Paymaster General.*

*Major.*

Washington Lee, 13 April, 1813. Northern Army.

*Assistant Deputy Paymaster Generals.*

*1st Lieutenants.*

J. H. Rees, 24 Sept., 1813. Frontiers of New York.
Philip D. Spencer, 30 Dec., 1813. Frontiers of New York.

*District Paymasters.*

Nehemiah Freeman, 16 March, 1802. 1st dist. Boston.

*Captains.*

Ambrose Whitlock, 13 June, 1805. 8th dist. Vincennes.
Simeon Knight, 24 March, 1808. 7th dist. Natchez.
Alpha Kingsley, 9 Feb., 1810. 7th dist. Nashville.
John T. Pemberton, 4 June, 1812. 7th dist. New Orleans.
Henry Phillips, 12 June, 1812. 4th dist. Philadelphia.
Satterlee Clark, 15 Aug., 1810. 5th dist. Washington.
Walter Sheldon, 4 Aug., 1813. 9th dist. Burlington, Vt.
Jacob W. Albright, 4 Sept., 1813. 4th dist. W. Pennsylvania.

*Citizens.*

James Taylor, 4 June, 1812. 8th dist. Newport.
Thompson Douglass, 12 June, 1813. 8th dist. St. Louis.
Samuel Turner, 12 June, 1813. 5th dist. Petersburg.
Joseph Watson, 25 July, 1813.
Jesse Hunt, 22 Sept., 1812. 8th dist. Cincinnati.
George Merchant, 29 Sept., 1812. 9th dist. Albany.
Samuel Huntington, 3 Oct., 1812. 8th dist. N. W. Army.
Joseph C. Boyd, 14 Jan., 1813. 1st dist. Portland.
Robert Gardner, 3 Aug., 1813. Quebec, to pay Prisoners.
George L. Perkins, 7 Sept., 1813. 2nd dist. New London.
John B. Cooper, 24 Dec., 1813. Norfolk.

*Assistant District Paymasters.*

Joseph E. Merritt, 19 Nov., 1812. Burlington, Vt.
David Clendenin, 19 April, 1814. Poland, Ohio.
James T. Eubank, 27 April, 1814. Newport, Ky.
Joseph H. Wendel, 4 May, 1814. Overton, Tenn.
Jacob Cutter, 14 May, 1814. Portsmouth, N. H.

---

## LINEAL RANK.

### Major Generals.

Henry Dearborn, 27 Jan., 1812.
Thomas Pinckney, 27 March, 1812.
James Wilkinson, 2 March, 1813.
Morgan Lewis, 2 March, 1813.
George Izard, 24 Jan., 1814.
Jacob Brown, 24 Jan., 1814.
Andrew Jackson, 1 May, 1814.

---

### Brigadier Generals.

Joseph Bloomfield, 27 March, 1812.
James Winchester, 27 March, 1812.
Thomas Flournoy, 18 June, 1812.
T. H. Cushing, 2 July, 1812.
John Chandler, 8 July, 1812.
John P. Boyd, 26 Aug., 1812.
W. H. Winder, 12 March, 1813.
D. M'Arthur, 12 March, 1813.
Benjamin Howard, 12 March, 1813.
A. Macomb, 24 Jan., 1814.
T. A. Smith, 24 Jan., 1814.
D. Bissell, 9 March, 1814.
E. P. Gaines, 9 March, 1814.
W. Scott, 9 March, 1814.
El. W. Ripley, 15 April, 1814.

---

### Colonels.

3 *May*, 1808.

Wm. Russell, 7th Infantry.

8 *July*, 1808.

Jonas Simonds, 6th Infantry.

18 *August*, 1808.

J. Kingsbury, 1st Infantry.

12 *March*, 1812.

M. Porter, Light Artillery. Brig. Gen. brevet.

6 *July*, 1812.

Richard Sparks, 2nd Infantry.
P. P. Schuyler, 13th Infantry.
Simon Larned, 9th Infantry.
James Burn, Light Dragoons.
Isaac Clark, 26th Infantry.
Hugh Brady, 22nd Infantry.
Wm. P. Anderson, 24th Infantry.
Cromwell Pearce, 16th Infantry.
Patrick Jack, 8th Infantry.
John Miller, 17th Infantry.
James Wellborn, 10th Infantry.

31 *July*, 1812.

Joseph G. Swift, Engineer. Brig. General brevet.

26 *August*, 1812.

Robert Purdy, 4th Infantry.

23 *February*, 1813.

D. Dana, 31st Infantry.
E. Fasset, 30th Infantry.
J. Lane, 33rd Infantry.
J. D. Larned, 34th Infantry.

3 *March*, 1813.

J. Goodwin, 35th Infantry.

11 *March*, 1813.

F. D. Owings, 28th Infantry.

12 *March*, 1813.

David Brearly, 15th Infantry.
J. A. Coles, 12th Infantry.

22 *March*, 1813.

H. Carberry, 36th Infantry.

12 *April*, 1813.

M. Smith, 29th Infantry.

6 *May*, 1813.

S. E. Fotterall, 32nd Infantry.

19 *May*, 1813.

P. Little, 38th Infantry.

18 *June*, 1813.

J. Williams, 39th Infantry.

20 *June*, 1813.

Charles G. Boerstler, 14th Infantry.

29 *June*, 1813.

G. Paull, 19th Infantry.

29 *July*, 1813.

R. Bogardus, 41st Infantry.

31 *July*, 1813.

J. Loring, 40th Infantry.

15 *August*, 1813.

H. V. Milton, 3rd Infantry.
James P. Preston, 23rd Infantry.

1 *August*, 1813.

G. T. Ross, 44th Infantry.

4 *August*, 1813.

N. Long, 43rd Infantry.
W. N. Irvine, 42nd Infantry.

24 *January*, 1814

G. W. Sevier, 1st Rifle.

21 *February*, 1814.
A. Butler, 2nd Rifle.
W. King, 3rd Rifle.
J. Gibson, 4th Rifle.

9 *March*, 1814.
C. C. Russell, 20th Infantry.
J. Miller, 24th Infantry.

13 *March*, 1814.
J. Bowyer, 25th Infantry.

26 *March*, 1814.
D. M'Cobb, 45th Infantry.

9 *April*, 1814.
J. B. Campbell, 11th Infantry.

15 *April*, 1814.
G. M'Feely, 5th Infantry.
H. Atkinson, 37th Infantry.

19 *April*, 1814.
R. Dennis, 18th Infantry.

---

LIEUTENANT COLONELS.

1 *April*, 1802.
Con. Freeman, Artillery. Colonel brevet.

12 *December*, 1811.
John R. Fenwick, Light Artillery.

6 *July*, 1812.
Benaja White, 18th Infantry.
Jonas Cutting, 25th Infantry.
Moody Bedel, 11th Infantry.
Andrew Pickens, 43rd Infantry.

31 *July*, 1812.
W. K. Armistead, Chief of Engineers.

15 *August*, 1812.
Robert C. Nicholas, 1st Infantry.

23 *February*, 1813.
M. Norton, 30th Infantry.
Huckens Storrs, 31st Infantry.
E. Smith, 34th Infantry.

3 *March*, 1813.
Geo. E. Mitchell, Artillery.
James R. Mullany, 22nd Infantry.
James House, Artillery.
F. K. Huger, Artillery.
Robert Pegram, 35th Infantry.

11 *March*, 1813.
Aaron Benjamin, 37th Infantry.

12 *March*, 1813.
Samuel S. Conner, 13th Infantry.
Timothy Upham, 21st Infantry.
Thos. Aspinwall, 9th Infantry.
Joseph L. Smith, 24th Infantry.
William Lindsay, Artillery.

25 *March*, 1813.
W. Scott, 36th Infantry.

9 *April*, 1813.
T. B. Van Horn, 19th Infantry.

12 *April*, 1813.
Gil. Young, 29th Infantry.

13 *April*, 1813.
Thornton Posey, 7th Infantry.

6 *May*, 1813.
S. B. Davis, 32nd Infantry.

19 *May*, 1813.
Wm. Stewart, 38th Infantry.

7 *June*, 1813.
Jacint Laval, Light Dragoons.

18 *June*, 1813.
T. H. Benton, 39th Infantry.

19 *July*, 1813.
J. Breck, 40th Infantry.

29 *July*, 1813.
J. W. Livingston, 41st Infantry.

1 *August*, 1813.
J. G. Forbes, 42nd Infantry.

4 *August*, 1813.
Dun. L. Clinch, 10th Infantry.

15 *August*, 1813.
George Gibson, 5th Infantry.
Robert Carr, 15th Infantry.
Lawrence Manning, 8th Infantry.

14 *November*, 1813.
Eph. L. Whitlock, 14th Infantry.

13 *December*, 1813.
W. R. Boote, 2nd Infantry.

24 *January*, 1814.
James M'Donald, 1st Rifle.

31 *January*, 1814.
John Campbell, 28th Infantry.

21 *February*, 1814.
Jno. T. Woodford, 20th Infantry.
Wm. S. Hamilton, 3rd Rifle.
G. Croghan, 2nd Rifle.
J. Snelling, 4th Rifle.
A. Davis, 45th Infantry.

9 *March*, 1814.
Matthew Arbuckle, 3rd Infantry.
Eli B. Clemson, 16th Infantry.

11 *March*, 1814.
R. Butler, 44th Infantry.

13 *March*, 1814.
George Todd, 17th Infantry.

15 *April*, 1814.
Ninian Pinkney, 22nd Infantry.
Benjamin Forsyth, 26th Infantry.
A. Dennison, 27th Infantry.

15 *April*, 1814.
W. S. Talmage, 46th Infantry.

19 *April*, 1814.
W. M'Rea, Artillery.
William Carson, 6th Infantry.

1 *May*, 1814.
Horatio Stark, 33rd Infantry.

MAJORS.

1800.

Z. Pike, 1st Infantry.

1810.

A. Eustis, Light Artillery. Lieut. Colonel brevet.

1812.

George Bomford, Engineer.
Samuel Nye, Artillery.
Daniel M. Forney, Artillery.
John V. H. Huyck, 13th Infantry.
William M'Ree, Engineer.
J. V. Ball, Light Dragoons. Lieut. Colonel brevet.

1813.

Stephen Ranney, 4th Infantry.
Thomas Pitts, Light Artillery.
D. Lane, 33rd Infantry.
T. M. Vinsen, 34th Infantry.
George Armistead, Artillery.
Washington Lee, 16th Infantry.
Samuel Lane, 14th Infantry.
John Stanard, 20th Infantry.
Richard M. Malcom, 13th Infantry.
Lewis L. Taylor, 20th Infantry.
Robert C. Nicholas, 12th Infantry.
Ralph Marlin, 22nd Infantry.
Orsa C Merrill, 11th Infantry.
A. C. Smith, 35th Infantry.
R. Lee, 37th Infantry.
Samuel Hoadley, 37th Infantry.
I. Smiley, 28th Infantry.
W. A. Trimble, 19th Infantry.
A. J. M'Connico, 35th Infantry.
William Cumming, 8th Infantry.
A. Stuart, 36th Infantry.
Richard Graham, 17th Infantry.
Thomas J. Jesup, 19th Infantry.
H. Lee, Jr., 36th Infantry.
H. B. Armstrong, 4th Rifle.
John E. Wooll, 29th Infantry.
Asa B. Sizer, 29th Infantry.
Benjamin Wallace, 5th Infantry.
James B. Many, Artillery.
G. H. Hunter, 32nd Infantry.
G. Keyser, 38th Infantry.
Thomas A. Helms, Light Dragoons.
Jacob Hindman, Artillery.
Charles K. Gardner, 25th Infantry.
Willo. Morgan, 12th Infantry.
Francis Armstrong, 24th Infantry.
Joseph Grafton, 21st Infantry.
Isaac D. Bernard, 14th Infantry.
Chester Lyman, 9th Infantry.
T. Rowland, 19th Infantry.
P. Putnam, 40th Infantry.
W. Peacock, 39th Infantry.
W. Clark, 44th Infantry.
I. D. Wallace, 41st Infantry.
I. Campbell, 43rd Infantry.
H. Piere, 44th Infantry.
D. Noon, 41st Infantry.
T. Riker, 42nd Infantry.
T. D. King, 43rd Infantry.
J. Bankhead, 7th Infantry.
Ang. L. Langham, 10th Infantry.
Hy. Leavenworth, 9th Infantry.
Daniel M'Farland, 23rd Infantry.
Robert Butler, 24th Infantry.
John M'Neal, Jr., 11th Infantry.
Robert Gray, 16th Infantry.
Philip Cook, 8th Infantry.
T. P. Moore, 18th Infantry.

13 *October*, 1813.

John Nicks, 7th Infantry.

19 *November*, 1813.

H. Grindage, 15th Infantry.

13 *December*, 1813.

Z. Rossell, 15th Infantry.
I. M'Clelland, 10th Infantry.
R. Pollard, 21st Infantry.

14 *January*, 1814.

L. Morgan, 1st Rifle.
S. Owings, 1st Rifle.
C. Buckner, 5th Infantry.

14 *February*, 1814.

J. Woodruff, 3rd Infantry.
D. Hughes, 2nd Infantry.
E. Beebe, 6th Infantry.
W. H. Overton, 3rd Rifle.
T. Chambers, 4th Rifle.
I. Selden, 3rd Rifle.
D. Gwynne, 2nd Rifle.
W. H. Puthuff, 2nd Rifle.

9 *March*, 1814.

Wm. Platt, 34th Infantry.
R. B Brown, 31st Infantry.
W Blue, 39th Infantry.

21 *March*, 1814.

J. Machesney, 6th Infantry.
J. T. Arrowsmith, 22nd Infantry.

9 *April*, 1814.

Richd. Oldham, 17th Infantry.
W. Buttler, 3rd Infantry.
H. Brevoort, 45th Infantry.
D. Baker, 45th Infantry.
D. Appling, 1st Rifle.
T. Stockton, 42nd Infantry.
E. G. Perlee, 46th Infantry.
I. D. Wadsworth, 27th Infantry.
I. Delafield, 46th Infantry.
C. Crolius, 27th Infantry.
G. Humphreys, 4th Infantry.
A. H. Holmes, 32nd Infantry.
W. Lawrence, 2nd Infantry.
I. S. Doherty, 28th Infantry.
L. Beall, Artillery.

14 *May*, 1814.

J. Walworth, 33rd Infantry.
G. M. Brooke, 23rd Infantry.
R. Whartonby, 40th Infantry.
R. B. Moore, 18th Infantry.
E. Cutler, 38th Infantry.
P. Muhlenburg, 31st Infantry.

---

CAPTAINS.

1797.

J. Whistler, 1st Infantry. Major brevet.

1800.

H. M'Call, 1st Infantry. Major brevet.

1804.

Samuel T. Dyson, Artillery.

1805.

Charles Wollstonecraft, Artillery.

1806.

J. B. Walbach, Artillery. Major brevet and Colonel, staff.

1807.

Moses Swett, Artillery.

1808.

Charles Gratiot, Engineer.
William Wilson, Artillery.

1809.

Henry R. Graham, Rifle.
Abraham A. Massias, Rifle.
Francis Newman, Artillery.

1810.

William Campbell, Light Artillery.
Robt. H. M'Pherson, Light Artillery. Major brevet.
Alden Partridge, Engineer.
T. Stith.
Z. Taylor, 7th Infantry. Major brevet.

1811.

James Denking, 3rd Infantry.
C. Nicholas, 1st Infantry. Major, staff.
William M'Clelland, 7th Infantry.
John N. M'Intosh, Light Artillery.
Hays G. White, 3rd Infantry.
Alexander A. White, 7th Infantry.
James Hanham, Artillery.
Samuel Price, Light Artillery.
Oliver G. Burton, 4th Infantry.
Alex. M'Ilhenny, 5th Infantry.
Michael Walsh, Artillery.
Alex. Cummings, Light Dragoons.
Charles Fuller, 4th Infantry.
James Dorman, 5th Infantry.

3 *January*, 1812.

R. Sterry, 6th Infantry. Major, staff.

12 *March*, 1812.

John Miller, 2nd Infantry.
James Reed, Artillery.

1 *April*, 1812.

Andrew M'Dowell, Light Artillery.

4 *June*, 1812.

J. E. A. Masters, 6th Infantry.

1 *July*, 1812.

E. D. Wood, Engineer. Major brevet.

6 *July*, 1812.

Reuben Chamberlain, 2nd Infantry.
Luther Leonard, Light Artillery.
Joshua Hamilton, 1st Rifle.
Ichabod B. Crane, Artillery.
Roger Jones, Artillery.
James H. Boyle, Artillery.
Alexander S. Brooks, Artillery.
Nathan Towson, Artillery.
Samuel B. Archer, Artillery.
William Nicholas, Artillery.
James H. Barker, Artillery.
Jacob B. I'on, Artillery.
Sanders Donoho, Artillery.
Samuel G. Hopkins, Light Dragoons.
Henry Hall, Light Dragoons.
Thomas Biddle, Jr., Artillery.
John W. Gookin, Artillery.
George Cloud, 10th Infantry.
Joseph Philips, 2nd Artillery.
Thomas M. Nelson, 10th Infantry.
John Sproull, 13th Infantry.
Josiah H. Vose, 21st Infantry.
William Bradford, 17th Infantry.
Peter Mills, 23rd Infantry.
Samuel D. Harris, Light Dragoons.
John A. Burd, Light Dragoons.
Turner Crooker, 9th Infantry.
John G. Blount, 18th Infantry.
Charles Quiray, 17th Infantry.
Jas. I. B. Romayne, Artillery.
George G. Steele, 16th Infantry.
Hugh R Martin, 13th Infantry.
David E. Twiggs, 8th Infantry.
Richard Hightower, 17th Infantry.
Charles W. Hunter, 15th Infantry.
Sampson S. King, 22nd Infantry.
George Howard, 25th Infantry.
John W. Weeks, 11th Infantry.
George Butler, 18th Infantry.
Dk. Van Veghten, 23rd Infantry.
Charles E. Tobey, 21st Infantry.
Thos. Montgomery, 14th Infantry.
James Paxton, 12th Infantry.
Har. H. Hickman, 19th Infantry.
Hor. H. Watson, Artillery.
Joseph Treat, 21st Infantry.
Alexander Gray, 24th Infantry.
Robert Cunningham, 8th Infantry.
Philip Brittain, 10th Infantry.
Mordecai Myers, 13th Infantry.
John Ritchie, Artillery.
Hodijah Meade, 20th Infantry.
Thomas Sangster, 12th Infantry.
John Goodall, Artillery.
Jacob Carmack, 22nd Infantry.
Myndert M. Dox, 13th Infantry.
William Chisholm, 8th Infantry.
Charles Proctor, 21st Infantry.
William S. Jett, Jr., 20th Infantry.
Wilson Elliott, 19th Infantry.
James M'Keon, Artillery.
White Youngs, 15th Infantry.
William M'Ilvain, 14th Infantry.
Rufus M'Intire, Artillery.
David Holt, 17th Infantry.
John A. Rodgers, 24th Infantry.
John Pentland, 22nd Infantry.
Felix W. Warley, 8th Infantry.
Robert Mitchell, 10th Infantry.
William Taylor, 18th Infantry.
Alexander M'Ewen, 16th Infantry.
James Herron, 19th Infantry.
William Jones, 8th Infantry.
William O. Allen, 24th Infantry.
John Macrae, Jr., 20th Infantry.
Philemon Hawkins, Artillery.
Edward King, 18th Infantry.
H. H. Van Dalsem, 15th Infantry.
W. D. Lawrence, 13th Infantry.
Emanuel I. Leigh, 10th Infantry.
Jeremiah Chapman, 21st Infantry.
Daniel Cushing, Artillery.
James Hunter, 17th Infantry.
James Charlton, 12th Infantry.
John Foster, 22nd Infantry.
James F. M'Elroy, 16th Infantry.
Robert Desha, 24th Infantry.
John T. Chunn, 19th Infantry.
Byrd C. Willis, 20th Infantry.
Stanton Sholes, Artillery.
Henry P. Taylor, 18th Infantry.
William J. Adair, 17th Infantry.
Mark Harden, 10th Infantry.
George W. Russell, Artillery.
Charles Page, 12th Infantry.
Andrew L. Madison, 12th Infantry.
Joseph Bryant, 10th Infantry.
Benj. S. Egerton, 11th Infantry.
Thomas W. Farrar, 8th Infantry.
Samuel Gordon, 11th Infantry.
Hugh Moore, 19th Infantry.
Frederick Evans, Artillery.
Benjamin Ropes, 21st Infantry.
James H. Campbell, 24th Infantry.
William M'Queen, 8th Infantry.
Josiah Woods, 10th Infantry.
Samuel Bradford, 21st Infantry.
Joseph Clay, 10th Infantry.
Asahel Nearing, 19th Infantry.
Owen Clinton, 18th Infantry.
James Duncan, 17th Infantry.
Silas Amberson, 22nd Infantry.
Matthew I. Keith, 8th Infantry.
Thomas I. Robeson, 18th Infantry.
Jesse Copeland, 10th Infantry.
Charles Crawford, 8th Infantry.
David Scott, 23rd Infantry.
Henry Fleming, 14th Infantry.
Ken. M'Kenzie, 14th Infantry.
Thomas Delano, 23rd Infantry.
Abraham F. Hull, 9th Infantry.

31 *July*, 1812.

J. G. Totten, Engineer. Major brevet.

*August*, 1812.

Thos. A. Patterson, 1st Rifle.
Benjamin Branch, Light Artillery.
George W. Melvin, Light Artillery.
Ambrose Whitlock, 1st Infantry.

*September*, 1812.

Charles Larrabee, 4th Infantry.
Samuel Babcock, Engineer.
Ho. G. Armstrong, 23rd Infantry.
Lizur B. Canfield, 23rd Infantry.
William Davenport, 16th Infantry.
Joseph L. Barton, 15th Infantry.

*October*, 1812.

Henry Phillips, 6th Infantry.

*November*, 1812.

Thomas Ramsey, 1st Rifle.

*December*, 1812.

W. M. Littlejohn, Light Dragoons.
William Whistler, 1st Infantry.

*January*, 1813.

Geo. W. Barker, 42nd Infantry.
John C. Symmes, 1st Infantry.
Simeon Knight, 1st Infantry.
Alpha Kingsley, 1st Infantry.
Hezekiah Johnson, 1st Infantry.
John T. Pemberton, 2nd Infantry.
Ebenezer Way, 4th Infantry.
George Haig, 1st Light Dragoons.
William Smith, 1st Rifle.
Arch. W. Thornton, Light Artillery.

*February*, 1813.

Thomas Murray, Artillery.

*March*, 1813.

William Gates, Artillery.
Alex. A. J. Williams, Artillery.
John Machesney, 16th Infantry.
James Hamilton, 18th Infantry.
David Cummings, 14th Infantry.
A. C. W. Fanning, Artillery.
John M. O'Conner, Artillery.
George H. Richards, Artillery.
Edmund Foster, 9th Infantry.
Jeremiah D. Hayden, 15th Infantry.
William S. Foster, 11th Infantry.
Joseph Kenney, 25th Infantry.
Sullivan Burbank, 21st Infantry.
J. Anderson, 19th Infantry.
Geo. F. Goodman, 32nd Infantry.
William Smyth, 32nd Infantry.
Caleb H. Holder, 17th Infantry.
Thomas Post, 12th Infantry.
D. C. Butts, 35th Infantry.
Samuel M'Guire, 35th Infantry.
M. Taliaferro, 35th Infantry.
I. Thorp, 35th Infantry.
Benjamin Hardaway, 35th Infantry.
Benj. B. Jones, 35th Infantry.
Francis E. Walker, 35th Infantry.
W. F. Cocke, 35th Infantry.
I. F. Preston, 35th Infantry.

*April*, 1813.

Stephen W. Kearney, 13th Infantry.
Samuel Haring, 13th Infantry.
William A. Shelton, 20th Infantry.
Thos. B. Randolph, 20th Infantry.
Isaac L. Baker, 44th Infantry.
William O. Butler, 44th Infantry.
Narcissus Broutin, 7th Infantry.
Isaac Roach, Jr., 23rd Infantry
David Espy, 22nd Infantry.
Israel Ingersoll, Jr., 9th Infantry.
Thomas M. Reed, 25th Infantry.
Miles Greenwood, 16th Infantry.
Charles Gee, 20th Infantry.
Bernard Peyton, 20th Infantry.
Benj. W. Sanders, 17th Infantry.
John B. Murdoch, 25th Infantry.
Joseph Henderson, 22nd Infantry.
Mar. L. Hawkins, 17th Infantry.
John Baldy, 16th Infantry.
William S. Henshaw, 5th Infantry.
D. A. A. Buck, 31st Infantry.
Benjn. Adams, 33rd Infantry.
Robert Douglass, 34th Infantry.
Joseph Hook, 36th Infantry.
E. Warner, 37th Infantry.
P. B. Van Beuren, 29th Infantry.
A. Aikin, 31st Infantry.
H. C. Neal, 36th Infantry.
S. Leland, 34th Infantry.
C. Ripley, 37th Infantry.
S. Clark, 30th Infantry.
Benjamin Dunn, 33rd Infantry.
Benjn. Schuyler, 29th Infantry.
R. K. Goodenow, 33rd Infantry.
David Sanford, 30th Infantry.
C. Ives, 37th Infantry.
R. R. Kendall, 34th Infantry.
M. D. Danvers, 29th Infantry.
Jos. S. Nelson, 36th Infantry.
R. Stewart, 31st Infantry.
D. Farrington, 30th Infantry.
E. Lyndes, 29th Infantry.
E. Burnap, 31st Infantry.
C. C. Randolph, 36th Infantry.
S. B. Northrop, 37th Infantry.
Isaac Hodston, 33rd Infantry.
V. Chadwick, 34th Infantry.
G. Spencer, Jr., 30th Infantry.
William Sweet, 34th Infantry.
I. C. Rochester, 29th Infantry.
R. Sweet, 37th Infantry.
Thomas Carbery, 36th Infantry.
J. Merrill, 31st Infantry.
Charles Lothrop, 33rd Infantry.
Thomas Dinsmore, 33rd Infantry.
S. Danforth, 30th Infantry.
Samuel Raisin, 36th Infantry.
J. B. Spencer, 39th Infantry.
S. Dickinson, 31st Infantry.
N. T. Ferry, 37th Infantry.
I. Carter, 34th Infantry.
S. D. Filden, 37th Infantry.
I. Curry, 33rd Infantry.
I. Taylor, 30th Infantry.
I. C. Adams, 34th Infantry.
Joseph I. Merrick, 36th Infantry.
M. D. Hall, 36th Infantry.
G. Gaylord, 37th Infantry.
H. W. Deneale, 36th Infantry.
Thomas Corcoran, 36th Infantry.

*May*, 1813.

Julius F. Helleman, Artillery.
William F. Ware, 2nd Infantry.
David S. Townsend, 9th Infantry.
Thomas Karney, 14th Infantry.
Minor Sturgus, 24th Infantry.
Aaron Sutphen, 15th Infantry.
Abraham Per Lee, 15th Infantry.
John K. Paige, 13th Infantry.
William B. Adams, 13th Infantry.
George Bender, Jr., 9th Infantry.
John Bliss, 11th Infantry.
Samuel Booden, 32nd Infantry.
Thomas Town, 32nd Infantry.
I. Steel, Jr., 32nd Infantry.
I. I. Robinson, 32nd Infantry.
I. B. Smith, 32nd Infantry.
H. Davis, 32nd Infantry.
Hopley Yeaton, Artillery.
John M. Davis, 2nd Infantry.
Chas. S. Todd, 28th Infantry.
Henry Northrup, 26th Infantry.
I. H. Hook, 38th Infantry.
I. Aldridge, 38th Infantry.

I. Swearingen, 19th Infantry.
George Stockton, 28th Infantry.
John Rothrock, 38th Infantry.
W. Gill, 19th Infantry.
George Kisling, 19th Infantry.
I. I. Robinson, 32nd Infantry.
H. C. Gist, 28th Infantry.
I. Brookes, 38th Infantry.
I. Collins, 19th Infantry.
I. Lowry, 28th Infantry.
I. Buck, 38th Infantry.
Henry O'Neal, 38th Infantry.
J. M'Gowen, 28th Infantry.
I. Van Horne, Jr., 19th Infantry.
R. C. Talbott, 19th Infantry.
N. H. Moore, 28th Infantry.
Chas. Stansbury, 38th Infantry.
S. C. Leakin, 38th Infantry.

*June,* 1813.

Samuel Maclay, Artillery.
Simon D. Wattles, 23rd Infantry.
Azariah W. Odell, 23rd Infantry.
Henry Dyer, 25th Infantry.
Thomas Lawrence, 22nd Infantry.
Leroy Opie, 5th Infantry.
Willis Foulke, 22nd Infantry.
Robert G. Hite, 12th Infantry.
Frank Hampton, 24th Infantry.
Ephraim F. Gilbert, 23rd Infantry.
Richard Baen, 11th Infantry.
Morrell Marston, 21st Infantry.
Reuben Gilder, 14th Infantry.
Minor Robins, 25th Infantry.
Val. R. Goodrich, 11th Infantry.
James F. Norris, 9th Infantry.

*July,* 1813.

J. B. Varnum, 40th Infantry.
Seth W. Nye, 40th Infantry.
J. Phagan, 39th Infantry.
William Walker, 39th Infantry.
Benjamin Reynolds, 39th Infantry.
J. B. Long, 39th Infantry.
A. H. Douglass, 39th Infantry.
Henry Henegar, 39th Infantry.
John Jones, 39th Infantry.
James Davis, 39th Infantry.
Thomas Steuart, 39th Infantry.
James Pery, 40th Infantry.
Jonathan Eastman, 21st Infantry.

*August,* 1813.

S. Berrian, 41st Infantry.
William G. Oliver, 42nd Infantry.
E. S. Mendenhall, 42nd Infantry.
Gilbert Seaman, 41st Infantry.
Mat. N. Sanborn, 40th Infantry.
A. Sherman, 41st Infantry.
R. Neale, Jr., 40th Infantry.
L. Ross, 40th Infantry.
A. Hamilton, 40th Infantry.
G. H. Manigault, 43rd Infantry.
I. I. Goodwyn, 43rd Infantry.
Theo. L. Gourdin, 43rd Infantry.
Wm. S. Radcliff, 41st Infantry.
Thomas Hanson, 42nd Infantry.
Thomas Hyde, 43rd Infantry.
E. B. Duvall, 42nd Infantry.
William R. Davis, 3rd Infantry.
E. F. Tatnall, 43rd Infantry.
H. Garrett, 43rd Infantry.
George Dubney, 43rd Infantry.
Robert Love, Jr., 43rd Infantry.
John Leonard, 40th Infantry.
Chas. Humphreys, 40th Infantry.
Samuel W. Butler, 3rd Infantry.
Michael Corning, 11th Infantry.
Richard H. Bell, 5th Infantry.
J. L. Eastman, 4th Infantry.
J. D. Howell, 15th Infantry.
Sylvester Churchill, Artillery.
Benjamin Watson, 25th Infantry.
John D. Coon, 16th Infantry.
William O. Winston, 24th Infantry
John Campbell, 13th Infantry.
Jonathan W. Aitkin, 16th Infantry.
George W. Jackson, 19th Infantry.
John A. Thomas, 25th Infantry.
George M'Glassin, 15th Infantry.
Walter Wilkinson, 24th Infantry.
Horace Hall, 11th Infantry.
Benjamin Smead, 11th Infantry.
Joseph Marshall, 14th Infantry.
Thomas Harrison, 9th Infantry.
F. Conkling, 4th Infantry.
Daniel Ketchum, 25th Infantry.
Benjamin K. Pierce, Artillery.

*September,* 1813.

John Baily, 40th Infantry.
Elisha W. Field, 40th Infantry.
I. Fillebrown, 40th Infantry.
A. Hawkins, 4th Infantry.
A. Brownlow, 2nd Infantry.
W. A. Blount, 18th Infantry.
Z. Morgan, 12th Infantry.
I. Larkin, 22nd Infantry.
Francis Allyn, 41st Infantry.

*October,* 1813.

Thos. Y. Sprogell, 22nd Infantry.
J. M'Donald, 14th Infantry.
James Biddle, 42nd Infantry.
Armstrong Irvine, 4th Rifle.
Henry Chotard, 3rd Infantry.
William Clarke, 28th Infantry.

*November,* 1813.

Francis Stribling, Light Artillery.
I. Milliken, 33rd Infantry.
John G. Camp, 12th Infantry.
R. Arell, 14th Infantry.
Thomas Barker, 42nd Infantry.
George Vashon, 10th Infantry.
George Strother, 10th Infantry.
E. Stallings, 1st Rifle.

*December,* 1813.

Hamlin Cook, 8th Infantry.
M. Lynch, 20th Infantry.
W. Sheldon, 11th Infantry.
A. B. Conant, 29th Infantry.
W. Barnet, 15th Infantry.
B. D. Herriott, 3rd Infantry.
George Newbegen, 33rd Infantry.

*January,* 1814.

I. P. Duvall, 20th Infantry.
N. M'Laughlin, 16th Infantry.
John Ingersoll, 41st Infantry.
M. M. Quackenbos, 41st Infantry.
I. S. Bicknell, 31st Infantry.
A. Arnold, 31st Infantry.
C. L. Rockwood, 31st Infantry.
John Jamison, 5th Infantry.
L. B. Willis, 12th Infantry.
I. Brownson, 1st Infantry.
I. M'Cullen, 41st Infantry.
J. Merrill, 34th Infantry.
William Miller, 30th Infantry.

*February,* 1814.

R. P. Johnson, 8th Infantry.
I. Burbridge, 25th Infantry.
A. Spencer, 29th Infantry.
George P. Peters, 4th Infantry.
E. Webb, 6th Infantry.
S. C. Mabson, 3rd Infantry.
I. Saunders, 5th Infantry.
Thomas Hamilton, 1st Infantry.
I. Robinson, 7th Infantry.
Adam Larrabee, Light Artillery.
D. Henderson, 21st Infantry.

*March,* 1814.

M. P. Payne, 20th Infantry.
S. Robinson, 30th Infantry.
I. Brown, 37th Infantry.
I. T. Wirt, 2nd Infantry.
I. Smith, 4th Infantry.
S. G. Earle, 43rd Infantry.
E. Beall, 43rd Infantry.
F. L. Amelung, 44th Infantry.
A. Peychard, 44th Infantry.
I. I. Miles, 44th Infantry.
Charles Tessier, 44th Infantry.
E. D. Mirepoix, 44th Infantry.
G. Winter, 44th Infantry.
I. M. Barclay, 44th Infantry.
C. Mulford, 44th Infantry.
I. S. Wade, 7th Infantry.
A. C. Spencer, 29th Infantry.
B. White, 25th Infantry.
Benjn. Birdsall, 4th Rifle.
H. Brackenridge, 2nd Rifle.
William Oliver, 2nd Rifle.
Thos. L. Beall, 4th Rifle.
Robert Fenner, 3rd Rifle.
Edward Carrington, 3rd Rifle.
Walter German, 4th Rifle.
John Lyttle, 4th Rifle.
Walter Coles, 3rd Rifle.
Jesse Kean, 4th Rifle.
Willie Martin, 3rd Rifle.
Hugh Innes, 2nd Rifle.
D. Kinchaloe, 3rd Rifle.
R. Scott, 4th Rifle.
S. Scott, 2nd Rifle.
Uriah Allison, 2nd Rifle.
Benjamin Desha, 2nd Rifle.
W. Green, 4th Rifle.
Benjn. Johnson, 2nd Rifle.
Batteal Harrison, 2nd Rifle.
Matthew I. Magee, 4th Rifle.
R. Campbell, 3rd Rifle.
I. M'Whorter, 3rd Rifle.
I. Morris, 4th Rifle.
I. E. Calhoun, 3rd Rifle.
William Pritchard, 2nd Rifle.
John O. Fallon, 2nd Rifle.
A. W. Brandon, 3rd Rifle.

*April,* 1814.

S. Vail, 7th Infantry.
E. Bogardus, 2nd Infantry.
Lina T. Helm, 1st Infantry.
W. Lavall, 3rd Infantry.
George Morley, 3rd Infantry.
G. C. Allen, 7th Infantry.
L. L. Bush, 6th Infantry.
H. Bradley, 2nd Infantry.
Thos. Traquair, 42nd Infantry.
I. S. Carty, 42nd Infantry.
Lewis Peckham, 4th Infantry.
I. Smith, 45th Infantry.
S. C. Cotton, 48th Infantry.
William Shotwell, 47th Infantry.
I. Lavaik, 48th Infantry.
I. Flanders, 45th Infantry.
I. Campbell, 48th Infantry.
B. Bradford, 45th Infantry.
S. Elkins, 45th Infantry.
Christopr. Hughes, 47th Infantry.
D. Holden, 45th Infantry.
Charles Hartell, 47th Infantry.
A. T. Crane, 47th Infantry.
W. Farnsworth, 48th Infantry.
I. Thompson, 48th Infantry.
M. Burnett, 46th Infantry.
N. Stanley, 45th Infantry.
B. Irvine, 47th Infantry.
T. Coleman, 48th Infantry.
S. Baker, 46th Infantry.
I. S. Suffern, 46th Infantry.
I. Williams, 48th Infantry.
I. Hedges, 48th Infantry.
Thomas Earle, 47th Infantry.
Robert Gourlay, Jr., 46th Infantry.
I. Danforth, 45th Infantry.
E. Hale, 45th Infantry.
A. D. Wilson, 46th Infantry.
I. Wright, 46th Infantry.
B. Wood, 47th Infantry.
A. Reynolds, 47th Infantry.
William Chappel, 45th Infantry.
D. Crawford, 46th Infantry.
I. Miller, 46th Infantry.
E. Boardman, 48th Infantry.
James Hall, 45th Infantry.
Thomas Bruyn, 46th Infantry.

*May,* 1814.

I. W. Stith, 35th Infantry.
J. Moulton, 33rd Infantry.
A. Ward, 29th Infantry.
E. Montgomery, 7th Infantry.
P. P. Walter, 32nd Infantry.
A. P. Thompson, 6th Infantry.
R. Patterson, 32nd Infantry.
I. S. Allison, 5th Infantry.
I. L. Carey, 3rd Infantry.
I. Smith, 38th Infantry.
I. Morton, 38th Infantry.
L. Powers, 31st Infantry.
R. W. Chick, 5th Infantry.
I. Gray, 39th Infantry.
I. Owens, 5th Infantry.

---

## Corps of Engineers.

*Colonel.*

Josh. G. Swift, 31 July, 1812. Brig. General brevet, 10 Feb.

*Lieut. Colonel.*

Walker K. Armistead, 31 July, 1812.

*Majors.*

G. Bomford, 6 July, 1812.
Wm. M'Ree, 31 July, 1812.

*Captains.*

Chs. Gratiot, 23 Feb., 1808.
A. Partridge, 23 July, 1810.
Elea. D. Wood, 1 July, 1812. Maj. brevet, 6 May, 1813. Killed.
J. G. Totten, 31 July, 1812. Maj. brevet, 6 June, 1813.
Saml. Babcock, 20 Sept., 1812.
Sylvs. Thayer, 13 Oct., 1813.

*1st Lieutenants.*

Wm. Cutbush, 1 July, 1812.
Ed. De Russey, 6 July, 1812.
Fredk. Lewis, 20 Sept., 1812. Aid to Maj. Gen. Dearborn.
Jas. Gadsden, 17 March, 1813.
T. W. Maurice, 13 Oct., 1813.
Hipolite Dumas, 20 Feb., 1814.

*2nd Lieutenants.*

D. B. Douglass, 1 Oct., 1813.
Geo. Trescott, 16 Oct., 1813.
J. L. Smith, 16 Oct., 1813.
Horace C. Story, 11 March, 1814.
John Wright, 30 March, 1814.

---

## Regiment of Light Artillery.

*Colonel.*

Moses Porter, 12 March, 1812. Brig. Gen. brevet, 10 Sept., 1813.

*Lieut. Colonel.*

J. R. Fenwick, 2 Dec., 1811.

*Majors.*

Abram. Eustis, 15 March, 1810. Lieut. Col. brevet, 10 Sept., 1813.
Thomas Pitts, 20 Jan., 1813.

*Captains.*

Wm. Campbell, 30 May, 1810.
Robert H. M'Pherson, 15 July, 1810. Maj. brevet, 30 March, 1814.
J. N. M'Intosh, 1 May, 1811.
Aw. M'Dowell, 1 April, 1812.
Luther Leonard, 6 July, 1812.
Benjn. Branch, 24 Aug., 1812.
G. W. Melvin, 24 Aug., 1812.
A. W. Thornton, 20 Jan., 1813.
Fras. Stribling, 1 Nov., 1813.
Adam Larrabee, 21 Feb., 1814.

*1st Lieutenants.*

Tho. Ketchum, 1 Sept., 1811.
John R. Bell, 24 Aug., 1812. Assistant Inspector General.
F. B. Murdoch, 24 Aug., 1812.
W. F. Hobart, 5 April, 1813.
W. Sumpter, 27 May, 1813.
G. W. Hight, 10 Aug., 1813.
G. N. Morris, 23rd Aug., 1813.
J. H. Wilkins, 3 Dec., 1813.
John Gates, Jr., 3 Dec., 1813. Paymaster.
Nelson Freeland, 21 Feb., 1814.

*2nd Lieutenants.*

J. T. M'Kinney, 5 April, 1813.
S. M. Mackay, 27 May, 1813. Adjutant.
B. F. Robb, 30 June, 1813.
G. E. Wells, 1 Oct., 1813.
Elijah Lyon, 23 Oct., 1813.
S. Washburn, 13 Dec., 1813.
Henry Stanton, 7 March, 1814.
Joseph Scott, 7 March, 1814.
Edm. M. Giles, 7 March, 1814.
Richd. W. Field, 17 March, 1814.

*3rd Lieutenant.*

Gustav. Drane, 15 April, 1814.

*Surgeon.*

Lewis Dunham, 12 Dec., 1808.

---

LIGHT DRAGOONS.

*Colonel.*

James Burn, 6 July, 1812.

*Lieut. Colonel.*

Jacint Laval, 7 June, 1813.

*Majors.*

James V. Ball, 16 Sept., 1812. Lieut Col. brevet, 18 Dec., 1812.
T. A. Helms, 7 June, 1813.

*Captains.*

A. P. Hayne, 10 Nov., 1809. Inspector General.
A. Cummings, 1 Nov., 1811.
S. G. Hopkins, 6 July, 1812.
Henry Hall, 6 July, 1812.
Saml. D. Harris, 6 July, 1812.
John A. Burd, 6 July, 1812.
W. M. Littlejohn, 1 Dec., 1812.
George Haig, 20 Jan., 1813.

*1st Lieutenants.*

H. Whiting, 20 Aug., 1811.
George Birch, 1 Nov., 1811.
Chas. J. Nourse, 7 May 1812.
Beverly Turpin, 6 July, 1812.
A. H. Sneed, 6 July, 1812.
F. S. Belton, 20 Jan., 1813. Paymaster.
Wm. Nielson, 7 June, 1813.
Louis Laval, 28 July, 1813.

*2nd Lieutenants.*

Robert H. Craig, 18 March, 1813. Adjutant.
Isaac Griffith, 18 March, 1813.
James Martin, 30 April, 1813.
George Watts, 1 Aug., 1813.
F. H. Lissenhoff, 1 Aug., 1813.
James Trippe, 1 May, 1814.
H. A. Hays, 1 May, 1814.
C. Wright, 1 May, 1814.

*3rd Lieutenants.*

Hugh Sterling, 29 April, 1813
John L. Elbert, 20 June, 1813.
L. P. Gustine, 29 July, 1813.
T. S. Bracken, 1 May, 1814.
Thos. Hogan, 1 May, 1814.
Philip Ansbach, 1 May, 1814.

*Cornets.*

Wm. Johnson, 11 Oct., 1813.
William Gale, 11 Oct., 1813.
Th. Robinson, 11 March 1814.
S. H. Cumming, 11 March, 1814.
I. Caldwell, 11 March, 1814.
Henry Stone, 11 March, 1814.

*Surgeon.*

W. H. Buckner, 6 July, 1812.

*Surgeon's Mate.*

S. H. Littlejohn, 3 April, 1813.

---

CORPS OF ARTILLERY.

*Lieut. Colonels.*

Cont Freeman, 1 April, 1802. Col. brevet.
G. E. Mitchell, 3 March, 1813.
James House, 3 March, 1813.
F. K. Huger, 3 March, 1813. Colonel, staff.
Wm. Lindsay, 12 March, 1813.
Wm. MacRea, 19 April, 1814.

*Majors.*

D. M. Forney, 6 July, 1812.
Samuel Nye, 6 July, 1812.
G. Armistead, 3 March, 1813.
Jas. B. Many, 5 May, 1813.
J. Hindman, 26 June, 1813.
Lloyd Beall, 21 April, 1814.

*Captains.*

S. T. Dyson, 15 Sept., 1804.
Charles Wollstonecraft, 15 March, 1805.
J. B. Walbach, 31 Jan., 1806. Major brevet, 13 Nov., and Colonel, staff.
Moses Swett, 30 June, 1807.
Wm. Wilson, 3 May 1808.
E. Humphreys, 9 Jan., 1809.
Frs. Newman, 1 Oct., 1809.
Jas. Hanham, 10 July, 1811.
Michl. Walsh, 31 Oct., 1811.
James Reed, 12 March, 1812.
Ichd. B. Crane, 6 July 1812.
Roger Jones, 6 July, 1812.
J. H. Boyle, 6 July, 1812.
A. S. Brookes, 6 July, 1812.
Nathan Towson, 6 July, 1812.
S. B. Archer, 6 July, 1812.
Wm. Nicholas, 6 July, 1812.
J. N. Barker, 6 July, 1812. Assistant Adjutant General.
J. R. I'on, 6 July, 1812.
Sanders Donoho, 6 July, 1812.
Thos. Biddle, Jr., 6 July, 1812.
J. W. Gookin, 6 July, 1812.

Joseph Philips, 6 July, 1812.
J. S. B. Romayne, 6 July, 1812.
Hor. H. Watson, 6 July, 1812.
James M'Keon, 6 July, 1812.
John Ritchie, 6 July, 1812.
John Goodall, 6 July, 1812.
Rufus M'Intyre, 6 July, 1812.
P. Hawkins, Jr., 6 July, 1812.
Danl. Cushing, 6 July, 1812.
Stanton Sholes, 6 July, 1812.
G. W. Russell, 6 July, 1812.
Fredk. Evans, 6 July, 1812.
Thos. Murray, 10 Feb., 1813.
Wm. Gates, 3 March, 1813.
A. J. Williams, 12 March, 1813.
A. C. W. Fanning, 13 March, 1813.
J. M. O'Connor, 13 March, 1813.
G. H. Richards, 13 March, 1813.
J. F. Heileman, 5 May, 1813.
Hopley Yeaton, 20 May, 1813.
Thos Bennett, 20 June, 1813.
S. Churchill, 15 Aug., 1813. Assistant Inspector General.
B. K. Pierce, 1 Oct., 1813.
Jas. Green, Jr., 29 Oct., 1813.
John S. Peyton, 15 Dec., 1813.
Hy. K. Craig, 23 Dec., 1813.

*1st Lieutenants.*

Ethan A. Allen, 1 Oct., 1809.
Archd. Darrah, 29 Jan., 1811.
M. P. Lomax, 30 June, 1811. Major, staff.
Justus Post, 1 July 1811.
S. Champlain, 31 Oct., 1811.
Heman A. Fay, 23 Dec., 1811.
Milo Mason, 29 Feb., 1812.
Chris. Vandeventer, 12 March, 1812.
J. L. Tracy, 6 July 1812.
Moses J. Chase, 6 July 1812.
Adrian Neil, 6 July, 1812
John Farley, 6 July, 1812
P. M'Donogh, 6 July, 1812
Wm. M. Read, 6 July, 1812.
Harold Smyth, 6 July, 1812.
Wm. J. Cohan, 6 July, 1812.
John Fontaine, 6 July 1812.
J. H. Larwill, 6 July, 1812.
L. Brown, 6 July, 1812.
Luther Scott, 6 July, 1812.
Robt. R. Ruffin, 6 July, 1812.
Hy. Slaughter, 6 July, 1812.
J. H. Daring, 6 July, 1812.
I. Erving, Jr., 16 Aug., 1812. Major, staff.
A. L. Sands, 10 Feb., 1813.
James Dalib, 3 March, 1812. Captain Ordnance.
Rich. A. Zantzinger, 13 March, 1813.
C. M. Macomb, 13 March 1813.
Jos. H. Rees, 13 March, 1813.
Robert Stewart, 13 March, 1813.
W. R. Duncan, 13 March, 1813.
Chester Root, 13 March, 1813.
Mw. Jenkins, 13 March, 1813.
J. L. Edwards 28 March, 1813.
Gus. Loomis, 5 May, 1813.
P. D. Spencer, 13 May, 1813.
R. H. Ashley, 20 May, 1813.
Jno. Mountfort, 20 May, 1813.
J. S. Brush, 20 June, 1813.
F. Whiting, 20 June, 1813.
Edwin Sharpe, 26 June, 1813.
G. Dearborn, 1 Oct., 1813.
Felix Ansart, 1 Oct., 1813.
Wm. King, 1 Oct., 1813.
T. C. Legate, 29 Oct., 1813.
Jacob Warley, 15 Dec., 1813.
Wm. Smith, 23 Dec., 1813.

*2nd Lieutenants.*

Saml. Spotts, 10 Feb., 1812.
Wm. Parker, 10 Feb., 1812.
Levi Whiting, 10 Feb., 1812.
J. W. Rouse, 27 March, 1812.
B. B. White, 14 April, 1812.
Abel B. Chase, 30 April, 1812.
James Baker, 1 May, 1812.
Joseph P. Bartlett, 6 July, 1812.
Lewis Morgan, 6 July, 1812.
W. H. Nicoll, 6 July, 1812.
John Ruffin, 6 July, 1812.
J. H. Gamble, 6 July, 1812.
Jno. W. Kincaid, 6 July, 1812.
Robert Goode, 6 July, 1812.
Francis O. Byrd, 6 July, 1812.
J. I. Cromwell, 23 Nov., 1812.
J. W. Lent, Jr., 12 March, 1813.
Charles Clark, 12 March, 1813.
Thos. Elfe, Jr., 17 March, 1813.
Thos Chrystie, 18 March, 1813.
S. Rockwell, 20 March, 1813.
J. Bosque, 12 April, 1813.
Thos. Clark, 16 April, 1813.
Cld. D. Cooper, 16 April, 1813.
Jos. P. Prince, 16 April, 1813.
G. Doneghey, 16 April, 1813.
P. J. Neville, 20 April, 1813.
A. W. Forbush, 5 May, 1813.
M. S. Massey, 13 May, 1813.
F. P. Woolsey, 20 May, 1813.
Ch. Anthony, 20 May, 1813.
W. M'Clintock, 20 June, 1813.
L. H. Osgood, 20 June, 1813.
J. P. Bunting, 26 June, 1813.
J. Henderson, 26 June, 1813.
Peter Melendy, 29 June, 1813.
B. C. Bartlett, 29 June, 1813.
Benjn. Lawson, 30 Sept., 1813.
R. M. Kirby, 1 Oct., 1813.
Wm. B. Read, 1 Oct., 1813.
Ed. Baynton, 1 Oct., 1813.
Wm. Lyon, 1 Oct., 1813.
H. M. Campbell, 12 Oct., 1813.
M. M. Russell, 20 Oct., 1813.
John Mitchell, 16 Nov., 1813.
Hy. L. Duffell, 15 Dec., 1813.
Wr. Berryman, 23 Dec., 1813.
J. Bennett, 24 Dec., 1813.
W. J. Sever, 31 Dec., 1813.
E. Hopkins, 31 Dec., 1813.
Jas. C. Pickett, 19 April, 1814.
Britton Evans, 19 April, 1814.
James Bailey, 19 April, 1814.
T. J. Harrison, 19 April, 1814.
J. Watmaugh, 19 April, 1814.
Wm. Kenny, 19 April, 1814.
C. Newkirk, 19 April, 1814.
Oliver Bangs, 19 April, 1814.
N. Henderson, 19 April, 1814.
G. W. Gardiner, 1 May, 1814.
C. S. Merchant, 1 May, 1814.
Nathl. G. Dana, 1 May, 1814.
John Monroe, 1 May, 1814.
J. S. Allanson, 1 May, 1814.
St. Birdsall, 1 May, 1814.
L. G. De Russy, 1 May, 1814.
Thomas Childs, 1 May, 1814.
Saml. L. Dana, 1 May, 1814.
J. S. Shoemick, 1 May, 1814.
S. G. Bloomfield, 1 May, 1814.
T. W. Freeman, 1 May, 1814.
Cassius Carter, 1 May, 1814.
Thos. V. Earle, 1 May, 1814.
Jonathan Pell, 1 May, 1814.
Chas. Mellon, 1 May, 1814.
Geo. H. Britt, 1 May, 1814.
James Hall, 1 May, 1814.
Aug. Aisquith, 1 May, 1814.
John S. Pierce, 1 May, 1814.
Elijah Brown, 1 May, 1814.
Joseph Gilbert, 1 May, 1814.
Eliud L. Davis, 1 May, 1814.
Allen Lowd, 1 May, 1814.
J. Armstrong, 19 May, 1814.
Jas. Scallan, 19 May, 1814.
Chas. W. Salter, 20 May, 1814.
P. A. Dennis, 20 May, 1814.

*3rd Lieutenants.*

D. S. Andrews, 19 April, 1814.
N. G. Wilkinson, 20 April, 1814.

D. C. Nicholls, 26 April, 1814.
David Telfair, 5 May, 1814.
William Elgin, 12 May, 1814.
Geo. Reardon, 18 May, 1814.
Ben.j Tennille, 23 May, 1814.
Hugh K. Meade, 23 May, 1814.
H. M. Simons, 23 May, 1814.
Thos. A. Linton, 9 June, 1814.

---

FIRST INFANTRY.

*New Jersey.*

*Colonel.*

J. Kingsbury, 18 Aug., 1808. Inspector. General.

*Lieut. Colonel.*

R. C. Nicholas, 15 Aug., 1812.

*Majors.*

*Z. Pike, 20 March, 1800. Lieut. Colonel. brevet, 10 July, 1812.
S. Owens, 31 Jan., 1814.

*Captains.*

John Whistler, 1 July, 1797. Major brevet, 10 July, 1812.
A. Whitlock, 26 Aug., 1812.
W. Whistler, 31 Dec., 1812.
J. C. Symmes, 20 Jan., 1813.
Simeon Knight, 20 Jan., 1813.
A. Kingsley, 20 Jan., 1813.
H. Johnson, 20 Jan., 1813.
J. Brownson, 31 Jan., 1814.
T. Hamilton, 21 Feb., 1814.
L. T. Helm, 15 April, 1814.

*1st Lieutenants.*

Benj. Marshall, 14 Oct., 1808.
J. W. Bryson, 20 Jan., 1813.
J. Campbell, 20 Jan., 1813.
D. Stansbury, 20 Jan., 1813.
B. Vasquez, 30 July, 1813.
Lewis Bissell, 31 Jan., 1814.
J. A. Shaw, 21 Feb., 1814.
Ormond Marsh, 30 March, 1814.
Danl. Curtis, 15 April, 1814.
R. A. M'Cabe, 1 May, 1814.

*2nd Lieutenants.*

N. E. Westfall, 20 Jan., 1813.
W. Anderson, 20 Jan., 1813.
L. Talliaferro, 14 Aug., 1813.
G. Harberger, 31 Jan., 1814.
Ph. Yost, 12 March, 1814.
C. Bertor, 19 April, 1814.
D. Trimble, 19 April, 1814.
W. Christie, 19 April, 1814.
E. J. Roberts, 1 May, 1814.

*3rd Lieutenants.*

J. Jeffries, 19 April, 1814.
Ste. Shea, 19 April, 1814.
T. Beauford, 19 April, 1814.
F. Bernard, 19 April, 1814.

*Surgeon.*

H. Catlett, 18 Feb., 1813.

*Surgeon's Mate.*

S. C. Muir, 7 April, 1813.

---

SECOND INFANTRY.

*Louisiana.*

*Colonel.*

Richard Sparks, 6 July, 1812.

*Lieut. Colonel.*

W. R. Boote, 13 Dec., 1813. Inspector General.

*Majors.*

Dan. Hughes, 21 Feb., 1814. Assistant Inspector General.
W. Lawrence, 19 April, 1814.

*Captains.*

Hugh, M'Call, 19 Aug., 1800. Major, brevet, 10 July, 1812.
John Miller, 12 March, 1812.
R. Chamberlain, 6 July, 1812.
J. T. Pemberton, 20 Jan., 1813.
Wm. F. Ware, 5 May, 1813.
John M. Davis, 30 May, 1813.
A. Brownlow, 7 Sept., 1813.
John T. Wirt, 9 March, 1814.
E. Bogardus, 15 April, 1814.
H. Bradley, 19 April, 1814.

*1st Lieutenants.*

P. Willis, 1 Nov., 1812.
H. H. Villard, 10 Jan., 1813.
H. A. Burchsted, 5 May, 1813.
J. Bell, 30 May, 1813. Aid to Maj. Gen. Wilkinson.
T. Doggett, 7 Sept., 1813.
R. Sturgus, 9 March, 1814.
Jas. Stuarte, 15 April, 1814.
H. Conway, 19 April, 1814.
N. Clarke, 1 May, 1814.

*2nd Lieutenants.*

W. M. Smith, 20 Jan., 1813.
T. F. Thomas, 9 July, 1813.
Beverly Roy, 25 Oct., 1813.
H. Saunders, 7 Sept., 1813.
L. M. Ayer, 9 March, 1814.
T. R. Saunders, 15 April, 1814.
W. Fuller, 19 April, 1814.
G. B. M'Claskey, 1 May, 1814.
John Darnell, 1 May, 1814.
E. Brooks, 1 May, 1814.

*3rd Lieutenants.*

J. R. Johnson, 1 May, 1814.
R. Davis, 1 May, 1814.
R. G. Saunders, 1 May, 1814.
John Saunders, 1 May, 1814.
Cy. Saunders, 1 May, 1814.

*Surgeon.*

Jabez W. Heustis, 2 April, 1814.

---

THIRD INFANTRY.

*Mississippi and Missouri Territories.*

*Colonel.*

H. V. Milton, 15 Aug., 1813.

*Lieut. Colonel.*

M. Arbuckle, 9 March, 1814.

*Majors.*

Jas. Woodruff, 21 Feb., 1814.
Wm. Butler, 15 April, 1814.

*Captains.*

J. Denking, 6 Feb., 1811.
H. G. White, 11 May, 1811.
W. R. Davis, 4 Aug., 1813.
S. W. Butler, 15 Aug., 1813.
H. Chotard, 9 Oct., 1813.
B. D. Herriot, 31 Dec., 1813.
S. C. Mabson, 21 Feb., 1814.
Wm. Laval, 15 April, 1814.
Geo. Marley, 15 April, 1814.
J. L. Carey, 1 May, 1814.

*1st Lieutenants.*

J. F. Everitt, 4 Aug., 1813.
Wm. Triplett, 15 Aug., 1813.
J. W. Hansell, 9 Oct., 1813.
T. Hunter, 1 Nov., 1813.
Wm. Christian, 31 Dec., 1813.
W. Bourke, 21 Feb., 1814.
John Tarrant, 15 April, 1814.
A. Donoh, 15 April, 1814.
Jas. Smith, 15 April, 1814.
T. Turner, 1 May, 1814.

*2nd Lieutenants.*

R. Goodwin, 15 Aug., 1813.
John Martin, 2 Sept., 1813.
W. L. Robeson, 9 Oct., 1813.
J. A. Watson, 1 Nov., 1813.
Jas. A. Hart, 31 Dec., 1813.
J. F. Ross, 21 Feb., 1814.
T. W. Barton, 15 April, 1814.
C. Stephens, 15 April, 1814.
Thos. Rogers, 15 April, 1814.
W. V. Cobbs, 1 May, 1814.

*3rd Lieutenants.*

R. Rackestraw, 1 May, 1814.
E. Basye, 1 May, 1814.
R. Miller, 1 May, 1814.
W. Mann, 1 May, 1814.
Th. S. Sydnor, 1 May, 1814.

*Surgeon.*

Isaac Davis, 21 May, 1814.

*Surgeon's Mate.*

Elisha Scott, 21 May, 1814.

---

FOURTH INFANTRY.

*New Hampshire.*

*Colonel.*

R. Purdy, 26 Aug., 1812.

*Majors.*

S. Ranney, 20 Jan., 1813.
G. Humphreys, 18 April, 1814.

*Captains.*

O. G. Burton, 25 Aug., 1811.
C. Fuller, 9 Nov., 1811.
C. Larrabee, 15 Sept., 1812.
E. Way, 20 Jan., 1813.
J. L. Eastman, 15 Aug., 1813.
F. Conkling, 2 Sept., 1813.
A. Hawkins, 2 Sept., 1813.
G. P. Peters, 21 Feb., 1814. Assistant Inspector General.
John Smith, 9 March, 1814.
L. Peckham, 28 April, 1814.

*1st Lieutenants.*

G. Gooding, 15 Feb., 1812.
Josiah Bacon, 15 Sept., 1812. Quartermaster.
P. Greenough, 20 Jan., 1813.
M. Bulley, 31 July, 1813.
J. Plymton, 15 Aug., 1813.
G. W. Hovey, 2 Sept., 1813.
P. Wheelock, 2 Sept., 1813.
S. Butterfield, 21 Feb., 1814.
S. Armstrong, 9 March, 1814.
S. Legate, 28 April, 1814.

*2nd Lieutenants.*

Paul Peckham, 19 May, 1813.
J. Ranney, 30 May, 1813.
E. Kerby, 31 July, 1813.
C. Monroe, 2 Sept., 1813.
J. P. Norton, 2 Sept., 1813.
A. Wilson, 7 March, 1814.
N. Wadhams, 7 March, 1814.
G. W. Boyd, 9 March, 1814.
Thos. Hunt, 9 April, 1814.
J. L. Gardner, 28 April, 1814.

*3rd Lieutenants.*

T. Green, Jr., 20 May, 1813.
I. Dean, 15 Aug., 1813.
C. Farnham, 1 May, 1814.
I. Pike, 1 May, 1814.
A. Neaf, 1 May, 1814.
I. H. Robbins, 1 May, 1814.
C. F. Sherburne, 20 May, 1814.

*Surgeon.*

Sylvester Day, 13 March, 1813.

*Surgeon's Mates.*

J. M. Harper, 19 Jan., 1813.
Jos. P. Russell, 25 May, 1814.

---

FIFTH INFANTRY.

*Pennsylvania.*

*Colonel.*

J. Bowyer, 13 March, 1814.

*Lieut. Colonel.*

Geo. Gibson, 15 Aug., 1813.

*Majors.*

Benj. Wallace, 30 April, 1813.
Colin Buckner, 31 Jan., 1814.

*Captains.*

Townsend Stith, 30 Sept., 1810.
A. M'Ilhenny, 1 Sept., 1811.
James Dorman, 9 Nov., 1811.
W. S. Henshaw, 30 April, 1813.
Leroy Opie, 26 June, 1813.
Richd. H. Bell, 15 Aug., 1813.
John Jamison, 31 Jan., 1814.
J. Saunders, 21 Feb., 1814.
J. Owens, 1 May, 1814.
R. W. Chick, 1 May, 1814.

*1st Lieutenants.*

J. S. Allison, 6 July, 1812.
J. R. Corbaly, 6 July, 1812.
Wm. C. Bird, 1 Sept., 1812.
P. B. Greenwell, 30 April, 1813.
J. G. Clark, 26 June, 1813.
John Gassaway, 15 Aug., 1813.
Henry O. Hill, 31 Jan., 1814.
J. M'Gunegle, 28 April, 1814. Quartermaster.
J. Cummings, 1 May, 1814.
S. W. Prestman, 1 May, 1814.

*2nd Lieutenants.*

G. D. Snyder, 1 Sept., 1812.
John Fendall, 30 April, 1813.
J. B. Taylor, 26 June, 1813.
Geo. Murray, 15 Aug., 1813.
Jas. Kearney, 1 Jan., 1814. Assistant Topographical Engineer.
Jas. Smith, 31 Jan., 1814.
J. A. Harding, 28 April, 1814.
George Rea, 1 May, 1814.
Jacob Swoyer, 1 May, 1814.
Wm. C. Yates, 1 May, 1814.

*3rd Lieutenants.*

T. Murphey, 14 Aug., 1813.
M. Fishback, 15 Aug., 1813.
George Brent, 1 Oct., 1813.
F. E. Hedges, 1 March, 1814.

A. Vincent, 1 March, 1814.
G. Leftwich, 31 March, 1814.
T. W. Morgan, 1 May, 1814.
R. Means, 1 May, 1814.
J. Wells, 1 May, 1814.
W. R. Richardson, 1 May, 1814.

*Ensigns.*

A, Whitehead, 15 Sept., 1813.
Azel Gates, 15 Sept., 1813.
J. M. Smith, 11 March, 1814.
N. H. Mason, 8 April, 1814.

*Surgeon.*

Alex. Blair, 30 March, 1814.

*Surgeon's Mate.*

Clajon Relly, 22 March, 1813.

---

SIXTH INFANTRY.

*New York.*

*Colonel.*

Jonas Simonds, 8 July, 1808.

*Lieut. Colonel.*

Wm. Carson, 19 April, 1814.

*Majors.*

Ebenr. Beebe, 21 Feb., 1814. Assistant Adjutant General.
J. Machesney, 21 March, 1814.

*Captains.*

Robert Sterry, 3 Jan., 1812. Assistant Inspector General.
J. E. A. Masters, 4 June, 1812.
Henry Phillips, 13 Oct., 1812.
Edwd. Webb, 21 Feb., 1814.
Henry Shell, 21 March, 1814.
James Bailey, 27 March, 1814.
Lond. L. Buck, 19 April, 1814.
A. R. Thompson, 1 May, 1814.
J. Chapman, 1 May, 1814.

*1st Lieutenants.*

Wm. Hazard, 13 Oct., 1812. Quartermaster.
G. D. Smith, 31 Oct., 1812. Adjutant.
Geo. W. Ten Broeck, 20 March, 1813.
R. B. Cuyler, 1 April, 1815.
G. W. Runk, 21 March, 1814.
H. R. Windle, 27 March, 1814.
Henry Cooke, 19 April, 1814.
N. Sherman, 1 May, 1814.
R. M'Clellan, 1 May, 1814. Paymaster.

*2nd Lieutenants.*

I. L. Dubois, 13 Oct., 1812.
George Keese, 1 Feb., 1813.
Wm. B. Staats, 20 March, 1813.
A. Quackinbush, 1 April, 1813.
James Young, 21 Feb., 1814.
John Sisk, 21 March, 1814.
Patrick Ford, 19 April, 1814.
John Harris, 1 May, 1814.
W. Bicker, Jr., 1 May, 1814.

*3rd Lieutenants.*

John Wood, 17 Jan., 1814.
John Grayson, 1 May, 1814.
E. P. Bacon, 1 May, 1814.
Waddy Bacon, 1 May, 1814.
Crom. Sprague, 1 May, 1814.
E. Roberts, 1 May, 1814.
Ch. Tallman, 1 May, 1814.
H. Barker, 1 May, 1814.
Louis Calame, 1 May, 1814.

*Surgeon.*

T. Lawson, 21 May, 1813.

*Surgeon's Mate.*

W. Beaumont, 2 Dec., 1812.

---

SEVENTH INFANTRY.

*Kentucky.*

*Colonel.*

Wm. Russell, 3 May, 1818.

*Lieut. Colonel.*

Thorn. Posey, 30 April, 1813.

*Majors.*

J. Bankhead, 15 Aug., 1813. Adjutant General.
J. Nicks, 9 Oct., 1813.

*Captains.*

Zach. Taylor, 30 Nov., 1810. Major, brevet, 5 Sept., 1812.
Carey Nicholas, 1 March, 1811. Assistant Adjutant General.
W. M'Clellan, 1 March, 1811.
Alex. A. White, 6 June, 1811.
Narcis. Broutin, 6 April, 1813.
J. Robertson, 21 Feb., 1814.
J. S. Wade, 13 March, 1814.
Samuel Vail, 9 April, 1814.
Geo. C. Allen, 19 April, 1814.
Elijah Montgomery, 1 May, 1814.

*1st Lieutenants.*

D. M'Clellan, 10 Feb., 1812. Quartermaster.
Jacob Miller, 10 Feb., 1812.
M. M'Clelland, 20 Jan., 1813.
E. Taylor, 20 June, 1813.
W. Snodgrass, 11 Oct., 1813.
Wm. Prosser, 21 Feb., 1814.
J. Forsythe, 13 March, 1814.
John Hays, 9 April, 1814.
John Meek, 19 April, 1814.
J. N. Carrick, 1 May, 1814.

*2nd Lieutenants.*

E. Hall, 20 June, 1813.
T. Blackstone, 26 Sept., 1813. Paymaster.
John Weaver, 11 Oct., 1813.
I. M. Rieley, 22 Jan., 1814.
A. Ross, 21 Feb., 1814.
John Noble, 13 March, 1814.
T. B. Rice, 9 April, 1814.
D. Burford, 19 April, 1814.
Wm. Query, 19 April, 1814.
A. Neilson, 1 May, 1814.

*3rd Lieutenants.*

Wilson Creed, 7 March, 1814.
F. S. Gray, 13 March, 1814.
B. B. De Witt, 13 March, 1814.
W. S. Doherty, 13 March, 1814.
R. O. Beall, 1 May, 1814.
I. C. Rainey, 1 May, 1814.
T. M'Clanahan, 1 May, 1814.
I. T. Rother, 1 May, 1814.
B. Scruggs, 14 May, 1814.

*Ensign.*

Jas. Brown, Jr., 23 May, 1814.

*Surgeon.*

A. G. Goodlet, 10 Feb., 1812.

EIGHTH INFANTRY.

*Georgia.*

*Colonel.*

Patrick Jack, 6 July, 1812.

*Lieut. Colonel.*

L. Manning, 15 Aug., 1813.

*Majors.*

W. Cummings, 25 March, 1813. Adjutant General.
Philip Cook, 15 Aug., 1813.

*Captains.*

D. E. Twiggs, 6 July, 1812.
W. Chisholm, 6 July, 1812.
F. B. Warley, 6 July, 1812.
W. Jones, 6 July, 1812.
T. W. Farrer, 6 July, 1812. Aid to Brigadiar General Flournoy.
W. M'Queen, 6 July, 1812. Brigade Major.
M. I. Keith, 6 July, 1812.
C. Crawford, 6 July, 1812.
Hamlin Cook, 2 Dec., 1813.
R. P. Johnson, 13 Feb., 1814.

*1st Lieutenants.*

T. C. Hunter, 6 July, 1812.
Otis Dyer, 6 July, 1812.
J. H. Mallory, 5 May, 1813.
M. A. Roberts, 5 May, 1813.
James Wilde, 5 July, 1813. Paymaster.
Wm. Bee, Jr., 14 Aug., 1813.
E. Halloway, 15 Aug., 1813.
J. A. Black, 2 Dec., 1813.
B. Martin, 2 Dec., 1813.
R. Lamar, 13 Feb., 1814.

*2nd Lieutenants.*

R. V. Marye, 25 March, 1813.
P. Lequex, 5 May, 1813.
J. Ferguson, 5 May, 1813. Aid to Major General Pinckney.
T. F. Wells, 5 May, 1813.
L. Gresham, 14 Aug., 1813.
W. W. Davis, 15 Aug., 1813.
S. Coleman, 2 Dec., 1813.
J. G. Bostwick, 13 Feb., 1814.
Wm. Wayne, 1 March, 1814.
A. Dousset, 1 May, 1814.

*3rd Lieutenants.*

R. J. Easter, 5 May, 1813.
J. A. Beaulard, 15 Aug., 1813.
H. L. Oneal, 2 Dec., 1813.
J. Gignilliat, 2 Dec., 1813.
J. G. Stallings, 7 March, 1813.
Wm. La Prade, 1 May, 1813.
Seaborn Burton, 1 May, 1813.
Joel Spencer, 1 May, 1813.
J. B. Hobkirk, 1 May, 1813.
J. Womack, 1 May, 1813.

*Ensign.*

Cuyler Lovett, 22 April, 1814.

*Surgeon.*

W. R. Waring, 11 April, 1813.

*Surgeon's Mates.*

J. W. Caldwell, 6 July, 1812.
Charles Lewis, 19 July, 1813.

---

NINTH INFANTRY.

*Massachusetts.*

*Colonel.*

Simon Larned, 6 July, 1812.

*Lieut. Colonel.*

T. Aspinwall, 12 March, 1813.

*Majors.*

C. Lyman, 26 June, 1813.
Henry Leavenworth, 15 Aug., 1813.

*Captains.*

T. Crooker, 6 July, 1812.
A. F. Hull, 6 July, 1812.
E. Foster, 13 March, 1813.
J. Ingersoll, Jr., 16 April, 1813.
D. S. Townsend, 13 May, 1813.
G. Bender, Jr., 13 May, 1813.
J. F. Norris, 26 June, 1813.
S. L. Allen, 15 Oct., 1813.
W. L. Foster, 15 Oct., 1813.

*1st Lieutenants.*

B. F. Greene, 30 March, 1813.
J. Fowle, Jr., 16 April, 1813. Paymaster.
S. Turner, 13 May, 1813.
E. Childs, 13 May, 1813.
Loring Palmer, 26 June, 1813.
David Perry, 30 June, 1813.
Aaron Lewis, 15 Aug., 1813.
J. H. Cranson, 15 Aug., 1813.
W. Browning, 15 Oct., 1813.
D. Chandler, 15 Oct., 1813.

*2nd Lieutenants.*

H. Wellington, 13 May, 1813.
W. Lyman, 26 June, 1813.
Otis Fisher, 30 June, 1813.
E. Norton, 15 July, 1813.
J. Gleason, 14 Aug., 1813. Adjutant.
J. Christie, 1 Nov., 1813.
David Foot, 23 Nov., 1813.
A. Burghardt, 15 Oct., 1813.
T. Childs, Jr., 15 Oct., 1813.
E. Badger, 5 April, 1813.

*3rd Lieutenants.*

F. S. Learned, 1 Jan., 1814.
E. Brinhall, 1 Jan., 1814.
I. Brigham, 1 May, 1814.
W. M. Dyer, 1 May, 1814.
B. C. Allen, 1 May, 1814.
C. Cushman, 1 May, 1814.
B. H. Scott, 1 May, 1814.
S. Chandler, 11 May, 1814.

*Ensign.*

Jas. G. Allen, 11 May, 1814.

*Surgeon.*

J. Lovell, 15 May, 1812.

*Surgeon's Mate.*

T. G. Mower, 2 Dec., 1812.

---

TENTH INFANTRY.

*North Carolina.*

*Colonel.*

James Welborn, 6 July, 1812.

*Lieut. Colonel.*

D. L. Clinch, 4 Aug., 1813.

*Majors.*

A. L. Langham, 15 Aug., 1813.
J. M'Clelland, 31 Dec., 1813.

*Captains.*

G. Cloud, 6 July, 1812.
T. M. Nelson, 6 July, 1812.
Philip Brittain, 6 July, 1812.

Robt. Mitchell, 6 July, 1812.
Eman. I. Leigh, 6 July, 1812.
Mark Harden, 6 July, 1812.
Josiah Woods, 6 July, 1812.
Joseph Clay, 6 July, 1812.
Geo. Vashon, 29 Nov., 1813.
Geo. Strother, 30 Nov., 1813.

*1st Lieutenants.*

Wm. Bailey, 6 July, 1812.
H. H. Carson, 6 July, 1812.
Abner S. Lewis, 6 July, 1812.
Chas. Lutterloh, 6 July, 1812.
Wm. Irvine, 14 Aug., 1813.
Jos. J. Clinch, 15 Aug., 1813.
Thos. C. Kelly, 3 Oct., 1813.
Jos. G. Wall, 29 Nov., 1813.
Arthur Fox, 30 Nov., 1813.
Lewis Yancey, 24 March, 1814. Paymaster.

*2nd Lieutenants.*

Jehu Bird, 15 April, 1813.
A. G. Glynn, 14 Aug., 1813.
James Roane, 15 Aug., 1813.
James Norris, 30 Nov., 1813.
Isaac Crayton, 26 Jan., 1814.
F. M'Rea, 26 Jan., 1814.
G. R. Bridges, 24 March, 1814.
W. Lancaster, 24 March, 1814.
James K. Hill, 24 March, 1814.

*3rd Lieutenants.*

S. Thomas, 14 Aug., 1813.
R. H. Goodwyn, 30 Nov., 1813.
M. Parkes, 26 Jan., 1814.
W. Pannill, 26 Jan., 1814.
John Carney, 24 March, 1814.
T. H. Ferguson, 24 March, 1814.
John Rice, 24 March, 1814.
Jas. Goodhue, 1 May, 1814.
I. Edney, 1 May, 1814.
A. M'Kenzie, 1 May, 1814.

*Ensigns.*

I. H. Pitts, 30 March, 1814.
F. Hannon, 30 March, 1814.
W. M'Kenzie, 15 April, 1814.
I. H. White, 15 April, 1814.
L. Coorpender, 15 April, 1814.
I. F. Clark, 15 April, 1814.
S. Beckham, Jr., 9 May, 1814.
M. Wilhight, 9 May, 1814.
Elisha Burnett, 23 May, 1814.
L. B. Phelps, 9 June, 1814.

*Surgeon.*

E. H. Bell, 30 March, 1814.

*Surgeon's Mate.*

H. Dade, 15 April, 1814.

---

### ELEVENTH INFANTRY.

*Vermont.*

*Colonel.*

I. B. Campbell, 9 April, 1814.

*Lieut. Colonel.*

Moody Bedel, 6 July, 1812.

*Major.*

J. M'Neal, Jr., 15 Aug., 1813.

*Captains.*

J. W. Weeks, 6 July, 1812.
Samuel Gordon, 6 July, 1812.
W. S. Foster, 13 March, 1813.
John Bliss, 13 May, 1813.
Richard Baen, 26 June, 1813.
V. R. Goodrich, 26 June, 1813.
Horace Hale, 15 Aug., 1813.
Benj. Smead, 15 Aug., 1813.
M. Corning, 15 Aug., 1813.
W. Sheldon, 12 Dec., 1813.

*1st Lieutenants.*

James Wells, 13 March, 1813.
Jas. Greene, 13 May, 1813.
H. J. Blake, 26 June, 1813.
D. Crawford, 26 June, 1813.
R. Bucklin, Jr., 15 Aug., 1813.
N. S. Clarke, 15 Aug., 1813. Adjutant.
Thos. Levake, 15 Aug., 1813.
W. Hale, 15 Aug., 1813.
E. Jewett, 19 Nov., 1813.
F. A. Sawyer, 12 Dec., 1813.

*2nd Lieutenants.*

T. Aldrich, 26 June, 1813.
J. V. Barron, 26 June, 1813.
T. Staniford, 26 June, 1813. Paymaster.
Isaac Clark, Jr., 14 Aug., 1813.
Wm. Risley, 15 Aug., 1813.
J. E. Merritt, 15 Aug., 1813.
Enoch Cooper, 15 Aug., 1813.
S. C. Cotton, 19 Nov., 1813.
J. C. Walker, 19 Nov., 1813.

*3rd Lieutenants.*

Jos. Hopkins, 19 Nov., 1813.
Thos. Tupper, 19 Nov., 1813.
P. S. Sanford, 12 Dec., 1813.
Hazen Bedel, 1 Jan., 1814.
B. Stevenson, 1 Jan., 1814.
H. Webster, 1 Jan., 1814.
James Brown, 1 May, 1814.
J. Shields, 1 May, 1814.
I. B. Davies, 1 May, 1814.
J. Grant, 1 May, 1814.

*Ensigns.*

A. M. Simonds, 18 April, 1814.
Ezra Dean, 20 April, 1814.

*Surgeon.*

G. P. Spencer, 7 April, 1813.

*Surgeon's Mates.*

T. Woodward, 9 Aug., 1813.
John Sackett, 9 Aug., 1813.

---

### TWELFTH INFANTRY.

*Virginia.*

*Colonel.*

Isaac A. Coles, 12 March, 1813.

*Majors.*

R. C. Nicholas, 3 March, 1813.
W. Morgan, 26 June, 1813.

*Captains.*

James Paxton, 6 July, 1812.
Thos. Sangster, 6 July, 1812.
James Charlton, 6 July, 1812.
Charles Page, 6 July, 1812.
A. L. Madison, 6 July, 1812.
Thomas Post, 29 March, 1813.
Robt. G. Hite, 26 June, 1813. Assistant Adjutant General.
Z. Morgan, 20 Sept., 1813.
J. G. Camp, 14 Nov., 1813.
L. B. Willis, 31 Jan., 1814.

*1st Lieutenants.*

A. M'Donald, 6 July, 1812.
John Key, Jr., 29 March, 1813.
Robt. Houston, 29 March, 1813.

Oth. W. Callis, 26 June, 1813. Quartermaster.
Wm. Stone, Jr., 26 June, 1813.
R. Harrison, 30 Sept., 1813.
John Fowles, 30 Sept., 1813.
Bailey Bruce, 31 Jan., 1814.
R. Booker, 17 March, 1814.
A. J. Bruce, 24 March, 1814.

*2nd Lieutenants.*

Jos. M'Gavock, 26 June, 1813.
David P. Polk, 30 Sept., 1813.
C. Randolph, 30 Sept., 1813.
P. C. Johnston, 14 Nov., 1813.
John Strother, 20 Nov., 1813.
F. S. Dade, 31 Jan., 1814.
Philip Wager, 17 March, 1814.
Jos. Shommo, 24 March, 1814.
Mw. M. Claiborne, Jr., 5 April, 1814.

*3rd Lieutenants.*

Geo. Eskridge, 20 Sept., 1813.
Mich. Crupper, 20 Sept., 1813.
John Robinson, 20 Nov., 1813.
S. Grantland, Jr., 31 Jan., 1814.
De La Fayette Johnston, 17 March, 1814.
Robert Call, 17 March, 1814.
R. Randolph, 24 March, 1814.
S. Bartlett, 1 April, 1814.
W. Wright, 5 April, 1814.

*Ensigns.*

Th. Gaultney, 4 Dec., 1813.
W. H. Curtis, 11 March, 1814.
T. C. Sumner, 17 March, 1814.
S. L. Meredith, 30 March, 1814.
R. Turner, 31 March, 1814.
T. K. Godfroy, 8 April, 1814.
John Hopewell, 20 April, 1814.

*Surgeon.*

J. Rogers, 15 April, 1814.

*Surgeon's Mate.*

T. Byrne, 8 April, 1814.

---

THIRTEENTH INFANTRY.

*New York.*

*Colonel.*

P. P. Schuyler, 6 July, 1812. Adjutant General.

*Lieut. Colonel.*

S. S. Conner, 12 March, 1813.

*Majors.*

J. V. H. Huyck, 6 July, 1812.
R. M. Malcom, 3 March, 1813.

*Captains.*

John Sproull, 6 July, 1812.
Hugh R. Martin, 6 July, 1812.
Mordecai Myers, 6 July, 1812.
Myndert M. Dox, 6 July, 1812.
W. D. Lawrence, 6 July, 1812.
S. W. Kearny, 1 April, 1813.
Samuel Haring, 1 April, 1813.
John K. Paige, 13 May, 1813.
W. B. Adams, 13 May, 1813.

*1st Lieutenants.*

R. S. Gardiner, 6 July, 1812. Paymaster.
W. Gansevoort, 6 July, 1812.
John L. Fink, 6 July, 1812.
Israel Turner, 6 July, 1812.
Daniel Hugunin, 1 April, 1813.
Wm. W. Carr, 13 May, 1813.
D. B. Wilcox, 15 Aug., 1813.
J. Sammons, 19 Jan., 1814.
J. H. Dwight, 31 Jan., 1814. Quartermaster.
John Williams, 31 Jan., 1814.

*2nd Lieutenants.*

John Kirby, 1 April, 1813.
Geo. Reab, Jr., 20 April, 1813.
T. W. Denton, 13 May, 1813.
John Graham, 20 June, 1813.
Mason Ronalds, 20 June, 1813.
John Haight, 15 Aug., 1813.
William Anderson, Jr., 15 Aug., 1813.
C. Harrison, 19 Jan., 1814.
M. C. Cantine, 31 Jan., 1814.
G. Helmbold, 31 Jan., 1814.

*3rd Lieutenants.*

R. Humphreys, 30 Sept., 1813.
R. M. Harrison, 30 Sept., 1813.
Jacob Meyers, 1 Oct., 1813.
A. Howard, 19 Jan., 1814.
E. Clarke, 31 Jan., 1814.
S. Johnson, 31 Jan., 1814.
H. H. Minton, 31 Jan., 1814.
C. F. Irvine, 1 May, 1814.
J. Clitz, 1 May, 1814.
L. Marsh, 1 May, 1814.

*Ensign.*

F. T. Helms, 8 April, 1814.
E. Gilbert, 8 April, 1814.
J. Claude, 15 April, 1814.
J. Murphy, 15 April, 1814.
C. Miller, 18 April, 1814.
F. T. Helm, 1 May, 1814.

*Surgeon.*

J. Y. Lancing, 15 Oct., 1812.

*Surgeon's Mate.*

John M'Call, 15 April, 1812.

---

FOURTEENTH INFANTRY.

*Maryland.*

*Colonel.*

C. G. Bœrstler, 20 June, 1813.

*Lieut. Colonel.*

E. L. Whitlock, 14 Nov., 1813.

*Majors.*

Samuel Lane, 3 March, 1813.
I. D. Barnard, 26 June, 1813.

*Captains.*

T. Montgomery, 6 July, 1812.
Henry Fleming, 6 July, 1812.
Wm. M'Ilvain, 6 July, 1812.
K. M'Kenzie, 6 July, 1812.
D. Cummings, 13 March, 1813.
Thos. Karney, 13 May, 1813.
Reuben Gilder, 26 June, 1813.
Jos. Marshall, 15 Aug., 1813.
J. M'Donald, 1 Oct., 1813.
Richard Arell, 14 Nov., 1813.

*1st Lieutenants.*

Peter Rich, 6 July, 1812.
John Waring, 13 March, 1813.
Thos. Randall, 13 March, 1813.
John Beckett, 13 March, 1813.
Edw. Wilson, 12 May, 1813.
A. Woodward, 13 May, 1813.
J. W. Thompson, 26 June, 1813.
James Christie, 1 Oct., 1813.
Geo. Murdock, 14 Nov., 1813.
Wm. G. Mills, 14 Nov., 1813. Aid to Brig. General Winder.

*2nd Lieutenants.*

James H. Gale, 13 March, 1813.
Kiml. Godwin, 13 March, 1813.
S. F. Donaldson, 13 March, 1813. Paymaster.
R. Bennett, 12 May, 1813.
N. N. Robinson, 12 May, 1813.
W. G. Sanders, 13 May, 1813.
Abraham Clark, 1 Oct., 1813.
Thos. Barton, 14 Nov., 1813.
Robert Beall, 14 Nov., 1813.
C. Comegys, Jr., 14 Nov., 1813.

*3rd Lieutenants.*

B. Ricketts, 12 May, 1813.
Massom Mudd, 12 May, 1813.
W. Thompson, 12 May, 1813.
D. M'Crimmin, 15 May, 1813.
W. G. Shade, 1 Oct., 1813.
Henry Parker, 14 Nov., 1813. Quartermaster.
J. W. Riddle, 14 Nov., 1813.
G. C. Clitherall, 1 May, 1814.
J. Beckwith, 1 May, 1814.

*Ensigns.*

J. Carr, 15 April, 1814.
J. S. Simpson, 11 May, 1814.
Hez. J. Balch, 21 May, 1814.

*Surgeon.*

John Young, 4 June, 1812.

*Surgeon's Mate.*

S. W. Magruder, 28 March, 1813.

---

FIFTEENTH INFANTRY.

*New Jersey.*

*Colonel.*

D. Brearley, 12 March, 1813.

*Lieut. Colonel.*

Robert Carr, 15 Aug., 1813.

*Majors.*

H. Grindage, 14 Nov., 1813.
Z. Rossell, 31 Dec., 1813.

*Captains.*

C. W. Hunter, 6 July, 1812. Brigade Major.
White Youngs, 6 July, 1812.
H. H. Van Dalsem, 6 July, 1812.
J. L. Barton, 30 July, 1812.
J. D. Hayden, 13 March, 1813.
Aaron Sutphen, 13 May, 1813.
Jb. D. Howell, 15 Aug., 1813.
G. M'Glassin, 15 Aug., 1813.
Wm. Barnet, 31 Dec., 1813.

*1st Lieutenants.*

James Platt, 6 July, 1812.
J. Schofield, 6 July, 1812.
R. L. Howell, 15 Sept., 1812. Brigade Major.
S. M'Dougall, 30 Sept., 1812.
David Riddle, 13 March, 1813.
A. Godwin, Jr., 13 May, 1813.
David Curtis, 13 May, 1813.
C. Stewart, 15 Aug., 1813.
John Scott, 15 Aug., 1813.
D. Fraser, 31 Dec., 1813. Assistant Deputy Paymaster General.

*2nd Lieutenants.*

J. Dickerson, 13 March, 1813.
Wm. Coffie, 13 March, 1813. Quartermaster.
C. Noyes, 13 May, 1813.
H. K. Mullin, 13 May, 1813. Adjutant.
J. T. David, 13 May, 1813.
C. H. Roberts, 13 May, 1813.
D. E. Burch, 15 Aug., 1813. Paymaster.
John Rose, 15 Aug., 1813.
Levi Heath, 31 Dec., 1813.
W. H. Howell, 17 March, 1814.

*3rd Lieutenants.*

Floreat Meline, 1 Oct., 1813.
J. Graison, 31 Dec., 1813.
J. C. Dehart, 17 March, 1814.
Chas. W. Lee, 17 March, 1814.
F. Walters, 17 March, 1814.
John Knapp, 17 March, 1814.
H. M. Mead, 1 May, 1814.
Z. S. Conger, 1 May, 1814.
H. F. Davis, 1 May, 1814.

*Ensign.*

Upton Fraser, 31 May, 1814.

*Surgeon.*

Fenn Deming, 14 April, 1812.

*Surgeon's Mates.*

R. T. Baker, 12 March, 1812.
R. Hampton, 30 March, 1814.

---

SIXTEENTH INFANTRY.

*Pennsylvania.*

*Colonel.*

C. Pearce, 6 July, 1812.

*Lieut. Colonel.*

E. B. Clemson, 9 March, 1814.

*Majors.*

W. Lee, 3 March, 1813.
Robert Gray, 15 Aug., 1813.

*Captains.*

G. G. Steele, 6 July, 1812.
A. M'Ewen, 6 July, 1812.
J. F. M'Elroy, 6 July, 1812.
W. Davenport, 28 Sept., 1812.
J. Machesney, 13 March, 1813.
M. Greenwood, 16 April, 1813.
John Baldy, 16 April, 1813.
J. W. Aitken, 15 Aug., 1813.
J. D. Coon, 15 Aug., 1813.
N. M'Laughlin, 1 Jan., 1814.

*1st Lieutenants.*

Thos. Horrell, 16 April, 1813.
T. M. Powers, 16 April, 1813. Paymaster.
Isaac Finch, 15 Aug., 1813.
Jacob Whisler, 15 Aug., 1813.
Thos. Mahon, 15 Aug., 1813.
Saml. Weigly, 15 Aug., 1813.
Thos. Evans, 15 Aug., 1813.
Chas. Fisler, 11 Nov., 1813.
T. P. M'Mahon, 1 Jan., 1814.
Wm. Downey, 22 Feb., 1814.

*2nd Lieutenants.*

S. Nicholson, 15 Aug., 1813.
S. Roberts, 15 Aug., 1813.
Thos. Lyon, 15 Aug., 1813.
John Williams, 1 Jan., 1814.
George Bryan, 22 Feb., 1814.
Hector Burns, 1 April, 1814.
Thos. Martin, 1 April, 1814.
L. Diffenbach, 1 April, 1814.

*3rd Lieutenants.*

Nathl. Young, 8 March, 1814.
G. R. Horter, 1 May, 1814.
J. White, 1 May, 1814.
G. Meson, 1 May, 1814.
T. Porter, 1 May, 1814.
J. M'Cartney, 1 May, 1814.
Fr. Kernan, 1 May, 1814.
J. A. Ramsey, 1 May, 1814.
M. Thomas, Jr., 1 May, 1814.

*Ensigns.*

James Aul, 15 April, 1814.
Jesse M'Ilvaine, 15 April, 1814.
George Reed, 15 April, 1814.

*Surgeon.*

S. Gilliland, 15 May, 1812.

*Surgeon's Mate.*

B. Delavan, 15 April, 1814.

---

SEVENTEENTH INFANTRY.

*Kentucky.*

*Colonel.*

John Miller, 6 July, 1812.

*Lieut. Colonel.*

George Todd, 13 March, 1814.

*Majors.*

Richd. Graham, 30 March, 1813.
Rich. Oldham, 9 April, 1814.

*Captains.*

H. H. Hickman, 6 July, 1812.
David Holt, 6 July, 1812.
Wm. J. Adair, 6 July, 1812.
James Herron, 6 July, 1812.
John T. Chunn, 6 July, 1812.
John Anderson, 16 March, 1813. Topographical Engineer.
C. H. Holder, 29 March, 1813.
B. W. Saunders, 16 April, 1813.
M. L. Hawkins, 16 April, 1813.
G. W. Jackson, 15 Aug., 1813.

*1st Lieutenants.*

H. Crittenden, 6 July, 1812.
Stephen Lee, 6 July, 1812.
James Campbell, 6 July, 1812.
James Morrow, 6 July, 1812.
J. Hackley, Jr., 13 March, 1813.
A. Garrett, 13 March, 1813. Paymaster.
T. Mountjoy, 13 March, 1813.
Philip P. Price, 30 March, 1813.
Jonathan Rees, 30 March, 1813.
Philip King, 15 Aug., 1813.

*2nd Lieutenants.*

Chesteen Scott, 30 March, 1813.
Geo. Atchison, 6 April, 1813.
A. E. Hoffman, 6 April, 1813.
Geo. W. Stall, 6 April, 1813.
Thos. Hawkins, 16 April, 1813.
James Gray, 16 April, 1813.
Asher Phillips, 20 May, 1813.
Wm. Baylor, 15 Aug., 1813.
Jac. Anderson, 20 Sept., 1813.

*3rd Lieutenants.*

D. L. Carney, 6 April, 1813.
John Hamilton, 6 April, 1813.
G. J. Floyd, 6 April, 1813.
Reuben Taylor, 12 April, 1813.
Wm. Eubank, 15 Aug., 1813.
John Taylor, 20 Sept., 1813.
John Cochran, 20 Sept., 1813.
G. M. Beall, 19 Jan., 1814.
John Simmons, 7 March, 1814.
T. R. M'Knight, 7 March, 1814.

*Ensigns.*

J. Mershon, 18 June, 1813.
Richard Doyle, 2 July, 1813.
And. Evans, 1 Aug., 1813.
Sam. M'Guire, 10 Aug., 1813.
C. B. Campbell, 24 Oct., 1813.
W. Featherston, 11 March, 1814.
Rice L. Stuart, 17 March, 1814.
Wm. Griffith, 26 March, 1814.
Wm. H. Shaug, 30 March, 1814.
O. Evans, 20 April, 1814.

*Surgeon.*

Wm. Turner, 7 April, 1813.

*Surgeon's Mates.*

W. S. Madison, 12 Dec., 1812.
Clayton Tiffin, 11 March, 1814.

---

EIGHTEENTH INFANTRY.

*South Carolina.*

*Colonel.*

R. Dennis, 19 April, 1814.

*Lieut. Colonel.*

Benajah White, 6 July, 1812.

*Majors.*

Ths. P. Moore, 20 Sept., 1813.
R. B. Moore, 1 May, 1814.

*Captains.*

J. G. Blount, Jr., 6 July, 1812.
George Butler, 6 July, 1812.
Wm. Taylor, 6 July, 1812.
H. P. Taylor, 6 July, 1812.
Owen Clinton, 6 July, 1812.
Jas. Hamilton, 13 March, 1813.
M. G. Waage, 26 June, 1813.
W. A. Blount, 14 Sept., 1813.
Robt. Fenner, 17 March, 1814.
B. T. Elmore, 31 March, 1814.

*1st Lieutenants.*

Elias D. Dick, 6 July, 1812.
J. W. Farrow, 6 July, 1812. Paymaster.
Alex. King, 6 July, 1812.
Wm. Tisdale, 6 July, 1812.
Thos. Reynolds, 13 March, 1813. Quartermaster.
T. C. Wilhight, 26 June, 1813.
E. S. Hawkins, 30 June, 1813.
W. N. Miller, 11 Sept., 1813.
R. Mebane, Jr., 14 Sept., 1813.
John Watkins, 31 March, 1814.

*2nd Lieutenants.*

H. Brown, 6 July, 1812.
R. Thurston, 6 July, 1812.
John Street, 6 July, 1812.
Alex. Pagan, 13 March, 1813.
John Peebles, 13 March, 1813.
W. D. Freeman, 30 June, 1813.
Fredk. Kinloch, 11 Sept., 1813.
S. W. Smith, 14 Sept., 1813.
John S. Todd, 1 Oct., 1813.
W. Whatley, 31 March, 1814.

*3rd Lieutenants.*

George Bruton, 14 Sept., 1813.
J. W. Allston, 1 Oct., 1813.
George Taylor, 20 Dec., 1813.
A. B. Addison, 31 March, 1814.
Wm. Smith, 31 March, 1814.

Th. B. Smith, 19 April, 1814.
Th. B. Guy, 19 April, 1814.
Jos. Jenkins, 19 April, 1814.

*Surgeon's Mate.*

James B. Hill, 6 July, 1812.

---

NINETEENTH INFANTRY.

*Ohio.*

*Colonel.*

George Paull, 29 June, 1813.

*Lieut. Colonel.*

T. B. Van Horne, 9 April, 1813.

*Majors.*

W. H. Trimble, 18 March, 1813.
Thos. Rowland, 29 June, 1813.

*Captains.*

Wm. Bradford, 6 July, 1812.
R. Hightower, 6 July, 1812.
Hugh Moore, 6 July, 1812.
Geo. Kisling, 20 May, 1813.
Hy. Northup, 20 May, 1813.
Joel Collins, 20 May, 1813.
Alex. Hill, 20 May, 1813.
William Gill, 20 May, 1813.
R. C. Talbot, 20 May, 1813.
J. Van Horne, Jr., 20 May, 1813.

*1st Lieutenants.*

A. P. Pinney, 20 May, 1813.
William Baird, 20 May, 1813.
George Will, 20 May, 1813.
Saml. Shannon, 20 May, 1813. Paymaster.
C. A. Trimble, 20 May, 1813.
W. Warner, 20 May, 1813.
Chas. A. Norton, 20 May, 1813.
N. Gregory, 20 May, 1813.
W. M'Donald, 20 May, 1813.
Chas. L. Cass, 20 May, 1813.

*2nd Lieutenants.*

James Blair, 20 May, 1813.
Jacob C. Leslie, 20 May, 1813.
Robt. Stockton, 20 May, 1813.
Saml. Coleman, 20 May, 1813.
John Carroll, 20 May, 1813.
Collin M'Cloud, 20 May, 1813.
T. C. Shields, 20 May, 1813.
Q. F. Atkins, 7 Aug., 1813.
Jas. Fisk, 10 Aug., 1813.

*3rd Lieutenants.*

A. Bushnell, 20 May, 1813.
Robert Nevill, 20 May, 1813.
J. Swearingen, 20 May, 1813.
James Nixon, 20 May, 1813.
O. Granger, 20 May, 1813.
John Goode, 20 May, 1813.
A. Patterson, 20 May, 1813.
John Hall, 20 May, 1813.
John Elvain, 20 May, 1813.
John Booten, 20 May, 1813.

*Ensigns.*

Jas. Shannon, 20 May, 1813.
Charles Cissna, 20 May, 1813.
Abijah Johns, 20 May, 1813.
John H. Simons, 20 May, 1813.
N. L. Reeves, 20 May, 1813.
Robert Young, 20 May, 1813.
Jno. Patterson, 20 May, 1813.
Robert Smith, 20 May, 1813.
N. M'Fadden, 20 May, 1813.
Thos. Riddle, 20 May, 1813.

*Surgeon.*

John Hamm, 16 April, 1813.

*Surgeon's Mate.*

Ed. B. Jackson, 28 April, 1813.

---

TWENTIETH INFANTRY.

*Virginia.*

*Colonel.*

G. C. Russell, 9 March, 1814.

*Lieut. Colonel.*

J. T. Woodford, 24 Feb., 1814.

*Majors.*

John Stanard, 3 March, 1813.
Lewis L. Taylor, 3 March, 1813.

*Captains.*

Wm. S. Jett, Jr., 6 July, 1812.
J. Macrae, Jr., 6 July, 1812.
T. B. Randolph, 5 April, 1813.
Charles Gee, 16 April, 1813.
Bernd. Peyton, 16 April, 1813.
M. Lynch, 11 Dec., 1813.
J. P. Duval, 31 Jan., 1814.
M. M. Payne, 2 March, 1814.
W. G. Hayes, 2 March, 1814.

*1st Lieutenants.*

R. Crawford, 6 July, 1812.
Clemt. White, 6 July, 1812.
Thos. Harris, 6 July, 1812.
Benjn. Smith, 5 April, 1813.
Thos. Howson, 16 April, 1813.
Thos. Monroe, 16 April, 1813.
Th. Blackwell, 11 Dec., 1813.
J. H. Howard, 2 March, 1814.
Geo. Evans, 2 March, 1814.
Wm. Ligon, 30 March, 1814.

*2nd Lieutenants.*

John B. Hogan, 16 April, 1813.
W. F. Pendleton, 16 April, 1813.
J. M. Glassell, 16 April, 1813.
E. B. Randolph, 14 Aug., 1813.
Daniel Booker, 15 Aug., 1813.
John Hill, 31 Jan., 1814.
Jacob Koontz, 2 March, 1814.
Thos. Rawlins, 2 March, 1814.
Frs. Callaway, 30 March, 1814.
Jos. Barnett, 30 March, 1814.

*3rd Lieutenants.*

Samuel Harris, 14 Aug., 1813.
G. M'Laughlin, 15 Aug., 1813. Quartermaster.
J. Pettipool, 11 Dec., 1813. Paymaster.
Dabney Morris, 31 Dec., 1813.
H. Lewis, 31 Jan., 1814.
Jas. Fuller, 2 March, 1814.
Robt. Carter, 2 March, 1814.
Jos. B. Scott, 30 March, 1814.
Ths. Rippets, 1 May, 1814.

*Ensigns.*

G. H. Rodgers, 11 March, 1814.
R. Dangerfield, 30 March, 1814.
Br. Davenport, 30 March, 1814.
C. H. Bradley, 31 March, 1814.
W. G. Wigginton, 31 March, 1814.
A. Douglas, 8 April, 1814.
J. A. Lewis, 18 April, 1814.
Drury Stith, 10 May, 1814.
Rt. W. Carr, 10 May, 1814.
Rt. M. Smith, 10 May, 1814.

*Surgeon.*

M. C. Buck, 2 July, 1813.

*Surgeon's Mate.*

W. I. Cocke, 15 April, 1814.

---

TWENTY-FIRST INFANTRY.

*Massachusetts.*

*Colonel.*

James Miller, 9 March, 1814.

*Lieut. Colonel.*

Tim. Upham, 12 March, 1813.

*Majors.*

Jos. Grafton, 26 June, 1813.
Rich. Pollard, 11 Dec., 1813.

*Captains.*

Josiah H. Vose, 6 July, 1812.
Joseph Treat, 6 July, 1812.
Chas. Procter, 6 July, 1812.
Benjn. Ropes, 6 July, 1812.
Leml. Bradford, 6 July, 1812.
S. Burbank, 13 March, 1813.
M. Marston, 26 June, 1813.
Peres Loring, 1 Feb., 1814.
Azor Orne, 28 Feb., 1814. Assistant Inspector.
Peter Pelham, 28 Feb., 1814.

*1st Lieutenants.*

Dan. Henderson, 6 July, 1812.
Henry Bender, 13 May, 1813. Aid to General Ripley.
J. Bartlett, 26 June, 1813.
Ira Drew, 30 July, 1813.
Wm. Bowman, 14 Aug., 1813.
James Pratt, 7 March, 1814.
N. N. Hall, 7 March, 1814. Assistant Inspector.
A. Bigelow, 7 March, 1814. Quartermaster.
Jos. Cilley, 7 March, 1814.
N. Blasdell, 7 March, 1814.

*2nd Lieutenants.*

Edward Hall, 15 Aug., 1813.
Brackett Paine, 7 March, 1814.
Daniel Rose, 7 March, 1814. Assistant Topographical Engineer.
J. A. Dix, 8 March, 1814.
H. C. Babcock, 8 March, 1814.
J. W. Holding, 8 March, 1814.
B. Jackson, 8 March, 1814.
B. F. Larned, 8 March, 1814.
N. G. Bean, 8 March, 1814.
B. Farnum, 8 March, 1814.

*3rd Lieutenants.*

N. Hinkley, 8 March, 1813.
J. Scribner, 8 March, 1813.
J. Craig, 8 March, 1813.
J. B. Fuller, 1 May, 1813.
G. H. Balding, 1 May, 1813.

*Ensigns.*

Fred. Merrill, 31 May, 1814.
P. R. Green, 31 May, 1814.
E. B. Lewis, 31 May, 1814.
H. W. Bettes, 31 May, 1814.

*Surgeon.*

A. Trowbridge, 1 Aug., 1813.

*Surgeon's Mates.*

Josiah Everett, 21 July, 1813.
Elisha Allen, 21 July, 1813.

TWENTY-SECOND INFANTRY.

*Pennsylvania.*

*Colonel.*

Hugh Brady, 6 July, 1812.

*Lieut. Colonel.*

N. Pinkney, 15 April, 1814.

*Majors.*

Ralph Marlin, 3 March, 1813.
J. T. Arrowsmith, 21 March, 1814.

*Captains.*

Sampson S. King, 6 July, 1812.
Jacob Carmack, 6 July, 1812.
John Pentland, 6 July, 1812.
Silas Amberson, 6 July, 1812.
David Espy, 16 April, 1813.
Jos. Henderson, 16 April, 1813.
Th. Lawrence, 20 June, 1813.
Willis Foulk, 20 June, 1813.
John Larken, 25 Sept., 1813.

*1st Lieutenants.*

Wm. Morrow, 6 July, 1812.
John Greene, 13 March, 1813. Adjutant.
S. A. Rippey, 16 April, 1813.
G. W. Ferguson, 16 April, 1813.
Wm. Sturgis, 20 June, 1813.
J. Culbertson, 1 Oct., 1813.
John D. Kehr, I Oct., 1813. Quartermaster.
Gideon Low, 8 Feb., 1814.
Th. Wright, 17 March, 1814.

*2nd Lieutenants.*

John R. Guy, 20 June, 1813.
Jno. Armstrong, 20 June, 1813.
John Fee, 26 June, 1813.
Jas. M'Kenney, 25 Sept., 1813.
Peleg Slocum, 1 Oct., 1813.
O. Martine, 8 Feb., 1814.
R. M. Davidson, 17 March, 1814.
Samuel Brady, 2 April, 1814.
John Arrison, 2 April, 1814.

*3rd Lieutenants.*

G. S. Wilkins, 29 July, 1813.
James Stewart, 25 Sept., 1813.
John Clark, 1 Sept., 1813.
J. Sample, 28 Feb., 1814.
C. F. Hennings, 17 March, 1814.
David Kizer, 31 March, 1814.
Chs. J. Brooke, 1 May, 1814.
J. Brady, 1 May, 1814.
J. S. Ashbridge, 1 May, 1814.

*Ensigns.*

Henry Fisher, 17 March, 1814.
H. F. Evans, 31 March, 1814.
J. Kline, 8 April, 1814.
R. Whiteside, 15 April, 1814.
I. F. Swift, 18 April, 1814.
W. Smith, 18 April, 1814.
I. Clements, 18 April, 1814.

*Surgeon.*

Edw. Scull, 8 April, 1814.

*Surgeon's Mate.*

M. I. Cunningham, 28 April, 1814.

---

TWENTY-THIRD INFANTRY.

*New York.*

*Colonel.*

Jas. P. Preston, 15 Aug., 1813.

*Lieut. Colonel.*

Jas. R. Mullany, 3 March, 1813.

*Majors.*

D. M'Farland, 15 Aug., 1813.
G. M. Brooke, 1 May, 1814.

*Captains.*

Peter Mills, 6 July, 1812.
Derick Van Veghten, 6 July, 1812.
Thomas Delano, 6 July, 1812.
Hor. G. Armstrong, 25 Sept., 1812. Assistant Inspector General.
L. B. Canfield, 25 Sept., 1812.
Isaac Roach, Jr., 13 April, 1813.
S. D. Wattles, 20 June, 1813.
A. W. Odell, 20 June, 1813.
E. F. Gilbert, 26 June, 1813.
Wm. Clarke, 15 Oct., 1813.

*1st Lieutenants.*

John M'Cartey, 6 July, 1812.
R. Goodell, 6 July, 1812.
W. J. Worth, 19 July, 1812. Aid to Major General Lewis.
H. Whiting, 20 June, 1812.
P. L. Hogeboom, 20 June, 1812. Paymaster.
Fred. Brown, 20 June, 1812.
Abijah Bennet, 20 June, 1812. Aid to Brig. General Cass.
R. Simons, 15 Oct., 1812.
J. P. Livingston, 19 Dec., 1812.

*2nd Lieutenants.*

Levi S. Burr, 18 March, 1813.
J. M'Auley, Jr., 16 April, 1813.
Jus. Ingersoll, 20 June, 1813. Quartermaster.
Saml. Tappan, 20 June, 1813.
I. H. Wats, 21 June, 1813.
Alph. Wetmore, 26 June, 1813.
W. G. Belknap, 15 Oct., 1813.
S. B. Griswold, 19 Dec., 1813.
Zadoc P. Morse, 19 April, 1814.
John Jones, 19 April, 1814.

*3rd Lieutenants.*

Rd. C. Smith, 3 May, 1813.
James S. Abeel, 3 May, 1813.
Abm. Cantine, 10 May, 1813.
J. P. Dieterich, 10 May, 1813.
Rd. Phillips, 13 May, 1813.
Samuel R. Hill, 21 June, 1813.
Ezra King, 15 Oct., 1813.
John B. Truax, 19 Dec., 1813.
Francis Blaize, 19 April, 1814.
Dudley Lamb, 19 April, 1814.

*Ensign.*

Isaac W. Webb, 3 Dec., 1813.

*Surgeon.*

Silas Fuller, 6 July, 1812.

*Surgeon's Mates.*

John Gale, 9 July, 1812.
Henry White, 28 July, 1813.

---

TWENTY-FOURTH INFANTRY.

*Tennessee.*

*Colonel.*

W. P. Anderson, 6 July, 1812.

*Lieut. Colonel.*

Jos. L. Smith, 12 March, 1813.

*Majors.*

F. W. Armstrong, 26 June, 1813.
Robert Butler, 15 Aug., 1813. Colonel, staff.

*Captains.*

Alexander Gray, 6 July, 1812.
Jno. A. Rodgers, 6 July, 1812.
Wm. O. Allen, 6 July, 1812.
Robert Desha, 6 July, 1812.
J. H. Campbell, 6 July, 1812.
Minor Sturgus, 13 May, 1813.
Frank Hampton, 26 June, 1813.
W. O. Winston, 15 Aug., 1813.
W. Wilkinson, 15 Aug., 1813.
Silas Stephens, 18 April, 1814.

*1st Lieutenants.*

James Stuart, 6 July, 1812.
Rt. Buntin, Jr., 26 June, 1813.
Caleb G. Fobes, 15 Aug., 1813.
Joseph Perkins, 15 Aug., 1813.
Abner Hynes, 30 Aug., 1813.
T. P. Favrot, 15 Oct., 1813.
Adam Peck, 15 Oct., 1813.
Litt. Johnson, 17 March, 1814.
Saml. Y. Balch, 17 March, 1814.
John Butler, 17 March, 1814.

*2nd Lieutenants.*

Jos. A. Martin, 14 Aug., 1813.
W. M. Crawford, 15 Aug., 1813.
J. S. Williamson, 15 Aug., 1813.
Francis Vallé, 30 Aug., 1813.
John Gilbreath, 15 Oct., 1813.
Rd. M. Woods, 18 Dec., 1813.
F. Baldridge, 19 Dec., 1813.
Ab. Brittain, 17 March, 1814.
I. S. Hackett, 17 March, 1814.
W. G. Childress, 17 March, 1814.

*3rd Lieutenants.*

W. K. Paulling, 15 Oct., 1813.
Wm. Johnson, 18 Dec., 1813.
Elijah Hayne, 14 May, 1814.
Benj. S. Rue, 14 May, 1814.
Elisha Walker, 14 May, 1814.
Benj. Davis, 14 May, 1814.
T. B. Young, 14 May, 1814.
Wm. S. Wells, 14 May, 1814.
Wm. Nelson, 14 May, 1814.
F. Woodward, 14 May, 1814.

*Ensigns.*

Wm. Jones, 15 April, 1814.
A. D. Masters, 18 April, 1814.

*Surgeon.*

Henry Skinner, 5 April, 1813.

*Surgeon's Mates.*

C. Humphries, 25 April, 1812.
Harry Bradford, 9 Aug., 1813.

---

TWENTY-FIFTH INFANTRY.

*Connecticut.*

*Colonel.*

G. M'Feeley, 15 April, 1814.

*Lieut. Colonel.*

Jonas Cutting, 6 July, 1812.

*Majors.*

T. S. Jesup, 6 April, 1813.
C. K. Gardner, 26 June, 1813. Adjutant General.

*Captains.*

Geo. Howard, 6 July 1812.
Joseph Kinney, 13 March, 1813.
T. M. Read, 16 April, 1813.
J. B. Murdoch, 16 April, 1813.
Henry Dyer, 20 June, 1813.
J. A. Thomas, 15 Aug., 1813.
Benj. Watson, 15 Aug., 1813.
D. Ketchum, 30 Sept., 1813.
J. Burbidge, 15 Feb., 1814.
Edward White, 14 March, 1814.

*1st Lieutenants.*

Daniel Forward, 16 April, 1813.
Archd. C. Crary, 16 April, 1813.
T. S. Seymour, 20 June, 1813.
Jesse Beach, 26 June, 1813.
E. Shaylor, 15 Aug., 1813.
Alex. T. F. Bill, 15 Aug., 1813.
John G. Munn, 15 Aug., 1813.
Geo. M'Chain, 30 Sept., 1813. Quartermaster.
J. Hutchinson, 15 Feb., 1814.
G. Talcott, Jr., 14 March, 1814.

*2nd Lieutenants.*

Russell Eddy, 13 July, 1813. Paymaster.
John Gifford, 13 July, 1813.
J. D. Brown 15 Aug., 1813.
S. H. Devotion, 28 Sept., 1813.
Henry De Witt, 15 Feb., 1814.
D. F. Wilcox, 14 March, 1814.
C. Burbridge, 14 March, 1814.
T. Pachin, 14 March, 1814.
Jas. Murphy, 1 May, 1814.
I. Holcomb, 1 May, 1814.

*Surgeon.*

P. Woodbury, 30 March, 1814.

---

TWENTY-SIXTH INFANTRY.

*Vermont.*

*Colonel.*

Isaac Clark, 6 July, 1812.

*Lieut. Colonel.*

Benj. Forsyth, 15 April, 1814.

*Major.*

Isaac Finch, 6 June, 1814.

*Captains.*

Elis Boarman, 21 April, 1814.
James. Hedges, 21 April, 1814.
Ira Williams, 21 April, 1814.
Th. Coleman, 21 April, 1814.
Jos Thompson, 21 April, 1814.
S. C. Cotton, 21 April, 1814.
I. Levake, 21 April, 1814.
W. Farnsworth, 21 April, 1814.
I. Campbell, 21 April, 1814.
G. H. Grosvenor, 21 April, 1814.

*1st Lieutenants.*

W. Bezeau, 17 March, 1814.
G. W. Templeton, 21 April, 1814.
Harvey Gilman, 21 April, 1814.
J. C. Walker, 21 April, 1814.
Phi. Smith, 21 April, 1814.
Ja. Wheepley, 21 April, 1814.
J. Morehouse, 21 April, 1814.
J. Boardman, 21 April, 1814.
P. Callan, 20 May, 1814.
J. A. Binns, 20 May, 1814.

*2nd Lieutenants.*

M. Scott, 21 April, 1814.
T. French, 21 April, 1814.
I. Black, 21 April, 1814.
Hor. Broughton, 21 April, 1814.
Seth Hall, 21 April, 1814.
Jacob Robinson, 21 April, 1814.

*3rd Lieutenants.*

Saml. Rich, 21 April, 1814.
Sl. Chittenton, 21 April, 1814.
Aug. Lavalk, 21 April, 1814.
W. T. Willard, 21 April, 1814.
Walter Thomas, 21 April, 1814.

*Ensigns.*

S. K. Gilchrist, 21 April, 1814.
Ths. Walde, 17 May, 1814.

*Surgeon.*

H. Stanard, 13 April, 1814.

*Surgeon's Mate.*

M. J. Cunningham, 27 April, 1814.

---

TWENTY-SEVENTH INFANTRY.

*New York.*

*Lieut. Colonel.*

Alex. Denniston, 15 April, 1814.

*Majors.*

J. D. Wadsworth, 15 April, 1814.
Clarks. Crolius, 15 April, 1814.

*Captains.*

C. Hartell, 21 April, 1814.
Ch. Hughes, 21 April, 1814.
Ben. Wood, 21 April, 1814.
Ths. Earle, 21 April, 1814.
A. Reynolds, 21 April, 1814.
A. T. Crane, 21 April, 1814.
Wm. Shotwell, 21 April, 1814.
Danl. Warren, 21 April, 1814.
Geo. Maxwell, 21 April, 1814.

*1st Lieutenants.*

Wm. Perron, 21 April, 1814.
Jas. Kerr, 21 April, 1814.
Rt. P. Ross, 21 April, 1814.
Danl. L. Scott, 21 April, 1814.
Jas. I. Ryan, 21 April, 1814.
Rt. M'Elworth, 21 April, 1814.
R. Hall, 21 April, 1814.

*2nd Lieutenants.*

T. Darling, 21 April, 1814.
Isaac Plesey, 21 April, 1814.
N. G. Carmer, 21 April, 1814.
Stew. Elder, 21 April, 1814.
Th. M'Conkey, 21 April, 1814.
Jacob S. Brown, 21 April, 1814.
Jas. Gary, 21 April, 1814.
T. Y. Spicer, 21 April, 1814.
Ol. Vance, 21 April, 1814.

*3rd Lieutenants.*

R. Geer, 21 April, 1814.
Jas. Mears, 21 April, 1814.
Const. Clifford, 21 April, 1814.
T. Crawford, 21 April, 1814.
D. M. Darrow, 21 April, 1814.
Pat. M'Keon, 17 May, 1814.

*Ensign.*

T. Behan, 21 April, 1814.

*Surgeon.*

A. M. Smith, 21 April, 1814.

TWENTY-EIGHTH INFANTRY.

*Kentucky.*

*Colonel.*

T. Deye Owings, 11 March, 1813.

*Lieut. Colonel.*

John Campbell, 31 Jan., 1814.

*Majors.*

James Smiley, 11 March, 1813.
Jas. Doherty, 19 April, 1814.

*Captains.*

Geo. Stockton, 20 May, 1813.
Henry C. Gist, 20 May, 1813.
John Lowrey, 20 May, 1813.
C. S. Todd, 20 May, 1813. Assistant Inspector General.
J. Megowan, 20 May, 1813.
N. H. Moore, 20 May, 1813.
Henry Daniel, 20 May, 1813.
T. L. Butler, 30 June, 1813.
Jos. C. Belt, 10 Oct., 1813.
David M'Nair, 20 Feb., 1814.

*1st Lieutenants.*

Mat. H. Jouitt, 20 May, 1813.
Jas. Hickman, 20 May, 1813.
John Mason, 20 May, 1813.
Th. Edmonson, 20 May, 1813.
Reasin H. Gist, 30 June, 1813.
D. G. Cowan, 1 Aug., 1813.
W. D. Hayden, 10 Oct., 1813.
John C. Kouns, 20 Feb., 1814.
W. Henry, 17 March, 1814.
Wm. Stewart, 17 March, 1814.

*2nd Lieutenants.*

John Trumbs, 30 June, 1813.
Joseph Taylor, 1 Aug., 1813.
John Wyatt, 1 Aug., 1813.
Robert Clark, 10 Oct., 1813.
Daniel Conner, 16 Oct., 1813.
Jonas Jordan, 20 Feb., 1814.
C. Harrison, 17 March, 1814.
John B. Clark, 9 April, 1814.
Peter Davis, 9 April, 1814.

*3rd Lieutenants.*

W. P. S. Blair, 1 June, 1813.
Jos. Dawson, 1 Aug., 1813.
J. Roads, 16 Oct., 1813.
D. Brown, 16 Oct., 1813.
Granv. N. Love, 14 May, 1814.
James Finley, 14 May, 1814.
John Harvey, 14 May, 1814.
Peter Bryan, 14 May, 1814.

*Ensigns.*

P. S. Richardson, 15 April, 1814.
Biram Williams, 15 April, 1814.
Richd. Mitchell, 15 April, 1814.

*Surgeon.*

N. L. Boulden, 15 April, 1814.

---

TWENTY-NINTH INFANTRY.

*New York.*

*Colonel.*

M. Smith, 12 April, 1813.

*Lieut. Colonel.*

G. D. Young, 12 April, 1813.

*Majors.*

John E. Wool, 13 April, 1813.
Asa B. Sizer, 13 April, 1813.

*Captains.*

P. B. Van Beuren, 30 April, 1813.
B. Schuyler, 30 April, 1813.
M. D. Danvers, 30 April, 1813.
Elam Lynds, 30 April, 1813.
J. C. Rochester, 30 April, 1813.
Jas. B. Spencer, 30 April, 1813.
A. Spencer, Jr., 20 Feb., 1814.
A. C. Spencer, 14 March, 1814.

*1st Lieutenants.*

G. Dumbleton, 30 April, 1813.
Joel Peebles, 30 April, 1813.
J. B. Stewart, 30 April, 1813.
Tennis Hanson, 30 April, 1813.
B. A. Boynton, 25 Nov., 1813.
T. Brownson, 25 Nov., 1813.
Daniel Adams, 20 Dec., 1813.
H. Van Antwerp, 20 Feb., 1814.
Th. Sutton, 14 March, 1814.
Sylvanus Mott, 1 May, 1814.

*2nd Lieutenants.*

S. D. Kellogg, 25 Nov., 1813.
Jas. Palmer, 20 Dec., 1813.
Daniel Smith, Jr., 11 Jan., 1814.
Alton Nelson, 31 Jan., 1814.
P. R. Halstead, 20 Feb., 1814.
T. Vail, 14 March, 1814.
S. Newcomb, 5 April, 1814.
T. Turner, Jr., 1 May, 1814.
J. R. Townsend, 1 May, 1814.

*3rd Lieutenants.*

Walter Smith, 7 Nov., 1813.
John Sing, 25 Nov., 1813.
John Wynkoop, 25 Nov., 1813.
J. W. Lansing, 30 Nov., 1813.
C. S. Stuart, 20 Dec., 1813.
M. A. Patrick, 1 May, 1814.
Saml. Burr, 1 May, 1814.
G. Bacon, 1 May, 1814.
C. Kelloog, 1 May, 1814.
M. Bowers, 1 May, 1814.

*Surgeon.*

Martin Jennison, 1 July, 1813.

*Surgeon's Mate.*

R. C. Walmsey, 1 July, 1813.

---

THIRTIETH INFANTRY.

*Vermont.*

*Colonel.*

Elias Fasset, 23 Feb., 1813.

*Lieut. Colonel.*

Martin Norton, 23 Feb., 1813.

*Major.*

John Bayley, 23 Feb., 1813.

*Captains.*

S. Wright, 30 April, 1813.
Salmon Clark, 30 April, 1813.
David Sanford, 30 April, 1813.
John Wires, 30 April, 1813.
D. Farrington, 30 April, 1813.
G. Spencer, Jr., 30 April, 1813.
S. Danforth, 30 April, 1813.
James Taylor, 30 April, 1813.
Wm. Miller, 31 Jan., 1814.
S. Robinson, 5 March, 1814.

*1st Lieutenants.*

Wm. Barney, 30 April, 1813.
Wm. Myrick, 30 April, 1813.
J. M. Young, 30 April, 1813.
G. W. Kendell, 30 April, 1813.
Israel Smith, 30 April, 1813. Paymaster.
G. Brownson, 15 Aug., 1813.
J. H. Burton, 31 Dec., 1813. Adjutant.
Steph. Rumsey, 31 Jan., 1814.
A. Bostwick, 18 Feb., 1814. Quartermaster.
Gideon Hawley, 5 March, 1814.

*2nd Lieutenants.*

Th. Stephens, 30 April, 1813.
Elisha Smith, 30 April, 1813.
Jas. Johnson, 30 April, 1813.
M. L. Selden, 15 Aug., 1813.
Benjn. Darby, 18 Sept., 1813.
Benjn. Fasset, 31 Dec., 1813.
Nat. Spalding, 31 Jan., 1814.
R. B. Hyde, 18 Feb., 1814.
Phelps Smith, 5 March, 1814.
Almerin Smith, 5 March, 1814.

*3rd Lieutenants.*

Return Strong, 30 April, 1813.
H. Wadams, 30 April, 1813.
James Smith, 30 April, 1813.
Th. Chittenden, 15 Aug., 1813.
Hen. Hendrix, 18 Sept., 1813.
S. Hatheway, 31 Dec., 1813.
A. B. Dake, 31 Jan., 1814.
J. R. Pettibone, 18 Feb., 1814.
R. R. Childs, 5 March, 1814.
Danl. Griswold, 5 March, 1814.

*Ensigns.*

W. B. Ferris, 30 April, 1813.
Stephen Webb, 30 April, 1813.
James Gilbert, 11 March, 1814.

*Surgeon's Mate.*

W. A. Needham, 19 July, 1813.

---

THIRTY-FIRST INFANTRY.

*Vermont.*

*Colonel.*

Danl. Dana, 23 Feb., 1813.

*Lieut. Colonel.*

Huckens Storrs, 23 Feb., 1813.

*Majors.*

R. B. Brown, 9 March, 1814.
P. Muhlenberg, 1 May, 1814.

*Captains.*

D. A. A. Buck, 30 April, 1813.
Asa Aikins, 30 April, 1813.
Rufus Stewart, 30 April, 1813.
Ethan Burnap, 30 April, 1813.
Joseph Morril, 30 April, 1813.
Silas Dickinson, 30 April, 1813.
C. L. Rockwood, 11 Jan., 1814.
Andw. Arnold, 11 Jan., 1814.
J. S. Bicknell, 11 Jan., 1814.
Levi Powers, 11 Jan., 1814.

*1st Lieutenants.*

D. C. Bryant, 30 April, 1813.
Levi Cox, 11 Jan., 1814.
A. W. Brown, 11 Jan., 1814.
Simon Brown, 11 Jan., 1814.
Asa Baker, 11 Jan., 1814.
John Farwell, 31 Jan., 1814.
John Hatch, 2 Feb., 1814.
E. Emmons, 1 May, 1814. Quartermaster.
Eleazer Davis, 1 May, 1814.

*2nd Lieutenants.*

John Pratt, Jr., 11 Jan., 1814.
Jonathan Eddy, 11 Jan., 1814.
S. Wetherbee, Jr., 11 Jan., 1814.
F. Nickinson, 11 Jan., 1814.
Harvey Gilman, 31 Jan., 1814.
Jeremiah York, 17 Feb., 1814.
S. M. Perkins, 21 Feb., 1814.
J. Y. Sawyer, 18 April, 1814.
S. Stevens, Jr., 1 May, 1814. Paymaster.
Isaac Briggs, 1 May, 1814.

*3rd Lieutenants.*

J. Greenleaf, 11 Jan., 1814.
Aaron Matson, 11 Jan., 1814.
Daniel Pearson, 1 May, 1814.
Clark Smith, 1 May, 1814.
J. E. Albro, 1 May, 1814.
L. P. Wheelock, 1 May, 1814.
Noadiah Kibby, 1 May, 1814.
E. Chase, 1 May, 1814.
E. W. Buchannon, 1 May, 1814.

*Ensigns.*

J. H. Atherton, 8 April, 1814.
H. S. Cabot, 8 April, 1814.

*Surgeon.*

P. S. Mason, 29 June, 1813.

*Surgeon's Mate.*

Wm. Paddock, 29 June, 1813.

---

THIRTY-SECOND INFANTRY.

*Delaware and Pennsylvania.*

*Colonel.*

S. E. Fotterall, 6 May, 1813.

*Lieut. Colonel.*

S. B. Davis, 6 May, 1813.

*Majors.*

Geo. H. Hunter, 6 May, 1813.
A. H. Holmes, 18 April, 1814. Major brevet, 4 March.

*Captains.*

G. F. Goodman, 18 March, 1813.
Wm. Smith, 18 March, 1813.
Samuel Borden, 17 May, 1813.
Thos. Town, 17 May, 1813.
Jno. Steele, Jr., 17 May, 1813.
J. J. Robinson, 17 May, 1813.
Jona. B. Smith, 17 May, 1813.
Horatio Davis, 17 May, 1813.
Robt. Patterson, 19 April, 1814.
Pr.-P. Walter, 19 April, 1814.

*1st Lieutenants.*

Claudius F. Le Grand, 17 April, 1813.
Richard Bache, 17 April, 1813.
Maskline Clark, 17 April, 1813.
John Suter, 17 April, 1813.
John Wilson, 16 July, 1813.
Jas. M'Karaher, 5 Oct., 1813.
C. B. Hopkins, 5 Oct., 1813.
Joseph Baldwin, 19 April, 1814.
Wm. Crosier, 19 April, 1814. Paymaster.

*2nd Lieutenants.*

Anthony Bonnaffon, 17 May, 1813.
Th. F. Hargis, 17 May, 1813.
Chas. Kean, 17 May, 1813.
De E. Sweeny, 16 July, 1813.
A. L. Gamble, 5 Oct., 1813.
H. M'Clelland, 5 Oct., 1813.
Geo. Dannaker, 19 April, 1814.

Thos. M'Elvee, 19 April, 1814.
John Stewart, 19 April, 1814.
Henry Wilson, 19 April, 1814.

*3rd Lieutenants.*

H. Gulick, 16 July, 1813.
Jas. M'Ilvaine, 5 Oct., 1813.
G. F. H. Crocket, 5 Oct., 1813.

*Ensign.*

J. W. Copes, 19 April, 1814.

*Surgeon.*

Frank Bache, 25 April, 1814.

---

THIRTY-THIRD INFANTRY.

*Massachusetts.*

*Colonel.*

Isaac Lane, 23 Feb., 1813.

*Lieut. Colonel.*

H. Stark, 1 May, 1814.

*Majors.*

Danl. Lane, 23 Feb., 1813.
J. Walworth, 1 May, 1814.

*Captains.*

Benjn. Adams, 30 April, 1813.
Benjn. Dunn, 30 April, 1813.
R. K. Goodenow, 30 April, 1813.
Isaac Hodsdon, 30 April, 1813.
Chas. Lothrop, 30 April, 1813.
Th. Dinsmore, 30 April, 1813.
James Curry, 30 April, 1813.
Joel Millikin, 3 Nov., 1813.
Josiah Moulton, 19 April, 1814.

*1st Lieutenants.*

Stephen Bean, 30 April, 1813.
Jere. Goodwin, 30 April, 1813. Paymaster.
Geo. Scammon, 30 April, 1813. Adjutant.
Eben. Seavey, 30 April, 1813.
Jos. Morrison, 30 April, 1813.
Isaac F. Snow, 3 Nov., 1813. Quartermaster.
Alx. Worster, 31 Dec., 1813.
T. Buckminster, 10 Feb., 1814.
James Willey, 19 April, 1814.

*2nd Lieutenants.*

M. M'Lane, 30 April, 1813.
S. Woodman, Jr., 30 April, 1813.
Wm. Cutts, 2 Nov., 1813.
Joseph Bryant, 3 Nov., 1813.
B. Palmer, Jr., 31 Dec., 1813.
Hanson Hayes, 10 Feb., 1814.
John Dunn, 19 April, 1814.
Rufus K. Lane, 29 April, 1814.
Jona. Goodwin, 29 April, 1814.

*3rd Lieutenants.*

James Walker, 2 Nov., 1813.
Nathl. Webster, 3 Nov., 1813.
James Banks, 31 Dec., 1813.
Geo. Dunham, 1 Jan., 1814.
J. B. Hartford, 10 Feb., 1814.
Joseph Snow, 31 March, 1814.
Samuel Powell, 29 April, 1814.

*Surgeon.*

Perl. F. Groves, 10 April, 1813.

*Surgeon's Mates.*

Ward Bassett, 10 April, 1813.
John P. Briggs, 10 April, 1813.

THIRTY-FOURTH INFANTRY.

*Massachusetts.*

*Colonel.*

J. D. Learned, 23 Feb., 1813.

*Majors.*

T. M. Vinson, 23 Feb., 1813.
Wm. Platt, 9 March, 1814.

*Captains.*

Peter Chadwick, 30 April, 1813.
Robt. Douglass, 30 April, 1813.
Benjn. Poland, 30 April, 1813.
Rbt. R. Kendall, 30 April, 1813.
Wm. Sweet, 30 April, 1813.
Isaac Carter, 30 April, 1813.
Jos. C. Adams, 30 April, 1813.
J. Merrill, 31 Jan., 1814.
Ths. Bailey, 24 March, 1814.

*1st Lieutenants.*

Jeremiah Edes, 30 April, 1813.
Edw. Barneville, 30 April, 1813.
Elihu Norton, 30 April, 1813.
Nathl. Gookin, 16 May, 1813.
W. A. Springer, 10 Nov., 1813.
Joseph Sumner, 31 Jan., 1814. Adjutant.
Nathl. Wilson, 24 March, 1814.
David Sherman, 24 March, 1814.

*2nd Lieutenants.*

S. Dearborn, 30 April, 1813.
Timothy Bacon, 30 April, 1813.
Calvin Crocker, 30 April, 1813.
Otis Robbins, 1 Nov., 1813.
Royal D. Simons, 10 Nov., 1813.
Thos. Johnson, 31 Jan., 1814.
Robert Gibson, 7 March, 1814.
Moses Clough, 8 March, 1814.
Jos. M'Clure, 24 March, 1814.
Edwd. Springer, 24 March, 1814.

*3rd Lieutenants.*

Isaac Townsend, 30 April, 1813.
Supply B. Gookin, 1 July, 1813.
Flavel Sabin, 15 Aug., 1813.
Henry Taylor, 1 Nov., 1813.
Steph. Merrill, 10 Nov., 1813.
D. Farnsworth, 31 Jan., 1814.
Josiah Parlin, 7 March, 1814.
Cotton Ward, 8 March, 1814.

*Surgeon.*

Jotham Forbes, 30 April, 1813.

*Surgeon's Mates.*

Charles Loring, 20 May, 1813.
Thad. Hubbard, 20 May, 1813.

---

THIRTY-FIFTH INFANTRY.

*Virginia.*

*Colonel.*

Jos. Goodwyn, 3 March, 1813.

*Lieut. Colonel.*

Robert Pegram, 3 March, 1813.

*Majors.*

Aug. C. Smith, 3 March, 1813.
A. I. M'Connico, 22 March, 1813.

*Captains.*

Danl. C. Butts, 31 March, 1813.
Saml. M'Guire, 31 March, 1813.

M. Taliaferro, 31 March, 1813.
John Thorp, 31 March, 1813.
B. Hardaway, 31 March, 1813.
Benj. B. Jones, 31 March, 1813.
F. E. Walker, 31 March, 1813.
W. T. Cocke, 31 March, 1813.
Isaac T. Preston, 31 March, 1813.
John W. Stith, 1 May, 1814.

*1st Lieutenants.*

Christn. Miller, 31 March, 1813.
James Belches, 31 March, 1813.
Th. J. Parker, 31 March, 1813.
John G. Crump, 31 March, 1813.
Blair Bolling, 31 March, 1813.
Edw. L. Pegram, 31 March, 1813.
John Garland, 31 March, 1813.
L. Dangerfield, 1 May, 1814.
Wm. Rivers, 1 May, 1814.
Henry Cook, 1 May, 1814.

*2nd Lieutenants.*

Wm. Loyall, 31 March, 1813.
S. C. Williams, 31 March, 1813.
David B. Stith, 31 March, 1813.
John B. Hall, 31 March, 1813.
Ch. R. Rose, 22 Jan., 1814.
D. Shelton, 3 March, 1814.
Ch. Hutchins, 8 March, 1814.
Th. K. Ball, 1 May, 1814.
Wm. Dunn, 1 May, 1814. Paymaster.
Fr. Charlton, 1 May, 1814.

*3rd Lieutenants.*

R. Crockwell, 31 March, 1813.
Winfield Jones, 31 March, 1813.
Samuel Kirby, 31 Dec., 1813.
Jno. Thompson, 22 Jan., 1814.
R. W. Scott, 3 March, 1814.
P. R. Burwell, 8 March, 1814.
John Huson, 1 May, 1814.
Lawr. M. Gale, 1 May, 1814.
Benj. Johnson, 1 May, 1814.
Fr. W. Brady, 1 May, 1814.

*Ensigns.*

Richard Watts, 8 April, 1814.
Ch. Daniel, 8 April, 1814.
H. Bibb, 3 May, 1814.
R. A. Crowder, 10 May, 1814.
Th. J. Wootton, 10 May, 1814.
E. Archer, 10 May, 1814.
H. F. Farley, 10 May, 1814.
P. H. Mann, 10 May, 1814.
L. P. Lanier, 10 May, 1814.

*Surgeon's Mates.*

W. W. Southall, 20 July, 1813.
L. R. Robinson, 8 April, 1814.

---

THIRTY-SIXTH INFANTRY.

*Maryland and Virginia.*

*Colonel.*

Henry Carbery, 22 March, 1813.

*Lieut. Colonel.*

William Scott, 25 March, 1813.

*Majors.*

Alex. Stuart, 25 March, 1813.
Henry Lee, Jr., 8 April, 1813.

*Captains.*

Joseph Hook, 30 April, 1813.
Henry C. Neale, 30 April, 1813.
Jos. S. Nelson, 30 April, 1813.
C. C. Randolph, 30 April, 1813.
Thos. Carbery, 30 April, 1813.
Samuel Rasin, 30 April, 1813.
J. J. Merrick, 30 April, 1813.
Mort. D. Hall, 30 April, 1813.
H. W. Deneale, 30 April, 1813.
Thos. Corcoran, 30 April, 1813.

*1st Lieutenants.*

Wm. C. Hobbs, 30 April, 1813.
James Neale, 30 April, 1813.
John Ricaud, 30 April, 1813. Paymaster.
James Ord, 30 April, 1813. ——
Fran. J. Neale, 30 April, 1813.
John Chauncey, 30 April, 1813.
Wm. N. Earle, 15 Aug., 1813.
W. L. Rogers, 1 May, 1814.
R. K. Watts, 1 May, 1814.
Cle. Sewell, 1 May, 1814.

*2nd Lieutenants.*

Chas. Queen, 30 April, 1813.
Wm. Merrick, 15 Aug., 1813.
Wm. A. Rind, 15 Aug., 1813.
George Slye, 21 Feb., 1814.
Wright Hall, 21 Feb., 1814.
Henry Redman, 1 May, 1814.
F. J. Wheeler, 1 May, 1814.
J. M. Burgess, 1 May, 1814.
Philip Fisher, 1 May, 1814.
John Clark, 1 May, 1814.

*3rd Lieutenants.*

Edward Scott, 15 Aug., 1813.
John Mansfield, 17 March, 1814.
H. Dunlap, 17 March, 1814. Quartermaster.
M. Latimore, 17 March, 1814.

*Ensigns.*

W. Washington, 23 April, 1814.
N. Bateman, 3 May, 1814.

*Surgeon.*

Thos. P. Hall, 10 July, 1813.

*Surgeon's Mate.*

Caleb Parker, 26 May, 1814.

---

THIRTY-SEVENTH INFANTRY.

*Connecticut.*

*Colonel.*

H. Atkinson, 15 April, 1814.

*Lieut. Colonel.*

A. Benjamin, 11 March, 1813.

*Majors.*

Roswell Lee, 3 March, 1813.
Saml. Hoadley, 11 March, 1813.

*Captains.*

Elizur Warner, 30 April, 1813.
Christ. Ripley, 30 April, 1813.
Chauncey Ives, 30 April, 1813.
S. B. Northrop, 30 April, 1813.
Riley Sweet, 30 April, 1813.
Noah T. Ferry, 30 April, 1813.
Steph. D. Tilden, 30 April, 1813.
Guy Gaylord, 31 May, 1813.
J. Brown, 9 March, 1814.
H. W. Huntington, 31 March, 1814.

*1st Lieutenants.*

David C. Welsh, 30 April, 1813. Paymaster.
Wm. Morgan, 30 April, 1813.
Step. Drummer, 30 April, 1813.
Elipha Ripley, 30 April, 1813.

Demas Deming, 30 April, 1813.
Chaun. Hosford, 30 April, 1813.
David Gibbs, 30 April, 1813.
Solomon Dewy, 31 May, 1813.
Henry Starr, 9 March, 1814.
Danl. Bicknell, 31 March, 1814.

*2nd Lieutenants.*

Jas. L. Reynolds, 30 April, 1813.
Eli Bradley, 30 April, 1813.
David Tracey, 30 April, 1813.
W. Wakeman, 30 April, 1813.
Nathan Clark, 19 May, 1813.
Samuel Keeler, 31 Jan., 1814.
Ralph Steel, 9 March, 1814.
J. R. Warren, 1 May, 1814.
Saml. Robinson, 1 May, 1814.

*3rd Lieutenants.*

Irad Storrs, 30 April, 1813.
Jno. Phelps, Jr., 3 June, 1813.
Saml. Keeler, Jr., 17 Dec., 1813.
Oren Hatch, 31 Jan., 1814.
Lyman Mallory, 31 Jan., 1814.
Henry Lord, 9 March, 1814.
Thomas Hewit, 31 March, 1814.
John Fellows, 1 May, 1814.
Ebenezer Fisk, 1 May, 1814.
Jas. Smith, Jr., 1 May, 1814.

*Surgeon.*

Elijah Butts, 20 May, 1813.

*Surgeon's Mate.*

Asahel Hall, 19 Sept., 1813.

---

THIRTY-EIGHTH INFANTRY.

*Maryland.*

*Colonel.*

Peter Little, 19 May, 1813.

*Lieut. Colonel.*

Wm. Steuart, 19 May, 1813.

*Majors.*

Geo. Keyser, 19 May, 1813.
E. Cutler, 1 May, 1814.

*Captains.*

James H. Hook, 20 May, 1813.
John Rothrock, 20 May, 1813.
Isaac Aldridge, 20 May, 1813.
John Brookes, 20 May, 1813.
John Buck, 20 May, 1813.
Henry O'Neal, 20 May, 1813.
Ch. Stansbury, 20 May, 1813.
S. C. Leakin, 20 May, 1813.
John Mowton, 1 May, 1814.
James Smith, 20 May, 1814.

*1st Lieutenants.*

William Ford, 20 May, 1813.
Henry S. Geyer, 20 May, 1813. Paymaster.
William Hall, 20 May, 1813.
Joshua Medtart, 15 Aug., 1813.
James Holmes, 31 Dec., 1813.
B. B. Sweeting, 22 April, 1814.
Jerem. Green, 1 May, 1814.
J. M. Barrett, 1 May, 1814.
Wm. Jones, 1 May, 1814.
Jas. S. Griffin, 20 May, 1814.

*2nd Lieutenants.*

Geo. Fletcher, 20 May, 1813.
John Sticher, 20 May, 1813.
Wm. H. Bates, 15 Aug., 1813.
D. W. Duncan, 3 Dec., 1813.
Peter Keyser, 22 April, 1814.
Saml. Barkley, 1 May, 1814.
Wm. Harwood, 1 May, 1814.
F. W. Hoffman, 1 May, 1814.
Henry Huber, 1 May, 1814.
Benj. P. Head, 20 May, 1814.

*3rd Lieutenants.*

Cassa. Watkins, 31 Dec., 1813.
John Savery, 7 Jan., 1814.
Rich. M. Sands, 22 April, 1814.
Jno. B. Martin, 1 May, 1814.
John Spicknall, 1 May, 1814.
J. Cochran, 20 May, 1814.

*Ensign.*

L. Bateman, 20 May, 1814.

*Surgeon.*

W. N. Mercer, 7 Aug., 1813.

*Surgeon's Mate.*

G. Berry, 8 April, 1814.

---

THIRTY-NINTH INFANTRY.

*Tennessee.*

*Colonel.*

John Williams, 18 June, 1813.

*Lieut. Colonel.*

Th. H. Benton, 18 June, 1813.

*Majors.*

Wm. Peacock, 29 July, 1813.
Uriah Blue, 13 March, 1814.

*Captains.*

John Phagan, 29 July, 1813.
William Walker, 29 July, 1813.
Benj. Reynolds, 29 July, 1813.
John R. Long, 29 July, 1813.
A. H. Douglass, 29 July, 1813.
Hen. Henniger, 29 July, 1813.
John Jones, 29 July, 1813.
James Davis, 29 July, 1813.
Thos. Stuart, 29 July, 1813.
James Gray, 1 May, 1814.

*1st Lieutenants.*

Rbt. M. Somerville, 29 July, 1813.
Benj. Wright, 29 July, 1813.
Samuel Wilson, 29 July, 1813.
Jas. M'Donald, 29 July, 1813.
Nath. Smith, 29 July, 1813.
Joel Denton, 29 July, 1813.
B. M. Patterson, 11 Jan., 1814.
M. C. Molton, 17 March, 1814.
James Leith, 1 May, 1814.

*2nd Lieutenants.*

Ashlay Stanfield, 29 July, 1813.
Jesse C. Tate, 29 July, 1813.
Jos. R. Henderson, 29 July, 1813.
Guy Smith, 29 July, 1813.
David M'Millen, 29 July, 1813.
Benjn. Duncan, 11 Jan., 1814.
M. W. M'Clellan, 17 March, 1814.
Isaac Paugle, 1 May, 1814.
Simpson Payne, 1 May, 1814.
R. Quarles, 1 May, 1814.

*3rd Lieutenants.*

S. Houston, 31 Dec., 1813.
T. C. Hindman, 11 Jan., 1814.
I. Parrish, 8 March, 1814.
A. Greer, 17 March, 1814.
J. K. Snap, 1 May, 1814.

N. Dortch, 1 May, 1814.
J. Corn, 1 May, 1814.
M. F. De Graffenreidt, 1 May, 1814.

*Ensigns.*

Cor. N. Lewis, 26 March, 1814.
D. Alexander, 31 March, 1814.
C. Summerville, 25 April, 1814.

*Surgeon's Mate.*

John H. Read, 2 July, 1813.

---

FORTIETH INFANTRY.

*Massachusetts.*

*Colonel.*

Jas. Loring, Jr., 31 July, 1813.

*Lieut. Colonel.*

John Breck, 19 July, 1813.

*Majors.*

Perley Putnam, 19 July, 1813.
R. Whartenby, 1 May, 1814.

*Captains.*

J. B. Varnum, 19 July, 1813.
Seth W. Nye, 19 July, 1813.
James Perry, 29 July, 1813.
Leonard Ross, 1 Aug., 1813.
M. N. Sanborn, 1 Aug., 1813.
Robert Neale, Jr., 1 Aug., 1813.
John Leonard, 6 Aug., 1813.
John Bailey, 1 Sept., 1813.
Elisha Field, 1 Sept., 1813.
John Fillebrown, 1 Sept., 1813.

*1st Lieutenants.*

Robt. Carter, 29 July, 1813.
Daniel P. Brown, 1 Aug., 1813.
J. Orne Bowden, 1 Sept., 1813.
Joseph M'Comb, 1 Sept., 1813.
Sam. Hodges, Jr., 1 Sept., 1813.
W. B. Parker, 11 March, 1814.
E. A. Clarey, 11 March, 1814.
I. T. Dixey, 11 March, 1814.
James Harris, 1 May, 1814.
Saml. C. Pope, 1 May, 1814.

*2nd Lieutenants.*

John Spalter, 1 Sept., 1813.
Elias Goodspeed, 1 Sept., 1813.
R. K. Blanchard, 1 Sept., 1813.
H. Loring, 11 March, 1814.
S. Twist, 11 March, 1814.
R. Lyman, 11 March, 1814.
Caleb Clapp, 11 March, 1814.
S. A. Morse, 11 March, 1814.
J. Parrott, 1 May, 1814.
S. H. Russell, 1 May, 1814.

*3rd Lieutenants.*

Enoch Manning, 1 Sept., 1813.
Andrew Lewis, 1 Sept., 1813.
Moses Aldrich, 1 Sept., 1813.
Caleb Lyman, Jr., 11 March, 1814.
L. Burrell, 11 March, 1814.
T. Shaw, 11 March, 1814.
M. Patrick, Jr., 11 March, 1814.
M. C. Pittsbury, 17 March, 1814.
J. Perry, Jr., 1 May, 1814.
N. B. Proctor, 1 May, 1814.

*Ensigns.*

Perez Alexander, 1 Sept., 1813.
Isaac Carpenter, 1 Sept., 1813.
C. H. George, 11 March, 1814.
E. Kendall, 11 March, 1814.
A. Clarke, 11 March, 1814.
D. Cops, 11 March, 1814.
Josh. Mason, 30 March, 1814.
Josh. Brown, 15 April, 1814.

*Surgeon.*

M. H. Elliott, 11 March, 1814.

*Surgeon's Mates.*

Wm. Stearne, 11 March, 1814.
E. Judson, 31 May, 1814.

---

FORTY-FIRST INFANTRY.

*New York.*

*Colonel.*

Rbt. Bogardus, 29 July, 1813.

*Lieut. Colonel.*

J. W. Livingston, 29 July, 1813.

*Majors.*

Darby Noon, 1 Aug., 1813.
Jas. D. Wallace, 1 Aug., 1813.

*Captains.*

Gilbert Seaman, 1 Aug., 1813.
Alex. Hamilton, 1 Aug., 1813.
Alphs. Sherman, 1 Aug., 1813.
Saml. Berrian, 1 Aug., 1813.
Wm. S. Radcliff, 3 Aug., 1813.
Chs. Humphrey, 7 Aug., 1813.
Francis Allyn, 30 Sept., 1813.
Mangle M. Quackenbos, 7 Jan., 1814.
John Ingersoll, 7 Jan., 1814.
Jas. M'Cullen, 26 Jan., 1814.

*1st Lieutenants.*

John L. Clark, 30 Sept., 1813.
John M. Schermerhorn, 30 Sept., 1813.
Chas. Conner, 11 Nov., 1813.
Wm. Hoffman, 11 Nov., 1813.
Daniel Sackett, 11 Nov., 1813.
Jud. Hammond, 7 Jan., 1814.
T. E. Beekman, 7 Jan., 1814.
Alex. Clinton, 26 Jan., 1814.
Danl. Wishart, 10 Feb., 1814.

*2nd Lieutenants.*

John Tabalee, 30 Sept., 1813.
Geo. Hamilton, 30 Sept., 1813.
Jno. H. Sims, 30 Sept., 1813.
Henry Brown, 30 Sept., 1813.
Luther Hand, 30 Sept., 1813.
Sol. Sutherland, 1 Nov., 1813.
C. S. M'Connell, 1 May, 1814.
George West, 1 May, 1814.
Wm. Hammell, 1 May, 1814.

*3rd Lieutenants.*

Isaac Miller, 1 May, 1814.
Asher Corles, 1 May, 1814.
John C. Hart, 1 May, 1814.

*Surgeon.*

John Nielson, 30 Sept., 1813.

*Surgeon's Mates.*

Fayette Cooper, 30 Sept., 1813.
Henry White, 30 Sept., 1813.

---

FORTY-SECOND INFANTRY.

*Pennsylvania and New York.*

*Colonel.*

Wm. N. Irvine, 4 Aug., 1813.

*Lieut. Colonel.*

Jas. G. Forbes, 1 Aug., 1813.

*Majors.*

Tunis Riker, 1 Aug., 1813.
Thos. Stockton, 15 April, 1814.

*Captains.*

Geo. W. Barker, 10 Jan., 1813.
E. S. Mendenhall, 1 Aug., 1813.
Wm. G. Oliver, 1 Aug., 1813.
Thos. Hanson, 4 Aug., 1813.
Edm. B. Duvall, 4 Aug., 1813.
John Biddle, 1 Oct., 1813.
T. Parker, 17 Nov., 1813.
J. F. De Peyster, 26 April, 1814.

*1st Lieutenants.*

Robt. Shaw, Jr., 15 April, 1814.
Joseph Hall, 20 April, 1814.
P. Mendenhall, 26 April, 1814.
Howerton Cross, 1 May, 1814.
P. S. Gilbert, 1 May, 1814.
J. B. Wilkinson, 1 May, 1814.
Daniel Saint, 1 May, 1814.

*2nd Lieutenant.*

Fredk. Lazarus, 1 May, 1814.

*3rd Lieutenants.*

Daniel Taylor, 1 May, 1814.
R. H. Hammon, 1 May, 1814.
J. Mullen, 1 May, 1814.
Lewis Lawshe, 1 May, 1814.
John Auld, 1 May, 1814.
T. Hunter, 1 May, 1814.
Charles Cooper, 1 May, 1814.

*Ensign.*

Truman Cross, 27 April, 1814.

*Surgeon.*

Henry Hall, 15 April, 1814.

*Surgeon's Mates.*

Js. M. Kelly, 6 Aug., 1813.
— Carpenter, 8 April, 1814.

---

## Forty-Third Infantry.

*North Carolina.*

*Colonel.*

Nicholas Long, 4 Aug., 1813.

*Lieut. Colonel.*

A. Pickens, Jr., 6 July, 1812.

*Majors.*

Jas. Campbell, 1 Aug., 1813.
Thomas D. King, 4 Aug., 1813.

*Captains.*

Jno. J. Goodwyn, 1 Aug., 1813.
Theo. L. Gourdin, 1 Aug., 1813. Aid to Major General Izard.
G. H. Manigault, 1 Aug., 1813.
Edw. F. Tattnall, 4 Aug., 1813.
Thomas Hyde, 4 Aug., 1813.
Henry Garrett, 4 Aug., 1813.
Robt. Love, Jr., 4 Aug., 1813.
George Dabney, 4 Aug., 1813.
Elias Beall, 11 March, 1814.
Saml. G. Earle, 11 March, 1814.

*1st Lieutenants.*

Abner H. Hicks, 1 Aug., 1813.
Saml. A. Taylor, 1 Aug., 1813.
W. Edmondson, 1 Aug., 1813.
Saml. Farrow, Jr., 1 Aug., 1813.
Charles Cantey, 3 Aug., 1813.
Jno. Smallwood, 4 Aug., 1813.
M. T. Alexander, 4 Aug., 1813.
Geo. R. Gilman, 4 Aug., 1813.
Wm. W. Holt, 4 Aug., 1813.
T. Lemar, 11 March, 1814.

*2nd Lieutenants.*

Robert Stark, 1 Aug., 1813.
Joshua Irby, 1 Aug., 1813. Paymaster.
Robt. H. Briggs, 1 Aug., 1813.
W. Timberlake, 4 Aug., 1813.
John M. Neel, 4 Aug., 1813.
Rbt. L. Coombs, 4 Aug., 1813.
Archd. Bigby, 4 Aug., 1813.
J. L. Thompson, 11 March, 1814.
William Miles, 1 May, 1814.

*3rd Lieutenants.*

M. Ayres, 1 Aug., 1813.
W. H. Norman, 4 Aug., 1813.
W. Welsh, 4 Aug., 1813.
W. Greer, 4 Aug., 1813.
C. C. Duncan, 17 March, 1814.
John Vereen, 1 May, 1814.
John H. Lawson, 1 May, 1814.
Joseph Oliver, 1 May, 1814.
Lar. L. Baldwin, 1 May, 1814.
W. H. Fairchild, 1 May, 1814.

*Ensigns.*

J. C. Bell, 11 March, 1814.
J. A. Mumford, 11 March, 1814.
Jas. Lawrence, 17 March, 1814.
Ira Conner, 30 March, 1814.
J. Stewart, 30 March, 1814.
Peter Simon, 30 March, 1814.
Geral. Buntin, 18 April, 1814.

*Surgeon's Mate.*

James W. Hunt, 18 April, 1814.

---

## Forty-Fourth Infantry.

*Louisiana.*

*Colonel.*

Geo. T. Ross, 1 Aug., 1813.

*Lieut. Colonel.*

Rich. Butler, 11 March, 1814.

*Majors.*

Henry D. Piere, 1 Aug., 1813.
Waters Clark, 1 Aug., 1813.

*Captains.*

Isaac L. Baker, 5 April, 1813.
Wm. O. Butler, 5 April, 1813.
J. M. Barclay, 11 March, 1814.
G. Winter, 11 March, 1814.
E. de Mirepoix, 11 March, 1814.
I. I. Miles, 11 March, 1814.
A. Peychand, 11 March, 1814.
T. L. Amelung, 11 March, 1814.

*1st Lieutenants.*

Nathanl. Pryor, 30 Aug., 1813.
S. Gordon, 11 March, 1814.
T. D. Kernion, 11 March, 1814.
L. F. de Marans, 11 March, 1814.
I. P. Thibault, 11 March, 1814.
G. Dupuy, 11 March, 1814.
T. Trudeau, 11 March, 1814.
Wm. Gibbs, 11 March, 1814.
M. Cox, 11 March, 1814.
Ch. Peters, 11 March, 1814.

*2nd Lieutenants.*

W. R. Willis, Jr., 11 March, 1814.
Ch. Smith, 11 March, 1814.
T. Montreuil, 11 March, 1814.
F. D. Morant, 11 March, 1814. Paymaster.
A. Dupuy, 11 March, 1814.
L. Allard, 11 March, 1814.

*3rd Lieutenants.*

E. de Flechier, 11 March, 1814.
J. Martin, 11 March, 1814.
C. Parent, 11 March, 1814.
Ed. Herries, 11 March, 1814.
Peter Hens, 11 March, 1814.
Chas. Dutillet, 11 March, 1814.
A. F. Duvall, 11 March, 1814.
J. B. Smith, 11 March, 1814.

*Ensigns.*

A. de Grandpre, 11 March, 1814.
A. M. Lamotte, 11 March, 1814.
G. de Grandpre, 11 March, 1814.

*Surgeon.*

Squire Lea, 1 Aug., 1813.

*Surgeon's Mates.*

R. S. Hall, 11 March, 1814.
C. G. Gerrard, 11 March, 1814.

---

FORTY-FIFTH INFANTRY.

*Massachusetts.*

*Colonel.*

Denny M'Cobb, 26 March, 1814.

*Lieut. Colonel.*

Aquila Davis, 21 April, 1814.

*Majors.*

H. B. Brevoort, 15 April, 1814.
Danl. Baker, 15 April, 1814.

*Captains.*

Elijah Hall, 21 April, 1814.
Benj. Bradford, 21 April, 1814.
Josh. Danforth, 21 April, 1814.
Daniel Holden, 21 April, 1814.
Nathan Stanley, 21 April, 1814.
Smith Elkins, 21 April, 1814.
Joseph Flanders, 21 April, 1814.
I. Hall, 21 April, 1814.
Wm. Chappel, 21 April, 1814.
J. Smith, 21 April, 1814.

*1st Lieutenants.*

Th. B. Sylvester, 21 April, 1814.
Jon. Butterfield, 21 April, 1814.
Danl M. Gregg, 21 April, 1814.
David Doane, 21 April, 1814.
A. P. Cochran, 21 April, 1814.
Henry Snow, 21 April, 1814.
I. Wingate, 21 April, 1814.

*2nd Lieutenants.*

Benj. White, 21 April, 1814.
Joseph Low, 21 April, 1814.
Marshall Baker, 21 April, 1814. Quartermaster.
Daniel Patch, 21 April, 1814.
Daniel Page, 21 April, 1814.
Saml. Sylvester, 21 April, 1814.
P. W. Cushing, 21 April, 1814.

*Ensigns.*

John Neal, Jr., 21 April, 1814.
Wm. Kendall, 21 April, 1814.
William Reed, 21 April, 1814.
Jonas G. Brooks, 21 April, 1814.
Enoch Page, 21 April, 1814.

*Surgeon.*

W. H. Wilson, 15 April, 1814.

---

FORTY-SIXTH INFANTRY.

*New York.*

*Lieut. Colonel.*

W. S. Tallmadge, 15 April, 1814.

*Majors.*

Edmd. G. Perlee, 15 April, 1814.
Joseph Delafield, 15 April, 1814.

*Captains.*

Thomas Bruyn, 21 April, 1814.
John S. Suffern, 21 April, 1814.
David Crawford, 21 April, 1814.
Peter Miller, 21 April, 1814.
Rob. Gourlay, Jr., 21 April, 1814.
Moses Burnet, 21 April, 1814.
Job Wright, 21 April, 1814.
A. D Willson, 21 April, 1814.
L. Austin, 21 April, 1814.
Saml. Baker, 21 April, 1814. Aid to Major General Brown.

*1st Lieutenants.*

Benjn. Smith, 19 April, 1814.
R. W. Nelson, 21 April, 1814.
Epens. Wheeler, 21 April, 1814.
Jesse Barlow, 21 April, 1814.
John Wilson, 21 April, 1814.
James M'Lean, 21 April, 1814.

---

FIRST RIFLE REGIMENT.

*Colonel.*

G. W. Sevier, 24 Jan., 1814.

*Lieut. Colonel.*

J. M'Donald, 24 Jan., 1814.

*Majors.*

L. Morgan, 24 Jan., 1814.
D. Appling, 15 April, 1814.

*Captains.*

H. R Graham, 8 March, 1809.
A. A. Massias, 1 July, 1809.
Joshua Hamilton, 6 July, 1812.
T. A. Patterson, 1 Aug., 1812.
T. Ramsay, 30 Nov., 1812.
William Smith, 20 Jan., 1813.
Elias Stallings, 30 Nov., 1813.
L. G. A. Armistead, 24 Jan., 1814.
W. E. Morris, 15 April, 1814. Aid to Major General Pinckney.
H. V. Swearingen, 11 May, 1814.

*1st Lieutenants.*

E. Wadsworth, 1 Aug., 1812.
Wm. Townly, 1 Aug., 1812.
W. C. Beard, 27 Sept., 1812.
James Ryan, 30 Nov., 1812.
George Gray, 20 Jan., 1813. Quartermaster.
H. Murray, 30 Nov., 1813.
J. S. M'Intosh, 31 Dec., 1813.
Jos. Calhoun, Jr., 24 Jan., 1814.
Hyem Cohen, 15 April, 1814.
Wm. Arnold, 11 May, 1814.

*2nd Lieutenants.*

J. Shortridge, 3 Dec., 1812.
John Hanson, 4 Dec., 1812.
John Harlee, 20 Jan., 1813.
Josiah Hill, 20 Jan., 1813.
S. V. Hamilton, 30 Nov., 1813.
R. M'Farland, 31 Dec., 1813.
Jacob Tipton, 1 Jan., 1814.
W Armstrong, 24 Jan., 1814.
Bennet Riley, 15 April, 1814.
L. Norton, 11 May, 1814.

*3rd Lieutenants.*

J. S Gray, 20 May, 1813.
T. F. Smith, 30 Nov., 1813.
Samuel Cobbs, 31 Dec., 1813.
G. Davidson, 31 Dec., 1813.
J. H. Stannon, 1 Jan., 1814.
Peter Albright, 24 Jan., 1814.
Edward Drake, 10 Feb., 1814.
Simon James, 18 March, 1814.
H. B. Austin, 15 April, 1814.
G. L. B. Duplessis, 11 May, 1814.

*Ensigns.*

John Page, Jr., 31 March, 1814.
Ll. Childress, 31 March, 1814.
L. W. Taylor, 8 April, 1814.

*Surgeon.*

Chas. Marvin, 15 April, 1814.

*Surgeon's Mate.*

Saml. P. Hugo, 12 March, 1812.

---

SECOND RIFLE REGIMENT.

*Colonel.*

A. Butler, 2 Feb., 1814.

*Lieut. Colonel.*

Geo. Groghan, 21 Feb., 1814. Brevet, 2 Aug., 1813.

*Majors.*

David Gwynne, 21 Feb., 1814.
W. H. Puthuff, 21 Feb., 1814.

*Captains.*

Benj. Johnson, 17 March, 1814.
Hugh Innes, 17 March, 1814.
Uriah Allison, 17 March, 1814.
Batteal Harrison, 17 March, 1814.
J. O'Fallon, 17 March, 1814.
Benjn. Desha, 17 March, 1814.
Wm. Oliver, 17 March, 1814.
Robt. Brackenridge, 17 March, 1814.
Wm. Pritchard, 17 March, 1814.
E. Shipp, 17 March, 1814.

*1st Lieutenants.*

Jas. Munday, 17 March, 1814.
Chs. Mitchell, 17 March, 1814.
E I. Langham, 17 March, 1814.
I. Stockton, 17 March, 1814.
I. Kennedy, 17 March, 1814
Benjn. Strother, 17 March, 1814.
Lewn. Hickman, 17 March, 1814.
Geo. Kennerly, 17 May, 1814.

*2nd Lieutenants.*

Josh. M'Lean, 17 March, 1814.
J. Swearingen, 17 March, 1814.
J. Heddelson, 17 March, 1814.
Thos. Griffith, 17 March, 1814.
Alln. C. Looker, 17 March, 1814.
R. B. De Witt, 17 March, 1814.
Ths. Berry, 17 March, 1814.
Wm. Scott, 17 March, 1814.
J. E. London, 17 March, 1814.

*3rd Lieutenants.*

W. N. Bryan, 1 Aug., 1814.
H Jackson, 15 Aug., 1814.
Cpl. L. Harrisson, 17 March, 1814.
O. W. Crocket, 17 March, 1814.
Cor. N. Lewis, 17 March, 1814.
W. Dougherty, 17 March, 1814.
Wm. P. S. Blair, 17 March, 1814.
E H. Miller, 17 March, 1814
Hor. Grooms, 17 March, 1814.
And. Johnston, 17 March, 1814.

*Ensigns.*

Patt. Clark, 17 March, 1814.
And. Gilmore, 17 March, 1814.
Wm. Chiton, 17 March, 1814.
Jas P. Hulee, 17 March, 1814.
W. G. Camp, 17 March, 1814.
Fras. Smith, 17 March, 1814.
M. A. Heard, 19 April, 1814.
J. Edmondson, Jr., 30 May, 1814
R. Crittenden, 30 May, 1813.

*Surgeon.*

Dan. Turney, 21 Feb., 1814.

*Surgeon's Mate.*

Dan. Smith, 17 May, 1814.

---

THIRD RIFLE REGIMENT.

*Colonel.*

Wm. King, 21 Feb., 1814.

*Lieut. Colonel.*

Wm. S. Hamilton, 21 Feb., 1814.

*Majors.*

W. H. Overton, 21 Feb., 1814.
Joseph Selden, 21 Feb., 1814.

*Captains.*

T. I. Robison, 6 July, 1812.
Willie Martin, 17 March, 1814.
E. Carrington, 17 March, 1814.
Walter Coles, 17 March, 1814.
Robt. Campbell, 17 March, 1814.
A. W. Brandon, 17 March, 1814.
J. E. Calhoun, 17 March, 1814.
J. M'Whorter, 17 March, 1814.
D. Kinchaloe, 17 March, 1814.

*1st Lieutenants.*

W. L. Dufphey, 15 April, 1813.
Wm. C. Parker, 17 March, 1814.
Wm. Hindman, 17 March, 1814.
Th. W. Blackledge, 17 March, 1814.
Jesse Maxwell, 17 March, 1814.
Ch. A. Sparks, 17 March, 1814.
J. H. Gillmeyer, 17 March, 1814.
Nath. Chapman, 17 March, 1814.
Wm. S. Gray, 26 March, 1814.
H. T. Crawford, 2 April, 1814.

*2nd Lieutenants.*

Wm. Alexander, 17 March, 1814.
Abrm. Fine, 17 March, 1814.
Willie I. Gordon, 17 March, 1814.
Ge. D. Barns, 17 March, 1814.
Gade Crawford, 17 March, 1814.
W. Meliver, 17 March, 1814.
Abn. Harrison, 17 March, 1814.
Jas. M'Dowell, 26 March, 1814.
I. Hollingsworth, 26 March, 1814.
R. I. Crockwell, 2 April, 1814.

*3rd Lieutenants.*

D. C. Hibbits, 17 March, 1814.
Robt. Love, 17 March, 1814.

John Jelks, 17 March, 1814.
James Green, 15 April, 1814.

*Ensigns.*

Ethelred Jelks, 17 March, 1814.
Duncan M'Rea, 17 March, 1814.
Wm. T. Scott, 17 March, 1814.
Joel Spencer, 17 March, 1814.
Solomon Chambliss, 17 March, 1814.
Ths. Ragland, 17 March, 1814.
Wm. H. Loftin, 17 March, 1814.

*Surgeon.*

T. G. Watkins, 30 March, 1814.

*Surgeon's Mates.*

Robt. C. Lane, 11 March, 1814.
C. Edmonds, 18 April, 1814.

---

FOURTH RIFLE REGIMENT.

*Colonel.*

J. Gibson, 21 Feb., 1814.

*Lieut. Colonel.*

J. Snelling, 21 Feb., 1814. Inspector General.

*Majors.*

H. B. Armstrong, 12 April, 1813.
T. Chambers, 21 Feb., 1814.

*Captains.*

Armst. Irvine, 1 Oct., 1813.
J. Kean, 17 March, 1814.
W. German, 17 March, 1814.
T. I. Beall, 17 March, 1814.
Benjn. Birdsall, 17 March, 1814.
John Lyttle, 17 March, 1814.
M. M. Magee, 17 March, 1814.
Robert Scott, 17 March, 1814.
J. Morris, 17 March, 1814.
Wm. G. Green, 17 March, 1814.

*1st Lieutenants.*

Jona. Kearsley, 6 July, 1812.
Dc. Cornyn, 20 June, 1813.
J. W. Smoot, 21 Feb., 1814.
J. H. Ballard, 17 March, 1814. Adjutant.
G. B. Sheldon, 17 March, 1814.
St. Gantt, 17 March, 1814.
G. Getz, 17 March, 1814.
Amos. Gustine, 17 March, 1814.
Sam. Burnett, 17 March, 1814.
T. Anderson, 17 March, 1814.

*2nd Lieutenants.*

John Ellison, 17 March, 1814.
R. R. Conrad, 17 March, 1814.
N. C. Kinney, 17 March, 1814.
Isaac Jaquett, 17 March, 1814.
Wm. Aull, 17 March, 1814.
R. N. Yates, 17 March, 1814.
J. Hays, 17 March, 1814.
Farley Eddy, 17 March, 1814.
J. Dawson, 18 April, 1814.

*3rd Lieutenants.*

J. Irvine, 1 Sept., 1813.
Ab. Schuyler, 17 Oct., 1813.
W. Gallop, 21 Feb., 1814.
G. Johnson, 21 Feb., 1814.
R. H. Lee, 17 March, 1814.
Sylv. Booth, 17 March, 1814.
Elias Smur, 17 March, 1814.
Abrm. Maury, 2 April, 1814.
John Maul, 1 May, 1814.

*Surgeon.*

Lewis L. Near, 17 March, 1814.

*Surgeon's Mates.*

W. H. Hemming, 20 April, 1814.
Henry Field, 23 April, 1814.

---

RANGERS.

*Captains.*

Piere André, 12 April, 1813.
Fredk. Shoults, 20 May, 1813.
Andw. Ramsey, 19 July, 1813.
David Musick, 19 July, 1813.
Danl. M. Boone, 19 July, 1813.
Jas. B. Moore, 1 Aug., 1813.
W. B. Whiteside, 1 Aug., 1813.
Jacob Short, 1 Aug., 1813.
Jas. Manary, Sen., 5 Aug., 1813.
Sam. M'Cormick, 7 Aug., 1813.

*1st Lieutenants.*

Henry Brinton, 12 April, 1813.
Hyacin. Lassell, 12 April, 1813.
John Carr, 30 April, 1813.
Jas. Morrison, 19 July, 1813.
P. K. Robbins, 19 July, 1813.
Wm. Massey, 19 July, 1813.
Jos. Borough, 1 Aug., 1813.
David Robinson, 1 Aug., 1813.
Nathl. Jurney, 1 Aug., 1813.
John Hopkins, 5 Aug., 1813.
John Knox, 30 May, 1814.

*2nd Lieutenants.*

Homer Johnson, 12 May, 1813.
James Curray, 30 May, 1813.
Sylvester Pattie, 19 July, 1813.
James Calloway, 19 July, 1813.
Peter Craig, 19 July, 1813.
Saml. Gilham, 1 Aug., 1813.
Arthur Morgan, 1 Aug., 1813.
Andw. Bankson, 1 Aug., 1813.
Brattn. Crawford, 5 Aug., 1813.
John Knox, 1 Oct., 1813.
W. G. Servess, 30 May, 1814.

*3rd Lieutenants.*

David Hillis, 12 April, 1813.
Jno. Hadden, Jr., 12 April, 1813.
W. P. Meredith, 30 April, 1813.
Wm. M'Henry, 1 Aug., 1813.
Stephn. Rector, 1 Aug., 1813.
Wm. Boon, 1 Aug., 1813.
David Steal, 5 Aug., 1813.
W. M. Rayburn, 30 May, 1814.

*Ensigns.*

Green B. Fields, 12 April, 1813.
David L. Gregg, 12 April, 1813.
Jno. Owens, Jr., 30 April, 1813.
David Bailey, 19 July, 1813.
John M'Nair, 19 July, 1813.
Drakford Gray, 19 July, 1813.
John Jurney, 1 Aug., 1813.
Aar. Armstrong, 1 Aug., 1813.
Eben. F. Seaman, 5 Aug., 1813.
Wm. Patterson, 1 Oct., 1813.
Abner Garrard, 30 May, 1814.

---

SEA FENCIBLES.

*Captains.*

Lemuel Morris, 4 Aug., 1813.
John Du Bose, 4 Aug., 1813.
Fredk. Brooks, 7 Aug., 1813.
M. S. Bunbury, 1 Oct., 1813.
W. H. Addison, 27 April, 1814.

*1st Lieutenants.*

Jas. J. Cumming, 1 Aug., 1813.
John J. Couturier, 4 Aug., 1813.
Richard Baynor, 7 Aug., 1813.
Gregory Foy, 1 Oct., 1813.
G. W. Green, 17 March, 1814.
Wm. Lytle, 5 April, 1814.

*2nd Lieutenants.*

Ferd. A. O'Neal, 1 Aug., 1813.
Byrd B. Mitchel, 7 Aug., 1813.
James Newman, 1 Oct., 1813.
C. P. Robinson, 17 March, 1814.
Edw. Thompson, 3 May, 1814.

*3rd Lieutenants.*

Henry B. Jones, 1 Aug., 1813.
John Hardwick, 4 Aug., 1813.
Gerard Gorsuch, 1 Oct., 1813.
G. M'Nair, 17 March, 1814.

---

# Brevets Conferred from 1776 to 1812.

Copied by permission of Brevet Major General J. B. Fry, U. S. A., from his work entitled "History of Brevets in the U. S. Army,"—this work being compiled from the Official Records of the War Department.

---

### ALLAIN.

January 13, 1779. The Board of War report, that the following named French gentlemen, having served as volunteers in Col. Armand's corps, with much reputation, as appears by the certificate of Col. Armand, and the recommendations of the Marquis de la Fayette and others are about to return to France, and therefore recommend that brevets be granted them, under the exceptions in the Resolutions against granting brevets, except to officers in the line, or in cases of merit, viz., to Monsieur Allain * * * the brevet of Lieutenant.

*Resolved*, That Congress agree to said report.

*Resolved*, That the sum of 400 dollars be paid to each of these gentlemen to enable them to prosecute their voyage to France.

### ALLEN, ETHAN.

May 14, 1778. *Resolved* That a brevet commission of colonel be granted to Ethan Allen, in reward of his firmness, fortitude and zeal in the cause of his country, manifested during the course of his long and cruel captivity, as well as on former occasions.

September 24, 1778. Whereas Congress did, on the 14th of May last, grant to Ethan Allen the rank of colonel by brevet in the army of the United States of America, in reward of his fortitude, firmness and zeal in the cause of his country, manifested during the course of his long and cruel captivity, as well as on former occasions; and whereas, on the 16th day of the same month, all the benefits and privileges of lieutenant colonel in the service of these States were granted to the said Ethan Allen during the time of his late captivity; and whereas it is represented to Congress that Colonel E. Allen's circumstances have been greatly reduced by his late long and cruel confinement, and his brevet commission does not entitle him to pay.

*Resolved*, That 75 dollars per month be allowed to Colonel E. Allen from the date of his brevet, during the pleasure of Congress, or until he shall be called into active service.

### ARCHER, JOHN.

June 26, 1779. *Resolved*, That the brevet of captain be given to Mr. Archer, the bearer of the general's letter, and volunteer aid to Brig. Gen. Wayne.

### BEAULIEU.

September 30, 1783. *Resolved*, That Lieutenant Beaulieu be promoted to the rank of captain by brevet in the army of the U. S.

### BRICE.

October 27, 1778. *Resolved*, That Mr. Brice, A. de C. to the Marquis de la Fayette, be promoted to the rank of lieutenant colonel by brevet in the service of the U. S.

### BRIFFAULT.

January 13, 1779. *Resolved*, That Congress agree to said report (cited in the case of *Allain*, and which recommends that the brevet of lieutenant be also granted to Monsieur Briffault).

*Resolved*, That the sum of 400 dollars be paid to each of these (French) gentlemen to enable them to prosecute their voyage to France.

January 15, 1786. *Resolved*, That Monsieur Briffault, who, on the 13th of January, 1779, was appointed to the brevet rank of lieutenant in the army of the U. S., receive a commission of lieutenant in Col. Armand's corps, to bear the date of his brevet.

### CAMBRAY.

May 2, 1783. *Resolved*, That Lieutenant Colonel Cambray, of the corps of engineers, be promoted to the rank of colonel by brevet.

### ÇAPITAINE.

November 5, 1778. *Resolved,* That the commission of major by brevet be granted to Monsieur Capitaine, a captain in the service of the U. S., and that a bill of exchange for 2400 *"livres tournois"* be drawn on the muster of the United States in favor of Monsieur Capitaine, for his expenses in coming to and returning from America.

### DE BEDAUX, FREDERICK.

September 15, 1777. *Resolved,* That Monsieur Frederick de Bedaux be appointed a captain by brevet, and receive the pay and rations annexed to that rank, from the 10th of May last.

### DE BERT.

February 6, 1784. *Resolved,* That the commission of major by brevet be issued to Captain de Bert.

### DE BOIS, PIERRE FRANCOIS.

October 7, 1776. *Resolved,* That Monsieur Pierre François de Bois be commissioned a major by brevet, and sent to General Mercer to be employed in such way as he shall think proper.

### DE BRAHM.

February 6, 1784. *Resolved,* That a brevet commission of lieutenant colonel be issued to Major de Brahm, of the late corps of engineers, and that he be informed that his further services are dispensed with.

### DE COLERUS, CHRISTIAN

September 19, 1776. *Resolved,* That Monsieur Christian de Colerus be appointed to the rank and pay of a major by brevet, and that his commission be forthwith given him.

### DE CORNEY, LOUIS ETHIS.

June 5, 1780. *Resolved,* That a brevet commission of lieutenant colonel of cavalry be granted to Monsieur Louis Ethis de Corney, and that the President furnish him with letters to the State Executives requesting their aid and advice in procuring provisions, etc., for French forces expected to arrive.

*Resolved,* That a brevet commission of colonel of cavalry be granted to Monsieur Louis Ethis de Corney.

### DE CREMIS.

November 9, 1778. A petition from the Chevalier de Cremis was read; whereupon *Resolved,* That a brevet commission of lieutenant colonel be granted to the Chevalier de Cremis.

### DE FONTEVIEU.

January 13, 1779. *Resolved,* That Congress agree to said report (cited in the case of *Allain,* and which recommends that the brevet of lieutenant be also granted to Monsieur de Fontevieu).

*Resolved,* That the sum of 400 dollars be paid to each of these (French) gentlemen to enable them to prosecute their voyage to France.

### DE FRANCHESSIN, JACQUES ANTOINE.

July 20, 1776. The Board of War brought in a report which was taken into consideration; whereupon,

*Resolved,* That a brevet commission of lieutenant colonel be granted to Monsieur Jacques Antoine de Franchessin, a Knight of the Order of St. Louis, an experienced officer in the French service, and who is well recommended in letters from abroad, and that he be ordered to join the flying camp.

July 25, 1776. It was ordered that two months' pay be advanced to Monsieur Jacques Antoine de Franchessin.

### DE GLASHEECH.

March 9, 1781. *Resolved,* That Baron de Glasheech, who served with Brig. Gen. Morgan, as a volunteer, have the brevet commission of a captain in the army of the U. S. in consideration of his merit and services.

### DE LAMNO.

January 13, 1779. *Resolved,* That Congress agree to said report (cited in the case of *Allain,* and which recommends that the brevet of lieutenant be also granted to Monsieur de Lamno).

*Resolved,* That the sum of 400 dollars be paid to each of these (French) gentlemen to enable them to prosecute their voyage to France.

### DE LA NEUVILLE, JR., NOIRMONT.

July 29, 1778. The Board of War report that Monsieur Noirmont de la Neuville, since the month of December, has acted as A. de C. to Major Gen. Conway, etc.; whereupon, *Resolved,* That Monsieur Noirmont de la Neuville have the rank of major by brevet in the American army.

October 18, 1779. *Resolved,* That Major de la Neuville, who has served two campaigns in the American army, and has obtained very honorable testimonials of his merit, valor and services in the several capacities in which he has been employed, be appointed a lieutenant colonel by brevet in the army of th U. S., and that Liutenant Colonel N. de la Neuville have permission to return to France.

## DE LA NEUVILLE, SR.

October 4, 1778. *Resolved,* That a brevet commission of brigadier be granted to Monsieur de la Neuville, the elder, in the army of the U. S. of America, to date August 14, 1778.

## DE MAFASTRAM.

January 13, 1779. *Resolved,* That Congress agree to said report (cited in the case of *Allain,* and which recommends that the brevet of lieutenant be also granted to Monsieur de Mafastram).

*Resolved,* That the sum of 400 dollars be paid to each of these (French) gentlemen to enable them to prosecute their voyage to France.

## DE MALMADY.

September 19, 1779. *Resolved,* That Monsieur Marquis de Malmady be appointed to the rank and pay of a major by brevet in the Continental army, and receive a commission accordingly.

## DE MONTFORT.

March 21, 1777. *Resolved,* That the Count de Montfort be recommended to General Washington for the brevet of lieutenant.

## DE PONCEAUX.

February 18, 1778. *Resolved,* That * * * * Monsieur de Ponceaux, Secretary to Baron Steuben, have the brevet rank of captain in the army of the U. S.

## DE PONTIERE.

February 18, 1778. *Resolved,* That Monsieur de Pontiere be appointed a captain of horse by brevet * * * *

September 13, 1783. *Resolved,* That Captain de Pontiere, late of Pulaski's Legion, be promoted to the rank of major by brevet in the army of the U. S., his relative rank to be settled by the date of his present commission.

## DERICK.

November 6, 1778. *Resolved,* That Major Derick be permitted to return to the U. S. of the Netherlands, and that he be promoted to the rank of lieutenant colonel by brevet, as a testimony of his merit and services in the army of the U. S.

December 29, 1779. *Resolved,* That in consideration of the peculiar circumstances attending the case of Lieutenant Colonel Derick, that gentleman receive the pay and subsistence of a lieutenant colonel in the army of the U. S. from the date of his brevet until the further order of Congress.

## DE TREUSON.

January 13, 1779. *Resolved,* That Congress agree to said report (cited in the case of *Allain,* and which recommends that the brevet of captain be granted to Monsieur de Treuson).

*Resolved,* That the sum of 400 dollars be paid to each of these (French) gentlemen to enable them to prosecute their voyage to France.

## DE VALCOUR, JOAN SIMONET.

December 1, 1778. A letter of November 11, from Elisha Sheldon, Colonel; Samuel Blackden, Lieutenant Colonel; Benjamin Talmud, Major, and Josiah Stoddard, Captain, of the 2nd Regiment of Light Dragoons, was read, representing that Lieutenant John Simonet de Valcour has served with reputation in the 2nd regiment of cavalry since its first establishment; that the rupture between France and England beginning to grow serious and interesting, Lieutenant Simonet is desirous of rejoining the army of His most Christian Majesty, and therefore requesting that Congress would promote Lieutenant Simonet to a captaincy in the cavalry, on condition of his leaving his present service, as an honorary compensation of his attachment and fidelity, with a saving to all his present senior officers, their superiority of rank and command, whereupon.

*Resolved,* That Lieutenant John Simonet de Valcour be promoted to the rank of captain by brevet, on the condition and with the saving in the above letter.

## DE VIENNE.

July 15, 1778. The Marquis de Vienne, a major in the service of the King of France, having served with reputation as a volunteer in the American army during the present campaign, and having requested Congress to honor him with the brevet commission of a colonel, without any pay annexed to the said rank,

*Resolved,* That the request of the Marquis de Vienne be complied with, and that a brevet commission of a colonel in the service of the U. S. be conferred on him.

## DE VERNEJOUX, JEAN LOUIS.

September 19, 1776. *Resolved,* That Jean Louis de Vernejoux be appointed to the rank and pay of a captain by brevet, and commissioned accordingly.

## DE PLESSIS, DE MAUDUIT.

January 19, 1778. *Resolved,* That a brevet of lieutenant colonel be granted to the Chevalier de Mauduit du Plessis, as a reward for his services and an encouragement to merit; and that his commission bear date the 26th of November, 1777, in order that the recompense may more immediately follow the services which he has done.

(*Mem.* On the 3rd of November, 1778, a resolution was introduced giving Du Plessis a brevet of colonel of artillery, but it was negatived.)

ELBERT, SAMUEL.

November 3, 1783. *Resolved,* That Colonel Samuel Elbert be promoted to the rank of brigadier by brevet.

FANEUIL.

March 24, 1777. *Resolved,* That Monsieur Faneuil have the rank of a colonel by brevet in the Continental army without pay or rations.

FONTIVIEUX.

February 6, 1784. *Resolved,* That the commission of captain by brevet be issued to Lieutenant Fontivieux.

FOUQUET.

FOUQUET, MARK.

January 15, 1778. *Resolved,* That in compliance with the said agreement (made by the Board engaging these persons in the service). Mr. Fouquet, the father, have the brevet rank of captain, and Mark Fouquet, the son, the brevet rank of lieutenant of artillery, in the army of the U. S.

FULLERTON, RICHARD.

November 1, 1783. Lieutenant Richard Fullerton, having acted as a volunteer at an early period of the war, particularly in the action on Long Island, and at the battles of Trenton and Princeton, and having discharged the several extra appointments of adjutant, major of brigade, and the important one of assistant adjutant general to the southern army, highly to the satisfaction of his general officers,

*Resolved,* That the Secretary of War issue to Lieutenant Fullerton the brevet commission of captain.

GERARD.

September 3, 1778. *Resolved,* That Mr. Gerard be appointed to the rank of a lieutenant of dragoons by brevet, and be permitted to join the army under General Washington, he having agreed to serve in that capacity at his own expense.

GIBBONS.

July 26, 1779. *Resolved,* unanimously, That Congress warmly approve and applaud the cool, determined spirit with which Lieutenant Gibbons and * * * led on the forlorn hope (at Stony Point), braving danger and death in the cause of their country.

*Resolved,* unanimously, That brevets of captain be given to Lieutenant Gibbons and * * * *

GILES, EDWARD.

March 9, 1781. *Resolved,* That Major Edward Giles, A. de C. of Brigadier General Morgan, have the brevet commission of major in the army of the U. S. in consideration of his merit and services.

GONVION.

November 16, 1781. *Resolved,* That Lieutenant Colonel Gonvion, of the corps of engineers, receive the brevet of colonel.

GOODALE.

October 16, 1783. Whereas it appears that Captain Goodale, lately promoted to the rank of major by brevet, has distinguished himself by extraordinary military services,

*Resolved,* That the Secretary of War issue to Captain Goodale a major's commission in the line of the army.

HARMAR, JOSIAH.

Lieut. Col. Comdt. Revol. Army. Lieut. Col. Comdt. Inf. reg., Sept. 29, 1789. General-in-chief of the army.

July 31, 1787. *Resolved,* That the Secretary of War transmit to Lieutenant Colonel Commandant Harmar, a brevet commission of brigadier general, and that he be allowed the emoluments but not the pay of the said rank. The allowance to commence with, and continue during his command on the frontier.

HASKELL.

September 30, 1783. *Resolved,* That the brevet commission of major in the army of the U. S. issue to Captain Haskell, A. de C. to Major General R. Howe.

HAY, UDNEY.

January 9, 1777. *Resolved,* That Udney Hay, Esq., be appointed a lieutenant colonel by brevet, and Asst. Dep. Q. M. General, and stationed at Ticonderoga.

May 29, 1778. *Resolved,* That Udney Hay, Esq., who, under the former arrangement of the said (Q. M. Gen.'s) department was appointed Asst. Dep. Q. M. General and a lieutenant colonel by brevet, cannot now hold that office by virtue of said appointment, nor be entitled to any privilege or emolument, which either does at present, or may hereafter, accrue to any officer of the same rank in the line.

HAZEN, MOSES.

June 29, 1781. *Resolved,* That Colonel Moses Hazen be, and he hereby is, appointed a brigadier in the army of the U. S. by brevet.

### HOUDIN, M. G.

February 6, 1784. *Resolved,* That the commission of major by brevet be issued to Captain M. G. Houdin.

### KNOX, HENRY.

July 26, 1779. *Resolved,* unanimously, That Congress warmly approve and applaud the cool, determined spirit with which Lieutenant Knox and * * * * led on the forlorn hope (at Stony Point), braving danger and death in the cause of their country.
*Resolved,* unanimously, That brevets of captain be given to Lieutenant Knox and * * * *

### KOSCIUSKO, THADDEUS.

October 13, 1783. *Resolved,* That the Secretary of War transmit to Colonel Kosciusko the brevet commission of brigadier general, and signify to that officer that Congress entertain a high sense of his long, faithful and meritorious services.

### LAUGHBURN, WILLIAM.

October 6, 1783. Whereas William Laughburn hath served from the commencement of the war with equal disinterestedness and reputation.
*Resolved,* That a brevet commission of lieutenant colonel be granted to the said William Laughburn.

### LE BRUN.

February 6, 1784. *Resolved,* That the commission of major by brevet be issued to Captain Le Brun.

### LE FIEVRE.

January 13, 1779. *Resolved,* That Congress agree to said report (cited in the case of *Allain,* and which recommends that the brevet of lieutenant be also granted to Monsieur Le Fievre).
*Resolved,* That the sum of 400 dollars be paid to each of these (French) gentlemen to enable them to prosecute their voyage to France.

### L'ENFANT, PIERRE CHARLES.

May 2, 1783. *Resolved,* * * * That Captain L'Enfant, of the engineer corps, be promoted to the rank of major by brevet.

### LE ROY.

February 6, 1784. *Resolved,* That the commission of captain by brevet be issued to Lieutenant Le Roy.

### LE TOURNEAU.

January 13, 1779. *Resolved,* That Congress agree to said report (cited in the case of *Allain,* and which recommends that the brevet of lieutenant be also granted to Monsieur Le Tourneau).
*Resolved,* That the sum of 400 dollars be paid to each of these (French) gentlemen to enable them to prosecute their voyage to France.

### MAC PHERSON, WILLIAM.

(Brig. Gen., Mar. 11, 1799.)

September 16, 1779. *Resolved,* That a brevet of major in the army of the U. S. be granted to William Mac Pherson, and that while in actual service he receive the pay and subsistence of major.

### MARCELLIN.

February 6, 1784. *Resolved,* That a commission of captain by brevet be issued to Lieutenant Marcellin.

### McCALLISTER.

September 24, 1779. *Resolved,* That Congress justly esteem the military caution so happily combined with daring activity by Lieutenant McCallister and * * *, in leading the forlorn hope (at Powle's Hook).
*Resolved,* That the brevet and pay and subsistence of captain be given to Lieutenant McCallister and * * *

### MORRIS.

September 9, 1778. *Resolved,* That Major Morris, A. de C. to Major General Sullivan, who brought forward to Congress the account of the repulse of the British forces on Rhode Island, on the 29th of August, and who, on the late expedition, as well as on several other occasions, behaved with great spirit and good conduct, be promoted to the rank of lieutenant colonel by brevet.

### MOYLAN, STEPHEN.

November 3, 1783. *Resolved,* That Colonel Stephen Moylan be promoted to the rank of brigadier by brevet.

### MULLENS, THOMAS.

June 11, 1778. The Board of War report that Major Thomas Mullens, late an A. de C. to Major General Coudray, is an old officer in the French service; that he served the last campaign in the main army, and for his bravery and good conduct at the battles of Brandywine and Germantown was honored with particular marks of approbation by the Commander-in-chief in General Orders and that he means to accompany General Coudray to France.
*Resolved,* That Major Thomas Mullens, who served with honor in the last campaign, have a brevet commission of lieutenant colonel in the armies of the U. S.

MURNAND, J. B.

September 15, 1783. *Resolved,* That the commission of lieutenant colonel by brevet in the army of the U. S. be issued to Major Murnand.

NEVILLE.

October 27, 1778. *Resolved,* That Mr. Neville, A. de C. to the Marquis de la Fayette, be promoted to the rank of lieutenant colonel in the service of the U. S. by brevet.

NORTH, WILLIAM.

(Adjt. Gen'l of the Army, (B. G.) July 19, 1798.)

September 11, 1783. *Resolved,* That the Secretary of War be, and he is hereby directed to issue to Captain North, A. de C. to Major General Steuben, the brevet commission of major in the army of the U. S.

OTTENDORF, N. D.

November 8, 1776. *Resolved,* That Mynheer N. D. Ottendorf be appointed a brevet captain in the service of the U. S.

November 9, 1776. Two months' pay advanced to Capt. Ottendorf, and ordered to repair to Headquarters and put himself under command of General Washington.

December 5, 1776. *Resolved,* That Captain Ottendorf be directed to raise an independent corps, consisting of 150 men (to be divided into three companies, etc.); that Captain Ottendorf have the rank of major, (and that he) be captain of the light infantry, and command.

PENET, P.

October 14, 1776. *Resolved,* That General Washington be informed the Congress approves of his appointing P. Penet his aid-de-camp by brevet, and that a commission of aid-de-camp be accordingly transmitted to him.

PINCKNEY, CHARLES COTESWORTH.

(Col. in the Revol. Army. Major General, July 1, 1798.)

November 3, 1783. *Resolved,* That Colonel Charles Cotesworth Pinckney be promoted to the rank of brigadier by brevet.

ROCHEFONTAINE.

November 16, 1781. *Resolved,* That Captain Rochefontaine, of the corps of engineers, receive the brevet of major.

ROGERS, NICHOLAS.

December 10, 1778. *Resolved,* That Major Nicholas Rogers, who came from France with Monsieur de Condray, has served as A. de C. to Major General De Kalb, and has obtained honorable testimonies of his conduct, but from the situation of his present affairs is obliged to leave the army, be promoted to the rank of lieutenant colonel by brevet, as a reward for his services.

RUDOLPH, MICHAEL.

(Adjt. and Insp. of the Army, February 22, 1793.)

September 24, 1779. *Resolved,* That Congress justly esteem the military caution so happily combined with daring activity by Lieutenants * * * Rudolph, in leading the forlorn hope (at Powle's Hook).

*Resolved,* That the brevet and pay and subsistence of a captain be given to * * * * Lieutenant Rudolph.

RUSSELL, WILLIAM

(Colonel 7th Infantry, March 3, 1808.)

November 3, 1783. *Resolved,* That Colonel William Russell be promoted to the rank of brigadier by brevet.

SARGENT, WINTHROP.

(Adjt. Gen. of the Army under Maj. Gen. St. Clair, 1791.)

August 28, 1783. *Resolved,* That Captain Winthrop Sargent be, and he is hereby, promoted to the rank of major by brevet in the army of the U. S.

SECOND.

September 30, 1783. *Resolved,* That Captain Second, late of Pulaski's Legion, be promoted to the rank of major by brevet in the army of the U. S., his relative rank to be settled by the date of his commission.

SMITH, FRANCIS J.

July 29, 1778. Whereas Monsieur Francis Joseph Smith has requested a commission to be made use of in case of his being made a prisoner while serving as a volunteer in the American Army.

*Resolved,* That Monsieur F. J. Smith have the commission of ensign by brevet in the army of the U. S.

ST. ELMO, GERARD DE.

February 13, 1779. The Board of War, to whom was referred the letter of February 3, from Monsieur Gerard de St. Elmo, having reported specially thereon, Congress took into consideration the said report, and thereupon came to the following *Resolution:* That Monsieur Gerard de St. Elmo, having manifested great zeal and encountered many difficulties to distinguish himself in the service of these States, (and) having also made a campaign here and behaved with bravery, and being about to return to France.

*Resolved,* That he be appointed to the rank of major by brevet, as a testimony of the approbation of Congress of his zeal and services.

STEVENS, EBENEZER.

May 27, 1777. *Resolved,* That Captain Stevens of the artillery have the brevet of a major, he having had that rank before his present appointment as a captain, and being a worthy, good officer, as General Schuyler represents.

April 30, 1778. *Resolved,* That Major Ebenezer Stevens, in consideration of his services, and the strict attention with which he discharged his duty as commanding officer of *artillery* in the Northern Department during two campaigns, take rank by brevet as a lieut. colonel of *Foot,* and that he be commissioned accordingly.

STEWART.

November 19, 1777. *Resolved,* That Major Stewart, who brought the late intelligence from General Gates, and who is recommended as a deserving officer, have the rank of lieut. colonel by brevet, and be presented with a sword of the value of $100.

STRUBING, PHILIP.

April 15, 1784. *Resolved,* That a brevet commission of captain in the army of the U. S. be issued to Lieutenant Philip Strubing, late of Van Heer's Corps.

TERNANT.

October 13, 1783. *Resolved,* That the Secretary of War issue to Lieut. Colonel Ternant the brevet commission of colonel.

TOUSARD, LEWIS.

(Lieut. Colonel Comdt. Art. and Eng., May 26, 1800.)

October 27, 1778. *Resolved,* That the gallantry of Monsieur Tousard in the late action on Rhode Island, is deserving of the highest applause, and that Congress, in consideration of his zeal and misfortune, do promote the said Monsieur Tousard to the rank of lieut. colonel by brevet, and that he do receive a pension of 30 dollars per month out of the Treasury of the U. S., during his life.

VERDI.

January 18, 1779. *Resolved,* That Congress agree to said report (cited in the case of *Allain,* and which recommends that the brevet of lieutenant be also granted to Monsieur Verdi).

*Resolved,* That the sum of $400 be paid to each of these (French) gentlemen, to enable them to prosecute their voyage to France.

VERDIER.

February 6, 1784. *Resolved,* That the commission of captain by brevet be issued to Lieut. Verdier.

VERMONET.

September 18, 1776. *Resolved,* That Monsieur Vermonet have rank and pay of a major by brevet, he being a gentleman of considerable military abilities.

VILLEFRANCHE.

May 2, 1783. *Resolved,* That Major Villefranche, of the corps of engineers, be promoted to the rank of lieut. colonel by brevet.

WILKINSON, JAMES.

Adjt. Gen. of Gates' Army, afterwards Lieut. Col. Comdt. 2d Inf., Nov. 7, 1791. Brig. Gen., March 5, 1792. Gen. in chief of the army, Dec., 1796. Maj. Gen., March 2, 1813.

November 6, 1777. *Resolved,* That Colonel James Wilkinson, Adjt. General in the Northern army, in consideration of his services in that Department, and being strongly recommended by General Gates as a gallant officer and a promising military genius, and having brought despatches to Congress giving an account of the surrender of Lieut. General Burgoyne and his army on the 17th of October last, be continued in his present employment with a brevet of brigadier general in the army of the U. S.

March 6, 1778. On account of dissatisfaction in the army, James Wilkinson relinquished his brevet of brigadier. Resignation accepted, brevet maj. general, July 10, 1812. (No record for what service.)

# List of Officers on whom Brevets were Conferred

By the President for "Gallant Actions, or Meritorious Conduct," during the War with Great Britain, showing the Regiment and Rank of the Officer at the time he received his Brevet.

---

## *1812.*

Lieut. Col. James Miller, 6th Infantry. Brevet Col. Aug. 9. Gallant conduct—battle of Brownstown.
Capt. Josiah Snelling, 4th Infantry. Brevet Maj. Aug. 9. Gallant conduct—Battle of Brownstown.
Capt. Daniel Baker, 1st Infantry. Brevet Maj. Aug. 9. Gallant conduct—Battle of Brownstown.
Capt. Charles Larrabee, 4th Infantry. Brevet Maj. Aug. 9. Gallant conduct—Battle of Brownstown.
Capt. Z. Taylor, 7th Infantry. Brevet Maj. Sept. 5. Gallant conduct in the defence of Fort Harrison.
Capt. Nathan Towson, 2nd Artillery. Brevet Maj. Oct. 8. Capturing the enemy's Brig Caledonia under the guns of Fort Erie.
Lieut. Col. John B. Campbell, 19th Infantry. Brevet Col. Dec. 18. Gallant conduct—Battle of Mississineway.
Maj. James V. Ball, 2nd Light Dragoons. Brevet Lieut. Col. Dec. 18. Gallant conduct—Battle of Mississineway.

## *1813.*

Lieut. Col. John R. Fenwick, Light Artillery. Brevet Col. March 18. Gallant conduct—Niagara Frontier.
Capt. Joseph G. Totten, Corps of Engineers. Brevet Maj. June 6. Meritorious services.
Capt. Eleazer D. Wood, Corps of Engineers. Brevet Maj. May 6. Distinguished services in the defence of Fort Meigs.
Capt. Samuel B. Archer, 2nd Artillery. Brevet Maj., May 27. Meritorious services in the bomb't of Fort George, U. C.
Capt. Arthur P. Hayne, 1st Light Dragoons. Brevet Maj. Aug. 1.
Maj. George Croghan, 17th Infantry. Brevet Lieut. Col. Aug. 2. Gallant conduct in the defence of Fort Sandusky.
1st Lieut. Charles J. Nourse, 2nd Light Dragoons. Brevet Capt. Aug. 15. Meritorious services.
Col. Moses Porter, Light Artillery. Brevet Brig. Gen., Sept. '10. Distinguished services in the campaign of 1813.
Maj. Abram Eustis, Light Artillery. Brevet Lieut. Col. Sept. 10. Meritorious services.
Capt. R. H. McPherson, Light Artillery. Brevet Maj. Nov. 11. Services in the campaign on the St. Lawrence in 1813.
Col. John B. Walbach, Adjutant General, (Capt.) 1st Artillery. Brevet Maj. Nov. 11. Gallant conduct—Battle of Crysler's Farm, St. Lawrence, U. C.
Capt. Ichabod B. Crane, 3d Artillery. Brevet Maj. Nov. 13. Meritorious services.

## *1814.*

Maj. Benjamin Forsyth, 1st Rifle. Brevet Lieut. Col. Feb. 6. Distinguished services.
Col. Joseph G. Swift, Engineers. Brevet Brig. Gen. Feb. 19. Meritorious services.
Capt. Joseph Selden, 2nd Light Dragoons. Brevet Maj. Feb. 21. Meritorious services.
Capt. Andrew H. Holmes, 24th Infantry. Brevet Maj. March 4. Gallant conduct.
1st Lieut. Henry Whiting, 1st Light Dragoons. Brevet Capt. March 17. Meritorious services.
Maj. R. H. McPherson, Light Artillery. Brevet Lieut. Col. March 30. Gallant conduct in the Battle of La Cole Mill.
Lieut. Col. George E. Mitchell, 3rd Artillery. Brevet Col. May 5. Gallant conduct—Battle of Otswego.
Capt. James H. Boyle, 3rd Artillery. Brevet Maj. May 5. Gallant conduct—Battle of Otswego.
Maj. Daniel Appling, 1st Rifle. Brevet Lieut. Col. May 30. Gallant conduct in defeating the enemy at Sandy Creek.
Capt. Turner Crooker, 9th Infantry. Brevet Maj. July 4. Gallant conduct in repelling a charge of British dragoons on the plains of Chippewa.
Maj. Thomas S. Jesup, 25th Infantry. Brevet Lieut. Col. July 5. Distinguished and meritorious services in the Battle of Chippewa.

Maj. Henry Leavenworth, 9th Infantry. Brevet Lieut. Col. July 5. Distinguished and meritorious services in the Battle of Chippewa.
Maj. John McNeil, 11th Infantry. Brevet Lieut. Col. July 5. Distinguished and meritorious services in the Battle of Chippewa.
Maj. Roger Jones, Assist. Adjutant General, (Capt.) Corps of Artillery. Brevet Maj. July 5. Distinguished services in the Battle of Chippewa.
Brevet Maj. Nathan Towson, Corps of Artillery. Brevet Lieut. Col. July 5. Distinguished and gallant conduct in the Battle of Chippewa.
Capt. Samuel D. Harris, Light Dragoons. Brevet Maj. July 5. Gallant conduct—Battle of Chippewa.
Capt. Thomas J. Harrison, 9th Infantry. Brevet Maj. July 5. Gallant conduct—Battle of Chippewa.
Capt. L. Austin, Aide-de-Camp, 46th Infantry. Brevet Maj. July 5. Gallant conduct—Battle of Chippewa.
1st Lieut. W. I. Worth, Aide-de-Camp, 23rd Infantry. Brevet Capt. July 5. Gallant and distinguished conduct—Battle of Chippewa.
2nd Lieut. George Watts, Light Dragoons. Brevet 1st Lieut. July 5. Gallant conduct—Battle of Chippewa.
2nd Lieut. H. M. Campbell, Corps of Artillery. Brevet 1st Lieut. July 5. Gallant conduct—Battle of Chippewa.
Brig. Gen. Winfield Scott, U. S. Army. Brevet Maj. Gen. July 25. Distinguished services in the successive Battles of Chippewa and Niagara and uniform gallantry and good conduct.
Brig. Gen. Eleazer W. Ripley, U. S. Army. Brevet Maj. Gen. July 25. Gallant conduct—Battle of Niagara.
Col. James Miller, 21st Infantry. Brevet Brig. Gen. July 25. Distinguished and meritorious services in the Battle of Niagara.
Brevet Lieut. Col. Thomas S. Jesup, 25th Infantry. Brevet Col. July 25. Gallant conduct and distinguished skill in the Battle of Niagara.
Brevet Lieut. Col. H. Leavenworth, 9th Infantry. Brevet Col. July 25. Gallant conduct—Battle of Niagara.
Brevet Lieut. Col. John M'Neil, Jr., 11th Infantry. Brevet Col. July 25. Gallant conduct—Battle of Niagara.
Maj. William McRee, Corps of Engineers. Brevet Lieut. Col. July 26. Gallant conduct—Battle of Niagara.
Brevet Maj. E. D. Wood, Corps of Engineers. Brevet Lieut. Col. July 25. Gallant conduct—Battle of Niagara.
Brevet Maj. Samuel D. Harris, Light Dragoons. Brevet Lieut. Col. July 25. Gallant conduct—Battle of Niagara.
Capt. Daniel Ketchum, 25th Infantry. Brevet Maj. July 25. Distinguished services and gallant conduct—Battle of Niagara.
Capt. John B. Murdock, 25th Infantry. Brevet Maj. July 25. Gallant conduct—Battle of Niagara.
Capt. Benjamin Watson, 25th Infantry. Brevet Maj. July 25. Gallant conduct—Battle of Niagara.
Capt. Gerard D. Smith, Brigade Major, 6th Infantry. Brevet Maj. July 25. Gallant conduct—Battle of Niagara.
Capt. John Pentland, 22nd Infantry. Brevet Maj. July 25. Gallant conduct—Battle of Niagara.
Capt. Azariah W. Odell, 23rd Infantry. Brevet Maj. July 25. Gallant conduct—Battle of Niagara.
Capt. William McDonald, 19th Infantry. Brevet Maj. July 25. Gallant conduct—Battle of Niagara.
Capt. Sullivan Burbank, 21st Infantry. Brevet Maj. July 25. Gallant conduct—Battle of Niagara.
Capt. W. J. Worth, Aide-de-Camp, 23rd Infantry. Brevet Maj. July 25. Distinguished and gallant conduct—Battle of Niagara.
1st Lieut. David Riddle, 15th Infantry. Brevet Capt. July 25. Gallant conduct—Battle of Niagara.
1st Lieut. Donald Frazer, Aide-de-Camp, 15th Infantry. Brevet Capt. July 25. Gallant conduct—Battle of Niagara.
1st Lieut. John P. Livingston, 23rd Infantry. Brevet Capt. July 25. Gallant conduct—Battle of Niagara.
1st Lieut. John W. Holding, 21st Infantry. Brevet Capt. July 25. Gallant conduct—Battle of Niagara.
1st Lieut. N. S. Clark, Brigade Major, 11th Infantry. Brevet Capt. July 25. Gallant conduct—Battle of Niagara.
2nd Lieut. Jacob Schmuck, Corps of Artillery. Brevet 1st Lieut. July 25. Gallant conduct—Battle of Niagara.
2nd Lieut. Edward B. Randolph, 20th Infantry. Brevet 1st Lieut. July 25. Gallant conduct—Battle of Niagara.
3rd Lieut. S. Rector, Rangers. Brevet 2nd Lieut. July 13.
Ensign John Riggs, Rangers. Brevet 3rd Lieut. July 13.
Capt. Robert Desha, 24th Infantry. Brevet Maj. Aug. 4. Gallant conduct in the attack on Fort Michilimacinac.
Brig. Gen. Edmund P. Gaines, U. S. Army. Brevet Maj. Gen. Aug. 15. Gallantry and good conduct in defeating the enemy in the assault upon Fort Erie, U. C.
Brevet Lieut. Col. William McRee, Corps of Engineers. Brevet Col. Aug. 15. Distinguished and meritorious services in the defence of Fort Erie.
Maj. George M. Brooke, 23rd Infantry. Brevet Lieut. Col. Aug. 15. Gallant conduct in the defence of Fort Erie.
Maj. Jacob Hindman, Corps of Artillery. Brevet Lieut. Col. Aug. 15. Gallant conduct in the defence of Fort Erie.
Maj. N. N. Hall, Assistant Inspector General, (1st Lieut.) 21st Infantry. Brevet Capt. Aug. 15. Gallant conduct in the defence of Fort Erie.
Capt. W. S. Foster, 11th Infantry. Brevet Maj. Aug. 15. Gallant conduct in the defence of Fort Erie.

Capt. A. C. W. Fanning, Corps of Artillery. Brevet Maj. Aug. 15. Gallant conduct in the defence of Fort Erie.
Capt. Thomas Biddle, Jr., Corps of Artillery. Brevet Maj. Aug. 15. Gallant conduct in the defence of Fort Erie.
Capt. Benjamin Birdsall, 4th Rifle. Brevet Maj. Aug. 15. Gallant conduct in the defence of Fort Erie.
Capt. John T. Chunn, 17th Infantry. Brevet Maj. Aug. 15. Gallant conduct in the defence of Fort Erie.
Capt. Morrill Marston, 21st Infantry. Brevet Maj. Aug. 15. Gallant conduct in the defence of Fort Erie.
1st Lieut. R. A. Zantzinger, Corps of Artillery. Brevet Capt. Aug. 15. Gallant conduct in the defence of Fort Erie.
1st Lieut. Jonathan Kearsly, 4th Rifle. Brevet Capt. Aug. 15. Gallant conduct in the defence of Fort Erie.
1st Lieut. Joseph Gleason, 9th Infantry. Brevet Capt. Aug. 15. Gallant conduct in the defence of Fort Erie.
2nd Lieut. R. M. Kirby, Aide-de-Camp, Corps of Artillery. Brevet 1st Lieut. Aug. 15. Gallant conduct in the defence of Fort Erie.
2nd Lieut. Benjamin F. Larned, 21st Infantry. Brevet 1st Lieut. Aug. 15. Gallant conduct in the defence of Fort Erie.
2nd Lieut. John Watmaugh, Corps of Artillery. Brevet 1st Lieut. Aug. 15. Gallant conduct in the defence of Fort Erie.
3rd Lieut. Richard H. Lee, 4th Rifle. Brevet 2nd Lieut. Aug. 15. Gallant conduct in the defence of Fort Erie.
3rd Lieut. Charles Cissna, 19th Infantry. Brevet 2nd Lieut. Aug. 15. Gallant conduct in the defence of Fort Erie.
Brig. Gen. Alexander Macomb, U. S. Army. Brevet Maj. Gen. Sept. 11. Distinguished and gallant conduct in defeating the enemy at Plattsburg.
Brevet Lieut. Col. Daniel Appling, 1st Rifle. Brevet Col. Sept. 11. Gallant conduct—Battle of Plattsburg.
Maj. John E. Wool, 29th Infantry. Brevet Lieut. Col. Sept. 11. Gallant conduct—Battle of Plattsburg.
Brevet Maj. Joseph G. Totten, Corps of Engineers. Brevet Lieut. Col. Sept. 11. Gallant conduct—Battle of Plattsburg.
Capt. Alexander S. Brooks, Corps of Artillery. Brevet Maj. Sept. 11. Gallant conduct—Battle of Plattsburg.
Capt. George McGlassin, 15th Infantry. Brevet Maj. Sept. 11. Gallant conduct—Battle of Plattsburg.
Capt. White Youngs, 15th Infantry. Brevet Maj. Sept. 11. Gallant conduct—Battle of Plattsburg.
1st Lieut. R. E. De Russey, Corps of Engineers. Brevet Capt. Sept. 11. Gallant conduct—Battle of Plattsburg.
1st Lieut. John Mountfort, Corps of Artillery. Brevet Capt. Sept. 11. Gallant conduct—Battle of Plattsburg.
1st Lieut. Harold Smyth, Corps of Artillery. Brevet Capt. Sept. 11. Gallant conduct—Battle of Plattsburg.
1st Lieut. Chester Root, Corps of Artillery. Brevet Capt. Sept. 11. Gallant conduct—Battle of Plattsburg.
2nd Lieut. George Trescott, Corps of Engineers. Brevet 1st Lieut. Sept. 11. Gallant conduct—Battle of Plattsburg.
2nd Lieut. J. G. Cromwell, Corps of Artillery. Brevet 1st Lieut. Sept. 11. Gallantry and good conduct during the battle of Plattsburg.
Maj. George Armistead, Corps of Artillery. Brevet Lieut. Col. Sept. 12. Gallant conduct in defence of Fort McHenry.
Maj. William Lawrence, 2nd Infantry. Brevet Lieut. Col. Sept. 15. Gallant conduct in the attack on Fort Boyer.
Lieut. Col. James McDonald, 1st Rifle. Brevet Col. Sept. 17. Distinguished and meritorious services in the Sortie from Fort Erie.
Lieut. Col. Thomas Aspinwall, 9th Infantry. Brevet Col. Sept. 17. Distinguished and meritorious services in the Sortie from Fort Erie.
Brevet Lieut. Col. George M. Brooke, 23rd Infantry. Brevet Col. Sept. 17. Distinguished and meritorious services in the Sortie from Fort Erie.
Maj. Roger Jones, Assistant Adjutant General, (Capt.) Artillery. Brevet Lieut. Col. Sept. 17. Gallantry and good conduct in the Sortie from Fort Erie.
Maj. Talbot Chambers, 4th Rifle. Brevet Lieut. Col. Sept. 17. Gallant conduct—Sortie from Fort Erie.
Maj. W. A. Trimble, 19th Infantry. Brevet Lieut. Col. Sept. 17. Gallant conduct—Sortie from Fort Erie.
Brevet Capt. David Riddle, 15th Infantry. Brevet Maj. Sept. 17. Gallant conduct—Sortie from Fort Erie.
Brevet Capt. D. Frazer, Aid-de-Camp, 15th Infantry. Brevet Maj. Sept. 17. Gallant conduct—Sortie from Fort Erie.
Brevet 1st Lieut. R. M. Kirkby, Aid-de-Camp, Corps of Artillery. Brevet Capt. Sept. 17. Gallant conduct—Sortie from Fort Erie.
1st Lieut. David B. Douglass, Corps of Engineers. Brevet Capt. Sept. 17. Gallant conduct—Sortie from Fort Erie.
2nd Lieut. Joshua B. Brant, 23rd Infantry. Brevet 1st Lieut. Sept. 17. Gallant conduct—Sortie from Fort Erie.
2nd Lieut. Horace C. Story, Corps of Engineers. Brevet 1st Lieut. Sept. 17. Gallant conduct in the defence of Fort Erie.
Brevet 2nd Lieut. Richard H. Lee, Aid-de-Camp, 4th Rifle. Brevet 1st Lieut. Sept. 17. Gallant conduct—Sortie from Fort Erie.
Brevet 2nd Lieut. Patrick O'Fling, 9th Infantry. Brevet 1st Lieut. Sept. 17. Gallant conduct—Sortie from Fort Erie.
3rd Lieut. Samuel Riddle, 15th Infantry. Brevet 2nd Lieut. Sept. 17. Gallant conduct—Sortie from Fort Erie.
Capt. John A. Burd, Light Dragoons. Brevet Maj. Oct. 31. Gallant conduct.

Capt. William Levall, 3rd Infantry. Brevet Maj. Nov. 7. Gallant conduct during the Siege of New Orleans.
1st Lieut. Richard K. Call, 44th Infantry. Brevet Capt. Nov. 7. Gallant conduct at Pensacola on the 7th Nov. and before New Orleans on the 23rd Dec.
Maj. George Bomford, Corps of Engineers. Brevet Lieut. Col. Dec. 22. Distinguished services in the Ordnance Department.
Col. Robert Butler, Adjutant General, (Maj.) 24th Infantry. Brevet Lieut. Col. Dec. 23. Gallant conduct during the Siege of New Orleans.
Maj. Henry D. Piere, 44th Infantry. Brevet Lieut. Col. Dec. 23. Gallant conduct during the Siege of New Orleans.
Maj. William Platt, 34th Infantry. Brevet Lieut. Col. Dec. 23. Gallant conduct during the Siege of New Orleans.
Col. A. P. Hayne, Inspector General, (Capt.) Light Dragoons. Brevet Lieut. Col. Dec. 23. Gallant conduct during the Siege of New Orleans.
Maj. Walter H. Overton, 3rd Rifle. Brevet Lieut. Col. Dec. 23. Gallant conduct during the Siege of New Orleans.
Maj. Alexander A. White, 12th Infantry. Brevet Lieut. Col. Dec. 23. Gallant conduct during the Siege of New Orleans.
Capt. John Reid, 44th Infantry. Brevet Maj. Dec. 23. Gallant conduct during the Siege of New Orleans.
Capt. W. O. Butler, 44th Infantry. Brevet Maj. Dec. 23. Gallant conduct during the Siege of New Orleans.
Capt. Isaac L. Baker, 44th Infantry. Brevet Maj. Dec. 23. Gallant conduct during the Siege of New Orleans.
Capt. Henry Chotard, 3rd Infantry. Brevet Maj. Dec. 23. Gallant conduct during the Siege of New Orleans.
Capt. John M. Davis, 2nd Infantry. Brevet Maj. Dec. 23. Gallant conduct during the Siege of New Orleans.
Capt. Enoch Humphreys, Corps of Artillery. Brevet Major. Dec. 23. Gallant conduct during the Siege of New Orleans.
1st Lieut. William Gibbs, 44th Infantry. Brevet Capt. Dec. 23. Gallant conduct during the Siege of New Orleans.
3rd Lieut. Joseph Leach, 7th Infantry. Brevet 2nd Lieut. Dec. 23. Gallant conduct during the Siege of New Orleans.

## 1815.

Capt. Thomas L. Butler, 28th Infantry. Brevet Maj. Jan. 8. Gallant conduct during the Siege of New Orleans.
Capt. Samuel Vail, 7th Infantry. Brevet Maj. Jan. 8. Gallant conduct during the Siege of New Orleans.
Capt. George C. Allen, 7th Infantry. Brevet Maj. Jan. 8. Gallant conduct during the Siege of New Orleans.
Capt. Elijah Montgomery, 7th Infantry. Brevet Maj. Jan. 8. Gallant conduct during the Siege of New Orleans.
1st Lieut. Samuel Spotts, Corps of Artillery. Brevet Capt. Jan. 8. Gallant conduct during the Siege of New Orleans.
Col. Charles K. Gardner, Adjutant General, (Maj.) 25th Infantry. Brevet Lieut. Col. Feb. 5. Distinguished and meritorious services.
2nd Lieut. John P. Dieterich, 23rd Infantry. Brevet 1st Lieut. Feb. 5. Gallant conduct.
2nd Lieut. John Brady, 22nd Infantry. Brevet 1st Lieut. Feb. 5. Gallant conduct.
Capt. Sylvanus Thayer, Corps of Engineers. Brevet Maj. Feb. 20. Distinguished and meritorious services at Norfolk.
1st Lieut. Luther Scott, Corps of Artillery. Brevet Capt. Feb. 20. Distinguished and meritorious services.
2nd Lieut. Francis O. Byrd, Corps of Artillery. Brevet 1st Lieut. Feb. 20. Distinguished and meritorious services.
Brevet Maj. John B. Walbach, Corps of Artillery. Brevet Lieut. Col. May 1. Meritorious services.
Brevet Maj. Joseph Selden, 3rd Rifle. Brevet Lieut. Col. May 1.
Brevet Lieut. Col. Jacob Hindman, Corps of Artillery. Brevet Col. May 17. Meritorious services.

# ARMY LIST

## 1815 to 1900.

# ARMY LIST,

## 1815 to 1900.

Graduates of the Military Academy are denoted by an asterisk(*).

---

ABADIE, EUGENE H. [Born in France. Appointed from Penn.]
Asst. Surg., 4 July, 1836. Maj. Surg., 24 July, 1853. Lieut. Col. Asst. Med. Pur., from 28 July, 1866, to 4 March, 1867. Died 22 Dec., 1874. Bvt. Lieut. Col. and Col., 13 March, 1865, for faithful and meritorious services during the war.

ABBOT, CHARLES W., JR. [Born in R. I. Appointed from R. I.]
2nd Lieut. 12th Inf., 16 Feb., 1881; eccepted 1 March, 1881. 1st Lieut., 1 Sept., 1887. Reg. Adj., 13 May, 1889. Capt., 26 April, 1898. Graduate of the Infantry and Cavalry School, 1883. Col. 1st R. I. Vols., 10 May, 1898, until muster out, 30 March, 1899.

ABBOT, FREDERICK V.* [Born in Mass. Appointed from N. Y.]
2nd Lieut. Eng., 13 June, 1879. 1st Lieut., 17 June, 1881. Capt., 22 July, 1888. Maj., 5 July, 1898.

ABBOT, HENRY.* [Born in Ind. Appointed from Ind.]
Addl. 2nd Lieut. 20th Inf., 11 June, 1897. Died 23 Dec., 1898.

ABBOT, HENRY L.* [Born in Mass. Appointed from Mass.]
Bvt. 2nd Lieut. Top. Eng., 1 July, 1854. 2nd Lieut., 2 Oct., 1855. 1st Lieut., 1 July, 1857. Bvt. Capt., 21 July, 1861, for gallant and meritorious services in the Battle of Bull Run, Va. Bvt. Maj., 4 May, 1862, for gallant and meritorious services in the Siege of Yorktown, Va. Capt. Top. Eng., 18 June, 1862. Col. 1st Conn. Art., 19 Jan., 1863. Trans. to Eng., 3 March, 1863. Bvt. Brig. Gen. Vols., 1 Aug., 1864, for gallant and distinguished services in the operations before Richmond, and especially in the lines before Petersburg, Va. Bvt. Lieut. Col., 13 March, 1865, for gallant and meritorious services during the Siege of Petersburg, Va. Bvt. Col., 13 March, 1865, for gallant and meritorious services during the war. Bvt. Brig. Gen., 13 March, 1865, for gallant and meritorious services in the field during the war. Bvt. Maj. Gen. Vols., 13 March, 1865, for gallant and meritorious services during the war. Mustered out of Vol. service, 25 Sept., 1865. Maj. Eng., 11 Nov., 1865. Lieut. Col., 31 March, 1880. Col., 12 Oct., 1886. Retired by operation of law, 13 Aug., 1895.

ABBOT, WILLIAM.* [Born in Ill. Appointed from Ill.]
2nd Lieut. 9th Inf., 14 June, 1872. Resigned 27 March, 1876.

ABBOTT, ASA T. [Born in Maine. Appointed from Minn.]
Priv. Co. E, 1st Minn. Vols., 29 April, 1861. Trans. to Sig. Corps, 12 Aug., 1863. 2nd Lieut. Sig. Corps, 31 Aug., 1863. Mustered out 29 Aug., 1865. 2nd Lieut. 28th Inf., 7 March, 1867. Bvt. 1st Lieut., 7 March, 1867, for faithful and meritorious services in the Sig. Corps during the war. Unassigned 31 March, 1869. Ass'd to 3rd Art., 14 July, 1869. 1st Lieut., 30 June, 1876. Retired 23 April, 1879. Graduate of the Artillery School, 1872.

ABBOTT, EDWARD F.* [Born in Ohio. Appointed from Ohio.]
Bvt. 2nd Lieut. 6th Inf., 1 July, 1847. 2nd Lieut. 5th Inf., 8 Sept., 1847. 1st Lieut., 4 Aug., 1851. R. Q. M., 17 Aug., 1851, to 31 Dec., 1854. Resigned 31 Dec., 1854.

ABBOTT, EDWARD S. [Born in Mass. Appointed from Army.]
2nd Lieut. 17th Inf., 10 Nov., 1862. 1st Lieut., 27 April, 1863. Killed at Battle of Gettysburg, Pa., 2 July, 1863. Bvt. Capt., 2 July, 1863, for gallant and meritorious service at the Battle of Gettysburg, Pa.

ABBOTT, LEMUEL A. [Born in Vt. Appointed from Vt.]
1st Sergt. Co. B, 10th Vt. Vols., 28 July, 1862. 2nd Lieut. 10th Vt. Vols., 20 March, 1863. 1st Lieut., 31 July, 1864. Capt., 5 Feb., 1865. Mustered out 22 June, 1865. 1st Lieut. 97th U. S. Col. Troops, 6 Nov., 1865. Mustered out 6 April, 1866. 2nd Lieut. 6th Cav., 2 July, 1867. 1st Lieut., 10 Sept., 1869. R. Q. M., 25 Nov., 1869, to 17 May, 1873. Capt., 3 June, 1880. Retired, for wounds received in line of duty, 3 Jan., 1885. Bvt. Maj., Feb. 27, 1890, for gallant services in action against Indians at Big Dry Wash, Ariz., 17 July, 1882.

ABBOTT, LUCIUS. [Born in Conn. Appointed from Conn.]
Asst. Surg., 15 Jan., 1828. Resigned 31 March, 1834.

ABBOTT, ROBERT O. [Born in Penn. Appointed from Penn.]
Asst. Surg., 23 Nov., 1849. Maj. Surg., 16 April, 1862. Died 16 June, 1867.. Bvt. Capt., 21 July, 1861, for gallant and meritoelous services at the Battle of Bull Run, Va. Bvt. Maj., 4 May, 1862, for gallant aed meritorious services at the Siege of Yorktown, Va. Bvt. Lieut. Col., 13 March, 1865, for gallant and meritorious services during the Siege of Petersburg, Va. Bvt. Col., 13 March, 1865, for gallant and meritorious services during the war. Bvt. Brig. Gen., 13 March, 1865, for gallant and meritorious services in the field during the war.

ABEEL, JAMES S. [Born in Penn. Appointed from N. Y.]
3rd Lieut. 23rd Inf., 13 May, 1813. 1st Lieut., 1 Oct., 1814. Disbanded 15 June, 1815. Reinstated 2 Dec., 1815, as 2nd Lieut. Corps Art. 1st Lieut., 20 April, 1818. Trans. to 1st Art., 1 June, 1821. Trans. to 2nd Art., 16 Aug., 1821. Resigned 31 Dec., 1834. Mil. Storekeeper, 6 Jan., 1838. Capt. O. S. K., 28 July, 1866. Retired 22 Feb., 1869. Died 1 Dec., 1870. Retained Jan., 1816, (in re-organization under Act of 3 March, 1815), as 2nd Lieut. of Art., with Bvt. of 1st Lieut. from 1 Oct., 1814. Bvt. Capt., 20 April, 1828, for ten years' faithful service in one grade.

ABELL, CORYDON S. [Born in N. Y. Appointed from Ky.]
Asst. Surg., 3 March, 1847. 3rd Drag., 9 April, 1847. Disbanded 31 July, 1848.

ABELL, HENRY H. [Born in Ohio. Appointed from Ohio.]
Priv. C, 19th Ohio Vols., 29 May, to 19 Aug., 1861. Priv. L, 6th Ohio Cav., 18 Oct., 1861. 2nd Lieut., 16 Dec., 1861. Hon. mustered out 25 Oct., 1864. 2nd Lieut., 26 Cav., 28 July, 1866. 1st Lieut., 21 Feb., 1867. Discharged 15 Dec., 1870.

ABERCROMBIE, JOHN J.* [Born in Tenn. Appointed from Tenn.]
Bvt. 2nd Lieut. 1st Inf., 1 July, 1822. 2nd Lieut., 1 July, 1822. 1st Lieut., 26 Sept., 1828. Reg. Adj., 1 Aug., 1825, to 1 March, 1833. Capt., 4 Sept., 1836. Maj. 5th Inf., 8 Sept., 1847. Lieut. Col. 2nd Inf., 1 May, 1852. Col. 7th Inf., 25 Feb., 1861. Retired 12 June, 1865. Died 3 Jan., 1877. Bvt. Maj., 25 Dec., 1837, for gallant and meritorious conduct in Florida. Bvt. Lieut. Col., 23 Sept., 1846, for gallant and meritorious conduct at Monterey. Bvt. Brig. Gen., 13 March, 1865, for long and faithful services in the army. Brig. Gen. Vols., 9 Sept., 1861. Mustered out of Vol. service, 24 June, 1864.

ABERCROMBIE, RALPH. [Born in Md. Appointed from Penn.]
2nd Lieut. 6th Inf., 30 June, 1855. Resigned 31 May, 1857. 1st Lieut., 13th Inf., 14 May, 1861. Resigned 15 Aug., 1862.

ABERCROMBIE, WM. R. [Born in Minn. Appointed from N. Y.]
2nd Lieut. 2nd Inf., 1 March, 1877. Accepted, 10 March, 1877. 1st Lieut., 20 March, 1885. Capt. 2nd Inf., 27 Aug., 1896.

ABERNETHY, ROBERT S.* [Born in Texas. Appointed from Texas.]
Addl. 2nd Lieut. 3rd Art., 11 June, 1897. 2nd Lieut., 10 Feb., 1898. 1st Lieut. 6th Art., 2 March, 1899. Capt. 36th U. S. Vol. Inf., 5 July, 1899.

ABERT, JAMES W.* [Born in N. J. Appointed at Large.]
Bvt. 2nd Lieut. 5th Inf., 1 July, 1842. Trans. to Top. Eng., 24 May, 1843. 2nd Lieut., 27 May, 1846. 1st Lieut., 3 March, 1853. Capt., 1 July, 1856. Maj. Eng., 3 March, 1863. Resigned 25 June, 1864. Bvt. Lieut. Col., 25 June, 1864, for faithful and meritorious service in the Valley of the Shenandoah from June, 1861, to Sept., 1862. Maj. U. S. A., 3 Jan., 1895, by Act of Congress, Aug. 17, 1894. Retired 14 Jan., 1895. Died Aug., 10, 1897.

ABERT, JOHN J.* [Born in Md. Appointed from Va.]
Cadet at Mil. Acad., 18 Jan., 1808, to 1 April, 1811, when he graduated but declined appointment. Bvt. Maj. Top. Eng., 22 Nov., 1814. Bvt. Lieut. Col. Top. Eng., 22 Nov., 1824. Col., 7 July, 1838. Retired 9 Sept., 1861. Died 27 Jan., 1863. Bvt. Lieut. Col., 22 Nov., 1824, for ten years' faithful service in one grade.

ABERT, WM. STRETCH. [Born in D. C. Appointed from D. C.]
2nd Lieut. 4th Art., 18 June, 1855. 1st Lieut., 31 March, 1857. Capt. 3rd Cav., 14 May, 1861; 6th Cav., 3 Aug., 1861. Lieut. Col. A. I. G., 17 Nov., 1862, to 6 Oct., 1864. Col. 3rd Mass. Art., 3 Dec., 1864, to 18 Sept., 1865. Maj. 7th Cav., 8 June, 1867. Died 25 Aug., 1867. Bvt. Maj., 27 May, 1862, for gallant and meritorious service at the Battle of Hanover C. H., Va. Bvt. Lieut. Col., 17 Sept., 1862, for gallant and meritorious service at the Battle of Antietam, Md., and Brig. Gen. Vols., 13 March, 1865, for gallant services during the war.

ABRAHAMS, BENJAMIN. [Born in Mass. Appointed from Mass.]
Corpl. Co. I, 21st Mass. Vols., 19 Aug., 1861, to 18 Aug., 1864. A. Asst. P. M. U. S. N., 14 Dec., 1864, to 24 Sept., 1865. 2nd Lieut. 39th Inf., 22 Jan., 1867. Died 13 Sept., 1867.

ABRAHAMS, DAVID B. [Born in Mass. Appointed from Mass.]
Priv. Co. G, 22nd Mass. Vols., 16 Sept., 1861, to 19 Aug., 1862. 2nd Lieut. 6th U. S. Col. Inf., 21 Oct., 1864. 1st Lieut., 24 Feb., 1866. Honorably mustered out 19 April, 1866. 2nd Lieut. 36th Inf., 24 Aug., 1867. Resigned 7 April, 1869.

ACKER, WM. H. [Born in N. Y. Appointed from Minn.]
Capt. 1st Minn. Vols., 29 April, 1861. Resigned 20 Aug., 1861. Capt. 16th Inf., 14 May, 1861. Killed at Battle of Shiloh, Tenn., 7 April, 1862. Bvt. Maj., 7 April, 1862, for gallant and meritorious service in the Battle of Shiloh, Tenn.

ADAIR, GEORGE W. [Born in Mich. Appointed from Mich.]
Asst. Surg., 10 Nov., 1874. Capt. Asst. Surg., 10 Nov., 1879. Maj. Surg., 11 Sept., 1891.

ADAIR, JOHN, JR.* [Born in Ky. Appointed from Oregon.]
2nd Lieut. 1st Drag., 6 May, 1861. 1st Cav., 3 Aug., 1861. 1st Lieut., 7 Sept., 1861. Dismissed 29 Dec., 1861.

ADAIR, JOHN I. [Born in Penn. Appointed from Army.]
Priv. and Sergt. Co. E, 3rd Batt. 18th Inf., 2 Nov., 1861, to 20 Aug., 1862. 2nd Lieut. 18th Inf., 14 July, 1862. 1st Lieut., 22 March, 1863. Reg. Adj., 29 July, to 14 Nov., 1866. Resigned 7 June, 1867. Bvt. 1st Lieut., 31 Dec., 1862, for gallant and meritorious service at the Battle of Murfreesboro', Tenn. Bvt. Capt., 1 Sept., 1864, for gallant and meritorious service during the Atlanta campaign at the Battle of Jonesboro', Ga.

ADAIR, LEWIS D. [Born in Ohio. Appointed from Ohio.]
1st Lieut. 26th Ohio Vols., 24 July, 1861. Capt., 1 Dec., 1861. Hon. mustered out 25 July, 1864. 1st Lieut. 22nd Inf., 28 July, 1866. Died 5 Oct., 1872, of wounds received in action with Indians in Dakota.

ADAIR, SAMUEL E.* [Born in Ohio. Appointed from W. Va.]
2nd Lieut. 5th Cav., 11 June, 1881. 1st Lieut. Cav. (9th), 25 Feb., 1891. Trans. to 5th Cav., 27 April, 1891. Resigned 5 Aug., 1897.

ADAIR, WM. I. [Born in Ky. Appointed from Ky.]
Capt. 17th Inf., 12 March, 1812. Trans. to 3rd Inf., 17 May, 1815. Resigned 17 March, 1817.

ADAM, EMIL. [Born in Germany. Appointed from Ill.]
2nd Lieut. 9th Ill. Vols., 25 April, 1861. 1st Lieut., 28 July, 1861. Capt., 14 Nov., 1861. Mustered out 20 Aug., 1864. Priv. Co. E, 144th Ill. Vols., 1 Sept., 1864. Capt. 144th Ill. Vols., 10 Sept., 1864. Maj., 18 March, 1865. Mustered out 14 July, 1865. 1st Lieut. 39th Inf., 28 July, 1866. Capt., 31 May, 1867. Unassigned 20 April, 1869. Ass'd to 5th Cav., 15 Dec., 1870. Bvt. Maj., 27 Feb., 1890, for gallant services in actions against Indians at Muchos Canons, Ariz., 25 Sept., 1872. Maj. 6th Cav., 11 June, 1886. Retired 8 March, 1893.

ADAMS, AXEL S. [Born in N. Y. Appointed from Army.]
Priv. and Sergt. Co. B, 2nd Batt., 14th Inf., 27 Feb., to 19 May, 1865. 2nd Lieut. 2nd Cav., 3 May, 1865. 1st Lieut., 6 July, 1865. Capt., 27 Nov., 1868. Resigned 26 Oct., 1869.

ADAMS, DANIEL M. [Born in N. H. Appointed from Kansas.]
Addl. P. M. Vols., 19 Feb., 1863, to 20 March, 1867. Bvt. Lieut. Col. Vols., 7 June, 1866, for faithful services in Pay Dept. Maj. P. M., 17 Jan., 1867. Resigned 1 May, 1867.

ADAMS, FRANK T. [Born in Penn. Appointed from N. J.]
Priv. Co. D, 15th Penn. Cav., 11 Aug., 1862. Trans. to Co. M, 1 March, 1863. Discharged 17 July, 1863. Recruiting 2nd Lieut. 2nd N. J. Cav., 23 July, 1863. 2nd Lieut. 2nd N. J. Cav., 2 Sept., 1863. 1st Lieut., 9 March, 1864. Mustered out 1 Nov., 1865. 2nd Lieut. 15th Inf., 23 Feb., 1866. Trans. to 33rd Inf., 21 Sept., 1866. 1st Lieut., 17 Jan., 1867. Reg. Adj., 24 Aug., 1868, to 3 May, 1869. Trans. to 8th Inf., 3 May, 1869. Died 26 July, 1880.

ADAMS, GEORGE F. [Born in Mass. Appointed from Army.]
2nd Lieut. 33rd Mass. Vols., 5 Aug., 1862. 1st Lieut., 15 Jan., 1863. Resigned 28 March, 1863. Priv., Corpl. and Sergt. Co. C, 2nd Batt., 17th Inf., 11 May, 1863 to 25 July, 1864. 2nd Lieut. 17th Inf., 30 June, 1864. 1st Lieut., 30 June, 1864. Dismissed 22 Feb., 1865. Bvt. Capt., 18 Aug., 1864, for gallant service at the Battle on the Weldon Railroad, Va.

ADAMS, GRANGER.* [Born in N. Y. Appointed from N. Y.]
2nd Lieut. 5th Art., 15 June, 1876. 1st Lieut., 30 March, 1884. Reg. Q. M., 4 Oct., 1889, to ——. Graduate of the Artillery School, 1882. Capt. 7th Art., 19 Sept., 1898.

ADAMS, HENRY H. [Born in Ohio. Appointed from Ohio.]
Priv. Co. C, 98th Ohio Vols., 2 Feb., 1864. Corpl., 20 March, 1865. Discharged 26 June, 1865. 2nd Lieut. 16th Inf., 23 Feb., 1866. Trans. to 25th Inf., 21 Sept., 1866. 1st Lieut., 21 Sept., 1866. Trans. to 18th Inf., 26 April, 1869. Capt. 18th Inf., 15 Oct., 1886. Maj. 18th Inf., 2 March, 1899.

ADAMS, HENRY M.* [Born in Mass. Appointed from Mass.]
2nd Lieut. Eng., 18 June, 1866. 1st Lieut., 10 July, 1866. Capt., 2 Sept., 1874. Maj., 10 Jan., 1887.

ADAMS, HENRY R.* [Born in Ohio. Appointed from Ohio.]
Addl. 2nd Lieut. 23rd Inf., 12 June, 1887. 2nd Lieut. 25th Inf., 1 Sept., 1887. Resigned 1 Sept., 1888.

ADAMS, ISAAC A.* [Born in Mass. Appointed from Maine.]
3rd Lieut. Corps Art., 17 July, 1817. 2nd Lieut., 29 Sept., 1817. 1st Lieut., 31 July, 1819. Trans. to 3rd Art., 1 June, 1821. Trans. to 4th Art., 3 Oct., 1821. Died 19 Oct., 1829.

ADAMS, JASPER. [Born in Mass. Appointed from S. C.]
Chaplain, Prof. at Mil. Acad., 1 Sept., 1838. Resigned 15 Nov., 1840.

ADAMS, JOHN.* [Born in Tenn. Appointed from Tenn.]
Bvt. 2nd Lieut. 1st Drag., 1 July, 1846. 2nd Lieut., 6 Dec., 1846. 1st Lieut., 9 Oct., 1851. Capt., 30 Nov., 1856. Resigned 31 May, 1861. Bvt. 1st Lieut., 16 March, 1848, for gallant and meritorious conduct at Santa Cruz de Rosales, Mexico.

ADAMS, JOHN Q. [Born in N. Y. Appointed from Ohio.]
Priv. Co. C, 88th Ohio Vols., 26 May, 1862. Discharged 26 Sept., 1862. Q. M. Sergt. Co. I, 10th Ohio Cav., 15 Oct., 1862. Priv. Co. B, Batt. Cav. Miss. Marine Brigade, 23 Feb., 1863. 2nd Lieut. Sig. Corps, 3 March, 1863. Mustered out 22 Aug., 1865. 2nd Lieut. 1st Cav., 17 Aug., 1867. Bvt. 1st Lieut., 17 Aug., 1867, for gallant and meritorious serivce in the Sig. Corps in the Battle of Alatoona, Ga. Bvt. Capt., 17 Aug., 1867, for gallant and meritorious service in the Sig. Corps at the capture of Fort McAllister and Savannah, Ga., and during the war. 1st Lieut., 14 Sept., 1869. Capt., 31 Oct., 1884. Retired (own request), 6 Nov., 1896.

ADAMS, JULIUS W.* [Born in Mass. Appointed from Ky.]
2nd Lieut. 4th Inf., 24 June, 1861. 1st Lieut., 24 June, 1861. Capt., 9 Aug., 1862. Resigned 29 June, 1864. Died 15 Nov., 1865.

ADAMS, MILTON B.* [Born in Penn. Appointed from Ohio.]
1st Lieut. Eng., 23 June, 1865. Capt., 6 Jan., 1870. Maj., 3 July, 1883. Lieut. Col., 5 July, 1898.

ADAMS, MOSES N. [Born in Ohio. Appointed from Minn.]
Post Chaplain, 14 Feb., 1876. Retired (op. law), 14 Feb., 1886.

ADAMS, SAML. [Born in Maine. Appointed from Md.]
Asst. Surg., 16 April, 1862. Died 9 Sept., 1867. Bvt. Capt., 13 March, 1865, for gallant and meritorious service during the operations in front of Petersburg, Va. Bvt. Maj., 13 March, 1865, for faithful and meritorious service during the war.

ADAMS, STERLING P.* [Born in Ala. Appointed from Ala.]
2nd Lieut. of Cav. (1st), 11 June, 1892. 1st Lieut. 9th Cav., 14 Dec., 1898.

ADAMS, THOS. B.* [Born in Mass. Appointed from Mass.]
Bvt. 2nd Lieut. Art., 1 July, 1828. 2nd Lieut. 2nd Art., 1 July, 1828. 1st Lieut., 1 Dec., 1834. Died 14 Dec., 1837.

ADAMS, THOS. R.* [Born in Ky. Appointed from Miss.]
2nd Lieut. 5th Art., 17 June, 1867. 1st Lieut., 2 March, 1871. Graduate of Artillery School, 1886. Capt., 8 March, 1898.

ADAMS, WM. [Born in Ireland. Appointed from Penn.]
Priv. Artif. and Armorer Ord. Dep., 19 Nov., 1838, to 19 Nov., 1848. Ord. Storekeeper, 13 Sept., 1862. Capt. Ord. Storekeeper, 28 July, 1866. Retired (op. law), 14 July, 1883. Died 25 Oct., 1888.

ADAMS, WM. A. [Born in Ga. Appointed from Army.]
Priv., Sergt. and 1st Sergt. C, 13th Inf., 2 April, 1847, to 3 May, 1848. 2nd Lieut. 13th Inf., 3 March, 1848. Disbanded 15 July, 1848.

ADAMS, WM. B. [Born in Pa. Appointed from N. Y.]
1st Lieut. 13th Inf., 12 March, 1812. Capt., 13 May, 1813. Disbanded 15 June, 1815. Re-instated 17 May, 1816, as 1st Lieut. 5th Inf. Resigned 1 May, 1817. 2nd Lieut. Corps Art., 31 Oct., 1818. Disbanded 1 June, 1821. Bvt. Capt., 13 May, 1815.

ADAMS, WYLY C. [Born in Ga. Appointed from Ga.]
2nd Lieut. 2nd Art., 31 May, 1848. 1st Lieut., 1 July, 1852. Dismissed 16 Aug., 1854.

ADDE, GEORGE J. [Born in Va. Appointed from La.]
2nd Lieut. Smith's Reg. Fla. Vols., 3 Feb., to 12 May, 1836. 1st Lieut. Adj. 1st La. Inf., 9 May, to 9 Aug., 1846. 1st Lieut. of Inf., 5 March, 1847. 3rd Drag., 9 April, 1847. Disbanded 8 Aug., 1848.

ADDISON, JOHN McL. [Born in Va. Appointed from D. C.]
2nd Lieut. Mounted Rifles, 14 June, 1848. Resigned 30 Nov., 1850.

ADDISON, OVERTON C. [Born in Md. Appointed from Md.]
Surg. Mate 1st Inf., 19 Feb., 1817. Resigned 18 March, 1818.

ADKINS, ISAAC L. [Born in Del. Appointed from Pa.]
Asst. Surg., 23 Nov., 1849. Resigned 9 Oct., 1852.

ADOLPHUS, PHILIP. [Born in Prussia. Appointed from Md.]
Asst. Surg., 5 Aug., 1861. Resigned 1 July, 1865.

ADMIRE, ELI LEWIS. [Born in Kansas. Appointed from Okla.]
2nd Lieut. 22nd Inf., 1 July, 1899.

AGER, WINTHROP D. [Born in Mass. Appointed from Army.]
Priv. and Sergt. 4th Inf., 9 Jan., 1811, to Jan., 1812. Ensign and 2nd Lieut. 4th Inf., 3 Jan., 1812. Resigned 31 May, 1813. Sergt. Capt. Gates' Co. —, Corps Art., 10 Feb., to 27 March, 1815. Sergt. and Q. M. Sergt. Corps Art., 15 Oct., 1817, to — Aug., 1819. 2nd Lieut. Corps Art., 13 Aug., 1819. Disbanded 1 June, 1821.

AGNEL, HYACINTH R. [Born in N. Y. Appointed from N. Y.]
Teacher and Prof. of French at Mil. Acad., 4 Feb., 1840, and Prof. 16 May, 1848, to 10 Feb., 1871. Died 10 Feb., 1871.

AHERN, GEORGE P.* [Born in N. Y. Appointed from N. Y.]
2nd Lieut. 25th Inf., 13 June, 1882. 1st Lieut. of Inf. (4th), 20 Feb., 1891. Trans. to 25th Inf., 20 July, 1891. Capt. of Inf. (9th), 30 June, 1898.

AIKEN, GERRITT V. S. [Born in N. Y. Appointed from Ohio.]
2nd Lieut. 2nd Ohio Vols., 17 April, 1861. Hon. mustered out 9 Aug., 1861. 2nd Lieut. 8th Inf., 5 Aug., 1861. 1st Lieut., 8 Oct., 1864. R. Q. M., 27 Aug., 1866, to 10 March, 1868. Dismissed 4 Jan., 1869.

AINSWORTH, FREDERICK C. [Born in Vt. Appointed from Vt.]
1st Lieut., Asst. Surg., 10 Nov., 1874. Capt. Asst. Surg., 10 Nov., 1879. Maj. Surg., 27 Feb., 1891. Col. Chief of Record and Pension office, 27 May, 1892. Brig. Gen. and Chf., 2 March, 1899.

AISQUITH, WM. E.* [Born in Md. Appointed from Va.]
Bvt. 2nd and 2nd Lieut. 2nd Art., 1 July, 1827. Dismissed 24 May, 1832. 2nd Lieut. 1st Art., 8 March, 1837. 1st Lieut., 7 July, 1838. Cashiered 24 Feb., 1845. 1st Sergt. Co. E, Batt. Md. and D. C. Vols., 8 June, 1846. 2nd Lieut., 1 Sept., 1846. Hon. mustered out 30 May, 1847. Priv. and Sergt. 1st Art., May to Dec., 1847. Capt. 1st Art., 20 Nov., 1847. Dropped 12 Jan., 1848.

ALBEE, GEORGE E. [Born in N. H. Appointed from Minn.]
Priv. Co. G, 1st U. S. Sharpshooters, 25 June, 1862. Discharged 22 Oct., 1862. Priv. 3rd Batty. Wis. Light Art., 23 Dec., 1863. 2nd Lieut. 36th Wis. Vols., 8 March, 1864. 1st Lieut., 16 Jan., 1865. Bvt. 1st Lieut. Vols., 13 March, 1865, for gallant and meritorious service during the war. Mustered out 12 July, 1865. 2nd Lieut. 36th U. S. Col. Troops, 18 Sept., 1865. Mustered out 28 Oct., 1866. 2nd Lieut. 41st Inf., 28 July, 1866. Bvt. 1st Lieut., 2 March, 1867, for gallant and meritorious service in the Battle of the Wilderness, Va. 1st Lieut. 41st Inf., 4 Nov., 1867. Trans. to 24th Inf., 11 Nov., 1869. Retired 28 June, 1878. Medal of Honor for distinguished gallantry in action against hostile Indians on the Brazos River, Tex., 28 and 29 Oct., 1869, while serving as 1st Lieut. 41st Inf. commanding Co. L, 9th Cav. Bvt. Capt., 27 Feb., 1890, for gallant services in the actions against Indians on the Brazos River, Tex., 16 Sept., 1869, and 28 and 29 Oct., 1869.

ALBERTI, EDWIN R. [Born in ——. Appointed from Penn.]
2nd Lieut. Light Art., 12 July, 1820. Trans. to 2nd Art., 1 June, 1821. Trans. to 4th Art., 22 May, 1822. Resigned 31 July, 1827.

ALBRIGHT, FRANK H.* [Born in Ohio. Appointed from Ohio.]
Addl. 2nd Lieut. 12th Inf., 12 June, 1887. 2nd Lieut. 9th Inf., 2 Oct., 1887. 1st Lieut. of Inf. (25th), 3 Jan., 1895. Capt., 2 March, 1899.

ALBRIGHT, JACOB W. [Born in ——. Appointed from Penn.]
Ensign 1st Inf., 6 March, 1806. 2nd Lieut., 15 Nov., 1807. 1st Lieut., 26 Aug., 1812. Dist. P. M., 4 Sept., 1813. Disbanded 15 June, 1815. P. M. 2nd Inf., 9 July, 1816. Maj. P. M., 1 June, 1821. Resigned 13 May, 1823.

ALBURTIS, WM. [Born in Va. Appointed from Va.]
2nd Lieut. 2nd Inf., 8 March, 1837. 1st Lieut., 1 July, 1839. Killed 11 March, 1847, in investment of Vera Cruz, Mexico. Bvt. Capt., 2 March, 1841, for gallantry and good conduct in war against the Florida Indians.

ALDEN, BRAD. R.* [Born in Penn. Appointed from N. Y.]
Bvt. 2nd Lieut. 4th Inf., 1 July, 1831. 2nd Lieut., 15 Sept., 1833. 1st Lieut., 13 Sept., 1836. Capt., 14 June, 1842. Resigned 29 Sept., 1853.

ALDEN, CHARLES H. [Born in Penn. Appointed from Penn.]
1st Lieut. Asst. Surg., 23 June, 1860. Bvt. Maj. and Lieut. Col., 13 March, 1865, for faithful and meritorious service during the war. Capt. Asst. Surg., 23 June, 1865. Maj. Surg., 28 July, 1866. Lieut. Col. Surg., 14 Nov., 1888. Col. Asst. Surg. Gen., 4 Dec., 1892. Retired by operation of law, 28 April, 1900.

ALDEN, GEORGE E. [Born in Mass. Appointed from Penn.]
Priv. Co. B, and Q. M. Sergt. Birge's S. S. Ill. Vols., 1 Dec., 1861, to 12 Aug., 1863. Capt. A. Q. M. Vols., 12 March, 1863, to 2 Dec., 1865. Capt. A. Q. M., 27 Nov., 1865.

Resigned 9 Dec., 1871. Bvt. Maj. 2 March, 1867, for faithful and meritorious service in the Q. M. D. during the war.

ALDEN, ROGER. [Born in N. Y. Appointed from N. Y.]
Ord. Storekeeper, 20 Jan., 1825. Died 5 Nov., 1836.

ALDRICH, BISHOP. [Born in N. Y. Appointed from Army.]
Priv., Corpl. and Sergt. Co. H, and Q. M. Sergt. 8th Inf., 29 July, 1855, to 6 Nov., 1863. 2nd Lieut. 8th Inf., 31 Oct., 1863. 1st Lieut., 28 July, 1866. R. Q. M., 7 Oct., 1869, to 16 May, 1877. Died 16 May, 1877. Bvt. 1st Lieut., 10 May, 1864, for gallant and meritorious service at the Battle of Spottsylvania, Va.

ALESHIRE, CHAS. C. [Born in Ohio. Appointed from Ohio.]
Capt. 18th Ohio Vols., 27 April, 1861. Hon. mustered out 28 Aug., 1861. Capt. 18th Ohio Batty 15 July, 1862. Hon. mustered out 29 June, 1865. 2nd Lieut. 3rd Art., 11 May, 1866. 1st Lieut., 5 Feb., 1867. Discharged 15 Nov., 1870. Bvt. Capt., 2 March, 1867, for gallant and meritorious service at the Battle of Peach Tree Creek, Ga.

ALESHIRE, JAMES B.* [Born in Ohio. Appointed from Ohio.]
2nd Lieut. 1st Cav., 12 June, 1880. 1st Lieut., 20 Sept., 1890. Capt. A. Q. M., 25 April, 1895. Maj. Q. M. Vols., 12 May, 1898. Lieut. Col. Q. M. (Act 7 July, 1898), 26 Nov., 1898. Honorably discharged 17 April, 1899. Maj. Q. M. Vols., 1 April, 1899.

ALEXANDER, ANDREW J. [Born in Ky. Appointed from Mo.]
2nd Lieut. and 1st Lieut. Mounted Rifles, 26 July, 1861. Bvt. Capt., 1 July, 1862, for gallant and meritorious service during the Peninsular Campaign in Virginia. Lieut. Col. A. A. G. (Act 17 July, 1862), 1 Jan., 1863. Bvt. Maj., 3 July, 1863, for gallant and meritorious service during the Gettysburg Campaign. Relieved as Lieut. Col. A. A. G., 10 Aug., 1863. Capt. 3rd Cav., 13 Sept., 1863. Lieut. Col. A. A. G. (Act 17 July, 1862), 23 April, 1864. Bvt. Lieut. Col., 20 July, 1864, for gallant and meritorious service during the Atlanta Campaign. Bvt. Col. and Brig. Gen. Vols., 5 Jan., 1865. Bvt. Col., 2 April, 1865, for gallant and meritorious service in the capture of Selma, Ala. Bvt. Brig. Gen., 16 April, 1865, for distinguished skill and gallantry in the Cavalry engagements at Ebenezer Church, Ala., and Columbus, Ga., and for steadfast devotion to duty in the field during the war. Relieved as Lieut. Col. A. A. G., 24 April, 1865. Maj. 8th Cav., 28 July, 1866. Lieut. Col. 2nd Cav., 20 March, 1879. Retired 3 July, 1885. Died 4 May, 1887.

ALEXANDER, BARTON S.* [Born in Ky. Appointed from Ky.]
Bvt. 2nd Lieut. Eng., 1 July, 1842. 2nd Lieut., 30 Sept., 1843. 1st Lieut., 3 March, 1853. Capt., 1 July, 1856. Lieut. Col. A. A. D. C., 28 Sept., 1861, to 31 May, 1866. Maj., 3 March, 1863. Lieut. Col., 7 March, 1867. Bvt. Maj., 21 July, 1861, for gallant and meritorious service at Battle of Bull Run, Va. Lieut. Col., 4 May, 1862, for gallant and meritorious service at Siege of Yorktown, Va. Bvt. Col. and Brig. Gen., 13 March, 1865, for meritorious services during the Rebellion. Died 15 Dec., 1878.

ALEXANDER, CHAS. T. [Born in Cherokee Nation. Appointed from Ark.]
1st Lieut. Asst. Surg., 1 Oct., 1856. Capt. Asst. Surg., 1 Oct., 1861. Maj. Surg., 9 Feb., 1863. Bvt. Lieut. Col., 13 March, 1865, for faithful and meritorious service during the war. Lieut. Col. and Surg., 26 July, 1886. Bvt. Col., 27 Feb., 1890, for gallant services in action against Indians, at the Clearwater, Idaho, 11 and 12 July, 1877. Col. Chief Med. Pur., 11 Sept., 1891. Retired (op. of law), 3 May, 1897.

ALEXANDER, EDMUND B.* [Born in Va. Appointed from Ky.]
Bvt. 2nd Lieut. 6th Inf., 1 July, 1823. 2nd Lieut. 3rd Inf., 1 July, 1823. 1st Lieut., 29 Dec., 1827. Capt., 7 July, 1838. Capt. A. Q. M., 7 July, 1838. Vacated Staff Commission, 18 June, 1846. Bvt. Maj., 18 April, 1847, for gallant and meritorious conduct in the Battle of Cerro Gordo. Bvt. Lieut. Col., 20 Aug., 1847, for gallant and meritorious conduct in the Battles of Contreras and Churubusco. Maj. 8th Inf., 10 Nov., 1851. Col. 10th Inf., 3 March, 1855. Bvt. Brig. Gen., 18 Oct., 1865, for meritorious service in the recruitment of the armies of the United States. Retired 22 Feb., 1869. Died 3 Jan., 1888.

ALEXANDER, ED. H. [Born in Va. Appointed from D. C.]
Cadet at Mil. Acad., 20 May, 1814, to 3 July, 1817. 2nd Lieut. 4th Inf., 22 May, 1818. 1st Lieut., 20 Aug., 1820. Resigned 29 Nov., 1826.

ALEXANDER, EDWARD P.* [Born in Ga. Appointed from Ga.]
Bvt. 2nd Lieut. Eng., 1 July, 1857. 2nd Lieut., 10 Oct., 1858. Resigned 1 May, 1861.

ALEXANDER, JAMES B. [Born in Ky. Appointed from Ky.]
Capt. C. S. Vols., 23 Sept., 1861, to 6 Dec., 1861. 2nd Lieut. 1st Cav., 26 Nov., 1861. Died 18 June, 1862.

ALEXANDER, JAMES B. S.* [Born in Va. Appointed from Va.]
Bvt. 2nd Lieut. 5th Inf., 1 July, 1856. 2nd Lieut. 9th Inf., 10 Sept., 1856. Resigned 9 May, 1861.

ALEXANDER, JAMES T. [Born in ——. Appointed from ——.]
Ord. Storekeeper, 19 Sept., 1822. Disbanded 10 May, 1824.

ALEXANDER, JOHN H.* [Born in Ark. Appointed from Ohio.]
2nd Lieut 9th Cav., 12 June, 1887. Died 26 March, 1894.

ALEXANDER, NEWTON F.* [Born in Tenn. Appointed from Tenn.]
Bvt. 2nd Lieut. Eng., 1 July, 1852. 2nd Lieut., 1 Aug., 1854. Died 10 Oct., 1858.

ALEXANDER, RICHARD H. [Born in Ill. Appointed from Ky.]
1st Lieut. Asst. Surg., 2 Dec., 1853. Capt. Asst. Surg., 2 Dec., 1858. Maj. Surg., 11 June, 1862. Bvt. Lieut. Col., 13 March, 1865, for faithful and meritorious service during the War. Lieut. Col. Asst. Med. Pur., 7 Dec., 1884. Died 29 March, 1889.

ALEXANDER, RICHARD H. L. [Born in Ky. Appointed from Ky.]
2nd Lieut. 7th Cav., 12 Dec., 1872. Died 9 Feb., 1875.

ALEXANDER, ROBERT. [Born in Md. Appointed from the Army.]
Priv., Sergt. and 1st Sergt. Co. G, 4th Inf., from 7 April, 1876, to 29 Jan., 1890. 2nd Lieut. 7th Inf., 17 Dec., 1889. 1st Lieut. 12th Inf., 7 Jan., 1897. Trans. to 11th Inf., 21 March, 1898. Capt. 14th Inf., 2 Oct., 1899. Trans. to 11th Inf., 17 Feb., 1900.

ALEXANDER, THOS. B. [Born in Ky. Appointed from Wash. Ter.]
2nd Lieut. 1st Cav., 21 Feb., 1861. 1st Lieut., 1 May, 1861. Trans. to 4th Cav., 3 Aug., 1861. Capt., 17 July, 1862. Dropped 4 March, 1865.

ALEXANDER, THOS. L.* [Born in Va. Appointed from Ky.]
Bvt. 2nd Lieut. 6th Inf., 1 July, 1830. 2nd Lieut., 1 July, 1830. 1st Lieut., 18 April, 1837. Capt., 7 July, 1838. Bvt. Maj., 20 Aug., 1847, for gallant and meritorious conduct in the Battles of Contreras and Churubusco. Maj. 8th Inf., 9 June, 1853. Lieut. Col. 5th Inf., 31 July, 1861. Retired 16 Oct., 1863. Died 11 March, 1881.

ALEXANDER, WALTER S.* [Born in Mass. Appointed at Large.]
2nd Lieut. 5th Inf., 13 June, 1879. Trans. to 4th Art., 11 July, 1879. 1st Lieut. 4th Art., 31 March, 1887. Capt., 2 March, 1899. Graduate of the Artillery School, 1890.

ALEXANDER, WM. [Born in Tenn. Appointed from Tenn.]
2nd Lieut. 6th Inf., 27 Oct., 1820. Trans. to 5th Inf., 1 June, 1821, 1st Lieut., 31 Oct., 1825. Capt., 18 Feb., 1836. Died 31 Oct., 1838.

ALEXANDER, WM. L. [Born in Iowa. Appointed from Iowa.]
1st Lieut. 30th Iowa Inf., 23 Sept., 1862. Capt., 1 Oct., 1863. Honorably mustered out 27 July, 1865. Capt. C. S., 4 Oct., 1889. Maj. C. S., 10 June, 1896. Lieut. Col. and C. S. Vols., 22 July, 1898. Col. C. S. Vols., 7 Oct., 1898, to 2 March, 1899.

ALEXANDER, WM. S. [Born in Mo. Appointed from Mo.]
Cadet at Mil. Acad., 1 July, 1865, to 23 Dec., 1865. 2nd Lieut. 8th Inf., 9 Oct., 1867. Died 29 March, 1869.

ALLAIRE, WM. H.* [Born in Ark. Appointed from Ill.]
2nd Lieut. 23rd Inf., 13 June, 1882. 1st Lieut., 15 July, 1890. Capt., 26 April, 1898.

ALLANSON, DUDLEY W. [Born in N. Y. Appointed from N. Y.]
Cadet at Mil. Acad., 6 Nov., 1818, to 4 Aug., 1823. 2nd Lieut. 5th Inf., 24 May, 1824. Resigned 8 Sept., 1827.

ALLANSON, JOHN S.* [Born in N. Y. Appointed from N. Y.]
3rd Lieut. 1st Art., 11 March, 1814. 2nd Lieut., 1 May, 1814. Trans. to Corps Art., 12 May, 1814. 1st Lieut., 20 April, 1818. Resigned 20 April, 1820.

ALLANSON, JOHN S. [Born in Mass. Appointed from Mass.]
2nd Lieut. 20th Inf., 7 March, 1867. 1st Lieut., 20 Oct., 1868. Discharged 1st Nov., 1870.

ALLEN, AUGUSTUS P.* [Born in N. Y. Appointed from N. Y.]
2nd Lieut. 3rd Art., 1 July, 1836. 1st Lieut., 23 Nov., 1837. 1st Lieut. Top. Eng., 7 July, 1838. Died 1 Sept., 1841.

ALLEN, AUSTIN W. [Born in Ky. Appointed from Ky.]
2nd Lieut. Marine Corps, 10 Feb., 1838. Trans. to Army, 26 Nov., 1838, to rank as 2nd Lieut. 5th Inf., 1 Aug., 1838. Dismissed 21 Oct., 1839.

ALLEN, CHAS. J.* [Born in N. Y. Appointed from N. Y.]
1st Lieut. Eng., 13 June, 1864. Bvt. Capt., 24 Aug., 1864, for highly meritorious services in the Sieges of Forts Gaines and Morgan, Ala. Bvt. Maj., 26 March, 1865, for gallant and meritorious services during the campaign against the city of Mobile and its defences. Capt. Eng., 7 March, 1867. Maj. Eng., 10 Jan., 1883. Lieut. Col. Eng., 5 Feb., 1897.

ALLEN, CYRUS M.* [Born in Ind. Appointed at Large.]
2nd Lieut. 2nd Cav., 23 June, 1865. 1st Lieut., 18 Jan., 1866. Reg. Com., 1 June, to 1 Dec., 1867. Resigned 5 July, 1868.

ALLEN, EBENEZER C. [Born in Mass. Appointed from Army.]
Priv., Sergt. and 1st Sergt. Co. A, 12th Inf., 16 Oct., 1861, to 26 June, 1862. 2nd Lieut. 12th Inf., 25 May, 1862. 1st Lieut., 19 Jan., 1863. Died 19 Dec., 1863.

ALLEN, ELISHA L. [Born in Mass. Appointed from Mass.]
Surg. Mate 21st Inf., 21 July, 1813. Trans. to 5th Inf., 17 May, 1815. Resigned 3 March, 1817. Hosp. Surg. Mate, 8 March, 1817. Died 5 Sept., 1817.

ALLEN, ETHAN A.* [Born in Vt. Appointed from Vt.]
2nd Lieut. Art., 14 Nov., 1806. 1st Lieut., 1 Oct., 1809. Trans. to Corps Art., 12 May, 1814. Capt., 25 June, 1814. Hon. discharged 15 June, 1815. Reinstated 17 May, 1816. Hon. discharged 1 June, 1821. Died 6 Jan., 1855.

ALLEN, GEORGE W. [Born in Mass. Appointed from Mass.]
2nd Lieut. 8th Inf., 13 Feb., 1818. 1st Lieut., 1 Jan., 1819. Trans. to 4th Inf., 1 June, 1821. Capt., 25 Jan., 1829. Maj. 2nd Inf., 9 Sept., 1846. Died 15 March, 1848. Bvt. Capt., 1 Jan., 1829, for ten years' faithful service in one grade. Bvt. Maj., 25 Dec., 1837, for gallant conduct on several occasions, and general efficiency in the war against Florida Indians. Bvt. Lieut. Col., 9 March, 1846, for gallant conduct in the Battles of Palo Alto and Resaca da la Palma.

ALLEN, HARRISON. [Born in Penn. Appointed from Penn.]
Asst. Surg., 30 July, 1862. Resigned 8 Dec., 1865. Bvt. Capt. and Maj., 13 March, 1865, for faithful and meritorious service during the War.

ALLEN, HARVEY A. [Born in N. C. Appointed from N. C.]
2nd Lieut. 2nd Art., 1 July, 1841. 1st Lieut., 3 March, 1847. Bvt. Capt., 8 Sept., 1847, for gallant and meritorious conduct in the Battle of Molino del Rey. Capt. 2nd Art., 25 Nov., 1854. Maj., 1 Aug., 1863. Lieut. Col., 2 July, 1877. Retired 10 April, 1879. Died 20 Sept., 1882.

ALLEN, HENRY T.* [Born in Ky. Appointed from Ky.]
2nd Lieut. 2nd Cav., 13 June, 1882. 1st Lieut., 22 June, 1889. Capt. 6th Cav., 10 Nov., 1898. Maj. and A. A. G. Vols., 3 June, 1898, to 13 June, 1899. Maj. 43rd U. S. Vols., 17 Aug., 1899.

ALLEN, JAMES.* [Born in Ind. Appointed from Ind.]
2nd Lieut. 3rd Cav., 14 June, 1872. 1st Lieut., 24 July, 1879. Capt., 29 Oct., 1888. Capt. Sig. Corps, 19 Dec., 1890. Maj., 8 July, 1898. Lieut. Col., 1 Dec., 1899. Lieut. Col. Chief Sig. Officer of Vols., 20 May, 1898. Col. Chief Sig. Officer Vols., 18 July, 1898, to 12 May 1899.

ALLEN, JAMES.* [Born in Ohio. Appointed from Ind.]
Bvt. 2nd Lieut. 5th Inf., 1 July, 1829. 2nd Lieut., 1 July, 1829. 2nd Lieut. 1st Drag., 4 March, 1833. 1st Lieut., 13 May, 1835. Capt., 30 June, 1837. Died 23 Aug., 1846.

ALLEN, JAMES.* [Born in N. C. Appointed from N. C.]
Bvt. 2nd Lieut. 4th Art., 1 July, 1831. 2nd Lieut., 1 July, 1831. Resigned 31 July, 1834.

ALLEN, JAS. B. [Born in Mass. Appointed from Mass.]
2nd Lieut. 3rd Inf., 27 Oct., 1820. Died 21 Aug., 1823.

ALLEN, JAMES G.* [Born in Tenn. Appointed from Tenn.]
Bvt. 2nd Lieut. 2nd Inf., 1 July, 1826. 2nd Lieut. 5th Inf., 1 July, 1826. Resigned 20 May, 1828.
ALLEN, JESSE K.* [Born in Tenn. Appointed from Ill.]
Bvt. 2nd Lieut. 5th Inf., 1 July, 1855. 2nd Lieut. 9th Inf., 16 Oct., 1855. Died 15 Aug., 1858, of wounds received in action with Indians in Washington Territory.
ALLEN, JOHN H.* [Born in Conn. Appointed from N. Y.]
Bvt. 2nd Lieut. 3rd Art., 1 July, 1833. 2nd Lieut., 28 Dec., 1835. Resigned 30 June, 1836.
ALLEN, JOSEPH C. [Born in Tenn. Appointed from Tenn.]
Cadet at Mil. Acad., 1 July, 1840, to 18 Sept., 1843. Capt. A. C. S. Vols., 21 June, 1847. Disbanded 20 July, 1848.
ALLEN, LEVEN C.* [Born in Mo. Appointed from Mo.]
2nd Lieut. 16th Inf., 14 June, 1872. 1st Lieut., 1 July, 1880. Reg. Adj., 26 April, 1883, to 26 April, 1887. Capt., 24 Feb., 1891. Maj. 12th Inf., 10 Oct., 1899.
ALLEN, LUCIUS H.* [Born in N. Y. Appointed from N. Y.]
2nd Lieut. 2nd Art., 1 July, 1839. Resigned 26 March, 1846. Died 5 Dec., 1887.
ALLEN, ROBERT.* [Born in Ohio. Appointed from Ind.]
Bvt. 2nd Lieut. 2nd Art., 1 July, 1836. 2nd Lieut. 1 Aug., 1836. 1st Lieut., 7 July, 1838. Capt. A. Q. M., 11 May, 1846. Bvt. Maj., 18 April, 1847, for gallant and meritorious conduct in the Battle of Cerro Gordo. Capt. 2nd Art., 19 Oct., 1847. Vacated Line Commission, 19 Oct., 1847. Maj. Q. M., 17 May, 1861. Col. Addl. A. deC., 19 Feb., 1862. Brig. Gen. Vols., 23 May, 1863. Bvt. Lieut. Col., Bvt. Col. and Brig. Gen., 4 July, 1864. Bvt. Maj. Gen., 13 March, 1865, for faithful and meritorious service during the war. Bvt. Maj. Gen. Vols., 13 March, 1865, for faithful and meritorious service during the war. Col. A. Q. M. G., 28 July, 1866. Mustered out of Vol. service, 1 Sept., 1866. Retired 21 March, 1878. Died 5 Aug., 1886.
ALLEN, ROBERT. [Born in Ky. Appointed from Ill.]
Maj. Q. M. Vols., 9 Sept., 1847. Disbanded 15 Oct., 1848.
ALLEN, ROBT. H. [Born in Va. Appointed from the Army.]
Priv. and Corpl. Troop D, 8th Cav., from 8 June, 1893, to 3 Nov., 1895. 2nd Lieut. 14th Inf., 31 Oct., 1895. 1st Lieut., 11 Aug., 1898.
ALLEN, ROBT., Jr. [Born in Maine. Appointed from Iowa.]
2nd Lieut. 1st Cav., 5 Aug., 1861. 1st Lieut., 29 Dec., 1861. Died 27 July, 1862, of wounds received in Battle of Gaines' Mill, Va.
ALLEN, ROBT. T. P.* [Born in Md. Appointed from Md.]
Bvt. 2nd Lieut. 1st Art., 1 July, 1834. 2nd Lieut., 6 April, 1835. Resigned 31 July, 1836.
ALLEN, SAMUEL E.* [Born in Ind. Appointed from Ind.]
2nd Lieut. 5th Art., 11 June, 1881. 1st Lieut., 26 Oct., 1886. Capt., 2 March, 1899. Graduate of the Artillery School, 1892.
ALLEN, VANDERBILT.* [Born in N. Y. Appointed from N. Y.]
1st Lieut. Eng., 13 June, 1864. Resigned 28 Sept., 1865. Bvt. Capt. and Maj., 13 March, 1865, for distinguished and meritorious services and great gallantry in action.
ALLEN, WATERS. [Born in ——. Appointed from La.]
Asst. Dist. P. M., 9 Aug., 1814. Died 27 March, 1815.
ALLEN, WM. [Born in Penn. Appointed from Army.]
Priv. Co. F, 29 Penn. Vols., 15 Aug., 1864. Discharged 7 June, 1865. Priv. Co. G, 2nd Batt. 14th Inf., 3 Aug., 1865. Trans. to 23rd Inf., 21 Sept., 1866. Corpl., 1 Nov., 1866. 1st Sergt., 11 Nov., 1867. Discharged 3 Aug., 1868. Priv. Co. I, 23rd Inf., 26 Feb., 1870. Corpl., 20 June, 1870. Sergt., 8 Nov., 1870. 1st Sergt., 7 Dec., 1871. Com. Sergt., U. S. A., 26 Feb., 1870, to 15 Dec., 1873. 2nd Lieut. 12th Inf., 1 Oct., 1873. 1st Lieut., 15 Dec., 1880. Died 8 Jan., 1882.
ALLEN, WM. O. [Born in Va. Appointed from La.]
Capt. 24th Inf., 14 April, 1812. Trans. to 35th Inf., 15 June, 1814. Trans. 17 May, 1815, to Corps Art. Resigned 20 March, 1818.
ALLEN, WM. T.* [Born in Va. Appointed from Va.]
Bvt. 2nd Lieut. 2nd Drag., 1 July, 1845. Died 6 Dec., 1845.
ALLENSWORTH, ALLEN. [Born in Ky. Appointed from Ky.]
Chaplain 24th Inf., 1 April, 1886.
ALLEY, JOHN W.* [Born in Maine. Appointed from Maine.]
Bvt. 2nd Lieut. 3rd Inf., 1 July, 1850. 2nd Lieut., 5 March, 1851. 1st Lieut., 31 Dec., 1856. Capt., 14 May, 1861. Dismissed 20 Oct., 1863.
ALLIGOOD, CHAS. A. [Born in Penn. Appointed from Penn.]
Mil. Storekeeper Ord. Dept., 27 March, 1861. Mil. Storekeeper Q. M. Dept., 19 Sept., 1861. Vacated as Mil. Storekeeper Ord. Dept., 27 Sept., 1861. Capt., 28 July, 1866, (Act 28 July, 1866.) Died 31 March, 1890.
ALLISON, JAMES B. [Born in S. C. Appointed from S. C.]
2nd Lieut. 7th Inf., 10 Oct., 1898. 1st Lieut. 6th Inf., 29 Jan., 1900. Trans. to 7th Inf., 16 April, 1900.
ALLISON, JAMES N.* [Born in Ky. Appointed from Ohio.]
Priv. Co. C, 39th Ky. Vols., 10 Aug., 1863. Discharged 3 June, 1865. Cadet at Mil. Acad., 1 Sept., 1867. 2nd Lieut. 2nd Cav., 12 June, 1871. 1st Lieut., 20 Dec., 1880. Capt., 15 Aug., 1892. Trans. to Sub. Dept., 31 Jan., 1893. Maj. and C. S., 11 May, 1898. Lieut. Col. Chief C. S. Vols., 9 May, 1898, to 12 April, 1899.
ALLISON, JOHN S. [Born in Va. Appointed from Va.]
2nd Lieut. 5th Inf., 3 Jan., 1812. 1st Lieut., 6 July, 1812. Capt., 25 June, 1814. Trans. to 7th Inf., 17 May, 1815. Resigned 31 Dec., 1822.
ALLISON, THOS. S. [Born in Penn. Appointed from N. J.]
Addl. P. M. Vols., 1 June, 1861, to 17 May, 1865. Bvt. Lieut. Col. Vols., 13 March, 1865, for faithful and meritorious service during the war. Maj. P. M., 1 April, 1867. Died 1 Feb., 1871.
ALLSTON, BENJAMIN.* [Born in S. C. Appointed from S. C.]
Bvt. 2nd Lieut. 1st Drag., 1 July, 1853. 2nd Lieut., 22 Oct., 1854. 1st Lieut., 8 Sept., 1855. Resigned 20 June, 1857.

ALLSTON, JOSEPH W. [Born in S. C. Appointed from S. C.]
Ensign 18th Inf., 29 June, 1813. 3rd Lieut., 1 Oct., 1813. 2nd Lieut., 30 June, 1814. Trans. to 7th Inf., 17 May, 1815. 1st Lieut., 20 Dec., 1816. Resigned 31 Aug., 1817.

ALLSTON, ROBT. F. W.* [Born in S. C. Appointed from S. C.]
Bvt. 2nd Lieut. 3rd Art., 1 July, 1821. Resigned 1 Feb., 1822.

ALLSTON, SAML. R.* [Born in R. I. Appointed from Mass.]
Bvt. 2nd Lieut. 6th Inf., 1 July, 1825. 2nd Lieut. 4th Inf., 1 July, 1825. Ist. Lieut., 28 Nov., 1835. Resigned 31 Jan., 1836. Died 14 Feb., 1836.

ALLSWORTH, EDWARD. [Born in N. Y. Appointed from Ky.]
Priv. Co. H, 2nd Art., 1 July, 1842. Trans. to Co. A, 2 Feb., 1847. Discharged 1 July, 1847. Priv. Co. H, 2nd Art., 27 July, 1847. Discharged 19 Aug., 1848. Priv. Co. C, 1st Art., 3 Nov., 1848. Corpl., 1 April, 1849. Priv., 2 Aug., 1849. Discharged 3 Nov., 1853. Priv. Co. G, 38th Mass. Vols., 5 Jan., 1865. Discharged 3 Jan., 1865. Capt., 119th U. S. Col. Troops, 20 Feb., 1865. Mustered out 27 April, 1866. 2nd Lieut. 40th Inf., 28 July, 1866. Bvt. 1st Lieut., 2 March, 1867, for gallant and meritorious service during the war. Trans. to 25th Inf., 20 April, 1869. 1st Lieut., 25 Jan., 1872. Retired 28 June, 1878. Died 22 Dec., 1891.

ALLYN, ARTHUR W. [Born in Conn. Appointed from Conn.]
Priv. Co. A, 1st Conn. Vols., 25 April, 1861. Discharged 26 June, 1861. 1st Lieut. 16th Inf., 14 May, 1861. Bvt. Capt., 31 Dec., 1862, for gallant and meritorious service in the Battles of Shiloh and Murfreesboro', Tenn. Capt. 16th Inf., 24 June, 1864. Bvt. Maj., 13 March, 1865, for faithful and meritorious service during the war. Trans. to 34th Inf., 21 Sept., 1866. Trans. to to 16th Inf., 14 April, 1869. Resigned 30 April, 1880.

ALMAN, JUSTINIAN. [Born in Ohio. Appointed from Penn.]
1st Lieut. 5th Pa. Cav., 17 Sept., 1861. Capt., 21 Nov., 1862. Maj., 25 April, 1865. Mustered out 6 June, 1865. 2nd Lieut. 4th Cav., 23 Feb., 1866. 1st Lieut., 28 July, 1866. Drowned 17 March, 1868.

ALMSTEDT, HENRY. [Born in Germany. Appointed from Mo.]
1st Lieut. Adj. St. Louis Legion, 18 May, to 25 Aug., 1846. 2nd Lieut. of Inf., 5 March, 1847; 12th Inf., 9 April, 1847. Discharged 25 July, 1848. Col. 1st Mo. Res. Corps, 7 May, 1861. Mustered out 20 Aug., 1861. Col. 2nd Mo. Light Art., 19 Sept., 1861. Resigned 27 Aug., 1863. Addl. P. M. Vols., 20 April, 1864. Bvt. Lieut. Col. Vols., 1 May, 1867, for faithful and meritorious services in the Pay Dept. Mustered out 1 Jan., 1868. Died 24 Nov., 1884.

ALMY, ALLEN. [Born in R. I. Appointed from Mass.]
Corpl. and Sergt. Co. D. 23rd Mass. Vols., 18 Sept., 1861, to 15 March, 1864. 2nd Lieut. 58th Mass. Vols., 21 March, 1864. 1st Lieut., 23 Aug., 1864. Mustered out 14 July, 1865. 2nd Lieut. 16th Inf., 23 Feb., 1866. 1st Lieut., 23 Feb., 1866. Trans. to 34th Inf., 21 Sept., 1866. Trans. to 16th Inf., 14 April, 1869. Cashiered 20 April, 1870.

ALMY, JACOB.* [Born in Mass. Appointed from Mass.]
2nd Lieut. 5th Cav., 17 June, 1867. 1st Lieut., 15 April, 1869. Reg. Com., 22 Nov., 1869, to 15 July, 1870. Killed by an Indian in Arizona, 27 May, 1873.

ALMY, WM. E.* [Born in D. C. Appointed at Large.]
2nd Lieut. 3rd Inf., 13 June, 1879. Trans. to 5th Cav., 4 Sept., 1879. 1st Lieut., 28 Aug., 1888. Trans. to 4th Cav., 23 June, 1898. Capt. 10th Cav., 5 July, 1898. Trans. to 5th Cav., 14 March, 1899. Graduate of the Infantry and Cavalry School, 1885. Maj. A. A. G. Vols., 20 June, 1898, to 5 April, 1899.

ALOE, ALFRED. [Born in Mo. Appointed from Pa.]
Priv. and Corp. Troop E, 8th Cav., from 25 Jan., 1897, to 18 Sept., 1898. 2nd Lieut. 18th Inf., 15 Feb., 1899. 1st Lieut. 12th Inf., 26 Dec., 1899.

ALSTON, THOMAS L. [Born in Mass. Appointed from Army.]
Priv., Corpl. and Sergt. Co. E. 3rd Inf., 8 June, 1853, to 8 June, 1858. Priv. and Sergt. Gen. Ser. and Co. C, 2nd Batt. 12th Inf., 16 April, 1861, to 6 June, 1863. 2nd Lieut. 12th Inf., 1 June, 1863. 1st Lieut., 9 Sept., 1863. Trans. to 21st Inf., 21 Sept., 1866. Unassigned 11 April, 1869. Discharged 31 Dec., 1870. Bvt. Capt., 1 Aug., 1864, for gallant service at the Battle of Spottsylvania, and during the campaign before Richmond.

ALTSTAETTER, FREDERICK W.* [Born in Ohio. Appointed from Ohio.]
Addl. 2nd Lieut. of Eng., 11 June, 1897. 2nd Lieut., 5 July, 1898. 1st Lieut., 29 Sept., 1899.

ALVORD, BENJAMIN.* [Born in Vt. Appointed from Vt.]
Bvt. 2nd Lieut. 4th Inf., 1 July, 1833. 2nd Lieut., 21 July, 1835. 1st Lieut., 23 Sept., 1836. Bvt. Capt., 9 May, 1846, for gallant conduct in the Battles of Palo Alto and Resaca de la Palma. Capt. 4th Inf., 9 Sept., 1846. Bvt. Maj., 15 Aug., 1847, for gallant conduct in several affairs with Guerilleros at Paso Ovejas, Natural Bridge and Cerro Gordo, Mex. Maj. P. M., 22 June, 1854. Brig. Gen. Vols., 15 April, 1862. Bvt. Lieut. Col. and Col., 13 March, 1865, and Bvt. Brig. Gen., 9 April, 1865, for faithful and meritorious service during the war. Resigned commission of Brig. Gen. Vols., 8 Aug., 1865. Col. P. M. G., 1 Jan., 1872 (Act 4 June, 1872.) Brig. Gen., P. M. G., 4 Aug., 1876, to rank from 22 July, 1876 (Act 22 July, 1876). Retired June 8, 1880, at his own request, having served over 46 consecutive years. Died 16 Oct., 1884.

ALVORD, BENJAMIN.* [Born in Washington. Appointed from D. C.]
2nd Lieut. 20th Inf., 13 June, 1882. 1st Lieut. 22nd Inf., 7 Jan., 1891. Trans. to 20th Inf., 20 July, 1891. Capt., 26 April, 1898. Graduate of the Infantry and Cavalry School, 1887. Capt. A. A. G. Vols., 12 May, 1898. (Declined) Maj. Chief Ord. Officer Vols., 18 July, 1898, to 16 Jan., 1899. Maj. A. A. G. Vols., 18 Oct., 1899.

ALVORD, CHAS. B.* [Born in N. Y. Appointed from N. Y.]
Bvt. 2nd Lieut. 8th Inf., 1 July, 1849. 2nd Lieut. 1st Inf., 26 Oct., 1850. Resigned 31 July, 1852.

ALVORD, HENRY E. [Born in Mass. Appointed from Mass.]
1st Sergt. Co. B. 7th squadron R. I. Cav., 24 June, 1862. Mustered out 2 Oct., 1862. 2nd Lieut. 2nd Mass. Cav., 21 Nov., 1862. 1st Lieut., 25 Jan., 1864. Capt.,

11 Dec., 1864. Mustered out 5 Aug., 1865. 1st Lieut. 10th Cav., 28 July, 1866. Reg. Adj., 1 June, to 31 July, 1867. Capt., 31 July, 1867. Trans. to unass'd, 5 Jan., 1870. Trans. to 9th Cav., 1 Jan., 1871. Resigned 9 Dec., 1871.

AMELUNG, FERDINAND L. [Born in Germany. Appointed from La.]
Capt. 44th Inf., 11 March, 1814. Trans. to 1st Inf., 17 May, 1815. Resigned 7 Jan., 1819.

AMES, ADELBERT.* [Born in Maine. Appointed from Maine.]
2nd Lieut. 2nd Art., 6 May, 1861. 1st Lieut. 5th Art., 14 May, 1861. Col. 20th Me. Vols., Aug., 1862. Brig. Gen. Vols., 20 May, 1863. Mustered out of Vol. service, 30 April, 1866. Capt., 11 June, 1864. Lieut. Col. 24th Inf., 28 July, 1866. Resigned 23 Feb., 1870. Bvt. Maj., 21 July, 1861, for gallant and meritorious service at the Battle of Bull Run, Va. Bvt. Lieut. Col., 1 July, 1862, for gallant and meritorious service at the Battle of Malvern Hill, Va. Bvt. Col., 1 July, 1863, for gallant and meritorious service at the Battle of Gettysburg, Penn. Bvt. Brig. Gen., 13 March, 1865, for gallant and meritorious service at the capture of Fort Fisher, N. C. Bvt. Maj. Gen., 13 March, 1865, for gallant and meritorious service in the field during the war.

AMES, BUTLER.* [Born in Mass. Appointed from Mass.]
2nd Lieut. 11th Inf., 12 June, 1894. Resigned 30 Sept., 1894.

AMES, EDWIN R. [Born in Ind. Appointed from Ind.]
Corpl. Co. B, 11th Ind. Vols., 22 April, 1861. Mustered out 4 Aug., 1861. 2nd Lieut. 7th Inf., 6 March, 1862. 1st Lieut., 28 Aug., 1863. Capt., 7 Oct., 1864. Unassigned 10 May, 1869. Ass'd to 6th Inf., 1 Jan., 1871. Resigned 31 Oct., 1876. 2nd Lieut. 6th Inf., 1 March, 1877. Resigned 20 April, 1877.

AMES, JOHN W. [Born in Mass. Appointed from Mass.]
Capt. 11th Inf., 14 May, 1861. Col. 6th U. S. Col. Inf., 28 Sept., 1863. Hon. mustered out of Vol. service 20 Sept., 1865. Resigned 4 Oct., 1866. Bvt. Maj., 27 June, 1862, for gallant and meritorious service at the Battle of Gaines Mills, Va. Bvt. Lieut. Col., 13 March, 1865, for gallant and meritorious service at the Battle of Gettysburg, Penn.

AMES, LUTHER S. [Born in N. Y. Appointed from Ill.]
Priv. Co. A, 64th Ill. Vols., 25 Sept., 1861. Q. M. Sergt., 1 Jan., 1862. Sergt. Maj., 1 Sept., 1862. 1st Lieut. 64th Ill. Vols., 10 Dec., 1863. Capt., 17 Sept., 1864. Mustered out 11 July, 1865. 2nd Lieut. 16th Inf., 11 May, 1866. Trans. to 2nd Inf., 17 April, 1869. 1st Lieut., 18 March, 1872. Capt., 27 Feb., 1887. Retired for disability 26 July, 1893.

AMES, ROBERT F. [Born in R. I. Appointed from N. Y.]
Cadet at Mil. Acad., 1 Sept., to 23 Dec., 1874. 2nd Lieut. 8th Inf., 1 Sept., 1879. 1st Lieut., 20 May, 1886. Capt. 8th Inf., 10 March, 1896.

AMES, THALES L.* [Born in Wis. Appointed from Wis.]
2nd Lieut. 3d Art., 12 June, 1895. 1st Lieut. Ord., 21 Nov., 1898.

AMET, ALBERT V. [Born in Mo. Appointed from Army.]
Priv. Co. F, 8th Ill. Cav., 2 Sept., 1861. Discharged 29 Jan., 1863. Priv. Co. E, and Hosp. Steward 17th Ill. Cav., 15 Dec., 1863. 1st Lieut., 7 July, 1865. Mustered out 18 Dec., 1865. Hosp. Steward U. S. A., 30 Sept., 1867, to 27 July, 1872. 2nd Lieut. 7th Inf., 27 July, 1872. Died 16 Dec., 1874.

AMICK, MYRON J. [Born in Ill. Appointed from Ill.]
Priv., Corpl. and Sergt. Co. K, 15th Ill. Cav., 23 Sept., 1861. Mustered out 15 July, 1865. 2nd Lieut. 10th Cav., 28 July, 1866. 1st Lieut., 31 July, 1867. Discharged 2 Dec., 1870.

AMMEN, JACOB.* [Born in Va. Appointed from Ohio.]
Bvt. 2nd Lieut. 1st Art., 1 July, 1831. 2nd Lieut., 1 July, 1831. 1st Lieut., 3 May, 1836. Resigned 30 Nov., 1837. Capt. 12th Ohio Vols., 18 April, 1861. Lieut. Col., 2 May, 1861. Col. 24th Ohio Vols., 22 June, 1861. Brig. Gen. Vols., 16 July, 1862. Resigned 4 Jan, 1865.

AMORY, COPLEY. [Born in Mass. Appointed from Mass.]
2nd Lieut. 4th Cav., 5 Aug., 1861. 1st Lieut., 17 Oct., 1862. Resigned 15 Dec., 1863.

AMORY, THOMAS J. C.* [Born in Mass. Appointed from Mass.]
Bvt. 2nd Lieut. 7th Inf., 1 July, 1851. 2nd Lieut., 24 Aug., 1851. 1st Lieut., 16 Oct., 1855. Capt., 7 May, 1861. Col. 17th Mass. Inf., 2 Sept., 1861. Bvt. Brig. Gen. Vols., 1 Oct., 1864, for gallant and meritorious services during the war. Maj. 8th Inf., 19 Sept., 1864. Died 8 Oct., 1864.

ANDERSON, ALLEN L.* [Born in Ohio. Appointed from Ohio.]
Bvt. 2nd Lieut. 2nd Inf., 1 July, 1859. 2nd Lieut. 5th Inf., 5 Sept., 1859. 1st Lieut., 14 May, 1861. Reg. Adj., 31 Dec., 1861, to 3 Dec., 1862. Capt., 3 Dec., 1862. Col. 8th Cal. Vols., 7 March, 1865. Mustered out of Vol. Service 10 Nov., 1865. Capt., 3 Dec., 1862. Resigned 7 Jan., 1867. Bvt. Maj., 21 Feb., 1862, for gallant and meritorious service at the Battle of Valverde, N. M. Bvt. Lieut. Col., 13 March, 1865, for gallant and meritorious services during the war, and Brig. Gen. Vols., 13 March, 1865, for faithful and meritorious services.

ANDERSON, ALVORD VAN F.* [Born in N. Y. Appointed from the Army.]
Priv. and Corpl. Troop G, 6th Cav., from 28 May, 1891, to 27 Aug., 1894. Priv. and Corpl. Troop B, 6th Cav., from 5 Nov., 1894, to 26 Feb., 1896. 2nd Lieut. 6th Cav., 5 Feb., 1896. 1st Lieut., 9 June, 1899.

ANDERSON, CALVIN A. [Born in Ohio. Appointed from Ind.]
Priv. Co. B, 7th Inf., 25 April, 1857, to 25 April, 1862. Priv., Sergt. and 1st Sergt. Co. C, 74th Ind. Vols., 12 Dec., 1862, to 24 July, 1865. 2nd Lieut. 15th Inf., 23 Feb., 1866. Trans. to 24th Inf., 21 Sept., 1866. Resigned 24 Jan., 1867.

ANDERSON, CHAS. D. [Born in S. C. Appointed from Texas.]
Cadet at Mil. Acad., 1 Sept., 1846, to 13 Nov., 1848. 2nd Lieut. 4th Art., 27 June, 1856. 1st Lieut., 6 July, 1859. Resigned 1 April, 1861.

ANDERSON, CHARLES L. G. [Born in Md. Appointed from Md.]
Asst. Surg., 5 Nov., 1886. Resigned 1 July, 1888.

ANDERSON, EDWARD.* [Born in Va. Appointed from Va.]
2nd Lieut. 15th Inf., 11 June, 1888. Trans. to 1st Cav., 11 Feb., 1889. 1st Lieut. 7th

Cav., 23 May, 1896. Honor graduate of the Infantry and Cavalry School, 1897. Capt. A. A. G. Vols., 30 June to 31 Dec., 1898.

ANDERSON, EDWARD D.* [Born in Tenn., Appointed from Tenn.]
2nd Lieut. 4th Cav., 12 June, 1891. 1st Lieut. 10th Cav., 6 Nov., 1897. Graduate of the Infantry and Cavalry School, 1895. Maj. 26th U. S. Vols., 5 July, 1899.

ANDERSON, GEORGE. [Born in Ireland. Appointed from Army.]
Priv., Corpl. and Sergt. Co. K, and Sergt. Maj. 6th Inf., 1 April, 1858, to 4 Oct., 1862. 2nd Lieut. 6th Inf., 18 July, 1862. Dropped 18 Sept., 1863.

ANDERSON, GEORGE B.* [Born in N. C. Appointed from N. C.]
Bvt. 2nd Lieut. 2nd Drag., 1 July, 1852. 2nd Lieut., 21 March, 1854. 1st Lieut., 13 Dec., 1855. Reg. Adj., 27 May, to 8 Sept., 1857, and 8 Aug., 1858, to 24 June, 1859. Resigned 25 April, 1861.

ANDERSON, GEORGE L.* [Born in Wis. Appointed from Wis.]
2nd Lieut. 4th Art., 17 June, 1874. 1st Lieut., 11 Nov., 1881. Capt. 7th Art., 8 March, 1898. Graduate of the Artillery School, 1876.

ANDERSON, GEORGE S.* [Born in N. J. Appointed from N. J.]
2nd Lieut. 6th Cav., 12 June, 1871. 1st Lieut., 20 Sept., 1874. Capt., 20 March, 1885. Maj 7th Cav., 10 Nov., 1898. Trans. to 6th Cav., 5 Jan., 1899. Maj. I. G. Vols., 12 May, 1898. (Declined). Col. 38th U. S. Vol. Inf., 17 August., 1899.

ANDERSON, GEORGE T. [Born in Ga. Appointed from Ga.]
2nd Lieut. Md. Co. Ga. Mounted Vols., 27 May, 1847. Discharged 10 July, 1848. Capt. 1st Cav., 3 March, 1855. Resigned 11 June, 1858.

ANDERSON, HARRY R. [Born in Ohio. Appointed from Ohio.]
Cadet at Mil. Acad., 1 July, 1864, to 18 Jan., 1865. Capt. 6th U. S. Vols., 28 April, 1865. Mustered out 12 June, 1866. 2nd Lieut. 6th Inf., 7 March, 1867. Unass'd 22 April, 1869. Ass'd to 4th Art., 14 July, 1869. 1st Lieut., 29 April, 1873. Capt., 6 June, 1896. Graduate of the Artillery School, 1875.

ANDERSON, JAMES. [Born in Penn. Appointed from Tenn.]
2nd Lieut. 3rd Drag., 9 Sept., 1847. Disbanded 31 July, 1848.

ANDERSON, JAMES J.* [Born in Ky. Appointed from Ky.]
Bvt. 2nd Lieut. 6th Inf., 1 July, 1825. 2nd Lieut. 4th Inf., 1 July, 1825. Resigned 1 July, 1830. Died 1 Oct., 1845.

ANDERSON, JAMES T. [Born in Germany. Appointed from Ohio.]
2nd Lieut. 16th Inf., 30 Oct., 1884. 1st Lieut. 25th Inf., 1 Nov., 1891. Graduate of the Infantry and Cavalry School, 1893. Retired for disability, 3 Jan., 1895.

ANDERSON, JAMES W.* Born in Va. Appointed from Va.]
Bvt. 2nd Lieut. 2nd Inf., 1 July, 1833. 2nd Lieut., 3 July, 1836. 1st Lieut., 4 Nov., 1838. Reg. Adj., 15 May, 1840, to 22 Sept., 1845. Capt., 16 Feb., 1847. Died 22 Aug., 1847, of wounds received at Churubusco, Mexico. Bvt. Capt., 23 Aug., 1841, for gallant and successful conduct in war against Florida Indians.

ANDERSON, JOHN. [Born in Mass. Appointed from Mass.]
Priv. Co. E, 1st Mich. Sharpshooters, 5 Jan., 1863. Discharged 12 Feb., 1864. 2nd Lieut. 57th Mass. Vols., 12 March, 1864. Discharged 21 Jan., 1865. Bvt. 1st Lieut. and Capt. Vols., 13 March, 1865, for gallant and meritorious services in the Battles before Petersburg, Va. 2nd Lieut. Vet. Res. Corps, 25 March, 1865. Mustered out 30 June, 1866. 2nd Lieut. 25th Inf., 10 Aug., 1867. Trans. to 18th Inf., 26 April, 1869. 1st Lieut., 17 Oct., 1878. Capt., 21 June, 1890. Retired for disability 6 June, 1894.

ANDERSON, JOHN.* [Born in Vt. Appointed from Vt.]
2nd Lieut. Art, 9 Dec., 1807. Resigned 1 May, 1811. 1st Lieut. 19th Inf., 6 July, 1812. Capt., 16 March, 1813. Bvt. Maj. Top. Eng., 12 April, 1813. Died 14 Sept., 1834. Bvt. Lieut. Col., 12 April, 1823, for ten years' faithful service in one grade.

ANDERSON, JOSEPH R.* [Born in Va. Appointed from Va.]
2nd Lieut. 3rd Art., 1 July, 1836. Trans. to Eng., 1 July, 1837, as Bvt. 2nd Lieut. to rank from 1 July, 1836. Resigned 30 Sept., 1837.

ANDERSON, MARCELLUS M. [Born in Va. Appointed from Va.]
2nd Lieut. 16th Inf., 9 April, 1847. Disbanded 7 Aug., 1848.

ANDERSON, PIERCE B. [Born in Tenn. Appointed from Tenn.]
Cadet at Mil. Acad., 1 July, 1823, to 31 Dec., 1825. Capt. of Inf., 5 March, 1847; 14th Inf., 9 April, 1847. Disbanded 26 July, 1848.

ANDERSON, RICHARD H.* [Born in S. C. Appointed from S. C.]
Bvt. 2nd Lieut. 1st Drag., 1 July, 1842. 2nd Lieut. 2nd Drag., 16 July, 1844. 1st Lieut., 13 July, 1848. Capt., 3 March, 1855. Resigned 3 March, 1861. Bvt. 1st Lieut., 20 Aug., 1847, for gallant and meritorious service at San Augustin, Mexico.

ANDERSON, ROBERT.* [Born in Ky. Appointed from Ky.]
Bvt. 2nd Lieut. 2nd Art., 1 July, 1825. 2nd Lieut. 3rd Art., 1 July, 1825. 1st Lieut., 30 June, 1833. (Bvt. Capt. A. A. G., 7 July, 1838, to 30 Nov., 1841.) Capt. 3rd Art., 23 Oct., 1841. Maj. 1st Art., 5 Oct., 1857. Brig. Gen., 15 May, 1861. Retired 27 Oct., 1863. Died 27 Oct., 1871. Bvt. Capt., 2 April, 1838, for gallantry and successful conduct in the war against Florida Indians. Bvt. Maj., 8 Sept., 1847, for gallant and meritorious conduct in the Battle of Molino del Rey, Mexico. Bvt. Maj. Gen., for gallant and meritorious service in the Harbor of Charleston, S. C.

ANDERSON, ROBERT H. [Born in Ga. Appointed from Ga.]
2nd Lieut. 9th Inf., 30 Oct., 1884. 1st Lieut., 28 Sept., 1889. Capt., 26 April, 1898.

ANDERSON, ROBERT H.* [Born in Ga. Appointed from Ga.]
Bvt. 2nd Lieut., 7th Inf., 1 July, 1857. 2nd Lieut. 9th Inf., 29 Dec., 1857. Resigned 17 May, 1861.

ANDERSON, SAMUEL H. [Born in Tenn. Appointed from Tenn.]
Capt. 2nd Drag., 8 June, 1836. Resigned 1 Oct., 1837.

ANDERSON, SAMUEL S.* [Born in Va. Appointed from Va.]
Bvt. 2nd Lieut. 2nd Art., 1 July, 1841. 2nd Lieut., 4 Jan., 1842. 1st Lieut., 3 March, 1847. Capt., 8 March, 1855. Resigned 27 April, 1861. Bvt. Capt., 8 Sept., 1847, for gallant and meritorious conduct at Molino del Rey. Bvt. Maj., 13 Sept., 1847, for gallant conduct at Chapultepec.

ANDERSON, THOS. M. [Born in Ohio. Appointed from Ohio.]
Priv. Co. A, 6th Ohio Vols., 20 April, 1861. Discharged 15 May, 1861. 2nd Lieut.

2nd Cav., 7 May, 1861. Capt. 12th Inf., 14 May, 1861. Bvt. Maj., 1 Aug., 1864, for gallant service in the Battle of the Wilderness. Bvt. Lieut. Col., 1 Aug., 1864, for gallant service in the Battle of Spottsylvania. Trans. to 21st Inf., 21 Sept., 1866. Maj., 26 March, 1868. Unassigned, 15 March, 1869. Ass'd to 10th Inf., 24 June, 1869. Lieut. Col. 9th Inf., 20 March, 1879. Col. 14th Inf., 6 Sept., 1886. Brig. Gen., 31 March, 1899. Brig. Gen. Vols., 4 May, 1898. Maj. Gen. Vols., 13 Aug., 1898, to 12 June, 1899. Retired Jan. 21, 1900, by operation of law.

ANDERSON, THOMAS M., Jr. [Born in Texas. Appointed from the Army.]
Priv. Corpl. and Sergt. Troop G, 4th Cav., 28 Aug., 1894, to 27 June, 1897. 2nd Lieut. 13th Inf., 8 June, 1897. 1st Lieut., 2 March, 1899.

ANDERSON, WM. [Born in ——. Appointed from Penn.]
3rd Lieut. 13th Inf., 13 May, 1813. 2nd Lieut., 15 Aug., 1813. 1st Lieut., 1 Oct., 1814. Trans. to Ord., 17 May, 1815. Dropped 1 Sept., 1818.

ANDERSON, WM. P. [Born in Penn. Appointed from Penn.]
2nd Lieut. 5th Inf., 5 Aug., 1861. 1st Lieut., 25 Sept., 1861. Dismissed 21 Oct. 1863.

ANDERSON, WM. T. [Born in Texas. Appointed from Ohio.]
Chaplain 10th Cav., 16 Aug., 1897.

ANDERSON, WM. W. [Born in S. C. Appointed from S. C.]
Asst. Surg., 29 June, 1849. Resigned 20 April, 1861.

ANDREWS, ALBERT H. [Born in Mass. Appointed from Mass.]
1st Lieut. 19th Inf., 14 May, 1861. Capt., 30 Jan., 1863. Trans. to 28th Inf., 21 Sept., 1866. Trans. to 19th Inf., 31 March, 1869. Unassigned 24 June, 1870. Mustered out 1 Jan., 1871. Bvt. Capt., 7 April, 1862, for gallant and meritorious service at the Battle of Shiloh, Tenn. Bvt. Maj., 31 Dec., 1862, for gallant and meritorious service at the Battle of Murfreesboro', Tenn.

ANDREWS, AVERY D.* [Born in N. Y. Appointed from N. Y.]
2nd Lieut. 5th Art., 1 July, 1886. 1st Lieut. 4th Art., 28 Nov., 1892. Trans. to 5th Art., 5 Dec., 1892. Resigned 2 Nov., 1893.

ANDREWS, CHRISTOPHER. Born in Ireland. Appointed from D. C.]
Maj. P. M., 24 Oct., 1836. Resigned 31 Dec., 1849.

ANDREWS, DAVID S. [Born in ——. Appointed from Penn.]
3rd Lieut. Corps Art., 20 April, 1814. 2nd Lieut., 22 July, 1814. 1st Lieut., 20 April, 1818. Disbanded 1 June, 1821.

ANDREWS, GEORGE.* [Born in D. C. Appointed from D. C.]
2nd Lieut. 6th Inf., 1 July, 1823. 1st Lieut., 11 Feb., 1827. Capt., 31 Dec., 1836. Maj. 7th Inf., 14 Aug., 1848. Lieut. Col. 6th Inf., 18 Oct., 1855. Retired 15 Feb., 1862. Died 13 Nov., 1873. Bvt. Maj., 25 Dec., 1837, for gallant and good conduct in war against Florida Indians.

ANDREWS, GEORGE.* [Born in R. I. Appointed from Ariz.]
2nd Lieut. 25th Inf., 15 June, 1876. 1st Lieut., 19 Feb., 1883. Reg. Adj., 17 Aug., 1886. Capt., 16 Sept., 1892. Maj. A. A. G., 26 Feb., 1898.

ANDREWS, GEORGE L.* [Born in Mass. Appointed from Mass.]
Bvt. 2nd Lieut. Eng., 1 July, 1851. 2nd Lieut., 2 Feb., 1854. Resigned 1 Sept., 1855. Lieut. Col. 2nd Mass. Vols., 25 May, 1861. Col., 13 June, 1862. Brig. Gen. Vols., 10 Nov., 1862. Bvt. Maj. Gen. Vols., March 26, 1865, for faithful and meritorious services during the campaign against the city of Mobile and its defences. Mustered out of Vol. service, 24 Aug., 1865. Appointed Professor of French in Mil. Acad., 28 Feb., 1871. Retired by op. of law 31 Aug., 1892. Died 4 April, 1899.

ANDREWS, GEORGE L. [Born in R. I. Appointed from Mo.]
Lieut. Col. 1st Mo. Vols., 24 April, 1861. Lieut. Col. 1st Mo. Light Art., 1 Sept., 1861. Discharged 5 Sept., 1861. Maj. 17th Inf., 14 May, 1861. Bvt. Lieut. Col., 30 Aug., 1862, for gallant and meritorious services in the Battle of Bull Run (2nd), Va. Bvt. Col., 3 May, 1863, for gallant and meritorious services in the Battle of Chancellorsville, Va. Lieut. Col. 13th Inf., 14 Oct., 1864. Unassigned, 15 March, 1869. Ass'd to 25th Inf., 15 Dec., 1870. Col., 1 Jan., 1871. Retired by op. of law 22 April, 1892.

ANDREWS, GEORGE P.* [Born in Conn. Appointed from N. C.]
Bvt. 2nd Lieut. 3rd Art., 1 July, 1845. 2nd Lieut., 16 Feb., 1847. 1st Lieut., 8 Sept., 1847. R. Q. M., 4 June, 1847, to 24 Oct., 1848. Bvt. Capt., 8 Sept., 1847, for gallant and meritorious conduct in the Battle of Molino del Rey. Bvt. Maj., 13 Sept., 1847, for gallant conduct at Chapultepec. Capt. 3rd Art., 12 Oct., 1858. Maj. 5th Art., 28 July, 1866. Lieut. Col. 4th Art., 1 July, 1880. Trans. to 1st Art., 27 Oct., 1881. Col. 3rd Art., 3 Nov., 1882. Trans. to 1st Art., 4 Nov., 1882. Retired by op. of law 22 March, 1885. Died 2 July, 1887.

ANDREWS, GEORGE T. [Born in D. C. Appointed from S. C.]
2nd Lieut. 3rd Art., 8 March, 1847. 1st Lieut., 19th Oct., 1847. Resigned 31 Dec., 1856.

ANDREWS, HENRY M.* [Born in N. Y. Appointed from N. Y.]
2nd Lieut. 1st. Art., 17 June, 1874. Ist. Lieut., 6 July, 1878. Capt., 8 March, 1898. Honor graduate of the Artillery School, 1876.

ANDREWS, JAMES M., Jr.* [Born in N. Y. Appointed from N. Y.]
Addl. 2nd Lieut. 5th Cav., 14 June, 1890. 2nd Lieut., 1st Cav., 20th Sept., 1890. Resigned 9 Nov., 1892.

ANDREWS, JOHN N.* [Born in Del. Appointed from Del.]
Bvt. 2nd Lieut. 4th Inf., 1 July, 1860. 2nd Lieut. 8th Inf., 28 Jan., 1861. 1st Lieut., 14 May, 1861. Bvt. Capt., 9 Aug., 1862, for gallant and meritorious service in the Battle of Cedar Mountain, Va. Capt. 8th Inf., 21 June, 1864. Bvt. Maj., 29 Nov., 1864, for gallant and meritorious services in the Battle of Franklin, Tenn. Bvt. Lieut. Col., 13 March, 1865, for gallant and meritorious services during the war. Maj. 21 Inf., 19 April, 1886. Lieut. Col. 25th Inf., 20 April, 1891. Col. 12th Inf., 1 Oct., 1895. Retired (over 30 years' service) 1 April, 1899. Brig. Gen. Vols., 3 June, 1898, to 24 Feb., 1899.

ANDREWS, LINCOLN C.* [Born in Minn. Appointed from N. Y.]
2nd Lieut. 3rd Cav., 12 June, 1893. 1st Lieut., 2 March, 1899. Maj. 43d U. S. Vols., 17 Aug., 1899.

**ANDREWS, PHINEHAS.** [Born in Conn. Appointed from the Army.]
Priv. and Sergt. 25th Inf., Oct., 1813, to July, 1814. 2nd Lieut. 25th Inf., 2 July, 1814. Trans. to 6th Inf., 17 May, 1815. Resigned 31 Oct., 1815. 2nd Lieut. 5th Inf., 27 Oct., 1820. 1st Lieut., 27 Sept., 1824. Died 21 Oct., 1826.

**ANDREWS, TIMOTHY P.** [Born in Ireland. Appointed from D. C.]
P. M., 22 May, 1822. (Col. Voltigeurs, 9 April, 1847, to 20 July, 1848.) Lieut. Col. Dep. P. M. G., 17 Dec., 1851. Col. P. M. G., 6 Sept., 1862. Retired 29 Nov., 1864. Died 11 March, 1868. Bvt. Brig. Gen., 13 Sept., 1847, for gallant and meritorious conduct in the Battle of Chapultepec.

**ANDREWS, WM. C. C.** [Born in Ohio. Appointed from Ohio.]
Asst. Surg., 5 Aug., 1876. Drowned, 19 April, 1877.

**ANDREWS, WM. H.** [Born in Mass. Appointed from N. Y.]
Capt. 108th N. Y. Vols., 18 Aug., 1862. Bvt. Maj. Vols., 13 March, 1865, for meritorious services during the war. Mustered out 28 May, 1865. Capt. 5th U. S. Vet. Vols., 11 Sept., 1865. Mustered out 1 May, 1866. 2nd Lieut. and 1st Lieut. 12th Inf., 23 Feb., 1866. Trans. to 30th Inf., 21 Sept., 1866. Unassigned, March 23, 1869. Ass'd to 3rd Cav., 15 Dec., 1870. Capt., 31 May, 1875. Retired for disability 30 Nov., 1879. Died 21 June, 1880.

**ANDREWS, WM. R.** [Born in Conn. Appointed from N. Y.]
Capt. of Inf., 18 March, 1847; 10th Inf., 9 April, 1847. Disbanded 16 Aug., 1848. Mil. Storekeeper Ord. Dept., 19 May, 1855. Died 2 Aug., 1858.

**ANDRUS, EDWIN P.*** [Born in N. Y. Appointed from N. Y.]
2nd Lieut. 5th Cav., 16 June, 1875. 1st Lieut., 29 March, 1883. Capt. 11 Feb., 1893.

**ANDRUS, FRANK B.*** [Born in Mich. Appointed from Ind.]
2nd Lieut. 4th Inf., 11 June, 1881. 1st Lieut., 2nd Inf., 12 Dec., 1890. Trans. to 4th Inf., 20 July, 1891. Capt., 26 April, 1898. Graduate of Infantry and Cavalry School, 1885.

**ANDRUSS, E. VAN ARSDALE.*** [Born in N. J. Appointed from N. J.]
2nd Lieut. 1st Art., 13 June, 1864. Bvt. 1st Lieut., 2 April, 1865, for gallant and meritorious service in the capture of Petersburg, Va. Bvt. Capt., 9 April, 1865, for gallant and meritorious service in the campaign ending with the surrender of the Rebel Army of Northern Virginia. 1st Lieut. 2nd Art., 10 May, 1865. Capt., 2 Jan., 1881. Graduate of the Artillery School, 1876. Maj. 4th Art., 10 Feb., 1898.

**ANGLUM, DANIEL F.** [Born in Mass. Appointed from the Army.]
Priv., Corpl., Sergt. and 1st Sergt., Co. C, 12th Inf., from 11 June, 1874, to 30 April, 1882. 2nd Lieut. 12th Inf., 27 March, 1882. 1st Lieut. 16th Inf., 1 Jan., 1891. Trans. to 12th Inf., 20 July, 1891. Capt. 26 April, 1898. Graduate of the Infantry and Cavalry School, 1885.

**ANSART, FELIX.** [Born in ——. Appointed from Mass.]
2nd Lieut. 3rd Art., 2 July, 1812. 1st Lieut., 1 Oct., 1813. Trans. to Corps Art., 12 May, 1814. Capt., 28 Nov., 1819. Trans. to 3rd Art., 1 June, 1821. Resigned 31 Aug., 1836. Bvt. Maj., 28 Nov., 1829, for ten years faithful service in one grade.

**ANSELL, SAMUEL T.*** [Born in N. C. Appointed from N. C.]
2nd Lieut. 11th Inf., 15 Feb., 1899.

**ANSON, WM. H. J.** [Born in Va. Appointed from Va.]
Maj. Surg., 2 Feb., 1847. Disbanded 3 Aug., 1848.

**ANTHONY, CHAS.** [Born in R. I. Appointed from N. Y.]
3rd Lieut. 3rd Art., 14 May, 1813. 2nd Lieut., 20 May, 1813. Trans. to Corps Art., 12 May, 1814. 1st Lieut., 28 Sept., 1817. Died 2 July, 1818.

**ANTHONY, JOSEPH B.** [Born in Mo. Appointed from Ark.]
Capt. of Inf., 6 March, 1847; 12th Inf., 9 April, 1847. Disbanded 20 July, 1848.

**APPEL, AARON H.** [Born in Penn. Appointed from Penn.]
Asst. Surg., 3 June, 1879. Capt. Asst. Surg., 3 June, 1884. Maj. Surg., 3 May, 1897.

**APPEL, DANIEL M.** [Born in Penn. Appointed from Penn.]
1st Lieut. Asst. Surg., 5 Aug., 1876. Capt. Asst. Surg., 5 Aug., 1881. Maj. Surg., 15 Nov., 1895.

**APPLETON, EDWARD L.** [Born in Maine. Appointed from Maine.]
2nd Lieut. 1st Art., 5 Aug., 1861. 1st Lieut., 5 Aug., 1861. Resigned 10 May, 1865.

**APPLETON, JOHN S.** [Born in Del. Appointed from Del.]
Priv. 1st Del. Inf., 2 Sept., 1861. Mustered out 30 Sept., 1864. 2nd Lieut. 31st U. S. Col Inf., 16 Oct., 1864. Resigned 30 April, 1865. 2nd Lieut. 5th U. S. Vet. Vols., 14 Sept., 1865. Mustered out 18 Feb., 1866. 2nd Lieut. 19th Inf., 19 April, 1866. 1st Lieut., 18 Nov., 1867. Unass'd 31 March, 1869. Mustered out 1 Jan., 1871.

**APPLETON, WM. E.** [Born in Del. Appointed from Del.]
2nd Lieut. 9th Inf., 5 Aug., 1861. 1st Lieut., 31 Dec., 1862. Capt., 24 May, 1864. Wholly retired 19 Oct., 1869.

**APPLEWHITE, HUGH LA F.*** [Born in Miss. Appointed from Miss.]
Addl. 2nd Lieut. 15th Inf., 11 June, 1897. 2nd Lieut. 22nd Inf., 26 Jan., 1898. Trans. to 6th Art., 8 March, 1898. 1st Lieut. 2nd Art., 19 Sept., 1899.

**APPLING, DANIEL.** [Born in Ga. Appointed from Ga.]
2nd Lieut. Rifles, 3 May, 1808. 1st Lieut., 1 July, 1809. Capt., 1 April, 1812. Maj. 1st Rifles, 15 April, 1814. Trans. to 7th Inf., 17 May, 1815. Resigned 1 June, 1816. Bvt. Lieut. Col., 30 May, 1814, for gallant conduct at Sandy Creek, N. Y. Bvt. Col., 11 Sept., 1814, for distinguished service at Plattsburg.

**ARBUCKLE, MATTHEW.** [Born in Va. Appointed from Va.]
Ensign 3rd Inf., 3 March, 1799. 1st Lieut., 24 Oct., 1799. Trans. to 2nd Inf., 1 April, 1802. Capt., 20 June, 1806. Maj. 3rd Inf., 15 Aug., 1812. Lieut. Col. 3rd Inf., 9 March, 1814. Col. 7th Inf., 16 March, 1820. Died 11 June, 1851. Bvt. Brig. Gen., 10 March, 1830, for ten years' faithful service in one grade.

**ARCHER, JAMES.** [Born in N. Y. Appointed from N. Y.]
3rd Lieut. 41st Inf., 17 July, 1814. 2nd Lieut., 1 Oct., 1814. Disbanded 15 June, 1815. Reinstated 2 Dec., 1815, in Corps Art. Resigned 1 Oct., 1816.

**ARCHER, JAMES J.** [Born in Md. Appointed from Md.]
Capt. Inf., 23 Feb., 1847; Voltigeurs, 9 April, 1847. Disbanded 31 Aug., 1848. Capt. 9th Inf., 3 March, 1855. Resigned 14 May, 1861. Bvt. Maj., 13 Sept., 1847, for gallant and meritorious conduct in the Battle of Chapultepec.

ARCHER, JAMES P. [Born in Md. Appointed from Md.]
2nd Lieut. Inf., 10 March, 1847; 9th Inf., 9 April, 1847. Disbanded 19 Aug., 1848.

ARCHER, JOHN.* [Born in Md. Appointed from Md.]
Bvt. 2nd Lieut. 7th Inf., 1 July, 1826. 2nd Lieut. 3rd Inf., 1 July, 1826. 1st Lieut., 31 Oct., 1833. Resigned 31 March, 1834.

ARCHER, ROBT. [Born in Va. Appointed from Va.]
Hosp. Surg. Mate, 13 May, 1814. Post. Surg., 18 April, 1818. Asst. Surg., 1 June, 1821. Maj. Surg., 9 May, 1825. Resigned 5 Aug., 1826. Asst. Surg., 5 Aug., 1826. Resigned 29 Feb., 1840. Died 19 May, 1877.

ARCHER, ROBT. H.* [Born in Md. Appointed from Md.]
Bvt. 2nd Lieut. 3rd Inf., 1 July, 1832. Trans. to 4th Art., 13 Nov., 1833. 2nd Lieut., 31 Dec., 1835. Resigned 31 Dec., 1837. 2nd Lieut. Voltigeurs, 9 April, 1847. Disbanded 31 Aug., 1848. Died 11 Aug., 1875.

ARCHER, SAML. [Born in Ohio. Appointed from Army.]
Corpl. and Sergt. Co. H, 5th Inf., 5 May, 1845, to 28 June, 1848. Bvt. 2nd Lieut. 5th Inf., 28 June, 1848. 2nd Lieut., 30 Jan., 1849. 1st Lieut., 3 March, 1855. Capt., 27 March, 1861. Maj. 3rd Inf., 30 March, 1864. Dropped 18 July, 1866. Supposed to have been drowned 9 April, 1866.

ARCHER, SAMUEL B. [Born in Va. Appointed from Va.]
Capt. 2nd Art., 12 March, 1812. Bvt. Maj., 27 April, 1813, for gallantry and good conduct in the cannonade and bombardment of Fort George, U. C. Trans. to Corps Art., 12 May, 1814. Trans. to 3rd Art., 1 June, 1821. Col. I. G., 16 Nov., 1821. Died 11 Dec., 1825.

ARDEN, THOS. B.* [Born in N. Y. Appointed from N. Y.]
Bvt. 2nd Lieut. 7th Inf., 1 July, 1835. 2nd Lieut., 26 Oct., 1836. 1st Lieut., 1 June, 1839. Resigned 31 Dec., 1842.

ARMES, GEORGE A. [Born in Va. Appointed from Va.]
Priv. Co. B, 16 Va. Vols., 1 Sept., 1862. 2nd Lieut. 16 Va. Vols., 8 Dec., 1862. Mustered out 10 June, 1863. 2nd Lieut. Veteran Reserve Corps, 1 July, 1863. Resigned 28 Oct., 1864. Capt. 2nd N. Y. Art., 7 Nov., 1864. Bvt. Maj. Vols., 13 March, 1865, for gallant and meritorious service during the campaigns of 1864 and 1865. Mustered out 8 Sept., 1865. 2nd Lieut. 2nd Cav., 19 April, 1866. Capt. 10th Cav., 28 July, 1866. Bvt. Maj., 2 March, 1867, for gallant and meritorious service in action at Hatcher's Run, Va., 9 Dec., 1864. Dismissed 7 June, 1870. Dismissal amended by Act of Congress, 8 June, 1874, so as to give him an honorable discharge, with same pay and allowances as if he had been discharged under section 3, Act 15 July, 1870. Capt. 10th Cav., 11 May, 1878, with former rank and date from 28 July 1866 (Act 23 April, 1878). Retired (disability) 15 Sept., 1883.

ARMISTEAD, CARROLL F. [Born in Ark. Appointed from Ark.]
2nd Lieut 2nd Art., 9 July, 1898. Capt. Co. D, 1st Ark. Vols., 14 May, to 25 July, 1898.

ARMISTEAD, FRANK S.* [Born in Va. Appointed at Large.]
Bvt. 2nd Lieut. 1st Inf., 1 July, 1856. 2nd Lieut. 10th Inf., 20 July, 1856. 1st Lieut., 3 March, 1861. Resigned 14 June, 1861.

ARMISTEAD, GEORGE. [Born in Va. Appointed from Va.]
2nd Lieut. 7th Inf., 8 Jan., 1799. 1st Lieut., 14 May, 1800. Trans. to Art. and Eng., 16 Feb., 1801. Trans. to Art., — April, 1802. Capt., 1 Nov., 1806. Maj. 3rd Art., 3 March, 1813. Trans. to Corps Art., 12 May, 1814. Died 25 April, 1818. Bvt. Lieut. Col., 12 Sept., 1814, for gallant conduct in defence of Fort McHenry.

ARMISTEAD, LEWIS A. [Born in N. C. Appointed from Va.]
Cadet at Mil. Acad., 1 Sept., 1834, to 15 Feb., 1836. 2nd Lieut. 6th Inf., 10 July, 1839. 1st Lieut., 30 March, 1844. Capt., 3 March, 1855. Resigned 26 May, 1861. Bvt. Capt., 20 Aug., 1847, for gallant and meritorious conduct at Contreras and Churubusco. Bvt. Maj., 8 Sept., 1847, for gallant and meritorious conduct at Molino del Rey.

ARMISTEAD, WILSON C. N. [Born in Va. Appointed from Va.]
Cadet at Mil. Acad., 15 April, 1813, to 7 Nov., 1817. 2nd Lieut. 4th Inf., 13 Feb., 1818. 1st Lieut., 24 Feb., 1818. Disbanded 1 June, 1821.

ARMISTEAD, WALKER K.* [Born in Va. Appointed from Va.]
2nd Lieut. Eng., 5 March, 1803. 1st Lieut., 11 June, 1805. Capt., 30 Oct., 1806. Maj., 23 July, 1810. Lieut. Col., 31 July, 1812. Col. Chief Eng., 12 Nov., 1818. Col. 3rd Art., 1 June, 1821. Died 13 Oct., 1845. Bvt. Brig. Gen., 12 Nov., 1828, for ten years' faithful service in one grade.

ARMSTRONG, BEZALEEL W.* [Born in Ohio. Appointed from Ohio.]
Bvt. 2nd Lieut. 1st Drag., 1 July, 1845. 2nd Lieut. 2nd Drag., 1 April, 1846. Died 17 Feb., 1849.

ARMSTRONG, FRANCIS C. [Born in Ark. Appointed from Texas.]
2nd Lieut. 2nd Drag., 7 June, 1855. 1st Lieut., 9 March, 1859. Capt., 6 June, 1861; 2nd Cav., 3 Aug., 1861. Resigned 13 Aug., 1861.

ARMSTRONG, FRANK S.* [Born in Ind. Appointed from Ind.]
2nd Lieut. 9th Cav., 12 June, 1891. 1st Lieut. 10th Cav., 1 July, 1898. Trans. to 9th Cav., 5 Oct., 1898.

ARMSTRONG, FRANCIS W. [Born in Va. Appointed from Tenn.]
Capt. 24th Inf., 12 March, 1812. Maj. 24th Inf., 26 June, 1813. Disbanded 15 June, 1815. Retained Dec., 1815 (in re-organization under Act of 3 March, 1815), as Capt. 7th Inf., with Bvt. of Maj., from 26 June, 1813. Resigned 30 April, 1817.

ARMSTRONG, GEORGE R. [Born in Tenn. Appointed from Tenn.]
2nd Lieut. 2nd Tenn. Vols., 18 May, 1898, to 8 Feb., 1899. 2nd Lieut. 5th Inf., 10 April, 1899.

ARMSTRONG, HORATIO G. [Born in N. Y. Appointed from N. Y.]
Capt. 23rd Inf., 25 Sept., 1812. Maj. A. I. G., 25 April, 1814. Disbanded 15 June, 1815.

ARMSTRONG, JOHN.* [Born in N. Y. Appointed from N. Y.]
3rd Lieut. Light Art., 19 April, 1814. Trans. to Corps Art., 12 May, 1814. 2nd Lieut. Corps Art., 19 May, 1814. 1st Lieut. 4th Rifle, 26 July, 1814. Resigned 15 June, 1815. Died 16 June, 1852.

ARMSTRONG, ROBT. G. [Born in Penn. Appointed from Penn.]
Priv. Co. G, 11th Penn. Res. Corps, 27 April, 1861. Discharged 13 June, 1864. 2nd

Lieut. 1st Inf., 22 Jan., 1867. Reg. Adj., 21 May, 1868, to 20 April, 1869. 1st Lieut., 29 May, 1874. Capt., 14 Dec., 1883. Died 30 Aug., 1893.

ARMSTRONG, ROBERT L.* [Born in N. Y. Appointed from N. Y.]
3rd Lieut. Light Art., 21 July, 1814. Trans. to Corps Art., 17 May, 1815. 2nd Lieut., 30 Aug., 1816. 1st Lieut., 2 July, 1818. Trans. to 2nd Art., 1 June, 1821. Reg. Adj., 1 June, 1821, to 30 April, 1826. Died 10 Oct., 1834. Bvt. Capt., 2 July, 1828, for ten years' faithful service in one grade.

ARMSTRONG, SAMUEL. [Born in Mass. Appointed from Mass.]
Ensign 4th Inf., 14 April, 1812. 2nd Lieut., 15 Sept., 1812. 1st Lieut., 9 March, 1814. Disbanded 15 June, 1815. Re-instated 16 May, 1816, in Corps Art. Died 8 Sept., 1819.

ARMSTRONG, SAMUEL E. [Born in Ind. Appointed from Ind.]
2nd Lieut. 1st Ind. Heavy Art., 24 July, 1861. Capt., 18 Nov., 1863. Mustered out 13 Feb., 1866. 2nd Lieut., 41st Inf., 28 July, 1866, and 1st Lieut., 2 May, 1867. Unassigned 11 Nov., 1869. Ass'd to 24th Inf., 3 May, 1870. Capt., 27 May, 1871. Retired 28 June, 1878.

ARMSTRONG, WM. [Born in Pa. Appointed from Ohio.]
Ensign 1st Rifles, 19 Jan., 1813. 3rd Lieut., 12 March, 1813. 2nd Lieut., 24 Jan., 1814. 1st Lieut., 1 Oct., 1816. Capt., 31 July, 1818. Trans. to 6th Inf., 1 June, 1821. Died 11 Feb., 1827.

ARMSTRONG, WM.* [Born in Ind. Appointed from Ind.]
2nd Lieut. 2nd Art., 1 July, 1837. 1st Lieut., 1 June, 1839. R. Q. M., 29 March, to 5 Aug., 1847. Capt. A. Q. M., 5 Aug., 1847. Killed 8 Sept., 1847, at Battle of Molino del Rey, Mexico.

ARMSTRONG, WM. K. [Born in Ala. Appointed from Ala.]
2nd Lieut. 23rd Inf., 1 Sept., 1899.

ARMSTRONG, WM. W. [Born in Penn. Appointed from N. Y.]
Priv. Co. F, 25th Pa. Vols., 2 May, 1861. Mustered out 26 July, 1861. Priv., Corpl. and Sergt. 15th Pa. Cav., 30 Nov., 1861, to 26 March, 1863. Capt. 65th U. S. Col. Inf., 22 Feb., 1864. Trans. to 92nd U. S. Col. Inf., 12 July, 1865. Mustered out 31 Dec., 1865. 2nd Lieut. 7th Inf., 23 Feb., 1866. 1st Lieut., 3 April, 1866. Unass'd 6 April, 1870. Ass'd to 16th Inf., 4 May, 1870. Dismissed 18 Nov., 1877.

ARNOLD, ABRAHAM K.* [Born in Penn. Appointed from Penn.]
Bvt. 2nd Lieut. 2nd Cav., 1 July, 1859. 2nd Lieut., 28 June, 1860. 1st Lieut., 6 April, 1861. Reg. Adj., 1 June, 1861, to 9 May, 1862. Bvt. Capt., 27 June, 1862, for gallant and meritorious service in the Battle of Gaines' Mill, Va. Capt. 5th Cav., 17 July, 1862. Bvt. Maj., 6 May, 1864, for gallant and meritorious service at the Battle of Todd's Tavern, Va. Maj. 6th Cav., 22 June, 1869. Lieut. Col. 1st Cav., 11 June, 1886. Col. 8th Cav., 7 Feb., 1891. Trans. to 1st Cav., 22 April, 1891. Brig. Gen. Vols., 4 May, 1898, to 12 May, 1899. Medal of honor for conspicuous gallantry in charge on the enemy in action at the Davenport Bridge, North Anna River, Va., 18 May, 1864; while serving as Capt. 5th U. S. Cav., commanding regiment.

ARNOLD, CONWAY H.* [Born in N. Y. Appointed from N. Y.]
Addl. 2nd Lieut. 5th Art., 12 June, 1895. 2nd Lieut. 2nd Art., 26 Nov., 1895. Trans. to 5th Art., 30 Jan., 1896. 1st Lieut., 2 March, 1899.

ARNOLD, FREDERICK T.* [Born in Iowa. Appointed from Iowa.]
Addl. 2nd Lieut. 6th Cav., 11 June, 1897. 2nd Lieut. 4th Cav., 15 Nov., 1897.

ARNOLD, ISAAC.* [Born in Conn. Appointed from Conn.]
2nd Lieut. 2nd Art., 17 June, 1862. Trans. to Ord., 27 April, 1863. 1st Lieut., 27 April, 1863. Bvt. Capt., 13 March, 1865, for faithful and meritorious service during the War. Capt. Ord., 7 March, 1867. Maj. Ord., 29 May, 1879. Lieut. Col., 2 Feb., 1897.

ARNOLD, LEWIS A. [Born in N. Y. Appointed from Mass.]
2nd Lieut. 1st Inf., 7 May, 1867. Died 25 Sept., 1867.

ARNOLD, LEWIS G.* [Born in N. J. Appointed from N. J.]
2nd Lieut. 2nd Art., 1 July, 1837. 1st Lieut., 9 July, 1838. Capt., 27 Oct., 1847. Maj. 1st Art., 15 May, 1861. Brig. Gen. Vols., 24 Jan., 1862; app't cancelled 8 Feb., 1864. Lieut. Col. 2nd Art., 1 Aug., 1863. Retired 1 Aug., 1864. Died 22 Sept., 1871. Bvt. Capt., 20 Aug., 1847, for gallant and mertorious service at Contreras and Churubusco, Mex. Bvt. Maj., 13 Sept., 1847, for gallant conduct at Chapultepec. Bvt. Lieut. Col., 22 Nov., 1861, for gallant and meritorious service during the bombardment of Fort Pickans, Fla.

ARNOLD, PERCY W. [Born in N. Y. Appointed from the Army.]
Priv. and Corpl. Troop F, 1st Cav., 31 Oct., 1896, to 5 July, 1898. 2nd Lieut. 7th Art., 23 June, 1898. Trans. to 5th Cav., 29 March, 1899.

ARNOLD, RICHARD.* [Born in R. I. Appointed from R. I.]
Bvt. 2nd Lieut. 1st Art., 1 July, 1850. 2nd Lieut. 3rd Art., 26 May, 1851. 1st Lieut., 17 March, 1854. Capt. 5th Art., 14 May, 1861. Bvt. Maj., 29 June, 1862, for gallant and meritorious service in the Battle of Savage Station, Va. Brig. Gen. Vols., 29 Nov., 1862. Bvt. Lieut. Col., 8 July, 1863, for gallant and meritorious service in the Siege of Port Hudson, La. Bvt. Col., 13 March, 1865, for gallant and meritorious service during the War. Bvt. Brig. Gen. and Maj. Gen., 13 March, 1865, for gallant and meritorious service in the field during the War. Bvt. Maj. Gen. Vols., 22 Aug., 1865, for gallant and meritorious service in the Sieges of Port Hudson, La., and Fort Morgan, Mobile Harbor. Mustered out Vol. service, 24 Aug., 1865. Maj. 5th Art., 1 May, 1875. Lieut. Col. 1st Art., 3 Nov., 1882. Died 8 Nov., 1882.

ARNOLD, RIPLEY A.* [Born in Miss. Appointed from Miss.]
2nd Lieut. 1st Drag., 1 July, 1838. 1st Lieut., 1 Feb., 1841. Capt. A. Q. M., 11 May, 1846, to 10 March, 1847. Capt. 1st Drag., 18 Aug., 1847. Murdered 6 Sept., 1853. Bvt. Capt., 19 April, 1842, for gallant conduct in war against Florida Indians. Bvt. Maj., 29 May, 1846, for gallant and meritorious conduct at Palo Alto and Resaca de la Palma.

ARNOLD, SAMUEL B.* [Born in N. Y. Appointed from N. Y.]
2nd Lieut. 1st Cav., 11 June, 1892. 1st Lieut., 2 March, 1899.

ARNOLD, SILAS R. [Born in N. Y. Appointed from N. Y.]
Asst. Surg., 1 July, 1837. Disbanded 23 Sept., 1842.

ARNOLD, WILBUR F. [Born in N. Y. Appointed from Army.]
Priv. and Q. M. Sergt. 18th Inf., 9 Aug., 1861, to 21 Dec., 1862. 2nd Lieut. 18th Inf., 21 Nov., 1862. 1st Lieut., 30 June, 1863. Capt. 41st Inf., 28 July, 1866. Died 12 Dec., 1867. Bvt. 1st Lieut., 31 Dec., 1862, for gallant and meritorious service at the Battle of Murfreesboro', Tenn. Bvt. Capt. 13 March, 1865, for gallant and meritorious service during the war.

ARNOLD, WM. [Born in ——. Appointed from Ky.]
2nd Lieut. 3rd Rifles, 3 Dec., 1812. 1st Lieut., 11 May, 1814. Disbanded 15 June, 1815. Re-instated 2 Dec., 1815, in 8th Inf. Capt., 5 Nov., 1817. Resigned 31 Oct., 1818.

ARNOLD, WM. W. [Born in N. Y. Appointed from Army.]
Priv. and Corpl. Co. B, 16th Inf., 9 Aug., to 26 Nov., 1861. 2nd Lieut. 16th Inf., 20 Nov., 1861. 1st Lieut., 21 Sept., 1846. Capt., 26 June, 1850. Died 11 Feb., 1856.

ARRASMITH, JAMES M. [Born in Iowa. Appointed from the Army.]
Priv., Corpl. and Sergt. Troop B, 4th Cav., 3 May, 1872, to 3 May, 1877. Priv. and Corpl. Troop C, 7th Cav., 22 July, 1880, to 5 July, 1883. 2nd Lieut. 2nd Inf., 3 July, 1883. 1st Lieut. 8th Inf., 9 March, 1891. Trans. to 2nd Inf., 20 July, 1891. Capt. 13th Inf., 7 Aug., 1898. Maj. Chief C. S. Vols., 7 Jan., to 13 June, 1899.

ARROWSMITH, GEORGE D. [Born in N. J. Appointed from N. J.]
2nd Lieut. 13th Inf., 9 July, 1898. 1st Lieut. 25th Inf., 2 March, 1899.

ARTHUR, BENJN. H. [Born in N. Y. Appointed from Vt.]
2nd Lieut. 1st Inf., 1 Dec., 1839. 1st Lieut., 21 Sept., 1846. Reg. Adj., 4 Oct., 1843, to 20 Sept., 1848. Capt., 26 June, 1850. Died 11 Feb., 1856.

ARTHUR, JOHN A. [Born in Ohio. Appointed from Ky.]
Priv. Co. D, 2nd Ohio Vols., 29 April, 1861. Mustered out 1 Aug., 1861. Capt. 8th Ky. Cav., 13 Sept., 1862. Mustered out 12 March, 1865. 2nd Lieut. 2nd Cav., 9 Aug., 1867. Resigned 26 March, 1868. Died 9 Feb., 1875.

ARTHUR, WM. [Born in Vt. Appointed from N. Y.]
1st Lieut. 4th N. Y. Art., 29 Jan., 1862. Capt., 1 Jan., 1863. Maj., 23 Dec., 1863. Bvt. Maj. Vols., 20 Feb., 1865. Bvt. Lieut. Col. Vols, 13 March, 1865, for gallant conduct in the Battles of Spottsylvania and Reams' Station, Va. Mustered out 6 April, 1865. Capt. Vet. Res. Corps, 19 Jan., 1865. Mustered out 22 Feb., 1866. 2nd Lieut. 3rd Art., 23 Feb., 1866. 1st Lieut., 28 July, 1866. Bvt. Capt., 2 March, 1867, for gallant and meritorious services in the Battle of Spottsylvania, Va. Bvt. Maj., 2 March, 1867, for gallant and meritorious service in the Battle of Reams' Station, Va. Maj. P. M., 26 July, 1875. Vacated commission of 1st Lieut. 3rd Art., 28 July, 1875. Retired (over 30 years' service) 30 April, 1898.

ARTHUR, WM. H. [Born in Pa. Appointed from Md.]
Asst. Surg., 18 Feb., 1881. Capt. Asst. Surg., 18 Feb., 1886. Maj. Surg., 23 Aug., 1898. Maj. Chief Surg. Vols., 4 June, 1898, to 30 Nov., 1898.

ARVIN, WM. B.* [Born in N. H. Appointed from N. H.]
Bvt. 2nd Lieut. 4th Art., 1 July, 1836. 2nd Lieut., 31 July, 1836. Resigned 30 Nov., 1836. Died — Oct., 1863.

ASBURY, GEORGE. [Born in Ill. Appointed from Ill.]
1st Lieut. 13th U. S. Col. Art., 31 Jan., 1865. Mustered out 16 March, 1866. 2nd Lieut. 1st Art., 23 Feb., 1866. 1st Lieut., 28 July, 1865. Drowned 4 May, 1871.

ASBURY, HENRY. [Born in Ill. Appointed from Ill.]
2nd Lieut. 3rd Inf., 5 Aug., 1861. 1st Lieut., 30 June, 1862. Capt., 31 Dec., 1864. Unassigned 11 Aug., 1869. Died 20 Oct., 1870. Bvt. Capt., 2 July, 1863, for gallant and meritorious service at the Battle of Gettysburg, Pa. Bvt. Maj., 13 March, 1865, for gallant and meritorious service during the war.

ASCH, MORRIS J. [Born in Penn. Appointed from Penn.]
Asst. Surg., 5 Aug., 1861. Resigned 31 March, 1873. Bvt. Capt. and Maj., 13 March, 1865, for faithful and meritorious service during the war.

ASH, JOSEPH P. [Born in Penn. Appointed from Penn.]
Corpl. Clay Batt. D. C. Vols., 18 April, 1861. 2nd Lieut. 2nd Cav., 30 April, 1861. 5th Cav., 3 Aug., 1861. 1st Lieut., 15 Jan., 1862. Capt., 25 Sept., 1863. Killed in action, 8 May, 1864, in or near Todd's Tavern, Va. Bvt. Maj., 8 Nov., 1862, for conspicuous gallantry at Warrentown, Va. Bvt. Lieut. Col., 8 May, 1864, for conspicuous gallantry at the Battle of Spottsylvania, Va.

ASH, NATHAN H. [Born in Ky. Appointed from Ill.]
Asst. Surg. Vols., 13 July, 1847. Died 7 Feb., 1848.

ASHBURN, PERCY M. [Born in Ohio. Appointed from Ohio.]
Asst. Surg., 12 Dec., 1898.

ASHBURN, THOMAS O.* [Born in Ohio. Appointed from Ohio.]
Addl. 2nd Lieut. 25th Inf., 11 June, 1897. 2nd Lieut. 7th Art., 8 March, 1898. Capt. 33rd U. S. Vols., 5 July, 1899. 1st Lieut. 6th Art., 1 March, 1900.

ASHE, RICHARD P. [Born in N. C. Appointed from Texas.]
Asst. Surg., 22 July, 1846. Disbanded 30 June, 1847.

ASHETON, ROBT. C. [Born in Eng. Appointed from Army.]
Priv. 1st Sergt. and Sergt. Maj. 1st Drag., 25 Oct., 1836, to Aug., 1838. 2nd Lieut. 2nd Drag., 31 July, 1838. Reg. Adj., 5 Sept., 1838, to 16 May, 1848. 2nd Lieut. 2nd Drag., 31 July, 1838. Dismissed 22 June, 1841.

ASHBY, JAMES A. [Born in N. Y. Appointed from S. C.]
Capt. 2nd Drag., 8 June, 1836. Resigned 15 Dec., 1841. Bvt. Maj., 19 July, 1836, for gallantry and good conduct in the affair at Welika.

ASHFORD, BAILEY K. [Born in D. C. Appointed from D. C.]
Asst. Surg., 6 Nov., 1897.

ASHLEY, RICHD. H.* [Born in Mass. Appointed from Mass.]
2nd Lieut. Art., 1 March, 1811. Capt. A. Dep. Q. M. G., 11 April, 1813. 1st Lieut. Art., 20 May, to 31 Dec., 1813. Disbanded 15 June, 1815. 2nd Lieut. 5th Inf., 30 July, 1817. Resigned 10 March, 1819.

ASPINWALL, JOHN.* [Born in Vt. Appointed from Wis.]
2nd Lieut. 7th Cav., 15 June, 1869. Dropped 12 July, 1874. Drowned 26 Dec., 1881.

ATCHESON, GEORGE. [Born in N. Y. Appointed from Army.]
Priv., Corpl. and Sergt. Co. I, 4th Inf., 2 Aug., 1859, to 27 March, 1863. 2nd Lieut. 4th Inf., 19 Feb., 1863. 1st Lieut., 20 Jan., 1865. Unass'd 25 March, 1869. Ass'd to 7th Inf., 1 Jan., 1871. Resigned 1 March, 1872. Bvt. 1st Lieut., 1 July, 1863, for gallant and meritorious service at the Battle of Gettysburg, Penn. Bvt. Capt., 5 May, 1864, for gallant and meritorious service at the Battle of the Wilderness, Va.

ATCHISON, CHAS. B. [Born in Ill. Appointed from Ill.]
2nd Lieut. 3rd Inf., 5 Aug., 1861. 1st Lieut., 9 Feb., 1863. Capt. A. A. de C., 11 July, 1862, to 1 Sept., 1866. Capt., 5 March, 1867. Unass'd 17 May, 1869. Ass'd to 14th Inf., 1 Jan., 1871. Wholly retired 25 Feb., 1876. Bvt. 1st Lieut., 1 July, 1862, for gallant and meritorious service at the Battle of Malvern Hill, Va. Bvt. Capt., 2 April, 1865, for gallant and meritorious service during operations resulting in the fall of Richmond. Bvt. Maj., 2 April, 1865, for gallant and meritorious service during the war. Bvt. Lieut. Col., 28 Oct., 1867, for faithful and meritorious service during the war. Died 10 May, 1876.

ATKINSON, BENJAMIN W. [Born in Mo. Appointed from Mo.]
2nd Lieut. 6th Inf., 10 Oct., 1883. 1st Lieut. 20th Inf., 12 March, 1891. Trans. to 6th Inf., 20 July, 1891. Capt., 11 Aug., 1898. Ass'd to 6th Inf., 1 Jan., 1899. Graduate of Infantry and Cavalry School, 1887.

ATKINSON, HENRY. [Born in N. C. Appointed from N. C.]
Capt., 3rd Inf., 1 July, 1808. Col. I. G., 25 April, 1813. Col. 4th Inf., 15 April, 1814. Trans. to 37th Inf., 22 April, 1814. Trans. to 6th Inf., 17 May, 1815. Brig. Gen., 13 May, 1820. Col. A. G., 1 June, 1821, which he declined, and on 16 Aug., 1821, was assigned as Col. 6th Inf. Retained as Col., 21 Aug., with Bvt. rank of Brig. Gen., 13 May, 1820. Died 14 June, 1842.

ATKINSON, JOHN R. [Born in Mo. Appointed from Mo.]
Maj. Surg. 3rd Drag., 16 March, 1848. Disbanded 31 July, 1848.

ATWELL, WM. P. [Born in Ohio. Appointed from Wis.]
1st Lieut. 37th Wis. Vols., 1 June, 1864. Mustered out 1 Dec., 1864. Bvt. Capt. and Maj. Vols., 13 March, 1865, for gallant and meritorious service in action before Petersburg, Va. 2nd Lieut. 43rd Inf., 22 Jan., 1867. Bvt. 1st Lieut., 2 March, 1867, for gallant and meritorious service in the assault on Petersburg, Va., 30 July, 1864. Bvt. Capt., 2 March, 1867, for gallant and meritorious service during the war. Unassigned 8 April, 1869. Retired with rank of Capt., 31 Dec., 1870.

ATWOOD, EDWIN B. [Born in Ohio. Appointed from Ohio.]
Sergt. Maj. 41st Ohio Vols., 19 Sept., 1861. Discharged 20 Jan., 1862. 2nd Lieut. 41st Ohio Vols., 21 Jan., 1862. 1st Lieut., 31 Oct., 1862. Capt., 1 May, 1864. Bvt. Maj. Vols., 13 March, 1865, for valuable and conspicuous service during the war. Mustered out 27 Nov., 1865. 2nd Lieut. 16th Inf., 11 May, 1866. Bvt. 1st Lieut., 2 March, 1867, for gallant and meritorious service in the Battle of Murfreesboro', Tenn. Bvt. Capt., 2 March, 1867, for gallant and meritorious service in the Battle of Chickamauga, Ga. Bvt. Maj., 2 March, 1867, for gallant and meritorious service in the Battle of Mission Ridge, Tenn. Trans. to 2nd Inf., 17 April, 1869. Trans. to 6th Inf., 31 Dec., 1870. 1st Lieut. 6th Inf., 1 March, 1872. Capt., A. Q. M., 24 April, 1875. Resigned Commission of 1st Lieut. 6th Inf., 28 April, 1875. Maj. Q. M., 10 July, 1890. Lieut. Col. D. Q. M. G., 11 Feb., 1897.

ATWOOD, GEORGE E. [Born in Maine. Appointed from Maine.]
2nd Lieut. 5th Me. Vols., 24 June, 1861. 1st Lieut., 7 March, 1862. Resigned 7 Oct., 1862. 1st Lieut. 24th Me. Vols., 16 Oct., 1862. Resigned 8 March, 1863. Capt. 87th U. S. Col. Inf., 19 Oct., 1863. Discharged 26 Nov., 1864. Capt. A. Q. M. Vols., 21 Jan., 1865. Bvt. Maj. and Lieut. Col. Vols., for gallant and meritorious services at the Battle of Gaines' Mill, Va. Mustered out 27 Jan., 1866. Capt. 27th Inf., 28 July, 1866. Resigned 5 March, 1867. Died 27 Oct., 1886.

ATWOOD, WM. [Born in Penn. Appointed from Penn.]
Priv. F. Batty Pa. Vols., 12 Aug., 1862. Discharged 4 Jan., 1864. Capt. A. A. G. Vols., 2 March, 1865. Bvt. Maj. Vols., 13 March 1865, for gallant and meritorious service during the war. Mustered out 31 Oct., 1866. 2nd Lieut. 19th Inf., 6 March, 1866. 1st Lieut., 23 July, 1867. Unass'd 31 March, 1869. Ass'd to 21st Inf., 15 Dec., 1870. Drowned 15 Oct., 1871.

AUDENRIED, JOSEPH C.* [Born in Penn. Appointed from Penn.]
2nd Lieut. 1st Cav., 24 June, 1861. 1st Lieut. 6th Cav., 24 June, 1861. Capt., A. de C. Vols., 20 Aug., 1862. Bvt. Capt., 17 Sept., 1862, for gallant and meritorious service in Battle of Antietam, Md. Mustered out of Vol. service, 15 Aug., 1863. Capt. A. de C. Vols., 27 Oct., 1863. Bvt. Major, 1 Sept., 1864, for gallant and meritorious service in the Atlanta Campaign. Bvt. Maj. Vols., 12 Jan., 1865. Bvt. Lieut. Col., 13 March, 1865, for gallant and meritorious service during the war. Capt. 6th Cav., 1 July, 1866. Vacated Commission of Capt. A. de C. Vols., 1 July, 1866. Lieut. Col. A. de C., 11 Aug., 1866, to March, 1869. Col. A. de C., 8 March, 1869. Died 3 June, 1880.

AUGUR, AMMON A.* [Born in Mich. Appointed from Mich.]
2nd Lieut. 24th Inf., 15 June, 1877. 1st Lieut., 18 June, 1880. Capt., 21 Jan., 1895.

AUGUR, CHRISTOPHER C.* [Born in N. Y. Appointed from Mich.]
Bvt. 2nd Lieut. 2nd Inf., 1 July, 1843. 2nd Lieut. 4th Inf., 12 Sept., 1845. 1st Lieut., 16 Feb., 1847. Capt., 1 Aug., 1852. Maj. 13th Inf., 14 May, 1861. Brig. Gen. Vols., 12 Nov., 1861. Appointed Maj. Gen. Vols., 9 Aug., 1862, for distinguished and meritorious service in the Battle of Cedar Mountain, Va. Bvt. Col., 9 Aug., 1862, for gallant and meritorious service in the Battle of Cedar Mountain, Va. Lieut. Col. 12th Inf., 1 July, 1863. Bvt. Brig. Gen., 13 March, 1865, for gallant and meritorious service at the capture of Port Hudson, La. Bvt. Maj. Gen., 13 March, 1865, for gallant and meritorious service in the field during the war. Col. 12th Inf., 15 March, 1866. Mustered out of Vol. service, 1 Sept., 1866. Brig. Gen. U. S. A., 4 March, 1869. Died 16 Jan., 1898.

AUGUR, COLON. [Born in N. Y. Appointed from D. C.]
2nd Lieut. 2nd Cav., 3 Aug., 1868. 1st Lieut., 15 Dec., 1873. Capt., 9 Jan., 1886. Retired (disability) 23 June, 1898.

AUGUR, JACOB A.* [Born in N. Y. Appointed at Large.]
2nd Lieut. 5th Cav., 15 June, 1869. 1st Lieut., 11 Jan., 1871. Capt., 14 June, 1879. Maj. 4th Cav., 2 June, 1897.

AULTMAN, DWIGHT E.* [Born in Pa. Appointed from Pa.]
2nd Lieut. 4th Cav., 12 June, 1894. Trans. to 2nd Art., 13 Sept., 1894. 1st Lieut. 2 March, 1899.

AUGUSTIN, JOSEPH W., Jr.* [Born in La. Appointed from Pa.]
2nd Lieut. 24th Inf., 12 June, 1895. Died of wounds received in action at Santiago, Cuba, 2 July, 1898.

AUMAN, WILLIAM. [Born in Pa. Appointed from Pa.]
Priv. Washington Art., Pottsville, Pa., 15 April, 1861. Mustered in as Co. B, 25th Pa. Vols., 18 April, 1861. Discharged 29 July, 1861. Corpl. Co. G, 48th Pa. Vols., 9 Sept., 1861. Sergt., 2 June, 1862. 2nd Lieut. 48th Pa. Vet. Vols., 28 June, 1864. 1st Lieut., 28 July, 1864. Capt., 3 March, 1865. Bvt. Capt. Vols., 2 April, 1865, for gallant and meritorious services before Petersburg, Va. 2nd Lieut. 13th U. S. Inf., 11 May, 1866. 1st Lieut., 5 Oct., 1867. Capt., 26 March, 1879. Maj., 26 April, 1898.

AUSTIN, ALBERT. [Born in Conn. Appointed from Conn.]
Corpl. Co. F, 8th Conn. Vols., 23 Sept., 1861. Sergt., 24 Dec., 1862. Sergt. Co. F, 8th Conn. Vols., 24 Dec., 1863. Discharged 12 May, 1865. 2nd Lieut. 11th Conn. Vols., 13 May, 1865. 1st Lieut., 2 Nov., 1865. Mustered out 21 Dec., 1865. 2nd Lieut. 14th Inf., 9 Aug., 1867. 1st Lieut., 23 Nov., 1874. Died 3 Dec., 1886.

AUSTIN, IVERS J.* [Born in Mass. Appointed from Mass.]
Bvt. 2nd Lieut. Art., 1 July, 1828. Resigned 8 Nov., 1828. Died 11 June, 1889.

AUSTIN, LORING. [Born in Mass. Appointed from Mass.]
2nd Lieut. 1st Light Drag., 28 Sept., 1812. 1st Lieut., 3 Sept., 1813. Capt. 46th Inf., 21 April, 1814. Trans. to 8th Inf., 17 May, 1815. Resigned 31 July, 1819. Bvt. Maj., 5 July, 1814, for gallant and distinguished conduct at the Battle of Chippewa. Died 28 Jan., 1827.

AUSTIN, WM. M. [Born in England. Appointed from N. Y.]
Asst. Surg., 28 Feb., 1866. Died 9 May, 1868. Bvt. Capt., 18 Dec., 1866, for meritorious and distinguished service at San Antonio, Texas, when cholera prevailed.

AUSTINE, WILLIAM.* [Born in Conn. Appointed from Conn.]
2nd Lieut. 2nd Drag., 1 July, 1838. Trans. to 3rd Art., 12 July, 1838. 1st Lieut., 5 Nov., 1839. Reg. Adj., 1 May, 1841, to 13 Aug., 1847. Capt., 13 Aug., 1847. Bvt. Maj., 20 Aug., 1847, for gallant and meritorious conduct in the Battles of Contreras and Churubusco. Maj. 3rd Art., 21 July, 1861. Retired 20 Feb., 1862. Bvt. Lieut. Col. and Col., 28 Sept., 1865, for long and faithful service.

AVERELL, WM. W.* [Born in N. Y. Appointed from N. Y.]
Bvt. 2nd Lieut. Mounted Rifle, 1 July, 1855. 2nd Lieut., 1 May, 1856. 1st Lieut., 14 May, 1861. 3rd Cav., 3 Aug., 1861. Capt., 17 July, 1862. Resigned 18 May, 1865. Bvt. Maj., 17 March, 1863, for gallant and meritorious service in action at Kelly's Ford, Va. Bvt. Lieut. Col., 6 Nov., 1863, for gallant and meritorious service in action at Droop Mountain, Va. Bvt. Col., 15 Dec., 1863, for gallant and meritorious service during the Salem expedition, in Va. Bvt. Brig. Gen., 13 March, 1865, for gallant servlee in the field of battle during the war. Bvt. Maj. Gen., 13 March, 1865, for gallant and meritorious service at the Battle of Moorfield, Va. Appointed Capt. U. S. Army, 17 Aug., 1888 (Act of 1 Aug., 1888). Retired 31 Aug., 1888.

AVERILL, NATHAN K.* [Born in Mich. Appointed from Mich.]
2nd Lieut. 7th Cav., 12 June, 1895. 1st Lieut., 2 March, 1899.

AVERY, FRANK F.* [Born in Mich. Appointed from Mich.]
Addl. 2nd Lieut. 3rd Inf., 14 June, 1878. 2nd Lieut., 28 June, 1878. 1st Lieut., 1 July, 1885. Capt., 26 April, 1898. Retired (disability) 8 Sept., 1898.

AVERY, HOWARD S. [Born in Cal. Appointed from Cal.]
Priv. and Corpl. Co. I, 14th Inf., 6 June, 1898, to 26 April, 1899. 2nd Lieut. 14th Inf., 10 April, 1899.

AVERY, ROBERT. [Born in Penn. Appointed from N. Y.]
Capt. 102nd N. Y. Vols., 17 Dec., 1861. Lieut. Col., 1 Jan., 1863. Mustered out 27 June, 1864. Bvt. Lieut. Col. Vols., 13 March, 1865, for gallant and meritorious service in the Battle of Chancellorsville, Va. Bvt. Col. and Bvt. Brig. Gen. Vols., 13 March, 1865, for gallant and meritorious service at the Battle of Lookout Mountain, Tenn. Bvt. Maj. Gen. Vols., 13 March, 1865, for gallant and meritorious service. Maj. Vet. Res. Corps, 27 April, 1865. Mustered out 8 Jan., 1867. 1st Lieut. 44th Inf., 28 July, 1866. Bvt. Capt., 2 March, 1867, for gallant and meritorious service in the Battle of Chancellorsville, Va. Bvt. Capt., 2 March, 1867, for gallant and meritorious service at the Battle of Lookout Mountain, Tenn. Reassigned 27 May, 1869. Retired with rank of Lieut. Col., 31 Dec., 1870.

AVIS, EDWARD S.* [Born in Va. Appointed from W. Va.]
2nd Lieut. 5th Inf., 12 June, 1880. 1st Lieut. 25th Inf., 11 Nov., 1890. Trans. to 18th Inf., 20 July, 1891. Retired (disability) with rank of Capt., 26 April, 1898.

AWL, FRANK A. [Born in Pa. Appointed from Pa.]
2nd Lieut. of Inf., (unass'd), 1 Dec., 1899.

AXT, GODFREY H. T. F. [Born in Germany. Appointed from N. Y.]
Priv. Co. G, 20th N. Y. Vols., 6 May, 1861. Mustered out 1 June, 1863. Asst. Surg., 9 Oct., 1867. Resigned 1 Feb., 1870.

AYER, SAMUEL. [Born in Mass. Appointed from Mass.]
Post Surg., 17 Feb., 1817. Resigned 9 March, 1818.

AYER, THOMAS J. [Born in Tenn. Appointed from Tenn.]
2nd Lieut. 1st Inf., 28 Jan., 1820. Reg. Adj. 15 Sept., 1821, to 14 Sept., 1823. Died 14 Sept., 1823.

AYER, WALDO E.* [Born in Mass. Appointed from Mass.]
2nd Lieut. 12th Inf., 15 June, 1884. 1st Lieut. 20th Inf., 19 May, 1891. Trans. to 11th Inf., 20 July, 1891. Trans. to 12th Inf., 16 April, 1894. Capt., 5 Oct., 1898. Ass'd to 12th Inf., 1 Jan., 1899.

AYERS, GEORGE W.* [Born in Penn. Appointed from Penn.]
2nd Lieut. 3rd Art., 1 July, 1841. 1st Lieut., 20 Dec., 1845. Killed 8 Sept., 1847, at Battle of Molino del Rey, Mexico. Bvt. Capt., 23 Sept., 1846, for gallant conduct in the several conflicts at Monterey, Mexico.

AYRES, CHARLES G. [Born in N. Y. Appointed from N. Y.]
2nd Lieut. 25th Inf., 31 Oct., 1874. Trans. to 10th Cav., 18 Sept., 1875, taking rank from 18 Sept., 1875. 1st Lieut., 21 Dec., 1882. Capt., 1 Jan., 1892. Maj. 29th U. S. Vols., 5 July, 1899 (declined).

AYRES, HENRY. [Born in N. Y. Appointed from N. Y.]
Ensign 23rd N. Y. Vols., 23 April, 1861. 1st Lieut., 9 Oct., 1862. 1st Lieut. Sig. Corps Vols., 3 March, 1863. Bvt. Capt. Vols., 26 March, 1865, for faithful and meritorious service during the campaign against the city of Mobile and its defences. Mustered out 1 May, 1866. 2nd Lieut. 3rd Cav., 7 March, 1867. 1st Lieut., 29 July, 1868. Trans. to Supernumerary, 15 Dec., 1870. Mustered out 1 Jan., 1871.

AYRES, JAMES C.* [Born in Wis. Appointed from Wis.]
2nd Lieut. 3rd Inf., 12 June, 1871. Trans. to Ord., 1 Nov., 1874. 1st Lieut., 1 Nov., 1874. Capt., 15 March, 1883.

AYRES, ROBERT. [Born in Penn. Appointed from Army.]
Priv., Corpl. and Sergt. Cos. A and D, Batt. Eng., 20 Dec., 1855, to 19 Dec., 1862. 2nd Lieut. 19th Inf., 29 Nov., 1862. 1st Lieut., 25 Nov., 1863. R. Q. M., 5 June, 1865, to 28 July, 1866. Capt., 28 July, 1866. Unass'd 31 March, 1869. Mustered out 1 Jan., 1871. Bvt. Capt., 25 Nov., 1863, for gallant and meritorious service at the Battle of Mission Ridge, Tenn.

AYRES, ROMEYN B.* [Born in N. Y. Appointed from N. Y.]
Bvt. 2nd Lieut. 4th Art., 1 July, 1847. 2nd Lieut. 3rd Art., 22 Sept., 1847. 1st Lieut., 16 March, 1852. Capt. 5th Art., 14 May, 1861. Brig. Gen. Vols., 29 Nov., 1862. Bvt. Maj., 2 July, 1863, for gallant and meritorious service in the Battle of Gettysburg, Pa. Bvt. Lieut. Col., 5 May, 1864, for gallant and meritorious service in the Battle of the Wilderness, Va. Bvt. Maj. Gen. Vols., 1 Aug., 1864, for conspicuous gallantry in the Battles of the Wilderness, Spottsylvania Court House, Jericho Mills, Bethesda Church, Petersburg and Globe Tavern (Weldon Railroad), and for faithful service in the campaign. Bvt. Col., 18 Aug., 1864, for gallant and meritorious service in the Battle on the Weldon Railroad, Va. Bvt. Brig. Gen., 13 March, 1865, for gallant and meritorious service in the Battle of Five Forks, Va. Bvt. Maj. Gen., 13 March, 1865, for gallant and meritorious service in the field during the war. Mustered out of Vol. service 30 April, 1866. Lieut. Col. 28th Inf., 28 July, 1866. Trans. to 19th Inf., 15 March, 1869. Trans. to 3rd Art., 15 Dec., 1870. Col. 2nd Art., 18 Jan., 1879. Died 4 Dec., 1888.

AZPELL, THOMAS F. [Born in Penn. Appointed from N. J.]
Maj. Surg. Vols., 7 Oct., 1861. Bvt. Lieut. Col. Vols., 18 Oct., 1865, for faithful and meritorious service. Mustered out 23 Oct., 1865. Capt. Asst. Surg., 14 May, 1867. Retired for disability 10 Aug., 1885.

BABBITT, EDWIN B.* [Born in Conn. Appointed from Ind.]
Bvt. 2nd and 2nd Lieut. 3rd Inf., 1 July, 1826. 1st Lieut., 31 March, 1834. A. Q. M., 10 March, 1836, to 7 July, 1838. Capt. A. Q. M., 7 July, 1838. Capt. 3rd Inf., 1 July, 1839. Vacated line commission, 18 June, 1846. Bvt. Maj., 30 May, 1848, for meritorious conduct while serving in the enemy's country. Maj. Q. M., 10 May, 1861. Lieut. Col. Dep. Q. M. G., 3 Aug., 1861. Bvt. Col., 13 March, 1865, for faithful and meritorious service during the war. Bvt. Brig. Gen., 13 March, 1865, for faithful and meritorious service in the Q. M. D. during the war. Col. A. Q. M. G., 29 July, 1866. Retired 29 July, 1866. Died 10 Dec., 1881.

BABBITT, EDWIN B.* [Born in N. Y. Appointed from Wash.]
2nd Lieut. 5th Art., 15 June, 1884. 1st Lieut. Ord., 15 April, 1889. Capt. (14 years' service) 15 June, 1898.

BABBITT, LAWRENCE S.* [Born in Mass. Appointed from Md.]
2nd Lieut. 3rd Art., 24 June, 1861. Bvt. 1st Lieut., 21 July, 1861, for gallant and meritorious service in the Battle of Bull Run, Va. Trans. to Ord., 26 Oct., 1861. 1st Lieut., 3 March, 1863. Bvt. Capt., 13 March, 1865, for faithful and meritorious service in the Ord. Dept. during the war. Capt. Ord., 22 Dec., 1866. Bvt. Maj., 27 Feb., 1890, for gallant services in action against Indians at the Clearwater, Idaho, 11 and 12 July, 1877. Maj., 10 May, 1878. Lieut. Col., 15 Sept., 1890. Col., 7 April, 1899.

BABCOCK, CAMPBELL E. [Born in Ill. Appointed from Ill.]
Priv. Troop K, 1st U. S. Vol. Cav., 21 May, 1898, to 1 Sept., 1898. 2nd Lieut. 12th Inf., 9 July, 1898. 1st Lieut. 7th Inf., 13 May, 1899.

BABCOCK, CONRAD S.* [Born in Conn. Appointed from N. Y.]
2nd Lieut. 2nd Inf., 26 April, 1898. Trans. to 6th Art., 8 June, 1898. Trans. to 1st Cav., 31 Oct., 1898.

BABCOCK, JOHN B. [Born in La. Appointed from Conn.]
Sergt. Co. G, 37th N. Y. State Militia, 29 May, 1862. Discharged 2 Sept., 1862. 2nd Lieut. 174th N. Y. Vols., 13 Nov., 1862. 1st Lieut., 1 Dec., 1863. Capt. 162nd N. Y. Vols., 9 Dec., 1864. Maj., 1 Jan., 1865. Resigned 23 July, 1865. 2nd Lieut. 5th Cav., 22 Jan., 1867. Bvt. 1st Lieut., Bvt. Capt. and Maj., 2 March, 1867, for gallant and meritorious service in the Battles of Sabine Cross-Roads, Pleasant Hill and Cane River Crossing, La. 1st Lieut. 5th Cav., 14 Feb., 1868. Capt., 9 May, 1877. Bvt. Lieut. Col., 27 Feb., 1890, for gallant services in actions against Indians at Tonto Creek, Ariz., 16 June, 1873, and at Four Peaks, Ariz., 16 Jan., 1874. Maj. A. A. G., 2 Feb., 1893. Lieut. Col. A. A. G., 25 Jan., 1897. Brig. Gen. of Vols., 3 June, to 30 Nov., 1898. Medal of Honor for most distinguished gallantry in action at Spring Creek, Nebr., 16 May, 1869; this officer, then a 1st Lieut. 5th U. S. Cav., and serving with a scouting column, while in advance with a troop of cavalry, was attacked by Indians outnumbering his force six times. Advancing to high ground, he dismounted his troop, himself remaining mounted to encourage his men, and there fought the Indians until relieved, his horse being wounded. Brig. Gen. Vols., 3 June, 1898. Honorably discharged 30 Nov., 1898. Was Chief of Staff Merritt's Expedition to Philippines.

BABCOCK, ORVILLE E.* [Born in Vt. Appointed from Vt.]
Bvt. 2nd Lieut. Eng., 6 May, 1861. 2nd Lieut., 6 May, 1861. 1st Lieut., 17 Nov., 1861. Bvt. Capt., 4 May, 1862, for gallant and meritorious service during the Siege

of Yorktown, Va. Lieut. Col. A. I. G. (Act 17 July, 1862), 1 Jan., 1863. Capt. Eng., 1 June, 1863. Bvt. Maj., 29 Nov., 1863, for gallant and meritorious service during the Siege of Knoxville, Tenn. Relieved as Lieut. Col. A. I. G. (Act 17 July, 1862), 28 March, 1864. Lieut. Col. A. de C. to the Lieut. Gen., 29 March, 1864. Bvt. Lieut. Col., 6 May, 1864, for gallant and eritorious service in the Battle of the Wilderness, Va. Bvt. Col. Vols., 24 Feb., 1865, for faithful and meritorious service. Bvt. Col., 13 March, 1865, for gallant and meritorious service during the war. Bvt. Brig. Gen., 13 March, 1865, for gallant and meritorious service in the field during the war. Relieved as Lieut. Col. A. de C., 24 July, 1866. Col. A. de C. to the Gen., 25 July, 1866. Maj. Eng., 21 March, 1867. Relieved as Col. A. de C., 4 March, 1869. Col. Superint. Pub. Buildings, 3 March, 1873, to 3 March, 1877. Drowned 2 June, 1884.

BABCOCK, SAMUEL.* [Born in Mass. Appointed from Mass.]
2nd Lieut. Eng., 23 Feb., 1808. 1st Lieut., 1 July, 1812. Capt., 20 Sept., 1812. Maj. 31 March, 1819. Resigned 22 Dec., 1830. Died 26 June, 1831.

BABCOCK, WALTER C.* [Born in Mass. Appointed from Mass.]
2nd Lieut. 8th Cav., 12 June, 1893. 1st Lieut., 2 March, 1899.

BABCOCK, WM. H. [Born in N. Y. Appointed from N. Y.]
Asst. Surg., 29 Aug., 1856. Died 3 Oct., 1859.

BACHE, ALEXR. D.* [Born in Penn. Appointed from Penn.]
Bvt. 2nd Lieut. Eng., 1 July, 1825. 2nd Lieut., 1 July, 1825. Resigned 1 June, 1829. Died 17 Feb., 1867.

BACHE, ALFRED B. [Born in Penn. Appointed from Penn.]
2nd Lieut. 5th Cav., 7 March, 1867. 1st Lieut., 20 July, 1868. Reg. Com., 25 April, to 2 Nov., 1876. Died 12 Nov., 1876.

BACHE, DALLAS. [Born in D. C. Appointed from Penn.]
1st Lieut. Asst. Surg., 28 May, 1861. Bvt. Capt. and Maj., 13 March, 1865, for faithful and meritorius service during the war. Capt. Asst. Surg., 28 May, 1866. Maj. Surg., 5 Aug., 1867. Lieut. Col. Surg., 9 Feb., 1890. Col. Asst. Surg. Gen., 18 April, 1895.

BACHE, FRANCIS M. [Born in Penn. Appointed at Large.]
1st Lieut. 16th Inf., 14 May, 1861. Capt., 25 Oct., 1861. Resigned 16 Nov., 1865. Bvt. Maj., 2 Dec., 1864, for faithful and meritorious service in the field. Bvt. Lieut. Col., 9 April, 1865, for gallant and meritorious service during the operations resulting in the fall of Richmond and surrender of General Lee.

BACHE, FRANKLIN. [Born in Penn. Appointed from Penn.]
Surg. Mate, 32nd Inf., 17 May, 1813. Maj. Surg. 42nd Inf., 25 April, 1814. Trans. to 2nd Inf., 17 May, 1815. Resigned 1 July, 1816. Died 19 March, 1864.

BACHE, HARTMAN.* [Born in Penn. Appointed from Penn.]
Bvt. Capt. Asst. Top. Eng., 24 July, 1818. Bvt. Maj. Top. Eng., 1 Aug., 1832. Maj. Top. Eng., 7 July, 1838. Lieut. Col., 6 Aug., 1861. Col. Eng., 3 March, 1863. Retired 7 March, 1867. Died 8 Oct., 1872. Bvt. Maj., 24 July, 1828, for ten years' faithful service in one grade. Bvt. Brig. Gen., 13 March, 1865, for long, faithful and meritorious service.

BACHE, RICHARD. [Born in Penn. Appointed from Penn.]
1st Lieut. 32nd Inf., 17 April, 1813. Retained 17 May, 1815, as 2nd Lieut. Corps Art. Capt. Ord., 30 May, 1832. Died 13 Jan., 1836. Retained May, 1815 (in reorganization under Act of 3 March, 1815), as 2nd Lieut. of Art., with Bvt. of 1st Lieut. from 17 April, 1813.

BACHELDER, DANIEL. [Born in Vt. Appointed from N. H.]
Capt. of Inf., 23 Feb., 1847; 9th Inf., 9 April, 1847. Resigned 17 Feb., 1848.

BACKENSTOS, JACOB B. [Born in Penn. Appointed from Ill.]
Capt. Mounted Rifles, 27 May, 1846. Resigned 30 June, 1851. Bvt. Maj., 20 Aug., 1847, for gallant and meritorious conduct in the Battles of Contreras and Churubusco, Mexico. Bvt. Lieut. Col., 13 Sept., 1845, for gallant and meritorious conduct in the Battle of Chapultepec, Mexico. Died 25 Sept., 1857.

BACKUS, CHRISTOPHER. [Born in La. Appointed from La.]
Asst. Apothecary Gen., 12 Aug., 1814. Resigned 15 Nov., 1819.

BACKUS, ELECTUS.* [Born in N. Y. Appointed from N. Y.]
Bvt. 2nd Lieut. 2nd Inf., 1 July, 1824. 2nd Lieut. 1st Inf., 1 July, 1824. 1st Lieut., 28 July, 1831. Capt., 17 Oct., 1837. Maj. 3rd Inf., 10 June, 1850. Lieut. Col., 19 Jan., 1859. Col. 6th Inf., 20 Feb., 1862. Died 7 June, 1862. Bvt. Maj., 23 Sept., 1846, for gallant and meritorious conduct at Monterey.

BACKUS, GEORGE B.* [Born in Penn. Appointed from Col.]
2nd Lieut. 1st Cav., 16 June, 1875. 1st Lieut., 12 Jan., 1880. Died 14 June, 1895.

BACON, ALEXANDER S.* [Born in Mich. Appointed from Mich.]
2nd Lieut. 1st Art., 15 June, 1876. Resigned 15 March, 1878.

BACON, CYRUS. [Born in Mich. Appointed from Mich.]
Asst. Surg. 7th Mich. Vols., 16 Aug., 1861, to 6 May, 1862. Asst. Surg., 16 April, 1862. Bvt. Capt. and Maj. for faithful and meritorious service during the war. Died 1 Sept., 1868.

BACON, GEORGE E.* [Born in N. Y. Appointed from N. Y.]
2nd Lieut. 16th Inf., 12 June, 1871. 1st Lieut., 7 Dec., 1879. Died 20 Dec., 1883.

BACON, GEORGE R.* [Born in Ill. Appointed from Ill.]
2nd Lieut. 1st Cav., 15 June, 1869. 1st Lieut., 28 May, 1875. Resigned 15 June, 1878.

BACON, HENRY. [Born in Mass. Appointed from Mass.]
2nd Lieut. 34th Mass. Vols., 31 July, 1862. 1st Lieut., 9 July, 1863. Discharged 28 Nov., 1864. 2nd Lieut. 23rd Inf., 7 March, 1867. Resigned 3 Oct., 1867.

BACON, JOHN D.* [Born in Maine. Appointed from Maine.]
Bvt. 2nd Lieut. 2nd Inf., 1 July, 1840. 2nd Lieut. 6th Inf., 3 Dec., 1840. 1st Lieut., 18 June, 1846. Died 12 Oct., 1847, of wounds received at the Battle of Churubusco, Mexico.

BACON, JOHN M. [Born in Ky. Appointed from Ky.]
2nd Lieut. 11th Ky. Cav., 22 Sept., 1862. 2nd Lieut. 4th Ky. Cav., 5 Nov., 1862. 1st Lieut., 1 Feb., 1863. Capt., 14 March, 1863. Maj., 20 Nov., 1864. Mustered out 21 Aug., 1865. Capt. 9th Cav., 28 July, 1866. Bvt. Maj., 2 March, 1867, for gallant and meritorious service in the Siege of Resaca, Ga. Col. A. de C., 1 Jan., 1871.

Maj. 7th Cav., 14 April, 1874. Bvt. Lieut. Col., 27 Feb., 1890, for gallant services in the actions against Indians on the Rio Pecos, Tex., 7 June, 1869, and near the headwaters of the Salt Fork of the Brazos River, Tex., 28 and 29 Oct., 1869. Lieut. Col. 1st Cav., 7 April, 1893. Col. 8th Cav., 29 June, 1897. Graduate of the Artillery School, 1872. Brig. Gen. of Vols., 4 May, 1898, to 24 Feb., 1899. Retired, over 30 years' service, 8 May, 1899.

BACON, RUFUS J.* [Born in Maine. Appointed from Maine.]
Bvt. 2nd Lieut. 4th Art., 1 July, 1846. Died 12 Aug., 1846.

BACOT, RICHARD H.* [Born in S. C. Appointed from S. C.]
2nd Lieut. 3rd Inf., 1 July, 1841. Resigned 31 Dec., 1843. Died 17 Aug., 1862.

BADEAU, ADAM. [Born in N. Y. Appointed from N. Y.]
Capt. Addl. A. de C., 29 April, 1862. Lieut. Col. Mil. Sec. to the Lieut. Gen., 29 March, 1864. Bvt. Col. Vols., 24 Feb., 1865, for faithful and meritorious service. Bvt. Brig. Gen. Vols., 9 April, 1865, for gallant and meritorious service during the campaign terminating with the surrender of the insurgent army, under General R. E. Lee. 2nd Lieut. 4th Inf., 22 March, 1866. Mustered out as Capt. Addl. A. de C., 1 July, 1866. Col. A. de C. to the Gen., 25 July, 1866. 1st Lieut., 28 July, 1866. Bvt. Capt., Maj., Lieut. Col., Col. and Brig. Gen., 2 March, 1867, for faithful and meritorious service during the war. Relieved as Col. A. de C. to the Gen., 4 March, 1869. Unassigned 23 March, 1869. Retired with rank of Capt., 18 May, 1869. Died 19 March, 1895.

BADEAU, ELIAS C. [Born in N. Y. Appointed from N. Y.]
Garrison Surg. Mate, 1 March, 1814. Surg. Mate 27th Inf., 21 April, 1814. Disbanded 15 June, 1815.

BADEN, JAMES T. [Born in Md. Appointed from Army.]
Priv., Corpl., Sergt. and 1st Sergt. Co. F, 5th Cav., 23 Oct., 1857, to 3 Oct., 1862. 2nd Lieut. 5th Cav., 17 July, 1862. 1st Lieut., 2 Nov., 1863. Resigned 12 Sept., 1864.

BADEN, NEHEMIAH. [Born in Md. Appointed from Va.]
1st Lieut. Asst. Dep. Com. of Ord., 6 Aug., 1813. Retained as 1st Lieut. Ord., 17 May, 1815. Trans. to 1st Art., 1 June, 1821. Capt., 1 April, 1824. Died 30 Nov., 1836. Bvt. Capt., 6 Aug., 1823, for ten years' faithful service in one grade. Bvt. Maj., 1 April, 1834, for ten years' faithful service in one grade.

BADGER, NICHOLAS D. [Born in N. Y. Appointed from Ohio.]
Priv. Co. F, 2nd Ohio Vols., 17 April, 1861. Discharged 31 July, 1861. 1st Lieut. 44th Ohio Vols., 18 Sept., 1861. Capt., 1 Oct., 1862. Capt. 8th Ohio Cav., 18 Jan., 1864. Maj., 13 June, 1865. Mustered out 30 July, 1865. 2nd Lieut. 10th Cav., 28 July, 1866. 1st Lieut., 29 May, 1867. Reg. Com., 11 Dec., 1867, to 2 April, 1870. Bvt. Capt., 29 May, 1867, for gallant and meritorious service during the war. Trans. to Inf. unass'd, 2 April, 1870. Ass'd to 22nd Inf., 1 Jan., 1871. Retired 28 June, 1878. Died 19 July, 1882.

BADGER, NORMAN. [Born in Mass. Appointed from Ky.]
Hosp. Chaplain Vols., 30 June, 1864. Mustered out 23 Sept., 1865. Chaplain post of Louisville, Ky., 24 Aug., 1865, to 30 April, 1867. Post Chaplain, 3 April, 1867. Died 5 June, 1876.

BADGER, WM. [Born in N. H. Appointed from N. H.]
Capt. 4th N. H. Vols., 18 Sept., 1861. Out of service 4 June, 1864. Bvt. Maj. Vols., 13 March, 1865, for gallant and meritorious service during the war. Capt. 9th U. S. Vet. Vols., 20 June, 1865. Mustered out 20 April, 1866. 2nd Lieut. 6th Inf., 19 May, 1866. 1st Lieut., 9 Feb., 1867. Bvt. Capt., 2 March, 1867, for gallant and meritorious service during the war. Retired 15 Jan., 1889. Died 11 May, 1897.

BADOLLET, JAMES F.* [Born in Penn. Appointed from Ind.]
3rd Lieut. Light Art., 21 July, 1814. Trans. to Corps Art., 17 May, 1815. 2nd Lieut., 1 Oct., 1816. Resigned 1 Aug., 1818. Died 8 May, 1878.

BAGBY, ARTHUR P.* [Born in Ala. Appointed at Large.]
Bvt. 2nd Lieut. 8th Inf., 1 July, 1852. Resigned 30 Sept., 1853.

BAGLEY, EDWARD F. [Born in Ga. Appointed from Ala.]
2nd Lieut. 13th Inf., 25 Sept., 1847. Disbanded 15 July, 1848. 2nd Lieut. 4th Art., 27 June, 1856. 1st Lieut., 17 Aug., 1857. Resigned 1 March, 1861.

BAILEY, ALBERT S.* [Born in Texas. Appointed from Texas.]
2nd Lieut. 9th Cav., 14 June, 1878. Trans. to 6th Cav., 9 Aug., 1878. Resigned 1 Nov., 1883. Died 31 March, 1889.

BAILEY, CHARLES J.* [Born in Pa. Appointed from N. Y.]
2nd Lieut. 1st Art., 12 June, 1880. 1st Lieut., 14 Jan., 1888. Graduate of the Artillery School, 1888. Capt. 7th Art., 2 March, 1899.

BAILEY, CLARENCE M. [Born in Ind. Appointed from Ind.]
2nd Lieut. 6th Inf., 5 Aug., 1861. 1st Lieut., 14 July, 1863. Capt., 28 July, 1866. Unassigned 22 April, 1869. Ass'd to 8th Inf., 15 Dec., 1870. Maj. 15th Inf., 10 July, 1891. Lieut. Col. 18th Inf., 25 April, 1895. Col. 16th Inf., 1 Nov., 1898. Retired (disability) 5 May, 1899.

BAILEY, EDWARD L. [Born in N. H. Appointed from N. H.]
Capt. 2nd N. H. Vols., 7 June, 1861. Maj., 26 July, 1862. Lieut. Col., 20 Feb., 1863. Col. 1 May, 1863. Mustered out 21 June, 1864. 2nd Lieut. 4th Inf., 7 March, 1867. Bvt. 1st Lieut., 6 Nov., 1867, for gallant and meritorious service in the Battle of Williamsburg, Va. Bvt. Capt., 6 Nov., 1867, for gallant and meritorious service in the Battle of Fair Oaks, Va. Bvt. Maj., 6 Nov., 1867, for gallant and meritorious service in the Battle of Bull Run (2nd), Va. Bvt. Lieut. Col., 6 Nov., 1867, for gallant and meritorious service in the Battle of Gettysburg, Penn. 1st Lieut. 4th Inf., 26 Feb., 1876. Capt., 4 Dec., 1891. Dismissed 15 Oct., 1893.

BAILEY, FREDK. W.* [Born in Ohio. Appointed at Large.]
2nd Lieut. 17th Inf., 23 June, 1865. 1st Lieut., 23 June, 1865. R. Q. M., 31 Dec., 1865, to 1 Aug., 1866. Trans. to 35th Inf., 21 Sept., 1866. Capt., 7 Oct., 1867. Dismissed 1 Sept., 1869. Reinstated as Capt. of Inf., 24 Jan., 1870. Unass'd 23 Feb., 1870. Discharged 19 Nov., 1870. Died 23 July, 1878.

BAILEY, GUILFORD D.* [Born in N. Y. Appointed from N. Y.]
2nd Lieut. 2nd Art., 1 July, 1856. 1st Lieut., 14 May, 1861. Capt. A. C. S., 3 Aug., 1861. Col. 1st N. Y. Light Art., 25 Sept., 1861. Killed 31 May, 1862, at Battle of Fair Oaks, Va.

BAILEY, HARRY L.* [Born in Ohio. Appointed from Ohio.]
2nd Lieut. 21st Inf., 15 June, 1876. Bvt. 1st Lieut., 27 Feb., 1890, for gallant services in action against Indians at the Clearwater, Idaho, 11 and 12 July, 1877. 1st Lieut., 25 March, 1884. R. Q. M., 24 Feb., 1889. Capt., 2 Dec., 1897.

BAILEY, HOBART K. [Born in Ind. Appointed from Miss.]
2nd Lieut. 5th Inf., 27 July, 1872. Bvt. 1st Lieut., 27 Feb., 1890, for gallant services in action against Indians on McClellan's Creek, Texas, 8 Nov., 1874. 1st Lieut., 17 Nov., 1879. Reg. Adj., 24 March, 1883, to 31 March, 1889. Capt. A. J. A. ass'd 12 Aug., 1887. Capt., 4 July, 1892.

BAILEY, JACOB W.* [Born in Mass. Appointed from R. I.]
Bvt. 2nd Lieut. 1st Art., 1 July, 1832. 2nd Lieut., 1 July, 1832. 1st Lieut., 6 Aug., 1836. Prof. Mil. Acad., 5 July, 1838. Died 26 Feb., 1857.

BAILEY, JAMES. [Born in N. Y. Appointed from N. Y.]
1st Lieut. 6th Inf., 3 Jan., 1812. Capt., 27 March, 1814. Disbanded 15 June, 1815. Reinstated as 1st Lieut. 2nd Inf., 17 May, 1816. Disbanded 1 June, 1821. Retained 17 May, 1816 (in re-organization under Act of 3 March, 1815), as 1st Lieut. 2nd Inf., with Bvt. of Capt. from 27 March, 1814. Capt., 17 June, 1816. Discharged 1 June, 1821. Died 24 July, 1821.

BAILEY, JOSEPH H. [Born in N. Y. Appointed from N. Y.]
Asst. Surg., 28 Nov., 1834. Capt., 28 Nov., 1839. Retired 27 Aug., 1862. Died 1 April, 1883.

BAILEY, LOUIS C. [Born in N. Y. Appointed from D. C.]
2nd Lieut. 2nd Cav., 8 June, 1861. 5th Cav., 3 Aug., 1861. Appointment expired 17 July, 1862. Capt. 1st D. C. Cav., 10 June, 1863. Resigned 29 Feb., 1864.

BAILEY, THOMAS C. J. [Born in Del. Appointed from Del.]
1st Lieut. 17th Inf., 14 May, 1861. Capt., 14 Dec., 1862. Bvt. Maj. 19 Aug., 1864, for gallant and meritorious service in the Battle of the Weldon Railroad, Va. Retired 18 Aug., 1865.

BAILEY, THOMAS N.* [Born in Tenn. Appointed at Large.]
2nd Lieut. Eng., 13 June, 1873. 1st Lieut., 16 Oct., 1877. Capt., 19 March, 1884. Died 20 April, 1886.

BAILEY, WM. [Born in Va. Appointed from Va.]
1st Lieut. 10th Inf., 12 March, 1812. Capt., 19 July, 1814. Disbanded 15 June, 1815. Reinstated 2 Dec., 1815, as 1st Lieut. 7th Inf., with Bvt. of Capt. from 19 July, 1814. Dismissed 31 May, 1817.

BAILY, CHAS. M. [Born in Ind. Ter. Appointed at Large.]
2nd Lieut. 8th Inf., 7 March, 1867. 1st Lieut., 30 May, 1877. R. Q. M., 1 Oct., 1878, to 28 Feb., 1882. Reg. Adj., 1 March, 1882, to 31 Dec., 1885. Died 31 Dec., 1885.

BAILY, ELISHA I. [Born in Penn. Appointed from Penn.]
1st Lieut. Asst. Surg., 16 Feb., 1847. Capt. Asst. Surg., 16 Feb., 1852. Maj. Surg., 15 May, 1861. Bvt. Lieut. Col., 13 March, 1865, for faithful and meritorious service during the war. Lieut. Col. Surg., 26 June, 1876. Col. Surg., 30 Jan., 1883. Retired (op. of law), 14 Nov., 1888.

BAILY, JOSEPH C. [Born in Penn. Appointed from Penn.]
1st Lieut. Asst. Surg., 27 Oct., 1857. Capt. Asst. Surg., 27 Oct., 1862. Maj. Surg., 1 Dec., 1864. Bvt. Lieut. Col., 13 March, 1865, for faithful and meritorious service during the war. Lieut. Col. Asst. Med. Pur., 18 Nov., 1886. Col. Surg., 9 March, 1892. Died 16 May, 1894.

BAINBRIDGE, AUGUSTUS H. [Born in N. Y. Appointed from Army.]
Priv. Gen. Ser., 11 Aug., 1858. Sergt. Co. A, 2nd Batt. 14th Inf., 14 June, 1862. 2nd Lieut. 14th Inf., 14 July, 1862. 1st Lieut., 9 June, 1864. Bvt. Capt., 18 Aug., 1864, for gallant services during the operations on the Weldon Railroad. Capt. 14th Inf., 11 Aug., 1866. Maj. 10th Inf., 14 Oct., 1892. Lieut. Col. 4th Inf., 17 April, 1897. Retired (at own request) 11 Aug., 1898.

BAINBRIDGE, EDMUND C.* [Born in Va. Appointed from N. Y.]
Bvt. 2nd Lieut. 3rd Art., 1 July, 1856. 2nd Lieut. 4th Art., 31 Oct., 1856. 1st Lieut., 2 Nov., 1859. Trans. to 5th Art., May 14, 1861. Capt. A. Q. M., 3 Aug., 1861. Capt. 5th Art., 30 Aug., 1862. Vacated commission of Capt. Q. M., 30 Aug., 1862. Maj. A. de C. Vols., 3 Sept., 1864. Bvt. Maj. and Lieut. Col., 13 March, 1865, for faithful and meritorious services during the war. Mustered out of Vol. service, 1 July, 1866. Col. 3rd Art., 12 Feb., 1895. Retired by direction of the President, being 62 years of age, 15 Oct., 1897.

BAINBRIDGE, HENRY.* [Born in N. Y. Appointed from Mass.]
2nd Lieut. 3rd Inf., 1 July, 1821. 1st Lieut., 6 June, 1827. Capt., 15 June, 1836. Maj. 7th Inf., 16 Feb., 1847. Lieut. Col. 1st Inf., 11 June, 1851. Drowned 31 May, 1857, by burning of steamer in Galveston Bay. Bvt. Maj., 23 Sept., 1846, for gallant and meritorious conduct at Monterey. Bvt. Lieut. Col., 20 Aug., 1847, for gallant and meritorious conduct at Contreras and Churubusco.

BAINBRIDGE, WM. P. [Born in Mich. Appointed from Ind.]
2nd Lieut. 101st Ind. Vols., 15 Feb., 1863. Capt. A. de C. Vols., 3 Sept., 1864. Mustered out 9 Feb., 1866. 2nd Lieut. 3rd Cav., 29 Nov., 1865. 1st Lieut., 28 July, 1866. Mustered out 28 Dec., 1870.

BAINBRIDGE, WM. P.* [Born in Ky. Appointed from Ky.]
Bvt. 2nd Lieut. 3rd Art., 1 July, 1824. 2nd Lieut. 4th Art., 1 July, 1824. 1st Lieut., 30 May, 1832. Capt., 19 March, 1842. Died 16 Sept., 1850. Bvt. Maj., 18 April, 1847, for gallant and meritorious conduct in the Battle of Cerro Gordo, Mexico.

BAIRD, ABSOLOM.* [Born in Penn. Appointed from Penn.]
Bvt. 2nd Lieut. 2nd Art., 1 July, 1849. 2nd Lieut. 1st Art., 1 April, 1850. 1st Lieut., 24 Dec., 1853. Bvt. Capt. A. A. G., 11 May, 1861. Vacated commission of 1st Lieut. Art., 14 May, 1861. Capt. A. A. G., 3 Aug., 1861. Vacated 14 Nov., 1861. Maj. A. I. G., 12 Nov., 1861. Brig. Gen. Vols., 28 April, 1862. Bvt. Lieut. Col., 20 Sept., 1863, for gallant and meritorious services in the Battle of Chickamauga, Ga. Bvt. Col., 24 Nov., 1863, for gallant and meritorious service in the Battle of Chattanooga, Tenn. Bvt. Maj. Gen. Vols., 1 Sept., 1864, for faithful services and discreet conduct during the Atlanta campaign, and particularly in the Battles of Resaca and Jonesboro, and for general good conduct in the command of his division

against Savannah. Bvt. Brig. G., 13 March, 1865, for gallant and meritorious service in the capture of Atlanta, Ga. Bvt. Maj. Gen., 13 March, 1865, for gallant and meritorious services in the field during the war. Mustered out of Vol. service, 1 Sept., 1866. Lieut. Col. A. I. G., 13 June, 1867, with pay from 16 June, 1874 (Act 16 June, 1874). Col. I. G., 11 March, 1885. Brig. Gen. I. G., 22 Sept., 1885. Retired (op. of law) 20 Aug., 1888. Medal of Honor for most distinguished gallantry in action at Jonesboro, Ga., Sept. 1, 1864, voluntarily leading a detached brigade in an assault upon the enemy's works; while serving as Brig. Gen. of Vols., commanding a division.

BAIRD, GEORGE W. [Born in Conn. Appointed from Conn.]
Priv. 1st Batty Conn. 1st Art., 25 Aug., 1862. Priv. Co. H., 13th Reg. Vet. Res. Corps, 19 Dec., 1863. Discharged, 14 March, 1864. Col. 32nd U. S. Col. Troops, 18 March, 1864. Mustered out, 22 Aug., 1865. 2nd Lieut. 19th Inf., 11 May, 1866. Trans. to 37th Inf., 21 Sept., 1866. 1st Lieut., 27 April, 1867. Trans. to 5th Inf., 19 May, 1869. Maj. P. M., 23 June, 1879. Bvt. Capt., 27 Feb., 1890, for gallant services in actions against Indians at Red River, Tex., 30 Aug., 1874, and at Bear Paw Mountain, Mont., 30 Sept., 1877, in which last named action he was severely wounded (declined). Lieut. Col. and Dep. P. M. G., 12 July, 1890. Medal of Honor for most distinguished gallantry in action against hostile Nez Perce Indians at Bear Paw Mountain, Mont., Sept. 30, 1877, where he was twice severely wounded while serving as 1st Lieut. and Adj. 5th Inf.

BAIRD, THOMAS J.* [Born in Ireland. Appointed from Penn.]
3rd Lieut. Light Art., 21 July, 1814. Trans. to Corps Art., 17 May, 1815. 2nd Lieut., 1 Aug., 1816. 1st Lieut., 2 June, 1818. Trans. to 3rd Art., 1 June, 1821. Capt., 28 Feb., 1827. Resigned 1 May, 1828. Died 5 April, 1842.

BAIRD, WM.* [Born in Penn. Appointed at Large.]
2nd Lieut. 6th Cav., 16 June, 1875. 1st Lieut., 15 Feb., 1881. Reg. Adj., 27 Nov., 1884, to 1 Nov., 1886. Capt., 24 Feb., 1891. Retired for disability, 3 Dec., 1897.

BAKER, CHAS. T.* [Born in Conn. Appointed at Large.]
Bvt. 2nd Lieut., 3rd Inf., 1 July, 1842. 2nd Lieut. 6th Inf., 30 March, 1844. 1st Lieut., 15 April, 1851. Resigned 31 Dec., 1851. Died 28 Feb., 1881.

BAKER, CHAUNCEY B.* [Born in Ohio. Appointed from Ohio.]
2nd Lieut. 7th Inf., 1 July, 1886. 1st Lieut., 29 Sept., 1892. Capt., 2 March, 1899. Honor graduate of the Infantry and Cavalry School, 1889. Capt. A. Q. M. Vols., 12 May to 30 Nov., 1898. Maj. Q. M. Vols., 7 Jan., 1899.

BAKER, DANIEL. [Born in N. H. Appointed from Vt.]
Ensign 16th Inf., 8 Jan., 1799. 2nd Lieut., 3 March, 1799. Discharged 15 June, 1800. 2nd Lieut. 3rd Inf., 16 Feb., 1801. Trans. to 1st Inf., 1 April, 1802. 1st Lieut., 11 Aug., 1806. Capt., 12 March, 1812. Maj. 45th Inf., 15 April, 1814. Retained Capt. 8th Inf., 17 May, 1815. Maj. 7th Inf., 1 June, 1819. Lieut. Col. 6th Inf., 1 May, 1829. Died 30 Oct., 1836. Bvt. Maj., 9 Aug., 1812, for gallant conduct at the Battle of Brownsville.

BAKER, DAVID. [Born in Ill. Appointed from Ill.]
Asst. Surg., 23 July, 1898.

BAKER, DAVID, J., Jr.* [Born in Ill. Appointed from Ill.]
2nd Lieut. 12th Inf., 1 July, 1886. 1st Lieut. 24th Inf., 9 July, 1892. Trans. to 12th Inf., 24 Feb., 1893. Capt., 2 March, 1899.

BAKER, EDWARD D. [Born in Ill. Appointed from Oregon.]
2nd Lieut. 1st Cav., 8 May, 1861. 1st Lieut. 4th Cav., 17 July, 1862. Reg. Adj., 30 Nov., 1862, to 1 April, 1863. Capt. A. Q. M., 13 March, 1863. Resigned commission 1st Lieut. 4th Cav., 12 Oct., 1864. Maj. Q. M., 21 April, 1879. Died 25 Jan., 1883.

BAKER, EUGENE M.* [Born in N. Y. Appointed from N. Y.]
Bvt. 2nd Lieut. 2nd Drag., 1 July, 1859. 2nd Lieut. 1st Drag., 28 Feb., 1860. 1st Lieut., 7 May, 1861. R. Q. M., Dec., 1861, to 16 Jan., 1862. Capt., 16 Jan., 1862. Bvt. Maj., 5 May, 1862, for gallant and meritorious services in the Battle of Williamsburg, Va. Bvt. Lieut. Col., 19 Sept., 1864, for gallant and meritorious service in the Battle of Winchester, Va. Bvt. Col., 1 Dec., 1868, for zeal and energy while in command of troops operating against hostile Indians in 1866, 1867 and 1868. Maj. 2nd Cav., 8 April, 1869. Died 19 Dec., 1884.

BAKER, FRANK.* [Born in Mass. Appointed from Mass.]
2nd Lieut. 13th Inf., 14 June, 1872. 1st Lieut., 1 Nov., 1874. Trans. to Ord., 18 April, 1879. Capt. (14 years' service), 14 June, 1886.

BAKER, HENRY. [Born in England. Appointed from Army.]
Priv., Corpl. and Sergt. Co. A. and Sergt. Maj. 5th Cav., 13 Aug., 1860, to 22 Sept., 1862. 2nd Lieut. 5th Cav., 17 July, 1862. 1st Lieut., 13 April, 1863. Dropped 12 Jan., 1866.

BAKER, HORATIO N. [Born in Vt. Appointed from Vt.]
2nd Lieut. 3rd Inf., 13 Aug., 1819. 1st Lieut., 3rd Sept., 1822. Died 13 Oct., 1823.

BAKER, ISAAC L. [Born in Ky. Appointed from Ky.]
2nd Lieut. 2nd Inf., 6 July, 1812. Trans. to 44th Inf., — Aug., 1813. Capt., 5th April, 1813. Trans. to 1st Inf., 17 May, 1815. Resigned 1 May, 1817. Bvt. Maj., 23 Dec., 1814, for gallant conduct at the Siege of New Orleans.

BAKER, JAMES. [Born in Conn. Appointed from D. C.]
1st Lieut. Asst. Dep. Com. Ord., 6 Aug., 1813. Retained as 1st Lieut. Ord., 8 Feb., 1815. Resigned 3 Dec., 1819. Mil. Storekeeper, 17 March, 1837. Died 20 March, 1844.

BAKER, JOHN P. [Born in Ill. Appointed from Ill.]
2nd Lieut. 1st Drag., 23 March, 1861. 1st Lieut., 13 May, 1861. 1st Cav., 3 Aug., 1861. Capt., 17 July, 1862. Capt. A. de C. Vols. 20 Aug., 1862, which was revoked 14 Feb., 1863. Resigned 1 July, 1868. Bvt. Maj., 9 April, 1864, for gallant and meritorious service at the Battle of Pleasant Hill, La. Bvt. Lieut. Col., 13 March, 1865, for gallant and meritorious service during the war. Appointed Maj. P. M., 8 Dec., 1882.

BAKER, JOSHUA.* [Born in Ky. Appointed from La.]
2nd Lieut. Corps Art., 1 July, 1819. Resigned 31 Oct., 1820. Died 15 April, 1885.

BAKER, LAWRENCE S.* [Born in N. C. Appointed from N. C.]
Bvt. 2nd Lieut. Mounted Rifle, 1 July, 1851. 2nd Lieut., 31 March, 1853. 1st Lieut., 22 Nov., 1859. Resigned 10 May, 1861.

BAKER, R. T. [Born in N. Y. Appointed from N. J.]
Surg. Mate 15th Inf., 12 March, 1812. Disbanded 15 June, 1815.

BAKER, ROBERT F.* [Born in N. Y. Appointed from N. Y.]
Bvt. 2nd Lieut. 7th Inf., 1 July, 1836. 2nd Lieut. 19 Jan., 1837. 1st Lieut., 26 Nov., 1841. Dismissed 16 March, 1844. Died 13 Dec., 1845.

BAKER, RUFUS L. [Born in Conn. Appointed from Conn.]
1st Lieut. Asst. Dep. Com. Ord., 12 March, 1813. Capt., 21 May, 1817. Trans. to 3rd Art., 1 June, 1821. Capt. Ord., 30 May, 1832. Maj., 6 July, 1838. Lieut. Col., 10 July, 1851. Resigned 31 Dec., 1854. Bvt. Maj., 21 May, 1827, for ten years' faithful service in one grade. Bvt. Lieut. Col., 30 May, 1848, for meritorious conduct, particularly in performing his duties in prosecuting war with Mexico.

BAKER, STEPHEN. [Born in Mich. Appointed from Army.]
Priv. Co. E, 6th Inf., 20 Aug., 1860. Corpl., 7 March, 1862. Sergt. Maj. 6th Inf., 1 April, 1863. Priv. Co. F, 6th Inf., 24 Aug., 1863. Sergt., 1 Sept., 1863. Sergt. Co. D, 6th Inf., 18 March, 1864. 1st Sergt., 20 March, 1864. Discharged 10 July, 1864. 1st Sergt. Co. D, 6th Inf., 11 July, 1864. Q. M. Sergt. 6th Inf., 6 Oct., 1864. 2nd Lieut. and 1st Lieut. 6th Inf., 3 May, 1865. Capt., 8 June, 1874. Maj. 4th Inf., 7 July, 1897. Retired (over 30 years' service) 11 Jan., 1899.

BAKER, WM. [Born in D. C. Appointed from D. C.]
Post Surg., 20 June, 1817. Resigned 12 Aug., 1818.

BAKER, WM. B. [Born in ——. Appointed from ——.]
2nd Lieut. of Inf., 1st Dec., 1899. Unassigned Jan. 1, 1900.

BAKER, WM. H.* [Born in Mich. Appointed from Vt.]
Bvt. 2nd Lieut. 4th Inf., 1 July, 1828. 2nd Lieut., 1 July, 1828. Resigned 20 May, 1831. Died in 1835.

BAKER, WM. L. [Born in Mass. Appointed from Mass.]
2nd Lieut. 4th Art., 5 Aug., 1861. 1st Lieut., 5 Aug., 1861. Killed at the Battle of Antietam, Md., 17 Sept., 1862.

BAKER, WM. P. [Born in Ark. Appointed from Ark.]
2nd Lieut. 10th Inf., 12 June, 1887. Resigned 16 Feb., 1889.

BALCH, GEORGE T.* [Born in Maine. Appointed from Ohio.]
Bvt. 2nd Lieut. Ord., 1 July, 1851. 2nd Lieut., 26 Feb., 1853. 1st Lieut., 1 July, 1854. Capt., 1 Nov., 1861. Resigned 1 Dec., 1865. Bvt. Maj. and Lieut. Col., 13 March, 1865, for faithful and meritorious service in the Ord. Dept.

BALDER, CHRISTIAN. [Born in Germany. Appointed from Army.]
Priv., Corpl. and Sergt. Co. A, 1st Cav., 13 April, 1855, to 26 Oct., 1861. 2nd Lieut. 6th Cav., 26 Oct., 1861. 1st Lieut., 23 Dec., 1862. Killed 3 July, 1863, at the Battle of Gettysburg, Penn.

BALDEY, GEORGE. [Born in Penn. Appointed from La.]
Priv. Co. G, 16th Inf., 14 April, 1847, to 5 Aug., 1848. Priv. and Sergt. 2nd Colo. Cav., 14 Sept., 1862. 1st Lieut. and Adj., 20 Nov., 1862. Maj. 65th U. S. Col. Inf., 28 Jan., 1864. Lieut. Col. 21 June, 1865. Bvt. Brig. Gen. Vols., 13 March, 1865, for faithful and meritorious service. Mustered out 8 Jan., 1867. 1st Lieut. 39th Inf., 28 July, 1866. Capt., 20 July, 1868. Unass'd 20 April, 1869. Discharged 5 Oct., 1870. Bvt. Capt., 2 March, 1867, for gallant and meritorious service in New Mexico, Colorado, and on the Plains, while Adj. of the 3rd Col. Vols.

BALDRIDGE, BENJ. L. [Born in Ohio. Appointed from Kansas.]
Post Chaplain, 8 June, 1876. Retired by op. of law 9 Feb., 1885.

BALDWIN, ALEXANDER G.* [Born in Va. Appointed from Va.]
Bvt. 2nd Lieut. 3rd Inf., 1 July, 1826. 2nd Lieut., 1 July, 1826. Died 25 July, 1835.

BALDWIN, BRISCOE G. [Born in Va. Appointed from Ala.]
Mil. Storekeeper, 3 Oct., 1851. Resigned 22 April, 1861.

BALDWIN, FRANK D. [Born in Mich. Appointed from Mich.]
2nd Lieut. Mich. Horse Guards, 19 Sept., 1861. Mustered out 22 Nov., 1861. 1st Lieut. 19th Mich. Vols., 5 Sept., 1862. Capt., 1 March, 1864. Mustered out 10 June, 1865. 2nd Lieut. and 1st Lieut. 19th Inf., 23 Feb., 1866. Trans. to 37th Inf., 21 Sept., 1866. Trans. to 5th Inf., 19 May, 1869. Capt., 20 March, 1879. Bvt. Capt., 27 Feb., 1890, for gallant services in actions against Indians on the Salt Fork of the Red River, Tex., 30 Aug., 1874, and on McLellan's Creek, Tex., 8 Nov., 1874. Bvt. Maj., 27 Feb., 1890, for gallant and successful attack on Sitting Bull's Camp of Indians, on Red Water River, Mont., 18 Dec., 1876, and conspicuous gallantry in action against Indians at Wolf Mountain, Mont., 8 Jan., 1877. Maj. 5th Inf., 26 April, 1898. Trans. to 3rd Inf., 3 Nov., 1899. Lieut. Col. I. G. Vols., 9 May, 1898, to 12 May, 1899. Medals of Honor for distinguished bravery in the Battle of Peach Tree Creek, Ga., July 20, 1864, while serving as Capt. 19th Mich. Inf.; for most distinguished gallantry in action against hostile Indians near McLellan's Creek, Tex., Nov. 8, 1874, in attacking the Indians with two companies, D, 6th Cav., and D, 5th Inf., forcing them from their strong position and pursuing them until they were utterly routed. Lieut. Col. 3rd Inf., 18 Dec., 1899.

BALDWIN, HENRY M. [Born in N. J. Appointed from N. J.]
2nd Lieut. 5th Art., 14 May, 1861. Died 8 Nov., 1864, of wounds received at the Battle of Cedar Creek, Va., 19 Oct., 1864.

BALDWIN, HOMER H. [Born in Ohio. Appointed from Ohio.]
Priv. and Sergt. Co. E, 1st Ohio Vols., 17 April to 26 June, 1861. 2nd Lieut. 5th Art., 14 May, 1861. 1st Lieut., 2 Dec., 1864. Died 11 June, 1870. Bvt. 1st Lieut., 6 July, 1863, for gallant and meritorious service at the Battle of Gettysburg, Penn. Bvt. Capt., 8 April, 1864, for gallant and meritorious service in the Red River campaign.

BALDWIN, ISAAC H. [Born in Va. Appointed from Va.]
Asst. Surg., 30 Aug., 1836. Resigned 31 May, 1841.

BALDWIN, JAMES H. [Born in Mass. Appointed from Mass.]
1st Lieut. 35th Mass. Vols., 16 Aug., 1862. 1st Lieut. 3rd Co. Mass. Heavy Art., 19 Jan., 1863. Capt. 1st Batty Mass. Heavy Art., 26 May, 1863. Mustered out 20

Oct., 1865. 2nd Lieut. 16th Inf., 30 March, 1866. Trans. to 25th Inf., 21 Sept., 1866. 1st Lieut., 31 July, 1867. Trans. to 18th Inf., 26 April, 1869. R. Q. M., 29 April, to 30 June, 1869. Capt., 6 Oct., 1887. Retired for disability 30 Nov., 1892. Died 11 Nov., 1894.

BALDWIN, JOHN A. [Born in Iowa. Appointed from N. Y.]
2nd Lieut. 9th Inf., 27 July, 1872. 1st Lieut., 9 May, 1881. Capt., 4 Nov., 1890. Graduate of the Infantry and Cavalry School, 1885. Maj. 22nd Inf., 2 June, 1899.

BALDWIN, JOHN M.* [Born in La. Appointed from La.]
2nd Lieut. 5th Art., 16 June, 1875. 1st Lieut., 26 June, 1882. Resigned 30 March, 1884.

BALDWIN, MURRAY. [Born in Cal. Appointed from the Army.]
Priv. and Corpl. Batty I, 2nd Art., 21 March, 1892, to 1 Nov., 1894. 2nd Lieut. 18th Inf., 31 Oct., 1894. 1st Lieut. 11th Inf., 27 May, 1898. Trans. to 18th Inf., 13 May, 1899.

BALDWIN, THEODORE A. [Born in N. J. Appointed from Army.]
Priv. 19th Inf., 3 May, 1862. Q. M. Sergt., 9 June, 1862. Discharged 3 May, 1865. 2nd Lieut. and 1st Lieut. 19th Inf., 9 Feb., 1865. R. Q. M., 23 Nov., 1866, to 23 July, 1867. Capt., 23 July, 1867. Unass'd 31 March, 1869. Ass'd to 10th Cav., 15 Dec., 1870. Maj. 7th Cav., 5 Oct., 1887. Lieut. Col. 10th Cav., 11 Dec., 1896. Col. 7th Cav., 6 May, 1899. Brig. Gen. Vols., 6 Oct., 1898, to 31 Jan., 1899.

BALDWIN, THEODORE A., Jr. [Born in Ind. T. Appointed from Mont.]
2nd Lieut. 24th Inf., 9 Sept., 1898. 1st Lieut., 20 Nov., 1899.

BALDWIN, WM. H.* [Born in Penn. Appointed from Penn.]
Addl. 2nd Lieut. 5th Cav., 15 June, 1877. 2nd Lieut. 7th Cav., 30 Sept., 1877. 1st Lieut. 9th Cav., 12 Dec., 1890. Trans. to 7th Cav., 9 Feb., 1892. Capt. C. S., 14 Oct., 1896. Maj. C. S., 9 Sept., 1898. Lieut. Col. Chief C. S. Vols., 9 May, 1898. Col. C. S. Vols., 22 July, 1898, to 2 March, 1899. Discharged from Vol. service, 7 March, 1899.

BALFE, JOHN E. [Born in Ireland. Appointed from Ind.]
Maj. 35th Ind. Vols., 11 Dec., 1861. Lieut. Col., 18 March, 1862. Resigned 6 April, 1862. Lieut. Col. 35th Ind. Vols., 29 Sept., 1862. Resigned 11 April, 1864. 2nd Lieut. 39th Inf., 28 July, 1866. Resigned 15 June, 1867.

BALK, STEPHEN S. [Born in England. Appointed from Army.]
Priv., Musician, Corpl. and Sergt. Batty A, 2nd Art., 15 Feb., 1845, to 15 Feb., 1850, and 13 Sept., 1850, to 13 Sept., 1855. Priv. and Sergt. Gen. Mounted Service, 21 June, 1856, to 21 June, 1861. and from 1 July to 24 Aug., 1861. 2nd Lieut. 6th Cav., 20 Aug., 1861. 1st Lieut., 17 July, 1862. Wholly retired 4 May, 1864.

BALL, CHAS. J. [Born in Ohio. Appointed from D. C.]
1st Lieut. 13th Inf., 14 May, 1861. Dismissed 10 Jan., 1864.

BALL, EDWARD. [Born in Penn. Appointed from Army.]
Entered service under name of David Rey. Priv. Co. H, 4th Inf., 25 Nov., 1844. Trans. to Co. E, 2 June, 1846. Discharged 25 Nov., 1849. Priv. Co. H, 1st Drag., 7 May, 1850. Corpl., 1 Jan., 1851. 1st Sergt., 1 June, 1851. Discharged 7 May, 1855. Priv. Co. H, 1st Drag., 7 March, 1856. Corpl., 1 Aug., 1856. 1st Sergt., 13 Aug., 1856. Priv., 16 July, 1857. Corpl. 27 March, 1858. 1st Sergt., 5 May, 1858. Discharged 7 Jan., 1861. 1st Sergt. Co. H, 1st Drag., 7 Jan., 1861. 2nd Lieut., 12th Inf., 14 May, 1861. Trans. to 2nd Cav., 20 Sept., 1861. 1st Lieut., 5 April, 1862. R. Q. M., 24 Sept., 1862, to 25 July, 1865. Capt., 25 July, 1865. Maj. 7th Cav., 1 April, 1880. Retired for disability 14 April, 1884. Died 22 Oct., 1884.

BALL, FRANK W. [Born in ——. Appointed from the Army.]
Priv. and Corpl. Co. A, 17th Inf., 18 Jan., 1897, to 24 Nov., 1899. 2nd Lieut. 18th Inf., 1st Oct., 1899.

BALL, GEORGE E. [Born in Mich. Appointed from Mich.]
1st Sergt. 35th Mich. Vols., 13 July to 12 Sept., 1898. 2nd Lieut., 13 Sept., 1898. 1st Lieut., 6 March to 31 March, 1899. 2nd Lieut. 21st Inf., 10 April, 1899.

BALL, JAMES V. [Born in Va. Appointed from Va.]
Cornet Light Drag., 1 May, 1794. Lieut. Drag., 19 Oct., 1795. Capt., 6 Feb., 1799. Disbanded 1 June, 1802. Capt. Light Drag., 28 April, 1812. Maj. 2nd Light Drag., 16 Sept., 1812. Disbanded 15 June, 1815. Reinstated as Maj. 6th Inf., 17 May, 1816. Lieut. Col. 1st Inf., 31 March, 1817. Died 24 Feb., 1818. Bvt. Lieut. Col. 18 Dec., 1812, for gallant conduct at the Battle of Misseneway River.

BALL, ROBT. M. Born in Va. Appointed from Penn.]
Surg. Mate 4th Inf., 17 Feb., 1817. Post Surg., 4 Dec., 1819. Died 13 Oct., 1820.

BALL, LOUIS R. [Born ——. Appointed from ——..
2nd Lieut. of Cav., 1 Dec., 1899.

BALL, ROBT. R. [Born in Va. Appointed from Va.]
Asst. Surg., 19 Nov., 1886. Capt. Asst. Surg., 19 Nov., 1891. Died 5 Oct., 1897.

BALLANCE, JOHN G.* [Born in Ill. Appointed from Ill.]
2nd Lieut. 16th Inf., 16 June, 1875. Trans. to 22nd Inf., 1 July, 1875. 1st. Lieut., 25 Feb., 1881. R. Q. M., 22 Sept., 1882, to 22 April, 1884. Capt. A. J. A., 17 Aug., 1884, to 1 April, 1890. Capt., 14 Jan., 1892. Maj. I. G. Vols., 17 May, 1898, to 20 Feb., 1899.

BALLANTINE, GEORGE W. [Born in Penn. Appointed from Penn.]
Priv. Co. I, 12th Pa. Vols., 25 April, 1861. Mustered out 24 July, 1861. Priv. and 1st Sergt. 9th Pa. Res. and Co. K, 190th Pa. Vols., 15 Aug., 1862, until mustered out 28 June, 1865. 2nd Lieut. 15th Inf., 23 Feb., 1866. 1st Lieut., 7 March, 1867. Capt., 25 Aug., 1868. Unass'd 12 Aug., 1869. Ass'd to 7th Inf., 1 Jan., 1871. Resigned 15 May, 1871.

BALLARD, JAMES H. [Born in ——. Appointed from Md.]
2nd Lieut. 36th Inf., 30 April, 1813. Reg. Adj., Aug., 1813, to March, 1814. 1st Lieut. 4th Rifle, 17 March, 1814. Reg. Adj., March, 1814, to June, 1815. Trans. to Rifle Reg. 17 May, 1815. Capt., 22 April, 1817. Trans. to 2nd Inf., 1 June, 1821. Trans. to 4th Art., 10 Oct., 1822. Died 15 Jan., 1823.

BALLARD, WM. [Born in Mass. Appointed from Mass.]
Garrison Surg. Mate, 24 March, 1812. Post Surg., 18 April, 1818. Asst. Surg., 1 June, 1821. Resigned 28 Feb., 1822.

BALLARD, WM. H. [Born in La. Appointed from La.]
Asst. Surg., 29 June, 1849. Resigned 30 April, 1850.

BALLOU, CHARLES C.* [Born in N. Y. Appoinetd from Ill.]
2nd Lieut. 16th Inf., 1 July, 1886. 1st Lieut. 12th Inf., 28 April, 1893. Capt., 2 March, 1899. Maj. 7th Ill. Vols., 8 July to 20 Oct., 1898.

BALTZELL, GEORGE F.* [Born in Fla. Appointed from Fla.]
Addl. 2nd Lieut. 12th Inf., 11 June, 1897. 2nd Lieut. 5th Inf., 16 Dec., 1897. 1st Lieut., 2 March, 1899.

BAMFORD, FRANK E. [Born in Wis. Appointed from the Army.]
Priv., Corpl. and Sergt. Co. E, and Sergt. Maj. 2nd Inf., 14 July, 1891, to 3 Nov., 1893. 2nd Lieut. 5th Inf., 7 Oct., 1893. 1st Lieut., 15th Inf., 26 April, 1898.

BANCROFT, EUGENE A. [Born in Mass. Appointed from Mass.]
Priv. Steel's Co., Sturgis Rifles, Ill. Vols., 6 May to 9 Nov., 1861. 2nd Lieut. 4th Art., 24 Oct., 1861. Bvt. 1st Lieut., 25 June, 1862, for gallant and meritorious service in action near Fair Oaks, Va. 1st Lieut. 4th Art., 13 Dec., 1862. R. Q. M., 12 July, 1865, to 26 April, 1873. Bvt. Capt., 3 July, 1863, for gallant and meritorious service in the Battle of Gettysburg, Penn. Capt. 15th Inf., 22 Jan., 1867, declined. Capt. 4th Art., 26 April, 1873. Retired by op. of law 17 June, 1889. Bvt. Maj., 27 Feb., 1890, for gallant services in actions against Indians at the Clearwater, Idaho, 11 and 12 July, 1877, where he was severely wounded.

BANDHOLTZ, HARRY H.* [Born in Mich. Appointed from Mich.]
2nd Lieut. 6th Inf., 12 June, 1890. 1st Lieut., 24th Inf., 12 Feb., 1897. Trans. to 7th Inf., 29 March, 1897. Maj. 35th Mich. Vols., 25 July, 1898, to 31 March, 1899. Capt. 2nd Inf., 15 Nov., 1899.

BANDY, WM. M. [Born in Ill. Appointed from Ill.]
2nd Lieut. 37th Ill. Vols., 18 Sept., 1861. 1st Lieut., 7 June, 1863. Resigned 17 Oct., 1864. 2nd Lieut. 28th Inf., 29 Aug., 1867. Trans. to 19th Inf., 31 March, 1869. Resigned 30 June, 1873. Died 8 May, 1884.

BANGS, OLIVER O. [Born in ——. Appointed from Army.]
Sergt. 3rd Art., 6 May, 1812, to Oct., 1813. 3rd Lieut. 3rd Art., 11 Oct., 1813. 2nd Lieut., 19 April, 1814. Trans. to Corps Art., 12 May, 1814. Resigned 30 Sept., 1814. 2nd Lieut. Ord., 2 Dec., 1815. 1st Lieut., 13 Aug., 1819. Disbanded 1 June, 1821.

BANISTER, JOHN M. [Born in Ala. Appointed from Ala.]
Asst. Surg., 3 June, 1879. Capt., 3 June, 1884. Maj. Surg., 26 Jan., 1897.

BANISTER, WM. B. [Born in Ala. Appointed from Ala.]
Asst. Surg., 26 Jan., 1886. Capt., 26 Jan., 1891. Maj. Brig. Surg. Vols., 4 June, 1898, to 30 April, 1899. Maj. Surg. Vols., 11 Nov., 1899.

BANKHEAD, HENRY C.* [Born in Md. Appointed at Large.]
Bvt. 2nd Lieut. 5th Inf., 1 July, 1850. 2nd Lieut., 4 Aug., 1851. 1st Lieut. 19 July, 1855. Capt., 25 June, 1861. Lieut. Col. A. I. G. (Act 17 July, 1862), 1 Jan., 1863. Bvt. Maj., 3 July, 1863, for gallant and meritorious service in the Battle of Gettysburg, Penn. Bvt. Lieut. Col., 8 May, 1864, for gallant and meritorious service in the Battle of Spottsylvania, Va. Brev. Col. Vols., 1 Aug, 1864, for brave conduct and efficient service in the battles and marches of the campaign. Bvt. Brig. Gen. Vols., 1 April, 1865, for gallant and meritorious service in the Battle of Five Forks, Va. Bvt. Col., 2 April, 1865, for gallant and meritorious service in front of Petersburg, Va. Relieved as Lieut. Col. A. I. G., 1 Aug., 1865. Bvt. Brig. Gen., 1 Oct., 1868, for the prompt, energetic, and meritorious service rendered by him during the present campaign against hostile Indians, and especially in the prompt relief of Col. Forsyth's beleaguered party on the Republican in Sept., 1868. Trans. to 8th Cav., 15 Dec., 1870. Maj. 4th Cav., 15 Jan., 1873. Retired 12 Nov., 1879. Died Jan. 9, 1894.

BANKHEAD, HENRY M. [Born in Ala. Appointed from Ala.]
Capt. 5th U. S. Vols., 15 July, 1898, to 31 May, 1899. 2nd Lieut. 20th Inf., 15 June, 1899.

BANKHEAD, JAMES. [Born in Va. Appointed from Va.]
Capt. 5th Inf., 18 June, 1808. Maj. A. A. G., 5 March, 1813. Maj. 7th Inf., 15 Aug., 1813. Col. A. G., 9 Sept., 1813. Disbanded 15 June, 1815. Reinstated as Maj. Corps Art., 2 Dec., 1815. Trans. to 3rd Art., 1 June, 1821. Lieut. Col., 26 April, 1832. Col. 2nd Art., 16 Sept., 1838. Died 11 Nov., 1856. Retained 17 May, 1815, (in re-organization under Act of 3 March, 1815), as Capt. 4th Inf., with Bvt. of Maj. from 15 Aug., 1813 (the date of his appointment as Maj. 4th Inf.) Bvt. Lieut. Col., 15 Aug., 1823, for ten years' faithful service in one grade. Bvt. Col., 7 July, 1838, for meritorious conduct in campaigns in Florida. Bvt. Brig. Gen., 29 March, 1847, for gallant and meritorious conduct at the Siege of Vera Cruz.

BANKS, CECIL R. [Born in Penn. Appointed from Penn.]
Priv. 22nd Pa. Cav., 23 Feb., to 5 March, 1865. 2nd Lieut. 21st Inf., 6 May, 1867. Resigned 21 April, 1868.

BANKS, SIDNEY. [Born in Penn. Appointed from Penn.]
2nd Lieut. 3rd Cav., 5 Aug., 1861. 1st Lieut., 5 Aug., 1861. Capt., 18 May, 1865. Resigned 7 Jan., 1866.

BANNISTER, DWIGHT. [Born in Ohio. Appointed from Ohio.]
Addl. P. M. Vols., 1 June, 1861, to 4 July, 1868. Maj. P. M., 3 March, 1868. Bvt. Lieut. Col. Vols., 13 March, 1865, for faithful and meritorious service during the war. Discharged 31 Dec., 1870.

BANNISTER, JOHN. [Born in N. Y. Appointed from N. Y.]
Priv. Co. K, 27th N. Y. Vols., 21 May, 1861. Corpl. 1 Dec., 1862. Discharged 31 May, 1863. Priv. Co. M, 24th N. Y. Cav., 8 Dec., 1863. 1st Sergt., 21 Jan., 1865. 1st Lieut., 19 July, 1865. Mustered out 21 July, 1865. 2nd Lieut. 43rd Inf., 22 Jan., 1867. Bvt. 1st Lieut., 2 March, 1867, for gallant and meritorious service in action at Petersburg, Va., 8 July, 1864. Unass'd 8 April, 1869. Ass'd to 20th Inf., 14 July, 1869. 1st Lieut., 12 July, 1873. Retired 30 Nov., 1879.

BANZHAF, CHAS. [Born in Prussia. Appointed from Mo.]
Priv. Co. G, and Musician 2nd Drag., 8 Jan., 1856, to 8 Jan., 1861. Maj. 1st Mo. Cav., 6 Sept., 1861. Resigned 20 April, 1863. Capt. Vet. Res. Corps, 1 Aug., 1863.

Mustered out 21 July, 1867. 1st Lieut. 10th Cav., 12 June, 1867. Discharged 30 Dec., 1870.

BARBARIN, FRANCIS N.* [Born in N. Y. Appointed from N. Y.]
3rd Lieut. Ord., 1 July, 1820. Trans. to 3rd Art., 1 June, 1821. 1st Lieut., 28 Feb., 1837. Resigned 16 Sept., 1836. Died 28 Feb., 1883.

BARBER, AMAZIAH J. [Born in N. Y. Appointed from Army.]
Priv., Corpl., Sergt. and 1st Sergt. Co. H, and Sergt. Maj. 11th Inf., 8 Jan., 1862, to 27 March, 1863. 2nd Lieut. 11th Inf., 19 Feb., 1863. Died 26 July, 1863, of wounds received at Battle of Gettysburg, Penn. Bvt. 1st Lieut., 2 July, 1863, for gallant and meritorious service at the Battle of Gettysburg, Penn.

BARBER, GEORGE C.* [Born in N. J. Appointed from N. J.]
Bvt. 2nd Lieut. 7th Inf., 1 July, 1848. 2nd Lieut. 8th Inf., 28 June, 1849. Died 11 Oct., 1853.

BARBER, HENRY A. [Born in Md. Appointed from the Army.]
Priv., Corpl., Sergt. and 1st Sergt. Troop E, 7th Cav., 5 March, 1885, to 3 March, 1889. 2nd Lieut. 1st Cav., 11 Feb., 1889. 1st Lieut. 9th Cav., 27 Aug., 1896. Graduate of the Infantry and Cavalry School, 1893.

BARBER, MERRITT. [Born in Vt. Appointed from Vt.]
Priv. Co. E, 10th Vt. Vols., 2 June, 1862. 1st Lieut. 10th Vt. Vols., 1 Sept., 1862. Capt., 31 July, 1864. Bvt. Maj. Vols., 19 Oct., 1864, for having borne himself with distinguished gallantry in every engagement since 5 May, and particularly in the engagement at Cedar Creek, Va. Capt. A. A. G., Vols., 13 Dec., 1864. Mustered out 19 Sept., 1865. 2nd Lieut. and 1st Lieut. 16th Inf., 23 Feb., 1866. Trans. to 34th Inf., 21 Sept., 1866. Bvt. Capt., 2 March, 1867, for gallant and meritorious service in the Battle of the Wilderness, Va. Bvt. Maj., 2 March, 1867, for gallant and meritorious service in the Battle of Cedar Creek, Va. Trans. to 16th Inf., 14 April, 1869. Capt., 4 March, 1879. Maj. A. A. G., 20 June, 1882. Lieut. Col. A. A. G., 2 Aug., 1890. Col. A. A. G., 15 Nov., 1896.

BARBER, THOS. H.* [Born in England. Appointed from N. Y.]
2nd Lieut. 1st Art., 17 June, 1867. 1st Lieut., 10 July, 1872. Resigned 1 July, 1885.

BARBOUR, JOHN L.* [Born in Mo. Appointed from Ohio.]
2nd Lieut. 7th Inf., 11 June, 1881. 1st Lieut., 23 July, 1889. Retired with rank of Capt., 26 April, 1898.

BARBOUR, PHILIP N.* [Born in Ky. Appointed from Ky.]
Bvt. 2nd Lieut. 3rd Inf., 1 July, 1834. 2nd Lieut., 1 April, 1836. 1st Lieut., 7 July, 1838. Capt., 26 Nov., 1845. Killed 21 Sept., 1846, at the Battle of Monterey, Mexico. Bvt. Capt., 15 April, 1842, for active and highly meritorious services in the war against the Florida Indians. Bvt. Maj., 9 May, 1846, for gallant and distinguished services in the Battles of Palo Alto and Resaca de la Palma.

BARBOUR, SAML. L. [Born in Ga. Appointed from Ga.]
Asst. Surg., 28 Aug., 1847. Resigned 31 Jan., 1850.

BARCLAY, THOS. J. [Born in Penn. Appointed from Penn.]
2nd Lieut. 11th Inf., 30 Dec., 1847. Resigned 6 May, 1848.

BARCLAY, WM. H. [Born in Penn. Appointed from Penn.]
2nd Lieut., 4th Inf., 18 April, 1818. 1st Lieut., 20 April, 1819. Disbanded 1 June, 1821.

BARD, ROBT. W. [Born in N. Y. Appointed from N. Y.]
1st Lieut. 95th N. Y. Vols., 10 Dec., 1861. Capt., 1 Sept., 1862. Maj., 29 Dec., 1863. Lieut. Col., 3 June, 1864. Mustered out 16 July, 1865. 2nd Lieut. 16th Inf., 23 Feb., 1866. 1st Lieut., 23 Feb., 1866. Trans. to 2nd Inf., 17 April, 1869. Dismissed 16 Aug., 1876.

BARDEN, TILSON C. [Born in N. Y. Appointed from Wis.]
2nd Lieut. 2nd Mich. Vols., 25 May, 1861. 1st Lieut., 22 Sept., 1861. Capt., 24 Sept., 1863. Mustered out 6 June, 1864. Priv. and Sergt. Batty L, 5th N. Y. Art., 6 Sept., 1864. Mustered out 23 June, 1865. 1st Lieut., 117th U. S. Col. Inf., 9 Aug., 1865. Capt., 30 Nov., 1865. Mustered out 10 Aug., 1867. 2nd Lieut. 9th Cav., 10 Sept., 1867. Resigned 18 March, 1869.

BARDEN, WM. J.* [Born in Conn. Appointed from Conn.]
Addl. 2nd Lieut. Eng., 12 June, 1894. 2nd Lieut., 31 March, 1896. 1st Lieut., 5 July, 1898.

BARKER, JAMES N. [Born in Penn. Appointed from Penn.]
Capt. 2nd Art., 27 May, 1812. Trans. to Corps Art., 12 May, 1814, and was Capt. of same to 15 June, 1815. Maj. A. A. G., 8 April, 1814. Discharged 15 June 1815. Reinstated as Maj. A. A. G., 17 May, 1816. Resigned 1 April, 1817. Died 9 March, 1815.

BARKER, JOHN W.* [Born in N. Y. Appointed from N. Y.]
2nd Lieut. 9th Inf., 12 June, 1894. Trans. to 3d Inf., 30 Aug., 1894. 1st Lieut., 26 April, 1898. Capt. C. S., 8 June, 1898 (declined). Maj. Chief Ord. Officer, 27 July to 30 Nov., 1898.

BARKER, THOMAS. [Born in N. Y. Appointed from N. Y.]
1st Lieut. 41st Inf., 1 Aug., 1813. Capt. 42nd Inf., 17 Nov., 1813. Disbanded 15 June, 1815. 2nd Lieut. 1st Inf., 3 Feb., 1819. 1st Lieut., 23 July, 1820. Capt., 31 May, 1829. Died 11 Nov., 1839.

BARKER, THOS. [Born in Minn. Appointed from Cal.]
2nd Lieut. 2nd Cal. Cav., 17 July, 1862. 1st Lieut., 13 March, 1863. Capt., 25 Feb., 1864. Bvt. Maj. Vols., 13 March, 1865, for gallant and meritorious service during the War. Resigned 30 Nov., 1864. 2nd Lieut. 23rd Inf., 28 July, 1866. 1st Lieut., 21 May, 1868. Died 17 Jan., 1869.

BARKSDALE, WM. [Born in Tenn. Appointed from Miss.]
Capt. A. C S., 18 Jan., 1847. Disbanded 31 Aug., 1848.

BARLOW, JOHN W.* [Born in N. Y. Appointed from Wis.]
2nd Lieut. 2nd Art., 6 May, 1861. 1st Lieut., 15 May, 1861. Bvt. Capt., 27 May, 1862, for gallant and meritorious service in the Battle of Hanover Court House, Va. Trans. to Top. Eng., 24 July, 1862. Trans. to Eng., 3 March, 1863. Capt., 3 July, 1863. Bvt. Maj., 22 July, 1864, for gallant and meritorious service in the Atlanta Campaign. Bvt. Lieut. Col., 13 March, 1865, for gallant and meritorious

service in the Battles before Nashville, Tenn. Maj. Eng., 23 April, 1869. Lieut. Col. 19 March, 1884. Col., 10 May, 1885.

BARLOW, WARREN S.* [Born in N. Y. Appointed from N. Y.]
Addl. 2nd Lieut. 9th Inf., 11 June, 1897. 2nd Lieut. 15th Inf., 8 March, 1898. 1st Lieut., 2 March, 1899.

BARNARD, ISAAC D. [Born in Penn. Appointed from Penn.]
Capt. 14th Inf., 12 March, 1812. Maj., 26 June, 1813. Disbanded 15 June, 1815. Reinstated 2 Dec., 1815, as Capt. 4th Inf., but declined. Died 19 Feb., 1834.

BARNARD, JOHN G.* [Born in Mass. Appointed from Mass.]
Bvt. 2nd Lieut. Eng., 1 July, 1833. 2nd Lieut., 15 May, 1835. Capt., 7 July, 1838. Bvt. Maj., 30 May, 1848, for meritorious conduct while serving in the enemy's country. Maj. Eng., 13 Dec., 1858. Brig. Gen. Vols., 23 Sept., 1861. Bvt. Col., 30 June, 1862, for gallant and meritorious service in the campaign of the Peninsula. Lieut. Col. Eng., 3 March, 1863. Bvt. Maj. Gen. Vols., 4 July, 1864, for meritorious and distinguished service during the present war. Bvt. Brig. Gen., 13 March, 1865, for gallant and meritorious service in the campaign terminating with the surrender of the insurgent army under Gen. Robt. E. Lee. Bvt. Maj. Gen., 13 March, 1865, for gallant and meritorious service in the field during the war. Col. Eng., 28 Dec., 1865. Mustered out of Vol. service 15 Jan., 1866. Retired 2 Jan., 1881. Died 14 May, 1882.

BARNARD, MOSES J. [Born in Mass. Appointed from Penn.]
Capt. Inf., 16 Feb., 1847. Capt. Voltigeurs, 9 April, 1847. Disbanded 31 Aug., 1848. Bvt. Maj., 13 Sept., 1817, for gallant and meritorious conduct at the Battle of Chapultepec.

BARNARD, PHINEAS P. [Born in N. Y. Appointed from Mich.]
Capt. A. Q. M. Vols., 13 May, 1863. Bvt. Maj. Vols., 13 March, 1865, for faithful and meritorious service. Mustered out 6 Dec., 1865. 2nd Lieut. 4th Inf., 7 March, 1867. Bvt. 1st Lieut. and Bvt. Capt., 7 March, 1867, for faithful and meritorious service during the war. Unassigned 23 March, 1869. Ass'd to 5th Cav., 14 July, 1869. 1st Lieut., 4 June, 1875. Retired 13 Oct., 1884. Died — —, 1898.

BARNARD, ROBT. W. [Born in D. C. Appointed from D. C.]
1st Lieut. 19th Inf., 14 May, 1861. Capt., 16 July, 1863. Col. 101st U. S. Col. Inf., 12 Nov., 1864. Mustered out of Vol. service 21 Jan., 1866. Trans. to 37th Inf., 21 Sept., 1866. Trans. to 28th Inf., 30 Nov., 1867. Trans. to 19th Inf., 31 March, 1869. Died 21 July, 1870. Bvt. Maj., 1 Sept., 1864, for gallant and meritorious service during the Atlanta campaign. Bvt. Lieut. Col., 13 March, 1865, for gallant and meritorious service during the war.

BARNES, EUGENE L. [Born in N. Y. Appointed from N. Y.]
Priv. Co. A, 151st N. Y. Vols., 22 Oct., 1862, to 14 Jan., 1864. 2nd Lieut. 26th U. S. Col. Inf., 14 Jan., 1864. 1st Lieut., 13 Dec., 1864. Capt. 128th U. S. Col. Inf., 30 March, 1865. Bvt. Maj. Vols., 13 March, 1865, for gallant and meritorious service. Mustered out 31 Oct., 1866. 2nd Lieut. 39th Inf., 28 July, 1866. Died 7 Oct., 1867.

BARNES, JAMES.* [Born in Mass. Appointed from Mass.].
Bvt. 2nd Lieut. 4th Art., 1 July, 1829. 2nd Lieut., 1 July, 1829. 1st Lieut., 30 June, 1836. Resigned 31 July, 1836. Col. 18th Mass. Vols., 26 July, 1861. Brig. Gen. Vols., 29 Nov., 1862. Bvt. Maj. Gen. Vols., 13 March, 1865, for meritorious service during the war. Mustered out 15 Jan., 1866. Died 12 Feb., 1869.

BARNES, JOHN W. [Born in Cal. Appointed from Cal.]
2nd Lieut. 18th Inf., 22 Sept., 1898. 1st Lieut. 24th Inf., 15 Nov., 1899.

BARNES, JOSEPH K. [Born in Penn. Appointed from Penn.]
Asst. Surg., 15 June, 1840. Capt. Asst. Surg., 11 Feb., 1847. Maj. Surg., 29 Aug., 1856. Lieut. Col. Med. Insp., 9 Feb., 1863. Col. Med. Insp. Gen., 10 Aug., 1863. Brig. Gen., Surg. Gen., 22 Aug., 1864. Vacated commission of Col. Med. Insp. Gen., 31 Aug., 1864. Bvt. Maj. Gen., 13 March, 1865, for faithful and meritorious service during the war. Retired 30 June, 1882. Died 5 April, 1883.

BARNETT, CHAS. R.* [Born in Mo. Appointed from Ky.]
2nd Lieut. 5th Art., 15 June, 1868. 1st Lieut., 1 May, 1875. Capt. A. Q. M., 18 Feb., 1881. Maj. Q. M., 11 Feb., 1894. Lieut. Col. and D. Q. M. G., 13 Nov., 1898. Graduate of the Artillery School, 1874. Lieut. Col. Chief Q. M. Vols., 16 July, to 15 Dec., 1898.

BARNETT, JOHN T.* [Born in Ind. Appointed from Ind.]
2nd Lieut. 5th Cav., 14 June, 1878. Retired for disability 10 Aug., 1886. Col. 150th Ind. Vols., 12 May, to 23 Nov., 1898.

BARNETT, RICHARDS. [Born in Miss. Appointed from Miss.]
1st Lieut. Asst. Surg., 26 June, 1875. Capt., 26 June, 1880. Died 27 March, 1889.

BARNETT, ROBT. J. [Born in Ky. Appointed from Mo.]
2nd Lieut. 3rd Drag., 9 Sept., 1847. Disbanded 31 July, 1848.

BARNETT, ROBERT W. [Born in Miss. Appointed from Miss.]
2nd Lieut. 12th Inf., 9 July, 1898. 1st Lieut. 13th Inf., 2 March, 1899.

BARNEY, GEORGE F.* [Born in Iowa. Appointed from Vt.]
2nd Lieut. 2nd Art., 13 June, 1882. 1st Lieut., 3 Sept., 1888. Graduate of the Artillery School, 1886. Capt. 2nd Art., 2 March, 1899.

BARNEY, JOSHUA.* [Born in Md. Appointed from Md.]
2nd Lieut. Corps Art., 1 July, 1820. Trans. to 2nd Art., 1 June, 1821. Resigned 31 July, 1832. Died 13 April, 1867.

BARNHARDT, GEORGE C.* [Born in N. C. Appointed from N. C.]
2nd Lieut. 6th Cav., 11 June, 1892. 1st Lieut. 4th Cav., 7 Nov., 1898. Trans. to 6th Cav., 6 Feb., 1899.

BARNHART, FRANK H. [Born in Penn. Appointed from Penn.]
Priv. Co. G, 6th Penn. Vols., 22 April, 1861. Discharged 26 July, 1861. Corpl. Co. A, 50th Penn. Vols., 19 Aug., 1861. Corpl. Co. A. 50th Penn. Vet. Vols., 31 Dec., 1863. Sergt. Maj. 50th Penn. Vet. Vols., 1 March, 1864. 1st Lieut. 50th Penn. Vet. Vols., 26 Nov., 1864. Capt., 21 March, 1865. Mustered out 30 July, 1865. 2nd Lieut. 25th Inf., 18 June, 1867. Trans. to 18th Inf., 26 April, 1869. 1st Lieut., 30 June, 1877. Retired 16 June, 1890, for disability. Died 28 Nov., 1896.

BARNHART, LEVANT W. [Born in Penn. Appointed from Mich.]
Priv. and Sergt. Co. E, 6th Mich. Cav., 25 Nov., 1862. 2nd Lieut., 9 May, 1863. Capt., 19 May, 1864. Capt. A. A. G. Vols., 22 May, 1865. Bvt. Maj. Vols, 13 March, 1865, for meritorious and distinguished service. Mustered out 20 March, 1866. 2 Lieut. 4th Cav., 2 May, 1866. 1st Lieut., 28 Nov., 1866. Dismissed 2 Sept., 1867. Restored 16 Feb., 1869. Dropped 25 July, 1870.

BARNITZ, ALBERT. [Born in Penn. Appointed from Ohio.]
Sergt. Co. G, 2nd Ohio Cav., 22 Aug., 1861. Discharged 1 June, 1862. 2nd Lieut. 2nd Ohio Cav., 1 June, 1862. 1st Lieut., 18 Feb., 1863. Capt., 26 Feb., 1863. Maj., 20 March, 1865. Mustered out 11 Sept., 1865. Capt. 7th Cav., 28 July, 1866. Bvt. Maj., 2 March, 1867, for gallant and meritorious service in action at Ashland Station, Va. Bvt. Lieut. Col., 2 March, 1867, for gallant and meritorious service in the Battle of Sailer's Creek, Va. Bvt. Col., 27 Nov., 1868, for distinguished gallantry in the Battle of Washita, Indian Ter., Nov., 1868, in which engagement he was severely wounded. Retired 15 Dec., 1870.

BARNUM, DAVID S. [Born in ——. Appointed from Mass.]
2nd Lieut. 1st Inf., 17 Oct., 1818. 1st Lieut., 5 Sept., 1819. Disbanded 1 June, 1821.

BARNUM, EPHRAIM K. [Born in Vt. Appointed from N. Y.]
2nd Lieut. 5th Inf., 11 June, 1817. 1st Lieut., 31 Dec., 1820. Trans. to 2nd Inf., 7 June, 1821. Capt., 28 Dec., 1832. Maj. 3rd Inf., 16 Feb., 1847. Died 26 Dec., 1847. Bvt. Capt., 31 Dec., 1830, for ten years' faithful service in one grade.

BARNUM, MALVERN HILL.* [Born in N. Y. Appointed from N. Y.]
2nd Lieut. 3rd Cav., 1 July, 1886. 1st Lieut. 5th Cav., 7 April, 1893. Trans. to 10th Cav., 22 March, 1894. Graduate of the Infantry and Cavalry School, 1893.

BARNWELL, THOS. O.* [Born in S. C. Appointed from S. C.]
Bvt. 2nd Lieut. 3rd Inf., 1 July, 1834. 2nd Lieut., 17 Oct., 1835. Resigned 31 Oct., 1837.

BARR, D. EGLINTON. [Born in Scotland. Appointed from N. Y.]
Chaplain 81st U. S. Col. Inf., 16 Sept., 1865. Mustered out 24 Oct., 1866. Chaplain 39th Inf., 28 July, 1866. Trans. to 25th Inf., 20 April, 1869. Resigned in Sept., 1872.

BARR, SAMUEL L. [Born in Del. Appointed from Del.]
2nd Lieut. 5th Inf., 24 Oct., 1861. 1st Lieut., 30 April, 1863. Capt., 31 Oct., 1866. Unassigned 19 May, 1869. Mustered out 1 Jan., 1871.

BARR, THOS. F. [Born in Mass. Appointed from Mass.]
Maj. J. A. Vols., 26 Feb., 1865. Bvt. Lieut. Col. Vols., 2 Dec., 1865, for faithful and meritorious service in his department. J. A., U. S. A., 25 Feb., 1867 (Act 25 Feb., 1867). Lieut. Col. D. J. A. G., 5 July, 1884. Col. A. J. A. G., 3 Aug., 1895.

BARRETT, ADDISON. [Born in Mass. Appointed from Mass.]
Sergt. Gen. Ser., 16 Aug., 1862. Discharged 1 April, 1863. Capt. A. C. S. Vols., 21 Dec., 1864. Bvt. Maj. Vols., 14 Sept., 1865, for faithful and meritorious service. Capt. Mil. Storekeeper, Q. M. D., 28 July, 1866. Mustered out of Vol. service 8 Dec., 1866. Died 22 Sept., 1896.

BARRETT, GREGORY, Jr. [Born in Md. Appointed from Md.]
Capt. 4th Md. Vols., 15 Aug., 1862. Lieut. Col., 9 March, 1864. Bvt. Col. Vols., 4 Jan., 1865. Mustered out 31 May, 1865. 1st Lieut. 26th Inf., 28 July, 1866. R. Q. M., 1 March to 19 May, 1869. Trans. to 10th Inf., 19 May, 1869. Capt., 8 April, 1884. Died 7 Aug., 1898.

BARRETT, JOHN M. [Born in Md. Appointed from Md.]
2nd Lieut. 38th Inf., 20 May, 1813. 1st Lieut., 1 May, 1814. Disbanded 15 June, 1815. 2nd Lieut. 4th Inf., 13 Aug., 1819. Died 16 Oct., 1819.

BARRETT, WALLACE W. [Born in N. Y. Appointed from Mich.]
Capt. 44th Ill. Vols., 13 Sept., 1861. Col., 1 Jan., 1863. Bvt. Brig. Gen. Vols., 13 March, 1865, for gallant and meritorious service during the war. Mustered out 14 Dec., 1865. 1st Lieut. 34th Inf., 28 July, 1866. Bvt. Capt., 2 March, 1867, for gallant and meritorious service in the Battle of Stone River, Tenn. Bvt. Maj., 2 March, 1867, for gallant and meritorious service in the Battle of Chickamauga, Ga. Bvt. Lieut. Col., 2 March, 1867, for gallant and meritorious service in the Battle of Peach Tree Creek, Ga. Trans. to 16th Inf., 14 April, 1869. Died 1 July, 1879.

BARRETTE, JOHN D. [Born in La. Appointed from Iowa.]
2nd Lieut. 3rd Art., 14 June, 1885. 1st Lieut. 3 June, 1892. Trans. to 7th Art., 8 March, 1898.

BARRI, THOS. O. [Born in Conn. Appointed from Mass.]
1st Lieut. Adj. 5th Mass. Vols., 1 May, 1861. Capt. 11th Inf., 14 May, 1861. Killed 2 July, 1863, at the Battle of Gettysburg. Bvt. Maj., 2 July, 1863, for gallant and meritorious service in the Battle of Gettysburg, Penn.

BARRIGER, JOHN W.* [Born in Ky. Appointed from Ky.]
2nd Lieut. 2nd Art., 1 July, 1856. 1st Lieut., 2 May, 1861. 1st Lieut. 5th Art., 14 May, 1861, declined. Bvt. Capt., 21 July, 1861, for gallant and meritorious service in the Battle of Bull Run, Va. Capt. C. S., 3 Aug., 1861. Lieut. Col. C. S. (Act 17 July, 1862), 17 Nov., 1863. Vacated commission of 1st Lieut. 2nd Art., 30 March, 1864. Bvt. Maj., Lieut. Col., Col. and Brig. Gen., 13 March, 1865, for faithful and meritorious service during the war. Relieved as Lieut. Col. C. S. (Act 17 July, 1862), 1 Aug., 1865. Maj. C. S., 21 Nov., 1875. Lieut. Col. A. C. G. S., 12 March, 1892. Col. A. C. G. S., 8 Oct, 1894. Retired, over 30 years' service, 1 June, 1896.

BARROLL, FRANKLIN H. [Born in N. Y. Appointed from Army.]
Priv., Corpl. and Sergt. Batty I, 1st Art., 30 Nov., 1857, to 22 May, 1861. 2nd Lieut. 2nd Inf., 22 May, 1861. 1st Lieut., 10 Aug., 1861. Capt., 27 Aug., 1862. Resigned 8 Aug., 1866.

BARROLL, MORRIS K.* [Born in Md. Appointed from Md.]
Addl. 2nd Lieut. 1st Art., 12 June, 1889. 2nd Lieut. 4th Art., 14 Aug., 1889. Trans. to 2nd Art., 23 Aug., 1894. 1st Lieut. 3rd Art., 29 Oct., 1896. Graduate of the Artillery School, 1894.

BARRON, WM. A. [Born in ——. Appointed from Mass.]
Capt. 2nd Art. and Eng., 14 May, 1800. Capt. Eng., 13 April, 1802. Maj., 11 June, 1805. Resigned 15 June, 1807. Capt. A. Dep. Q. M. G., 18 April, 1818. Disbanded 1 June, 1821. Died 19 July, 1828.

BARROWS, CHARLES C. [Born in Miss. Appointed from Miss.]
Asst. Surg., 23 May, 1882. Resigned 17 Feb., 1887.

BARRY, GARRETT.* [Born in Md. Appointed from Md.]
2nd Lieut. 1st Inf., 1 July, 1839. 1st Lieut., 31 Jan., 1844. Resigned 31 March, 1847. Drowned 2 Sept., 1860.

BARRY, JOHN. [Born in Ireland. Appointed from Army.]
Priv., Corpl., Sergt. and 1st Sergt. Co. E, 2nd Drag., 7 May, 1857, to 7 May, 1862. 2nd Lieut. 1st Cav., 19 Feb., 1863. 1st Lieut., 2 April, 1864. Reg. Com., 14 Aug., 1864, to 20 July, 1866. Capt., 1 July, 1868. Trans. to Supernumerary, 14 Sept., 1870. Mustered out 1 Jan., 1871. Bvt. Capt., 6 March, 1864, for gallant and meritorious service at the Battle of Todd's Tavern, Va. Died 2 May, 1880.

BARRY, JOHN W.* [Born in Ky. Appointed from Ky.]
Bvt. 2nd Lieut. 1st Art., 1 July, 1830. 2nd Lieut., 1 July, 1830. 1st Lieut., 31 Dec., 1835. Resigned 30 Nov., 1836. Died 2 June, 1837.

BARRY, PAUL A. [Born in Tenn. Appointed from Tenn.]
Priv. Troop F, 1st Cav., and Hosp. Corps, 30 Aug., 1895, to 6 Oct., 1897. Priv. and Corpl. Cos. B and L, 20th Inf., 1 Sept., 1898, to 23 Nov., 1899. 2nd Lieut. 4th Inf., 1 Oct., 1899. 2nd Lieut. 4th Inf., 5 Oct., 1899. Capt. Co. L, 3rd Ala. Vols., 5 Aug., 1898. Mustered out 20 March, 1899.

BARRY, ROBERT P. [Born in N. Y. Appointed from N. Y.]
Priv. Co. H, 7th N. Y. State Militia, 26 April, 1861, to 3 June, 1861. Capt. 16th Inf., 14 May, 1861. Resigned 30 Sept., 1864. Bvt. Maj., 31 Dec., 1862, for gallant and meritorious services at the Battle of Murfreesboro', Tenn.

BARRY, THOMAS H.* [Born in N. Y. Appointed from N. Y.]
2nd Lieut. 7th Cav., 15 June, 1877. Trans. 1st Inf., 31 Aug., 1880. 1st Lieut., 11 March, 1882. Capt., 25 Feb., 1891. Maj. A. A. G., 29 Jan., 1897. Lieut. Col. A. A. G. Vols., 22 June, 1898.

BARRY, THOMAS W. [Born in Canada. Appointed from Kan.]
Post Chaplain, 3 Aug., 1882.

BARRY, WM. F.* [Born in N. Y. Appointed from N. Y.]
Bvt. 2nd Lieut. 4th Art., 1 July, 1838. 2nd Lieut., 7 July, 1838. Trans. to 2nd Art., 12 July, 1838. 1st Lieut., 17 Aug., 1842. Capt., 1 July, 1852. Maj. 5th Art., 14 May, 1861. Brig. Gen. Vols., 20 Aug., 1861. Lieut. Col. 1st Art., 1 Aug., 1863. Bvt. Col., 1 Sept., 1864, for gallant and meritorious service in the capture of Atlanta, Ga. Bvt. Maj. Gen. Vols., 1 Sept., 1864, for gallant and meritorious service in the campaign of Atlanta. Bvt. Brig. Gen., 13 March, 1865, for gallant and meritorious service in the campaign terminating with the surrender of the insurgent army under Gen. J. E. Johnson. Bvt. Maj. Gen., 13 March, 1865, for gallant and meritorious service in the field during the war. Col. 2nd Art., 11 Dec., 1865. Mustered out of Vol. service 15 Jan., 1866. Died 18 July, 1879.

BARRY, WM. J. [Born in Md. Appointed from Md.]
Maj. Surg. 11th Inf., 9 April, 1847. Disbanded 14 Aug., 1848.

BARSTOW, ELIJAH W. [Born in Mass. Appointed from Mass.]
2nd Lieut. 3rd Mass. Art., 2 Nov., 1863. 1st Lieut., 6 Feb., 1865. Mustered out 18 Sept., 1865. 2nd Lieut. 5th Art., 5 May, 1866. 1st Lieut., 7 March, 1867. Died 6 June, 1867.

BARSTOW, GEORGE F. [Born in Mass. Appointed from Mass.]
2nd Lieut. and 1st Lieut. 3rd Art., 30 Nov., 1861. Bvt. Capt., 3 July, 1863, for gallant and meritorious service in the Battle of Gettysburg, Penn. Bvt. Maj., 25 Aug., 1864, for gallant and meritorious service in action at Kearneysville, Va. Capt. 3rd Art., 20 Dec., 1875. Honor graduate of the Artillery School, 1871. Retired for disability 10 Dec., 1889.

BARSTOW, SIMON F. [Born in Mass. Appointed from Mass.]
Capt. A. A. G. Vols., 6 March, 1862. Capt. A. A. de C., 18 March, 1862. Vacated appointment of Capt. A. A. de C. Vols., 2 July, 1862. Maj. A. A. G. Vols,, 15 July, 1862. Bvt. Lieut. Col. Vols., 1 Aug., 1864, for faithful and meritorious service in the field. Bvt. Col. Vols., 9 April, 1865, for gallant and meritorious service during the recent operations resulting in the fall of Richmond, Va., and the surrender of the insurgent army under Gen. R. E. Lee. Bvt. Brig. Gen. Vols. 13 March, 1865, for faithful and meritorious service. Capt. A. Q. M., 11 May, 1866. Mustered out of Vol. service 31 July, 1866. Bvt. Maj., 2 March, 1867, for gallant and meritorious service at the Battle of Gettysburg, Pa. Bvt. Lieut. Col., 2 March, 1867, for gallant and meritorious service at the fall of Petersburg, Va. Retired 7 June, 1879. Died 31 July, 1882.

BARTH, CHARLES H.* [Born in Iowa. Appointed from Kan.]
2nd Lieut. 12th Inf., 11 June, 1881. 1st Lieut., 23 April, 1890. Capt., 26 April, 1898. Honor graduate of the Infantry and Cavalry School, 1891.

BARTHOLF, JOHN H. [Born in N. J. Appointed from N. Y.]
Asst. Surg. 18th N. Y. Vols., 5 Nov., 1862. Mustered out 28 May, 1863. Asst. Surg. Vols., 12 Jan., 1865. Bvt. Capt. Vols., 6 Oct., 1865, for faithful and meritorious service. Mustered out 9 Oct., 1865. 1st Lieut. Asst. Surg., 14 May, 1867. Capt. Asst. Surg., 23 May, 1869. Maj. Surg., 4 Jan., 1886. Retired by operation of law, 13 March, 1894.

BARTHOLOW, ROBERTS. [Born in Md. Appointed from Md.]
Asst. Surg., 4 June, 1857. Resigned 11 May, 1864.

BARTHOLOMEW, WM. H. [Born in Penn. Appointed from Penn.]
Priv. Co. H, 25th Pa. Vols., 19 April, to 19 June, 1861. 2nd Lieut. 16th Inf., 14 May, 1861. 1st Lieut., 19 Nov., 1861. Capt., 4 Jan., 1865. Trans. to 34th Inf., 21 Sept., 1866. Trans. to 16th Inf., 14 April, 1869. Died 25 Dec., 1874. Bvt. Capt. and Maj., 3 Dec., 1862, for gallant and meritorious service at the Battle of Murfreesboro', Tenn.

BARTLETT, CHAS. G. [Born in N. Y. Appointed from N. Y.]
Capt. 5th N. Y. Vols., 9 May, 1861. Mustered out 8 Sept., 1861. Capt. 12th Inf., 5 Aug., 1861. Lieut. Col. 150th N. Y. Vols., 29 Sept., 1862. Bvt. Maj., 14 May, 1864, for gallant and meritorious service in the Battle of Resaca, Ga. Mustered out of Vol. service 31 Dec., 1864. Bvt. Brig. Gen. Vols., 13 March, 1865, for gallant

and meritorious service during the war. Bvt. Lieut. Col., 13 March, 1865, for gallant and meritorious service during the war. Col. 119th U. S. Col. Troops, 10 May, 1865. Mustered out of Vol. service 27 April, 1866. Trans. to 30th Inf., 21 Sept., 1866. Trans. to 4th Inf., 23 March, 1869. Maj. 11th Inf., 10 Jan., 1876. Lieut. Col. 1st Inf., 10 March, 1883. Col. 9th Inf., 23 April, 1890. Retired, over 30 years' service, 1 May, 1896.

BARTLETT, EDWARD C. [Born in N. Y. Appointed from N. Y.]
2nd Lieut. 2nd Cav., 20 June, 1868. Trans. to 1st Cav., 29 Oct., 1870. 1st Lieut., 9 Aug., 1871. Resigned 15 Nov., 1871.

BARTLETT, GEORGE T.* [Born in N. H. Appointed from Kan.]
2nd Lieut. 3rd Art., 11 June, 1881. 1st Lieut., 10 Dec., 1889. Capt., 2 March, 1899. Graduate of the Artillery School, 1890. Maj. C. S. Vols., 3 June, 1898. Discharged from Vols., 13 June, 1899.

BARTLETT, WM. C.* [Born in N. Y. Appointed at Large.]
2nd Lieut. 3rd Art., 17 June, 1862. Bvt. 1st Lieut., 17 Sept., 1862, for gallant and meritorious service in the Battle of Antietam, Md. Bvt. Capt., 16 Nov., 1863, for gallant and meritorious service in action at Campbell's Station, Tenn. Capt. A. de C. Vols., 19 March, 1864. Bvt. Maj., 1 Sept., 1864, for gallant and meritorious service during the Atlanta Campaign. 1st Lieut. 3rd Art., 14 Oct., 1864. Lieut. Col. 2nd N. C. Mounted Inf., 17 Nov., 1864. Bvt. Brig. Gen. Vols., 13 March, 1865, for meritorious service. Mustered out of Vol. service 16 Aug., 1865. Trans. to 3rd Inf., 5 Feb., 1872, taking rank from 2 Feb., 1867. Capt., 12 Sept., 1885. Retired, over 30 years' service, 29 Nov., 1892.

BARTLETT, WM. H. C.* [Born in Penn. Appointed from Mo.]
Bvt. 2nd Lieut. Eng., 1 July, 1826. 2nd Lieut., 1 July, 1826. Prof. Mil. Acad., 20 April, 1836. Retired with pay of Col., 14 Feb., 1871. Died 11 Feb., 1893.

BARTON, ALBERT G. [Born in Maine. Appointed from Maine.]
Priv., Sergt. and 1st Sergt. Co. G., 9th Inf., 8 March, 1847, to 8 May, 1848. 2nd Lieut. 9th Inf., 29 March, 1848. Disbanded 26 Aug., 1848.

BARTON, EDWARD H. [Born in Md. Appointed from La.]
Maj. Surg. 3rd Drag., 9 April, 1847. Resigned 29 Jan., 1848.

BARTON, FRANK A. [Born in D. C. Appointed from D. C.]
2nd Lieut. 24th Inf., 1 Aug.,1891. Trans. to 10th Cav., 1 June, 1892. 1st Lieut. 3rd Cav., 16 Oct., 1898.

BARTON, IRA McL. [Born in N. H. Appointed from N. H.]
Capt 1st N. H. Vols., 27 April, 1861. Mustered out 9 Aug., 1861. Capt. 5th N. H. Vols., 19 Oct., 1861. Resigned 6 Sept., 1862. Capt. 1st N. H. Art., 17 Sept., 1863. Lieut. Col., 29 Sept., 1864. Bvt. Col. Vols., 13 March, 1865, for faithful and meritorious service. Mustered out 15 June, 1865. 2nd Lieut. 19th Inf., 11 May, 1866. Trans. to 28th Inf., 21 Sept., 1866. 1st Lieut., 20 Aug., 1867. Unass'd 31 March, 1869. Discharged 25 Oct., 1870.

BARTON, SETH M.* [Born in Va. Appointed from Va.]
Bvt. 2nd Lieut. 3rd Inf., 1 July, 1849. 2nd Lieut. 1st Inf., 19 April, 1850. 1st Lieut., 1 June, 1853. Reg. Adj., 1 May, 1855, to 31 Oct., 1857. Capt., 31 Oct., 1857. Resigned 11 June, 1861.

BASCOM, GEORGE N.* [Born in Ky. Appointed from Ky.]
Bvt. 2nd Lieut. 9th Inf., 1 July, 1858. 2nd Lieut. 7th Inf., 23 April, 1859. 1st Lieut. 16th Inf., 14 May, 1861. Capt., 24 Oct., 1861. Killed 21 Feb., 1862, at Battle of Val Verde, N. M.

BASCOM, GUSTAVUS M. [Born in Ohio. Appointed from Ohio.]
Capt. A. de C. Ohio Vols., 23 April, 1861. Mustered out 15 Aug., 1861. Capt. A. A. G. Vols., 20 Aug., 1861. Maj. A. A. G. Vols., 7 Oct., 1862. Lieut. Col. A. A. G. Vols. (Act 17 July, 1862), 25 Jan., 1864, to 31 Jan., 1865. Bvt. Lieut. Col. and Col. Vols., 4 Nov., 1865, for faithful and meritorious service. Mustered out 1 July, 1866. 1st Lieut. 17th Inf., 22 Jan., 1867. Bvt. Capt., 2 March, 1867, for gallant and meritorious service in the Battle of Antietam, Md. Bvt. Maj., 2 March, 1867, for gallant and meritorious service in the Battle of Resaca, Ga. Unassigned 27 May, 1869. Ass'd to 13th Inf., 14 July, 1869. R. Q. M., 1 Aug., 1871, to 11 Dec., 1873. Capt., 11 Dec., 1873. Died 16 Aug., 1884.

BASH, DANIEL N. [Born in Ohio. Appointed from Ill.]
Maj. P. M., 18 Feb., 1881. Retired by direction of the President, being over 62 years of age, 2 July, 1892.

BASH, LOUIS H.* [Born in Ill. Appointed from Ill.]
Addl. 2nd Lieut. 13th Inf., 12 June, 1895. 2nd Lieut., 5 July, 1895. 1st Lieut. Inf. (25th), 4 Aug., 1898. Trans. to 13th Inf., 23 March, 1899.

BASINGER, WM. E.* [Born in Ga. Appointed from Ga.]
Bvt. 2nd Lieut. 2nd Art., 1 July, 1830. 2nd Lieut., 1 July, 1830. Killed 28 Dec., 1835, at Dade's Massacre, in Fla.

BASS, EDGAR W.* [Born in Wis. Appointed from Minn.]
Bvt. 2nd Lieut. Eng., 15 June, 1868. 2nd Lieut., 15 Feb., 1869. 1st Lieut., 14 Feb., 1871. Prof. of Math., 17 April, 1878. Retired, over 30 years' service, 7 Oct., 1898.

BASSEL, JAMES.* [Born in Va. Appointed from Va.]
2nd Lieut. 2nd Art., 17 June, 1867. Discharged 4 Nov., 1870.

BASSETT, BRADFORD S. [Born in Penn. Appointed from Kansas.]
Corpl. Co. D. 1st Ill. Cav., 15 July, 1861, to 5 April, 1862. 2nd Lieut. 2nd Kan. Batty, 15 May, 1862. 1st Lieut., 26 Jan., 1864. Mustered out 19 Jan., 1865. Capt. 16th Kan. Cav., 17 May, 1865. Mustered out 6 Dec., 1865. 2nd Lieut. 7th Cav., 18 June, 1867. 1st Lieut., 31 July, 1868. Died 11 March, 1869.

BASSETTE, BUELL B.* [Born in ——. Appointed from ——.]
2nd Lieut. 16th Inf., — June, 1893. Resigned 27 Sept., 1893.

BASSFORD, ABRAHAM. [Born in N. Y. Appointed from N. Y.]
Priv. Co. F, 8th N. Y. Militia, 25 April, 1861. Mustered out 2 Aug., 1861. 1st Lieut. 14th N. Y. Cav., 16 Dec., 1862. Maj., 10 July, 1863. Col., 3 Oct., 1864. Mustered out 12 June, 1865. Capt. 8th Cav., 28 July, 1866. Resigned 9 Nov., 1869. Bvt. Maj., 2 March, 1867, for gallant and meritorious service in action at Morganza, La.

BATCHELDER, JAMES E.* [Born in Vt. Appointed from Vt.]
2nd Lieut. 2nd Cav., 15 June, 1868. 1st Lieut., 4 May, 1870. Resigned 4 Dec., 1871.

BATCHELDER, RICHARD N. [Born in N. H. Appointed from N. H.]
1st Lieut. R. Q. M. 1st N. H. Vols., 2 May, 1861. Mustered out 9 Aug., 1861. Capt. A. Q. M., Vols., 3 Aug., 1861. Lieut. Col. Q. M. (Act 17 July, 1862), 1 Jan., 1863, to 1 Aug., 1864. Col. Q. M. (Act 4 July, 1864), 2 Aug., 1864. Capt. A. Q. M., U. S. A., 16 Feb., 1865. Vacated commission of Capt. A. Q. M. Vols., 8 June, 1865. Bvt. Maj., Lieut. Col., Col. and Brig. Gen. Vols., 13 March, 1865, for faithful and meritorious service during the war. Bvt. Maj. Lieut. Col. and Col., 13 March, 1865, for faithful and meritorious service during the war. Relieved as Col. Q. M. (Act 4 July, 1864), 5 Sept., 1865. Maj. Q. M., 18 Jan., 1867. Vacated commission of Capt. A. Q. M., 23 March, 1867. Lieut. Col. D. Q. M. G., 10 March, 1882. Brig. Gen. Q. M. G., 26 June, 1890. Retired by operation of law 27 July, 1896. Medal of Honor for most distinguished gallantry in action against Mosby's guerrillas, between Catlett's and Fairfax Stations, Va., 13 and 15 Oct., 1863; while serving as Lieut. Col. and Q. M. Vols., C. Q. M., 2nd Army Corps.

BATCHELOR, JOSEPH B., Jr. [Born in N. C. Appointed from N. C.]
Cadet at Mil. Acad., 14 June, 1876, to 15 June, 1880. 2nd Lieut. 24th Inf., 29 Nov., 1880. 1st Lieut., 30 Aug., 1890. Capt., 26 April, 1898. Graduate of the Infantry and Cavalry Schools, 1891.

BATEMAN, CEPHAS C. [Born in Mich. Appointed from Ore.]
Post Chaplain, 6 Dec., 1890.

BATEMAN, HARRY F. [Born in Ohio. Appointed from the Army.]
Priv., Corpl., Farrier, Sergt. and 1st Sergt. Troop C, and Sergt. Maj. 8th Cav., 2 Jan., 1882, to 22 Oct., 1885. 2nd Lieut. 10th Inf., 22 Oct., 1886. Dropped, in accordance to Sec. 1229 Rev. Sta., 2 March, 1889.

BATEMAN, JOHN C. [Born in Ohio. Appointed from Ohio.]
Corpl. and Sergt. Co. E, and Sergt. Maj. 90th Ohio Vols., 26 Aug., 1862. 1st Lieut., 26 May, 1865. Mustered out 26 June, 1865. 2nd Lieut. 2nd Inf., 7 March, 1867. Resigned 1 July, 1872.

BATES, ALFRED E.* [Born in Mich. Appointed from Mich.]
2nd Lieut. 2nd Cav., 23 June, 1865. 1st Lieut., 19 Oct., 1865. Capt., 26 Jan., 1869. Maj. P. M., 3 March, 1875. Vacated commission of Capt. 2nd Cav., 9 April, 1875. Lieut. Col. and D. P. M. G., 7 Jan., 1897. Brig. Gen. Vols., 4 May to 31 Oct., 1898. Col. Asst. P. M. G., 31 March, 1899. Brig. Gen. P. M. G., 12 July, 1899.

BATES, CHARLES F. [Born in Mich. Appointed from N. Y.]
Priv. Co. B, 71st N. Y. Vols., 16 June to 8 July, 1898. Priv. Co. A., 8th Inf., 2 May to 7 June, 1898. 2nd Lieut. 25 Inf., 9 July, 1898. 1st Lieut., 2 March, 1899.

BATES, DORUS E. [Born in Ill. Appointed from Ill.]
Bugler Co. K. 2nd Ill. Cav., 12 Aug., 1861. Discharged 17 March, 1862. 2nd Lieut. 13th Inf., 19 Feb., 1862. 1st Lieut., 14 May, 1862. Retired 25 Jan., 1865. Bvt. Capt., 13 March, 1865, for gallant and meritorious service during the war. Died 17 Aug., 1880.

BATES, FRANCIS H.* [Born in Md. Appointed from Mass.]
Bvt. 2nd Lieut. 4th Inf., 1 July, 1850. 2nd Lieut., 15 April, 1852. 1st Lieut., 22 Nov., 1854. Capt. 17th Inf., 14 May, 1861, declined. Capt. 4th Inf., 14 May, 1861. Bvt. Maj., 27 June, 1862, for gallant and meritorious service in the Battle of Gaines' Mill, Va. Retired 19 Oct., 1863. Died 12 Aug., 1895.

BATES, JAMES A. [Born in Scotland. Appointed from N. Y.]
Priv. Co. F, 12th N. Y. State Militia, 19 April, 1861. Discharged 5 Aug., 1861. 1st Lieut. 12th N. Y. Vols., 10 Dec., 1861. Capt., 29 Dec., 1862. Mustered out 21 April, 1864. 1st Lieut. Vet. Res. Corps, 3 June, 1864. Bvt. Maj. Vols., 13 March, 1865, for gallant and meritorious service during the war. Capt. Vet. Res. Corps, 15 March, 1865. Bvt. Lieut. Col. Vols., 19 March, 1865, for faithful and meritorious service. Mustered out 2 Oct., 1866. Capt. 43rd Inf., 28 July, 1866. Bvt. Maj., 2 March, 1867, for gallant and meritorious service in the Battle of Gaines' Mill, Va. Bvt. Lieut. Col., 2 March, 1867, for gallant and meritorious service in the Battle of Malvern Hill,, Va. Unassigned 8 April, 1869. Retired 15 Dec., 1870.

BATES, JOHN C. [Born in Mo. Appointed from Mo.]
1st Lieut. 11th Inf., 14 May, 1861. Capt., 1 May, 1863. Bvt. Maj., 1 Aug., 1864, for faithful and meritorious service in the field. Bvt. Lieut. Col., 9 April, 1865, for gallant and meritorious service during the recent operations resulting in the fall of Richmond, Va., and the surrender of the insurgent army under Gen. R. E. Lee. Trans. to 20th Inf., 21 Sept., 1866. Maj. 5th Inf., 6 May, 1882. Trans. to 20th Inf., 24 May, 1882. Lieut. Col. 13th Inf., 19 Oct., 1886. Trans. to 20th Inf., 10 Dec., 1890. Col. 2nd Inf., 25 April, 1892. Brig. Gen. Vols., 4 May, 1898. Maj. Gen. Vols., 8 July, 1898. Discharged from Vols., 13 April, 1899. Brig. Gen. Vols., 13 April, 1899.

BATES, JOSHUA H.* [Born in Mass. Appointed from Mass.]
2nd Lieut. 4th Art., 1 July, 1837. 1st Lieut., 31 Jan., 1842. Resigned 20 July, 1842. Brig. Gen. Ohio Vols., 27 April, 1861. Mustered out 27 Aug., 1861.

BATES, KINZIE. [Born in Mich. Appointed from Mich.]
Priv. Co. A, 1st Mich. Vols., 1 May, 1861. Corpl., 13 June, 1861. Discharged 7 Aug., 1861. 2nd Lieut. 1st Inf., 5 Aug., 1861. 1st Lieut., 23 Nov., 1861. R. Q. M., 9 March, 1862, to 27 Jan., 1864. Reg. Adj., 27 Jan., 1864, to 15 March, 1866. Bvt. Capt., 4 Oct., 1862, for gallant and meritorious service in the Battle of Corinth, Miss. Bvt. Maj., 4 July, 1863, for gallant and meritorious service during the Siege of Vicksburg, Miss. Capt. 1st Inf., 15 March, 1866. Died 20 Feb., 1884.

BATES, ROBERT F. [Born in N. Y. Appointed from Penn.]
Priv. Co. D, 53rd N. Y. Vols., 16 Sept., 1861. Discharged 21 March, 1862. Sergt. Co. D, 121st Penn. Vols., 13 Aug., 1862. Discharged 29 Feb., 1864. 1st Lieut., 121st Penn. Vols., 1 March, 1864. Mustered out 2 June, 1865. 2nd Lieut. 18th Inf., 7 March, 1867. Bvt. 1st Lieut., 7 March, 1867, for gallant and meritorious service in the Battle of Gettysburg, Penn. 1st Lieut. 18th Inf., 28 March, 1873. Reg. Adj., 1 July, 1879, to 26 May, 1886. Capt., 26 Dec., 1888. Maj. 22nd Inf., 2 March, 1899. Retired, over 30 years' service, 2 June, 1899.

BATMAN, MARK W.* [Born in Penn. Appointed from Penn.]
2nd Lieut. 6th Inf., 1 July, 1823. 1st Lieut., 20 Dec., 1826. Capt., 16 Nov., 1836. Died 31 July, 1837.

BATSON, MATTHEW A. [Born in Ill. Appointed from the Army.]
Priv. and Corpl. Troops M and G, 2nd Cav., 9 April, 1888, to 1 Aug., 1891. 2nd Lieut. 9th Cav., 31 July, 1891. 1st Lieut. 4th Cav., 9 July, 1898. Graduate of the Infantry and Cavalry School, 1895.

BATTEE, JOHN S. [Born in Md. Appointed from Md.]
Asst. Surg., 5 Oct., 1847. Resigned 28 July, 1848.

BATTEY, FREDK. A. [Born in R. I. Appointed from Iowa.]
Sergt. Co. F, 57th Ill. Vols., 12 Sept., 1861. Capt., 26 Dec., 1861. Maj., 11 Feb., 1865. Lieut. Col., 6 June, 1865. Mustered out 7 July, 1865. 1st Lieut. 40th Inf., 28 July, 1866. Unass'd 20 April, 1869. Discharged 16 Oct., 1870.

BATTLE, JOHN S.* [Born in N. C. Appointed from N. C.]
2nd Lieut. 11th Inf., 1 June, 1894. 1st Lieut., 26 April, 1898. R. C. S., 12 May, 1899.

BAXLEY, JOSEPH M. [Born in Md. Appointed from Md.]
Ensign 38th Inf., 7 July, 1814. 3rd Lieut., 1 Oct., 1814. Disbanded 15 June, 1815. 2nd Lieut. 5th Inf., 13 Aug., 1819. 1st Lieut., 1 May, 1824. Capt., 4 March, 1833. Resigned 1 April, 1836. Died 14 Dec., 1839.

BAXTER, ANDREW J. [Born in Ohio. Appointed from Ohio.]
Asst. Surg., 5 Aug., 1861. Dismissed 19 Jan., 1863.

BAXTER, GEORGE W.* [Born in N. C. Appointed from Tenn.]
Addl. 2nd Lieut. 5th Cav., 15 June, 1877. 2nd Lieut. 3rd Cav., 16 Sept., 1877. Resigned 1 July, 1881.

BAXTER, JEDEDIAH H. [Born in Vt. Appointed from Vt.]
Maj. Surg. 12th Mass. Vols., 26 June, 1861. Discharged 17 April, 1862. Maj. Surg. U. S. Vols., 4 April, 1862. Bvt. Lieut. Col., 30 March, 1865, for meritorious and faithful service in recruitment of the armies of the United States. Bvt. Col. Vols., 13 March, 1865, for faithful and meritorious service during the war. Lieut. Col. Asst. Med. Pur., 20 July, 1867. Vacated commission of Surg. U. S. Vols., 30 July, 1867. Bvt. Col., 20 July, 1867, for faithful and meritorious service during the war. Lieut. Col. Chief Med. Pur., 12 March, 1872 (Act 12 March, 1872). Col. Chief Med. Pur., 23 June, 1874. Brig. Gen. Surg. Gen., 16 Aug., 1890. Died 4 Dec., 1890.

BAXTER, JOHN, Jr.* [Born in N. J. Appointed from N. J.]
Addl. 2nd Lieut. 19th Inf., 15 June, 1877. 2nd Lieut. 9th Inf., 1 July, 1877. 1st Lieut., 3 Feb., 1885. Capt. A. Q. M., 15 Oct., 1897.

BAYARD, ALBERT F. [Born in N. Y. Appointed from N. Y.]
Priv. 7th R. I. Cav., 24 June, to 2 Oct., 1862. Priv. and Sergt. Troop G, 5th Cav., and Gen. Ser., 11 April, 1865, to 13 Sept., 1867. 2nd Lieut. 4th Cav., 11 Sept., 1867. Discharged 29 Oct., 1870.

BAYARD, GEORGE D. [Born in N. Y. Appointed at Large.]
2nd Lieut. 1st Cav., 1 July, 1856. 1st Lieut., 16 March, 1861. Trans. to 4th Cav., 3 Aug., 1861. Capt., 20 Aug., 1861. Col. 1st Pa. Cav., 14 Sept., 1861. Brig. Gen. Vols., 28 April, 1862. Died 14 Dec., 1862, of wounds received in Battle of Fredericksburg, Va.

BAYARD, JOHN A. [Born in Penn. Appointed from Army.]
Priv. and Corpl. Co. D, 11th Inf., 17 March, 1847, to 18 Nov., 1847. 2nd Lieut. 11th Inf., 4 Aug., 1847. Discharged 15 Aug., 1848. Sergt. Troop E, 1st Pa. Cav., 27 Aug., 1861. 1st Lieut., 12 Nov., 1861. Resigned 26 Feb., 1862. Priv. and Sergt. Co. H., 148th Pa. Vols., 16 Aug., 1862. 2nd Lieut., 1 Nov., 1862. Died 3 Aug., 1863, of wounds received at the Battle of Gettysburg, Pa.

BAYARD, WM. [Born in N. Y. Appointed from Army.]
2nd Lieut. 1st Pa. Cav., 1 March, 1862. Discharged 1 Sept., 1862. Priv. and Corpl. Troop G, 4th Cav., 2 Feb., to 23 Nov., 1863. 2nd Lieut. 4th Cav., 31 Oct., 1863. 1st Lieut., 10 Aug., 1865. Capt. 9th Cav., 28 July, 1866. Mustered out 1 Jan., 1871. Bvt. 1st Lieut., 16 Dec., 1864, for gallant and meritorious services in pursuit of Rebel forces under Gen. Hood. Bvt. Capt., 2 April, 1865, for gallant and meritorious services at the capture of Selma, Ala. Bvt. Maj., 2 April, 1865, for gallantry during pursuit of Hood after the Battle of Nashville, and in charge of his regiment against the earthwork at Selma, Ala.

BAYER, FERDINAND. [Born in Germany. Appointed from Ohio.]
2nd Lieut. 38th U. S. Col. Inf., 17 April, 1865. 1st Lieut., 17 Jan., 1866. Mustered out 19 April, 1866. 2nd Lieut. 15th Inf., 23 Feb., 1866. 1st Lieut., 31 Aug., 1866. Resigned 18 Aug., 1868.

BAYLIES, JAMES. [Born in Mass. Appointed from the Army.]
Priv. Corpl. and Sergt. Cos. B and A, 5th Inf., 7 Feb., 1883, to 19 March, 1888. 2nd Lieut. 5th Inf., 6 Feb., 1888. 1st Lieut. 18th Inf., 30 Jan., 1895. Trans. to 10th Inf., 16 May, 1895. Capt., 2 March, 1899. Graduate of the Infantry and Cavalry School, 1891.

BAYLISS, WM. C. [Born in D. C. Appointed from D. C.]
2nd Lieut. 4th Cav., 17 May, 1867. 1st Lieut., 17 March, 1868. Mustered out 1 Jan., 1871. Died 28 Jan., 1872.

BAYLOR, JOHN W. [Born in Va. Appointed from Ky.]
Asst. Surg., 8 July, 1824. Dismissed 28 May, 1825. Restored 11 July, 1825. Dropped 20 May, 1833. Died — Jan., 1834.

BAYLOR, THOS. G.* [Born in Va. Appointed from Va.]
Bvt. 2nd Lieut. Ord., 1 July, 1857. 2nd Lieut., 25 Jan., 1861. 1st Lieut., 1 Feb., 1861. Capt. 12th Inf., 14 May, 1861, declined. Capt. Ord., 3 March, 1863. Bvt. Maj., 1 Sept., 1864, for gallant service in the capture of Atlanta. Bvt. Lieut. Col., 21 Dec., 1864, for gallant service in the capture of Savannah. Bvt. Col., 13 March, 1865, for meritorious service in the recent campaigns of Atlanta, Savannah, and the Carolinas. Maj. Ord., 7 March, 1867. Lieut. Col., 29 May, 1879. Col., 4 Dec., 1882. Died 15 Sept., 1890.

BAYNE, ANDREW C. [Born in Scotland. Appointed from N. Y.]
Sergt. Co. G, 16th N. Y. Vols., 15 May, 1861. 2nd Lieut. 16th N. Y. Vols., 13 Sept., 1862. 1st Lieut., 11 Feb., 1863. Mustered out 3 June, 1863. 1st Lieut. Vet. Res.

BECKETT, FRANCIS O. Born in Maine. Appointed from Iowa.]
2nd Lieut. Inf., 8 March, 1847; 15th Inf., 9 April, 1847. 1st Lieut., 6 May, 1848. Disbanded 4 Aug., 1848. Bvt. 1st Lieut., 20 Aug., 1847, for gallant and meritorious conduct at Contreras and Churubusco.

BECKHAM, ROBT. F.* [Born in Va. Appointed from Va.]
Bvt. 2nd Lieut. Top. Eng., 1 July, 1859. Resigned 3 May, 1861.

BECKLEY, ALFRED.* [Born in D. C. Appointed from Ky.]
Bvt. 2nd Lieut. 3rd Art., 1 July, 1823. 2nd Lieut. 4th Art., 1 July, 1823. 1st Lieut., 31 July, 1831. Resigned 24 Oct., 1836. Died 26 May, 1888.

BECKURTS, CHARLES L. [Born in Ky. Appointed from Ky.]
2nd Lieut. 6th Inf., 30 Oct., 1884. 1st Lieut. 14th Inf., 29 Sept., 1891. Trans. to 6th Inf., 6 Oct., 1891. Capt. 16th Inf., 11 Jan., 1899. Graduate of the Infantry and Cavalry School, 1889.

BECKWITH, AMOS.* [Born in Vt. Appointed from Vt.]
Bvt. 2nd Lieut. 1st Art., 1 July, 1850. 2nd Lieut., 22 Feb., 1851. 1st Lieut., 21 Aug., 1854. Capt. C. S., 10 May, 1861. Vacated commission of 1st Lieut. 1st Art., 14 May, 1861. Maj. C. S., 29 Sept., 1861. Col. A. A. de C., 1 Jan., 1862. Bvt. Lieut. Col., 1 Sept., 1864, for gallant and meritorious service in the Atlanta campaign. Bvt. Col., 1 Sept., 1864, for gallant and meritorious service in the campaign against Atlanta. Bvt. Brig. Gen. Vols., 12 Jan., 1865. Bvt. Brig. Gen., 13 March, 1865, for gallant and meritorious service in the campaign terminating in the surrender of the insurgent army under Gen. Jos. E. Johnston. Bvt. Maj. Gen., 13 March, 1865, for faithful and meritorious service in the Sub. Dept. during the war. Mustered out as Col. A. A. de C., 31 May, 1866. Lieut. Col. A. G. S., 23 June, 1874. Lieut. Col. A. C. G., 23 June, 1874. Col. A. C. G., 28 Aug., 1888. Retired by op. of law 4 Oct., 1889. Died 26 Oct., 1894.

BECKWITH, EDWARD G.* [Born in N. Y. Appointed from N. Y.]
2nd Lieut. 3rd Art., 1 July, 1842. 1st Lieut., 18 June, 1846. Capt., 12 May, 1855. Col. A. A. de C., 5 July, 1862. Maj. 2nd Art., 8 Feb., 1864. Bvt. Lieut. Col., and Brig. Gen., 13 March, 1865, for faithful and meritorious service during the war. Mustered out as Col. A. A. de C., 31 May, 1866. Retired 20 March, 1879. Died 22 June, 1881.

BECKWITH, JENNINGS. [Born in Md. Appointed from Md.]
Ensign 14th Inf., 15 April, 1814. 3rd Lieut., 1 May, 1814. 2nd Lieut. 1 Dec., 1814. Disbanded 15 June, 1815. Reinstated 2 Dec., 1815, in 3rd Inf. Resigned 30 June, 1816.

BEDAL, SYLVESTER S. [Born in Canada. Appointed from Minn.]
Asst. Surg., 10 Nov., 1874. Dismissed 10 Feb., 1877.

BEDEL, HAZEN. [Born in Me. Appointed from Army.]
Priv. and Sergt. 11th Inf., 27 Aug., 1812, to Sept., 1813. Ensign 11th Inf., 21 Sept., 1813. 3rd Lieut., 1 Jan., 1814. 2nd Lieut., 15 June, 1814. Trans. to 6th Inf., 17 May, 1815. 1st Lieut., 19 Oct., 1818. Disbanded 1 June, 1821.

BEDELL, JOHN. [Born in N. H. Appointed from N. H.]
2nd Lieut. 9th Inf., 30 Dec., 1847. Disbanded 26 Aug., 1848. Maj. 3rd N. H. Vols., 26 Aug., 1861. Lieut. Col., 27 June, 1862. Col., 6 April, 1864. Bvt. Brig. Gen. Vols., 13 March, 1865, for gallant and meritorious service. Mustered out 20 July, 1865. Died 26 Feb., 1875.

BEDFORD, ROBT. W. [Born in Tenn. Appointed from Tenn.]
2nd Lieut. 14th Inf., 9 April, 1847. Died 13 June, 1848.

BEDINGER, DANIEL. [Born in Va. Appointed from Va.]
Ord. Storekeeper, 22 Oct., 1830. Died 19 Dec., 1838.

BEE, BARNARD E.* [Born in S. C. Appointed at Large.]
Bvt. 2nd Lieut. 3rd Inf., 1 July, 1845. 2nd Lieut., 21 Sept., 1846. 1st Lieut., 5 March, 1851. Reg. Adj., July, 1848, to 3 March, 1855. Capt. 10th Inf., 3 March, 1855. Resigned 3 March, 1861. Bvt. 1st Lieut., 18 April, 1847, for gallant and meritorious conduct at Cerro Gordo. Bvt. Capt., 13 Sept., 1847, for gallant and meritorious conduct at Chapultepec.

BEE, RICHARD J. R. [Born in Ga. Appointed from Ga.]
Mil. Storekeeper Ord., 4 April, 1844. Resigned 31 Dec., 1854.

BEE, WM., Jr. [Born in S. C. Appointed from S. C.]
2nd Lieut. 8th Inf., 15 May, 1812. 1st Lieut. 14 Aug., 1813. Trans. to 7th Inf., 17 May, 1815. Capt., 30 April, 1817. Resigned 13 June, 1820.

BEEBE, WM. M., Jr. [Born in Ohio. Appointed from Ohio.]
1st Lieut. 41st Ohio Vols., 7 June, 1862. Capt. 1 May, 1864. Lieut. Col. 128th U. S. Col. Inf., 16 March, 1865. Bvt. Maj. Vols., 13 March, 1865, for gallant and meritorious service on the 27th of May, 1864, and for meritorious services during the Atlanta campaign. Mustered out 18 April, 1867. Capt. 38th Inf., 7 March, 1867. Unassigned 11 Nov., 1869. Mustered out 1 Jan., 1871. Bvt. Maj., 7 March, 1867, for gallant and meritorious service in the Battle of Stone River, Tenn.

BEEBE, WM. S.* [Born in N. Y. Appointed from Pa.]
2nd Lieut. Ord., 11 June, 1863. 1st Lieut., 30 July, 1863. Resigned 1 Jan., 1874. Bvt. Capt., 6 July, 1864, for gallant and meritorious service, and for intrepidity, daring and skill in handling men in the face of the enemy. Bvt. Maj., 23 Aug., 1864, for gallant and meritorious service at the Siege of Fort Morgan, Ala.

BEECHER, FREDK. H. [Born in La. Appointed from Mass.]
Sergt. Co. B., 16th Me. Inf., 14 Aug., 1862. 2nd Lieut. 1 Feb., 1863. Resigned 20 Sept., 1864. 2nd Lieut. Vet. Res. Corps, 22 Aug., 1864. Bvt. 1st Lieut. and Capt. Vols. 5 Dec., 1865, for gallant and meritorious service. Mustered out 3 March, 1866. 2nd Lieut. 3rd Inf., 29 Nov., 1865. 1st Lieut., 28 July, 1866. Killed 17 Sept., 1868, in action with Indians in Kansas.

BEECHER, HENRY B. [Born in Ind. Appointed from N. Y.]
1st Lieut. 67th N. Y. Vols., 20 June, 1861. Resigned 14 Nov., 1861. 2nd Lieut. 4th Art., 30 Nov., 1861. 1st Lieut., 11 Aug., 1863. Resigned 4 Oct., 1866. Bvt. Capt., 3 June, 1864, for gallant and meritorious service in the Battle of Cold Harbor, Va. Bvt. Maj., 1 Nov., 1865, for faithful and meritorious service during the war.

BEEKMAN, STEPHEN DE W. [Born in N. Y. Appointed from Army.]
Cadet at Mil. Acad., 1 July, 1854, to 30 June, 1856. 1st Lieut. 71st Pa. Vols., 1 July, 1861. Resigned 28 July, 1862. Sergt. Gen. Mtd. Ser., 11 Jan. to 5 June, 1864. 2nd Lieut. 2nd Cav., 18 May, 1864. Died 7 July, 1864.

BELCHER, JOHN H. [Born in Mass. Appointed from Cal.]
Capt. A. Q. M. Vols., 14 Oct., 1864. Bvt. Maj. Vols., 13 March, 1865, for faithful service during the war. Capt. A. Q. M., 16 June, 1866. Vacated commission of Capt. A. Q. M. Vols., 2 Aug., 1866. Bvt. Maj., 2 March, 1867, for meritorious service in the Q. M. Dept. during the war. Maj. Q. M., 2 July, 1883. Retired by op. of law 20 April, 1892.

BELDEN, GEORGE P. [Born in Ohio. Appointed from Neb.]
2nd Lieut. 2nd Cav., 10 June, 1867. 1st Lieut., 3 Nov., 1868. Cashiered, 4 Nov., 1869.

BELDING, GODFREY H. [Born in ——. Appointed from Army.]
Priv. and Sergt. 11th and 21st Inf. 20 Sept., 1812, to April, 1814. Ensign 21st Inf., 30 March, 1814. 3rd Lieut., 1 May, 1814. 2nd Lieut., 25 July, 1814. Trans. to 5th Inf., 17 May, 1815. Resigned 15 July, 1816.

BELGER, EDWARD A. [Born in Va. Appointed from Army.]
1st Lieut. 70th N. Y. Vols., 25 June, 1862. Mustered out 1 July, 1864. Priv. and Sergt. Co. A, 3rd Inf., 22 Feb. to 2 April, 1865. 2nd Lieut. 3rd Inf., 12 March, 1865. 1st Lieut., 25 April, 1865. Capt. 41st Inf., 28 July, 1866, declined. Bvt. Capt., 2 March, 1867, for gallant service in Battle of Chancellorsville, Va., 3 May, 1863. Bvt. Maj., 2 March, 1867, for gallantry in the Battle of Gettysburg, 2 July, 1863. Unassigned 11 Aug., 1869. Ass'd to 3rd Inf., 1 Jan., 1871. Died 8 Oct., 1879.

BELGER, JAMES. [Born in N. Y. Appointed from Army.]
Priv. Co. H, 2nd Inf., 7 Nov., 1832. Corpl., 27 Aug., 1833. Sergt., 22 Aug., 1835. Sergt., Maj., 23 May, 1837. Discharged 6 Nov., 1837. Sergt. Maj. 2nd Inf., 7 Nov., 1837. 2nd Lieut. 6th Inf., 15 Oct., 1838. 1st Lieut., 27 Feb., 1843. Reg. Adj., 1 Feb., 1840, to 1 Jan., 1846. Capt. A. Q. M., 18 June, 1846. Bvt. Maj., 30 May, 1848, for meritorious conduct, particularly in the performance of his duty in the prosecution of the war with Mexico. Vacated commission of 1st Lieut. 6th Inf., 9 June, 1853. Maj. Q. M., 3 Aug., 1861. Col. A. A. de C., 11 July, 1862. Out of service, 30 Nov., 1863. Maj. Q. M., 3 March, 1871 (Act 3 March, 1871). Retired 19 June, 1879. Died 10 Dec., 1891.

BELKNAP, HENRY. [Born in Mass. Appointed from Mass.]
Capt. 11th Inf., 14 May, 1861. Resigned 30 May, 1863.

BELKNAP, WM. G. [Born in N. Y. Appointed from N. Y.]
3rd Lieut. 23rd Inf., 5 April, 1813. 2nd Lieut., 15 Oct., 1813. 1st Lieut., 19 Aug., 1814. Trans. to 2nd Inf., 17 May, 1815. Trans. to 3rd Inf., 1 June, 1821. Capt., 1 Feb., 1822. Maj. 8th Inf., 31 Jan., 1842. Lieut. Col. 5th Inf., 26 Sept., 1847. Died 10 Nov., 1851. Bvt. Maj., 1 Feb., 1832, for ten years' faithful service in one grade. Bvt. Lieut. Col., 15 March, 1842, for general good conduct in war against Florida Indians, and for securing by military operations and negotiations a great number of prisoners. Bvt. Col., 9 May, 1846, for gallant and distinguished service at Palo Alto and Resaca de la Palma. Bvt. Brig. Gen., 23 Feb., 1847, for gallant and meritorious conduct at Buena Vista.

BELL, BENJ. F. [Born in N. Y. Appointed from Ill.]
Priv. and Sergt. Co. B, 17th Ill. Cav., 22 Jan., 1864, to 28 Aug., 1865. 2nd Lieut. U. S. Col. Inf. 10 Sept., 1865. Bvt. 1st Lieut. and Capt. Vols., 13 March, 1865, for meritorious services during the war. Mustered out 28 Feb., 1867. 2nd Lieut. 10th Cav., 18 June, 1867. 1st Lieut., 10 April, 1869. Dismissed 1 Sept., 1869.

BELL, DAVID.* [Born in Ohio. Appointed from Iowa.]
Bvt. 2nd Lieut. 2nd Drag., 1 July, 1851. 2nd Lieut., 9 Oct., 1852. 1st Lieut. 1st Cav., 3 March, 1855. Died 2 Dec., 1860.

BELL, EDWIN.* [Born in D. C. Appointed from N. Y.]
2nd Lieut. 8th Inf., 12 June, 1894. 1st Lieut., 26 April, 1898.

BELL, EGBERT H. [Born in N. C. Appointed from N. C.]
Surg. Mate, 10th Inf., 12 March, 1812. Maj. Surg., 30 March, 1814. Disbanded 15 June, 1815. Hosp. Surg., 29 April, 1816. Maj. Surg. 8th Inf., 18 April, 1818. Post Surg., 28 Jan., 1820. Asst. Surg., 1 June, 1821. Resigned 16 July, 1821. Died 27 Aug., 1821.

BELL, GEORGE.* [Born in Md. Appointed from Md.]
Bvt. 2nd Lieut. 4th Art., 1 July, 1853. 2nd Lieut. 1st Art., 31 Oct., 1853. 1st Lieut., 30 June, 1855. Capt. 14th Inf., 14 May, 1861, declined. Capt. C. S., 3 Aug., 1861. Vacated commission of 1st Lieut. 1st Art., 14 May, 1861, but served as such to 22 Aug., 1861. Lieut. Col. C. S. (Act 17 July, 1862), 20 Aug., 1862. Bvt. Maj., 13 March, 1865, for faithful and meritorious service during the war. Bvt. Lieut. Col., 13 March, 1865, for meritorious service during the war. Bvt. Col., 13 March, 1865, for faithful and meritorious service during the war. Bvt. Brig. Gen., 9 April, 1865, for faithful and meritorious service in the Sub. Dept. during the war. Maj. C. S., 25 April, 1865. Relieved as Lieut. Col. C. S. (Act 17 July, 1862), 1 Aug., 1865. Lieut. Col. A. C. G., 9 Nov., 1884. Col. A. C. G., 4 Oct., 1889. Retired by op. of law 12 March, 1892.

BELL, GEORGE, Jr. [Born in Md. Appointed from D. C.]
2nd Lieut. 3rd Inf., 12 June, 1880. 1st Lieut., 24 April, 1886. Capt., 1st Inf., 26 April, 1898. R. Q. M., 7 Nov., 1899.

BELL, JACOB B. [Born in Penn. Appointed from Penn.]
Capt. 15th Inf., 14 May, 1861. Killed 31 Dec., 1862, at Battle of Murfreesboro', Tenn. Bvt. Maj., 7 April, 1862, for gallant and meritorious service in the Battle of Shiloh, Tenn. Bvt. Lieut. Col., 31 Dec., 1862, for gallant and meritorious service at the Battle of Stone River, Tenn. (where he was killed.)

BELL, JAMES E.* [Born in Tenn. Appointed from Tenn.]
2nd Lieut., 1st Art., 17 June, 1867. 1st Lieut., 28 June, 1872. Died 11 Sept., 1873.

BELL, JAMES E. [Born in Ill. Appointed from Ill.]
Priv. Co. C, 1st Ill. Vols., 13 May to 26 July, 1898. 2nd Lieut. 12th Inf., 9 July, 1898. 1st Lieut. 17th Inf., 9 Sept., 1899.

Lieut. Col. and Col., 13 March, 1865, for faithful and meritorious service during the war. Mustered out of Vol. service, 27 Oct., 1865. Lieut. Col. 4th Inf., 7 Oct., 1868. Unassigned 15 March, 1869. Ass'd to 18th Inf., 1 July, 1870. Col. 23rd Inf., 6 Feb., 1882. Retired 15 Jan., 1891. Died 5 Aug., 1893.

BLACK, SAML. W. [Born in Penn. Appointed from Army.]
Cadet Mil. Acad., 1 July, 1863, to 15 Nov., 1864. Priv. 17th Inf., 28 Nov. to 2 Dec., 1864. 2nd Lieut. 17th Inf., 2 Dec., 1864. 1st Lieut., 2 Dec., 1864. Capt., 6 July, 1867. Died 29 Sept., 1867.

BLACK, WM. M.* [Born in Penn. Appointed from Penn.]
2nd Lieut. Eng., 15 June, 1877. 1st Lieut., 31 March, 1880. Capt., 31 Dec., 1886. Maj., 18 May, 1898. Lieut. Col. Chief Eng. Vols., 9 May, 1898. Discharged Vol. service 13 June, 1899.

BLACK, WILLIAM. [Born in Iowa. Appointed from Iowa.]
2nd Lieut. 24th Inf., 1 Sept., 1879. 1st Lieut., 11 March, 1885. Capt., 26 April, 1898. Graduate of the Infantry and Cavalry School, 1895.

BLACKALLER, HENRY M. [Born in Mass. Appointed from Ohio.]
1st Lieut. 6th U. S. Col. Cav., 1 Nov., 1864. Capt. 9 March, 1866. Mustered out 15 April, 1866. 1st Lieut. 9th Cav., 7 March, 1867. Died 12 July, 1867.

BLACKBURN, JAMES. [Born in La. Appointed from La.]
1st Lieut. of Inf., 5 March, 1847; 14th Inf., 9 April, 1847. Capt., 1 Oct., 1847. Disbanded 25 July, 1848. Bvt. Capt., 13 Sept., 1847, for gallant and meritorious conduct at Chapultepec.

BLACKSTONE, THOMAS. [Born in Va. Appointed from Tenn.]
Ensign 7th Inf., 10 Feb., 1812. 3rd Lieut., 12 March, 1813. 2nd Lieut., 26 Sept., 1813. 1st Lieut., 15 May, 1814. Trans. to 7th Inf., 17 May, 1815. Capt., 31 May, 1817. Disbanded 1 June, 1821.

BLAINE, EPHRAIM. [Born in ——. Appointed from ——.]
Asst. Surg., 17 Nov., 1829. Died 13 March, 1835.

BLAINE, JOHN E. [Born in Penn. Appointed from Penn.]
Mil. Storekeeper Q. M. Dept., 16 June, 1868. Resigned 1 May, 1870. Maj. P. M., 3 March, 1875. Died 21 April, 1887.

BLAINE, MALNOR C. [Born in Ky. Appointed from Pa.]
Priv. Co. H, 54th Ky. M. Inf., 1 Sept., 1864. Discharged 1 Sept., 1865. Post Chaplain, 16 June, 1880. Died 30 Nov., 1896.

BLAIR, FRANCIS P.* [Born in Mo. Appointed from Mo.]
Addl. 2nd Lieut. 3rd Art., 15 June, 1877. 2nd Lieut., 13 June, 1878. Resigned 1 Sept., 1882.

BLAIR, JAMES D. [Born in Ky. Appointed from Miss.]
Capt. of Inf., 23 Feb., 1847; Voltigeurs, 9 April, 1847. Disbanded 31 Aug., 1848.

BLAIR, MONTGOMERY.* [Born in Ky. Appointed from Ky.]
Bvt. 2nd Lieut. 4th Art., 1 July, 1835. Trans. to 2nd Art., 14 Aug., 1835. Resigned 20 May, 1836. Died 27 July, 1883.

BLAIR, THOMAS. [Born in Scotland. Appointed from Army.]
Priv. Co. A, Batt. Eng., 7 April, 1865. Trans. to Co. D, 31 Aug., 1865. Artificer, 1 Sept., 1865. 2nd Lieut. 15th Inf., 22 May, 1867. 1st Lieut., 13 Oct., 1867. Capt., 25 Aug., 1877. Dismissed 5 Aug., 1879.

BLAIR, WM. B.* [Born in Va. Appointed from Va.]
2nd Lieut. 2nd Art., 1 July, 1838. 1st Lieut. 4 Nov., 1840. Capt. C. S., 27 Sept., 1850. Resigned 14 May, 1861. Bvt. Capt., 18 April, 1847, for gallant and meritorious conduct at Cerro Gordo.

BLAIR, WM. P. S. [Born in ——. Appointed from Ky.]
Ensign 28th Inf., 20 May, 1813. 3rd Lieut. 2nd Rifles, 17 March, 1814. 2nd Lieut., 21 July, 1814. Disbanded 15 June, 1815. 2nd Lieut. Rifles, 17 Feb., 1817. 1st Lieut., 15 July, 1817. Disbanded 1 June, 1821. Died 3 Aug., 1828.

BLAKE, CHESLEY. [Born in Me. Appointed from Army.]
Priv. and Sergt. 9th Inf., 18 March, 1813, to July, 1814. Ensign 9th Inf., 12 July, 1814. 3rd Lieut., 25 July, 1814. 2nd Lieut., 31 Oct., 1814. Trans. to 5th Inf., 17 May, 1815. Resigned 1 May, 1816.

BLAKE, CHAS. M. [Born in Maine. Appointed from Penn.]
Chaplain U. S. Vols., 13 Aug., 1861. Hosp. Chaplain Vols., 4 June, 1862. Resigned 21 July, 1863. Capt. 3rd U. S. Col. Troops, 26 July, 1863. Discharged 11 Aug., 1864. Hosp. Chaplain Vols., 26 Sept., 1864. Discharged 10 May, 1865. Post Chaplain, Fort Whipple, Arizona, Ter., 17 May, 1866, to 10 June, 1867. Post Chaplain, 3 April, 1867. Resigned 17 March, 1869. Restored to service, 2 Oct., 1878. Died 3 June, 1893.

BLAKE, EDMUND M.* [Born in S. C. Appointed from N. C.]
2nd Lieut. 5th Art., 12 June, 1889. 1st Lieut. 4th Art., 21 Dec., 1895.

BLAKE, EDWARD D.* [Born in S. C. Appointed from S. C.]
Bvt. 2nd Lieut. 2nd Inf., 1 July, 1847. 2nd Lieut. 8th Inf., 17 Sept., 1847. 1st Lieut., 15 May, 1851. Capt., 17 Oct., 1860. Resigned 11 June, 1861.

BLAKE, GEORGE A. H. [Born in Penn. Appointed from Penn.]
1st Lieut. 2nd Drag., 11 June, 1836. Capt., 3 Dec., 1839. Bvt. Maj., 17 Aug., 1847, for gallant and meritorious conduct in the affair of San Augustine, Mexico. Maj. 1st Drag., 23 July, 1850. Lieut. Col., 13 May, 1861. Col. 1st Cav., 15 Feb., 1862. Bvt. Brig. Gen., 13 March, 1865, for gallant and effective service during the Gettysburg campaign. Retired 15 Dec., 1870. Died 27 Oct., 1884.

BLAKE, HENRY J. [Born in Vt. Appointed from Vt.]
2nd Lieut. 11th Inf., 1 May, 1812. 1st Lieut., 26 June, 1813. Capt., 1 Sept., 1814. Trans. to Corps Art., 17 May, 1815. Resigned 8 Feb., 1816.

BLAKE, JACOB E.* [Born in Penn. Appointed from Penn.]
Bvt. 2nd Lieut. 6th Inf., 1 July, 1833. 2nd Lieut., 31 July, 1836. 1st Lieut., 6 Sept., 1837. 1st Lieut. Top. Eng., 7 July, 1838. Accidentally killed 9 May, 1846.

BLAKE, JOHN Y. F.* [Born in Mo. Appointed from Ark.]
2nd Lieut. 6th Cav., 12 June, 1880. 1st Lieut., 5 Oct., 1887. Resigned 19 Aug., 1889.

BLAKER, JOHN D. [Born in Penn. Appointed from Penn.]
Priv. and Corpl. Co. C, 3rd Pa. Res., 28 July, 1861, to 24 Nov., 1862. 2nd Lieut., 3rd

U. S. Col. Inf., 26 July, 1863. Resigned 28 May, 1864. 2nd Lieut. 9th Inf., 23 Feb., 1866. 1st Lieut., 28 July, 1866. Resigned 21 April, 1868.

BLAKEY, JOHN M. [Born in Va. Appointed from Va.]
1st Lieut. of Inf., 23 Feb., 1847; Voltigeurs 9 April, 1847. Disbanded 20 July, 1848.

BLAKELEY, GEORGE.* [Born in Pa. Appointed from Pa.]
2nd Lieut. 2nd Art., 11 June, 1892. 1st Lieut., 13 Feb., 1899. Graduate of the Artillery School, 1896.

BLANCHARD, ALBERT G.* [Born in Mass. Appointed from Mass.]
Bvt. 2nd Lieut. 3rd Inf., 1 July, 1829. 2nd Lieut., 31 Aug., 1833. 1st Lieut., 30 Oct., 1836. Resigned 1 Oct., 1840. Capt. Ind. Co., La., Vols., 15 May, 1846. Mustered out 16 May, 1847. Maj. 12th Inf., 27 May, 1847. Disbanded 25 July, 1848.

BLANCHARD, SAWYER.* [Born in N. H. Appointed from N. H.]
Addl. 2nd Lieut. of Art. (1st), 11 June, 1892. 2nd Lieut. of Art. (1st), 23 Dec., 1892, to rank from 11 June, 1892.

BLANCHARD, WM. [Born in Penn. Appointed from Penn.]
2nd Lieut. 2nd Cav., 14 Nov., 1861. 1st Lieut., 17 July, 1862. Resigned 6 July, 1865.

BLANDING, JAMES D. [Born in S. C. Appointed from S. C.]
2nd Lieut. S. C. Vols., 6 Dec., 1846. Capt. A. C. S., 4 Jan., 1847. Disbanded 31 Aug., 1848.

BLANDING, ORMSBY. [Born in S. C. Appointed from S. C.]
2nd Lieut. of Inf., 5 March, 1847; 12th Inf., 9 April, 1847. Disbanded 25 July, 1848.

BLANEY, GEORGE.* [Born in Mass. Appointed from Mass.]
Bvt. 2nd Lieut. Eng., 4 March, 1815. 2nd Lieut., 31 Oct., 1816. 1st Lieut., 12 Nov., 1818. Capt., 1 July, 1824. Died 15 May, 1835. Bvt. Maj., 1 July, 1834, for ten years' faithful service in one grade.

BLANEY, JAMES R.* [Born in Del. Appointed from Del.]
2nd Lieut. Corps Art., 1 July, 1819. Trans. to 4th Art., 1 June, 1821. 1st Lieut., 11 Aug., 1823. Dismissed 27 Nov., 1826. Died in 1840.

BLANTON, ALEXR. M. [Born in Ky. Appointed from Ky.]
Asst. Surg., 14 July, 1846. Disbanded 30 June, 1847.

BLATCHFORD, RICHARD M. [Born in N. Y. Appointed from N. Y.]
2nd Lieut. 11th Inf., 10 Oct., 1883. 1st Lieut., 7 Dec., 1887. Capt., 26 April, 1898. Graduate of the Infantry and Cavalry School, 1887.

BLAUVELT, WM. F. [Born in N. Y. Appointed from the Army.]
Priv., Corpl. and Sergt. Batty. D, 4th Art., 28 Feb., 1878, to 7 July, 1880. 2nd Lieut. 15th Inf., 24 June, 1880. 1st Lieut., 26 Aug., 1890. Capt., 26 April, 1898. Graduate of the Infantry and Cavalry School, 1891. R. Q. M., 28 Aug., 1899.

BLEDSOE, ALBERT T.* [Born in Ky. Appointed from Ky.]
Bvt. 2nd Lieut. 7th Inf., 1 July, 1830. Resigned 31 Aug., 1832.

BLISS, ALEXANDER. [Born in Mass. Appointed from N. Y.]
Capt. A. Q. M. Vols., 3 Feb., 1862. Capt. A. Q. M., 13 March, 1863. Lieut. Col. Q. M. Vols., 20 April, 1863. Col. Q. M. Vols., 7 May, 1866, to 1 Jan., 1867. Resigned 30 March, 1868. Bvt. Maj. Lieut. Col. and Col., 13 March, 1865, for faithful and meritorious service during the war.

BLISS, HORACE.* [Born in N. H. Appointed from N. H.]
2nd Lieut. 4th Art., 1 July, 1822. 1st Lieut., 31 Dec., 1827. Resigned 10 June, 1836. Died 7 Nov., 1878.

BLISS, JOHN.* [Born in N. H. Appointed from N. H.]
Ensign 2nd Inf., 1 March, 1811. 2nd Lieut. 2nd Inf., 1 March, 1811. 1st Lieut., 20 Jan., 1813. Capt. A. Dep. Q. M. G., 25 April, 1813. Disbanded 15 June, 1815. Died 6 Dec., 1822.

BLISS, JOHN. [Born in N. H. Appointed from N. H.]
1st Lieut. 11th Inf., 12 March, 1812. Capt. 13 May, 1813. Trans. to 6th Inf., 17 May, 1815. Trans. to 3rd Inf., 31 Dec., 1821. Maj. 1st Inf., 15 July, 1830. Lieut. Col. 6th Inf., 30 Sept., 1836. Resigned 6 Sept., 1837. Bvt. Maj., 13 May, 1823, for ten years' faithful service in one grade. Died 22 Nov., 1854.

BLISS, TASKER H.* [Born in Penn. Appointed from Penn.]
2nd Lieut. 1st Art., 16 June, 1875. 1st Lieut., 1 July, 1880. Capt. C. S., 20 Dec., 1892. Maj. C. S., 30 April, 1898. Honor graduate of the Artillery School, 1884. Lieut. Col. Chief C. S. Vols., 9 May, 1898. Discharged 13 June, 1899.

BLISS, WM. W. S.* [Born in N. Y. Appointed from N. H.]
Bvt. 2nd Lieut. 4th Inf., 1 July, 1833. 2nd Lieut., 31 March, 1834. 1st Lieut., 21 Sept., 1836. Bvt. Capt. A. A. G., 26 Oct., 1839. Capt. 4th Inf., 12 June, 1846. Bvt. Maj. A. A. G., 12 June, 1846. Died 5 Aug., 1853. Bvt. Maj. 9 May, 1846, for gallant and meritorious conduct at Palo Alto and Resaca de la Palma. Bvt. Lieut. Col., 23 Feb., 1847, for gallant and meritorious conduct at Buena Vista.

BLISS, ZENAS R.* [Born in R. I. Appointed from R. I.]
Bvt. 2nd Lieut. 1st Inf., 1 July, 1854. 2nd Lieut. 8th Inf., 3 March, 1855. 1st Lieut., 17 Oct., 1860. Capt., 14 May, 1861. Col. 10th R. I. Vols., 26 May, 1862. Col. 7th R. I. Vols., 21 Aug., 1862. Bvt. Maj., 13 Dec., 1862, for gallant and meritorious service in the Battle of Fredericksburg, Va. Bvt. Lieut. Col., 7 May, 1864, for gallant and meritorious service in the Battle of the Wilderness, Va. Mustered out of Vol. service, 9 June, 1865. Maj. 39th Inf., 6 Aug., 1867. Trans. to 25th Inf., 15 March, 1869. Lieut. Col. 19th Inf., 4 March, 1879. Col. 24th Inf., 20 April, 1886. Brig. Gen., 25 April, 1895. Maj. Gen., 14 May, 1897. Retired on his own request after 40 years' service, 22 May, 1897. Medal of Honor for most distinguished gallantry in action at the Battle of Fredericksburg, Va., 13 Dec., 1862, on which occasion, to encourage his regiment (never before in action and ordered to lie down to partially protect itself from a deadly fire), he arose to his feet, advanced in front of the line and fired several shots at the enemy at short range, being fully exposed to their fire at the time; while serving as Col. 7th Rhole Island Vol Inf.

BLOCKSOM, AUGUSTUS P.* [Born in Ohio. Appointed from Ohio.]
2nd Lieut. 6th Cav., 15 June, 1877. 1st Lieut., 15 Jan., 1884. Capt., 10 Nov., 1894. Bvt. 1st Lieut., 27 Feb., 1890, for gallant services in action against Indians at Ash Creek, Arizona, 7 May, 1880. Maj. 27th U. S. Vols., 5 July, 1899. (declined).

BRIGHAM, HENRY A. [Born in Mass. Appointed from N. Y.]
Mil. Storekeeper Ord., 6 March, 1862. Died 15 Nov., 1870.

BRIGHAM, HENRY O. [Born in Vt. Appointed from Mass.]
Priv. Co. D, and Princ. Musician 9th Inf., 10 April, 1847, to 26 Aug., 1848. Addl. P. M. Vols., 1 June, 1861. Resigned 30 April, 1864. Maj. and P. M., 17 Jan., 1867. Died 22 Jan., 1868.

BRIGHTLY, CHAS. H.* [Born in Penn. Appointed from Penn.]
2nd Lieut. 4th Inf., 24 June, 1861. 1st Lieut., 24 June, 1861. Capt., 16 Sept., 1862. Died 9 June, 1864, of wounds received in Battle of Wilderness, Va. Bvt. Maj., 3 May, 1863, for gallant and meritorious service in the Battle of Chancellorsville, Va. Bvt. Lieut. Col., 5 May, 1864, for gallant and meritorious service at the Battle of the Wilderness, Va.

BRIMHALL, ELISHA. [Born in Mass. Appointed from Me.]
Supt. Artificers, July, 1812, to Dec., 1813. Ensign 9th Inf., 4 Dec., 1813. 3rd Lieut., 1 Jan., 1814. 2nd Lieut., 1 Sept., 1814. 1st Lieut., 1 Sept., 1814. Disbanded 15 June, 1815. Reinstated 2 Dec., 1815, as 2nd Lieut. Corps Art. 1st Lieut., 20 April, 1818. Resigned 30 Nov., 1820. Retained — Jan., 1816 (in re-organization under Act of 3 March, 1815), as 2nd Lieut. Art., with Bvt. of 1st Lieut. from 1 Sept., 1814.

BRINCKLE, JOHN R. [Born in Penn. Appointed from Del.]
2nd Lieut. 5th Art., 14 May, 1861. 1st Lieut., 18 Sept., 1862. Bvt. Capt., 6 April, 1865, for gallant and meritorious service in the Battle of Sailor's Creek, Va. Bvt. Maj., 9 April, 1865, for gallant and meritorious service in the campaign terminating with the surrender of the insurgent forces under Gen. R. E. Lee. Capt. 5th Art., 7 Oct., 1874. Retired for disability, with the rank of Maj., 27 Aug., 1896. Graduate of the Artillery School, 1870.

BRINDLEY, RICHD. [Born in Del. Appointed from Del.]
2nd Lieut. 2nd Inf., 3 May, 1861. 1st Lieut., 14 May, 1861. Capt., 15 March, 1862. Killed 27 June, 1862, in Battle of Gaines' Mill, Va. Bvt. Maj., 27 June, 1862, for gallant and meritorious service at the Battle of Gaines' Mills, Va.

BRINKERHOFF, HENRY R. [Born in Ohio. Appointed from Mo.]
1st Lieut. 30th Ohio Vols., 29 Aug., 1861. Lieut. Col. 52nd U. S. Col. Troops, 27 July, 1863. Resigned 20 June, 1865. Lieut. Col. 52nd U. S. Col. Troops, 16 Sept., 1865. Mustered out 5 May, 1866. 2nd Lieut. 15th Inf., 3 June, 1867. 1st Lieut., 7 Nov., 1867. Capt., 18 Sept., 1878. Maj. 3rd Inf., 26 April, 1898. Lieut. Col. 11th Inf., 8 Sept., 1899.

BRINTON, JEREMIAH B. [Born in Penn. Appointed from Penn.]
Asst. Surg., 16 April, 1862. Resigned 17 Nov., 1865. Bvt. Capt. and Bvt. Maj., 13 March, 1865, for faithful and meritorious service during the war.

BRISBANE, ABBOTT H.* [Born in S. C. Appointed from S. C.]
Bvt. 2nd Lieut. 3rd Art., 1 July, 1825. 2nd Lieut., 1 July, 1825. Resigned 1 Jan., 1828. Died 28 Sept., 1861.

BRISBIN, JAMES S. [Born in Penn. Appointed from Penn.]
2nd Lieut. 1st Drag., 26 April, 1861. Capt. 6th Cav., 5 Aug., 1861. Bvt. Maj., 9 June, 1863, for gallant and meritorious service in the Battle of Beverly Ford, Va. Col. 5th U. S. Col. Cav., 1 March, 1864. Bvt. Brig. Gen. Vols., 12 Dec., 1864. Bvt. Lieut. Col., 19 Dec., 1864, for gallant and meritorious service in action at Marion, E. Tenn. Bvt. Col., 13 March, 1865, for gallant and meritorious service during the war. Bvt. Maj. Gen. Vols., 13 March, 1865, for meritorious service during the war. Brig. Gen. Vols., 1 May, 1865. Mustered out of Vol. service, 15 Jan., 1866. Trans. to 9th Cav., 8 Sept., 1866. Maj. 2nd Cav., 1 Jan., 1869. Lieut. Col. 9th Cav., 6 June, 1885. Col. 1st Cav., 20 Aug., 1889. Trans. to 8th Cav., 22 April, 1891. Died 14 Jan., 1892.

BRISTOL, HENRY B. [Born in Mich. Appointed from Mich.]
2nd Lieut. 5th Inf., 15 May, 1857. 1st Lieut., 13 May, 1861. Capt., 1 June, 1862. Bvt. Maj., 13 March, 1865, for faithful and meritorious service in New Mexico. Bvt. Lieut. Col., 13 March, 1865, for faithful and meritorious service in New Mexico, and particularly for his untiring zeal and energy in controlling the Navajoe tribe of Indians at the Bosque Redondo, and for his praise-worthy efforts in advancing their condition from that of savages to that of civilized men. Retired 20 March, 1879.

BRITT, GEORGE H. [Born in Va. Appointed from Va.]
2nd Lieut. 2nd Art., 1 May, 1814. Trans. to Corps Art., 12 May, 1814. Died 31 Jan., 1816.

BRITTON, FORBES.* [Born in Va. Appointed from Va.]
Bvt. 2nd Lieut. 7th Inf., 1 July, 1834. 2nd Lieut., 18 Nov., 1835. 1st Lieut., 7 July, 1838. Capt., 16 Feb., 1847. Resigned 16 July, 1850. Died 14 Feb., 1861.

BRITTON, THOS. [Born in England. Appointed from Army.]
Priv. Co. I, 4th Ky. Vols., 26 Oct., 1847, to 25 July, 1848. Priv. Co. D, 6th Inf., 22 Dec., 1848. Corpl., 1 Sept., 1849. Out of service 3 March, 1850. Priv. Gen. Ser., 25 May, 1850. Priv. Co. D, 6th Inf., 11 Oct., 1850. Discharged 3 July, 1854. Priv. Co. H, 6th Inf., 3 Oct., 1854 Corpl., 5 April, 1855. Sergt., 1 Oct., 1856. 1st Sergt., 9 Nov., 1858. Discharged 3 Aug., 1859. 1st Sergt. Co. H, 6th Inf., 3 Aug., 1859 Ord. Sergt. U. S. A., 11 Nov., 1862 2nd Lieut. 6th Inf., 18 Nov., 1862. Bvt. 1st Lieut., 2 July, 1863, and Bvt. Capt., 13 March, 1865, for gallant and meritorious service in the Battle of Gettysburg, Penn. 1st Lieut. 6th Inf., 23 March, 1865. Capt. 39th Inf., 28 July, 1866, declined. Capt. 6th Inf., 1 March, 1872 Retired, over 30 years' service, 16 July, 1889. Died 18 Sept., 1896.

BROADUS, WM. [Born in Va. Appointed from Va.]
Mil. Storekeeper Ord., 2 April, 1824. Died 5 Oct., 1830.

BROATCH, WM. J. [Born in Conn. Appointed from Army.]
Priv. and Sergt. Co. A, 8th Conn. Vols., 25 Sept., 1861. 2nd Lieut., 28 March, 1862. 1st Lieut., 18 Sept., 1862. Resigned 24 Oct., 1863. 1st Sergt. Co. F, and Sergt. Maj. 14th Inf, 1 Nov., 1863, to 10 June, 1864. 2nd Lieut. 10th Inf., 18 May, 1864. 1st Lieut., 3 Oct., 1864 Capt. 40th Inf., 28 July, 1866. Unass'd 20 April, 1869. Discharged 31 Dec., 1870. Bvt. 1st Lieut., 1 Oct., 1864, for gallant service at the Battle of Chapel House, Va.

BROCK, JOHN P. [Born in Va. Appointed from Va.]
2nd Lieut. 11th Inf., 21 June, 1848. Disbanded 15 Aug., 1848.

BROCKENBROUGH, AUSTIN.* [Born in Va. Appointed from Va.]
2nd Lieut. Corps Art., 1 July, 1819. Trans. to 3rd Art., 1 June, 1821. 1st Lieut., 1 Oct., 1826. Resigned 30 June, 1833. Died 6 Sept., 1842.

BROCKWAY, THOS. C.* [Born in Conn. Appointed from Conn.]
Bvt. 2nd Lieut. 7th Inf., 1 July, 1828. 2nd Lieut., 1 July, 1828. Died 28 Sept., 1831.

BRODHEAD, DANIEL M. [Born in Penn. Appointed from N. Y.]
1st Lieut. 14th Inf., 14 May, 1861. Capt., 9 June, 1864. Died 10 June, 1864, of wounds received in Battle of Wilderness, Va. Bvt. Capt., 5 May, 1864, for gallant and meritorious service at the Battle of the Wilderness, Va.

BRODHEAD, JOSIAH A. [Born in N. H. Appointed from Mass.]
Capt. A. Q. M. Vols., 14 April, 1862. Addl. P. M., 26 Nov., 1862. Resigned commission of Capt. A. Q. M., 8 Dec., 1862. Bvt. Lieut. Col. Vols., 27 Dec., 1865, for faithful service in his department. Mustered out 1 April, 1869. Maj. P. M., 25 July, 1875. Died 3 April, 1884.

BRODHEAD, THORNTON F. [Born in N. H. Appointed from Mich.]
1st Lieut. 15th Inf., 9 April, 1847. Capt., 2 Dec., 1847. Bvt. Capt., 20 Aug., 1847. Disbanded 31 July, 1848. Bvt. Capt., 20 Aug., 1847, for gallant and meritorious conduct at Contreras and Churubusco.

BRODIE, ALEXR. O.* [Born in N. Y. Appointed from N. Y.]
2nd Lieut. 1st Cav., 15 June, 1870 1st Lieut., 25 May, 1875. Reg. Adj., 1 Sept., 1874, to 1 April, 1875. Resigned 30 Sept., 1877. Priv. Troop M, 6th Cav., 6 Aug., 1883, to 4 Feb., 1884. Maj. in Wood's Rough Riders in Spanish War of 1898.

BRODIE, ROBT. L. [Born in S. C. Appointed from S. C.]
Asst. Surg., 15 May, 1854. Resigned 7 May, 1861.

BRODRICK, PATRICK T.* [Born in Ireland. Appointed from Ind.]
2nd Lieut. 25th Inf., 15 June, 1868. Unass'd 26 April, 1869. Ass'd to 23rd Inf., 14 July, 1869. 1st Lieut., 24 July, 1874. Reg. Adj., 1 Oct., 1876, to date of death. Died 28 March, 1886.

BROMWELL, CHARLES S.* [Born in Ky. Appointed from Ohio.]
Addl. 2nd Lieut. Eng., 12 June, 1890. 2nd Lieut., 18 May, 1893. 1st Lieut., 12 Oct., 1895.

BRONAUGH, JOHN M. [Born in D. C. Appointed from M. O.]
2nd Lieut. Inf., 22 March, 1847; 12th Inf., 9 April, 1847. Reg. Adj., 1 May, to 31 Dec., 1847. Bvt. 1st Lieut., 20 Aug., 1847, for gallant and meritorious conduct in the Battles of Contreras and Churubusco, Mex. Mustered out 25 July, 1848. Died 23 March, 1889.

BRONAUGH, WM. N. [Born in Va. Appointed from Va.]
2nd Lieut. 7th Inf., 18 April, 1818. 1st Lieut., 31 Dec., 1819. Reg. Adj., 1 Sept., 1819, to 1 Aug., 1821. Resigned 1 March, 1824.

BRONAUGH, JAMES C. [Born in Va. Appointed from Va.]
Maj. and Surg. 12th Inf., 28 April, 1812. Hosp. Surg., 15 April, 1814. Asst. Surg. Gen., 18 April, 1818. Disbanded 1 June, 1821.

BRONSON, NELSON. [Born in Conn. Appointed from Conn.]
1st Sergt. Co. E, 8th Conn. Vols., 25 Sept., 1861. 1st Lieut. 8th Conn. Vols., 18 March, 1862. Mustered out 17 Jan., 1863. 1st Lieut. Vet. Res. Corps, 19 Aug., 1863. Mustered out 15 Oct., 1866. 2nd Lieut. 42nd Inf., 28 July, 1866. Trans. to 6th Inf., 22 April, 1869. 1st Lieut., 8 June, 1874. Retired 30 Nov., 1879.

BROOKE, BENJAMIN. [Born in Pa. Appointed from Pa.]
Asst. Surg., 4 May, 1891. Retired for disability, with the rank of Capt., 10 April, 1898.

BROOKE, EDMUND H. [Born in Md. Appointed from Md.]
Addl. P. M., 1 April, 1865. Bvt. Lieut. Col. Vols., 1 April, 1865, for faithful and meritorious service. Maj. P. M., 17 Jan., 1867. Vacated commission of Addl. P. M., 17 Jan., 1867. Retired 30 June, 1882. Died 26 March, 1890

BROOKE, EDWARD H. [Born in Ore. Appointed from Ore.]
Cadet Mil. Acad., 1 July, 1875, to 26 June, 1877. 2nd Lieut 21st Inf., 28 Nov., 1879. 1st Lieut., 6 March, 1888. Died 11 Nov., 1896.

BROOKE, FRANCIS J.* [Born in Va. Appointed from Va.]
Bvt. 2nd Lieut. 7th Inf., 1 July, 1826. 2nd Lieut. 6th Inf., 1 July, 1826. Reg. Adj., 1 April, 1833, to 1 Aug., 1836. 1st Lieut., 6 May, 1835. Killed 25 Dec., 1837, in Battle at Okeechobee Lake, Fla.

BROOKE, GEO. M. [Born in Va. Appointed from Va.]
1st Lieut. 5th Inf., 3 May, 1808. Capt., 1 May, 1810. Maj. 23rd Inf., 1 May, 1814. Trans. to 4th Inf., 17 May, 1815. Trans. to 8th Inf., 27 Jan., 1819. Lieut. Col., 1 March, 1819. Trans. to 4th Inf., 13 Aug., 1819. Col. 5th Inf., 15 July, 1831. Died 9 March, 1851. Bvt. Lieut. Col., 15 Aug., 1814, for gallant conduct in the defence of Fort Erie, U. C. Bvt. Col., 17 Sept., 1814, for distinguished and meritorious service in the Sortie from Fort Erie, U. C. Bvt. Brig. Gen., 17 Sept., 1824, for ten years' faithful service in one grade. Bvt. Maj. Gen., 30 May, 1848, for meritorious conduct, particularly in the performance of his duties in prosecuting the war with Mexico

BROOKE, GEORGE M. [Born in Va. Appointed from the Army.]
Priv., Corpl. and Sergt. Batteries I and O, 1st Art., 6 Aug., 1897, to 22 Nov., 1899. 2nd Lieut. 5th Inf., 1 Oct., 1899.

BROOKE, JOHN. [Born in Penn. Appointed from Penn.]
1st Lieut. Asst. Surg., 22 Nov., 1862. Bvt. Capt. and Maj., 13 March, 1865, for faithful and meritorious service during the War. Capt. Asst. Surg., 28 July, 1866. Maj and Surg., 2 March, 1882. Retired, operation of law, 22 Feb., 1894.

BROOKE, JOHN M. [Born in Va. Appointed from Va.]
2nd Lieut. Corps Art., 13 Aug., 1819. Resigned 12 June, 1820.

BROOKE, JOHN R. [Born in Penn. Appointed from Penn.]
Capt. 4th Penn. Vols., 20 April, 1861. Mustered out 27 July, 1861. Col. 53rd Penn. Vols., 7 Nov., 1861. Brig. Gen. Vols., 12 May, 1864, for distinguished service during the recent Battles of the Old Wilderness and Spottsylvania Court House, Va. Bvt.

BELL, JAMES F.* [Born in Ky. Appointed from Ky.]
Addl. 2nd Lieut. 9th Cav., 14 June, 1878. 2nd Lieut., 28 June, 1878. Trans. to 7th Cav., 9 Aug., 1878. 1st Lieut., 29 Dec., 1890. Capt., 2 March, 1899. Maj. and Eng. Officer Vols., 17 May, 1898. Discharged 17 April, 1899. Maj. A. A. G., 17 April, 1899. Vacated 12 July, 1899. Lieut. Col., 32nd U. S. Vols., 5 July, 1899 (declined). Col., 36th U. S. Vols., 5 July, 1899.

BELL, JAMES M. [Born in Va. Appointed from Va.]
Asst. Surg., 30 Jan., 1847. Disbanded 3 Aug., 1848.

BELL, JAMES M. [Born in Penn. Appointed from Penn.]
1st Lieut. 86th Ohio Vols., 10 June, 1862. Mustered out 25 Sept., 1862. Capt. Independent Co. Penn. Cav., 30 June, 1863. Mustered out 9 Aug., 1863. Capt. 13th Penn. Cav., 8 Oct., 1863. Mustered out 14 July, 1865. 2nd Lieut. 7th Cav., 28 July, 1866. Bvt. 1st Lieut. and Capt., 2 March, 1867, for gallant and meritorious service in the Battle of the Wilderness, Va. Bvt. Maj., 2 March, 1867, for gallant and meritorious service in the Battle of Ream's Station, Va. 1st Lieut. 7th Cav., 2 April, 1867. Capt., 25 June, 1876. Bvt. Lieut. Col., 27 Feb., 1890, for gallant services in action against Indians at Canon Creek, Mont., 13 Sept., 1877. Maj. 1st Cav., 23 May, 1896. Col. 27th U. S. Vols., 5 July, 1899. Lieut. Col. 8th Cav., 10 Jan., 1900.

BELL, JOHN. [Born in N. H. Appointed from N. H.]
Asst. Surg., 26 Aug., 1861. Resigned 24 June, 1867. Bvt. Capt. and Maj., 13 March, 1865, for faithful and meritorious service during the war.

BELL, JOHN R.* [Born in N. Y. Appointed from N. Y.]
2nd Lieut. Light Art., 3 Jan., 1812. 1st Lieut., 24 Aug., 1812. Maj. A. I. G., 29 July, 1813. Capt. Light Art., 10 Oct., 1814. (Col. I. G., 28 Oct., 1814, to 15 June, 1815.) Trans. to 4th Art., 1 June, 1821. Died 11 April, 1825. Bvt. Maj., 10 Oct., 1824, for ten years' faithful service in one grade.

BELL, JONATHAN. [Born in ——. Appointed from N. Y.]
Ensign 2nd Inf., 14 April, 1812. 2nd Lieut., 14 April, 1812. 1st Lieut., 30 May, 1813. Asst. Dep. P. M. G., 1 Aug., 1814. Disbanded 24 April, 1816.

BELL, OLA W.* [Born in Mich. Appointed from Mich.]
Addl. 2nd Lieut. 3rd Cav., 12 June, 1896. 2nd Lieut., 11 Dec., 1896.

BELL, RICHARD H. [Born in Va. Appointed from Va.]
2nd Lieut. 5th Inf., 3 May, 1808. 1st Lieut., 1 Sept., 1809. Capt., 15 Aug., 1813. Trans. to 7th Inf., 17 May, 1815. Resigned 31 May, 1817.

BELL, SAMUEL H. [Born in N. C. Appointed from Pa.]
Post Chaplain, 20 Jan., 1897.

BELL, WM. H.* [Born in Penn. Appointed from Penn.]
Bvt. 2nd Lieut. 3rd Inf., 1 July, 1858. 2nd Lieut., 6 Dec., 1858. 1st Lieut., 14 May, 1861. Capt. C. S., 11 June, 1862. Vacated commission of 1st Lieut. 3rd Inf., 12 March, 1862, but served as such to 17 June, 1862. Bvt. Maj., 13 March, 1865, for faithful and meritorious service in New Mexico. Maj. C. S., 14 Aug., 1883. Lieut. Col. A. C. G., 27 Dec., 1892. Col. A. C. G., 10 June, 1896. Brig. Gen. C. G. S., 14 Nov., 1897. Retired by op. of law 28 Jan., 1898.

BELL, WM. H.* [Born in N. C. Appointed from N. C.]
3rd Lieut. Ord., 1 July, 1820. Trans. to 3rd Art., 1 June, 1821. Capt. A. Q. M., 1 Nov., 1830, to 31 July, 1831. Capt. Ord., 30 May, 1832. Maj., 25 March, 1848. Resigned 28 May, 1861.

BELL, WM. W. Born in Canada. Appointed from Army.]
Priv. Sergt. and 1st Sergt. Co. H, 1st Battalion and G, 2nd Battalion 18th Inf., 1 April, 1862, to 1 April, 1865. Sergt. Co. G, 2nd Battalion, 1 May to 13 May, 1865. 2nd Lieut. 18th Inf., 21 Feb., 1865. 1st Lieut., 21 Feb., 1865. Died 14 June, 1868.

BELLAS, HENRY H. [Born in Penn. Appointed from Va.]
2nd Lieut. 4th Cav., 1 Oct., 1873. 1st Lieut., 2 April, 1879. Retired 26 May, 1886, for disability. Appointed Capt. of Cav., 2nd Oct., 1890, with rank from 24 April, 1886. Retired 3 Oct., 1890.

BELLINGER, JOHN B.* [Born in S. C. Appointed from S. C.]
2nd Lieut., 7th Cav., 15 June, 1884. Trans. to 5th Cav., 13 Oct., 1884. 1st Lieut. 3rd Cav., 22 April, 1891. Trans. to 5th Cav., 27 April, 1891. Capt. A. Q. M., 11 Aug., 1894. Maj. Q. M. Vols., 16 July, 1898. Lieut. Col. Q. M. Vols., 10 Aug., 1898, to 2 March, 1899.

BELLOWS, ALONZO J. [Born in Mass. Appointed from Army.]
Priv. and Corpl. Co. F, 2nd Drag., 7 Jan., 1856, to 7 Jan., 1861. Priv. and 1st Sergt. Co. D., 14th Inf., 10 Aug. to 25 Nov., 1861. 2nd Lieut. 14th Inf., 20 Nov., 1861. 1st Lieut., 17 Sept., 1862. Resigned 28 Sept., 1865.

BELTON, FRANCIS S. [Born in Md. Appointed from Md.]
2nd Lieut. Light Drag., 27 March, 1812. 1st Lieut., 20 Jan., 1813. Maj. A. A. G., 18 Oct., 1814. Disbanded 15 June, 1815. Reinstated 3 May, 1816, as Maj. A. I. G., to rank from 18 Oct., 1814. Reinstated 20 May, 1820, to the lineal rank of Capt. in the 4th Inf., to rank from 31 July, 1817, but served as Maj. A. I. G. to 1 June, 1821. Trans. to 2nd Art. as Capt., 1 June, 1821. Maj. 1st Art., 7 to 30 July, 1838. Maj. 4th Art., 16 Sept., 1838. Lieut. Col. 3rd Art., 13 Oct., 1845. Col. 4th Art., 10 June, 1857. Retired 28 Aug., 1861. Bvt. Col. 20 Aug., 1847, for gallant and meritorious conduct in the Battles of Contreras and Churubusco, Mex. Died 10 Sept., 1861.

BELTON, WM. H. [Born in Md. Appointed from Md.]
2nd Lieut. 4th Inf., 9 Sept., 1818. Died 10 April, 1819.

BELTZHOOVER, DANIEL M.* Born in Penn. Appointed at Large.]
Bvt. 2nd Lieut. 1st Art., 1 July, 1847. 2nd Lieut., 20 Aug., 1847. 1st Lieut., 22 Feb., 1851. Resigned 6 Dec., 1855.

BENDER, GEORGE. [Born in Mass. Appointed from Mass.]
1st Lieut. 9th Inf., 15 May, 1812. Capt., 13 May, 1813. Trans. to 5th Inf., 17 May, 1815. Capt. A. D. Q. M. G., 18 April, 1818. Retained as A. Q. M., 1 June, 1821. Maj. Q. M., 22 May, 1826. Maj. 5th Inf., 23 April, 1830. Resigned 31 Oct., 1833. Bvt. Maj. 13 May, 1823, for ten years' faithful service in one grade. Died 21 Aug., 1865.

BENDIRE, CHARLES. [Born in Germany. Appointed from Army.]
Priv. Co. D, 1st Drag., 10 June, 1854. Corpl., 1 Dec., 1855. Priv., 17 Aug., 1856. Discharged 10 June, 1859. Priv. Co. D, 1st Cav., 8 June, 1860. Corpl., 16 March, 1861. Sergt. Co. D, 4th Cav., 21 Nov., 1861. Hosp. Steward 4th Cav., 3 Nov., 1862. Discharged 1 July, 1864. Hosp. Steward 4th Cav., 1 July, 1864. 2nd Lieut. 2nd Inf., 18 May, 1864. Bvt. 1st Lieut., 11 June, 1864, for gallant and meritorious service in the Battle of Trevillian Station, Va. Trans. to 1st Cav., 9 Sept., 1864. 1st. Lieut., 12 Nov., 1864. Capt., 21 Feb., 1873. Retired 24 April, 1886. Died 4 Feb., 1897.

BENEDICT, ABNER R. [Born in N. Y. Appointed from N. Y.]
2nd Lieut. 4th Inf., 5 Aug., 1861. 1st Lieut., 5 Aug., 1861. Capt., 8 June, 1863. Died 15 May, 1867. Bvt. Capt., 27 June, 1862, for gallant and meritorious services at Battle of Gaines' Mill, Va. Bvt. Maj., 13 Dec., 1862, for gallant and meritorious service at Battle of Fredericksburg, Va.

BENET, J. WALKER.* [Born in Ky. Appointed from D. C.]
2nd Lieut. 15th Inf., 12 June, 1880. Trans. to 5th Art., 18 March, 1881. 1st Lieut., 18 July, 1886. Trans. to Ord., 26 Oct., 1886. Capt. (14 years' service), 12 June, 1894. Graduate of the Artillery School, 1884.

BENET, STEPHEN V.* [Born in Fla. Appointed from Fla.]
Bvt. 2nd Lieut. Ord., 1 July, 1849. 2nd Lieut., 10 July, 1851. 1st Lieut., 1 July, 1853. Capt., 3 Aug., 1861. Bvt. Maj. and Lieut. Col., 13 March, 1865, for faithful and meritorious service in the Ord. Dept. Maj. Ord., 22 Dec., 1866. Brig. Gen. Chief of Ord., 23 June, 1874. Retired 22 Jan., 1891. Died 22 Jan., 1895.

BENHAM, DANIEL W. [Born in Ohio. Appointed from Ohio.]
Priv. Co. B, 6th Ohio Vols., 20 April, 1861. Discharged 21 Aug., 1861. 2nd Lieut. 18th Inf., 24 Oct., 1861. 1st Lieut., 19 Feb., 1862. Bvt. Capt., 31 Dec., 1861, for gallant and meritorious service in the Battle of Murfreesboro', Tenn. Capt. 18th Inf., 8 Feb., 1865. Bvt. Maj., 13 March, 1865, for gallant and meritorious service during the Atlanta campaign. Trans. to 36th Inf., 21 Sept., 1866. Trans. to 7th Inf., 19 May, 1869. Maj., 16 Dec., 1888. Lieut. Col., 4 July, 1892. Col., 7 July, 1897. Retired for disability 23 July, 1898.

BENHAM, HENRY H. [Born in Mass. Appointed from N. Y.]
Cadet at Mil. Acad., 1 July, 1875, to 17 Aug., 1876. 2nd Lieut. 2nd Inf., 1 Sept., 1879. 1st Lieut., 15 June, 1889. Capt., 1 Feb., 1898. Graduate of the Infantry and Cavalry School, 1893. Maj. Chief Ord. Officers Vols., 18 July, 1898. Discharged 12 May, 1899.

BENHAM, ROBERT B. [Born in Ohio. Appointed from Pa.]
Asst. Surg., 16 June, 1880. Capt. Asst. Surg., 16 June, 1885. Retired for disability 7 Jan., 1897.

BENHAM, HENRY W.* [Born in Conn. Appointed from Conn.]
Bvt. 2nd Lieut. Eng., 1 July, 1837. 1st Lieut., 7 July, 1838. Bvt. Capt., 23 Feb., 1847, for gallant and meritorious conduct in the Battles of Buena Vista. Capt. Eng., 24 May, 1848. Maj. 9th Inf., 3 March, 1855, declined. Bvt. Col., 13 July, 1861, for gallant and meritorious service in the Battle of Carrick's Ford, Va. Maj. Eng., 6 Aug., 1861. Brig. Gen. Vols., 13 Aug., 1861. Lieut. Col. Eng., 3 March, 1863. Bvt. Brig. Gen., 13 March, 1865, for gallant and meritorious service in the campaign terminating with the surrender of the insurgent army under Gen. Robt. E. Lee. Bvt. Maj. Gen., 13 March, 1865, for gallant and meritorious service during the War. Bvt. Maj. Gen. Vols., 13 March, 1865, for faithful and meritorious service during the War. Mustered out of Vol. service, 15 Jan., 1866. Col. Eng., 7 March, 1867. Retired 30 June, 1882. Died 1 June, 1884.

BENHAM, JOHN H., Jr. [Born in Conn. Appointed from Conn.]
Sergt. Maj. 99th N. Y. Vols., 28 May, 1861. 2nd Lieut., 6 July, 1862. Resigned 14 Jan., 1863. 2nd Lieut. 79th U. S. Col. Inf., 2 March, 1863. Resigned 7 March, 1864. 2nd Lieut. 1st U. S. Vet. Vols., 24 Dec., 1864. 1st Lieut., 27 Sept., 1865. Mustered out 10 Feb., 1866. 2nd Lieut. 24th Inf., 16 Oct., 1867. Trans. to 11th Inf., 25 April, 1869. Unassigned 23 July, 1870. Mustered out 1 Jan., 1871.

BENJAMIN, CALVIN.* [Born in N. Y. Appointed from Ind.]
2nd Lieut. 4th Art., 1 July, 1842. 1st Lieut., 16 Feb., 1847. Killed 13 Sept., 1847, in the assault on City of Mexico.

BENJAMIN, EDWARD A. [Born in Conn. Appointed from La.]
2nd Lieut. 6th Cav., 12 Dec., 1872. Trans. to 3rd Inf., 13 Oct., 1873. Retired 28 June, 1878.

BENJAMIN, EVERETT E. [Born in N. Y. Appointed from N. Y.]
Cadet Mil. Acad., 1 July, 1879, to 15 Jan., 1880. 2nd Lieut. 1st Inf., 30 Oct., 1884. 1st Lieut. 4th Inf., 4 Dec., 1891. Trans. to 1st Inf., 8 Dec., 1891. Capt., 2 March, 1899. Graduate of the Infantry and Cavalry School, 1889.

BENJAMIN, SAML. N.* [Born in N. Y. Appointed from N. Y.]
2nd Lieut. 2nd Art., 6 May, 1861. 1st Lieut., 15 May, 1861. Capt., 13 June, 1864. Bvt. Maj, 1 Aug., 1864, for good conduct and gallant service in the Battle of, Spottsylvania. Bvt. Lieut. Col., 13 March, 1865, for good conduct and gallant service during the War. Maj. A. A. G., 3 March, 1875. Resigned commission of Capt. 2nd Art., 16 March, 1875. Died 15 May, 1886.

BENNER, HIRAM H. [Born in Penn. Appointed from Ill.]
Priv. and Sergt. Co. E, 34th Ill. Vols., 24 Sept., 1861. Trans. to 78th Ill. Vols., Jan., 1864. Mustered out 8th Feb., 1865. Capt. 18th Ill. Vols., 25 March, 1865. Mustered out 16 Dec., 1865. 2nd Lieut. 18th Inf., 18 June, 1867. 1st Lieut., 1 May, 1875. Died 17 Oct., 1878.

BENNET, JOHN B.* [Born in N. J. Appointed from Colo.]
2nd Lieut. 7th Inf., 12 June, 1891. 1st Lieut. 2nd Inf., 3 Dec., 1897. Trans. to 7th Inf., 11 Jan., 1898. Capt. Act. J. A., 2 Nov., 1899. Trans. to 6th Inf., 16 April, 1900.

BENNETT, ALBERT G. [Born in Del. Appointed from Miss.]
Addl. P. M., 14 Aug., 1846. Maj. P. M., 2 March, 1849. Died 28 Feb., 1857. Bvt. Lieut. Col., 11 June, 1847, for gallant and meritorious conduct in affairs with Guerillas at National Bridge, Mexico.

10 May, 1861. Capt. A. Q. M., 3 Aug., 1861. Resigned 9 Oct., 1865. Bvt. Maj., Lieut. Col. and Col., 13 March, 1865, for faithful and meritorious services during the war. Capt., under Act of Congress 18 Jan., 1883. Retired 5 Feb., 1883. Died 11 Oct., 1887.

BILL, EDMUND B. [Born in N. Y. Appointed from Ill.]
Capt. of Inf., 23 Feb., 1847; 16th Inf., 9 April, 1847. Died 12 Oct., 1847.

BILL, JOSEPH H. [Born in Penn. Appointed from Penn.]
1st Lieut. A. Surg., 13 April, 1860. Bvt. Maj. and Lieut. Col., 13 March, 1865, for faithful and meritorious service during the war. Capt. Asst. Surg., 13 April, 1865. Maj. Surg., 28 July, 1866. Died 21 July, 1885.

BILLINGS, AMOS A. [Born in Me. Appointed from Me.]
1st Sergt. Co. E, 9th Inf., 23 March, 1847, to 4 May, 1848. 2nd Lieut. 9th Inf., 29 March, 1848. Disbanded 20 July, 1848.

BILLINGS, JOHN S. [Born in Ind. Appointed from Ohio.]
1st Lieut. Asst. Surg., 16 April, 1862. Bvt. Capt., Maj. and Bvt. Lieut. Col., 13 March, 1865, for faithful and meritorious service during the war. Capt. Asst. Surg., 28 July, 1866. Maj. Surg., 2 Dec., 1876. Lieut. Col. and D. S. G., 6 June, 1894. Retired for over 30 years' service 1 Oct., 1895.

BINCKLEY, OHIO HARRISON. [Born in Ohio. Appointed from Army.]
Served as an enlisted man under the name of George Binckley. Priv. Troop D, 5th Cav., 10 July, 1860, to 2 Dec., 1861. 2nd Lieut. 15th Inf., 24 Oct., 1861. Resigned 10 June, 1862.

BINGHAM, GONZALES S. [Born in Fla. Appointed from Ind.]
2nd Lieut. 7th Inf., 10 Oct., 1883. Trans. to 9th Cav., 4 Aug., 1884. 1st Lieut. 6th Cav., 1 July, 1891. Trans. to 9th Cav., 20 July, 1891. Capt. A. Q. M., 18 May, 1895. Maj. Chief Q. M. of Vols., 26 Nov., 1898.

BINGHAM, HORATIO S. [Born in Canada. Appointed from Minn.]
2nd Lieut. 2nd Minn. Cav., 23 Dec., 1863. Capt., 4 Jan., 1864. Mustered out 19 April, 1866. 2nd Lieut. 2nd Cav., 23 Feb., 1866. Killed 6 Dec., 1866, in action with Indians near Fort Phil. Kearny, Dakota Ter.

BINGHAM, JAMES W. [Born in Mich. Appointed from Mich.]
1st Lieut. 16th Inf., 14 May, 1861. Died 9 Nov., 1862.

BINGHAM, JUDSON D.* [Born in N. Y. Appointed from Ind.]
2nd Lieut. 2nd Art., 1 July, 1854. 1st Lieut., 12 March, 1856. Capt. A. Q. M., 13 May, 1861. Lieut. Col. Q. M. (Act 17 July, 1862), 1 Jan., 1863. Vacated commission of 1st Lieut. 2nd Art., 1 Aug., 1863. Relieved as Lieut. Col. Q. M. (Act 17 July, 1862), 1 Aug., 1864. Col. Q. M. (Act 4 July, 1864), 2 Aug., 1864. Bvt. Maj., Lieut. Col. and Col., 13 March, 1865, for faithful and meritorious service during the war. Bvt. Brig. Gen., 9 April, 1865, for faithful and meritorious service in the field during the war. Maj. Q. M., 29 July, 1866. Relieved as Col. Q. M. (Act 4 July, 1864), 1 Jan., 1867. Lieut. Col. Dep. Q. M. Gen., 3 March, 1875. Col. Asst. Q. M. G., 2 July, 1883. Retired by operation of law 16 May, 1895.

BINGHAM, THEODORE A.* [Born in Conn. Appointed at Large.]
2nd Lieut. Eng., 13 June, 1879. 1st Lieut., 17 June, 1881. Capt., 2 July, 1889. Maj., 5 July, 1898. In charge of Public Buildings and Grounds, D. C., with rank of Col., 9 March, 1897.

BINGHAM, THOMAS.* [Born in Penn. Appointed from Penn.]
Bvt. 2nd Lieut. 2nd Drag., 1 July, 1850. 2nd Lieut., 10 Nov., 1851. Resigned 21 March, 1854. Died in 1872.

BINNEY, HORACE. [Born in Penn. Appointed from Penn.]
2nd Lieut. 118th Pa. Inf., 23 Aug., 1862. 1st Lieut., 20 Sept., 1862. Capt., 9 Aug., 1864. Bvt. Maj. Vols., 1 June, 1865, for gallant conduct during the war. Mustered out 1 June, 1865. 2nd Lieut. 20th Inf., 22 Jan., 1867. Resigned 24 June, 1867.

BINNING, WM. [Born in Scotland. Appointed from Army.]
Priv., Corpl. and Sergt., Gen. Mtd. Ser., 14 March to 13 Oct., 1865. 2nd Lieut. 5th Cav., 9 Oct., 1865. 1st Lieut., 28 July, 1866. Died 1 Jan., 1868.

BINNS, JOSEPH R. [Born in Minn. Appointed from Army.]
Priv., Corpl. and Sergt. Co. D, 7th Inf., 7 March, 1890, to 3 Nov., 1893. 2nd Lieut. of Inf. (1st), 7 Oct., 1893. Resigned 26 Oct., 1896.

BIRCH, GEORGE. [Born in ——. Appointed from Penn.]
Cornet Light Drag., 12 Dec., 1808. 2nd Lieut., 1 Oct., 1809. 1st Lieut., 1 Nov., 1811. Trans. to 7th Inf., 17 May, 1815. Capt., 31 Aug., 1816. Maj. 4th Inf., 8 June, 1836. Died 26 Sept., 1837. Bvt. Maj., 31 Aug., 1826, for ten years' faithful service in one grade.

BIRD, CHAS. [Born in Del. Appointed from Del.]
1st Lieut. 1st Del. Vols., 20 May, 1861. Mustered out 16 Aug., 1861. 2nd Lieut. 2nd Del. Vols., 11 April, 1862. 1st Lieut., 1 Oct., 1862. Capt., 15 March, 1863. Mustered out 30 June, 1864. Lieut. Col. 9th Del. Vols., 3 Sept., 1864. Mustered out 23 Dec., 1864. Lieut. Col. 1st U. S. Vet. Vols., 25 Jan., 1865. Col., 30 May, 1865. Mustered out 19 Jan., 1866. 2nd Lieut. 14th Inf., 11 May, 1866. Trans. to 23rd Inf., 21 Sept., 1866. Bvt. 1st Lieut. and Bvt. Capt., 2 March, 1867, for gallant and meritorious service in the Battle of Fredericksburg, Va. Bvt. Maj., 2 March, 1867, for gallant and meritorious service in the Battle of Spottsylvania, Va. Bvt. Lieut. Col., 2 March, 1867, for gallant and meritorious service in the Battle of Petersburg, Va., 20 June, 1864. 1st Lieut., 23 May, 1867. Capt. A. Q. M., 14 March, 1882. Maj. Q. M., 14 Jan., 1895. Lieut. Col. Chief Q. M. Vols., 9 May, 1898. Col. Q. M. Vols., 10 July, 1898. Discharged Vol. service, 13 May, 1899.

BIRDSALL, BENJAMIN. [Born in ——. Appointed from N. Y.]
Capt. 4th Rifles, 17 March, 1814. Trans. to Rifle Regiment, 17 May, 1815. Killed by a soldier, 12 July, 1818. Bvt. Maj., 15 Aug., 1814, for gallant conduct at the defence of Fort Erie.

BIRDSALL, EGBERT B.* [Born in N. Y. Appointed from N. Y.]
Bvt. 2nd Lieut. 3rd Inf., 1 July, 1823. 2nd Lieut., 1 July, 1823. 1st Lieut., 17 Feb., 1829. Capt. 8th Inf., 7 July, 1838. Died 4 March, 1845.

BIRDSALL, LEWIS A. [Born in N. Y. Appointed from N. Y.]
Asst. Surg., 29 Dec., 1834. Discharged 23 Sept., 1842.

BIRDSALL, STEPHEN.* [Born in N. Y. Appointed from N. Y.]
3rd Lieut. 1st Art., 11 March, 1814. 2nd Lieut., 1 May, 1814. Trans. to Corps Art., 12 May, 1814. Disbanded 15 June, 1815. Died 10 Feb., 1858.

BIRKHIMER, WM. E.* [Born in Ohio. Appointed from Iowa.]
Priv. Co. M, 4th Iowa Cav., 21 March, 1864. Discharged 8 Aug., 1865. Cadet Mil. Acad., 1 Sept., 1866. 2nd Lieut. 3rd Art, 15 June, 1870. 1st Lieut., 10 April, 1879. Capt., 10 Feb., 1898. Honor graduate of the Artillery School, 1873. Col. 28th U. S. Vols., 5 July, 1899.

BIRMINGHAM, HENRY P. [Born in N. Y. Appointed from Minn.]
Asst. Surg., 18 Feb., 1881. Capt. Asst. Surg., 18 Feb., 1886. Maj. Surg., 15 Dec., 1898. Maj. Brig. Surg. Vols., 4 June, 1898. Discharged 20 Feb., 1899.

BIRNEY, JAMES G. [Born in Conn. Appointed from Mich.]
Sergt. Co. C, 7th Mich. Cav., 13 Nov., 1862. 2nd Lieut. 24 Jan., 1863. Capt. 31 March, 1864. Trans. to 1st Mich. Cav., 9 Oct., 1865. Mustered out 6 June, 1866. 2nd Lieut. 9th Cav., 28 July, 1866. 1st Lieut., 14 April, 1867. Capt., 1 Dec., 1869. Died 16 Jan., 1870. Bvt. 1st Lieut. and Capt., 2 March, 1867, for gallant and meritorious service at the Battle of Gettysburg, Pa.

BIRNIE, ROGERS.* [Born in Md. Appointed from Md.]
2nd Lieut. 13th Inf., 14 June, 1872. 1st Lieut., 18 Feb., 1874. R. Q. M., 27 March to 1 Aug., 1874. Trans. to Ord., 13 June, 1878. Capt. (14 years' service), 14 June, 1886. Lieut. Col. Chief Ord. Officer Vols., 18 July, 1898. Discharged Vol. service 10 April, 1899.

BISBEE, WM. H. [Born in R. I. Appointed from Army.]
Priv. Co. A, 2nd Batt. 18th Inf., 2 Sept., 1861. 1st Sergt., 2 Sept., 1861. Q. M. Sergt. 2nd Batt. 18th Inf., 1 Nov., 1861. 2nd Lieut. 18th Inf., 9 June, 1862. Bvt. 1st Lieut., 31 Dec., 1862, for gallant and meritorious service at the Battle of Murfreesboro', Tenn. 1st Lieut. 18th Inf., 31 Dec., 1862. Bvt. Capt., 1 Sept., 1864, for gallant and meritorious service during the Atlanta campaign, and in the Battle of Jonesboro', Ga. Trans. to 27th Inf., 21 Sept., 1866. Capt., 21 Dec., 1866. Unassigned 14 June, 1869. Ass'd to 25th Inf., 5 July, 1870. Trans. to 4th Inf., 27 Oct., 1870. Maj. 17th Inf., 18 May, 1893. Trans. to 8th Inf., 7 Aug., 1895. Lieut. Col. 1st Inf., 4 May, 1897. Col. 13th Inf., 16 June, 1899.

BISHOP, AUGUSTUS H. [Born in Del. Appointed from Del.]
2nd Lieut. 2nd Inf., 1 July, 1899.

BISHOP, HARRY G.* [Born in Mich. Appointed from Ind.]
Addl. 2nd Lieut. 19th Inf., 11 June, 1897. 2nd Lieut. 6th Art., 17 Oct., 1899. 1st Lieut. 2nd Art., 17 Oct., 1899. Trans. to 6th Art., 29 Nov., 1899.

BISHOP, HOEL S.* [Born in Wis. Appointed from Wis.]
2nd Lieut. 5th Cav., 13 June, 1873. 1st Lieut., 14 June, 1879. Capt., 12 Dec., 1892.

BISHOP, JOHN S. [Born in Penn. Appointed from Ind.]
Sergt. Co. A, 68th Ill. Vols., 27 May, 1862. 1st Lieut. and Adj. 68th Ill. Vols., June 4, 1862. Mustered out 26 Sept., 1862. Lieut. Col. 108th U. S. Col. Troops, 1 July, 1864. Col., 16 Oct., 1865. Mustered out 21 March, 1866. 2nd Lieut. 30th Inf., 7 March, 1867. Trans. to 4th Inf., 23 March, 1869. Unassigned 17 June, 1869. Ass'd to 13th Inf., 22 Nov., 1869. 1st Lieut., 19 Jan., 1872. Capt., 1 March, 1887. Retired by operation of law 23 March, 1898.

BISHOP, PERCY P. [Born in Tenn. Appointed from Tenn.]
2nd Lieut. 4th Art., 9 July, 1898.

BISSELL, CHAS. T. [Born in Mich. Appointed from Army.]
1st Lieut. 5th Mich. Vols., 8 Dec., 1861. Resigned 16 July, 1864. 1st Lieut. 1st Mich. Cav., 3 Aug., 1864. Bvt. Capt. Vols., 1 Aug., 1864, for gallant and distinguished services at the Battle of Gettysburg, Pa., and in the lines before Petersburg, Va. Resigned 10 March, 1865. Priv. 5th Art., 20 March to 9 April, 1865. 2nd Lieut. 2nd Art., 9 April, 1865. 1st Lieut., 21 Nov., 1865. Discharged 23 Dec., 1870. Bvt. 1st Lieut. and Capt., 9 April, 1865, for good conduct and gallant services during the war.

BISSELL, DANIEL. [Born in Conn. Appointed from Conn.]
Ensign 1st Inf., 11 April, 1792. In 1st Sub. Legion, — Dec., 1792. Lieut., — Jan., 1794. In 1st Inf., 1 Nov., 1796. Capt. 1 Jan., 1799. Lieut. Col. 1st Inf., 18 Aug., 1808. Col. 5th Inf., 15 Aug., 1812. Brig. Gen., 9 March, 1814. Retained 17 May, 1815, as Col. 1st Inf. Disbanded 1 June, 1821. Retained — May, 1815 (in re-organization under Act of 3 March, 1815), as Col. 1st Inf., with Bvt. of Brig. Gen. from 9 March, 1814.

BISSELL, GEORGE R.* [Born in Conn. Appointed from Mo.]
Bvt. 2nd Lieut. 4th Art., 1 July, 1853. 2nd Lieut. 3rd Art., 2 Oct., 1853. 1st Lieut., 12 May, 1855. Resigned 1 Sept., 1856.

BISSELL, LEWIS. [Born in ——. Appointed from ——.]
Ensign 1st Inf., 12 Dec., 1808. 2nd Lieut., 12 March, 1812. 1st Lieut., 30 March, 1814. Capt., 30 June, 1814. Trans. to 3rd Inf., 17 May, 1815. Resigned 31 March, 1817.

BISSELL, LYMAN. [Born in Conn. Appointed from Conn.]
1st Lieut. — Inf., 24 Feb., 1847. 1st Lieut. 9th Inf., 9 April, 1847. Capt., 8 Sept., 1847. Disbanded 26 Aug., 1848. 1st Lieut. 9th Inf., 3 March, 1855. Capt., 15 March, 1861. Maj. 11th Inf., 4 March, 1864. Trans. to 29th Inf., 21 Sept., 1866. Trans. to 11th Inf., 15 March, 1869. Retired 31 Dec., 1870. Died 22 Dec., 1888.

BIXLEY, WM. H.* [Born in Mass. Appointed from Mass.]
2nd Lieut. Eng., 13 June, 1873. 1st Lieut., 9 Dec., 1875. Capt., 16 April, 1883. Maj., 2 Oct., 1895.

BLACK, CHARLES S. [Born in Ireland. Appointed from N. Y.]
Ast. Surg., 3 Dec., 1883. Resigned 30 April, 1890.

BLACK, HANSON B. [Born in Md. Appointed from W. Va.]
2nd Lieut. 4th Art., 9 July, 1898.

BLACK, HENRY, M.* [Born in Penn. Appointed from Penn.]
Bvt. 2nd Lieut. 4th Inf., 1 July, 1847. 2nd Lieut. 7th Inf., 20 Aug., 1847. R. Q. M., 10 Sept., 1850, to 14 April, 1855. 1st Lieut. 9th Inf., 3 March, 1855. Capt., 10 Sept., 1856. Col. 6th Cal. Vols., 1 Feb., 1863. Maj. 7th Inf., 25 July, 1863. Bvt.

June, 1878, and at Birch Creek, Oregon, 8 July, 1878. Retired by operation of law 14 Oct., 1896.

BERNARD, SIMON. [Born in France. Appointed from ——.]
Brig. Gen. Asst. Eng., 16 Nov., 1816. Resigned 10 Aug., 1831.

BERRIEN, JAMES H. [Born in Ga. Appointed from Ga.]
Asst. Surg., 8 June, 1860. Resigned 17 March, 1861.

BERRIEN, JOHN M.* [Born in N. J. Appointed from Penn.]
Bvt. 2nd Lieut. 2nd Inf., 1 July, 1826. 2nd Lieut. 5th Inf., 1 July, 1826. 1st Lieut., 31 Dec., 1830. Resigned 31 Dec., 1836. Died 12 Oct., 1876.

BERRIEN, WM. D. [Born in Ga. Appointed from Ga.]
2nd Lieut. 6th Inf., 16 Oct., 1837. 1st Lieut., 7 July, 1838. Died 2 Dec., 1840.

BERRY, ALGA P.* [Born in Kan. Appointed from Kan.]
2nd Lieut. 10th Inf., 12 June, 1896. 1st Lieut. of Inf., 16 Sept., 1898. Ass'd to 10th Inf., 1 Jan., 1899.

BERRY, BENJN. A.* [Born in S. C. Appointed from S. C.]
Bvt. 2nd Lieut. 4th Inf., 1 July, 1841. 2nd Lieut., 14 June, 1842. Accidentally killed 12 Sept., 1845.

BERRY, DANIEL G.* [Born in Ill. Appointed from Ill.]
2nd Lieut. 1st Inf., 26 April, 1898. 1st Lieut., 2 March, 1899.

BERRY, EDWARD C. [Born in Ky. Appointed from Ky.]
2nd Lieut. 16th Inf., 9 April, 1847. 1st Lieut., 12 Oct., 1847. Disbanded 7 Aug., 1848.

BERRY, GEORGE. [Born in Va. Appointed from Ind.]
Maj. Surg. 3 March, 1847; 16th Inf., 9 April, 1847. Disbanded 5 Aug., 1848.

BERRY, GEORGE H. [Born in ——. Appointed from ——.]
Chaplain post of Fort Steilacoom, Wash. Ter., 22 Oct., 1856, to 28 Feb., 1860.

BERRY, LUCIEN G.* [Born in N. Y. Appointed from N. Y.]
2nd Lieut. 4th Art., 1 July, 1886. 1st Lieut. 5th Art., 28 Nov., 1892. Trans. to 4th Art., 5 Dec., 1892. Trans. to 7th Art., 8 March, 1898. Graduate of the Artillery School, 1892. Capt. A. A. G. Vols., 12 May, 1898. Discharged 31 May, 1899.

BERRY, MATTHEW. [Born in Ireland. Appointed from N. J.]
Priv. Troop H, 2nd Cav., 25 May, 1857, to 12 Dec., 1861. 2nd Lieut. 5th Pa. Cav., 12 Dec., 1861. 1st Lieut., 26 Dec., 1863. Discharged 3 Feb., 1864. Capt. 20th Pa. Cav., 17 Feb., 1864. Mustered out 13 Jan., 1865. 1st Lieut. 7th Cav., 28 July, 1866. Capt., 5 Dec., 1868. Trans. to unassigned 9 Aug., 1869. Discharged 31 Dec., 1870. Bvt. Capt., 2 March, 1867, for gallant and meritorious service in the Battle of Antietam, Md.

BERRY, THOS. J.* [Born in Ga. Appointed from Ga.]
Bvt. 2nd Lieut. 1st Drag., 1 July, 1857. Trans. to 2nd Drag., — April, 1858. 2nd Lieut. 2nd Drag., 4 June, 1858. Resigned 28 Jan., 1861.

BERRY, WM. A. [Born in ——. Appointed from ——.]
Asst. Surg., 25 April, 1831. Resigned 19 Nov., 1836.

BERRYMAN, HENRY.* [Born in Va. Appointed from Va.]
3rd Lieut. Corps Art., 17 July, 1817. 2nd Lieut. 7th Inf., 13 Feb., 1818. 1st Lieut., 31 Dec., 1818. Capt., 6 Oct., 1822. Resigned 30 April, 1833. Died 20 July, 1859.

BERTRAND, EUGENE P. [Born in France. Appointed from Md.]
Priv. Co. C, 18th Pa. Vols., 24 April, 1861. Mustered out 6 Aug., 1861. Sergt. Troop B, 6th Pa. Cav., 29 Aug., 1861. 2nd Lieut., 20 Nov., 1862. 1st Lieut., 1 March, 1863. Mustered out 31 Oct., 1864. 2nd Lieut. 4th Cav., 23 March, 1866. Died 21 Sept., 1866.

BERTSCH, WM. H.* [Born in Mich. Appointed from Mich.]
2nd Lieut. 15th Inf., 12 June, 1891. 1st Lieut., 6 Oct., 1897.

BEST, CLERMONT L.* [Born in N. Y. Appointed from N. Y.]
Bvt. 2nd Lieut. 1st Art., 1 July, 1847. 2nd Lieut. 4th Art., 13 Sept., 1847. 1st Lieut., 12 Sept., 1850. Capt., 29 April, 1861. Bvt. Maj., 3 May, 1863, for gallant and meritorious service in the Battle of Chancellorsville, Va. Lieut. Col. A. I. G. (Act 17 July, 1862), 15 May, 1863. Bvt. Lieut. Col., 3 July, 1863, for gallant and meritorious service in the Battle of Gettysburg, Penn. Relieved as Lieut. Col. A. I. G., 4 April, 1864. Bvt. Col., 13 March, 1865, for good conduct and gallant service during the War. Maj. 1st Art., 5 Feb., 1867. Lieut. Col., 15 March, 1881. Trans. to 4th Art., 27 Oct., 1881. Col., 2 Oct., 1883. Retired by operation of law 25 April, 1888. Died 7 April, 1897.

BEST, CLERMONT L., Jr. [Born in N. Y. Appointed from N. Y.]
2nd Lieut. 1st Art., 3 Oct., 1867. 1st Lieut., 7 Feb., 1875. R. Q. M., 30 June, 1882, to 5 May, 1887. Capt., 1 June, 1897. Graduate of the Artillery School, 1874.

BETHEL, WALTER A.* [Born in Ohio. Appointed from Ohio.]
Addl. 2nd Lieut. 4th Art., 12 June, 1889. 2nd Lieut., 17 June, 1889. 1st Lieut. 3rd Art., 1 Sept., 1896. Capt. A. A. G. Vols., 12 May, 1898. Honorably discharged 31 May, 1898.

BETHELL, THOS. F. [Born in Ind. Appointed from Ind.]
Capt. Inf., 23 Feb., 1847; 16th Inf., 9 April, 1847. Disbanded 20 July, 1848. Capt. 25th Ind. Vols., 19 Aug., 1861. Resigned 6 Sept., 1861. Died 25 March, 1873.

BETTENS, PHILIP A., Jr.* [Born in Ind. Appointed from Ind.]
2nd Lieut. 9th Cav., 14 June, 1885. 1st Lieut., — ——, 1892. Died 27 March, 1892.

BETTS, CHAS. [Born in Va. Appointed from Va.]
3rd Lieut. Corps Art., 11 Aug., 1814. 2nd Lieut., 17 Nov., 1814. Disbanded 15 June, 1815. 2nd Lieut., 7th Inf., 19 Feb., 1817. 1st Lieut., 31 May, 1817. Resigned 31 Dec., 1818. Died 7 Jan., 1822.

BETTS, WM. H.* [Born in Va. Appointed from Ga.]
Bvt. 2nd Lieut. 7th Inf., 1 July, 1835. Trans. to 1st Art., 28 Sept., 1835. 2nd Lieut. 1st Art., 29 Feb., 1836. 1st Lieut., 30 Nov., 1837. Resigned 20 June, 1839. Died Jan., 1841.

BEYER, CHAS. D. [Born in N. Y. Appointed from La.]
Musician Gen. Ser., 12 Aug., 1858. Musician Co. B, 1st Inf., 25 May, 1860. Discharged 14 July, 1863. Musician Co. B, 1st Inf., 14 July, 1863. Principal Musician 1st Inf., 25 Jan., 1864. Discharged 14 Oct., 1865. 2nd Lieut. 81st U. S. Col.

Troops, 17 Oct., 1865. Mustered out 15 July, 1867. Capt. 41st Inf., 6 June, 1867. Trans. to 24th Inf., 11 Nov., 1869. Trans. to 9th Cav., 1 Jan., 1871. Dismissed 21 Nov., 1884.

BIART, VICTOR. [Born in Belgium. Appointed from Kan.]
1st Lieut. Asst. Surg., 6 June, 1878. Capt. Asst. Surg., 6 June, 1883. Retired for disability 21 Oct., 1891.

BIBB, JOHN J. C.* [Born in Ky. Appointed at Large.]
Bvt. 2nd Lieut. 3rd Inf., 1 July, 1844. 2nd Lieut., 18 June, 1846. Resigned 31 Dec., 1846. Died 29 Sept., 1854.

BIBB, LUCIEN I.* [Born in Ky. Appointed from Ky.]
Bvt. 2nd Lieut. of Art., 1 July, 1827. 2nd Lieut. 1st Art., 1 July, 1827. Died 7 Sept., 1831.

BIBBY, GEORGE A. [Born in N. Y. Appointed from N. Y.]
Maj. P. M., 13 May, 1823. Died 12 Feb., 1824.

BICKER, WALTER, Jr. [Born in ——. Appointed from N. Y.]
Ensign 6th Inf., 29 July, 1813. 3rd Lieut., 10 Aug., 1813. 2nd Lieut., 1 May, 1814. 1st Lieut., 1 Sept., 1814. Trans. to 2nd Inf., 17 May, 1815. Resigned 1 May, 1828. Bvt. Capt., 1 Sept., 1824, for ten years' faithful service in one grade. Died 3 June, 1886.

BICKHAM, THOS. H. Y. [Born in Ohio. Appointed from Ohio.]
Priv. Co. D, 2nd Ohio Vols., 17 April to 24 June, 1861. 1st Lieut. 19th Inf., 14 May, 1861. Dismissed 5 Jan., 1865.

BICKLEY, ABRAM W. [Born in Penn. Appointed from Penn.]
Priv. Commonwealth Pa. Art., 24 April to 27 May, 1861. 2nd Lieut. 6th Inf., 5 Aug., 1861. 1st Lieut., 20 Sept., 1863. Dismissed 28 March, 1865.

BICKLEY, WM.* [Born in Ky. Appointed from Ky.]
Bvt. 2nd Lieut. 6th Inf., 1 July, 1824. 2nd Lieut. 7th Inf., 1 July, 1824. Resigned 15 Jan., 1825. Died 21 July, 1877.

BICKNELL, JOHN Y.* [Born in Tenn. Appointed from Tenn.]
Bvt. 2nd Lieut. 2nd Drag., 1 July, 1844. 2nd Lieut., 31 March, 1846. Died 11 Nov., 1849.

BIDDLE, CHAS. J. [Born in Penn. Appointed from Penn.]
Capt. Inf., 16 Feb., 1847; Voltigeurs, 9 April, 1847. Disbanded 29 Aug., 1848. Bvt. Maj., 13 Sept., 1847, for gallant and meritorious conduct at Chapultepec. Col. 13th Pa. Res., 21 June, 1861. Resigned 11 Dec., 1861. Died 28 Sept., 1873.

BIDDLE, DAVID W. [Born in Penn. Appointed from Penn.]
2nd Lieut. 9th Inf., 26 April, 1861. 1st Lieut., 14 May, 1861. Capt., 25 July, 1863. Resigned 24 May, 1864.

BIDDLE, JAMES. [Born in Mich. Appointed from Mich.]
Capt. 16th Inf., 5 Aug., 1861. Resigned 30 Sept., 1864. Bvt. Maj., 1 Sept., 1864, for gallant and meritorious service during the Atlanta campaign.

BIDDLE, JAMES. [Born in Penn. Appointed from N. Y.]
1st Lieut. 10th N. Y. Vols., 2 May, 1861. Mustered out 31 Aug., 1861. Capt. 15th Inf., 5 Aug., 1861. Bvt. Maj., 1 Sept., 1862, for gallant and meritorious service in the Battle of Richmond, Ky. Col. 6th Ind. Cav., 11 Nov., 1862. Bvt. Lieut. Col., 16 Dec., 1864, for gallant and meritorious service in the Battle of Nashville, Tenn. Bvt. Brig. Gen. Vols., 13 March, 1865, for long, gallant and meritorious service during the war. Mustered out of Vol. service, 27 June, 1865. Trans. to 24th Inf., 21 Sept., 1866. Trans. to 11th Inf., 25 April, 1869. Trans. to 1st Cav., 1 Jan., 1871. Maj. 6th Cav., 21 Feb., 1873. Lieut. Col. 5th Cav., 10 Oct., 1887. Col. 9th Cav., 1 July, 1891. Retired by operation of law 11 Dec., 1896.

BIDDLE, JOHN. [Born in Penn. Appointed from Penn.]
2nd Lieut. 3rd Art., 6 July, 1812. 1st Lieut., 13 March, 1813. Capt. 42nd Inf., 1 Oct., 1813. Trans. to Corps Art., 17 May, 1815. Maj. A. I. G., 19 June, 1817. Disbanded 1 June, 1821. Died 21 Aug., 1859.

BIDDLE, JOHN.* [Born in Mich. Appointed from Mich.]
2nd Lieut. Eng., 11 June, 1881. 1st Lieut., 10 Jan., 1883. Capt., 11 Oct., 1892. Lieut. Col. Chief Eng. of Vols., 9 May, 1898. Discharged from Vols., 12 May, 1899.

BIDDLE, J. WILLIAMS. [Born in Penn. Appointed from Penn.]
2nd Lieut. 7th Cav., 31 Aug., 1876. Killed in action with Indians at Snake River, Montana Ter., 30 Sept., 1877.

BIDDLE, THOMAS, Jr. [Born in Penn. Appointed from Penn.]
Capt. Inf., 9 April, 1812. Trans. to 2nd Art., 6 July, 1812. Trans. to Corps Art., 12 May, 1814. Trans. to Rifle regiment, 7 Jan., 1820. Maj. P. M., 7 Aug., 1820. Killed in duel, 29 Aug., 1831. Bvt. Maj., 15 Aug., 1814, for gallant conduct in the defence of Fort Erie.

BIDDLE, WM. S.* [Born in Mich. Appointed from Mich.]
2nd Lieut. 13th Inf., 14 June, 1885. 1st Lieut. 14th Inf., 23 March, 1892. Capt., 2 March, 1899. R. Q. M., 1 Aug., 1899.

BIGELOW, CHAS. H.* [Born in Mass. Appointed from Mass.]
Bvt. 2nd Lieut. Eng., 1 July, 1835. 2nd Lieut., 30 June, 1837. 1st Lieut., 7 July, 1838. Capt., 16 June, 1839. Resigned 25 April, 1846. Died 15 April, 1862.

BIGELOW, EDWARD P. [Born in N. Y. Appointed from N. Y.]
Cadet at Mil. Acad., 1 July, 1861, to 23 Jan., 1862. 2nd Lieut. 1st Cav., 14 July, 1862. 1st Lieut., 1 Oct., 1862. Retired 10 Sept., 1863.

BIGELOW, JOHN, Jr.* [Born in N. Y. Appointed from N. Y.]
2nd Lieut. 10th Cav., 15 June, 1877. 1st Lieut., 24 Sept., 1883. Capt., 15 April, 1893. Lieut. Col. 47th U. S. Vol. Inf., 17 Aug., 1899 (declined).

BIGELOW, MORTIMER O.* [Born in Mich. Appointed from Mich.]
Addl. 2nd Lieut. 10th Cav., 12 June, 1895. 2nd Lieut., 13 June, 1895. Trans. to 8th Cav., 22 June, 1895. 1st Lieut., 2 March, 1899.

BIGGER, SAML. S. [Born in Ind. Appointed from Ind.]
2nd Lieut. 19th Inf., 24 Oct., 1861. Resigned 7 July, 1862.

BIGGS, HERMAN.* [Born in N. Y. Appointed from N. Y.]
Bvt. 2nd Lieut. Inf., 1 July, 1856. 2nd Lieut. 1st Inf., 31 July, 1856. 1st Lieut.,

Corps, 16 July, 1863. Capt., 24 May, 1864. Mustered out 14 Sept., 1866. 2nd Lieut. 42d Inf., 28 July, 1866. Bvt. 1st Lieut., 2 March, 1867, for gallant and meritorious service in the Battle of Marye's Heights. Bvt. Capt., 2 March, 1867, for gallant and meritorious service during the war. Trans. to 6th Inf., 22 April, 1869. Retired 25 March, 1871. Died 12 Oct., 1893.

BEACH, FRANCIS.* [Born in Conn. Appointed from Conn.]
Bvt. 2nd Lieut. 2nd Art., 1 July, 1857. 2nd Lieut. 4th Art., 29 Dec., 1857. 1st Lieut., 29 April, 1861. Reg. Adj., 14 May, to 30 Dec., 1861. Capt., 14 Aug., 1862. Col. 16th Conn. Vols., 24 Aug., 1862. Mustered out of Vol. service 24 June, 1865. Retired 22 Aug., 1871. Died 5 Feb., 1873. Bvt. Maj., 17 Sept., 1862, for gallant and meritorious service at the Battle of Antietam, Md. Bvt. Lieut. Col., 20 April, 1864, for gallant and meritorious service during the Siege of Plymouth, N. C.

BEACH, FRANCIS H.* [Born in N. Y. Appointed from N. Y.]
Addl. 2nd Lieut. 1st Cav., 12 June, 1887. 2nd Lieut. 6th Cav., 5 Oct., 1887. 1st Lieut. 7th Cav., 24 Jan., 1895. Graduate of the Infantry and Cavalry School, 1893.

BEACH, JOHN.* [Born in Mass. Appointed from N. H.]
Bvt. 2nd Lieut. 1st Inf., 1 July, 1832. 2nd Lieut., 25 Oct., 1835. 1st Lieut., 31 Dec., 1837. Resigned 30 June, 1838. Died 31 Aug., 1874.

BEACH, LANSING H.* [Born in Iowa. Appointed from Iowa.]
Addl. 2nd Lieut. Eng., 13 June, 1882. 2nd Lieut., 30 June, 1882. 1st Lieut., 10 Jan., 1884. Capt., 4 Oct., 1894.

BEACH, SAML. E. [Born in N. Y. Appointed from Mich.]
2nd Lieut. Inf., 2 March, 1847. 15th Inf., 9 April, 1847. 1st Lieut., 23 Feb., 1848. Disbanded 4 Aug., 1848. Bvt. 1st Lieut., 20 Aug., 1847, for gallant and meritorious conduct in the Battles of Contreras and Churubusco. Lieut. Col. 5th Mich. Vols., 10 June, 1861. Col. 18 July, 1862. Mustered out 10 June, 1864.

BEACH, WARREN C.* [Born in N. Y. Appointed from N. Y.]
2nd Lieut. and 1st Lieut. 15th Inf., 23 June, 1865. Trans. to 24th Inf., 21 Sept., 1866. Reg. Adj. 13 Dec., 1866, to 25 April, 1869. Trans. to 11th Inf., 25 April, 1869. Reg. Adj., 25 April, 1869, to 23 Jan., 1871. Capt., 29 Oct., 1873. Resigned 1 June, 1886.

BEACH, WILLIAM D.* [Born in N. Y. Appointed from N. Y.]
2nd Lieut. 3rd Cav., 13 June, 1879. 1st Lieut., 17 Nov., 1883. Capt., 16 Aug., 1892. Maj. and Eng. Officer of Vols., 19 May, 1898. Honorably discharged 12 May, 1899. Maj. I. G. Vols., 6 Sept., 1899.

BEACHAM, JOSEPH W., Jr. [Born in N. Y. Appointed from N. Y.]
Priv. and Sergt. Astor (Vol.) Batty, 30 May, 1898, to 2 Feb., 1899. 2nd Lieut., 1st Inf., 10 April, 1899.

BEACOM, EDGAR S.* [Born in Penn. Appointed from Penn.]
2nd Lieut. 24th Inf., 13th June, 1873. Resigned 31 March, 1877.

BEACOM, JOHN H.* [Born in Ohio. Appointed from Ohio.]
2nd Lieut. 18th Inf., 13 June, 1882. Trans. to 3rd Inf., 19 April, 1883. 1st Lieut., 20 Jan., 1888. Capt., 6th Inf., 26 April, 1898. Capt. A. A. G. Vols., 12 May, 1898. Lieut. Col. A. A. G. Vols., 27 Aug., 1898. Discharged 22 April, 1899. Lieut. Col. 45th U. S. Vols., 17 Aug., 1899. Trans. to 42nd U. S. Vols., 1 Sept., 1899.

BEALE, ROBT. G. [Born in Va. Appointed from La.]
Capt. 14th Inf., 9 April, 1847. Maj. 16th Inf., 3 Dec., 1847. Disbanded 8 Aug., 1848.

BEALL, BENJ. L. [Born in D. C. Appointed from D. C.]
Cadet at Mil. Acad. 1 Jan., 1814, to 15 Oct., 1818. Capt. Washington City Vols. Fla. War, 1 June, 1836. Capt. 2nd Drag., 8 June, 1836. Maj. 1st Drag., 16 Feb., 1847. Lieut. Col. 3 March, 1855. Col. 13 May, 1861. Retired 15 Feb., 1862. Died 16 Aug., 1863. Bvt. Maj., 15 March, 1837, for gallant and successful service in the war against Florida Indians. Bvt. Lieut. Col., 16 March, 1848, for gallant and meritorious conduct in the Battle of Santa Cruz de Rosales.

BEALL, FIELDER M. M. [Born in Md. Appointed from the Army.]
Priv. and Sergt. Sig. Corps, 1 Sept., 1870, to 14 Oct., 1883. 2nd Lieut. Sig. Corps, 15 Oct., 1883. 2nd Lieut. 5th Inf., 4 Feb., 1891, to rank from 15 Oct., 1883. 1st Lieut. 25th Inf., 17 April, 1891. Trans. to 18th Inf., 20 July, 1891. Capt. of Inf., 30 Aug., 1898. Ass'd to 3rd Inf., 1 Jan., 1899.

BEALL, GEORGE T. [Born in D. C. Appointed from N. M.]
Capt. Med. Storekeeper, 28 July, 1866. Retired by op. of law 13 Feb., 1894.

BEALL, LLOYD. [Born in D. C. Appointed from Mo.]
2nd Lieut. 2nd Art., 29 March, 1848. 1st Lieut., 30 June, 1851. Trans. to 2nd Inf., 21 Oct., 1859. Capt., 30 April, 1861. Dismissed 12 Sept., 1862.

BEALL, LLOYD. [Born in Md. Appointed from Md.]
Capt. in Revol. Army. Capt 9th Inf., 8 Jan., 1799. Discharged 15 June, 1800. Capt. 2nd Art. and Eng., 1 April, 1802. Trans. to Corps. Art. 12 May, 1814, to rank as Maj. from 21 April, 1814. Bvt. Maj. 10 July, 1812. Discharged 15 June, 1815. M. S. K. Ord. Dept., 20 June, 1815. Died 5 Oct., 1817.

BEALL, LLOYD J.* [Born in R. I. Appointed from Md.]
Bvt. 2nd Lieut. 1st Inf., 1 July, 1830. 2nd Lieut., 1 July, 1830. Reg. Adj., 1 March, 1833, to 11 June, 1836. 1st Lieut. 2nd Drag., 11 June, 1836. Capt., 19 Oct., 1836. Maj. P. M., 13 Sept., 1844. Resigned 22 April, 1861.

BEALL, ROBERT. [Born in Md. Appointed from Md.]
3rd Lieut. 14th Inf., 30 March, 1813. 2nd Lieut., 14 Nov., 1813. Trans. to Corps Art., 17 May, 1815. 1st Lieut., 20 March, 1818. Cashiered 4 Dec., 1819.

BEALL, THOMAS J.* [Born in D. C. Appointed from Md.]
2nd Lieut. Art., 1 March, 1811. 1st Lieut., 3 March, 1813. Capt., 4th Rifles, 17 March, 1814. Disbanded, 1 June, 1815. Reinstated 1 Jan., 1816, as 1st Lieut. Corps Art. Capt., 26 Sept., 1818. Trans. to 2nd Inf., 1 June, 1821. Trans. to 1st Inf., 1 Jan., 1829. Died 26 Oct., 1832. Retained Jan., 1816 (in re-organization under Act of 3 March, 1815), as 1st Lieut. Art., with Bvt. of Capt. from 17 March, 1814. Bvt. Maj., 26 Sept., 1828, for ten years' faithful service in one grade.

BEALL, WM. N. R.* [Born in Ky. Appointed from Ark.]
Bvt. 2nd Lieut. 4th Inf., 1 July, 1848. 2nd Lieut. 5th Inf., 30 April, 1849. 1st Lieut. 1st Cav., 3 March, 1855. Capt., 27 March, 1855. Resigned 20 Aug., 1861.

BEAMAN, CHARLES C. [Born in ——. Appointed from ——.]
Chaplain post of Hancock Bks., Mo., 20 Oct., 1838, to 31 Aug., 1840.

BEAMAN, JENKS.* [Born in Vt. Appointed from Vt.]
Bvt. 2nd Lieut. 8th Inf., 1 July, 1842. 2nd Lieut. 4th Inf., 31 Dec., 1842. 1st Lieut., 27 Nov., 1846. Died 6 May, 1848.

BEAN, JESSE. [Born in Tenn. Appointed from Tenn.]
Capt. Mtd. Rangers, 16 June, 1832. Capt. 1st Drag., 15 Aug., 1833. Resigned 31 May, 1835.

BEAN, JOHN W. [Born in Vt. Appointed from N. H.]
2nd Lieut. 5th N. H. Vols., 15 Oct., 1861. 1st Lieut., 31 July, 1862. Capt., 1 Jan., 1863. Mustered out 20 Sept., 1864. 2nd Lieut. 35th Inf., 22 Jan., 1867. Bvt. 1st Lieut., 2 March, 1867, for gallant and meritorious service in the Battle of Fredericksburg, Va. Bvt. Capt., 2 March, 1867, for gallant and meritorious service in the Battle of Cold Harbor, Va. Trans. to 15th Inf., 12 Aug., 1869. 1st Lieut., 13 Dec., 1871. Capt., 5 March, 1879. Retired for disability 29 Sept., 1890.

BEAN, JONATHAN L. [Born in R. I. Appointed from Penn.]
Cadet at Mil. Acad. 2 Sept., 1818, to 26 Dec., 1820. Capt. 2nd Drag., 8 June, 1836. Resigned 1 Oct., 1837.

BEAN, WM. H.* [Born in Penn. Appointed from Penn.]
2nd Lieut. 2nd Cav., 1 July, 1886. 1st Lieut. 8th Cav., 5 Oct., 1892. Trans. to 2nd Cav., 5 Dec., 1892.

BEARD, WM. C. [Born in Md. Appointed from Md.]
2nd Lieut. Rifles, 19 May, 1812. 1st Lieut., 27 Sept., 1812. Capt. 1st Rifles, 20 Aug., 1814. Disbanded 15 June, 1815. Reinstated 17 May, 1816, as 1st Lieut. 1st Inf. Capt., 1 May, 1817. Resigned 1 Feb., 1822. Retained, 1 May, 1816 (in re-organization under Act of 3 March, 1815), as 1st Lieut. 1st Inf., with Bvt. of Capt. from 20 Aug., 1814. Died 18 April, 1837.

BEARDSLEE, GUY R.* [Born in N. Y. Appointed from Ala.]
2nd Lieut. 9th Inf., 29 Aug., 1879. Resigned 27 Dec., 1880.

BEARDSLEY, JOHN.* [Born in N. Y. Appointed from N. Y.]
Bvt. 2nd Lieut. 8th Inf., 1 July, 1841. 2nd Lieut., 31 Aug., 1841. 1st Lieut., 18 June, 1846. Capt., 28 June, 1849. Resigned 31 Dec., 1853. Bvt. Capt., 8 Sept., 1847, for gallant and meritorious conduct in the Battle of Molino del Rey, Mex. Col. 9th N. Y. Cav., Nov., 1861. Resigned 8 April, 1863.

BEARDSLEY, JOSEPH C. [Born in Ohio. Appointed from the Army.]
Priv., Corpl. and Sergt. Co. B, 4th Inf., 12 Jan., 1885, to 21 March, 1888. 2nd Lieut., 8th Inf., 6 Feb., 1888. Resigned 1 July, 1893.

BEAUMONT, EUGENE B.* [Born in Penn. Appointed from Penn.]
2nd Lieut. 1st Cav. (4th Cav.), 6 May, 1861. 1st Lieut. 4th Cav., 14 Sept., 1861. Capt. A. de C. Vols., 13 May, 1863. Bvt. Capt., 7 Nov., 1863, for gallant and meritorious service in the Battle of Rappahannock Station, Va. Maj. A. A. G. Vols., 20 Oct., 1864. Bvt. Lieut. Col. Vols., 13 March, 1865, for gallant and meritorious service during the recent campaign in Tennessee. Bvt. Col. Vols., 2 April, 1865, for gallant and distinguished service in the Battle of Selma, Ala. Bvt. Maj. 2 April, 1865, for gallant and meritorious service in the capture of Selma, Ala. Bvt. Lieut. Col., 2 April, 1865, for gallant and meritorious service during the war. Capt. 4th Cav., 25 July, 1865. Mustered out of Vol. service, 19 March, 1866. Maj. 4th Cav., 12 Nov., 1879. Lieut. Col. 3rd Cav., 14 Jan., 1892. Retired, over 30 years' service, 6 May, 1892. Medal of Honor for most distinguished gallantry in action at the Harpeth River, Tenn., Dec. 17, 1864, where he led the attack upon a battery and captured the guns; and at Selma, Ala., April 2, 1865, where he charged with his regiment into the enemy's works, while Maj. and Asst. Adj. Gen. of Vols., serving with the Cav. Corps, Army of the Mississippi.

BEAUMONT, WM. [Born in Conn. Appointed from N. Y.]
Surg. Mate 16th Inf., 2 Dec., 1812. Trans. to 6th Inf., 30 Jan., 1813. Disbanded 15 June, 1815. Post Surg., 4 Dec., 1819. Asst. Surg., 1 June, 1821. Maj. Surg., 26 Nov., 1827. Resigned 31 Dec., 1839. Died 25 April, 1853.

BEAUREGARD, PETER G. T.* [Born in La. Appointed from La.]
2nd Lieut. 1st Art., 1 July, 1838. 2nd Lieut. Eng., 7 July, 1838. 1st Lieut., 16 June, 1839. Capt., 3 March, 1853. Resigned 20 Feb., 1861. Bvt. Capt., 20 Aug., 1847, for gallant and meritorious conduct at Contreras and Churubusco. Bvt. Maj., 13 Sept., 1847, for gallant and meritorious conduct at Chapultepec.

BECK, HENRY L. [Born in Penn. Appointed from Army.]
1st Lieut. Ulman's Batty Pa. Art., 14 Feb., 1862. Mustered out 17 March, 1862. Priv. Troop K, 15th Pa. Cav., 30 Aug., to 30 Oct., 1862. Priv. and Sergt. Batty G, 5th Art., 30 Oct., 1862, to 15 Jan., 1863. 2nd Lieut. 13th Inf., 26 Nov., 1862. 1st Lieut., 28 June, 1863. Trans. to 22nd Inf., 21 Sept., 1866. Capt., 31 July, 1867. Unass'd 15 May, 1869. Mustered out 1 Jan., 1871. Bvt. 1st Lieut., 10 Jan., 1863, for gallant and meritorious service at the Battle of Arkansas Post, Ark. Bvt. Capt., 4 July, 1863, for gallant and meritorious service during the Siege of Vicksburg, Miss.

BECK, PAUL W. [Born in Texas. Appointed from Colo.]
2nd Lieut. 5th Inf., 1 Sept., 1899.

BECK, WM. BUTLER. [Born in Penn. Appointed from Penn.]
Cadet at Mil. Acad., 1 July, 1855, to 24 Oct., 1856. 1st Lieut. 11th Penn. Vols., 24 April, 1861. 2nd Lieut., 5th Art., 14 May, 1861. Bvt. 1st Lieut., 10 May, 1864, for gallant and meritorious service in the battle near the crossing of the Po River, Va. Bvt. Capt., 27 Oct., 1864, for gallant and meritorious service in the Battle on the Boydton Plank Road, Va. 1st Lieut. 5th Art., 26 Jan., 1865. Bvt. Maj. 13 March, 1865, for gallant and meritorious service during the Seige of Petersburg, Va. Bvt. Lieut. Col., 13 March, 1865, for gallant and meritorious service during the war. R. Q. M., 1 Oct., 1867, to 30 Oct., 1876. Capt. 5th Art., 30 Oct., 1876. Retired, over 30 years' service, 24 April, 1891.

BECK, WM. H. [Born in Penn. Appointed from Ill.]
Corpl. Co. B, 10th Ill. Vols., 16 April, 1861. Discharged 29 July, 1861. Q. M. Sergt., 6th Ill. Cav., 21 Sept., 1861. 1st Lieut. 6th Ill. Cav., 1 Nov., 1862. Resigned 28 Feb., 1863. 2nd Lieut. 10th Cav., 18 June, 1867. R. Q. M., 1 Sept., 1867, to 31 Dec., 1874. 1st Lieut., 11 Dec., 1867. Capt., 23 Dec., 1887. Col. 49th U. S. Vols., 9 Sept., 1899.

BOTHWELL, JOHN R. [Born in Ill. Appointed from Army.]
Priv. and Corpl. Co. H, 2nd Batt. 12th Inf., 21 Nov., 1861, to 11 June, 1864. 2nd Lieut. 4th Inf., 18 May, 1864. 1st Lieut., 11 Feb., 1865. Unassigned 23 March, 1869. Ass'd to 8th Inf., 10 Dec., 1869. Trans. to 5th Inf., 18 Jan., 1870. Cashiered 29 Dec., 1870.

BOTTOMS, SAM. F.* [Born in Ky. Appointed from Texas.]
Addl. 2nd Lieut. 10th Inf., 11 June, 1897. 2nd Lieut. 6th Art., 8 March, 1898. 1st Lieut. 7th Art., 5 April, 1900.

BOTTS, ARCHIBALD B.* [Born in Va. Appointed at Large.]
Bvt. 2nd Lieut. 4th Inf., 1 July, 1846. Died 1 Jan., 1847.

BOTTSFORD, CHAS. E. [Born in N. Y. Appointed from Army.]
Priv. Co. D, 18th N. Y. Cav., 17 Aug., 1863. Discharged 23 June, 1864. Priv., Corpl. and Sergt. Co. A, 10th Inf., 4 Jan., 1865, to 13 June, 1867. 2nd Lieut. 10th Inf., 20 May, 1867. 1st Lieut., 28 June, 1878. Died 29 Nov., 1884.

BOUGHTON, DANIEL H.* [Born in Minn. Appointed from Iowa.]
2nd Lieut. 3rd Cav., 11 June, 1881. 1st Lieut., 27 Jan., 1885. Capt., 5 April, 1899. Honor graduate of the Infantry and Cavalry School, 1887.

BOULD, JOSEPH. [Born in England. Appointed from Army.]
Priv., Corpl. and 1st Sergt. Troop A, 6th Cav., 29 Aug., 1861, to 8 June, 1863. 2nd Lieut. 6th Cav., 1 June, 1863. Resigned 25 Feb., 1865.

BOURKE, JAMES C.* [Born in Wis. Appointed from Mo.]
Addl. 2nd Lieut. 2nd Art., 12 June, 1887. 2nd Lieut. 5th Art., 9 Dec., 1887. Resigned 15 June, 1889.

BOURKE, JOHN G.* [Born in Penn. Appointed at Large.]
Priv. Co. E, 15th Penn. Cav., 12 Aug., 1862. Trans. to Co. D, 1 March, 1863. Discharged 5 July, 1865. Cadet Mil. Acad., 17 Oct., 1865. 2nd Lieut. 3rd Cav., 15 June, 1869. 1st Lieut., 17 May, 1876. Capt. 26 June, 1882. Died 8 June, 1896.

BOURNE, WM. R. [Born in N. Y. Appointed from N. Y.]
Priv. Co. C, 44th N. Y. Vols., 26 Aug., 1861. 1st Sergt. Co. K, 1 Oct., 1861. 2nd Lieut. 44th N. Y. Vols., 14 May, 1862. 1st Lieut., 18 Dec., 1862. Capt., 11 Jan., 1863. Mustered out 9 Oct., 1863. Capt. Vet. Res. Corps, 30 Oct., 1863. Bvt. Maj. Vols., 13 March, 1865, for gallant and meritorious service during the War. Mustered out 10 Jan., 1867. 2nd Lieut. 42nd Inf., 28 July, 1866. Bvt. 1st Lieut., 2 March, 1867, for gallant and meritorious service in the Battle of Gettysburg, Penn. 1st Lieut. 42nd Inf., 10 Sept., 1868. Unassigned 22 April, 1869. Retired with rank of Capt., 15 Dec., 1870.

BOUTELLE, FRAZIER A. [Born in N. Y. Appointed from the Army.]
Q. M. Sergt. Co. A, 5th N. Y. Cav., 15 Aug., 1861. 2nd Lieut. 5th N. Y. Cav., 5 Nov., 1862. 1st Lieut., 2 April, 1864. Discharged 31 Aug., 1864. Capt. 5th N. Y. Cav., 10 Jan., 1865. Discharged 19 July, 1865. Priv., Corpl., Sergt. and Sergt. Maj. 1st Cav., 12 Feb., 1866, to 12 Feb., 1869. 2nd Lieut. 1st Cav., 2 Jan., 1869. 1st Lieut., 31 July, 1873. Capt., 24 April, 1886. Retired for disability 27 Aug., 1895. Bvt. 1st Lieut. for gallantry in actions against Indians at Lost River, Ore., 29 29 Nov., 1872, and conspicuous gallantry and meritorious conduct during the whole Modoc War.

BOUTELLE, HENRY M. [Born in Wash'n. Appointed from Wash'n.]
2nd Lieut., 3rd Art., 9 July, 1898. Trans. to 14th Inf., 24 Dec., 1898. Trans. to 3rd Art. — ——, 1899. Killed in action 2 Nov., 1899, near Manila, Philippine Islands.

BOUTON, ROBT. A. [Born in N. Y. Appointed from N. Y.]
1st. Lieut. of Inf., 23 Feb., 1847; 10th Inf., 9 April, 1847. Disbanded 24 Aug., 1848.

BOWDOIN, GEORGE R. J.* [Born in Mass. Appointed from Mass.]
(Graduate as George R. Sullivan.) Bvt. 2nd Lieut. 1st Inf., 1 July, 1829. Resigned 31 Aug., 1832. Died 14 March, 1870.

BOWEN, ACHILLES.* [Born in Ky. Appointed from Tenn.]
Bvt. 2nd Lieut. 1st Art., 1 July, 1850. Resigned 1 Dec., 1850.

BOWEN, EDWARD C.* [Born in N. Y. Appointed from Wis.]
2nd Lieut. and 1st Lieut. 12th Inf., 23 June, 1865. R. Q. M., 16 Oct., 1865, to 11 Aug., 1866. Trans. to 30th Inf., 21 Sept., 1866. Reg. Adj., 1 Sept. to 10 Nov., 1868. Capt., 22 Feb., 1869. Unassigned 23 March, 1869. Ass'd to 11th Inf., 1 Jan., 1871. Retired 7 June, 1879.

BOWEN, ISAAC.* [Born in N. Y. Appointed from N. Y.]
Bvt. 2nd Lieut. 4th Art., 1 July, 1842. 2nd Lieut. 1st Art., 7 Oct., 1842. 1st Lieut., 3 March, 1847. Capt. C. S., 27 Sept., 1850. Died 3 Oct., 1858. Bvt. 1st Lieut., 23 Sept., 1846, for gallant and meritorious conduct at Monterey. Bvt. Capt., 23 Feb., 1847, for gallant and meritorious conduct at Buena Vista.

BOWEN, JOHN S.* [Born in Ga. Appointed from Ga.]
Bvt. 2nd Lieut. Mounted Rifles, 1 July, 1853. 2nd Lieut., 20 July, 1854. Resigned 1 May, 1856.

BOWEN, NICOLAS.* [Born in N. Y. Appointed from N. Y.]
Bvt. 2nd Lieut. Top. Eng., 1 July, 1860. 2nd Lieut., 15 May, 1861. 1st Lieut., 6 Aug., 1861. Lieut. Col. A. A. G. Vols., 23 Jan., 1863, to 3 July, 1865. Capt. Eng., 3 March, 1863. Maj., 7 March, 1867. Died 11 July, 1871. Bvt. Capt., 24 May, 1862, for gallant and meritorious service during the reconnaissance near New Bridge, Va. Bvt. Maj., 25 Nov., 1863, for gallant and meritorious service during the Siege of Knoxville, Tenn. Bvt. Lieut. Col., 3 June, 1864, for gallant and meritorious service at the Battle of Cold Harbor, Va. Bvt. Col., 13 March, 1865, for gallant and meritorious service during the war.

BOWEN, WM. H. C. [Born in N. Mex. Appointed from Maine.]
2nd Lieut. 5th Inf., 15 Oct., 1875. 1st Lieut., 30 Nov., 1879. Capt., 7 March, 1893.

BOWER, WM. H. [Born in N. Y. Appointed from N. Y.]
Sergt. Batty L, 1st N. Y. Light Art., 18 Sept., 1861. Discharged 10 Nov., 1862. 2nd Lieut. N. Y. Light Art., 5 June, 1863. Resigned 31 Oct., 1863. 2nd Lieut. Vet. Res. Corps, 15 Nov., 1863. 1st Lieut, 21 Feb., 1865. Mustered out 30 June, 1866. 2nd Lieut. 45th Inf., 22 Jan., 1867. Unassigned 22 July, 1869. Ass'd to 14th Inf., 5 Aug., 1869. Dismissed 3 Aug., 1871.

BOWERMAN, RICHD. N. [Born in Md. Appointed from Md.]
Corpl. Co. G, 7th N. Y. Militia, 26 April to 3 June, 1861. 1st Lieut. 11th N. Y. Vols., 11 July, 1861. Capt., 4 Oct., 1861. Mustered out 19 April, 1862. Lieut. Col. 4th Md. Vols., 1 Aug., 1862. Col., 4 April, 1863. Bvt. Brig. Gen. Vols., 1 April, 1865, for gallantry and good conduct at the Battle of Five Forks, Va. Mustered out 31 May, 1865. Lieut. Col. 31st Inf., 28 July, 1866. Resigned 6 June, 1867.

BOWERS, GEORGE. [Born in N. H. Appointed from N. H.]
Cadet Mil. Acad., 1 July to 30 Nov., 1834. 1st Lieut. of Inf., 11 March, 1847; 9th Inf., 9 April, 1847. Capt., 4 Dec., 1847. Disbanded 26 Aug., 1848. Bvt. Capt., 20 Aug., 1847, for gallant and meritorious conduct at Contreras and Churubusco. Lieut. Col. 13th N. H. Vols., 23 Sept., 1862. Resigned 30 May, 1863. Maj. Vet. Res. Corps, 15 Nov., 1863. Mustered out 7 Nov., 1865. Died 14 Feb., 1883.

BOWERS, THEODORE S. [Born in Penn. Appointed from Ill.]
Priv. Co. G, 48th Ill. Vols., 25 Oct., 1861. 1st Lieut., 24 March, 1862. Capt A. de C. Vols., 1 Nov., 1862. Maj. J. A. Vols., 19 Feb., 1863. Lieut. Col. A. A. G. Vols., 30 Aug., 1863, to 6 March, 1866. Capt. A. Q. M., 29 July, 1864. Maj. A. A. G., 6 Jan., 1865. Killed by railroad accident, 6 March, 1866. Bvt. Lieut. Col. and Col., 13 March, 1865; for faithful and meritorious services during the war. Bvt. Brig. Gen., 9 April, 1865, for gallant and meritorious service in the field during the war.

BOWES, JOHN R.* [Born in Mass. Appointed from Mass.]
3rd Lieut. Ord., 1 July, 1819. 2nd Lieut., 10 Oct., 1819. Trans. to 2nd Art., 1 June, 1821. Trans. to 4th Art., 16 Aug., 1821. Resigned 1 Aug., 1822. Died in 1825.

BOWIE, GEORGE W. [Born in Md. Appointed from Iowa.]
1st Lieut. 8th Inf., March, 1847. 1st Lieut. 15th Inf., 9 April, 1847. Capt., 20 July, 1847. Disbanded 4 Aug., 1848. Bvt. Maj., 20 Aug., 1847, for gallant and meritorious conduct at Contreras and Churubusco. Col. 5th Cal. Vols., 8 Nov., 1861. Bvt. Brig. Gen. Vols., 13 March, 1865, for faithful and meritorious service. Mustered out 14 Dec., 1864.

BOWKER, HUGH D. [Born in Ohio. Appointed from Ohio.]
Priv. Co. C, 13th Ohio Vols., 6 May, 1861. Discharged 6 June, 1861. Corpl. Co. D, 8th Ohio Vols., 7 June, 1861. Discharged 26 Aug., 1862. Priv. and Sergt. Vet. Res. Corps, 24 July, 1863, to 16 Jan., 1865. 1st Lieut. 122nd U. S. Col. Troops, 17 Jan., 1865. R. Q. M., 8 Dec., 1865, to 8 Feb., 1866. Mustered out 8 Feb., 1866. 1st Lieut. 45th Inf., 22 April, 1867. Unassigned 22 July, 1869. Ass'd to 13th Inf., 1 Sept., 1869. Unassigned 7 May, 1870. Retired 15 Dec., 1870.

BOWLEY, ALBERT J.* [Born in Cal. Appointed from Cal.]
Addl. 2nd Lieut. 4th Art., 11 June, 1897. 2nd Lieut. 5th Art., 10 Feb., 1898. Trans. to 4th Art., 12 April, 1898. 1st Lieut., 2 March, 1899.

BOWMAN, ALEXR. H.* [Born in Penn. Appointed from Penn.]
Bvt. 2nd Lieut. Eng., 1 July, 1825. 2nd Lieut., 1 July, 1825. 1st Lieut., 21 Jan., 1835. Capt., 7 July, 1838. Maj., 5 Jan., 1857. Lieut. Col., 3 March, 1863. Died 11 Nov., 1865.

BOWMAN, ALPHEUS H. [Born in Va. Appointed from Va.]
Capt. 91st Penn. Vols., 3 Dec., 1861. Out of service 12 Sept., 1862. Capt. 91st Penn. Vols., 22 Dec., 1862. Discharged 23 Sept., 1863. Priv. Co. L, 3rd Penn. Art., 24 Dec., 1863. 1st Sergt., 24 Jan., 1864. Discharged 21 March, 1864. 2nd Lieut. 2nd Penn. Vol. Art., 21 March, 1864. 1st Lieut., 1 Sept., 1864. Mustered out 9 Nov., 1865. 2nd Lieut. 27th Inf., 28 July, 1866. 1st Lieut., 5 March, 1867. Trans. to 9th Inf., 14 June, 1869. Capt., 19 May, 1881. Maj. 2nd Inf., 30 June, 1898.

BOWMAN, ANDREW W.* [Born in Penn. Appointed from Penn.]
Bvt. 2nd Lieut. 1st Inf., 1 July, 1841. 2nd Lieut. 3rd Inf., 30 April, 1842. 1st Lieut., 21 Sept., 1846. R. Q. M., 28 March, 1847, to 30 April, 1852. Capt., 6 June, 1852. Maj. 9th Inf., 7 June, 1862. Lieut. Col. 31st Inf., 6 June, 1867. Died 17 July, 1869. Bvt. Capt., 18 April, 1847, for gallant and meritorious conduct in the Battle of Cerro Gordo, Mexico.

BOWMAN, CHAS. S.* [Born in Fla. Appointed at Large.]
Bvt. 2nd Lieut. 1st Cav., 1 July, 1860. 2nd Lieut., 2 Dec., 1860. 1st Lieut., 25 April, 1861. 4th Cav., 3 Aug., 1861. Capt., 17 July, 1862. Died 13 Jan., 1868. Bvt. Maj., 20 Feb., 1864, for gallant and meritorious service in the Cavalry Expedition in Miss.

BOWMAN, FRANCIS L. [Born in Penn. Appointed from Penn.]
1st Lieut. Pa. Vols., 16 Dec., 1846. Maj. 18 Dec., 1846. Mustered out 8 Aug., 1848. Capt. 9th Inf., 3 March, 1855. Resigned 10 Sept., 1856.

BOWMAN, JAMES M.* [Born in Penn. Appointed from Penn.]
Bvt. 3rd Lieut. Mounted Rangers, 1 July, 1832 Bvt. 2nd Lieut., 1st Drag., 14 Aug., 1833. 2nd Lieut., 30 June, 1835. 1st Lieut., 15 Oct., 1836. Died 21 July, 1839.

BOWMAN, WILLIAM. [Born in Penn. Appointed from Army.]
2nd Lieut. 21st Inf., 12 March, 1812. 1st Lieut., 4 Aug., 1814. Discharged 15 June, 1815. Priv. and Sergt. Troop D and Sergt. Maj. 1st Drag., 25 March, 1835, to 26 Aug., 1837. 2nd Lieut. 1st Drag., 1 Aug., 1837. 1st Lieut., 27 June, 1842. Died 8 Oct., 1844.

BOYCE, MICHAEL C. [Born in Maine. Appointed from Army.]
Priv., Corpl., Sergt. and 1st Sergt. Cos. E and A. 10th Inf., 23 March, 1858, to 17 July, 1862. 2nd Lieut. 10th Inf., 17 July, 1862. Died 28 July, 1863, of wounds received in Battle of Gettysburg, Penn.

BOYCE, PATRICK, [Born in Ireland. Appointed from Army.]
Priv., Corpl. and Sergt. Co. F, 8th Inf., 15 April, 1861, to 1 April, 1863. 2nd Lieut. 8th Inf., 19 Feb., 1863. 1st Lieut., 14 Jan., 1866. Resigned 19 July, 1866.

BOYCE, WM. M.* [Born in Md. Appointed from Penn.]
2nd Lieut. 1st Inf., 1 July, 1822. 1st Lieut., 30 June, 1825. Capt., 25 Oct., 1835. Resigned 14 Nov., 1836. Killed 29 Aug., 1855, in a railroad accident.

BOYD, AUGUSTUS. [Born in Penn. Appointed from Penn.]
1st Lieut. 19th Inf., 14 May, 1861. Capt. A. Q. M., 30 May, 1861. Resigned 15 Oct., 1864. Bvt. Maj., 10 Oct., 1864, for faithful and valuable service during the War. Bvt. Lieut. Col., 13 March, 1865, for faithful and valuable service during the war.

BROWN, HENRY L. [Born in Ind. Appointed from Army.]
Bvt. 2nd Lieut. 3rd Inf., 28 June, 1848. Resigned 31 March, 1850.

BROWN, HORACE. [Born in Me. Appointed from Me.]
Priv., Corpl., Sergt. and 1st Sergt. 2nd Me. Vols., 28 May, 1861. 2nd Lieut., 4 Sept., 1861. Dischraged 9 Nov., 1861. 1st Lieut. 18th Inf., 26 Oct., 1861. Resigned 28 July, 1864

BROWN, HUGH G. [Born in Penn. Appointed from Iowa.]
2nd Lieut. 15th Iowa Vols., 1 Dec., 1861. 1st Lieut., 9 July, 1862. Capt. A. de C. Vols., 28 Aug., 1863. Bvt. Maj. Vols., 29 Sept., 1864, for gallant and meritorious service in the campaign of 1864. Bvt. Lieut. Col. Vols., 31 March, 1865, for gallant conduct in the field. 2nd Lieut. 18th Inf., 2 May, 1866. Mustered out of Vol. service, 10 July, 1866. Trans. to 36th Inf., 21 Sept., 1866. 1st Lieut., 25 Nov., 1866. Bvt. Capt., 2 March, 1867, for gallant and meritorious service in the Siege of Vicksburg, Miss. Bvt. Maj., 2 March, 1867, for gallant and meritorious service in the capture of Fort Harrison, Va. Unass'd 19 May, 1869. Ass'd to 12th Inf., 15 Dec., 1870. Capt., 20 March, 1879. Maj., 26 April, 1898. Retired, over 30 years' service, 16 May, 1899.

BROWN, JACOB. [Born in Penn. Appointed from N. Y.]
Brig. Gen. N. Y. Vols., June, 1812, to July, 1813. Brig. Gen., 19 July, 1813. Maj. Gen., 24 Jan., 1814. Brig. Gen. N. Y. Vols , June, 1812, to July, 1813. Commander-in-chief of the Army, 1 June, 1821, to 24 Feb., 1828. Received the thanks of Congress 3 Nov., 1814, for his gallantry and good conduct in the successive Battles of Chippewa, Niagara and Erie, U. C., in which British veteran troops were beaten and repulsed by equal or inferior numbers; and with the presentation of a gold medal emblematic of these triumphs. Died 24 Feb., 1828.

BROWN, JACOB. [Born in Mass. Appointed from Army.]
Priv. and Sergt. 11th Inf., 3 Aug., 1812, to April, 1814. Ensign 11th Inf., 15 April, 1814. 3rd Lieut., 1 May, 1814. 2nd Lieut., 1 Sept., 1814. Trans. to 6th Inf., 17 May, 1815 R. Q. M., April, 1816, to 1 June, 1821. 1st Lieut., 18 Aug , 1819. Capt., 7 April, 1825. Capt. A. Q. M., 23 Aug., to — Oct., 1839. Maj. 7th Inf., 27 Feb., 1843. Died 9 May, 1846, of wounds received in defense of Fort now known as Fort Brown, Texas.

BROWN. JACOB.* [Born in N. Y. Appointed from N. Y.]
Bvt. 2nd Lieut. 2nd Inf., 1 July,1832. 2nd Lieut., 21 July, 1834. Resigned 31 July, 1836. Maj. Addl. P. M., 4 Jan., 1840. Died 24 Oct., 1841. Maj. 7th Inf., 27 Feb., 1843.

BROWN, JAMES D. [Born in Conn. Appointed from Conn.]
Ensign 25th Inf., 22 Jan., 1813. 2nd Lieut., 15 Aug., 1813. 1st Lieut., 2 May, 1814. Disbanded 15 June, 1815. Reinstated as 2nd Lieut. Corps Art., 2 Dec., 1815. Died 13 May, 1817. Retained 2 Dec., 1815 (in re-organization under Act of 3 March, 1815), as 2nd Lieut. Art., with Bvt. of 1st Lieut. from 2 May, 1814.

BROWN, JAMES. P. [Born in Ohio. Appointed from Army.]
Priv. Co. C, 8th Ohio Vols., 29 April, to 16 Aug., 1861. Priv., Corpl. and 1st Sergt. Co. E, 15th Inf., 4 Sept., 1861, to 21 Aug., 1863. 2nd Lieut. 15th Inf., 10 Aug., 1863. 1st Lieut., 15 Aug , 1864. Capt., 15 Aug., 1867. Died 9 June, 1875. Bvt. 1st Lieut., 20 Sept., 1863, for gallant and meritorious service at the Battle of Chickamauga, Ga.

BROWN, JOHN A.* [Born in Md. Appointed from Md.]
Bvt. 2nd Lieut. 4th Art., 1 July, 1846. 2nd Lieut., 3 March, 1847. 1st Lieut., 20 Aug., 1848. Capt., 31 Oct., 1856. Resigned 3 July, 1861. Died 8 Oct., 1877.

BROWN, JOHN T. [Born in N. Y. Appointed from Mich.]
1st Lieut. Inf., 9 March, 1847; 3rd Drag., 9 April, 1847. Disbanded 20 July, 1848.

BROWN, JOSEPH B. [Born in N. Y. Appointed from Mich.]
1st Lieut. Asst. Surg , 29 June, 1849. Maj. and Surg., 4 July, 1861. Bvt. Lieut. Col. and Bvt Col., 13 March, 1865, for faithful and meritorious service during the war. Bvt. Brig. Gen., 28 Sept., 1866, for meritorious and distinguished service at Fort Columbus, N. Y. Harbor, where cholera prevailed. Lieut. Col. Surg., 30 June, 1882. Col. Surg., 24 Jan., 1886. Retired by operation of law 26 July, 1886 Died 21 Oct., 1891.

BROWN, JUSTUS M. [Born in Ohio. Appointed from Ohio.]
1st Lieut. Asst. Surg., 11 July, 1862. Bvt. Capt. and Bvt. Maj., 13 March, 1865, for faithful and meritorious service during the War. Capt. Asst. Surg., 28 July, 1866. Maj. Surg., 13 April, 1881. Lieut. Col. Dep. Surg. Gen., 15 Nov., 1895.

BROWN, LAWRENCE C. [Born in N. Y. Appointed from the Army.]
Priv. Troop F, 7th Cav., 20 April, 1894, to 19 July, 1897, and Priv. and Corpl. Batty. D, 4th Art., 1 Oct., 1897, to 6 July, 1898. 2nd Lieut. 6th Art., 22 June, 1898. Trans. to 2nd Art., 4 April, 1899.

BROWN, LOWNDES. [Born in S. C. Appointed from S. C.]
1st Lieut. 2nd Art., 12 March, 1812. Trans. to Corps Art., 12 May, 1814. Capt., 28 Sept., 1817. Resigned 30 Sept., 1819.

BROWN, LUCIUS F. [Born in Ohio. Appointed from Army.]
Priv. and Sergt. Co C, 3rd Batt. 18th Inf., 7 Oct., 1861, to 9 June, 1862. 2nd Lieut. 18th Inf., 9 June, 1862. 1st Lieut., 14 Jan., 1863. Died 10 Oct , 1863, of wounds received at the Battle of Chickamauga. Bvt. Capt., 19 Sept., 1863, for gallant and meritorious service at the Battle of Chickamauga, Ga.

BROWN, LYTLE.* [Born in Tenn. Appointed from Tenn.]
Addl. 2nd Lieut. Eng., 26 April, 1898. 2nd Lieut. 5 July, 1898.

BROWN, MANNING. [Born in S. C. Appointed from S. C.]
2nd Lieut. 12th Inf., 30 Dec., 1847. Disbanded 25 July, 1848.

BROWN, MICAH R.* [Born in Mass. Appointed from Mass.]
1st Lieut. Eng., 23 June, 1865. Capt., 23 April, 1869. Died 9 April, 1880.

BROWN, NATHAN W. [Born in N. Y. Appointed from N. Y.]
Maj. P. M., 5 Sept., 1849. Lieut. Col. Dep. P. M. Gen., 4 April, 1864. Bvt. Col., 13 March, 1865, for faithful and meritorious service during the war. Col. A. P. M., G., 28 July, 1866. Bvt. Brig. Gen., 15 Oct., 1867, for faithful and meritorious service

during the war. Brig. Gen. and P. M. G., 8 June, 1880. Retired, over 62 years of age, 6 Feb., 1882. Died 4 March, 1893.

BROWN, OSCAR J.* [Born in Ga. Appointed from Ga.]
Addl. 2nd Lieut. 3rd Cav., 15 June, 1877. 2nd Lieut. 1st Cav., 30 Sept., 1877. 1st Lieut., 24 April, 1886. Capt., 11 Dec., 1896. Col. 2nd Ga. Vols., 14 May, 1898. Mustered out Vols., 30 Nov., 1898.

BROWN, PAUL R. [Born in N. Y. Appointed from N. Y.]
1st Lieut. Asst. Surg., 10 Nov., 1874. Capt. Asst. Surg., 10 Nov., 1879. Maj. Surg., 3 Dec., 1891. Retired for disability 1 Oct., 1897.

BROWN, PRESTON. [Born in Ky. Appointed from the Army.]
Priv. and Corpl. Batty A. 5th Art., 1 Sept., 1894, to 26 March, 1897. 2nd Lieut. 2nd Inf., 2 March, 1897. 1st Lieut., 27 Feb., 1899.

BROWN, ROBERT A.* [Born in Pa. Appointed from Pa.]
2nd Lieut. 4th Cav., 14 June, 1885. 1st Lieut. 7th Cav., 28 Nov., 1891. Graduate of the Infantry and Cavalry School, 1889. Trans. to 4th Cav., 1 Dec., 1891. Capt. 8th Cav., 14 Sept., 1899. Maj. I. G. Vols., 7 June, 1898. Discharged Vols., 12 May, 1899. Maj. I.G. Vols., 30 Sept., 1899.

BROWNE, JESSE B. [Born in N. C. Appointed from Ill.]
2nd Lieut. 4th Inf., 18 June, 1866. 1st Lieut., 10 June, 1876. R. Q. M , 1 Nov., 1887, to 14 July, 1890. Capt , 14 July, 1890. Died 14 Sept., 1892.

BROWN, SAML. [Born in Penn. Appointed from N. Y.]
Maj. Dep. Q. M. G., 26 March, 1813. Resigned 18 June, 1816.

BROWN, SEWELL H. [Born in Penn. Appointed from Penn.]
1st Lieut. 6th Cav., 14 May, 1861. Resigned 25 Jan., 1864. Died 9 May, 1887.

BROWN, STANLEY A. [Born in Penn. Appointed from Wis.]
Priv. Co. D, 5th Wis Vols., 12 July, 1861, to 27 Aug., 1864. 2nd Lieut. 5th U. S. Vet. Vols., 19 Jan., 1865. 1st Lieut , 31 Oct., 1865. Mustered out 1 April, 1866. 2nd Lieut. 3rd Inf., 23 Feb., 1866. 1st Lieut., 1 Aug., 1866. Died 13 May, 1868.

BROWN, THEOPHILUS B.* [Born in Conn. Appointed from N. Y.]
Bvt. 2nd Lieut. 4th Art., 1 July, 1826. 2nd Lieut. 3rd Art., 1 July, 1826. Died 14 Sept., 1834.

BROWN, THOMPSON S.* [Born in N. Y. Appointed from N. Y.]
Bvt. 2nd Lieut Eng., 1 July, 1825. 2nd Lieut., 1 July, 1825. 1st Lieut., 15 May, 1835. Resigned 31 Oct., 1836.

BROWN, WALTER S.* [Born in Me. Appointed from Me.]
2nd Lieut. 3rd Inf., 15 Feb., 1899.

BROWN, WM. A.* [Born in Conn. Appointed from Conn.]
Changed name to Wm. Austine,—which see.

BROWN, WM. C.* [Born in Minn. Appointed from Minn.]
Addl. 2nd Lieut. 2nd Cav., 15 June, 1877. 2nd Lieut. 1st Cav.,3 July, 1877. 1st Lieut., 19 Dec., 1884. Capt., 6 Nov., 1896. Graduate of the Infantry and Cavalry School, 1883. Maj. 45th U. S. Vols., 17 Aug., 1899. Trans. to 42nd U. S. Vols., 14 Sept., 1899. Bvt. 1st Lieut., 27 Feb., 1890, for gallant services in actions against Indians at Big Creek, Idaho, 19 Aug., 1879, and in the reconnaissances of 17 Aug., and 25 Sept., 1879.

BROWN, WM. H. [Born in Md. Appointed from Army.]
Priv., Corpl. and Sergt. Troop C, 2nd Cav., 1 March, 1858, to 12 June, 1861 2nd Lieut. 11th Inf., 14 May, 1861. 1st Lieut., 9 Sept., 1861. Resigned 23 Oct., 1861. 2nd Lieut. 5th Cav., 23 Oct., 1861. R. Q M., 13 Nov., 1861, to 1 Dec , 1862. 1st Lieut., 17 July, 1862. Capt. A. Q. M. Vols., 20 Oct., 1862. Mustered out of Vols., 25 Aug., 1865. Capt 5th Cav., 1 April, 1865. Bvt Capt., 18 June, 1864, for gallant and meritorious service during the Piedmont and Lynchburg expeditions. Bvt. Maj., 1 April, 1865. for gallant and meritorious service at the Battle of Five Forks, Va. Bvt. Maj. Vols., 13 March, 1865, for faithful and meritorious service during the war. Committed suicide 4 June, 1875.

BROWN, WM. H. [Born in Penn. Appointed from Penn.]
Capt. 14th Inf., 14 May, 1861. Bvt. Maj., 17 Sept., 1863, for gallant and meritorious service at the Battle of Antietam, Md. Bvt. Lieut. Col., 13 March, 1865, for gallant and meritorious service during the war. Trans. to 23rd Inf., 21 Sept., 1866. Trans. to 21st Inf., 19 April, 1869. Maj. 18th Inf., 16 Aug., 1871. Lieut. Col. 1st Inf., 15 Dec., 1880. Died 10 March, 1883.

BROWN, WM. R. [Born in Penn. Appointed from Penn.]
Capt. 15th Inf., 14 May, 1861. Resigned 21 Aug., 1865.

BROWN, WM. S.* [Born in N. Y. Appointed from N. Y.]
Bvt. 2nd Lieut. 3rd Art., 1 July, 1835. Resigned 31 Dec., 1835.

BROWN, WM. S. [Born in N. Y. Appointed from Mich.]
Capt. Asst. C. S., 14 Feb., 1848. Disbanded 29 July, 1848.

BROWNE, EDWARD H.* [Born in Mich. Appointed from Mich.]
2nd Lieut. 4th Inf., 13 June, 1879. 1st Lieut., 17 July, 1890. Capt., 10 April, 1897.

BROWNE, JESSE B [Born in N. C. Appointed from Ill ]
Capt. Mounted Rangers, 16 June, 1832. Capt. 1st Drag., 15 Aug., 1833. Resigned 30 June, 1837.

BROWNE, WM. C. [Born in Md. Appointed from Penn.]
2nd Lieut. 8th Inf., 7 July, 1838. 1st Lieut., 1 Oct., 1840. Resigned 31 Dec., 1845.

BROWNELL, FRANCIS E. [Born in N. Y. Appointed from N. Y.]
Priv. Co. A, 11th N. Y. Vols., 20 April, 1861. Discharged 4 July, 1861. 2nd Lieut. 11th Inf., 14 May, 1861. 1st Lieut., 24 Oct., 1861. Retired 4 Nov., 1863. Died 15 March, 1894.

BROWNELL, THOMAS S. [Born in Conn. Appointed from Conn.]
2nd Lieut. 5th Inf., 30 Dec., 1839. Died 5 May, 1841.

BROWNING, GEORGE L. [Born in N. Y. Appointed from Army.]
Priv. Co. F, 7th N. Y. State Militia, 26 April, 1861. Discharged 3 June, 1861. Priv. Co. F, 1st Batt. 14th Inf., 29 Sept., 1862. Sergt., 29 Dec., 1862. 2nd Lieut. 14th Inf., 27 Feb., 1863. 1st Lieut., 15 Aug., 1864. Trans. to 23rd Inf., 21 Sept., 1866. Capt., 7 Feb., 1867. Unass'd 23 July, 1869. Ass'd to 7th Inf., 1 Jan., 1871. Died 1 May, 1882.

BROWNING, WM. [Born in Mass. Appointed from Mass.]
Ensign 9th Inf., 12 March, 1812. 2nd Lieut., 13 March, 1813. 1st Lieut., 15 Oct., 1813. Capt., 31 Oct., 1814. Retained 17 May, 1815, as 1st Lieut. 2nd Inf. Capt., 1 Nov., 1817. Retained 17 May, 1815, (in re-organization under Act of 3 March, 1815), as 1st Lieut. 2nd Inf., with Bvt. of Capt. from 31 Oct., 1814. Resigned 23 Sept., 1827.

BROWNLOW, ALEXR. [Born in Va. Appointed from Va.]
Ensign 2nd Inf., 10 June, 1807. 2nd Lieut., 30 Sept., 1808. 1st Lieut., 1 Jan., 1810. Reg. Adj., Oct., to 10 Sept, 1813. Capt., 7 Sept, 1813. Disbanded 15 June, 1815. Reinstated 2 Dec., 1815, in 8th Inf. Died 5 Nov., 1817.

BROWNLOW, JAMES P. [Born in Tenn Appointed from Tenn.]
Capt. 1st Tenn. Cav., 1 April, 1862. Lieut. Col., 1 Aug., 1862. Col., 15 June, 1864. Bvt. Brig. Gen. Vols, 13 March, 1865, for gallant and meritorious service during the war. Mustered out 11 April, 1865. Capt. 8th Cav., 28 July, 1866. Resigned 26 March, 1868. Died 26 April, 1879.

BROWNSON, HENRY F. [Born in Mass. Appointed from N. Y.]
1st Lieut. 15th N. Y. Eng., 17 June, 1861. Resigned 2 Jan., 1862. 2nd Lieut., 3rd Art., 1 Dec., 1861. 1st Lieut., 28 Feb., 1862. Capt. A. A. G. Vols., 3 April, 1863. Resigned from Vols., 2 July, 1865. Capt. 43rd Inf., 28 July, 1866. Unass'd 8 April, 1869. Ass'd to 25th Inf., 15 Dec., 1870. Discharged 29 Dec., 1870. Bvt. Capt., 1 July, 1862, for gallant and meritorious service at the Battle of Malvern Hill, Va. Chancellorsville, Va.

BRUA, JACOB. [Born in Penn. Appointed from Penn.]
2nd Lieut. 11th Inf., 25 May, 1847. Died 3 July, 1847.

BRUA, JOHN P. [Born in Penn. Appointed from Penn.]
Addl. P. M. Vols., 1 June, 1861. Vacated commission, 23 Feb., 1864. Maj. P. M. U. S. A., 23 Feb., 1864. Bvt. Lieut. Col., 13 March, 1865, for faithful and meritorious service during the war. Retired 8 Feb, 1875. Died 26 May, 1888.

BRUCE, GEORGE. [Born in Scotland. Appointed from Army.]
Priv., Corpl. and Sergt. Co. H, 1st Inf., 17 April, 1838, to 17 April, 1841. Priv., Corpl. and Sergt. Co. H, 2nd Inf., 8 July, 1841, to 8 July, 1848. Bvt. 2nd Lieut. 2nd Inf, 28 June, 1848. 2nd Lieut., 28 June, 1848. Resigned 19 Aug., 1848.

BRUCE, WM. E.* [Born in Pa. Appointed from Ohio.]
2nd Lieut. 22nd Inf., 12 June, 1887. Died 27 Feb., 1892.

BRUEN, LUTHER P. [Born in Ohio. Appointed from Ohio.]
Maj. 12th Inf., 14 May, 1861. Died 21 June, 1864, of wounds received in Battle of Laurel Hill, Va., 13 May, 1864.

BRUFF, LAWRENCE L.* [Born in Md. Appointed from Md.]
2nd Lieut. 3rd Art., 15 June, 1876. Trans. to Ord., 30 Oct., 1879. 1st Lieut., 30 Oct., 1879. Capt. (14 years' service) 15 June, 1890.

BRUMBACH, VIRGIL J.* [Born in Ind. Appointed from Idaho.]
2nd Lieut. 2nd Inf., 11 June, 1881. 1st Lieut., 25 Sept., 1890. Resigned 18 May, 1893.

BRUMBY, ARNOLDUS V.* [Born in S. C. Appointed from N. C.]
Bvt. 2nd Lieut. 1st Art., 1 July, 1835. 2nd Lieut., 31 Dec., 1835. Resigned 30 June, 1836.

BRUNCK, FRANK C. [Born in N. Y. Appointed from N. Y.]
1st Lieut. 100th N. Y. Vols., 7 Jan, 1862. Capt., 15 Nov., 1862. Mustered out 9 Jan., 1865. 2nd Lieut 15th Inf., 28 July, 1866. 1st Lieut., 27 Aug., 1867. Died 7 Nov., 1867.

BRUNOT, HILLARY.* [Born in Penn. Appointed from Penn.]
3rd Lieut. 1st Inf., 21 July, 1814. 2nd Lieut., 22 July, 1814. Disbanded 15 June, 1815. Reinstated 2 Dec, 1815, in 3rd Inf. 1st Lieut., 31 Dec., 1818. Disbanded 1 June, 1821. Died 26 March, 1872.

BRUNTON, WM. B. [Born in Penn. Appointed from Iowa.]
2nd Lieut. 2nd Iowa Cav., 1 Dec., 1861 1st Lieut., 4 June, 1862. Capt., 5 April, 1864. Mustered out 19 Sept., 1865. 2nd Lieut. 9th Cav., 18 June, 1867. 1st Lieut., 13 Sept., 1867. Resigned 24 May, 1873. Bvt. 1st Lieut, 18 June, 1867, for gallant conduct at the Battle of Corinth, Miss., 2 Oct., 1862. Bvt. Capt., 18 June, 1867, for gallant conduct at the Battle of Nashville, Tenn., 14 Dec, 1864.

BRUSH, ALFRED.* [Born in Mich. Appointed from Mich.]
Bvt. 2nd Lieut. 4th Art., 1 July, 1832. 2nd Lieut., 14 Sept., 1834. Resigned 28 July, 1836. Died 12 April, 1870.

BRUSH, DANIEL H.* [Born in Ill. Appointed from Ill.]
Priv. Co. F, 145th Ill. Vols., 22 May, to 23 Sept., 1864. Cadet Mil Acad., 1 Sept., 1867. 2nd Lieut. 17th Inf., 12 June, 1871. 1st Lieut., 4 Aug., 1876. Capt, 2 May, 1892.

BRUYERE, PETER H. [Born in N. J. Appointed from N. Y.]
2nd Lieut. Inf., 23 Feb., 1847; 10th Inf., 9 April, 1847. 1st Lieut., 6 March, 1848. Disbanded 22 Aug., 1848.

BRYAN, EDWARD B.* [Born in S. C. Appointed at Large.]
Bvt. 2nd Lieut 1st Art., 1 July, 1848. Resigned 5 Oct., 1848. Died 28 April, 1861.

BRYAN, FRANCIS T.* [Born in N. C. Appointed from N. C.]
Bvt. 2nd Lieut. Top. Eng., 1 July, 1846. 2nd Lieut., 24 April, 1851. 1st Lieut., 1 July, 1855. Capt., 1 July, 1860. Resigned 10 June, 1861. Bvt. 1st Lieut., 23 Feb., 1847, for gallant and meritorious conduct at Buena Vista.

BRYAN, GOODE.* [Born in Ga. Appointed from Ga.]
Bvt. 2nd Lieut 5th Inf., 1 July, 1834. Resigned 30 April, 1835. Maj. 1st Ala. Vols., 27 June, 1846. Mustered out 28 May, 1847.

BRYAN, GUY, Jr. [Born in Penn. Appointed from N. J.]
1st Sergt. Co. I, 5th N. J. Vols., 4 Aug., 1861. 2nd Lieut., 20 March, 1863. Resigned 13 May, 1863. 1st Lieut. 18th Pa. Cav., 12 June, 1863. Capt., 18 May, 1865. 3rd Pa. Prov Cav., 24 June, 1865. Mustered out 31 Oct., 1865. 2nd Lieut. 25th Inf., 22 Jan., 1867. Died 18 July, 1868.

BRYAN, ROGER B.* [Born in Tenn. Appointed from Mass.]
2nd Lieut. 2nd Cav., 13 June, 1883. 1st Lieut., 18 Sept., 1890. Capt. 5th Cav., 2

March, 1899. Reg'l Q. M., 3 Aug., 1899. Graduate of the Infantry and Cavalry School, 1889.

BRYAN, TIMOTHY M.* [Born in Penn. Appointed from Penn.]
Bvt. 2nd Lieut. 9th Inf., 1 July, 1855. 2nd Lieut. 10th Inf., 25 Aug., 1855. Resigned 1 Jan., 1857. Lieut. Col. 12th Mass. Vols., 26 June, 1861. Resigned 7 Oct., 1862. Col. 18th Pa. Cav., 24 Dec., 1862. Discharged 29 Dec., 1864. Died 8 April, 1881.

BRYANT, CULLEN.* [Born in Ill. Appointed from Ill.]
2nd Lieut. Ord., 13 June, 1864. 1st Lieut., 5 July, 1867. Capt., 23 June, 1874. Maj., 31 Jan., 1891. Retired, over 30 years' service, 2 Sept., 1894.

BRYANT, MONTGOMERY. [Born in Kan. Appointed from Mo.]
2nd Lieut. 6th Inf., 21 Feb., 1857. 1st Lieut., 3 May, 1861. 1st Lieut. 16th Inf., 14 May, 1861, declined. Capt. 6th Inf., 10 June, 1861. Bvt. Maj., 13 Dec., 1862, for gallant and meritorious service in the Battle of Fredericksburg, Va. Maj. 14th Inf., 7 Oct., 1874. Lieut. Col. 8th Inf., 22 June, 1882. Col. 13th Inf., 16 Dec., 1888. Retired, over 30 years' service, 1 March, 1894.

BRYANT, THOS. S. [Born in Penn. Appointed from Penn.]
Asst. Surg., 5 Oct., 1825. Resigned 31 Dec., 1835. 1st Lieut. 2nd Drag., 11 June, 1836. Capt., 26 Sept., 1837. Resigned 2 Dec., 1839. Addl. P. M., 28 Dec., 1846. Disbanded 1 July, 1849.

BRYANT, WM.* [Born in Va. Appointed from Va.]
Bvt. 2nd Lieut. 1st Art., 1 July, 1826. 2nd Lieut. 3rd Art., 1 July, 1826. Resigned 31 Aug., 1835. Died 15 Aug., 1846.

BUBB, JOHN W. [Born in Penn. Appointed from Army.]
Priv. Co. E, 1st Batt. 12th Inf., 13 Sept., 1861. Sergt., 1 Jan., 1862. 1st Sergt., 1 Dec., 1862. Discharged 10 Feb., 1864. 1st Sergt. Co. E, 1st Batt. 12th Inf., 10 Feb., 1864. 2nd Lieut. and 1st Lieut. 12th Inf., 5 Feb., 1866. Trans. to 30th Inf., 21 Sept., 1866. Trans. to 4th Inf., 23 March, 1869. Capt., 16 March, 1879. Maj., 26 April, 1898. Lieut. Col. 12th Inf., 20 Oct., 1899.

BUCHAN, FRED E. [Born in Kan. Appointed from Kan.]
Capt. Co. B, 20th Kan. Vols., 9 May, 1898. Mustered out 30 July, 1899. 2nd Lieut. 6th Cav., 1 June, 1899.

BUCHANAN, JAMES A. [Born in Md. Appointed from Md.]
2nd Lieut. 14th Inf., 7 March, 1867. 1st Lieut., 10 Dec., 1873. Capt., 10 June, 1890. Trans. to 11th Inf., 21 July, 1893. Maj. 15th Inf., 4 May, 1899. Lieut. Col. Porto Rico Batt. of Vols., — Feb., 1900.

BUCHANAN, ROBERT C.* [Born in Md. Appointed from D. C.]
Bvt. 2nd Lieut. 4th Inf., 1 July, 1830. 2nd Lieut., 1 July, 1830. Reg. Adj., 4 Feb., 1835, to 30 Nov., 1838. 1st Lieut., 16 March, 1836. Capt., 1 Nov., 1838. Maj., 3 Feb., 1855. Lieut. Col., 9 Sept., 1861. Brig. Gen. Vols., 29 Nov., 1862. Appointment expired 4 March, 1863. Col. 1st Inf., 8 Feb., 1864. Retired 31 Dec., 1870. Died 29 Nov., 1878. Bvt. Maj., 9 May, 1846, for gallant and distinguished service in the Battles of Palo Alto and Resaca de la Palma. Bvt. Lieut. Col., 8 Sept., 1847, for gallant and meritorious conduct in the Battle of Molino del Rey, Mexico. Bvt. Col., 27 June, 1862, for gallant and meritorious service at the Battle of Gaines' Mill, Va. Bvt. Brig. Gen., 13 March, 1865, for gallant and meritorious service at the Battle of Malvern Hill, Va. Bvt. Maj. Gen., 13 March, 1865, for gallant and distinguished service at the Battles of Manassas and Fredericksburg, Va.

BUCHANAN, WM. F. [Born in Penn. Appointed from Penn.]
Asst. Surg., 30 March, 1864. Capt. Asst. Surg., 30 March, 1869. Resigned 1 April, 1878. Bvt. Capt., 13 March, 1865, for faithful and meritorious service.

BUCHANAN, WM. P.* [Born in Va. Appointed from Va.]
3rd Lieut. Ord., 1 July, 1820. Trans. to 2nd Art., 1 June, 1821. Resigned 31 March, 1822. 2nd Lieut. 6th Inf., 21 June, 1822. Drowned 20 Sept., 1822.

BUCK, BEAUMONT B.* [Born in Miss. Appointed from Tex.]
2nd Lieut. 16th Inf., 14 June, 1885. 1st Lieut. 19th Inf., 4 May, 1892. Trans. to 16th Inf., 12 Aug., 1892. Capt., 2 March, 1899. Maj. 2nd Tex. Vols., 13 May, 1898. Mustered out 9 Nov., 1898.

BUCK, DANIEL A. A.* [Born in Vt. Appointed from Vt.]
2nd Lieut. Eng., 23 Feb., 1808. Resigned 31 Aug., 1811. 2nd Lieut. 3rd Art., 17 Oct., 1812. Capt. 31st Inf., 30 April, 1813. Disbanded 15 June, 1815. Died 24 Dec., 1841.

BUCK, MARCUS C. [Born in Va. Appointed from Va.]
Maj. and Surg. 20th Inf., 2 July, 1813. Trans. to 4th Inf., 17 May, 1815. Resigned 4 Sept., 1815. Mil. Storekeeper, 25 April, 1831. Died 7 May, 1845.

BUCK, WM. L.* [Born in Ala. Appointed from Ala.]
2nd Lieut. 13th Inf., 14 June, 1878. 1st Lieut., 4 Feb., 1888. Capt., 23 March, 1898.

BUCKEY, MERVYN C.* [Born in Md. Appointed from D. C.]
Addl. 2nd Lieut. 5th Art., 11 June, 1897. 2nd Lieut. 6th Art., 8 March, 1898. Trans. to 5th Art., 22 April, 1898. 1st Lieut. 3rd Art., 18 March, 1899.

BUCKINGHAM, CATHARINUS P.* [Born in Ohio. Appointed from Ohio.]
Bvt. 2nd Lieut. 3rd Art., 1 July, 1829. 2nd Lieut., 1 July, 1829. Resigned 30 Sept., 1831. Brig. Gen. Vols., 16 July, 1862. Resigned 11 Feb., 1863. Died 30 Aug., 1888.

BUCKLEY, JOSEPH. [Born in N. Y. Appointed from N. Y.]
3rd Lieut. 38th Inf., 1 May, 1814. Trans. to Corps Art., 12 May, 1814. 2nd Lieut., 22 July, 1814. Disbanded 15 June, 1815. 3rd Lieut. Ord., 13 Aug., 1819. Retained as 2nd Lieut. 6th Inf., 1 June, 1821. Resigned 1 July, 1822.

BUCKLIN, BENJN. F. [Born in R. I. Appointed from R. I.]
Capt. C. S. Vols., 26 Nov., 1862. Bvt. Maj. Vols., 2 Aug., 1865, for faithful service in the Sub. Dept. Lieut. Col. Vols., 2 Aug., 1865, for faithful, gallant and meritorious service. Mustered out 3 Aug., 1865. 2nd Lieut. 34th Inf., 22 Jan., 1867. Dismissed 18 Sept., 1867.

BUCKLIN, CHAS. M. [Born in Vt. Appointed from Vt.]
Priv. 2nd Vt. Batty., 5 Aug., 1864. Discharged 9 March, 1865. Sergt. Maj. 81st U. S. Col. Inf., 14 March, 1865. 2nd Lieut., 12 Aug., 1865. Mustered out 22 March, 1867. 1st Lieut. 39th Inf., 12 June, 1867. Died 5 Oct., 1867.

1874. Capt., 22 June, 1889. Retired for disability, with the rank of Maj., 16 March, 1899. Medal of Honor for gallantry at the Battle of Newmarket, Va., 15 May, 1864, while Sergt. Co. B, 1st W. Va. Vols.; under a heavy fire of musketry from the enemy, he voluntarily assisted a wounded comrade from the field of battle, thereby saving him from capture by the enemy.

BURNS, THOS. [Born in Ireland. Appointed from Army.]
Priv., Corpl. and Sergt. Gen. Mtd. Ser., 2 Jan., 1858, to 29 June, 1861. Priv., Corpl. and 1st Sergt. Troop I, 1st Cav., 4 July, 1862, to 4 April, 1863. 2nd Lieut. 1st Cav., 1 April, 1863. Dropped 13 April, 1864.

BURNS, WM. [Born in N. Y. Appointed from N. Y.]
Corpl. and Sergt. Co. K, 34th N. Y. Vols., 15 June, 1861. 2nd Lieut., 23 Dec., 1862. 2nd Lieut. Vet. Res. Corps, 28 May, 1863. 1st Lieut., 7 Sept., 1864. Bvt. Capt. Vols., 13 March, 1865, for gallant and meritorious service at the Battle of White Oak Swamp, Va.; and Bvt. Maj. Vols., 13 March, 1865, for gallant and meritorious service during the war. Mustered out 20 Oct., 1866. 1st Lieut. 44th Inf., 28 July, 1866. Trans. to 17th Inf., 27 May, 1869. Retired 15 Dec., 1870. Died 7 Dec., 1874. Bvt. Capt., 2 March, 1867, for gallant and meritorious service at the Battle of White Oak Swamp, Va.

BURNS, WM. W.* [Born in Ohio. Appointed from Ohio.]
Bvt. 2nd Lieut. 3rd Inf., 1 July, 1847. 2nd Lieut. 5th Inf., 8 Sept., 1847. 1st Lieut., 12 Aug., 1850. Capt. C. S., 3 Nov., 1858. Vacated commission of 1st Lieut. 5th Inf., 19 Jan., 1859. Maj. C. S., 3 Aug., 1861. Brig. Gen. Vols., 28 Sept., 1861. Bvt. Lieut. Col., 29 June, 1862, for gallant and meritorious service in the Battle of Savage Station, Va. Bvt. Col., 30 June, 1862, for gallant and meritorious service in the Battle of Glendale, Va. Resigned commission of Brig. Gen. Vols., 20 March, 1863. Bvt. Brig. Gen., 13 March, 1865, for gallant and meritorious service during the war. Lieut. Col. A. C. G. S., 23 June, 1874. Col. A. C. G. S., 9 Nov., 1884. Retired 3 Sept., 1889. Died 19 April, 1892.

BURNSIDE, AMBROSE E.* [Born in Ind. Appointed from Ind.]
Bvt. 2nd Lieut. 2nd Art., 1 July, 1847. 2nd Lieut. 3rd Art., 8 Sept., 1847. 1st Lieut., 12 Dec., 1851. Resigned 2 Oct., 1853. Col. 1st R. I. Vols., 2 May, to 2 Aug., 1861. Brig. Gen. Vols., 6 Aug., 1861. Maj. Gen. Vols., 18 March, 1862. Resolution of 28 Jan., 1864, that the thanks of Congress be and they are presented to Maj. Gen. Ambrose E. Burnside, and through him to the officers and men who fought under his command, for their gallantry, good conduct and soldier-like endurance. Resigned 15 April, 1865. Died 13 Sept., 1881.

BURNSIDE, WM. A.* [Born in Ohio. Appointed from Ohio.]
Addl. 2nd Lieut. 17th Inf., 12 June, 1896. 2nd Lieut. 14th Inf., 1 Nov., 1896. 1st Lieut. of Inf., 15 Dec., 1898. Ass'd to 17th Inf., 1 Jan., 1899. Trans. to 14th Inf., 6 April, 1899. Capt. and A. Q. M. Vols., 18 Sept., 1899.

BURR, EDWARD.* [Born in Mo. Appointed from Mo.]
2nd Lieut. Eng., 13 June, 1882. 1st Lieut., 16 April, 1883. Capt., 18 Sept., 1894. Lieut. Col. 2nd Vol. Eng., 7 June, 1898. Mustered out Vols., 16 May, 1899.

BURR, FRANK S. [Born in Neb. Appointed from Neb.]
Priv. Co. M, 2nd Neb. Vols., 12 May, 1898, to 29 July, 1898. 2nd Lieut. 3rd Inf., 9 July, 1898. 1st Lieut. 21st Inf., 25 May, 1899. Trans. to 11th Inf., 23 Oct., 1899.

BURR, GEORGE W.* [Born in Ill. Appointed from Mo.]
2nd Lieut. 1st Art., 11 June, 1888. 1st Lieut. of Ord., 10 Jan., 1893. Capt., 7 April, 1899.

BURROUGHS, GEORGE.* [Born in N. J. Appointed from Mass.]
2nd Lieut. Eng., 17 June, 1862. 1st Lieut., 3 March, 1863. Capt., 5 June, 1864. Died 22 Jan., 1870. Bvt. Capt., 20 Sept., 1863, for gallant and meritorious service at the Battle of Chickamauga, Ga. Bvt. Maj., 13 March, 1865, for gallant and meritorious service during the War.

BURROWES, THOMAS B. [Born in Penn. Appointed from Penn.]
1st Lieut. 18th Inf., 14 May, 1861. Dismissed 17 June, 1863. Reinstated 27 Feb., 1864. Capt., 13 Nov., 1863. Bvt. Maj., 1 Sept., 1864, for gallant and meritorious service in the Battle of Jonesboro', Ga. Trans. to 27th Inf., 21 Sept., 1866. Trans. to 9th Inf., 14 June, 1869. Retired 20 March, 1879 Died 12 Oct., 1885.

BURROWS, CHAS. W.* [Born in Me. Appointed from Me.]
2nd Lieut. 3rd Art., 15 June, 1870. Resigned 10 Oct., 1872.

BURT, ANDREW S. [Born in Ohio. Appointed from Ohio.]
Sergt. Co. A, 1st Ohio Vols., 20 April, to 15 July, 1861. 1st Lieut. 18th Inf., 14 May, 1861. Capt. A. A. de C., 3 April, 1862. Bvt. Capt., 19 June, 1862, for gallant and meritorious service in the Battle of Mill Spring, Ky. Capt. 18th Inf., 30 May, 1863. Vacated commission of Capt. A. A. de C., 30 May, 1863. Bvt. Maj., 1 Sept., 1864, for gallant and meritorious service during the Atlanta campaign, and in the Battle of Jonesboro', Ga. Trans. to 27th Inf., 21 Sept, 1866. Trans. to 9th Inf., 14 June, 1869. Maj 8th Inf., 26 Jan., 1883. Lieut. Col. 7th Inf., 1 Jan., 1888. Col. 25th Inf., 4 July, 1892. Brig. Gen. of Vols., 4 May, 1898. Discharged from Vols., 31 Dec., 1898.

BURT, REYNOLDS J.* [Born in Neb. Appointed from Ohio.]
Addl. 2nd Lieut. 25th Inf., 12 June, 1896. 2nd Lieut. 10th Inf., 4 Nov., 1896. Trans. to 25th Inf., 4 Feb., 1897. 1st Lieut. of Inf., 20 Dec., 1898. Ass'd to 25th Inf., 1 Jan., 1899. Reg'l Com., 20 March, 1899.

BURTON, GEORGE H.* [Born in Del. Appointed from Del.]
2nd Lieut. and 1st Lieut. 12th Inf., 23 June, 1865. Trans. to 21st Inf., 21 Sept., 1866. Reg. Adj., 9 Dec., 1866, to 2 June, 1868, and from 5 April, 1869, to 16 Aug., 1871. Capt., 16 Aug., 1871. Maj. and I. G., 27 March, 1885. Lieut. Col. and I. G., 31 Aug., 1888. Col. and I. G., 2 Jan., 1895. Bvt. Maj., 27 Feb., 1890, for gallant services in actions against Indians in the Lava Beds, Cal., 17 Jan., 1873, and at the Clearwater, Idaho, 11 and 12 July, 1877.

BURTON, HENRY G. [Born in Vt. Appointed from Vt.]
1st Lieut. Asst. Surg., 5 Aug., 1876. Capt. and Asst. Surg., 5 Aug., 1881. Retired for disability 5 Feb., 1892.

BURTON, HENRY S.* [Born in N. Y. Appointed from Vt.]
2nd Lieut. 3rd Art., 1 July, 1839. 1st Lieut., 11 Nov., 1839. Capt., 22 Sept., 1847. Maj., 14 May, 1861. Lieut. Col. 4th Art., 25 July, 1863. Col. 5th Art., 11 Aug., 1863. Died 4 April, 1869. Bvt. Brig. Gen., 13 March, 1865, for gallant and meritorious service at the capture of Petersburg, Va.

BURTON, OLIVER G.* [Born in Vt. Appointed from Vt.]
1st Lieut. 4th Inf., 18 June, 1808. Capt., 25 Aug., 1811. Maj. 33rd Inf., 15 June, 1814. Disbanded 15 June, 1815. M. S K., at West Point, 1816 to 1820. Died 22 Feb., 1821.

BURTON, THOS. W. [Born in N. Y. Appointed from Army.]
Priv. and Corpl. Cos. G, C, A and E, and Sergt. Maj. 2nd Drag., 26 March, 1852, to 2 Nov., 1861. 2nd Lieut. 2nd Cav., 24 Oct., 1861. 1st Lieut., 17 July, 1862. Dismissed 25 Nov., 1862

BURTT, WILSON B.* [Born in Ill. Appointed from Ill.]
2nd Lieut. 8th Inf., 15 Feb., 1899.

BURTWELL, JOHN R. B. [Born in Ala. Appointed from Ala.]
Bvt. 2nd Lieut. 1st Cav., 1 July, 1860. 2nd Lieut., 30 Oct., 1860. Resigned 21 March, 1861.

BURTWELL, WM. T.* [Born in Va. Appointed from Va.]
Bvt. 2nd Lieut. 6th Inf., 1 July, 1844. 2nd Lieut. 5th Inf., 18 May, 1846. Killed 8 Sept., 1847, at Battle of Molino del Rey, Mexico.

BUSH, ASAHEL K. [Born in N. Y. Appointed from Ind.]
1st Lieut. 9th Ind. Vols., 19 April, 1861. Mustered out 29 July, 1861. Capt. 4th Ind. Batty Art., 30 Sept., 1861, to 25 Sept., 1863. Capt. Vet. Res. Corps, 5 Sept., 1863. Bvt. Maj. and Lieut. Col. Vols., 13 March, 1865, for faithful and meritorious service during the war. Mustered out 29 Nov., 1865. 2nd Lieut. 2nd Art., 22 Ja 1867. Resigned 28 Feb., 1869.

BUSH, EDWARD G.* [Born in Ill. Appointed from Ill.]
Bvt. 2nd Lieut. 6th Inf., 1 July, 1859. 2nd Lieut. 10th Inf., 7 Aug., 1859. 1st Lieut. 12th Inf., 14 May, 1861, declined. 1st Lieut. 10th Inf., 14 May, 1861. Reg. Adj., 1 Aug., 1861, to 13 March, 1863. Capt., 13 March, 1863. Bvt. Maj., 2 July, 1863, for gallant and meritorious service in the Battle of Gettysburg, Penn. Maj. 6th Inf., 11 April, 1882. Lieut. Col. 11th Inf., 13 Oct., 1886. Col. 25th Inf., —, 1892. Died, 1892.

BUSH, JAMES C.* [Born in Conn. Appointed from Conn.]
2nd Lieut. 5th Art., 16 June, 1875. 1st Lieut., 1 Nov., 1882. Capt. 7th Art., 8 March, 1898. Graduate of the Artillery School, 1880.

BUSH, JOHN G. [Born in Va. Appointed from Army.]
2nd Lieut. 13th Inf., 3 March, 1848. Disbanded 15 July, 1848.

BUSH, JOSEPH. [Born in Mass. Appointed from Vt.]
Capt. 1st Vt. Vols., 9 May, 1861. Mustered out 15 Aug., 1861. Capt. 13th Inf., 5 Aug., 1861. Bvt. Maj., 4 July, 1863, for gallant and meritorious service in the Siege of Vicksburg, Miss. Trans. to 22nd Inf., 21 Sept., 1866. Maj. 25th Inf., 4 March, 1879. Retired for disability 2 April, 1883. Died 30 Nov., 1884.

BUSH, ROSS L.* [Born in Ill. Appointed from Ill.]
2nd Lieut. 15th Inf., 12 June, 1891. 1st Lieut. 25th Inf., 15 Nov., 1897.

BUSHFIELD, LLEWELLYN N.* [Born in Tenn. Appointed from Ky.]
2nd Lieut. 17th Inf., 15 Feb., 1899.

BUSHNELL, GEORGE E. [Born in Mass. Appointed from Wis.]
Asst. Surg., 18 Feb., 1881. Capt. Asst. Surg., 18 Feb., 1886. Maj. Surg., 10 Dec., 1898. Maj. Chief Surg. Vols., 4 June, 1898. Discharged 23 Jan., 1899.

BUSSEY, THOS. H. [Born in Md. Appointed from Army.]
Priv. Co. C, 14th Inf., 24 June, 1847, to 29 Feb., 1848. 2nd Lieut. 4th Inf., 30 Dec., 1847. Cashiered 11 April, 1848.

BUTLER, BENJ. I.* [Born in Mass. Appointed from Mass.]
2nd Lieut. 9th Cav., 15 June, 1877. Resigned 1 June, 1878. Died 1 Sept., 1881.

BUTLER, CHRISTOPHER R. P. [Born in S. C. Appointed from S. C.]
2nd Lieut. Inf., 5 March, 1847; 12th Inf., 9 April, 1847. 1st Lieut., 23 May, 1848. 2nd Lieut. 2nd Art., 27 June, 1848. 1st Lieut., 28 Sept., 1852. Died 1 Nov., 1853.

BUTLER, DAVID. [Born in N. Y. Appointed from N. Y.]
Mil. Storekeeper Ord. Dept., 1 Sept., 1837. Dismissed 29 March, 1850.

BUTLER, EDMOND. [Born in Ireland. Appointed from N. Y.]
2nd Lieut. 5th Inf., 7 Oct., 1861. 1st Lieut., 20 Feb., 1862. Capt., 14 May, 1864. Maj. 2nd Inf., 8 Oct., 1885. Lieut. Col. of Inf. (17th), 9 March, 1891. Retired 19 March, 1891. Died 21 Aug., 1895.

BUTLER, EDWARD G. W.* [Born in Tenn. Appointed from Tenn.]
2nd Lieut. Corps Art., 1 July, 1820. Trans. to 4th Art., 1 June, 1821. 1st Lieut., 6 Nov., 1823. Resigned 28 May, 1831. Col. 3rd Drag., 9 April, 1847. Disbanded 31 July, 1848 Died 6 Sept., 1888.

BUTLER, GEORGE B. [Born in N. Y. Appointed from N. Y.]
2nd Lieut. 3rd Inf., 5 Aug., 1861. 1st Lieut., 7 June, 1862. Resigned 24 Nov., 1863.

BUTLER, GEORGE H. [Born in Mo. Appointed from Cal.]
2nd Lieut. 10th Inf., 16 May, 1861. R. Q. M., 6 Nov., 1862, to 12 June, 1863. 1st Lieut., 15 July, 1861. Resigned 12 June, 1863. Died 11 May, 1886.

BUTLER, JAMES. [Born in England. Appointed from Army.]
Priv. and Corpl. Co. B, 4th Inf., 30 Nov., 1848, to 19 Nov., 1851. Priv, Sergt. and 1st Sergt. Co. C, 2nd Inf., 11 March, 1854, to 2 Dec., 1862. 2nd Lieut. 2nd Inf., 26 Nov., 1862. 1st Lieut., 16 Nov., 1863. Dismissed 21 April, 1864. Reinstated 22 July, 1864 Unass'd 17 April, 1869. Discharged 20 Nov., 1870. Bvt. 1st Lieut., 3 May, 1863, for gallant and meritorious service at the Battle of Chancellorsville, Va. Bvt. Capt., 2 July, 1863, for gallant and meritorious service at the Battle of Gettysburg, Penn.

BUTLER, JAMES R. [Born in Penn. Appointed from Penn.]
Capt. Pittsburg Blues, Pa. Vols., 14 Aug., 1812, to Oct., 1814. Mil. Storekeeper Ord., 28 March, 1826. Died 29 April, 1842.

BUTLER, JOHN. [Born in Penn. Appointed from Penn.]
Capt. Inf., 16 Feb., 1847; Capt. 3rd Drag., 9 April, 1847. Died 23 Dec, 1847.

BUTLER, JOHN B. [Born in N. Y. Appointed from Penn.]
Maj. and P. M., 25 June, 1846. Mil. Storekeeper Ord., 30 June, 1847. Retired 1 Oct., 1863. Died 7 Dec., 1870.

BUTLER, JOHN B. [Born in Va. Appointed from Va.]
Asst. Surg. 12th Inf., 3 Aug., 1847. Disbanded 25 July, 1848.

BUTLER, JOHN G.* [Born in Penn. Appointed from Penn.]
2nd Lieut. 4th Art., 11 June, 1863. Bvt. 1st Lieut., 26 Sept., 1863, for gallant and meritorious service in the Battle of Chickamauga, Ga. Trans. to Ord., 29 Jan., 1864. 1st Lieut., 7 March, 1867. Capt., 23 June, 1874. Maj., 15 Sept., 1890.

BUTLER, JOHN H. [Born in Mass. Appointed from Conn.]
2nd Lieut. 2nd Art., 22 May, 1861. 1st Lieut., 10 June, 1861. Bvt. Capt., 30 June, 1862, for gallant and meritorious service in the Battle of Glendale, Va. Bvt. Maj., 8 Nov., 1863, for gallant and meritorious service in action near Culpeper, Va. Retired 7 Feb., 1865. Capt. 42nd Inf., 22 Jan., 1867. Unass'd 22 April, 1869. Retired with rank of Capt. Mounted, 14 May, 1870.

BUTLER, JOHN J. [Born in Md. Appointed from D. C.]
Asst. Surg., 5 Aug, 1861. Dropped 17 May, 1862. Died 19 Feb., 1866.

BUTLER, JOHN R. [Born in Ky. Appointed from Ky.]
2nd Lieut. 2nd Inf., 22 May, 1847. Resigned 11 Sept., 1848.

BUTLER, MATTHEW C., Jr.* [Born in S. C. Appointed from S. C.]
Addl. 2nd Lieut. 14th Inf., 11 June, 1888. 2nd Lieut. 9th Inf., 17 Oct., 1888. Trans. to 5th Cav., 11 Feb., 1889. 1st Lieut. 7th Cav., 27 Aug., 1896. Maj. Chief Ord. Officer Vols., 19 July, 1898. Discharged from Vols., 12 May, 1899.

BUTLER, PIERCE M. [Born in S. C. Appointed from S. C.]
2nd Lieut. 4th Inf., 13 Aug., 1819. Trans. to 7th Inf., 13 Dec., 1819. 1st Lieut., 1 March, 1822. Capt., 16 Dec, 1825. Resigned 1 Oct., 1829. Col. Palmetto Reg. S. C. Vols., 22 Dec., 1846. Killed 20 Aug., 1847, at the ttle of Churubusco, Mex.

BUTLER, ROBERT. [Born in Penn. Appointed from Tenn.]
Capt. 24th Inf., 12 March, 1812. Maj., 15 Aug., 1813. (Col. A. G., 5 March, 1814, to 16 Aug., 1821.) Lieut. Col. 1st Inf., 24 Feb., 1818. Col. 4th Inf., 1 June, 1821. Assigned to 1st Inf., 16 Aug., 1821, as Lieut. Col. Resigned 16 Nov., 1821.

BUTLER, ROBT. Q.* [Born in Va. Appointed from Va.]
2nd Lieut. Eng., 1 July, 1839. Died 3 April, 1843.

BUTLER, WM. [Born in S. C. Appointed from Kan.]
2nd Lieut. 2nd Art., 7 June, 1855. Resigned 1 Feb., 1861.

BUTLER, WM. O. [Born in Ky. Appointed from Ky.]
Sergt. Ky. Vols., 1812. Capt. 17th Inf., 5 April, 1813. Trans. to 44th Inf., 3 Aug., 1813. Trans. to 1st Inf., 17 May, 1815. Bvt. Maj., 23 Dec., 1814, for gallant conduct at New Orleans, La. Resigned 31 May, 1817. Maj. Gen. Vols., 29 June, 1846. Received by resolution of Congress 2 March, 1847, the presentation of a sword in testimony of the high sense entertained by Congress of his gallantry and good conduct in the storming of Monterey, Mex. Discharged 15 Aug., 1848. Died 6 Aug., 1880.

BUTLER, WM. P.* [Born in Ky. Appointed from Ky.]
2nd Lieut. Ord., 18 June, 1866. Resigned 12 July, 1873.

BUTNER, HENRY W.* [Born in N. C. Appointed from N. C.]
2nd Lieut. 3rd Art., 26 April, 1898.

BUTTLER, WM. C.* [Born in N. J. Appointed from N. J.]
2nd Lieut. 3rd Inf., 15 June, 1876. 1st Lieut., 16 April, 1885. Capt., 26 April, 1898.

BUTTERFIELD, DANIEL [Born in N. Y. Appointed from N. Y.]
1st Sergt. Clay Guards, D. C. Vols., 16 April, 1861. Col. 12th N. Y. Militia, 2 May, 1861. Mustered out 5 Aug., 1861. Brig. Gen. Vols., 7 Sept., 1861. Maj. Gen. Vols., 29 Nov., 1862. Mustered out 24 Aug., 1865. Lieut. Col. 12th Inf., 14 May, 1861. Col. 5th Inf., 1 July, 1863. Unass'd 15 March, 1869. Resigned 14 March, 1870. Bvt. Brig. Gen., 13 March, 1865, for gallant and meritorious service during the war. Bvt. Maj. Gen., 13 March, 1865, for gallant and meritorious service in the field during the war.

BUTTERFIELD, SHUBAEL. [Born in N. H. Appointed from N. H.]
Ensign and 2nd Lieut. 4th Inf., 3 Jan., 1812. 1st Lieut., 21 Feb., 1814. Disbanded 15 June, 1815. Reinstated 2 Dec., 1815, as 2nd Lieut. 5th Inf. P. M. 2nd Inf., 21 May, 1816. Resigned 4 Oct., 1816. Retained — Jan., 1816, (in re-organization under Act of 3 March, 1815), as 2nd Lieut. 5th Inf., with Bvt. of 1st Lieut. from 21 Feb., 1814 Died 16 Oct., 1824.

BUTTS, EDMUND L.* [Born in Minn. Appointed from Minn.]
2nd Lieut. 21st Inf., 14 June, 1890. 1st Lieut., 27 June, 1897. Trans. to 5th Inf., 21 July, 1897. Capt. and A. A. G. Vols., 12 May, 1898, to 15 Nov., 1898. Capt. 18th Inf., 18 Jan., 1900.

BYERS, JOSEPH K. [Born in Penn. Appointed from Penn.]
1st Lieut. 121st Pa. Vols, 3 Sept., 1862. to 14 Oct., 1863. 1st Lieut. Vet. Res. Corps, 20 Sept., 1863. Bvt. Capt. Vols., 13 March, 1865, for gallant and meritorious service at the Battle of Fredericksburg, Va. Mustered out 12 July, 1866. 1st Lieut. 42nd Inf, 7 March, 1867. Unass'd 22 April, 1869. Retired 15 Dec., 1870. Died 30 Nov., 1878. Bvt. Capt, 7 March, 1867, for gallant and meritorious service in the Battle of Fredericksburg, Va. Bvt. Maj., 7 March, 1867, for gallant and meritorious service during the war.

BYRAM, GEORGE L.* [Born in Miss. Appointed from Ala.]
2nd Lieut. 1st Cav., 14 June, 1885. 1st Lieut., 4 Feb., 1892. Maj. 27th U. S. Vols., 5 July, 1899. Capt. 6th Cav., 23 Jan., 1900.

BYRD, FRANCIS O. [Born in Va. Appointed from Va.]
2nd Lieut. 2nd Art., 6 July, 1812. Trans. to Corps Art., 12 May, 1814. 1st Lieut., 30 Aug., 1816. Resigned 23 March, 1818. Bvt. 1st Lieut., 20 Feb., 1815, for distinguished and meritorious service.

BYRNE, BERNARD A. [Born in Ky. Appointed from D. C.]
2nd Lieut. 6th Inf., 15 Oct., 1875. 1st Lieut., 31 Dec., 1882. Capt., 9 Nov., 1894. Maj. Vol. Inf., 10 Aug., 1899 (declined). Lieut. Col. 40th U. S. Vols., 17 Aug., 1899.

BYRNE, BERNARD M. [Born in Ireland. Appointed from Md.]
Asst. Surg., 20 May, 1836. Maj. and Surg., 31 March, 1853. Died 6 Sept., 1860.

BYRNE, CHAS. [Born in Washington Ter. Appointed from D. C.]
2nd Lieut. 6th Inf., 9 Jan., 1877. 1st Lieut., 31 Oct., 1883. Reg. Adj., 1 April, 1890. Capt., 27 Aug., 1896. Graduate of the Infantry and Cavalry School, 1883.

BYRNE, CHAS. B. [Born in Md. Appointed from Md.]
1st Lieut. Asst. Surg., 16 Nov., 1868. Capt. Asst. Surg., 16 Nov., 1871. Maj. and Surg., 2 Jan., 1891.

BYRNE, CHAS. C. [Born in Md. Appointed from Md.]
1st Lieut. Asst. Surg., 23 June, 1860. Bvt. Maj. and Bvt. Lieut. Col., 13 March, 1865, for faithful and meritorious service during the War. Capt. Asst. Surg., 23 June, 1865. Maj. and Surg., 28 July, 1866. Lieut. Col. and Surg., 29 March, 1889. Col. and Asst. Surg. Gen., 4 Dec., 1893.

BYRNE, EDWARD. [Born in Ireland. Appointed from N. Y.]
2nd Lieut. 11th N. Y. Vols., 1 Aug., 1861. 1st Lieut., 15 Feb., 1862. Resigned 17 April, 1862. 1st Lieut 170th N Y. Vols., 7 Oct., 1862. Capt., 28 Jan., 1863. Discharged 21 Aug., 1863. Maj. 18th N. Y. Cav., 26 Aug., 1863. Lieut. Col., 11 Oct., 1865. Mustered out 31 May, 1866. Capt. 10th Cav., 28 July, 1866. Mustered out 1 Jan., 1871

BYRNE, JOHN. [Born in Md. Appointed from Md.]
Asst. Surg., 2 Aug., 1838. Resigned 23 Dec., 1846. Asst. Surg., 2 March, 1849. Resigned 11 Oct., 1857.

BYRNE, ROGERS M. [Born in N. Y. Appointed from N. Y.]
Maj. and Surg. 47th Inf., 20 July, 1814. Trans. to 30th Inf., 9 Nov., 1814. Disbanded 15 June, 1815. Surg. Mate 5th Inf., 6 Nov., 1817. Resigned 30 Nov., 1819.

BYRNE, THOMAS. [Born in Ireland. Appointed from Army.]
Priv. Co. A, 2nd Inf., 14 Dec., 1854. Corpl., 1 June, 1855. 1st Sergt., 15 Sept., 1856. Discharged 3 Nov., 1859. 1st Sergt. Co. A, 2nd Inf., 3 Nov., 1859. 2nd Lieut. 2nd Inf., 18 July, 1862. 1st Lieut., 9 June, 1863. Bvt. Capt., 2 July, 1863, for gallant and meritorious service in the Battle at Gettysburg, Pa. Capt. 2nd Inf., 15 Aug., 1867. Unass'd 17 April, 1869. Ass'd to 12th Inf., 1 Jan., 1871. Died 11 Jan., 1881.

BYRNES, RICHD. [Born in Ireland. Appointed from Army.]
Priv., Corpl. and Sergt. Co G, and Sergt. Maj. 1st Cav., 21 May, 1856, to 9 July, 1861. 2nd Lieut. 17th Inf., 14 May, 1861. Trans. to 5th Cav, 21 Sept., 1861. 1st Lieut., 17 July, 1862. Col. 28th Mass. Vols., 18 Oct., 1862. Died 12 June, 1864, of wounds received at the Battle of Cold Harbor, Va.

BYROADE, GEORGE L. [Born in Penn. Appointed from Army.]
Priv., Corpl. and Sergt. Batty. F, 1st Art., 23 Jan., 1894, to 26 April, 1897. 2nd Lieut. 3rd Inf., 13 April, 1897. 1st Lieut., 2 March, 1899. Trans. to 1st Inf., 20 May, 1899.

BYRON, JOSEPH C.* [Born in N. Y. Appointed from N. Y.]
2nd Lieut. 8th Cav., 1 July, 1886. 1st Lieut. 2nd Cav., 18 Jan., 1893. Trans. to 8th Cav., 23 May, 1894. Capt. and A. Q. M., 12 Nov., 1898.

CABANISS, ARCHIBALD A. [Born in Cal. Appointed from the Army.]
Priv., Corpl. and Sergt. Troop B, 4th Cav., 3 Jan., 1885, to 14 March, 1888. 2nd Lieut. 20th Inf., 6 Feb., 1888. 1st Lieut. 24th Inf., 25 April, 1895. Capt., 2 March, 1899. Graduate of the Infantry and Cavalry School, 1893.

CABANISS, CHAS. H., Jr.* [Born in Va. Appointed from Va.]
2nd Lieut. 18th Inf., 17 June, 1874. 1st Lieut., 18 Nov., 1883. Retired 10 July, 1891. Graduate of the Infantry and Cavalry School, 1887.

CABANNE, LUCIEN D. [Born in D. C. Appointed from Mo.]
Cadet at Mil. Acad., 1 July, 1831, to 30 June, 1835. 2nd Lieut. 1st Inf., 8 March, 1837. Resigned 21 Aug., 1837. Died 10 April, 1875.

CABELL, DE ROSEY C.* [Born in Ark. Appointed from Ark.]
2nd Lieut. 8th Cav., 15 June, 1884. 1st Lieut. 5th Cav., 17 April, 1891. Trans. to 8th Cav., 27 April, 1891. Capt. 6th Cav., 23 April, 1899. Capt. and A. A. G. Vols., 12 May, 1898 (declined). Lieut. Col. 2nd Ark. Vols., 18 May, 1898, to 25 Feb., 1899.

CABELL, HENRY C.* [Born in Va. Appointed from Va.]
2nd Lieut. 14th Inf., 13 June, 1883. 1st Lieut. 13th Inf., 24 Feb., 1891. Trans. to 14th Inf., 6 Oct., 1891. Capt. of Inf., 10 July, 1898. Ass'd to 3rd Inf., 1 Jan., 1899. Capt. and A. A. G. Vols., 12 May, 1898, to 10 July, 1898.

CABELL, WM. L.* [Born in Va. Appointed from Va.]
Bvt. 2nd Lieut. 7th Inf., 1 July, 1850. 2nd Lieut. 7th Inf., 9 March, 1851. 1st Lieut., 3 March, 1855. R. Q. M., 16 April, 1855, to 8 March, 1858. Capt. Asst. Q. M., 8 March, 1858 Resigned 20 April, 1861.

CABELL, JULIAN M. [Born in Va. Appointed from Va.]
Asst. Surg., 14 April, 1887. Capt. and Asst. Surg., 14 April, 1892. Retired for disability 29 March, 1897. Surg. 69th N. Y. Vols., 9 May, 1898. Mustered out 31 Jan., 1899.

CABELL, LAWRENCE D.* [Born in Tex. Appointed from Tex.]
2nd Lieut. 5th Inf., 15 Feb., 1899.

CADLE, JOSEPH.* [Born in N. Y. Appointed from N. Y.]
Bvt. 2nd Lieut. 7th Inf., 1 July, 1824. 2nd Lieut., 1 July, 1824. Dismissed 7 April, 1830. Died 10 March, 1835

CADY, ALBERMARLE.* [Born in N. H. Appointed from N. H.]
Bvt. 2nd Lieut. 6th Inf., 1 July, 1829. 2nd Lieut., 1 July, 1829. 1st Lieut., 31 Dec., 1836. Capt., 7 July, 1838. Bvt. Maj., 8 Sept., 1847, for gallant and meritorious service in the Battle of Molino del Rey. Maj. 6th Inf., 27 Jan., 1853. Lieut. Col. 7th Inf., 6 June, 1861. Col. 8th Inf., 20 Oct., 1863. Retired 18 May, 1864. Bvt. Brig Gen., 13 March, 1865, for long and faithful service in the army. Died 14 March, 1888.

CADY, HEMAN M. [Born in N. Y. Appointed from Wis.]
2nd Lieut. Inf., 6 March, 1847; 15th Inf., 9 April, 1847. R. Q. M., 1 Sept., 1847, to

BOYD, CARLILE. [Born in Ireland. Appointed from N. Y.]
2nd Lieut. 5th N. Y. Vols., 9 May, 1861. 1st Lieut., 5 Sept., 1861. Capt., 6 Dec., 1861. Maj., 1 Jan., 1863. Mustered out 14 May, 1863. Maj. Vet. Res. Corps, 17 Sept., 1863. Lieut. Col., 29 Sept., 1863. Mustered out 30 June, 1866. Capt. 44th Inf., 28 July, 1866. Bvt. Maj., 2 March, 1867, for gallant and meritorious service in the Battle of Gaines' Mill, Va. Bvt. Lieut. Col., 2 March, 1867, for gallant and meritorious service in the Battle of Groveton, Va. Trans. to 17th Inf., 27 May, 1869. Wholly retired 22 March, 1879. Died 22 March, 1883.

BOYD, CHARLES T.* [Born in Iowa. Appointed from Iowa.]
Addl. 2nd Lieut. 7th Cav., 12 June, 1896. 2nd Lieut. 4th Cav., 14 Jan., 1897. Maj. 37th U. S. Vols., 5 July, 1899.

BOYD, GEORGE W. [Born in N. H. Appointed from N. H.]
3rd Lieut. 4th Inf., 16 April, 1813. 2nd Lieut., 9 March, 1814. Trans. to 1st Inf., 17 May, 1815. Trans. to Corps Art., 20 June, 1816. 1st Lieut., 20 April, 1818. Resigned 2 June, 1818.

BOYD, JOSEPH B.* [Born in Tenn. Appointed from Tenn.]
2nd Lieut. 3rd Art., 1 July, 1839. Resigned 31 Dec., 1841. Died 17 June, 1845.

BOYD, ORSEMUS B.* [Born in N. Y. Appointed from N. Y.]
Corpl. Co. I, 89th N. Y. Vols., 16 Sept., 1861. 2nd Lieut. 144th N. Y. Vols., 27 Sept., 1862. Resigned 14 Feb., 1863. Cadet Mil. Acad., 1 July, 1863. 2nd Lieut. 8th Cav., 17 June, 1867. 1st Lieut., 13 Oct., 1868. R. Q. M., 1 Sept., 1880, to 1 Sept., 1881. Capt. 26 June, 1882. Died 23 July, 1885.

BOYLE, ARCHIBALD. [Born in Scotland. Appointed from Mass.]
1st Lieut. 39th Inf., 21 May, 1867. Trans. to 25th Inf., 20 April, 1869. Dismissed 20 Dec., 1871.

BOYLE, JUAN A. [Born in Md. Appointed from Neb.]
Priv., Corpl. and Sergt. Co. B, 22nd Inf., 31 Aug., 1897, to 23 Jan., 1899. 2nd Lieut. 15th Inf., 7 Jan., 1899. Trans. to 21st Inf., 30 March, 1899.

BOYLE, LLEWELLYN. [Born in Md. Appointed from Md.]
2nd Lieut. of Inf., 20 March, 1847; 15th Inf., 9 April, 1847. 1st Lieut., 23 May, 1848. Disbanded 20 July, 1848.

BOYLE, WM. H. [Born in N. Y. Appointed from N. Y..
2nd Lieut. 5th N. Y. Art., 28 June, 1862. 1st Lieut., 27 Dec., 1864. Mustered out 9 March, 1865. Capt. 5th N. Y. Art., 25 March, 1865. Maj., 20 May, 1865. Mustered out 19 July, 1865. 2nd Lieut. 2nd Inf., 10 May, 1866. 1st Lieut., 15 Aug., 1867. Unassigned 17 April, 1869. Ass'd to 21st Inf., 15 Dec., 1870. Capt., 23 April, 1877. Maj. 9th Inf., 25 March, 1898. Trans. to 21st Inf., 26 Sept., 1898. Lieut. Col. 19th Inf., 5 May, 1899.

BOYNTON, BENJAMIN A. [Born in N. Y. Appointed from N. Y.]
2nd Lieut. 29th Inf., 30 April, 1813. 1st Lieut., 25 Nov., 1813. Reg. Adj., March, 1814, to June, 1815. Trans. to 2nd Inf., 17 May, 1815. Capt. 8 Jan., 1823. Died 19 Feb., 1837. Bvt. Maj., 8 Jan., 1833, for ten years' faithful service in one grade.

BOYNTON, EDWARD C.* [Born in Vt. Appointed from Vt.]
Bvt. 2nd Lieut. 2nd Art., 1 July, 1846. 2nd Lieut. 1st Art., 16 Feb., 1847. 1st Lieut., 20 Aug., 1847. Resigned 16 Feb., 1856. Capt. 11th Inf., 23 Sept., 1861. Trans. to 29th Inf., 21 Sept., 1866. Unassigned 25 April, 1869. Ass'd to 3rd Art., 15 Dec., 1870. Resigned 1 Dec., 1872. Bvt. Capt., 20 Aug., 1847, for gallant and meritorious service at Contreras and Churubusco. Bvt. Maj., 13 March, 1865, for faithful service during the war.

BOZEMAN, JAMES F. [Born in Ga. Appointed from Ga.]
Asst. Surg., 8 Sept., 1847. Disbanded 20 July, 1848.

BRACKETT, ALBERT G. [Born in N. Y. Appointed from Ind.]
2nd Lieut. 4th Ind. Vols., 1 June, 1847. 1st Lieut., 18 June, 1847. Mustered out 16 July, 1848. Capt. 2nd Cav., 3 March, 1855. Col. 9th Ill. Cav., 26 Oct., 1861. Bvt. Maj., 28 June, 1862, for gallant and meritorious service in the campaign in Arkansas. Maj. 1st Cav., 17 July, 1862. Bvt. Lieut. Col. 1 Sept., 1864, for gallant and meritorious service during the Atlanta campaign. Mustered out of Vol. service 26 Oct., 1864. Bvt. Col., 13 March, 1865, for gallant and meritorious service during the war. Lieut. Col. 2nd Cav., 9 June, 1868. Col. 3rd Cav., 20 March, 1879. Retired, over 30 years' service, 18 Feb., 1891. Died 25 June, 1896.

BRACKETT, JOHN E.* [Born in N. Y. Appointed from N. Y.]
Bvt. 2nd Lieut. 2nd Art., 1 July, 1832. Resigned 31 Aug., 1833. Capt. 2nd N. Y. Vols., 1 Aug., 1846. Mustered out 15 Aug., 1848. Died 25 Jan., 1855.

BRADBURY, LUCIUS.* [Born in Maine. Appointed from Maine.]
Bvt. 2nd Lieut. 7th Inf., 1 July, 1835. Resigned 1 Oct., 1835. Died 25 June, 1850.

BRADEN, CHAS.* [Born in Mich. Appointed from Mich.]
2nd Lieut. 7th Cav., 15 June, 1869. 1st Lieut., 9 Dec., 1875. Retired 28 June, 1878. Bvt. 1st Lieut., 27 Feb., 1890, for gallant and meritorious services against Indians in the Big Horn River, Mont., 11 Aug., 1873, where he was severely wounded.

BRADFORD, EDMUND.* [Born in Penn. Appointed from Penn.]
2nd Lieut. 4th Art., 1 July, 1837. 1st Lieut., 25 June, 1841. Resigned 20 May, 1849.

BRADFORD, EDMUND G. [Born in Tenn. Appointed from Miss.]
2nd Lieut. 1st Inf., 27 June, 1848. Resigned 30 June, 1849.

BRADFORD, HENRY C. [Born in Ala. Appointed from Ala.]
1st Lieut. of Inf., 8 March, 1847; 13th Inf., 9 April, 1847. Resigned 31 Dec., 1847. Died 3 April, 1879.

BRADFORD, JAMES A. J.* [Born in Tenn. Appointed from Ky.]
Bvt. 2nd Lieut. Art., 1 July, 1827. 2nd Lieut. 3rd Art., 1 July, 1827. Capt. Ord., 30 May, 1832. Resigned 1 May, 1861.

BRADFORD, JAMES H. [Born in Del. Appointed from Army.]
Priv. 1st Batty 1st Del. Light Art., 20 Oct., 1862. Discharged 18 Nov., 1862. Priv. Co. ——, 17th Inf., 18 Nov., 1862. 2nd Lieut. 17th Inf., 18 Nov., 1862. 1st Lieut., 1 May, 1863. Bvt. Capt., 1 Aug., 1864, for gallant service in the Battle of Spottsylvania and during the campaign before Richmond, Va. Capt. 17th Inf., 1 Dec., 1865. Trans. to 26th Inf., 21 Sept., 1866. Unassigned 19 May, 1869. Ass'd to 19th Inf.,

16 Aug., 1869. Maj. 11th Inf., 24 Feb., 1891. Lieut. Col. 17th Inf., 16 Aug., 1894. Retired for disability 27 Aug., 1896.

BRADFORD, JAMES H. [Born in Mass. Appointed from Mass.]
Surg. Mate 9th Inf., 14 April, 1812. Maj. Surg. 3rd Art., 3 Oct., 1813. Rejected by Senate in 1814. 2nd Lieut. Light Art., 28 Oct., 1818. Dismissed 13 Aug., 1819. Died 28 Feb., 1863.

BRADFORD, JAMES H., Jr.* [Born in La. Appointed from Ariz.]
2nd Lieut. 19th Inf., 26 April, 1898. 1st Lieut., 2 March, 1899.

BRADFORD, ROBT. E. [Born in Ohio. Appointed from Ohio.]
Priv. Co. F, 2nd Ohio Vols., 17 April to 31 July, 1861. Priv. 16th Ohio Batty, 20 Aug., 1861, to 2 Aug., 1865. 2nd Lieut. 15th Inf., 6 June, 1867. 1st Lieut., 14 May, 1868. Dismissed 13 Dec., 1871.

BRADFORD, THOMAS C.* [Born in R. I. Appointed from R. I.]
Bvt. 2nd Lieut. Ord., 24 June, 1861. 1st Lieut., 3 Aug., 1861. Capt., 3 March, 1863. Died 12 Jan., 1872. Bvt. Maj., 13 March, 1865, for faithful and meritorious service in the Ord. Dept.

BRADFORD, WM. [Born in Va. Appointed from Ky.]
Capt. 17th Inf., 12 March, 1812. Maj. 21st Inf., 20 Aug., 1814. Maj., 10 Nov., 1818. Retained as Capt. 7th Inf., 1 June, 1821. Maj. 4th Inf., 6 Oct., 1822. Resigned 1 May, 1824. Retained 17 May, 1815 (under Act of 3 March, 1815), as Capt. of Rifles, with Bvt. of Maj., from 20 Aug., 1814.

BRADFORD, WM. [Born in N. C. Appointed from N. C.]
2nd Lieut. Mounted Rangers, 6 Nov., 1832. 2nd Lieut., 1st Drag., 19 Sept., 1833. Accidentally killed himself 17 March, 1834.

BRADFORD, WM. S. [Born in N. H. Appointed from Army.]
Priv., Corpl. and Sergt. of Co. H, 5th Inf., 17 April, 1834, to 11 April, 1837. Priv., Corpl. and Sergt. Co. A, 6th Inf., 27 Aug., 1838, to 22 Aug., 1843. Priv. and Sergt. Co. E and Q. M. Sergt. 7th Inf., 1 Jan., 1844, to 31 July, 1848. Bvt. 2nd Lieut. 7th Inf., 28 June, 1848. Resigned 31 Oct., 1848.

BRADFORD, WM. S. [Born in Del. Appointed from Del.]
2nd Lieut. 17th Inf., 10 April, 1899.

BRADFUTE, WM. R. [Born in Tenn. Appointed from Tenn.]
1st Lieut. 1st Tenn. Vols., 28 May, 1846. Mustered out 23 May, 1847. Capt. 3rd Tenn. Vols., 24 Sept., 1847. Mustered out 24 July, 1848. Capt. 2nd Cav., 3 March, 1855. Resigned 21 March, 1861.

BRADLEY, ALFRED E. [Born in N. Y. Appointed from N. Y.]
Asst. Surg., 29 Oct., 1888. Capt. Asst. Surg., 29 Oct., 1893. Maj. Brig. Surg. Vols., 4 June, 1898. Discharged from Vols. 01 Nov., 1899.

BRADLEY, BRADFORD. [Born in La. Appointed from La.]
2nd Lieut. 1st Inf., 3 March, 1819. 1st Lieut., 30 Nov., 1820. Disbanded 1 June, 1821.

BRADLEY, CHAS. A.* [Born in N. Y. Appointed from Ill.]
2nd Lieut. 9th Cav., 15 June, 1877. Resigned 1 June, 1880.

BRADLEY, CHAS. O. [Born in N. H. Appointed from N. H.]
1st Sergt. Co. I, N. H. Vols., 20 April, 1861. Discharged 9 Aug., 1861. Capt. 13th N. H. Vols., 19 Sept., 1862. Mustered out 10 June, 1864. Capt. 1st N. H. Art., 17 Sept., 1864. Mustered out 15 June, 1865. 2nd Lieut. and 1st Lieut. 11th Inf., 23 Feb., 1866. Trans. to 20th Inf., 21 Sept., 1866. Capt., 25 Aug., 1874. Died 14 May, 1887.

BRADLEY, GEORGE W. [Born in N. Y. Appointed from N. Y.]
Capt. A. Q. M. Vols., 26 Nov., 1862. Lieut. Col. Q. M. (Act 17 July, 1862), 17 Sept., 1864, to 6 Nov., 1864. Col. Q. M. (Act 4 July, 1864), 7 Nov., 1864. Bvt. Maj. Lieut. Col. and Col., 13 March, 1865, for faithful and meritorious service during the war. Capt. A. Q. M., 4 Nov., 1865. Vacated commission of Capt. A. Q. M. Vols., 14 Nov., 1865. Relieved as Col. Q. M. (Act 4 July, 1864), 18 Oct., 1866. Died 20 Feb., 1882.

BRADLEY, HEZEKIAH. [Born in Va. Appointed from Ind.
Ensign 2nd Inf., 12 Dec., 1808. 2nd Lieut., 1 Jan., 1810. 1st Lieut., 15 Aug., 1812. Capt., 19 April, 1814. Trans. to 3rd Inf., 17 May, 1815. Died 18 March, 1826. Bvt. Maj., 19 April, 1824, for ten years' faithful service in one grade.

BRADLEY, JAMES H. [Born in Ohio. Appointed from Ohio.]
Priv. 14th Ohio Vols., 23 April to 13 Aug., 1861. Priv., Corpl. and Sergt. Co. F, 45th Ohio Vols., 19 Aug., 1862. Mustered out 5 July, 1865. 2nd Lieut. 18th Inf., 23 Feb., 1866. 1st Lieut., 29 July, 1866. Trans. to 7th Inf., 28 Nov., 1871. Killed in action with Indians in Montana Ter., 9 Aug., 1877.

BRADLEY, JOHN. [Born in N. Y. Appointed from Army.]
Priv. and Sergt. 11th Inf. and Sergt. Maj. 6th Inf., 11 Oct., 1814, to 19 Oct., 1819. 2nd Lieut. 6th Inf., 28 Jan., 1820. 1st Lieut., 2 Oct., 1822. Trans. to 2nd Inf., 30 July, 1823. Capt., 21 July, 1834. Resigned 30 June, 1839. Bvt. Capt., 2 Oct., 1832, for ten years' faithful service in one grade.

BRADLEY, JOHN J.* [Born in Ill. Appointed from Ill.]
2nd Lieut. 14th Inf., 12 June, 1891. 1st Lieut., 26 April, 1898. Capt. A. Q. M. Vols., 16 July, 1898.

BRADLEY, LUTHER P. [Born in Conn. Appointed from Ill.]
Lieut. Col. 51st Ill. Vols., 15 Oct., 1861. Col., 15 Oct., 1862. Brig. Gen. Vols., 30 July, 1864. Resigned 30 June, 1865. Lieut. Col. 27th Inf., 28 July, 1866. Bvt. Col., 2 March, 1867, for gallant and meritorious service in the Battle of Chickamauga, Ga. Bvt. Brig. Gen., 2 March, 1867, for gallant and meritorious service in the Battle of Resaca, Ga. Trans. to 9th Inf., 15 March, 1869. Col. 3rd Inf., 20 March, 1879. Trans. to 13th Inf., 14 June, 1879. Retired by op. of law 8 Dec., 1886.

BRADLEY, THEODORE. [Born in N. Y. Appointed from N. J.]
Priv. and Corpl. Co. F, 8th Inf., 6 May to 1 Nov., 1861. 2nd Lieut. 2nd Art., 24 Oct., 1861. 1st Lieut., 25 July, 1863. Resigned 6 May, 1864.

BRADLEY, THOS. H. [Born in Ill. Appointed from Mo.]
Priv. Co. F, 2nd Mo. Cav., 16 Dec., 1861. Capt. A. A. G. Vols., 6 June, 1863. Maj. A. A. G. Vols., 1 May, 1865. 2nd Lieut. 11th Inf., 11 May, 1866. Mustered out of Vol. service, 1 Sept., 1866. Bvt. 1st Lieut. and Bvt. Capt., 2 March, 1867, for faith-

BENNETT, ANDREW S. [Born in N. Y. Appointed from Wis.]
2nd Lieut. 5th Wis. Vols., 12 July, 1861. 1st Lieut., 25 Dec., 1862. Mustered out 2 Aug., 1864. 1st Lieut. 15th Inf., 7 March, 1867. Capt., 28 Feb., 1869. Unassigned 12 Aug., 1869. Ass'd to 5th Inf., 1 Jan., 1871. Killed 4 Sept., 1878, in action with Indians in Montana.

BENNETT, CHAS. [Born in N. J. Appointed from N. J.]
2nd Lieut. of Inf., 8 March, 1847; 10th Inf., 9 April, 1847. Disbanded 24 Aug., 1848.

BENNETT, CHARLES A.* [Born in N. J. Appointed from N.
2nd Lieut. 3rd Art., 11 June, 1881. 1st Lieut., 16 Dec., 1889. Capt., 2 March, 1899. Graduate of the Artillery School, 1886.

BENNETT, CLARENCE E.* Born in N. Y. Appointed from N. Y.]
Bvt. 2nd Lieut. 3rd Inf., 1 July, 1855. 2nd Lieut. 10th Inf., 13 Aug., 1855. Reg. Adj., 1 Oct., 1858, to 30 April, 1860. R. Q. M., 30 April to 16 July, 1860. Resigned 10 Sept., 1860. Maj. 1st Cal. Cav., 9 Feb., 1868. Lieut. Col., 31 Dec., 1863. Bvt. Col. Vols., 13 March, 1865, for faithful and meritorious service. Mustered out 15 Aug., 1866. 2nd Lieut. 6th Cav., 23 Feb., 1866. 1st Lieut., 28 July, 1866. Capt. 17th Inf., 22 Jan., 1867. Maj. 19th Inf., 28 Nov., 1893. Lieut. Col. 11th Inf., 27 June, 1897. Retired, by operation of law, 2 Dec., 1897.

BENNETT, FRANK T. [Born in Ohio. Appointed from Army.]
Priv. Co. H, 3rd Batt. 18th Inf., 29 April, 1862. Q. M. Sergt., 1 Aug., 1862. 2nd Lieut. 18th Inf., 19 Feb., 1863. Bvt. 1st Lieut., 26 June, 1863, for gallant and meritorious service in action at Hoover's Gap, Tenn. Bvt. Capt., 20 Sept., 1863, for gallant and meritorious service in the Battle of Chickamauga, Ga. 1st Lieut. 18th Inf., 6 Jan., 1864. Trans. to 36th Inf., 21 Sept., 1866. Resigned 15 Oct., 1866. Reinstated 4 Dec., 1866. Capt. 30th Inf., 23 Jan., 1867. Unassigned 20 April, 1869. Ass'd to 9th Cav., 15 Dec., 1870. Maj. 2nd Cav., 6 June, 1885. Retired for disability 23 Jan., 1889. Died 21 June, 1894.

BENNETT, JOHN.* [Born in Ohio. Appointed from Ohio.]
2nd Lieut. 4th Art., 1 July, 1856. Died 24 Feb., 1859.

BENNETT, JOHN E. [Born in N. Y. Appointed from Ill.]
2nd Lieut. 19th Inf., 23 Feb., 1866. 1st Lieut., 23 Feb., 1866. Trans. to 28th Inf., 21 Sept., 1866. Resigned 8 Aug., 1868. Bvt. Capt., 2 March, 1867, for gallant and meritorious service in the Battle of Lookout Mountain, Tenn. Bvt. Maj., 2 March, 1867, for gallant and meritorious service in the Battle of Franklin, Tenn. Bvt. Lieut. Col., 2 March, 1867, for gallant and meritorious service in the Battle of Nashville, Tenn.

BENNETT, JOHN R. [Born in Md. Appointed from Iowa.]
2nd Lieut. of Inf., 8 March, 1847; 15th Inf., 9 April, 1847. Bvt. 1st Lieut., 13 Sept., 1847, for gallant and meritorious conduct in the Battle of Chapultepec, Mex. Mustered out 4 Aug., 1848. Capt. 3rd Minn. Inf., 25 Oct., 1861. Resigned, 27 Feb., 1862.

BENNETT, NAPOLEON B.* [Born in Del. Appointed from Penn.
Bvt. 2nd Lieut. 3rd Art., 1 July, 1824. 2nd Lieut., 1 July, 1824. Died 2 Nov., 1832.

BENNETT, RICHARD. [Born in Md. Appointed from Md.]
Ensign and 3rd Lieut. 14th Inf., 12 March, 1812. 2nd Lieut., 12 May, 1813. 1st. Lieut., 1 Dec., 1814. Disbanded 15 June, 1815. 2nd Lieut. 1st Inf., 9 Jan., 1837. 1st Lieut., 7 July, 1838. Resigned 13 March, 1839. Addl. P. M., 13 March, 1839. Resigned 16 March, 1840. Died 8 Oct., 1843.

BENNETT, THOMAS.* [Born in N. J. Appointed from N. J.]
2nd Lieut. Art., 14 Nov., 1806. 1st Lieut., 1 Aug., 1809. Capt., 20 June, 1815. Trans. to Corps Art., 12 May, 1814. Died 26 Sept., 1818.

BENNETT, WM. C. [Born in Cal. Appointed from the Army.]
Priv., Corpl. and Sergt. Co. H, 17th Inf., 30 Nov., 1885, to 7 March, 1889. 2nd Lieut. 6th Inf., 11 Feb., 1889. 1st Lieut. 12th Inf., 9 Jan., 1896. Trans. to 6th Inf., 7 May, 1897. Capt. 16th Inf., 16 May, 1899. Graduate of the Infantry and Cavalry School, 1893.

BENNETT, WM. E., Jr. [Born in ——. Appointed from ——.]
2nd Lieut. of Inf. (unassigned), 1 Oct., 1899.

BENSON, HARRY C.* [Born in Ohio. Appointed from Ohio.]
2nd Lieut. 1st Art., 13 June, 1882. Trans. to 4th Cav., 31 Jan., 1884. 1st Lieut., 4 March, 1888. Capt., 21 Nov., 1897. Maj. I. G., 12 May, 1898. Discharged 12 May, 1899.

BENSON, HENRY. [Born in N. J. Appointed from Army.]
Priv., Corpl., Sergt. and 1st Sergt. Batty A, 2nd Art., 6 June, 1845, to 2 Aug., 1848. Bvt. 2nd Lieut. 2nd Art., 28 June, 1848. 2nd Lieut., 26 Jan., 1849. 1st Lieut., 2 March, 1853. Capt., 14 May, 1861. Died 11 Aug., 1862, of wounds received at Malvern Hill, Va.

BENSON, HENRY M. [Born in Mo. Appointed from Cal.]
1st Lieut. 1st Cal. Vols., 27 Aug., 1861. Capt., 1 March, 1863. Mustered out 31 Aug., 1864. Maj. 4th Cal. Vols., 22 May, 1865. Mustered out 31 Jan., 1866. 2nd Lieut., and 1st Lieut. 18th Inf., 23 Feb., 1866. Trans. to 36th Inf., 21 Sept., 1866. Trans. to 7th Inf., 19 May, 1869. Bvt. Capt., 27 Feb., 1890, for gallant services in action against Indians at Camas Meadows, Idaho, 20 Aug., 1877, where he was severely wounded. Capt., 1 May, 1882. Retired for disability 14 Nov., 1885.

BENT, CHARLES L.* [Born in Mass. Appointed from Mass.]
2nd Lieut. 1st Inf., 12 June, 1894. 1st Lieut. 7th Inf., 26 April, 1898.

BENTEEN, FRED'K W. [Born in Ga. Appointed from Ga.]
2nd Lieut. 2nd Inf., 1 June, 1899.

BENTEEN, FRED'K W [Born in Va. Appointed from Mo.]
1st Lieut. 10th Mo. Cav., 1 Sept., 1861. Capt., 1 Oct., 1861. Maj., 19 Dec., 1862. Lieut. Col., 27 Feb., 1864. Mustered out 30 June, 1865. Col. 138th U. S. Col. Troops, 15 July, 1865. Mustered out 6 Jan., 1866. Capt. 7th Cav., 28 July, 1866. Bvt. Maj., 2 March, 1867, for gallant and meritorious service in the Battle of the Osage. Bvt. Lieut. Col., 2 March, 1867, for gallant and meritorious service in the charge of Columbus, Ga. Bvt. Col., 13 Aug., 1868, for gallant and meri-

torious conduct in an engagement with hostile Indians on the Saline River, Kansas, 13 Aug., 1868. Maj. 9th Cav., 17 Dec., 1882. Retired for disability 7 July, 1888. Died 22 June, 1898.

BENTLEY, EDWIN. [Born in Conn. Appointed from Conn.]
Asst. Surg. 4th Conn. Vols., 6 June, 1861. Discharged 1 Oct., 1861. Maj. and Surg. Vols., 4 Sept., 1861. Bvt. Lieut. Col. Vols., 13 March, 1865, for faithful and meritorious service during the War. Mustered out 4 June, 1866. 1st Lieut. Asst. Surg., 28 Feb., 1866. Capt. Asst. Surg., 28 July, 1866. Maj. Surg., 12 July, 1879. Retired by operation of law 3 July, 1888.

BENTON, EDWARD T. [Born in Md. Appointed from Md.]
2nd Lieut. 1st Cav., 19 Feb., 1862. 1st Lieut., 17 July, 1862. Resigned 2 April, 1864.

BENTON, ELISHA S.* [Born in Mass. Appointe from Mass.]
2nd Lieut. 3rd Art., 15 June, 1884. 1st Lieut., 31 July, 1891. Trans. to 1st Art., 24 July, 1897. Trans. to 7th Art., 8 March, 1898. Graduate of the Artillery School, 1898.

BENTON, JAMES G.* [Born in N. H. Appointed from N. H.]
Bvt. 2nd Lieut. Ord., 1 July, 1842. 2nd Lieut., 3 March, 1847. 1st Lieut., 25 March, 1848. Capt., 1 July, 1856. Maj., 15 Sept., 1863. Bvt. Lieut. Col. and Col., 13 March, 1865, for faithful service in the Ord. Dept. Lieut. Col. Ord., 23 June, 1874. Col., 29 May, 1879. Died 31 Aug., 1881.

BENTON, JAMES W.* [Born in D. C. Appointed from Mass.]
2nd Lieut. 9th Cav., 14 June, 1885. 1st Lieut. of Cav. (7th), 22 March, 1892. Trans. to 9th Cav., 12 April, 1892. R. Q. M., 12 April, 1895. Died 2 Sept., 1896.

BENTZONI, CHAS. [Born in Prussia. Appointed from Army.]
Priv. Gen. Ser., 12 May, 1857. Corpl., 1 Nov., 1857. Sergt., 24 Sept., 1859. Sergt. Co. D, 1st Batt. 11th Inf., 29 Aug., 1861. 1st Sergt., 1 Sept., 1861. 2nd Lieut. 11th Inf., 20 Nov., 1861. 1st Lieut., 17 March, 1862. Bvt. Capt., 30 Sept., 1864, for gallant and meritorious service in the Battle of Poplar Spring Church, Va. Col. 56th U. S. Col. Troops, 29 Jan., 1865. Bvt. Maj. and Lieut. Col., 13 March, 1865, for gallant and meritorious service during the War. Mustered out of Vol. service, 15 Sept., 1866. Trans. to 29th Inf., 21 Sept., 1866. Capt. 40th Inf., 28 July, 1866. Trans. to 25th Inf., 20 April, 1869. Maj. 1st Inf., 4 Dec., 1891. Retired by operation of law 11 Oct., 1894.

BENYAURD, WM. H. H.* [Born in Penn. Appointed from Penn.]
1st Lieut. Eng., 11 June, 1863. Bvt. Capt., 1 Aug., 1864, for gallant and meritorious service during the campaign before Richmond, Va. Bvt. Maj., 1 April, 1865, for gallant and meritorious service in the Battle of Five Forks, Va. Capt. Eng., 1 May, 1866. Maj., 4 March, 1879. Lieut. Col., 2 July, 1889. Died 16 Feb., 1900. Medal of Honor for most distinguished gallantry in action at Five Forks, Va., 1 April, 1865, Maj. Gen. Warren, commanding 5th Army Corps, seeing his troops wavering, seized his headquarter's flag, rode to the front, accompanied by Lieut. Benyaurd, Corps of Eng., and calling on his men to follow, the troops resumed the advance and were successful. Also, in the same action, Lieut. Benyaurd, with one companion, voluntarily advanced beyond the skirmishers, where he was exposed to imminent peril. In his reconnaissance seven prisoners were captured; while serving as 1st Lieut., Corps of **Eng.**

BERARD, ACHILLE. [Born in La. Appointed from La.]
2nd Lieut. 14th Inf., 3 March, 1848. Disbanded 20 July, 1848.

BERARD, CLAUDIUS. [Born in France. Appointed from Penn.]
Teacher of French at Mil. Acad., 3 Jan., 1815. Prof. of French, 8 Aug., 1846. Died 6 May, 1848.

BEREMAN, ALVAH H. [Born in Ky. Appointed from Iowa.]
Capt. 18th Inf., 14 May, 1861. Resigned 22 July, 1862. Col. 45th Iowa Vols., 25 May, 1864. Mustered out 16 Sept., 1864.

BERG, CHAS. [Born in Penn. Appointed from Army.]
Sergt. Maj. 2nd Ohio Vols., 17 April to 25 June, 1861. Sergt. Maj. 19th U. S. Inf., 25 June to Nov., 1861. 2nd Lieut. 19th Inf., 20 Nov., 1861. Resigned 27 May, 1862.

BERGLAND, ERIC.* [Born in Sweden. Appointed from Ill.]
2nd Lieut. 57th Ill. Vols., 26 Dec., 1861. 1st Lieut. 57th Ill. Vols., 20 July, 1862. Mustered out 7 July, 1865. Cadet at Mil. Acad. 1 July, 1865. 2nd Lieut. 5th Art., 15 June, 1869. Trans. to Eng., 10 June, 1872. 1st Lieut., 10 June, 1872. Capt. (14 years' service), 10 Jan., 1884. Maj. 12 Oct., 1895. Retired, over 30 years' service, 31 March, 1896.

BERIER, FRANCIS N.* [Born in Md. Appointed from N. Y.]
3rd Lieut. Corps Art., 2 March, 1815. 2nd Lieut., 19 June, 1817. Resigned 31 March, 1818. Died 26 Oct., 1822.

BERKELEY, HUGH D.* [Born in Va. Appointed from Miss.]
Addl. 2nd Lieut. 1st Cav., 12 June, 1894. 2nd Lieut., 18 Aug., 1894. 1st Lieut., 2 March, 1899.

BERNARD, JOHN J. [Born in Cal. Appointed from the Army.]
Priv., Corpl. and Sergt. Troop I, 1st Cav., 20 Aug., 1894, to 13 April, 1897. 2nd Lieut. 4th Inf., 25 March, 1897. Killed in action at San Juan, Santiago, Cuba, 1 July, 1898.

BERNARD, REUBEN F. [Born in Tenn. Appointed from Army.]
Priv. Co. D, 1st Drag., 19 Feb., 1855. Corpl., 1 June, 1857. Priv., 1 May, 1858. Corpl., 1 March, 1859. Sergt., 5 May, 1859. 1st Sergt., 6 June, 1859. Discharged 19 Dec., 1859. 1st Sergt. Co. D, 1st Drag., 19 Dec., 1859. Priv., 5 Jan., 1862. 2nd Lieut. 1st Cav., 17 July 1862. 1st Lieut., 21 June, 1863. Bvt. Capt., 6 May, 1864, for gallant and meritorious service in the Battle of Todd's Tavern, Va. Bvt. Maj., 28 Aug., 1864, for gallant and meritorious service in action at Smithfield, Va. Bvt. Lieut. Col. and Bvt. Col., 13 March, 1865, for gallant and meritorious service during the War. Capt. 1st Cav., 28 July, 1866. Maj. 8th Cav., 1 Nov., 1882. Lieut. Col. 9th Cav., 22 July, 1892. Bvt. Brig. Gen., Feb. 27, 1890, for gallant services in action against Indians at Chericahua Pass, Arizona, 20 Oct., 1869, and in the actions against Indians near the Silver River, Oregon, 23

Maj. Gen. Vols., 1 Aug., 1864, for gallant and meritorious service in the Battles of Tolopotomy and Cold Harbor, Va. Resigned 1 Feb., 1866. Lieut. Col. 37th Inf., 28 July, 1866. Bvt. Col., 2 March, 1867, for gallant and meritorious service in the Battle of Gettysburg, Penn. Bvt. Brig. Gen., 2 March, 1867, for gallant and meritorious service in the Battle of Spottsylvania Court House, Va. Trans. to 3rd Inf., 15 March, 1869. Col. 13th Inf., 20 March, 1879. Trans. to 3rd Inf., 14 June, 1879. Brig. Gen., 6 April, 1888. Maj. Gen., 22 May, 1897.

BROOKE, LEONARD O.* [Born in Md. Appointed from Md.]
2nd Lieut. 4th Inf., 24 July, 1818. Disbanded 1 June, 1821. Died in 1821.

BROOKE, ROBT. L. [Born in Penn. Appointed from Penn.]
2nd Lieut. 5th Inf., 1 July, 1839. Resigned 18 May, 1846.

BROOKE, ROBT. S.* [Born in Va. Appointed from Va.]
3rd Lieut. Ord., 1 July, 1820. Resigned 1 Dec., 1820. Died 14 May, 1851.

BROOKE, WM. [Born in Pa. Appointed from Pa.]
2nd Lieut. 4th Inf., 7 Oct., 1891. 1st Lieut., 26 April, 1898. Trans. to 15th Inf., 21 Nov., 1899. Capt. 35th U. S. Vol. Inf., 5 July, 1899. Vacated 22 Sept., 1899. Maj. 46th U. S. Vol. Inf., 17 Aug., 1899.

BROOKES, ALBERT S.* [Born in Ark. Appointed from Ark.]
2nd Lieut. 18th Inf., 12 June, 1895. 1st Lieut. of Inf., 10 July, 1898. Ass'd to 18th Inf., 1 Jan., 1899. Capt. and C. S. Vols., 13 June, 1898. Discharged 7 March, 1899.

BROOKFIELD, ROBERT M.* [Born in Pa. Appointed from Pa.]
Addl. 2nd Lieut. of Inf., 12 June, 1896. 2nd Lieut. 2nd Inf., 12 June, 1896. 1st Lieut. of Inf., 28 Sept., 1898. Ass'd to 23rd Inf., 1 Jan., 1899. Trans. to 11th Inf., 28 Feb., 1899.

BROOKS, ALEXANDER S. [Born in Mass. Appointed from Mass.]
1st Lieut Light Art., 3 May, 1808. Capt., 11 June, 1809. Resigned 2 May, 1810. Capt. 3rd Art., 12 March, 1812. Trans. to Corps Art., 12 May, 1814. Trans. to Light Art., 17 May, 1816. Trans. to 1st Art., 1 June, 1821. Maj. 3rd Art., 26 April, 1832. Lieut. Col. 4th Art., 6 April, 1835. Killed 17 Dec., 1836, by steamboat explosion Bvt. Maj., 11 Sept., 1814, for gallant conduct at the Battle of Plattsburg

BROOKS, CHAS. S. [Born in Ill. Appointed from Cal.]
Capt. 4th Cal. Vols., 1 Oct., 1861. Resigned 3 April, 1862. 2nd Lieut. 5th Cav., 24 March, 1862. Died 7 July, 1862.

BROOKS, DAVID. [Born in N. Y. Appointed from N. Y.]
2nd Lieut. 2nd Inf., 28 Jan., 1820. Died 16 May, 1827.

BROOKS, EDWARD. [Born in Mass. Appointed from N. Y.]
Asst. Surg., 19 Aug., 1862. Died 19 April, 1866. Bvt. Capt. and Maj., 13 March, 1865, for faithful and meritorious services during the War.

BROOKS, EDWARD C.* [Born in Ore. Appointed from Ore.]
2nd Lieut. 8th Cav., 1st July, 1886. 1st Lieut. 6th Cav., 8 March, 1893. Capt. A. A. G. Vols., 17 Sept., 1898. Discharged from Vols., 12 May, 1899. Maj. 46th U. S. Vol. Inf., 17 Aug., 1899 (declined).

BROOKS, EDWARD E. [Born in N. J. Appointed from Ky.]
3rd Lieut. 2nd Inf., 8 April, 1814. 2nd Lieut., 1 May, 1814. Trans. to 3rd Inf., 17 May, 1815. 1st Lieut., 1 June, 1817. Capt., 28 April, 1826. Resigned 6 June, 1827.

BROOKS, EDWARD J. [Born in Mich. Appointed from Mich.]
2nd Lieut. 7th Inf., 30 June, 1855. Reg Adj., 1 July, 1856, to 31 Aug., 1859. 1st Lieut., 26 Feb., 1861. Resigned 16 May, 1861.

BROOKS, HORACE.* [Born in Mass. Appointed from Mass.]
Bvt. 2nd Lieut. 2nd Art., 1 July, 1835. 2nd Lieut., 28 Dec., 1835. Bvt. 1st Lieut., 31 Dec., 1835, for gallantry and good conduct in the war against the Florida Indians. 1st Lieut. 2nd Art., 8 Feb., 1837. Capt., 18 June, 1846. Bvt. Maj., 20 Aug., 1847, for gallant and meritorious conduct in the Battles of Contreras and Churubusco. Bvt. Lieut. Col., 8 Sept., 1847, for gallant and meritorious conduct in the Battle of Molino del Rey. Maj. 2nd Art., 28 April, 1861. Lieut. Col., 26 Oct., 1861. Col. 4th Art., 1 Aug., 1863. Bvt. Brig. Gen., 13 March, 1865, for meritorious service during the war. Retired 10 Jan., 1877. Died 13 Jan., 1894.

BROOKS, JEHIEL. [Born in Ky. Appointed from Ky.]
2nd Lieut. 1st Inf., 13 Feb., 1818. 1st Lieut., 16 March, 1819. Resigned 30 Nov., 1820.

BROOKS, JOHN C. W.* [Born in N. Y. Appointed from Pa.]
2nd Lieut. 4th Art., 14 June, 1885. 1st Lieut., 14 Aug., 1889. Capt. 6th Art., 2 March, 1899. Trans. to 4th Art., 21 April, 1899. Graduate of the Artillery School, 1888. Capt. and A. Q. M. Vols., 17 May, 1898. Maj. and Q. M. Vols., 12 Nov., 1898.

BROOKS, LORENZO L. C.* [Born in Iowa. Appointed from Iowa.]
2nd Lieut. 5th Cav., 13 June, 1879. Resigned 30 June, 1883.

BROOKS, WHITFIELD B. [Born in S. C. Appointed from S. C.]
2nd Lieut. 12th Inf., 4 Aug., 1847. Died 2 Oct., 1847, of wounds received in action at Churubusco, Mexico.

BROOKS, WM. T. H.* [Born in Ohio. Appointed from Ohio.]
Bvt. 2nd Lieut. 3rd Inf., 1 July, 1841. 2nd Lieut., 31 Jan., 1842. 1st Lieut., 21 Sept., 1846. Capt., 10 Nov , 1851. Brig. Gen. Vols., 28 Sept., 1861. Maj. Gen , 10 June, 1863. Appointment as Maj. Gen. revoked 18 April, 1864. Resigned from Vol. service 14 July, 1864. Maj. 18th Inf., 12 March, 1862. Resigned 14 July, 1864. Bvt. Capt., 23 Sept., 1846, for gallant and meritorious conduct at Monterey. Bvt. Maj., 20 Aug., 1847, for gallant and meritorious conduct at Contreras and Churubusco Died 19 July, 1870.

BROOM, JAMES M. [Born in Penn. Appointed from Penn.]
2nd Lieut. 7th Inf., 26 April, 1861. 1st Lieut., 30 May, 1861. Discharged 10 Sept., 1863. 2nd Lieut. 9th Inf., 7 June, 1864. 1st Lieut., 7 June, 1864. Dismissed 21 May, 1869.

BROOM, THOMAS R. [Born in N. Y. Appointed from N. Y.]
3rd Lieut. Light Art , 21 July, 1814. Trans. to Corps Art., 17 May, 1815. Batt. Adj., 1 May, to 1 Nov., 1816. Resigned 1 Nov., 1816. P. M. 4th Inf., 13 Feb , 1818. Trans. to 7th Inf., 10 June, 1818. Disbanded 1 June, 1821. Died 4 Feb., 1829.

BROPHY, WM. [Born in Ireland. Appointed from Army.]
Priv. and Sergt. Troop D, 2nd Cav., 14 May, 1855, to 14 May, 1860. Priv., Corpl., Sergt. and 1st Sergt. Troop D, 5th Cav., 25 June, 1860, to 25 March, 1863. 2nd Lieut. 5th Cav., 19 Feb., 1863. Resigned 12 Sept., 1863.

BROTHERTON, DAVID H.* [Born in Penn. Appointed from Penn.]
Bvt. 2nd Lieut. 5th Inf., 1 July, 1854. 2nd Lieut., 3 March, 1855. 1st Lieut., 22 Aug., 1859. Capt., 25 Sept., 1861. Bvt. Maj., 21 Feb., 1862, for gallant and meritorious service in the Battle of Valverde, New Mexico. Maj. 5th Inf., 20 March, 1879. Trans. to 7th Inf., 18 Dec., 1879. Lieut. Col. 25th Inf., 3 July, 1883. Retired for disability 14 April, 1884. Died 17 Sept., 1889.

BROUGHTON, HORACE. [Born in Vt. Appointed from Vt.]
2nd Lieut. 26th Inf., 21 April, 1814. 1st Lieut., 10 Dec., 1814. Disbanded 15 June, 1815. 2nd Lieut. 6th Inf., 19 Feb., 1817. Trans. to Rifle Reg., 8 May, 1817. 1st Lieut., 31 July, 1817. Resigned 5 April, 1818.

BROWER, CHAS. B. [Born in N. Y. Appointed from N. Y.]
2nd Lieut. N. Y. Vols., 5 Dec., 1846, to Jan., 1848. 2nd Lieut. 3rd Inf., 30 Dec., 1847. Died 24 July, 1851.

BROWER, RALPH P. [Born in Ill. Appointed from Ill.]
2nd Lieut. 7th Art., 9 July, 1898. Trans. to 3rd Art., 4 April, 1899.

BROWN, A. BENSON. [Born in N. J. Appointed from N. J.]
Sergt. and 1st Sergt. Co. C, 9th N. J. Vols., 29 Sept., 1861. 2nd Lieut., 9 March, 1862. 1st Lieut., 13 April, 1863. Capt., 8 Sept., 1864. Capt. Vet. Res. Corps, 3 Dec., 1864. Mustered out 6 Jan., 1867. 1st Lieut. 43rd Inf., 28 July, 1866. Trans. to 1st Inf., 8 April, 1869. Retired 13 Feb., 1873. Died 6 May, 1875. Bvt. Capt., 2 March, 1867, for gallant and meritorious service in the Battle of Drury's Bluff, Va.

BROWN, ANDREW M. [Born in Ill. Appointed from Ill.]
2nd Lieut. Mo. Vols., 11 June, 1861. Mustered out 14 Nov., 1861. 1st Lieut. 15th Inf., 26 Oct., 1861. Capt., 21 Aug., 1865. Trans. to 24th Inf., 21 Sept., 1866. Unass'd 25 April, 1869. Ass'd to 13th Inf., 14 July, 1869. Retired 31 Aug., 1871.

BROWN, ARTHUR W. [Born in ——. Appointed from ——.]
2nd Lieut. of Inf., 1 Dec., 1899. Unass'd.

BROWN, AUSTIN H.* [Born in Ill. Appointed from Ill.]
2nd Lieut. 4th Inf., 14 June, 1885. 1st Lieut. 22nd Inf., 16 Jan., 1892. Trans. to 4th Inf., 27 Dec., 1892. Capt., 2 March, 1899. Adj., 1 Sept., 1899.

BROWN, EARL I.* [Born in Ga. Appointed from Ga.]
Addl. 2nd Lieut. Eng., 26 April, 1898. 2nd Lieut., 5 July, 1898.

BROWN, EDWARD O. [Born in Wis. Appointed from Wis.]
Addl. 2nd Lieut. Eng., 11 June, 1881. 2nd Lieut., 14 June, 1881. Resigned 1 July, 1882.

BROWN, EDWARD T.* [Born in Me. Appointed from Me.]
2nd Lieut. 5th Art., 13 June, 1873. 1st Lieut., 13 June, 1882. Graduate of the Artillery School, 1876. Cap. 7th Art., 8 March, 1898.

BROWN, FREDK. H. [Born in N. Y. Appointed from Army.]
2nd Lieut. 18th Inf., 30 Oct., 1861. 1st Lieut., 24 March, 1862. Capt., 15 May, 1866. Killed 21 Dec., 1866, in action with Indians, in Dakota. Bvt. Capt., 1 Sept., 1864, for gallant and meritorious service during the Atlanta campaign.

BROWN, FRED R.* [Born in Ill. Appointed from Ill.]
2nd Lieut. 9th Inf., 15 Feb., 1899.

BROWN, GEORGE Le R.* [Born in Mich. Appointed from Mich.]
2nd Lieut. 11th Inf., 14 June, 1872. 1st Lieut., 23 Oct., 1882. Capt., 29 Dec., 1890. Maj. 10th Inf., 12 July, 1899. Col. 4th Tenn., Vols., 13 July, 1898. Mustered out Vols., 6 May, 1899.

BROWN, GEORGE M.* [Born in Mo. Appointed from Mo.]
2nd Lieut. 16th Inf., 12 June, 1890. Resigned 13 April, 1893.

BROWN, GUSTAVUS.* [Born in Va. Appointed from Ky.]
Bvt. 2nd Lieut. 3rd Art., 1 July, 1829. 2nd Lieut., 1 July, 1829. Died 12 July, 1832.

BROWN, HACHALIAH.* [Born in N. Y. Appointed from N. Y.]
Bvt. 2nd Lieut. 4th Art., 1 July, 1842. 2nd Lieut. 3rd Art., 1 March, 1845. 1st Lieut., 3 March, 1847. Reg. Adj., 1 Dec., 1848, to 10 Oct., 1850. Died 22 Aug., 1853. Bvt. Capt., 25 March, 1847, for gallant and meritorious conduct in the affair at Medelin, Mexico.

BROWN, HARVEY.* [Born in N. J. Appointed from N. J.]
2nd Lieut. Light Art., 24 July, 1818. Trans. to 1st Art., 1 June, 1821. Trans. to 4th Art., 16 Aug., 1821. 1st Lieut., 23 Aug., 1821. Capt., 10 April, 1835. Maj. 2nd Art., 9 Jan., 1851. Lieut. Col. 4th Art., 28 April, 1861. Col. 5th Art., 14 May, 1861. Retired 1 Aug., 1863. Died 31 March, 1874. Bvt. Capt., 23 Aug., 1831, for ten years' faithful service in one grade. Bvt. Maj., 21 Nov., 1836, for gallant conduct on several occasions and general efficiency in the war against Florida Indians. Bvt. Lieut. Col., 20 Aug., 1847, for gallant and meritorious conduct in the Battle of Contreras. Bvt. Col., 13 Sept., 1847, for gallant conduct at the Gate of Belen, City of Mexico. Bvt. Brig. Gen., 23 Nov., 1861, for gallant and good conduct during the engagement of 22 and 23 Nov., 1861, between Fort Pickens and the rebel batteries. Bvt. Maj. Gen., 2 Aug., 1866, for distinguished services in the suppression of riot in New York City.

BROWN, HARVEY E. [Born in N. Y. Appointed from Mass.]
Asst. Surg. 70th N. Y. Vols., 29 June, 1861. Maj. and Surg. 70th N. Y. Vols., 27 July, 1861. Resigned 10 Dec., 1862. 1st Lieut. Asst. Surg., 13 April, 1863. Bvt. Capt. and Bvt. Maj., 13 March, 1865, for faithful and meritorious service during the War. Capt. Asst. Surg., 28 July, 1866. Died 20 Aug., 1889.

BROWN, EDWARD O.* [Born in Wis. Appointed from Wis.]
Addl. 2nd Lieut. Eng., 11 June, 1881. 2nd Lieut., 14 June, 1881. Resigned 1 July, 1882.

BROWN, HENRY A. [Born in Ohio. Appointed from Ariz.]
Post Chap., 4 April, 1898.

BUCKNER, SIMON B.* [Born in Ky. Appointed from Ky.]
Bvt. 2nd Lieut 2nd Inf., 1 July, 1844. 2nd Lieut. 6th Inf., 9 May, 1846. R. Q. M., 8 Aug., to 17 Dec., 1847. 1st Lieut., 31 Dec., 1851. Capt. C. S., 3 Nov., 1852. Resigned 26 March, 1855. Bvt. 1st Lieut., 20 Aug., 1847, for gallant conduct at Churubusco. Bvt. Capt., 8 Sept., 1847, for gallant conduct at Molino del Rey.

BUCKNER, WM. H. [Born in Va. Appointed from Va.]
Maj. and Surg. 2nd Light Drag., 6 July, 1812. Disbanded 15 June, 1815. Restored as Hosp. Surg. Mate, 13 Sept., 1815. Trans. to 4th Inf., — Sept., 1816. Post Surg., 18 April, 1818. Died 2 Oct., 1820.

BUDD, GEORGE W. [Born in N. Y. Appointed from N. Y.]
1st Sergt. Co. G, 2nd Iowa Cav., 30 Aug., 1861. 2nd Lieut. 2nd Iowa Cav., 1 June, 1862. Capt., 7 Feb., 1865. Mustered out 19 Sept., 1865. 2nd Lieut. 9th Cav., 17 Aug., 1867. 1st Lieut., 20 April, 1872. Retired 28 June, 1878.

BUDD, OTHO W. [Born in Penn. Appointed from Md.]
2nd Lieut. 4th Cav., 8 Dec., 1868. 1st Lieut., 5 Jan., 1874. Capt., 28 Dec., 1882. Retired for disability 22 April, 1891.

BUDLONG, ALTON H. [Born in R. I. Appointed from the Army.]
Served under name of Chas. A. Howard as Priv. and Corpl. Co. I, 3rd Inf., 9 July, 1870, to 2 Nov., 1872. Priv., Corpl. and Sergt. Co. C, and Q. M. Sergt. 6th Cav., 14 Jan., 1873, to 14 Jan., 1878. Q. M. Sergt. and Sergt. Maj. 6th Cav., 28 Jan., 1878, to 5 Sept., 1880. 2nd Lieut. 9th Cav., 24 June, 1880. Name changed to Budlong by Act of Congress 15 May, 1882. 1st Lieut. 9th Cav., 3 July, 1885. Resigned 12 Jan., 1886.

BUEL, DAVID H.* [Born in Mich. Appointed from N. Y.]
Bvt. 2nd and 2nd Lieut. 1st Drag., 24 June, 1861. 1st Cav., 3 Aug., 1861. Trans. to 3rd Art., 23 Oct., 1861. Trans. to Ord., 24 Oct., 1861. 1st Lieut., 3 March, 1863. Capt., 30 July, 1863. Assassinated 22 July, 1870. Bvt. Maj., 22 July, 1864, for gallant and meritorious service in action in front of Atlanta, Ga. Bvt. Lieut. Col., 13 March, 1865, for meritorious and distinguished service in the campaign from Atlanta, Ga., to Goldsboro', N. C.

BUELL, DON CARLOS.* [Born in Ohio. Appointed from Ind.]
2nd Lieut. 3rd Inf., 1 July, 1841. 1st Lieut., 18 June, 1846. Reg. Adj., 15 Feb., 1847. to 25 Jan., 1848. Bvt. Capt. A. A. G., 25 Jan., 1848. Maj. A. A. G., 25 Feb., 1861. Lieut. Col., 11 May, 1861. Col., 17 July, 1862. Brig. Gen. Vols., 17 May, 1861. Maj. Gen. Vols., 21 March, 1862. Mustered out of Vols., 23 May, 1864. Resigned 1 June, 1864. Bvt. Capt., 23 Sept., 1864, for gallant and meritorious conduct at Monterey. Bvt. Maj., 20 Aug., 1847, for gallant and meritorious conduct at Contreras and Churubusco.

BUELL, GEORGE P. [Born in Ind. Appointed from Ind.]
Lieut. Col. 58th Ind. Vols., 17 Dec., 1861. Col., 24 June, 1862. Bvt. Brig. Gen. Vols., 12 Jan., 1865, for long, faithful and most valuable service, and for able management of pontoon trains. Mustered out 25 July, 1865. Lieut. Col. 29th Inf., 28 July, 1866. Bvt. Col., 2 March, 1867, for gallant and meritorious service in the Battle of Missionary Ridge, Tenn. Bvt. Brig. Gen., 2 March, 1867, for gallant and meritorious service during the War. Trans. to 11th Inf., 15 March, 1869. Col. 15th Inf., 20 March, 1879. Died 31 May, 1883.

BUELL, JAMES W. [Born in N. Y. Appointed from N. Y.]
1st Lieut. Asst. Surg., 5 Aug., 1876. Capt. and Asst. Surg., 5 Aug., 1881. Retired for disability 2 July, 1891. Died 5 Oct., 1897.

BUELL, JOHN L. [Born in Ind. Appointed from Col.]
2nd Lieut 4th Inf., 5 Aug., 1861. R. Q. M., 1 April, to 31 July, 1862. 1st Lieut., 25 Nov., 1861. Resigned 6 Nov., 1862.

BUFFINGTON, ABRAHAM P. [Born in Iowa. Appointed from Iowa.]
2nd Lieut. 7th Inf., 30 Oct., 1884. 1st Lieut. 1st Inf., 10 Sept., 1891. Trans. to 13th Inf., 6 Oct., 1891. Capt. 1st Inf., 7 Jan., 1899. Reg'l Adj., 1 May, 1899. Graduate of the Infantry and Cavalry School, 1887.

BUFFINGTON, ADELBERT R.* [Born in Va. Appointed from Va.]
Bvt. 2nd Lieut. Ord., 6 May, 1861. 2nd Lieut., 14 May, 1861. 1st Lieut., 22 July, 1861. Capt., 3 March, 1863. Bvt. Maj., 13 March, 1865, for faithful and meritorious service in the Ord. Dept. Maj. Ord., 23 June, 1874. Lieut. Col., 1 June, 1881. Col., 28 Feb., 1889. Brig. Gen. and Chief of Ord., 5 April, 1899.

BUFFUM, MARTIN P. [Born in R. I. Appointed from R. I.]
Priv. Co. C, 1st R. I. Vols., 2 May, to 2 Aug., 1861. Capt. 4th R. I. Vols., 30 Oct., 1861. Maj., 10 Oct., 1862. Lieut. Col., 24 Dec., 1862. Resigned 17 Dec., 1864. Lieut. Col. 9th U. S. Vet. Vols., 1 June, 1865. Bvt. Col. Vols., 13 March, 1865, for gallant and meritorious service during the war. Mustered out 10 May, 1866. 2nd Lieut. 15th Inf., 16 March, 1866. 1st Lieut., 11 May, 1867. Resigned 22 Feb., 1877. Bvt. 1st Lieut. and Bvt. Capt., 2 March, 1867, for gallant and meritorious service in the assault after the explosion of the mine in front of Petersburg, Va. Bvt. Maj., 2 March, 1867, for gallant and meritorious service during the war. Died 20 April, 1884.

BUFORD, ABRAM.* [Born in Ky. Appointed from Ky.]
Bvt. 2nd Lieut. 1st Drag., 1 July, 1841. 2nd Lieut., 12 April, 1842. 1st Lieut., 6 Dec., 1846. Capt., 15 July, 1853. Resigned 22 Oct., 1854. Bvt. Capt., 23 Feb., 1847, for gallant and meritorious conduct at Buena Vista.

BUFORD, JOHN, JR.* [Born in Ky. Appointed from Ill.]
Bvt. 2nd Lieut. 1st Drag., 1 July, 1848. 2nd Lieut. 2nd Drag., 17 Feb., 1849. 1st Lieut., 9 July, 1853. R. Q. M., 9 May, 1855. to 4 Aug., 1858. Capt., 9 March, 1859. Maj. A. I. G., 12 Nov., 1861. Brig. Gen. Vols., 27 July, 1862. Maj. Gen. Vols., 1 July, 1863. Died 16 Dec., 1863.

BUFORD, NAPOLEON B.* [Born in Ky. Appointed from Ky.]
Bvt. 2nd Lieut. Art., 1 July, 1827. 2nd Lieut. 3rd Art., 1 July, 1827. Resigned 31 Dec., 1835. Col. 27th Ill. Vols., 10 Aug., 1861. Brig. Gen. Vols., 15 April, 1862. Maj. Gen. Vols., 29 Nov., 1862. Appointment as Maj. Gen. expired 4 March, 1863. Bvt. Maj. Gen. Vols., 13 March, 1865, for gallant and meritorious service during the war. Mustered out 24 Aug., 1865. Died 28 March, 1883.

BUFORD, TEMPLE. [Born in Me. Appointed from Army.]
2nd Lieut. 5th Cav., 19 Feb., 1863. Resigned 11 Jan., 1864.

BUGGE, JENS.* [Born in Wis. Appointed from Minn.]
2nd Lieut. 3rd Inf., 12 June, 1895. 1st Lieut. of Inf., 1 July, 1898. Ass'd to 3rd Inf., 1 Jan., 1899.

BUIST, GEORGE. [Born in S. C. Appointed from S. C.]
Asst. Surg., 12 July, 1842. Resigned 23 Sept., 1842. Asst. Surg., 5 June, 1844. Resigned 31 Dec., 1845.

BULLARD, ROBERT L.* [Born in Ala. Appointed from Ala.]
2nd Lieut. 10th Inf., 14 June, 1885. 1st Lieut. 6th Inf., 2 April, 1892. Trans. to 10th Inf., 28 Sept., 1892. Capt. and C. S., 22 June, 1898. Maj. 1st Batt. Ala. Col. Inf., 2 June, 1898. Col. 3rd Ala. Vols., 6 Aug., 1898. Mustered out 20 March, 1899. Col. 39th U. S. Vols., 17 Aug., 1899.

BULLIS, JOHN L. [Born in N. Y. Appointed from Ark.]
Corpl. Co. H, 126th N. Y. Vols., 8 Aug., 1862. Discharged 17 Aug., 1864. Capt. 118th U. S. Col Troops, 18 Aug., 1864. Mustered out 6 Feb., 1866. 2nd Lieut. 41st Inf., 3 Sept., 1867. Trans. to 24th Inf., 11 Nov., 1869. 1st Lieut., 20 June, 1873. Bvt. Capt., 27 Feb., 1890, for gallant services in action against Indians at Remolina, Mexico, 18 May, 1873, and on the Pecos River, Tex.,26 April, 1875. Bvt. Maj., 27 Feb., 1890, for gallant services in action against Indians near Saragossa, Mexico, 30 July, 1876, and in action against Indians in the Burro Mountains, Mexico, 3 May, 1881. Capt., 29 April, 1886. Maj. and P. M., 29 Jan., 1897.

BULLOCK, EDWIN C.* [Born in N. J. Appointed from N. J.]
2nd Lieut. 7th Cav., 13 June, 1883. 1st Lieut. of Cav. (4th), 25 Feb., 1891. Trans. to 7th Cav., 1 Dec., 1891. Died 15 Dec., 1896.

BULLOCK, ERASMUS D. [Born in N. C. Appointed from N. C.]
1st Lieut. 2nd Drag., 11 June, 1836. Capt., 29 Jan., 1838. Resigned 1 Feb., 1841.

BUMPUS, EDWARD A. [Born in Mass. Appointed from Mass.]
Priv. Co. A, 1st Mass. Heavy Art., 8 May, 1898, to 4 Aug., 1898. 2nd Lieut. 21st Inf., 9 July, 1898. 1st Lieut. 9th Inf., 8 July, 1899.

BUNDEL, CHARLES M.* [Born in Pa. Appointed from Pa.]
2nd Lieut. 4th Inf., 15 Feb., 1899.

BUNDY, OMAR.* [Born in Ind. Appointed from Ind.]
2nd Lieut. 2nd Inf., 13 June, 1883. Trans. to 3rd Inf., 13 May, 1884. 1st Lieut., 26 May, 1890. Capt. 6th Inf., 26 April, 1898. Reg. Q. M., 10 March, 1899. Graduate of the Infantry and Cavalry School, 1887. Capt. C. S., 12 May, 1898 (declined).

BUNNELL, GEORGE W., Jr.* [Born in Cal. Appointed from Cal.]
2nd Lieut. 4th Art., 15 Feb., 1899.

BUNTING, JOSEPH P. [Born in Pa. Appointed from Pa.]
Ensign Rifles, 4 Jan., 1813. 3rd Lieut. 2nd Art., 14 May, 1813. 2nd Lieut., 26 June, 1813. Trans. to Corps Art., 12 May, 1814. Disbanded 15 June, 1815. 2nd Lieut. 4th Inf., 13 Feb., 1818. 1st Lieut., 24 Feb., 1818. Dismissed 8 Jan., 1819.

BURBANK, CLAYTON S. [Born in Ky. Appointed from Ky.]
2nd Lieut. 10th Inf., 7 March, 1867. 1st Lieut., 24 March, 1878. Capt., 21 Aug., 1888. Died 8 March, 1898.

BURBANK, JACOB E. [Born in Penn. Appointed from Ind.]
Addl. P. M. Vols., 19 Feb., 1863. Vacated commission 17 Jan., 1867. Maj. and P. M. U. S. A., 17 Jan., 1867. Retired 3 March, 1875.

BURBANK, JAMES B. [Born in Conn. Appointed from the Army.]
Asst. Q. M. G., State of Conn., Oct., 1861, to 24 Nov., 1862. 1st Lieut. and Adj. 20th Conn. Vols., 24 Nov., 1862. Capt., 4 June, 1863. Resigned 17 Dec., 1863. Priv. 3rd Art., 14 May, 1864. Sergt. Maj., 19 May, 1864. 2nd Lieut. 3rd Art., 12 March, 1865. Bvt. 1st Lieut., 13 March, 1865, for gallant and meritorious service during the war. Bvt. Maj. Vols., 13 March, 1865, for gallant conduct in the Battle of Chancellorsville and Gettysburg. 1st Lieut., 28 July, 1866. Capt. 3rd Art., 3 Nov., 1882. Maj. 5th Art., 8 March, 1898. Graduate of the Artillery School, 1872.

BURBANK, JOHN G.* [Born in Mass. Appointed from Mass.]
2nd Lieut. 8th Inf., 1 July, 1841. 1st Lieut., 31 Dec., 1845. R. Q. M., 31 March, to 10 Sept., 1847. Died 10 Sept., 1847, of wounds received in Battle of Molino del Rey, Mex.

BURBANK, NATHANIEL. [Born in Me. Appointed from Mass.]
Priv. Co. B, 15th Mass. Vols , 8 July, 1863. to 15 Sept., 1864. 2nd Lieut. 10th U. S. Col. Art., 17 Sept., 1864. 1st Lieut., 27 Sept., 1864. Bvt. Capt. Vols., 13 March, 1865, for gallant and meritorious service during the war. Mustered out 22 Feb , 1867. 2nd Lieut. 37th Inf., 22 Jan., 1867. Unass'd 19 May, 1869 Ass'd to 5th Inf., 14 July, 1869. Resigned 1 Aug., 1869. Bvt. 1st Lieut., 2 March, 1867, for gallant and meritorious service at the Battle of Bristow Station, Va.

BURBANK, SIDNEY.* [Born in Mass. Appointed from Mass.]
Bvt. 2nd Lieut. 1st Inf., 1 July, 1829. 2nd Lieut., 1 July, 1829. 1st Lieut., 29 Oct., 1836. Capt., 8 Nov., 1839. Maj. 2nd Inf., 8 Dec., 1855. Trans. to 1st Inf., 2 July, 1856. Lieut. Col. 13th Inf., 14 May, 1861. Col. 2nd Inf., 16 Sept., 1862. Bvt. Brig. Gen., 13 March, 1865, for gallant and meritorious service in the Battle of Gettysburg, Pa. Unass'd 15 March, 1869. Retired 1 May, 1870. Died 7 Dec., 1882.

BURBANK, SIDNEY S. [Born in Tex. Appointed from the Army.]
Priv., Corpl. and Sergt. Cos. H and K, 19th Inf., 6 Sept., 1897, to 16 Nov., 1899. 2nd Lieut. 6th Inf., 1 Oct., 1899.

BURBANK, SULLIVAN. [Born in Mass. Appointed from Mass.]
Sergt. Maj., 15th Inf., Aug., 1799, to June, 1800. 1st Lieut. 21st Inf., 12 March, 1812 Capt., 13 March, 1813. Trans to 5th Inf., 17 May, 1815. Maj. 7th Inf., 20 Aug., 1828. Lieut. Col. 5th Inf., 21 Sept., 1836 Resigned 30 June, 1839. Bvt. Maj., 25 July, 1814, for gallant conduct at the Battle of Niagara. Died 30 Sept., 1862.

BURBANK, SULLIVAN W. [Born in N. Y. Appointed from Ky.]
2nd Lieut. 2nd Cav., 27 March, 1861. 1st Lieut., 10 May, 1861. Trans. to 14th Inf., 22 June, 1861. Capt., 3 March, 1862. Died 9 June, 1864, of wounds received in Battle of Wilderness, Va.

BURBRIDGE, CHARLES. [Born in Conn. Appointed from Army.]
Sergt. 25th Inf., 8 March, 1813, to Nov., 1813. Ensign 25th Inf., 24 Nov., 1813. 2nd

CAMP, FREDK. E. [Born in Conn. Appointed from Conn.]
2nd Lieut. 14th Conn. Vols., 18 Nov., 1862. 1st Lieut., 6 April, 1863. Mustered out 30 Sept., 1863. Capt. 29th Conn. Vols., 23 Jan., 1864. Maj. 24 Nov., 1864. Lieut. Col., 1 Jan., 1865. Mustered out 6 Nov., 1865. 2nd Lieut. 14th Inf., 23 Feb., 1866. 1st Lieut., 23 Feb., 1866. Trans. to 32nd Inf., 21 Sept., 1866. Capt., 12 Dec., 1868. Unass'd 19 April, 1869. Ass'd to 2nd Inf., 1 Jan., 1871. Resigned 20 July, 1875.

CAMP, WM. H.* [Born in Wis. Appointed from Wis.]
2nd Lieut. 17th Inf., 1 July, 1886. Resigned 14 Sept., 1889.

CAMP, WM. G. [Born in ——. Appointed from Army.]
Sergt. 19th Inf., 3 Feb., 1813, to March, 1814. Ensign 2nd Rifles, 17 March, 1814. 3rd Lieut., 1 Oct., 1814. Disbanded 15 June, 1815. 2nd Lieut. 5th Inf., 13 Feb., 1818. R. Q. M., 1 Aug., 1819, to 1 June, 1821. Disbanded 1 June, 1821.

CAMPBELL, ANDREW. [Born in Ireland. Appointed from Tenn.]
Priv. Co. G, 13th Tenn. Cav., 6 April, 1864. 1st Lieut., 13 Oct., 1864 Mustered out 28 Nov., 1865. 2nd Lieut. 19th Inf., 23 Feb., 1866. 1st Lieut., 23 Nov., 1866. Resigned 14 May, 1868.

CAMPBELL, ARCHIBALD.* [Born in N. Y. Appointed from N. Y.]
Bvt. 2nd Lieut. 6th Inf., 1 July, 1835. Resigned 30 Sept., 1836. Died 26 July, 1887.

CAMPBELL, ARCHIBALD.* [Born in Pa. Appointed from N. Y.]
Addl. 2nd Lieut. 5th Art., 12 June, 1889. 2nd Lieut. 3rd Art., 10 Dec., 1889. 1st Lieut., 7 June, 1897. Graduate of the Artillery School, 1894.

CAMPBELL, ARCHIBALD B. [Born in Penn. Appointed from Penn.]
Asst. Surg. Vols., 12 July, 1847. Discharged 25 Aug., 1848. Maj. Surg. 20th Pa. Vols., 30 April, 1861. Mustered out 6 Aug., 1861. Surg. U. S. Vols., 2 Sept., 1861. Mustered out 28 Nov., 1865. Asst. Surg., 14 Oct., 1867. Capt. and Surg., 14 Oct., 1872. Died 1 Sept., 1878.

CAMPBELL, CALEB B. [Born in ——. Appointed from Ohio.]
Ensign 19th Inf., 24 Oct., 1813. Trans. to 25th Inf., — Aug., 1814. 2nd Lieut., 1 Oct., 1814. Trans. to 6th Inf., 17 May, 1815. Resigned 10 Sept., 1816.

CAMPBELL, CHAS. C.* [Born in Mo. Appointed from Mo.]
2nd Lieut. 1st Cav., 6 May, 1861. Dismissed 6 June, 1861.

CAMPBELL, CHAS. E. [Born in Prince Edward's Island. Appointed from N. Y.]
Priv. 83rd N. Y. Vols., 27 March, 1862. Discharged 6 March, 1863. 2nd Lieut. Vet. Res. Corps, 30 Oct., 1863. 1st Lieut., 10 May, 1865. Mustered out 27 Nov., 1865. 2nd Lieut. 42nd Inf., 28 July, 1866. Cashiered 30 July, 1868. 2nd Lieut. 42nd Inf., 6 Jan., 1869. Unassigned 22 April, 1869. Ass'd to 3rd Inf., 22 July, 1869. Resigned 15 July, 1872.

CAMPBELL, CHAS. H. [Born in D. C. Appointed from D. C.]
Cadet Mil. Acad., 1 July, 1863, to 25 July, 1864. 2nd Lieut. 1st N. Y. Art., 4 Feb., 1865. Bvt. 1st Lieut. Vols., 9 April, 1865, for meritorious service during the campaign terminating with the surrender of the insurgent army under Gen. R. E. Lee. Capt. A. A. G. Vols., 1 June, 1865. Mustered out 11 May, 1866. 2nd Lieut. 6th Cav., 25 July, 1866. Bvt. 1st Lieut. and Bvt. Capt., 2 March, 1867, for gallant and meritorious service in the Battle of Petersburg, Va. 1st Lieut. 6th Cav., 7 May, 1867. Capt., 20 Sept., 1874. Resigned 15 Feb., 1881.

CAMPBELL, CHAS. T. [Born in Penn. Appointed from Penn.]
1st Lieut. Inf., 11 Feb., 1847; 11th Inf., 9 April, 1847. Capt., 12 Aug., 1847. Discharged 14 Aug., 1848. Capt. Batty A, Pa. Light Art., 29 May, 1861. Lieut. Col. 1st Pa. Art., 5 Aug., 1861. Col., 13 Sept., 1861. Brig. Gen. Vols., 29 Nov., 1862. Appointment expired 4 March, 1863. Brig. Gen. Vols., 13 March, 1863. Mustered out 15 Jan., 1866.

CAMPBELL, DANIEL H. [Born in Va. Appointed from Ky.]
2nd Lieut. Rifles, 18 April, 1818. 1st Lieut., 25 April, 1819. Resigned 2 Nov., 1819.

CAMPBELL, GEORGE J. [Born in Scotland. Appointed from Army.]
Priv. Drag., Mil. Acad., 13 Jan., 1851. Priv. Co. A, Eng. Batt., 24 May, 1853. Artificer, 1 Jan., 1854. Discharged 28 Nov., 1855. Artificer Co. A, Eng. Batt., 28 Nov., 1855. Discharged 28 Nov., 1860. Priv. Co. C, 3rd Art., 11 Dec., 1860. Corpl., 1 Oct., 1861. Sergt., 1 Jan., 1862. Q. M. Sergt., 1 Jan., 1863. 2nd Lieut. 3rd Cav., 18 May, 1864. 1st Lieut., 7 Jan., 1866. Retired 29 July, 1868.

CAMPBELL, HARRY R. [Born in Ind. Appointed from Ind.]
2nd Lieut. 22nd Inf., 9 July, 1898. 1st Lieut. 8th Inf., 14 May, 1899. Trans. to 1st Inf., 17 Feb., 1900.

CAMPBELL, HENRY M. [Born in Md. Appointed from Md.]
3rd Lieut. 2nd Art., 19 July, 1813. 2nd Lieut., 12 Oct., 1813. Trans. to Corps Art., 12 May, 1814. Resigned 1 May, 1817. Bvt. 1st Lieut., 5 July, 1814, for distinguished service at the Battle of Chippewa. Bvt. Capt., 25 July, 1814, for distinguished service at the Battle of Niagara Falls. Died 12 May, 1824.

CAMPBELL, JOHN. [Born in N. Y. Appointed from N. Y.]
Asst. Surg., 13 Dec., 1847. Maj. and Surg., 21 May, 1861. Col. Med. Direc. (Act 25 Feb., 1865), 25 Feb., 1865. Bvt. Lieut. Col. and Bvt. Col., 13 March, 1865, for faithful and meritorious service during the war Relieved as Col. Med. Direc., 30 June, 1865. Lieut. Col. Surg., 8 Nov., 1877. Col. and Surg., 7 Dec., 1884. Retired by operation of law 16 Sept., 1885.

CAMPBELL, JOHN A.* [Born in N. Y. Appointed from S. C.]
Priv. Co. K, 5th Mo. Vols., 10 May, to 26 Aug., 1861. Priv. Co. H, and Com. Sergt. 3rd Mo. Vols., 7 Nov., 1861, to 6 Oct., 1863. Cadet at Mil. Acad., 19 Oct., 1863. 2nd Lieut. 2nd Art., 17 June, 1867. 1st Lieut., 24 July, 1874. Died 29 Oct., 1875.

CAMPBELL, JOHN A. [Born in Ohio. Appointed from Ohio.]
1st Lieut. 1st Ohio Vols., 31 Oct., 1861. Maj. A. A. G. Vols., 27 Oct., 1862. Lieut. Col. A. A. G. Vols., 31 Jan., to 1 Aug., 1865. Bvt. Col. Vols., 13 March, 1865, for gallant and meritorious service, and Bvt. Brig. Gen. Vols., 13 March, 1865, for courage in the field and marked ability and fidelity. Mustered out 1 Sept., 1866. 2nd Lieut. 5th Art., 10 Oct., 1867. Resigned 15 April, 1869. Bvt. 1st Lieut., 10 Oct., 1867, for gallant and meritorious service during the war, especially in the Battle of Shiloh, Tenn. Bvt. Capt., 10 Oct., 1867, for gallant and meritorious service during

the war, especially in the Battle of Stone River, Tenn. Bvt. Maj., 10 Oct., 1867, for gallant and meritorious service during the war, especially in the Battle of Resaca, Ga. Bvt. Lieut. Col., 10 Oct., 1867, for gallant and meritorious service during the war, especially in the Battle of Franklin, Tenn. Died 15 July, 1880.

CAMPBELL, JOHN B. [Born in S. C. Appointed from Ga.]
Capt. 13th Inf., 9 April, 1847. Disbanded 15 July, 1848.

CAMPBELL, JOHN M. [Born in Mich. Appointed from N. Y.]
Priv. Co. B, 71st N. Y. Vols., 10 May, 1898, to 18 Sept., 1898. 2nd Lieut. 25th Inf., 9 Sept., 1898. 1st Lieut. 5th Inf., 18 Jan., 1900.

CAMPBELL, JOHN S. [Born in Penn. Appointed from Penn.]
1st Lieut. 12th Inf., 14 May, 1861. Resigned 19 Jan., 1863.

CAMPBELL, JOSEPH B.* [Born in Penn. Appointed from N. H.]
Bvt. 2nd Lieut., 2nd Lieut. and 1st Lieut. 4th Art., 24 June, 1861. Bvt. Capt., 30 Aug., 1862, for gallant and meritorious service in the Battle of Bull Run (2nd), Va. Bvt. Maj., 17 Sept., 1862, for gallant and meritorious service in the Battle of Antietam, Md. Capt. A. A. de C., 16 May, 1862. Mustered out as Capt. A. A. de C., 10 July, 1865. Capt. 16th Inf., 28 July, 1866, declined. Capt. 4th Art., 5 Feb., 1867. Maj. 2nd Art., — ——, 1891. Died 28 Aug., 1891.

CAMPBELL, LAFAYETTE E. [Born in Ohio. Appointed from Ohio.]
Priv. Co. F, 3rd Iowa Cav., 20 July, 1862. Mustered out 22 Feb., 1865. 1st Lieut. 3rd U. S. Vols., 22 Feb., 1865. Mustered out 29 Nov., 1865. 2nd Lieut. 15th Inf., 11 May, 1866. Trans. to 33rd Inf., 21 Sept., 1866. 1st Lieut., 11 Oct., 1868. Unass'd 3 May, 1869. Ass'd to 22nd Inf., 23 July, 1869. Capt. A. Q. M., 29 May, 1876. Resigned commission of 1st Lieut. 22nd Inf., 28 June, 1876. Retired for disability, with rank of Maj., 11 Dec., 1892.

CAMPBELL, NEIL A. [Born in R. I. Appointed from R. I.]
2nd Lieut. 19th Inf., 10 April, 1899.

CAMPBELL, NICHOLAS L. [Born in N. Y. Appointed from N. Y.]
Asst. Surg., 23 Aug., 1847. Dismissed 4 Aug., 1852.

CAMPBELL, PETER. [Born in Canada. Appointed from the Army.]
Priv. and Corpl. Co. G, 33rd N. Y. Vols., 22 May, 1861, to 24 March, 1862. Corpl. and Sergt. H, and Sergt. Maj. 14th N. Y. Art., 13 Nov., 1863, to 23 June, 1865. 2nd Lieut. 14th N. Y. Art., 24 June, 1865. Mustered out 26 Aug., 1865. Priv., Cor-Sergt. and 1st Sergt., D, and Q. M. Sergt. and Sergt. Maj. 18th Inf., 12 Jan., 1871, to 11 July, 1880. 2nd Lieut. 18th Inf., 24 June, 1880. Died 27 Jan., 1887.

CAMPBELL, QUINTIN.* [Born in Mo. Appointed from Mo.]
2nd Lieut. 5th Inf., 18 June, 1866. Reg. Adj., 5 Aug., 1869, to 31 Jan., 1870. 1st Lieut., 1 Jan., 1871. Resigned 31 Aug., 1875.

CAMPBELL, REUBEN P.* [Born in N. C. Appointed from N. C.]
2nd Lieut. 2nd Drag., 1 July, 1840. 1st Lieut., 3 Nov., 1845. Capt., 8 Aug., 1851. Resigned 11 May, 1861. Bvt. Capt., 23 Feb., 1847, for gallant and meritorious conduct at Buena Vista, Mex.

CAMPBELL, STEPHEN H.* [Born in Vt. Appointed from Vt.]
2nd Lieut. 2nd Art., 1 July, 1838. 2nd Lieut. Eng., 7 July, 1838. 1st Lieut., 1 July, 1839. Died 1 Jan., 1845.

CAMPBELL, THOMAS L. [Born in Scotland. Appointed from N. Y.]
1st Lieut. Asst. Dep. Com. Ord., 12 Aug., 1812. Capt., 5 Aug., 1813. Dismissed 21 May, 1817.

CAMPBELL, THOMPSON, Jr. [Born in Cal. Appointed from Army.]
2nd Lieut. 17th Inf., 17 Aug., 1864. 1st Lieut., 17 Aug., 1864. Wholly retired 19 Feb., 1866.

CAMPBELL, WM. A. [Born in N. J. Appointed from the Army.]
Priv., Corpl. and Sergt. Co. K, 12th Inf., 13 Oct., 1885, to 5 March, 1889. 2nd Lieut. 9th Inf., 11 Feb., 1889. 1st Lieut. 22nd Inf., 16 Feb., 1896. Capt., 16 May, 1899. Graduate of the Infantry and Cavalry School, 1893.

CAMPBELL, WM. J. [Born in Ireland. Appointed from Penn.]
Priv. Co. A, 18th Penn. Vols., 24 April, 1861. Discharged 5 Aug., 1861. Priv. Co. A, 95th Penn. Vols., 21 Aug., 1861. Com. Sergt., 16 Oct., 1861. Sergt. Maj., 21 July, 1862. Discharged 10 Feb., 1863. 1st Lieut. 95th Penn. Vols., 10 Feb., 1863. Mustered out 2 Nov., 1864. 2nd Lieut. 22nd Inf., 21 May, 1867. 1st Lieut., 12 May, 1875. Died 17 Dec., 1886.

CAMPION, WM. H. [Born in N. J. Appointed from N. J.]
2nd Lieut. 5th N. J. Vols., 24 Aug., 1861. Resigned 11 May, 1862. 2nd Lieut. Vet. Res. Corps, 1 Oct., 1863. 1st Lieut., 25 March, 1865. Mustered out 30 June, 1866 2nd Lieut. 18th Inf., 22 Jan., 1867. 1st Lieut., 24 Oct., 1867. Unass'd 26 April, 1869. Ass'd to 4th Inf., 15 Dec., 1870. Cashiered 17 May, 1872.

CANBY, EDWARD R. S.* [Born in Ky. Appointed from Ind.]
2nd Lieut. 2nd Inf., 1 July, 1839. 1st Lieut., 18 June, 1846. Bvt. Capt. A. A. G., 3 March, 1847. Maj. 10th Inf., 3 March, 1855. Col. 19th Inf., 14 May, 1861. Brig. Gen., 28 July, 1866. Murdered by Modoc Indians in Oregon, 11 April, 1873. Bvt. Maj., 20 Aug., 1847, for gallant and meritorious conduct at Contreras and Churubusco. Bvt. Lieut. Col., 13 Sept., 1847, for gallant conduct at Belen Gate of the City of Mexico. Bvt. Brig. Gen., 13 March, 1865, for gallant and meritorious sevice at the Battle of Valverde, N. Mex. Bvt. Maj. Gen., 13 March, 1865, for gallant and meritorious service in the capture of Fort Blakely and Mobile, Ala.

CANBY, JAMES P. [Born in Del. Appointed from Del.]
Addl. P. M., 28 May, 1864. Bvt. Lieut. Col. Vols., 8 Jan., 1867, for faithful service in the Pay Dept. Maj. and P. M., 17 Jan., 1867. Vacated commission of Addl. P. M., 17 Jan., 1867. Lieut. Col. and Dep. P. M. G., 6 Jan., 1893. Col. and Asst. P. M. G., 24 Feb., 1896. Retired by operation of law 7 Jan., 1897.

CANBY, SAML. [Born in Del. Appointed from Del.]
1st Sergt. Co. I, 4th N. J. Vols., 20 May, to 25 July, 1861. 1st Lieut. and Adj. 2nd Del. Inf., 25 July, 1861, to 28 Nov., 1861. 2nd Lieut. 4th Art., 21 Oct., 1861. 1st Lieut., 5 Aug., 1862. Resigned 1 July, 1868. Bvt. 1st Lieut., 7 April, 1862, for gallant and meritorious service at the Battle of Shiloh, Tenn. Bvt. Capt., 3 July, 1863,

for gallant and meritorious service at the Battle of Gettysburg, Penn. Bvt. Maj., 13 March, 1865, for gallant and meritorious service at the Battle of Franklin, Tenn.

CANDEE, GEORGE W. [Born in N. J. Appointed from Ill.]
Addl. P. M., 23 Feb., 1864. Mustered out 15 Jan., 1866. Maj. and P. M., 17 Jan., 1867. Lieut. Col. and D. P. M. G., 22 Jan., 1893. Col. and Asst. P. M. G., 7 Jan., 1897. Died 10 June, 1898.

CANFIELD, ANDREW N. [Born in Penn. Appointed from Iowa.]
Priv. Co. D, and Sergt. Maj. 5th Iowa Vols., 15 July, 1861, to 1 Sept., 1864. 1st Sergt. Troop G, 5th Iowa Cav., 1 Sept., 1864. 1st Lieut., 22 Feb., 1865. Mustered out 11 Aug., 1865. 2nd Lieut. 13th Inf., 23 Feb., 1866. 1st Lieut., 7 April, 1866. Resigned 10 April, 1869.

CANFIELD, AUGUSTUS.* [Born in N. J. Appointed from N. J.]
Bvt. 2nd Lieut. 1st Art., 1 July, 1822. 2nd Lieut., 1 July, 1822. Trans. to ——. 4th Art., 18 Feb., 1823. 1st Lieut., 1 March, 1830. Bvt. Capt. Asst. Top. Eng., 14 Sept., 1834. Capt. Top. Eng., 7 July, 1838. Died 18 April, 1854.

CANFIELD, CHAS. W. [Born in N. J. Appointed from N. J.]
Cadet at Mil. Acad., 1 July, 1853, to 26 April, 1854. 2nd Lieut. 2nd Drag., 26 April, 1861. 1st Lieut., 14 May, 1861. Trans. to 2nd Cav., 3 Aug., 1861. Maj. 6th Mo. State Militia Cav., 22 April, 1862. Lieut. Col., 29 April, 1862. Resigned Vol. service 10 June, 1862. Capt., 17 July, 1862. Killed 9 June, 1863, at the Battle of Beverly Ford, Va.

CANTON, THOS. M. [Born in Ireland. Appointed from N. Y.]
2nd Lieut. 69th N. Y. Militia, 9 May, to 3 Aug., 1861 1st Lieut. 69th N. Y. Vols., 26 May, 1862. 1st Lieut. 182nd N. Y. Vols, 17 Nov., 1862. Capt., 12 Feb., 1863. Mustered out 15 May, 1865. Capt. 4th U. S. Vet. Vols., 5 Aug., 1865. Mustered out 16 March, 1866. 2nd Lieut 25th Inf., 28 July, 1866. Trans. to 18th Inf., 26 April, 1869 Cashiered 17 July, 1873. Bvt. 1st Lieut., 2 March, 1867, for gallant and meritorious service at the Battle of Spottsylvania, Va. Bvt. Capt., 2 March, 1867, for gallant and meritorious service at the Battle of Reams' Station, Va.

CANTWELL, EDWARD. [Born in S. C. Appointed from N. C.]
2nd Lieut. Inf., 17 March, 1847; 12th Inf., 9 April, 1847. Resigned 21 Feb., 1848.

CANTWELL, JOHN T.* [Born in N. Y. Appointed from N. Y.]
1st Lieut. Eng., 13 June, 1864. Accidentally killed 18 April, 1865.

CAPRON, ALLYN.* [Born in Fla. Appointed from N. C.]
2nd Lieut. 1st Art., 17 June, 1867. 1st Lieut., 19 Aug., 1873. Capt., 4 Dec., 1888. Honor graduate of the Artillery School, 1873. Died 18 Sept., 1898.

CAPRON, ALLYN K. [Born in N. Y. Appointed from the Army.]
Priv., Corpl. and Sergt. Troop B, 4th Cav., 20 Oct., 1890, to 3 Nov., 1893. 2nd Lieut. of Inf. (5th), 7 Oct., 1893. Trans. to 7th Cav., 30 Nov., 1894. Killed in action at La Quasima, Cuba, 24 June, 1898.

CAPRON, ERASTUS A.* [Born in Conn. Appointed from N. Y.]
Bvt. 2nd Lieut. 1st Art., 1 July, 1833. 2nd Lieut., 31 May, 1834. 1st Lieut., 19 Nov., 1836. Capt., 16 Feb., 1847. Killed in Battle of Churubusco, Mexico, 20 Aug., 1847.

CAPRON, SETH M.* [Born in R. I. Appointed from N. Y.]
Bvt. 2nd and 2nd Lieut. 5th Inf., 1 July, 1821. 1st Lieut., 21 Oct., 1826. Resigned 31 May, 1827. Died 30 Nov, 1878.

CAPRON, THADDEUS H. [Born in Wis. Appointed from Ill.]
Priv. Co. C, 55th Ill. Vols., 9 Sept., 1861. Q. M. Sergt., 25 Nov., 1862. 2nd Lieut. 55th Ill. Vols., 1 March, 1863. 1st Lieut., 10 Oct., 1863. Capt. A. Q. M., Vols., 1 June, 1865. Maj. Q. M. Vols., 6 June, to 1 Aug., 1865. Mustered out 31 Oct., 1865. 2nd Lieut. 9th Inf., 22 Jan., 1867. 1st Lieut., 8 Nov., 1871. Retired for disability, 30 Aug., 1887.

CARAHER, ANDREW P. [Born in Ireland. Appointed from Mass.]
Capt. 28th Mass. Vols., 13 Dec., 1861. Maj., 15 Nov., 1862. Maj. Vet. Res. Corps, 21 Sept., 1863. Lieut. Col., 1 Oct., 1863. Col. 2nd U. S. Vols., 18 Feb., 1865. Mustered out as Col. 2nd U. S. Vols., 7 Nov., 1865. Mustered out of Vet. Res. Corps, 6 Jan., 1867. 1st Lieut. 43rd Inf., 28 July, 1866. Bvt. Capt., 2 March, 1867, for gallant and meritorious service in the Battle of Fredericksburg, Va. Bvt. Maj., 2 March, 1867, for gallant and meritorious service in the Battle of Gettysburg, Penn. Trans. to 1st Inf., 8 April, 1869. Trans. to 8th Cav., 1 Jan., 1871. Capt., 15 Jan., 1873. Died 4 April, 1885.

CARBAUGH, HARVEY C.* [Born in Pa. Appointed from Ill.]
2nd Lieut. 5th Art., 13 June, 1882. 1st Lieut., 25 April, 1888. Capt. 4th Art., 2 March, 1899. Graduate of the Art. School, 1896. Capt. and A. A. G. Vols., 12 May, 1898. Lieut. Col. and J. A. Vols., 15 Nov., 1898, to 17 April, 1899. Maj. and J. A. Vols., 17 April, 1899.

CARD, BENJAMIN C. [Born in R. I. Appointed from Kansas.]
1st Lieut. 12th Inf., 27 Sept., 1861. Capt. A. Q. M., 27 Sept., 1861. Resigned commission of 1st Lieut. 12th Inf., 11 June, 1864. Col. Q. M. (Act 4 July, 1864), 2 Aug., 1864. Bvt. Maj., Lieut. Col., and Col., 13 March, 1865, for faithful and meritorious service during the war. Bvt. Brig. Gen., 13 March, 1865, for faithful and meritorious service in the Q. M. Dept. during the war. Relieved as Col. Q. M. (Act 4 July 1864), 1 Jan., 1867. Maj. Q. M., 6 June, 1872. Lieut. Col. and D. Q. M. G., 31 Aug., 1883. Retired by operation of law, 15 Feb., 1889.

CAREY, ASA B.* [Born in Conn. Appointed from Conn.]
Bvt. 2nd Lieut. 6th Inf., 1 July, 1858. 2nd Lieut. 7th Inf., 22 Oct., 1858. 1st Lieut. 13th Inf., 14 May, 1861. Capt. 24 Oct., 1861. Bvt. Maj., 28 March, 1862, for gallant and meritorious service at the Battle of Apache Canon, New Mexico. Bvt. Lieut. Col., 13 March, 1865, for gallant and meritorious service in the war against the Navajo Indians. Maj. and P. M., 5 Oct., 1867. Vacated commission of Capt. 13th Inf., 11 Oct., 1867. Lieut. Col. and D. P. M. G., 27 March, 1895. Col. and Asst. P. M. G., 10 June, 1898. Brig. Gen. and P. M. G., 30 Jan., 1899. Retired by operation of law, 12 July, 1899.

CAREY, EDWARD C.* [Born in N. Mex. Appointed from N. Mex.]
2nd Lieut. 16th Inf., 12 June, 1893. 1st Lieut., 26 April, 1898. Capt. and A. A. G. Vols., 9 Nov., 1898, to 7 April, 1899. Maj. 42nd U. S. Vols., 17 Aug., 1899.

CAREY, STEPHEN H. [Born in Ohio. Appointed from Ohio.]
Priv. and Sergt. Co. K, 57th Ohio Inf. Vols., 18 Oct., 1861. 2nd Lieut., 1 Jan., 1863. 1st Lieut., 3 June, 1864. Bvt. Capt. Vols., 13 March, 1865, for gallant and meritorious services during the war. Mustered out 11 Nov., 1864. 2nd Lie . 2nd Inf., 23 Feb., 1866. 1st Lieut., 8 Aug., 1866. Cashiered 29 Dec., 1868.

CARGILL, NATHL. E. [Born in Va. Appointed from Va.]
2nd Lieut. 11th Inf., 10 May, 1848. Disbanded 15 Aug., 1848.

CARLAND, JOHN. [Born in Ireland. Appointed from Mich.]
2nd Lieut. 23rd Mich. Vols., 22 July, 1862. Capt., 12 Sept., 1862. Maj., 25 March, 1865. Mustered out 28 June, 1865. 2nd Lieut. 6th Inf., 7 March, 1867. 1st Lieut., 31 Dec., 1868. Unass'd 22 April, 1869. Ass'd to 6th Inf., 18 Oct., 1869. Capt., 25 Jan., 1889. Retired 3 Jan., 1890. Died 24 Feb., 1890.

CARLETON, GUY.* [Born in Tex. Appointed from Tex.]
2nd Lieut. 2nd Cav., 11 June, 1881. 1st Lieut., 24 July, 1888. Capt. 10th Cav., 1 July, 1898. Adj., 30 April, 1899. Graduate of the Infantry and Cavalry School, 1887.

CARLETON, HENRY G. [Born in N. Mex. Appointed from Cal.]
2nd Lieut. 8th Cav., 1 Oct., 1873. Resigned 1 Aug., 1876.

CARLIN, WM. D. [Born in Ohio. Appointed from Ohio.]
Asst. Surg. 15th Inf., 9 April, 1847. Disbanded 7 Aug., 1848.

CARLIN, WM. P.* [Born in Ill. Appointed from Ill.]
Bvt. 2nd Lieut. 6th Inf., 1 July, 1850. 2nd Lieut., 15 April 1851. 1st Lieut., 3 March, 1855. Capt., 2 March, 1861. Col. 38th Ill. Vols., 15 Aug., 1861. Brig. Gen. Vols., 29 Nov., 1862 Bvt. Lieut. Col., 24 Nov., 1863, for gallant and meritorious service in the Battle of Chattanooga, Tenn. Maj. 16th Inf., 8 Feb., 1864. Bvt. Col., 1 Sept., 1864, for gallant and meritorious service in the Battle of Jonesboro', Ga. Bvt. Brig. Gen., 13 March, 1865, for gallant and meritorious service in the Battle of Bentonville, N. C. Bvt. Maj. Gen., 13 March, 1865, for gallant and meritorious service in the field during the war. Bvt. Maj. Gen. Vols., 19 March, 1865, for gallant and meritorious service during the war. Mustered out of Vol. service, 24 Aug., 1865. Trans. to 34th Inf., 21 Sept., 1866. Trans. to 16th Inf., 15 March, 1869. Lieut. Col. 17th Inf., 1 July, 1872. Col. 4th Inf., 11 April, 1882. Brig. Gen., 17 May, 1893. Retired by operation of law 24 Nov., 1893.

CARLING, ELIAS B.* [Born in Md. Appointed from Md.]
Bvt. 2nd Lieut. 2nd Art., 1 July, 1859. 2nd Lieut. 3rd Art., 31 Dec., 1859. 1st Lieut., 14 May, 1861. Capt. A. Q M., 20 Aug., 1862. Died 1 July, 1875. Bvt. Maj. and Bvt. Lieut. Col., 13 March, 1865, for valuable and faithful service as Chf. Q. M. of the Cav. of the Mil. Div. of Mississippi.

CARLISLE, JOSIAH H.* [Born in Maine. Appointed from Maine.]
Bvt 2nd Lieut. 2nd Art., 1 July, 1845. 2nd Lieut. 3rd Art., 18 June, 1846. Trans. to 2nd Art., 19 Oct., 1846 1st Lieut., 12 Oct., 1847. Capt. 3 March, 1857. Retired 4 Nov., 1863. Died 16 Dec., 1866. Bvt. Maj., 1 July, 1862, for gallant and meritorious service during the Peninsular campaign in Virginia.

CARLTON, CALEB H.* [Born in Ohio. Appointed from Ohio.]
Bvt. 2nd Lieut. 7th Inf., 1 July, 1859. 2nd Lieut. 4th Inf., 12 Oct., 1859. 1st Lieut., 14 May, 1861. Capt., 30 June, 1862. Bvt. Maj., 4 July, 1862, for gallant and meritorious service in the Peninsular campaign. Col. 89th Ohio Vols., 7 July, 1863. Bvt. Lieut. Col. 20 Sept., 1863, for gallant and meritorious service in the Battle of Chickamauga, Ga. Mustered out of Vol. service, 23 June, 1865. Unass'd 23 March, 1869. Ass'd to 10th Cav., 15 Dec., 1870. Maj. 3rd Cav., 17 May, 1876. Lieut. Col. 7th Cav., 11 April, 1889. Col. 8th Cav., 30 Jan., 1892. Brig. Gen., 28 June, 1897. Retired, over 30 years' service, 30 June, 1897.

CARLTON, JAMES H. [Born in Me. Appointed from Me.]
2nd Lieut. 1st Drag., 18 Oct., 1839. 1st Lieut., 17 March, 1845. Capt., 16 Feb., 1847. 1st Cav., 3 Aug., 1861. Maj. 6th Cav., 7 Sept., 1861. Lieut. Col. 4th Cav., 31 July, 1866. Died 7 Jan., 1873. Bvt. Maj., 23 Feb., 1847, for gallant and meritorious conduct at Buena Vista. Bvt. Lieut. Col., 13 March, 1865, for service in New Mexico. Bvt. Col., 13 March, 1865, for meritorious service in New Mexico. Bvt. Brig. Gen., 13 March, 1865, for gallant and meritorious service in New Mexico. Bvt. Maj. Gen., 13 March, 1865, for meritorious service during the war.

CARMICHAEL, RODERICK L.* [Born in S. C. Appointed from S. C.]
Addl. 2nd Lieut. 11th Inf., 11 June, 1897. 2nd Lieut. 7th Art., 8 March, 1898. 1st Lieut. 6th Art., 16 Oct., 1899. Trans. to 2nd Art., 29 Nov., 1899.

CARNAHAN, EARL C. [Born in Miss. Appointed from the Army.]
Priv. and Corpl. Co. G, 16th Inf., 10 Oct., 1883, to 22 March, 1888. 2nd Lieut. 12th Inf., 6 Feb., 1888. 1st Lieut. 5th Inf., 18 April, 1895 Capt., 2 March, 1899. Graduate of the Infantry and Cavalry School, 1895.

CARNCROSS, SEPTIMUS E. [Born in England. Appointed from N. Y.]
Priv. Co C, 3rd Art., 24 June, 1850, to 24 June, 1855. Priv. Co. F, 6th Inf., 20 July, 1855. Trans. to gen ser., 1 Dec., 1858. Trans. to Co. A, 1st Art., 1 March, 1859. Trans. to Co. K, 3rd Art., 1 Sept., 1861. Discharged 7 Oct., 1861. 1st Lieut. 10th N. Y. Vols., 7 Oct., 1861. Capt. A. D. C. Vols., 17 Sept., 1862. Capt. A. A. G. Vols., 4 Sept., 1863. Maj. A. A. G. Vols., 29 April, 1864. Resigned 21 March, 1865. 2nd Lieut. 11th Inf., 11 May, 1866. Trans. to 20th Inf., 21 Sept., 1866. 1st Lieut., 3 Oct., 1867. Died 4 Nov., 1873. Bvt. Capt., 3 Oct., 1867, for gallant and meritorious service in the Battle of Hatcher's Run, Va.

CARNEY, BARNARD. [Born in Ireland. Appointed from Army.]
Priv. and Corpl. Co. A, and Sergt. Maj. Eng. Batt., 16 March, 1859, to 12 Feb., 1867. 2nd Lieut. 20th Inf., 3 Jan., 1867. 1st Lieut., 20 Jan., 1868. Resigned 1 Feb., 1869.

CARNEY, JOSEPH D. [Born in Penn. Appointed from Kansas.]
1st Lieut. 17th Inf., 14 May, 1861. Capt., 1 May, 1863. Died 8 Feb., 1866. Bvt. Maj., 13 March, 1865, for gallant and meritorious service at the Battle of Gettysburg, Penn.

CHASE, WM. H.* [Born in Mass. Appointed from Mass.]
Bvt. 2nd Lieut. Eng., 4 March, 1815. 2nd Lieut., 15 April, 1818. 1st Lieut., 31 March, 1819. Capt., 1 Jan., 1825. Maj., 7 July, 1838. Resigned 31 Oct., 1856.

CHASE, WM. H.* [Born in Penn. Appointed from Penn.]
2nd Lieut. 1st Art., 23 June, 1865. 1st Lieut., 14 Dec., 1865. Trans. to Eng., 1 May, 1866. Died 24 June, 1871.

CHASE, WILSON. [Born in Tenn. Appointed from Army.]
Priv., Corpl. and Sergt. Troop B, 7th Cav., 18 March, 1885, to 4 March, 1889. 2nd Lieut. 20th Inf., 11 Feb., 1889. 1st Lieut. 22nd Inf., 1 May, 1896. Capt. 21st Inf., 8 June, 1899. Graduate of the Infantry and Cavalry School, 1895.

CHATFIELD, WALTER H. [Born in Conn. Appointed from the Army.]
Priv. and Corpl. Co. G, and Q. M. Sergt. 7th Cav., 4 Oct., 1878, to 16 Oct., 1880. 2nd Lieut. 5th Inf., 4 Oct., 1880. 1st Lieut. 18th Inf., 20 Nov., 1890. Trans. to 5th Inf., 20 July, 1891. Capt., 26 April, 1898.

CHAYTOR, GEORGE W. [Born in Md. Appointed from Del.]
Capt. 11th Inf., 9 April, 1847. Disbanded 20 July, 1848.

CHEEK, DAVIS W. [Born in Ind. Appointed from Ind.]
Sergt. Co. K, 4th Ind. Vols., 15 May, 1847, to 20 July, 1848. Capt. 13th Inf., 5 Aug., 1861. Retired 9 April, 1864. Resigned 4 May, 1865.

CHEEVER, BENJN. H., Jr. [Born in D. C. Appointed from D. C.]
2nd Lieut. 6th Cav., 15 Aug., 1876. 1st Lieut., 30 Dec., 1881. Capt., 8 March, 1893. Maj. and I. G. Vols., 12 May, 1898, to 12 May, 1899. Graduate of the Infantry and Cavalry School, 1883. Medal of Honor for gallantry in action against hostile Sioux Indians on the north bank of the White River, near the mouth of Little Grass Creek, S. Dak., 1 Jan., 1891, in heading the advance across the White River, partly frozen, in a spirited movement to the effective assistance of Troop K, 6th Cav.; while serving as 1st Lieut. 6th Cav.

CHENEY, GEORGE W. [Born in La. Appointed from La.]
2nd Lieut. 14th Inf., 9 April, 1847. Resigned 23 Feb., 1848.

CHENEY, SHERWOOD A.* [Born in Conn. Appointed from Conn.]
Addl. 2nd Lieut. Eng., 11 June, 1897. 2nd Lieut., 5 July, 1898. 1st Lieut., 26 Jan., 1899.

CHENEY, WARD. [Born in Conn. Appointed from Conn.]
2nd Lieut. 4th Inf., 9 July, 1898. 1st Lieut. 15th Inf., 2 June, 1899. Trans. to 4th Inf., 21 Nov., 1899

CHERBONNIER, ANDREW V. [Born in La. Appointed from Md.]
Capt. Med. Storekeeper, 28 July, 1866. Retired by operation of law, 12 Oct., 1890.

CHERRY, SAML. A.* [Born in Ind. Appointed from Ind.]
2nd Lieut. 23rd Inf., 16 June, 1875. Trans. to 5th Cav., 28 July, 1876, taking rank from 28 July, 1876. Murdered by a soldier 11 May, 1881.

CHERRY, WM. B. [Born in N. C. Appointed from Tenn.]
Capt. A. C. S., 26 June, 1846. Resigned 6 April, 1847.

CHESEBROUGH, WM. H. [Born in N. Y. Appointed from N. Y.]
1st Lieut. 11th Inf., 14 May, 1861. Resigned 26 April, 1864.

CHESTER, ELIPHALET N.* [Born in N. Y. Appointed from Ark.]
Mus. and Priv. Cos. F and D, 94th N. Y. Vols., 23 Aug., 1862, to 23 Aug., 1863. 2nd Lieut. 4th Art., 17 June, 1867. Discharged 22 Oct., 1870.

CHESTER, JAMES. [Born in Scotland. Appointed from Army.]
Priv. Co. E, 1st Art., 1 Dec., 1854. Corpl., 1 July, 1855. Sergt., 29 May, 1856. 1st Sergt., 1 Oct., 1857. Discharged 1 Oct., 1859. 1st Sergt. Co. E, 1st Art., 1 Oct., 1859. Sergt., 3 Nov., 1859. 1st Sergt., 15 Jan., 1862. Bvt. 2nd Lieut. 1st Art., 19 Feb., 1863. 2nd Lieut. 3rd Art., 17 April, 1863. Bvt. 1st Lieut., 3 July, 1863, for gallant and meritorious service in the Gettysburg campaign. Bvt. Capt., 25 Aug., 1864, for gallant and meritorious service in action at Kearneysville, Va. 1st Lieut. 3rd Art., 14 Jan., 1865. Capt., 20 Sept., 1880. Maj., 7 June, 1897. Honor graduate of the Artillery School, 1872. Retired by operation of law, 10 Feb., 1898.

CHESTER, JOHN. [Born in Tenn. Appointed from Tenn.]
2nd Lieut. 14th Inf., 9 April, 1847. Disbanded 26 July, 1848.

CHESTER, ROBERT. [Born in Scotland. Appointed from Penn.]
Capt. 17th Inf., 5 Aug., 1861. Dismissed 4 May, 1863.

CHETWOOD, BRADBURY C. [Born in N. J. Appointed from N. J.]
1st Lieut. 2nd N. J. Vols., 2 May, 1861. Resigned 12 Dec., 1861. Maj. A. D. C. Vols., 20 Aug., 1862. Resigned 16 April, 1863. Lieut. Col. A. I. G., 16 April, to 10 Aug., 1863. 2nd Lieut. 1st Art., 24 Oct., 1861. 1st Lieut., 5 May, 1863. Resigned 1 Sept., 1863.

CHEVERS, MARK L. [Born in N. Y. Appointed from Va.]
Capt. Post Chap., 3 April, 1867. Died 13 Sept., 1875.

CHICKERING, JOHN W. [Born in Ill. Appointed from Ill.]
Capt. 88th Ill. Vols., 27 Aug., 1862. Bvt. Maj. Vols., 13 March, 1865, for gallant and meritorious services in the Battle of Chickamauga, Ga. Mustered out 17 Nov., 1865. 2nd Lieut. 13th Inf., 11 May, 1866. Trans. to 22nd Inf., 21 Sept., 1866. 1st Lieut., 1 Feb., 1868. Unassigned 15 May, 1869. Ass'd to 6th Cav., 1 Jan., 1871. Cashiered 27 Jan., 1875. Bvt. 1st Lieut. and Capt., 2 March, 1867, for gallant and meritorious service at the Battle of Chickamauga, Ga.

CHIFFELLE, THOS. P.* [Born in S. C. Appointed from S. C.]
Bvt. 2nd Lieut. 7th Inf., 1 July, 1836. Resigned 30 Sept., 1836.

CHILDE, JOHN.* [Born in Mass. Appointed from Mass.]
Bvt. 2nd Lieut. Art., 1 July, 1827. 2nd Lieut. 3rd Art., 1 July, 1827. Resigned 31 Dec., 1835.

CHILDS, BILLINGS B. [Born in N. Y. Appointed from Penn.]
2nd Lieut. 6th Inf., 5 Aug., 1861. 1st Lieut., 5 Aug., 1861. Resigned 8 Aug., 1863.

CHILDS, EBENEZER. [Born in Mass. Appointed from Mass.]
Sergt. 4th Inf., 11 Oct., 1808. 2nd Lieut. 9th Inf., 12 March, 1812. 1st Lieut., 13 May, 1813. Capt., 20 July, 1814. Trans. to 5th Inf., 17 May, 1815. Resigned 3 March, 1817.

CHILDS, FREDERICK L.* [Born in Maine. Appointed at Large.]
Bvt. 2nd Lieut. 2nd Art., 1 July, 1855. 2nd Lieut. 1st Art., 14 July, 1855. Resigned 4 March, 1861.

CHILDS, MARSHALL. [Born in Pa. Appointed from Pa.]
2nd Lieut. 6th Inf., 9 July, 1898. 1st Lieut. 12th Inf., 19 Aug., 1899.

CHILDS, THOMAS.* [Born in Mass. Appointed from Mass.]
3rd Lieut. 1st Art., 11 March, 1814. 2nd Lieut., 1 May, 1814. Trans. to Corps Art., 12 May, 1814. 1st Lieut., 20 April, 1818. Trans. to 3rd Art., 1 June, 1821. Capt., 1 Oct., 1826. Maj. 1st Art., 16 Feb., 1847. Died 8 Oct., 1853. Bvt. Maj., 21 Aug., 1836, for planning the attack on the Indians at Fort Drane, Fla., and good conduct in that affair. Bvt. Lieut. Col., 1 Feb., 1841, for gallant conduct and repeated successes in the war against Florida Indians. Bvt. Col., 9 May, 1846, for gallant conduct at Palo Alto and Resaca de la Palma.

CHILES, SEABORN G.* [Born in Fla. Appointed from Fla.]
Addl. 2nd Lieut. 12th Inf., 11 June, 1897. 2nd Lieut. 11th Inf., 8 March, 1898. 1st Lieut., 2 March, 1899.

CHILSON, GEORGE W. [Born in Mich. Appointed from Mich.]
Corpl. Co. F, 24th Mich. Vols., 30 July, 1862. Sergt., 1 May, 1864. 1st Lieut., 24th Mich. Vols., 14 Aug., 1864. Mustered out 30 June, 1865. 2nd Lieut. 14th Inf., 23 Feb., 1866. 1st Lieut., 9 July, 1866. Trans. to 32nd Inf., 21 Sept., 1866. Trans. to 21st Inf., 19 April, 1869. Unass'd 16 Aug., 1869. Ass'd to 8th Cav., 15 Dec., 1870. Capt., 28 Dec., 1871. Died 18 Jan., 1881.

CHILTON, ROBERT H.* [Born in Va. Appointed from Va.]
2nd Lieut. 1st Drag., 1 July, 1837. 1st Lieut., 21 Feb., 1842. Capt., 6 Dec., 1846. Capt. A. Q. M., 11 May, 1846. Maj. and P. M., 25 July, 1854. Resigned 29 April, 1861. Bvt. Maj., 23 Feb., 1847, for gallant and meritorious conduct at Buena Vista.

CHILTON, THOS. J. [Born in Ala. Appointed from Ala.]
Asst. Surg. 13th Inf., 29 March, 1848. Disbanded 20 July, 1848.

CHIPMAN, HENRY L. [Born in N. Y. Appointed from Mich.]
Capt. 11th Inf., 14 May, 1861. Lieut. Col. 2nd Mich. Vols., 25 May, 1861. Resigned Vol. commission, 24 June, 1861. Bvt. Maj., 3 May, 1863, for gallant and meritorious service in the Battle of Chancellorsville, Va. Bvt. Lieut. Col., 2 July, 1863, for gallant and meritorious service in the Battle of Gettysburg, Penn. Col. 102nd U. S. Colored Troops, 15 April, 1864. Bvt. Brig. Gen. Vols., 13 March, 1865, for gallant and meritorious service during the war. Mustered out of Vol. service, 30 Sept., 1865. Trans. to 29th Inf., 21 Sept., 1866. Trans. to 11th Inf., 25 April, 1869. Maj. 3rd Inf., 29 Oct., 1873. Lieut. Col. 7th Inf., 19 May, 1881. Retired by operation of law, 1 Feb., 1887.

CHITTENDEN, HIRAM M.* [Born in N. Y. Appointed from N. Y.]
2nd Lieut. Eng., 15 June, 1884. 1st Lieut., 31 Dec., 1886. Capt., 2 Oct., 1895. Lieut. Col. and Chief Eng., 9 May, 1898, to 25 Feb., 1899.

CHITTY, WM. D.* [Born in Mo. Appointed from Mo.]
Addl. 2nd Lieut. 8th Cav., 12 June, 1896. 2nd Lieut. 3rd Cav., 6 Feb., 1897.

CHOISY, GEORGE L. [Born in S. C. Appointed from Army.]
Priv. Co. F, 2nd Batt. 14th Inf., 28 Nov., 1861. 1st Sergt., 1 Dec., 1861. 2nd Lieut. 14th Inf., 9 June, 1862. 1st Lieut., 30 April, 1863. Bvt. Capt., 1 Aug., 1864, for gallant service in the Battle of the North Anna River, Va. Bvt. Maj., 18 Aug., 1864, for gallant service in battle on the Weldon Railroad, Va. Trans. to 23rd Inf., 21 Sept., 1866. Capt. 40th Inf., 28 July, 1866. Trans. to 25th Inf., 20 April, 1869. Unass'd 24 June, 1870. Ass'd to 11th Inf., 1 Jan., 1871. Died 21 Dec., 1880.

CHOTARD, HENRY. [Born in ——. Appointed from Ga.]
2nd Lieut. 3rd Inf., 3 May, 1808. 1st Lieut., 31 Dec., 1809. Capt., 9 Oct., 1813. (Maj. A. A. G., 17 Oct., 1814, to 15 June, 1815.) Trans. to 1st Inf., 17 May, 1815. Resigned 1 Dec., 1820. Bvt. Maj., 23 Dec., 1814, for gallant conduct at the Siege of New Orleans.

CHRISMAN, EDWARD R.* [Born in Ind. Appointed from Ind.]
2nd Lieut. 2nd Inf., 11 June, 1888. 1st Lieut. 20th Inf., 31 May, 1895. Trans. to 6th Inf., 23 July, 1895. Capt. 20th Inf., 16 March, 1899. Trans. to 16th Inf., 23 Oct., 1899.

CHRISTIAN, BENJN. R. [Born in ——. Appointed from ——.]
Ensign 7th Inf., 9 July, 1814. 3rd Lieut., 1 Sept., 1814. 2nd Lieut. 7th Inf., 31 Oct., 1816. 1st Lieut., 30 April, 1817. Disbanded 15 June, 1815. 2nd Lieut. 7th Inf., 31 Oct., 1816. Disbanded 1 June, 1821.

CHRISTIAN, JNO. B.* [Born in Mo. Appointed from Mo.]
2nd Lieut. 2nd Cav., 12 June, 1896. 1st Lieut. 9th Cav., 31 Aug., 1899.

CHRISTIAN, WM. [Born in ——. Appointed from ——.]
2nd Lieut. 3rd Inf., 3 Jan., 1812. 1st Lieut., 31 Dec., 1813. Capt., 31 May, 1814. Trans. to 1st Inf., 17 May, 1815. Disbanded 1 June, 1821.

CHRISTIE, WM. [Born in ——. Appointed from Ky.]
2nd Lieut. 1st Inf., 9 March, 1814. Resigned 1 Oct., 1816.

CHRISTOPHER, JOHN. [Born in Penn. Appointed from Penn.]
1st Lieut. 16th Inf., 14 May, 1861. Capt., 21 Feb., 1862. Trans. to 25th Inf., 21 Sept., 1866. Trans. to 18th Inf., 26 April, 1869. Died 4 May, 1874. Bvt. Maj., 20 Sept., 1863, for gallant and meritorious service at the Battle of Chickamauga, Ga. Bvt. Lieut. Col., 13 March, 1865, for gallant and meritorious service during the war.

CHUBB, CHAS. St. J. [Born in D. C. Appointed from Army.]
Priv. Gen. Ser., 6 Oct., 1873, to 6 Feb., 1875. 2nd Lieut. 17th Inf., 20 Jan., 1875. 1st Lieut., 11 Sept., 1880. Capt., 28 Nov., 1893. Reg. Q. M., — Nov., 1899.

CHUNN, JOHN T. [Born in ——. Appointed from Ohio.]
Capt. 19th Inf., 14 April, 1812. Trans. to 17th Inf., 12 May, 1814. Trans. to 3rd Inf., 17 May, 1815. Disbanded 1 June, 1821. Bvt. Maj., 15 Aug., 1814, for gallant conduct in defence of Fort Erie.

CHURCH, ALBERT E.* [Born in Conn. Appointed from Conn.]
Bvt. 2nd Lieut. Art., 1 July, 1828. 2nd Lieut. 3rd Art., 1 July, 1828. 1st Lieut., 13 Jan., 1836. Prof. at Mil. Acad., 13 March, 1838. Died 30 March, 1878.

CHURCH, JAMES R. [Born in Ill. Appointed from D. C.]
Asst. Surg., 12 Dec., 1898.

CHURCH, JOHN R.* [Born in Ga. Appointed from Ga.]
Bvt. 2nd Lieut. 1st Cav., 1 July, 1855. 2nd Lieut., 27 Aug., 1855. Resigned 30 Oct., 1860.

CHURCHILL, ALEXR. P. [Born in Ky. Appointed from Ky.]
Capt. Voltigeurs, 9 April, 1847. Disbanded 31 Aug., 1848.

CHURCHILL, CHARLES A. [Born in Mo. Appointed from Ky.]
2nd Lieut. 5th Inf., 1 Sept., 1879. 1st Lieut., 12 May, 1886. Died 1 March, 1894.

CHURCHILL, CHAS C. [Born in Penn. Appointed from Penn.]
2nd Lieut. 3rd Art., 3 March, 1848. 1st Lieut., 30 June, 1852. Capt., 14 May, 1861. Retired 28 Feb., 1862, for disability.

CHURCHILL, JOHN L. [Born in N. Y. Appointed from N. Y.]
Sergt. Co. A, 3rd Inf., 29 May, to 29 June, 1865. 2nd Lieut. 15th Inf., 23 Feb., 1866. Trans. to 24th Inf., 21 Sept., 1866. 1st Lieut., 30 Sept., 1866. Died 14 Oct., 1868.

CHURCHILL, MARLBOROUGH.* [Born in R. I. Appointed from Mass.]
2nd Lieut. 1st Art., 1 July, 1836. Resigned 19 Nov., 1836.

CHURCHILL, RICHARD C.* [Born in Ga. Appointed from D. C.]
2nd Lieut. 4th Art., 18 June, 1866. 1st Lieut., 28 July, 1866. Resigned 1 Sept., 1872.

CHURCHILL, SYLVESTER. [Born in Vt. Appointed from Vt.]
1st Lieut. 3rd Art., 12 March, 1812. Capt., 15 Aug., 1813. Trans. to Corps Art., 12 May, 1814. (Maj. A. I. G., 29 Aug., 1813. Disbanded 15 June, 1815.) Trans. to 1st Art., 1 June, 1821. Maj. 3rd Art., 6 April, 1835. Col. I. G., 25 June, 1841. Disbanded 29 April, 1845. Reinstated 20 Jan., 1846. Retired 25 Sept., 1861. Died 7 Dec., 1862. Bvt. Maj., 15 Aug., 1823, for ten years' faithful service in one grade. Bvt. Brig. Gen., 23 Feb., 1847, for gallant and meritorious conduct at Buena Vista.

CHURCHILL, WM. H.* [Born in N. Y. Appointed at Large.]
2nd Lieut. 3rd Art., 1 July, 1840. 1st Lieut., 27 June, 1843. Capt. A. Q. M., 3 March, 1847. Died 19 Oct., 1847. Bvt. Capt., 9 May, 1846, for gallant and distinguished service at Palo Alto and Resaca de la Palma.

CHURCHILL, WM. H. [Born in Ind. Appointed from Army.]
Priv., Corpl., Sergt. and 1st Sergt. Co. K, 2nd and 5th Cav., 3 July, 1855, to 18 July, 1864. 2nd Lieut. 5th Cav., 7 June, 1864. 1st Lieut., 3 Aug., 1865. Died 20 Aug., 1866. Bvt. 1st Lieut. and Bvt. Capt., 9 April, 1865, for gallant and meritorious conduct during the campaign terminating with the surrender of General Lee's army.

CHURCHMAN, CLARKE. [Born in ——. Appointed from ——.]
2nd Lieut. 12th Inf., — ——, 1898. Died 2 July, 1898, of wounds received in battle.

CHYNOWETH, EDWARD.* [Born in N. Y. Appointed from Wis.]
2nd Lieut. 17th Inf., 15 June, 1877. 1st Lieut., 26 Nov., 1884. Capt., 26 April, 1898.

CILLEY, GREENLEAF. [Born in Ohio. Appointed from Ohio.]
Corpl. Co. B, and Q. M. Sergt. 4th Ohio Cav., 23 Nov., 1861. 2nd Lieut., 9 May, 1863. 1st Lieut., 1 Jan., 1864. Capt., 18 Dec., 1864. Mustered out 15 July, 1865. 2nd Lieut. 1st Cav., 23 Feb., 1866. 1st Lieut., 11 April, 1867. Trans. to 12th Inf., 19 Feb., 1870. Discharged 30 Aug., 1870. Bvt. 1st Lieut. and Capt., 2 March, 1867, for gallant and meritorious service at the Battle of Chickamauga, Ga.

CILLEY, JOSEPH. [Born in N. H. Appointed from N. H.]
Ensign 21st Inf., 12 March, 1812. 2nd Lieut., 13 May, 1813. 1st Lieut., 7 March, 1814. Trans. to 5th Inf., 17 May, 1815. Resigned 30 June, 1816.

CLAFLIN, IRA W.* [Born in Vt. Appointed from Iowa.]
Bvt. 2nd Lieut. Mtd. Rifles, 1 July, 1857. 2nd Lieut., 14 June, 1858. 1st Lieut. 6th Cav., 14 May, 1861. Capt., 23 Dec., 1862. Died 18 Nov., 1867. Bvt. Capt., 21 Feb., 1862, for gallant and meritorious service at the Battle of Valverde, New Mexico. Bvt. Maj., 7 July, 1863, for gallant and meritorious service during the Gettysburg campaign.

CLAGGETT, J. ROZIER. [Born in D. C. Appointed from D. C.]
2nd Lieut. 23rd Inf., 29 Nov., 1875. 1st Lieut., 9 April, 1884. Capt., 28 June, 1892.

CLAGUE, JOHN J. [Born in England. Appointed from Minn.]
Priv. Co. F, 6th Minn. Vols., 28 June, 1862. Sergt., 22 Aug., 1862. Capt. 18th U. S. Colored Troops, 11 Oct., 1864. Mustered out 21 Feb., 1866. 2nd Lieut. 40th Inf., 7 March, 1867. Unass'd 20 April, 1869. Ass'd to 12th Inf., 3 Aug., 1870. 1st Lieut., 1 Sept., 1873. Capt. and C. S., 30 Aug., 1880. Maj. and C. S., 8 Oct., 1894. Lieut. Col. and Asst. C. G., 11 March, 1898. Col. and C. S. Vols., 22 July, to 5 Aug., 1898.

CLAIBORNE, MATTHEW M. [Born in Va. Appointed from Va.]
Ensign 12th Inf., 13 Jan., 1813. 3rd Lieut., 14 Aug., 1813. 2nd Lieut., 5 April, 1814. Disbanded 15 June, 1825.

CLAIBORNE, THOS., Jr. [Born in Tenn. Appointed from Tenn.]
2nd Lieut. Mtd. Rifles, 27 May, 1846. 1st Lieut., 16 Feb., 1847. Capt., 30 Aug., 1853. Resigned 14 May, 1861. Bvt. Capt., 9 Oct., 1847, for gallant and meritorious conduct at the Battle of Huamantla.

CLAPP, WM. H. [Born in Ohio. Appointed from Ohio.]
Priv. Co. A, 71st N. Y. State Mil., 19 April, 1861. Discharged 30 July, 1861. 2nd Lieut. 42nd Ohio Vols., 25 Sept., 1861. 1st Lieut., 14 March, 1862. Capt. A. A. G. Vols., 15 May, 1863. Bvt. Maj. Vols. and Bvt. Lieut. Col. Vols., 13 March, 1865, for faithful and meritorious service during the war. Mustered out 5 Dec., 1865. 2nd Lieut. and 1st Lieut. 11th Inf., 23 Feb., 1866. Trans. to 16th Inf., 14 April, 1869. Capt., 25 Dec., 1874. Maj. 24th Inf., 7 Aug., 1897. Trans. to 11th Inf., 6 Aug., 1898. Lieut. Col. 21st Inf., 1 April, 1899.

CLARK, BAYARD. [Born in N. Y. Appointed from N. Y.]
2nd Lieut. 8th Inf., 3 March, 1841. Trans. to 2nd Drag., 28 Sept., 1841. Resigned 15 Dec., 1843.

CLARK, CHAS. B. [Born in N. Y. Appointed from N. Y.]
1st Sergt. Co. I, 122nd N. Y. Vols., 1 Aug., 1862. 2nd Lieut., 17 March, 1864. 1st Lieut., 8 July, 1864. Capt., 20 April, 1865. Mustered out, 23 June, 1865. 2nd Lieut. 11th Inf., 11 May, 1866. Trans. to 20th Inf., 21 Sept., 1866. 1st Lieut., 3 Oct., 1867. Unass'd 3 Sept., 1869. Resigned 1 Dec., 1869.

CLARK, CHARLES B.* [Born in Mass. Appointed from Mass.]
2nd Lieut. 23rd Inf., 15 Feb., 1899.

CLARK, CHARLES C.* [Born in Pa. Appointed from Pa.]
2nd Lieut. 9th Inf., 12 June, 1890. 1st Lieut. 5th Inf., 1 June, 1897. Capt. Vol. Sig. Corps, 2 June, to 30 Nov., 1898. Capt., 20th Inf., 12 Jan., 1897. Trans. to 5th Inf., 17 Feb., 1900.

CLARK, CHAS. H.* [Born in Mass. Appointed from Mass.]
2nd Lieut. 1st Art., 16 June, 1875. 1st Lieut. of Ord., 16 June, 1880. Capt. (14 years' service), 15 June, 1890. Honor graduate of the Artillery School, 1880.

CLARK, C. J. [Born in S. C. Appointed from Ala.]
Asst. Surg., 16 July, 1846. Maj. and Surg., 28 June, 1847. Disbanded 20 July, 1848.

CLARK, DARIUS D.* [Born in N. Y. Appointed from N. Y.]
Bvt. 2nd Lieut. 2nd Inf., 1 July, 1849. 2nd Lieut. 6th Inf., 7 Jan., 1851. 1st Lieut., 3 March, 1855. Died 2 Dec., 1859.

CLARK, DILLARD H.* [Born in Ky. Appointed from Ky.]
Priv. Co. D, 14th Ky. Cav., 20 Aug., 1862. Discharged 16 Sept., 1863. 2nd Lieut. 15th Inf., 13 June, 1873. 1st Lieut., 29 Feb., 1876. Retired with the rank of Capt., 15 June, 1891.

CLARK, EDWIN R. [Born in N. H. Appointed from Mass.]
Capt. 30th Mass. Vols., 12 May, 1862. Mustered out 25 April, 1865. Capt. 30th Mass. Vet. Vols., 3 May, 1865. Mustered out 5 July, 1866. 2nd Lieut. 26th Inf., 16 May, 1867. Trans. to 10th Inf., 19 May, 1869. Dismissed 12 July, 1876. 2nd Lieut. 10th Inf., 12 June, 1879, with rank from 16 May, 1867. 1st Lieut., 14 Dec., 1881. Retired 17 March, 1883.

CLARK, ELISHA. [Born in ——. Appointed from Army.]
Ensign 13th Inf., 27 Oct., 1813. 3rd Lieut., 31 Jan., 1814. 2nd Lieut., 25 July, 1814. Disbanded 15 June, 1815. Reinstated in 2nd Inf., 2 Dec., 1815. Resigned 1 Dec., 1819.

CLARK, ELMER W.* [Born in Penn. Appointed from Iowa.]
2nd Lieut., 14th Inf., 12 June, 1893. 1st Lieut. 18th Inf., 26 April, 1898.

CLARK, HARTFORD T. [Born in R. I. Appointed from R. I.]
1st Lieut. 1st Cav., 3 March, 1855. Discharged 1 May, 1856.

CLARK, HENRY.* [Born in Conn. Appointed from Conn.]
Bvt. 2nd Lieut. 5th Inf., 1 July, 1822. 2nd Lieut., 1 July, 1822. 1st Lieut., 16 Aug., 1828. Died 14 Oct., 1830.

CLARK, HENRY B.* [Born in Wis. Appointed from Ill.]
2nd Lieut. 3rd Art., 15 Feb., 1899.

CLARK, HENRY E. W. [Born in Ga. Appointed from Fla.]
Capt. 13th Inf., 9 April, 1847. Disbanded 15 July, 1848.

CLARK, HOLLIS C.* [Born in Ill. Appointed from N. Y.]
2nd Lieut. 23rd Inf., 12 June, 1891. 1st Lieut. 10th Inf., 8 March, 1898. Trans. to 25th Inf., 18 April, 1898.

CLARK, HOMER H. [Born in N. Y. Appointed from Army.]
Priv. Gen. Ser., 16 April, 1860. 1st Sergt. Co. A, 16th Inf., 7 Sept., 1861, to 26 Nov., 1861. 2nd Lieut. 16th Inf., 20 Nov., 1861. 1st Lieut., 21 Feb., 1862. Died 21 Oct., 1863, of wounds received at the Battle of Chickamauga, Ga. Bvt. Capt., 19 Sept., 1863, for gallant and meritorious conduct at the Battle of Chickamauga, Ga.

CLARK, ISAAC, Jr. [Born in Vt. Appointed from Vt.]
Ensign 11th Inf., 31 Dec., 1812. 3rd Lieut., 1 May, 1813. 2nd Lieut., 14 Aug., 1813. 1st Lieut., 1 Sept., 1814. Disbanded 15 June, 1815. Reinstated 2 Dec., 1815, in 5th Inf. Trans. to 6th Inf., 17 May, 1816. Capt., 27 Aug., 1822. Maj. Q. M., 7 July, 1838. Drowned 22 July, 1842. Bvt. Maj., 7 Aug., 1832, for 10 years' faithful service in one grade.

CLARK, JAMES.* [Born in Penn. Appointed from Penn.]
Bvt. 2nd Lieut. 4th Inf., 1 July, 1829. Resigned 18 Aug., 1830.

CLARK, JOHN. [Born in Md. Appointed from Md.]
Ensign 36th Inf., 30 April, 1813. 3rd Lieut., 15 Aug., 1813. 1st Lieut., 1 May, 1814. Disbanded 15 June, 1815. 2nd Lieut. Rifles, 20 June, 1817. 1st Lieut., 12 July, 1818. Died 16 March, 1820.

CLARK, JOHN. [Born in Penn. Appointed from Penn.]
Ensign 22nd Inf., 29 July, 1813. 3rd Lieut., 1 Sept., 1813. Resigned 18 June, 1814. 2nd Lieut. Rifle Regiment, 28 Jan., 1820. Disbanded 1 June, 1821.

CLARK, JOHN B. [Born in Ky. Appointed from Ky.]
Ensign 28th Inf., 20 May, 1813. 2nd Lieut., 9 April, 1814. Trans. to 3rd Inf., 17 May, 1815. 1st Lieut., 7 May, 1817. Capt., 18 May, 1826. A. Q. M., 19 May, 1826, to Sept., 1829. Maj. 1st Inf., 26 Nov., 1845. Died 23 Aug., 1847.

CLARK, JOHN D.* [Born in N. C. Appointed from N. C.]
Bvt. 2nd Lieut. 4th Inf., 1 July, 1842. 2nd Lieut. 8th Inf., 31 Dec., 1842. 1st Lieut., 21 July, 1846. Drowned 2 Aug., 1848. Bvt. Capt., 8 Sept., 1847, for gallant and meritorious conduct at Molino del Rey.

CLARK, JOHN R. [Born in N. C. Appointed from N. C.]
Ensign 10th Inf., 15 April, 1814. 3rd Lieut., 10 Dec., 1814. Disbanded 15 June, 1815. 2nd Lieut. 4th Inf., 19 Feb., 1817. 1st Lieut. 31 Oct., 1817. Dismissed 23 July, 1818.

CLARK, JOSEPH C., Jr.* [Born in N. J. Appointed from N. J.]
Bvt. 2nd Lieut. 3rd Art., 1 July, 1848. 2nd Lieut. 4th Art., 6 Jan., 1849. 1st Lieut.,

Lieut., 14 March, 1814. Disbanded 15 June, 1815. 2nd Lieut. 6th Inf., 16 June, 1818. Trans. to 5th Inf., 1 June, 1821. 1st Lieut., 1 June, 1821. Resigned 31 Oct., 1825. Died 7 Aug., 1831.

BURBRIDGE, GEORGE S. [Born in Ky. Appointed from Ky.]
Maj. Mounted Rifles, 27 May, 1846. Resigned 8 Jan., 1848.

BURCH, DANIEL E. [Born in N. J. Appointed from N. J.]
Ensign 15th Inf., 7 Oct., 1812. 3rd Lieut., 13 March, 1813. 2nd Lieut., 15 Aug., 1813. Reg. P. M., 12 March, 1814, to 15 June, 1815. Disbanded 15 June, 1815. 2nd Lieut. 7th Inf., 5 Jan., 1817. 1st Lieut., 7 June, 1817. Capt., 30 June, 1820. Capt. A. Q. M., 25 Oct., 1822, to 27 June, 1831. Resigned 30 April, 1833. Died 8 May, 1833.

BURCHSTED, HENRY.* [Born in N. Y. Appointed from N. Y.]
Ensign 2nd Inf., 1 March, 1811. 2nd Lieut., 13 March, 1811. 1st Lieut., 5 May, 1813. Killed, 30 Nov., 1813, in action with Indians in Ala.

BURD, BENJAMIN E. [Born in Penn. Appointed from Penn.]
1st Lieut. 45th Inf., 16 Sept., 1814. Disbanded 15 June, 1815. 2nd Lieut. 3rd Inf., 21 Nov., 1817. Died 30 Oct., 1818.

BURD, JOHN A. [Born in Penn. Appointed from Penn.]
Capt. 2nd Light Drag., 16 March, 1812. Trans. to 4th Inf., 17 May, 1815. Trans. to Corps Art., 7 Jan., 1820. Trans. to 3rd Art., 1 June, 1821. Died 28 Feb., 1827. Bvt. Maj., 31 Oct., 1814, for gallant conduct.

BURDINE, CLARK.* [Born in Ga. Appointed from Ga.]
Bvt. 2nd and 2nd Lieut. 4th Art., 1 July, 1821. Resigned 1 June, 1825. Died 10 Aug., 1836.

BURGESS, HARRY.* [Born in Miss. Appointed from Miss.]
Addl. 2nd Lieut. Eng., 12 June, 1895. 2nd Lieut., 5 Feb., 1897. 1st Lieut., 5 July, 1898.

BURGESS, LOUIS R.* [Born in Wis. Appointed from Iowa.]
Addl. 2nd Lieut. 5th Art., 11 June, 1892. 2nd Lieut., 28 Nov., 1892. 1st Lieut., 2 March, 1899.

BURGOYNE, EDMUND. [Born in Mass. Appointed from Army.]
Priv., Corpl. and Sergt. of Cos. G and A, and Sergt. Maj. 11th Inf., 14 Aug., 1861, to 1 April, 1865. 2nd Lieut. 14th Inf. 12 March, 1865. 1st Lieut., 12 March, 1865. Trans. to 32nd Inf., 21 Sept., 1866. Resigned 14 Jan., 1867.

BURGWIN, JOHN H. K.* [Born in N. C. Appointed from N. C.]
Bvt. 2nd Lieut. 2nd Inf., 1 July, 1830. 2nd Lieut. 1st Drag., 4 March, 1833. 1st Lieut., 30 June, 1835. Capt., 31 July, 1837. Died 7 Feb., 1847, of wounds received in Battle at Pueblo de Taos, New Mexico.

BURKE, DANIEL W. [Born in Conn. Appointed from Army.]
Priv. Co. E, 2nd Inf., 10 June, 1858. Corpl., 1 Nov., 1859. Priv., 31 Dec., 1860. Corpl., 19 Sept., 1861. 1st Sergt. Co. B, 2nd Inf., 1 Dec., 1861. 2nd Lieut. 2nd Inf., 18 July, 1862. 1st Lieut., 2 July, 1863. Bvt. Capt., 2 July, 1863, for gallant and meritorious service in the Battle of Gettysburg, Pa. Capt. 45th Inf., 22 Jan., 1867. Bvt. Maj., 22 Jan., 1867, for gallant and meritorious service in the Battle of Gettysburg, Penn. Trans. to 14th Inf., 22 July, 1869. Maj. 23rd Inf., 13 Aug., 1894. Lieut. Col. 11th Inf., 2 Dec., 1897. Col. 17th Inf., 8 Sept., 1899. Brig. Gen., 20 Oct., 1899. Retired, over 30 years' service, 21 Oct., 1899. Medal of Honor for distinguished gallantry in action at Shepherdstown Ford, W. Va., 20 Sept., 1862, voluntarily attempting to spike a gun in the face of the enemy; while serving as 1st Sergt. Co. B, 2nd Inf.

BURKE, JOHN. [Born in Ireland. Appointed from La.]
Chaplain Fort Washita, Ark., Nov., 1850, to 16 April, 1861, and at Fort Hamilton, N. Y., 18 Jan., 1862, to 28 April, 1867. Post Chap., 3 April, 1867. Retired 20 July, 1867. Accidentally killed 24 Dec., 1873.

BURKE, MARTIN. [Born in Md. Appointed from D. C.]
2nd Lieut. 8th Inf., 28 Jan., 1820. Trans. to 1st Inf., 1 June, 1821. Trans. to 3rd Art., 12 June, 1823. 1st Lieut., 1 May, 1828 Capt., 1 Dec., 1838. Bvt. Maj., 12 Aug., 1847, for gallant and meritorious conduct in the Battles of Contreras and Churubusco. Bvt. Lieut. Col., 8 Sept., 1847, for gallant and meritorious conduct in the Battle of Molino del Rey. Maj. 2nd Art., 11 Nov., 1856. Lieut. Col. 3rd Art., 28 Aug., 1861. Retired 1 Aug., 1863. Bvt. Col. and Bvt. Brig. Gen., 13 March, 1865, for faithful service to his country. Died 24 April, 1882.

BURKE, MARTIN J.* [Born in N. Y. Appointed from N. Y.]
Bvt. 2nd Lieut. 1st Art., 1 July, 1836. 2nd Lieut., 31 Aug., 1836. 1st Lieut., 7 July, 1838. Reg. Adj., 11 May, 1846, to 3 March, 1847. Capt., 3 March, 1847. Killed 20 Aug., 1847, at Battle of Churubusco, Mexico.

BURKE, ORVILLE. [Born in Ohio. Appointed from Ill.]
1st Sergt. Co. H, 14th Iowa Vols., 6 Nov., 1861. 2nd Lieut., 2 Feb., 1863. Capt., 19 Nov., 1864. Mustered out 8 Aug., 1865. Capt. 41st Inf., 28 July, 1866. Unass'd 15 May, 1869. Ass'd to 10th Cav., 5 Jan., 1870. Mustered out 1 Jan., 1871.

BURKE, PATRICK E. [Born in Ireland. Appointed from Mo.]
Capt. 1st Mo. Vols., 18 May, 1861, to 5 July, 1861. 1st Lieut. 13th Inf., 14 May, 1861. Capt., 24 Oct., 1861 Col. 66th Ill. Vols., 24 June, 1862. Bvt. Maj, 14 May, 1864, for gallant and meritorious services in the Battle of Resaca, Ga. Died 19 May, 1864, of wounds received in the Battle of Resaca.

BURKE, THOS. P. [Born in Ireland. Appointed from Penn.]
2nd Lieut. 8th Inf., 27 Oct., 1820. Trans. to 4th Inf., 1 June, 1821. Trans. to 2nd Art., 29 Aug., 1822. Trans. to Marine Corps, 20 Nov., 1830. Died in 1834

BURKHARDT, SAMUEL, Jr.* [Born in Ill. Appointed from Ill.]
2nd Lieut. 25th Inf., 12 June, 1889. 1st Lieut. 10th Inf., 1 Jan., 1897. Capt. 19th Inf., 16 Sept., 1899.

BURNES, THOMAS. [Born in Ireland. Appointed from the Army.]
Priv., Sergt. and 1st Sergt. Batty. L, 5th Art., 7 Sept., 1861, to 6 Nov., 1863. 2nd Lieut. 5th Art., 31 Oct., 1863 Trans. to 2nd Art., 13 Sept., 1864. Died 28 Oct., 1864, of wounds received, 27 Oct., 1864, at Battle of Hatcher's Run, Va.

BURNET, ROBT. W.* [Born in Ohio. Appointed from Ohio.]
Bvt. 2nd Lieut. 4th Inf., 1 July, 1829. 2nd Lieut., 1 July, 1829. Resigned 31 March, 1833.

BURNET, WM. E. [Born in Texas. Appointed from Texas.]
2nd Lieut. 1st Inf., 21 Feb., 1857. Resigned 17 July, 1861.

BURNETT, GEORGE R.* [Born in Pa. Appointed from Pa.]
2nd Lieut. 9th Cav., 12 June, 1880. 1st Lieut., 6 June, 1885. Graduate of the Infantry and Cavalry School, 1885. Retired for disability 20 Feb., 1891. Medal of Honor for most distinguished gallantry in action at Cuchillo Negro, N. Mex., 16 Aug., 1881, in saving the life of a dismounted soldier, who was in imminent danger of being cut off, by galloping quickly to the assistance of the man, under a heavy fire, and escorting him to a place of safety; while serving as 2nd Lieut. 9th Cav.

BURNETT, ISAAC R. D.* [Born in Va. Appointed from Ind.]
Bvt. 2nd Lieut. 2nd Inf., 1 July, 1833. 2nd Lieut., 28 June, 1836. 1st Lieut., 7 July, 1838. Reg. Adj., 3 Oct., 1845, to 15 March, 1846. Died 15 March, 1846.

BURNETT, LEVI F. [Born in N. Y. Appointed from N. Y.]
Priv. Co. A, 84th N. Y. Vols., 16 Aug., 1862. Trans. to Co. A, 21st Reg. Vet. Res. Corps, 15 Aug., 1863. 2nd Lieut. Vet. Res. Corps, 12 May, 1864. Bvt. 1st Lieut. and Capt. Vols., 13 March, 1865, for gallant and meritorious service in the Battles of South Mountain and Antietam, Md. Mustered out 9 June, 1867. 2nd Lieut. 36th Inf., 25 May, 1867. Bvt. 1st Lieut., 25 May, 1867, for gallant and meritorious service in the Battle of Antietam, Md. Bvt. Capt., 25 May, 1867, for gallant and meritorious service during the war. Trans. to 7th Inf., 19 May, 1869. 1st Lieut., 10 May, 1873. Reg. Adj., 5 Nov., 1874, to 1 Oct., 1880. Capt., 28 April, 1889. Retired for disability 31 July, 1894

BURNETT, ROBERT L. [Born in N. Y. Appointed from Penn.]
1st Lieut. 12th Inf, 14 May, 1861. R. Q. M., 9 April, to 19 Nov., 1863. Capt., 24 Dec., 1864. Trans. to 21st Inf., 21 Sept., 1866. Discharged 2 Sept., 1870. Bvt. Capt., 27 June, 1862, for gallant and meritorious service at the Battle of Gaines' Mills, Va. Bvt. Maj., 2 July, 1863, for gallant and meritorious service at the Battle of Gettysburg, Penn.

BURNETT, WARD B.* [Born in Penn. Appointed from Penn.]
Bvt. 2nd Lieut. 2nd Art., 1 July, 1832. 2nd Lieut., 1 April, 1834. Resigned 31 July, 1836 Col. 1st N. Y. Vols., 3 Dec., 1846. Mustered out 1 Aug., 1848. Died 27 June, 1884.

BURNETT, WELLINGTON C. [Born in N. Y. Appointed from Army.]
Priv. and Sergt. Cos. D and E, 15th Inf., 19 April, 1847, to 17 July, 1848. 2nd Lieut. 15th Inf., 17 June, 1848. Disbanded 30 Aug., 1848.

BURNHAM, ARTHUR H.* [Born in Vt. Appointed from Mass.]
1st Lieut. Eng., 13 June, 1864. Capt., 6 March, 1867. Died 12 Sept., 1877. Bvt. Capt., 23 Aug., 1864, for highly meritorious services at the Siege of Forts Gaines and Morgan, Ala. Bvt. Maj., 26 March, 1865, for gallant and meritorious service during the campaign against the city of Mobile and its defences. Died 12 Sept., 1877.

BURNHAM, DAVID R. [Born in Penn. Appointed from N. Y.]
1st Lieut. 67th Penn. Vols., 28 Aug., 1861. Capt., 7 Jan., 1864. Mustered out 15 Sept., 1864. 2nd Lieut. 35th Inf., 18 June, 1867. Trans. to 15th Inf., 12 Aug., 1869. 1st Lieut., 1 Jan., 1875. Capt., 31 Oct., 1884. Retired for disability 15 June, 1891.

BURNHAM, FRANK. [Born in N. Y. Appointed from Army.]
(Proper name, Frank Burnham Woodhouse.) Priv. Co. I, 1st Cav., and Sergt Maj. 4th Cav, 23 Nov., 1859, to 1 May, 1862. 2nd Lieut. 2nd Cav., 1 May, 1862. 1st Lieut., 25 April, 1863. Dismissed 25 Nov., 1863. Re-entered service as Priv. Co. I, 2nd Mo. Cav., under name of Charles C. Canfield. Mustered out 19 Sept, 1865. Died 21 Dec., 1885.

BURNHAM, HORACE B. [Born in N. Y. Appointed from Penn.]
Lieut. Col. 67th Penn. Vols., 31 Oct., 1861. Mustered out 31 Oct., 1864. Maj. J. A. Vols., 31 Oct., 1864. Bvt. Lieut. Col. and Col. Vols., 13 March, 1865, for faithful and meritorious service during the war. J. A. U. S. Army, 25 Feb., 1867 (Act 25 Feb., 1867). Lieut. Col. and D. J. A. Gen., 5 July, 1884. Retired by operation of law 10 Sept., 1888. Died 10 April, 1894.

BURNHAM, HOWARD M. [Born in Mass. Appointed from Mass.]
2nd Lieut. 5th Art., 14 May, 1861. 1st Lieut., 27 April, 1863. Killed at Battle of Chickamauga, Ga., 19 Sept., 1863.

BURNHAM, JAMES D.* [Born in N. Y. Appointed from N. Y.]
Trans. from Marines to 2nd Art., 28 June, 1826, as 2nd Lieut., to rank from 1 July, 1825. Died 6 March, 1828.

BURNHAM, WM. P. [Born in Pa. Appointed from the Army.]
Cadet at Mil. Acad., 1 July, 1877, to 30 June, 1880. Priv., Corpl. and Sergt. gen. service and Co. E, 14th Inf., 26 April, 1881, to 5 July, 1883. 2nd Lieut. 6th Inf., 3 July, 1883. 1st Lieut. 11th Inf., 25 Feb., 1891. Trans. to 6th Inf., 20 July, 1891. Trans. to 20th Inf., 22 July, 1895. Capt. of Inf., 4 Aug., 1898. Ass'd to 5th Inf., 1 Jan., 1899. Graduate of the Infantry and Cavalry School, 1889. Lieut. Col. 4th Missouri Vols., 16 May, 1898. Mustered out Vols., 10 Feb., 1899.

BURNS, GEORGE H. [Born in Penn. Appointed from Army.]
Priv 15th Inf., 4 to 13 Nov., 1861. 2nd Lieut. 15th Inf., 12 Nov., 1861. R. Q. M., 1 Dec., 1861, to 8 May, 1862. 1st Lieut., 22 Dec., 1862. Died 13 Oct., 1865. Bvt. Capt., 31 Dec., 1862, for gallant and meritorious services at the Battle of Murfreesboro', Tenn.

BURNS, JAMES. [Born in Ireland. Appointed from Army.]
Priv. Troop H and Com. Sergt. 5th Cav., 28 July, 1858, to 28 July, 1863. Priv. and Sergt. Troop K, 5th Cav., 10 Sept., 1864, to 11 Aug, 1865. 2nd Lieut. 5th Cav., 9 Aug., 1865. 1st Lieut., 28 July, 1866. Capt., 1 March, 1872. Died 15 Aug., 1874.

BURNS, JAMES D.* [Born in Ky. Appointed from Ill.]
Bvt. 2nd Lieut. 3rd Art., 1 July, 1853. 2nd Lieut. 2nd Art., 1 Nov., 1853. Died 2 Oct., 1854.

BURNS, JAMES M. [Born in Ohio. Appointed from Ohio.]
Priv. Co. B, 1st W. Va. Vols., 3 Oct., 1861. Sergt., 1 Nov., 1863. Sergt. Co. B, 1st W. Va. Vet. Vols., 23 Jan., 1864. Trans. to Co. D, 2nd W. Va. Vols., 10 Dec., 1864. Discharged 17 July, 1865. 2nd Lieut. 17th Inf., 21 Sept., 1867. 1st Lieut., 25 July,

12 Jan., 1848. 1st Lieut., 22 Dec., 1847. Resigned 23 Feb., 1848. 2nd Lieut. 15th Inf., 21 June, 1848. Disbanded 5 Aug., 1848. Capt. 17th Inf., 5 Aug., 1861. Resigned 27 May, 1863.

CAHILL, JAMES. [Born in Ireland. Appointed from Army.]
Priv., Corpl. and Sergt. Co. B, 2nd Drag, 16 Jan, 1845, to 16 Jan., 1850, and 12 Oct., 1850, to 12 Oct., 1855. Priv., Corpl., Sergt. and 1st Sergt. Co. C, 2nd Cav., 1 April, 1856, to 6 Sept., 1862. Ord. Sergt., 6 Sept., 1862, to 10 Aug., 1863. 2nd Lieut. 2nd Cav., 10 Aug., 1863. 1st Lieut., 11 June, 1864. Capt., 1 Nov., 1867. Died 5 Feb., 1868. Bvt. 1st Lieut., 6 May, 1864, for gallant and meritorious service at the Battle of Todd's Tavern, Va.

CAIN, AVERY B. [Born in Vt. Appointed from Vt.]
2nd Lieut. and 1st Lieut. 4th Inf., 5 Aug., 1861. Bvt. Capt., 3 May, 1863, for gallant and meritorious service in the Battle of Chancellorsville, Va. Capt. 4th Inf., 19 Oct., 1863. Bvt. Maj., 24 May, 1864, for gallant and meritorious service in the Battle of North Anna River, Va. Died 16 March, 1879.

CAIN, WM. J. [Born in Vt. Appointed from Army.]
Priv. Co. M, 2nd Art., 9 Oct., 1862, to 14 April, 1863. 2nd Lieut. 3rd Inf., 19 Feb., 1863. Resigned 23 April, 1863. 2nd Lieut. 3rd Cav., 23 April, 1863. 1st Lieut., 9 Oct., 1865. Mustered out 31 Dec, 1870. Bvt. 1st Lieut., 15 Nov., 1863, for gallant and meritorious service in action near Tuscumbia, Ala. Bvt. Capt., 13 March, 1865, for gallant and meritorious service in the Battle of Mission Ridge and in the Atlanta campaign. Died 15 Jan., 1879.

CAIRNS, ROBT. [Born in Ireland. Appointed from Ky.]
2nd Lieut. 28th Ky. Vols., 30 April, 1862. 1st Lieut., 27 June, 1863. Resigned 4 Nov., 1864. 2nd Lieut. 17th Inf., 16 Oct., 1867. 1st Lieut, 1 June, 1875. Died 4 Aug., 1876.

CALDWELL, DANIEL G. [Born in Penn. Appointed from Penn.]
Asst. Surg. 74th Penn. Vols., 4 Aug., 1862. Mustered out 21 Oct., 1863. 1st Lieut. Asst. Surg., 28 Feb., 1866. Capt., 11 Dec., 1867. Maj. and Surg., 14 Dec., 1882. Retired for disability 2 May, 1896.

CALDWELL, EDWIN A. [Born in N. Y. Appointed from N. Y.]
2nd Lieut. 3rd Inf., 27 Oct., 1820. Resigned 1 Sept., 1821.

CALDWELL, FRANK M.* [Born in N. Y. Appointed from Wis.]
2nd Lieut. 3rd Cav., 12 June, 1890. 1st Lieut. 7th Cav., 6 Feb., 1891. Lieut. Col. 4th Wis. Vols., 11 July, 1898. Mustered out Vols., 28 Feb., 1899.

CALDWELL, GEORGE. [Born in ——. Appointed from Ohio]
3rd Lieut. Mounted Rangers, 30 July, 1832. Disbanded 1 Oct., 1833.

CALDWELL, GEORGE A. [Born in Ky. Appointed from K—]
Maj. Q. M. Vols., 28 June, 1846. Maj. Inf., 3 March, 1847; Voltigeurs, 9 April, 1847. Disbanded 25 Aug., 1848. Bvt. Lieut. Col., 13 Sept., 1847, for gallant and meritorious conduct at Chapultepec.

CALDWELL, GREEN W. [Born in N. C. Appointed from N. C.]
Asst. Surg., 13 July, 1832. Resigned 19 Oct, 1832. Capt. Inf., 3 March, 1847; 3rd Drag., 9 April, 1847. Disbanded 20 July, 1848.

CALDWELL, JAMES N.* [Born in Ohio. Appointed from Ohio.]
Bvt. 2nd Lieut. 2nd Inf., 1 July, 1840. 2nd Lieut. 1st Inf., 5 Aug., 1840. 1st Lieut., 31 March, 1847. Capt., 26 Oct., 1850. Maj. 18th Inf., 27 Feb., 1862. Bvt. Lieut. Col., 31 Dec., 1862, for gallant and meritorious service in the Battle of Murfreesboro', Tenn. Retired 29 Dec., 1863. Died 12 March, 1886.

CALDWELL, VERNON A.* [Born in Mo. Appointed from Ind.]
2nd Lieut. 25th Inf., 12 June, 1890. 1st Lieut. 5th Inf., 7 June, 1897. Trans. to 25th Inf., 24 June, 1897. Capt. 7th Inf., 15 Feb., 1900.

CALEF, JOHN H.* [Born in Mass. Appointed from Mass.]
2nd Lieut. 5th Art., 17 June, 1862. Trans. to 2nd Art., 6 Oct., 1862. 1st Lieut., 4 Nov., 1863 Reg. Adj., 18 Nov., 1864, to 16 March, 1875. Bvt. Capt., 6 July, 1864, for gallantry and good conduct in the Battle of Gettysburg, and in the campaign from the Rapidan to Petersburg, Va. Bvt. Maj., 13 March, 1865, for good conduct and gallant service during the war. Capt. 10th Cav., 12 June, 1867, declined. Capt. 2nd Art., 16 March, 1875. Maj. 1st Art., 27 Aug., 1896. Lieut. Col. 3rd Art., 6 June, 1900.

CALHOUN, FRED S. [Born in Ohio. Appointed from Dakota.]
Priv. Co. B, 137th Ohio Vols., 12 May, 1864. Discharged 19 Aug., 1864. 2nd Lieut. 14th Inf., 10 March, 1875. 1st Lieut., 3 Dec., 1886. Retired for disability 6 May, 1890.

CALHOUN, JAMES. [Born in Ohio. Appointed from Army.]
Priv. and Sergt. Co. D, 23rd Inf., 22 Feb., 1865, to 24 Oct., 1867. 2nd Lieut. 32nd Inf., 31 July, 1867. Trans. to 21st Inf., 19 April, 1869. Unass'd 29 Oct., 1870. Ass'd to 7th Cav., 1 Jan., 1871. 1st Lieut., 9 Jan., 1871. Killed 25 June, 1876, in action with Indians in Montana.

CALHOUN, JAMES T. [Born in N. J. Appointed from N. J.]
Asst. Surg 74th N. Y. Vols., 15 Oct., 1861 Maj. Surg., 1 Nov., 1861. Asst. Surg., 13 April, 1863. Bvt. Capt. and Bvt. Maj., 13 March, 1865, for faithful and meritorious service during the war. Bvt. Lieut. Col., 19 July, 1866, for distinguished and meritorious service at Hart's Island, N. Y., where cholera prevailed, and of which he died 19 July, 1866.

CALHOUN, JOSEPH, Jr. [Born in S C. Appointed from S. C.]
2nd Lieut. 1st Rifles, 2 Dec., 1812. 1st Lieut. 1st Rifles, 24 Jan., 1814. Trans. to Rifle Regt., 17 May, 1815. Capt., 31 March, 1817. Resigned 15 April, 1818.

CALHOUN, PATRICK.* [Born in D. C. Appointed from S. C.]
Bvt. 2nd Lieut. 2nd Drag., 1 July, 1841. 2nd Lieut., 15 Dec., 1841. 1st Lieut., 29 July, 1847. Capt., 6 Sept., 1853. Died 4 June, 1858.

CALHOUN, WM. R.* [Born in S. C. Appointed at Large.]
Bvt. 2nd Lieut. 1st Drag., 1 July, 1850. Resigned 26 April, 1851.

CALIFF, JOSEPH M. [Born in Penn. Appointed from Penn.]
Cadet Naval Acad., 27 Sept, 1860, to 13 Nov., 1861. 2nd Lieut. 7th U. S. Col. Troops,

8 Oct., 1863. 1st Lieut., 5 March, 1865. Bvt. Capt. Vols., 13 March, 1865, for gallant and meritorious service. Mustered out 13 Oct., 1866. 2nd Lieut. 3rd Art., 17 Aug., 1867. 1st Lieut., 21 May, 1875. Capt., 29 Oct., 1896. Honor graduate of Artillery School, 1871.

CALL, RICHD. K. [Born in Ky. Appointed from Ky.]
1st Lieut. 44th Inf., 15 July, 1814. Trans. to 1st Inf., 17 May, 1815. Capt., 1 July, 1818. Resigned 1 May, 1822. Bvt. Capt., 7 Nov., 1814, for gallant conduct at Pensacola and New Orleans. Died 14 Sept., 1862.

CALLAHAN, CHAS. M. [Born in Ireland. Appointed from Mo.]
Sergt. Co. K, 1st Mo. Vols., 26 April, 1861. Discharged 9 Aug., 1861. 2nd Lieut. 1st Mo. Light Art., 9 Aug., 1861. 2nd Lieut., 1 Sept., 1861. Capt., 26 Jan., 1865. Mustered out 16 June, 1865. 2nd Lieut. 3rd Art., 23 Feb., 1866. 1st Lieut., 28 July, 1866. Bvt. Capt., 2 March, 1867, for gallant and meritorious service in the Battle of Bentonville, N. C. Trans. to 4th Cav., 13 Jan., 1874, taking rank from 15 Feb., 1868. Capt., 2 April, 1879. Retired 11 Feb., 1887. Died 17 May, 1895.

CALLAN, ROBERT E.* [Born in Md. Appointed from Tenn.]
Addl. 2nd Lieut. 5th Art., 12 June, 1896. 2nd Lieut., 27 Aug., 1896. 1st Lieut., 2 March, 1899.

CALLEHAN, JAMES. [Born in N. Y. Appointed from Army.]
Priv., Corpl. and Sergt. Troop D, 4th Cav., 25 July, 1860, to 28 Aug., 1863. 2nd Lieut. 4th Cav., 10 Aug., 1863. 1st Lieut., 25 July, 1865. Died 25 March, 1870. Bvt. 1st Lieut., 16 Dec., 1864, for gallant and meritorious service in pursuit of rebel forces under Gen. Hood. Bvt. Capt., 2 April, 1865, for gallant and meritorious service at the capture of Selma, Ala. Bvt. Maj., 2 April, 1865, for gallantry during the pursuit of Hood after the Battle of Nashville, and in the charge of his regiment against the earthworks at Selma, Ala.

CALLENDER, FRANKLIN D.* [Born in N. Y. Appointed from N. Y.]
Bvt. 2nd Lieut. Ord., 1 July, 1839. 2nd Lieut., 16 Nov., 1839. Bvt. 1st Lieut., 1 May, 1842, for active and highly meritorious service in the war against the Florida Indians. 1st Lieut. Ord., 3 March, 1847. Bvt. Capt., 20 Aug., 1847, for gallant and meritorious conduct in the Battles of Contreras and Churubusco. Capt. Ord., 1 July, 1853. Bvt. Maj., 14 April, 1862, for faithful and meritorious service in his department. Maj. Ord., 3 March, 1863. Bvt. Lieut. Col., 13 March, 1865, for faithful and meritorious service during the Siege of Corinth, Miss. Bvt. Col., 13 March, 1865, for faithful and meritorious service in the Ord. Dept. at St. Louis, Mo. Bvt. Brig. Gen., 9 April, 1865, for faithful and meritorious service in the Ord. Dept. Lieut. Col. Ord., 6 April, 1866. Col., 23 June, 1874. Retired 29 May, 1879. Died 13 Dec., 1882.

CALLINAN, DANIEL F. [Born in Ireland. Appointed from Army.]
Priv. Co. E, 1st Inf., 5 Sept., 1860. Corpl., 1 Aug., 1861. 1st Sergt., 21 Jan., 1862. Sergt., 20 Feb., 1863. 2nd Lieut. 1st Inf., 10 Aug., 1863. 1st Lieut., 28 July, 1866. Capt., 1 July, 1879. Retired for disability 22 Oct., 1891.

CALLIS, JOHN B. [Born in N. C. Appointed from Wis.]
Capt. 7th Wis. Vols., 30 Aug., 1861. Maj., 5 Jan., 1863. Discharged 29 Nov., 1863. Maj. Vet. Res. Corps, 24 May, 1864. Lieut. Col., 11 Feb., 1865. Bvt. Col. and Brig. Gen. Vols., 13 March, 1865, for efficient and meritorious service. Mustered out 14 May, 1867. Capt. 45th Inf., 7 March, 1867. Resigned 4 Feb., 1868. Bvt. Maj., 7 March, 1867, for gallant and meritorious service in the Battle of Gettysburg, Penn.

CALLIS, OTHO W. [Born in Va. Appointed from Va.]
2nd Lieut. 12th Inf., 14 May, 1812. 1st Lieut., 26 June, 1813. Reg. Adj., May, 1813, to June, 1815. Trans. to 4th Inf., 17 May, 1815. Capt., 12 May, 1817. Resigned 31 May, 1817. Died 13 May, 1831.

CALVERT, ROBERT B.* [Born in Ind. Appointed from Ind.]
2nd Lieut. 18th Inf., 15 Feb., 1899.

CALVERT, WM. J.* [Born in Ky. Appointed from Ky.]
Asst. Surg., 30 Jan., 1899.

CALWELL, JAMES H. [Born in Md. Appointed from Va.]
Capt. Inf., 23 Feb., 1847; Voltigeurs, 9 April, 1847. Died 18 Sept., 1847, of wounds received at Paso Ovigas, Mexico.

CAMBRIDGE, TOBIA P. [Born in Penn. Appointed from Penn.]
Hosp. Surg. Mate, 2 July, 1812. Resigned 20 Dec., 1812. Surg. Light Art., 20 March, 1813. Hosp. Surg. Mate, 12 Sept., 1814. Disbanded 15 June, 1815. Reinstated 3 Sept., 1815. Resigned 1 May, 1816.

CAMERON, BRUA. [Born in Penn. Appointed from Penn.]
Maj. and P. M., 1 May, 1861. Retired 4 Nov., 1863. Died 13 Jan., 1864.

CAMERON, GEORGE H.* [Born in Ill. Appointed from Ill.]
2nd Lieut. 7th Cav., 13 June, 1883. 1st Lieut. 4th Cav., 9 March, 1891. Capt., 2 March, 1899.

CAMERON, WM. A. [Born in England. Appointed from D. C.]
Capt. 16th N. Y. Cav., 6 Dec., 1864. Mustered out 23 June, 1865. 2nd Lieut. 5th Art., 29 Nov., 1865. 1st Lieut., 25 Oct., 1866. Discharged 25 Oct., 1870. Died 2 May, 1873.

CAMP, ELISHA E. [Born in N. Y. Appointed from Army.]
(Served as enlisted man under name of Henry Leon.) Priv. Gen. Ser., 4 to 31 Aug., 1847. 2nd Lieut. 3rd Drag., 28 Aug., 1847. Resigned 4 Feb., 1848. 2nd Lieut. 9th Inf., 14 May, 1857. 1st Lieut., 14 May, 1861. Capt. A. Q. M., 3 Aug., 1861. Died 4 Aug., 1867. Bvt. Maj. and Lieut. Col., 13 March, 1865, for faithful and meritorious service during the war.

CAMP, ERSKINE M. [Born in N. Y. Appointed from N. Y.]
Capt 35th N. Y. Vols., 11 June, 1861. Capt. A. Q. M., Vols., 19 May, 1863. Bvt. Maj. Vols., 13 March, 1865, for faithful and meritorious service. Mustered out 31 July, 1866. 1st Lieut. 40th Inf., 10 June, 1867. Unass'd 20 April, 1869. Ass'd to 12th Inf., 1 Jan., 1871. Died 28 Dec., 1876. Bvt. Capt., 10 June, 1867, for gallant and meritorious service at the Battle of Cedar Mountain, Va. Died 28 Dec., 1876.

Sergt. Co. D, 9 Sept., 1864. 2nd Lieut. and 1st Lieut., 7th Inf., 12 Nov., 1864. Bvt. Capt., 2 March, 1867, for gallant and meritorious service in the Battle of Antietam, Md. Bvt. Maj., 2 March, 1867, for gallant and meritorious service in the Battle of Fredericksburg, Va. Trans. to 18th Inf., 28 Nov., 1871, taking rank from 28 July, 1866. Capt., 6 Feb., 1882. Retired for disability 21 June, 1890. Died 5 Sept., 1897.

BOMFORD, GEORGE N. [Born in S. C. Appointed from the Army.]
Priv. Cos. D and M, 5th Inf., 15 May, 1896, to 6 July, 1898. 2nd Lieut. 5th Inf., 22 June, 1898. 1st Lieut., 2 March, 1899.

BOMFORD, JAMES V.* [Born in N. Y. Appointed from D. C.]
Bvt. 2nd Lieut. 2nd Inf., 1 July, 1832. 2nd Lieut., 6 Oct., 1834. 1st Lieut. 8th Inf., 7 July, 1838. Capt., 4 March, 1845. Bvt. Maj., 20 Aug., 1847, for gallant and meritorious conduct in the Battles of Contreras and Churubusco. Bvt. Lieut. Col., 8 Sept., 1847, for gallant and meritorious conduct in the Battle of Molino del Rey. Maj. 6th Inf., 17 Oct., 1860. Lieut. Col. 16th Inf., 10 Jan., 1862. Bvt. Col., 8 Oct., 1862, for gallant and meritorious service in the Battle of Perryville, Ky. Col. 8th Inf., 18 May, 1864. Bvt. Brig. Gen., 13 March, 1865, for faithful and effective service. Retired 8 June, 1874. Died 6 Jan., 1892.

BOMUS, PETER S.* [Born in N. Y. Appointed from N. Y.]
2nd Lieut. 1st Cav., 15 June, 1870. 1st Lieut., 5 June, 1876. Bvt. 1st Lieut., 27 Feb., 1890, for gallant services in action against Indians at the Mazatzal Mountains, Arizona, 13 Dec., 1872. Capt., 26 March, 1888.

BONAPARTE, JEROME N.* [Born in Md. Appointed from Md.]
Bvt. 2nd Lieut. Mounted Rifles, 1 July, 1852. 2nd Lieut., 3 Aug., 1853. Resigned 16 Aug., 1854.

BOND, ADOLPHUS F.* [Born in N. Y. Appointed from Ohio.]
Bvt. 2nd Lieut. 2nd Inf., 1 July, 1851. 2nd Lieut., 23 Feb., 1852. 1st Lieut., 3 March, 1855. Capt., 6 June, 1861. Retired 1 Dec., 1863. Died 16 April, 1866.

BOND, JOHN L. [Born in Ohio. Appointed from Ohio.]
2nd Lieut. 19th Inf., 1 May, 1899.

BONESTEEL, CHAS. H.* [Born in Conn. Appointed from Dakota.]
2nd Lieut. 21st Inf., 15 June, 1876. 1st Lieut., 17 July, 1883. R. Q. M., 25 March, 1888, to 28 Feb., 1889. Capt., 27 June, 1897.

BONHAM, MILLEDGE L. [Born in S. C. Appointed from S. C.]
Capt. S. C. Vol. in Fla. war, 9 April to 7 July, 1836. Lieut. Col. Inf., 3 March, 1847; 12th Inf., 9 April, 1847. Col., 12 Aug., 1847. Disbanded 25 July, 1848.

BONIFACE, JOHN J. [Born in N. Y. Appointed from the Army.]
Priv., Corpl. and Sergt. Troops A and K, 6th Cav., 22 Jan., 1892, to 30 May, 1894. Priv. Troops A and I, 6th Cav., and H, 4th Cav., 22 Jan., 1896, to 6 July, 1898. 2nd Lieut. 17th Inf., 22 June, 1898. Trans. to 4th Cav., 7 Jan., 1899.

BONNAFFON, AUGUSTUS B. [Born in Penn. Appointed from Penn.]
Corpl. 12th Pa. Vols., 25 April, 1861. Maj. 78th Pa. Vols., 18 Oct., 1861. Lieut. Col., 25 July, 1864. Col., 26 March, 1865. Discharged 27 Dec., 1865.

BONNAFFON, SYLVESTER, Jr. [Born in Pa. Appointed from Pa.]
Priv., Corpl. and Sergt. 99th Pa. Vols., 14 Dec., 1861, to 1 Aug., 1862. 2nd Lieut. 99th Pa. Vols., 1 Aug., 1862. 1st Lieut., 18 June, and Capt., 10 Oct., 1864. Bvt. Maj. U. S. Vols., 13 March, 1865, for gallant and meritorious services at the Battle of Boydton Plank Road, Va. Bvt. Lieut. Col., 13 March, 1865, for gallant and meritorious service during the war. Discharged 1 July, 1867. 2nd Lieut. 31st U. S. Inf., 22 May, 1867. (declined). Awarded Medal of Honor for "distinguished gallantry in action at the Battle of Boydton Plank Road, Va.," 10 Oct., 1864.

BONNAFFON, SYLVESTER, 3rd. [Born in Pa. Appointed from Pa.]
2nd Lieut. 13th Inf., 1 Aug., 1899.

BONNEAU, RICHARD V.* [Born in S. C. Appointed from Ala.]
Bvt. 2nd Lieut. 3rd Inf., 1 July, 1852. 2nd Lieut., 3 March, 1855. Resigned 2 March, 1861.

BONNELL, JOSEPH.* [Born in Penn. Appointed from Penn.]
Bvt. 2nd Lieut. 5th Inf., 1 July, 1825. 2nd Lieut. 3rd Inf., 1 July, 1825. 1st Lieut., 15 July, 1831. Capt. 8th Inf., 7 June, 1838. Died 27 Sept., 1840.

BONNEVILLE, BENJAMIN L. E.* [Born in France. Appointed from N. Y.]
Bvt. 2nd Lieut. Light Art., 11 Dec., 1815. 2nd Lieut., 15 Jan., 1817. 2nd Lieut. 8th Inf., 10 March, 1819. 1st Lieut., 9 July, 1820. Trans. to 7th Inf., 1 June, 1821. Dropped 31 May, 1834. Reinstated 19 April, 1836. Maj. 6th Inf., 15 July, 1845. Lieut. Col. 4th Inf., 7 May, 1849. Col. 3rd Inf., 3 Feb., 1855. Retired 9 Sept., 1861. Died 12 June, 1878. Bvt. Lieut. Col., 20 Aug., 1847, for gallant and meritorious service at Contreras and Churubusco. Bvt. Brig. Gen., 13 March, 1865, for long and faithful service in the army.

BONNEY, SETH. [Born in Mass. Appointed from Mass.]
Priv. Co. C, 6th Mass. Vols., 16 May, 1861. Mustered out 2 Aug., 1861. 2nd Lieut., 26th Mass. Vols., 3 Sept., 1861. 1st Lieut., 11 Feb., 1863. Capt. 11 Dec., 1864. Mustered out 26 Aug., 1865. 1st Lieut. 27th Inf., 28 July, 1866. Capt., 11 Nov., 1868. Unassigned 14 June, 1869. Ass'd to 13th Inf., 1 Jan., 1871. Resigned 1 April, 1872. Priv. Co. I, 13th Inf., 24 Jan., 1879. Discharged 11 Nov., 1879.

BONNYCASTLE, HENRY C. [Born in Ky. Appointed from Ky.]
2nd Lieut. 20th Inf., 9 July, 1898. 1st Lieut. 23rd Inf., 26 March, 1899.

BONNYCASTLE, JOHN C. [Born in Va. Appointed from Va.]
Cadet Mil. Acad., 1 July, 1843, to 9 July, 1846. 1st Lieut., Adj. Cal. Vols., 1 Aug., 1846. 2nd Lieut. 4th Inf., 27 June, 1848. 1st Lieut., 5 Aug., 1853. Capt. A. Q. M., 1 Feb., 1861. Resigned 30 May, 1861. Died 29 Oct., 1884.

BONSALL, SAMUL. W. [Born in Ind. Appointed from Ind.]
2nd Lieut. 3rd Inf., 9 April, 1866. 1st Lieut., 1 Oct., 1867. Resigned 1 Nov., 1872.

BOOGE, AARON J. [Born in Conn. Appointed from N. Y.]
Chaplain, 16 June, 1813. Disbanded 1 June, 1815. Reinstated 3 May, 1816. Disbanded 14 April, 1818.

BOOKER, JACOB J.* [Born in Ind. Appointed from Ind.]
Bvt. 2nd Lieut. 1st Inf., 1 July, 1843. 2nd Lieut. 8th Inf., 1 June, 1845. 1st Lieut., 10 Sept., 1847. Died 26 June, 1849.

BOOKMILLER, EDWIN V.* [Born in Ohio. Appointed from Ohio.]
2nd Lieut. 2nd Inf., 12 June, 1889. 1st Lieut. 9th Inf., 10 July, 1896. Capt. 16th Inf., 8 July, 1899. Trans. to 9th Inf., 29 Aug., 1899.

BOONE, NATHAN. [Born in Ky. Appointed from Mo.]
Capt. Mo. Rangers, 25 March, 1812. Maj., 10 Dec., 1813. Discharged June, 1815. Capt. Mounted Rangers, 16 June, 1832. Capt. 1st Drag., 15 Aug., 1833. Maj., 16 Feb., 1847. Lieut. Col. 2nd Drag., 25 July, 1850. Resigned 15 July, 1853. Died 12 Jan., 1857.

BOOTE, WM. R. [Born in N. H. Appointed from ——.]
Ensign and 2nd Lieut. 3rd Inf., 10 July, 1797. 1st Lieut., 16 July, 1798. Capt., 15 Nov., 1800. Trans. to 2nd Inf., 1 April, 1802. Maj. 6 July, 1812. Col. I. G., 6 April, 1813. Lieut. Col. 2nd Inf., 13 Dec., 1813. Disbanded 15 June, 1815.

BOOTES, JOHN S. [Born in D. C. Appointed from D. C.]
1st Lieut. 12th Inf., 14 May, 1861. Resigned 7 Feb., 1863.

BOOTES, LEVI C. [Born in D. C. Appointed from Army.]
Priv. Co. F, Mounted Rifles, 19 June, 1846. Sergt., 1 Aug., 1846. Bvt. 2nd Lieut. 6th Inf., 28 June, 1848. 2nd Lieut., 28 Sept., 1848. 1st Lieut., 9 June, 1853. Capt., 5 June, 1860. Bvt. Maj., 1 July, 1862, for gallant and meritorious service in the Battle of Malvern Hill, Va. Bvt. Lieut. Col., 13 Dec., 1862, for gallant and meritorious service in the Battle of Fredericksburg, Va. Bvt. Col., 2 July, 1863, for gallant and meritorious service in the Battle of Gettysburg, Pa. Maj. 17th Inf., 20 Sept., 1863. Trans. to 26th Inf., 21 Sept., 1866. Unassigned 15 March, 1869. Ass'd to 20th Inf., 15 Dec., 1870. Lieut. Col. 25th Inf., 1 Jan., 1871. Retired 7 Oct., 1874. Died 18 April, 1896.

BOOTH, CHAS. A. [Born in N. Y. Appointed from N. Y.]
Capt. A. A. G. Vols., 20 June, 1863. Bvt. Maj. Vols. and Bvt. Lieut. Col. Vols., 13 March, 1865, for faithful and meritorious service during the war. Mustered out 10 Feb., 1866. 2nd Lieut. 1st Inf., 7 March, 1867. 1st Lieut., 1 March, 1878. Capt. A. Q. M., 9 Feb., 1883. Maj. Q. M., 21 Aug., 1896.

BOOTH, CHAS. A.* [Born in Vt. Appointed from Vt.]
2nd Lieut. 7th Inf., 14 June, 1872. 1st Lieut., 15 April, 1878. Capt., 19 June, 1891. Maj. 6th Inf., 15 Jan., 1900.

BOOTH, JOHN C.* [Born in Ga. Appointed at Large.]
Bvt. 2nd Lieut. 2nd Art., 1 July, 1848. 2nd Lieut. 4th Art., 31 May, 1849. 1st Lieut., 25 Nov., 1853. Resigned 1 May, 1856. Died 6 Sept., 1862.

BOOTH, OLIN R. [Born in Conn. Appointed from the Army.]
Priv. and Corpl. Troop E, 7th Cav., 10 Oct., 1895, to 9 Oct., 1898. Priv. Gen. Ser., 17 Oct., 1898, to 12 April, 1899. 2nd Lieut. 11th Inf., 5 April, 1899.

BOOTH, WM. L.* [Born in Va. Appointed from D. C.]
3rd Lieut. Corps Art., 21 July, 1814. Trans. to Corps Art., 17 May, 1815. 2nd Lieut., 16 July, 1816. 1st Lieut., 25 April, 1818. Trans. to 3rd Art., 1 June, 1821. Trans. to 4th Art., 16 Aug., 1821. Resigned 21 July, 1822. Died 20 Oct., 1868.

BOOTH, WM. L. [Born in Conn. Appointed from Ky.]
Asst. Surg. 10th Inf., 22 May, 1847. Disbanded 28 Dec., 1849.

BORDEN, GEORGE P. [Born in Ind. Appointed from Ind.]
Priv. Co. C, 121st N. Y. Vols., 25 July, 1862. Discharged 12 Oct., 1863. Cadet Mil. Acad., 16 Sept., 1863, to 23 Jan., 1864. 2nd Lieut. 5th Inf., 1 Oct., 1866. 1st Lieut., 4 Sept., 1878. Capt., 20 Feb., 1891. Maj. 3rd Inf., 8 Sept., 1899. Trans. to 5th Inf., 3 Nov., 1899.

BORDEN, WM. C. [Born in N. Y. Appointed from N. Y.]
Asst. Surg., 3 Dec., 1883. Capt. A. Surg., 3 Dec., 1888. Maj. Brig. Surg. Vols., 4 June, 1898. Honorably discharged from Vols., 31 March, 1899.

BORLAND, HAROLD.* [Born in N. C. Appointed from Ark.]
Bvt. 2nd Lieut. 5th Inf., 1 July, 1860. Resigned 31 March, 1861.

BORROWE, WM. [Born in N. Y. Appointed from N. Y.]
2nd Lieut. 2nd Art., 15 Nov., 1861. 1st Lieut., 1 Aug., 1863. Dismissed 8 March, 1865. Reinstated 26 July, 1865. Mustered out 1 Jan., 1871.

BORTHWICK, WM. A. [Born in Penn. Appointed from Penn.]
2nd Lieut. 6th Cav., 9 May, 1867. 1st Lieut., 25 Nov., 1867. Died 12 June, 1872.

BORUP, HENRY D.* [Born in Minn. Appointed from Minn.]
2nd Lieut. 2nd Art., 15 June, 1876. Trans. to Ord., 13 Sept., 1879. 1st Lieut., 13 Sept., 1879. Capt., 15 June, 1890. (14 years' service). Lieut. Col. Ch. Ord. Off. Vols., 18 July, 1898, to 16 March, 1899.

BOSQUE, JOSEPH. [Born in ——. Appointed from La.]
2nd Lieut. 1st Art., 12 April, 1813. Trans. to Corps Art., 12 May, 1814. Resigned 28 Feb., 1815. 2nd Lieut. Marine Corps, 28 Feb., 1815. Reinstated as 2nd Lieut. Corps Art., 2 Dec., 1815, to rank from 12 April, 1813. Dropped 8 Sept., 1817. Reinstated 3 Feb., 1818. Resigned 31 Aug., 1818.
Trans. to Corps Art., 17 May, 1815. Resigned 30 Sept., 1815.

BOSWELL, BENJN. D. [Born in Ind. Appointed from Iowa.]
1st Sergt. Co. I, W. Va. Vols., 1 Aug., 1861. 2nd Lieut. 4th W. Va. Vols., 11 Nov., 1861. 1st Lieut., 8 Dec., 1862. Capt., 1 March, 1863. Maj. 2nd W. Va. Vet. Vols., 29 Dec., 1864. Mustered out 16 July, 1865. 2nd Lieut. 29th Inf., 18 June, 1867. Bvt. 1st Lieut., 18 June, 1867, for gallant and meritorious service in the Siege of Vicksburg, Miss. Bvt. Capt., 18 June, 1867, for meritorious service during the war. Trans. to 11th Inf., 25 April, 1869. 1st Lieut., 8 Feb., 1877. Retired 28 June, 1878.

BOSWORTH, FELIX G. [Born in La. Appointed from La.]
Maj. P. M., 3 March, 1847. Died 9 June, 1847.

BOSWORTH, GEORGE B. [Born in N. Y. Appointed from N. Y.]
Priv. Co. B, 8th N. Y. Militia, 24 May to 2 Aug., 1861. Maj. 87th N. Y. Vols., 15 Oct., 1861. Resigned 15 July, 1862. Maj. 16th N. Y. Cav., 9 Jan., 1864. 3rd N. Y. Prov. Cav., 23 June, 1865. Mustered out 21 Sept., 1865. 1st Lieut. 9th Cav., 31 July, 1867. Mustered out 1 Jan., 1871.

BLODGETT, GARDNER S. [Born in Vt. Appointed from Vt.]
Capt. A. Q. M. Vols., 3 Aug., 1861. Capt. A. Q. M., 2 July, 1864. Resigned 14 Oct., 1865. Bvt. Maj. and Lieut. Col., 13 March, 1865, for faithful and meritorious service during the war.

BLOOD, HOSEA. [Born in Ky. Appointed from Ky.]
Hosp. Surg. Mate, 6 July, 1812. Hosp. Surg., 5 May, 1813. Disbanded 15 June, 1815. Reinstated 3 May, 1816, as Post Surg. Died 12 Sept., 1816.

BLOOD, WM. [Born in N. Y. Appointed from Ind.]
2nd Lieut. 3rd Drag., 9 April, 1847. Disbanded 31 July, 1848.

BLOODGOOD, EDWARD. [Born in Me. Appointed from Wis.]
Sergt. Maj. 1st Wis. Inf., 17 May, 1861. Mustered out 21 Aug., 1861. Capt. 1st Wis. Inf., 18 Oct., 1861. Resigned 4 Aug., 1862. Lieut. Col. 22nd Wis. Inf., 1 Sept., 1862. Dismissed 9 Oct., 1863. Reinstated 28 Dec., 1863. Col. 12 May, 1865. Mustered out 12 June, 1865. Capt. 38th Inf., 28 July, 1866. Trans. to 24th Inf., 11 Nov., 1869. Dismissed 6 Dec., 1869. Reinstated 28 March, 1870. Mustered out 1 Jan., 1871. Bvt. Maj., 2 March, 1867, for gallant and meritorious service in the Battle of Resaca, Ga. Bvt. Lieut. Col., 2 March, 1867, for gallant and meritorious service in the Savannah campaign.

BLOODGOOD, WM.* [Born in N. Y. Appointed from N. Y.]
Bvt. 2nd Lieut. 1st Inf., 1 July, 1824. 2nd Lieut. 2nd Inf., 1 July, 1824. 1st Lieut., 28 Dec., 1832. Resigned 31 Dec., 1836. Died 1 Aug., 1874.

BLOOM, JACOB E.* [Born in Ohio. Appointed from Ohio.]
2nd Lieut. 4th Art., 13 June, 1873. 1st Lieut., 28 April, 1875. Resigned 1 Jan., 1880.

BLOW, WM. N., Jr. [Born in Va. Appointed from Va.]
2nd Lieut. 15th Inf., 30 Oct., 1884. 1st Lieut. 1st Inf., 22 Oct., 1891. Trans. to 15th Inf., 5 Nov., 1891. Capt., 2 March, 1899.

BLUE, URIAH. [Born in Va. Appointed from Va.]
2nd Lieut. 8th Inf., 12 July, 1799. Discharged 15 June, 1800. In 2nd Inf., 16 Feb., 1801. Disbanded 1 June, 1802. 1st Lieut. 7th Inf., 3 May, 1808. Capt., 9 May, 1809. Maj. 39th Inf., 13 March, 1814. Disbanded 15 June, 1815. Reinstated 2 Dec., 1815, as Capt. 8th Inf. Resigned 3 Dec., 1816. Retained 2 Dec., 1815 (in re-organization under Act of 3 March, 1815), as Capt. 8th Inf., with Bvt. of Maj. from 13 March, 1814. Died May, 1836.

BLUNT, ALBERT C.* [Born in N. Y. Appointed from Texas.]
Addl. 2nd Lieut. 3rd Art., 11 June, 1881. 2nd Lieut. 5th Art., 30 Oct., 1881. 1st Lieut., 10 Aug., 1887. Capt., 2 March, 1899. Graduate of the Artillery School, 1886.

BLUNT, ASA P. [Born in Vt. Appointed from Vt.]
1st Lieut. Adj. 3rd Vt. Vols., 20 June, 1861. Mustered out 31 Aug., 1861. Lieut. Col. 6th Vt. Vols., 15 Oct., 1861. Mustered out 18 Sept., 1862. Col. 12th Vt. Vols., 4 Oct., 1862. Mustered out 14 July, 1863. Capt. A. Q. M. Vols., 29 Feb., 1864. Bvt. Maj., Lieut. Col. and Col Vols., 9 June, 1865, for faithful and meritorious service. Bvt. Brig. Gen. Vols., 13 March, 1863, for faithful and meritorious service. Col. Q. M. (Act 4 July, 1864), 31 July, 1866, to 1 Jan., 1867. Capt. A. Q. M., 28 March, 1867. Vacated commission of Capt. A. Q. M. Vols., 9 April, 1867. Bvt. Maj., 28 March, 1867, for gallant and meritorious service in the Battle of Lee's Mill, 16 April, 1862. Bvt. Lieut. Col., 28 March, 1867, for gallant and meritorious service in the Battle of Savage Station, Va. Bvt. Col., 28 March, 1867, for meritorious service during the war. Maj. Q. M., 30 Sept., 1889. Died 4 Oct., 1889.

BLUNT, CHAS. E.* [Born in N. H. Appointed at Large.]
Bvt. 2nd Lieut. Eng., 1 July, 1846. 2nd Lieut., 28 Feb., 1848. 1st Lieut., 2 Feb., 1854. Capt., 1 July, 1860. Maj., 3 March, 1863. Bvt. Lieut. Col., 30 June, 1866, for long and faithful service. Bvt. Col., 30 June, 1866, for meritorious service during the war. Lieut. Col. Eng., 7 March, 1867. Col., 30 June, 1882. Retired, over 30 years' service, 10 Jan., 1887. Died 10 July, 1892.

BLUNT, J. Y. MASON. [Born in D. C. Appointed from Md.]
2nd Lieut. 10th Inf., 26 Feb., 1885. Trans. to 5th Cav., 4 Nov., 1886. 1st Lieut., 11 Dec., 1893. Trans. to 3rd Cav., 24 Oct., 1896. Graduate of the Infantry and Cavalry School, 1887. Capt. A. Q. M. Vols., 26 Nov., 1898.

BLUNT, MATTHEW M.* [Born in N. Y. Appointed from N. Y.]
Bvt. 2nd Lieut. 1st Art., 1 July, 1853. 2nd Lieut. 2nd Art., 30 Sept., 1853. 1st Lieut., 31 March, 1855. Capt. 12th Inf., 14 May, 1861. Bvt. Maj., 1 July, 1862, for gallant and meritorious service in the Battle of Malvern Hill, Va. Bvt. Lieut. Col., 13 Dec., 1862, for gallant and meritorious service in the Battle of Fredericksburg, Va. Bvt. Col., 19 June, 1864, for gallant and meritorious service in front of Petersburg, Va. Maj. 7th Inf., 30 July, 1865. Trans. to 14th Inf., 15 March, 1869. Lieut. Col. 25th Inf., 7 Oct., 1874. Col. 16th Inf., 3 July, 1883. Retired, operation of law, 13 Aug., 1894.

BLUNT, STANHOPE E.* [Born in Mass. Appointed from N. Y.]
2nd Lieut. 13th Inf., 14 June, 1872. 1st Lieut., 27 March, 1874. Trans. to Ord., 1 Nov., 1874. Capt., 24 April, 1880. Maj., 7 July, 1898.

BOARD, BUCKNER.* [Born in Ky. Appointed from Ky.]
2nd Lieut. 3rd Art., 1 July, 1838. 1st Lieut., 1 Aug., 1838. Resigned 31 March, 1840. Col. 2nd Ky. Cav., 9 Sept., 1861. Resigned 25 Dec., 1862.

BOARDMAN, ELIJAH. [Born in Conn. Appointed from Conn.]
Cornet Lieut. Drag., 13 June, 1808. 2nd Lieut., 15 Feb., 1809. 1st Lieut., 3 May, 1810. Capt., 1 Aug., 1813. Trans. to 26th Inf., 21 April, 1814. Disbanded 15 June, 1815. Reinstated 2 Dec., 1815, as 1st Lieut. 6th Inf. Capt., 31 March, 1817. Trans. to 2nd Inf., 1 June, 1821. Died 22 March, 1832. Retained 2 Dec., 1815, (in reorganization under Act of 3 March, 1815), as 1st Lieut. 6th Inf., with Bvt. of Capt. from 1 Aug., 1813. Bvt. Maj., 31 March, 1827, for ten years' faithful service in one grade.

BODAMER, JOHN A. [Born in N. Y. Appointed from N. Y.]
Musician and Priv. Co. B, 21st N. Y. Vols., 12 May, 1861. Mustered out 18 May, 1863. Priv. and Sergt. Co. B, and Sergt. Maj. 24th N. Y. Cav., 22 Dec., 1863, to 24 May, 1865. 2nd Lieut. 1st Prov. N. Y. Cav., 24 May, 1865. Mustered out 19

July, 1865. 2nd Lieut. 10th Cav., 7 March, 1867. 1st Lieut., 11 Dec., 1867. Discharged 1 Dec., 1870.

BODFISH, CHAS. N. [Born in Me. Appointed from Me.]
Capt. of Inf., 23 Feb., 1847; 9th Inf., 9 April, 1847. Bvt. Maj. 20 Aug., 1847. Disbanded 26 Aug., 1848. Bvt. Maj., 20 Aug., 1847, for gallant and meritorious conduct at Contreras and Churubusco. Died 16 March, 1865.

BODFISH, SUMNER H.* [Born in Mass. Appointed from Ga.]
Priv. Co. D, 46th Mass. Vols., 25 Sept., 1862, to 30 May, 1863. Priv. Co. A, 2nd Mass. Art., 28 April to 16 Sept., 1863. Cadet Mil. Acad., 16 Sept., 1863. 2nd Lieut. 6th Cav., 15 June, 1868. Reg. Adj., 27 Nov., 1869, to 31 Aug., 1870. Discharged 1 Jan., 1871.

BOECKLIN, WERNER. [Born in Switzerland. Appointed from N. Y.]
Capt. 19th Inf., 28 Oct., 1861. Resigned 7 July, 1864.

BOEHM, PETER M. [Born in N. Y. Appointed from Montana Ter.]
Priv. Gen. Mounted Ser., 3 July, 1858. Bugler Co. B, 2nd Cav., 20 April, 1861. Discharged 3 July, 1863. Priv. Gen. Ser., 3 Sept., 1863. Discharged 1 March, 1865. 2nd Lieut. 15th N. Y. Cav., 1 March, 1865. Mustered out 4 Oct., 1865. 2nd Lieut. 4th Cav., 1 May, 1866. 1st Lieut., 27 Sept., 1866. Capt., 1 May, 1873. Retired 1 March, 1878. Medal of Honor for most distinguished gallantry in action at Dinwiddie Court House, Va., 31 March, 1865, while acting as A. de C. to Gen. Custer, in taking a flag from the hands of the color bearer, riding in front of a line that was being driven back by the enemy, and, under a heavy fire, rallying the men, re-forming the line, and repulsing the charge; while serving as 2nd Lieut. 15 New York. Cav. Vols. Bvt. Capt., 27 Feb., 1890, for gallant services in action against Indians on the Brazos River, Texas., 28 and 29 Oct., 1869; special gallantry in action on the same river, 10 Oct., 1871; and gallant conduct in action against Indians on the Red River, Tex., 29 Sept., 1872.

BOGARDUS, EDGAR. [Born in N. Y. Appointed from Ill.]
Capt. of Inf., 23 Feb., 1847; 14th Inf., 9 April, 1847. Disbanded 25 July, 1848.

BOGARDUS, STEPHEN H. [Born in N. Y. Appointed from N. Y.]
Corpl. and Sergt. Co. C, 5th N. Y. Vols., 9 May to 16 Dec., 1861. 2nd Lieut. Purnell Legion Md. Vols., 30 Nov., 1861. 1st Lieut., 2 Jan., 1863. Mustered out 24 Oct., 1864. Capt. 192nd N. Y. Vols., 28 March, 1865. Bvt. Maj. Vols., 13 March, 1865, for faithful and meritorious service during the war. Mustered out 28 Aug., 1865. 2nd Lieut. 4th Inf., 4 May, 1866. Unassigned 23 March, 1869. Re-ass'd to 4th Inf., 14 July, 1869. Mustered out 1 Jan., 1871.

BOGART, ISAAC H. [Born in N. Y. Appointed from N. Y.]
Mil. Storekeeper Ord. Dept., 24 May, 1837. Resigned 1 April, 1841.

BOGGS, WM. M. [Born in Penn. Appointed from Penn.]
Priv. Co. F, 114th Pa. Vols., 30 July, 1862, to 14 Feb., 1865. 2nd Lieut. 57th U. S. Col. Inf., 15 Feb., 1865. Resigned 4 April, 1865. 2nd Lieut. 38th Inf., 28 July, 1866. Resigned 17 July, 1867.

BOGGS, FRANK C., Jr.* [Born in N. J. Appointed from Pa.]
Addl. 2nd Lieut. Eng., 26 April, 1898. 2nd Lieut., 5 July, 1898. 1st Lieut., 7 Feb., 1900.

BOGGS, WM. R.* [Born in Ga. Appointed from Ga.]
Bvt. 2nd Lieut. Top. Eng., 1 July, 1853. Trans. to Ord., 28 June, 1854. 2nd Lieut., 31 Dec., 1854. 1st Lieut., 7 Nov., 1856. Resigned 1 Feb., 1861.

BOICE, THEODORE A. [Born in N. Y. Appointed from N. Y.]
Sergt. Co. A, 5th N. Y. Cav., 15 Aug., 1861. 1st Lieut., 2 Jan., 1863. Capt., 2 April, 1864. Maj., 13 Oct., 1864. Lieut. Col., 30 Jan., 1865. Mustered out 19 July, 1865. Served as Priv., Sergt. and 1st Sergt. Troop G, 2nd Cav., 30 Sept., 1865, to 14 May, 1867, under name of Guy Traver. 1st Lieut. 9th Cav., 28 July, 1866. Capt., 31 July, 1867. Cashiered 16 July, 1869.

BOIES, JUSTUS A. [Born in Mass. Appointed from N. Y.]
Priv. Co. A, 71st N. Y. Militia, 20 April to 21 June, 1861. 1st Lieut. 13th Inf., 14 May, 1861. Died 28 June, 1863, of wounds received at Vicksburg. Bvt. Capt., 28 June, 1863, for gallant and meritorious service in action in front of Vicksburg, Miss.

BOLD, JOHN. [Born in S. C. Appointed from S. C.]
2nd Lieut. 8th Inf., 27 June, 1848. Died 25 May, 1852.

BOLLES, ASA.* [Born in Ohio. Appointed from Ohio.]
2nd Lieut. 3rd Art., 17 June, 1862. Died 21 April, 1863.

BOLLES, FRANK C.* [Born in Ill. Appointed from Mo.]
Cadet at Mil. Acad., 17 June, 1891, to 19 Jan., 1894. Re-appointed 17 Feb., 1894. Addl. 2nd Lieut. 6th Inf., 12 June, 1896. 2nd Lieut. 18th Inf., 6 Jan., 1897. 1st Lieut. 6th Inf., 11 Jan., 1899.

BOLTON, EDWARD C. [Born in N. Y. Appointed from the Army.]
Priv., Corpl. and Sergt. Co. G, 23rd Inf., 21 Aug., 1891, to 20 Aug., 1894. Priv. and Corpl. Co. H, 19th Inf., 7 Oct., 1894, to 16th Nov., 1899. 2nd Lieut. 17th Inf., 1 Oct., 1899.

BOLTON, EDWIN B.* [Born in Miss. Appointed from Miss.]
2nd Lieut. 23rd Inf., 16 June, 1875. 1st Lieut., 15 Feb., 1884. Reg. Adj. 1 April, 1886, to 31 March, 1890. Capt. 23rd Inf., 21 Oct., 1891. Trans. to 16th Inf., 28 Oct., 1899.

BOMFORD, GEORGE.* [Born in N. Y. Appointed from N. Y.]
Cadet Mil. Acad., 24 Oct., 1804, to 30 June, 1805. 2nd Lieut. Eng., 1 July, 1805. 1st Lieut., 30 Oct., 1806. Capt., 23 Feb., 1808. Maj. A. C. O., 18 June, 1812. Maj. Eng., 6 July, 1812. Lieut. Col. Ord., 9 Feb., 1815. Trans. to 1st Art., 1 June, 1821. Col. Chief of Ord., 30 May, 1832. Died 25 March, 1848. Bvt. Lieut. Col., 22 Dec., 1814, for distinguished service in the Ord. Dept. Bvt. Col., 9 Feb., 1825, for ten years' faithful service in one grade.

BOMFORD, GEORGE N. [Born in N. Y. Appointed from Army.]
1st Lieut. 42nd N. Y. Vols., 28 June, 1861. Capt., 19 Feb., 1862. Lieut. Col., 2 Aug., 1862. Mustered out 16 March, 1863. Priv. Co. D, 1st Batt. 15th Inf., 25 Aug., 1864.

CAROLIN, ALEXR. [Born in N. Y. Appointed from N. Y.]
2nd Lieut. 4th Inf., 5 Aug., 1861. 1st Lieut., 25 Sept., 1861. Capt., 9 June, 1864. Died 23 Sept., 1865. Bvt. Maj., 13 March, 1865, for gallant and meritorious service.

CAROLIN, DENIS. [Born in N. Y. Appointed from N. Y.]
1st Lieut. 155th N. Y. Vols., 18 Nov., 1862. Capt., 9 Feb., 1863. Resigned 14 Oct., 1864. 2nd Lieut. 19th Inf., 23 Feb., 1866. 1st Lieut., 28 July, 1866. Discharged 10 Dec., 1870.

CARPENTER, ARTHUR B. [Born in Mass. Appointed from Army.]
Priv. and Sergt. Co. D, 19th Inf., 14 Oct., 1861, to 25 Dec., 1862. 2nd Lieut. 19th Inf., 29 Nov., 1862. 1st Lieut., 20 Sept., 1863. Capt., 29 Jan., 1866. Trans. to 37th Inf., 21 Sept., 1866. Unass'd 18 May, 1869 Mustered out 1 Jan., 1871. Bvt. Capt., 1 Sept., 1864, for gallant and meritorious service during the Atlanta campaign and at the Battle of Jonesboro', Ga.

CARPENTER, EDWARD. [Born in Mass. Appointed from Pa.]
Priv. 1st Troop Phila. City Cav., 7 May, 1898, to 22 July, 1898. 2nd Lieut. 2nd Art., 9 July, 1898.

CARPENTER, GILBERT S. [Born in Ohio. Appointed from Army.]
2nd Lieut. 19th Ohio Vols, 22 April, 1861. Mustered out 31 Aug., 1861. Priv. Co. F, 2nd Batt 18th Inf., 14 Sept., 1861. 1st Sergt., 31 Oct., 1861. Sergt., 1 Feb., 1862. 2nd Lieut. 18th Inf., 9 June, 1862. 1st Lieut., 25 Nov., 1862. Bvt. Capt., 31 Dec., 1862, for gallant and meritorious service in the Battle of Murfreesboro', Tenn. Capt. 18th Inf., 21 Dec., 1866. Capt. 45th Inf., 22 Jan., 1867. Trans. to 14th Inf., 22 July, 1869. Maj. 4th Inf., 1 March, 1894. Lieut. Col. 7th Inf., 7 July, 1897. Col. 18th Inf., 29 June, 1899. Brig. Gen. Vols., 21 Sept., 1898, to 12 May, 1899.

CARPENTER, JOHN. [Born in ——. Appointed from N. Y.]
Hosp. Surg. Mate, 9 April, 1817. Resigned 1 March, 1818.

CARPENTER, LOUIS H. [Born in N. J. Appointed from Army.]
Priv. Co. C, 6th Cav., — Nov., 1861. Sergt., 1 Jan., 1862. Trans. to Co. L, 19 May, 1862. Corpl., 5 June, 1862. Sergt., 1 July, 1862. Discharged 20 Sept., 1862. 2nd Lieut. 6th Cav., 17 July, 1862. Bvt. 1st Lieut., 3 July, 1863, for gallant and meritorious service in the Battle of Gettysburg, Penn. Bvt. Capt., 19 Sept., 1864, for gallant and meritorious service in the Battle of Winchester, Va. 1st Lieut. 6th Cav., 28 Sept., 1864. Lieut. Col. 5th U. S. Colored Cav., 1 Oct., 1864. Bvt. Maj. and Bvt. Lieut. Col., 13 March, 1865, for gallant and meritorious service during the war. Bvt. Col. Vols., 28 Sept., 1865, for meritorious service during the war. Col. 5th U. S. Colored Cav., 2 Nov., 1865. Mustered out of Vol. service, 16 March, 1866. Capt. 10th Cav., 28 July, 1866. Bvt. Col., 18 Oct., 1868, for gallant and meritorious service in the engagement with Indians on Beaver Creek, Kansas, 18 Oct., 1868. Maj. 5th Cav., 17 Feb., 1883. Lieut. Col. 2nd Cav., 28 July, 1892. Trans. to 5th Cav., 12 Aug., 1892. Trans. to 7th Cav., 22 Sept., 1894. Col. 5th Cav., 2 June, 1897. Brig. Gen. Vols., 4 May, 1898, to 12 June, 1899. Brig. Gen., 18 Oct., 1899. Retired, over 30 years' service, 19 Oct., 1899. Medal of Honor for distinguished conduct during the Indian campaign in Kansas and Colorado, Sept. and Oct., 1868, and in the forced march 23-25 Sept., 1868, to the relief of Forsyth's scouts; while serving as Capt. 10th Cav., commanding Troop H.

CARPENTER, SETH L. [Born in Maine. Appointed from Maine.]
1st Lieut. 17th Inf., 14 May, 1861. Dismissed 25 Nov., 1862.

CARPENTER, STEPHEN D.* [Born in Maine. Appointed from Maine.]
Bvt 2nd Lieut 1st Inf., 1 July, 1840. 2nd Lieut., 12 Oct., 1840. 1st Lieut., 8 Sept., 1847. Capt., 17 Oct., 1851. Maj. 19th Inf., 14 May, 1861. Killed at the Battle of Murfreesboro', Tenn., 31 Dec., 1862. Bvt. Lieut. Col., 7 April, 1862, for gallant and meritorious service at the Battle of Shiloh, Tenn. Bvt. Col., 31 Dec., 1862, for gallant and meritorious conduct at the Battle of Murfreesboro', Tenn.

CARPENTER, THOS. H. [Born in Penn. Appointed from Iowa.]
1st Lieut. 17th Inf., 14 May, 1861. Capt., 4 May, 1863. Resigned 1 March, 1866. Bvt. Maj., 13 March, 1865, for gallant and meritorious service at the Battle of Gettysburg, Penn.

CARPENTER, WM. L. [Born in N. Y. Appointed from Army.]
Priv. Co. D, 2nd Art., 29 July, 1864. Trans to Co L, 25 Sept., 1865. Corpl., 28 Sept., 1866. Sergt., 29 Jan., 1867. 2nd Lieut. 9th Inf., 5 April, 1867. 1st Lieut., 31 Dec., 1873. Capt., 2 Oct., 1887. Died 10 July, 1898.

CARR, CAMILLO C C [Born in Va. Appointed from Army.]
Priv. Co. F, 1st Cav., 15 Aug., 1862. Corpl., 1 Sept., 1862. Sergt., 26 Dec., 1862. 1st Sergt., 11 April, 1863. Sergt. Maj. 1st Cav., 1 Sept., 1863. Sergt. Co. F, 1st Cav, 28 Oct., 1863. 1st Sergt., 29 Oct., 1863. Discharged 31 Oct., 1863. 2nd Lieut., 31 Oct., 1863. Bvt. 1st Lieut., 6 May, 1864, for gallant and meritorious service in the Battle of Todd's Tavern, Va. 1st Lieut. 1st Cav., 28 June, 1864. Bvt. Capt., 19 Sept., 1864, for gallant and meritorious service in the Battle of Winchester, Va. Capt. 1st Cav., 8 April, 1869. Bvt. Maj., 27 Feb., 1890, for gallant and meritorious services in action against Indians at Camas Meadows, Idaho, 20 Aug., 1877. Maj. 8th Cav., 7 Feb., 1891. Lieut. Col. 5th Cav., 16 Oct., 1898. Col. 4th Cav., 23 Jan., 1900.

CARR, DAVID W. [Born in N. J. Appointed from Army.]
Priv, Corpl. and Sergt. Co. B, 2nd Batt. 12th Inf., 12 May, 1862, to 22 March, 1863. 2nd Lieut. 12th Inf., 19 Feb., 1863. 1st Lieut., 16 June, 1863. Resigned 28 Oct., 1863.

CARR, EUGENE A.* [Born in N. Y. Appointed from N Y.]
Bvt. 2nd Lieut. Mounted Rifles, 1 July, 1850. 2nd Lieut., 30 June, 1851. 1st Lieut. 1st Cav., 3 March, 1855. Capt., 11 June, 1858. Bvt. Lieut. Col., 10 Aug., 1861, for gallant and meritorious service in the Battle of Wilson's Creek, Mo. Col. 3rd Ill. Cav., 16 Aug., 1861. Brig. Gen. Vols., 7 March, 1862, for distinguished service in the Battle of Pea Ridge. Maj. 5th Cav., 17 July, 1862. Bvt. Col., 17 May, 1863, for gallant and meritorious service in the action of Black River Bridge, Miss. Bvt. Maj Gen. Vols., 11 March, 1865. Bvt. Brig. Gen., 13 March, 1865, for gallant

and meritorious service in the capture of Little Rock, Arkansas. Bvt. Maj. Gen., 13 March, 1865, for gallant and meritorious service in the field during the war. Mustered out of Vol service, 15 Jan., 1866. Lieut. Col. 4th Cav., 7 Jan., 1873. Trans. to 5th Cav., 10 April, 1873. Col. 6th Cav., 29 April, 1879. Brig. Gen., 19 July, 1892. Retired by direction of the President, being over 62 years of age, 15 Feb., 1893. Medal of Honor for distinguished gallantry in the Battle of Pea Ridge, Ark., 7 March, 1862, directing the deployment of his command and holding his ground, under a brisk fire of shot and shell, in which he was several times wounded; while serving as Col. 3rd Ill. Cav.

CARR, GEORGE W. [Born in Va. Appointed from Va.]
2nd Lieut. Voltigeurs, 9 April, 1847. Disbanded 31 Aug., 1848. 1st Lieut. 9th Inf., 3 March, 1855. Resigned 20 Feb., 1861.

CARR, IRVING J. [Born in Wis. Appointed from Tex.]
2nd Lieut. 17th Inf., 9 July, 1898. 1st Lieut., 16 March, 1899.

CARR, LEWIS. [Born in Penn. Appointed from Penn.]
1st Lieut. Inf., 16 Feb., 1847. Capt., 5 March, 1847; 11th Inf., 9 April, 1847. Disbanded 17 Aug., 1848.

CARR, MILTON T.* [Born in Va. Appointed from Va.]
Bvt. 2nd Lieut. 1st Drag., 1 July, 1854. 2nd Lieut., 3 March, 1855. 1st Lieut., 20 June, 1857. Capt., 31 May, 1861. 1st Cav., 3 Aug., 1861. Wholly retired 29 Dec., 1863.

CARR, OVERTON, Jr.* [Born in Penn. Appointed at Large.]
2nd Lieut. 12th Inf., 14 June, 1872. Resigned 21 Sept., 1872.

CARR, ROYAL S. [Born in N. H. Appointed from Mass.]
Priv. Co. E. 5th Mass Mil., 1 May, 1861, to 1 Aug., 1861. Priv. Corpl. and Sergt Co. C, 39th Mass. Vols., 14 Aug., 1862, to 2 June, 1865. 2nd Lieut. 18th Inf., 28 July, 1866. 1st Lieut., 25 Feb., 1867. Resigned 12 Aug., 1867.

CARR, SAML. I. [Born in S. C. Appointed from Md.]
Mil Storekeeper, 7 Feb., 1842. Died 24 Oct., 1847.

CARR, WINFRED B. [Born in Vt. Appointed from Vt.]
2nd Lieut. 2nd Art., 9 July, 1898.

CARR, WM. W. [Born in Ind. Appointed from Ind.]
2nd Lieut. 16th Inf., 9 April, 1847. Resigned 25 Oct., 1847.

CARRICK, ROBT. [Born in Ireland. Appointed from Mo.]
Priv. Co. I, Mtd Rifle, 19 March, 1851, to 19 March, 1856. Priv., Corpl. and Sergt Cos. G and H, 2nd Drag., 15 April, 1856, to 18 April, 1861. Maj. 3rd Mo. Cav., 26 Nov., 1861. Lieut. Col., 2 Feb., 1863. Resigned 26 June, 1863. 2nd Lieut. 8th Cav., 7 March, 1867. 1st Lieut., 9 Oct., 1867. Mustered out 28 Dec., 1870.

CARRINGTON, FRANK DE L.* [Born in Ga. Appointed from Ga.]
Addl. 2nd Lieut. 1st Inf., 14 June, 1878 2nd Lieut. 23rd Inf., 25 June, 1878. Trans. to 1st Inf., 28 June, 1878. 1st Lieut., 7 March, 1883. Capt., 30 Aug., 1893. Lieut. Col. 8th Cal. Vols., 8 July, 1898, to muster out, 6 Feb., 1899.

CARRINGTON, HENRY B. [Born in Conn. Appointed from Ohio.]
Col. 18th Inf., 14 May, 1861. Brig. Gen. Vols., 29 Nov., 1862. Mustered out of Vol. service, 24 Aug., 1865. Unass'd 15 March, 1869. Retired 15 Dec., 1870.

CARROLL, CHAS. H. [Born in D. C Appointed from D. C]
2nd Lieut. 5th Art., 5 Aug., 1861. 1st Lieut., 31 July, 1865. Resigned 30 Nov., 1865. Bvt. 1st Lieut., 9 April, 1865, for gallant and meritorious service at the Battle of Sailor's Creek, Va.

CARROLL, EDWIN E. [Born in N. Mex. Appointed from Kan.]
2nd Lieut 1st Inf., 5 Oct., 1899.

CARROLL, GEORGE A. [Born in Md. Appointed from Md.]
Post Surg., 17 Feb., 1817. Resigned 24 Oct., 1818.

CARROLL, HENRY. [Born in N. Y. Appointed from Army.]
Priv. Co. E, 3rd Art., 13 Jan., 1859. Corpl., 1 Dec., 1859. Sergt., 13 Oct., 1860. 1st Sergt., 1 July, 1861. Discharged 13 Jan., 1864. Priv. Co. G, 3rd Art., 3 Feb., 1864. Sergt., 18 March, 1864. 2nd Lieut. 3rd Cav., 18 May, 1864. 1st Lieut., 14 April, 1866. Capt. 9th Cav., 22 Jan., 1867. Bvt. Maj., 27 Feb., 1890, for gallant services in actions against Indians on the main fork of the Brazos River, Tex., 16 Sept., 1869, and against Indians in the San Andreas Mountains, N. M., 7 April, 1880, where he was severely wounded. Maj. 1st Cav., 3 July, 1885. Lieut. Col. 6th Cav., 23 May, 1896. Col. 7th Cav., 29 March, 1899. Brig. Gen. Vols., 8 June, 1898, to 30 Nov., 1898. Retired for over 30 years' service 6 May, 1899.

CARROLL, JOHN C. [Born in Ky. Appointed from Ky.]
1st Sergt. 15th Ky. Vols., 14 Dec., 1861. 2nd Lieut., 25 April, 1862. 1st Lieut., 11 Dec., 1862. Capt., 17 March, 1863. Mustered out 14 Jan., 1865. 2nd Lieut. 14th Inf., 23 Feb., 1866. 1st Lieut., 23 Feb., 1866. Trans. to 32nd Inf., 21 Sept., 1866. Died 5 Nov., 1867.

CARROLL, SAML. S.* [Born in D. C. Appointed from D C.]
Bvt. 2nd Lieut. 9th Inf., 1 July, 1856. 2nd Lieut. 10th Inf., 1 Oct., 1856. 1st Lieut., 25 April, 1861. 1st Lieut. 19th Inf., 14 May, 1861, declined. Capt., 10th Inf., 1 Nov., 1861. Col. 8th Ohio Vols., 15 Dec., 1861. Bvt. Maj., 3 May, 1863, for gallant and meritorious service in the Battle of Chancellorsville, Va. Bvt. Lieut. Col., 3 July, 1863, for gallant and meritorious service in the Battle of Gettysburg, Penn. Bvt. Col., 5 May, 1864, for gallant and meritorious service in the Battle of the Wilderness, Va. Bvt. Brig. Gen. Vols., 12 May, 1864, for gallant and distinguished service in the eight days Battles in the old Wilderness, and at Spottsylvania, C. H., Va. Bvt. Brig. Gen., 13 March, 1865, for gallant and meritorious service in the Battle of Spottsylvania, Va. Bvt. Maj Gen., 13 March, 1865, for gallant and meritorious service in the field during the war. Bvt. Maj. Gen. Vols., 13 March, 1865, for gallant and meritorious service during the war. Mustered out of Vol. service, 15 Jan., 1866. Lieut. Col. 21st Inf., 22 Jan., 1867. Retired with rank of Maj. Gen., 9 June, 1869. Died 28 Jan., 1893

CARROW, CHARLES M.* [Born in Penn. Appointed from Penn.]
Addl. 2nd Lieut. 7th Cav., 14 June, 1878. 2nd Lieut., 28 June, 1878. Died 19 May, 1879.

CARSE, GEORGE B. [Born in N. J. Appointed from Penn.]
2nd Lieut. 40th N. Y. Vols., 14 June, 1861. 1st Lieut., 1 Oct., 1861. Capt., 1 May, 1862. Mustered out 15 Dec., 1863. Capt. Vet. Res. Corps, 25 Jan., 1864. Bvt. Maj. Vols., 13 March, 1865, for gallant and meritorious service in the Battle of Chancellorsville, Va. Bvt. Lieut. Col. Vols. and Bvt. Col. Vols., 13 March, 1865, for gallant and meritorious service during the war. Mustered out 17 June, 1867. Capt. 45th Inf., 21 May, 1867. Unass'd 22 July, 1869. Retired 15 Dec., 1870. Died 28 Nov., 1883.

CARSEN, CHRISTOPHER. [Born in Ky. Appointed from Mo.]
2nd Lieut. Mtd. Rifles, 9 June, 1847. Rejected by Senate, 28 Jan., 1848.

CARSON, JOHN M., Jr.* [Born in Pa. Appointed from Pa.]
2nd Lieut. 5th Cav., 14 June, 1885. 1st Lieut. 7th Cav., 3 Dec., 1891. Trans. to 5th Cav., 9 Feb., 1892. Capt. and A. Q. M., 11 Feb., 1897. Maj. and Chf. Q. M. Vols., 17 May, 1898.

CARSON, THOMAS G.* [Born in Ill. Appointed from Ill.]
2nd Lieut. 4th Inf., 12 June, 1894. Trans. to 4th Cav., 19 Oct., 1894. 1st Lieut., 2 March, 1899. Maj. 11th U. S. Vol. Cav., 10 Aug., 1899.

CARSWELL, WM. A. [Born in S. C. Appointed from S. C.]
Asst Surg., 29 Nov., 1859. Resigned 25 March, 1861.

CARTER, CLIFTON C.* [Born in Ky. Appointed from Ky.]
2nd Lieut. 6th Art., 15 Feb., 1899. Trans. to 2nd Art., 4 April, 1899.

CARTER, EDWARD C. [Born in Va. Appointed from Va.]
Surg. Mate 8th Inf., 15 March, 1819. Resigned 16 Oct., 1819

CARTER, EUGENE.* [Born in Maine. Appointed from Maine.]
Bvt. 2nd Lieut. 8th Inf., 24 June, 1861. 2nd Lieut., 24 June, 1861. 1st Lieut., 26 Oct., 1861. Capt. 29th Inf., 28 July, 1866. Trans. to 11th Inf., 25 April, 1869. Mustered out 1 Jan., 1871. Bvt. Capt., 4 July, 1862, for gallant and meritorious service during the Peninsular campaign in Va. Bvt. Maj., 13 Dec., 1862, for gallant and meritorious service at the Battle of Fredericksburg, Va. Died 10 Feb., 1877.

CARTER, EDWARD CHAMPE. [Born in Va. Appointed from Va.]
Asst. Surg., 22 Oct., 1881. Capt. and Asst. Surg., 22 Oct., 1886. Maj. Surg., 21 Dec., 1898. Maj. Brig. Surg. of Vols., 4 June, 1898, to 22 Feb., 1899.

CARTER, JESSIE McI.* [Born in Mo. Appointed from Mo.]
2nd Lieut. 3rd Cav., 1 July, 1886 1st Lieut. 5th Cav., 11 Feb., 1893.

CARTER, JOHN W. [Born in Mass. Appointed from Army.]
Priv and Corpl. Co. A, and Q. M Sergt. 17th Inf., 5 Nov., 1862, to 10 Aug., 1863. 2nd Lieut. 17th Inf., 10 Aug., 1863. 1st Lieut., 25 Sept., 1863. Resigned 9 Dec., 1864.

CARTER, LAWRENCE F.* [Born in Va. Appointed from Va.]
Bvt. 2nd Lieut. 4th Inf., 1 July, 1825. 2nd Lieut. 7th Inf., 1 July, 1825. 1st Lieut., 15 Dec., 1833. Died 19 Jan., 1837.

CARTER, MASON. [Born in Ga. Appointed from Army.]
(Entered service as Mason Howard.) Priv. Co. B, 1st Inf., 1 Feb., 1860. Corpl., 17 June, 1861. Discharged 21 May, 1862. 2nd Lieut. 5th Inf., 12 May, 1862. 1st Lieut., 14 May, 1864. Bvt. Capt., 18 Oct., 1867, for gallant and meritorious service in an affair with Indians en route from Fort Hays to Fort Harker, Kansas. Capt. 5th Inf., 4 Sept., 1878. Bvt. Maj., 27 Feb., 1890, for gallant services in action against Indians at Bear Paw Mountain, Mont., 30 Sept., 1877. Retired by operation of law 26 Jan., 1898. Medal of Honor for most distinguished gallantry in action against hostile Nez Perce Indians at Bear Paw Mountain, Mont., 30 Sept., 1877, in leading a charge under a galling fire, in which he inflicted great loss upon the enemy; while 1st Lieut. 5th Inf.

CARTER, OBERLIN M.* [Born in Ohio. Appointed from Ohio.]
2nd Lieut. Eng., 12 June, 1880. 1st Lieut., 15 June, 1882. Capt., 26 Feb., 1891. Dismissed 29 Sept., 1899.

CARTER, ROBT. G.* [Born in Maine. Appointed from Mass.]
Priv Co. H, 22nd Mass. Vols., 15 Aug., 1862. Discharged 14 Oct., 1864. 2nd Lieut. 4th Cav., 15 June, 1870. 1st Lieut., 21 Feb, 1875. Retired 28 June, 1876. Bvt. 1st Lieut., 27 Feb., 1890, for specially gallant conduct in action against Indians on the Brazos River, Tex., 10 Oct., 1871. Bvt. Capt., 27 Feb., 1890, for gallant services in action against Kickapoo, Lipan and Mescalero Indians at Remotina, Mexico, 18 May, 1873.

CARTER, W. FITZHUGH. [Born in Va. Appointed from Va.]
1st Lieut. Asst. Surg., 3 June, 1879. Capt. Asst. Surg., 3 June, 1884. Maj. Surg., 30 Nov., 1897.

CARTER, WM. H.* [Born in Tenn. Appointed at Large.]
2nd Lieut. 8th Inf., 13 June, 1873. Trans. to 6th Cav., 28 Nov., 1874, taking rank from 28 Nov., 1874. 1st Lieut., 14 April, 1879 Capt., 20 Nov., 1889. Maj. and A. A. G., 29 Jan., 1897. Lieut. Col. and A. A. G., 18 May, 1898. Medal of Honor for distinguished bravery in action against hostile Apache Indians in rescuing, with the voluntary assistance of two soldiers, the wounded from under a heavy fire of hostile Indians, at Cibicu Creek, Ariz., 30 Aug., 1881; while serving as 1st Lieut. and Regimental Q. M. and Acting Adj. 6th Cav.

CARTWRIGHT, GEORGE S [Born in N. Y. Appointed from N. Y.]
2nd Lieut. 24th Inf., 14 June, 1885. 1st Lieut. 16th Inf., 2 April, 1892. Trans. to 24th Inf., 12 Aug., 1892. Capt., 2 March, 1899. Capt. and A. Q. M. Vols., 19 May, 1898, to 19 June, 1899. Maj. Q. M. Vols., 11 July, 1899.

CARVALLO, CARLOS. [Born in South America. Appointed from D. C.]
1st Lieut. Asst. Surg, 14 May, 1867. Capt. Asst. Surg., 14 May, 1870. Died 23 July, 1882.

CASEY, EDWARD W.* [Born in Cal. Appointed at Large.]
2nd Lieut. 22nd Inf, 13 June, 1873. 1st Lieut., 11 Jan., 1880. Murdered by a Brule Indian, 7 Jan., 1891.

CASEY, JAMES S. [Born in Penn. Appointed from N. Y.]
Priv. Co. H, 7th N. Y. State Militia, 26 April, 1861. Discharged 3 June, 1861. 2nd Lieut. 5th Inf., 5 Aug., 1861. 1st Lieut., 25 Sept., 1861. Capt , 1 Dec., 1863. Bvt. Maj., 25 March, 1865, for gallant and meritorious service during the attack by the enemy on Port Steedman, Va. Maj. 17th Inf., 27 June, 1884. Lieut. Col. 1st Inf., 23 April, 1890. Cal. 22nd Inf., 21 Jan., 1895. Retired by operation of law 28 Jan , 1897. Medal of Honor for most distinguished gallantry in action against hostile Indians at Wolf Mountain, Mont., 8 Jan., 1877, in leading his command in a successful charge against superior numbers of the enemy strongly posted; while Capt. 5th Inf. Bvt. Lieut. Col., 27 Feb , 1890, for conspicuous gallantry in leading his command in a successful charge against a superior number of Indians, strongly posted, at Wolf Mountain, Mont., 6 Jan., 1877.

CASEY, JOHN C.* [Born in England. Appointed from N. J ]
Bvt. 2nd Lieut. 2nd Art., 1 July, 1829. 2nd Lieut., 1 July, 1829. 1st Lieut., 30 April, 1835. Capt. C. S., 7 July, 1838. Capt. 2nd Art., 4 Jan., 1842. Trans. to 3rd Inf, 15 May, 1844. Vacated line commission 18 July, 1846. Died 25 Dec., 1856.

CASEY, JOHN J.* [Born in N. Y. Appointed from N. Y.]
2nd Lieut. 4th Art , 15 June, 1868. Died 24 March, 1869.

CASEY, SILAS.* [Born in R. I. Appointed from R. I.]
Bvt. 2nd Lieut. 7th Inf., 1 July, 1826. 2nd Lieut 2nd Inf., 1 July, 1826. 1st Lieut., 28 June, 1836. Capt., 1 July, 1839. Bvt. Maj., 20 Aug., 1847, for gallant and meritorious conduct in the Battles of Contreras and Churubusco. Bvt Lieut. Col., 13 Sept., 1847, for gallant and meritorious conduct at the Battle of Chapultepec. Lieut. Col. 9th Inf., 3 March, 1855. Brig. Gen. Vols., 31 Aug , 1861. Col. 4th Inf., 9 Oct., 1861. Bvt. Brig. Gen., 31 May, 1862, for gallant and meritorious conduct in the Battle of Fair Oaks, Va. Maj. Gen. Vols., 31 May, 1862. Bvt. Maj. Gen., 13 March, 1865, for gallant and meritorious service during the war. Mustered out of Vol. service, 24 Aug., 1865. Retired 8 July, 1868. Died 22 Jan., 1882.

CASEY, THOS.* [Born in S. C. Appointed from Ala.]
2nd Lieut. 3rd Art., 1 July, 1838. 1st Lieut., 1 Aug., 1838 Resigned 28 Feb., 1839.

CASEY, THOS. L.* [Born in N. Y. Appointed at Large.]
Bvt. 2nd Lieut. Eng , 1 July, 1852. 2nd Lieut., 22 June, 1854. 1st Lieut., 1 Dec., 1856. Capt., 6 Aug , 1861. Maj., 2 Oct., 1863. Bvt. Lieut. Col. and Bvt. Col., 13 March, 1865, for faithful and meritorious service during the war. Lieut. Col. Eng., 2 Sept., 1874. Col and Superintendent of Public Buildings, 3 March, 1877, to 1 April, 1881. Col. Eng., 12 March, 1884. Brig. Gen. and Chief of Eng., 6 July, 1888. Retired by operation of law 10 May, 1895. Died 25 March, 1896.

CASEY, THOS. L., Jr.* [Born in N. Y. Appointed at Large.]
2nd Lieut. Eng., 13 June, 1879. 1st Lieut., 17 June, 1881. Capt., 23 July, 1888. Maj., 5 July, 1898.

CASH, ANDREW D., Jr. [Born in Penn. Appointed from Penn.]
Priv. Commonwealth Pa. Art., 24 April, to 20 June, 1861. 1st Lieut. 18th Inf., 14 May, 1861. Died 24 March, 1862.

CASS, CHAS. L. [Born in N. H. Appointed from Ohio.]
1st Lieut. 27th Inf., 20 May, 1813. Trans. to 19th Inf., 12 May, 1814. Disbanded 15 June, 1815. Reinstated 2 Dec., 1815, in 3rd Inf., Capt., 31 Dec., 1818. Resigned 1 May, 1824.

CASS, GEORGE W.* [Born in Ohio. Appointed from Ohio.]
Bvt. 2nd Lieut. 7th Inf., 1 July, 1832. 2nd Lieut., 4 March, 1833. 1st Lieut., 3 Dec., 1835. Resigned 26 Oct., 1836.

CASS, LEWIS. [Born in Ohio. Appointed from Mich.]
Maj. 3rd Drag., 9 April, 1847. Disbanded 20 July, 1848.

CASSATT, EDWARD B.* [Born in Pa. Appointed from Pa.]
2nd Lieut. 9th Cav., 12 June, 1893. Trans. to 4th Cav., 5 Aug., 1893. 1st Lieut., 2 March, 1899. Capt. and A. A. G. Vols., 12 May, 1898, to 12 May, 1899. Maj. 27th U. S. Vols., 5 July, 1899.

CASSELS, ARTHUR F. [Born in D. C. Appointed from D. C.]
2nd Lieut. 7th Art., 9 July, 1898.

CASTLE, CHARLES W.* [Born in Minn. Appointed from Minn.]
2nd Lieut. 16th Inf., 12 June, 1894. 1st Lieut., 26 April, 1898.

CASTLE, JOSEPH C. [Born in Penn. Appointed from Penn.]
Priv. Co. I, 29th Pa. Vols., 20 July, to 11 Sept., 1861. Corpl. Co. I, 118th Pa. Vols., 16 Aug., 1862. 1st Lieut. 19th Penn. Cav., 29 Jan., 1864. Mustered out 2 March, 1866. 2nd Lieut. 21st Inf., 28 July, 1866. Unass'd 8 April, 1869. Resigned 18 Nov., 1870.

CASTNER, JOSEPH C. [Born in N. J. Appointed from N. J.]
2nd Lieut. 4th Inf., 1 Aug., 1891. 1st Lieut., 26 April, 1898. Graduate of the Infantry and Cavalry School, 1895. Capt. 4th Inf., 3 April, 1900.

CASTOR, THOS. F.* [Born in Penn. Appointed from Penn.]
Bvt. 2nd Lieut. 2nd Drag., 1 July, 1846. 2nd Lieut. 1st Drag., 6 Dec., 1846. 1st Lieut., 9 Oct., 1851. Died 8 Sept., 1855.

CATE, THOS. J. [Born in N. H. Appointed from Mass.]
2nd Lieut. 6th Mass. Mil., 22 April, to 2 Aug., 1861. 1st Lieut. 16th Inf., 5 Aug., 1861. Resigned 31 Aug., 1863.

CATLETT, GEORGE F. [Born in Ky. Appointed from Ky.]
2nd Lieut. Rifles, 18 April, 1818. Resigned 8 Aug., 1818.

CATLETT, HANSON. [Born in Ky. Appointed from Ky.]
Garrison Surg. Mate, 26 March, 1804. Resigned 23 Nov., 1804. Garrison Surg. Mate, 18 Feb., 1813. Surg. 1st Inf., 9 Sept., 1814. Disbanded 15 June, 1815. Post Surg., 3 May, 1816. Retained as Asst. Surg., 1 June, 1821. Died 21 Oct., 1824.

CATLEY, HENRY. [Born in Ohio. Appointed from Oregon.]
Priv. Co. K, 9th Inf., 3 July, 1855. Corpl., 1 Oct., 1855. Priv., 7 Feb., 1857. Hosp. Stwd. U. S. A., 15 July, 1857. Discharged 21 June, 1860. Hosp. Stwd. U. S. A., 21 June, 1860. Discharged 31 Dec., 1864. 1st Lieut. 1st Oregon Vols., 2 Jan., 1865. Mustered out 9 Feb., 1866. 2nd Lieut. 16th Inf., 23 Feb., 1866. 1st Lieut., 5 Aug.,

1866. Trans. to 2nd Inf., 17 April, 1869. Capt., 22 June, 1882. Retired, over 30 years' service, 17 April, 1891.

CATLIN, EDWARD H.* [Born in N. H. Appointed from N. H.]
2nd Lieut. 2nd Art., 12 June, 1880. 1st Lieut., 4 Nov., 1886. Capt., 2 March, 1899. Graduate of the Artillery School, 1884.

CATLIN, GEORGE DE G. [Born in N. Y. Appointed from N. Y.]
2nd Lieut. 10th Inf., 9 July, 1898. 1st Lieut. 2nd Inf., 15 July, 1899. Capt. 42nd U. S. Vols., 17 Aug., 1899.

CATLIN, ISAAC S. [Born in N. Y. Appointed from N. Y.]
Capt. 3rd N. Y. Vols., 14 May, 1861. Resigned 14 March, 1862. Lieut. Col. 109th N. Y. Vols., 28 Aug., 1862. Col., 29 July, 1864. Bvt. Brig. Gen. Vols., 13 March, 1865, for gallant and meritorious service during the war. Bvt. Maj. Gen. Vols., 13 March, 1865, for gallant and meritorious service in the Battles before Petersburg, Va. Mustered out 4 June, 1865. Capt. 45th Inf., 6 May, 1867. Bvt. Maj., 6 May, 1867, for gallant and meritorious service in the Battle of the Wilderness, Va. Bvt. Lieut. Col., 6 May, 1867, for gallant and meritorious service in the Battle of Petersburg, Va. Unass'd 22 July, 1869. Retired with rank of Col., 6 May, 1870. Medal of Honor for most distinguished gallantry in action at the explosion of the mine, Petersburg, Va., 30 July, 1864, in a heroic and desperate effort to rally the broken and disorganized troops under his command, on which occasion he was disabled by a wound in the side, and while being carried from the field he recovered somewhat, and bravely started to return to his command, when he received another severe wound, which necessitated the amputation of his right leg; while serving as Col. 109th N. Y. Vol. Inf.

CATLIN, JULIUS.* [Born in Penn. Appointed from Penn.]
Bvt. 2nd Lieut. 7th Inf., 1 July, 1824. 2nd Lieut. 1st Inf., 1 July, 1824. Resigned 8 Sept., 1826.

CATLIN, LYNDE. [Born in N. Y. Appointed from N. Y.]
Capt. 15th Inf., 26 Oct., 1861. Lieut. Col. A. I. G. (Act 17 July, 1862), April, 1864. Bvt. Maj., 13 March, 1865, for faithful and meritorious service during the war. Relieved as Lieut. Col. A. I. G., 1 Aug., 1865. Trans. to 24th Inf., 21 Sept., 1866. Trans. to 11th Inf., 25 April, 1869. Retired 28 June, 1878.

CATLIN, ROBERT.* [Born in Ind. Appointed from Wash. Ter.]
2nd Lieut. 5th Art., 11 June, 1863. Bvt. 1st Lieut., 18 Aug., 1864, for gallant and meritorious service during the operations on the Weldon Railroad, Va. Bvt. Capt., 21 Aug., 1864, for gallant and meritorious service in the Battle on the Weldon Railroad, Va. Retired 26 April, 1865. Capt. 43rd Inf., 28 July, 1866. Unass'd 8 April, 1869. Retired 15 Dec., 1870.

CAULFIELD, JAMES D. [Born in Va. Appointed from Miss.]
Asst. Surg., 8 Sept., 1847. Disbanded 20 July, 1848.

CAUSTEN, MANUEL C. [Born in D. C. Appointed from D. C.]
1st Lieut. 19th Inf., 14 May, 1861. Capt., 28 July, 1864. Resigned 15 Feb., 1865. Died — ——, 1878.

CAVANAUGH, JAMES B.* [Born in Ill. Appointed from Wash.]
Addl. 2nd Lieut. Eng., 11 June, 1892. 2nd Lieut., 31 March, 1895. 1st Lieut., 5 Feb., 1897.

CAVENAUGH, HARRY G. [Born in Penn. Appointed from Del.]
Corpl. Co. I, 1st Del. Vols., 19 Sept., 1861. Sergt., 13 Nov., 1862. Sergt. Co. I, 1st Del. Vet. Vols., 19 Dec., 1863. 1st Lieut. 1st Del. Vet. Vols., 26 July, 1864. Capt., 26 Dec., 1864. Mustered out 12 July, 1865. 2nd Lieut. 37th Inf., 28 July, 1866. Trans. to 5th Inf., 19 May, 1869. Unass'd 5 June, 1869. Ass'd to 13th Inf., 31 March, 1870. 1st Lieut., 4 Sept., 1871. Capt., 16 Aug., 1884. Maj. 13th Inf., 17 Sept., 1898. Retired for disability 16 Sept., 1899.

CAVENAUGH, HARRY LA T.* [Born in Utah. Appointed from Okla.]
2nd Lieut. 9th Cav., 12 June, 1895. 1st Lieut. 10th Cav., 2 March, 1899.

CAVENAUGH, WM. A. [Born in Colo. Appointed from the Army.]
Priv. and Corpl. Co. D, 20th Inf., 1 Aug., 1896, to 8 July, 1898. 2nd Lieut. 22nd Inf., 23 June, 1898. Trans. to 20th Inf., 27 Aug., 1898. 1st Lieut., 2 March, 1899.

CAZIARC, LOUIS V. [Born in Mass. Appointed from Mass.]
Sergt. Co. I, 38th Mass. Vols., 16 Aug., 1862. 1st Sergt., 2 Nov., 1862. Discharged 19 April, 1864. 1st Lieut. 89th U. S. Colored Troops, 24 April, 1864. Mustered out 11 Aug., 1864. 1st Lieut. 81st U. S. Colored Troops, 30 Aug., 1864. 1st Lieut. 73rd U. S. Colored Troops, 12 Oct., 1864. Bvt. Capt. Vols., 26 March, 1865, for faithful and meritorious service during the campaign against the City of Mobile and its defences. 1st Lieut. 81st U. S. Colored Troops, 22 Aug., 1865. Mustered out 9 Sept., 1866. 2nd Lieut. 11th Inf., 20 July, 1866. 1st Lieut., 23 Nov., 1868. Unass'd 14 April, 1869. Ass'd to 2nd Art., 1 Jan., 1871. Capt., 22 May, 1891. Maj. and A. A. G. Vols., 12 May, 1898, to 12 May, 1899.

CECIL, GEORGE R.* [Born in Va. Appointed from Va.]
2nd Lieut. 13th Inf., 17 June, 1874. 1st Lieut., 24 July, 1883. Capt., 1 Oct., 1895. Lieut. Col. and A. A. G. Vols., 9 May, 1898, to 13 June, 1899.

CECIL, JOSEPHUS S. [Born in Tenn. Appointed from Tenn.]
2nd Lieut. 19th Inf., 1 May, 1899.

CENTER, ALEXR. J.* [Born in N. Y. Appointed from N. Y.]
Bvt. 2nd Lieut. Inf., 1 July, 1827. 2nd Lieut. 5th Inf., 1 July, 1827. 1st Lieut., 31 Dec., 1834. Resigned 31 Dec., 1836.

CENTER, JOHN P.* [Born in Mass. Appointed from Mass.]
Bvt. 2nd Lieut. 6th Inf., 1 July, 1833. 2nd Lieut., 10 Aug., 1836. 1st Lieut., 26 Sept., 1837. Killed in Battle of Okeechobee, Fla., 25 Dec., 1837.

CHADBOURNE, JOSIAH P. [Born in Maine. Appointed from Army.]
Priv. Co. A, Engs., 18 Aug., 1846. to 31 March, 1847. 2nd Lieut. 9th Inf., 9 April, 1847. Resigned 4 Nov., 1847.

CHADBOURNE, THEODORE L.* [Born in Maine. Appointed at Large.]
Bvt. 2nd Lieut. 2nd Inf., 1 July, 1843. 2nd Lieut. 8th Inf., 10 Sept., 1845. Killed 9 May, 1846, at the Battle of Resaca de la Palma, Mexico.

CHAFFEE, ADNA R. [Born in Ohio. Appointed from Army.]
Priv. Co. K, 6th Cav., 22 July, 1861. Sergt., 1 Oct., 1861. 1st Sergt., 26 Sept., 1862. 2nd Lieut. 6th Cav., 13 March, 1863. Bvt. 1st Lieut., 3 July, 1863, for gallant and meritorious service in the Battle of Gettysburg, Penn. Reg. Adj., 11 Nov., 1864, to 12 Dec., 1866. Reg. Q. M., 12 Dec., 1866, to 12 Oct., 1867. 1st Lieut. 6th Cav., 22 Feb., 1865. Resigned 13 March, 1867. Reinstated 8 April, 1867. Bvt. Capt., 31 March, 1865, for gallant and meritorious service in the Battle of Dinwiddle, C. H., Va. Capt. 6th Cav., 12 Oct., 1867. Bvt. Maj., 7 March, 1868, for gallant and efficient service in an engagement with Comanche Indians on Paint Creek, Tex., 7 March, 1868. Bvt. Lieut. Col., 27 Feb., 1890, for gallant services in leading a cavalry charge over rough and precipitious bluffs held by Indians on the Red River, Texas, 30 Aug., 1874, and gallant services, in action against Indians at the Big Dry Wash, Ariz., 17 July, 1882. Maj. 9th Cav., 7 July, 1888. Lieut. Col. 3rd Cav., 1 June, 1897. Col. 8th Cav., 8 May, 1899. Brig. Gen. Vols., 4 May, 1898. Maj. Gen. Vols., 8 July, 1898, to 13 April, 1899. Brig. Gen. Vols., 13 April, 1899.

CHAFFEE, CLEMENS C.* [Born in N. Y. Appointed from Mass.]
2nd Lieut. Ord., 17 June, 1862. 1st Lieut., 3 March, 1863. Capt., 7 March, 1867. Died 5 July, 1867. Bvt. Capt., 4 July, 1863, for gallant and meritorious service during the Siege of Vicksburg, Miss.

CHAFFEE, JOHN.* [Born in Mass. Appointed from Mass.]
Mil. Storekeeper, — ——, 1813. Disbanded 1 June, 1821.

CHALFIN, SAMUEL F.* [Born in Ill. Appointed from Ill.]
2nd Lieut. 1st Art., 1 July, 1847. 1st Lieut., 6 Nov., 1849. Capt., 27 April, 1861. Trans. to 5th Art., 14 May, 1861. Maj. A. A. G., 17 June, 1863. Resigned 20 Sept., 1869. Bvt. Lieut. Col., 24 Sept., 1864, for meritorious and faithful service during the war. Bvt. Col., 13 March, 1865, for diligent, faithful and meritorious service in the A. G. Dept. during the war.

CHALMERS, CHAS. B.* [Born in D. C. Appointed from D. C.]
Bvt. 2nd Lieut. 1st Art., 1 July, 1834. 2nd Lieut., 31 Aug., 1835. 1st Lieut., 4 Feb., 1837. Dropped 14 Feb., 1838.

CHALONER, AARON D. [Born in Penn. Appointed from Penn.]
Asst. Surg. Voltigeurs, 9 April, 1847. Resigned 12 July, 1847.

CHAMBERLAIN, BENJN. F.* [Born in N. Y. Appointed from N. Y.]
Bvt. 2nd Lieut. 1st Inf., 1 July, 1853. Resigned 30 Jan., 1854.

CHAMBERLAIN, FRED VAN S. [Born in N. J. Appointed from Ill.]
Cadet at Mil. Acad., 15 June, 1895, to 24 Jan., 1896. 2nd Lieut. Co. H, 2nd Ill. Inf., 16 July, 1898, to 26 April, 1899. 2nd Lieut. 2nd Inf., 1 Aug., 1899.

CHAMBERLAIN, HENRY B. [Born in Conn. Appointed from Conn.]
Priv. and Corpl. Marine Corps, Feb., 1857, to Sept., 1859. 1st Lieut. 34th N. Y. Vols., 15 June, 1861. Resigned 22 Nov., 1861. Priv. and Sergt. Co. I, 97th N. Y. Vols., 18 Feb., 1862. 1st Lieut., 12 Feb., 1863. Capt., 4 Jan., 1864, to 25 Feb., 1865. 2nd Lieut. 108th U. S. Col. Inf., 17 Aug., 1865. 1st Lieut., 1 Jan., 1866. Mustered out 21 March, 1866. 2nd Lieut. 26th Inf., 18 June, 1867. Trans. to 10th Inf., 19 May, 1869. Died 20 June, 1877.

CHAMBERLAIN, JOHN L.* [Born in N. Y. Appointed from N. Y.]
2nd Lieut. 1st Art., 12 June, 1880. 1st Lieut., 14 Aug., 1887. Capt., 2 March, 1899. Maj. and Chief O. O., 18 July, 1898, to 12 April, 1899. Adj., 18 April, 1899. Graduate of the Artillery School, 1890.

CHAMBERLAIN, WARREN W. [Born in N. Y. Appointed from N. Y.]
1st Lieut. 14th Inf., 14 May, 1861. Killed 30 Aug., 1862, at the Battle of Bull Run, Va. Bvt. Capt., 30 Aug., 1862, for gallant and meritorious service at the Battle of Bull Run, Va.

CHAMBERLAIN, WESTON P. [Born in Me. Appointed from Me.]
Asst. Surg., 23 July, 1898.

CHAMBERLAINE, WM.* [Born in Va. Appointed from Va.]
Addl. 2nd Lieut. 2nd Art., 11 June, 1892. 2nd Lieut. 1st Art., 23 Dec., 1892. 1st Lieut., 2 March, 1899. Honor graduate of the Artillery School, 1896.

CHAMBERLIN, LOWELL A. [Born in Mass. Appointed from Mass.]
1st Sergt. 2nd Independent Batty Mass. Light Art., 5 July, 1861. Discharged 11 Dec., 1861. 2nd Lieut. 1st Md. Light Art., 16 Dec., 1861. 1st Lieut., 21 Jan., 1863. Mustered out 3 July, 1865. 1st Lieut. 5th U. S. Vet. Vols., 31 July, 1865. Mustered out 20 July, 1866. 2nd Lieut. 1st Art., 11 May, 1866. 1st Lieut., 28 Aug., 1867. Resigned 17 Nov., 1873. Reinstated 23 March, 1875, (joint resolution 3 March, 1875). Capt., 25 Nov., 1886. Died 9 Aug., 1889.

CHAMBERLIN, SIMON E. [Born in Vt. Appointed from N. Y.]
2nd Lieut. 118th N. Y. Vols., 29 Aug., 1862. 1st Lieut., 1 Jan., 1863. Capt. 25th N. Y. Cav., 16 May, 1864. Mustered out 27 June, 1865. 1st Lieut. 8th Cav., 28 July, 1866. Resigned 9 Oct., 1867.

CHAMBERLIN, WM. H. [Born in Maine. Appointed from Army.]
Priv., Corpl. and Sergt. Co. A, 17th Inf., 19 Aug., 1861, to 2 Aug., 1862. 2nd Lieut. 17th Inf., 19 July, 1862. 1st Lieut., 16 Aug., 1862. Killed 2 July, 1863, at the Battle of Gettysburg, Penn. Bvt. Capt., 2 July, 1863, for gallant and meritorious service at the Battle of Gettysburg, Penn.

CHAMBERS, ALEXR.* [Born in N. Y. Appointed from N.
Bvt. 2nd Lieut. 5th Inf., 1 July, 1853. 2nd Lieut., 3 March, 1855. 1st Lieut., 19 Jan., 1859. Capt. 18th Inf., 14 May, 1861. Col. 16th Iowa Vols., 24 March, 1862. Bvt. Maj., 7 April, 1862, for gallant and meritorious service in the Battle of Shiloh, Tenn. Bvt. Lieut. Col., 19 Sept., 1862, for gallant and meritorious service in the Battle of Iuka, Miss. Bvt. Col., 4 July, 1863, for gallant and meritorious service during the Siege of Vicksburg, Miss. Brig. Gen. Vols., 11 Aug., 1863. Negatived and revoked, 6 April, 1864. Bvt. Brig. Gen. Vols., 13 March, 1865, for gallant and meritorious service in the Battles of Champion Hills, Miss., 4 Feb., 1864, and Meridian, Miss., 14 Feb., 1864. Trans. to 27th Inf., 21 Sept., 1866. Maj. 22nd Inf., 5 March, 1867. Trans. to 10th Inf., 15 March, 1869. Unass'd 24 June, 1869. Ass'd

to 4th Inf., 4 Feb., 1870. Lieut. Col. 21st Inf., 22 Oct., 1876. Col. 17th Inf., 1 March, 1886. Died 2 Jan., 1888.

CHAMBERS, JAMES A.* [Born in Md. Appointed from Md.]
2nd Lieut. Light Art., 1 July, 1820. Trans. to Corps Art., 2 Aug., 1820. Trans. to 2nd Art., 1 June, 1821. 1st Lieut., 28 Jan., 1832. Capt., 7 July, 1838. Capt. A. Q. M., 7 July, 1838. Died 10 Dec., 1838. Bvt. 1st Lieut., 1 July, 1830, for faithful service 10 years in one grade.

CHAMBERS, JOSEPH N.* [Born in Md. Appointed from Md.]
2nd Lieut. Corps Art., 24 July, 1818. Trans. to 4th Art., 1 June, 1821. 1st Lieut., 21 May, 1822. Resigned 6 Nov., 1823.

CHAMBERS, TALBOT. [Born in, ——. Appointed from Penn.]
1st Lieut. 5th Inf., 18 June, 1808. Capt., 31 Oct., 1811. Maj. A. A. G., 2 April, 1813. Maj. 4th Rifles, 21 Feb., 1814. Trans. to Rifle Reg., 17 May, 1815. Lieut. Col., 8 March, 1817. Col., 10 Nov., 1818. Trans. to 1st Inf., 1 June, 1821. Dismissed 28 April, 1826. Bvt. Lieut. Col., 17 Sept., 1814, for gallant conduct in the Sortie from Fort Erie.

CHAMBLISS, JOHN R., Jr.* [Born in Va. Appointed from Va.]
Bvt. 2nd Lieut. Mtd. Rifles, 1 July, 1853. Resigned 4 March, 1854.

CHAMBLISS, NATHL. R.* [Born in Va. Appointed from Tenn.]
2nd Lieut. 3rd Art., 6 May, 1861. Dismissed 25 May, 1861.

CHAMBLISS, NATHANIEL R.* [Born in Ala. Appointed from Ala.]
Cadet Mil. Acad., 15 June, 1894, to 23 June, 1898. 1st Lieut. and Adj. 3rd Ala. Vols., 6 Aug., 1898, to muster out, 20 March, 1899. 2nd Lieut. 8th Inf., 10 April, 1899.

CHAMBLISS, SOLOMON. [Born in N. C. Appointed from N. C.]
Ensign 3rd Rifles, 17 March, 1814. 3rd Lieut., 1 Oct., 1814. Disbanded 15 June, 1815. 2nd Lieut. 7th Inf., 3 Mrach, 1819. Dismissed 13 May, 1820.

CHAMBLISS, WM. P. [Born in Va. Appointed from Tenn.]
2nd Lieut. 1st Tenn. Mtd. Vols., 23 May, 1846, to 23 May, 1847. Capt. 3rd Tenn. Vols., 7 Oct., 1847, to 24 July, 1848. 1st Lieut. 2nd Cav., 3 March, 1855. Capt., 6 April, 1861. (5th Cav., 3 Aug., 1861.) Maj. 4th Cav., 30 March, 1864. Resigned 1 Nov., 1867. Bvt. Maj., 4 May, 1862, for gallant and meritorious service in action at Warwick's Creek, Va. Bvt. Lieut. Col., 28 June, 1862, for gallant and meritorious service at the Battle of Gaines' Mills, Va. Reinstated as Maj. and retired 21 Dec., 1886 (Act 21 Dec., 1886), Died 22 Feb., 1887.

CHAMPLIN, SAMUEL.* [Born in Conn. Appointed from Conn.]
2nd Lieut. Reg. of Artillerists, 9 Dec., 1807. District P. M., 14 June, 1811. 1st Lieut. Reg. of Artillerists, 31 Oct., 1811. Trans. to Corps Art., 12 May, 1814: Maj. D. Q. M. G., 18 March, 1813. Disbanded 21 May, 1816.

CHANCE, JESSE C. [Born in Ohio. Appointed from Ohio.]
Priv. Co. E, 25th Ohio Vols., 18 Aug., 1862. 2nd Lieut. 103rd U. S. Colored Troops, 17 March, 1865. Mustered out 16 April, 1866. 2nd Lieut. 13th Inf., 22 Jan., 1867. Unass'd 20 July, 1869. Ass'd to 13th Inf., 4 March, 1870. 1st Lieut., 18 Oct., 1871. Capt., 16 Oct., 1884. Maj. 5th Inf., 28 Sept., 1898.

CHANCE, JOSIAH. [Born in Ohio. Appointed from Ohio.]
Priv. Co. H, 13th Ohio Vols., 28 June, 1861. Trans. to Band, 2 July, 1861. Discharged 3 Sept., 1862. Bugler Independent Co. Union Light Guard, Ohio Cav., 4 Dec., 1863. Discharged 11 Sept., 1864. Capt. 127th U. S. Colored Troops, 13 Sept., 1864. Mustered out 20 Oct., 1865. 2nd Lieut. 17th Inf., 22 July, 1867. 1st Lieut., 23 Dec., 1873. Died 12 Dec., 1885.

CHANDLER, DANIEL T. [Born in D. C. Appointed from La.]
2nd Lieut. 3rd Inf., 1 Aug., 1838. 1st Lieut., 30 Sept., 1841. Capt., 21 Sept., 1846. Maj. 5th Inf., 20 May, 1861. Retired 27 Feb., 1862. Resigned 24 Sept., 1862. Bvt. Maj., 23 Sept., 1846, for gallant and meritorious conduct at Monterey. Bvt. Lieut. Col., 20 Aug., 1847, for gallant and meritorious conduct at Contreras and Churubusco.

CHANDLER, ELIAS.* [Born in Ill. Appointed from Ill.]
2nd Lieut. 16th Inf., 12 June, 1880. 1st Lieut., 14 April, 1887. Capt. 1st Inf., 26 April, 1898. Col. 1st Ark. Vols., 20 May, until muster out, 25 Oct., 1898.

CHANDLER, JOHN G.* [Born in Mass. Appointed from Mass.]
Bvt. 2nd Lieut. 3rd Art., 1 July, 1853. 2nd Lieut., 24 Dec., 1853. 1st Lieut., 31 May, 1856. Capt. A. Q. M., 17 May, 1861. Vacated commission of 1st Lieut. 3rd Art., 1 Nov., 1861. Lieut. Col. Q. M. (Act 17 July, 1862), 1 Jan., 1863. Bvt. Maj., Lieut. Col., and Col., 13 March, 1865, for faithful and meritorious service during the war. Relieved as Lieut. Col. Q. M. (Act 17 July, 1862), 1 Aug., 1865. Maj. Q. M., 18 Jan., 1867. Vacated commisssion of Capt. A. Q. M., 13 April, 1867. Lieut. Col. D. Q. M. G., 4 March, 1879. Col. Asst. Q. M. G., 11 Dec., 1892. Retired by operation of law, 31 Dec., 1894.

CHANDLER, ROBT. [Born in N. Y. Appointed from Wis.]
Capt. A. A. G. Vols., 28 Aug., 1861. Bvt. Maj. and Lieut. Col. Vols., 13 March, 1865, for faithful and meritorious service during the war. Mustered out 1 Sept., 1866. Capt. 13th Inf., 28 July, 1866. Trans. to 7th Inf., 19 May, 1870. Died 10 May, 1873. Bvt. Maj., 2 March, 1867, for gallant and meritorious service in the Battle of Antietam, Md.

CHANDLER, WALTER S.* [Born in D. C. Appointed from D. C.]
Bvt. 2nd Lieut. 2nd Art., 1 July, 1830. 2nd Lieut., 1 July, 1830. Drowned 25 Jan., 1835.

CHAPIN, ALONZO R. [Born in Ill. Appointed from Ill.]
Asst. Surg., 3 Dec., 1883. Capt. Asst. Surg., 3 Dec., 1888. Retired for disability 10 May, 1895.

CHAPIN, EDWARD S.* [Born in Conn. Appointed from Iowa.]
2nd Lieut. 4th Art., 15 June, 1870. 1st Lieut., 19 Nov., 1873. Trans. to 15th Inf., 12 Aug., 1882. Capt., 27 Feb., 1888. Graduate of the Artillery School, 1874. Retired, over 30 years' service, 7 Nov., 1896. Died 3 May, 1899.

CHAPIN, GURDEN.* [Born in D. C. Appointed from Va.]
Bvt. 2nd Lieut. 7th Inf., 1 July, 1851. 2nd Lieut., 24 Aug., 1851. 1st Lieut., 3 March,

1855. Capt., 22 April, 1861. Maj. 14th Inf., 18 May, 1864. Trans. to 32nd Inf., 21 Sept., 1866. Retired 27 Jan., 1869. Died 22 Aug., 1875. Bvt. Maj., 15 April, 1862, for gallant and meritorious service at the Battle of Peralta, N. Mex. Bvt. Lieut. Col., 13 March, 1865, for faithful and meritorious service during the war. Bvt. Col., 13 March, 1865, for meritorious service during the war.

CHAPIN, ROBT. H. [Born in N. Y. Appointed from N. Y.]
2nd Lieut. 3rd N. Y. Vols., 14 May, 1861. 1st Lieut., 12 Aug., 1861. Resigned 31 Oct., 1861. 2nd Lieut. 2nd Art., 24 Oct., 1861. 1st Lieut., 25 Aug., 1862. Capt. 8th Cav., 28 July, 1866. Cashiered 26 May, 1870. Bvt. 1st Lieut., 27 May, 1862, for gallant and meritorious service at the Battle of Hanover C. H., Va. Bvt. Capt., 17 Sept., 1862, for gallant and meritorious service at the Battle of Antietam, Md. Bvt. Maj., 13 March, 1865, for good conduct and gallant service during the war.

CHAPLIN, WINFIELD S.* [Born in Maine. Appointed from Maine.]
2nd Lieut. 5th Art., 15 June, 1870. Resigned 6 April, 1872.

CHAPMAN, ALFRED B.* [Born in Ala. Appointed from Ala.]
Bvt. 2nd Lieut. 2nd Art., 1 July, 1854. 2nd Lieut. 3rd Art., 15 Feb., 1855. Trans. to 1st Drag., 3 March, 1855. 1st Lieut., 6 Jan., 1859. Resigned 14 May, 1861.

CHAPMAN, JAMES R.* [Born in Ill. Appointed from Ill.]
2nd Lieut. 22nd Inf., 12 June, 1880. Resigned 10 Jan., 1884.

CHAPMAN, LESLIE A. I. [Born in Wis. Appointed from Iowa.]
2nd Lieut. 1st Cav., 1 July, 1899.

CHAPMAN, ORREN.* [Born in N. Y. *Appointed from N. Y.]
Bvt. 2nd Lieut. 2nd Drag., 1 July, 1846. 2nd Lieut. 1st Drag., 7 Feb., 1847. 1st Lieut., 1 Feb., 1853. Died — Jan., 1859. Bvt. 1st Lieut., 25 March, 1847, for gallant and meritorious conduct at Medelin, near Vera Cruz, Mexico.

CHAPMAN, WM.* [Born in Md. Appointed from Md.]
Bvt. 2nd Lieut. 5th Inf., 1 July, 1831. 2nd Lieut., 4 March, 1833. 1st Lieut., 31 Dec., 1836. Capt., 8 June, 1845. Bvt. Maj., 20 Aug., 1847, for gallant and meritorious conduct in the Battles of Contreras and Churubusco. Bvt. Lieut. Col., 8 Sept., 1847, for gallant and meritorious conduct in the Battle of Molino del Rey. Maj. 2nd Inf., 25 Feb., 1861. Lieut. Col. 3rd Inf., 20 Feb., 1862. Bvt. Col., 30 Aug., 1862, for gallant and meritorious service in the Battle of Bull Run (2nd), Va. Retired 26 Aug., 1863. Died 17 Dec., 1887.

CHAPMAN, WM. H. H.* [Born in Wis. Appointed from Wis.]
2nd Lieut. 20th Inf., 12 June, 1891. 1st Lieut., 26 April, 1898. Reg. Com., 22 April, 1899.

CHAPMAN, WM. W.* [Born in Mass. Appointed from Mass.]
2nd Lieut. 2nd Art., 1 July, 1837. 1st Lieut., 7 July, 1838. Capt. A. Q. M., 11 May, 1846. Died 27 Sept., 1859. Bvt. Maj., 23 Feb., 1847, for gallant and meritorious conduct at Buena Vista.

CHARLES, OSCAR J.* [Born in Ill. Appointed from Ill.]
Addl. 2nd Lieut. 10th Inf., 12 June, 1895. 2nd Lieut., 31 July, 1895. 1st Lieut. of Inf., 8 Aug., 1898. Ass'd to 10th Inf., 1 Jan., 1899.

CHASE, ARTHUR W.* [Born in Iowa. Appointed from Iowa.]
Addl. 2nd Lieut. 2nd Art., 11 June, 1892. 2nd Lieut., 1 July, 1892. 1st Lieut., 23 Feb., 1899. Graduate of the Artillery School, 1896.

CHASE, CONSTANTINE. [Born in Mass. Appointed from Mass.]
2nd Lieut. 3rd Mass. Art., 9 Sept., 1863. 1st Lieut., 15 Oct., 1864. Bvt. Capt. Vols., 13 March, 1865, for faithful and meritorious service during the war. Mustered out 18 Sept., 1865. 2nd Lieut. 1st Art., 11 May, 1866. Trans. to 3rd Art., 28 Sept., 1866. Bvt. 1st Lieut., 2 March, 1867, for gallant and meritorious service during the war. 1st Lieut. 3rd Art., 26 March, 1868. Capt. and A. Q. M., 13 April, 1891. Trans. to 4th Art., 20 April, 1892. Graduate of the Artillery School, 1876.

CHASE, DANIEL. [Born in Conn. Appointed from Ohio.]
Capt. 15th Inf., 9 April, 1847. Disbanded 15 Aug., 1848. Mil. Storekeeper Ord., 16 April, 1856. Maj. 13th Inf., 26 Oct., 1861. Retired 31 Dec., 1864. Died 24 June, 1877. Bvt. Maj., 20 Aug., 1847, for gallant and meritorious conduct at Contreras and Churubusco. Bvt. Lieut. Col., 29 Dec., 1862, for gallant and meritorious service at the Battle of Chickasaw Bluffs, Miss. Bvt. Col., 11 Jan., 1863, for gallant and meritorious service at the Battle of Arkansas Post, Ark.

CHASE, DUDLEY. [Born in Conn. Appointed from Cal.]
Hosp. Chap., 7 April, 1864. Mustered out 21 Aug., 1865. Chap. Post of Alcatraz Island, Cal., 17 April, 1866, to 15 July, 1867. Post Chap., 3 April, 1867. Retired by operation of law, 30 June, 1882.

CHASE, DUDLEY H. [Born in Ind. Appointed from Ind
Capt. 9th Ind. Vols., 24 April, 1861. Mustered out 29 July, 1861. Capt. 17th Inf., 5 Aug., 1861. Resigned 14 Feb., 1864.

CHASE, GEORGE E.* [Born in Mass. Appointed from Mass.]
Bvt. 2nd Lieut. 3rd Art., 1 July, 1828. 2nd Lieut., 1 July, 1828. Resigned 31 Aug., 1833.

CHASE, GEORGE F.* [Born in Ill. Appointed from Ill.]
2nd Lieut. 9th Inf., 12 June, 1871. Trans. to 3rd Cav., 8 May, 1872. 1st Lieut., 20 March, 1879. Capt., 25 Nov., 1887. Graduate of the Artillery School, 1882.

CHASE, GEORGE N.* [Born in Wis. Appointed from Mo.]
Addl. 2nd Lieut. 1st Inf., 15 June, 1877. 2nd Lieut. 4th Inf., 1 July, 1877. 1st Lieut., 10 Nov., 1886. Retired for disability 20 Feb., 1891.

CHASE, LESLIE.* [Born in N. Y. Appointed from N. Y.]
Bvt. 2nd Lieut. 2nd Art., 1 July, 1838. 2nd Lieut., 7 July, 1838. 1st Lieut., 16 April, 1846. Capt. A. Q. M., 10 April, 1847. Died 15 April, 1849. Bvt. Capt., 9 May, 1846, for gallant and meritorious conduct at Palo Alto and Resaca de la Palma.

CHASE, LEWIS S. [Born in Md. Appointed from N. Y.]
Corpl. Co. C. 10th Md. Vols., 18 June, 1863, to 29 Jan., 1864. 2nd Lieut. 24th Inf., 7 March, 1867. Resigned 20 April, 1869.

BRECKINRIDGE, JOSEPH C. [Born in Md. Appointed from Ky.]
1st Lieut. A. de C., 30 Aug., 1861, to June, 1862. 2nd Lieut. 2nd Art., 14 April, 1862. 1st Lieut., 1 Aug., 1863. Bvt. Capt., 22 July, 1864, for gallant and meritorious service in Battle in front of Atlanta, Ga. Bvt. Maj., 13 March, 1865, for gallant and meritorious service during the War. Capt. 2nd Art., 17 June, 1874. Maj. A. I. G., 19 Jan., 1881. Lieut. Col. I. G., 5 Feb., 1885. Col. I. G., 22 Sept., 1885. Brig. Gen. I. G., 30 Jan., 1889. Graduate of the Artillery School, 1871. Maj. Gen. Vols., 4 May, 1898. Hon. discharged from Vols., 30 Nov., 1898.

BREEDLOVE, JULIAN P. [Born in La. Appointed from La.]
Maj. Walton's Reg. La Vols., 26 May, to 25 Nov., 1846. Capt. of Inf., 5 March, 1847; 14th Inf., 9 April, 1847. Disbanded 20 July, 1848.

BREES, HERBERT J. [Born in Wyo. Appointed from Wyo.]
1st Lieut. Troop C, 2nd U. S. Vol Cav., 23 May, to 28 July, 1898. 2nd Lieut. 4th Art., 9 July, 1898. Trans. to 9th Cav., 29 March, 1899.

BREESE, WM. M. [Born in Ill. Appointed from Ill.]
2nd Lieut. 16th Inf., 24 Oct., 1861. 1st Lieut., 15 Jan., 1862. Resigned 24 May, 1864.

BRENEMAN, EDWARD De W. [Born in Penn. Appointed from Penn.]
Asst. Surg. 1st Pa. Res., 26 July, 1861. Resigned 5 Dec., 1861. Asst Surg., 16 April, 1862. Resigned 1 April, 1867. Bvt. Capt. and Bvt. Maj., 31 March, 1865, for faithful and meritorious service during the war.

BRENNAN, JAMES. [Born in England. Appointed from Army.]
Priv. Co. K, 7th N. Y. Heavy Art., 14 Jan., 1864. Trans. to 138th Co. 2nd Batt. Vet. Res. Corps, 17 April, 1865. Discharged 9 Aug., 1865. Hosp. Stwrd. U. S. Army, 31 Dec., 1866, to 2 Jan., 1875. 2nd Lieut. 17th Inf., 20 Jan., 1875. 1st Lieut., 22 March, 1879. Died 15 July, 1888.

BRENNER, EDWARD F. [Born in Penn. Appointed from Army.]
Priv., Corpl. and Sergt. Co. H, 5th Inf., 24 May, 1839, to 24 May, 1844. Priv., Corpl. and Sergt. Cos. D and F, 8th Inf., 17 June, 1844, to 14 Sept., 1853 Ord. Sergt., 14 Sept., 1853, to 31 March, 1862. 2nd Lieut. 4th Inf., 19 Feb., 1862. Dismissed 24 Oct., 1862.

BRENT, GEORGE. [Born in Va. Appointed from Va.]
Ensign 5th Inf., 2 July, 1813. 3rd Lieut., 1 Oct., 1813. 2nd Lieut., 1 Aug., 1814. Trans. to 7th Inf., 17 May, 1815. Resigned 30 Nov., 1815. Died 7 April, 1845.

BRENT, ROBERT. [Born in Md. Appointed from D. C.]
P. M. of the Army, 1 July, 1808. Resigned 28 Aug., 1819. Died 8 Sept., 1819.

BRENT, ROBERT C.* [Born in Va. Appointed from Md.]
3rd Lieut. Corps Art., 2 March, 1815. 2nd Lieut., 13 May, 1817. 1st Lieut., 5 March, 1819. Trans. to 1st Art., 1 June, 1821. Trans. to 1st Inf., 16 Nov., 1821. Trans. to 1st Art., 21 Dec., 1822. Resigned 1 Nov., 1823. Died 15 May, 1837.

BRENT, THOS. L.* [Born in Va. Appointed from Va.]
Bvt. 2nd Lieut. 6th Inf., 1 July, 1835. 2nd Lieut. 4th Art., 1 Nov., 1836. 1st Lieut., 1 Aug., 1839. Capt. A. Q. M., 3 March, 1847. Died 11 Jan., 1858. Bvt. Capt., 23 Feb., 1847, for gallant and meritorious conduct at Buena Vista.

BRENT, THOS. L.* [Born in Penn. Appointed at Large.]
2nd Lieut. and 1st Lieut. 18th Inf., 23 June, 1865. R. Q. M., 25 Feb., 1867, to 11 July, 1868. Capt., 11 July, 1868. Unass'd 26 April, 1869. Ass'd to 3rd Cav., 1 Jan., 1871. Retired 17 May, 1876. Died 24 May, 1880.

BRERETON, JOHN A. [Born in Md. Appointed from Md.]
Asst. Surg., 1 July, 1821. Died 22 April, 1839.

BRERETON, JOHN J.* [Born in N. J. Appointed from N. J.]
2nd Lieut. 24th Inf., 15 June, 1877. 1st Lieut., 20 May, 1882. Capt., 25 April, 1895. Maj. Chief. Q. M. Vols., 15 Nov., 1898. Discharged from Vols., 20 May, 1899. Lieut. Col. 33rd U. S. Vol. Inf., 5 July, 1899. Died — ——, 1900.

BRERETON, THOS. J.* [Born in D. C. Appointed at Large.]
Bvt. 2nd Lieut. 4th Art., 1 July, 1843. Trans. to Ord., 20 July, 1843. 2nd Lieut., 3 March, 1847. 1st Lieut., 31 Oct., 1851. Capt., 1 July, 1857. Resigned 20 Dec., 1858. Bvt. 1st Lieut., 9 May, 1846, for gallant and meritorious conduct at Palo Alto and Resaca de la Palma. Died 18 Sept., 1870.

BRESLIN, PATRICK H. [Born in N. Y. Appointed from Ohio.]
Capt. 18th Inf., 14 May, 1861. Dismissed 25 Nov., 1862. 2nd Lieut. 12th Inf., 9 April, 1866. Trans. to 30th Inf., 21 Sept., 1866. 1st Lieut., 17 Feb., 1868. Trans. to 4th Inf., 23 March, 1869. Died 26 Feb., 1876.

BRETT, JAMES E. [Born in N. C. Appointed from the Army.]
Priv. Co. K, 12th Inf., and Hosp. Stwrd., 23 Sept., 1870, to 12 July, 1880. 2nd Lieut. 24th Inf., 24 June, 1880. 1st Lieut., 22 Dec., 1887. Capt., 26 April, 1898.

BRETT, LLOYD M.* [Born in Me. Appointed from Mass.]
2nd Lieut. 2nd Cav., 13 June, 1879. 1st Lieut., 4 May, 1886. Capt., 13 Jan., 1897. Maj. 31st U. S. Vol. Inf., 5 July, 1899. Medal of Honor for most distinguished gallantry in action against hostile Sioux Indians near O'Fallons Creek, Mont., 1 April, 1880, by fearless exposure and dashing bravery, cutting off the Indians' pony herd and greatly crippling the hostiles; while 2nd Lieut. 2nd Cav.

BREWER, ALONZO.* [Born in Vt. Appointed from Vt.]
3rd Lieut. Corps Art., 2 March, 1815. Resigned 16 Oct., 1816. Died in 1823.

BREWER, CHAS. [Born in Md. Appointed from Md.]
Asst. Surg., 29 Aug., 1856. Resigned 7 May, 1861.

BREWER, EDWIN P. [Born in Ohio. Appointed from Ohio.]
Cadet at Mil. Acad., 1 July, 1871, to 14 Nov., 1871. 2nd Lieut. 7th Cav., 31 Aug., 1876. 1st Lieut., 28 Sept., 1885. Capt., 8 Dec., 1896.

BREWER, GEORGE E. [Born in Ohio. Appointed from Ohio.]
Priv. Co. E, 19th Ohio Vols., 28 June, 1862, to 4 Sept., 1863. 2nd Lieut. 18th Inf., 30 June, 1866 Trans. to 27th Inf., 21 Sept., 1866. Resigned 11 March, 1867

BREWER, JOHN W. [Born in Md. Appointed from Md.]
Asst. Surg. Vols., 4 Oct., 1862. 1st Lieut. Asst. Surg., 22 Nov., 1862. Vacated commission of Asst. Surg. Vols., 26 Nov., 1862. Bvt. Capt. and Bvt. Maj., 13 March,

1865, for faithful and meritorious service during the War. Capt. Asst. Surg., 28 July, 1866. Died 15 Nov., 1880.

BREWER, MADISON M. [Born in Kan. Appointed from D. C.]
Priv. Sig. Corps, 22 Sept., 1882, to 24 Oct., 1887. Asst. Surg., 5 May, 1892. Capt. and Asst. Surg., 5 May, 1897. Died 4 Oct., 1898.

BREWER, RICHARD H.* [Born in Md. Appointed from Md.]
Bvt. 2nd Lieut. 1st Drag., 1 July, 1858. 2nd Lieut., 29 March, 1859. 1st Lieut., 26 April, 1861. Resigned 13 May, 1861.

BREWER, THOMAS L. [Born in Md. Appointed from Md.]
Priv. and Q. M. Sergt. Co. A, 1st Md. Vols., 4 May to 5 July, 1898. 2nd Lieut., 6 July, 1898. Mustered out 28 Feb., 1899. 2nd Lieut. 21st Inf., 10 April, 1899.

BREWERTON, GEORGE D. [Born in R. I. Appointed from N. Y.]
2nd Lieut. 2nd N. Y. Vols., 15 Aug., 1846. 2nd Lieut. 1st Inf., 22 May, 1847. 1st Lieut., 26 June, 1850. Resigned 31 Dec., 1852.

BREWERTON, HENRY.* [Born in N. Y. Appointed from N. Y.]
Bvt. 2nd Lieut. Eng., 1 July, 1819. 2nd Lieut., 1 July, 1819. 1st Lieut., 1 Jan., 1825. Capt., 21 Sept., 1836. Maj., 23 Aug., 1856. Lieut. Col., 6 Aug., 1861. Col., 22 April, 1864. Bvt. Brig. Gen., 13 March, 1865, for long, faithful and meritorious service. Retired 7 March, 1867. Died 17 April, 1879.

BREWERTON, HENRY F. [Born in N. Y. Appointed at Large.]
2nd Lieut. 5th Art., 14 May, 1861. 1st Lieut., 1 March, 1862. Bvt. Capt., 19 Oct., 1864, for gallant and meritorious service in the Battle of Cedar Creek, Va. Capt. 5th Art., 18 Sept., 1868. Retired for disability, with the rank of Maj. 28 Nov., 1892.

BREWSTER, ANDRE W. [Born in N. J. Appointed from Pa.]
2nd Lieut. 10th Inf., 19 Jan., 1885. 1st Lieut. 22nd Inf., 17 Dec., 1891. Trans. to 9th Inf., 9 Feb., 1892. Capt., 2 March, 1899. Capt. A. Q. M. Vols., 15 Oct, 1898. Discharged 12 May, 1899.

BREWSTER, CHAS. [Born in N. Y. Appointed from N. Y.]
Capt. C. S. Vols , 26 Nov., 1862. Appointment expired 4 March, 1863. 1st Lieut. 13th N. Y. Cav., 10 July, 1863. Capt. C. S. Vols., 2 March, 1864. Bvt. Maj. Vols., 15 July, 1865, for efficient and meritorious services. Mustered out 15 July, 1865. 2nd Lieut. 7th Cav., 28 July, 1866. 1st Lieut , 24 Feb., 1867. Discharged 18 Nov., 1870. Bvt. Capt., 2 March, 1867, for gallant and meritorious service during the war.

BREWSTER, WM. B. [Born in Penn. Appointed from Penn.]
1st Lieut. Asst. Surg., 3 June, 1879. Resigned 8 Feb., 1884.

BREYFOGLE, ROLAND C. [Born in Ohio. Appointed from Ohio.]
Priv. and Corpl. Co. C, 8th Ohio Vols., 4 May, 1861, to 21 June, 1864. Capt 186th Ohio Vols., 27 Feb., 1865. Mustered out 18 Sept., 1865. 2nd Lieut 12th Inf., 28 July, 1866. Unass'd 22 Sept., 1869. Retired 14 May, 1870. Died 28 July, 1870. Bvt. 1st Lieut., 2 March, 1867, for gallant and meritorious service at the Battle of Spottsylvania, Va.

BRICE, BENJN. W.* [Born in Va. Appointed from Ohio.]
Bvt. 2nd Lieut. 3rd Inf., 1 July, 1829. Resigned 13 Feb., 1832. Maj. and P. M., 3 March, 1847. Disbanded 4 March, 1849. Maj. and P. M., 9 Feb., 1852. Col. P. M. G., 8 Feb., 1866, to rank from 29 Nov., 1864. Bvt. Lieut. Col., Col. and Brig. Gen., 2 Dec., 1864. Bvt. Maj. Gen., 13 March, 1865, for faithful, meritorious and distinguished service in the Pay Dept. during the War. Brig. Gen. and P. M. G., 28 July, 1866. Retired 1 Jan., 1872. Died 4 Dec., 1892.

BRICKER, EDWIN D.* [Born in Pa. Appointed from Pa.]
2nd Lieut. 17th Inf., 26 April, 1898. 1st Lieut., 2 March, 1899.

BRIDGES, CHARLES H.* [Born in Ill. Appointed from Ill.]
Addl. 2nd Lieut. 6th Inf., 11 June, 1897. 2nd Lieut. 22nd Inf., 8 March, 1898. 1st Lieut., 2 March, 1899.

BRIDGES, EDWIN T. [Born in N. Y. Appointed from Ill.]
Capt. C. S. Vols., 17 March, 1863. Bvt. Maj. Vols , 13 March, 1865, for meritorious service in his department during the war. Mustered out 31 July, 1866. 2nd Lieut. 5th Inf., 23 Feb., 1866. 1st Lieut., 28 July, 1866. Unass'd 19 May, 1869. Ass'd to 13th Inf., 26 July, 1870. Discharged 31 Dec., 1870.

BRIDGES, GEORGE R [Born in N. C. Appointed from N. C.]
3rd Lieut. 10th Inf., 24 March, 1813. 2nd Lieut., 24 March, 1814. Trans. to 7th Inf., 17 May, 1815. Killed 21 Feb., 1816, by a deserter.

BRIDGMAN, FRANK. [Born in Mass. Appointed from Iowa.]
Addl. P. M., 5 Sept., 1861. Bvt. Lieut. Col. Vols., 24 Nov., 1865, for faithful and meritorious service. Mustered out 1 Jan., 1869. Maj. and P. M., 3 Feb., 1869. Retired by operation of law 10 July, 1884.

BRIDGMAN, VICTOR H.* [Born in Vt. Appointed from Vt.]
2nd Lieut. 2nd Art., 16 June, 1875. 1st Lieut., 9 Aug., 1883. Capt. 6th Art., 8 March, 1898. Honor graduate of the Artillery School, 1878.

BRIGGS, FRANK O.* [Born in N. H. Appointed from N. H.]
2nd Lieut. 2nd Inf., 14 June, 1872. Resigned 16 Dec., 1877. Graduated as Obadiah F. Briggs.

BRIGGS, OBADIAH F.* [Born in N. H. Appointed from N. H.]
Changed name to Frank O. Briggs—which see.

BRIGGS, THOS. B. [Born in R. I. Appointed from Conn.]
Priv. Co. G, 4th Ill. Vols., 17 June, 1846. Discharged 26 May, 1847. 1st Sergt. Co. A, 1st R. I. Vols., 2 May, 1861. Discharged 2 Aug., 1861. Capt. 3rd R. I. Vols., 29 Aug., 1861. Mustered out 22 May, 1863. 1st Lieut. 11th U. S. Col. Troops, 22 Sept., 1863. Mustered out 2 Oct., 1865. 2nd Lieut. 3rd Inf., 18 June, 1867. Unass'd 11 Aug., 1869. Ass'd to 14th Inf., 27 April, 1870. 1st Lieut., 9 Feb., 1874. Retired for disability 15 March, 1883.

BRIGHAM, ELIJAH D. [Born in Mass. Appointed from Army.]
Capt. C. S. Vols., 30 Sept., 1861, to 9 Feb., 1863. Priv. Gen. Ser., 28 Nov., 1862. 2nd Lieut. 10th Inf., 28 Nov., 1862. 1st Lieut , 4 Nov., 1863. Capt. C. S., 9 Feb., 1863. Resigned 25 Feb., 1867. Bvt. Maj. Lieut. Col., 13 March, 1865, for faithful and meritorious service during the war.

ful and meritorious service during the war. 1st Lieut. 11th Inf., 12 Aug., 1868. Unass'd 14 April, 1869. Ass'd to 21st Inf., 15 Dec., 1870. Capt., 17 Sept., 1883. Retired, over 30 years' service, 15 Dec., 1892.

BRADLEY, WM. A. [Born in D. C. Appointed from D. C.]
Asst. Surg., 22 Oct., 1861. Died 27 Feb., 1869. Bvt. Capt. and Bvt. Maj., 13 March, 1865, for faithful and meritorious service during the War.

BRADY, ABRAM. [Born in Penn. Appointed from Penn.]
2nd Lieut. Corps Art., 13 Aug., 1819. Disbanded 1 June, 1821.

BRADY, ALLEN G. [Born in Mass. Appointed from Conn.]
Lieut. Col. 3rd Conn. Vols., 14 May to 12 Aug., 1861. Capt. 17th Conn. Vols., 28 Aug., 1862. Maj., 29 Aug., 1862. Resigned 21 Oct., 1863. Maj. Vet. Res. Corps, 23 Nov., 1863. Bvt. Lieut. Col. and Col. Vols., 7 Aug., 1865, for meritorious service during the war. Mustered out 15 Dec., 1866. 1st Lieut. 43rd Inf., 28 July, 1866. Appointment expired 4 March, 1867.

BRADY, CHAS. B. [Born in N. Y. Appointed from N. Y.]
Priv. and Corpl. Co. I and Com. Sergt. 2nd Drag., 8 March, 1858, to 8 March, 1863. Sergt. Gen. Serv., 18 April, 1863, to 1 April, 1864. 2nd Lieut. 5th Cav., 16 Nov., 1866. 1st Lieut., 11 Aug., 1867. Discharged 30 Nov., 1870. Died 8 Jan., 1885.

BRADY, EBENEZER W. [Born in Ohio. Appointed from Iowa.]
Chap. 116th Ohio Vols., 27 Sept., 1862. Resigned 18 Oct., 1864. Post Chap., 19 Feb., 1884. Died 9 Sept., 1886.

BRADY, EDWARD W.* [Born in Ind. Appointed from Ind.]
2nd Lieut. 6th Cav., 15 June, 1869. Discharged 29 Dec., 1870.

BRADY, FRANCIS W. [Born in ——. Appointed from Penn.]
Ensign 35th Inf., 5 April, 1814. 3rd Lieut., 1 May, 1814. Disbanded 15 June, 1815. 2nd Lieut. 4th Inf., 19 Feb., 1817. 1st Lieut., 31 July, 1817. R. Q. M., Oct., 1817, to 2 Sept., 1818. Capt., 31 Dec., 1820. Resigned 30 April, 1831.

BRADY, GEORGE K. [Born in Penn. Appointed from Penn.]
Priv. Co. B, 12th Penn. Vols., 25 April, 1861. Discharged 8 July, 1861. 1st Lieut. 14th Inf., 14 May, 1861. R. Q. M., 1 Jan., 1862, to 10 June, 1864. Capt., 10 June, 1864. Bvt. Maj., 18 Aug., 1864, for gallant service during the operations on the Weldon Railroad, Va. Bvt. Lieut. Col., 13 March, 1865, for gallant and meritorious service during the war. Trans. to 23rd Inf., 21 Sept., 1866. Maj. 18th Inf., 1 March, 1886. Lieut. Col. 17th Inf., 19 March, 1891. Retired, over 30 years' service, 16 Aug., 1894. Died 19 Jan., 1899.

BRADY, HUGH. [Born in Penn. Appointed from Penn.]
Ensign Inf., 7 March, 1792. 4th Sub-Legion, 4th Sept., 1792. Lieut., 10 Feb., 1794. Discharged 1 Nov., 1796. Capt. 10th Inf., 8 Jan., 1799. Disbanded 15 June, 1800. Col. 22nd Inf., 6 July, 1812. Trans. to 2nd Inf., 17 May, 1815. Died 15 April, 1851. Bvt. Brig. Gen., 6 July, 1822, for 10 years' faithful service in one grade. Bvt. Maj. Gen., 30 May, 1848, for meritorious conduct.

BRADY, JAMES F.* [Born in N. Y. Appointed from N. Y.]
Addl. 2nd Lieut. 13th Inf., 11 June, 1897. 2nd Lieut. 19th Inf., 16 Jan., 1898. Trans. to 7th Art., 8 March, 1898. 1st Lieut., 28 Aug., 1899.

BRADY, JASPER E. [Born in Pa. Appointed from the Army.]
Priv. and Corpl. Co. D, 18th Inf., 17 Sept., 1888, to 1 Aug., 1891. 2nd Lieut. 19th Inf., 31 July 1891. 1st Lieut., 26 April, 1898. Capt. Vol. Sig. Corps, 20 May, 1898. Trans. to 1st Inf., —, 1899. Resigned 30 Sept., 1899. Graduate of the Infantry and Cavalry School, 1895.

BRADY, JOHN. [Born in Penn. Appointed from Penn.]
Ensign 22nd Inf., 31 March, 1814. 3rd Lieut., 1 May, 1814. 2nd Lieut., 25 Sept., 1814. Trans. to 8th Inf., 17 May, 1815. Resigned 15 Oct., 1817. Bvt. 1st Lieut., 5 Feb., 1815, for gallant conduct.

BRADY, JOSEPH C. [Born in Mo. Appointed from Mo.]
2nd Lieut. 4th Inf., 1 Sept., 1899.

BRADY, SAMUEL. [Born in Penn. Appointed from Penn.]
Ensign 22nd Inf., 20 May, 1813. 3rd Lieut., 26 June, 1813. 2nd Lieut., 2 April, 1814. 1st Lieut., 1 Oct., 1814. Trans. to 8th Inf., 17 May, 1815. Died 17 Feb., 1816.

BRAGG, BRAXTON.* [Born in N. C. Appointed from N. C.]
2nd Lieut. 3rd Art., 1 July, 1837. Reg. Adj. 19 Nov., 1837, to 8 March, 1838. 1st Lieut., 7 July, 1838. Capt., 18 June, 1846. Resigned 3 Jan., 1856. Bvt. Capt., 9 May, 1846, for gallant and distinguished conduct in defence of Fort Brown, Texas. Bvt. Maj., 23 Sept., 1846, for gallant conduct at Monterey. Bvt. Lieut. Col., 23 Feb., 1847, for gallant and meritorious conduct at Buena Vista. Died 27 Sept., 1876.

BRAGG, HENRY M. [Born in N. Y. Appointed from N. Y.]
1st Lieut. 139th N. Y. Vols., 9 Sept., 1862. Capt. A. de C. Vols., 17 Aug., 1863. Bvt. Maj. Vols., 13 March, 1865, for faithful and meritorious service. Mustered out 3 Nov., 1865. 2nd Lieut. 2nd Inf., 8 May, 1866. Trans. to 3rd Cav., 28 Sept., 1866. Resigned 17 Nov., 1869.

BRAGG, JAMES F. [Born in Me. Appointed from Me.
1st Lieut. 9th Inf., 19 April, 1847. Dropped 19 Jan., 1848.

BRAINARD, DAVID L. [Born in N. Y. Appointed from N. Y.]
Priv., Corpl. and Sergt. Troop L, 2nd Cav., 18 Sept., 1876, to 31 July, 1884. Sergt. Sig. Corps, 1 Aug., 1884, to 21 Oct., 1886. 2nd Lieut. 2nd Cav., 22 Oct., 1886. 1st Lieut., 26 Oct., 1886. Capt. C. S., 14 Oct., 1896. Lieut. Col. Chief C. S. Vols., 9 May, 1898. Col. C. S. Vols., 8 Nov., 1898, to 2 March, 1899. Maj. C. S. Vols., 17 April, 1899. Maj. C. S., 12 Feb., 1900.

BRAINERD, THOS. C. [Born in Penn. Appointed from Penn.]
Asst. Surg., 5 Aug., 1861. Resigned 28 May, 1866. Bvt. Capt. and Bvt. Maj., 13 March, 1865, for faithful and meritorious service during the War.

BRAMBILA, ROBERT M. [Born in Mexico. Appointed from Nev.]
2nd Lieut. 23rd Inf., 9 July, 1898. 1st Lieut. 14th Inf., 30 June, 1899.

BRANNAGAN, PATRICK. [Born in Ireland. Appointed from Army.]
Priv. and Corpl. C and F., 4th Art., 19 June, 1854, to 24 Oct., 1859. Priv., Corpl. and

1st Sergt. 1st Inf., 29 May, 1860, to 12 April, 1863. 2nd Lieut. 1st Inf., 19 Feb., 1863. 1st Lieut., 29 Dec., 1865. Died 13 March, 1868. Bvt. 1st Lieut., 4 July, 1863, for gallant and meritorious service during the Siege of Vicksburg, Miss.

BRANCH, R. H. [Born in Va. Appointed from Va.]
2nd Lieut. 7th Inf., 3 Feb., 1819. 1st Lieut., 10 Oct., 1820. Disbanded 1 June, 1821.

BRAND, THOS. T. [Born in Ohio. Appointed from Ohio.]
1st Lieut. 2nd Ohio Vols., 17 April, 1861. Resigned 22 June, 1861. 1st Lieut. 18th Inf., 14 May, 1861. Capt., 11 Sept., 1863. Retired 31 Dec., 1864. Bvt. Maj., 13 March, 1865, for gallant and meritorious service in the Battles of Stone River, Tenn., and Chickamauga, Ga.

BRANDT, MARTIN L. [Born in Md. Appointed from Army.]
Priv. and Sergt. Co. C, 2nd Batt. and Sergt. Maj. 15th Inf., 30 April, 1862, to 30 April, 1865. Priv. Co. A, and Sergt. Maj. 36th Inf., 24 March, 1866, to 18 Nov., 1867. 2nd Lieut. 36th Inf., 6 Nov., 1867. Trans. to 7th Inf., 19 May, 1869. Unass'd 21 April, 1870. Cashiered 26 July, 1870.

BRANNAN, JOHN M.* [Born in D. C. Appointed from Ind.]
Bvt. 2nd Lieut. 1st Art., 1 July, 1841. 2nd Lieut., 16 May, 1842. 1st Lieut., 3 March, 1847. Reg. Adj., 17 April, 1847, to 4 Nov., 1854 Bvt. Capt., 20 Aug., 1847, for gallant and meritorious conduct in the Battles of Contreras and Churubusco. Capt. 1st Art., 4 Nov., 1854. Brig. Gen. Vols., 28 Sept., 1861. Bvt. Lieut. Col., 25 Sept., 1862, for gallant and meritorious service in the Battle of Jacksonville, Fla. Maj. 1st Art., 1 Aug., 1863. Bvt. Col., 20 Sept., 1863, for gallant and meritorious service in the Battle of Chickamauga, Ga. Bvt. Maj. Gen. Vols., 23 Jan., 1865. Bvt. Brig. Gen., 13 March, 1865, for gallant and meritorious service in the campaign against Atlanta, Ga. Bvt. Maj. Gen., 13 March, 1865, for gallant and meritorious service in the field during the war. Mustered out of Vol. service, 31 May, 1866. Lieut. Col. 22nd Inf., 28 July, 1866, declined. Lieut. Col. 4th Art., 10 Jan., 1877. Trans. to 1st Art., 16 March, 1877. Col. 4th Art., 15 March, 1881. Retired 19 April, 1882, being over 62 years of age. Died 16 Dec., 1892.

BRANNON, JAMES W. [Born in Va. Appointed from Ky.]
Capt. of Inf., 3 March, 1847; 16th Inf., 9 April, 1847. Disbanded 2 Aug., 1848.

BRANSFORD, SAML. J.* [Born in Va. Appointed from Va.]
2nd Lieut. 2nd Art., 1 July, 1836. 1st Lieut., 14 Dec., 1837. Killed 3 Nov., 1840, accidentally.

BRANT, JOSHUA B. [Born in Conn. Appointed from Army.]
Priv., Sergt. and Sergt. Maj. 23rd Inf., 26 Feb., 1813, to July, 1814. Ensign 23rd Inf., 15 July, 1814. 2nd Lieut., 1 Oct., 1814. Trans. to 2nd Inf., 17 May, 1815. R. Q. M., 10 June, 1815, to 9 Dec., 1819. Capt. A. Dep. Q. M. G., 30 Nov., 1819. Capt. A. Q. M., 22 March, 1832. Maj. Q. M., 28 Dec., 1832. Lieut. Col. Dep. Q. M. G., 7 July, 1838. Resigned 7 Nov., 1839. Bvt. 1st Lieut., 17 Sept., 1814, for gallant conduct in the sortie from Fort Erie.

BRANT, LOUIS P.* [Born in Ohio. Appointed from Washington Ter.]
2nd Lieut. 21st Inf., 13 June, 1873. Resigned 31 March, 1870. 2nd Lieut. 1st Inf., 7 Aug., 1879. 1st Lieut., 20 Feb., 1884. Capt., 6 Feb., 1897. Retired for disability 7 Jan., 1899.

BRATT, JOHN.* [Born in N. Y. Appointed from N. Y.]
2nd Lieut. 3rd Art., 1 July, 1837. Resigned 1 Aug., 1837. Died 21 May, 1890.

BRATTON, THOMAS S. [Born in S. C. Appointed from S. C.]
Asst. Surg., 26 Oct., 1893. Capt. Asst. Surg., 8 April, 1899.

BRAYTON, CHAS. R. [Born in R. I. Appointed from R. I.]
1st Lieut. 3rd R. I. Art., 27 Aug., 1861. Capt., 28 Nov., 1862. Lieut. Col., 17 Nov., 1863. Col., 1 April, 1864. Bvt. Brig. Gen. Vols., 13 March, 1865, for faithful and meritorious service during the war. Capt. 17th Inf., 7 March, 1867. Resigned 6 July 1867.

BRAYTON, GEORGE M. [Born in Mass. Appointed from Ohio.]
1st Lieut. 15th Inf., 14 May, 1861. R. Q. M., 8 May, to 3 Oct., 1862. Capt., 3 Jan., 1863. Bvt. Maj., 13 March, 1865, for gallant and meritorious service in the Battle of Missionary Ridge, Tenn. Trans. to 33rd Inf., 21 Sept., 1866. Trans. to 8th Inf., 3 May, 1869. Bvt. Lieut. Col., 27 Feb., 1890, for gallant services in action against Indians in Ariz., 25 June, 1875; 4 July, 1875; 10 Jan., 1877; 21 Jan., 1877, and 30 Jan., 1877 Maj. 15th Inf., 6 Feb., 1882. Lieut. Col. 9th Inf., 6 Sept., 1886. Col. 19th Inf., 23 March, 1892. Retired, over 30 years' service, 16 Sept., 1892.

BREARLEY, DAVID. [Born in N. J. Appointed from N. J.]
Capt. Light Drag., 3 May, 1808. Resigned 31 May, 1811. Lieut. Col. 15th Inf., 12 March, 1812. Col., 12 March, 1813. Disbanded 15 June, 1815. Reinstated 1 Jan., 1816, as Lieut. Col. 7th Inf. Col., 30 April, 1817. Resigned 16 March, 1820. Retained 1 Jan., 1816, (under Act of 3 March, 1815), as Lieut. Col. 7th Inf., with Bvt. of Col. from 12 March, 1813. Died in 1837.

BRECHEMIN, LOUIS. [Born in Penn. Appointed from Penn.]
1st Lieut. Asst. Surg., 6 June, 1878. Capt. Asst. Surg., 6 June, 1883. Maj. Surg., 9 Nov., 1896.

BRECK, SAMUEL.* [Born in Mass. Appointed from Mass.]
Bvt. 2nd Lieut. 1st Art., 1 July, 1855. 2nd Lieut., 1 July, 1855. 1st Lieut., 11 April, 1861. Capt. A. A. G., 29 Nov., 1861. Vacated commission of 1st Lieut. 1st Art., 20 Feb., 1862. Maj. A. A. de C., 23 May, 1862. Maj. A. A. G., 17 July, 1862. Vacated commission of Maj. A. A. de C., 17 July, 1862. Bvt. Lieut. Col., 24 Sept. 1864, for faithful and meritorious service during the War. Bvt. Col. and Bvt. Brig. Gen., 13 March, 1865, for diligent, faithful and meritorious service in the A. G.'s Dept. during the war. Lieut. Col. and A. A. G., 28 Feb., 1887. Col. and A. A. G., 31 Aug., 1893. Brig. Gen. and A. G., 11 Sept., 1897. Retired, by operation of law, 25 Feb., 1898.

BRECKINRIDGE, CHAS. H.* [Born in Md. Appointed at Large.]
2nd Lieut. 15th Inf., 23 June, 1865. 1st Lieut., 23 June, 1865. Died 27 Aug., 1867.

BRECKINRIDGE, ETHELBERT L. D. [Born in Ky. Appointed from Ky.]
2nd Lieut. 7th Inf., 10 Oct., 1898. 1st Lieut. 10th Inf., 5 Feb., 1900.

11 Dec., 1850. Capt., 14 May, 1861. Bvt. Maj., 9 June, 1862, for gallant and meritorious service in the campaign of the Shenandoah Valley, Va. Bvt. Lieut. Col., 17 Sept., 1862, for gallant and meritorious service in the Battle of Antietam, Md. Retired 11 May, 1864. Bvt. Col., 13 March, 1865, for gallant and meritorious service during the war. Capt. 42nd Inf., 28 July, 1866, declined. Retired with rank of Maj., 28 July, 1866. (Act 28 July, 1866, sec. 32).

CLARK, JOSEPH N. [Born in N. Y. Appointed from N. Y.]
Surg. Mate 4th Inf., 28 Jan., 1820. Died 8 March, 1821.

CLARK, LEMUEL B. [Born in Md. Appointed from Md.]
Garrison Surg. Mate, 4 Jan., 1808. Post Surg., 24 April, 1816. Resigned 18 Oct., 1817.

CLARK, MERIWETHER L.* [Born in Mo. Appointed from Mo.]
Bvt. 2nd Lieut. 6th Inf., 1 July, 1830. Resigned 31 May, 1833.

CLARK, MICHAEL M.* [Born in Va. Appointed from Va.]
Bvt. 2nd Lieut. 2nd Art., 1 July, 1826. 2nd Lieut., 1 July, 1826. (Asst. Q. M., 4 April, 1832, to 7 July, 1838.) 1st Lieut., 31 Dec., 1833. Capt. Asst. Q. M., 7 July, 1838. Maj. Q. M., 1 Aug., 1856. Died 10 May, 1861.

CLARK, NATHAN. [Born in Ga. Appointed from Conn.]
2nd Lieut. 37th Inf., 19 May, 1813. Trans. to 5th Inf., 17 May, 1815. 1st Lieut., 3 March, 1817. Capt., 29 June, 1824. Died 18 Feb., 1836. Bvt. Maj., 29 June, 1834, for 10 years' faithful service in one grade.

CLARK, NATHANIEL. [Born in ——. Appointed from Ga.]
Ensign 2nd Inf., 7 Oct., 1812. 2nd Lieut., 20 Jan., 1813. 1st Lieut., 1 May, 1814. Trans. to Light Art., 17 May, 1815. Resigned 15 Nov., 1817.

CLARK, NELSON N.* [Born in Vt. Appointed from N. Y.]
Bvt. 2nd Lieut. Inf., 1 July, 1827. 2nd Lieut. 4th Inf., 1 July, 1827. Died 11 July, 1832.

CLARK, PEYTON G. [Born in La. Appointed from Ala.]
2nd Lieut. 13th Inf., 9 July, 1898. 1st Lieut., 2 March, 1899.

CLARK, RICHD. [Born in N. Y. Appointed from N. Y.]
Asst. Surg., 2 March, 1833. Maj. Surg., 7 July, 1838. Died 29 June, 1839.

CLARK, ROBERT S. [Born in N. Y. Appointed from N. Y.]
2nd Lieut. 9th Inf., 1 Sept., 1899.

CLARK, SIDNEY E. [Born in Conn. Appointed from Conn.]
Priv. Co. G, 2nd Conn. Vols., 7 May, 1861. Discharged 7 Aug., 1861. Capt. 12th Conn. Vols., 1 Jan., 1862. Maj. 13th Oct., 1864. Mustered out 12 Aug., 1865. 2nd Lieut. 16th Inf., 28 July, 1866. Bvt. 1st Lieut., 2 March, 1867, for gallant and meritorious service in the Battle of Winchester, Va. Bvt. Capt., 2 March, 1867, for gallant and meritorious service during the war. Trans. to 2nd Inf., 17 April, 1869. 1st Lieut., 1 Aug., 1875. Capt., 25 Sept., 1890. Retired by operation of law, 1 Feb., 1898.

CLARK, SATTERLEE.* [Born in Vt. Appointed from Vt.]
2nd Lieut. Reg. of Artillerists, 9 Dec., 1807. Dist. P. M., 15 Aug., 1810. (1st Lieut. Reg. of Artillerists, 10 July, 1811, to 31 Dec., 1813.) Disbanded 15 June, 1815. Batt. Dist. P. M., 29 April, 1816. Dismissed 5 Aug., 1824.

CLARK, WALLIS O.* [Born in Mass. Apointed from Mass.]
Addl. 2nd Lieut. 7th Cav., 15 June, 1877. 2nd Lieut. 6th Cav., 31 Dec., 1877. Trans. to 12th Inf., 13 Feb., 1882. 1st Lieut., 12 Feb., 1886. Capt., 12 April, 1898.

CLARK, WM. A. [Born in Iowa. Appointed from Iowa.]
1st Lieut. 35th Iowa Vols., 17 Sept., 1862. Capt., 28 June, 1864. Hon. mustered out, 10 Aug., 1865. 2nd Lieut. 30th Inf., 18 June, 1867. Resigned 26 March, 1868.

CLARK, WM. B. [Born in N. Y. Apointed from Kansas.]
Priv. Co. E, 2nd Mass. Cav., 7 March to 3 Sept., 1863. 2nd Lieut. 14th Kans. Cav., 16 Sept., 1863. Hon. mustered out 25 June, 1865. 2nd Lieut. 7th Cav., 18 June, 1867. Resigned 1 May, 1869.

CLARK, WM. F.* [Born in Ind. Appointed from Minn.]
Addl. 2nd Lieut. 7th Cav., 12 June, 1890. 2nd Lieut., 22 July, 1890. 1st Lieut. 2nd Cav., 13 June, 1897. Graduate of the Inf. and Cav. School, 1893.

CLARK, WM. J. [Born in Penn. Appointed from Penn.]
Hosp. Surg. Mate, 26 April, 1817. Post. Surg., 18 April, 1818. Resigned 1 June, 1819.

CLARK, WM. J. [Born in N. C. Apointed from N. C.]
Capt. 12th Inf., 9 April, 1847. Disbanded 25 July, 1848. Bvt. Maj. 15 Aug., 1847, for gallant and meritorious conduct in several affairs with Guerillas at Paso Ovejas, National Bridge, and Cerro Gordo.

CLARK, WM. P.* [Born in N. Y. Apointed from N. Y.]
2nd Lieut. 2nd Cav., 15 June, 1868. 1st Lieut., 10 July, 1869. Adj., 31 July, 1869, to 1 July, 1876. Capt., 25 Jan., 1881. Died 22 Sept., 1884.

CLARKE, ALEXR. S.* [Born in Mo. Appointed at Large.]
2nd Lieut. 2nd Art., 13 June, 1864. Trans. to 1st Cav., 21 Nov., 1864. 1st Lieut., 6 Feb., 1865. Capt., 44th Inf., 28 July, 1866. Unassigned 27 May, 1869. Ass'd to 5th Cav., 15 Dec., 1870. Resigned 1 March, 1872. Bvt. Capt., 2 April, 1865, for gallant and meritorious service at the Battle of Five Forks, Va.

CLARKE, ALPHEUS E. [Born in Penn. Appointed from Wis.]
Capt. C. S. Vols., 28 Sept., 1862. Bvt. Maj. and Lieut. Col. Vols., 13 March, 1865, for meritorious service in his department during the war. Mustered out 19 Dec., 1865. 2nd Lieut. 3rd Art., 23 Feb., 1866. 1st Lieut., 28 July, 1866. Resigned 14 April, 1873.

CLARKE, CHAS. E. [Born in Conn. Appointed from Mich.]
Capt. 6th Mich. Vols., 20 Aug., 1861. Maj. 21 June, 1862. Lieut. Col., 1 May, 1864. Mustered out 7 Sept., 1865. Capt. 38th Inf., 28 July, 1866. Bvt. Maj., 2 March, 1867, for gallant and meritorious service in the Siege of Port Hudson, La. Unassigned 11 Nov., 1869. Ass'd to 17th Inf., 25 April, 1870. Retired 28 June, 1878.

CLARKE, CHARLES J. T. [Born in N. Y. Appointed from the Army.]
Priv. band 22nd Inf., 15 Nov., 1870, to 15 Nov., 1875. Private and princ. mus. band and Corpl. and Sergt. Co. K, 22nd Inf., 15 Dec., 1875, to 27 April, 1882. 2nd Lieut. 10th Inf., 27 March, 1882. 1st Lieut., 1 Aug., 1886. Capt., 26 April, 1898. Graduate of the Inf. and Cav. School, 1885.

CLARKE, CHAS. M. [Born in Sweden. Appointed from Ohio.]
Capt. 6th Ohio Vols., 18 June, 1861. Bvt. Maj. Vols., 13 March, 1865, for faithful and meritorious services. Resigned 8 Sept., 1862. 2nd Lieut. 19th Inf., 15 May, 1866. 1st Lieut., 13 Jan., 1868. Drowned 6 May, 1868.

CLARKE, ELISHA. [Born in Conn. Appointed from Army.]
Priv. and Sergt. Capt. Sproul's Co. 13th Inf., 1 Oct., 12 to 27 Oct., 1813. Ensign 13th Inf., 27 Oct., 1813. 3rd Lieut., 31 Jan., 1814. 2nd Lieut., 25 July, 1814. Discharged 15 June, 1815. Reinstated in 2nd Inf., 2 Dec., 1815. Resigned 1 Dec., 1819.

CLARKE, FRANCIS. [Born in Ireland. Appointed from Army.]
Priv. Co. G, 3rd Inf., 4 June, 1850. Corpl., 1 Jan., 1853. Sergt., 1 March, 1853. Discharged 4 April, 1855. Sergt. Co. G, 3rd Inf., 4 April, 1855. Discharged 15 Feb., 1860. Sergt. Co. G, 3rd Inf., 15 Feb., 1860. 1st Sergt., 8 Dec., 1860. 2nd Lieut. 13th Inf., 14 May, 1861. 1st Lieut., 24 Oct., 1861. Bvt. Capt., 4 July, 1863, for gallant and meritorious service in the Siege of Vicksburg, Miss. Bvt. Maj., 25 Nov., 1863, for gallant and meritorious service in the Battle of Mission Ridge, Tenn. Capt. 13th Inf., 10 Oct., 1865. Trans. to 31st Inf., 21 Sept., 1866. Trans. to 22nd Inf., 15 May, 1869. Retired by operation of law 2 June, 1889. Died 13 Feb., 1898.

CLARKE, FRANCIS N.* [Born in N. Y. Appointed at Large.]
2nd Lieut. 4th Art., 1 July, 1840. 1st Lieut., 13 Oct., 1845. Capt., 15 July, 1852. Maj. 5th Art., 5 Aug., 1862. Died 13 Aug., 1866. Bvt. Lieut. Col. and Col., 1 Feb., 1865. (Services not specified.)

CLARKE, GEORGE R. [Born in D. C. Appointed from D. C.]
Asst. Surg., 1 Nov., 1834. Resigned 17 June, 1840.

CLARKE, HENRY.* [Born in Conn. Appointed from Conn.]
Bvt. 2nd Lieut. and 2nd Lieut. 5th Inf., 1 July, 1822. 1st Lieut., 16 Aug., 1828. Died 14 Oct., 1830.

CLARKE, HENRY D. [Born in Iowa. Apointed from Iowa.]
Priv. Co. A, 11th Pa. Cav., 29 Oct., 1861, to 22 Sept., 1864. Priv. and Sergt. Co. A, 11th Penn. Cav., 27 March, 1865. Mustered out 13 Aug., 1865. 2nd Lieut. 11th Inf., 23 Feb., 1866. Resigned 27 April, 1866.

CLARKE, HENRY F.* [Born in Penn. Appointed from Penn.]
Bvt. 2nd Lieut. 2nd Art., 1 July, 1843. 2nd Lieut., 18 June, 1846. 1st Lieut., 8 Sept., 1847. Bvt. Capt., 13 Sept., 1847, for gallant and meritorious conduct in the Battle of Chapultepec. Capt. C. S., 12 Jan., 1857. Vacated commission of 1st Lieut. 2nd Art., 3 March, 1857. Maj. C. S., 3 Aug., 1861. Col. Addl. A. de C., 28 Sept., 1861. Bvt. Col., 11 Sept., 1863, for gallant and meritorious service during the Maryland campaign. Lieut. Col. Asst. C. G. S. 29 June, 1864. Bvt. Brig. Gen., 13 March, 1865, for gallant and meritorious service in the Battle of Gettysburg, Penn. Bvt. Maj. Gen., 13 March, 1865, for faithful and meritorious service in the Subsistence Department during the war. Mustered out as Col. Addl. A. de C., 31 May, 1866. Col. and Asst. C. G. S., 20 May, 1882. Retired by operation of law, 9 Nov., 1884. Died 10 May, 1887.

CLARKE, JAMES L. [Born in Va. Apointed from Va.]
Asst. Surg. Voltigeurs, 9 April, 1847. Disbanded 25 Aug., 1848.

CLARKE, JOHN B. [Born in Ky. Appointed from Ky.]
Ensign 28th Inf., 20 May, 1813. 2nd Lieut., 9 April, 1814. Trans. to 3rd Inf., 17 May, 1815. 1st Lieut., 7 May, 1817. Capt., 18 March, 1826. (Asst. Q. M., 19 May, 1826, to — Oct., 1830.) Maj. 1st Inf., 26 Nov., 1845. Died 23 Aug., 1847.

CLARKE, JOSEPH T. [Born in D. C. Appointed from N. Y.]
Cadet at Mil. Acad., 1 July, 1883, to 19 June, 1885. Asst. Surg., 6 June, 1890. Capt. and Asst. Surg., 6 June, 1895. Major and Surg., 47th U. S. Vols., 17 Aug., 1899.

CLARKE, LUKE. [Born in Ireland. Appointed from Army.]
Priv. Co. A, 1st Batt. 13th Inf., 8 July, 1862. Sergt., 1 May, 1863. 1st Sergt., 1 Aug., 1863. 2nd Lieut. 2nd Inf., 7 June, 1864. Retired 28 Feb., 1865. Died 19 Nov., 1881.

CLARKE, NEWMAN S. [Born in Conn. Appointed from Vt.]
Ensign 11th Inf., 12 March, 1812. 2nd Lieut., — March, 1813. 1st Lieut., 15 Aug., 1813. Capt., 1 Oct., 1814. Trans. to 6th Inf., 17 May, 1815. Maj. 2nd Inf., 21 July, 1834. Lieut. Col. 8th Inf., 7 July, 1838. Col. 6th Inf., 29 June, 1846. Died 17 Oct., 1860. Bvt. Capt., 25 July, 1814, for gallant conduct at the Battle of Niagara. Bvt. Maj., 25 July, 1824, for 10 years' faithful service in one grade. Bvt. Brig. Gen., 29 March, 1847, for gallant and meritorious conduct at the Siege of Vera Cruz.

CLARKE, POWHATAN H.* [Born in La. Appointed from La.]
2nd Lieut. 10th Cav., 15 June, 1884. 1st Lieut. of Cav. (9th), 27 April, 1891. Trans. to 10th Cav., 9 Feb., 1892. Accidentally drowned 21 July, 1893.

CLARKE, RICHARD. [Born in N. Y. Appointed from N. Y.]
Asst. Surg., 2 March, 1833. Maj. Surg., 7 July, 1838. Died 29 June, 1839.

CLARKE, ROBERT. [Born in Penn. Appointed from Pa.]
2nd Lieut. 8th Pa. Res., 1 May to 28 Sept., 1861. 2nd Lieut. 2nd Art., 23 Sept., 1861. 1st Lieut., 24 July, 1862. Resigned 9 Feb., 1865.

CLARKE, ROBERT D. [Born in Penn. Appointed from Penn.]
Addl. P. M., 12 Aug., 1863. Bvt. Lieut. Col. Vols., 13 March, 1865, for faithful and meritorious service in the Pay Department. Maj. P. M., 17 Jan., 1867. Vacated commission of Addl. P. M., 17 Jan., 1867. Retired 30 June, 1882. Died 7 April, 1891.

CLARKE, WILLIAM L. [Born in Del. Appointed from Del.]
2nd Lieut. 36th Inf., 20 Nov., 1867. Unassigned 19 May, 1869. Ass'd to 23rd Inf., 3 Aug., 1870. 1st Lieut., 6 Sept., 1873. Dismissed 15 Feb., 1884.

CLARY, ROBERT E.* [Born in Mass. Appointed from Mass.]
Bvt. 2nd Lieut. Inf., 1 July, 1828. 2nd Lieut. 5th Inf., 1 July, 1828. 1st Lieut., 1 April, 1836. Capt. Asst. Q. M., 7 July, 1838. Capt. 5th Inf., 3 April, 1839. Vacated line commission, 18 June, 1846. Maj. Q. M., 17 May, 1861. Col. Addl. A. de C., 5 July, 1862. Lieut. Col. Dep. Q. M. Gen., 15 April, 1864. Bvt. Col. and Brig. Gen.,

13 March, 1865, for faithful and meritorious service during the war. Mustered out as Col. Addl. A. de C., 31 May, 1866. Col. Asst. Q. M. Gen., 29 July, 1866. Retired 22 Feb., 1869. Died 19 Jan., 1890.

CLARY, ROBT. E. [Born in Mich. Appointed from Mich.]
2nd Lieut. 2nd Drag., 26 April, 1861. 1st Lieut., 30 May, 1861. 2nd Cav., 3 Aug., 1861. Capt. 25 Aug., 1862. Dismissed 13 Feb., 1864.

CLAY, CHARLES D. [Born in Ky. Appointed from Ky.]
2nd Lieut. 17th Inf., 10 Oct., 1883. 1st Lieut. 11th Inf., 19 March, 1891. Trans. to 17th Inf., 5 Nov., 1896. Capt. of Inf., 15 Aug., 1898. Ass'd to 17th Inf., 1 Jan., 1899. Graduate of the Inf. and Cav. School, 1887.

CLAY, HENRY.* [Born in Ky. Appointed from Ky.]
Bvt. 2nd Lieut. 2nd Art., 1 July, 1831. Resigned 1 Nov., 1831.

CLAY, HENRY DE B. [Born in Ohio. Appointed from Ohio.]
Capt. 14th Inf., 14 May, 1861. Trans. to 23rd Inf., 21 Sept., 1866. Discharged 25 Nov., 1870.

CLAY, HUGH L. [Born in Ala. Appointed from Ala.]
Capt. 13th Inf., 9 April, 1847. Disbanded 15 July, 1848.

CLAY, JOHN K. [Born in Ohio. Appointed from Army.]
Priv. and Sergt. Co. A., 2nd Batt. 14th Inf., 1 May to 1 Aug., 1862. 2nd Lieut. 14th Inf., 30 June, 1862. 1st Lieut., 14 May, 1864. Died 14 May, 1864, of wounds received in Battle of the Wilderness, Va. Bvt. Capt., 5 May, 1864, for gallant and meritorious service at the Battle of the Wilderness, Va.

CLAY, JOSEPH.* [Born in Ga. Appointed from Ga.]
Bvt. 2nd Lieut. 6th Inf., 1 July, 1825. 2nd Lieut. 4th Inf., 1 July, 1825. Died 8 July, 1832.

CLAY, THOS. J. [Born in Ky. Appointed from Ky.]
2nd Lieut. 10th Inf., 25 April, 1877. Expired by Constitutional Limitation, 3 Dec., 1877. 2nd Lieut. 10th Inf., 26 Jan., 1878, with rank from 25 April, 1877. 1st Lieut., 15 Sept., 1884. Graduate of the Inf. and Cav. School, 1883. Retired for disability, 22 March, 1894.

CLAY, RALPH A. [Born in N. Y. Appointed from the Army.]
Priv., Corpl. and Sergt. Co. B, 5th Inf., 25 May, 1895, to 6 July, 1898. 2nd Lieut. 13th Inf., 22 June, 1898. 1st Lieut. 14th Inf., 2 March, 1899. Died 30 Aug., 1899.

CLAYTON, BERTRAM T.* [Born in Ala. Appointed from Ala.]
2nd Lieut. 11th Inf., 1 July, 1886. Resigned 31 May, 1888.

CLAYTON, HENRY. [Born in Del. Appointed from Md.]
1st Lieut. Purnell Legn. Md. Cav., 14 Nov., 1861. Mustered out 26 Oct., 1864. Capt. 19th Inf., 28 July, 1866. Unassigned 31 March, 1869. Ass'd to 17th Inf., 5 July, 1870. Resigned 31 Dec., 1872. Appointed Maj. and P. M., 7 Sept., 1882. Died 26 Dec., 1888.

CLAYTON, JERE B. [Born in Pa. Appointed from Cal.]
Asst. Surg., 6 Nov., 1897.

CLAYTON, POWELL, Jr. [Born in Ark. Appointed from Ark.]
2nd Lieut. 5th Cav., 13 Jan., 1892. 1st Lieut., 16 Oct., 1898. Graduate of the Inf. and Cav. School, 1897.

CLEARY, PETER J. A. [Born in Malta. Appointed from N. Y.]
Asst. Surg. Vols., 4 Oct., 1862. Maj. Surg. Vols., 13 April, 1863. Bvt. Lieut. Col. Vols., 9 Aug., 1865, for faithful and meritorious service. Mustered out 10 Aug., 1865. 1st Lieut. Asst. Surg., 9 Oct., 1867. Capt. Asst. Surg., 26 Dec., 1867. Out of service 2 July, 1868. Reinstated 8 March, 1869. Maj. and Surg., 30 Jan., 1883. Lieut. Col. and Dep. Surg. Gen., 15 Nov., 1897.

CLEGHORN, JOHN F. [Born in Canada. Appointed from Ill.]
2nd Lieut. 20th Ill. Vols., 22 April, 1861. 1st Lieut., 13 June, 1861. Capt., 28 Feb., 1862. Resigned 4 July, 1863. 1st Lieut. V. R. C., 22 Jan., 1864. Capt., 21 Feb., 1865. Bvt. Maj. Vols., 22 June, 1865, for faithful and arduous service during the war, both in the field and in the recruitment of the armies of the U. S. Bvt. Lieut. Col. Vols., 16 March, 1866, for faithful and meritorious service connected with the mustering out and disbanding of the Volunteer armies of the U. S. Mustered out 11 Sept., 1866. 1st Lieut. 45th Inf., 28 July, 1866. Bvt. Capt., 2 March, 1867, for gallant and meritorious service in the capture of Vicksburg, Miss. Unassigned 22 July, 1869. Retired with rank of Capt., 15 Dec., 1870. Died 24 May, 1898.

CLEM, JOHN L. [Born in Ohio. Appointed from Ohio.]
Musician Co. C, 22nd Mich. Vols., 1 May, 1863. Lance Sergt., 20 Sept., 1863. Discharged 19 Sept., 1864. 2nd Lieut. 24th Inf., 18 Dec., 1871. 1st Lieut., 5 Oct., 1874. Capt. and A. Q. M., 4 May, 1882. Maj. and Q. M., 16 May, 1895. Graduate of the Artillery School, 1875.

CLEMENS, JEREMIAH. [Born in Ala. Appointed from Ala.]
Maj. 13th Inf., 9 April, 1847. Lieut. Col. 9th Inf., 16 July, 1847. Disbanded 20 July, 1848.

CLEMENS, WM. W. [Born in Penn. Appointed from Penn.]
Priv. Co. H, 25th Pa. Vols., 18 April to 29 July, 1861. 2nd Lieut. Sig. Corps, 3 March, 1863. Bvt. 1st Lieut. and Capt. Vols., 13 March, 1865, for faithful and meritorious services during the war. Mustered out 12 Aug., 1865. 2nd Lieut., 17th Inf., 23 Feb., 1866. Trans. to 35th Inf., 21 Sept., 1866. 1st Lieut., 1 Feb, 1867. Trans. to 15th Inf., 12 Aug., 1869. Discharged 5 Oct., 1870. Bvt. Capt., 2 March, 1867, for gallant and meritorious service in the capture of Fort Fisher, N. C. Bvt. Maj., 2 March, 1867, for meritorious service in the Signal Corps during the war.

CLEMENT, HENRY C., Jr. [Born in Va. Appointed from the Army.]
Priv., Corpl. and Sergt. Troop K, 5th Cav., 25 April, 1889, to 2 Nov., 1894. 2nd Lieut. 22nd Inf., 31 Oct., 1894. 1st Lieut. 21st Inf., 26 April, 1898.

CLEMENTS, BENNETT A. [Born in D. C. Appointed from N. Y.]
1st Lieut. Asst. Surg., 4 Nov., 1856. Capt. Asst. Surg., 4 Nov., 1861. Maj. Surg., 27 Feb., 1863. Bvt. Lieut. Col., 13 March, 1865, for faithful and meritorious service during the war. Died 1 Nov., 1886.

CLEMENTS, GEORGE A. H. [Born in D. C. Appointed from D. C.]
2nd Lieut. 1st Md. Cav., 6 May, 1864. Discharged 14 March, 1865. 1st Lieut. 44th Inf., 28 July, 1866. Unassigned 27 May, 1869. Died 20 June, 1870.

CLEMSON, ELI B. [Born in ——. Appointed from Penn.]
2nd Lieut. 1st Inf., 3 March, 1799. 1st Lieut., 30 April, 1800. Capt., 4 March, 1807. Maj. 1st Inf., 20 Jan., 1813. Lieut. Col. 16th Inf., 5 March, 1814. Disbanded 15 June, 1815. Asst. Commissary of Issues, 25 Aug., 1816. Resigned 1 Dec., 1819.

CLENDENIN, DAVID R. [Born in Penn. Appointed from Ill.]
Capt. and Maj. 8th Ill. Cav., 18 Sept., 1861. Lieut. Col., 5 Dec., 1862. Bvt. Col. Vols., 20 Feb., 1865. Bvt. Brig. Gen. Vols., 11 July, 1865, for meritorious service. Mustered out 17 July, 1865. Maj. 8th Cav., 22 Jan., 1867. Lieut. Col. 3rd Cav., 1 Nov., 1882. Col. 2nd Cav., 29 Oct., 1888. Retired for disability, 20 April, 1891. Died 5 March, 1895.

CLENDENIN, JOHN M.* [Born in Penn. Appointed from Md.]
Bvt. 2nd Lieut. 2nd Inf., 1 July, 1830. 2nd Lieut., 4 March, 1833. 1st Lieut., 26 April, 1838. Died 17 Oct., 1842.

CLENDENIN, PAUL. [Born in Ill. Appointed from Ill.]
Asst. Surg., 5 Nov., 1886. Capt. and Asst. Surg., 5 Nov., 1891. Maj. Brigade Surg. of Vols., 4 June, 1898. Died 4 July, 1899.

CLIFFORD, JAMES A. [Born in Ireland. Appointed from Mo.]
Capt. 1st Mo. Cav., 6 Sept., 1861, to 4 Jan., 1865. Priv. Mtd. Ser., 18 Jan. to 8 May, 1865. 2nd Lieut. 3rd Cav., 31 March, 1866. 1st Lieut., 22 Jan., 1867. Cashiered 9 June, 1868.

CLIFFORD, JOSEPH C. [Born in Mass. Appointed from N. H.]
1st Sergt. Co. B, 42nd Mass. Vols., 3 Sept., 1862. Discharged 12 Nov., 1862. 2nd Lieut. 42nd Mass. Vols., 12 Nov., 1862. Mustered out 20 Aug., 1863. 1st Lieut. 1st N. H. Art., 8 Sept., 1864. Mustered out 15 June, 1865. 2nd Lieut. Ordnance, 9 June, 1865. 1st Lieut., 23 June, 1874. Capt., 14 April, 1875. Died 12 Nov., 1890.

CLIFFORD, WALTER. [Born in N. Y. Appointed from Army.]
Priv. and Corpl. General Service and Co. A, 1st Batt and Sergt. Maj. 16th Inf., 19 March, 1860, to 10 June, 1863. 2nd Lieut. 16th Inf., 10 Aug., 1863. Bvt. 1st Lieut., 19 Sept., 1863, for gallant and meritorious service in the Battle of Chickamauga, Ga. 1st Lieut. 16th Inf., 14 May, 1864. Trans. to 34th Inf., 21 Sept., 1866. Capt., 31 July, 1867. Unassigned, 14 April, 1869. Ass'd to 7th Inf., 1 Jan., 1871. Died 23 Feb., 1883.

CLIFT, EMORY W. [Born in N. Y. Appointed from Mich.]
1st Lieut. 13th Inf., 14 May, 1861. Capt. 20 Sept., 1864. Retired for disability, 16 Oct., 1884. Died 30 April, 1886.

CLINCH, CHARLES N. [Born in Conn. Appointed from N. Y.]
2nd Lieut. 24th Inf., 10 Oct., 1883. Trans. to 3rd Cav., 4 Jan., 1887 (to rank in Cav., 15 June, 1884). Died 12 June, 1890.

CLINCH, DUNCAN L. [Born in N. C. Appointed from N. C.]
1st Lieut. 3rd Inf., 1 July, 1808. Capt. 31 Dec., 1810. Lieut. Col. 43rd Inf., 4 Aug., 1813. Trans. to 4th Inf., 17 May, 1815. Col. 8th Inf., 20 April, 1819. Resigned 21 Sept., 1836. Bvt. Brig. Gen., 20 April, 1829, for 10 years' faithful service in one grade.

CLINCH, DUNCAN L., Jr. [Born in Fla. Appointed from Ga.]
1st Lieut. 13th Inf., 9 April, 1847. Capt., 30 July, 1847. Disbanded 15 July, 1848.

CLINCH, JOSEPH J. [Born in N. C. Appointed from N. C.]
2nd Lieut. 10th Inf., 22 April, 1812. 1st Lieut., 15 Aug., 1813. Trans. to 7th Inf., 17 May, 1815. Capt., 31 May, 1817. Resigned 31 Oct., 1820.

CLINTON, DE WITT. [Born in N. Y. Appointed from N. Y.]
2nd Lieut. 10th Inf., 9 April, 1847. Disbanded 23 Aug., 1848. 2nd Lieut. 10th N. Y. Vols., 1 Nov., 1861. Capt. A. de C. Vols., 9 Oct., 1862. Bvt. Lieut. Vol. Vols. 13 March, 1865, for meritorious service in the Mil. Div. West Minn. and La. Maj. J. A., 27 May, 1864. Died 14 Aug., 1873.

CLINTON, JAMES W. [Born in N. C. Appointed from the Army.]
Priv., Corpl. and Sergt. Troop F, 4th Cav., 17 Aug., 1893, to 3 March, 1897. 2nd Lieut. 7th Inf., 16 Feb., 1897. 1st Lieut. 22nd Inf., 16 Jan., 1899.

CLINTON, WM. [Born in Penn. Appointed from Penn.]
Priv. Co. D, 1st Pa. Vols., 14 Dec., 1846. 2nd Lieut., 16 Dec., 1846. 1st Lieut., 20 July, 1848. Mustered out 8 Aug., 1848. 1st Lieut. 10th Inf., 3 March, 1855. Capt., 3 March, 1861. Maj. 13th Inf., 17 Feb., 1864. Unassigned 15 March, 1869. Mustered out 1 Jan., 1871. Bvt. Maj., 2 July, 1863, for gallant and meritorious service at the Battle of Gettysburg, Penn.

CLITHERALL, GEORGE C. [Born in N. C. Appointed from N. C.]
Hosp. Surg. Mate, 8 March, 1817. Post Surg., 18 April, 1818. Asst. Surg., 1 June, 1821. Died 10 Nov., 1829.

CLITZ, EDWARD M. [Born in Wis. Appointed from N. Y.]
2nd Lieut. 10th Inf., 3 March, 1848. Disbanded 10 Sept., 1848.

CLITZ, HENRY B.* [Born in N. Y. Appointed at Large.]
Bvt. 2nd Lieut. 7th Inf., 1 July, 1845. 2nd Lieut. 3rd Inf., 21 Sept., 1846. Bvt. 1st Lieut., 18 April, 1847, for gallant and meritorious conduct in the Battle of Cerro Gordo. 1st Lieut. 3rd Inf., 5 March, 1851. Capt., 6 Dec., 1858. Maj. 12th Inf., 14 May, 1861. Bvt. Lieut. Col., 27 June, 1862, for gallant and meritorious service in the Battle of Gaines' Mill, Va. Lieut. Col. 6th Inf., 4 Nov., 1863. Bvt. Col., 13 March, 1865, for gallant and meritorious service during the war. Bvt. Brig. Gen., 13 March, 1865, for gallant and distinguished service in the field. Col. 10th Inf., 22 Feb., 1869. Retired 1 July, 1885. Supposed to have been drowned, 30 Oct., 1888.

CLITZ, JOHN. [Born in N. Y. Appointed from N. Y.]
Ensign 13th Inf., 30 March, 1814. 3rd Lieut., 1 May, 1814. 2nd Lieut., 19 Oct., 1814. Trans. to 2nd Inf., 17 May, 1815. 1st Lieut., 31 Dec., 1819. Capt., 4 April, 1832. Died 6 Nov., 1836. Bvt. 1st Lieut., 17 Sept., 1814, for distinguished service at Brown's Sortie from Fort Erie. Bvt. Capt., 31 Dec., 1829, for 10 years' faithful service in one grade.

CLOKE, HAROLD E.* [Born in N. J. Appointed from N. J.]
Addl. 2nd Lieut. 3rd Inf., 11 June, 1897. 2nd Lieut. 6th Art., 8 March, 1898. Trans. to 3rd Art., 4 April, 1899. Capt. C. S. Vols., 12 May, 1898, to 17 Dec., 1898.

CLOMAN, SYDNEY A.* [Born in Ohio. Appointed from Ohio.]
2nd Lieut. 1st Inf., 12 June, 1889. 1st Lieut. 15th Inf., 7 Nov. 1896. Capt. 23rd Inf., 7 Sept., 1899. Maj. Chief C. S., 28 May, 1898, to 13 June, 1899. Capt. A. Q. M. Vols., 18 July, 1899. Vacated 7 Sept., 1899.

CLOSSON, HENRY W.* [Born in Vt. Appointed from Vt.]
2nd Lieut. 1st Art., 1 July, 1854. 1st Lieut., 31 Oct., 1856. Capt. 19th Inf., 14 May, 1861, declined. Capt. 1st Art., 14 May, 1861. Bvt. Maj., 8 July, 1863, for gallant and meritorious service in the capture of Port Hudson, La. Bvt. Lieut. Col., 23 Aug., 1864, for gallant and meritorious service in the capture of Fort Morgan, Ala. Maj. 5th Art., 1 Nov., 1876. Lieut Col. 5th Art., 14 Sept., 1883. Col. 4th Art., 25 April, 1888. Retired by operation of law, 6 June, 1896.

CLOUD, MARSHALL M. [Born in Va. Appointed from Kan.]
Asst. Surg., 13 Nov., 1896.

CLOUS, JOHN W. [Born in Germany. Appointed from Army.]
Priv. Co. K, 9th Inf., 2 Feb., 1857. Trans. to Band, 9th Inf., 1 May, 1859. Discharged 5 Nov., 1860. Priv. Co. K, 6th Inf., 9 Feb., 1861. Corpl., 1 May, 1861. Q. M. Sergt. 6th Inf., 1 Aug., 1862. 2nd Lieut. 6th Inf., 29 Nov., 1862. Bvt. 1st Lieut., 2 July, 1863, and Bvt. Capt., 13 March, 1865, for gallant and meritorious service in the Battle of Gettysburg, Penn. 1st Lieut. 6th Inf., 28 March, 1865. Capt. 38th Inf., 22 Jan., 1867. Trans. to 24th Inf., 11 Nov., 1869. Maj. J. A., 1 April, 1886. Lieut. Col. Dep. J. A. Gen., 12 Feb., 1892. Brig. Gen. Vols., 21 Sept., 1898, to 24 March, 1899.

CLULEY, JOHN F. [Born in Penn. Appointed from Mo.]
Priv., Corpl. and Sergt. Co. F, 2nd Ill. Art., 11 Dec., 1861. Mustered out 27 July, 1865. 2nd Lieut. 12th Inf., 23 Feb., 1866. Trans. to 21st Inf., 21 Sept., 1866. 1st Lieut., 9 Dec., 1866. Discharged 2 Dec., 1870.

CLUTTER, GEORGE W. [Born in Va. Appointed from Va.]
2nd Lieut. of Inf., 23 Feb., 1847. 1st Lieut. 13th Inf., 9 April, 1847. Disbanded 15 July, 1848.

CLYMAN, JAMES. [Born in ——. Appointed from Mo.]
2nd Lieut. Mounted Rangers, 23 July, 1832. 2nd Lieut. 1st Drag., 19 Sept., 1833. Resigned 31 May, 1834.

COALE, JOHN H. [Born in Md. Appointed from Md.]
Capt. C. S. Vols., 30 Aug., 1862. Lieut. Col. C. S. Vols. (Act 17 July, 1862), 1 Jan., 1863, to 10 May, 1865. Bvt. Maj. Vols., 24 June, 1865, for faithful and meritorious service. Mustered out 26 June, 1865. 2nd Lieut. 27th Inf., 2 Oct., 1867. Trans. to 9th Inf., 14 June, 1869. Trans. to 2nd Cav., 17 March, 1873. 1st Lieut., 25 June, 1877. R. Q. M., 1 June, 1880, to 1 Feb., 1881. Died 27 March, 1883.

COATES, EDWIN M. [Born in N. Y. Appointed from Ill.]
1st Lieut. 11th N. Y. Vols., 7 May, 1861. Resigned 4 Aug., 1861. 2nd Lieut. 2nd Cav., 5 Aug., 1861. Trans. to 12th Inf., 20 Sept., 1861. 1st Lieut., 24 Oct., 1861. Bvt. Capt., 1 Aug., 1864, for gallant service in the Battle of the Wilderness, Va., and during campaign before Richmond, Va. Capt. 12th Inf., 11 April, 1865. Trans. to 30th Inf., 21 Sept., 1866. Trans. to 4th Inf., 23 March, 1869. Maj. 19th Inf., 14 July, 1890. Lieut. Col. 16th Inf., 28 Nov., 1893. Col. 7th Inf., 23 July, 1898. Retired by operation of law, 29 Jan., 1900.

COATS, ALBERT. [Born in Ohio. Appointed from Army.]
Priv., Corpl. and Sergt. Co. C, 1st Cav., 8 Dec., 1856, to 7 Nov., 1861. 2nd Lieut. 6th Cav., 26 Oct., 1861. 1st Lieut., 23 Dec., 1862. Resigned 25 Jan., 1866. Bvt. Capt., Maj. and Lieut. Col., 13 March, 1865, for gallant and meritorious service during the war.

COBB, EDMUND M.* [Born in Mass. Appointed from Cal.]
2nd Lieut. 8th Cav., 15 June, 1870. Trans. to 2nd Art., 7 Oct., 1871. 1st Lieut., 7 June, 1878. Died 28 Oct., 1883.

COBB, JAMES D.* [Born in Vt. Appointed from Vt.]
2nd Lieut. Light Art., 1 March, 1811. 1st Lieut. Light Art., 1 April, 1812. Discharged by order of the President, 9 March, 1814.

COBB, SAML. K.* [Born in S. C. Appointed from Ala.]
Bvt. 2nd Lieut. 3rd Inf., 1 July, 1828. 2nd Lieut., 1 July, 1828. Died 11 Jan., 1834.

COBBS, WADDY V. [Born in Va. Appointed from Va.]
Ensign 3rd Inf., 4 Aug., 1813. 2nd Lieut., 1 May, 1814. Disbanded 15 June, 1815. Reinstated in 8th Inf., 2 Dec., 1815. Trans. to 1st Inf., — Aug., 1816. 1st Lieut., 15 April, 1817. Capt., 31 March, 1819. Maj. 5th Inf., 26 April, 1838. Trans. to 4th Inf., 22 Oct., 1845. Died 1 Jan., 1848. Bvt. Maj., 31 March, 1829, for 10 years' faithful service in one grade.

COBURN, HAROLD D. [Born in ——. Appointed from Wyo.]
1st Lieut. 1st Wyo. Inf., 8 May, 1898, to muster out 23 Sept., 1898. 2nd Lieut. 25th Inf., 5 Oct., 1899.

COBURN, JOSEPH L.* [Born in Vt. Appointed from Vt.]
Bvt. 2nd Lieut. 3rd Inf., 1 July, 1834. 2nd Lieut., 31 Oct., 1835. 1st Lieut., 7 July, 1838. Capt., 3 Nov., 1845. Resigned 18 May, 1846.

COCHEN, FRANK S.* [Born in N. Y. Appointed from N. Y.]
2nd Lieut. 12th Inf., 12 June, 1894. 1st Lieut., 26 April, 1898.

COCHRAN, C. H.* [Born in Ohio. Appointed from Ohio.]
2nd Lieut. 7th Inf., 13 June, 1883. 1st Lieut. of Inf. (7th), 20 Feb., 1891. Died 29 Sept., 1892.

COCHRAN, JOHN J. [Born in Mass. Appointed from N. Y.]
Asst. Surg., 17 Feb., 1880. Capt. Asst. Surg., 17 Feb., 1885. Died 5 Aug., 1891.

COCHRAN, MELVILLE A. [Born in Maine. Appointed from Me.]
Capt. 16th Inf., 5 Aug., 1861. Bvt. Maj., 20 Sept., 1863, for gallant and meritorious service in the Battle of Chickamauga, Ga. Trans. to 2nd Inf., 17 April, 1869. Maj.

12th Inf., 4 March, 1879. Lieut. Col. 5th Inf., 31 May, 1883. Col. 6th Inf., 14 July, 1890. Retired for disability, 30 June, 1898.

COCHRAN, PERCY M. [Born in Fla. Appointed from the Army.]
Priv. and Corpl. Co. B, 2nd Inf. Priv., Corpl. and Sergt. Co. G, 6th Inf., 15 Aug., 1895, to 6 July, 1898. 2nd Lieut. 7th Inf., 22 June, 1898. 1st Lieut., 2 March, 1899.

COCHRAN, ROBT. M.* [Born in Del. Appointed at Large.]
2nd Lieut. 4th Inf., 1 July, 1838. 1st Lieut., 4 Oct., 1840. Cashiered 29 Nov., 1844.

COCHRAN, THEODORE D. [Born in Del. Appointed from Penn.]
2nd Lieut. Voltigeurs, 9 April, 1847. Disbanded 31 Aug., 1848. Capt. 15th Inf., 14 May, 1861. Resigned 3 Jan., 1862.

COCHRAN, WM. B. [Born in Va. Appointed from the Army.]
Priv., Corpl. and Sergt. Co. B, 5th Inf., 11 Sept., 1892, to 5 April, 1896. 2nd Lieut. 25th Inf., 23 March, 1896. 1st Lieut. of Inf., 30 Aug., 1898. Ass'd to 25th Inf., 1 Jan., 1899. Trans. to 16th Inf., 21 April, 1899.

COCHRANE, ALEXANDER F.* [Born in D. C. Appointed from D. C.]
3rd Lieut. Corps Art., 2 March, 1815. 2nd Lieut., 5 Aug., 1817. 1st Lieut., 7 April, 1819. Disbanded 1 Jan., 1821.

COCHRANE, RICHD. E. [Born in Del. Appointed from Del.]
2nd Lieut. 4th Inf., 18 Sept., 1838. 1st Lieut., 31 Dec., 1842. Killed in the Battle of Resaca de la Palma, 9 May, 1846.

COCKE, PHILIP ST. GEORGE.* [Born in Va. Appointed from Va.]
Bvt. 2nd Lieut. 2nd Art., 1 July, 1832. 2nd Lieut., 1 July, 1832. Resigned 1 April, 1834.

CODDING, MARTIN O. [Born in Penn. Appointed from Penn.]
Sergt. and 1st Sergt., Co. B, and Sergt. Maj. and Q. M. Sergt. 141st Pa. Vols., 22 Aug., 1862. Mustered out 28 May, 1865. 2nd Lieut. 13th Inf., 23 Feb., 1866. 1st Lieut., 28 July, 1866. Unassigned 13 July, 1869. Discharged 15 Dec., 1870.

CODMAN, R. A. L. [Born in ——. Appointed from Conn.]
2nd Lieut. 1st Inf., 13 Aug., 1819. Disbanded 1 June, 1821.

COE, FRANK W.* [Born in Kan. Appointed from Kan.]
Addl. 2nd Lieut. 1st Art., 11 June, 1892. 2nd Lieut., 13 July, 1892. 1st Lieut., 2 March, 1899. Graduate of the Artillery School, 1896.

COE, JOHN N. [Born in Maine. Appointed from Army.]
Priv. Co. H, 1st Batt. 11th Inf., 14 April, 1862. Corpl., 17 May, 1862. Sergt. 1 Jan., 1863. 1st Sergt., 1 Jan., 1863. Com. Sergt. 11th Inf., 1 April, 1863. Q. M. Sergt. 11th Inf., 11 Jan., 1865. 2nd Lieut. and 1st Lieut. 11th Inf., 12 March, 1865. Trans. to 20th Inf., 21 Sept., 1866. Capt. 19 June, 1868. Maj. 21st Inf., 26 April, 1895. Lieut. Col. 13th Inf., 11 Aug., 1898. Retired for disability, 12 July, 1899.

COENZLER, PETER J. [Born in Prussia. Appointed from Army.]
Priv. and 1st Sergt. Co. B, 16th Inf., 16 Oct., 1861, to Aug., 1863. 2nd Lieut. 16th Inf., 10 Aug., 1863. Killed 25 Nov., 1863, at the Battle of Mission Ridge, Tenn. Bvt. 1st Lieut., 25 Nov., 1863, for gallant and meritorious service at the Battle of Mission Ridge, Tenn.

COFFEE, ANDREW J. [Born in Tenn. Appointed from Ala.]
Addl. P. M., 24 June, 1846. Maj. P. M., 23 Feb., 1847. Resigned 31 July, 1859. Bvt. Lieut. Col., 23 Feb., 1847, for gallant and meritorious conduct at Buena Vista.

COFFEE, JOHN T. [Born in Tenn. Appointed from Mo.]
Capt. 1st Cav., 3 March, 1855. Resigned 20 Dec., 1855.

COFFIE, WM. [Born in Ireland. Appointed from N. J.]
Ensign 15th Inf., 12 March, 1812. 2nd Lieut., 16 March, 1813. 1st Lieut., 21 Sept., 1814. Disbanded 15 June, 1815. Reinstated 17 May, 1816, as 2nd Lieut. Corps Art. Died — Sept., 1817. Retained 17 May, 1816 (re-organization under Act of 3 March, 1815), as 2nd Lieut. Art., with Bvt. of 1st Lieut. from 21 Sept., 1814.

COFFIN, WM. H.* [Born in D. C. Appointed at Large.]
2nd Lieut. 5th Art., 13 June, 1873. 1st Lieut., 6 March, 1882. Capt. 8 March, 1898. Grad. of the Artillery School, 1875. Maj. 26th U. S. Vols., 5 July, 1899 (declined).

COFFMAN, JOSEPH C. [Born in Ohio. Appointed from Ohio.]
Priv. Co. I, 36th Ohio Vols., 13 Aug., 1861. Corpl., 12 April, 1862. Priv. — Oct., 1862. Discharged 22 Sept., 1864. 2nd Lieut. 173rd Ohio Vols., 29 Sept., 1864. Mustered out 26 June, 1865. 2nd Lieut. 19th Inf., 23 Feb., 1866. Trans. to 37th Inf., 21 Sept., 1866. 1st Lieut., 14 Dec., 1866. Retired 21 July, 1868. Died 23 Dec., 1895.

COGSWELL, MILTON.* [Born in Ind. Appointed from Ind.]
Bvt. 2nd Lieut. 4th Inf., 1 July, 1849. 2nd Lieut. 8th Inf., 4 Aug., 1849. 1st Lieut., 15 Aug., 1855. Capt., 13 May, 1861. Col. 42nd N. Y. Vols., 21 July, 1861. Bvt. Maj., 21 Oct., 1861, for gallant and meritorious service in the Battle of Ball's Bluff, Va. Col. 2nd N. Y. Heavy Art., 1 Oct., 1862. Mustered out of Vol. service 7 April, 1863. Bvt. Lieut. Col., 30 July, 1864, for gallant and meritorious service in front of Petersburg, Va. Maj. 8th Inf., 8 Oct., 1864. Bvt. Col., 13 March, 1865, for gallant and meritorious service during during the war. Unassigned 15 March, 1869. Ass'd to 21st Inf., 26 March, 1869. Retired 5 Sept., 1871. Died 20 Nov., 1882.

COIT, DANIEL R. [Born in Conn. Appointed from Wis.]
1st Lieut. 11th Inf., 14 May, 1861. Resigned 20 June, 1863.

COLBURN, ALBERT V.* [Born in Vt. Appointed from Vt.]
Bvt. 2nd Lieut. 2nd Cav., 1 July, 1855. 2nd Lieut. 1st Cav., 1 Oct., 1855. 1st Lieut., 31 Jan., 1861. Bvt. Capt. A. A. G., 1 July, 1861. Capt. A. A. G., 3 Aug., 1861. Maj., 17 July, 1862. Died 17 June, 1863.

COLBY, EDWARD P. [Born in Vt. Appointed from Vt.]
Priv. Co. D, Pa. Art., 20 Feb. to 13 Aug., 1864. 2nd Lieut. 11th Inf., 13 April, 1866. Trans. to 29th Inf., 21 Sept., 1866. Trans. to 11th Inf., 25 April, 1869. Died 31 Dec., 1869.

COLCOCK, RICHARD W.* [Born in S. C. Apointed from S. C.]
Bvt. 2nd Lieut. 4th Inf., 1 July, 1826. 2nd Lieut. 3rd Inf., 1 July, 1826. 1st Lieut., 31 May, 1835. Resigned 1 April, 1836.

COLCORD, AUSTIN N.* [Born in Mass. Appointed from Penn.]
Bvt. 2nd Lieut. 4th Inf., 1 July, 1850. Trans. to 2nd Inf., 11 Feb., 1851. 2nd Lieut., 11 June, 1851. Resigned 31 May, 1855.

COLE, ALONZO A. [Born in Ohio. Appointed from Ind.]
2nd Lieut. 7th Inf., 24 Oct., 1861. 1st Lieut., 2 Jan., 1863. Capt. 8 May, 1864. Mustered out 1 Jan., 1871. Bvt. Capt., 2 July, 1863, for gallant and meritorious service at the Battle of Gettysburg, Pa. Bvt. Maj., 13 March, 1865, for gallant and meritorious service at the Battle of Gettysburg, Penn.

COLE, CHAS. [Born in Md. Appointed from Md.]
Chaplain 1st Potomac Home Brigade Md. Cav., 23 April, 1864, to 28 June, 1865. Post Chaplain, 3 April, 1867. Resigned 1 Jan., 1869.

COLE, EDWIN T.* [Born in Md. Appointed from Penn.]
2nd Lieut. 8th Inf., 12 June, 1889. 1st Lieut. 6th Inf., 27 Aug., 1896. Capt. 11th Inf., 12 July, 1899. Maj. 45th U. S. Vol., 17 Aug., 1899. Trans. to 6th Inf., 24 Jan., 1900.

COLE, GEORGE W. [Born in Mo. Appointed from Mo.]
Cadet Mil. Acad., 1 July, 1882, to 19 June, 1885. 2nd Lieut. 7th Cav., 7 Oct., 1891. 1st Lieut. 1st Cav., 23 Aug., 1898. Trans. to 7th Cav., 3 Oct., 1898.

COLE, HAYDN S.* [Born in N. Y. Appointed from Ill.]
2nd Lieut. 3rd Inf., 14 June, 1885. Retired with rank of 1st Lieut. for disability in line of duty, 9 Jan., 1892.

COLE, HENRY G.* [Born in Ga. Appointed from Ga.]
2nd Lieut. 23rd Inf., 11 June, 1892. 1st Lieut., 26 April, 1898. Com. 2 Aug., 1899.

COLE, JAMES A.* [Born in N. Y. Appointed from Wis.]
2nd Lieut. 6th Cav., 15 June, 1884. 1st Lieut. 9th Cav., 1 April, 1891. Trans. to 6th Cav., 20 July, 1891. Capt. 9th Cav., 8 April, 1899. Trans. to 6th Cav., 10 April, 1900.

COLE, JAMES B.* [Born in Ohio. Appointed from Ohio.]
2nd Lieut. 4th Cav., 18 June, 1866. 1st Lieut., 25 Aug., 1867. Discharged 13 Dec., 1870.

COLE, ROBERT G.* [Born in Va. Appointed at Large.]
Bvt. 2nd Lieut. 5th Inf., 1 July, 1850. Trans. to 8th Inf., 11 Feb., 1851. 2nd Lieut., 25 May, 1852. 1st Lieut., 4 Sept., 1855. Resigned 28 Jan., 1861.

COLE, WILLIAM E.* [Born in Utah. Appointed from Utah.]
2nd Lieut. 1st Art., 26 April, 1898.

COLEMAN, FREDK. W. [Born in N. Y. Appointed from Md.]
Capt. 151st N. Y. Vols., 22 Oct., 1862, to 17 Oct., 1864. 2nd Lieut. 15th Inf., 23 Feb., 1866. 1st Lieut., 23 Feb., 1866. Capt., 22 Oct., 1867. Resigned 31 March, 1874. Bvt. Capt., 2 March, 1867, for gallant and meritorious service in the Battle of Spottsylvania, Va. Bvt. Maj., 2 March, 1867, for gallant and meritorious service in the Battle of Cold Harbor, Va.

COLEMAN, FREDERICK W., Jr. [Born in Md. Appointed from D. C.]
2nd Lieut. 13th Inf., 9 Sept., 1898. 1st Lieut. 8th Inf., 11 Oct., 1899.

COLEMAN, RICHARD M. [Born in Ky. Appointed from Ky.]
Surg. Mate 2nd Inf., 10 Aug., 1818. Asst. Surg., 1 June, 1821. Maj. Surg., 13 July, 1832. Died 2 Sept., 1832.

COLEMAN, WM. I. [Born in Va. Appointed from Army.]
Priv., Corpl. and Sergt. 1st Mtd. Rifles, 4 Aug., 1846, to 20 Sept., 1847. 2nd Lieut. 12th Inf., 4 Aug., 1847. Disbanded 25 July, 1848.

COLEMAN, WILLIS F. [Born in La. Appointed from La.]
2nd Lieut. 9th Inf., 1 July, 1899.

COLERICK, CHAS.* [Born in Penn. Appointed from Penn.]
Bvt. 2nd Lieut. 6th Inf., 1 July, 1826. Died 9 Jan., 1828.

COLLADAY, SAML. R. [Born in Penn. Appointed from Penn.]
Priv. Co. F, 19th Penn. Vols., 27 April, 1861. Discharged 9 Aug., 1861. Corpl. Co. B, 6th Penn. Cav., 29 Aug., 1861. Sergt., 1 June, 1862. 2nd Lieut. 6th Penn. Cav., 24 Jan., 1863. Mustered out 3 June, 1864. 1st Lieut. 6th Penn. Cav., 1 March, 1865. Capt., 23 March, 1865. Mustered out 7 Aug., 1865. 2nd Lieut. 10th Cav., 9 Aug., 1867. 1st Lieut., 1 Jan., 1871. Died 14 Jan., 1884.

COLLETT, JOSHUA W. [Born in N. J. Appointed from N. J.]
Capt. 10th Inf., 9 April, 1847. Killed in a duel, 21 Jan., 1848.

COLLIER, GEORGE W. [Born in Ohio. Appointed from Ohio.]
Chaplain 34th Ohio Vols., 14 Sept., 1861. Trans. to 36th Ohio Vols. Mustered out 27 July, 1865. Post Chaplain, 23 June, 1879. Retired 29 Aug., 1889.

COLLIER, WM. S. [Born in Md. Appointed from Pa.]
2nd Lieut. 12th Penn. Vols., 25 April, 1861. Mustered out 5 Aug., 1861. 2nd Lieut. 4th Inf., 5 Aug., 1861. 1st Lieut., 25 Nov., 1861. Bvt. Capt., 3 May, 1863, for gallant and meritorious service in the Battle of Chancellorsville, Va. Capt. 4th Inf., 29 June, 1864. Bvt. Maj., 2 April, 1865, for gallant and meritorious service in front of Petersburg, Va. Wholly retired, 27 April, 1880. Died 15 June, 1889.

COLLINS, CHRISTOPHER C. [Born in Va. Appointed from Va.]
Asst. Surg., 30 Jan., 1899.

COLLINS, CHARLES L.* [Born in Ky. Appointed from Ohio.]
2nd Lieut. 24th Inf., 13 June, 1882. 1st Lieut. 19th Inf., 20 Feb., 1891. Trans. to 11th Inf., 20 July, 1891. Capt. 23rd Inf., 27 May, 1898. Adj., 17 Oct., 1894. Died 7 Sept., 1899.

COLLINS, CHAS. O.* [Born in ——. Appointed from N. Y.]
Bvt. 2nd Lieut. 4th Art., 1 July, 1828. 2nd Lieut., 1 July, 1828. 1st Lieut., 11 June, 1836. Capt. A. Q. M., 7 July, 1838. Died 17 Aug., 1846.

COLLINS, EDGAR T.* [Born in Pa. Appointed from Pa.]
Addl. 2nd Lieut. 8th Inf., 11 June, 1897. 2nd Lieut. 23rd Inf., 8 March, 1898. Trans. to 8th Inf., 29 April, 1898. 1st Lieut., 2 March, 1899.

COLLINS, CHAS. R.* [Born in Penn. Appointed from Penn.]
Bvt. 2nd Lieut. Top. Eng., 1 July, 1859. Resigned 10 June, 1861.

COLLINS, EDWARD. [Born in Mass. Appointed from Army.]
Priv. Co. A, Batt. Eng., 4 June, 1846. Artificer, 1 Sept., 1846. Corpl., 18 May, 1848. Sergt., 1 Feb., 1849. Discharged 4 June, 1851. Sergt. Co. A, Batt. Eng., 11 June, 1851. Discharged 11 June, 1856. Sergt. Co. A, Batt. Eng., 11 June, 1856. Discharged 11 June, 1861. 1st Lieut. 17th Inf., 14 May, 1861. Capt., 25 May, 1863.

Maj. 1st Inf., 26 June, 1882. Lieut. Col. 7th Inf., 1 Feb., 1887. Retired at his own request, after 40 years' service, 1 Jan., 1888.

COLLINS, FRANCIS.* [Born in N. Y. Appointed from N. Y.]
Bvt. 2nd Lieut. 4th Art., 1 July, 1845. 2nd Lieut., 18 Aug., 1846. 1st Lieut., 13 Sept., 1847. Resigned 11 Dec., 1850. Bvt. 1st Lieut., 20 Aug., 1847, for gallant and meritorious conduct at Contreras and Churubusco.

COLLINS, GAMALIEL. [Born in Mass. Appointed from Penn.]
Chaplain 72nd Penn. Vols., 10 Aug., 1861. Mustered out 24 Aug., 1864. Post Chaplain, 10 Oct., 1867. Retired 30 Oct., 1879.

COLLINS, JAMES. [Born in Penn. Appointed from Penn.]
Priv. Co. K, 11th Pa. Cav., 31 Aug., 1861, to 1 Sept., 1864. 2nd Lieut. 36th U. S. C. Inf., 22 Nov., 1864. 1st Lieut., 12 Aug., 1865, to 4 Dec., 1865. 2nd Lieut. 19th Inf., 23 Feb., 1866. 1st Lieut., 2 Sept., 1866. Trans. to 28th Inf., 21 Sept., 1866. Trans. to 19th Inf., 31 March, 1869. Unassigned 1 Sept., 1869. Ass'd to 1st Cav., 1 Jan., 1871. Dismissed 9 Aug., 1871.

COLLINS, JAMES. [Born in Ireland. Appointed from Army.]
Priv. and Sergt. 7th Inf., 27 Aug., 1808, to 27 Aug., 1813, and from 14 Nov., 1813, to Dec., 1814. 3rd Lieut., 44th Inf., 20 Dec., 1814. Disbanded 15 June, 1815. 2nd Lieut. 1st Inf., 19 Feb., 1817. 1st Lieut., 1 March, 1818. Resigned 1 Oct., 1818.

COLLINS, JOSEPH B. [Born in D. C. Appointed from D. C.]
Priv. Co. F, Mtd. Rifles, 9 July, 1846, to 19 May, 1847. 2nd Lieut. 4th Inf., 29 March, 1848. 1st Lieut., 7 July, 1853. Capt., 14 May, 1861. Bvt. Maj., 27 June, 1862, for gallant and meritorious service in the Battle of Gaines' Mill, Va. Bvt. Lieut. Col., 30 Aug., 1862, for gallant and meritorious service in the Battle of Bull Run (2nd), Va. Maj. 2nd Inf., 20 Jan., 1865. Bvt. Col., 9 April, 1865, for gallant and meritorious service during the operations resulting in the fall of Richmond, Va., and the surrender of the insurgent army under Gen. R. E. Lee. Unassigned 15 March, 1860. Mustered out 1 Jan., 1871 (sec. 12, 15 July, 1870). Restored to the Army, 8 March, 1879, and placed on the retired list to date from 1 Jan., 1871 (Act 3 March, 1879). Died 20 Dec., 1888.

COLLINS, PATRICK. [Born in Ireland. Appointed from Army.]
Priv. Gen. Mtd. Ser., 14 Feb., 1855. Priv. Co. I, 2nd Cav., 5 June, 1855. Corpl., 4 Dec., 1858. Discharged 14 Nov., 1859. Corpl. Co. I, 2nd Cav., 14 Nov., 1859. Sergt. 21 Dec., 1860. 2nd Lieut. 14th Inf., 14 May, 1861. 1st Lieut., 24 Oct., 1861. Bvt. Capt., 30 Aug., 1862, for gallant and meritorious service in the Battle of Bull Run (2nd), Va. Bvt. Maj., 17 Sept., 1862, for gallant and meritorious service in the Battle of Antietam, Md. Capt. 14th Inf., 22 July, 1865. Trans. to 32nd Inf., 21 Sept., 1866. Trans. to 21st Inf., 19 April, 1869. Died 11 Nov., 1879.

COLLINS, RICHARD D. C.* [Born in N. Y. Appointed from N. Y.]
2nd Lieut. 4th Inf., 1 July, 1823. 1st Lieut., 3 Nov., 1829. Capt., 2 Nov., 1836. (Capt. A. Q. M., 15 Oct., 1830, to 21 Nov., 1836.) Dismissed 24 Feb., 1841.

COLLINS, THOS. E. [Born in N. Y. Appointed from Army.]
Priv. and Sergt. Maj. 2nd Batt. 14th Inf., 18 March to 30 July, 1862. 2nd Lieut. 14th Inf., 14 July, 1862. Supposed to have been killed 5 May, 1864, at Battle of Wilderness, Va.

COLLINSWORTH, JOHN T.* [Born in Tenn. Appointed from Tenn.]
Bvt. 2nd Lieut. 5th Inf., 1 July, 1830. 2nd Lieut., 1 July, 1830. Resigned 31 July, 1836.

COLQUHOUN, WM. S. [Born in Va. Appointed from Va.]
2nd Lieut. 7th Inf., 4 Dec., 1819. 1st Lieut., 31 Dec., 1822. Dismissed 10 Nov., 1829.

COLTON, CHAS. M. [Born in Ohio. Appointed from Penn.]
Asst. Surg., 11 July, 1862. Died 29 Feb., 1864.

COMBA, RICHARD. [Born in Ireland. Appointed from Army.]
Priv. Co. K, 7th Inf., 30 Jan., 1855. Corpl., 18 March, 1858. Priv., 1 July, 1859. Discharged 1 Dec., 1859. Priv. Co. K, 7th Inf., 1 Dec., 1859. Sergt., 15 Feb., 1860. 1st Sergt., 6 June, 1860. Sergt. Co. B, 7th Inf., 8 Dec., 1861. Sergt. Co. E, 7th Inf., 13 Dec., 1861. 1st Sergt., 17 March, 1862. 2nd Lieut. 7th Inf., 19 Feb., 1863. Bvt. 1st Lieut., 2 July, 1863, for gallant and meritorious service in the Battle of Gettysburg, Penn. 1st Lieut. 7th Inf., 30 Oct., 1863. Bvt. Capt. and Maj., 13 March, 1865, for gallant and meritorius service in the Battle of Gettysburg, Penn. Capt. 7th Inf., 14 March, 1865. Maj. 9th Inf., 15 May, 1889. Lieut. Col. 12th Inf., 7 March, 1893. Col. 5th Inf., 30 June, 1898. Brig. Gen. Vols., 7 Sept., 1898, to 15 April, 1899. Bvt. Lieut. Col., Feb. 27, 1890, for gallant services in action against Indians at the Big Hole, Montana, 9 Aug., 1877.

COMEGYS, CORNELIUS, Jr. [Born in ——. Appointed from Md.]
3rd Lieut. 14th Inf., 10 May, 1813. 2nd Lieut., 14 Nov., 1813. Trans. to 4th Inf., 17 May, 1815. Died in 1815.

COMEGYS, EDWARD T. [Born in Ohio. Appointed from Ohio.]
1st Lieut. Asst. Surg., 26 June, 1875. Capt. Asst. Surg., 26 June, 1880. Maj. Surg., 26 Oct., 1893.

COMEGYS, WILLIAM H. [Born in Ohio. Appointed from Ohio.]
Maj. P. M., 18 Feb., 1881.

COMER, JAMES McD. [Born in Ala. Appointed from Ala.]
2nd Lieut. 16th Inf., 9 July, 1898. 1st Lieut. 25th Inf., 20 June, 1899.

COMO, JAMES H. [Born in Canada. Appointed from the Army.]
Priv. and Corpl. Batty L, 2nd Art., 20 Jan., 1891, to 29 Apr., 1894. Priv. Co. H, 11th Inf. and Priv. and Corpl. Co. A, 15th Inf., 9 Dec., 1895, to 8 Dec., 1898. Priv. Batty I, 3rd Art., 17 May, 1899, to 20 Nov., 1899. 2nd Lieut. 25th Inf., 1 Oct., 1899.

COMLY, CLIFTON.* [Born in Ohio. Appointed from Ohio.]
2nd Lieut. 1st Cav., 17 June, 1862. 1st Lieut., 27 July, 1862. Trans. to Ord., 26 May, 1863. Bvt. Capt., 13 March, 1865, for faithful and meritorious service in the Ord. Dept. Capt. Ord., 15 Dec., 1867. Maj. 2 Aug., 1879. Died 17 April, 1894.

COMMAGERE, FRANK Y. [Born in Ohio. Appointed from Ohio.]
Priv. Co. A, 14th Ohio Vols., 27 April, 1861, to 13 Aug., 1861. 2nd Lieut. 67th N. Y. Vols., 13 Oct., 1862. Dismissed 30 Nov., 1863. Maj. 6th U. S. Col. Cav., 18 Jan., 1864, to 15 April, 1866. 1st Lieut. 7th Cav., 28 July, 1866. Resigned 1 Feb., 1868.

COMPTON, BEALL C. [Born in D. C. Appointed from N. Y.]
2nd Lieut. 4th Inf., 30 June, 1855. Dropped 17 May, 1856.

COMPTON, CHAS. E. [Born in N. J. Appointed from Iowa.]
1st Sergt. Co. A, 1st Iowa Vols., 7 May, 1861. Sergt. Maj., 24 May, 1861. Discharged 21 Aug., 1861. Capt. 11th Iowa Vols., 19 Oct., 1861. Maj. 47th U. S. Col. Troops, 5 May, 1863. Lieut. Col. 53rd U. S. Col. Troops, 9 Dec., 1864. Mustered out 8 March, 1866. Maj., 40th Inf., 28 July, 1866. Bvt. Lieut. Col., 2 March, 1867, for gallant and meritorious service in the campaign against Mobile, Ala. Unassigned 15 March, 1869. Ass'd to 6th Cav., 15 Dec., 1870. Bvt. Col., 27 Feb., 1890, for distinguished services in leading cavalry battalion in a gallant and successful charge in action against Indians on the Red River, Texas, 30 Aug., 1874. Lieut. Col. 5th Cav., 29 April, 1879. Col. 4th Cav., 19 Oct., 1887. Bvt. Col., Feb. 27, 1890. Brig. Gen. Vol., 4 May, 1898, to 6 Dec., 1898. Retired, over 62 years of age, 9 June, 1899.

COMSTOCK, CYRUS B.* [Born in Mass. Appointed from Mass.]
Bvt. 2nd Lieut. Eng., 1 July, 1855. 2nd Lieut., 1 Sept., 1855. 1st Lieut., 1 July, 1860. Capt., 3 March, 1863. Bvt. Maj., 4 July, 1863, for gallant and meritorious service in the Siege of Vicksburg, Miss. Lieut. Col. Asst. I. G. (Act 17 July, 1862), 19 Nov., 1863, to 28 March, 1864. Lieut. Col. A. de C., 29 March, 1864. Bvt. Lieut. Col., 6 May, 1864, for gallant and meritorious service in the Battle of the Wilderness, Va. Bvt. Col., 15 Jan., 1865, for gallant and meritorious service in the capture of Fort Fisher, N. C. Bvt. Col. and Brig. Gen. Vols., 15 Jan., 1865, for gallant service in the capture of Fort Fisher. Bvt. Brig. Gen., 13 March, 1865, for gallant and meritorious service in the campaign ending with the capture of Mobile, Ala. Bvt. Maj. Gen. Vols., 26 March, 1865, for faithful and meritorious service during the campaign against the city of Mobile and its defences. Maj. Eng., 28 Dec., 1865. Relieved as Lieut. Col. A. de C., 24 July, 1866. Col. A. de C., 25 July, 1866. Relieved as Col. A. de C., 3 May, 1870. Lieut. Col., 17 July, 1881. Col., 7 April, 1888. Retired by operation of law, 3 Feb., 1895.

COMSTOCK, JOHN M. [Born in N. Y. Appointed from N. Y.]
Military Storekeeper Ord., 10 March, 1851. Resigned 15 July, 1853.

COMSTOCK, WALTER. [Born in Mass. Appointed from Mass.]
1st Lieut. 16th Inf., 29 Nov., 1865. Trans. to 25th Inf., 21 Sept., 1866. Died 9 Aug., 1867.

COMSTOCK, WM. S. [Born in R. I. Appointed from R. I.]
Surg. 3rd Inf., 21 April, 1818. Post Surg., 12 Oct., 1821. Asst. Surg., 1 June, 1821. Died 15 June, 1825.

COMPSTON, SAML. L. [Born in Ireland. Appointed from Army.]
Priv., Corpl. and Sergt. Co. E and Q. M. Sergt. 5th Inf., 30 Aug., 1856, to 19 March, 1863. 2nd Lieut. 5th Inf., 19 Feb., 1863. Died 31 Oct., 1863.

CONANT, ROSWELL.* [Born in Vt. Appointed from Vt.]
2nd Lieut. Rifles, 1 Jan., 1819. Resigned 30 Sept., 1820.

CONE, AURELIUS F.* [Born in Ga. Appointed from Ga.]
Bvt. 2nd Lieut. 6th Inf., 1 July, 1857. 2nd Lieut. 1st Inf., 1 July, 1857. Resigned 13 May, 1861.

CONGER, ARTHUR L. [Born in Ohio. Appointed from Ohio.]
Corpl. and Sergt. Co. M., 12th N. Y. Inf., 2 May, 1898, to 20 Sept., 1898. 2nd Lieut. 18th Inf., 9 Sept., 1898. 1st Lieut. 4th Inf., 2 Dec., 1899.

CONGER, JOHN. [Born in N. Y. Appointed from N. Y.]
Asst. Surg. 10th Inf., 9 April, 1847. Disbanded 26 Aug., 1848.

CONKLIN, ARTHUR S.* [Born in N. Y. Appointed from N. Y.]
Addl. 2nd Lieut. 21st Inf., 11 June, 1897. 2nd Lieut. 20th Inf., 8 Aug., 1897. Trans. to 7th Art., 8 March, 1898. 1st Lieut., 20 April, 1899.

CONKLIN, JOHN Jr.* [Born in N. Y. Appointed from N. Y.]
2nd Lieut. 2nd Art., 15 June, 1884. 1st Lieut., 29 May, 1891. Capt. 5th Art., 17 Oct., 1899. Graduate of the Artillery School, 1890.

CONKLING, BARNABUS.* [Born in N. Y. Appointed from N. Y.]
2nd Lieut. 2nd Art., 1 July, 1836. 1st Lieut., 31 Dec., 1837. Died 18 April, 1839.

CONKLING, SOLOMON G.* [Born in N. Y. Appointed from Vt.]
2nd Lieut. Regiment of Art., 24 Jan., 1809. Died 9 Aug., 1810.

CONLEY, EDGAR T.* [Born in Md. Appointed from Md.]
Addl. 2nd Lieut. 15th Inf., 11 June, 1897. 2nd Lieut. 21st Inf., 1 Feb., 1898. 1st Lieut., 2 March, 1899.

CONLINE, JOHN.* [Born in Vt. Appointed from Ga.]
Priv. Co. E, 1st Vt. Vol., 2 May, 1861. Discharged 15 Aug., 1861. Priv. Co. E, 4th Vt. Vols., 1 March, 1862. Discharged 5 Sept., 1863. 2nd Lieut. 9th Cav., 15 June, 1870. 1st Lieut., 15 Nov., 1875. Capt., 11 Feb., 1887. Bvt. Capt., Feb. 27, 1890, for gallant services in action against Indians in the San Andreas Mountains, N. M., 7 April, 1880. Retired for disability, 25 Feb., 1891.

CONNELL, THOMAS W.* [Born in N. Y. Appointed from N. Y.]
2nd Lieut. 5th Inf., 12 June, 1894. Trans. to 9th Inf., 18 Sept., 1894. 1st Lieut., 26 April, 1898.

CONNELLY, TIMOTHY. [Born in Ireland. Appointed from Army.]
Priv. and Corpl. Co. C, 6th Inf., 20 Aug., 1849, to 20 Aug., 1854. Priv., Corpl. and Sergt. Co. A, 1st Inf., 14 Sept., 1854, to 16 Jan., 1863. Ord. Sergt., 16 Jan. to June, 1863. 2nd Lieut. 9th Inf., 1 June, 1863. 1st Lieut., 29 Dec., 1863. Capt., 10 Sept., 1867. Dismissed 25 June, 1869.

CONNER, EDWARD J.* [Born in N. H. Appointed from N. H.]
Bvt. 2nd Lieut. 5th Inf., 1 July, 1857. 2nd Lieut. 4th Inf., 22 Oct., 1857. 1st Lieut. 17th Inf., 14 May, 1861. Capt., 24 Oct., 1861. Wholly retired, 8 Dec., 1863.

CONNER, JOHN C. [Born in Ind. Appointed from Ind.]
Capt. 41st Inf., 28 July, 1866. Unassigned 11 Nov., 1869. Resigned 29 Nov., 1869.

CONNER, PHINEAS S. [Born in Penn. Appointed from Ohio.]
Asst. Surg., 16 April, 1862. Resigned 1 Aug., 1866. Bvt. Capt. and Maj., 13 March, 1865, for faithful and meritorious service during the war.

CONNELL, THOMAS W.* [Born in N. Y. Appointed from N. Y.]
2nd Lieut. 5th Inf., 12 June, 1894. Trans. to 9th Inf., 18 Sept., 1894. 1st Lieut., 26 April, 1898.

CONNOLLY, PATRICK A. [Born in Ireland. Appointed from the Army.]
Priv. Co. F, 21st Inf., 24 July, 1893, to 23 Oct., 1896. Priv. and Corpl. Co. F, 21st Inf., 7 Nov., 1896, to 6 July, 1898. 2nd Lieut. 5th Art., 22 June, 1898. Trans. to 21st Inf., 24 Dec., 1898. 1st Lieut., 2 March, 1899.

CONNOLLY, THOMAS. [Born in Ireland. Appointed from Army.]
Priv., Corpl. and Sergt. Co. C, 19th Inf., 12 June, 1871, to 12 June, 1876. Priv., Corpl. and Sergt. Co. H, and Sergt. Maj. 21st Inf., and Q. M. Sergt., 12 July, 1876, to 13 July, 1880. 2nd Lieut. 1st Inf., 24 June, 1880. 1st Lieut., 23 April, 1889. Graduate of in the Inf. and Cav. School, 1883. Retired with rank of Capt., for disability, 26 April, 1898.

CONNOLLY, THOS. [Born in Ireland. Appointed from N. H.]
Capt. 8th N. H. Vols., 23 Dec., 1861. Maj. 24 March, 1864, to 18 Jan., 1865. 2nd Lieut. 27th Inf., 22 June, 1867. 1st Lieut, 1 July, 1867. Unassigned, 14 June, 1869. Ass'd to 13th Inf., 15 Dec., 1870. Discharged 31 Dec., 1870. Bvt. 1st Lieut. and Capt., 2 March, 1867, for gallant and meritorious service during the Siege of Port Hudson, La.

CONNOR, JOHN. [Born in N. Y. Appointed from N. Y.]
2nd Lieut. 5th Inf., 8 March, 1837. Died 24 Feb., 1838.

CONNOR, WILLIAM D.* [Born in Wis. Appointed from Iowa.]
Addl. 2nd Lieut. Eng., 11 June, 1897. 2nd Lieut., 5 July, 1898. 1st Lieut., 5 July, 1898.

CONRAD, BRYAN. [Born in Va. Appointed from Mont.]
Priv. Troops A and D, 4th Cav., 23 April, 1892, to 22 July, 1895. 2nd Lieut. 18th Inf., 9 July, 1898. 1st Lieut. Co. M, 1st Mont. Vols., 8 May, 1898, to 1 Sept., 1898. 1st Lieut. 18th Inf., 2 March, 1899.

CONRAD, CASPER H. [Born in N. Y. Appointed from D. C.]
Priv. Co. I, 120th N. Y. Vols., 18 Aug., 1862. Priv. Co. B, 1st Regt. V. R. C., 8 April, 1864. Discharged 31 July, 1865. 1st Lieut. 35th Inf., 7 March, 1867. Trans. to 15th Inf., 12 Aug., 1869. Capt., 25 Jan., 1876. Maj. 8th Inf., 6 Oct., 1897. Died 15 Aug., 1898.

CONRAD, CASPER H, Jr.* [Born in Ohio. Appointed from S. Dak.]
2nd Lieut. 6th Cav., 12 June, 1895. Trans. to 5th Cav., 30 July, 1895. 1st Lieut. 7th Cav., 2 March, 1899.

CONRAD, JAMES R. [Born in Va. Appointed from Va.]
Asst. Surg., 21 Aug., 1838. Dropped 28 June, 1853.

CONRAD, JOHN.* [Born in Penn. Appointed from Penn.]
Bvt. 2nd Lieut. 5th Inf., 1 July, 1831. Trans. to 6th Inf., 20 Oct., 1831. 2nd Lieut., 18 April, 1835. 1st Lieut., 31 July, 1837. Died 10 Aug., 1838.

CONRAD, JOSEPH. [Born in Germany. Appointed from Mo.]
Capt. 3rd Mo. Vols., 22 April, 1861. Maj., 31 July, 1861. Mustered out 25 May, 1862. Lieut. Col. 15th Mo. Vols., 26 May, 1862. Col., 29 Nov., 1862. Bvt. Brig. Gen. Vols., 13 March, 1865, for gallant and meritorious conduct throughout the Atlanta campaign. Mustered out 3 Feb., 1866. Capt. 29th Inf., 28 July, 1866. Bvt. Maj., 2 March, 1867, for gallant and meritorious service in the Atlanta campaign. Bvt. Lieut. Col., 2 March, 1867, for gallant and meritorious service in the Battle of Franklin, Tenn. Bvt. Col., 2 March, 1867, for gallant and meritorious service in the Battle of Nashville, Tenn. Trans. to 11th Inf., 25 April, 1869. Retired with rank of Col., 23 Oct., 1882. Died 16 July, 1897.

CONRAD, JOSEPH S.* [Born in N. Y. Appointed from N. Y.]
Bvt. 2nd Lieut. 4th Inf., 1 July, 1857. 2nd Lieut. 2nd Inf., 12 Oct., 1857. 1st Lieut., 14 May, 1861. 1st Lieut. 12th Inf., 14 May, 1861 (declined). Capt., 1 Nov., 1861. Lieut. Col. A. A. de C., 5 May, 1862. Mustered out as A. A. de C. 21 Jan., 1864. Bvt. Maj., 1 Aug., 1864, for gallant service in the Battle of the Wilderness, Va. Bvt. Lieut. Col., 1 Aug., 1864, for gallant service in the Battle of North Anna River, Va. Bvt. Col., 13 March, 1865, for gallant and meritorious service in the campaign under Gen. W. S. Hancock in 1864. Maj. 17th Inf., 27 April, 1879. Lieut. Col. 22nd Inf., 27 June, 1884. Col. of Inf. (21st), 24 Feb., 1891. Died 4 Dec., 1891.

CONRAD, JULIUS T.* [Born in W. Va. Appointed from D. C.]
Addl. 2nd Lieut. 3rd Cav., 11 June, 1892. 2nd Lieut., 2 July, 1892. 1st Lieut., 2 March, 1899.

CONRAD, WILLIAM D. [Born in N. Mex. Appointed from Army.]
Priv. and Corpl. Troops C and I, 5th Cav., 16 Aug., 1893, to 29 March, 1897. 2nd Lieut. 14th Inf., 2 March, 1897. Trans. to 23rd Inf., 4 May, 1898. 1st Lieut., 2 March, 1899.

CONSTABLE, NATHANIEL S. [Born in England. Appointed from Mo.]
1st Lieut. 19th Mo. Vols., 15 Oct., 1861. Discharged 29 Sept., 1862. Capt. Asst. Q. M. Vols., 23 Sept., 1862. Bvt. Maj. Vols. and Bvt. Lieut. Col. Vols., 13 March, 1865, for faithful service during the war. Mustered out of Volunteer service 4 Aug., 1865. Capt. A. Q. M., 18 Jan., 1867. Died 29 Feb., 1880.

CONVERSE, GEORGE L., Jr.* [Born in Ohio. Appointed from Ohio.]
2nd Lieut. 3rd Cav., 12 June, 1880. 1st Lieut., 15 Feb., 1884. Bvt. 1st Lieut., Feb. 27, 1890, for gallant services in action against Indians at Big Dry Wash, Arizona, 17 July, 1882, where he was severely wounded. Retired with rank of Capt., owing to wounds in line of duty, 8 Aug., 1895. Capt. Co. G, 1st Ohio Cav., 11 May to 22 Oct., 1898.

CONVERSE, OSCAR I. [Born in N. H. Appointed from N. H.]
Priv. 1st Batty N. H. Light Art., 24 Aug., 1861. Discharged 26 May, 1863. 2nd Lieut. 1st N. H. Cav., 21 July, 1864. Mustered out 15 Nov., 1865. 2nd Lieut. 14th Inf., 23 Feb., 1866. 1st Lieut., 31 May, 1866. Retired 19 Oct., 1868.

CONWAY, EDWIN J. [Born in Ireland. Appointed from Mo.]
Priv. Co. H, 1st Drag., 22 April, 1852. Corpl., 1 Nov., 1854. Priv., 15 Jan., 1855. Corpl., 1 May, 1856. Priv., 14 Jan., 1857. Discharged 22 April, 1857. Priv. Co. B,

1st Cav., 28 Nov., 1859. Discharged 4 Dec., 1862. 1st Lieut. 18th Mo. Vols., 4 Dec., 1862. Mustered out 7 April, 1863. 2nd Lieut. 4th Cav., 19 Feb., 1863. 1st Lieut., 7 Sept., 1864. Bvt. Capt., 2 April, 1865, for gallant and meritorious service in the capture of Selma, Ala. Capt. 4th Cav., 16 Aug., 1867. Retired 31 Dec., 1870.

CONWAY, HENRY. [Born in ——. Appointed from Tenn.]
Ensign 2nd Inf., 28 Sept., 1812. 2nd Lieut., 10 Jan., 1813. 1st Lieut., 19 April, 1814. Trans. to 3rd Inf., 17 May, 1815. Reg. Adjt., 1 Nov., 1815, to 1 June, 1817. Resigned 1 Dec., 1820.

CONWAY, THOS. T. [Born in Mo. Appointed from Ark.]
2nd Lieut. 12th Inf., 9 April, 1847. 1st Lieut., 22 Dec., 1847. Disbanded 25 July, 1848.

CONWAY, WM. [Born in N. Y. Appointed from N. Y.]
1st Lieut. 74th N. Y. Vols., 27 June, 1861. Capt., 14 Jan., 1863. Mustered out 19 June, 1864. 2nd Lieut. 16th Inf., 22 March, 1866. Trans. to 15th Inf., 21 Sept., 1866. 1st Lieut., 4 April, 1867. Unassigned 26 April, 1869. Ass'd to 22nd Inf., 6 April, 1870. Capt., 4 July, 1879. Bvt. Capt., 27 Feb., 1890, for gallant service in action against Indians at Spring Creek, Mont., 15 and 16 Oct., 1876. Retired for disability 6 June, 1894.

CONYNGHAM, JOHN B. [Born in Penn. Appointed from Penn.]
2nd Lieut. 8th Pa. Vols., 22 April, 1861, to 29 July, 1861. Maj. 52nd Pa. Vols., 5 Nov., 1861. Lieut. Col., 9 Jan., 1864. Col., 3 June, 1865, to 12 July, 1865. Capt. 38th Inf., 7 March, 1867. Trans. to 24th Inf., 11 Nov., 1869. Died 27 March, 1871. Bvt. Maj. 7 March, 1867, for gallant and meritorious service in the Siege of Yorktown, Va. Bvt. Lieut. Col., 7 March, 1867, for gallant and meritorious service at the Battle of Fair Oaks, Va.

CONYNGHAM, JOHN F. [Born in N. Y. Appointed from Iowa.]
2nd Lieut. 16th Iowa Vols., 18 Jan., 1862. 1st Lieut., 20 July, 1862. Capt., 4 Jan., 1865. Bvt. Maj. Vols., 13 March, 1865, for faithful and meritorious services during the war. Mustered out 19 July, 1865. 2nd Lieut. 15th Inf., 23 Feb., 1866. 1st Lieut., 23 Feb., 1866. Trans. to 24th Inf., 21 Sept., 1866. Died 7 Feb., 1868. 1st Capt., 2 March, 1867, for gallant and meritorious service during the war.

COOK, ANSON J.* [Born in Mass. Appointed at Large.]
Bvt. 2nd Lieut. 2nd Art., 1 July, 1847. 2nd Lieut., 8 Sept., 1847. 1st Lieut., 15 April, 1849. Died 18 Oct., 1853.

COOK, AUGUSTUS.* [Born in Conn. Appointed from Ky.]
Bvt. 2nd Lieut. 2nd Drag., 1 July, 1844. Died 1 Nov., 1845.

COOK, FRANKLIN. [Born in N. H. Appointed from Army.]
Priv. Co. E, 8th Inf., 4 Oct., 1855, to 6 Oct., 1856. Priv., Corpl., Sergt. and 1st Sergt. Co. E, 8th Inf., 1 Nov., 1856, to 30 Oct., 1861. 2nd Lieut. 5th Inf., 24 Oct., 1861. 1st Lieut., 3 Dec., 1862. Resigned 20 Feb., 1865.

COOK, GEORGE H. [Born in N. Y. Appointed from N. Y.]
1st Lieut. 109th U. S. Col. Troops, 8 July, 1864. Capt. 8th U. S. Col. Art., 13 Feb., 1865. Bvt. Maj. and Lieut. Col. Vols., 10 March, 1866, for faithful and meritorious service. Mustered out 10 March, 1866. 2nd Lieut. 28th Inf., 22 Jan., 1867. Trans. to 19th Inf., 31 March, 1869. 1st Lieut., 7 Oct., 1873. Capt. A. Q. M., 10 Feb., 1882. Died 4 Oct., 1889.

COOK, GEORGE T. [Born in N. Y. Appointed from N. Y.]
Corpl., Sergt. and 1st Sergt. Co. C, 21st N. Y. Vols., 20 May, 1861, to 30 Aug., 1862. 2nd Lieut., 30 Aug., 1862, to 18 May, 1863. 2nd Lieut. V. R. C., 3 Nov., 1863. 1st Lieut., 3 Dec., 1864, to 15 April, 1867. 2nd Lieut. 6th Inf., 7 March, 1867. 1st Lieut., 31 Dec., 1868. Unassigned 22 April, 1869. Discharged 31 Dec., 1870.

COOK, HENRY C. [Born in Mass. Appointed from Mass.]
2nd Lieut. 2nd R. I. Vols., 5 June, 1861. Mustered out 7 Aug., 1861. 1st Lieut., 16th Inf., 5 Aug., 1861. Reg. Adj., 15 March, 1862, to 7 Nov., 1863. Bvt. Capt., 1 Sept., 1864, for gallant and meritorious service during the Atlanta campaign and in the Battle of Jonesboro', Ga. Captain 16th Inf., 24 Sept., 1864. Trans. to 2nd Inf., 17 April, 1869. Maj. 13th Inf., 27 Feb., 1897. Lieut. Col. 4th Inf., 2 Jan., 1892. Col. 5th Inf., 17 April, 1897. Retired, for disability, 30 June, 1898.

COOK, WM.* [Born in N. J. Appointed from N. J.]
2nd Lieut. 4th Art., 1 July, 1822. 1st Lieut., 15 May, 1829. Resigned 31 Jan., 1832.

COOK, WM. B. [Born in Va. Appointed from Ala.]
1st Lieut. 3rd Drag., 9 April, 1847. Resigned 8 Jan., 1848.

COOK, WM. I. [Born in Ky. Appointed from Army.]
Corpl. and Sergt. Co. D, 15th Inf., 30 April, 1872, to 2 Dec., 1876. 2nd Lieut. 17th Inf., 15 Nov., 1876. Resigned 15 May, 1878.

COOKE, ELEUTHEROS H. [Born in D. C. Appointed from Minn.]
Sergt. and 1st Sergt. Co. I, 14th Minn. Vols., 8 May, 1898, to 18 Sept., 1898. 2nd Lieut. 10th Inf., 9 Sept., 1898. 1st Lieut. 21st Inf., 26 Nov., 1899. Trans. to 10th Inf., 26 March, 1900.

COOKE, FRANCIS N.* [Born in N. C. Appointed from N. C.]
2nd Lieut. 5th Art., 15 Feb., 1899.

COOKE, FRANK A.* [Born in R. I. Appointed from R. I.]
2nd Lieut. 4th Cav., 14 June, 1885. Resigned 28 May, 1886.

COOKE, GEORGE F. [Born in Ohio. Appointed from Ohio.]
2nd Lieut. 15th Inf., 15 Oct., 1875. 1st Lieut. 3 Nov., 1879. Capt., 30 Oct., 1893.

COOKE, JAMES H.* [Born in N. C. Appointed from N. C.]
Bvt. 2nd Lieut. 1st Art., 1 July, 1822. 2nd Lieut., 1 July, 1822. 1st Lieut., 26 April, 1832. Resigned 31 Jan., 1833.

COOKE, JOHN R. [Born in Mo. Appointed from Mo.]
2nd Lieut., 8th Inf., 30 June, 1855. 1st Lieut., 28 Jan., 1861. Resigned, 30 May, 1861.

COOKE, LORENZO W. [Born in N. Y. Appointed from Kansas.]
Priv. Co. H, 27th Wis. Vols., 26 July, 1862. Corpl., 22 Oct., 1862. Trans. to Priv. Co. E, 1st Batt. 13th U. S. Inf., 11 Dec., 1862. Discharged 11 Dec., 1865. Priv. Gen.

Ser., 13 Dec., 1865. 2nd Lieut. 3rd Inf., 21 Sept., 1866. 1st Lieut., 17 Sept., 1868. Mustered out 1 Jan., 1871. 2nd Lieut. 3rd Inf., 13 Oct., 1871. 1st Lieut., 31 May, 1883. Capt of Inf. (3rd), 29 Nov., 1892.

COOKE, PHILIP ST. GEORGE.* [Born in Va. Appointed from Va.]
Bvt. 2nd Lieut. Inf., 1 July, 1827. 2nd Lieut. 6th Inf., 1 July, 1827. 1st Lieut. 1st Drag., 4 March, 1833. Capt., 31 May, 1835. Maj. 2nd Drag., 16 Feb., 1847. Bvt. Lieut. Col., 20 Feb., 1847, for meritorious conduct in California. Lieut. Col. 2nd Drag., 15 July, 1853. Col., 14 June, 1858. Brig. Gen. Vols., 12 Nov., 1861. Brig. Gen. U. S. A., 12 Nov., 1861. Bvt. Maj. Gen., 13 March, 1865, for gallant and meritorious service during the war. Retired 29 Oct., 1873. Died 20 March, 1895.

COOKE, WM. W. [Born in Canada. Appointed from N. Y.]
2nd Lieut. 24th N. Y. Cav., 26 Jan., 1864. 1st Lieut., 14 Dec., 1864, to 25 June, 1865. 2nd Lieut. 7th Cav., 28 July, 1866. 1st Lieut., 31 July, 1867. Killed 25 June, 1876, in action with Indians in Montana. Bvt. Capt., 2 March, 1867, for gallant and meritorious service in the Battle of Petersburg, Va., 17 June, 1864. Bvt. Maj., 2 March, 1867, for gallant and meritorious service in the Battle of Dinwiddie C. H., Va., 29 March, 1865. Bvt. Lieut. Col., 2 March, 1867, for gallant and meritorious service in the Battle of Sailor's Creek, Va., 6 April, 1865.

COOL, JONATHAN S. [Born in ——. Appointed from N. J.]
Garrison Surg. Mate, 28 Jan., 1811. Post Surg., 24 April, 1816. Resigned 1 Sept., 1816.

COOLEY, FRANCIS M. [Born in N. Y. Appointed from Penn.]
Capt. 5th Pa. Vols., 19 April, to 22 June, 1861. Capt. 11th Inf., 14 May, 1861. Trans. to 16th Inf., 14 April, 1869. Unass'd 29 Jan., 1870. Discharged 1 Sept., 1870. Bvt. Maj., 1 Aug., 1864, for gallant service at Spottsylvania, Va. Bvt. Lieut. Col., 1 Aug., 1864, for gallant service in Battle before Petersburg, Va.

COOLEY, JAMES C. [Born in Mass. Appointed from Army.]
1st Sergt. Co. D, 133rd N. Y. Vols., 15 Aug., 1862. 2nd Lieut., 24 Sept., 1862. 1st Lieut., 26 Jan., 1863. Capt., 24 July, 1864, to 27 Feb., 1865. Priv. Co. G, 5th Cav., 24 March, to 3 May, 1865. 2nd Lieut. 5th Cav., 3 May, 1865. 1st Lieut., 28 July, 1866. Resigned 1 March, 1867. Bvt. 1st Lieut. and Capt., 3 May, 1865, for gallant and meritorious service during the war.

COOLEY, JOHN. [Born in N. Y. Appointed from N. Y.]
1st Lieut. 148th N. Y. Vols., 14 Sept., 1862. Capt., 14 May, 1864. Maj., 7 Dec., 1864, to 22 June, 1865. 2nd Lieut. 13th Inf., 23 Feb., 1866. 1st Lieut., 23 Feb., 1866. Trans. to 22nd Inf., 21 Sept., 1866. Resigned 25 Feb., 1869.

COOLIDGE, CHAS. A. [Born in Mass. Appointed from Army.]
Priv. 16th Inf. and Priv. Co. H, 3rd Batt. 16th Inf., 23 April, 1862, to 21 July, 1864. 2nd Lieut. 7th Inf., 18 May, 1864, and 1st Lieut., 20 July, 1864. Capt., 9 Aug., 1877. Bvt. Maj., 27 Feb., 1890, for gallant services in action against Indians at the Big Hole, Mont., 9 Aug., 1877, where he was three times wounded. Maj. 7th Inf., 26 April, 1898. Lieut. Col. 9th Inf., 16 May, 1899.

COOLIDGE, RICHD. H. [Born in N. Y. Appointed from N. Y.]
Asst. Surg., 16 Aug., 1841. Maj. Surg., 26 June, 1860. (Lieut. Col. Medical Inspector, 11 June, 1862, to 31 Oct., 1865.) Died 23 Jan., 1866. Bvt. Lieut. Col., 13 March, 1865, for faithful and meritorious service during the war.

COOLIDGE, SIDNEY. [Born in Mass. Appointed from Mass.]
Maj. 16th Inf., 14 May, 1861. Killed 19 Sept., 1863, at Battle of Chickamauga, Ga. Bvt. Lieut. Col., 19 Sept., 1863, for gallant and meritorious service at the Battle of Chickamauga, Ga.

COOMB, ROBT. L. [Born in Ga. Appointed from Ga.]
2nd Lieut. 43rd Inf., 4 Aug., 1813. Trans. to 1st Inf., 17 May, 1815. 1st Lieut., 31 Aug., 1816. Capt., 7 Jan., 1819. Disbanded 1 June, 1821.

COOMBS, WM. H.* [Born in Cal. Appointed from Cal.
2nd Lieut. 8th Cav., 15 June, 1868. Resigned 18 March, 1869.

COONEY, MICHAEL. [Born in Ireland. Appointed from N. Y.]
Priv. Co. A, 1st Cav., 4 Dec., 1856. Corpl., 1 May, 1859. Sergt., 10 March, 1860. Discharged 4 Dec., 1861. Priv. Co. M, 6th Cav., 18 Dec., 1861. 1st Sergt., 1 Jan., 1862. Saddler Sergt. 6th Cav., 20 Jan., 1863. Q. M. Sergt. — ——, 1863. Discharged 22 March, 1864. Q. M. Sergt. 6th Cav., 22 March, 1864. Discharged 30 Dec., 1864. Capt. 5th U. S. Col. Cav., 1 Jan., 1865. Mustered out 16 March, 1866. 1st Lieut. 9th Cav., 28 July, 1866. Capt., 1 Jan., 1868. Maj. 4th Cav., 10 Dec., 1888. Lieut. Col. 7th Cav., 2 June, 1897. Col. 4th Cav., 9 June, 1899. Retired, over 30 years' service, 14 Sept., 1899.

COOPER, CHAS. [Born in Penn. Appointed from Penn.]
Ensign 42nd Inf., 30 March, 1814. 3rd Lieut., 1 May, 1814. 2nd Lieut., 1 Oct., 1814. Trans. to 1st Inf., 17 May, 1815. Resigned 28 Feb., 1817.

COOPER, COLDEN D. [Born in N. Y. Appointed from N. Y.]
2nd Lieut. 2nd Art., 16 April, 1813. Trans. to Corps Art., 12 May, 1814. Resigned 1 Jan., 1816.

COOPER, CHAS. L. [Born in N. Y. Appointed from Penn.]
Priv. Co. B, 71st N. Y. State Militia, 27 May, 1862. Discharged 2 Sept., 1862. Priv. Co. A, 21st N. Y. State Militia, 27 June, 1863. Discharged 6 Aug., 1863. 2nd Lieut. 127th U. S. Col. Troops, 5 Sept., 1864. 1st Lieut., 5 March, 1865. Mustered out 20 Oct., 1865. 2nd Lieut. 39th Inf., 28 July, 1866. 1st Lieut., 5 Oct., 1867. Unass'd 20 April, 1869. Ass'd to 10th Cav., 1 Jan., 1871. Capt., 15 Sept., 1883. Maj. 5th Cav., 5 July, 1898.

COOPER, GEORGE.* [Born in N. Y. Appointed from N. Y.]
3rd Lieut. Corps Art., 2 March, 1815. Resigned 15 Feb., 1817.

COOPER, GEORGE A. [Born in La. Appointed from La.]
2nd Lieut. 15th Inf., 1 Sept., 1899.

COOPER, GEORGE E. [Born in Penn. Appointed from Penn.]
1st Lieut. Asst. Surg., 28 Aug., 1847. Capt. Asst. Surg., 28 Aug., 1852. Maj. Surg., 21 May, 1861. Bvt. Lieut. Col., 1 Sept., 1864. Col. Medical Director, (Act 25 Feb., 1865), 25 Feb., 1865. Bvt. Col., 13 March, 1865, for faithful and meritorious ser-

vice during the war. Relieved as Col. Medical Director (Act 25 Feb., 1865), 30 June, 1865. Lieut. Col. Asst. Medical Purveyor, 2 Dec., 1876. Died 13 April, 1881.

COOPER, JAMES F.* [Born in N. Y. Appointed from Penn.]
Bvt. 2nd Lieut. 3rd Inf., 1 July, 1834. 2nd Lieut., 31 May, 1835. Resigned 25 Aug., 1837.

COOPER, JAMES F. [Born in Penn. Appointed from Penn.]
2nd Lieut. 10th Inf., 5 Aug., 1861. Dismissed 2 July, 1862.

COOPER, JOHN E. S. [Born in Mo. Appointed from Wis.]
Priv. and Corpl. Co. G, and Sergt. Maj. 5th Wis. Vols., 5 May, 1861, to 26 Sept., 1864. 2nd Lieut. 5th Wis. Vols., 26 Sept., 1864. Capt. C. S. Vols., 2 Feb., 1865. Bvt. Maj. Vols., 5 Dec., 1865, for faithful service in the Sub. Dept. Mustered out 13 Dec., 1865. 2nd Lieut. 19th Inf., 23 Feb., 1866. 1st Lieut., 23 Feb., 1866. Died 2 Sept., 1866.

COOPER, SAMUEL.* [Born in N. Y. Appointed from N. Y.]
Bvt. 2nd Lieut. Light Art., 11 Dec., 1815. 2nd Lieut., 15 Nov., 1817. Trans. to 1st Art., 1 June, 1821. 1st Lieut. 2nd Art., 6 July, 1821. Trans. to 4th Art., 31 Dec., 1824. Capt., 11 June, 1836. Bvt. Maj. A. A. G., 7 July, 1838. Lieut. Col. A. A. G., 3 March, 1847. Col. A. G., 15 July, 1852. Resigned 7 March, 1861. Bvt. Capt., 6 July, 1831, for ten years' faithful service in one grade. Bvt. Col., 30 May, 1848, for meritorious conduct in the war with Mexico.

COOPER, SAML. M. [Born in Va. Appointed from D. C.]
2nd Lieut. 1st Art., 21 Feb., 1857. Resigned 5 April, 1861.

COOPER, SIDNEY W. [Born in N. Y. Appointed from Penn.]
2nd Lieut. 8th Inf., 5 Aug., 1861. Resigned 28 July, 1864.

COOPER, THOMAS A. [Born in N. Y. Appointed from N. Y.]
Mil. Storekeeper Ord., 18 April, 1841, to 1 Oct., 1842.

COOPER, WICKLIFF. [Born in Ky. Appointed from Ky.]
Sergt. Co. K, 20th Ky. Vols., 15 Nov., 1861. 2nd Lieut., 24 Jan., 1862. Lieut. Col. 4th Ky. Cav., 13 April, 1863. Col., 29 May, 1863. Mustered out 21 Aug., 1865. Maj. 7th Cav., 28 July, 1866. Died 8 June, 1867. Bvt. Lieut. Col., 2 March, 1867, for gallant and meritorious service at the Battle of Resaca, Ga. Bvt. Col., 2 March, 1867, for gallant and meritorious service in the capture of Montgomery, Ala.

COOPER, WM. [Born in Ind. Appointed from Ind.]
2nd Lieut. 16th Inf., 9 April, 1847. Disbanded 7 Aug., 1848.

COPP, WM. M. [Born in Conn. Appointed from N. Y.]
2nd Lieut. 6th Art., 9 July, 1898.

COPPEE, HENRY.* [Born in Ga. Appointed from Ga.]
Bvt. 2nd Lieut. 2nd Art., 1 July, 1845. 2nd Lieut., 1st Art., 18 June, 1846. 1st Lieut., 20 Aug., 1847. Resigned 30 June, 1855. Bvt. Capt., 20 Aug., 1847, for gallant and meritorious conduct at Contreras and Churubusco.

COPPINGER, JOHN J. [Born in Ireland. Appointed from N. Y.]
Capt. 14th Inf., 30 Sept., 1861. Bvt. Maj., 12 June, 1864, for gallant and meritorious service in the Battle of Trevillian Station, Va. Bvt. Lieut. Col., 19 Oct., 1864, for gallant and meritorious service in the Battle of Cedar Creek, Va. Col. 15th N. Y. Cav., 27 Jan., 1865. Mustered out of Vol. service, 17 June, 1865. Trans. to 23rd Inf., 21 Sept., 1866. Bvt. Col., 1 Dec., 1868, for zeal and energy while in command of troops operating against hostile Indians in 1866, 1867 and 1868. Maj. 10th Inf., 20 March, 1879. Lieut. Col. 18th Inf., 31 Oct., 1883. Col. 23rd Inf., 15 Jan., 1891. Brig. Gen., 25 April, 1895. Maj. Gen. Vols., 4 May, to 31 Oct., 1898. Retired, by operation of law, 11 Oct., 1898.

CORBIN, HENRY C. [Born in Ohio. Appointed from Ohio.]
Recruiting 2nd Lieut. 83rd Ohio Vols., 28 July, 1862. 2nd Lieut. 79th Ohio Vols., 29 Aug., 1862. 1st Lieut., 11 May, 1863. Maj. 14th U. S. Col. Troops, 14 Nov., 1863. Lieut. Col., 4 March, 1864. Bvt. Brig. Gen. Vols., 13 March, 1865, for meritorious service. Col. 14th U. S. Col. Troops, 23 Sept., 1865. Mustered out 26 March, 1866. 2nd Lieut. 17th Inf., 11 May, 1866. Capt. 38th Inf., 28 July, 1866. Bvt. Maj., 2 March, 1867, for gallant and meritorious service in action at Decatur, Ala. Bvt. Lieut Col., 2 March, 1867, for gallant and meritorious service in Battle of Nashville, Tenn. Trans. to 24th Inf., 11 Nov., 1869. Maj. A. A. G., 16 June, 1880. Lieut. Col. A. A. G., 7 June, 1889. Col. A. A. G., 26 May, 1896. Brig. Gen. A. G., 25 Feb., 1898. Maj. Gen. Vols., 13 Aug., 1898 (declined). Maj. Gen. and A. G., by special act of Congress, 6 June, 1900, this grade to expire with the termination of office of the present incumbent.

CORBOLEY, JOHN R. [Born in Md. Appointed from Md.]
2nd Lieut. 5th Inf., 3 Jan., 1812. 1st Lieut., 6 July, 1812. Capt., 28 June, 1814. Disbanded 15 June, 1815. Reinstated 2 Dec., 1815, as 1st Lieut. 7th Inf. Capt., 18 Sept., 1816. Resigned 31 May, 1819. Retained, 2 Dec., 1815 (in re-organization under Act of 3 March, 1815), as 1st Lieut. 7th Inf., with Bvt. of Capt. from 28 June, 1814.

CORBUSIER, WILLIAM H. [Born in N. Y. Appointed from Cal.]
1st Lieut. Asst. Surg., 5 Aug., 1876. Capt. Asst. Surg., 5 Aug., 1881. Maj. Surg., 17 Oct., 1895.

CORCORAN, THOMAS M.* [Born in Mass. Appointed from Mass.]
2nd Lieut. 7th Cav., 12 June, 1891. Trans. to 9th Cav., 23 July, 1897. Trans. to 10th Cav., 11 Aug., 1897. 1st Lieut. 6th Cav., 26 Feb., 1898.

CORDIER, CONSTANT. [Born in ——. Appointed from ——.]
2nd Lieut. Inf., 1 Dec., 1899. Ass'd to 5th Inf., 1 Jan., 1900.

CORDRAY, DAVID P.* [Born in Ohio. Appointed from Ohio.]
2nd Lieut. 8th Inf., 29 Aug., 1891. Trans. to 17th Inf., 3 Jan., 1895. 1st Lieut., 26 April, 1898.

CORLEY, JAMES L.* [Born in S. C. Appointed from S. C.]
Bvt. 2nd Lieut. 6th Inf., 1 July, 1850. 2nd Lieut., 6 May, 1851. 1st Lieut., 3 March, 1855. Resigned 4 May, 1861.

CORLISS, AUGUSTUS W. [Born in Maine. Appointed from Army.]
Maj. R. I. Cav., 24 June, 1862. Mustered out 2 Oct., 1862. Maj. 2nd R. I. Cav., 24 Dec., 1862. Lieut. Col., 19 Jan., 1863. Resigned 11 July, 1863. Priv. Co. H, 2nd Batt. 15th Inf., 14 March, 1865. 1st Sergt., 1 April, 1865. 2nd Lieut. and 1st Lieut. 15th Inf., 21 July, 1865. Trans. to 33rd Inf., 21 Sept., 1866. Trans. to 8th Inf., 3 May, 1869. Capt., 29 May, 1873. Maj. 17th Inf., 4 Feb., 1897. Trans. to 7th Inf., 23 Feb., 1897. Lieut. Col. 2nd Inf., 6 Feb., 1899.

CORNICK, WM. F. [Born in Va. Appointed from Va.]
Asst. Surg., 31 Oct., 1860. Resigned 9 Oct., 1865.

CORNING, CLARENCE H. [Born in N. Y. Appointed from N. Y.]
1st Lieut. 17th Inf., 14 May, 1861. Capt., 11 Dec., 1862. Lieut. Col. 14th N. Y. Art., 4 Sept., 1863, to 8 March, 1865. Resigned 1 Dec., 1865.

CORNISH, GEORGE A.* [Born in Ala. Appointed from Ala.]
2nd Lieut. 15th Inf., 13 June, 1873. 1st Lieut., 25 Jan., 1876. Capt., 29 Sept., 1890. Maj., 25 May, 1899.

CORNISH, LESTER W.* [Born in Mass. Appointed from Mass.]
2nd Lieut. 5th Cav., 11 June, 1881. 1st Lieut., 16 Jan., 1889. Capt. 9th Cav., 16 Oct., 1898.

CORNMAN, DANIEL.* [Born in Penn. Appointed from Penn.]
2nd Lieut. 21st Inf., 13 June, 1873. 1st Lieut., 17 June, 1877. Capt., 6 March, 1888. Maj., 2 March, 1899.

CORPREW, GEORGE W.* [Born in Va. Appointed from Va.]
2nd Lieut. Corps Art., 24 July, 1818. Trans. to 3rd Art., 1 June, 1821. 1st Lieut. 3rd Art., 6 Aug., 1822. Resigned 30 June, 1833.

CORSON, JOSEPH K. [Born in Penn. Appointed from Penn].
Corpl. Co. K, 4th Penn. Vols., 20 April, 1861. Sergt., 30 May, 1861. Discharged 26 July, 1861. Asst. Surg., 35th Penn. Vols., 26 March, 1863. Mustered out 11 June, 1864. 1st Lieut. Asst. Surg., 9 Oct., 1867. Capt. Asst. Surg., 23 July, 1869. Maj. Surg., 14 Nov., 1888. Retired, over 30 years' service, 30 Nov., 1897.

CORTELYOU, DAVID H. [Born in N. Y. Appointed from W. Va.]
Corpl. Co. E, 6th N. Y. Cav., 18 Sept., 1861. Sergt., 23 May, 1862. Sergt. Maj., 6 Oct., 1863. 1st Lieut. 6th N. Y. Cav., 6 April, 1864. Mustered out 16 March, 1865. 2nd Lieut. 9th Cav., 15 May, 1867. 1st Lieut., 31 July, 1867. Retired with rank of Capt. Mounted, 15 Dec., 1870. Reduced to 1st Lieut., 3 March, 1875.

CORTHELL, CHARLES.* [Born in Mass. Appointed from Mass.]
2nd Lieut. 4th Art., 15 June, 1884. 1st Lieut., 24 April, 1889. Died 14 Nov., 1893.

CORY, WM. O. [Born in Ohio. Appointed from Army.]
Priv. Co. H, 7th Inf., 5 Oct., 1864. Corpl., 21 Oct., 1864. Sergt., 1 June, 1866. Com. Sergt., 20 Feb., 1867. 2nd Lieut. 24th Inf., 22 Jan., 1867. 1st Lieut., 16 July, 1868. Unassigned 25 April, 1869. Ass'd to 24th Inf., 15 Dec., 1870. Mustered out 1 Jan., 1871. 2nd Lieut. 15th Inf., 1 Oct., 1873. 1st Lieut., 22 Feb., 1877. Retired, with the rank of Capt., for disability 15 June, 1891.

COSBY, GEORGE B.* [Born in Ky. Appointed from Ky.]
Bvt. 2nd Lieut. Mtd. Rifles, 1 July, 1852. 2nd Lieut., 16 Sept., 1853. Trans. to 2nd Cav., 3 March, 1855. 1st Lieut., 1 May, 1856. Capt., 9 May, 1861. Resigned 10 May, 1861.

COSBY, SPENCER.* [Born in Md. Appointed from Ky.]
Addl. 2nd Lieut. Eng., 12 June, 1891. 2nd Lieut., 12 April, 1894. 1st Lieut., 13 Oct., 1895. Maj. Chief Eng. Vols., 13 June, to 31 Dec., 1898.

COSTER, CHAS. R. [Born in N. Y. Appointed from N. Y.]
Priv. Co. K, 7th N. Y. State Mil., 14 May, to 3 June, 1861. 1st Lieut. 12th Inf., 14 May, 1861. Capt., 30 Aug., 1862. Col. 134th N. Y. Vols., 8 Oct., 1862, to 12 Nov., 1863. Resigned 31 Dec., 1863.

COSTER, JOHN H. [Born in N. Y. Appointed from N. Y.]
Priv. Co. K, 7th N. Y. State Militia, 26 April, 1861. Discharged 3 June, 1861. Capt. 1st N. Y. Vols., 12 Sept., 1861. Mustered out 3 March, 1863. Bvt. Maj. Vols., 13 March, 1865, for gallant and meritorious service during the war. 1st Lieut. 6th Cal. Vols., 20 Sept., 1865. Mustered out 25 Oct., 1865. 1st Lieut. 7th Cal. Vols., 18 Nov., 1865. Capt. 1st Ariz. Vols., 1 April, 1866. Mustered out 13 June, 1866. 2nd Lieut. 14th Inf., 28 July, 1866, declined. 1st Lieut. 30th Inf., 7 March, 1867. Bvt. Capt., 7 March, 1867, for gallant and meritorious service in action at Glendale, Va. Unass'd 23 March, 1869. Ass'd to 8th Cav., 15 Dec., 1870. Capt., 29 March, 1873. Retired for disability 26 June, 1882. Died 7 Dec., 1895.

COTTELL, HAMPDEN S. [Born in Maine. Appointed from Ill.]
Sergt. Co. C, 15th Ill. Vols., 24 May, 1861. 2nd Lieut. 15th Ill. Vols., 11 Dec., 1862. Capt., 20 Aug., 1863. Mustered out 3 June, 1864. 1st Sergt. 9th U. S. Vet. Vols., 12 April, 1865. Discharged 19 July, 1865. 2nd Lieut. 30th U. S. Col. Troops, 17 Aug., 1865. 1st Lieut., 26 Oct., 1865. Mustered out 10 Dec., 1865. 2nd Lieut. 39th Inf., 18 June, 1867. Unass'd 20 April, 1869. Ass'd to 15th Inf., 3 Aug., 1870. 1st Lieut., 3 March, 1875. Retired 29 Feb., 1876. Died 6 July, 1894.

COTTER, JOHN. [Born in Ireland. Appointed from the Army.]
Priv., Corpl., Sergt. and 1st Sergt. Batty A, 2nd Art., 27 March, 1877, to 20 April, 1882. 2nd Lieut. 15th Inf., 27 March, 1882. 1st Lieut. 2nd Inf., 6 Jan., 1891. Trans. to 15th Inf., 20 July, 1891. Capt., 26 April, 1898. Graduate of the Infantry and Cavalry School, 1887.

COTTON, GILBERT P.* [Born in Ohio. Appointed from La.]
2nd Lieut. 1st Art., 17 June, 1867. 1st Lieut., 11 Sept., 1873. Capt., 2 March, 1889. Graduate of the Artillery School, 1873. Retired, over thirty years' service, 26 Aug., 1897.

COTTON, JOHN W.* [Born in Mass. Appointed from Mass.]
Bvt. 2nd Lieut. 5th Inf., 1 July, 1823. 2nd Lieut. 3rd Inf., 1 July, 1823. 1st Lieut., 4 Oct., 1827. Capt., 15 Nov., 1836. Resigned 3 Nov., 1845.

COUCH, DARIUS N.* [Born in N. Y. Appointed from N. Y.]
Bvt. 2nd Lieut. 4th Art., 1 July, 1846. 2nd Lieut., 16 Feb., 1847. 1st Lieut., 4 Dec., 1847. Resigned 30 April, 1855. Bvt. 1st Lieut., 23 Feb., 1847, for gallant and meritorious conduct at Buena Vista.

COUES, ELLIOTT. [Born in N. H. Appointed from D. C.]
1st Lieut. Asst. Surg., 30 March, 1864. Bvt. Capt., 13 March, 1865, for faithful and meritorious service during the war. Capt. Asst. Surg., 30 March, 1867. Resigned 7 Nov., 1881.

COULTER, WILL. A. [Born in Penn. Appointed from Penn.]
Priv. and 1st Sergt. Co. C, 3rd Batt. 18th Inf.,4 Oct.,1861, to 15 June, 1864. Capt. 100th U. S. C. Inf., 16 June, 1864, to 25 May, 1865. Capt. A. A. G. Vols., 27 Feb., 1865. Bvt. Maj. Vols., 13 March, 1865, for faithful services during the war. Mustered out 25 Nov., 1865. 2nd Lieut. 12th Inf., 11 May, 1866. 1st Lieut., 22 Feb., 1869. Unass'd 28 May, 1869. Discharged 1 Nov., 1870. Bvt. 1st Lieut. and Capt., 2 March, 1867, for gallant and meritorious service at the Battle of Nashville, Tenn.

COUNSELMAN, JACOB H.* [Born in Md. Appointed from Md.]
2nd Lieut. 1st Art., 11 June, 1863. Lieut. Col. 1st Md. Cav., 8 June, 1864. Mustered out of Vol. service, 8 Aug., 1865. 1st Lieut., 16 Aug., 1864. Died 21 Feb., 1875. Bvt. 1st Lieut., 1 Aug., 1863, for gallant and meritorious service at Battle of Brandy Station, Va. Bvt. Capt., 14 Aug., 1864, for gallant and meritorious service in action at Deep Bottom, Va. Bvt. Maj. and Lieut. Col., 13 March, 1865, for gallant and meritorious service during the war.

COUNSELMAN, THOS. H. B. [Born in Md. Appointed from Md.]
2nd Lieut. 1st Md. Cav., 12 Jan., 1865. Mustered out 8 Aug., 1864. 2nd Lieut. 18th Inf., 30 March, 1866. 1st Lieut., 7 Jan., 1867. Trans. to 1st Art., 3 Aug., 1869. Resigned 10 July, 1872.

COURTENAY, EDWARD H.* [Born in Md. Appointed from Md.]
Bvt. 2nd Lieut. Eng., 1 July, 1821. 2nd Lieut., 1 July, 1821. Resigned 16 Feb., 1829. Prof. at Mil. Acad., 16 Feb., 1829. Resigned 31 Dec., 1834.

COURTNEY, MICHL. L. [Born in Ireland. Appointed from Ill.]
Sergt. Co. I, 102nd Ill. Vols., 26 July, 1862. 2nd Lieut. 102nd Ill. Vols., 9 April, 1863. 1st Lieut., 9 Aug., 1863. Lieut. Col. 16th U. S. Col. Troops, 21 Dec., 1863. Mustered out 30 April, 1866. 2nd Lieut. 39th Inf., 28 July, 1866. Bvt. 1st Lieut. and Capt., 2 March, 1867, for gallant and meritorious service in action at Pulaski, Ga. Bvt. Maj., 2 March, 1867, for gallant and meritorious service in the Battle of Nashville, Tenn. 1st Lieut. 39th Inf., 31 May, 1867. Trans. to 25th Inf., 20 April, 1869. Capt., 3 March, 1875. Died 16 July, 1886.

COUTS, CAVE J.* [Born in Tenn. Appointed from Tenn.]
Bvt. 2nd Lieut. Rifles, 1 July, 1843. 2nd Lieut. 1st Drag., 31 March, 1845. 1st Lieut., 16 Feb., 1847. Resigned 9 Oct., 1851.

COVEY, EDWARD N. [Born in Md. Appointed from Md.]
Asst. Surg., 29 Aug., 1856. Resigned 1 June, 1861.

COVINGTON, ERASMUS F.* [Born in Ky. Appointed from Ky.]
Bvt. 2nd Lieut. 1st Inf., 1 July, 1831. 2nd Lieut., 11 July, 1833. Resigned 30 Sept., 1833.

COWAN, ARTHUR S.* [Born in Me. Appointed from Me.]
2nd Lieut. 15th Inf., 15 Feb., 1899.

COWAN, STEWART. [Born in ——. Appointed from Tenn.]
2nd Lieut. 3rd Inf., 12 July, 1820. 1st Lieut., 18 March, 1826. Dismissed 29 Dec., 1827.

COWAN, WM. J. [Born in N. C. Appointed from N. C.]
1st Lieut. 2nd Art., 12 March, 1812. Maj. A. A. I. G., 17 Oct., 1814. Disbanded 15 June, 1815. Mil. Storekeeper Ord., 21 Feb., 1838. Removed 1 April, 1841.

COWDREY, STEVENS G. [Born in N. H. Appointed from N. H.]
1st Lieut. Asst. Surg., 16 Nov., 1868. Capt. Asst. Surg., 16 Nov., 1871. Maj. Surg., — ——, 1891. Died 22 Feb., 1891.

COWIN, WM. B. [Born in Ohio. Appointed from Neb.]
2nd Lieut. 3rd Cav., 1 June, 1899.

COWLES, CALVIN D.* [Born in N. C. Appointed from N. C.]
2nd Lieut. 23rd Inf., 13 June, 1873. 1st Lieut., 20 March, 1879. Capt., 31 Jan., 1891. Maj. 17th Inf., 14 Aug., 1899. Lieut. Col. 1st N. C. Vols., 11 May, 1898, to muster out 22 April, 1899.

COWLES, EDWARD. [Born in Vt. Appointed from Vt.]
Asst. Surg., 13 June, 1863. Resigned 1 March, 1872. Bvt. Capt., 13 March, 1865, for faithful and meritorious service.

COWLES, WARREN H.* [Born in Pa. Appointed from Dak.]
2nd Lieut. 16th Inf., 12 June, 1880. 1st Lieut., 6 Sept., 1886. Capt. 4th Inf., 26 April, 1898.

COX, CHAS. G. [Born in Maine. Appointed from Colorado.]
Priv. Co. G, 40th Mass. Vols., 10 Sept., 1862. 2nd Lieut., 13 Nov., 1862. 1st Lieut., 1 Sept., 1863. Capt., 26 March, 1864. Maj., 25 Nov., 1864. Resigned 2 Dec., 1864. 1st Lieut. 26th N. Y. Cav., 18 Jan., 1865, to 22 Feb., 1865. Capt. 3rd Mass. Cav., 1 March, 1865, to 28 Sept., 1865. 2nd Lieut. 7th Cav., 7 March, 1867. Capt. 10th Cav., 12 June, 1867. Cashiered 11 Aug., 1870. Bvt. Maj., 12 June, 1867, for gallant and meritorious service in the Battle of Cold Harbor, Va.

COX, JOHN L.* [Born in Iowa. Appointed from Iowa.]
Addl. 2nd Lieut. 20th Inf., 14 June, 1878. 2nd Lieut., 28 June, 1878. Resigned 30 July, 1879.

COX, WITTINGHAM. [Born in N. Y. Appointed from Army.]
Priv. Co. K, 7th N. Y. State Mil., 25 May, to 5 Sept., 1862. Priv. Co. B, and Sergt. Maj. 14th Inf., 11 April, 1863, to 20 June, 1864. 2nd Lieut. 4th Inf., 18 May, 1864. 1st Lieut., 23 Sept., 1865. Discharged 1 Nov., 1870.

COX, WALTER. [Born in Md. Appointed from Md.]
Asst. Surg., 12 Dec., 1898.

COXE, FERDINAND. [Born in Penn. Appointed from Penn.]
2nd Lieut. 1st Inf., 1 Aug., 1838. 1st Lieut., 5 Aug., 1840. Resigned 31 Jan., 1844.

COXE, FRANK M. [Born in Penn. Appointed from Penn.]
2nd Lieut. 87th U. S. Col. Troops, 2 Nov., 1863. 1st Lieut., 9 May, 1864. 1st Lieut. 81st U. S. Col. Troops, 1 Dec., 1864. Bvt. Maj., Lieut. Col. and Col. Vols., 13 March,

1865, for faithful and meritorious service during the war. Capt. 87th U. S. Col. Troops, 7 July, 1865. Capt. 84th U. S. Col. Troops, 31 Aug., 1865. Mustered out 14 March, 1866. Capt. 40th Inf., 28 July, 1866. Trans. to 25th Inf., 20 April, 1869. Maj. P. M., 3 March, 1875. Vacated commission of Capt. 25th Inf., 29 April, 1875. Lieut. Col. Dep. P. M. G., 24 Feb., 1896. Col. Asst. P. M. G., 1 Feb., 1899.

COXE, ROBT. E.* [Born in Ala. Appointed from Ky.]
2nd Lieut. 8th Cav., 15 June, 1870. Resigned 3 Sept., 1874.

CRABB, GEORGE W. [Born in Penn. Appointed from Penn.]
Priv. Co. I, 2nd Penn. Vols., 20 April, 1861. Discharged 2 July, 1861. 2nd Lieut. 5th Art., 14 May, 1861. Bvt. 1st Lieut., 17 Sept., 1862, for gallant and meritorious service in the Battle of Antietam, Md. 1st Lieut. 5th Art., 22 Feb., 1865. Bvt. Capt., 2 April, 1865, for gallant and meritorious service during the Siege of Petersburg, Va. Capt., 17 April, 1881. Graduate of the Artillery School, 1872. Retired with rank of Maj., for disability, 8 March 1898.

CRABBS, JOSEPH T.* [Born in Ind. Appointed from Ill.]
2nd Lieut. 8th Cav., 12 June, 1891. 1st Lieut. 9 Cav., 1 July, 1898. Trans. to 8th Cav., 31 Aug., 1899.

CRADELBAUGH, GEORGE W.* [Born in Ohio. Appointed from Nevada.]
Sergt. Co. F, 68th Ill. Vols., 20 April to 14 July, 1862. Cadet at Mil. Acad., 1 July, 1863. 2nd Lieut. 3rd Cav., 17 June, 1867. Reg. Adj., 7 Sept. to 27 Dec., 1868. 1st Lieut., 6 May, 1869. Mustered out 1 Jan., 1871. Died 25 Nov., 1875.

CRAFT, DAVID L. [Born in Penn. Appointed from Penn.]
Priv. Co. D, 8th Penn. Res. Corps, 1 May, 1861. Trans. to Sig. Corps, 1 Aug., 1863. 2nd Lieut. Sig. Corps, 2 Sept., 1863. Mustered out 4 Sept., 1865. 2nd Lieut. 6th Inf., 24 Aug., 1867. Bvt. 1st Lieut., 24 Aug., 1867, for gallantry in maintaining his position under great exposure on the Appomattox signal tower during the Siege of Petersburg, Va., in the late war, while his station was for some time deliberately cannonaded by the rebel batteries. Bvt. Capt., 24 Aug., 1867, for faithful and meritorious service in the Sig. Corps, during the war. 1st Lieut., 6th Inf., 31 Oct., 1876. Died 12 Nov., 1890.

CRAFT, ELIJAH R. [Born in N. Y. Appointed from N.
2nd Lieut. 5th Art., 14 May, 1861. 1st Lieut., 22 Sept., 1864. Resigned 17 Jan., 1866. Bvt. Capt., 13 March, 1865, for gallant and highly meritorious service at Port Hudson, La. Bvt. Maj., 13 March, 1865, for gallant and meritorious service at Fort Morgan, Ala.

CRAFTS, WELCOME A. [Born in N. H. Appointed from N. H.]
1st Sergt. Co. F, 2nd N. H. Vols., 27 May, to 3 Oct., 1861. 1st Lieut. 5th N. H. Vols., 23 Oct., 1861. Capt., 11 Sept., 1862. Maj., 14 Oct., 1864. Lieut. Col., 13 Nov., 1864. Bvt. Col. Vols., 13 March, 1865, for gallant and meritorious conduct during the war. Mustered out 28 June, 1865. 2nd Lieut. 17th Inf., 6 April, 1866. Capt. 26th Inf., 28 July, 1866. Unass'd 19 May, 1869. Mustered out 1 Jan., 1871. Bvt. Maj., 2 March, 1867, for gallant and meritorious service in the Battle of Fredericksburg, Va. Bvt. Lieut. Col., 2 March, 1867, for gallant and meritorious service in the Battle of Gettysburg, Penn.

CRAIG, HENRY K. [Born in Penn. Appointed from Penn.]
1st Lieut. 2nd Art., 17 March, 1812. Capt., 23 Dec., 1813. Trans. to Corps Art., 12 May, 1814. Trans. to Light Art., 17 May, 1815. Trans. to 3rd Art., 1 June, 1821. Maj. Ord., 30 May, 1832. Lieut. Col., 25 March, 1848. Col. Chief of Ord., 10 July, 1851. Retired 1 June, 1863. Died 7 Dec., 1869. Bvt. Maj., 23 Dec., 1823, for ten years' faithful service in one grade. Bvt. Lieut. Col., 23 Sept., 1846, for gallant and meritorious conduce in several conflicts at Monterey. Bvt. Brig. Gen., 13 March, 1865, for long and faithful service in the army.

CRAIG, ISAAC E.* [Born in Penn. Appointed from Penn.]
2nd Lieut. Corps Art., 21 July, 1814. 1st Lieut. 20 April, 1818. Died 26 June, 1819.

CRAIG, JAMES. [Born in ——. Appointed from Army.]
Priv. and Sergt. 21st Inf., 18 Nov., 1812, to 24 Nov., 1813. Ensign 21st Inf., 24 Nov., 1813. 3rd Lieut., 8 March, 1814. 2nd Lieut., 23 June, 1814. Trans. to 5th Inf., 17 May, 1815. Dropped 14 May, 1816.

CRAIG, JOHN. [Born in Penn. Appointed from Penn.]
Mil. Storekeeper Q. M. D., 31 Jan., 1865. Capt., 28 July, 1866. Discharged 31 Dec., 1870. Bvt. Maj. Vols., 13 March, 1865, for faithful and meritorious service.

CRAIG, JOHN N. [Born in Mass. Appointed from D. C.]
Capt. A. A. G. Vols., 3 Oct., 1862. Bvt. Maj. Vols., 1 Aug., 1864, for gallant and distinguished service in the Battle of Gettysburg, and in the operations before Richmond, Va. Bvt. Lieut. Col., 9 April, 1865, for good conduct and meritorious service during the recent operations resulting in the fall of Richmond, Va., and the surrender of the insurgent army under Gen. R. E. Lee. Mustered out 19 May, 1866. Capt. 38th Inf., 28 July, 1866. Bvt. Maj., 2 March, 1867, for gallant and distinguished service in the Battle of Gettysburg, Penn., and for good conduct and meritorious service during the operations resulting in the fall of Richmond, Va., and the surrender of the insurgent army under Gen. R. E. Lee. Unass'd 11 Nov., 1869. Ass'd to 10th Inf., 15 Dec., 1870. Died 6 Dec., 1884.

CRAIG, JOHN W. [Born in Ala. Appointed from Ala.]
2nd Lieut. 5th Cav., 12 June, 1894. 1st Lieut. 1st Cav., 2 March, 1899.

CRAIG, LOUIS A.* [Born in Mo. Appointed from Mo.]
2nd Lieut. 9th Inf., 17 June, 1874. Trans. to 6th Cav., 25 May, 1875, taking rank from 25 May, 1875. 1st Lieut., 30 Nov., 1879. Capt., 24 Feb., 1899. Maj. A. A. G. Vols., 20 May, 1898, to 7 April, 1899. Col. 32nd U. S. Vols., 5 July, 1899.

CRAIG, LEWIS S. [Born in Va. Appointed from Va.]
2nd Lieut. 2nd Drag., 14 Oct., 1837. Trans. to 3rd Inf., — Aug., 1838. 1st Lieut., 1 June, 1840. Capt., 18 June, 1846. Killed 6 June, 1852, by deserters. Bvt. Maj., 27 Sept., 1846, for gallant and meritorious conduct at Monterey. Bvt. Lieut. Col., 20 Aug., 1847, for gallant and meritorious conduct at Contreras and Churubusco.

CRAIG, MALIN.* [Born in Mo. Appointed from Pa.]
2nd Lieut. 4th Inf., 26 April, 1898. Trans. to 4th Cav., 23 June, 1898. Trans. to 6th Cav., 31 Dec., 1898.

CRAIG, PRESLEY H. [Born in Penn. Appointed from Penn.]
Surg. Mate 6th Inf., 12 April, 1820. Asst. Surg., 1 June, 1821. Maj. Surg., 13 July, 1832. Died 8 Aug., 1848.

CRAIG, PRESLEY O. [Born in Mass. Appointed from Penn.]
2nd Lieut. 2nd Art., 14 May, 1857. Killed 21 July, 1861, at the Battle of Bull Run, Va.

CRAIG, ROBT.* [Born in Penn. Appointed from Penn.]
2nd Lieut. 4th Art., 18 June, 1866. 1st Lieut., 5 Feb., 1867. Capt. A. Q. M., 10 Dec., 1888. Capt. Sig. Corps, 18 Dec., 1890. Maj., 29 March, 1897. Lieut. Col., 8 July, 1898. Retired for disability, 1 Dec., 1899.

CRAIG, ROBT. ORR. [Born in N. Y. Appointed from N. Y.]
Asst. Surg., 29 Aug., 1856. Resigned 7 April, 1863.

CRAIG, SAML. [Born in N. J. Appointed from N. J.]
Priv. and Sergt. Cos. L and K, 1st N. J. Cav., 16 Dec., 1862, to 2 Jan., 1864. 2nd Lieut., 2 Jan., 1864. 1st Lieut., 3 Sept., 1864. Capt., 11 Dec., 1864. Mustered out 24 July, 1865. 2nd Lieut. 16th Inf., 11 May, 1866. Trans. to 25th Inf., 21 Sept., 1866. 1st Lieut., 22 June, 1868. Unass'd 26 April, 1869. Ass'd to 8th Inf., 14 Oct., 1869. Resigned 26 March, 1878.

CRAIG, WM.* [Born in Ind. Appointed from Ind.]
Bvt. 2nd Lieut. 3rd Inf., 1 July, 1853. 2nd Lieut. 8th Inf., 3 March, 1855. 1st Lieut., 19 Oct., 1858. Capt. A. Q. M., 17 May, 1861. Resigned 5 April, 1864.

CRAIGHILL, WILLIAM E.* [Born in Md. Appointed from W. Va.]
2nd Lieut. Eng., 14 June, 1885. 1st Lieut., 22 July, 1888. Capt., 5 Feb., 1897. Maj. Chf. Eng., 16 July, 1898 (declined). Maj. 40th U. S. Inf., 17 Aug., 1899.

CRAIGHILL, WM. P.* [Born in Va. Appointed from Va.]
Bvt. 2nd Lieut. Eng., 1 July, 1853. 2nd Lieut., 3 March, 1855. 1st Lieut., 1 July, 1859. Capt., 3 March, 1863. Bvt. Lieut. Col., 13 March, 1865, for faithful and meritorious service during the war, and particularly for his services in the defence of Cumberland Gap and the ulterior operations of Gen. Morgan's forces. Bvt. Col., 13 March, 1865, for gallant and meritorious service during the war (declined). Maj. Eng., 23 Nov., 1865. Lieut. Col., 2 Jan., 1881. Col., 10 Jan., 1887. Brig. Gen. Chf. Eng., 10 May, 1895. Retired at his own request, after 40 years' service, 1 Feb., 1897.

CRAIGHILL, WM. P. [Born in ——. Appointed from ——.]
Mil. Storekeeper Ord., 9 Aug., 1823. Died — March, 1824.

CRAIGIE, DAVID J. [Born in Scotland. Appointed from Iowa.]
1st Lieut. 8th Iowa Vols., 12 Sept., 1861. Capt. A. A. G., 2 July, 1864. Mustered out 19 Sept., 1865. 2nd Lieut. 12th Inf., 11 May, 1866. Bvt. 1st Lieut., 2 March, 1867, for gallant and meritorious service in the Battle of Shiloh, Tenn. Bvt. Capt., 2 March, 1867, for gallant and meritorious service in the Battle of Iuka. 1st Lieut. 12th Inf., 17 Oct., 1867. Capt., 16 Dec., 1880. Maj. 25th Inf., 26 April, 1898.

CRAIGIE, WALLACE M. [Born in Cal. Appointed from Pa.]
2nd Lieut. 7th Inf., 10 April, 1899.

CRAIN, CHARLES F.* [Born in Ill. Appointed from Ill.]
2nd Lieut. 10th Inf., 12 June, 1894. Trans. to 19th Inf., 17 Aug., 1894. 1st Lieut. 15th Inf., 26 April, 1898.

CRALLE, G. MAURY.* [Born in Va. Appointed from Va.]
2nd Lieut. 20th Inf., 26 April, 1898. 1st Lieut., 2 March, 1899.

CRAM, DANL. H. [Born in N. H. Appointed from N. H.]
2nd Lieut. 9th Inf., 9 April, 1847. 1st Lieut., 8 Sept., 1847. Resigned 4 Dec., 1847.

CRAM, GEORGE C. [Born in N. Y. Appointed from N. Y.]
Capt. 6th Cav., 14 May, 1861. Maj. 4th Cav., 12 Oct., 1867. Resigned 26 Jan., 1869. Bvt. Maj., 9 June, 1863, for gallant and meritorious service at the Battle of Beverly Ford, Va.

CRAM, GEORGE H. [Born in Penn. Appointed from Ky.]
Capt. 9th Ky. Vols., 26 Nov., 1861. Lieut. Col., 10 May, 1862. Col., 10 March, 1863. Bvt. Brig. Gen. Vols., 13 March, 1865, for gallant and meritorious services in the Battles of Stone River, Chickamauga and Mission Ridge, in campaign in east Tenn., in winter of 1863 and 1864, and throughout the Atlanta campaign. Mustered out 15 Dec., 1864. 2nd Lieut. 17th Inf., 23 Feb., 1866. 1st Lieut., 23 Feb., 1866. Capt., 8 Oct., 1867. Unass'd 27 May, 1869. Ass'd to 22nd Inf., 1 Jan., 1871. Died 5 Aug., 1872. Bvt. Capt., 2 March, 1867, for gallant and meritorious service at the Battle of Shiloh, Tenn. Bvt. Maj., 2 March, 1867, for gallant and meritorious service in the Battle of Mission Ridge, Tenn. Bvt. Lieut. Col., 2 March, 1867, for gallant and meritorious service in the Battle of Atlanta, Ga.

CRAM, THOS. J.* [Born in N. H. Appointed from N. H.]
Bvt. 2nd Lieut. 2nd Art., 1 July, 1826. 2nd Lieut. 4th Art., 1 July, 1826. 1st Lieut., 10 April, 1835. Resigned 16 Sept., 1836. Capt. Top. Eng., 7 July, 1838. Maj., 6 Aug., 1861. Lieut. Col., 9 Sept., 1861. Col. A. A. de C., 25 Sept., 1861. Trans. to Eng., 3 March, 1863. Bvt. Brig. Gen. Vols., 13 March, 1865, for faithful and meritorious service during the war. Col. Eng., 23 Nov., 1865. Mustered out as Col. A. A. de C., 23 Nov., 1865. Bvt. Brig. Gen. and Bvt. Maj. Gen., 13 Jan., 1866, for faithful and meritorious service during the war. Retired 22 Feb., 1869. Died 20 Dec., 1883.

CRAMPTON, LOUIS W. [Born in Md. Appointed from Penn.]
1st Lieut. Asst. Surg., 26 June, 1875. Capt. Asst. Surg., 26 June, 1880. Maj. Surg., 6 Sept., 1895.

CRANDAL, FREDK. M. [Born in Penn. Appointed from Md.]
1st Lieut. 33rd Ill. Vols., 15 Aug., 1861. Capt. A. A. G. Vols., 2 Oct., 1862. Col. 48th U. S. Col. Troops, 8 Aug., 1863. Bvt. Brig. Gen. Vols., 24 Oct., 1865, for gallant and meritorious service. Mustered out 4 Jan., 1866. 1st Lieut. 38th Inf., 28 July, 1866. Bvt. Capt. and Maj., 2 March, 1867, for gallant and meritorious service in the Battle of Arkansas Post, Ark. Bvt. Lieut. Col., 2 March, 1867, for gallant and meritorious service in the capture of Fort Blakely, Ala. Capt. 41st Inf., 12 June, 1867. Trans. to 24th Inf., 11 Nov., 1869. Maj. 3rd Inf., 21 Jan., 1895. Retired by operation of law 12 May, 1895.

CRANE, CHAS. H. [Born in R. I. Appointed from Mass.]
Asst. Surg., 14 Feb., 1848. Capt. A. Surg., 14 Feb., 1853. Maj. Surg., 21 May, 1861. Bvt. Lieut. Col. and Bvt. Col., 1 Jan., 1865. Bvt. Brig. Gen., 13 March, 1865, for faithful and meritorious service during the war. Col. A. Surg. G., 28 July, 1866. Died 10 Oct., 1883.

CRANE, CHAS. J.* [Born in Miss. Appointed from Texas.]
2nd Lieut. 24th Inf., 15 June, 1877. 1st Lieut., 20 March, 1879. Capt., 4 July, 1892. Col. 9th U. S. C., Inf., 31 May, 1898, until 25 May, 1899. Lieut. Col. 38th U. S. Vols., 17 Aug., 1899.

CRANE, ICHABOD B. [Born in N. J. Appointed from N. Y.]
2nd Lieut. Marine Corps, 26 Jan., 1899. 1st Lieut., — May, 1809. Capt., 3rd Art., 25 April, 1812. Trans. to Corps Art., 12 May, 1814. Trans. to 1st Art., 1 June, 1821. Maj. 4th Art., 15 Sept., 1825. Lieut. Col. 2nd Art., 3 Nov., 1832. Col. 1st Art., 27 June, 1843. Died 5 Oct., 1857. Bvt. Maj., 13 Nov., 1813, for meritorious service.

CRANE, JOSEPH G. [Born in Ohio. Appointed from Ind.]
Capt. C. S. Vols., 28 June, 1861. Lieut. Col. C. S. Vols., 27 Jan., 1863, to 1 Aug., 1865. Capt. C. S., 25 April, 1865. Died 8 June, 1869. Bvt. Maj., 25 April, 1865, for faithful and meritorious service in the Subsistence Department during the war.

CRANSTON, ARTHUR.* [Born in Mass. Appointed from Ohio.]
2nd Lieut. 4th Art., 17 June, 1867. 1st Lieut., 30 Nov., 1871. Killed 26 April, 1873, in action with Indians in Oregon.

CRANSTON, ARTHUR.* [Born in D. C. Appointed from D. C.]
2nd Lieut. 17th Inf., 9 July, 1898. 1st Lieut. 4th Inf., 2 March, 1899. Trans. to 17th Inf., 31 Aug., 1899.

CRANSTON, JAMES R. [Born in Mass. Appointed from Mass.]
Corpl. Co. E, 24th Mass. Vols., 9 Sept., 1861. Sergt., 9 Aug., 1862. Capt. 119th U. S. Col. Troops, 31 Aug., 1864. Mustered out 27 April, 1866. 2nd Lieut. 10th Inf., 24 Aug., 1867. 1st Lieut., 20 March, 1879. R. Q. M., 7 May, 1884, to 7 May, 1888. Died 23 Aug., 1888.

CRAVEN, AUGUSTUS C. [Born in N. Y. Appointed at Large.]
2nd Lieut. 4th Art., 24 Oct., 1861. Died 19 March, 1863.

CRAWFORD, ALEXR. McL. [Born in Penn. Appointed from Penn.]
1st Lieut. 12th Penn. Vols., 22 April, 1862. Mustered out 21 Nov., 1864. Bvt. Capt. Vols., 13 March, 1865, for faithful and meritorious service during the war. Bvt. Maj. Vols., 13 March, 1865, for meritorious conduct in the Battle of the Wilderness and that campaign. 2nd Lieut. Vet. Res. Corps, 21 Feb., 1865. Mustered out 3 Jan., 1867. 2nd Lieut. 38th Inf., 28 July, 1866. 1st Lieut., 29 March, 1867. Unass'd 11 Nov., 1869. Retired 31 Dec., 1870. Died 19 Oct., 1899.

CRAWFORD, CHAS. [Born in ——. Appointed from Ga.]
Capt. 8th Inf., 6 July, 1812. Disbanded 15 June, 1815. Reinstated 17 May, 1816. Resigned 1 Dec., 1816.

CRAWFORD, CHARLES.* [Born in Ohio. Appointed from Kans.]
2nd Lieut. 10th Inf., 12 June, 1889. 1st Lieut 21st Inf., 11 Nov., 1896. Capt. 5th Inf., 8 Sept., 1899. Trans. to 20th Inf., 17 Feb., 1900.

CRAWFORD, EMMET. [Born in Penn. Appointed from Penn.]
Priv. Co. F, 71st Penn. Vols., 28 May, 1861. Discharged 2 July, 1864. 1st Sergt. Co. K, 197th Penn. Vols., 11 July, 1864. Discharged 11 Nov., 1864. 1st Lieut. 13th U. S. Col. Troops, 23 Nov., 1864. Bvt. Capt. and Maj. Vols., 13 March, 1865, for meritorious service during the war. Mustered out 18 Nov., 1865. 2nd Lieut. 37th U. S. Col. Troops, 16 Feb., 1866. Mustered out 19 May, 1867. 2nd Lieut. 39th Inf., 22 Jan., 1867. 1st Lieut., 5 June, 1868. Trans. to 25th Inf., 20 April, 1869. Unassigned 17 June, 1869. Ass'd to 3rd Cav., 1 Jan., 1871. Capt., 20 March, 1879. Died of wounds received from Mexican troops near Nacori, Mex., while in pursuit of Indians, 18 Jan., 1886.

CRAWFORD, MEDOREM, Jr.* [Born in Oregon. Appointed from Oregon.]
2nd Lieut. 2nd Art., 17 June, 1867. 1st Lieut., 17 June, 1874. Capt., 8 March, 1898. Graduate of the Artillery School, 1875, 1890.

CRAWFORD, RICHARD R. [Born in D. C. Appointed from Conn.]
1st Lieut. 1st Conn. Cav., 26 Nov. to 4 Dec., 1861. 2nd Lieut. 7th Inf., 29 Nov., 1861. 1st Lieut., 2 July, 1863. Died 30 Oct., 1863, of wounds received at Battle of Gettysburg. Bvt. Capt., 2 July, 1863, for gallant and meritorious service at the Battle of Gettysburg, Penn.

CRAWFORD, SAMUEL W. [Born in Penn. Appointed from Penn.]
Asst. Surg., 10 March, 1851. Maj. 13th Inf., 14 May, 1861. Brig. Gen. Vols., 25 April, 1862. Bvt. Col., 2 July, 1863, for gallant and meritorious service in the Battle of Gettysburg, Penn. Lieut. Col. 2nd Inf., 17 Feb., 1864. Bvt. Maj. Gen. Vols., 1 Aug., 1864, for conspicuous gallantry in the Battles of the Wilderness, Spottsylvania C. H., Jericho Mills, Bethesda Church, Petersburg, and Globe Tavern (Weldon Railroad), and for faithful service in the campaign. Bvt. Brig. Gen., 13 March, 1865, for gallant and meritorious service in the Battle of Five Forks, Va. Bvt. Maj. Gen., 13 March, 1865, for gallant and meritorious service in the field during the war. Mustered out of Vol. service, 15 Jan., 1866. Col. 16th Inf., 22 Feb., 1869. Trans. to 2nd Inf., 15 March, 1869. Retired 19 Feb., 1873, for wounds received in line of duty. Retired with rank of Brig. Gen. to date from 19 Feb., 1873, with pay as such from 3 March, 1875 (Act 3 March, 1875). Died 3 Nov., 1892.

CRAYCROFT, WM T.* [Born in Ky. Appointed from Ky.]
2nd Lieut. 7th Cav., 15 June, 1869. 1st Lieut., 2 Dec., 1875. Retired 28 June, 1878, for disability.

CREAMER, ROBT T. [Born in N. J. Appointed from N. Y.]
Med. Storekeeper, 13 Aug., 1862. Mustered out 9 Dec., 1865.

CREANOR, CHAS. M. [Born in Penn. Appointed from Texas.]
2nd Lieut. 12th Inf., 9 April, 1847. 1st Lieut., 27 June, 1847. Disbanded 25 July, 1848. Bvt. Capt., for gallant and meritorious conduct in several affairs with guerillas, at Paso Ovejas, National Bridge, and Cerro Gordo, 10, 11 and 15 Aug., 1847.

CREARY, WILLIAM E. [Born in N. Y. Appointed from Mich.]
Priv. Co. F, 3rd Mich. Vols., 13 May, 1861. Trans. to 2nd Batt. Vet. Res. Corps, 19 Oct., 1863. Discharged 10 June, 1864. Priv. 2nd Batt. Vet. Res. Corps, 13 June, 1864. Discharged 23 Aug., 1866. Maj. and P. M., 23 June, 1879. Retired for disability, 22 Dec., 1892. Died 29 July, 1899.

CREARY, WILLIAM F. [Born in D. C. Appointed from the Army.]
Pvt., Corpl. and Sergt. Co. C, 3rd Inf., 19 Jan., 1893, to 23 March, 1896. 2nd Lieut. 2nd Inf., 5 March, 1896. 1st Lieut. 12th Inf., 12 Aug., 1898. Reg. Com., 15 June, 1899.

CREDEN, SAMUEL G.* [Born in Me. Appointed from ——.]
2nd Lieut. of Inf. (25th), 12 June, 1895. Died 9 Feb., 1896.

CREE, JOHN K.* [Born in Pa. Appointed from Pa.]
2nd Lieut. 3rd Art., 14 June, 1885. 1st Lieut., 13 July, 1892. Trans. to 6th Art., 8 March, 1898. Graduate of the Art. School, 1898.

CREEL, HEBER M.* [Born in Mo. Appointed from Mo.]
Addl. 2nd Lieut. 8th Cav., 15 June, 1877. 2nd Lieut. 7th Cav., 30 Sept., 1877. Resigned 1 July, 1882.

CRESS, GEORGE O.* [Born in Ill. Appointed from Ill.]
2nd Lieut. 7th Cav., 15 June, 1884. 1st Lieut. 8th Cav., 20 April, 1891. Trans. to 4th Cav., 27 April, 1891. Capt., 1 July, 1899.

CRESSY, EDWARD P.* [Born in N. Y. Appointed from N. Y.]
Bvt. 2nd Lieut. Mtd. Rifles, 1 July, 1858. 2nd Lieut., 22 Nov., 1859. 1st Lieut., 14 May, 1861. 3rd Cav., 3 Aug., 1861. Capt. 17 July, 1862. Mustered out 1 Jan., 1871. Bvt. Maj. and Lieut. Col., 13 March, 1865, for faithful service during the war.

CRESSON, CHAS. C. [Born in Penn. Appointed from Penn.]
2nd Lieut. 66th Penn. Vols., 3 Aug., 1861. 1st Lieut. 73rd Penn. Vols., 13 March, 1862. Capt. 30 Aug., 1862. Maj., 1 Jan., 1864. Lieut. Col., 24 Dec., 1864. Mustered out 24 Aug., 1865. 2nd Lieut. 17th Inf., 11 May, 1866. Trans. to 35th Inf., 21 Sept., 1866. Bvt. 1st Lieut., 2 March, 1867, for gallant and meritorious service in the Battle of Mill Creek, Ga. Bvt. Capt., 2 March, 1867, for gallant and meritorious service in the Battle of Resaca., Ga. Bvt. Maj., 2 March, 1867, for gallant and meritorious service in the Battle of Kenesaw Mountain, Ga. 1st Lieut. 35th Inf., 7 Oct., 1867. Unassigned, 12 Aug., 1869. Ass'd to 7th Cav., 15 Dec., 1870. Trans. to 1st Cav., 23 Dec., 1870. Retired 4 April, 1879. Bvt. Lieut. Col., Feb. 27, 1890, for gallant and meritorious services in action against Indians at the Lava Beds, California, 17 April, 1873, and gallant services in action against Indians at Camas Meadows, Idaho, 20 Aug., 1877.

CREWS, HANSON H. [Born in Ill. Appointed from Ill.]
Priv. Co. G, 39th Ill. Vols., 9 Aug., 1861. Discharged 19 Feb., 1864. 2nd Lieut. 64th Ill. Vols., 20 Feb., 1864. 1st Lieut., 20 Sept., 1864. Capt., 8 April, 1865. Mustered out 11 July, 1865. 1st Lieut. 28th Inf., 28 July, 1866. Bvt. Capt., 2 March, 1867, for gallant and meritorious service in the Battle of Kenesaw Mountain. Trans. to 19th Inf., 31 March, 1869. Trans. to 4th Cav., 10 July, 1873, taking rank from 13 Jan., 1868. Reg. Adj., 1 March, 1878, to 17 May, 1878. Capt., 20 March, 1879. Resigned 28 Dec., 1882.

CRILLY, FRANCIS J.* [Born in Penn. Appointed from Penn.]
Bvt. 2nd Lieut. 5th Inf., 1 July, 1859. 2nd Lieut. 7th Inf., 31 Aug., 1859. 1st Lieut., 7 May, 1861. Capt. A. Q. M., 19 Feb., 1863. Resigned 8 Feb., 1869. Bvt. Maj., Lieut. Col. and Col., 13 March, 1865, for faithful and meritorious service during the war.

CRIMMINS, MARTIN L. [Born in N. Y. Appointed from N. Y.]
Priv. Troop B, 1st U. S. Cav. and Co. B, 69th N. Y. Vols., 23 May, 1898, to 29 July, 1898. 2nd Lieut. Co. B, 69th N. Y. Vols., 1 Aug. to 20 Sept., 1898. 2nd Lieut. 18th Inf., 9 Sept., 1898. 1st Lieut. 6th Inf., 1 Oct., 1899.

CRISPIN, SILAS.* [Born in Penn. Appointed from Penn.]
Bvt. 2nd Lieut. Ord., 1 July, 1850. 2nd Lieut., 31 Oct., 1851. 1st Lieut., 1 July, 1854. Capt., 3 Aug., 1861. Bvt. Maj. and Bvt. Lieut Col., 13 March, 1865, for faithful and meritorious service in the Ord. Dept. Bvt. Col., 13 March, 1865, for faithful and meritorious service in the Ord. Dept. during the war. Maj. Ord., 7 March, 1867. Lieut. Col., 14 April, 1875. Col., 23 Aug., 1881. Died 28 Feb., 1889.

CRITCHLOW, BENJN. D.* [Born in Penn. Appointed from Penn.]
2nd Lieut. 13th Inf., 23 June, 1865. 1st Lieut., 23 June, 1865. Trans. to 22nd Inf., 21 Sept., 1866. Resigned 5 Jan., 1869.

CRITTENDEN, ALEXANDER P.* [Born in Ky. Appointed from Ky.]
Bvt. 2nd Lieut. 1st Art., 1 July, 1836. 2nd Lieut., 31 July, 1836. Resigned 30 Sept., 1836.

CRITTENDEN, A. BURNLEY. [Born in Ky. Appointed from Ky.]
2nd Lieut. 4th Inf., 31 Oct., 1874. Resigned 18 March, 1880.

CRITTENDEN, EUGENE W. [Born in Ky. Appointed from Ky.]
2nd Lieut. 1st Cav., 3 March, 1855. 1st Lieut., 4 May, 1859. Capt., 7 May, 1861. 4th Cav., 3 Aug., 1861. Maj. 5th Cav., 28 July, 1866. Died 1 Aug., 1874.

CRITTENDEN, GEORGE B.* [Born in Ky. Appointed from Ky.]
Bvt. 2nd Lieut., 4th Inf., 1 July, 1832. Resigned 30 April, 1833. Capt. Mtd. Rifles, 27 May, 1846. Maj., 15 March, 1848. Lieut. Col., 30 Dec., 1856. Resigned 10 June, 1861. Bvt. Maj., 20 Aug., 1847, for gallant and meritorious conduct at Contreras and Churubusco.

CRITTENDEN, JOHN J. [Born in Ky. Appointed from Ky.]
2nd Lieut. 20th Inf., 15 Oct., 1875. Killed 25 June, 1876, in action with Indians in Montana Ter.

CRITENDEN, JOHN J. [Born in Ky. Appointed from Ky.]
2nd Lieut. 22nd Inf., 14 Dec., 1876. 1st Lieut., 20 July, 1882. Capt., 6 July, 1894. Graduate of the Inf. and Cav. School, 1883.

CRITTENDEN, THOS. L. [Born in Ky. Appointed from Ky.]
Priv. Ky. Vols., 17 Aug. to 18 Sept., 1836. Lieut. Col. 3rd Ky. Vols., 4 Oct., 1847, to 21 July, 1848. Brig. Gen. Vols., 27 Sept., 1861. Maj. Gen. Vols., 17 July, 1862.

Resigned 13 Dec., 1864. Col. 32nd Inf., 28 July, 1866. Bvt. Brig. Gen., 2 March, 1867, for gallant and meritorious service in the Battle of Stone River, Tenn. Trans. to 17th Inf., 15 March, 1869. Retired 19 May, 1881. Died 23 Oct., 1893.

CRITTENDEN, WM. L.* [Born in Ky. Appointed from Ky.]
Bvt. 2nd Lieut. 5th Inf., 1 July, 1845. 2nd Lieut. 1st Inf., 21 Sept., 1846. Resigned 1 March, 1849.

CROCKER, GEORGE D. [Born in Conn. Appointed from Mass.]
Chaplain 6th N. Y. Cav., 14 Dec., 1861. Mustered out 9 Aug., 1865. Post Chaplain, 3 Oct., 1867. Retired 25 Dec., 1886. Died 21 April, 1888.

CROFT, EDWARD. [Born in S. C. Appointed from S. C.]
2nd Lieut. 19th Inf., 9 July, 1898. 1st Lieut. 14th Inf., 31 March, 1899. Trans. to 19th Inf., 6 July, 1899.

CROFTON, ROBT. E. A. [Born in Ireland. Appointed from Del.]
Capt. 16th Inf., 14 May, 1861. Bvt. Maj., 7 April, 1862, for gallant and meritorious service in the Battle of Shiloh, Tenn. Bvt. Lieut. Col., 25 Nov., 1863, for gallant and meritorious service in the Battles of Chickamauga, Ga., and Mission Ridge, Tenn. Maj. 14th Inf., 25 Sept., 1868. Trans. to 17th Inf., 15 March, 1869. Lieut. Col. 13th Inf., 27 April, 1879. Col. 15th Inf., 19 Oct., 1886. Retired by direction of the President, being 62 years of age, 4 Feb., 1897. Died 21 June, 1898.

CROFTON, WILLIAM M. [Born in Va. Appointed from Ill.]
2nd Lieut. 1st Inf., 7 Oct., 1891. 1st Lieut., 26 April, 1898. Graduate of the Inf. and Cav. School., 1897. Reg. Com., 19 Aug., 1899.

CROGHAN, GEORGE. [Born in Ky. Appointed from Ky.]
Capt. 17th Inf., 12 March, 1812. Maj. 30 March, 1813. Lieut Col. 2nd Rifles, 21 Feb., 1814. Trans. to 1st Inf., 17 May, 1815. Resigned 31 March, 1817. Col. I. G., 21 Dec., 1825. Died 8 Jan., 1849. Bvt. Lieut. Col., 2 Aug., 1813, for gallant conduct in defence of Fort Sandusky. Presented with gold medal, with suitable emblems and devices, in testimony of the high sense entertained by Congress of his gallantry and good conduct in the defence of Fort Stephenson, Ohio (Act of Congress 13 Feb., 1835).

CROLLY, JAMES D. [Born in Ireland. Appointed from N. Y.]
Priv. Co. B., 2nd Art., 26 July, 1860, to 11 Aug., 1862. 2nd Lieut. 5th Inf., 17 July, 1862. Resigned 19 Jan., 1863.

CRONE, LOUIS E. [Born in Saxony. Appointed from Mass.]
Corpl. Co. E, 22nd Mass. Vols., 20 Sept., 1861. Discharged 4 Sept., 1862. 2nd Lieut. 22nd Mass. Vols., 31 Oct., 1862. 1st Lieut., 16 Dec., 1862. Mustered out 20 June, 1863. 2nd Lieut. Vet. Res. Corps, 15 June, 1863. Mustered out 3 July, 1866. Capt. 42nd Inf., 28 July, 1866. Unassigned 22 April, 1869. Retired 15 Dec., 1870. Died 22 Aug., 1891.

CRONIN, MARCUS D.* [Born in Mass. Appointed from Mass.]
2nd Lieut. 20th Inf., 12 June, 1887. 1st Lieut. 25th Inf., 15 July, 1894. Capt., 2 March, 1899. Maj. 33rd U. S. Vols., 5 July, 1899.

CRONKHITE, ADELBERT.* [Born in N. Y. Appointed from Ariz.]
2nd Lieut. 4th Art., 12 June, 1882. 1st Lieut., 25 Jan., 1889. Capt., 2 March, 1899. Graduate of the Artillery School, 1886.

CRONKHITE, HENRY M. [Born in N. Y. Appointed from Cal.]
Priv. Co. C, 26th N. Y. Vols., 29 July, 1861, to 28 May, 1863. 1st Lieut. Asst. Surg., 14 May, 1867. Capt. Asst. Surg., 14 May, 1870. Maj. Surg., 26 July, 1886. Retired for disability in line of duty, 17 Oct., 1895.

CROOK, GEORGE.* [Born in Ohio. Appointed from Ohio.]
Bvt. 2nd Lieut. 4th Inf., 1 July, 1852. 2nd Lieut., 7 July, 1853. 1st Lieut., 11 March, 1856. Capt., 14th Inf., 14 May, 1861 (declined). Capt. 4th Inf., 14 May, 1861. Col. 36th Ohio Vols., 13 Sept., 1861. Bvt. Maj., 23 May, 1862, for gallant and meritorious service in the Battle of Lewisburg, Va. Brig. Gen. Vols., 7 Sept., 1862, for gallant and meritorious service in the field. Bvt. Lieut. Col., 17 Sept., 1862, for gallant and meritorious service in the Battle of Antietam, Md. Bvt. Col., 7 Oct., 1863, for gallant and meritorious service in the Battle of Farmington, Tenn. Bvt. Maj. Gen. Vols., 18 July, 1864, for gallant and distinguished service in W. Va. Maj. Gen. Vols., 21 Oct., 1864. Bvt. Brig. Gen., 13 March, 1865, for gallant and meritorious service in the campaign in 1864, in W. Va. Bvt. Maj. Gen., 13 March, for gallant and meritorious service in the Battle of Fisher's Hill, Va. Mustered out of Vol. service, 15 Jan., 1866. Maj. 3rd Inf., 18 July, 1866. Lieut. Col. 23rd Inf., 28 July, 1866. Brig. Gen. U. S. A., 29 Oct., 1873. Maj. Gen., 6 April, 1888. Died 21 March, 1890.

CROOKER, TURNER. [Born in Mass. Appointed from Mass.]
Capt. 9th Inf., 14 May, 1812. Maj., 1 Sept., 1814. Disbanded 15 June, 1815. Reinstated as Capt. 6th Inf., 2 Dec., 1815. Dismissed 18 Aug., 1819. Mil. Storekeeper, 10 Dec., 1819. Disbanded 1 June, 1821. Bvt. Maj., 4 July, 1814, for distinction in command of advanced guard near Chippewa, N. C. Died 31 May, 1833.

CROSBY, EBEN. [Born in Maine. Appointed from Maine.]
Priv., Sergt. and 1st Sergt. Co. I, 6th Me. Vols., 15 July, 1861, to 17 Jan., 1864. 2nd Lieut. Vet. Res. Corps, 30 March, 1864. Mustered out 30 June, 1866. 2nd Lieut. 44th Inf., 28 July, 1866. Trans. to 17th Inf., 27 May, 1869. 1st Lieut., 30 June, 1872. Killed 3 Oct., 1872, by Indians in Dakota.

CROSBY, FRANKLIN B. [Born in N. Y. Appointed from N. Y.]
2nd Lieut. 4th Art., 8 Aug., 1861. 1st Lieut., 8 Aug., 1861. Killed 3 May, 1863, at the Battle of Chancellorsville, Va.

CROSBY, HENRY R. [Born in Penn. Appointed from Va.]
2nd Lieut. 12th Inf., 21 July, 1847. Disbanded 25 July, 1848. 1st Lieut. 3rd Md. Cav., 9 Nov., 1863. Capt., 9 Jan., 1864. Resigned 10 Oct., 1864.

CROSBY, HERBERT B.* [Born in Kans. Appointed from Ill.]
2nd Lieut. 8th Cav., 12 June, 1893. 1st Lieut., 2 Mar., 1899.

CROSBY, JOHN S. [Born in N. Y. Appointed from N. Y.]
2nd Lieut. 1st Art., 5 Aug., 1861. 2nd Lieut., 28 Aug., 1861. Capt. A. de C. Vols., 3 June, 1863. Mustered out of Vols. 1 Aug., 1866. Lieut. Col. A. de C. to Lieut. Gen. Sheridan, 13 March, 1869, to 31 July, 1870. Bvt. Maj. and Lieut. Col. Vols., 15

Feb., 1865, for gallant and meritorious service during the war. Discharged 31 Dec., 1870. Bvt. Capt., 12 April, 1863, for gallant and meritorious service in action at Fort Bisland, La. Bvt. Maj., 9 April, 1864, for gallant and meritorious service at the Battle of Pleasant Hill, La. Bvt. Lieut. Col., 13 March, 1865, for gallant and meritorious service during the war.

CROSBY, OSCAR T.* [Born in La. Appointed from Miss.]
Addl. 2nd Lieut. Eng., 13 June, 1882. 2nd Lieut. 23rd June, 1882. 1st Lieut., 3 July, 1883. Resigned 22 Oct., 1887.

CROSBY, THOMPSON H. [Born in Maine. Appointed from Maine.]
2nd Lieut. of Inf., 23 Feb., 1847; 9th Inf., 9 April, 1847. 1st Lieut., 4 Dec., 1847. Disbanded 26 Aug., 1848. Bvt. 1st Lieut., 13 Sept., 1847, for gallant and meritorious conduct at Chapultepec, Mex.

CROSBY, WM. [Born in Maine. Appointed from Maine.]
Sergt. Co. H, 7th Me. Vols., 22 Aug., 1861. 2nd Lieut., 18 Sept., 1862. 1st Lieut., 15 March, 1864. Mustered out 5 Sept., 1864. Capt. 1st Me. Vet. Inf., 10 Dec., 1864. Resigned 6 May, 1865. Capt. 2nd U. S. Vet. Vols., 5 Oct., 1865. Mustered out 20 March, 1866. 2nd Lieut. 12th Inf., 23 Feb., 1866. 1st Lieut., 23 Feb., 1866. Trans. to 21st Inf., 21 Sept., 1866. Unassigned 8 April, 1869. Mustered out 1 Jan., 1871.

CROSBY, WILLIAM D. [Born in Mass. Appointed from N. Y.]
Asst. Surg., 3 Dec., 1883. Capt. Asst. Surg., 3 Dec., 1888. Maj. Brig. Surg., 4 June, 1898.

CROSMAN, FREDERICK E. [Born in Mass. Appointed from Penn.]
1st Lieut. 17th Inf., 26 Oct., 1861. Killed 19 Aug., 1864, at the Battle of Weldon Railroad, Va. Bvt. Capt., Maj. and Lieut. Col., 19 Aug., 1864, for gallant conduct in the Battles on the Weldon Railroad, 17, 18 and 19 Aug., 1864.

CROSMAN, GEORGE H. [Born in Penn. Appointed at Large.]
Cadet at Mil. Acad., 1 July, 1854, to 13 July, 1855. 2nd Lieut. 10th Inf., 5 Aug., 1861. 1st Lieut., 1 Nov., 1861. Capt., 4 Nov., 1863. Unassigned 26 Sept., 1870. Mustered out 1 Jan., 1871. Bvt. Capt., 3 May, 1863, for gallant and meritorious service at the Battle of Chancellorsville, Va. Bvt. Maj., 2 July, 1863, for gallant and meritorious service at the Battle of Gettysburg, Pa.

CROSMAN, GEORGE H.* [Born in Mass. Appointed from Mass.]
Bvt. 2nd Lieut. 3rd Inf., 1 July, 1823. 2nd Lieut. 6th Inf., 1 July, 1823. 1st Lieut., 30 Aug., 1828. Capt., 30 April, 1837. Capt. A. Q. M., 7 July, 1838. Bvt. Maj., 8 May, 1846, for gallant and meritorious conduct in the Battle of Palo Alto. Vacated line commission, 18 June, 1846. Maj. Q. M., 3 March, 1847. Lieut. Col. Dep. Q. M. G., 22 Dec., 1856. Col. A. Q. M. G., 26 Feb., 1863. Bvt. Brig. Gen. and Maj. Gen., 13 March, 1865, for faithful and meritorious service during the war. Retired 29 July, 1866. Died 28 May, 1882.

CROSS, ALEXANDER H. [Born in D. C. Appointed from D. C.]
1st Lieut. Inf., 24 Feb., 1847; Voltigeurs, 9 April, 1847. Disbanded 31 Aug., 1848. 1st Lieut. 2nd Cav., 3 March, 1855. Appointment expired 1 May, 1856. Died in 1869.

CROSS, CHARLES E.* [Born in Mass. Appointed from Mass.]
Bvt. 2nd Lieut. Eng., 6 May, 1861. 2nd Lieut., 6 May, 1861. 1st Lieut., 6 Aug., 1861. Capt., 3 March, 1863. Killed 5 June, 1863, in action at the passage of the Rappahannock, Va. Bvt. Maj., 1 July, 1862, for gallant and meritorious service in the Virginia Peninsular campaign. Bvt. Lieut. Col., 17 Sept., 1862, for gallant and meritorious service at the Battle of Antietam, Md. Bvt. Col., 5 June, 1863, for gallant and meritorious service while assisting to throw a bridge across the Rappahannock at Fredericksburg, in the face of the enemy, when he was killed.

CROSS, OSBORN.* [Born in Md. Appointed from Md.]
Bvt. 2nd Lieut. 1st Inf., 1 July, 1825. 2nd Lieut., 4th Inf., 1 July, 1825. Trans. to 1st Inf., 29 Sept., 1827. 1st Lieut., 31 Dec., 1831. Capt., 7 July, 1838. Capt. A. Q. M., 7 July, 1838. Maj. Q. M., 24 July, 1847. Lieut. Col. Dep. Q. M. G., 26 Feb., 1863. Col. A. Q. M. G., 29 July, 1866. Retired 29 July, 1866. Died 15 July, 1876. Bvt. Brig. Gen., 13 March, 1865, for faithful and meritorious service in the Q. M. D. during the war.

CROSS, TRUEMAN. [Born in Md. Appointed from Md.]
Ensign 42nd Inf., 27 April, 1814. 2nd Lieut., 1 Oct., 1814. Trans. to 1st Inf., 17 May, 1815. 1st Lieut., 2 Jan., 1818. R. Q. M., 1 April, 1816, to 20 June, 1818. Capt. 27 Sept., 1819. Capt. A. Dep. Q. M. G., 16 June, 1818. Bvt. Maj. Asst. I. G., 17 Oct., 1820. Retained as Capt. 1st Inf., 1 June, 1821. Trans. to 7th Inf., 1 June, 1821. Maj. Q. M., 22 May, 1826. Col. A. Q. M. G., 7 July, 1838. Killed 21 April, 1846, by Mexicans, near the present Fort Brown, Texas.

CROWDER, ENOCH H.* [Born in Mo. Appointed from Mo.]
2nd Lieut. 8th Cav., 11 June, 1881. 1st Lieut., 5 July, 1886. Maj. J. A., 11 Jan., 1895. Lieut. Col. J. A. Vols., 22 June, 1898, to 18 Aug., 1899. Lieut. Col. 39th U. S. Vols., 17 Aug., 1899.

CROWELL, NATHL. S. [Born in S. C. Appointed from S. C.]
Asst. Surg., 8 Nov., 1854. Resigned 17 May, 1861.

CROWELL, WM. H. H. [Born in Ohio. Appointed from Ohio.]
Priv. Batty F, 1st Ohio Art., 21 April to 27 July, 1861. 2nd Lieut. 15th Ohio Batty, 12 Dec., 1861. Resigned 15 Dec., 1862. Capt. 2nd Ohio Art., 9 Sept., 1863. Mustered out 23 Aug., 1865. 2nd Lieut. 17th Inf., 22 Jan., 1867. 1st Lieut., 17 Dec., 1867. Unassigned 27 May, 1869. Ass'd to 6th Inf., 15 Dec., 1870. Capt., 31 Oct., 1883. Maj. 11th Inf., 22 Aug., 1898. Trans. to 6th Inf., 4 Oct., 1898. Retired, over 30 years' service, 15 Jan., 1900.

CROWLEY, MATTHIAS.* [Born in Ireland. Appointed from N. Y.]
2nd Lieut. 5th Inf., 12 June, 1891. 1st Lieut., 26 April, 1898. Trans. to 7th Inf., 20 Sept., 1899.

CROWLEY, SAMUEL T. [Born in D. C. Appointed from D. C.]
2nd Lieut. 4th Inf., 19 Feb., 1862. 1st Lieut., 8 June, 1863. Died 10 March, 1866. Bvt. 1st Lieut., 27 June, 1862, for gallant and meritorious service at the Battle of Gaines' Mills, Va. Bvt. Capt., 30 Aug., 1862, for gallant and meritorious service at the Battle of Bull Run (2nd), Va.

CROXTON, RICHARD C.* [Born in Va. Appointed from Va.]
2nd Lieut. 5th Inf., 1 July, 1896. 1st Lieut. 1st Inf., 1 Sept., 1898. Capt., 2 March, 1899. Trans. to 23rd Inf., 31 Oct., 1899. Lieut. Col. 6th Va. Col. Inf., 30 July, 1898, to 28 Jan., 1899.

CROZET, ALFRED.* [Born in N. Y. Appointed at Large.]
(Changed name to A. St. Amand Crozet,—which see.)

CROZET, A. ST. AMAND.* [Born in N. Y. Appointed at Large.]
(Graduated as Alfred Crozet.) Bvt. 2nd Lieut. 7th Inf., 1 July, 1843. 2nd Lieut. 8th Inf., 31 Dec., 1845. 1st Lieut., 27 Jan., 1848. R. Q. M., 9 July, 1849, to 4 July, 1852. Died 23 April, 1855.

CROZET, CLAUDE. [Born in France. Appointed from N. Y.]
Asst. Prof. at Mil. Acad., 1 Oct., 1816. Prof., 6 March, 1817. Resigned 28 April, 1823. Died in 1863.

CROZIER, WM.* [Born in Ohio. Appointed from Kansas.]
2nd Lieut. 4th Art., 15 June, 1876. 1st Lieut. Ord., 11 July, 1881. Capt. (14 years' service), 15 June, 1890. Maj. I. G., 17 May, 1898, to 30 Nov., 1898.

CRUGER, NICHOLAS.* [Born in N. Y. Appointed from N. Y.]
2nd Lieut. 2nd Inf., 1 July, 1820. Trans. to 7th Inf., 15 July, 1820. Trans. to 6th Inf., 25 July, 1820. 1st Lieut., 28 Feb., 1823. Capt., 11 Feb., 1827. Resigned 31 Oct., 1827. Died 3 June, 1868.

CRUGER, WM. E. [Born in N. Y. Appointed from N. Y.]
Cadet at Mil. Acad., 22 Dec., 1814, to 11 Sept., 1819. 2nd Lieut. 5th Inf., 12 July, 1820. 1st Lieut., 29 June, 1824. Capt., 1 Oct., 1833. Resigned 1 Oct., 1836. Died in 1841.

CRUICE, ROBT. B. [Born in Ireland. Appointed from Pa.]
Asst. Surg. 12th Pa. Cav., 28 Jan. to 22 July, 1862. Asst. Surg., 16 April, 1862. Resigned 17 Aug., 1863. K

CRUIKSHANK, WILLIAM M.* [Born in D. C. Appointed from D. C.]
2nd Lieut. 1st Art., 12 June, 1893. 1st Lieut., 2 March, 1899.

CRUMBAUGH, SAML. R. [Born in Ky. Appointed from Ky.]
Cadet at Naval Acad., 20 Feb., 1863, to 2 June, 1868. 2nd Lieut. 2nd Inf., 5 June, 1868. Reg. Adj., 20 April to 8 Nov., 1869. Resigned 1 Jan., 1870.

CRUMP, SAML. H. [Born in Ga. Appointed from Ga.]
2nd Lieut. Inf., 4 March, 1847; 13th Inf., 9 April, 1847. Disbanded 15 July, 1848.

CRUPPER, MICAJAH. [Born in Va. Appointed from Va.]
Ensign 12th Inf., 29 March, 1813. 3rd Lieut., 30 Sept., 1813. 2nd Lieut., 24 June, 1814. Disbanded 15 June, 1815. Reinstated 2 Dec., 1815, in 7th Inf. 1st Lieut., 15 Oct., 1816. Capt., 31 May, 1819. Disbanded 1 June, 1821.

CRUSE, THOMAS.* [Born in Ky. Appointed from Ky.]
2nd Lieut. 6th Cav., 13 June, 1879. Bvt. 1st Lieut., 27 Feb., 1890, for gallant service in action against Indians at Big Dry Wash, Ariz., 17 July, 1882. 1st Lieut., 28 Sept., 1887. Capt. A. Q. M., 1 Dec., 1896. Capt. A. Q. M., 22 Dec., 1896. Maj. Q. M., 12 May, 1898. Honor graduate of the Infantry and Cavalry School, 1891. Medal of Honor for distinguished conduct in action against hostile Apache Indians at the Big Dry Wash, Ariz., July 17, 1882, gallantly charging the enemy, and also with his carbine compelling a party of them to keep under cover of their breast works, thus being enabled to recover a soldier severely wounded; while serving as 2nd Lieut., 6th Cav.

CRUTCHFIELD, PETER T. [Born in Va. Appointed from Ark.]
Maj. and P. M., 3 March, 1847. Resigned 15 June, 1848.

CRUTTENDEN, HENRY E. [Born in D. C. Appointed from N. Y.]
Asst. Surg., 22 June, 1839. Resigned 25 June, 1846.

CULBERTSON, HOWARD. [Born in Ohio. Appointed from Wis.]
Maj. Surg. U. S. Vols., 7 Nov., 1862. Bvt. Lieut. Col. Vols., 6 Oct., 1865, for faithful and meritorious service. Mustered out 7 Oct., 1865. 1st Lieut. Asst. Surg., 28 Feb., 1866. Capt., 8 July, 1866. Retired 8 Jan., 1869. Died 18 June, 1890.

CULBERTSON, JACOB.* [Born in Ky. Appointed from Ky.]
Bvt. 2nd Lieut. 4th Art., 1 July, 1850. 2nd Lieut., 11 Dec., 1850. 1st Lieut., 14 Feb., 1856. Resigned 10 Jan., 1857.

CULBERTSON, JOHN. [Born in Pa. Appointed from Pa.]
Ensign 22nd Inf., 17 March, 1812. 2nd Lieut., 13 March, 1813. 1st Lieut., 1 Oct., 1813. Trans. to 8th Inf., 17 May, 1815. Trans. to 3rd Inf., 17 May, 1816. Capt., 1 June, 1819. Disbanded 1 June, 1821.

CULBERTSON, MICHAEL S.* [Born in Penn. Appointed from Penn.]
2nd Lieut. 1st Art., 1 July, 1839. Resigned 15 April, 1841. Died 25 Aug., 1862.

CULBERTSON, SAML. S. [Born in Ohio. Appointed from Army.]
Priv. and Sergt. Co. C. 19th Inf., 26 Sept. to 26 Nov., 1861. 2nd Lieut. 19th Inf., 20 Nov., 1861. 1st Lieut., 30 June, 1863. Capt., 26 Sept., 1865. Trans. to 28th Inf., 21 Sept., 1866. Trans. to 19th Inf., 31 March, 1869. Unassigned 16 Aug., 1869. Mustered out 1 Jan., 1871. Bvt. Capt., 2 April, 1865, for gallant and meritorious service at the Battle of Selma, Ala. Bvt. Maj., 2 April, 1865, for gallant and meritorious service during the war.

CULLEN, DORSEY. [Born in Va. Appointed from the Army.]
Priv., Corpl., Sergt. and 1st Sergt. Troop B, 3rd Cav., 5 Aug., 1895, to 14 Nov., 1899. 2nd Lieut. 9th Cav., 1 Oct., 1899.

CULLEN, EDGAR M. [Born in N. Y. Appointed from N. Y.]
2nd Lieut. 1st Inf., 24 March, 1862. 1st Lieut., 29 Sept., 1863. Col. 96th N. Y. Vols., 26 Dec., 1862. Mustered out Vols., 21 March, 1865. Resigned 9 April, 1865.

CULLEN, JAMES. [Born in Del. Appointed from Del.]
2nd Lieut. 7th Inf., 5 Aug., 1861. 1st Lieut., 2 Jan., 1863. Capt., 3 Dec., 1863. Resigned 12 Oct., 1867. Bvt. Capt., 2 July, 1863, for gallant and meritorious service in the Battle of Gettysburg, Pa. Bvt. Maj., 13 March, 1865, for gallant and meritorious service in the Battle of Gettysburg, Pa.

CULLISON, JESSE M. [Born in Md. Appointed from the Army.]
Priv., Corpl. and Sergt. Batty C, 5th Art., 21 May, 1897, to 16 Nov., 1899. 2nd Lieut. 2nd Inf., 1 Oct., 1899.

CULLOM, ALVAN. [Born in Tenn. Appointed from Army.]
Priv. Co. E, 14th Inf., 22 April, 1847, to 3 July, 1848. 2nd Lieut. 14th Inf., 14 June, 1848. Disbanded 24 July, 1848.

CULLOM, TILMAN. [Born in Tenn. Appointed from Tenn.]
1st Lieut. 14th Inf., 30 Dec., 1847. Died 25 Jan., 1848.

CULLUM, GEORGE W.* [Born in N. Y. Appointed from Pa.]
Bvt. 2nd Lieut. Eng., 1 July, 1833. 2nd Lieut., 20 April, 1836. Capt., 7 July, 1838. Maj., 6 Aug., 1861. Lieut. Col. A. de C., to Bvt. Lieut. Gen Scott, 9 April to 6 Aug., 1861. and Col. and A. A. de C., 6 Aug., 1861. Brig. Gen. Vols., 1 Nov., 1861. Lieut. Col. Eng., 3 March, 1863. Bvt. Col. and Bvt. Brig. Gen., 13 March, 1865, for faithful and meritorious service during the war. Bvt. Maj. Gen., 13 March, 1865, for faithful, meritorious and distinguished service during the war. Mustered out of Vol. service. 1 Sept., 1866. Col. Eng., 7 March, 1867. Retired 13 Jan., 1874. Died 28 Feb., 1892.

CULLY, MERVIN E. [Born in Ohio. Appointed from Ohio.]
2nd Lieut. 4th Inf., 27 June, 1856. Dropped 18 Feb., 1857.

CUMING, THOS. B., Jr. [Born in N. Y. Appointed from Mich.
2nd Lieut. 15th Inf., 3 March, 1848. Disbanded 4 Aug., 1848.

CUMMING, ALFRED.* [Born in Ga. Appointed from Ga.]
Bvt. 2nd Lieut. 8th Inf., 1 July, 1849. 2nd Lieut. 7th Inf., 16 July, 1850. 1st Lieut. 10th Inf., 3 March, 1855. Capt., 20 July, 1856. Resigned 19 Jan., 1861.

CUMMINGS, ALEXANDER. [Born in Ireland. Appointed from Pa.]
2nd Lieut. Light Drag., 3 May, 1808. 1st Lieut., 30 Sept., 1809. Capt., 1 Nov., 1811. Trans. to 4th Inf., 17 May, 1815. Maj. 6th Inf., 20 April, 1819. Lieut. Col. 2nd Inf., 20 Aug., 1828. Col. 4th Inf., 1 Dec., 1839. Died 31 Jan., 1842.

CUMMINGS, ARTHUR C. [Born in Va. Appointed from Va.]
Capt. Inf., 23 Feb., 1847; 11th Inf., 9 April, 1847. Disbanded 17 Aug., 1848. Bvt. Maj., 15 Aug., 1847, for gallant and meritorious conduct in several affairs with Guerillas at Paso Ovejas, National Bridge and Cerro Gordo.

CUMMINGS, JOHN P. [Born in Scotland. Appointed from Army.]
Priv., Corpl and Sergt. Co. I, 157th N. Y. Vols., 24 Oct., 1863, to 15 June, 1865. Capt. 104th U. S. Col. Inf., 21 July, 1865. Mustered out 5 Feb., 1866. Priv. Troop K, 5th Cav., 8 Aug., 1866, to 21 March, 1867. 2nd Lieut. 5th Cav., 5 Feb., 1867. Cashiered 18 Aug., 1868.

CUMMINGS, JOSEPH F.* [Born in Texas. Appointed from Texas.]
2nd Lieut. 10th Cav., 15 June, 1876. Trans. to 3rd Cav., 28 July, 1876. 1st Lieut., 30 Jan., 1881. Dismissed 15 Feb., 1884.

CUMMINGS, THOS. [Born in Pa. Appointed from Pa.]
1st Lieut. 19th Inf., 14 May, 1861. Capt., 9 Feb., 1863. Cashiered 31 Dec., 1869. Reinstated on unassigned list, 28 March, 1870. Resigned 15 July, 1870. Bvt. Maj., 20 Sept., 1863, for gallant and meritorious service at the Battle of Chickamauga, Ga.

CUMMINGS, WILBUR F. [Born in Ohio. Appointed from Ohio.]
Capt. 44th Ohio Vols., 9 Oct., 1861, to 30 Jan., 1864. Maj. 176th Ohio Vols., 24 Sept., 1864. Mustered out 14 June, 1865. Capt. 15th Inf., 7 March, 1867. Died 2 Oct., 1867.

CUMMINS, ALBERT S.* [Born in Mich. Appointed from Mich.]
2nd Lieut. 4th Art., 13 June, 1873. 1st Lieut., 29 May, 1875. Capt., 8 March, 1898. Lieut. Col. 27th U. S. Inf., 5 July, 1899. Graduate of the Artillery School, 1884.

CUMMINS, FRANCIS M. [Born in N. Y. Appointed from N. Y.]
1st Lieut. of Inf., 24 Feb., 1847; 10th Inf., 9 April, 1847. Capt., 6 March, 1848. Disbanded 22 Aug., 1848. Lieut. Col. 124th N. Y. Vols., 5 Sept., 1862. Col., 11 Feb., 1864. Resigned 19 Sept., 1864. Died 26 March, 1884.

CUMMINS, RICHARD W. [Born in Ind. Appointed from Ind.]
2nd Lieut. 35th Ind. Vols., 21 Jan., 1862. Resigned 8 April, 1862. 1st Lieut. and Adj. 99th Ind. Vols., 1 Nov., 1862. Dismissed 15 Sept., 1863. 2nd Lieut. 7th Inf., 22 Jan., 1867. Resigned 15 Aug., 1871.

CUNNINGHAM, ARTHUR S.* [Born in Va. Appointed at Large.]
2nd Lieut. 10th Inf., 1 Jan., 1857. 1st Lieut., 1 May, 1861. Resigned 25 June, 1861. Died 28 July, 1885.

CUNNINGHAM, CHAS. N. W. [Born in Ohio. Appointed from Mass.]
Priv., Corpl. and Sergt. 13th Mass. Vols., 16 July, 1861. to 25 Oct., 1863. 1st Lieut. U. S. Col. Inf., 25 Oct., 1863. Capt. 38th U. S. Col. Inf., 13 Jan., 1865. Mustered out 17 Oct., 1866. Capt. 38th Inf., 28 July, 1866. Trans. to 24th Inf., 11 Nov., 1869. Dismissed 23 Dec., 1878.

CUNNINGHAM, CORNELIUS. [Born in D. C. Appointed from D. C.]
Garrison Surg. Mate, 15 Oct., 1810. Retained as Post Surg., 17 May, 1815. Resigned 31 March, 1820.

CUNNINGHAM, FRANCIS A. [Born in S. C. Appointed from Ohio.]
Addl. P. M., 30 Dec., 1847. P. M., 2 March, 1849. Retired 27 Aug., 1863. Died 16 Aug., 1864.

CUNNINGHAM, GEORGE A.* [Born in Ga. Appointed from Ala.]
Bvt. 2nd Lieut. 1st Cav., 1 July, 1857. 2nd Lieut. 2nd Cav., 1 Oct., 1858. Resigned 27 Feb., 1861.

CUNNINGHAM, JOHN M. [Born in Ill. Appointed from Ill.]
2nd Lieut. 19th Inf., 1 Sept., 1879. Wholly retired 22 May, 1890.

CUNNINGHAM, NATHL. F. [Born in Ind. Appointed from Army.]
Cadet at Mil. Acad., 1 July, 1865, to 15 March, 1866. Priv. Co. A, 12th Inf., 20 Jan., 1869. Priv. Gen. Ser., 21 June, 1870. Discharged 20 Jan., 1872. Priv. Gen. Ser., 21 Jan., 1872. Discharged 31 March, 1872. Priv. Gen. Ser., 1 April, 1872. Corpl., 1 Nov., 1872. Sergt., 1 Feb., 1874. 2nd Lieut. 8th Inf., 20 Jan., 1875. Dismissed 20 Feb., 1879.

CUNNINGHAM, THOS. A. [Born in Va. Appointed from Va.]
1st Lieut. Asst. Surg., 5 Aug., 1876. Capt. Asst. Surg., 5 Aug., 1881. Died 12 Oct., 1887.

CURD, EDWARD. [Born in Ky. Appointed from Ky.]
1st Lieut. of Inf., 5 March, 1847; 16th Inf., 9 April, 1847. Capt., 12 Oct., 1847. Disbanded 5 Aug., 1848.

CURD, THOS. J.* [Born in Ky. Appointed from Ky.]
Bvt. 2nd Lieut. 1st Art., 1 July, 1844. 2nd Lieut. 4th Art., 18 June, 1846. 1st Lieut., 3 March, 1847. Resigned 4 Dec., 1847. Died 12 Feb., 1850.

CURRIER, JACOB. [Born in N. H. Appointed from N. H.]
Cadet Mil. Acad., 1 July, 1833, to 18 June, 1835. 2nd Lieut. 3rd Inf., 31 July, 1838. 1st Lieut., 1 Dec., 1840. Resigned 30 Sept., 1841.

CURRIER, JOHN C. [Born in N. H. Appointed from N. H.]
2nd Lieut. 12th N. H. Vols., 2 Sept., 1862. Capt., 12 Aug., 1864. Discharged 18 Jan., 1865. 2nd Lieut. 21st Inf., 22 Jan., 1867. Unassigned 12 May, 1869. Ass'd to 12th Inf., 14 July, 1869. Resigned 27 Aug., 1869. Bvt. 1st Lieut., 2 March, 1867, for gallant and meritorious service in the Battle of the Wilderness, Va. Bvt. Capt., 2 March, 1867, for gallant and meritorious service in the Battle of Poplar Grove Church, Va.

CURRY, JAMES. [Born in England. Appointed from Va.]
Priv. Co. I, 2nd Art., 1 Sept., 1849. Corpl., 1 June, 1851. Priv., 28 Aug., 1851. Discharged 1 Sept., 1854. Priv. Co. E, 2nd Art., 11 Sept., 1854. Trans. to Co. G, 22 Nov., 1856. Q. M. Sergt., 2nd Art., 22 Dec., 1856. Discharged 11 June, 1859. Q. M. Sergt. 2nd Art., 11 July, 1859. Discharged 5 June, 1861. Capt. C. S. Vols., 25 July, 1862. Bvt. Maj. and Lieut. Col. Vols., 9 March, 1865, for long, faithful, and arduous service. Col. C. S. Vols. (Act 3 March, 1865), 23 June, 1865, to 31 Oct., 1866. Mustered out 13 March, 1867. 2nd Lieut. 5th Art., 18 June, 1867. 1st Lieut., 12 April, 1871. Retired for disability 23 Sept., 1885. Died 8 Aug., 1889.

CURTENIUS, EDWARD A. [Born in N. Y. Appointed from Mich.]
1st Lieut. 15th Inf., 14 May, 1861. Died 9 Nov., 1862. Bvt. Capt., 7 April, 1862, for gallant and meritorious service in the Battle of Shiloh, Tenn.

CURTIS, ALFRED. [Born in Ohio. Appointed from Army.]
Priv. and Sergt. Co. D, 19th Inf., 10 Oct., 1861, to 29 June, 1862. 2nd Lieut. 19th Inf., 19 Feb., 1862. 1st Lieut., 9 Feb., 1863. Capt., 9 Jan., 1866. Resigned 19 Sept., 1866. Bvt. Capt., 1 Sept., 1864, for gallant and meritorious service during the Atlanta campaign and at the Battle of Jonesboro', Ga.

CURTIS, ARTHUR F.* [Born in N. Y. Appointed from N. J.]
2nd Lieut. 2nd Art., 14 June, 1885. 1st Lieut. 3rd Art., 17 Dec., 1891. Trans. to 2nd Art., 9 Feb., 1892. Trans. to 6th Art., 8 March, 1898. Honor graduate of the Artillery School, 1892.

CURTIS, CHAS. A. [Born in Maine. Appointed from Maine.]
2nd Lieut. 7th Inf., 14 April, 1862. Trans. to 5th Inf., 28 April, 1862. 1st Lieut., 30 March, 1864. Bvt. Capt., 27 Sept., 1865, for meritorious service during the war. Unassigned 19 May, 1869. Retired 15 Dec., 1870.

CURTIS, DANIEL. [Born in N. H. Appointed from Mich.]
Ensign 1st Inf., 3 Jan., 1812. 2nd Lieut., 31 Dec., 1812. 1st Lieut., 15 April, 1814. Reg. Adjt., Aug., 1814, to June, 1815. Trans. to 3rd Inf., 17 May, 1815. Capt., 17 Oct., 1820. Trans. to 2nd Inf., 1 June, 1821. Dismissed 16 Oct., 1821. Reinstated 8 April, 1822. Dismissed 8 Jan., 1823.

CURTIS, EDWARD. [Born in R. I. Appointed from N. Y.]
Asst. Surg., 30 March, 1864. Resigned 7 June, 1870. Bvt. Capt. and Maj., 13 March, 1865, for faithful and meritorious service during the war.

CURTIS, EDWARD M. [Born in N. Y. Appointed from N. Y.]
1st Lieut. 7th Inf., 5 Aug., 1861. Capt., 23 July, 1862. Resigned 20 July, 1864.

CURTIS, EDWIN S.* [Born in N. Y. Appointed from Va.]
Priv. Co. D, 48th N. Y. Vols., 1 Sept., 1861. Discharged 16 Sept., 1863. 2nd Lieut. 2nd Art., 17 June, 1867. 1st Lieut., 10 Feb., 1873. Capt., 27 Aug., 1896. Graduate of the Artillery School, 1872.

CURTIS, HERBERT P. [Born in Mass. Appointed from Mass.]
2nd Lieut. 1st Mass. Cav., 4 Jan., 1862. 1st Lieut., 19 July, 1862. Capt., 6 Feb., 1864. Mustered out 26 June, 1865. Maj. J. A. Vols., 21 June, 1865. Bvt. Lieut. Col. and Col. Vols., 2 Dec., 1865, for faithful and meritorious service in his department. J. A. U. S. A., 25 Feb., 1867. Lieut. Col. Dep. J. A. Gen., 10 Sept., 1888. Died 12 Feb., 1892.

CURTIS, JAMES.* [Born in Maine. Appointed from Ill.]
Bvt. 2nd Lieut. 2nd Inf., 1 July, 1851. 2nd Lieut., 30 Jan., 1852. 1st Lieut., 3 March, 1855. Resigned 15 Jan., 1857. 1st Lieut., 15th Inf., 14 May, 1861. Capt., 25 Oct., 1861. Unassigned 12 Aug., 1869. Ass'd to 3rd Cav., 15 Dec., 1870. Maj. 10th Cav., 31 May, 1875. Retired 17 May, 1876. Died 19 Jan., 1878. Bvt. Maj., 1 Sept., 1864, for gallant and meritorious service at the Battle of Shiloh, Tenn., and during the Atlanta campaign.

CURTIS, LAURENCE A. [Born in Vt. Appointed from Wis.]
Priv. Co. G, 1st Wis. Inf., 14 May, 1898, to 2 July, 1898. 2nd Lieut. 12th Inf., 9 July, 1898. 1st Lieut. 2nd Inf., 2 March, 1899.

CURTIS, SAML. R.* [Born in Ohio. Appointed from Ohio.]
Bvt. 2nd Lieut. 7th Inf., 1 July, 1831. Resigned 30 June, 1832.

CURTISS, AMBROSE B. [Born in Mich. Appointed from Mich.]
Corpl. and Sergt. Co. G, 4th Mich. Vols., 20 June, 1861. Mustered out 20 June, 1864. 2nd Lieut. 8th Cav., 19 Aug, 1867. 1st Lieut., 31 Oct., 1869. Trans. to Supernumerary, 12 Aug., 1870. Discharged 13 Oct., 1870.

CUSACK, JOHN. [Born in Ireland. Appointed from Army.]
Priv. and Corpl. Co. E, 2nd Art., 5 Jan., 1854, to 24 Oct., 1861. 2nd Lieut. 1st Inf., 24 Oct., 1861. 1st Lieut., 27 Feb., 1862. Capt. C. S. Vols., 1 Aug., 1863, to 31 May, 1866 Capt., 18 Sept., 1867. Unass'd 8 April, 1869. Died 14 Jan., 1870. Bvt. Capt. and Maj., 28 Oct., 1865, for faithful and meritorious service.

CUSACK, JOSEPH E. [Born in N. Y. Appointed from Army.]
Priv. and Corpl. Troop C, 5th Cav., 13 Jan., 1890, to 21 Nov., 1892. 2nd Lieut. 5th Cav., 19 Nov., 1892. 1st Lieut., 2 March, 1899.

CUSACK, PATRICK. [Born in Ireland. Appointed from N. Y.]
Priv. Co. K, 4th Art., 8 Sept., 1855. Corpl., 1 May, 1856. Priv., 10 Nov., 1857. Corpl., 1 July, 1858. Sergt., 9 Aug., 1859. Priv., 30 Sept., 1859. Discharged 9 July, 1860. Priv. Co. K, 4th Art., 9 July, 1860. Trans. to 6th Cav., 4 Nov., 1861. Sergt. Co. B,

6th Cav., 4 Nov., 1861. 1st Sergt., 1 Dec., 1862. Sergt. Maj., 23 June, 1863. Discharged 19 Jan., 1865. Capt. 6th U. S. Col. Cav., 1 March, 1865. Mustered out 15 April, 1866. 2nd Lieut. 9th Cav., 7 March, 1867. Bvt. Capt., 12 Sept., 1868, for conspicuous gallantry in an engagement with Indians at Horse-Head Hills, 12 Sept., 1868. 1st Lieut. 9th Cav., 31 July, 1867. Capt., 20 Jan., 1883. Retired for disability 21 April, 1891. Died 9 Jan., 1894.

CUSHING, ALONZO H.* [Born in Wis. Appointed from N. Y.]
2nd Lieut. 4th Art., 24 June, 1861. 1st Lieut., 24 June, 1861. Killed 3 July, 1863, at the Battle of Gettysburg, Pa. Bvt. Capt., 13 Dec., 1862, for gallant and meritorious service at the Battle of Fredericksburg, Va. Bvt. Maj., 2 May, 1863, for gallant and meritorious service at the Battle of Chancellorsville, Va. Bvt. Lieut. Col., 1 July, 1863, for conspicuous gallantry at the Battle of Gettysburg, Pa.

CUSHING, HARRY C. Born in Md. Appointed from R. I.]
Corpl. Co. A, 1st R. I. Art., 6 June, 1861. Sergt., 16 Sept., 1861. 2nd Lieut. 4th Art., 24 Oct., 1861. Bvt. 1st Lieut., 9 Aug., 1862, for gallant and meritorious service in the Battle of Cedar Mountain, Va. 1st Lieut. 4th Art., 17 Sept., 1862. Bvt. Capt., 20 Sept., 1863, for gallant and meritorious service in the Battle of Chickamauga, Ga. Bvt. Maj., 28 Aug., 1864, for gallant and meritorious service in the Battle of Smithfield, Va. Capt. 38th Inf., 28 July, 1866 (declined). Capt. 4th Art., 22 Aug., 1871. Graduate of the Artillery School, 1870. Retired for disability, with the rank of Maj., 12 Feb., 1895.

CUSHING, HOWARD B. [Born in Wis. Appointed from Army.]
Priv. Co. B, 1st Ill. Art., 24 March, 1862, to 30 Nov., 1863. Priv. Co. B, 4th Art., 30 Nov., 1863. 2nd Lieut. 4th Art., 30 Nov., 1863. Trans. to 3rd Cav., 7 Sept., 1867. 1st Lieut., 16 Dec., 1867. Killed 5 May, 1871, in action with the Indians in Ariz.

CUSHING, SAMUEL T.* [Born in R. I. Appointed from R. I.]
Bvt. 2nd Lieut. 10th Inf., 1 July, 1860. 2nd Lieut. 2nd Inf., 19 Jan., 1861. 1st Lieut., 14 May, 1861. Capt., 15 Feb., 1862. Capt. C. S., 9 Feb., 1863. Vacated commission of Capt. 2nd Inf., 12 May, 1863. Bvt. Maj., 13 March, 1865, for faithful and meritorious service during the war. Maj. and C. S., 28 Aug., 1888. Lieut. Col. and Asst. C. G. S., 11 Nov., 1895. Col. and Asst. C. G. S., 26 Jan., 1897. Brig. Gen. and C. G. S., 28 Jan., 1898. Retired for disability 21 April, 1898.

CUSHMAN, GUY. [Born in R. I. Appointed from Mo.]
Priv. and Corpl. Co. M, 1st Mo. Vols., 13 May, 1898. Trans. to Troop D, 1st Ohio Cav., 12 July, 1898. Mustered out 23 Oct., 1898. 2nd Lieut. 2nd Cav., 10 April, 1899.

CUSHMAN, C. SETH. [Born in Me. Appointed from Wis.]
1st Lieut. 14th Inf., 5 Aug., 1861. Reg. Adj., 15 Oct., 1863, to 6 Dec., 1864. Resigned 6 Dec., 1864.

CUSHMAN, EUGENE. [Born in Pa. Appointed from Pa.]
2nd Lieut. 16th Inf., 17 Dec., 1872. 1st Lieut., 15 March, 1883. Resigned 1 Oct., 1888.

CUSHMAN, HERBERT. [Born in Pa. Appointed from Pa.]
Cadet Naval Acad., 23 Sept., 1862, to 7 April, 1864. 2nd Lieut. 20th Inf., 23 June, 1868. 1st Lieut., 22 Oct., 1876. Retired for disability 27 April, 1891.

CUSICK, CORNELIUS C. [Born in N. Y. Appointed from N. Y.]
2nd Lieut. 132nd N. Y. Vols., 14 Aug., 1862. 1st Lieut., 1 July, 1863. Mustered out 29 June, 1865. 2nd Lieut. 13th Inf., 20 June, 1866. Trans. to 31st Inf., 21 Sept., 1866. Trans. to 22nd Inf., 15 May, 1869. 1st Lieut., 5 Aug., 1872. Capt., 1 Jan., 1888. Retired for disability 14 Jan., 1892.

CUSTER, BETHEL M. [Born in Pa. Appointed from Pa.]
Priv. Co. C, 19th Pa. Vols., 18 April, 1861. Discharged 9 Aug., 1861. Corpl. Co. C, 90th Pa. Vols., 17 Sept., 1861. Sergt., 1 March, 1863. Discharged 27 Feb., 1864. 2nd Lieut. 32nd U. S. Col. Troops, 4 March, 1864. 1st Lieut., 26 Nov., 1864. Mustered out 22 Aug., 1865. 1st Lieut. 11th U. S. Col. Troops, 22 Oct., 1865. Mustered out 12 Jan., 1866. 2nd Lieut. 38th Inf., 28 July, 1866. Bvt. 1st Lieut., 2 March, 1867, for gallant and meritorious service at James Island, S. C. Trans. to 24th Inf., 11 Nov., 1869. 1st Lieut., 1 March, 1871. R. Q. M., 15 May, 1877, to 30 April, 1880. Capt., 18 June, 1880. Died 22 Dec., 1887.

CUSTER, GEORGE A.* [Born in Ohio. Appointed from Ohio.]
2nd Lieut. 2nd Cav., 24 June, 1861. 5th Cav., 3 Aug., 1861. 1st Lieut., 17 July, 1862. Capt. A. A. de C., 5 June, 1862, to 31 March, 1863. Brig. Gen. Vols., 29 June, 1863. Maj. Gen. Vols., 15 April, 1865. Mustered out Vol. Service, 1 Feb., 1866. Capt., 8 May, 1864. Lieut. Col. 7th Cav., 28 July, 1866. Killed 25 June, 1876, in action with Indians in Montana Ter. Bvt. Maj., 3 July, 1863, for gallant and meritorious service at the Battle of Gettysburg, Pa. Bvt. Lieut. Col., 11 May, 1864, for gallant and meritorious service at the Battle of Yellow Tavern, Va. Bvt. Col., 19 Sept., 1864, for gallant and meritorious service at the Battle of Winchester, Va. Bvt. Brig. Gen., 13 March, 1865, for gallant and meritorious service at the Battle of Five Forks, Va. Bvt. Maj. Gen., 13 March, 1865, for gallant and meritorious service during the campaign ending with the surrender of the insurgent army of Northern Virginia.

CUSTER, THOS. W. [Born in Ohio. Appointed from Mich.]
Priv. Co. H, 21st Ohio Vols., 2 Sept., 1861, to 10 Oct., 1864. 2nd Lieut. 6th Mich. Cav., 8 Nov., 1864. Bvt. 1st Lieut., Capt. and Maj. Vols., 13 March, 1865, for distinguished and gallant conduct. Mustered out 24 Nov., 1865. 2nd Lieut. 1st Inf., 23 Feb., 1866. 1st Lieut. 7th Cav., 28 July, 1866. Capt., 2 Dec., 1875. Killed 25 June, 1876, in action with Indians in Montana Ter. Bvt. Capt., 2 March, 1867, for gallant and distinguished conduct in the engagement with the enemy at Waynesboro', Va., 2 March, 1865. Bvt. Maj., 2 March, 1867, for distinguished conduct in the engagement with the enemy near Namozine Church, Va., 3 April, 1865. Bvt. Lieut. Col., 2 March, 1867, for distinguished courage and service at the Battle of Sailor's Creek, Va.

CUTBUSH, JAMES. [Born in Pa. Appointed from Pa.]
Asst. Apothecary Gen., 12 Aug., 1814. Post Surg., 16 May, 1820. Asst. Surg., 1 June, 1821. Died 15 Dec., 1823.

CUTBUSH, WM.* [Born in Pa. Appointed from Pa.]
2nd Lieut. Eng., 27 March, 1812. 1st Lieut., 1 July, 1812. Capt., 17 Sept., 1814. Resigned 1 Oct., 1817.

CUTLER, ENOS. [Born in Mass. Appointed from Ohio.]
1st Lieut. 7th Inf., 3 May, 1808. Capt., 3 Sept., 1810. Maj. A. A. G., 15 Feb., 1813. Maj. A. I. G., 18 March, 1813. Maj. 38th Inf., 1 May, 1814. Retained as Capt. 4th Inf., 17 May, 1815. Maj. 2nd Inf., 10 Feb., 1818. Lieut. Col. 3rd Inf., 28 April, 1826. Col. 4th Inf., 21 Sept., 1836. Resigned 30 Nov., 1839. Retained — May, 1815 (in re-organization under Act of 3 March, 1815), as Capt. 4th Inf., with Bvt. of Maj., from 1 May, 1814 (the date of his appointment as Maj. of the 38th Inf.).

CUTTING, HEYWARD. [Born in N. Y. Appointed from N. Y.]
2nd Lieut. 10th Inf., 27 May, 1861. 1st Lieut., 7 Sept., 1861. Resigned 9 April, 1864.

CUTTS, JAMES M., Jr. [Born in D. C. Appointed from Ill.]
Priv. Co. I, R. I. Vols., 2 May to 23 June, 1861. Capt. 11th Inf., 14 May, 1861. Trans. to 20th Inf., 21 Sept., 1866. Resigned 19 June, 1868. Bvt. Maj., 1 Aug., 1864, for gallant service at Spottsylvania, and during the present campaign before Richmond, Va. Bvt. Lieut. Col., 1 Aug., 1864, for distinguished service in the Battle of the Wilderness, Va.

CUTTS, THOS.* [Born in D. C. Appointed from Me.]
Bvt. 2nd Lieut. 3rd Inf., 1 July, 1828. 2nd Lieut., 1 July, 1828. 1st Lieut., 15 June, 1836. Died 2 Sept., 1838.

CUYLER, JAMES W.* [Born in D. C. Appointed at Large.]
1st Lieut. Eng., 13 June, 1864. Bvt. Capt., 13 March, 1865, for faithful and meritorious service during the war. Capt. Eng., 7 March, 1867. Maj., 17 July, 1881. Died 16 April, 1883.

CUYLER, JOHN M. [Born in Ga. Appointed from Ga.]
Asst. Surg., 1 April, 1834. Capt. Asst. Surg., 11 Feb., 1847. Maj. Surg., 16 Feb., 1847. Lieut. Col. Med. Inspector, 11 June, 1862. Bvt. Col., 29 Nov., 1864. Bvt. Brig. Gen., 13 March, 1865, for faithful and meritorious service during the war. Mustered out as Lieut. Col. Med. Inspector, 31 Oct., 1865. Col. Surg., 26 June, 1876. Retired 30 June, 1882. Died 26 April, 1884.

CUYLER, WM. C. [Born in Ga. Appointed at Large.]
2nd Lieut. 3rd Art., 19 Feb., 1862. 1st Lieut., 17 April, 1863. Died 2 Nov., 1869. Bvt. Capt. 18 Oct., 1864, for gallant and distinguished service in the Battles of Winchester and Cedar Creek, Va. Bvt. Maj., 13 March, 1865, for good conduct and gallant service during the war.

DADE, ALEXANDER L.* [Born in Ky. Appointed from Ky.]
2nd Lieut. 13th Inf., 12 June, 1887. Trans. to 10th Cav., 27 Feb., 1888. 1st Lieut. 2nd Cav., 13 June, 1895. Trans. to 3rd Cav., 7 Nov., 1895. Graduate of the Infantry and Cavalry School, 1893. Maj. 48th U. S. Vols., 9 Sept., 1899.

DADE, FRANCIS L. [Born in Va. Appointed from Va.]
3rd Lieut. 12th Inf., 29 March, 1813. 2nd Lieut., 31 Jan., 1814. Trans. to 4th Inf., 17 May, 1815. 1st Lieut., 4 Sept., 1816. Capt., 24 Feb., 1818. Massacred by Indians in Fla., 28 Dec., 1835. Bvt. Maj., 24 Feb., 1828, for ten years' faithful service in one grade.

DADE TOWNSHEND. [Born in Va. Appointed from Va.]
1st Lieut. 2nd Drag., 11 June, 1836. Capt., 1 Oct., 1837. Dismissed 17 Feb. 1840.

DAGGETT, AARON S. [Born in Me. Appointed from Me.]
1st Lieut. 5th Me. Vols., 25 June, 1861. Capt., 15 Aug., 1861. Maj., 14 April, 1863. Mustered out 27 July, 1864. Lieut. Col. 5th U. S. Vet. Vols., 23 Jan., 1865. Bvt. Col. Vols. and Bvt. Brig. Gen. Vols., 13 March, 1865, for gallant and meritorious service during the war. Mustered out 10 May, 1866. Capt. 16th Inf., 28 July, 1866. Bvt. Maj., 2 March, 1867, for gallant and meritorious service in the Battle of Rappahannock Station, Va., 7 Nov., 1863. Bvt. Lieut. Col., 2 March, 1867, for gallant and meritorious service in the Battle of the Wilderness, Va. Trans. to 2nd Inf., 17 April, 1869. Maj. 13th Inf., 2 Jan, 1892. Lieut. Col. 25th Inf., 1 Oct., 1895. Col. 14th Inf., 31 March, 1899. Brig. Gen. Vols., 21 Sept., 1898, to 30 Nov., 1898.

DAHLGREN, PAUL.* [Born in Del. Appointed at Large.]
2nd Lieut. 3rd Art., 15 June, 1868. Resigned 12 June, 1870.

DAINGERFIELD, JOSEPH F.* [Born in Va. Appointed from Va.]
2nd Lieut. Corps Art., 24 July, 1818. Resigned 20 Dec., 1820

DAKE, ARNOLD B. [Born in Vt. Appointed from Vt.]
Ensign 30th Inf., 30 April, 1813. 3rd Lieut., 31 Jan., 1814. 2nd Lieut, 13 Sept., 1814. Trans. to 5th Inf., 17 May, 1815. Resigned, 1 Jan., 1817.

DAKIN, GEORGE K. [Born in N. H. Appointed from N. H.]
Corpl., Sergt. and 1st Sergt. 1st N. H. Batty., 26 Sept., 1861, to 18 Oct., 1864. 1st Lieut., 18 Oct., 1864. Capt., 18 Feb., 1865. Mustered out 9 June, 1865. 2nd Lieut. 3rd Art., 23 Feb., 1866. 1st Lieut., 28 July, 1866. Died 21 Sept., 1871. Bvt. Capt., 2 March, 1867, for gallant and meritorious service at the Battle of Sutherland Station, 2 May, 1865.

DALLAM, SAMUEL F.* [Born in Pa. Appointed from Pa.]
Addl. 2nd Lieut. 1st Cav., 12 June, 1896. 2nd Lieut. 8th Cav., 22 Dec., 1896.

DALLAS, ALEXR. J. [Born in D. C. Appointed at Large.]
Priv. Co. H, 3rd Batt. D. C. Vols., 27 April, 1861. Discharged 11 June, 1861. Capt. 12th Inf., 14 May, 1861. Bvt. Maj., 30 July, 1864, for gallant and meritorious service in front of Petersburg, Va. Trans. to 30th Inf., 21 Sept., 1866. Maj. 23rd Inf., 22 Feb., 1869. Lieut. Col. 22nd Inf., 8 Feb., 1880. Retired 27 June, 1884. Died 19 July, 1895.

DALLIBA, JAMES.* [Born in Conn. Appointed from Conn.]
2nd Lieut. Reg. of Art., 1 March, 1811. 1st Lieut, 3 March, 1813. Capt. Dep. Com. Ord., 5 Aug., 1813. Maj. A. C. G. Ord., 9 Feb., 1815. Retained 1 June, 1821, as Capt. 1st Art. Resigned 1 May, 1824. Retained 21 May, 1821, in re-organization, with Bvt. of Maj. from 19 Feb., 1815.

DALTON, ALBERT C. [Born in Ind. Appointed from the Army.]
Priv., Corpl. and Sergt. Co. A, 22nd Inf., 18 Jan., 1889, to 1 Aug., 1891. 2nd Lieut. 22nd Inf., 31 July, 1891. 1st Lieut., 26 April, 1898. Graduate of the Infantry and Cavalry School, 1895.

DALTON, HARRY F. [Born in Mass. Appointed from Mass.]
2nd Lieut. 9th Inf., 9 July, 1898. 1st Lieut. 19th Inf., 11 July, 1899.

DALTON, SAML. W. [Born in N. Y. Appointed from N. Y.]
Asst. Surg., 16 July, 1829. Resigned 31 Dec., 1833.

DAMRELL, ANDREW N.* [Born in Mass. Appointed from Mass.]
1st. Lieut. Eng., 13 June, 1864. Bvt. Capt., 13 March, 1865, for meritorious service in the Battle of Franklin, Tenn. Bvt. Maj., 13 March, 1865, for meritorious service in the Battles before Nashville, Tenn. Capt. Eng., 7 March, 1867. Maj., 8 Aug., 1882. Lieut. Col., 12 Oct., 1895.

DANA, JAMES J. [Born in Mass. Appointed from N. Y.]
2nd Lieut. 4th Art., 18 June, 1855. 1st Lieut., 10 Jan., 1857. Capt. A. Q. M., 3 Aug., 1861. Vacated commission of 1st Lieut. 4th Art., 3 Sept., 1861. Lieut. Col. Q. M. (Act 17 July, 1862), 1 Jan., 1863, to 7 July, 1863. Col. Q. M. (Act 4 July, 1864), 2 Aug., 1864. Bvt. Maj., Lieut. Col. and Col., 13 March, 1865, for faithful and meritorious service during the war. Bvt. Brig. Gen., 13 March, 1865, for faithful and meritorious service in the Q. M. Dept. during the war. Relieved as Col. Q. M. (Act 4 July, 1864), 1 Jan., 1867. Maj. Q. M., 18 Jan., 1867. Lieut. Col. Dept. Q. M. G., 13 Feb., 1882. Retired by operation of law 9 April, 1885. Died 15 Sept., 1898.

DANA, NAPOLEON J. T.* [Born in Me. Appointed at Large.]
2nd Lieut. 7th Inf., 1 July, 1842. 1st Lieut., 16 Feb., 1847. Capt. A. Q. M., 3 March, 1848. Bvt. Capt., 18 April, 1847, for gallant and meritorious conduct in the Battle of Cerro Gordo, Mexico. Resigned 1 March, 1855. Capt. and A. Q. M., 2 Aug., 1894 (Act 1 Aug., 1894). Retired by said act 11 Aug., 1894.

DANA, NATHANIEL G.* [Born in Mass. Appointed from Mass.]
3rd Lieut. 1st Art., 11 March, 1814. 2nd Lieut., 1 May, 1814. Trans. to Corps Art., 12 May, 1814. 1st Lieut., 20 April, 1818. Capt., 15 Sept., 1825. Died 4 Feb., 1833.

DANA, SAML. [Born in Mass. Appointed from Mass.]
Corpl. Co. K, 7th N. Y. State Mil., 26 April to 3 June, 1861. Capt. 17th Inf., 5 Aug., 1861. Trans. to 26th Inf., 21 Sept., 1866. Maj. and P. M., 7 March, 1867. Died 27 Sept., 1870. Bvt. Maj., 2 July, 1863, for gallant and meritorious service at the Battle of Gettysburg, Pa. Bvt. Lieut. Col., 13 March, 1865, for faithful and meritorious service connected with the organization of the Volunteer armies of the U. S. during the war.

DANCY, FRANCIS L.* [Born in N. C. Appointed from N. C.]
Bvt. 2nd Lieut. 2nd Art., 1 July, 1826. 2nd Lieut., 1 July, 1826. 1st Lieut., 3 Nov., 1832. Resigned 11 Sept., 1836.

DANDY, GEORGE B. [Born in Ga. Appointed from Army.]
Cadet at Mil. Acad., 1 July, 1849, to 10 July, 1852. Priv. Co. A, 1st Art., 14 Nov., 1854. Sergt., 15 Jan., 1855. 1st Sergt., to 22 March, 1857. 2nd Lieut. 3rd Art., 21 Feb., 1857. 1st Lieut., 3 March, 1861. Capt. A. Q. M., 24 March, 1862. Col. 100th N. Y. Vols., 29 Aug., 1862. Bvt. Maj., 6 Sept., 1863, for gallant and meritorious service in the Siege of Fort Wagner, S. C. Vacated commission 1st Lieut. 3rd Art., 8 Feb., 1864. Bvt. Lieut. Col., 14 Aug., 1864, for gallant and meritorious service in action at Deep Bottom, Va. Bvt. Col., 13 March, 1865, for gallant and meritorious service in the capture of Fort Gregg, Va. Bvt. Brig. Gen., 13 March, 1865, for gallant and meritorious service in the field during the war. Bvt. Brig. Gen. Vols., 13 March, 1865, for gallant and meritorious service at Fort Gregg, Va. Mustered out of Vol. service, 28 Aug., 1865. Maj. Q. M., 3 March, 1875. Lieut. Col. and Dep. Q. M. G., 11 Nov., 1887. Retired by operation of law, 11 Feb., 1894.

DANES, HENRY C.* [Born in N. Y. Appointed from N. Y.]
2nd Lieut. 3rd Art., 17 June, 1867. 1st Lieut., 20 Dec., 1872. Capt., 12 Feb., 1895. Graduate of the Artillery School, 1869, 1890.

DANFORTH, JOSHUA N. [Born in Mass. Appointed from Mass.]
Priv. Co. F, 5th Mass. Vols., 16 July to 16 Nov., 1864. 2nd Lieut. 7th U. S. Col. Inf., 15 June, 1865, to 13 Oct., 1866. 2nd Lieut. 2nd Inf., 7 March, 1867. Unassigned 17 April, 1869. Ass'd to 13th Inf., 3 Aug., 1870. Discharged 10 Sept., 1870.

DANIEL, BYRON G. [Born in N. Y. Appointed from N. Y.]
1st Lieut. 19th Inf., 14 May, 1861. Capt., 30 Sept., 1862. Resigned 13 Sept., 1864.

DANIEL, LUNSFORD. [Born in Ga. Appointed from the Army.]
Priv., Corpl. and Sergt. H Batt., 2nd Art., 16 Sept., 1886, to 30 Jan., 1890. 2nd Lieut. 6th Cav., 17 Dec., 1889. Died 31 May, 1894.

DANIEL, J. TOWNSEND. [Born in England. Appointed from Md.]
Capt. 36th N. Y. Vols., 17 June, 1861, to 28 April, 1863. Maj. 10th Md. Vols., 30 July, 1863, to 29 Jan., 1864. Maj. 1st Potomac Home Brig., Md. Cav., 19 March, 1864, to 28 June, 1865. 2nd Lieut. 7th Cav., 28 July, 1866. Appointment expired 20 July, 1867.

DANIEL, JUNIUS.* [Born in N. C. Appointed at Large.]
Bvt. 2nd Lieut. 3rd Inf., 1 July, 1851. 2nd Lieut., 10 Nov., 1851. 1st Lieut., 31 May, 1857. Resigned 14 Jan., 1858.

DANIELS, CHAS. B.* [Born in N. H. Appointed from N. H.]
Bvt. 2nd Lieut. 2nd Art., 1 July, 1836. 2nd Lieut., 11 Sept., 1836. 1st Lieut., 7 July, 1838. Capt., 19 Oct., 1847. Died 27 Oct., 1847, of wounds received at Battle of Molino del Rey, Mexico.

DANIELS, NAPOLEON H. [Born in La. Appointed from Ind.]
Sergt. Co. B, 18th Ind. Vols., 16 Aug., 1861. 1st Lieut. 12 Feb., 1863. Mustered out 28 Aug., 1865. 2nd Lieut. 18th Inf., 23 Feb., 1866. Killed 21 July, 1866, in action with Indians in Dakota.

DANILSON, WM. H. [Born in N. Y. Appointed from N. Y.]
Priv. Co. E, 13th N. Y. Vols., 23 April to 6 Aug., 1861. Sergt. Co. E, 48th N. Y. Vols., 27 Sept., 1861. 1st Lieut. 33rd U. S. Col. Inf., 31 Jan., 1863. Capt., 26 Aug., 1863. Maj. 128th U. S. Col. Inf., 28 March, 1865. Mustered out 28 Jan., 1867. 1st Lieut. 40th Inf., 28 July, 1866. Unassigned 20 April, 1869. Discharged 31 Dec., 1870.

DAPRAY, JOHN A. [Born in S. C. Appointed from D. C.]
2nd Lieut. 23rd Inf., 24 Nov., 1880. 1st. Lieut., 28 June, 1889. Capt., 26 April, 1898. Capt. and A. A. G. Vols., 12 May, 1898, to 31 Aug., 1898.

DARKEN, EDWARD J. [Born in Conn. Appointed from N. Y.]
Asst. Surg., 13 April, 1863. Resigned 2 April, 1868. Bvt. Capt., 13 March, 1865, for gallant and meritorious service during the war.

DARLING, JOHN. [Born in Vt. Appointed from Army.]
Priv., Corpl. and Sergt. Co. H, and Q. M. Sergt. 4th Art., 22 Jan., 1830, to 22 June, 1838. 2nd Lieut. 5th Inf., 31 July, 1838. Resigned 15 Aug., 1839.

DARLING, JOHN A. [Born in Me. Appointed from Me.]
2nd Lieut. 2nd Art., 5 Aug., 1861. 1st Lieut., 31 May, 1862. Maj. 3rd Pa. Heavy Art., 31 March, 1863. Bvt. Capt. and Bvt. Maj., 13 March, 1865, for gallant and meritorious service during the war. Mustered out of Vol. service, 1 Sept, 1865. Capt. 2nd Art., 9 Dec., 1867. Mustered out 1 Jan., 1871. Capt. Art., 24 April, 1878, with rank from 9 Dec., 1867 (Act 8 April, 1878). Ass'd to 1st Art., 20 March, 1879. Maj. 5th Art., 1 July, 1892. Trans. to 3 Art., 7 Oct., 1896. Retired, over 30 years' service, 7 June, 1897.

DARLING, NATHAN. [Born in N. Y. Appointed from N. Y.]
2nd Lieut. 2nd Drag., 23 Nov., 1836. 1st Lieut., 1 March, 1838. Reg. Adjt., 3 Feb. to 5 Sept., 1838. Capt., 15 Dec., 1841. Resigned 31 Aug., 1843.

D'ARMIT, ALBERT M.* [Born in Pa. Appointed from Iowa.]
Addl. 2nd Lieut. Eng., 12 June, 1889. 2nd Lieut., 5 Oct., 1889, to rank from 12 June, 1889. 1st Lieut., 18 Sept., 1894. Died 13 Oct., 1895.

DARNALL, CARL R. [Born in Tex. Appointed from N. J.]
Asst. Surg., 26 Oct., 1896.

DARNE, ALEXR. C. H.* [Born in Md. Appointed from Md.]
Bvt. 2nd Lieut. 8th Inf., 1 July, 1841. 2nd Lieut., 7 Sept., 1841. Resigned 10 Sept., 1845.

DARR, FRANCIS J. A.* [Born in Ohio. Appointed from N. Y.]
2nd Lieut. 12th Inf., 12 June, 1880. 1st Lieut. 26 May, 1886. Resigned 1 Sept, 1887.

DARRAGH, ARCHIBALD. [Born in Pa. Appointed from Pa.]
2nd Lieut. Light Art., 27 Feb., 1807. 1st Lieut., 29 Jan., 1811. Trans. to Corps. Art., 12 May, 1814. Capt., 15 Aug., 1814. Disbanded 15 June, 1815. Capt. A. Dep. Q. M. G., 18 April, 1818. Disbanded 1 June, 1821.

DARRAH, THOMAS W.* [Born in Kan. Appointed from Kan.]
2nd Lieut. 9th Inf., 12 June, 1895. 1st Lieut. of Inf., 1 July, 1898. Ass'd to 20th Inf., 1 Jan., 1899, Capt. 35th U. S. Vols., 5 July, 1899.

DARROW, GEORGE. [Born in Ind. Appointed from Ind.]
Sergt. Co. H, 55th Ind. Vols., 15 July to 18 Sept., 1862. Priv. Co. C, 132nd Ind. Vols., 7 May to 7 Sept., 1864. Capt. 148th Ind. Vols., 15 Feb., 1865. Mustered out 5 Sept., 1865. 2nd Lieut. 4th Inf., 24 Sept., 1867. Resigned 26 March, 1868.

DARROW, WALTER N. P.* [Born in N. Y. Appointed from N. Y.]
2nd Lieut. 4th Art., 1 July, 1886. Resigned 26 Oct., 1891.

DASHIELL, JEREMIAH Y. [Born in Md. Appointed from La.]
Addl. P. M., 2 July, 1846. Maj. and P. M., 2 March, 1849. Dismissed 10 July, 1858.

DASHIELL, WM. R.* [Born in Va. Appointed from Va.]
Addl. 2nd Lieut. 8th Inf., 11 June, 1888. 2nd Lieut. 17th Inf., 15 July, 1888. Trans. to 8th Inf. 3 Jan., 1895. 1st Lieut. 24th Inf., 4 Dec., 1895. Capt., 25 April, 1899.

DAUGHERTY, WILL W. [Born in Ind. Appointed from Ind.]
Priv. Co. G, 27th Ind. Vols., 19 Aug., 1861. Sergt. Maj., 1 June, 1862. 2nd Lieut. 27th Ind. Vols., 14 Nov., 1862. 1st Lieut., 7 March, 1863. Mustered out 4 Nov., 1864. 2nd Lieut. 18th Inf., 7 March, 1867. 1st Lieut., 2 Jan., 1869. Unassigned 26 April, 1869. Ass'd to 22nd Inf., 1 Jan., 1871. Capt., 7th Sept., 1882. Retired for disability 1 Feb., 1893.

DAVANT, WM. M.* [Born in S. C. Appointed from S. C.]
Bvt. 2nd Lieut. Mounted Rifles, 1 July, 1854. 2nd Lieut., 3 March, 1855. Drowned 1 Oct., 1855.

DAVENPORT, THOS. C.* [Born in D. C. Appointed at Large.]
2nd Lieut. 9th Cav., 14 June, 1872. 1st. Lieut., 28 June, 1878. Trans. to 4th Art., 8 Feb., 1886. Died 6 May, 1887.

DAVENPORT, WM. [Born in Pa. Appointed from N. C.]
Capt. 16th Inf., 28 Sept., 1812. Trans. to 8th Inf., 17 May, 1815. Maj. 6th Inf., 16 Dec., 1825. Lieut. Col. 1st Inf., 4 April, 1832. Col. 6th Inf., 14 June, 1842. Trans. to 1st Inf., 7 July, 1843. Resigned 31 Jan., 1850. Bvt. Maj., 28 Sept., 1822, for ten years' faithful service in one grade. Bvt. Col., 7 July, 1838, for meritorious service in Florida.

DAVID, VIRGIL. [Born in ——. Appointed from Md.]
Mil. Storekeeper Ord., 22 Dec., 1837. Died 28 Nov. 1838.

DAVIDSON, BENJ. K. [Born in Scotland. Appointed from Ind.]
Priv. Ind. Reg. Mexican War, 1847 to 1848. Priv. Co. C, 25th Ind. Vols., 19 Aug., 1861, to 22 Aug., 1864. Asst. Surg. 143rd Ind. Vols., 27 Feb., 1865. Mustered out 17 Oct., 1865. 2nd Lieut. 12th Inf., 5 March, 1866. Trans. to 30th Inf., 21 Sept., 1866. Resigned 8 June, 1867.

DAVIDSON, DELOZIER. [Born in D. C. Appointed from D. C.]
2nd Lieut. 2nd Inf., 31 July, 1838. 1st Lieut., 11 March, 1846. Capt., 1 Jan., 1849. Maj. 4th Inf., 1 Nov., 1861. Resigned 9 March, 1863. Bvt. Capt., 20 Aug., 1847, for gallant and meritorious conduct at Contreras and Churubusco.

DAVIDSON, EDWARD C. [Born in N. C. Appointed from N. C.]
1st Lieut. 3rd Drag., 9 April, 1847. Disbanded 31 July, 1848.

DAVIDSON, FRANCIS S. [Born in Mass. Appointed from Mass.]
2nd Lieut. 5th Mass. Cav., 9 June, 1865. Mustered out 1 Oct., 1865. 2nd Lieut. 9th Cav., 7 March, 1867. Dismissed 8 Dec., 1875.

DAVIDSON, GEORGE. [Born in Ky. Appointed from Ky.]
1st Lieut. 11th Inf., 9 April, 1847. Disbanded 15 Aug., 1848.

DAVIDSON, HENRY B.* [Born in Tenn. Appointed from Tenn.]
Bvt. 2nd Lieut. 1st Drag., 1 July, 1853. 2nd Lieut., 20 Jan., 1855. 1st Lieut., 30 Nov., 1856. Capt., 13 May, 1861. Dropped 30 July, 1861.

DAVIDSON, JAMES. [Born in Scotland. Appointed from Army.] 2nd Lieut. 19th Co. Me. Vols., 21 March, 1865, to 23 May, 1865. Priv., Corpl., Sergt. and 1st Sergt. Co. D, Eng. Batt., 12 June, 1865, to 1 June, 1867. 2nd Lieut. 29th Inf., 22 May, 1867. Trans. to 11th Inf., 25 April, 1869. Discharged 6 Sept., 1870.

DAVIDSON, JOHN T. [Born in Md. Appointed from Md. 2nd Lieut. Light Art., 27 Oct., 1820. Trans. to 4th Art., 1 June, 1821. Died 12 Nov., 1824.

DAVIDSON, JOHN W.* [Born in Va. Appointed at Large.] Bvt. 2nd Lieut. 1st Drag., 1 July, 1845. 2nd Lieut., 21 April, 1846. 1st Lieut., 8 Jan., 1848. Reg. Adjt., 4 Jan., 1851, to 30 Sept., 1851. Capt. 1st Drag. (1st Cav.), 20 Jan., 1855. Maj. 2nd Cav., 14 Nov., 1861. Brig. Gen. Vols., 3 Feb., 1862. Bvt. Lieut. Col., 27 June, 1862, for gallant and meritorious service in the Battle of Gaines' Mills, Va. Bvt. Col., 28 June, 1862, for gallant and meritorious service in the Battle of Golding's Farm, Va. Bvt. Brig. Gen., 13 March, 1865, for gallant and meritorious service in the capture of Little Rock, Ark. Bvt. Maj. Gen., 13 March, 1865, for gallant and meritorious service in the field during the war. Bvt. Maj. Gen. Vols., 13 March, 1865, for gallant and meritorious service during the war. Mustered out of Vol. service 15 Jan., 1866. Lieut. Col. 10th Cav., 1 Dec., 1866. Col. 2nd Cav., 20 March, 1879. Died 26 June, 1881.

DAVIDSON, LEVI P.* [Born in N. Y. Appointed from N. Y.] 2nd Lieut. 1st Drag., 1 July, 1837. 1st Lieut., 31 Dec., 1840. Died 27 June, 1842.

DAVIDSON, WM. B.* [Born in Va. Appointed from Va.] 3rd Lieut. Ord., 2 Dec., 1815. 2nd Lieut., 1 Sept., 1818. Trans. to 1st Art., 1 June, 1821. Trans. to 3rd Art., 16 Aug., 1821. Capt., 7 July, 1838. Died 25 Dec., 1840.

DAVIDSON, WM. T. [Born in Pa. Appointed from Pa.] Garrison Surg. Mate, 13 June, 1808. Post Surg., 18 April, 1818. Resigned 1 May, 1820.

DAVIES, CHARLES.* [Born in Conn. Appointed from N. Y.] Bvt. 2nd Lieut. Light Art., 11 Dec., 1815. Trans. to Eng., 31 Aug., 1816. Resigned 1 Dec., 1816. Prof. at Mil. Acad., 1 Dec., 1816. Resigned 31 May, 1837. Maj. and P. M., 17 Nov., 1841. Resigned 30 Sept., 1845.

DAVIES, FIELDING L. [Born in Ohio. Appointed from Ohio.] Priv. Co. F, 3rd Ohio Vols., 15 June, 1861. Capt. 15th U. S. Col. Troops, 13 Jan., 1864. Mustered out 7 April, 1866. 2nd Lieut. 22nd Inf., 17 July, 1867. 1st Lieut., 10 March, 1877. Dismissed 25 Jan., 1881.

DAVIES, FRANCIS A.* [Born in Pa. Appointed from Pa. 2nd Lieut. 2nd Art., 6 May, 1861. 1st Lieut., 17 May, 1861. Capt. 16th Inf., 27 Sept., 1861. Trans. to 25th Inf., 21 Sept., 1866. Resigned 21 Nov., 1868. Bvt. Maj., 30 Aug., 1862, for gallant and meritorious service at the Battle of Bull Run (2nd), Va. Died 22 Jan., 1889.

DAVIES, THOS. A.* [Born in N. Y. Appointed from N. Y.] Bvt. 2nd Lieut. 1st Inf., 1 July, 1829. Resigned 31 Oct., 1831. Col. 16th N. Y. Vols., 15 May, 1861. Brig. Gen. Vols., 7 March, 1862. Bvt. Maj. Gen. Vols., 11 July, 1865, for gallant and meritorious service. Mustered out 24 Aug., 1865.

DAVIES, WM. F. [Born in Ireland. Appointed from N. Y.] 2nd Lieut. 62nd N. Y. Vols., 30 June, 1861. 1st Lieut., 31 May, 1862. Capt. 2 Nov., 1863. Mustered out 1 Feb., 1865. 2nd Lieut. 18th Inf., 11 May, 1866. Trans. to 36th Inf., 21 Sept., 1866. Dismissed 16 Aug., 1867.

DAVIES, WM. S.* [Born in N. Y. Appointed from Cal.] 2nd Lieut. 13th Inf., 17 June, 1874. 1st Lieut., 16 Aug., 1884. Died 4 Feb., 1888.

DAVIESS, CAMILLUS C.* [Born in Ky. Appointed from Ky.] Bvt. 2nd Lieut. 5th Inf., 1 July, 1830. 2nd Lieut., 1 July, 1830. 1st Lieut., 31 Dec., 1836. Resigned 30 Sept., 1838. Died in 1842.

DAVIS, ALEXANDER M.* [Born in R. I. Appointed from D. C.] 2nd Lieut. 8th Cav., 11 June, 1892. 1st Lieut. 4th Cav., 20 Jan., 1899.

DAVIS, BENJN. F.* [Born in Ala. Appointed from Miss.] Bvt. 2nd Lieut. 5th Inf., 1 July, 1854. 2nd Lieut. 1st Drag., 3 March, 1855. 1st Lieut., 9 Jan., 1860. Capt., 30 July, 1861. Trans. to 1st Cav., 3 Aug., 1861. Lieut. Col. 1st Cal. Cav., 19 Aug., 1861. Resigned from Vols., 1 Nov., 1861. Col. 8th N. Y. Cav., 25 June, 1862. Killed 9 June, 1863, in the Battle at Beverly Ford, Va. Bvt. Maj., 15 Sept., 1862, for meritorious service in the withdrawal of the Cavalry force from Harper's Ferry at the surrender of that place.

DAVIS, BRITTON.* [Born in Tex. Appointed from Tex.] Addl. 2nd Lieut. 5th Cav., 11 June, 1881. Resigned 1 June, 1886.

DAVIS, CHAS. E. L. B.* [Born in Conn. Appointed from Conn.] 2nd Lieut. Eng., 18 June, 1866. 1st Lieut., 7 March, 1867. Capt., 12 Sept., 1877. Maj., 7 April, 1888.

DAVIS, CHARLES L. [Born in Pa. Appointed from Del.] Priv. Commonwealth Art. Pa. Vols., 24 April, 1861. Discharged 5 Aug., 1861. 2nd Lieut. 31st Pa. Vols., 20 Aug., 1861. 1st Lieut., 1 Sept., 1861. Capt., 4 Feb., 1863. Trans. to 82nd Pa. Vols., 1 Sept., 1861. Mustered out 19 June, 1863. Capt. Sig. Corps, 3 March, 1863. Bvt. Maj. Vols., 9 April, 1865, for gallant and meritorious service during the recent operations resulting in the fall of Richmond, Va., and the surrender of the insurgent army under Gen. R. E. Lee. Mustered out 18 Aug., 1865. 2nd Lieut. and 1st Lieut. 10th Inf., 23 Feb., 1866. Bvt. Capt., 2 March, 1867, for gallant and meritorious service in the campaign from the Rapidan to the James. Bvt. Maj., 2 March, 1867, for gallant and meritorious service in the Siege of Petersburg, Va. Capt. 10th Inf., 20 March, 1879. Maj. 6th Inf., 26 April, 1898. Trans. to 11th Inf., 4 Oct., 1898. Lieut. Col. 6th Inf., 15 Dec., 1899.

DAVIS, EDWARD.* [Born in Ky. Appointed from Ky.] 2nd Lieut. 5th Ky. Cav., 20 Sept., 1862. Resigned 2 Nov., 1863. Cadet at Mil. Acad., 20 Oct., 1863. 2nd Lieut. 3rd Art., 17 June, 1867. Bvt. 1st Lieut., 17 June, 1867, for gallant and meritorious service in the Battle of Chickamauga, Ga. 1st Lieut. 3rd Art., 14 April, 1873. R. Q. M., 1 May, 1880, to 22 April, 1884. Capt., 1 Sept., 1896. Graduate of the Artillery School, 1876. Maj. and A. A. G. Vols., 12 May, 1898, to 15 April, 1899. R. Q. M., 7 June, 1899.

DAVIS, ELIJAH. [Born in Pa. Appointed from Pa.]
2nd Lieut. 1st Inf., 3 Feb., 1819. 1st Lieut., 3 Oct., 1820. Died 18 Nov., 1822.

DAVIS, GEORGE B.* [Born in Mass. Appointed from Mass.]
Q. M. Sergt. Co. I and Q. M. Sergt. 1st Mass. Cav., 10 Sept., 1863. 2nd Lieut. 1st Mass. Cav., 17 June, 1865. Mustered out 26 June, 1865. Cadet at Mil. Acad., 1 July, 1867. 2nd Lieut. 5th Cav., 12 June, 1871. 1st Lieut., 9 May, 1877. Capt., 21 Aug., 1888. Maj. and J. A., 10 Dec., 1888. Lieut. Col. and Dep. J. A. G., 3 Aug., 1895. Professor of Law at Mil. Acad., 20 Aug., 1895.

DAVIS, GEORGE B.* [Born in N. Y. Appointed from N. Y.]
2nd Lieut. 23rd Inf., 1 July, 1886. 1st Lieut. 5th Inf., 7 March, 1893. Trans. to 4th Inf., 10 July, 1893. Capt. and C. S., 29 Jan., 1897. Graduate of the Infantry and Cavalry School, 1891. Col. and C. S. Vols., 22 July, 1898, to 2 March, 1899. Maj. and C. S. Vols., 17 April, 1899.

DAVIS, GEORGE W. [Born in Conn. Appointed from Conn.]
Q. M. Sergt. 11th Conn. Vols., 27 Nov., 1861. Discharged 3 April, 1862. 1st Lieut. 11th Conn. Vols., 5 April, 1862. Bvt. Maj. Vols., 13 March, 1865, for faithful and meritorious service during the war. Capt. A. Q. M. Vols., 22 May, 1865. Maj. Q. M. (Act. 4 July, 1864), 31 May, 1865, to 5 Feb., 1866. Mustered out 20 April, 1866. Capt. 14th Inf., 22 Jan., 1867. Lieut. Col. and A. de C. to Lieut. Gen. Sheridan, 15 April to 10 Oct., 1885. Maj. 11th Inf., 16 Aug., 1894. Trans. to 9th Inf., 29 May, 1897. Lieut. Col. 14th Inf., 26 April, 1898. Col. 23rd Inf., 19 Oct., 1899. Brig. Gen. Vols., 4 May, 1898, to 14 April, 1899, and from that date to ——.

DAVIS, GLENN H.* [Born in Ohio. Appointed from Ohio.]
2nd Lieut. 12th Inf., 12 June, 1895. 1st Lieut., 3 July, 1898.

DAVIS, HENRY C.* [Born in S. C. Appointed from S. C.]
2nd Lieut. 3rd Art., 13 June, 1883. 1st Lieut. 10 Feb., 1891. Trans. to 7th Art., 8 March, 1898. Capt., 15 March, 1899. Graduate of the Artillery School, 1892. Maj. 3rd Vol. Eng., 22 June, 1898, until mustered out, 17 May, 1899.

DAVIS, HENRY T. [Born in Mass. Appointed from Mass.]
2nd Lieut. 1st Mass. Cav., 31 Oct., 1861. 1st Lieut., 1 May, 1862. Bvt. Capt. Vols., 13 March, 1865, for gallant and meritorious service. Resigned 9 April, 1864. Capt. 10th Cav., 28 July, 1866. Died 10 April, 1869. Bvt. Maj., 2 March, 1867, for gallant and meritorious service at the Battle of Chancellorsville, Va.

DAVIS, JACKMAN J.* [Born in N. H. Appointed from N. H.]
2nd Lieut. Corps Art., 21 July, 1814. 1st Lieut., 20 April, 1818. Trans. to 1st Art., 16 Aug., 1821. A. Q. M., 19 May, 1826, to 20 Feb., 1828. Died 20 Feb., 1828.

DAVIS, JAMES. [Born in S. C. Appointed from S. C.]
Maj. and Surg., 4 Jan., 1847. Resigned 28 June, 1847.

DAVIS, JAMES L.* [Born in Va. Appointed from Va.]
Bvt. 2nd Lieut., 4th Art., 1 July, 1833. 2nd Lieut., 10 April, 1835. Resigned 11 Sept., 1836. Died 11 May, 1871.

DAVIS, JEFFERSON.* [Born in Ky. Appointed from Miss.]
Bvt. 2nd Lieut. 1st Inf., 1 July, 1828. 2nd Lieut., 1 July, 1828. 1st Lieut. 1st Drag., 4 March, 1833. Reg. Adj., 30 Aug., 1833, to 5 Feb., 1834. Resigned 30 June, 1935. Col. 1st Miss. Rifles, 18 July, 1846. Mustered out 12 July, 1847. Secretary of War, 7 March, 1853, to 6 March, 1857.

DAVIS, JEFFERSON C. [Born in Ind. Appointed from Ind.]
Corpl. and Sergt. Co. I. 3rd Ind. Vols., 22 June, 1846, to 27 June, 1847. 2nd Lieut. 1st Art., 17 June, 1848. 1st Lieut., 29 Feb., 1852. Capt., 14 May, 1861. Col. 22nd Ind. Vols., 1 Aug., 1861. Brig. Gen. Vols., 18 Dec., 1861. Bvt. Maj., 9 March, 1862, for gallant and meritorious service in the Battle of Pea Ridge, Ark. Bvt. Lieut. Col., 15 May, 1864, for gallant and meritorious service in the Battle of Resaca, Ga. Bvt. Col., 20 May, 1864, for gallant and meritorious service in the capture of Rome, Ga. Bvt. Maj. Gen. Vols., 8 Aug., 1864. Bvt. Brig. Gen., 13 March, 1865, for gallant and meritorious service in the Battle of Kenesaw Mountain, Ga. Bvt. Maj. Gen., 13 March, 1865, for gallant and meritorious service in the Battle of Jonesboro', Ga. Col. 23rd Inf., 28 July, 1866. Mustered out of Vol. service, 1 Sept., 1866. Died 30 Nov., 1879.

DAVIS, JOHN M. [Born in Pa. Appointed from Pa.]
Ensign 2nd Inf., 27 Feb., 1807. 2nd Lieut., 3 May, 1808. 1st Lieut., 1 Jan., 1810. Reg. P. M., March, 1812, to May, 1813. Capt., 30 May, 1813, to 15 June, 1815. Maj. A. I. G., 1 Oct., 1814. Bvt. Maj., 23 Dec., 1814, for gallant conduct at the Siege of New Orleans, La. Discharged 15 June, 1815. Reinstated 3 May, 1816, as Maj. A. I. G. Discharged 1 June, 1821.

DAVIS, JOHN M. K.* [Born in D. C. Appointed from Ark.]
2nd Lieut. 1st Art., 17 June, 1867. 1st Lieut., 23 Dec., 1871. Reg. Adj., 17 Aug., 1877, to 15 April, 1887. Capt. 14 Jan., 1888. Maj. 5th Art., 16 Oct., 1899. Trans. to 1st Art., 28 Oct., 1899. Honor graduate of the Artillery School, 1869. Maj. and I. G. Vols., 12 May, 1898, to 7 March, 1899.

DAVIS, JOHN P.* [Born in Me. Appointed from Me.]
Bvt. 2nd Lieut. 7th Inf., 1 July, 1829. 2nd Lieut., 1 July, 1829. 1st Lieut., 31 Dec., 1834. Capt., 7 July, 1838. Capt. A. Q. M., 7 July, 1838. Dismissed 18 April, 1845.

DAVIS, JOSEPH D., Jr. [Born in Pa. Appointed from Pa.]
2nd Lieut. 11th Inf., 29 March, 1848. Disbanded 15 Aug., 1848. 1st Lieut. 177th Pa. Vols., 3 Dec., 1862, to 5 Aug., 1863. 1st Lieut. 103rd Pa. Vols., 12 April, 1865. Mustered out 25 June, 1865.

DAVIS, MATTHEW L.* [Born in N. C. Appointed from N. C.]
Bvt. 2nd Lieut. 3rd Inf., 1 July, 1852. 2nd Lieut., 1 July, 1852. 1st Lieut., 14 Jan., 1858. Resigned 13 May, 1861.

DAVIS, MILTON F.* [Born in Minn. Appointed from Ore.]
2nd Lieut. 4th Cav., 12 June, 1890. 1st Lieut. 2nd Cav., 14 Jan., 1897. Trans. to 1st Cav., 10 March, 1897.

DAVIS, MURRAY. [Born in Ohio. Appointed from Ohio.]
Priv. Co. H, 95th Ohio Vols., 19 Aug., 1862. 2nd Lieut., 31 Dec., 1862. 1st Lieut. Adj., 9 Nov., 1863. Capt. A. A. G. Vols., 17 Aug., 1864. Maj. A. A. G. Vols., 15

Feb., 1865. Bvt. Lieut. Col. and Col. Vols., 13 March, 1865, for faithful and meritorious service during the war. Mustered out 1 Oct., 1866. 2nd Lieut. 1st Cav., 17 March, 1866. Capt. 8th Cav., 28 July, 1866. Resigned 23 May, 1870. Bvt. Maj. 2 March, 1867, for gallant and meritorious service in the Battle of Guntown, Miss.

DAVIS, NELSON H.* [Born in Mass. Appointed from Mass.]
Bvt. 2nd Lieut. 3rd Inf., 1 July, 1846. 2nd Lieut. 2nd Inf., 16 Feb., 1847. Bvt. 1st Lieut., 20 Aug., 1847, for gallant and meritorious conduct in the Battles of Contreras and Churubusco. 1st Lieut. 2nd Inf., 8 June, 1849. Capt., 3 March, 1855. Col. 7th Mass. Vols., 4 Sept., 1861. Resigned Vol. commission, 12 Nov., 1861. Maj. A. I. G., 12 Nov., 1861. Bvt. Lieut. Col., 3 July, 1863, for gallant and meritorious service in the Battle of Gettysburg, Pa. Bvt. Col., 29 May, 1864, for gallant and meritorious service in action with Apache Indians in Arizona. Bvt. Brig. Gen., 13 March, 1865, for meritorious and efficient service during the war. Lieut. Col. A. I. G., 13 June, 1867. Col. I. G., 25 June, 1872, to rank from 23 March, 1864. Brig. Gen. I. G., 11 March, 1885. Retired 20 Sept., 1885. Died 15 May, 1890.

DAVIS, NICHOLAS, Jr. [Born in Ala. Appointed from Ala.]
2nd Lieut. of Inf., 8 March, 1847; 13th Inf., 9 April, 1847. 1st Lieut., 28 May, 1847. Resigned 31 March, 1848.

DAVIS, ORRIN E. [Born in Ohio. Appointed from Army.]
2nd Lieut. 17th Ohio Vols., 5 June, 1861, to 15 Aug., 1861. Priv. and Sergt. Co. H, 2nd Batt. 18th Inf., 17 March, 1862, to 27 March, 1863. 2nd Lieut. 18th Inf., 19 Feb., 1863. 1st Lieut., 24 Jan., 1864. Resigned 12 Oct., 1864.

DAVIS, PHILIP C. [Born in Va. Appointed from D. C.]
Asst. Surg., 28 May, 1861. Maj. Surg., 17 Oct., 1868. Died 2 Oct., 1871. Bvt. Capt. and Bvt. Maj., 13 March, 1865, for faithful and meritorious service during the war.

DAVIS, RICHARD D. [Born in ——. Appointed from Ohio.]
2nd Lieut. 7th Inf., 18 April, 1818. 1st Lieut., 15 Sept., 1820. Disbanded 1 June, 1821.

DAVIS, RICHMOND P.* [Born in N. C. Appointed from N. C.]
2nd Lieut. 2nd Art., 12 June, 1887. 1st Lieut., 23 March, 1893.

DAVIS, ROBERT. [Born in ——. Appointed from Miss.]
Ensign 2nd Inf., 26 March, 1814. 3rd Lieut., 1 May, 1814. 2nd Lieut., 30 June, 1814. Trans. to 3rd Inf., 17 May, 1815. Trans. to 1st Inf., 2 Dec., 1815. Resigned 6 March, 1816.

DAVIS, ROBERT. [Born in Mass. Appointed from Army.]
Priv. 1st Mass. Vols., 31 Jan., 1848. Discharged 15 July, 1848. Priv. Co. I, 2nd Inf., 11 June, 1858. Corpl., 1 Sept., 1859. Sergt., 1 June, 1861. 2nd Lieut. 2nd Inf., 18 July, 1862. 1st Lieut., 20 Oct., 1863. Bvt. Capt., 1 Aug., 1864, for gallant service in the Battle of Spottsylvania and during the campaign before Richmond, Va. Retired with rank of Capt., 28 July, 1866. Reduced to 1st Lieut., 3 March, 1875. Died 29 Dec., 1889.

DAVIS, ROBERT C.* [Born in Pa. Appointed from Pa.]
2nd Lieut. 17th Inf., 26 April, 1898. 1st Lieut., 2 March, 1899.

DAVIS, ROBT. H. [Born in Miss. Appointed from Miss.]
1st Lieut. 9th Inf., 3 March, 1855. Resigned 1 Aug., 1857.

DAVIS, SAML. B. [Born in La. Appointed from La.]
Cadet at Mil. Acad., 1 July, 1844, to 7 Jan., 1845. 2nd Lieut. of Inf., 5 March, 1847; 14th Inf., 9 April, 1847. 1st Lieut., 3 Dec., 1847. Reg. Adj., 1 Nov., 1847, to 29 July, 1848. Disbanded 29 July, 1848. Bvt. 1st Lieut., 20 Aug., 1847, for gallant and meritorious conduct at Contreras and Churubusco, Mex.

DAVIS, THOS. [Born in Va. Appointed from Ill.]
2nd Lieut. Mtd. Rifles, 27 May, 1846. Killed at the Battle of Cerro Gordo, Mex., 18 April, 1847.

DAVIS, THOS. [Born in Pa. Appointed from Army.]
Priv. and 1st Sergt. Co. C, 19th Inf., 21 Sept., 1861, to 12 Nov., 1863. 2nd Lieut. 19th Inf., 31 Oct., 1863. 1st Lieut., 1 April, 1864. Resigned 12 Oct., 1864.

DAVIS, THOS. F.* [Born in N. Y. Appointed from N. Y.]
2nd Lieut. 15th Inf., 16 June, 1875. 1st Lieut., 5 March, 1879. Reg. Adj., 3 Nov., 1879, to 1 Nov., 1880. R. Q. M., 31 March, 1887, to 31 March, 1890. Capt. 25 April, 1892.

DAVIS, THOS. O. [Born in Me. Appointed from D. C.]
2nd Lieut. 6th Inf., 30 Dec., 1847. Dismissed 15 May, 1851.

DAVIS, WIRT. [Born in Va. Appointed from Army.]
Priv. Co. K, 1st Cav., 12 May, 1860. Corpl., 12 March, 1862. Sergt. Co. L, 4th Cav., 1 Nov., 1862. 2nd Lieut. 4th Cav., 22 April, 1863. Bvt. 1st Lieut., 19 Sept., 1863, for gallant and meritorious service in the Battle of Chickamauga, Ga. Bvt. Capt., 20 Feb., 1864, for gallant and meritorious service during the Cav. expedition in Mississippi. Bvt. Maj., 2 April, 1865, for gallant and meritorious service in the capture of Selma, Ala. 1st Lieut. 4th Cav., 2 April, 1865. Reg. Adj., 1 March, 1865, to 19 June, 1868. Capt., 19 June, 1868. Maj. 5th Cav., 15 April, 1890. Bvt. Lieut. Col., 27 Feb., 1890, for gallant services in action against Indians, on the North Fork of Red River, Tex., 29 Sept., 1872, and in action against Indians in the Big Horn Mountains, Mont., 25 Nov., 1876. Lieut. Col. 8th Cav., 5 July, 1898. Col. 3rd Cav., 10 Jan., 1900.

DAVIS, WM., Jr. [Born in Ind. Appointed from Ind.]
1st Lieut. 1st Mo. Cav., 7 June, 1862. Mustered out 1 Sept., 1865. 2nd Lieut. 10th Cav., 17 Aug., 1867. 1st Lieut., 3 March, 1873. R. Q. M., 1 Sept., 1878, to 30 Sept., 1881. Capt., 10 May, 1888. Retired, over 30 years' service, 6 Nov., 1897.

DAVIS, WM. B. [Born in Va. Appointed from Va.]
1st Lieut. Asst. Surg., 9 Jan., 1877. Capt. Asst. Surg., 9 Jan., 1882. Maj. Surg., 11 Aug., 1896.

DAVIS, WILLIAM C.* [Born in N. Y. Appointed from N. Y.]
Addl. 2nd Lieut. 5th Art., 12 June, 1890. 2nd Lieut. 3rd Art., 22 May, 1891. Trans. to 5th Art., 12 Aug., 1891. 1st Lieut. 6th Art., 8 March, 1898. Graduate of the Artillery School, 1896.

**DAVIS, WILLIAM D.*** [Born in Mich. Appointed from Mo.]
2nd Lieut. 17th Inf., 11 June, 1892. 1st Lieut., 26 Apr., 1898.

**DAVISON, JAMES.** [Born in England. Appointed from Army.]
Priv. Co. B, 3rd Art., 22 March, 1854. Corpl., 1 March, 1856. Sergt., 16 Oct., 1856. 1st Sergt., 15 Sept., 1857. Discharged 22 Feb., 1859. 1st Sergt. Co. B, 3rd Art., 22 Feb., 1859. Q. M. Sergt., 1 Sept., 1861. Bvt. 2nd Lieut. 3rd Art. and 2nd Lieut. 5th Art., 22 Oct., 1862. Bvt. 1st Lieut., 13 Dec., 1862, for gallant and meritorious service in the Battle of Fredericksburg, Va. Bvt. Capt., 2 July, 1863, for gallant and meritorious service in the Battle of Gettysburg, Pa. Retired 13 Jan., 1864. Retired with rank of 2nd Lieut. Mtd., 28 July, 1866. Reduced to 2nd Lieut., 3 March, 1875.

**DAVISON, LORENZO P.*** [Born in Wis. Appointed from Iowa.]
2nd Lieut. 7th Cav., 28 Aug., 1885. Trans. to 11th Inf., 12 March, 1886. 1st Lieut., 28 July, 1890. Capt. 5th Inf., 26 April, 1898. Maj. Puerto Rico Batt., 5 June, 1899, to 1 Dec., 1899.

**DAVISON, PETER W.*** [Born in Wis. Appointed from Wis.]
2nd Lieut. 22nd Inf., 11 June, 1892. 1st Lieut., 26 April, 1898.

**DAWES, WM. J.** [Born in Ohio. Appointed from Wis.]
Capt. 8th Wis. Vols., 25 Sept., 1861. Mustered out 31 March, 1864. Capt. Vet. Res. Corps, 25 March, 1864. Bvt. Maj. Vols., 13 March, 1865, for gallant and meritorious service. Mustered out 16 Jan., 1867. 2nd Lieut. 43rd Inf., 28 July, 1866. Bvt. 1st Lieut., 2 March, 1867, for gallant and meritorious service in the Battle of Corinth, Miss. (declined). 1st Lieut. 43rd Inf., 20 July, 1867. Unassigned 8 April, 1869. Retired with rank of Capt., 15 Dec., 1870. Died 19 Aug., 1887.

**DAWSON, BYRON.** [Born in Ind. Appointed from Ind.]
1st Sergt. Co. L, 3rd Ind. Cav., 5 Sept., 1862. 2nd Lieut. 3rd Ind. Cav., 1 Sept., 1864. Trans. to 8th Ind. Cav., 1 April, 1865. Capt. 8th Ind. Cav., 4 May, 1865. Mustered out 20 July, 1865. 2nd Lieut. 9th Cav., 28 July, 1866. 1st Lieut., 31 July, 1867. Capt., 4 April, 1879. Retired for disability in line of duty, 15 June, 1888. Bvt. Capt., 27 Feb., 1890, for gallant services in the actions against Indians on the River Pecos, Tex., 7 June, 1869, and on the Brazos River, Tex., 28 and 29 Oct., 1869.

**DAWSON, JAMES L.** [Born in Md. Appointed from Md.]
3rd Lieut. Ord., 13 Aug., 1819. Retained as 2nd Lieut. 7th Inf., 1 June, 1821. Reg. Adj., 1 Dec., 1821, to 16 May, 1825. 1st Lieut., 1 May, 1824. Capt., 30 April, 1833. Resigned 31 Dec., 1835.

**DAWSON, SAML. K.*** [Born in Pa. Appointed from Pa.]
2nd Lieut. 1st Art., 1 July, 1839. 1st Lieut., 18 June, 1846. R. Q. M., 30 April, 1847, to 1 Dec., 1848. Bvt. Capt., 18 April, 1847, for gallant and meritorious conduct in the Battle of Cerro Gordo. Capt. 1st Art., 31 March, 1853. Maj. 19th Inf., 14 May, 1861. Lieut. Col. 15th Inf., 4 July, 1863. Bvt. Col., 20 Sept., 1863, for gallant and meritorious service in the Battle of Chickamauga, Ga. Bvt. Brig. Gen., 13 March, 1865, for faithful and meritorious service during the war. Col. 19th Inf., 28 July, 1866. Unassigned 15 March, 1869. Retired 11 May, 1870. Died 17 April, 1889.

**DAY, CLARENCE R.*** [Born in Va. Appointed from Ky.]
Addl. 2nd Lieut. 7th Cav., 11 June, 1897. 2nd Lieut. 10th Cav., 27 May, 1898. Trans. to 7th Cav., 17 Aug., 1898.

**DAY, FREDERICK R.** [Born in N. Y. Appointed from the Army.]
Priv. and Sergt. Sig. Corps., 6 Aug., 1880, to 24 July, 1884. 2nd Lieut. Sig. Corps, 15 July. 2nd Lieut. 22nd Inf., 4 Feb., 1891 (to rank from 15 July, 1884). 1st Lieut. 9th Inf., 15 June, 1891. Trans. to 20th Inf., 20 July, 1891. Capt. of Inf., 1 Nov., 1898. Ass'd to 3rd Inf., 1 Jan., 1899.

**DAY, EDWARD H.*** [Born in Va. Appointed from Tenn.]
Bvt. 2nd Lieut. 2nd Art., 1 July, 1851. 2nd Lieut. 3rd Art., 30 June, 1852. 1st Lieut., 3 March, 1855. Died 2 Jan., 1860.

**DAY, HANNIBAL.*** [Born in Vt. Appointed from Vt.]
2nd Lieut. 2nd Inf., 1 July, 1823. 1st Lieut., 4 April, 1832. Capt., 7 July, 1838. Maj., 23 Feb., 1852. Lieut. Col., 25 Feb., 1861. Col. 6th Inf., 7 June, 1862. Retired 1 Aug., 1863. Bvt. Brig. Gen., 13 March, 1865, for long and faithful service in the army. Died 26 March, 1891.

**DAY, MATTHIAS W.*** [Born in Ohio. Appointed from Ohio.]
Addl. 2nd Lieut. 10th Cav., 15 June, 1877. 2nd Lieut. 9th Cav., 1 March, 1878. 1st Lieut., 31 Aug., 1883. R. Q. M., 1 March, 1889. Bvt. Capt., 27 Feb., 1890, for gallant services in action against Indians during the attack on Geronimo's stronghold in the Sierra Madre Mountains, Mexico, 7 Aug., 1885, and in the Terres Mountains, Mexico, 22 Sept., 1885. Capt., 21 April, 1891. Lieut. Col. 1st Ohio Cav., 9 May, 1898, to 22 Oct., 1898. Medal of Honor for bravery in action against hostile Apache Indians at Las Animas Canon, N. Mex., September 18, 1879, in singly advancing into the enemy's line and carrying a wounded soldier of his command on his back down a rocky trail, under a hot fire, after he had been ordered to retreat, while serving as 2nd Lieut., 9th Cav.

**DAY, RUSSELL H.** [Born in N. Y. Appointed from N. Y.]
2nd Lieut. 16th N. Y. Art., 19 Jan., 1864. 1st Lieut., 1 July, 1865. Mustered out 21 Aug., 1865. 2nd Lieut. 6th Inf., 30 May, 1866. 1st Lieut., 25 Feb., 1867. Died 18 Oct., 1882.

**DAY, SELDEN A.** [Born in Ohio. Appointed from Army.]
Priv. Co. C, 7th Ohio Vols., 20 June, 1861. Corpl., 20 Nov., 1861. Sergt., 24 March, 1862. Discharged 4 Feb., 1863. Hosp. Steward U. S. A., 4 Feb., 1863. 2nd Lieut. 5th Art., 7 April, 1864. Bvt. 1st Lieut., 3 June, 1864, for gallant and meritorious service in the Battle of Cold Harbor, Va. Bvt. Capt., 13 March, 1865, for gallant and meritorious service during the war. 1st Lieut. 5th Art., 28 July, 1866. Capt., 18 July, 1886. Trans. to 1st Art., 7 May, 1898. Maj. 5th Art., 14 May, 1898. Graduate of the Artillery School in 1874.

**DAY, SYLVESTER.** [Born in Vt. Appointed from Vt.]
Garrison Surg. Mate, 9 Dec., 1807. Maj. and Surg. 4th Inf., 13 March, 1813. Trans. to 5th Inf., 17 May, 1815. Post Surg., 18 April, 1818. Asst. Surg., 1 June, 1821. Died 20 Feb., 1851.

DAY, WM. [Born in N. Y. Appointed from N. Y.]
2nd Lieut. 1st Inf., 27 Oct., 1820. 1st Lieut., 25 Dec., 1823. Capt., 26 Oct., 1832. Died 4 Aug., 1840.

DAYTON, LEWIS M. [Born in N. Y. Appointed from N. Y.]
Capt. A. de C. Vols., 11 March, 1863. Maj. A. A. G. Vols., 12 Jan., 1865. Bvt. Lieut. Col. Vols., 13 March, 1865, for meritorious service in the campaign of Atlanta and Savannah, and in the Carolinas. Mustered out 1 Sept., 1866. 2nd Lieut. 2nd Inf., 24 July, 1866. Capt. 7th Cav., 6 March, 1867. Lieut. Col. Mil. Sec. to Lieut. Gen. Sherman, 11 Aug., 1866, to 8 March, 1869. Col. A. de C. to Gen. Sherman, 8 March, 1869, to 31 Dec., 1870. Discharged 31 Dec., 1870. Bvt. 1st Lieut., Capt. and Maj., 2 March, 1867, for gallant and meritorious service in the Atlanta campaign. Bvt. Lieut. Col., 2 March, 1867, for gallant and meritorious service in the campaign through the Carolinas.

DEAKYNE, HERBERT.* [Born in Del. Appointed from Del.]
Addl. 2nd Lieut. Eng., 12 June, 1890. 2nd Lieut., 11 Oct., 1892. 1st Lieut., 2 Oct., 1895. Capt., 2 April, 1900.

DEAN, ALEX. T. [Born in N. J. Appointed from Pa.]
2nd Lieut. 25th Inf., 26 Nov., 1880. Trans. to 4th Cav., 13 Feb., 1882. 1st Lieut., 11 Feb., 1887. Resigned 30 April, 1898.

DEAN, ELMER A. [Born in Tenn. Appointed from Tenn.]
Asst. Surg., 12 Dec., 1898.

DEAN, JAMES. [Born in N. H. Appointed from Vt.]
Ensign 4th Inf., 19 July, 1813. 3rd Lieut., 15 Aug., 1813. 2nd Lieut., 28 June, 1814. Disbanded 15 June, 1815. Reinstated 1 Jan., 1816, in 3rd Inf. 1st Lieut., 31 Oct., 1818. Reg. Adj., Aug., 1817, to 19 Dec., 1826. Capt., 4 Oct., 1827. Resigned 15 Nov., 1836.

DEAN, JAMES T.* [Born in Ohio. Appointed from Ohio.]
2nd Lieut. 3rd Inf., 12 June, 1887. 1st Lieut. 14th Inf., 14 Aug., 1894. Capt. 10th Inf., 2 March, 1899. Maj. Chf. Ord. Vols., 18 July, 1898, to 12 May, 1899.

DEAN, WARREN. [Born in Wis. Appointed from N. Y.]
Priv., Corpl. and Sergt. Troop C, 1st Ill. Cav., 26 April, 1898, to 21 Oct., 1898. 2nd Lieut. 11th Inf., 9 Sept., 1898. Trans. to 6th Cav., 7 Jan., 1899.

DEAN, WM. [Born in Pa. Appointed from Army.]
2nd Lieut. 1st Cav., 17 July, 1862. 1st Lieut., 9 June, 1863. Priv., Corpl. and Sergt. Cos. B and I, 1st Drag., 6 June, 1854, to 16 Jan., 1862. Ord. Sergt., 16 Jan. to 20 Sept., 1862. R. Q. M., 18 Oct., 1863, to 2 Feb., 1865. Capt., 6 Feb., 1865. Retired 11 April, 1867. Died 27 Aug., 1870. Bvt. Capt., 11 June, 1864, for gallant and meritorious service at the Battle of Trevillian Station, Va. Bvt. Maj., 1 April, 1865, for gallant and meritorious service at the Battle of Five Forks, Va.

DEANE, THOS. M. [Born in N. Y. Appointed from N. Y.]
Mil. Storekeeper Ord. Dept., 7 April, 1864. Capt., 28 July, 1866. Died 21 Jan., 1877.

DEANE, WM. W. [Born in Me. Appointed from Me.]
1st Lieut. 12th Me. Vols., 15 Nov., 1861. Reg. Adj., 31 July, 1862. Capt. A. A. G. Vols., 29 Feb., 1864. Bvt. Maj. and Lieut. Col. Vols., 4 June, 1866, for faithful and meritorious services. Mustered out 1 Nov., 1866. 2nd Lieut. 12th Inf., 28 July, 1866. Unassigned 27 March, 1869. Died 22 July, 1870. Bvt. 1st Lieut., 2 March, 1867, for gallant and meritorious service in the Siege of Port Hudson, La. Bvt. Capt., 2 March, 1867, for faithful and meritorious service during the war.

DEANEY, JAMES A. [Born in Pa. Appointed from Pa.]
2nd Lieut. 1st Pa. Vols., 16 Dec., 1846. 2nd Lieut. 8th Inf., 29 March, 1848. Died 24 Dec., 1848.

DEARBORN, ALEXANDER H.* [Born in N. Y. Appointed from N. Y.]
2nd Lieut. 2nd Art., 1 July, 1838. 2nd Lieut. Ord., 9 July, 1838. 1st Lieut., 3 March, 1847. Died 26 Feb., 1853.

DEARBORN, GREENLEAF. [Born in Mass. Appointed from Mass.]
2nd Lieut. 3rd Art., 12 March, 1812. 1st Lieut., 1 Oct., 1813. Trans. to Corps Art., 12 May, 1814. Capt., 30 Sept., 1819. Trans. to 2nd Inf., 1 June, 1821. Maj. 1st Inf., 27 Nov., 1839. Lieut. Col. 7th Inf., 26 Nov., 1845. Died 9 Sept., 1846. Bvt. Maj., 30 Sept., 1829, for 10 years' faithful service in one grade.

DEARING, HENRY P. [Born in N. C. Appointed from N. C.]
M. S. K., 28 March, 1813. Discharged 1 June, 1821.

DEARING, JAMES H. [Born in N. C. Appointed from N. C.]
1st Lieut. 2nd Art., 15 May, 1812. Trans. to Corps. Art., 12 May, 1814. Resigned 1 April, 1816.

DEARING, ST. CLAIR. [Born in Ga. Appointed from Ga.]
2nd Lieut. 4th Inf., 7 June, 1855. Trans. to 2nd Art., 17 March, 1858. Resigned 7 Feb., 1861.

DEARY, THOS. V. [Born in Ohio. Appointed from Ohio.]
2nd Lieut. 1st Art., 14 Sept., 1867. Discharged 1 Nov., 1870.

DEAS, EDWARD.* [Born in S. C. Appointed from S. C.]
Bvt. 2nd Lieut. 4th Art., 1 July, 1832. 2nd Lieut., 31 Oct., 1833. 1st Lieut., 24 Oct., 1836. Capt., 16 Feb., 1847. Dismissed 11 April, 1848. Restored 15 June, 1848. Drowned 16 May, 1849.

DEAS, GEORGE. [Born in Pa. Appointed from Pa.]
2nd Lieut. 5th Inf., 1 Aug., 1838. 1st Lieut., 17 Nov., 1845. Reg. Adj., 13 April, 1841, to 1 Feb., 1847. Capt., 9 Dec., 1847. Bvt. Capt. A. A. G., 29 Dec., 1846. Bvt. Maj. A. A. G., 13 Dec., 1855 Resigned 25 Feb., 1861. Bvt. Maj., 20 Aug., 1847, for gallant and meritorious conduct at Contreras and Churubusco, Mex.

DE BEAUMONT, ADRIAN V. L. R. [Born in La. Appointed from Army.]
Priv. Co. E, 21st Inf., and Priv. and Sergt. Sig. Corps from 1 April, 1896, to 31 March, 1899. Priv. Co. C, 7th Inf., 30 June to 16 Nov., 1899. 2nd Lieut. 8th Inf., 1 Oct., 1899.

DE CAMP, SAML. G. I. [Born in N. J. Appointed from N. J.]
Ast. Surg., 10 Oct., 1823. Maj. Surg., 1 Dec., 1833. Retired 27 Aug., 1862. Died 8 Sept., 1871.

DECKER, JOHN P. [Born in Ohio. Appointed from Army.]
Priv. 15th Inf., 14 Sept., 1861, to 8 July, 1862. 2nd Lieut. 15th Inf., 11 June, 1862. Resigned 7 Feb., 1863.

DECKER, THEODORE. [Born in Germany. Appointed from Army.]
Priv., Corpl., Sergt. and 1st Sergt. Battery F 4th Art., 20 Feb., 1875, to 20 Aug., 1879. 2nd Lieut. 24th Inf., 9 Aug., 1879. Dismissed 4 Sept., 1880.

DE COURCY, FERDINAND E. [Born in Ireland. Appointed from Army.]
Priv. Co. K, 2nd Inf., 22 Dec., 1857. Corpl., 14 June, 1859. Sergt., 1 Nov., 1859. 2nd Lieut. 13th Inf., 14 May, 1861. 1st Lieut., 24 Oct., 1861. Reg. Adj., 1 Oct., 1862, to 12 Nov., 1864. Capt., 21 Nov., 1865. Retired with rank of Maj. for disability in line of duty, 24 Feb., 1891.

DEEMS, CLARENCE.* [Born in Va. Appointed from Md.]
2nd Lieut. 4th Art., 17 June, 1874. 1st Lieut., 14 Sept., 1883. Capt. 6th Art., 8 March, 1898. Graduate of the Artillery School, 1878, 1892.

DE FOREST, WM. H.* [Born in N. Y. Appointed from N. Y.]
Bvt. 2nd Lieut. 6th Inf., 1 July, 1835. 2nd Lieut., 18 April, 1836. Resigned 30 Sept., 1837. Capt. 13th Inf., 19 Aug., 1861. Resigned 4 Jan., 1862.

DEFREES, THOMAS M. [Born in Ind. Appointed from W. Va.]
2nd Lieut. 5th Inf., 13 Jan., 1880. 1st Lieut., 14 Oct., 1885. Graduate of the Infantry and Cavalry School, 1883. Retired for disability in line of duty, 7 June, 1897.

DE FUNIAK, FREDERICK R., Jr. [Born in Ala. Appointed from Ky.]
Capt. Co. M, 1st Ky. Vols., 13 May, 1898, to 24 Feb., 1899. 2nd Lieut. 11th Inf., 10 April, 1899.

DE GRAFFENREID, MATTHEW F. [Born in ——. Appointed from Tenn.]
Ensign 39th Inf., 26 March, 1814. 3rd Lieut., 1 May, 1814. 2nd Lieut., 26 Nov., 1814. Disbanded 15 June, 1815. Reinstated in Corps Art., 2 Dec., 1815. Resigned 31 Oct., 1817.

DE GRAW, CHAS. S. [Born in N. Y. Appointed from N. Y.]
Asst. Surg., 8th N. Y. Militia, 25 April, 1861, to 25 Oct., 1861. Asst. Surg., 11 July, 1862. Resigned 1 Jan., 1878. Bvt. Capt. and Maj., 13 March, 1865, for faithful and meritorious service during the war.

DE GRESS, JACOB C. [Born in Prussia. Appointed from Mo.]
Capt. 6th Mo. Cav., 1 April, 1862. Mustered out 21 May, 1865. Bvt. Lieut. Col., 13 March, 1865, for meritorious service at the Bayou de Glaze, La. Maj. A. de C. Vols., 12 May, 1865. Mustered out 1 Sept., 1866. 1st Lieut. 9th Cav., 28 July, 1866. Bvt. Capt. and Maj., 2 March, 1867, for gallant and meritorious service during the Siege of Vicksburg, Miss. Bvt. Lieut. Col., 2 March, 1867, for gallant and meritorious service in the Battle of Bayou de Glaze, La. Capt. 9th Cav., 31 July, 1867. Retired 31 Dec., 1870. Died 21 March, 1894.

DE HANNE, J. VICTOR. [Born in N. Y. Appointed from N. Y.]
Priv. Co. B, 176th N. Y. Vols., 7 Oct., 1862, to 22 Sept., 1863. Asst. Surg. Vols., 21 Dec., 1864. 1st Lieut. Asst. Surg., 14 May, 1867. Vacated commission of Asst. Surg. Vols., 28 May, 1867. Bvt. Capt. and Maj. Vols., 3 June, 1867, for faithful and meritorious service. Capt. Asst. Surg., 12 May, 1868. Retired for disability in line of duty, 26 Feb., 1891.

DE HART, HENRY V.* [Born in N. Y. Appointed at Large.]
2nd Lieut. 3rd Art., 1 July, 1856. 1st Lieut., 3 Dec., 1858. Capt., 5th Art., 14 May, 1861. Died 13 July, 1862, of wounds received at Battle of Gaines' Mills, Va.

DE HART, JOHN C. [Born in N. J. Appointed from N. J.]
Ensign 15th Inf., 9 Sept., 1813. 3rd Lieut., 17 March, 1814. 2nd Lieut., 1 Aug., 1814. Disbanded 15 June, 1815. Reinstated — Jan., 1816, in Ord. Resigned 1 Oct., 1818.

DE HART, WM. C.* [Born in N. Y. Appointed from N. Y.]
3rd Lieut. Ord., 1 July, 1820. Trans. to 2nd Art., 1 June, 1821, to rank as 2nd Lieut. from 1 July, 1820. 1st Lieut., 10 Oct., 1831. Capt., 3 April, 1838. Died 21 April, 1848. Bvt. 1st Lieut., 1 July, 1830, for 10 years' faithful service in one grade.

DEISS, GEORGE. [Born in ——. Appointed from Army.]
Priv., Corpl. and Sergt. Batty D, 1st Art., 2 June, 1891, to 31 Jan., 1896. Priv. Batty K, 1st Art., 11 July, 1898, to 23 Feb., 1899. Priv. Batty D, 6th Art., 8 June, 1899, to 23 Nov., 1899. 2nd Lieut. 25th Inf., 1 Oct., 1899.

DE JANON, PATRICE. [Born in South America. Appointed from N. Y.]
Sword Master at Mil. Acad., 6 Jan., 1848. Prof. of Spanish, 1 July, 1857. Out of service from 16 Sept., 1863, to 4 March, 1865. Retired with pay of Col., 30 June, 1882. Died 15 Jan., 1892.

DE KAY, DRAKE. [Born in N. J. Appointed from N. Y.]
1st Lieut. 14th Inf., 14 May, 1861. Capt., 14 May, 1864. Resigned 18 Jan., 1865. Bvt. Maj., 1 Aug., 1864, for gallant service at the Battle of the Wilderness, Va. Bvt. Lieut. Col., 1 Aug., 1864, for gallant service at the Battle of Spottsylvania, Va.

DELAFIELD, RICHARD.* [Born in N. Y. Appointed from N. Y.]
2nd Lieut. Eng., 24 July, 1818. 1st Lieut., 29 Aug., 1820. Capt., 24 May, 1828. Maj., 7 July, 1838. Lieut. Col., 6 Aug., 1861. Col., 1 June, 1863. Brig. Gen. Chief of Eng., 22 April, 1864. Retired 8 Aug., 1866. Died 5 Nov., 1873. Bvt. Maj. Gen., 13 March, 1865, for faithful, meritorious and distinguished service in the Engineer Department during the war.

DE LAGNEL, JULIUS A.* [Born in N. Y. Appointed from N. Y.]
Bvt. 2nd Lieut. and 2nd Lieut. 5th Inf., 1 July, 1821. Trans. to 2nd Art., 30 Dec., 1825. 1st Lieut., 30 May, 1832. Capt. Ord., 1 Nov., 1836. Bvt. 1st Lieut., 1 July, 1831, for 10 years' faithful service in one grade. Died 21 May, 1840.

DE LAGNEL, JULIUS A. [Born in N. J. Appointed from Va.]
2nd Lieut. 2nd Art., 8 March, 1847. 1st Lieut., 26 Jan., 1849. Resigned 17 May, 1861.

DE LAMOS, FERNANDO G. [Born in ——. Appointed from La.]
2nd Lieut. 44th Inf., 7 July, 1814, to 15 June, 1815. Reinstated in Corps. Art., 2 Dec., 1815. Trans. to 1st Inf., 20 June, 1816. Resigned 1 Oct., 1816.

DE LANO, HORACE F.* [Born in Conn. Appointed from N. Y.]
Bvt. 2nd Lieut. 1st Drag., 1 July, 1849. 2nd Lieut. 2nd Drag., 13 Jan., 1850. Died 24 May, 1854.

DELANY, ALFRED. [Born in Pa. Appointed from Pa.]
Asst. Surg. Vols., 26 Jan., 1864. Bvt. Capt. Vols., 21 Dec., 1865, for faithful service. Mustered out 10 Jan., 1866. Asst. Surg., 9 Oct., 1867. Died 14 Feb., 1876.

DE LANY, CYRUS M. [Born in Ohio. Appointed from Ohio.]
Priv. and Corpl. Co. B, 30th Ohio Vols., 30 July, 1861. Sergt., 27 April, 1863. Sergt. Co. B, 30th Ohio Vet. Vols., 1 Feb., 1864. Sergt. Maj., 15 April, 1864. 2nd Lieut., 30th Ohio Vet. Vols., 25 Sept., 1864. 1st Lieut., 28 Dec., 1864. Capt., 1 April, 1865. Mustered out 13 Aug., 1865. 2nd Lieut. 35th Inf., 30 Oct., 1867. Trans. to 15th Inf., 12 Aug., 1869. 1st Lieut., 9 June, 1875. Capt., 23 Sept., 1885. Died 27 Feb., 1888.

DE LANY, HAYDEN. [Born in Ohio. Appointed from Ohio.]
Priv. Co. B, 30th Ohio Vols., 31 Dec., 1861. Priv. Co. B, 30th Ohio Vet. Vols., 1 Feb., 1864. Corpl., 1 Oct., 1864. Discharged 31 May, 1865. Cadet at Mil. Acad., 1 July, 1865, to 5 Sept., 1867. 2nd Lieut. 9th Inf., 11 Sept., 1867. Bvt. 1st Lieut., 1 May,, 1868, for gallant and meritorious service in action with the Pah-Ute Indians in Warner Valley, Ore., 1 May, 1868. 1st Lieut. 9th Inf., 28 June, 1878. Capt., 28 Sept., 1889. Died Nov. 4, 1890.

DE LAUBENFELS, JOHN L. [Born in Poland. Appointed from Iowa.]
Served under name of John Rziha to 3 May, 1874. Capt. 19th Inf., 5 Aug., 1861. Trans. to 37th Inf., 21 Sept., 1866. Unassigned 11 Aug., 1869. Ass'd to 4th Inf., 22 March, 1870. Dismissed 31 Dec., 1875. Bvt. Maj., 27 Feb., 1865. Died 18 March, 1881.

DELAVAN, BENJAMIN. [Born in N. Y. Appointed from N. J.]
Surg. Mate 16th Inf., 15 April, 1814, to 15 June, 1815. Reinstated 17 May, 1816, as Hosp. Surg. Mate, Post Surg., 18 April, 1818. Asst. Surg., 1 June, 1821. Maj. Surg., 27 Jan., 1823. Died 26 Nov., 1827.

DE LEON, DAVID C. [Born in S. C. Appointed from S. C.]
Asst. Surg., 21 Aug., 1838. Maj. Surg., 29 Aug., 1856. Resigned 19 Feb., 1861.

DE LOFFRE, AUGUSTUS A. [Born in France. Appointed from La.]
1st Lieut. Asst. Surg., 10 Nov., 1874. Capt. Asst. Surg., 10 Nov., 1879. Maj. Surg., 1 June, 1892. Died 4 Sept., 1899.

DEMENT, JOHN. [Born in D. C. Appointed from Army.]
Priv., Corpl. and Sergt. Co. F, Mtd. Rifles, 11 July, 1846, to 25 July, 1848. Bvt. 2nd Lieut. 1st Art., 28 June, 1848. 2nd Lieut., 29 Oct., 1848. 1st Lieut., 31 March, 1853. Resigned 30 April, 1854.

DE MEULEN, EMILIUS. [Born in Italy. Appointed from R. I.]
1st Lieut. 5th R. I. Vols., 28 Nov., 1862. Capt., 25 Aug., 1863. Bvt. Maj. Vols., 13 March, 1865, for meritorious service in the line of his duty. Mustered out 26 June, 1865. 2nd Lieut. 2nd Art., 11 May, 1866. 1st Lieut., 9 Dec., 1867. Cashiered 25 July, 1870.

DE MOTTE, LUTHER M. [Born in Ind. Appointed from Ill.]
2nd Lieut. 38th Ill. Vols., 19 Aug., 1861. Resigned 21 March, 1864. Capt. 5th U. S. Vet. Vols., 14 Jan., 1865. Mustered out 26 March, 1866. 2nd Lieut. 19th Inf., 2 May, 1866. Trans. to 28th Inf., 21 Sept., 1866. 1st Lieut., 7 March, 1867. Resigned 31 Oct., 1867.

DEMPSEY, CHAS. A.* [Born in Va. Appointed from Va.]
2nd Lieut. 17th Inf., 23 June, 1865. 1st Lieut., 23 June, 1865. Trans. to 35th Inf., 21 Sept., 1866. Unassigned 12 Aug., 1869. Ass'd to 2nd Inf., 3 June, 1870. Reg. Adj., 21 Dec., 1871, to 9 Feb., 1878. Capt., 9 Feb., 1878. Maj. 2nd Inf., 26 April, 1898. Lieut. Col. 1st Inf., 16 June, 1899.

DENISON, CHAS. E. [Born in Vt. Appointed from Ill.]
Capt. 8th Ill. Vols., 25 April, 1861, to 1 July, 1861. Capt. 18th Inf., 14 May, 1861. Died 15 Jan., 1863, of wounds received at Battle of Murfreesboro', Tenn. Bvt. Maj., 31 Dec., 1862, for gallant and meritorious service at the Battle of Murfreesboro', Tenn.

DENISON, DAVID S.* [Born in Md. Appointed from Md.]
2nd Lieut. 5th Art., 15 June, 1868. 1st Lieut., 11 March, 1876. Resigned 9 April, 1877.

DENMAN, CHAS. L. [Born in England. Appointed from N. Y.]
Cadet at Mil. Acad., 1 July to 31 Dec., 1837. 2nd Lieut. Mtd. Rifles, 27 May, 1846. 1st Lieut., 15 May, 1847. Resigned 30 Nov., 1850.

DENMAN, FREDK. J.* [Born in N. Y. Appointed from N. Y.]
2nd Lieut. 1st Inf., 1 July, 1842. 1st Lieut., 31 Aug., 1849. Reg. Adj., 21 Sept., 1848, to 2 March, 1853. Died 2 March, 1853.

DENNIS, EDGAR W. [Born in N. Y. Appointed from N. Y.]
Priv. Co. H, 4th N. Y. Art., 27 Dec., 1861. 1st Lieut., 20 Feb., 1862. Capt. A. A. de C., 11 July, 1862. Maj. J. A. Vols., 19 Jan., 1865. Trans. to U. S. A., 25 Jan., 1867. Bvt. Lieut. Col. and Col. Vols., 2 Dec., 1865, for meritorious service in his department. Resigned 22 May, 1869. Died 2 April, 1878.

DENNIS, PETER A. [Born in ——. Appointed from Army.]
Priv., Corpl. and Sergt. 20th Inf., 19 May, 1813, to May, 1814. 2nd Lieut. Corps Art., 20 May, 1814. Dismissed 5 Aug., 1817.

DENNEY, JEREMIAH C. [Born in Ireland. Appointed from Army.]
2nd Lieut. 5th Cav., 17 July, 1862. 1st Lieut., 17 July, 1862. Capt., 28 July, 1866. Died 12 June, 1869. Bvt. Capt., 19 Oct., 1864, for gallant and meritorious service at the Battle of Cedar Creek, Va.

DENNEY, WM. F. [Born in Ohio. Appointed from Tenn.]
2nd Lieut. 32nd Inf., 24 Aug., 1867. Resigned 10 Oct., 1868.

DENNISON, JAMES A.* [Born in Ind. Appointed from Mo.]
Priv. 15th Mo. Vols., Sept., 1861, to Jan., 1862. Priv. Co. E., 8th Mo. Militia Cav., 13 April, 1862, to 12 April, 1865. Cadet at Mil. Acad., 1 Sept., 1866. 2nd Lieut. 2nd Art., 15 June, 1870. Trans. to 8th Cav., 7 Oct., 1871. Resigned 31 Aug., 1872.

DENNISON, WM. N. [Born in Ohio. Appointed from Ohio.]
2nd Lieut. 2nd Art., 5 Aug., 1861. 1st Lieut., 12 Nov., 1861. Capt., 3 Jan., 1867. Discharged 31 Dec., 1870. Bvt. Capt., 6 July, 1864, for gallant and good conduct in the Battle of Antietam, and the Maryland campaign of September, 1862. Bvt.

Maj., 6 July, 1864, for gallant and good conduct in the Battles of Gaines' Mills and Malvern Hill, Va. Bvt. Lieut. Col., 13 March, 1865, for good conduct and gallant service during the war.

DENNY, ST. CLAIR.* [Born in Pa. Appointed from Pa.]
2nd Lieut. 5th Inf., 1 July, 1822. 1st lieut., 30 Nov., 1827. (A. Q. M., 15 Oct., 1830, to 28th Jan., 1834.) Capt., 1 April, 1836. Trans. to 8th Inf., 7 July, 1838. Resigned 30 April, 1839. Maj. P. M., 15 Oct., 1841. Died 18 Aug., 1858.

DENT, FREDK. T.* [Born in Mo. Appointed from Mo.]
Bvt. 2nd Lieut. 6th Inf., 1 July, 1843. 2nd Lieut. 5th Inf., 30 March, 1846. Bvt. 1st Lieut., 20 Aug., 1847, for gallant and meritorious conduct in the Battles of Contreras and Churubusco. Bvt. Capt., 8 Sept., 1847, for gallant and meritorious conduct in the Battle of Molino del Rey. 1st Lieut. 5th Inf., 11 Sept., 1847. Capt. 9th Inf., 3 March, 1855. Maj. 4th Inf., 9 March, 1863. Lieut. Col. A. de C. to the Lieut. Gen., 29 March, 1864. Bvt. Lieut. Col., 7 May, 1864, for gallant and meritorious service in the Battle of the Wilderness, Va. Bvt. Col., 30 July, 1864, for gallant and meritorious service in front of Petersburg, Va. Bvt. Col. Vols., 24 Feb., 1865, for faithful and meritorious service. Bvt. Brig. Gen., 13 March, 1865, for gallant and meritorious service in the field during the war. Brig. Gen. Vols., 5 April, 1865. Mustered out of Vol. service 30 April, 1866. Trans. to 14th Inf., 21 Aug., 1866. Lieut. Col. 32nd Inf., 31 Dec., 1867. Unassigned 15 March, 1869. Ass'd to 5th Art., 15 Dec., 1870. Col. 1st Art., 2 Jan., 1881. Trans. to 3rd Art., 4 Nov., 1882. Retired 1 Dec., 1883. Died 23 Dec., 1892.

DENT, JAMES T. [Born in ——. Appointed from Ga.]
J. A., 19 July, 1813. Disbanded 14 April, 1818.

DENT, JOHN C. [Born in Oregon. Appointed at Large.]
2nd Lieut. 20th Inf., 15 Aug., 1876. 1st Lieut., 6 May, 1882. Capt., 19 May, 1891. Maj. 11th Inf., 15 Dec., 1899. Trans. to 24th Inf., 17 Feb., 1900.

DENTLER, CLARENCE E.* [Born in Pa. Appointed from Pa.]
2nd Lieut. 6th Inf., 15 June, 1884. 1st Lieut. 20th Inf., 27 April, 1891. Trans. to 11th Inf., 20 July, 1891. Capt. of Inf., 21 Sept., 1898. Ass'd to 5th Inf., 1 Jan., 1899. Trans. to 11th Inf., 6 April, 1899.

DENTON, ANSEL B. [Born in N. Y. Appointed from Mich.]
1st Lieut. 18th Inf., 14 May, 1861. Capt., 22 July, 1862. Resigned 9 Sept., 1864.

DENTON, THOS. W. [Born in N. Y. Appointed from N. Y.]
Ensign 13th Inf., 1 June, 1812. 3rd Lieut., 1 April, 1813. 2nd Lieut., 13 May, 1813. 1st Lieut., 30 June, 1814. Disbanded 15 June, 1815. Reinstated 17 May, 1816, as 2nd Lieut. Corps Art. Dismissed 11 Aug., 1820. Retained 17 May, 1816 (in reorganization under Act of 3 March, 1815), as 2nd Lieut. Art., with Bvt. of 1st Lieut. from 30 June, 1814. Dismissed 11 Aug., 1820.

DENVER, JAMES W. [Born in Va. Appointed from Mo.]
Capt. of Inf., 5 March, 1847; 12th Inf., 9 April, 1847. Disbanded 25 July, 1848. Brig. Gen. Vols., 14 Aug., 1861. Resigned 5 March, 1863.

DERBY, GEORGE H.* [Born in Mass. Appointed from Mass.]
Bvt. 2nd Lieut. Ord., 1 July, 1846. Trans. to Top. Eng., 12 Aug., 1846. 2nd Lieut., 4 Aug., 1851. 1st Lieut., 2 Oct., 1855. Capt., 1 July, 1860. Died 15 May, 1861. Bvt. 1st Lieut., 18 April, 1847, for gallant and meritorious conduct at Cerro Gordo, Mex.

DERBY, GEORGE McC.* [Born at Sea. Appointed at Large.]
2nd Lieut. Eng., 14 June, 1878. 1st Lieut., 2 Jan., 1881. Capt., 7 April, 1888. Maj., 5 July, 1898. Lieut. Col. Chf. Eng., 9 May, 1898, to 12 May, 1899.

DERBY, LOUIS P. [Born in Ill. Appointed from Utah.]
Priv. Co. B, 68th Ohio Vols., 7 Oct., 1861. Mustered out 10 July, 1865. 2nd Lieut. 14th Inf., 23 Feb., 1866. 1st Lieut., 28 July, 1866. Unass'd 22 July, 1869. Ass'd to 11th Inf., 31 Jan., 1870. Discharged 12 Oct., 1870.

DERRICK, CLARENCE.* [Born in D. C. Appointed at Large.]
Bvt. 2nd Lieut. Eng., 24 June, 1861. Dismissed 16 July, 1861.

DERICKSON, RICHD. W. [Born in Pa. Appointed from Pa.]
1st Lieut. 15th Inf., 14 May, 1861. Resigned 23 July, 1864.

DE RUDIO, CHAS. C. [Born in Italy. Appointed from N. Y.]
Priv. Co. A, 79th N. Y. Vols., 25 Aug., 1864. Discharged 17 Oct., 1864. 2nd Lieut. U. S. Col. Troops, 11 Nov., 1864. Mustered out 5 Jan., 1866. 2nd Lieut. 2nd Inf., 31 Aug., 1867. Appointment cancelled, 20 Sept., 1867. Appointment renewed, 25 Oct., 1867. Unass'd 17 April, 1869. Ass'd to 7th Cav., 14 July, 1869. 1st Lieut., 15 Dec., 1875. Capt., 17 Dec., 1882. Retired by operation of law 26 Aug., 1896.

DE RUSSY, GUSTAVUS A. [Born in N. Y. Appointed from Va.]
Cadet at Mil. Acad., 1 July, 1835, to 15 June, 1838. 2nd Lieut. 4th Art., 8 March, 1847. Bvt. 1st Lieut., 20 Aug., 1847, for gallant and meritorious conduct in the Battles of Contreras and Churubusco. Bvt. Capt., 13 Sept., 1847, for gallant conduct at Chapultepec. R. Q. M., 15 Feb., 1849, to 9 Aug., 1857. 1st Lieut. 4th Art., 16 May, 1849. Capt., 17 Aug., 1857. Bvt. Maj., 25 June, 1862, for gallant and meritorious service in action near Fair Oaks, Va. Bvt. Lieut. Col., 1 July, 1862, for gallant and meritorious service in the Battle of Malvern Hill, Va. Col. 4th N. Y. Art., 17 March, 1863. Brig. Gen. Vols., 23 May, 1863. Bvt. Col., 13 March, 1865, for gallant and meritorious service during the war. Bvt. Brig. Gen., 13 March, 1865, for gallant and meritorious service in the field during the war. Mustered out of Vol. ser., 15 Jan., 1866. Maj. 3rd Art., 26 July, 1866. Lieut. Col., 25 Aug., 1879. Col. 4th Art., 30 June, 1882. Trans. to 3rd Art., 17 July, 1882. Retired by operation of law 3 Nov., 1882. Died 29 May, 1891.

DE RUSSY, ISAAC D. [Born in Va. Appointed from N. Y.]
2nd Lieut. 1st Inf., 26 April, 1861. 1st Lieut., 14 May, 1861. Capt., 27 Feb., 1862. Bvt. Maj., 13 March, 1865, for faithful and meritorious service during the war. Maj. 4th Inf., 29 Sept., 1879. Lieut. Col. 14th Inf., 1 July, 1885. Col. 11th Inf., 19 May, 1891.

DE RUSSY, JOHN.* [Born in N. Y. Appointed at Large.]
Bvt. 2nd Lieut. 6th Inf., 1 July, 1847. 2nd Lieut., 16 Sept., 1847. Trans. to 2nd Inf., 30 Sept., 1848. Trans. to 2nd Art., 24 April, 1849. Died 8 July, 1850.

DE RUSSY, LEWIS G.* [Born in N. Y. Appointed from N. Y.]
3rd Lieut. 1st Art., 11 March, 1814. 2nd Lieut., 1 May, 1814. Trans. to Corps Art., 12 May, 1814. Batt. Adj., 1 Nov., 1816, to 20 May, 1819. 1st Lieut., 20 April, 1818. Trans. to 2nd Art., 1 June, 1821. Trans. to 3rd Art., 16 Aug., 1821. Capt., 11 Dec., 1825. Maj. P. M., 21 Sept., 1826. Dropped 28 July, 1842. Col. 1st La. Vols., 26 Dec., 1846. Mustered out 10 July, 1848.

DE RUSSY, RENE E.* [Born in N. Y. Appointed from N. Y.]
2nd Lieut. Eng., 10 June, 1812. 1st Lieut., 6 July, 1812. Capt., 9 Feb., 1815. Maj., 22 Dec., 1830. Lieut. Col., 7 Dec., 1838. Col., 3 March, 1863. Died 23 Nov., 1865. Bvt. Capt., 11 Sept., 1814, for gallant conduct at the Battle of Plattsburg. Bvt. Maj., 11 Sept., 1814, for ten years' faithful service in one grade. Bvt. Lieut. Col., 30 June, 1834, for faithful service and meritorious conduct. Bvt. Brig. Gen., 13 March, 1865, for long and faithful service in the army.

DE RUSSY, RENE E. [Born in Va. Appointed from N. J.]
2nd Lieut. 4th N. Y. Art., 21 Dec., 1863. Resigned 24 Feb., 1865. 2nd Lieut. 2nd Art, 25 April, 1866. 1st Lieut., 1 May, 1867. Resigned 16 Nov., 1874.

DE SAUSSURE, WM. D. [Born in S. C. Appointed from S. C.]
Capt. Palmetto Reg. S. C. Vols., 15 Dec., 1846. Mustered out 30 June, 1848. Capt. 1st Cav., 3 March, 1855. Resigned 1 March, 1861.

DESHLER, GEORGE W.* [Born in N. J. Appointed from N. J.]
2nd Lieut. 1st Art., 15 June, 1868. 1st Lieut., 1 March, 1875. Died 28 July, 1875.

DESHLER, JAMES.* [Born in Ala. Appointed from Ala.]
Bvt. 2nd Lieut. 3rd Art., 1 July, 1854. Trans. to 10th Inf., 3 March, 1855. 1st Lieut., 17 Sept., 1858. Dropped 15 July, 1861.

DESHON, GEORGE.* [Born in Conn. Appointed from Conn.]
Bvt. 2nd Lieut. Top. Eng., 1 July, 1843. Trans. to Ord., 20 July, 1843. 2nd Lieut., 3 March, 1847. 1st Lieut., 10 July, 1851. Resigned 31 Oct., 1851.

DE SHON, GEORGE D.* [Born in Mass. Appointed from Mass.]
2nd Lieut. 23rd Inf., 1 July, 1886. Resigned 21 March, 1890. App. Asst. Surg., 5 May, 1892. Capt. Asst. Surg., 5 May, 1897. Maj. Surg. 11th U. S. Vol. Cav., 10 Aug., 1899.

DESPINVILLE, CHAS.* [Born in N. Y. Appointed from N. Y.]
3rd Lieut. Corps Art., 17 July, 1817. 2nd Lieut., 24 Oct., 1817. 1st Lieut., 10 Sept., 1819. Trans. to 4th Art., 1 June, 1821. Resigned 1 March, 1830. Died 18 May, 1830.

DETCHEMENDY, GEORGE A. [Born in Mo. Appointed from Army.]
Priv. and Corpl. Co. G, 3rd Inf., 20 March, 1877, to 19 March, 1882. Priv. Co. B, Sig. Corps, 15 April, 1885, to 12 Nov., 1885. Priv. and Corpl. Co. G and Q. M. Sergt. 3rd Inf., 23 Nov., to 19 March, 1888. 2nd Lieut. 6th Inf., 6 Feb., 1888. 1st Lieut. 1st Inf., 6 April, 1895. Capt., 2 March, 1899. Trans. to 22 Inf., 5 May, 1899. Graduate of the Infantry and Cavalry School, 1891.

DE TREVILLE, RICHARD* [Born in S. C. Appointed from S. C.]
Bvt. 2nd Lieut. 3rd Art., 1 July, 1823. 2nd Lieut., 1 July, 1823. Resigned 30 April, 1825. Died 25 Nov., 1874.

DE TROBRIAND, PHILIP R. [Born in France. Appointed from N. Y.]
Col. 55th N. Y. Vols., 28 Aug., 1861. Col. 38th N. Y. Vols., 21 Dec., 1862. Mustered out 21 Nov., 1863. Brig. Gen. Vols., 5 Jan., 1864. Bvt. Maj. Gen. Vols., 9 April, 1865, for highly meritorious service during the campaign terminating with the surrender of the insurgent army under Gen. R. E. Lee. Mustered out 15 Jan., 1866. Col. 31st Inf., 28 July, 1866. Bvt. Brig. Gen., 2 March, 1867, for gallant and meritorious service during the war. Trans. to 13th Inf., 15 March, 1869. Retired 20 March, 1879. Died 15 July, 1897.

DE VEUVE, HENRY.* [Born in La. Appointed from N. J.]
Bvt. 2nd Lieut. 1st Art., 1 July, 1852. 2nd Lieut., 3 Aug., 1852. Resigned 31 Aug., 1853.

DEVIN, JOHN D. [Born in Me. Appointed from N. H.]
2nd Lieut. 9th Inf., 26 April, 1861. 1st Lieut., 14 May, 1861. Capt., 9 March, 1863. Bvt. Maj. and Lieut. Col., 13 March, 1865, for gallant and meritorious service during the war. Retired 27 March, 1879. Died 31 Dec., 1882.

DEVIN, THOS C. [Born in N. Y. Appointed from N. Y.]
Capt. 1st N. Y. Cav., 19 July, 1861. Mustered out 19 Oct., 1861. Col. 6th N. Y. Cav., 18 Nov., 1861. Brig. Gen. Vols., 19 Oct., 1864. Bvt. Brig. Gen. Vols., 15 Aug., 1864, for gallant and distinguished service in the field during the Civil War and especially in the recent brilliant engagement near Port Royal, where his command captured two stands of colors from the Rebels; and Maj. Gen. Vols., 13 March, 1865, for gallant and meritorious service during the war. Mustered out 15 Jan., 1866. Lieut. Col. 8th Cav., 28 July, 1866. Col. 3rd Cav., 25 June, 1877. Died 4 April, 1878. Bvt. Col., 2 March, 1867, for gallant and meritorious service at the Battle of Fisher's Hill, Va. Bvt. Brig. Gen., 2 March, 1867, for gallant and meritorious service at the Battle of Sailor's Creek, Va.

DEVINE, WM. [Born in Ireland. Appointed from Army.]
Priv. Batty I, 4th Art., 19 Sept., 1856, to 19 Sept., 1861. Priv., Corpl. and Sergt. Co. G, 11th Inf., 16 Oct., 1861, to 27 March, 1863. Capt. 79th U. S. Col. Inf., 27 March, 1863. Resigned 11 Sept., 1863. 2nd Lieut. 9th Inf., 22 April, 1863. Resigned 7 Nov., 1863. Died 2 May, 1884.

DEVOE, FREDK. [Born in N. Y. Appointed from Army.]
Priv. Co. A, and Sergt. Maj. 3rd Inf., 26 July, 1858, to 24 Oct., 1861. 2nd Lieut. 3rd Inf., 24 Oct., 1861. Reg. Adj., 1 Dec., 1861, to 12 Dec., 1862. Dismissed 12 Dec., 1862.

DEVOL, CARROLL A. [Born in Ohio. Appointed from Ohio.]
2nd Lieut. 25th Inf., 1 Sept., 1879. 1st Lieut., 19 Oct., 1886. R. Q. M., 1 April, 1887. Capt. A. Q. M., 21 Aug., 1896. Maj. Q. M. Vol., 17 Oct., 1898.

DEVORE, DANIEL B.* [Born in Ohio. Appointed from Ohio.]
2nd Lieut. 23rd Inf., 14 June, 1885. 1st Lieut. 17th Inf., 2 May, 1892. Trans. to 23rd Inf., 12 Aug., 1892. Capt. A. A. G. Vols., 12 May, 1898, to 28 Feb., 1899. Capt. 23rd Inf., 2 March, 1899.

DEWEES, JOHN T. [Born in Ind. Appointed from Ind.]
2nd Lieut. 24th Ind. Vols., 31 July, 1861. Resigned 15 Feb., 1862. Capt. 4th Ind. Cav., 8 Aug., 1862. Maj., 24 April, 1863. Lieut. Col. 7 May, 1863. Resigned 11 March, 1864. 2nd Lieut. 8th Inf., 24 July, 1866. Resigned 14 Aug., 1867.

DEWEES, THOS. B. [Born in Penn. Appointed from Army.]
Priv. Co. B, 2nd Drag., 9 March, 1858. Corpl., 17 July, 1860. Sergt., 1 Feb., 1861. 1st Sergt., 1 May, 1861. Discharged 24 Oct., 1861. 2nd Lieut. 2nd Cav., 24 Oct., 1861. 1st Lieut., 17 July, 1862. Bvt. Capt., 9 June, 1863, for gallant and meritorious service in the Battle of Beverly Ford, Va. Capt. 2nd Cav., 10 July, 1866. Maj. 9th Cav., 28 Oct., 1881. Died 5 July, 1886.

DEWEY, ISRAEL O. [Born in Vt. Appointed from N. H.]
Addl. P. M., 28 May, 1864. Mustered out 1 Dec., 1865. Maj. P. M., 17 Jan., 1867. Retired 9 Jan., 1888. Died 12 May, 1888.

DEWEY, ORVILLE S. [Born in N. Y. Appointed from N. Y.]
Priv. Co. D, 21st N. Y. Vols., 20 May, 1861. 2nd Lieut. 49th N. Y. Vols., 15 May, 1862, to 27 Nov., 1862. 2nd Lieut. 27th N. Y. Batty, 25 Jan., 1863. 1st Lieut. 33rd N. Y. Batty, 7 Dec., 1863. Resigned 9 Oct., 1864. 2nd Lieut. 4th Cav., 22 Jan., 1867. Died 30 June, 1867.

DEWEY, WM. W. [Born in Ohio. Appointed from Iowa.]
1st Lieut. 12th Inf., 30 Sept., 1861. Cashiered 10 April, 1863.

DE WITT, CALVIN. [Born in Pa. Appointed from Pa.]
Capt. 49th Pa. Vols., 24 Oct., 1861. Resigned 18 Jan., 1863. 1st Lieut. Asst. Surg., 14 May, 1867. Capt. Asst. Surg., 14 May, 1870. Maj. Surg., 21 July, 1885. Lieut. Col. Dep. Surg. Gen., 21 Dec., 1898.

DE WITT, DAVID P.* [Born in N. J. Appointed from N. Y.]
Bvt. 2nd Lieut. 2nd Art., 1 July, 1836. Resigned 31 Oct., 1836. Maj. 2nd Md. Vols., 21 Sept., 1861. Col. 3rd Md. Vols., 29 March, 1862. Resigned 8 Oct., 1862. Col. 2nd N. Y. Vols., 8 Oct., 1862. Resigned 30 April, 1863. Maj. Vet. Res. Corps, 9 June, 1863. Col. Vet. Res. Corps, 29 Sept., 1863. Bvt. Brig. Gen. Vols., 13 March, 1865, for faithful and meritorious service. Mustered out 6 June, 1866.

DEWITT, HENRY. [Born in Conn. Appointed from Conn.]
3rd Lieut. 25th Inf., 17 Oct., 1813. 2nd Lieut., 15 Feb., 1814. 1st Lieut., 25 July, 1814. Trans. to 6th Inf., 17 May, 1815. Resigned 17 Oct., 1815.

DE WITT, JOHN L. [Born in Neb. Appointed from Va.]
2nd Lieut. 20th Inf., 10 Oct., 1898. 1st Lieut. 25th Inf., 29 Jan., 1900.

DE WITT, THEODORE F. [Born in N. J. Appointed from N. J.]
Asst. Surg., 7 June, 1889. Resigned 16 May, 1892.

DE WOLFE, HENRY. [Born in R. I. Appointed from R. I.]
2nd Lieut. Inf., 8 March, 1847. 9th Inf., 9 April, 1847. 1st Lieut., 6 May, 1848. Disbanded 9 Aug., 1848.

DEY, GUSTAV. [Born in Prussia. Appointed from Army.]
Priv., Corpl. Sergt. and 1st Sergt. Cos. I and F, 2nd Art., 18 Dec., 1854, to 26 Nov., 1863. 2nd Lieut. 2nd Art., 31 Oct., 1863. 1st Lieut., 15 June, 1864. Dropped 6 Oct., 1865.

DEYERLE, CHARLES P. [Born in Va. Appointed from Va.]
Asst. Surg., 16 Feb., 1847. Died 30 Oct., 1853.

DIBBLE, CHAS. E. [Born in Conn. Appointed from Conn.]
Priv. and Corpl. Co. E, 8th Conn. Vols., 25 Sept., 1861, to 18 April, 1865. 2nd Lieut. 11th Conn. Vols., 18 April, 1865. 1st Lieut. and Adj., 12 May, 1865. Mustered out 28 Dec., 1865. 2nd Lieut. 18th Inf., 23 Feb., 1866. 1st Lieut., 21 July, 1866. Trans. to 27th Inf., 21 Sept., 1866. Resigned 17 Jan., 1867.

DIBBLE, FREDK. H. [Born in England. Appointed from Idaho.]
Priv., Corpl. and Sergt. 15th Ohio Batty, 1 Oct., 1862. Mustered out 20 June, 1865. 2nd Lieut. 13th Inf., 23 Feb., 1866. Trans. to 22nd Inf., 21 Sept., 1866. 1st Lieut., 1 Jan., 1867. Unass'd 15 May, 1869. Ass'd to 12th Inf., 14 July, 1869. Discharged 31 Dec., 1870.

DICHMANN, HENRY M.* [Born in Wis. Appointed from Wis.]
Addl. 2nd Lieut. 22nd Inf., 11 June, 1897. 2nd Lieut. 7th Inf., 3 Dec., 1897. 1st Lieut., 2 March, 1899.

DICK, GEORGE McG.* [Born in Pa. Appointed from Pa.]
Bvt. 2nd Lieut. 8th Inf., 1 July, 1855. 2nd Lieut. 1st Inf., 26 Oct., 1855. Died 31 July, 1856.

DICK, SAML. J. [Born in Pa. Appointed from Army.]
Priv. and 1st Sergt. Co. B, 18th Inf., 24 July, 1861, to Nov., 1861. 2nd Lieut. 18th Inf., 30 Oct., 1861. 1st Lieut., 30 June, 1862. Died 28 Dec., 1864.

DICKERSON, FRANK W. [Born in Me. Appointed from Me.]
2nd Lieut. 5th Cav., 19 Feb., 1862. 1st Lieut., 17 July, 1862. Died 17 Feb., 1866. Bvt. Capt. and Maj., 13 March, 1865, for gallant and meritorious service during the war.

DICKERSON, JOHN H.* [Born in Ohio. Appointed from Ind.]
Bvt. 2nd Lieut. 4th Art., 1 July, 1847. 2nd Lieut. 1st Art., 19 Aug., 1847. 1st Lieut., 1 April, 1850. R. Q. M., 9 Oct., 1852, to 18 June, 1856. Capt. A. Q. M., 18 June, 1856. Resigned 31 March, 1864. Bvt. Maj., 13 March, 1865, for efficient and meritorious service in the Department of the Ohio.

DICKEY, CHAS. J. [Born in Pa. Appointed from Pa.]
1st Lieut. 13th Inf., 14 May, 1861. Bvt. Capt., 4 July, 1863, for gallant and meritorious service in the Siege of Vicksburg, Miss. Bvt. Maj., 1 Sept., 1864, for gallant and meritorious service during the Atlanta campaign and in the Battle of Jonesboro', Ga. Capt. 13th Inf., 5 Nov., 1864. Trans. to 31st Inf., 21 Sept., 1866. Trans. to 22nd Inf., 15 May, 1869. Maj. 8th Inf., 1 Jan., 1888. Retired for disability in line of duty 26 Dec., 1888. Died 30 Nov., 1893.

DICKINSON, GEORGE. [Born in Mo. Appointed from Mo.]
2nd Lieut. 4th Art., 21 Oct., 1861. 1st Lieut., 29 Nov., 1861. Killed 13 Dec., 1862, at Battle of Fredericksburg, Va.

DICKINSON, JOSEPH W. [Born in Ireland. Appointed from Ill.]
Priv. 39th Ill. Vols., 11 Oct., 1861, to 2 June, 1864. Capt. 21st U. S. Col. Inf., 24

Aug., 1864. Mustered out 25 April, 1866. 2nd Lieut. 17th Inf., 11 May, 1866. Trans. to 26th Inf., 21 Sept., 1866. 1st Lieut., 4 Nov., 1867. Unass'd 19 May, 1869. Discharged 31 Dec., 1870.

DICKINSON, SAML. [Born in N. J. Appointed from N. J.]
Capt. of Inf., 22 March, 1847; 10th Inf., 9 April, 1847. Disbanded 22 Aug., 1848.

DICKINSON, WALTER M.* [Born in Mass. Appointed from Mass.]
2nd Lieut. 4th Cav., 12 June, 1880. 1st Lieut., 1 Sept., 1886. Capt., 9 April, 1898. Died 2 July, 1898, of wounds received in Battle of San Juan, Santiago, Cuba.

DICKINSON, WM. [Born in Conn. Appointed from Conn.]
2nd Lieut. 3rd Inf., 21 Feb., 1857. 1st Lieut., 10 May, 1861. Bvt. Maj., 21 July, 1861, for gallant and meritorious service in the Battle of Bull Run, Va. Capt. 3rd Inf., 31 July, 1861. Retired 3 Oct., 1863. Died 7 Aug., 1887.

DICKMAN, JOSEPH T.* [Born in Ohio. Appointed from Ohio.]
2nd Lieut. 3rd Cav., 11 June, 1881. 1st Lieut., 18 Jan., 1886. Capt. 8th Cav., 27 May, 1898. Maj. 26th U. S. Vols., 5 July, 1899. Lieut. Col. Vols., 13 Sept., 1899. Honor graduate of the Infantry and Cavalry School, 1883.

DICKSON, JAMES N. [Born in Pa. Appointed from Pa.]
Priv. Commonwealth Pa. Art., 24 April, to 5 Aug., 1861. 2nd Lieut. 6th Pa. Cav., 4 Oct., 1861. R. C. S., 8 April, 1862, to 1 March, 1863. Capt., 1 March, 1863. Resigned 17 Jan., 1864. 2nd Lieut. 3rd Art., 6 March, 1862. Resigned 27 April. 1863.

DICKSON, JOHN M. [Born in Pa. Appointed from Pa.]
Asst. Surg. 93rd Pa. Vols., 14 March, 1863. Mustered out 29 Oct., 1864. Maj. Surg., 213th Pa. Vols., 18 March, 1865. Mustered out 18 Nov., 1865. 1st Lieut. Asst. Surg., 16 Nov., 1868. Capt. Asst. Surg., 31 July, 1869. Died 7 Aug., 1887.

DICKSON, TRACY C.* [Born in Iowa. Appointed from Tex.]
2nd Lieut. 2nd Art., 11 June, 1892. 1st Lieut. Ord., 19 June, 1894.

DIEFFENDORF, OLIVER. [Born in N. Y. Appointed from Ill.]
2nd Lieut. of Inf., 23 Feb., 1847; 16th Inf., 9 April, 1847. 1st Lieut., 18 Nov., 1847. Disbanded 31 Aug., 1848.

DIETERICH, JOHN P. [Born in Germany. Appointed from N. Y.]
3rd Lieut. 23rd Inf., 10 May, 1813. 2nd Lieut., 14 June, 1814. Trans. to 4th Inf., 17 May, 1815. Resigned 4 Oct., 1816. 2nd Lieut. Corps Art., 31 Oct., 1818. Resigned 29 July, 1820. Bvt. 1st Lieut., 5 Feb., 1815, for distinguished and meritorious service.

DIETZ, WM. D. [Born in Ga. Appointed from N. Y.]
Asst. Surg., 3 Dec., 1883. Capt. and Asst. Surg., 3 Dec., 1888. Died 28 Jan., 1891.

DILLAHUNTY, JOHN N.* [Born in Miss. Appointed from Miss.]
Bvt. 2nd Lieut. 4th Art., 1 July, 1824. 2nd Lieut. 1st Art., 1 July, 1824. Resigned 14 April, 1832.

DILLENBACK, JOHN W. [Born in N. Y. Appointed from N. Y.]
Priv. Co. G, 10th N. Y. Heavy Art., 7 Aug., 1862. Corpl., 11 Sept., 1862. Discharged 21 Aug., 1863. Capt. 4th U. S. Col. Troops, 22 Aug., 1863. Bvt. Maj. and Lieut. Col. Vols., 13 March, 1865, for gallant and meritorious service during the war. Mustered out 11 April, 1866. 2nd Lieut. 1st Art., 23 Feb., 1866. 1st Lieut., 1 May, 1866. R. Q. M., 1 March, 1875, to 30 June, 1882. Capt., 30 June, 1882. Maj. 2nd Art., 8 March, 1898. Graduate of the Artillery School, 1869. Retired for over 30 years' service, 31 March, 1899.

DILLINGHAM, ALBERT R. [Born in Va. Appointed from Pa.]
Priv. Co. —, 14th Inf., 2 June, 1898, to 16 June, 1899. 2nd Lieut. 13th Inf., 1 May, 1899.

DILLINGHAM, LUCIUS A. [Born in N. Y. Appointed from N. Y.]
1st Lieut. 122nd N. Y. Vols., 8 Oct., 1862. 2nd Lieut. Sig. Corps, 3 March, 1863. Bvt. Capt. Vols., 2 April, 1865, for meritorious services in the campaign before Petersburg, Va. Mustered out 11 Aug., 1865.

DILWORTH, RANKIN.* [Born in Ohio. Appointed from Ohio.]
Bvt. 2nd Lieut. 1st Inf., 20 Aug., 1844. 2nd Lieut., 18 June, 1846. Died 27 Sept., 1846, of wounds received at Monterey, Mex.

DIMICK, JUSTIN.* [Born in Conn. Appointed from Vt.]
2nd Lieut. Light Art., 1 July, 1819. Trans. to 1st Art., 1 June, 1821. 1st Lieut., 1 May, 1824. Capt., 6 April, 1835. Maj., 1 April, 1850. Lieut. Col. 2nd Art., 5 Oct., 1857. Col. 1st Art., 26 Oct., 1861. Retired 1 Aug., 1863. Died 13 Oct., 1871. Bvt. Capt., 1 May, 1834, for ten years' faithful service in one grade. Bvt. Maj., 8 May, 1836, for gallant and meritorious conduct in the war against Florida Indians. Bvt. Lieut. Col., 20 Aug., 1847, for gallant and meritorious conduct at Contreras and Churubusco. Bvt. Col., 13 Sept., 1847, for gallant and meritorious conduct at Chapultepec. Bvt. Brig. Gen., 13 March, 1865, for long, gallant and faithful service to his country.

DIMICK, JUSTIN E.* [Born in N. H. Appointed at Large.]
2nd Lieut. 6th Inf., 24 June, 1861. 1st Lieut., 24 June, 1861. Trans. to 1st Art., 14 Aug., 1861. Reg. Adj., 1 Feb., 1862, to 3 May, 1863. Died 5 May, 1863, of wounds received at the Battle of Chancellorsville, Va.

DIMMICK, EUGENE D. [Born in N. Y. Appointed from N. Y.]
Priv. Co. G, 2nd N. J. State Militia, 26 April, 1861. Discharged 31 July, 1861. 1st Sergt. Co. M, 5th N. Y. Cav., 7 Oct., 1861. 2nd Lieut. 5th N. Y. Cav., 9 May, 1862. 1st Lieut., 10 Oct., 1862. Mustered out 6 Nov., 1863. 2nd Lieut. Vet. Res. Corps, 3 Feb., 1864. Mustered out 30 June, 1866. 2nd Lieut. 9th Cav., 9 Aug., 1867. 1st Lieut., 16 Jan., 1870. Capt., 25 Oct., 1883. Bvt. Capt., 27 Feb., 1890, for gallant services in action against Indians in the Black Range Mountains, N. M., 23 Sept., 1879. Maj. 5th Cav., 13 July, 1898.

DIMMOCK, CHAS.* [Born in Mass. Appointed from Mass.]
Bvt. 2nd Lieut. 1st Art., 1 July, 1821. 2nd Lieut., 1 July, 1821. 1st Lieut., 20 Feb., 1828. A. Q. M., 18 Aug., 1831, to 20 Aug., 1836. Capt. 1st Art., 6 Aug., 1836. Resigned 30 Sept., 1836.

DIMON, GEORGE D.* [Born in Conn. Appointed from Conn.]
Bvt. 2nd Lieut. 1st Inf., 1 July, 1833. Died 16 Sept., 1834.

DIMPFEL, GEORGE H. A. [Born in N. Y. Appointed from Cal.]
Mil. Storekeeper Q. M. D., 19 Feb., 1863. Capt., 28 July, 1866. Wholly retired 16 Aug., 1872.

DINWIDDIE, WM. A. [Born in Ind. Appointed from Iowa.]
Hosp. Steward 40th Iowa Vols., 13 Aug., 1862. Asst. Surg., 22nd Iowa Vols., 16 May, 1863. Mustered out 21 Feb., 1865. 2nd Lieut. 8th Cav., 20 June, 1868. Trans. to 2nd Cav., 22 March, 1869. 1st Lieut., 3 March, 1875. Retired for disability 26 July, 1886.

DINKINS, JAMES E. [Born in S. C. Appointed from S. C.]
1st Lieut. 3rd Inf., 1 July, 1808. Capt., 6 Feb., 1811. Maj. 44th Inf., 15 May, 1814. Trans. to 36th Inf., 18 Nov., 1814. Retained 17 May, 1815, as Capt. 4th Inf. Maj., 8 May, 1818. Died 6 Oct., 1822. Retained 17 May, 1815 (in re-organization under Act of 3 March, 1815), as Capt. 4th Inf., with Bvt. of Maj. from 15 May, 1814.

DINKINS, SIMEON M.* [Born in Ala. Appointed from Ala.]
Addl. 2nd Lieut. 11th Inf., 11 July, 1881. 2nd Lieut. 6th Inf., 31 July, 1881. Resigned 1 Feb., 1883.

DISAY, ISAAC. [Born in Netherlands. Appointed from Army.]
Priv. Co. A, 14th Ohio Vols., 27 April, to 13 Aug., 1861. Priv. Sergt. and 1st Sergt. Co. A, and Sergt. Maj. 18th Inf., 24 Sept., 1861, to Nov., 1863. 2nd Lieut. 18th Inf., 31 Oct., 1863. 1st Lieut., 31 Jan., 1864. Trans. to 27th Inf., 21 Sept., 1866. Capt., 5 March, 1867. Unass'd 14 June, 1869. Discharged 31 Dec., 1870.

DITCH, WM. T.* [Born in Ill. Appointed from Ill.]
2nd Lieut. 1st Cav., 15 June, 1868. R. C. S., 23 Feb., 1869, to 15 July, 1870. 1st Lieut., 1 March, 1870. Discharged 7 Sept., 1870.

DIVVER, JOSEPH A. [Born in N. Y. Appointed from N. Y.]
1st Lieut. of Inf., 2 March, 1847; 3rd Drag., 9 April, 1847. Disbanded 31 July, 1848.

DIX, CHAS. T. [Born in N. Y. Appointed from N. Y.]
1st Lieut. 14th Inf., 14 May, 1861. Resigned 7 Feb., 1863. Maj. A. A. de C., 20 June, 1862. Bvt. Lieut. Col. Vols., 13 March, 1865, for faithful and meritorious services during the war. Resigned 15 March, 1865.

DIX, JOHN A. [Born in N. H. Appointed from N. Y.]
Ensign 14th Inf., 10 May, 1813. 3rd Lieut. 21st Inf., 7 March, 1814. 2nd Lieut., 8 March, 1814. Trans. to Corps Art., 9 Aug., 1814. 1st Lieut., 23 March, 1818. Trans. to 1st Art., 1 June, 1821. Trans. to 3rd Art., 16 Aug., 1821. Capt., 30 Aug., 1825. Resigned 31 Dec., 1828. Maj. Gen. Vols., 16 May, 1861. Resigned 30 Nov., 1865. Died 21 April, 1879.

DIX, ROGER S.* [Born in N. H. Appointed from N. H.
Bvt. 2nd Lieut. 7th Inf., 1 July, 1832. 2nd Lieut., 28 Jan., 1834. 1st Lieut., 31 July, 1836. Capt., 15 July, 1845. Capt. A. Q. M., 7 July, 1838. Maj. P. M., 30 Sept., 1845. Died 7 Jan., 1849. Bvt. Lieut. Col., 23 Feb., 1847, for gallant and meritorious conduct at Buena Vista.

DIXON, HENRY B.* [Born in Iowa. Appointed from Iowa.]
Addl. 2nd Lieut. 10th Cav., 12 June, 1895. 2nd Lieut. 4th Cav., 21 Dec., 1895. Trans. to 10th Cav., 1 Feb., 1896. 1st Lieut. 8th Cav., 6 May, 1899.

DIXON, JAMES W. [Born in D. C. Appointed from Conn.]
1st Lieut. 2nd Conn. Art., 11 Feb., 1865. Mustered out 20 July, 1865. 2nd Lieut. 3rd Cav., 7 May, 1866. Trans. to 4th Art., 7 Sept., 1867. 1st Lieut., 7 Dec., 1867. Discharged 4 Aug., 1870. Bvt. 1st Lieut. and Capt., 2 March, 1867, for gallant and meritorious service in the capture of Petersburg, Va.

DIXON, JOSEPH.* [Born in Tenn. Appointed from Tenn.]
Bvt. 2nd Lieut. Top. Eng., 1 July, 1858. Resigned 28 June, 1861.

DIXON, WM. P.* [Born in N. Y. Appointed from Ill.]
2nd Lieut. 6th Cav., 18 June, 1866. Died 6 Oct., 1866.

D'LAGNEL, JULIUS A.* [Born in N. Y. Appointed from N. Y.]
Bvt. 2nd Lieut. 5th Inf., 1 July, 1821. 2nd Lieut., 1 July, 1821. Trans. to 2nd Art., 30 Dec., 1825. 1st Lieut., 30 May, 1832. Capt. Ord., 1 Nov., 1836. Died 21 May, 1840. Bvt. 1st Lieut., 1 July, 1831, for faithful service of ten years in one grade.

D'LAGNEL, JULIUS A. [Born in N. J. Appointed from Va.]
2nd Lieut. 2nd Art., 8 March, 1847. 1st Lieut., 26 Jan., 1849. Resigned 17 May, 1861.

DOANE, GUSTAVUS C. [Born in Ill. Appointed from D. C.]
Priv. and Sergt. Cos. I and A, 2nd Mass. Cav., 30 Oct., to 22 March, 1864. 1st Lieut. Cav., Miss. Marine Brigade, 23 March, 1864. Mustered out 23 Jan., 1865. 2nd Lieut. 2nd Cav., 5 July, 1868. 1st Lieut., 4 Dec., 1871. Capt., 22 Sept., 1884. Died 5 May, 1892.

DOBBINS, STEPHEN D. [Born in Pa. Appointed from Pa.]
Cadet Mil. Acad., 1 July, to 30 Sept., 1830, and 1 July, 1834, to 10 July, 1835. 2nd Lieut. 3rd Inf., 29 Sept., 1838. 1st Lieut., 31 Jan., 1842. Capt., 16 Feb., 1847. Dismissed 21 March, 1847. Reinstated 24 May, 1847. Dismissed 1 Dec., 1847.

DOCKERY, OLIVER H., Jr. [Born in N. C. Appointed from N. C.]
2nd Lieut. Co. K, 1st N. C. Vols., 6 Dec., 1898, to 22 April, 1899. 2nd Lieut. 3rd Inf., 10 April, 1899.

DOD, ALBERT B. [Born in N. J. Appointed from N. J.]
Priv. Co. A, National Guard N. J. Vols., 16 April, to July, 1861. Capt. 15th Inf., 14 May, 1861. Resigned 15 Aug., 1864.

DODD, ALBERT. [Born in Mass. Appointed from Mass.]
Capt. 3rd Batt. Mass. Vols., 19 May, 1861. Capt. 17th Inf., 14 May, 1861. Killed 27 June, 1862, at Battle of Gaines' Mills, Va. Bvt. Maj., 27 June, 1862, for gallant and meritorious service at the Battle of Gaines' Mills, Va.

DODD, GEORGE A.* [Born in Pa. Appointed from Pa.]
2nd Lieut. 3rd Cav., 15 June, 1876. 1st Lieut., 29 Feb., 1880. Capt., 31 Aug., 1889.

DODD, STEPHEN G. [Born in N. J. Appointed from N. J.]
Chap. 25th Mass. Vols., 28 May, 1864, to muster out 13 July, 1865. Post Chap., 23 June, 1879. Retired, operation of law, 24 March, 1890.

DODDS, FRANK L.* [Born in Pa. Appointed from Ill.]
2nd Lieut. 9th Inf., 23 June, 1879. 1st Lieut., 15 June, 1887. Capt., 26 April, 1898.

DODGE, CHARLES, Jr. [Born in D. C. Appointed from Army.]
Priv. Gen. Ser., 14 June, 1875. Sergt., 1 Dec., 1876. 2nd Lieut. 24th Inf., 25 Oct., 1878. 1st Lieut., 30 June, 1883. Adj., 1 Jan., 1884, to 30 April, 1886. Graduate of the Infantry and Cavalry School, 1883. Capt. of Inf. (24th), 4 Dec., 1895. Died 30 July, 1898.

DODGE, FRANCIS S. [Born in Mass. Appointed from Mass.]
Priv. and Corpl. Co. F, 23rd Mass. Vols., 9 Oct., 1861, to 19 Dec., 1863. 1st Lieut. 2nd U. S. Col. Cav., 20 Dec., 1863. Capt., 6 July, 1865. Mustered out 12 Feb., 1866. 1st Lieut. 9th Cav., 28 July, 1866. Capt., 31 July, 1867. Bvt. Maj., 27 Feb., 1890, for gallant services in action against Indians at Milk Creek, Col., 29 and 30 Sept., and 1 Oct., 1879. Maj. P. M., 13 Jan., 1880. Medal of Honor for most distinguished gallantry against hostile Indians near White River Agency, Colo., in voluntarily marching with his force of forty men to the relief of Maj. Thornburgh and his command, reaching the field 2 Oct., 1879, joining in the action, and fighting for three days until relief arrived; while serving as Capt., 9th Cav., commanding Troop. D.

DODGE, FREDERICK. [Born in Ind. Appointed from N. Y.]
1st Lieut. 3rd Cav., 14 May, 1861. 6th Cav., 3 Aug., 1861. R. C. S., 5 Sept., to 20 Oct., 1862. Dropped 20 Oct., 1862.

DODGE, FREDK. L. [Born in N. H. Appointed from N. H.]
Priv. Co. F, 44th Mass. Vols., 29 Aug., 1862. Discharged 18 June, 1863. 1st Lieut. 18th N. H. Vols., 22 March, 1865. Mustered out 29 July, 1865. 2nd Lieut. 23rd Inf., 7 March, 1867. 1st Lieut., 22 Jan., 1873. Capt., 22 June, 1889. Retired for disability — ——, 1891. Died 11 Sept., 1891.

DODGE, HENRY. [Born in Ind. Appointed from Wis.]
Capt., Maj. and Lieut. Col. Mo. Vols., 1812 to 1815. Col. Mich. Mtd. Vols., 15 April, to 1 July, 1832. Maj. Mtd. Rangers, 21 June, 1832. Col. 1st Drag., 4 March, 1833. Resigned 4 July, 1836.

DODGE, HENRY C.* [Born in N. Y. Appointed from N. Y.]
2nd Lieut. 2nd Art., 11 June, 1863. 1st Lieut., 11 June, 1864. Lost at sea, 27 Jan., 1873. Bvt. Capt., 13 March, 1865, for gallant and meritorious service at the Battle of Cold Harbor, Va.

DODGE, JAMES E. [Born in Minn. Appointed from Army.]
Priv., Corpl. and Sergt. Co. D, 11th Inf., 16 Feb., 1887, to 9 Nov., 1890. 2nd Lieut. of Inf. (14th), 6 Nov., 1890. Dismissed 31 Jan., 1893.

DODGE, RICHD. I.* [Born in N. C. Appointed from N. C.]
Bvt. 2nd Lieut. 8th Inf., 1 July, 1848. 2nd Lieut., 24 Dec., 1848. 1st Lieut., 3 March, 1855. Reg. Adj., 1 Sept., 1854, to 1 Oct., 1855. Capt., 3 May, 1861. Lieut. Col. A. I. G., 1 Jan., 1863, to 24 Feb., 1863. Maj. 12th Inf., 21 June, 1864. Bvt. Lieut. Col., 30 March, 1865, for meritorious and faithful service in the recruitment of the armies of the United States. Bvt. Col., 30 March, 1865, for faithful and meritorious service connected with the organization of the Vol. armies of the United States during the war. Trans. to 30th Inf., 21 Sept., 1866. Trans. to 3rd Inf., 15 March, 1869. Lieut. Col. 23rd Inf., 29 Oct., 1873. Col. A. de C. to Gen. Sherman, 1 Jan., 1881, to 26 June, 1882. Col. 11th Inf., 26 June, 1882. Retired, operation of law, 19 May, 1891. Died 16 June, 1895.

DODGE, THEODORE A. [Born in Mass. Appointed from Mass.]
1st Lieut. 101st N. Y. Vols., 13 Feb., 1862. 1st Lieut. 119th N. Y. Vols., 17 Oct., 1862. Capt. Vet. Res. Corps, 12 Nov., 1863. Maj., 17 Aug., 1864. Bvt. Lieut. Col. and Col. Vols., 2 Dec., 1865, for gallant and meritorious service. Capt. 44th Inf., 28 July 1866. Mustered out of Vet. Res. Corps, 1 Dec., 1866. Bvt. Maj., 2 March, 1867, for gallant and meritorious service in the Battle of Gettysburg, Pa. Bvt. Lieut. Col., 2 March, 1867, for gallant and meritorious service during the war. Unass'd 27 May, 1869. Retired 28 April, 1870.

DODGE, WM. T. [Born in Me. Apointed from Me.]
Priv. Co. E, 1st Me. Vols., 3 May, to 5 Aug., 1861. Priv. Cos. K and A, 10th and 29th Me. Vols., 15 Oct., 1862, to 17 Oct., 1864. 2nd Lieut. 16th Me. Vols., 19 Nov., 1864. Bvt. 1st Lieut. and Capt. Vols., 13 March, 1865, for gallant and meritorious service during the war. Mustered out 5 June, 1865. 2nd Lieut. 7th Inf., 23 Feb., 1866. 1st Lieut., 28 July, 1866. Unass'd 19 May, 1869. Ass'd to 21st Inf., 14 July, 1869. Discharged 25 Oct., 1870.

DODT, HELENUS. [Born in Germany. Appointed from N. Y.]
2nd Lieut. 29th N. Y. Vols., 23 Dec., 1862, to 20 June, 1863. 2nd Lieut. 7th N. Y. Vols., 17 Sept., 1864. Capt., 25 Feb., 1865. Bvt. Maj. Vols., 9 April, 1865, for conspicuous gallantry during the war. Mustered out 4 Aug., 1865. 2nd Lieut. 15th Inf., 11 May, 1866. Trans. to 33rd Inf., 21 Sept., 1866. 1st Lieut., 24 Aug., 1868. Unass'd 3 May, 1869. Ass'd to 24th Inf., 1 Jan., 1871. Reg. Adj., 1 Aug., 1872, to 30 Dec., 1878. Died 30 Dec., 1878. Bvt. 1st Lieut., 2 March, 1867, for gallant and meritorious service in the Battle of Sutherland Station, Va.

DOEBLER, THOS. S. [Born in Pa. Appointed from Army.]
Cadet Mil. Acad., 1 July to 25 Sept., 1859. Priv. Co. E, 2nd Batt. 14th Inf., 1 May, to 13 July, 1862. 2nd Lieut. 14th Inf., 30 June, 1862. 1st Lieut., 31 July, 1863. Retired 25 Dec., 1865. Died 12 May, 1874. Bvt. Capt., 13 March, 1865, for gallant and meritorious service in the Battle of Snicker's Gap, Va.

DOGGETT, THOS. [Born in Va. Appointed from Army.]
Priv., Corpl., Sergt. and Sergt. Maj., 2nd Inf., 14 Nov., 1807, to Sept., 1812. Ensign 2nd Inf., 28 Sept., 1812. 2nd Lieut. 28 Sept., 1812. 1st Lieut., 7 Sept., 1813. Trans. to 1st Inf., 17 May, 1815. Resigned 10 Oct., 1815.

DOHERTY, EDWARD P. [Born in Canada. Appointed from N. Y.]
Priv. Co. A, 71st N. Y. State Mil., 20 April to 9 Aug., 1861. 1st Lieut. 16th N. Y. Cav., 12 Sept., 1863. Capt., 23 April, 1865. Trans. to 3rd Provisional N. Y. Cav., 23 June. 1865. Mustered out 21 Sept., 1865. 2nd Lieut. 5th Cav., 19 April, 1866. 1st Lieut., 1 March, 1867. Mustered out 27 Dec., 1870.

DOLAN, MICHAEL. [Born in Ireland. Appointed from Army.]
Priv. Co. E, 2nd Inf., 22 April, 1856. Corpl., 1 Aug., 1858. Discharged 15 April, 1861. Corpl. Co. E, 2nd Inf., 15 April, 1861. Sergt., 1 May, 1861. 1st Sergt., 1 Oct., 1861. 2nd Lieut. 2nd Inf., 19 Feb., 1863. 1st Lieut., 31 Jan., 1866. Unass'd 17 April, 1869. Retired 15 Dec., 1870. Died 2 May, 1882.

DOLPH, CYRUS A. [Born in Ore. Appointed from Ore.]
Priv. Hosp. Corps, 7 June, 1898, to 3 April, 1899. 2nd Lieut. 4th Inf., 1 June, 1899.

DOLPHIN, JOHN F. [Born in Mass. Appointed from Minn.]
Post Chap., 5 March, 1888. Resigned 24 Jan., 1893.

DONALDSON, CHARLES V.* [Born in Sweden. Appointed from Iowa.]
2nd Lieut. 24th Inf., 11 June, 1888. Drowned 15 July, 1890.

DONALDSON, THOMAS Q.* [Born in S. C. Appointed from S. C.]
Addl. 2nd Lieut. 3rd Cav., 12 June, 1887. 2nd Lieut. 7th Cav., 1 Sept., 1887. 1st Lieut. 8th Cav., 3 Jan., 1895.

DONALDSON, JAMES L.* [Born in Md. Appointed from Md.]
2nd Lieut. 3rd Art., 1 July, 1836. Trans. to 1st Art., 25 May, 1837. 1st Lieut., 7 July, 1838. Capt. A. Q. M., 3 March, 1847. Maj. Q. M., 3 Aug., 1861. Col. A. Q. M. G., 28 July, 1866. Retired 15 March, 1869. Resigned 1 Jan., 1874. Bvt. Capt., 23 Sept., 1846, for gallant and meritorious conduct at Monterey. Bvt. Maj., 23 Feb., 1847, for gallant and meritorious conduct at Buena Vista. Bvt. Lieut. Col., 14 May, 1861 (services not specified). Bvt. Col. and Bvt. Brig. Gen., 17 Sept., 1864, for distinguished and important service in the Q. M. D. in the campaign terminating in the capture of Atlanta, Ga. Bvt. Maj. Gen., 13 March, 1865, for faithful and meritorious service in the Q. M. D. during the war.

DONELSON, ANDREW J., Jr.* [Born in Tenn. Appointed from Tenn.]
Bvt. 2nd Lieut. Eng., 1 July, 1820. 2nd Lieut., 1 Oct., 1820. Resigned 1 Feb., 1822.

DONELSON, ANDREW J, Jr., [Born in Tenn. Appointed from Tenn.]
Bvt. 2nd Lieut. Eng., 1 July, 1848. 2nd Lieut., 16 Oct., 1852. 1st Lieut., 3 March, 1855. Died 20 Oct., 1859.

DONELSON, DANIEL S.* [Born in Tenn. Appointed from Tenn.]
2nd Lieut. 3rd Art., 1 July, 1825. Resigned 22 Jan., 1826.

DONOHO, ARCHIMEDES. [Born in N. C. Appointed from N. C.]
Ensign 3rd Inf., 3 Jan., 1812. 2nd Lieut., 1 Nov., 1812. 1st Lieut., 15 April, 1814. Reg. Adj., July, 1814, to June, 1815. Trans. to 1st Inf., 17 May, 1815. Reg. Adj., 1 Sept., 1815, to 2 Nov., 1816. Resigned 31 Jan., 1819.

DONOHO, SANDERS. [Born in N. C. Appointed from N. C.]
Capt. 2nd Art., 6 July, 1812. Trans. to Corps Art., 12 May, 1814. Disbanded 15 June, 1815. Reinstated 2 Dec., 1815. Trans. to 4th Inf., 7 Jan., 1820. Maj., 1 May, 1824. Killed 7 July, 1826, by a Sergt. Bvt. Maj., 6 July, 1822, for ten years' faithful service in one grade.

DONAVAN, EDWARD. [Born in Ireland. Appointed from Neb.]
Priv. Co. A and Hosp. Stwd. 1st Neb. Vols., 11 June, 1861, to 1 Oct., 1861. 2nd Lieut., 1 Oct., 1861. 1st Lieut., 1 June 1862. Capt., 25 Dec., 1865. Mustered out 1 July, 1866. 2nd Lieut. 41st Inf., 28 July, 1866. 1st Lieut., 1 July, 1867. Reg. Adj., 31 March, 1862, to 11 Nov., 1862. Trans. to 24th Inf., 11 Nov., 1869. Reg. Adjt., 11 Nov., 1869, to 31 July, 1872. Resigned 9 July, 1878.

DONOVAN, JOHN H. [Born in Ireland. Appointed from N. Y.]
1st Lieut. 69th N. Y. Vols., 5 Jan., 1862. Capt., 17 Sept., 1862. Mustered out 12 June, 1863. Capt. Vet. Res. Corps, 28 Aug., 1863. Maj., 4 Dec., 1863. Bvt. Lieut. Col. and Col. Vols., 13 March, 1865, for gallant and meritorious service during the war, especially in the Battles of Malvern Hill and Fredericksburg, Va. Mustered out 23 Nov., 1866. Capt. 44th Inf., 28 July, 1866. Bvt. Maj., 2 March, 1867, for gallant and meritorious service in the picket attack near Fair Oaks, Va., — June, 1862. Trans. to 17th Inf., 27 May, 1869. Retired 28 June, 1878. Died 16 April, 1882.

DONOVAN, JOSEPH L.* [Born in Ky. Appointed from Ky.]
2nd Lieut. 17th Inf., 12 June, 1891. Trans. to 21st Inf., 31 Aug., 1897. 1st Lieut., 2 Dec., 1897. Trans. to 11th Inf., 23 Oct., 1899. Lieut. Col. 69th N. Y. Vols., 21 May, 1898, until mustered out 31 Jan., 1899. Trans. to 16th Inf., 17 March, 1900.

DOOLITTLE, ANSON O. [Born in N. Y. Appointed from Wis.]
1st Lieut. 2nd Wis. Vols., 11 June, 1861. Mustered out 7 Aug., 1861. 2nd Lieut. 4th Cav., 5 Aug., 1861. 1st Lieut., 17 July, 1862. Lieut. Col. 37th Wis. Vols., 13 April, 1864. Bvt. Col. Vols., 13 March, 1865, for conspicuous gallantry in front of Petersburg, 18 June, 1864. Resigned from Vol. ser. and U. S. Army 7 Sept., 1864.

DOORES, WM. R. [Born in D. C. Appointed from N. Y.]
2nd Lieut. 5th Art., 9 July, 1898.

DORCY, BEN. H. [Born in Ore. Appointed from Army.]
2nd Lieut. 3rd Pa. Vols., 11 May to 22 Oct., 1898. Priv. and Corpl. Batty G, 4th Art., 1 March, to 13 April, 1899. 2nd Lieut. 4th Cav., 5 April, 1899.

D'OREMIEUIX, THEOPHILUS. [Born in France. Appointed from N. Y.]
2nd Lieut. 1st Inf., 1 July, 1840. 1st Lieut., 31 Oct., 1846. Capt., 31 Oct., 1856. Resigned 8 Dec., 1856.

DOREY, HALSTEAD.* [Born in Mo. Appointed from Mo.]
Addl. 2nd Lieut. 23rd Inf., 11 June, 1897. 2nd Lieut. 4th Inf., 16 Dec., 1897. 1st Lieut. 2 March, 1899.

DORMAN, JAMES. [Born in Va. Appointed from Va.]
1st Lieut. 5th Inf., 1 July, 1808. Capt., 9 Nov., 1811. Maj. 34th Inf., 28 June, 1814. Retained 17 May, 1815 (in re-organization under Act of 3 March, 1815), as Capt. 8th Inf., with Bvt. of Maj. from 28 June, 1814. Died 11 April, 1819.

DORN, ANDREW J. [Born in N. Y. Appointed from Mo.]
1st Lieut. Clark's Batt. Mo. Vols., 19 June, 1846. Mustered out 24 June, 1847. 2nd Lieut. 3rd Drag., 28 Aug., 1847. Disbanded 31 July, 1848.

DORR, GUSTAVUS.* [Born in Mass. Appointed from Mass.]
Bvt. 2nd Lieut. 2nd Inf., 1 July, 1825. 2nd Lieut. 6th Inf., 1 July, 1825. 1st Lieut., 4 March, 1833. Capt., 26 Sept., 1837. Dropped 22 Nov., 1843.

DORST, JOSEPH H.* [Born in Ky. Appointed from Ind.]
2nd Lieut. 4th Cav., 13 June, 1873. 1st Lieut., 20 March, 1879. Capt., 2 March, 1885.

Maj. 2nd Cav., 7 Nov., 1898. Lieut. Col. and A. A. G. Vols., 9 May, 1898, to 12 May, 1899. Col. 45th U. S. Inf., 17 Aug., 1899.

DOST, GEORGE W. [Born in Germany. Appointed from Army.]
Priv., Corpl., Sergt. and 1st Sergt., Co. B, and Sergt. 7th Inf., 11 Aug., 1852, to 23 March, 1863. 2nd Lieut. 4th Inf., 19 Feb., 1863. 1st Lieut., 9 June, 1864. Reg. Adj., 1 Jan. to 31 Aug., 1865. Capt., 15 May, 1867. Unass'd 23 March, 1869. Ass'd to 14th Inf., 15 Dec., 1870. Cashiered 23 Nov., 1874. Bvt. Capt., 2 April, 1865, for gallant and meritorious service in front of Petersburg, Va.

DOSTER, CHASE. [Born in Kan. Appointed from Kan.]
Maj. 22nd Kan. Vols., 18 May, 1898, until muster out 3 Nov., 1898. Cadet at Mil. Acad., 21 June, 1893, to 25 June, 1895. 2nd Lieut. 21st Inf., 10 April, 1899.

DOUBLEDAY, ABNER.* [Born in N. Y. Appointed from N. Y.]
Bvt. 2nd Lieut. 3rd Art., 1 July, 1842. 2nd Lieut. 1st Art., 24 Feb., 1845. 1st Lieut., 3 March, 1847. Capt., 3 March, 1855. Maj. 17th Inf., 14 May, 1861. Brig. Gen. Vols., 3 Feb., 1862. Bvt. Lieut. Col., 17 Sept., 1862, for gallant and meritorious service in the Battle of Antietam, Md. Maj. Gen. Vols., 29 Nov., 1862. Bvt. Col., 2 July, 1863, for gallant and meritorious service in the Battle of Gettysburg, Pa. Lieut. Col. 17th Inf., 20 Sept., 1863. Bvt. Brig. Gen. and Bvt. Maj. Gen., 13 March, 1865, for gallant and meritorious service during the war. Mustered out of Vol. service, 24 Aug., 1865. Col. 35th Inf., 15 Sept., 1867. Unass'd 15 March, 1869. Ass'd to 24th Inf., 15 Dec., 1870. Retired 11 Dec., 1873. Died 26 Jan., 1893.

DOUGHERTY, ANDREW J. [Born in Ill. Appointed from Army.]
Priv., Corpl. and Sergt. Troop B, 3rd Cav., 12 Feb., 1897, to 14 April, 1899. 2nd Lieut. 17th Inf., 5 April, 1899.

DOUGHERTY, JOHN J.* [Born in Ill. Appointed from Ill.]
2nd Lieut. 11th Inf., 14 June, 1872. 1st Lieut., 21 Dec., 1880. Retired for disability, with rank of Capt., 29 Dec., 1890. Died 11 Aug., 1899.

DOUGHERTY, WM. E. [Born in Ireland. Appointed from Army.]
Priv. Gen. Ser., 10 April, 1860. Priv. Co. K, 1st Inf., 10 Dec., 1860. Corpl., 1 July, 1861. Trans. to Co. G, 8 Nov., 1861. Sergt., 20 Nov., 1861. 1st Sergt., 1 May, 1862. 2nd Lieut. 1st Inf., 19 Feb., 1863. Bvt. 1st Lieut., 4 July, 1863, for gallant and meritorious service during the Siege of Vicksburg, Miss. 1st Lieut. 1st Inf., 9 April, 1865. Capt., 1 March, 1878. Maj., 26 April, 1898. Lieut. Col. 7th Inf., 20 June, 1899.

DOUGLAS, JOSEPH B. [Born in Md. Appointed from Md.]
2nd Lieut. 5th Art., 9 July, 1898.

DOUGLAS, SAML. R.* [Born in Scotland. Appointed from Montana Ter.]
2nd Lieut. 7th Inf., 15 June, 1876. Resigned 3 June, 1883.

DOUGLAS, WM. O. [Born in N. Y. Appointed from Army.]
Cadet at Mil. Acad., 1 July, 1861, to 23 Jan., 1862. Priv. Co. F, 2nd Batt. 14th Inf., 10 March, 1862. Sergt., 30 April, 1862. 2nd Lieut. 14th Inf., 30 June, 1862. Bvt. Capt., 2 July, 1863, for gallant and meritorious service in the Battle of Gettysburg, Pa. 1st Lieut. 14th Inf., 14 May, 1864. Retired 31 Dec., 1864.

DOUGLASS, DAVID B. [Born in N. J. Appointed from N. Y.]
2nd Lieut. Eng., 1 Oct., 1813. 1st Lieut., 17 Sept., 1814. Capt., 31 March, 1819. Prof. at Mil. Acad., 29 Aug., 1820. Resigned 1 March, 1831. Bvt. Capt., 17 Sept., 1814, for gallant conduct in the Sortie from Fort Erie. Died 19 Oct., 1849.

DOUGLASS, HENRY.* [Born in N. Y. Appointed from N. Y.]
Bvt. 2nd Lieut. 7th Inf., 1 July, 1852. 2nd Lieut. 8th Inf., 31 Dec., 1853. 2nd Lieut. 9th Inf., 3 March, 1855. 1st Lieut., 10 Sept., 1856. Capt., 18th Inf., 14 May, 1861. Bvt. Maj., 31 Dec., 1862, for gallant and meritorious service in the Battle of Murfreesboro', Tenn. Maj. 3rd Inf., 28 July, 1866. Unass'd 15 March, 1869. Ass'd to 11th Inf., 31 Dec., 1870. Lieut. Col. 14th Inf., 10 Jan., 1876. Col. 10th Inf., 1 July, 1885. Retired by operation of law, 9 March, 1891. Died 19 June, 1892.

DOUGLASS, RICHARD. [Born in Penn. Appointed from Army.]
Priv., Corpl. and Sergt. 5th Inf., and Light Art., 25 June, 1812, to 25 June, 1817. 2nd Lieut. 2nd Inf., 15 June, 1817. Disbanded 1 June, 1821.

DOVE, WILBUR E. [Born in Cal. Appointed from Army.]
Priv., Corpl. and Sergt. Co. E, 12th Inf., 28 Jan., 1889, to 1 Aug., 1892. 2nd Lieut. 12th Inf., 18 July, 1892. 1st Lieut., 26 April, 1898.

DOVE, WM. E. [Born in Ohio. Appointed from Ohio.]
Priv. Co. B, 126th Ohio Vols., 8 Aug., 1862. Corpl., 1 Feb., 1863. Sergt., 24 Sept., 1863. 1st Lieut. 196th Ohio Vols., 24 March, 1865. Mustered out 11 Sept., 1865. 2nd Lieut. 12th Inf., 23 Feb., 1866. 1st Lieut., 28 July, 1866. Capt., 1 Sept., 1873. Drowned 28 May, 1884.

DOWD, HEMAN.* [Born in N. Y. Appointed from N. Y.]
2nd Lieut. 3rd Art., 15 June, 1876. 1st Lieut., 1 Nov., 1881. Resigned 1 June, 1883.

DOWDY, ROBT. W.* [Born in Miss. Appointed from Ark.]
2nd Lieut. 17th Inf., 13 June, 1879. 1st Lieut., 12 Dec., 1885. Retired with rank of Capt., 26 April, 1898. Restored to active list, Act of 9 Feb., 1899. Capt. of Inf., (22nd), 26 April, 1898. Accepted 11 March, 1899.

DOWLING, JOHN T. [Born in Ireland. Appointed from Army.]
Priv., Corpl. and 1st Sergt. Co. D, 6th Inf., 25 Oct., 1857, to 25 Oct., 1862. Priv., Sergt. and 1st Sergt. Co. E, 13th Inf., 15 Jan., to 24 Nov., 1863. 2nd Lieut., 17th Inf., 31 Oct., 1863. 1st Lieut., 8 Dec., 1863. Died 1 June, 1864, of wounds received in the Battle of Laurel Hill, Va. Bvt. Capt., 5 May, 1864, for gallant and meritorious service at the Battle of the Wilderness, Va.

DOWNES, EDWARD E. [Born in Tex. Appointed from Tex.]
Cadet at Mil. Acad., 15 June, 1896, to 25 Jan., 1898. 2nd Lieut. 1st Inf., 9 July, 1898. 1st Lieut., 2 March, 1899.

DOWNEY, GEORGE M. [Born in Md. Appointed from Va.]
1st Lieut. 14th Inf., 26 Oct., 1861. Reg. Adj., 11 Dec., 1864, to 5 Oct., 1865. Bvt. Capt., 2 July, 1863, and Bvt. Maj., 13 March, 1865, for gallant and meritorious service in the Battle of Gettysburg, Pa. Capt. 14th Inf., 5 Oct., 1865. Trans. to 32nd Inf., 21 Sept., 1866. Trans. to 21st Inf., 19 April, 1869. Retired for disability, 6 March, 1888.

DOWNEY, WM. [Born in Pa. Appointed from Pa.]
Ensign 16th Inf., 14 July, 1813. 2nd Lieut., 15 Aug., 1813. 1st Lieut., 22 Feb., 1814. Disbanded 15 June, 1815. 2nd Lieut. 5th Inf., 3 Sept., 1816. Disbanded 1 June, 1821.

DOWNING, DENNIS J. [Born in Ireland. Appointed from N. Y.]
Sergt. Maj. 42nd N. Y. Vols., 21 May, 1861. 2nd Lieut., 25 July, 1861. Resigned 17 Sept., 1861. Priv. Co. B, 97th N. Y. Vols., 14 Nov., 1861. 1st Lieut., 1 Nov., 1862. Capt., 8 Jan., 1863. Discharged 12 Feb., 1864. Capt. Vet. Res. Corps, 1 Feb., 1864. Bvt. Maj. and Lieut. Col. Vols., 13 March, 1865, for gallant and meritorious service during the war. 1st Lieut. 44th Inf., 28 July, 1866. Unass'd 27 May, 1869. Retired as Capt., 15 Dec., 1870. Died 14 May, 1871. Bvt. Capt., 2 March, 1867, for gallant and meritorious service at the Battle of Bull Run (2nd), Va. Bvt. Maj., 2 March, 1867, for gallant and meritorious service at the Battle of Gettysburg, Pa.

DOWNING, JOHN C. C. [Born in Pa. Appointed from D. C.]
Asst. Surg., 5 Aug., 1861. Resigned 27 March, 1865.

DOYLE, MICHAEL P. [Born in Ireland. Appointed from Mich.]
2nd Lieut. of Inf., March, 1847; 15th Inf., 9 April, 1847. Died 23 Oct., 1847.

DOYLE, WM. E. [Born in Pa. Appointed from Ky.]
Priv. Co. B, and Sergt. Maj. 15th Ind. Vols., 14 June, 1861, to 2 March, 1864. 1st Lieut. Adj. 15th Ind. Vols., 2 March, 1864. Mustered out 25 June, 1864. 1st Lieut. Adj. 17th Ind. Vols., 13 July, 1864. Mustered out 8 Aug., 1865. 2nd Lieut. 10th Cav., 1 Sept., 1868. Mustered out 31 Dec., 1870.

DRAKE, ALEXR. E. [Born in N. Y. Appointed from Ky.]
Midshipman U. S. N., 26 June, 1834. Resigned 28 Jan., 1837. 2nd Lieut. 2nd Inf., 21 Feb., 1857. 1st Lieut., 14 May, 1861. Capt., 9 Oct., 1861. Retired 27 Aug., 1862. Bvt. Maj., Lieut. Col. and Col., 31 May, 1865, for faithful and meritorious service. Died 31 March, 1897.

DRAKE, CHARLES B.* [Born in Pa. Appointed from Pa.]
Addl. 2nd Lieut. 1st Cav., 12 June, 1896. 2nd Lieut. 5th Cav., 27 Aug., 1896. 1st Lieut. 4th Cav., 13 Dec., 1899. Trans. to 1st Cav., 23 Feb., 1900.

DRAKE, GEORGE B. [Born in Mass. Appointed from Mass.]
2nd Lieut. 12th Mass. Vols., 26 June, 1861, to 26 Aug., 1861. 2nd Lieut. 6th Inf., 5 Aug., 1861. 1st Lieut., 20 Sept., 1863. Capt. A. A. de C., 22 May, 1862. Maj. A. A. G. Vols., 11 March, 1863. Lieut. Col. A. A. G. Vols., 4 Nov., 1863, to 23 March, 1865. Bvt. Col. and Brig. Gen. Vols., 13 March, 1865, for faithful, efficient and meritorious service during the war. Resigned 23 March, 1865.

DRANE, ANTHONY.* [Born in Md. Appointed from Md.]
Bvt. 2nd Lieut. 7th Inf., 1 July, 1824. 2nd Lieut. 5th Inf., 1 July, 1824. 1st Lieut., 20 Aug., 1828. A. Q. M., 18 April, 1829. Resigned 25 Nov., 1835. Reinstated 17 March, 1842, to rank as Capt. 5th Inf., from 31 Oct, 1836. Cashiered 10 July, 1846. Died 5 April, 1850.

DRANE, GUSTAVUS S. [Born in Md. Appointed from the Army.]
Priv., Corp. and Sergt. Light Art., 21 April, 1812, to April, 1814. 3rd Lieut. Light Art., 15 April, 1814. 2nd Lieut., 17 March, 1814. 1st Lieut., 15 Nov., 1817. Trans. to 2nd Art., 1 June, 1821. Capt., 30 May, 1822. Died 16 April, 1846. Bvt. Capt., 15 Nov., 1827, for ten years' faithful service in one grade.

DRAPER, PAUL. [Born in ——. Appointed from Army.]
Priv., Corpl., Sergt and 1st Sergt. Co. D, 16th Inf., 27 July, 1897, to 23 Nov., 1899. 2nd Lieut. 22nd Inf., 1 Oct., 1899.

DRAVO, EDWARD E.* [Born in Pa. Appointed from Pa.]
2nd Lieut. 6th Cav., 15 June, 1876. 1st Lieut., 30 Aug., 1881. Capt. and C. S., 28 March, 1892. Major and C. S., 4 Feb., 1898. Lieut. Col. and Chief C. S. Vols., 9 May, 1898. Col. and C. S., 22 July, 1898, to 2 March, 1899. Discharged 7 March, 1899.

DRAYTON, THOS. F.* [Born in S. C. Appointed from S. C.]
Bvt. 2nd Lieut. 6th Inf., 1 July, 1828. 2nd Lieut., 1 July, 1828. Resigned 15 Aug., 1836.

DRESSER, GEORGE W.* [Born in Conn. Appointed from Mass.]
2nd Lieut. 4th Art., 6 May, 1861. 1st Lieut., 14 May, 1861. R. Q. M., 1 Aug., 1862, to 1 Oct., 1863. Resigned 13 Oct., 1865. Bvt. Capt., 18 Aug., 1864, for gallant services during the operations on the Weldon Railroad, Va. Bvt. Maj., 13 March, 1865, for good conduct and gallant service during the war. Died 27 May, 1883.

DREW, ALFRED.* [Born in Tex. Appointed from Tex.]
2nd Lieut. 12th Inf., 12 June, 1891. 1st Lieut., 26 April, 1898. Maj. 3rd Tex. Vols., 14 May, 1898. Killed in action near Angeles, P. I., 19 Aug., 1899.

DREW, CHAS. E. [Born in N. H. Appointed from Mass.]
Sergt. Co. F, 6th Mass. Mil., 16 April to 2 Aug., 1861. 1st Lieut. 26th Mass. Vols., 23 Sept., 1861. Mustered out 7 Nov., 1864. 2nd Lieut. 16th Inf., 8 March, 1866. Trans. to 34th Inf., 21 Sept., 1866. 1st Lieut., 31 July, 1867. Unassigned 14 April, 1869. Died 5 June, 1870.

DREW, GEORGE A. [Born in Mich. Appointed from Mich.]
Capt. 6th Mich. Cav., 11 Oct., 1862. Maj., 24 Sept. 1863. Bvt. Lieut. Col. 13 March, 1865, for highly distinguished and meritorious service in the Shenandoah Valley. Bvt. Col. Vols., 9 April, 1865, for highly distinguished and meritorious service in the campaign against Richmond, Va. Mustered out 11 Oct., 1865. 2nd Lieut. 10th Inf., 15 May, 1866. Bvt. 1st Lieut., 2 March, 1867, for gallant and meritorious service in the campaigns in the Shenandoah Valley, in 1864. Bvt. Capt., 2 March, 1867, for gallant and meritorious service in the campaign against Richmond, Va., in 1865, 1st Lieut., 26 March, 1868. Unassigned 19 May, 1869. Ass'd to 3rd Cav., 31 Dec,. 1870. Capt., 20 March, 1879. Retired by operation of law, 15 March, 1896.

DRIGGS, WM. J. [Born in N. Y. Appointed from Mich.]
Corpl. Troop L, 6th Mich. Cav., 11 Oct., 1862, to 20 Dec., 1862. 1st Lieut. 1st Mich. S. S., 22 July, 1863. Resigned 6 July, 1864. 2nd Lieut. 11th Inf., 23 Feb., 1866. 1st Lieut., 28 July, 1866. Trans. to 20th Inf., 21 Sept., 1866. Mustered out 1 Jan., 1871.

DRIPS, JOSEPH. [Born in Iowa. Appointed from the Army.]
Priv., Corpl. and Sergt. Troop D, 8th Cav., 9 May, 1893, to 23 March, 1896. 2nd Lieut. of Inf. (8th), 5 March, 1896. Dropped 17 April, 1898.

DRISCOLL, JOHN J. [Born in Ireland. Appointed from the Army.]
Priv., Corpl., Sergt. and 1st Sergt. Batty. A, 1st Art., 12 June, 1855, to 28 June, 1864. 2nd Lieut. 2nd Inf., 7 June, 1864. Trans. to 1st Art., 22 Aug., 1864. 1st Lieut., 1 Dec., 1865. Mustered out 5 Dec., 1870.

DROUILLARD, JAMES P.* [Born in Ohio. Appointed from Ohio.]
2nd Lieut. 6th Inf., 24 June, 1861. 1st Lieut., 24 June, 1861. Capt. A. A. de C., 23 May, 1862. Resigned 1 Feb., 1865.

DROUILLARD, JAMES F. [Born in Tenn. Appointed from Tenn.]
1st Lieut. 4th Tenn. Vols., 13 July, 1898. Resigned 19 Sept., 1898. 2nd Lieut. 6th Inf., 9 Sept., 1898. 1st Lieut. 1st Inf., 30 Sept., 1899. Trans. to 9th Inf., 23 April, 1900.

DRUIEN, JAMES L.* [Born in Ky. Appointed from Ky.]
2nd Lieut. 17th Inf., 1 July, 1886. 1st Lieut. of Inf. (19th), 30 Nov., 1892. Trans. to 17th Inf., 15 Dec., 1892. Resigned 30 April, 1895.

DRUM, HUGH A. [Born in Mich. Appointed from Mass.]
2nd Lieut. 12th Inf., 9 Sept., 1898. 1st Lieut. 25th Inf., 15 Jan., 1900.

DRUM, JOHN. [Born in Ireland. Appointed from Cal.]
1st Lieut. 8th Cal. Vols., 5 Dec., 1864. Mustered out 24 Oct., 1865. 2nd Lieut. 14th Inf., 28 July, 1866. 1st Lieut., 31 July, 1867. Unassigned 22 July, 1869. Ass'd to 10th Inf., 15 Dec., 1870. Capt., 15 Sept., 1884. Killed in action at San Juan, Santiago, Cuba, 1 July, 1898.

DRUM, RICHARD C. [Born in Pa. Appointed from Pa.]
Priv. Co. K, 1st Penn. Vols., 16 Dec., 1846. 2nd Lieut. of Inf., 18 Feb., 1847; 9th Inf., 9 April, 1847. Bvt. 1st Lieut., 13 Sept., 1847, for gallant and meritorious conduct in the Battle of Chapultepec. Trans. to 4th Art., 8 March, 1848. 1st Lieut., 16 Sept., 1850. Bvt. Capt. A. A. G., 16 March, 1861. Vacated commission of 1st Lieut. 4th Art., 14 May, 1861. Maj. A. A. G., 3 Aug., 1861. Lieut. Col. A. A. G., 17 July, 1862. Bvt. Col., 24 Sept., 1864, for meritorious and faithful service during the war. Bvt. Brig. Gen., 13 March, 1865, for faithful and meritorious service in the A. G.'s Dept. during the war. Col. A. A. G., 22 Feb., 1869. Brig. Gen. A. G., 15 June, 1880. Retired by operation of law 28 May, 1889.

DRUM, SIMON H.* [Born in Pa. Appointed from Pa.]
Bvt. 2nd Lieut. 4th Art., 1 July, 1830. 2nd Lieut., 1 July, 1830. 1st Lieut., 31 Aug., 1836. Capt. A. Q. M., 29 June to 18 Aug., 1846. Capt. 4th Art., 18 Aug., 1846. Killed 13 Sept., 1847, in the assault on City of Mexico.

DRUM, WM. F. [Born in N. Y. Appointed from Minn.]
Cadet at Mil. Acad., 1 July, 1850, to 29 May, 1851, and from 1 July, 1851, to 11 May, 1852. Priv. Co. F, 3rd Ohio Vols., 1 June to 31 July, 1861. 2nd Lieut. 2nd Inf., 5 Aug., 1861. 1st Lieut., 9 Oct., 1861. Capt., 1 May, 1863. Bvt. Maj., 2 Dec., 1864, for gallant service during the campaign before Richmond, Va. Bvt. Lieut. Col., 1 April, 1865, for gallant and meritorious service in the Battle of Five Forks, Va. Lieut. Col. 5th N. Y. Vols., 1 April, 1865. Col., 29 May, 1865. Mustered out of Vol. service, 21 Aug., 1865. Maj. 14th Inf., 22 June, 1882. Lieut. Col. 12th Inf., 8 Dec., 1886. Col. of Inf., 4 July, 1892. Died 4 July, 1892.

DRUMMOND, THOS. [Born in Va. Appointed from Iowa.]
2nd Lieut. 2nd Cav., 26 April, 1861. 1st Lieut., 30 May, 1861. 5th Cav., 3 Aug., 1861. Lieut. Col. 4th Iowa Cav., 31 Dec., 1861. Resigned from Vols., 3 June, 1862. Capt. 5th Cav., 17 July, 1862. Died 1 April, 1865, of wounds received in action at Five Forks, Va.

DRURY, THOS. [Born in Ireland. Appointed from Army.]
Priv. Co. A, 1st Inf., 7 Jan., 1842. Corpl., 1 Jan., 1844. Sergt., 26 July, 1845. Discharged 14 Nov., 1846. Sergt. Co. A, 1st Inf., 14 Nov., 1846. 1st Sergt., 1 Jan., 1848. Discharged, 16 Sept., 1851. 1st Sergt. Co. A, 1st Inf., 16 Sept., 1851. Ord. Sergt. U. S. A., 1 Dec., 1852. Discharged 16 July, 1856. Ord. Sergt. U. S. A., 16 July, 1850. Discharged 16 May, 1861. Ord. Sergt. U. S. A., 16 May, 1864, for 2nd Lieut. 2nd Inf., 10 Aug., 1863. Bvt. 1st Lieut., 5 May, 1864, for gallant and meritorious service in the Battle of the Wilderness, Va. 1st Lieut. 2nd Inf., 28 Feb., 1866. Capt. 39th Inf., 28 July, 1866 (declined). Capt. 2nd Inf., 27 April, 1879. Died 26 Sept., 1881.

DRY, THOS. [Born in England. Appointed from Army.]
Priv. Co. I, 2nd Inf., 11 Sept., 1854, to 1 July, 1859. Priv., Corpl. and Sergt. Cos. D and F, and Sergt. Maj. 7th Inf., 1 July, 1859, to 6 Nov., 1863. 2nd Lieut. 1st Inf., 31 Oct., 1863. 1st Lieut., 28 July, 1866. Resigned 30 June, 1869.

DRYER, HIRAM. [Born in N. Y. Appointed from Army.]
Priv., Sergt. and 1st Sergt. Co. H, Mounted Rifles, 31 Oct., 1846, to 24 July, 1848. Bvt. 2nd Lieut. 4th Inf., 28 June, 1848. 2nd Lieut., 31 July, 1848. 1st Lieut., 29 Sept., 1853. Capt., 14 May, 1861. Maj. 13th Inf., 2 Feb., 1865. Trans. to 22nd Inf., 21 Sept., 1866. Died 5 March, 1867. Bvt. Maj., 13 Dec., 1862, for gallant and meritorious service at the Battle of Fredericksburg, Va. Bvt. Lieut. Col., 3 May, 1863, for gallant and meritorious service at the Battle of Chancellorsville, Va.

DRYSDALE, JOHN. [Born in Fla. Appointed from Fla.]
2nd Lieut. 3rd Art., 30 June, 1855. 1st Lieut., 5 Oct., 1857. Dropped 27 Sept., 1860.

DUANE, JAMES C.* [Born in N. Y. Appointed from N. Y.]
Bvt. 2nd Lieut. Eng., 1 July, 1848. 2nd Lieut., 16 March, 1853. 1st Lieut., 1 July, 1855. Capt. 12th Inf., 14 May, 1861 (declined). Capt. Eng., 6 Aug., 1861. Maj., 3 March, 1863. Bvt. Lieut. Col. and Bvt. Col., 6 July, 1864, for meritorious and faithful service in the field in the campaign from the Rapidan to the James, and particularly for distinguished professional service in the operations before Petersburg, Va. Bvt. Brig. Gen., 13 March, 1865, for gallant and meritorious service during the Siege of Petersburg, Va., and in the campaign terminating with the surrender of the insurgent army under Gen. Robt. E. Lee. Lieut. Col. Eng., 7 March, 1867. Col., 10 Jan., 1883. Brig. Gen. Chief of Eng., 11 Oct., 1886. Retired by operation of law 30 June, 1888. Died 8 Nov., 1897.

DU BARRY, BEEKMAN.* [Born in N. J. Appointed from D. C.]
Bvt. 2nd Lieut. 1st Art., 1 July, 1849. 2nd Lieut. 3rd Art., 13 Feb., 1850. 1st Lieut., 24 Dec., 1853. Capt. C. S., 11 May, 1861. Vacated commission of 1st Lieut. 3rd Art., 14 May, 1861, but served as such to 20 May, 1861. Maj. C. S., 9 Feb., 1863. Lieut. Col., 13 March, 1865, for meritorious service during the war. Bvt. Col., 13 March, 1865, for faithful and meritorious service during the war. Lieut. Col. A. C. G. S., 20 May, 1882. Brig. Gen. C. G. S., 10 July, 1890. Retired by operation of law 4 Dec., 1892.

DU BOIS, HENRY A. [Born in N. Y. Appointed from N. Y.]
Asst. Surg., 26 Aug., 1861. Resigned 1 April, 1868. Bvt. Capt. and Maj., 13 March, 1865, for faithful and meritorious service during the war.

DU BOIS, JOHN V. D.* [Born in N. Y. Appointed from N. Y.]
Bvt. 2nd Lieut. Mounted Rifles, 1 July, 1855. 2nd Lieut., 1 Oct., 1855. 1st Lieut. 13 May, 1861. Capt. 15th Inf., 14 May, 1861 (declined). Bvt. Capt., 10 Aug., 1861, for gallant and meritorious service in the Battle of Wilson's Creek, Mo. (declined). Maj. 1st Mo. Light Art., 1 Sept., 1861. Capt. 3rd Cav., 21 Feb., 1862. Mustered out of Vol. service, 24 Feb., 1862. Col. A. A. de C., 19 Feb., 1862. Col. 1st Mo. Light Art., 7 Aug., 1862. Bvt. Maj., 4 Oct., 1862, for gallant and meritorious service in the Battle of Corinth, Miss. (declined). Resigned commission of Col. 1st Mo. Light Art., 14 Oct., 1862. Bvt. Lieut. Col., 13 March, 1865, for gallant and meritorious service during the war (declined). Mustered out as Col. A. A. de C., 9 Feb., 1866. Maj. 3rd Cav., 6 May, 1869. Retired 17 May, 1876. Died 31 July, 1879.

DU BOIS, RICHD. C. [Born in Pa. Appointed from Army.]
Sergt. Co. K, 6th Pa. Res. Corps, 23 April, 1861. Discharged 27 Jan., 1862. Sergt. Co. B, 17th Pa. Cav., 15 Sept. to 29 Nov., 1862. Discharged 12 Aug., 1863. Priv. Gen. Ser., 6 March, 1864. 2nd Lieut. and 1st Lieut. 14th Inf., 9 Oct., 1865. Retired 15 Dec., 1870.

DU BOIS, WM. A. [Born in Ill. Appointed from Ill.]
Sergt. Co. I, 7th Ill. Vols., 22 April to 25 July, 1861. 2nd Lieut. 3rd Cav., 5 Aug., 1861. 1st Lieut., 17 July, 1862. Resigned from Vols. 18 July, 1863, and from U. S. A. 10 Dec. 1863.

DU BOIS, WILBUR F. [Born in Mich. Appointed from Mich.]
2nd Lieut. 15th Inf., 22 Jan., 1867. 1st Lieut., 17 Sept., 1867. Resigned 22 June, 1869.

DU BOSE, BENJN. E.* [Born in S. C. Appointed from S. C.]
Bvt. 2nd Lieut. 3rd Inf., 1 July, 1833. Dropped 1 Oct., 1833.

DUCAT, ARTHUR C., Jr.* [Born in Ill. Appointed from Ill.]
2nd Lieut. 11th Inf., 13 June, 1879. Trans. to 3rd Cav., 8 Sept., 1879, taking rank from 8 Sept., 1879. 1st Lieut., 3 Nov., 1883. Trans. to 24th Inf., 23 Feb., 1887 (to rank in Inf., 26 Nov., 1884.) Capt., 17 April, 1897. Lieut. Col. 49th U. S. Vols., 9 Sept., 1899. Graduate of the Infantry and Cavalry School 1885.

DU COMMUN, JOSEPH. [Born in France. Appointed from N. Y.]
Teacher of French at Military Academy, 1 March, 1818. Resigned 31 Aug., 1831.

DUDLEY, CLARK D. [Born in Mo. Appointed from the Army.]
Mus., Priv., Corpl. and Sergt. Batty. I, 1st Art., and Batty H, 6th Art., 5 March, 1889, to 20 April, 1899. 2nd Lieut. 4th Cav., 5 April, 1899.

DUDLEY, EDGAR S.* [Born in N. Y. Appointed from N. Y.]
2nd Lieut. 1st N. Y. Light Art., 28 May, 1864. Mustered out 28 Nov., 1864. Cadet at Mil. Acad., 1 Sept., 1876. 2nd Lieut. 2nd Art., 15 June, 1870. 1st Lieut., 29 Oct., 1875. Capt. A. Q. M., 20 Dec., 1892. Lieut. Col. J. A. Vols., 9 May, 1898, to 17 April, 1899. Maj. J. A. Vols., 7 April, 1899.

DUDLEY, JAMES S. [Born in Vt. Appointed from Vt.]
2nd Lieut. 2nd Art., 24 Oct., 1861. 1st Lieut., 23 May, 1863. Discharged 1 Oct., 1870. Bvt. 1st Lieut., 30 June, 1862, for gallant and meritorious service at the Battle of Glendale, Va. Bvt. Capt., 1 July, 1862, for gallant and distinguished service at the Battle of Malvern Hill, Va. Bvt. Maj., 13 March, 1865, for gallant and meritorious service during the war.

DUDLEY, NATHAN A. M. [Born in Mass. Appointed from Mass.]
1st Lieut. 10th Inf., 3 March, 1855. Capt., 7 May, 1861. Col. 30th Mass. Vols., 1 March, 1862. Bvt. Maj., 5 Aug., 1862, for gallant and meritorious service in the Battle of Baton Rouge, La. Bvt. Lieut. Col., 14 June, 1863, for gallant and meritorious service in the Siege of Port Hudson, La. Maj. 15th Inf., 13 Sept., 1864. Bvt. Brig. Gen. Vols., 19 Jan., 1865. Mustered out of Vol. service 16 Feb., 1865. Bvt. Col., 13 March, 1865, for gallant and meritorious service during the war. Trans. to 24th Inf., 21 Sept., 1866. Unassigned 15 March, 1869. Ass'd to 3rd Cav., 15 Dec., 1870. Lieut. Col. 9th Cav., 1 July, 1876. Col. 1st Cav., 6 June, 1885. Retired by operation of law 20 Aug., 1889.

DUER, EDWARD A. [Born in N. J. Appointed from N. J.]
2nd Lieut. 1st Art., 24 Oct., 1861. 1st Lieut., 11 Oct., 1862. Resigned 15 April, 1867. Bvt. Capt., 3 June, 1864, for gallant and meritorious service at the Battle of Cold Harbor, Va. Bvt. Maj., 13 March, 1865, for gallant and meritorious service during the war.

DUFF, GEORGE. [Born in Scotland. Appointed from Pa.]
Priv. Co. D, 102nd Pa. Vols., 16 Aug., 1861. Corpl., 1 Nov, 1861. 1st Sergt., 1 July, 1862. 2nd Lieut. 102nd Pa. Vols., 1 Jan., 1863. 2nd Lieut. Vet. Res. Corps, 15 Sept., 1864. Mustered out 23 Nov., 1866. 2nd Lieut. 43rd Inf., 28 July, 1866. Bvt. 1st. Lieut., 2 March, 1867, for gallant and meritorious service during the war. Trans. to 1st Inf., 8 April, 1869. 1st Lieut. 13 Feb., 1873. Retired 28 June, 1878. Died 22 Sept., 1896.

DUFF, ROBERT J.* [Born in Pa. Appointed from Mich.]
2nd Lieut. 8th Cav., 13 June, 1883. 1st Lieut. 6th Cav., 24 Feb., 1891. Trans. to 8th Cav., 27 April, 1891. Capt. 5th Cav., 2 March, 1899. Trans. to 8th Cav., 3 May, 1899. Adj., 5 Sept., 1899.

DUFF, WM. H. [Born in England. Appointed from N. Y.]
Capt. of Inf., 2 March, 1847; 3rd Drag., 9 April, 1847. Died 16 July, 1847.

DUFFY, JOHN M. [Born in Ireland. Appointed from R. I.]
Sergt. Co. C, 2nd R. I. Vols., 5 June, 1861. 2nd Lieut., 22 July, 1861. 1st Lieut., 13 Nov., 1861. Discharged 27 Nov., 1861. 1st Lieut. 13th Inf., 5 Aug., 1861. Capt., 8 Nov., 1864. Trans. to 22nd Inf., 21 Sept., 1866. Unassigned 15 May, 1869. Discharged 25 Oct., 1870. Died 24 Feb., 1881.

DUFPHEY, WM. L. [Born in N. C. Appointed from N. C.]
2nd Lieut. 10th Inf., 5 June, 1812. Trans. to 3rd Rifle, — March, 1813. 1st Lieut., 15 April, 1813. Capt., 12 Aug., 1814. Trans. to Rifle regiment, 17 May, 1815. Resigned 15 Feb., 1818.

DUGAN, JAMES. [Born in Ohio. Appointed from Ill.]
Corpl. Co. B, 14th Ill. Vols., 25 May, 1861, to 30 Nov., 1863. 2nd Lieut. 8th U. S. Vet. Vols., 28 May, 1865. 1st Lieut., 1 Sept., 1865. Resigned 28 Oct., 1865. 2nd Lieut. 5th Inf., 23 Feb., 1866. Resigned 17 Dec., 1866.

DUGAN, THOMAS B.* [Born in Md. Appointed from Md.]
Addl. 2nd Lieut. 10th Cav., 13 June, 1882. 2nd Lieut. 3rd Cav., 26 June, 1882. 1st Lieut., 29 Oct., 1888. Capt. 7th Cav., 9 July, 1899.

DUGGAN, WALTER T. [Born in England. Appointed from Army.]
Priv. Co. B, 5th Wis. Vols., 13 June, 1861. Discharged 31 Aug., 1863. Hosp. Steward U. S. A., 7 Sept., 1863. 2nd Lieut. 10th Inf., 3 Jan., 1867. 1st Lieut., 13 Nov., 1874. Capt., 1 Aug., 1886. Maj., 2 March, 1899.

DUKE, JAMES W. [Born in Ky. Appointed from Ky.]
2nd Lieut. 2nd Cav., 5 Aug., 1861. 1st Lieut., 17 July, 1862. Died 28 Oct., 1862.

DULANY, EDWARD N. [Born in Md. Appointed from Md.]
2nd Lieut. 4th Inf., 27 Oct., 1820. Resigned 1 May, 1823.

DULANY, HENRY R.* [Born in Va. Appointed from Md.]
3rd Lieut. Light Art., 2 March, 1815. Trans. to Corps Art., 17 May, 1815. Batt. Adj., 15 Aug., 1815, to 5 March, 1817. 2nd Lieut. 4th Inf., 5 March, 1817. 1st Lieut., 10 Feb., 1818. Reg. Adj., 20 April to 10 Oct., 1819. Capt., 3 Feb., 1822. Resigned 31 May, 1825. Died 27 Nov., 1838.

DULANY, WM. [Born in Md. Appointed from Md.]
2nd Lieut. 5th Cav., 12 Dec., 1872. Resigned 3 June, 1873. Died 25 Feb., 1888.

DUMAS, HIPOLITE. [Born in France. Appointed from Pa.]
2nd Lieut. Eng., 3 Aug., 1813. 1st Lieut. 20 Feb., 1814. Capt., 31 March, 1819. Resigned 1 Jan., 1825. Died 7 Feb., 1841.

DUMESTE, JACOB A.* [Born in Md. Appointed from Md.]
2nd Lieut. Corps Art., 1 July, 1819. Trans. to 2nd Art., 1 June, 1821. 1st Lieut., 1 Jan., 1831. Died 10 Oct., 1831.

DUMMER, SAMUEL R. [Born in N. J. Appointed from N. J.]
1st Lieut. of Inf., 8 March, 1847; 10th Inf., 9 April, 1847. Capt., 21 Jan., 1848. Disbanded 24 Aug., 1848.

DUMMETT, EDWARD J. [Born in Fla. Appointed from Fla.]
2nd Lieut. of Inf., 8 March, 1847; 13th Inf., 9 April, 1847. 1st Lieut., 31 March, 1848. Disbanded 15 July, 1848. 1st Lieut. 1st Cav., 3 March, 1855. Died 1 Oct., 1855.

DUMREICHER, CONRAD C. [Born in Germany. Appointed from Ill.]
Asst. Surg. Vols., 11 Sept., 1862. Surg. Vols., 27 May, 1863. Bvt. Lieut. Col. Vols., 1 June, 1865, for faithful and meritorious service. Mustered out 27 July, 1865. Asst. Surg., 28 Feb., 1866. Cashiered 17 June, 1868.

DUNBAR, GEORGE W. [Born in N. Y. Appointed from Wis.]
Post Chaplain, 15 Aug., 1876. Retired by operation of law, 8 March, 1897.

DUNCAN, DANIEL.* [Born in Ky. Appointed from Ky.]
Addl. 2nd Lieut. of Inf., 12 June, 1895. 2nd Lieut. 6th Inf., 5 Aug., 1895. Trans. to 4th Inf., 11 Sept., 1895. Drowned 8 Aug., 1897.

DUNCAN, GEORGE B.* [Born in Ky. Appointed from Ky.]
2nd Lieut. 9th Inf., 1 July, 1886. 1st Lieut. 4th Inf., 18 May, 1893. Capt., 2 March, 1899. Capt. A. A. G. Vols., 12 May, 1898, to 20 Feb., 1899.

DUNCAN, JAMES.* [Born in N. Y. Appointed from N. Y.]
Bvt. 2nd Lieut. 2nd Art., 1 July, 1834. 2nd Lieut., 17 Nov., 1834. 1st Lieut., 30 Nov., 1836. Capt., 16 April, 1846. Col. I. G., 26 Jan., 1849. Died 3 July, 1849. Bvt. Maj., 8 May, 1846, for gallant and distinguished services at Palo Alto. Bvt. Lieut. Col., 9 May, 1846, for gallant and highly distinguished conduct at Resaca de la Palma. Bvt. Col., 23 Sept., 1846, for gallant and meritorious conduct at Monterey, Mex.

DUNCAN, JOHN. [Born in Pa. Appointed from Pa.]
2nd Lieut. Rifle Reg., 4 Dec., 1819. Trans. to 6th Inf., 1 June, 1821. Resigned 4 Dec., 1821.

DUNCAN, JOHNSON K.* [Born in Pa. Appointed from Ohio.]
Bvt. 2nd Lieut. 2nd Art., 1 July, 1849. 2nd Lieut. 3rd Art., 31 Oct., 1849. 1st Lieut., 24 Dec., 1853. Resigned 31 Jan., 1855. Died 18 Dec., 1862.

DUNCAN, JOSEPH W. [Born in Tex. Appointed from Mo.]
2nd Lieut. 21st Inf., 1 Oct., 1873. 1st Lieut., 10 May, 1878. Capt., 24 April, 1888. Maj. 13th Inf., 2 March, 1899. Bvt. 1st Lieut., 27 Feb., 1890, for gallant services in action against Indians at the Clearwater, Idaho, 11 and 12 July, 1877.

DUNCAN, MATTHEW. [Born in Penn. Apointed from Ill.]
Capt. Mounted Rangers, 4 Oct., 1832. Capt. 1st Drag., 15 Aug., 1833. Resigned 15 Jan., 1837.

DUNCAN, THOS. [Born in Ill. Appointed from Ill.]
1st Lieut. Mtd. Rifles, 27 May, 1846. Capt., 15 March, 1848. Maj., 10 June, 1861; 3rd Cav., 3 Aug., 1861. Bvt. Lieut. Col., 8 April, 1862, for gallant and meritorious service in action near Albuquerque, N. Mex. Bvt. Col. and Brig. Gen., 13 March, 1865, for meritorious service during the war. Lieut. Col. 5th Cav., 28 July, 1866. Retired 15 Jan., 1873. Died 7 Jan., 1887.

DUNCAN, WM. R. [Born in Pa. Appointed from Pa.]
2nd Lieut. 3rd Art., 9 April, 1812. 1st Lieut., 13 March, 1813. Trans. to Corps Art., 12 May, 1814. Capt., 31 Dec., 1818. Died 17 May, 1820.

DUNGAN, HUGH E.* [Born in Pa. Appointed from Pa.]
Bvt. 2nd Lieut. 4th Art., 1 July, 1850. 2nd Lieut., 15 July, 1852. Died 11 Nov., 1853.

DUNHAM, CURTIS. [Born in N. Y. Appointed from Kan.]
2nd Lieut. 10th Inf., 3 March, 1855. Resigned 1 Oct., 1856.

DUNHAM, LEWIS. [Born in N. J. Appointed from N. J.]
Maj. Surg. Light Drag., 12 Dec., 1808. Trans. to Light Art., 12 May, 1814. Resigned 21 Sept., 1819.

DUNKELBERGER, ISAAC R. [Born in Pa. Appointed from Pa.]
1st Sergt. Co. E, 1st Pa. Vols., 20 April to 13 May, 1861. 2nd Lieut. 1st Drag., 26 April, 1861. 1st Cav., 3 Aug., 1861. 1st Lieut., 7 Aug., 1861. Capt., 9 June, 1863. Mustered out 1 Jan., 1871. Bvt. Maj., 11 June, 1864, for gallant and meritorious service at the Battle of Trevillian Station, Va. Bvt. Lieut. Col., 13 March, 1865, for gallant and meritorius service during the war.

DUNLOP, SAMUEL R. [Born in N. Y. Appointed from N. Y.]
Asst. Surg., 31 Oct., 1891. Resigned 21 Jan., 1893.

DUNN, BEVERLY W.* [Born in La. Appointed from La.]
2nd Lieut. 3rd Art., 13 June, 1883. 1st Lieut. Ord., 8 July, 1890. Capt. (14 years' service), 15 June, 1898. Honor graduate of the Artillery School, 1888.

DUNN, FRANCIS J. [Born in Ohio. Appointed from Ohio.]
Priv., Corpl. and Sergt. Co. G, 61st Ohio Vols., 4 March, 1862, to 31 March, 1865, when mustered out. 2nd Lieut. 11th Inf., 23 Feb., 1866. 1st Lieut., 28 July, 1866. Unassigned 14 April, 1869. Ass'd to 22nd Inf., 14 July, 1869. Resigned 31 Jan., 1870.

DUNN, JOHN G. [Born in Ind. Appointed from Ind.]
Asst. Surg., 14 July, 1846. Resigned 19 Aug., 1847. Died 10 June, 1857.

DUNN, THOS. [Born in Scotland. Appointed from Army.]
Priv. Batty M, 4th Art., 13 April, 1862, to 13 April, 1865, and Priv. Co. K, 2nd Inf., 9 Jan.,, 1866, to 23 Nov., 1867. 2nd Lient. 15th Inf., 19 Nov., 1867. 1st Lieut., 28 Feb., 1869. Unassigned 12 Aug., 1869. Discharged 5 Nov., 1870. Priv. Co. C, 19th Inf., 6 July, 1871, and Priv. and Sergt. Gen. Ser., 4 Dec., 1871, to 28 March, 1885.

DUNN, THOS. S. [Born in Ind. Appointed from Ind.]
Priv. Co. G, 1st Ind. Vols., 14 June, 1846. Discharged 15 June, 1847. Capt. 9th Ind. Vols., 24 April, 1861. Mustered out 29 July, 1861. Capt. 12th Inf., 14 May, 1861. Bvt. Maj., 1 Aug., 1864, for gallant service in the Battle of the Wilderness, and during the campaign before Richmond, Va. Bvt. Lieut. Col., 13 March, 1865, for gallant and meritorious service during the war. Trans. to 21st Inf., 21 Sept., 1866. Maj. 8th Inf., 19 Feb., 1873. Trans. to 12th Inf., 14 May, 1877. Retired 29 June, 1878. Died 14 Nov., 1895.

DUNN, WM. McK., Jr. [Born in Ind. Appointed from Ind.]
Priv. Co. K, 6th Ind. Vols., 18 April, 1861. Discharged 2 Aug., 1861. Priv. Co. C, 67th Ind. Vols., 8 Aug., 1862. 2nd Lieut. 83rd Ind. Vols., 19 Nov., 1862. 1st Lieut., 4 Oct., 1863. Capt. A. A. Gen. Vols., 9 April, 1865. 1st Lieut. 10th Inf., 29 Nov., 1865. Mustered out of Vol. service 3 May, 1866. Capt. 21st Inf., 28 July, 1866. Bvt. Maj., 2 March, 1867, for gallant and meritorious service in the campaigns and Battles of Vicksburg, Miss.; Chattanooga., Tenn.; Richmond and Petersburg, Va. Unassigned 19 April, 1869. Ass'd to 2nd Art., 31 Dec., 1870. Died 30 Sept. 1891.

DUNN, WM. McK. [Born in Ind. Appointed from Ind.]
Vol. A. de C. to Gen. McClellan, 19 June to Aug., 1861. Maj. J. A. Vols., 13 March, 1863. Col. A. J. A. G., 22 June, 1864. Bvt. Brig. Gen., 13 March, 1865, for faithful, meritorious and distinguished service in his Dept. Brig. Gen. J. A. G., 1 Dec., 1875. Retired 22 Jan., 1881. Died 24 July, 1887.

DUNNING, SAMUEL W.* [Born in N. Y. Appointed from N. Y.]
2nd Lieut. 16th Inf., 12 June, 1880. 1st Lieut., 1 July, 1885. Capt., 26 April, 1898.

DUNOVANT, JOHN. [Born in S. C. Appointed from S. C.]
Sergt. Co. B, Palmetto Reg. S. C. Vols., 14 Dec., 1846, to muster out, 7 Dec., 1847. Capt. 10th Inf., 3 March, 1855. Resigned 29 Dec., 1860. Killed 1 Oct., 1864, in Confederate service.

DUNSTER, EDWARD S. [Born in Me. Appointed from N. Y.]
Asst. Surg., 5 Aug., 1861. Resigned 1 Feb., 1866. Bvt. Capt. and Maj., 13 March, 1865, for faithful and meritorious service during the war. Died 4 May, 1888.

DUNTON, WARREN R. [Born in Vt. Appointed from Vt.]
1st Sergt. Co. E, 5th Vt. Vols., 16 Sept., 1861. 2nd Lieut. 5th Vt. Vols., 21 June, 1862. 1st Lieut., 14 Dec., 1862. Mustered out 31 March, 1863. 1st Lieut. Vet. Res. Corps, 15 Oct., 1863. Capt., 5 Jan., 1865. Bvt. Maj. Vols., 13 March, 1865, for gallant and meritorious service during the war. Mustered out 30 June, 1866. 2nd Lieut. 2nd Inf., 22 Jan., 1867. Bvt. 1st Lieut., 2 March, 1867, for gallant and meritorious service in the Battle of Fredericksburg, Va. Unassigned 28 March, 1870. Ass'd to 19th Inf., 3 Aug., 1870. 1st Lieut., 31 Dec., 1872. Retired 28 June, 1878.

DUNWOODY, HENRY H. C.* [Born in Ohio. Appointed from Iowa.]
2nd Lieut. 4th Art., 18 June, 1866. 1st Lieut., 5 Feb., 1867. Capt., 17 June, 1889. Maj. Sig. Corps, 18 Dec., 1890. Lieut. Col., 15 March, 1897. Col., 8 July, 1898. Col. Chf. Sig Off. Vols., 20 May, 1898, to 20 July, 1898.

DUPERU, ALPHONSE M. [Born in Va. Appointed from La.]
Capt. of Inf., 5 March, 1847; 3rd Drag., 9 April, 1847. Disbanded 20 July, 1848.

DU PONT, HENRY A.* [Born in Del. Appointed at Large.]
Bvt. 2nd Lieut. Eng., 6 May, 1861. 2nd Lieut., 6 May, 1861. 1st Lieut. 5th Art., 14 May, 1861. Reg. Adj., 6 July, 1861, to 24 March, 1864. Capt., 24 March, 1864. Resigned 1 March, 1875. Bvt. Maj., 19 Sept., 1864, for gallant service at Opequan and Fisher's Hill, Va. Bvt. Lieut. Col., 19 Oct., 1864, for distinguished service at Cedar Creek, Va.

DU PONT, HENRY.* [Born in Del. Appointed from Del.]
Bvt. 2nd Lieut. 4th Art., 1 July, 1833. Resigned 15 June, 1834. Died 8 Aug., 1889.

DURAND, C. F. L. [Born in N. Y. Appointed from N. Y.]
2nd Lieut. 6th Inf., 13 Feb., 1818. 1st Lieut., 27 May, 1820. Disbanded 1 June, 1821.

DURFEE, LUCIUS L.* [Born in Ohio. Appointed from Ohio.]
2nd Lieut. 17th Inf., 1 July, 1886. 1st Lieut. 10th Inf., 19 May, 1893. Trans. to 17th Inf., 17 April, 1895. Capt., 2 March, 1899.

DURHAM, CASS.* [Born in Ind. Appointed from Ind.]
2nd Lieut. and 1st Lieut. 16th Inf., 23 June, 1865. Trans. to 25th Inf., 21 Sept., 1866. Trans. to 18th Inf., 26 April, 1869. Capt., 30 June, 1877. Retired for disability in line of duty 15 June, 1887. Died 3 April, 1898.

DURKEE, RICHD. P. H. [Born in N. Y. Appointed from N. Y.]
1st Lieut. 14th Inf., 14 May, 1861. Reg. Adj., 13 Sept. to 25 Oct., 1861. Capt., 25 Oct., 1861. Resigned 11 July, 1863.

DURNIN, THOS. J. [Born in Pa. Appointed from Army.]
Priv., Corpl., Sergt. and 1st Sergt. Troop G, 2nd Drag., 14 June, 1855, to 1 Aug., 1861. 2nd Lieut. 16th Inf., 14 May, 1861. 1st Lieut., 24 Oct., 1861. R. Q. M., 21 Nov., 1862, to 3 March, 1863. Capt., 8 Dec., 1864. Trans. to 25th Inf., 21 Sept., 1866. Cashiered 21 Sept., 1867. Bvt. Capt., 19 Sept., 1863, for gallant and meritorious service at the Battle of Chickamauga, Ga.

DURYEA, RICHARD C.* [Born in N. Y. Appointed from N. Y.]
Bvt. 2nd Lieut. 4th Art., 1 July, 1853. 2nd Lieut. 1st Art., 24 Dec., 1853. 1st Lieut., 6 Dec., 1855. Capt., 14 May, 1861. Col. 7th N. Y. Art., 26 Dec., 1864. Mustered out of Vols., 3 July, 1865. Bvt. Maj., 8 July, 1863, for gallant and meritorious service at the capture of Port Hudson, La. Bvt. Lieut. Col., 13 March, 1865, for gallant and meritorious service during the war. Mustered out of Vols. 15 Dec., 1870.

DUSENBERRY, SAMUEL B.* [Born in N. C. Appointed from N. C.]
2nd Lieut. Corps Art., 1 July, 1820. Trans. to 4th Art., 1 June, 1821. 1st Lieut., 1 March, 1825. Capt., 7 July, 1838. A. Q. M., 15 Feb., 1833, to 7 July, 1838. Maj. Q. M., 3 March, 1847. Died 5 April, 1855.

DUTCHER, BASIL H. [Born in N. J. Appointed from N. Y.]
Asst. Surg., 26 Oct., 1896.

DUTTON, ARTHUR H.* ]Born in Conn. Appointed from Conn.]
Bvt. 2nd Lieut. Eng., 24 June, 1861. 2nd Lieut., 3 Aug., 1861. 1st Lieut., 3 March, 1863. Capt., 2 Oct., 1863. Col. 21st Conn. Vols., 5 Sept., 1862. Died 5 June, 1864, of wounds received in action near Bermuda Hundred, Va. Bvt. Maj., 13 Dec., 1862, for gallant and meritorious service at the Battle of Fredericksburg, Va. Bvt. Lieut. Col., 3 May, 1863, for gallant and meritorious service in defence of Suffolk, Va. Bvt. Col., 26 May, 1864, for gallant and meritorious service while reconnoitering the enemy's works near Bermuda Hundred, Va., where he was wounded. Bvt. Brig. Gen. Vols., 16 May, 1864, for gallant and meritorious conduct in reconnaissances in front of Bermuda Hundred, Va., where he was wounded, 26 May, 1864, and of which he died.

DUTTON, CLARENCE E. [Born in Conn. Appointed from Conn.]
1st Lieut. Adj. 21st Conn. Vols., 5 Sept., 1862. Capt., 1 March, 1863. Mustered out 1 June, 1864. 2nd Lieut. Ord., 29 Jan., 1864. 1st Lieut., 7 March, 1867. Capt., 23 June, 1874. Maj., 1 May, 1890.

DUTTON, GEORGE.* [Born in Conn. Appointed from Conn.]
Bvt. 2nd Lieut. and 2nd Lieut. Eng., 1 July, 1822. 1st Lieut., 22 Dec., 1830. Capt., 7 July, 1838. Maj., 31 Oct., 1856. Died 5 Jan., 1857.

DUTTON, WM.* [Born in Conn. Appointed from N. Y.]
Bvt. 2nd Lieut. 1st Art., 1 July, 1846. Resigned 18 Sept., 1846.

DUVAL, DOUGLAS F. [Born in Md. Appointed from Md.]
Asst. Surg., 23 July, 1898.

DUVAL, JOHN H. [Born in D. C. Appointed from Pa.]
Priv. Sig. Corps, 10 Aug., 1880, to 29 Oct., 1880. 2nd Lieut. 18th Inf., 10 Oct., 1883. 1st Lieut., 16 Dec., 1889. Capt. C. S., 15 Nov., 1897. Maj. C. S. Vols., 22 July, 1898, to 5 Aug., 1898, and from 7 Aug., 1898, to 9 Sept., 1898. Graduate of Infantry and Cavalry School, 1889.

DUVALL, WM. P.* [Born in Md. Appointed from Md.]
2nd Lieut. 5th Art., 15 June, 1869. 1st Lieut., 9 April, 1877. Capt. 1st Art., 8 March, 1898. Maj. I. G. Vols., 12 May, 1898. Lieut. Col. Chf. Ord. Off. Vols., 18 July, 1898, to 12 May, 1899. Lieut. Col. 26th U. S. Vols., 5 July, 1899, to 13 Sept., 1899. Col. 48th U. S. Vols., 9 Sept., 1899.

DUVILLARD, JOHN A. [Born in N. Y. Appointed from N. Y.]
2nd Lieut. 12th Inf., 24 Oct., 1861. 1st Lieut., 11 Aug., 1862. Died 8 May, 1865.

D'WOLF, WM.* [Born in Ill. Appointed from Ill.]
2nd Lieut. 3rd Art., 19 Feb., 1862. Died 3 June, 1862, of wounds received at the Battle of Williamsburg, Va.

DWYER, CHARLES G.* [Born in Tex. Appointed from Tex.]
2nd Lieut. 21st Inf., 1 July, 1886. 1st Lieut. 3rd Inf., 22 May, 1893. Capt., 2 March, 1899. Maj. 1st Tex. Inf., 20 May, 1898. Lieut. Col., 2 Sept., 1898. Col., 19 Jan., 1899, to 18 Apr., 1899.

DWYER, PHILIP. [Born in Ireland. Appointed from Army.]
Priv., Corpl. and Sergt. Co. B, and Q. M. Sergt. 2nd (5th) Cav., 21 Aug., 1858, to 22 Sept., 1862. 2nd Lieut. 5th Cav., 17 July, 1862. 1st Lieut., 17 July, 1862. Reg. Com. Sergt., 29 Nov., 1862, to 31 July, 1866. Capt., 31 July, 1866. Died 29 Aug., 1872. Bvt. Capt., 11 June, 1864, for gallant and meritorious service at the Battle of Trevillian Station, Va.

DWYER, THOMAS F.* [Born in Ireland. Appointed from N. Y.]
2nd Lieut. 9th Inf., 12 June, 1895. 1st Lieut. of Inf., 10 July, 1898. Ass'd to 9th Inf., 1 Jan., 1899. Trans. to 18th Inf., 29 Aug., 1899.

DYE, JAMES M. [Born in Ga. Appointed from Ga.]
1st Lieut. of Inf., March, 1847; 13th Inf., 9 April, 1847. Disbanded 15 July, 1848.

DYE, WM. McE.* [Born in Pa. Appointed from O.]
Bvt. 2nd Lieut. 4th Inf., 1 July, 1853. 2nd Lieut. 8th Inf., 9 Nov., 1854. 1st Lieut., 1 Feb., 1856. Reg. Adj., 1 Oct., 1855, to 10 Oct., 1859. R. Q. M., 10 Oct., 1859, to 14 May, 1861. Capt., 14 May, 1861. Col. 20th Iowa Vols., 25 Aug., 1862. Mustered out of Vols. 8 July, 1865. Maj. 4th Inf., 14 Jan., 1866. Unassigned 4 Feb., 1870. Discharged 30 Sept., 1870. Bvt. Maj., 4 July, 1863, for gallant and meritorious service during the Siege of Vicksburg, Miss. Bvt. Lieut. Col., 28 May, 1864, for gallant and meritorious service during the Red River campaign. Bvt. Col., 9 April,

1865, for gallant and meritorious service during the campaign aginst Mobile, Ala. Bvt. Brig. Gen. Vols., 13 March, 1865, for gallant and meritorious service during the war.

DYER, ALEXANDER B.* [Born in Va. Appointed from Mo.]
2nd Lieut. 3rd Art., 1 July, 1837. 2nd Lieut. Ord., 9 July, 1838. 1st Lieut., 3 March, 1847. Capt., 3 March, 1853. Maj., 3 March, 1863. Brig. Gen. Chief of Ord., 12 Sept., 1864. Died 20 May, 1874. Bvt. Capt., 16 March, 1848, for gallant and meritorious conduct in the Battle of Santa Cruz de Rosales, Mex. Bvt. Maj. Gen., 13 March, 1865, for faithful and meritorious and distinguished service in the Ord. Dept. during the rebellion.

DYER, ALEXANDER B.* [Born in N. C. Appointed at Large.]
2nd Lieut. 4th Art., 13 June, 1873. 1st Lieut., 13 Aug., 1875. Reg. Adj., 6 Sept., 1879. Capt. 6th Art., 8 March, 1898. Maj. 32nd U. S. Vols., 5 July, 1899 (declined). Graduate of the Artillery School, 1878.

DYER, S. ALLEN. [Born in Ark. Appointed from D. C.]
2nd Lieut. 23rd Inf., 31 Aug., 1876. 1st Lieut., 10 April, 1885. Resigned 16 April, 1894.

DYERLE, CHARLES P. [Born in Va. Appointed from Va.]
Asst. Surg., 16 Feb., 1847. Died 30 Oct., 1853.

DYKEMAN, NEWTON L. [Born in N. Y. Appointed from Iowa.]
1st Lieut. 2nd Iowa Vols., 27 May, 1861, to 4 July, 1861. 1st Lieut. 16th Inf., 14 May, 1861. Reg. Adj., 2 Sept., 1861, to 15 Feb., 1862. Capt., 15 Feb., 1862. Trans. to 34th Inf., 21 Sept., 1866. Resigned 31 July, 1867. Bvt. Maj., 31 Dec., 1862, for gallant and meritorious service at the Battle of Murfreesboro', Tenn.

DYKMAN, WM. N.* [Born in N. Y. Appointed from N. Y.]
2nd Lieut. 22nd Inf., 16 June, 1875. Resigned 1 Oct., 1876.

EAGAN, CHAS. P. [Born in Ireland. Appointed from Washington Ter.]
1st Lieut. 1st Wash. Ter. Vols., 21 June, 1862. Mustered out 1 April, 1865. 2nd Lieut. 9th Inf., 30 Aug., 1866. 1st Lieut., 2 Jan., 1869. Unassigned 14 June, 1869. Ass'd to 12th Inf., 1 Jan., 1871. Bvt. Capt., 27 Feb., 1890, for gallant services in action against Indians in the Lava Beds, Cal., 17 April, 1873, where he was wounded. Capt. C. S., 23 June, 1874. Maj. C. S., 12 March, 1892. Lieut. Col. A. C. G., 26 Jan., 1897. Col. A. C. G., 11 March, 1898. Brig. Gen. C. G. S., 3 May, 1898.

EAGLE, ROBERT N. [Born in N. Y. Appointed from Tex.]
1st Lieut. 2nd Cav., 3 March, 1855. Capt., 25 April, 1861. 5th Cav., 3 Aug., 1861. Resigned 15 Jan., 1862.

EAKIN, CHANDLER P. [Born in Pa. Appointed from Pa.]
Priv. Montgomery's Co. Commonwealth Art. Penn. Vols., 24 April, 1861. Discharged 25 June, 1861. 2nd Lieut. 1st Art., 5 Aug., 1861. 1st Lieut., 26 Oct., 1861. Bvt. Capt., 5 May, 1862, for gallant and meritorious service in the Battle of Williamsburg, Va. Bvt. Maj., 3 July, 1863, for gallant and meritorious service in the Battle of Gettysburg, Pa. Capt. 42nd Inf., 28 July, 1866 (declined). Capt. 1st Art., 1 Oct., 1874. Graduate of the Artillery School 1869. Retired for disability from wounds in line of duty 14 Jan. 1888.

EAKIN, CONSTANTINE M.* [Born in N. Y. Appointed from N. Y.]
3rd Lieut. Corps Art., 17 July, 1817. 2nd Lieut., 20 March, 1818. 1st Lieut., 13 May, 1820. Trans. to 2nd Art., 1 June, 1821. Resigned 27 Oct., 1828. Col. 25th Pa. Militia, 15 Sept. to 1 Oct., 1862. Died 2 Oct., 1869.

EAKIN, HARRY P. [Born in Pa. Appointed from Pa.]
Priv. Commonwealth Pa. Art., 24 April to 5 Aug., 1861. 1st Lieut. 3rd Md. Cav., 15 Sept., 1863. Capt., 1 Dec., 1863. Dismissed 8 June, 1864. 2nd Lieut. 6th Cav., 15 Oct., 1867. Discharged 29 Oct., 1870.

EAKIN, SAMUEL H. [Born in Penn. Appointed from Penn.]
Dist. P. M., 3 June, 1812. Disbanded 15 June, 1815. Mil. Storekeeper, 9 March, 1819. Disbanded 1 June, 1821.

EAKINS, DAVID W. [Born in Pa. Appointed from Pa.]
Post Chaplain, 2 July, 1870. Died 5 March, 1876.

EAMES, HENRY E. [Born in Mo. Appointed from the Army.]
Priv. and Corpl. Troop E, 4th Cav., 20 July, 1893, to 3 March, 1897. 2nd Lieut. 19th Inf., 16 Feb., 1897. 1st Lieut. 14th Inf., 6 Feb., 1899. Trans. to 11th Inf., 14 March, 1899.

EARLE, MADISON.* [Born in N. Y. Appointed from Army.]
Priv., Corpl. and Sergt. Co. G. 12th Inf., 10 Nov. to 27 Nov., 1862. 2nd Lieut. 12th Inf., 6 Nov., 1862. 1st Lieut., 27 April, 1863. Trans. to 21st Inf., 21 Sept., 1866. Capt., 26 March, 1868. Unassigned 19 April, 1869. Mustered out 1 Jan., 1871. Bvt. Capt., 18 Aug., 1864., for gallant service during the operations on the Weldon Railroad, Va. Died 26 Dec., 1880.

EARLE, RICHARD T. [Born in Md. Appointed from D. C.]
Cadet M. A., 1 Sept., 1864, to 26 Dec., 1867. 2nd Lieut. 2nd Inf., 5 Nov., 1875. 1st Lieut., 22 June, 1882. Died 12 Nov., 1890.

EARLE, THOMAS V. [Born in N. Y. Appointed from N. Y.]
3rd Lieut. 3rd Art., 17 March, 1814. 2nd Lieut., 1 May, 1814. Trans. to Corps. Art., 12 May, 1814. Died 14 Oct., 1817.

EARLY, JUBAL A.* [Born in Va. Appointed from Va.]
2nd Lieut. 3rd Art., 1 July, 1837. 1st Lieut., 7 July, 1838. Resigned 31 July, 1838. Maj. 1st Va. Vols., 7 Jan., 1847. Mustered out, 3 Aug., 1848.

EARNEST, CYRUS A. [Born in Ohio. Appointed from Ohio.]
Priv. Co. G, 2nd Ohio Vols., 17 April, 1861. Discharged 31 July, 1861. Sergt. Co. H, 30th Ohio Vols., 21 Aug., 1861. 2nd Lieut. 30th Ohio Vols., 20 Dec., 1861. 1st Lieut., 12 Aug., 1862 Capt., 1 Sept., 1863. Bvt. Lieut. Col. Vols., 13 March, 1865, for valuable and constant service during the war. Mustered out 13 Aug., 1865. 2nd Lieut. 33rd Inf., 28 July, 1866. Bvt. 1st Lieut., 2 March, 1867, for gallant and meritorious service in the Siege of Vicksburg, Miss. Bvt. Capt., 2 March, 1867, for gallant and meritorious service during the Atlanta campaign. Bvt. Maj., 2 March, 1867, for gallant and meritorious service in the capture of Fort McAllister, Ga. Trans. to 8th Inf., 3 May, 1869. 1st Lieut., 1 Aug., 1872. Capt., 19 April, 1886. Died 16 Sept., 1893.

EASLEY, THOS.* [Born in Va. Appointed from Va.]
Bvt. 2nd Lieut. 8th Inf., 1 July, 1846. 2nd Lieut., 16 Feb., 1847. Killed 20 Aug., 1847, at the Battle of Churubusco, Mexico.

EASTER, RICHD J. [Born in Ga. Appointed from Ga.]
Ensign 8th Inf., 25 March, 1813. 3rd Lieut., 5 May, 1813. 2nd Lieut., 11 June, 1814. Reg. P. M., June, 1814, to June, 1815. Disbanded 15 June, 1815. 1st Lieut. 7th Inf., 18 Feb., 1818. Capt. A. Dep. Q. M. G., 18 April, 1818, to 25 April, 1820. Capt. 7th Inf., 31 Oct., 1820. Resigned 1 April, 1821.

EASTERLY, JAMES. [Born in N. Y. Appointed from Army.]
1st Sergt. 10th Inf., 3 May to 30 Dec., 1847. 2nd Lieut. 10th Inf., 30 Dec., 1847. Disbanded 15 Aug., 1848.

EASTIN, RICHARD T. [Born in La. Appointed from La.]
2nd Lieut. of Inf., 5 March, 1847; 14th Inf., 9 April, 1847. 1st Lieut., 21 Oct., 1847. Disbanded 25 July, 1848.

EASTMAN, AHIRA G. [Born in Vt. Appointed from Mich.]
1st Lieut. of Inf., 1 March, 1847; 15th Inf., 9 April, 1847. Resigned 31 May, 1847.

EASTMAN, ELBRIDGE G.* [Born in N. H. Appointed from N. H.]
Bvt. 2nd Lieut. 2nd Inf., 1 July, 1831. 2nd Lieut., 4 March, 1833. Died 6 Oct., 1834.

EASTMAN, FRANK F.* [Born in Ill. Appointed from Ill.]
2nd Lieut. 14th Inf., 13 June, 1879. 1st Lieut., 1 July, 1890. Capt., 14 Aug., 1894.

EASTMAN, JAMES E.* [Born in Mass. Appointed from Mass.]
2nd Lieut. 2nd Art., 18 June, 1866. 1st Lieut., 6 May, 1869. Capt., 28 Nov. 1892. Graduate of the Artillery School 1878, 1892. Died 28 Aug., 1899.

EASTMAN, JOHN L. [Born in N. H. Appointed from N. H.]
2nd Lieut. 4th Inf., 12 Dec., 1808. 1st Lieut., 9 June, 1810. Reg. Adj., June, 1812, to July, 1813. Capt., 31 July, 1813. Maj. A. I. G., 27 July, 1814. Disbanded 15 June, 1815. Reinstated 17 May, 1816, as Capt. Light Art. Trans. to 1st Art., 1 June, 1821. Dismissed 4 Nov., 1823. Died 12 June, 1865.

EASTMAN, LEWIS M. [Born in Md. Appointed from Md.]
Asst. Surg., 5 Aug., 1861. Resigned 19 Jan., 1863.

EASTMAN, ROBT. L.* [Born in Md. Appointed at Large.]
2nd Lieut. 6th Inf., 6 May, 1861. 1st Lieut., 17 May, 1861. Capt., 8 Feb., 1864. Died 7 Nov., 1865. Bvt. Capt., 27 June, 1862, for gallant and meritorious service at the Battle of Gaines' Mills, Va. Bvt. Maj., 1 July, 1862, for gallant and meritorious service at the Battle of Malvern Hill.

EASTMAN, SETH.* [Born in Me. Appointed from Me.]
Bvt. 2nd Lieut. 1st Inf., 1 July, 1829. 2nd Lieut., 1 July, 1829. 1st Lieut., 14 Nov., 1836. Capt., 12 Nov., 1839. Maj. 5th Inf., 31 Oct., 1856. Lieut. Col. 1st Inf., 9 Sept., 1861. Retired 3 Dec., 1863. Died 31 Aug., 1875. Bvt. Col., 9 April, 1865, for meritorious service during the war. Bvt. Brig. Gen., 9 Aug., 1866, for meritorious service during the war.

EASTON, LANGDON C.* [Born in Mo. Appointed from Mo.]
2nd Lieut. 6th Inf., 1 July, 1838. 1st Lieut., 23 July, 1839. Capt. Asst. Q. M., 3 March, 1847. Vacated commission of 1st Lieut. 6th Inf., 15 April, 1851. Maj. Q. M., 3 Aug., 1861. Lieut. Col. Q. M. (Act 17 July, 1862), 13 Nov., 1863, to 1 Aug., 1864. Col. Q. M. (Act 4 July, 1864), 2 Aug., 1864. Bvt. Lieut. Col., Col. and Brig. Gen., 17 Sept., 1864, for distinguished and important service in the Q. M. Dept. in the campaign terminating in the capture of Atlanta, Ga. Bvt. Maj. Gen., 13 March, 1865, for meritorious service during the war. Lieut. Col. Dep. Q. M. G., 29 July, 1866. Relieved as Col. Q. M. (Act 4 July, 1864), 1 Jan., 1867. Col. Asst. Q. M. G., 6 June, 1872. Retired, over 62 years of age, 24 Jan., 1881. Died 29 April, 1884.

EATON, AMOS B.* [Born in N. Y. Appointed from N. Y.]
Bvt. 2nd Lieut. 4th Inf., 1 July, 1826. 2nd Lieut. 2nd Inf., 1 July, 1826. 1st Lieut., 21 July, 1834. Capt., 1 March, 1839. Capt. C. S., 7 July, 1838. Maj., 9 May, 1861. Lieut. Col. A. C. G. S., 29 Sept., 1861. Col., 9 Feb., 1863. Brig. Gen. C. G. S., 29 June, 1864. Retired 1 May, 1874. Died 21 Feb., 1877. Bvt. Maj., 23 Feb., 1847, for gallant and meritorious conduct at Buena Vista. Bvt. Maj. Gen., 13 March, 1865, for faithful, meritorious and distinguished service in the Subsistence Department during the war.

EATON, GEORGE O.* [Born in Me. Appointed from Me.]
2nd Lieut. 5th Cav., 13 June, 1873. 1st Lieut., 1 May, 1879. Resigned 29 March, 1883.

EATON, HARRY A. [Born in Ind. Appointed from W. Va.]
Sergt. Maj. 1st W. Va. Vols., 14 May, 1898. 1st Lieut. 1st W. Va. Vols., 23 May to 25 July, 1898. 2nd Lieut. 8th Inf., 9 July, 1898. 1st Lieut., 2 March, 1899.

EATON, JOHN B. [Born in N. Y. Appointed from N. Y.]
Capt. 27th N. Y. Art., 17 Dec., 1862. Bvt. Maj. Vols., 13 March, 1865, for gallant and meritorious conduct in action before Petersburg, Va., 17 June, 1864. Bvt. Lieut. Col., 2 April, 1865, for gallant and meritorious conduct in action before Petersburg, Va. Mustered out 22 June, 1865. 2nd Lieut. 3rd Art., 27 May, 1867. Bvt. 1st Lieut., 27 May, 1867, for gallant and meritorious conduct in action before Petersburg, 17 June, 1864. Bvt. Capt., 27 May, 1867, for gallant and meritorious service in action before Petersburg, 2 April, 1865. 1st Lieut. 3rd Art., 7 April, 1870. Capt. A. Q. M., 20 Dec., 1892. Died 14 Aug., 1893.

EATON, JOSEPH. [Born in Mass. Appointed from Mass.]
Surg. Mate 3rd Art., 14 April, 1812. Resigned 12 Dec., 1813. Hosp. Surg. Mate, 15 April, 1814. Post Surg., 18 April, 1818. Asst. Surg., 1 June, 1821. Died 16 March, 1860.

EATON, JOSEPH H.* [Born in Mass. Appointed at Large.]
Bvt. 2nd Lieut. 3rd Inf., 1 July, 1835. 2nd Lieut., 30 Oct., 1836. 1st Lieut., 3 Sept., 1838. Capt., 18 June, 1846. Bvt. Maj., 23 Sept., 1846, for gallant and meritorious conduct in the several conflicts at Monterey. Bvt. Lieut. Col., 23 Feb., 1847, for gallant and meritorious conduct in the Battle of Buena Vista, Mexico. Resigned 31 Dec., 1856. Addl. P. M., 1 June, 1861. Maj. P. M., 21 April, 1864. Bvt. Lieut. Col., 13 March, 1865, for meritorious and valuable service in the Pay Department during the war. Bvt. Col., 13 March, 1865, for meritorious and valuable service as Asst.

to the Paymaster Gen. Bvt. Brig. Gen., 13 March, 1865. for faithful and meritorious service in the Pay Department. Retired, over 62 years of age, 24 Jan., 1881. Died 20 Jan., 1896.

EATON, NATHL. J.* [Born in Mass. Appointed from Mass.]
Bvt. 2nd Lieut. 6th Inf., 1 July, 1827. 2nd Lieut., 1 July, 1827. 1st Lieut., 31 July, 1836. Dropped 18 April, 1837. Died 29 March, 1883.

EATON, WM. W.* [Born in Mass. Appointed from Mass.]
Bvt. 2nd Lieut. 6th Inf., 1 July, 1824. 2nd Lieut., 1 July, 1824. Died 10 May, 1828.

EBBETS, GEORGE A. [Born in N. Y. Appointed from Army.]
Sergt. Co. I. and Sergt. Maj. 31st N. Y. Vols., 3 June, 1861, to 9 May, 1862. 2nd Lieut., 9 May, 1862. 1st Lieut., 27 Nov., 1862. Capt., 18 Jan., 1863. Mustered out 4 June, 1863. Priv., Corpl. and Sergt. Maj. 2nd Batt. 17th Inf., 26 Sept., 1863, to 7 Nov., 1866. 2nd Lieut. 17th Inf., 7 Nov., 1866. Trans. to 26th Inf., 23 Nov., 1866. 1st Lieut., 2 Oct., 1868. Unassigned 19 May, 1869. Resigned 31 Dec., 1869.

EBERT, RUDOLPH G. [Born in N. Y. Appointed from Ore.]
Asst. Surg., 16 June, 1880. Capt. Asst. Surg., 16 June, 1885. Maj. Surg., 17 April, 1898.

EBSTEIN, FREDERICK H. E. [Born in Prussia. Appointed from Army.]
Priv. Co. H. 4th Inf., 18 Nov., 1864. Corpl., 7 Aug., 1865. Sergt., 16 Jan., 1866. Priv., 31 July, 1866. 2nd Lieut. 18th Inf., 12 Sept., 1867. Unassigned 26 April, 1869. Ass'd to 21st Inf., 14 July, 1869. 1st Lieut., 19 Feb., 1873. Capt., 1 April, 1885. Maj. 19th Inf., 16 Jan., 1899. Retired, over 30 years' service, 8 July, 1899.

ECHOLS, CHARLES P.* [Born in Ala. Appointed from Ala.]
Addl. 2nd Lieut. Eng., 12 June, 1891. 2nd Lieut., 4 Oct., 1894, to rank from 12 June, 1891. 1st Lieut., 6 Jan., 1896. Asst. Prof. Mil. Acad. since 7 Oct., 1898.

ECHOLS, ROBT. M. [Born in Ga. Appointed from Ga.]
Col. Inf., 3 March, 1847; 13th Inf., 9 April, 1847. Killed in action at National Bridge, Mexico, 3 Dec., 1847.

ECHOLS, WILLIAM H.* [Born in Ala. Appointed from Ala.]
Bvt. 2nd Lieut. Top. Eng., 1 July, 1858. Resigned 21 March, 1861.

ECKELS, WM. H. [Born in Pa. Appointed from Pa.]
1st Lieut. 9th Pa. Cav., 17 Oct., 1861. Capt. 9th Pa. Cav., 22 May, 1863. Mustered out 25 Nov., 1864. Maj. P. M., 3 March, 1875. Retired by operation of law 11 Feb., 1895. Died 13 Feb., 1896.

ECKERSON, EDWIN P. [Born in Washington Ter. Appointed from Va.]
2nd Lieut. 5th Cav., 12 Dec., 1872. Dismissed 15 July, 1875. 2nd Lieut. 7th Cav., 2 May, 1876. 1st Lieut., 25 June, 1876. Dismissed 30 June, 1878. Died 17 Aug., 1885.

ECKERSON, THEODORE H.* [Born in Ore. Appointed at Large.]
2nd Lieut. 6th Inf., 17 June, 1874. Resigned 15 Sept., 1875. 2nd Lieut. 19th Inf., 15 Aug., 1876. 1st Lieut., 11 Oct., 1882. Capt., 30 Nov., 1892. Retired for disability 3 Jan., 1895.

ECKERSON, THEODORE J. [Born in N. Y. Appointed from Washington Ter.]
Priv. Co. I. 3rd Inf., 20 Dec., 1838. Trans. to Co. C, 2 Oct., 1841. Discharged 20 Dec., 1843. Priv. Co. C, 3rd Inf., 25 Dec., 1843. Discharged 21 Jan., 1848. Priv. Co. H, 1st Art., 15 Sept., 1848. Trans. to Co. L, 28 Sept., 1848. Corpl., 1 Oct., 1849. Sergt., 7 Feb., 1850. 1st Sergt., 7 Oct., 1851. Sergt., 17 Oct., 1852. Discharged 17 Feb., 1853. Mil. Storekeeper Ord. Dept., 16 Sept., 1853. Capt. A. Q. M., 21 March, 1865. Bvt. Maj., 21 March, 1865, for faithful and meritorious service in the Q. M. D. Maj. Q. M., 24 Jan., 1881. Retired by operation of law 22 Jan., 1885.

ECKERT, GEORGE B. [Born in Pa. Appointed from Pa.]
2nd Lieut. 3rd Inf., 5 Aug., 1861. 1st Lieut., 12 March, 1862. Resigned 10 Nov., 1864.

ECKHART, CHAS. G.* [Born in La. Appointed from La.]
2nd Lieut. 4th Art., 17 June, 1867. Discharged 1 Sept., 1870.

ECKLES, JOHN W. [Born in Del. Appointed from Del.]
Sergt. and Sergt. Maj. 1st Del. Vols., 19 Sept., 1861, to 17 Dec., 1862. 2nd Lieut., 17 Dec., 1862. 1st Lieut., 16 Jan., 1863. Resigned 5 Sept., 1864. 2nd Lieut. 1st U. S. Vet. Vols., 27 Dec., 1864. 1st Lieut., 18 Sept., 1865. Mustered out 13 Feb., 1866. 2nd Lieut. 17th Inf., 23 Feb., 1866. 1st Lieut., 1 March, 1866. Trans. to 35th Inf., 21 Sept., 1866. R. Q. M., 1 Feb., to 12 Aug., 1869. Trans. to 15th Inf., 12 Aug., 1869. R. Q. M., 6 Sept., 1870, to 1 Oct., 1871. Capt., 3 March, 1875. Dismissed 23 Aug., 1877. Bvt. Capt., 2 March, 1867, for gallant and meritorious service in the Battle of Fredericksburg, Va. Bvt. Maj., 2 March, 1867, for gallant and meritorious service in the Battle of Gettysburg, Pa.

ECKLEY, WM. J. [Born in Ohio. Appointed from Ohio.]
Priv. Co. D, and Q. M. Sergt. 80th Ohio Vols., 10 Feb. to 28 June, 1862. 1st Lieut., 28 June, 1862. Capt., 30 Sept., 1863. Mustered out 21 Sept., 1864. 2nd Lieut. 5th Inf., 22 May, 1866. Died 20 June, 1867.

ECTOR, WALTON.* [Born in Ga. Appointed from Ga.]
Capt. of Inf., 8 March, 1847; 13th Inf., 9 April, 1847. Disbanded 15 July, 1848. Died 1 Feb., 1862.

EDDY, ASHER R.* [Born in R. I. Appointed from R. I.]
Bvt. 2nd Lieut. 1st Art., 1 July, 1844. 2nd Lieut., 18 June, 1846. 1st Lieut., 19 Aug., 1847. Capt. A. Q. M., 12 Feb., 1861. Bvt. Maj., Lieut. Col. and Col., 13 March, 1865, for faithful and meritorious service during the war. Maj. Q. M., 29 July, 1866. Lieut. Col. Dep. Q. M. G., 6 June, 1872. Died 27 Jan., 1879.

EDDY, FARLEY. [Born in N. Y. Appointed from N. Y.]
2nd Lieut. 4th Rifles, 17 March, 1814. Disbanded 15 June, 1815. 2nd Lieut. 8th Inf., 11 Aug., 1817. 1st Lieut., 12 Sept., 1817. Dismissed 19 March, 1819.

EDELIN, THOS. B. [Born in Md. Appointed from Md.]
2nd Lieut. 7th Inf., 7 June, 1855. 1st Lieut., 20 Dec., 1860. Resigned 30 May, 1861.

EDES, BENJN. C. [Born in Md. Appointed from Md.]
2nd Lieut. 6th Inf., 1 Aug., 1838. 1st Lieut., 10 Feb., 1842. Died 30 March, 1844.
EDGAR, JAMES C. [Born in Mo. Appointed from N. Mex.]
2nd Lieut. 1st N. M. Cav., 22 Jan., 1864. 1st Lieut., 14 Feb., 1865. Resigned 7 June, 1866. 2nd Lieut. 9th Cav., 12 Sept., 1867. Cashiered 14 July, 1868.
EDGAR, WILLIAM F. [Born in Ky. Appointed from Mo.]
Asst. Surg., 2 March, 1849. Maj. Surg., 21 May, 1861. Retired 27 Aug., 1862. Died 23 Aug., 1897.
EDGER, BENJAMIN J., Jr. [Born in Pa. Appointed from Pa.]
Asst. Surg., 14 June, 1899.
EDGERLY, WINFIELD S.* [Born in N. H. Appointed from N. H.]
2nd Lieut. 7th Cav., 15 June, 1870. 1st Lieut., 25 June, 1876. R. Q. M., 25 June to 14 Nov., 1876. Capt., 22 Sept., 1883. Maj. 6th Cav., 9 July, 1898. Trans. to 7th Cav., 5 Jan., 1899. Lieut. Col. I. G. Vols., 8 June, 1898, to 12 April, 1899.
EDGERTON, EDWARD C.* [Born in Ind. Appointed from Ind.]
2nd Lieut. 5th Cav., 15 June, 1870. Resigned 31 Dec., 1872.
EDGERTON, WM. G. [Born in Vt. Appointed from Vt.]
Capt. 11th Inf., 5 Aug., 1861. Trans. to 29th Inf., 21 Sept., 1866. Wholly retired 2 Nov., 1867. Bvt. Maj., 2 April, 1863, for gallant and meritorious service in front of Petersburg, Va.
EDGERTON, WRIGHT P.* [Born in Ohio. Appointed from Ohio.]
2nd Lieut. 2nd Art., 17 June, 1874. 1st Lieut., 23 March, 1881. Asso. Prof. Mil. Acad. since 1894.
EDIE, GUY L. [Born in Va. Appointed from Va.]
Asst. Surg., 3 Dec., 1883. Capt. Asst. Surg., 3 Dec., 1888. Maj. Brig. Surg. Vols., 4 June, 1898.
EDIE, JOHN R.* [Born in Pa. Appointed from Pa.]
2nd Lieut. 2nd Cav., 24 June, 1861. 5th Cav., 3 Aug., 1861. Trans. to 3rd Art., 23 Oct., 1861. Trans. to Ord., 24 Oct., 1861. 1st Lieut., 3 March, 1863. Capt., 12 Sept., 1864. Died 29 Oct., 1874. Bvt. Capt., 1 Aug., 1864, for faithful and meritorious service in the field. Bvt. Maj., 13 March, 1865, for faithful and meritorious service in the Ord. Dept. and in the field.
EDIE, JOHN R. [Born in Pa. Appointed from Pa.]
Cadet at Mil. Acad., 1 July, 1828, to 15 Jan., 1829. Maj. 15th Inf., 14 May, 1861. Lieut. Col. 8th Inf., 13 Sept., 1864. Mustered out 1 Jan., 1871. Bvt. Lieut. Col., 25 Nov., 1863, for gallant and meritorious service at the Battle of Mission Ridge, Tenn. Bvt. Col., 1 Sept., 1864, for gallant and meritorious service during the Atlanta campaign and at the Battle of Jonesboro', Ga.
EDMONDSON, JOHN. [Born in Pa. Appointed from Army.]
Sergt. Rifles, Jan., 1812, to June, 1814. Ensign 2nd Rifles, 30 May, 1814. Discharged 15 June, 1815. 2nd Lieut. Rifles, 22 March, 1819. Discharged 1 June, 1821.
EDMUNDS, FRANK H.* [Born in Mich. Appointed from Dakota.]
2nd Lieut. 1st Inf., 12 June, 1871. 1st Lieut., 6 May, 1879. Capt., 24 Jan., 1889. Maj. 15th Inf., 2 March, 1899. Trans. to 1st Inf., 18 May, 1899. Maj. Chf. Ord. Off. Vols., 18 July, 1898, to 12 May, 1899. Died at Havana, Cuba, 18 June, 1900.
EDSON, JOHN H.* [Born in N. Y. Appointed at Large.]
Bvt. 2nd Lieut. Mtd. Rifles, 1 July, 1853. 2nd Lieut., 16 Aug., 1854. Resigned 1 Sept., 1860. Maj. 1st Mass. Cav., 4 Nov., 1861. Resigned 7 Jan., 1862.
EDSON, THEODORE.* [Born in Mass. Appointed from Mass.]
Bvt. 2nd Lieut. Ord., 1 July, 1860. 2nd Lieut., 22 April, 1861. 1st Lieut., 1 July, 1861. Capt., 3 March, 1863. Maj., 15 Dec., 1867. Died 17 Nov., 1870. Bvt. Capt., 31 Dec., 1862, for gallant and meritorious service at the Battle of Stone River, Tenn. Bvt. Maj., 13 March, 1865, for faithful and meritorious service in the Ord. Dept.
EDWARDS, ALBERT G.* [Born in Ill. Appointed from Ill.]
Bvt. 3rd Lieut. Mtd. Rangers, 1 July, 1832. Bvt. 2nd Lieut. 1st Drag., 14 Aug., 1833, to rank from 1 July, 1832. Resigned 2 May, 1835.
EDWARDS, ARTHUR M.* [Born in N. Y. Appointed from Neb.]
2nd Lieut. 3rd Inf., 12 June, 1893. 1st Lieut., 26 April, 1898. Trans. to 14th Inf., 11 Oct., 1899.
EDWARDS, CHAS. M. [Born in Ill. Appointed from Ill.]
Priv. 8th Ill. Vols., 18 May, 1861. 2nd Lieut., 13 Dec., 1862. 1st Lieut., 22 Aug., 1863. Mustered out 11 June, 1864. 2nd Lieut. 18th Ill. Vols., 13 Dec., 1862. 1st Lieut., 22 Aug., 1863. Mustered out 11 June, 1864. 2nd Lieut. 10th Inf., 23 Feb., 1866. 1st Lieut., 28 July, 1866. Retired 28 Jan., 1871. Died 30 July, 1879.
EDWARDS, CLARENCE R.* [Born in Ohio. Appointed from Ohio.]
2nd Lieut. 23rd Inf., 13 June, 1883. 1st Lieut. 1st Inf., 25 Feb., 1891. Trans. to 23rd Inf., 20 July, 1891. Capt. of Inf., 30 July, 1898. Ass'd to 10th Inf., 1 Jan., 1899. Maj. A. A. G. Vols., 12 May, 1898, to 1 Oct., 1899. Lieut. Col. 47th U. S. Vols., 17 Aug., 1899.
EDWARDS, DOUGLAS. [Born in Scotland. Appointed from Army.]
Priv. and Sergt. Maj. 4th Art., 10 Nov., 1856, to 13 Sept., 1861. Priv., Sergt. and 1st Sergt. Co. E, 19th Inf., 24 Jan. to 29 Nov., 1862. 2nd Lieut. 19th Inf., 29 Nov., 1862. 1st Lieut., 7 Nov., 1863. Died 24 Dec., 1865. Bvt. Capt., 13 March, 1865, for meritorious service at the Battle of Atlanta, Ga.
EDWARDS, EATON A. [Born in Ireland. Appointed from Army.]
Priv. Co. K, 10th Conn. Vols., 16 Oct., 1861, to 25 Aug., 1864. Hosp. Stwd., 26 Aug., 1864, to 16 July, 1880. 2nd Lieut. 25th Inf., 24 June, 1880. 1st Lieut., 1 Sept., 1887. Capt., 10 March, 1898.
EDWARDS, FRANK A. [Born in Pa. Appointed from D. C.]
2nd Lieut. 1st Cav., 1 Oct., 1873. 1st Lieut., 7 Sept., 1879. Capt., 9 March, 1891.
EDWARDS, GEORGE.* [Born in England. Appointed from N. Y.]
Bvt. 2nd Lieut. 2nd Art., 1 July, 1845. 2nd Lieut., 18 June, 1846. 1st Lieut., 19 Oct., 1847. Resigned 30 June, 1851. Bvt. 1st Lieut., 12 Oct., 1847, for gallant and meritorious conduct in defence of Puebla, Mexico.
EDWARDS, JAMES L. [Born in Va. Appointed from Va.]
2nd Lieut. Marine Corps, 18 June, 1811. 2nd Lieut. 2nd Art., 7 May, 1812. Resigned

8 July, 1812. 1st Lieut. 2nd Art., 28 March, 1813. Trans. to Corps Art., 12 May, 1814. Resigned 1 April, 1816.

EDWARDS, JOHN.* [Born in Me. Appointed from Me.]
Bvt. 2nd Lieut. 3rd Art., 1 July, 1851. 2nd Lieut., 16 March, 1852. 1st Lieut., 15 Feb., 1855. Capt., 23 July, 1861. Unassigned 11 Aug., 1870. Discharged 7 Nov., 1870. Bvt. Maj., 27 June, 1862, for gallant and meritorious service at the Battle of Gaines' Mills, Va. Bvt. Lieut. Col., 17 Sept., 1862, for gallant and meritorious service at the Battle of Antietam, Md.

EDWARDS, JOHN M.* [Born in Va. Appointed from Va.]
2nd Lieut. Light Art., 1 July, 1819. Trans. to 3rd Art., 1 June, 1821. Trans. to 1st Art., 16 Aug., 1821. Resigned 1 Nov., 1824. Died 14 Feb., 1836.

EDWARDS, LEWIS A. Born in D. C. Appointed from D. C.]
Asst. Surg., 27 Aug., 1846. Maj. and Surg., 19 Feb., 1861. Lieut. Col., 26 June, 1876. Died 8 Nov., 1877. Bvt. Lieut. Col. and Col., 13 March, 1865, for faithful and meritorious service during the war.

EDWARDS, LYNN S. [Born in N. Y. Appointed from Army.]
Priv., Corpl. and Sergt. Batty I and Sergt. Maj. 2nd Art., 28 Aug., 1897, to 2 Nov., 1899. 2nd Lieut. 8th Inf., 1 Oct., 1899.

EDWARDS, OLIVER.* [Born in Mass. Appointed from Mass.]
2nd Lieut. 11th Inf., 12 June, 1894. 1st Lieut., 26 April, 1898. Trans. to 6th Inf., 28 April, 1899.

EDWARDS, OSCAR E. [Born in Va. Appointed from Va.]
Capt. Inf., 23 Feb., 1847; Voltigeurs, 9 April, 1847. Disbanded 31 July, 1848. Bvt. Maj., 13 Sept., 1847, for gallant and meritorious conduct at Chapultepec.

EDWARDS, ROBT. A. [Born in Pa. Appointed from D. C.]
2nd Lieut. 13th Inf., 22 Jan., 1867. Trans. to 5th Cav., 4 Aug., 1868. Resigned 31 Oct., 1870.

EGAN, JAMES. [Born in Ireland. Appointed from Army.]
Priv. Troop H, 2nd Cav., 13 Sept., 1856, to 21 June, 1858.r Priv. Co. E 1st Cav., 1 March, 1860. Corpl., 1 Dec., 1860. Sergt. 1 Dec., 1861. 1st Sergt., 8 Jan., 1863. 2nd Lieut. 2nd Cav., 10 Aug., 1863. Bvt. 1st Lieut., 31 May, 1864, for gallant and meritorious service in the Battle of Cold Harbor, Va. 1st Lieut. 2nd Cav., 15 Oct., 1864. Capt., 5 Feb., 1868. Retired 9 May, 1879. Died 14 April, 1883.

EGAN, JOHN.* [Born in N. Y. Appointed from N. Y.]
2nd Lieut. 1st Art., 17 June, 1862. Bvt. 1st Lieut., 17 Sept., 1862, for gallant and meritorious service in the Battle of Antietam, Md. Bvt. Capt., 3 July, 1863, for gallant and meritorious service in the Battle of Gettysburg, Pa. 1st Lieut. 1st Art., 19 May, 1864. Bvt. Maj., 1 June, 1864, for gallant and meritorious service in the Battle of Cold Harbor, Va. Capt. 11th Inf., 28 July, 1866. Unassigned 14 April, 1869. Ass'd to 23rd Inf., 1 Sept., 1869. Trans. to 4th Art., 1 Jan.. 1871. Maj. 1st Art., 25 Jan., 1889. Retired for over thirty years' service, 1 Sept., 1896.

EGAN, PETER R. [Born in Ireland. Appointed from N. Y.]
Asst. Surg., 23 May, 1882. Capt. Asst. Surg., 23 May, 1887. Maj. Brig. Surg. Vols., 4 June, 1898, to 22 March, 1899. Maj. Surg., 2 Feb., 1900.

EGAN, WM. [Born in Ireland. Appointed from Army.]
Priv., Serg. and 1st Sergt. Batty H, 5th Art., 23 Feb., 1861, to 27 Feb., 1863. Bvt. 2nd Lieut. 5th Art., 27 Feb., 1863. 2nd Lieut. 2nd Art., 27 April, 1863. 1st Lieut., 11 June, 1864. Resigned 28 March, 1866. Bvt. Capt., 11 June, 1864, for gallant and meritorious service at the Battle of Trevillian Station, Va.

EGBERT, AUGUSTUS R. [Born in N. J. Appointed from N. J.]
Maj. Surg. U. S. Vols., 5 Nov., 1861. Bvt. Lieut. Col. Vols., 6 Oct., 1865, for faithful and meritorious service. Mustered out 7 Oct., 1865. 2nd Lieut. 21st Inf., 28 July, 1866. Unassigned 19 April, 1869. Ass'd to 8th Inf., 14 July, 1869. Trans. to 2nd Inf., 26 May, 1870. 1st Lieut., 18 Dec., 1873. Capt., 27 May, 1889. Died 25 Sept., 1890.

EGBERT, HARRY C. [Born in Pa. Appointed from Pa.]
1st Lieut. 12th Inf., 23 Sept., 1861. Bvt. Capt., 1 Aug., 1864, for gallant service in the Battle of North Anna, Va. Bvt. Maj., 1 Aug., 1864, for gallant service in the Battle of Bethesda Church, Va. Capt., 12th Inf., 1 April, 1865. Maj. 17th Inf., 23 April, 1890. Lieut. Col. 6th Inf., 18 May, 1893. Col. 22nd Inf., 1 July, 1898. Brig. Gen. Vols., 1 Oct., 1898, to 1 Dec., 1898. Killed in action at Malinta, Philippine Islands, 26 March, 1899.

EGELSTON, ROUSE S. [Born in N. Y. Appointed from N. Y.]
Capt. 97th N. Y. Vols., 18 Feb., 1862. Lieut. Col., 17 Feb., 1865. Mustered out 18 July, 1865. 2nd Lieut. 25th Inf., 28 July, 1866. Trans. to 18th Inf., 26 April, 1869. Mustered out 1 Jan., 1871.

EGGEMEYER, AUGUST. [Born in Germany. Appointed from Army.]
Priv. Gen. Ser. and Sergt. and 1st Sergt. Co. H, 12th Inf., 27 Feb., 1860, to 6 Nov., 1863. 2nd Lieut. 12th Inf., 31 Oct., 1863. 1st Lieut., 7 May, 1864. Killed 1 June, 1864, at the Battle of Bethesda Church, Va. Bvt. Capt., 29 Aug., 1864, for gallant and meritorious service at the Battle of Bethesda Church, Va.

EGGLESTON, MILLARD F.* [Born in Ind. Appointed from Ind.]
2nd Lieut. 10th Cav., 15 June, 1877. 1st Lieut., 30 April, 1885. Resigned 7 June, 1890.

EGGLESTON, VIRGIL S. [Born in N. Y. Appointed from N. Y.]
Maj. P. M., 22 Feb., 1869. Cashiered 4 Nov., 1874.

EHNINGER, HENRY A.* [Born in N. Y. Appointed from N. Y.]
Bvt. 2nd Lieut. 4th Art., 1 July, 1846. 2nd Lieut., 3 March, 1847. Resigned 6 Jan., 1849.

EKIN, JAMES A. [Born in Pa. Appointed from Pa.]
1st Lieut. 12th Pa. Vols., 25 April, 1861. Mustered out 5 Aug., 1861. Capt. A. Q. M. Vols., 7 Aug., 1861. Capt. A. Q. M. U. S. A., 13 March, 1863. Lieut. Col. Q. M. (Act. 17 July, 1862), 15 Feb., 1864, to 1 Aug., 1864. Col. Q. M. (Act. 4 July, 1864), 2 Aug., 1864. Bvt. Brig. Gen. Vols., 8 March, 1865. Bvt. Maj., Lieut. Col. and Col., 13 March, 1865, for faithful and meritorious service during the war. Bvt.

Brig. Gen., 13 March, 1865, for faithful and meritorious service in the Q. M. Dept. during the war. Lieut. Col. Dep. Q. M. G., 29 July, 1866. Relieved as Col. Q. M., 1 Jan., 1867. Retired 31 Aug., 1883. Died 27 March, 1891.

ELBERT, JOHN L. [Born in Md. Appointed from Md.]
Cornet 2nd Light Drag., 28 April, 1813. 3rd Lieut., 20 June, 1813. Retained in Light Drag., 12 May, 1814. 2nd Lieut., 18 July, 1814. Disbanded 15 June, 1815. Reinstated in 4th Inf., 17 May, 1816. Resigned 1 May, 1817. 2nd Lieut. 2nd Inf., 18 April, 1818. Resigned 5 July, 1819.

ELBERT, LEROY S.* [Born in Ohio. Appointed from Iowa.]
Bvt. 2nd and 2nd Lieut. Mounted Rifles, 24 June, 1861. 1st Lieut., 24 June, 1861; 3rd Cav., 3 Aug., 1861. Capt., 11 March, 1863. Died 13 Sept., 1863.

ELBRY, FREDK. W. [Born in Va. Appointed from N. Y.]
1st Lieut. Asst. Surg., 16 Nov., 1868. Capt. Asst. Surg. 16 Nov., 1871. Retired with rank of Maj. for disability 24 Feb., 1891.

ELDER, JAMES. [Born in Pa. Appointed from D. C.]
2nd Lieut. 11th Inf., 24 July, 1847. Discharged 17 Aug., 1848. Capt. Camero . Guards, D. C. V., 20 April to 20 July, 1861. Capt. 11th Inf., 14 May, 1861. Dismissed 6 Jan., 1864.

ELDER, MATTHEW. [Born in Mich. Appointed from Mich.]
Capt. 8th Mich. Vols., 12 Aug., 1861, to 1 March, 1862. 1st Lieut. 11th Inf., 5 Aug., 1861. Died 25 July, 1863, of wounds received at the Battle of Gettysburg, Pa. Bvt. Capt., 2 July, 1863, for gallant and meritorious service at the Batti eof Gettysburg, Pa.

ELDER, SAML. S. [Born in Pa. Appointed from Pa.]
Priv. Co. C, 2nd Art., 1 June, 1853. Corpl., 1 May, 1854. Sergt., 15 June, 1855. 1st Serg., 12 June, 1857. Discharged 31 May, 1858. 2nd Lieut. 1st Art., 23 March, 1861. 1st Lieut., 14 May, 1861. Bvt. Capt., 17 Sept., 1862, for gallant and meritorious service in the Battle of Antietam, Md. Capt. 1st Art., 1 Aug., 1863. Bvt. Maj., 20 Feb., 1864, for gallant and meritorious service in the Battle of Olustee, Fla. Bvt. Lieut. Col., 15 May, 1864, for gallant and meritorious service in the Battle of Drury's Bluff, Va. Maj. 2nd Art., 30 June, 1882. Died 6 April, 1885.

ELDERKIN, WM. A.* [Born in N. Y. Appointed from N. Y.]
2nd Lieut. 1st Art., 6 May, 1861. 1st Lieut., 14 May, 1861. Capt. C. S., 4 July, 1864. Bvt. Maj., 13 March, 1865, for faithful and meritorious service during the war. Maj. C. S., 3 Sept., 1889. Lieut. Col. A. C. G. S., 1 June, 1896. Col. A. C. G. S., 15 Nov,, 1897. Retired 11 March, 1898.

ELDRIDGE, BOGARDUS. [Born in Ala. Appointed from Mass.]
2nd Lieut. 10th Inf., 31 Aug., 1876. 1st Lieut., 21 May, 1883. Capt. 14th Inf., 7 Sept., 1897. Died of wounds received in action near Bacoor, Philippine Islands, 2 Oct., 1899.

ELGIN, WM. [Born in Va. Appointed from Va.]
3rd Lieut. Corps Art., 12 May, 1814. 2nd Lieut., 29 July, 1814. Disbanded 15 June, 1815. 2nd Lieut. 8th Inf., 3 Sept., 1816. Resigned 30 April, 1817.

ELIASON, WM. A.* [Born in D. C. Appointed from D. C.]
2nd Lieut. Eng., 1 July, 1819. 1st Lieut., 28 July, 1823. Capt., 5 March, 1832. Died 15 June, 1839.

ELLICOTT, ANDREW. [Born in Pa. Appointed from Pa.]
Prof. at Mil. Acad., 1 Sept., 1813. Died 29 Aug., 1820.

ELLINWOOD, RALPH E. [Born in Ohio. Appointed from Army.]
Priv. and Corpl. Co. I, 8th Inf., 21 Sept., 1858, to 30 Oct., 1861. 2nd Lieut. 2nd Inf., 24 Oct., 1861. 1st Lieut., 27 June, 1862. Died 25 Sept., 1862, of wounds received at the Battle of Bull Run, Va. Bvt. Capt., 30 Aug., 1862, for gallant and meritorious service in the Battle of Bull Run (2nd), Va.

ELLIOT, GEORGE H.* [Born in Mass. Appointed from Mass.]
Bvt. 2nd Lieut. 4th Art., 1 July, 1855. 2nd Lieut. 1st Art., 1 July, 1855. Trans. to Eng., 26 Jan., 1857. 1st Lieut., 3 Aug., 1861. Capt., 3 March, 1863. Bvt. Maj., 13 March, 1865, for meritorious service during the war. Maj. Eng., 7 March, 1867. Lieut. Col., 8 Aug., 1882. Col., 18 May, 1893. Retired by operation of law 31 March, 1895.

ELLIOT, WILLIAM G.* [Zorn in Me. Appointed from Me.]
2nd Lieut. 9th Inf., 1 July, 1886. 1st Lieut. 12th Inf., 19 Oct., 1893. Graduate of the Infantry and Cavalry School 1891. Died Aug. 11, 1898.

ELLIOTT, CHARLES P.* [Born in S. C. Appointed from S. C.]
2nd Lieut. 13th Inf., 13 June, 1882. Trans. to 4th Cav., 7 June, 1883 (to rank in Cav., 28 June, 1882). 1st Lieut., 2 Oct., 1888. Retired for disability with rank of Capt., 9 July, 1898.

ELLIOTT, EDWARD G. [Born in D. C. Appointed from D. C.]
2nd Lieut. 4th Inf., 1 Nov., 1838. 1st Lieut., 29 Nov., 1844. Capt., 1 Jan., 1848. Capt. A. Q. M., 3 March, 1847. Resigned Reg. Com., 1 Jan., 1848. Died 5 Jan., 1849.

ELLIOTT, JARED L. [Born in D. C. Appointed from D. C.]
Chaplain Post of Fort Atkinson, 3 Sept., 1845, to 23 Jan., 1849. Chaplain Post of Fort Washington, 25 March, 1867. Post Chaplain U. S. A., 3 April, 1867. Retired 24 Nov., 1868. Died 16 April, 1881.

ELLIOTT, JOEL H. [Born in Ind. Appointed from Ind.]
Priv. Co. C, 2nd Ind. Cav., 13 Sept., 1861, to 25 June, 1863. 2nd Lieut. 7th Ind. Cav., 25 June, 1863. Capt., 23 Oct., 1863. Mustered out 18 Feb., 1866. Maj. 7th Cav., 7 March, 1867. Killed 27 Nov., 1868, in action with Indians in Indian Ter.

ELLIOTT, JOHN.* [Born in Pa. Appointed from Pa.]
2nd Lieut. 2nd Art., 13 June, 1864. Retired 1 Feb., 1865. Capt. 43rd Inf., 28 July, 1866. Unassigned 8 April, 1869. Retired 15 Dec., 1870. Died 18 April, 1871. Bvt. 1st Lieut., 21 Aug., 1864, for gallant services during campaign before Richmond, Va.

ELLIOTT, JOHN W. [Born in Pa. Appointed from Pa.]
Post Chaplain, 14 June, 1867. Died 12 March, 1868.

ELLIOTT, MILTON A. [Born in Ark. Appointed from Ark.]
1st Sergt. Co. H, 1st Ark. Vols., 17 May to 26 Aug., 1898. 2nd Lieut., 27 Aug. to 25 Oct., 1898. 2nd Lieut. 13th Inf., 10 April, 1899.

ELLIOTT, MOSES H. [Born in Mass. Appointed from Mass.]
Maj. Surg. 40th Inf., 11 March, 1814. Disbanded 15 June, 1815. Post Surg., 7 Nov., 1816. Maj. Surg. 4th Inf., 31 Oct., 1817. Asst. Surg., 1 June, 1821. Died 8 Sept., 1822.

ELLIOTT, ROBT. [Born in Ireland. Appointed from D. C.]
Chap., 20 May, 1813. Disbanded 14 April, 1818.

ELLIOTT, STEPHEN H.* [Born in Ga. Appointed from Tex.]
Addl. 2nd Lieut. 4th Cav., 1 July, 1886. 2nd Lieut. 8th Cav., 5 July, 1886. Trans. to 5th Cav., 20 June, 1887. 1st Lieut. 10th Cav., 12 Feb., 1894. Trans. to 5th Cav., 22 March, 1894. Honor graduate of the Infantry and Cavalry School 1893.

ELLIOTT, THOS. I. [Born in Ky. Appointed from Ky.]
2nd Lieut. 2nd Ky. Vols., 9 Oct., 1862. Mustered out 19 June, 1864. 2nd Lieut. 13th Inf., 23 Feb., 1866. Trans. to 22nd Inf., 21 Sept., 1866. 1st Lieut., 1 Jan., 1867. Unassigned 15 May, 1869. Ass'd to 20th Inf., 14 July, 1869. Died 19 March, 1870.

ELLIOTT, WASHINGTON L. [Born in Pa. Appointed from Pa.]
Cadet Mil. Acad., 1 July, 1841, to 30 June, 1844. 2nd Lieut. Mounted Rifles, 27 May, 1846. 1st Lieut., 20 July, 1847. R. Q. M., 1 April, 1852, to 20 July, 1854. Capt. Mtd. Rifles (3rd Cav.), 20 July, 1854. Col. 2nd Iowa Cav., 14 Sept., 1861. Maj. 1st Cav., 5 Nov., 1861. Bvt. Lieut. Col., 7 April, 1862, for gallant and meritorious service in the capture of Island No. 10, on the Mississippi River. Bvt. Col., 30 May, 1862, for gallant and meritorious service in the raid on the Mississippi and Ohio Railroad, and in the Siege of Corinth, Miss. Brig. Gen. Vols., 11 June, 1862. Bvt. Brig. Gen., 13 March, 1865, for gallant and meritorious service in the Battle of Nashville, Ten- Bvt. Gen. Vols., 13 March, 1865, for gallant and meritorious service in the Battles before Nashville, Tenn. Bvt. Maj. Gen., 13 March, 1865, for gallant and meritorious service in the field during the war. Mustered out of Vol. service, 1 March, 1866. Lieut. Col. 1st Cav., 31 Aug., 1866. Col. 3rd Cav., 4 April, 1878. Retired 20 March, 1879. Died 29 June, 1888.

ELLIOTT, WILLIAM J.* [Born in Pa. Appointed from Md.]
Addl. 2nd Lieut. 8th Cav., 14 June, 1878. 2nd Lieut., 28 June, 1878. Resigned 1 June, 1881.

ELLIS, EUGENE A.* [Born in N. Y. Appointed from N. Y.]
2nd Lieut. 8th Cav., 15 June, 1876. 1st Lieut., 9 Oct., 1882. Capt., 20 April, 1891.

ELLIS, FRANK W. [Born in Tex. Appointed from the Army.]
Priv. and Sergt. Sig. Corps, 5 Jan., 1882, to 16 Aug., 1885. 2nd Lieut. Sig. Corps, 15 Aug., 1885. 2nd Lieut. 2nd Inf., 4 Feb., 1891 (to rank from 15 Aug., 1885). Retired for disability 22 Oct., 1891

ELLIS, HENRY A. [Born in N. Y. Appointed from N. Y.]
Capt. 17th Inf., 30 Nov., 1861. Trans. to 35th Inf., 21 Sept., 1866. Trans. to 15th Inf., 12 Aug., 1869. Dismissed 7 Oct., 1871. Reinstated 28 May, 1872. Died 25 Jan., 1876.

ELLIS, JAMES N.* [Born in Va. Appointed from Va.]
Bvt. 2nd Lieut. 1st Art., 1 July, 1835. Resigned 19 Oct., 1835.

ELLIS, PHILIP H. [Born in Md. Appointed from Md.]
Priv. Co. L, 6th Pa. Cav., 11 Nov., 1862. Sergt., 1 Dec., 1862. 2nd Lieut. 6th Pa. Cav., 1 May, 1863. 1st Lieut., 12 March, 1864. Mustered out 3 Nov., 1864. 2nd Lieut. 13th Inf., 23 Feb., 1866. Trans. to 31st Inf., 21 Sept., 1866. 1st Lieut., 28 Dec., 1866. Unassigned 21 June, 1869. Ass'd to 13th Inf., 1 Jan., 1871. Capt., 1 April, 1872. Maj. 13th Inf., 1 Oct., 1895. Lieut. Col. 8th Inf., 17 Sept., 1898.

ELLIS, WILMOT E.* [Born in N. J. Appointed from N. J.]
2nd Lieut. 5th Art., 12 June, 1889. 1st Lieut. 4th Art., 6 June, 1896. Graduate of the Artillery School 1898.

ELLISON, JOHN. [Born in Ireland. Appointed from Army.]
Priv., Corpl. and Sergt. Capt. Walbach's Co. Artillerists, 8 Sept., 1806, to Sept, 1813. 3rd Lieut. 1st Art., 1 July, 1813. 2nd Lieut. 4th Rifles, 17 March, 1814. Disbanded 15 June, 1815. Reinstated in 6th Inf., 2 Dec., 1815. Resigned 1 March, 1820.

ELLSWORTH, EDWARD A. [Born in Me. Appointed from Wis.]
2nd Lieut. 11th Inf., 24 Oct., 1861. 1st Lieut., 24 Oct., 1861. Trans. to 29th Inf., 21 Sept., 1866. Resigned 18 Dec., 1866. Bvt. Capt., 1 Aug., 1864, for gallant service at the Battle of the Wilderness, and during the campaign before Richmond, Va.

ELLSWORTH, EPHRAIM D. [Born in N. Y. Appointed from N. Y.]
Ord. Storekeeper, 16 Nov., 1861. Capt. Ord. Storekeeper, 28 July, 1866. Retired 30 June, 1882. Died 6 Nov., 1889.

ELTING, FRANK M. [Born in Pa. Appointed from Pa.]
Maj. and P. M., 13 April, 1867. Discharged 31 Dec., 1870.

ELTING, NORMAN.* [Born in N. Y. Appointed from N. Y.]
Bvt. 2nd Lieut. 6th Inf., 1 July, 1843. 2nd Lieut. 4th Inf., 9 May, 1846. Resigned 29 Oct., 1846.

ELTING, OSCAR. [Born in N. Y. Appointed from N. Y.]
Corpl. Co. A, 1st N. Y. Cav., 30 July, 1861. Priv., 1 April, 1863. Re-enlisted 1 Jan., 1864. Discharged 22 Aug., 1866. 2nd Lieut. 3rd Cav., 22 July, 1867. 1st Lieut., 17 Nov., 1869. Capt., 30 Jan., 1881. Retired by operation of law, 8 Aug., 1895.

ELTINGE, LEROY.* [Born in N. Y. Appointed from N. Y.]
2nd Lieut. 4th Cav., 12 June, 1896. 1st Lieut. 6th Cav., 15 July, 1899.

ELTONHEAD, FRANCIS E.* [Born in Pa. Appointed from Pa.]
2nd Lieut. 21st Inf., 16 June, 1875. 1st Lieut., 15 Aug., 1880. Capt., 15 Dec., 1892. Bvt. 1st Lieut., 27 Feb., 1890, for distinguished services and conspicuous gallantry in action against Indians at the Clearwater, Idaho, 11 and 12 July, 1877.

ELWES, ALFRED W. [Born in Md. Appointed from Md.]
Asst. Surg., 9 May, 1825. Maj. and Surg., 4 July, 1836. Died 12 June, 1842.

ELWOOD, JOHN. [Born in Ohio. Appointed from Ky.]
2nd Lieut. 5th Inf., 14 May, 1857. 1st Lieut., 7 May, 1861. Capt., 20 Feb., 1862. Died 3 Dec., 1862.

ELY, FRANK D.* [Born in Ill. Appointed from Ill.]
2nd Lieut. 6th Inf., 12 June, 1894. Trans. to 13th Inf., 10 Sept., 1895. 1st Lieut. 9th Inf., 26 April, 1898. Trans. to 2nd Inf., 23 Feb., 1899.

ELY, HANSON E.* [Born in Iowa. Appointed from Iowa.]
2nd Lieut. 22nd Inf., 12 June, 1891. 1st Lieut., 26 April, 1898.

ELY, JOHN F. [Born in Pa. Appointed from Pa.]
1st Lieut. 19th Inf., 14 May, 1861. Died 19 Jan., 1863.

ELZEY, ARNOLD. [Born in D. C. Appointed from D. C.]
Garrison Surg.'s Mate, 15 April, 1814. Post Surg., 10 April, 1816. Died 6 June, 1818.

ELZEY, ARNOLD.* [Born in Md. Appointed from Md.]
(Changed name from A. E. Jones.) 2nd Lieut. 2nd Art., 1 July, 1837. 1st Lieut., 12 Nov., 1839. Reg. Adj., 8 Dec., 1847, to 11 Jan., 1848. Capt., 14 Feb., 1849. Resigned 25 April, 1861. Bvt. Capt., 20 Aug., 1847, for gallant and meritorious conduct at Contreras and Churubusco.

EMBICK, STANLEY D.* [Born in Pa. Appointed from Pa.]
2nd Lieut. 2nd Art., 15 Feb., 1899.

EMBURY, PETER.* [Born in N. Y. Appointed from N. Y.]
Bvt. 2nd Lieut. Light Art., 11 Dec., 1815. Resigned 1 Nov., 1816.

EMERSON, FRANK. [Born in N. H. Appointed from Ind.]
2nd Lieut. 3rd Drag., 29 March, 1848. Disbanded 20 July, 1848. Col. 67th Ind. Vols., 22 Aug., 1862. Resigned, 30 Sept., 1864.

EMERSON, JAMES J. [Born in N. Y. Appointed from Army.]
Priv., Corpl. and Sergt. Co. C, 17th Inf., 13 Sept., 1861, to 24 March, 1863. 2nd Lieut., 17th Inf., 19 Feb., 1863. 1st Lieut., 4 May, 1863. Capt., 8 Jan., 1866. Trans. to 26th Inf., 21 Sept., 1866. Cashiered 2 Oct., 1868. Bvt. Capt., 1 Aug., 1864, for gallant service at the Battle of North Anna River, and during the campaign before Richmond, Va.

EMERSON, JOHN. [Born in Pa. Appointed from Pa.]
Asst. Surg., 1 Dec., 1833. Disbanded 23 Sept., 1842.

EMERY, JONAS A.* [Born in Ind. Appointed from Ind.]
2nd Lieut. 11th Inf., 11 June, 1881. 1st Lieut., 8 Dec., 1886. Capt., 16 Dec., 1897.

EMMET, ROBT. T.* [Born in N. Y. Appointed at Large.]
2nd Lieut. 9th Cav., 15 June, 1877. 1st Lieut., 20 Jan., 1883. Resigned 1 April, 1891.

EMORY, CAMPBELL D.* [Born in Pa. Appointed at Large.]
2nd Lieut. 6th Inf., 6 May, 1861. Trans. to 9th Inf., 25 May, 1861. 1st Lieut., 25 June, 1861. Reg. Adj., 21 July, 1862, to 29 Dec., 1863. Capt., 29 Dec., 1863. Died 11 March, 1878. Bvt. Maj., 2 April, 1865, for gallant and meritorious service in front of Petersburg, Va. Bvt. Lieut. Col. 9 April, 1865, for faithful and distinguished service in the field during the war.

EMORY, JOHN R. [Born in Md. Appointed from Md.]
2nd Lieut. 6th Inf., 21 Oct., 1839. Resigned 9 Feb., 1843.

EMORY, WM. H.* [Born in Md. Appointed from Md.]
Bvt. 2nd Lieut. 4th Art., 1 July, 1831. 2nd Lieut., 1 July, 1831. Resigned 30 Sept., 1836. 1st Lieut. Top. Eng., 7 July, 1838. Bvt. Capt., 6 Dec., 1846, for gallant and meritorious service in the Battle of San Pasqual. Bvt. Maj., 9 Jan., 1847, for gallant and meritorious service in the Battles of San Gabriel and the Plains of Mesa. Capt. Top. Eng., 24 April, 1851. Maj. 2nd Cav., 3 March, 1855. Trans. to 1st Cav., 26 May, 1855. Bvt. Lieut. Col., 19 Oct., 1857, for meritorious and distinguished service as commissioner for running the boundary line between United States and the Republic of Mexico. Lieut. Col. 1st Cav., 31 Jan., 1861. Resigned 9 May, 1861. Lieut. Col. 6th Cav., 14 May, 1861. Brig. Gen. Vols March, 1862. Bvt. Col., 27 May, 1862, for gallant and meritorious service in the Battle of Hanover, C. H., Va. Col. 5th Cav., 27 Oct., 1863. Bvt. Brig. Gen., 13 March, 1865, for gallant and meritorious service in the Battle of Fisher's Hill, and in the campaign of Shenandoah Valley, Va. Bvt. Maj. Gen., 13 March, 1865 for gallant and meritorious service in the Battle of Cedar Creek, Va. Maj. Gen. Vols., 25 Sept., 1865. Mustered out of Vol. service, 15 Jan., 1866. Retired with rank of Brig. Gen., 1 July, 1876. Died 1 Dec., 1887.

EMPIE, ADAM. [Born in N. C. Appointed from N. C.]
Chaplain and Prof. at Mil. Acad., 9 Aug., 1813. Resigned 30 April, 1817.

ENGELS, PETER. [Born in Prussia. Appointed from Tenn.]
Priv. Co. L, 1st Tenn. Vols., 28 May to 12 Nov., 1846. Priv. and Sergt. Co. C, 3rd Drags., 23 April, 1847, to 31 July, 1848. 1st Lieut. 10th Tenn. Vols., 1 July, 1862. Capt., 1 May, 1863. Mustered out 23 June, 1865. 2nd Lieut. 24th Inf., 28 July, 1866. 1st Lieut., 14 Sept., 1867. Resigned 27 July, 1869.

ENGLAND, GEORGE A. [Born in Vt. Appointed from Col.]
Post Chap., 1 Feb., 1876. Died 4 Dec., 1883.

ENGLAND, LLOYD.* [Born in Ark. Appointed from Ark.]
Addl. 2nd Lieut. 3rd Art., 12 June, 1896. 2nd Lieut. 5th Art., 1 June, 1897. Trans. to 3rd Art., 24 June, 1897. 1st Lieut., 2 March, 1899. Capt. 11th U. S. Vol. Cav., 12 Aug., 1899.

ENGLE, ARCHIBALD H. [Born in Mo. Appointed from Mo.]
Priv. Co. F, 17th Pa. Vols., 25 April to 27 June, 1861. 1st Lieut. 13th Inf., 14 May, 1861. Capt., 3 May, 1864. Killed 14 May, 1864, at the Battle of Resaca, Ga. Bvt. Maj., 14 May, 1864, for gallant and meritorious service at the Battle of Resaca, Ga.

ENGLE, JAMES.* [Born in N. J. Appointed from N. J.]
Bvt. 2nd Lieut. 7th Inf., 1 July, 1825. 2nd Lieut. 4th Inf., 1 July, 1825. Trans. to 5th Inf., 25 Jan., 1827. 1st Lieut., 14 Oct., 1830. Resigned 31 Dec., 1834.

ENGLE, JOHN B. [Born in Ind. Appointed from Ind.]
Corpl. Co. K, 86th Ind. Vols., 4 Sept., 1862. Mustered out 6 June, 1865. 2nd Lieut. 17th Inf., 23 Feb., 1866. Trans. to 35th Inf., 21 Sept., 1866. 1st Lieut., 2 Feb., 1867. Trans. to 15th Inf., 12 Aug., 1869. Capt., 9 June, 1875. Resigned 18 Sept., 1878.

ENGLISH, THOMAS C.* [Born in Pa. Appointed from Pa.]
Bvt. 2nd Lieut. 5th Inf., 1 July, 1849. 2nd Lieut., 31 July, 1850. 1st Lieut. 9th Inf., 3 March, 1855. Reg. Adjt., 18 April, 1855, to 31 May, 1856. Capt., 29 Dec., 1857. Maj. 5th Inf., 27 Aug., 1863. Lieut. Col. 2nd Inf., 22 Feb., 1869. Died 10 June, 1876. Bvt. Lieut. Col., 13 March, 1865, for faithful and meritorious service during the war.

ENGLISH, WILLIAM. [Born in Va. Appointed from Pa.]
Cadet Mil. Acad., 1 July, 1875, to 24 June, 1876. Priv. Gen. Ser., 23 April, 1879. Discharged 31 Aug., 1879. 2nd Lieut. 17th Inf., 1 Sept., 1879. Dismissed 11 March, 1885.

ENGLISH, WM. L. [Born in Ill. Appointed from Ill.]
1st Sergt. Co. E, 101st Ill. Vols., 2 Sept., 1862. 2nd Lieut., 1 May, 1863. 1st Lieut., 5 March, 1864. Mustered out 7 June, 1865. 2nd Lieut. 7th Inf., 18 June, 1867. 1st Lieut., 24 Oct., 1874. Died 20 Aug., 1877, of wounds received in action with Indians in Montana Ter.

ENNIS, JOSEPH J. [Born in Ireland. Appointed from Ky.]
Sergt. Co. K, 12th Ohio Vols., 25 April to 18 Aug., 1861. Priv. Co. G, 20th Ky. Vols., 12 Oct, 1863, to 27 May, 1864. 1st Lieut. and Adjt. 54th Ky. Vols., 28 May, 1864. Mustered out 11 July, 1864. Priv. and Comsy. Sergt. 6th U. S. Vet. Vols., 10 March to Aug., 1865. 2nd Lieut. 6th U. S. Vet. Vols., 14 Aug., 1865. Mustered out 22 March, 1866. 2n2d Lieut. 3rd Cav., 18 April, 1866. 1st Lieut., 14 Nov., 1867. Died 12 Aug., 1869.

ENNIS, WM.* [Born in R. I. Appointed from R. I.]
2nd Lieut. 4th Art., 13 June, 1864. Bvt. 1st Lieut., 30 Nov., 1864, for gallant and meritorious service in the Battle of Franklin, Tenn. Bvt. Capt., 13 March, 1865, for gallant service at Nashville, Tenn., 15 and 16 Dec., 1864. 1st Lieut. 4th Art., 8 May, 1866. Reg. Adj., 1 April, to 5 Aug., 1887. Capt., 5 Oct., 1887. Maj. 6th Art., 18 March, 1899. Graduate of the Artillery School, 1876. Lieut. Col. and Chief Ord. Officer, 18 July to 31 Dec., 1898.

ENOCHS, BERKELEY.* [Born in Ohio. Appointed from Ohio.]
2nd Lieut. 25th Inf., 26 April, 1898. 1st Lieut., 2 March, 1899.

ENOS, HERBERT M.* [Born in N. Y. Appointed from N. Y.]
Bvt. 2nd Lieut. Mounted Rifles, 1 July, 1856. 2nd Lieut., 26 Jan., 1857. 1st Lieut. 6th Cav., 14 May, 1861. Capt. Asst. Q. M., 3 Aug., 1861. Maj. Q. M. Vols. (Act 4 July, 1864), 2 Aug., 1864, to 3 June, 1865. Bvt. Maj., Lieut. Col. and Col., 13 March, 1865, for faithful and meritorious service during the war. Col. Q. M. Vols. (Act 4 July, 1864), 3 June, 1865, to 8 Jan., 1866. Maj. Q. M., 6 June, 1872. Retired 29 May, 1876.

EPFLEY, KURTZ. [Born in N. J. Appointed from N. J.]
Priv. Troop D, U. S. Cav., 17 June to 15 Sept., 1898. 2nd Lieut. 15th Inf., 10 April, 1899.

ERICKSON, HJALMER. [Born in Norway. Appointed from the Army.
Priv., Corpl. and Sergt. Troop B, 8th Cav., 6 Feb., 1893, to 5 Feb., 1898. Priv., Corpl. and Sergt. Troop B, Sergt. and 1st Sergt. Troop M., 8th Cav., 28 March, 1898, to 21 April, 1899. 2nd Lieut. 15th Inf., 5 April, 1899. Trans. to 7th Inf., 29 March, 1900.

ERNST, OSWALD H.* [Born in Ohio. Appointed from Mass.]
1st Lieut. Eng., 13 June, 1864. Bvt. Capt., 13 March, 1865, for faithful and meritorious service. Capt. Eng., 7 March, 1867. Maj., 5 May, 1882. Lieut. Col., 31 March, 1895. Brig. Gen. Vols., 27 May, 1898, to 12 June, 1899.

ERNST, RUDOLPH F.* [Born in Ill. Appointed from Ill.]
Bvt. 2nd Lieut. 6th Inf., 1 July, 1841. 2nd Lieut., 9 Feb., 1843. Died 22 Sept., 1847, of wounds received at the Battle of Molino del Rey.

ERVING, JOHN. [Born in Mass. Appointed from Mass.]
2nd Lieut. Artillerists, 9 Jan., 1809. 1st Lieut., 16 Aug., 1812. Maj. A. A. G., 6 April, 1813, to 15 June, 1815. Trans. to Corps Art. as 1st Lieut., 17 May, 1815. Capt., 25 April, 1818. Maj. 3rd Art., 25 June, 1841. Trans. to 4th Art., 1 June, 1821. Trans. to 2nd Art., 2 Dec., 1843. Lieut. Col., 18 Aug., 1846. Col. 1st Art., 5 Oct., 1857. Retired 26 Oct., 1861. Died 26 Oct., 1862. Bvt. Maj., 25 April, 1828. for ten years' faithful service in one grade.

ERWIN, ISAAC.* [Born in Fla. Appointed from Fla.]
2nd Lieut. 16th Inf., 11 June, 1892. 1st Lieut., 26 April, 1898.

ERWIN, JAMES B.* [Born in Ga. Appointed from Ga.]
2d Lieut. 4th Cav., 12 June, 1880. 1st Lieut., 24 April, 1886. Capt., 25 Feb., 1896. Honor graduate of the Infantry and Cavalry School, 1883.

ESCHENBURG, JOHN R. [Born in South America. Appointed from Cal.]
Priv. Co. I, 2nd Cal. Vols., 30 Sept., 1864. Mustered out 10 May, 1866. 2nd Lieut. 14th Inf., 23 Feb., 1866. 1st Lieut., 28 July, 1866. Trans. to 23rd Inf., 21 Sept., 1866. Mustered out 1 Jan., 1871.

ESKRIDGE, OLIVER S. [Born in Mass. Appointed from Army.]
Priv., Mus., Corpl. and Sergt. Co. E, 18th Inf., 13 July, 1895, to 24 April, 1899. 2nd Lieut. 18th Inf., 5 April, 1899.

ESKRIDGE, RICHD. I. [Born in Mo. Appointed from Mo.]
1st class Mus., Band 2nd Iowa Vols., 10 Sept., 1861. Discharged 1 May, 1862. Priv. 2nd Mo. Cav., 9 Jan., 1864. Sergt., 1 March, 1864. 1st Lieut. 14th Mo. Cav., 8 Feb., 1865. Capt., 28 Aug., 1865. Mustered out 17 Nov., 1865. 2nd Lieut. 14th Inf., 23 Feb., 1866, and 1st Lieut., 22 March, 1866. Trans. to 23rd Inf., 21 Sept., 1866. Bvt. Capt., 26 Sept., 1867, for conspicuous gallantry in charging a large band of Indians strongly fortified in the Infernal Caverns, Pitt River, Cal., 26 Sept., 1867. Capt. 23rd Inf., 1 Sept., 1873. Maj. 10th Inf., 17 April, 1897. Lieut. Col. 23rd Inf., 26 March, 1899.

ESTERLY, CALVIN.* [Born in Ohio. Appointed from Kan.]
2nd Lieut. 10th Cav., 15 June, 1877. Resigned 30 June, 1883.

ESTES, CHAS. A. M. [Born in Wis. Appointed from Army.]
Priv., Sergt. and 1st Sergt. Co. H, 16th Inf., 13 July, 1861, to 9 Sept., 1862. 2nd Lieut. 16th Inf., 13 Aug., 1862. 1st Lieut., 13 Jan., 1863. Capt., 20 Oct., 1865. Trans. to

25th Inf., 21 Sept., 1866. Trans. to 18th Inf., 26 April, 1869. Mustered out 1 Jan., 1871. Bvt. Capt., 1 Sept., 1864, for gallant and meritorious service during the Atlanta campaign, and at the Battle of Jonesboro, Ga.

ESTES, GEORGE H., JR.* [Born in Ala. Appointed from Ga.]
2nd Lieut. 20th Inf., 12 June, 1894. 1st Lieut., 20 April, 1898.

EUSTIS, ABRAM. [Born in Va. Appointed from Mass.]
Capt. Light Art., 3 May, 1808. Maj., 15 March, 1810. Trans. to 4th Art., 1 June, 1821. Lieut. Col. 2nd Art., 8 May, 1822. Trans. to 4th Art., 2 Aug., 1822. Col. 1st Art., 17 Nov., 1834. Died 27 June, 1843. Bvt. Lieut. Col., 10 Sept., 1813, for meritorious service. Bvt. Col., 10 Sept., 1823, for 10 years' faithful service in one grade. Bvt. Brig. Gen., 30 June, 1834.

EUSTIS, HENRY L.* [Born in Mass. Appointed from Mass.]
2nd Lieut. Eng., 1 July, 1842. Resigned 30 Nov., 1849. Col. 10th Mass. Vols., 21 Aug., 1862. Brig. Gen. Vols., 12 Sept., 1863. Resigned, 27 June, 1864. Died 11 Jan., 1885.

EUSTIS, WM.* [Born in R. I. Appointed from Mass.]
Bvt. 2nd Lieut. 3rd Inf., 1 July, 1830. Trans. to 1st Drag., 14 Aug., 1833. 2nd Lieut., 17 March, 1834. 1st Lieut., 15 June, 1836. Capt., 17 March, 1845. Resigned, 4 Aug., 1849.

EVANS, ALEXR. [Born in Ky. Appointed from Ky.]
2nd Lieut. of Inf., 4 March, 1847; 16th Inf., 9 April, 1847. R. Q. M., 9 April to 25 July, 1847. 1st Lieut., 13 May, 1848. Disbanded 7 Aug., 1848.

EVANS, ANDREW W.* [Born in Md. Appointed from Md.]
Bvt. 2nd Lieut. 7th Inf., 1 July, 1852. 2nd Lieut., 3 March, 1855. 1st Lieut., 20 Sept., 1856. Capt. 3rd Cav., 14 May, 1861; 6th Cav., 3 Aug., 1861. Bvt. Maj., 21 Feb., 1862, for gallant and meritorious service in the Battle of Valverde, N. Mex. Col. 1st Md. Cav., 15 April, 1864. Bvt. Lieut. Col., 9 April, 1865, for gallant and meritorious service in the Cav. action at Appomattox C. H., Va. Mustered out of Vol. service 8 Aug., 1865. Maj. 3rd Cav., 10 May, 1867. Bvt. Col., 25 Dec., 1868, for gallant and meritorious service resulting in the capture and destruction of a Comanche Indian village at the western base of the Wichita Mountains, 25 Dec., 1868. Lieut. Col. 7th Cav., 2 April, 1883. Retired over 30 years' service, 22 Sept., 1883.

EVANS, BRITTON. [Born in Pa. Appointed from Pa.]
3rd Lieut. 2nd Art., 17 Aug., 1813. 2nd Lieut., 19 April, 1814. Trans. to Corps Art., 12 May, 1814. Disbanded 15 June, 1815. 2nd Lieut. 3rd Inf., 30 Aug., 1816. 1st Lieut., 1 April, 1819. Disbanded 1 June, 1821.

EVANS, CLAIBORNE E. [Born in Ala. Appointed from Ala.]
2nd Lieut. 13th Inf., 27 June, 1848. Disbanded 15 July, 1848.

EVANS, COLUMBUS P. [Born in Pa. Appointed from Del.]
2nd Lieut. of Inf., 5 March, 1847; 11th Inf., 9 April, 1847. 1st Lieut., 29 July, 1847. R. Q. M., 17 June to 14 Aug., 1848. Disbanded 14 Aug, 1848. Bvt. Capt., 20 Aug., 1847, for gallant and meritorious conduct at Contreras and Churubusco. Died 19 Feb., 1854.

EVANS, ELLWOOD W.* [Born in Md. Appointed from Md.]
2nd Lieut. 8th Cav., 12 June, 1887. 1st Lieut. 5th Cav., 25 Aug., 1894. Trans. to 8th Cav., 20 Feb., 1895. Maj. 1st Md. Vols., 17 May, 1898. Lieut. Col. 6th July, 1898, to muster out, 28 Feb., 1899.

EVANS, FREDERICK D.* [Born in Ill. Appointed from Ill.]
Addl. 2nd Lieut. 22nd Inf., 1 July, 1887. 2nd Lieut. 18th Inf., 6 Oct., 1887. 1st Lieut. 24th Inf., 21 Jan., 1895. Trans. to 18th Inf., 16 May, 1895. Capt., 2nd March, 1899. Reg. Adjt., 2 March, 1899.

EVANS, GEORGE F.* [Born in Me. Appointed from Me.]
Bvt. 2nd Lieut. 1st Drag., 1 July, 1846. 2nd Lieut., 18 Oct., 1847. Died 29 March, 1859. Bvt. 1st Lieut., 23 Feb., 1847, for gallant and meritorious conduct at Buena Vista, Mex.

EVANS, GEORGE H.* [Born in Pa. Appointed from Pa.]
2nd Lieut. 10th Cav., 14 June, 1872. 1st Lieut., 18 Nov., 1881. Capt., 20 Oct., 1892. Retired for disability 11 March, 1898.

EVANS, GEORGE W. [Born in Md. Appointed from Md.]
Capt. 1st Md. Vols., 23 Dec., 1861. Mustered out 23 Dec., 1864. 2nd Lieut. 32nd Inf., 22 Jan., 1867. Bvt. 1st Lieut. and Bvt. Capt., 2 March, 1867, for gallant and meritorious service during the war. 1st Lieut. 32nd Inf., 9 Dec., 1867. Unassigned 19 April, 1869. Ass'd to 21st Inf., 21 Oct., 1869. Reg. Adjt., 31 Aug., 1871, to 20 March, 1879. Capt., 20 March, 1879. Retired for disability 24 April, 1886. Died 11 Aug., 1896.

EVANS, HENRY C., Jr. [Born in N. Y. Appointed from Tenn.]
2nd Lieut. 3rd Art., 9 July, 1898.

EVANS, HENRY F. [Born in Md. Appointed from Pa.]
Ensign 22nd Inf., 31 March, 1814. 3rd Lieut., 2 June, 1814. 2nd Lieut., 2 June, 1814. Trans. to Corps. Art., 17 May, 1815. Trans. to Light Art., 23 Dec., 1815. 1st Lieut., 8 Aug., 1819. Trans. to 3rd Art., 1 June, 1821. Trans. to 1st Art., 16 Aug., 1821. Cashiered 11 Feb., 1825.

EVANS, HOUSTON V.* [Born in Mo. Appointed from Mo.]
Addl. 2nd Lieut. 14th Inf., 12 June, 1896. 2nd Lieut. 6th Inf., 7 Dec., 1896. 1st Lieut. of Inf., 28 Dec., 1898. Ass'd to 6th Inf., 1 Jan., 1899.

EVANS, JAMES P. [Born in Tenn. Appointed from Tenn.]
Maj. and Surg., 28 Sept., 1847. Disbanded 20 July, 1848.

EVANS, JOHN E. [Born in D. C. Appointed from Md.]
1st Lieut. 11th Inf., 26 Oct., 1861. Cashiered 10 May, 1862.

EVANS, JOHN S. [Born in Ky. Appointed from Ky.]
Mil. Storekeeper, 7 May, 1851. Removed 18 Nov., 1851.

EVANS, NATHAN G.* [Born in S. C. Appointed from S. C.]
Bvt. 2nd Lieut. 1st Drag., 1 July, 1848. 2nd Lieut. 2nd Drag., 30 Sept., 1849. 1st Lieut. 2nd Cav., 3 March, 1855. Capt., 1 May, 1856. Resigned 27 Feb., 1861. Died 20 Nov., 1868.

EVANS, ROBT. K.* [Born in Miss. Appointed from Miss.]
2nd Lieut. 12th Inf., 16 June, 1875. 1st Lieut., 8 Jan., 1882. Capt., 19 Oct., 1893.

EVANS, THOS. H. [Born in Eng. Appointed from Army.]
Priv. and Serg. Gen. Ser., 2 Oct., 1849, to 2 Oct., 1859. Priv. and Sergt. Gen. Ser. and Sergt. Maj. 12th Inf., 1 Nov., 1861, to 30 June, 1862. 2nd Lieut. 12th Inf., 25 May, 1862. 1st Lieut., 30 Aug., 1862. Resigned 17 Feb., 1863. Sergt. Gen. Ser., 4 June, 1863, to 1 Dec., 1865. Died 9 Sept., 1895.

EVANS, WILLIAM P.* [Born in Wis. Appointed from Wis.]
2nd Lieut. 19th Inf., 14 June, 1878. 1st Lieut., 13 Oct., 1886. R. Q. M., 1 July, 1887. Capt., 7 June, 1894.

EVELETH, WM. S.* [Born in D. C. Appointed from D. C.]
Bvt. 2nd Lieut. Eng., 4 March, 1815. 2nd Lieut., 31 Oct., 1816. Died 4 Oct., 1818, by shipwreck.

EVERETT, JOSIAH. [Born in N. H. Appointed from Mass.]
Surg. Mate 21st Inf., 21 July, 1813. Disbanded 15 June, 1815. Reinstated in 2nd Inf., 13 Sept., 1815. Post Surg., 10 Aug., 1818. Maj. and Surg., Light Art., 28 Jan., 1820. Retained as Maj. and Surg., 1 June, 1821. Died 14 July, 1832.

EVERETT, THORNLEY S. [Born in Va. Appointed from Army.]
Priv. and Corpl. Co. K, 4th Art., 10 Oct., 1841, to 1 Oct., 1843. Sergt. Co. E, 2nd Inf., to 10 Oct., 1846, and Sergt. Co. A, Eng., to 14 July, 1848. Bvt. 2nd Lieut. 1st Art., 28 June, 1848. 2nd Lieut., 22 Sept., 1848. Resigned 30 June, 1852. Capt. A. A. G. Vols., 5 Aug., 1861. Resigned 1 April, 1862.

EVERETT, WILLIAM.* [Born in Me. Appointed from N. H.]
2nd Lieut. 4th Art, 15 June, 1868. 1st Lieut., 26 April, 1873. Capt., 12 Feb., 1895. Graduate of the Artillery School, 1873, 1886. Died 15 March, 1899.

EVERTS, EDWARD. [Born in Tex. Appointed from Cal.]
Asst. Surg., 23 May, 1882. Capt. and Asst. Surg., 23 May, 1887.

EWELL, BENJAMIN S.* [Born in D. C. Appointed from Va.]
Bvt. 2nd Lieut. 4th Art., 1 July, 1832. 2nd Lieut., 1 July, 1832. Resigned 30 Sept., 1836.

EWELL, RICHARD S.* [Born in Va. Appointed from Va.]
Bvt. 2nd Lieut. 1st Drag., 1 July, 1840. 2nd Lieut., 1 Nov., 1840. 1st Lieut. 18 Sept., 1845. Capt., 4 Aug., 1849. Resigned 7 May, 1861. Bvt. Capt., 20 Aug., 1847. for gallant and meritorious conduct at Contreras and Churubusco, Mex. Died 25 Jan., 1872.

EWELL, THOS. [Born in Va. Appointed from Tenn.]
2nd Lieut. Mounted Rifles, 27 May, 1846. Killed 18 April, 1847, at the Battle of Cerro Gordo, Mexico.

EWEN, CLARENCE. [Born in N. Y. Appointed from N. Y.]
Asst. Surg. 53rd N. Y. Vols., 8 Sept., 1862. Mustered out 13 Sept., 1862. Asst. Surg. 182nd N. Y. Vols., 13 Dec., 1862. Resigned 27 Oct., 1863. Asst. Surg. 29th U. S. Col. Troops, 2 Nov., 1864. Mustered out 6 Nov., 1865. 1st Lieut. Asst. Surg., 16 Nov., 1868. Capt. Asst. Surg., 23 Dec., 1869. Maj. Surg., 15 April, 1889. Retired for over 30 years' service, 26 Jan., 1897.

EWERS, EZRA P. [Born in N. Y. Appointed from Army.]
Priv. Co. E, 1st Batt. 19th Inf., 18 Jan., 1862. Sergt., 15 March, 1862. 1st Sergt., 1 March, 1863. Bvt. 1st Lieut., 26 June, 1863, for gallant service in action at Hoover's Gap, Tenn. 2nd Lieut. 19th Inf., 31 Oct., 1863. Bvt. Capt., 25 Nov., 1863, for gallant and meritorious service in the Battle of Chattanooga, Tenn. 1st Lieut. 19th Inf., 16 March, 1864. Trans. to 37th Inf., 21 Sept., 1866. Capt., 12 Sept., 1866. Trans. to 5th Inf., 19 May, 1869. Maj. 9th Inf., 7 March, 1893. Lieut. Col., 30 April, 1897. Col. 10th Inf., 16 May, 1899. Brig. Gen. Vols., 12 July, 1898, to 20 April, 1899. Bvt. Maj., 27 Feb., 1890, for gallant services in action against Indians under Crazy Horse, on Tongue River, Mont., Jan. 8, 1877.

EWING, CHAS. [Born in Ohio. Appointed from Ohio.]
Capt. 13th Inf., 14 May, 1861. Lieut. Col. A. I. G., 22 June, 1863, to 1 April, 1865. Brig. Gen. Vols., 8 March, 1865. Resigned 1 Dec., 1865. Trans. to 22nd Inf., 21 Sept., 1866. Resigned 31 July, 1867. Bvt. Maj., 4 July, 1863, for gallant and meritorious service during the Siege of Vicksburg, Miss. Bvt. Lieut. Col., 1 Sept., 1864, for gallant and meritorious service during the Atlanta campaign. Bvt. Col., 13 March, 1865, for gallant and meritorious service during the war. Died 20 June, 1883.

EWING, CHARLES B. [Born in Mo. Appointed from Mo.]
Cadet at Mil. Acad., 14 June, 1876, to 31 Oct., 1876. Asst. Surg., 5 July, 1884. Capt. and Asst. Surg., 5 July, 1889. Maj. Brig. Surg. Vols., 4 June to 30 Nov., 1898. Maj. Surg. Vols., 1 Nov., 1899.

EWING, EVARTS S. [Born in Tenn. Appointed from Mo.]
Bugler Co. D, 1st Iowa Cav., 29 July, 1861. Q. M. Sergt., 8 Aug., 1861. Chief Bugler, 7 Oct., 1861. Com. Sergt., 1 Jan., 1862. Priv. Co. D, ———. Discharged 12 Sept., 1863. Capt. C. S. Vols., 31 Jan., 1865. Bvt. Maj., Lieut. Col. and Col. Vols., 6 Oct., 1865, for faithful and meritorious service. Mustered out 9 Oct., 1865. 2nd Lieut. 16th Inf., 23 Feb., 1866. 1st Lieut., 19 March, 1866. Tran. to 34th Inf., 21 Sept., 1866. Bvt. Capt. and Maj., 2 March, 1867, for gallant and meritorious service during the war. Trans. to 16th Inf., 14 April, 1869. R. Q. M., 9 March to 30 April, 1880. Capt., 30 April, 1880. Retired 20 March, 1885.

EWING, MASKELL C.* [Born in Pa. Appointed from Pa.]
Bvt. 2nd Lieut. 3rd Art., 1 July, 1826. 2nd Lieut. 4th Art., 1 July, 1826. 1st Lieut., 31 Dec., 1835. Resigned 15 Aug., 1836. Died 20 Nov., 1849.

EWING, ROBERT W. [Born in ——. Appointed from Ky.]
Ensign 17th Inf., 16 June, 1813. 3rd Lieut., 7 March, 1814. Disbanded 15 June, 1815. 2nd Lieut. 1st Inf., 17 June, 1816. Resigned 1 Dec., 1817.

EWING, WM. [Born in Scotland. Appointed from Army.]
Priv. and Q. M. Sergt. 17th Inf., 1 Aug., 1862, to 13 May, 1863. 2nd Lieut. 17th Inf., 12 May, 1863. 1st Lieut., 2 July, 1863. Retired 15 Feb., 1864. Resigned 28 Feb., 1865.

EWING, WM. [Born in Ireland. Appointed from Army.]
Priv., Corpl. and Sergt. Co. C, Mtd. Rifles (3rd Cav.), 24 Jan., 1859, to 17 Dec., 1862. 2nd Lieut. 3rd Cav., 17 July, 1862. Dropped 9 Aug., 1863, having deserted to the enemy.

EXTON, CHARLES W.* [Born in N. J. Appointed from N. J.]
2nd Lieut. 20th Inf., 26 April, 1898. 1st Lieut., 2 March, 1899.

EYSTER, JACOB M. [Born in Pa. Appointed from Pa.]
Capt. 18th Inf., 14 May, 1861. Discharged 8 Feb., 1865.

EYRE, MANUEL. [Born in Pa. Appointed from Del.]
Sergt. Co. I, 3rd Del. Vols., 8 March, 1862. 2nd Lieut., 24 Sept., 1862. 1st Lieut., 15 Aug., 1864. Mustered out 3 June, 1865. Lieut. Col. 6th U. S. Vet. Vols., 22 Sept., 1865. Mustered out 12 June, 1866. 1st Lieut. 14th Inf., 28 July, 1866. Dismissed 18 May, 1869. Bvt. Capt., 2 March, 1867, for gallant and meritorious service in the Battle of Cold Harbor, Va. Bvt. Maj., 2 March, 1867, for gallant and meritorious service in front of Petersburg, Va., 18 June, 1864. Bvt. Lieut. Col., 2 March, 1867, for gallant and meritorious service in the Battle of Hatcher's Run, Va. Bvt. Col., 2 March, 1867, for gallant and meritorious service during the war.

EZEKIEL, DAVID I. [Born in Ohio. Appointed from Ohio.]
Corpl. Co. E, 5th, and B, 7th Ohio Vols., and Sergt. and 1st Sergt. Co. G, 10th W. Va. Vols., 20 April, 1861, to 11 Sept., 1862. 2nd Lieut. 10th W. Va. Vols., 12 Sept., 1862. Mustered out 9 March, 1865. Capt. 6th U. S. Vet. Vols., 28 April, 1865. Mustered out 15 Oct., 1866. 1st Lieut. 38th Inf., 28 July, 1866. Bvt. Capt., 2 March, 1867, for gallant and meritorious service in action at Harper's Ferry, Va., 7 July, 1864. Unassigned 11 Nov., 1869. Assigned to 4th Inf., 6 April, 1870. Retired 28 June, 1878. Died 17 March, 1895.

FAHNESTOCK, SIMON S.* [Born in Pa. Appointed from Pa.]
Bvt. 2nd Lieut. 4th Art., 1 July, 1841. 2nd Lieut., 1 July, 1841. 1st Lieut., 18 June, 1846. Resigned 30 April, 1850. Died 15 June, 1876.

FAIN, RICHD. G.* [Born in Tenn. Appointed from Tenn.]
Bvt. 2nd Lieut. 1st Art., 1 July, 1832. Resigned 31 Dec., 1832. Died 12 Sept., 1878.

FAIRCHILD, LUCIUS. [Born in Ohio. Appointed from Wis.]
Capt. 1st Wis. Vols., 17 May, 1861. Mustered out 17 Aug., 1861. Lieut. Col. 2nd Wis. Vols., 20 Aug., 1861. Col., 1 Sept., 1862. Resigned 20 Aug., 1863. Capt. 16th Inf., 5 Aug., 1861. Resigned 19 Aug., 1863. Brig. Gen. Vols., 19 Oct., 1863. Resigned 2 Nov., 1863.

FAIRFAX, RAYMOND. [Born in Va. Appointed from Va.]
2nd Lieut. 2nd Art., 30 June, 1855. Resigned 6 Dec., 1855.

FAIRLY, DAVID. [Born in Ireland. Appointed from N. J.]
2nd Lieut. 3rd N. J. Vols., 4 June, 1861. 1st Lieut. Adj., 1 July, 1862. Mustered out 23 June, 1864. Capt. 3rd N. J. Cav., 21 Oct., 1864. Bvt. Maj. and Lieut. Col. Vols., 9 April, 1865, for gallant conduct in the closing battles around Richmond, Va., particularly in the Battle of Namozine Church, Va. Mustered out 1 Aug., 1865. 1st Lieut. 7th Cav., 22 Jan., 1867. Killed 2 April, 1867, by railroad accident.

FAISON, SAMSON L.* [Born in N. C. Appointed from N. C.]
2nd Lieut. 1st Inf., 13 June, 1883. 1st Lieut. 13th Inf., 24 Feb., 1891. Trans. to 1st Inf., 28 July, 1891. Capt. of Inf., 1 July, 1898. Ass'd to 13th Inf., 1 Jan., 1899.

FALCK, WM. [Born in Germany. Appointed from Army.]
Priv. Co. F, 2nd Inf., 14 June, 1858. Corpl., 1 April, 1860. Sergt. Maj. 2nd Inf., 1 Nov., 1861. 2nd Lieut. 2nd Inf., 18 July, 1862. 1st Lieut., 9 Feb., 1863. Reg. Adj., 1 Nov., 1863, to 30 Nov., 1864. Bvt. Capt., 1 Aug., 1864, for gallant service in the Battle of Spottsylvania and during the campaign before Richmond, Va. Bvt. Maj., 13 March, 1865, for gallant and meritorious service in the Battle of Chancellorsville, Va. Bvt. Lieut. Col., 13 March, 1865, for gallant and meritorious service in the Battle of Spottsylvania C. H., Va. Capt. 2nd Inf., 18 April, 1866. Retired for disability from wound in line of duty, 15 March, 1883.

FALLS, MOOR N. [Born in N. C. Appointed from N. C.]
2nd Lieut. 18th Inf., 9 July, 1898. 1st Lieut. 12th Inf., 2 March, 1899.

FALVEY, JOHN. [Born in Ireland. Appointed from Army.]
Corpl., Sergt. and 1st Sergt. Co. G, Mtd. Rifles (3rd Cav.), 16 April, 1856, to 16 Dec., 1862. 2nd Lieut. 3rd Cav., 17 July, 1862. 1st Lieut., 25 June, 1865. Capt., 16 Dec., 1867. Cashiered 9 July, 1868. Bvt. 1st Lieut., 15 Nov., 1863, for gallant and meritorious service in action near Tuscumbia, Ala.

FANNING, ALEXANDER C. W.* [Born in Mass. Appointed from Mass.]
1st Lieut. 3rd Art., 12 March, 1812. Capt., 13 March, 1813. Trans. to Corps Art., 12 May, 1814. Trans. to 2nd Art., 1 June, 1821. Maj. 4th Art., 3 Nov., 1832. Lieut. Col., 16 Sept., 1838. Trans. to 2nd Art., 24 May, 1841. Died 18 Aug., 1846. Bvt. Maj., 15 Aug., 1814, for gallant conduct in defence of Fort Erie. Bvt. Lieut. Col., 15 Aug., 1824, for 10 years' faithful service in one grade. Bvt. Col., 31 Dec., 1835, for gallant and meritorious conduct in the Battle of the Withlacoochee, Fla., etc.

FARBER, CHARLES W. [Born in Ohio. Appointed from the Army.]
Priv., Sergt. and 1st Sergt. Gen. Mtd. Ser. and Priv., Corpl., Sergt. and 1st Sergt. Troop H, 8th Cav., 14 Oct., 1879, to 16 Aug., 1885. 2nd Lieut. 8th Cav., 15 Aug., 1885. 1st Lieut. 6th Cav., 5 April, 1892. Trans. to 8th Cav., 22 April, 1892.

FARLEY, JOHN. [Born in Mass. Appointed from Mass.]
1st Lieut. 3rd Art., 12 March, 1812. Trans. to Corps. Art., 12 May, 1814. Disbanded 15 June, 1815. Reinstated 2 Dec., 1815. Capt., 19 June, 1817. Disbanded 1 June, 1821. Died 5 Feb., 1831.

FARLEY, JOHN.* [Born in Mass. Appointed from Mich.]
Bvt. 2nd Lieut. 2nd Art., 1 July, 1823. 2nd Lieut. 1st Art., 1 July, 1823. 1st Lieut., 1 Aug., 1832. Resigned 29 Feb., 1836. Died 31 July, 1874.

FARLEY, JOSEPH P.* [Born in D. C. Appointed at Large.]
Bvt. 2nd Lieut. 2nd Art., 24 June, 1861. 2nd Lieut., 24 June, 1861. Trans. to Ord., 24 Oct., 1861. 1st Lieut., 3 March, 1863. Bvt. Capt., 13 March, 1865, for meritorious service in the Ord. Dept. during the war. Capt. Ord., 6 April, 1866. Maj., 25 March, 1876. Lieut. Col., 28 Feb., 1889. Col., 7 July, 1898.

FARMER, CHARLES C., Jr. [Born in Ill. Appointed from Ill.]
2nd Lieut. 10th Cav., 15 Feb., 1899.

FARNSWORTH, ALFRED B. [Born in Mich. Appointed from Mich.]
2nd Lieut. 11th Inf., 17 July, 1862. Dismissed 1 Jan., 1864.

FARNSWORTH, CHARLES S.* [Born in Penn. Appointed from Penn.]
2nd Lieut. 25th Inf., 12 June, 1887. 1st Lieut. 7th Inf., 31 July, 1894. Capt., 13 March, 1899.

FARNSWORTH, HENRY J. [Born in N. Y. Appointed from N. Y.]
Capt. A. Q. M. Vols., 8 July, 1864. Bvt. Maj. and Lieut. Col. Vols., 13 March, 1865, for faithful and meritorious service during the war. 1st Lieut. 34th Inf., 14 June, 1867. Bvt. Capt., 14 June, 1867, for faithful and efficient service during the war. Mustered out of Vol. service, 1 Sept., 1867. Unassigned 14 April, 1869. Ass'd to 8th Cav., 15 Dec., 1870. Capt., 17 May, 1876. Maj. I. G., 22 Sept., 1885. Died 19 Nov., 1888.

FARQUHAR, FRANCIS U.* [Born in Pa. Appointed from Pa.]
Bvt. 2nd Lieut. Eng., 24 June, 1861. 2nd Lieut., 29 June, 1861. Bvt. 1st Lieut., 5 May, 1862, for gallant and meritorious service in the Battle of Williamsburg, Va. 1st Lieut. Eng., 3 March, 1863. Capt., 1 Aug., 1863. Bvt. Maj., 1 June, 1864, for gallant and meritorious service in the Battle of Cold Harbor, Va. Bvt. Lieut. Col., 13 March, 1865, for gallant and meritorious service during the war. Maj. Eng., 11 July, 1871. Died 3 July, 1883.

FARQUHAR, JOHN H. [Born in Md. Appointed from Md.]
Capt. 19th Inf., 14 May, 1861. Resigned 9 Aug., 1864.

FARR, OTHO W. B.* [Born in Me. Appointed from Me.]
Addl. 2nd Lieut. 2nd Art., 12 June, 1893. 2nd Lieut. 4th Art., 14 Nov., 1893. Trans. to 2nd Art., 29 Nov., 1893. 1st Lieut., 2 March, 1899.

FARRAGUT, LOYALL.* [Born in Va. Appointed from Va.]
2nd Lieut. 21st Inf., 15 June, 1868. Trans. to 5th Art., 13 April, 1869. Resigned 25 April, 1872.

FARRAND, CHARLES E.* [Born in N. Y. Appointed from N. Y.]
Bvt. 2nd Lieut. 2nd Inf., 1 July, 1857. 2nd Lieut. 7th Inf., 2 Jan., 1858. Trans. to 1st Inf., 24 June, 1858. 1st Lieut. 11th Inf., 14 May, 1861. Capt., 24 Oct., 1861. Trans. to 20th Inf., 21 Sept., 1866. Unassigned 11 May, 1869. Mustered out 1 Jan., 1871.

FARRAND, DAVID O. [Born in Mich. Appointed from Mich.]
Asst. Surg., 15 Feb., 1865. Resigned 1 July, 1866. Bvt. Capt., 13 March, 1865, for faithful and meritorious service during the war. Died in 1883.

FARRAR, HENRY B.* [Born in Mo. Appointed from Mo.]
2nd Lieut. 4th Art., 15 Feb., 1899.

FARRELLY, PATRICK A.* [Born in Pa. Appointed at Large.]
Bvt. 2nd Lieut. 4th Inf., 1 July, 1845. 2nd Lieut. 5th Inf., 10 July, 1846. 1st Lieut., 9 Dec., 1847. Bvt. 1st Lieut., 20 Aug., 1847, for gallant and meritorious conduct at Contreras and Churubusco, Mex. Accidentally killed 4 Aug., 1851.

FARROW, EDWARD S.* [Born in Md. Appointed from Md.]
2nd Lieut. 21st Inf., 15 June, 1876. 1st Lieut., 17 Sept., 1883. Resigned 24 Feb., 1892.

FARROW, SAML., Jr. [Born in S. C. Appointed from S. C.]
1st Lieut., 43rd Inf., 1 Aug., 1813. Trans. to 1st Inf., 17 May, 1815. Resigned 18 May, 1816.

FARRY, JOSEPH F.* [Born in Pa. Appointed from Pa.]
Bvt. 2nd Lieut. 4th Art., 1 July, 1845. 2nd Lieut. 3rd Art., 17 Oct., 1846. 1st Lieut., 13 Aug., 1847. Killed 8 Sept., 1847, at the Battle of Molino del Rey, Mex.

FASSETT, WILLIAM M.* [Born in N. H. Appointed from N. H.]
Addl. 2nd Lieut. 4th Inf., 11 June, 1897. 2nd Lieut. 21st Inf., 2 Dec., 1897. 1st Lieut., 2 March, 1899.

FAST, EDWARD G. [Born in Prussia. Appointed from D. C.]
2nd Lieut. 2nd Art., 17 Aug., 1867. Resigned 18 Aug., 1868.

FATHERLY, RICHD. [Born in Va. Appointed from Ark.]
Mil. Storekeeper Ord., 9 Aug., 1858. Resigned 1 May, 1861.

FAULKNER, CHARLES P. [Born in W. Va. Appointed from W. Va.]
2nd Lieut. 4th Art., 9 July, 1898. Trans. to 14th Inf., 9 March, 1899. 1st Lieut. 8th Inf., 19 July, 1899.

FAULKNER, PETER. [Born in Pa. Appointed from Pa.]
Capt. 11th Inf., 8 Jan., 1799. Disbanded 15 June, 1800. Mil. Storekeeper Ord., 19 Aug., 1818. Dismissed 20 June, 1820. Died 20 Sept., 1823.

FAUNTLEROY, ARCHIBALD McG. [Born in Va. Appointed from Va.]
Asst. Surg., 23 June, 1860. Resigned 9 May, 1861. Died 19 June, 1886.

FAUNTLEROY, THOS. T. [Born in Va. Appointed from Va.]
Maj. 2nd Drag., 8 June, 1836. Lieut. Col., 30 June, 1846. Col. 1st Drag., 25 July, 1850. Resigned 13 May, 1861. Died 12 Sept., 1883.

FAUNTLEROY, POWELL C. [Born in Va. Appointed from Va.]
Asst. Surg., 15 Nov., 1895.

FAY, HEMAN A.* [Born in Vt. Appointed from Vt.]
2nd Lieut. Art., 13 June, 1808. 1st Lieut., 23 Dec., 1811. In 1st Art., — March, 1812. Trans. to Corps Art., 12 May, 1814. Disbanded 15 June, 1815. M. S. K., Q. M. D., 3 Jan., 1818. Removed 1 July, 1842. Died 20 Aug., 1865.

FAY, JOHN J. [Born in N. Y. Appointed from N. Y.]
Lieut. Col. of Inf., 18 March, 1847; 10 Inf., 9 April, 1847. Col. 13th Inf., 3 Dec., 1847. Disbanded 15 July, 1848.

FAYSSOUX, EDWARD S. [Born in S. C. Appointed from S. C.]
Mil. Storekeeper, 24 Aug., 1833. Died 16 Sept., 1852.

FAYSSOUX, PETER. [Born in S. C. Appointed from S. C.]
Mil. Storekeeper, 4 Dec., 1819. Removed in 1833.

FEALY, THOMAS J. [Born in D. C. Appointed from D. C.]
2nd Lieut. 5th Inf., 9 Sept., 1898. 1st Lieut. 4th Inf., 7 Jan., 1900.

FEBIGER, GEORGE L. [Born in Pa. Appointed from Del.]
Maj. and P. M., 3 May, 1861. Bvt. Lieut. Col., 13 March, 1865, for faithful and meritorious service during the war. Lieut. Col. Dept. Pm. Gen., 31 Dec., 1879. Col. Asst. P. M. Gen., 24 Jan., 1881. Retired by operation of law 8 Dec., 1886. Died 22 Jan., 1891.

FEBIGER, LEA. [Born in Ohio. Appointed at Large.]
2nd Lieut. 23rd Inf., 15 Aug., 1876. 1st Lieut., 9 June, 1884. Capt., 11 Oct., 1894. Q. M., 2 Aug., 1899.

FECHET, EDMOND G. [Born in Mich. Appointed from Mich.]
Sergt. and 1st Sergt. Co. A, 7th Mich. Vols., 19 June, 1861, to 17 Sept., 1862. 2nd Lieut. 7th Mich. Vols., 17 Sept., 1862. 1st Lieut., 18 June, 1863. Discharged 31 July, 1863. Q. M. Sergt. Co. G, 10th Mich. Cav., 13 Oct., 1863. 2nd Lieut. 10th Mich. Cav., 23 Jan., 1864. 1st Lieut., 1 April, 1865. Mustered out 21 Nov., 1865. 2nd Lieut. 8th Cav., 28 July, 1866. Bvt. 1st Lieut. and Bvt. Capt., 2 March, 1867, for gallant and meritorious service in the Battle of Antietam, Md. 1st Lieut. 8th Cav., 31 July, 1867. Capt., 23 May, 1870. Maj. 6th Cav., 20 April, 1891. Retired for disability 9 July, 1898.

FECHET, EUGENE O.* [Born in Mich. Appointed from Mich.]
Sergt. 2nd Mich Batty, 10 Sept., 1861, to 10 April, 1864. Cadet at Mil. Acad., 1 July, 1864. 2nd Lieut. 2nd Art., 15 June, 1868. Resigned 15 March, 1875.

FEETER, GEORGE I. [Born in N. Y. Appointed from N. Y.]
2nd Lieut. 19th Inf., 1 May, 1899.

FEILNER, JOHN. [Born in Germany. Appointed from Army.]
Priv., Corpl., Sergt. and 1st Sergt. Co. F, 1st Drag., 16 June, 1856, to 30 May, 1861. 2nd Lieut. 1st Drag., 26 April, 1861. 1st Lieut., 14 May, 1861. Capt., 17 July, 1862. Killed in action with Indians in Dakota, 28 June, 1864.

FELCH, JOHN H. H. [Born in Mass. Appointed from Ark.]
Capt. Gray's Batt. Ark. Vols., 19 July, 1846, to 15 April, 1847. 1st Lieut. Inf., 6 March, 1847; 12th Inf., 9 April, 1847. R. Q. M., 1 Aug., 1847, to 23 May, 1848. Capt., 23 May, 1848. Disbanded 25 July, 1848. Died 4 March, 1851.

FELL, ADALBERT. [Born in Germany. Appointed from N. Y.]
1st Sergt. Co. B, 7th N. Y. Vols., 23 April, 1861. 2nd Lieut., 1 Aug., 1862. 1st Lieut., 1 Nov., 1862. Capt., 1 Jan., 1863. Mustered out 8 May, 1863. 1st Lieut. Vet. Res. Corps, 30 Sept., 1863. Capt., 12 Dec., 1863. Mustered out 1 Sept., 1866. 2nd Lieut. 21st Inf., 7 March, 1867. Unassigned 19 April, 1869. Ass'd to 2nd Art., 14 July, 1869. Cashiered 28 Dec., 1869. Bvt. 1st Lieut., 7 March, 1867, for gallant and meritorious service in the Battle of Fredericksburg, Va.

FELL, JESSE W. [Born in Pa. Appointed from Ill.]
Maj. and P. M., 30 June, 1862. Resigned 26 Dec., 1863.

FELLOWES, BENJN. F. [Born in N. H. Appointed from N. H.]
Asst. Surg., 2 March, 1833. Resigned 30 May, 1839.

FELLOWS, JOHN. [Born in Mass. Appointed from N. Y.]
Mil. Storekeeper, 15 June, 1812. Disbanded 1 June, 1821. Died 3 Jan., 1844.

FELTUS, HENRY J.* [Born in Pa. Appointed from N. Y.]
2nd Lieut. Corps Art., 1 July, 1820. Trans. to 3rd Art., 1 June, 1821. Trans. to 1st Art., 16 Aug., 1821. 1st Lieut., 15 Sept., 1825. Resigned 31 March, 1827. Died 12 June, 1871.

FENNER, ROBERT. [Born in N. C. Appointed from Ala.]
Capt. 3rd Rifles, 17 March, 1814. Trans. to 18th Inf., 14 May, 1814. Disbanded 15 June, 1815. Capt. A. C. S. Vols., 26 June, 1846. Died 19 Sept., 1847.

FENNO, DARWIN G. [Born in Ill. Appointed from Wis.]
Priv., Sergt. and 1st Sergt. Troops G and M, 1st Wis. Cav., 31 Oct., 1861, to 7 Dec., 1863. 1st Lieut. 62nd U. S. Col. Inf., 7 Dec., 1863. Reg. Adj., 24 Dec., 1863. Mustered out 31 March, 1866. 2nd Lieut. 17th Inf., 30 Sept., 1867. Cashiered 15 Sept., 1871.

FENTON, CHARLES W.* [Born in Mich. Appointed from Mich.]
2nd Lieut. 9th Inf., 11 June, 1888. Trans. to 7th Cav., 22 March, 1891. 1st Lieut. 5th Cav., 5 Aug., 1897. Capt. A. A. G. Vols., 12 May, 1898, to 12 May, 1899.

FENTON, REUBEN N. [Born in N. Y. Appointed from N. Y.]
Priv. and Sergt. Co. C, 9th N. Y. Cav., 2 Oct., 1861, to 16 Jan., 1863. 2nd Lieut. 9th N. Y. Cav., 16 Jan., 1863. Resigned 31 March, 1863. 2nd Lieut. 18th Inf., 23 Feb., 1866. 1st Lieut., 28 July, 1866. Trans. to 27th Inf., 21 Sept., 1866. Capt., 8 Jan., 1868. Unassigned 14 June, 1869. Ass'd to 6th Cav., 1 Jan., 1871. Cashiered 22 May, 1872.

FENWICK, JOHN R. [Born in S. C. Appointed from S. C.]
2nd Lieut. Marine Corps, 10 Nov., 1799. 1st Lieut., 1 Dec., 1801. Capt., 13 Aug., 1809. Resigned 1 April, 1811. Lieut. Col. Light Art., 2 Dec., 1811. Col. A. G., 18 March, 1813, to 17 May, 1815, when retained in Light Art. Trans. to 4th Art., 1 June, 1821. Col., 8 May, 1822. Bvt. Col., 18 March, 1813, for gallant conduct on the Niagara frontier. Bvt. Brig. Gen., 18 March, 1823, for 10 years' faithful service in one grade. Died 19 March, 1842.

FERGUS, ROBERTSON S. [Born in Scotland. Appointed from Army.]
Priv. and Corpl. Co. B, 2nd Batt. 14th Inf., 20 May, 1863, to 6 April, 1865. 2nd Lieut. 14th Inf., 23 March, 1865. 1st Lieut., 23 March, 1865. Trans. to 32nd Inf., 21 Sept., 1866. Capt., 5 Nov., 1866. Resigned 30 Sept., 1868.

FERGUSON, COLIN B. [Born in Scotland. Appointed from Army.]
Priv. and Corpl. Co. A and Sergt. Maj. 2nd Art., 3 Aug., 1850, to June, 1861. 2nd Lieut. 19th Inf., 14 May, 1861. 1st Lieut., 24 Oct., 1861. Capt. A. Q. M., 28 April, 1862. Dismissed 30 May, 1864. Died in Dec., 1869.

FERGUSON, HARLEY B.* [Born in N. C. Appointed from N. C.]
Addl. 2nd Lieut. Eng., 11 June, 1897. 2nd Lieut., 5 July, 1898.

FERGUSON, HENRY T.* [Born in Wis. Appointed from Fa.]
2nd Lieut. 7th Inf., 12 June, 1890. Trans. to 23rd Inf., 11 June, 1891. 1st Lieut. 13th Inf., 15 Feb., 1897. Capt. 18th Inf., 15 Nov., 1899.

FERGUSON, SAML. W.* [Born in S. C. Appointed from S. C.]
Bvt. 2nd Lieut. 2nd Drag., 1 July, 1857. 2nd Lieut. 1st Drag., 14 June, 1858. Resigned 1 March, 1861.

FERGUSSON, FRANK K.* [Born in Tenn. Appointed from Tenn.]
Addl. 2nd Lieut. 3rd Art., 12 June, 1896. 2nd Lieut. 1st Art., 25 Dec., 1897. 1st Lieut., 2 March, 1899.

FERRIS, FRANK O. [Born in N. Y. Appointed from the Army.]
Priv. and Corpl. Batty L, 3rd Art., 6 Dec., 1881, to 6 Aug., 1884. 2nd Lieut. 1st Inf., 4 Aug., 1884. 1st Lieut. 18th Inf., 10 July, 1891. Trans. to 20th Inf., 20 July, 1891. Retired with rank of Capt. for disability 15 Dec., 1898. Graduate of Infantry and Cavalry School, 1887.

FERRIS, SAMUEL P.* [Born in Conn. Appointed from Conn.]
Bvt. 2nd Lieut. and 2nd Lieut. 8th Inf., 24 June, 1861. R. Q. M., 1 Oct., 1861, to 15 Nov., 1862, and 2 Feb., 1864, to 13 Aug., 1866. 1st Lieut., 19 Feb., 1862. Col. 28th Conn. Vols., 15 Nov., 1862. Bvt. Capt., 14 June, 1863, for gallant and meritorious service in the campaign against Port Hudson, La. Mustered out of Vol. service 28 Aug., 1863. Bvt. Maj., 28 Oct., 1864, for gallant and meritorious service in the Battle of Hatcher's Run, Va. Capt. 30th Inf., 28 July, 1866. Trans. to 4th Inf., 23 March, 1869. Died 4 Feb., 1882.

FESSENDEN, FRANCIS. [Born in Me. Appointed from Me.]
Capt. 19th Inf., 14 May, 1861. Col. 25th Me. Vols., 29 Sept., 1862. Mustered out 10 July, 1863. Col. 30th Me. Vols., 11 Jan., 1864. Brig. Gen. Vols., 10 May, 1864. Bvt. Maj. and Lieut. Col., 6 July, 1864, for gallant service at Shiloh and Montell's Bluff, on Red River. Bvt. Brig. Gen., 13 March, 1865, for gallant and meritorious service in the field during the war. Bvt. Maj. Gen., 13 March, 1865, for gallant and meritorious service during the war. Maj. Gen. Vols., 9 Nov., 1865. Lieut. Col. 45th Inf., 28 July, 1866 (declined). Mustered out of Vol. service 1 Sept., 1866. Trans. to 28th Inf., 21 Sept., 1866. Retired with rank of Brig. Gen., 1 Nov., 1866.

FESSENDEN, JOHN M.* [Born in R. I. Appointed from Mass.]
Bvt. 2nd Lieut. 1st Art., 1 July, 1824. 2nd Lieut. 4th Art., 1 July, 1824. Resigned 30 Nov., 1831. Died 8 Feb., 1883.

FESSENDEN, JOSHUA A. [Born in Me. Appointed from Me.]
Sergt. Co. B, 1st Me. Cav., 18 Sept., 1861. 2nd Lieut. 1st Cav., 24 March, 1862. Resigned 6 Aug., 1862. 2nd Lieut. 5th Art., 6 Sept., 1862. Bvt. 1st Lieut., 31 Dec., 1862, for gallant and meritorious service in the Battle of Stone River, Tenn. Bvt. Capt., 20 Sept., 1863, for gallant and meritorious service in the Battle of Chickamauga, Ga. 1st Lieut. 5th Art., 30 Nov., 1865. Capt., 26 June, 1882. Retired for disability 3 Jan., 1894.

FETTERMAN, GEORGE.* [Born in Pa. Appointed from Pa.]
Bvt. 2nd Lieut. Art., 1 July, 1827. 2nd Lieut. 3rd Art., 1 July, 1827. Resigned 31 May, 1836. Died 27 June, 1844.

FETTERMAN, GEORGE W. [Born in Conn. Appointed from Pa.]
1st Lieut. 15th Inf., 5 Aug., 1861. Capt., 25 Feb., 1865. Cashiered 15 Aug., 1867. Restored 20 Sept., 1867. Died 13 Oct., 1867. Bvt. Capt., 16 Dec., 1864, for gallant and meritorious service at the Battle of Nashville, Tenn. Bvt. Maj., 12 April, 1865, for gallant and meritorious service at the capture of Mobile, Ala.

FETTERMAN, WM. J. [Born in Conn. Appointed from Del.]
1st Lieut. 18th Inf., 14 May, 1861. Capt., 25 Oct., 1861. Trans. to 27th Inf., 21 Sept., 1866. Killed 21 Dec., 1866, in action with Indians in Dakota. Bvt. Maj., 31 Dec., 1862, for gallant and meritorious service at the Battle of Murfreesboro', Tenn. Bvt. Lieut. Col., 1 Sept., 1864, for gallant and meritorious service during the Atlanta campaign, and in the Battle of Jonesboro', Tenn.

FIEBEGER, GUSTAV J.* [Born in Ohio. Appointed from Ohio.]
Addl. 2nd Lieut. Eng., 13 June, 1879. 2nd Lieut., 31 Oct., 1879. 1st Lieut., 15 June, 1882. Capt., 22 Feb., 1891. Prof. Mil. Acad., 1897.

FIELD, ANDREW J. [Born in Md. Appointed from Md.]
2nd Lieut. 6th Inf., 1 Aug., 1838. Resigned 11 May, 1841.

FIELD, CHAS. W.* [Born in Ky. Appointed at Large.]
Bvt. 2nd Lieut. 2nd Drag., 1 July, 1849. 2nd Lieut., 30 June, 1851. R. Q. M., 9 Sept., 1853, to 3 March, 1855. 1st Lieut. 2nd Cav., 3 March, 1855. Capt., 31 Jan., 1861. Resigned 30 May, 1861.

FIELD, EDWARD. [Born in N. J. Appointed from N. J.]
2nd Lieut 1st N. J. Cav., 15 Aug., 1861. Mustered out 28 Feb., 1862. 2nd Lieut. 4th Art., 19 Feb., 1862. Bvt. 1st Lieut., 30 June, 1862, for gallant and meritorious service in the Battle of White Oak Swamp, Va. 1st Lieut. 4th Art., 11 Aug., 1863. Bvt. Capt., 11 May, 1864, for gallant and meritorious service in action at Meadow Bridge, Va. Capt. 4th Art., 29 April, 1873. Maj. 2nd Art., 6 June, 1896. Lieut. Col. 3rd Art., 17 Oct., 1899. Graduate of the Artillery School, 1870.

FIELD, FRANCIS A. [Born in Ohio. Appointed from Army.]
Priv. and 1st Sergt. Co. A, 8th Inf., 29 Aug., 1859, to 8 May, 1862. 2nd Lieut. 11th Inf., 14 April, 1862. 1st Lieut., 20 June, 1863. Reg. Adj., 5 Dec., 1863, to 5 Dec., 1866. Capt., 23 Nov., 1868. Unassigned 14 April, 1869. Discharged 1 Oct., 1870. Bvt. Capt., 2 July, 1863, for gallant and meritorious service at the Battle of Gettysburg, Pa.

FIELD, GABRIEL. [Born in ——. Appointed from Mo.]
2nd Lieut. Rifles, 24 May, 1817. 1st Lieut., 15 April, 1818. Trans. to 6th Inf., 1 June, 1821. Died 16 April, 1823.

FIELD, GEORGE P.* [Born in N. Y. Appointed from N. Y.]
Bvt. 2nd Lieut. 3rd Inf., 1 July, 1834. 2nd Lieut., 25 July, 1835. 1st Lieut., 7 July, 1838. Capt., 29 Feb., 1844. Killed at Battle of Monterey, Mex., 21 Sept., 1846.

FIELD, HORACE B.* [Born in N. Y. Appointed from N. Y.]
2nd Lieut. 3rd Art., 1 July, 1840. 1st Lieut., 27 June, 1844. Drowned 24 Dec., 1853. Bvt. Capt., 9 Oct., 1847, for gallant and meritorious conduct at Huamantla, Mex.

FIELD, JOSIAH H. V.* [Born in Fla. Appointed from Mass.]
1st Lieut. Ord., 11 June, 1863. Died 16 July, 1864.

FIELD, ROBERT. [Born in D. C. Appointed from Army.]
Priv., Corpl. and Sergt. Troop H, 8th Cav., 7 Jan., 1894, to 1 March, 1897. 2nd Lieut. 14th Inf., 16 Feb., 1897. 1st Lieut. 11th Inf., 13 Feb., 1899. Trans. to 14th Inf., 14 March, 1899.

FILLER, JOHN H. [Born in Pa. Appointed from Pa.]
Maj. 55th Pa. Vols., 4 Dec., 1861. Mustered out 25 April, 1865. 2nd Lieut. 29th Inf., 6 June, 1867. Resigned 21 April, 1868.

FILLMORE, GEORGE M. [Born in N. Y. Appointed from Minn.]
Priv. and Corpl. Co. D, 2nd Minn. Vols., 5 July to 12 Dec., 1861. 2nd Lieut. 3rd Art., 30 Nov., 1861. 1st Lieut., 28 Feb., 1862. Resigned 17 April, 1863.

FINDLEY, JOHN K.* [Born in Pa. Appointed from Pa.]
Bvt. 2nd Lieut. 3rd Art., 1 July, 1824. 2nd Lieut. 1st Art., 1 July, 1824. Resigned 13 May, 1828. Died 13 Sept., 1885.

FINE, ABRAHAM. [Born in ——. Appointed from Tenn.]
Ensign 24th Inf., 1 Oct., 1813. 2nd Lieut. 3rd Rifles, 17 March, 1814. 1st Lieut., 17 Sept., 1814. Disbanded 15 June, 1815. Reinstated in Rifle Regiment, 2 Dec., 1815. Resigned 1 Oct., 1816.

FINE, LOUIS H. [Born in N. Y. Appointed from Mo.]
Priv. and Sergt. Co. H, 25th Mo. Vols., 25 June, 1861, to 3 June, 1862. 2nd Lieut. 3rd Art., 19 Feb., 1862. 1st Lieut., 25 June, 1863. Resigned 26 March, 1868. Priv. Co. H, 1st Art., 22 March, 1873, to 8 Oct., 1881, under name of Louis Hasbrouck. Died 22 Dec., 1886.

FINK, THEODORE. [Born in Germany. Appointed from Army.]
Priv. and Corpl. Co. C, and Sergt. Maj. 8th Inf., 16 June, 1841, to 4 Aug., 1848. Bvt. 2nd Lieut. 8th Inf., 28 June, 1848. 2nd Lieut., 2 Aug., 1848. 1st Lieut., 7 Dec., 1852. Capt., 31 Dec., 1860. Died 3 May, 1861.

FINLEY, CLEMENT A. [Born in Ohio. Appointed from Ohio.]
Surg. Mate 1st Inf., 10 Aug., 1818. Asst. Surg., 1 June, 1821. Maj. and Surg., 13 July, 1832. Surg. Gen., 15 May, 1861. Retired 14 April, 1862. Bvt. Brig. Gen., 13 March, 1865, for long and faithful service in the army. Granted the retired pay of a Brig. Gen. from 10 July, 1876. Died 8 Sept., 1879.

FINLEY, JAMES A. [Born in Ky. Appointed from Pa.]
1st Lieut. Asst. Surg., 10 Nov., 1874. Capt. Asst. Surg., 10 Nov., 1879. Wholly retired 26 Feb., 1891. Reappointed Capt. Asst. Surg., 13 Feb., 1893, to rank from 10 Nov., 1879. Retired 16 Feb., 1893.

FINLEY, JOHN P. [Born in Mich. Appointed from Army.]
Priv., Corpl. and Sergt. Sig. Corps., 8 March, 1877, to 10 July, 1884. 2nd Lieut. Sig. Corps, 1 July, 1884. 2nd Lieut. 19th Inf., 7 Feb., 1891 (to rank from 1 July, 1894). 1st Lieut. 15th Inf., 15 June, 1891. Trans. to 9th Inf., 20 July, 1891. Capt. 9th Inf., 1 Nov., 1898. R. Q. M., 1896 to 1898, and from March 16, 1899.

FINLEY, LEIGHTON. [Born in S. C. Appointed from S. C.]
2nd Lieut. 15th Inf., 1 Sept., 1879. Trans. to 10th Cav., 11 Nov., 1879, taking rank from 11 Nov., 1879. 1st Lieut., 5 Oct., 1887. R. Q. M., 20 Aug., 1889. Died 12 Feb., 1894.

FINLEY, WALTER L.* [Born in Pa. Appointed from Pa.]
2nd Lieut. 9th Cav., 13 June, 1879. 1st Lieut., 25 Oct., 1883. Reg. Adj., 1 Feb., 1889, to 22 April, 1891. Capt., 22 April, 1891.

FISCUS, WILLIAM W., Jr.* [Born in Pa. Appointed from Pa.]
2nd Lieut. 2nd Inf., 26 April, 1898. Trans. to 19th Inf., 1 Dec., 1898. 1st Lieut., 2 March, 1899.

FISH, JOHN F. [Born in N. Y. Appointed from Mo.]
Chaplain Posts of San Antonio, Fort McKavett, and Jefferson Bks., 23 Feb., 1849, to 2 May, 1867. Post Chap., 3 April, 1867. Died 21 Oct., 1878.

FISH, OLIVER H.* [Born in Ky. Appointed from Ky.]
Bvt. 2nd Lieut. 1st Cav., 1 July, 1857. 2nd Lieut., 11 June, 1858. Resigned 1 May, 1861. Died 18 Feb., 1865.

FISH, SEWALL L.* [Born in Vt. Appointed from N. H.]
Changed name to Sewall L. Fremont,—which see.

FISH, WILLISTON.* [Born in Ohio. Appointed from Ohio.]
2nd Lieut. 4th Art., 11 June, 1881. Resigned 31 Dec., 1887.

FISHER, CAESAR R. [Born in Pa. Appointed from Pa.]
2nd Lieut. 1st Cav., 12th Nov., 1861. 1st Lieut., 17 July, 1862. Died 21 June, 1863, of wounds received in action at Ashby's Gap, Va.

FISHER, CHAS. G. [Born in D. C. Appointed from D. C.]
2nd Lieut. 4th Art., 24 Oct., 1867. Resigned 20 Oct., 1868.

FISHER, HENRY C. [Born in Md. Appointed from Md.]
Asst. Surg., 31 Oct., 1891. Capt. Asst. Surg., 31 Oct., 1896. Maj. Surg. Vols., 1 Oct., 1899.

FISHER, OTIS. [Born in Mass. Appointed from Mass.]
Ensign 9th Inf., 12 March, 1812. 2nd Lieut., 30 June, 1813. 1st Lieut., 20 July, 1814. Trans. to 5th Inf., 17 May, 1815. R. Q. M., 20 Feb., 1816, to March, 1819. Died 3 May, 1820.

FISHER, OTIS. [Born in Me. Appointed from N. J.]
2nd Lieut. 8th Inf., 5 Aug., 1861. 1st Lieut., 19 Sept., 1863. Died 3 Oct., 1864, of wounds received in action at Poplar Spring Church, Va. Bvt. Capt., 9 Aug., 1862, for gallant and meritorious service at the Battle of Cedar Mtn., Va. Bvt. Maj., 30 Sept., 1864, for gallant and meritorious service at the Battle of Poplar Spring Church, Va.

FISHER, THOMAS H. [Born in N. Y. Appointed from N. Y.]
2nd Lieut. N. Y. Vols., 1 Sept., 1861. 1st Lieut., 31 Dec., 1862. Mustered out 26 May, 1863. 1st Lieut. 8th N. J. Vols., 31 Aug., 1863. Mustered out 1 Oct., 1864. 1st Lieut. 22nd Inf., 28 July, 1866. Bvt. Capt., 2 March, 1867, for gallant and meritorious service in the Battle of Deep Bottom, Va. Capt. 22nd Inf., 4 March, 1879. Died 4 July, 1879.

FISHER, THOMAS M. [Born in Pa. Appointed from Pa.]
Corpl. Co. G, 2nd Pa. Res., 30 May, 1862, to 19 June, 1864. 1st Lieut. 190th Pa. Vols., 20 June, 1864. Mustered out 28 June, 1865. 2nd Lieut. 23rd Inf., 7 March, 1867. Resigned 15 Sept., 1872.

FISHER, WALTER W. R. [Born in Va. Appointed from Va.]
Ast. Surg., 3 Dec., 1883. Capt. and Asst. Surg., 3 Dec., 1888. Died 8 June, 1896.

FISHER, WILLIAM J. [Born in Del. Appointed from Del.]
2nd Lieut. 10th Inf., 5 Aug., 1861. 1st Lieut., 4 March, 1863. Killed 2 July, 1863, at Battle of Gettysburg, Pa. Bvt. Capt., 2 July, 1863, for gallant and meritorious service at the Battle of Gettysburg, Pa.

FISK, WALTER L.* [Born in Ill. Appointed from Iowa.]
2nd Lieut. Eng., 15 June, 1877. 1st Lieut., 9 April, 1880. Capt., 10 Jan., 1887. Maj., 5 July, 1898.

FISKE, HAROLD B.* [Born in Ore. Appointed from Ore.]
Addl. 2nd Lieut. 14th Inf., 11 June, 1897. 2nd Lieut. 18th Inf., 7 Aug., 1897. 1st Lieut., 2 March, 1899.

FITCH, BENJAMIN. [Born in Conn. Appointed from Army.]
Priv., Corpl. and Sergt. Capt. White's Co. 25th Inf., 25 Aug., 1812, to July, 1814. 2nd Lieut. 25th Inf., 25 July, 1814. Trans. to 6th Inf., 17 May, 1815. 1st Lieut., 30 June, 1819. Disbanded 1 June, 1821.

FITCH, CHAUNCEY W. [Born in N. Y. Appointed from Mich.]
Hosp. Chaplain Vols., 26 Oct., 1863. Mustered out 20 Nov., 1865. Chaplain Post of Fort Wayne, Mich., 7 Feb., 1866, to 27 April, 1867. Post Chap., 3 April, 1867. Died 13 July, 1878.

FITCH, GRAHAM D.* [Born in Ill. Appointed from Ill.]
2nd Lieut. 5th Art., 13 June, 1882. Trans. to Eng., 7 June, 1883. 1st Lieut., 17 March, 1884. Capt., 26 Jan., 1895. Maj. Chf. Eng. Vols., 20 June, 1898, to 31 Dec., 1898.

FITCH, JULIAN R. [Born in Ohio. Appointed from Kan.]
Priv. Co. I, 6th Ohio Vols., 16 May to 21 Aug., 1861. 2nd Lieut. 35th Ohio Vols., 9 Sept., 1861. 1st Lieut., 4 Sept., 1863. Mustered out 1 Sept., 1864. 2nd Lieut. Sig. Corps, 3 March, 1863. Bvt. 1st Lieut. and Capt. Vols., 13 March, 1865, for distinguished service during the war. Mustered out 25 Nov., 1865. 2nd Lieut. 17th Inf., 23 Feb., 1866. Trans. to 35th Inf., 21 Sept., 1866. 1st Lieut., 1 Nov., 1866. Trans. to 15th Inf., 12 Aug., 1869. Cashiered 15 Jan., 1873.

FITCH, ROGER S. [Born in N. Y. Appointed from N. Y.]
Priv. Troop G, 1st U. S. Vol. Cav., 27 May to 15 Sept., 1898. 2nd Lieut. 1st Cav., 1 June, 1899.

FITCH, WM. G. [Born in Conn. Appointed from Conn.]
1st Lieut. 4th Conn. Vols., 22 May, 1861. Mustered out 7 Aug., 1861. 2nd Lieut. 2nd Inf., 29 Oct., 1861. 1st Lieut., 12 Sept., 1862. Retired 16 Nov., 1863.

FITZGERALD, EDWARD. [Born in Ireland. Appointed from Army.]
Priv., Corpl. and 1st Sergt. Troop E, 1st Cav. (4th), 8 Jan., 1858, to 8 Jan., 1863. 2nd Lieut. 4th Cav., 19 Feb., 1863. 1st Lieut., 9 May, 1864. Died 16 Feb., 1865, of wounds received, 17 Dec., 1864, at Battle of Franklin, Tenn.

FITZGERALD, EDWARD H. [Born in Pa. Appointed from Va.]
2nd Lieut. 6th Inf., 20 Oct., 1839. 1st Lieut., 7 Nov., 1845. Capt. A. Q. M., 5 Aug., 1847. Trans. to 9th Inf., 26 Aug., 1847. Capt., 8 Sept., 1847, which he vacated same date. Trans. to 1st Drag., 23 Aug., 1849, to rank as Capt. from 5 Aug., 1847. Died 9 Jan., 1860. Bvt. Maj., 13 Sept., 1847, for gallant and meritorious conduct at Chapultepec, Mex.

FITZGERALD, EDWARD H. [Born in Ireland. Appointed from Mo.]
Post Chaplain, 27 Oct., 1897.

FITZGERALD, GEORGE B. [Born in ——. Appointed from Va.]
2nd Lieut. of Inf., 8 March, 1847; 11th Inf., 9 April, 1847. 1st Lieut., 29 June, 1848. Disbanded 14 Aug., 1848.

FITZGERALD, JAMES G. [Born in Ky. Appointed from La.]
2nd Lieut. of Inf., 5 March, 1847; 14th Inf., 9 April, 1847. 1st Lieut., 22 Oct., 1847. Disbanded 25 July, 1848.

FITZGERALD, JENKINS A. [Born in Ind. Appointed from Ind.]
Asst. Surg. 70th Ind. Vols., 22 Oct., 1863. Mustered out 8 June, 1865. 1st Lieut. Asst. Surg., 9 Oct., 1867. Capt. Asst. Surg., 22 Feb., 1869. Died 11 Aug., 1879.

FITZGERALD, JOHN. [Born in Ireland. Appointed from Army.]
Priv., Corpl., Sergt. and 1st Sergt. Batty M, 4th Art., 1 Nov., 1856, to 31 Oct., 1863. 2nd Lieut. 2nd Art., 31 Oct., 1863. 1st Lieut., 12 Aug., 1864. Died 21 April, 1870. Bvt. Capt., 19 Sept., 1864, for gallant and meritorious service at the Battle of Winchester, Va.

FITZGERALD, MICHAEL J. [Born in Ireland. Appointed from Army.]
Priv. Co. E, 1st Art., 5 Jan., 1855. Corpl., 1 Nov., 1858. Priv., 10 July, 1859. Discharged 5 Nov., 1859. Priv. Co. E, 1st Art., 5 Nov., 1859. Trans. to Ord., 1 Dec., 1859. Artificer Ord., 1 June, 1860. Discharged 23 Feb., 1861. Hosp. Steward U. S. A., 14 March, 1861. 2nd Lieut. 9th Inf., 1 June, 1863. 1st Lieut., 4 March, 1864. Capt., 31 Dec., 1873. Retired 1 May, 1879.

FITZGERALD, RICHARD. [Born in Ireland. Appointed from Army.]
Priv., Corpl. and Sergt. Gen. Mtd. Ser., 20 Jan., 1859, to 8 Nov., 1863. 2nd Lieut. 5th Cav., 31 Oct., 1863. 1st Lieut., 12 June, 1864. Killed 19 Sept., 1864, in action near Winchester, Va.

FITZ GERALD, WM. G.* [Born in N. Y. Appointed from N. Y.]
2nd Lieut. of Cav. (7th), 11 June, 1892. Resigned 30 Sept., 1896.

FITZHUGH, CHAS. L. [Born in N. Y. Appointed from N. Y.]
Cadet at Mil. Acad., 1 July, 1859, to 4 Sept., 1861. 1st Lieut. 4th Art., 24 Oct., 1861. Col. 6th N. Y. Cav., 18 Feb., 1865. Trans. to 2nd N. Y. Prov. Cav., 17 June, 1865. Mustered out of Vols. 9 Aug., 1865. Bvt. Capt., 7 April, 1862, for gallant and meritorious service at the Battle of Shiloh, Tenn. Bvt. Maj., 28 Aug., 1864, for gallant and meritorious service at the Battle of Smithfield, Va. Bvt. Lieut. Col., 13 March, 1865, for gallant and meritorious service at the Battle of Five Forks, Va. Bvt. Col. and Brig. Gen., 13 March, 1865, for gallant and meritorious service in the field during the war. Resigned 21 May, 1868.

FITZHUGH, FRANK W. [Born in Ind. Appointed from Army.]
Priv., Corpl. and Sergt. Co. A, and Sergt. Maj. 2nd Batt. 11th Inf., 28 Nov., 1861, to 4 June, 1863. 2nd Lieut. 11th Inf., 11 March, 1863. Dismissed 16 July, 1864.

FITZHUGH, HENRY W.* [Born in Va. Appointed from D. C.]
2nd Lieut. Corps Art., 21 July, 1814. 1st Lieut., 20 April, 1818. Batt. Q. M., 1 July, 18— to 1 July, 1821. Trans. to 2nd Art., 1 June, 1821. A. Q. M., 19 May, 1826, to 28 June, 1836. Resigned 28 June, 1836. Bvt. Capt., 20 April, 1828, for 10 years' faithful service in one grade. Died 10 June, 1876.

FITZHUGH, WM. H. [Born in Md. Appointed from Md.]
Priv., Corpl. and Sergt. Co. I, Voltigeurs, 28 April, 1847, to 29 April, 1848. 2nd Lieut. Voltigeurs, 29 March, 1848. Disbanded 31 Aug., 1848.

FITZPATRICK, PATRICK.* [Born in Ohio. Appointed from Ohio.]
2nd Lieut. 43rd Inf., 15 June, 1868. Unassigned 8 April, 1869. Ass'd to 13th Inf., 14 July, 1869. 1st Lieut., 1 April, 1872. Retired 29 June, 1872. Died 23 Sept., 1884.

FITZSIMMONS, WM. C.* [Born in Mich. Appointed from Mich.]
2nd Lieut. 4th Art., 15 June, 1869. Resigned 13 Dec., 1869.

FLAGG, CHARLES E. B. [Born in S. C. Appointed from S. C.]
Asst. Surg., 12 May, 1893. Capt. and Asst. Surg., 12 May, 1898.

FLAGLER, CLEMENT A. F.* [Born in Ga. Appointed from Iowa.]
Addl. 2nd Lieut. Eng., 12 June, 1889. 2nd Lieut., 1 April, 1890. 1st Lieut., 4 Oct., 1894. Capt., 5 July, 1898. Maj. and Chief. Eng. Vols., 17 May, 1898, to 31 Dec., 1898.

FLAGLER, DANIEL W.* [Born in N. Y. Appointed from N. Y.]
Bvt. 2nd Lieut. Ord., 24 June, 1861. 2nd Lieut., 24 June, 1861. 1st Lieut., 3 Aug., 1861. Bvt. Capt., 14 March, 1862, for gallant and meritorious service in the Battle of Newbern, N. C. Bvt. Maj., 26 April, 1862, for gallant and meritorious service in the Siege of Fort Macon, N. C. Capt. Ord., 3 March, 1863. Bvt. Lieut. Col., 13 March, 1865, for distinguished service in the field, and faithful service in the Ord. Dept. during the war. Maj. Ord., 23 June, 1874. Lieut. Col., 23 Aug., 1881. Col., 15 Sept., 1890. Brig. Gen. and Chief of Ordnance, 23 Jan., 1891. Died 29 March, 1899.

FLANAGAN, WM.* [Born in Ky. Appointed from Ky.]
Bvt. 2nd Lieut. Inf., 1 July, 1827. Resigned 20 May, 1828. Died 1 Sept., 1851.

FLEESON, REESE E. [Born in Pa. Appointed from Pa.]
2nd Lieut. 10th Inf., 5 Aug., 1861. 1st Lieut., 27 June, 1862. Cashiered 4 March, 1863.

FLEMING, ADRIAN S.* [Born in Ky. Appointed from Ky.]
Addl. 2nd Lieut. 5th Art., 12 June, 1895. 2nd Lieut. 4th Art., 1 Feb., 1896. Trans. to 6th Art., 18 June, 1898. 1st Lieut., 2 March, 1899.

FLEMING, GEORGE M. [Born in Pa. Appointed from Pa.]
Priv. Co. E, and Q. M. Sergt. 137th Pa. Vols., 22 Aug., 1862. Priv. Co. G, and Q. M. Sergt. 21st Pa. Cav., 7 July, 1863, to 1 March, 1864. Mustered out 8 July, 1865. 2nd Lieut. 11th Inf., 23 Feb., 1866. 1st Lieut., 28 May, 1866. Unassigned 14 April, 1869. Discharged 10 Dec., 1870.

FLEMING, HUGH B.* [Born in Pa. Appointed from Pa.]
Bvt. 2nd Lieut. 6th Inf., 1 July, 1852. 2nd Lieut., 9 June, 1853. 2nd Lieut. 9th Inf., 3 March, 1855. 1st Lieut., 7 June, 1856. Capt. 16th Inf., 14 May, 1861 (declined). Capt. 9th Inf., 14 May, 1861. Maj. 19th Inf., 28 July, 1866. Trans. to 37th Inf., 21 Sept., 1866. Trans. to 5th Inf., 15 March, 1869. Unassigned 9 June, 1869. Retired 15 Dec., 1870. Died 9 April, 1895.

FLEMING, LAWRENCE J.* [Born in Ga. Appointed from Ga.]
2nd Lieut. 10th Cav., 12 June, 1890. 1st Lieut. 5th Cav., 1 June, 1897.

FLEMING, ROBERT J.* [Born in Ireland. Appointed from Mich.]
2nd Lieut. 7th Cav., 12 June, 1891. 1st Lieut. 10th Cav., 11 March, 1898.

FLEMING, WM. W.* [Born in Ky. Appointed from Mo.]
2nd Lieut. 6th Inf., 18 June, 1866. 1st Lieut., 1 April, 1867. Unassigned 22 April, 1869. Ass'd to 12th Inf., 1 Jan., 1871. Dismissed 30 June, 1877.

FLETCHER, BIRD L. [Born in Vt. Appointed from Army.]
Priv. and Corpl. Troop I, 1st Cav., 27 Dec., 1859, to 26 March, 1863. 2nd Lieut. 4th Cav., 19 Feb., 1863. 1st Lieut., 12 Oct., 1864. Capt., 25 Aug., 1867. Retired 19 June, 1868. Dismissed 24 July, 1872. Bvt. 1st Lieut., 10 May, 1863, for gallant and meritorious service in the Cavalry action at Franklin, Tenn.

FLETCHER, CHAS. H. [Born in Ohio. Appointed from Iowa.]
Cadet at Mil. Acad., 1 July, 1856, to 8 Jan., 1857. Capt. 1st Iowa Batty, 17 Aug., 1861. Resigned 14 Jan., 1862. 2nd Lieut. 1st Inf., 5 Aug., 1861. 1st Lieut., 9 Sept., 1861. Capt., 1 Aug., 1863. Resigned 19 April, 1866. Bvt. Maj., 18 Oct., 1865, for meritorious service in the recruitment of the armies of the United States.

FLETCHER, CRAWFORD. [Born in Tenn. Appointed from Ark.]
1st Lieut. Miss. Rifles, 6 June, 1846. Mustered out 11 June, 1847. Capt. 9th Inf., 3 March, 1855. Resigned 1 March, 1861. Died 4 Sept., 1876.

FLETCHER, EDMUND L. [Born in N. Y. Appointed from Army.]
Priv. Co. E, 15th Inf., 2 Aug., 1872. 2nd Lieut. 13th Inf., 9 Jan., 1873. 1st Lieut., 30 June, 1879. Retired for disability with rank of Capt., 5 July, 1895.

FLETCHER, JOHN C.* [Born in Pa. Appointed from Pa.]
2nd Lieut. 6th Inf., 1 July, 1838. 1st Lieut., 1 Nov., 1838. Reg. Adj., 28 May, 1839, to 1 Feb., 1840. Resigned 10 Nov., 1840.

FLETCHER, JOSHUA S., Jr. [Born in Pa. Appointed from Pa.]
1st Lieut. 11th Inf., 14 May, 1861. Capt., 17 March, 1862. Bvt. Maj., 1 Aug., 1864, for gallant and meritorious service in the Battle of the Wilderness, Va. Bvt. Lieut. Col., 18 Aug., 1864, for gallant service in Battle on the Weldon Railroad, Va. Trans. to 16th Inf., 14 April, 1869. Maj. 23rd Inf., 8 Feb., 1880. Lieut. Col. 2nd Inf., 10 July, 1885. Retired, over 30 years' service, 19 June, 1891. Died 3 Jan., 1899.

FLETCHER, ROBT.* [Born in N. Y. Appointed from N. Y.]
2nd Lieut. 1st Art., 15 June, 1868. Discharged 31 Dec., 1870.

FLETCHER, ROBT. H. [Born in Ohio. Appointed from Ohio.]
2nd Lieut. 21st Inf., 27 July, 1872. 1st Lieut., 23 April, 1877. Retired for disability 21 Oct., 1886.

FLETCHER, ROBERT S. [Born in D. C. Appointed from D. C.]
2nd Lieut. 8th Inf., 3 Sept., 1867. Mustered out 27 Dec., 1870.

FLETCHER, WM. [Born in N. Y. Appointed from Army.]
Priv. Co. G, 1st Ohio Vols., 10 June, 1846. Discharged 14 June, 1847. Priv. Co. A, 2nd Ohio Vols., 31 July, 1847. Corpl., 27 Sept., 1847. Priv., 30 Nov., 1847. Discharged 26 July, 1848. Priv. Co. F, 1st Art., 9 Dec., 1848. Discharged 9 Oct., 1853. Priv. Co. F, 1st Art., 9 Oct., 1853. Corpl., 20 June, 1854. Priv., 3 Sept., 1855. Corpl., 5 Feb., 1856. Priv., 1 July, 1858. Discharged 9 Oct., 1858. Priv. Co. F, 8th Inf., 23 June, 1859. Sergt., 14 July, 1861. 2nd Lieut. 11th Inf., 29 Oct., 1861. 1st Lieut., 12 March, 1862. Bvt. Capt., 30 Aug., 1862, for gallant and meritorious service in the Battle of Bull Run (2nd), Va. Trans. to 20th Inf., 21 Sept., 1866. Capt., 2 Nov., 1866. Retired, over 30 years' service, 31 Aug., 1887.

FLEWELLEN, JAMES P.* [Born in Ga. Appointed from Ga.]
Bvt. 2nd Lieut. 2nd Art., 1 July, 1850. 2nd Lieut. 1st Art., 22 Feb., 1851. Resigned 2 Nov., 1854.

FLINT, FRANKLIN F.* [Born in N. H. Appointed from Mass.]
2nd Lieut. 6th Inf., 1 July, 1841. 1st Lieut., 12 Oct., 1847. Capt., 16 Sept., 1856. Maj. 16th Inf., 14 May, 1861. Lieut. Col. 7th Inf., 20 Oct., 1863. Col. 4th Inf., 8 July, 1868. Retired, over 40 years' service, 11 April, 1882. Died 15 Sept., 1891.

FLIPPER, HENRY O.* [Born in Ga. Appointed from Ga.]
2nd Lieut. 10th Cav., 15 June, 1877. Dismissed 30 June, 1882.

FLOOD, PATRICK H. [Born in N. Y. Appointed from Army.]
Priv., Sergt. and 1st Sergt. Co. D, Eng. Batt., 22 Nov., 1860, to 8 June, 1864. 2nd Lieut. 2nd Inf., 18 May, 1864. 1st Lieut., 18 July, 1866. Unass'd 28 April, 1870. Discharged 30 Sept., 1870.

FLOYD, DANIEL H.* [Born in Md. Appointed from Ind.]
2nd Lieut. 9th Cav., 15 June, 1870. Trans. to 18th Inf., 18 Sept., 1875. 1st Lieut., 1 July, 1879. Capt. and A. Q. M., 2 May, 1883. Died 10 March, 1894.

FLOYD, GABRIEL J. [Born in ——. Appointed from Ky.]
3rd Lieut. 17th Inf., 16 April, 1813. 2nd Lieut., 1 Oct., 1814. Trans. to 3rd Inf., 17 May, 1815. Resigned 9 Oct., 1818.

FLOYD-JONES, DE LANCEY.* [Born in N. Y. Appointed from N. Y.]
Bvt. 2nd Lieut. 7th Inf., 1 July, 1846. 2nd Lieut. 4th Inf., 27 Nov., 1846. Bvt. 1st Lieut., 8 Sept., 1847, for gallant and meritorious conduct in the Battle of Molino del Rey. 1st Lieut. 4th Inf., 1 Jan., 1848. Capt., 31 July, 1854. Maj. 11th Inf., 14 May, 1861. Bvt. Lieut. Col., 4 July, 1862, for gallant and meritorious service during the Peninsular campaign in Va. Bvt. Col., 2 July, 1863, for gallant and meritorious service in the Battle of Gettysburg, Pa. Lieut. Col. 19th Inf., 1 Aug., 1863. Col. 6th Inf., 25 June, 1867. Unass'd 15 March, 1869. Ass'd to 3rd Inf., 31 Dec., 1870. Retired 20 March, 1879.

FLOYD, ROBT. [Born in Ireland. Appointed from Army.]
Priv., Corpl. and Sergt. Batty M, 4th Art., 8 Nov., 1856, to 23 April, 1863. Bvt. 2nd Lieut. 4th Art., 27 Feb., 1863. 2nd Lieut. 3rd Art., 27 April, 1863. Died 23 Sept., 1863, of wounds received at the Battle of Chickamauga, Ga.

FLYNN, DANIEL. [Born in Ireland. Appointed from Army.]
Priv., Corpl. and Sergt. Troop E, 2nd Drag., 10 March, 1858, to 8 Oct., 1862. 2nd Lieut. 2nd Cav., 17 July, 1862. Retired 30 Sept., 1863. Died 4 May, 1875. Bvt. 1st Lieut., 9 June, 1863, for gallant and meritorious service at the Battle of Beverly Ford, Va.

FLYNN, WM. F.* [Born in Conn. Appointed from Conn.]
2nd Lieut. 8th Cav., 13 June, 1883. 1st Lieut., 20 Jan., 1890. Capt., 2 March, 1899. R. Q. M., 25 April, 1899.

FOARD, ANDREW J. [Born in Ga. Appointed from Ga.]
Asst. Surg., 11 May, 1853. Resigned 1 April, 1861. Died in 1867.

FOGARTY, MICHL. B. [Born in Ireland. Appointed from Il'
1st Lieut. 19th Inf., 14 May, 1861. Reg. Adj., 20 July, 1862, to 26 July, 1863. Killed 20 Sept., 1863, at the Battle of Chickamauga, Ga. Bvt. Capt., 19 Sept., 1863, for gallant and meritorious service at the Battle of Chickamauga, Ga.

FOGG, LEANDER W. [Born in Me. Appointed from N. H.]
1st Lieut. 7th N. H. Vols., 11 Dec., 1861. Capt., 7 Nov., 1863. Mustered out 22 Dec., 1864. 2nd Lieut. 12th Inf., 11 May, 1866. Trans. to 21st Inf., 21 Sept., 1866. Died 11 Nov., 1866.

FOLEY, HAMILTON. [Born in D. C. Appointed from N. Y.]
Cadet at Mil. Acad., 1 Sept., 1893, to 19 Jan., 1894, and from 15 June, 1894, to 10 Feb., 1895. 2nd Lieut. 5th Cav., 10 April, 1899. 2nd Lieut. 14th N. Y. Vols., 16 May, 1898. 1st Lieut., 23 July, 1898. Mustered out 27 Oct., 1898. 1st Lieut. 203rd N. Y. Vols., 28 Oct., 1898, to muster out 25 March, 1899.

FOLGER, GEORGE W.* [Born in Mass. Appointed from Mass.]
Bvt. 2nd and 2nd Lieut. 2nd Inf., 1 July, 1822. Trans. to 6th Inf., 5 June, 1823. 1st Lieut. 6th Inf., 1 Aug., 1825. Resigned 20 Dec., 1826. Died in 1845.

FOLLETT, FREDK. M.* [Born in N. Y. Appointed from N. Y.]
Bvt. 2nd Lieut. 3rd Inf., 1 July, 1850. Trans. to 8th Inf., 11 Feb., 1851. 2nd Lieut., 13 Sept., 1852. Resigned 9 Oct., 1855. 2nd Lieut. 4th Art., 27 June, 1856. 1st Lieut., 10 Sept., 1857. Capt., 3 Sept., 1861. Cashiered 3 Sept., 1867. Reinstated 9 Oct., 1867. Expired 4 March, 1869. Bvt. Maj., 30 Jan., 1863, for gallant and meritorious service at the Siege of Suffolk, Va. Bvt. Lieut. Col., 13 March, 1865, for gallant and meritorious service during the war. Died 9 April, 1869.

FOLSOM, JOSEPH L.* [Born in N. H. Appointed from N. H.]
Bvt. 2nd Lieut. 8th Inf., 1 July, 1840. 2nd Lieut. 5th Inf., 3 Nov., 1840. 1st Lieut., 29 June, 1846. Capt. A. Q. M., 10 Sept., 1846. Died 19 July, 1855.

FOLTZ, FREDERICK S.* [Born in Pa. Appointed at Large.]
2nd Lieut. 1st Cav., 13 June, 1879. 1st Lieut., 26 March, 1888. Capt. 2nd Cav., 23 June, 1898.

FOLWELL, WM. B. [Born in Minn. Appointed from Minn.]
1st Lieut. 14th Minn. Vols., 8 May, 1898, to 28 July, 1898. 2nd Lieut. 1st Inf., 9 July, 1898. 1st Lieut., 2 March, 1899.

FOOT, ALFRED. [Born in N. Y. Appointed from N. Y.]
1st Lieut. 14th Inf., 14 May, 1861. Capt., 18 Jan., 1865. Trans. to 32nd Inf., 21 Sept., 1866. Retired as Maj., 5 Nov., 1866. Died 1 Sept., 1869. Bvt. Capt., 5 May, 1864, for gallant and meritorious service at the Battle of the Wilderness, Va. Bvt. Maj., 8 Nov., 1865, for gallant and meritorious service during the war.

FOOT, FRANK W. [Born in Fla. Appointed from N. Y.]
2nd Lieut. 121st N. Y. Vols., 20 July, 1863. 1st Lieut., 19 April, 1864. Resigned 24 Sept., 1864. 2nd Lieut. Vet. Res. Corps, 15 May, 1865. Mustered out 30 Oct., 1866. 2nd Lieut. 45th Inf., 28 July, 1866. Resigned 10 Jan., 1868.

FOOT, ISAAC. [Born in N. Y. Appointed from N. Y.]
Hosp. Surg. Mate, 22 Nov., 1814. Disbanded 15 June, 1815. Reinstated 1 Jan., 1816. Resigned 16 May, 1816.

FOOT, LYMAN. [Born in Conn. Appointed from Conn.]
Surg. Mate 2nd Inf., 10 Aug., 1818. Post Surg., 12 Dec., 1820. Asst. Surg., 1 June, 1821. Maj. Surg., 5 March, 1831. Died 24 Oct., 1846.

FOOTE, GEORGE F. [Born in N. Y. Appointed from Tenn.]
Priv. Co. E, 14th Mich. Vols., 2 Jan., 1862. 1st Sergt., 7 Jan., 1862. 2nd Lieut. 14th Mich. Vols., 15 March, 1863. 1st Lieut., 1 Sept., 1864. Bvt. Maj. and Lieut. Col. Vols., 13 March, 1865, for gallant and meritorious service during the war. Capt. 14th Mich. Vols., 26 May, 1865. Mustered out 18 July, 1865. 2nd Lieut. 9th Inf., 28 July, 1866. Bvt. 1st Lieut., 2 March, 1867, for gallant and meritorious service in the Battle of Stone River, Tenn. Bvt. Capt., 2 March, 1867, for gallant and meritorious service in the Battle of Jonesboro, Ga. 1st Lieut. 9th Inf., 21 April, 1868. Unassigned 14 June, 1869. Ass'd to 9th Inf., 17 Dec., 1869. Trans. to 8th Cav., 1 Feb., 1870. Capt., 18 Jan., 1881. Retired for disability 24 April, 1886.

FOOTE, MORRIS C. [Born in N. Y. Appointed from N. Y.]
Priv. Co. C, 44th N. Y. Vols., 3 Sept., 1861. Discharged 20 June, 1862. 2nd Lieut. 92nd N. Y. Vols., 21 June, 1862. Mustered out 31 Dec., 1864. 1st Lieut. 121st N. Y. Vols., 26 March, 1865. Bvt. Capt. Vols., 6 April, 1865, for gallant and meritorious service before Petersburg and in the Battle of Little Sailor's Creek, Va. Mustered out 17 July, 1865. 2nd Lieut. 9th Inf., 7 May, 1866. 1st Lieut., 7 March, 1867. Capt., 26 Jan., 1883. Maj., 11 Aug., 1898. Maj. and C. S. Vols., 16 July, 1898. Resigned Vols., 27 Sept., 1898.

FOOTE, RENSSELAER W. [Born in N. Y. Appointed from N. Y.]
Cadet at Mil. Acad., 1 Sept., 1834, to 1 June, 1835. 2nd Lieut. 6th Inf., 1 Nov., 1838. 1st Lieut., 22 Nov., 1843. Capt., 9 June, 1853. Killed 27 June, 1862, at the Battle of Gaines' Mills, Va. Bvt. Maj., 27 June, 1862, for gallant and meritorious service at the Battle of Gaines' Mills, Va.

FOOTE, STEPHEN M.* [Born in Mich. Appointed from Vt.]
2nd Lieut. 4th Art., 15 June, 1884. 1st Lieut., 17 June, 1889. Capt. 6th Art., 2 March, 1899. Graduate of the Artillery School, 1888.

FORBES, JOSEPH C. [Born in Sandwich Islands. Appointed from Army.]
Priv. and Sergt. Co. C, 2nd Batt. 15th Inf., 28 Sept., 1861, to 30 March, 1863. 2nd Lieut. 15th Inf., 19 Feb., 1863. Killed 31 May, 1864, at the Battle of New Hope Church, Ga. Bvt. 1st Lieut., 31 May, 1864, for gallant and meritorious service at the Battle of New Hope Church, Ga.

FORBES, THEODORE F. [Born in Sandwich Islands. Appointed from Pa.]
Corpl. Co. G, 102nd N. Y. Vols., 9 Nov., 1861. Sergt., 12 Aug., 1862. 2nd Lieut. 102nd N. Y. Vols., 12 Nov., 1862. Mustered out 7 March, 1863. 2nd Lieut. Vet. Res. Corps, 13 Aug., 1863. Mustered out 12 Oct., 1866. 2nd Lieut. 42nd Inf., 28 July, 1866. Reg. Adj., 1 Jan. to 15 June, 1867. Bvt. 1st Lieut., 2 March, 1867, for gallant and meritorious service in the Battle of Cedar Mountain, Va. Unassigned 22 April, 1869. Ass'd to 5th Inf., 15 Nov., 1869. 1st Lieut., 31 Aug., 1875. Reg. Q. M., 14 March, 1882, to 8 Oct., 1885. Capt., 8 Oct., 1885. Maj. 4th Inf., 27 Feb., 1899. Trans. to 5th Inf., 20 March, 1899.

FORBUSH, WM. C.* [Born in Mass. Appointed from Mass.]
2nd Lieut. 5th Cav., 15 June, 1868. 1st Lieut., 19 March, 1870. Reg. Adj., 12 July, 1869, to 5 Oct., 1876. Capt., 1 May, 1879. Maj. 9th Cav., 1 June, 1897.

FORD, CLYDE S. [Born in Ohio. Appointed from W. Va.]
Asst. Surg., 12 Dec., 1898.

FORD, JOSEPH H.* [Born in D. C. Appointed from D. C.]
Asst. Surg., 12 Dec., 1898.

FORD, GEORGE E. [Born in Pa. Appointed from Pa.]
Priv. Co. B, 4th Iowa Vols., 10 July, 1861. Sergt., 8 Aug., 1861. 1st Sergt., 10 Oct., 1861. Discharged 22 Jan., 1862. 2nd Lieut. 4th Iowa Vols., 23 Jan., 1862. Capt., 15 Sept., 1862. Capt. A. de C. Vols., 2 Feb., 1865. Bvt. Maj. and Lieut. Col. Vols., 13 March, 1865, for gallant and meritorious service during the war. Bvt. Col. Vols., 13 March, 1865, for gallant service in the Battle of Ringgold, Ga. Mustered out 12 Jan., 1866. 1st Lieut. 39th Inf., 12 June, 1867. Unassigned 20 April, 1869. As to 3rd Cav., 1 Jan., 1871. Capt., 14 Dec., 1877. Retired 20 March, 1879. Died 28 April, 1893.

FORD, JOHN A. [Born in Md. Appointed from Va.]
1st Lieut. 13th Inf., 5 Aug., 1861. Died 2 Oct., 1862.

FORD, LEMUEL. [Born in Va. Appointed from Ind.]
Capt. Mtd. Rangers, 16 June, 1832. Capt. 1st Drag., 15 Aug., 1833. Resigned 31 July, 1837. Capt. 3rd Drag., 9 April, 1847. Disbanded 31 July, 1848. Bvt. Maj., 19 Oct., 1847, for gallant and meritorious conduct in the affair of Atlixco, Mexico.

FORD, STANLEY H. [Born in Ohio. Appointed from Ohio.]
2nd Lieut. 16th Inf., 9 July, 1898. 1st Lieut. 25th Inf., 16 June, 1899.

FORNANCE, JAMES.* [Born in Pa. Appointed from Pa.]
2nd Lieut. 13th Inf., 12 June, 1871. 1st Lieut., 29 June, 1872. Reg. Adj., 24 July, 1879, to 5 March, 1887. Capt., 16 Dec., 1889. Died 3 July, 1898, of wounds received at Battle of San Juan, Santiago, Cuba.

FORNEY, JOHN H.* [Born in N. C. Appointed from Ala.]
Bvt. 2nd Lieut. 7th Inf., 1 July, 1852. 2nd Lieut., 24 Oct., 1853. Trans. to 10th Inf., 3 March, 1855. 1st Lieut., 25 Aug., 1855. Resigned 23 Jan., 1861.

FORNEY, PHILIP R. [Born in Pa. Appointed from Pa.]
2nd Lieut. 9th Inf., 5 Aug., 1861. 1st Lieut., 6 Sept., 1861. Capt. 18th Inf., 19 Feb., 1862. Trans. to 14th Inf., 21 March, 1866. Dismissed 31 May, 1866. Died 14 July, 1870.

FORRY, SAML. [Born in Pa. Appointed from Pa.]
Asst. Surg., 30 Aug., 1836. Resigned 31 Oct., 1840. Died 8 Nov., 1844.

FORSE, ALBERT G.* [Born in Pa. Appointed from Ohio.]
2nd Lieut. 1st Cav., 23 June, 1865. 1st Lieut., 15 Oct., 1866. Capt., 4 March, 1879. Maj. 7th Cav., 11 Dec., 1896. Trans. to 1st Cav., 7 Jan., 1897. Killed in action at the Battle of San Juan, Santiago, Cuba, 1 July, 1898.

FORSE, WM. [Born in Ky. Appointed from Army.]
Priv. and Corpl. Cos. D and B, 3rd Inf., 5 March, 1896, to 6 July, 1898. 2nd Lieut. 3rd Art., 22 June, 1898.

FORSTER, WEIDMAN. [Born in Pa. Appointed from Pa.]
2nd Lieut. of Inf., 16 Feb., 1847; 11th Inf., 9 April, 1847. 1st Lieut., 4 Dec., 1847. Disbanded 15 Aug., 1848.

FORSYTH, GEORGE. [Born in Mich. Appointed from Mich.]
2nd Lieut. 2nd Drag., 8 June, 1836. 1st Lieut., 26 Sept., 1837. Resigned 31 Dec., 1837.

FORSYTH, GEORGE A. [Born in Pa. Appointed from Ill.]
Priv. Chicago Drag., 19 April to 18 Aug., 1861. 1st Lieut. 8th Ill. Cav., 18 Sept., 1861. Capt., 12 Feb., 1862. Maj., 1 Sept., 1863. Bvt. Col. Vols., 19 Oct., 1864, for gallant and meritorious service in the Battles of Opequan and Middletown, Va. Bvt. Brig. Gen. Vols., 13 March, 1865, for distinguished service and conspicuous gallantry. Mustered out 1 Feb., 1866. Maj. 9th Cav, 28 July, 1866. Bvt. Lieut. Col., 2 March, 1867, for gallant and meritorious service in the Battle of Dinwiddie C. H., Va. Bvt. Col., 2 March, 1867, for gallant and meritorious service in the Battle of Five Forks, Va. Bvt. Brig. Gen., 17 Sept., 1868, for gallant conduct and meritorious service in an engagement with hostile Indians, on the Arickaree Fork of the Republican River, on the 17, 18, 19 and 20 Sept., 1868. Lieut. Col. Mil. Sec'ry to Lieut. Gen. Sheridan, 13 March, 1869. Relieved 17 March, 1873. Lieut. Col. A. de C., 9 April, 1878. Lieut. Col. 4th Cav., 26 June, 1881. Retired for disability 25 March, 1890.

FORSYTH, JAMES W.* [Born in Ohio. Appointed from Ohio.]
2nd Lieut. 9th Inf., 1 July, 1856. 1st Lieut., 15 March, 1861. Trans. to 18th Inf., 14 May, 1861. Capt., 24 Oct., 1861. Bvt. Maj., 20 Sept., 1863, for gallant and meritorious service in the Battle of Chickamauga, Ga. Maj. A. A. G. Vols., 7 April, 1864. Lieut. Col. A. I. G. (Act 17 July, 1862), 19 April, 1864. Bvt. Lieut. Col., 19 Oct., 1864, for gallant and meritorious service in the Battle of Cedar Creek, Va. Bvt. Brig. Gen. Vols., 19 Oct., 1864, for gallant and meritorious service in the Battles of Opequan, Fisher's Hill and Middletown, Va. Bvt. Col., 1 April, 1865, for gallant and meritorious service in the Battle of Five Forks, Va. Bvt. Brig. Gen., 9 April, 1865, for gallant and meritorious service in the field during the war. Relieved as Lieut. Col. A. I. G. (Act 17 July, 1862), 19 May, 1865. Brig. Gen. Vols., 19 May, 1865, for gallant and meritorious service. Mustered out of Vol. service, 15 Jan., 1866. Maj. 10th Cav., 28 July, 1866. Lieut. Col. A. de C., 13 March, 1869, to 17 March, 1873. Lieut. Col. Mil. Sec'ry, 17 March, 1873, to 4 April, 1878. Lieut. Col. 1st Cav., 4 April, 1878. Col. 7th Cav., 11 June, 1886. Brig. Gen., 9 Nov., 1894. Maj. Gen., 11 May, 1897. Retired, over 30 years' service, 14 May, 1897.

FORSYTH, JOHN. [Born in N. Y. Appointed from N. Y.]
Chap. 19th N. Y. State Militia, 2 July, 1862. Mustered out 6 Sept., 1862. Appointed Chap. and Prof. Ethics and Law, 28 July, 1871. Retired, over 62 years of age, with pay of Col., 12 Dec., 1881. Died 17 Oct., 1886.

FORSYTH, LEWIS C. [Born in Mich. Appointed from D. C.]
Capt. A. Q. M. Vols., 11 June. 1862. Mustered out 3 Nov., 1866. Capt. A. Q. M., 11 March, 1867. Bvt. Maj., 11 March, 1867, for faithful and meritorious service during the war. Maj. and Q. M., 19 Oct., 1888. Lieut. Col. and Dep. Q. M. G., 22 Sept., 1896. Retired by operation of law 11 June, 1897.

FORSYTH, ROBT. A. [Born in Mich. Appointed from Mich.]
Cadet at Mil. Acad., 23 Sept., 1814, to 28 Feb., 1817. Maj. and P. M., 10 Sept., 1831. Dismissed 6 Dec., 1839. Maj. and P. M., 8 Aug., 1846. Died 21 Oct., 1849.

FORSYTH, ROBT. C. [Born in Ga. Appointed from Ga.]
Cadet at Mil. Acad., 1 July, 1842, to 20 Jan., 1843. 2nd Lieut. Voltigeurs, 9 April, 1847. 1st Lieut., 18 Sept., 1847. Disbanded 30 Aug., 1848. Bvt. 1st Lieut., 13 Sept., 1847, for gallant and meritorious conduct at Chapultepec, Mex.

FORSYTH, ROBT. M.* [Born in Ga. Appointed from Ga.]
3rd Lieut. Corps Art., 2 March, 1815. 2nd Lieut., 8 Sept., 1817. Dismissed 1 Dec., 1818. Died in 1819.

FORSYTH, WM. D. [Born in Ill. Appointed from Ohio.]
1st Lieut. 1st Ohio Cav., 9 May to 20 Sept., 1898. 2nd Lieut. 19th Inf., 9 Sept., 1898. Trans. to 5th Cav., 25 Oct., 1898.

FORSYTH, WM. W.* [Born in Ga. Appointed from Ga.]
2nd Lieut. 6th Cav., 13 June, 1882. 1st Lieut., 20 Nov., 1889. Capt., 2 March, 1899. R. Q. M., 26 April, 1899.

FORSYTHE, BENJAMIN D.* [Born in Ky. Appointed from Ill.]
Bvt. 2nd Lieut. 3rd Inf., 1 July, 1848. 2nd Lieut. 4th Inf., 8 Oct., 1848. 1st Lieut., 27 March, 1854. Reg. Adj., 12 June, 1854, to 1 Sept., 1855. Died 31 Jan., 1861.

FORTUNE, J. CAMPBELL. [Born in Pa. Appointed from Pa.]
Midshipman U. S. N., 27 Sept., 1859, to 15 March, 1861. 2nd Lieut. Miss. Marine Brig., 9 Feb., 1863. Mustered out 18 Jan., 1865. 2nd Lieut. 19th Inf., 7 March, 1867. Mustered out 1 Jan., 1871.

FORWOOD, WM. H. [Born in Del. Appointed from Pa.]
1st Lieut. Asst. Surg., 5 Aug., 1861. Bvt. Capt. and Maj., 13 March, 1865, for faithful and meritorious service during the war. Capt. Asst. Surg., 28 July, 1866. Maj. Surg., 26 June, 1876. Lieut. Col. Surg., 15 June, 1891. Col. and Asst. Surg. Gen., 3 May, 1897.

FOSDICK, HARRISON. [Born in N. Y. Appointed from Army.]
Priv. and Sergt. Gen. Mtd. Ser., 1 Dec., 1858, to 9 Nov., 1861. 2nd Lieut. 5th Cav., 26 Oct., 1861. 1st Lieut., 17 July, 1862. Resigned 10 Oct., 1862. Sergt. Gen. Ser., 26 Nov., 1862, to 31 March, 1863. Died 2 Aug., 1866.

FOSDICK, WM. [Born in Va. Appointed from Ind.]
Asst. Surg., 14 July, 1846. Disbanded 30 June, 1847. Asst. Surg., 8 Sept., 1847. Discharged 22 Sept., 1847.

FOSTER, AMOS.* [Born in N. H. Appointed from N. H.]
Bvt. 2nd Lieut. 5th Inf., 1 July, 1828. 2nd Lieut., 1 July, 1828. Killed by a soldier, 7 Feb., 1832.

FOSTER, ARTHUR B.* [Born in Ill. Appointed from Ill.]
2nd Lieut. 19th Inf., 12 June, 1887. 1st Lieut. 2nd Inf., 5 July, 1894. Trans. to 19th Inf., 8 Dec., 1894. Capt., 2 March, 1899. Graduate of the Infantry and Cavalry School, 1893. R. Q. M., 5 May, 1899.

FOSTER, CHAS. G. [Born in ——. Appointed from La.]
Asst. Apoth. Gen., 28 Jan., 1820. Disbanded 1 June, 1821.

FOSTER, CHARLES S. [Born in Ill. Appointed from N. D.]
Q. M. Sergt. Co. B, 1st N. D. Vols., 14 May, 1898, to 28 April, 1899. 2nd Lieut. 9th Inf., 10 April, 1899. Resigned 24 Jan., 1900.

FOSTER, CHAS. W. [Born in Mass. Appointed from N. H.]
Priv. Co. A, Eng., 1 June, 1846. Artificer, 1 Aug., 1848. Corpl., 1 March, 1849. Sergt., — ——, 1850. Discharged 1 June, 1851. Priv. Co. A, Eng., 26 Aug., 1851. Sergt., 1 Sept., 1851. Discharged 26 Aug., 1856. Capt. A. A. G. Vols., 19 Sept., 1861. Maj. A. A. G. Vols., 24 Aug., 1863. Bvt. Lieut. Col. Vols. and Bvt. Col. Vols., 24 Sept., 1864, for faithful and meritorious service during the war. Capt. A. Q. M., 4 Nov., 1865. Bvt. Maj., Lieut. Col. and Col., 4 Nov., 1865, for faithful and meritorious service in the A. G. Dept. during the war. Mustered out of Vol. service, 1 Sept., 1867. Maj. and Q. M., 15 March, 1883. Retired, over 30 years' service, 24 Sept., 1891.

FOSTER, CHAS. W.* [Born in Mich. Appointed from Mich.]
2nd Lieut. 4th Inf., 15 June, 1876. Trans. to 3rd Art., 15 Aug., 1876, taking rank from 15 Aug., 1876. 1st Lieut., 1 June, 1883. Capt. 6th Art., 8 March, 1898. Graduate of the Artillery School, 1878.

FOSTER, CLAIBORNE L.* [Born in La. Appointed from La.]
2nd Lieut. 5th Cav., 11 June, 1888. Died 10 Aug., 1890.

FOSTER, FRED W.* [Born in Pa. Appointed from N. Y.]
2nd Lieut. 5th Cav., 15 June, 1877. 1st Lieut., 1 April, 1885. Capt., 14 Oct., 1896.

FOSTER, HERBERT S.* [Born in Vt. Appointed from Vt.]
2nd Lieut. 20th Inf., 15 June, 1876. 1st Lieut., 4 June, 1881. Capt., 20 April, 1891. Maj. 12th Inf., 15 Nov., 1899.

FOSTER, JAMES E. H. [Born in Pa. Appointed from Pa.]
Priv. Co. A, Independent Batty Pa. Art., 19 May, 1864. Discharged 29 Aug., 1864. Priv. Co. F, 155th Pa. Vols., 21 March, 1865. Trans. to Co. G, 191st Pa. Vols., 23 June, 1865. Discharged 23 June, 1865. 2nd Lieut. 3rd Cav., 1 Oct., 1873. 1st Lieut., 30 Nov., 1879. Died 8 May, 1883.

FOSTER, JOHN G.* [Born in N. H. Appointed from N. H.]
Bvt. 2nd Lieut. Eng., 1 July, 1846. 2nd Lieut., 24 May, 1848. 1st Lieut., 1 April, 1854. Capt., 1 July, 1860. Brig. Gen. Vols., 23 Oct., 1861. Maj. Gen. Vols., 18 July, 1862. Mustered out Vols., 1 Sept., 1866. Maj., 3 March, 1863. Lieut. Col., 7 March, 1867. Died 2 Sept., 1874. Bvt. 1st Lieut., 20 Aug., 1847, for gallant and meritorious conduct at Contreras and Churubusco. Bvt. Capt., 8 Sept., 1847, for gallant and meritorious conduct at Molino del Rey. Bvt. Maj., 26 Dec., 1860, for distinguished part taken in the transfer of the garrison of Fort Moultrie to Fort Sumter, S. C. Bvt. Lieut. Col., 8 Feb., 1862, for gallant and meritorious service in the capture of Roanoke Island, N. C. Bvt. Col., 12 March, 1862, for gallant and meritorious service in the capture of Newbern, N. C. Bvt. Brig. Gen., 13 March, 1865, for gallant and meritorious service in the capture of Savannah, Ga. Bvt. Maj. Gen., 13 March, 1865, for gallant and meritorious service in the field during the war.

FOSTER, JOSEPH T. [Born in Ohio. Appointed from Iowa.]
Sergt. and 1st Sergt. Co. B, 1st Iowa Cav., 31 July, 1861, to 7 Feb., 1863. 1st Lieut. 1st Iowa Cav., 7 Feb., 1863. Capt., 1 Oct., 1864. Mustered out 15 Feb., 1866. 1st Lieut. 8th Cav., 28 July, 1866. Dismissed 28 Dec., 1868.

FOSTER, PIERCE C. [Born in ——. Appointed from ——.]
2nd Lieut. 3rd Inf., — ——, 1899. Died 22 May, 1899.

FOSTER, SAML. A.* [Born in Me. Appointed from Me.]
Bvt. 2nd Lieut. 1st Inf., 1 July, 1860. 2nd Lieut. 6th Inf., 20 Aug., 1860. 1st Lieut., 14 May, 1861. Col. 5th Mo. Vols., 23 Oct., 1862. Mustered out Vols., 22 Nov., 1862. Col. 35th Mo. Vols., 3 Dec., 1862. Resigned from Vols., 1 Aug., 1863. Capt. C. S., 9 Feb., 1863. Died 2 Feb., 1871. Bvt. Capt., 27 June, 1862, for gallant and meritorious service at the Battle of Gaines' Mills, Va. Bvt. Maj., 13 March, 1865, for faithful and meritorious service during the war.

FOSTER, WM. L. [Born in Mass. Appointed from Mass.]
2nd Lieut. 9th Inf., 12 March, 1812. 1st Lieut., 23 March, 1813. Capt., 15 Oct., 1813. Trans. to 5th Inf., 17 May, 1815. Disbanded 1 June, 1821. Died Nov., 1821.

FOSTER, WM. S. [Born in N. H. Appointed from N. H.]
1st Lieut. 11th Inf., 12 March, 1812. Capt., 13 March, 1813. Trans. to 6th Inf., 17 May, 1815. Maj. 4th Inf., 7 July, 1826. Lieut. Col., 8 June, 1836. Died 26 Nov., 1839. Bvt. Maj., 15 Aug., 1814, for gallant conduct in the defence of Fort Erie. Bvt. Col., 25 Dec., 1837, for distinguished service in Florida and particularly in the Battle of Kissimmee, Fla.

FOULK, WM. L. [Born in Pa. Appointed from Pa.]
2nd Lieut. 7th Pa. Vols., 23 April, 1861. 1st Lieut., 11 June, 1861. Mustered out 5 Aug., 1861. Capt., 46th Pa. Vols., 26 Aug., 1861. Lieut. Col., 9 June, 1863. Mustered out 29 July, 1865. 2nd Lieut. 18th Inf., 11 May, 1866. Trans. to 36th Inf., 21 Sept., 1866. 1st Lieut., 1 March, 1867. Unassigned 19 May, 1869. Ass'd to 10th Cav.,

15 Dec., 1870. Capt., 3 March, 1873. Out of service, 6 Dec., 1873. Capt. of Cav., 14 June, 1878, to rank from 3 March, 1873. Ass'd to 6th Cav., 10 Aug., 1878. Retired for disability 15 Jan., 1884. Died 28 March, 1886.

FOULK, WILLIS. [Born in Pa. Appointed from Pa.]
1st Lieut. 22nd Inf., 12 March, 1812. Capt., 20 June, 1813. Trans. to 8th Inf., 17 May, 1815. Disbanded 1 June, 1821. Died 7 June, 1856.

FOUNTAIN, SAML. W.* [Born in Va. Appointed from Ohio.]
Priv. Co. K, 140th Ohio Vols., 2 May, 1864. Discharged 3 Sept., 1864. Cadet at Mil. Acad., 1 July, 1866. 2nd Lieut. 8th Cav., 15 June, 1870. 1st Lieut., 22 Oct., 1878. Capt., 11 April, 1889.

FOWLE, JOHN. [Born in Mass. Appointed from Mass.]
2nd Lieut. 9th Inf., 9 April, 1812. Reg. P. M., 3 July to 12 June, 1814. 1st Lieut., 16 April, 1813. Capt., 10 June, 1814. Trans. to 5th Inf., 17 May, 1815. Maj. 3rd Inf., 4 March, 1833. Lieut. Col. 6th Inf., 25 Dec., 1837. Killed 25 April, 1838, by steamboat explosion. Bvt. Maj., 10 June, 1824, for 10 years' faithful service in one grade.

FOWLER, ABRAM C. [Born in N. Y. Appointed from Army.]
Priv. and Sergt. 30th Inf., 5 Nov., 1813, to 24 Aug., 1814. 3rd Lieut. Corps Art., 2 July, 1814. 2nd Lieut., 30 Sept., 1814. Resigned 31 Oct., 1816. 2nd Lieut. Corps Art., 3 March, 1819. Trans. to 2nd Art., 1 June, 1821. 1st Lieut., 20 Feb., 1827. Died 30 April, 1834.

FOWLER, CHARLES S. [Born in Me. Appointed from Army.]
Priv., Saddler, Corpl., Sergt. and Priv. Co. E, 4th Cav., 14 Nov., 1872, to 14 Nov., 1877. Priv., Corpl. and Sergt. Co. C, 19th Inf., 22 Aug., 1878, to 6 July, 1882. 2nd Lieut. 19th Inf., 7 June, 1882. Graduate of the Infantry and Cavalry School, 1885. Retired for disability, with the rank of 1st Lieut., 7 Jan., 1891.

FOWLER, FRANK B.* [Born in Texas. Appointed from Texas.]
2nd Lieut. 4th Cav., 1 July, 1886. Resigned 30 Oct., 1888.

FOWLER, HENRY W. [Born in N. Y. Appointed from N. Y.]
2nd Lieut. Marine Corps, 26 May, 1824. 1st Lieut., 2 May, 1834. Resigned 8 June, 1836. Capt. 2nd Drag., 8 June, 1836. Resigned 31 March, 1841. Maj. 3rd La. Vols., 21 May, 1846. Mustered out 21 Aug., 1846.

FOWLER, JOSHUA L.* [Born in N. Y. Appointed from N. Y.]
2nd Lieut. 2nd Cav., 15 June, 1868. 1st Lieut., 4 Nov., 1869. R. Q. M., 15 Sept., 1874. Capt., 26 Oct., 1881. Maj. 10th Cav., 1 July, 1898. Died 11 July, 1899.

FOWLER, STERNE H. [Born in Conn. Appointed from Conn.]
2nd Lieut. 5th Inf., 12 Nov., 1838. 1st Lieut., 18 May, 1846. R. Q. M., 1 Sept. to 9 Dec., 1847. Capt., 9 Dec., 1847. Resigned 1 April, 1857. Bvt. Capt., 20 Aug., 1847, for gallant and meritorious conduct at Contreras and Churubusco. Bvt. Maj., 8 Sept., 1847, for gallant conduct at Molino del Rey.

FOWLER, WM. H.* [Born in Md. Appointed from D. C.]
2nd Lieut. 1st Art., 1 July, 1837. 1st Lieut., 1 May, 1839. Capt., 29 Oct., 1848. Died 4 Sept., 1851. Bvt. 1st Lieut., 15 Jan., 1838, for gallant and good conduct in the war against the Florida Indians.

FOX, JOSEPH C.* [Born in Pa. Appointed from Pa.]
2nd Lieut. 13th Inf., 12 June, 1890. Retired for disability, with rank of 1st Lieut., 7 June, 1897.

FOX, WARREN B. [Born in Wis. Appointed from Army.]
Priv., Corpl. and Sergt. Co. A, 20th Inf., 21 May, 1889, to 27 Nov., 1892. 2nd Lieut. of Inf. (10th), 19 Nov., 1892. Dropped 15 Sept., 1893.

FOY, ROBERT C.* [Born in Ala. Appointed from Ala.]
2nd Lieut. 8th Inf., 15 Feb., 1899. Trans. to 1st Cav., 26 Dec., 1899.

FRANCIS, SIMEON. [Born in Conn. Appointed from Ore.]
Maj. and P. M., 3 Aug., 1861. Retired 18 Oct., 1867. Died 25 Oct., 1872.

FRANK, ROYAL T.* [Born in Me. Appointed from Me.]
Bvt. 2nd Lieut. 5th Inf., 1 July, 1858. 2nd Lieut. 8th Inf., 19 Oct., 1858. 1st Lieut., 14 May, 1861. Capt., 27 Feb., 1862. Bvt. Maj., 3 July, 1862, for gallant and meritorious service during the Peninsular campaign. Bvt. Lieut. Col., 13 Dec., 1862, for gallant and meritorious service in the Battle of Fredericksburg, Va. Trans. to 1st Art., 15 Dec., 1870. Maj., 2 Jan., 1881. Lieut. Col. 2nd Art., 25 Jan., 1889. Col. 1st Art., 25 Oct., 1894. Brig. Gen. Vols., 4 May, 1898, to 12 May, 1899. Brig. Gen., 17 Oct., 1899. Retired, over 30 years' service, 18 Oct., 1899.

FRANKLIN, THOMAS. [Born in Md. Appointed from Army.]
Priv., Corpl., Sergt. and 1st Sergt. Co. A, and Sergt. Maj. 18th Inf., 10 Dec., 1892, to 28 March, 1897. 2nd Lieut. 23rd Inf., 2 March, 1897. 1st Lieut., 2 March, 1899.

FRANKLIN, WALTER S. [Born in Pa. Appointed from Pa.]
1st Lieut. 12th Inf., 14 May, 1861. R. Q. M., 29 July, 1862, to 6 Feb., 1863. Lieut. Col. A. I. G., 1 March to 28 July, 1865. Capt. 12th Inf., 6 Feb., 1863. Trans. to 21st Inf., 21 Sept., 1866. Unassigned 24 June, 1869. Discharged 30 Sept., 1870. Bvt. Maj., 19 Oct., 1864, for faithful and meritorious service in the field during the campaign before Richmond and in the Shenandoah Valley. Bvt. Lieut. Col., 2 April, 1865, for meritorious service at the capture of Petersburg, Va.

FRANKLIN, WM. B.* [Born in Pa. Appointed from Pa.]
Bvt. 2nd Lieut. Top. Eng., 1 July, 1843. 2nd Lieut., 21 Sept., 1846. 1st Lieut., 3 March, 1853. Capt., 1 July, 1857. Col. 12th Inf., 14 May, 1861. Brig. Gen. Vols., 17 May, 1861. Maj. Gen. Vols., 4 July, 1862. Resigned from Vols., 10 Nov., 1865. Resigned 15 March, 1866. Bvt. 1st Lieut., 23 Feb., 1847, for gallant and meritorious conduct at Buena Vista. Bvt. Brig. Gen., 30 June, 1862, for gallant and meritorious conduct in the Battle before Richmond, Va. Bvt. Maj. Gen., 13 March, 1865, for gallant and meritorious service in the field during the war.

FRANKS, SAML. J. [Born in Pa. Appointed from Pa.]
2nd Lieut. 8th Inf., 6 March, 1862. Resigned 15 Aug., 1864.

FRANTZ, JOHN H. [Born in Pa. Appointed from Md.]
1st Lieut. Asst. Surg., 28 May, 1861. Bvt. Capt., Maj. and Lieut. Col., 13 March,

1865, for faithful and meritorious service during the war. Capt. Asst. Surg., 28 May, 1866. Maj. Surg., 19 Dec., 1867. Died 2 March, 1882.

FRASER, DONALD. [Born in N. Y. Appointed from N. Y.]
Ensign 15th Inf., 12 March, 1812. 2nd Lieut., 13 March, 1813. Asst. D. P. M. G., 4 Aug., 1813, to 17 March, 1814. 1st Lieut. 15th Inf., 31 Dec., 1813. Trans. to 8th Inf., 17 May, 1815. Trans. to Corps Art., 13 March, 1816. Resigned 1 Nov., 1816. Maj. P. M., 29 Oct., 1836. Resigned 17 Nov., 1841. Bvt. Capt., 25 July 1814, for gallant conduct at the Battle of Niagara. Bvt. Maj., 17 Sept., 1814, for gallant and meritorious conduct in the Sortie from Fort Erie.

FRASER, UPTON S. [Born in N. Y. Appointed from N. J.]
Ensign 15th Inf., 31 May, 1814. 3rd Lieut., 1 Oct., 1814. Trans. to Corps Art., 17 May, 1815. 2nd Lieut., 1 Dec., 1816. 1st Lieut., 20 Oct., 1818. Trans. to 3rd Art., 1 June, 1821. Capt., 1 May, 1828. Massacred 28 Dec., 1835, by Indians in Florida.

FRASER, WM. D.* [Born in N. Y. Appointed from N. Y.]
(Graduated as Wm. Smith.) Bvt. 2nd Lieut. Eng., 1 July, 1834. 2nd Lieut., 21 Sept., 1836. Capt., 7 July, 1838. Died 27 July, 1856. Bvt. Maj., 30 May, 1848, for gallant and meritorious conduct while serving in the enemy's country.

FRAZER, JOHN W.* [Born in Tenn. Appointed from Miss.]
Bvt. 2nd Lieut. 2nd Inf., 1 July, 1849. 2nd Lieut., 30 June, 1850. 1st Lieut. 9th Inf., 3 March, 1855. Capt., 1 May, 1857. Resigned 15 March, 1861.

FRAZER, WM.* [Born in Pa. Appointed from Pa.]
Bvt. 2nd Lieut. 3rd Art., 1 July, 1836. 2nd Lieut., 31 Aug., 1836. 1st Lieut., 7 July, 1838. Died 27 June, 1844.

FRAZIER, JOSEPH.* [Born in Mo. Appointed from Mo.]
2nd Lieut. 19th Inf., 12 June, 1891. 1st Lieut. 9th Inf., 16 Jan., 1898. Graduate of the Infantry and Cavalry School, 1897.

FREDBERG, ALFRED. [Born in Denmark. Appointed from N. Y.]
Ensign 1st N. Y. Vols., 24 April, 1861. 1st Lieut., 5 Nov., 1861. Capt., 13 Sept., 1862. Mustered out 25 May, 1863. Capt. 84th U. S. Col. Inf., 29 Oct., 1863, to 23 May, 1865. Maj. A. A. G. Vols., 31 Dec., 1864. Bvt. Lieut. Col. Vols., 26 March, 1865, for faithful and meritorious services during campaign against City of Mobile. Mustered out 12 Jan., 1866. 2nd Lieut. 19th Inf., 23 Feb., 1866. 1st Lieut., 23 Feb., 1866. Reg. Adj., 14 May, 1870, to 7 Oct., 1873. Died 7 Oct., 1873.

FREDERICK, CALVIN H. [Born in N. Y. Appointed from Mo.]
Lieut. Col. 59th Ill. Vols., 17 June, 1861. Resigned 23 Jan., 1863. Lieut. Col. Vet. Res. Corps, 25 Sept., 1863. Bvt. Col. Vols., 13 March, 1865, for faithful and meritorious service in all the campaigns of the Southwest and for conspicuous discipline and gallantry at the Battle of Pea Ridge, Ark. Mustered out 19 Nov., 1866. 1st Lieut. 45th Inf., 28 July, 1866. Trans. to 14th Inf., 22 July, 1869. Discharged 1 Dec., 1870. Bvt. Capt., 2 March, 1867, for gallant and meritorious service in the Battle of Pea Ridge, Ark. Bvt. Maj., 2 March, 1867, for gallant and meritorious service in the Battle of Stone River, Tenn.

FREDERICK, DANIEL A.* [Born in Ga. Appointed from Ga.]
Addl. 2nd Lieut. 10th Inf., 15 June, 1877. 2nd Lieut. 7th Inf., 9 Aug., 1877. 1st Lieut., 14 Nov., 1885. Capt., 28 Jan., 1897. Maj. 45th U. S. Vols., 17 Aug., 1899.

FREEDLEY, HENRY W.* [Born in Pa. Appointed from Pa.]
Bvt. 2nd Lieut. 9th Inf., 1 July, 1855. 2nd Lieut. 3rd Inf., 30 Sept., 1855. 1st Lieut., 31 March, 1861. Capt. 16th Inf., 14 May, 1861 (declined). Capt. 3rd Inf., 14 May, 1861. Bvt. Maj., 3 May, 1863, for gallant and meritorious service in the Battle of Chancellorsville, Va. Bvt. Lieut. Col., 2 July, 1863, for gallant and meritorious service in the Battle of Gettysburg, Pa. Maj. 39th Inf., 28 July, 1863 (declined). Maj. 14th Inf., 31 Dec., 1867. Retired with rank of Col., 25 Sept., 1868, and with rank of Maj., 3 March, 1875. Died 3 Nov., 1889.

FREELAND, CHARLES W. [Born in Canada. Appointed from Va.]
Post Chap., 18 July, 1892.

FREELAND, HARRY.* [Born in Md. Appointed from Md.]
2nd Lieut. 3rd Inf., 1 July, 1886. 1st Lieut. 5th Inf., 4 July, 1892. Trans. to 3rd Inf., 12 Aug., 1892. Capt., 2 March, 1899.

FREELAND, NELSON. [Born in Va. Appointed from Va.]
2nd Lieut. Light Art., 4 April, 1813. 1st Lieut., 21 Feb., 1814. Resigned 30 Sept., 1816.

FREELON, THOS. H. [Born in Vt. Appointed from Mich.]
1st Lieut. of Inf., 2 March, 1847; 15th Inf., 9 April, 1847. R. Q. M., 1 July, to 1 Sept., 1847. Capt., 4 Dec., 1847. Disbanded 6 Aug., 1848. Bvt. Capt., 13 Sept., 1847, for gallant and meritorious conduct at Chapultepec, Mex.

FREEMAN, ALEXR. H. [Born in Pa. Appointed from Pa.]
2nd Lieut. 6th Inf., 5 Aug., 1861. 1st Lieut., 27 June, 1862. Resigned 31 Oct., 1866. Bvt. Capt., 3 May, 1863, for gallant and meritorious service at the Battle of Chancellorsville, Va.

FREEMAN, CHAS. M. [Born in N. Y. Appointed from N. Y.]
2nd Lieut. 2nd Inf., 5 Aug., 1861. 1st Lieut., 1 Nov., 1861. Capt., 20 Oct., 1863. Wholly retired 18 April, 1866. Bvt. Maj., 13 Oct., 1865, for faithful service.

FREEMAN, CONSTANT.* [Born in Md. Appointed from Md.]
2nd Lieut. 4th Inf., 1 July, 1838. Died 17 Sept., 1839.

FREEMAN, EDMUND. [Born in Mass. Appointed from Mass.]
2nd Lieut. 5th Inf., 7 June, 1855. 1st Lieut., 27 March, 1861. Retired 26 Oct., 1861. Died 18 Sept., 1865.

FREEMAN, GEORGE D., Jr. [Born in Ohio. Appointed from Ohio.]
2nd Lieut. 19th Inf., 10 April, 1899.

FREEMAN, HENRY B. [Born in Ohio. Appointed from Army.]
Priv. Co. G, 10th Inf., 16 July, 1855. Discharged 5 Feb., 1856. Priv. Co. B, 2nd Batt. 18th Inf., 8 July, 1861. 1st Sergt., — —, —. 2nd Lieut. 18th Inf., 30 Oct., 1861. 1st Lieut., 30 May, 1862. Bvt. Capt., 31 Dec., 1862, for gallant and meritorious service in the Battle of Murfreeboro', Tenn. Adj. 1st Batt. 18th Inf., 16 March, 1863, to 1 Nov., 1865. Bvt. Maj., 20 Sept., 1863, for gallant and meritorious

service in the Battle of Chickamauga, Ga. Capt. 18th Inf., 28 July, 1866. Trans. to 27th Inf., 21 Sept., 1866. Unassigned 14 June, 1869. Ass'd to 7th Inf., 7 Jan., 1870. Maj. 16th Inf., 19 June, 1891. Lieut. Col. 5th Inf., 30 Jan., 1895. Col. 24th Inf., 4 Oct., 1898. Medal of Honor for distinguished gallantry in the Battle of Stone River, Tenn., 31 Dec., 1862, voluntarily going to the front and picking up and carrying to a place of safety, under a heavy fire from the advancing enemy, an acting field officer who had been wounded and was about to fall into the enemy's hands; while serving as 1st Lieut. 18th Inf.

FREEMAN, JONATHAN.* [Born in N. J. Appointed from N. J.]
Bvt. 2nd Lieut. 6th Inf., 1 July, 1829. 2nd Lieut., 1 July, 1829. Resigned 15 May, 1837. Died 1854.

FREEMAN, SAMUEL D.* [Born in Va. Appointed from N. C.]
2nd Lieut. 10th Cav., 13 June, 1883. 1st Lieut., 20 Aug., 1889. Capt. 5th Cav., 14 Feb., 1899. Trans. to 10th Cav., 14 March, 1899.

FREEMAN, WM. G.* [Born in Va. Appointed from Va.]
Bvt. 2nd Lieut. 4th Art., 1 July, 1834. 2nd Lieut., 8 June, 1836. Capt. Creek Vols., 1 Sept., 1836. Maj. Creek Vols., 1 June to 18 Sept., 1837. 1st Lieut., 7 July, 1838. Capt., 13 Sept., 1847. Bvt. Capt. A. A. G., 2 Dec., 1841. Bvt. Maj. A. A. G., 3 March, 1847. Resigned 31 March, 1856. Bvt. 1st Lieut., 21 Nov., 1836, for gallant services in the war against the Florida Indians. Bvt. Lieut. Col., 30 May, 1848, for meritorious conduct in the war with Mexico. Died 12 Nov., 1866.

FREMONT, FRANCIS P. [Born in D. C. Appointed from Ariz.]
2nd Lieut. 3rd Inf., 1 Sept., 1879. 1st Lieut., 20 April, 1886. Reg. Adj., 24 May, 1888, to — —, —. Capt. 2nd Inf., 26 April, 1898. Capt. A. A. G. Vols., 12 May, 1898, to 9 Oct., 1898.

FREMONT, JOHN C. [Born in S. C. Appointed from S. C.]
2nd Lieut. Top. Engs., 7 July, 1838. Maj. Batty Cal. Vols., 23 July to 27 Oct., 1840. Lieut. Col. Mtd. Rifles, 27 May, 1846. Resigned 15 March, 1848. Maj. Gen., 14 May, 1861. Resigned 4 June, 1864. Bvt. Capt., 31 July, 1844, for gallant and highly meritorious services in two expeditions commanded by himself—the first to the Rocky Mountains, which terminated 17 Oct., 1842,—the second, beyond those mountains, which terminated 31 July, 1844. Maj. Gen. retired, 28 April, 1890. Died 13 July, 1890.

FREMONT, SEWALL L.* [Born in Vt. Appointed from N. H.]
(Graduated as Sewall L. Fish.) 2nd Lieut. 3rd Art., 1 July, 1841. 1st Lieut., 11 May, 1846. Capt. A. Q. M., 3 March, 1847, to 19 Feb., 1849. Resigned 5 April, 1854. Died 1 May, 1886.

FRENCH, CHARLES G.* [Born in Mass. Appointed from Mass.]
Addl. 2nd Lieut. 20th Inf., 11 June, 1888. 2nd Lieut. 25th Inf., 1 Sept., 1888. 1st Lieut. 15th Inf., 31 Dec., 1895. Capt. 7th Inf., 5 May, 1899.

FRENCH, DANIEL. [Born in Ohio. Appointed from Ohio.]
2nd Lieut. 15th Inf., 9 April, 1847. 1st Lieut., 20 July, 1847. Disbanded 4 Aug., 1848. Bvt. Capt., 13 Sept., 1847, for gallant and meritorious conduct at Chapultepec. 2nd Lieut. 65th Ohio Vols., 4 Oct., 1861. Capt., 6 Nov., 1861. Lieut. Col., 30 Nov., 1861. Resigned 8 Aug., 1862. Col. 120th Ohio Vols., 17 Oct., 1862. Resigned 18 Feb., 1863.

FRENCH, EDMUND.* [Born in Conn. Appointed from Conn.]
Bvt. 2nd Lieut. 1st Art., 1 July, 1828. 2nd Lieut., 1 July, 1828. 1st Lieut., 25 Feb., 1835. Resigned 3 May, 1836. Died 7 July, 1860.

FRENCH, FRANCIS H.* [Born in Ind. Appointed from Ind.]
2nd Lieut. 19th Inf., 13 June, 1879. 1st Lieut., 24 March, 1888. Capt., 26 Nov., 1894.

FRENCH, F. HALVERSON.* [Born in Va. Appointed at Large.]
Addl. 2nd Lieut. 3rd Cav., 15 June, 1877. 2nd Lieut., 18 May, 1878. 1st Lieut., 26 June, 1881. Wholly retired 27 Jan., 1885.

FRENCH, FRANK S. [Born in Me. Appointed at Large.]
2nd Lieut. 1st Art., 27 Sept., 1861. 1st Lieut., 20 Feb., 1862. Died 4 Sept., 1865. Bvt. Capt., 13 March, 1865, for gallant and good conduct at the Battle of Fair Oaks, Va. Bvt. Maj., 13 March, 1865, for gallant and good conduct at the Battle of Antietam, Md. Bvt. Lieut. Col., 13 March, 1865, for gallant and good conduct at the Battle of Cold Harbor, Va.

FRENCH, GEORGE E. [Born in Mass. Appointed from Army.]
Priv., Corpl. and Sergt. Co. A. 1st Inf., 14 April, 1884, to 22 Oct., 1886. 2nd Lieut. 4th Inf., 22 Oct., 1886. 1st Lieut. 5th Inf., 1 March, 1894. Trans. to 4th Inf., 12 April, 1894. Capt. 16th Inf., 2 March, 1899. Graduate of the Infantry and Cavalry School, 1891.

FRENCH, HOWARD W. [Born in N. Y. Appointed from Army.]
Priv. and Corpl. Troop G. 1st Cav., 7 Sept., 1892, to 24 March, 1896. 1st Lieut. of Inf., 15 Aug., 1898. Ass'd to 17th Inf., 1 Jan., 1899.

FRENCH, J. HANSELL.* [Born in Pa. Appointed from La.]
2nd Lieut. 9th Cav., 17 June, 1874. Resigned 31 Aug., 1876. 2nd Lieut. 9th Cav., 10 Aug., 1878. Killed 17 Jan., 1880, in action with Indians in New Mexico.

FRENCH, JOHN T., Jr.* [Born in Mass. Appointed from Mass.]
2nd Lieut. 4th Art., 15 June, 1876. 1st Lieut., 23 Sept., 1885. Capt. A. Q. M., 25 April, 1895. Maj. Q. M. Vols., 6 July, 1899. Graduate of the Artillery School, 1880.

FRENCH, JOHN W. [Born in D. C. Appointed at Large.]
Priv. Co. F, 7th N. Y. State Militia, 17 April, 1861. Discharged 3 June, 1861. 2nd Lieut. 8th Inf., 24 Oct., 1861. Bvt. 1st Lieut., 19 Aug., 1864, for gallant and meritorious service in Battle on Weldon Railroad, Va. Bvt. Capt., 28 Oct., 1864, for gallant and meritorious service in the Battle of Hatcher's Run, Va. 1st Lieut. 8th Inf., 9 Jan., 1866. R. Adj., 31 Jan., 1866, to 20 Nov., 1866. Capt. 40th Inf., 28 July, 1866. Trans. to 25th Inf., 20 April, 1869. Maj. 14th Inf., 1 Nov., 1891. Lieut. Col. 23rd Inf., 5 July, 1895. Col. 22nd Inf., 26 March, 1899.

FRENCH, JOHN W. [Born in Tex. Appointed from Army.]
Priv., Corpl. and Sergt. Co. C, 21st Inf., 16 May, 1895, to 17 July, 1898. 2nd Lieut. 11th Inf., 22 June, 1898. 1st Lieut., 2 March, 1899. Trans. to 19th Inf., 4 May, 1899.

FRENCH, ROBT. [Born in D. C. Appointed from D. C.]
Post Surg., 12 April, 1820. Asst. Surg., 1 June, 1821. Died 13 Aug., 1835.

FRENCH, SAML. G.* [Born in N. J. Appointed from N. J.]
Bvt. 2nd Lieut. 3rd Art., 1 July, 1843. 2nd Lieut., 18 June, 1846. 1st Lieut., 3 March, 1847. Capt. A. Q. M., 12 Jan., 1848. Resigned 31 May, 1856. Bvt. 1st Lieut., 23 Sept., 1846, for gallant and meritorious conduct at Monterey. Bvt. Capt., 23 Feb., 1847, for gallant and meritorious conduct at Buena Vista.

FRENCH, THOS. H. [Born in Md. Appointed from Army.]
Priv. 10th Inf., 13 Jan., 1864, to 9 June, 1864. 2nd Lieut. 10th Inf., 18 May, 1864. 1st Lieut., 23 June, 1864. Bvt. Capt., 18 Aug., 1864, for gallant service during the operations on the Weldon Railroad. Capt. 44th Inf., 28 July, 1866 (declined). Capt. 10th Inf., 26 March, 1868. Unassigned 19 May, 1869. Ass'd to 7th Cav., 1 Jan., 1871. Retired 5 Feb., 1880. Died 27 March, 1882.

FRENCH, WILLIAM E. P. [Born in N. Y. Appointed from N. Y.]
2nd Lieut. 3rd Inf., 1 Sept., 1879. 1st Lieut., 12 Sept., 1885. Capt., 26 April, 1898. Trans. to 2nd Inf., 15 Nov., 1899. Retired for disability, 2 Feb., 1900.

FRENCH, WM. H.* [Born in Md. Appointed from D. C.]
2nd Lieut. 1st Art., 1 July, 1837. 1st Lieut., 9 July, 1838. Bvt. Capt., 18 April, 1847, for gallant and meritorious conduct in the Battle of Cerro Gordo. Bvt. Maj., 20 Aug., 1847, for gallant and meritorious conduct in the Battles of Contreras and Churubusco. Capt. 1st Art., 22 Sept., 1848. Brig. Gen. Vols., 28 Sept., 1861. Maj. 2nd Art., 26 Oct., 1861. Bvt. Lieut. Col., 1 June, 1862, for gallant and meritorious service in the Battle of Fair Oaks, Va. Bvt. Col., 17 Sept., 1862, for gallant and meritorious service in the Battle of Antietam, Md. Maj. Gen. Vols., 29 Nov., 1862. Lieut. Col. 2nd Art., 8 Feb., 1864. Mustered out of Vol. service, 6 May, 1864. Bvt. Brig. Gen., 13 March, 1865, for gallant and meritorious service in the Battle of Chancellorsville, Va. Bvt. Maj. Gen., 13 March, 1865, for gallant and meritorious service during the war. Col. 4th Art., 2 July, 1877. Retired 1 July, 1880. Died 2 May, 1881.

FRENCH, WM. H., Jr. [Born in R. I. Appointed from Del.]
1st Lieut. 57th N. Y. Vols., 8 March, 1862. Trans. to 61st N. Y. Vols., 2 Dec., 1864. Mustered out 12 March, 1865. 2nd Lieut. 19th Inf., 28 July, 1866. 1st Lieut., 6 May, 1868. Unassigned 31 March, 1869. Discharged 15 Oct., 1870. Bvt. Capt., 2 March, 1867, for gallant and meritorious service in the Battle of Cold Harbor, Va.

FREUDENBERG, CHARLES G. [Born in Germany. Appointed from N. Y.]
Capt. 52nd N. Y. Vols., 1 Nov., 1861. Maj., 2 Nov., 1861. Lieut. Col., 24 Nov., 1862. Maj. Vet. Res. Corps, 26 Nov., 1863. Resigned as Lieut. Col. 52nd N. Y. Vols., 11 Dec., 1863. Lieut. Col. Vet. Res. Corps, 22 April, 1864. Bvt. Col. Vols., 13 March, 1865, for gallant and meritorious service during the war. Mustered out 9 March, 1866. Capt. 45th Inf., 28 July, 1866. Bvt. Maj., 2 March, 1867, for gallant and meritorious service in the Battle of Fair Oaks, V. Bvt. Lieut. Col., 2 March, 1867, for gallant and meritorious service in the Battle of Gettysburg, Pa. Trans. to 14th Inf., 22 July, 1869. Retired 15 Dec., 1870. Retired, with rank of Lieut. Col., 3 March, 1877. Died 28 Aug., 1885.

FRICK, EUCLID B. [Born in Pa. Appointed from Pa.]
Asst. Surg., 29 Oct., 1889. Capt. Asst. Surg., 29 Oct., 1894.

FRICK, JACOB G. [Born in Pa. Appointed from Pa.]
2nd Lieut. 3rd Ohio Vols., 25 June, 1846. Mustered out 23 June, 1847. 2nd Lieut. 11th Inf., 29 March, 1848. Disbanded 14 Aug., 1848. Lieut. Col. 96th Pa. Vols., 3 Sept., 1861. Resigned 29 July, 1862. Col. 129th Pa. Vols., 15 Aug., 1862. Mustered out 18 May, 1863.

FRIER, JAMES H.* [Born in Mo. Appointed from Mo.]
2nd Lieut. 17th Inf., 1 July, 1886. 1st Lieut. 12th Inf., 26 Jan., 1893. Trans. to 17th Inf., 24 Feb., 1893. Capt., 2 March, 1899.

FRIES, AMOS A. [Born in Wis. Appointed from Ore.]
Addl. 2nd Lieut. Eng., 26 April, 1898. 2nd Lieut., 5 July, 1898.

FRISSELL, THOMAS T.* [Born in Mo. Appointed from Mo.]
Addl. 2nd Lieut. 23rd Inf., 11 June, 1897. 2nd Lieut. 3rd Inf., 15 Oct., 1897. 1st Lieut., 2 March, 1899.

FRITH, ROBERT E. [Born in Ill. Appointed from Ill.]
2nd Lieut. 24th Inf., 9 July, 1898.

FROHOCK, WM. T. [Born in Maine. Appointed from Ill.]
Priv. Co. F, 3rd Batt. D. C. Vols., 29 April, 1861. Mustered out 24 July, 1861. 1st Lieut. and Adj. 45th Ill. Vols., 26 Dec., 1861. Capt., 18 May, 1863. Col. 66th U. S. Col. Inf., 13 Jan., 1864. Resigned 20 Sept., 1864. Maj. 7th U. S. Vet. Vols., 26 March, 1865. Bvt. Lieut. Col. and Col. of Vols., 13 March, 1865, for gallant and meritorious service during the war, and Brig. Gen. Vols., 13 March, 1865, for faithful and meritorious services during the war. Mustered out 10 April, 1866. 1st Lieut. 15th Inf., 28 July, 1866. Capt. 9th Cav., 7 March, 1867. Resigned 31 May, 1870. Bvt. Capt. and Bvt. Maj., 2 March, 1867, for gallant and meritorious service in the Battle of Shiloh, Tenn. Bvt. Lieut. Col., 2 March, 1867, for gallant and meritorious service in the Siege of Vicksburg, Miss.

FROST, ALFRED S. [Born in Ill. Appointed from Army.]
Priv., Corpl. and Sergt. Co. A, 11th Inf., 13 Sept., 1881, to 6 Aug., 1884. 2nd Lieut. 25th Inf., 4 Aug., 1884. 1st Lieut. 7th Inf., 10 July, 1891. Trans. to 25th Inf., 20 July, 1891. Capt. of Inf., 14 Dec., 1898. Ass'd to 22nd Inf., 1 Jan., 1899. Col. 1st S. Dak. Inf., 19 May, 1898, to 5 Oct., 1899. Maj. 39th U. S. Inf., 17 Aug. (declined). Graduate of the Infantry and Cavalry School, 1891. Maj. P. M., 3 Feb., 1900. Retired for disability, 14 Feb., 1900.

FROST, DANIEL M.* [Born in N. Y. Appointed from N. Y.]
Bvt. 2nd Lieut. 1st Art., 1 July, 1844. Trans. to Mtd. Rifles, 17 July, 1846. 2nd Lieut., 16 Feb., 1847. R. Q. M., 18 March, 1847, to 4 Nov., 1851. 1st Lieut., 31 Oct., 1848. Expired 3 March, 1849. 1st Lieut., 30 Nov., 1850. Resigned 31 May, 1853. Bvt. 1st Lieut., 18 April, 1847, for gallant and meritorious conduct at Cerro Gordo.

FROST, JAMES A. [Born in Md. Appointed from Md.]
2nd Lieut. of Inf., 23 Feb., 1847; Voltigeurs, 9 April, 1847. 1st Lieut., 31 Dec., 1847. Disbanded 25 Aug., 1848.

FRY, BIRKETT D. [Born in Va. Appointed from Va.]
1st Lieut. of Inf., 24 Feb., 1847; Voltigeurs, 9 April, 1847. Reg. Adj., 15 June to 20 Aug., 1847. Disbanded 31 Aug., 1848.

FRY, CARY H.* [Born in Ky. Appointed from Ky.]
Bvt. 2nd Lieut. 3rd Inf., 1 July, 1834. 2nd Lieut., 31 Aug., 1835. Resigned 31 Oct., 1836. Maj. 2nd Ky Vols., 9 June, 1846. Mustered out 9 June, 1847. Maj. and P. M., 7 Feb., 1853. Lieut. Col. D. P. M. G., 28 July, 1866. Died 5 March, 1873. Bvt. Lieut. Col., 13 March, 1865, for faithful and meritorious service during the war. Bvt. Col. and Bvt. Brig. Gen., 15 Oct., 1867, for faithful and meritorious service during the war.

FRY, JAMES B.* [Born in Ill. Appointed from Ill.]
Bvt. 2nd Lieut. 3rd Art., 1 July, 1847. 2nd Lieut. 1st Art., 20 Aug., 1847. 1st Lieut., 22 Feb., 1851. Bvt. Capt. A. A. G., 16 March, 1861. Vacated commission of 1st Lieut. 1st Art., 14 May, 1861. Capt. A. A. G., 3 Aug., 1861. Col. A. A. de C., 14 Nov., 1861. Maj. A. A. G., 22 April, 1862. Lieut. Col. A. A. G., 31 Dec., 1862. Col. Provost Marshal Gen., 17 March, 1863. Brig. Gen. Provost Marshal Gen., 21 April, 1864. Bvt. Col., 13 March, 1865, for gallant and meritorious service in the Battle of Bull Run (1st), Va. Bvt. Brig. Gen., 13 March, 1865, for gallant and meritorious service in the Battles of Shiloh, Tenn., and Perryville, Ky. Bvt. Maj. Gen., 13 March, 1865, for faithful, meritorious and distinguished service in the Provost Marshal Gen. Dept. during the war. Commission of Provost Marshal Gen. expired by law, 27 Aug., 1866. Col. A. A. G., 3 March, 1875. Retired, for over 30 years' service, 1 July, 1881. Died 11 July, 1894.

FRYER, BLENCOWE E. [Born in England. Appointed from Pa.]
1st Lieut. Asst. Surg., 28 May, 1861. Bvt. Capt. and Bvt. Maj., 13 March, 1865, for faithful and meritorious service during the war. Capt. Asst. Surg., 28 May, 1866. Maj. and Surg., 30 Oct., 1867. Lieut. Col. A. M. P., 28 Aug., 1890. Retired, for disability in line of duty, 24 Feb., 1891.

FUGER FREDK. [Born in Germany. Appointed from Army.]
Priv. Co. A, 4th Art., 21 Aug., 1856. Corpl., 1 Aug., 1859. Discharged 21 July, 1861. Corpl. Co. A, 4th Art., 21 July, 1861. Sergt., 6 Nov., 1861. 1st Sergt., 16 July, 1862. 2nd Lieut. 4th Art., 31 Oct., 1863. Bvt. 1st Lieut., 11 May, 1864, for gallant and meritorious service in the Battle of Yellow Tavern, Va. Bvt. Capt., 31 March, 1865, for gallant and meritorious service in the Battle of Dinwiddie Court House, Va. 1st Lieut. 4th Art., 21 Dec., 1865. R. Q. M., 1 Aug., 1875. Capt., 5 March, 1887. Maj., 13 Feb., 1899. Medal of Honor for most distinguished gallantry in action at Gettysburg, Pa., 3 July, 1863; this officer, then a Sergt. with field Batty A, 4th U. S. Art., succeeded to the command of the Batty; all its officers having been killed or wounded and five of its guns disabled in Pickett's assault; with the most distinguished gallantry he fought the remaining guns until the Batty was ordered to be withdrawn.

FUGER, FREDERICK W. [Born in N. Y. Appointed from Mass.]
2nd Lieut. 13th Inf., 1 Aug., 1891. 1st Lieut., 26 April, 1898. Graduate of the Infantry and Cavalry School, 1895.

FULLER, ALFRED M.* [Born in Pa. Appointed from Pa.]
2nd Lieut. 10th Cav., 15 June, 1876. Trans. to 2nd Cav., 28 July, 1876. 1st Lieut., 27 March, 1883. Capt., 14 Aug., 1893. Bvt. 1st Lieut., 27 Feb., 1890.

FULLER, ALVARADO M. [Born in R. I. Appointed from Army.]
Priv. Co. B, 2nd Cav., 1 Jan., 1870. Corpl., 1 Sept., 1872. Sergt., 1 March, 1873. Discharged 1 Jan., 1875. Priv. 2nd Cav., 1 April, 1876. Sergt. Maj., 6 April, 1876. 2nd Lieut., 28 June, 1879. 1st Lieut., 28 Dec., 1888. Capt. 9th Cav., 13 July, 1898. Graduate of the Infantry and Cavalry School, 1885.

FULLER, CHAS. A.* [Born in Mass. Appointed from Mass.]
Bvt. 1st Lieut. 3rd Art., 1 July, 1834. 2nd Lieut. 2nd Art., 28 Feb., 1835. 1st Lieut., 31 Dec., 1836. Resigned 31 May, 1837.

FULLER, EZRA B.* [Born in Ill. Appointed from Ill.]
Priv. Co. E, 141st Ill. Vols., 17 May, 1864. Discharged 10 Oct., 1864. Priv. Co. M, 8th Ill. Cav., 26 Feb., 1865. Discharged 17 July, 1865. Cadet Mil. Acad., 1 July, 1869. 2nd Lieut. 8th Cav., 13 June, 1873. Trans. to 7th Cav., 26 June, 1876. 1st Lieut., 30 Sept., 1877. R. Q. M., 7 Nov., 1887, to ———. Capt., 22 March, 1892. Bvt. 1st Lieut., 27 Feb., 1890.

FULLER, LAWSON M.* [Born in Wis. Appointed from Wis.]
2nd Lieut. 9th Cav., 12 June, 1891. 1st Lieut. Ord., 10 Oct., 1894.

FULLER, LEIGH A. [Born in N. J. Appointed from N. J.]
Asst. Surg., 26 Oct., 1896.

FULTON, DAVID W.* [Born in Ohio. Appointed from Ill.]
2nd Lieut. 24th Inf., 1 July, 1886. Died 28 March, 1889.

FULLER, WM. D.* [Born in Me. Appointed from Me.]
Bvt. 2nd Lieut. and 2nd Lieut. 3rd Art., 24 June, 1861. 1st Lieut., 24 June, 1861. Capt., 1 Nov., 1867. Trans. to 21st Inf., 1 Jan., 1871. Resigned 22 July, 1872. Bvt. Capt., 5 May, 1862, for gallant and meritorious service at the Battle of Williamsburg, Va. Bvt. Maj., 3 July, 1863, for gallant and meritorious service at the Battle of Gettysburg, Pa. Died 11 March, 1886.

FULLWOOD, WM. E. [Born in Ga. Appointed from Ga.]
Asst. Surg., 1 Oct., 1840. Died 17 April, 1850.

FULMER, JESSE. [Born in Penn. Appointed from Penn.]
Priv. Co. A, 11th Pa. Vols., 24 April to 31 July, 1861. Capt. 15th Inf., 14 May, 1861. Resigned 28 March, 1866. Bvt. Maj., 7 June, 1865, for gallant service at the Battle of Stone River, Tenn.

FULTON, BENJAMIN F. [Born in La. Appointed from La.]
Capt. of Inf., 5 March, 1847; 14th Inf., 9 April, 1847. Resigned 21 Oct., 1847.

FULTON, WM. M. [Born in Va. Appointed from Va.]
Capt. 2nd Drag., 6 Oct., 1836. Resigned 31 March, 1846. Died 28 June, 1853.

FUNK, AUGUSTUS. [Born in Fla. Appointed from N. Y.]
Ensign 38th N. Y. Vols., 3 June, 1861. 1st Lieut., 6 Aug., 1861. Capt., 11 Jan., 1862. Maj., 19 Jan., 1863. Mustered out 22 June, 1863. Col. 39th N. Y. Vols., 20 Jan., 1864. Mustered out 1 July, 1865. 1st Lieut. 41st Inf., 28 July, 1866. R. Q. M., 2 May, 1867, to 31 May, 1868. Resigned 20 Nov., 1868. Bvt. Capt., 2 March, 1867, for gallant and meritorious service in the Battle of the Wilderness, Va. Bvt. Maj. and Lieut. Col., 2 March, 1867, for gallant and meritorious service during the war.

FUREY, JOHN V. [Born in N. Y. Appointed from N. Y.]
Priv. Co. C, 84th N. Y. Vols., 18 April, 1861. Mustered out 28 Sept., 1862. Capt. A. Q. M. Vols., 7 April, 1864. Bvt. Maj. Vols., 13 March, 1865, for meritorious service in the Q. M. D. during the war. Capt. A. Q. M., 18 Jan., 1867. Vacated commission of Capt. A. Q. M. Vols., 25 March, 1867. Maj. Q. M., 11 Nov., 1887. Lieut. Col. D. Q. M. G., 21 Aug., 1896. Col. Q. M. Vols., 12 July, 1898, to 2 March, 1899.

FURLONG, JOHN W.* [Born in N. J. Appointed from Pa.]
2nd Lieut. 1st Cav., 12 June, 1891. 1st Lieut. 6th Cav., 11 Dec., 1897.

FURLOW, JAMES W. [Born in Ga. Appointed from Army.]
Cadet Mil. Acad., 15 June, 1894, to 24 Jan., 1895. Priv. Troop K, 1st Cav. and Co. B, 5th Inf., 8 March, 1897, to 23 May, 1898. 1st Class Priv. and Corpl. Sig. Corps, 23 May, 1898, to 1 May, 1899. 2nd Lieut. 11th Inf., 5 April, 1899.

FURMAN, JOHN G.* [Born in S. C. Appointed from S. C.]
Bvt. 2nd Lieut. of Inf., 1 July, 1827. 2nd Lieut. 5th Inf., 1 July, 1827. Died 29 Aug., 1830.

GADSDEN, JAMES. [Born in S. C. Appointed from S. C.]
2nd Lieut. Eng., 2 Dec., 1812. 1st Lieut., 17 March, 1813. Capt., 15 April, 1818. Col. I. G., 1 Oct., 1820. Col. A. G., 13 Aug., 1821, which was not confirmed by Senate, and appointment expired 22 May, 1822. Asst. Eng., 10 Aug., 1831. Office abolished 1 Oct., 1833. Q. M. G. Fla. Vols., 1 Feb. to 30 April, 1836. Died 26 Dec., 1858.

GAEBEL, FREDERICK A. H. [Born in Prussia. Appointed from N. Y.]
Capt. 7th N. Y. Vols., 23 April, 1861. Maj., 8 Feb., 1862. Lieut. Col., 1 Nov., 1862. Mustered out 8 May, 1863. Maj. Vet. Res. Corps, 12 Nov., 1863. Bvt. Lieut. Col. Vols., 10 Dec., 1864. Mustered out 4 Jan., 1867. 1st Lieut. 45th Inf., 28 July, 1866. Died 12 Dec., 1868. Bvt. Capt., 2 March, 1867, for gallant and meritorious service at the Battle of Malvern Hill, Va. Bvt. Maj., 2 March, 1867, for gallant and meritorious service at the Battle of Fredericksburg, Va.

GAENSLEN, JOHN J. [Born in N. Y. Appointed from Va.]
Asst. Surg., 16 May, 1856. Resigned 17 Aug., 1861.

GAGEBY, JAMES H. [Born in Pa. Appointed from Army.]
Sergt. Co. K, 3rd Pa. Vols., 19 April, 1861. Discharged 30 July, 1861. 1st Sergt. Co. G, 1st Batt. 19th Inf., 25 Oct., 1861. 2nd Lieut. 19th Inf., 1 June, 1863. Bvt. 1st Lieut., 26 June, 1863, for gallant and meritorious service in action at Hoover's Gap, Tenn. Bvt. Capt., 25 Nov., 1863, for gallant and meritorious service in the Battle of Chattanooga, Tenn. 1st Lieut. 19th Inf., 28 Dec., 1863. Capt. 37th Inf., 28 July, 1866. Trans. to 3rd Inf., 11 Aug., 1869. Maj. 12th Inf., 4 July, 1892. Died 13 July, 1896.

GAILLARD, DAVID DuB.* [Born in S. C. Appointed from S. C.]
2nd Lieut. Eng., 15 June, 1884. 1st Lieut., 22 Oct., 1887. Capt., 25 Oct., 1895. Col. 3rd Vol. Eng., 7 June, 1898, to 17 May, 1899.

GAILLARD, JOHN S. [Born in S. C. Appointed from S. C.]
Mil. Storekeeper, 5 Dec., 1827. Died 12 Jan., 1834.

GAILLARD, PETER C.* [Born in S. C. Appointed from S. C.]
Bvt. 2nd Lieut. 1st Inf., 1 July, 1835. 2nd Lieut., 29 Oct., 1836. Resigned 30 April, 1838. Died 11 Jan., 1889.

GAILLARD, WM. W.* [Born in S. C. Appointed from S. C.]
Bvt. 2nd Lieut. 4th Inf., 1 July, 1821. Trans. to 6th Inf., 1 July, 1821. Died 11 Oct., 1822.

GAINES, AUGUSTUS W. [Born in Ky. Appointed from Ky.]
Maj. and P. M. Vols., 20 July, 1846. Maj. and P. M. U. S. A., 2 March, 1849. Died 19 Feb., 1860.

GAINES, EDMUND P. [Born in Va. Appointed from Tenn.]
Ensign 6th Inf., 10 Jan., 1799. 2nd Lieut., 3 March, 1799. Discharged 15 June, 1800. 2nd Lieut. 4th Inf., 16 Feb., 1801. Trans. to 2nd Inf., 1 April, 1802. 1st Lieut., 27 April, 1802. Capt., 28 Feb., 1807. Maj. 8th Inf., 24 March, 1812. Lieut. Col. 24th Inf., 6 July, 1812. Col. 25th Inf., 12 March, 1813. Col. and A. G., 1 Sept., 1813. Brig. Gen., 9 March, 1814. Bvt. Maj. Gen., 15 Aug., 1814, for his gallantry and good conduct in defeating the enemy at Fort Erie. Received the thanks of Congress 3 Nov., 1814, for gallantry and good conduct in defeating the enemy at Erie on the 15 Aug., in repelling with great slaughter the attack of the British veteran army, superior in numbers, and with the presentation of a gold medal emblematical of this triumph. Died 6 June, 1849.

GAINES, FRANCIS Y. [Born in Ala. Appointed from Ala.]
2nd Lieut. of Inf., 5 March, 1847; 3rd Drag., 9 April, 1847. Disbanded 31 July, 1848.

GAITHER, EDGAR B.* [Born in Ky. Appointed from Ky.]
2nd Lieut. 1st Drag., 1 July, 1839. Resigned 31 Oct., 1840. Capt. of Drag., 5 March, 1847; 3rd Drag., 9 April, 1847. Disbanded 31 July, 1848. Died 17 Sept., 1855.

GALBRAITH, JACOB G.* [Born in Minn. Appointed from Pa.]
2nd Lieut. 1st Cav., 15 June, 1877. 1st Lieut., 31 Oct., 1884. Capt., 27 Aug., 1895.

GALBRAITH, WM. W.* [Born in Pa. Appointed from Pa.]
2nd Lieut. 5th Art., 15 June, 1877. 1st Lieut., 23 Sept., 1885. Graduate of the Artillery School, 1884. Retired, with rank of Capt. for disability, 2 March, 1899.

GALBRAITH, ALVAN S. [Born in Ohio. Appointed from Ohio.]
Sergt. Co. F, 124th Ohio Vols., 12 Sept., 1862. 1st Lieut., 17 April, 1863. Capt., 8 Aug., 1864. Mustered out 9 July, 1865. 2nd Lieut. 18th Inf., 11 May, 1866. 1st Lieut., 22 Jan., 1867. Unassigned 26 April, 1869. Ass'd to 2nd Inf., 18 July, 1870. Resigned 18 Dec., 1873. Bvt. Capt., 2 March, 1867, for gallant and meritorious service in the action at Brown's Ferry, Tenn., 27 Oct., 1863. Bvt. Maj., 2 March, 1867, for gallant and meritorious service at the Battle of Nashville, Tenn.

GALE, GEORGE H. G.* [Born in Me. Appointed from Mass.]
2nd Lieut. 4th Cav., 13 June, 1879. 1st Lieut., 26 Nov., 1884. Capt., 2 July, 1892.

GALE, JAMES H. [Born in Md. Appointed from Md.]
Ensign 14th Inf., 12 March, 1812. 2nd Lieut., 13 March, 1813. 1st Lieut., 29 June, 1814. Trans. to 4th Inf., 17 May, 1815. Capt., 31 July, 1817. Trans. to 1st Inf., 1 June, 1821. Resigned 28 July, 1831.

GALE, JOHN. [Born in N. H. Appointed from N. H.]
Surg. Mate 23rd Inf., 6 July, 1812. Surg. 34th Inf., 31 Aug., 1814. Disbanded 15 June, 1815. Reinstated as Surg. Mate 3rd Inf., 13 Sept., 1815. Surg. Rifle Regiment, 18 April, 1818. Maj. and Surg., 1 June, 1821. Died 27 July, 1830.

GALE, LEVIN.* [Born in Md. Appointed from Md.]
Bvt. 2nd Lieut. 1st Inf., 1 July, 1827. 2nd Lieut., 1 July, 1827. Died 1 Sept., 1832.

GALLAGER, JOHN H. [Born in Pa. Appointed from Pa.]
Priv. Co. I, 18th Pa. Vols., 24 April to 6 Aug., 1861. Sergt. and 1st Sergt. Co. A, 106th Pa. Vols., 17 Aug., 1861, to 15 June, 1864. 1st Lieut. 106th Pa. Vols., 15 June, 1864. Capt., 26 Jan., 1865. Mustered out 30 June, 1865. 2nd Lieut. 14th Inf., 23 Feb., 1866. 1st Lieut., 23 Feb., 1866. Trans. to 32nd Inf., 21 Sept., 1866. Capt., 30 Sept., 1868. Unassigned 19 April, 1869. Mustered out 1 Jan., 1871. Died 2 Jan., 1872.

GALLAGHER, HUGH J.* [Born in Canada. Appointed from Iowa.]
2nd Lieut. 6th Cav., 15 June, 1884. 1st Lieut. 8th Cav., 20 April, 1891. Trans. to 6th Cav., 27 April, 1891. Capt. 3rd Cav., 8 May, 1899. Maj. C. S. Vols., 20 May, 1898. Lieut. Col. C. S. Vols., 9 Sept., 1898, to 2 March, 1899.

GALLAGHER, JOSEPH S. [Born in N. Y. Appointed from N. Y.]
2nd Lieut. Corps Art., 4 Oct., 1820. Trans. to 2nd Inf., 1 June, 1821. 1st Lieut., 2 Feb., 1830. Resigned 28 June, 1836. Died 12 April, 1877.

GALLAGHER, M. FRANK. [Born in Mich. Appointed from Mich.]
1st Lieut. 1st Mich. Cav., 8 Aug., 1861. Capt., 5 July, 1862. Maj. 9th Mich. Cav., 12 Nov., 1862. Discharged 9 Feb., 1864. Lieut. Col. 7th U. S. Vet. Vols., 27 March, 1865. Bvt. Col. Vols., 13 March, 1865, for distinguished gallantry and efficient service. Mustered out 8 May, 1866. 2nd Lieut. 16th Inf., 11 May, 1866. Trans. to 2nd Inf., 17 April, 1869. R. Q. M., 20 April, 1869, to 26 Dec., 1870, and Reg. Adj., 26 Dec., 1870, to 21 Dec., 1871. Dismissed 19 July, 1873. Bvt. 1st Lieut. and Bvt. Capt., 2 March, 1867, for distinguished gallantry and good service during the war.

GALLOUPE, DWIGHT E. [Born in ——. Appointed from N. J.]
Post Chap., — May, 1898. Resigned 27 Oct., 1898.

GALLOWAY, JAMES P. [Born in Ohio. Appointed from Army.]
Priv. 18th Inf., 5 Sept. to 4 Nov., 1861. 2nd Lieut. 18th Inf., 30 Oct., 1861. Rejected by Senate, 26 March, 1862.

GALLOWAY, WM. G. [Born in Ohio. Appointed from Army.]
Priv. 15th Inf., 11 Sept., 1861, to 19 May, 1862. 2nd Lieut. 15th Inf., 24 March, 1862. 1st Lieut., 31 Dec., 1862. Capt., 23 April, 1867. Discharged 15 Aug., 1867. Bvt. Capt., 20 Sept., 1863, for gallant and meritorious service at the Battle of Chickamauga, Ga.

GALLUP, CHARLES C.* [Born in N. Y. Appointed from N. Y.]
2nd Lieut. 5th Art., 11 June, 1888. 1st Lieut. of Art. (3rd), 28 May, 1894. Trans. to 5th Art., 10 Oct., 1896. Died 23 Sept., 1897.

GALLUP, FRED H.* [Born in Iowa. Appointed from Iowa.]
2nd Lieut. 4th Art., 15 Feb., 1899.

GALLUPE, GEORGE S. [Born in N. Y. Appointed from Pa.]
1st Lieut. 8th Pa. Res. Vet. Corps, 17 April, 1861. Capt., 29 July, 1861. Maj., 2 Nov., 1863. Mustered out 24 May, 1864. Col. 5th Pa. Art., 10 Sept., 1864. Mustered out 30 June, 1865. Capt. 43rd Inf., 28 July, 1866. Appointment revoked 30 Nov., 1866. Capt. 43rd Inf., 15 March, 1867, to rank from 28 July, 1866. Bvt. Maj., 2 March, 1867, for gallant and meritorious service in the Battle of Gaines' Mills, Va. Bvt. Lieut. Col., 2 March, 1867, for gallant and meritorious service in the Battle of Charles City Cross-Roads, Va. Unassigned 8 April, 1869. Ass'd to 1st Inf., 7 June, 1869. Retired 1 March, 1878.

GALT, JOHN M. [Born in Va. Appointed from Va.]
Mil. Storekeeper, 28 Dec., 1842. Resigned 28 Feb., 1861.

GALT, PATRICK H. [Born in Va. Appointed from Va.]
3rd Lieut. Corps Art., 16 Sept., 1814. 2nd Lieut., 1 Nov., 1816. 1st Lieut., 26 Sept., 1818. Trans. to 2nd Art., 1 June, 1821. Trans. to 4th Art., 16 Aug., 1821. Capt., 15 May, 1829. Maj. 2nd Art., 16 Feb., 1847. Died 9 Jan., 1851. Bvt. Capt., 26 Sept., 1828, for 10 years' faithful service in one grade. Bvt. Lieut. Col., 20 Aug., 1847, for gallant and meritorious conduct at Contreras and Churubusco, Mex.

GAMBLE, GEORGE H. [Born in Mo. Appointed from Ill.]
Priv. Co. A, 1st Ill. light Art., 25 Aug., 1861. Trans. to Troop L, 8th Ill. Cav., 23 Dec., 1861. Sergt. Maj., 1 Feb., 1862. 1st Lieut. Adj., 10 Feb., 1863. Mustered out 3 July, 1865. Capt. 9th Cav., 28 July, 1866. Resigned 1 Dec., 1869.

GAMBLE, WM. [Born in Ireland. Appointed from Ill.]
Priv., Corpl. and Sergt. Co. H and Sergt. Maj. 1st Drag., 10 March, 1839. Discharged 6 Aug., 1843. Lieut. Col. 8th Ill. Cav., 18 Sept., 1861. Col., 5 Dec., 1862. Mustered

out 17 July, 1865. Brig. Gen. Vols., 25 Sept., 1865. Bvt. Brig. Gen. Vols., 14 Dec., 1864. Mustered out 13 March, 1866. Maj. 8th Cav., 28 July, 1866. Died 20 Dec., 1866.

GAME, CLYFFARD.* [Born in England. Appointed from Minn.]
2nd Lieut. 11th Inf., 15 Feb., 1899.

GANDY, CHARLES M. [Born in N. J. Appointed from N. J.]
Asst. Surg., 3 Dec., 1883. Capt. Asst. Surg., 3 Dec., 1888. Maj. Brig. Surg. Vols., 4 June, 1898. Maj. and Chf. Surg. Vols., 7 Jan., 1899.

GANNETT, THOS. B. [Born in Mass. Appointed from Mass.]
2nd Lieut. 7th Inf., 1 July, 1839. Died 30 Oct., 1841.

GANO, AARON G.* [Born in Ohio. Appointed from Ohio.]
3rd Lieut. Corps Art., 2 March, 1815. Resigned 1 Oct., 1817. Died 2 Dec., 1854.

GANSEVOORT, HENRY S. [Born in N. Y. Appointed from N. Y.]
Priv. 7th N. Y. Mil., 19 April, 1861. 2nd Lieut. 5th Art., 14 May, 1861. 1st Lieut., 1 March, 1862. Lieut. Col. 13th N. Y. Cav., 20 June, 1863. Col., 28 March, 1864. Mustered out Vols. 17 Aug., 1865. Capt., 13 Aug., 1866. Died 12 April, 1871. Bvt. Capt., 17 Sept., 1862, for gallant and meritorious service at the Battle of Antietam, Md. Bvt. Maj., 14 Oct., 1864, for gallant and meritorious service in action near Manassas Gap, Va. Bvt. Lieut. Col., 13 March, 1865, for gallant and meritorious service during the war. Bvt. Brig. Gen. Vols., 24 June, 1865, for faithful and meritorious service.

GANTT, EDWARD S. [Born in Va. Appointed from Va.]
Cadet at Mil. Acad., 26 July, 1814, to 11 Dec., 1815. Bvt. 2nd Lieut. Light Art., 11 Dec., 1815. 2nd Lieut. Rifles, 2 Nov., 1817. Resigned 25 April, 1818. Died 30 March, 1844.

GANTT, JOHN. [Born in Va. Appointed from Ky.]
2nd Lieut. Rifles, 24 May, 1817. 1st Lieut., 5 April, 1818. Trans. to 6th Inf., 1 June, 1821. Capt., 28 Feb., 1823. Dismissed 12 May, 1829.

GANTT, LEVI.* [Born in D. C. Appointed from Md.]
Bvt. 2nd Lieut. 2nd Inf., 1 July, 1841. 2nd Lieut. 7th Inf., 30 April, 1842. 1st Lieut., 16 Feb., 1847. Killed 13 Sept., 1847, in Battle of Chapultepec, Mexico.

GANTT, STOUGHTON. [Born in Va. Appointed from Ky.]
Surg. Mate Rifle Regiment, 2 June, 1813. 1st Lieut. 4th Rifles, 17 March, 1814. Trans. to Rifle Regiment, 17 May, 1815. Reg. P. M., 4 March, 1816, to 15 April, 1818. Capt., 15 April, 1818. Resigned 25 April, 1819.

GAPEN, HENRY CLAY. [Born in Pa. Appointed from Pa.]
1st Lieut. 15th Inf., 14 May, 1861. Capt., 17 Dec., 1863. Retired 25 Feb., 1865. Died 13 Jan., 1869.

GARBER, HEZEKIAH H.* [Born in Ohio. Appointed from Ill.]
Bvt. 2nd Lieut. 5th Inf., 1 July, 1852. 2nd Lieut. 4th Inf., 31 July, 1854. Died 12 Oct., 1859.

GARDENER, CORNELIUS.* [Born in Netherlands. Appointed from Mich.]
2nd Lieut. 19th Inf., 13 June, 1873. 1st Lieut., 19 June, 1879. Capt. 19th Inf., 24 Feb., 1891. Maj. 13th Inf., 16 Sept., 1899. Col. 31st Mich. Inf., 11 May, 1898, to 17 March, 1899. Col. 30th U. S. Vols., 5 July, 1899.

GARDENIER, JOHN R. B.* [Born in N. Y. Appointed from N. Y.]
Bvt. 2nd Lieut. 1st Inf., 1 July, 1828. 2nd Lieut., 1 July, 1828. 1st Lieut., 4 Sept., 1836. Capt., 11 June, 1839. Died 26 June, 1850.

GARDINER, ASA B. [Born in N. Y. Appointed from N. Y.]
1st Lieut. 31st N. Y. Vols., 27 May, 1861. Mustered out 7 Aug., 1861. Capt. 22nd N. Y. Vols., 31 May, 1862. Mustered out 5 Sept., 1862. Capt. 22nd N. Y. Vols., 18 June, 1863. Mustered out 24 July, 1863. Bvt. Capt. Vols., 13 March, 1865, for gallant and meritorious service during the war. 1st Lieut. Vet. Res. Corps., 11 Feb., 1865. Reg. Adj. 7th Vet. Res. Corps, 29 May, 1865, to 13 Aug., 1866. Mustered out 13 Aug., 1866. 2nd Lieut. 9th Inf., 20 July, 1866. 1st Lieut., 14 Feb., 1868. Trans. to 1st Art., 3 April, 1869. Maj. J. A., 18 Aug., 1873. Resigned commission of 1st Lieut. 1st Art., 19 Aug., 1873. Prof. of Law at Mil. Acad., 29 July, 1874, to 28 Aug., 1878. Retired for disability, 8 Dec., 1888. Medal of Honor for distinguished services performed during the recent war while serving as Capt. 22nd N. Y. State Mil. Inf.

GARDINER, GEO. W.* [Born in D. C. Appointed from D. C.]
3rd Lieut. 1st Art., 11 March, 1814. 2nd Lieut., 1 May, 1814. Trans. to Corps Art., 12 May, 1814. 1st Lieut., 20 April, 1818. Trans. to 2nd Art., 1 June, 1821. Trans. to 2nd Art., 16 Aug., 1821. Capt., 3 Nov., 1832. Massacred by Indians in Florida, 28 Dec., 1835. Bvt. Capt., 20 April, 1828, for 10 years' faithful service in one grade.

GARDINER, GUSTAVUS F. [Born in R. I. Appointed from R. I.]
2nd Lieut. 9th Inf., 30 Dec., 1847. Died 16 March, 1848.

GARDINER, JOHN DE B. W. [Born in Md. Appointed from Md.]
1st Lieut. Asst. Surg., 26 June, 1875. Capt. Asst. Surg., 26 June, 1880. Retired for disability, 25 Feb., 1891.

GARDINER, JOHN W. T.* [Born in Me. Appointed from Me.]
Bvt. 2nd Lieut. 1st Drag., 1 July, 1840. 2nd Lieut., 31 Dec., 1840. 1st Lieut., 21 April, 1846. Capt., 9 Oct., 1851. Maj. 2nd Cav., 26 Oct., 1861. Retired 14 Nov., 1861. Bvt. Lieut. Col., 13 March, 1865, for meritorious service during the war. Died 27 Sept., 1879.

GARDNER, CHARLES K. [Born in N. J. Appointed from N. Y.]
Ensign 6th Inf., 3 May, 1808. Reg. Adj., 20 May, 1809, to April, 1811. 2nd Lieut., 10 June, 1809. Capt. 3rd Art., 6 July, 1812. Maj. A. A. G., 18 March, 1813. Trans. to 23rd Inf., 15 April, 1813. Maj. 25th Inf., 26 June, 1813. Trans. to 3rd Inf., 17 May, 1815. Col. A. G., 12 April, 1814. Resigned 17 March, 1818. Died 1 Nov., 1869.

GARDNER, EDWIN F. [Born in Me. Appointed from Me.]
Priv. Co. A, 1st Batt. Me. Vols., 22 March, 1865. Discharged 5 April, 1866. 1st Lieut. Asst. Surg., 5 Aug., 1876. Capt. and Asst. Surg., 5 Aug., 1881. Maj. Surg., 1 Oct., 1895.

GARDNER, FRANKLIN.* [Born in N. Y. Appointed from Iowa.]
Bvt. 2nd Lieut. 7th Inf., 1 July, 1843. 2nd Lieut., 12 Sept., 1845. 1st Lieut., 13 Sept.,

1847. Reg. Adj., 14 July, 1847, to 16 Nov., 1853. Capt., 10th Inf., 3 March, 1855. Dropped 7 May, 1861. Bvt. 1st Lieut., 23 Sept., 1846, for gallant and meritorious conduct at Monterey. Bvt. Capt., 18 April, 1847, for gallant and meritorious conduct at Cerro Gordo, Mex. Died 29 April, 1873.

GARDNER, GEORGE W.* [Born in Mass. Appointed from Mass.]
3rd Lieut. Light Art., 21 July, 1814. Trans. to Corps Art., 17 May, 1815. 2nd Lieut., 1 Oct., 1816. 1st Lieut., 30 Aug., 1818. Resigned 31 July, 1819. Died in 1820.

GARDNER, HEZEKIAH. [Born in Ill. Appointed from N. Y.]
Priv. 100th Ill. Vols., 5 to 18 Aug., 1862. Capt. 100th Ill. Vols., 30 Aug., 1862. Mustered out 18 Aug., 1864. Capt. Vet. Res. Corps, 15 Sept., 1864. Bvt. Maj. and Lieut. Col. Vols., 13 March, 1865, for meritorious conduct in the Battle of Chattanooga and in the charge on Mission Ridge. Mustered out 28 Oct., 1866. Capt. 44th Inf., 28 July, 1866. Bvt. Maj., 2 March, 1867, for gallant and meritorious service in the Battle of Mission Ridge, Tenn. Unassigned 27 May, 1869. Retired, from loss of right leg from wound, 15 Dec., 1870.

GARDNER, JOHN H.* [Born in Ill. Appointed from Ill.]
Addl. 2nd Lieut. 8th Cav., 11 June, 1881. 2nd Lieut. 9th Cav., 19 Aug., 1881. 1st Lieut., 15 June, 1888. Capt. 2nd Cav., 30 June, 1898.

GARDNER, JOHN L. [Born in Mass. Appointed from Mass.]
3rd Lieut. 4th Inf., 20 May, 1813. 2nd Lieut., 28 March, 1814. Trans. to Corps Art., 17 May, 1815. 1st Lieut., 20 April, 1818. A. Q. M., 18 May, 1820, to — Oct., 1830. Trans. to 3rd Art., 1 June, 1821. Trans. to 4th Art., 16 Aug., 1821. Capt., 1 Nov., 1823. Maj., 13 Oct., 1845. Lieut. Col. 1st Art., 3 Aug., 1852. Col. 2nd Art., 23 July, 1861. Retired 1 Nov., 1861. Died 19 Feb., 1869. Bvt. Maj., 1 Nov., 1833, for 10 years' faithful service in one grade. Bvt. Lieut. Col., 18 April, 1847, for gallant and meritorious conduct at Cerro Gordo. Bvt. Col., 20 Aug., 1847, for gallant and meritorious conduct at Contreras. Bvt. Brig. Gen., 13 March, 1865, for long and faithful service in the Army.

GARDNER, JOHN M. [Born in Ga. Appointed from Ga.]
Asst. Surg., 9 Aug., 1833. Resigned 30 Nov., 1834.

GARDNER, RICHARD W. [Born in Tenn. Appointed from Tenn.]
Asst. Surg. Vols., 28 Sept., 1847. Disbanded 20 July, 1848.

GARDNER, ROGERS F.* [Born in N. Y. Appointed from Mass.]
2nd Lieut. 15th Inf., 12 June, 1894. Trans. to 3rd Art., 25 Feb., 1895. 1st Lieut., 2 March, 1899.

GARDNER, SYMMES. [Born in Vt. Appointed from N. Y.]
1st Lieut. 18th Inf., 14 May, 1861. (Capt. A. Q. M., 12 Aug., 1861. Appointment revoked 6 Feb., 1862.) Capt. 18th Inf., 30 June, 1863. Dropped 13 Nov., 1863.

GARDNER, THOMAS J.* [Born in N. Y. Appointed from N. Y.]
Bvt. 2nd Lieut. Light Art., 11 Dec., 1815. 2nd Lieut., 1 Jan., 1817. 1st Lieut., 31 Dec., 1819. Trans. to 4th Art., 1 June, 1821. Died 20 July, 1822.

GARDNER, WM. F. [Born in Pa. Appointed from Pa.]
1st Sergt. Troop B, 2nd Pa. Cav., 14 Dec., 1861, to 18 Sept., 1862. 2nd Lieut. 118th Pa. Vols., 18 Sept., 1862. 1st Lieut., 1 Nov., 1862. Mustered out 1 June, 1865. 2nd Lieut. 38th Inf., 7 March, 1867. Trans. to 24th Inf., 11 Nov., 1869. Died 9 Sept., 1872.

GARDNER, WM. H. [Born in N. C. Appointed from D. C.]
1st Lieut. Asst. Surg., 22 Nov., 1862. Bvt. Capt. and Bvt. Maj., 13 March, 1865, for faithful and meritorious service during the war. Capt. Asst. Surg., 28 July, 1866. Maj. Surg., 23 June, 1882. Lieut. Col. Dep. Surg. Gen., 10 Oct., 1896. Retired, over 30 years' service, 10 Dec., 1898.

GARDNER, WM. M.* [Born in Ga. Appointed from Ga.]
Bvt. 2nd Lieut. 1st Inf., 1 July, 1846. 2nd Lieut. 7th Inf., 16 Feb., 1847. Trans. to 2nd Inf., 13 July, 1847. 1st Lieut., 16 Oct., 1849. Capt., 3 March, 1855. Resigned 19 Jan., 1861. Bvt. 1st Lieut., 20 Aug., 1847, for gallant and meritorious conduct at Contreras and Churubusco, Mex.

GARESCHE, JULIUS P.* [Born in Cuba. Appointed from Del.]
2nd Lieut. 4th Art., 1 July, 1841. 1st Lieut., 18 June, 1846. Bvt. Capt. A. A. G., 9 Nov., 1855. Bvt. Maj. A. A. G., 14 May, 1861. Maj. A. A. G., 3 Aug., 1861. Lieut. Col., 17 July, 1862. Killed 31 Dec., 1862, at Battle of Murfreesboro,' Tenn.

GAREY, GEORGE W.* [Born in Md. Appointed from Md.]
Bvt. 2nd Lieut. 7th Inf., 1 July, 1825. 2nd Lieut. 1st Inf., 1 July, 1825. 1st Lieut., 26 Oct., 1832. Died 10 Dec., 1834.

GARLAND, JOHN. [Born in Va. Appointed from Va.]
1st Lieut. 35th Inf., 31 March, 1813. Trans. to 3rd Inf., 17 May, 1815. Capt., 7 May, 1817. Capt. A. Q. M., 31 May, 1826, to 10 July, 1832. Maj. 1st Inf., 30 Oct., 1836. Lieut. Col. 4th Inf., 27 Nov., 1839. Col. 8th Inf., 7 May, 1849. Died 5 June, 1861. Bvt. Maj., 7 May, 1827, for 10 years' faithful service in one grade. Bvt. Col., 9 May, 1846, for gallant conduct at Palo Alto and Resaca de la Palma. Bvt. Brig. Gen., 20 Aug., 1847, for gallant and meritorious conduct at Contreras and Churubusco, Mex.

GARLAND, JOHN S. [Born in Mich. Appointed from Mich.]
2nd Lieut. 4th Art., 8 March, 1847. 1st Lieut., 20 May, 1849. Capt., 29 Dec., 1857. Retired 29 Nov., 1861. Died 6 Oct., 1897.

GARLAND, ROBERT R. [Born in Va. Appointed from Mo.]
2nd Lieut. 7th Inf., 30 Dec., 1847. 1st Lieut., 3 March, 1855. R. Q. M., 1 May, 1858, to 1 April, 1860. Capt., 23 March, 1861. Dropped 23 May, 1861.

GARLAND, WM. A.* [Born in Vt. Appointed from N. H.]
2nd Lieut. 19th Inf., 23 June, 1865. 1st Lieut., 23 June, 1865. Died 1 Dec., 1865.

GARLINGTON, ERNEST A.* [Born in S. C. Appointed from Ga.]
2nd Lieut. 7th Cav., 15 June, 1876. 1st Lieut., 25 June, 1876. Reg. Adj., 6 June, 1877, to 30 Nov., 1881. Capt., 3 Dec., 1891. Maj. and Ins. Gen., 2 Jan., 1895. Lieut. Col. Ins. Gen., 7 July, 1898. Medal of Honor for distinguished gallantry in action against hostile Sioux Indians on Wounded Knee Creek, S. Dak., December 29, 1890, where he was severely wounded while serving as 1st Lieut. 7th Cav.

GARNER, GEORGE G. [Born in Mass. Appointed from Md.]
Cadet at Mil. Acad., 1 July, 1847, to 23 June, 1849. 2nd Lieut. 2nd Art., 30 June, 1855. Resigned 31 Oct., 1856.

GARNER, HEZEKIAH. [Born in Md. Appointed from Md.]
2nd Lieut. Corps Art., 28 Jan., 1820. Trans. to 3rd Art., 1 June, 1821. 1st Lieut., 26 Feb., 1827. Reg. Adj., 15 March, 1827, to 16 Nov., 1837. Capt., 7 July, 1838. Died 23 Oct., 1841.

GARNETT, RICHARD B.* [Born in Va. Appointed from Va.]
2nd Lieut. 6th Inf., 1 July, 1841. 1st Lieut., 16 Feb., 1847. Capt., 9 May., 1855. Resigned 17 May, 1861.

GARNETT, ROBERT S.* [Born in Va. Appointed from Va.]
Bvt. 2nd Lieut. 4th Art., 1 July, 1841. 2nd Lieut., 31 Jan., 1842. 1st Lieut., 18 Aug., 1846. Trans. to 7th Inf., 31 Aug., 1848. Capt., 9 March, 1851. Trans. to 1st Cav., 3 March, 1855. Maj. 9th Inf., 27 March, 1855. Resigned 30 April, 1861. Bvt. Capt., 23 Sept., 1846, for gallant conduct at Monterey. Bvt. Maj., 23 Feb., 1847, for gallant and meritorious conduct at Buena Vista.

GARNSLEN, JOHN J. [Born in N. Y. Appointed from Va.]
Asst. Surg., 16 May, 1856. Resigned 17 Aug., 1861.

GARRARD, ALEXANDER B. [Born in La. Appointed from La.]
2nd Lieut. 1st Inf., 18 April, 1818. R. Q. M., 25 Oct., 1818, to 3 Oct., 1820. 1st Lieut., 26 July, 1819. Died 3 Oct., 1820.

GARRARD, CUTHBERT G. [Born in La. Appointed from La.]
Surg. Mate 44th Inf., 11 March, 1814. Disbanded 15 June, 1815. Reinstated in 1st Inf., 13 Sept., 1815. Post Surg., 19 Feb., 1817. Died 23 March, 1818.

GARRARD, JOSEPH.* [Born in Ky. Appointed from Ky.]
2nd Lieut. 4th Art., 13 June, 1873. 1st Lieut., 1 Aug., 1875. Trans. to 9th Cav., 8 Feb., 1886. Reg. Adj., 9 May, 1888, to 10 Dec., 1888. Capt., 10 Dec., 1888. Graduate of the Artillery School, 1884.

GARRARD, KENNER.* [Born in Ky. Appointed at Large.]
Bvt. 2nd Lieut. 4th Art., 1 July, 1851. Trans. to 1st Drag., 20 Feb., 1852. 2nd Lieut., 31 Oct., 1853. 1st Lieut., 2nd Cav., 3 March, 1855. Reg. Adj., 20 April, 1855, to 31 May, 1858. Capt., 27 Feb., 1861. 5th Cav., 3 Aug., 1861. Maj. 3rd Cav., 2 Nov., 1863. Col. 146th N. Y. Vols., 23 Sept., 1862. Brig. Gen. Vols., 23 July, 1863. Mustered out Vols. 24 Aug., 1865. Bvt. Maj. Gen. Vols., 15 Dec., 1864, for conspicuous gallantry and efficiency during the battles of the 15th and 16th Dec., 1864, before Nashville, Tenn. Bvt. Lieut. Col., 2 July, 1863, for gallant and meritorious service at the Battle of Gettysburg, Pa. Bvt. Col., 22 July, 1864, for gallant and meritorious service in the expedition to Covington, Ga. Bvt. Brig. Gen., 13 March, 1865, for gallant and meritorious service at the Battle of Nashville, Tenn. Bvt. Maj. Gen., 13 March, 1865, for gallant and meritorious service in the field during the war. Resigned 9 Nov., 1866. Died 15 May, 1879.

GARRARD, THEOPHILUS T. [Born in Ky. Appointed from Ky.]
Capt. of Inf., 5 March, 1847; 16th Inf., 9 April, 1847. Disbanded 5 Aug., 1848. Col. 7th Ky. Vols., 22 Sept., 1861. Brig. Gen. Vols., 29 Nov., 1862. Mustered out 4 April, 1864.

GARRARD, WM. [Born in Ky. Appointed from Ky.]
Capt. A. C. S. Vols., 26 June, 1846. Resigned 11 Nov., 1846. Priv. and Sergt. 16th Inf., 24 April, 1847, to 28 Feb., 1848. 2nd Lieut. 16th Inf., 30 Dec., 1847. Disbanded 7 Aug., 1848.

GARRETSON, CHAS. [Born in Md. Appointed from Pa.]
Com. Sergt. 16th Pa. Vols., 3 May to 2 Aug., 1861. 1st Lieut. R. Q. M. 76th Pa. Vols., 13 Nov., 1861, to 28 July, 1862. Capt. A. Q. M. Vols., 11 June, 1862. Mustered out 5 March, 1864. 2nd Lieut. 17th Inf., 3 March, 1866. 1st Lieut., 1 Sept., 1867. R. Q. M., 1 Nov., 1866, to 27 May, 1869. Unassigned 27 May, 1869. Mustered out 1 Jan., 1871. Died 2 Sept., 1871.

GARRETSON, GEORGE A.* [Born in Ohio. Appointed from Ohio.]
Priv. Co. E, 84th Ohio Vols., 26 May to 20 Sept., 1862. Cadet at Mil. Acad., 1 July, 1863. 2nd Lieut. 4th Art., 17 June, 1867. Resigned 1 Jan., 1870.

GARRETT, ALBERT J. [Born in D. C. Appointed from D. C.]
2nd Lieut. 27th Inf., 1 Nov., 1867. Trans. to 1st Cav., 20 Nov., 1867. 1st Lieut., 1 March, 1870. Discharged 31 Dec., 1870.

GARRETT, BERNARD H. [Born in Ky. Appointed from Ky.]
2nd Lieut. of Inf., 5 March, 1847; 16th Inf., 9 April, 1847. Disbanded 5 Aug., 1848.

GARRETT, ISAIAH.* [Born in Tenn. Appointed from Mo.]
Bvt. 2nd Lieut. 2nd Art., 1 July, 1833. Resigned 15 Nov., 1833. Died 5 May, 1874.

GARRETTY, FRANK D. [Born in Ireland. Appointed from Ky.]
2nd Lieut. 15th Ky. Vols., 14 Dec., 1861. Mustered out 27 June, 1863. 1st Lieut. Vet. Res. Corps, 2 Oct., 1863. Mustered out 13 Dec., 1866. 2nd Lieut. 43rd Inf., 28 July, 1866. Bvt. 1st Lieut., 2 March, 1867, for gallant and meritorious service during the war. 1st Lieut. 43rd Inf., 11 Jan., 1868. Unassigned 8 April, 1869. Ass'd to 17th Inf., 15 Dec., 1870. Capt., 26 June, 1882. Retired 4 Feb., 1893.

GARST, CHAS. E.* [Born in Ohio. Appointed from Iowa.]
2nd Lieut. 15th Inf., 15 June, 1876. Resigned 10 Jan., 1884.

GARVEY, THOS. [Born in Ireland. Appointed from Army.]
Priv. Co. A, 2nd Art., 10 Aug., 1863. Corpl., 7 June, 1865. Trans. to Co. K, 25 Sept., 1865. Trans. to Co. A, 2 Jan., 1866. Sergt., 1 Sept., 1866. Discharged 10 Aug., 1868. 2nd Lieut. 1st Cav., 7 Oct., 1868. 1st Lieut., 20 June, 1872. Capt., 19 Dec., 1884. Dismissed 26 March, 1888.

GARVIN, EDWIN L. [Born in Pa. Appointed from N. Y.]
2nd Lieut. 52nd N. Y. Vols., 24 Sept., 1861, to 18 July, 1862. 2nd Lieut. 1st Art., 19 Feb., 1862. 1st Lieut., 4 July, 1863. Resigned 20 March, 1866. Bvt. Capt., 13 March, 1865, for good conduct and gallant service during the war.

GASKILL, CHAS. B. [Born in N. Y. Appointed from N. Y.]
Priv. Co. A, 44th N. Y. Vols., 30 Aug., 1861. 2nd Lieut., 23 Dec., 1861. 1st Lieut., 16 Oct., 1862. Resigned 18 Dec., 1862. Capt. 78th U. S. Col. Inf., 27 March, 1863. Maj. 81st U. S. Col. Inf., 8 April, 1864. Lieut. Col., 5 Oct., 1864. Col., 30 Oct., 1865. Mustered out 31 Dec., 1865. Capt. 40th Inf., 28 July, 1866. Trans. to 25th Inf., 20 April, 1869. Discharged 1 Dec., 1870. Bvt. Maj., 2 March, 1867, for gallant and

meritorious service at the Battle of Gaines' Mills, Va. Bvt. Lieut. Col., 2 March, 1867, for gallant and meritorious service at the Battle of Fredericksburg, Va., 13 Dec., 1862.

GASKILL, EDWIN C. [Born in Mass. Appointed from Mass.]
Priv. Co. B, 25th Mass. Vols., 12 Oct., 1861. Discharged 17 Jan., 1864. Priv. Co. F, 25th Mass. Vet. Vols., 18 Jan., 1864. Discharged 29 Feb., 1864. 2nd Lieut. 36th U. S. Col. Troops, 21 April, 1864. 1st Lieut., 11 July, 1864. Capt., 21 Oct., 1864. Mustered out 28 Oct., 1866. 1st Lieut. 43rd Inf., 21 May, 1867. Unassigned 8 April, 1869. Retired with rank of Capt., 15 Dec., 1870. Died 17 June, 1889.

GASMANN, HANS. J. [Born in Wis. Appointed from Wis.]
Cadet at Mil. Acad., 1 July, 1869, to 19 Jan., 1871. 2nd Lieut. 10th Cav., 1 Oct., 1873. Died 4 Sept., 1879.

GASSAWAY, JOHN. [Born in Md. Appointed from Md.]
2nd Lieut. Marine Corps, 18 June, 1810. Resigned 29 Dec., 1810. Ensign and 2nd Lieut. 5th Inf., 3 Jan., 1812. 1st Lieut., 15 Aug., 1813. Disbanded 15 June, 1815. Reinstated 2 Dec., 1815, in 7th Inf. Resigned 1 Feb., 1817. 2nd Lieut. Corps Art., 20 April, 1818. Resigned 28 Sept., 1819.

GASTON, JOSEPH A.* [Born in Pa. Appointed from Pa.]
2nd Lieut. 8th Cav., 11 June, 1881. 1st Lieut., 24 April, 1886. Capt., 3 Jan., 1895.

GASTON, WM.* [Born in N. C. Appointed at Large.]
Bvt. 2nd Lieut. 2nd Drag., 1 July, 1856. 2nd Lieut. 1st Drag., 30 Nov., 1856. Killed 17 May, 1858, in action with Indians in Washington Ter.

GATCHELL, GEORGE W.* [Born in R. I. Appointed from R. I.]
Addl. 2nd Lieut. 5th Art., 12 June, 1887. 2nd Lieut., 10 Aug., 1887. Trans. to 4th Art., 12 Nov., 1887. 1st Lieut. 5th Art., 11 Dec., 1893.

GATES, COLLINSON R.* [Born in N. Y. Appointed at Large.]
Bvt. 2nd Lieut. 4th Inf., 1 July, 1836. 2nd Lieut., 21 Sept., 1836. 1st Lieut., 7 July, 1838. Capt., 18 June, 1846. Died 28 June, 1849. Bvt. Capt., 9 May, 1846, for gallant conduct at Palo Alto and Resaca de la Palma. Bvt. Maj., 8 Sept., 1847, for gallant conduct at Molino del Rey, Mex.

GATES, CORNELIUS. [Born in N. Y. Appointed from N. Y.]
2nd Lieut. 8th Inf., 13 Feb., 1818. Cashiered 13 Aug., 1819.

GATES, JOHN A. [Born in Mich. Appointed from Army.]
Priv. and Sergt. Co. C. and Q. M. Sergt. 13th Inf., 2 Oct., 1861, to 18 May, 1863. 2nd Lieut. 13th Inf., 22 April, 1863. Rejected by Senate 18 March, 1864.

GATES, JOHN, Jr. [Born in N. Y. Appointed from N. Y.]
Ensign 13th Inf., 1 May, 1812. 2nd Lieut., Light Art., 1 April, 1813. 1st Lieut., 3 Dec., 1813. Reg. P. M., 26 Jan., 1814, to 13 Feb., 1818. Resigned 5 June, 1819.

GATES, J. GRANVILLE. [Born in R. I. Appointed from N. Y.]
2nd Lieut. 20th Inf., 1 Oct., 1873. 1st Lieut., 30 Nov., 1879. Dismissed 1 June, 1880.

GATES, LEMUEL. [Born in Md. Appointed from Md.]
2nd Lieut. Corps Art., 13 Aug., 1819. Trans. to 2nd Art., 1 June, 1821. Trans. to 1st Art., 16 Aug., 1821. 1st Lieut., 11 Feb., 1825. Capt., 1 Oct., 1835. Died 6 Aug., 1836.

GATES, RUFUS C. [Born in Vt. Appointed from Army.]
Priv., Corpl. and Sergt. Co. A, 3rd, and A, 2nd Batt. 18th Inf., 22 Oct., 1861, to 2 April, 1863. 2nd Lieut. 18th Inf., 19 Feb., 1863. 1st Lieut., 12 Dec., 1863. Resigned 5 June, 1865.

GATES, WILLIAM.* [Born in Mass. Appointed from Mass.]
2nd Lieut. Art., 6 March, 1806. 1st Lieut., 3 Nov., 1807, in 1st Art., — March, 1812. Capt., 3 March, 1813. Trans. to Corps Art., 12 May, 1814. Trans. to 2nd Art., 1 June, 1821. Maj. 1st Art., 30 May, 1832. Dismissed 11 June, 1836. Reinstated as Maj. 2nd Art., 7 Jan., 1837. Lieut. Col. 3rd Art., to rank from 17 Dec., 1836. Col., 13 Oct., 1845. Retired 1 June, 1863. Died 7 Oct., 1868. Bvt. Maj., 3 March, 1823, for 10 years' faithful service in one grade. Bvt. Brig. Gen., 13 March, 1865, for long and faithful service in the army.

GATEWOOD, CHAS. B.* [Born in Va. Appointed from Va.]
2nd Lieut. 6th Cav., 15 June, 1877. 1st Lieut., 3 Jan., 1885. Died 20 May, 1896.

GATLEY, GEORGE G.* [Born in Me. Appointed from Me.]
Addl. 2nd Lieut. 5th Art., 12 June, 1890. 2nd Lieut. 3rd Art., 31 July, 1891. Trans. to 5th Art., 12 Aug., 1891. 1st Lieut. 2nd Art., 21 March, 1898. Trans. to 5th Art., 4 May, 1898.

GATLIN, JOHN S. [Born in N. C. Appointed from N. C.]
Asst. Surg., 3 Aug., 1834. Massacred by Indians in Florida, 28 Dec., 1835.

GATLIN, RICHARD C.* [Born in N. C. Appointed from N. C.]
Bvt. 2nd Lieut. 7th Inf., 1 July, 1832. 2nd Lieut., 31 May, 1834. 1st Lieut., 31 Aug., 1836. Reg. Adj., 13 Dec., 1838, to 30 Sept., 1845. Capt., 30 Sept., 1845. Maj., 5th Inf., 26 Feb., 1861. Resigned 20 May, 1861. Bvt. Maj., 23 Sept., 1846, for gallant and meritorious conduct at Monterey, Mex.

GAVITT, HALSEY C. [Born in Ohio. Appointed from Ill.]
Post Chap., 2 March, 1898.

GAY, EBENEZER.* [Born in N. H. Appointed from N. H.]
Bvt. 2nd Lieut. 1st Drag., 1 July, 1855. 2nd Lieut., 2nd Drag., 1 July, 1855. 1st Lieut., 31 March, 1861. Capt. 16th Inf., 14 May, 1861. Trans. to 34th Inf., 21 Sept., 1866. Maj. 17th Inf., 16 Sept., 1867. Dismissed 3 June, 1869. Reinstated 24 Jan., 1870, as Maj. of Inf. Mustered out 1 Jan., 1871. Bvt. Maj., 8 Oct., 1862, for gallant and meritorious service at the Battle of Perryville, Ky. Bvt. Lieut. Col., 1 Sept., 1864, for gallant and meritorious services during the Atlanta campaign. Died 11 Sept., 1871.

GAYLE, EDWARD E.* [Born in Va. Appointed from N. C.]
2nd Lieut. 2nd Art., 15 June, 1876. 1st Lieut. 18 Mar., 1885. Capt., 13 Feb., 1899. Graduate of the Artillery School, 1888.

GEAR, EZEKIEL G. [Born in Conn. Appointed from Minn.]
Chap. Post of Fort Snelling, Minn, 2 Oct., 1838, to 1 June, 1858, and Fort Ripley, Minn., 1 Jan., 1860, to 12 May, 1867. Post. Chap., 3 April, 1867. Retired 19 Aug., 1867. Died 13 Oct., 1873.

GEARY, BENJN. H. [Born in Pa. Appointed from the Army.]
Priv. and Sergt. Co. H, 13th Inf., 12 Aug., 1861, to 3 Sept., 1862. 2nd Lieut. 13th Inf., 13 Aug., 1862. 1st Lieut., 15 April, 1863. Dismissed 21 July, 1863.

GEARY, JOHN T. [Born in Ky. Appointed from Ky.]
2nd Lieut. 7th Art., 9 July, 1898. Trans. to 5th Art., 4 April, 1899.

GEARY, WM. L.* [Born in Cal. Appointed at Large.]
Musician, band 28th Penn. Vols., 17 July, 1861. Discharged 9 Sept., 1862. Cadet Mil. Acad., 1 Sept., 1870. 2nd Lieut. 12th Inf., 17 June, 1874. Reg. Adj., 20 Feb., 1875, to 17 Nov., 1878. 1st Lieut., 16 Dec., 1880. Resigned 15 Oct., 1884.

GEARY, WOODBRIDGE.* [Born in Ore. Appointed from Ore.]
Addl. 2nd Lieut. 19th Inf., 13 June, 1882. 2nd Lieut., 15 June, 1882. 1st Lieut. 19th Inf., 20 Feb., 1891. Capt. of Inf., 30 June, 1898. Ass'd to 13th Inf., 1 Jan., 1899. Died of wounds received in action in Philippine Islands, 11 Oct., 1899.

GEDDES, ANDREW. [Born in Canada. Appointed from Iowa.]
Priv. Co. K, 1st Iowa Vols., 14 May to 20 Aug., 1861. Capt. 8th Iowa Vols., 1 Oct., 1861. Lieut. Col., 11 Nov., 1865. Mustered out 20 April, 1866. 1st Lieut. 40th Inf., 12 June, 1867. Reg. Adjt., 15 Sept., 1868, to 20 Apr., 1869. Bvt. Capt., 12 June, 1867, for gallant and meritorious service in the siege of Vicksburg, Miss. Bvt. Maj., 2 March, 1867, for gallant and meritorious service in the capture of Spanish fort. Trans. to 25th Inf., 20 April, 1869. Reg Adj., 24 April to 29 July, 1869. Capt., 11 April, 1878. Dismissed 31 Dec., 1880.

GEIGER, WM. C. [Born in Va. Appointed from Army.]
Priv. and 1st Class Priv. Co. E ,Batt. Eng., 9 July, 1896, to 27 July, 1898. 2nd Lieut. 24th Inf., 23 June, 1898. 1st Lieut. 14th Inf., 2 March, 1899.

GEISSE, PAUL D. [Born in Pa. Appointed from Pa.]
2nd Lieut. 7th Inf., 23 Oct., 1839. Trans. to 5th Inf., 6 May, 1843. Resigned 30 March, 1846.

GELRAY, JOSEPH W. [Born in England. Appointed from Mass.]
Priv. Co. A., 2nd Mass. Vols., 25 May, 1861. Corpl., 25 May, 1861. Sergt. Co. H, 2nd Mass. Vols., 22 Dec., 1861. 2nd Lieut. 2nd Mass. Vols., 12 Feb., 1863. 1st Lieut. 23rd Mass. Vols., 23 July, 1863. Mustered out 13 Oct., 1864. Capt. 57th Mass. Vols., 19 Oct., 1864. Mustered out 14 Nov., 1864. Maj. 4th Mass Heavy Art., 7 Dec., 1864. Mustered out 17 June, 1865. Capt. 45th Inf., 28 July, 1866. Bvt. Maj., 2 March, 1867, for gallant and meritorious service in the Battle of Cedar Mountain, Va. Bvt. Lieut. Col., 2 March, 1867, for gallant and meritorious service in the Battle of Gettysburg, Penn. Unassigned 22 July, 1869. Retired 15 Dec., 1870.

GENSEL, IRA F. [Born in Pa. Appointed from Pa.]
2nd Lieut. 4th Inf., 15 Aug., 1861. 1st Lieut., 9 Aug., 1862. Died 28 Dec., 1862, of wounds received at the Battle of Fredericksburg, Va. Bvt. Capt., 13 Dec., 1862, for gallant and meritorious service at the Battle of Fredericksburg, Va.

GENTRY, WM. T.* [Born in Ind. Appointed from Ind.]
Bvt. 2nd Lieut. 4th Inf., 1 July, 1856. 2nd Lieut., 1 Aug., 1856. 1st Lieut. 17th Inf., 14 May, 1861. Capt., 24 Oct., 1861. Bvt. Maj., 6 July, 1864, for gallant service at the crossing of the North Anna and during the present campaign before Richmond, Va. Bvt. Lieut. Col., 1 April, 1865, for gallant and meritorious service in the Battle of Five Forks, Va. Unassigned 27 May, 1869. Ass'd to 19th Inf., 15 Feb., 1870. Maj. 9th Inf., 20 March, 1879. Lieut. Col. 25th Inf., 14 April, 1884. Died 28 June, 1885.

GEOGHEGAN, JOHN D. [Born in Ireland. Appointed from Army.]
Priv., Corpl. and Sergt. Co. H. 18th Inf., 24 April, 1862, to 24 April, 1865. Priv., Sergt. and 1st Sergt. Co. C, 10th Inf., 16 Dec., 1865, to 10 June, 1866. 2nd Lieut. 10th Inf., 20 April, 1866. 1st Lieut., 28 July, 1866. Resigned 11 Sept., 1869.

GEORGE, CHARLES P. [Born in N. H. Appointed from N. H.]
2nd Lieut. 16th Inf., 10 Oct., 1883. 1st Lieut. 8th Inf., 9 March, 1891. Trans. to 16th Inf., 20 July, 1891. Capt. of Inf., 11 Aug., 1898. Ass'd to 16th Inf., 1 Jan., 1899.

GERHARD, WM.* [Born in Pa. Appointed at Large.]
2nd Lieut. 9th Cav., 15 June, 1869. 1st Lieut., 19 Nov., 1873. Resigned 30 Sept., 1874.

GERHARDT, CHARLES.* [Born in Md. Appointed from N. C.]
2nd Lieut. 20th Inf., 12 June, 1887. 1st Lieut. 8th Inf., 1 Aug., 1894. Capt., 2 March, 1899.

GERLACH, WM. [Born in Germany. Appointed from Army.]
Priv. Co. H, 4th Art., 26 Feb., 1856. Discharged 26 Dec., 1860. Priv. Co. H, 4th Art., 26 Dec., 1860. Hosp. Stew. U. S. A., 29 Aug., 1861. Discharged 19 July, 1864. Hosp. Stew. U. S. A., 19 July, 1864. 2nd Lieut. 37th Inf., 22 May, 1867. Trans. to 3rd Inf., 11 Aug., 1869. 1st Lieut., 8 Oct., 1879. R. Q. M., 20 Jan., 1888, to 23 April, 1890. Capt., 23 April, 1890. Maj. 10th Inf., 25 April, 1899. Trans. to 12th Inf., 31 May, 1899. Retired by operation of law 15 Nov., 1899.

GETTY, GEORGE W.* [Born in D. C. Appointed from D. C.]
2nd Lieut. 4th Art., 1 July, 1840. 1st Lieut., 31 Oct., 1845. Bvt. Capt., 20 Aug., 1847, for gallant and meritorious conduct in the Battles of Contreras and Churubusco. Capt. 4th Art., 4 Nov., 1853. Trans. to 5th Art., 14 May, 1861. Lieut. Col. A. A. de C., 28 Sept., 1861. Brig. Gen. Vols., 25 Sept., 1862. Bvt. Lieut. Col., 19 April, 1863, for gallant and meritorious service during the siege of Suffolk, Va. Maj. 5th Art., 1 Aug., 1863. Bvt. Col., 5 May, 1864, for gallant and meritorious service in the Battle of the Wilderness, Va. Bvt. Maj. Gen. Vols., 1 Aug., 1864, for gallant and meritorious service in the Battles of Winchester and Fisher's Hill, Va. Bvt. Brig. Gen., 13 March, 1865, for gallant and meritorious service in the capture of Petersburg, Va. Bvt. Maj. Gen., 13 March, 1865, for gallant and meritorious service in the field during the war. Col. 37th Inf., 28 July, 1866. Mustered out of Vol. service 9 Oct., 1866. Trans. to 3rd Inf., 15 March, 1869. Trans. to 3rd Art., 1 Jan., 1871. Trans. to 4th Art., 17 July, 1882. Retired 2 Oct., 1883.

GETTY, ROBERT N.* [Born in N. Y. Appointed at Large.]
Addl. 2nd Lieut. 22nd Inf., 14 June, 1878. 2nd Lieut., 28 June, 1878. 1st Lieut., 17 Dec., 1886. Capt. 22nd Inf., 17 March, 1896. Trans. to 1st Inf., 23 Jan., 1899.

GETTY, THOMAS M. [Born in Md. Appointed from Va.]
Asst. Surg., 23 Nov., 1849. Maj. and Surg., 16 April, 1862. Died 30 Oct., 1867. Bvt. Lieut. Col., 13 March, 1865, for faithful and meritorious service during the war.

GHISELIN, JAMES T. [Born in Md. Appointed from Md.]
Asst. Surg., 1 June, 1855. Maj. and Surg., 14 June, 1862. Resigned 6 June, 1874. Bvt. Lieut. Col., 13 March, 1865, for faithful and meritorious service during the war. Bvt. Col., 9 April, 1865, for meritorious service during the campaign from Winchester to Appomattox Court House, Va.

GIBBES, WADE H.* [Born in S. C. Appointed from S. C.]
Bvt. 2nd Lieut. 2nd Cav., 1 July, 1860. Resigned 1 Jan., 1861.

GIBBON, DAVID J. [Born in Ohio. Appointed from Army.]
Priv. Co. K, 5th Ohio Vols., 20 June, 1861. Discharged 13 Oct., 1862. Sergt. Sig. Corps., 12 September, 1870. 2nd Lieut. 9th Cav., 4 March, 1872. 1st Lieut., 28 June, 1878. Retired for disability 16 July, 1888.

GIBBON, JOHN.* [Born in Pa. Appointed from N. C.]
Bvt. 2nd Lieut. 3rd Art., 1 July, 1847. 2nd Lieut. 4th Art., 13 Sept., 1847. 1st Lieut. 12 Sept., 1850. Capt., 2 Nov., 1859. Brig. Gen. Vols., 2 May, 1862. Bvt. Maj., 17 Sept., 1862, for gallant and meritorious service in the Battle of Antietam, Md. Bvt. Lieut. Col., 13 Dec., 1862, for gallant and meritorious service in the Battle of Fredericksburg, Va. Bvt. Col., 4 July, 1863, for gallant and meritorious service in the Battle of Gettysburg, Pa. Maj. Gen. Vols., 7 June, 1864. Bvt. Brig. Gen., 13 March, 1865, for gallant and meritorious service in the Battle of Spottsylvania, Va. Bvt. Maj. Gen., 13 March, 1865, for gallant and meritorious service in the capture of Petersburg, Va. Mustered out of Vol. service, 15 Jan., 1866. Col. 36th Inf., 28 July, 1866. Trans. to 7th Inf., 15 March, 1869. Brig. Gen., 10 July, 1885. Died 6 Feb., 1896.

GIBBS, ALFRED.* [Born in N. Y. Appointed from N. Y.]
Bvt. 2nd Lieut. Mtd. Rifles, 1 July, 1846. 2nd Lieut., 31 Dec., 1847. 1st Lluet., 31 May, 1853. Reg. Adj., 24 March to 15 Sept., 1858. Capt., 13 May, 1861. 3rd Cav., 3 Aug., 1861. Col. 130th N. Y. Vols., 6 Sept., 1862. 19th N. Y. Cav., 11 Aug., 1863. Brig. Gen. Vols., 19 Oct., 1864. Mustered out of Vols. 11 Feb., 1866. Maj. 7th Cav., 28 July, 1866. Died 26 Dec., 1868. Bvt. 1st Lieut., 18 April, 1847, for gallant and meritorious conduct at Cerro Gordo. Bvt. Capt., 13 Sept., 1847, for gallant conduct at Garita de Belen, City of Mexico. Bvt. Maj., 11 June, 1864, for gallant and meritorious service at the Battle of Trevillian Station, Va. Bvt. Lieut. Col., 19 Sept., 1864, for gallant and meritorious service at the Battle of Winchester, Va. Bvt. Col., 13 March, 1865, for gallant and meritorious service at the Battle of Five Forks, Va. Bvt. Brig. Gen. and Bvt. Maj. Gen. U. S. A. and Vols., 13 March, 1865, for gallant and meritorious service in the field during the war.

GIBBS, EUGENE B. [Born in R. I. Appointed from R. I.]
Capt. 2nd Cal. Vols., 17 Sept., 1861. Mustered out 6 May, 1866. 2nd Lieut. 8th Inf., 22 Jan., 1867. 1st Lieut., 18 Feb., 1869. Unassigned, 3 May, 1869. Ass'd to 6th Inf., 1 Jan., 1871. Capt. A. Q. M., 23 March., 1880. Died 25 April, 1882.

GIBBS, JOHN S. [Born in Maine. Appointed from Maine.]
Priv. Co. A, 3rd Mass. Vols., 19 April to 3 Aug., 1861. 2nd Lieut. 1st Art., 5 Aug., 1861. 1st Lieut., 5 Aug., 1861. Resigned 19 May, 1864. Capt. 38th U. S. Col. Inf., 27 March, 1865. Bvt. Maj. Vols., 13 March, 1865, for gallant and meritorious service during the war. Mustered out 15 March, 1866.

GIBBS, ROBT. T. [Born in Ala. Appointed from Ala.]
Asst. Surg., 3 March, 1847 ; 13th Inf., 9 April, 1847. Disbanded 15 July, 1848.

GIBBS, THEODORE K. [Born in R. I. Appointed from R. I.]
2nd Lieut. 1st Art., 24 Oct., 1861. 1st Lieut., 20 Feb., 1862. Resigned 1 May, 1870. Bvt. Capt., 20 Feb., 1864, for gallant and meritorious service at the Battle of Olustee, Fla. Bvt. Maj., 3 June, 1864, for gallant and meritorious service at the Battle of Cold Harbor, Va.

GIBBS, WM. [Born in ——. Appointed from La.]
1st Lieut. 44th Inf., 11 March, 1814. Reg. Adj., May, 1814, to June, 1815. Trans. to 1st Inf., 17 May, 1815. Reg. P. M., 15 July, 1866, to 13 July, 1818. Died 5 Sept., 1819. Bvt. Capt., 23 Dec., 1814, for gallant conduct at the Siege of New Orleans, La.

GIBSON, ARCHIE.* [Born in Mo. Appointed from Mo.]
2nd Lieut. 7th Cav., 13 June, 1879. Died 26 January, 1881.

GIBSON, AUGUSTUS A.* [Born in Maine. Appointed from Maine.]
2nd Lieut. 2nd Art., 1 July, 1839. 1st Lieut., 18 June, 1846. Capt., 9 July, 1853. Col. 2nd Penn. Heavy Art., 25 June, 1862. Maj. 3rd Art., 25 July, 1863. Mustered out of Vol. service 22 July, 1864. Lieut. Col. 3rd Art., 4 April, 1869. Retired 15 Dec., 1870. Died 11 Feb., 1893.

GIBSON, CHAS. H.* [Born in Pa. Appointed from Pa.]
2nd Lieut. 2nd Drag., 6 May, 1861. 2nd Cav., 3 Aug., 1161. 1st Lieut., 12 Nov., 1861. Resigned 30 May, 1864.

GIBSON, DAVID.* [Born in Va. Appointed from Va.]
Bvt. 2nd Lieut. 3rd Art., 1 July, 1842. 2nd Lieut. 2nd Art., 1 June, 1844. Died 6 Feb., 1847.

GIBSON, EASTON R. [Born in Mo. Appointed from the Army.]
Priv. and Corpl. Co. D, 20th Inf., 28 Aug., 1897, to 1 Sept., 1898. 2nd Lieut. 9th Inf., 9 July, 1898. 1st Lieut., 16 March, 1899.

GIBSON, EDWIN O. [Born in N. Y. Appointed from N. Y.]
2nd Lieut. 114th N. Y. Vols., 3 Sept., 1862. 1st Lieut., 1 Nov., 1863. Mustered out 8 June, 1865. 2nd Lieut. 17th Inf., 23 Feb., 1866. Trans. to 26th Inf., 21 Sept.,

1866. 1st Lieut., 28 July, 1866. Trans. to 10th Inf., 19 May, 1869. Reg. Adj., 13 Dec., 1871, to 1 June, 1879. Capt., 21 May, 1883. Retired for loss of right leg in line of duty 16 Feb., 1885.

GIBSON, FRANCIS M. [Born in Pa. Appointed from Pa.]
2nd Lieut. 7th Cav., 5 Oct., 1867. 1st Lieut., 11 July, 1871. Capt. 5 Feb., 1880. Retired for disability 3 Dec., 1891.

GIBSON, GEORGE. [Born in Pa. Appointed from Pa.]
Capt. 5th Inf., 3 May, 1808. Maj. 7th Inf., 9 Nov., 1811. Lieut. Col. 5th Inf., 15 August, 1813. Disbanded 15 June, 1815. Col. Q. M. Gen., 29 April, 1816. Com. G. of S., 18 April, 1818. Died 28 Sept., 1861. Bvt. Brig. Gen., 29 April, 1826, for ten years' faithful service in one grade. Bvt. Maj. Gen., 30 May, 1848, for meritorious conduct, particularly in performing his duties in prosecuting the war with Mexico.

GIBSON, GEORGE. [Born in Pa. Appointed from Pa.]
Mil. S. Q. M. Dept., 9 April, 1853. Capt. 11th Inf., 14 May, 1861. Bvt. Maj., 13 March, 1865, for gallant conduct in the Battle of Gettysburg, Penn. Bvt. Lieut. Col., 9 April, 1865, for gallant and meritorious service during the operations resulting in the fall of Richmond, Va., and the surrender of the insurgent army under Gen. R. E. Lee. Maj. 1st Inf., 12 Jan., 1869. Unassigned 15 March, 1869. Ass'd to 5th Inf., 9 June, 1869. Lieut Col. 3rd Inf., 20 March, 1879. Col. 5th Inf., 1 Aug., 1886. Died 5 Aug., 1888.

GIBSON, HORATIO G.* Born in Md. Appointed from Pa.]
Bvt. 2nd Lieut. 2nd Art., 1 July, 1847. 2nd Lieut. 3rd Art., 8 Sept., 1847. 1st Lieut., 26 May, 1851. R. Q. M., 1 Nov., 1858, to 14 May, 1861. Capt., 14 May, 1861. Bvt. Maj., 5 May, 1862, for gallant and meritorious service in the Battle of Williamsburg, Va. Bvt. Lieut. Col., 17 Sept., 1862, for gallant and meritorious service in the Battle of Antietam, Md. Lieut. Col. 2nd Ohio Art., 1 Aug., 1863. Col., 15 Aug., 1863. Bvt. Col., 13 March, 1865, for gallant and meritorious service in the field during the war. Bvt. Brig. Gen. Vols., 13 March, 1865, for gallant and meritorious service during the war. Mustered out of Vol. service, 23 Aug., 1865. Maj. 3rd Art., 5 Feb., 1867. Lieut. Col., 2nd Art., 19 April, 1882. Col. 3rd Art., 1 Dec., 1883. Retired 22 May, 1891.

GIBSON, JAMES.* [Born in Md. Appointed from Del.]
1st Lieut. Light Art., 12 Dec., 1808. Capt., 2 May, 1810. Maj. A. I. G., 2 April, 1813. Col. I. G., 13 July, 1813. Col. 4th Rifles, 21 Feb., 1814. Killed 17 Sept., 1814, in the assault on Fort Erie.

GIBSON, JAMES. [Born in Ireland. Appointed from Pa.]
Capt. 12th Inf., 12 March, 1812. Resigned 31 Jan., 1814. Mil. Storekeeper 1 March, 1814. Disbanded 1 June, 1821.

GIBSON, JOHN. [Born in ——. Appointed from Ind.]
1st Lieut. Mtd Rangers, 1 July, 1832. Disbanded 1 Oct., 1833.

GIBSON, JOHN B. [Born in Pa. Appointed from Pa.]
2nd Lieut. 1st Art., 8 March, 1847. 1st Lieut., 12 Jan., 1848. Resigned 21 Aug., 1854. Bvt. 1st Lieut., 20 Aug., 1847, for gallant and meritorious conduct at Contreras and Churubusco. Died 15 Jan., 1856.

GIBSON, JOSEPH R. [Born in Pa. Appointed from Pa.]
1st Lieut. Asst. Surg., 16 April, 1862. Bvt. Capt. and Bvt. Maj., 13 March, 1865, for faithful and meritorious service during the war. Capt. Asst. Surg., 28 July, 1866. Bvt. Lieut. Col., 28 Sept., 1866, for meritorious and distinguished service at Hart's Island, New York Harbor, where cholera prevailed. Maj. and Surg., 19 March, 1877. Lieut. Col. Dep. Surg. Gen., 28 June, 1894. Retired for disability 15 Nov., 1895.

GIBSON, ROBT. A. [Born in Pa. Appointed from Iowa.]
Sergt. Co. G, 12th Iowa Vols., 25 Nov., 1861. 1st Lieut., 16 Jan., 1865. Capt., 6 Feb., 1865. Mustered out 20 Jan., 1866. 2nd Lieut., 13th Inf., 9 April, 1866. Trans. to 22nd Inf., 21 Sept., 1866. Died 23 Sept., 1867.

GIBSON, ROBERT J. [Born in Conn. Appointed from Conn.]
Asst. Surg., 16 June, 1880. Capt. and Asst. Surg., 16 June, 1885. Maj. and Surg., 23 April, 1898.

GIBSON, THOMAS W. [Born in Ind. Appointed from Ind.]
Priv. Co. E, 54th Ind. Vols., 10 June to 16 Sept., 1862. Sergt. Co. B, 7th Ind. Cav., 19 Sept., 1863. Mustered out 18 Feb., 1866. 2nd Lieut. 8th Cav., 25 May, 1867. 1st Lieut., 4 Nov., 1867. Mustered out 1 Jan., 1871.

GIBSON, WILLIAM R. [Born in S. C. Appointed from Oregon.]
Mil. S. Q. M. Dept., 14 March, 1857. Addl. P. M., 1 June, 1861. Bvt. Lieut. Col. Vols., 13 March, 1865, for faithful and valuable service in the Pay Department. Maj. and P. M., 17 Jan., 1867. Lieut. Col. Dep. P. M. G., 8 Dec., 1886. Col. Asst. P. M. G., 3 Jan., 1893. Retired for disability 6 Jan., 1893. Died 1 March, 1899.

GIBSON, WM. R. [Born in Ohio. Appointed from Iowa.]
2nd Lieut. 3d Inf., 1 June, 1899.

GIBSON, WILLIAM W.* [Born in Conn. Appointed from Conn.]
2nd Lieut. 5th Inf., 13 June, 1879. Trans. to 3rd Art., 11 July, 1879. 1st Lieut. Ord., 10 Jan., 1887. Capt. (14 years' service) 12 June, 1894.

GIDDINGS, GROTIUS R. [Born in Ohio. Appointed from Ohio.]
Capt. 23rd Ohio Vols., 11 June, 1861, to 23 July, 1861. Maj. 14th Inf., 14 May, 1861. Lieut. Col., 16th Inf., 18 May, 1864. Died 21 June, 1867. Bvt. Lieut. Col., 2 July, 1863, for gallant and meritorious service at the Battles of Chancellorsville, Va., and Gettysburg, Penn. Bvt. Col., 13 March, 1865, for gallant and meritorious service at the Battle of Gettysburg, Penn.

GIDDINGS, PAUL. [Born in Minn. Appointed from Army.]
Priv., Corpl., Sergt. and 1st Sergt. Troop E, 8th Cav., 5 July, 1892, to 19 April, 1897. 2nd Lieut. 3rd Inf., 25 March, 1897. 1st Lieut., 2 March, 1899.

GIFFORD, JOHN H.* [Born in Ind. Appointed from Ind.]
Priv. Co. E, 16th Ind. Vols., 23 April, 1861. Discharged 14 May, 1862. Cadet.

Mil. Acad., 1 July, 1863. 2nd Lieut. 2nd Art., 17 Juns, 1867. 1st Lieut., I Nov., 1874. Graduate of the Art. School, 1873 and 1890. Retired with rank of Capt. for disability 8 March, 1898.

GIGNILIAT, JAMES. [Born in Ga. Appointed from Ga.]
Ensign 8th Inf., 20 May, 1813. 3rd Lieut., 2 Dec., 1813. 2nd Lieut., 4 Oct., 1814. Disbanded 15 June, 1815. Reinstated in Corps Art., 2 Dec., 1815. Resigned 31 Oct., 1817.

GILBERT, BERTRAM C.* [Born in Cal. Appointed from N. M.]
Addl. 2nd Lieut. 1st Art., 11 June, 1897. 2nd Lieut., 2nd Art., 10 Feb., 1898. 1st Lieut. 6th Art., 2 March, 1899.

GILBERT, CHARLES C.* [Born in Ohio. Appointed from Ohio.]
Bvt. 2nd Lieut. 3rd Inf., 1 July, 1846. 2nd Lieut. 1st Inf., 27 Sept., 1846. 1st Lieut., 10 June, 1850. Capt., 8 Dec., 1855. Bvt. Maj., 7 April, 1862, for gallant and meritorious service in the Battle of Shiloh, Tenn. Bvt. Lieut. Col., 1 Sept., 1862, for gallant and meritorious service in the Battle of Richmond, Ky. Brig. Gen. Vols., 9 Sept., 1862, for gallant conduct at Springfield, Mo., and Pittsburg Landing, Tenn. Bvt. Col., 8 Oct., 1862, for gallant and meritorious service in the Battle of Perryville, Ky. Appointment of Brig. Gen. Vols., expired by Constitutional limitation, 4 March, 1863. Maj. 19th Inf., 2 July, 1863. Trans. to 28th Inf., 21 Sept., 1866. Lieut. Col. 7th Inf., 8 July, 1868. Col. 17th Inf., 19 May, 1881. Retired by operation of law, 1 March, 1886.

GILBERT, HENRY.* [Born in N. Y. Appointed from N. Y.]
2nd Lieut. Corps Art., 1 July, 1819. Trans. to 2nd Art., 1 June, 1821. Died 26 June, 1827.

GILBERT, WM. W. [Born in N. Y. Appoined from N. Y.]
1st Lieut. 19th Inf., 14 May, 1861. Reg. Adj., 4 August, 1861, to 7 July, 1864. Capt., 7 July, 1864. Resigned 9 Jan., 1866. Maj. and P. M., 3 Nov., 1898.

GILBREATH, ERASMUS C. [Born in Ohio. Appointed from Ind.]
1st Lieut. 20th Ind. Vols., 22 July, 1861. Capt., 7 Dec., 1862. Maj., 27 July, 1863. Mustered out 19 Oct., 1864. Capt. A. Q. M. Vols., 23 Jan., 1865. Mustered out 28 July, 1864. 2nd Lieut. and 1st Lieut. 15th Inf., 23 Feb., 1866. Trans. to 24th Inf., 21 Sept., 1866. Trans. to 11th Inf., 25 April, 1869. Capt. 23 Dec., 1873. Maj. 9th Inf., 30 April, 1897. Trans. to 11th Inf., 29 May, 1897. Died 22 Aug., 1898.

GILBRETH, BENJAMIN H. [Born in Maine. Appointed from Maine.]
Ord. Storekeeper, 11 May, 1861. Capt. Ord. Storekeeper, 28 July, 1866. Retired by operation of law, 30 June, 1882.

GILBRETH, JOSEPH L. [Born in Ark. Appointed from Idaho.]
2nd Lieut. 14th Inf., 9 July, 1898. 1st Lieut., 2 March, 1899.

GILE, GEORGE W. [Born in N. H. Appointed from Pa.]
1st Lieut. 22nd Penn. Vols., 23 April, 1861. Mustered out 7 Aug., 1861. Maj. 88th Penn. Vols., 18 Sept., 1861. Lieut. Col., 1 Sept., 1862. Col., 24 Jan., 1863. Mustered out 2 March, 1863. Maj. Veteran Reserve Corps, 22 May, 1863. Col., 29 Sept., 1863. Bvt. Brig. Gen. Vols., 6 May, 1865, for energy and good conduct in assisting to repel the attack on Fort Slocum, D. C. Mustered out 4 Jan., 1867. 1st Lieut. 45th Inf., 28 July, 1866. Bvt. Capt., 2 March, 1867, for gallant and meritorious service in the Battle of Bull Run (2nd), Va. Bvt. Maj., 2 March, 1867, for gallant and meritorious service in the Battle of South Mountain, Md. Bvt. Lieut. Col., 2 March, 1867, for gallant and meritorious service in the Battle of Antietam, Md. Capt. 45th Inf., 4 Feb., 1868. Unassigned 22 July, 1869. Retired with rank of Col., 15 Dec., 1870. Reduced to Lieut. Col., 3 March, 1875. Died 26 Feb., 1896.

GILES. AQUILA. [Born in N. Y. Appointed from N. Y.]
Maj. in Revolutionary Army. Mil. Storekeeper, 1 Nov., 1817. Died 8 April, 1822.

GILES. HENRY.* [Born in N. Y. Appointed from N. Y.]
2nd Lieut. 5th Inf., 24 July, 1818. Reg. Adj., 4 Jan. to 4 June, 1819. Resigned 1 Jan., 1820. Died 27 March, 1877.

GILES, WM. B. [Born in Va. Appointed from Mo.]
1st Lieut. of Inf., 4 March, 1847; 12th Inf., 9 April, 1847. Disbanded 25 July, 1848. Bvt. Capt., 20 Aug., 1847, for gallant and meritorious conduct at Contreras and Churubusco.

GILES, WM. M. [Born in Ireland. Appointed from N. Y.]
Med. Storekeeper, 20 June, 1863. Resigned 10 Sept., 1863.

GILHAM. WM.* [Born in Ind. Appointed from Ind.]
2nd Lieut. 3rd Art., 1 July, 1840. 1st Lieut., 23 Oct., 1841. Resigned 17 Oct., 1846. Died 16 Nov., 1872.

GILL, JOHN U. [Born in Pa. Appointed rom Army.]
Priv. 13th Penn. Vols., 20 April to 21 July, 1861. Priv. and Com. Sergt. 3rd Batt. and Sergt. Maj. 2nd Batt. 18th Inf., 4 Oct., 1861 to 13 Nov., 1863. 2nd Lieut. 18th Inf., 31 Oct., 1863. 1st. Lieut., 28 July, 1864. Trans. to 36th Inf., 21 Sept., 1866. Resigned 21 May, 1868. Bvt. Capt., 1 Sept., 1864, for gallant and meritorious service during the Atlanta campaign, and at the Battle of Jonesboro', Ga.

GILL, NATHANIEL J. [Born in Mass. Appointed from Mass.]
2nd Lieut. 9th Inf., 30 Dec., 1847. Disbanded 26 Aug., 1848.

GILL, SAMUEL.* [Born in Ky. Appointed from Ky.]
Bvt. 2nd Lieut. 4th Art., 1 July, 1844. 2nd Lieut., 18 June, 1846. 1st Lieut., 3 March, 1847. Resigned 29 May, 1847. Died 18 Jan., 1876.

GILL, THOS. H. [Born in Mass. Appointed from Mass.]
2nd Lieut. Voltigeurs. 30 Dec., 1847. Trans. to 9th Inf., 24 March, 1848. Disbanded 26 Aug., 1848.

GILL, WM. G.* [Born in N. J. Appointed from Pa.]
Bvt. 2nd Lieut. 3rd Art., 1 July, 1848. 2nd Lieut. 4th Art., 28 Feb., 1849. 1st Lieut., 9 Jan., 1851. Resigned 4 Feb., 1861. Died 7 Jan., 1862.

GILL, WM. H.* [Born in Pa. Appointed from Ohio.]
Mil. Storekeeper Q. M. D., 12 June, 1858. Capt. and M. S. K., 28 July, 1866.

Discharged 16 Dec., 1870. Reinstated 25 March, 1882, with same grade and rank held at date of discharge, under act of Congress 4 March, 1882. Died 21 Aug., 1886.

GILLEM, ALVAN C.* [Born in Tenn. Appointed from Tenn.]
Bvt. 2nd Lieut. 1st Art., 1 July, 1851. 2nd Lieut., 31 Dec., 1851. 1st Lieut., 3 March, 1855. Capt. A. Q. M., 12 July, 1861. Col. 10th Tenn. Vols., 13 May, 1862. Brig. Gen. Vols., 17 Aug., 1863. Maj. Gen. Vols., 3 Nov., 1865. Mustered out Vols., 1 Sept., 1866. Col. 24th Inf., 28 July, 1866. Trans. to 11th Inf., 15 March, 1869. Trans. to 1st Cav., 15 Dec., 1870. Died 2 Dec., 1875. Bvt. Maj., 19 Jan., 1862, for gallant and meritorious service at the Battle of Mill Spring, Ky. Bvt. Lieut. Col., 16 Dec., 1864, for gallant and meritorious service in action at Marion, Va. Bvt. Col., 13 March, 1865, for gallant and meritorious service during the war. Bvt. Brig. Gen., 13 March, 1865, for gallant and meritorious service in the field during the war. Bvt. Maj. Gen., 12 April, 1865, for gallant conduct at the Battle of Salisbury, N. C.

GILLESPIE, GEORGE L.* [Born in Tenn. Appointed from Tenn.]
2nd Lieut. Eng., 17 June, 1862. 1st Lieut., 3 March, 1863. Capt., 22 April, 1864. Bvt. Maj., 1 Aug., 1864, for gallant and meritorious service during the campaign before Richmond, Va. Bvt. Lieut. Col., 9 April, 1865, for gallant and meritorious service in the campaign from Winchester to Appomattox Court House, Va. Maj. Eng., 5 Sept., 1871. Lieut. Col., 12 Oct., 1886. Col., 2 Oct., 1895. Medal of honor for most distinguished gallantry in action near Bethesda Church, Va., 31 May, 1864. He went through the enemy's lines to communicate with General Sheridan and verify his presence; was seized as a prisoner, but escaped; again ordered to surrender, but dashed away under fire, reached General Sheridan's command, and thence immediately returned to General Meade with very valuable information; while serving as 1st Lieut., Corps of Eng. Brig. Gen. Vols., 7 May to 30 Nov., 1898.

GILLETT, CORNELIUS. [Born in Conn. Appointed from Conn.]
Priv., Corpl. and Sergt., Co. A, 1st Conn. Art., 22 May, 1861, to 21 Feb., 1863. 2nd Lieut. 1st Conn. Art., 21 Feb., 1863. 1st Lieut., 2 Apr., 1864. Capt., 24 May, 1865. Bvt. Capt. Vols., 9 April, 1865, for efficient services during the recent operations resulting in the fall of Richmond, Va., and in the surrender of the Insurgent army under Gen. R. E. Lee. Mustered out 25 Sept., 1865. 2nd Lieut. 2nd Art., 23 Feb., 1866. 1st Lieut., 28 July, 1866. Drowned 24 Dec., 1866.

GILLETTE, CASSIUS E.* [Born in N. Y. Appointed from Pa.]
2nd Lieut. Eng., 15 June, 1884. 1st Lieut., 10 Jan., 1887. Capt., 12 Oct., 1895.

GILLETTE, JAMES. [Born in Pa. Appointed from Md.]
Priv. Co. F, 71st N. Y. Mil., 20 April, 1861, to 11 Jan., 1862. 1st Lieut. 3rd Md. Vols., 7 May, 1862, to 2 Oct., 1862. Capt. C. S. Vols., 10 Sept., 1862. Bvt. Maj. Vols., 13 March, 1865, for meritorious services in his Dept. Lieut. Col. Vols., 30 Nov., 1865, for faithful service in Subs. Dept. Mustered out 27 Dec., 1866. Capt. 15th Inf., 7 March, 1867. Resigned 11 March, 1869. Bvt. Maj., 7 March, 1867, for gallant and meritorious service in the Battle of Chancellorsville, Va. Died 24 Nov., 1881.

GILLETTE, LEE P. [Born in Ohio. Appointed from Neb.]
1st Lieut. 1st Neb. Cav., 15 June, 1861. Capt., 1 Sept., 1862. Mustered out, 1 July, 1866. 1st Lieut. 7th Cav., 28 July, 1866. Capt., 8 June, 1867. Resigned 5 Dec., 1868.

GILLISS, JAMES. [Born in D. C. Appointed from D. C.]
2nd Lieut. 5th Art., 14 May, 1861. Bvt. 1st Lieut., 1 July, 1862, for gallant and meritorious service in the Battle of Malvern Hill, Va. 1st Lieut. 5th Art., 27 April, 1863. Bvt. Capt., 12 May, 1864, for gallant and meritorious service in the Battle of Spottsylvania Court House, Va. Capt. A. Q. M., 10 Aug., 1864. Maj. and Q. M., 22 Jan., 1881. Lieut Col. and Dep. Q. M. G., 11 Feb., 1894. Col. Asst. Q. M. G., 15 Oct., 1897. Died 13 Nov., 1898.

GILLMORE, QUINCY A.* [Born in Ohio. Appointed from Ohio.]
Bvt. 2nd Lieut. Eng., 1 July, 1849. 2nd Lieut., 5 Sept., 1853. 1st Lieut., 1 July, 1856. Capt., 6 Aug., 1861. Bvt. Lieut. Col., 11 April, 1862, for gallant and meritorious service in the capture of Fort Pulaski, Ga. Brig. Gen. Vols., 28 April, 1862. Bvt. Col., 30 March, 1863, for gallant and meritorious service in the Battle of Somerset, Ky. Maj. Eng., 1 June, 1863. Maj. Gen. Vols., 10 July, 1863, for the distinguished skill, ability and gallantry displayed in the operations under his charge in Charleston Harbor; the descent upon Morris Island; the reduction of Fort Sumter, and the taking of Fort Wagner and Battery Gregg. Bvt. Brig. Gen., 13 March, 1865, for gallant and meritorious service in the capture of Fort Wagner, S. C. Bvt. Maj. Gen., 13 March, 1865, for gallant and meritorious service in the assault on Morris Island, S. C., 10 July, 1863, and the bombardment and demolition of Fort Sumter. Resigned as Maj. Gen. Vols., 5 Dec., 1865. Lieut. Col. Eng., 13 Jan., 1874. Col., 20 Feb., 1883. Died 7 April, 1888.

GILLMORE, QUINCEY O'M.* [Born in N. Y. Appointed from N. Y.]
2nd Lieut. 10th Cav., 13 June, 1873. Resigned 12 Nov., 1874. 2nd Lieut. 8th Cav., 19 March, 1875. 1st Lieut., 26 June, 1882. R. Q. M., 5 July, 1886. Capt., 20 Feb., 1891. Retired for disability 31 May, 1896. Lieut. Col. 4th N. J. Vols., 4 July, 1898, to muster out 6 April, 1899.

GILMAN, BENJ. H.* [Born in N. H. Appointed from Ill.]
2nd Lieut. 13th Inf., 14 June, 1872. 1st Lieut., 13 June, 1878. R. Q. M., 1 Sept., 1886, to 15 March, 1889. Capt. of Inf. (13th), 24 Feb., 1891. Died 26 July, 1898.

GILMAN, EDWARD R.* [Born in Pa. Appointed from Maine.]
2nd Lieut. 5th Inf., 14 June, 1885. Resigned 5 Jan., 1888.

GILMAN, JEREMIAH H.* [Born in Maine. Appointed from Maine.]
Bvt. 2nd Lieut. 1st Art., 1 July, 1856. 2nd Lieut., 31 Oct., 1856. 1st Lieut., 27 April, 1861. Capt. 19th Inf., 14 May, 1861. Bvt. Maj., 7 April, 1862, for gallant

and meritorious service in the Battle of Shiloh, Tenn. Bvt. Lieut. Col., 31 Dec., 1862, for gallant and meritorious service in the Battle of Stone River, Tenn. Capt. C. S., 9 Feb., 1863. Maj. and C. S., 9 Nov., 1884. Lieut. Col. and Asst. C. G., 8 Oct., 1894. Retired by operation of law 11 Nov., 1895.

GILMAN, SAML. [Born in N. Y. Appointed from Army.]
Priv. Co. I, 5th Art. and Gen. Ser., 3 Feb., 1862, to 23 May, 1864. 2nd Lieut. 5th Art., 7 April, 1864. Dismissed 6 Dec., 1864.

GILMER, JEREMY F.* [Born in N. C. Appointed from N. C.]
2nd Lieut. Eng., 1 July, 1839. 1st Lieut., 29 Dec., 1845. Capt., 1 July, 1853. Resigned 29 June, 1861. Died 1 Dec., 1883.

GILMORE, ALEXR. [Born in N. J. Appointed from N. J.]
Post Chap., 2 July, 1870. Retired 17 May, 1879.

GILMORE, JOHN C. [Born in Canada. Appointed from N. Y.]
Capt. 16th N. Y. Vols., 15 May, 1861. Maj., 29 Sept., 1862. Mustered out 22 May, 1863. Lieut. Col. 193rd N. Y. Vols., 28 March, 1865. Bvt. Col. Vols., 14 Nov., 1865, for gallant and meritorious service. Mustered out 18 Jan., 1866. 2nd Lieut. 12th Inf., 11 May, 1866. Trans. to 30th Inf., 21 Sept., 1866. Reg. Adj., 10 Dec., 1866, to 9 Feb., 1867. Capt. 38th Inf., 22 Jan., 1867. Bvt. Maj., 2 March, 1867, for gallant and meritorious service in the Battle of Antietam, Md. Bvt. Lieut. Col., 2 March, 1867, for gallant and meritorious service in the Battle of Fredericksburg, Va. Trans. to 24th Inf., 11 Nov., 1869. Maj. and A. A. G., 14 Aug., 1890. Lieut. Col. and A. A. G., 15 Nov., 1896. Col. A. A. G., 28 April, 1900. Brig. Gen. Vols., 27 May, 1898, to 12 June, 1899. Medal of Honor for distinguished conduct in the Battle of Salem Heights, Va., 3 May, 1863, seizing the colors of his regiment and gallantly rallying his men under a very severe fire of the enemy while serving as Maj. 16th N. Y. Inf.

GILMORE, JOHN C., JR.* [Born in N. M. Appointed from N. Y.]
2nd Lieut. 4th Cav., 12 June, 1894. Trans. to 4th Art., 12 Oct., 1894. 1st Lieut., 2 March, 1899. Capt. and A. A. G. Vols., 12 May, 1898, to 13 June, 1899. Capt. and A. Q. M., 14 June to 18 Aug., 1899. Maj. 43rd U. S. Vols., 17 Aug., 1899, to ——.

GILPIN, WM. [Born in Pa. Appointed from Pa.]
Cadet at Mil. Acad., 1 July, 1834, to 15 Feb., 1835. 2nd Lieut. 2nd Drag., 8 June, 1836. 1st Lieut., 19 Oct., 1836. Resigned 30 April, 1838.

GIMBREDE, THOS. [Born in France. Appointed from N. Y.]
Teacher Drawing, Mil. Acad., 6 Jan., 1819. Died 25 Dec., 1832.

GIRARD, ALFRED C. [Born in Switzerland. Appointed from N. Y.]
1st Lieut. Asst. Surg., 14 May, 1867. Capt. Asst. Surg., 14 May, 1870. Maj. and Surg., 17 Nov., 1887. Lieut. Col. and Chf. Surg. Vols., 9 May, 1898, to 12 April, 1899.

GIRARD, JOSEPH B. [Born in France. Appointed from Mich.]
1st Lieut. Asst. Surg., 14 May, 1867. Capt. Asst. Surg., 14 May, 1870. Maj. and Surg., 22 March, 1888.

GIRD, HENRY H.* [Born in N. Y. Appointed from N. Y.]
Bvt. 2nd Lieut. 4th Art., 1 July, 1822. 2nd Lieut., 1 July, 1822. Trans. to 2nd Art., 14 Sept., 1827. Resigned 30 Nov., 1829. Died 1 June, 1845.

GITTINGS, ERSKINE.* [Born in Md. Appointed from Md.]
2nd Lieut. 3rd Art., 6 May, 1861. 1st Lieut., 14 May, 1861. Bvt. Capt., 22 Oct., 1862, for gallant and meritorious service in action at Pocotaligo, S. C. Bvt. Maj., 29 Nov., 1863, for gallant and meritorious service during the Siege of Knoxville, Tenn. Capt. 13th Inf., 28 July, 1866, declined. Capt. 3rd Art., 5 Feb., 1867. Died 20 Sept., 1880.

GIVENS, NEWTON C.* [Born in Ky. Appointed from Ind.]
Bvt. 2nd Lieut. 1st. Drag., 1 July, 1845. 2nd Lieut. 2nd Drag., 9 May, 1846. 1st Lieut., 25 July, 1850. Capt., 28 Feb., 1857. Died 9 March, 1859. Bvt. 1st Lieut., 23 Feb., 1847, for gallant and meritorious conduct at Buena Vista.

GIVENS, WM. C. [Born in N. Y. Appointed from N. Y.]
2nd Lieut. 6th Inf., 4 Dec., 1818. Disbanded 1 June, 1821.

GLACKIN, JOHN. [Born in Mass. Appointed from R. I.]
2nd Lieut. of Inf., 23 Feb. 1847; 9th Inf., 9 April, 1847. 1st Lieut., 4 Dec., 1847. Disbanded 26 Aug., 1848. Bvt. 1st Lieut., 13 Sept., 1847, for gallant and meritorious conduct to Chapultepec, Mex.

GLASS, JOHN N.* [Born in Tenn. Appointed from Tenn.]
Addl. 2nd Lieut. 10th Cav., 14 June, 1878. 2nd Lieut., 25 June, 1878. Trans. to 6th Cav., 9 Aug., 1878. 1st Lieut., 20 March, 1885. Died 15 Aug., 1892.

GLASGOW, WM. J.* [Born in Mo. Appointed from Mo.]
2nd Lieut. 1st Cav., 12 June, 1891. 1st Lieut 2nd Cav., 1 July, 1898. Capt. and Act. J. A., 4 Oct., 1899.

GLASSELL, JAMES M. [Born in Va. Appointed from Va.]
Ensign 20th Inf., 1 May, 1812. 2nd Lieut., 16 April, 1813. 1st Lieut., 12 July, 1814. Reg. Adj., July, 1814, to June, 1815. Trans. to 4th Inf., 17 May, 1815. Reg. Adj., 1 Oct., 1815, to 7 Sept., 1816. Capt., 10 Feb., 1818. Maj. A. A. G., 22 May, 1818, to 1 June, 1821. Maj. 6th Inf., 6 Sept., 1837. Died 3 Nov., 1838. Bvt. Maj., 10 Feb., 1828, for ten years' faithful service in one grade.

GLASSFORD, WILLIAM A. [Born in Ind. Appointed from Army.]
Cadet at Naval Acad., 27 Sept., 1871, to 13 June, 1873. Priv. Sig. Corps, 20 Nov., 1874. Sergt., 1 Nov., 1877. Discharged 13 Nov., 1879. 2nd Lieut. Sig. Corps, 1 Nov., 1879. 1st Lieut., 19 Dec., 1890. Capt. (14 years' service), 14 Nov., 1893. Maj. and Chief Sig. Off. Vols., 20 May, 1898. Lieut. Col. and Chief Sig. Off. Vols., 18 July, 1898, to 17 April, 1899. Maj. and Sig. Off. Vols., 17 April, 1899, to —.

GLEASON, JOSEPH. [Born in Mass. Appointed from Mass.]
Ensign 9th Inf., 22 Jan., 1813. 3rd Lieut., 17 March, 1813. 2nd Lieut., 14 Aug., 1813. Reg. Adj., May, 1813, to Aug., 1814. 1st Lieut., 25 July, 1814. Trans. to 5th Inf., 17 May, 1815. Died 27 March, 1820. Bvt. Capt., 15 Aug., 1814, for gallant conduct in defence of Fort Erie.

GLEASON, WILLARD E.* [Born in Ohio. Appointed from Ohio.]
2nd Lieut. 6th Inf., 11 June, 1892. 1st Lieut., 26 April, 1898.

GLEN, JOHN C. [Born in S. C. Appointed from S. C.]
Asst. Surg., 22 June, 1839. Died 14 Feb., 1848.

GLEN, THOS. B. [Born in Ga. Appointed from Ga.]
2nd Lieut. 3rd Inf., 15 Oct., 1838. Died 9 June, 1841.

GLENN, EDWIN F.* [Born in N. C. Appointed from N. C.]
2nd Lieut. 25th Inf., 15 June, 1877. 1st Lieut., 4 Dec., 1884. Capt., 5 July, 1895.

GLENN, GEORGE E. [Born in Ohio. Appointed from Ohio.]
Addl. P. M., 24 Nov., 1862. Maj. and P. M., 17 Jan., 1867. Lieut. Col. and Dep. P. M. G., 3 Jan., 1893. Col. and Asst. P. M. G., 27 March, 1895. Died 31 March, 1899.

GLENN, THOS. [Born in Del. Appointed from La.]
Capt. of Inf., 5 March, 1847; 14th Inf., 9 April, 1847. Disbanded 26 July, 1848. Bvt. Maj., 13 Sept., 1847, for gallant and meritorious conduct at Chapultepec, Mex.

GLENNAN, JAMES D. [Born in N. Y. Appointed from D. C.]
Asst. Surg., 29 Oct., 1888. Capt. and Asst. Surg., 29 Oct., 1893. Maj. and Brigade Surg. Vols., 4 June. 1898, to 12 May, 1899. Maj. and Surg. 38th U. S. Vols., 17 Aug., 1899, to —.

GLIDDEN, JOSEPH W. [Born in Mass. Appointed from Maine.]
2nd Lieut. 4th Inf., 9 July, 1898. 1st Lieut., 2 March, 1899. Capt. 46th U. S. Vols., 17 Aug., 1899, to —.

GLISAN, RODNEY. [Born in Md. Appointed from Md.]
Asst. Surg., 2 May, 1850. Resigned 7 June, 1861.

GLOVER, ELISHA V., Jr. [Born in Mass. Appointed from N. J.]
1st Lieut. 34th N. J. Vols., 3 Sept., 1863. Capt., 15 May, 1864. Bvt. Maj. and Lieut. Col. Vols., 11 Nov., 1865, for gallant and meritorious service. Mustered out 30 April, 1866 2nd Lieut. 29th Inf., 22 Jan., 1867. Dismissed 9 June, 1868.

GODDARD, CHAS. C. [Born in Ohio. Appointed from Ohio.]
Capt. 17th Inf., 20 Sept., 1861. Resigned 26 May, 1864.

GODDARD, CHAS. E. [Born in N. Y. Appointed from N. Y.]
1st Lieut. Asst. Surg., 28 May, 1861. Bvt. Capt. and Bvt. Maj., 13 March, 1865, for faithful and meritorious service during the war. Capt. Asst. Surg., 28 May, 1866. Maj. and Surg., 6 Jan., 1868. Died 4 Jan., 1886.

GODDARD, VINTON A.* [Born in N. Y. Appointed at Large.]
2nd Lieut. 6th Cav., 12 June, 1871. Resigned 17 Jan., 1873. 2nd Lieut. 4th Art., 27 Sept., 1873. Died 2 March, 1877.

GODFREY, EDWARD S.* [Born in Ohio. Appointed from Ohio.]
Priv. Co. D., 21st Ohio Vols., 26 April, 1861. Discharged 12 Aug., 1861. Cadet at Mil. Acad., 1 July, 1863. 2nd Lieut. 7th Cav., 17 June, 1867. 1st Lieut., 1 Feb., 1868. Capt., 9 Dec., 1876. Maj. 1st Cav., 8 Dec., 1896. Trans. to 7th Cav., 7 Jan., 1897. Bvt. Maj., 27 Feb., 1890, for gallant services in action against Indians at Bear Paw Mountain, Mont., Sept. 30, 1877, where he was wounded. Medal of honor for most distinguished gallantry in action against hostile Nez Perce Indians at Bear Paw Mountain, Mont., Sept. 30, 1877, in leading his command into action, where he was severely wounded.

GODFREY, GEORGE J.* [Born in N. Y. Appointed from N. Y.]
2nd Lieut. 12th Inf., 1 July, 1886. 1st Lieut. 22nd Inf., 1 Feb., 1893. Capt., 2 March, 1899.

GODFREY, GUY M. C. [Born in Ohio. Appointed from Ohio.]
Asst. Surg., 12 May, 1893. Capt. Asst. Surg., 24 Oct., 1898.

GODMAN, JOHN W. [Born in Ohio. Appointed from Ohio.]
Sergt. and 1st Sergt. Co. C, 96th Ohio Vols., 19 Aug., 1862, to 27 March, 1863. 1st Lieut. 96th Ohio Vols., 27 March, 1863. Mustered out 7 July, 1865. 2nd Lieut. 6th Inf., 23 Feb., 1866. Dropped 8 Jan., 1867.

GODWIN, EDWARD A.* [Born in Va. Appointed from W. Va.]
Priv. Co. A, 1st W. Va. Cav., 13 Feb., 1865. Discharged 8 July, 1865. Cadet at Mil. Acad. 17 Oct., 1865. 2nd Lieut. 8th Cav., 15 June, 1870. 1st Lieut., 3 Oct., 1876. R. Q. M., 23 May, 1883, to 5 July, 1886. Capt., 5 July, 1886. Maj. 7th Cav., 1 July, 1899. Col. 7th U. S. Vols., 21 May, 1898, to 28 Feb., 1899. Col. 40th U. S. Vols., 17 Aug., 1899.

GODWIN, WM. T. [Born in Pa. Appointed from Pa.]
2nd Lieut. 10th Inf., 15 May, 1861. 1st Lieut., 1 July, 1861. Dismissed 13 Sept., 1862. Priv. and Serg. Co. F, 118th Pa. Vols., 17 July, 1863, to 29 Dec., 1864. 1st Lieut 118th Pa. Vols., 29 Dec., 1864. Mustered out 1 June, 1865.

GOE, JAMES B.* [Born in Ohio. Appointed from Ohio.]
2nd Lieut. 13th Inf., 16 June, 1875. 1st Lieut., 16 Oct., 1884. Capt., 4 May, 1897.

GOETHALS, GEORGE W.* [Born in N. Y. Appointed from N. Y.]
2nd Lieut. Eng., 12 June, 1880. 1st Lieut., 15 June, 1882. Capt., 14 Dec., 1891. Lieut. Col. and Chf. Eng. Vols., 9 May, 1898, to 31 Dec., 1898. Maj. Eng., 7 Feb., 1900.

GOHN, JOSEPH F.* [Born in Ill. Appointed from Ill.]
2nd Lieut. 14th Inf., 26 April, 1898. 1st Lieut., 2 Mar., 1899.

GOLDMAN, HENRY J.* [Born in Germany. Appointed from N. Y.]
2nd Lieut. 5th Cav., 15 June, 1877. 1st Lieut., 24 April, 1886. Capt., 1 June, 1897.

GONZALES, MANUEL J. [Born in Maderia. Appointed from D. C.]
Hosp. Chap. Vols., 6 Aug., 1862. Mustered out 15 Sept., 1863. Hosp. Chap. Vols., 17 Oct., 1863. Mustered out 4 Aug., 1865. Chap. 9th Cav., 26 Dec., 1868. Retired 30 June, 1882. Died 22 Sept., 1885.

GOODALE, GEORGE S.* [Born in Ore. Appointed from Ore.]
Addl. 2nd Lieut. 23rd Inf., 12 June, 1896. 2nd Lieut. 25th Inf., 1 Jan., 1897. Trans. to 23rd Inf., 4 Feb., 1897. 1st Lieut. 11th Inf., 7 Jan., 1899. Trans. to 23rd Inf., 28 Feb., 1899.

GOODALE, GREENLEAF A. [Born in Maine. Appointed from Maine.]
Priv. Co. E, 6th Maine Vols., 7 May, 1861. Corp., ———, Serg., 5 May, 1863. 1st Lieut. 77th U. S. Col. Troops, 2 Jan., 1864. Capt., 24 May, 1864. Bvt. Maj. Vols., 13 March, 1865, for faithful and meritorious service during the war. Mustered out 14 November, 1866. 1st Lieut. 23rd Inf., 28 July, 1866. Bvt. Capt., 2 March, 1867, for gallant and meritorious service at the Battle of Gettysburg. Capt. 23rd Inf., 25 June, 1878. Maj., 26 April, 1898. Lieut. Col. 3rd Inf., 19 July, 1899.

GOODE, GEORGE W.* [Born in Mo. Appointed from Mo.]
2nd Lieut. 1st Cav., 12 June, 1880. 1st Lieut. 3rd Cav., 1 Feb., 1891. Trans. to 1st Cav., 27 April, 1891. Capt., 2 March, 1899.

GOODE, JOHN THOMAS. [Born in Va. Appointed from Va.]
2nd Lieut. 4th Art., 18 June, 1855. 1st Lieut., 10 June, 1857. Dismissed 3 July, 1861.

GOODE, ROBERT. [Born in Va. Appointed from Va.]
2nd Lieut. 2nd Art., 6 July, 1812. Trans to Corps Art., 12 May, 1814. 1st Lieut., 15 July, 1815. Dismissed 5 Aug., 1817. Died 3 March, 1837.

GOODFELLOW, HENRY. [Born in Pa. Appointed from Pa.]
Capt. 26th Penn. Vols., 5 May, 1861. Mustered out 18 June, 1864. Bvt. Lieut. Col. Vols., 13 March, 1865, for gallant and meritorious conduct in the Battle of Gettysburg, Penn. Bvt. Col. Vols., 13 March, 1865, for gallant and meritorious conduct in the Battles of the Wilderness and Spottsylvania, Va. Maj. J. A. Vols., 28 Nov., 1865. 2nd Lieut. 31st Inf., 11 May, 1866, declined. J. A. U. S. A., 25 Feb., 1867. Died 29 Dec., 1885.

GOODFELLOW, JOHN C. [Born in D. C. Appointed from D. C.]
2nd Lieut. 7th Art., 9 July, 1898. Trans. to 4th Art., 4 April, 1899.

GOODHUE, JOHN M. [Born in Mass. Appointed from Mass.]
1st Lieut., Adj. 3rd Batt. Mass. Vols., 19 April to 30 June, 1861. Capt. 11th Inf., 14 May, 1861. Maj. 23rd Inf., 23 Nov., 1868. Trans. to 11th Inf., 24 Dec., 1868. Trans. to 21st Inf., 15 March, 1869. Unassigned 26 March, 1869. Mustered out 1 Jan., 1871. Bvt. Maj., 13 March, 1865, for gallant and meritorious service at the Battle of Gettysburg, Penn.

GOODHUE, JOSEPH. [Born in Vt. Appointed from Vt.]
Garrison. Surg. Mate, 8 Feb., 1803. Post Surg., 5 Aug., 1816. Asst. Surg., 1 June, 1821. Resigned 31 Dec., 1824.

GOODIN, JAMES A.* [Born in Ky. Appointed from Ky.]
2nd Lieut. 7th Inf., 13 June, 1882. 1st Lieut. 19th Inf., 20 Feb., 1891. Trans. to 7th Inf., 20 July, 1891. Capt. 25th Inf., 2 May, 1898. Trans. to 7th Inf., 16 Sept., 1898. Graduate of the Infantry and Cavalry School, 1891.

GOODING, GEORGE. [Born in Mass. Appointed from Mass.]
Ensign 4th Inf., 12 Dec., 1808. 2nd Lieut., 9 June, 1810. 1st Lieut., 15 Feb., 1812. Capt., 15 June, 1814. Disbanded 15 June, 1815. Reinstated 2 Dec., 1815, as 1st Lieut. 5th Inf. Capt., 31 Dec., 1820. Disbanded 1 June, 1821. Retained — Dec., 1815 (in reorganization under Act of 3 March, 1815), as 1st Lieut. 5th Inf., with Bvt. of Capt. from 15 June, 1814. Died 20 March, 1830.

GOODING, OLIVER P.* [Born in Ind. Appointed from Ind.]
Bvt. 2nd Lieut. 4th Inf., 1 July, 1858. 2nd Lieut. 10th Inf., 5 Feb., 1859. 1st Lieut., 7 May, 1861. Capt., 27 June, 1862. Col. 31st Mass. Vols., 18 Feb., 1862. Mustered out Vols., 26 Nov., 1864. Bvt. Brig. Gen., Vols., 13 March, 1865, for meritorious service. Bvt. Maj. Gen. Vols., 13 March, 1865, for gallant conduct in the assault on the enemy's works at Port Hudson, La., in 1863, and for gallant and distinguished conduct throughout the Red River campaign in 1864. Resigned 20 March, 1865.

GOODLET, ADAM G. [Born in ——. Appointed from Ky.]
Surg. Mate 7th Inf., 12 Dec., 1808. Surg. 7th Inf., 10 Feb., 1812. Trans. to 3rd Inf., 17 May, 1815. Trans. to 4th Inf., 2 Oct., 1816. Resigned 1 Oct., 1817. Died 19 April, 1848.

GOODLOE, ARCHIBALD H.* [Born in Ky. Appointed from Ky.]
2nd Lieut. and 1st Lieut. 13th Inf., 23 June, 1865. Trans. to 22nd Inf., 21 Sept., 1866. R. Q. M., 1 Jan., 1867, to 31 Jan., 1868. Reg. Adj., 31 Jan., 1868, to 1 March, 1869. R. Q. M., 30 July, 1869, to 1 July, 1872. Capt., 1 July, 1872. Retired for disability 24 April, 1883. Died 27 Nov., 1899.

GOODLOE, WM. H. H. [Born in Ohio. Appointed from Ohio.]
2nd Lieut. of Inf., 24 March, 1847; 15th Inf., 9 April, 1847. Resigned 4 Dec., 1847.

GOODMAN, JOHN B. [Born in Pa. Appointed from Mich.]
2nd Lieut. of Inf., 2 March, 1847; 15th Inf., 9 April, 1847. 1st Lieut., 31 May, 1847. Killed 20 Aug., 1847, in Battle of Churubusco, Mexico.

GOODNOW, HAROLD P. [Born in N. Y. Appointed from the Army.]
Priv., Corpl. and Sergt. Co. H, 3rd Inf., 3 Feb., 1896, to 6 July, 1898. 2nd Lieut. 2nd Art., 22 June, 1898. Trans. to 8th Inf., 10 Sept., 1899 (to rank from 10 Sept., 1899).

GOODRICH, FRANK C. [Born in N. H. Appointed from Mass.]
Cadet at Mil. Acad., 1 July to 22 Oct., 1854. Sergt. Co. D, 3d Mass. Vols., 23 April to 22 July, 1861. 2nd Lieut. 2nd Inf., 5 Aug., 1861. 1st Lieut., 19 Nov., 1861. Cashiered 21 July, 1862. Restored 11 Dec., 1862. Killed 2 July, 1863, at Battle of Gettysburg, Penn. Bvt. Capt., 3 May, 1863, for gallant and meritorious service at the Battle of Chancellorsville, Va.

GOODWIN, MILLARD F.* [Born in N. Y. Appointed from N. Y.]
2nd Lieut. 9th Cav., 14 June, 1872. 1st Lieut., 4 April, 1879. R. Q. M., 1 Jan., 1881, to 1 May, 1883. Resigned 31 Aug., 1883.

GOODWIN, WM. F. [Born in Maine. Appointed from N. H.]
1st Lieut. 16th Inf., 14 May, 1861. Capt., 14 May, 1864. Retired 11 Feb., 1865. Died 12 March, 1872. Bvt. Capt., 20 Sept., 1863, for gallant and meritorious service at the Battle of Chickamauga, Ga.

GOODWIN, WM. P. [Born in Ill. Appointed from Ohio.]
2nd Lieut. 14th Inf., 15 Aug., 1876. 1st Lieut., 8 April, 1889. Capt., 1 March, 1894. Retired for disability 8 Sept., 1898.

GOODWYN, ROBERT H. [Born in S. C. Appointed from S. C.]
Ensign 10th Inf., 24 March, 1813. 3rd Lieut., 10 Nov., 1813. 2nd Lieut., 24 July, 1814. Reg. Adj., Aug., 1814, to June, 1815. Trans. to 7th Inf., 17 May, 1815. 1st Lieut., 1 Feb., 1817. Resigned 30 April, 1817. Col. S. C. Vols., 17 Feb., to 15 May, 1836.

GOOLRICH, JOHN C. [Born in ———. Appointed from Ala.]
2nd Lieut. Corps Art., 28 Jan., 1820. Disbanded 1 June, 1821.

GORDON, ABRAM M E. [Born in Md. Appointed from Md.]
1st Lieut. 4th N. Y. Art., 18 Jan., 1864. Bvt. Capt. Vols., 13 March, 1865, for faithful and meritorious service during the war. Mustered out 26 Sept., 1865. 2nd Lieut. 5th Art., 11 May, 1866. 1st Lieut., 1 April, 1867. Died 28 Sept., 1867.

GORDON, CHAS. G. [Born in N. C. Appointed from Cal.]
Corp. Co. B, 2nd Cal. Cav., 14 Sept., 1861. Priv., 30 Sept., 1862. Discharged 25 April, 1864. 2nd Lieut. 6th Cav., 26 Sept., 1867. 1st Lieut., 21 Feb., 1870. R. Q. M., 4 April, 1874, to 3 Sept., 1878. Capt., 30 Aug., 1881. Retired for disability, 5 Oct., 1887. Died 26 Oct., 1898.

GORDON, CHARLES M., JR. [Born in Mo. Appointed from Mo.]
2nd Lieut 16th Inf., 1 Aug., 1899.

GORDON, DAVID S. [Born in Penn. Appointed from Kansas.]
2nd Lieut. 2nd Drag., 26 April, 1861. 1st Lieut., 1 June, 1861. 2nd Cav., 3 Aug., 1861. Capt., 25 April, 1863. Bvt. Maj., 3 July, 1863, for gallant and meritorious service in the Gettysburg campaign. Major 2nd Cav., 25 June, 1877. Lieut. Col., 20 Nov., 1889. Col. 6th Cav., 28 July, 1892. Retired 23 May, 1896. Bvt. Lieut. Col., 27 Feb., 1890, for gallant services in action against Indians at Miners' Delight, Wyoming, 4 May, 1870.

GORDON, GEORGE A.* [Born in Va. Appointed at Large.]
Bvt. 2nd Lieut. 3rd Art., 1 July, 1854. 2nd Lieut. 2nd Art., 20 Feb., 1855. Trans. to 2nd Drag., 3 March, 1855. 1st Lieut., 4 June, 1858. Capt., 30 May, 1861. 2nd Cav., 3 Aug., 1861. Maj. 4th Cav., 1 Nov., 1867. Mustered out 1 Jan., 1871. Reappointed Maj. 5th Cav., 27 Jan., 1873, to rank from 1 Nov., 1867. Died 26 Oct., 1878. Bvt. Maj., 24 March, 1862, for gallant and meritorious service on the reconnaissance near New Bridge, Va. Bvt. Lieut. Col., 11 June, 1864, for gallant and meritorious service at the Battle of Trevillian Station, Va.

GORDON, GEORGE H.* [Born in Mass. Appointed from Mass.]
Bvt. 2nd Lieut. Mounted Rifles, 1 July, 1846. 2nd Lieut., 8 Jan., 1848. 1st Lieut., 30 Aug., 1853. Resigned 31 Oct., 1854. Bvt. 1st Lieut., 18 April, 1847, for gallant and meritorious conduct at Cerro Gordo, Mex. Col. 2nd Mass. Vols., 25 May, 1861. Brig. Gen. Vols., 9 June, 1862. Bvt. Maj. Gen. Vols., 9 April, 1865, for meritorious and distinguished service. Mustered out 24 Aug., 1865. Died 30 Aug., 1886.

GORDON, HENRY. [Born in Ireland. Appointed from Army.]
Priv. Co. F, 2nd Drag., 1 Dec., 1849, to 1 Dec., 1854. Priv., Sergt. and 1st Sergt. Co. I, 2nd Cav., 13 July, 1855, to 13 July, 1860, and of Co. I, 4th Cav., 26 July, 1860, to 8 Dec., 1861. 2nd Lieut. 4th Cav., 24 Oct., 1861. Dismissed 2 Dec., 1862.

GORDON, JONATHAN W. [Born in Penn. Appointed from Ind.]
Maj. 9th Ind. Vols., 27 April to 26 June, 1861. Maj. 11th Inf., 14 May, 1861. Resigned 4 March, 1864. Died 8 April, 1887.

GORDON, RAY T. [Born in N. Y. Appointed from N. Y.]
Priv. Co. A, 71st N. Y. Militia, 20 April to 30 July, 1861. 2nd Lieut. 53rd N. Y. Vols., 16 Nov., 1861. Mustered out 16 Nov., 1862. Priv. Co. M, 3rd N. Y. Cav., 15 Oct., 1864. 2nd Lieut. 2nd N. Y. Cav., 23 Dec., 1864. Mustered out 23 June, 1865. 2nd Lieut 8th Cav., 25 March, 1868. 1st Lieut., 26 May, 1870. Resigned 31 July, 1873.

GORDON, WALTER H.* [Born in Miss. Appointed from La.]
2nd Lieut. 12th Inf., 1 July, 1886. 1st Lieut. 18th Inf., 30 Nov., 1892. Capt., 2 March, 1899. Maj. 1st Del. Inf., 29 June, 1898. Col., 21 Sept., 1898, to 16 Nov., 1898.

GORDON, WILLIE J. [Born in N. C. Appointed from N. C.]
3rd Lieut. 10th Inf., 24 March, 1813. 2nd Lieut. 3rd Rifle Reg., 17 March, 1814. Retained in Rifle Reg., 17 May, 1815. Resigned 10 Sept., 1816.

GORDON, WM. [Born in Ky. Appointed from Ill.]
Capt. 2nd Drag., 8 June, 1836. Resigned 26 Sept., 1837.

GORDON, WM. B.* [Born in Pa. Appointed from Pa.]
2nd Lieut. 4th Art., 15 June, 1877. 1st Lieut. Ord., 4 Nov., 1881. Capt. (14 years' service), 15 June, 1891.

GORDON, WM. H. [Born in Va. Appointed from Va.]
2nd Lieut. 3rd Inf., 31 July, 1838. 1st Lieut., 21 June, 1841. Capt. 21 Sept., 1846. Maj. 8th Inf., 31 July, 1861. Retired 15 March, 1862. Died 7 Dec., 1865. Bvt. Maj., 20 August, 1847, for gallant conduct at Churubusco, Mex.

GORDON, WM. W.* [Born in Ga. Appointed from Ga.]
3rd Lieut. Ord, 2 March, 1815. Resigned 15 Oct., 1815. Died 20 March, 1842.

GORE, JAMES M. [Born in Mich. Appointed from Ky.]
2nd Lieut. 22nd Inf., 6 Jan., 1873. 1st Lieut., 4 July, 1879. Resigned 30 June, 1881.

GORE, JOHN H. [Born in Md. Appointed from Md.]
2nd Lieut. 4th Inf., 1 Aug., 1838. 1st Lieut., 14 June, 1842. Capt., 26 Dec., 1847. Died 1 Aug., 1852. Bvt. Capt., 20 Aug., 1847, for gallant and meritorious conduct at Contreras and Churubusco. Bvt. Maj., 8 Sept., 1847, for gallant conduct at Molino del Rey, Mex.

GORGAS, JOSIAH.* [Born in Pa. Appointed from N. Y.]
Bvt. 2nd Lieut. Ord., 1 July, 1841. 1st Lieut., 3 March, 1847. Capt., 1 July, 1855. Resigned 3 April, 1861.

GORGAS, WILLIAM C. [Born in Ala. Appointed from Ala.]
Asst. Surg., 16 June, 1880. Capt. and Asst. Surg., 16 June, 1885. Maj. and Surg., 6 July, 1898. Maj. and Brig. Surg. Vols., 4 June, 1898, to 6 July, 1898.

GORHAM, BENJ.* [Born in Mass. Appointed from Mass.]
2nd Lieut. Light Art., 1 July, 1820. Trans. to 5th Inf., 1 June, 1821. Died 15 Oct., 1821.

GORRINGE, CHRISTOPHER H. [Born in W. Indies. Appointed from Ohio.]
2nd Lieut. 11th Inf., 31 Oct., 1874. Resigned 1 Aug., 1876.

GOSE, ERNEST B.* [Born in Ill. Appointed from Ill.]
2nd Lieut. 8th Inf., 12 June, 1890. 1st Lieut. 13th Inf., 4 May, 1897. Capt. 24th Inf., 23 Dec., 1899.

GOTSHALL, JOHN. [Born in Penn. Appointed from Penn.]
Priv. Co. F, 25th Pa Vols., 2 May to 26 July,1861. 1st Lieut. 55th Pa. Vols., 28 Aug., 1861. Reg. Adj., 3 Aug., 1863. Mustered out 30 Aug., 1865. 2nd Lieut. 26th Inf., 7 March, 1867. Trans. to 10th Inf., 19 May, 1869. Cashiered 18 Oct., 1873.

GOULD, WM. P. [Born in R. I. Appointed from Nev.]
Addl. P. M., 1 June, 1861. Bvt. Lieut. Col. Vols., 13 March, 1865, for faithful and meritorious service during the war. Mustered out 1 July, 1867. Maj. and P. M., 18 Oct., 1867, Rejected by the Senate, 25 July, 1868, and revoked 1 Aug., 1868. Reappointed 8 March, 1869, to rank from 18 Oct., 1867. Retired, having served over 20 years, 10 Aug., 1885.

GOULEY, JOHN W. S. [Born in La. Appointed from N. Y.]
Asst. Surg., 28 May, 1861. Resigned 18 Feb., 1864.

GOUVERNEUR, SAML. L. [Born in N. Y. Appointed from D. C.]
2nd Lieut. 4th Art., 8 March, 1847. Resigned 31 May, 1849. Bvt. 1st Lieut., 20 Aug., 1847, for gallant and meritorious conduct at Contreras and Churubusco, Mex.

GOVE, JESSE A. [Born in N. H. Appointed from N. H.]
2nd Lieut. of Inf., 8 March, 1847; 9th Inf., 9 April, 1847. 1st Lieut., 4 Dec., 1847. Disbanded 26 Aug., 1848. Capt. 10th Inf., 3 March, 1855. Col. 22nd Mass. Vols. 9 Nov., 1861. Killed at the Battle of Gaines' Mill, Va., 27 June, 1862.

GOWEN, JAMES B.* [Born in N. Y. Appointed fromN. Y.]
2nd Lieut. 16th Inf., 26 April, 1898. 1st Lieut., 2 March, 1899.

GRACIE, ARCHIBALD, JR.* [Born in N. Y. Appointed from N. J.]
Bvt. 2nd Lieut. 4th Inf., 1 July, 1854. 2nd Lieut. 5th Inf., 3 March, 1855. Resigned 3 May, 1856.

GRAFFAM, GEORGE W. [Born in Mass. Appointed from Army.]
Sergt. Co. C, 1st Maine Vols., 3 May to 5 Aug., 1861. 1st Lieut. Adj. 5th Maine Vols., 8 Oct., 1861 Resigned 18 Oct., 1863. Priv. and Sergt. Co. G, and Sergt. Maj. 2nd Batt. 16th Inf., 6 June to 1 Dec., 1865. 2nd Lieut. 16th Inf., 24 Nov., 1865. 1st Lieut., 24 Nov., 1865. Trans. to 34th Inf., 21 Sept., 1866. Unassigned 14 April, 1869. Mustered out 1 Jan., 1871. Died 11 Aug., 1882.

GRAFIUS, ABRAHAM. [Born in Penn. Appointed from Penn.]
2nd Lieut. 2nd Inf., 26 Nov., 1861. 1st Lieut., 25 Sept., 1862. Died 9 June, 1863.

GRAFTON, BENJAMIN F. [Born in Ohio. Appointed from Ohio.]
Priv. and Corpl. Co. H, 26th Ohio Vols., 29 July, 1861, to 15 March, 1862. 2nd Lieut. 26th Ohio Vols., 15 March, 1862. 1st Lieut., 17 March, 1863. Resigned 6 Nov., 1864. 2nd Lieut. 29th Inf., 6 May, 1867. Trans. to 11th Inf., 25 April, 1869. Unassigned 29 March, 1870. Ass'd to 19th Inf., 3 Aug., 1870. Discharged 1 Sept., 1870. Bvt. 1st Lieut., 6 May, 1867, for gallant and meritorious service in the Battle of Atlanta, Ga. Bvt. Capt., 6 May, 1867, for gallant and meritorious service in the Battle of Jonesboro, Ga. Died 29 July, 1883.

GRAFTON, HENRY D.* [Born in Mass. Appointed from Mass.]
2nd Lieut. 1st Art., 1 July, 1839. 1st Lieut., 24 Feb., 1845. Capt., 4 Sept., 1851. Resigned 4 Nov., 1854. Bvt. Capt., 20 Aug., 1847, for gallant and meritorious conduct at Contreras and Churubusco, Mex. Died 13 April, 1855.

GRAHAM, CAMPBELL.* [Born in Va. Appointed from Va.]
Bvt. 2nd Lieut. 3rd Art., 1 July, 1822. 2nd Lieut., 1 July, 1822. 1st Lieut., 11 Sept., 1828. Bvt. Capt. Asst. Topographical Eng., 23 Nov., 1837. Capt. Topographical Eng., 7 July, 1838. Maj., 9 Dec., 1857. Retired 9 Sept., 1861. Died 8 Nov., 1866. Bvt. Capt., 31 Dec., 1835, for gallant and good conduct in the affair of the Withlacoochee, Fla.

GRAHAM, GEORGE W. [Born in N. Y. Appointed from N. Y.]
2nd Lieut. 24th N. Y. Batty, 7 Dec., 1861. Trans. to 3rd N. Y. Cav., 24 Dec., 1862. Discharged 30 April, 1863. 1st. Lieut. 1st N. C. Vols., 1 May, 1863. Capt., 19 Oct., 1863. Mustered out 27 June, 1865. 1st Lieut. 10th Cav., 28 July, 1866. Capt., 29 May, 1867. Cashiered 16 Aug., 1870. Bvt. Maj., 17 Sept., 1868, for gallant and meritorious service at the affair with Indians on the Big Sandy, C. T., 17 Sept., 1868. Killed 12 Oct. 1875.

GRAHAM, JAMES D.* [Born in Va. Appointed from Va.]
3rd Lieut. Corps. Art., 17 July, 1817. 2nd Lieut., 14 Oct., 1817. 1st Lieut., 8 Sept., 1819. Trans. to 4th Art., 1 June, 1821. Trans. to 3rd Art., 16 Aug., 1821. Bvt. Capt. Asst. Top. Eng., 15 Jan., 1829. Bvt. Maj. Top. Eng., 14 Sept., 1834. Maj. Top. Eng., 7 July, 1838. Lieut. Col., 6 Aug., 1861. Trans. to Eng., 3 March, 1863. Col., 1 June, 1863. Died 28 Dec., 1865. Bvt. Lieut. Col., 1 Jan., 1847, for valuable and highly distinguished service, particularly on the boundary line between the United States and British Provinces,etc.

GRAHAM, JAMES D.* [Born in La. Appointed at Large.]
2nd Lieut. 13th Inf., 23 June, 1865. 1st Lieut., 23 June, 1865. Trans. to 2nd Cav., 13 Feb., 1867. Died 18 June, 1868.

GRAHAM, JAMES L. [Born in Penn. Appointed from Penn.]
2nd Lieut. 5th Inf., 9 July, 1898. Resigned 4 Oct., 1899.

GRAHAM, JAMES M. [Born in Mass. Appointed from Cal.]
2nd Lieut. 11th Inf., 9 July, 1898. 1st Lieut. 19th Inf., 2 March, 1899.

GRAHAM, JOHN* [Born in Penn. Appointed from N. Y.]
Bvt. 2nd Lieut. 4th Inf., 1 July, 1834. 2nd Lieut., 31 Jan., 1836. 1st Lieut. 2nd Drag., 11 June, 1836. Capt., 1 Oct., 1837. Resigned 28 Jan., 1838. Died 20 July, 1841.

GRAHAM, JOHN C. [Born in Penn. Appointed from Penn.]
2nd Lieut. 3rd Cav., 25 Feb., 1868. Discharged 31 Dec., 1870.

GRAHAM, JOHN L. [Born in Ireland. Appointed from Ky.]
Priv. 13th N. Y. Vols., April to Aug., 1861. 1st Sergt. Co. K, 108th N. Y. Vols., 28 July, 1862. 2nd Lieut., 31 Dec., 1862. Discharged 14 Nov., 1863. 2nd Lieut. Vet. Res. Corps, 20 Feb., 1864. Bvt. 1st Lieut. and Capt. Vols., 13 March, 1865, for gallant conduct in the Battles of Antietam, Fredericksburg, and Gettysburg. Mustered out 1 Jan., 1868. 2nd Lieut. 45th Inf., 7 Jan., 1869. Unassigned 22 July, 1869. Ass'd to 13th Inf., 1 Jan., 1871. Died 12 Nov., 1872.

GRAHAM, LAWRENCE P. [Born in Va. Appointed from Va.]
2nd Lieut. 2nd Drag., 13 Oct., 1837. 1st Lieut., 1 Jan., 1839. Capt., 31 Aug., 1843. Bvt. Maj., 9 May, 1846, for gallant conduct in the Battles of Palo Alto and Resaca de la Palma. Maj. 2nd Drag., 14 June, 1858. Brig. Gen. Vols., 31 Aug., 1861. Lieut. Col. 5th Cav., 1 Oct., 1861. Col. 4th Cav., 9 May, 1864. Bvt. Brig. Gen., 13 March, 1865, for gallant and meritorious service during the war. Mustered out of Vol. service, 24 Aug., 1865. Retired 15 Dec., 1870.

GRAHAM, LORIMER. [Born in N. Y. Appointed from N. Y.]
2nd Lieut. of Inf., 25 Feb., 1847; 10th Inf., 9 April, 1847. Trans. to 1st Drag., 2 Feb., 1848. Resigned 31 Oct., 1853. Bvt. 1st Lieut., 13 Aug., 1847, for gallant and meritorious conduct in the affair at Mira Flores, Mex. Bvt. Capt., 20 Aug., 1847, for gallant and meritorious conduct at Churubusco, Mex.

GRAHAM, RICHARD H.* [Born in Ky. Appointed from Ky.]
2nd Lieut. 2nd Drag., 1 July, 1838. Trans. to 4th Inf., 9 Aug., 1838. 1st Lieut., 25 Feb., 1841. Died 12 Oct., 1846, of wounds received in Battle of Monterey, Mex.

GRAHAM, SAML. [Born in Ireland. Appointed from Army.]
Priv., Corpl. and Sergt. Co. D. Eng. Batt., 14 April, 1863, to 27 Jan., 1867. 2nd Lieut. 11th Inf., 21 July, 1866. Trans. to 29th Inf., 21 Sept., 1866. 1st Lieut., 18 July, 1868. Unassigned 25 April, 1869. Dismissed 3 June, 1869.

GRAHAM, WM. M.* [Born in Va. Appointed from D. C.]
3rd Lieut. Corps Art., 17 July, 1817. 2nd Lieut., 30 Sept., 1817. 1st Lieut., 11 Aug., 1819. Trans. to 8th Inf., 20 Oct., 1820. Trans. to 4th Inf., 1 June, 1821. Capt., 4 April, 1832. Maj. 2nd Inf., 16 Feb., 1847. Lieut. Col. 11th Inf., 9 April, 1847. Killed 8 Sept., 1847, in the Battle of Molino del Rey, Mex. Bvt. Capt., 11 Aug., 1829, for ten years' faithful service in one grade. Bvt. Maj., 31 Dec., 1835, for gallant and good conduct in the affair of the Withlacoochee, Fla.

GRAHAM, WM. M. [Born in D. C. Appointed from D. C.]
2nd Lieut. 1st Art., 7 June, 1855. 1st Lieut., 1 March, 1861. Capt., 26 Oct., 1861. Bvt. Maj., 1 July, 1862, for gallant and meritorious service during the Peninsular campaign in Virginia. Bvt. Lieut. Col., 17 Sept., 1862, for gallant and meritorious service at the Battle of Antietam, Md. Bvt. Col., 3 July, 1863, for gallant and meritorious service in the Battle of Gettysburg, Penn. Bvt. Brig. Gen., 13 March, 1865, for gallant and meritorious service in the field during the war. Col. 2nd D. C. Vols., 7 April, 1865. Mustered out of Vol. service, 12 Sept., 1865. Maj. 4th Art., 18 July, 1879. Lieut. Col. 1st Art., 10 Aug., 1887. Trans. to 5th Art., 1 May, 1890. Col. 5th Art., 1 July, 1891. Brig. Gen., 26 May, 1897. Retired 28 Sept., 1898.

GRANDIN, WM. G.* [Born in N. Y. Appointed from N. Y.]
2nd Lieut. 4th Inf., 1 July, 1837. 1st Lieut., 1 April, 1840. Resigned 3 Oct., 1840. Capt. C. S. Vols., 3 Sept., 1861. Appointment negatived by Senate, 3 Feb., 1862. Died 4 Aug., 1863.

GRANGER, GORDON.* [Born in N. Y. Appointed from N. Y.]
Bvt. 2nd Lieut. 2nd Inf., 1 July, 1845. Trans. to Mounted Rifles, 17 July, 1846. 2nd Lieut., 29 May, 1847. 1st Lieut., 24 May, 1852. Capt., 5 May, 1861. 3rd Cav., 3 Aug., 1861. Col. 2nd Mich. Cav. to Sept., 1861. Brig. Gen. Vols., 26 March, 1862. Maj. Gen. Vols., 17 Sept., 1862. Mustered out of Vols., 15 Jan., 1866. Col. 25th Inf., 28 July, 1866. Unassigned 15 March, 1869. Ass'd to 15th Inf., 20 Dec., 1870. Died 10 Jan., 1876. Bvt. 1st Lieut., 20 Aug., 1847, for gallant and meritorious conduct at Contreras and Churubusco. Bvt. Capt., 13 Sept., 1847, for gallant and meritorious conduct at Chapultepec. Bvt. Maj., 10 Aug., 1861, for gallant and meritorious service at the Battle of Wilson's Creek, Mo. Bvt. Lieut. Col., 20 Sept., 1863, for gallant and meritorious service at the Battle of Chickamauga, Ga. Bvt. Col., 24 Nov., 1863, for gallant and meritorious service at the Battle of Chattanooga, Tenn. Bvt. Brig. Gen., 13 March, 1865, for gallant and meritorious service at the capture of Mobile, Ala. Bvt. Maj. Gen., 13 March, 1865, for distinguished gallantry and good conduct at the capture of Forts Gaines and Morgan, Ala.

GRANGER, LOUIS E. [Born in Mass. Appointed from Mass.]
Priv. 4th Batt. Rifles Mass. Militia, 19 April, to 15 July, 1861. Priv. Co. A. 13th Mass. Vols., 16 July, 1861, to 4 March, 1863. 2nd Lieut. 80th U. S. Col. Inf., 4 March, 1863. 1st Lieut., 18 Feb., 1864. Capt., 18 July, 1865. Bvt Mj. Vols., 13 March, 1865, for gallant and meritorious service during the war. Mustered out 1 March, 1867. 2nd Lieut. 40th Inf., 7 March, 1867. Reg. Adj., 27 May, 1867, to 3 Sept., 1868. Trans. to 25th Inf., 20 April, 1869. Dismissed 1 Sept., 1869. Bvt. 1st Lieut., 7 March, 1867, for gallant and meritorious service at the Battle of Antietam, Md. Bvt. Capt., 7 March, 1867, for gallant and meritorious service at the Siege of Port Hudson, La.

GRANGER, MOSES M. [Born in Ohio. Appointed from Ohio.]
Capt. 18th Inf., 14 May, 1861. Resigned 30 May, 1862. Maj. 122nd Ohio Vols., 8 Oct., 1862. Lieut. Col., 1 May, 1863. Bvt. Col. Vols., 19 Oct., 1864, for gallant and meritorious conduct in the campaign before Richmond, Va., and in the Shenandoah Valley. Resigned 10 Dec., 1864.

GRANGER, RALPH S.* [Born in Conn. Appointed from Conn.]
2nd Lieut. 4th Art., 15 Feb., 1899.

GRANGER, ROBERT S.* [Born in Ohio. Appointed from Ohio.]
2nd Lieut. 1st Inf., 1 July, 1838. 1st Lieut., 14 March, 1839. Capt., 8 Sept., 1847.

Maj. 5th Inf., 9 Sept., 1861. Bvt. Col., 9 Oct., 1862, for gallant and meritorious service in the Battle of Lawrenceburg, Ky. Brig. Gen. Vols., 20 Oct., 1862. Bvt. Brig. Gen., 13 March, 1865, for gallant and meritorious service in the defence of Decatur, Ala. Bvt. Maj. Gen., 13 March, 1865, for gallant and meritorious service during the war. Lieut. Col. 11th Inf., 12 June, 1865. Mustered out of Vol. service, 24 Aug., 1865. Trans. to 16th Inf., 15 March, 1869. Col. 21st Inf., 16 Aug., 1871. Retired 10 Dec., 1873. Died 25 April, 1894.

GRANT, ALEX'R. [Born in Canada. Appointed from Army.]
Priv. Co. I, 1st Art., 11 April, 1861, to 11 April, 1864. Priv. and Corpl. Ord. Dept., 4 May, 1864, to 25 April, 1865, when trans. to Co. I, 1st Art. Sergt., 17 Aug., 1865. Sergt. Maj., 4 Sept., 1865, to 5 Oct., 1866. His proper name was Alexander Grant Skene. 2nd Lieut. 1st Cav., 10 Sept., 1866. 1st Lieut., 1 July, 1868. Died 28 March, 1875.

GRANT, FREDK. D.* [Born in Mo. Appointed at Large.]
2nd Lieut 4th Cav., 12 June, 1871. Lieut. Col. A. de C. to the Lieut Gen., 17 March, 1873. 1st Lieut. 4th Cav., 28 June, 1876. Resigned 1 Oct., 1881. Brig. Gen. Vols., 1898.

GRANT, NATHL. [Born in Ga. Appointed from Ga.]
2nd Lieut. of Inf., 20 March, 1847; 13th Inf., 9 April, 1847. 1st Lieut., 29 Feb., 1848. Disbanded 15 July, 1848. Died 1 Feb., 1865

GRANT, ULYSSES S.* [Born in Ohio. Appointed from Ohio.]
Bvt. 2nd Lieut. 4th Inf., 1 July, 1843. 2nd Lieut. 7th Inf., 30 Sept. 1845. Trans. to 4th Inf., 15 Nov., 1845. 1st Lieut., 16 Sept., 1847. R. Q. M., 1 April, 1847, to 23 July, 1848, and 17 Nov., 1848, to 5 Aug., 1853. Capt., 5 Aug., 1853. Resigned 31 July, 1854. Col. 21st Ill. Vols., 17 June, 1861. Brig. Gen. Vols., to rank from 17 May, 1861. Maj. Gen. Vols., 16 Feb., 1862. Maj. Gen. U. S. A., 4 July, 1863. Lieut. Gen. U. S. A., 2 March, 1864. Gen. U. S. A., 25 July, 1866, to 4 March, 1869. Sec. of War *ad interim*, 12 Aug., 1867, to 14 Jan., 1868. President of the U. S., 4 March, 1869, to 4 March, 1877. Gen. on the retired list, 3 March, 1885. (Act of 3 March, 1885.) Received the thanks of Congress and the presentation of a gold medal by joint resolution 17 Dec., 1863, as follows: "Be it resolved by the Senate and House of Representatives in Congress Assembled. That the thanks of Congress be and they hereby are presented to Maj. Gen. Ulysses S. Grant, and through him to the officers and soldiers who fought under his command during this Rebellion, for their gallantry and good conduct in the battles in which they have been engaged; and that the President of the U. S. be requested to cause a gold medal to be struck, with suitable emblems, devices and inscriptions, to be presented to Maj. Gen. Grant. Sec. 2. And be it further resolved, That when the said medal shall have been struck, the President shall cause a copy of this joint resolution to be engrossed on parchment, and shall transmit the same, together with the said medal, to Maj. Gen. Grant, to be presented to him in the name of the people of the United States of America." Bvt. 1st Lieut., 8 Sept., 1847, for gallant and meritorious conduct at Molino del Rey. Bvt. Capt., 13 Sept., 1847, for gallant conduct at Chapultepec. Died 23 July, 1885.

GRATIOT, CHAS.* [Born in Mo. Appointed from Mo.]
2nd Lieut. Eng., 30 Oct., 1806. Capt., 23 Feb., 1808. Maj., 9 Feb., 1815. Lieut. Col., 31 March, 1819. Col. and Chief Eng., 24 May, 1828. Dismissed 6 Dec., 1838. Bvt. Brig. Gen, 24 May, 1828, for meritorious service and general good conduct. Died 18 May, 1855.

GRATTAN, JOHN L.* [Born in Vt. Appointed from N. H.]
Bvt. 2nd Lieut. 6th Inf., 1 July, 1853. Killed 19 Aug., 1854, in action with Indians in Nebraska

GRAVES, CHAS. H. [Born in Mass. Appointed from Mass.]
Sergt. Co. H, 40th N. Y. Vols., 27 June, 1861. 2nd Lieut., 4 Nov., 1861. 1st Lieut., 8 July, 1862. Capt., 1 Jan. to 1 May, 1864. Capt. A. A. G. Vols., 29 Feb., 1864. Maj. A. A. G. Vols, 15 Jan., 1865. Bvt. Lieut. Col. and Col. Vols., 13 March, 1865, for faithful and efficient service during the war and gallant conduct in the field. Mustered out 1 Sept., 1866. 1st Lieut. 14th Inf., 29 Nov., 1865. Capt. 34th Inf., 28 July, 1866. Unassigned 14 April, 1869. Discharged 29 Dec., 1870. Bvt. Maj., 2 March, 1867, for gallant and meritorious service in the Battle of Gettysburg, Penn. Bvt. Lieut. Col., 2 March, 1867, for gallant and meritorious service in the assault on Fort Fisher, N. C.

GRAVES, EDWARD A. [Born in Ky. Appointed from Ky.]
Capt. of Inf., 5 March, 1847; 16th Inf., 9 April, 1847. Disbanded 5 Aug., 1848.

GRAVES, WILLIAM P. [Born in D. C. Appointed from Ky.]
2nd Lieut. 2nd Art., 24 March, 1862. Bvt. 1st Lieut., 1 July, 1862, for gallant and meritorious service in the Battle of Malvern Hill, Va. Bvt. Capt., 29 Aug., 1862, for gallant and meritorious service in the Battle of Manassas, Va. 1st Lieut. 2nd Art., 1 Aug., 1863. Bvt. Maj., 29 Nov., 1863, for gallant and meritorious service during the defence of Fort Saunders, Tenn. Capt. 2nd Art., 25 March, 1873. Died 20 Jan., 1889.

GRAVES, WILLIAM S.* [Born in Texas. Appointed from Texas.]
2nd Lieut. 7th Inf., 12 June, 1889. 1st Lieut. 6th Inf., 19 Nov., 1896. Trans. to 7th Inf., 23 Nov., 1896. Capt. 5th Inf., 8 Sept., 1899. Trans. to 20th Inf., 24 Oct., 1899.

GRAY, ALEXANDER. [Born in ——. Appointed from Tenn.]
Capt. 24th Inf., 12 March, 1812. Disbanded 15 June, 1815. Reinstated as Capt. 1st Inf., 2 Dec., 1815. Resigned 6 March, 1819. Died Aug., 1823.

GRAY, ALONZO.* [Born in Wis. Appointed from Iowa.]
Addl. 2nd Lieut. 5th Cav., 12 June, 1887. 2nd Lieut. 6th Cav., 19 Oct., 1887. 1st Lieut. 8th Cav., 24 Jan., 1895. Trans. to 5th Cav., 20 Feb., 1895.

GRAY, CHAS. C. [Born in N. Y. Appointed from N. Y.]
1st Lieut. Asst. Surg., 28 May, 1861. Bvt. Capt., Maj. and Lieut. Col., 13 March, 1865, for faithful and meritorious service during the war. Capt. Asst. Surg., 28 May, 1866. Maj. Surg., 28 July, 1866. Retired 10 Jan., 1879. Died 22 Nov., 1884.

GRAY, CYRUS N. [Born in Ind. Appointed from Minn.]
Priv. Co. C, 22nd Ind. Vols., 15 Aug., 1861. Sergt. Maj., 1 Sept., 1862. 2nd Lieut. 15th U. S. Colored Troops, 3 Feb., 1864. 1st Lieut., 25 March, 1864. Capt., 11 April, 1865. Resigned 21 Nov., 1865. 1st Lieut. 39th Inf., 12 June, 1867. Trans. to 25th Inf., 26 April, 1869. Reg. Adj., 9 Aug., 1869, to 1 Jan., 1876. Capt., 20 March, 1879. Dismissed 1 Sept., 1887.

GRAY, FRENCH S. [Born in Va. Appointed from Ky.]
Ensign 7th Inf., 6 Aug., 1813. 3rd Lieut., 13 March, 1814. 2nd Lieut., 2 May, 1814. 1st Lieut., 18 Sept., 1816. Capt., 1 June, 1817. Died 15 June, 1819.

GRAY, GEORGE. [Born in Va. Appointed from Ky.]
2nd Lieut. 1st Rifles, 4 June, 1812. 1st Lieut., 20 Jan., 1813. R. Q. M., May, 1813, to Sept., 1814. Capt., 17 Sept., 1814. Disbanded 15 June, 1815. Reinstated as Capt. 3rd Inf., 17 May, 1816. Resigned 9 Jan., 1820.

GRAY, JAMES S. [Born in Va. Appointed from Ky.]
3rd Lieut. 1st Rifles, 20 May, 1813. 2nd Lieut., 11 May, 1814. Retained in Rifle Reg., 17 May, 1815. 1st Lieut., 31 March, 1817. R. Q. M., 1 Jan. to 10 Nov., 1818. Capt., 10 Nov., 1818. Trans. to 6th Inf., 1 June, 1821. Dismissed 15 Feb., 1826.

GRAY, JOHN W. [Born in Mo. Appointed from Cal.]
1st Lieut. 11th Inf., 14 May, 1861. Died 15 Dec., 1862.

GRAY, ROBERT. [Born in Ireland. Appointed from Penn.]
Lieut. Light Drag., 8 Jan., 1799. Discharged 15 June, 1800. 2nd Lieut. 1st Artillerists and Engs., 16 Feb., 1801. Discharged 1 June, 1802. Capt. 16th Inf., 14 April, 1812. Maj., 15 Aug., 1813. Disbanded 15 June, 1815. Reinstated 2 Dec., 1815, as Capt. 2nd Inf. Disbanded 1 June, 1821. Retained 15 Dec. (in reorganization under Act of 3 March, 1815), as Capt. 2nd Inf., with Bvt. of Maj., from 15 Aug. 1813. Died 14 Jan., 1831.

GRAY, ROBT. [Born in England. Appointed form Ill.]
Priv. Co. F and Com. Sergt. 12th Ill. Cav., 7 Oct., 1861, to 25 Feb., 1864. 1st Lieut. 12th Ill. Cav., 25 Feb., 1864. Capt., 20 May, 1865. Mustered out 29 May, 1866. 1st Lieut. 10th Cav., 28 July, 1866. Capt., 31 July, 1867. Discharged 31 Dec., 1870.

GRAY, ROMAN H. [Born in Ohio. Appointed from Army.]
Priv. and Sergt. Co. E, 15th Inf., 27 Sept., 1861, to 8 Sept., 1862. 2nd Lieut. 15th Inf., 7 April, 1862. 1st Lieut., 3 Jan., 1863. Trans. to 24th Inf., 21 Sept., 1866. Capt., 30 Sept., 1866. Died 14 Sept., 1867. Bvt. Capt., 20 Sept., 1863, for gallant and meritorious service at the Battle of Chickamauga, Ga.

GRAY, WM. H. [Born in Penn. Appointed from Penn.]
2nd Lieut. of Inf., 16 Feb., 1847; 11th Inf., 9 April, 1847. 1st Lieut., 13 June, 1847. Disbanded 14 Aug., 1848. Col. 20th Pa. Vols., 30 April, 1861, to 3 Aug., 1861.

GRAY, WM. M'C. [Born in Penn. Appointed from Penn.]
2nd Lieut. 2nd Inf., 19 Feb., 1818. Disbanded 1 June, 1821.

GRAY, WM. W. [Born in Tenn. Appointed from Tenn.]
1st Lieut. Asst. Surg., 6 June, 1878. Capt. Asst. Surg., 6 June, 1883. Maj. Surg., 10 Oct., 1896.

GRAYSON, JOHN B.* [Born in Ky. Appointed from Ky.]
Bvt. 2nd Lieut. 3rd Art., 1 July, 1826. 2nd. Lieut. 2nd Art., 1 July, 1826. 1st Lieut., 30 April, 1834. Capt., 11 Dec., 1838. Resigned Reg. Commission, 18 June, 1846. Capt. C. S., 7 July, 1838. Maj., 21 Oct., 1852. Resigned 1 July, 1861. Bvt. Maj., 20 Aug., 1847, for gallant and meritorious conduct at Contreras and Churubusco. Bvt. Lieut. Col., 13 Sept., 1847, for gallant and meritorious conduct at Chapultepec. Died 21 Oct., 1861.

GRAYSON, PETER W. [Born in Va. Appointed from Va.]
2nd Lieut. 3rd Inf., 10 Feb., 1818. Dismissed 5 Feb., 1820.

GREALISH, MICHAEL J. [Born in Ireland. Appointed from Kan.]
Ord. Storekeeper, 4 June, 1866. Capt. Ord. Storekeeper, 28 July, 1866. Died 1 May, 1897.

GREBLE, EDWIN ST. J.* [Born in N. Y. Apointed from Pa.]
2nd Lieut. 2nd Art., 11 June, 1881. 1st Lieut., 2 May, 1887. Capt., 2 March, 1899. Capt. A. A. G. Vols., 12 May, 1898, to 12 May, 1899. Maj. A. A. G. Vols., 5 Sept., 1899. Honor graduate of the Artillery School, 1892.

GREBLE, JOHN T.* [Born in Penn. Appointed from Penn.]
Bvt. 2nd Lieut. 2nd Art., 1 July, 1854. 2nd Lieut., 27 Sept., 1854. 1st Lieut. 2 March, 1857. Killed 10 June, 1861, in action at Big Bethel, Va. Bvt. Capt., Maj., and Lieut. Col., 10 June, 1861, for conspicuous gallantry and meritorious conduct in the Battle of Big Bethel, Va.

GREELY, ADOLPHUS W. [Born in Mass. Appointed from La.]
Priv. Co. B, 19th Mass. Vols., 26 July, 1861. Corpl. 15 May, 1862. 1st Sergt., 1 Jan., 1863. 2nd Lieut. 81st U. S. Col. Troops, 18 March, 1863. 1st Lieut., 26 April, 1864. Bvt. Maj. Vols., 13 March, 1865, for faithful and meritorious service during the war. Capt. 81st U. S. Col. Troops, 4 April, 1865. Mustered out 22 March, 1867. 2nd Lieut. 36th Inf., 7 March, 1867. Unassigned 19 May, 1869. Ass'd to 5th Cav., 14 July, 1869. 1st Lieut., 27 May, 1873. Capt., 11 June, 1886. Brig. Gen. and Chf. Sig. Off., 3 March, 1887.

GREELEY, WM. F. [Born in N. H. Appointed from N. H.]
1st Lieut. 1st N. H. Vols., 30 April to 9 Aug., 1861. 1st Lieut. 11th Inf., 5 Aug., 1861. Reg., Adj., 1 July to 5 Dec., 1863. Resigned 30 May, 1865.

GREEN, CHAS. H. [Born in N. Y. Appointed from the Army.]
Priv., Corpl. and Sergt. Co. B, 1st Art., 18 Nov., 1848, to 18 Nov., 1853. Priv. and Sergt. Gen. Service, 13 Oct., 1855, to 14 Aug., 1863. 2nd Lieut. 5th Art., 10 Aug., 1863. Resigned 19 Dec., 1863.

GREEN, DUFF C.* [Born in D. C. Appointed at Large.]
Bvt. 2nd Lieut. 5th Inf., 1 July, 1849. 2nd Lieut. 3rd Inf., 22 May, 1850. Resigned 31 Dec., 1856.

GREEN, GEORGE W. [Born in Penn. Appointed from Penn.]
1st Lieut. 17th Inf., 14 May, 1861. Capt., 11 Oct., 1864. Died 8 Jan., 1866. Bvt. Capt., 3 May, 1863, for gallant and meritorious service at the Battle of Chancellorsville, Va. Bvt. Maj., 2 July, 1863, for gallant and meritorious service at the Battle of Gettysburg, Pa. Bvt. Lieut. Col, 13 March, 1865, for gallant and meritorious service during the war.

GREEN, HENRY H. [Born in Ill. Appointed from Ky.]
Cadet Mil. Acad., 1 July, 1841, to 30 June, 1843. 2nd Lieut. 15th Inf., 3 Aug., 1847. Disbanded 4 Aug., 1848.

GREEN, JAMES. [Born in Mass. Appointed from Mass.]
1st Lieut. 3rd Art., 12 March, 1812. Capt., 29 Oct, 1813. Trans. to Corps Art., 12 May, 1814. Disbanded 15 June, 1815. 2nd Lieut. Corps Art., 11 Sept., 1818. Trans. to 2nd Art., 1 June, 1821. Capt., A. D. Q. M. G., 11 Sept., 1818, to 1 June, 1821, and A. Q. M., 1 June, 1821, to 17 May, 1824. 1st Lieut., 31 May, 1826. Reg. Adj., 1 May, 1826, to 20 June, 1837. Capt., 20 June, 1837. Died 17 Aug., 1842.

GREEN, JAMES O.* [Born in Wis. Appointed from Wis.]
2nd Lieut. 25th Inf., 13 June, 1882. 1st Lieut., 30 June, 1890. Retired for disability 15 Nov., 1897.

GREEN, JOHN. [Born in Germany. Appointed from Army.]
Sergt. Co. B, Mounted Rifles, 1 July, 1846. 1st Sergt., 7 Feb., 1847. Sergt. Maj., 1 May, 1848. Discharged, 27 Aug., 1848. Priv. Co. B, Mounted Rifles, 18 Sept., 1852. 1st Sergt., 5 Oct., 1852. 2nd Lieut. 2nd Drag., 18 June, 1855. 1st Lieut., 3 March, 1861; 2nd Cav., 3 Aug., 1861. Capt. 2nd Cav., 13 Aug., 1861. Bvt. Maj., 3 July, 1863, for gallant and meritorious service in the Gettysburg campaign. Bvt. Lieut. Col., 15 April, 1865, for faithful and meritorious service during the war. Maj. 1st Cav., 9 June, 1868. Lieut. Col. 2nd Cav., 3 July, 1885. Retired 20 Nov., 1889. Bvt. Col., 27 Feb., 1890, for gallant services in action against Indians at Mount Turnbull, Ariz., April 30, 1869. Bvt. Brig. Gen., 27 Feb., 1890, for gallant services against Indians in the Lava Beds, Cal., 17 Jan, 1873, and conspicuous gallantry in the several actions during the Modoc war. Medal of honor for most distinguished gallantry in action against hostile Modoc Indians at the Lava Beds, Cal., Jan. 17, 1873, in exposing himself in the most fearless manner to very great danger by walking in front of the line when the men hesitated to go forward as ordered, and reassuring the command, which then advanced upon the Indians, who were concealed among the rocks and fighting from behind their natural fortifications, while serving as Maj., 1st Cav.

GREEN, JOHN A. [Born in Penn. Appointed from Md.]
Mil. S. Ord. Dept., 27 Sept., 1861. Resigned 27 June, 1862.

GREEN, JOHN M. Born in Ohio. Appointed from Ill.]
Priv. Co. H, 40th Ill. Vols., 10 Aug., 1861, to 18 May, 1863. 2nd Lieut. 58th Ill. Vols., 18 May, 1863. 1st Lieut., 17 Oct., 1864. Capt., 7 Nov., 1865. Mustered out 1 April, 1866. 2nd Lieut. 13th Inf., 23 Feb., 1866. 1st Lieut., 23 Feb., 1866. Resigned 10 Feb., 1869.

GREEN, MOSES C. [Born in N. Y. Appointed from N. Y.]
Capt. 15th N. Y. Eng., 15 Jan., 1862. Resigned 8 July, 1862. 1st Lieut. 13th Inf., 14 June, 1862. Resigned 20 Feb., 1864.

GREEN, PLATT R. [Born in N. Y. Appointed from Pa.]
Ensign 21st Inf., 31 May, 1814. 2nd Lieut., 1st Oct., 1814. Trans. to 5th Inf., 17 May, 1815. Reg. Adjt., 4 June, 1819, to 1 Sept., 1821. 1st Lieut., 27 March, 1820. Died 30 June, 1828.

GREEN, TIMOTHY. [Born in Mass. Appointed from Mass.]
3rd Lieut. 4th Inf., 20 May, 1813. 2nd Lieut., 15 June, 1814. Reg. P. M., 4 Feb. to June, 1815. Disbanded 15 June, 1815. Reinstated 2 Dec., 1815, in Corps Art. Trans. to 1st Art., 1 June, 1821. 1st Lieut., 20 April, 1818. Died 23 Dec., 1847. Bvt. Capt., 20 April, 1828, for ten years' faithful service in one grade.

GREEN, WM. C. [Born in Penn. Appointed from Penn.]
2nd Lieut. 1st Inf., 27 Sept., 1861. 1st Lieut., 10 Jan., 1862. Capt., 1 Jan., 1867. Died 18 Sept., 1867. Bvt. Capt., 4 July, 1863, for gallant and meritorious service during the Siege of Vicksburg, Miss.

GREENE, AUGUSTUS P. [Born in N. Y. Appointed from N. Y.]
1st Lieut. 15th N. Y. Eng., 17 June, 1861. Capt., 14 March, 1863. Mustered out 25 June, 1863. 2nd Lieut. 14th Inf., 20 July, 1866. 1st Lieut., 24 May, 1867. Unassigned 22 July, 1869. Ass'd to 4th Art., 15 Dec., 1870. Dismissed 28 March, 1873.

GREENE, BENJN. D.* [Born in Mass. Appointed from Maine.]
2nd Lieut. Eng., 18 June, 1866. 1st Lieut., 7 March, 1867. Capt., 16 Oct., 1877. Resigned 31 Dec., 1882.

GREENE, CHAS. H. [Born in R. I. Appointed from R. I.]
2nd Lieut. 4th R. I. Vols., 30 Oct., 1861. 1st Lieut., 20 Nov., 1861. Capt., 11 Aug., 1862. Mustered out 30 Sept., 1862. Capt. 4th R. I. Vols., 2 May, 1863. Mustered out 15 Oct., 1864. 2nd Lieut. 17th Inf., 22 Jan., 1867. 1st Lieut., 1 Nov., 1867. Capt., 19 May, 1881. Retired for over 30 years' service, 1 Jan., 1896.

GREENE, CHAS. T. [Born in Md. Appointed fgom N. Y.]
Priv. Co. G, 22nd N. Y. State Militia, 28 May, 1862. Discharged 8 Aug., 1862. 2nd Lieut. 60th N. Y. Vols., 21 Aug., 1862. 1st Lieut., 10 Aug., 1863. Capt. A. A. G. Vols., 4 Sept., 1863. Bvt. Maj. Vols., 13 March, 1865, for meritorious service during the war. Mustered out of Vol. Service 19 Sept., 1865. Capt. 42nd Inf., 28 July, 1866. Bvt. Maj., 2 March, 1867, for gallant and meritorious service in the Battle of Ringgold, Ga., 27 Nov., 1863. Unassigned 22 April, 1869. Retired with rank of Capt., mounted, 15 Dec., 1870.

GREENE, CHAS. W. [Born in R. I. Appointed from R. I.]
Capt. 19th Inf., 17 May, 1861. Resigned 30 Sept., 1862.

GREENE, CHRISTOPHER A.* [Born in R. I. Appointed from R. I.]
Bvt. 2nd Lieut. 3rd Art., 1 July, 1836. 2nd Lieut., 13 Aug., 1836. Resigned 30 April, 1837. Died 28 Nov., 1853.

GREENE, DUANE M. [Born in N. Y. Appointed from Ohio.]
Capt. 6th Cal. Vols., 10 July, 1863. Resigned 1 Feb., 1865. 2nd Lieut. 3rd Inf., 27 July, 1872. Trans. to 6th Cav., 13 Oct., 1873. Resigned 31 Dec., 1877.

GREENE, FRANCIS V.* [Born in R. I. Appointed from D. C.]
2nd Lieut. 4th Art., 15 June, 1870. Trans. to Eng., 10 June, 1872. 1st Lieut., 13 Jan., 1874. Capt., 20 Feb., 1883. Resigned 31 Dec., 1886.

GREENE, FRANK. [Born in Penn. Appointed from the Army.]
Priv. and Sergt. Sig. Corps, 3 March, 1876, to 4 April, 1882. 2nd Lieut. Sig. Corps, 27 Jan., 1882. 1st Lieut., 20 Dec., 1890. Capt. (14 years' service), 22 July, 1898. Maj. and Chief Sig. Off. Vols., 20 May, 1898. Lieut. Col. Chief Sig. Off. Vols., 18 July, 1898, to 31 Dec., 1898.

GREENE, GEORGE S.* [Born in R. I. Appointed from R. I.]
Bvt. 2nd Lieut. 1st Art., 1 July, 1823. 2nd Lieut. 3rd Art., 1 July, 1823. 1st Lieut., 31 May, 1829. Resigned 30 June, 1836. Col. 60th N. Y. Vols., 18 Jan., 1862. Brig. Gen. Vols., 28 April, 1862. Bvt. Maj. Gen. Vols., 13 March, 1865, for gallant and meritorious service during the war. Mustered out 30 April, 1866. Appointed 1st. Lieut. of Art., 2 Aug., 1894. Retired 11 Aug., 1894. Died 28 Jan., 1899.

GREENE, HENRY A.* [Born in N. Y. Appointed from N. Y.]
2nd Lieut. 20th Inf., 13 June, 1879. 1st Lieut., 24 July, 1886. Reg. Adj., 22 Oct., 1886. Capt., 14 Oct., 1891.

GREENE, LEWIS D.* [Born in N. Y. Appointed from N. Y.]
2nd Lieut. 7th Inf., 14 June, 1878. 1st Lieut., 16 Dec., 1888. R. Q. M., 13 June, 1889. Retired for disability, with rank of Capt., 26 April, 1898.

GREENE, JAMES B.* [Born in N. Y. Appointed from N. Y.]
Bvt. 2nd Lieut. 1st Inf., 1 July, 1851. 2nd Lieut., 1 May, 1852. 1st Lieut., 11 Feb., 1856. Died 24 June, 1861.

GREENE, JAMES D. [Born in Mass. Appointed from Mass.]
Lieut. Col. 5th Mass. Vols., 1 May, 1861. Lieut. Col. 17th Inf., 14 May, 1861. Col. 6th Inf., 20 Sept., 1863. Resigned 25 June, 1867. Bvt. Brig. Gen., 13 March, 1865, for gallant and meritorious service during the war.

GREENE, JOHN. [Born in Ireland. Appointed from Penn.]
2nd Lieut. 22nd Inf., 12 March, 1812. 1st Lieut., 13 March, 1813. Reg. Adj., May, 1813, to 25 Sept., 1814. Capt., 25 Sept., 1814. Trans. to 8th Inf., 17 May, 1815. Trans. to 3rd Inf., 12 Aug., 1815. Maj. 5th Inf., 31 Oct., 1833. Lieut. Col. 6th Inf., 26 April, 1838. Died 21 Sept., 1840. Bvt. Maj., 23 Sept., 1824, for two years' faithful service in one grade.

GREENE, OLIVER D.* [Born in N. Y. Appointed from N. Y.]
Bvt. 2nd Lieut. 3rd Art., 1 July, 1854. 2nd Lieut. 2nd Art., 25 Nov., 1854. 1st Lieut., 25 April, 1861. Bvt. Capt., 21 July, 1861, for gallant and meritorious service in the Battle of Bull Run, Va. Capt. A. A. G., 3 Aug., 1861. Maj. A. A. G., 17 July, 1862. Lieut. Col. A. A. G. (Act 17 July, 1862), 20 Aug., 1862, to 31 Dec., 1862. Capt. 2nd Art., 1 Oct., 1863. Resigned commission of Capt. 2nd Art., 13 June, 1864. Bvt. Lieut. Col., 13 March, 1865, for gallant and meritorious service in the Battle of Crampton's Gap, Md. Bvt. Col., 13 March, 1865, for gallant and meritorious service in the Battle of Antietam, Md. Bvt. Brig. Gen., 13 March, 1865, for gallant and meritorious service during the war. Lieut. Col. A. A. G., 28 Feb., 1887. Col. A. A. G., 9 July, 1892. Retired 25 Jan., 1897. Medal of honor for distinguished gallantry at the Battle of Antietam, Md., Sept. 17, 1862, while serving as Lieut. Col. A. A. G., and Chief of Staff to the Commanding General, 6th Army Corps.

GREENE, SAML. C. [Born in Penn. Appointed from N. Y.]
Priv., Corpl., Sergt. and 1st Sergt. Co. D, and Sergt. Maj. 2nd Inf., 10 Aug., 1840, to 27 Aug., 1847. Sergt. Clay Guards, D. C. Vols., 23 to 26 April, 1861. 1st Lieut. 15th Inf., 14 May, 1861. Capt. C. S. Vols., 5 Aug., 1862. Mustered out Vols., 25 Aug., 1865. Capt., 21 Dec., 1864. Trans. to 24th Inf., 21 Sept., 1866. Trans. to 11th Inf., 25 April, 1869. Unassigned 10 Dec., 1869. Retired 15 Dec., 1870. Died 28 Aug., 1875. Bvt. Maj., 13 March., 1865, for meritorious service in the Sub. Dept. during the war. Bvt. Maj. of Vols., 13 March, 1865, for meritorious service during the war.

GREENE, WM. B. [Born in Mass. Appointed from Mass.]
Cadet at Mil. Acad., 1 July, 1835, to 15 Nov., 1837. 2nd Lieut. 7th Inf., 1 July, 1839. Resigned 20 Nov., 1841. Col. 1st Mass. Art., 5 July, 1861. Resigned 11 Oct., 1862.

GREENLEAF, CHAS. R. [Born in Penn. Appointed from Ohio.]
Asst. Surg. 5th Ohio Vols., 9 May, 1861. Discharged 18 July, 1861. 1st Lieut. Asst. Surg., 5 Aug., 1861. Bvt. Capt. and Maj., 13 March, 1865, for faithful and meritorious service during the war. Capt. Asst. Surg., 28 July, 1866. Maj. Surg., 26 June, 1876. Lieut. Col. and Asst. Med. Pur., 24 Feb., 1891. Col. and Asst. Surg. Gen., 10 Oct., 1896.

GREENLEAF, HENRY S. [Born in Idaho. Appointed from Cal.]
Asst. Surg., 7 Jan., 1899.

GREENOUGH, GEORGE G.* [Born in D. C. Appointed from N. Y.]
2nd Lieut. and 1st Lieut. 12th Inf., 23 June, 1865. Trans. to 21st Inf., 21 Sept., 1866. Unassigned 19 April, 1869. Ass'd to 4th Art., 15 Dec., 1870. Capt., 1 Dec., 1883. Maj. 7th Art., 8 March, 1898. Graduate of the Artillery School, 1882.

GREENOUGH, JONATHAN K.* [Born in Maine. Appointed from Mass.]
Bvt. 2nd Lieut. 1st Inf., 1 July, 1827. 2nd Lieut., 1 July, 1827. 1st Lieut., 10 Dec., 1834. Resigned 17 Dec., 1836. Died 22 Aug., 1858.

GREER, ALLEN J. [Born in Tenn. Appointed from Tenn.]
Capt. Co. L, 3rd Ala. Inf., 5 Aug., 1898, to 20 March, 1899. 2nd Lieut. 4th Inf., 5 Oct., 1899.

GREER, JOHN E.* [Born in Penn. Appointed from Penn.]
2nd Lieut. Ord., 17 June, 1867. 1st Lieut., 23 June, 1874. Capt., 10 May, 1878. Maj., 17 April, 1894.

GREGG, DAVID McM.* [Born in Penn. Appointed from Penn.]
Bvt. 2nd Lieut. 2nd Drag., 1 July, 1855. 2nd Lieut. 1st Drag., 4 Sept., 1855. 1st Lieut., 21 March, 1861. Reg. Adj., 12 April to 14 May, 1861. Capt. 3rd Cav., 14 May, 1861; 6th Cav., 3 Aug., 1861. Col. 8th Pa. Cav., 24 Jan., 1862. Brig. Gen. Vols., 29 Nov., 1862. Bvt. Maj. Gen. Vols., 1 Aug., 1864, for highly meritorious and distinguished conduct throughout the campaign, particularly in the reconnaissance on the Charles City Road, Va. Resigned from U. S. A. and U. S. V., 3 Feb., 1865.

GREGG, JOHN C.* [Born in Penn. Appointed from Penn.]
2nd Lieut. 16th Inf., 12 June, 1887. 1st Lieut. 18th Inf., 6 June, 1894. Trans. to 4th Inf., 24 May, 1897. Graduate of the Infantry and Cavalry School, 1897. Killed in action in the Philipine Islands, 31 March, 1899.

GREGG, JOHN I. [Born in Penn. Appointed from Penn.]
Priv. Co. D, 2nd Penn. Vols., 29 Dec., 1846. 1st Lieut. Inf., 18 Feb., 1847. 1st Lieut. 11th Inf., to rank from 9 April, 1847. Capt., 5 Sept., 1847. Disbanded 14 Aug., 1848. Capt. 3rd Cav., 14 May, 1861; 6th Cav., 3 Aug., 1861. Col. 16th Penn. Cav., 14 Nov., 1862. Bvt. Maj., 17 March, 1863, for gallant and meritorious service in the Battle of Kelly's Ford, Va. Bvt. Lieut. Col., 12 Oct., 1863, for gallant and meritorious service in action at Sulphur Springs, Va. Bvt. Brig. Gen. Vols., 1 Aug., 1864, for gallant and distinguished service in the engagement at the defences of Richmond on the Brock Turnpike, and at the Trevillian Station. Bvt. Col., 7 Oct., 1864, for gallant and meritorious service in the Battle of Deep Bottom, Va. Bvt. Brig. Gen., 13 March, 1865, for gallant and meritorious service in the field during the war. Bvt. Maj. Gen. Vols., 13 March, 1865, for gallant and meritorious service. Mustered out of Vol. service 11 Aug., 1865. Col. 8th Cav., 28 July, 1866. Retired 2 April, 1879. Died 6 Jan., 1892.

GREGG, MAXCY. [Born in S. C. Appointed from S. C.]
Maj. of Inf., 24 March, 1847; 12th Inf., 9 April, 1847. Disbanded 25 July, 1848.

GREGG, THOMAS J. [Born in Penn. Appointed from Penn.]
Priv. 125th Penn. Vols., 7 Aug., 1862. Corp., 20 Aug., 1862. Discharged 30 Oct., 1862. 2nd Lieut. 6th Penn. Cav., 1 Nov., 1862. Mustered out 3 Oct., 1864. Capt. 8th Penn. Cav., 24 June, 1865. Trans. to 16th Penn. Cav., 24 July, 1865. Mustered out 11 Aug., 1865. 2nd Lieut. 2nd Cav., 23 Feb., 1866. 1st Lieut., 1 Sept., 1866. Reg. Commissary, 3 Nov., 1868, to 15 July, 1870. Bvt. Capt. and Bvt. Maj., 2 March, 1867, for gallant and meritorious service during the war. Capt. 2nd Cav., 25 June, 1877. Retired for disability 24 March, 1890.

GREGORY, A. PARK.* [Born in Penn. Appointed from Penn.]
2nd Lieut. 4th Art., 1 July, 1837. Resigned 31 Dec., 1838. Died 19 Nov., 1840.

GREGORY, JAMES F.* [Born in N. Y. Appointed from N. Y.]
2nd Lieut. 5th Art., 23 June, 1865. Trans. to Eng., 1 May, 1866. 1st Lieut., 1 May, 1866. Capt., 13 Jan., 1874. Lieut. Col. A. de C. to Lieut. Gen. Sheridan, 15 July, 1881, to 10 Oct., 1885. Maj., 12 Oct., 1886. Died 31 July, 1897.

GRELAUD, JOHN H.* [Born in Penn. Appointed from Penn.]
Bvt. 2nd Lieut. 1st Art., 1 July, 1843. 2nd Lieut. 4th Art., 31 Oct., 1845. 1st Lieut., 3 March, 1847. Capt., 31 March, 1856. Died 17 Aug., 1857.

GRESHAM, JOHN C.* [Born in Va. Appointed from Va.]
2nd Lieut. 3rd Cav., 15 June, 1876. Trans. to 7th Cav., 26 June, 1876. 1st Lieut., 28 June, 1878. Capt., 8 April, 1892. Medal of honor for distinguished gallantry in voluntarily leading a party into a ravine to dislodge Indians concealed therein, in action at Wounded Knee Creek, S. Dak., Dec. 29, 1890, while serving as 1st Lieut. 7th Cav.

GREY, THOS. [Born in Ireland. Appointed from Army.]
Priv., Corpl., Sergt. and 1st Sergt. Batty E, 2nd Art., 17 Aug. 1837, to 19 April, 1848. 2nd Lieut. 9th Inf., 30 Dec., 1847. Disbanded 26 Aug., 1848. Priv. and 1st Sergt. Co. E. and Sergt. Maj. 2nd Art., 5 Oct., 1848, to 7 June, 1855. 2nd Lieut. 2nd Art., 7 June, 1855. 1st Lieut., 27 April, 1861. Reg. Adj., 1 Dec., 1861, to 4 Nov., 1863. Capt., 4 Nov., 1863. Retired 15 Dec., 1870. Died 7 Aug., 1872. Bvt. Maj. and Lieut. Col., 13 March, 1865, or faithful and meritorious service.

GREY, WILLIAM D. [Born in S. C. Appointed from Ga..
2nd Lieut. of Inf., 20 March, 1847; 13th Inf., 9 April, 1847. Died 7 April, 1848.

GRIER, JAMES.* [Born in N. Y. Appointed from N. Y.]
2nd Lieut. 2nd Art., 1 July, 1821. Trans. to 5th Inf., 30 Dec., 1824. 1st Lieut. 5th Inf., 31 May, 1827. Died 22 Aug., 1828.

GRIER, MATTHEW C. [Born in Penn. Appointed from Penn.]
1st Lieut. and Adj. 82nd Pa. Vols., 27 July, 1861. Resigned 6 Feb., 1863. 1st Lieut. 3rd Pa. Art., 28 July, 1863. Mustered out 16 Oct., 1865. 2nd Lieut. 5th Art., 11 May, 1866. Trans. to 4th Art, 23 Oct., 1866. 1st Lieut., 1 July, 1868. Resigned 7 March, 1874.

GRIER, WM. N.* [Born in Penn. Appointed from Penn.]
Bvt. 2nd Lieut. 1st Drag., 1 July, 1835. 2nd Lieut., 15 June, 1836. 1st Lieut. 14 April, 1838. Capt., 23 Aug., 1846. Bvt. Maj., 16 March, 1848, for gallant and meritorious conduct in the Battle of Santa Cruz de Rosales. Maj. 2nd Drag., 20 April, 1861. 2nd Cav., 3 Aug., 1861. Lieut. Col. 1st Cav., 15 Feb., 1862. Bvt. Col., 5 May, 1862, for gallant and meritorious service in the Battle of Williamsburg, Va. Bvt. Brig. Gen., 13 March, 1865, for faithful and meritorious service during the war. Col. 3rd Cav., 31 Aug., 1866. Retired 15 Dec., 1870. Died 8 July, 1885.

GRIER, WM. P. [Born in Penn. Appointed from Penn.]
Asst. Surg., 30 July, 1862. Killed 8 Jan., 1866, by explosion of steamer on Arkansas River.

GRIERSON, BENJAMIN H. [Born in Penn. Appointed from Ill.]
Vol. A. de C. to Gen. Prentiss, 8 May, 1861. Maj. 6th Ill. Cav., 24 Oct., 1861. Col., 12 April, 1862. Brig. Gen. Vols., 3 June, 1863, for gallant and distinguished service. Bvt. Maj. Gen. Vols., 10 Feb., 1865. Maj. Gen. Vols., 27 May, 1865. Mustered out of Vol. service, 30 April, 1866. Col. 10th Cav., 28 July, 1866. Bvt. Brig. Gen., 2 March, 1867, for gallant and meritorious service in the raid

through Mississippi in 1863. Bvt. Maj. Gen., 2 March, 1867, for gallant and meritorious service in the raid through Mississippi in 1864. Brig. Gen., 5 April, 1890. Retired by operation of the law, 8 July, 1890.

GRIERSON, CHARLES H.* [Born in Ill. Appointed from Mo.]
2nd Lieut. 10th Cav., 13 June, 1879. 1st Lieut., 6 July, 1886. R. Q. M., 22 April to 30 Sept., 1887. Reg. Adj., 1 Oct., 1887, to 30 Nov., 1888. Capt., 6 Nov., 1897. Lieut. Col. and Chief C. S. Vols., 9 May, 1898, to 17 March, 1899.

GRIFFIN, CHAS.* [Born in Ohio. Appointed from Ohio.]
Bvt. 2nd Lieut. 4th Art., 1 July, 1847. 2nd Lieut. 2nd Art., 12 Oct., 1847. 1st Lieut., 30 June, 1849. Capt., 25 April, 1861. Trans. to 5th Art., 14 May, 1861. Brig. Gen. Vols., 9 June, 1862. Maj. Gen. Vols., 2 April, 1865. Mustered out of Vols., 15 Jan., 1866. Col. 35th Inf., 28 July, 1866. Died 15 Sept., 1867. Bvt. Maj., 21 July, 1861, for gallant and meritorious service at the Battle of Bull Run, Va., Bvt. Lieut. Col., 6 May, 1864, for gallant and meritorious service at the Battle of the Wilderness, Va. Bvt. Col., 18 Aug., 1864, for gallant and meritorious service at the Battle on the Weldon R. R., Va. Bvt. Brig. Gen., 13 March, 1865, for gallant and meritorious service at the Battle of Five Forks, Va. Bvt. Maj. Gen., 13 March, 1865, for gallant and meritorious service in the field during the war.

GRIFFIN, EUGENE.* [Born in Maine. Appointed from Maine.]
2nd Lieut. Eng., 16 June, 1875. 1st Lieut., 30 June, 1879. Capt., 16 Sept., 1886. Resigned 5 Oct., 1889.

GRIFFIN, GEORGE H.* [Born in Va. Appointed from Va.]
Bvt. 2nd Lieut. 6th Inf., 1 July, 1832. 2nd Lieut., 6 May, 1835. 1st Lieut., 31 July, 1837. Bvt. Capt. A. A. G., 7 July, 1838. Died 8 Oct., 1839.

GRIFFIN, HENRY J.* [Born in Va. Appointed from Va.]
Bvt. 2nd Lieut. 5th Inf., 1 July, 1826. 2nd Lieut., 1 July, 1826. Drowned 20 Feb., 1828.

GRIFFIN, JOHN S. [Born in Va. Appointed from Ky.]
Asst. Surg., 18 June, 1840. Resigned 14 Sept., 1854.

GRIFFIN, SETH E. [Born in N. Y. Appointed from N. Y.]
1st Sergt. Co. C, 43rd N. Y. Vols., 28 Aug., 1861. 2nd Lieut., 9 Sept., 1861. 1st Lieut., 6 Nov., 1861. Resigned 16 July, 1862. 1st Lieut. 20th N. Y. Cav., 1 Nov., 1863. Capt., 1 July, 1865. Mustered out 31 July, 1865. 1st Lieut. 9th Cav., 28 July, 1866. Died 14 April, 1867.

GRIFFIN, WM. [Born in Ireland. Appointed from Army.]
Priv., Corpl., Sergt. and 1st Sergt. Co. B, 2nd Inf., 21 Jan., 1854, to 14 Nov., 1861. 2nd Lieut. 13th Inf., 24 Oct., 1861. 1st Lieut., 25 April, 1862. Died 6 Nov., 1864.

GRIFFIN, WM. H.* [Born in S. C. Appointed from S. C.]
Bvt. 2nd Lieut. 7th Inf., 1 July, 1835. 2nd Lieut., 31 July, 1836. Resigned 30 April, 1837.

GRIFFING, THOS. S. [Born in N. Y. Appointed from N. Y.]
2nd Lieut. of Inf., 2 March, 1847; 10th Inf., 9 April, 1847. 1st Lieut., 8 May, 1848. Disbanded 23 Aug., 1848.

GRIFFITH, DAVID A. [Born in Md. Appointed from Penn.]
2nd Lieut. Co. H, Md. and D. C. Vols., 30 Sept., 1847. Mustered out 15 July, 1848. Capt. 14th Penn. Vols., 25 April, 1861. Mustered out 7 Aug., 1861. Capt. 88th Penn. Vols., 14 Sept., 1861. Maj., 1 Sept., 1862. Resigned 31 Dec., 1862. Capt. 31st Penn. Vols., 19 June, 1863. Lieut. Col. 27 June, 1863. Mustered out 8 Aug., 1863. 2nd Lieut. 30th Inf., 22 Jan., 1867. 1st Lieut., 29 Oct., 1868. Unassigned 23 March, 1869. Ass'd to 3rd Inf., 31 Dec., 1870. Retired for disability 15 March, 1883.

GRIFFITH, EMERSON.* [Born in Penn. Appointed from Penn.]
2nd Lieut. 13th Inf., 14 June, 1872. 1st Lieut., 10 June, 1876. Retired for disability, with rank of Capt., 24 Feb., 1891.

GRIFFITH, FREDERICK L.* [Born in Va. Appointed from Va.]
3rd Lieut. Corps Art., 17 July, 1817. 2nd Lieut., 9 Dec., 1817. 1st Lieut., 28 Nov., 1819. Batt. Adj., 1 June, 1818, to 1 June, 1821. Trans. to 3rd Art., 1 June, 1821. Trans. to 2nd Art., 16 Aug., 1821. Died 28 Jan., 1832.

GRIFFITH, GEORGE R. [Born in Ohio. Appointed from Ohio.]
1st Lieut. 9th Inf., 29 Nov., 1865. Resigned 1 July, 1877.

GRIFFITH, JOSEPH E.* [Born in Wales. Appointed from N. C.]
Sergt. Co. I, 22nd Iowa Vols., 5 Aug., 1862. 2nd Lieut. 22nd Iowa Vols., 4 June, 1863. 1st Lieut., 31 Aug., 1863. Resigned 11 Oct., 1863. Cadet at Mil. Acad., 19 Oct., 1863. 2nd Lieut. Eng., 17 June, 1867. Discharged 25 Dec., 1870. Died 7 July, 1877.

GRIFFITH, ORLANDO B. [Born in Penn. Appointed from Army.]
Priv. Co. A, Eng., 2 Aug., 1846, to 13 April, 1847. 2nd Lieut. 16th Inf., 9 April, 1847. 1st Lieut., 20 Aug., 1847. Disbanded 7 Aug., 1848. 1st Lieut. 82nd Pa. Vols., 20 Aug., 1861. Capt., 27 Dec., 1862. Bvt. Maj. and Lieut. Col. Vols., 13 March, 1865, for gallant and meritorious service during the war. Mustered out 16 Sept., 1864. Died 6 June, 1877.

GRIFFITH, STEPHEN. [Born in Md. Appointed from Md.]
3rd Lieut. 1st Inf., 16 Sept., 1814. Disbanded 15 June, 1815. 2nd Lieut. 2nd Inf., 19 Feb., 1817. Died 23 July, 1818.

GRIFFITH, THOMAS. [Born in ———. Appointed from Ky.]
3rd Lieut. 28th Inf., 20 May, 1813. 2nd Lieut. 2nd Rifles, 17 March, 1814. Trans. to Rifle Reg., 17 May, 1815. Resigned 28 Feb., 1817.

GRIFFITH, THOMAS W.* [Born in Penn. Appointed from Penn.]
2nd Lieut. 18th Inf., 13 June, 1883. 1st Lieut., 16 Nov., 1889. Capt., 26 April, 1898.

GRIFFITHS, ALBERT J.* [Born in ———. Appointed from ———.]
2nd Lieut. 2nd Cav., — June, 1882. Killed by a fall 6 Nov., 1882.

GRIMES, EDWARD B. [Born in Md. Appointed from Kansas.]
Capt. A. Q. M. Vols., 29 Sept., 1862. Capt. A. Q. M., 26 May, 1865. Bvt. Maj., 26 May, 1865, for faithful and meritorious service in the Q. M. Dept. during the war. Maj. and Q. M., 10 March, 1882. Died 11 Oct., 1883.

GRIMES, GEORGE M. [Born in Va., Appointed from Army.]
Priv., Corpl. and Sergt. Troop B, 2nd Cav., 4 June, 1896, to 6 July, 1898. 2nd Lieut. 20th Inf., 23 June, 1898. 1st Lieut., 2 March, 1899.

GRIMES, GEORGE S. [Born in England. Appointed from N. Y.]
Priv. Co. G, 116th N. Y. Vols., 16 Aug., 1862. Sergt. Maj. 89th U. S. Col. Troops, 1 Dec., 1863. Trans. to 93rd U. S. Col. Troops, 5 Aug., 1864. 2nd Lieut. 81st U. S. Col. Troops, 30 March, 1865. 1st Lieut., 6 Jan., 1866. Mustered out 30 Nov., 1866. 2nd Lieut. 39th Inf., 22 Jan., 1867. 1st Lieut., 20 July, 1868. Trans. to 25th Inf., 20 April, 1869. Unassigned 13 July, 1869. Ass'd to 2nd Art., 15 Dec., 1870. Graduate of the Artillery School, 1886. Capt., 20 Nov., 1887. Maj., 31 March, 1899.

GRIMES, JAMES F. [Born in N. H. Appointed from N. H.]
Capt. 17th Inf., 5 Aug., 1861. Trans. to 26th Inf., 21 Sept., 1866. Trans. to 10th Inf., 19 May, 1869. Unassigned 2 June, 1870. Discharged 31 Dec., 1870. Bvt. Maj., 1 Aug., 1864, for gallant services at Spottsylvania, and during the campaign before Richmond, Va. Bvt. Lieut. Col., 13 March, 1865, for gallant and meritorious service during the war.

GRIMES, WASHINGTON M. [Born in Ohio. Appointed from Ohio.]
Chap. 92nd Ohio Vols., 1 Dec., 1862. Resigned 9 Sept., 1863. Hosp. Chap. Vols., 29 Feb., 1864. Mustered out 24 June, 1865. Chap. 10th Cav., 7 Feb., 1867. Resigned 19 March, 1869.

GRIMSHAW, JAMES. [Born in Penn. Appointed from Penn.]
Asst. Surg. 11th Inf., 29 March, 1848. Disbanded 14 Aug., 1848.

GRISARD, JNO. S.* [Born in Ohio. Appointed from Ohio..
2nd Lieut. 13th Inf., 11 June, 1888. 1st Lieut. 7th Inf., 12 May, 1895. Capt., 13th March, 1899.

GRISWOLD, EDMUND B. [Born in N. Y. Appointed from N. Y.
2nd Lieut. 2nd Inf., 13 Aug., 1819. 1st Lieut., 10 Feb., 1825. Died 17 Sept., 1828.

GRISWOLD, GAYLORD H. [Born in N. Y. Appointed from N. Y.]
2nd Lieut. 10th Inf., 13 May, 1847. Resigned 21 Sept., 1847.

GRISWOLD, HENRY W.* [Born in Ohio. Appointed from Ohio.]
3rd Lieut. Corps. Art., 2 March, 1815. 2nd Lieut., 1 May, 1817. 1st Lieut., 12 Dec., 1818. Trans. to 1st Art., 1 June, 1821. Reg. Adj., 25 Sept., 1822, to 11 Oct., 1831. Capt., 26 April, 1832. Died 23 Oct., 1834. Bvt. Capt., 12 Dec., 1828, for faithful service, ten years in one grade.

GRISWOLD, SAMUEL B. [Born in N. Y. Appointed from N. Y.]
3rd Lieut. 23rd Inf., 5 April, 1813. 2nd Lieut., 19 Dec., 1813. 1st Lieut., 1 Sept., 1814. Trans. to 2nd Inf., 17 May, 1815. Trans. to 5th Inf., 7 June, 1821. Resigned 1 Nov., 1821. Died 4 Sept., 1830.

GROESBECK, STEPHEN W. [Born in N. Y. Appointed from Ill.]
Q. M. Serg. Co. H. 4th Iowa Cav., 28 Oct., 1861. 2nd Lieut. 4th Iowa Cav., 1 Nov., 1862. Mustered out 4 April, 1863. 2nd Lieut. Vet. Res. Corps, 16 Sept., 1864. Mustered out 14 Jan., 1867. 2nd Lieut. 42nd Infantry, 28 July, 1866. Trans. to 6th Inf., 22 April, 1869. 1st Lieut., 7 Oct., 1874. Reg. Adj., 1 Feb., 1875, to 30 March, 1880, and from 31 Oct., 1883, to 31 Oct., 1886. Capt., 16 July, 1889. Capt. A. J. A., 5 Oct., 1886. Maj. and J. A., 23 March, 1892.

GROSS, FRANK P. [Born in Penn. Appointed from Ind..
Sergt. Maj. 9th Ind. Vols., 27 Aug., 1861. 1st Lieut. 9th Ind. Vols., 8 Oct., 1861. Resigned 25 April, 1863. 1st Lieut. Vet. Res. Corps, 24 Oct., 1863. Mustered out 25 Aug., 1867. 2nd Lieut. 9th Cav., 9 Aug., 1867. 1st Lieut., 22 Dec., 1869. Retired 28 June, 1878.

GROSS, LOUIS H. [Born in Ill. Appointed from the Army.]
Priv. and Corpl. Co. G, 5th Inf., 6 Oct., 1893, to 28 March, 1897. 2nd Lieut. 6th Inf., 2 March, 1897. Retired for disability, with rank of 1st Lieut., 2 March, 1899.

GROSSMAN, FREDK. E. [Born in Germany. Appointed from the Army.]
Priv., Corpl., Sergt. and 1st Sergt. Co. G., and Sergt. Maj. 7th Inf., 3 Feb., 1855, to 24 April, 1863. 2nd Lieut. 7th Inf., 22 April, 1863. 1st Lieut., 4 Nov., 1863. Capt., 12 Oct., 1867. Unassigned 19 May, 1869. Ass'd to 17th Inf., 1 Jan., 1871. Resigned 1 June, 1875. Bvt. 1st Lieut. 2 July, 1863, for gallant and meritorious service at the Battle of Gettysburg, Pa. Bvt. Capt., 13 March, 1865, for gallant and meritorious service at the Battle of Gettysburg, Pa. Died 30 Sept., 1877.

GROSVENOR, GEORGE H. [Born in N. Y. Appointed from N. Y.]
Capt. 26th Inf., 21 April, 1814. Trans. to 8th Inf., 17 May, 1815. Trans. to 3rd Inf., 8 July, 1815. Disbanded 1 June, 1821.

GROSVENOR, OLIVER. [Born in N. Y. Appointed from Ill.]
Priv. and Sergt. Maj. 12th Ill. Cav., 1 June to 8 Oct., 1862. 2nd Lieut. 12th Ill. Cav., 8 Oct., 1862. 1st Lieut., 1 Nov., 1863. Capt., 2 March, 1864. Mustered out 31 March, 1865. 2nd Lieut. 4th Cav., 20 Sept., 1867. Mustered out 1 Jan., 1871.

GROTE, WM. F.* [Born in Ill. Appointed from Ill.]
2nd Lieut. 18th Inf., 12 June, 1891. 1st Lieut., 26 April, 1898.

GROVER, CUVIER.* [Born in Maine. Appointed from Maine.]
Bvt. 2nd Lieut. 1st Art., 1 July, 1850. 2nd Lieut. 4th Art., 16 Sept., 1850. 1st Lieut. 10th Inf., 3 March, 1855. Capt., 17 Sept., 1858. Brig. Gen. Vols., 14 April, 1862. Bvt. Lieut. Col., 5 May, 1862, for gallant and meritorious service in the Battle of Williamsburg, Va. Bvt. Col., 31 May, 1862, for gallant and meritorious service in the Battle of Fair Oaks, Va. Maj. 3rd Inf., 31 Aug., 1863. Bvt. Maj. Gen. Vols., 19 Oct., 1864, for gallant and meritorious service in the Battles of Winchester and Fisher's Hill, Va. Bvt. Brig. Gen., 13 March, 1865, for gallant

and meritorious service in the Battle of Cedar Creek, and in the campaign of the Shenandoah Valley, Va. Bvt. Maj. Gen., 13 March, 1865, for gallant and meritorious service in the field during the war. Mustered out of Vol. Service 24 Aug., 1865. Lieut. Col. 38th Inf., 28 July, 1866. Trans. to 24th Inf., 15 Mar., 1869. Unassigned 14 April, 1869. Ass'd to 3rd Cav., 15 Dec., 1870. Col. 1st Cav., 2 Dec., 1875. Died 6 June, 1885.

GROVES, LESLIE R. [Born in N. Y. Appointed from N. Y.]
Post Chap., 26 Oct., 1896.

GRUBBS, HAYDON Y.* [Born in Ky. Appointed from Ky.]
2nd Lieut. of Inf. (18th), 12 June, 1896. 1st Lieut., 26 April, 1898. Killed in action, in the island of Cebu (Philippines], 1 Oct., 1899.

GRUGAN, FRANK C. [Born in Penn. Appointed from Penn.
Priv. Commonwealth Penn. Heavy Art., 4 June, 1861. Discharged 5 Aug., 1861. 2nd Lieut. 114th Penn. Vols., 15 Aug., 1862. 1st Lieut., 1 Sept., 1863. 1st Lieut. 3rd Penn. Cav., 19 Dec., 1864. Trans. to 5th Penn. Cav., 8 May, 1865. Mustered out 7 Aug., 1865. Priv. Gen. Ser., 18 Aug., 1865. Discharged 15 May, 1866. 2nd Lieut. 2nd Cav., 25 April, 1866. Reg. Q. M., 1 Nov., 1867, to 15 July, 1870. 1st Lieut., 1 Nov., 1867. Trans. to 2nd Art., 11 April, 1879. Graduate of the Artillery School, 1882. Capt., 18 March, 1885. Maj. 6th Art., 8 March, 1898. Retired, over 30 years' service, 18 March, 1899.

GRUMLEY, EDWARD I. [Born in Ohio. Appointed from the Army.]
Priv. 13th Batty Wis. Light Art., 16 Nov., 1863, to 27 July, 1864. 1st Lieut. 37th Wis. Vols., 28 Oct., 1864, to 27 July, 1865. Priv., Corpl. and Sergt. Co. A, 21st Inf., 13 Aug., 1870, to 13 Aug., 1875. Priv., Corpl., Sergt. and 1st Sergt. Co. G, 21st Inf., 1 Sept., 1875, to 13 July, 1880. 2nd Lieut. 17th Inf., 24 June, 1880. 1st Lieut., 15 July, 1888. Retired for disability, with rank of Capt., 26 April, 1898.

GRUMMOND, GEORGE W. [Born in Mich. Appointed from Mich.]
1st Sergt. Co. A, 1st Mich Vols., 1 May to 7 Aug., 1861. Capt. 1st Mich. Vols., 12 Sept., 1861. Resigned 14 July, 1862. Maj. 14th Mich. Vols., 9 March, 1863. Lieut. Col., 20 April, 1863. Mustered out 18 July, 1865. 2nd Lieut. 18th Inf., 7 May, 1866. Killed 21 Dec., 1866, in action with Indians near Fort Phil. Kearney, Dakota.

GUARD, ALEXANDER McC.* [Born in Ill. Appointed from Ohio.]
2nd Lieut. 19th Inf., 12 June, 1871. 1st Lieut., 20 March, 1879. Capt., 20 Feb., 1891. Trans. to 5th Inf., 11 Aug., 1899. Retired for disability, with rank of Maj., 8 Sept., 1899.

GUENTHER, FRANCIS L.* [Born in N. Y. Appointed from N. Y.]
Bvt. 2nd Lieut. 1st Art., 1 July, 1859. 2nd Lieut. 4th Art., 2 Nov., 1859. 1st Lieut. 5th Art., 14 May, 1861. Bvt. Capt., 7 April, 1862, for gallant and meritorious service in the Battle of Shiloh, Tenn. Bvt. Maj. 31 Dec., 1862, for gallant and meritorious service in the Battle of Stone River, Tenn. Capt. 5th Art., 2 July, 1863. Bvt. Lieut. Col. and Col. 13 March, 1865, for gallant and meritorious service during the war. Maj. 2nd Art., 26 June, 1882. Lieut. Col. 5th Art., 1 July, 1891. Col. 4th Art., 6 June, 1896. Brig. Gen. Vols., 4 May to 30 Nov., 1898.

GUERRANT, CHAS.* [Born in Va. Appointed from Va.]
2nd Lieut. 7th Inf., 1 July, 1820. Resigned 13 Aug., 1820. Died 5 Sept., 1852.

GUEST, JOHN. [Born in Penn. Appointed from Md.]
2nd Lieut. 8th Cav., 15 Aug., 1876. 1st Lieut., 16 Jan., 1884. Capt. 8th Cav., 20 April, 1891. Retired for disability 3 Jan., 1895.

GUIGNARD, WM. S.* [Born in S. C. Appointed from S. C.]
Addl. 2nd Lieut. 4th Art., 12 June, 1896. 2nd Lieut., 1 Sept., 1896. 1st Lieut., 2 March, 1899.

GUILD, LA FAYETTE. [Born in Ala. Appointed from Ala.]
Asst. Surg., 2 March, 1849. Dismissed 1 July, 1861.

GUILFOYLE, JOHN F.* [Born in Md. Appointed from Md.]
2nd Lieut. 9th Cav., 15 June, 1877. 1st Lieut., 1 Nov., 1881. R. Q. M., 7 May, 1884, to 8 Jan., 1885. Reg. Adj., 8 Jan., 1885, to 9 May, 1888. Capt., 25 Feb., 1891. Bvt. 1st Lieut., Feb. 27, 1890, for gallant services in action against Indians at White Sands, N. M., 19 July, 1881; in the San Andreas Mountains, N. M., 25 July, 1881; and at Monica Springs, N. M., 3 Aug., 1881.

GUINEY, PATRICK W.* [Born in Mass. Appointed from Mass.]
2nd Lieut. 6th Cav., 15 Feb., 1899.

GUION, ELIJAH. [Born in N. Y. Appointed from La.]
Chap. 1st N. O. Vols., 27 Feb., 1865. Mustered out 1 June, 1866. Chap. 41st Inf., 28 July, 1866. Unassigned 11 Nov., 1869. Ass'd to 10th Cav., 31 Dec., 1870. Died 17 Jan., 1879.

GUION, FREDERICK L.* [Born in Miss. Appointed from Miss..
Bvt. 2nd Lieut. 4th Art., 1 July, 1823. 2nd Lieut., 1 July, 1823. Died 4 April, 1824.

GUION, WALTER B. [Born in Miss. Appointed from Miss.]
Cadet Mil. Acad., 1 July, 1824, to 9 May, 1827. Capt. Top. Eng., 7 July, 1838. Resigned 31 March, 1842.

GUNN, GEORGE H. [Born in Mass. Appointed from Md.]
Asst. Surg., 14 May, 1867. Died 29 May, 1871.

GUNNISON, JOHN W.* [Born in N. H. Appointed from N. H.]
2nd Lieut. 2nd Art., 1 July, 1837. 2nd Lieut. Top. Eng., 7 July, 1838. 1st Lieut., 9 May, 1846. Capt., 3 March, 1853. Massacred 26 Oct., 1853, by Mormons and Indians in Utah.

GUNTHER, SEBASTIAN. [Born in Germany. Appointed from Army.]
Priv. Co. B, 1st Cav., 27 Aug., 1855. Corpl., 1 Dec., 1857. Sergt., 1 April, 1858. Discharged 27 June, 1860. Sergt. Co. B, 1st Cav., 27 June, 1860. Com. Sergt. 4th Cav., 17 Oct., 1862. 2nd Lieut. 4th Cav., 10 Aug., 1863. Bvt. 1st Lieut., 16 Dec., 1864, for gallant and meritorious service in the pursuit of the rebel forces

under Gen. Hood. Bvt. Capt., 2 April, 1865, for gallant and meritorious service in the capture of Selma, Ala. 1st Lieut. 4th Cav., 25 July, 1865. Reg. Com., 31 Dec., 1863, to 30 Nov., 1867. Capt., 10 Feb., 1870. Retired for disability, 26 Nov., 1884.

GURLEY, CHAS. L. [Born in Ind. Appointed from Dakota.]
2nd Lieut. 6th Inf., 27 July, 1872. 1st Lieut., 19 July, 1881. Resigned 31 Dec., 1882.

GURNEY, JOHN A.* [Born in Mich. Appointed from Mich.]
2nd Lieut. of Inf. (5th), 12 June, 1895. Trans. to 24th Inf., 1 Oct., 1896. 1st Lieut., 2 April, 1898. Killed in action at Santiago, Cuba, 1 July, 1898.

GURNEY, SMITH J. [Born in N. Y. Appointed from N. Y.]
Priv. Co. G, 30th N. Y. Vols., 7 May, 1861, to 21 Nov., 1862. 1st Lieut. 2nd N. Y. Cav., 9 Sept., 1863. Capt., 18 Dec., 1863. Mustered out 8 Nov., 1865. 2nd Lieut. 45th Inf., 28 July, 1866. Trans. to 14th Inf., 22 July, 1869. Mustered out 23 Dec., 1870. Died 3 Dec., 1878.

GUROVITS, ODON. [Born in Hungary. Appointed from the Army.]
Priv., Corpl. and Sergt. Co. C, and Sergt. Maj. 6th Inf., 16 March, 1880, to 22 Oct., 1886. 2nd Lieut. 11th Inf., 22 Oct., 1886. 1st Lieut. 12th Inf., 15 Dec., 1893. Trans. to 11th Inf., 16 April, 1894. Capt., 2 March, 1899. Graduate of the Infantry and Cavalry School, 1889.

GUSTIN, JOSEPH H.* [Born in Ohio. Appointed from Ohio.]
2nd Lieut. 14th Inf., 16 June, 1875. 1st Lieut., 15 June, 1887. R. Q. M., 1 July, 1888. Retired for disability, with rank of Capt., 1 March, 1894.

GUTHRIE, EDWARD A. [Born in Ind. Appointed from Army.]
Priv. and Corpl. Co. C, 11th Inf., 7 Dec., 1861, to 17 July, 1862. 2nd Lieut. 11th Inf., 11 June, 1862. 1st Lieut., 2 July, 1863. Cashiered 28 Aug., 1865.

GUTHRIE, EDWIN. [Born in N. Y. Appointed from Iowa.]
Capt. of Inf., 8 March, 1847; 15th Inf., 9 April, 1847. Died 20 July, 1847, of wounds received in action at La Hoya, Mexico.

GUTHRIE, JOHN B. [Born in Ohio. Appointed from Ohio.]
1st Lieut. 8th Tenn. Cav., 1 May, 1863. Resigned 14 Dec., 1863. 2nd Lieut. 11th Inf., 9 May, 1866. Trans. to 29th Inf., 21 Sept., 1866. 1st Lieut., 18 Dec., 1866. Trans. to 11th Inf., 25 April, 1869. Died 30 Dec., 1871.

GUTHRIE, JOHN B. [Born in Ohio. Appointed from Ohio.]
Corpl. Co. C, 1st Ky. Vols., 7 June, 1861. 1st Sergt., 1 April, 1862. 2nd Lieut. 1st Ky. Vols., 7 Dec., 1862. Mustered out 18 June, 1864. 2nd Lieut. 13th Inf., 28 July, 1866. 1st Lieut., 1 Sept., 1871. Capt., 7 May, 1882. Major 15th Inf., 8 Aug., 1898. Died in 1900.

GUTHRIE, PRESLEY N. [Born in Penn. Appointed from Penn.]
Capt. of Inf., 16 Feb., 1847; 11th Inf., 9 April, 1847. Disbanded 20 July, 1848. Bvt. Maj., 20 Aug., 1847. Capt. 9th Inf., 3 March, 1855. Died 29 Dec., 1857. Bvt. Maj., 20 Aug., 1847, for gallant and meritorious conduct at Contreras and Churubusco.

GUTHRIE, SHELDON. [Born in Ohio. Appointed from La.]
1st Sergt. Co. G., 32nd Ohio Vols., 1 Aug., 1861. 2nd Lieut., 2 April, 1862. 1st Lieut. 1 Nov., 1862. Capt., 1 Jan., 1863. Lieut. Col., 2 May, 1865. Mustered out 20 July, 1865. 2nd Lieut. 32nd Inf., 28 July, 1866. 1st Lieut., 5 Nov., 1867. Unassigned 19 April, 1869. Ass'd to 23rd Inf., 1 Sept., 1869. Discharged 30 Dec., 1870.

GUY, JOHN R. [Born in Md. Appointed from Penn.]
Ensign 16th Inf., 15 May, 1812. Trans. to 22nd Inf., 12 Sept., 1812. 2nd Lieut., 20 June, 1813. 1st Lieut., 3 May, 1814. Trans. to 8th Inf., 17 May, 1815. Resigned 20 Aug., 1817.

GUYER, GEORGE D. [Born in N. Y. Appointed form N. Y.]
2nd Lieut. 16th Inf., 12 June, 1891. 1st Lieut., 26 April, 1898. Graduate of the Inf. and Cav. School, 1897.

GWYNN, WALTER.* [Born in Va. Appointed from Va.]
Bvt. 2nd Lieut. 3rd Art., 1 July, 1822. 2nd Lieut. 3rd Art., 1 July, 1822. Trans. to 4th Art., 18 Feb., 1823. 1st Lieut., 19 Oct., 1829. Resigned 2 Feb., 1832. Died 6 Feb., 1882.

GWYNNE, DAVID. [Born in Md. Appointed from Ohio.]
1st Lieut. 19th Inf., 12 March, 1812. Reg. P. M., 1 Oct., 1812, to 30 March, 1813. Capt., 30 March, 1813. Maj. 2nd Rifles, 21 Feb., 1814. Disbanded 15 June, 1815. Maj. and P. M., 29 April, 1816. Resigned 29 April, 1830. Died 1849.

GWYNNE, THOS P. [Born in Va. Appointed from Va.]
Cadet at Mil. Acad., 19 June, 1813, to 30 Sept., 1818. 2nd Lieut. 1st Inf., 12 Dec., 1820. 1st Lieut., 31 Dec., 1824. Capt., 4 March, 1833. Trans. to 8th Inf., 7 July, 1838. Maj. 6th Inf., 16 Feb., 1847. Trans. to 5th Inf., 20 Feb., 1852. Died 26 Feb., 1861.

HAAN, WM. G.* [Born in Ind. Appointed from Ind.]
2nd Lieut. 1st Art., 12 June, 1889. Trans. to 5th Art., 29 Jan., 1891. 1st Lieut., 27 Aug., 1896. Trans. to 3rd Art., 10 Oct., 1896. Capt. and A. Q. M. Vols., 17 Oct., 1898.

HACKETT, GEORGE. [Born in Penn. Appointed from Penn.]
Mil. Storekeeper, March, 1814. Disbanded 1 June, 1821.

HACKLEY, CHAS. W.* [Born in N. Y. Appointed from N. Y.]
Bvt. 2nd Lieut. 3rd Art., 1 July, 1829. 2nd Lieut., 1 July, 1829. Resigned 30 Sept., 1833. Died 10 Jan., 1861.

HACKLEY, JAMES, Jr. [Born in Ky. Appointed from Ky.]
2nd Lieut. 17th Inf., 12 March, 1812. 1st Lieut., 13 March, 1813. Trans. to 3rd Inf., 17 May, 1815. Capt., 17 May, 1816. Resigned 31 Dec., 1818. Died 1831.

HACKNEY, STEPHEN M. [Born in Ala. Appointed from Army.]
Priv. and Corpl. Co. G, 16th Inf., 24 April, 1883, to 22 Oct., 1886. 2nd Lieut. 16th Inf., 22 Oct., 1886. 1st Lieut. 4th Inf., 3 Feb., 1894. Trans. to 5th Inf., 12 April, 1894. Capt., 2 March, 1899. Adj., 15 Sept., 1899. Graduate at the Inf. and Cav. School, 1889.

HADEN, JOHN J.* [Born in Mo. Appointed from Texas.]
2nd Lieut. 8th Inf., 15 June, 1877. 1st Lieut., 8 April, 1885. Capt., 16 Sept., 1893. Retired for disability 27 Aug., 1896.

HADEN, JOHN M. [Born in Miss. Appointed from Miss.]
Asst. Surg., 13 Dec., 1847. Resigned 25 April, 1861.

HADEN, PORTER. [Born in Ky. Appointed from Cal.]
1st Lieut. 1st Cal. Cav., 7 Sept., 1861. Mustered out 7 Sept., 1864. 2nd Lieut. 8th Cav., 10 Aug., 1867. Resigned 26 March, 1868.

HADLEY, HENRY C. [Born in N. Y. Appointed from Wis.]
Priv. Co. D, 16th Wis. Vols., 5 Dec., 1861, to 9 Aug., 1862. Priv. Co. B, 29th Wis. Vols., 18 Feb., 1864. 1st Lieut. and Adj., 10 April, 1864. Mustered out 22 June, 1865. 2nd Lieut. 6th Inf., 7 March, 1867. Resigned 20 Nov., 1868.

HADSELL, G. ARTHUR. [Born in Conn. Appointed from Conn.]
2nd Lieut. 19th Inf., 1 May, 1899.

HAGADORN, CHARLES B.* [Born in N. Y. Appointed from N. Y.]
2nd Lieut. 23rd Inf., 12 June, 1889. 1st Lieut. 17th Inf., 23 May, 1896. Trans. to 23rd Inf., 5 Nov., 1896. Capt. 12th Inf., 16 June, 1899. Graduate of the Infantry and Cavalry School, 1893. Trans. to 23rd Inf., 23 Feb., 1900.

HAGAN, JAMES. [Born in Ireland. Appointed from Ala.]
Capt. of Inf., 5 March, 1847; 3rd Drag., 9 April, 1847. Disbanded 31 July, 1848.

HAGAN OSCAR. [Born in Prussia. Appointed from Army.]
Priv. Gen. Ser., 26 May, 1857. Corpl., 9 June, 1858. Priv. Co. C, 2nd Inf., 1 Jan., 1860. Sergt., 1 Jan., 1860. 1st Sergt., 1 May, 1860. 2nd Lieut. 11th Inf., 20 Nov., 1861. 1st Lieut., 3 April, 1862. Reg. Q. M., 15 April, 1862, to 12 Jan., 1868. Bvt. Capt. 13 March, 1865, for gallant and meritorious service in the field during the war. Capt. 11th Inf., 12 Jan., 1868. Unassigned 14 April, 1869. Ass'd to 9th Cav., 1 Jan., 1871. Retired 4 April, 1879. Died 30 Dec. 1880.

HAGAN, ROBERT. [Born in Ireland. Appointed from La.]
Ast. Surg. 14th Inf., 9 Nov., 1847. Disbanded 29 July, 1848.

HAGEDORN, ERNST. [Born in Germany. Appointed from Army.]
Priv., Corpl. and Sergt. Co. E, 8th Inf., 23 June, 1896, to 26 May, 1899. 2nd Lieut. 16th Inf., 5 April, 1899.

HAGER, JONATHAN B. [Born in Md. Appointed from Ind.]
Cadet at Mil. Acad, 1 July, 1840, to 1 July, 1842. Capt. 14th Ind. Vols., 7 June to 5 July, 1861. Capt. 14th Inf., 14 May, 1861. Resigned 9 July, 1866.

HAGOOD, JOHNSON.* [Born in S. C. Appointed from S. C.]
Addl. 2nd Lieut. 2nd Art., 12 June, 1896. 2nd Lieut. 1st Art., 26 Aug., 1897. 1st Lieut., 2 March, 1899.

HAGNER, CHAS N. [Born in D. C. Appointed from D. C.]
2nd Lieut. Top. Eng., 7 July, 1838. 1st Lieut., 3 March, 1847. Died 14 July, 1849.

HAGNER, JOHN R. [Born in D. C. Appointed from D. C.]
Maj. and P. M., 9 Jan., 1850. Died 6 Dec., 1856.

HAGNER, PETER V.* [Born in D. C. Appointed from D. C.]
Bvt. 2nd Lieut. 1st Art., 1 July, 1836. 2nd Lieut., 6 Aug., 1836. 2nd Lieut. Ord., 9 July, 1838. 1st Lieut., 22 May, 1840. Bvt. Capt., 18 April, 1847, for gallant and meritorious conduct in the Battle of Cerro Gordo. Bvt. Maj., 13 Sept., 1847, for gallant and meritorious conduct in the Battle of Chapultepec. Capt. Ord., 10 July, 1851. Maj., 3 Aug., 1861. Lieut. Col., 1 June, 1863. Bvt. Col. and Brig. Gen., 13 March, 1865, for faithful and meritorious service in the Ord. Dept. Col. Ord., 7 March, 1867. Retired, over 40 years' service, 1 June, 1881. Died 11 March, 1893.

HAIGHT, CHARLES S. [Born in N. Y. Appointed from N. Y.]
Corpl. Troop A, N. Y. Cav., 2 May to 28 July, 1898. 2nd Lieut. 4th Art., 9 July, 1898. Trans. to 4th Cav., 1 April, 1899.

HAIGHT, EDWARD. [Born in N. Y. Appointed from N. Y.]
1st Lieut. 16th Inf., 14 May, 1861. Capt., 16 June, 1864. Resigned 13 Feb., 1866. Bvt. Maj. and Lieut. Col., 5 May, 1865, for meritorious service during the war.

HAILE, CHRISTOPHER M. [Born in R. I. Appointed from R. I.]
Cad. Mil. Acad., 1 July, 1836, to 4 Oct., 1837. 1st Lieut. of Inf., 11 March, 1847; 14th Inf., 9 April, 1847. Capt., 22 May, 1847. Disbanded 20 July, 1848.

HAILE, JOSEPH T.* [Born in R. I. Appointed from La.]
Bvt. 2nd Lieut. 1st Inf., 1 July, 1850. Trans. to 2nd Inf., 11 Feb., 1851. 2nd Lieut., 11 June, 1851. Died 31 July, 1853.

HAILE, WILLIAM F. [Born in Vt. Appointed from Vt.]
Ensign 11th Inf., 27 May, 1812. 2nd Lieut., 13 March, 1813. 1st Lieut., 15 Aug., 1813. Trans. to 6th Inf., 17 May, 1815. Capt., 14 May, 1818. Resigned 28 Feb., 1823.

HAINES, ABNER, Jr. [Born in Ohio. Appointed from Ohio.]
Corpl. Co. C, 20th Ohio Vols., 17 April, 1861. Discharged 18 Aug., 1861. Priv. Co. F, 87th Ohio Vols., 2 June, 1862. Discharged 3 Oct., 1862. 2nd Lieut. 54th Ohio Vols., 2 April, 1864. 1st Lieut., 1 Jan., 1865. Capt., 28 March, 1865. Mustered out 15 Aug., 1865. 2nd Lieut., 16th Inf., 28 March, 1866. Trans. to 2nd Inf., 17 April, 1869. 1st Lieut., 1 Jan., 1871. Capt., 15 March, 1883. Died 22 Jan., 1892.

HAINES, JOHN T.* [Born in Mo. Appointed from N. Y..
2nd Lieut. 5th Cav., 1 July, 1886. 1st Lieut. 1st Cav., 22 July, 1892. Trans. to 5th Cav., 27 Dec., 1892. Graduate of the Infantry and Cavalry School, 1889.

HAINES, THOS J.* [Born in N. H. Appointed from N. H.]
Bvt. 2nd Lieut. 1st Art., 1 July, 1849. 2nd Lieut. 2nd Art., 1 July, 1849. 1st Lieut., 9 July, 1853. Reg. Adj., 1 Oct., 1855, to 3 Aug., 1861. Capt. 13th Inf., 14 May, 1861, declined. Capt. C. S., 3 Aug., 1861. Col. A. A. de C., 1 May, 1862. Maj. C. S., 9 Feb., 1863. Bvt. Lieut. Col., Col., Brig. Gen., 13 March, 1865, for faithful and meritorious service during the war Mustered out as Col. A. A. de C., 31 May, 1866. Died 14 Aug., 1883.

HAINS, JOHN P.* [Born in Penn. Appointed from D. C.]
Addl. 2nd Lieut. 1st Art., 12 June, 1889. 2nd Lieut. 3rd Art., 16 Dec., 1889. 1st Lieut. 1st Art., 17 June, 1897. Trans. to 3rd Art., 24 July, 1897. Graduate of the Artillery School, 1894.

HAINS, PETER C.* [Born in Penn. Appointed from N. J.]
2nd Lieut. 2nd Art., 24 June, 1861. 1st Lieut., 24 June, 1861. Bvt. Capt., 27 May, 1862, for gallant and meritorious service in the Battle of Hanover Court House, Va. Trans. to Top. Eng., 24 July, 1862. Trans. to Eng., 3 March, 1863. Bvt. Maj., 4 July, 1863, for gallant and meritorious service during the Siege of Vicksburg, Miss. Capt. Eng., 18 July, 1863. Bvt. Lieut. Col., 13 March, 1865, for gallant and meritorious service during the war. Maj. Eng., 22 Sept., 1870. Lieut. Col., 16 Sept., 1886. Col., 13 Aug., 1895. Brig. Gen. Vols., 27 May to 30 Nov., 1898.

HAINS, PETER C., JR. [Born in Md. Appointed from Md.]
2nd Lieut. 7th Art., 9 July, 1898.

HALDEMAN, HORACE. [Born in Penn. Appointed from Penn.]
2nd Lieut. of Inf., 16 Feb., 1847; 11th Inf., 9 April, 1847. 1st Lieut., 25 Sept., 1847. Trans. to 8th Inf., 29 June, 1848, to rank as 2nd Lieut. from 9 April, 1847. 1st Lieut., 13 Sept., 1852. Resigned 1 Feb., 1856. Died 10 Sept., 1883.

HALE, CHAS. H. [Born in Penn. Appointed from Penn.]
1st Lieut. 19th Inf., 5 Aug., 1861. Capt. A. A. de C., 25 June, 1862. Capt., 20 Feb., 1865. Resigned 28 April, 1865. Died 3 Oct., 1872.

HALE, CLAYTON. [Born in Penn. Appointed from Ill.]
Capt. 59th Ill. Vols., 17 July, 1861. Maj., 1 April, 1863. Lieut. Col., 5. Dec., 1863. Mustered out 8 Dec., 1865. 2nd Lieut. and 1st Lieut. 16th Inf., 23 Feb., 1866. Trans. to 34th Inf., 21 Sept., 1866. R. Q. M., 10 Feb., 1867 to 14 April, 1869. Bvt. Capt., 2 March, 1867, for gallant and meritorious service in the Battle of Stone River, Tenn. Bvt. Maj., 2 March, 1867, for gallant and meritorious service in the Battle of Missionary Ridge, Tenn. Bvt. Lieut. Col., 2 March, 1867, for gallant and meritorious service in the Battle of Franklin, Tenn. Trans. to 16th Inf., 14 April, 1869. Capt., 24 Sept., 1871. Retired for disability 29 Dec., 1890. Died 19 Jan., 1896.

HALE, DAVID E.* [Born in N. H. Appointed from N. H.]
Bvt. 2nd Lieut. 1st Art., 1 July, 1833. 2nd Lieut., 23 Oct., 1834. 1st Lieut., 30 Nov., 1836. Died 30 April, 1839.

HALE, HARRY C.* [Born in Ill. Appointed from Ill.]
2nd Lieut. 12th Inf., 13 June, 1883. 1st Lieut. 18th Inf., 20 Feb., 1891. Trans. to 20th Inf., 20 July, 1891. Capt. of Inf., 1 July, 1898. Ass'd. to 20th Inf., 1 Jan., 1899. Maj. and A. A. G. of Vols., 20 May, 1898, to 7 April, 1899. Maj. 44th U. S. Vols., 17 Aug., 1899, to —

HALE, IRVING.* [Born in N. Y. Appointed from Colo.]
2nd Lieut. Eng., 15 June, 1884. 1st Lieut., 16 Sept., 1886. Resigned 1 April, 1890.

HALE, JOHN S. [Born in Tenn. Appointed from Ala.]
1st Lieut. of Inf., 8 March, 1847; 13th Inf., 9 April, 1847. Disbanded 15 July, 1848.

HALE, JOSEPH. [Born in Mass. Appointed from Army.]
Priv. Co. I, 5th Mass. Vols., 19 April, 1861. Discharged 31 July, 1861. Priv. Co. B, 11th Inf., 10 Aug., 1861. Priv. Co. B, 2nd Batt. 11th Inf., 8 Sept., 1862. Corp., 11 Sept., 1862. Sergt., 1 Oct., 1862. 1st Sergt., 30 Dec., 1862. 1st Sergt. Co. B, 1st Batt. 11th Inf., 1 March, 1863. Discharged 10 Feb., 1864. 1st Sergt. Co. B, 1st Batt. 11th Inf., 10 Feb., 1864. Discharged 25 May, 1864. 2nd Lieut. 3rd Inf., 18 May, 1864. 1st Lieut., 21 March, 1865. Reg. Adj., 5 May, 1872, to 2 March, 1885. Capt., 2 March, 1885. Died 12 Oct., 1898.

HALE, MORDECAI. [Born in N. Y. Appointed from N. Y.]
Post Surg., 13 Feb., 1818. Disbanded 1 June, 1821. Asst. Surg., 27 Oct., 1821. Died 9 Dec., 1832.

HALE, OWEN. [Born in N. Y. Appointed from N. Y.]
Sergt. Maj. 7th N. Y. Cav., 23 Oct., 1861, to 31 March, 1862. Priv. Co. B, and Sergt. Maj. 7th N. Y. Cav., 14 Aug., 1862, to 9 May, 1863. 2nd Lieut. 7th N. Y. Cav., 9 May, 1863. 1st Lieut., 19 Oct., 1864. Bvt. Capt. Vols., 13 March, 1865, for gallant and meritorious service during the war. Mustered out 29 Nov., 1865. 1st Lieut. 7th Cav., 28 July, 1866. Capt., 1 March, 1869. Killed 30 Sept., 1877, in action with Indians in Montana Ter.

HALES, SAML. W. [Born in Ohio. Appointed from Ky.]
Asst. Surg., 23 July, 1833. Died 30 Jan., 1835.

HALFORD, ELIJAH W. [Born in England. Appointed from Ind.]
Maj. and P. M., 10 Jan., 1893.

HALL, ABEL W. [Born in Ohio. Appointed from Ohio.]
Capt. 15th Inf., 5 Aug., 1861. Resigned 22 Dec., 1862.

HALL, ANSON.* [Born in Vt. Appointed from Vt.]
Ensign 4th Inf., 27 Jan., 1809. Resigned 16 Feb., 1810. Died — 1837.

HALL, CHALMERS G.* [Born in N. C. Appointed from N. C.]
Addl. 2nd Lieut. 5th Cav., 11 June, 1897. 2nd Lieut., 30 April, 1898.

HALL, CHARLES BADGER. [Born in Maine. Appointed from Maine.]
2nd Lieut. 25th Maine Vols., 29 Sept., 1862. 1st Lieut., 6 March, 1863. 1st Lieut. 30th Maine Vet. Vols., 1 Jan., 1864. Mustered out 2 Sept., 1865. 2nd Lieut. 28th Inf., U. S. A., 22 Jan., 1867. Bvt. 1st Lieut., 2 March, 1867, for gallant and meritorious service in the Battle of Sabine Cross Roads, La. Bvt. Capt., 2 March, 1867, for gallant and meritorious service at the Battle of Pleasant Hill, La. 1st Lieut. 28th U. S. Inf., 28 Dec., 1868. Unassigned 31 March, 1869, and attached to the 1st U. S. Inf. until assigned to the 19th U. S. Inf., 23 Dec., 1870. R. Q. M., 1 May, 1876, to 23 Feb., 1882. Reg. Adj., 24 Feb., 1882, to 31 March, 1887. Capt. U. S. Inf., 24 March, 1888. Maj. U. S. Inf., 2 March, 1899.

HALL, CHAS. S.* [Born in Ind. Appointed from Ind.]
2nd Lieut. 13th Inf., 15 June, 1876. 1st Lieut., 1 March, 1887. Graduate of the Infantry and Cavalry School 1885. Resigned 15 Feb., 1897.

HALL, CHRISTOPHER T.* [Born in Ky. Appointed from Ill.]
2nd Lieut. 2nd Cav., 15 June, 1868. 1st Lieut., 3 July, 1869. Resigned 17 Nov., 1880. Died 31 Jan., 1887.

HALL, CYRUS.* [Born in N. Y. Appointed from Ohio.]
Bvt. 2nd Lieut. 1st Inf., 1 July, 1842. 2nd Lieut. 8th Inf., 1 July, 1843. Trans. to 1st Inf., 8 July, 1844. Died 11 April, 1849.

HALL, EDMUND. [Born in Maine. Appointed from Maine.]
Ensign 28th Inf., 20 May, 1813. 2nd Lieut., 19 April, 1814. Disbanded 15 June, 1815. Reinstated 2 Dec., 1815, in 7th Inf. 1st Lieut., 31 Aug., 1816. Resigned 20 Dec., 1816.

HALL, HARRISON. [Born in Ohio. Appointed from Ohio.]
2nd Lieut. 5th Art., 9 July, 1898.

HALL, HENRY F. [Born in Penn. Appointed from Del.]
Surg. Mate 3rd Inf., 23 July, 1819. Asst. Surg., 1 June, 1821. Resigned 30 June, 1823.

HALL, HENRY H. [Born in Ohio. Appointed from Cal.]
Priv. Batty B, Ind. Pa. Light Art., 5 Jan., 1864, to 12 Oct., 1865. Post Chap., 7 Sept., 1889. Retired for disability 25 Oct., 1899.

HALL, HERMAN.* [Born in Ill. Appointed from Mo.]
2nd Lieut. 4th Inf., 12 June, 1887. 1st Lieut. 11th Inf., 8 June, 1894. Trans. to 22nd Inf., 22 June, 1894. Capt. 21st Inf., 2 March, 1899.

HALL, JAMES. [Born in Penn. Appointed from Penn.]
3rd Lieut 2nd Art., 30 March, 1814. 2nd Lieut., 1 May, 1814. Trans. to Corps Art., 12 May, 1814. Trans. to Ord., 1 Jan., 1816. 1st Lieut., 17 May, 1816. Resigned 30 June, 1818.

HALL, JAMES A. [Born in Texas. Appointed from Army.]
Priv. and Corpl. Co. A, Mtd. Rifle, 13 Jan., 1852, to 22 Aug., 1854. Sergt and 1st Sergt. Co. C, and Q. M. Sergt. 1st Drag., 22 Aug., 1854, to 10 Dec., 1861. 2nd Lieut. 1st Cav., 24 Oct., 1861. 1st Lieut., 16 Jan., 1862. R. Q. M., 19 March, to 18 June, 1862, and 30 Jan., to 21 May, 1863. Capt., 3 June, 1864. Mustered out 1 Jan., 1871. Bvt. Capt., 6 May, 1864, for gallant and meritorious service at the Battle of Todd's Tavern, Va. Bvt. Maj., 1 April, 1865, for gallant and meritorious service at the Battle of Five Forks, Va.

HALL, JOHN D. [Born in N. H. Appointed from N. Y.]
1st Lieut. Asst. Surg., 16 Nov., 1868. Capt. Asst. Surg., 16 Nov., 1871. Maj. and Surg., 20 Aug., 1889.

HALL, J. DE CAMP. [Born in — Appointed from —]
2nd Lieut. Inf., 1 Dec., 1899.

HALL, JONATHAN N.* [Born in N. Y. Appointed from Mich.]
Changed name to Norman J. Hall—which see.

HALL, JOSEPH.* [Born in England. Appointed from Mich.]
Priv. Co. A, 22nd Mich. Vols., 22 Oct., 1862. Trans. to Co. A, 29th Mich. Vols., 30 June, 1865. Discharged 6 Sept., 1865. Cadet Mil. Acad., 1 July, 1868. 2nd Lieut. 14th Inf., 14 June, 1872. Resigned 26 May, 1879.

HALL, J. HARRISON.* [Born in Ohio. Appointed at Large.]
2nd Lieut. 1st Cav., 23 June, 1865. 1st Lieut., 15 Oct., 1866. Reg. Adj., 7 Sept., 1866, to 7 Nov., 1869. Resigned 1 March, 1870.

HALL, NATHANIEL N. [Born in Mass. Appointed from Mass.]
Ensign 21st Inf., 12 March, 1812. 2nd Lieut., 13 March, 1813. 1st Lieut., 7 March, 1814. Capt., 30 Sept., 1814. (Maj. A. I. G., 25 April, 1814, to 15 June, 1815.) Trans. to Corps Art., 17 May, 1815. Resigned 5 March, 1819. Bvt. Capt., 15 Aug., 1814, for gallant conduct in the defence of Fort Erie. Died — 1850.

HALL, NORMAN J.* [Born in N. Y. Appointed from Mich.]
Graduated as Jonathan N. Hall. Bvt. 2nd Lieut. 4th Art., 1 July, 1859. 2nd Lieut. 1st Art., 10 Jan., 1860. 1st Lieut. 5th Art., 14 May, 1861. Col. 7th Mich. Vols., 14 July, 1862. Mustered out Vol. Ser., 4 June, 1864. Capt., 1 Aug., 1863. Retired 22 Feb., 1865. Died 26 May, 1867. Bvt. Capt., 17 Sept., 1862, for gallant and meritorious service at the Battle of Antietam, Md. Bvt. Maj., 13 Dec., 1862, for gallant and meritorious service at the Battle of Fredericksburg, Va. Bvt. Lieut. Col., 3 July, 1863, for gallant and meritorious service at the Battle of Gettysburg, Pa. Died 26 May, 1867.

HALL, PETER P. G. [Born in Penn. Appointed from Penn.]
2nd Lieut. 26th Penn. Vols., 31 May, 1861. 1st Lieut. 26th Penn. Vols., 25 Aug., 1861. Discharged 16 Feb., 1863. Addl. P. M., 6 Nov., 1863. Mustered out 15 Nov., 1865. Maj. and P. M., 17 Jan., 1867. Retired, having served over 20 years (Act 5 July, 1884), 2 July, 1891.

HALL, ROBT. H.* [Born in Mich. Appointed from Ill.]
Bvt. 2nd Lieut. 5th Inf., 1 July, 1860. 2nd Lieut. 10th Inf., 23 Jan., 1861. 1st Lieut., 1 June, 1861. Capt., 31 Aug., 1863. Maj. 22nd Inf., 21 May, 1883. Lieut. Col. 6th Inf., 5 Aug., 1888. Col. 4th Inf., 18 May, 1893. Brig. Gen. Vols., 27 May, 1898, to 15 April, 1899. Brig. Gen. Vols., 15 April, 1899. Bvt. Maj., 24 Nov., 1863, for gallant and meritorious service in the Battle of Lookout Mountain, Tenn. Bvt. Lieut. Col., 19 Aug., 1864, for gallant and meritorious service on the Weldon Railroad, Va.

HALL, ROBT. M. [Born in Scotland. Appointed from Army.]
Priv., Corpl. and Sergt. Co. M, 1st Art., 12 April, 1848, to 19 Feb., 1853. Sergt. and 1st Sergt. Co. M, 1st Art., 11 April, 1853, to 13 Nov., 1861. 2nd Lieut. 1st Art., 24 Oct., 1861. 1st Lieut., 20 Feb., 1862. Col. 38th U. S. Col. Inf., 31 Dec., 1864. Mustered out of Vol. Ser., 25 Jan., 1867. Reg. Adj. 1st Art., 13 Feb., 1868, to 18 Jan., 1869, and R. Q. M., 1 Feb., 1869, to 18 July, 1874. Bvt. Capt., 28 May, 1864, for gallant and meritorious service in action at Bermuda Hundred, Va. Bvt. Maj., 7 Oct., 1864, for gallant and meritorious service in action on the Darbytown Road, near Richmond, Va. Bvt. Lieut. Col. and Col., 13 March, 1865, for gallant and meritorious service during the war. Bvt. Brig. Gen. Vols., 13 March, 1865, for gallant, faithful and meritorious service during the war, and for completeness as an officer during the time he held a command in the army. Died 18 July, 1874.

HALL, SAML. D. [Born in —. Appointed from Mass.]
Maj. and P. M., 7 Feb., 1821. Disbanded 1 June, 1821.

HALL, THOMAS P. [Born in Md. Appointed from Md.]
Maj. and Surg. 36th Inf., 10 July, 1813. Disbanded 15 June, 1815. Post Surg., 12 Dec., 1820. Asst. Surg., 1 June, 1821. Died 21 Sept., 1825.

HALL, THOMAS W.* [Born in N. Y. Appointed from Ill.]
Addl. 2nd Lieut. 4th Cav., 12 June, 1887. 2nd Lieut. 10th Cav., 5 Oct., 1887. Resigned 1 Jan., 1889.

HALL, WM. P.* [Born in Mo. Appointed from Mo.]
2nd Lieut. 19th Inf., 15 June, 1868. Unassigned 31 March, 1869. Ass'd to 5th Cav., 14 July, 1869. 1st Lieut., 1 July, 1876. R. Q. M., 5 Oct., 1876, to 8 March, 1887. Capt., 8 March, 1887. Maj. A. A. G., 6 Nov., 1893. Lieut. Col. A. A. G., 11 Sept., 1897. Medal of Honor for most distinguished gallantry in action near camp on White River, Colo., 20 Oct., 1879; this officer, then a 1st Lieut. 5th U. S. Cav., in command of a reconnoitering party of three men, and while going to the rescue of a brother officer who had been attacked by Indians, was himself attacked by about thirty-five warriors. During the engagement he several times exposed himself in order to draw the fire of his assailants and locate their position so his small party could reply with effect. Lieut. Weir, Ord. Dept., and a scout who accompanied him, were both killed by the Indians at this time.

HALL, WILLIAM R. [Born in Mo. Appointed from Mo.]
1st Lieut. Asst. Surg., 26 June, 1875. Capt. Asst. Surg., 26 June, 1880. Bvt. Capt., 27 Feb., 1890, for gallant services in action against Indians in attending to his professional duty under fire at the Clearwater, Idaho, 11 and 12 July, 1877. Maj. Surg., 16 May, 1894.

HALLECK, HENRY W.* [Born in N. Y. Appointed from N. Y.]
2nd Lieut. Eng., 1 July, 1839. 1st Lieut., 1 Jan., 1845. Capt., 1 July, 1853. Resigned 1 Aug., 1854. Maj. Gen., 19 Aug., 1861. Commander-in-Chief of the army, 23 July, 1862, to 9 March, 1864. Died 9 Jan., 1872. Bvt. Capt., 1 May, 1847, for gallant conduct in affairs with the enemy, 19 and 20 Nov., 1847, and for meritorious service in California.

HALLECK, WALTER F. [Born in Mich. Appointed from Mich.]
Priv. Co. I, 11th Mich. Vols., 25 July, 1862. Discharged 13 Aug., 1863. 2nd Lieut. Vet. Res. Corps, 14 April, 1864. Mustered out 6 Sept., 1865. 2nd Lieut. 18th Inf., 30 May, 1866. Trans. to 27th Inf., 21 Sept., 1866. 1st Lieut., 31 Jan., 1867. Retired 29 Sept., 1868.

HALLER, GEORGE. [Born in Prussia. Appointed from Army.]
Priv., Corpl. and Sergt. Gen. Ser. and Co. K, 10th Inf., 22 Sept., 1851, to 22 Sept., 1856. Priv., Corpl. and Sergt. Co. I, 7th Inf., 22 July, 1857, to 22 July, 1862. Priv. and 1st Sergt. Co. F, 2nd Batt. 15th Inf., 25 Nov., 1862, to 15 May, 1865. 2nd Lieut. 15th Inf., 23 Dec., 1864. 1st Lieut., 23 Dec., 1864. Trans. to 24th Inf., 21 Sept., 1866. R. Q. M., 13 Dec., 1866, to 1 Feb., 1867. Capt., 16 July, 1868. Died 8 June, 1869.

HALLER, GRANVILLE O. [Born in Penn. Appointed from Penn.]
2nd Lieut. 4th Inf., 17 Nov., 1839. Reg. Adj., 1 Jan., 1843, to 19 Sept., 1845. 1st Lieut., 12 July, 1846. Bvt. Capt., 8 Sept., 1847, for gallant and meritorious conduct in the Battle of Molino del Rey. Bvt. Maj., 13 Sept., 1847, for gallant and meritorious conduct in the Battle of Chapultepec. Capt. 4th Inf., 1 Jan., 1848. Maj. 7th Inf., 25 Sept., 1861. Dismissed 25 July, 1863. Col. of Inf., 1 July, 1879, to rank 19 Feb., 1873, (Joint Resolution 3 March, 1879). Ass'd to 23rd Inf., 11 Dec., 1879. Retired, over 62 years of age, 6 Feb., 1882. Died 2 May, 1897.

HALLOCK, HARRY M. [Born in N. J. Appointed from N. J.]
Asst. Surg., 4 Nov., 1892. Capt. Asst. Surg., 4 Nov., 1897.

HALLONQUIST, JAMES H.* [Born in S. C. Appointed from S. C.]
Bvt. 2nd Lieut. 3rd Art., 1 July, 1858. 2nd Lieut. 4th Art., 24 Feb., 1859. Resigned 1 Jan., 1861.

HALLORAN, JAMES. [Born in Ireland. Appointed from Oregon.]
Musician Co. K, 9th Inf., 18 April, 1855. Discharged 18 April, 1860. 2nd Lieut. 1st Wash. Ter. Vols., 17 Sept., 1862. Mustered out 17 March, 1865. 2nd Lieut. 12th Inf., 1 Dec., 1866. 1st Lieut., 30 Aug., 1871. Capt., 16 Oct., 1882. Died 12 April, 1898.

HALSEY, SILAS. [Born in Conn. Appointed from D. C.]
2nd Lieut. Light Drag., 3 May, 1808. 1st Lieut., 15 Feb., 1809. Capt., 31 May, 1811. Trans. to 46th Inf., 11 May, 1814. Maj. 32nd Inf., 7 June, 1814. Discharged 15 June, 1815. Mil. Storekeeper, 16 Dec., 1816. Disbanded 1 June, 1821. Mil. Storekeeper Ord., 24 Feb., 1837. Died 7 Nov., 1848.

HALSEY, THOS H. [Born in N. J. Appointed from Vt.]
Addl. P. M. Vols., 8 June, 1861. Maj. and P. M., 17 Jan., 1867. Retired 9 Feb., 1877. Bvt. Lieut. Col. Vols., 15 June, 1866, for faithful and meritorious conduct. Died 19 Nov., 1877.

HALSTEAD, FRANK. [Born in France. Appointed from Ohio.]
2nd Lieut. 4th Inf., 9 July, 1898. 1st Lieut. 24th Inf., 4 May, 1899.

HALSTEAD, LAWRENCE.* [Born in Ohio. Appointed from Ohio.]
2nd Lieut. 11th Inf., 15 Feb., 1899.

HAM, SAMUEL V.* [Born in Ind. Appointed from Ind.]
2nd Lieut. 24th Inf., 11 June, 1892. Trans. to 5th Inf., 1 Oct., 1896. 1st Lieut., 26 April, 1898. Capt. A. Q. M., 20 June, 1898, to ——.

HAMBRICK, PAUL R. [Born in Va. Appointed from N. J.]
1st Lieut. 1st N. J. Vols., 9 Dec., 1861. Capt., 5 Jan., 1863. Mustered out 27 June, 1863. Capt. Vet. Res. Corps, 23 Oct., 1863. Bvt. Maj. Vols., 13 March, 1865, for gallant and meritorious service during the war. Mustered out 25 Oct., 1866. 2nd Lieut. 45th Inf., 28 July, 1866. 1st Lieut., 4 Feb., 1868. Unassigned 22 July, 1869. Resigned 9 Aug., 1870. Bvt. 1st Lieut., 2 March, 1867, for gallant and meritorious service in action at Salem Church, Va.

HAMBRIGHT, HENRY A. [Born in Penn. Appointed from Penn.]
1st Sergt. Co. G, 2nd Penn. Vols., 6 Dec., 1846. Discharged 10 Aug., 1847. 1st Lieut. 2nd Penn. Vols., 10 Aug., 1847. Mustered out 12 July, 1848. 2nd Lieut. 6th Inf., 23 March, 1861, declined. Capt. 1st Penn. Vols., 20 April, 1861. Mustered out 26 July, 1861. Capt. 11th Inf., 14 May, 1861. Col. 79th Penn. Vols., 18

Oct., 1861. Bvt. Maj., 31 Dec., 1862, for gallant and meritorious service in the Battle of Murfreesboro, Tenn. Bvt. Lieut. Col., 20 Sept., 1863, for gallant and meritorious service in the Battle of Chickamauga, Ga. Bvt. Col., 1 Sept., 1864, for gallant and meritorious service during the Atlanta campaign. Bvt. Brig. Gen. Vols., 7 June, 1865, for meritorious service. Mustered out of Vol. Service, 20 July, 1865. Trans. to 29th Inf., 21 Sept., 1866. Maj. 32nd Inf., 27 Jan., 1869. Trans. to 19th Inf., 15 March, 1869. Retired 6 May, 1879. Died 19 Feb., 1893.

HAMBRIGHT, HORACE G.* [Born in Tenn. Appointed from Tenn.]
Cadet at Mil. Acad., 16 June, 1887, to 15 Nov., 1887. Reappointed 1888. 2nd Lieut. of Inf. (22nd), 11 June, 1892. Died 15 April, 1896.

HAMER, WM. [Born in Ohio. Appointed from Ind.]
1st Lieut. 16th Inf., 16 April, 1847. Resigned 6 Nov., 1847.

HAMILTON, ALSTON.* [Born in N. C. Appointed from Va.]
2nd Lieut. 5th Cav., 12 June, 1894. Trans. to 1st Art., 4 Oct., 1894. 1st Lieut., 2 March, 1899.

HAMILTON, ARCHIBALD W. [Born in N. Y. Appointed from N. Y.]
Capt. A. D. Q. M. G., 13 Feb., 1818. Disbanded 1 June, 1821.

HAMILTON, CHAS. S.* [Born in N. Y. Appointed from N. Y.]
Bvt. 2nd Lieut. 2nd Inf., 1 July, 1843. 2nd Lieut. 5th Inf., 17 Nov., 1845. 1st Lieut., 30 June, 1847. R. Q. M., 1 March to 18 Sept., 1848. Resigned 30 April, 1853. Bvt. Capt., 20 Aug., 1847, for gallant and meritorious conduct at Contreras and Churubusco, Mex. Col. 3rd Wis. Vols., 11 May, 1861. Brig. Gen. Vols., 17 May, 1861. Maj. Gen. Vols., 19 Sept., 1862. Resigned 13 April, 1863.

HAMILTON, FOWLER.* [Born in N. Y. Appointed from N. J.]
2nd Lieut. 2nd Drag., 1 July, 1840. 1st Lieut., 31 Aug., 1843. (Maj. 10th Inf., 9 April, 1847, and Lieut. Col. 16th Inf., 23 May, 1848, to 20 July, 1848.) Capt. 2nd Drag., 25 July, 1850. Died 8 Aug., 1851.

HAMILTON, FRANK B.* [Born in Ohio. Appointed from Ohio.]
2nd Lieut. 3rd Art., 17 June, 1862. Bvt. 1st Lieut., 17 Sept., 1862, for gallant and meritorious service in the Battle of Antietam, Md. Bvt. Capt., 3 July, 1863, for gallant and meritorious service in the Battle of Gettysburg, Penn. 1st Lieut. 3rd Art., 18 June, 1864. Capt. 14th Inf., 28 July, 1866. Trans. to 2nd Art., 15 Dec., 1870. Maj. 3rd Art., — —, 1891. Died 29 May, 1891.

HAMILTON, GEORGE. [Born in Scotland. Appointed from Army.]
Priv., Corpl., Sergt. and 1st Sergt. Co. B, 10th Inf., 29 May, 1859, to 1 Dec., 1862. 2nd Lieut. 10th Inf., 18 July, 1862. 1st Lieut., 19 Sept., 1863. Dropped 28 Jan., 1864.

HAMILTON, GEORGE F.* [Born in Maine. Appointed from Maine.]
2nd Lieut. 9th Cav., 12 June, 1894. 1st Lieut. 10th Cav., 2 March, 1899.

HAMILTON, JAMES.* [Born in Ireland. Appointed from Mass.]
Addl. 2nd Lieut. 2nd Art., 12 June, 1890. 2nd Lieut. 3rd Art., 10 Feb., 1891. Retired for disability, with rank of Capt., 10 Feb., 1898.

HAMILTON, JAMES W. [Born in Ark. Appointed from Mo.]
Cadet Mil. Acad., 8 Dec., 1824, to 12 June, 1827. 1st Lieut. Mounted Rangers, 16 July, 1832. 1st Lieut. 1st Drag., 19 Sept., 1833. Reg. Adjt., 5 Feb., 1834, to 8 Aug., 1835. Cashiered, 15 Aug., 1835. 1st Lieut. 2nd Drag., 11 June, 1836. Died 26 Nov., 1837.

HAMILTON, JOHN.* [Born at Sea. Appointed from Ind.]
2nd Lieut. 3rd Art., 1 July, 1847. 1st Lieut., 13 Feb., 1850. Capt., 27 April, 1861. Bvt. Maj., 11 April, 1862, for gallant and meritorious service during the investment of Fort Pulaski, Ga. Bvt. Lieut. Col., 17 June, 1862, for gallant and meritorious service in action at Secessionville, James Island, S. C., Bvt. Col., 20 Feb., 1864, for gallant and meritorious service in the Battle of Olustee, Fla. Maj. 1st Art., 13 Aug., 1866. Lieut. Col. 5th Art., 2 Jan., 1881. Col. 14 Sept., 1883. Retired by operation of law, 10 Aug., 1887.

HAMILTON, JOHN. [Born in Ireland. Appointed from Army.]
Priv. Co. A, 1st Inf., 14 Oct., 1850. Corpl., 1 June, 1854. Discharged 1 Sept., 1855. Corpl. Co. A, 1st Inf., 1 Sept., 1855. Sergt., 1 Sept., 1856. 1st Sergt., 22 Dec., 1858. Discharged 1 July, 1860. 1st Sergt. Co. A, 1st Inf., 1 July, 1860. Ord. Sergt. U. S. A., 27 April, 1863. 2nd Lieut. 1st Inf., 12 May, 1863. Bvt. 1st Lieut., 4 July, 1863, for gallant and meritorious service during the Siege of Vicksburg, Miss. 1st Lieut. 1st Inf., 15 March, 1866. Capt., 6 May, 1879. Retired for disability, 14 April, 1887.

HAMILTON, JOHN B. [Born in Ill. Appointed from Ill.]
Asst. Surg., 10 Nov., 1874. Resigned 31 May, 1876.

HAMILTON, JOHN M. [Born in Canada. Appointed from N. Y.]
Priv. Co. H, 33rd N. Y. Vols., 1 May, 1861. Corpl., 1 Sept., 1861. Discharged 2 June, 1863. 2nd Lieut. 9th U. S. Col. Troops, 24 Dec., 1863. Bvt. Capt. Vols., 13 March, 1865, for faithful and meritorious service during the war. 1st Lieut. 9th U. S. Col. Troops, 15 May, 1865. Mustered out 20 June, 1867. Capt. 39th Inf., 6 June, 1867. Unassigned 20 April, 1869. Ass'd to 5th Cav., 30 Dec., 1870. Maj. 1st Cav., 21 April, 1887. Lieut. Col. 9th Cav., 8 Dec., 1896. Killed in action 1 July, 1898.

HAMILTON, JOHN W. [Born in Ill. Appointed from Ill.]
1st Lieut. 18th Inf., 14 May, 1861. Rejected by Senate, 5 Aug., 1861. 1st Lieut. 68th Ill. Vols., 20 June, 1862. Mustered out 26 Sept., 1862.

HAMILTON, LOUIS McL. [Born in N. Y. Appointed from Army.]
Priv. Co. G, 22nd N. Y. Militia, 21 July to 5 Sept., 1862. Priv. 14th Inf., 23 Sept., 1862. 2nd Lieut. 3rd Inf., 27 Sept., 1862. 1st Lieut., 6 May, 1864. R. Q. M., 8 June, 1865, to 21 May, 1866. Capt. 7th Cav., 28 July, 1866. Killed 27 Nov., 1868, in action with Indians in Indian Territory. Bvt. 1st Lieut., 3 May, 1863, for gallant and meritorious service at the Battle of Chancellorsville, Va. Bvt. Capt., 2 July, 1863, for gallant and meritorious service at the Battle of Gettysburg, Pa. Bvt. Maj., 27 Nov., 1868, for gallant and meritorious services in

engagements with the Indians, particularly in the battle with the Cheyennes on the Washita River, 27 Nov., 1868, where he fell while gallantly leading his command.

HAMILTON, LOUIS McL. [Born in Tenn. Appointed from N. Y.]
2nd Lieut. Co. M, 6th U. S. Vols., 7 Jan. to 15 March, 1899. 2nd Lieut. 14th Inf., 5 Oct., 1899.

HAMILTON, OLIVER P. [Born in S. C. Appointed from S. C.]
Cadet at Mil. Acad., 1 July, 1840, to 13 Jan., 1841. Capt. of Inf., 5 March, 1847; 12th Inf., 9 April, 1847. Disbanded, 25 July, 1848.

HAMILTON, ROBERT L.* [Born in W. Va. Appointed from W. Va.]
2nd Lieut. 22nd Inf., 12 June, 1891. 1st Lieut. 5th Inf., 26 Jan., 1898. Graduate of the Infantry and Cavalry School, 1895.

HAMILTON, SAML. T. [Born in Penn. Appointed from Penn.]
Priv. Co. I, 15th Penn. Cav., 22 Aug., 1862. Corpl., 30 Oct., 1862. Sergt., 1 Nov., 1862. Trans. to Co. B, 1 March, 1863. Com. Sergt. 15th Penn. Cav., 10 Nov., 1864. Q. M. Sergt., 16 March, 1865. Discharged, 21 June, 1865. 2nd Lieut. 2nd Cav., 18 June, 1867. 1st Lieut., 27 Nov., 1868. Capt., 14 June, 1879. Retired 15 Aug., 1892.

HAMILTON, SAML. V. [Born in Va. Appointed from Va.]
Ensign 1st Rifles, 4 Dec., 1812. 3rd Lieut., 12 March, 1813. 2nd Lieut., 30 Nov., 1813. 1st Lieut., 17 Sept., 1814. Trans. to Rifle Reg., 17 May, 1815. Resigned 1 July, 1817.

HAMILTON, SCHUYLER.* [Born in N. Y. Appointed from N. Y.]
2nd Lieut. 1st Inf., 1 July, 1841. R. Q. M., 19 April to 7 May, 1847. 1st Lieut., 15 March, 1848. Resigned 31 March, 1855. Bvt. 1st Lieut., 23 Sept., 1846, for gallant and meritorious conduct at Monterey. Bvt. Capt., 13 Aug., 1847, for gallant and meritorious conduct at Mil Flores, Mexico. Priv. 7th N. Y. Militia, 19 April to 9 May, 1861. Lieut. Col. Mil. Sec. to Bvt. Lieut. Gen. Scott, 9 May, to 7 Aug., 1861. Col. A. A. de C., 7 Aug., 1861. Brig. Gen. Vols., 12 Nov., 1861. Maj. Gen. Vols., 17 Sept., 1862. Resigned 27 Feb., 1863.

HAMILTON, THOMAS. [Born in N. Y. Appointed from Army.]
Priv. and Sergt. 1st Inf., 2 June, 1802, to March, 1806. Ensign 1st Inf., 6 March, 1806. 2nd Lieut., 1 June, 1807. 1st Lieut., 15 Dec., 1808. Capt., 21 Feb., 1814. Disbanded 15 June, 1815. Reinstated in 6th Inf., 17 May, 1816. Trans. to 5th Inf., 29 April, 1823. Resigned 16 Aug., 1828. Bvt. Maj., 21 Feb., 1824, for ten years' faithful service in one grade.

HAMILTON, WM. J.* [Born in Penn. Appointed from N. J.]
2nd Lieut. 4th Art., 15 June, 1868. Died 22 Jan., 1872.

HAMILTON, WM. R.* [Born in Wis. Appointed at Large.]
2nd Lieut. 5th Art., 15 June, 1876. 1st Lieut., 18 April, 1883. Capt. 7th Art., 8 March, 1898. Graduate of the Artillery School, 1894.

HAMILTON, WM. S. [Born in N. C. Appointed from N. C.]
1st Lieut. 3rd Inf., 1 July, 1808. Resigned 1 Nov., 1812. Maj. 10th Inf., 3 March, 1813. Maj. A. I. G., 4 March, 1813. Lieut. Col. 3rd Rifles, 21 Feb., 1814. Trans. to Rifle Reg., 17 May, 1815. Resigned 8 March, 1817.

HAMILTON, WM. W.* [Born in Ga. Appointed from Ga.]
2nd Lieut. 6th Art., 26 April, 1898. Trans. to 2nd Art., 4 April, 1899.

HAMLETT, JAMES E. [Born in Va. Appointed from Va.]
1st Lieut. of Inf., 24 Feb., 1847; 11th Inf., 9 April, 1847. Resigned 29 July, 1847.

HAMMER, JOHN S. [Born in Ky. Appointed from Ky.]
2nd Lieut. 16th Ky. Vols., 27 Jan., 1862. 1st Lieut., 20 July, 1862. Capt., 2 Nov., 1864. Lieut. Col., 10 June, 1865. Mustered out 15 July, 1865. 2nd Lieut. 19th Inf., 23 Feb., 1866. 1st Lieut., 23 Feb., 1866. R. Q. M., 23 July, 1867, to 31 March, 1869. Unassigned 31 March, 1869. Ass'd to 14th Inf., 13 Jan., 1870. Discharged 30 Nov., 1870.

HAMMON, SETH L. [Born in Maine. Appointed from Minn.]
Sergt. Co. D, 1st Minn. Vols., 29 April, 1861. 2nd Lieut., 8 Aug., 1861. 1st Lieut., 1 Jan., 1862. Resigned 13 Sept., 1862. 2nd Lieut. Vet. Res. Corps, 24 June, 1863. Bvt. 1st Lieut. and Capt. Vols., 18 July, 1865, for faithful service. Mustered out 29 Nov., 1865. 2nd Lieut. 12th Inf., 26 March, 1866. 1st Lieut., 11 Aug., 1866. Cashiered 15 Aug., 1867.

HAMMOND, ANDREW G.* [Born in Conn. Appointed from Conn.]
2nd Lieut. 8th Cav., 11 June, 1881. 1st Lieut., 11 April, 1889. Capt., 31 May, 1896. Graduate of the Infantry and Cavalry School, 1891. Lieut. Col. 1st Conn. Vols., 26 May, to 31 Oct., 1898.

HAMMOND, BRANT C. [Born in Penn. Appointed from Iowa.]
Chaplain 5th Wis. Vols., from 1 Oct., 1864, to 20 June, 1865. Post Chaplain, 26 Feb., 1885.

HAMMOND, CHAS. L.* [Born in N. Y. Appointed from N. Y.]
2nd Lieut. 9th Cav., 15 June, 1876. Trans. to 3rd Cav., 28 July, 1876. Resigned 16 Sept., 1877.

HAMMOND, GEORGE. [Born in Md. Appointed from Md.]
Asst. Surg., 28 June, 1856. Maj. and Surg., 27 Aug., 1862. Drowned 14 Aug., 1863.

HAMMOND, HAROLD.* [Born in Ill. Appointed from Ill.]
2nd Lieut. 9th Inf., 26 April, 1898. 1st Lieut., 2 March, 1899.

HAMMOND, HARRY T.* [Born in Cal. Appointed from Idaho.]
2nd Lieut. 9th Cav., 15 June, 1877. Resigned 1 March, 1878. Died 8 Feb., 1883.

HAMMOND, JOHN F. [Born in S. C. Appointed from S. C.]
1st Lieut. Asst. Surg., 16 Feb., 1847. Capt. Asst. Surg., 16 Feb., 1852. Maj. Surg., 26 Feb., 1861. Bvt. Lieut. Col., 13 March, 1865, for faithful and meritorious service during the war. Lieut. Col. Surg., 26 June, 1876. Col. Surg., 14 Dec., 1882. Retired by operation of law, 7 Dec., 1884. Died 29 Sept., 1886.

HAMMOND, LAFAYETTE. [Born in Penn. Appointed from Cal.]
1st Lieut. 1st Cal. Vols., 15 Aug., 1861. Capt., 25 Aug., 1862. Resigned 19 Sept., 1863. Maj. 2nd Ohio Art., 8 Oct., 1863. Mustered out 23 Aug., 1865. 1st Lieut., 23rd Inf., 28 July, 1866. Reg. Adj., 22 Jan. to 1 Aug., 1873. Died 6 Sept., 1873.

HAMMOND, MARCUS C. M.* [Born in S. C. Appointed from S. C.]
Bvt. 2nd Lieut. 4th Inf., 1 July, 1836. 2nd Lieut., 23 Sept., 1836. 1st Lieut., 7 Nov., 1839. Reg. Adj., 1 April, 1841, to 31 Dec., 1842. Resigned 31 Dec., 1842. Addl. P. M., 25 June, 1846. Resigned 15 April, 1847. Died 23 Jan., 1876.

HAMMOND, RICHARD P.* [Born in Md. Appointed from Ark.]
Bvt. 2nd Lieut. 3rd Art., 1 July, 1841. 2nd Lieut. 3rd Art., 10 Sept., 1841. 1st Lieut., 28 May, 1846. Reg. Adj., 1 Oct. to 1 Dec., 1848. Resigned 26 May, 1851. Bvt. Capt., 18 April, 1847, for gallant and meritorious service at Cerro Gordo. Bvt. Maj., 20 Aug., 1847, for gallant and meritorious conduct at Contreras and Churubusco, Mex.

HAMMOND, ROBERT H. [Born in Penn. Appointed from Penn.]
Ensign 42nd Inf., 11 March, 1814. 3rd Lieut., 1 May, 1814. 2nd Lieut., 1 Oct., 1814. Disbanded 15 June, 1815. Reinstated in 5th Inf., 17 May, 1816. 1st Lieut., 11 Nov., 1818. Resigned 15 Oct., 1820. Addl. P. M., 30 May, 1846. M P. M., 29 June, 1846. Died 2 June, 1847.

HAMMOND, THOMAS C.* [Born in Penn. Appointed from Penn.]
Bvt. 2nd Lieut. 2nd Drag., 1 July, 1842. Trans. to 1st Drag., 6 March, 1843. 2nd Lieut., 4 March, 1845. Killed 6 Dec., 1846, in action at San Pasqual, California.

HAMMOND, WM. [Born in Md. Appointed from Md.]
Asst. Surg., 1 June, 1834. Maj Surg., 7 Aug., 1847. Died 13 Feb., 1851.

HAMMOND, WM., Jr. [Born in Md. Appointed from Mo.]
Asst. Surg., 2 March, 1848. Resigned 15 Sept., 1853.

HAMMOND, WM. A. [Born in Md. Appointed from Md.]
1st Lieut. Asst. Surg., 29 June, 1849. Capt. Asst. Surg., 29 June, 1854. Resigned 31 Oct., 1860. 1st Lieut. Asst. Surg., 28 May, 1861. Brig. Gen., Surg. Gen., 25 April, 1862. Dismissed 18 Aug., 1864. Restored to the army and placed on the retired list as Surg. Gen., Brig. Gen., 27 Aug., 1879., without pay or allowances, under Act of Congress approved 15 March, 1878. Retired [illegible] Aug., 1879.

HAMNER, WM. H. [Born in Tenn. Appointed from N. Y.]
Priv. Co. H, 1st Art., 13 Feb., 1856. Corpl., 1 Nov., 1856. Sergt., 21 March, 1857. 1st Sergt., 26 May, 1858. Q. M. Sergt. 1st Art., 1 Feb., 1860. Discharged 20 Dec., 1860. Q. M. Sergt. 1st Art., 20 Dec., 1860. Discharged 14 Oct., 1861. 2nd Lieut. 3rd R. I. Art., 17 Oct., 1861. 1st Lieut., 8 May, 1863. Capt., 9 June, 1863. Mustered out 9 Aug., 1865. 2nd Lieut. 20th Inf., 16 Oct., 1867. 1st Lieut., 27 July, 1875. Capt., 31 Aug., 1887. Maj. and P. M., 17 May, 1893.

HAMPSON, JESSE A. P. [Born in Penn. Appointed from Iowa.]
Priv. Co. M, 4th Iowa Cav., 6 Nov., 1861, to 1 April, 1862. 2nd Lieut. 10th Inf., 19 Feb., 1862. Bvt. 1st Lieut., 3 May, 1863, for gallant and meritorious service in the Battle of Chancellorsville, Va. Bvt. Capt., 2 July, 1863, for gallant and meritorious service in the Battle of Gettysburg, Penn. 1st Lieut. 10th Inf., 31 Aug., 1863. Capt., 3 Feb., 1865. Bvt. Maj., 13 March, 1865, for gallant and meritorious service in the Battle of Gettysburg, Penn. Maj. 12th Inf., 21 Aug., 1888. Lieut. Col. 12th Inf., 4 July, 1892. Died 2 Aug., 1892.

HAMPTON, CELWYN E.* [Born in Ohio. Appointed from Ohio.]
Cadet at Mil. Acad. from 17 June, 1890, to 29 Jan., 1891. Reappointed and graduated in 1896. 2nd Lieut. 23rd Inf., 12 June, 1896. 1st Lieut. of Inf., 17 Sept., 1898. Ass'd to 23rd Inf., 1 Jan., 1899.

HAMTRAMCK, JOHN F.* [Born in Ind. Appointed from Ind.]
Sergt. 1st Inf. in 1813-14. Cadet at Mil. Acad., 26 Sept., 1815. 2nd Lieut. Corps Art., 1 July, 1819. Trans. to 3rd Art., 1 June, 1821. Resigned 1 March, 1822. Col. 1st Va. Vols., 31 Dec., 1846, to 20 June, 1848. Died 21 April, 1858.

HANCOCK, BENJAMIN F. [Born in Penn. Apppointed from Penn.]
2nd Lieut. 2nd Inf., 23 Jan., 1878. Died 20 Oct., 1882.

HANCOCK, DAVID P.* [Born in Penn. Appointed from Penn.]
Bvt. 2nd Lieut. 7th Inf., 1 July, 1854. 2nd Lieut., 3 March, 1855. 1st Lieut., 20 April, 1858. Capt., 27 May, 1861. Bvt. Maj., 2 July, 1863, and Lieut. Col., 13 March, 1865, for gallant and meritorious service in the Battle of Gettysburg, Penn. Maj. 2nd Inf., 24 Oct., 1874. Died 21 May, 1880.

HANCOCK, GWYNN R.* [Born in Mo. Appointed at Large.]
2nd Lieut. 6th Art., 15 Feb., 1899.

HANCOCK, WM. F.* [Born in Ohio. Appointed from Ohio.]
2nd Lieut. 5th Art., 13 June, 1883. 1st Lieut., 4 Oct., 1889. Trans. to 6th Art., 29 April, 1898. Capt., 2 March, 1899. Graduate of the Artillery School, 1888. Capt. A. A. G., 12 May, 1898, to 14 April, 1899.

HANCOCK, WINFIELD S.* [Born in Penn. Appointed from Penn.]
Bvt. 2nd Lieut. 6th Inf., 1 July, 1844. 2nd Lieut., 18 June, 1846. Bvt. 1st Lieut., 20 Aug., 1847, for gallant and meritorious conduct in the Battles of Contreras and Churubusco, Mexico. Reg. Q. M., 30 June, 1848, to 1 Oct., 1849. Reg. Adj., 1 Oct., 1849, to 7 Nov., 1855. 1st Lieut. 6th Inf., 27 Jan., 1853. Capt. A. Q. M., 7 Nov., 1855. Brig. Gen. Vols., 23 Sept., 1861. Maj. Gen. Vols., 29 Nov., 1862. Maj. Q. M., 30 Nov., 1863. App'd Brig. Gen. U. S. A., 12 Aug., 1864, for gallant and distinguished services in the Battles of the Wilderness, Spottsylvania, and Cold Harbor, and in all the operations of the army in Virginia, under Lieut. Gen. Grant. Bvt. Maj. Gen., 13 March, 1865, for gallant and meritorious service in the Battle of Spottsylvania, Va. Tendered the thanks of Congress—in addition to the thanks heretofore voted by joint resolution, approved 28 Jan., 1864, to * * * * and the officers and soldiers of the Army of the Potomac—by joint resolution approved 21 April, 1866, for the skill and heroic valor, which, at Gettysburg, repulsed, defeated, and drove back, broken and

dispirited, the veteran army of the rebellion, the gratitude of the American people, and the thanks of their Representatives in Congress, are likewise due, and are hereby tendered, to Maj. Gen. Winfield S. Hancock, for his gallant, meritorious, and conspicuous share in that great and decisive victory. Maj. Gen. U. S. A., 26 July, 1866. Died 9 Feb., 1886.

HAND, LUTHER. [Born in N. Y. Appointed from N. Y.]
2nd Lieut. 41st Inf., 30 Sept., 1813. Trans. to 8th Inf., 17 May, 1815. 1st Lieut., 1 June, 1816. Died 1 Dec., 1818.

HAND, ZEBULON M. P. [Born in Ind. Appointed from Ind.]
Priv., Sergt. and 1st Sergt. Co. D, Mounted Rifles, 17 July, 1846, to 5 May, 1848. Discharged 20 July, 1848. 2nd Lieut. 16th Inf., 29 March, 1848. Discharged 20 July, 1848. 1st Lieut. 10th Ind. Vols., 25 April, 1861. Mustered out 6 Aug., 1861. Died 8 July, 1870.

HANDBURY, THOS. H.* [Born in Penn. Appointed from Penn.]
2nd Lieut. 2nd Art., 23 June, 1865. Trans. to Eng., 1 May, 1866. 1st Lieut., 1 May, 1866. Capt., 5 Sept., 1871. Maj., 2 June, 1884.

HANDFORTH, BENJAMIN F.* [Born in Ill. Appointed from N. J.]
2nd Lieut. 11th Inf., 11 June, 1881. 1st Lieut., 5 Sept., 1886. Dismissed 7 Dec., 1887.

HANDY, CHAS. W. [Born in Md. Appointed from Md.]
Asst. Surg., 11 May, 1833. Resigned 31 May, 1834.

HANDY, JAMES O.* [Born in R. I. Appointed from R. I.]
Bvt. 2nd Lieut. 5th Inf., 1 July, 1842. 2nd Lieut. 8th Inf., 30 May, 1845. Died 26 Sept., 1845.

HANEY, WM. W.* [Born in Mo. Appointed from Ark.]
2nd Lieut. of Inf. (8th), 11 June, 1892. Retired for disability, 6 Sept., 1895. Died 9 March, 1897.

HANHAM, JAMES R. [Born in England. Appointed from Md.]
2nd Lieut. Art., 17 Jan., 1805. 1st Lieut., 1 Nov., 1806. Capt., 10 July, 1811. In 1st Art., — March, 1812. Trans. to Corps Art., 12 May, 1814. Disbanded 15 June, 1815. Mil. Storekeeper Ord. Dept., 23 July, 1838. Dismissed 13 Sept., 1862. Died 2 Nov., 1865.

HANIGAN, HENRY A. [Born in Tex. Appointed from the Army.]
Priv., Corpl. and Sergt. Troop B, 3rd Cav., 9 Aug., 1893, to 19 July, 1896. Priv. and Corpl. Troop G, 8th Cav., 6 Aug., 1896, to 19 April, 1899. 1st Lieut. 4th Texas Vols., 22 July, 1898, to muster out, 10 March, 1899. 2nd Lieut. 6th Inf., 5 April, 1899.

HANLY, JOHN H.* [Born in Ky. Appointed from Ky.]
Bvt. 2nd Lieut. 1st Drag., 1 July, 1835. 2nd Lieut., 5 March, 1836. Died 26 May, 1836.

HANNA, MATTHEW E.* [Born in Ohio. Appointed from Ohio.]
Addl. 2nd Lieut. 4th Cav., 11 June, 1897. 2nd Lieut. 2nd Cav., 28 June, 1897.

HANNA, ROBT.* [Born in Ind. Appointed from Ind.]
2nd Lieut. 6th Cav., 14 June, 1872. 1st Lieut., 11 July, 1878. Capt., 7 July, 1888. Retired for disability, 24 Feb., 1891.

HANNA, VALENTINE C. [Born in Ind. Appointed from Ind.]
Addl. P. M. Vols., 15 Aug., 1861. Bvt. Lieut. Col. Vols., 13 March, 1865, for faithful and meritorious service during the war. Mustered out 20 July, 1866. Maj. P. M. U. S. A., 17 Jan., 1867. Retired 11 Jan., 1877. Died 10 Nov., 1884.

HANNAY, JOHN R. R. [Born in La. Appointed from Minn.]
2nd Lieut. 3rd Inf., 9 July, 1898. 1st Lieut. 22nd Inf., 2 March, 1899.

HANNAY, JOHN W. [Born in England. Appointed from Penn.]
1st Lieut. 198th Penn. Vols., 29 Oct., 1864. Resigned 15 Feb., 1865. 1st Lieut. 8th U. S. Col. Heavy Art., 10 March, 1865. Mustered out 10 Feb., 1866. 2nd Lieut. 3rd Inf., 28 Sept., 1866. 1st Lieut., 15 Feb., 1873. Capt., 1 Feb., 1887. Maj., 2 March, 1899.

HANNON, FERDINAND. [Born in Ga. Appointed from N. C.]
Ensign 10th Inf., 30 March, 1814. 3rd Lieut., 24 July, 1814. Disbanded 15 June, 1815. 2nd Lieut. 7th Inf., 25 Aug., 1819. Resigned 1 Nov., 1819.

HANNON, MARSHALL. [Born in Penn. Appointed from Penn.]
1st Lieut. of Inf., 16 Feb., 1847; 11th Inf., 9 April, 1847. Died 6 Dec., 1847.

HANSON, CHAS. [Born in D. C. Appointed from D. C.]
2nd Lieut. 7th Inf., 6 Sept., 1838. 1st Lieut., 16 March, 1844. Capt., 16 Feb., 1847. Killed 20 Aug., 1847, at the Battle of Contreras, Mexico.

HANSON, GRAFTON D. [Born in D. C. Appointed from D. C.]
2nd Lieut. 8th Inf., 10 Dec., 1839. 1st Lieut., 31 Dec., 1845. Resigned 4 Aug., 1849.

HANSON, JAMES.* [Born in Sweden. Appointed from S. D.]
Cadet at Mil. Acad., 15 June, 1894, to 25 June, 1895. Reappointed 2 Sept., 1895, and graduated in 1899. 2nd Lieut. 14th Inf., 15 Feb., 1899.

HANSON, JOHN M. [Born in N. Y. Appointed from N. Y.]
2nd Lieut. 8th Inf., 13 Feb., 1818. 2nd Lieut. Corps Art., 21 April, 1818. 1st Lieut., 1 Oct., 1820. Disbanded 1 June, 1821. Capt. Fla. Vols., 3 Nov., 1836. Lieut. Col., 20 Oct., 1837. Mustered out 8 Feb., 1838. Died 10 May, 1871.

HANSON, JONATHAN B. [Born in Mass. Appointed from Mass.]
Sergt. 1st Mass. Art., 5 July, 1861. 2nd Lieut., 22 Sept., 1861. 1st Lieut., 18 Jan., 1862. Mustered out 12 March, 1865. 2nd Lieut. 39th Inf., 7 March, 1867. 1st Lieut., 1 Jan., 1869. Unassigned 20 April, 1869. Ass'd to 10th Inf., 1 Jan., 1871. Died 2 Nov., 1876.

HANSON, THOMAS. [Born in Md. Appointed from Md.]
Capt. 42nd Inf., 4 Aug., 1813. Disbanded 15 June, 1815. J. A., 29 April, 1816. Disbanded 14 April, 1818.

HANSON, THOMAS G.* [Born in Cal. Appointed from Cal.]
2nd Lieut. 19th Inf., 12 June, 1887. 1st Lieut., 7 June, 1894. Capt., 2 March, 1899. Graduate of the Infantry and Cavalry School, 1891.

HANSON, WEIGHTMAN K.* [Born in D. C. Appointed from D. C.]
Bvt. 2nd Lieut. 7th Inf., 1 July, 1835. 2nd Lieut., 8 June, 1836. 1st Lieut., 7 July, 1838. Died 21 July, 1844. Bvt. Capt., 3 Aug., 1839, for meritorious conduct and gallantry in the war in Florida.

HAPPERSETT, JOHN C. G. [Born in Penn. Appointed from Penn.]
1st Lieut. Asst. Surg., 26 Aug., 1861. Bvt. Capt. and Maj., 13 March, 1865, for faithful and meritorious service during the war. Capt. Asst. Surg., 28 July, 1866. Maj. Surg., 26 June, 1876. Died 7 April, 1893.

HARBACH, ABRAM A. [Born in Penn. Appointed from Army.]
Sergt. Co. E, 1st Iowa Vols., 7 May, 1861. Discharged 20 Aug., 1861. Priv. Co. —, 11th Inf., 7 Dec., 1861. Corpl. Co. H, 1st Batt. 11th Inf., ——. 2nd Lieut. 11th Inf., 11 June, 1862. 1st Lieut., 2 July, 1863. Bvt. Capt., 2 July, 1863, for gallant and meritorious service in the Battle of Gettysburg, Penn. Adj. 2nd Batt. 11th Inf., 10 June, 1866, to 21 Sept., 1866. Trans. to 20th Inf., 21 Sept., 1866. Reg. Adj., 6 Dec., 1866, to 1 March, 1867. Capt., 22 Jan., 1867. Maj. 18th Inf., 12 March, 1894. Lieut. Col. 3rd Inf., 8 Aug., 1897. Col. 1st Inf., 19 July, 1899.

HARBESON, JAMES P.* [Born in Ky. Appointed from Ky.]
2nd Lieut. 12th Inf., 12 June, 1895. 1st Lieut., 3 July, 1898.

HARBORD, JAMES G. [Born in Ill. Appointed from the Army.]
Priv., Corpl. and Sergt. Co. A, and Q. M. Sergt. 4th Inf., 10 Jan, 1889, to 1 Aug., 1891. 2nd Lieut. 5th Cav., 31 July, 1891. 1st Lieut. 10th Cav., 1 July, 1898. Maj. 2nd U. S. Vol. Cav., 24 May, 1898, to 24 Oct., 1898. Graduate of the Infantry and Cavalry School, 1895.

HARDAWAY, BENJAMIN F. [Born in Ky. Appointed from the Army.]
Priv., Corpl. and Sergt. Co. C, 17th Inf., 28 April, 1886, to 1 Aug., 1891. 2nd Lieut. 17th Inf., 31 July, 1891. 1st Lieut., 26 April, 1898. Graduate of the Infantry and Cavalry School, 1895.

HARDCASTLE, AARON B. [Born in Md. Appointed from Md.]
2nd Lieut. 6th Inf., 7 June, 1855. 1st Lieut., 18 July, 1860. Resigned 7 May, 1861.

HARDCASTLE, EDMUND L. F.* [Born in Md. Appointed from Md.]
Bvt. 2nd Lieut. Top. Eng., 1 July, 1846. 2nd Lieut., 26 Sept., 1849. 1st Lieut., 1 July, 1853. Resigned 30 April, 1856. Bvt. 1st Lieut., 20 Aug., 1847, for gallant and meritorious conduct at Contreras and Churubusco. Bvt. Capt., 8 Sept., 1847, for gallant and meritorious conduct at Molino del Rey.

HARDEE, WM. J.* [Born in Ga. Appointed from Ga.]
2nd Lieut. 2nd Drag., 1 July, 1838. 1st Lieut., 3 Dec., 1839. Capt., 13 Sept., 1844. Maj. 2nd Cav., 3 March, 1855. Lieut. Col. 1st Cav., 28 June, 1860. Resigned 31 Jan., 1861. Bvt. Maj., 25 March, 1847, for gallant and meritorious conduct at Medelin, near Vera Cruz, Mexico. Bvt. Lieut. Col., 20 Aug., 1847, for gallant and meritorious conduct at San Augustine, Mexico.

HARDEMAN, LETCHER.* [Born in Mo. Appointed from Mo.]
2nd Lieut. 4th Inf., 1 July, 1886. 1st Lieut. 10th Inf., 15 April, 1893. Maj. 2nd Mo. Inf., 23 May, 1898, to 22 July, 1898.

HARDEN, MARK. [Born in N. C. Appointed from N. C.]
Capt. 10th Inf., 12 March, 1812. Disbanded 15 June, 1815. Capt. A. Q. M. G., 20 April, 1816. Resigned 30 Nov., 1817. Died in 1840.

HARDENBERGH, EVERT W. [Born in N. Y. Appointed from N. Y.]
2nd Lieut. 2nd Inf., 18 Sept., 1838. Resigned 31 May, 1840.

HARDENBERGH, J. RICHMOND. [Born in N. J. Appointed from Cal.]
2nd Lieut. 2nd Cal. Cav., 8 June, 1865. Mustered out 2 June, 1866. 2nd Lieut. 9th Inf., 5 April, 1866. 1st Lieut., 28 July, 1866. Discharged 7 Sept., 1870.

HARDENBERG, RAYMOND W. [Born in Penn. Appointed from Penn.]
Corpl. Co. E, 13th Pa. Vols., 12 May, 1898, to 14 July, 1898. Priv. and Batt. Sergt. Maj. 3rd U. S. Eng., 15 July to 4 Oct., 1898. 2nd Lieut. 3rd U. S. Vol. Eng., 5 Oct., 1898. 1st Lieut., 16 March, 1899, to 17 May, 1899. 2nd Lieut. 4th Inf., 1 June, 1899.

HARDIA, WM.* [Born in Va. Appointed from Va.]
2nd Lieut. 1st Drag., 1 July, 1837. 1st Lieut., 1 Dec., 1838. Dismissed 17 Feb., 1840. Died 4 March, 1842.

HARDIE, FRANCIS H. [Born in Cal. Appointed at Large.]
Cadet at Mil. Acad., 1 July, 1872, to 10 Jan., 1873, and from 10 Feb., 1873, to 26 May, 1875. 2nd Lieut. 3rd Cav., 28 July, 1876. 1st Lieut., 21 Feb., 1881. R. Q. M., 22 Nov., 1884, to 31 Aug., 1888. Capt., 31 Jan., 1891.

HARDIE, JAMES A.* [Born in N. Y. Appointed at Large.]
Bvt. 2nd Lieut. 1st Art., 1 July, 1843. 2nd Lieut. 3rd Art., 28 May, 1846. Maj. 1st N. Y. Vols., 1 Aug., 1846, to 26 Oct., 1848. 1st Lieut. 3rd Art., 3 March, 1847. Reg. Adj., 1 Nov., 1851, to 1 Dec., 1853, and 3 May, 1855, to 5 Oct., 1857. Capt., 5 Oct., 1857. Trans. to 5th Art., 14 May, 1861. Lieut. Col. A. A. de C., 28 Sept., 1861, to 24 March, 1864. Brig. Gen. Vols., 29 Nov., 1862. Appointment as Brig. Gen. revoked 22 Jan., 1863. Maj. A. A. G., 19 Feb., 1863. Col. I. G., 24 March, 1864. Died 14 Dec., 1876. Bvt. Brig. Gen., 3 March, 1865, for diligent and faithful service during the war. Bvt. Maj. Gen., 13 March, 1865, for faithful, meritorious and distinguished service in the I. G. Dept. Died 14 Dec., 1876.

HARDIE, JOHN H. [Born in N. Y. Appointed from Army.]
Priv. Co. I, 79th N. Y. Vols., 27 May to 16 Oct., 1861. Priv. Co. A, 9th Inf., 28 Sept., 1863. 2nd Lieut. 9th Inf., 28 Sept., 1863. 1st Lieut., 20 April, 1864. Mustered out 31 Dec., 1870. Died 12 Aug., 1873.

HARDIN, CHARLES B. [Born in Ill. Appointed from the Army.]
Priv. and Corpl. Co. G, 1st Cav., 17 Aug., 1872, to 6 June, 1877. Priv., Corpl. and Sergt. Co. G, 1st Cav., 15 Oct., 1878, to 23 April, 1882. 2nd Lieut. 18th Inf., 27 March, 1882. 1st Lieut., 26 Dec., 1888. Capt., 26 April, 1898. Graduate of the Infantry and Cavalry School, 1885.

HARDIN, EDWARD E.* [Born in Ky. Appointed from Ky.]
2nd Lieut. 7th Inf., 17 June, 1874. 1st Lieut., 4 March, 1881. Capt., 31 July, 1894. Col. 2nd N. Y. Vols., 17 May, 1898, to 25 Oct., 1898. Col. 29th U. S. Vols., 5 July, 1899. Bvt. 1st Lieut. for gallant services against Indians at Big Hole, Mont., 9 Aug., 1877.

HARDIN, JAMES P.* [Born in Ky. Appointed from Ky.]
Bvt. 2nd Lieut. 4th Inf., 1 July, 1832. Resigned 15 Dec., 1832. Died 26 Oct., 1842.

HARDIN, MARTIN D.* [Born in Ill. Appointed from Ill.]
Bvt. 2nd Lieut. 3rd Art., 1 July, 1859. 2nd Lieut., 2 Jan., 1860. 1st Lieut., 14 May, 1861. Lieut. Col. 12th Penn. Res. Vet. Corps, 8 July, 1862. Bvt. Capt., 29 Aug., 1862, for gallant and meritorious service in the Batte of Groveton, Va. Bvt. Maj., 30 Aug., 1862, for gallant and meritorious service in the Battle of Bull Run (2nd), Va. Col. 12th Pa. Res. Vet. Corps, 1 Sept., 1862. Bvt. Lieut. Col., 14 Dec., 1863, for gallant and meritorious service in an encounter with a band of guerillas. Bvt. Col., 23 May, 1864, for gallant and meritorious service in the Battle of North Anna River, Va. Mustered out of Vol. Serv.., 15 Jan., 1866. Brig. Gen. Vols., 2 July, 1864. Bvt. Brig. Gen., 13 March, 1865, for gallant and meritorious service in the field during the war. Maj. 43rd Inf., 28 July, 1866. Trans. to 1st Inf., 15 March, 1869. Retired with rank of Brig. Gen., 15 Dec., 1870.

HARDING, CHESTER.* [Born in Miss. Appointed from Ala.]
Addl. 2nd Lieut. Eng., 12 June, 1889. 2nd Lieut., 12 Aug., 1890. 1st Lieut., 26 Jan., 1895. Capt., 5 July, 1898.

HARDING, EBENEZER D. [Born in Penn. Appointed from Army.]
Priv. and Sergt. Co. C, 3rd Batt. 18th Inf., 25 Sept., 1861, to 1 July, 1862. 2nd Lieut. 18th Inf., 9 June, 1862. 1st Lieut., 15 Jan., 1863. Trans. to 27th Inf., 21 Sept., 1866. Capt., 7 Jan., 1867. Wholly retired 19 Oct., 1867. Bvt. Capt., 25 Nov., 1863, for gallant and meritorious service at the Battle of Mission Ridge, Tenn. Died 28 Dec., 1868.

HARDING, EDWARD.* [Born in Md. Appointed from Md.]
2nd Lieut. Corps Art., 24 July, 1818. Trans. to 2nd Art., 1 June, 1821. 1st Lieut., 10 May, 1826. Capt. Ord., 30 May, 1832. Maj., 10 July, 1851. Died 15 Feb., 1855.

HARDING, JOHN A. B. [Born in Va. Appointed from Va.]
3rd Lieut. 5th Inf., 25 April, 1813. 2nd Lieut., 28 April, 1814. Disbanded 15 June, 1815. Reinstated in 6th Inf., 2 Dec., 1815. Resigned 15 July, 1816.

HARDING, WILLIAM WILKINS. [Born in Ala. Appointed from Penn.]
2nd Lieut. 3rd Art., 7 June, 1855. Resigned 19 Oct., 1855.

HARDY, ARTHUR S.* [Born in Mass. Appointed from Mass.]
2nd Lieut. 3rd Art., 15 June, 1869. Discharged 12 Nov., 1870.

HARE, JOSEPH. [Born in Penn. Appointed from Penn.]
2nd Lieut. 5th Inf., 28 Jan., 1820. Disbanded 1 June, 1821.

HARE, LUTHER R.* [Born in Ind. Appointed from Texas.]
2nd Lieut. 7th Cav., 17 June, 1874. 1st Lieut., 25 June, 1876. R. Q. M., 14 Aug., 1886, to 20 July, 1887. Capt., 29 Dec., 1890. Lieut. Col. 1st Tex. Cav., 15 May, 1898. Col., 2 June, 1898, to 14 Nov., 1898. Col. 33rd U. S. Vols., 5 July, 1899.

HARFORD, WM. H.* [Born in Ga. Appointed from Ga.]
Bvt. 2nd Lieut. 4th Inf., 1 July, 1829. 2nd Lieut., 1 July, 1829. Resigned 15 Sept., 1833. Died 19 Jan., 1836.

HARGOUS, CHAS. E. [Born in N. Y. Appointed from N. Y.]
1st Lieut. 15th N. Y. Eng., 1 Dec., 1862. Mustered out 25 June, 1863. 1st Lieut., 15th N. Y. Eng., 22 July, 1864. Capt., 17 Jan., 1865. Mustered out 13 June, 1865. 2nd Lieut. 40th Inf., 28 July, 1866. R. Q. M., 15 May to 24 Dec., 1865. Bvt. 1st Lieut., 2 March, 1867, for gallant and meritorious service at Sedgwick's Crossing, Va. Bvt. Capt., 2 March, 1867, for gallant and meritorious service during the war. Unassigned 20 April, 1869. Ass'd to 5th Inf., 9 Dec., 1869. 1st Lieut., 21 June, 1878. Capt., 12 May, 1886. Died 10 March, 1891.

HARGRAVE, RICHD. W. [Born in Ireland. Appointed from Army.]
1st Lieut. 17th Ind. Vols., 12 June, 1861. Resigned 19 Sept., 1861. Priv., Corpl. and Sergt. Co. A, 2nd Batt. 17th Inf., 7 Feb., 1862, to 28 April, 1863. 2nd Lieut. 17th Inf., 22 April, 1863. 1st Lieut., 2 July, 1863. Resigned 29 March, 1865.

HARISON, GEORGE S.* [Born in N. Y. Appointed from N. J.]
2nd Lieut. of Inf. (10th), 11 June, 1892. Died 2 June, 1894.

HARKER, CHAS. G.* [Born in N. J. Appointed from N. J.]
Bvt. 2nd Lieut. 2nd Inf., 1 July, 1858. 2nd Lieut. 9th Inf., 15 Aug., 1858. 1st Lieut. 15th Inf., 14 May, 1861. Capt., 24 Oct., 1861. Col. 65th Ohio Vols., 11 Nov., 1861. Brig. Gen. Vols., 20 Sept., 1863. Killed 27 June, 1864, in Battle at Kenesaw Mountain, Ga.

HARKER, THOMAS R. [Born in Ill. Appointed from Army.]
Priv., Corpl. and Sergt. Co. D, 20th Inf., 31 Jan., 1891, to 1 March, 1898. 2nd Lieut. 15th Inf., 23 June, 1898. 1st Lieut., 2 March, 1899.

HARKINS, CHAS. [Born in Ireland. Appointed from Nev.]
Priv. Co. H, 6th Inf., 3 Dec., 1853. Corpl., 1 Oct., 1856. Sergt., 1 May, 1857. Discharged 3 Dec., 1858. Priv. Co. F, 2nd Mass. Cav., 26 March, 1863, to 9 Jan., 1865. 1st Lieut. 124th U. S. Col. Troops, 10 Jan., 1865. Mustered out 24 Oct., 1865. 2nd Lieut. 2nd Inf., 23 Feb., 1866. 1st Lieut., 28 July, 1866. Capt., 26 Sept., 1881. Retired for disability, 20 March, 1885.

HARLEY, BENJAMIN F. [Born in Penn. Appointed from Penn.]
2nd Lieut. of Inf., 2 March, 1847; 11th Inf., 9 April, 1847. 1st Lieut., 12 Aug., 1847. Disbanded 13 Aug., 1848. Bvt. Capt., 20 Aug., 1847, for gallant and meritorious conduct in the Battles of Contreras and Churubusco, Mexico.

HARLOW, FRANK S.* [Born in Vt. Appointed from Vt.]
2nd Lieut. 9th Inf., 13 June, 1879. Trans. to 1st Art., 11 Aug., 1879. 1st Lieut., 7 July, 1886. Capt., 2 March, 1899. Honor graduate of the Artillery School, 1890.

HARMAN, JOHN A.* [Born in Va. Appointed from Va.]
Addl. 2nd Lieut. 7th Cav., 12 June, 1887. 2nd Lieut., 5 July, 1887. 1st Lieut. 6th Cav., 10 Nov., 1894. Maj. Chf. Ord. Off. Vols., 17 Sept., 1898, to May, 1899. Resigned 1 March, 1900.

HARMON, MILLARD F.* [Born in Pa. Appointed from Pa.]
2nd Lieut., 5th Inf., 12 June, 1880. Trans. to 1st Art., 21 July, 1880. 1st Inf., 4 Dec., 1888. Capt. 2nd Art., 2 March, 1899. Honor graduate of the Artillery School, 1890.

HARMON, WM. [Born in Maine. Appointed from Minn.]
Sergt. Co. D, 1st Minn. Vols., 29 April, 1861. 2nd Lieut., 13 Sept., 1862. 1st Lieut., 27 March, 1863. Mustered out 5 May, 1864. 2nd Lieut. 18th Inf., 21 July, 1866. Trans. to 36th Inf., 21 Sept., 1866. 1st Lieut., 14 Nov., 1867. Unassigned 19 May, 1869. Discharged 31 Dec., 1870.

HARMON, WM. R. [Born in Ohio. Appointed from Ohio.]
2nd Lieut. 70th Ohio Vols., 6 Jan., 1862. 1st Lieut., 11 Feb., 1862. Resigned 3 Sept., 1862. 2nd Lieut. 10th Cav., 17 Aug., 1867. 1st Lieut., 6 Dec., 1873. Died 6 July, 1886.

HARNEY, BENJAMIN F. [Born in Del. Appointed from Miss.]
Maj. Surg. 3rd Inf., 17 Aug., 1814. Disbanded 15 June, 1815. Reinstated in 1st Inf., 17 May, 1816. Maj. Surg., 1 June, 1821. Died 29 Aug., 1858.

HARNEY, WM. S. [Born in La. Appointed from La.]
2nd Lieut. 1st Inf., 13 Feb., 1818. 1st Lieut., 7 Jan., 1819. Trans. to 1st Art., 16 Nov., 1821. Trans. to 1st Inf., 21 Dec., 1822. Capt., 14 May, 1825. Maj. P. M., 1 May, 1833. Lieut. Col. 2nd Drag., 15 Aug., 1836. Bvt. Col., 7 Dec., 1840, for gallant and meritorious conduct in several successive engagements with the hostile Indians in Florida. Col. 2nd Drag., 30 June, 1846. Bvt. Brig. Gen., 18 April, 1847, for gallant and meritorious conduct in the Battle of Cerro Gordo. Brig. Gen., 14 June, 1858. Retired 1 Aug.,1863. Bvt. Maj. Gen., 13 March, 1865, for long and faithful service. Died 9 May, 1889.

HAROLD, JOHN. [Born in Tenn. Appointed from Tenn.]
Priv. Co. A. 4th Tenn. Vols., 12 Aug., 1862. 1st Lieut., 9 Sept., 1863. Capt., 14 Oct., 1864. Mustered out 2 Aug., 1865. 2nd Lieut. 19th Inf., 23 Feb., 1866. 1st Lieut., 23 Feb., 1866. Trans. to 28th Inf., 21 Sept., 1866. Trans. to 19th Inf., 31 March, 1869. Died 27 Nov., 1878.

HARPER, ROY B.* [Born in Ill. Appointed from Ill.]
Addl. 2nd Lieut. 7th Cav., 11 June, 1897. 2nd Lieut. 10th Cav., 11 Jan., 1898. Trans to 7th Cav., 4 May, 1898. Lieut. Col. 1st Ill. Cav., 21 May, 1898, to 11 Oct., 1898.

HARPER, WM., JR. [Born in Penn. Appointed from Penn.]
2nd Lieut. 1st N. J. Cav., 11 Feb., 1862. 1st Lieut., 1 May, 1862. Capt., 26 Oct., 1863. Maj., 27 April, 1865. Bvt. Maj. and Lieut. Col. Vols., 13 March, 1865, for gallant and efficient service during the war. Mustered out 24 July, 1865. 2nd Lieut. 6th Cav., 18 Oct., 1866. 1st Lieut., 10 May, 1867. Capt., 27 Jan., 1875. Dismissed 15 Nov., 1876. Bvt. 1st Lieut., Capt. and Maj., 2 March, 1867, for gallant and meritorious service during the war.

HARPSTER, ISAAC. [Born in Ohio. Appointed from Army.]
1st Sergt. Co. I, 15th Inf., 24 March, 1847, to 1 March, 1848. 2nd Lieut. 15th Inf., 30 Dec., 1847. Resigned 6 May., 1848. Capt. 102nd Ohio Vols., 6 Sept., 1862. Resigned 19 March, 1863.

HARRINGTON, EDWARD J. [Born in D. C. Appointed from D. C.]
Capt. A. A. G. Vols.,7 March, 1865. Mustered out 4 Aug., 1866. 2nd Lieut. 1st Cav., 2 April, 1866. Resigned 16 Nov., 1867. Died 7 Feb., 1877.

HARRINGTON, GEORGE. [Born in Ireland. Appointed from Army.]
Priv., Corpl. and Sergt. Co. D, and Sergt. Maj. Mtd. Rifles (3rd Cav.), 16 Oct., 1855, to 20 Dec., 1863. 2nd Lieut. 3rd Cav., 31 Oct., 1863. Killed 21 Aug., 1864, in attack on Memphis, Tenn.

HARRINGTON, HENRY M.* [Born in N. Y. Appointed from Mich.]
2nd Lieut. 7th Cav., 14 June, 1872. Killed 25 June, 1876, in action with Indians at Little Big Horn River, Mont.

HARRINGTON, JEREMIAH. [Born in Ireland. Appointed from Army.]
Priv., Corpl. and Sergt. Gen. Mtd. Ser., 3 Aug., 1860, to 7 Dec., 1862. 2nd Lieut. 1st Cav., 29 Nov., 1862. Dismissed 26 June, 1863.

HARRIS, ARCHIE J. [Born in Iowa. Appointed from Col.]
2nd Lieut. 2nd Inf., 9 July, 1898. 1st Lieut., 16 May, 1899.

HARRIS, ARNOLD.* [Born in N. Y. Appointed from N. Y.]
Bvt 2nd Lieut. 7th Inf., 1 July, 1854. 2nd Lieut., 1 June, 1835. Resigned 8 March, 1837. Died 2 April, 1866.

HARRIS, DAVID B.* [Born in Va. Appointed from Va.]
Bvt. 2nd Lieut. 1st Art., 1 July, 1833. 2nd Lieut., 6 March, 1834. Resigned 31 Aug., 1835 Died 10 Oct., 1864.

HARRIS, EDWARD. [Born in Va. Appointed from Army.]
Priv. Co. F, 5th Cav., 19 Oct., 1860, to 11 July, 1864. 2nd Lieut. 5th Cav., 7 June, 1864. 1st Lieut., 29 Sept., 1864. Resigned 31 Oct., 1866. Bvt. 1st Lieut., 6 May, 1864, for gallant and meritorious service at the Battle of Todd's Tavern, Va. Bvt. Capt., 19 Sept., 1864, for gallant and meritorious service at the Battle of Winchester, Va.

HARRIS, FLOYD W.* [Born in W. Va. Appointed from W. Va.]
2nd Lieut. 4th Cav., 1 July, 1886. 1st Lieut. 2nd Cav., 15 Aug., 1892. Trans. to 4th Cav., 5 Dec., 1892. Graduate of Infantry and Cavalry School, 1891.

HARRIS, FRANK E.* [Born in Poland. Appointed from Iowa.]
2nd Lieut. 1st Art., 11 June, 1892. 1st Lieut. 3rd Art., 13 Feb., 1899. Honor graduate of the Artillery School, 1896.

HARRIS, GEORGE M.* [Born in Penn. Appointed from Ga.]
2nd Lieut. 10th Inf., 15 June, 1868. Unassigned 19 May, 1869. Ass'd to 4th Art., 14 July, 1869. 1st Lieut., 1 May, 1873. Died 12 May, 1873, of wounds received in action with Indians at the Lava Beds, Ore.

HARRIS, HENRY L.* [Born in Penn. Appointed from N. J.]
2nd Lieut. 1st Art., 15 June, 1869. 1st Lieut., 1 Nov., 1876. Reg. Adj., 15 April, 1887, to —. Capt., 26 Aug., 1897. Graduate of the Artillery School, 1880.

HARRIS, HENRY, Jr.* [Born in N. Y. Appointed from N. J..
2nd Lieut. 20th Inf., 15 Feb., 1899.

HARRIS, HENRY S. T. [Born in Va. Appointed from Va.]
Asst. Surg., 5 Jan., 1886. Capt. Asst. Surg., 5 Jan., 1891. Maj. Brig. Surg. Vols., 4 June, 1898.

HARRIS, JOSEPH W.* [Born in N. H. Appointed from N. H.]
Bvt. 2nd Lieut. 4th Art., 1 July, 1825. 2nd Lieut. 3rd Art., 1 July, 1825. 1st Lieut., 30 June, 1833. Died 18 May, 1837.

HARRIS, JOSIAH D. [Born in N. Y. Appointed from N. Y.]
Asst. Surg., 2 March, 1833. Died 26 Sept., 1833.

HARRIS, MATTHIAS. [Born in Md. Appointed from Md.]
Chap. Post of Fort Moultrie, S. C., 21 June, 1849, to 23 Dec., 1860. At Fort Washington, Md., 22 Jan., 1861, to 28 Jan., 1864, and at Fort Foote, Md., 10 Oct., 1864, to 26 April, 1867. Capt. Post Chap., 3 April, 1867. Retired 20 July, 1867. Died 10 July, 1871.

HARRIS, MOSES. [Born in N. H. Appointed from Army.]
Priv. Co. G, 1st Cav., 19 March, 1857. Corpl., 16 April, 1860. Sergt., 13 July, 1861. Discharged 20 Jan., 1862. Sergt. Co. G, 4th Cav., 20 Jan., 1862. 1st Sergt., 19 April, 1863. 2nd Lieut. 1st Cav., 18 May, 1864. 1st Lieut., 15 Aug., 1864. Bvt. Capt., 19 Sept., 1864, for gallant and meritorious service in the Battle of Winchester, Va. Capt. 1st Cav., 20 June, 1872. Maj. 8th Cav., 22 June, 1892. Retired for over 30 years' service 7 March, 1893. Medal of Honor for most distinguished gallantry in action at Smithfield, W. Va., 28 Aug., 1864, where, in an attack upon a largely superior force, his personal gallantry was so conspicuous as to inspire the men to extraordinary effort, resulting in the complete rout of the enemy; while serving as 1st Lieut. 1st Cav.

HARRIS N. SAYRE.* [Born in N. J. Appointed from N. J.]
Bvt. 2nd Lieut. 5th Inf., 1 July, 1825. 2nd Lieut. 3rd Inf., 1 July, 1825. 1st Lieut., 11 Sept., 1829. Reg. Adj., 10 Feb., 1827, to 19 Oct., 1830. Resigned 31 May, 1835. Died 22 April, 1886.

HARRIS, PATRICK H. [Born in Ky. Appointed from Ky.]
1st Lieut. of Inf., 5 March, 1847; 16th Inf., 9 April, 1847. Capt., 14 June, 1847. Disbanded 7 Aug., 1848.

HARRIS, PETER C.* [Born in Ga. Appointed from Ga.]
2nd Lieut. 13th Inf., 11 June 1888. 1st Lieut., 5 July, 1895. Capt. 9th Inf., 16 March, 1899. Honor graduate of the Infantry and Cavalry School, 1895.

HARRIS, SAMUEL D. [Born in Mass. Appointed from Mass.]
Capt. 2nd Light Drag., 21 March, 1812. Trans. to Reg. Light Drag., 12 May, 1814. Trans. to Light Art., 17 May, 1815. Resigned 31 Dec., 1819. Bvt. Maj., 5 July, 1814, for gallant conduct at Battle of Chippewa. Bvt. Lieut. Col., 25 July, 1814, for distinguished service at the Battle of Niagara. P. M. 7th Inf., 7 Feb., 1821. Resigned 2 March, 1821.

HARRIS, THOS. A. [Born in Va. Appointed from Mo.]
Cadet Mil. Acad., 1 Sept., 1843, to 3 May, 1845. 2nd Lieut. 12th Inf., 31 May, 1848. Disbanded 1 Aug., 1848.

HARRIS, WM. H.* [Born in N. Y. Appointed from N. Y.]
Bvt. 2nd Lieut. Ord., 24 June, 1861. 2nd Lieut., 3 Aug., 1861. 1st Lieut., 14 Sept., 1862. Capt., 1 June, 1863. Discharged 21 Sept., 1870. Bvt. Maj. and Lieut. Col., 1 Aug., 1864, for gallant and efficient service in the Battles from the Rapidan to Petersburg, Va., Died 20 Feb., 1837.

HARRIS WM. L.* [Born in Va. Appointed from Va.]
Bvt. 2nd Lieut. 4th Inf., 1 July, 1824. 2nd Lieut., 1st Inf., 1 July, 1824. 1st Lieut., 31 Dec., 1830. Dismissed 29 Oct., 1836.

HARRISON, ABNER. [Born in ——. Appointed from Tenn.]
2nd Lieut. 3rd Rifle Reg., 17 March, 1814. Disbanded 15 June, 1815. Reinstated in Rifle Reg., 2 Dec., 1815. Dropped 15 July, 1817.

HARRISON, ARCHIBALD I. [Born in Ohio. Appointed from Ohio.]
2nd Lieut. 6th Inf., 21 Feb., 1857. Resigned 5 Sept., 1859. 1st Lieut. and Adj. 8th Ind. Vols., 27 April, 1861. Mustered out 6 Aug., 1861. Lieut Col. 27th Ind. Vols., 12 Sept., 1861. Resigned 29 Oct., 1861. Died — Dec., 1870.

HARRISON ARCHIBALD I. [Born in Mo. Appointed from Mo.]
2nd Lieut. 25th Inf., 9 July, 1898. 1st Lieut. 21st Inf., 8 Sept., 1899.

HARRISON, CHARLES. [Born in N. Y. Appoited from N. Y.]
3rd Lieut. 13th Inf., 16 May, 1813. 2nd Lieut., 19 Jan., 1814. 1st Lieut., 19 Oct., 1814. Disbanded 15 June, 1815. 2nd Lieut. 3rd Inf., 26 Oct., 1818. Disbanded 1 June, 1821. Died 17 July, 1821.

HARRISON, GEORGE F. E.* [Born in Cal. Appointed from Cal.]
2nd Lieut. 2nd Art., 13 June, 1873. 1st Lieut. 20 Jan., 1881. Capt. 7th Art., 8 March, 1898. Graduate of the Artillery School, 1882.

HARRISON, JAMES E. [Born in Va. Appointed from D. C.]
2nd Lieut. 2nd Cav., 27 June, 1856. 1st Lieut., 27 Feb., 1861. Capt., 30 May, 1861. 5th Cav., 3 Aug., 1861. Died 4 Nov., 1867. Bvt. Maj., 27 May, 1862, for gallant and meritorious service at the Battle of Hanover C. H., Va. Bvt. Lieut. Col., 17 Sept., 1862, for gallant and meritorious service at the Battle of Antietam, Md.

HARRISON, JAMES FINDLEY. [Born in Ohio. Appointed from Ohio.]
Cad. Mil. Acad., 1 Sept., 1841, to 10 April, 1845. 2nd Lieut 1st Ohio Vols., 31 Aug., 1846. Mustered out 12 June, 1847. 1st Lieut. 10th Inf., 3 March, 1855. Resigned 8 Aug., 1855. Col. 11th Ohio Vols., 25 April, 1861. Resigned 29 May, 1861.

HARRISON, JOHN K. [Born in N. C. Appointed from N. C.]
2nd Lieut. 3rd Inf., March, 1847; 3rd Drag., 9 April, 1847. Disbanded 31 July, 1848.

HARRISON, JOSEPH P.* [Born in Ga. Appointed from Ala.]
Bvt. 2nd Lieut. 6th Inf., 1 July, 1833. 2nd Lieut., 16 Nov., 1836. 1st Lieut., 31 Oct., 1837. Reg. Adj., 1 Jan. to 19 Sept., 1838. Resigned 22 July, 1839. Died 11 Oct., 1839.

HARRISON, LLOYD M. [Born in Va. Appointed from D. C.]
2nd Lieut. 5th Art., 14 May, 1861. 1st Lieut., 16 June, 1863. Dismissed 22 Sept., 1864. Died 15 Oct., 1880.

HARRISON, MASSILLON.* [Born in Md. Appointed at Large.]
2nd Lieut. Eng., 1 July, 1841. 1st Lieut., 24 May, 1848. Died 2 Feb., 1854.

HARRISON, MATTHEW R. T.* [Born in Ga. Appointed from Ga.]
Changed name to M. J. Williams,—which see.

HARRISON, MONROE. [Born in Mo. Appointed from Mo.]
1st Lieut. 7th Mo. Vols., 13 May, 1861. Capt., 1 March, 1862. Mustered out 14 June, 1864. 2nd Lieut. 40th Mo. Vols., 10 Aug., 1864. Capt., 7 Sept., 1864. Mustered out 8 Aug., 1865. 2nd Lieut. 19th Inf., 18 June, 1867. Died 5 July, 1869.

HARRISON, MONTGOMERY P.* [Born in Ind. Appointed at Large.]
Bvt. 2nd Lieut., 7th Inf., 1 July, 1847. 2nd Lieut. 5th Inf., 11 Sept., 1847. Killed 7 Oct., 1849, by Indians in Texas.

HARRISON, RALPH.* [Born in Mo. Appointed from Mo.]
Addl. 2nd Lieut. 2nd Cav., 12 June, 1889. 2nd Lieut., 22 June, 1889. 1st Lieut. 1st Cav., 6 Nov., 1896. Trans. to 2nd Cav., 10 March, 1897. Maj. 2nd Mo. Inf., 22 July, 1898, to 3 March, 1899.

HARRISON, ROBT. [Born in Mass. Appointed from Army.]
Priv. and Sergt. Co. A, 2nd Batt. 15th Inf., 3 Feb., 1862, to 30 March, 1863. 2nd Lieut. 15th Inf., 19 Feb., 1863. 1st Lieut., 11 June, 1864. Trans. to 33rd Inf., 21 Sept., 1866. Capt., 7 March, 1867. Died 11 Oct., 1868. Bvt. Capt., 1 Sept., 1864, for gallant and meritorious service during the Atlanta campaign.

HARRISON, ROBERT M. [Born in N. Y. Appointed from N. Y.]
Ensign 13th Inf., 29 July, 1813. 3rd Lieut., 30 Sept., 1813. 2nd Lieut., 30 June, 1814. Trans. to 2nd Inf., 17 May, 1815. 1st Lieut., 1 Nov., 1817. Died 10 Feb., 1825.

HARRISON, THOMAS. [Born in Mass. Appointed from Mass.]
2nd Lieut. 21st Inf., 15 May, 1812. 1st Lieut. 9th Inf., 20 March, 1813. Capt., 15 Aug., 1813. Trans. to 42nd Inf., 10 June, 1814. Disbanded 15 June, 1815. Mil. S. Q. M. Dept., 25 Dec., 1817. Resigned 28 March, 1826.

HARRISON, THOMAS J. [Born in Va. Appointed from Va.]
3rd Lieut. 1st Light Drag., 15 Aug., 1813. 2nd Lieut., 19 April, 1814. Trans. to Corps Art., 12 May, 1814. 1st Lieut., 20 April, 1818. Trans. to 3rd Inf., 1 June, 1821. Capt., 23 Sept., 1827. Died 15 June, 1836.

HARRISON, WM. H. [Born in Penn. Appointed from Penn..
2nd Lieut. 2nd Cav., 30 Nov., 1861. 1st. Lieut., 25 Aug., 1862. Col. 214th Pa. Vols., 6 April, 1865. Mustered out of Vol. Ser., 21 March, 1866. Capt., 28 July, 1866. Resigned 17 Nov., 1866. Bvt. Capt., 6 May, 1864, for gallant and meritorious service at the Battle of Todd's Tavern, Va. Bvt. Maj., 19 Sept., 1864, for gallant and meritorious service at the Battle of Winchester, Va.

HARROLD, CHRISTOPHER W. [Born in N. H. Appointed from Mass.]
Priv. Co. B, 17th N. H. Vols., 7 Nov., 1862. Sergt., 13 Nov., 1862. Discharged 16 April, 1863. 2nd Lieut. 1st N. H. Art., 25 Aug., 1863. 1st Lieut., 14 Nov., 1864. Mustered out 11 Sept., 1865. 2nd Lieut. 3rd Art., 7 Nov., 1866. 1st Lieut., 21 Sept., 1868. Graduate of the Artillery School, 1880. Retired with rank of Capt. for disability, 13 July, 1892.

HART, DANIEL. [Born in N. J. Appointed from N. J.]
2nd Lieut. 7th N. J. Vols., 24 Aug., 1861. 1st Lieut., 27 May, 1862. Capt., 5 Sept., 1862. Maj., 17 March, 1865. Lieut. Col., 1 April, 1865. Bvt. Lieut. Col. Vols., 9 April, 1865, for meritorious service during the recent campaign terminating with the surrender of the insurgent army under Gen. R. E. Lee. Mustered out, 17 July, 1865. 1st Lieut. 40th Inf., 22 Jan., 1867. Trans. to 25th Inf., 20 April, 1869. Capt., 30 Nov., 1873. Died 11 April, 1878. Bvt. Capt., 2 March, 1867, for gallant and meritorious service in the Battle of Gettysburg, Pa.. Bvt. Maj., 2 March, 1867, for gallant and meritorious service in the Battle of the Wilderness, Va.

HART, PATRICK J. [Born in Ohio. Appointed from Minn.]
Post Chap., 2 Feb., 1893.

HART, THOS. [Born in Ky. Appointed from Ill.]
2nd Lieut. 14th Inf., 9 Sept., 1847. Disbanded 25 July, 1848.

HART, VERLING K. [Born in Ind. Appointed from Ind.]
Capt. 19th Inf., 30 Oct., 1861. Bvt. Maj., 20 Sept., 1863, for gallant and meritorious service in the Battle of Chickamauga, Ga. Bvt. Lieut. Col., 13 March, 1865, for gallant and mertorious service during the war. Trans. to 37th Inf., 21 Sept., 1866. Trans. to 3rd Inf., 11 Aug., 1869. Trans. to 7th Cav., 1 Jan., 1871. Maj. 5th Cav., 2 Dec., 1875. Died 17 Feb., 1883.

HART, VERLING K.* [Born in Kan. Appointed from Wyo.]
2nd Lieut. 16th Inf., 12 June, 1893. Trans to 17th Inf., 4 Aug., 1893. 1st Lieut., 26 April, 1898.

HART, WILLIAM H.* [Born in Minn. Appointed from Dak.]
2nd Lieut. 20th Inf., 11 June, 1888. Trans. to 4th Cav., 11 Feb., 1889. 1st Lieut. 7th Cav., 23 May, 1896.

HARTE, EDWARD. [Born in N. Y. Appointed from N. Y.]
2nd Lieut. of Inf., 13 March, 1847; 10th Inf., 9 Aprl, 1847. R. Q. M., 1 May to 13 Oct., 1847. Resigned 3 Feb., 1848.

HARTLEY, JOHN. [Born in Maine. Appointed from Minn.]
Priv. Co. E. 8th Minn. Vols., 14 Aug., 1862. Sergt. Maj. 8th Minn. Vols., 1 Jan., 1863. Capt. C. S. Vols., 27 Jan., 1865. Bvt. Maj. Vols., 11 July, 1865, for efficient and meritorious service. Mustered out 12 July, 1865. Capt. 22nd Inf., 28 July, 1866. Resigned 7 Sept., 1882. Died 10 March, 1883.

HARTMAN, JOHN D. L.* [Born in Penn. Appointed from Penn.]
2nd Lieut. 4th Cav., 11 June, 1888. 1st Lieut., 27 Aug., 1895.

HARTMANN, EDWARD T. [Born in Ill. Appointed from Army.]
Priv., Corpl. and Sergt. Co. H, 7th Inf., 29 Aug., 1893, to 23 March, 1896. 2nd Lieut. 15th Inf., 5 March, 1896. 1st Lieut. of Inf., 15 Aug., 1898. Ass'd to 19th Inf., 1 Jan., 1899.

HARNETT, EUGENE H. [Born in N. Y. Appointed from N. J.]
Asst. Surg., 23 July, 1898.

HARTS, WILLIAM W.* [Born in Ill. Appointed from Ill.]
Addl. 2nd Lieut. Eng., 12 June, 1889. 2nd Lieut., 22 Feb., 1891. Capt., 26 Oct., 1898. Maj. Chf. Eng. Vol., 13 July to 30 Nov., 1898.

HARTSHORNE, BENJ. M., Jr.* [Born in N. J. Appointed from N. J.]
Addl. 2nd Lieut. 9th Inf., 12 June, 1896. 2nd Lieut. 23rd Inf., 6 Jan., 1897. Trans. to 10th Inf., 4 Feb., 1897. 1st Lieut. 9th Inf., 7 Jan., 1899.

HARTSOCK, FREDERICK M. [Born in Md. Appointed from D. C.]
Asst. Surg., 23 July, 1898.

HARTSUFF, ALBERT. [Born in N. Y. Appointed from Mich.]
1st Lieut. Asst. Surg., 5 Aug., 1861. Bvt. Capt. and Maj., 13 March, 1865, for faithful and meritorious service during the war. Capt. Asst. Surg., 28 July, 1866. Bvt. Lieut. Col., 26 Nov., 1866, for meritorious and distinguished service during the outbreak and continuance of cholera in New Orleans, La. Maj. Surg., 26 June, 1876. Lieut. Col. Dep. Surg. Gen., 4 Dec., 1892.

HARTSUFF, GEORGE L.* [Born in N. Y. Appointed from Mich.]
Bvt. 2nd Lieut. 4th Art., 1 July, 1852. 2nd Lieut. 2nd Art., 12 June, 1853. 1st Lieut., 8 March, 1855. Capt., 23 May, 1863, to 15 June, 1864. Bvt. Capt. A. A. G., 22 March, 1861. Capt. A. A. G., 3 Aug., 1861. Maj., 17 July, 1862. Brig. Gen. Vols., 15 April, 1862. Maj. Gen. Vols., 29 Nov., 1862. Brig. Gen. Vols., 15 April, 1862. Maj. Gen. Vols., 29 Nov., 1862. Mustered out of Vol. Service, 24 Aug., 1865. Lieut. Col., 1 June, 1864. Retired as Maj. Gen., 29 June, 1871. Died 16 May, 1874. Bvt. Col., 17 Sept., 1862, for gallant and meritorious service atthe Battle of Antietam, Md. Bvt. Brig. Gen., 13 March, 1865, for gallant and meritorious service in the campaign terminating in the surrender of Lee's Army. Bvt. Maj. Gen., 13 March, 1865, for gallant and meritorious service in the field during the war.

HARTWELL, CHAS. A. [Born in Mass. Appointed from Mass.]
1st Lieut. 11th Inf., 5 Aug., 1861. Col. 77th U. S. Col. Inf., 8 Dec., 1863. Trans. to 10th U. S. Col. Art., 1 Oct., 1865. Mustered out of Vol. Service, 22 Feb., 1867. Capt. 11th Inf., 4 Oct., 1866. Unassigned 14 April, 1869. Ass'd to 8th Cav., 15 Dec., 1870. Died 3 Oct., 1876. Bvt. Capt., 27 June, 1862, for gallant and meritorious service at the Battle of Gaines' Mills, Va. Bvt. Maj., 14 June, 1863, for gallant and meritorious service at the Siege of Port Hudson, La. Bvt. Lieut. Col., 13 March, 1865, for gallant and meritorious service during the war.

HARTWELL, GEORGE. [Born in Vt. Appointed from Wis.]
2nd Lieut. 2nd Cav., 3 March, 1855. Resigned 21 Aug., 1855.

HARTWICK, EDWARD E.* [Born in Mich. Appointed from Mich.]
Addl. 2nd Lieut. 3rd Cav., 12 June, 1893. 2nd Lieut. 4th Cav., 26 July, 1893. Trans. to 9th Cav., 5 Aug., 1893. Resigned. 31 Aug., 1899.

HARTZ, EDWARD L.* [Born in Pa. Appointed from Pa.]
Bvt. 2nd Lieut. 7th Inf., 1 July, 1855. 2nd Lieut. 8th Inf., 15 Aug., 1855. Reg. Adj., 27 March to 31 May, 1861. 1st Lieut., 28 Feb., 1861. Capt. A. Q. M., 17 May, 1861. Dropped 29 July, 1864. Capt. 27th Inf., 28 July, 1866. Died 11 Nov., 1868.

HARTZ, WILSON T. [Born in Penn. Appointed from Penn.]
Sergt. Maj. 6th Penn. Vols., 22 April, 1861. Discharged 27 July, 1861. 1st Lieut. 70th N. Y. Vols., 22 Oct., 1861. Capt. A. A. G. Vols., 23 Oct., 1862. Bvt. Maj. Vols., 13 March, 1865, for faithful and meritorious service. 2nd Lieut. 15th Inf., 11 May, 1866. Bvt. 1st Lieut. and Capt., 2 March, 1867, for gallant and meritorious service in the Battle of Fair Oaks, Va. Bvt. Maj., 2 March, 1867, for gallant and meritorious service in the Battle of Fredericksburg, Va. 1st Lieut. 15th Inf., 17 June, 1867. Mustered out of Vol. Ser., 1 Sept., 1867. Capt. 15th Inf., 23 Aug., 1877. Maj., 26 April, 1898. Lieut. Col. 22nd Inf., 25 May, 1899.

HARVEY, JOHN G.* [Born in N. C. Appointed from N. C.]
Bvt. 2nd Lieut. 2nd Inf., 1 July, 1831. Resigned 15 Feb., 1833.

HARVEY, PHILIP F. [Born in Ohio. Appointed from Iowa.]
1st Lieut. Asst. Surg., 16 Nov., 1868. Capt. Asst. Surg., 16 Nov., 1871. Maj. Surg., 9 Feb., 1890. Lieut. Col. Chf. Surg. Vol., 8 July, 1898, to 31 July, 1898.

HARVIE, EDWIN J. [Born in Va. Appointed from Va.]
2nd Lieut. 9th Inf., 3 March, 1855. 1st Lieut., 29 Dec., 1857. Resigned 15 March, 1861.

HARVIE, JOHN M.* [Born in Va. Appointed from Va.]
2nd Lieut. 2nd Inf., 1 July, 1837. 1st Lieut. 8th Inf., 7 July, 1838. Died 7 Sept., 1841.

HARWOOD, FRANKLIN.* [Born in R. I. Appointed at Large.]
2nd Lieut. 3rd Art., 6 May, 1861. 1st Lieut., 14 May, 1861. Trans. to Top. Eng., 24 July, 1862. Trans. to Eng., 3 March, 1863. Capt., 5 June, 1863. Bvt. Maj., 1 Aug., 1864, for gallant and meritorious service during the campaign before Richmond, Va. Bvt. Lieut. Col., 9 April, 1865, for faithful and meritorious service during the operations resulting in the fall of Richmond, Va., and the surrender of the insurgent army under Gen. Robert E. Lee. Maj. Eng., 22 Feb., 1869. Died 26 March, 1883.

HARWOOD, PAUL. [Born in Penn. Appointed from Conn.]
Priv. Co. E, 8th N. Y. State Militia, 20 April, 1861. Discharged 2 Aug., 1861. 2nd Lieut. 1st Conn. Art., 20 April, 1862. 1st Lieut., 11 Dec., 1863. Mustered out 8 June, 1864. Maj. 57th U. S. Col. Troops, 20 July, 1864. Col., 9 Jan., 1865. Mus-

tered out 19 Oct., 1866. 2nd Lieut. 27th Inf., 7 March, 1867. 1st Lieut., 8 Jan., 1868. Unassigned 14 June, 1869. Ass'd to 20th Inf., 3 Sept., 1869. Capt., 19 Sept., 1884. Retired for disability 20 April, 1891. Died 7 Aug., 1899.

HASBROUCK, ALFRED, Jr.* [Born in N. Y. Appointed from N. Y.]
2nd Lieut. 14th Inf., 13 June, 1883. 1st Lieut. 13th Inf., 24 Feb., 1891. Trans. to 14th Inf., 20 July, 1891. Capt. of Inf., 2 July, 1898. Ass'd to 14th Inf., 1 Jan., 1899.

HASBROUCK, HENRY C.* [Born in N. Y. Appointed from N. Y.]
2nd Lieut. 4th Art., 6 May, 1861. 1st Lieut., 14 May, 1861. Bvt. Capt., 25 Oct., 1862, for gallant and meritorious service in action at Blackwater Bridge, near Suffolk, Va. Capt. 4th Art., 26 July, 1866. Lieut. Col. Commandant of Cadets, 22 Aug., 1882, to 1 Feb., 1888. Bvt. Maj., 27 Feb., 1900, for gallant service in the action against Indians at Sorass Lake, Cal., 10 May, 1873. Maj. 4th Art., 5 March, 1887. Lieut. Col., 29 Oct., 1896. Col. 7th Art., 13 Feb., 1899. Brig. Gen. Vols., 27 May, 1898, to 12 June, 1899.

HASCALL, HERBERT A.* [Born in N. Y. Appointed from N. Y.]
2nd Lieut. 4th Art., 1 July, 1856. 1st Lieut., 27 Sept., 1859. Trans. to 5th Art., 14 May, 1861. Capt. A. Q. M., 3 Aug., 1861. Capt. 5th Art., 13 July, 1862. Bvt. Maj. and Lieut. Col., 13 March, 1865, for faithful and meritorious service during the war. Retired 10 Nov., 1874. Died 14 Oct., 1890

HASCALL, MILO S.* [Born in N. Y. Appointed from Ind.]
Bvt. 2nd Lieut. 3rd Art., 1 July, 1852. 2nd Lieut. 2nd Art., 31 March, 1853. Resigned 30 Sept., 1853. Col. 17th Ind. Vols., 12 June, 1861. Brig. Gen. Vols., 25 April, 1862. Resigned 27 Oct. 1864.

HASE, WM. F. Born in Wis. Appointed from Wis.]
2nd Lieut. 6th Art., 9 July, 1898. Trans. to 4th Art., 31 March, 1899.

HASKELL, ALEX. M. [Born in D. C. Appointed from Ind.]
2nd Lieut. 1st Inf., 27 June, 1856. Resigned 1 May, 1861.

HASKELL, ERNEST E. [Born in Mass. Appointed from Mass.]
Cadet at Mil. Acad., 15 June, 1896, to 12 April, 1899. 2nd Lieut. 21st Inf., 10 April, 1899.

HASKELL, HARRY L. [Born in Maine. Appointed from N. Y.]
Priv. Co. A, 125th N. Y. Vols., 26 Aug., 1862. Sergt. Maj., 26 Aug, 1862. 2nd Lieut. 125th N. Y. Vols., 16 March, 1863. Capt., 7 Dec., 1863. Mustered out 22 Sept., 1864. Capt. 7th U. S. Vet. Vols., 10 May, 1865. Mustered out 27 April, 1866. 2nd Lieut. 12th Inf., 30 Aug., 1867. Unass'd 3 June, 1869. Ass'd to 12th Inf., 3 Aug., 1870. 1st Lieut., 30 June, 1877. Capt., 2 Jan., 1888. Maj., 2 March, 1899.

HASKELL, JOSEPH T. [Born in Ohio. Appointed from Ohio.]
Capt. C. S. Vols., 19 Feb., 1863. Bvt. Maj. Vols., 13 March, 1865, for meritorious service in his department during the war. Bvt. Lieut. Col., 2 April, 1866, for faithful and zealous service in the Subsist. Dept. Capt. 23rd Inf., 28 July, 1866. Bvt. Col. Vols., 26 Nov., 1866, for faithful service in the Subsist. Dept. Mustered out of Vol. Service 8 Dec., 1866. Maj. of Inf. (24th), 28 June, 1892. Lieut. Col. of Inf. (17th), 27 Aug., 1896. Died 16 Sept., 1898.

HASKIN, JOSEPH A.* [Born in N. Y. Appointed from N. Y.]
2nd Lieut. 1st Art., 1 July, 1839. 1st Lieut., 31 Aug., 1844. Capt. A. Q. M., 12 Aug., 1848, to 22 Feb., 1851. Capt. 1st Art., 22 Feb., 1851. Maj. 3rd Art., 20 Feb., 1862. Lieut. Col. A. A. de C., 26 June, 1862. Brig. Gen. Vols., 5 Aug., 1864. Mustered out Vols., 30 April, 1866. Lieut. Col. 1st Art., 26 July, 1866. Retired 15 Dec., 1870. Died 3 Aug., 1874. Bvt. Capt., 18 April, 1847, for gallant and meritorious conduct at Cerro Gordo. Bvt. Maj., 13 Sept., 1847, for gallant and meritorious conduct at Chapultepec. Bvt. Lieut. Col., Col. and Brig. Gen., 13 March, 1865, or faithful and meritorious service during the war.

HASKIN, PETER V. [Born in N. Y. Appointed from N. Y.]
Priv. Co. I, 6th N. Y. Cav., 13 Feb., 1864. 1st Lieut., 1 Dec., 1864. Mustered out 9 Aug., 1865. 2nd Lieut. 5th Cav., 13 June, 1867. 1st Lieut., 22 Dec., 1868. Resigned 19 March, 1870

HASKIN, WILLIAM L. [Born in Maine. Appointed from N. Y.]
2nd Lieut. and 1st Lieut. 1st Art., 5 Aug., 1861. Bvt. Capt., 8 July, 1863, for gallant and meritorious service in the capture of Port Hudson, La. Bvt. Maj., 13 March, 1865, for good conduct and gallant service during the war. Capt. 1st Art., 28 July, 1866. Maj., 11 Aug., 1887. Lieut. Col. 2nd Art., 1 June, 1897. Col. 16 Oct., 1899.

HASKINS, THOMAS W. [Born in Mass. Appointed from Utah.]
Capt. Post Chap., 16 Nov., 1868. Resigned 27 April, 1872.

HASLITT, ROBT. E. [Born in Md. Appointed from Md.]
2nd Lieut. 3rd Drag., 21 July, 1847. Disbanded 20 July, 1848.

HASSAUREK, FRANK. [Born in Ohio. Appointed from Ohio.]
2nd Lieut. 17th Inf., 9 July, 1898. Died 19 May, 1899.

HASSLER, FERDINAND R. [Born in Switzerland. Appointed from Penn.]
Prof. Mil. Acad., 14 Feb., 1807. Resigned 14 Feb., 1810. Died 20 Nov., 1843.

HASSLER, JOHN J. S. [Born in D. C. Appointed from Army.]
Capt. 31st N. Y. Vols., 24 May, 1861. Dismissed 23 Jan., 1863. Priv. Gen. Ser., 24 Dec., 1862, to 19 Feb., 1863. 2nd Lieut. 4th Inf., 19 Feb., 1863. 1st Lieut., 25 Aug., 1864. Unassigned 21 April, 1869. Discharged 15 Oct., 1870. Bvt. Capt., 2 April, 1865, for gallant and meritorious service in front of Petersburg, Va.

HASSON, ALEXANDER B. [Born in Md. Appointed from Md.]
Asst. Surg., 29 June, 1849. Maj. Surg., 17 Aug., 1861. Died 19 March, 1877. Bvt. Lieut. Col., 13 March, 1865, for faithful and meritorious service during the war.

HASSON, PATRICK. [Born in Ireland. Appointed from Pa.]
Priv. Co. F, 4th Inf., 12 Jan., 1856. Corpl., 1 July, 1857. Sergt., 23 July, 1858. Discharged 12 Jan., 1861. 2nd Lieut. 14th Inf., 22 Jan., 1867. 1st Lieut., 12 April, 1872. Bvt. 1st Lieut., 27 Feb., 1890, for gallant service in action against Indians near Willows, Ariz., 8 Nov., 1867, where he was wounded. Capt. 14th Inf., 8 April, 1889. Retired, over 30 years' service, 28 March, 1892.

HASTINGS, DAVID H. [Born in Ireland. Appointed from Army.]
Priv. Co. B, 2nd Inf., 19 July, 1837. Corpl., 21 April, 1838. Sergt., 10 Nov., 1838. Discharged 18 July, 1840. 1st Sergt. Co. B, 2nd Inf., 18 Nov., 1840. Discharged 17 Nov., 1845. Priv. Co. K, 3rd Art., 1 Dec., 1845. Corpl., 1 July, 1846. Sergt., 18 July, 1846. 1st Sergt., 1 Aug., 1846. Trans. to Co. A, Batt. of Eng., 25 April, 1847. Bvt. 2nd Lieut. 1st Drag., 28 June, 1848. 2nd Lieut., 27 Dec., 1848. 1st Lieut., 22 Oct., 1854. Capt., 9 Jan., 1860. Maj. 5th Cav., 23 Sept., 1863. Retired 7 Dec., 1863. Died 22 Sept., 1882.

HASTINGS, JAMES. [Born in England. Appointed from Army.]
Priv., Corpl. and Sergt. Co. E, 2nd (5th) Cav., 13 July, 1858, to 22 Sept., 1862. 2nd Lieut. 5th Cav., 17 July, 1862. 1st Lieut., 25 Sept., 1863. Reg. Adj., 1 Dec., 1862, to 15 Aug., 1866. Capt., 11 Aug., 1867. Wholly retired 22 Dec., 1868. Bvt. Capt., 19 Sept., 1864, for gallant and meritorious service at the Battle of Winchester, Va. Bvt. Maj., 31 March, 1865, for gallant and meritorious service at the Battle of Dinwiddie C. H., Va.

HATCH, EDWARD. [Born in Maine. Appointed from Iowa.]
Capt. 2nd Iowa Cav., 12 Aug., 1861. Maj., 5 Sept., 1861. Lieut. Col., 11 Sept., 1861. Col., 13 June, 1862. Brig. Gen. Vols., 27 April, 1864. Bvt. Maj. Gen., 15 Dec., 1864, for gallant and meritorious service in the battle, before Nashville, Tenn. Mustered out of Vol. Service 15 Jan., 1866. Col. 9th Cav., 28 July, 1866. Bvt. Brig. Gen., 2 March, 1867, for gallant and meritorious service in the Battle of Franklin, Tenn. Bvt. Maj. Gen., 2 March, 1867, for gallant and meritorious service in the Battle of Nashville, Tenn., — Dec., 1864. Died 11 April, 1889.

HATCH, EVERARD E.* [Born in Maine. Appointed from Maine.]
2nd Lieut. 18th Inf., 15 June, 1884. 1st Lieut., 16 June, 1890. Capt., 26 April, 1898.

HATCH, HENRY J. [Born in Mich. Appointed from Mich.]
2nd Lieut. 2nd Art., 9 July, 1898. Trans. to 4th Art., 27 Dec., 1898.

HATCH, JOHN P.* [Born in N. Y. Appointed from N. Y.]
Bvt. 2nd Lieut. 3rd Inf., 1 July, 1845. Trans. to Mounted Rifles, 17 July, 1846. 2nd Lieut., 18 April, 1847. Reg. Adj., 1 Nov., 1847, to 1 May, 1850. Bvt. 1st Lieut., 20 Aug., 1847, for gallant and meritorious service in the Battles of Contreras and Churubusco. Bvt. Capt., 13 Sept., 1847, for gallant and meritorious service in the Battle of Chapultepec. 1st Lieut. Mounted Rifles, 30 June, 1851. Capt., 13 Oct., 1860; 3rd Cav., 3 Aug., 1861. Brig. Gen. Vols., 28 Sept., 1861. Bvt. Maj., 30 Aug., 1862, for gallant and meritorious service in the Battle of Manassas, Va.. Bvt. Lieut. Col., 14 Sept., 1862, for gallant and meritorious service in the Battle of South Mountain, Md. Maj. 4th Cav., 27 Oct., 1863. Bvt. Col., 13 March, 1865, for gallant and meritorious service during the war. Bvt. Brig. Gen., 13 March, 1865, for gallant and meritorious service in the field during the war. Bvt. Maj. Gen. Vols., 13 March, 1865, for gallant and meritorious service during the war. Mustered out of Vol. Service 15 Jan., 1866. Lieut. Col. 5th Cav., 15 Jan., 1873. Trans. to 4th Cav., 10 April, 1873. Col. 2nd Cav., 26 June, 1881. Retired by operation of law, 9 Jan., 1886. Medal of Honor for distinguished gallantry in the Battle of South Mountain, Md., 14 Sept., 1862, where he was severely wounded while leading one of his brigades in the attack under a severe fire from the enemy; while serving as Brig. Gen. of Vols., commanding division.

HATFIELD, CHAS. A. P.* [Born in Ala. Appointed from Md.]
2nd Lieut. 4th Cav., 14 June, 1872. 1st Lieut., 28 June, 1878. Capt., 26 Nov., 1884. Maj. 8th Cav., 16 Oct., 1898. Bvt. Maj., 27 Feb., 1890, for gallant services in action against Indians in the attack on Geronimo's Camp, in the Santa Cruz Mountains, Mexico, 16 May, 1886.

HATHAWAY, FORREST H. [Born in Vt. Appointed from Vt.]
Priv. Co. G, 16th Vt. Vols., 4 Sept., 1862. Discharged 10 Aug., 1863. Capt. 107th U. S. Col. Troops, 30 June, 1864. Bvt. Maj. Vols., 25 July, 1866, for faithful service. Mustered out 20 Feb., 1867. 2nd Lieut. 41st Inf., 7 March, 1867. Bvt. 1st Lieut., 7 March, 1867, for gallant and meritorious service in the Battle of Fair Oaks, Va., 27 Oct., 1864. Bvt. Capt., 7 March, 1867, for gallant and meritorious service in the Battle of Newmarket, Va. Trans. to 40th Inf., 27 Nov., 1867. R. Q. M., 24 Dec., 1867, to 20 April, 1869. Unassigned 20 April, 1869. Ass'd to 5th Inf., 17 Dec., 1869. Reg. Adj., 31 Jan. to 10 June, 1870. 1st Lieut., 4 Sept., 1878. R. Q. M., 10 June, 1870, to 22 Feb., 1882. Capt. A. Q. M., 13 Feb., 1882. Maj. Q. M., 12 Sept., 1894. Lieut. Col. Q. M. Vols., 3 Sept., 1898, to 2 March, 1899.

HATHEWAY, JOHN M. [Born in Conn. Appointed from Conn.]
2nd Lieut. 9th Inf., 24 April, 1847. Resigned 31 March, 1848. Bvt. 1st Lieut., 13 Sept., 1847, for gallant and meritorious conduct in Battle of Chapultepec. Died 17 Jan., 1890.

HATHEWAY, JOHN S.* [Born in N. Y. Appointed from N. Y.]
Bvt. 2nd Lieut. 1st Art., 1 July, 1836. 2nd Lieut., 31 Aug., 1836. 1st Lieut., 7 July, 1838. Capt., 3 March, 1847. Died 31 March, 1853. Bvt. Maj., 20 Aug., 1847, for gallant and meritorious conduct at Contreras and Churubusco, Mex.

HAUGHEY, JAMES A. [Born in Del. Appointed from Del.]
1st Lieut. 3rd Del. Vols., 7 Nov., 1861. Capt., 1 Dec., 1862. Mustered out 6 Dec., 1864. Capt. 8th U. S. Vet. Vols., 21 Aug., 1865. Mustered out 28 April, 1866. 2nd Lieut. 36th Inf., 28 July, 1866. 1st Lieut., 21 May, 1868. Unassigned 19 May, 1869. Ass'd to 21st Inf., 15 Dec., 1870. Capt., 15 Aug., 1880. Died 18 July, 1890.

HAUGHEY, JOHN V. [Born in Ireland. Appointed from Del.]
Capt. 15th Inf., 14 May, 1861. Resigned 27 May, 1862.

HAUPT, HERMAN.* [Born in Penn. Appointed from Penn.]
Bvt. 2nd Lieut. 3rd Inf., 1 July, 1835. Resigned 30 Sept., 1835. Col. A. A. de C., 27 April, 1862. Brig. Gen. Vols., 5 Sept., 1862. Declined 5 Sept., 1863.

HAUPT, LEWIS M.* [Born in Penn. Appointed from Ga.]
2nd Lieut. Eng., 17 June, 1867. Resigned 20 Sept., 1869.

HAVARD, VALERY. [Born in France. Appointed from N. Y.]
1st Lieut. Asst. Surg., 10 Nov., 1874. Capt. Asst. Surg., 10 Nov., 1879. Maj. Surg., 27 Feb., 1891. Lieut. Col. Chief Surg. Vols., 1 Aug. to 5 Nov., 1898.

HAVILAND, JOHN V. S. [Born in Penn. Appointed from Penn.]
2nd Lieut. o Inf., 5 March, 1847; 3rd Drag., 9 April, 1847. Reg. Adj., 15 June to 20 Dec., 1847. Resigned 20 Dec., 1847.

HAWES, JAMES M.* [Born in Ky. Appointed from Ky.]
Bvt. 2nd Lieut. 2nd Drag., 1 July, 1845. 2nd Lieut., 25 April, 1846. 1st Lieut., 13 Jan., 1850. Capt., 13 Dec., 1855. Resigned 9 May, 1861. Bvt. 1st Lieut., 1 Aug., 1847, for gallant and meritorious conduct at San Juan de los Llamos, Mexico. Died 22 Nov., 1889.

HAWES, JOHN J. [Born in Ky. Appointed from Ky.]
2nd Lieut. 7th Ind. Batty, 9 Jan., 1862. 1st Lieut., 1 Sept., 1862. Resigned 23 Dec., 1862. 2nd Lieut. 1st Ky. Art., 17 June, 1863. 1st Lieut., 30 Oct., 1863. Capt., 1 Jan., 1864. Mustered out 20 Jan., 1865. 2nd Lieut. 1st Art., 23 April, 1866. 1st Lieut., 28 July, 1866. Discharged 31 Dec., 1870.

HAWK, ADAM. [Born in Penn. Appointed from Ala.]
1st Lieut. of Inf., 8 March, 1847; 13th Inf., 9 April, 1847. Capt., 28 May, 1847. Disbanded 15 July, 1848.

HAWKINS, CLYDE E.* [Born in Penn. Appointed from Penn.]
Addl. 2nd Lieut. 3rd Cav., 12 June, 1895. 2nd Lieut., 8 Aug., 1895. 1st Lieut. 7th Cav., 29 March, 1899.

HAWKINS, EDGAR S.* [Born in N. Y. Appointed from N. Y.]
2nd Lieut. 3rd Inf., 1 July, 1820. Trans. to 7th Inf., 24 July, 1820. 1st Lieut., 22 Jan., 1824. Capt., 10 Nov., 1829. Maj. 1st Inf., 16 Feb., 1847. Trans. to 2nd Inf., 2 July, 1856. Retired 26 Oct., 1861. Died 5 Nov., 1865. Bvt. Maj., 9 May, 1846, for gallant and distinguished service in defence of Fort Brown, Tex.

HAWKINS, FRANK B. [Born in Penn. Appointed from Penn.]
1st Lieut. 10th Penn. Vols., 11 May, 1898. Capt., 12 May, 1898, to muster out, 17 June, 1899. 2nd Lieut. 3rd Inf., 1 May, 1899. Trans. to 15th Inf., 31 Oct., 1899.

HAWKINS, GEORGE W.* [Born in N. C. Appointed from N. C.]
Bvt. 2nd Lieut. 1st Inf., 1 July, 1844. Trans. to Mounted Rifles, 17 July, 1846. 2nd Lieut., 18 April, 1847. 1st Lieut., 30 June, 1851. Dismissed 27 Jan., 1853.

HAWKINS, HAMILTON S. [Born in Md. Appointed from Md.]
Asst. Surg., 22 Nov., 1824. Maj. Surg., 4 July, 1836. Died 7 Aug., 1847.

HAWKINS, HAMILTON S. [Born in S. C. Appointed from N. Y.]
Cadet at Mil. Acad., 1 July, 1852, to 31 Jan., 1855. 2nd Lieut. 6th Inf., 26 April, 1861, and 1st Lieut., 14 May, 1861. R. Q. M., 25 Dec., 1861, to 20 Sept., 1863. Bvt. Capt., 2 July, 1863, for gallant and meritorious service in the Battle of Gettysburg, Penn., declined. Capt. 6th Inf., 20 Sept., 1863. Bvt. Maj., 11 Oct., 1865, for meritorious servive, declined. Maj. 10th Inf., 31 Oct., 1883. Lieut. Col. Commandant Cadets 1 Feb., 1888, to ——. Lieut. Col. 23rd Inf., 17 Feb., 1889. Col. 16th Inf., 13 Aug., 1894. Trans. to 20th Inf., 15 Sept., 1894. Brig. Gen. Vols., 4 May, 1898. Maj. Gen. Vols., 8 July, to 30 Nov., 1898. Brig. Gen., 28 Sept., 1898. Retired, after 40 years' service, 4 Oct., 1898.

HAWKINS, HAMILTON S.* [Born in Dak. Appointed from Del.]
Addl. 2nd Lieut. 4th Cav., 12 June, 1894. 2nd Lieut. 10th Cav., 30 Aug., 1894. Trans. to 4th Cav., 18 Sept., 1894. 1st Lieut., 2 March, 1899.

HAWKINS, JOHN P.* [Born in Ind. Appointed from Ind.]
Bvt. 2nd Lieut. 6th Inf., 1 July, 1852. 2nd Lieut. 2nd Inf., 23 June, 1854. 1st Lieut., 12 Oct., 1857. R. Q. M., 1 Oct., 1858, to 10 Aug., 1861. 1st Lieut. 14th Inf., 14 May, 1861, declined. Capt. C. S., 3 Aug., 1861. Lieut. Col. C. S. (Act 17 July, 1862), 1 Nov., 1862, to 13 April, 1863. Brig. Gen. Vols., 13 April, 1863. Bvt. Maj., 13 March, 1865, for gallant and meritorious service during the Siege of Mobile, Ala., Bvt. Lieut. Col. and Col., 13 March, 1865, for gallant and meritorious service during the war. Bvt. Brig. Gen. and Maj. Gen., 13th March, 1865, for gallant and meritorious service in the field during the war. Bvt. Maj. Gen. Vols., 30 June, 1865, for gallant and meritorious service during the war. Mustered out of Vol. Service 1 Feb., 1866. Maj. C. S., 23 June, 1874. Lieut. Col. Asst. C. G. S., 3 Sept., 1889. Col. Asst. C. G. S., 12 March, 1892. Brig. Gen. C. G. S., 22 Dec., 1892. Retired, by operation of law, 29 Sept., 1894.

HAWKINS, THOS. T. [Born in Ky. Appointed from Ky.]
2nd Lieut. 16th Inf., 9 April, 1847. Disbanded 10 Aug., 1848.

HAWKINS, THOS. L. [Born in N. C. Appointed from N. C.]
1st Lieut. Asst. Dep. Com. of Ord., 6 Aug., 1813. Retained as 1st Lieut. Ord., 6 Aug., 1813. Resigned 31 Jan., 1816.

HAWLEY, PHILIP. [Born in ——. Appointed from ——.]
2nd Lieut. 16th Inf., —— ——, 1892. Dropped 10 June, 1892.

HAWLEY, WM. [Born in D. C. Appointed from D. C.]
Priv. Co. H, 3rd Batt. D. C. Vols., 15 April, 1861. Discharged 15 July, 1861. 2nd Lieut. and 1st Lieut. 3rd Cav., 5 Aug., 1861. Capt., 15 Feb., 1864. Maj. 4th Cav., 20 March, 1879. Retired 14 June, 1879.

HAWLEY, WM. [Born in N. Y. Appointed from Wis.]
Priv., Corpl. and Sergt. Batty M, 3rd Art., 26 July, 1847, to 27 July, 1848. Capt. 3rd Wis. Vols., 24 April, 1861. Lieut. Col., 14 Nov., 1862. Col., 29 June, 1864. Bvt. Brig. Gen. Vols., 16 March, 1865, for gallant service in the campaign in Ga. and S. C. Mustered out 18 July, 1865. 2nd Lieut. 11th Inf., 11 May, 1866. Trans. to 20th Inf., 21 Sept., 1866. 1st Lieut., 6 Dec., 1866. Died 15 Jan., 1873.

HAWTHORNE, HARRY L. [Born in Minn. Appointed from Ky.]
2nd Lieut. 2nd Art., 30 Oct., 1884. 1st Lieut. 4th Art., 28 Aug., 1891. Medal of Honor for gallantry, coolness, discretion, and effect in handling and serving the guns of his command in action against hostile Sioux Indians on Wounded Knee

Creek, S. Dak., 29 Dec., 1890, where he was severely wounded; while 2nd Lieut. 2nd Art., and commanding platoon of light Batty E, 1st Art. (two Hotchkiss mountain howitzers). Graduate of the Artillery School, 1888. Capt. A. Q. M. Vols., 17 Oct., 1898, declined. Maj. 29th U. S. Vols., 5 July, 1899, to ——.

HAY, CHAS. [Born in Ohio. Appointed from Ohio.]
Priv. Co. C, 8th Ohio Vols., 23 April, 1861. Discharged 23 July, 1861. Priv. Co. H, 23rd Ohio Vols., 24 July, 1861. Corpl., 28 April, 1862. Com. Sergt., 21 Jan., 1863. Priv. Co. B, 1 July, 1864. Discharged 24 July, 1864. Capt. 5th U. S. Vet. Vols., 20 Feb., 1865. Mustered out 28 May, 1866. 2nd Lieut. 36th Inf., 22 Jan., 1867. Unassigned 19 May, 1869. Ass'd to 23rd Inf., 14 July, 1869. 1st Lieut., 1 Jan., 1871. Capt. C. S., 10 Dec., 1888. Died 27 June, 1892.

HAY, CHAS. E. [Born in Ind. Appointed from Mo.]
2nd Lieut. 3rd Cav., 5 Aug., 1861. 1st Lieut., 5 Nov., 1861. Resigned 9 Oct., 1865. Bvt. Capt., 22 June, 1865, for meritorious service during the war.

HAY, CHARLES E. Jr. [Born in Ill. Appointed from Ill.]
2nd Lieut. 24th Inf., 10 April, 1899.

HAY, LEONARD. [Born in Ind. Appointed from Army.]
Priv. Co. D, 3rd Batt., 5th Inf., 18 June, 1864. 2nd Lieut. 9th Inf., 2 July, 1864. 1st Lieut., 29 Sept., 1864. Reg. Adj., 1 July, 1865, to 11 March, 1878. Capt., 11 March, 1878. Retired for disability, 15 June, 1891.

HAY, THOS. H. [Born in N. Y. Appointed from N. Y.]
1st Lieut. 54th N. Y. Vols., 1 Dec., 1862. Mustered out 31 May, 1864. 1st Lieut. Vet. Res. Corps, 30 May, 1864. Bvt. Maj. Vols., 13 March, 1865, for gallant and meritorious service in the Battles of Chancellorsville, Va., and Gettysburg, Pa. Capt. Vet. Res. Corps, 21 Feb., 1865. Mustered out 31 March, 1867. 1st Lieut. 42nd Inf., 22 Jan., 1867. Bvt. Capt., 2 March, 1867, for gallant and meritorious service in the Battle of Chancellorsville, Va. Bvt. Maj., 2 March, 1867, for gallant and meritorious service in the Battle of Gettysburg, Pa. Unassigned 22 April, 1869. Retired with rank of Capt., 31 Dec., 1870. Died 7 Dec., 1881.

HAY, WM. H.* [Born in Fla. Appointed from Fla.]
2nd Lieut. 3rd Cav., 1 July, 1886. 1st Lieut. 10th Cav., 21 July, 1893. Graduate of the Infantry and Cavalry School, 1891. Capt. A. Q. M. Vols., 26 Nov., 1898, to——.

HAYCOCK, JUDSON. [Born in Maine. Appointed from Cal.]
Cadet Mil. Acad., 1 July, 1855, to 30 June, 1856. 2nd Lieut. 1st Cav., 26 Aug., 1861. 1st Lieut., 13 Jan., 1862. Capt., 29 Dec., 1863. Dismissed 12 Nov., 1864.

HAYDEN, HORACE J. [Born in Mass. Appointed from Mass.]
2nd Lieut. 3rd Art., 5 Aug., 1861. 1st Lieut., 5 Aug., 1861. Resigned 31 Oct., 1868. Bvt. Capt., 27 June, 1862, for gallant and meritorious service at the Battle of Gaines' Mills, Va. Bvt. Maj., 13 March, 1865, for good conduct and gallant service during the war.

HAYDEN, JEREMIAH D. [Born in N. J. Appointed from N. J.]
1st Lieut. 15th Inf., 12 March, 1812. Capt., 13 March, 1813. Disbanded 15 June, 1815. Reinstated in Corps Art. as 1st Lieut., 2 Dec., 1815, with Bvt. rank of Capt. from 13 March, 1813. Capt. Ord., 1 Jan., 1816, to rank from 9 Feb., 1815. Trans. to 4th Art., 1 June, 1821. Resigned 21 May, 1822. Maj. P. M., 1 July, 1824. Died 10 June, 1826.

HAYDEN, JNO. L.* [Born in Ill. Appointed from Wash.]
2nd Lieut. 1st Art., 11 June, 1888. 1st Lieut., 2 Oct., 1894. Graduate of the Artillery School, 1898.

HAYDEN, JULIUS. [Born in N. Y. Appointed from Fla.]
2nd Lieut. 2nd Inf. 16 Jan., 1839. 1st Lieut., 18 June, 1846. Capt., 30 June, 1850. Maj. 10th Inf., 15 Feb., 1862. Lieut. Col. A. I. G., 13 March, to 31 Oct., 1863. Lieut. Col., 15th Inf., 28 July, 1866. Unassigned 15 March, 1869. Retired 6 May, 1870. Died 29 Oct., 1878. Bvt. Capt., 20 Aug., 1847, for gallant and meritorious conduct at Contreras and Churubusco. Bvt. Lieut. Col., 1 Aug., 1864, for faithful and meritorious service. Bvt. Col., 23 Jan., 1865, for faithful service in action at Chancellorsville, Va. Bvt. Brig. Gen., 13 March, 1865, for gallant and distinguished service in the field.

HAYES, EDMUND.* [Born in Pa. Appointed from Pa.]
Bvt. 2nd Lieut. 1st Art., 1 July, 1846. 2nd Lieut. 4th Art., 16 Feb., 1847. 1st Lieut., 13 Sept., 1847. Died 25 Nov., 1853.

HAYES, EDWARD M. [Born in N. Y. Appointed from N. J.]
Musician Gen. Mtd. Ser., 28 Aug., 1855. Bugler Co. H, 2nd Cav., 15 Feb., 1857. Trans. to Co. B, 1 July, 1859. Discharged 28 Aug., 1860. 1st Lieut. 10th Ohio Cav., 15 Jan., 1863. Capt., 24 March, 1864. Bvt. Maj. Vols., 13 March, 1865, for gallant and meritorious service during the campaigns in Georgia and the Carolinas. Mustered out 24 July, 1865. 2nd Lieut. 5th Cav., 23 Feb., 1866. 1st Lieut., 20 Aug., 1866. R. Q. M., 20 June, 1869, to 1 May, 1872. Capt., 15 Aug., 1874. Bvt. Capt., Feb. 27, 1890, for gallant service in action against Indians at Beaver Creek, Kans., 25 and 26 Oct., 1868. Maj. 7th Cav., 7 April, 1893. Lieut. Col. 4th Cav., 1 July, 1899.

HAYES, JACK. [Born in Neb. Appointed at Large.]
2nd Lieut. 16th Inf., 10 April, 1899.

HAYMAN, SAML. B.* [Born in Penn. Appointed from Penn.]
Bvt. 2nd Lieut. 1st Inf., 1 July, 1842. 2nd Lieut. 7th Inf., 21 July, 1844. 1st Lieut., 16 Feb., 1847. Capt., 3 March, 1855. Col. 37th N. Y. Vols., 28 Sept., 1861. Maj. 10th Inf., 21 Jan., 1863. Bvt. Lieut. Col., 3 May, 1863, for gallant and meritorious service in the Battle of Chancellorsville, Va. Mustered out of Vol. Service, 22 June, 1863. Bvt. Col., 6 May, 1864, for gallant and meritorious service in the Battle of the Wilderness, Va. Bvt. Brig. Gen. Vols., 13 March, 1865, for gallant service in the Battle of Fair Oaks, Va. Lieut. Col. 17th Inf., 15 Sept., 1867. Retired 1 July, 1872. Died 1 May, 1895.

HAYMOND, HENRY. [Born in Va. Appointed from Va.]
Capt. 18th Inf., 26 Oct., 1861. Trans. to 27th Inf., 21 Sept., 1866. Unassigned 14 June, 1869. Discharged 1 Nov., 1870. Bvt. Maj., 20 Sept., 1863, for gallant and

meritorious service at the Battle of Murfreeboro, Tenn., and Chickamauga, Ga. Bvt. Lieut. Col., 13 March, 1865, for gallant and meritorious service during the war.

HAYNE, ARTHUR P. [Born in S. C. Appointed from S. C.]
1st Lieut. Light Drag., 3 May, 1808. Capt., 10 Nov., 1809. Maj. 1st Light Drag., 1 Aug., 1813. Col. I. G., 12 April, 1814. Col. A. G., 1 March, 1815. Disbanded 15 June, 1815. Restored as Col. I. G., 3 May, 1816. Resigned 20 Sept., 1820. Maj. and P. M., 4 July, 1836. Resigned 25 Oct., 1836. Bvt. Lieut. Col., 23 Dec., 1814, for gallant conduct at New Orleans.

HAYNE, PAUL T., Jr. [Born in S. C. Appointed from S. C.]
Priv. and Corpl. Troop K, 5th Cav., 30 Aug., 1897, to 30 April, 1899. 2nd Lieut. 8th Cav., 1 May, 1899.

HAYNES, IRA A.* [Born in Ky. Appointed from Ky.]
2nd Lieut. 3rd Art., 13 June, 1883. 1st Lieut. 4th Art., 1 April, 1891. Capt. 6th Art., 10 July, 1899. Graduate of the Artillery School, 1888. Capt. A. Q. M. Vols., 26 Nov., 1898, declined.

HAYNES, JAMES M.* [Born in Tenn. Appointed from Ala.]
Bvt. 2nd Lieut. 4th Art., 1 July, 1848. 2nd Lieut. 1st Art., 29 Oct., 1848. Died 16 Sept., 1850.

HAYNES, MILTON A.* [Born in Tenn. Appointed from Tenn.]
Bvt. 2nd Lieut. 3rd Art., 1 July, 1838. 2nd Lieut., 7 July, 1838. Resigned 30 Sept., 1839. Capt. 1st Tenn. Cav., 9 June, 1846. Mustered out 31 May, 1847.

HAYNES, PRESTON G. [Born in Tenn. Appointed from Tenn.]
1st Lieut. of Inf., 22 March, 1847; 14th Inf., 9 April, 1847. Resigned 21 Dec., 1847.

HAYNSWORTH, HENRY J. [Born in S. C. Appointed from N. Y.]
Capt. A. Q. M., 26 Feb., 1885. Retired by operation of law 25 Oct., 1891. Died 4 Feb., 1892.

HAYS, ALEXANDER.* [Born in Penn. Appointed from Penn.]
Bvt. 2nd Lieut. 4th Inf., 1 July, 1844. 2nd Lieut. 8th Inf., 18 June, 1846. Resigned 12 April, 1848. Maj. 12th Pa. Vols., 25 April, 1861. Mustered out 5 Aug., 1861. Capt. 16th Inf., 14 May, 1861. Col. 63rd Pa. Vols., 9 Oct., 1861. Brig. Gen. Vols., 29 Sept., 1862. Bvt. Maj. Gen. Vols., 5 May, 1865, for gallant and distinguished conduct at the Battles of the Peninsula, Gettysburg, and the Wilderness. Killed 5 May, 1864, at Battle of Wilderness, Va. Bvt. 1st Lieut., 9 May, 1846, for gallant conduct at Palo Alto and Resaca de la Palma. Bvt. Maj., 30 June, 1862, for gallant and meritorious service at the Battles of Fair Oaks, Peach Orchard, and Glendale, Va. Bvt. Lieut. Col., 1 July, 1862, for gallant and meritorious service at the Battle of Malvern Hill, Va. Bvt. Col., 2 July, 1863, for gallant and meritorious service at the Battle of Gettysburg, Pa.

HAYS, CHARLES E. [Born in Ill. Appointed from the Army.]
Priv. and Corpl. Co. F, 18th Inf., 26 Sept., 1888, to 1 Aug., 1891. 2nd Lieut. of Inf. (18th), 31 July, 1891. Resigned 6 Jan., 1897.

HAYS, HENRY B. [Born in Penn. Appointed from Penn.]
Capt. 3rd Cav., 14 May, 1861; 6th Cav., 3 Aug., 1861. Rejected by Senate, 5 Aug., 1861. Capt. 6th Cav., 5 Aug., 1861. Resigned 5 July, 1864. Died 10 Aug., 1881.

HAYS, JAMES C. C. [Born in Tenn. Appointed from Miss.]
2nd Lieut. 14th Inf., 12 April, 1847. Disbanded 25 July, 1848.

HAYS, JOHN B. [Born in Penn. Appointed from Penn.]
2nd Lieut. 19th Inf., 24 Oct., 1861. 1st Lieut., 5 April, 1862. Capt., 28 April, 1865. Bvt. Maj., 8 June, 1865, for faithful service during the war. Resigned 19 Sept., 1865.

HAYS, JOSEPH H. [Born in Vt. Appointed from N. Y.]
2nd Lieut. 142nd N. Y. Vols., 29 Sept., 1862. 1st Lieut., 22 Jan., 1863. Mustered out 22 Dec., 1864. 2nd Lieut. 12th Inf., 23 Feb., 1866. Trans. to 30th Inf., 21 Sept., 1866. 1st Lieut., 28 July, 1866. Bvt. Capt., 2 March, 1867, for gallant and meritorious service in the Battle of Drury's Farm. Unassigned 23 March, 1869. Retired 31 Dec., 1870. Died 8 April, 1894.

HAYS, STOKELY D. [Born in ——. Appointed from Tenn.]
Q. M. G. Tenn. Vols., 1812 to 1814. J. A., 10 Sept., 1818. Disbanded 1 June, 1821.

HAYS, WM.* [Born in Va. Appointed from Tenn.]
2nd Lieut. 2nd Art., 1 July, 1840. 1st Lieut., 3 March, 1847. Capt., 8 Oct., 1853. Maj. 5th Art., 1 Aug., 1863. Lieut. Col. A. A. de C., 28 Sept., 1861. Brig. Gen. Vols., 29 Nov., 1862. Mustered out of Vol. Ser., 15 Jan., 1866. Died 7 Feb., 1875. Bvt. Capt., 20 Aug., 1847, for gallant and meritorious conduct at Contreras and Churubusco. Bvt. Maj., 13 Sept., 1847, for gallant and meritorious conduct at Chapultepec. Bvt. Lieut. Col., 1 July, 1862, for gallant and meritorious service during the Peninsula campaign in Virginia. Bvt. Col., 13 March, 1865, for gallant and meritorious service during the war. Bvt. Brig. Gen., 13 March, 1865, for gallant and meritorious service in the field during the war.

HAYWARD, JAMES C. [Born in Md. Appointed from Md.]
2nd Lieut. Corps Art., 28 Jan., 1820. Trans. to 3rd Inf., 1 June, 1821. Resigned 1 Sept., 1821.

HAYWARD, ROBERT S. [Born in Md. Appointed from Fla.]
1st Lieut. of Inf., 8 March, 1847; 13th Inf., 9 April, 1847. Disbanded 15 July, 1848.

HAYWARD, SAMUEL. [Born in Ohio. Appointed from Ohio.]
Capt. 13th Inf., 14 May, 1861. Resigned 14 May, 1862.

HAYWARD, WM. B. [Born in Md. Appointed from Army.]
Priv., Corpl. and Sergt. Co. A, and Sergt. Maj. 1st Art., 21 July, 1831, to 7 July, 1838. 2nd Lieut. 8th Inf., 7 July, 1838. 1st Lieut., 31 Aug., 1841. Resigned 31 Dec., 1842. Col. 60th N. Y. Vols., 25 Oct., 1861. Resigned 8 Jan., 1862. Lieut. Col. 102nd N. Y. Vols., 7 March, 1862. Resigned 16 July, 1872. Died 26 Jan., 1888.

HAZARD, WM. W. [Born in R. I. Appointed from Mass.]
Hosp. Surg.'s Mate, 14 May, 1813. Resigned 20 Sept., 1816.

HAZELTON, JAMES B. [Born in N. Y. Appointed from N. Y.]
Sergt. Co. C, 1st N. Y. Light Art., 6 Sept., 1861. 2nd Lieut., 15 Sept., 1862. 1st

Lieut., 14 April, 1864. Capt., 22 Dec., 1864. Mustered out 16 June, 1865. 2nd Lieut. 4th Art., 11 May, 1866. 1st Lieut., 28 July, 1866. Dismissed 19 Nov., 1873. Bvt. 1st Lieut. and Capt., 2 March, 1867, for gallant and meritorious service during the war.

HAZEN, HENRY E. [Born in Vt. Appointed from Ohio.]
2nd Lieut. 8th Inf., 5 Aug., 1861. 1st Lieut., 3 Oct., 1864. Capt., 18 Feb., 1869. Unassigned 3 May, 1869. Died 14 Aug., 1869. Bvt. 1st Lieut., 4 July, 1862, for gallant and meritorious service during the Peninsular campaign in Virginia. Bvt. Capt., 13 Dec., 1862, for gallant and meritorious service at the Battle of Fredericksburg, Va.

HAZEN, WM. B.* [Born in Vt. Appointed from Ohio.]
Bvt. 2nd Lieut. 4th Inf., 1 July, 1855. 2nd Lieut., 8th Inf., 4 Sept., 1855. Bvt. 1st Lieut., 16 May, 1859, for gallant conduct in two several engagements with Indians in Texas. 1st Lieut. 8th Inf., 1 April, 1861. Capt., 14 May, 1861. Capt. 17th Inf., 14 May, 1861, declined. Col. 41st Ohio Vols., 29 Oct., 1861. Brig. Gen. Vols., 29 Nov., 1862. Bvt. Maj., 20 Sept., 1863, for gallant and meritorious service in the Battle of Chickamauga, Ga. Bvt. Lieut. Col., 24 Nov., 1863, for gallant and meritorious service in the Battle of Chattanooga, Tenn. Bvt. Col., 1 Sept., 1864, for gallant and meritorious service in the capture of Atlanta, Ga. Bvt. Brig. Gen., 13 March, 1865, for gallant and meritorious service in the capture of Fort McAllister, Ga. Bvt. Maj. Gen., 13 March, 1865, for gallant and meritorious service in the field during the war. Maj. Gen. Vols., 13 Dec., 1864, for long and continued service of the highest character and for special gallantry and service at Fort McAllister. Mustered out of Vol. Service, 15 Jan., 1866. Col. 38th Inf., 28 July, 1866. Trans. to 6th Inf., 15 March, 1869. Brig. Gen. Chf. Sig. Off., 15 Dec., 1880. Died 16 Jan., 1887.

HAZLETT, CHAS. E.* [Born in Ohio. Appointed from Ohio.]
2nd Lieut. 2nd Cav., 6 May, 1861. 1st Lieut. 5th Art., 14 May, 1861. Killed 2 July, 1863, at the Battle of Gettysburg, Pa.

HAZLITT, ROBT.* [Born in Penn. Appointed from Ohio.]
Bvt. 2nd Lieut., 4th Inf., 1 July, 1843. 2nd Lieut. 3rd Inf., 3 Nov., 1845. Killed 21 Sept., 1846, in the Battle of Monterey, Mexico.

HAZZARD, DAVID. [Born in Del. Appointed from Army.]
Priv. and Sergt. Co. F, 11th Inf., 5 Dec., 1861, to 23 Feb., 1863. 2nd Lieut. 11th Inf., 19 Feb., 1863. 1st Lieut., 12 July, 1864. Resigned 28 May,, 1866. Bvt. Capt., 1 Oct., 1864, for gallant service at the Battle of the Wilderness and during the campaign before Richmond, Va.

HAZZARD. GEORGE W.* [Born in Del. Appointed from Ind.]
2nd Lieut. 4th Art., 1 July, 1847. 1st Lieut., 31 March, 1850. Reg. Adj., 13 April, 1855, to 14 Dec., 1857. Capt., 6 July, 1859. Col. 37th Ind. Vols., 17 Oct., 1861. Resigned from Vols., 5 March, 1862. Died 14 Aug., 1862, of wounds received in the Battle of White Oak Swamp, Va.

HAZZARD, R. EDWARD.* [Born in S. C. Appointed from S. C.]
Bvt. 2nd Lieut. 4th Art., 1 July, 1824. 2nd Lieut. 2nd Art., 1 July, 1824. Resigned 30 Sept., 1829. Died 9 Aug., 1831.

HAZZARD, SAMUEL C.* [Born in Penn. Appointed from Penn.]
Addl. 2nd Lieut. 1st Art., 12 June, 1893. 2nd Lieut. 5th Art., 10 Sept., 1893. Trans. to 1st Art., 27 Oct., 1893. 1st Lieut., 2 March, 1899.

HEAD, GEORGE E. [Born in Mass. Appointed from Mass.]
1st Lieut. 11th Inf., 14 May, 1861. Reg. Adj., 1 Oct., 1862, to 24 April, 1863. Capt., 12 July, 1864. Bvt. Maj., 1 Aug., 1864, for gallant conduct in the Battle of Spottsylvania. Trans. to 29th Inf., 21 Sept., 1866. Unassigned 25 April, 1869. Ass'd to 3rd Inf., 1 Jan., 1871. Maj., 20 April, 1886. Lieut. Col. 14th Inf., 19 May, 1891. Retired for over 30 years' service, 10 July, 1891.

HEAD, JOHN F. [Born in Mass. Appointed from Mass.]
Asst. Surg., 6 Aug., 1846. Capt. Asst. Surg., 6 Aug., 1851. Maj. and Surg., 6 Sept., 1860. Bvt. Lieut. Col., 13 March, 1865, for faithful and meritorious service during the war. Lieut. Col. Surg., 26 June, 1876. Col. Surg., 30 June, 1882. Retired 9 Jan., 1885.

HEADLEY, IVORY H. B. [Born in Mass. Appointed from Mass.]
Post. Chap., 8 May, 1896.

HEALY, FRANCIS W. [Born in Wash. Appointed from Idaho.]
2nd Lieut. 8th Inf., 1 June, 1899.

HEALY, THOS. [Born in N. Y. Appointed from Army.]
Priv., Corpl. and Sergt. Co. E, 2nd Drag., 29 June, 1848, to 5 July, 1856, and from 1 Nov., 1856, to 23 Sept., 1861. Ord. Sergt., 23 Sept., 1861, to 29 Sept., 1862. 2nd Lieut. 4th Cav., 17 July, 1862. Died 23 April, 1863, of wounds received in action at Franklin, Tenn.

HEAP, DAVID P.* [Born in Asia. Appointed from Penn.]
1st Lieut. Eng., 13 June, 1864. Bvt. Capt., 2 April, 1865, for gallant and meritorious service during the Siege of Petersburg, Va. Capt. Eng., 7 March, 1867. Maj., 23 June. 1882. Lieut. Col., 10 May, 1895.

HEARD, JOHN W.* [Born in Miss. Appointed from Miss.]
2nd Lieut. 3rd Cav., 13 June, 1883. 1st Lieut., 31 Aug., 1889. Capt., 2 March, 1899. Medal of Honor for distinguished gallantry in action at the mouth of the Manimani River, west of Bahia Honda, Cuba, after two men had been shot down by Spaniards, while transmitting orders to the engine room on board the S. S. Wanderer; the ship having become disabled, Lieut. Heard took the position held by them and personally transmitted orders, remaining at his post until the ship was out of danger.

HEARN, CLINT. C.* [Born in Tex. Appointed from Tex.]
Addl. 2nd Lieut. 4th Art., 12 June, 1890. 2nd Lieut. 2nd Art., 24 April, 1891. Trans. to 4th Art., 23 Aug., 1894. 1st Lieut. 7th Art., 8 March, 1898. Graduate of the Artillery School, 1894.

HEARN, JAMES A. [Born in Ireland. Appointed from Army.]
Priv. Co. G, 5th Inf., 20 Aug., 1844. Corpl., 1 Feb., 1848. Sergt., 1 May, 1849. Discharged 9 July, 1849. Sergt. Co. G, 5th Inf., 9 July, 1849. Discharged 15 June, 1854. Sergt. Co. G, 5th Inf., 15 June, 1854. 1st Sergt., 1 May, 1855. Ord. Sergt., U. S. A., 1 Aug., 1857. Discharged 16 May, 1859. Ord. Sergt., 16 May, 1859. 2nd Lieut. 16th Inf., 27 Feb., 1863. 1st Lieut., 31 Aug., 1863. Capt., 2 April, 1866. Trans. to 34th Inf., 21 Sept., 1866. Bvt. Maj., 2 March, 1866, for faithful and meritorious service during the war. Unassigned 14 April, 1869. Retired 31 Dec., 1870. Died 20 July, 1890.

HEARN, LAWRENCE J. [Born in Tex. Appointed from Ky.]
2nd Lieut. 21st Inf., 24 Nov., 1880. 1st Lieut., 10 July, 1888. Capt., 26 April, 1898. Graduate of Infantry and Cavalry School, 1885.

HEATH, FRANK.* [Born in England. Appointed from N. Y.]
2nd Lieut. 3rd Art., 15 June, 1868. Trans. to Ord., 1 Nov., 1874. 1st Lieut., 1 Nov., 1874. Capt., 18 Dec., 1880. Maj., 7 July, 1898.

HEATON, EDWARD. [Born in Ohio. Appointed from Ohio.]
2nd Lieut. 2nd Art., 23 Aug., 1861. 1st Lieut., 24 July, 1862. Resigned 1 March, 1865.

HEAVEY, JOHN W.* [Born in Ill. Appointed from Ill.]
2nd Lieut. 5th Inf., 12 June, 1891. 1st Lieut. 11th Inf., 16 Dec., 1897.

HEBERT, LOUIS.* [Born in La. Appointed from La.]
Bvt. 2nd Lieut. Eng., 1 July, 1845. Resigned 15 Feb., 1846.

HEBERT, PAUL O.* [Born in La. Appointed from La.]
2nd Lieut. Eng., 1 July, 1840. Resigned 31 March, 1845. Lieut. Col. of Inf., 3 March, 1847; 14th Inf., 9 April, 1847. Disbanded 25 July, 1848. Bvt. Col., 8 Sept., 1847, for gallant and meritorious conduct at Molino del Rey.

HECK, JOHN H. [Born in Md. Appointed from Army.]
Priv. and Corpl. Battys B and G, 3rd Art., 24 July, 1844, to 9 Aug., 1848. Bvt. 2nd Lieut. 3rd Art., 28 June, 1848. 2nd Lieut., 28 June, 1848. Resigned 27 July, 1850.

HECKSCHER, JOHN G. [Born in N. Y. Appointed from N. Y.]
1st Lieut. 12th Inf., 14 May, 1861. Resigned 11 Aug., 1862.

HEDBERG, ALFRED. [Born in Sweden. Appointed from Army.]
Priv. 15th Inf., 19 Nov., 1862, to 21 July, 1863. 2nd Lieut. 15th Inf., 21 July, 1863. 1st Lieut., 11 Aug., 1864. Capt., 17 June, 1867. Cashiered 15 Jan., 1873. App. Capt. 15th Inf., 1 March, 1889 (Act. 16 April, 1888). Died 19 Oct., 1893.

HEDDLESON, JOHN. [Born in ——. Appointed from ——.]
3rd Lieut. 28th Inf., 20 May, 1813. 2nd Lieut. 2nd Rifle Reg., 17 March, 1814. 1st Lieut., 30 Sept., 1814. Trans. to Rifle Reg., 17 May, 1815. Resigned 31 March, 1817.

HEDEKIN, CHARLES A.* [Born in Ind. Appointed from Ind.]
2nd Lieut. 3rd Cav., 11 June, 1888. 1st Lieut, 8 Aug., 1895.

HEDGES, JOSEPH. [Born in Ohio. Appointed from Ohio.]
1st Sergt. Co. I, 1st Ohio Vols., 17 April to 2 Aug., 1861. 2nd Lieut. 4th Cav., 5 Aug., 1861. 1st Lieut., 17 July, 1862. Capt., 28 July, 1866. Resigned 31 July, 1867. Bvt. 1st Lieut., 10 May, 1863, for gallant and meritorious service in Cav. action at Franklin, Tenn. Bvt. Capt., 16 Dec., 1864, for gallant and meritorious service during the pursuit of the rebel forces under Gen. Hood. Bvt. Maj., 13 March, 1865, for gallant and meritorious service during the war.

HEDGES, JOSEPH S. [Born in Del. Appointed from Del.]
1st Lieut. of Inf., 5 March, 1847; 11th Inf., 9 April, 1847. Resigned 4 Dec., 1847.

HEGER, ANTHONY. [Born in Austria. Appointed from Penn.]
1st Lieut. Asst Surg., 29 Aug., 1856. Maj. Surg., 17 Sept., 1862. Bvt. Lieut. Col., 13 March, 1865, for faithful and meritorious service during the war. Lieut. Col. Surg., 24 Jan., 1886. Col. Surg., 2 Jan., 1891. Retired 4 Dec., 1892.

HEGEWALD, JOHN F. C.* [Born in Ind. Appointed from Ind.]
Addl. 2nd Lieut. 11th Inf., 15 June, 1877. 2nd Lieut. 15th Inf., 25 Aug., 1877. Resigned 22 May, 1880.

HEIBERG, ELVIN R. [Born in Minn. Appointed from Wis.]
Addl. 2nd Lieut. 3rd Cav., 12 June, 1896. 2nd Lieut. 6th Cav., 8 Dec., 1896. 1st Lieut. 2nd Cav., 1 March, 1900. Trans. to 6th Cav., 2 April, 1900.

HEIDT, GRAYSON V.* [Born in Ga. Appointed from Ga.]
2nd Lieut. 3rd Cav., 15 Feb., 1899.

HEIDT, JAMES V. [Born in Ga. Appointed from Army.]
Cadet M. A., 15 June, 1892, to 2 July, 1894. Priv. and Corpl. Co. E, and Sergt. Maj. 13th Inf. and Priv. Gen. Ser., 30 Aug., 1894, to 28 April, 1898. 2nd Lieut., 6th Inf., 12 April, 1898. 1st Lieut., 2 March, 1899.

HEILEMAN, JOHN F. [Born in Germany. Appointed from Mass.]
Garrison Surg. Mate, 2 June, 1802. Post Surg., 20 April, 1816. Died 9 Oct., 1816.

HEILEMAN, JULIUS F.* [Born in Mass. Appointed from Vt.]
2nd Lieut. Art., 6 March, 1806. 1st Lieut., 30 April, 1808. Trans. to 1st Art., 12 March, 1812. Capt., 5 May, 1813. Trans. to Corps Art., 12 May, 1814. Trans. to 2nd Art., 1 June, 1821. Maj., 17 Nov., 1834. Died 27 June, 1836. Bvt. Maj., 5 May, 1823, for ten years' faithful service in one grade. Bvt. Lieut. Col., 9 June, 1836, for gallant and good conduct in the affair of Micanopy, Fla.

HEILMAN, WM. H. [Born in Penn. Appointed from Army.]
Priv. 15th Inf., 30 Dec., 1861, to 22 Aug., 1862. 2nd Lieut. 15th Inf., 13 Aug., 1862. 1st Lieut., 3 Oct., 1863. Capt., 11 May, 1867. Resigned 25 Aug., 1868. Bvt. 1st Lieut., 20 Sept., 1863, for gallant and meritorious service at the Battle of Chickamauga, Ga.

HEIN, OTTO L.* [Born in D. C. Appointed from D. C.]
2nd Lieut. 1st Cav., 15 June, 1870. 1st Lieut., 30 Sept., 1877. Capt., 16 Jan., 1889. Commandant of Cadets, with rank of Lieut. Col., 15 June, 1897.

HEINER, GORDON G.* [Born in D. C. Appointed from Penn.]
2nd Lieut. 2nd Art., 12 June, 1893. Trans. to 4th Art., 29 Nov., 1893. 1st Lieut., 2 March, 1899.

HEINER, ROBT. G. [Born in Penn. Appointed from Penn.]
2nd Lieut. 22nd U. S. Col. Troops, 26 Dec., 1863. 1st Lieut., 25 Jan., 1865. Mustered out 16 Oct., 1865. 2nd Lieut. 11th Inf., 23 Feb., 1866. Trans. to 29th Inf., 21 Sept., 1866. 1st Lieut., 28 July, 1866. Unassigned 25 April, 1869. Ass'd to 1st Inf., 14 July, 1869. Capt., 29 Sept., 1879. Died 27 Nov., 1890.

HEINTZELMAN, CHAS. S.* [Born in Mich. Appointed at Large.]
2nd Lieut. 3rd Art., 17 June, 1867. 1st Lieut., 20 April, 1870. Capt. A. Q. M., 29 May, 1876. Died 27 Feb., 1881.

HEINTZELMAN, SAML. P.* [Born in Penn. Appointed from Penn.]
Bvt. 2nd Lieut. 3rd Inf., 1 July, 1826. 2nd Lieut. 2nd Inf., 1 July, 1826. 1st Lieut., 4 March, 1833. Capt. A. Q. M., 7 July, 1838. Capt. 2nd Inf., 4 Nov., 1838. Vacated Staff Commission, 18 June, 1846. Bvt. Maj., 9 Oct., 1847, for gallant and meritorious conduct in the Battle of Huamantla. Bvt. Lieut. Col., 19 Dec., 1851. Maj. 1st Inf., 3 March, 1855. Col. 17th Inf., 14 May, 1861. Brig. Gen. Vols., 17 May, 1861. Maj. Gen. Vols., 5 May, 1862. Bvt. Brig. Gen., 31 May, 1862, for gallant and meritorious conduct in the Battle of Fair Oaks, Va. Bvt. Maj. Gen., 13 March, 1865, for gallant and meritorious service in the Battle of Williamsburg, Va. Mustered out of Vol. Service 24 Aug., 1865. Retired as Col. 17th Inf., 22 Feb., 1869. Retired with rank of Maj. Gen., 29 April, 1869, to date from 22 Feb. 1869. Died 1 May, 1880.

HEINTZELMAN, STUART.* [Born in N. Y. Appointed at Large.]
2nd Lieut. 6th Cav., 15 Feb., 1899.

HEISKELL, HENRY L. [Born in Va. Appointed from Va..
Asst. Surg., 13 July, 1832. Maj. Surg., 7 July, 1838. Died 12 Aug., 1855.

HEISTAND, HENRY O. S.* [Born in Ohio. Appointed from Ohio.]
Addl. 2nd Lieut. 11th Inf., 14 June, 1878. 2nd Lieut., 28 June, 1878. 1st Lieut., 1 June, 1886. Capt., 19 March, 1891. Maj. A. A. G., 11 Sept., 1897.

HEIZMAN, CHAS. L. [Born in Penn. Appointed from Penn.]
1st Lieut. Asst. Surg., 14 May, 1867. Capt. Asst. Surg., 14 May, 1870. Maj. Surg., 18 Nov., 1886.

HELM, BEN HARDIN.* [Born in Ky. Appointed from Ky.]
Bvt. 2nd Lieut. 2nd Drag., 1 July, 1851. 2nd Lieut., 31 March, 1852. Resigned 9 Oct., 1852. Died of wounds, 21 Sept., 1863.

HELM, CHAS. J. [Born in N. Y. Appointed from Ky.]
1st Lieut. of Inf., 8 March, 1847; 16th Inf., 9 April, 1847. Reg. Adj., 1 May, 1847, to 15 March, 1848. Disbanded 16 Aug., 1848.

HELM, ISAAC A. [Born in Ind. Appointed from Ind.]
2nd Lieut. 3rd Inf., 5 Aug., 1861. 1st Lieut., 11 Sept., 1863. Reg. Adj., 28 Aug., 1863, to 31 Jan., 1866. Died 24 July, 1867. Bvt. 1st Lieut., 3 May, 1863, for gallant and meritorious service in the Battle of Chancellorsville, Va. Bvt. Capt., 2 July, 1863, for gallant and meritorious service at the Battle of Gettysburg, Pa.

HELMICK, ELI A.* [Born in Ind. Appointed from Kan.]
Addl. 2nd Lieut. 11th Inf., 11 June, 1888. 2nd Lieut. 4th Inf., 5 Aug., 1888. Trans. to 6th Inf., 11 Sept., 1895. Trans. to 2nd Inf., 2 Dec., 1895. 1st Lieut. 10th Inf., 21 Dec., 1895. Capt. 15th Inf., 4 May, 1899. Trans. to 10th Inf., 3 July, 1899.

HELMS, GEORGE W.* [Born in Va. Appointed from Va.]
Addl. 2nd Lieut. 22nd Inf., 11 June, 1897. 2nd Lieut. 19th Inf., 7 Sept., 1897. 1st Lieut., 2 March, 1899.

HELSBY, THOS. H. [Born in Md. Appointed from Md.]
Asst. Surg., 5 Aug., 1861. Resigned 1 Oct., 1865.

HEMPHILL, WM. C. [Born in Va. Appointed from Army.]
Priv. Co. D, 2nd Cav., 1 July, 1855. Corpl. 6 Nov., 1855. Sergt., 18 Jan., 1856. Priv., Band 2nd Cav., 1 Aug., 1857. Priv. Co. D, 2nd Cav., 1 March, 1858. Corp., 15 Aug., 1858. Priv., 24 Nov., 1858. Discharged 1 May, 1860. Corp. Co. D, 2nd Cav., 1 May, 1860. Sergt., 1 July, 1860. 1st Sergt., 15 March, 1861. Out of service, 21 Oct., 1861. Priv. Co. D, 5th Cav., 22 March, 1863. Corp., 1 Oct., 1863. Sergt., 1 May, 1864. Discharged 11 July, 1864. Sergt. Co. D, 5th Cav., 11 July, 1864. 2nd Lieut. 4th Cav., 25 May, 1866. 1st Lieut., 22 Jan., 1867. Capt., 17 May, 1876. Dismissed 1 Nov., 1881.

HEMPSTEAD, THOS. [Born in ———. Appointed from Ind.]
Asst. Dist. P. M., 15 June, 1814. Disbanded 15 June, 1815. Mil. Storekeeper, 9 March, 1819. Disbanded 1 June, 1821.

HENDEE, OSCAR P. [Born in Mich. Appointed from Mich..
Priv., Corpl. and 1st Sergt. Co. I, 8th Mich. Vols., 23 Sept., 1861, to 21 July, 1864. 2nd Lieut. 1st Mich. Vols., 21 July, 1864. 1st Lieut., 5 May, 1865. Mustered out 31 July, 1865. 2nd Lieut. 18th Inf., 11 May, 1866. Trans. to 36th Inf., 21 Sept., 1866. 1st Lieut., 22 Jan., 1867. Wholly retired 14 Nov., 1867.

HENDERSHOTT, HENRY B.* [Born in Ky. Appointed from Ohio.]
Bvt. 2nd Lieut. 5th Inf., 1 July, 1847. 2nd Lieut. 2nd Inf., 20 Aug., 1847. 1st Lieut., 30 June, 1850. Trans. to 2nd Art., 21 Oct., 1859. Capt., 27 April, 1861. Retired 30 March, 1864. Bvt. Maj., Lieut. Col. and Col., 13 March, 1865, for faithful and meritorious service connected with the recruitment and organization of the Vol. armies of the U. S. during the war.

HENDERSON, BENNETT H.* [Born in Tenn. Appointed from N. C.]
Bvt. 2nd Lieut. 4th Art., 1 July, 1826. 2nd Lieut. 3rd Art., 1 July, 1826. Resigned 30 June, 1832. Accidentally killed 8 July, 1832.

HENDERSON, JOHN. [Born in Ireland. Appointed from Army.]
Sergt. 2nd Art., Aug., 1812, to May, 1813. 3rd Lieut. 2nd Art., 20 May, 1813. 2nd Lieut., 26 June, 1813. Trans. to Corps Art., 12 May, 1814. Disbanded 15 June, 1815. Reinstated 2 Dec., 1815. Dismissed 2 April, 1818.

HENDERSON, JOHN E.* [Born in Tenn. Appointed from Tenn.]
Bvt. 2nd Lieut. 2nd Art., 1 July, 1834. 2nd Lieut., 31 Dec., 1834. Died 4 July, 1836.

HENDERSON, RICHARD.* [Born in Tenn. Appointed from Tenn.]
Bvt. 2nd Lieut. 2nd Art., 1 July, 1835. Massacred by Indians in Florida, 28 Dec., 1835.

HENDERSON, THOS. [Born in Va. Appointed from Va.]
Asst. Surg., 31 Dec., 1833. Died 11 Aug., 1854.

HENDERSON, TIPPO S. [Born in Va. Appointed from Va.]
2nd Lieut. Rifles., 22 July, 1818. Dropped 31 Oct., 1818.

HENDERSON, WASHN. I. [Born in Mo. Appointed from Oregon.]
Priv. Co. G., 1st Ore. Cav., 10 Aug., 1863. Mustered out 10 Feb., 1866. 2nd Lieut. 12th Inf., 23 Feb., 1866. Trans. to 1st Cav., 21 April, 1866. 1st Lieut., 14 Oct., 1867. Wholly retired 14 Sept., 1869.

HENDREN, CORNELIUS D. [Born in Va. Appointed from Miss.]
2nd Lieut. 3rd Inf., 21 Feb., 1857. Resigned 30 June, 1860.

HENDRICKS, JOHN A. [Born in Ind. Appointed from Ind.]
Capt. of Inf., 23 Feb., 1847; 16th Inf., 9 April, 1847. Resigned 14 June, 1847. Lieut. Col. 22nd Ind. Vols., 15 Aug., 1861. Killed 7 March, 1862, at the Battle of Pea Ridge, Ark.

HENDRICKSON, THOMAS. [Born in Penn. Appointed from Mo.]
Priv. Co. D, 4th Batty. Corps Art., 13 Dec., 1819, to 18 July, 1821. Priv. and Sergt. Co. F, and Sergt. Maj. 3rd Inf., 20 July, 1823, to 20 July, 1828. Priv. and Sergt. Cos. E and G, and Sergt. Maj. 6th Inf., 28 July, 1828, to 25 April, 1833. Ord. Sergt., 25 April, 1833, to 10 June, 1836. 2nd Lieut. 6th Inf., 31 July, 1838. 1st Lieut., 3 Dec., 1840. Capt., 27 Jan., 1853. Maj. 3rd Inf., 27 June, 1862. Retired 31 Aug., 1863. Died 24 Oct., 1878. Bvt. Capt., 20 Aug., 1847, for gallant and meritorious conduct at Contreras and Churubusco. Bvt. Lieut. Col., 1 July, 1862, for gallant and meritorious service at the Battle of Malvern Hill, Va. Bvt. Col., 13 March, 1865, for gallant and meritorious conduct during the war.

HENELY, AUSTIN.* [Born in Ireland. Appointed at Large.]
2nd Lieut. 6th Cav., 14 June, 1872. 1st Lieut., 15 Nov., 1876. Drowned 11 July, 1878.

HENLEY, JOSEPH P. [Born in Ireland. Appointed from Army.]
Priv., Corpl., Sergt. and 1st Sergt. Co. G, 5th Cav., 16 Nov., 1860, to 25 April, 1863. 2nd Lieut. 5th Cav., 22 April, 1863. 1st Lieut., 30 March, 1864. Killed 12 June, 1864, in action at Trevillian Station, Va.

HENNING, WM. H. [Born in Penn. Appointed from Penn.]
Maj. and Sergt. 4th Mounted Rifles, 20 April, 1814. Trans. to Rifle Regiment, 17 May, 1815. Resigned 10 March, 1816.

HENNISEE, ARGALUS G. [Born in Md. Appointed from Md.]
1st Lieut. 1st E. S. Md. Vols., 30 Sept., 1861. Capt., 24 July, 1862. Discharged 11 Feb., 1865. 2nd Lieut. 19th Inf., 22 Jan., 1867. 1st Lieut., 14 May, 1868. Unassigned 31 March, 1869. Ass'd to 8th Cav., 1 Jan., 1871. Reg. Adj., 22 Oct., 1878, to 16 March, 1881. Capt., 16 March, 1881. Maj. 2nd Cav., 31 May, 1898.

HENRY, ADDIS M.* [Born in Ohio. Appointed from Ohio.]
2nd Lieut. 3rd Inf., 14 June, 1872. Resigned 29 Nov., 1882.

HENRY, FRANCIS. [Born in Ill. Appointed from Wis.]
2nd Lieut. of Inf., 9 March, 1847; 3rd Drag., 9 April, 1847. Disbanded 20 July, 1848.

HENRY, GUY V.* [Born in Indian Ter. Appointed from N. Y.]
2nd Lieut. 1st Art., 6 May, 1861. 1st Lieut., 14 May, 1861. Bvt. Capt., 22 Oct., 1862, for gallant and meritorious service in action near Pocotaligo River, S. C. Col. 40th Mass. Vols., 9 Nov., 1863. Bvt. Maj., 20 Feb., 1864, for gallant and meritorious service in the Battle of Olustee, Fla. Bvt. Lieut. Col., 29 Sept., 1864, for gallant and meritorious service in front of Petersburg, Va. Bvt. Brig. Gen. Vols., 25 Oct., 1864, for gallant and meritorious service during the campaign in front of Petersburg, Va. Bvt. Col., 13 March, 1865, for gallant and meritorious service during the war. Mustered out of Vol. Service, 30 June, 1865. Capt. 1st Art., 1 Dec., 1865. Trans. to 3rd Cav., 15 Dec., 1870. Maj. 9th Cav., 26 June, 1881. Lieut. Col. 7th Cav., 30 Jan., 1892. Trans. to 5th Cav., 22 Sept., 1894. Trans. to 3rd Cav., 15 Oct., 1895. Col. 10th Cav., 1 June, 1897. Brig. Gen., 11 Oct., 1898. Brig. Gen. Vols., 4 May, 1898. Maj. Gen. Vols., 7 Dec., 1898. Bvt. Brig. Gen., Feb. 27, 1890. Medal of honor for noteworthy and conspicuous gallantry while Col. 40th Mass. Vols., leading the assaults of his brigade upon the enemy's works at Cold Harbor, Va., 1 June, 1864, where he had two horses shot under him—one while in the act of leaping over the breastworks of the enemy. Died 27 Oct., 1899.

HENRY, GUY V., Jr.* [Born in Neb. Appointed from Va.]
2nd Lieut. 4th Inf., 26 April, 1898. Trans. to 1st Cav., 26 Sept., 1898. Capt. 26th U. S. Vols., 5 July, 1899. Maj., 13 Sept., 1899.

HENRY, JAMES. [Born in Ireland. Appointed from Army.]
Priv. and Sergt. Co. C, 11th Inf., 24 Aug., 1863, to 26 May, 1864. 2nd Lieut. 10th Inf., 18 May, 1864. Died May 26, 1864, of wounds received in battle.

HENRY, JAMES M. L.* [Born in Ky. Appointed from D. C.]
Bvt. 2nd Lieut. 7th Inf., 1 July, 1844. 2nd Lieut. 2nd Inf., 18 June, 1846. Trans. to 4th Inf., 30 Sept., 1848. Resigned 13 July, 1852.

HENRY, MATHIAS W.* [Born in Ky. Appointed from Ky.]
Bvt. 2nd and 2nd Lieut. Mounted Rifles, 6 May, 1861; 3rd Cav., 3 Aug., 1861. Resigned 19 Aug., 1861. Died 28 Nov., 1877.

HENRY, THOS. [Born in N. Y. Appointed from Army.]
Priv., Corpl. and Sergt. Co. I, and Q. M. Sergt. 7th Inf., 8 Feb., 1838, to 20 May, 1847. 2nd Lieut. 7th Inf., 20 May, 1847. 1st Lieut., 24 Oct., 1853. Resigned 16 Oct., 1855. Bvt. 1st Lieut., 20 Aug., 1847, for gallant and meritorious conduct at Contreras and Churubusco, Mex.

HENRY, THOMAS C. [Born in S. C. Appointed from S. C.]
Asst. Surg., 1 March, 1853. Resigned 25 April, 1859. Asst. Surg. Vols., 30 June, 1864. Surg. Vols., 23 Feb., 1865. Bvt. Lieut. Col. Vols., 22 Aug., 1865, for faithful and meritorious service. Mustered out 25 Aug., 1865. Died 6 Jan., 1877.

HENRY, WM. S.* [Born in N. Y. Appointed from N. Y.]
Bvt. 2nd Lieut. 3rd Inf., 1 July, 1835. 2nd Lieut., 15 June, 1836. 1st Lieut., 7 July, 1838. Capt., 18 May, 1846. Bvt. Maj., 23 Sept., 1846, for gallant and meritorious conduct in several conflicts at Monterey, Mex. Died 5 March, 1851.

HENSHAW, EDWARD C. [Born in Vt. Appointed from Ill.]
Capt. Ill. Batty, 3 Dec., 1862. Cashiered 14 Dec., 1864. Restored 4 April, 1865. Mustered out 18 July, 1865. 2nd Lieut. 15th Inf., 3 Sept., 1867. 1st Lieut., 18 Aug., 1868. Unassigned 12 Aug., 1869. Ass'd to 24th Inf., 15 Dec., 1870. Died 14 Sept., 1872.

HENSHAW, JAMES.* [Born in Va. Appointed from Va.]
Bvt. 2nd Lieut. 7th Inf., 1 July, 1821. Resigned 1 Dec., 1821.

HENSHAW, JOHN C. [Born in N. Y. Appointed from N. Y.]
2nd Lieut. 7th Inf., 1 July, 1839. 1st Lieut., 21 July, 1844. Capt., 3 March, 1847. Dismissed 9 Jan., 1856. Bvt. Maj., 20 Aug., 1847, for gallant and meritorious conduct at Contreras and Churubusco, Mex.

HENSLEY, ALEX. C. [Born in Ky. Appointed from Ky.]
Maj. Surg. Vols., 14 July, 1846. Disbanded 30 June, 1847. Asst. Surg. 16th Inf., 7 July, 1847. Disbanded 10 Aug., 1848.

HENTIG, EDMUND C. [Born in Mich. Appointed from Mich.]
2nd Lieut. 6th Cav., 12 June, 1867. 1st Lieut., 23 Dec., 1868. Capt., 15 Nov., 1876. Killed in action with Apache Indians at Cibicu Creek, Ariz., 30 Aug., 1881.

HENTON, JAMES. [Born in England. Appointed from Army.]
Priv. Co. D, 6th Inf., 22 Nov., 1853. Corpl., 1 July, 1855. Sergt., 1 June, 1856. 1st Sergt., 17 March, 1858. Discharged 22 Nov., 1858. Priv. Gen. Service., 14 May, 1860. Trans. to 14th Inf., 1 Sept., 1861. 1st Sergt. Co. H, 3rd Batt. 14th Inf., ———, 1861. 2nd Lieut. 14th Inf., 5 Oct., 1861. 1st Lieut., 19 Feb., 1862. Bvt. Capt., 13 March, 1865, for gallant and meritorious service in the Battle of Gettysburg, Pa. Capt. 14th Inf., 4 Nov., 1865. Trans. to 23rd Inf., 21 Sept., 1866. Maj. of Inf. (23rd Inf.), 31 Jan., 1891. Lieut. Col., 13 Aug., 1894. Died 5 July, 1895.

HEPBURNE, JAMES S.* [Born in N. Y. Appointed from N. Y.]
2nd Lieut. Corps Art., 1 July, 1819. Trans. to 4th Art., 1 June, 1821. Trans. to 2nd Art., 16 Aug., 1821. Resigned 1 Oct., 1824. Died 2 May, 1833.

HEQUEMBOURG, CHAS. L. [Born in Conn. Appointed from N. Y.]
Post Chap., 2 July, 1870. Died 24 Dec., 1875.

HERBERT, ALFRED.* [Born in Md. Appointed from Md.]
Bvt. 2nd Lieut. 1st Art., 1 July, 1835. 2nd Lieut., 1 Dec., 1835. Resigned 30 June, 1837. Bvt. 1st Lieut., 27 July, 1836, for gallantry and good conduct on several occasions in Florida.

HERKNESS, BERNARD H. [Born in Penn. Appointed from Penn.]
Priv. Co. A., 20th Pa. Vols., 30 April to 6 Aug., 1861. Sergt. Co. C, 6th Pa. Cav., 10 Sept., 1861. 2nd Lieut., 1 April, 1863. 1st Lieut., 20 Feb., 1864. Capt., 24 Dec., 1864. Maj., 22 March, 1865. Mustered out 7 Aug., 1865. 2nd Lieut. 17th Inf., 11 May, 1866. Trans. to 35th Inf., 21 Sept., 1866. Killed 23 April, 1869, by deserters.

HERMAN, HENRY M. [Born in N. Y. Appointed from N. Y.]
1st Lieut. 15th Inf., 14 May, 1861. Appointment expired 6 Aug., 1861. 1st Lieut. 5th U. S. Vols., 18 Sept., 1865. Discharged 8 Feb., 1866.

HERNDON, DABNEY. [Born in Va. Appointed from Va.]
Asst. Surg., 30 Sept., 1841. Disbanded 23 Sept., 1842.

HERNDON, JAMES C. [Born in Va. Appointed from Va.]
Asst. Surg., 22 Feb., 1856. Dropped 27 Nov., 1861.

HERO, ANDREW, Jr.* [Born in La. Appointed from La.]
2nd Lieut. 12th Inf., 12 June, 1891. Trans. to 4th Art., 14 Nov., 1891. 1st Lieut. 5th Art., 19 Sept., 1898. Graduate of the Artillery School, 1896.

HERON, JAMES E. [Born in Penn. Appointed from N. Y.]
Asst. Com. of Purchases, 10 Sept., 1813. Disbanded 1 June, 1821. Died 1845.

HERONIUS, QUIN B. [Born in ———. Appointed from D. C.]
2nd Lieut. 4th Inf., 19 Feb., 1818. 1st Lieut., 8 May, 1818. Died 20 Aug., 1820.

HERR, HIERO B.* [Born in Penn. Appointed from Penn.]
2nd Lieut. 1st Art., 18 June, 1866. 1st Lieut., 17 Feb., 1868. Resigned 15 May, 1870.

HERRICK, OSGOOD E. [Born in Vt. Appointed from Fla.]
Chap. Post of Key West, Fla., 4 Nov., 1864, to 7 May, 1867. Post Chap., 3 April, 1867. Retired 25 April, 1890.

HERRING, DANL. S.* [Born in Va. Appointed from Va.]
Bvt. 2nd Lieut. 4th Art., 1 July, 1826. 2nd Lieut. 3rd Art., 1 July, 1826. 1st Lieut., 28 Dec., 1835. Died 22 June, 1836.

HERRING, ELBERT. [Born in Conn. Appointed from N. Y.]
Maj. P. M., 4 July, 1836. Dismissed 14 Oct., 1841.

HERRING, JOSEPH. [Born in S. C. Appointed from the Army.]
Priv., Corpl. and Sergt. Batty E, 3rd Art., 13 Aug., 1893, to 21 April, 1899. 2nd Lieut. 24th Inf., 5 April, 1899.

HERRON, CHARLES D.* [Born in Ind. Appointed from Ind.]
2nd Lieut. 18th Inf., 15 Feb., 1899.

HERRON, JOSEPH S.* [Born in Ohio. Appointed from Ohio.]
Addl. 2nd Lieut. 1st Cav., 12 June, 1895. 2nd Lieut., 27 Aug., 1895. 1st Lieut. 8th Cav., 23 April, 1899.

HERSEY, MARK L.* [Born in Maine. Appointed from Maine.]
Addl. 2nd Lieut. 19th Inf., 12 June, 1887. 2nd Lieut. 9th Inf., 30 Aug., 1887. 1st Lieut. 12th Inf., 16 Dec., 1894. Capt. 9th Inf., 2 March, 1899.

HERSHLER, FRED W. [Born in Ill. Appointed from D. C.]
2nd Lieut. 7th Inf., 10 April, 1899. Trans. to 14th Inf., 4 Oct., 1899.

HESS, FRANK W. [Born in Penn. Appointed from Penn.]
Capt. 15th Penn. Vols., 23 April, 1861. Mustered out 7 Aug., 1861. 1st Lieut. 3rd

Penn. Cav., 9 Nov., 1861. Capt., 8 July, 1862. Maj., 31 Oct., 1864. Trans. to 5th Penn. Cav., 8 May, 1865. Mustered out 7 Aug., 1865. 2nd Lieut. and 1st Lieut. 11th Inf., 23 Feb., 1866. Trans. to 29th Inf., 21 Sept., 1866. Trans. to 11th Inf., 25 April, 1869. Trans. to 3rd Art., 15 Dec., 1870. Capt., 15 March, 1881. Maj., 10 Feb., 1898. Graduate of the Artillery School, 1873.

HESS, LOUIS T. [Born in Penn. Appointed from Penn.]
Asst. Surg., 30 Jan., 1899.

HESSELBERGER, GUSTAVUS A. [Born in Germany. Appointed from Dak.
1st Lieut. 6th Iowa Cav., 31 Jan., 1863. Resigned 26 May, 1865. 2nd Lieut. 3rd Inf., 23 Feb., 1866. 1st Lieut., 7 May, 1867. Unassigned, 11 Aug., 1869. Mustered out 1 Jan., 1871.

HETH, HENRY.* [Born in Va. Appointed from Va.]
Bvt. 2nd Lieut. 1st Inf., 1 July, 1847. 2nd Lieut. 6th Inf., 22 Sept., 1847. 1st Lieut., 9 June, 1853. R. Q. M., 24 Nov., 1854, to 3 March, 1855. Capt. 10th Inf., 3 March, 1855. Resigned 25 April, 1861.

HETZEL, ABNER R.* [Born in Penn. Appointed from Penn.]
Bvt. 2nd Lieut. and 2nd Lieut. 2nd Inf., 1 July, 1827. 1st Lieut., 28 June, 1836. Capt. A. Q. M., 7 July, 1838. Died 20 July, 1847.

HETZEL, CALVIN. [Born in Penn. Appointed from Penn.]
2nd Lieut. 8th Inf., 22 Oct., 1839. 1st Lieut., 30 May, 1845. Resigned 31 Dec., 1845.

HEUER, WM. H.* [Born in Mo. Appointed from Mo.]
1st Lieut. Eng., 23 June, 1865. Capt., 22 Sept., 1870. Maj., 17 March, 1884.

HEUSTIS, JABEZ W. [Born in La. Appointed from La.]
Maj. Surg. 2nd Inf., 2 April, 1814. Disbanded 15 June, 1815. Post Surg., 12 Nov., 1817. Resigned 31 Dec., 1819.

HEWIT, AUGUSTINE F.* [Born in N. Y. Appointed at Large.]
2nd Lieut. 22nd Inf., 13 June, 1879. Died 3 June, 1882.

HEWIT, HENRY S. [Born in Conn. Appointed from Conn.]
Asst. Surg., 2 March, 1849. Resigned 30 April, 1851. Surg. U. S. Vols., 3 Aug., 1861. Bvt. Lieut. Col. and Col. Vols., 13 March, 1865, for faithful and meritorious service during the war. Mustered out 7 Oct., 1865. Died 19 Aug., 1873.

HEWITT, CHRISTIAN C.* [Born in Va. Appointed from W. Va.]
2nd Lieut. 19th Inf., 17 June, 1874. 1st Lieut., 15 June, 1882. Reg. Adj., 31 March, 1887, to March, 1891. Capt., 4 June, 1892.

HEYL, ASHTON B. [Born in Penn. Appointed from Penn.]
Asst. Surg., 6 June, 1890. Capt. Asst. Surg., 6 June, 1895. Resigned 28 Feb., 1900.

HEYL, CHAS. H. [Born in Penn. Appointed from N. J.]
2nd Lieut. 23rd Inf., 1 Oct., 1873. 1st Lieut., 20 March, 1882. Reg. Adj., 1 April, 1890, to 18 April, 1891. Capt., 18 April, 1891. Maj. A. A. G., 19 May, 1898. Maj. I. G. Vols., 8 July, 1898. Lieut. Col. 1st D. C. Vols., 14 May, 1898 (declined). Lieut. Col. I. G. Vols., 30 Sept., 1899. Graduate of the Infantry and Cavalry School, 1883. Bvt. 1st Lieut., Feb. 27, 1890, for gallant services in action against Indians near the Verde River, Ariz., 24 May, 1874, and gallantry in action against Indians near Grace Creek, Neb., 28 April, 1876. Medal of Honor for most distinguished gallantry in action near Fort Hartsuff., Neb., 28 April, 1876, while in command of a small scouting party, in charging with three men upon six Indians, who were intrenched upon a hilltop, while serving as 2nd Lieut. 23rd Inf.

HEYL, EDWARD M. [Born in Penn. Appointed from Penn.]
Q. M. Sergt. Co. E, 3rd Penn. Cav., 12 Aug., 1861. 1st Sergt., 16 Oct., 1861. Discharged 8 Sept., 1862. 2nd Lieut. 3rd Pa. Cav., 8 Sept., 1862. 1st Lieut., 1 May, 1863. Capt., 2 May, 1864. Mustered out 24 Aug., 1864. 1st Lieut. 9th Cav., 28 July, 1866. Capt., 31 July, 1867. Trans. to 4th Cav., 1 Jan., 1871. Maj. I. G., 19 Feb., 1885. Lieut. Col. I. G., 12 Feb., 1889. Died 2 Jan., 1895.

HEYWARD, WM. C.* [Born in N. Y. Appointed from N. Y.]
Bvt. 2nd Lieut. 3rd Inf., 1 July, 1830. Resigned 6 Feb., 1832.

HEZLEP, JOHN K.* [Born in Ohio. Appointed from Minn.]
2nd Lieut. 7th Inf., 23 June, 1865. 1st Lieut., 23 June, 1865. Trans. to Eng., 1 June, 1866. Died 13 Aug., 1867.

HICK, WM. H. [Born in N. J. Appointed from N. J.]
2nd Lieut. 1st N. J. Cav., 28 Dec., 1861. 1st Lieut., 1 May, 1862. Capt., 19 May, 1863. Mustered out 7 Oct, 1864. Priv. Troop L, 1st N. J. Cav., 31 Oct., 1864. Capt., 1 Jan., 1865. Maj., 9 June, 1865. Mustered out 24 July, 1865. 2nd Lieut. 4th Cav., 7 March, 1867. 1st Lieut., 2 Sept., 1867. Mustered out 1 Jan., 1871.

HICKEY, JAMES B.* [Born in Md. Appointed from N. Y.]
2nd Lieut. 8th Cav., 12 June, 1871. 1st Lieut., 23 April, 1879. Reg. Adj., 9 Oct., 1882, to 31 March, 1887. Capt., 20 Jan., 1890. Maj. A. A. G. Vols., 5 Sept., 1899.

HICKMAN, EDWIN A. [Born in Mo. Appointed from Mo.]
1st Lieut. 6th Mo. Inf., 12 July, 1898. Maj., 6 Dec., 1898, to 10 May, 1899. 2nd Lieut. 1st Cav., 10 April, 1899.

HICKMAN, LLEWELLIN. [Born in Va. Appointed from Ky.]
1st Lieut. 2nd Rifles, 17 March, 1814. Retained in Rifle Reg., 17 May, 1815. Capt., 15 Feb., 1818. Resigned 20 May, 1820.

HICKMAN, PHILANDER A. [Born in Va. Appointed from La.]
1st Lieut. of Inf., 5 March, 1847; 14th Inf., 9 April, 1847. Capt., 22 Oct., 1847. Disbanded 25 July, 1848.

HICKOK, HOWARD R.* [Born in Mo. Appointed from Mo.]
2nd Lieut. 9th Cav., 11 June, 1892. 1st Lieut., 2 March, 1899.

HICKOX, CHAS. R. [Born in Ohio. Appointed from Ohio.]
2nd Lieut. 5th Art., 14 May, 1861. 1st Lieut., 11 June, 1864. Resigned 2 Dec., 1864.

HICKS, JOHN W. [Born in Penn. Appointed from Penn.]
1st Lieut. 3rd Pa. Vols., 20 April, 1861, to 30 July, 1861. Capt. 76th Pa. Vols., 17 Oct., 1861. Maj., 1 May, 1863. Lieut. Col., 13 Feb., 1864. Discharged 1 June, 1864. Capt. 9th U. S. Vet. Vols., 10 Aug., 1865. Bvt. Maj., Lieut. Col. and Col. Vols., 13 March, 1865, for gallant and meritorious service during the war. Mustered out 24 April, 1866. 1st Lieut. 20th Inf., 28 July, 1866. Died 22 Oct., 1867. Bvt. Capt., 2 March, 1867, for gallant and meritorious service in the assault on Fort Wagner, S. C.

HIGBEE, GEORGE H. [Born in Ohio. Appointed from N. J.]
1st Lieut. 11th Inf., 14 May, 1861. Capt., 19 Feb., 1866. Unassigned 14 April, 1869. Ass'd to 13th Inf., 14 July, 1869. Unassigned, 16 April, 1870. Discharged 31 Dec., 1870. Bvt. Capt., 5 May, 1864, for gallant and meritorious service at the Battle of the Wilderness, Va. Bvt. Maj., 13 March, 1865, for gallant and meritorious service in front of Petersburg, Va. Bvt. Lieut. Col., 13 March, 1865, for meritorious service in the battles before Petersburg and on the Weldon Railroad, Va.

HIGGINS, HIRAM H. [Born in Ky. Appointed from Ala.]
Capt. 13th Inf., 9 April, 1847. Disbanded 15 July, 1848.

HIGGINS, SILAS P.* [Born in Ala. Appointed from Ala.]
Bvt. 2nd Lieut. 8th Inf., 1 July, 1853. 2nd Lieut. 6th Inf., 3 March, 1855. 1st Lieut., 24 Dec., 1856. Died 18 July, 1860.

HIGGINS, THADDEUS.* [Born in Penn. Appointed from Penn.]
2nd Lieut. 4th Inf., 1 July, 1840. Accidentally killed 12 Sept., 1845.

HIGGS, AUGUSTUS F. [Born in West Indies. Appointed from Ill.]
Priv. and 1st Sergt. Co. E, 67th Ill. Vols., 31 May to 27 Sept., 1862. 1st Lieut. 127th Ill. Vols., 22 Oct., 1862. Resigned 10 March, 1863. 1st Lieut. Vet. Res. Corps, 28 Oct., 1863. Mustered out 14 July, 1867. 2nd Lieut. 16th Inf., 18 June, 1867. Resigned 6 Jan., 1869. Bvt. 1st Lieut., 18 June, 1867, for gallant and meritorious service in the Siege of Vicksburg, Miss. Died 21 Dec., 1887.

HIGHT, THOS.* [Born in Ind. Appointed from Ind.]
Bvt. 2nd Lieut. 1st Drag., 1 July, 1853. 2nd Lieut. 2nd Drag., 24 May, 1854. 1st Lieut., 2 Feb., 1857. Capt., 13 May, 1861; 2nd Cav., 3 Aug., 1861. Lieut. Col. 1st Maine Cav., 19 Oct., 1861. Resigned from Vols., 14 March, 1862, and from the U. S. Army 27 April, 1863. Lieut. Col. 31st Maine Vols., 12 March, 1864. Col., 29 April, 1864. Discharged 2 July, 1864. Died 17 Oct., 1867.

HIGLEY, BRAINERD S., Jr. [Born in Ohio. Appointed from Ohio.]
Asst. Surg., 6 Nov., 1897.

HILDEBURN, SAML. [Born in Penn. Appointed from Army.]
Priv. Gen. Ser., 28 Jan. to 13 March, 1863. 2nd Lieut. 3rd Cav., 19 Feb., 1863. 1st Lieut., 28 Sept., 1865. Capt., 3 Jan., 1869. Mustered out 1 Jan., 1871. Bvt. 1st Lieut., 15 Nov., 1863, for gallant and meritorious service in action near Tuscumbia, Ala.

HILDT, JOHN McL.* [Born in Penn. Appointed at Large.]
Bvt. 2nd Lieut. 6th Inf., 1 July, 1856. 2nd Lieut. 1st Inf., 31 Oct., 1856. Trans. to 3rd Inf., 13 Feb., 1857. 1st Lieut., 17 April, 1861. Capt., 30 May, 1861. Resigned 20 April, 1870. Bvt. Maj., 1 July, 1862, for gallant and meritorious services at the Battles of Gaines' Mills and Malvern Hill, Va. Bvt. Lieut. Col., 13 March, 1865, for gallant and meritorious service during the war. Died 25 April, 1877.

HILL, AMBROSE P.* [Born in Va. Appointed from Va.]
Bvt. 2nd Lieut. 1st Art., 1 July, 1847. 2nd Lieut., 26 Aug., 1847. 1st Lieut., 4 Sept., 1851. Resigned 1 March, 1861. Killed in battle 2 April, 1865.

HILL, BENNETT H.* [Born in D. C. Appointed from D. C.]
2nd Lieut. 1st Art., 1 July, 1837. 1st Lieut., 9 July, 1838. Capt., 12 Jan., 1848. Maj. 2nd Art., 28 Aug., 1861. Lieut. Col. 5th Art., 1 Aug., 1863. Bvt. Col. and Brig. Gen., 31 Jan., 1865. Retired 15 Dec., 1870. Died 24 March, 1886.

HILL, DANIEL H.* [Born in S. C. Appointed from S. C.]
Bvt. 2nd Lieut. 1st Art., 1 July, 1842. Trans. to 3rd Art., 20 Oct., 1843. 2nd Lieut. 4th Art., 13 Oct., 1845. 1st Lieut., 3 March, 1847. Resigned 28 Feb., 1849. Bvt. Capt., 20 Aug., 1847, for gallant and meritorious conduct at Contreras and Churubusco, Mex. Bvt. Maj., 13 Sept., 1847, for gallant and meritorious conduct in the storming of Chapultepec. Died 24 Sept., 1889.

HILL, EDWARD B. [Born in N. Y. Appointed from N. Y.]
2nd Lieut. 1st Art., 26 April, 1861. 1st Lieut., 14 May, 1861. Died 13 July, 1862, of wounds received at the Battle of White Oak Swamp, Va.

HILL, GABRIEL H. [Born in N. C. Appointed from N. C.]
2nd Lieut. 3rd Art., 21 Feb., 1857. Resigned 29 April, 1861.

HILL, GEORGE D. [Born in Ohio. Appointed from Mich.]
Priv. Co. D, 3rd Mich. Vols., 13 May, 1861. Principal Musician, 1 Sept., 1861. Discharged 15 Jan., 1863. 1st Sergt. Co. I, 1st Mich. Cav., 23 Oct., 1863. 2nd Lieut. 1st Mich Cav., 2 Jan., 1865. 1st Lieut., 1 May, 1865. Mustered out 7 Nov., 1865. 1st Lieut. 42nd Inf., 28 July, 1866. Bvt. Capt., 2 March, 1867, for gallant and meritorious service in the Battle of Appomattox C. H., Va. Unassigned 22 April, 1869. Retired with rank of Capt. Mounted, 31 Dec., 1870. Drowned 4 Dec., 1890.

HILL, GEORGE W. [Born in N. H. Appointed from Mass.]
1st Lieut. 13th Inf., 14 May, 1861. Capt., 20 May, 1863. Trans. to 31st Inf., 21 Sept., 1866. Trans. to 22nd Inf., 15 May, 1869. Mustered out 1 Jan., 1871.

HILL, HENRY. [Born in Va. Appointed from Va.]
Maj. P. M., 6 Nov., 1847. Resigned 14 June, 1861.

HILL, JAMES B. [Born in N. C. Appointed from N. C.]
Surg. Mate 18th Inf., 6 July, 1812. Trans. to 3rd Inf., 17 May, 1815. Trans. to 4th Inf., 21 Oct., 1815. Resigned 14 Oct., 1816.

HILL, JAMES F. [Born in Ireland. Appointed from N. Y.]
Priv., Corpl. and Sergt. Co. D, 2nd N. Y. Vols., 14 May, 1861, to 1 Sept., 1862. 2nd Lieut., 1 Sept., 1862. 1st Lieut., 9 March, 1863. Mustered out 26 May, 1863. 1st

Lieut. 24th N. Y. Cav., 29 June, 1863. Mustered out 11 Sept., 1866. 2nd Lieut. 6th Cav., 22 Jan., 1867. 1st Lieut., 17 Sept., 1867. Reg. Adj., 16 Aug., 1868, to 27 Nov., 1869. Drowned 27 April, 1870.

HILL, JAMES H.* [Born in Maine. Appointed from N. Y.]
Bvt. 2nd Lieut. 10th Inf., 1 July, 1855. 2nd Lieut., 8 Aug., 1855. 1st Lieut., 27 Feb., 1861. Reg. Adj., 16 July, 1860, to 1 May, 1861. Resigned 1 May, 1861.

HILL, JAMES M.* [Born in N. H. Appointed from Maine.]
Bvt. 2nd Lieut. 2nd Inf., 1 July, 1830. 2nd Lieut., 1 July, 1830. 1st Lieut., 31 Dec., 1836. Reg. Adj., 8 May to 5 July, 1838. Trans. to 8th Inf., 7 July, 1838. Capt., 28 Sept., 1840, to 18 June, 1846. Capt. A. Q. M., 7 July, 1838. Died 29 Jan., 1849.

HILL, JOHN H.* [Born in Penn. Appointed from Penn.]
2nd Lieut. 2nd Drag., 1 July, 1839. 1st Lieut., 8 Oct., 1841. Died 29 July, 1847.

HILL, LOUIS E. [Born in Ohio. Appointed from Ohio.]
Sergt. Troop A. 1st Ohio Cav., 9 May to 24 July, 1898. 2nd Lieut. 4th Inf., 9 July, 1898. 1st Lieut., 11 July, 1899.

HILL, RICHD. M.* [Born in D. C. Appointed at Large.]
Bvt. 2nd Lieut. Ord., 24 June, 1861. 2nd Lieut., 24 June, 1861. 1st Lieut., 1 Nov., 1861. Capt., 3 March, 1863. Maj., 23 June, 1874. Died 25 March, 1876. Bvt. Maj., 13 March, 1865, for faithful and meritorious service in the Ord. Dept.

HILL, ROBERT C.* [Born in N. C. Appointed from N. C.]
Bvt. 2nd Lieut. 6th Inf., 1 July, 1855. 2nd Lieut. 5th Inf., 18 Oct., 1855. Resigned 3 March, 1861.

HILL, ROWLAND G.* [Born in Iowa. Appointed from Iowa.]
2nd Lieut. 20th Inf., 11 June, 1881. Capt. A. J. A., 28 Sept., 1886, to 7 Nov., 1887. 1st Lieut., 15 July, 1890. Graduate of the Infantry and Cavalry School, 1883. Capt. 25th Inf., 26 April, 1898. Died 2 May, 1898.

HILL, THOS. M.* [Born in Maine. Appointed from Maine.]
Bvt. 2nd Lieut. 1st Inf., 1 July, 1832. 2nd Lieut., 10 Dec., 1834. 1st Lieut., 3 Oct., 1837. Died 10 July, 1838.

HILLARY, MICHAEL. [Born in Ireland. Appointed from N. Y.]
Asst. Surg. 50th N. Y. Eng., 5 July, 1862. Resigned 5 Feb., 1863. Asst. Surg., 13 June, 1863. Dismissed 11 Nov., 1867. Bvt. Capt., 13 March, 1865, for faithful and meritorious service.

HILLHOUSE, JOHN.* [Born in N. Y. Appointed from N. Y.]
Bvt. 2nd Lieut. 4th Art., 1 July, 1842. 2nd Lieut. 3rd Art., 30 April, 1844. Resigned 1 March, 1845. Capt. A. A. G. Vols., 11 Sept., 1861. Resigned 6 Nov., 1861. Died 29 March, 1882.

HILLMAN, JAMES W. [Born in N. Y. Appointed from N. Y.]
Post Chap., 4 Jan., 1894.

HILLS, ELBRIDGE R.* [Born in Ohio. Appointed from Ohio.]
2nd Lieut. 5th Art., 18 June, 1866. 1st Lieut., 28 Sept., 1867. Reg. Adj., 1 Sept., 1870, to 15 April, 1887. Capt., 28 Nov., 1892. Graduate of the Artillery School, 1890.

HILLS, FRANCIS L.* [Born in Mass. Appointed from Mass.]
2nd Lieut. 5th Art., 18 June, 1866. Trans. to 3rd Art., 23 Oct., 1866. 1st Lieut., 2 April, 1868. Resigned 7 April, 1870.

HILLS, JOHN.* [Born in Mass. Appointed from Mass.]
3rd Lieut. Ord., 2 March, 1815. 2nd Lieut., 1 Jan., 1818. 1st Lieut., 31 Dec., 1819. Trans. to 3rd Art., 1 June, 1821. Resigned 6 Aug., 1822. 2nd Lieut. 6th Inf., 25 June, 1827. Resigned 17 Dec., 1831. 2nd Lieut. 4th Art., 17 Dec., 1831. Capt. Ord., 13 July, 1832. Died 25 Feb., 1835.

HINDMAN, JACOB. [Born in Md. Appointed from Md.]
2nd Lieut. 5th Inf., 3 May, 1808. 1st Lieut., 1 May, 1810. Capt. 2nd Art., 2 July, 1812. Maj. 2nd Art., 26 June, 1813. Trans. to Corps Art., 12 May, 1814. Trans. to 2nd Art., 1 June, 1821. Died 17 Feb., 1827. Bvt. Lieut. Col., 15 Aug., 1814, for distinguished service in defence of Fort Erie. Bvt. Col., 17 May, 1815, for distinguished service.

HINDMAN, THOMAS C. [Born in Tenn. Appointed from Tenn.]
Ensign 39th Inf., 29 July, 1813. 3rd Lieut., 11 Jan., 1814. 2nd Lieut., 20 May, 1814. Reg. Adj., May, 1814, to June, 1815. Trans. to 1st Inf., 17 May, 1815. R. Q. M., 1 Jan. to 31 March, 1816. Trans. to 8th Inf., 8 May, 1816. Resigned 30 June, 1816.

HINDS, ERNEST.* [Born in Ala. Appointed from Ala.]
2nd Lieut. 2nd Art., 12 July, 1887. 1st Lieut., 1 July, 1893. Honor graduate of the Artillery School, 1898. Maj. 49th U. S. Vols., 9 Sept., 1899.

HINE, CHARLES DeL.* [Born in Va. Appointed from Va.]
2nd Lieut. of Inf. (6th), 12 June, 1891. Resigned 5 Aug., 1895.

HINES, JOHN L.* [Born in W. Va. Appointed from W. Va.]
2nd Lieut. 2nd Inf., 12 June, 1891. 1st Lieut., 26 April, 1898.

HINES, JOHN W. [Born in Va. Appointed from Va.]
Priv. Co. C, 1st Ky. Vols., 8 June, 1861, to 15 May, 1863. Priv. Co. B, 59th Ohio Vols., 19 Jan. to 17 June, 1864. 1st Lieut. Adj. 4th Tenn. Vols., 18 June, 1864. Resigned 24 April, 1865. 2nd Lieut. 10th Inf., 22 Jan., 1867. Resigned 1 March, 1870.

HINKLE, FRANK S. [Born in Ohio. Appointed from Army.]
Priv., Corpl. and Sergt. Co. A. 5th Inf., 20 Sept., 1871, to 31 Oct., 1873. 2nd Lieut. 5th Inf., 1 Oct., 1873. Resigned 31 Jan., 1877. Died 9 June, 1888.

HINKLEY, JAMES W., Jr.* [Born in N. Y. Appointed from N. Y.]
Addl. 2nd Lieut. 3rd Art., 12 June, 1896. Trans. to 5th Art., 27 Feb., 1897. 2nd Lieut. 3rd Art., 7 June, 1897. Trans. to 5th Art., 24 June, 1897. 1st Lieut., 2 March, 1899.

HINKS, EDWARD W. [Born in Maine. Appointed from Mass.]
2nd Lieut. 2nd Cav., 26 April, 1861. Lieut. Col. 8th Mass. Vols., 30 April, 1861. Col. 16th May, 1861. Resigned commission of 2nd Lieut. 2nd Cav., 4 June, 1861. Mustered out of Vol. Service 1 Aug., 1861. Col. 19th Mass. Vols., 3 Aug., 1861.

Brig. Gen. Vols., 29 May, 1862. Bvt. Maj. Gen. Vols., 13 March, 1865, for gallant and meritorious service. Resigned 30 June, 1865. Lieut. Col. 40th Inf., 28 July, 1866. Bvt. Col., 2 March, 1865, for gallant and meritorious service in the Battle of Antietam, Md. Bvt. Brig. Gen., 2 March, 1867, for gallant and meritorious service in the assault on Petersburg, Va. Trans. to 25th Inf., 15 March, 1869. Retired with the rank of Col., 15 Dec., 1870. Died 14 Feb., 1894.

HINMAN, FREDK. A.* [Born in Mich. Appointed from Va.]
2nd Lieut. Eng., 1 June, 1867. 1st Lieut., 1 Oct., 1869. Capt. (14 years' service), 17 June, 1881. Retired for disability 26 Feb., 1891.

HINTON, CHAS. B. [Born in D. C. Appointed from D. C.]
2nd Lieut. 25th Inf., 6 May, 1867. Trans. to 18th Inf., 26 April, 1869. 1st Lieut., 4 May, 1874. R. Q. M., 22 Dec., 1888, to 8 Nov., 1889. Capt., 8 Nov., 1889. Maj., 26 March, 1899. Retired for over 30 years' service, 8 Sept., 1899.

HIRSCH, HARRY J.* [Born in Penn. Appointed from Penn.]
2nd Lieut. 15th Inf., 12 June, 1891. 1st Lieut. 18th Inf., 16 Dec., 1897.

HIRST, ROBERT L.* [Born in Penn. Appointed from Penn.]
2nd Lieut. 11th Inf., 1 July, 1886. 1st Lieut., 19 Sept., 1890. Capt. 12th Inf., 26 April, 1898.

HITT, PARKER. [Born in Ind. Appointed from Ind.]
Sergt. Co. D, 2nd U. S. Eng., 1 July, 1898, to 16 May, 1899. 2nd Lieut. 25th Inf., 1 Sept., 1899. Trans. to 22nd Inf., 12 Oct., 1899.

HITCHCOCK, CHAS M. [Born in Md. Appointed from Md.]
Asst. Surg., 17 Aug., 1835. Maj. Surg., 13 Feb., 1851. Resigned 31 March, 1853. Died 3 April, 1885.

HITCHCOCK, DANIEL. [Born in N. Y. Appointed from N. Y.]
Priv. Co. F, 71st N. Y. Militia, 20 April to 30 July, 1861. Com. Sergt. 5th N. Y. Cav., 25 Nov., 1861, to 22 Sept., 1862. 1st Lieut. R. Q. M. 15th N. Y. Art., 31 July, 1863. Resigned 7 Nov., 1863. Priv. and Serg. Co. B, 15th N. Y. Cav., 14 Sept., 1864, to 16 June, 1865. 2nd Lieut. 2nd U. S. Col. Cav., 30 July, 1865. Bvt. 1st Lieut., 13 March, 1865, for highly meritorious service during the war. Mustered out 12 Feb., 1866. 2nd Lieut. 5th Cav., 2 March, 1867. Resigned 10 July, 1868.

HITCHCOCK, ETHAN A.* [Born in Vt. Appointed from Vt.]
3rd Lieut. Corps Art., 17 July, 1817. 2nd Lieut. 8th Inf., 13 Feb., 1818. 1st Lieut., 31 Oct., 1818. Reg. Adj., July, 1819, to 1 June, 1821, and from 16 July to 15 Sept., 1821. Trans. to 1st Inf., 1 June, 1821. Capt., 31 Dec., 1824. Maj. 8th Inf., 7 July, 1838. Lieut. Col. 3rd Inf., 31 Jan., 1842. Col. 2nd Inf., 15 April, 1851. Resigned 18 Oct., 1855. Bvt. Col., 20 Aug., 1847, for gallant and meritorious conduct at Contreras and Churubusco, Mex. Bvt. Brig. Gen., 8 Sept., 1847, for gallant and meritorious conduct at Molino del Rey. Maj. Gen. Vols., 10 Feb., 1862. Mustered out 1 Oct., 1867. Died 5 Aug., 1870.

HITCHCOCK, JOHN F. [Born in Ohio. Appointed from Army.]
Priv.,Corpl., Sergt. and 1st Sergt. Cos. F and A, 2nd Batt. 18th Inf., 14 Sept., 1861, to 24 July, 1862. 2nd Lieut. 18th Inf., 9 June, 1862. Killed 31 Dec., 1862, at Battle of Murfreesboro, Tenn. Bvt. 1st Lieut., 31 Dec., 1862, for gallant and meritorious service at the Battle of Murfreesboro, Tenn.

HITCHCOCK, SAML.* [Born in Vt. Appointed from Ala.]
Bvt. 2nd Lieut. of Inf,. 1 July, 1827. Resigned 19 Dec., 1827. Died 1 Aug., 1851.

HITE, ROBERT G. [Born in Va. Appointed from Va.]
1st Lieut. 12th Inf., 30 April, 1812. Reg. Adj., 4 Aug., 1812, to 26 June, 1813. Capt., 26 June, 1813. Maj. A. A. G., 6 Aug., 1813. Retained as Capt. Corps Art., 17 May, 1815. Resigned 1 Dec., 1816. Died 2 Dec., 1823.

HOAG, JOHN MURRAY. [Born in N. Y. Appointed from N. Y.]
Priv. Co. B, 138th N. Y. Vols. (9th N. Y. Heavy Art.). 11 Aug., 1862. Corpl., 4 May, 1863. Discharged 29 Aug., 1863. 2nd Lieut. 4th U. S. Col. Troops, 2 Sept., 1863. 1st Lieut., 24 Sept., 1864. Capt., 19 Nov., 1864. Bvt. Maj. and Lieut. Col. Vols., 13 March, 1865, for gallant and meritorious service during the war. 1st Lieut. 44th Inf., 28 July, 1866. Mustered out of Vol. Service, 28 Jan., 1867. Bvt. Capt., 2 March, 1867, for gallant and meritorious service in action at Chapin's Farm, Va. Unassigned 27 May, 1869. Retired with rank of Capt., 15 Dec., 1870.

HOAG, WM. R.* [Born in Penn. Appointed from N. Y.]
2nd Lieut. 21st Inf., 12 June, 1871. Died 16 Jan., 1875.

HOAGLAND, MOSES. [Born in Ohio. Appointed from Ohio.]
Capt. of Inf., 8 March, 1847; 15th Inf., 9 April, 1847. Disbanded 4 Aug., 1848. Bvt. Maj., 20 Aug., 1847, for gallant and meritorious conduct at Contreras and Churubusco.

HOBART, CHAS. [Born in Mass. Appointed from Oregon.]
2nd Lieut. 1st Ore. Cav., 16 Jan., 1862. 1st Lieut., 12 Oct., 1865. Mustered out 25 July, 1866. 1st Lieut. 8th Cav., 28 July, 1866. Reg. Adj., 10 June, 1867, to 20 March, 1868. Capt., 26 March, 1868. Trans to 3rd Inf., 29 Dec., 1873. Maj. 15th Inf., 25 April, 1895. Lieut. Col. 8th Inf., 8 Aug., 1898. Retired, over 30 years' service, 17 Sept., 1898.

HOBART, CHRISTOPHER C. [Born in Mass. Appointed from Mass.]
2nd Lieut. Light Art., 8 Oct., 1818. Trans. to 5th Inf., 1 June, 1821. 1st Lieut., 1 April, 1822. Dismissed 30 Nov., 1827.

HOBART, HENRY A.* [Born in Maine. Appointed from Maine.]
2nd Lieut. Light Art., 1 March, 1811. 1st Lieut. Light Art., 15 Aug., 1811. Killed 27 May, 1813, in the capture of Fort George, U. C.

HOBART, WM. F.* [Born in N. H. Appointed from Maine.]
2nd Lieut. Light Art., 3 Jan., 1812. 1st Lieut., 5 April, 1813. (Maj. A. I. G., 27 July, 1814, to 1 June, 1815.) Capt. Light Art., 1 Jan., 1817. Trans. to 4th Art., 1 June, 1821. Trans. to 2nd Inf., 10 Oct., 1822. Resigned 25 Jan., 1823. Died 14 Aug., 1825.

HOBBS, CHAS. W. [Born in N. Y. Appointed from N. Y.]
2nd Lieut. 113th N. Y. Vols., 19 Aug., 1862. Trans. to 7th N. Y. Art., 19 Dec., 1862. 1st Lieut. 7th N. Y. Art., 13 July, 1863. Capt., 12 Nov., 1864. Maj., 22 March, 1865. Mustered out 3 July, 1865. 2nd Lieut. 3rd Art., 21 Sept., 1867. Bvt. 1st Lieut., 21 Sept., 1867, for gallant and meritorious service in the Battle of Spottsylvania, Va. Bvt. Capt., 21 Sept., 1867, for gallant and meritorious service in the Battle of Cold Harbor, Va. 1st Lieut. 3rd Art., 20 [illegible] 1875. Capt., 30 Apr., 1897. Graduate of the Artillery School 1871 and 1888.

HOBBS, FRANK E.* [Born in Maine. Appointed from Maine.]
2nd Lieut. 2nd Art., 14 June, 1878. 1st Lieut. Ord., 16 Dec., 1882. Capt., 14 years' service, 14 June, 1892.

HOBBS, HORACE P. [Born in Pa. Appointed from Pa.]
2nd Lieut. 17th Inf., 10 April, 1899.

HOBKIRK, JOHN B. [Born in Ga. Appointed from Ga.]
Ensign 8th Inf., 8 April, 1814. 3rd Lieut., 1 May, 1814. Disbanded 15 June, 18[illegible] 3rd Lieut. Ord., 18 April, 1818. 2nd Lieut. 7th Inf., 24 July, 1819. 1st L[illegible] 31 Oct., 1820. Dismissed 22 Jan., 1824.

HOCK, ORMENTIZ J. C.* [Born in Penn. Appointed from Wis.]
Addl. 2nd Lieut., 17th Inf., 14 June, 1878. 2nd Lieut., 28 June, 1878. Died 5 June, 1883.

HOCKER, WOODSON. [Born in Ky. Appointed from Mo.]
Priv. Co. K, 3rd Mo. Inf., 14 May to 9 July, 1898. 2nd Lieut. 5th Art., 9 July, 1898. Trans. to 11th Inf., 21 Nov., 1898 (to rank from 11 Oct., 1898).

HODGE, JOHN L. [Born in Penn. Appointed from Penn.]
Addl. P. M. Vols., 1 June, 1861. Maj. P. M. U. S. A., 17 Jan., 1867. Bvt. Lieut. Col. Vols., 13 March, 1865, for faithful and meritorious service as Asst. to P. M. Gen. Cashiered 9 Oct., 1871.

HODGE, JUSTIN. [Born in Conn. Appointed from Conn.]
1st Lieut. Inf., 16 March, 1847; 9th Inf., 9 April, 1847. R. Q. M., 9 April, 1847, to 1 April, 1848. Resigned 6 May, 1848.

HODGES, CHAS. L. [Born in R. I. Appointed from Army.]
Priv., Corpl. and Sergt. Cos. H, E and G, and Sergt. Maj. 65th N. Y. Vols., 20 Aug., to 17 July, 1865. Priv. Co. D, 18th Inf., 17 Nov., 1869. Corpl., 15 Aug., 1870. 1871. Discharged 17 Nov., 1874. Priv. Gen. Ser., 17 Nov., 1874. Corpl., 24 Nov., 1874. 2nd Lieut. 25th Inf., 20 Jan., 1875. 1st Lieut., 1 June, 1880. R. Q. M., 1 Jan., 1882, to 31 March, 1887. Capt., 1 Nov., 1891.

HODGES, GEORGE T. [Born in Vt. Appointed from Vt.]
2nd Lieut. 6th Inf., 5 Aug., 1861. Reg. Adj., 22 Aug., 1863, to 1 April, 1865. 1st Lieut., 27 June, 1862. Resigned 1 April, 1865.

HODGES, HARRY F.* [Born in Mass. Appointed from Mass.]
Addl. 2nd Lieut. Eng., 11 June, 1881. 2nd Lieut., 17 July, 1881. 1st Lieut., 20 Feb., 1883. Capt., 18 May, 1893. Lieut. Col., 1st Vol. Eng., 10 June, 1898, until mustered out, 25 Jan., 1899.

HODGES, HENRY C.* [Born in Vt. Appointed from Vt.]
Bvt. 2nd Lieut. 4th Inf., 1 July, 1851. 2nd Lieut., 1 Aug., 1852. 1st Lieut., 23 May, 1855. Reg. Adj., 1 Oct., 1855, to 25 June, 1861. Capt. A. Q. M., 17 May, 1861. Lieut. Col. Q. M. (Act 17 July, 1862), 1 Jan., 1863, to 11 Feb., 1863. Lieut. Col. Q. M. (Act 17 July, 1862,) 1 Aug., 1863, to 13 Nov., 1863. Bvt. Maj. and Lieut. Col., 13 March, 1865, for faithful and meritorious service during the war. Maj. Q. M., 29 July, 1866. Lieut. Col. Dep. Q. M. G., 29 May, 1876. Col. and Asst. Q. M. G., 19 Oct., 1888. Retired, by operation of law, 14 Jan., 1895.

HODGES, HENRY C., Jr. [Born in Wash. Appointed from D. C.]
2nd Lieut. 22nd Inf., 11 June, 1881. 1st Lieut., 30 Aug., 1890. Capt., 26 April, 1898. Reg. Adj., 29 July, 1899.

HODGES, WM. G. [Born in Mass. Appointed from Mass.]
Mil. Storekeeper, Q. M. Dept., 30 Sept., 1864. Capt. Mil. Storekeeper, 28 July, 1866. Cashiered 4 Nov., 1871.

HODGSON, BENJN. H.* [Born in Penn. Appointed from Penn.]
2nd Lieut. 7th Cav., 15 June, 1870. Killed 25 June, 1876, in action with Indians in Mont. Ter.

HODGSON, FREDERICK G.* [Born in Ga. Appointed from Ga.]
2nd Lieut. 6th Cav., 11 June, 1881. 1st Lieut., 7 July, 1888. Capt. A. Q. M., 13 March, 1894. Maj. Q. M. Vols., 12 May, 1898. Lieut. Col. Q. M. Vols., 10 Aug., 1898, to 2 March, 1899.

HOELCKE, WM. [Born in Germany. Appointed from Wis.]
Capt. A. A. de C., 19 Aug., 1861. Mustered out 12 March, 1866. Capt. 5th U. S. Vols., 1 April, 1866. Mustered out 3 Nov., 1866. 2nd Lieut. 39th Inf., 28 July, 1866. 1st Lieut., 5 Jan., 1867. Unassigned 20 April, 1869. Discharged 1 Sept., 1870.

HOF, SAMUEL.* [Born in Wis. Appointed from Wis.]
2nd Lieut. 6th Cav., 12 June, 1894. 1st Lieut. Ord., 4 Oct., 1898.

HOFF, ALEXR. H. [Born in Penn. Appointed from N. Y.]
Surg. 3rd N. Y. Vols., 14 May to 1 Sept., 1861. Surg. U. S. Vols., 3 Aug., 1861. Bvt. Lieut. Col. and Col. Vols., 13 March, 1865, for faithful and meritorious service during the war. Mustered out 1 March, 1866. Asst. Surg., 14 May, 1867. Died 19 Aug., 1876.

HOFF, JOHN J. [Born in Penn. Appointed from N. J.]
2nd Lieut. 1st N. J. Art., 12 Aug., 1861. 1st Lieut., 1 Dec., 1861. Resigned [illegible] Nov., 1862. Capt. C. S. Vols., 26 Nov., 1862. Bvt. Maj. Vols., 13 March, 1865, for meritorious service in his Dept. during the war. Mustered out 1 Nov., 1866. Capt. 20th Inf., 28 July, 1866. Unassigned 1 Sept., 1869. Died 20 July, 1870.

HOFF, JOHN VAN R. [Born in N. Y. Appointed from N. Y.]
1st Lieut. Asst. Surg., 10 Nov., 1874. Capt. Asst. Surg., 10 Nov., 1879. Maj. Surg., 15 June, 1891. Lieut. Col. Chief Surg. Vols., 9 May, 1898, to 5 Nov., 1898.

HOFFER, JAY E.* [Born in Penn. Appointed from Penn.]
2nd Lieut. 3rd Art., 11 June, 1892. 1st Lieut. Ord., 4 Oct., 1898. Graduate of the Artillery School, 1896.

HOFFMAN, ADAM E. [Born in Germany. Appointed from Ohio.]
2nd Lieut. 19th Inf., 6 April, 1813. Trans. to 17th Inf., 12 May, 1814. 1st Lieut., 1 Oct., 1814. Resigned 4 Jan., 1815. 2nd Lieut. 1st Inf., 13 Aug., 1819. Disbanded 1 June, 1821.

HOFFMAN, ALEXR. T. [Born in N. Y. Appointed from N. Y.]
2nd Lieut. 2nd Inf., 1 Aug., 1838. Died 25 Jan., 1844.

HOFFMAN, ALEX. W.* [Born in N. Y. Appointed from Dak.]
2nd Lieut. 10th Inf., 23 June, 1865. R. Q. M., 12 May, 1866, to 12 July, 1869. 1st Lieut., 23 June, 1865. Resigned 13 Nov., 1874.

HOFFMAN, GEORGE M.* [Born in Penn. Appointed from Penn.]
Addl. 2nd Lieut. Eng., 12 June, 1896. 2nd Lieut., 18 May, 1898. 1st Lieut., 5 July, 1898.

HOFFMAN, SATTERLEE. [Born in Mich. Appointed from Mich.]
2nd Lieut. 1st Art., 8 March, 1847. Killed 20 Aug., 1847, in the Battle of Churubusco, Mex.

HOFFMAN, WM. [Born in N. Y. Appointed from N. Y.]
1st Lieut. 41st Inf., 11 Nov., 1813. Trans. to 2nd Inf., 17 May, 1815. Capt., 1 May, 1819. Maj. 6th Inf., 4 Nov., 1838. Lieut. Col. 7th Inf., 15 July, 1845. Died 26 Nov., 1845. Bvt. Maj., 1 May, 1829, for ten years' faithful service in one grade.

HOFFMAN, WM.* [Born in N. Y. Appointed from N. Y.]
Bvt. 2nd Lieut. 6th Inf., 1 July, 1829. 2nd Lieut., 1 July, 1829. 1st Lieut., 16 Nov., 1836. Capt., 1 Feb., 1838. Bvt. Maj., 20 Aug., 1847, for gallant and meritorious conduct in the Battles of Contreras and Churubusco. Bvt. Lieut. Col., 8 Sept., 1847, for gallant and meritorious conduct in the Battle of Molino del Rey. Maj. 5th Inf., 15 April, 1851. Trans. to 6th Inf., 20 Feb., 1852. Lieut. Col. 8th Inf., 17 Oct., 1860. Col. 3rd Inf., 25 April, 1862. Bvt. Brig. Gen., 7 Oct., 1864, for faithful and meritorious service during the war. Bvt. Maj. Gen., 13 March, 1865, for faithful, meritorious and distinguished service as Commissary General of Prisoners during the war. Unassigned 15 March, 1869. Retired 1 May, 1870. Died 12 Aug., 1884.

HOFFMAN, WM. [Born in Maine. Appointed from Maine.]
Sergt. Co. G, 5th N. Y. Vols., 9 May, 1861. 2nd Lieut., 26 July, 1862. 1st Lieut., 24 Sept., 1862. Capt., 23 Jan., 1863. Mustered out 14 May, 1863. Capt. 13th N. Y. Art., 29 Aug., 1863. Mustered out 24 Aug., 1865. 2nd Lieut. 11th Inf., 11 May, 1866. Trans. to 29th Inf., 21 Sept., 1866. 1st Lieut., 25 June, 1867. Trans. to 11th Inf., 25 April, 1869. Capt., 24 April, 1886. Retired for disability 8 June, 1894.

HOFFMAN, WM. G. [Born in Va. Appointed from Va.]
2nd Lieut. 3rd Cav., 24 Oct., 1861. 1st Lieut., 17 July, 1862. Dismissed 31 Dec., 1864. Reinstated 14 Feb., 1865. Casiered 6 Sept., 1865.

HOFMAN, WM. E. [Born in Ohio. Appointed from Ill.]
1st Lieut. 98th Ill. Vols., 3 Sept., 1862. Capt., 1 May, 1863. Mustered out 27 June, 1865. 1st Lieut. 31st Inf., 12 June, 1867. Unassigned 15 May, 1869. Ass'd to 9th Inf., 4 May, 1870. Capt., 3 Feb., 1885. Retired for disability not incident to the service, 28 Sept., 1889.

HOFFMANN, ERNEST F. [Born in Prussia. Appointed from Iowa.]
Maj. A. A. de C., 31 May, 1862. Mustered out 5 July, 1866. 2nd Lieut. 35th Inf., 24 Oct., 1867. Unassigned 12 Aug., 1869. Ass'd. to 23rd Inf., 3 Aug., 1870. Discharged 31 Dec., 1870. Died 14 Aug., 1884.

HOGAN, BENJ. R. [Born in S. C. Appointed from Ala.]
Asst. Surg., 13 July, 1832. Resigned 30 April, 1835.

HOGAN, JOHN B. [Born in Va. Appointed from Va.]
Ensign 20th Inf., 12 March, 1812. 2nd Lieut., 16 April, 1813. Maj. Dep. Q. M. G., 25 June, 1814. Disbanded 15 June, 1815. P. M. 7th Inf., 25 Sept., 1817. Trans. to 4th Inf., 10 June, 1818. Disbanded 1 June, 1821. Adjt. and A. I. G. Ala. Vols., 21 May, 1836. Brig. Gen. Ala. Vols., 9 June to 10 Aug., 1836. Died 17 May, 1845.

HOGAN, MARTIN E. [Born in Ind. Appointed from Ind.]
Priv. Co. I, Ind. Cav., 4 July, 1861, to 11 Feb., 1865. 2nd Lieut. 13th Inf., 23 Feb., 1866. Trans. to 31st Inf., 21 Sept., 1866. 1st Lieut., 28 Dec., 1866. Trans. to 22nd Inf., 15 May, 1869. Dismissed 12 May, 1875.

HOGAN, PATRICK H. [Born in Ireland. Appointed from Vt.]
2nd Lieut., 1st Cav., 27 July, 1872. Died 21 Nov., 1873.

HOGARTY, MICHAEL J. [Born in Ireland. Appointed from N. Y.]
Priv. Co. I, 141st N. Y. Vols., 30 Dec., 1863. Discharged 1 Sept., 1864. Priv. Co. I, 141st N. Y. Vols., 16 Sept., 1864. 1st Lieut. 141st N. Y. Vols., 23 April, 1865. Mustered out 8 June, 1865. 1st Lieut. 42nd Inf., 28 July, 1866. Trans. to 6th Inf., 22 April, 1869. Unassigned 8 July, 1870. Retired 15 Dec., 1870.

HOGARTY, WM. P. [Born in N. Y. Appointed from N. Y.]
Priv. Co. D, 23rd N. Y. Vols., 16 May, 1861. Trans. to Light Batty B, 4th U. S. Art., 4 Dec., 1861. Discharged 29 Jan., 1863, on acount of physical disability resulting from the loss of left arm incurred in the Battle of Fredericksburg, Va., 13 Dec., 1862. Appointed 2nd Lieut. Vet. Res. Corps, 30 Jan., 1865. Bvt. 1st Lieut. and Capt. U. S. Vols., 13 March, 1865, for gallant and meritorious conduct during the war. Mustered out of Vol. Service, 16 Oct., 1866. Appointed 2nd Lieut. 45th Reg. U. S. Army, 28 July, 1866. Bvt. 1st Lieut. U. S. Army, 2 March, 1867, for gallant and meritorious services in the Battle of Fredericksburg, Va. In command of Co. B, 21st Reg. Vet. Res. Corps at Trenton Barracks, N. J., from — June, 1865, to 8 Dec., 1865. Awaiting orders from 8 Dec., 1865, to 2 April, 1866. On duty in the Bureau Refugees, Freedman and Abandoned Lands at Louisville, Ky., from 12 May, 1866, to 30 Oct., 1866, capturing guerillas and

desperadoes in different parts of the State, establishing colored schools, paying bounties and back-pay to discharged colored soldiers. On recruiting service, and in command of a detachment of U. S. Troops at Covington, Ky., from 30 Oct., 1866, to 17 April, 1867. In command of Co. E, 45th Reg. U. S. Inf., and the Post of Chattanooga, Tenn., also the Post of Pulaska, Tenn., from 17 April, 1867, to 30 Aug., 1867. On duty in the Bureau Refugees, Freedman and Abandoned Lands, at Louisville, Ky., from 30 Aug., 1867, to 4 June, 1868. On leave of absence in Europe on surgeon's certificate of disability, undergoing special treatment for partial deafness, from 4 June, 1868, to 23 Jan., 1869. On duty with Reg. at Nashville, Tenn., and Union, W. Va., from 23 Jan., 1869, to 18 Sept., 1869. On recruiting service at Fort Leavenworth, Kan., from 18 Sept., 1869, to 31 Dec., 1870. Retired from active service, 31 Dec., 1870, on account of physical disability resulting from loss of left arm and partial deafness incurred in line of duty. Awarded the Medal of Honor for distinguished gallantry in the Battle Antietam, Md., 17 Sept., 1862; and in the Battle of Fredericksburg, Va., 13 Dec., 1862, in which last named Battle he was severely wounded (loss of left arm): while a private in Co. D, 23rd N. Y. Vol. Inf., serving in Light Batty B, 4th U. S. Art. Gen. Jeff. C. Davis, commanding the Mil. District of Ky., referring to the services of Lieutenant Hogarty while under his command, in a communication to the War Department, says: "Lieutenant Hogarty has been rendering gallant and signal service, capturing guerillas and desperadoes in different parts of the State."

HOGE, GEORGE B. [Born in Penn. Appointed from Ill.]
Capt. 25th Mo. Vols., 25 July, 1861. Col. 113th Ill. Vols., 1 Oct., 1862. Bvt. Brig. Gen. Vols., 13 March, 1865, for gallant and meritorious service during the war. Mustered out 20 June, 1865. Capt. 41st Inf., 17 July, 1867. Unassigned 12 Nov., 1869. Ass'd to 12th Inf., 1 Jan., 1871. Wholly retired 30 Aug., 1871. Capt. 12th Inf., 3 March, 1873. Resigned 31 Jan., 1874.

HOGE, SOLOMON L. [Born in Ohio. Appointed from Ohio.]
1st Lieut. 82nd Ohio Vols., 14 Nov., 1861. Capt., 18 March, 1862. Resigned 25 April, 1863. 1st Lieut. Vet. Res. Corps, 18 June, 1864. Bvt. Capt. and Maj. Vols., 9 Nov., 1865, for meritorious service. Mustered out 19 April, 1866. 2nd Lieut. 6th Inf., 23 Feb., 1866. 1st Lieut., 28 July, 1866. Resigned 1 Sept., 1868. Bvt. Capt., 2 March, 1867, for gallant and meritorious service in the Battle of Bull Run (2nd), Va.

HOKE, JOHN F. [Born in N. C. Appointed from N. C.]
1st Lieut. Inf., 8 March, 1847; 12th Inf., 9 April, 1847. Capt., 27 June, 1847. Disbanded 25 July, 1848.

HOLABIRD, SAML. B.* [Born in Conn. Appointed from Conn.]
Bvt. 2nd Lieut. 1st Inf., 1 July, 1849. 2nd Lieut., 10 June, 1850. 1st Lieut., 31 May, 1855. R. Q. M., 1 July, 1852, to 31 May, 1858. Capt. A. Q. M., 13 May, 1861. Maj. A. A. de C., 2 July, 1862. Col. A. A. de C., 11 July, 1862. Bvt. Maj., Lieut. Col., Col. and Brig. Gen., 13 March, 1865, for gallant and meritorious service during the war. Mustered out as Col. A. A. de C., 31 May, 1866. Lieut. Col. Dep. Q. M. G., 29 July, 1866. Col. Ass't Q. M. G., 22 Jan., 1881. Brig. Gen., Q. M. G., 1 July, 1883. Retired by operation of law, 16 June, 1890.

HOLBROOK, LUCIUS R.* [Born in Wis. Appointed from Minn.]
Addl. 2nd Lieut. 4th Cav., 12 June, 1896. 2nd Lieut., 14 Oct., 1896. 1st Lieut. 1st Cav., 23 Jan., 1900.

HOLBROOK, SAML. S. [Born in Penn. Appointed from the Army.]
Priv. Co. F, 1st Pa. Vols., 20 April to 23 July, 1861. Priv. 15th Inf., 8 Oct., to 2 Nov., 1861. 2nd Lieut. 15th Inf., 13 Oct., 1861. 1st Lieut., 3 Jan., 1862. R. Q. M., 1 Dec., 1862, to 29 June, 1863. Resigned 2 April, 1866. Bvt. Capt., 20 Sept., 1863, for gallant and meritorious service at the Battle of Chickamauga, Ga.

HOLBROOK, WILLARD A.* [Born in Wis. Appointed from Wis.]
2nd Lieut. 1st Cav., 14 June, 1885. 1st Lieut. 7th Cav., 17 Dec., 1891. Capt. 5th Cav., 18 Oct., 1899. Honor graduate of the Inf. and Cav. School 1891. Capt. A. A. G. Vols., 12 May, 1898. Capt. A. Q. M. Vols., 1 April to 19 Aug., 1899. Maj. 38th U. S. Vols., 17 Aug., 1899, to ——.

HOLCOMB, FREEBORN P. [Born in N. Y. Appointed from Army.]
Priv., Corpl. and Sergt. Troops B and L, 8th Cav., 5 Sept., 1895, to 23 Nov., 1899. 2nd Lieut. 2nd Cav., 1 Oct., 1899.

HOLCOMB, PYTHAGORAS E. [Born in Ohio. Appointed from Army.]
Priv. Co. E, 3rd Art., 3 Oct., 1845. Corpl., 24 Sept., 1846. Priv., 11 Nov., 1847. 2nd Lieut. 16th Inf., 30 Dec., 1847. Disbanded 2 Aug., 1848. 1st Lieut. 17th Inf., 14 May, 1861. Capt. 2nd Batty Vt. Light Art., 22 March, 1862. Bvt. Capt., 14 June, 1863, for gallant and meritorious service in the Siege of Port Hudson, La. Mustered out of Vol. Service, 19 Aug., 1863. Maj. 1st Texas Cav., 20 Aug., 1863. Capt. 17th Inf., 26 Jan., 1864. Resigned Vol. commission, 5 Oct., 1864. Bvt. Maj., 13 March, 1865, for faithful and meritorious service during the war. Trans. to 35th Inf., 21 Sept., 1866. Retired 30 Jan., 1869. Died 20 Nov., 1884.

HOLDEN, EDWARD S.* [Born in Mo. Appointed from Mo.]
2nd Lieut. 4th Art., 15 June, 1870. Trans. to Eng., 10 June, 1872. Resigned 28 March, 1873.

HOLDEN, GEORGE J. [Born in Vt. Appointed from Vt.]
2nd Lieut. 10th Inf., 9 July, 1898. 1st Lieut., 2 March, 1899.

HOLDEN, LEVI H. [Born in R. I. Appointed from R. I.]
Asst. Surg., 15 June, 1840. Maj. Surg., 23 April, 1860. Retired 27 Oct., 1868. Died 12 May, 1874. Bvt. Lieut. Col., 13 March, 1865, for faithful and meritorious service during the war.

HOLDEN, NATHL. B. [Born in N. Y. Appointed from Mo.]
Capt. Inf., 5 March, 1847; 12th Inf., 9 April, 1847. Disbanded 25 July, 1848. Murdered 21 Sept., 1863. Bvt. Maj., 20 Aug., 1847, for gallant and meritorious conduct at Contreras and Churubusco, Mex.

HOLDING, JOHN W. [Born in Md. Appointed from Army.]
Sergt. Maj. 21st Inf., 18 May, 1812, to — Aug., 1813. Ensign 21st Inf., 5 Aug., 1813. 2nd Lieut., 8 March, 1814. 1st Lieut., 31 July, 1814. Trans. to 5th Inf., 17 May, 1815. Dropped 11 Nov., 1818. Died — Oct., 1821. Bvt. Capt., 25 July, 1814, for gallant conduct at the Battle of Niagara.

HOLGATE, ASA H.* [Born in N. Y. Appointed from Ohio.]
1st Lieut. Eng., 11 June, 1863. Capt., 28 July, 1866. Resigned 9 Dec., 1875. Bvt. Capt., 13 March, 1865, for meritorious service during the war. Died Sept., 1880.

HOLLAND, JOHN C.* [Born in S. C. Appointed from S. C.]
Bvt. 2nd Lieut. 3rd Art., 1 July, 1821. 2nd Lieut. 4th Art., 1 July, 1821. Trans. to 4th Art., 1 Jan., 1822. Died 10 Oct., 1825.

HOLLENBUSH, CALVIN G. [Born in Penn. Appointed from Penn.]
Asst. Surg., 4 June, 1857. Died 6 Aug., 1861.

HOLLEY, DWIGHT E.* [Born in Conn. Appointed from Conn.]
2nd Lieut. 1st Inf., 1 July, 1886. 1st Lieut. 4th Inf., 15 Oct., 1893. Capt., 2 March, 1899.

HOLLIDAY, JONAS P.* [Born in N. Y. Appointed from N. Y.]
Bvt. 2nd Lieut. 2nd Drag., 1 July, 1850. 2nd Lieut., 11 Oct., 1851. 1st Lieut., 3 March, 1855. R. Q. M., 4 Aug., 1858, to 5 July, 1859. Capt., 9 May, 1861. 2nd Cav., 3 Aug., 1861. Col. 1st. Vt. Cav., 14 Feb., 1862. Died 5 April, 1862.

HOLLINGSWORTH, JOHN. [Born in Va. Appointed from Va.]
2nd Lieut. 3rd Rifle Reg., 26 March, 1814. Retained in Rifle Reg., 17 May, 1815. R. Q. M., — May, 1816, to 31 July, 1817. 1st Lieut., 8 March, 1817. Resigned 31 July, 1817.

HOLLIS, MAGNUS O.* [Born in Ga. Appointed from Ga.]
2nd Lieut. 4th Inf., 13 June, 1882. 1st Lieut. 23rd Inf., 31 Jan., 1891. Trans. to 4th Inf., 20 July, 1891. Capt., 26 April, 1898. Died 15 Nov., 1899.

HOLLISTER, GEORGE S.* [Born in N. Y. Appointed from N. Y.]
Bvt. 2nd Lieut. 1st Inf., 1 July, 1860. 2nd Lieut. 7th Inf., 26 Feb., 1861. 1st Lieut., 14 May, 1861. Capt., 21 Jan., 1863. Lieut. Col. 16th N. Y. Cav., 30 Dec., 1863. Dismissed from Vol. Service and U. S. A., 7 Oct., 1864. Reinstated as Capt. 7th Inf., 25 Jan., 1866. Mustered out 1 Jan., 1871.

HOLLOWAY, EDMUNDS B.* [Born in Ky. Appointed from Ky.]
Bvt. 2nd Lieut. 4th Inf., 1 July, 1843. 2nd Lieut. 8th Inf., 26 Sept., 1845. 1st Lieut., 17 Sept., 1847. R. Q. M., 1 July, 1852, to 31 Dec., 1853. Capt., 31 Dec., 1853. Resigned 14 May, 1861. Bvt. 1st Lieut., 20 Aug., 1847, for gallant and meritorious conduct at Contreras and Churubusco, Mex. Accidentally killed 17 June, 1861.

HOLLOWAY, JUNIUS B. [Born in Ky. Appointed from Ky.]
2nd Lieut. 2nd Cav., 26 April, 1861. 1st Lieut., 21 May, 1861; 5th Cav., 3 Aug., 1861. Capt., 17 July, 1862. Dismissed 6 Dec., 1862.

HOLMAN, CHAS. [Born in England. Appointed from Army.]
Priv., Corpl, Sergt. and 1st Sergt. Co. K, 5th Art., 1 Aug., 1861, to 28 Oct., 1862. 2nd Lieut. 5th Art., 22 Oct., 1862. Resigned 14 Nov., 1864.

HOLMAN, JAS. H. [Born in Tenn. Appointed from Tenn.]
2nd Lieut. 1st Inf., 21 Feb., 1857. Resigned 17 April, 1861.

HOLMES, CHAS. [Born in N. H. Appointed from N. H.]
1st Sergt. Co. B, 2nd N. H. Vols., 27 May, 1861. 2nd Lieut. 2nd N. H. Vols., 1 July, 1861. Mustered out 11 Nov., 1861. Capt. 17th Inf., 26 Oct., 1861. Retired 28 Nov., 1863.

HOLMES, JAMES.* [Born in N. C. Appointed from N. C.]
Bvt. 2nd Lieut. 2nd Art., 1 July, 1848. 2nd Lieut. 4th Art., 24 April, 1849. 1st Lieut., 15 July, 1852. Died 27 May, 1854.

HOLMES, NORMAN. [Born in Penn. Appointed from Md.]
Cadet Mil. Acad., 20 May, 1818, to 25 Aug., 1819. 2nd Lieut. Corps Art., 28 Jan., 1820. Trans. to 7th Inf., 1 June, 1821. Died 18 Dec., 1821.

HOLMES, REUBEN.* [Born in Conn. Appointed from Conn.]
2nd Lieut. 6th Inf., 1 July, 1823. 1st Lieut., 15 Feb., 1826. Capt. 1st Drag., 4 March, 1833. Died 4 Nov., 1833.

HOLMES, ROBT. S. [Born in Penn. Appointed from Penn.]
Asst. Surg., 16 Aug., 1841. Resigned 4 Oct., 1847.

HOLMES, SAML. N.* [Born in Penn. Appointed from N. J.]
2nd Lieut. 13th Inf., 13 June, 1873. 1st Lieut., 24 July, 1879. Dismissed 24 July, 1883. Burned to death 15 July, 1884.

HOLMES, THEOPHILUS H.* [Born in N. C. Appointed from N. C.]
Bvt. 2nd Lieut. 7th Inf., 1 July, 1829. 2nd Lieut., 1 July, 1829. 1st Lieut., 26 March, 1835. Reg. Adj., 9 Aug. to 9 Dec., 1838. Capt., 9 Dec., 1838. Maj. 8th Inf., 3 March, 1855. Resigned 22 April, 1861. Bvt. Maj., 23 Sept., 1846, for gallant conduct at Monterey. Died 20 June, 1880.

HOLT, CHAS.* [Born in N. Y. Appointed from N. Y.]
Bvt. 2nd Lieut. 2nd Inf., 1 July, 1823. 2nd Lieut. 1st Inf., 1 July, 1823. Died 14 Sept., 1824.

HOLT, GEORGE W.* [Born in Ala. Appointed from Ala.]
Bvt. 2nd Lieut. 9th Inf., 1 July, 1857. 2nd Lieut. 3rd Inf., 28 Sept., 1857. Resigned 28 Feb., 1861. Died 23 Jan., 1876.

HOLT, HARRISON. [Born in N. Y. Appointed from Mass.]
1st Sergt. Co. F and Sergt. Maj. 30th N. Y. Vols., 1 June, 1861, to 1 Nov., 1862. 1st Lieut. 30th N. Y. Vols., 1 Nov., 1862. Resigned 13 March, 1863. 2nd Lieut. 55th Mass. Vols., 16 May, 1863. 1st Lieut., 24 June, 1863. Resigned 14 Oct., 1863. 1st Lieut. Mass. Cav., 13 Jan., 1864. Resigned 26 July, 1864. 2nd Lieut. 6th Cav., 15 May, 1867. 1st Lieut., 18 Aug., 1868. Died 21 Feb., 1870.

HOLT, HENRY. [Born in N. Y. Appointed from N. Y.]
Asst. Surg., 31 Dec., 1833. Resigned 30 Sept., 1841.

HOLT, JOSEPH. [Born in Ky. Appointed from D. C.]
Sec. of War, 18 Jan. to 5 March, 1861. Col. J. A. G., 3 Sept., 1862. Brig. Gen.

J. A. G., 22 June, 1864. Bvt. Maj. Gen., 13 March, 1865, for faithful, meritorious and distinguished service in the Bureau of Military Justice during the war. Retired 1 Dec., 1875. Died 1 Aug., 1894.

HOLTON, FREDERICK D.* [Born in Vt. Appointed from Vt.]
2nd Lieut. 2nd Cav., 12 June, 1880. 1st Lieut., 12 Dec., 1886. Died 18 Sept., 1890.

HOMANS, JOHN, Jr. [Born in Mass. Appointed from Mass.]
Asst. Surg., 22 Nov., 1862. Resigned 5 June, 1865.

HOMER, WILLIAM B.* [Born in Mass. Appointed from Mass.]
2nd Lieut. 5th Art., 15 June, 1870. 1st Lieut., 17 April, 1881. Capt. 6th Art., 8 March, 1898. Graduate of the Artillery School, 1875 and 1890.

HONEY, ROBERTSON.* [Born in Ala. Appointed from R. I.
Addl. 2nd Lieut. of Art. (3rd), 12 June, 1893. 2nd Lieut. of Art. (4th), 11 Dec., 1893, to rank from 12 June, 1893. Resigned 28 Feb., 1898.

HONEY, SAMUEL R. [Born in England. Appointed from Army.]
Priv. Gen. Ser. and Sergt. Maj. 2nd Batt. 15th Inf., 20 Aug., 1860, to 22 Aug., 1862. 2nd Lieut. 15th Inf., 13 Aug., 1862. 1st Lieut., 17 Feb., 1863. Trans. to 33rd Inf., 21 Sept., 1866. Capt., 1 Nov., 1866. Unassigned 3 May, 1869. Discharged 7 Oct., 1870. Bvt. Capt., 1 Sept., 1864, for gallant and meritorious service during the Atlanta campaign, and at the Battle of Jonesboro, Ga.

HONEYCUTT, JOHN T.* [Born in Miss. Appointed from Miss.]
2nd Lieut. 1st Art., 17 June, 1874. 1st Lieut., 18 July, 1879. Graduate of the Artillery School, 1878. Capt. 6th Art., — ———, 1898. Died 7 Oct., 1898.

HOOD, CHAS. C. [Born in Ohio. Appointed from Ohio.]
Priv. Co. G, 31st Ohio Vols., 20 Aug., 1861. Corpl., 24 Sept., 1861. Sergt., 1 June, 1862. 1st Lieut. 31st Ohio Vols., 3 Feb., 1864. Capt., 26 Oct., 1864. Mustered out 20 July, 1865. Capt. 41st Inf., 28 July, 1866. Trans. to 24th Inf., 11 Nov., 1869. Maj. 7th Inf., 4 July, 1892. Lieut. Col. 19th Inf., 28 Jan., 1897. Col. 10th Inf., 5 May, 1899.

HOOD, JOHN B.* [Born in Ky. Appointed from Ky.]
Bvt. 2nd Lieut. 4th Inf., 1 July, 1853. 2nd Lieut. 2nd Cav., 3 March, 1855. 1st Lieut., 18 Aug., 1858. Resigned 16 April, 1861. Died 30 Aug., 1879.

HOOD, WASHINIGTON.* [Born in Penn. Appointed from Penn.]
Bvt. 2nd Lieut. 4th Inf., 1 July, 1827. 2nd Lieut., 1 July, 1827. 1st Lieut., 28 Dec., 1835. Resigned 7 Aug., 1836. Capt. Top. Eng., 7 July, 1838. Died 17 July, 1840.

HOOE, ALEXANDER S.* [Born in Va. Appointed from Va.]
Bvt. 2nd Lieut. Inf., 1 July, 1827. 2nd Lieut. 5th Inf., 1 July, 1827. 1st Lieut., 1 Oct., 1833. Reg. Adj., 1 to 7 July, 1838. Capt., 7 July, 1838. Died 9 Dec., 1847. Bvt. Maj., 9 May, 1846, for gallant and distinguished conduct at Palo Alto and Resaca de la Palma.

HOOK, CORNELIUS J.* [Born in Ill. Appointed from Ill.]
Bvt. 2nd Lieut. 1st Art., 1 July, 1860. 2nd Lieut., 22 Nov., 1860. 1st Lieut., 14 May, 1861. Capt., 1 June, 1863. Retired 4 Nov., 1863. Died 19 June, 1864.

HOOK, JAMES H. [Born in Md. Appointed from Md.]
Ensign 5th Inf., 30 April, 1812. 2nd Lieut., 1 Sept., 1812. Capt. 38th Inf., 20 May, 1813. Disbanded 15 June, 1815. Reinstated in 4th Inf., 2 Dec., 1815. Maj. C. S., 10 March, 1829. Lieut. Col. A. C. G. S., 7 July, 1838. Died 30 Nov., 1841. Bvt. Maj., 20 May, 1823, for ten years' faithful service in one grade.

HOOKER, AMBROSE E. [Born in N. Y. Appointed from Cal.]
Lieut. Col. 6th Cal. Vols., 16 Feb., 1863. Bvt. Col. and Brig. Gen. Vols., 13 March, 1865, for faithful and meritorious service. Mustered out 31 Oct., 1865. Lieut. Col. 2nd Cal. Cav., 1 Nov., 1865. Mustered out 13 June, 1866. 1st Lieut. 8th Cav., 28 July, 1866. Capt. 9th Cav., 6 March, 1867. Died 20 Jan., 1883.

HOOKER, JOSEPH.* [Born in Mass. Appointed from Mass.]
2nd Lieut. 1st Art., 1 July, 1837. 1st Lieut., 1 Nov., 1838. Reg. Adj., 1 Sept., 1841, to 11 May, 1846. Bvt. Capt., 23 Sept., 1846, for gallant and meritorious conduct in the several conflicts at Monterey. Bvt. Capt. A. A. G., 3 March, 1847. Bvt. Maj., 11 June, 1847, for gallant and meritorious conduct in the affair at the National Bridge. Bvt. Lieut. Col., 13 Sept., 1847, for gallant and meritorious conduct in the Battle of Chapultepec. Capt. 1st Art., 29 Oct., 1848. Vacated Line Commission, 29 Oct, 1848. Resigned 21 Feb., 1853. Brig. Gen. Vols., 17 May, 1861. Maj. Gen. Vols., 5 May, 1862. Brig. Gen. U. S. A., 20 Sept., 1862. Bvt. Maj. Gen., 13 March, 1865, for gallant and meritorious service in the Battle of Chattanooga, Tenn. Mustered out of Vol. Service, 1 Sept., 1866. Retired with rank of Maj. Gen., 15 Oct., 1868. Died 31 Oct., 1879.

HOOPER, GEORGE F. [Born in Va. Appointed from Ill.]
Cadet Mil. Acad., 1 July, 1842, to 7 Aug., 1844. 2nd Lieut. 15th Inf., 4 Aug., 1847. Disbanded 4 Aug., 1848.

HOOPER, JOHN L.* [Born in Mass. Appointed from Mass.]
Bvt. 2nd Lieut. 4th Inf., 1 July, 1833. 2nd Lieut., 28 Nov., 1835. Dismissed 2 May, 1836. 1st Lieut. 4th Inf., 2 Nov., 1836. Resigned 31 March, 1840. Died 9 Aug., 1840.

HOOPER, MICHAEL H. [Born in Md. Appointed from Md.]
2nd Lieut. of Inf., 8 March, 1847; Voltigeurs, 9 Apri, 1847. Disbanded 31 Aug., 1848.

HOOTON, MOTT. [Born in Penn. Appointed from Penn.]
1st Sergt. Co. A. 1st Pa. Res., 4 June, 1861. 2nd Lieut. Pa. Res. Corps, 11 June, 1861. Capt., 16 Oct., 1861. Mustered out 13 June, 1864. Bvt. Maj. Vols., 13 March, 1865, for gallant and meritorious service in the Wilderness campaign. 2nd Lieut. and 1st Lieut. 13th Inf., 23 Feb., 1866. Trans. to 31st Inf., 21 Sept., 1866. Trans. to 22nd Inf., 15 May, 1869. Capt., 5 Aug., 1872. Bvt. Maj., 27 Feb., 1890, for gallant services in action against Indians at Spring Creek, Mont., 15 and 16 Oct., 1876. Maj. 25th Inf., 1 May, 1896. Lieut. Col. 5th Inf., 4 Oct., 1898.

HOOVER, GEORGE W. [Born in D. C. Appointed from D. C.]
2nd Lieut. 14th Inf., 24 Oct., 1861. Died 1 July, 1862, of wounds received at Battle of Gaines' Mill, Va. Bvt. 1st Lieut., 27 June, 1862, for gallant and meritorious service at the Battle of Gaines' Mills, Va.

HOPKINS, CHAS. B. [Born in Penn. Appointed from Penn.]
2nd Lieut. 32nd Inf., 17 May, 1813. 1st Lieut., 5 Oct., 1813. Trans. to 42nd Inf., 25 June, 1814. Trans. to 8th Inf., 17 May, 1815. R. Q. M., June, 1816, to 26 June, 1817. Died 26 June, 1817.

HOPKINS, DAVID. [Born in Mass. Appointed from Md.]
Maj. 9th Inf., 8 Jan., 1799. Disbanded 15 June, 1800. Mil. Storekeeper, 26 May, 1816. Disbanded 1 June, 1821.

HOPKINS, EDMUND. [Born in Penn. Appointed from Penn.]
Ensign 16th Inf., 19 July, 1813. 3rd Lieut. 1st Art., 1 Aug., 1813. 2nd Lieut., 31 Dec., 1813. Trans. to Corps Art., 12 May, 1814. Disbanded 15 June, 1815. 2nd Lieut. 3rd Inf., 1 July, 1816. 1st Lieut., 31 Oct., 1818. Disbanded 1 June, 1821.

HOPKINS, EDWARD R.* [Born in N. Y. Appointed from N. Y.]
Bvt. 2nd Lieut. 2nd Inf., 1 July, 1860. 2nd Lieut. 3rd Inf., 1 July, 1860. 1st Lieut., 14 May, 1861. Capt., 7 June, 1862. Capt. C. S., 9 Feb., 1863. Resigned 13 May, 1865. Bvt. Maj., 13 March, 1865, for faithful and meritorious service during the war.

HOPKINS, JAMES A. [Born in N. H. Appointed from Army.]
Priv., Sergt. and 1st Sergt. Co. F, 13th Inf., 1 May, 1862, to 23 Dec., 1863. 2nd Lieut. 17th Inf., 31 Oct., 1863. 1st Lieut., 11 Jan., 1864. Capt., 1 March, 1866. Trans. to 35th Inf., 21 Sept., 1866. Wholly retired 15 July, 1869. Bvt. Capt., 19 Aug., 1864, for gallant and meritorious service in the Battle of the Weldon Railroad, Va.

HOPKINS, JOHN W. [Born in Maine. Appointed from Ore.]
2nd Lieut. 1st Ore. Cav., 27 Nov., 1861. 1st Lieut., 30 March, 1863, to 21 Sept., 1865. Capt. C. S. Vols., 7 March, 1865. Mustered out 8 Dec., 1865. 2nd Lieut. 1st Cav., 7 March, 1867. Resigned 1 Feb., 1869. Died 12 May, 1877.

HOPKINS, JOSEPH. [Born in Penn. Appointed from Penn.]
Ensign 11th Inf., 4 Aug., 1813. 3rd Lieut., 19 Nov., 1813. 2nd Lieut., 2 May, 1814. Trans. to 2nd Inf., 17 May, 1815. Resigned 1 Dec., 1816. 2nd Lieut. Corps Art., 3 March, 1819. Trans. to 3rd Art., 1 June, 1821. Trans. to 4th Art., 16 Aug., 1821. Resigned 30 April, 1822.

HOPKINS, ROBERT. [Born in Ky. Appointed from Vt.]
2nd Lieut. of Inf., 8 March, 1847; 9th Inf., 9 April, 1847. 1st Lieut., 19 Jan., 1848. Disbanded 26 Aug., 1848.

HOPKINS, WM. D. [Born in Ga. Appointed from Ga.]
2nd Lieut. 7th Inf., 24 March, 1818. 1st Lieut., 15 June, 1819. Dismissed 25 Sept., 1819.

HOPKINS, WM. E. [Born in Va. Appointed from Cal.]
Asst. Surg., 23 May, 1882. Capt. Asst. Surg., 23 May, 1887. Resigned 5 April, 1892.

HOPKINS, WM. F.* [Born in Conn. Appointed from Conn.]
Bvt. 2nd Lieut. 2nd Art., 1 July, 1825. 2nd Lieut. 4th Art., 1 July, 1825. 1st Lieut., 14 Sept., 1834. Resigned 30 June, 1836. Died 13 July, 1859.

HOPPIN, CURTIS B.* [Born in N. Y. Appointed from N. Y.]
Addl. 2nd Lieut. 1st Cav., 15 June, 1877. 2nd Lieut. 2nd Cav., 25 June, 1877. 1st Lieut 22 Sept., 1884. Capt., 10 June, 1895. R. Q. M., 15 March, 1899.

HOPPY, EDWARD. [Born in Germany. Appointed from N. Y.]
Priv. Co. D, 2nd Art., 31 May, 1854. Trans. to Co. E, 8th Inf., 7 May, 1857. Discharged 31 May, 1859. Priv. Co. D, 2nd Art., 11 June, 1859. Discharged 24 Feb., 1862. 2nd Lieut. Vet. Res. Corps, 23 July, 1863. Bvt. 1st Lieut. Vols. and Bvt. Capt. Vols., 13 March, 1865, for gallant service in the Battle of Bull Run, Va., and for faithful and meritorious service during the war. Mustered out 26 Dec., 1866. 2nd Lieut. 44th Inf., 28 July, 1866. Bvt. 1st Lieut., 2 March, 1867, for gallant and meritorious service in the Battle of Bull Run (1st), Va. Unassigned 27 May, 1869. Ass'd to 9th Inf., 3 Aug., 1870. 1st Lieut., 15 Sept., 1871. Retired 8 Nov., 1871.

HOPSON, JOHN D.* [Born in Vt. Appointed from Vt.]
2nd Lieut. 3rd Inf., 1 July, 1822. 1st Lieut., 23 Sept., 1827. Died 17 Feb., 1829.

HOPSON, NEVIL.* [Born in Ky. Appointed from Ky.]
2nd Lieut. 7th Inf., 1 July, 1837. 1st Lieut., 31 Dec., 1842. Dismissed 22 Aug., 1846. Died ——— 1847.

HOPWOOD, THOMAS H. [Born in Penn. Appointed from R. I.]
1st Sergt. Co. F, 11th Pa. Res., 23 May, 1861. 1st Lieut., 23 Sept., 1861. Resigned 25 Dec., 1862. 1st Lieut. Vet. Res. Corps, 9 June, 1863. Capt., 25 March, 1865. Bvt. Maj. Vols., 7 Nov., 1865, for meritorious service. Mustered out 6 July, 1866. 2nd Lieut. 10th Inf., 11 May, 1866. Wholly retired 16 Aug., 1867. Died 31 Dec., 1867.

HORN, TIEMANN N.* [Born in N. Y. Appointed from N. J.]
2nd Lieut. 3rd Cav., 12 June, 1891. Trans. to 2nd Art., 15 Dec., 1891. 1st Lieut. 1st Art., 7 Oct., 1898. Graduate of Artillery School, 1898.

HORNBROOK, JAMES J.* [Born in Ind. Appointed from Ind.]
Addl. 2nd Lieut. 2nd Cav., 12 June, 1890. 2nd Lieut., 19 June, 1890. 1st Lieut. 5th Cav., 2 June, 1897. Graduate of the Infantry and Cavalry School, 1895.

HORNE, WM. J. D.* [Born in Ore. Appointed from Ariz.]
Addl. 2nd Lieut. 9th Cav., 11 June, 1888. 2nd Lieut., 15 June, 1888. 1st Lieut., 21 Dec., 1895. Reg. Commissary, 17 Apri, 1899.

HORNER, SAMUEL H. [Born in N. J. Appointed from Penn.]
Asst. Surg., 16 April, 1862. Resigned 31 March, 1867. Bvt. Capt. and Maj., 13 March, 1865, for faithful and meritorious service during the war.

HORNEY, ODUS C.* [Born in Ill. Appointed from Ohio.]
2nd Lieut. 7th Inf., 12 June, 1891. 1st Lieut. Ord., 2 May, 1894.

HORNSBY, C. C. [Born in N. C. Appointed from Texas.]
Capt. of Inf., 1 April, 1847; 12th Inf., 9 April, 1847. Resigned 31 Dec., 1847.

HORR, JOSEPH L. [Born in Canada. Appointed from Army.]
Priv. and Sergt. Co. C, 13th Inf., 30 Aug., 1861, to 29 Aug., 1862. 2nd Lieut. 13th Inf., 29 Aug., 1862. 1st Lieut., 20 May, 1863. Capt., Oct., 1867. Unassigned 10 Aug., 1869. Discharged 31 Dec., 1870. Bvt. Capt., 10 Jan., 1863, for gallant and meritorious service at the Battle of Arkansas Post, Ark. Bvt. Maj., 4 July, 1863, for gallant and meritorious service during the Siege of Vicksburg, Miss.

HORRIGAN, PATRICK W. [Born in Ireland. Appointed from the Army.]
Priv., Corpl., Sergt. and 1st Sergt. Co. B, 2nd Drag. (2nd Cav.), 4 March, 1860, to 14 Nov., 1863. 2nd Lieut. 2nd Cav., 31 Oct., 1863. 1st Lieut., 5 Jan., 1865. Trans. to 13th Inf., 13 Feb., 1867. Unassigned 8 June, 1869. Mustered out 1 Jan., 1871. Bvt. 1st Lieut., 11 June, 1864, for gallant and meritorious service at the Battle of Trevillian Station, Va.

HORTON, SAML. M. [Born in Penn. Appointed from Penn.]
1st Lieut. Asst. Surg., 26 Aug., 1861. Bvt. Capt. and Maj., 13 March, 1865, for faithful and meritorious service during the war. Capt. Asst. Surg., 28 July, 1866. Maj. Surg., 26 June, 1876. Lieut. Col. Dept. Surg. Gen., 4 Dec., 1893. Retired for disability, 6 June, 1894.

HORTON, WM. E. [Born in Conn. Appointed from Conn.]
Sergt. and 1st Sergt. Co. H, 11th Conn. Vols., 16 Dec., 1861, to 9 April, 1864. 1st Lieut. 11th Conn. Vols., 9 April, 1864. Resigned 5 Oct., 1864. 1st Lieut. 8th U. S. Vet. Vols., 22 March, 1865, for meritorious and distinguished service at the Battle of Cold Harbor, Va., 3 June, 1864. Cashiered 2 Feb., 1866. 1st Lieut. 41st Inf., 12 June, 1867. Trans. to 24th Inf., 11 Nov., 1869. Unassigned 16 Nov., 1870. Mustered out 1 Jan., 1871.

HOSEA, LOUIS M. [Born in Ala. Appointed from Ohio.]
Priv. Co. A, 6th Ohio Vols., 12 May to 3 July, 1861. 1st Lieut. 16th Inf., 14 May, 1861. R. Q. M., 3 March, 1863, to 19 Oct., 1863Septapt., 19 Oct., 1863. Resigned 20 Oct., 1865. Bvt. Maj., 2 April, 1865, for gallant and meritorious service at the capture of Selma, Ala.

HOSKINS, CHARLES.* [Born in N. C. Appointed from N. C.]
Bvt. 2nd Lieut. 4th Inf., 1 July, 1836. 2nd Lieut., 13 Sept., 1836. 1st Lieut., 30 Dec., 1838. Reg. Adj., 10 Sept., 1845, to 21 Sept., 1846. Killed 21 Sept., 1846, at the Battle of Monterey, Mex.

HOSKINS, JOHN D. C.* [Born in Mo. Appointed from N. Y.]
2nd Lieut. 1st Inf., 15 June, 1868. Trans. to 3rd Art., 13 May, 1869. 1st Lieut., 20 Dec., 1875. R. Q. M., 31 July, 1875, to 1 Nov., 1877. Reg. Adj., 1 Nov., 1877, to 12 April, 1887. Capt., 7 June, 1897. Graduate of the Artillery School, 1874.

HOSMER, CHAS. H. [Born in N. Y. Appointed from Ill.]
2nd Lieut. 1st Inf., 5 Aug., 1861. 1st Lieut., 23 Nov., 1861. R. Q. M., 27 Jan., 1864, to 8 May, 1865. Capt., 19 April, 1866. Died 1 Jan., 1867. Bvt. Capt., 4 Oct., 1862, for gallant and meritorious service at the Battle of Corinth, Miss. Bvt. Maj., 4 July, 1863, for gallant and meritorious conduct during the Siege of Vicksburg, Miss.

HOSMER, JOHN E.* [Born in Mass. Appointed from Mass.]
2nd Lieut. 16th Inf., 23 June, 1865. 1st Lieut., 23 June, 1865. Reg. Adj., 27 Dec., 1865, to 8 Aug., 1868. Unassigned 17 April, 1869. Ass'd to 13th Inf., 7 Jan., 1870. Died 13 July, 1870.

HOTSENPILLER, CHAS. W. [Born in Ohio. Appointed from Army.]
Priv. Co. A, 2nd Batt. 16th Inf., 21 March, 1862. Sergt., 15 May, 1862. 1st Sergt., 15 May, 1862. 2nd Lieut. 16th Inf., 10 Aug., 1863. 1st Lieut., 24 May, 1864. Bvt. Capt., 1 Sept., 1864, for gallant and meritorious service during the Atlanta campaign and in the Battle of Jonesboro, Ga. Adj. 1st Batt. 16th Inf., 23 Nov., 1864, to 15 Aug., 1866. Capt., 25 Sept., 1868. Unassigned 17 April, 1869. Ass'd to 19th Inf., 1 Jan., 1871. Retired 19 June, 1879. Died 30 Sept., 1896.

HOUGH, ALFRED L. [Born in N. J. Appointed from Penn.]
Sergt. Co. F, 17th Penn. Vols., 18 April, 1861. Discharged 29 June, 1861. Capt. 19th Inf., 14 May, 1861. Bvt. Maj., 20 Sept., 1863, for gallant and meritorious service in the Battle of Chickamauga, Ga. Bvt. Lieut. Col., 13 March, 1865, for faithful service in connection with the mustering of troops. Bvt. Col., 13 March, 1865, for gallant and meritorious service during the war. Trans. to 28th Inf., 21 Sept., 1866. Unassigned 31 March, 1869. Ass'd to 13th Inf., 16 April, 1870. Maj. 22nd Inf., 18 Feb., 1874. Lieut. Col. 16th Inf., 20 Feb., 1882. Col. 9th Inf., 21 Aug., 1888. Retired by operation of law, 23 April, 1890.

HOULE, GEORGE E.* [Born in Canada. Appointed from Mass.]
2nd Lieut. 3rd Inf., 12 June, 1893. 1st Lieut., 26 April, 1898.

HOULIHAN, PATRICK W. [Born in Ireland. Appointed from Army.]
Priv., Corpl., Sergt. and 1st Sergt. Co. A, 16th Inf., 31 July, 1861, to 5 July, 1862. 2nd Lieut. 16th Inf., 7 April, 1862. 1st Lieut., 23 Dec., 1862. Capt., 10 Oct., 1865. Unassigned 17 April, 1869. Died 5 Oct., 1870. Bvt. Capt., 20 Sept., 1863, for gallant and meritorious service at the Battle of Chickamauga, Ga.

HOUSE, JAMES. [Born in Conn. Appointed from Penn.]
Lieut. 1st Art. and Eng., 22 Feb., 1799. Reg. P. M., 18 Oct., 1799. Dist. P. M., 16 March, 1802. Retained 1 April, 1802, as 1st Lieut. Reg. of Art. Capt., 1 Nov., 1805. A. D. Q. M. G., 3 April, 1812. Lieut. Col. 3rd Art., 3 March, 1813. Trans. to Corps Art., 12 May, 1814. Trans. to 2nd Art., 1 June, 1821. Col. 1st Art., 8 May, 1822. Died 17 Nov., 1834. Bvt. Brig. Gen., 8 May, 1832, for ten years' faithful service in one grade.

HOUSTON, ALEX. M. [Born in Va. Appointed from Tenn.]
2nd Lieut. 7th Inf., 24 March, 1818. R. Q. M., 1 Oct., 1818, to 31 Dec., 1818. 1st Lieut., 31 Aug., 1819. Resigned 1 March, 1822. Capt. 2nd Ill. Vols., 19 June to 15 Aug., 1822.

HOUSTON, DAVID C.* [Born in N. Y. Appointed from N. Y.]
Bvt. 2nd Lieut. Eng., 1 July, 1856. 2nd Lieut., 31 Oct., 1856. 1st Lieut., 2 May,

1861. Maj. A. A. de C., 16 May, 1862. Bvt. Capt., 10 Aug., 1862, for gallant and meritorious service in the Battle of Cedar Mountain, Va. Bvt. Maj., 17 Sept., 1862, for gallant and meritorious service during the Maryland campaign. Capt. Eng., 3 March, 1863. Bvt. Lieut. Col., 17 June, 1863, for gallant and meritorious service in action at Port Hudson, La. Bvt. Col., 13 March, 1865, for gallant and meritorious service during the war. Mustered out as Maj. A. A. de C., 31 May, 1866. Maj. Eng., 7 March, 1867. Lieut. Col., 30 June, 1882. Col., 2 July, 1889. Died 19 May, 1893.

HOUSTON, JOHN S. [Born in Tenn. Appointed from Ark.]
2nd Lieut. 12th Inf., 3 March, 1848. Disbanded 25 July, 1848.

HOUSTON, ROBERT. [Born in Va. Appointed from Va.]
2nd Lieut. 12th Inf., 12 March, 1812. 1st Lieut., 29 March, 1813. Disbanded 15 June, 1815. Reinstated in 8th Inf., 17 May, 1816. Capt., 31 March, 1817. Died 24 Dec., 1818.

HOUSTON, SAMUEL. [Born in Va. Appointed from Tenn.]
Priv. and Sergt. 7th Inf., 24 March to Aug., 1813. Ensign 39th Inf., 29 July, 1813. 3rd Lieut., 31 Dec., 1813. 2nd Lieut., 20 May, 1814. Trans. to 1st Inf., 17 May, 1815. 1st Lieut., 1 May, 1817. Resigned 1 March, 1818. Died 25 July, 1863.

HOUSTON, WM. F. [Born in Penn. Appointed from Penn.]
Priv. Co. F, 25th Pa. Vols., 2 May to 26 July, 1861. Priv. Co. E, 2nd U. S. Cav., 1 Jan., 1862, to 18 July, 1863. 1st Lieut. and Adj. 2nd Ohio Art., 18 July, 1863. Capt., 2 Aug., 1864. Mustered out 23 Aug., 1865. 2nd Lieut. 23rd Inf., 22 Jan., 1867. 1st Lieut., 17 Jan., 1869. Cashiered 12 Aug., 1869.

HOUTTARD, EDWARD. [Born in Prussia. Appointed from Army.]
Priv. Co. G, 8th N. Y. Vols., 23 May, 1861. 2nd Lieut., 16 Feb., 1862. 1st Lieut., 14 Oct., 1862. Mustered out 23 April, 1863. Priv., Corpl. and Sergt. Cos. I and G, and Sergt. Maj. 6th Inf., 11 Feb., 1864, to 7 Sept., 1866. 2nd Lieut. 14th Inf., 2 Aug., 1866. Trans. to 32nd Inf., 21 Sept., 1866. Dismissed 31 Aug., 1867.

HOVEY, GEORGE W. [Born in Mass. Appointed from Mass.]
2nd Lieut. 4th Inf., 3 Jan., 1812. 1st Lieut., 15 Aug., 1813. Disbanded 15 June, 1815. Reinstated in 5th Inf., 2 Dec., 1815. Resigned 1 July, 1817.

HOVEY, HENRY W. [Born in Maine. Appointed from N. Y.]
2nd Lieut. 24th Inf., 23 Nov., 1880. 1st Lieut., 15 May, 1888. Capt., 26 April, 1898.

HOW, JOHN C. [Born in N. Y. Appointed from Army.]
Priv. Co. H, 16th Inf., 16 April to 3 Aug., 1847. 2nd Lieut. 16th Inf., 3 Aug., 1847. Resigned 6 Nov., 1847.

HOWARD, ALFRED G. [Born in S. C. Appointed from S. C.]
Asst. Surg., 3 March, 1847; 12th Inf., 9 April, 1847. Disbanded 22 Aug., 1848.

HOWARD, BENJAMIN. [Born in England. Appointed from N. Y.]
Asst. Surg. 3rd N. Y. Art., 22 May to 14 Sept., 1861. Asst. Surg. U. S. A., 26 Aug., 1861. Resigned 28 Dec., 1864.

HOWARD, CHAS. [Born in Mass. Appointed from Mass.]
Mil. Storekeeper Ord., 17 Nov., 1829. Removed 15 July, 1841.

HOWARD, CHAS. O. [Born in Ohio. Appointed from Ind.]
Capt. 8th Ind. Vols., 25 April to 21 June, 1861. 1st Lieut. Adj. to 6 Aug., 1861. 1st Lieut. and Adj. 8th Ind. Vols., 5 Sept., 1861, to 25 June, 1862. Capt. 18th Inf., 12 May, 1862. Resigned 15 Feb., 1866. Bvt. Maj., 13 March, 1865, for gallant and valuable service.

HOWARD, CLARENCE O.* [Born in Mass. Appointed from Mass.]
2nd Lieut. 2nd Art., 15 June, 1868. 1st. Lieut., 26 April, 1875. Reg. Adj., 24 March, 1877, to 27 Jan., 1881. Resigned 29 Jan., 1882.

HOWARD, COLUMBUS W. [Born in N. C. Appointed from Army.]
Priv. and Sergt. Co. C, and Sergt. Maj. 13th Inf., 13 May, 1847, to 3 July, 1848. 2nd Lieut. 4th Inf., 17 June, 1848. Resigned 6 Nov., 1848.

HOWARD, DEANE C. [Born in Mass. Appointed from Mass.]
Asst. Surg., 26 Oct., 1893. Capt. Asst. Surg., 26 Oct., 1898.

HOWARD, DOUGLAS A.* [Born in Ill. Appointed at Large.]
2nd Lieut. 9th Inf., 14 June, 1878. Trans. to 3rd Art., 13 June, 1879. 1st Lieut. Ord., 17 April, 1883. Retired for disability, with rank of Capt., 14 June, 1892.

HOWARD, EDWIN T.* [Born in Mo. Appointed from Mo.]
2nd Lieut. 12th Inf., 13 June, 1873. Resigned 1 Jan., 1875.

HOWARD, GUY. [Born in Maine. Appointed at Large.]
2nd Lieut. 12th Inf., 31 Aug., 1876. 1st Lieut., 19 July, 1882. Reg. Adj., 1 July, 1888, to 13 May, 1889. Capt. C. S., 7 Jan., 1893. Trans. to Q. M. D., 31 Jan., 1893. Graduate of the Artillery School, 1882. Maj. Q. M., 12 May, 1898. Lieut. Col. Chief Q. M., 11 Aug., 1898. Killed in action near Arayat, P. I., 22 Oct., 1899.

HOWARD, HAROLD P.* [Born in Minn. Appointed from Minn.]
2nd Lieut. 6th Cav., 12 June, 1891. 1st Lieut. 3rd Cav., 31 May, 1898.

HOWARD, JAMES. [Born in Md. Appointed from Md.]
2nd Lieut. 3rd Art., 21 Feb., 1857. Resigned 3 April, 1861.

HOWARD, JOHN. [Born in D. C. Appointed from N. Y.]
2nd Lieut. 19th Inf., 1 Aug., 1891. 1st Lieut., 26 April, 1898. Graduate of the Infantry and Cavalry School, 1895.

HOWARD, JOHN C. [Born in D. C. Appointed from Texas.]
1st Lieut. of Inf., 17 March, 1847; 12th Inf., 9 April, 1847. Disbanded 25 July, 1848. 1st Lieut. 9th Inf., 28 Aug., 1855. Resigned 6 Sept., 1861. Died 23 Dec., 1885.

HOWARD, JOHN E. [Born in Md. Appointed from Md.]
Capt. of Inf., 23 Feb., 1847; Voltigeurs, 9 April, 1847. Disbanded 25 Aug., 1848. Bvt. Maj., 13 Sept., 1847, for gallant and meritorious conduct at Chapultepec.

HOWARD, JOSEPH H. [Born in N. Y. Appointed from N. Y.]
1st Lieut. of Inf., 12 March, 1847; 10th Inf., 9 April, 1847. Disbanded 23 Aug., 1848.

HOWARD, JOSHUA. [Born in Mass. Appointed from Mass.]
3rd Lieut. 9th Inf., 17 March, 1813. 2nd Lieut., 31 Aug., 1813. Resigned 5 April, 1814. 3rd Lieut. Ord., 2 Dec., 1815. 2nd Lieut., 1 Sept., 1818. Trans. to 1st Art., 1 June, 1821. 1st Lieut., 1 Nov., 1823. Capt., 6 March, 1834. Resigned 31 Dec., 1835. Lieut. Col. 15th Inf., 9 April, 1847. Disbanded 7 Aug., 1848. Bvt. Capt., 1 Nov., 1833, for ten years' faithful service in one grade. Bvt. Col., 13 Sept., 1847, for gallant and meritorious conduct at Chapultepec. Died 12 July, 1868.

HOWARD, MASON. [Born in Ga. Appointed from Army.]
(Changed name to Mason Carter)—which see.

HOWARD, OCRAN H. [Born in Mass. Appointed from Mass.]
2nd Lieut. 2nd Mass. Vols., 25 May, 1861. 1st Lieut., 22 Dec., 1861. Capt., 10 Aug., 1862, to 11 Sept., 1863. Capt. Sig. Corps, 3 March, 1863. Bvt. Maj. Vols., 9 April, 1865, for gallant and meritorious service during the campaign terminating with the surrender of the insurgent army under Gen. R. E. Lee, and Lieut. Col. Vols., 9 April, 1865, for gallant and meritorious service at the Battle of Five Forks, Va. Mustered out 20 June, 1866. 2nd Lieut. 5th Art., 3 Sept., 1867. 1st Lieut., 1 Sept., 1871. Dropped 11 March, 1876. Bvt. 1st Lieut., 3 Sept., 1867, for gallant and meritorious service in the Sig. Corps in the cavalry campaign from Winchester to Petersburg and in the Battles of Dinwiddie C. H. and Appomattox C. H., Va. Bvt. Capt., 3 Sept., 1867, for gallant and meritorious service in the Sig. Corps at the Battle of Five Forks, Va., and during the war. Bvt. Maj., 3 Sept., 1867, for meritorious service in the Sig. Corps during the war at the Battle of Port Royal Ferry, S. C., and while Chief Sig. Off. of the Dept. and Army of the Tenn., Mid. Mil. Div. and Mil. Div. of the Gulf.

HOWARD, OLIVER O.* [Born in Maine. Appointed from Maine.]
Bvt. 2nd Lieut. Ord., 1 July, 1854. 2nd Lieut., 15 Feb., 1855. 1st Lieut., 1 July, 1857. Resigned 7 June, 1861. Col. 3rd Maine Vols., 4 June, 1861. Brig. Gen. Vols., 3 Sept., 1861. Maj. Gen. Vols., 29 Nov., 1862. The gratitude of the American people, and the thanks of their Representatives in Congress tendered to . . . . . . . Maj. Gen. Oliver O. Howard, and the officers and soldiers of the Army of the Potomac, by joint resolution approved 28 Jan., 1864, for the skill and heroic valor which, at Gettysburg, repulsed, defeated and drove back, broken and dispirited, beyond the Rappahannock, the veteran army of the rebellion. Brig. Gen. U. S. A., 21 Dec., 1864. Bvt. Maj. Gen., 13 March, 1865, for gallant and meritorious service in the Battle of Ezra Church, and during the campaign against Atlanta, Ga. Mustered out of Vol. Service, 1 Jan., 1869. Maj. Gen., 19 March, 1886. Medal of Honor for distinguished bravery in the Battle of Fair Oaks, Va., June 1, 1862, leading the 61st N. Y. Vol. Inf. in the charge across the enemy's line, where he was twice severely wounded in the right arm, necessitating its amputation, while serving as Brig. Gen. of Vols., commanding brigade. Retired by operation law 8 Nov., 1894.

HOWARD, ROBERT V. W. [Born in Ireland. Appointed from Army.]
Priv., Corpl., Sergt. and 1st Sergt. Co. A. and Sergt. Maj. 4th Art., 22 April, 1839, to 28 June, 1848. Bvt. 2nd Lieut. 4th Art., 28 June, 1848. 2nd Lieut., 20 Aug., 1848. 1st Lieut., 20 Sept., 1850. Capt., 14 May, 1861. Maj. 3rd Art., 4 April, 1869. Died 1 Feb., 1875. Bvt. Maj., 22 Oct., 1863, for gallant and meritorious service in action at Blackwater Bridge, near Suffolk, Va. Bvt. Lieut. Col., 13 March, 1865, for faithful and meritorious service during the war.

HOWARD, SUMNER. [Born in N. Y. Appointed from Mich.]
Sergt. Co. F, 2nd Mich. Vols., 25 May to 3 Oct., 1861. 1st Lieut. 17th Inf., 14 May, 1861. Resigned 25 Sept., 1863.

HOWARD, THOMAS F. [Born in Eng. Appointed from Texas.]
2nd Lieut. 2nd Cav., 12 June, 1896. Trans to 7th Cav., 21 April, 1898. Retired for disability, with the rank of Capt., 14 Sept., 1899.

HOWARD, WM. T.* [Born in S. C. Appointed from S. C.]
2nd Lieut. 2nd Art., 15 June, 1876. 1st Lieut., 16 Oct., 1884. Died 3 Sept., 1878.

HOWE, ALBION. [Born in Fla. Appointed from N. Y.]
2nd Lieut. 14th N. Y. Art., 16 Dec., 1863. 1st Lieut., 3 May, 1865. Maj., 26 July, 1865. Mustered out 26 Aug., 1865. 2nd Lieut. 4th Art., 1 Dec., 1866. 1st Lieut., 18 Nov., 1869. Killed 26 April, 1873, in action with Indians at Lava Beds, Cal. Bvt. 1st Lieut., 2 March, 1867, for gallant and distinguished service in the Battle of Cold Harbor, Va. Bvt. Capt., 2 March, 1867, for gallant and distinguished service in the Battle of Petersburg, Va.

HOWE, ALBION P.* [Born in Maine. Appointed from Maine.]
2nd Lieut. 4th Art., 1 July, 1841. 1st Lieut., 18 June, 1846. Reg. Adj., 1 Oct., 1846, to 2 March, 1855. Bvt. Capt., 20 Aug., 1847, for gallant and meritorious conduct in the Battles of Contreras and Churubusco. Capt. 4th Art., 2 March, 1855. Bvt. Maj., 1 July, 1862, for gallant and meritorious service in the Battle of Malvern Hill, Va. Brig. Gen. Vols., 11 June, 1862. Bvt. Lieut. Col., 3 May, 1863, for gallant and meritorious service in action at Salem Heights, Va. Maj. 4th Art., 11 Aug., 1863. Bvt. Col., 7 Nov., 1863, for gallant and meritorious service in the Battle of Rappahannock Station, Va. Bvt. Brig. Gen. and Maj. Gen., 13 March, 1865, for gallant and meritorious service during the war. Bvt. Maj. Gen. Vols., 13 July, 1865, for faithful and meritorious service. Mustered out of Vol. Service, 15 Jan., 1866. Lieut. Col. 20th Inf., 28 July, 1866, declined. Lieut. Col. 2nd Art., 10 April, 1879. Col. 4th Art., 19 April, 1882. Retired 30 June, 1882. Died 25 Jan.,1897.

HOWE, CHILEAB S.* [Born in Mass. Appointed from N. Y.]
Bvt. 2nd Lieut. 4th Inf., 1 July, 1829. 2nd Lieut., 1 July, 1829. Reg. Adj., 1 Nov., 1833, to 4 Feb., 1835. 1st Lieut., 31 Jan., 1836. Resigned 28 Feb., 1838.

HOWE, EDGAR W.* [Born in Mass. Appointed from Iowa.]
2nd Lieut. 17th Inf., 1 June, 1878. 1st Lieut., 30 Jan., 1885. Capt., 20 April, 1898.

HOWE, EDWIN.* [Born in N. Y. Appointed at Large.]
Bvt. 2nd Lieut. 5th Inf., 1 July, 1843. 2nd Lieut. 6th Inf., 7 Nov., 1845. Died 31 March, 1850. Bvt. 1st Lieut., 8 Sept., 1847, for gallant and meritorious conduct at Molino del Rey.*

HOWE, HENRY S. [Born in Mass. Appointed from Minn.]
Priv. Co. B, Hatche's Ind. Batt. Minn. Cav., 1 July, 1863. 1st Sergt., 10 Aug., 1863. 2nd Lieut., 29 June, 1864. 1st Lieut., 6 July, 1865. Mustered out 30 May, 1866. 2nd Lieut. 17th Inf., 23 Feb., 1866. 1st Lieut., 28 July, 1866. Capt., 1 June, 1875. Retired for disability 2 May, 1892.

HOWE, MARSHALL S. [Born in Maine. Appointed from Maine.]
Cadet at Mil. Acad., 1 July, 1823, to 1 July, 1827. 1st Lieut. 2nd Drag., 11 June, 1836. Capt., 1 Jan., 1839. Maj., 13 July, 1848. Lieut. Col., 14 June, 1858. Col. 3rd Cav., 28 Sept., 1861. Retired 31 Aug., 1866. Died 8 Dec., 1878.

HOWE, MYRON W.* [Born in Mass. Appointed from Mass.]
2nd Lieut. 4th Art., 16 June, 1875. Died 16 June, 1879.

HOWE, WALTER.* [Born in Ind. Appointed from N. M.]
2nd Lieut. 4th Art., 17 June, 1867. 1st Lieut., 1 Sept., 1872. Capt., 1 Jan., 1891. Graduate of Artillery School, 1873.

HOWELL, CHAS. W.* [Born in Ind. Appointed from Ind.]
1st Lieut. Eng., 11 June, 1863. Bvt. Capt., 1 Aug., 1864, for gallant and meritorious service during the campaign before Richmond, Va. Bvt. Maj., 1 Aug., 1864, for gallant and meritorious service during the campaign from the Rapidan to the James, and in front of Petersburg, Va. Capt. Eng., 10 July, 1866. Maj., 30 June, 1879. Died 5 April, 1882.

HOWELL, DANIEL L.* [Born in Iowa. Appointed from Iowa.]
2nd Lieut. 7th Lnf., 13 June, 1879. 1st Lieut., 23 April, 1889. Capt., 26 April, 1898.

HOWELL, ELY P. [Born in N. C. Appointed from Ga.]
1st Lieut. 13th Inf., 9 April, 1847. Capt., 20 Aug., 1847. Disbanded 15 July, 1848.

HOWELL, FRANKLIN D. [Born in Penn. Appointed from N. J.]
1st Lieut. 17th Inf., 14 May, 1861. Resigned 27 April, 1863.

HOWELL, GEORGE P. [Born in N. C. Appointed from N. C.]
Addl. 2nd Lieut. Eng., 12 June, 1893. 2nd Lieut., 13 Aug., 1895. 1st Lieut., 18 May, 1898.

HOWELL, JAMES F. [Born in Iowa. Appointed from Iowa.]
2nd Lieut. 6th Art., 9 July, 1898.

HOWELL, JOHN H. [Born in Ohio. Appointed from N. Y.]
1st Sergt. Co. A, 1st N. Y. Light Art., 17 Sept., 1861. 1st Lieut., 1 March, 1862. Mustered out 16 Sept., 1862. Capt. 3rd N. Y. Art., 22 Nov., 1862. Mustered out 26 June, 1865. 2nd Lieut. 2nd Art., 23 Feb., 1866. Resigned 3 Sept., 1866.

HOWELL, LEWIS* [Born in Penn. Appointed from Penn.]
Bvt. 2nd Lieut. 7th Inf., 1 July, 1832. Resigned 31 Oct., 1833. Died 23 Sept., 1854.

HOWELL, REZIN G.* [Born in Ky. Appointed from Ky.]
2nd Lieut. 2nd Art., 13 June, 1864. 1st Lieut., 1 March, 1865. Capt., 8 Nov., 1882. Died 2 May, 1887.

HOWELL, RICHARD L. [Born in N. J. Appointed from N. J.]
2nd Lieut. 15th Inf., 12 March, 1812. 1st Lieut., 15 Sept., 1812. Capt., 26 Sept., 1814. Trans. to Corps Art., 17 May, 1815. Resigned 25 Sept., 1815. Died in 1834.

HOWELL, WILLEY. [Born in Ark. Appointed from Army.]
Priv. and Corpl. Co. G, 16th Inf., 26 June, 1897, to 1 Sept., 1898. 2nd Lieut. 4th Inf., 9 July, 1898. 1st Lieut., 2 March, 1899.

HOWELL, WM. T. [Born in Penn. Appointed from Penn.]
Capt. A. Q. M. Vols., 5 Aug., 1863. Bvt. Lieut. Col. Vols., 11 May, 1865, for long and faithful service during the war. Capt. A. Q. M., 26 Oct., 1865. Bvt. Maj., 2 March, 1867, for faithful and meritorious service in the Q. M. Dept. during the war. Wholly retired 10 Feb., 1882. Found drowned 20 Aug., 1883.

HOWES, LEANDER T.* [Born in N. Y. Appointed from N. Y.]
2nd Lieut. 1st Art., 17 June, 1867. Resigned 1 May, 1869.

HOWGATE, HENRY W. [Born in Eng. Appointed from Mich.]
2nd Lieut. 22nd Mich Vols., 14 Aug., 1862. 1st Lieut., 17 Jan., 1863. 1st. Lieut. Sig. Corps, 3 March, 1863. Bvt. Capt. Vols., 13 March, 1865, for gallant and meritorious service in the Battle of Chickamauga, Ga. Bvt. Maj. Vols., 13 March, 1865, for gallant and meritorious service in the Atlanta campaign. Mustered out 20 June, 1866. 2nd Lieut. 20th Inf., 22 Oct., 1867. Bvt. 1st Lieut., 22 Oct., 1867, for gallant and meritorious service in the Battle of Chickamauga, Ga. Bvt. Capt., 22 Oct., 1867, for gallant and meritorious service in the Atlanta campaign. Unassigned 28 July, 1869. Ass'd to 20th Inf., 3 Aug., 1870. 1st Lieut., 4 Aug., 1875. Resigned 18 Dec., 1880.

HOWLAND, CARVER.* [Born in R. I. Appointed from R. I.]
2nd Lieut. 4th Inf., 15 June, 1876. 1st Lieut., 1 Oct., 1886. Reg. Adj., 1 Nov., 1887, to ——. Capt., 3 Feb., 1894.

HOWLAND, CHARLES R.* [Born in Ohio. Appointed from Ohio.]
2nd Lieut. 20th Inf., 12 June, 1895. 1st Lieut. of Inf., 1 July, 1898. Ass'd to 20th Inf., 1 Jan., 1899. Capt. 28th U. S. Inf., 5 July, 1899.

HOWLAND, GEORGE W.* [Born in R. I. Appointed at Large.]
Bvt. 2nd Lieut. Mtd Rifles, 1 July, 1848. 2nd Lieut., 30 June, 1851. 1st Lieut., 3 March, 1855. Capt., 14 May, 1861; 3rd Cav., 3 Aug., 1861. Maj. 2nd Cav., 1 Dec., 1866. Wholly retired 8 April, 1869. Bvt. Maj., 21 Feb., 1862, for gallant and meritorious service at the Battle of Val Verde, N. M. Died 21 Dec., 1886.

HOWLAND, HARRY S. [Born in Sweden. Appointed from Ill.]
2nd Lieut. 23rd Inf., 9 Sept., 1898. 1st Lieut. 13th Inf., 23 Dec., 1899.

HOWLAND, JAMES C. [Born in Ind. Appointed from Ind.]
2nd Lieut. 16th Inf., 19 Feb., 1862. 1st Lieut., 7 April, 1862. Resigned 19 Feb., 1863.

HOWLAND, STANLEY. [Born in Cal. Appointed from R. I.]
2nd Lieut. 24th Inf., 9 July, 1898. 1st Lieut., 8 June, 1899.

HOWZE, ROBERT L.* [Born in Tex. Appointed from Tex.]
Addl. 2nd Lieut. 5th Cav., 11 June, 1888. 2nd Lieut. 6th Cav., 7 July, 1888. 1st Lieut. 9th Cav., 9 Jan., 1896. Trans. to 6th Cav., 14 March, 1896. Capt. A. A. G. Vols., 12 May, 1898, to 31 Dec., 1898. Lieut. Col. 34th U. S. Vols., 5 July, 1899. Medal of Honor for gallantry in repulsing the attacks of hostile Sioux Indians on the north bank of White River, near the mouth of Little Grass Creek, S. Dak., 1 Jan., 1891.

HOXIE, RICHARD L.* [Born in N. Y. Appointed from Iowa.]
Bugler, Priv. and Corpl. Co. F, 1st Iowa Cav., 13 June, 1861, to 9 June, 1864. Appointed Cadet at Mil. Acad., 1 July, 1864. 2nd Lieut. Eng., 15 June, 1868. 1st Lieut., 22 Sept., 1870. Capt. (14 years' service), 15 June, 1882. Maj., 31 March, 1895.

HOXTON, LLEWELLYN G.* [Born in D. C. Appointed at Large.]
Bvt. 2nd Lieut. Ord., 6 May, 1861. Dismissed 25 May, 1861.

HOXTON, WM. W. [Born in D. C. Appointed from D. C.]
Asst. Surg., 24 Aug., 1835. Resigned 30 Sept., 1841. Died 23 Aug., 1855.

HOYER, JACOB C. [Born in Penn. Appointed from Penn.]
1st Lieut. 12th Inf., 14 May, 1861. Resigned 27 April, 1863.

HOYER, JOSEPH S. [Born in Penn. Appointed from Penn.]
2nd Lieut. 1st Cav., 6 March, 1862. 1st Lieut., 18 July, 1862. Killed 29 Aug., 1864, in action at Smithfield, Va.

HOYLE, ELI D.* [Born in Ga. Appointed from Ala.]
2nd Lieut. 2nd Art., 16 June, 1875. 1st Lieut., 28 Oct., 1883. Capt. 1st Art., 18 Sept., 1898. Capt. C. S. Vols., 12 May, 1898 (declined). Maj. Chf. Ord. Off., 18 Ju.yl 1898, to 12 May, 1899.

HOYLE, GEORGE S.* [Born in Ga. Appointed from Ga.]
2nd Lieut. 1st Cav., 13 June, 1873. 1st Lieut., 29 April, 1879. Capt., 7 Feb., 1891.

HOYT, CHAS. H. [Born in Conn. Appointed from N. Y.]
1st Lieut. 37th N. Y. Vols., 8 June, 1861. Discharged 8 June, 1862. Capt. A. Q. M. Vols., 12 May, 1862. Col. Q. M. (Act 4 July, 1864), 2 Aug., 1864. Bvt. Maj., Lieut. Col. and Col. Vols., 13 March, 1865, for faithful and meritorious service during the war. Bvt. Brig. Gen. Vols., 13 March, 1865, for meritorious service in the Northern Department. Relieved as Col. Q. M. (Act of 4 July, 1864), 31 Dec., 1866. Capt. A. Q. M., 22 March, 1867. Maj. Q. M., 15 Feb., 1889. Retired 30 Sept., 1889. Died 17 Nov., 1887.

HOYT, EDWIN C. [Born in ——. Appointed from ——.]
2nd Lieut. 11th Inf., —— ——, 1898. Resigned 30 Sept., 1898.

HOYT, GEORGE S. [Born in N. H. Appointed from Wis.]
Sergt. Co. K, 7th Wis. Vols., 7 Aug., 1861. 1st Sergt., 22 March, 1862. 2nd Lieut. 7th Wis. Vols., 5 Oct., 1862. 1st Lieut., 1 March, 1863. Capt., 1 June, 1863. Capt. 7th Wis. Vet. Vols., 1 Jan., 1864. Maj., 9 Jan., 1865. Mustered out 3 July, 1865. 2nd Lieut. 18th Inf., 18 June, 1867. 1st Lieut., 5 Oct., 1874. Capt. A. Q. M., 25 Feb., 1889. Died 17 Sept., 1896.

HOYT, JAMES T. [Born in N. Y. Appointed from Cal.]
Capt. A. Q. M. Vols., 17 Nov., 1863. Bvt. Maj. Vols., 13 March, 1865, for faithful and efficient service. Capt. A. Q. M., 18 Jan., 1867. Resigned 3 April, 1869. Died 18 July, 1879.

HOYT, RALPH W.* [Born in N. Y. Appointed from N. Y.]
2nd Lieut. 11th Inf., 14 June, 1872. Reg. Q. M., 7 June, 1879. 1st Lieut., 7 June, 1879. Capt., 19 Sept., 1890. Maj. 10th Inf., 16 May, 1899.

HUBBARD, EDWARD B. [Born in Ohio. Appointed from Ohio.]
Cadet at Mil. Acad., 1 July, 1860, to 6 July, 1861. Priv. 14th Ind. Batty Ohio Light Art., 20 Aug., 1861. 2nd Lieut. 2nd Ohio Cav., 17 Oct., 1861. 1st Lieut., 15 July, 1862. Trans. to 25th Ohio Batty, 17 Feb., 1863. Mustered out 12 Sept., 1864. 2nd Lieut. 32nd Inf., 22 Jan., 1867. 1st Lieut., 30 Sept., 1868. Unassigned 19 April, 1869. Ass'd to 2nd Art., 1 Jan., 1871. Capt. and A. Q. M., 22 March, 1881. Dismissed 31 Oct., 1883.

HUBBARD, ELMER W.* [Born in Conn. Appointed from Conn.]
2nd Lieut. 1st Art., 14 June, 1885. 1st Lieut. 3rd Art., 13 July, 1892. Trans. to 7th Art., 8 March, 1898. Graduate of the Artillery School, 1896.

HUBBARD, VAN BUREN. [Born in Ohio. Appointed from Ohio.]
1st Lieut. Asst. Surg., 11 July, 1862. Bvt. Capt. and Maj., 13 March, 1865, for faithful and meritorious service during the war. Capt. Asst. Surg., 28 July, 1866. Maj. Surg., 10 Aug., 1881. Died 6 Sept., 1895.

HUBBARD, WILLIAM F. [Born in N. Y. Appointed from N. Y.]
Priv. Co. D, 149th N. Y. Vols., 4 Sept., 1862, to 8 June, 1864. Post Chap., 20 July, 1891. Retired 26 March, 1898.

HUBBELL, HENRY W., Jr. [Born in N. Y. Appointed from N. Y.]
Priv. Co. H, 7th N. Y. Militia, 17 April to 3 June, 1861. 2nd Lieut. 40th N. Y. Vols., 4 Dec., 1861. Mustered out 4 Oct., 1863. 2nd Lieut. 1st Art., 18 June, 1867. 1st Lieut., 17 Nov., 1873. Capt., 9 Aug., 1899. Graduate of the Artillery School 1872 and 1888.

HUBBELL, SHADRACH. [Born in Ohio. Appointed from Ohio.]
2nd Lieut. 186th Ohio Vols., 27 Feb., 1865. 1st Lieut., 26 June, 1865. Mustered out 18 Sept., 1865. 2nd Lieut. 1st Inf., 12 May, 1866. Died 30 Sept., 1867.

HUBBS, WM. H. [Born in Ind. Appointed from Ind.]
1st Lieut. 13th Inf., 14 May, 1861. Capt., 9 April, 1864. Dismissed 10 Oct., 1865.

HUBERT, EDGAR.* [Born in Ga. Appointed from Ga.]
2nd Lieut. 8th Inf., 12 June, 1880. 1st Lieut. 29 Oct., 1887. Capt., 4 Feb., 1897. Died 4 Aug., 1898.

HUDDLESTON, CREED T. [Born in Tenn. Appointed from Tenn.]
Capt. of Inf., 22 March, 1847; 14th Inf., 9 April, 1847. Died 1 Oct., 1847.

HUDSON, ANDREW J. [Born in Tenn. Appointed from Tenn.]
2nd Lieut. of Inf., 22 March, 1847; 14th Inf., 9 April, 1847 Disbanded 26 July, 1848.

HUDSON, CHAS. L. [Born in Canada. Appointed from Ohio.]
Priv. Co. A and Q. M. Sergt. and Sergt. Maj. 72nd Ohio Vols., 8 Nov., 1861, to 29

Nov., 1864. 2nd Lieut., 22 Nov., 1864. 1st Lieut., 11 April, 1865. Mustered out 11 Sept., 1865. 2nd Lieut. 15th Inf., 19 Nov., 1867. 1st Lieut., 14 Jan., 1869. Unassigned 12 Aug., 1869. Ass'd to 4th Cav., 1 Jan., 1871. Died 5 Jan., 1874. Bvt. 1st Lieut., 19 Nov., 1867, for gallant and meritorious service in the Battle of Tupelo, Miss. Bvt. Capt., 19 Nov., 1867, for gallant and meritorious service in the Battle of Nashville, Tenn.

HUDSON, EDWARD McK.* [Born in Conn. Appointed from Conn.]
Bvt. 2nd Lieut. 3rd Art., 1 July, 1849. 2nd Lieut. 4th Art., 12 Sept., 1850. 1st Lieut., 30 April, 1855. Capt. 14th Inf., 14 May, 1861. Lieut. Col. A. A. de C., 28 Sept., 1861. Discharged as Lieut. Col. A. A. de C., 31 March, 1863. Bvt. Maj., 1 Aug., 1864, for gallant service in the Battle of the Wilderness, and during the campaign before Richmond, Va. Bvt. Lieut. Col., 13 March, 1865, for gallant and meritorious service during the war. Maj. 15th Inf., 4 Nov., 1865. Unassigned 15 March, 1869. Retired 15 Dec., 1870. Died 20 July, 1892.

HUDSON, WALTER W. [Born in Ky. Appointed from Army.]
Priv., Sergt. and 1st Sergt. Co. K, 15th Inf., 12 April, 1847, to 18 July, 1848. Bvt. 2nd Lieut. 1st Inf., 28 June, 1848. 2nd Lieut., 1 March, 1849. Died 19 April, 1850, of wounds received in action with Indians in Texas, 7 April, 1850.

HUGER, BENJAMIN.* [Born in S. C. Appointed from S. C.]
Bvt. 2nd Lieut. 3rd Art., 1 July, 1825. 2nd Lieut., 1 July, 1825. Capt. Ord., 30 May, 1832. Maj., 15 Feb., 1855. Resigned 22 April, 1861. Bvt. Maj., 29 March, 1847, for gallant and meritorious conduct at the Siege of Vera Cruz. Bvt. Lieut. Col., 8 Sept., 1847, for gallant and meritorious conduct at Molino del Rey. Bvt. Col., 13 Sept., 1847, for gallant and meritorious conduct at Chapultepec. Died 7 Dec., 1877.

HUGER, FRANK.* [Born in Va. Appointed at Large.]
Bvt. 2nd Lieut. 3rd Inf., 1 July, 1860. 2nd Lieut. 10th Inf., 19 Jan., 1861. Resigned 21 May, 1861.

HUGGINS, ELI L. [Born in Ill. Appointed from Minn.]
Priv. Co. E, 2nd Minn. Vols., 5 July, 1861. Corpl., 19 Nov., 1862. Discharged 14 July, 1864. Priv. Co. K, 1st Minn. Art., 16 Feb., 1865. 1st Lieut. 1st Minn. Art., 1 March, 1865. Mustered out 27 Sept., 1865. 2nd Lieut. 2nd Art., 23 Feb., 1866. 1st Lieut., 24 Dec., 1866. Trans. to 2nd Cav., 11 April, 1879. Capt., 23 April, 1879. Maj. 6th Cav., 13 Jan., 1897. Col. 28th U. S. Vols., 24 May, 1898. Graduate of the Artillery School, 1872. Medal of Honor for most distinguished gallantry in action against hostile Ogaliala Sioux Indians near O'Fallon's Creek, Mont., 1 April, 1880, with his troop, surprising the Indians in their strong position and fighting until dark with great boldness.

HUGHES, CHAS. J.* [Born in Md. Appointed from Md.]
2nd Lieut. 6th Inf., 1 July, 1838. Died 22 Aug., 1839.

HUGHES, DANIEL W. [Born in Penn. Appointed from Penn.]
1st Lieut. 17th Inf., 14 May, 1861. Rejected by Senate, 6 Aug., 1861. Capt. A. A. de C., 15 May, 1862. Mustered out 31 May, 1866. Died 3 March, 1883.

HUGHES, ELLIS. [Born in Md. Appointed from Md.]
Asst. Surg., 21 Aug., 1838. Resigned 31 July, 1840.

HUGHES, GEORGE W. [Born in N. Y. Appointed from N. Y.]
Cadet Mil. Acad., 1 July, 1823, to 16 June, 1827. Capt. Top. Eng., 7 July, 1838. Lieut. Col. Md. and D. C. Vols., 4 Aug., 1847. Col., 1 Oct., 1847. Mustered out of Vol. Service 24 July, 1848. Resigned 4 Aug., 1851. Bvt. Maj., 18 April, 1847, for gallant and meritorious conduct at Cerro Gordo. Bvt. Lieut. Col., 30 May, 1848, for meritorious conduct while serving in the enemy's country. Died 4 Dec., 1870.

HUGHES, JAMES. [Born in Md. Appointed from Ind.]
Cadet Mil. Acad., 1 July, 1844, to 26 Oct., 1844. 1st Lieut. of Inf., 24 Feb., 1847; 16th Inf., 9 April, 1847. Resigned 6 July, 1848.

HUGHES, JAMES B.* [Born in N. C. Appointed from N. C.]
2nd Lieut. 10th Cav., 15 June, 1884. 1st Lieut., 23 April, 1891. Capt. 1st Cav., 11 June, 1899. Trans. to 4th Cav., 9 Aug., 1899.

HUGHES, JOHN H.* [Born in N. Y. Appointed from N. Y.]
Addl. 2nd Lieut. 17th Inf., 11 June, 1897. 2nd Lieut. 4th Inf., 8 Aug., 1897. 1st Lieut., 2 March, 1899.

HUGHES, JOHN T. [Born in Ky. Appointed from Ind.]
1st Lieut of Inf., 24 Feb., 1847; 16th Inf., 9 April, 1847. Capt., 12 Feb., 1848. Disbanded 7 Aug., 1848.

HUGHES, LOUIS M. [Born in Md. Appointed from Md.]
Priv. Co. I, 7th Md. Vols., 15 Aug., 1862, to 31 May, 1865. 2nd Lieut. 36th Inf., 28 July, 1866. 1st Lieut., 22 Feb., 1869. Unassigned 19 May, 1869. Died 14 Feb., 1870.

HUGHES, MARTIN B.* [Born in Penn. Appointed from Penn.]
2nd Lieut. 9th Cav., 15 June, 1869. 1st Lieut., 24 May, 1873. Capt., 6 June, 1885. Maj., 29 March, 1899. Graduate of the Infantry and Cavalry School, 1883. Bvt. Capt., 27 Feb., 1890, for gallant service in action against Indians in the San Andreas Mountains, New Mexico, 7 April, 1890.

HUGHES, ROBT. P. [Born in Penn. Appointed from Penn.]
Priv. Co. E, 12th Penn. Vols., 25 April, 1861. Discharged 5 Aug., 1861. 1st Lieut. 85th Penn. Vols., 11 Oct., 1861. Capt., 20 May, 1862. Lieut. Col. 199th Penn. Vols., 7 Dec., 1864. Bvt. Col. Vols., 2 April, 1865, for gallant and distinguished service at Fort Gregg, Va. Mustered out 28 June, 1865. Capt. 18th Inf., 28 July, 1866. Bvt. Maj., 2 March, 1867, for gallant and meritorious service in the assault on Fort Gregg, Va. Unassigned 26 April, 1869. Ass'd to 3rd Inf., 5 July, 1870. Maj. I. G., 19 Feb., 1885. Lieut. Col. I. G., 11 March, 1885. Col. I. G., 31 Aug., 1888. Brig. Gen. Vols., 3 June, 1898, to 19 April, 1899. Brig. Gen. Vols., 16 April, 1899, to ——.

HUGHES, WM. B.* [Born in Tenn. Appointed from Tenn.]
Bvt. 2nd Lieut. 4th Inf., 1 July, 1856. 2nd Lieut. 9th Inf., 30 Sept., 1856. 1st Lieut., 1 April, 1861. 1st Lieut. 18th Inf., 14 May, 1861, declined. Capt. 18th Inf., 24th

Oct., 1861, declined. Capt. A. Q. M., 19 Feb., 1863. Maj. Q. M., 29 May, 1876. Lieut. Col. D. Q. M. G., 15 Feb., 1889. Died Sept. 22, 1896.

HUGHES, WM. N. [Born in Tenn. Appointed from Tenn.]
2nd Lieut. 13th Inf., 1 Sept., 1879. 1st Lieut. 9th Inf., 4 Nov., 1890. Trans. to 13th Inf., 20 July, 1891. Capt., 20 April, 1890. Graduate of the Infantry and Cavalry School, 1897.

HUGHES, WM. N., Jr. [Born in Tenn. Appointed from Penn.]
2nd Lieut. 13th Inf., 1 Aug., 1899.

HUGO, SAMUEL P. [Born in ——. Appointed from Md.]
Surg. Mate 14th Inf., 12 March, 1812. Trans. to 1st Rifles, 26 Jan., 1814. Retained in Rifle Reg., 17 May, 1815. Post Surg., 27 Aug., 1818, which appointment was revoked. Dismissed 7 Sept., 1818.

HUGO, WM. H. [Born in N. Y. Appointed from Mich.]
Capt. 70th N. Y. Vols., 21 June, 1861. Mustered out 1 July, 1864. 2nd Lieut. 16th Inf., 11 May, 1866. Trans. to 25th Inf., 21 Sept., 1866. 1st Lieut., 21 Nov., 1868. Unassigned 26 April, 1869. Ass'd to 9th Cav., 1 Jan., 1871. Dismissed 1 Nov., 1881.

HUGHEY, WILLISON. [Born in Penn. Appointed from Penn].
Asst. Surg., 25 Oct., 1833. Killed by explosion on steamer, 25 April, 1838.

HUGUET, ADOLPHE H. [Born in La. Appointed from La.]
2nd Lieut. 21st Inf., 9 July, 1898. 1st Lieut. 22nd Inf., 31 March, 1899.

HULBERT, WM.* [Born in N. Y. Appointed from N. Y.]
2nd Lieut. 6th Inf., 1 July, 1838. Killed by Indians in Florida, 2 May, 1839.

HULINGS, THOS. M. [Born in Penn. Appointed from Penn.]
1st Lieut. 25th Pa. Vols., 18 April, 1861. Capt., 28 May, 1861. Mustered out 29 July, 1861. Capt. 12th Inf., 19 Feb., 1862. Maj. 49th Pa. Vols., 31 July, 1861. Lieut. Col., 16 Oct., 1862. Col., 22 April, 1864. Killed 10 May, 1864, at Battle of Spottsylvania Court House, Va.

HULL, GUSTAVUS A. [Born in N. Y. Appointed from Ky.]
Mil. Storekeeper Q. M. D., 21 July, 1862. Capt., 28 July, 1866. Died 27 Sept., 1891.

HULL, JOHN. [Born in Ky. Appointed from Ala.]
2nd Lieut. 4th Inf., 24 March, 1818. 1st Lieut., 1 March, 1819. Disbanded 1 June, 1821.

HULL, ROBT. B. [Born in N. Y. Appointed from N. Y.]
1st Lieut. 18th Inf., 14 May, 1861. Capt., 25 Oct., 1861. Unassigned 4 March, 1870. Discharged 28 Aug., 1870. Bvt. Maj., 31 Dec., 1862, for gallant and meritorious service at the Battle of Mufreesboro, Tenn. Bvt. Lieut. Col., 1 Sept., 1864, for gallant and meritorious service during the Atlanta campaign, and in the Battle of Jonesboro, Ga.

HULL, WM. H. [Born in N. J. Appointed from the Army.]
Priv. Co. A Engs., 9 July, 1846, to 19 April, 1848. 2nd Lieut. 10th Inf., 3 March, 1848. Disbanded 24 Aug., 1848. Died 12 Nov., 1883.

HULSE, ISAAC, Jr. [Born in Md. Appointed from Fla.]
2nd Lieut. of Inf., 8 March, 1847; 13th Inf., 9 April, 1847. Disbanded 15 July, 1848.

HUMASON, STANLEY D. [Born in Ohio. Appointed from Ohio.]
Sergt. Co. B, and Sergt. Maj. 104th Ohio Vols., 30 Aug., 1862, to 1 July, 1863. 2nd Lieut. 104th Ohio Vols., 1 July, 1863. 1st Lieut., 14 Sept., 1864. Mustered out 17 June, 1865. 2nd Lieut. 34th Inf., 7 March, 1867. Trans. to 16th Inf., 14 April, 1869. Cashiered 2 March, 1870.

HUMBER, CHAS. H.* [Born in Mass. Appointed from Mass.]
2nd Lieut. 7th Inf., 1 July, 1840. 1st Lieut., 30 Sept., 1845. Capt., 16 July, 1850. Died 2 Jan., 1858. Bvt. Capt., 18 April, 1847, for gallant and meritorious conduct at Cerro Gordo.

HUMBER, ROBERT C. [Born in Ga. Appointed from Ga.]
2nd Lieut. 10th Inf., 1 Aug., 1899.

HUMBERT, JAMES. [Born in Penn. Appointed from Penn.]
2nd Lieut. 8th Inf., 1 Nov., 1866. 1st Lieut., 10 June, 1868. Unassigned 3 May, 1869. Ass'd to 17th Inf., 15 Dec., 1870. Trans. to 1st Inf., 23 April, 1878. Capt., 15 Sept., 1882. Died 20 Sept., 1883.

HUMPHREY, BALLARD S. [Born in Va. Appointed from Army.]
Priv. Co. I, 1st Art., 1 Dec., 1857. Artificer, 30 Nov., 1859. Trans. to Ord. Dept., 1 Aug., 1860. Trans. to Co. I, 1st Art., ——. 1st Sergt., ——, 1861. 2nd Lieut. 1st Art., 22 Oct., 1862. Bvt. 1st Lieut., 26 May, 1863, for gallant and meritorious service in an assault on Port Hudson, La. 1st Lieut. 1st Art., 4 June, 1864. Bvt. Capt., 13 March, 1865, for good and gallant service during the war. Mustered out 1 Jan., 1871. 2nd Lieut. 9th Cav., 12 Dec., 1872. 1st Lieut., 24 June, 1879. Died 28 Oct., 1889.

HUMPHREY, CHAS. F. [Born in N. Y. Appointed from Army.]
Priv. Co. E, 5th Art., 17 March, 1863. Corpl., 9 Nov., 1863. Sergt., 1 Oct., 1864. 1st Sergt., 3 Nov., 1865. 2nd Lieut. 5th Art., 8 May, 1866. Trans. to 4th Art., 23 Oct., 1866. 1st Lieut., 21 May, 1868. Capt. A. Q. M., 23 June, 1879. Maj. Q. M., 11 Dec., 1892. Lieut. Col. D. Q. M. G., 15 Oct., 1897. Col. Q. M. Vols., 7 July, 1898, to 20 Sept., 1898. Brig. Gen. Vols., 21 Sept., 1898, to 12 June, 1899 Bvt. Capt., 27 Feb., 1890, for gallant services in action against Indians at Clear Water, Idaho, July 11, 1877. Medal of Honor for most distinguished gallantry in action at the Clear Water, Idaho, July 11, 1877, where he voluntarily and successfully conducted, in the face of a withering fire, a party which recovered the possession of an abandoned howitzer and two gatling guns lying between the lines and within a few yards of the Indians, while serving as 1st Lieut., 4th U. S. Art.

HUMPHREY, CHARLES F., Jr. [Born in D. C. Appointed from D. C.]
2nd Lieut. 17th Inf., 9 July, 1898. 1st Lieut. 12th Inf., 2 March, 1899. Trans. to 17th Inf., 2 Oct., 1899.

HUMPHREY, CHAUNCEY B.* [Born in Kans. Appointed from Kans.]
2nd Lieut. 3rd Inf., 26 April, 1898. 1st Lieut., 2 March, 1899.

HUMPHREY, EVANS.* [Born in N. Y. Appointed from N. Y.]
2nd Lieut. Corps Art., 21 July, 1814. 1st Lieut., 20 April, 1818. Disbanded 1 June, 1821. Died 11 April, 1833.

HUMPHREY, EVAN H.* [Born in Cal. Appointed from Neb.]
2nd Lieut. 7th Cav., 15 Feb., 1899.

HUMPHREY, HARRY D. [Born in Wis. Appointed from Idaho.]
Cadet Mil. Acad., 1 July, 1881, to 14 June, 1882. 2nd Lieut. 20th Inf., 10 Jan., 1887. 1st Lieut. 10th Inf., 22 March, 1894. Trans. to 20th Inf., 5 May, 1894. Capt., 2 March, 1899.

HUMPHREY, ROMAN B. [Born in Ohio. Appointed from Army.]
Priv., Sergt. and 1st Sergt. Co. A, 13th Inf., 15 Aug., 1861, to 13 June, 1863. 2nd Lieut. 13th Inf., 1 June, 1863. 1st Lieut., 20 Feb., 1864. Died 4 Oct., 1864.

HUMPHREYS, ANDREW A.* [Born in Penn. Appointed from Penn.]
Bvt. 2nd Lieut. 2nd Art., 1 July, 1831. 2nd Lieut., 1 July, 1831. 1st Lieut., 16 Aug., 1836. Resigned 30 Sept., 1836. 1st Lieut. Top. Eng., 13 Feb., 1839, to rank from 7 July, 1838. Capt., 31 May, 1848. Maj., 6 Aug., 1861. Col. A. A. de C., March, 1862. Brig. Gen. Vols., 28 April, 1862. Bvt. Col., 13 Dec., 1862, for gallant and meritorious service in the Battle of Fredericksburg, Va. Lieut. Col. Eng., 3 March, 1833. Maj. Gen. Vols., 8 July, 1863. Bvt. Brig. Gen., 13 March, 1865, for gallant and meritorious service in the Battle of Gettysburg, Penn. Bvt. Maj. Gen., 13 March, 1865, for gallant and meritorious service in the Battle of Sailor's Creek, Va. Brig. Gen. Chief of Eng., 8 Aug., 1866. Mustered out of Vol. Service, 1 Sept., 1866. Retired 30 June, 1879. Died 27 Dec., 1883.

HUMPHREYS, CHAS. [Born in Penn. Appointed from D. C.]
2nd Lieut. 1st N. Y. Art., 14 Feb., 1865. Mustered out 16 June, 1865. 2nd Lieut. 3rd Art., 9 May, 1867. 1st Lieut., 1 Jan., 1870. Capt., 30 June, 1893. Graduate of the Artillery School, 1890 and 1892.

HUMPHREYS, ENOCH. [Born in Conn. Appointed from Conn.]
Lieut. 1st Art. and Eng., 16 Feb., 1801. Retained 1 April, 1802, in Art. Capt., 9 Jan., 1809, in 1st Art., — March, 1812. Trans. to Corps Art., 12 May, 1814. Trans. to 4th Art., 1 June, 1821. Died 1 Aug., 1825. Bvt. Maj., 23 Dec., 1814, for gallant conduct at the Siege of New Orleans.

HUMPHREYS, FREDERICK C. [Born in Mass. Appointed from Fla.]
Mil. Storekeeper, 30 Jan., 1855. Resigned 22 May, 1861.

HUMPHREYS, GAD. [Born in Conn. Appointed from N. Y.]
1st Lieut 6th Inf., 3 May, 1808. Capt., 31 Dec., 1809. Maj. 4th Inf., 18 April, 1814. Disbanded 15 June, 1815. Reinstated as Capt. 6th Inf. with Bvt. of Maj. from 18 April, 1814, to 2 Dec., 1815. Maj., 31 March, 1817. Lieut. Col. 2nd Inf., 13 May, 1820. Disbanded 1 June, 1821.

HUMPHREYS, GEORGE S.* [Born in Conn. Appointed from Md.]
Bvt. 2nd Lieut. 2nd Inf., 1 July, 1846. Trans. to 2nd Drag., 17 Aug., 1846. Died 9 Nov., 1847.

HUMPHREYS, HENRY H. [Born in Penn. Appointed from Penn.]
1st Lieut. 2nd Pa. Art., 3 Oct., 1862, to 26 April, 1865. Maj. A. de C. Vols., 5 April, 1865. Bvt. Lieut. Col. Vols., 9 April, 1865, for valuable and meritorious service during the campaign, terminating with the surrender of the insurgent army under Gen. R. E. Lee. Mustered out 10 Nov., 1865. 2nd Lieut. and 1st Lieut. 17th Inf., 23 Feb., 1866. Trans. to 35th Inf., 21 Sept., 1866. Bvt. Capt., 2 March, 1867, for gallant and meritorious service in the Battle of Fredericksburg, Va. Bvt. Maj., 2 March, 1867, for gallant and meritorious service in the Battle of Gettysburg, Pa. Bvt. Lieut. Col., 2 March, 1867, for gallant and meritorious service at the fall of Petersburg, and in the pursuit of the rebel army under Gen. R. E. Lee. Trans. to 15th Inf., 12 Aug., 1869. Capt., 15 Jan., 1873. Maj. 12th Inf., 13 July, 1896. Lieut. Col. 22nd Inf., 23 Dec., 1898. Retired for over 30 years' service 25 May, 1899.

HUMPHREYS, REUBEN. [Born in N. Y. Appointed from N. Y.]
Ensign 13th Inf., 19 July, 1813. 3rd Lieut., 30 Sept., 1813. 2nd Lieut., 19 May, 1814. Disbanded 15 June, 1815. Reinstated in 8th Inf., 2 Dec., 1815. Capt., 24 Dec., 1818. Trans. to 3rd Inf., 1 June, 1821. Trans. to 4th Inf., 4 June, 1821. Died 3 Feb., 1822.

HUMPHREYS, ROBERT. [Born in Tenn. Appointed from Tenn.]
1st Lieut. of Inf., 20 March, 1847; 14th Inf., 9 April, 1847. Disbanded 25 July, 1848.

HUMPHREVILLE, J. LEE. [Born in Ohio. Appointed from Ohio.]
2nd Lieut. 9th Cav., 28 July, 1866. 1st Lieut., 12 July, 1867. Capt., 31 May, 1870. Dismissed 3 April, 1874.

HUN, LEONARD G.* [Born in N. Y. Appointed from N. Y.]
2nd Lieut. 5th Art., 15 June, 1869. Discharged 2 Aug., 1870.

HUNT, EDWARD B.* [Born in N. Y. Appointed from N. Y.]
Bvt. 2nd Lieut. Eng., 1 July, 1845. 2nd Lieut., 29 Dec., 1845. 1st Lieut., 1 July, 1853. Capt., 1 July, 1859. Maj., 3 March, 1863. Died 2 Oct., 1863.

HUNT, FRANKLIN E.* [Born in N. J. Appointed from N. J.]
Bvt. 2nd Lieut. 4th Art., 1 July, 1829. 2nd Lieut., 1 July, 1829. 1st Lieut., 15 Aug., 1836. Capt., 18 June, 1846. Maj. P. M., 2 March, 1855. Bvt. Lieut. Col., 13 March, 1865, for faithful and meritorious service during the war. Lieut. Col. D. P. M. Gen., 3 March, 1878. Retired 7 June, 1879. Died 2 Feb., 1881.

HUNT, HENRY J.* [Born in Mich. Appointed from Ohio.]
2nd Lieut. 2nd Art., 1 July, 1839. 1st Lieut., 18 June, 1846. Bvt. Capt., 20 Aug., 1847, for gallant and meritorious conduct in the Battles of Contreras and Churubusco. Bvt. Maj., 13 Sept., 1847, for gallant and meritorious conduct in the Battle of Chapultepec. Capt. 2nd Art., 28 Sept., 1852. Maj. 5th Art., 14 May, 1861. Col. A. A. de C., 28 Sept., 1861. Brig. Gen. Vols., 15 Sept., 1862, for meritorious service. Bvt. Col., 3 July, 1863, for gallant and meritorious service in the Battle of Gettysburg, Pa. Lieut. Col. 3rd Art., 1 Aug., 1863. Bvt. Maj. Gen.

Vols., 6 July, 1864, for gallant and distinguished conduct in the Battle of Gettysburg, Penn., and for faithful and highly meritorious service in the campaign from the Rapidan to Petersburg, Va. Bvt. Brig. Gen., 13 March, 1865, for gallant and meritorious service during the Siege of Petersburg, and in the campaign terminating with the surrender of the insurgent army under Gen. R. E. Lee. Bvt. Maj. Gen., 13 March, 1865, for gallant and meritorious service in the field during the war. Mustered out of Vol. Service, 30 April, 1866. Col. 5th Art., 4 April, 1869. Retired 14 Sept., 1883. Died 11 Feb., 1889.

HUNT, HENRY J. [Born in La. Appointed from the Army.]
Priv. and Corpl. Co. I, 14th Inf., 14 Dec., 1887, to 7 Nov., 1890. 2nd Lieut. 15th Inf., 6 Nov., 1890. 1st Lieut., 6th Inf., 7 July, 1897. Graduate of the Infantry and Cavalry School, 1895. Capt. 11th Inf., 29 Jan., 1900. Trans. to 24th Inf., 17 Feb., 1900.

HUNT, IRWIN L.* [Born in Cal. Appointed from Cal.]
2nd Lieut. 19th Inf., 15 Feb., 1899.

HUNT, JAMES C. [Born in N. J. Appointed from N. J.]
1st Lieut. 1st N. J. Cav., 15 Aug., 1861, to 22 March, 1862. 2nd Lieut. 1st Cav., 19 Feb., 1862. 1st Lieut., 17 July, 1862. R. Q. M., 18 June, 1862, to 30 Jan., 1863, and 21 May to 18 Oct., 1863. Capt., 28 June, 1864. Resigned 20 June, 1872. Bvt. Capt., 6 May, 1864, for gallant and meritorious service at the Battle of Todd's Tavern, Va. Bvt. Maj., 1 April, 1865, for gallant and meritorious service at the Battle of Five Forks, Va. Bvt. Lieut. Col., 29 Jan., 1867, for gallantry in an engagement with a band of Indians at Steer's Mountain, Ore., 29 Jan., 1867.

HUNT, JAMES L. [Born in Maine. Appointed from Maine.
Capt. 21st Maine Vols., 14 Oct., 1862. Mustered out 25 Aug., 1863. Capt. 32nd Maine Vols., 16 April, 1864. Lieut. Col., 18 Oct., 1864. Mustered out 12 Dec., 1864. Capt. Maine Coast Guards, 26 April, 1865. Mustered out 7 July, 1865. 2nd Lieut. 32nd Inf., 7 March, 1867. Trans. to 21st Inf., 19 April, 1869. Resigned 27 Aug., 1869.

HUNT, JOHN E. [Born in R. I. Appointed from Army.]
Cadet Mil. Acad., 15 June, 1892, to 19 Jan., 1894. Priv., Corpl and Sergt. Troop H, 8th Cav., 30 Aug., 1894, to 25 June, 1897. 2nd Lieut. 25th Inf., 8 June, 1897. 1st Lieut., 2 March, 1899.

HUNT, JOHN S. [Born in N. Y. Appointed from N. Y.]
1st Lieut. 2nd N. Y. Art., 2 Oct. to 12 Nov., 1861. 2nd Lieut. 4th Art., 21 Oct., 1861. 1st Lieut., 25 Oct., 1861. Drowned 29 May, 1864.

HUNT, LEVI P.* [Born in Mo. Appointed from Mo.]
2nd Lieut. 10th Cav., 15 June, 1870. 1st Lieut., 30 June, 1875. Capt., 25 March, 1890.

HUNT, LEWIS C.* [Born in Wis. Appointed from Mo.]
Bvt. 2nd Lieut. 3rd Inf., 1 July, 1847. 2nd Lieut. 4th Inf., 13 Sept., 1847. 1st Lieut., 15 April, 1852. Capt., 23 May, 1855. Col. 92nd N. Y. Vols., 25 May, 1862. Bvt. Maj., 31 May, 1862, for gallant and meritorious service in the Battle of Fair Oaks, Va. Bvt. Lieut. Col., 14 Dec., 1862, for gallant and meritorious service in the Battle of Kingston, N. C. Brig. Gen. Vols., 24 Dec., 1862. Maj. 14th Inf., 8 June, 1863. Bvt. Col., 13 March, 1865, for gallant and meritorious service during the war. Bvt. Brig. Gen., 13 March, 1865, for gallant and meritorious service in the field during the war. Mustered out of Vol. Service 15 Jan., 1866. Trans. to 4th Inf., 21 Aug., 1866. Lieut. Col. 20th Inf., 29 March, 1868. Trans. to 4th Inf., 25 Feb., 1881. Col. 14th Inf., 19 May, 1881. Died 16 Sept., 1886.

HUNT, ORA E.* [Born in Cal. Appointed from Cal.]
2nd Lieut. 14th Inf., 12 June, 1894. 1st Lieut. 18th Inf., 26 April, 1898.

HUNT, SAML. W. [Born in N. Y. Appointed from N. Y.
Cadet Mil. Acad., 2 May, 1814, to Jan., 1819. 2nd Lieut. 3rd Inf., 3 Feb., 1819. 1st Lieut., 1 Feb., 1822. Died 11 Sept., 1829.

HUNT, THOMAS. [Born in Mass. Appointed from Mass.]
3rd Lieut. 4th Inf., 6 May, 1813. 2nd Lieut., 9 March, 1814. Trans. to 8th Inf., 17 May, 1815. Trans. to 5th Inf., 1 Jan., 1816. 1st Lieut., 1 July, 1817. R. Q. M., 1 March to 31 July, 1819. Capt., 27 Sept., 1824. Resigned 31 Oct., 1836. Died 16 Feb., 1838.

HUNT, THOS. B. [Born in Canada. Appointed from Minn.]
1st Lieut. R. Q. M., 4th Minn. Vols., 23 Dec., 1861. Capt. A. Q. M. Vols., 26 Nov., 1862. Bvt. Maj. and Lieut. Col. Vols., 28 July, 1865, for meritorious service in his department. Capt. A. Q. M., 18 Jan., 1867. Bvt. Maj. and Lieut. Col., 2 March, 1867, for faithful and meritorious service in the Q. M. D. during the war. Vacated commission of Capt. A. Q. M. Vols., 2 April, 1867. Cashiered 26 Feb., 1874. Re-appointed 12 June, 1879, with former rank and date of commission. Retired 20 Feb., 1885. Died 7 Sept., 1891.

HUNT, THOS. F. [Born in N. C. Appointed from N. C.]
3rd Lieut. 1st Light Drag., 2 July, 1813. 2nd Lieut. 3rd Rifles, 29 June, 1814. Disbanded 15 June, 1815. Reinstated 2 Dec., 1815, in 3rd Inf. Trans. to Rifle Reg., 1 Jan., 1816. 1st Lieut., 1 July, 1817. Capt. A. Dep. Q. M. Gen., 16 June, 1818. Capt. Rifle Reg., 20 May, 1820. Trans. to 5th Inf., 1 June, 1821. A. Q. M., 1 June, 1821. Maj. Q. M., 7 July, 1838. Lieut. Col. Dep. Q. M. Gen., 8 Nov., 1839. Col. Asst., Q. M. G., 16 Sept., 1851. Bvt. Maj., 16 June, 1828, for ten years' faithful service in one grade. Bvt. Col., 30 May, 1848, for meritorious conduct during the war with Mexico. Died 22 Dec., 1856.

HUNT, WILLIAM E. [Born in N. H. Appointed from N. H.]
2nd Lieut. 19th Inf., 10 April, 1899.

HUNTER, ALFRED M.* [Born in Ill. Appointed from Ill.]
2nd Lieut. 5th Cav., 12 June, 1887. Trans. to 4th Art., 3 April, 1888. 1st Lieut. 1st Art., 22 March, 1894. Trans. to 4th Art., 27 April, 1894. Graduate of the Artillery School, 1896.

HUNTER, CHARLES H.* [Born in Penn. Appointed from Penn.]
2nd Lieut. 19th Inf., 12 June, 1880. Trans. to 1st Art., 18 March, 1881. 1st Lieut.,

2 March, 1889. Capt., 3rd Art., 2 March, 1899. Graduate of the Artillery School, 1886.

HUNTER, DAVID.* [Born in D. C. Appointed from Ill.]
2nd Lieut. 5th Inf., 1 July, 1822. 1st Lieut., 30 June, 1828. Capt. 1st Drag., 4 March, 1833. Resigned 4 July, 1836. Addl. P. M., 13 Nov., 1841. Maj. P. M., 14 March, 1842. Col. 3rd Cav., 14 May, 1861; 6th Cav., 3 Aug., 1861. Brig. Gen. Vols., 17 May, 1861. Maj. Gen. Vols., 13 Aug., 1861. Bvt. Brig. Gen., 13 March, 1865, for gallant and meritorious service in the Battle of Piedmont, and during the campaign in the Valley of Virginia. Bvt. Maj. Gen., 13 March, 1865, for gallant and meritorious service during the war. Mustered out of Vol. Service 15 Jan., 1866. Retired 31 July, 1866. Died 2 Feb., 1886.

HUNTER, EDWARD.* [Born in Maine. Appointed from Maine.]
2nd Lieut. and 1st Lieut. 12th Inf., 23 June, 1865. R. Q. M., 11 Aug., 1866, to 28 April, 1869. Reg. Adj., 31 Oct., 1869, to 9 Feb., 1870. Trans. to 1st Cav., 19 Feb., 1870. R. Q. M., 19 Sept., 1870, to 1 May, 1873. Reg. Adj., 26 Nov., 1877, to 21 Aug., 1879. Capt., 21 Aug., 1879. Maj. J. A., 10 Dec., 1888. Lieut. Col. Dep. J. A. G., 3 Jan., 1895.

HUNTER, GEORGE K. [Born in Ohio. Apointed from Ohio.]
Addl. 2nd Lieut. 4th Cav., 15 June, 1877. 2nd Lieut. 3rd Cav., 14 Dec., 1877. 1st Lieut., 24 May, 1881. Reg. Adjt., 27 Nov., 1885, to 25 Aug., 1886. Capt., 1 Feb., 1891.

HUNTER, JOHN. [Born in N. Y. Appointed from the Army.]
Priv., Corpl. and Sergt. Cos. I and G, and Q. M. Sergt. and Sergt. Maj. 4th Art., 29 Sept., 1858, to 9 June, 1864. 2nd Lieut. 10th Inf., 18 May, 1864. 1st Lieut., 20 March, 1865. Unassigned 19 May, 1869. Discharged 1 Jan., 1871. Bvt. 1st Lieut., 1 Oct., 1864, for gallant service at the Battle of Chapel House, Va.

HUNTER, JOHN F. [Born in S. C. Appointed from Penn.]
Capt. of Inf., 16 Feb., 1847. Maj., 3 March, 1847; 11th Inf., 9 April, 1847. Disbanded 14 Aug., 1848. Bvt. Lieut. Col., 20 Aug., 1847, for gallant and meritorious conduct at Contreras and Churubusco, Mex.

HUNTER, MANN P. [Born in Va. Appointed from Va.]
2nd Lieut. Inf., 8 March, 1847; 13th Inf., 9 April, 1847. Disbanded 15 July, 1848.

HUNTER, NATHL. W.* [Born in Ga. Appointed from G
Bvt. 2nd Lieut. 7th Inf., 1 July, 1833. Resigned 1 Oct., 1833. 2nd Lieut. 2nd Drag., 6 Oct., 1836. 1st Lieut., 31 Dec., 1837. Capt., 1 April, 1841. Died 25 April, 1849.

HUNTER, PENDLETON. [Born in Mich. Appointed from Mich.]
2nd Lieut. 8th Cav., 12 Oct., 1867. 1st Lieut., 1 May, 1870. Mustered out 1 Ja 1871.

HUNTER, ROBERT F.* [Born in Ohio. Appointed from Ohio.]
Bvt. 2nd Lieut. 2nd Inf., 1 July, 1853. 2nd Lieut., 3 March, 1855. 1st Lieut., 19 Jan., 1861. Cashiered 19 Nov., 1861.

HUNTING, GEORGE F. [Born in Vt. Appointed from Army.]
Priv. 12th Inf., 1 Nov., 1861, to 19 Feb., 1862. 2nd Lieut. 3rd Art., 19 Feb., 1862. 1st Lieut., 8 Feb., 1864. Resigned 21 Sept., 1868.

HUNTINGTON, DAVID L. [Born in Mass. Appointed from Penn.]
1st Lieut. Asst. Surg., 11 July, 1862. Col. Med. Director (Act 25 Feb., 1865), 25 Feb., 1865. Bvt. Capt. and Bvt. Maj., 13 March 1865, for faithful and meritorious service during the war. Bvt. Lieut. Col., 13 March, 1865, for gallant and meritorious service during the war. Relieved as Col. Med. Director (Act 25 Feb., 1865), 30 June, 1865. Capt. Asst. Surg., 28 July, 1866. Maj. Surg., 28 April, 1877. Lieut. Col. Dep. Surg. Gen., 18 Apr., 1885. Retired 10 April, 1898.

HUNTINGTON, EDWARD S. [Born in Mass. Appointed from Army.]
Priv., Sergt. and 1st Sergt. Co. D, 11th Inf., 8 Aug., 1861, to 4 May, 1862. 2nd Lieut. 11th Inf., 14 April, 1862. 1st Lieut., 1 May, 1863. Trans. to 29th Inf., 21 Sept., 1866. Capt., 25 Jan., 1867. Resigned 1 Aug., 1869. Bvt. Capt., 2 July, 1863, for gallant and meritorious service at the Battle of Gettysburg, Penn.

HUNTINGTON, HENRY A. [Born in Ill. Appointed from Ill.]
2nd Lieut. 9th Ill. Cav., 9 Oct. to 6 Nov., 1861. 2nd Lieut. 4th Art., 24 Oct., 1861. 1st Lieut., 3 May, 1863. Resigned 19 Nov., 1869. Bvt. 1st Lieut., 7 April, 1862, for gallant and meritorious service at the Battle of Shiloh, Tenn. Bvt. Capt., 31 Dec., 1862, for gallant and meritorious service at the Battle of Stone River, Tenn. Bvt. Maj., 13 March, 1865, for gallant and meritorious service during the war.

HUNTINGTON, HENRY D.* [Born in Vt. Appointed from Iowa.]
2nd Lieut. 2nd Cav., 16 June, 1875. 1st Lieut., 26 Oct., 1881. Died 4 May, 1886.

HUNTON, THOMAS.* [Born in Ky. Appointed from Ky.]
2nd Lieut. 2nd Drag., 1 July, 1839, declined. Died 11 May, 1890.

HUNTT, GEORGE G. [Born in D. C. Appointed from D. C.]
2nd Lieut. 1st Cav., 27 March, 1861. 1st Lieut., 2 May, 1861; 4th Cav., 3 Aug., 1861. Reg. Adj., 14 Sept., 1861, to 17 July, 1862. Capt. 4th Cav., 17 July, 1862. Maj. 1st Cav., 10 Feb., 1870. Lieut. Col. 10th Cav., 21 April, 1887. Col. 2nd Cav., 20 April, 1891. Retired, for over 30 years' service, 31 May, 1898.

HURLBURT, JOSEPH. [Born in Conn. Appointed from Conn.]
Chap. Post of Ft. Trumbull, Conn., 26 March, 1863, to 27 Aug., 1867. Post Chap., 3 April, 1867. Retired 19 Aug., 1867. Died 5 June, 1875.

HURST, JOSEPH H. [Born in England. Appointed from Penn.]
Sergt. Co. A, 141st Penn. Vols., 7 Aug., 1862. 1st Lieut. 141st Penn. Vols., 16 Feb., 1863. Capt., 21 April, 1865. Mustered out 28 May, 1865. 2nd Lieut. 12th Inf., 7 March, 1867. Bvt. 1st Lieut., 7 March, 1867, for gallant and meritorious service in the Battle of Chancellorsville, Va. Bvt. Capt., 7 March, 1867, for gallant and meritorious service in the Battle of Spottsylvania, Va. 1st Lieut. 12th Inf., 31 Jan., 1874. Capt., 28 May, 1884. Retired 15 March, 1893. Died 24 Jan., 1896.

HURST, PAUL. [Born in N. J. Appointed from D. C.]
2nd Lieut. 3rd Inf., 10 April, 1899.

HUSE, CALEB.* [Born in Mass. Appointed from Mass.]
Bvt. 2nd Lieut. 1st Art., 1 July, 1851. 2nd Lieut., 4 Sept., 1851. 1st Lieut., 4 Nov., 1854. Resigned 25 Feb., 1861.

HUSE, GUY E.* [Born in N. Y. Appointed at Large.]
2nd Lieut. 4th Cav., 13 June, 1879. 1st Lieut., 26 Nov., 1884. Resigned 1 Sept., 1886.

HUSTON, DANL., Jr.* [Born in Maine. Appointed from N. Y.]
Bvt. 2nd Lieut. 8th Inf., 1 July, 1848. 2nd Lieut. 1st Inf., 30 June, 1849. 1st Lieut., 31 Dec., 1852. Capt., 8 Dec., 1856. Bvt. Maj., 10 Aug., 1861, for gallant and meritorious service in the Battle of Wilson's Creek, Mo. Col. 7th Mo. Cav., 21 Feb., 1862. Bvt. Lieut. Col., 4 July, 1863, for gallant and meritorious service during the Siege of Vicksburg, Miss. Maj. 11th Inf., 1 Aug., 1863. Mustered out of Vol. Service, 30 Dec., 1864. Bvt. Col., 13 March, 1865, for gallant and meritorious service during the war. Trans. to 23rd Inf., 24 Dec., 1868. Lieut. Col. 6th Inf., 22 Feb., 1869. Col. 5th Inf., 6 Feb., 1882. Retired 22 June, 1882. Died 2 Dec., 1884.

HUSTON, JOSEPH F.* [Born in N. Y. Appointed from N. Y.]
2nd Lieut. 20th Inf., 13 June, 1873. 1st Lieut., 28 June, 1878. R. Q. M., 30 June, 1883, to 1 Sept., 1887. Capt., 15 July, 1890. Maj. 19th Inf., 5 May, 1899.

HUTCHINS, BENJAMIN T. [Born in N. H. Appointed from N. H.]
Priv. Co. A, Nat. Rifles D. C. Vols., 15 April to 20 June, 1861. 1st Lieut. 3rd Cav., 14 May, 1861; 6th Cav., 14 May, 1861. R. Q. M., 1 July to 1 Oct., 1861. Capt., 19 Nov., 1863. Lieut. Col. 1st N. H. Cav., 18 March, 1864. Mustered out of Vol. Service, 15 July, 1865. Resigned 10 Sept., 1869. Bvt. Maj., 13 March, 1865, for gallant and meritorious service during the war.

HUTCHESON, GROTE.* [Born in Ohio. Appointed from Ohio.]
2nd Lieut. 9th Cav., 15 June, 1884. 1st Lieut. 8th Cav., 20 April, 1891. Trans. to 9th Cav., 27 April, 1891. Capt. 6th Cav., 9 June, 1899. Capt. A. A. G. Vol., 12 May, 1898, to 13 April, 1899.

HUTCHINSON, MERRILL N. [Born in N. H. Appointed from Army.]
Priv. Co. G, 1st Batt. 18th Inf., 12 Oct., 1861. Sergt., 1 Jan., 1862. 2nd Lieut. 18th Inf., 9 June, 1862. 1st Lieut., 14 Jan., 1863. Bvt. Capt., 20 Sept., 1863, for gallant and meritorious service in the Battle of Chickamauga, Ga. Retired 6 Jan., 1864. Died 23 Jan., 1896.

HUTTER, GEORGE C. [Born in Penn. Appointed from Penn.]
2nd Lieut. Corps Art., 28 Jan., 1820. Trans. to 4th Art., 1 June, 1821. 1st Lieut., 30 Sept., 1823. Trans. to 6th Inf., 30 July, 1824. Capt., 12 May, 1829. Dropped 22 June, 1841. Reinstated 6 Aug., 1841. Rejected by Senate, 10 Feb., 1842. Re-appointed Capt. 6th Inf., 1 April, 1847. Maj. 1st Inf., to rank from 16 Feb., 1847. Rejected by Senate, 12 Jan., 1848. A. P. M., 10 May, 1848. Maj. P. M., 2 March, 1849. Resigned 30 April, 1861. Died 31 July, 1879.

HUTTON, FRANKLIN S.* [Born in N. Y. Appointed from N. Y.]
2nd Lieut. 2nd Inf., 12 June, 1895. 1st Lieut. of Inf., 9 July, 1898. Ass'd to 4th Inf., 1 Jan., 1899.

HUTTON, JAMES A.* [Born in Cal. Appointed from Cal.]
2nd Lieut. 8th Inf., 15 June, 1876. 1st Lieut., 23 May, 1884. Capt. of Inf. (8th Inf.), 10 July, 1891. Died 31 July, 1894.

HUXFORD, WM. P. [Born in N. Y. Appointed from N. Y.]
Priv. and Corpl. Co. D, 4th Mich. Vols., 10 June, 1861, to 15 Aug., 1862. Priv. Co. B, and Sergt. Maj. 162nd N. Y. Vols., 6 Sept., 1862, to 3 Jan., 1863. Capt. 162nd N. Y. Vols., 3 Jan., 1863. Mustered out 12 Oct., 1865. Capt. 42nd Inf., 28 July, 1866. Bvt. Maj., 2 March, 1867, for gallant and meritorious service in the assault on Port Hudson, La. Retired 10 Sept., 1868.

HYATT, CHAS. C. [Born in Ill. Appointed from N. Y.]
1st Lieut. 6th N. Y. Art., 2 Sept., 1862. Resigned 4 March, 1864. 1st Lieut. Vet. Res. Corps, 29 Feb., 1864. Mustered out 19 April, 1866. 2nd Lieut. 11th Inf., 23 Feb., 1866. Capt. 24th Inf., 28 July, 1866. Died 5 Oct., 1867.

HYDE, JOHN McE. [Born in N. Y. Appointed from N. Y.]
Priv. Co. A, 71st N. Y. State Militia, 16 June, 1861. Discharged 30 July, 1861. 2nd Lieut. 38th N. Y. Vols., 11 Jan., 1862. 1st Lieut., 1 Nov., 1862. Mustered out 22 June, 1863. 1st Lieut. 38th N. Y. Vols., 29 June, 1863. Mustered out 14 Oct., 1863. 1st Lieut. 39th N. Y. Vols., 22 Dec., 1863. Maj., 27 Jan., 1865. Bvt. Lieut. Col. Vols., 13 March, 1865, for gallant and meritorious service in the Battle of Cold Harbor, Va. Bvt. Col. Vols., 13 March, 1865, for gallant and meritorious service in front of Petersburg, Va. Mustered out 15 May, 1865. 2nd Lieut. 33rd Inf., 3 Sept., 1867. Trans. to 8th Inf., 3 May, 1869. 1st Lieut., 26 March, 1878. Reg. Adj., 20 May, 1886, to 23 Oct., 1889. Capt. A. Q. M., 22 Oct., 1889. Maj. Q. M., 13 July, 1899. Maj. Q. M. Vols., 10 Aug., 1898, to 2 March, 1899.

HYDE, RUSSEL B. [Born in Vt. Appointed from Vt.]
3rd Lieut. 30th Inf., 30 April, 1813. 2nd Lieut., 18 Feb., 1814. Dismissed 25 Oct., 1814. Restored 10 Dec., 1814. Trans. to 1st Inf., 17 May, 1815. Trans. to 8th Inf., 17 May, 1816. 1st Lieut., 1 July, 1816. Capt., 31 Oct., 1818. Trans. to 7th Inf., 1 June, 1821. Resigned 31 Dec., 1834. Bvt. Maj., 31 Oct., 1828, for ten years' faithful service in one grade.

HYER, BENJAMIN B.* [Born in N. Y. Appointed from N. Y.]
2nd Lieut. 6th Cav., 12 June, 1893. 1st Lieut., 2 March, 1899.

HYER, JOSEPH K.* [Born in Wis. Appointed from Wis.]
2nd Lieut. and 1st Lieut. 18th Inf., 23 June, 1865. Capt., 4 May, 1874. Retired 20 March, 1879. Died 12 Feb., 1882.

HYNES, JOHN R. [Born in N. H. Appointed from N. H.]
2nd Lieut. 3rd N. H. Vols., 23 Aug., 1861. 1st Lieut., 1 May, 1862, to 28 Sept., 1864. Capt. A. Q. M. Vols., 20 Sept., 1864. Bvt. Maj. and Lieut. Col. Vols.,

13 March, 1865, for faithful and meritorious service during the war. Mustered out 1 May, 1867. 2nd Lieut. 24th Inf., 22 Jan., 1867. 1st Lieut., 5 Oct., 1867. Unassigned 25 April, 1869. Died 31 Oct., 1870.

HYNES, THOS. [Born in Ireland. Appointed from Mo.]
Priv., Corpl., Sergt. and 1st Sergt. Co. B. 2nd Inf., 17 Nov., 1853, to 1 June, 1861. 2nd Lieut. 1st Mo. Vols., 11 June, 1861. Trans. to 1st Mo. Light Art., 1 Sept., 1861. Resigned 9 March, 1862. 1st Lieut. Adj. 10th Mo. Cav., 23 July to 20 Aug., 1862. 2nd Lieut. 1st Inf., 21 April, 1862. 1st Lieut., 28 May, 1864. Lieut. Col. 28th Mo. Vols., 20 Sept. to 3 Dec., 1862. Maj. 4th Mo. Cav., 4 Dec., 1862. Dismissed from Vols. and U. S. A., 2 Sept., 1864, to date from 28 May, 1864. Hosp. Steward 13 Sept., 1871, to 30 June, 1874.

IAEGER, GEORGE A. [Born in Penn. Appointed from Penn.]
2nd Lieut. 12th Inf., 17 Dec., 1872. Resigned 31 July, 1876.

IDE, WM. C. [Born in Mass. Appointed from Mass.]
1st Lieut. 13th Inf., 14 May, 1861. Capt., 14 May, 1862. Dismissed 14 May, 1869. Bvt. Maj., 13 March, 1865, for meritorious service during the war.

IHRIE, GEORGE P. [Born in Penn. Appointed from N. J.]
Cadet at Mil. Acad., 1 July, 1845, to 16 Jan., 1847. 2nd Lieut. 3rd Art., 18 June, 1855. 1st Lieut., 28 Feb., 1857. Resigned 31 Dec., 1859. Lieut. Col. 3rd Cal. Vols., 4 Sept., 1861. Resigned 11 Dec., 1861. Col. A. A. de C., 7 May, 1862. Bvt. Brig. Gen. Vols., 13 March, 1865, for gallant and meritorious service during the late rebellion at the Siege of Corinth, at Iuka, Battle of Corinth, Tallahatchie, advance on Grenada, Jackson, Humboldt and Siege of Vicksburg. Discharged 18 Aug., 1863. Maj. P. M., 14 April, 1866. Resigned 1 July, 1873. Bvt. Lieut. Col., Col. and Brig. Gen., 2 March, 1867, for gallant and meritorious service during the war, at the Siege of Corinth, at Iuka, Battle of Corinth, Tallahatchie, advance on Grenada, Jackson, Humboldt, and Siege of Vicksburg.

ILGES, GUIDO. [Born in Prussia. Appointed from Ind.]
Capt. 14th Inf., 14 May, 1861. Bvt. Maj., 1 Aug., 1864, for gallant service in the Battle of the Wilderness, Va. Bvt. Lieut. Col., 1 Aug., 1864, for gallant service in the Battle of Spottsylvania, Va. Maj. 7th Inf., 10 Dec., 1873. Trans. to 5th Inf., 18 Dec., 1879. Lieut. Col. 18th Inf., 6 Feb., 1882. Dismissed 31 Oct., 1883.

ILIFF, JAMES A. [Born in N. J. Appointed from Ind.]
Priv. and Sergt. Co. A, 132nd Ind. Vols., 18 May to 7 Sept., 1864. Sergt. Maj. 109th U. S. Col. Inf., 1 Feb., 1865. 2nd Lieut., 8 Nov., 1865. Mustered out 6 Feb., 1866. 2nd Lieut. 41st Inf., 2 Nov., 1867. Trans. to 24th Inf., 11 Nov., 1869. Unassigned 1 Feb., 1870. Mustered out 1 Jan., 1871.

ILSLEY, CHAS. S. [Born in Maine. Appointed from Maine.]
Priv. Co. C, 71st N. Y. State Militia, 20 April, 1861. Discharged 30 July, 1861. Capt. 15th Maine Vols., 23 Dec., 1861. Mustered out 25 March, 1865. Capt. 5th N. Y. Art., 3 April, 1865. Mustered out 19 July, 1865. 2nd Lieut. and 1st Lieut. 16th Inf., 23 Feb., 1866. Bvt. Capt., 2 March, 1867, for gallant and meritorious service during the war. Unassigned 17 April, 1869. Ass'd to 1st Cav., 15 Dec., 1870. Trans. to 7th Cav., 23 Dec., 1870. Capt., 11 July, 1871. Maj. 30 Jan., 1892. Retired ——, 1899. Died 17 April, 1899.

INGALLS, CHAS. H. [Born in Maine. Appointed from Maine.]
2nd Lieut. 6th Inf., 29 Feb., 1876. 1st Lieut., 26 June, 1883. Capt. A. Q. M., 2 July, 1883. Retired with rank of Maj., 22 Sept., 1896.

INGALLS, JAMES M. [Born in Vt. Appointed from Army.]
Priv. Co. A, 2nd Batt. 16th Inf., 2 Jan., 1864. Corpl., 1 April, 1864. Com. Sergt. 16th Inf., 1 Sept., 1864. Q. M. Sergt. 16th Inf., 1 March, 1865. 2nd Lieut. and 1st Lieut. 16th Inf., 3 May, 1865. Trans. to 2nd Inf., 17 April, 1869. Trans. to 1st Art., 31 Dec., 1871. Capt., 1 July, 1880. Maj., 1 June, 1897. Trans. to 5th Art., 28 Oct., 1899. Graduate of the Artillery School, 1872.

INGALLS, RUFUS.* [Born in Maine. Appointed from Maine.]
Bvt. 2nd Lieut. Rifles, 1 July, 1843. 2nd Lieut. 1st Drag., 17 March, 1845. Bvt. 1st Lieut., 4 Feb., 1847, for gallant and meritorious conduct in the conflicts of Embudo and Taos, New Mexico. 1st Lieut. 1st Drag., 16 Feb., 1847. Capt. A. Q. M., 12 Jan., 1848. Capt. 1st Drag., 22 Oct., 1854. Lieut. Col. A. A. de C., 28 Sept., 1861. Maj. Q. M., 12 Jan., 1862. Brig. Gen. Vols., 23 May, 1863. Bvt. Lieut. Col., Col. and Brig. Gen., 6 July, 1864, for meritorious and distinguished service during the war. Bvt. Maj. Gen., 13 March, 1865, for faithful and meritorious service during the war. Bvt. Maj. Gen. Vols., 13 March, 1865, for faithful and meritorious service during the war. Lieut. Col. Dep. Q. M. Gen., 28 July, 1866. Col. A. Q. M. G., 29 July, 1866. Mustered out of Vol. Service, 1 Sept., 1866. Brig. Gen. Q. M. G., 23 Feb., 1882. Retired, for over 40 years' service, 1 July, 1883. Died 15 Feb., 1893.

INGALLS, THOS. R.* [Born in N. Y. Appointed from N. Y.]
2nd Lieut. 2nd Art., 1 July, 1822. Resigned 31 Dec., 1829. Died 26 July, 1864.

INGE, JOHN M. [Born in Tenn. Appointed from Ala.]
2nd Lieut. 13th Inf., 30 Dec., 1847. Disbanded 15 July, 1848.

INGE, ZEBULON M. P.* [Born in Ala. Appointed from Ala.]
2nd Lieut. 2nd Drag., 1 July, 1838. 1st Lieut., 2 Feb., 1841. Killed 9 May, 1846, at the Battle of Resaca da la Palma, Mex.

INGERSOLL, EDWARD. [Born in Mass. Appointed from Mass.]
Ord. Storekeeper, 24 May, 1841. Capt. Ord. Storekeeper, 28 July, 1866. Maj. P. M. Springfield Armory, 28 July, 1866. Retired 30 June, 1882. Died 28 Jan., 1891.

INGERSOLL, JUSTUS. [Born in N. Y. Appointed from N. Y.]
Ensign 23rd Inf., 12 March, 1812. 2nd Lieut., 20 June, 1813. 1st Lieut., 1 June, 1814. R. Q. M., May, 1813, to June, 1815. Disbanded 15 June, 1815. Mil. Storekeeper, 15 July, 1820. Disbanded 1 June, 1821.

INGERSOLL, STEPHEN M. [Born in N. Y. Appointed from Conn.]
Surg. Mate 37th Inf., 16 Sept., 1814. Disbanded 15 June, 1815. Reinstated in 7th Inf., 13 Sept., 1815. Resigned 1 Sept., 1816.

INGERTON, WM. H. [Born in Ohio. Appointed from Army.]
Priv. Co. K, 3rd Inf., 12 Aug., 1850, to 12 Aug., 1855. Priv., Corpl., Sergt. and 1st Sergt. Co. I, and Sergt. Maj. 1st Drag., 13 Aug., 1855, to 15 July, 1861. 2nd Lieut. 16th Inf., 14 May, 1861. 1st Lieut., 24 Oct., 1861. Capt., 15 Oct., 1864. Lieut. Col. 13th Tenn. Cav., 11 May, 1864. Died 8 Dec., 1864. Bvt. Capt., 7 April, 1862, for gallant and meritorious service at the Battle of Shiloh, Tenn. Bvt. Maj., 31 Dec., 1862, for gallant and meritorious service at the Battle of Murfreesboro, Tenn.

INGHAM, GEORGE T. [Born in N. J. Appointed from N. J.]
1st Lieut. 4th N. J. Vols., 25 April to 2 June, 1861. 1st Lieut. 11th Inf., 14 May, 1861. Resigned 9 Aug., 1864. Bvt. Capt. and Maj., 13 March, 1865, for faithful and meritorious service.

INGRAHAM, CHAS. H.* [Born in Ohio. Appointed from Mass.]
2nd Lieut. 8th Inf., 1 July, 1858. Trans. to 7th Inf., 30 Nov., 1858. 1st Lieut., 7 May, 1861. Trans. to 14th Inf., 14 May, 1861. Capt., 24 Oct., 1861. Resigned 6 May, 1865. 1st Lieut. 41st Inf., 7 March, 1867. Died 20 Sept., 1867.

INGRAHAM, EDWARD. [Born in Penn. Appointed from Miss.]
2nd Lieut. 1st Cav., 27 June, 1856. 1st Lieut., 27 Feb., 1861. Resigned 2 May, 1861.

INGRAM, ALEXR. [Born in Scotland. Appointed from Ohio.]
Asst. Surg., 28 May, 1861. Lost at Sea, 30 July, 1865.

INGRAM, RALPH E.* [Born in Mass. Appointed from Mass.]
2nd Lieut. 5th Inf., 26 April, 1898. 1st Lieut., 2 March, 1899.

INMAN, HENRY. [Born in N. Y. Appointed from Army.]
Priv. and Corpl. Co. G, 9th Inf., 9 March, 1857, to 8 Aug., 1861. 2nd Lieut. 17th Inf., 14 May, 1861. 1st Lieut., 24 Oct., 1861. R. Q. M., 2 Jan., 1863, to 27 April, 1864. Capt. A. Q. M., 18 March, 1864. Cashiered 24 July, 1872. Bvt. Capt., 27 June, 1862, for gallant and meritorious service at the Battle of Gaines' Mills, Va. Bvt. Maj., 27 Nov., 1866, for faithful and meritorious service in the Q. M. D. Bvt. Lieut. Col., 11 Feb., 1869, for meritorious service during the campaign against Indians.

INSLEY, MERRITT H. [Born in Ind. Appointed from Kansas.]
Capt. A. Q. M. Vols., 6 Aug., 1861, to 13 Aug., 1863. Capt. A. Q. M., 13 March, 1863. Resigned 26 May, 1865.

IRELAND, DAVID. [Born in Scotland. Appointed from N. Y.]
1st Lieut. and Adj. 79th N. Y. Vols., 29 May to 18 Sept., 1861. Capt. 15th Inf., 5 Aug., 1861. Col. 137th N. Y. Vols., 25 Sept., 1862. Died 10 Sept., 1864. Bvt. Maj., 3 May, 1863, for gallant and meritorious service at the Battle of Chancellorsville, Va. Bvt. Lieut. Col., 1 Sept., 1864, for gallant and meritorious service during the Atlanta campaign.

IRELAND, MERRITTE W. [Born in Ind. Appointed from Ind.]
Asst. Surg., 4 May, 1891. Capt. Asst. Surg., 4 May, 1896. Maj. Surg. 45th U. S. Vols., 17 Aug., 1899.

IRGENS, HENRY A. [Born in Norway. Appointed from Army.]
Sergt. and 1st Sergt. Co. A, 17th N. Y. Vols., 7 Aug., 1863, to 2 Aug., 1865. Priv., Corpl. and Sergt. Co. B, Eng. Batt., 30 Aug., 1865, to 26 Nov., 1867. 2nd Lieut. 27th Inf., 20 Nov., 1867. Unassigned 14 June, 1869. Ass'd to 7th Inf., 21 April, 1870. Resigned 31 Dec., 1875.

IRISH, DALLAS C. [Born in Penn. Appointed from Penn.]
Capt. 13th Inf., 5 Aug., 1861. Resigned 7 April, 1866. Bvt. Maj., 10 Jan., 1863, for gallant and meritorious service at the Battle of Arkansas Post, Ark. Bvt. Lieut. Col., 4 July, 1863, for gallant and meritorious service during the Siege of Vicksburg, Miss.

IRISH, JOSEPH E. [Born in N. Y. Appointed from Wis.]
Post Chap., 20 July, 1892. Retired 7 Aug., 1897. Died 2 May, 1899.

IRONS, JAMES A.* [Born in Penn. Appointed from Penn.]
2nd Lieut. 20th Inf., 13 June, 1879. 1st Lieut., 14 May, 1887. Capt., 25 Aug., 1893. Maj. Vol. Eng., 13 June, 1898, to 16 Feb., 1899. Graduate of the Infantry and Cavalry School, 1885.

IRONS, JOSEPH F.* [Born in Penn. Appointed from Penn.]
2nd Lieut. 1st Art., 1 July, 1841. 1st Lieut., 3 March, 1847. Died 26 Aug., 1847, of wounds received, 20 Aug., 1847, in Battle of Churubusco, Mex.

IRVAN, BURWELL B. [Born in Ky. Appointed from Ky.]
2nd Lieut. of Inf., 5 March, 1847; 16th Inf., 9 April, 1847. 1st Lieut., 12 Feb., 1848. Disbanded 2 Aug., 1848.

IRVIN, WILLIAM.* [Born in Ohio. Appointed from Ohio.]
2nd Lieut. 4th Art., 1 July, 1839. Resigned 31 March, 1841. Lieut. Col. 2nd Ohio Vols., 23 June, 1846. Col., 15 Sept., 1847. Mustered out 26 July, 1848. Died 4 Oct., 1852.

IRVINE, ARMSTRONG.* [Born in Penn. Appointed from Penn.]
2nd Lieut. Light Art., 1 March, 1811. 1st Lieut., 6 July, 1812. Capt. 42nd Inf., 1 Oct., 1813. Trans. to 4th Rifles, 15 April, 1814. Trans. to Light Art., 17 May, 1815. Died 15 Jan., 1817.

IRVINE, CALEB E. [Born in Tenn. Appointed from Army.]
Priv., Corpl., Sergt. and 1st Sergt. Co. D, Mtd. Rifles, 14 July, 1846, to 24 July, 1848. Bvt. 2nd Lieut. Mtd. Rifles, 28 June, 1848. 2nd Lieut., 31 Oct., 1848. Appointment expired 3 March, 1849. 2nd Lieut. Mtd. Rifles, 30 Nov., 1850. Resigned 30 June, 1851.

IRVINE, CALLENDER. [Born in Penn. Appointed from Penn.]
Capt. 2nd Art. and Eng., 1 June, 1798. Resigned 20 May, 1801. Supt. Mil. Stores, 24 Oct., 1804. Com. Gen. Purchases, 8 Aug., 1812. Died 9 Oct., 1841.

IRVINE, JAMES. [Born in Penn. Appointed from Penn.]
Ensign 32nd Inf., 17 May, 1813. 3rd Lieut., 1 Sept., 1813. Trans. to 42nd Inf.,

11 Jan., 1814. Trans. to 4th Rifles, 15 April, 1814. 2nd Lieut., 1 Sept., 1814. Disbanded 15 June, 1815. Reinstated in Corps Art., 2 Dec., 1815. Trans. to Light Art., 23 Dec., 1815. Resigned 1 March, 1818. Died —, 1831.

IRVINE, JAVAN B. [Born in N. Y. Appointed from Minn.]
Priv. Co. A, 1st Minn. Vols., 29 April, 1861. Discharged 15 May, 1861. Priv. Co. A, 1st Minn. Vols., 9 July, 1861. Discharged 2 Dec., 1861. 1st Lieut. 13th Inf., 26 Oct., 1861. R. Q. M., 1 Nov., 1862, to 1 March, 1865. Capt., 7 April, 1866. Trans. to 22nd Inf., 21 Sept., 1866. Retired with rank of Maj., 19 May, 1891.

IRVINE, ROBERT. [Born in Ireland. Appointed from Penn.]
A. C. Purchases, 15 May, 1813. Disbanded 1 June, 1821.

IRVINE, ROBT. J. C. [Born in Canada. Appointed from Ga.]
2nd Lieut. 11th Inf., 1 Sept., 1879. 1st Lieut., 24 Aug., 1886. Reg. Adj., 5 Sept., 1866, to 30 Nov., 1889. Capt., 8 June, 1894. Graduate of the Infantry and Cavalry School, 1883.

IRVINE, WM. [Born in Va. Appointed from Va.]
2nd Lieut. 10th Inf., 12 March, 1812. 1st Lieut., 14 Aug., 1813. Trans. to 7th Inf., 17 May, 1815. Resigned 25 Sept., 1815.

IRWIN, BERNARD J. D. [Born in Ireland. Appointed from N. Y.]
1st Lieut. Asst. Surg., 28 Aug., 1856. Capt. Asst. Surg., 28 Aug., 1861. Maj. Surg., 16 Sept., 1862. Bvt. Lieut. Col. and Col., 13 March, 1865, for faithful and meritorious service during the war. Lieut. Col. Asst. Med. Pur., 16 Sept., 1885. Col. Surg., 28 Aug., 1890. Retired 28 June, 1894. Medal of Honor for distinguished gallantry in action against hostile Chiricahua Apache Indians, near Apache Pass, Ariz., 13 and 14 Feb., 1861, while serving as Asst. Surg.; voluntarily taking command of troops and attacking and defeating the hostile Indians he met on the road.

IRWIN, DAVID A. [Born in Penn. Appointed from Penn.]
2nd Lieut. 12th Penn. Cav., 18 March, 1862. 1st Lieut., 7 Oct., 1862. Capt., 2 May, 1864. Mustered out 20 July, 1865. 2nd Lieut. 4th Cav., 28 May, 1866. 1st Lieut., 31 July, 1867. R. C. S., 30 Nov., 1867, to 15 July, 1870. R. Q. M., 1 April, 1875, to 1 Sept., 1876. Capt., 1 March, 1878. Retired 2 April, 1879.

IRWIN, DOUGLASS S.* [Born in D. C. Appointed at Large.]
Bvt. 2nd Lieut. 6th Inf., 1 July, 1840. 2nd Lieut. 3rd Inf., 18 Nov., 1840. 1st Lieut., 18 May, 1846. Reg. Adj., 12 Oct., 1845, to 21 Sept., 1846. Killed 21 Sept., 1846, in the Battle at Monterey, Mex. Bvt. 1st Lieut., 7 Sept., 1841, for gallant and good conduct in the war against the Florida Indians.

IRWIN, FRANCIS G., Jr.* [Born in Ky. Appointed from Tenn.]
2nd Lieut. 2nd Cav., 13 June, 1882. 1st Lieut., 24 March, 1890. Capt., 2 March, 1899. Graduate of the Infantry and Cavalry School, 1887.

IRWIN, GEORGE LeR.* [Born in Mich. Appointed from Ill.]
Addl. 2nd Lieut. 5th Art., 12 June, 1889. 2nd Lieut. 3rd Art., 11 Feb., 1890. 1st Lieut. 5th Art., 23 Sept., 1897. Capt. A. Q. M. Vols., 13 July, 1899. Graduate of the Artillery School, 1894.

IRWIN, JAMES R.* [Born in Penn. Appointed from Penn.]
Bvt. 2nd Lieut. 2nd Art., 1 July, 1825. 2nd Lieut. 1st Art., 1 July, 1825. 1st Lieut., 31 May, 1833. Reg. Adj., 10 Oct., 1836, to 23 May, 1838. Capt., 16 May, 1842. Resigned Reg. commission, 18 June, 1846. Capt. A. Q. M., 7 July, 1838. Died 10 Jan., 1848. Bvt. Capt., 21 Aug., 1836, for gallant and good conduct in the war against the Florida Indians.

IRWIN, JOHN A. [Born in Ireland. Appointed from Army.]
Priv., Corpl., Sergt. and 1st Sergt. Co. C, 1st (4th) Cav., 16 Feb., 1857, to 16 Feb., 1862. Priv. and 1st Sergt. Co. E, 6th Cav., 21 May to 22 Sept., 1862. 2nd Lieut. 6th Cav., 17 July, 1862. 1st Lieut., 28 Sept., 1864. R. Q. M., — Feb to 18 May, 1863, and 22 Aug., 1863, to 5 Nov., 1865. Capt., 8 June, 1867. Dismissed 27 Jan., 1875. Bvt. Capt., 30 March, 1865, for gallant and meritorious service in the Battle of the White Oak Road, Va.

IRWIN, WM. H. [Born in Penn. Appointed from Penn.]
Capt. of Inf., 16 Feb., 1847; 11th Inf., 9 April, 1847. Disbanded 16 Aug., 1848. Bvt. Maj., 20 Aug., 1847, for gallant and meritorious conduct in the Battles of Contreras and Churubusco, Mex. Col. 7th Penn. Vols., 23 April, 1861. Mustered out 23 July, 1861. Col. 49th Penn. Vols., 28 Feb., 1862. Bvt. Brig. Gen. Vols., 13 March, 1865, for gallant conduct in the Battle of Antietam, Md. Resigned 24 Oct., 1863. Died 17 Jan., 1886.

ISAACS, ANDREW J. [Born in N. Y. Appointed from La.]
2nd Lieut. of Inf., 18 March, 1847; 14th Inf., 9 April, 1847. Disbanded 25 July, 1848. Bvt. 1st Lieut., 13 Sept., 1847, for gallant and meritorious conduct at Chapultepec.

ISAACS, CHAS. E. [Born in N. Y. Appointed from Miss.]
Asst. Surg., 16 Aug., 1841. Resigned 24 July, 1846.

ISETT, SAMUEL L. [Born in ——. Appointed from Md.]
2nd Lieut. 1st Inf., 20 Oct., 1818. 1st Lieut., 27 Sept., 1819. Reg. Adj., 10 Jan. to 1 June, 1821. Resigned 1 Jan., 1823.

ISHAM, PIERREPONT.* [Born in Germany. Appointed from Ill.]
Addl. 2nd Lieut. 7th Cav., 12 June, 1887. 2nd Lieut. 3rd Cav., 25 Nov., 1887. Resigned 1 June, 1888.

IVERSON, ALFRED. [Born in Ga. Appointed from Ga.]
2nd Lieut. Seymour's Batt. Ga. Vols., 20 Aug., 1847. Mustered out 11 July, 1848. 1st Lieut. 1st Cav., 3 March, 1855. Resigned 21 March, 1861. Died 4 March, 1873.

IVES, BRAYTON C.* [Born in N. Y. Appointed from N. Y.]
Bvt. 2nd Lieut. 3rd Inf., 1 July, 1856. 2nd Lieut. 1st Inf., 8 Dec., 1856. Died 27 June, 1857.

IVES, EDWARD B.* [Born in D. C. Appointed from N. Y.]
2nd Lieut. 19th Inf., 14 June, 1878. 1st Lieut., 18 Dec., 1886. Resigned 3 Dec., 1889.

IVES, FRANCIS J. [Born in Mass. Appointed from N. Y.]
Asst. Surg., 25 July, 1885. Capt. Asst. Surg., 25 July, 1890. Maj. Brig. Surg. Vols., 4 June, 1898.

IVES, JOSEPH C.* [Born in N. Y. Appointed from Conn.]
Bvt. 2nd Lieut. Ord., 1 July, 1852. Trans. to Top. Eng., 18 March, 1853. 2nd Lieut., 30 April, 1855. 1st Lieut., 1 July, 1857. Dismissed 26 Dec., 1861.

IVES, ROLLIN A.* [Born in N. Y. Appointed from N. Y.]
2nd Lieut. 5th Art., 15 June, 1870. Died 29 Oct., 1881.

IZARD, J. ALLEN SMITH. [Born in Penn. Appointed from Penn.]
(Graduated as J. Allen Smith.) Bvt. 2nd Lieut. 3rd Art., 1 July, 1829. 2nd Lieut., 1 July, 1829. 1st Lieut., 30 June, 1836. Resigned 30 April, 1837. Died 26 July, 1879.

IZARD, JAMES F.* [Born in Penn. Appointed from Penn.]
Bvt. 2nd Lieut. 2nd Inf., 1 July, 1828. 2nd Lieut., 1 July, 1828. 1st Lieut. 1st Drag., 4 March, 1833. Died 5 March, 1836, from wounds received 28 Feb., 1836, in action with Indians in Florida, at Camp Izard.

JACK, JOSEPH L. [Born in Penn. Appointed from Penn.]
Priv. and 1st Sergt. Co. H, 201st Penn. Vols., 26 Aug., to 15 Dec., 1864. 2nd Lieut., 15 Dec., 1864. Mustered out 23 June, 1865. 2nd Lieut. 14th Inf., 23 Feb., 1866. 1st Lieut., 28 July, 1866. Trans. to 23rd Inf., 21 Sept., 1866. Resigned 21 May, 1868.

JACK, MATTHEW. [Born in Penn. Appointed from Penn.]
1st Lieut. 19th Inf., 14 May, 1861. Resigned 1 April, 1864. Died 26 Dec., 1871.

JACKSON, ALFRED B.* [Born in N. Y. Appointed from Mass.]
2nd Lieut. 9th Cav., 13 June, 1883. 1st Lieut., 1 Feb., 1889. Died 1897, or 1898.

JACKSON, ALLAN H. [Born in N. Y. Appointed from N. Y.]
Capt. 91st N. Y. Vols., 18 Dec., 1861. Mustered out 23 Feb., 1863. Lieut. Col. 134th N. Y. Vols., 3 April, 1863. Mustered out 10 June, 1865. 2nd Lieut. 7th Inf., 11 May, 1866. Bvt. 1st Lieut., 2 March, 1867, for gallant and meritorious service in the Battle of Chancellorsville, Va. Bvt. Capt., 2 March, 1867, for gallant and meritorious service in the Battle of Gettysburg, Penn. Bvt. Maj., 2 March, 1867, for gallant and meritorious service in the Battle of Chattanooga, Tenn. 1st Lieut. 7th Inf., 1 Jan., 1871. Reg. Adj., 31 March, 1882, to 1 Oct., 1885. Capt. A. J. A., 1 Oct., 1855, to 1 June, 1886. Capt., 14 Nov., 1885. Maj. P. M., 17 Nov., 1896. Retired, over 30 years' service, 29 Oct., 1898. Bvt. Lieut. Col., 27 Feb., 1890, for gallant services in action against Indians at the Big Hole, Mont., 9 Aug., 1877.

JACKSON, ANDREW. [Born in S. C. Appointed from Tenn.]
Brig. Gen., 19 April, 1814. Maj. Gen., 1 May, 1814. Received the thanks of Congress 27 Feb., 1815, as follows: "That the thanks of Congress be, and they are hereby given to Maj. Gen. Jackson, and through him to the officers and soldiers of the regular army, of the Militia, and of the volunteers, under his command, the greater proportion of which troops consisted of Militia and volunteers suddenly collected together, for their uniform gallantry and good conduct conspicuously displayed against the enemy from the time of his landing before New Orleans until his final expulsion therefrom; and particularly for their valor, skill and good conduct on the 8th of January last in repulsing, with great slaughter a numerous British army of chosen veteran troops when attempting, by a bold and daring attack to carry by storm the works hastily thrown up for the protection of New Orleans; and thereby obtaining a most signal victory over the enemy, with a disparity of loss on his part unexampled in military annals.

"*Resolved*, That the President of the United States be requested to cause to be struck a gold medal, with devices emblematical of this splendid achievement, and presented to Maj. Gen. Jackson as a testimony of the high sense entertained by Congress of his judicious and distinguished conduct on that memorable occasion.

"*Resolved*, That the President of the United States be requested to cause the foregoing resolution to be communicated to Maj. Gen. Jackson, in such terms as he may deem best calculated to give effect to the objects thereof." Disbanded 1 June, 1821. President of the United States, 4 March, 1829, to 4 March, 1837. Died 8 June, 1845.

JACKSON, ANDREW. [Born in Va. Appointed from Va.]
2nd Lieut. 3rd Inf., 30 Dec., 1847. 1st Lieut., 3 March, 1855. Dismissed 6 June, 1861.

JACKSON, ANDREW, Jr.* [Born in Tenn. Appointed at Large.]
Bvt. 2nd Lieut. 1st Cav., 1 July, 1858. 2nd Lieut., 4 May, 1859. Resigned 7 May, 1861.

JACKSON, DONALD. [Born in Canada. Appointed from Texas.]
Asst. Surg., 10 Nov., 1874. Died 22 Sept., 1876.

JACKSON, GEORGE.* [Born in Va. Appointed from Va.]
Bvt. 2nd Lieut. 1st Drag., 1 July, 1856. 2nd Lieut. 2nd Drag., 2 Feb., 1857. 1st Lieut., 25 April, 1861. Resigned 1 June, 1861.

JACKSON, HAROLD L. [Born in Penn. Appointed from Army.]
Priv. and Corpl. Co. F, 13th Inf., and Priv. and Corpl. Co. F, 15th Inf., from 1 April, 1885, to 5 March, 1889. 2nd Lieut. 5th Inf., 11 Feb., 1889. 1st Lieut. 22nd Inf., 17 March, 1896. Capt. 1st Inf., 25 May, 1899. Graduate of the Inf. and Cav. Sch., 1893.

JACKSON, HARRY F.* [Born in Mo. Appointed from Mo.]
Addl. 2nd Lieut. 2nd Art., 12 June, 1896. 2nd Lieut., 29 June, 1896. 1st Lieut., 2 March, 1899. Capt. Acting J. A., 31 Aug., 1899.

JACKSON, HENRY. [Born in England. Appointed from Ill.]
Priv. Co. A, 14th Ill. Cav., 28 Dec., 1863. Corpl., 1 June, 1864. Sergt. Maj. 5th U. S. Col. Cav., 2 Jan., 1865. 2nd Lieut. 5th U. S. Col. Cav., 14 May, 1865. 1st Lieut., 28 Dec., 1865. Mustered out 16 March, 1866. 2nd Lieut. 7th Cav., 28

July, 1866. 1st Lieut., 31 July, 1867. Capt., 25 June, 1876. Maj. 3rd Cav., 27 Aug., 1896. Lieut. Col. 5th Cav., 23 Feb., 1900.

JACKSON, JAMES. [Born in N. J. Appointed from Army.]
Priv. 12th Inf., 8 Nov., 1861. Sergt., 1 July, 1862. Sergt. Co. C, 2nd Batt. 12th Inf., 6 Sept., 1862. 2nd Lieut., 12th Inf., 22 April, 1863. 1st Lieut., 31 Aug., 1863. Bvt. Capt., 1 Aug., 1864, for gallant service in the Battle of the North Anna River, Va. Bvt. Maj., 18 Aug., 1864, for gallant service in the Battle of the Weldon Railroad, Va. Trans. to 30th Inf., 21 Sept., 1866. Capt., 17 Feb., 1868. Unassigned 23 March, 1869. Ass'd to 1st Cav., 31 Dec., 1870. Maj. 2nd Cav., 23 Jan., 1889. Lieut. Col., 4th Cav., 19 June, 1897. Trans. to 1st Cav., 11 Aug., 1897. Bvt. Lieut. Col., 27 Feb., 1890, for gallant and meritorious services in action against Indians during the Modoc war, especially in the action on Lost River, Ore., 29 Nov., 1872; and gallant services in action against Indians, at the Clearwater, Idaho, 12 July, 1877. Medal of Honor for most distinguished gallantry in action against hostile Indians at Camas Meadows, Idaho, 20 Aug., 1877, under heavy fire from the enemy securing the body of a soldier of his command who had been killed in action, and with the aid of one or two men conveying it to a place of safety; while serving as Capt. Troop B, 1st Cav.

JACKSON, JAMES B.* [Born in Ky. Appointed at Large.]
Addl. 2nd Lieut. 5th Inf., 15 June, 1877. 2nd Lieut. 7th Inf., 9 Aug., 1877. 1st Lieut., 18 April, 1884. Capt., 22 Dec., 1896.

JACKSON, JOHN. [Born in Denmark. Appointed from Army.]
Priv. and Corpl. Co. C, 2nd Inf., 29 May, 1858, to 1 Nov., 1861. 2nd Lieut. 7th Inf., 31 Oct., 1861. 1st Lieut., 2 May, 1863. R. Q. M., 1 March, 1863, to 18 May, 1864. Capt., 18 May, 1864. Resigned 27 June, 1866. Bvt. Maj., 13 March, 1865, for gallant and meritorious service at the Battle of Gettysburg, Penn.

JACKSON, JOHN H. [Born in N. H. Appointed from N. H.]
1st Lieut. of Inf., 10 March, 1847; 9th Inf., 9 April, 1847. Capt., 4 Dec., 1847. Disbanded 26 Aug., 1848. Bvt. Capt., 20 Aug., 1847, for gallant and meritorious conduct at Contreras and Churubusco. Lieut. Col. 3rd N. H. Vols., 26 Aug., 1861. Col., 28 June, 1862. Resigned 24 Feb., 1864.

JACKSON, JOHN J.* [Born in Va. Appointed from Va.]
2nd Lieut. Corps Art., 24 July, 1818. Trans. to 4th Inf., 1 Dec., 1819. Reg. Adj., 10 Feb., 1821, to 30 Sept., 1822. Resigned 1 Jan., 1823. Died 1 Jan., 1877.

JACKSON, JOHN S. [Born in N. C. Appointed from N. C.]
Surg. Mate 4th Inf., 12 Dec., 1820. Asst. Surg., 1 June, 1821. Died 31 Jan., 1832.

JACKSON, JOHN W. [Born in Penn. Appointed from Penn.]
Post Chap., 3 March, 1877. Retired, by operation of law, 20 March, 1888.

JACKSON, MASON. [Born in Ohio. Appointed from Army.]
Priv. Co. C, Fremont's Body Guard, 20 Aug., 1861. Discharged 30 Nov., 1861. Priv. Co. —, 15th Inf., 17 Dec., 1861. 2nd Lieut. 15th Inf., 24 Nov., 1862. 1st Lieut., 17 Dec., 1863. Bvt. Capt., 1 Sept., 1864, for gallant and meritorious service during the Atlanta campaign. Trans. to 24th Inf., 21 Sept., 1866. Capt., 14 Sept., 1867. Trans. to 11th Inf., 25 April, 1869. Retired, for wound and disability, 24 April, 1886.

JACKSON, RHEES. [Born in Oreg. Appointed from Oreg.]
2nd Lieut. 12th Inf., 1 Aug., 1899.

JACKSON, RICHARD H. [Born in Ireland. Appointed from Army.]
Priv. Co. L, 4th Art., 12 Dec., 1851. Corpl., 23 April, 1852. Priv., 18 May, 1853. Corpl., 9 Feb., 1854. Sergt., 9 April, 1856. Discharged 30 Sept., 1856. Sergt. Co. L, 4th Art., 30 Sept., 1856. 1st Sergt., 28 Dec., 1856. Bvt. 2nd Lieut. 4th Art., 13 Sept., 1859. 2nd Lieut. 1st Art., 13 July, 1860. 1st Lieut., 14 May, 1861. Capt., 20 Feb., 1862. Lieut. Col. A. I. G. (Act 17 July, 1862), 15 April, 1863. Bvt. Maj., 15 May, 1864, for gallant and meritorious service in the Battle of Drury's Bluff, Va. Bvt. Lieut. Col., 7 Oct., 1864, for gallant and meritorious service in action at Newmarket Heights, Va. Bvt. Brig. Gen. Vols., 1 Jan., 1865, for gallant and meritorious service in the campaign of 1864. Bvt. Col., 13 March, 1865, for gallant and meritorious service during the war. Bvt. Brig. Gen., 13 March, 1865, for gallant and meritorious service in the field during the war. Relieved as Lieut. Col. A. I. G., 23 May, 1865. Brig. Gen. Vols., 19 May, 1865. Bvt. Maj. Gen. Vols., 24 Nov., 1865, for gallant and meritorious service during the war. Mustered out of Vol. Service, 1 Feb., 1866. Maj. 5th Art., 1 July, 1880. Lieut. Col. 4th Art., 4 Dec., 1888. Died 28 Nov., 1892.

JACKSON, THOMAS H.* [Born in Canada. Appointed from Mich.]
Addl. 2nd Lieut. Eng., 15 Feb., 1899. 2nd Lieut., 29 Feb., 1900.

JACKSON, THOS. J.* [Born in Va. Appointed from Va.]
Bvt. 2nd Lieut. 1st Art., 1 July, 1846. 2nd Lieut., 3 March, 1847. 1st Lieut., 20 Aug., 1847. Resigned 19 Feb., 1852. Bvt. Capt., 20 Aug., 1847, for gallant and meritorious conduct at Contreras and Churubusco. Bvt. Maj., 13 Sept., 1847, for gallant and meritorious conduct at Chapultepec.

JACKSON, THOS. K.* [Born in S. C. Appointed from S. C.]
Bvt. 2nd Lieut. 5th Inf., 1 July, 1848. 2nd Lieut. 8th Inf., 22 Jan., 1849. 1st Lieut., 3 March, 1855. Resigned 1 April, 1861.

JACKSON, WM. H.* [Born in Tenn. Appointed from Tenn.]
Bvt. 2nd Lieut. Mounted Rifles, 1 July, 1856. 2nd Lieut., 30 Dec., 1856. Resigned 16 May, 1861.

JACKSON, WILLIAM P.* [Born in Mo. Appointed from Mo.]
2nd Lieut. 24th Inf., 12 June, 1891. 1st Lieut. 1st Inf., 29 March, 1898. Trans. to 24th Inf., 17 Nov., 1898.

JACOB, RICHD. T., Jr. [Born in Ky. Appointed from Ky.]
2nd Lieut. 6th Inf., 1 Oct., 1867. 1st Lieut., 30 Nov., 1879. Dismissed 19 July, 1881.

JACOBI, JOHN C. [Born in Poland. Appointed from Conn.]
Sergt. Muskogee Blues in 1837 (Creek War). Chap. 4th N. Y. Cav., 14 Oct., 1862.

Discharged 11 June, 1863. Hosp. Chap. U. S. V., 18 March, 1864. Mustered out 15 Nov., 1866. Chap. 9th Cav., 9 March, 1867. Retired 29 July, 1868. Died 9 Feb., 1874.

JACOBS, GEORGE W. [Born in Mass. Appointed from Army.]
Priv., Corpl. and Sergt. 9th Inf., 8 Jan., 1813, to Aug., 1814. Ensign 9th Inf., 12 July, 1814. 3rd Lieut., 20 July, 1814. 2nd Lieut., 1 Sept., 1814. Trans. to 5th Inf., 17 May, 1815. Resigned 1 Dec., 1815. Died 2 Oct., 1828.

JACOBS, JOSEPH K. [Born in Vt. Appointed from Army.]
Priv. and Sergt. 9th Inf., 8 Jan., 1813, to — July, 1814. Ensign 9th Inf., 12 July, 1814. 2nd Lieut., 1 Sept., 1814. Trans. to 5th Inf., 17 May, 1815. Resigned 1 Dec., 1815.

JACOBS, JOSHUA W. [Born in Ky. Appointed from Ky.]
Priv. Co. K, 4th Ky. Vols., 10 Nov., 1861. Sergt. Maj., 1 Jan., 1862. 1st Lieut. 4th Ky. Vols., 25 Sept., 1862. Capt., 1 Sept., 1863. Mustered out 15 May, 1865. Maj. 4th Ky. Vols., 1 July, 1865. Mustered out 17 Aug., 1865. 2nd Lieut. 18th Inf., 28 June, 1866. Trans. to 36th Inf., 21 Sept., 1866. 1st Lieut., 1 March, 1867. Trans. to 7th Inf., 19 May, 1869. R. Q. M., 1 June, 1869, to 20 March, 1872. Capt. A. Q. M., 8 March, 1882. Maj. Q. M., 31 Dec., 1894. Lieut. Col. Chf. Q. M. Vols., 11 Aug., 1898, to 12 May, 1899. Bvt. Capt., 27 Feb., 1890, for gallant and meritorious services in reconnaissance and action against Indians at the Big Hole, Mont., 9 Aug., 1877, preceded by important and hazardous service on 8 Aug., 1877, in a reconnaissance which led to the action (declined).

JADWIN, EDGAR.* [Born in Penn. Appointed from Penn.]
Addl. 2nd Lieut. Eng., 12 June, 1890. 2nd Lieut., 14 Dec., 1891. 1st Lieut., 10 May, 1895. Maj. 3rd Vol. Eng., 20 June, 1898. Lieut. Col., 15 Sept., 1898, to 17 May, 1899.

JAMAR, MITCHELL F.* [Born in Md. Appointed from Md.]
2nd Lieut. 13th Inf., 14 June, 1872. 1st Lieut., 26 March, 1879. Capt. 14th Inf., 6 Aug., 1894. Dismissed 27 Aug., 1896.

JAMERSON, GEORGE H.* [Born in Va. Appointed from Va.]
2nd Lieut. 7th Inf., 12 June, 1893. 1st Lieut., 26 April, 1898.

JAMES, EDWIN. [Born in N. Y. Appointed from N. Y.]
Asst. Surg., 27 Jan., 1823. Resigned 31 Dec., 1833.

JAMES, FREDERICK J.* [Born in N. Y. Appointed from N. Y.]
2nd Lieut. 3rd Cav., 17 June, 1862. 1st Lieut., 27 Oct., 1863. Accidentally killed, 4 Aug., 1864.

JAMES, GEORGE S. [Born in S. C. Appointed from S. C.]
2nd Lieut. 4th Art., 27 June, 1856. 1st Lieut., 29 Dec., 1857. Resigned 1 Feb., 1861. Killed 14 Sept., 1862.

JAMES, HARRY L. [Born in Wis. Appointed from Wis.]
2nd Lieut. 3rd Art., 9 July, 1898.

JAMES, JOHN F. [Born in Va. Appointed from Va.]
2nd Lieut. 8th Inf., 10 April, 1899.

JAMES, ROBERT. [Born in Ireland. Appointed from Ar[illegible]
Priv., Corpl. and Sergt. Co. F, 3rd Art., 24 Oct., 1856, to 20 March, 1860. Priv., Sergt. and 1st Sergt. Co. K, 4th Art., 10 Jan., 1861, to 17 April, 1863. Bvt. 2nd Lieut. 4th Art., 19 Feb., 1863. 2nd Lieut. 3rd Art., 21 April, 1863. Cashiered 19 Aug., 1866.

JAMES, WM. H. W.* [Born in Tenn. Appointed from Tenn.]
2nd Lieut. 24th Inf., 14 June, 1872. 1st Lieut., 9 July, 1878. Reg. Adj., 7 Jan., 1879, to 31 Dec., 1883. Capt., 30 Aug., 1890. Maj. 23rd Inf., 16 May, 1899.

JAMIESON, CHARLES C.* [Born in Vt. Appointed from Vt.]
2nd Lieut. 15th Inf., 11 June, 1892. 1st Lieut. Ord., 9 April, 1895.

JAMISON, JOHN. [Born in Va. Appointed from Va.]
Ensign 5th Inf., 1 July, 1808. 2nd Lieut., 10 July, 1809. 1st Lieut., 31 Oct., 1811. Capt., 31 Jan., 1814. Maj. A. A. G., 20 June, 1814. Disbanded 15 June, 1815.

JAMISON, JOHN. [Born in Md. Appointed from Md.]
Mil. Storekeeper Ord. Dept., 14 July, 1862. Dismissed 27 May, 1863.

JAMISON, LOUIS T.* [Born in Va. Appointed from La.]
Bvt. 2nd Lieut. 5th Inf., 1 July, 1824. 2nd Lieut., 1 July, 1824. Resigned 30 April, 1825. 2nd Lieut. 5th Inf., 1 May, 1825. 1st Lieut., 23 April, 1830. Capt., 31 Oct., 1836. Dismissed 31 Dec., 1838. Died 23 June, 1858.

JAMISON, TITUS T. [Born in Va. Appointed from Va.]
Cadet at Mil. Acad., 3 June, 1814, to 7 Nov., 1817. 2nd Lieut. 8th Inf., 31 July, 1818. Resigned 30 June, 1819.

JANDA, JOSEPH F.* [Born in Wis. Appointed from Wis.]
2nd Lieut. 8th Inf., 26 April, 1898. 1st Lieut., 2 March, 1899.

JANES, HENRY W. [Born in N. Y. Appointed from N. J.]
1st Lieut. and R. Q. M., 55th Ill. Vols., 31 Oct., 1861. Discharged 10 Aug., 1863. Capt. A. Q. M. Vols., 31 July, 1863. Capt. A. Q. M., 30 Oct., 1863. Bvt. Maj. and Lieut. Col., 13 March, 1865, for faithful and meritorious service during the war. Maj. Q. M., 19 June, 1879. Retired 2 July, 1879. Died 16 Feb., 1883.

JANES, LEROY L.* [Born in Ohio. Appointed from Ohio.]
2nd Lieut. 2nd Art., 6 May, 1861. 1st Lieut., 10 June, 1861. Capt., 15 June, 1864. Resigned 9 Dec., 1867.

JANEWAY, JOHN H. [Born in Penn. Appointed from Penn.]
1st Lieut. Asst. Surg., 26 Aug., 1861. Bvt. Capt., 29 Feb., 1863, for gallant and meritorious service during the war. Bvt. Maj. and Lieut. Col., 13 March, 1865, for faithful and meritorious service during the war. Capt. Asst. Surg., 28 July, 1866. Maj. Surg., 26 June, 1876. Lieut. Col. Dep. Surg. Gen., 31 May, 1893. Retired 12 Aug., 1893.

JAQUETT, GEORGE P. [Born in N. J. Appointed from N. J.]
1st Lieut. Asst. Surg., 23 Oct., 1861. Bvt. Capt. and Maj., 13 March, 1865, for faithful and meritorious service during the war. Capt. Asst. Surg., 28 July, 1866. Maj. Surg., 14 May, 1880. Died 6 Oct., 1882.

JANUARY, PETER T. [Born in Ky. Appointed from Ky.]
2nd Lieut. 4th Inf., 3 March, 1819. Resigned 31 May, 1820.

JARRETT, GEORGE D.* [Born in Ga. Appointed from Ga.]
2nd Lieut. 10th Inf., 15 Feb., 1899.

JARVIS, CHARLES E.* [Born in Maine. Appointed from Maine.]
Bvt. 2nd Lieut. 3rd Inf., 1 July, 1843. 2nd Lieut. 2nd Inf., 11 March, 1846. 1st Lieut., 12 Jan., 1848. Died 8 June, 1849. Bvt. 1st Lieut., 20 Aug., 1847, for gallant and meritorious conduct at Contreras and Churubusco.

JARVIS, MELVILLE S.* [Born in W. Va. Appointed from W. Va.]
2nd Lieut. 4th Inf., 12 June, 1891. 1st Lieut. 5th Inf., 16 Dec., 1897.

JARVIS, NATHAN S. [Born in N. Y. Appointed from N. Y.]
Asst. Surg., 2 March, 1833. Surg., 7 July, 1838. Died 12 May, 1862.

JARVIS, NATHAN S. [Born in Md. Appointed from N. Y.]
Asst. Surg., 14 Oct., 1887. Capt. Asst. Surg., 14 Oct., 1892. Resigned 1 July, 1897.

JEFFERSON, JOHN P.* [Born in Del. Appointed from Del.]
2nd Lieut. 5th Art., 16 June, 1875. Resigned 15 Feb., 1882.

JENIFER, WALTER H. [Born in Md. Appointed from Md.]
Cadet Mil. Acad., 1 July, 1841, to 20 Jan., 1843. 1st Lieut. of Inf., 16 Feb., 1847; 3rd Drag., 9 April, 1847. Capt., 16 July, 1847. Disbanded 31 July, 1848. 1st Lieut. 2nd Cav., 3 March, 1855. Resigned 30 April, 1861. Died 9 April, 1878.

JENKINS, ALBERT G. [Born in England. Appointed from Army.]
Priv., Corpl. and Sergt. Cos. A and I, 18th Inf., 6 Nov., 1895, to 8 July, 1898. 2nd Lieut. 1st Art., 22 June, 1898.

JENKINS, JOHN M.* [Born in S. C. Appointed from S. C.]
2nd Lieut. 5th Cav., 12 June, 1887. 1st Lieut. 9th Cav., 16 Feb., 1894. Trans. to 3rd Cav., 9 July, 1896. Trans. to 5th Cav., 24 Oct., 1896. Graduate of the Infantry and Cavalry School, 1891.

JENKINS, LEONIDAS.* [Born in N. Y. Appointed from N. Y.]
Bvt. 2nd Lieut. 1st Drag., 1 July, 1841. 2nd Lieut., 31 Dec., 1841. 1st Lieut., 30 June, 1846. Died 18 Oct., 1847.

JENKINS, MICAH J.* [Born in S. C. Appointed from S. C.]
2nd Lieut. 4th Cav., 13 June, 1879. 1st Lieut., 2 March, 1885. Resigned 1 March, 1886. Died 14 May, 1874.

JENKINS, WALWORTH.* [Born in N. Y. Appointed at Large.]
Bvt. 2nd Lieut. 1st Art., 1 July, 1853. 2nd Lieut., 24 Dec., 1853. 1st Lieut., 16 Feb., 1856. Capt. A. Q. M., 3 Aug., 1861. Resigned 7 Oct., 1863.

JENKS, ISAAC C.* [Born in Mass. Appointed from Mass.]
2nd Lieut. 24th Inf., 12 June, 1891. 1st Lieut., 26 April, 1898.

JENNESS, JOHN C. [Born in Vt Appointed from N. H.]
Priv. and Sergt. Co. A, and Q. M. Sergt. 17th N. H. Vols., 25 Nov., 1862, to 16 April, 1863. 1st Lieut. N. H. Vols., 19 Sept., 1864. Mustered out 15 June, 1865. 2nd Lieut. 27th Inf., 28 July, 1866. 1st Lieut., 5 March, 1867. Killed 2 Aug., 1867, in action with Indians in Dakota.

JENNINGS, GILBERT S. [Born in N. Y. Appointed from N. Y.]
Maj. 26th N. Y. Vols., 21 May, 1861. Lieut. Col., 20 Sept., 1862. Mustered out 28 May, 1863. Maj. Vet. Res. Corps., 16 July, 1863. Lieut. Col., 25 Sept., 1863. Bvt. Col. Vols., 13 March, 1865, for gallant and meritorious service during the war. Mustered out 11 Sept., 1866. 2nd Lieut. 43rd Inf., 22 Jan., 1867. Bvt. 1st Lieut., 2 March, 1867, for gallant and meritorious service in the Battle of Groveton, Va. Bvt. Capt., 2 March, 1867, for gallant and meritorious service in the Battle of Fredericksburg, Va. Trans. to 1st Inf., 8 April, 1869. 1st Lieut., 4 May, 1873. Retired 28 June, 1878. Died 1 Nov., 1893.

JENNINGS, GUILFORD D. [Born in Canada. Appointed from Wis.]
Priv. and Corpl. Co. C, 3rd Wis. Vols., 1 May, 1861, to 28 June, 1864. 2nd Lieut. Vet. Res. Corps, 1 July, 1864. Bvt. 1st Lieut. Vols., 13 March, 1865, for gallant service at the Battle of Winchester, Va., 3 May, 1863. Mustered out 5 April, 1867. 2nd Lieut. 21st Inf., 22 Jan., 1867. Unassigned 8 June, 1869. Ass'd to 3rd Art., 14 July, 1869. Died 6 Nov., 1871.

JENNINGS, ROWLEY S.* [Born in Tenn. Appointed from Tenn.]
Bvt. 2nd Lieut. 3rd Art., 1 July, 1838. 2nd Lieut., 7 July, 1838. Died 12 Nov., 1839.

JEROME, AARON B. [Born in Ala. Appointed from N. J.]
1st Sergt. Co. B, 1st N. Y. Vols., 21 May, 1861. 2nd Lieut., 31 Aug., 1861. 1st Lieut., 16 April, 1863, to 9 Nov., 1863. 1st Lieut. Sig. Corps, 3 March, 1863. Resigned 20 Sept., 1864. 2nd Lieut 8th Cav., 18 June, 1867. 1st Lieut., 10 Aug., 1869. Discharged 1 Dec., 1870. Bvt. 1st Lieut., 18 June, 1867, for gallant and meritorious service during the war. Bvt. Capt., 18 June, 1867, for gallant and meritorious service in the Sig. Corps during the war. Died 17 April, 1881.

JEROME, LOVELL H.* [Born in N. Y. Appointed at Large.]
2nd Lieut. 2nd Cav., 15 June, 1870. Resigned 12 April, 1879. Priv. and Corpl. Co. H, 8th Cav., 16 March, 1880, to 31 Jan., 1882.

JERVEY, EUGENE P., Jr.* [Born in S. C. Appointed from S. C.]
2nd Lieut. 5th Cav., 12 June, 1896. 1st Lieut. 10th Cav., 11 June, 1899.

JERVEY, HENRY.* [Born in Va. Appointed from S. C.]
Addl. 2nd Lieut. Eng., 11 June, 1888. 2nd Lieut., 15 June, 1888. 1st Lieut., 14 Dec., 1891. Capt., 5 July, 1898.

JERVEY, JAMES P.* [Born in Va. Appointed from Ga.]
Addl. 2nd Lieut. Eng., 11 June, 1892. 2nd Lieut., 10 May, 1895. 1st Lieut., 31 July, 1897.

JESSOP, SAML. S. [Born in Ireland. Appointed from N. Y.]
Asst. Surg. U. S. Vols., 20 Sept., 1864. Bvt. Capt. Vols., 16 Nov., 1865, for faithful and meritorious service. Mustered out 27 Nov., 1865. Asst. Surg., 28 Feb., 1866. Resigned 30 June, 1878.

JESUP, CHAS. E.* [Born in D. C. Appointed at Large.]
Bvt. 2nd Lieut. 10th Inf., 1 July, 1858. 2nd Lieut. 6th Inf., 31 May, 1859. Resigned 20 Aug., 1860. Died 22 April, 1861.

JESUP, THOMAS S. [Born in Va. Appointed from Ohio.]
2nd Lieut. 7th Inf., 3 May, 1808. 1st Lieut., 1 Dec., 1809. Capt., 20 Jan., 1813. Maj. 19th Inf., 6 April, 1813. Trans to 25th Inf., 18 April, 1814. Trans. to 1st Inf., 17 May, 1815. Lieut. Col 3rd Inf., 30 April, 1817. Col. Adj. Gen., 27 March, 1818. Brig. Gen. Q. M. G., 8 May, 1818. Died 10 June, 1860. Bvt. Lieut. Col., 5 July, 1814, for distinguished and meritorious service at the Battle of Chippewa. Bvt. Col., 25 July, 1814, for gallant conduct at the Battle of Niagara. Bvt. Maj. Gen., 8 May, 1828, for ten years' faithful service in one grade. Died 10 June, 1860.

JEWELL, FRANK C.* [Born in Ill. Appointed from Wis.]
2nd Lieut. 5th Art., 15 Feb., 1899.

JEWETT, CHAS. E. [Born in Vt. Appointed from Wis.]
Priv., Corpl. and Sergt. Co. F, 2nd Wis. Vols., 11 June, 1861, to 24 April, 1864. 1st Lieut. 39th Wis. Vols., 3 June, 1864. Mustered out 22 Sept., 1864. 2nd Lieut. 10th Inf., 23 Feb., 1866. 1st Lieut., 28 July, 1866. Resigned 25 April, 1877. Bvt. Capt., 2 March, 1867, for gallant and meritorious service in the Battle of Gettysburg, Penn.

JEWETT, HORACE. [Born in Maine. Appointed from Maine.]
1st Lieut. 15th Inf., 14 May, 1861. Bvt. Capt., 31 Dec., 1862, for gallant and meritorious conduct in the Battles of Shiloh and Murfreesboro, Tenn. Capt. 15th Inf., 31 Dec., 1862. Bvt. Maj., 1 Sept., 1864, for gallant and meritorious service during the Atlanta campaign, and in the Battle of Jonesboro, Ga. Maj. 16th Inf., 31 Jan., 1882. Lieut. Col. 3rd Inf., 1 Aug., 1886. Col. of Inf. (21st Inf.), 4 Dec., 1891. Died 30 April, 1897.

JOCELYN, STEPHEN P. [Born in Vt. Appointed from Vt.]
Priv. Co. A, 6th Vt. Vols., 22 Aug., 1863. Discharged 6 July, 1864. 1st Lieut. 115th U. S. Col. Troops, 1 Aug., 1864. Mustered out 10 Feb., 1866. 2nd Lieut. 6th Inf., 23 Feb., 1866. 1st Lieut., 28 July, 1866. Mustered out 1 Jan., 1871. 2nd Lieut. 21st Inf., 9 March, 1871. 1st Lieut. 21st Inf., 14 April, 1873, with rank from 28 July, 1866. Capt., 19 May, 1874. Maj. 19th Inf., 27 June, 1897. Lieut. Col. 25th Inf., 31 March, 1899. Bvt. Maj., 27 Feb., 1890, for conspicuous gallantry in action against Indians at the Clearwater, Idaho, 11 and 12 July, 1877.

JOHNS, EDWARD W. [Born in Md. Appointed from Md.]
Asst. Surg., 29 June, 1849. Resigned 22 April, 1861.

JOHNS, THOMAS.* [Born in D. C. Appointed from D. C.]
Bvt. 2nd Lieut. 2nd Inf., 1 July, 1833. 2nd Lieut., 31 July, 1836. 1st Lieut. 8th Inf., 7 July, 1838. Resigned 31 Aug., 1841. Col. 2nd Potomac Home Brig. Md. Vols., 11 Oct., 1861. Resigned 1 Jan., 1862. Died 18 June, 1882.

JOHNS, THOS. D.* [Born in Penn. Appointed from Penn.]
Bvt. 2nd Lieut. 1st Inf., 1 July, 1848. 2nd Lieut. 2nd Inf., 8 June, 1849. Resigned 3 Dec., 1851. Col 7th Mass. Vols., 28 March, 1863. Bvt. Brig. Gen. Vols., 13 March, 1865, for gallant conduct at the Battle of Fredericksburg, Va., and for gallant and meritorious service during the war. Mustered out 27 June, 1864. Died 31 July, 1883.

JOHNS, WM. B.* [Born in D. C. Appointed from D. C.]
Bvt 2nd Lieut. 8th Inf., 1 July, 1840. 2nd Lieut. 3rd Inf., 18 Nov., 1840. 1st Lieut. 26 Nov., 1845. Capt., 4 Dec., 1847. Dropped 11 April, 1861. Bvt. Capt., 18 April, 1847, for gallant and meritorious conduct at Cerro Gordo.

JOHNSON, ALFRED B. [Born in Texas. Appointed from Minn.]
2nd Lieut. 7th Inf., 15 Oct., 1875. 1st Lieut., 1 May, 1882 Reg. Adj., 1 Sept., 1889, to —. Capt. 14th Inf., 27 Aug., 1896. Died 18 March, 1897.

JOHNSON, ALLEN G. [Born in Ga. Appointed from Fla.]
Maj. of Inf., 3 March, 1847; 13th Inf., 9 April, 1847. Resigned 22 Dec. 1847.

JOHNSON, ARTHUR.* [Born in Minn. Appointed from Minn.]
2nd Lieut. 11th Inf., 28 Aug., 1886. 1st Lieut. 17th Inf., 28 Nov., 1893. Capt. 13th Inf., 2 March, 1899. Reg. Adj., 2 Aug., 1899.

JOHNSON, BEN.* [Born in Miss. Appointed from Miss.]
Addl. 2nd Lieut. 4th Art., 12 June, 1889. 2nd Lieut. 1st Art., 9 Aug., 1889. Resigned 30 Sept., 1889.

JOHNSON, BUSHROD R.* [Born in Ohio. Appointed from Ohio.]
2nd Lieut. 3rd Inf., 1 July, 1840. 1st Lieut., 29 Feb., 1844. Resigned 22 Oct., 1847. Died 7 Sept., 1880.

JOHNSON, CARTER P. [Born in Va. Appointed from Army.]
Priv., Corpl. and Sergt. Co. F, 3rd Cav., 12 Sept., 1876, to 24 April, 1882. 2nd Lieut. 4th Inf., 27 March, 1882. Trans. to 10th Cav., 19 Sept., 1883. 1st Lieut., 7 June, 1890. Capt., 2 March, 1899. Maj. 49th U. S. Vols., 9 Sept., 1899.

JOHNSON, CHAS. A. [Born in N. Y. Appointed from N. Y.]
2nd Lieut. of Inf., 1 April, 1847; 10th Inf., 9 April, 1847. Discharged 14 Aug., 1848. Maj. 17th N. Y. Vols., 24 May, 1861. Lieut. Col. 25th N. Y. Vols., 4 Oct., 1861. Col., 1 April, 1862. Bvt. Brig. Gen. Vols., 13 March, 1865, for gallant and meritorious service in the Battle of Hanover C. H., Va. Mustered out 10 July, 1863.

JOHNSON, CHAS. A. [Born in Penn. Appointed from Wis.]
Priv. Co. B, 1st Wis. Vols., 20 April, 1861. Discharged 21 Aug., 1861. Priv. 13th Batty Wis. Light Art., 4 July, 1863. 1st Sergt., 31 Dec., 1863. Sergt., 21 Feb., 1864. Priv., 30 Aug., 1864. Discharged 22 March, 1865. 2nd Lieut. 51st Wis. Vols., 6 April, 1865. Mustered out 6 May, 1865. 2nd Lieut. 14th Inf., 9 Aug., 1867. 1st Lieut., 23 Jan., 1876. Retired, with rank of Capt. for disability, 9 Jan., 1892. Died 22 Dec., 1893.

JOHNSON, CHAS. J. [Born in N. Y. Appointed from N. Y.]
Sergt. Co. A, 148th N. Y. Vols., 5 Sept., 1862. 2nd Lieut., 2 Feb., 1864. 1st Lieut., 15 Oct., 1864. Resigned 14 May, 1865. 2nd Lieut. 15th Inf., 11 May, 1866. 1st Lieut., 15 Aug., 1867. Resigned 14 Jan., 1869.

JOHNSON, DAVID. D.* [Born in Penn. Appointed from Penn.]
2nd Lieut. 5th Art., 15 June, 1868. 1st Lieut., 1 March, 1875. Graduate of the Artillery School, 1886. Retired for disability 1 Feb., 1896.

JOHNSON, EDWARD.* [Born in Ky. Appointed from Ky.]
2nd Lieut. 6th Inf., 1 July, 1838. 1st Lieut., 9 Oct., 1839. Capt., 15 April, 1851. Resigned 10 June, 1861. Bvt. Capt., 8 Sept., 1847, for gallant and meritorious conduct at Molino del Rey. Bvt. Maj., 13 Sept., 1847, for gallant conduct at Chapultepec. Died 22 Feb., 1893.

JOHNSON, EVAN M., Jr. [Born in N. Y. Appointed from Army.]
Priv., Corpl. and Sergt. Co. F, 10th Inf., 12 June, 1882, to 16 Aug., 1885. 2nd Lieut. 10th Inf., 15 Aug.,1885. 1st Lieut. 23rd Inf., 28 June, 1892. Trans. to 17th Inf., 12 Aug., 1892. Trans. to 19th Inf., 15 Dec., 1892. Capt., 2 March, 1899. Maj. 29th U. S. Vols., 5 July, 1899. Graduate of the Infantry and Cavalry School, 1889.

JOHNSON, FRANKLIN O.* [Born in Minn. Appointed from Minn.]
2nd Lieut. 3rd Cav., 11 June, 1881. 1st Lieut., 31 Jan., 1885. Capt., 8 June, 1896.

JOHNSON, FREDERICK C. [Born in Wyo. Appointed from Army.]
Priv., Corpl. and Sergt. Troop L, 7th Cav., 28 Aug., 1898, to 2 June, 1899. 2nd Lieut. 2nd Cav., 10 April, 1899.

JOHNSON, GEORGE W. [Born in Penn. Appointed from Army.]
Priv., Sergt. and 1st Sergt. Co. D, 19th Inf., 12 Aug., 1861, to 12 Dec., 1862. 2nd Lieut. 19th Inf., 29 Nov., 1862. 1st Lieut., 20 Sept., 1863. Resigned 30 Aug., 1864. Died 6 Sept., 1878.

JOHNSON, GRAHAM L. [Born in Ala. Appointed from Ga.]
2nd Lieut. 11th Inf., 10 April, 1899.

JOHNSON, HARRY C. [Born in Penn. Appointed from Penn.]
2nd Lieut. 2nd Inf., 27 July, 1872. Trans. to 1st Inf., 14 July, 1873. Resigned 31 March, 1878. Died 23 July, 1879.

JOHNSON, HENRY. [Born in South America. Appointed from Penn.]
Med. Storekeeper Vols., 13 Aug., 1862. Capt. Med. Storekeeper, 28 July, 1866. Died 11 June, 1891.

JOHNSON, HENRY, Jr. [Born in Del. Appointed from Cal..
2nd Lieut. 8th Inf., 15 Oct., 1875. 1st Lieut., 3 July, 1883. Resigned 2 July, 1886. Died 8 Aug., 1886.

JOHNSON, HENRY C. [Born in Ohio. Appointed from Kan.]
Priv. Co. I, 69th Ohio Vols., 10 March, 1862. Discharged 10 March, 1864. Priv. Co. I, 69th Ohio Vols., 10 March, 1864. Discharged 10 May, 1865. 2nd Lieut. 45th Inf., 19 Feb., 1868. Unassigned 22 July, 1869. Ass'd to 23rd Inf.,, 3 Aug., 1870. Retired 4 Oct., 1872. Dismissed 12 Nov., 1881.

JOHNSON, HEZEKIAH. [Born in Md. Appointed from Md.]
Ensign 1st Inf., 26 March, 1804. 2nd Lieut., 20 June, 1806. 1st Lieut., 18 Aug., 1808. Capt., 20 Jan., 1813. Disbanded 15 June, 1815. Capt. Asst. Dep. Q. M. G., 16 June, 1818. Disbanded 1 June, 1821. Mil. Storekeeper, 26 Sept., 1821. Died 8 Sept., 1837.

JOHNSON, HUGH. [Born in N. Y. Appointed from N. Y.]
Ensign 21st N. Y. Vols., 20 May, 1861. 1st Lieut., 2 Jan., 1862, to 6 May, 1862. 2nd Lieut. 5th Inf., 19 Feb., 1862. 1st Lieut., 21 Oct., 1863. Resigned 15 Nov., 1869.

JOHNSON, JACOB C.* [Born in Ohio. Appointed form Mo.]
2nd Lieut. 4th Art., 26 April, 1898.

JOHNSON, JOHN B. [Born in Penn. Appointed from Penn.]
Capt. 11th Pa. Vols., 23 April to 13 July, 1861. 1st Lieut. 3rd U. S. Cav., 14 May, 1861; 6th Cav., 3 Aug., 1861. Capt., 3 Feb., 1865. Bvt. Maj. and Lieut. Col., 13 March, 1865, for meritorious service during the war. Wholly retired, 31 Dec., 1870. Died 24 June, 1871.

JOHNSON, JOHN B. [Born in Mass. Apointed from Mass.]
2nd Lieut. 6th U. S. Col. Troops, 8 Sept. 1863. Discharged 20 Jan., 1865. 1st Lieut. 6th U. S. Col. Troops, 15 Feb., 1865. Mustered out 20 Sept., 1865. 2nd Lieut. 7th Inf., 23 April, 1866. 1st Lieut., 12 Oct., 1867. Unassigned 19 May, 1869. Ass'd to 3rd Cav., 1 Jan., 1871. Reg. Adj., 15 May, 1871, to 4 April, 1878. Capt., 4 April, 1878. Died 5 April, 1896.

JOHNSON, JOHN M.* [Born in Iowa. Appointed from S. C.]
Priv. Co. B, 20th Iowa Vols., 14 Aug., 1862, to 3 Oct., 1863. Cadet Mil. Acad., 7 Nov., 1863. 2nd Lieut. 7th Cav., 17 June, 1867. 1st Lieut., 1 Nov., 1867. Discharged 31 Dec., 1870.

JOHNSON, LANGDON C. [Born in S. C. Appointed from S. C.]
2nd Lieut. of Inf., 4 March, 1847; 3rd Drag., 9 April, 1847. Resigned 31 Aug., 1847.

JOHNSON, LEWIS. [Born in Germany. Appointed from Ind.]
Priv. Co. E, 10th Ind. Vols., 18 April, 1861. Discharged 6 Aug., 1861. 1st Lieut. 10th Ind. Vols., 18 Sept., 1861. Capt., 29 Aug., 1862. Col. 44th U. S. Col. Troops, 16 Sept., 1864. Bvt. Brig. Gen. Vols., 13 March, 1865, for gallant and meritorious service during the war. Mustered out 30 April, 1866. 1st Lieut. 41st Inf., 28 July, 1866. Bvt. Capt., 2 March, 1867, for gallant and meritorious service in the Battle of Mill Springs, Ky. Bvt. Maj., 2 March, 1867, for gallant and meritorious service in the Siege of Corinth, Miss. Bvt. Lieut. Col., 2 March, 1867. for gallant and meritorious service in the Battle of Mission Ridge, Tenn. Capt. 41st Inf., 12 Dec., 1867. Trans. to 24th Inf., 11 Nov., 1869. Retired for disability, with rank of Maj., 25 April, 1895.

JOHNSON, LORENZO. [Born in Conn. Appointed from Conn.]
Capt. of Inf., 23 Feb., 1847; 9th Inf., 9 April, 1847. Resigned 4 Dec., 1847.

JOHNSON, MILO,* [Born in Vt. Appointed from N. Y.]
3rd Lieut. Corps Art., 2 March, 1815. 2nd Lieut., 5 Aug., 1817. Resigned 1 March, 1818.

JOHNSON, ORRIMEL. [Born in ——. Appointed from Ky.]
Surg.'s Mate Rifle Reg., 3 March, 1819. Died 4 Feb., 1820.

JOHNSON, RICHARD W.* [Born in Ky. Appointed from Ky.]
Bvt. 2nd Lieut. 6th Inf., 1 July, 1849. 2nd Lieut. 1st Inf., 10 June, 1850. Reg. Adj., 3 March, 1853, to 12 April, 1855. 1st Lieut. 2nd Cav., 3 March, 1855. R. Q. M., 12 June, 1855, to 30 Sept., 1856. Capt., 1 Dec., 1856. 5th Cav., 3 Aug., 1861. Brig. Gen. Vols., 11 Oct., 1861. Maj. 4th Cav., 17 July, 1862. Bvt. Lieut. Col., 20 Sept., 1863, for gallant and meritorious service in the Battle of Chickamauga, Ga. Bvt. Col., 24 Nov., 1863, for gallant and meritorious service in the Battle of Chattanooga, Tenn. Bvt. Brig. Gen., 13 March, 1865, for gallant and meritorious service in the Battle of Nashville, Tenn. Bvt. Maj. Gen., 13 March, 1865, for gallant and meritorious service in the field during the war. Bvt. Maj. Gen. Vols., 13 March, 1865, for gallant and meritorious service in the battles before Nashville, Tenn. Mustered out of Vol. Service 15 Jan., 1866. Retired with rank of Maj. Gen., 12 Oct., 1867, and with rank of Brig. Gen., 3 March, 1875. Died 21 April, 1897.

JOHNSON, RICHARD W. [[Born in Texas. Appointed from Minn.]
Asst. Surg., 22 Oct., 1881. Capt., Asst. Surg., 22 Oct., 1886. Maj. Surg., 6 Nov., 1899. Maj. Brig. Surg. Vols., 4 June, 1898, to 11 Jan., 1899.

JOHNSON, SAML. [Born in Va. Appointed from Army.]
Priv., Corpl. and Sergt. 15th Inf., 4 Dec., 1813, to June, 1815. Sergt. and Sergt. Maj. Light Art., June, 1815, to 11 May, 1818. 2nd Lieut. Light Art., 18 April, 1818. Resigned 9 Oct., 1818. Died ——, 1827.

JOHNSON, SETH. [Born in N. J. Appointed from Army.]
Priv., Corpl. and Sergt. 13th Inf., 5 May, 1812, to Nov., 1813. Ensign 13th Inf., 27 Oct., 1813. 3rd Lieut., 31 Jan., 1814. 2nd Lieut., 20 Aug., 1814. Trans. to 2nd Inf., 17 May, 1815. 1st Lieut., 1 May, 1819. Capt., 13 Sept., 1831. Resigned 28 June, 1836. Bvt. Capt., 1 May, 1829, for ten years' faithful service in one grade.

JOHNSON, THOS. R. [Born in Md. Appointed from Md.]
Asst. Surg., 4 July, 1836. Died 11 July, 1837.

JOHNSON, THOS. S. J. [Born in Penn. Appointed from Mo.]
2nd Lieut. 8th Inf., 7 July, 1838. 1st Lieut., 31 Dec., 1842. Dismissed 30 May, 1845. Capt. 1st Md. Vols., 28 May, 1861. Died 20 Nov., 1864, while prisoner of war.

JOHNSON, WAIT C. [Born in Vt. Appointed from Vt..
Sergt. Co. A, 1st Vt. Vols., 16 May, 1898, to 3 Nov., 1898. 2nd Lieut. 15th Inf., 1 May, 1899.

JOHNSON, WM. F. [Born in Vt. Appointed from Ohio.]
Maj. C. S. Vols., 26 June, 1846. Resigned 11 Nov., 1846.

JOHNSON, WILLIAM O.* [Born in Ky. Appointed from Ky.]
2nd Lieut. 19th Inf., 12 June, 1890. 1st Lieut. 7th Inf., 29 Jan., 1897. Trans. to 2nd Inf., 11 Jan., 1898. Capt. 16th Inf., 10 Oct., 1899.

JOHNSON, WM. S. [Born in Ill. Appointed from Mich.]
Priv. Co. A, 4th Batt. D. C. Vols., 17 April, 1861. Discharged 10 July, 1861. 1st Lieut. 1st Ark. Cav., 1 Oct., 1862. Capt., 5 Feb., 1863. Mustered out 21 July, 1864. 1st Lieut. Vet. Res. Corps, 15 Sept., 1864. Bvt. Capt. and Maj. Vols., 13 March, 1865, for gallant and meritorious service during the war. Mustered out 20 Aug., 1866. 1st Lieut. 43rd Inf., 12 June, 1867. R. Q. M., 20 July, 1867, to 8 April, 1869. Unassigned 8 April, 1869. Dismissed 4 Oct., 1869. 1st Lieut. Inf., 24 Jan., 1870. Mustered out 1 Jan. 1871. 2nd Lieut. 24th Inf., 9 March, 1871. Retired with rank of Capt. Mounted, 20 May, 1871. Dismissed 31 Oct., 1894.

JOHNSTON, ABRAHAM R.* [Born in Ohio. Appointed from Ohio.]
Bvt. 2nd Lieut. 1st Drag., 1 July, 1835. 2nd Lieut., 31 March, 1836. 1st Lieut., 15 June, 1837. Reg. Adj., 17 June to 30 June, 1846. Capt., 30 June, 1846. Killed 6 Dec., 1846, in the Battle of San Pasqual, Cal.

JOHNSTON, ALBERT S.* [Born in Ky. Appointed from La.]
Bvt. 2nd Lieut. 2nd Inf., 1 July, 1826. 2nd Lieut. 6th Inf., 1 July, 1826. Reg. Adj., 14 Sept., 1828, to 7 Sept., 1832. Resigned 31 May, 1834. Col. 1st Texas Rifles, 8 July to 24 Aug., 1846. Maj. P. M., 31 Oct., 1849. Col. 2nd Cav., 3 March, 1855. Resigned 3 May, 1861. Bvt. Brig. Gen., 18 Nov., 1857, for meritorious conduct in the ability, zeal, energy and prudence displayed by him in command of the Army in Utah.

JOHNSTON, ALEXR.* [Born in Penn. Appointed from Penn.]
Bvt. 2nd Lieut. 5th Inf., 1 July, 1824. 2nd Lieut., 1 July, 1824. 1st Lieut., 22 Aug., 1828. Capt., 31 Oct., 1836. Died 8 June, 1845.

JOHNSTON, ALEXR. [Born in Penn. Appointed from Penn.]
(Served also under names of John Alexander and Edward Blunt). 1st Sergt. Co. F, 7th Penn. Vols., 22 April, to 5 Aug., 1861. Capt. 16th Inf., 14 May, 1861. Resigned 19 Nov., 1861. Priv. Co. B, 2nd Batt. 17th Inf., 8 Sept., 1862, to 20 Feb., 1863. Priv. Co. A, Pa. Art., July to Nov., 1863. Priv. Co. F, 15th N. Y. Art., 2 Jan., 1864, to 22 Aug., 1865. 2nd Lieut. 11th Inf., 24 Nov., 1865. 1st Lieut., 24 Nov., 1865. Resigned 1 May, 1866.

JOHNSTON, FREDERICK E.* [Born in Iowa. Appointed from Iowa.]
Addl. 2nd Lieut. 1st Inf., 11 June, 1897. 2nd Lieut. 11th Inf., 7 Aug., 1897. Trans. to 7th Art., 8 March, 1898. 1st Lieut., 26 March, 1899.

JOHNSTON, JOHN A.* [Born in Penn. Appointed from Penn.]
2nd Lieut. 8th Cav., 13 June, 1879. 1st Lieut., 20 Jan., 1886. Capt., 3 Jan., 1895. Maj. A. A. G. Vols., 19 May, 1898. Lieut. Col. A. A. G. Vols., 9 May, 1898, declined. Honor graduate of the Infantry and Cavalry School, 1883.

JOHNSTON, JOHN L. [Born in Penn. Appointed from Penn.]
Corpl. Co. H, 2nd Penn. Vols., 20 April, 1861. Discharged 26 July, 1861. 1st Sergt. Co. H, 148th Penn. Vols., 8 Aug., 1862. 1st Lieut. 148th Penn. Vols., 8 Sept., 1862. Capt., 15 Nov., 1863. Mustered out 1 June, 1865. Capt. 3rd U. S. Vet. Vols., 8 Aug., 1865. Mustered out 21 April, 1866. 1st Lieut. 21st Inf., 28 July, 1866. Reg. Adj., 2 June, 1868, to 5 April, 1869. R. Q. M., 5 April, 1869, to 29 May, 1874. Bvt. Capt., 2 March, 1867, for gallant and meritorious service in the

first assault on Petersburg, Va. Capt. 21st Inf., 29 May, 1874. Retired 28 June, 1878.

JOHNSTON, JOSEPH E.* [Born in Va. Appointed from Va.]
Bvt. 2nd Lieut. 4th Art., 1 July, 1829. 2nd Lieut., 1 July, 1829. 1st Lieut., 31 July, 1836. Resigned 31 May, 1837. 1st Lieut. Top. Eng., 7 July, 1838. Capt., 21 Sept., 1846. Lieut. Col. Voltigeurs, 9 April, 1847, to 19 July, 1848. Lieut. Col. 1st Cav., 3 March, 1855. Brig. Gen. Q. M. G., 28 June, 1860. Resigned 22 April, 1861. Bvt. Capt., 7 July, 1838, for gallantry on several occasions in war with the Florida Indians. Bvt. Maj. and Col., 12 April, 1847, for gallant and meritorious conduct at Cerro Gordo. Bvt. Lieut. Col., 13 Sept., 1847, for gallant and meritorious conduct at Chapultepec.

JOHNSTON, RICHARD H. L. [Born in Penn. Appointed from Penn.]
2nd Lieut. of Inf., 5 March, 1847; 11th Inf., 9 April, 1847. Killed 8 Sept., 1847, at Molino del Rey, Mex.

JOHNSTON, RICHARD W.* [Born in Va. Appointed from Va.]
Bvt. 2nd Lieut. 3rd Art., 1 July, 1842. 2nd Lieut., 19 Nov., 1843. 1st Lieut., 27 Oct., 1846. Resigned 4 Dec., 1847. Died 25 Jan., 1854.

JOHNSTON, ROBT.* [Born in Va. Appointed from Va.]
Bvt. 2nd Lieut. 1st Drag., 1 July, 1850. 2nd Lieut., 1 Feb., 1853. 1st Lieut., 3 March, 1855. Resigned 25 April, 1861.

JOHNSTON, ROBT. E. [Born in Va. Appointed from W. Va.]
Capt. 8th Penn. Res. Vet. Corps., 20 April, 1861. Maj., 10 March, 1863. Capt. Vet. Res. Corps., 11 Sept., 1863. Maj., 15 Oct., 1863. Lieut. Col., 4 Dec., 1863. Bvt. Col. Vols., 13 March, 1865, for gallant and meritorious service. Mustered out 7 Oct., 1866. Capt. 43rd Inf., 28 July, 1866. Bvt. Maj., 2 March, 1867, for gallant and meritorious service in the Battle of Gaines' Mill, Va. Bvt. Lieut. Col., 2 March, 1867, for gallant and meritorious service in the Battle of Fredericksburg, Va. Trans. to 1st Inf., 8 April, 1869. Died 8 Jan., 1880.

JOHNSTON, ROBERT P.* [Born in N. C. Appointed from N. C.]
Addl. 2nd Lieut. Eng., 12 June, 1893. 2nd Lieut., 13 Oct., 1895. 1st Lieut., 5 July, 1898. Capt. 2nd Vol. Eng., 8 June, 1898, to 16 May, 1899.

JOHNSTON, THOMAS. [Born in Md. Appointed from Md.]
2nd Lieut. 4th Inf., 16 June, 1818. R. Q. M., 1 Jan. to 2 April, 1819. 1st Lieut., 31 Dec., 1820. Dismissed 25 March, 1826.

JOHNSTON, THOS.* [Born in Penn. Appointed from Penn.]
2nd Lieut. 7th Inf., 1 July, 1822. 1st Lieut., 16 Dec., 1825. A. Q. M., 17 July, to 4 Dec., 1834. Dropped 4 Dec., 1834. Died 2 Feb., 1835.

JOHNSTON, WM. H. [Born in Ohio. Appointed from Ohio.]
Addl. P. M., 5 Sept., 1861. Bvt. Lieut. Col. Vols., 13 March, 1865, for faithful service in the Pay Dept. Mustered out as Addl. P. M. Vols., 20 July, 1866. Maj. P. M., 28 July, 1866. Bvt. Lieut. Col., 2 March, 1867, for faithful and meritorious service in the Pay Dept. during the war. Lieut. Col. Dep. P. M. Gen., 5 July, 1884. Retired 6 Sept., 1888. Died 6 Jan., 1896.

JOHNSTON, WILLIAM H. [Born in Ohio. Appointed from Ohio.]
2nd Lieut. 16th Inf., 10 Oct., 1883. 1st Lieut. 5th Inf., 9 March, 1891. Trans. to 16th Inf., 20 July, 1891. Capt. of Inf., 8 Aug., 1898. Ass'd to 16th Inf., 1 Jan., 1899. Capt. and A. A. G. Vols., 12 May, 1898, to 8 July, 1898. Maj. 46th U. S. Vols., 17 Aug., 1899. Honor graduate of the Infantry and Cavalry School, 1887.

JOHNSTON, WILLIAM T.* [Born in Pa. Appointed from Mo.]
2nd Lieut. 10th Cav., 12 June, 1891. 1st Lieut. 3rd Cav., 27 May, 1898.

JOHNSTON, WM W. [Born in Ohio. Appointed from Ohio.]
2nd Lieut. 2nd Inf., 27 June, 1848. Died 10 March, 1849.

JOHNSTONE, JOHN P.* [Born in Va. Appointed from Va.]
Bvt. 2nd Lieut. 4th Art., 1 July, 1843. 2nd Lieut. 1st Art., 21 April, 1846. 1st Lieut., 3 March, 1847. Killed 19 Aug., 1847, in an attack on Contreras, Mexico.

JONES, ARNOLD E.* [Born in Md. Appointed from Md..
(Changed name to Arnold Elzey)—which see.

JONES, CAVE. [Born in N. Y. Appointed from N. Y.]
Chap. at Mil. Acad., 29 April, 1816. Resigned 18 April, 1818. Died Jan., 1829.

JONES, CHARLES R. [Born in Penn. Appointed from N. C.]
1st Lieut. of Inf., 15 March, 1847; 12th Inf., 9 April, 1847. Capt., 16 July, 1847. Disbanded 25 July, 1848.

JONES, CLARENCE N. [Born in Mich. Appointed from Army.]
Priv. Troop B, 5th Cav., 11 Aug., 1896, to 20 April, 1898. Sergt. Sig. Corps, 21 April, 1898, to 27 Nov., 1899. 2nd Lieut. 10th Inf., 1 Oct., 1899.

JONES, DAVID R.* [Born in S. C. Appointed from Ga.]
Bvt. 2nd Lieut. 2nd Inf., 1 July, 1846. 2nd Lieut., 23 Nov., 1846. Reg. Adj., 15 April, 1847, to 29 Dec., 1848. 1st Lieut., 7 May, 1849. Bvt. Capt. A. A. G., 16 March, 1853. Resigned 15 Feb., 1861. Bvt. 1st Lieut., 20 Aug., 1847, for gallant and meritorious conduct at Contreras and Churubusco. Died 16 June, 1863.

JONES, DELANCY F.* [Born in N. Y. Appointed from N. Y.]
(Changed name to De Lancey Floyd-Jones)—which see.

JONES, E. PENROSE. [Born in Penn. Appointed from Ohio.]
Mil. Storekeeper Ord. Dept., 9 Feb., 1865. Died 3 Dec., 1871.

JONES, EDMUND C.* [Born in Ind. Appointed from Ind.]
Bvt. 2nd Lieut. 2nd Inf., 1 July, 1853. 2nd Lieut. 7th Inf., 3 March, 1855. 1st Lieut., 1 Aug., 1857. Capt., 23 May, 1861. Cashiered 9 July, 1862. Died 24 May, 1869.

JONES, EDWARD N., Jr.* [Born in Ala. Appointed from Ala.]
2nd Lieut. 8th Inf., 1 July, 1886. 1st Lieut., 16 Sept., 1893. Capt., 2 March, 1899.

JONES, EGBERT I. [Born in Ala. Appointed from Ala.]
Capt. 13th Inf., 22 July, 1847. Disbanded 15 July, 1848.

JONES, FRANCIS B. [Born in Penn. Appointed from Penn.]
1st Lieut. 149th Penn. Vols., 30 Aug., 1862. Capt., 25 March, 1863. Mustered out 6 April, 1865. Lieut. Col. 215th Penn. Vols., 16 April, 1865. Mustered out 31

July, 1865. 2nd Lieut. 19th Inf., 11 May, 1866. Trans. to 37th Inf., 21 Sept., 1866. 1st Lieut., 21 July, 1868. R. Q. M., 31 Dec., 1868, to 11 Aug., 1869. Trans. to 3rd Inf., 11 Aug., 1869. R. Q. M., 11 Aug., 1869, to 16 April, 1885. Capt. A. Q. M., 16 April, 1885. Maj. Q. M., 15 Oct., 1897. Lieut. Col. Chf. Q. M. Vols., 9 May, 1898, to 13 May, 1899.

JONES, FRANK B.* [Born in Miss. Appointed from Miss.]
2nd Lieut. 22nd Inf., 13 June, 1879. 1st Lieut., 1 Jan., 1888. Capt., 1 May, 1896.

JONES, FRANCIS L.* [Born in N. C. Appointed from Tenn.]
Bvt. 2nd Lieut. 4th Art., 1 July, 1824. 2nd Lieut. 2nd Art., 1 July, 1824. Trans. to 4th Art., 14 Sept., 1827. 1st. Lieut., 31 Jan., 1832. Resigned 10 June, 1842. Died ——, 1846.

JONES, HENRY. [Born in Ireland. Appointed from Army.]
Priv., Corpl., Sergt. and 1st Sergt., Co. G, 2nd Cav. (5th), 19 July, 1855, to 22 Sept., 1862. 2nd Lieut. 5th Cav., 17 July, 1862. 1st Lieut., 10 Oct., 1862. Dismissed 19 Nov., 1863.

JONES, HENRY P. [Born in Ohio. Appointed from Ohio.]
Cadet Mil. Acad., 1 July, 1854, to 17 Jan., 1855. Priv. Cos. D and K, 79th Ohio Vols., 5 Sept., 1863, to 20 July, 1865. 2nd Lieut. 37th Inf., 28 July, 1866. Resigned 20 March, 1867.

JONES, HENRY R. [Born in Conn. Appointed from Conn.]
1st Sergt. Co. C, 8th Conn. Vols., 25 Sept., 1861. 2nd Lieut. 8th Conn. Vols., 5 June, 1862. Mustered out 17 Jan., 1863. 2nd Lieut. Vet. Res. Corps, 16 July, 1863. 1st Lieut., 11 Nov., 1864. Capt., 3 April, 1865. Mustered out 30 June, 1866. 1st Lieut. 43rd Inf., 28 July, 1866. Trans. to 1st Inf., 8 April, 1869. Retired 28 June, 1878, for wound in line of duty.

JONES, HORATIO M.* [Born in Penn. Appointed from N. C.]
2nd Lieut. 4th Art., 17 June, 1867. Resigned 1 June, 1873. Died 2 June, 1887.

JONES, JACOB D. [Born in Penn. Appointed from Penn.]
1st Lieut. 19th Inf., 14 May, 1861. R. Q. M., 19 Jan. to 1 July, 1864. Capt., 1 July, 1864. Trans. to 37th Inf., 21 Sept., 1866. Trans. to 5th Inf., 19 May, 1869. Mustered out 1 Jan., 1871. Bvt. Capt. and Bvt. Maj., 31 Dec., 1862, for gallant and meritorious service at the Battle of Murfreesboro, Tenn.

JONES, JAMES A. [Born in N. Y. Appointed from Ohio.]
Capt. of Inf., 8 March, 1847; 15th Inf., 9 April, 1847. Disbanded 3 Aug., 1848. Bvt. Maj., 20 Aug., 1847, for gallant and meritorious conduct at Contreras and Churubusco. Lieut. Col. 25th Ohio Vols., 10 June, 1861. Col., 26 July, 1861. Resigned 16 May, 1862.

JONES, JAMES H.* [Born in N. Y. Appointed at Large.]
2nd Lieut. 4th Cav., 15 June, 1868. 1st Lieut., 21 April, 1872. Resigned 29 Sept., 1874.

JONES, JAMES M.* [Born in Ohio. Appointed from Ohio.
2nd Lieut. 4th Art., 16 June, 1875. 1st Lieut., 1 Dec., 1883. Died 2 Jan., 1886.

JONES, JOEL W. [Born in N. Y. Appointed from D. C.]
Mil. Storekeeper Ord., 19 June, 1846. Resigned 30 Aug., 1852.

JONES, JOHN. [Born in Ga. Appointed from Ga.]
Cadet Mil. Acad., 1 July, 1832, to Feb., 1833. Capt. of Inf., 23 Feb., 1847; Voltigeurs, 9 April, 1847. Disbanded 30 Aug., 1848.

JONES, JOHN. [Born in ———. Appointed from Tenn.]
Capt. 39th Inf., 29 July, 1813. Trans. to 1st Inf., 17 May, 1815. Trans. to 7th Inf., 14 Dec., 1821, and belonged to it to 1 May, 1824. Capt. A. D. Q. M. G., 26 Aug., 1818. A. Q. M., 1 June, 1821, to 1 May, 1824. Resigned 1 May, 1824. Bvt. Maj., 29 July, 1823, for ten years' faithful service in one grade.

JONES, JOHN M.* [Born in Va. Appointed from Va.]
Bvt. 2nd Lieut. 5th Inf., 1 July, 1841. 2nd Lieut. 7th Inf., 18 April, 1845. 1st Lieut., 20 Aug., 1847. Capt., 3 March, 1855. Resigned 27 May, 1861. Killed 10 May, 1864.

JONES, JOHN W. [Born in Mass. Appointed from Mass.]
1st Lieut. 12th Inf., 14 May, 1861. Dismissed 4 May, 1863.

JONES, JOSEPH P. [Born in N. C. Appointed from N. C.]
Cadet Mil. Acad., 1 July, 1849, to 10 Jan., 1850. 2nd Lieut. 2nd Art., 27 June, 1856. Resigned 28 Jan., 1861.

JONES, LLEWELLYN. [Born in N. Y. Appointed from N. Y.]
Cadet Mil. Acad., 1 July, 1828, to 30 April, 1831. 1st Lieut. Mounted Rifles, 27 May, 1846. Reg. Adj., 13 Nov., 1846, to 1 Nov., 1847. Capt., 31 Dec., 1847; 3rd Cav., 3 Aug., 1861. Maj. 1st Cav., 28 Sept., 1861. Retired 5 Nov., 1861. Died 17 July, 1873. Bvt. Lieut. Col. and Col., 13 March, 1865, for meritorious service during the war.

JONES, ROBERT T.* [Born in Va. Appointed from Va.]
2nd Lieut. 3rd Art., 1 July, 1837. 1st Lieut., 7 July, 1838. Resigned 31 July, 1838. Killed 31 May, 1862.

JONES, ROGER. [Born in Va. Appointed from Va.]
2nd Lieut. Marine Corps, 26 Jan., 1809. 1st Lieut., 28 June, 1809. Resigned 7 July, 1812. Capt. 3rd Art., 12 July, 1812. Trans. to Corps Art., 12 May, 1814. Trans. to 3rd Art., 1 June, 1821. Maj. 2nd Art., 17 Feb., 1827. Lieut. Col. 4th Art., 17 Nov., 1834. Resigned from Line, 6 April, 1835. Brig. Maj., 27 May, 1813. Maj. A. A. G., 3 Aug., 1813. Reverted to Line, 15 Aug., 1815. Col. Adj. Gen., 10 Aug., 1818. Reverted to Line, 1 June, 1821. Col. Adj. Gen., 7 March, 1825. Died 15 July, 1852. Bvt. Maj., 5 July, 1814, for distinguished service at the Battle of Chippewa. Bvt. Lieut. Col., 17 Sept., 1814, for gallant and good conduct in the sortie from Fort Erie. Bvt. Col., 17 Sept., 1824, for ten years' faithful service in one grade. Bvt. Brig. Gen., 7 June, 1832, for ten years' faithful service in one grade. Bvt. Maj Gen., 30 May, 1848, for meritorious conduct during the war with Mexico.

JONES, ROGER.* [Born in D. C. Appointed from D. C.]
Bvt. 2nd Lieut. Mounted Rifles, 1 July, 1851. 2nd Lieut., 24 May, 1852. 1st Lieut.,

26 Jan., 1857. Reg. Adj., 1 July, 1854, to 24 March, 1858. Capt., A. Q. M., 23 April, 1861. Maj. A. I. G., 12 Nov., 1861. Lieut. Col. A. I. G., 13 June, 1867. Col. I. G., 5 Feb., 1885. Brig. Gen. I. G., 20 Aug., 1888. Died 26 Jan., 1889.

JONES, SAML.* [Born in Va. Appointed from Va.]
Bvt. 2nd Lieut. 1st Art., 1 July, 1841. 2nd Lieut., 28 Sept., 1841. 1st Lieut., 3 March, 1847. Capt., 24 Dec., 1853. Resigned 27 April, 1861. Died 31 July, 1887.

JONES, SAMUEL G.* [Born in Ala. Appointed from Ala.]
Addl. 2nd Lieut. 5th Cav., 12 June, 1890. 2nd Lieut., 10 Aug., 1890. Trans. to 2nd Cav., 8 Jan., 1897. 1st Lieut. 4th Cav., 19 June, 1897. Trans. to 5th Cav., 23 June, 1898.

JONES, SAML. R* [Born in Penn. Appointed from Penn.]
2nd Lieut. 4th Art., 17 June, 1867. 1st Lieut., 22 Aug., 1871. R. Q. M., 9 Dec., 1887, to —. Capt., 24 Jan., 1891. Trans. to Q. M. D., 20 April, 1892. Maj. Chf. Q. M. Vols., 12 May, 1898. Graduate of the Artillery School, 1876.

JONES, THADDEUS W.* [Born in N. C. Appointed from N. C.]
2nd Lieut. 10th Cav., 14 June, 1872. 1st Lieut., 20 Nov., 1879. R. Q. M., 1 Oct., 1887, to 1 Dec., 1888. Capt., 14 Jan., 1891. Col. 10th U. S. Vols., 13 July, 1898, to 8 March, 1899. Lieut. Col. 48th U. S. Vols., 9 Sept., 1899.

JONES, THOS. M.* [Born in Va. Appointed from Va.]
Bvt. 2nd Lieut. 8th Inf., 1 July, 1853. 2nd Lieut., 3 March, 1855. R. Q. M., 5 March, 1857, to 10 Oct., 1859. Reg. Adj., 10 Oct., 1859, to 13 Dec., 1860. 1st Lieut., 19 July, 1858. Resigned 28 Feb., 1861.

JONES, WALTER. [Born in D. C. Appointed from Va.]
2nd Lieut. 1st Inf., 30 June, 1855. 1st Lieut., 31 Oct., 1857. Resigned 10 May, 1861.

JONES, WM. A.* [Born in Mo. Appointed from Ill.]
1st Lieut. Eng., 13 June, 1864. Capt., 7 March, 1867. Maj., 30 June, 1882. Lieut. Col., 2 Oct., 1895.

JONES, WM. A. B. [Born in Wis. Appointed from Iowa.]
2nd Lieut. 1st Cav., 3 March, 1855. Resigned 30 April, 1856.

JONES, WM. E.* [Born in Va. Appointed from Va.]
Bvt. 2nd Lieut. Mounted Rifles, 1 July, 1848. 2nd Lieut., 30 Nov., 1850. 1st Lieut., 31 Oct., 1854. Resigned 26 Jan., 1857. Killed 5 June, 1864.

JONES, WM. G.* [Born in Ohio. Appointed from Ohio.]
Bvt. 2nd Lieut. 8th Inf., 1 July, 1860. 2nd Lieut. 10th Inf., 29 Dec., 1860. 1st Lieut., 14 May, 1861. Lieut. Col. 71st Pa. Vols., 1 March to 6 April, 1863. Capt. 10th U. S. Cav., 1 June, 1863. Col. 36th Ohio Vols., 30 April, 1863. Killed 19 Sept., 1863, in Battle of Chickamauga, Ga.

JONES, WILLIAM K.* [Born in Iowa. Appointed from Iowa.]
Addl. 2nd Lieut. 14th Inf., 12 June, 1887. 2nd Lieut., 15 June, 1887. 1st Lieut. 6th Inf., 9 Nov., 1894. Capt., 2 March, 1899.

JONES, WM. P* [Born in N. Y. Appointed at Large.]
2nd Lieut. 3rd Art., 1 July, 1840. Accidentally killed 9 Sept., 1841.

JORDAN, ALLEN R.* [Born in S. C. Appointed from S. C..
2nd Lieut. 3rd Cav., 13 June, 1879. Died 13 Dec., 1882.

JORDAN, CHAS. [Born in N. Y. Appointed from Army.]
Priv., Corpl. and Sergt. Co. H, and Q. M. Sergt. 2nd Batt. 11th Inf., 18 Aug., 1864, to 30 Dec., 1866. 2nd Lieut. 11th Inf., 14 Nov., 1866. Trans. to 16th Inf., 14 April, 1869. Cashiered 12 Sept., 1872.

JORDAN, CHAS. D.* [Born in Mass. Appointed at Large.]
Bvt. 2nd Lieut. 8th Inf., 1 July, 1842. 2nd Lieut. 1st Inf., 31 Jan., 1844. Trans. to 8th Inf., 8 July, 1844. 1st Lieut., 21 Sept., 1846. Capt., 15 May, 1851. Maj. 5th Inf., 27 Feb., 1862. Retired 27 Aug., 1863. Died 5 Jan., 1876. Bvt. 1st Lieut., 9 May, 1846, for gallant and meritorious conduct at Palo Alto and Resaca de la Palma.

JORDAN, JOHN W. [Born in Md. Appointed from Md.]
Priv. Co. D, 3rd Md. Vols., 30 Sept., 1861. 2nd Lieut., 25 Nov., 1861. Mustered out 15 May, 1862. 2nd Lieut. 2nd Potomac Home Brig. Md. Vols., 24 May, 1862. Mustered out 29 Sept., 1864. 2nd Lieut. 37th Inf., 6 May, 1867. Unassigned 21 April, 1869. Resigned 10 Feb., 1870. Died 24 Dec., 1889.

JORDAN, LAMBERT W., Jr.* [Born in S. C. Appointed from S. C.]
2nd Lieut. 1st Inf., 26 April, 1898. 1st Lieut., 2 March, 1899.

JORDAN, LEWIS W. [Born in Tenn. Appointed from Tenn.]
Maj. Surg., 3 March, 1847; 14th Inf., 9 April, 1847. Disbanded 20 July, 1848.

JORDAN, SIDNEY S.* [Born in N. J. Appointed from N. J.]
Addl. 2nd Lieut. 5th Art., 12 June, 1889. 2nd Lieut., 15 June 1889. 1st Lieut. 2nd Art., 27 Aug., 1896. Graduate of the Artillery School, 1896.

JORDAN, THOMAS.* [Born in Va. Appointed from Va.]
Bvt. 2nd Lieut. 5th Inf., 1 July, 1840. 2nd Lieut. 3rd Inf., 1 Dec., 1840. 1st Lieut., 18 June, 1846. Capt. A. Q. M., 3 March, 1847. Resigned 21 May, 1861.

JORDAN, WM. H.* [Born in Ohio. Appointed from Ohio.]
Bvt. 2nd Lieut. 2nd Inf., 1 July, 1860. 2nd Lieut. 9th Inf., 20 Feb., 1861. 1st Lieut., 14 May, 1861. Bvt. Capt., 27 June, 1862, for gallant and meritorious service in the Battle of Gaines' Mill, Va. Capt. 9th Inf., 31 Dec., 1862. Maj. 8th Cal. Vols., 3 Feb., 1865. Mustered out of Vol. Service 24 Oct., 1865. Maj. 3rd Inf., 19 May, 1881. Lieut. Col. 19th Inf., 20 April, 1886. Col., 1 Nov., 1891. Retired for over 30 years' service, 23 March, 1892.,

JORDAN, WILLIAM H., Jr. [Born in Neb. Appointed form Ore.]
Priv. Co. H, 2nd Ore. Vols., 13 May to 2 Sept., 1898. 2nd Lieut. 18th Inf., 9 July, 1898. 1st Lieut., 2 March, 1899.

JOUETT, JAMES S. [Born in Ky. Appointed from Md.]
2nd Lieut. 10th Inf., 20 Jan., 1875. Trans. to 10th Cav., 6 Feb., 1877. 1st Lieut., 17 Feb., 1883. Dismissed 30 April, 1885. 1st Lieut. 10th Cav., 12 May, 1888, to rank from 17 Feb., 1883. Resigned 15 Jan., 1889.

JOUETT, WM. R. [Born in Tenn. Appointed from Tenn.]
2nd Lieut. 1st Inf., 19 Feb., 1818. 1st Lieut., 31 March, 1819. Capt., 1 May, 1829. Maj. 3rd Inf., 31 Oct., 1846. Lieut. Col. 2nd Inf., 31 Jan., 1850. Died 1 May, 1852.

JOYES, JAMES. [Born in Ireland. Appointed from N. Y.]
Sergt. Co. I, 182nd N. Y. Vols., 30 Sept., 1862. Trans. to Vet. Res. Corps., 6 Aug., 1863. 2nd Lieut. Vet. Res. Corps., 23 Feb., 1864. 1st Lieut., 19 Jan., 1865. Mustered out 25 June, 1866. 1st Lieut. 42nd Inf., 28 July, 1866. R. Q. M., 4 Jan., 1867, to 22 April, 1869. Unassigned 22 April, 1869. Ass'd to 17th Inf., 1 Jan., 1871. Resigned 30 June, 1872.

JOYES, JOHN W.* [Born in N. Y. Appointed from Cal.]
2nd Lieut. 5th Art., 12 June, 1894. 1st Lieut. Ord., 13 April, 1897.

JUDAH, HENRY M.* [Born in Md. Appointed from N. Y.]
Bvt. 2nd Lieut. 8th Inf., 1 July, 1843. 2nd Lieut. 4th Inf., 19 April, 1846. 1st Lieut., 26 Sept., 1847. Capt., 29 Sept., 1853. Maj., 30 June, 1862. Col. 4th Cal. Vols., 6 Sept., 1861. Resigned from Vol. Service, 8 Nov., 1861. Brig. Gen. Vols., 21 March, 1862. Mustered out of Vol. Service 24 Aug., 1865. Died 14 Jan., 1866. Bvt. 1st Lieut., 8 Sept., 1847, for gallant and meritorious conduct at Molino del Rey. Bvt. Capt., 13 Sept., 1847, for gallant and meritorious conduct at Chapultepec. Bvt. Col. and Lieut. Col., 13 March, 1865, for gallant and meritorious service during the war.

JUDD, EDWIN D. [Born in Conn. Appointed from Conn.]
Addl. P. M. Vols., 1 June, 1861. Bvt. Lieut. Col. Vols., 13 March, 1865, for faithful and meritorious service during the war. Mustered out 20 July, 1866. Maj. P. M. U. S. A., 17 Jan., 1867. Retired 4 June, 1879.

JUDD, GEORGE E. [Born in Mass. Appointed from Mich.]
1st Sergt. Co. A, 3rd Mich Vols., 10 June, 1861. Discharged 1 Aug., 1861. 2nd Lieut. 3rd Mich., Vols., 10 Aug., 1861. 1st Lieut., 28 Oct., 1861. Capt., 23 June, 1862. Mustered out 7 Feb., 1864. Capt. Vet. Res. Corps, 29 Jan., 1864. 2nd Lieut. 45th Inf., 19 Aug., 1868. Mustered out as Capt. Vet. Res. Corps, 27 Aug., 1868. Trans. to 14th Inf., 14 Aug., 1869. Unassigned 27 Sept., 1869. Retired with rank of Capt., 28 May, 1870.

JUDD, HENRY B.* [Born in Conn. Appointed from Conn.]
2nd Lieut. 3rd Art., 1 July, 1839. 1st Lieut., 26 Dec., 1840. Reg. Adj., 20 Jan. to 1 June, 1848. Bvt. Capt., 25 March, 1847, for gallant and meritorious conduct in the affair at Medelin. Capt. 3rd Art., 13 Feb., 1850. Maj. 4th Art., 1 Nov., 1861. Retired 21 Nov., 1861. Bvt. Lieut. Col., 13 Nov., 1865, for faithful and meritorious service connected with the mustering and disbanding of the Vol. armies of the United States. Bvt. Col., 13 Nov., 1865, for faithful and meritorious service connected with the organization of the Vol. armies of the United States during the war. Died 27 July, 1892.

JUDSON, JOHN W.* [Born in Conn. Appointed from Conn.]
Bvt. 2nd Lieut. 2nd Art., 1 July, 1836, declined. Died 30 May, 1878.

JUDSON, WILLIAM V.* [Born in Ind. Appointed from Ind.]
Addl. 2nd Lieut. Eng., 11 June, 1888. 2nd Lieut., 23 July, 1888. 1st Lieut., 18 May, 1893. Capt., 5 July, 1898.

JUSTICE, JAMES.* [Born in Texas. Appointed from Texas.]
2nd Lieut. 22nd Inf., 15 Feb., 1899.

KAISER, AUGUST [Born in France. Appointed from Army.]
Priv., Corpl., Sergt. and 1st Sergt. Co. G, and Sergt. Maj. 3rd Inf., 4 Jan., 1858, to 18 July, 1862. 2nd Lieut. 3rd Inf., 18 July, 1862. 1st Lieut., 24 Nov., 1863. Unassigned 11 Aug., 1869. Mustered out 1 Jan., 1871. Priv., Corpl., Sergt. and 1st Sergt. Cos. E and D, and Q. M. Sergt. 1st Inf., 12 June, 1871, to 12 June, 1876. Died 20 Oct., 1881.

KALK, FRANK G.* [Born in Wis. Appointed from Wis.]
2nd Lieut. 3rd Inf., 1 July, 1886. 1st Lieut. of Inf. (24th), 4 July, 1892. Trans. to 5th Inf., 12 Aug., 1892. Graduate of the Infantry and Cavalry School, 1893. Died 5 March, 1898.

KANE, DELANCEY A.* [Born in R. I. Appointed from Utah.]
2nd Lieut. 1st Cav., 15 June, 1868. Resigned 8 Dec., 1869.

KANE, ELIAS K.* [Born in Ill. Appointed from Ill.]
Bvt. 2nd Lieut. 2nd Drag., 1 July, 1841. Reg. Adj., 16 April to 17 Sept., 1842. 2nd Lieut., 10 July, 1843. 1st Lieut., 18 Aug., 1847. Capt. A. Q. M., 12 Jan., 1848. Died 9 July, 1863.

KANE, JOHN H. [Born in Ireland. Appointed from Army.]
Priv., Corpl. and Sergt. Co. D, 2nd (5th) Cav., 6 June, 1855, to 2 April, 1863. 2nd Lieut. 5th Cav., 19 Feb., 1863. 1st Lieut., 19 Nov., 1863. Capt., 22 Dec., 1868. Discharged 31 Aug., 1870. Bvt. Capt., 9 April, 1865, for gallant and meritorious service in the battles terminating with the surrender of Gen. Lee's army.

KANE, JOHN I. [Born in N. Y. Appointed from N. Y.]
2nd Lieut. 24th Inf., 31 Oct., 1874. 1st Lieut., 23 Dec., 1878. R. Q. M., 6 May, 1880, to 1 Nov., 1882. Resigned 30 June, 1883.

KANE, JOHN J. [Born in Ky. Appointed from Penn.]
1st Lieut. Asst. Surg., 3 June, 1879. Resigned 13 April, 1887.

KAPUS, WM. [Born in Germany. Appointed from Ore.]
1st Lieut. 1st Wash. Ter. Inf., 20 Sept., 1862. Mustered out 24 July, 1865. 2nd Lieut. 13th Inf., 7 March, 1867. R. Q. M., 3 Dec., 1868, to 1 May, 1869. Resigned 1 May, 1869.

KARGE, JOSEPH. [Born in Prussia. Appointed from N. J.]
Lieut Col. 1st N. J. Cav., 18 Oct., 1861. Resigned 22 Dec., 1862. Col. 2nd N. J. Cav., 25 Sept., 1863. Bvt. Brig. Gen. Vols., 13 March, 1865, for gallant and meritorious service during the war. Mustered out 1 Nov., 1865. 1st Lieut. 8th Cav., 12 June, 1867. Trans. to 9th Inf., 1 Feb., 1870. Unassigned 4 May, 1870. Mustered out 1 Jan., 1871.

KARNES, WILLIAM L. [Born in ——. Appointed from ——.]
2nd Lieut. Cav., 1 Dec., 1899. [Unassigned.]

KARNEY, THOS. [Born in Ireland. Appointed from Md.]
1st Lieut. 14th Inf., 12 March, 1812. Capt., 13 May, 1813. Disbanded 15 June, 1815. Retained 17 May, 1816 (in reorganization under Act of 3 March, 1815), as 1st Lieut. 4th Inf., with Bvt. of Capt., from 13 May, 1813. Resigned 31 Dec., 1816. Died 18 July, 1834.

KARPLES, HENRY M. [Born in Austria. Appointed from N. Y.]
Priv. Co. C, 12th N. Y. State Mil., 11 June to 5 Aug., 1861. 1st Lieut. 52nd N. Y. Vols., 9 March, 1862. Capt., 1 Nov., 1862. Maj., 1 Sept., 1863. Lieut. Col., 1 Nov., 1864. Mustered out 1 July, 1865. 2nd Lieut. 19th Inf., 11 May, 1866. Trans. to 37th Inf., 21 Sept., 1866. Cashiered 9 June, 1868.

KAUFFMAN, ALBERT B. [Born in Penn. Appointed from Mo.]
Priv. Co. D, 11th Inf., 18 March, 1847. Corpl., 1 Jan., 1848. Sergt., 1 May, 1848. Discharged 16 Aug., 1848. Priv. Co. F, 6th Inf., 11 Jan., 1850. Corpl., 12 Nov., 1850. Sergt., 1 May, 1851. 1st Sergt., 1 Oct., 1851. Discharged 21 Nov., 1854. 1st Sergt. Co. F, 6th Inf., 21 Nov., 1854. Discharged 21 Nov., 1859. Priv. Co. I, 1st Cav., 12 Sept., 1860. Corpl. Co. I, 4th Cav., 4 Oct., 1861. 1st Sergt., 1 April, 1862. Sergt., 31 Aug., 1862. Priv., 1 May, 1863. Discharged 14 Sept., 1863. Capt. 11th Mo. Cav., 14 Sept., 1863. Maj., 21 March, 1865. Mustered out 27 July, 1865. 1st Lieut. 8th Cav., 28 July, 1866. R. Q. M., 26 Aug., 1867, to 13 May, 1869. Capt., 13 May, 1869. Maj. 8th Cav., 18 Feb., 1891. Trans. to 4th Cav., 8 July, 1891. Retired, after 40 years' service, 1 Jan., 1892.

KAUTZ, AUGUST V.* [Born in Germany. Appointed from Ohio.]
Priv. Co. G, 1st Ohio Vols., 8 June, 1846. Discharged 14 June, 1847. Cadet Mil. Acad., 1 July, 1848. Bvt. 2nd Lieut. 4th Inf., 1 July, 1852. 2nd Lieut., 24 March, 1853. 1st Lieut., 4 Dec., 1855. Capt. 3rd Cav., 14 May, 1861. 6th Cav., 3 Aug., 1861. Col. 2nd Ohio Cav., 2 Sept., 1862. Bvt. Maj., 9 June, 1863, for gallant and meritorious service in action at Monticello, Ky. Brig. Gen. Vols., 7 May, 1864. Bvt. Lieut. Col., 9 June, 1864, for gallant and meritorious service in an attack on Petersburg, Va. Bvt. Col., 7 Oct., 1864, for gallant and meritorious service in action on the Darbytown Road, Va. Bvt. Maj. Gen. Vols., 28 Oct., 1864, for gallant and meritorious service during the campaign against Richmond, Va. Bvt. Brig. Gen. and Bvt. Maj. Gen., 13 March, 1865, for gallant and meritorious service in the field during the war. Mustered out of Vol. Service, 15 Jan., 1866. Lieut. Col. 34th Inf., 28 July, 1866. Trans. to 15th Inf., 15 March, 1869. Col. 8th Inf., 8 June, 1874. Brig. Gen., 20 April, 1891. Retired, by operation of law, 5 Jan., 1892. Died 4 Sept., 1895.

KAVENAUGH, THOMAS W. [Born in Ky. Appointed from Ky.]
2nd Lieut. Rifles, 13 Feb., 1818. 1st Lieut., 10 Nov., 1818. Trans. to 6th Inf., 1 June, 1821. Died 29 May, 1823.

KEAIS, JOHN L.* [Born in N. C. Appointed from N. C.]
Bvt. 2nd Lieut. 3rd Art., 1 July, 1835. Massacred by Indians in Florida, 28 Dec., 1835.

KEAN, JEFFERSON R. [Born in Va. Appointed from Va.]
Asst. Surg., 8 Dec., 1884. Capt. Asst. Surg., 8 Dec., 1889. Maj. Brig. Surg. Vols., 4 June, 1898. Maj. Chf. Surg. Vols., 30 Jan., 1899. Lieut. Col. Chf. Surg. Vols., 21 Feb., 1899, to 17 April, 1899. Maj. Surg. Vols., 17 April, 1899, to ——.

KEAN, JOSEPH. [Born in Va. Appointed from Va.]
Cornet Light Drag., 1 July, 1808. 2nd Lieut., 4 July, 1809. 1st Lieut., 31 May, 1811. Reg. Adj., July, 1812, to March, 1814. Capt. 4th Rifles, 17 March, 1814. Retained in Rifle Reg., 17 May, 1815. Resigned 31 March, 1817.

KEARNEY, JAMES. [Born in Ireland. Appointed from D. C.]
3rd Lieut. 5th Inf., 12 April, 1813. 2nd Lieut., 1 June, 1814. 1st Lieut., 13 Aug., 1814, to 15 June, 1815. Capt. Asst. Top. Eng., 12 April, 1813. Discharged 15 June, 1815. Maj. Top. Eng., 29 April, 1816. Lieut. Col. Top. Eng., 7 July, 1838. Retired 9 Sept., 1861. Died 10 Jan., 1862. Bvt. Lieut. Col., 29 April, 1826, for ten years' faithful service in one grade.

KEARNY, PHILIP. [Born in N. Y. Appointed from N. Y.]
2nd Lieut. 1st Drag., 8 March, 1837. 1st Lieut., 22 July, 1839. Resigned 6 April, 1846. Reinstated 11 May, 1846. Capt. 1st Drag., 6 Dec., 1846. Resigned 9 Oct., 1851. Bvt. Maj., 20 Aug., 1847, for gallant and meritorious conduct at Contreras and Churubusco. Brig. Gen. Vols., 17 May, 1861. Maj. Gen. Vols., 4 July, 1862. Killed, 1 Sept., 1862, at the Battle of Chantilly, Va.

KEARNY, STEPHEN W. [Born in N. J. Appointed from N. Y.]
1st Lieut. 13th Inf., 12 March, 1812. Capt., 1 April, 1813. Trans. to 2nd Inf., 17 May, 1815. Trans. to 3rd Inf., 1 June, 1821. Trans. to 1st Inf., 4 June, 1821. Maj. 3rd Inf., 1 May, 1829. Lieut. Col. 1st Drag., 4 March, 1833. Col. 1st Drag., 4 July, 1836. Brig. Gen., 30 June, 1846. Died 31 Oct., 1848. Bvt. Maj., 1 April, 1823, for ten years' faithful service in one grade. Bvt. Maj. Gen., 6 Dec., 1846, for gallant and meritorious conduct in New Mexico and California, to date from the Battle of San Pasqual.

KEARNY, WM. [Born in N. Y. Appointed from Mo.]
Cadet Mil. Acad., 1 July, 1849, to 19 Jan., 1852. 2nd Lieut. 10th Inf., 3 March, 1855. 1st Lieut., 23 Jan., 1861. Resigned 1 June, 1861.

KEECH, FRANK B.* [Born in Md. Appointed from Md.]
2nd Lieut. 5th Inf., 12 June, 1890. Resigned 30 April, 1893.

KEEFER, FRANK R. [Born in Penn. Appointed from Penn.]
Asst. Surg., 6 June, 1890. Capt. Asst. Surg., 6 June, 1895. Maj. Surg. Vols., 1 Oct., 1899.

KEEFER, JOHN B. [Born in Penn. Appointed from Penn.]
Maj. P. M., 13 Feb., 1877. Retired by operation of law 10 April, 1896.

KEEFFE, JOSEPH. [Born in Ireland. Appointed from Army.]
Priv. Co. E, 2nd Art., 5 Dec., 1853. Corpl., 2 May, 1855. Sergt., 9 July, 1856. Priv., 3 March, 1857. Discharged 5 Dec., 1858. Priv. Co. E, 2nd Art., 5 Dec., 1858. Corpl., 20 Dec., 1858. Sergt., 5 Aug., 1861. 1st Sergt., 29 Jan., 1862. Bvt. 2nd Lieut. 2nd Art., 22 Oct., 1862. 2nd Lieut. 5th Art., 22 Oct., 1862. Bvt. 1st Lieut., 29 Nov., 1863, for gallant and meritorious service during the defence of Fort

Saunders, Tenn. Bvt. Capt., 23 Sept., 1864, for gallant and meritorious service in the Battle of Fisher's Hill, Va. 1st Lieut. 5th Art., 28 July, 1866. Capt. 9th Cav., 12 June, 1867, declined. Trans. to 4th Inf., 22 May, 1875. Capt., 4 Feb., 1882. Died 4 Dec., 1891.

KEELER, BIRNEY B. [Born in N. Y. Appointed from N. Y.]
1st Lieut. 142nd N. Y. Vols., 29 Sept., 1862. Capt., 18 May, 1864. Trans. to 169th N. Y. Vols., 7 June, 1865. Mustered out 7 July, 1865. Bvt. Maj. Vols., 13 March, 1865, for gallant and meritorious conduct at the storming of Fort Fisher, N. C. Bvt. Lieut. Col. Vols., 13 March, 1865, for gallant and distinguished service in the field during the campaign of 1864. Maj. J. A. Vols., 26 June, 1865. Mustered out 31 May,, 1866. 1st Lieut. 39th Inf., 28 July, 1866. R. Q. M., 5 Jan., 1867, to 17 Jan., 1868. Bvt. Capt., 2 March, 1867, for gallant and meritorious service in action at Chapin's Farm, Va. Bvt. Maj., 2 March, 1867, for gallant and meritorious service in the assault on Fort Fisher, N. C. Capt. 39th Inf., 5 June, 1868. Unassigned 20 April, 1869. Ass'd to 18th Inf., 1 Jan., 1871. Died 15 Oct., 1886.

KEELER, SAML. [Born in Conn. Appointed from Conn..
3rd Lieut. 37th Inf., 30 April, 1813. 2nd Lieut., 31 Jan., 1814. Trans. to 5th Inf., 17 May, 1815. Resigned 1 May, 1816.

KEELER, SAML., Jr. [Born in Conn. Appointed from Conn.]
Ensign 37th Inf., 30 April, 1813. 3rd Lieut., 17 Dec., 1813. R. Q. M., Aug., 1813, to June, 1815. 2nd Lieut., 7 June, 1814. Disbanded 15 June, 1815. Reinstated 2 Dec., 1815, in 3rd Inf. Trans. to 6th Inf., 15 March, 1816. 1st Lieut., 14 May, 1818. Died 27 May, 1820.

KEELING, WM. H. [Born in Vt. Appointed from Army.]
Priv., Sergt. and 1st Sergt. Co. H, 13th Inf., 16 Sept., 1861, to 23 Nov., 1863. 2nd Lieut. 13th Inf., 31 Oct., 1863. 1st Lieut., 30 March, 1864. Resigned 30 June, 1867.

KEENAN, JAMES, Jr. [Born in Penn. Appointed from Penn.]
2nd Lieut. 11th Inf., 6 Sept., 1847. Disbanded 16 Aug., 1848.

KEENE, HENRY C., Jr.* [Born in S. A. Appointed from Mass.]
2nd Lieut. 24th Inf,, 1 July, 1886. 1st Lieut. 17th Inf., 4 Feb., 1893. Trans. to 24th Inf., 24 Feb., 1893. Capt., 2 March, 1899.

KEENEY, CHAS. C. [Born in N. Y. Appointed from Mich.]
Asst. Surg., 12 July, 1842. Disbanded 23 Sept., 1842. Reappointed 19 March, 1845. Capt. Asst. Surg., 19 March, 1850. Maj. Surg., 23 June, 1860. Lieut. Col. Med. Ins., 11 June, 1862. Bvt. Lieut. Col., 13 March, 1865, for faithful and meritorious service during the war. Mustered out as Col. Med. Ins., 31 Oct., 1865. Lieut. Col. Surg., 26 June, 1876. Col. Surg., 30 June, 1882. Died 30 Jan., 1883.

KEISER, CHRISTOPHER. [Born in Md. Appointed from Penn.]
1st Lieut. Asst. Dep. Com. Ord., 6 Aug., 1813. Died 10 Oct., 1819.

KEITH, DANIEL. [Born in Va. Appointed from Army.]
Priv., Corpl. and Sergt. 35th Inf., 16 Feb. to July, 1814. Ensign 35th Inf., 14 July, 1814. Disbanded 15 June, 1815. 2nd Lieut. Rifle Reg., 13 Feb., 1819. 1st Lieut., 20 May, 1820. Disbanded 1 June, 1821.

KELL, WM. H. [Born in Ohio. Appointed from Ohio.]
Priv. Co. F, 1st Ohio Vols., 17 April, 1861. Discharged 16 Aug., 1861. Priv. Co. I, 2nd Ohio Vols., 15 Sept., 1862. Trans. to Co. E, 18th Ohio Vols., 10 Nov., 1864. Discharged 10 June, 1865. 2nd Lieut. 22nd Inf., 12 Dec., 1872. 1st Lieut., 25 June, 1879. Reg. Adj., 1 Feb., 1887, to —. Capt., 19 May, 1891. Bvt. 1st Lieut., 27 Feb., 1890, for gallant services in action against Indians at Spring Creek, Mont., Oct. 15 and 16, 1876. Retired with rank of Maj., 15 Dec., 1899.

KELLER, CHAS.* [Born in Penn. Appointed from Penn.]
2nd Lieut. and 1st Lieut. 16th Inf., 23 June, 1865. Trans. to 2nd Inf., 17 April, 1869. R. Q. M., 20 Aug., 1873, to 20 July, 1875. Capt., 20 July, 1875. Maj. 18th Inf., 8 Aug., 1897. Lieut. Col. 24th Inf., 25 April, 1899.

KELLER, CHARLES.* [Born in N. Y. Appointed from N. Y.]
Addl. 2nd Lieut. Eng., 12 June, 1890. 2nd Lieut., 20 Sept., 1892. 1st Lieut., 13 Aug., 1895.

KELLER, DANIEL F. [Born in Penn. Appointed from Penn.]
Priv., Corpl. and Sergt. Troop A, 8th Cav., 1 Feb., 1896, to 3 Aug., 1898. 2nd Lieut. 24th Inf., 9 July, 1898. 1st Lieut., 16 May, 1899.

KELLER, JACOB W. [Born in Prussia. Appointed from Conn.]
Priv. Co. K, 6th Mass. Vols., 22 April, 1861. Discharged 2 Aug., 1861. 1st Lieut. 5th N. H. Vols., 12 Oct., 1861. Capt., 1 May, 1863. Mustered out 26 Jan., 1864. Capt. Vet. Res. Corps, 22 Jan., 1864. Mustered out 11 Jan., 1867. 2nd Lieut. 42nd Inf., 28 July, 1866. 1st Lieut., 20 March, 1867. Unassigned 22 April, 1869. Retired with rank of Capt., 15 Dec., 1870.

KELLEY, ANDREW J. [Born in Tenn. Appointed from Tenn.]
Priv. Co. I, 1st Tenn. Cav., 1 Aug., 1862, to 5 June, 1865. 2nd Lieut. 33rd Inf., 13 June, 1867. Resigned 2 Oct., 1868.

KELLEY, JOSEPH M. [Born in N. Y. Appointed from Penn.]
Priv. Co. G, 19th Pa. Vols., 18 April, 1861. Discharged 8 Aug., 1861. 1st Lieut. 69th Pa. Vols., 26 Aug., 1861. Mustered out 4 March, 1863. 1st Lieut. Vet. Res. Corps, 8 March, 1864. Capt., 3 April, 1865. Mustered out 20 Nov., 1865. 1st Lieut. 38th Inf., 7 March, 1867. Unassigned 11 Nov., 1869. Ass'd to 10th Cav., 15 Dec., 1870. Capt., 15 April, 1875. Maj., 15 April, 1893. Retired for over thirty years' service, 24 Oct., 1898.

KELLEY, MOSES J. [Born in Maine. Appointed from Maine.]
Chap. 6th Maine Vols., 14 Aug., 1862. Mustered out 15 Aug., 1864. Post Chap., 2 July, 1870. Retired 3 October, 1879. Died 25 Aug., 1898.

KELLIHER, JOHN. [Born in New Brunswick. Appointed from Mass.]
Sergt. Co. F, 20th Mass. Vols., 26 July, 1861. 1st Sergt., 16 Dec., 1861. 2nd Lieut. 20th Mass. Vols., 14 Dec., 1862. 1st Lieut., 5 Sept., 1863. Capt., 11 Nov., 1863. Maj., 24 Dec., 1864. Mustered out 16 July, 1865. 1st Lieut. 42nd Inf., 28 July, 1866. Bvt. Capt., 2 March, 1867, for gallant and meritorious service in the Battle of Gettysburg, Pa. Bvt. Maj., 2 March, 1867, for gallant and meritorious

service in the Battle of Spottsylvania, Va. Unassigned 22 April, 1869. Retired with rank of Capt., 15 Dec., 1870.

KELLIHER, PATRICK. [Born in Ireland. Appointed from Army.]
Priv. 2nd Inf., 9 July, 1866. Hosp. Steward, 27 May, 1867, to 19 Nov., 1868. 2nd Lieut. 39th Inf., 6 Nov., 1868. Trans. to 25th Inf., 20 April, 1869. Died 12 Feb., 1876.

KELLO, WM. O.* [Born in Va. Appointed from Va.]
Bvt. 2nd Lieut. 3rd Inf., 1 July, 1832. 2nd Lieut., 11 Jan., 1834. 1st Lieut., 15 Nov., 1836. Trans. to 8th Inf., 7 July, 1838. Capt., 1 May, 1839. Died 27 Jan., 1848.

KELLOGG, EDGAR R. [Born in N. Y. Appointed from Army.]
Sergt. Co. A, 24th Ohio Vols., 6 June, 1861. Sergt. Maj. 24th Ohio Vols., 19 June, 1861. Discharged 23 July, 1861. 2nd Lieut. 24th Ohio Vols., 23 July, 1861. Resigned 28 Oct., 1861. Priv. Co. B, 1st Batt. 16th Inf., 29 Nov., 1861. Sergt. Maj. 1st Batt. 16th Inf., 18 Dec., 1861. Discharged 1 Aug., 1862. 2nd Lieut. 16th Inf., 7 April, 1862. 1st Lieut., 3 May, 1862. Bvt. Capt., 31 Dec., 1862, for gallant and meritorious service in the Battle of Murfreesboro, Tenn. Bvt. Maj., 1 Sept., 1864, for gallant and meritorious service during the Atlanta campaign and in the Battle of Jonesboro, Ga. Capt. 16th Inf., 16 Feb., 1865. Trans. to 25th Inf., 21 Sept., 1866. Trans. to 18th Inf., 26 April, 1869. Maj. 8th Inf., 26 Dec., 1888. Lieut. Col. 10th Inf., 16 Sept., 1892. Col. 6th Inf., 30 June, 1898. Brig. Gen. Vols., 1 Oct., 1898, to 24 Feb., 1899.

KELLOGG, JOHN.* [Born in Mass. Appointed from Mass.]
Bvt. 2nd Lieut. 4th Art., 1 July, 1849. 2nd Lieut. 3rd Art., 7 Sept., 1850. 1st Lieut., 24 Dec., 1853. Reg. Adj., 17 June to 17 Sept., 1861. Capt. C. S., 3 Aug., 1861. Col. 5th Cal. Vols., 12 Sept., 1861. Resigned from Vol. Service, 8 Nov., 1861. Maj. C. S., 29 June, 1864. Lieut. Col. C. S. Ass'd 12 Aug., 1864. Died 25 April, 1865.

KELLOGG, JOSEPH. [Born in N. Y. Appointed from Ill.]
1st Lieut. of Inf., 24 Feb., 1847; 16th Inf., 9 April, 1847. R. Q. M., 25 July to 18 Oct., 1847. Resigned 18 Nov., 1847. Capt. 12th Ill. Vols., 2 May, 1861. Mustered out 1 Aug., 1861.

KELLOGG, JOSIAH H.* [Born in Penn. Appointed from Penn.]
Bvt. 2nd Lieut. 1st Drag., 1 July, 1860. 2nd Lieut., 8 Jan., 1861. 1st Lieut., 13 May, 1861. 1st Cav., 3 Aug., 1861. Reg. Adj., 13 Jan. to 20 May, 1862. Capt. 1st Cav., 20 May, 1862. Col. 17th Penn. Cav., 19 Nov., 1862. Bvt. Maj., 3 July, 1863, for gallant and meritorious service in the Battle of Gettysburg, Pa. Mustered out of Vol. Service 17 Dec., 1864. Retired 6 Feb., 1865.

KELLOGG, LYMAN M.* [Born in N. Y. Appointed from N. Y.]
Bvt. 2nd Lieut. 2nd Inf., 1 July, 1852. 2nd Lieut., 28 Feb., 1854. 2nd Lieut. 10th Inf., 3 March, 1855. Resigned 16 Aug., 1855. 2nd Lieut. 3rd Art., 27 June, 1856. 1st Lieut., 31 July, 1858. Cashiered 30 May, 1860. Capt. 18th Inf., 14 May, 1861. Dismissed 11 Aug., 1862. Reinstated 1 June, 1864. Unassigned 26 April, 1869. Ass'd to 20th Inf., 11 May, 1869. Unassigned 14 July, 1870. Discharged 31 Dec., 1870. Bvt. Maj., 1 Sept., 1864, for gallant and meritorious services during the Atlanta campaign, and at the Battle of Jonesboro, Ga. Died 31 Jan., 1877.

KELLOGG, SANFORD C. [Born in N. Y. Appointed from N. Y.]
Sergt. Co. G, 37th N. Y. State Mil., 29 May, 1862. Priv., 19 July, 1862. Discharged 2 Sept., 1862. Capt. A. A. de C. Vols., 11 March, 1863. Bvt. Maj. Vols., 3 June, 1865, for faithful service. Bvt. Lieut. Col. and Col. Vols., 3 June, 1865, for gallant and meritorious service during the Atlanta campaign, and in the Battle of Nashville, Tenn. 2nd Lieut. 18th Inf., 23 Feb., 1866. 1st Lieut., 15 May, 1866. Mustered out of Vol. Service 10 July, 1866. Bvt. Capt., 2 March, 1867, for gallant and meritorious service in the Battle of Chattanooga, Tenn. Bvt. Maj., 2 March, 1867, for gallant and meritorious service in the Battle of Atlanta, Ga. Bvt. Lieut. Col., 2 March, 1867, for gallant and meritorious service in the Battle of Nashville, Tenn. Unassigned 26 April, 1869. Ass'd to 5th Cav., 15 Dec., 1870. Capt., 11 Jan., 1871. Lieut. Col. A. de C. to Lieut. Gen. Sheridan, 6 Nov., 1885, to 1 June, 1888, and Col. A. de C. to Gen. Sheridan, 1 June to 5 Aug., 1888. Maj. 4th Cav., 14 Jan., 1892. Retired, over thirty years' service, 23 Sept., 1898.

KELLOGG, WM. L. [Born in Ohio. Appointed from Ohio.]
2nd Lieut. 10th Inf., 5 Aug., 1861. 1st Lieut., 13 March, 1863. Bvt. 1st Lieut., 3 May, 1863, for gallant and meritorious service in the Battle of Chancellorsville, Va. Bvt. Capt., 2 July, 1863, for gallant and meritorious service in the Battle of Gettysburg, Pa. Capt. 10th Inf., 1 Jan., 1864. Bvt. Maj., 13 March, 1865, for gallant and meritorious service in the Battle of Gettysburg, Pa. Maj. 19th Inf., 15 Sept., 1884. Lieut. Col. 5th Inf., 14 July, 1890. Col. of Inf (5th), 30 Jan., 1895. Died 17 April, 1897.

KELLY, BERNARD. [Born in Va. Appointed from Kan.]
1st Lieut. Co. F, 103rd Ill. Vols., 2 Oct., 1962. Capt., 1 May, 1863. Discharged 13 Oct., 1864. Post Chap., 27 Oct., 1897.

KELLY, HENRY B. [Born in Ala. Appointed at Large.]
1st Lieut. of Inf., 5 March, 1847; 14th Inf., 9 April, 1847. Disbanded 27 July, 1848. 1st Lieut. 10th Inf., 3 March, 1855. Resigned 27 Feb., 1861.

KELLY, JAMES. [Born in Ireland. Appointed from N. Y.]
Capt. 69th State Mil., 9 May, 1861. Mustered out 3 Aug., 1861. Lieut. Col. 69th N. Y. Vols., 8 Nov., 1861. Mustered out 12 June, 1863. Capt. 16th Inf., 26 Oct., 1861. Dismissed 24 June, 1864. Dismissal revoked and reinstated 16 Sept., 1867, as Capt. 34th Inf. Trans. to 16th Inf., 14 April, 1869. Died 24 Sept., 1871.

KELLY, JAMES R. [Born in Ireland. Appointed from Army.]
Priv. Co. A, Eng., 28 Feb., 1854. Artificer, 1 July, 1855. Corpl., 1 July, 1857. Artificer, 17 May, 1858. Discharged 28 Feb., 1859. Priv. Co. D, 4th Art., 3 Aug., 1859. Corpl., 1 Sept., 1859. Sergt., 4 June, 1861. 2nd Lieut. and 1st Lieut. 3rd

Art., 29 Nov., 1861. Bvt. Capt., 27 June, 1862, for gallant and meritorious service in the Battle of Gaines' Mill, Va. Bvt. Maj., 13 Dec., 1862, for gallant and meritorious service in the Battle of Fredericksburg, Va. Capt. 3rd Art., 20 Dec., 1872. Died 3 Dec., 1884.

KELLY, MICHAEL J. [Born in Ireland. Appointed from D. C.]
2nd Lieut. 1st Cav., 8 May, 1861. 4th Cav., 3 Aug., 1861. 1st Lieut., 17 July, 1862. Capt., 21 April, 1866. Died 13 Aug., 1867. Bvt. Capt., 31 Dec., 1862, for gallant and meritorious service at the Battle of Stone River, Tenn. Bvt. Maj., 1 Sept., 1864, for gallant and meritorious service during the Atlanta campaign.

KELLY, PATRICK. [Born in Ireland. Appointed from N. Y.]
Capt. 69th N. Y. State Mil., 9 May, 1861. Mustered out 3 Aug., 1861. Capt. 16th Inf., 26 Oct., 1861. Lieut. Col. 88th N. Y. Vols., 14 Sept., 1861. Col., 20 Oct., 1862. Killed 16 June, 1864, in action before Petersburg, Va. Bvt. Maj., 7 April, 1862, for gallant and meritorious service at the Battle of Shiloh, Tenn.

KELLY, WM. [Born in Ireland. Appointed from Wash. Ter.]
Priv. Co. F, 3rd Inf., 14 Dec., 1843. Trans. to Co. E, 4th Inf., 1847. Discharged 14 Dec., 1848. Priv., Corpl. and Sergt. Co. G, 4th Inf., 16 Dec., 1848, to 16 Dec., 1853. 1st Lieut. 1st Ore. Cav., 20 Dec., 1861. Capt., 21 March, 1862. Mustered out 28 July, 1866. Capt. 8th Cav., 28 July, 1866. Died 28 Dec., 1871. Bvt. Maj., 5 April, 1868, for gallantry in an engagement with a large band of Indians on Malheur River, Ore., 5 April, 1868.

KELLY, WM.* [Born in N. Y. Appointed from Wis.]
2nd Lieut. Eng., 15 Feb., 1899.

KELLY, WM., Jr.* [Born in Texas. Appointed from Texas.]
Addl. 2nd Lieut. 5th Cav., 12 June, 1896. 2nd Lieut. 2nd Cav., 4 Jan., 1897.

KELTON, DWIGHT H. [Born in Vt. Appointed from Vt.]
Priv. Co. B, 98th N. Y. Vols., 29 Jan., 1864. Discharged 14 Oct., 1864. Capt. 115th U. S. Col. Troops, 15 Oct., 1864. Mustered out 10 Feb., 1866. 2nd Lieut. 10th Inf., 20 July, 1866. 1st Lieut., 26 March, 1868. Unassigned 19 May, 1869. Ass'd to 10th Inf., 15 Dec., 1870. Capt., 16 Feb., 1885. Retired for disability 6 March, 1888.

KELTON, JOHN C.* [Born in Penn. Appointed from Penn.]
Bvt. 2nd Lieut. 6th Inf., 1 July, 1851. 2nd Lieut., 31 Dec., 1851. 1st Lieut., 9 May, 1855. R. Q. M., 27 Nov., 1855, to 15 Feb., 1867. Bvt. Capt. A. A. G., 11 May, 1861. Capt. A. A. G., 3 Aug., 1861. Col. 9th Mo. Vols., 19 Sept., 1861. Col. A. A. de C., 4 Jan., 1862. Resigned Vol. commission, 1 March, 1862. Maj. A. A. G., 17 July, 1862. Bvt. Lieut. Col. and Col., 13 March, 1865, for most valuable and arduous service, both in the field and at headquarters. Bvt. Brig. Gen., 13 March, 1865, for valuable and arduous service during the war, both in the field and at headquarters. Lieut. Col. A. A. G., 23 March, 1866. Mustered out as Col. A. A. de C., 21 May, 1866. Col. A. A. G., 15 June, 1880. Brig. Gen. A. G., 7 June, 1889. Retired by operation of law, 24 June, 1892. Died 15 July, 1894.

KELTON, ROBERT H. C. [Born in Cal. Appointed from Conn.]
2nd Lieut. 1st Art., 9 July, 1898.

KEMBLE, JAMES R. [Born in Penn. Appointed from Penn.]
2nd Lieut. 3rd Cav., 5 Aug., 1861. 1st Lieut., 28 Sept., 1861. Capt., 7 Jan., 1866. Died 3 Jan., 1869. Bvt. Capt., 30 March, 1865, for meritorious and faithful service in the recruitment of the armies of the United States.

KEMP, FRANKLIN M. [Born in N. Y. Appointed from N. Y.]
Asst. Surg., 26 Oct., 1896.

KEMP, ULYSSES G. [Born in Ohio. Appointed from Ohio.]
Addl. 2nd Lieut. 4th Cav., 12 June, 1889. 2nd Lieut. 8th Cav., 28 Sept., 1889. 1st Lieut. 7th Cav., 15 Dec., 1896. Died 16 July, 1898.

KEMPER, JAMES B. [Born in Ohio. Appointed from Ohio.]
2nd Lieut. 14th Inf., 9 Sept., 1898. 1st Lieut. 6th Inf., 8 Dec., 1899.

KENASTON, HERBERT. [Born in N. Y. Appointed from Ohio.]
1st Lieut. 11th Inf., 14 May, 1861. Killed 2 July, 1863, at Battle of Gettysburg. Bvt. Capt., 2 July, 1863, for gallant and meritorious service at the Battle of Gettysburg, Pa.

KENDALL, FREDERIC A. [Born in N. H. Appointed from N. H.]
Priv. Co. B, 11th Ind. Vols., 18 June, 1861. Trans. to Co. I, N. H. Vols., 23 July, 1861. Discharged 9 Aug., 1861. 2nd Lieut. 4th N. H. Vols., 18 Sept., 1861. 1st Lieut., 1 Jan., 1863. Capt., 27 Sept., 1864. Mustered out 23 Aug., 1865. Capt. 8th U. S. Col. Art., 9 Oct., 1865. Mustered out 10 Feb., 1866. 2nd Lieut. 40th Inf., 28 July, 1866. Bvt. 1st Lieut. and Bvt. Capt., 2 March, 1867, for gallant and meritorious service at Fort Harrison, Va. 1st Lieut. 40th Inf., 31 July, 1867. Trans. to 25th Inf., 20 April, 1869. Capt., 22 March, 1879. Retired for disability 4 Dec., 1884.

KENDALL, HENRY F.* [Born in France. Appointed from Texas.]
Addl. 2nd Lieut. 3rd Inf., 14 June, 1878. 2nd Lieut., 28 June, 1878. Trans. to 20th Inf., 9 Sept., 1878. Trans. to 8th Cav., 3 June, 1879. 1st Lieut., 4 April, 1885. Capt., 1 July, 1891.

KENDALL, HENRY M. [Born in Mass. Appointed from Ind.]
Priv. and Corpl. 5th Batty Ind. Light Art., 23 Sept., 1861. Discharged 5 Jan., 1863. 2nd Lieut. 6th Cav., 17 July, 1862. 1st Lieut., 11 Sept., 1869. Capt., 15 Feb., 1881. Retired for disability, with rank of Maj., 31 May, 1898.

KENDALL, THEODORE. [Born in N. Y. Appointed from Army.]
Priv. Artificer, Corpl. and Sergt. Co. A, Eng., 25 July, 1853, to 13 May, 1863. 2nd Lieut. 15th Inf., 12 May, 1863. 1st Lieut., 11 June, 1864. Trans. to 33rd Inf., 21 Sept., 1866. Resigned 1 July, 1868. Bvt. 1st Lieut., 20 Sept., 1863, for gallant and meritorious service at the Battle of Chickamauga, Ga.

KENDALL, WM. [Born in Mass. Appointed from Mass.]
Ensign McCobb's Reg., Maine and N. H. Vols., 16 Nov., 1812. Ensign 45th Inf., 21 April, 1814. 3rd Lieut. 4th Rifle Reg., 13 June, 1814. 2nd Lieut., 16 June, 1814. 1st Lieut. 45th Inf., 1 Jan., 1815. Disbanded 15 June, 1815. Reinstated

in 2nd Inf., 2 Dec., 1815 (in reorganization under Act of 3 March, of that year) as 2nd Lieut. 2nd Inf., with Bvt. of 1st Lieut., from 1 Jan., 1815. Resigned 16 Oct., 1816. Died 5 May, 1872.

KENDALL, WM. P. [Born in Mass. Appointed from Mass.]
Asst. Surg., 12 Aug., 1885. Capt. Asst. Surg., 12 Aug., 1890. Maj. Brig. Surg., 4 June to 17 June, 1898.

KENDIG, DANIEL. [Born in Penn. Appointed from Cal.]
Chap. Posts of Fort Steilacoom, Wash. Ter., and Presidio, San Francisco, Cal., 13 Dec., 1859, to 27 May, 1867. Post. Chap., 3 April, 1867. Retired 10 Nov., 1888.

KENDRICK, FREDK. M. H. [Born in N. Y. Appointed from Tenn.]
2nd Lieut. 31st Mass. Vols., 19 Feb., 1862. Mustered out 7 Aug., 1862. Capt. 1st La. Vols., 8 Aug., 1862. Mustered out 20 July, 1863. Capt. Vet. Res. Corps, 25 March, 1864. Mustered out 31 Oct., 1867. 2nd Lieut. 7th Inf., 22 Oct., 1867. 1st Lieut., 9 Aug., 1877. Capt., 15 May, 1889. Maj., 2 March, 1899.

KENDRICK, HENRY L.* [Born in N. H. Appointed from N. H.]
Bvt. 2nd Lieut. 2nd Inf., 1 July, 1835. 2nd Lieut., 1 April, 1836. Trans. to 2nd Art., 16 June, 1836. 1st Lieut., 20 June, 1837. Capt., 18 June, 1846. Bvt. Maj., 12 Oct., 1847, for gallant and meritorious conduct in defence of Puebla. Prof. Mil. Acad., 3 March, 1857. Brig. Gen. Vols., 23 Sept., 1861, declined. Retired, with the pay of Col., at his own request, being over sixty-two years of age and forty-five years' service. Died 24 May, 1891.

KENLY, WM. L.* [Born in Md. Appointed from Md.]
2nd Lieut. 4th Art., 12 June, 1889. 1st Lieut. 1st Art., 29 June, 1896. Graduate of the Artillery School, 1894.

KENNEDY, ALFRED W. [Born in Ky. Appointed from Ky.]
Asst. Surg., 15 June, 1840. Died 3 June, 1851.

KENNEDY, CHASE W.* [Born in Ohio. Appointed from Ohio.]
2nd Lieut. 3rd Inf., 13 June, 1883. 1st Lieut., 13 Nov., 1889. Capt. 8th Inf., 26 April, 1898.

KENNEDY, JAMES M. [Born in S. C. Appointed from S. C.]
Asst. Surg., 12 May, 1893. Capt., 24 Oct., 1898.

KENNEDY, JOHN F.* [Born in Md. Appointed from Md.]
Bvt. 2nd Lieut. 1st Art., 1 July, 1829. 2nd Lieut., 1 July, 1829. 1st Lieut., 1 Oct., 1835. Died 19 May, 1837.

KENNEDY, JOHN S. [Born in Penn. Appointed from Penn.]
Capt. 17th Inf., 5 Aug., 1861. Resigned 16 Aug., 1862.

KENNEDY, JOSEPH M. [Born in Penn. Appointed from N. Y.]
Capt. 9th N. Y. Cav., 27 Nov., 1861. Maj., 25 June, 1864. Bvt. Lieut. Col. Vols., 13 March, 1865, for faithful and efficient service during the war. Mustered out 26 Aug., 1865. 2nd Lieut. 16th Inf., 11 May, 1866. Trans. to 25th Inf., 21 Sept., 1866. 1st Lieut., 9 Aug., 1867. Unassigned 26 April, 1869. Resigned 3 July, 1869.

KENNEDY, JOSIAH F. [Born in Penn. Appointed from Iowa.]
Asst. Surg., 5 Aug., 1861. Resigned 10 Oct., 1862.

KENNEDY, WM. B. [Born in Ireland. Appointed from Cal.]
1st Lieut. 1st Cal. Cav., 13 June, 1863. Capt., 12 Nov., 1863. Mustered out 22 May, 1866. 1st Lieut. 10th Cav., 22 Jan., 1867. Capt., 7 June, 1870. Maj. 4th Cav., 1 Jan., 1892. Retired for over thirty years' service, 13 Jan., 1897.

KENNERLY, GEORGE H. [Born in Va. Appointed from Mo.]
1st Lieut. 19th Inf., 6 April, 1813. Negatived by Senate, 29 July, 1813. 1st Lieut. 26th Inf., 17 May, 1814. Trans. to 2nd Rifle Reg., 20 May, 1814. Disbanded 15 June, 1815. Reinstated as 2nd Lieut. 8th Inf., 17 May, 1816, with Bvt. of 1st Lieut. from 17 May, 1814. 1st Lieut., 15 Jan., 1817. Reg. Adj., 1 Nov., 1816, to 1 Jan., 1819. Resigned 1 Jan., 1819. Capt. A. Q. M. Vols., 26 June, 1846. Disbanded 15 Oct., 1848.

KENNICOTT, RANSOM. [Born in Ill. Appointed from Ill.]
Capt. 37th Ill. Vols., 18 Sept., 1861. Maj., 8 March, 1864. Lieut. Col., 30 July, 1865. Mustered out 19 April, 1866. 2nd Lieut. and 1st Lieut. 19th Inf., 23 Feb., 1866. Trans. to 37th Inf., 21 Sept., 1866. Retired 5 Nov., 1868.

KENNINGTON, ALFRED E.* [Born in Wyo. Appointed from Wash'n.]
Addl. 2nd Lieut. 7th Cav., 12 June, 1896. 2nd Lieut. 10th Cav., 2 March, 1897.

KENNINGTON, JAMES. [Born in Ireland. Appointed from Army.]
Priv. Co. K, 2nd Inf., 20 Oct., 1851. Corpl., 17 Nov., 1853. Sergt., 21 July, 1855. Discharged 20 Aug., 1856. Sergt. Co. K, 2nd Inf., 20 Aug., 1856. 1st Sergt., 5 Sept., 1858. Sergt., 10 Oct., 1860. Discharged 20 June, 1861. Sergt. Co. K, 2nd Inf., 20 June, 1861. Sergt. Co. —, 1st Batt. 11th Inf., 16 Aug., 1861. Sergt. Maj. 1st Batt. 11th Inf., 1 March, 1862. Com. Sergt. 1st Batt. 11th Inf., 23 Sept., 1862. 2nd Lieut. 11th Inf., 26 Nov., 1862. Bvt. 1st Lieut., 13 Dec., 1862, for gallant and meritorious service in the Battle of Fredericksburg, Va. 1st Lieut. 11th Inf., 5 May, 1864. Bvt. Capt., 13 March, 1865, for general good conduct in the field. Unassigned 14 April, 1869. Ass'd to 14th Inf., 1 Jan., 1871. Capt., 10 Dec., 1873. Retired for disability 15 June, 1887. Died 22 April, 1897.

KENNON, LYMAN W. V.* [Born in R. I. Appointed from R. I.]
Addl. 2nd Lieut. 1st Inf., 11 June, 1881. 2nd Lieut. 6th Inf., 19 July, 1881. 1st Lieut., 16 July, 1889. Capt., 7 July, 1897. Maj. A. A. G. Vols., 26 Nov., 1898, to 19 July, 1899. Col. 34th U. S. Vols., 5 July, 1899, to—.

KENSEL, GEORGE A.* [Born in Penn. Appointed from Ky.]
Bvt. 2nd Lieut. 4th Art., 1 July, 1857. 2nd Lieut., 17 Aug., 1857. 1st Lieut., 1 March, 1861. Trans. to 5th Art., 14 May, 1861. Capt. A. Q. M., 3 Aug., 1861. Capt. 5th Art., 8 Oct., 1862. Vacated commission of Capt. A. Q. M., 8 Oct., 1862. Bvt. Maj., 20 Sept., 1863, for gallant and meritorious service in the Battle of Chickamauga, Ga. Lieut. Col. A. I. G. (Act 17 July, 1862), 9 Nov., 1863. Bvt. Lieut. Col., 13 March, 1865, for meritorious service while serving as Chief of Art. of the Dept. of the Gulf and of Virginia and North Carolina, and for gallant conduct in action at Drury's Bluff, Va. Bvt. Col. Vols., 13 March, 1865, for

gallant and meritorious service during the war. Relieved as Lieut. Col. A. I. G., 1 Aug., 1865. Died 17 April, 1881.

KENT, JACOB F.* [Born in Penn. Appointed from Penn.]
2nd Lieut. 3rd Inf., 6 May, 1861. 1st Lieut., 31 July, 1861. Lieut. Col. A. I. G., 1 Jan., 1863. Bvt. Maj., 3 May, 1863, for gallant and meritorious service in the Battle of Marye's Heights, Va. Capt. 3rd Inf., 8 Jan., 1864. Bvt. Lieut. Col., 12 May, 1864, for gallant and meritorious service in the Battle of Spottsylvania, Va. Bvt. Col., 19 Oct., 1864, for faithful and meritorious service in the field during the campaign before Richmond, Va. Relieved as Lieut. Col. A. I. G., 31 Aug., 1865. Maj. 4th Inf., 1 July, 1885. Lieut. Col. 18th Inf., 15 Jan., 1891. Col. 24th Inf., 25 April, 1895. Brig. Gen. Vols., 4 May, 1898. Maj. Gen. Vols., 8 July to 30 Nov., 1898. Brig. Gen., 4 Oct., 1898. Retired after forty years' service 15 Oct., 1898.

KENT, WM. A. [Born in D. C. Appointed from D. C.]
Sergt. Co. E, 1st D. C. Vols., 15 May, 1898. Trans. to 3rd U. S. Vol. Eng., 23 June, 1898. Sergt. Maj., 30 June, 1898. 2nd Lieut., 14 Sept., 1898. Mustered out 17 May, 1899. 2nd Lieut. 23rd Inf., 1 June, 1899.

KEOGH, MYLES W. [Born in Ireland. Appointed from D. C.]
Capt. A. A. de C., 9 April, 1862. Maj. A. de C. Vols., 7 April, 1864. Bvt. Lieut. Col. Vols., 13 March, 1865, for uniform gallantry and good conduct during the war. Mustered out 1 Sept., 1866. 2nd Lieut. 4th Cav., 4 May, 1866. Capt. 7th Cav., 28 July, 1866. Killed 25 June, 1876, in action with Indians in Montana Territory. Bvt. Maj., 2 March, 1867, for gallant and meritorious service in the Battle of Gettysburg, Pa. Bvt. Lieut. Col., 2 March, 1867, for gallant and meritorious service in the Battle of Dallas, Ga.

KEPHART, SAMUEL A.* [Born in Penn. Appointed from Penn.]
Addl. 2nd Lieut. 3rd Art., 11 June, 1892. 2nd Lieut. 4th Art., 28 Nov., 1892. 1st Lieut., 2 March, 1899. Graduate of the Artillery School, 1896.

KER, CROGHAN. [Born in La. Appointed from La.]
2nd Lieut. 2nd Drag., 8 June, 1836. 1st Lieut., 6 Oct., 1836. Capt., 8 March, 1840. Resigned 10 Nov., 1851.

KER, DAVID C. [Born in Va. Appointed from Va.]
Hosp. Surg., 30 April, 1812. Post Surg., 18 April, 1818, declined 5 June, 1818.

KER, WM. H. [Born in Va. Appointed rfom La.]
2nd Lieut. 1st Inf., 14 Aug., 1817. 1st Lieut., 31 March, 1818. Capt., 1 Dec., 1820. Resigned 21 May, 1829.

KERIN, JOSEPH. [Born in Ireland. Appointed from Army.]
Priv. Co. B, 2nd Drag., 3 Jan., 1853. Discharged 3 Jan., 1858. Priv. Gen. Mounted Ser., 5 Aug., 1858. Corpl., 15 Nov., 1858. Sergt., 1 Jan., 1859. 2nd Lieut. 6th Cav., 26 Oct., 1861. Bvt. 1st Lieut., 27 May, 1862, for gallant and meritorious service in the Battle of Hanover C. H., Va. 1st Lieut. 6th Cav., 23 Dec., 1862. Reg. Adj., 18 May to 25 Oct., 1863. Bvt. Capt., 1 April, 1865, for gallant and meritorious service in the Battle of Beverly Ford, Va., 9 June, 1863. Capt. 6th Cav., 28 July, 1866. Retired 28 June, 1878. Died 24 Sept., 1890.

KERNAN, FRANCIS J.* [Born in Fla. Appointed from Fla.]
2nd Lieut. 21st Inf., 11 June, 1881. 1st Lieut., 28 Sept., 1889. Capt. 2nd Inf., 26 April, 1898.

KERR, FREDERICK B.* [Born in Penn. Appointed from Penn.]
2nd Lieut. 22nd Inf., 15 Feb., 1899.

KERR, JAMES C. [Born in Del. Appointed from Del.]
Post Chap., 8 April, 1890. Died 2 March, 1896.

KERR, JAMES T. [Born in Ohio. Appointed from Ohio.]
2nd Lieut. 17th Inf., 11 June, 1881. 1st Lieut., 30 Aug., 1890. Capt., 26 April, 1898. Honor graduate of the Infantry and Cavalry School, 1897.

KERR, JOHN B.* [Born in Ky. Appointed from Ky.]
2nd Lieut. 6th Cav., 15 June, 1870. 1st Lieut., 1 Aug., 1874. Capt., 3 Jan., 1885. Maj. 10th Cav., 24 Oct., 1898. Medal of Honor for distinguished bravery in command of his troop in action against hostile Sioux Indians on the north bank of the White River, near the mouth of Little Grass Creek, S. Dak., Jan. 1, 1891, while Capt. of 6th Cav.

KERR, JOHN M.* [Born in N. C. Appointed from N. C.]
Bvt. 2nd Lieut. Mounted Rifles, 1 July, 1860. Dropped 13 July, 1861.

KERR, ROBERT D. [Born in ———. Appointed from ———.]
Addl. 2nd Lieut. Eng., 26 April, 1898. Died at sea 21 July, 1898.

KERR, ROBT. E. [Born in D. C. Appointed from D. C.]
Asst. Surg., 2 May, 1826. Resigned 31 Aug., 1833.

KERR, WM. H. [Born in D. C. Appointed from D. C.]
Cadet at Mil. Acad., 24 Feb., 1815, to 31 Aug., 1819. 2nd Lieut. Corps Art., 27 Oct., 1820. Trans. to 3rd Art., 1 June, 1821. Died 21 Jan., 1827.

KERTH, MONROE C.* [Born in Ill. Appointed from Ill.]
2nd Lieut. 23rd Inf., 26 April, 1898. 1st Lieut. 2 March, 1899.

KERWIN, ARTHUR R.* [Born in N. Y. Appointed from N. Y.]
Addl. 2nd Lieut. 25th Inf., 12 June, 1896. 2nd Lieut. 24th Inf., 22 Dec., 1896. 1st Lieut. 13th Inf., 7 Jan., 1899.

KESSLER, PERCY M.* [Born in Ind. Appointed from Ind.]
Addl. 2nd Lieut. 2nd Art., 12 June, 1896. 2nd Lieut. 3rd Art., 17 June, 1897. 1st Lieut., 2 March, 1899.

KETCHAM, DANIEL W.* [Born in Ind. Appointed from Ind.]
Addl. 2nd Lieut. 2nd Art., 12 June, 1890. 2nd Lieut., 15 June, 1891. 1st Lieut. 6th Art., 8 March, 1898. Graduate of the Artillery School, 1894.

KETCHAM, CORNELIUS. [Born in N. Y. Apointed from Ohio.]
2nd Lieut. of Inf., 8 March, 1847; 13th Inf., 9 April, 1847. 1st Lieut., 31 Dec., 1847. Disbanded 4 Aug., 1848.

KETCHUM, DANIEL. [Born in Conn. Appointed from Conn.]
2nd Lieut. 25th Inf., 6 July, 1812. 1st Lieut., 13 March, 1813. Capt., 30 Sept.,

1813. Trans. to 6th Inf., 17 May, 1815. Died 30 Aug., 1828. Bvt. Maj., 25 July, 1814, for distinguished service and gallant conduct at the Battle of Niagara.

KETCHUM, HIRAM H. [Born in Canada. Appointed from N. Y.]
Priv. Co. K, 16th N. Y. Vols., 20 Sept., 1861. Discharged 29 Sept., 1862. Priv. Co. I, 1st N. Y. Eng., 10 Sept., 1864. Discharged 30 May, 1865. 2nd Lieut. 13th Inf., 23 Feb., 1866. Trans. to 22nd Inf., 21 Sept., 1866. 1st Lieut., 31 July, 1867. Reg. Adj., 1 March, 1869, to 1 Oct., 1881. Capt., 20 July, 1882. Maj., 26 April, 1898. Died 12 Aug., 1898.

KETCHUM, JAMES M.* [Born in N. Y. Appointed at Large.]
2nd Lieut. 3rd Art., 1 July, 1838. 1st Lieut., 1 Dec., 1838. Resigned 30 April, 1844. Died 8 June, 1844.

KETCHUM, THOMAS.* [Born in N. Y. Appointed from N. Y.]
2nd Lieut. Light Art., 1 March, 1811. 1st Lieut., 1 Sept., 1811. Capt., 31 Aug., 1814. Disbanded 15 June, 1815.

KETCHUM, WM. S.* [Born in Conn. Appointed from Conn.]
Bvt. 2nd Lieut. 6th Inf., 1 July, 1834. 2nd Lieut., 31 Dec., 1836. 1st Lieut., 25 Dec., 1837. Reg. Adj., 1 Oct., 1838, to 28 Feb., 1839. Capt. A. Q. M., 28 Feb., 1839, to 2 April, 1846. Capt. 6th Inf., 10 Feb., 1842. Maj. 4th Inf., 5 June, 1860. Lieut. Col. 10th Inf., 1 Nov., 1861. Brig. Gen. Vols., 3 Feb., 1862. Mustered out of Vol. Service, 30 April, 1866. Col. 11th Inf., 6 May, 1864. Unassigned 15 March, 1869. Retired 15 Dec., 1870. Died 28 June, 1871. Bvt. Col., 1 Feb., 1863, for meritorious service in Missouri in the line of the army. Bvt. Brig. Gen., 13 March, 1865, for faithful and meritorious service during the war. Bvt. Maj. Gen., 13 March, 1865, for diligent, faithful and meritorious service in the War Dept.

KETELTAS, HENRY. [Born in N. Y. Appointed from N. Y.]
Capt. 15th Inf., 5 Aug., 1861. Resigned 17 June, 1867. Bvt. Maj., 7 April, 1862, for gallant and meritorious service at the Battle of Shiloh, Tenn. Bvt. Lieut. Col., 25 Nov., 1863, for gallant and meritorious service at the Battle of Chickamauga, Ga., and Mission Ridge, Tenn.

KEYE, FREDK. [Born in Germany. Appointed from Army.]
Priv., Corpl. and Sergt. Co. K, 1st Art., 18 April, 1861, to 15 July, 1867. 2nd Lieut. 10th Inf., 2 July, 1867. Resigned 6 May, 1869. Priv., Sergt. and 1st Sergt. Co. D, 20th Inf., 12 March, 1870, to 12 March, 1875.

KEYES, ALEXR. S. B. [Born in Mass. Appointed from Mass.]
Priv. Co. A, 59th Mass. Vols., 31 Oct., 1863. Sergt., ———. Sergt. Maj., 1 May, 1864. Discharged 30 June, 1864. 2nd Lieut. 1st Mass. Art., 5 July, 1864. Mustered out 20 Oct., 1865. 2nd Lieut. 12th Inf., 23 Feb., 1866. Trans. to 30th Inf., 21 Sept., 1866. 1st Lieut., 9 Feb., 1867. Reg. Adj., 10 Nov., 1868, to 23 March, 1869. Bvt. Capt., 2 March, 1867, for gallant and meritorious service during the war. Unassigned 23 March, 1869. Ass'd to 10th Cav., 2 April, 1870. Capt., 6 Dec., 1873. Maj. 3rd Cav., 20 Oct., 1892. Retired for disability 27 Aug., 1896.

KEYES, CHAS. W. [Born in Maine. Appointed from Maine.]
Sergt. Co. B, 28th Maine Vols., 10 Sept., 1862. Hosp. Steward 28th Maine Vols., 1 March, 1863. Discharged 31 Aug., 1863. Priv. 2nd Maine Cav., 10 Nov., 1863. Discharged 27 Feb., 1864. 1st Lieut. 32nd Maine Vols., 2 April, 1864. Mustered out 27 Sept., 1864. 2nd Lieut. Maine Coast Guard, 20 Jan., 1865. Mustered out 7 July, 1865. 2nd Lieut. 44th Inf., 28 July, 1866. Bvt. 1st Lieut., 2 March, 1867, for gallant and meritorious service in action at Fort Buker, La. Bvt. Capt., 2 March, 1867, for gallant and meritorious service in the Battle of Spottsylvania C. H., Va. Unassigned 27 May, 1869. Retired with rank of 1st Lieut., 31 Dec., 1870.

KEYES, EDWARD L. [Born in Mass. Appointed from Mass.]
2nd Lieut. 5th Cav., 27 July, 1872. Dismissed 28 April, 1877.

KEYES, ERASMUS D.* [Born in Mass. Appointed from Maine.]
Bvt. 2nd Lieut. 3rd Art., 1 July, 1832. 2nd Lieut., 1 Aug., 1833. 1st Lieut., 16 Sept., 1836. Capt. A. A. G., 7 July to 16 Nov., 1838. Capt. 3rd Art., 30 Nov., 1841. Maj. 1st Art., 12 Oct., 1858. Lieut. Col. Mil. Sec. to Bvt. Lieut. Scott, 1 Jan., 1860, to 19 April, 1861. Brig. Gen. Vols., 17 May, 1861. Maj. Gen. Vols., 5 May, 1862. Col. 11th Inf., 14 May, 1861. Resigned 6 May, 1864. Bvt. Brig. Gen., 31 May, 1862, for gallant and meritorious conduct at the Battle of Fair Oaks, Va.

KEYES, HAMLIN W. [Born in Conn. Appointed from Mass.]
Maj. 5th Mass. Vols., 1 May to 26 June, 1861. Capt. 14th Inf., 14 May, 1861. Died 18 June, 1864, of wounds received at Battle of Laurel Hill, Va. Bvt. Maj., 5 May, 1864, for gallant and meritorious service at the Battle of the Wilderness, Va.

KEYES, MAXWELL. [Born in ———. Appointed from ———.]
2nd Lieut. 3rd Inf., — ———, 1899. Killed in action in Ildefonso, Philippine Islands, 24 Nov., 1899.

KEYES, PATRICK T. [Born in Penn. Appointed from Penn.]
1st Lieut. 16th Inf., 14 May, 1861. Capt., 24 Dec., 1861. Died 3 May, 1862, of wounds received at the Battle of Shiloh, Tenn.

KIBBY, EPAPHRAS.* [Born in Mo. Appointed from Ohio.]
Bvt. 2nd Lieut. 1st Art., 1 July, 1834. 2nd Lieut. 2nd Art., 25 Jan., 1835. 1st Lieut., 31 Dec., 1836. Resigned 31 Dec., 1837. Died 15 Sept., 1839.

KIDD, MEREDITH H. [Born in Ind. Appointed from Ind.]
Maj. 10th Cav., 6 March, 1864. Discharged 31 Dec., 1870.

KIDD, WM. [Born in N. Y. Appointed from N. Y.]
2nd Lieut. 2nd Inf., 26 Nov., 1861. Killed 30 Aug., 1862, Battle of Bull Run, Va. Bvt. 1st Lieut., 27 June, 1862, for gallant and meritorious service at the Battle of Gaines' Mills, Va. Bvt. Capt., 30 Aug., 1862, for gallant and meritorious service at the Battle of Bull Run (2nd), Va.

KIDDER, LYMAN S. [Born in Vt. Appointed from Dak.]
Corpl. K, 5th Iowa Cav., 1 Nov., 1861. 1st Lieut. 1st Minn. Cav., 6 June, 1863. Mustered out 28 Nov., 1863. Priv., Sergt. and 1st Sergt. Co. E, Hatch's Batt.

Minn. Cav., 20 Aug., 1864. Mustered out 1 May, 1866. 2nd Lieut. 2nd Cav., 22 Jan., 1867. Killed by Indians in Kansas, 21 July, 1867.

KIDDOO, JOSEPH B. [Born in Penn. Appointed from Penn.. Priv. Co. K, 12th Penn. Vols., 25 April, 1861. Discharged 5 Aug., 1861. Priv. Co. F, 63rd Penn. Vols., 1 Nov., 1861. Corpl., 22 Nov., 1861. Sergt., 1 June, 1862. 1st Sergt., 10 July, 1862. Lieut. Col. 137th Penn. Vols., 25 Aug., 1862. Col., 15 March, 1863. Mustered out 1 June, 1863. Maj. 6th U. S. Col. Troops, 5 Oct., 1863. Col. 22nd U. S. Col. Troops., 6 Jan., 1864. Bvt. Brig. Gen. Vols., 15 June, 1865, and Bvt. Maj. Gen. Vols., 4 Sept., 1865, for gallant and meritorious service during the war. Lieut. Col. 43rd Inf., 28 July, 1866. Mustered out of Vol. Service, 28 Jan, 1867. Bvt. Col., 2 March, 1867, for gallant and meritorious service in the assault on Petersburg, Va., 15 June, 1864. Bvt. Brig. Gen., 2 March, 1867, for gallant and meritorious service in action at Fair Oaks, Va., 27 Oct., 1864. Unassigned 15 March, 1869. Retired with rank of Brig. Gen., 15 Dec., 1870. Died 19 Aug., 1880.

KIEFFER, CHARLES F. [Born in Penn. Appointed from Penn.] Asst. Surg., 31 Oct., 1891. Capt. Asst. Surg., 31 Oct., 1896. Maj. Surg. 48th U. S. Vols., 9 Sept., 1899, to —.

KIGER, GEORGE R. [Born in Va. Appointed from Miss.] 2nd Lieut. of Inf., 2 March, 1847; Voltigeurs, 9 April, 1847. Disbanded 31 Aug., 1848.

KILBOURNE, CHAS. E.* [Born in Ohio. Appointed from Ohio.] 2nd Lieut. 2nd Art., 18 June, 1866. 1st Lieut., 3 Dec., 1868. Honor graduate of the Artillery School, 1870. Capt. Sig. Corps., 20 Dec., 1890. Maj. P. M., 6 Nov., 1893.

KILBOURNE, CHARLES E., Jr. [Born in Va. Appointed from Ore.] 2nd Lieut. Vol. Sig. Corps, 20 May, 1898. 1st Lieut., 1 July, 1898. 2nd Lieut. 14th Inf., 1 Aug., 1899.

KILBOURNE, HENRY S. [Born in N. Y. Appointed from Wis.] 1st Lieut. Asst. Surg., 26 June, 1875. Capt., Asst. Surg., 26 June, 1880. Maj. Surg., 22 Feb., 1894.

KILBOURNE, LINCOLN F.* [Born in Cal. Appointed from Ohio.] 2nd Lieut. 1st Inf., 12 June, 1893. 1st Lieut., 26 April, 1898. Trans. to 3rd Inf., 20 May, 1899.

KILBRETH, JOHN W., Jr. [Born in N. Y. Appointed from N. Y.] 2nd Lieut. 4th Art., 9 Sept., 1898.

KILBURN, CHAS. L.* [Born in Penn. Appointed from Penn.] Bvt. 2nd Lieut. 1st Art., 1 July, 1842. Trans. to 3rd Art., 1 July, 1843. 2nd Lieut., 27 June, 1844. Bvt. 1st Lieut., 23 Sept., 1846, for gallant and meritorious conduct at Monterey. 1st Lieut. 3rd Art., 16 Feb., 1847. Bvt. Capt., 23 Feb., 1847, for gallant and meritorious conduct in the Battle of Buena Vista. Capt. C. S., 13 Sept., 1853. Vacated commission of 1st Lieut. 3rd Art., 11 Nov., 1856. Maj. C. S., 11 May, 1861. Lieut. Col. A. C. G. S., 9 Feb., 1863. Col. A. C. G. S., 29 June, 1864. Bvt. Brig. Gen., 13 March, 1865, for faithful and meritorious service during the war. Retired 20 May, 1882. Died 17 March, 1899.

KILBURN, DANA W.* [Born in Penn. Appointed from Ill.] Cadet at Mil. Acad., 15 June, 1889, to 17 Jan., 1890. Reappointed 17 June, 1890. 2nd Lieut. 1st Inf., 12 June, 1894. 1st Lieut. 3rd Inf., 26 April, 1898. Trans. to 8th Inf., 14 Aug., 1899.

KILGOUR, WM. M. [Born in Penn. Appointed from Ill.] 2nd Lieut. 13th Ill. Vols., 24 May, 1861. Resigned 3 Feb., 1862. Maj. 75th Ill. Vols., 2 Sept., 1862. Lieut. Col., 3 Feb., 1863. Bvt. Lieut. Col. and Brig. Gen. Vols., 20 June, 1865, for meritorious service. Mustered out 12 June, 1865. Capt. 41st Inf., 28 July, 1866. Bvt. Maj., 2 March, 1867, for gallant and meritorious service in the Battle of Mission Ridge, Tenn. Bvt. Lieut. Col., 2 March, 1867, for gallant and meritorious service in the Battle of Atlanta, Ga. Bvt. Col., 2 March, 1867, for gallant and meritorious service in the Battle of Nashville, Tenn. Wholly retired 16 Dec., 1867. Reinstated as Capt. 24th Inf., 8 March, 1873. Retired 20 June, 1873. Died 29 May, 1885.

KILPATRICK, ANDREW E. [Born in Miss. Appointed from Miss.] 2nd Lieut. 17th Inf., 15 Oct., 1875. Resigned 30 June, 1880.

KILPATRICK, JUDSON.* [Born in N. J. Appointed from N. J.] 2nd Lieut. 1st Art., 6 May, 1861. 1st Lieut., 14 May, 1861. Capt. 5th N. Y. Vols., 9 May to 6 Sept., 1861. When he resigned from Vol. Service Lieut. Col. A. A. de C., 29 Jan., 1862. Discharged 21 March, 1862. Lieut. Col. 2nd N. Y. Cav., 25 Sept., 1861. Col., 6 Dec., 1862. Brig. Gen. Vols., 13 June, 1863. Maj. Gen. Vols., 18 June, 1865. Resigned from Vol. Service 1 Jan., 1866. Capt. 1st Art., 30 Nov., 1864. Resigned 1 Dec., 1865. Bvt. Maj., 17 June, 1863, for gallant and meritorious service at the Battle of Aldie, Va. Bvt. Lieut. Col., 3 July, 1863, for gallant and meritorious service at the Battle of Gettysburg, Pa. Bvt. Col., 13 May, 1864, for gallant and meritorious service at the Battle of Resaca, Ga. Bvt. Brig. Gen., 13 March, 1865, for gallant and meritorious service in the capture of Fayetteville, N. C. Bvt. Maj. Gen., 13 March, 1865, and Bvt. Maj. Gen. Vols., 12 Jan., 1865, for gallant and meritorious service during the campaign in the Carolinas. Died 2 Dec., 1881.

KILPATRICK, ROBT. L. [Born in Scotland. Appointed from Ohio.] Capt. 5th Ohio Vols., 9 May, 1861. Lieut. Col., 8 April, 1863. Mustered out 17 Aug., 1864. Capt. Vet. Res. Corps, 28 Sept., 1864. Bvt. Maj. and Lieut. Col. Vols., 13 March, 1865, for gallant and meritorious service during the war. Mustered out 30 June, 1866. Capt. 42nd Inf., 28 July, 1866. Bvt. Maj., 2 March, 1867, for gallantry in the Battle of Port Republic, 9 June, 1862. Bvt. Lieut. Col., 2 March, 1867, for gallantry in the Battle of Chancellorsville, Va. Unassigned 22 April, 1869. Retired with rank of Col., 15 Dec., 1870. Died 8 May, 1895.

KIMBALL, AMOS S. [Born in N. Y. Appointed from N. Y.] 1st Lieut. 98th N. Y. Vols., 27 Nov., 1861. Discharged 1 May, 1864. Capt. A. Q. M.

Vols., 7 April, 1864. Bvt. Maj. Vols., 1 Feb., 1866, for faithful and efficient service in the Q. M. Dept. Capt. A. Q. M. U. S. A., 19 Nov., 1866. Maj. Q. M., 11 Oct., 1883. Lieut. Col. Dep. Q. M. Gen., 31 Dec., 1894. Col. A. Q. M. G., 13 Nov., 1898. Col. Q. M. Vols., 12 July, 1898, to 28 Nov., 1898.

KIMBALL, EDGAR A. [Born in N. H. Appointed from Vt.]
Capt. of Inf., 8 March, 1847; 9th Inf., 9 April, 1847. Disbanded 26 Aug., 1848. Bvt. Maj., 20 Aug., 1847, for gallant and meritorious conduct at Contreras and Churubusco, Mex. Maj. 9th N. Y. Vols., 4 May, 1861. Lieut. Col., 14 Feb., 1862. Killed 12 April, 1863, by Gen. Michael Corcoran.

KIMBALL, FREDERICK C.* [Born in Maine Appointed from Maine.]
2nd Lieut. 5th Inf., 1 July, 1886. 1st Lieut. of Inf. (4th), 4 April, 1893. Trans. to 5th Inf., 10 July, 1893. R. Q. M., 21 Sept., 1893. Died 11 Sept., 1897.

KIMBALL, JAMES P. [Born in N. Y. Appointed from N. Y.]
Asst. Surg. 121st N. Y. Vols., 16 Jan., 1865. Trans. to 65th N. Y. Vols., 26 June, 1865. Mustered out 17 July, 1865. 1st Lieut. Asst. Surg., 14 May, 1867. Capt. Asst. Surg., 12 Nov., 1869. Maj. Surg., 24 Jan., 1886. Lieut. Col. Surg, 1900.

KIMBALL, WM. A. [Born in Ind. Appointed from Utah.]
Cadet at Mil. Acad., 1 July, 1872, to 14 Jan., 1873. 2nd Lieut. 14th Inf., 31 Aug., 1876. 1st Lieut., 6 May, 1890. Graduate of Infantry and Cavalry School, 1883. Retired, with the rank of Capt., 13 Aug., 1894.

KIMMEL, MANNING M.* [Born in Mo. Appointed from Mo.]
Bvt. 2nd Lieut. 2nd Cav., 1 July, 1857. 2nd Lieut., 18 Aug., 1858. 1st Lieut., 1 April, 1861. Resigned 14 Aug., 1861.

KIMMEL, EDWARD. [Born in Iowa. Appointed from Wash'n..
1st Sergt. Co. K, 1st Wash'n Vols., 12 May to 4 Aug., 1898. 2nd Lieut. 3rd Art., 9 July, 1898.

KINCAID, JOHN W. [Born in Va. Appointed from Va.]
2nd Lieut. 2nd Art., 15 May, 1812. Trans. to Corps Art., 12 May, 1814. 1st Lieut., 17 May, 1816. Resigned 20 April, 1817.

KING, ALBERT A. [Born in Iowa. Appointed from the Army.]
Priv., Corpl. and Sergt. Troop I, 1st Cav., 6 Jan., 1896, to 17 Nov., 1899. 2nd Lieut. 7th Cav., 1 Oct., 1899.

KING, ALBERT D. [Born in Ohio. Appointed from Ohio.]
Priv. Co. F, 2nd Cav., 15 Aug., 1864. Discharged 27 June, 1866. 2nd Lieut. 3rd Cav., 5 Oct., 1867. 1st Lieut., 8 July, 1870. Capt., 26 June, 1881. Retired for disability 22 April, 1891.

KING, BENJN. [Born in Md. Appointed from Md..
Surg. Mate. 7th Inf., 14 Oct., 1818. Asst. Surg., 1 June, 1821. Retired 9 Nov., 1863. Died 24 June, 1888.

KING, CAMPBELL. [Born in N. C. Appointed from Ga.]
Priv. and Corpl. Troop K, 5th Cav., 31 July, 1897, to 25 July, 1898. 2nd Lieut. 1st Inf., 9 July, 1898. 1st Lieut., 2 March, 1899.

KING, CHARLES.* [Born in N. Y. Appointed at Large.]
2nd Lieut. 1st Art., 18 June, 1866. 1st Lieut., 15 May, 1870. Trans. to 5th Cav., 1 Jan., 1871. Reg. Adj., 5 Oct., 1876, to 28 Jan., 1878. Capt., 1 May, 1879. Retired 14 June, 1879. Bvt. Capt., 27 Feb., 1890, for gallant and distinguished services in action against Indians near Diamond Butte, Ariz., 21 May, 1874 (declined). Brig. Gen. Vols., 27 May, 1898, to 15 April, 1899, and same from 15 April to 2 Aug., 1899.

KING, CORNELIUS L. [Born in N. Y. Appointed from N. Y.]
1st Lieut. 14th Inf., 14 May, 1861. R. Q. M., 8 July to 31 Dec., 1861. Capt., 19 Feb., 1862. Trans. to 30th Inf., 21 Sept., 1866. Resigned 30 July, 1868. Bvt. Maj. 1 Aug., 1864, for gallant service at the Battle of the Wilderness, Va. Bvt. Lieut. Col., 1 Aug., 1864, for gallant and meritorious service at the Battle of Spottsylvania, Va.

KING, DAVID M.* [Born in Ohio. Appointed from Ohio.]
Addl. 2nd Lieut. 4th Art., 12 June, 1893. 2nd Lieut., 1 Aug., 1893. 1st Lieut. Ord., 21 Nov., 1898.

KING, EDWARD A. [Born in N. Y. Appointed from Ohio.]
Capt. of Inf., 9 March, 1847; 15th Inf., 9 April, 1847. Disbanded 4 Aug., 1848. Col. Ohio Vols., 17 April to 24 June, 1861. Lieut. Col. 19th Inf., 14 May, 1861. Col. 6th Inf., 1 Aug., 1863. Killed 20 Sept., 1863, at Battle of Chickamauga, Ga.

KING, EDWARD L.* [Born in Mass. Appointed from Mass.]
Addl. 2nd Lieut. 8th Cav., 12 June, 1896. Trans. to 7th Cav., 18 Aug., 1896. 2nd Lieut. 9th Cav., 22 Dec., 1896. Trans. to 7th Cav., 23 July, 1897. Trans. to 8th Cav., 19 Aug., 1898. Capt. 11th U. S. Vol. Cav., 11 Aug., 1899.

KING, JAMES S. [Born in West Indies. Appointed from N. Y.]
Priv. Co. B, 7th N. Y. State Militia, 26 April to 3 June, 1861. 2nd Lieut. 65th N. Y. Vols., 2 July, 1861. 1st Lieut., 11 Jan., 1862. Mustered out 9 July, 1862. Capt. 162nd N. Y. Vols., 14 Oct., 1862. Mustered out 14 Aug., 1863. 1st Lieut. 79th N. Y. Vols., 7 Oct., 1864. Capt., 1 July, 1865. Mustered out 14 July, 1865. 2nd Lieut. 13th Inf., 11 May, 1866. Trans. to 31st Inf., 21 Sept., 1866. Unassigned 15 May, 1869. Ass'd to 12th Inf., 14 July, 1869. 1st Lieut., 7 Feb., 1871. Capt., 11 Jan., 1881. Died 16 Oct., 1882.

KING, JOHN C. [Born in Penn. Appointed from Penn.]
1st Lieut. 16th Inf., 14 May, 1861. Capt., 7 April, 1862. Resigned 24 Sept., 1864. Capt. C. S. Vols., 21 Jan., 1865. Mustered out 28 June, 1865.

KING, JOHN H. [Born in Mich. Appointed from Mich.]
2nd Lieut. 1st Inf., 2 Dec., 1837. 1st Lieut., 2 March, 1839. Capt., 31 Oct., 1846. Maj. 15th Inf., 14 May, 1861. Brig. Gen. Vols., 29 Nov., 1862. Lieut. Col. 14th Inf., 1 June, 1863. Bvt. Col., 20 Sept., 1863, for gallant and meritorious service in the Battle of Chickamauga, Ga. Bvt. Brig. Gen., 13 March, 1865, for gallant and meritorious service in the Battle of Ruff's Station, Ga. Bvt. Maj. Gen., 13 March, 1865, for gallant and meritorious service in the field during the war. Bvt. Maj. Gen. Vols., 31 May, 1865, for gallant and meritorious ser-

vice during the war. Col. 9th Inf., 30 July, 1865. Mustered out of Vol. Service, 15 Jan., 1866. Retired at his own request, for over 62 years of age, 20 Feb., 1882. Died 7 April, 1888.

KING, JOSEPH H. T. [Born in England. Appointed from N. Y.]
1st Lieut. Asst. Surg., 9 Oct., 1867. Capt. Asst. Surg., 9 Oct., 1870. Resigned 30 June, 1881.

KING, JOSIAH H. [Born in Penn. Appointed from Penn.]
Cadet at Mil. Acad., 1 July, 1871, to 28 June, 1873. 2nd Lieut. 8th Cav., 15 Aug., 1876. 1st Lieut., 23 May, 1883. Graduate of the Infantry and Cavalry School. 1883. Retired with rank of Capt., for disability, 20 April, 1891.

KING, JOSIAS R. [Born in D. C. Appointed from Minn.]
Priv. and 1st Sergt. Co. A, 1st Minn. Vols., 29 April, 1861. 2nd Lieut., 18 Sept., 1861. 1st Lieut., 10 July, 1862. Capt., 2 July, 1863. Mustered out 5 May, 1864. Lieut. Col. 2nd U. S. Vol. Inf., 1 March, 1865. Mustered out 7 Nov., 1865. 2nd Lieut. 2nd Inf., 26 May, 1866. 1st Lieut., 1 Oct., 1868. Unassigned 17 April, 1869. Discharged 31 Dec., 1870.

KING, ROBT. [Born in ——. Appointed from Mo.]
2nd Lieut. Mounted Rangers, 30 July, 1832. Disbanded — March, 1833.

KING, ROBT. P., Jr. [Born in Penn. Appointed from Army.]
Priv. Co. C, 19th Penn. Vols., 27 April to 30 June, 1861. 1st Lieut. 15th Inf., 14 May, 1861. Rejected by Senate, 5 Aug., 1861. Priv. 15th Inf., 11 Oct. to 30 Oct., 1861. 2nd Lieut. 15th Inf., 30 Oct., 1861. 1st Lieut., 27 May, 1862. Resigned 30 Jan., 1865.

KING, RUFUS.* [Born in N. Y. Appointed from N. Y.]
Bvt. 2nd Lieut. Eng., 1 July, 1833. Resigned 30 Sept., 1836. Brig. Gen. Vols., 17 May, 1861. Resigned 20 Oct., 1863. Died 13 Oct., 1876.

KING, RUFUS, Jr. [Born in N. Y. Appointed from N. Y.]
Priv. Co. F, 7th N. Y. Militia, 26 April to 3 June, 1861. 2nd Lieut. 4th Art., 5 Aug., 1861. 1st Lieut., 5 Aug., 1861. Capt., 4 April, 1869. Mustered out 1 Jan., 1871. Bvt. Capt., 30 June, 1862, for gallant and meritorious service at the Battle of White Oak Swamp, Va. Bvt. Maj., 13 March, 1865, for good conduct and gallant service during the war.

KING, THOS. GROSVENOR. [Born in N. Y. Appointed from N. Y.]
Mil. Storekeeper Q. M. Dept., 24 July, 1843. Cashiered 23 Dec., 1847.

KING, WM. [Born in Del. Appointed from Md.]
2nd Lieut. 5th Inf., 3 May, 1808. 1st Lieut., 30 Sept., 1810. Reg. Adj., March, 1811, to July, 1812. Capt. 15th Inf., 2 July, 1812. Maj., 3 March, 1813. Maj. A. A. G., 28 April, 1813. Col. A. G., 18 July, 1813. Col. 3rd Rifle, 21 Feb., 1814. Trans. to 4th Inf., 17 May, 1815. Disbanded 1 June, 1821. Died 1 Jan., 1826.

KING, WM. [Born in Mass. Appointed from Mass.]
2nd Lieut. 3rd Art., 12 March, 1812. 1st Lieut., 1 Oct., 1813. Trans. to Corps Art., 12 May, 1814. Disbanded 15 June, 1815. Reinstated 2 Dec., 1815. Trans. to 8th Inf., 13 March, 1816. Resigned 1 July, 1816. Died — July, 1827.

KING, WM. H. [Born in Penn. Appointed from Penn.]
Asst. Surg. 149th Penn. Vols., 23 May, 1863. Mustered out 30 July, 1863. Maj. Surg. 21st Penn. Cav., 5 Aug., 1863. Mustered out 8 July, 1865. 1st Lieut. Asst. Surg., 16 Nov., 1868. Capt. Asst. Surg., 6 Oct., 1869. Died 23 Aug., 1883.

KING, WM. H. [Born in N. Y. Appointed from N. Y.]
Capt. 34th N. Y. Vols., 15 June, 1861. Resigned 1 Jan., 1863. Capt. Vet. Res. Corps, 11 Aug., 1863. Bvt. Maj. and Lieut. Col. Vols., 13 March, 1865, for faithful and meritorious service. Mustered out 19 April, 1866. 2nd Lieut. 10th Inf., 23 Feb., 1866. 1st Lieut., 14 March, 1866. Died 23 Aug., 1870. Bvt. Capt., 2 March, 1867, for gallant and meritorious service at the Battle of Fair Oaks, Va., in May, 1862.

KING, WM. R.* [Born in N. Y. Appointed from N. Y.]
1st Lieut. Eng., 11 June, 1863. Bvt. Capt., 1 Dec., 1864, for gallant and meritorious service during the campaign of 1864 in the district of North Carolina. Bvt. Maj., 9 April, 1865, for gallant conduct in the field. Capt. Eng., 31 Dec., 1865. Maj., 4 March, 1879. Lieut. Col., 23 July, 1888. Died 18 May, 1898.

KING, WM. S. [Born in Penn. Appointed from Penn.]
Asst. Surg., 29 July, 1837. Capt. Asst. Surg., 11 Feb., 1847. Maj. Surg., 29 Aug., 1856. Bvt. Lieut. Col. and Col., 13 March, 1865, for faithful and meritorious service during the war. Lieut. Col. Surg., 26 June, 1876. Col. Surg., 17 March, 1880. Retired, by operation of law, 30 June, 1882. Died 2 Aug., 1895.

KING, WM. W. [Born in ——. Appointed from ——.]
2nd Lieut. 1st Inf., 28 Jan., 1820. Dismissed 21 Nov., 1820.

KINGMAN, DANIEL C.* [Born in N. H. Appointed from N. H.]
2nd Lieut. Eng., 16 June, 1875. 1st Lieut., 4 March, 1879. Capt., 20 April, 1886. Maj., 31 July, 1897.

KINGSBURY, CHAS E. [Born in Conn. Appointed from Conn.]
2nd Lieut. 2nd Drag., 8 June, 1836. Died 9 June, 1837.

KINGSBURY, CHARLES P.* [Born in N. Y. Appointed from N. C.]
2nd Lieut. Ord., 1 July, 1840. Bvt. 1st Lieut., 23 Feb., 1847, for gallant and meritorious conduct in the Battle of Buena Vista. 1st Lieut. Ord., 3 March, 1847. Capt., 1 July, 1854. Col. A. A. de C., 28 Sept., 1861. Appointment of A. A. de C. expired by constitutional limitation 17 July, 1862. Maj. Ord., 3 March, 1863. Bvt. Lieut. Col. and Col., 13 March, 1865, for faithful and meritorious service during the war. Bvt. Brig. Gen., 13 March, 1865, for gallant and meritorious service during the war. Lieut. Col. Ord., 22 Dec., 1866. Retired 31 Dec., 1870. Died 25 Dec., 1879.

KINGSBURY, FREDERICK W.* [Born in Ohio. Appointed from Wis.]
2nd Lieut. 2nd Cav., 15 June, 1870. 1st Lieut., 1 April, 1880. R. Q. M., 1 April, 1887. Capt. of Cav. (2nd Cav), 5 May, 1892. Died 13 June, 1897.

KINGSBURY, GAINES P.* [Born in Ohio. Appointed from Ohio.]
Bvt. 3rd Lieut. Mounted Rangers, 1 July, 1832. Trans. to 1st Drag., 14 Aug., 1833. 2nd Lieut., 31 May, 1835. 1st Lieut., 4 July, 1836. Resigned 15 Oct., 1836. Died 15 Aug., 1839.

KINGSBURY, GEORGE W. [Born in Vt. Appointed from Vt.]
Priv. Co. K, 16th Vt. Vols., 15 Sept., 1862. Corpl., 1 Oct., 1862. Discharged 10 Aug., 1863. Priv. Co. F, 17th Vt. Vols., 2 Jan., 1864. 2nd Lieut. 17th Vt. Vols., 9 April, 1864. Mustered out 5 Oct., 1864. 2nd Lieut. Vet. Res. Corps, 25 Oct., 1864. Bvt. 1st Lieut. and Capt. Vols., 13 March, 1865, for faithful and meritorious service. Mustered out 5 June, 1867. 2nd Lieut. 43rd Inf., 31 May, 1867. Bvt. 1st Lieut., 31 May, 1867, for gallant and meritorious service in the Battle of the Wilderness, Va. Unassigned 8 April, 1869. Ass'd to 12th Inf. 5 Jan., 1870. 1st Lieut., 3 July, 1874. Reg. Q. M., 1 Feb., 1876, to 1 July, 1879. Retired 26 May, 1886. Appointed Capt. of Inf., 2 Oct., 1890, with rank from 12 Feb., 1886. Retired, for disability from wound, 3 Oct., 1890. Died 22 June, 1897.

KINGSBURY, HENRY P.* [Born in N. C. Appointed at Large.]
2nd Lieut. 6th Cav., 12 June, 1871. 1st Lieut., 27 Jan., 1875. Capt., 5 Oct., 1887. Maj. 3rd Cav., 23 Jan., 1900.

KINGSBURY, HENRY W.* [Born in Ill. Appointed from N. Y.]
Bvt. 2nd Lieut. Ord., 6 May, 1861. 2nd Lieut., 6 May, 1861. 1st Lieut. 5th Art., 14 May, 1861. Col. 11th Conn. Vols., 25 April, 1862. Died 18 Sept., 1862, of wounds received at the Battle of Antietam, Md.

KINGSBURY, JAMES W. [Born in Conn. Appointed from Co[illegible]
Cadet Mil. Acad., 28 Aug., 1819, to 19 June, 1823. 2nd Lieut. 1st Inf., 19 Aug., 1823. 1st Lieut., 1 Aug., 1830. Capt., 3 Oct., 1837. Resigned 17 Oct., 1837. Resigned 17 Oct., 1837. Mil. Storekeeper, 17 Oct., 1837. Resigned 15 July, 1843. Died 25 June, 1853.

KINGSBURY, JULIUS J. B.* [Born in Conn. Appointed from Conn.]
2nd Lieut. 2nd Inf., 1 July, 1823. 1st Lieut., 13 Sept., 1831. Capt., 13 Feb., 1837. Maj. 6th Inf., 7 May, 1849. Dismissed 27 Jan., 1853. Bvt. Maj., 20 Aug., 1847, for gallant and meritorious conduct at Contreras and Churubusco. Died 26 June, 1856.

KINGSBURY, WILLIAM E. [Born in Penn. Appointed from Conn.]
Cadet Mil. Acad., 1 July, 1852, to 29 June, 1853. Priv. Co. I, 7th Inf., 16 Oct., 1857. Discharged 16 Oct., 1862. 1st Lieut. 13th N. Y. Art., 17 Nov., 1863. Mustered out 24 Aug., 1865. 1st Lieut., 24th Inf., 22 Jan., 1867. Trans. to 11th Inf., 25 April, 1869. Capt., 23 Oct., 1882. Retired for disability, 9 Oct., 1885. Died 4 Oct., 1887.

KINLOCH, FREDERICK. [Born in S. C. Appointed from S. C.]
Ensign 18th Inf., 22 Jan., 1813. 3rd Lieut., 13 March, 1813. 2nd Lieut., 11 Sept., 1813. 1st Lieut., 10 Oct., 1814. Trans. to Light Art., 17 May, 1815. Resigned 1 May, 1816.

KINNARD, ANDREW.* [Born in Penn. Appointed from Penn.]
Bvt. 2nd Lieut. 1st Art., 1 July, 1823. 2nd Lieut., 1 July, 1823. Resigned 31 Oct., 1830. Died —, 1831.

KINNEY, CLIFTON C. [Born in Tex. Appointed from Tex.]
2nd Lieut. 13th Inf., 9 July, 1898.

KINNEY, ERNEST L. [Born in N. Y. Appointed from Army.]
2nd Lieut. 54th N. Y. Vols., 9 Jan., 1863. Resigned 14 Nov., 1864. Priv. and Sergt. Co. C, 1st Cav., 17 Nov., 1864, to 20 April, 1865. 2nd Lieut. 1st Cav., 2 Jan., 1865. 1st Lieut., 1 July, 1865. Resigned 8 Aug., 1866. Bvt. 1st Lieut., 1 April, 1865, for gallant and meritorious service at the Battle of Five Forks, Va. Bvt. Capt. and Maj., 25 Oct., 1865, for meritorious service.

KINNEY, NATHANIEL C. [Born in N. Y. Appointed from N. Y.]
1st Lieut. 18th Inf., 14 May, 1861. Reg. Q. M., 5 Oct. to 4 Nov., 1861. Capt., 25 Nov., 1862. Trans. to 27th Inf., 21 Sept., 1866. Resigned 7 Jan., 1867. Bvt. Maj., 31 Dec., 1862, for gallant and meritorious service at the Battle of Murfreesboro, Tenn. Bvt. Lieut. Col., 25 Oct., 1865, for meritorious service during the war.

KINNEY, SAML.* [Born in Ill. Appointed from Ill.]
Bvt. 2nd Lieut. 7th Inf., 1 July, 1830. 2nd Lieut., 1 July, 1830. 1st Lieut., 4 May, 1835. Died 3 Dec., 1835.

KINNEY, SAML. H.* [Born in Ohio. Appointed from Utah.]
2nd Lieut. 2nd Art., 13 June, 1864. 1st Lieut., 6 Oct., 1865. Died 3 Dec., 1868. Bvt. 1st Lieut., 9 April, 1865, for gallant and meritorious service in action at Appomattox C. H., Va. Bvt. Capt., 9 April, 1865, for gallant and meritorious service.

KINNISON, HENRY L. [Born in Mo. Appointed from Army.]
Priv., Corpl. and Sergt. Cos. I and B, 7th Inf., 14 Nov., 1888, to 23 Nov., 1892. 2nd Lieut. 25th Inf., 19 Nov., 1892. 1st Lieut., 26 April, 1898. Capt. A. Q. M. Vols., 18 Sept., 1899.

KINSEY, SAML.* [Born in Penn. Appointed from Penn.]
Bvt. 2nd Lieut. 1st Art., 1 July, 1854. 2nd Lieut., 2 Nov., 1854. Died 14 July, 1855.

KINSIE, HUNTER. [Born in Wis. Appointed from S. C.]
2nd Lieut. 20th Inf., 1 Aug., 1899.

KINSLEY, ZEBINA J. D.* [Born in N. Y. Appointed from N. Y.]
2nd Lieut. Light Art., 1 July, 1819. Trans. to 1st Art., 1 June, 1821. Trans. to 3rd Art., 16 Aug., 1821. 1st Lieut., 30 Aug., 1825. Resigned 1 Dec., 1835. Died 24 Aug., 1849.

KINSMAN, BENJ. W.* [Born in Maine. Appointed from Maine.]
Bvt. 2nd Lieut. 7th Inf., 1 July, 1828. 2nd Lieut., 1 July, 1828. Died 14 May, 1832.

KINSMAN, JOHN H. [Born in Mass. Appointed from N. Y.]
1st Lieut. Asst. Surg., 30 March, 1864. Bvt. Capt., 13 March, 1865, for faithful and meritorious service during the war. Capt. Asst. Surg., 30 March, 1867. Resigned 21 Sept., 1879.

KINTZING, GUSTAVUS S. [Born in Penn. Appointed from Penn.]
2nd Lieut. of Inf., 3 March, 1847; Voltigeurs, 9 April, 1847. Disbanded 29 Aug., 1848. Died 6 Dec., 1884.

KINZIE, DAVID H. [Born in Ill. Appointed from Kansas.]
Cadet at Mil. Acad., 1 July, 1859, to 6 Feb., 1861. 2nd Lieut. 5th Art., 14 May, 1861. Bvt. 1st Lieut., 30 June, 1862, for gallant and meritorious service in the Battle of White Oak Swamp, Va. 1st Lieut. 5th Art., 30 Aug., 1862. Bvt. Capt., 17 Sept., 1862, for gallant and meritorious service in the Battle of Antietam, Md. Bvt. Maj., 13 March, 1865, for good conduct and gallant service during the war. Capt. 39th Inf., 28 July, 1866, declined. Capt., 5th Art., 12 April, 1871. Maj. 1st Art., 25 Oct., 1894. Trans. to 5th Art., 22 Dec., 1894. Trans. to 3rd Art., 5 Oct., 1896. Lieut. Col. 1st Art., 23 Feb., 1899. Graduate of the Artillery School, 1870.

KINZIE, FRANK X. [Born in Ill. Appointed from Ill.]
2nd Lieut. 20th Inf., 31 Oct., 1874. Resigned 1 Jan., 1879.

KINZIE, GEORGE H. [Born in Ill. Appointed from Ill.]
Priv. Co. D, 134th Ill. Vols., 16 May, 1864. Discharged 25 Oct., 1864. 2nd Lieut. 15th Inf., 1 Oct., 1873. 1st Lieut., 18 Sept., 1878. Reg. Adj., 1 Nov., 1880, to 1 Sept., 1886. Died 26 Aug., 1890.

KINZIE, JOHN. [Born in Kansas. Appointed from Ill.]
2nd Lieut. 2nd Inf., 27 July, 1872. 1st Lieut., 7 June, 1877. Reg. Adj., 8 March, 1887. Capt., 2 Jan., 1892. Retired for disability, 3 Dec., 1897.

KINZIE, ROBT. A. [Born in Ill. Appointed from Kansas.]
Maj. P. M., 2 May, 1861. Died 13 Dec., 1873. Bvt. Lieut. Col., 13 March, 1865, for 1865, for faithful and meritorious service during the war.

KIP, LAWRENCE. [Born in N. Y. Appointed from Cal.]
Cadet at Mil. Acad., 1 July, 1853, to 31 May, 1854. 2nd Lieut. 4th Art., 30 June, 1857. Trans. to 3rd Art., 27 Aug., 1857. 1st Lieut., 14 May, 1861. Reg. Adj., 27 Sept. to 30 Nov., 1861. Maj. A. de C. Vols., 20 Aug., 1862. Resigned from Vols., 15 Aug., 1863. Capt., 13 Aug., 1866. Resigned 1 Nov., 1867. Bvt. Capt., 11 June, 1864, for gallant and meritorious service at the Battle of Trevillian Station, Va. Bvt. Maj., 31 March, 1865, for gallant and meritorious service in the Cav. campaign from Winchester to Petersburg, and at the Battle of Dinwiddie C. H., Va. Bvt. Lieut. Col., 1 April, 1865, for gallant and meritorious service at the Battle of Five Forks, Va.

KIRBY, BYRON. [Born in Ohio. Appointed from Ohio.]
Priv. and Sergt. Co. B, 6th Cav., 6 Sept. to 29 Nov., 1861. 2nd Lieut. 6th Inf., 24 Oct., 1861. 1st Lieut., 23 Feb., 1864. Maj. 3rd Md. Cav., 26 Sept., 1863. Lieut. Col., 23 Jan., 1864. Mustered out Vols., 7 Sept., 1865. Bvt. 1st Lieut., 31 Dec., 1862, for gallant and meritorious service at the Battle of Murfreesboro, Tenn. Bvt. Capt. and Maj., 13 March, 1865, for meritorious service during the war. Bvt. Col. and Brig. Gen. Vols., 6 Sept., 1865, for gallant and meritorious service during the war. Resigned from U. S. A., 7 Nov., 1865. Died 29 Nov., 1881.

KIRBY, DENNIS T. [Born in N. Y. Appointed from Mo.]
Capt. 8th Mo. Vols., 25 June, 1861. Maj., 15 July, 1862. Mustered out 7 July, 1864. Lieut. Col. 27th Mo. Vols., 6 Nov., 1864. Bvt. Col. and Brig. Gen. Vols., 13 March, 1865, for gallant and meritorious service during the war. Mustered out 13 June, 1865. Capt. 39th Inf., 28 July, 1866. Cashiered 1 Oct., 1868. Bvt. Maj., 2 March, 1867, for gallant and meritorious service in the Battle of Chickasaw Bayou, Miss. Bvt. Lieut. Col., 2 March, 1867, for gallant and meritorious service in the assault of Vicksburg, Miss. Bvt. Col., 2 March, 1867, for gallant and meritorious service in the Battles of Chickamauga, Mission Ridge, and River's Bridge.

KIRBY, EDMUND. [Born in Conn. Appointed from Conn.]
Ensign 4th Inf., 6 July, 1812. 3rd Lieut., 12 March, 1813. 2nd Lieut., 31 July, 1813. Reg. Adj., Sept., 1813, to June, 1815. Trans. to Corps Art., 17 May, 1815. Trans. to 5th Inf., 2 Dec., 1815. 1st Lieut., 1 May, 1817. Reg. Adj., Sept., 1816, to 4 Jan., 1819. Trans. to 2nd Art., 1 June, 1821. Trans. to 1st Art., 16 Aug., 1821. Capt., 1 May, 1824. Maj. P. M., 5 Aug., 1824. Died 20 Aug., 1849. Bvt. Lieut. Col., 20 Aug., 1847, for gallant and meritorious conduct at Contreras and Churubusco. Bvt. Col., 13 Sept., 1847, for gallant and meritorious conduct at Chapultepec.

KIRBY, EDMUND.* [Born in N. Y. Appointed at Large.]
2nd Lieut. 1st Art., 6 May, 1861. 1st Lieut., 14 May, 1861. Brig. Gen. Vols., 28 May, 1863. Died 28 May, 1863, of wounds in Battle of Chancellorsville, Va.

KIRBY, HENRY.* [Born in N. C. Appointed from N. C.]
Addl. 2nd Lieut. 12th Inf., 15 June, 1877. 2nd Lieut. 10th Inf., 20 June, 1877. 1st Lieut., 1 Jan., 1885. Capt., 20 April, 1898.

KIRBY, JOHN. [Born in N. Y. Appointed from N. Y.]
Ensign 13th Inf., 12 March, 1812. 2nd Lieut., 1 April, 1813. 1st Lieut., 19 May, 1814. Trans. to 2nd Inf., 17 May, 1815. Reg. Adj., Sept., 1815, to 26 July, 1816. Resigned 30 Sept., 1816.

KIRBY, REYNOLD M. [Born in Conn. Appointed from Conn.]
3rd Lieut. 3rd Art., 6 July, 1813. 2nd Lieut., 1 Oct., 1813. Trans. to Corps Art., 12 May, 1814. 1st Lieut., 23 March, 1818. Trans. to 1st Art., 1 June, 1821. Reg. Adj., 1 June, 1821, to 1 July, 1822. (Maj. A. A. G., 29 April, 1816, to 20 May, 1820.) Capt. 1st Art., 5 Aug., 1824. Died 7 Oct., 1842. Bvt. 1st Lieut., 15 Aug., 1814, for gallant conduct in defence of Fort Erie. Bvt. Capt., 17 Sept., 1814, for gallant and good conduct in the sortie from

Fort Erie, and Bvt. Maj., 17 Sept., 1824, for ten years' faithful service in one grade.

KIRBY, SELAH. [Born in ——. Appointed from N. Y.]
Post Surg., 27 July, 1819. Died 5 Oct., 1819.

KIRK, EZRA B. [Born in Ohio. Appointed from Ohio.]
Priv. Co. H, 71st N. Y. State Militia, 20 April, 1861. Mustered out 30 J 1861. 1st Lieut. 14th Ohio Vols., 15 Aug., 1861. Discharged 9 Feb., 1864. Capt. A. Q. M. Vols., 5 Dec., 1863, to 13 Dec., 1866. Bvt. Maj. Vols., 19 Aug., 1865, for faithful and meritorious service. Bvt. Lieut. Col. Vols., 19 Aug., 1865, for faithful and meritorious service in the Q. M. Dept. and in the f Capt. A. Q. M., U. S. A., 28 July, 1866. Maj. Q. M., 31 Aug., 1883. Retired by operation of law, 8 Aug., 1894.

KIRK, JOHN C.* [Born in N. Y. Apointed from N. Y.]
3rd Lieut. Corps Art., 17 July, 1817. 2nd Lieut., 31 Oct., 1817. 1st Lieut., 30 Sept., 1819. Trans. to 1st Art., 1 June, 1821. Trans. to 3rd Art., 16 Aug., 1821. Trans. to 4th Art., 5 Dec., 1821. Resigned 30 Sept., 1823. Died ——, 1825.

KIRKHAM, RALPH W.* [Born in Mass. Appointed from Mass.]
Bvt. 2nd Lieut. 2nd Inf., 1 July, 1842. 2nd Lieut. 6th Inf., 27 Feb., 1843. Reg. Adj., 1 Jan., 1846, to 1 Oct., 1849. R. Q. M., 1 Oct., 1849, to 16 Nov., 1854. 1st Lieut., 7 Jan., 1851. Capt. A. Q. M., 16 Nov., 1854. Maj. Q. M., 26 Feb., 1863. Lieut. Col. Dep. Q. M. G., 29 July, 1866. Resigned 10 Feb., 1870. Bvt. 1st Lieut., 20 Aug., 1847, for gallant and meritorious conduct at Contreras and Churubusco. Bvt. Capt., 13 Sept., 1847, for gallant and meritorious conduct at Chapultepec. Bvt. Lieut. Col. and Col., 13 March, 1865, for faithful and meritorious service during the war. Bvt. Brig. Gen., 13 March, 1865, for faithful and meritorious service in the Q. M. Dept. during the war.

KIRKMAN, GEORGE W.* [Born in Tex. Appointed from Ill.]
2nd Lieut. 1st Inf., 12 June, 1889. 1st Lieut. 8th Inf., 27 Aug., 1896. Capt. 23rd Inf., 19 July, 1899. Maj. 49th U. S. Vols., 9 Sept., 1899. Trans. to 12th Inf., 17 Feb., 1900.

KIRKMAN, JOEL T. [Born in Ill. Appointed from Ill.]
2nd Lieut. 21st Ill. Vols., 28 June, 1861. 1st Lieut., 13 Nov., 1862. Capt., 1 Jan., 1864. Mustered out 7 June, 1864. Capt. 6th U. S. Vet. Vols., 19 Feb., 1865. Mustered out 9 April, 1866. 2nd Lieut. and 1st Lieut. 17th Inf., 23 Feb., 1866. Trans. to 26th Inf., 21 Sept., 1866. Trans. to 10th Inf., 19 May, 1869. Capt., 11 April, 1882. Maj. 16th Inf., 23 July, 1898.

KIRKPATRICK, DANIEL. [Born in Ga. Appointed from Ga.
2nd Lieut. of Inf., 3 March, 1847; 13th Inf., 9 April, 1847. 1st Lieut., 31 Jan., 1848. Disbanded 15 July, 1848.

KIRKPATRICK, GEORGE W.* [Born in S. C. Appointed from S. C.]
2nd Lieut. 10th Inf., 11 June, 1892. Trans. to 4th Cav., 17 Aug., 1892. Trans. to 8th Cav., 31 Aug., 1892. 1st Lieut., 2 March, 1899. Graduate of the Infantry and Cavalry School, 1897.

KIRKPATRICK, N. D.* [Born in Va. Appointed from Va.]
2nd Lieut. Cav. (1st Cav.), 12 June, 1896. Died 7 Sept., 1898.

KIRKPATRICK, THOMAS J. [Born in Va. Appointed from Pe
Asst. Surg., 6 Nov., 1895.

KIRTLAND, THADDEUS S. [Born in Conn. Appointed from Army.]
Priv. 18th Inf., 1 Oct., 1861. 2nd Lieut. 18th Inf., 30 Oct., 1861. 1st Lieut., 22 July, 1862. Trans. to 36th Inf., 21 Sept., 1866. Capt., 28 July, 1866. Trans. to 7th Inf., 19 May, 1869. Retired with rank of Maj., for disability, 10 July, 1891.

KISE, REUBEN C. [Born in Ind. Appointed from Ind.]
Capt. 10th Inf. Vols., 23 April, 1861. Mustered out 6 Aug., 1861. 1st Lieut. and Adj. 10th Ind. Vols., 18 Sept., 1861. Capt. A. A. G. Vols., 21 June, 1862. Resigned 16 March, 1864. Maj. 120th Ind. Inf., 16 March, 1864. Lieut. Col., 15 Sept., 1864. Col., 9 Sept., 1865. Bvt. Brig. Gen. Vols., 13 March, 1865, for gallant and distinguished service during the war. Mustered out 6 Jan., 1866. 1st Lieut. 25th Inf., 28 July, 1866. Resigned 4 April, 1867. Died 22 Nov., 1872.

KISLINGBURY, FREDK. F. [Born in England. Appointed from Mich.]
Priv. Co. E, 54th N. Y. State Militia, 26 July, 1864. Discharged 10 Nov., 1864. Priv. Co. D, 4th Inf., 3 June, 1865. Discharged 3 June, 1868. Priv. Co. K, 4th Inf., 3 July, 1868. Trans. to Gen. Ser., 4 Jan., 1869. Discharged 9 June, 1869. Priv. Gen. Ser., 2 Feb., 1870. Corpl., 1 Aug., 1870. Sergt., 1 Aug., 1872. Discharged 1 Feb., 1873. 2nd Lieut. 11th Inf., 1 Oct., 1873. Died 1 June, 1884, at Camp Clay, Grinnell Land, in the Arctic regions, while on expedition under Lieut. Greely.

KISTLER, AMANDUS C. [Born in Penn. Appointed from Army.]
Priv. and Sergt. Co. G, 14th Inf., 1 Nov., 1864, to 7 Aug., 1865. 2nd Lieut. 14th Inf., 21 July, 1865. 1st Lieut., 21 July, 1865. Trans. to 23rd Inf., 21 Sept., 1866. Capt., 16 Dec., 1867. Discharged 30 Dec., 1870.

KLINE, JACOB. [Born in Penn. Appointed from Penn.]
1st Lieut. 16th Inf., 9 Sept., 1861. Bvt. Capt., 7 April, 1862, for gallant and meritorious service in the Battle of Shiloh, Tenn. Bvt. Maj., 1 Sept., 1864, for gallant and meritorious service during the Atlanta campaign. Capt. 16th Inf., 30 Sept., 1864. Trans. to 25th Inf., 21 Sept., 1866. Trans. to 18th Inf., 26 April, 1869. Maj. 24th Inf., 6 Oct., 1887. Lieut. Col. 9th Inf., 23 March, 1892. Col. 21st Inf., 30 April, 1897. Brig. Gen. Vols., 27 May, 1898, to 15 March, 1899.

KNABENSHUE, FREDERICK G. [Born in Ohio. Appointed from Ohio.]
2nd Lieut. 4th Inf., 9 July, 1898. 1st Lieut. 15th Inf., 7 Sept., 1899.

KNAPP, JOHN S. [Born in Ill. Appointed from Ill.]
Priv. Co. K, 14th Ill. Vols., 25 May to 25 Nov., 1861. 2nd Lieut. 17th Inf., 24 Oct., 1861. 1st Lieut., 27 June, 1862. Resigned 11 Jan., 1864.

KNAPP, JOSHUA L.* [Born in N. Y. Appointed from Ill.]
2nd Lieut. 4th Art., 13 June, 1873. 1st Lieut., 10 Jan., 1877. Drowned 19 April, 1877.

KNAPP, ORSON C. [Born in Ohio. Appointed from Army.]
Priv. Co. A, 13th Ohio Vols., 3 May to 5 Aug., 1861. Priv. and Sergt. Co. A, and Sergt. Maj. 2nd Batt. 15th Inf., 6 Aug., 1861, to 24 Aug., 1863. 2nd Lieut. 15th Inf., 10 Aug., 1863. 1st Lieut., 10 Sept., 1864. Trans. to 33rd Inf., 21 Sept., 1866. Reg. Adj., 17 Jan. to 24 Aug., 1867. Capt., 24 Aug., 1867. Unassigned 3 May, 1869. Discharged 25 Oct., 1870. Bvt. 1st Lieut., 1 Sept., 1864, for gallant and meritorious services at the Battle of Mission Ridge, and during the Atlanta campaign. Bvt. Capt., 13 March, 1865, for meritorious service at the Battle of Mission Ridge, Tenn. Died 16 April, 1877.

KNEASS, CHAS. L. [Born in Penn. Appointed from Penn.]
1st Lieut. 18th Inf., 14 May, 1861. Reg. Adj., 1 July, 1861, to 16 Jan., 1862. Capt., 30 May, 1862. Killed 31 Dec., 1862, at the Battle of Murfreesboro, Tenn. Bvt. Maj., 31 Dec., 1862, for gallant and meritorious service at the Battle of Murfreesboro, Tenn.

KNEEDLER, WILLIAM L. [Born in Penn. Appointed from Penn.]
Asst. Surg., 3 Dec., 1883. Capt. Asst. Surg., 3 Dec., 1888. Maj. Brig. Surg. Vols., 30 July, 1898, to 30 June, 1899.

KNICKERBOCKER, BOLIVAR. [Born in N. Y. Appointed from Penn.]
Asst. Surg., 5 Aug., 1861. Resigned 1 July, 1876. Bvt. Capt. and Maj., 13 March, 1865, for faithful and meritorious service during the war.

KNIGHT, HARRY E. [Born in N. J. Appointed from N. Y.]
Priv. Co. K, 14th N. Y. Vols., 13 May, 1898, to 20 July, 1898. 2nd Lieut. 1st Inf., 9 July, 1898. 1st Lieut. 5th Inf., 5 May, 1899.

KNIGHT, JOHN G. D.* [Born in England. Appointed from Mo.]
2nd Lieut. Eng., 15 June, 1868. 1st Lieut., 22 Jan., 1870. Capt. (14 years' ser.), 15 June, 1882. Maj., 3 Feb., 1895.

KNIGHT, JOHN H. [Born in Del. Appointed from Del.]
1st Lieut. 1st Del. Vols., 22 May, 1861, to 30 Aug., 1861. Capt. A. A. G. Vols., 20 Aug., 1861, to 18 April, 1862. Capt. 18th Inf., 19 Feb., 1862. Trans. to 36th Inf., 21 Sept., 1866. Unassigned 19 May, 1869. Discharged 1 Oct., 1870. Bvt. Maj., 13 March, 1865, for faithful and meritorious service during the war. Bvt. Lieut. Col., 13 March, 1865, for faithful and meritorious service connected with organization of the Vol. armies of the United States during the war.

KNIGHT, JOHN T.* [Born in Va. Appointed from Va.]
2nd Lieut. 3rd Cav., 15 June, 1884. 1st Lieut. 4th Cav., 23 April, 1891. Trans. to 3rd Cav., 27 April, 1891. Capt. A. Q. M., 14 Oct., 1896. Capt. A. Q. M., 22 Dec., 1896. Maj. Q. M. Vols., 6 Sept., 1898, to 2 March, 1899. Maj. Q. M. Vols., 6 July, 1899.

KNIGHT, SIMEON. [Born in Vt. Appointed from Vt.]
Ensign 1st Inf., 29 April, 1802. 2nd Lieut., 1 April, 1805. 1st Lieut., 9 Dec., 1807. District P. M., 24 March, 1808. Capt. 1st Inf., 20 Jan., 1813. Col. Q. M. G., 7 Feb., 1815. Disbanded 15 June, 1815. Batt. P. M., 16 May, 1817. Resigned 30 Nov., 1820.

KNOWER, EDWARD C. [Born in N. Y. Appointed from N. Y.]
2nd Lieut. 4th N. Y. Art., 3 Feb., 1862. 1st Lieut., 11 July, 1862. Capt., 20 Nov., 1863. Mustered out 3 Sept., 1864. Capt. Vet. Res. Corps, 3 Dec., 1864. Mustered out 31 Dec., 1866. 2nd Lieut. 45th Inf., 28 July, 1866. Bvt. 1st Lieut. and Capt., 2 March, 1867, for gallant and meritorious service in front of Petersburg, Va., 18 July, 1864. 1st Lieut. 45th Inf., 25 March, 1867. Unassigned 22 July, 1869. Ass'd to 3rd Art., 15 Dec., 1870. Capt., 7 May, 1887. Graduate of the Art. Sch., 1874. Retired for disability, 30 June, 1893. Died 5 Feb., 1897.

KNOWLES, ALDEN C. [Born in N. Y. Appointed from Army.]
Priv. and Corpl. Co. F. and Batt. Sergt. Maj. 13th Inf., 20 Aug., 1896, to 12 April, 1899. 2nd Lieut. 13th Inf., 5 April, 1899.

KNOWLTON, JOSEPH L.* [Born in Ill. Appointed from Ill.]
2nd Lieut. 2nd Art., 12 June, 1895. 1st Lieut., 2 March, 1899.

KNOWLTON, MINOR.* [Born in Conn. Appointed from Conn.]
Bvt. 2nd Lieut. 1st Art., 1 July, 1829. 2nd Lieut., 1 July, 1829. 1st Lieut., 23 July, 1835. Capt., 21 April, 1846. Retired 26 Oct., 1861. Died 24 Dec., 1870.

KNOX, EDWARD B. [Born in Maine. Appointed from Army.]
1st Lieut. 11th N. Y. Vols., 7 May, 1861. Mustered out 4 Aug., 1861. 1st Lieut. and Adj. 44th N. Y. Vols., 25 Sept., 1861. Capt., 4 July, 1862. Maj., 14 July, 1862. Mustered out 11 Oct., 1864. Priv. Co. D, 1st Batt. 12th Inf., 21 April, 1865. 1st Sergt., 29 April, 1865. 2nd Lieut. and 1st Lieut. 12th Inf., 16 June, 1865. Trans. to 21st Inf., 21 Sept., 1866. R. Q. M., 1 Jan., 1867, to 5 April, 1869. Bvt. Capt., 2 March, 1867, for gallant and meritorious service in the Battle of Hanover C. H., Va. Bvt. Maj., 2 March, 1867, for gallant and meritorious service in the Battle of Gettysburg, Penn. Bvt. Lieut. Col., 2 March, 1867, for gallant and meritorious service in the Battle of Spottsylvania C. H., Va. Unassigned 19 April, 1869. Retired with rank of 1st Lieut. Mounted, 7 May, 1870. Reduced to 1st Lieut., 3 March, 1875. Died 9 April, 1890.

KNOX, GEORGE H. [Born in N. Y. Appointed from N. Y.]
2nd Lieut. 20th Inf., 9 July, 1898. 1st Lieut. 7th Inf., 8 Sept., 1899.

KNOX, KILBURN. [Born in Penn. Appointed from Penn.]
Entered as Ira Kilburn Knox. Priv. Commonwealth Art. Penn. Vols., 24 April to 9 June, 1861. 1st Lieut. 13th Inf., 14 May, 1861. Capt., 14 May, 1864.

Trans. to 22nd Inf., 21 Sept., 1866. Resigned 1 April, 1869. Bvt. Maj., 22 July, 1864. for gallant and efficient services in the attack on Atlanta. Bvt. Lieut. Col., 13 March, 1865, for faithful and meritorious service.

KNOX, THOMAS T.* [Born in Tenn. Appointed from Tenn.]
2nd Lieut. 1st Cav., 12 June, 1871. R. Q. M., 1 Oct., 1873, to 11 Nov., 1875. 1st Lieut., 4 March, 1879. Capt., 23 Jan., 1889. Maj. I. G. Vols., 25 July, 1898.

KNOX, WILLIAM M. [Born in Ill. Appointed from Wash. Ter.]
1st Lieut. 1st Wash. Ter. Vols., 10 May, 1862. Capt., 19 June, 1862. Mustered out 11 Dec., 1865. 2nd Lieut. 18th Inf., 23 Feb., 1866. 1st Lieut., 23 Feb., 1866. Trans. to 36th Inf., 21 Sept., 1866. Died 25 Nov., 1866.

KNUDSEN, FREDRIK L. [Born in Norway. Appointed from Army.]
Priv., Corpl. and Sergt. and 1st Sergt. Cos. K and F, 13th Inf., 30 Jan., 1889, to 3 Nov., 1893. 2nd Lieut. 8th Inf., 7 Oct., 1893. 1st Lieut., 26 April, 1898.

KNUDSON, KNUD. [Born in Mo. Appointed from Wis.]
2nd Lieut. 7th Inf., 1 June, 1899.

KOBBE, FERDINAND W. [Born in N. Mex. Appointed from Va.]
2nd Lieut. 22nd Inf., 7 Oct., 1891. Trans. to 23rd Inf., 6 April, 1892. 1st Lieut., 26 April, 1898.

KOBBE, WM. A., Jr. [Born in N. Y. Appointed from N. Y.]
Priv. Co. K, 7th N. Y. State Militia, 5 June, 1862. Discharged 5 Sept., 1862. Priv. Co. G, 178th N. Y. Vols., 29 May, 1863. Discharged 18 Oct., 1863. 1st Lieut. 178th N. Y. Vols., 18 Oct., 1863. Bvt. Maj. Vols. and Bvt. Lieut. Col. Vols., 13 March, 1865, for distinguished and faithful service throughout the war. Capt. 178th N. Y. Vols., 2 Aug., 1865. Mustered out 1 March, 1866. 2nd Lieut. 19th Inf., 17 March, 1866. Trans. to 37th Inf., 21 Sept., 1866. 1st Lieut., 2 Feb., 1867. Bvt. Capt., 2 March, 1867, for gallant and meritorious service in the Battle of Nashville, Tenn. Bvt. Maj., 2 March, 1867, for gallant and meritorious service in the capture of Fort Blakely, Ala. Reg. Adj. 37th Inf., 31 Oct., 1868, to 11 Aug., 1869. Trans. to 3rd Inf., 11 Aug., 1869. Reg. Adj., 11 Aug., 1869, to 5 Feb., 1872. Trans. to 3rd Art., 5 Feb., 1872. Reg. Adj., 1 May, 1873, to 10 Oct., 1877. Capt., 6 April, 1885. Maj., 8 March, 1898. Col. 35th U. S. Vols., 5 July, 1899. Graduate of the Artillery School, 1873.

KOCHERSPERGER, S. M.* [Born in Penn. Appointed from Penn.]
Addl. 2nd Lieut. 2nd Cav., 12 June, 1896. 2nd Lieut. 10th Cav., 11 Dec., 1896. Trans. to 7th Cav., 16 Feb., 1897. Trans. to 2nd Cav., 21 April, 1898.

KOEHLER, BENJAMIN M.* [Born in Ill. Appointed from Nebr.]
Addl. 2nd Lieut. 7th Inf., 11 June, 1897. 2nd Lieut. 15th Inf., 16 Dec., 1897. Trans. to 6th Art., 8 March, 1898. 1st Lieut. 4th Art., 10 July, 1899. Capt. 37th U. S. Vols., 5 July, 1899.

KOEHLER, EDGAR F. [Born in Ill. Appointed from Army.]
Priv. and Corpl. Co. C, 8th Inf., 8 Nov., 1891, to 1 Nov., 1894. 2nd Lieut. 11th Inf., 31 Oct., 1894. Trans. to 9th Inf., 27 Sept., 1897. 1st Lieut., 12 May, 1898. Reg. Adj., 22 Sept., 1898, until reorganization of Regiment 2 March, 1899. Killed in action at Tinuba, Luzon, Philippine Islands, 4 March, 1900.

KOEHLER, LEWIS M.* [Born in Ill. Appointed from Iowa.]
2nd Lieut. 6th Cav., 14 June, 1885. 1st Lieut. 10th Cav., 1 Jan., 1892. Trans. to 9th Cav., 9 Feb., 1892. Capt. 4th Cav., 9 Aug.,1899. Graduate of the Infantry and Cavalry School, 1889.

KOERPER, EGON A. [Born in Prussia. Appointed from Penn.]
Asst. Surg. 75th Penn. Vols., 11 Sept., 1861. Mustered out 11 Sept., 1862. Asst. Surg. 75th Penn. Vols., 25 July, 1864. Maj. Surg. 75th Penn. Vols., 8 Oct., 1864. Mustered out 1 Sept., 1865. 1st Lieut. Asst. Surg., 14 May, 1867. Capt. Asst. Surg., 6 April, 1868. Maj. Surg., 9 Jan., 1885. Lieut. Col. Dep. Surg. Gen., 10 April, 1898. Retired by operation of law, 21 Feb., 1900.

KOESTER, FRANCIS J.* [Born in Penn. Appointed from Penn.]
2nd Lieut. 10th Cav., 11 June, 1888. 1st Lieut. 3rd Cav., 8 Aug., 1895.

KONOVER, IRA S. [Born in N. J. Appointed from N. J.]
2nd Lieut. of Inf., 8 March, 1847; 10th Inf., 9 April, 1847. Disbanded 24 Aug., 1848.

KOOPS, CARL. [Born in Germany. Appointed from Army.]
Priv., Corpl. and Sergt. Troop C, 2nd Cav., 17 Nov., 1881, to 22 Oct., 1886. 2nd Lieut. 13th Inf., 22nd Oct., 1886. 1st Lieut. of Inf. (14th), 1 March, 1894. Trans. to 10th Inf., 5 May, 1894. Graduate of the Infantry and Cavalry School, 1889. Died 6 Aug., 1898.

KOPP, FREDERICK. [Born in Germany. Appointed from Army.]
Priv., Corpl. and Sergt. Co. D, 5th Inf., 14 Aug., 1848, to 15 June, 1858, and from 14 July, 1858, to 4 March, 1863. 2nd Lieut. 13th Inf., 19 Feb., 1863. 1st Lieut., 21 July, 1863. Dismissed 13 Nov., 1863.

KORN, WM. H.* [Born in Penn. Appointed from Penn.]
2nd Lieut. 1st Inf., 1 July, 1839. Resigned 15 March, 1840. Died 24 Sept., 1842.

KOWNS, JOHN C. [Born in ——. Appointed from Ky.]
2nd Lieut. 28th Inf., 20 May, 1813. 1st Lieut., 20 Feb., 1814. Trans. to 1st Inf., 17 May, 1815. Resigned 31 Oct., 1817.

KRAMER, ADAM. [Born in Germany. Appointed from Penn.]
Priv. Co. F, 2nd Drag., 16 May, 1857. Discharged 16 May, 1862. Priv. Co. I, 15th Penn. Cav., 25 Aug., 1862. Sergt., 30 Oct., 1862. 1st Sergt., 1 Nov., 1862. 1st Lieut., 15th Penn. Cav., 1 March, 1863. Capt., 8 May, 1863. Mustered out 21 June, 1865. 2nd Lieut. 2nd U. S. Col. Cav., 7 Dec., 1865. Mustered out 12 Feb., 1866. 2nd Lieut. 6th Cav., 27 April, 1866. 1st Lieut., 12 Dec., 1866. Capt., 1 Aug., 1874. Maj., 8 March, 1893. Retired, for over 30 years' service, 13 Jan., 1897. Bvt. Maj., 27 Feb., 1890, for gallant services in action against Indians at Ash Creek, Ariz., 6 May, 1880, and at Big Dry Wash, Ariz., 7 July, 1882.

KRASZYNSKI, MAURICE. [Born in Poland. Appointed from Conn.] Priv. Co. E, 1st Conn. Vols., 19 April to 31 July, 1861. Sergt. Co. K, 11th Conn. Vols., 24 Oct., 1861. 2nd Lieut., 1 Sept., 1862. Capt., 22 Aug., 1864. Resigned 25 May, 1865. 2nd Lieut. 12th Inf., 22 Jan., 1867. Dismissed 6 Dec., 1872.

KRAUSE, DAVID. [Born in Penn. Appointed from Penn.] 1st Lieut. 14th Inf., 14 May, 1861. Capt., 31 July, 1863. Bvt. Maj., 13 March, 1865, for gallant and meritorious service in the Battle of Gettysburg, Penn. Maj. 5th Inf., 2 April, 1883. Trans. to 11th Inf., 17 May, 1883. Died 12 Sept., 1885.

KRAUSE, WILLIAM.* [Born in Pa. Appointed from Pa.] 2nd Lieut. and 1st Lieut. 19th Inf., 23 June, 1865. Trans. to 37th Inf., 21 Sept., 1866. Trans. to 3rd Inf., 11 Aug., 1869. Capt., 1 July, 1885. Retired for disability, 23 April, 1890.

KRAUTHOFF, CHARLES R. [Born in Mo. Appointed from Army.] Priv., Corpl., Sergt. and 1st Sergt. Batty F, 2nd Art., 13 Aug., 1884, to 1 Aug., 1891. 2nd Lieut. 14th Inf., 31 July, 1891. 1st Lieut., 26 April, 1898. Graduate of the Infantry and Cavalry School, 1895. Capt. A. C. S., 11 March, 1900.

KREBS, WM. H. W. [Born in Md. Appointed from Md.] Priv. and Sergt. Co. F, 12th Inf., 26 Oct., 1861, to 27 May, 1862. Capt. A. A. G. C, 3 May, 1862. Mustered out 6 Sept., 1865. 2nd Lieut. and 1st Lieut. Inf., 23 Feb., 1866. Mustered out 1 Jan., 1871.

KREMS, JOHN. [Born in Md. Appointed from Md.] 2nd Lieut. 8th Inf., 4 Dec., 1818. 1st Lieut., 8 May, 1819. Trans. to Corps Art., 20 Oct., 1820. Resigned 28 Feb., 1821.

KREPPS, SOLOMON G. [Born in Penn. Appointed from Penn.] Sergt. and 1st Sergt. Co. D, Penn. Res., 29 July, 1861. 2nd Lieut., 1 Oct., 1861, to 18 April, 1862. 2nd Lieut. 4th Inf., 19 Feb., 1862. Resigned 16 Aug., 1862.

KREPS, JACOB F.* [Born in Penn. Appointed from Penn.] 2nd Lieut. 22nd Inf., 13 June, 1883. 1st Lieut. 13th Inf., 24 Feb., 1891. Trans. to 22nd Inf., 20 July, 1891. Capt., 3 July, 1898.

KRESS, JOHN A. [Born in Penn. Appointed from N. Y.] Maj. 94th N. Y. Vols., 9 July, 1862. Lieut. Col., 1 Nov., 1862. 2nd Lieut. Ord., 24 Nov., 1863. Resigned Vol. commission, 11 Dec., 1863. 1st Lieut. Ord., 16 July, 1864. Bvt. Capt., 2 April, 1865, for gallant and meritorious service during the Siege of Richmond and Petersburg, Va. Bvt. Maj., 3 April, 1865, for meritorious and distinguished services as Chief of Ord. of the 25th Army Corps. Capt. Ord., 23 June, 1874. Maj., 3 Jan., 1887. Bvt. Lieut. Col., 27 Feb., 1890, for gallant services in action against Indians, on the Columbia River, Ore., 8 July, 1878.

KROMER, LEON B.* [Born in Mich. Appointed from Mich.] 2nd Lieut. 10th Cav., 15 Feb., 1899.

KROUTINGER, ADOLPH W. [Born in Germany. Appointed from Army.] Priv. Co. D, 2nd Inf., 15 Nov., 1848. Corpl., 1 April, 1852. 1st Sergt., 1 May, 1852. Discharged 19 Oct., 1853. 1st Sergt. Co. D, 2nd Inf., 19 Oct., 1853. Sergt. Maj. 2nd Inf., 5 April, 1855. Discharged 20 Aug., 1858. Sergt. Maj. 2nd Inf., 20 Aug., 1858. 2nd Lieut. 2nd Inf., 24 Oct., 1861. Reg. Adj., 16 Nov., 1861, to 20 Nov., 1863. 1st Lieut., 15 March, 1862. Bvt. Capt., 3 May, 1863, for gallant and meritorious service in the Battle of Chancellorsville, Va. Bvt. Maj., 2 uly, 1863, for gallant and meritorious service in the Battle of Gettysburg, Penn. Capt. 2nd Inf., 11 April, 1864. Retired 7 June, 1879. Died 17 Feb., 1893.

KRUG, FREDERICK V. [Born in Penn. Appointed from D. C.] 2nd Lieut. 8th Inf., 30 Oct., 1884. 1st Lieut. 23rd Inf., 21 Oct., 1891. Trans. to 20th Inf., 5 Nov., 1891. Capt. 27 Feb., 1899.

KUHN, HENRY H. [Born in Penn. Appointed from Penn.] Priv., Corpl. and Sergt. Co. A, 10th Penn. Res. Corps, 20 June, 1861, to 2 April, 1864. 1st Lieut. 23rd U. S. Col. Troops, 4 April, 1864. Mustered out 22 Nov., 1864. 2nd Lieut. Vet. Res. Corps, 5 Jan., 1865. Mustered out 31 Oct., 1866. 2nd Lieut. 42nd Inf., 22 Jan., 1867. Unassigned 22 April, 1869. Retired with rank of Captain, 31 Dec., 1870. Reduced to 1st Lieut., 3 March, 1875.

KUHN, JOSEPH E.* [Born in Kan. Appointed from Kan.] 2nd Lieut. Eng., 14 June, 1885. 1st Lieut., 15 June, 1888. Capt., 26 May, 1896. Maj. Chief Eng. Vols., 31 May, 1898, to 12 April, 1899.

KUHNS, HENRY B. [Born in Penn. Appointed from Penn.] 2nd Lieut. Inf., 5 March, 1847; 11th Inf., 9 April, 1847. Resigned 4 Sept., 1847.

KULP, JOHN S. [Born in Penn. Appointed from Penn.] Asst. Surg., 12 May, 1893. Capt. Asst. Surg., 12 May, 1898.

KURTZ, JOHN D.* [Born in D. C. Appointed from D. C.] 2nd Lieut. Eng., 1 July, 1842. 1st Lieut., 3 March, 1853. Capt., 1 July, 1856. Maj. 3 March, 1863. Lieut. Col., 8 Aug., 1866. Died 16 Oct., 1877. Bvt. Lieut. Col., 13 March, 1865, for faithful and meritorious service in the Eng. Dept. Bvt. Col., 13 March, 1865, for meritorious service during the war.

KUTZ, CHARLES W.* [Born in Penn. Appointed from Penn.] Add'l 2nd Lieut. Eng., 12 June, 1893. 2nd Lieut. 2 Oct., 1895. 1st Lieut., 5 July, 1898.

KYLE, JOHN G.* [Born in Ohio. Appointed from Ohio.] 2nd Lieut. 1st Cav., 15 June, 1870. 1st Lieut., 3 Sept., 1876. Died 30 March, 1877.

KYLE, WM. J. [Born in Ohio. Appointed from Ohio.] Priv., Corpl. and Sergt. Co. G, 25th Ohio Vols., 18 June, 1861, to 1 Jan., 1865. 2nd Lieut., 1 Jan., 1865. 1st Lieut., 27 Sept., 1865. Mustered out 18 June, 1866. 2nd Lieut. 16th Inf., 23 Feb., 1866. 1st Lieut., 2 April, 1866. Trans. to 25th

Inf., 21 Sept., 1866. Unassigned 26 April, 1869. Ass'd to 11th Inf., 1 Jan., 1871. Dropped 8 Feb., 1877.

LACEY, EDGAR M.* [Born in N. Y. Appointed from N. Y.]
Bvt. 2nd Lieut. Inf., 1 July, 1827. 2nd Lieut. 5th Inf., 1 July, 1827. 1st Lieut., 25 Nov., 1835. Capt., 1 Nov., 1838. Died 2 April, 1839.

LACEY, FRANCIS E. [Born in Ireland. Appointed from Army.]
Priv. Co. I, 2nd Inf., 10 May, 1858. Corpl., 1 Sept., 1859. Sergt., 1 July, 1860. 1st Sergt., 1 July, 1860. 2nd Lieut. 2nd Inf., 18 July, 1862. 1st Lieut., 1 May, 1863. Bvt. Capt., 2 July, 1863, for gallant and meritorious service in the Battle of Gettysburg, Penn. Dismissed 21 April, 1864. Reinstated 22 July, 1864. Capt. 2nd Inf., 8 Aug., 1866. Unassigned 17 April, 1869. Ass'd to 10th Inf., 5 July, 1870. Maj. 8th Inf., 16 Sept., 1892. Trans. to 17th Inf., 7 Aug., 1895. Lieut. Col. 3rd Inf., 4 Feb., 1897. Retired by operation of law, 8 Aug., 1897.

LACEY, FRANCIS E. Jr.* [Born in W. Va. Appointed from Mich.]
2nd Lieut. 10th Inf., 12 June, 1889. 1st Lieut. 1st Inf., 4 Nov., 1896. Capt. 23rd Inf., 14 Aug., 1899. Trans. to 1st Inf.

LACOCK, ALLAS. [Born in S. C. Appointed from S. C.]
Mil. Storekeeper, 9 March, 1819. Disbanded 1 June, 1821.

LACY, WESTWOOD, A.* [Born in Va. Appointed from Va.]
2nd Lieut. 4th Inf., 1 July, 1822. 1st Lieut., 31 Oct., 1826. Died 3 Nov., 1829.

LADD, EUGENE F.* [Born in Vt. Appointed from Vt.]
2nd Lieut. 9th Cav., 15 June, 1884. 1st Lieut., 28 Oct., 1889. Capt., 2 March, 1899. Maj. Chief Q. M. Vols., 12 May, 1898.

LADLEY, OSCAR D. [Born in Ohio. Appointed from Ohio.]
Priv. Co. E, 16th Ohio Vols., 23 April, 1861, to 18 Aug., 1861. Priv. Co. G, 75th Ohio Vols., 28 Aug., 1861. Sergt., 4 Dec., 1861. 1st Sergt., 31 July, 1862. 2nd Lieut. 75th Ohio Vols., 1 Nov., 1862. 1st Lieut., 19 Jan., 1863. Capt., 12 May, 1864. Mustered out 17 Jan., 1865. 2nd Lieut. 22nd Inf., 2 Oct., 1867. 1st Lieut., 28 June, 1878. Died 11 Jan., 1880.

LADUE, WILLIAM B.* [Born in Mich. Appointed from Ore.]
Addl. 2nd Lieut. Eng., 12 June, 1894. 2nd Lieut., 6 Jan., 1896. 1st Lieut., 5 July, 1898.

LAFFERTY, HERBERT A. [Born in ——. Appointed from ——.]
2nd Lieut. 7th Inf., — April, 1898. Died 17 Sept., 1898.

LAFFERTY, JOHN. [Born in N. Y. Appointed from Cal.]
1st Lieut. 1st Batt. Cal. Cav., 21 July, 1864. Mustered out 15 March, 1866. 2nd Lieut. 8th Cav., 28 July, 1866. 1st Lieut., 31 July, 1867. Capt., 3 Oct., 1876. Retired 28 June, 1878. Died 15 Oct., 1899.

LAFITTE, JACQUES DE L.* [Born in La. Appointed from La.]
2nd Lieut. 8th Inf., 12 June, 1891. Trans. to 1st Inf., 12 Dec., 1896. 1st Lieut., 26 April, 1898. Capt. A. Q. M. Vols., 10 June, 1898.

LA GARDE, LOUIS A. [Born in La. Appointed from Ky.]
Asst. Surg., 16 June, 1878. Capt. Asst. Surg., 6 June, 1883. Maj. Surg., 13 Nov., 1896.

LAGNEL, JULIUS A. D.* [Born in N. Y. Appointed from N. Y.]
Bvt. 2nd Lieut. 5th Inf., 1 July, 1821. 2nd Lieut., 1 July, 1821. Trans. to 2nd Art., 30 Dec., 1825. 1st Lieut., 30 May, 1832. Capt. Ord., 1 Nov., 1836. Died 21 May, 1840. Bvt. 1st Lieut., 1 July, 1831, for 10 years' faithful service in one grade.

LAIDLEY, THEODORE T. S.* [Born in Va. Appointed from Va.]
Bvt. 2nd Lieut. Ord., 1 July, 1842. 1st Lieut., 3 March, 1847. Bvt. Capt., 18 April, 1847, for gallant and meritorious conduct in the Battle of Cerro Gordo. Bvt. Maj., 12 Oct., 1847, for gallant and meritorious conduct in the defence of Puebla. Capt. Ord., 1 July, 1856. Maj., 1 June, 1863. Bvt. Lieut. Col. and Col., 13 March, 1865, for faithful and meritorious service in the Ord. Dept. Lieut. Col. Ord., 7 March, 1867. Col., 14 April, 1875. Retired for over 40 years' service 4 Dec., 1882. Died 4 April, 1886.

LALLY, FOLLIOTT T. [Born in N. Y. Appointed from Maine.]
Maj. of Inf., 3 March, 1847; 9th Inf., 9 April, 1847. Disbanded 26 Aug., 1848. Bvt. Lieut. Col., for gallant and meritorious conduct in several affairs at Paso Ovejas, National Bridge and Cerro Gardo, 10, 12 and 15 Aug., 1847.

LAMAR, JOHN T. [Born in Ga. Appointed from Ga.]
Maj. Surg. 13th Inf., 9 April, 1847. Disbanded 15 July, 1848.

LAMBERT, EDWARD J.* [Born in D. C. Appointed from D. C.]
3rd Lieut. Corps Art., 17 July, 1817. 2nd Lieut., 1 March, 1818. 2nd Lieut. 8th Inf., 10 March, 1819. Trans. to 1st Inf., 1 June, 1821. 1st Lieut., 1 May, 1822. Resigned 30 Sept., 1823. Died 4 Dec., 1832.

LAMBERT, JOHN J. [Born in Ireland. Appointed from Iowa.]
1st Lieut. 9th Iowa Cav., 30 Nov., 1863. Capt., 6 May, 1865. Mustered out 15 March, 1866. 2nd Lieut. 5th Inf., 7 March, 1867. Resigned 31 March, 1872.

LAMBERT, LOUIS J. [Born in France. Appointed from N. Y.]
Capt. A. A. G. Vols., 29 Jan., 1862. Bvt. Maj. Vols., 13 March, 1865, for repeated acts of gallantry on the field. Bvt. Lieut. Col. Vols., 13 March, 1865, for long and faithful service and repeated acts of gallantry on the field. Bvt. Col. Vols., 13 March, 1865, for gallant and meritorious service at the Battles of Chickamauga, Ga., and Chatanooga, Tenn. Mustered out 12 June, 1866. 1st Lieut. 17th Inf., 28 July, 1866. Died 13 Sept., 1867. Bvt. Capt., 2 March, 1867, for gallant and meritorious service in the Battle of Chickamauga, Ga. Bvt. Maj., 2 March, 1867, for gallant and meritorious service in the Battle of Chattanooga, Tenn. Bvt. Lieut. Col., 2 March, 1867, for gallant and meritorious service in the Battle of Pocotaligo River, S. C.

LAMONION, GEORGE. [Born in N. Y. Appointed from Army.]
Priv. Co. A, 2nd Drag., 16 Sept., 1846, to 1 Oct., 1851. Priv. Cos. K and H, 2nd

Drag., 1 Oct., 1851, to 1 Oct., 1856. Priv. and Corpl. Co. H, 2nd Art., 9 Oct., 1856, to 9 Oct., 1861. Priv., Sergt. and 1st Sergt. Co. H, 12th Inf., 1 Nov., 1861, to 28 Nov., 1862. 2nd Lieut. 12th Inf., 6 Nov., 1862. 1st Lieut., 17 Feb., 1863. Retired 4 Nov., 1865. Died 5 Oct., 1866.

LAMOREUX, THOMAS B.* [Born in Mich. Appointed from Mich.]
Addl. 2nd Lieut. 4th Art., 12 June, 1890. 2nd Lieut. 2nd Art., 28 Aug., 1891. Trans. to 4th Art., 16 Sept., 1891. 1st Lieut. 2nd Art., 14 May, 1898. Graduate of the Artillery School, 1894.

LA MOTTE, CLARENCE K. [Born in ——. Appointed from ——.]
2nd Lieut. Inf., 1 Dec., 1899. Unasigned.

LAMOTTE, JOSEPH H.* [Born in N. C. Appointed from N. C.]
Bvt. 2nd Lieut. Inf., 1 July, 1827. 2nd Lieut. 1st Inf., 1 July, 1827. 1st Lieut., 11 July, 1833. Capt., 7 July, 1838. Maj. 5th Inf., 1 May, 1952. Resigned 31 Oct., 1856. Bvt. Maj., 23 Sept., 1846, for gallant and meritorious conduct at Monterey. Died 15 Nov., 1888.

LA MOTTE, ROBERT S. [Born in Penn. Appointed from Del.]
Capt. 1st Del. Vols., 2 May, 1861. Maj., 12 June, 1861. Mustered out 24 June, 1861. Capt. 13th Inf., 14 May, 1861. Maj. 12th Inf., 3 Dec., 1868. Trans. to 13th Inf., 15 March, 1869. Lieut. Col. 12th Inf., 7 June, 1879. Col. 13th Inf., 8 Dec., 1886. Died 16 Dec., 1888.

LANCASTER, GEORGE. [Born in Maine. Appointed from Army.]
Priv. 17th Inf., 14 April, 1862, to 16 May, 1863. 2nd Lieut 17th Inf., 13 March, 1863. 1st Lieut., 14 May, 1863. Capt., 6 Feb., 1866. Retired 6 May, 1870. Died 26 Sept., 1875.

LANCASTER, JAMES M.* [Born in Ky. Appointed from Ky.]
2nd Lieut. 3rd Art., 17 June, 1862. 1st Lieut., 24 June, 1864. Reg. Adj., 26 March to 24 Sept., 1867. Bvt. Capt., 13 March, 1865, for good conduct and gallant service during the war. Capt. 3rd Art., 20 March, 1879. Maj. of Art. (4th Art.), 29 Oct., 1896.

LANCASTER, JOB R. H.* [Born in Ohio. Appointed from Ohio.]
2nd Lieut. 1st Inf., 1 July, 1840. Died 5 July, 1841.

LANDERS, GEORGE F.* [Born in Md. Appointed from Md.]
2nd Lieut. 4th Art., 12 June, 1887. 1st Lieut., 14 Nov., 1893. Graduate of the Artillery School, 1892.

LANDIS, J. F. REYNOLDS.* [Born in Penn. Appointed at Large.]
Addl. 2nd Lieut. 1st Cav., 14 June, 1878. 2nd Lieut., 15 June, 1878. Capt. 6th Cav., 31 May, 1898. Trans. to 1st Cav., 19 Oct., 1898. Graduate of the Infantry and Cavalry School, 1885.

LANDON, EDWIN.* [Born in Minn. Appointed from Mich.]
Addl. 2nd Lieut. 4th Art., 12 June, 1896. 2nd Lieut. 2nd Art., 29 Oct., 1896. 1st Lieut. 4th Art., 2 March, 1899.

LANDON, HENRY H.* [Born in N. Y. Appointed from N. Y.]
2nd Lieut. 25th Inf., 14 June, 1872. 1st Lieut., 28 June, 1878. Resigned 1 June, 1880.

LANDON, WM. D. F. [Born in Ky. Appointed from ]
Sergt. Co. G, 14th Ind. Vols., 7 June, 1861. 1st Sergt., 1 March, 1862. 2nd Lieut., 11 Aug., 1862. Mustered out 16 June, 1864. Priv. and Sergt. Co. E, 1st U. S. Vet. Vols., 20 Dec., 1864, to 14 Sept., 1865. 2nd Lieut. 3rd U. S. Col. Inf., 22 Oct., 1865. Mustered out 31 Oct., 1865. 2nd Lieut. 18th Inf., 23 Feb., 1866. Drowned 8 July, 1866.

LANE, JAMES H. [Born in Ind. Appointed from Kan.]
2nd Lieut. 25th Inf., 15 Oct., 1875. 1st Lieut., 31 Dec., 1880. Dismissed 4 April, 1881.

LANE, JOHN. [Born in Mich. Appointed from Army.]
Cadet at Mil. Acad., 1 July, 1857, to 20 Feb., 1861. Priv., Corpl. and Sergt. Co. B, 18th Inf., 31 July, 1861, to 1 June, 1863. 2nd Lieut. 18th Inf., 1 June, 1865. Died 15 Oct., 1863, from wounds received in Battle of Chickamauga, Ga. Bvt. 1st Lieut., 19 Sept., 1863, for gallant and meritorious service in the Battle of Chickamauga, Ga.

LANE, JOHN F.* [Born in Ky. Appointed from Ind.]
Bvt. 2nd Lieut. 4th Art., 1 July, 1828. 2nd Lieut., 1 July, 1828. A. Q. M., 28 June, 1834, to 17 March, 1835. Capt. 2nd Drag., 8 June, 1836. Col. Creek Vols., 1 Sept., 1836. Died 19 Oct., 1836.

LANE, ROBERT C. [Born in Va. Appointed from Va.]
Surg.'s Mate 3rd Rifles, 11 March, 1814. Disbanded 1 June, 1815. Reinstated in 4th Inf., 13 Sept., 1815. Resigned 1 June, 1818.

LANE, SAMUEL. [Born in Md. Appointed from Md.]
2nd Lieut. 3rd Inf., 3 March, 1799. 1st Lieut., 12 May, 1799. Trans. to 2nd Inf., 1 April, 1802. Resigned 12 Aug., 1802. Capt. 14th Inf., 12 March, 1812. Maj. 14th Inf., 3 March, 1813. Lieut. Col. 32nd Inf., 15 June, 1814. Discharged 15 June, 1815. M. S. K., 6 Jan., 1816. Resigned 29 April, 1816. Died 10 Sept., 1822.

LANE, WM. B. [Born in Ky. Appointed from Army.]
Priv. Co. D, Mtd Rifles, 17 July, 1846. Corpl., 2 Dec., 1846. Sergt., 1 Feb., 1847. 1st Sergt., 25 Feb., 1847. Sergt., 16 Nov., 1847. Trans. to Priv. Co. A, 4th Ky. Vols., 21 Jan., 1848. Bvt. 2nd Lieut. Mtd. Rifles, 28 June, 1848. 2nd Lieut., 31 Oct., 1848. 1st Lieut., 16 Sept., 1853. Capt., 14 May, 1861. 3rd Cav., 3 Aug., 1861. Bvt. Maj., 30 March, 1865, for meritorious and faithful service in recruitment of the armies of the United States. Bvt. Lieut. Col., 13 Nov., 1865, for faithful and meritorious service in connection with the mustering out of service and disbanding of the Vol. Army of the United States. Maj. 3rd Cav., 9 Nov., 1866. Retired 15 Dec., 1870. Died 28 June, 1898.

LANE, WILLIAM C. [Born in Ind. Appointed from Ind.]
Garrison Surg. Mate, 15 Sept., 1814. Post Surg., 24 April, 1816. Resigned 14 Nov., 1818.

LANG, CLARENCE E.* [Born in Ohio. Appointed from Ohio.]
2nd Lieut. 2nd Art., 12 June, 1894. Dismissed 1 May, 1899.

LANG, FRANK R. [Born in Maine. Appointed from Maine.]
Sergt. Maj. 1st Maine Vols., 13 May, 1898. 2nd Lieut. Co. H., 5 July to 30 Oct., 1898. 2nd Lieut. 9th Inf., 10 April, 1899.

LANGDON, LOOMIS L.* [Born in N. Y. Appointed from N. Y.]
Bvt. 2nd Lieut. 4th Art., 1 July, 1854. 2nd Lieut. 1st Art., 21 Aug., 1854. 1st Lieut., 13 July, 1860. Capt., 28 Aug., 1861. Bvt. Maj., 20 Feb., 1864, for gallant and meritorious service in the Battle of Olustee, Fla. Bvt. Lieut. Col., 29 Sept., 1864, for gallant and meritorious service in the attack on Fort Gilmer, Va. Maj. 2nd Art., 20 March, 1879. Lieut. Col., 1 Dec., 1883. Col. 1st Art., 25 Jan., 1889. Retired by operation of law, 25 Oct., 1895.

LANGDON, RUSSELL C.* [Born in N. Y. Appointed from N. Y.]
Addl. 2nd Lieut. 8th Inf., 12 June, 1896. 2nd Lieut. 1st Inf., 7 Nov., 1896. Trans. to 8th Inf., 12 Dec., 1896. 1st Lieut. of Inf., 20 Dec., 1898. Ass'd to 8th Inf., 1 Jan., 1899. Trans. to 3rd Inf., 14 Aug., 1899.

LANGDON, WILLIAM E. [Born in N. H. Appointed from N. H.]
Asst. Surg., 8 May, 1822. Resigned 1 May, 1826.

LANGFITT, WILLIAM C.* [Born in Va. Appointed form Ohio.]
Cadet at Mil. Acad., 1 July, 1878, to 25 July, 1879. Reappointed 26 July, 1880. 2nd Lieut. Eng., 13 June, 1883. 1st Lieut., 30 Sept., 1884. Capt., 31 March, 1895. Maj. 2nd Vol. Eng., 7 June, 1898, to 16 May, 1899.

LANGHAM, AUGUST L. [Born in Va. Appointed from Ohio.]
Ensign Rifles, 3 May, 1808. Resigned 15 April, 1809. Capt. 19th Inf., 12 March, 1812. Maj. 10th Inf., 15 Aug., 1813. Disbanded 15 June, 1815. Reinstated 2 Dec., 1815, as Capt. 7th Inf. Resigned 15 Oct., 1817. Retained Dec., 1815 (in reorganization under Act of 3 March, of that year), as Capt. 7th Inf., with Bvt. of Maj., from 15 Aug., 1813. Died 28 Aug., 1834.

LANGHORNE, GEORGE T.* [Born in Ky. Appointed from Va.]
Addl. 2nd Lieut. 5th Cav., 12 June, 1889. 2nd Lieut. 3rd Cav., 31 Aug., 1889. 1st Lieut. 1st Cav., 11 Dec., 1896. Capt. 27 U. S. Vols., 5 July, 1899, to 2 Nov., 1899. Maj. 39th U. S. Vols., 17 Aug., 1899.

LANGWORTHY, ELISHA P. [Born in N. Y. Appointed from N. Y.]
Asst. Surg., 16 May, 1850. Resigned 30 April, 1861. Died 8 March, 1862.

LANSING, ARTHUR B.* Born in N. Y. Appointed from N. Y.]
Bvt. 2nd Lieut. 1st Art., 1 July, 1836. Resigned 30 Sept., 1836. 2nd Lieut. 2nd Art., 13 Nov., 1839. 1st Lieut., 18 June, 1846. Capt. A. Q. M., 18 Jan., 1847, to 30 June, 1851. Resigned 1 Sept., 1851. Died 9 Feb., 1880.

LANSING, HENRY S. [Born in N. Y. Appointed from N. Y.]
Col. 17th N. Y. Vols., 24 May, 1861. Bvt. Brig. Gen. Vols., 13 March, 1865, for faithful and meritorious service during the war. Mustered out 2 June, 1863. Capt. 12th Inf., 5 Aug., 1861. Resigned 17 July, 1863. Died 13 April, 1882.

LANSING, SANDERS. [Born in N. Y. Appointed from N. Y.]
Mil. Storekeeper Ord., 19 July, 1834. Removed 10 March, 1851. Mil. Storekeeper Ord., 9 April, 1853. Removed 6 March, 1862.

LANTZ, PETER A. [Born in Penn. Appointed from Penn.]
Priv. Co. A, 25th Penn. Vols., 18 April to 23 July, 1861. 1st Lieut. 50th Penn. Vols., 13 Sept., 1861. Resigned 18 Jan., 1862. Sergt. Co. H, 128th Penn. Vols., 15 Aug., 1862. 2nd Lieut., 21 Feb., 1863. Mustered out 19 May, 1863. 2nd Lieut. 205th Penn. Vols., 31 Aug., 1864. Mustered out 12 May, 1865. 2nd Lieut. 30th Inf., 22 Jan., 1867. 1st Lieut., 22 Feb., 1869. Unassigned 23 March, 1869. Cashiered 14 Feb., 1870.

LANZA, CONRAD H. [Born in N. Y. Appointed from D. C.]
2nd Lieut. 3rd Art., 9 July, 1898.

LA POINT, HENRY C.* [Born in Vt. Appointed from Vt.]
2nd Lieut. 2nd Cav., 13 June, 1873. 1st Lieut., 25 Jan., 1881. Dismissed 24 July, 1888.

LARKE, ALURED. [Born in Eng. Appointed from Wis.]
Priv. Co. A, 2nd Wis. Vols., 27 May, 1861. Sergt., 1 Dec., 1861. 2nd Lieut. 2nd Wis. Vols., 20 Feb., 1863. 1st Lieut., 21 Aug., 1863. Capt., 24 March, 1864. Mustered out 14 Dec., 1864. Capt. 5th U. S. Vet. Vols., 9 Jan., 1865. Mustered out 20 July, 1866. 2nd Lieut. 26th Inf., 7 March, 1867. Trans. to 10th Inf., 19 May, 1869. 1st Lieut., 25 April, 1877. Died 14 Dec., 1881.

LARKIN, WILLIAM J. [Born in Ireland. Appointed from Ill.]
Post Chap., 10 Dec., 1888.

LARNARD, CHAS. H.* [Born in R. I. Appointed from R. I.]
Bvt. 2nd Lieut. 4th Inf., 1 July, 1831 2nd Lieut., 1 July, 1831. 1st Lieut., 7 Aug., 1836. Capt., 25 Feb., 1841. Drowned 27 March, 1854. Bvt. Maj., 9 May, 1846, for gallant and meritorious conduct at Palo Alto and Resaca de la Palma.

LARNED, BENJAMIN F. [Born in Mass. Appointed from Mass.]
Ensign 21st Inf., 1 Oct., 1813. 3rd Lieut., 7 March, 1814. 2nd Lieut., 8 March, 1814. Reg. P. M., 20 Jan. to June, 1815, and from 24 Nov., 1815, to 1 June, 1821. 1st Lieut., 4 Aug., 1814. Trans. to 5th Inf., 17 May, 1815. Maj. P. M., 24 Nov., 1815. Lieut. Col. Dep. P. M. G., 3 March, 1847. Col. P. M. G., 20 July, 1854. Died 6 Sept., 1862. Bvt. Capt., 15 Aug., 1814, for gallant conduct in defence of Fort Erie.

LARNED, CHAS. H.* [Born in R. I. Appointed from R. I.]
(Changed name to Chas. H. Larnard)—which see.

LARNED, CHAS. T. [Born in Mich. Appointed from Mich.]
Cadet at Mil. Acad., 1 July, 1851, to 29 June, 1854. Addl. P. M., 1 June, 1861. Maj. P. M., 30 Aug., 1861. Bvt., Lieut. Col., 13 March, 1865, for faithful and meritorious service during the war. Lieut. Col. Dep. P. M. Gen., 8 June, 1880. Died 17 March, 1882.

LARNED, CHAS. W.* [Born in N. Appointed at Large.]
2nd Lieut. 3rd Cav., 15 June, 1870. Trans. to 7th Cav., 10 Oct., 1870. 1st Lieut., 25 June, 1876. Prof. of Drawing at Mil. Acad., 25 July, 1876.

LARNED, DANIEL R. [Born in Conn. Appointed from Conn.]
Capt. A. A. G. Vols., 13 March, 1863. Bvt. Maj. Vols., 1 Aug., 1864, for gallant and meritorious service during the campaign in East Tenn.; at the Siege of Knoxville, and in the Battles of the late campaign from the Rapidan to Petersburg. Bvt. Lieut. Col. Vols., 13 March, 1865, for gallant and meritorious service in the campaign form the Rapidan to Petersburg, Va. Resigned 1 June, 1865. Maj. P. M., 23 June, 1879. Retired by operation of law, 26 July, 1892.

LARNED, FRANK H. [Born in Mich. Appointed from Mich.]
2nd Lieut. Inf., 8 March, 1847. 2nd Lieut. Voltigeurs, 9 April, 1847. Trans. to 2nd Art., 27 June, 1848. 1st Lieut., 1 July, 1852. Capt., 28 April, 1861. Maj. 1st Art., 3 Jan., 1867. Retired 5 Feb., 1867. Died 8 Jan., 1891.

LARNED, FREDERIC S. [Born in Mass. Appointed from Mo.]
Capt. 12th Inf., 14 May, 1861. Dropped 31 Aug., 1863.

LARRABEE, CHARLES. [Born in Conn. Appointed from Conn.]
2nd Lieut. Light Drag., 13 June, 1808. 1st Lieut. 4th Inf., 12 June, 1809. Capt., 12 Sept., 1812. Maj. A. I. G., 9 Nov., 1814, to 15 June, 1815. Retained as Capt. 8th Inf., 17 May, 1815. Trans. to 3rd Inf., 2 Dec., 1815. Trans. to 5th Inf., 31 Dec., 1821. Trans. to 6th Inf., 29 April, 1823. Resigned 7 April, 1825. Bvt. Maj., 9 Aug., 1812, for gallant conduct in the Battle of Brownstown, Mich., where he lost his left arm.

LARRABEE, CHAS. F. [Born in Maine. Appointed from Maine.]
Sergt. Maj. 30th Maine Vols., 11 Jan., 1864. 1st Lieut., 1 Sept., 1864. Bvt. Capt. and Maj. Vols., 13 March, 1865, for gallant and distinguished service at the Battles of Sabine Cross Roads, Pleasant Hill and Monet's Bluff, La., 8, 9 and 23 April, 1864. Mustered out 12 Aug., 1865. 2nd Lieut. 7th Inf., 23 Feb., 1866. 1st Lieut., 28 July, 1866. Mustered out 1 Jan., 1871. Bvt. Capt., 2 March, 1867, for gallant and meritorious service in the Battle of Pleasant Hill, La.

LASSEIGNE, ARMAND I.* [Born in La. Appointed from La.]
2nd Lieut. 7th Inf., 1 July, 1886. 1st Liuet. 21st Inf., 15 Dec., 1892. Trans. to 14th Inf., 27 Dec., 1892. Capt., 2 March, 1899.

LASSITER, WILLIAM. [Born in N. C. Appointed from N. C.]
Cadet at Mil. Acad., 1 Sept., 1868, to 19 July, 1871. 2nd Lieut. 16th Inf., 1 Oct., 1873. 1st Lieut., 26 April, 1883. R. Q. M., 1 July, 1885, to 1 Aug., 1889. Capt., 7 Aug., 1897.

LASSITER, WILLIAM.* [Born in Va. Appointed from Va.]
Addl. 2nd Lieut. 4th Art., 12 June, 1889. 2nd Lieut. 5th Art., 10 Feb., 1890. Trans. to 1st Art., 29 Jan., 1891. 1st Lieut., 26 Aug., 1897. Graduate of the Artillery School, 1894.

LATCHFORD, THOS. [Born in Mass. Appointed from Md.]
1st Lieut. 8th Md. Vols., 31 Oct., 1862, to 11 March, 1864. 1st Lieut. 28th U. S. Col. Inf., 28 Aug., 1864. Capt., 18 Nov., 1864. Mustered out 8 Nov., 1865. 2nd Lieut. 11th Inf., 6 April, 1866. Trans. to 20th Inf., 21 Sept., 1866. 1st Lieut., 2 Nov., 1866. R. Q. M., 20 Aug., 1868, to 31 Dec., 1870. Died 12 July, 1873.

LATHROP, SOLON H. [Born in N. H. Appointed from N. M.]
Capt. 17th Inf., 5 Aug., 1861. Lieut. Col. A. I. G. Vols., 20 Aug., 1862, to 1 Aug., 1865. Bvt. Col. Vols., 13 March, 1865, for meritorious service in the Northern Dept. Trans. to 35th Inf., 21 Sept., 1866. Died 7 Oct., 1867.

LATIMER, ALFRED E.* [Born in S. C. Appointed from S. C.]
Bvt. 2nd Lieut. 4th Inf., 1 July, 1853. 2nd Lieut. 2nd Inf., 5 Feb., 1855. 1st Lieut., 18 April, 1859. Capt. 11th Inf., 14 May, 1861. Bvt. Maj., 13 March, 1865, for gallant and meritorious service. Trans. to 29th Inf., 21 Sept., 1866. Maj. 19th Inf., 25 June, 1867. Unassigned 15 March, 1869. Ass'd to 4th Cav., 15 Dec., 1870. Retired 20 March, 1879.

LA TOURRETTE, JAMES A. M. [Born in N. Y. Appointed from N. Y.]
Chap. Post of Fort Columbus, N. Y. Harbor, 6 Feb., 1865, to 27 April, 1867. Post Chap., 3 April, 1867. Retired 23 March, 1890. Died 23 Sept., 1891.

LATTIMORE, WALTER O. [Born in Ind. Appointed from Ind.]
Sergt. Co. K, 12th Ind. Vols., 24 July to 1 Sept., 1861. 1st Lieut. 19th Inf., 5 Aug., 1861. Capt., 18 March, 1865. Discharged 10 Dec., 1870. Bvt. Capt., 1 Sept., 1864, for gallant and meritorious service during the Atlanta campaign, and at the Battle of Jonesboro, Ga.

LAUB, CHAS H. [Born in D. C. Appointed from D. C.]
Asst. Surg., 30 Nov., 1836. Maj. Surg., 17 Oct., 1854. Lieut. Col. Asst. Med. Pur., 26 June, 1876. Died 2 Dec., 1876. Bvt. Lieut. Col., 13 March, 1865, for gallant and meritorious service during the war.

LAUBACH, HOWARD L.* [Born in Penn. Appointed from Ind.]
2nd Lieut. 23rd Inf., 12 June, 1893. 1st Lieut., 26 April, 1898.

LAUDERDALE, JOHN V. [Born in N. Y. Appointed from N. Y.]
1st Lieut. Asst. Surg., 14 May, 1867. Capt. Asst. Surg., 14 May, 1870. Maj. Surg., 3 July, 1888. Retired by operation of law 13 Nov., 1896.

LAUFFER, SAMUEL B. [Born in Penn. Appointed from Penn.]
Capt. A. Q. M. Vols., 14 Aug., 1863. Mustered out 30 April, 1866. Capt. A. Q. M., 18 Jan., 1867. Discharged 1 Jan., 1871. Died 15 June, 1876.

LAUMAN, GEORGE S. [Born in Penn. Appointed from Penn.]
Priv. Ringgold Batty Penn. Vols., 18 April to 29 April,1861. 2nd Lieut. 10th Inf., 26 April, 1861. 1st Lieut., 25 June, 1861. Capt., 16 Oct., 1863. Died 3 Oct., 1864.

LAUTZ, HENRY H. [Born in Penn. Appointed from Army.]
Priv. Co. C, 7th Penn. Res., 27 July, 1861. 2nd Lieut., 7 Nov., 1861. Discharged 10 Nov., 1862. Priv. and Corpl. Co. F, 4th Inf., 21 July, 1865. 2nd Lieut. 4th Inf., 21 July, 1865. 1st Lieut., 10 March, 1866. Dropped 16 Nov., 1866. Died 24 Oct., 1889.

LAVAL, JACINT. [Born in France. Appointed from S. C.]
Capt. Light Drag., 3 May, 1808. Maj., 15 Feb., 1809. Lieut. Col. 1st Light Drag., 7 June, 1813. Col., 1 Aug., 1813. Retained 12 May, 1814, as Lieut. Col. Light

Drag. Disbanded 15 June, 1815. Mil. Storekeeper, 21 May, 1816. Died 2 Sept., 1822.

LAVAL, LOUIS. [Born in S. C. Appointed from S. C.]
2nd Lieut. Light Drag., 1 May, 1812. 1st Lieut. Rifles, 28 July, 1813. Trans. to Rifle Reg., 17 May, 1815. Resigned 1 March, 1817. Died 10 Sept., 1832.

LAVAL, WM. [Born in S. C. Appointed from S. C.]
Ensign 3rd Inf., 12 Dec., 1808. 2nd Lieut., 1 Jan., 1810. 1st Lieut., 11 May, 1811. Capt., 15 Feb., 1814. Trans. to 1st Inf., 17 May, 1815. Trans. to 3rd Art., 1 June, 1821. Resigned 31 Dec., 1822. Bvt. Maj., 7 Nov., 1814, for gallant conduct during the Siege of New Orleans. Died — Aug., 1865.

LAVERTY, JAMES C. [Born in Ireland. Appointed from Penn.]
Chap. 24th Inf., 15 March, 1876. Retired 5 Feb., 1886. Died 20 Jan., 1887.

LAW, EDWARD. [Born in Penn. Appointed from Penn.]
2nd Lieut. 7th Cav., 15 Aug., 1867. 1st Lieut., 11 March, 1869. Resigned 22 March, 1870. Drowned 5 Oct., 1881.

LAWDER, RYND E. [Born in Ohio. Appointed from Mo.]
Priv. Co. B, 11th Ohio Vols., 20 April, 1861, to 18 Aug., 1861. 1st Lieut. 2nd Ohio Cav., 18 Dec., 1862. Capt., 19 Dec., 1864. Maj., 1 Sept., 1865. Mustered out 11 Sept., 1865. 2nd Lieut. 7th Cav., 28 July, 1866. Resigned 4 April, 1867.

LAWLESS, MICHAEL. [Born in Ireland. Appointed from Army.]
Priv., Corpl., Sergt. and 1st Segt. Troop H, 2nd Drag.(2nd Cav.), 13 March, 1855, to 23 Sept., 1862. 2nd Lieut. 2nd Cav., 17 July, 1862. 1st Lieut., 9 June, 1863. Killed 11 June, 1864, in action at Trevillian Station, Va.

LAWRENCE, JAMES K. [Born in Penn. Appointed from Penn.]
Capt. 11th Inf., 5 Aug., 1861. Trans. to 29th Inf., 21 Sept., 1866. Trans. to 11th Inf., 25 April, 1869. Resigned 1 Jan., 1870. Bvt. Maj., 13 Dec., 1862, for gallant and meritorious service at the Battle of Fredericksburg, Va.

LAWRENCE, SAML. B. [Born in N. Y. Appointed from N. Y.]
Priv. Co. F, 7th N. Y. State Militia, 26 April to 3 June, 1861. 1st Lieut. 16th Inf., 14 May, 1861. Capt., 3 May, 1862. Lieut. Col. A. A. G., 18 March, 1864, to 3 Aug., 1865. Resigned 14 Aug., 1865. Bvt. Capt., 7 April, 1862, for gallant and meritorious service at the Battle of Shiloh, Tenn. Bvt. Maj., 13 March, 1865, for gallant and meritorious service during the war.

LAWRENCE, WM. [Born in Md. Appointed from Md.]
2nd Lieut. 4th Inf., 8 June, 1801. Trans. to 2nd Inf., 1 April, 1802. 1st Lieut., 12 Oct., 1804. Reg. Adj., Jan., 1807, to Jan., 1810. Capt., 1 Jan., 1810. Maj., 19 April, 1814. Trans. to 8th Inf., 17 May, 1815. Lieut. Col. 3rd Inf., 8 May, 1818. Trans. to 1st Inf., 12 Dec., 1820. Trans. to 2nd Inf., 1 June, 1821. Col. 5th Inf., 20 Aug., 1828. Resigned 15 July, 1831. Bvt. Lieut. Col., 15 Sept., 1814, for gallant conduct in the attack on Fort Bowyer. Bvt. Col., 15 Sept., 1824, for ten years' faithful service in one grade. Died 7 Jan., 1841.

LAWRENCE, WM. D. [Born in R. I. Appointed from N. Y.]
Capt. 13th Inf., 12 March, 1812. Disbanded 15 June, 1815. Batt. P. M. Corps Art., 29 April, 1816. Disbanded 20 Nov., 1817. Died 26 Feb., 1833.

LAWRENCE, WM. H. [Born in N. J. Appointed from N. Y.]
Priv. Co. F, 7th N. Y. State Militia, 29 April, 1861. Mustered out 3 June, 1861. 1st Lieut. 14th Inf., 14 May, 1861. Capt., 25 Oct., 1861. Col. 34th N. J. Vols., 9 Nov., 1863. Bvt. Maj. and Lieut. Col., 13 March, 1865, for gallant and meritorious service during the war, and Brig. Gen. Vols., 13 March, 1865, for faithful and meritorious service during the war. Resigned from Vol. Service 3 Aug., 1865, and from U. S. A., 14 Aug., 1865.

LAWS, ALBERT.* [Born in Md. Appointed from Md.]
2nd Lieut. 24th Inf., 12 June, 1893. 1st Lieut., 26 April, 1898. Maj. 35th U. S. Vols., 5 July, 1899.

LAWSHE, LEWIS. [Born in Penn. Appointed from Penn.]
Ensign 42nd Inf., 11 March, 1814. 3rd Lieut., 1 May, 1814. 2nd Lieut., 1 Oct., 1814. Trans. to 7th Inf., 17 May, 1815. R. Q. M., Feb., 1816, to 1 Nov., 1818. 1st Lieut., 30 April, 1817. Resigned 31 Aug., 1819.

LAWSON, GAINES. [Born in Tenn. Appointed from Tenn.]
Priv. Co. D, 4th Tenn. Vols., 21 Dec., 1862. 1st Sergt., 15 April, 1863. Capt. 4th Tenn. Vols., 10 Aug., 1864. Maj., 5 June, 1865. Mustered out 2 Aug., 1865. Capt. 39th Inf., 28 July, 1866. Bvt. Maj. and Lieut. Col., 2 March, 1867, for faithful and meritorious service. Trans. to 25th Inf., 20 April, 1869. Retired with rank of Maj. by operation of law 16 Sept., 1892. Medal of Honor for most distinguished gallantry in action at McMinnville, Tenn., 3 Oct., 1863, while serving as 1st Sergt. Co. D, 4th Tenn. Inf., in trying to save the life of a comrade who lay wounded between the lines.

LAWSON, GEORGE W.* [Born in Tenn. Appointed from Tenn.]
Bvt. 2nd Lieut. 2nd Art., 1 July, 1830. Resigned 30 June, 1831. Died in 1832.

LAWSON, JOSEPH. [Born in Ireland. Appointed from Ky.]
2nd Lieut. 11th Ky. Cav., 3 Oct., 1862. Capt., 28 Nov., 1862. Mustered out 17 July, 1865. 2nd Lieut. 3rd Cav., 23 Feb., 1866. 1st Lieut., 28 July, 1866. Capt., 25 Sept., 1876. Died 30 Jan., 1881.

LAWSON, THOS. [Born in Va. Appointed from Va.]
Surg. Mate U. S. N., 1 March, 1809. Resigned 12 Jan., 1811. Garrison Surg. Mate, 8 Feb., 1811. Maj. Surg. 6th Inf., 21 May, 1813. Trans. to 7th Inf., 17 May, 1815. Maj. Surg., 1 June, 1821. Surg. Gen., 30 Nov., 1836. Died 15 May, 1861. Bvt. Brig. Gen., 30 May, 1848, for meritorious conduct in the Mexican war.

LAWSON, THOMAS E. [Born in Ky. Appointed from Ky.]
Priv. Co. A, 3rd Ky. Cav., 11 Dec., 1861, to 11 July, 1865. 2nd Lieut. 12th Inf., 23 Feb., 1866. Trans. to 21st Inf., 21 Sept., 1866. 1st Lieut., 1 Jan., 1867. Unassigned 8 April, 1869. Discharged 14 Nov., 1870.

LAWTON, ALEXR. R.* [Born in S. C. Appointed from S. C.]
2nd Lieut. 1st Art., 1 July, 1839. Resigned 31 Dec., 1840.

LAWTON, EDWARD P.* [Born in Ga. Appointed from Ga.]
2nd Lieut. 13th Inf., 14 June, 1885. 1st Lieut. 19th Inf., 4 June, 1892. Capt., 2 March, 1899.

LAWTON, FRANK H. [Born in Iowa. Appointed from Army.]
Priv., Corpl. and Sergt. Co. F, 14th Inf., 1 Aug., 1891, to 1 Nov., 1893. 2nd Lieut. 21st Inf., 2 Oct., 1893. 1st Lieut., 26 April, 1898.

LAWTON, FREDERICK G.* [Born in Miss. Appointed from Miss.]
2nd Lieut. 19th Inf., 12 June, 1894. 1st Lieut., 26 April, 1898.

LAWTON, HENRY W. [Born in Ohio. Appointed from Ind.]
Sergt. Co. E, 9th Ind. Vols., 18 April, 1861. Discharged 29 July, 1861. 1st Lieut. 30th Ind. Vols., 20 Aug., 1861. Capt., 17 May, 1862. Lieut. Col., 15 Nov., 1864. Bvt. Col. Vols., 13 March, 1865, for gallant and meritorious service during the war. Mustered out 25 Nov., 1865. 2nd Lieut. 41st Inf., 28 July, 1866. 1st Lieut., 31 July, 1867. R. Q. M., 1 June, 1868, to 11 Nov., 1869. Trans. to 24th Inf., 11 Nov., 1869. R. Q. M., 11 Nov., 1869, to 1 Jan., 1871. Trans. to 4th Cav., 1 Jan., 1871. R. Q. M., 1 May, 1872, to 20 March, 1875, and 1 Sept., 1876, to 15 March, 1879. Capt., 20 March, 1879. Maj. I. G., 17 Sept., 1888. Lieut. Col. I. G., 12 Feb., 1889. Col. I. G., 7 July, 1898. Brig. Gen. Vols., 4 May, 1898. Maj. Gen. Vols., 11 July, 1898. Medal of Honor for distinguished gallantry in leading a charge of skirmishers against the enemy's rifle pits, taking them with their occupants and stubbornly and successfully resisting two determined attacks of the enemy to retake the works; in front of Atlanta, Ga., 3 Aug., 1864; while serving as Capt. Co. A, 30th Ind. Vols., and Brigade Officer of the Day.

LAWTON, LOUIS B.* [Born in Iowa. Appointed from N. Y.]
2nd Lieut. 9th Inf., 12 June, 1893. 1st Lieut., 26 April, 1898.

LAWTON, ROBERT B. [Born in R. I. Appointed from R. I.]
2nd Lieut. 2nd Drag., 12 Oct., 1836. 1st Lieut., 29 Jan., 1838. Resigned 8 Oct., 1841. Col. R. I. Cav., 14 Dec., 1861. Discharged 5 July, 1862. Died — May, 1876.

LAY, GEORGE W.* [Born in Va. Appointed from Va.]
Bvt. 2nd Lieut. 6th Inf., 1 July, 1842. 2nd Lieut., 22 Nov., 1843. 1st Lieut., 15 April, 1851. Capt., 24 Dec., 1856. Lieut. Col. A. A. de C. to Bvt. Lieut. Gen. Scott, 7 March, 1855, to 2 March, 1861. Resigned 2 March, 1861. Bvt. 1st Lieut., 23 Sept., 1846, for gallant and meritorious conduct at Monterey. Bvt. Capt., 20 Aug., 1847, for gallant and meritorious conduct at Contreras and Churubusco. Died 7 May, 1867.

LAY, J. CARBERRY. [Born in D. C. Appointed from D. C.]
Priv. National Rifles D. C. Vols., 15 April, to 2 July, 1861. 1st Lieut. 12th Inf., 14 May, 1861. Capt., 24 Oct., 1861. Cashiered 21 July, 1862. 2nd Lieut. 17th Inf., 30 Oct., 1863. 1st Lieut., 28 Nov., 1863. Resigned 12 Sept., 1864.

LAY, RICHARD G. [Born in D. C. Appointed from D. C.]
2nd Lieut. 3rd Inf., 20 June, 1859. 1st Lieut., 14 May, 1861. Capt., 12 March, 1862. Unassigned 23 April, 1869. Discharged 19 Aug., 1870. Bvt. Maj., 2 July, 1863, for gallant and meritorious service at the Battle of Gettysburg, Penn. Bvt. Lieut. Col., 13 March, 1865, for gallant and meritorious service at the Battle of Gettysburg, Penn.

LAYNE, ALEX. C. [Born in Va. Appointed from Va.]
2nd Lieut. of Inf., 1 March, 1847; 14th Inf., 9 April, 1847. Disbanded 25 July, 1848.

LAYTON, CALEB R. [Born in Del. Appointed from Del.]
Cadet Mil. Acad., 1 July, 1843, to 1 July, 1845. Capt. 1st Del. Vols., 16 May, 1861. Maj., 1 July, 1861. Mustered out 17 Aug., 1861. Capt. 11th Inf., 5 Aug., 1861. Bvt. Maj., 2 July, 1863, for gallant and meritorious service in the Battle of Getysburg, Penn. Trans. to 16th Inf., 14 April, 1869. Maj. 20th Inf., 4 March, 1879. Trans. to 5th Inf., 24 May, 1882. Lieut. Col. 20th Inf., 2 April, 1883. Retired for disability 8 Oct., 1885. Died 20 Aug., 1887.

LAZARUS, FREDERICK. [Born in Penn. Appointed from Penn.]
3rd Lieut. 42nd Inf., 1 Oct., 1813. 2nd Lieut., 1 May, 1814. 1st Lieut., 11 May, 1814. Disbanded 15 June, 1815. 2nd Lieut. 8th Inf., 3 Feb., 1819. 1st Lieut., 1 Jan., 1820. Disbanded 1 June, 1821.

LAZELLE, HENRY M.* [Born in Mass. Appointed from Mass.]
Bvt. 2nd Lieut. 1st Inf., 1 July, 1855. 2nd Lieut., 8th Inf., 9 Oct., 1855. 1st Lieut., 27 April, 1861. Capt., 11 June, 1861. Col. 16th N. Y. Cav., 23 Oct., 1863. Bvt. Maj., 19 Sept., 1864, for gallant and meritorious service in action near Culpeper, Va. Resigned Vol. Com., 19 Oct., 1864. Maj. 1st Inf., 15 Dec., 1874. Lieut. Col. 23rd Inf., 26 June, 1882. Col. 18th Inf., 17 Feb., 1889. Retired for disability 26 Nov., 1894.

LAZELLE, JACOB H. G.* [Born in Md. Appointed from Minn.]
2nd Lieut. 18th Inf., 11 June 1892. Died 12 July, 1898.

LAZENBY, HENRY. [Born in D. C. Appointed from D. C.]
2nd Lieut. 6th Cav., 11 Oct., 1867. Appointment rejected by Senate and revoked, 1 Aug., 1868. Died 28 June, 1888.

LEA, ALBERT M.* [Born in Tenn. Appointed from Tenn.]
Bvt. 2nd Lieut. 1st Art., 1 July, 1831. Trans. to 7th Inf., 11 Aug., 1831. 2nd Lieut., 4 March, 1833. 2nd Lieut. 2nd Drag., 4 March, 1833. Resigned 31 May, 1836.

LEA, SAMUEL. [Born in N. Y. Appointed from N. Y.]
1st Lieut. of Inf., 2 March, 1847; 10th Inf., 9 April, 1847. Reg. Adj., 1 May, 1847, to 26 Aug., 1848. Disbanded 26 Aug., 1848.

LEA, SQUIRE. [Born in La. Appointed from La.]
Maj. Surg. 44th Inf., 1 Aug., 1813. Disbanded 15 June, 1815. Post Surg., 15 May, 1818. Asst. Surg., 1 June, 1821. Died 5 Feb., 1826.

LEACH, GEORGE. [Born in Ohio. Appointed from Ind.]
2nd Lieut. Mounted Rangers, 6 July, 1832. Resigned 1 Feb., 1833.

LEACH, SMITH S.* [Born in Ind. Appointed from Ind.]
2nd Lieut. Eng., 16 June, 1875. 1st Lieut., 4 March, 1879. Capt., 30 Sept., 1884. Maj., 5 Feb., 1897.

LEADBETTER, DANVILLE.* [Born in Maine. Appointed from Maine.]
Bvt. 2nd Lieut. 1st Art., 1 July, 1836. Trans. to Eng., 1 Nov., 1836. Trans. to 1st Art., 31 Dec., 1836. Trans. to Eng., 31 July, 1837. 1st Lieut., 7 July, 1838. Capt., 16 Oct., 1852. Resigned 31 Dec., 1857. Died 26 Sept., 1866.

LEAHY, MICHAEL. [Born in Ireland. Appointed from Army.]
Priv. Co. B, 3rd Art., 15 July, 1853. Trans. to Co. C, 1st Art., 3 Dec., 1853. Corpl., 10 July, 1857. Discharged 15 May, 1858. Corpl. Co. C, 1st Art., 15 May, 1858. Sergt., 1 Sept., 1862. 1st Sergt., 22 Oct., 1862. Discharged 15 March, 1863. 1st Sergt. Co. C, 1st Art., 15 March, 1863. 2nd Lieut. 1st Art., 31 Oct., 1863. Bvt. 1st Lieut., 20 Feb., 1864, for gallant and meritorious service in the Battle of Olustee, Fla. Bvt. Capt., 7 Oct., 1864, for gallant and meritorious service in action on the Darbytown Road, near Richmond, Va. 1st Lieut., 1st Art., 14 Oct., 1864. Trans. to 18th Inf., 3 Aug., 1869. R. Q. M., 31 March to 15 June, 1887. Capt., 15 June, 1887. Retired for disability 8 Nov., 1889.

LEAMY, WM. H. [Born in Penn. Appointed from Army.]
Priv. and Corpl. Co. A. Mounted Rifles, 5 Aug., 1857, to 18 Aug., 1861. 2nd Lieut. 19th Inf., 14 May, 1861. 1st Lieut., 24 Oct., 1861. Died 11 July, 1864.

LEAR, CLINTON W. [Born in Ala. Appointed from Ala.]
2nd Lieut. 5th Inf., 3 March, 1847. 1st Lieut., 30 April, 1849. Died 26 Oct., 1854. Bvt. 1st Lieut., 15 Aug., 1847, for gallant and meritorious conduct at Paso Ovejas, National Bridge and Cerro Gordo.

LEAR, WM. K. [Born in Florida. Appointed from Texas.]
2nd Lieut. 3rd Art., 7 June, 1855. Resigned 1 April, 1856.

LEAR, WM. W. [Born in Md. Appointed from Army.]
Priv., Corpl. and Sergt. Light Drag., 18 May, 1812, to 15 June, 1815, and in 4th Inf. to March, 1818. 2nd Lieut. 4th Inf., 13 Feb., 1818. 1st Lieut., 24 Feb., 1818. Capt. 1 May, 1824. Maj. 3rd Inf., 14 June, 1842. Died 31 Oct., 1846, of wounds received in the Battle of Monterey, Mexico. Bvt. Maj., 1 May, 1834, for ten years' faithful service in one grade.

LEARNARD, HENRY G.* [Born in Mo. Appointed from Mich.]
2nd Lieut. 19th Inf., 12 June, 1890. 1st Lieut. 14th Inf., 1 March, 1897. Capt. 4th Inf., 15 Nov., 1899. Trans. to 14th Inf., 3 Feb., 1900.

LEARY, EDMUND M.* [Born in Mass. Appointed from Maine.]
2nd Lieut. 2nd Cav., 11 June, 1892. 1st Lieut., 2 March, 1899.

LEARY, PETER, Jr. [Born in Md. Appointed from Md.]
2nd Lieut. Md. Independent Light Art., 18 Aug., 1862. 1st Lieut., 8 April, 1865. Mustered out 17 June, 1865. 2nd Lieut. 4th Art., 2 April, 1867. 1st Lieut., 24 Jan., 1873. Capt., 28 Aug., 1891. Graduate of the Artillery School, 1880. Bvt. Capt., 27 Feb., 1890, for gallant and meritorious service in action against Indians in the Lava Beds, Cal., 15 and 16 April, 1873.

LEAS, EDWIN J. [Born in Ohio. Appointed from Ind.]
2nd Lieut. 5th Cav., 17 Aug., 1867. Resigned 13 Aug., 1869.

LEAVELL, BENJAMIN W.* [Born in Ohio. Appointed from Ohio.]
2nd Lieut. 24th Inf., 13 June, 1879. 1st Lieut., 7 Oct., 1884. Capt., 12 Feb., 1897.

LEAVENWORTH, HENRY. [Born in Conn. Appointed from N. Y.]
Capt. 25th U. S. Inf., 25 April, 1812. Maj. 9th Inf., 15 Aug., 1813. Trans. to 2nd Inf., 17 May, 1815. Lieut. Col. 5th Inf., 10 Feb., 1818. Trans. to 6th Inf., 1 Oct., 1821. Col. 3rd Inf., 16 Dec., 1825. Died 21 July, 1834. Bvt. Lieut. Col., 15 July, 1814, for distinguished and meritorious service at the Battle of Chippewa. Bvt. Col., 25 July, 1814, for distinguished service at Niagara Falls. Bvt. Brig. Gen., 25 July, 1824, for ten years' faithful service in one grade.

LEAVENWORTH, JESSE H.* [Born in Vt. Appointed from Vt.]
Bvt. 2nd Lieut. 4th Inf., 1 July, 1830. 2nd Lieut., 1 July, 1830. Trans. to 2nd Inf., 18 Aug., 1831. Resigned 31 Oct., 1836. Col. 2nd Col. Vols., 17 Feb., 1862. Discharged 26 Sept., 1863. Died 12 March, 1885.

LEAVENWORTH, MARK F. [Born in Vt. Appointed from N. Y.]
Cadet Mil. Acad., 1 Sept., 1849, to 24 June, 1850. 1st Lieut. 3rd Cav., 14 May, 1861. 6th Cav., 3 Aug., 1861. Appointment expired 6 Aug., 1861. Capt. 18th Inf., 19 Feb., 1862. Resigned 27 April, 1863. Died 18 March, 1864.

LEAVENWORTH, MELINAS C. [Born in Conn. Appointed from Conn..
Asst. Surg., 1 Sept., 1833. Resigned 30 Sept., 1840. Died 16 Nov., 1862.

LEAVITT, EDWARD H. [Born in Ohio. Appointed from Ohio.]
Chap. Posts of San Diego and Drum Barracks, Cal., 14 Aug., 1866, to 15 July, 1867. Post Chap., 3 April, 1867. Resigned 15 Sept., 1869.

LEAVY, JAMES T. [Born in Ky. Appointed from Ky.]
Sergt. Co. H, 3rd Ky. Cav., 1 Oct., 1861. 2nd Lieut. 3rd Ky. Cav., 8 April, 1862. Mustered out 26 Dec., 1864. 2nd Lieut. 7th Cav., 22 Jan., 1867. Bvt. 1st Lieut., 2 March, 1867, for gallant and meritorious service in the Battle of Shiloh, Tenn. Bvt. Capt., 2 March, 1867, for gallant and meritorious service in the capture of Savannah, Ga. 1st Lieut., 7th Cav., 31 July, 1867. Retired 31 July, 1868. Wholly retired 1 July, 1869. Restored to retired list 2 April, 1878, to date from 31 July, 1868. Died 8 Jan., 1893.

LE BARRON, FRANCIS. [Born in Mass. Appointed from Mass.]
Surg. Mate U. S. N., 31 Jan., 1800. Resigned 1 March, 1802. Garrison Surg. Mate, 26 March, 1802. Maj. Surg., 12 Dec., 1808. Apoth. Gen., 11 June, 1813. Disbanded 1 June, 1821. Died 20 June, 1829.

LEBO, THOS. C. [Born in Penn. Appointed from Penn.]
2nd Lieut. 11th Penn. Vols., 26 April, 1861. Mustered out 1 Aug., 1861. 2nd Lieut. 1st Penn. Cav., 28 Nov., 1861. 1st Lieut., 12 Feb., 1863. Capt., 13 Dec., 1864. Trans. to 2nd Penn. Provincial Cav., 17 June, 1865. Mustered out 7 Aug., 1865. 1st Lieut. 10th Cav., 12 June, 1867. Capt., 17 May, 1876. Maj. 6th Cav., 26 July, 1893. Lieut. Col. 1st Cav., 14 Sept., 1899.

LE CONTE, JOHN. [Born in N. Y. Appointed from N. Y.]
Capt. Asst. Top. Eng., 18 April, 1818. Resigned 20 Aug., 1831. Bvt. Maj., 18 April, 1828, for ten years' faithful service in one grade. Died 21 Nov., 1860.

LEDGERWOOD, WASHINGTON L. [Born in Tenn. Appointed from Tenn.]
Priv. Co. B, 1st Tenn. Vols., 16 Aug., 1861. 1st Lieut., 10 Feb., 1862. Trans. to 3rd Tenn. Vols., 8 April, 1862. Capt., 1 Nov., 1863. Mustered out 23 Feb., 1865. 2nd Lieut. 18th Inf., 30 July, 1868. Unassigned 26 April, 1869. Ass'd to 8th Cav., 14 July, 1869. Resigned 1 March, 1870.

LEDYARD, AUGUSTUS C. [Born in Ill. Appointed from Mich.]
Priv. 1st Conn. Art., 19 May, to 20 July, 1898. 2nd Lieut. 2nd Inf., 9 July, 1898. 1st Lieut. 6th Inf., 13 March, 1899.

LEDYARD, HENRY B.* [Born in France. Appointed at Large.]
2nd Lieut. 19th Inf., 23 June, 1865. 1st Lieut., 23 June, 1865. R. Q. M., 20 Nov., 1865, to 6 Sept., 1866. Trans. to 37th Inf., 21 Sept., 1866. R. Q. M., 14 Dec., 1866, to 25 Feb., 1867. Trans. to 4th Art., 25 Feb., 1867. Discharged 18 Oct., 1870.

LEE, A. NISBET.* [Born in Md. Appointed at Large.]
2nd Lieut. 5th Art., 23 June, 1865. Trans. to 1st Art., 29 Nov., 1865. 1st Lieut., 28 Feb., 1866. Trans. to Eng., 2 June, 1866. Capt., 11 July, 1871. Died 31 Oct., 1879.

LEE, A. TRACY.* [Born in Mass. Appointed at Large.]
2nd Lieut. 5th Art., 17 June, 1867. Died 19 Feb., 1870.

LEE, ARTHUR T. [Born in Penn. Appointed from Penn.]
2nd Lieut. 5th Inf., 8 Oct., 1838. Trans. to 8th Inf., 1 Nov., 1838. 1st Lieut., 4 March, 1845. Capt., 27 Jan., 1848. Maj. 2nd Inf., 26 Oct., 1861. Bvt. Lieut. Col., 2 July, 1863, for gallant and meritorious service in the Battle of Gettysburg, Penn. Retired 20 Jan., 1865. Retired with rank of Col., 28 July, 1866. Died 29 Dec., 1879.

LEE, CHAS. C.* [Born in S. C. Appointed from N. C.]
Bvt. 2nd Lieut. Ord., 1 July, 1856. 2nd Lieut., 20 Dec., 1858. Resigned 31 July, 1859. Killed 30 June, 1862.

LEE, CHAS. C. [Born in Penn. Appointed from Penn.]
Asst. Surg. 1st Md. Cav., 1 Oct., 1861. Discharged 4 March, 1862. Asst. Surg., 22 Nov., 1862. Resigned 16 May, 1866. Bvt. Capt. and Maj., 13 March, 1865, for faithful and meritorious service during the war.

LEE, D. MORTIMER. [Born in Conn. Appointed from Conn.]
Priv. Co. E, 2nd Conn. Vols., 7 May, 1861. Discharged 7 Aug., 1861. Sergt. Co. K, 1st Conn. Heavy Art., 4 April, 1862. Discharged 31 Dec., 1863. 2nd Lieut. 29th Conn. Colored Vols., 1 Jan., 1864. 1st Lieut., 1 Feb., 1865. Mustered out 24 Oct., 1865. 2nd Lieut. 19th Inf., 23 Feb., 1866. Trans. to 37th Inf., 21 Sept., 1866. 1st Lieut., 12 Sept., 1866. Trans. to 5th Inf., 19 May, 1869. Unassigned 22 June, 1869. Ass'd to 6th Inf., 1 Jan., 1871. Capt., 31 Oct., 1876. Retired for disability 26 June, 1883.

LEE, DANIEL S. [Born in Va. Appointed from Va.]
1st Lieut. of Inf., 24 Feb., 1847; 11th Inf., 9 April, 1847. Reg. Adj., 9 April, 1847, to 14 Aug., 1848. Disbanded 14 Aug., 1848. Bvt. Capt., 20 Aug., 1847, for gallant and meritorious conduct in Battles of Contreras and Churubusco. Died 15 Aug., 1857.

LEE, FITZHUGH.* [Born in Va. Appointed from Va.]
Bvt. 2nd Lieut. 2nd Cav., 1 July, 1856. 2nd Lieut., 1 Jan., 1858. 1st Lieut., 31 March, 1861. Resigned 21 May, 1861. Brig. Gen. Vols., May, 1898.

LEE, FITZHUGH, Jr. [Born in Va. Appointed from Va.]
2nd Lieut. 1st Cav., 8 Jan., 1899.

LEE, FRANCIS.* [Born in Penn. Appointed from Penn.]
2nd Lieut. 7th Inf., 1 July, 1822. 1st Lieut., 24 Sept., 1824. Capt. A. Q. M., 22 May, 1826, to 31 May, 1834. Capt., 31 May, 1834. Maj. 4th Inf., 16 Feb., 1847. Lieut. Col. 6th Inf., 9 March, 1851. Col. 2nd Inf., 18 Oct., 1855. Died 19 Jan., 1859. Bvt., Lieut. Col., 20 Aug., 1847, for gallant and meritorious conduct at Contreras and Churubusco. Bvt. Col., 8 Sept., 1847, for gallant and meritorious conduct at Molino del Rey.

LEE, GEORGE. [Born in N. Y. Appointed from Mich.]
1st Lieut. 2nd Mich. Cav., 25 Oct., 1861. Reg. Adj., 1 Aug., 1862, to 23 April, 1863. Capt. A. A. G. Vols., 11 March, 1863. Maj. A. A. G. Vols., 19 May, 1865. Bvt. Lieut. Col. Vols., 13 March, 1865, for faithful and meritorious service during the war. Mustered out 31 Oct., 1866. 1st Lieut. 21st Inf., 28 July, 1866. Died 29 Oct., 1867. Bvt. Capt., 2 March, 1867, for gallantry at Battles of New Madrid, Boonsville and Perrysville. Bvt. Maj., 2 March, 1867, for gallantry at Battles of Stone River and Chickamauga. Bvt. Lieut. Col., 2 March, 1867, for faithful service in the field during the war.

LEE ,GEORGE W. CUSTIS.* [Born in Va. Appointed at Large.]
Bvt, 2nd Lieut. Eng., 1 July, 1854. 2nd Lieut., 3 March, 1855. 1st Lieut., 20 Oct., 1859. Resigned 2 May, 1861.

LEE, HARRY R.* [Born in R. I. Appointed from R. I.]
2nd Lieut. 11th Inf., 12 June, 1889. 1st Lieut. 2nd Inf., 8 June, 1896. Trans. to 6th Inf., 3 Aug., 1896. Capt. 11th Inf., 20 June, 1899.

LEE, JAMES G. C. [Born in Canada. Appointed from Ohio.]
Capt. A. Q. M. Vols., 26 Nov., 1862. Capt. A. Q. M., 2 July, 1864. Bvt. Maj., 31 July, 1865, for faithful and meritorious service during the war. Bvt. Lieut. Col., 31 July, 1865, for faithful and meritorious service. Maj. Q. M., 2 July, 1879. Lieut. Col. Dep. Q. M. G., 11 Dec., 1892. Col. A. Q. M. G., 18 Feb., 1897.

LEE, JESSE M. [Born in Ind. Appointed from Ind.]
Priv. Co. B, 59th Ind. Vols., 13 Nov., 1861. Com. Sergt., 15 Nov., 1861. 2nd Lieut. 59th Ind Vols., 13 Oct., 1862. 1st Lieut., 14 Feb., 1863. Capt., 11 Aug., 1863. Mustered out 17 July, 1865. Capt. 38th U. S. Colored Troops, 23 Aug., 1865. Mustered out 25 Jan., 1867. 2nd Lieut. 39th Inf., 28 July, 1866. 1st Lieut., 7

Jan., 1867. Reg. Adj., 1 Jan. to 20 April, 1869. Trans. to 25th Inf., 20 April, 1869. Reg. Adj., 20 April to 24 April, 1869. Unassigned 24 April, 1869. Ass'd to 9th Inf., 1 Jan., 1871. Reg. Adj., 11 March, 1878, to 1 May, 1879. Capt., 1 May, 1879. Maj., 26 April, 1898. Maj. I. G., 12 May, 1898, declined. Col. 10th U. S. Vols., 31 May to 8 July, 1898.

LEE, JOEL R. [Born in Ala. Appointed from Army.]
Priv. and Corpl. Batty A, 4th Art., 6 Aug., 1892, to 5 Nov., 1895. Priv. Batty I, 1st Art., Act. Hosp. Steward and Hosp. Steward Hosp. Corps, 22 Sept., 1896, to 18 April, 1899. 2nd Lieut. 10th Inf., 5 April, 1899.

LEE, JOHN. [Born in Ireland. Appointed from Army.]
Priv. Co. I, 2nd Drag., 12 Aug., 1850. Corpl., 29 March, 1853. Discharged 12 Aug., 1855. Priv. Gen. Mounted Ser., 21 Nov., 1855. Corpl., 1 Dec., 1855. Sergt., 16 Jan., 1857. Priv., 19 March, 1860. Discharged 10 Oct., 1860. Priv. Gen. Mounted Ser., 10 Oct., 1860. Corpl., 1 Nov., 1861. Trans. to 6th Cav., 2 Dec., 1861. Sergt. Maj., 8 Dec., 1861. Sergt. Co. K, 12 May, 1862. 1st Sergt., 1 June, 1862. 2nd Lieut. 4th Cav., 17 July, 1862. 1st Lieut., 5 Nov., 1863. R. Q. M., 10 Aug., 1865, to 11 Aug., 1866. Bvt. Capt., 2 April, 1865, for gallant and meritorious service in the capture of Selma, Ala. Capt. 4th Cav., 31 July, 1867. Retired for disability, 26 Nov., 1884. Died 24 April, 1890.

LEE, JOHN D. [Born in N. Y. Appointed from N. Y.]
Sergt. Co. A, 1st N. Y. Mounted Rifles, 31 Aug., 1861. 2nd Lieut., 6 Feb., 1862. 1st Lieut. R. Q. M. 13 Aug., 1862. Dismissed 6 March, 1863. 1st Lieut. 20th N. Y. Cav., 15 Oct., 1863. Capt., 15 May, 1865. Mustered out 31 July, 1865. 2nd Lieut. 3rd Cav., 3 May, 1866. Died 13 June, 1867.

LEE, JOHN F.* [Born in Va. Appointed from Va.]
Bvt. 2nd Lieut. 1st Art., 1 July, 1834. 2nd Lieut., 23 July, 1835. 1st Lieut., 17 Dec., 1836. 1st Lieut. Ord., 9 July, 1838. Capt., 3 March, 1847. Bvt. Maj. J. A. of Army, 2 March, 1849. Resigned 4 Sept., 1862. Bvt. Capt., 27 Jan., 1837, for gallant and good conduct in the war against the Fla. Indians. Died 17 June, 1884.

LEE, PHILIP L. [Born in Va. Appointed from Va.]
Priv. Co. F, 2nd N. Y. Cav., 28 Aug., 1862. Discharged 7 April, 1865. 1st Lieut. 16th N. Y. Cav., 7 April, 1865. Mustered out 7 Oct., 1865. 1st Lieut. 10th Cav., 28 July, 1866. Capt., 10 April, 1869. Died 25 Dec., 1889.

LEE, RICHARD B.* [Born in Va. Appointed from Va.]
3rd Lieut. Corps Art., 17 July, 1817. 2nd Lieut., 24 Nov., 1817. 1st Lieut., 31 Oct., 1819. Trans. to 3rd Art., 1 June, 1821. Capt., 31 Aug., 1836. Capt. C. S., 7 July, 1838. Maj., 30 Nov., 1841. Resigned 9 May, 1861. Bvt. Capt., 31 Oct., 1829, for ten years' faithful service in one grade. Bvt. Maj., 9 June, 1836, for gallant and good conduct in the affair of Micanopy, Fla. Died 2 Aug., 1875.

LEE, RICHARD H. [Born in Md. Appointed from Md.]
Ensign 36th Inf., 30 April, 1813. 3rd Lieut. 4th Rifles, 17 March, 1814. Trans. to Corps Art., 17 May, 1815. 2nd Lieut., 17 May, 1816. 1st Lieut., 20 April, 1818. Resigned 1 Jan., 1820. Bvt. 2nd Lieut., 15 Aug., 1814, for gallant conduct in defence of Fort Erie. Bvt. 1st Lieut., 17 Sept., 1814, for gallant conduct in sortie from Fort Erie.

LEE, ROBERT E.* [Born in Va. Appointed from Va.]
Bvt. 2nd Lieut. Eng., 1 July, 1829. 2nd Lieut., 1 July, 1829. 1st Lieut., 21 Sept., 1836. Capt., 7 July, 1838. Lieut. Col. 2nd Cav., 3 March, 1855. Col. 1st Cav., 16 March, 1861. Resigned 25 April, 1861. Bvt. Maj., 18 April, 1847, for gallant and meritorious conduct at Cerro Gordo. Bvt. Lieut. Col., 20 Aug., 1847, for gallant and meritorious conduct at Contreras and Churubusco, Mex. Bvt. Col., 13 Sept., 1847, for gallant and meritorious conduct at Chapultepec. Died 12 Oct., 1870.

LEE, ROSSWELL W.* [Born in Mass. Appointed from Mass.]
Bvt. 2nd Lieut. 3rd Art., 1 July, 1833. 2nd Lieut., 14 Sept., 1834. 1st Lieut., 18 May, 1837. Cashiered 16 July, 1838. Died 20 Dec., 1873.

LEE, SAML. P. [Born in Maine. Appointed from Maine.]
1st Lieut. 3rd Maine. Vols., 31 July, 1861. Capt., 1 Sept., 1862. Maj., 14 Nov., 1862. Mustered out 12 Nov., 1863. Maj. Vet. Res. Corps, 9 Nov., 1863. Bvt. Lieut. Col. and Col. Vols., 13 March, 1865, for distinguished gallantry in the Battles of Fredericksburg, Va., and Gettysburg, Pa. Mustered out 19 Oct., 1866. Capt. 45th Inf., 28 July, 1866. Bvt. Maj., 2 March, 1867, for gallant and meritorious service in the Battle of Fredericksburg, Va. Bvt. Lieut. Col., 2 March, 1867, for gallant and meritorious service in the Battle of Gettysburg, Pa. Unassigned 22 July, 1869. Retired with rank of Maj., 15 Dec., 1870. Died 20 Oct., 1890.

LEE, STEPHEN D.* [Born in S. C. Appointed from S. C.]
2nd Lieut. 4th Art., 1 July, 1854. 1st Lieut., 31 Oct., 1856. R. Q. M., 18 Sept., 1857, to 8 Feb., 1861. Resigned 20 Feb., 1861.

LEE, THOS. [Born in N. J. Appointed from N. J.]
Asst. Surg., 1 Jan., 1836. Died 6 Sept., 1838.

LEE, THOMAS J.* [Born in France. Appointed from D. C.]
Bvt. 2nd Lieut. 4th Art., 1 July, 1830. 2nd Lieut., 1 July, 1830. Resigned 31 Aug., 1836. 1st Lieut. Top. Eng., 7 July, 1838. Capt., 3 March, 1847. Resigned 30 April, 1855.

LEE, THOS. J.* [Born in Ind. Appointed from Ind.]
Bvt. 2nd Lieut. 10th Inf., 1 July, 1857. 2nd Lieut. 3rd Inf., 14 Jan., 1858. Resigned 20 June, 1859. Capt. 8th Ind. Vols., 27 April, 1861. Resigned 25 July, 1861. Priv. Co. D, 5th Ind. Vols., 25 June, 1863, to 30 Sept., 1864. Died 28 Nov., 1888.

LEE ,WASHINGTON. [Born in Va. Appointed from Penn.]
2nd Lieut. 5th Inf., 3 May, 1808. 1st Lieut., 4 May, 1810. Capt. 16th Inf., 12 March, 1812. A. A. G., 12 July, 1812. Maj., 16th Inf., 3 March, 1813. Lieut. Col. 11th Inf., 9 June, 1814, to 15 June, 1815. Dep. P. M. G., 13 April, 1813. Disbanded 29 April, 1816.

LEE, WM. F. [Born in Va. Appointed from Va.]
2nd Lieut. 2nd Inf., 30 June, 1855. Resigned 30 April, 1861.

LEE, WM. H. F. [Born in Va. Appointed from Va.]
2nd Lieut. 6th Inf., 31 May, 1857. Resigned 31 May, 1859.

LEEFE, JOHN G. [Born in England. Appointed from N. Y.]
1st Lieut. 162nd N. Y. Vols., 14 Oct., 1862. Capt., 1 July, 1864. Bvt. Maj. Vols., 13 March, 1865, for gallant service in the Battle of the Opequan, Va. Bvt. Lieut. Col. Vols., 13 March, 1865, for gallant service in the Battle of Fisher's Hill, Va. Capt. A. A. G. Vols., 15 June, 1865. Mustered out 22 Nov., 1865. 2nd Lieut. 19th Inf., 11 May, 1866. Reg. Adj., 23 Nov., 1866, to March 31, 1869. Bvt. 1st Lieut., 2 March, 1867, for gallant and meritorious service in the Battle of the Opequan. Bvt. Capt., 2 March, 1867, for gallant and meritorious service in the Battle of Fisher's Hill. 1st Lieut. 19th Inf., 18 Nov., 1867. R. Q. M., 12 April, 1869, to 1 May, 1876. Capt., 13 Oct., 1886. Maj., 2 March, 1899.

LEEPER, MATTHEW, Jr. [Born in Ark. Appointed from Texas.]
2nd Lieut. 4th Cav., 27 July, 1872. 1st Lieut., 20 March, 1879. Resigned 5 May, 1880.

LEET, GEORGE K. [Born in Pa. Appointed from Ill.]
Priv. Chicago Mercantile Batty, 7 Aug., 1862, to 29 Oct., 1863. Capt. A. A. G. Vols., 3 Oct., 1863. Maj. A. A. G. Vols., 25 Feb., 1865, to 25 May, 1866. Capt. A. Q. M., 23 March, 1866. Maj. A. A. G., 23 March, 1866. Discharged 1 Aug., 1870. Bvt. Lieut. Col., 2 March, 1867, for faithful and meritorious service during the war. Died 26 March, 1881.

LEFTWICH, GRANVILLE. [Born in Va. Appointed from Va.]
Ensign 5th Inf., 19 July, 1813. 3rd Lieut., 31 March, 1814. 2nd Lieut., 13 Aug., 1814. Trans. to 7th Inf., 17 May, 1815. Reg. Adj., Feb., 1816, to 31 Aug., 1819. 1st Lieut., 30 April, 1817. Capt., 15 June, 1819. Died 24 Sept., 1824.

LEGATE, GEORGE M.* [Born in N. Y. Appointed from N. Y.]
Bvt. 2nd Lieut. 2nd Art., 1 July, 1835. 2nd Lieut., 31 Oct., 1835. Resigned 1 April, 1836. Died 9 Nov., 1837.

LEGATE, STEPHEN B.* [Born in Mass. Appointed from N. Y.]
Bvt. 2nd Lieut. 3rd Inf., 1 July, 1830. 2nd Lieut., 31 Oct., 1833. Resigned 31 Aug., 1835. Died 12 Nov., 1835.

LEGATE, THOS. C. [Born in Mass. Appointed from Mass.]
2nd Lieut. 3rd Art., 30 April, 1812. 1st Lieut., 29 Oct., 1813. Trans. to Corps Art., 12 May, 1814. Disbanded 15 June, 1815. Reinstated 2 Dec., 1815. Trans. to 2nd Art., 1 June, 1821. Capt., 13 May, 1820. Resigned 31 Dec., 1836. Bvt. Maj., 13 May, 1830, for ten years' faithful service in one grade.

LEGGETT, HENRY F. [Born in Ohio. Appointed from Ohio.]
Priv. Co. H, 12th Ohio Vols., 4 June, 1861. Discharged 20 Oct., 1861. 1st Lieut. 59th Ohio Vols., 20 Oct., 1861. Resigned 18 April, 1862. Capt. 9th Ky. Vols., 18 April, 1862. Mustered out 15 Dec., 1864. 2nd Lieut. 38th Inf., 17 July, 1867. Bvt. 1st Lieut., 17 July, 1867, for gallant and meritorious service in the Battle of Mission Ridge, Tenn. Bvt. Capt., 17 July, 1867, for gallant and meritorious service in the Battle of Peach Tree Creek, Ga. Trans. to 24th Inf., 11 Nov., 1869. 1st Lieut., 14 Sept., 1872. Capt., 26 Nov., 1884. Died 15 May, 1888.

LEGGETT, WELLS W.* [Born in Ohio. Appointed at Large.]
Capt. A. de C. Vols., 16 Aug., 1864, to 11 July, 1865. Cadet at Mil. Acad., 1 Sept., 1865. 2nd Lieut. 8th Cav., 15 June, 1869. Resigned 10 Jan., 1870.

LEIB, CHAS. [Born in Penn. Appointed from Ill.]
1st Lieut. 11th Inf., 21 May, 1861. Rejected by Senate, 5 Aug., 1861. 1st Lieut. 11th Inf., 20 Aug., 1861. Appointment revoked, 12 March, 1862. Capt. A. Q. M., 20 Aug., 1861. Rejected by Senate, 19 Feb., 1862. Died 21 Jan., 1865.

LEIB, EDWARD H. [Born in Penn. Appointed from Penn.]
Priv. Co. B, 25th Pa. Vols., 18 to 29 April, 1861. 2nd Lieut. 2nd Cav., 26 April, 1861. 1st Lieut., 10 June, 1861; 5th Cav., 3 Aug., 1861. Capt., 13 April, 1863. Dismissed 9 May, 1877. Bvt. Capt., 13 June, 1862, for gallant and meritorious service in the Cav. action at Old Church, Va. Bvt. Maj., 1 April, 1865, for gallant and meritorious service at the Battle of Five Forks, Va. Bvt. Lieut. Col., 1 April, 1865, for gallant and meritorious service during the war.

LEIB, GEORGE. [Born in Penn. Appointed from Penn.]
Cadet at Mil. Acad., 18 Feb., 1815, to 30 Sept., 1816. 2nd Lieut. Corps Art., 31 July, 1818. Disbanded 1 June, 1821.

LEIGH, JOHN W. [Born in Va. Appointed from Va.]
1st Lieut. of Inf., 25 Feb., 1847; Voltigeurs, 9 April, 1847. Disbanded 31 Aug., 1848. Bvt. Capt. for gallant and meritorious conduct in several affairs with guerillas at Paso Ovejas, National Bridge, and Cerro Gerdo, on 10, 12 and 15 Aug., 1847.

LEITCH, JOSEPH D.* [Born in Mich. Appointed from Neb.]
2nd Lieut. 24th Inf., 12 June, 1889. 1st Lieut. 7th Inf., 22 Dec., 1896. Trans. to 24th Inf., 29 March, 1897. Capt. 25th Inf., 8 Sept., 1899.

LEMLY, HENRY R.* [Born in N. C. Appointed from N. C.]
2nd Lieut. 3rd Cav., 14 June, 1872. Trans. to 3rd Art., 7 Oct., 1878. 1st Lieut., 23 Feb., 1880. Capt., 6 Feb., 1897. Retired for over thirty years' service, 20 April, 1899.

LENDRUM, JOHN H. [Born in Conn. Appointed from Md.]
2nd Lieut. 3rd Art., 8 March, 1847. 1st Lieut., 24 March, 1848. Capt., 3 Dec., 1858. Died 26 Oct., 1861. Bvt. 1st Lieut., 20 Aug., 1847, for gallant and meritorious conduct in the Battles of Contreras and Churubusco, Mex. Bvt. Capt., 13 Sept., 1847, for gallant and meritorious conduct at Chapultepec.

LENDRUM, THOS. W.* [Born in D. C. Appointed from Va.]
3rd Lieut. Corps Art., 2 March, 1815. 2nd Lieut., 28 Sept., 1817. Batt. Adj., Sept., 1816, to 14 May, 1818. 1st Lieut., 30 May, 1819. Trans. to 3rd Art., 1 June, 1821. Capt., 31 Dec., 1828. Maj. C. S., 7 July, 1838. Died 21 Oct., 1852.

L'ENGLE, JOHN.* [Born in S. C. Appointed from S. C.]
2nd Lieut. Corps Art., 1 July, 1819. Trans. to 3rd Art., 1 June, 1821. 1st Lieut., 11 Dec., 1825. Capt., 7 July, 1838. Resigned 30 Nov., 1838. Died 19 Sept., 1864.

L'ENGLE, WM. J. [Born in Fla. Appointed from S. C.]
Asst. Surg., 28 Aug., 1856. Resigned 30 April, 1861.

LENIHAN, MICHAEL J.* [Born in Mass. Appointed from Mass.]
Addl. 2nd Lieut. 25th Inf., 12 June, 1887. 2nd Lieut. 20th Inf., 25 Aug., 1887. 1st Lieut. 19th Inf., 27 Nov., 1894. Trans. to 2nd Inf., 8 Dec., 1894. Capt. 25th Inf., 2 March, 1899. Graduate of the Infantry and Cavalry School, 1891. R. Q. M., 4 June, 1899.

LENNOX, ROBERT. [Born in Ireland. Appointed from Army.]
Priv., Corpl., Sergt. and 1st Sergt. Co. D, and Sergt. Maj. 2nd Drag. (2nd Cav.), 16 Oct., 1854, to 23 Sept., 1862. 2nd Lieut. 2nd Cav., 17 July, 1862. 1st Lieut., 27 April, 1863. Reg. Adj., 17 Oct., 1863, to 1 July, 1865. Resigned 18 Jan, 1866. Died 8 June, 1875.

LENT, JAMES W., Jr. [Born in N. Y. Appointed from N. Y.]
Ensign 13th Inf., 1 May, 1812. 2nd Lieut. 1st Art., 12 March, 1813. Trans. to Corps Art., 12 May, 1814. 1st Lieut., 1 Nov., 1816. Batty Q. M. May to Oct., 1816. Dismissed 24 Oct., 1817. Died 8 Dec., 1824.

LENTZ, ASHLEY R. [Born in Ala. Appointed from Army.]
Priv. Co. F, 13th Inf., 8 May, 1847, to 15 July, 1848. 2nd Lieut. 13th Inf., 27 June, 1848. Disbanded 15 July, 1848.

LEONARD, CHAS. H. [Born in N. Y. Appointed from Penn.]
2nd Lieut. Adj. 6th N. Y. Art., 2 Sept., 1862. 1st Lieut., 29 Oct., 1862, to 23 May, 1863. Capt. A. A. G. Vols., 15 May, 1863. Bvt. Maj. Vols., 19 Oct., 1864, for gallant and meritorious conduct during the campaign before Richmond, and more especially in the battles of Cold Harbor, Va., Monocacy, Md., and in the several engagements in the valley of the Shenandoah; and Bvt. Lieut. Col. Vols., 2 April, 1865, for gallant and meritorious service before Petersburg, Va. Mustered out 12 Jan., 1866. 2nd Lieut. 31st Inf., 7 March, 1867. Unassigned 15 May, 1869. Ass'd to 13th Inf., 14 July, 1869. Unassigned 1 July, 1870. Resigned 31 Dec., 1870.

LEONARD, HIRAM. [Born in Vt. Appointed from N. Y.]
Addl. P. M., 24 Nov., 1846. Maj. P. M., 2 March, 1849. Lieut. Col. Dep. P. M. G., 6 Sept., 1862. Bvt. Col., 13 March, 1865, for faithful and meritorious services during the war. Bvt. Brig. Gen., 13 March, 1865, for faithful and meritorious service in the Pay Dept. during the war. Retired 1 Jan., 1872. Died 21 Dec., 1883.

LEONARD, IVERS W. [Born in Ind. Appointed from Ind.]
2nd Lieut. 22nd Inf., 9 July, 1898. 1st Lieut., 2 March, 1899.

LEONARD, JOHN. [Born in Ireland. Appointed from N. J.]
Priv. Co. F, 9th Inf., 17 May, 1855. Corpl., 6 Sept., 1855. Sergt., 6 Feb., 1856. 1st Sergt., 5 June, 1856. Discharged 15 May, 1860. Capt. 72nd N. Y. Vols., 21 June, 1861. Maj., 27 April, 1863. Lieut. Col., 4 May, 1863. Mustered out 19 June, 1864. Capt. Vet. Res. Corps, 26 Aug., 1864. Bvt. Maj. Vols., 7 Nov., 1865, for gallant and meritorious service. Mustered out 2 Jan., 1867. 1st Lieut. 43rd Inf., 28 July, 1866. Bvt. Capt., 2 March, 1867, for gallant and meritorious service in the Battle of Fredericksburg, Va. Bvt. Maj., 2 March, 1867, for gallant and meritorious service in the Battle of Gettysburg, Pa. Trans. to 1st Inf., 8 April, 1869. Retired 15 Dec., 1870.

LEONARD, LUTHER.* [Born in Vt. Appointed from Vt.]
2nd Lieut. Light Art., 12 Dec., 1808. 1st Lieut., 1 Sept., 1809. Capt. Light Art., 6 July, 1812. Disbanded 15 June, 1815. Reinstated 17 May, 1816. Disbanded 1 June, 1821. Mil. Storekeeper Ord. Dept., 31 Dec., 1845. Retired 29 Nov., 1861. Died 11 Feb., 1865.

LEONARD, WM. T. [Born in Md. Appointed from Md.]
Asst. Surg., 21 Aug., 1838. Resigned 23 Sept., 1842.

LEONHAEUSER, HARRY A.* [Born in Penn. Appointed from Penn.]
2nd Lieut. 25th Inf., 11 June, 1881. 1st Lieut., 31 Jan., 1889. Capt., 26 April, 1898. Lieut. Col. 15th Minn. Vols., 14 July, 1898. Col., 17 Aug., 1898, to 27 March, 1899.

LEOSER, CHAS. McK.* [Born in Penn. Appointed from Penn.]
2nd Lieut. 2nd Drag., 6 May, 1861. 2nd Cav., 3 Aug., 1861. 1st Lieut., 8 Aug., 1861. Col. 11th N. Y. Vols., 20 Aug., 1861. Resigned from Vols., 17 April, 1862. Capt., 9 June, 1863. Resigned 19 Oct., 1865.

LESLIE, CHAS. R. [Born in England. Appointed from England.]
Teacher of Drawing at Mil. Acad., 2 March, 1833. Resigned 15 April, 1834.

LESLIE, THOS. J.* [Born in England. Appointed from Penn.]
Bvt. 2nd Lieut. Eng., 4 March, 1815. 2nd Lieut., 31 Oct., 1816. 1st Lieut., 31 March, 1819. P. M. of Eng., 27 Nov., 1815, to 7 July, 1838. Maj. and P. M., 7 July, 1838. Retired 3 Feb., 1869. Died 25 Nov., 1874. Bvt. Capt., 31 March, 1829, for ten years' faithful service in one grade. Bvt. Lieut. Col., Col. and Brig. Gen., 13 March, 1865, for faithful and meritorious performance of duty in the Pay Dept. during fifty years' service.

LESTER, CHAS. H.* [Born in Conn. Appointed from Conn..
2nd Lieut. 2nd Cav., 11 June, 1863. Bvt. 1st Lieut., 6 May, 1864, for gallant and meritorious service in the Battle of Todd's Tavern, Va. 1st Lieut. 2nd Cav., 30 May, 1864. Reg. Adj., 6 March to 1 July, 1866. Bvt. Capt., 27 July, 1864, for gallant and meritorious service in action at Deep Bottom, Va. Capt. 8th Cav., 28 July, 1866. Resigned 13 May, 1869. 2nd Lieut. 24th Inf., 6 Aug., 1873. Trans. to 8th Cav., 31 Oct., 1876. 1st Lieut., 4 April, 1884. Retired with rank of Capt. for disability, 1 July, 1891. Died 27 Oct., 1899.

LETHERBURY, JAMES W. [Born in Del. Appointed from Del.]
Sergt. Co. A, 2nd Del. Vols., 21 May, 1861. 2nd Lieut., 26 April, 1862. Discharged 24 Sept., 1862. 1st Lieut. 1st Del. Vols., 7 May, 1863. Mustered out 1 July, 1864. 2nd Lieut. 17th Inf., 7 March, 1867. Resigned 3 June, 1871.

LETTERMAN, JONATHAN. [Born in Penn. Appointed from Penn.]
Asst. Surg., 29 June, 1849. Maj. Surg., 16 April, 1862. Resigned 22 Dec., 1864. Died 15 March, 1872.

LEVELY, WM. [Born in Md. Appointed from Md.]
Asst. Surg., 30 Sept., 1841. Died 24 Nov., 1848.

LEWIS, ANDREW. [Born in Mass. Appointed from Mass.]
3rd Lieut. 40th Inf., 1 Sept., 1813. 2nd Lieut., 2 May, 1814. Disbanded 15 June, 1815. Reinstated 17 May, 1816, in 3rd Inf. 1st Lieut., 10 Feb., 1818. Capt., 6 June, 1827. Died 30 Nov., 1840.

LEWIS, CHAS. [Born in N. Y. Appointed from Army.]
Priv., Corpl. and Sergt. Co. C, 2nd Drag. (2nd Cav.), 17 Oct., 1855, to 23 Sept., 1862. 2nd Lieut. 2nd Cav., 17 July, 1862. Dismissed 3 June, 1864. He was sentenced to be hanged 15 Oct., 1864, but made his escape and joined the Confederate Army. His proper name was Denis Daily.

LEWIS, CHAS. H. [Born in Maine. Appointed from Maine.]
Capt. 16th Inf., 5 Aug., 1861. Resigned 28 July, 1864.

LEWIS, EDSON A.* [Born in Canada. Appointed from Mich.]
Addl. 2nd Lieut. 18th Inf., 12 June, 1887. 2nd Lieut., 15 June, 1887. 1st Lieut. 23rd Inf., 11 Oct., 1894. Trans. to 18th Inf., 8 June, 1895. Capt., 2 March, 1899.

LEWIS, EDWARD M.* [Born in Ind. Appointed from Ind.]
2nd Lieut. 11th Inf., 1 July, 1886. 1st Lieut. 20th Inf., 31 Aug., 1893. Capt., 2 March, 1899. Adj., 2 March, 1899.

LEWIS, FISHER A.* [Born in Va. Appointed from Va.]
2nd Lieut. 1st Art., 1 July, 1836. Resigned 15 Feb., 1838. Died 19 Sept., 1883.

LEWIS, FREDERICK. [Born in N. Y. Appointed from N. Y.]
Cadet at Mil. Acad., 25 Jan., 1803, to 18 May, 1805. 2nd Lieut. Eng., 6 July, 1812. 1st Lieut., 20 Sept., 1812. Capt., 1 Oct., 1817. Resigned 1 July, 1824.

LEWIS, FREDERICK W.* [Born in N. Y. Appointed from N. Y.]
Addl. 2nd Lieut. 13th Inf., 12 June, 1896. 2nd Lieut. 22nd Inf., 27 Aug., 1896. 1st Lieut. of Inf., 1 Nov., 1898. Ass'd to 17th Inf., 1 Jan., 1899. Trans. to 12th Inf., 2 Oct., 1899.

LEWIS, GRANVILLE. [Born in Penn. Appointed from Penn.]
Priv. Co. D, Mounted Rifles, 16 Oct., 1855. Trans. to Band, 1 Nov., 1857. Trans. to Co. K, 1 June, 1859. Discharged 30 Sept., 1860. Priv. Co. A, 4th N. Y. Vols., 8 Feb., 1862. Sergt., 14 April, 1862. Sergt. Maj., 3 May, 1862. 1st Lieut. 4th N. Y. Vols., 28 May, 1862. Mustered out 25 May, 1863. Priv. Gen. Ser., U. S. A., 9 Feb., 1864. Discharged 1 Feb., 1865. 2nd Lieut. 5th Inf., 11 May, 1866. 1st Lieut., 29 Jan., 1867. Retired 30 Nov., 1879.

LEWIS, ISAAC N.* [Born in Penn. Appointed from Kan.]
2nd Lieut. 2nd Art., 15 June, 1884. 1st Lieut., 15 June, 1891. Trans. to 6th Art., 8 March, 1898. Trans. to 7th Art., 23 Aug., 1899. Capt. 6th Art., 5 April, 1900.

LEWIS, JOHN F. [Born in Ohio. Appointed from Ill.]
2nd Lieut. 14th Inf., 23 Feb., 1866. 1st Lieut., 28 July, 1866. Trans. to 32nd Inf., 21 Sept., 1866. Trans. to 21st Inf., 19 April, 1869. Mustered out 1 Jan., 1871.

LEWIS, JOHN J. H. [Born in Va. Appointed from Va.]
2nd Lieut. Rifles, 12 Nov., 1818. Resigned 10 June, 1819.

LEWIS,*JOHN R. [Born in Penn. Appointed from Vt.]
Sergt. Co. H, 1st Vt. Vols., 2 May, 1861. Discharged 15 Aug., 1861. Capt. 5th Vt. Vols., 16 Sept., 1861. Maj., 16 July, 1862. Lieut. Col., 6 Oct., 1862. Col., 5 June, 1864. Mustered out 11 Sept., 1864. Col. Vet. Res. Corps, 8 Sept., 1864. Bvt. Brig. Gen. Vols., 13 March, 1865, for gallant service in the Wilderness, Va. Mustered out 31 March, 1867. Maj. 44th Inf., 22 Jan., 1867. Bvt. Lieut. Col., 2 March, 1867, for gallant and meritorious service in the Battle of White Oak Swamp, Va. Bvt. Col., 2 March, 1867, for gallant and meritorious service in the Battle of the Wilderiness, Va. Unassigned 15 March, 1869. Retired with rank of Col., 28 April, 1870.

LEWIS, JOHN V. [Born in Mass. Appointed from N. Y.]
Post Chap., 12 Dec., 1883. Wholly retired 10 May, 1890.

LEWIS, JOHN W. [Born in Md. Appointed from Ky.]
2nd Lieut. 4th Ky. Vols., 17 July, 1861. Capt. 4th Ky. Cav., 23 June, 1863. Resigned 14 Jan., 1865. 2nd Lieut. 14th Inf., 20 July, 1866. Trans. to 23rd Inf., 21 Sept., 1866. 1st Lieut., 8 June, 1867. Mustered out 1 Jan., 1871.

LEWIS, LOUIS H.* [Born in N. Y. Appointed from N. Y.]
2nd Lieut. 9th Inf., 12 June, 1895. Killed in action at San Juan, Santiago, Cuba, 1 July, 1898.

LEWIS, MARTIN V. B.* [Born in N. Y. Appointed from Ohio.]
Bvt. 2nd Lieut. 7th Inf., 1 July, 1860. 2nd Lieut. 8th Inf., 1 Dec., 1860. 1st Lieut., 14 May, 1861. Died 29 June, 1862.

LEWIS, THEODORE. [Born in Ky. Appointed from La.]
Mil. Storekeeper Ord., 31 Aug., 1852. Resigned 18 Feb., 1861.

LEWIS, THOMAS J.* [Born in La. Appointed from La.]
2nd Lieut. 2nd Cav., 13 June, 1879. 1st Lieut., 26 July, 1886. Capt., 13 June, 1897.

LEWIS, WM. A. H. [Born in Penn. Appointed from Penn.]
1st Lieut. 1st Pa. Vols., 20 April, 1861, to 26 July, 1861. 1st Lieut. Adj. 93rd Pa. Vols., 28 Oct., 1861. Resigned 5 May, 1863. 2nd Lieut. 15th Inf., 9 April, 1866. Died 3 Sept., 1866.

LEWIS, WM. C. M. [Born in N. J. Appointed from N. J.]
1st Lieut. 10th Inf., 15 April, 1847. Died 19 Nov., 1847.

LEWIS, WILLIAM F. [Born in Va. Appointed from N. C.]
Asst. Surg., 12 May, 1893. Capt. Asst. Surg., 12 May, 1898.

LEWIS, WM. H.* [Born in Ala. Appointed from N. Y.]
Bvt. 2nd Lieut. 4th Inf., 1 July, 1849. 2nd Lieut. 1st Inf., 7 Oct., 1849. Trans. to 5th Inf., 7 Aug., 1850. 1st Lieut., 3 March, 1855. Reg. Adj., 1 Nov., 1856, to

6 June, 1857. Capt., 7 May, 1861. Maj. 18th Inf., 14 July, 1864. Trans. to 36th Inf., 21 Sept., 1866. Trans. to 7th Inf., 15 March, 1869. Lieut. Col. 19th Inf., 10 Dec., 1873. Died 28 Sept., 1878, of wounds received in action with Indians in Kansas. Bvt. Maj., 28 March, 1862, for gallant and meritorious service at the Battle of Apache Canon, N. M. Bvt. Lieut. Col., 15 April, 1862, for gallant and meritorious service at the Battle of Peralta, N. M.

LEYDEN, JAMES A.* [Born in Tenn. Appointed from Pa.]
2nd Lieut. 4th Inf., 13 June, 1879. 1st Lieut., 16 Dec., 1889. Capt. of Inf. (4th), 22 April, 1896. Died 10 April, 1897.

L'HOMMEDIEU, TILLINGHAST. [Born in Ohio. Appointed from Ohio.]
2nd Lieut. 6th Inf., 26 April, 1861. Trans. to 1st Cav., 7 May, 1861; 4th Cav., 3 Aug., 1861. 1st Lieut., 20 Aug., 1861. Reg. Com., 17 Oct., 1862, to 31 Dec., 1863. Died 31 Dec., 1863.

LIDDELL, OLIVER B. [Born in Ind. Appointed from Ind.]
Sergt. 68th Ind. Vols., 19 Aug., 1862. 1st Lieut., 22 April, 1864. Mustered out 20 June, 1865. 2nd Lieut. 18th Inf., 23 Feb., 1866. Trans. to 36th Inf., 21 Sept., 1866. Resigned 1 Jan., 1867.

LIEBER, G. NORMAN. [Born in S. C. Appointed from N. Y.]
1st Lieut. 11th Inf., 14 May, 1861. Reg. Adj., 18 Sept., 1861, to 1 Oct., 1862. Bvt. Capt., 27 June, 1862, for gallant and meritorious service in the Battle of Gaines' Mills, Va. Maj. J. A. Vols., 13 Nov., 1862. Capt. 11th Inf., 2 July, 1863. Bvt. Maj., 28 May, 1864, for gallant and meritorious service in the Red River campaign. Bvt. Lieut. Col., 13 March, 1865, for faithful and meritorious service during the war. Trans. to 29th Inf., 21 Sept., 1866. J. A. U. S. A., 25 Feb., 1867. Resigned commission of Capt. 29th Inf., 25 April, 1869. Prof. of Law at Mil. Acad., 28 Aug., 1878. Col. A. J. A. G., 5 July, 1884. Brig. Gen., J. A. G., 3 Jan., 1895.

LIEBER, HAMILTON. [Born in Penn. Appointed from N. Y.]
2nd Lieut. 9th Ill. Cav., 25 April, 1861. 1st Lieut., 28 July, 1861. Resigned 4 March, 1863. Capt. Vet. Res. Corps, 2 June, 1863. Bvt. Maj. Vols., 13 March, 1865, for meritorious service during the war, and Lieut. Col. Vols., 13 March, 1865, for gallant and meritorious service at the Battle of Fort Donelson, Tenn. Mustered out 30 June, 1866. Capt. Mil. Storekeeper, Q. M. Dept., 28 July, 1866. Retired 13 Dec., 1875. Died 18 Oct., 1876.

LIEBER, WILLIAM A. [Born in Minn. Appointed from D. C.]
2nd Lieut. 23rd Inf., 9 July, 1898. 1st Lieut. 24th Inf., 8 Sept., 1899.

LIEDTKE, FREDERICK W. [Born in Prussia. Appointed from Penn.]
Priv. Co. I, 97th Penn. Vols., 27 Aug., 1862. 2nd Lieut. 11th Penn. Vols., 28 Aug., 1862. Resigned 6 Nov., 1863. 1st Lieut. Vet. Res. Corps, 23 Nov., 1863. Capt., 25 March, 1865. Mustered out 7 Jan., 1867. 2nd Lieut. 43rd Inf., 28 July, 1866. Trans. to 1st Inf., 8 April, 1869. Mustered out 1 Jan., 1871.

LIGGETT, HUNTER.* [Born in Penn. Appointed from Penn.]
2nd Lieut. 5th Inf., 13 June, 1879. 1st Lieut., 27 June, 1884. Capt., 1 June, 1897. Maj. A. A. G. Vols., 3 June, 1898, to 12 April, 1899. Maj. 31st U. S. Vols., 5 July, 1899.

LILLY, FORTUNATUS. [Born in Va. Appointed from Army.]
Priv. and Sergt. Cos. D and E, 15th Inf., 2 April, 1847, to 22 July, 1848. Bvt. 2nd Lieut. 4th Inf., 28 June, 1848. Resigned 31 Oct., 1848.

LINCOLN, ABRAM B.* [Born in N. Y. Appointed from N.
Bvt. 2nd Lieut. 1st Inf., 1 July, 1845. 2nd Lieut. 4th Inf., 12 July, 1846. 1st Lieut., 24 Nov., 1847. Died 15 April, 1852. Bvt. 1st Lieut., 8 Sept., 1847, for gallant and meritorious conduct in the Battle of Molino del Rey, Mex.

LINCOLN, ALBERT.* [Born in Conn. Appointed from Conn.]
2nd Lieut. 5th Inf., 1 July, 1822. Died 13 Oct., 1822.

LINCOLN, CHARLES S. [Born in Iowa. Appointed from Army.]
Priv., Corpl. and Sergt. Co. B, 2nd Inf., 5 Jan., 1895, to 29 April, 1898. 2nd Lieut. 24th Inf., 12 April, 1898. 1st Lieut., 2 March, 1899.

LINCOLN, GEORGE. [Born in Mass. Appointed from Mass.]
2nd Lieut. 4th Inf., 14 Sept., 1837. Trans. to 8th Inf., 12 July, 1838. 1st Lieut., 28 Sept., 1840. Reg. Adj., 1 Sept., 1842, to 1 Nov., 1843. Capt., 16 Feb., 1847. Bvt. Capt. A. A. G., 7 July, 1846. Killed 23 Feb., 1847, in Battle of Buena Vista, Mex. Bvt. Capt., 9 May, 1846, for gallant conduct in Battles of Palo Alto and Resaca de la Palma.

LINCOLN, SUMNER H. [Born in Mass. Appointed from Vt.]
Priv. Co. B, 1st Vt. Vols., 2 May, 1861. Discharged 15 Aug., 1861. Corpl. Co. B, 6th Vt. Vols., 15 Oct., 1861. 1st Lieut. and Reg. Adj., 21 Feb., 1863. Mustered out 28 Oct., 1864. Maj. 6th Vt. Vols., 10 Nov., 1864. Lieut. Col., 6 Feb., 1865. Mustered out 26 June, 1865. 2nd Lieut. and 1st Lieut. 17th Inf., 23 Feb., 1866. Trans. to 26th Inf., 21 Sept., 1866. Reg. Adj., 1 May, 1868, to 19 May, 1869. Trans. to 10th Inf., 19 May, 1869. Capt., 24 March, 1878. Maj., 26 April, 1898. Lieut. Col. 13th Inf., 12 July, 1899. Trans. to 10th Inf., 12 Aug., 1899.

LIND, JOHN S. [Born in Penn. Appointed from Army.]
Priv. and Sergt. Co. E, and Sergt. Maj. 2nd Batt. 18th Inf., 29 Sept., 1861, to 30 March, 1863. 2nd Lieut. 18th Inf., 19 Feb., 1863. 1st Lieut., 11 Sept., 1863. Resigned 12 Oct., 1864.

LINDEN, HENRY ST. J.* [Born in Md. Appointed from Md.]
(Graduated as James S. Thompson.) Bvt. 2nd Lieut. 2nd Inf., 1 July, 1825. 2nd Lieut. 6th Inf., 1 July, 1825. 1st Lieut., 4 March, 1833. Died 10 Aug., 1836.

LINDENBERGER, V. H. [Born in Md. Appointed from La.]
2nd Lieut. 3rd Inf., 1 July, 1839. Dropped 18 Nov., 1840.

LINDESMITH, ELI W. J. [Born in Ohio. Appointed from Ohio.]
Post Chap., 19 June, 1880. Retired by operation of law 7 Sept., 1891.

LINDSAY, ANDREW J. [Born in Ala. Appointed from M[illegible]
Cadet Mil. Acad., 1 July, 1839, to 28 Aug., 1841. 1st Lieut. Mtd. Rifles, 27 May,

1846. Capt., 31 Oct., 1848. Appointment as Capt. expired by limitation, 3 March, 1849. Capt., 30 June, 1851. Resigned 5 May, 1861.

LINDSAY, GEORGE F.* [Born in Va. Appointed from D. C.]
2nd Lieut. 7th Inf., 1 July, 1820. Trans. to 2nd Inf., 15 July, 1820. Resigned 1 July, 1822. 2nd Lieut. Marines, 1 April, 1823. 1st Lieut., 19 Sept., 1831. Capt. A. Q. M. Marine Corps, 12 March, 1838. Maj. Q. M. Marines, 19 July, 1855. Died 27 Sept., 1857.

LINDSAY, JAMES R.* [Born in Ill. Appointed from I[llegible]
2nd Lieut. 14th Inf., 12 June, 1890. 1st Lieut. 8th Inf., 4 Feb., 1897. Capt. 13th Inf., 11 Oct., 1899. Graduate of the Infantry and Cavalry School, 1897.

LINDSAY, WM. [Born in Va. Appointed from Va.]
Maj. 2nd Art., 14 May, 1812. Lieut. Col., 12 March, 1813. Trans. to Corps Art., 12 May, 1814. Trans. to 7th Inf., 1 June, 1821. Trans. to 3rd Art., 16 Aug., 1821. Col. 2nd Art., 26 April, 1832. Died 15 Sept., 1838. Bvt. Col., 12 March, 1823, for 10 years' faithful service in one grade.

LINDSEY, JULIAN R.* [Born in Ga. Appointed from Ga.]
2nd Lieut. 9th Cav., 11 June, 1892. 1st Lieut. 10th Cav., 14 Feb., 1899.

LINDSEY, REMEMBRANCE H.* [Born in Penn. Appointed from Penn.]
2nd Lieut. 3rd Art., 15 June, 1869. Discharged 1 Nov., 1870.

LINDSLEY, ELMER.* [Born in N. Y. Appointed from N. [illegible]
2nd Lieut. 6th Cav., 12 June, 1891. Trans. to 4th Cav., 24 June, 1897. 1st Lieut. 1st Cav., 23 June, 1898.

LINDSLEY, WEBSTER. [Born in D. C. Appointed from D. C.]
Asst. Surg., 28 May, 1861. Died 8 Aug., 1866. Bvt. Capt. and Maj., 13 March, 1865, for faithful and meritorious service during the war.

LINING, THOS. [Born in S. C. Appointed from S. C.]
Asst. Surg., 1 Sept., 1827. Resigned 10 Dec., 1832.

LINK, HENRY H. [Born in Mo. Appointed from W. Va.]
Sergt. Co. G, 6th W. Va. Vols., 25 June, 1861. 2nd Lieut., 23 Sept., 1862. 1st Lieut., 3 Oct., 1862. Mustered out 12 Aug., 1864. 2nd Lieut. 18th Inf., 23 Feb., 1866. 1st Lieut., 28 July, 1866. Trans. to 36th Inf., 21 Sept., 1866. Trans. to 7th Inf., 19 May, 1869. Mustered out 1 Jan., 1871.

LINN, WM. A. [Born in Mo. Appointed from Mo.]
2nd Lieut. Inf., 5 March, 1847; 12th Inf., 9 April, 1847. Disbanded 25 July, 1848.

LINNARD, THOS. B.* [Born in Penn. Appointed from Penn.]
Bvt. 2nd Lieut. 2nd Art., 1 July, 1830. 2nd Lieut., 1 July, 1830. 1st Lieut., 28 Dec., 1835. 1st Lieut. Top. Eng., 7 July, 1838. Capt., 31 March, 1842. Died 24 April, 1851. Bvt. Capt., 30 Sept., 1836, for galant conduct, activity and enterprise in the war against the Florida Indians. Bvt. Maj., 23 Feb., 1847, for gallant and meritorious conduct in the Battle of Buena Vista.

LINNARD, WM. [Born in Penn. Appointed from Penn.]
Mil. Agt. Middle Dept., 29 April, 1802. Maj. Dep. Q. M. G., 3 April, 1812. Col. Q. M. G., 12 April, 1813. Retained 15 June, 1815, as Maj. and Dep. Q. M. G. Retained as Maj. Q. M. in the reorganization of 1 June, 1821. Died 20 Sept., 1835. Bvt. Lieut. Col., 15 June, 1825, for 10 years' faithful service in one grade.

LIPPINCOTT, AUBREY. [Born in N. Y. Appointed from Colo.]
2nd Lieut. 1st Cav., 1 Aug., 1899.

LIPPINCOTT, HENRY. [Born in Nova Scotia. Appointed from Cal.]
Asst. Surg. 6th Cal. Vols., 18 May, 1865. Mustered out 31 Oct., 1865. 1st Lieut. Asst. Surg., 28 Feb., 1866. Capt. Asst. Surg., 11 Nov., 1868. Maj. Surg., 17 Aug., 1884. Lieut. Col. D. S. G., 10 April, 1898.

LIPPITT, WILLIAM J., Jr. [Born in W. Va. Appointed from W. Va.]
Asst. Surg., 4 May, 1891. Capt. Asst. Surg., 4 May, 1896. Maj. Surg. 44th U. S. Vols., 17 Aug., 1899.

LISCUM, EMERSON H. [Born in Vt. Appointed from Army.]
Corpl. Co. H, 1st Vt. Vols., 2 May, 1861. Discharged 15 Aug., 1861. Priv. Co. E, 2nd Batt. 12th Inf., 1 Feb., 1862. Corpl., 24 May, 1862. Sergt., 1 June, 1862. 1st Sergt., 1 June, 1862. Trans. to Co. A, 3 March, 1863. 2nd Lieut. 12th Inf., 19 Feb., 1863. 1st Lieut., 4 May, 1863. R. Q. M., 5 Feb. to 16 Oct., 1865. Bvt. Capt., 1 Aug., 1864, for gallant service in the Battle of Bethesda Church, and during the present campaign before Richmond, Va. Trans. to 30th Inf., 21 Sept., 1866. Capt. 45th Inf., 28 July, 1866, declined. Capt. 25th Inf., 28 July, 1866. Unassigned 26 April, 1869. Ass'd to 19th Inf., 5 July, 1870. Maj. 22nd Inf., 4 May, 1892. Lieut. Col. 24th Inf., 23 May, 1896. Col. 9th Inf., 25 April, 1899. Brig. Gen. Vols., 12 July, 1898, to 31 Dec., 1898. Killed in action at Tien Tsin, China, 13 July, 1900.

LISSAK, ORMOND M.* [Born in Cal. Appointed from Cal.]
2nd Lieut. 4th Art., 13 June, 1882. 1st Lieut., 16 Jan., 1889. Trans. to Ord., 24 April, 1889. Capt. (14 years' service), 15 June, 1898. Maj. Chf. Ord. Off. Vols., 18 July, 1898, to 12 May, 1899.

LISSENHOFF, FREDERICK H. [Born in ——. Appointed from Ga.]
Cornet 1st Light Drag., 20 May, 1813. 3rd Lieut., 20 May, 1813. 2nd Lieut., 1 Aug., 1813. Trans. to 4th Inf., 17 May, 1815. Resigned 10 Jan., 1816. Died — Dec., 1819.

LITCHFIELD, HENRY G. [Born in N. Y. Appointed from Army.]
Priv. Co. G, 2nd Batt. 18th Inf., 21 March, 1862. 1st Sergt., 24 March, 1862. Discharged 31 July, 1862. 2nd Lieut. 18th Inf., 14 July, 1862. 1st Lieut., 27 April, 1863. Bvt. Capt., 20 Sept., 1863, for gallant and meritorious service in the Battle of Chickamauga, Ga. Bvt. Maj., 1 Sept., 1864, for gallant and meritorious service during the Atlanta campaign and in the Battle of Jonesboro, Ga. Lieut. Col. A. I. G. (Act 17 July, 1862), 6 Dec., 1864. Bvt. Lieut. Col., 13 March, 1865, for gallant and meritorious service in the Battle of Ben-

tonville, N. C. Relieved as Lieut. Col. A. I. G., 1 Aug., 1865. Trans. to 36th Inf., 21 Sept., 1866. Capt., 22 Feb., 1869. Unassigned 19 May, 1869. Ass'd to 2nd Art., 1 Jan., 1871. Retired for disability, with rank of Maj., 28 Nov., 1892.

LITTEBRANT, WILLIAM I.* [Born in Cal. Appointed from Cal.]
Addl. 2nd Lieut. 19th Inf., 11 June, 1888. 2nd Lieut. 10th Cav., 23 Aug., 1888. Trans. to 10th Cav., 11 Feb., 1889. 1st Lieut. 7th Cav., 26 Aug., 1896.

LITTELL, ISAAC W.* [Born in N. J. Appointed from N. J.]
2nd Lieut. 10th Inf., 13 June, 1883. 1st Lieut., 21 Aug., 1888. Capt. A. Q. M., 25 April, 1895.

LITTLE, CHAS. L. [Born in Penn. Appointed from Penn.]
Mil. Storekeeper, 1 Nov., 1833. Resigned 3 March, 1837.

LITTLE, HENRY. [Born in Md. Appointed from Md.]
2nd Lieut. 5th Inf., 1 July, 1839. Trans. to 7th Inf., 6 May, 1843. 1st Lieut., 18 April, 1845. Capt., 20 Aug., 1847. Resigned 7 May, 1861. Bvt. Capt., 23 Sept., 1846, for gallant and meritorious conduct at Monterey.

LITTLE, J. MILLARD. [Born in Ga. Appointed from Ga.]
2nd Lieut. 19th Inf., 1 May, 1899.

LITTLE, JOHN. [Born in Conn. Appointed from Wis.]
Sergt. Co. D. 17th Wis. Vols., 20 Oct., 1861. 2nd Lieut., 23 Sept., 1862. 1st Lieut., 6 Nov., 1863. Mustered out 31 March, 1865. 2nd Lieut. 35th Inf., 6 May, 1867. Trans. to 15th Inf., 12 Aug., 1869. Capt., 15 Jan., 1873. Dismissed 2 Nov., 1875.

LITTLE, JOHN.* [Born in Tenn. Appointed from Tenn.]
2nd Lieut. 24th Inf., 14 June, 1885. 1st Lieut. 14th Inf., 28 March, 1892. Capt. C. S., 3 May, 1898. Maj. C. S. Vols., 22 July to 13 Sept., 1898, and from 9 Nov., 1898, to 2 March, 1899.

LITTLE, REUBEN F. [Born in England. Appointed from Army.]
Priv. and Sergt. Co. C. and Sergt. Maj. 18th Inf., 8 Aug., 1861, to 26 March, 1863. 2nd Lieut. 18th Inf., 19 Feb., 1863. 1st Lieut., 12 Aug., 1863. Resigned 25 Sept., 1865.

LITTLE, THOS. [Born in Ireland. Appointed from Army.]
Priv., Corpl., Sergt. and 1st Sergt. Batty H, 4th Art., 29 Sept., 1856, to 13 Oct., 1861. Sergt. Co. C. 1st Batt. 13th Inf., 8 Nov., 1861, to 2 July, 1862. 2nd Lieut. 13th Inf., 31 May, 1862. 1st Lieut., 15 Aug., 1862. Trans. to 31st Inf., 21 Sept., 1866. Capt., 1 Nov., 1867. Unassigned 24 July, 1869. Ass'd to 10th Cav., 1 Jan., 1871. Dismissed 20 Dec., 1877. Bvt. Capt., 4 July, 1863, for gallant and meritorious service during the Siege of Vicksburg, Miss. Bvt. Maj., 25 Nov., 1863, for gallant and meritorious service at the Battle of Mission Ridge, Tenn.

LITTLE, WM. [Born in Va. Appointed from Va.]
Mil. Storekeeper Harper's Ferry Armory, 20 Dec., 1820. Resigned 14 Feb., 1822.

LITTLEJOHN, SAML. H. [Born in Va. Appointed from Va.]
Surg.'s Mate 35th Inf., 3 April, 1813. Trans. to 1st Light Drag., 12 May, 1813. Disbanded 15 June, 1815. Reinstated in 2nd Inf., 13 Sept., 1815. Asst. Surg., 1 June, 1821. Died 8 Sept., 1824.

LIVERMORE, BENJAMIN W. [Born in N. Y. Appointed from Ind.]
1st Sergt. 16th Ind. Batty, 20 Feb., 1862. 2nd Lieut., 1 Jan., 1863. 1st Lieut., 1 May, 1863. Capt., 10 June, 1865. Mustered out 5 July, 1865. 2nd Lieut. 2nd Art., 11 May, 1866. Accidentally killed 20 June, 1868.

LIVERMORE, RICHARD L.* [Born in N. Y. Appointed from N. J.]
2nd Lieut. 8th Cav., 12 June, 1891. Trans. to 10th Cav., 22 June, 1895. 1st Lieut., 11 Jan., 1898.

LIVERMORE, WM. R.* [Born in Mass. Appointed from Mass.]
1st Lieut. Eng., 23 June, 1865. Capt., 22 Jan., 1870. Maj., 12 March, 1884. Lieut. Col., 5 July, 1898. Lieut. Col. Chf. Eng. Vols., 9 May to 5 July, 1898.

LIVERS, JOHN. [Born in Md. Appointed from Penn.]
Priv. Co. E, 4th Art., 11 Feb., 1828. Corpl., 1 Aug., 1829. Sergt., 1 March, 1831. Out of service 9 July, 1832. Priv. Co. E. 4th Art., 18 June, 1833. Discharged 20 Nov., 1836. Hosp. Stwd., 12 June, 1837. Discharged 9 Oct., 1837. Priv. Co. E, 4th Art., 1 Nov., 1839. Corpl., — —, —. Sergt., 27 Dec., 1839. 1st Sergt., 1 May, 1840. Sergt., 5 Jan., 1844. Discharged 1 Sept., 1844. Sergt. Co. E. 4th Art., 1 Sept., 1844. Trans. to Co. D. 31 Aug., 1846. Q. M. Sergt., 25 Aug., 1847. Discharged 1 July, 1849. Q. M Sergt. 4th Art., 1 July, 1849. Discharged 1 May, 1854. Q. M. Sergt. 4th Art., 1 May, 1854. Ord. Sergt., 8 Jan., 1859. Discharged 1 March, 1859. Ord. Sergt., 1 March, 1859. Discharged 17 Nov., 1862. 1st Lieut. 3rd Penn. Art., 17 Nov., 1862. Mustered out 25 Nov., 1865. Mil. Storekeeper Q. M. Dept., 27 Nov., 1865. Capt., 28 July, 1866. Retired 30 June, 1882. Died 12 Sept., 1885.

LIVINGSTON, HENRY B. [Born in N. Y. Appointed from N. Y.]
1st Lieut. and R. Q. M., 12th N. Y. State Mil., 27 April to 29 Oct., 1861. 1st Lieut. 11th Inf., 28 Oct., 1861. Rejected by Senate, 3 April, 1862.

LIVINGSTON, HENRY B. [Born in N. Y. Appointed from N. Y.]
2nd Lieut. 2nd Drag., 18 June, 1855. 1st Lieut., 28 Jan., 1861. 2nd Cav., 3 Aug., 1861. Capt., 8 Aug., 1861. Wholly retired 25 Aug., 1862. Died— ——, 1865.

LIVINGSTON, JAMES. [Born in N. Y. Appointed from N. Y.]
1st Lieut. Asst. Dep. Comsy. of Ord., 5 March, 1814. Retained as 1st Lieut. of Ord., 8 Feb., 1815, with rank from 5 March, 1814. Resigned 1 Sept., 1818.

LIVINGSTON, JOHN P. [Born in N. Y. Appointed from N. Y.]
2nd Lieut. 23rd Inf., 25 Sept., 1812. 1st Lieut., 19 Dec., 1813. Trans. to 6th Inf., 17 May, 1815. Capt., 18 Aug., 1819. Resigned 1 March, 1820. Bvt. Capt., 25 July, 1814, for gallant conduct at the Battle of Niagara.

LIVINGSTON, LA RHETT L.* [Born in N. Y. Appointed from N. Y.]
Bvt. 2nd Lieut. 1st Art., 1 July, 1853. 2nd Lieut. 3rd Art., 24 Dec., 1853. 1st Lieut., 3 Jan., 1856. Capt., 26 Oct., 1861. Bvt. Maj., 1 July, 1862, for gallant and meritorious service in the Battle of Malvern Hill, Va. Bvt. Lieut. Col. 28 Aug., 1864, for gallant and meritorious service in the Battle of Smithfield, Va. Maj. 4th Art., 10 April, 1879. Lieut. Col. 3rd Art., 5 March, 1887. Col. 3rd Art., 22 May, 1891. Retired by operation of law, 12 Feb., 1895.

LIVINGSTON, MANNING. [Born in N. Y. Appointed from N. Y.]
2nd Lieut. 3rd Art., 19 Feb., 1862. Bvt. 1st Lieut. and Bvt. Capt., 2 July, 1863, for gallant and meritorious service in the Battle of Gettysburg, Penn., where he was killed, 2 July, 1863.

LIVINGSTON, WALTER H. [Born in N. Y. Appointed from N. Y.]
Surg.'s Mate Light Art., 26 July, 1814. Post Surg., 3 Feb., 1819. Asst. Surg., 1 June, 1821. Died 5 April, 1822.

LLOYD, CHAS. F.* [Born in Sweden. Appointed from Iowa.]
2nd Lieut. 14th Inf., 17 June, 1874. Resigned 10 June, 1883.

LLOYD, CHARLES R., Jr. [Born in England. Appointed from Cal.]
Priv. Batty A, Conn. Vol. Lt. Art., 19 May to 24 July, 1898. 2nd Lieut. 6th Art., 9 July, 1898.

LLOYD, EDWARD. [Born in Va. Appointed from D. C.]
Priv. and Sergt. Sig. Corps, 22 July, 1871, to 26 Nov., 1880. 2nd Lieut. 15th Inf., 26 Nov., 1880. 1st Lieut., 29 Sept., 1890. Capt., 26 April, 1898.

LLOYD, THOMAS J.* [Born in Penn. Appointed from Penn.]
2nd Lieut. and 1st Lieut. 13th Inf., 23 June, 1865. Reg. Adj., 15 July, 1866, to 1 June, 1868. Capt., 3 Dec., 1868. Unassigned 11 June, 1869. Ass'd to 1st Inf., 1 Jan., 1871. Retired for disability, with rank of Maj., 12 May, 1895.

LOCHRIDGE, P. D.* [Born in Ala. Appointed from Miss.]
2nd Lieut. 2nd Cav., 12 June, 1887. 1st Lieut. 8th Cav., 2 April, 1894. Trans. to 2nd Cav., 23 May, 1894. Honor graduate of the Infantry and Cavalry School, 1893.

LOCKE, JOSEPH L.* [Born in Maine. Appointed from Maine.]
Bvt. 2nd Lieut. 2nd Art., 1 July, 1828. 2nd Lieut., 1 July, 1828. 1st Lieut., 17 Nov., 1834. Resigned 16 Aug., 1836. Died 5 Oct., 1864.

LOCKE, JOSEPH M. [Born in Ohio. Appointed from Ohio.]
Capt. 14th Inf., 19 Sept., 1861. Resigned 22 July, 1865. Bvt. Maj., 30 Aug., 1862, for gallant and meritorious service at the Battle of Bull Run (2nd), Va. Bvt. Lieut. Col., 2 July, 1863, for gallant and meritorious conduct at the Battle of Gettysburg, Penn.

LOCKETT, JAMES.* [Born in Ga. Appointed from Ga.]
2nd Lieut. 4th Cav., 13 June, 1879. 1st Lieut., 1 March, 1886. Capt., 14 April, 1894. Col. 11th U. S. Vol. Cav., 10 Aug., 1899.

LOCKETT, SAML. H.* [Born in Va. Appointed from Ala.]
Bvt. 2nd Lieut. Eng., 1 July, 1859. Resigned 1 Feb., 1861.

LOCKWOOD, BENJAMIN C. [Born in Ky. Appointed from Ky.]
Priv. Co. F, 6th Ky. Vols., 2 Oct., 1861. Discharged 7 April, 1863. 2nd Lieut. 54th Ky. Vols., 30 Sept., 1864. Mustered out 1 Sept., 1865. 2nd Lieut. 31st Inf., 7 March, 1867. Trans. to 22nd Inf., 15 May, 1869. 1st Lieut., 5 Oct., 1872. Capt., 2 June, 1889. Maj. 21st Inf., 13 March, 1899.

LOCKWOOD, DANIEL W.* [Born in N. Y. Appointed from N. Y.]
2nd Lieut. Eng., 18 June, 1866. 1st Lieut., 7 March, 1867. Capt., 30 June, 1879. Maj., 23 July, 1888.

LOCKWOOD, HENRY H.* [Born in Del. Appointed from D[illegible]
Bvt. 2nd Lieut. 2nd Art. 1 July, 1836. 2nd Lieut., 20 July, 1836. Resigned [illegible] Sept., 1837. Col. 1st Del. Vols., 25 May, 1861. Brig. Gen. Vols., 8 Aug., 1861. Mustered out 24 Aug., 1865. Prof. Naval Acad., 4 Nov., 1841. Retired 18 Aug., 1876.

LOCKWOOD, JAMES B. [Born in Md. Appointed from Md.]
2nd Lieut. 23rd Inf., 1 Oct., 1873. 1st Lieut., 15 March, 1883. Died at Camp Clay, Grinnell Land, Arctic Regions, while on the Lady Franklin expedition under Lieut. Greely, 9 April, 1884.

LOCKWOOD, JOHN A. [Born in Saxony. Appointed from D. C.]
2nd Lieut. 17th Inf., 23 Nov., 1880. 1st Lieut., 22 June, 1889. Trans. to 4th Cav., 4 Oct., 1891. Capt., 7 Nov., 1898. Graduate of the Infantry and Cavalry School, 1893.

LODER, SAML. H.* [Born in N. J. Appointed from N. J.]
Addl. 2nd Lieut. 9th Inf., 15 June, 1877. 2nd Lieut. 7th Inf., 20 Aug., 1877. Died 30 June, 1879.

LODER, RICHARD.* [Born in N. Y. Appointed from N. J.]
Bvt. 2nd Lieut. 4th Art., 1 July, 1856. 2nd Lieut., 31 Oct., 1856. 1st Lieut., 1 Feb., 1861. Capt., 29 Nov., 1861. Bvt. Maj., 31 Dec., 1862, for gallant and meritorious service in the Battle of Stone River, Tenn. Lieut. Col. A. I. G. (Act 17 July, 1862), 20 Jan., 1863, to 10 Nov., 1863. Bvt. Lieut. Col. and Col., 13 March, 1865, for gallant and meritorious service during the war. Maj. 3 Art., 25 Aug., 1879. Lieut. Col. 5th Art., 25 April, 1888. Trans. to 1st Art., 1 May, 1890. Col. 2nd Art., 1 July, 1892. Retired by operation of law, 29 Oct., 1896.

LOEB, ABRAHAM U. [Born in ——. Appointed from ——.]
2nd Lieut. of Inf., 1 Dec., 1899. (Unassigned.)

LOEFFLER, CHARLES D. A. [Born in Germany. Appointed from D. C.]
Priv. Troop H, 2nd and 5th Cav., 10 July, 1858, to 14 March, 1863. Priv. and Sergt. Gen. Ser., 7 Aug., 1863, to 17 July, 1872. Capt. M. S. K., 5 July, 1898.

LOESER, LUCIEN.* [Born in Penn. Appointed from Penn.]
Bvt. 2nd Lieut. 2nd Art., 1 July, 1842. 2nd Lieut. 3rd Art., 31 May, 1845. 1st Lieut., 3 March, 1847. Reg. Adj., 1 March to 4 April, 1854. Capt., 11 Nov.,

1856. Resigned 3 Dec., 1858. Lieut. Col. 7th W. Va. Cav., 27 Nov., 1861. Dismissed 24 Aug., 1862.

LOFLAND, PURNELL. [Born in Del. Appointed from Del.]
2nd Lieut. 11th Inf., 4 May, 1847. Resigned 5 Feb., 1848.

LOGAN, THOS. H. [Born in Ohio. Appointed from Ind.]
1st Lieut. 20th Ind. Vols., 22 July, 1861. Capt., 15 Nov., 1862. Mustered out 26 Aug., 1864. Maj. 28th U. S. Col. Troops, 29 Aug., 1864. Lieut. Col., 18 Oct., 1864. Mustered out 8 Nov., 1865. 1st Lieut. 40th Inf., 28 July, 1866. R. Q. M., 1 Dec., 1866, to 22 April, 1867. Bvt. Capt., 2 March, 1867, for gallant and meritorious service in the Battle of Gettysburg, Penn. Bvt. Maj., 2 March, 1867, for gallant and meritorious service in the Battle of the Wilderness, Va. Unassigned 20 April, 1869. Ass'd to 5th Inf., 26 Nov., 1869. Capt., 21 Oct., 1881. Retired for disability, 20 Feb., 1891.

LOGAN, WM. [Born in Ireland. Appointed from Army.]
Priv., Corpl. and Sergt. Co. I, 7th Inf., 27 Dec., 1850, to 12 Jan., 1863, and Hosp. Stwd. to 4 June, 1864. 2nd Lieut. 7th Inf., 18 May, 1864. 1st Lieut., 18 May, 1864. R. Q. M., 23 Sept., 1864, to 19 May, 1869. Capt., 24 Oct., 1874. Killed 9 Aug., 1877, in action with Indians in Montana.

LOMAX, LUNSFORD L.* [Born in R. I. Appointed at Large.]
Bvt. 2nd Lieut. 2nd Cav., 1 July, 1856. 2nd Lieut. 1st Cav., 30 Sept., 1856. 1st Lieut., 21 March, 1861. Resigned 25 April, 1861.

LOMAX, MANN P. [Born in Va. Appointed from Va.]
2nd Lieut. Art., 10 June, 1807. 1st Lieut., 30 June, 1811. Trans. to 1st Art., — March, 1812. Trans. to Corps Art., 12 May, 1814. (Maj. A. A. G., 3 March, 1814, to 15 June, 1815.) Capt. Corps Art., 17 Nov., 1814. Trans. to 3rd Art., 1 June, 1821. Maj. Ord., 7 July, 1838. Died 27 March, 1842. Bvt. Maj., 17 Nov., 1824, for ten years' faithful service in one grade.

LOMIA, LUIGI.* [Born in Italy. Appointed from Tenn.]
2nd Lieut. 5th Art., 17 June, 1867. 1st Lieut., 24 March, 1869. Capt., 3 Feb., 1894. Graduate of the Artilery School, 1876.

LONDON, ROBT.* [Born in N. C. Appointed from N. C.]
2nd Lieut. 5th Cav., 13 June, 1873. 1st Lieut., 1 May, 1879. R. Q. M., 11 March, 1887, to ——. Died 12 Dec., 1892.

LONG, ANDREW K. [Born in Ill. Appointed from Tenn.]
Priv. Co. C, 9th Penn. Vols., 23 April to 26 July, 1861. Priv. Co. A, 7th Penn. Res., 25 Oct., 1861, to 14 Dec., 1863. 1st Lieut. 12th Tenn. Cav., 1 Feb., 1864, to 4 Oct., 1865. Maj. A. A. G. Vols., 4 Sept., 1865. Bvt. Capt. and Maj. Vols., 13 March, 1865, for faithful and meritorious conduct during the war, and Lieut. Col. and Col. Vols., 13 March, 1865, for gallant and meritorious service during the war. Mustered out 31 Jan., 1867. 2nd Lieut. 6th Inf., 20 Nov., 1865. 1st Lieut., 20 Nov., 1865. Capt. C. S., 25 Feb., 1867. Died 22 Jan., 1878. B Maj. and Bvt. Lieut. Col., 2 March, 1867, for gallant and meritorious service during the yar.

LONG, ARMISTEAD, L.* [Born in Va. Appointed from Va.]
Bvt. 2nd Lieut. 2nd Art., 1 July, 1850. Trans. to 3rd Art., 11 Feb., 1851. 2nd Lieut. 2nd Art., 30 June, 1851. 1st Lieut., 1 July, 1854. Resigned 10 June, 1861.

LONG, EDWIN R.* [Born in N. C. Appointed from N. C.]
Bvt. 2nd Lieut. 2nd Inf., 1 July, 1829. 2nd Lieut., 1 July, 1829. 1st Lieut., 6 Nov., 1836. Died 11 March, 1846.

LONG, ELI. [Born in Ky. Appointed from Ky.]
2nd Lieut. 1st Cav., 27 June, 1856. 1st Lieut., 1 March, 1861. Capt., 24 May, 1861. 4th Cav., 3 Aug., 1861. Bvt. Maj., 7 Oct., 1862, for gallant and meritorious service in the Battle of Farmington, Tenn. Col. 4th Ohio Cav., 23 Feb., 1862. Bvt. Lieut. Col., 3 Dec., 1863, for gallant and meritorious service during the defence of Knoxville, Tenn. Bvt. Col., 21 Aug., 1864, for gallant and meritorious service in the Battle of Lovejoy's Station, Ga. Brig. Gen. Vols., 18 Aug., 1864. Bvt. Brig. Gen., 13 March, 1865, for gallant and meritorious service in the Battle and Capture of Selma, Ala. Bvt. Maj. Gen., 13 March, 1865, for gallant and meritorious service in the field during the war. Bvt. Maj. Gen. Vols., 13 March, 1865, for gallant and meritorious service in action. Mustered out of Vol. Service 15 Jan., 1866. Retired with rank of Maj. Gen., 16 Aug., 1867, and with rank of Brig. Gen., 3 March, 1875.

LONG, GEORGE W.* [Born in N. H. Appointed from N
Bvt. 2nd Lieut. 1st Art., 1 July, 1824. 2nd Lieut. 4th Art., 1 July, 1824. 1st Lieut., 2 Feb., 1832. Resigned 31 Dec., 1835. Died 7 July, 1880.

LONG, JAMES W. [Born in N. C. Appointed from N.
2nd Lieut. 2nd Inf., 5 Aug., 1861. 1st Lieut., 10 Aug., 1861. Capt., 9 Feb., 1 Unassigned 17 April, 1869. Ass'd to 25th Inf., 15 Dec., 1870. Discharged Dec., 1870. Bvt. Capt., 27 June, 1862, for gallant and meritorious service at the Battle of Gaines' Mills, Va. Bvt. Maj., 5 May, 1864, for gallant and meritorious service at the Battle of the Wilderness, Va.

LONG, JOHN C. [Born in Ill. Appointed from Ill.]
2nd Lieut. 19th Ill. Vols., 17 June to 31 Aug., 1861. 2nd Lieut. 9th Inf., 5 Aug., 1861. Dismissed 25 Nov., 1862. 1st Lieut. Adj. 147th Ill. Vols., 1 Feb., 1865. Bvt. Capt. Vols., 16 Feb., 1866, for faithful service. Mustered out 20 Jan., 1866.

LONG, JOHN D.* [Born in Ind. Appointed from Ind.]
2nd Lieut. 7th Cav., 15 Feb., 1899.

LONG, JOHN O.* [Born in Ill. Appointed at Large.]
Bvt. 2nd Lieut. 2nd Inf., 1 July, 1854. 2nd Lieut., 3 March, 1855. 1st Lieut., 19 Jan., 1861. Resigned 2 May, 1861. Died 3 April, 1875.

LONG, OSCAR F.* [Born in N. Y. Appointed from N. Y.]
2nd Lieut. 5th Inf., 15 June, 1876. 1st Lieut., 21 Oct., 1881. Reg. Adj., 31 March, 1887, to 29 Oct., 1889. Capt. A. Q. M., 26 May, 1892. Maj. Q. M.

Vols., 12 May, 1898. Lieut. Col. Q. M. Vols., 10 Aug., 1898, to 2 March, 1899. Medal of Honor for most distinguished gallantry in action against Indians at Bear Paw Mountain, Mont., 30 Sept., 1877; having been directed to order a troop of Cav. to advance, and having found both officers killed, he voluntarily assumed command, and, under a heavy fire from the Indians, advanced the troop to its proper position; while 2nd Lieut. 5th Inf., and acting A. de C. to the Col. commanding.

LONG, RICHARD H.* [Born in Penn. Appointed at Large.]
2nd Lieut. 5th Inf., 1 July, 1847. Died 30 Jan., 1849.

LONG, STEPHEN H. [Born in N. H. Appointed from N. H.]
2nd Lieut. Eng., 12 Dec., 1814. Bvt. Maj. Top. Eng., 29 April, 1816. Maj. T Eng., 7 July, 1838. Col., 9 Sept., 1861. Trans. to Eng., 3 March, 1863. Retired 1 June, 1863. Died 4 Sept., 1864. Bvt. Lieut. Col., 29 April, 1826, for ten years' faithful service in one grade.

LONG, WALTER S. [Born in Md. Appointed from Md.]
Capt. 95th U. S. Col. Inf., 26 Aug., 1863. Mustered out 29 Jan., 1866. 2nd Lieut. 40th Inf., 28 July, 1866. 1st Lieut., 31 July, 1867. Unassigned 13 April, 1869. Cashiered 30 Sept., 1869. Bvt. 1st Lieut. and Capt., 2 March, 1867, for gallant and meritorious service in the Battle of Antietam, Md.

LONG, WM. ST. CLAIR. [Born in Penn. Appointed from Penn.]
2nd Lieut. 7th Inf., 1 Oct., 1873. Dismissed 9 Dec., 1875.

LONGAN, OLIVER W. [Born in Penn. Appointed from Penn.]
Priv. and Sergt. Co. G, and Sergt. Maj. 13th Penn. Cav., 12 Aug., 1862, to 13 March, 1864. 2nd Lieut. 7th Cav., 20 Nov., 1867. Resigned 30 June, 1869.

LONGAN, RUFUS E.* [Born in Mo. Appointed from Mo.]
Addl. 2nd Lieut. 18th Inf., 11 June, 1897. 2nd Lieut. 9th Inf., 16 Sept., 1897. Trans. to 11th Inf., 27 Sept., 1897. 1st Lieut., 2 March, 1899.

LONGNECKER, HENRY C. [Born in Penn. Appointed from Penn.]
1st Lieut. of Inf., 16 Feb., 1847; Voltigeurs, 9 April, 1847. Reg. Adj., 27 Aug. to 22 Oct., 1847. Discharged 29 Aug., 1848. Col. 9th Penn. Vols., 24 April, 1861. Mustered out 29 July, 1861. Col. 5th Penn. Mil., 11 Sept., 1862. Mustered out 27 Sept., 1862. Died 16 Sept., 1871.

LONGSHAW, LUTHER M. [Born in Va. Appointed from F
2nd Lieut. 30th Inf., 18 June, 1867. Trans. to 4th Inf., 23 March, 1869. Resigned 21 Sept., 1874.

LONGSTREET, JAMES.* [Born in S. C. Appointed from Ala
Bvt. 2nd Lieut. 4th Inf., 1 July, 1842. 2nd Lieut. 8th Inf., 4 March, 1845. 1st Lieut., 23 Feb., 1847. Reg. Adj., 8 June, 1847, to 1 July, 1849. Capt., 7 Dec., 1852. Maj. P. M., 19 July, 1858. Resigned 1 June, 1861. Bvt. Capt., 20 Aug., 1847, for gallant and meritorious conduct at Contreras and Churubusco. Bvt. Maj., 8 Sept., 1847, for gallant and meritorious conduct at Molino del Rey.

LOOMIS, GUSTAVUS.* [Born in Vt. Appointed from Vt.]
2nd Lieut. Art., 1 March, 1811. Trans. to 1st Art., — March, 1812. 1st Lieut., 5 May, 1813. Trans. to Corps Art., 12 May, 1814. Capt., 7 April, 1819. Trans. to 1st Inf., 1 June, 1821. Maj. 2nd Inf., 7 July, 1838. Lieut. Col. 6th Inf., 22 Sept., 1840. Col. 5th Inf., 9 March, 1851. Retired 1 June, 1863. Died 5 March, 1872. Bvt. Maj., 7 April, 1829, for ten years' faithful service in one grade. Bvt. Brig. Gen., 13 March, 1865, for long and faithful service in the army.

LOOSELEY, DANIEL. [Born in England. Appointed from Army.]
Priv., Corpl. and Sergt. Co. C. 4th Inf., 31 March, 1855, to 31 March, 1860. Priv. Gen. Ser. and Corpl. and 1st Sergt. Co. H, 3rd Batt. 14th Inf., 3 Dec., 1860, to 25 Nov., 1861. 2nd Lieut. 14th Inf., 20 Nov., 1861. 1st Lieut., 30 Aug., 1862. Capt., 31 May, 1866. Trans. to 23rd Inf., 21 Sept., 1866. Resigned 7 Feb., 1867. Bvt. Capt., 17 Sept., 1862, for gallant and meritorious service at the Battle of Antietam, Md.

LORAIN, LORENZO.* [Born in Penn. Appointed from Penn.]
2nd Lieut. 3rd Art., 1 July, 1856. 1st Lieut, 2 Jan., 1860. Bvt. Capt., 18 July, 1861, for gallant and meritorious service in the Battle of Blackburn's Ford, Va. Capt. 3rd Art., 28 Feb., 1862. Bvt. Maj., 13 March, 1865, for good conduct and gallant service during the war. Maj. 1st Art., 15 March, 1881. Died 6 March, 1882.

LORD, CHAS. McC. [Born in Conn. Appointed from Conn.]
1st Lieut. 15th Inf., 14 May, 1861. Capt., 10 Sept., 1864. Trans. to 33rd Inf., 21 Sept., 1866. Unassigned 3 May, 1869. Discharged 26 Oct., 1870. Died 2 Feb., 1877.

LORD, GEORGE E. [Born in Mass. Appointed from Mass.]
Asst. Surg., 26 June, 1875. Killed 25 June, 1876, in action with Sioux Indians on Little Big Horn River, Mont.

LORD, JAMES H.* [Born in Penn. Appointed from Penn.]
Bvt. 2nd Lieut. 2nd Art., 17 June, 1862. Bvt. 1st Lieut., 1 July, 1862, for gallant and meritorious service in the Battle of Malvern Hill, Va. 2nd Lieut. 2nd Art., 24 July, 1862. Bvt. Capt., 17 Sept., 1862, for gallant and meritorious service in the Battle of Antietam, Md. 1st Lieut. 2nd Art., 30 March, 1864. Bvt. Maj., 9 April, 1865, for gallant and meritorious service in action at Appomattox C. H., Va. Capt. A. de C. Vols., 26 June, 1865. Mustered out of Vol. Ser., 25 Aug., 1865. R. Q. M., 1 May, 1867, to 28 April, 1875. Capt. A. Q. M., 24 April, 1875. Maj. Q. M., 4 Oct., 1889. Retired for disability, 6 Sept., 1893. Died 21 Feb., 1896.

LORD, RICHARD S. C.* [Born in Ohio. Appointed from Ohio.]
Bvt. 2nd Lieut. 7th Inf., 1 July, 1856. 2nd Lieut. 3rd Art., 31 Oct., 1856. Trans. to 1st Drag., 22 June, 1857. 1st Lieut., 23 April, 1861. 1st Cav., 3 Aug., 1861. Capt., 26 Oct., 1861. Died 15 Oct., 1866. Bvt. Maj., 7 July, 1863, for gallant and meritorious service during the Gettysburg campaign. Bvt. Lieut. Col., 1 April, 1865, for gallant and meritorious serivce at the Battle of Five Forks, Va.

LORD, ROBT. C. [Born in Mass. Appointed from Army.]
Priv. and Sergt. Co. C, 11th Inf., 7 March, 1864, to 3 April, 1865. 2nd Lieut. 14th Inf., 12 March, 1865. 1st Lieut., 12 March, 1865. Trans. to 23rd Inf., 21 Sept., 1866. Resigned 4 Oct., 1866.

LORD, THOS. W. [Born in Mass. Appointed from Maine.]
Sergt. Co. K. 17th Maine Vols., 21 July, 1862. Discharged 23 Feb., 1863. 2nd Lieut. 17th Maine Vols., 23 Feb., 1863. Mustered out 8 Sept., 1863. 2nd Lieut. Vet. Res. Corps, 8 Dec., 1863. Bvt. Capt. Vols., 13 March, 1865, for gallant and meritorious service in the Battle of Chancellorsville, Va. 1st Lieut. Vet. Res. Corps, 5 June, 1865. Mustered out 3 Oct., 1866. 2nd Lieut. 43rd Inf., 28 July, 1866. Reg. Adj., 12 Jan., 1867, to 8 April, 1869. Bvt. 1st Lieut., 2 March, 1867, for gallant and meritorious service in the Battle of Chancellorsville, Va. Unassigned 8 April, 1869. Ass'd to 20th Inf., 14 July, 1869. Reg. Q. M., 1 Oct., 1871, to 30 June, 1883. 1st Lieut., 1 Oct., 1871. Retired 25 Aug., 1887. Appointed Capt. of Cav., 2 Oct., 1890, with rank from 24 April, 1886. Retired for loss of leg from wound in line of duty, 28 Jan., 1890.

LORD, WM. P. [Born in Del. Appointed from Del.]
Capt. 1st Del. Vols., 8 Sept., 1862. Maj., 18 April, 1864. Mustered out 26 June, 1865. 2nd Lieut. 2nd Art., 4 Sept., 1867. Resigned 28 May, 1868.

LORENTZ, ANTONE. [Born in France. Appointed from N. Y.]
Sword Master at the U. S. Mil. Acad., 13 April, 1858. Died 25 Dec., 1884.

LORING, ALONZO. [Born in N. Y. Appointed from Va.]
2nd Lieut. of Inf., 8 March, 1847; 11th Inf., 9 April, 1847. 1st Lieut., 9 Dec., 1847. Disbanded 15 Aug., 1848. Bvt. 1st Lieut., for gallant and meritorious conduct in several affairs with Guerilleros, at Paso Ovejas, Natural Bridge and Cerro Gordo on the 10, 12 and 15 Aug., 1847.

LORING, AUSTIN. [Born in Mass. Appointed from Mass.]
2nd Lieut. 1st Light Drag., 28 Sept., 1812. 1st Lieut., 3 Sept., 1813. Capt. 46th Inf., 21 April, 1814. Trans. to 8th Inf., 17 May, 1815. Bvt. Maj., 5 July, 1814. for gallant and distinguished conduct at the Battle of Chippewa. U. C. Resigned 31 July, 1819. Died 28 Jan., 1827.

LORING, CHAS. [Born in Maine. Appointed from Mass.]
Surg. Mate 34th Inf., 20 May, 1813. Trans. to 6th Inf., 17 May, 1815. Resigned 1 Oct., 1816.

LORING, HENRY H.* [Born in Mass. Appointed from Mass.]
2nd Lieut. 6th Inf., 24 July, 1818. Trans. to Light Art., 27 Aug., 1818. Trans. to 3rd Inf., 20 Oct., 1818. 1st Lieut., 17 Oct., 1820. Capt., 15 July, 1831. Resigned 31 Oct., 1835. Bvt. Capt., 17 Oct., 1830, for ten years' faithful service in one grade. Died 16 July, 1840.

LORING, LEONARD Y. [Born in Mo. Appointed from Mo.]
1st Lieut. Asst. Surg., 14 May, 1867. Capt. Asst. Surg., 14 May, 1870. Maj. Surg., 9 Oct., 1888. Retired for disability, 27 Feb., 1891.

LORING, WM. W. [Born in N. C. Appointed from Fla.]
2nd Lieut. Fla. Vols., 16 June to 16 Aug., 1837. Capt. Mounted Rifles, 27 May, 1846. Maj., 16 Feb., 1847. Lieut. Col., 15 March, 1848. Col., 30 Dec., 1856. Resigned 13 May, 1861. Bvt. Lieut. Col., 20 Aug., 1847, for gallant and meritorious conduct at Contreras and Churubusco. Bvt. Col., 13 Sept., 1847, for gallant and meritorious conduct at Chapultepec. Died 30 Dec., 1886.

LOSHE, CHAS. F. [Born in Germany. Appointed from Army.]
Priv., Corpl. and Sergt. Cos. K, 1st Inf. and K, 4th Inf., 13 Sept., 1858, to 13 Sept., 1863. 1st Lieut. and Adj. 38th Iowa Vols., 23 Oct., 1863. Mustered out 15 Aug., 1865. Priv. and Corpl. Co. C, 8th Inf., 26 Sept. to 26 Oct., 1865. 2nd Lieut. 8th Inf., 19 Oct., 1865. 1st Lieut., 28 July, 1866. Resigned 31 Dec., 1875. Died — Oct., 1878.

LOTHROP, WARREN L. [Born in Maine. Appointed from Army.]
Priv., Corpl., Sergt. and 1st Sergt. Co. A, Eng., 23 June, 1846, to 20 March, 1857. 2nd Lieut. 4th Art., 21 Feb., 1857. 1st Lieut., 20 Feb., 1861. Capt. A. Q. M., 3 Aug., 1861. Died 31 Oct., 1866. Bvt. Maj., 14 March, 1862, for gallant and meritorious service in action at New Madrid, Mo. Bvt. Lieut. Col., 13 March, 1865, for gallant and meritorious service during the war.

LOTT, ABRAHAM G.* [Born in Penn. Appointed from Kans.]
Addl. 2nd Lieut. 6th Cav., 12 June, 1896. 2nd Lieut. 8th Cav., 15 Dec., 1896.

LOTT, GEORGE G. [Born in Penn. Appointed from Ohio.]
Cadet Mil. Acad., 1 July, 1861, to 23 June 1862. Capt. A. A. de C., 2 July, 1862. Mustered out 31 May, 1866. 2nd Lieut. 24th Inf., 7 March, 1867. 1st Lieut., 14 Oct., 1868. Trans. to 11th Inf., 25 April, 1869. Capt., 1 June, 1886. Retired for disability, 25 Feb., 1891. Reg. Adj., 11 Nov., 1874, to 31 May, 1886.

LOUCKS, MELVILLE R.* [Born in N. Y. Appointed from N. Y.]
2nd Lieut. 2nd Art., 13 June, 1864. 1st Lieut., 9 Feb., 1865. Mustered out 10 Dec., 1870. Died 20 Feb., 1872.

LOUD, JAMES M. [Born in ——. Appointed from ——.]
2nd Lieut. of Inf., 1 Dec., 1899. (Unassigned.)

LOUD, JOHN S. [Born in N. Y. Appointed from N. Y.]
Priv. Co. E, 7th N. Y. National Guard, 25 May, 1862. Discharged 5 Sept., 1862. 1st Lieut. 12th N. Y. Cav., 5 Jan., 1863. Capt., 20 Nov., 1863. Mustered out 24 June, 1865. 2nd Lieut. 9th Cav., 22 Jan., 1867. Bvt. 1st Lieut. and Capt., 2 March, 1867, for meritorious service during the war. 1st Lieut. 9th Cav., 31 July, 1867. Reg. Adj. 9th Cav., 13 Sept., 1867. Capt., 13 Jan., 1880. Maj. 3rd Cav., 29 June, 1897. Retired for disability, 30 June, 1898.

LOUGHBOROUGH, HARRISON.* [Born in Ky. Appointed from Ky.]
Bvt. 2nd Lieut. 2nd Art., 1 July, 1834. 2nd Lieut., 10 Oct., 1834. Died 20 July, 1836.

LOUGHBOROUGH, ROBT. H. R. [Born in Va. Appointed from Va.]
2nd Lieut. 25th Inf., 15 Oct., 1875. 1st Lieut., 6 Aug., 1881. Capt., 4 Dec., 1891.

LOVE, GEORGE M. [Born in N. Y. Appointed from N. Y.]
1st Sergt. Co. D, 21st N. Y. Vols., 13 May, 1861. Sergt. Maj., 13 May, 1861. Discharged 23 Aug., 1861. 1st Lieut. 44th N. Y. Vols., 23 Aug., 1861. Capt., 2 Jan., 1862. Mustered out 4 Sept., 1862. Maj. 116th N. Y. Vols., 5 Sept., 1862. Col., 16 July, 1863. Bvt. Brig. Gen. Vols., 7 March, 1865. Mustered out 8 June, 1865. 2nd Lieut. 11th Inf., 7 March, 1867. Bvt. 1st Lieut., 7 March, 1867, for gallant and meritorious service in action at Plain's Store. Bvt. Capt., 7 March, 1867, for gallant and meritorious service in the assault on Port Hudson, La. Bvt. Maj., 7 March, 1867, for gallant and meritorious service in the Battle of Cedar Creek, Va. Bvt. Lieut. Col., 7 March, 1867, for gallant and meritorious service during the war. Trans. to 16th Inf., 14 April, 1869. 1st Lieut., 1 March, 1875. Retired 15 March, 1883. Died 15 March, 1887.

LOVE, HARRY. [Born in Vt. Appointed from Cal.]
1st Lieut. 1st Cav., 3 March, 1855. Resigned 28 Feb., 1856.

LOVE, JAMES M., Jr. [Born in Va. Appointed from Va.]
2nd Lieut. 21st Inf., 9 Sept., 1898. 1st Lieut. 5th Inf., 8 Oct., 1899.

LOVE, JOHN.* [Born in Va. Appointed from Tenn.]
Bvt. 2nd Lieut. 1st Drag., 1 July, 1841. 2nd Lieut., 21 Feb., 1842. 1st Lieut., 30 June, 1846. R. Q. M., 12 March, 1849, to 1 Dec., 1850. Resigned 1 Feb., 1853. Bvt. Capt., 16 March, 1848, for gallant and meritorious conduct in the Battle of San Cruz de Rosales, Mex. Maj. I. G. Ind. Vols., 27 April to 29 July, 1861, and Maj. Gen. Ind. Legn. Mil., 1 Aug. to 10 Sept., 1861, and 4 Sept., 1862, to 1 Jan., 1863. Died 29 Jan., 1881.

LOVE, SAML. T. [Born in Va. Appointed from Tenn.]
2nd Lieut. 14th Inf., 15 April, 1847. Resigned 8 Feb., 1848.

LOVELL, CHAS. S. [Born in Mass. Appointed from Army.]
Priv. Co. D. 2nd Art., 30 Dec., 1830, to 5 Jan., 1832. Priv. Co. F, and Q. M. Sergt. and Sergt. Maj. 2nd Art., 25 April, 1832, to — Oct., 1837. 2nd Lieut. 6th Inf., 13 Oct., 1837. 1st Lieut., 7 July, 1838. Capt., 18 June, 1846. Maj. 10th Inf., 14 May, 1861. Lieut. Col. 18th Inf., 21 Jan., 1863. Col. 14th Inf., 16 Feb., 1865. Retired 15 Dec., 1870. Died 3 Jan., 1871. Bvt. Lieut. Col., 27 June, 1862, for gallant and meritorious service at the Battle of Gaines' Mill, Va. Bvt. Col., 1 July, 1862, for gallant and meritorious service at Battle of Malvern Hill, Va. Bvt. Brig. Gen., 13 March, 1865, for gallant service at the Battle of Antietam, Md.

LOVELL, CHRISTOPHER S. [Born in S. C. Appointed from S. C.]
2nd Lieut. 2nd Inf., 31 July, 1838. 1st Lieut., 17 Oct., 1842. Capt., 12 Jan., 1848. Maj. 3rd Inf., 9 Oct., 1861. Retired 23 Nov., 1861. Died 16 Aug., 1868. Bvt. Capt., 20 Aug., 1847, for gallant and meritorious conduct at Contreras and Churubusco.

LOVELL, JAMES. [Born in Mass. Appointed from Mass.]
2nd Lieut. Corps Art., 13 Aug., 1819. Disbanded 1 June, 1821.

LOVELL, JOSEPH. [Born in Mass. Appointed from Mass.]
Maj. Surg. 9th Inf., 15 May, 1812. Hosp. Surg., 30 June, 1814. Surg. Gen., 18 April, 1818. Died 17 Oct., 1836.

LOVELL, MANSFIELD.* [Born in D. C. Appointed from D. C.]
2nd Lieut. 4th Art., 1 July, 1842. 1st Lieut., 16 Feb., 1847. Resigned 18 Dec., 1854. Bvt. Capt., 13 Sept., 1847, for gallant and meritorious conduct at Chapultepec. Died 1 June, 1884.

LOVELL, ROBT. A. [Born in Kansas. Appointed from Ky.]
2nd Lieut. 14th Inf., 27 July, 1872. 1st Lieut., 2 April, 1883. Resigned 1 July, 1890.

LOVERING, LEONARD A.* [Born in Vt. Appointed from N. H.]
2nd Lieut. 4th Inf., 15 June, 1876. 1st Lieut., 3 Jan., 1885. Capt., 15 Oct., 1893. Maj. 30th U. S. Vols., 5 July, 1899.

LOW, CHAS. F. [Born in N. H. Appointed from N. H.]
2nd Lieut. of Inf., 11 March, 1847; 9th Inf., 9 April, 1847. Disbanded 26 Aug., 1848. Drowned 16 Jan., 1874.

LOW, EPHRAIM W.* [Born in Mass. Appointed from Mass.]
Bvt. 2nd Lieut. 3rd Inf., 1 July, 1824. 2nd Lieut. 1st Inf., 1 July, 1824. Drowned 8 July, 1825.

LOW, WM. H., Jr.* [Born in N. Y. Appointed from Ill.]
2nd Lieut. 20th Inf., 14 June, 1872. 1st Lieut., 7 April, 1877. Died 24 July, 1886.

LOWD, ALLEN. [Born in Mass. Appointed from Mass.]
2nd Lieut. Corps Art., 1 May, 1814. 1st Lieut., 20 April, 1818. Trans. to 2nd Art., 1 June, 1821. Capt. 2nd Art., 30 Nov., 1836. Maj. 1st Art., 8 Oct., 1853. Died 25 Nov., 1854. Bvt. Capt., 20 April, 1828, for ten years' faithful service in one grade. Bvt. Maj., 9 May, 1846, for gallant conduct in defence of Fort Brown.

LOWE, BRADLEY S. A.* [Born in Md. Appointed from D. C.]
3rd Lieut. Light Art., 21 July, 1814. Trans. to Corps Art., 17 May, 1815. 2nd Lieut., 31 Oct., 1816. 1st Lieut., 17 Sept., 1818. Resigned 30 Sept., 1819. Died 9 Aug., 1857.

LOWE, CARLETON. [Born in Ohio. Appointed from Iowa.]
Priv. Co. D, 2nd Iowa Vols., 27 May to 13 Nov., 1861. 2nd Lieut. 2nd Art., 24 Oct., 1861. Cashiered 1 June, 1862. Priv. Md. Vols., 1863, to 1865. Died 15 Dec., 1885.

LOWE, GIDEON. [Born in Penn. Appointed from Penn.]
Ensign 22nd Inf., 1 June, 1812. 2nd Lieut., 16 April, 1813. 1st Lieut., 8 Feb., 1814. Discharged 15 June, 1815. 2nd Lieut. Rifles, 3 Feb., 1819. 1st Lieut., 16 March, 1820. Trans. to 5th Inf., 1 June, 1821. Capt. 5th Inf., 20 Aug., 1828. Resigned 29 Feb., 1840.

LOWE, JOHN.* [Born in Md. Appointed from D. C.]
(For record, see Bradley S. A. Lowe.)

LOWE, PERCIVAL G. [Born in Kansas. Appointed from Army.]
Priv., Corpl. and Sergt. Co. B, 18th Inf., 29 Sept., 1885, to 4 March, 1889. 2nd Lieut. 18th Inf., 11 Feb., 1889. 1st Lieut. 4th Inf., 22 April. 1896. Trans. to 18th Inf., 24 May, 1897. Capt. 25th Inf., 8 June, 1899. Graduate of the Infantry and Cavalry School, 1895.

LOWE, WM. B. [Born in Ohio. Appointed from Ohio.]
Capt. 11th Inf., 14 May, 1861. Retired 19 Feb., 1865. Died 11 Sept., 1889.

LOWE, WM. R. [Born in Ohio. Appointed from Army.]
Priv. and Q. M. Sergt. 16th Inf., 1 to 26 Nov., 1861. 2nd Lieut. 19th Inf., 20 Nov., 1861. 1st Lieut., 19 Jan., 1863. Capt., 19 Sept., 1865. Unassigned 31 March, 1869. Resigned 2 Sept., 1869. Bvt. Capt., 1 Sept., 1864, for gallant and meritorious service during the Atlanta campaign, and at the Battle of Jonesboro, Ga. Bvt. Maj., 13 March, 1865, for long and meritorious service.

LOWE, WM. W.* [Born in Ind. Appointed from Iowa.]
Bvt. 2nd Lieut. 2nd Drag., 1 July, 1853. 2nd Lieut. 1st Drag., 22 Oct., 1854. Trans. to 2nd Cav., 3 March, 1855. 1st Lieut., 1 Dec., 1856. Reg. Adj., 31 May, 1858, to 9 May, 1861. Capt., 9 May, 1861; 5th Cav., 3 Aug., 1861. Col. 5th Iowa Cav., 1 Jan., 1862. Mustered out Vols., 24 Jan., 1865. Maj. 6th Cav., 31 July, 1866. Resigned 22 June, 1869. Bvt. Maj., 9 Oct., 1863, for gallant and meritorious service in the cavalry engagement near Chickamauga, Ga. Bvt. Lieut. Col., 15 Dec., 1863, for gallant and meritorious service in the cavalry action near Huntsville, Ala. Bvt. Col., 13 March, 1865. for gallant and meritorious service during the war. Bvt. Brig. Gen., 13 March, 1865, for gallant and meritorious service in the field during the war.

LOWELL, CHAS. R. [Born in Mass. Appointed from Mass.]
Capt. 6th Cav., 14 May, 1861. Col. 2nd Mass. Vols., 10 May, 1863. Brig. Gen. Vols., 19 Oct., 1864. Died 20 Oct., 1864, of wounds received in action at Middletown, Va.

LOWELL, DELMAR R. [Born in Vt. Appointed from N. Y.]
Priv. Co. G, 121st N. Y. Vols., 2 Sept., 1864, to 19 June, 1865. Post Chap., 19 April, 1890. Retired for disability, 18 Sept., 1897.

LOWNDES, RAWLINS.* [Born in S. C. Appointed from S. C.]
2nd Lieut. Corps Art., 1 July, 1820. Trans. to 3rd Art., 1 June, 1821. Trans. to 1st Inf., 12 June, 1823. 1st Lieut., 7 Aug., 1823. Resigned 31 Dec., 1830. Died 10 Aug., 1877.

LOWRY, ALBERT. [Born in Penn. Appointed from Penn.]
2nd Lieut. 2nd Drag., 19 Oct., 1839. 1st Lieut., 15 Dec., 1841. Capt. A. Q. M., 10 March, 1847, to 31 March, 1849. Resigned 30 Sept., 1849. Bvt. Maj., 25 March, 1847, for gallant and meritorious conduct in affair at Medelin, Mex.

LUCAS, EDWARD. [Born in Va. Appointed from Va.]
P. M. and Mil. Storekeeper Ord., 12 May, 1847. Died 5 March, 1858.

LUCAS, E. W. VAN C.* [Born in N. Y. Appointed from Conn.]
2nd Lieut. 1st Art., 12 June, 1887. Trans. to Eng., 14 May, 1888. 1st Lieut., 26 Feb., 1891. Capt., 5 July, 1898. Maj. Chf. Eng. Vols., 31 May, 1898, to 2 March, 1899.

LUCAS, MICHAEL E. [Born in Ireland. Appointed from Ohio.]
Mil. Storekeeper Q. M. D., 13 March, 1863. Capt., 28 July, 1866. Died 26 March, 1868.

LUCE, CHAS. F. [Born in Mass. Appointed from Mass.]
Asst. Surg., 22 Sept., 1823. Died 30 Sept., 1827.

LUDINGTON, ELISHA H. [Born in Penn. Appointed from Va.]
Capt. 17th Inf., 5 Aug., 1861. Bvt. Maj., 2 July, 1863. for gallant and meritorious service in the Battle of Gettysburg, Penn. Maj. A. I. G., 20 April, 1864. Bvt. Lieut. Col., 13 March, 1865, for meritorious service during the war. Bvt. Col., 13 March, 1865, for faithful and meritorious service in his department. Retired for disability, 27 March, 1879. Died 21 Jan., 1891.

LUDINGTON, MARSHALL I. [Born in Penn. Appointed from Penn.]
Capt. A. Q. M. Vols., 20 Oct., 1862. Maj. Q. M. (Act 4 July, 1864), 2 Aug. to 23 Oct., 1864. Col. Q. M. (Act 4 July, 1864), 24 Oct., 1864. Bvt. Maj., Lieut. Col. and Col. Vols., 13 March, 1865, for faithful and meritorious service during the war. Bvt. Brig. Gen. Vols., 13 March, 1865, for faithful and meritorious service in the Q. M. D. during the war. Relieved as Col. Q. M. (Act 4 July, 1864), 1 Jan., 1867. Maj. Q. M., 18 Jan., 1867. Vacated commission of Capt. A. Q. M. Vols., 14 March, 1867. Bvt. Lieut. Col., 2 March, 1867, for faithful and meritorious service in the Q. M. D. during the war. Lieut. Col. Q. M. G., 15 March, 1883. Col. A. Q. M. G., 31 Dec., 1894. Brig. Gen. Q. M. G., 3 Feb., 1898.

LUDLOW, HENRY H.* [Born in Penn. Appointed from Tenn.]
2nd Lieut. 3rd Art., 15 June, 1876. 1st Lieut., 3 Nov., 1882. Capt. 6th Art., 8 March, 1898. Graduate of the Artillery School, 1888.

LUDLOW, ISRAEL. [Born in Ohio. Appointed from Ohio.]
2nd Lieut. 5th Art., 14 May, 1861. 1st Lieut., 24 March, 1864. Resigned 31 July, 1865. Bvt. Capt., 13 March, 1865, for good conduct and gallant service during the war. Died 28 April, 1873.

LUDLOW, WM.* [Born in N. Y. Appointed from N. Y.]
1st Lieut. Eng., 13 June, 1864. Bvt. Capt., 20 July, 1864, for gallant and meritorious service in the defence of Allatoona Pass. Bvt. Maj., 21 Dec., 1864, for meritorious service in the campaign through Georgia in 1864. Bvt. Lieut. Col., 13 March, 1865, for gallant and meritorious conduct in the campaign of the Carolinas. Capt. Eng., 7 March, 1867. Maj., 30 June, 1882. Lieut. Col., 13 Aug., 1895. Brig. Gen. Vols., 4 May, 1898. Maj. Gen. Vols., 7 Sept., 1898, to 13 April, 1899. Brig. Gen. Vols., 13 April, 1899.

LUFF, EDMUND. [Born in N. Y. Appointed from Ill.]
Priv. Board of Trade Batty, Ill. Art., 22 July, 1862. Corpl., 4 April, 1863. Discharged 20 Feb., 1864. 1st Lieut. 12th Ill. Cav., 25 Feb., 1864. Capt., 13 Oct., 1864. Mustered out 2 Oct., 1865. 2nd Lieut. 8th Cav., 20 Nov., 1867. 1st Lieut., 23 May, 1870. R. Q. M., 1 Sept., 1881, to 2 April, 1883. Capt., 2 April, 1883. Retired for disability, 3 Jan., 1895.

LUGENBEEL, PINKNEY.* [Born in Md. Appointed from Ohio.]
Bvt. 2nd Lieut. 5th Inf., 1 July, 1840. 2nd Lieut., 22 Sept., 1840. 1st Lieut., 29 June, 1846. Reg. Adj., 1 Feb., 1847, to 15 April, 1855. Bvt. Capt., 20 Aug., 1847, for gallant and meritorious conduct in the Battles of Contreras and Churubusco. Bvt. Maj., 13 Sept., 1847, for gallant and meritorious service in the Battle of Chapultepec. Capt. 9th Inf., 3 March, 1855. Maj. 19th Inf., 31 Dec., 1862. Lieut. Col., 25 June, 1867. Trans. to 1st Inf., 15 March, 1869. Col. 5th Inf., 15 Dec., 1880. Retired 6 Feb., 1882. Died 18 March, 1886.

LUHN, GERHARD L. [Born in Germany. Appointed from Army.]
Priv. Co. E, 6th Inf., 10 Jan., 1853. Corpl., 1 July 1855. Discharged 16 Nov., 1857. Corpl. Co. E, 6th Inf., 16 Nov., 1857. Sergt., 18 March, 1859. 1st Sergt., 1 Nov., 1859. Sergt., 8 Dec., 1861. Discharged 16 Nov., 1862. 2nd Lieut. 4th Inf., 19 Feb., 1863. 1st Lieut., 29 June, 1864. R. Q. M., 31 Jan., 1869, to 1 Jan, 1871. Bvt. Capt., 2 April, 1865, for gallant and meritorious service in front of Petersburg, Va. Capt. 4th Inf., 31 Dec., 1875. Retired by operation of law, 19 Feb., 1895.

LUMPHREY, OLIVER. [Born in Canada. Appointed from D. C.]
Priv. Co. C, 1st N. Y. Cav., 19 Aug., 1861. 1st Lieut., 20 March, 1865. Mustered out 24 July, 1865. 2nd Lieut. 43rd Inf., 22 Jan., 1867. Unassigned 8 April, 1869. Mustered out 1 Jan., 1871.

LUNDEEN, JOHN A.* [Born in Sweden. Appointed from Minn.]
2nd Lieut. 4th Art., 13 June, 1873. 1st Lieut., 7 March, 1874. Capt. 7th Art., 8 March, 1898. Honor graduate of the Artillery School, 1882.

LUNING, ADOLPH. [Born in Germany. Appointed from Army.]
Priv., Corpl., Sergt. and 1st Sergt. Co. C, 10th Inf., 6 Jan., 1859, to 6 June, 1863. 2nd Lieut. 10th Inf., 1 June, 1863. Reg. Adj., 1 Sept. to 8 Nov., 1863. 1st Lieut., 28 Nov., 1863. Capt., 20 March, 1865. Dropped 7 Nov., 1865.

LUPTON, LANCASTER P.* [Born in N. Y. Appointed from N. Y.]
Bvt. 2nd Lieut. 3rd Inf., 1 July, 1829. 2nd Lieut. 1st Drag., 4 March, 1833. 1st Lieut., 4 March, 1833. Resigned 31 March, 1836.

LUSK, JAMES L.* [Born in Penn. Appointed from Penn.]
2nd Lieut. Eng., 14 June, 1878. 1st Lieut. 14 June, 1881. Capt., 15 June, 1888. Maj., 5 July, 1898. Lieut. Col. Chf. Eng., Vols., 9 May, 1898, to 7 Dec., 1898.

LUTHER, HENRY E. [Born in Ind. Appointed from Ind.]
Priv. Co. F, 11th Ky. Cav., 22 Sept., 1862, to 3 Jan., 1863. Priv. Co. G, 7th Ind. Cav., 5 Sept., 1863, to 12 July, 1864. Q. M. Sergt. 3rd U. S. Col. Art., 13 July, 1864, to 5 June, 1865. Capt. A. Q. M. Vols., 27 Feb., 1865. Mustered out 4 Aug., 1865. 2nd Lieut. 18th Inf., 22 Jan., 1867. 1st Lieut., 14 June, 1868. Resigned 2 Jan., 1869.

LUTHER, ROLAND A.* [Born in Penn. Appointed from Penn.]
2nd Lieut. 2nd Art., 1 July, 1836. 1st Lieut., 3 April, 1838. Capt., 3 March, 1847. Died 9 July, 1853.

LUTZ, WILLIAM J. [Born in Ind. Appointed from Army.]
Priv., Corpl. and Sergt. Batty F, 1st Art., 16 Jan., 1890, to 24 Nov., 1892. 2nd Lieut. 2nd Inf., 19 Nov., 1892. 1st Lieut., 26 April, 1898.

LYDECKER, GARRETT J.* [Born in N. J. Appointed from N. Y.]
1st Lieut. Eng., 13 June, 1864. Bvt. Capt., 2 April, 1865, for gallant and meritorious service in the Siege of Petersburg, Va. Capt. Eng., 8 Aug., 1866. Maj., 31 March, 1880. Lieut. Col., 14 Dec., 1891.

LYFORD, STEPHEN C.* [Born in N. H. Appointed from N. H.]
Bvt. 2nd Lieut. 1st Drag., 24 June, 1861. 2nd Lieut., 24 June, 1861. Trans. to 3rd Art., 23 Oct., 1861, and to Ord., 24 Oct., 1861. 1st Lieut., 3 March, 1863. Bvt. Capt., 4 July 1863, for gallant and meritorious service during the Siege of Vicksburg, Miss. Capt. Ord., 15 Sept., 1863. Bvt. Maj., 13 March, 1865, for faithful and meritorious service in the Ord. Dept. and in the field during the war. Bvt. Lieut. Col., 13 March, 1865, for gallant and meritorious service during the war. Maj. Ord., 23 June, 1874. Died 9 May, 1885.

LYLE, DAVID A.* [Born in Ohio. Appointed from Ohio.]
2nd Lieut. 2nd Art., 15 June, 1869. Trans. to Ord., 1 Nov., 1874. 1st Lieut., 1 Nov., 1874. Capt., 23 Aug., 1881. Maj., 7 April, 1899.

LYLE, DAVID E. W.* [Born in Ohio. Appointed from Mich.]
2nd Lieut. 18th Inf., 26 April, 1898. 1st Lieut., 2 March, 1899. Capt. 37th U. S. Vols., 5 July, 1899.

LYMAN, CHARLES G.* [Born in N. Y. Appointed from N. Y.]
2nd Lieut. 5th Inf., 1 July, 1886. Trans. to 2nd Cav., 7 Jan., 1889 (to rank in Cav., 29 Dec., 1888). Retired for disability, with rank of 1st Lieut., 23 May, 1896.

LYMAN, JOEL H. [Born in N. Y. Appointed from N. Y.]
Priv. Cos. E and B, 9th N. Y. Cav., 7 Oct., 1861, to 11 Oct., 1864. 2nd Lieut. 7th Inf., 8 May, 1866. 1st Lieut., 12 Oct., 1867. Unassigned 19 May, 1869. Discharged 30 Nov., 1870.

LYMAN, ROBERT. [Born in Mass. Appointed from Mass.]
2nd Lieut. 40th Inf., 11 March, 1814. R. Q. M., July, 1814, to June, 1815. Trans. to Corps Art., 17 May, 1815. 1st Lieut. 7th Inf., 13 Feb., 1818. Died 10 Oct., 1820.

LYMAN, WM. [Born in Mass. Appointed from Mass.]
Ensign 9th Inf., 25 April, 1812. 2nd Lieut., 26 June, 1813. 1st Lieut., 10 June, 1814. Trans. to Light Art., 17 May, 1815. Reg. Adj., — June, 1816, to 31 Dec., 1819. Capt., 31 Dec., 1819. Disbanded 1 June, 1821.

LYMAN, WM. C. [Born in Mass. Appointed from Mass.]
1st Lieut. Ord., 19 April, 1813. Resigned 31 March, 1819.

LYMAN, WYLLYS. [Born in Vt. Appointed from Vt.]
1st Lieut. Adj. 10th Vt. Vols., 15 Aug., 1862. Maj., 24 Feb., 1865. Mustered out 28 June, 1865. Capt. 40th Inf., 28 July, 1866. Bvt. Maj., 2 March, 1867, for gallant and meritorious service in the Battle of the Opequan, Va. Trans. to 25th Inf., 20 April, 1869. Trans. to 5th Inf., 15 Dec., 1870. Retired for disability, with rank of Maj., 4 July, 1892. Bvt. Lieut. Col., 27 Feb., 1890, for gallant services in the actions against Indians on the Upper Washita River, Texas, 9, 10 and 11 Sept., 1874.

LYNCH, CHARLES. [Born in N. Y. Appointed from N. Y.]
Asst. Surg., 12 May, 1893. Capt. Asst. Surg., 12 May, 1898.

LYNCH, DOMINICK, Jr. [Born in Va. Appointed from N. Y.]
2nd Lieut. 4th Cav., 3 Sept., 1867. 1st Lieut., 10 June, 1870. Died 21 Feb., 1875.

LYNCH, EDWARD. [Born in Ireland. Appointed from Army.]
Priv. Band 3rd Inf., 21 July, 1858. Sergt. Maj. 3rd Inf., 1 Oct., 1862. Discharged 14 Oct., 1863. 2nd Lieut. Vet. Res. Corps., 14 Dec., 1863. Mustered out 30 June, 1866. Sergt. Co. F, 3rd Batt. 16th Inf., 3 Aug., 1866. Trans. to 34th Inf., 21 Sept., 1866. Sergt. Maj. 34th Inf., 1 Dec., 1866. 2nd Lieut. 33rd Inf., 9 July, 1868. Trans. to 8th Inf., 3 May, 1869. 1st Lieut., 4 July, 1879. Retired for disability with rank of Capt., 9 March, 1891.

LYNCH, JAMES A. [Born in N. Y. Appointed from Army.]
Priv., Corpl. and Sergt. Troop H, 8th Cav., 17 July, 1891, to 30 Oct., 1894. 2nd Lieut. 15th Inf., 31 Oct., 1894. 1st Lieut., 26 April, 1898.

LYNCH, WM. F. [Born in N. Y. Appointed from Ill.]
Sergt. Maj. 23rd Ill. Vols., 18 June to 25 Sept., 1861. Col. 58th Ill. Vols., 25 Jan., 1862. Bvt. Brig. Gen. Vols., 31 Jan., 1865. Mustered out 7 Feb., 1865. 1st Lieut. 42nd Inf., 28 July, 1866. Capt., 20 March, 1867. Unassigned 22 April, 1869. Retired with rank of Brig. Gen., 15 Dec., 1870. Died 29 Dec., 1876. Bvt. Capt. and Maj.. 2 March, 1867, for gallant and meritorious service in the Battle of Pleasant Hill, La. Bvt. Lieut. Col., 2 March, 1867, for gallant and meritorious service in the Battle of Yellow Bayou, La.

LYNDE, CHAS. J. [Born in Mich. Appointed from Texas.]
2nd Lieut. 5th Inf., 30 June, 1855. Dismissed 5 Sept., 1859.

LYNDE, FREDERICK M. [Born in Mich. Appointed from Wis.]
Sergt. Co. B, 4th Vt. Vols., 20 Aug., 1861. 2nd Lieut. 4th Vt. Vols., 20 Jan., 1862. Mustered out 31 July, 1862. Priv. Co. C. 1st Wis. Heavy Art., 18 Aug., 1863. Priv. to 21 Aug., 1864. Sergt., 17 Feb., 1865. Discharged 21 Sept., 1865. 2nd Lieut. 22nd Inf., 28 July, 1866. 1st Lieut., 25 Feb., 1869. Unassigned 15 May, 1869. Ass'd to 1st Inf., 31 Dec., 1870. Capt., 20 Sept., 1883. Retired for disability 23 Sept., 1885. Died 26 Dec., 1898.

LYNDE, ISAAC.* [Born in Vt. Appointed from Vt.]
Bvt. 2nd Lieut. 5th Inf., 1 July, 1827. 2nd Lieut., 1 July, 1827. 1st Lieut., 18 Feb., 1836. Capt., 1 Jan., 1839. Maj. 7th Inf., 18 Oct., 1855. Dropped 25 Nov., 1861. Restored to service as Maj. 18th Inf., 27 Nov., 1866, to date from 28 July, 1866. Retired 27 Nov., 1866, to date from 28 July, 1866. Died 10 April, 1886.

LYNDE, RICHARD D. [Born in Mich. Appointed from Md.]
Asst. Surg., 29 Aug., 1856. Resigned 31 Aug., 1862. Asst. Surg. Vols., 19 Feb., 1863. Surg. Vols., 2 Sept., 1863. Bvt. Lieut. Col. Vols., 9 Jan., 1866, for faithful and meritorious service. Mustered out 18 Jan., 1866. Died 12 Feb., 1876.

LYNN, DANIEL D.* [Born in Ind. Appointed from Ind.]
Bvt. 2nd Lieut. 3rd Inf., 1 July, 1860. 2nd Lieut. 6th Inf., 18 July, 1860. 1st Lieut., 14 May, 1861. Capt., 14 June, 1863. Unassigned 5 Jan., 1870. Discharged 1 Nov., 1870. Bvt. Capt., 2 July, 1863, for gallant and meritorious service at the Battle of Gettysburg, Penn. Bvt. Maj., 13 March, 1865, for gallant and meritorious service at the Battle of Gettysburg, Penn.

LYON, A. McD. [Born in Penn. Appointed from Penn.]
1st Lieut. Erie Regt. Penn. Vols., 21 April to 25 July, 1861. Addl. P. M. Vols., 1 June, 1861. Maj. P. M. U. S. A., 3 Sept., 1863. Appointment revoked 14 July, 1864. Resigned from Vols., 1 June, 1865. Died 6 Nov., 1869.

LYON, CHAS. D. [Born in Penn. Appointed from D. C.]
Cadet Mil. Acad., 1 July, 1855, to 30 June, 1856. Priv. Co. B, 102nd Penn. Vols., 19 Aug., 1861. Trans. to Sig. Corps, 12 Aug., 1863. Sergt., 1 Oct., 1863. Discharged 19 Aug., 1864. 2nd Lieut. 6th Inf., 13 April, 1866. 1st Lieut., 28 July, 1866. Resigned 31 Dec., 1868.

LYON, DUPONT B. [Born in Tex. Appointed from Tex.]
2nd Lieut. 16th Inf., 1 July, 1899.

LYON, ELIJAH. [Born in Mass. Appointed from Army.]
Sergt. Light Art., 15 Oct., 1808, to May, 1813. 3rd Lieut. Light Art., 20 May, 1813. 2nd Lieut., 23 Oct., 1813. Trans. to Corps Art., 17 May, 1815. 1st Lieut., 1 Jan., 1817. Trans. to 2nd Art., 1 June, 1821. Capt., 20 Feb., 1827. Trans. to 3rd Art., 18 March, 1829. Died 19 Nov., 1843. Bvt. Capt., 1 Jan., 1827, for ten years' faithful service in one grade.

LYON, HENRY G.* [Born in N. Y. Appointed from N. Y.]
2nd Lieut. 17th Inf., 12 June, 1890. 1st Lieut. 24th Inf., 17 April, 1897. Capt. 22nd Inf., 15 Dec., 1899.

LYON, HYLAN B.* [Born in Ky. Appointed from Ky.]
Bvt. 2nd Lieut. 2nd Art., 1 July, 1856. 2nd Lieut. 3rd Art., 1 Oct., 1856. 1st Lieut., 27 Sept., 1860. Resigned 30 April, 1861.

LYON, LEROY S.* [Born in Va. Appointed from Va.]
2nd Lieut. 7th Cav., 12 June, 1891. Trans. to 2nd Art., 1 Oct., 1891. 1st Lieut., 18 Sept., 1898. Graduate of the Artillery School, 1898.

LYON, MARCUS W.* [Born in N. J. Appointed from N. J.]
2nd Lieut. 13th Inf., 14 June, 1872. Trans. to Ord., 1 Nov., 1874. 1st Lieut., 1 Nov., 1874. Capt., 9 May, 1885. Resigned 8 March, 1894.

LYON, NATHANIEL.* [Born in Conn. Appointed from Conn.]
2nd Lieut. 2nd Inf., 1 July, 1841. 1st Lieut., 16 Feb., 1847. Capt., 11 June, 1851. Brig. Gen. Vols., 17 May, 1861. Killed 10 Aug., 1861, in the Battle of Wilson's Creek, Mo. Bvt. Capt., 20 Aug., 1847, for gallant and meritorious conduct at Contreras and Churubusco. Joint resolution of Congress, approved 24 Dec., 1861:

"*Resolved* by the Senate and House of Representatives of the United States of America, in Congress assembled, 1. That Congress deems it just and proper to enter upon its records a recognition of the eminent and patriotic services of the late Brig. Gen. Nathaniel Lyon. The country to whose service he devoted his life will guard and preserve his fame as a part of its own glory,

"2. That the thanks of Congress are hereby given to the brave officers and soldiers who, under the command of the late Gen. Lyon, sustained the honor of the flag and achieved victory against overwhelming numbers, at the Battle of Springfield, Mo.: and that, in order to commemorate an event so honorable to the country and to themselves, it is ordered that each regiment engaged shall be authorized to bear upon its colors the word 'Springfield,' embroidered in letters of gold. And the President of the United States is hereby requested to cause these resolutions to be read at the head of every regiment in the army of the United States."

LYON, SAMUEL P. [Born in N. J. Appointed from Army.]
Priv., Corpl. and Sergt. Troop A, 1st Cav., 30 Jan., 1890, to 1 Nov., 1894. 2nd Lieut. 25th Inf., 31 Oct., 1894. 1st Lieut. 16th Inf., 30 June, 1898. Trans. to 25th Inf., 21 April, 1899.

LYON, WILBERFORCE W. [Born in Penn. Appointed from Penn.]
2nd Lieut. 14th Inf., 24 Oct., 1861. 1st Lieut. 3 March, 1862. Resigned 15 Aug., 1864. Died 19 Oct., 1868.

LYONS, ROBT. T. [Born in Ireland. Appointed from Del.]
Priv. Co. F, 1st Del. Vols., 28 Sept., 1861, to 30 Sept., 1864. Priv., Corpl. and Sergt. Troops M (2nd) and K (5th) Cav., 28 Sept., 1865, to 12 June, 1868. 2nd Lieut. 17th Inf., 17 Dec., 1872. Died 10 July, 1875.

LYSTER, WM. J. [Born in Mich. Appointed from Mich.]
2nd Lieut. and Adj. 2nd Mich. Vols., 25 May, 1861. Discharged 21 June, 1861. 1st Lieut. 19th Inf., 14 May, 1861. Bvt. Capt., 7 April, 1862, for gallant and meritorious service in the Battle of Shiloh, Tenn. Bvt. Maj., 20 Sept., 1863, for gallant and meritorious service in the Battle of Chickamauga, Ga. Capt. 19th Inf., 9 Aug., 1864. Bvt. Lieut. Col., 1 Sept., 1864, for gallant and meritorious service in the Battle of Mission Ridge, Tenn., and during the Atlanta campaign. Maj. 6th Inf., 13 Oct., 1886. Lieut. Col. of Inf. (21st), 1 Aug., 1891. Col. of Inf. (9th), 1 May, 1896. Retired 27 June, 1897. Died 3 Sept., 1897.

LYTLE, JOHN S. [Born in Ky. Appointed from Ohio.]
Maj. P. M., 17 Feb., 1834. Died 10 Dec., 1839.

MACADAMS, JAMES G. [Born in Canada. Appointed from Ky.]
2nd Lieut. 6th Ky. Cav., 6 Feb., 1863. Mustered out 14 July, 1865. Capt., 6th Ky. Cav., 1 Aug., 1865. Mustered out 6 Sept., 1865. 2nd Lieut. 2nd Cav., 7 March, 1867. 1st Lieut., 18 June, 1868. Capt., 9 May, 1879. Died 19 June, 1890.

MACARTHUR, ARTHUR. [Born in Mass. Appointed from Wis.]
1st Lieut. and Adj. 24th Wis. Vols., 4 Aug., 1862. Maj., 25 Jan., 1864. Bvt. Lieut. Col. Vols., 13 March, 1865, for gallant and meritorious service in the Battles of Perryville, Ky., Stone River, Tenn., Mission Ridge and Danridge, Ga. Bvt. Col. Vols., 13 March, 1865, for gallant and meritorious service in the Battle of Franklin, Tenn., and the Atlanta campaign. Lieut. Col. 24th Wis. Vols., 18 May, 1865. Mustered out 10 June, 1865. 2nd Lieut. and 1st Lieut. 17th Inf., 23 Feb., 1866. Trans. to 26th Inf., 21 Sept., 1866. Capt. 36th Inf., 28 July, 1866. Unassigned 19 May, 1869. Ass'd to 13th Inf., 5 July, 1870. Maj. A. A. G., 1 July, 1889. Lieut. Col. A. A. G., 26 May, 1896. Brig. Gen. Vols., 27 May, 1898. Maj. Gen. Vols., 13 Aug., 1898. Col. A. A. G., 28 April, 1900. Medal of Honor for coolness and conspicuous bravery in action in seizing the colors of his regt. at a critical moment and planting them on the captured works on the crest of Missionary Ridge, Tenn., 25 Nov., 1863; while serving as 1st Lieut. and Adj. 24th Wis. Inf.

MACAULEY, C. N. BERKELEY. [Born in Minn. Appointed from Mass.]
Asst. Surg., 10 Aug., 1882. Capt. Asst. Surg., 10 Aug., 1887. Died 6 Feb., 1896.

MACAULEY, PATRICK. [Born in Ireland. Appointed from Penn.]
Garrison Surg. Mate, 8 April, 1814. Resigned 10 Jan., 1816.

MACCONNELL, CHAS. C. [Born in Penn. Appointed from Penn.]
2nd Lieut. 5th Art., 14 May, 1861. Bvt. 1st Lieut., 27 June, 1862, for gallant and meritorious service in the Peninsular campaign in Va. Bvt. Capt., 2 July, 1863, for gallant and meritorious service in the Battle of Gettysburg, Penn. 1st Lieut. 5th Art., 1 Aug., 1863. Bvt. Maj., 25 March, 1865, for gallant and meritorious service during the attack on Fort Steedman, Va. Capt. 5th Art., 1 May, 1875. Graduate of the Art. School 1872. Retired for disability 18 April, 1883.

MACCALLA, WILLIAM L. [Born in Ky. Appointed from Ohio.]
Chap. 29 April, 1816. Disbanded 14 April, 1818.

MACDONALD, GODFREY H.* [Born in Ill. Appointed from Ill.]
2nd Lieut 1st Cav., 13 June, 1883. 1st Lieut., 9 March, 1891. Graduate of the Infantry and Cavalry School, 1889. Capt. 10th Cav., 2 March, 1899. Capt. A. A. G. Vols., 12 May, 1898. Maj. Chief Ord. Officer, 13 Aug., 1898, to 12 May, 1899.

MACE, EDWARD H. [Born in Ind. Appointed from Ind.]
2nd Lieut. 1st Inf., 24 Oct., 1861. 1st Lieut., 25 April, 1862. Dismissed 28 May, 1864.

MACFEELY, ROBT.* [Born in Penn. Appointed from Penn.]
Bvt. 2nd Lieut. 4th Inf., 1 July, 1850. 2nd Lieut., 13 July, 1852. 1st Lieut., 3 Feb., 1855. R. Q. M., 10 Sept., 1856, to 18 May, 1861. Capt. C. S., 11 May, 1861. Lieut. Col. C. S. (Act 17 July, 1862), 1 Jan., 1863. Maj. C. S., 9 Feb., 1863. Relieved as Lieut. Col. C. S. (Act 17 July, 1862), 3 Sept., 1864. Bvt. Lieut. Col. and Col, 13 March, 1865, for faithful and meritorious service during the war. Brig. Gen. C. G. S., 14 April, 1875. Retired by operation of law, 1 July, 1890.

MacGOWAN, ALEXR. B. [Born in Scotland. Appointed from Cal.]
1st Lieut. 1st Cal. Vols., 16 Aug., 1861. Capt. 6th Cal. Vols., 11 July, 1863. Mustered out 31 Oct., 1865. 2nd Lieut. and 1st Lieut. 12th Inf., 23 Feb., 1866. Capt., 30 Aug., 1871. Bvt. Maj., 27 Feb., 1890, for gallant services against Indians in their attack on Fort Apache, Ariz., 1 Sept., 1881. Retired by operation of law, 16 Dec., 1894.

MACHESNEY, JOHN. [Born in N. J. Appointed from N. J.]
1st Lieut. 6th Inf., 3 May, 1808. Capt. 7th Inf., 10 June, 1809. Maj., 21 March, 1814. Retained 17 May, 1815, (in reorganization under Act of 3 March, 1815), as Capt. 7th Inf., with Bvt. of Maj., from 21 March, 1814. Died 18 Sept., 1816.

MACK, OSCAR A.* [Born in N. H. Appointed from N. H.]
Bvt. 2nd Lieut. 3rd Art., 1 July, 1850. 2nd Lieut. 4th Art., 9 Jan., 1851. 1st Lieut., 14 Feb., 1856. Capt. 13th Inf., 14 May, 1861. Maj. A. A. de C., 11 March, 1863, to 19 June, 1866. Maj. 9th Inf., 19 June, 1866. Unassigned 15 March, 1869. Ass'd to 1st Inf., 15 Dec., 1870. Lieut. Col. 21st Inf., 15 Dec., 1874. Died 22 Oct., 1876. Bvt. Maj., 10 Sept., 1861, for gallant service at the Battle of Carnifex Ferry, Va. Bvt. Lieut. Col., 31 Dec., 1862, for gallant and distinguished service at the Battle of Murfreesboro, Tenn. Bvt. Col., 13 March, 1865, for gallant and meritorious service during the war.

MACKALL JAMES B.* [Born in Ohio. Appointed from Ohio.]
Bvt. 2nd Lieut. Eng., 15 June, 1868. Died 18 April, 1871.

MACKALL, WM. W.* [Born in D. C. Appointed from Md.]
2nd Lieut. 1st Art., 1 July, 1837. 1st Lieut., 9 July, 1838. Reg. Adj., 20 Jan., 1840, to 31 Aug., 1841. Capt., 20 Aug., 1847. Vacated same date. Bvt. Capt. A. A. G., 29 Dec., 1846. Bvt. Maj. A. A. G., 5 Aug., 1853. Resigned 3 July, 1861. Bvt. Capt., 23 Sept., 1846, for gallant and meritorious conduct in the several conflicts at Monterey, Mex. Bvt. Maj., 20 Aug., 1847, for gallant and meritorious conduct in the Battles of Contreras and Churubusco, Mex.

MACKAY, ÆNEAS. [Born in N. Y. Appointed from N. Y.]
Asst. Dep. Com. of Ord., 12 March, 1813. Retained as 1st Lieut. of Ord., 8 Feb., 1815, to rank from 12 March, 1813. Discharged 15 June, 1815. Reinstated as 2nd Lieut. Ord., 2 Dec., 1815, with Bvt. of 1st Lieut. from 12 March, 1813. Trans. to Corps Art., 17 May, 1816. 1st Lieut., 1 Dec., 1816. Trans. to 3rd Art., 1 June, 1821. Capt., 31 Dec., 1822, to 7 July, 1838. Capt. A. Q. M., 15 July, 1824. Maj. Q. M., 7 July, 1838. Lieut. Col. Dep. Q. M. G., 21 April, 1846 Died 23 May, 1850. Retained—May, 1816, (in reorganization under Act of 3 March, 1815), as 2nd Lieut. of Art., with Bvt. of 1st Lieut., from 12 March, 1813. Bvt. Maj., 31 Dec., 1832, for ten years' faithful service in one grade. Bvt. Col., 30 May, 1848, for meritorious conduct, particularly in performing his duties in prosecuting war with Mex.

MACKAY, ALEXR. D.* [Born in N. Y. Appointed from N. Y.]
Bvt. 2nd Lieut. 3rd Art., 1 July, 1825. 2nd Lieut. 1st Art., 1 July, 1825. 1st Lieut., 4 Feb., 1833. Killed by steamboat explosion, 17 Dec., 1836.

MACKAY, JAMES O.* [Born in Nova Scotia. Appointed from Nev.]
2nd Lieut. 3rd Cav., 13 June, 1879. 1st Lieut., 8 May, 1883. Graduate of the Infantry and Cavalry School, 1885. Capt., 22 April, 1891.

MACKAY, JOHN.* [Born in Ga. Appointed from Ga.]
Bvt. 2nd Lieut. 2nd Art., 1 July, 1829. 2nd Lieut., 1 July, 1829. 1st Lieut., 31 Dec., 1834. Reg. Adj., 27 Jan. to 7 July, 1838. Capt. Top. Eng., 7 July, 1838. Died 31 May, 1848.

MACKAY, SAMUEL M. [Born in Vt. Appointed from Mass.]
3rd Lieut. Light Art., 4 April, 1813. 2nd Lieut. 27 May, 1813. 1st Lieut., 10 Oct., 1814. Resigned 31 Oct., 1819.

MACKAY, UNIACKE C. [Born in Ireland. Appointed from N. Y.]
1st Lieut. 100th N. Y. Vols., 7 Jan., 1862, to 10 March, 1862. 2nd Lieut. 10th Inf., 19 Feb., 1862. 1st Lieut., 2 July, 1863. Capt., 3 Oct., 1864. Dismissed 3 Feb., 1865.

MACKAY, WM. S. [Born in England. Appointed from Army.]
(Proper name was William Mackey Porter.) Priv. and Corpl. and Q. M. Sergt. and Sergt. Maj. 3rd Mass. Cav., 21 July, 1865. Mustered out 28 Sept., 1865. Priv. and Sergt. Co. D, 11th Inf., 24 Oct., 1865, to 11 Sept., 1866. 2nd Lieut. 11th Inf., 19 Aug., 1866. Trans. to 29th Inf., 21 Sept., 1866. Unassigned 21 Dec., 1869. Ass'd to 3rd Inf., 22 March, 1870. 1st Lieut., 1 Nov., 1872. Resigned 15 Feb., 1873. Died 20 Sept., 1889.

MACKENZIE, ALEXR.* [Born in Wis. Appointed from Ill.]
1st Lieut. Eng., 13 June, 1864. Bvt. Capt., 13 March, 1865, for gallant and meritorious serviec during the war. Capt. Eng., 7 March, 1867. Maj., 5 April, 1882. Lieut. Col., 3 Feb., 1895.

MACKENZIE, JOHN.* [Born in N. C. Appointed from N. C.]
2nd Lieut. 8th Inf., 1 July, 1819. Trans. to 1st Inf., 1 June, 1821. 1st Lieut., 18 Nov., 1822. Killed by a soldier, 26 Sept., 1828.

MACKENZIE, RANALD S.* [Born in N. Y. Appointed from N. J.]
2nd Lieut. Eng., 17 June, 1862. Bvt. 1st Lieut., 29 Aug., 1862, for gallant and meritorious service in the Battle of Manassas, Va. 1st Lieut. Eng., 3 March, 1863.

Bvt. Capt., 3 March, 1863, for gallant and meritorious service in the Battle of Chancellorsville, Va. Bvt. Maj., 4 July, 1863, for gallant and meritorious service in the Battle of Gettysburg, Penn. Capt. Eng., 6 Nov., 1863. Bvt. Lieut. Col., 18 June, 1864, for gallant and meritorious service before Petersburg, Va. Col. 2nd Conn. Art., 10 July, 1864. Bvt. Col., 19 Oct., 1864, for gallant and meritorious service in the Battle of Cedar Creek, Va. Brig. Gen. Vols., 19 Oct., 1864, for gallant and meritorious service in the Battles of Opequan, Fisher's Hill and Middletown Va. Bvt. Brig. Gen., 13 March, 1865, for gallant and meritorious service in the field during the war. Bvt. Maj. Gen. Vols., 31 March, 1865, for gallant and meritorious service during the war. Mustered out of Vol. Service 15 Jan., 1866. Col. 41st Inf., 6 March, 1867. Trans to 24th Inf., 15 Mach, 1869. Trans. to 4th Cav., 15 Dec., 1870. Brig. Gen., 26 Oct., 1882. Retired for disability 10 July, 1885. Died 19 Jan., 1889.

MACKENZIE, SAMUEL,* [Born in N. C. Appointed from N. C.]
2nd Lieut. Corps Art., 24 July, 1818. Trans. to 3rd Art., 1 June, 1821. Trans. to 2nd Art., 16 Aug., 1821. 1st Lieut., 20 Feb., 1825. Capt., 8 Feb., 1837. Died 1 Jan., 1867.

MACKENZIE, THOS. G. [Born in Md. Appointed from Md.]
Asst. Surg., 16 April, 1862. Died 1 Jan., 1867. Bvt. Capt. and Maj., 13 March, 1865, for faithful and meritorious service during the war.
1 June, 1863. 1st Lieut., 5 May, 1864. Trans. to 25th Inf., 21 Sept., 1866. Capt. Chickamauga, Ga. Died 25 May, 1888.

MACKEY, JOHN T. [Born in Va. Appointed from Army.]
Priv. and Sergt. 16th Inf., 14 Feb., 1862, to 10 June, 1863. 2nd Lieut. 16th Inf., 21 Sept., 1867. Unassigned 26 April, 1869. Discharged 31 Dec., 1870. Bvt. 1st Lieut., 19 Sept., 1863, for gallant and meritorious service at the Battle of Chickamauga, Ga. Died 25 May, 1888.

MACKIN, CHAS., Jr. [Born in Mass. Appointed from Mass.]
Asst. Surg., 14 May, 1867. Resigned 29 April, 1873.

MACKLIN, EDGAR A. [Born in N. D. Appointed from Mo.]
Priv., Corpl. and Sergt. Co. A. and Col. Sergt 5th Art., 4 Oct., 1889, to 5 Feb., 1896. 2nd Lieut. 11th Inf., 9 July, 1898. 1st Lieut., 19th Inf., 2 March, 1899. Trans. to 11th Inf., 4 May, 1899..

MACKLIN, JAMES E. [Born in N. Y. Appointed from Ind.]
Priv. Co. B, 16th Ind. Vols., 22 April, 1861. Corpl., ———. Discharged 23 May, 1862. 2nd Lieut. 16th Ind. Vols., 19 Aug., 1862. 1st Lieut., 1 March, 1863. Capt., 20 Dec., 1864. Mustered out 30 June, 1865. 2nd Lieut. 31st Inf., 9 Aug., 1867. Unassigned 15 May, 1869. Ass'd to 22nd Inf., 14 July, 1869. Dismissed 20 Nov., 1876. 2nd Lieut. 11th Inf., 12 Jan., 1877. 1st Lieut., 24 April, 1886. R. Q. M., 15 Feb., 1889, to ———. Capt., 25 Feb., 1891. Maj. 24th Inf., 19 Oct., 1899. Trans. to 11th Inf., 17 Feb., 1900.

MACLAY, A. B. [Bron in ——. Appointed from ——.]
2nd Lieut. 5th Inf., — ——, 1898. Resigned 19 Aug., 1898.

MACLAY, ISAAC W.* [Born in N. Y. Appointed from N. Y.]
2nd Lieut. 1st Art., 13 June, 1864. Trans. to Ord., 23 Jan., 1865. 1st Lieut., 13 Nov., 1868. Resigned 15 Nov., 1873.

MACLAY, ROBT. P.* [Born in Penn. Appointed from Penn.]
Bvt. 2nd Lieut. 6th Inf., 1 July, 1840. 2nd Lieut. 8th Inf., 1 Oct., 1840. 1st Lieut., 31 Dec., 1845. Capt., 22 Jan., 1849. Resigned 31 Dec., 1860.

MACLIN, SACKFIELD. [Born in Tenn. Appointedfrom Ark.]
Addl. P. M., 2 July, 1846. Maj. P. M., 2 March, 1849. Resigned 1 March, 1861.

MacMURRAY, JUNIUS W. [Born in Mo. Appointed from Mo.]
2nd Lieut. 1st Mo. Vols., 9 May, 1861. 2nd Lieut. 1st Mo. Light Art., 10 June, 1861. 1st Lieut., 1 Sept., 1861. Capt., 1 Nov., 1863. Mustered out 20 July, 1865. Bvt. Maj. and Lieut. Col. Vols., 13 March, 1865, for gallant and meritorious service during the war.. Capt. 2nd Mo. Light Art., 21 July, 1865. Mustered out 20 Nov., 1865. 2nd Lieut. 1st Art., 23 Feb., 1866. 1st Lieut., 20 March, 1866. Bvt. Capt., 2 March, 1867, for gallant and meritorious service in the Siege of Corinth, Miss. Bvt. Maj., 2 March, 1867, for gallant and meritorious service in the Siege of Vicksburg, Miss. Capt., 19 April, 1882. Maj. 5th Art.,— ——, 1898. Died 14 May, 1898.

MACNAB, ALEXANDER J. [Born in Idaho. Appointed from Idaho.]
Sergt. Co. D, 1st Idaho Vols., 12 May to 26 July, 1898. 2nd Lieut. 23rd Inf., 9 July, 1898. 1st Lieut. 10th Inf., 19 May, 1899.

MACNUTT, IRA.* [Born in Penn. Appointed from Penn.]
2nd Lieut. 3rd Art., 15 June, 1870. Trans. to Ord., 13 June, 1878. 1st Lieut., 13 June, 1878. Honor graduate of the Artillery School, 1875. Capt. (14 years' service), 14 June, 1886.

MACOMB, ALEXANDER. [Born in Mich. Appointed from N. Y.]
Cornet Cav., 10 Jan., 1799. 2nd Lieut., 2 March, 1799. Discharged 15 June, 1800. 2nd Lieut. 2nd Inf., 16 Feb., 1801. 1st Lieut. Eng., 12 Oct., 1802. Capt., 11 June, 1805. Maj. 23 Feb., 1808. Lieut. Col., 23 July, 1810. Col. 3rd Art., 6 July, 1812. Brig. Gen., 24 Jan., 1814. Retained as Col. and Chf. Eng. in the reorganization of the Army, 1 June, 1821. Maj. Gen. and Gen.-in-Chf. of the Army, 24 May, 1828. Died 25 June, 1841. Bvt. Maj. Gen., 11 Sept., 1814, for distinguished and gallant conduct in defeating the enemy at Plattsburg, N. Y.; by resolution of Congress of 3 Nov., 1814 it was "*Resolved*, That the thanks of Congress be, and they are hereby, presented to Maj. Gen. Macomb, and through him to the officers and men of the Regular Army under his command, and to the Militia and Vols. of N. Y. and Vt. for their gallantry and good conduct in defeating the enemy at Plattsburg, Sept., 1811, repelling, with 1500 men, aided by a body of Militia and Vols. from N. Y. and Vt., a British Vet. Army greatly superior in numbers; and that the President of the U. S. be requested to cause a gold medal to be struck emblematical of this triumph, and presented to Maj. Gen. Macomb.

MACOMB, ALEXR. S.* [Born in N. J. Appointed from N. J.]
Bvt. 2nd Lieut. 1st Drag., 1 July, 1835. 2nd Lieut., 1 March, 1836. 1st Lieut. 2nd

Drag., 6 Oct., 1836. Reg. Adj., 1 March to 1 April, 1837. Capt. 2nd Inf., 18 Feb., 1840. Resigned 31 Jan., 1841. Died 8 May, 1876.

MACOMB, AUGUSTUS C. [Born in Mich. Appointed at Large.]
2nd Lieut. 4th Inf., 23 Jan., 1878. Trans. to 5th Cav., 3 June, 1879. 1st Lieut., 11 March, 1887. Capt., 2 June, 1897.

MACOMB, EDWARD. [Born in N. Y. Appointed from N. Y.]
Asst. Surg., 20 Jan., 1824. Maj. Surg., 1 Nov., 1834. Died 26 March, 1844.

MACOMB, HENRY H. [Born in N. Y. Appointed from N. Y.]
2nd Lieut. Corps Art., 28 Jan., 1820. Disbanded 1 June, 1821.

MACOMB, JASPER. [Born in N. Y. Appointed from N. Y.]
Cadet Mil. Acad., 1 Sept., 1818, to 22 June, 1822. Bvt. 2nd Lieut. 4th Inf., 1 July, 1823. 2nd Lieut. 7th Inf., 24 May, 1824. 1st Lieut., 10 Nov., 1829. Died 15 Dec., 1833.

MACOMB, JOHN N.* [Born in N. Y. Appointed from N. Y.]
Bvt. 2nd Lieut. 4th Art., 1 July, 1832. 2nd Lieut., 30 Sept., 1833. 1st Lieut., 15 Oct., 1836. 1st Lieut. Top. Eng., 7 July, 1838. Capt., 4 Aug., 1851. Maj., 6 Aug., 1861. Lieut. Col. A. A. de C., 28 Sept., 1861. Col. A. A. de C., 15 May, 1862. Lieut. Col. Eng., 3 March, 1863. Bvt. Col., 13 March, 1865, for faithful and meritorious service during the war. Mustered out as Col. A. A. de C., 31 May, 1866. Col. Eng., 7 March, 1867. Retired by operation of law, 30 June, 1882. Died 16 March, 1889.

MACOMB, MONTGOMERY M.* [Born in Mich. Appointed at Large.]
2nd Lieut. 4th Art., 17 June, 1874. 1st Lieut., 6 Sept., 1879. Graduate of the Artillery School, 1886. Capt. 7th Art., 8 March, 1898.

MACOMBER, GEORGE. [Born in Mass. Appointed from Mass.]
1st Lieut. 34th Mass. Vols., 31 July, 1862. Capt., 14 Oct., 1864. Trans. to 24th Mass. Vols., 16 June, 1865. Bvt. Maj. Vols., 13 March, 1865, for gallant and meritorious service during the war. Mustered out 20 Jan., 1866. 2nd Lieut. 14th Inf., 11 May, 1866. Trans. to 32nd Inf., 21 Sept., 1866. 1st Lieut., 14 Jan., 1867. Trans. to 21st Inf., 19 April, 1869. Died 9 Sept., 1869.

MACOMBER, JOHN H. [Born in N. Y. Appointed from Minn.]
Corpl. and Sergt. Co. C, 1st Vt. Heavy Art., 12 Aug., 1862, to 10 July, 1863. 1st Lieut. 1st Vt. Heavy Art., 11 July, 1863. Bvt. Capt. Vols., 2 April, 1865. Capt. 1st Vt. Heavy Art., 23 May, 1865. Mustered out 25 Aug., 1865. Post Chap., 16 June, 1880.

MACRAE, NATHL. C.* [Born in Va. Appointed from Va.]
Bvt. 2nd Lieut. 1st Inf., 1 July, 1826. 2nd Lieut. 3rd Inf., 1 July, 1826. 1st Lieut., 31 Oct., 1835. Capt., 18 Dec., 1839. Maj., 31 May, 1857. Retired 25 Sept., 1861. Died 5 Feb., 1878. Bvt. Lieut. Col. and Col., 13 March, 1865, for long and faithful service.

MACREA, WM. [Born in Va. Appointed from Va.]
Lieut. Inf., 16 March, 1792. In 3rd Sub. Legion, 4 Sept., 1792. Capt., 11 Oct., 1794. Disbanded 1 Nov., 1796. Capt. Art. and Eng., 1 June, 1798. Maj., 2nd Art. and Eng., 31 July, 1800. Trans. to 1st Art., — March, 1812. Lieut. Col., 19 April, 1814. Trans. to Corps Art., 12 May, 1814. Trans. to 4th Art., 1 June, 1821. Died 3 Nov., 1832. Bvt. Lieut. Col., 10 July, 1812. Bvt. Col., 18 April, 1824, for ten years' faithful service in one grade.

MACY, JOHN P. [Born in Canada. Appointed from Army.]
Priv. Cos. I (7th) and I (10th) Inf., 22 Jan., 1858, to 1 Oct., 1862. Sergt. Gen. Ser., 19 May to 10 Aug., 1863. 2nd Lieut. 10th Inf., 10 Aug., 1863. 1st Lieut., 17 Feb., 1864. Capt., 29 Dec., 1865. Resigned 26 March, 1868.

MADDEN, DANIEL. [Born in England. Appointed from Army.]
Priv. Co. E, 2nd Drag., 9 Dec., 1850. Trans. to Co. H, 1st Drag., 22 Aug., 1854. Discharged 9 Dec., 1855. Priv. Co. B, 2nd Drag., 1 May, 1856. Corpl., 1 Jan., 1857. Sergt., 15 June, 1857. 1st Sergt., 1 April, 1859. Discharged 28 April, 1861. Com. Sergt., 4 Aug., 1861. Discharged 4 Nov., 1861. 2nd Lieut. 6th Cav., 1 Nov., 1861. Bvt. 1st Lieut., 9 June, 1863, for gallant and meritorious service in the Battle of Beverly Ford, Va. 1st Lieut. 6th Cav., 4 May, 1864. R. C. S., 6 Aug. to 3 Nov., 1865. Bvt. Capt., 9 April, 1865, for gallant and meritorious service in the campaign terminating with the surrender of the insurgent army under Gen. R. E. Lee. Capt. 6th Cav., 10 May, 1867. Maj. 7th Cav., 21 May, 1886. Retired for over thirty years' service, 5 Oct., 1887.

MADDEN, FRANK. [Born in Ireland. Appointed from N. Y.]
Priv. Co. B, 55th N. Y. Vols., 1 March, 1862. Trans. to Co. K, 38th N. Y. Vols., 21 Dec., 1862. Trans. to Co. H, 40th N. Y. Vols., 28 May, 1863. Discharged 23 April, 1864. Priv. Gen. Ser., 19 July, 1865. Trans. to Co. K, 44th Inf., 1 Oct., 1866. 2nd Lieut. 42nd Inf., 28 July, 1866. Unassigned 22 April, 1869. Retired 31 Dec., 1870.

MADDEN, GEORGE J. [Born in Conn. Appointed from Army.]
Priv., Sergt. and 1st Sergt. Cos. H and E, and Sergt. Maj. 3rd Batt. 16th Inf., 15 March, 1864, to 25 April, 1866. 2nd Lieut. 16th Inf., 24 Jan., 1866. 1st Lieut., 24 Jan., 1866. Trans. to 25th Inf., 21 Sept., 1866. Reg. Adj., 15 Dec., 1866, to 26 April, 1869. Trans. to 18th Inf., 26 April, 1869. Dropped 28 March, 1873.

MADDEN, JOHN F. [Born in Cal. Appointed from Cal.]
2nd Lieut. 5th Inf., 7 Oct., 1891. Graduate of the Infantry and Cavalry School, 1897. 1st Lieut. 5th Inf., 26 April, 1898.

MADDOX, JOSEPH H. [Born in Md. Appointed from Md.]
2nd Lieut. of Inf., 16 Feb., 1847; 3rd Drag., 9 April, 1847. Disbanded 20 July, 1848.

MADDOX, THOMAS J. C. [Born in Md. Appointed from Md.]
Asst. Surg., 22 Oct., 1881. Killed 19 Dec., 1885, in an affair with Apache Indians, near the White House N. M.

MADIGAN, JOHN. [Born in Ireland. Appointed from N. J.]
Priv. Co. G, 88th N. Y. Vols., 12 Oct., 1861. Com. Sergt., 20 Feb., 1862. 2nd Lieut., 13 Dec., 1862. Mustered out 12 June, 1863. 1st Lieut. 2nd N. J. Cav., 12 Aug., 1863. Mustered out 1 Nov., 1865. 2nd Lieut. 1st Cav., 23 Feb., 1866. 1st Lieut.,

25 April, 1867. Bvt. Capt., 27 Sept., 1867, for conspicuous gallantry in charging a large band of Indians strongly fortified in the Infernal Caverns, Pitt River, Cal., where killed, 27 Sept., 1867.

MADISON, AMBROSE.* [Born in Va. Appointed from Va.]
2nd Lieut. Marine Corps., 17 July, 1817. Resigned 21 July, 1818. Died ——, 1823.

MADISON, THOS. C. [Born in Va. Appointed from Va.]
Asst. Surg., 27 Feb., 1840. Maj. Surg., 29 Aug., 1856. Resigned 17 Aug., 1861. Died 7 Nov., 1866.

MADISON, WM. S. [Born in ——. Appointed from Ky.]
Surg. Mate 17th Inf., 2 Dec., 1812. Trans. to 1st Inf., 17 May, 1815. Resigned 1 Nov., 1815. Maj. Surg. 3rd Inf., 5 Oct., 1816. Killed by Indians 14 May, 1821.

MAFFITT, WM. [Born in Va. Appointed from Va.]
Asst. Surg., 1 Jan., 1836. Resigned 31 Oct., 1843. Died 27 Oct., 1864.

MAGEE, JOHN. [Born in N. Y. Appointed from N. Y.]
2nd Lieut. Inf., 1 April, 1847; 10th Inf., 9 April, 1847. Mustered out 15 Aug., 1848.

MAGEE, MATTHEW I. [Born in Penn. Appointed from Penn.]
Capt. Pittsburg Blues Penn. Vols., Aug. 1812 to Dec., 1813. Capt. 4th Rifle Reg., 17 March, 1814. Disbanded 15 June, 1815. Reinstated as 1st Lieut. of Ord., 1 Jan., 1816. Capt., to rank from 10 Feb., 1815. Trans. to Rifle Reg., 11 Sept., 1818. Trans. to 6th Inf., 1 June, 1821. Trans. to 5th Inf., 3 Oct., 1821. Died 29 June, 1824. Retained 1 Jan., 1816 (in reorganization under Act of 3 March, 1815], as 1st Lieut. of Ord., with Bvt. of Capt. from 17 March, 1814. Died 29 June, 1824.

MAGILL, WM J. [Born in S. C. Appointed from S. C.]
2nd Lieut. of Inf., 2 March, 1847; 3rd Drag., 9 April, 1847. R. Q. M., 13 Oct., 1847, to 15 Jan., 1848. Resigned 3 May, 1848.

MAGILTON, ALBERT S.* [Born in Del. Appointed from Penn.]
Bvt. 2nd Lieut. 4th Art., 1 July, 1846. 2nd Lieut., 3 March, 1847. 1st Lieut., 28 Feb., 1849. Capt., 10 June, 1857. Resigned 29 Dec., 1857. Bvt. 1st Lieut., 20 Aug., 1847, for gallant and meritorious conduct at Contreras and Churubusco. Lieut. Col. 2nd Penn. Res., 21 June, 1861. Col. 4th Penn. Res., 4 Oct., 1861. Resigned 23 Dec., 1862. Died 28 Dec., 1875.

MAGINNIS, THOMAS F.* [Born in Minn. Appointed from Minn..
2nd Lieut. 11th Inf., 26 April, 1898. 1st Lieut., 2 March, 1899. Capt. Porto Rican Batt. Vols., 13 May, 1899, to ——.

MAGNITZKY, GUSTAVE. [Born in Prussia. Appointed from Mass.]
Sergt. Co. C. 20th Mass. Vols., 18 July, 1861. Priv., 15 June, 1862. Trans. to Co. G, 4 Aug., 1862. Sergt., — ——, —. 1st Sergt., — ——, —. Trans. to Co. E, 21st Vet. Res. Corps, 3 Dec., 1863. Trans. to Co. C. 20th Mass. Vols., 12 Feb., 1864. 1st Lieut. 20th Mass. Vols., 6 May, 1864. Capt., 12 Sept., 1864. Mustered out 16 July, 1865. 2nd Lieut. 39th Inf., 7 March, 1867. Bvt. 1st Lieut., 7 March, 1867, for gallant and meritorious service in the Battle of Gettysburg, Pa. Bvt. Capt., 7 March, 1867. for galant and meritorious service in the Battle of Petersburg, Va. Unassigned 20 April, 1869. Ass'd to 14th Inf., 3 Aug., 1870. Retired 14 Nov., 1871.

MAGRUDER, DAVID L. [Born in Md. Appointed from Va.]
1st Lieut. Asst. Surg., 1 Feb., 1850. Capt. Asst. Surg., 1 Feb., 1855. Maj. Surg., 16 April, 1862. Bvt. Lieut. Col., 13 March, 1865, for faithful and meritorious service during the war. Lieut. Col. Surg., 30 June, 1882. Col. Surg., 26 July, 1886. Retired by operation of law, 23 April, 1889.

MAGRUDER, LLOYD. [Born in Md. Appointed from Ark.]
2nd Lieut. 12th Inf., 9 April, 1847. Resigned 31 March, 1848.

MAGRUDER, JOHN B.* [Born in Va. Appointed from Va.]
Bvt. 2nd Lieut. 7th Inf., 1 July, 1830. 2nd Lieut., 1 July, 1830. Trans. to 1st Art., 11 Aug., 1831. 1st Lieut., 31 March, 1836. Capt., 18 June, 1846. Resigned 20 April, 1861. Bvt. Maj., 18 April, 1847, for gallant and meritorious conduct at Cerro Gordo. Bvt. Lieut. Col., 13 Sept., 1847, for gallant and meritorious conduct at Chapultepec. Died 19 Feb., 1871.

MAGRUDER, JOHN T.* [Born in Va. Appointed at Large.]
Bvt. 2nd Lieut. 2nd Cav., 1 July, 1857. Trans. to 1st Cav., 24 April, 1858. Died 28 June, 1858.

MAGRUDER, JOHN W. [Born in Md. Appointed from D. C.]
2nd Lieut. 7th Inf., 26 April, 1861. 1st Lieut., 27 May, 1861. Capt., 4 July, 1863. Wholly retired 4 Nov., 1863.

MAGRUDER, WM. B.* [Born in Va. Appointed from Va.]
Bvt. 2nd Lieut. Inf., 1 July, 1827. Resignd 25 Oct., 1827. Died 4 Aug., 1877.

MAGRUDER, WM. T.* [Born in Md. Appointed from Md.]
Bvt. 2nd Lieut. 1st Drag., 1 July, 1850. 2nd Lieut., 9 Oct., 1851. 1st Lieut., 3 March, 1855. R. Q. M., 1 May to 26 Sept., 1860. Capt., 8 Jan., 1861. 1st Cav., 3 Aug., 1861. Resigned 1 Oct., 1862. Killed in Confed. Ser., 3 July, 1863.

MAGUIRE, CHAS. F. [Born in Penn. Appointed from Penn.]
Priv., Sergt. and 1st Sergt. Co. B. 3rd Drag., 18 Feb., 1847, to 1 May, 1848. 2nd Lieut. 3rd Drag., 29 March, 1848. Disbanded 8 Aug., 1848. Capt. 90th Penn. Vols., 1 Oct., 1861. Trans. to 186th Penn. Vols., 25 May, 1864. Mustered out 15 Aug., 1865.

MAGUIRE, EDWARD.* [Born in Tenn. Appointed from Tenn.]
2nd Lieut. Eng., 17 June, 1867. 1st Lieut., 15 Feb., 1869. Capt., 14 June, 1881. Died 11 Oct., 1892.

MAHAN, DENNIS H.* [Born in N. Y. Appointed from Va.]
Bvt. 2nd Lieut. Eng., 1 July, 1824. 2nd Lieut., 1 July, 1824. Resigned 1 Jan., 1832. Prof. of Eng. at the U. S. Mil. Acad., 1 Jan., 1832. Drowned 16 Sept., 1871.

MAHAN. FREDK. A.* [Born in N. Y. Appointed at Large.]
2nd Lieut. Eng., 17 June, 1867. 1st Lieut., 22 Feb., 1869. Capt. (fourteen years' service), 17 June, 1881. Maj. 18 Sept. 1894, Retired over thirty years' service, 2 April, 1900.

MAHAN, MARTIN. [Born in Ireland. Appointed from Army.]
Priv., Corpl. and Sergt. Co. K, 1st Inf., 21 Dec., 1857, to 21 Dec., 1862. Priv., Sergt. and 1st Sergt. Co. D, 2nd Batt. 16th Inf., 1 Jan. to 8 June, 1863. 2nd Lieut. 16th Inf., 1 June, 1863. 1st Lieut., 21 Oct., 1863. Dismissed 8 Nov., 1864.

MAHNKEN, JOHN H. [Born in Germany. Appointed from N. Y.]
1st Sergt. Devin's Indep. Co. Cav. N. Y. State Militia, 14 July, 1861. Discharged 23 Oct., 1861. 1st Lieut. 6th N. Y. Cav., 27 Nov., 1861. Capt., 1 May, 1864. Capt. A. A. G. Vols., 18 May, 1864. Bvt. Maj. Vols., 31 March, 1865, for gallant and meritorious service in the vicinity of Five Forks, Va. Mustered out 15 Sept., 1866. 1st Lieut. 8th Cav., 7 Aug., 1867. Reg. Adj., 13 Oct., 1868, to 28 June, 1878. Bvt. Capt., 7 Aug., 1867, for gallant and meritorious service in the Battle of Cedar Creek, Va. Bvt. Maj., 7 Aug., 1867, for gallant and meritorious service in the Battle of Five Forks, Va. Capt. 8th Cav., 28 June, 1878. Died 16 March, 1881.

MAHON, STEPHEN K. [Born in Ireland. Appointed from Iowa.]
Priv. Co. E, 36th Iowa Vols., 14 Aug., 1862. Sergt. Maj., 5 Oct., 1862. 1st Lieut., 11 Aug., 1863. Mustered out 24 Aug., 1865. 2nd Lieut. 11th Inf., 23 Feb., 1866. 1st Lieut., 28 July, 1866. Bvt. Capt., 2 March, 1867, for gallant and meritorious service in the defence of Helena, Ark. Trans. to 16th Inf., 14 April, 1869 Capt., 8 July, 1882. Retired for disability 11 April, 1883. Died 11 Jan., 1885.

MAHON, THOMAS. [Born in Penn. Appointed from Penn.]
Ensign 16th Inf., 12 Oct., 1812. 3rd Lieut., 19 April, 1813. 2nd Lieut., 19 May, 1813. 1st Lieut., 15 Aug., 1813. Disbanded 15 June, 1815. 2nd Lieut. Rifle Reg., 22 July, 1818. Resigned 20 Nov., 1819.

MAHONY, ANDREW. [Born in Ireland. Appointed from Mass.]
Capt. 19th Mass. Vols., 28 Aug., 1861. Trans. to Vet. Res. Corps, 8 Aug., 1863. Bvt. Maj., Lieut. Col. and Col. Vols., 13 March, 1865, for gallant conduct at the Battle of Gettysburg, and for meritorious service during the war. Mustered out 19 May, 1867. 1st Lieut. 45th Inf., 7 March, 1867. Trans. to 14th Inf., 22 July, 1869. Died 12 April, 1872.

MAITLAND, WM. S.* [Born in N. Y. Appointed from N. Y.]
2nd Lieut. 3rd Inf., 1 July, 1820. Trans. to Corps Art., 24 Aug., 1820. Trans. to 4th Art., 1 June, 1821. Trans. to 2nd Art., 28 May, 1822. Trans. to 3rd Art., 22 July, 1826. 1st Lieut., 31 Dec., 1828. Drowned 19 Aug., 1837. Bvt. Capt., 31 Dec., 1835, for gallant and meritorious conduct in the affair of the Withlacoochee and Welika Rivers, Fla.

MAIZE, WM. R. [Born in Penn. Appointed from Penn.]
Priv. Co. K, 19th Penn. Vols., 18 April, 1861. Discharged 9 Aug., 1861. 2nd Lieut. 78th Penn. Vols., 14 Oct., 1861. 1st Lieut., 1 Sept., 1863. Mustered out 4 Nov., 1864. 2nd Lieut. 2nd Inf., 23 April, 1866. 1st Lieut., 22 Jan., 1867. Bvt. Capt., 2 March, 1867, for gallant and meritorious service in the Battle of Stone River, Tenn. Unassigned 17 April, 1869. Ass'd to 20th Inf., 2 April, 1870. Capt., 6 May, 1882. Retired for disability 24 Feb., 1891.

MAJOR, DUNCAN K., Jr.* [Born in N. Y. Appointed from N. Y.]
2nd Lieut. 14th Inf., 15 Feb., 1899.

MAJOR, JAMES P.* [Born in Mo. Appointed from Mo.]
Bvt. 2nd Lieut. 1st Cav., 1 July, 1856. 2nd Lieut. 2nd Cav., 1 Dec., 1856. Resigned 21 March, 1861.

MAJTHENY, THEODORE. [Born in Hungary. Appointed from Iowa.]
1st Sergt. Co. C, 2nd Iowa Vols., 28 May, 1861. Trans. to Fremont's Body Guard, 21 Aug., 1861. 2nd Lieut., 15 Sept., 1861. Mustered out 30 Nov., 1861. Capt. 1st Ind. Cav., 18 April, 1862. Mustered out 13 Dec., 1864. 2nd Lieut. 6th Cav., 23 Feb. 1866. 1st Lieut., 20 Oct., 1866. Resigned 23 Dec., 1868.

MALCOLM, WM.* [Born in Mass. Appointed from Mass.]
2nd Lieut. 8th Inf., 1 July, 1819. Trans. to 1st Inf., 1 June, 1821. 1st Lieut., 1 June, 1822. Died 7 Aug., 1823.

MALE, WM. H. [Born in N. Y. Appointed from N. Y.]
Priv. Co. A, 71st N. Y. Militia, 20 April to 30 July, 1861. Priv., Sergt. and 1st Sergt. Co. K, 139th N. Y. Vols., 25 Aug. to 19 Dec., 1862. 2nd Lieut. 139th N. Y. Vols., 19 Dec., 1862. 1st Lieut., 22 Dec., 1863. Capt., 1 Sept., 1864, to 19 June, 1865. Capt., A. de C. Vols., 10 June, 1865. Bvt. Maj. Vols., 9 April, 1865, for gallant conduct in the field. Mustered out 2 Feb., 1866. 1st Lieut. 36th Inf., 28 July, 1866. R. Q. M., 1 June, 1868, to 19 May, 1869. Trans. to 7th Inf., 18 May, 1869. R. Q. M., 19 to 31 May, 1869. Unassigned 31 May, 1869. Discharged 15 Sept., 1870. Bvt. Capt., 2 March, 1867, for gallant and meritorious service during the war.

MALEY, THOS. E. [Born in Ireland. Appointed from Ill.]
Priv. and Sergt. Co. I, 2nd Cav., 15 May, 1855. Sergt. and Q. M. Sergt., 1 Feb., 1857. Discharged 15 April, 1860. 1st Lieut. R. Q. M. 6th Penn. Cav., 12 Sept., 1861. Resigned 22 April, 1862. 2nd Lieut. 5th Cav., 14 April, 1862. Bvt. 1st Lieut., 27 June, 1862, for gallant and meritorious service in the Battle of Gaines' Mill, Va. 1st Lieut. 5th Cav., 17 July, 1862. Reg. Adj., 9 May to 1 Dec., 1862. R. Q. M., 1 Dec., 1862, to 30 Nov., 1864. Bvt. Capt., 17 Sept., 1862, for gallant and meritorious service in the Battle of Antietam, Md. Bvt. Maj., 28 July, 1864, for gallant and meritorious service in the Battle of Deep Bottom, Va. Capt. 5th Cav., 28 July, 1866. Retired with rank of Lieut. Col., 15 Dec., 1870, for wounds in line of duty. Reduced to rank of Capt., 3 March, 1875. Raised to rank of Lieut. Col., 3 March, 1877. Died 1 July, 1896.

MALIN, JOSEPH. [Born in Ind. Appointed from Mo.]
Asst. Surg. Vols., 17 Sept., 1847. Disbanded 26 Oct., 1848.

MALLAROY, HENRY S. [Born in ——. Appointed from Ky.]
Appointed under the name of H. S. Mallory. Ensign 17th Inf., 12 Dec., 1814. 3rd Lieut., 4 Jan., 1815. Disbanded 15 June, 1815. 3rd Lieut. Corps Art., 15 Nov., 1817. 2nd Lieut. 7th Inf., 13 Feb., 1818. 1st Lieut., 31 May, 1819. Trans. to 2nd Art., 1 June, 1821. Capt., 31 Dec., 1836. Resigned 30 June, 1837. Bvt. Capt., 31 May, 1829, for ten years' faithful service in one grade. Died in Aug., 1849.

MALLERY, GARRICK. [Born in Penn. Appointed from Penn.]
Capt. 71st Penn. Vols., 4 June, 1861. Lieut. Col. 13th Penn. Cav., 17 Feb., 1863. Lieut. Col. Vet. Res. Corps, 1 July, 1864. Bvt. Col. Vols., 13 March, 1865, for gallant and meritorious service during the war. Capt. 43rd Inf., 28 July, 1866. Mustered out of Vet. Res. Corps., 5 Nov., 1866. Bvt. Maj., 2 March, 1867, for gallant and meritorious service in a skirmish at Garnett's Farm. Bvt. Lieut. Col., 2 March, 1867, for gallant and meritorious service in the Battle of Peach Orchard, Va. Unassigned 8 April, 1869. Ass'd to 1st Inf., 15 Dec., 1870. Retired 1 July, 1879. Died 24 Oct., 1894.

MALLERY, JOHN C.* [Born in Penn. Appointed from Ala.]
2nd Lieut. Eng., 17 June, 1867. 1st Lieut., 17 June, 1867. Capt., 31 March, 1880. Maj., 14 Dec., 1891. Retired for disability 26 Jan., 1895.

MALLORY, FRANCIS. [Born in Va. Appointed from Va.]
2nd Lieut. 4th Inf., 27 June, 1856. Resigned 10 July, 1861.

MALLORY, GILBERT A. [Born in N. Y. Appointed from Ohio.]
2nd Lieut. 15th Inf., 24 Oct., 1861. Resigned 10 June, 1862.

MALLORY, JOHN H. [Born in Va. Appointed from Ga.]
2nd Lieut. 8th Inf., 12 March, 1812. 1st Lieut., 5 May, 1813. Reg. Adj., Aug., 1814, to June, 1815. Trans. to 7th Inf., 17 May, 1815. Reg. P. M., 21 Dec., 1815, to 30 April, 1817. Capt., 30 April, 1817. Resigned 1 June, 1817.

MALLORY, JOHN S.* [Born in Va. Appointed from Va.]
2nd Lieut. 2nd Inf., 13 June, 1879. 1st Lieut., 10 April, 1888. Capt., 3 Dec., 1897. Maj. I. G. Vols., 20 June, 1898, to 17 Aug., 1899. Lieut. Col. 41st U. S. Vols., 17 Aug., 1899.

MALLOY, ADAM G. [Born in Ireland. Appointed from Wis.]
Capt. 6th Wis. Vols., 16 July, 1861, to 2 Feb., 1862. Lieut. Col. 17th Wis. Vols., 3 March, 1862. Col., 1 Dec., 1862. Bvt. Brig. Gen. Vols., 13 March, 1865, for gallant and meritorious services. Mustered out 14 July, 1865. 2nd Lieut. 17th Inf., 23 Feb., 1866. 1st Lieut., 23 Feb., 1866. Trans. to 35th Inf., 21 Sept., 1866. Unassigned 12 Aug., 1869. Bvt. Capt., 2 March, 1867, for gallant and meritorious service in the Siege of Vicksburg, Miss. Bvt. Maj., 2 March, 1867, for gallant and meritorious service at the Battle of Kenesaw Mountain, Ga. Bvt. Lieut. Col., 2 March, 1867, for gallant and meritorious service in the Battle of Atlanta, Ga. Bvt. Col., 2 March, 1867, for gallant and meritorious service in the Battle of Nashville, Tenn.

MALONE, FRANKLIN J. [Born in Ala. Appointed from Ala.]
Asst. Surg., 3 March, 1847; 13th Inf., 9 April, 1847. Resigned 30 Dec., 1847.

MALONE, PAUL B.* [Born in N. Y. Appointed from N. Y.]
2nd Lieut. 13th Inf., 12 June, 1894. 1st Lieut., 26 April, 1898.

MALONEY, HUNDLEY S. [Born in Tenn. Appointed from Tenn.]
Priv. and Corpl. Co. D, 4th Tenn. Vols., 7 May, 1864, to 2 Aug., 1865. 2nd Lieut. 33rd Inf., 22 July, 1867. Unassigned 8 May, 1869. Ass'd to 15th Inf., 3 Aug., 1870. Discharged 6 Sept., 1870.

MALONEY, MAURICE. [Born in Ireland. Appointed from Army.]
Priv., Corpl., Sergt. and 1st Sergt. Co. D, and Sergt. Maj. 4th Inf., 5 Nov., 1836, to 27 Nov., 1846. 2nd Lieut. 4th Inf., 27 Nov., 1846. 1st Lieut, 6 May, 1848. Reg. Adj., 27 Oct., 1847, to 1 Feb., 1849. Capt., 22 Nov., 1854. Col. 13th Wis. Vols., 15 Oct., 1861. Discharged from Vols., 1 Aug., 1862. Maj. 1st Inf., 16 Sept., 1862. Lieut. Col. 16th Inf., 21 June, 1867. Unassigned 15 March, 1869. Retired 15 Dec., 1870. Died 8 Jan., 1872. Bvt. 1st Lieut., 8 Sept., 1847, for gallant and meritorious conduct at Molino del Rey. Bvt. Capt., 13 Sept., 1847, for gallant and meritorious conduct at Chapultepec. Bvt. Lieut. Col., 4 July, 1863, for gallant and meritorious service during the Siege of Vicksburg. Bvt. Col., 13 March, 1865, for ~allant and meritorious service during the war. Died 8 Jan., 1872.

MANEY, GEORGE E. [Born in Tenn. Appointed from Tenn.]
1st Lieut. of Inf., 6 March, 1847; 3rd Drag, 9 April, 1847. Disbanded 31 July, 1848.

MANEY, JAMES A.* [Born in Tenn. Appointed from Tenn.]
Addl. 2nd Lieut., 16th Inf., 15 June, 1877. 2nd Lieut. 15th Inf., 23 Aug., 1877. 1st Lieut., 23 Sept., 1885. Capt., 6 Oct., 1897.

MANGAN, MICHAEL. [Born in Ireland. Appointed from Wis.]
Priv. Co. E, 6th Wis. Vols., 28 June, 1861. Corpl., 23 Oct., 1861. Sergt., 19 Dec., 1861. 2nd Lieut. 6th Wis. Vols., 1 July, 1863. 1st Lieut., 8 Aug, 1863. Mustered out 3 April, 1864. 2nd Lieut. Vet. Res. Corps, 18 March, 1864. Mustered out 6 Sept., 1866. 2nd Lieut. 45th Inf., 22 Jan., 1867. Unassigned 22 July, 1869. Retired 31 Dec., 1870, for loss of right leg from wound.

MANGHAM, JOHN C., Jr.* [Born in Ga. Appointed from Ga.]
2nd Lieut. of Inf., 10 March, 1847; 13th Inf., 9 April, 1847. Reg. Adj., 1 Feb. to 15 July, 1848. Disbanded 15 July, 1848.

MANIGAULT, EDWARD. [Born in S. C. Appointed from S. C.]
Capt. of Inf., 5 March, 1847; 12th Inf., 9 April, 1847. Maj. 13th Inf., 16 July, 1847. Disbanded 15 July, 1848.

MANIGAULT, GABRIEL H. [Born in S. C. Appointed from S. C.]
Capt. 43rd Inf., 1 Aug., 1813. Maj. A. I. G., 9 Sept., 1814. Disbanded 15 June, 1815. Reinstated 17 May, 1816. Resigned 13 June, 1817.

MANLEY, CHAS., Jr. [Born in N. C. Appointed from N. C.]
2nd Lieut. 12th Inf., 3 March, 1848. Disbanded 25 July, 1848.

MANLEY, JOHN A. [Born in N. Y. Appointed from N. Y.]
Corpl. Co. F, 64th N. Y. Vols., 20 Aug., 1861. Sergt., 27 Nov., 1862. 1st Lieut. 64th N. Y. Vols, 1 March, 1863. Capt., 18 Oct., 1863. Mustered out 16 Dec., 1864. 2nd Lieut. 18th Inf., 7 March, 1867. 1st Lieut., 21 Aug., 1868. Unassigned 26 April, 1869. Ass'd to 20th Inf., 15 Dec., 1870. Capt., 14 May, 1887. Died 15 July, 1890.

MANLY, CLARENCE J. [Born in Ky. Appointed from N. Y.]
Asst. Surg., 23 July, 1898.

MANN, JAMES. [Born in Mass. Appointed from Mass.]
Hosp. Surg., 9 April, 1812. Disbanded 15 June, 1815. Reinstated 3 May, 1816. Post Surg., 18 April, 1818. Asst. Surg., 1 June, 1821. Died 7 Nov., 1832.

MANN, JAMES D.* [Born in Ind. Appointed from Ind.]
2nd Lieut. 7th Cav., 15 June, 1877. 1st Lieut. 7th Cav., — ——, 1890. Died of wounds received in action with Indians near White Clay Creek, S. D., 15 Jan., 1891.

MANN, WM. A.* [Born in Penn. Appointed from Penn.]
2nd Lieut. 17th Inf., 16 June, 1875. 1st Lieut., 19 May, 1881. Reg. Adj., 30 Jan., 1885, to 30 Jan., 1889. Capt., 1 Jan., 1896.

MANN, WM. H. [Born in Ga. Appointed from Ga.]
2nd Lieut. 4th Inf., 3 Feb., 1819. 1st Lieut., 1 Jan., 1823. Dismissed 25 April, 1823.

MANNING, DAVID A.* [Born in N. C. Appointed from N. C.]
Bvt. 2nd Lieut. 4th Inf., 1 July, 1830. 2nd Lieut., 1 July, 1830. Died 21 July, 1835.

MANNING, ELBRIDGE G. [Born in Mass. Appointed from La.]
Corpl. Co. F, 19th Mass. Vols., 28 Aug., 1861, to 27 Feb., 1863. 1st Lieut. Adj. 81st U. S. Col. Inf., 28 Feb., 1863. Capt., 14 Feb., 1866. Bvt. Capt. Vols., 13 March, 1865, for gallant and meritorious service during the war. Mustered out 30 Nov., 1866. 2nd Lieut. 5th Inf., 22 Jan., 1867. Died 31 May, 1869.

MANNING, WM. C. [Born in N. Y. Appointed from Maine.]
Priv., Musician and Corpl. Co. D, and Sergt. Maj. 1st Mass. Vols., 22 May, 1861, to 20 Feb., 1863. 1st Lieut. Adj. 35th U. S. Col. Troops, 18 May, 1863. Capt., 6 Aug., 1864. Maj. 103rd U. S. Col. Troops, 27 Feb., 1865. Mustered out 5 May, 1866. 2nd Lieut. 14th Inf., 11 May, 1866. Trans. to 23rd Inf., 21 Sept., 1866. 1st Lieut., 7 Feb., 1867. Reg. Adj., 8 July, 1868, to 7 Dec., 1869. Capt., 1 March, 1886. Trans. to 14th Inf., 19 Nov., 1898. Retired for disability, with rank of Maj., 2 March, 1899. Bvt. Capt., 27 Feb., 1890, for gallant service in action against Indians at Mazatzal Mountains, Ariz., 13 Dec., 1872.

MANSFIELD, EDWARD D.* [Born in Conn. Appointed from N. Y.]
2nd Lieut. Eng., 1 July, 1819, declined. Died 27 Oct., 1880.

MANSFIELD, FRANCIS W.* [Born in Ohio. Appointed from Ohio.]
2nd Lieut. 11th Inf., 12 June, 1871. 1st Lieut., 28 June, 1878. Capt., 13 April, 1889. Maj., 2 March, 1899. Graduate of the Infantry and Cavalry School, 1885.

MANSFIELD, JARED. [Born in Conn. Appointed from Conn.]
Capt. Eng., 3 May, 1802. Maj., 11 June, 1805. Lieut. Col., 25 Feb., 1808. Resigned 23 July, 1810. Prof. at the U. S. Mil. Acad., 7 Oct., 1812. Resigned 31 Aug., 1828. Died 3 Feb., 1830.

MANSFIELD, JOHN. [Born in Md. Appointed from Md.]
Ensign 36th Inf., 30 April, 1813. 3rd Lieut., 17 March, 1814. 2nd Lieut., 30 Sept., 1814. Disbanded 15 June, 1815. Reinstated 2 Dec., 1815, in 6th Inf. 1st Lieut., 25 Dec., 1819. Disbanded 1 June, 1821.

MANSFIELD, JOSEPH K. F.* [Born in Conn. Appointed from Conn.]
Bvt. 2nd Lieut. and 2nd Lieut. Eng., 1 July, 1822. 1st Lieut., 5 March, 1832. Capt., 7 July, 1838. Col. I. G., 28 May, 1853. Brig. Gen., 14 May, 1861. Maj. Gen. Vols., 18 July, 1862. Died 18 Sept., 1862, of wounds received at the Battle of Antietam, Md. Bvt. Maj., 9 May 1846, for gallant and distinguished service in defence of Fort Brown. Bvt. Lieut. Col., 23 Sept., 1846, for gallant and meritorious conduct at Monterey. Bvt. Col., 23 Feb., 1847, for gallant and meritorious conduct at the Battle of Buena Vista. Bvt. Brig. Gen., 6 May, 1861.

MANSFIELD, SAMUEL M.* [Born in Conn. Appointed at Large.]
2nd Lieut. Eng., 17 June, 1862. Col. 24th Conn. Vols., 18 Nov., 1862. 1st Lieut. Eng., 3 March, 1863. Bvt. Capt., 14 June, 1863, for gallant and meritorious service in action at Port Hudson, La. Mustered out of Vol. Service, 30 Sept., 1863. Capt. Eng., 15 Aug., 1864. Bvt. Maj. and Lieut. Col., 13 March, 1865, for gallant and meritorious service during the war. Maj. Eng., 2 Sept., 1874. Lieut. Col., 22 July, 1888. Col., 5 July, 1898.

MANY, JAMES B. [Born in Del. Appointed from Del.]
1st Lieut. 2nd Art. and Eng., 4 June, 1798. Capt., 1 Oct., 1804. In 1st Art., — March, 1812. Maj., 5 May, 1813. Trans. to Corps Art., 12 May, 1814. Trans. to 4th Inf., 1 June, 1821. Trans. to 5th Inf., 24 Oct., 1821. Lieut. Col. 7th Inf., 1 June, 1821. Col. 3rd Inf., 21 July, 1834. Died 23 Feb., 1852. Bvt. Col., 1 June, 1831, for ten years' faithful service in one grade.

MAPES, CHAS. [Born in N. Y. Appointed from N. Y.]
Maj. P. M., 7 Jan., 1835. Resigned 23 Sept., 1842. Died 29 June, 1852.

MARCH, PEYTON C.* [Born in Penn. Appointed from Penn.]
Addl. 2nd Lieut. 3rd Art., 11 June, 1888. 2nd Lieut., 30 Nov., 1888. 1st Lieut. 5th Art., 25 Oct., 1894. Maj. 33rd U. S. Vol., 5 July, 1899. Graduate of the Artillery School, 1898.

MARCH, THOS. J.* [Born in Penn. Appointed from Penn.]
2nd Lieut. 7th Cav., 15 June, 1868. Resigned 10 March, 1872.

MARCOTTE, HENRY. [Born in England. Appointed from N. Y.]
Corpl. Co. I, 2nd N. Y. Vols., 14 May, 1861. Sergt., 23 Sept., 1861. 1st Sergt., 12 Aug., 1862. 2nd Lieut. 2nd N. Y. Vols., 12 Feb., 1863. Mustered out 26 May, 1863. 2nd Lieut. Vet. Res. Corps, 12 Oct., 1863. Bvt. 1st Lieut. and Capt. Vols., 13 March, 1865, for gallant and meritorious service in the Battles of Big Bethel, White Oak Swamp, Malvern Hill, Fredericksburg and Chancellorsville, Va. Mustered out 23 Nov., 1866. 2nd Lieut. 44th Inf., 28 July, 1866. Bvt. 1st Lieut. and Bvt. Capt., 2 March, 1867, for gallant and meritorious service in the Battle of Chancellorsville, Va. 1st Lieut. 44th Inf., 5 June, 1867. Trans. to 17th Inf., 27 May, 1869. Retired 28 June, 1878, for wound in line of duty.

MARCY, RANDOLPH B.* [Born in Mass. Appointed from Mass.]
Bvt. 2nd Lieut. 5th Inf., 1 July, 1832. 2nd Lieut., 25 Nov., 1835. 1st Lieut., 22 June, 1837. Capt., 18 May, 1846. Maj. P. M., 22 Aug., 1859. Col. I. G., 9 Aug., 1861. Brig. Gen. Vols., 23 Sept., 1861. Appt. expired by constitutional limitation, 4 March, 1863. Bvt. Brig: Gen., 13 March, 1865, for gallant and meritorious service in the field during the war. Bvt. Maj. Gen., 13 March, 1865, for faithful and meritorious service during the war. Brig. Gen. I. G., 12 Dec., 1878. Retired for over forty years' service 2 Jan., 1881. Died 22 Nov., 1887.

MARGART, JOHN H. [Born in S. C. Appointed from S. C.]
Capt. Dep. Com. Ord., 31 Dec., 1812. Disbanded 1 June, 1821.

MARKHAM, EDWARD M.* [Born in N. Y. Appointed from N. Y.]
Addl. 2nd Lieut. Eng., 15 Feb., 1899. 2nd Lieut., 29 Sept., 1899.

MARKLAND, MATTHEW. [Born in Ky. Appointed from Ky.]
Priv. Co. F, 22nd Ky. Vols., 2 Dec., 1861. Discharged 20 Jan., 1865. 2nd Lieut., 1st Inf., 24 Oct., 1867. 1st Lieut., 28 June, 1878. Capt., 23 Sept., 1885. Retired for disability 25 Feb., 1891.

MARKLAND, WILLIAMSON. [Born in Mich. Appointed from Army.]
Priv. and Corpl. Co. B, 9th Inf., 23 Jan., 1890, to 23 Nov., 1892. 2nd Lieut. of Inf. (12th), 19 Nov., 1892. Died 24 Feb., 1895.

MARKLE, WILLIAM, Jr. [Born in Canada. Appointed from Canada.]
2nd Lieut. Canadian Vols., 19 April, 1814. Trans. to Rifle Reg., 17 May, 1815. Resigned 10 Feb., 1817.

MARKLEY, ALFRED C. [Born in Penn. Appointed from Penn.]
Sergt. Co. K, 197th Penn. Vols., 11 July, 1864. Discharged 5 Sept., 1864. 2nd Lieut. 127th U. S. Col. Troops, 9 Sept., 1864. 1st Lieut., 5 March, 1865. Mustered out 20 Oct., 1865. 2nd Lieut. 41st Inf., 28 July, 1866. Reg. Adj., 25 Dec., 1866, to 14 June, 1867. 1st Lieut., 31 March, 1868. Trans. to 24th Inf., 11 Nov., 1869. Capt., 20 March, 1879. Maj. 11th Inf., 26 April, 1898. Trans. to 24th Inf., 6 Aug., 1898.

MARKLEY, JOHN A. [Born in Ky. Appointed from Ind.]
2nd Lieut. 16th Inf., 14 April, 1847. R. Q. M., 18 Oct., 1847, to 10 Aug., 1848. Disbanded 10 Aug., 1848.

MARKLEY, JOHN H. [Born in Penn. Appointed from Penn.]
2nd Lieut. 2nd Inf., 26 Nov., 1861. 1st Lieut., 8 Jan., 1863. Resigned 31 Jan., 1866. Bvt. 1st Lieut., 27 June, 1862, for gallant and meritorious service at the Battle Gaines' Mill, Va. Bvt. Capt., 30 Aug., 1862, for gallant and meritorious service at the Battle of Bull Run (2nd), Va. Died 18 Jan., 1890.

MARMADUKE, JOHN S.* [Born in Mo. Appointed from Mo.]
Bvt. 2nd Lieut. 1st Inf., 1 July, 1857. 2nd Lieut. 7th Inf., 1 Aug., 1857. Resigned 17 April, 1861. Died 28 Dec., 1887.

MARQUART, PETER E. [Born in Mo. Appointed from Army.]
Priv. and Mus. Gen. Ser., Priv. Det. of Art. and Priv. Corpl. and Sergt. Co. G, 3rd Inf., 25 Nov., 1885, to 1 Oct., 1891. 2nd Lieut. 2nd Inf., 1 Oct., 1891. 1st Lieut., 26 April, 1898. Graduate of the Infantry and Cavalry School, 1897.

MARR, JAMES. [Born in Canada. Appointed from Mo.]
2nd Lieut. 1st Mo. Art., 9 May, 1861. 1st Lieut., 2 Sept., 1861. Capt., 6 Feb., 1863. Bvt. Maj. Vols., 3 June, 1865, for meritorious service. Mustered out 4 Aug., 1865. 2nd Lieut. 4th Art., 23 Feb., 1866. Resigned 7 April, 1866.

MARRAST, JOHN C. [Born in Ala. Appointed from Ala.]
1st Lieut. of Inf., 5 March, 1847; 13th Inf., 9 April, 1847. Disbanded 15 July, 1848.

MARRIOTT, JAMES C. [Born in Md. Appointed from Md.]
1st Lieut. of Inf., 24 Feb., 1847; Voltigeurs, 9 April, 1847. Capt., 18 Sept., 1847. Disbanded 31 Aug., 1848.

MARROW, CHARLES E. [Born in Va. Appointed from Va.]
Asst. Surg., 12 Dec., 1898.

MARSH, ELIAS J. [Born in N. J. Appointed from N. J.]
Asst. Surg., 5 Aug., 1861. Discharged 17 Aug., 1870. Bvt. Capt. and Maj., 13 March, 1865, for faithful and meritorious service during the war.

MARSH, FREDK.* [Born in N. Y. Appointed from Mo.]
Addl. 2nd Lieut. 2nd Art., 15 June, 1877. 2nd Lieut. 1st Art., 15 March, 1878. 1st Lieut., 9 July, 1884. Capt. 6th Art., 7 Oct., 1898. Graduate of the Artillery School, 1886.

MARSH, ORMAND.* [Born in Conn. Appointed from Conn.]
Ensign 1st Inf., 1 March, 1811. 2nd Lieut. 2nd Inf., 30 Oct., 1812. 1st Lieut., 30 March, 1814. Disbanded 15 June, 1815. Died 18 Jan., 1854.

MARSH, SALEM S.* [Born in Mass. Appointed from Mass.]
Bvt. 2nd Lieut. 9th Inf., 1 July, 1860. 2nd Lieut. 2nd Inf., 19 Jan., 1861. 1st Lieut., 14 May, 1861. Capt., 12 Nov., 1861. Killed 1 May, 1863, at the Battle of Chancellorsville, Va. Bvt. Maj., 13 Dec., 1862, for gallant and meritorious service at the Battle of Fredericksburg, Va. Bvt. Lieut. Col., 3 May, 1863, for gallant and meritorious service at the Battle of Chancellorsville, Va.

MARSHALL, EDWARD C. [Born in Ky. Appointed from Ohio.]
1st Lieut. Inf., 11 March, 1847; 15th Inf., 9 April, 1847. R. Q. M., 9 April to 17 May, 1847. Capt., 6 May, 1848. Dismissed 22 May, 1848. Bvt. Capt., 13 Sept., 1847, for gallant and meritorious conduct at Chapultepec.

MARSHALL, ELISHA G.* [Born in N. Y. Appointed from N. Y.]
Bvt. 2nd Lieut. 4th Inf., 1 July, 1850. 2nd Lieut. 6th Inf., 15 May, 1851. 1st Lieut., 26 March, 1855. Capt., 14 May, 1861. Col. 13th N. Y. Vols., 20 April, 1862. Bvt. Maj., 27 June, 1862, for gallant and meritorious service in the Battle of Gaines' Mill, Va. Bvt. Lieut. Col., 13 Dec., 1862, for gallant and meritorious service in the Battle of Fredericksburg, Va. Bvt. Brig. Gen. Vols., 13 Dec., 1862, for gallant and meritorious service in the Battle of Fredericksburg, Va. Mustered out of Vol. Service, 23 May, 1863. Col. 14th N. Y. Art., 4 Jan., 1864. Bvt. Col., 30 July, 1864, for gallant and meritorious service in the action which succeeded the explosion of the Petersburg mine. Bvt. Brig. Gen., 13 March, 1865, for gallant and meritorious service during the war. Bvt. Maj. Gen. Vols., 13 March, 1865, for gallant and meritorious service during the war. Maj. 5th Inf., 12 June, 1865. Mustered out of Vol. Service, 26 Aug., 1865. Retired with rank of Col., 11 Sept., 1867. Died 3 Aug., 1883.

MARSHALL, FRANCIS C.* [Born in Ill. Appointed from Wis.]
2nd Lieut. 8th Cav., 12 June, 1890. 1st Lieut. 6th Cav., 5 Jan., 1897.

MARSHALL, FRANK B. [Born in Ill. Appointed from Ill.]
Sergt. Co. A, 11th N. Y. Vols., 30 April to — June, 1861. 1st Lieut. Adj. 39th

Ill. Vols., 5 Oct., 1861. Resigned 15 July, 1862. 2nd Lieut. 13th Inf., 7 March, 1867. Resigned 21 Dec., 1867.

MARSHALL, HUMPHREY.* [Born in Ky. Appointed from Ky.]
Bvt. 3rd Lieut. Mtd. Rangers, 1 July, 1832. Trans. to 1st Drag., 4 March, 1833. Resigned 30 April, 1833. Col. 1st Ky. Cav., 9 June, 1846. Mustered out 7 July, 1847.

MARSHALL, JAMES M.* [Born in Ill. Appointed at Large.]
2nd Lieut. 13th Inf., 23 June, 1865. 1st Lieut., 23 June, 1865. Trans. to 31st Inf., 21 Sept., 1866. R. Q. M., 28 Dec., 1866, to 31 March, 1867. Reg. Adj., 31 March, 1867, to 15 May, 1869. Trans. to 22nd Inf., 15 May, 1869. Trans. to 4th Art., 15 Dec., 1870. Capt. A. Q. M., 24 April, 1875. Mustered out 7 July, 1847. Maj. Q. M., 24 Sept., 1891. Lieut. Col. D. Q. M. G., 18 Feb., 1897.

MARSHALL, JOSEPH. [Born in Ind. Appointed from Ind.]
1st Lieut. 13th Inf., 14 May, 1861. Capt., 30 March, 1864. Trans. to 22nd Inf., 21 Sept., 1866. Died 15 Sept., 1867.

MARSHALL, JOSEPH G. [Born in Ind. Appointed from Ind.]
2nd Lieut. 9th Inf., 5 Aug., 1861. Cashiered 25 June, 1863.

MARSHALL, LOUIS H.* [Born in Va. Appointed at Large.]
Bvt. 2nd Lieut. 3rd Inf., 1 July, 1849. 2nd Lieut., 5 March, 1851. 1st Lieut. 10th Inf., 3 March, 1855. R. Q. M., 16 July to 29 Dec., 1860. Capt., 29 Dec., 1860. Col. A. A. de C., 30 June, 1862, to 28 July, 1865. Maj. 14th Inf., 16 Oct., 1863. Trans. to 23rd Inf., 21 Sept., 1866. Resigned 23 Nov., 1868. Bvt. Lieut. Col., 13 March, 1865, for gallant and meritorious service during the war.

MARSHALL, WM. L.* [Born in Ky. Appointed from Ky.]
Priv. Co. A, 10th Ky. Cav., 16 Aug., 1862, to 17 Sept., 1863. Cadet at Mil. Acad., 1 July, 1864. Bvt. 2nd Lieut. Eng., 15 June, 1868. 2nd Lieut., 22 Feb., 1869. 1st Lieut., 21 June, 1871. Capt., 14 years' service, 15 June, 1882. Maj., 10 May, 1895.

MARSHALL, WM. P. [Born in S. C. Appointed from S. C.]
Hosp. Surg.'s Mate, 30 March, 1814. Post Surg., 18 April, 1818. Disbanded 1 June, 1821.

MARSTELLER, JAMES S. [Born in Va. Appointed from W. Va.]
2nd Lieut. 24th Inf., 20 Jan., 1875. 1st Lieut., 7 Jan., 1879. Accidentally killed while hunting, 7 Oct., 1884.

MARSTON, MATTHEW R. [Born in Penn. Appointed from Penn.]
2nd Lieut. 1st Inf., 26 April, 1861. 1st Lieut., 14 May, 1861. Capt., 10 Jan., 1862. Died 13 Jan., 1869, from injuries received by explosion of steamboat boiler. Bvt. Maj., 4 July, 1863, for gallant and meritorious service during the Siege of Vicksburg, Miss.

MARSTON, MORRELL. [Born in Mass. Appointed from Mass.]
1st Lieut. 21st Inf., 12 March, 1812. Capt., 26 June, 1813. Trans. to 5th Inf., 17 May, 1815. Dismissed 27 Sept., 1824. Bvt. Maj., 15 Aug., 1814, for gallant conduct in defence of Fort Erie. Died 9 March, 1831.

MARTIN, AMOS H.* [Born in Penn. Appointed from Penn.]
2nd Lieut. 1st Inf., 12 June, 1893. 1st Lieut., 26 April, 1898. Trans. to 19th Inf., 9 Sept., 1899.

MARTIN, CARL A. [Born in Kan. Appointed from Kan.]
Cadet at Mil. Acad., 15 June, 1893, to 2 July, 1894. 2nd Lieut. 21st Inf., 9 July, 1898. 1st Lieut. 25th Inf., 2 March, 1899.

MARTIN, CHANCELLOR.* [Born in Ill. Appointed from Ill.]
2nd Lieut. 3rd Inf., 15 June, 1868. Unassigned 23 April, 1869. Ass'd to 24th Inf., 3 Aug., 1870. Discharged 1 Sept., 1870.

MARTIN, CHARLES H.* [Born in Ill. Appointed from Ill.]
2nd Lieut. 14th Inf., 12 June, 1887. 1st Lieut. 23rd Inf., 16 April, 1894. Trans. to 14th Inf., 5 May, 1894. Capt., 2 March, 1899. Capt. A. Q. M. Vols., 17 Oct., 1898, to 13 June, 1899.

MARTIN, EDWARD H.* [Born in N. Y. Appointed from N. Y.]
2nd Lieut. 21st Inf., 26 April, 1898. Trans. to 5th Art., 24 Dec., 1898.

MARTIN, GEORGE C. [Born in Vt. Appointed from D. C.]
2nd Lieut. 21st Inf., 9 July, 1898. 1st Lieut. 2nd Inf., 9 March, 1899.

MARTIN, GEORGE W. [Born in Penn. Appointed from Penn.]
Mil. Storekeeper Q. M. D., 21 July, 1862. Appointment expired 4 March, 1863.

MARTIN, GEORGE W. [Born in Miss. Appointed from Army.]
Priv., Corpl. and Sergt. Co. G, 2nd Inf., 23 June, 1880, to 22 June, 1885. Priv. and Corpl. Co. H, 1st Inf., 18 July, 1885, to 22 Oct., 1886. 2nd Lieut. 18th Inf., 22 Oct., 1886. 1st Lieut. 20th Inf., 12 March, 1894. Trans. to 23rd Inf., 5 May, 1894. Trans. to 18th Inf., 22 May, 1894. Capt., 2 March, 1899. Reg. Q. M., 2 March, 1899.

MARTIN, JAMES G.* [Born in N. C. Appointed from N. C.]
2nd Lieut. 1st Art., 1 July, 1840. 1st Lieut., 16 Feb., 1847. Capt. A. Q. M., 5 Aug., 1847. Resigned 4 June, 1861. Bvt. Maj., 20 Aug., 1847, for gallant and meritorious conduct at Contreras and Churubusco, Mex.

MARTIN, JAMES P.* [Born in Ky. Appointed at Large.]
Bvt. 2nd Lieut. 6th Inf., 1 July, 1860. 2nd Lieut. 7th Inf., 20 Dec., 1860. 1st Lieut., 14 May, 1861. Capt., 2 Jan., 1863. Bvt. Maj., 2 July, 1863, for gallant and meritorious service in the Battle of Gettysburg, Penn. Bvt. Lieut. Col., 22 July, 1865, for faithful and meritorious service. Maj. A. A. G., 10 April, 1869. Lieut. Col. A. A. G., 28 Feb., 1887. Died 19 Feb., 1895.

MARTIN, JOEL. [Born in Va. Appointed from Va.]
Asst. Surg., 15 Aug., 1825. Died 10 Dec., 1854.

MARTIN, JOHN J. [Born in S. C. Appointed from S. C.]
1st Lieut. Inf., 5 March, 1847; 12th Inf., 9 April, 1847. Capt., 31 Dec., 1847. Resigned 31 March, 1848.

MARTIN, JOHN T.* [Born in Ohio. Appointed from Ohio.]
2nd Lieut. 4th Art., 12 June, 1889. 1st Lieut. 5th Art., 1 Feb., 1896. Trans. to 1st Art., 9 July, 1897.

MARTIN, JOHN W. [Born in Va. Appointed from Va.]
2nd Lieut. 2nd Inf., 1 July, 1839. Resigned 23 Nov., 1846. 2nd Lieut. 3rd Drag. 21 July, 1847. Died 18 June, 1848. Bvt. 1st Lieut., 19 Oct., 1847, for gallant and meritorious conduct at Atlixco.

MARTIN, JOHN W. [Born in N. Y. Appointed from N. Y.]
Cadet at Mil. Acad., 1 July, 1869, to 15 Feb., 1871. 2nd Lieut. 4th Cav., 27 July, 1872. 1st Lieut., 4 Jan., 1879. Capt. 26 Nov., 1884. Retired for disability 25 Feb., 1891.

MARTIN, LEONARD.* [Born in Wis. Appointed from Wis.]
2nd Lieut. 4th Art., 6 May, 1861. 1st Lieut. 5th Art., 14 May, 1861. Col. 51st Wis. Vols., 29 April, 1865. Mustered out of Vol. Service., 25 Aug., 1865. Resigned 3 April, 1866. Died 14 April, 1890.

MARTIN, MEDAD C.* [Born in Vt. Appointed from Vt.]
2nd Lieut. 22nd Inf., 15 June, 1877. 1st Lieut., 24 April, 1883. R. Q. M., 22 May, 1888, to 2 Nov., 1891. Capt. A. Q. M., 2 Nov., 1891. Maj. Q. M. Vols., 12 May, 1898. Lieut. Col. Q. M. Vols., 10 Aug., 1890

MARTIN, OLIPHANT. [Born in Penn. Appointed from Penn.]
Ensign 22nd Inf., 20 May, 1813. 3rd Lieut., 26 June, 1813. 2nd Lieut., 8 Feb., 1814. 1st Lieut., 25 Sept., 1814. Disbanded 15 June, 1815. Retained 17 May, 1816 (in reorganization under Act of 3 March, 1815), as 2nd Lieut. 5th Inf., with Bvt. of 1st Lieut. from 25 Sept., 1814. 1st Lieut., 1 July, 1817. Dropped 20 Feb., 1818.

MARTIN, SAML. H. [Born in Ky. Appointed from Ill.]
2nd Lieut Inf., 23 Feb., 1847; 14th Inf., 9 April, 1847. Resigned 31 May, 1848.

MARTIN, THOS. [Born in Va. Appointed from Va.]
2nd Lieut. Rifles, 18 April, 1818. 1st Lieut., 15 Dec., 1818. Dropped 23 Feb., 1820.

MARTIN, THOS. A. [Born in Penn. Appointed from Penn.]
2nd Lieut. and 1st Lieut. 4th Inf., 5 Aug., 1861. Capt., 14 July, 1863. Dismissed 25 Aug., 1864.

MARTIN, WM. [Born in Penn. Appointed from Penn.]
2nd Lieut. 8th Inf., 27 Oct., 1820. Trans. to 4th Inf., 1 June, 1821. Reg. Adj., 1 Oct., 1822, to 1 March, 1828, and 15 Feb., 1831, to 1 Nov., 1833. 1st Lieut., 25 March, 1826. Capt., 28 Dec., 1835. Resigned 31 Dec., 1835. Restored 20 May, 1836. Resigned 23 Sept., 1836.

MARTIN, WILLIAM. F.* [Born in Ohio. Appointed from Ohio.]
2nd Lieut. 25th Inf., 14 June, 1885. 1st Lieut. 5th Inf., 3 June, 1892. Capt., 2 March, 1899.

MARTIN, WM. J. [Born in Penn. Appointed from Penn.]
2nd Lieut., 5 March, 1847; Voltigeurs, 9 April, 1847. Disbanded 31 Aug., 1848. Bvt. 1st Lieut., 13 Sept., 1847, for gallant and meritorious conduct at Chapultepec.

MARTIN, WM. P. [Born in Ireland. Appointed from Conn.]
Priv. Co. K, 1st Art., 28 March, 1839. Corpl., 4 June, 1841. Sergt., 1 Jan., 1842. Discharged 28 Jan., 1844. Sergt. Co. K, 1st Art., 28 Jan., 1844. Discharged 8 Dec., 1847. Priv. Gen. Ser., 21 Aug., 1850. Ord. Sergt., 20 Oct., 1850. Discharged 21 Aug., 1855. Ord. Sergt., 21 Aug., 1855. Discharged 21 June, 1860. Ord. Sergt., 21 June, 1860. Discharged 9 Oct., 1861. 1st Lieut and R. Q. M. 3rd R. I. Art., 9 Oct., 1861. Resigned 12 Sept., 1862. Capt. C. S. Vols., 30 Aug., 1862. Bvt. Maj. Vols., 13 March, 1865, for faithful service during the war. Bvt. Lieut. Col. Vols., 15 May, 1866, for faithful and meritorious service in the Subsist. Dept. Bvt. Col. Vols., 11 Dec., 1866, for faithful service in the S. Dept. Mustered out of Vol. Service, 27 Dec., 1866. Capt. Mil. Storekeeper Q. M. D., 5 March, 1867. Retired 20 March, 1885. Died 19 March, 1896.

MARTIN, WM. T.* [Born in N. J. Appointed from N. J.]
Bvt. 2nd Lieut. 4th Art., 1 July, 1837. Resigned 15 June, 1838.

MARTIN, WILMOT. [Born in Penn. Appointed from Penn.]
2nd Lieut. 3rd Inf., 8 March, 1837. 1st Lieut., 1 July, 1839. Resigned 31 May, 1840.

MARTIN, WYLY. [Born in ——. Appointed from Tenn.]
3rd Lieut. 24th Inf., 9 Aug., 1813. 1st Lieut. 39th Inf., 29 July, 1813. Capt., 17 March, 1814. Disbanded 15 June, 1815. Reinstated in Rifle Reg., 2 Dec., 1815. Trans. to 6th Inf., 1 June, 1821. Resigned 21 July, 1823.

MARTINDALE, ELIJAH B., Jr. [Born in Ind. Appointed from Ind.]
Priv. 27th Batty Ind. Light Art., 18 June, 1898, to 24 July, 1898. 2nd Lieut. 2nd Art., 9 July, 1898.

MARTINDALE, JOHN H.* [Born in N. Y. Appointed from N. Y.]
Bvt. 2nd Lieut. 1st Drag., 1 July, 1835. Resigned 10 March, 1836. Brig. Gen. Vols., 9 Aug., 1861. Bvt. Maj. Gen. Vols., 13 March, 1865, for gallant and distinguished service at the Battle of Malvern Hill, Va. Resigned 13 Sept., 1864. Died 13 Dec., 1881.

MARVIN, EDWIN C. [Born in Conn. Appointed from Pa.]
2nd Lieut. Inf., 25 March, 1847; Voltiguers, 9 April, 1847. R. Q. M., 15 Sept., 1847, to 29 Aug., 1848. Disbanded 29 Aug., 1848.

MARVINE, WALTER. [Born in Pa. Appointed from N. Y.]
Post Chap., 6 Dec., 1890.

MARYE, WM. A.* [Born in Md. Appointed from Cal.]
2nd Lieut. Ord., 17 June, 1862. 1st Lieut., 3 March, 1863. Capt., 7 May, 1867. Maj., 27 May, 1878. Lieut. Col., 31 Jan., 1891.

MASON, CHAS.* [Born in N. Y. Appointed from N. Y.]
Bvt. 2nd Lieut. Eng., 1 July, 1829. Resigned 31 Dec., 1831. Died 25 Feb., 1882.

MASON, CHARLES F. [Born in Va. Appointed from Va.]
Asst. Surg., 5 May, 1886. Resigned 5 March, 1887. Reappointed Asst. Surg., 2 July, 1888. Capt. Asst. Surg., 2 July, 1893. Maj. Brig. Surg. Vols., 4 June, 1898, to 22 March, 1899. Maj. Surg. 26th U. S. Vols., 5 July, 1899.

MASON, CHAS. W. [Born in Cal. Appointed from Ohio.]
2nd Lieut. 13th Inf., 20 Jan., 1875. Trans. to 4th Inf., 15 Feb., 1875. 1st Lieut., 4 Feb., 1882. Capt., 18 May, 1893. Graduate of the Infantry and Cavalry School, 1887.

MASON, EDWIN C. [Born in Ohio. Appointed from Ohio.]
Capt. 2nd Ohio Vols., 29 April, 1861. Mustered out 24 June, 1861. Capt. 17th Inf., 14 May, 1861. Col. 7th Maine Vols., 22 Aug., 1861. Bvt. Maj., 13 Dec., 1862, for gallant and meritorious service in the Battle of Fredericksburg, Va. Bvt. Lieut. Col., 6 May, 1864, for gallant and meritorious service in the Battle of the Wilderness, Va. Bvt. Col., 10 May, 1864, for gallant and meritorious service in the Battle of Spottsylvania, Va. Mustered out of Vol. Service, 5 Sept., 1864. Col. 176th Ohio Vols., 23 Sept., 1864. Bvt. Brig. Gen. Vols., 3 June, 1865, for faithful service. Mustered out of Vol. Service, 14 June, 1865. Trans. to 35th Inf., 21 Sept., 1866. Unassigned 12 Aug., 1869. Ass'd to 20th Inf., 14 Oct., 1869. Maj. 21st Inf., 5 Sept., 1871. Lieut. Col. 4th Inf., 19 May, 1881. Col. 3rd Inf., 24 April, 1888. Retired, by operation of law, 31 May, 1895. Bvt. Brig. Gen., 27 Feb., 1890, for gallant and meritorious services in action against Indians in the Lava Beds, Cal., 17 April, 1873, and gallant services in action against Indians at Clearwater, Idaho, 11 and 12 July, 1877. Died 30 April, 1898.

MASON, GEORGE F. [Born in D. C. Appointed from Mich.]
2nd Lieut. 5th Cav., 19 Aug., 1867. 1st Lieut., 22 June, 1869. Died 1 March, 1870.

MASON, GEORGE T.* [Born in Va. Appointed from Va.]
Bvt. 2nd Lieut. 2nd Drag., 1 July, 1842. Trans. to 1st Drag., 6 March, 1843. 2nd Lieut. 2nd Drag., 13 Sept., 1844. Killed in action near Fort Brown, Texas, 25 April, 1846.

MASON, JAMES L.* [Born in R. I. Appointed at Large.]
Bvt. 2nd Lieut. Eng., 1 July, 1836. 1st Lieut., 7 July, 1838. Capt., 24 April, 1847. Died 5 Sept., 1853. Bvt. Maj., 20 Aug., 1847, for gallant and meritorious conduct at Contreras and Churubusco. Bvt. Lieut. Col., 8 Sept., 1847, for gallant and meritorious conduct at Molino del Rey.

MASON, JOHN S.* [Born in Ohio. Appointed from Ohio.]
2nd Lieut. 3rd Art., 1 July, 1847. 1st Lieut., 7 Sept., 1850. R. Q. M., 27 June, 1854, to 1 June, 1858. Capt. 11th Inf., 14 May, 1861. Col. 4th Ohio Vols., 3 Oct., 1861. Bvt. Maj., 17 Sept., 1862, for gallant and meritorious service in the Battle of Antietam, Md. Bvt. Lieut. Col., 13 Sept., 1862, for gallant and meritorious service in the Batle of Fredericksburg, Va. Brig. Gen. Vols., 29 Nov., 1862. Maj. 17th Inf., 14 Oct., 1864. Bvt. Col., 13 March, 1865, for gallant and meritorious service during the war. Bvt. Brig. Gen., 13 March, 1865, for gallant and meritorious service in the field during the war. Mustered out of Vol. Service, 30 April, 1866. Trans. to 35th Inf., 21 Sept., 1866. Trans. to 15th Inf., 15 March, 1869. Lieut. Col., 4th Inf., 11 Dec., 1873. Trans. to 20th Inf., 25 Feb., 1881. Col. 9th Inf., 2 April, 1883. Retired, by operation of law, 21 Aug., 1888. Died 29 Nov., 1897.

MASON, JOHN S., Jr. [Born in Cal. Appointed from Texas.]
2nd Lieut. 1st Inf., 1 Sept., 1879. 1st Lieut., 20 April, 1886. Died 13 Feb., 1891.

MASON, JULIUS W. [Born in Penn. Appointed from Penn.]
2nd Lieut. 2nd Cav., 26 April, 1861. 1st Lieut., 1 June, 1861; 5th Cav., 3 Aug., 1861. Capt., 6 Dec., 1862. Bvt. Maj., 9 June, 1863, for gallant and meritorious service in the Battle of Beverly Ford, Va. Bvt. Lieut. Col., 1 Aug., 1863, for gallant and meritorious service in the Battle of Brandy Station, Va. Maj. 3rd Cav., 1 July, 1876. Died 19 Dec., 1882.

MASON, MILO.* [Born in Vt. Appointed from Vt.]
Ensign 4th Inf., 18 June, 1808. 2nd Lieut. Art., 9 Jan., 1809. 1st Lieut., 29 Feb., 1812. In 1st Art., — March, 1812. Trans. to Corps Art., 12 May, 1814. (Capt. A. Dept. Q. M. G., 29 April, 1816. Maj. Dep. Q. M. G., 13 Feb., 1818, to 1 May, 1820.) Capt. Corps Art., 17 May, 1816. Trans. to 1st Art., 1 June, 1821. Died 4 Feb., 1837. Bvt. Maj., 17 May, 1826, for ten years' faithful service in one grade. Died 4 Feb., 1837.

MASON, PHILIP D. [Born in Mass. Appointed from Mass.]
2nd Lieut. 1st Art., 18 March, 1862. 1st Lieut., 1 Sept., 1863. Died 18 July, 1864, of wounds received in action at Trevillian Station, Va.

MASON, RICHD. B. [Born in Va. Appointed from Va.]
2nd Lieut. 8th Inf., 2 Sept., 1817. 1st Lieut., 25 Sept., 1817. Capt., 31 July, 1819. Trans. to 3rd Inf., 1 June, 1821. Trans. to 1st Inf., 14 Dec., 1821. Maj. 1st Drag., 4 March, 1833. Lieut. Col., 4 July, 1836. Col., 30 June, 1846. Died 25 July, 1850. Bvt. Maj., 31 July, 1829, for ten years' faithful service in one grade. Bvt. Brig. Gen., 30 May, 1848, for meritorious conduct.

MASON, STANTON A.* [Born in N. Y. Appointed from N. Y.]
2nd Lieut. 4th Cav., 16 June, 1875. 1st Lieut., 2 April, 1879. Capt., 24 April, 1886. Died 9 March, 1891.

MASON, STEVENS T. [Born in Va. Appointed from Va.]
Mil. Storekeeper Ord., 15 May, 1845. Capt. Mtd Rifles, 27 May, 1846. Died 15 May, 1847, of wounds received in the Battle of Cerro Gordo, Mex., 19 April, 1847.

MASON, THOS. J. [Born in Md. Appointed from Fla.]
2nd Lieut. 3rd Inf., 3 March, 1848. Drowned 22 May, 1850.

MASSEY, MATTHEW S. [Born in Penn. Appointed from Penn.]
3rd Lieut. and 2nd Lieut. 2nd Art., 13 May, 1813. Trans. to Corps Art., 12 May, 1814. 1st Lieut., 5 Aug., 1817. Trans. to 4th Art., 1 June, 1821. Capt., 15 Jan., 1823. Died 11 Aug., 1823.

MASSEY, SOLON F.* [Born in N. Y. Appointed from Ohio.]
2nd Lieut. 5th Art., 15 June, 1877. 1st Lieut., 31 Oct., 1885. Retired for disability 20 Feb., 1891. Graduate of the Artillery School, 1886.

MASSIAS, ABRAHAM A. [Born in N. Y. Appointed from N. Y.]
1st Lieut. Rifles, 3 May, 1808. Capt., 1 July, 1809. Maj. 4th Rifles, 17 Sept., 1814, which was rejected by Senate, 10 Dec., 1814. Disbanded 15 June, 1815. Maj. P. M., 12 Dec., 1820. Disbanded 23 Sept., 1842.

MASSIE, ROBT. F. [Born in Va. Appointed from Va.]
3rd Lieut. Light Art., 2 July, 1814. 2nd Lieut., 31 Aug., 1814. Killed in a duel, 25 Dec., 1817.

MAST, JAMES L. [Born in South America. Appointed from Penn.]
Priv. Co. A, 25th Pa. Vols., 18 April, to 23 July, 1861. Corpl. Co. D, Pa. Art., 24 Sept., 1861. 2nd Lieut., 24 Nov., 1864. Mustered out 13 June, 1865. 2nd Lieut. 2nd Art., 23 Feb., 1866. 1st Lieut., 3 Jan., 1867. Dropped 7 June, 1878.

MASTEN, FREDK. H. [Born in N. Y. Appointed from N. Y.]
2nd Lieut. 1st Inf., 25 Sept., 1838. 1st Lieut., 1 May, 1841. Capt. A. Q. M., 3 March, 1847. Resigned 31 Dec., 1857. Died 8 Sept., 1874.

MATHER, WM. W.* [Born in Conn. Appointed from Conn.]
Bvt. 2nd Lieut. 7th Inf., 1 July, 1828. 2nd Lieut., 1 July, 1828. 1st Lieut., 4 Dec., 1834. Resigned 31 Aug., 1836. Died 27 Feb., 1859.

MATHEWS, ALMERON S. [Born in Mich. Appointed from Mich.]
1st Lieut. 7th Mich. Vols., 24 June, 1861. Resigned 11 Dec., 1861. 1st Lieut. 22nd Mich. Vols., 14 Aug., 1862. Capt., 30 July, 1864. Mustered out 26 June, 1865. 2nd Lieut. 14th Inf., 20 July, 1866. Trans. to 32nd Inf., 21 Sept., 1866. 1st Lieut., 15 Sept., 1867. Resigned 9 Dec., 1867.

MATTHEWS, JOHN H.* [Born in N. Y. Appointed from N. Y.]
2nd Lieut. 1st Inf., 1 July, 1838. Died 15 Aug., 1838.

MATHEY, EDWARD G. [Born in France. Appointed from Ind.]
1st Sergt. Co. C, 17th Ind. Vols., 31 May, 1861. Discharged 21 May, 1862. 2nd Lieut. 17th Ind. Vols., 1 May, 1862. Resigned 10 Aug., 1862. 2nd Lieut. 81st Ind. Vols., 1 Sept., 1862. 1st Lieut., 21 March, 1863. Capt., 8 Nov., 1863. Maj., 12 Sept., 1864. Mustered out 13 June, 1865. 2nd Lieut. 7th Cav., 24 Sept., 1867. 1st Lieut., 10 May, 1870. Capt., 30 Sept., 1877. Retired for disability with rank of Maj., 11 Dec., 1896.

MATILE, LEON A. [Born in Switzerland. Appointed from Army.]
Priv. Co. A, 3rd Batt. 15th Inf., 3 Dec., 1863. Corpl., 26 Aug., 1866. Trans. to 33rd Inf., 21 Sept., 1866. 2nd Lieut. 24th Inf., 7 March, 1867. Trans. to 11th Inf., 25 April, 1869. 1st Lieut., 23 Dec., 1873. Reg. Adj., 1 June to 7 Aug., 1886. Capt., 7 Aug., 1886. Trans. to 14th Inf., 21 July, 1893. Maj., 2 March, 1899.

MATSON, WINFIELD S. [Born in Ind. Appointed from Ind.]
Priv. Cos. C and F, 6th Ind. Cav., 25 Feb., 1863, to 15 Sept., 1865. 2nd Lieut. 18th Inf., 9 April, 1866. Trans. to 27th Inf., 21 Sept., 1866. 1st Lieut., 21 Dec., 1866. Trans. to 9th Inf., 14 June, 1869. Resigned 1 Jan., 1870.

MATTHEWS, WASHINGTON. [Born in Ireland. Appointed from Iowa.]
1st Lieut. Asst. Surg., 16 Nov., 1868. Capt. Asst. Surg., 16 Nov., 1871. Maj. Surg., 10 July, 1889. Retired for disability 26 Sept., 1895.

MAUCK, CLARENCE. [Born in Ind. Appointed from Penn.]
2nd Lieut. 1st Cav., 27 March, 1861. 1st Lieut., 9 May, 1861. 4th Cav., 3 Aug., 1861. Bvt. Capt., 31 Dec., 1862, for gallant and meritorious service in the Battle of Stone River, Tenn. Capt. 4th Cav., 5 Nov., 1863. Bvt. Maj., 11 Oct., 1864, for gallant and meritorious service during the Atlanta campaign. Maj. 9th Cav., 20 March, 1879. Died 25 Jan., 1881.

MAUCK, EDWIN.* [Born in Penn. Appointed from Penn.]
2nd Lieut. 6th Cav., 23 June, 1865. 1st Lieut., 1 July, 1866. Capt., 10 Sept., 1869. Mustered out 1 Jan., 1871. Died 16 Aug., 1880.

MAUL, JOHN. [Born in Penn. Appointed from D. C.]
Ensign 5th Inf., 29 July, 1813. 3rd Lieut., 1 May, 1814. Trans. to 4th Rifle, 16 May, 1814. Disbanded 15 June, 1815. 2nd Lieut. 8th Inf., 17 June, 1816. R. Q. M., — Sept., 1817, to 8 May, 1819. 1st Lieut., 20 Aug., 1817. Capt., 8 May, 1819. Disbanded 1 June, 1821.

MAULDIN, FRANK G.* [Born in S. C. Appointed from S. C.]
Addl. 2nd Lieut. 3rd Art., 12 June, 1890. 2nd Lieut. 2nd Art., 29 May, 1891. Trans. to 3rd Art., 12 Aug., 1891. 1st Lieut. 7th Art., 8 March, 1898.

MAULSBY, WM. P. [Born in Md. Appointed from Md.]
Mil. Storekeeper Ord., 1 Nov., 1847. Resigned 30 June, 1849. Col. 1st Potomac Home Brig. Md. Vols., 29 Nov., 1861. Resigned 25 Aug., 1864.

MAUPIN, GEORGE W. [Born in Va. Appointed from Va.]
Garrison Surg. Mate, 5 Nov., 1802. Post Surg., 18 April, 1818. Asst. Surg., 1 June, 1821. Died 18 June, 1825.

MAURICE, THEODORE W. [Born in Va. Appointed from Penn.]
2nd Lieut. Eng., 1 Aug., 1813. 1st Lieut., 13 Oct., 1813. Capt., 12 Nov., 1818. Died 5 March, 1832. Bvt. Maj., 12 Nov., 1828, for ten years' faithful service in one grade.

MAURICE, THOMAS D. [Born in N. Y. Appointed from Mo.]
Capt. 1st Mo. Vols., 23 April, 1861. Trans. to 1st Mo. Light Art., 1 Sept., 1861. Maj. 1st Mo. Light Art., 1 Jan., 1863. Mustered out 29 July, 1865. 2nd Lieut. 2nd Art., 23 Feb., 1866. 1st Lieut., 28 July, 1866. Capt., 16 Oct., 1884. Died 18 March, 1885.

MAURY, DABNEY H.* [Born in Va. Appointed at Large.]
Bvt. 2nd Lieut. Mtd. Rifles, 1 July, 1846 2nd Lieut. 3rd Art., 1 July, 1847. Trans. to Mtd. Rifles, 19 Feb., 1848. 1st Lieut., 27 Jan., 1853. Reg. Adj., 15 Sept., 1858, to 10 April, 1860. Bvt. Capt., A. A. G., 17 April, 1860. Dismissed 25 June, 1861. Bvt. 1st Lieut., 18 April, 1847, for gallant and meritorious conduct at Cerro Gordo.

MAURY, ZEB. M. P. [Born in Va. Appointed from Va.]
2nd Lieut. 2nd Drag., 8 June, 1836. 1st Lieut., 1 Oct., 1837. Resigned 28 Feb., 1838.

MAUS, LOUIS M. [Born in Md. Appointed from Md.]
1st Lieut. Asst. Surg., 10 Nov., 1874. Capt. Asst. Surg., 10 Nov., 1879. Maj. Surg., 4 Dec., 1892. Lieut. Col. Chf. Surg. Vols., 9 May, 1898, to 21 April, 1899.

MAUS, MARION P.* [Born in Md. Appointed from Md.]
2nd Lieut. 1st Inf., 17 June, 1874. 1st Lieut., 29 Sept., 1879. Capt. 1st Inf., 27 Nov.,

1890. Maj. 2nd Inf., 16 June, 1899. Lieut. Col. I. G. Vols., 9 May, 1898. Medal of Honor for most distinguished gallantry in action against hostile Apache Indians, led by Geronimo and Natchez, in the Sierra Madre Mountains, N. Mex., 11 Jan., 1866, while 1st Lieut., 1st Inf., and commanding the expedition.

MAXEY, ROBERT J.* [Born in Miss. Appointed from Ark.]
2nd Lieut. 6th Inf., 26 April, 1898. 1st Lieut., 2 March, 1899.

MAXEY, SAML. B.* [Born in Ky. Appointed from Ky.]
Bvt. 2nd Lieut. 7th Inf., 1 July, 1846. 2nd Lieut. 8th Inf., 23 Feb., 1847. Trans. to 7th Inf., 18 July, 1847. Resigned 17 Sept., 1849. Bvt. 1st Lieut., 20 Aug., 1847, for gallant and meritorious conduct at Contreras and Churubusco, Mex.

MAXFIELD, JOSEPH E. [Born in Mass. Appointed from the Army.]
Priv. and Sergt. Sig. Corps, 4 Jan., 1882, to 21 July, 1884. 2nd Lieut. Sig. Corps, 14 July, 1884. 1st Lieut., 19 Dec., 1890. Capt. (14 years' ser.), 22 July, 1898. Maj. Chf. Sig. Off. Vols., 20 May, 1898. Lieut. Col. Chf. Sig. Off. Vols., 18 July, 1898, to 17 April, 1899. Maj. Chf. Sig. Off. Vols., 17 April, 1899.

MAXON, MASON M.* [Born in Wis. Appointed from Wis.]
2nd Lieut. 10th Cav., 15 June, 1869. 1st Lieut., 24 April, 1875. R. Q. M., 1 Oct., 1881, to 21 April, 1887. Capt., 25 Dec., 1889. Retired for disability, 14 Jan., 1891.

MAXWELL, CHAS. D. [Born in Del. Appointed from Del.]
Asst. Surg., 30 Nov., 1836. Resigned 30 June, 1837.

MAXWELL, ERASTUS W. [Born in Maine. Appointed from Mass.]
2nd Lieut. 20th Inf., 13 June, 1877. Dismissed 26 Aug., 1878.

MAXWELL, JOSEPH E.* [Born in Ga. Appointed from Ga.]
Bvt. 2nd Lieut. 3rd Inf., 1 July, 1850. 2nd Lieut., 5 March, 1851. Killed 30 June, 1854, in action with Indians in New Mexico.

MAXWELL, MARCUS.* [Born in Ark. Appointed from Ark.]
2nd Lieut. 15th Inf., 1 July, 1886. 1st Lieut. of Inf., (15th), 30 Oct., 1893. Trans. to 2nd Inf., 13 Dec., 1893. Dismissed 5 July, 1894.

MAXWELL, PHILIP. [Born in Vt. Appointed from Vt.]
Asst. Surg., 13 July, 1832. Maj. Surg., 7 July, 1838. Disbanded 23 Sept., 1842.

MAXWELL, RALPH. [Born in Penn. Appointed from Penn.]
Capt. 57th Pa. Vols., 11 Dec., 1861. Resigned 8 Feb., 1863. 2nd Lieut. 11th Inf., 23 Feb., 1866. 1st Lieut., 1 May, 1866. Trans. to 20th Inf., 21 Sept., 1866. Resigned 1 Nov., 1867.

MAY, CHAS. A. [Born in D. C. Appointed from D. C.]
2nd Lieut. 2nd Drag., 8 June, 1836. 1st Lieut., 15 Dec., 1837. Capt., 2 Feb., 1841. Maj. 1st Drag., 3 March, 1855. Trans. to 2nd Drag., 23 Oct., 1855. Resigned 20 April, 1861. Bvt. Maj., 8 May, 1846, for gallant and distinguished service in the Battle of Palo Alto. Bvt. Lieut. Col., 9 May, 1846, for gallant and highly distinguished conduct at the Battle of Resca de la Palma. Bvt. Col., 23 Feb., 1847, for gallant and meritorious conduct at the Battle of Buena Vista.

MAY, CHAS. O.* [Born in Vt. Appointed from Vt.]
Bvt. 2nd Lieut. 6th Inf., 1 July, 1829. Killed in a duel, 19 Jan., 1830.

MAY, DANIEL O. [Born in ——. Appointed from Ind.]
2nd Lieut. 16th Inf., 22 May, 1847. Disbanded 20 July, 1848.

MAY, GEORGE W. [Born in England. Appointed from Army.]
Priv. Co. I, 5th Inf., 17 Aug., 1844, to 17 April, 1847. 2nd Lieut. of Inf., 8 March, 1847; 9th Inf., 9 April, 1847. 1st Lieut., 17 Feb., 1848. Disbanded 20 July, 1848.

MAY, JAMES H. [Born in Ind. Appointed from Army.]
Priv. Co. G, 9th Ind. Vols., 24 April to 29 July, 1861. Priv. and Corpl. Co. A, 2nd Batt., and Co. E, 1st Batt. 11th Inf., 12 Nov., 1861, to 1 Oct., 1863. 2nd Lieut. 12th Inf., 10 Aug., 1863. 1st Lieut., 31 Dec., 1863. Discharged 31 Dec., 1870. Bvt. Capt., 5 May, 1864, for gallant and meritorious service at the Battle of the Wilderness, Va.

MAY, JAMES R. [Born in Va. Appointed from Va.]
Cadet at Mil. Acad., 1 July, 1841, to 28 June, 1844. 2nd Lieut. of Inf., 4 March, 1847; Voltigeurs, 9 April, 1847. Disbanded 31 Aug., 1848.

MAY, JULIAN. [Born in D. C. Appointed from D. C.]
2nd Lieut. Mounted Rifles, 27 May, 1846. 1st Lieut., 31 Oct., 1848. R. Q. M., 1 Feb., 1855, to 22 May, 1859. Died 22 Nov., 1859. Bvt. 1st Lieut., 20 Aug., 1847, for gallant and meritorious conduct at Contreras and Churubusco, Mex.

MAY, WILL. T.* [Born in Ind. Appointed from Ind.]
2nd Lieut. 15th Inf., 13 June, 1879. 1st Lieut., 27 Feb., 1888. Capt., 26 April, 1898. Lieut. Col. 157th Ind. Vols., 10 May, 1898.

MAYER, BRANTZ. [Born in Md. Appointed from Md.]
Addl. P. M. Vols., 19 Feb., 1863. Bvt. Lieut. Col., 24 Nov., 1865, for faithful and meritorious service. Maj. P. M. U. S. A., 17 Jan., 1867. Retired 15 June, 1875. Died 23 Feb., 1879.

MAYER, MARTIN. [Born in Germany. Appointed from N. Y.]
Capt. 12th Inf., 14 May, 1861. Dismissed 16 June, 1863.

MAYNADIER, HENRY E.* [Born in Va. Appointed at Large.]
Bvt. 2nd Lieut. 1st Art., 1 July, 1851. 2nd Lieut., 29 Feb., 1852. 1st Lieut. 10th Inf., 3 March, 1855. R. Q. M., 7 April to 20 Oct., 1855. Reg. Adj., 20 Oct., 1855, to 1 Oct., 1858. Capt., 19 Jan., 1861. Maj. 12th Inf., 4 Nov., 1863. Col. 5th U. S. Vet. Vols., 27 March, 1865. Mustered out Vols., 30 Aug., 1866. Died 3 Dec., 1868. Bvt. Lieut. Col., 13 March, 1865, for faithful and meritorious service during the war. Bvt. Brig. Gen. Vols., 13 March, 1865, for gallant and meritorious service during the war, and particularly while commanding the Mortar flotilla under Admiral Foote, U. S. N., during operations upon Island No. 10 and other rebel forts on the Mississippi River. Bvt. Maj. Gen. Vols., 13 March, 1865, for distinguished service on the frontier while operating against hostile Indians, and accomplishing much toward bringing about peace with late hostile tribes.

MAYNADIER, WM.* [Born in Md. Appointed from D. C.]
Bvt. 2nd Lieut. Art., 1 July, 1827. 2nd Lieut. 1st Art., 1 July, 1827. 1st Lieut.,

31 May, 1834. Capt. Ord., 7 July, 1838. Maj., 5 May, 1861. Lieut. Col., 3 Aug., 1861. Col., 1 June, 1863. Died 3 July, 1871. Bvt. Brig. Gen., 13 March, 1865, for faithful and meritorious service in the Ord. Dept.

MAYNADIER, WM. M. [Born in Md. Appointed at Large.]
2nd Lieut. 1st Art., 1 May, 1861. 1st Lieut., 14 May, 1861. Bvt. Capt., 17 Sept., 1862, for gallant and meritorious service in the Battle of Antietam, Md. Capt. 1st Art., 4 June, 1864. Bvt. Maj., 13 March, 1865, for good conduct and gallant service during the war. Mustered out 8 Dec., 1870. Maj. P. M., 26 April, 1875. Retired for disability, 26 Sept., 1895. Died 19 June, 1898.

MAYS, JAMES F. [Born in Va. Appointed from Mo.]
Priv. Co. I, 2nd Drag., 17 Feb., 1858, to 9 March, 1859. Priv. Co. C, 45th and 48th Mo. Vols., 16 Sept., 1864, to Aug., 1865. 2nd Lieut. 14th Inf., 23 Feb., 1866. Died 21 July, 1866.

McADAM, WILLIAM T. [Born in Ohio. Appointed from Iowa.]
Chap. 57th Penn. Vols., 14 Dec., 1861, to 29 June, 1865. Post Chap., 16 June, 1880. Retired by operation of law, 5 Aug., 1887. Died 19 Feb., 1893.

McALESTER, MILES D.* [Born in N. Y. Appointed from Mich.]
Bvt. 2nd Lieut. Eng., 1 July, 1856. 2nd Lieut., 1 Dec., 1856. 1st Lieut., 2 May, 1861. Capt., 3 March, 1863. Maj., 7 March, 1867. Died 23 April, 1869. Bvt. Maj. and Lieut. Col., 1 July, 1862, for gallant and meritorious service in Peninsular campaign of 1862. Bvt. Col., 23 Aug., 1864, for highly meritorious service as Chief Eng. of Mil. Div. of West Miss., etc. Bvt. Brig. Gen., 9 April, 1865, for gallant and meritorious service at the Siege of Mobile, Ala.

McALEXANDER, ULYSSES G.* [Born in Minn. Appointed from Kans.]
2nd Lieut. 25th Inf., 12 June, 1887. 1st Lieut. 13th Inf., 16 Aug., 1894. Capt., 2 March, 1899. Capt. A. Q. M. Vols., 12 May, 1898, to 12 May, 1899.

McALISTER, JAMES. [Born in Tenn. Appointed from Tenn.]
2nd Lieut. 1st Inf., 3 Sept., 1837. 1st Lieut., 7 July, 1838. Resigned 10 June, 1839. Capt. 4th Tenn. Vols., 5 Oct., 1847, to 31 July, 1848. Died 30 Nov., 1849.

McALLISTER, JULIAN.* [Born in N. Y. Appointed at Large.]
2nd Lieut. 2nd Art., 1 July, 1847. Trans. to Ord., 13 April, 1848. 1st Lieut., 3 March, 1853. Capt., 1 July, 1861. Bvt. Maj. and Lieut. Col., 13 March, 1865, for faithful and meritorious service in the Ord. Dept. Bvt. Col., 13 March, 1865, for zeal, ability and faithfulness in the discharge of his duties as Senior Ord. Off. in the Dept. of the Pacific. Maj. Ord., 6 April, 1866. Lieut. Col., 23 June, 1874. Col., 1 June, 1881. Died 3 Jan., 1887.

McALLON, ANDREW J. [Born in Tenn. Appointed from Tenn.]
2nd Lieut. of Inf., 5 March, 1847; 14th Inf., 9 April, 1847. 1st Lieut., 22 May, 1847. Resigned 23 May, 1848.

McANANEY, WILLIAM D. [Born in N. Y. Appointed from Army.]
Priv., Blacksmith, Corpl., Sergt. and 1st Sergt. Troop M, 8th Cav., 11 June, 1879, to 6 Aug., 1884, under the name of William M. Clare. 2nd Lieut. 9th Cav., 4 Aug., 1884. 1st Lieut. of Cav. (8th), 1 July, 1891. Died 2 April, 1894.

McANDREW, JAMES W.* [Born in Penn. Appointed from Penn.]
2nd Lieut. 21st Inf., 11 June, 1888. 1st Lieut. 3rd Inf., 1 May, 1895. Capt., 2 March, 1899. Reg. Q. M., 2 March, 1899.

McARTHUR, JOHN C.* [Born in Minn. Appointed from S. Dak.]
2nd Lieut. 2nd Inf., 12 June, 1894. 1st Lieut. 3rd Inf., 26 April, 1898.

McARTHUR, JOSEPH H.* [Born in Mo. Appointed from Mo.]
Bvt. 2nd Lieut. 2nd Inf., 1 July, 1849. 2nd Lieut. 5th Inf., 12 Aug., 1850. 1st Lieut. 2nd Cav., 3 March, 1855. Capt., 28 June, 1860. 5th Cav., 3 Aug., 1861. Lieut. Col. 6th Pa. Cav., 11 Sept., 1861. Mustered out of Vol. Service, 3 Feb., 1862. Maj. 3rd Cav., 25 Sept., 1863. Retired 2 Nov., 1863, for disability.

McARTHUR, MALCOLM.* [Born in Maine. Appointed from Maine.]
2nd Lieut. and 1st Lieut. 17th Inf., 23 June, 1865. Adj. 1st Batt., 1 Jan., 1866, to 21 Sept., 1866. Capt., 18 Sept., 1867. Retired for disability, 26 Nov., 1884. Died 12 Jan., 1886.

McARTHUR, THOMAS.* [Born in Ohio. Appointed from Ohio.]
2nd Lieut. 6th Inf., 1 July, 1820. Resigned 24 Oct., 1820. Died 21 Feb., 1833.

McAULIFFE, JAMES R.* [Born in N. Y. Appointed from N. Y.]
2nd Lieut. 5th Art., 16 June, 1875. Died 21 Feb., 1882.

McBLAIN, JOHN F. [Born in Penn. Appointed from Army.]
Priv., Corpl. and Sergt. Co. L, 2nd Cav., 7 Oct., 1872, to 29 June, 1877. Priv., Corpl. and Sergt. Co. L, 2nd Cav., 22 Oct., 1878, to 16 July, 1880. 2nd Lieut. 9th Cav., 24 June, 1880. 1st Lieut., 11 Feb., 1887. Capt., 29 June, 1897.

McBLAIR, JOHN H., Jr. [Born in D. C. Appointed from D. C.]
1st Lieut. 15th Inf., 14 May, 1861. Wholly retired 6 Oct., 1863. Placed on retired list, 9 April, 1864, to date from 6 Oct., 1863; dropped from retired list 12 Nov., 1884. Appointed 1st Lieut. of Inf., 2 March, 1891, to rank from 14 May, 1861. Retired 4 March, 1891. Died 3 Dec., 1899.

McBRIDE, JAMES D. [Born in Ohio. Appointed from Ohio.]
Sergt. Co. I, 1st Ohio Vols., 16 April to 2 Aug., 1861. 2nd Lieut. 5th W. Va. Vols., 10 April, 1862. Resigned 8 Jan., 1863. Maj. 8th U. S. Col. Art., 20 Aug., 1864. Lieut. Col., 9 Feb., 1865. Bvt. Col. and Brig. Gen. Vols., 13 March, 1865, for gallant and meritorious service during the war. 2nd Lieut. 1st Cav., 20 Nov., 1867. Resigned 10 Sept., 1868.

McBRIDE, JOHN K. [Born in Ala. Appointed from Army.]
Priv. and Corpl. Co. H, 13th Inf., 6 May, 1847, to 10 May, 1848. 2nd Lieut. 13th Inf., 29 March, 1848. Disbanded 15 July, 1848.

McBRIDE, JOSEPH C. [Born in Ohio. Appointed from Iowa.]
Corpl. Co. B, 48th Ind. Vols., 16 Dec., 1861. 1st Lieut., 4 Nov., 1864. Capt., 21 May, 1865. Mustered out 15 July, 1865. 1st Lieut. 38th Inf., 22 Jan., 1867. Unassigned 11 Nov., 1869. Discharged 1 Oct., 1870. Bvt. Capt., 2 March, 1867, for gallant and meritorious service during the war.

McBROOM, WALTER S.* [Born in Ind. Appointed from Ind.]
2nd Lieut. 18th Inf., 12 June, 1895. 1st Lieut. of Inf., 12 July, 1898. Ass'd to 18th Inf., 1 Jan., 1899.

McCABE, ROBERT A. [Born in Penn. Appointed from Ind.]
Ensign 1st Inf., 3 Jan., 1812. 2nd Lieut., 31 Dec., 1812. 1st Lieut., 1 May, 1814. Disbanded 15 June, 1815. Reinstated as 2nd Lieut. 5th Inf., 17 May, 1816. 1st Lieut., 16 Oct., 1816. Capt., 1 May, 1824. Resigned 1 Oct., 1833. Retained — May, 1816 (in reorganization under Act of 3 March, 1815), as 2nd Lieut. 5th Inf., with Bvt. of 1st Lieut., from 1 May, 1814.

McCAFFERTY, NEIL J. [Born in Ireland. Appointed from Army.]
Priv., Corpl., Sergt. and 1st Sergt. Co. A, 1st (4th) Cav., 26 April, 1858, to 27 March, 1863. 2nd Lieut. 4th Cav., 19 Feb., 1863. 1st Lieut., 16 Feb., 1865. Capt., 13 Jan., 1868. Drowned 10 June, 1870. Bvt. 1st Lieut., 10 May, 1863, for gallant and meritorious service in Cav. action at Franklin, Tenn.

McCAIN, HENRY P.* [Born in Miss. Appointed from Miss.]
2nd Lieut. 3rd Inf., 14 June, 1885. 1st Lieut. 21st Inf., 24 Feb., 1892. Trans. to 14th Inf., 14 March, 1892. Capt., 2 March, 1899. Capt. A. J. A., 6 Jan., 1899.

McCALEB, THOS. S.* [Born in Va. Appointed from Va.]
2nd Lieut. 9th Inf., 16 June, 1875. 1st Lieut., 4 March, 1883. Capt., 22 April, 1892.

McCALL, CHAS. A. [Born in Mex. Appointed from Penn.]
Asst. Surg., 5 Aug., 1861. Resigned 1 Nov., 1865. Bvt. Capt. and Maj., 13 March, 1865, for faithful and meritorious service during the war.

McCALL, GEORGE A.* [Born in Penn. Appointed from Penn.]
2nd Lieut. 1st Inf., 1 July, 1822. Trans. to 4th Inf., 23 Dec., 1822. 1st Lieut., 25 Jan., 1829. Capt., 21 Dec., 1836. Bvt. Maj. A. A. G., 7 July, 1846, to 26 Dec., 1847. Maj. 3rd Inf., 26 Dec., 1847. Col. I. G., 10 June, 1850. Resigned 29 April, 1853. Bvt. Maj. and Lieut. Col., 9 May, 1846, for gallant conduct at Palo Alto and Resaca de la Palma. Maj. Gen. Penn. Vols., 15 May to 23 July, 1861. Brig. Gen. Vols., 17 May, 1861. Resigned 31 March, 1863. Died 25 Feb., 1868.

McCALL, HUGH. [Born in N. C. Appointed from S. C.]
Ensign 3rd Sub. Legion, 12 May, 1794. In 3rd Inf., 1 Nov., 1796. 1st Lieut., 1 July, 1798. Dep. P. M. G., 31 Jan., 1800. Capt., 19 Aug., 1800. Trans. to 2nd Inf., — April, 1802. Disbanded 15 June, 1815. Mil. Storekeeper, 31 March, 1818. Died 10 June, 1824. Bvt. Maj., 10 July, 1812.

McCALL, JAMES K. [Born in Tenn. Appointed from Tenn.]
2nd Lieut. 4th Inf., 27 June, 1856. Resigned 25 April, 1861.

McCALL, JOHN. [Born in ——. Appointed from N. Y.]
Surg. Mate 13th Inf., 15 April, 1812. Maj. Surg. 13th Inf., 21 Sept., 1814. Disbanded 15 June, 1815.

McCALL, JOHN D. [Born in South America. Appointed from Iowa.]
2nd Lieut. 1st Inf., 18 June, 1855. Died 26 Oct., 1855.

McCALL, WILLIAM C. [Born in N. J. Appointed from N. J.]
Capt. 14th Inf., 19 Sept., 1861. Resigned 31 July, 1863.

McCALLA, ROBT. P. [Born in Penn. Appointed from Penn.]
Asst. Apothecary Gen., 16 May, 1820. Disbanded 1 June, 1821.

McCALLA, WM. L. [Born in ——. Appointed from Ohio.]
Chap., 29 April, 1816. Disbanded 14 April, 1818.

McCALLUM, WM. B.* [Born in N. Y. Appointed from Tenn.]
2nd Lieut. 5th Art., 17 June, 1867. 1st Lieut., 1 Jan., 1871. Adj., 15 April, 1887. Died 26 March, 1889.

McCALMONT, JOHN S.* [Born in Penn. Appointed from Penn.]
Bvt. 2nd Lieut. 3rd Inf., 1 July, 1842. 2nd Lieut. 8th Inf., 10 Oct., 1842. Resigned 1 July, 1843. Col. 10th Penn. Res., 20 July, 1861. Resigned 9 Maj., 1862.

McCAMMON, WM. W. [Born in Ohio. Appointed from Mo.]
1st Lieut. 22nd Mo. Vols., 15 Oct., 1861. Capt., 24th Mo. Vols., 22 July, 1862. Capt. A. A. G. Vols., 3 Feb., 1865. Bvt. Maj. Vols., 13 March, 1865, for gallant and meritorious service during the war. Mustered out 2 Feb., 1866. 2nd Lieut. 14th Inf., 18 June, 1867. Reg. Adj., 23 July, 1869. 1st Lieut., 10 Dec., 1873. Capt., 29 Sept., 1891. Maj. A. A. G. Vols., 12 May, 1898, to 30 Nov., 1898. Medal of Honor for most distinguished gallantry in action at Corinth, Miss., in voluntarily assuming command of his company, then under fire, on 3 Oct., 1862, and so continuing in command of the same until the repulse and retreat of the enemy on 4 Oct., 1862; while 1st Lieut. Co. E, 24th Mo. Inf., and on duty as Provost Marshal 3rd Div. Army of the Miss.

McCAMMON, WILLIAM W., Jr. [Born in Utah. Appointed at Large.]
Priv. and Corpl. Co. E, 14th Inf., 16 May, 1898, to 11 June, 1899. 2nd Lieut. 23rd Inf., 1 June, 1899. Trans. to 4th Inf., 3 Feb., 1900.

McCANDLESS, IGNATIUS F. [Born in Va. Appointed from Va.]
2nd Lieut. Rifles, 22 July, 1818. Resigned 1 Jan., 1819.

McCARTHY, DANIEL E.* [Born in N. Y. Appointed from N. Y.]
2nd Lieut. 12th Inf., 11 June, 1881. 1st Lieut., 2 Jan., 1888. Capt. A. Q. M., 14 Oct., 1896. Capt. A. Q. M., 22 Dec., 1896. Graduate of the Infantry and Cavalry School, 1887.

McCARTHY, FLORENCE L. [Born in N. Y. Appointed from N. Y.]
Priv. Co. G, 22nd N. Y. Vols., 18 June to 24 July, 1863. 1st Lieut. 59th N. Y. Vols., 3 Jan., 1865. Capt., 18 May, 1865. Mustered out 30 June, 1865. 2nd Lieut. 27th Inf., 22 Jan., 1867. 1st Lieut., 4 Nov., 1867. Dismissed 8 April, 1869.

McCARTY, JAMES M. [Born in Penn. Appointed from Penn.]
2nd Lieut. 9th Inf., 16 Feb., 1881. Wholly retired 13 July, 1885.

McCARTNEY, JOHN. [Born in Ireland. Appointed from Penn.]
Ensign 16th Inf., 17 March, 1814. 3rd Lieut., 1 May, 1814. 2nd Lieut., 6 Nov., 1814. Disbanded 15 June, 1815. 2nd Lieut. 5th Inf., 16 July, 1816. 1st Lieut., 3 May, 1820. Disbanded 1 June, 1821.

McCARTY, JAMES C. [Born in Tenn. Appointed from Tenn.]
Capt. of Inf., 27 Fem., 1847. Mil. Storekeeper Q. M. D., 14 June, 1858. Died 25 Nov., 1862. *u*

McCARTY, JOHN. [Born in N. Y. Appointed from Wash. Ter.]
Brigade Chap. Mexican War, 11 April, 1847, to 6 July, 1848. Chap. Post of Jefferson Barracks, 18 Sept., 1848. Resigned 31 Dec., 1852. Chap. Post of Columbia Barracks, 31 Jan., 1853; of Fort Steilacoom, 19 Dec., 1864; and of Fort Vancouver, 26 Nov., 1865. Post Chap. U. S. A., 3 April, 1867. Retired 16 Sept., 1867. Died 10 May, 1881.

McCARTY, JUSTUS I. [Born in N. Y. Appointed from N. Y.]
Maj. 10th Inf., 9 April, 1847. Disbanded 26 Aug., 1848. Died 8 June, 1881.

McCASKEY, DOUGLAS. [Born in Minn. Appointed from Army.]
Priv. and Corpl. Troop H, 4th Cav., 27 April, 1894, to 26 April, 1897. Priv., Corpl. and Sergt. Troop K, 6th Cav., 14 May, 1898, to 16 Nov., 1899. 2nd Lieut. 4th Cav., 1 Oct., 1899.

McCASKEY, EDWARD W.* [Born in Penn. Appointed from Penn.]
2nd Lieut. 21st Inf., 1 July, 1886. 1st Lieut. 4th Inf., 17 Sept., 1892. Trans. to 21st Inf., 27 Dec., 1892. Capt., 2 March, 1899. Graduate of the Infantry and Cavalry School, 1889.

McCASKEY, GARRISON. [Born in Minn. Appointed from Army.]
2nd Lieut. 25th Inf., 10 Oct., 1898.

McCASKEY, WALTER B. [Born in Penn. Appointed from Penn.]
Priv. and 1st Sergt. Co. L, 4th Penn. Vols., 2 July to 6 July, 1898. 2nd Lieut., 7 July, 1898, to 16 Nov., 1898. 2nd Lieut. 21st Inf., 10 April, 1899.

McCASKEY, WM. S. [Born in Penn. Appointed from Penn.]
Priv. Co. F, 1st Penn. Vols., 20 April, 1861. Discharged 26 July, 1861. 1st Sergt. Co. B, 79th Penn. Vols., 5 Sept., 1861. 2nd Lieut. 79th Penn. Vols., 9 Oct., 1862. 1st Lieut., 10 April, 1863. Capt., 1 July, 1863. Mustered out 12 July, 1865. 2nd Lieut. and 1st Lieut. 13th Inf., 23 Feb., 1866. Adj. 2nd Batt., 20 July, 1866, to 21 Sept., 1866. Trans. to 22nd Inf., 21 Sept., 1866. Reg. Adj., 1 Jan., 1867, to 12 May, 1867. R. Q. M., 1 Feb., 1868, to 14 July, 1869. Trans. to 20th Inf., 14 July, 1869. R. Q. M., 1 Jan., 1871, to 5 Sept., 1871. Capt., 5 Sept., 1871. Maj., 31 May, 1895. Lieut. Col. 2nd Inf., 30 Aug., 1898. Trans. to 20th Inf., 30 Dec., 1898. Col. 7th Inf., 29 Jan., 1900. Trans. to 20th Inf., 3 Feb., 1900.

McCAULEY, CHAS. A. H.* [Born in Md. Appointed from Penn.]
2nd Lieut. 3rd Art., 15 June, 1870. Trans. to 3rd Cav., 7 Oct., 1878. 1st Lieut., 5 May, 1879. Capt. A. Q. M., 18 Feb., 1881. Maj. Q. M., 8 Aug., 1894. Lieut. Col. D. Q. M. G., 13 July, 1899.

McCAULLAY, EDMUND L. [Born in Ohio. Appointed from Ohio.]
Corpl. Co. D, 93rd Ohio Vols., 19 Aug., 1862, to 19 March, 1864. 2nd Lieut. 27th U. S. Col. Inf., 19 March, 1864. 1st Lieut., 1 Oct., 1864. Mustered out 21 Sept., 1865. 2nd Lieut. 27th Inf., 28 July, 1866. 1st Lieut., 5 March, 1867. Trans. to 9th Inf., 14 June, 1869. Unassigned 4 April, 1870. Discharged 31 Dec., 1870.

McCAULY, JOHN. [Born in Md. Appointed from Md.]
2nd Lieut. 7th Inf., 28 Jan., 1820. Died 4 Sept., 1821.

McCAW, WALTER D. [Born in Va. Appointed from Va.]
Asst. Surg., 20 Aug., 1884. Capt. Asst. Surg., 20 Aug., 1889. Maj. Brig. Surg. Vols., 4 June, 1898, to 30 Nov., 1898. Maj. Surg. 42nd Vols., 17 Aug., 1899.

McCAWLEY, HENRY M. [Born in Va. Appointed from Va.]
2nd Lieut. 3rd Penn. Cav., 19 Aug., 1861. Mustered out 18 Jan., 1862. 2nd Lieut. 117th U. S. Col. Troops, 6 March, 1865. Mustered out 9 May, 1865. 2nd Lieut. 25th U. S. Col. Troops, 16 June, 1865. Mustered out 6 Dec., 1865. 2nd Lieut. 13th Inf., 22 Jan., 1867. 1st Lieut., 10 Oct., 1871. Died 30 June, 1879.

McCHAIN, GEORGE. [Born in N. Y. Appointed from N. Y.]
Ensign 25th Inf., 14 April, 1812. 2nd Lieut., 16 April, 1813. 1st Lieut., 30 Sept., 1813. R. Q. M., — Sept., 1813, to June, 1815. Trans. to 6th Inf., 17 May, 1815. Died 19 Oct., 1818.

McCLANNAHAN, NELSON. [Born in Tenn. Appointed form Tenn.]
1st Lieut. of Inf., 3 March, 1847; 14th Inf., 9 April, 1847. Disbanded 25 July, 1848.

McCLASKEY, GEORGE B. [Born in ——. Appointed from Tenn.]
3rd Lieut. 2nd Inf., 30 March, 1814. 2nd Lieut., 1 May, 1814. Disbanded 15 June, 1815. Reinstated in 4th Inf., 17 May, 1816. 1st Lieut., 31 Dec., 1816. Dismissed 23 July, 1818.

McCLEARY, DANIEL. [Born in Ohio. Appointed from Ohio.]
2nd Lieut. of Inf., 8 March, 1847; 15th Inf., 9 April, 1847. R. Q. M., 17 May to 29 June, 1847. Died 29 June, 1847.

McCLEARY, JOHN.* [Born in Ohio. Appointed from Ohio.]
Bvt. 2nd Lieut. 3rd Inf., 1 July, 1854. 2nd Lieut. 6th Inf., 26 March, 1855. 1st Lieut., 5 June, 1860. Capt., 17 May, 1861. Died 25 Feb., 1868. Bvt. Maj., 2 July, 1863, for gallant and meritorious service at the Battle of Gettysburg, Penn.

McCLEAVE, ROBERT. [Born in N. M. Appointed from Army.]
Priv. and Corpl. Co. G, and Corpl. Co. C, and Sergt. Maj. 1st Inf., 15 Aug., 1894, to 3 May, 1898. 2nd Lieut. 7th Art., 12 April, 1898. Trans. to 2nd Inf., 8 June, 1898 (to rank from 26 April), 1st Lieut., 2 March, 1899.

McCLEAVE, WM. [Born in Ireland. Appointed from Cal.]
Priv. Co. K, 1st Drag., 7 Oct., 1850. Sergt., 1 Aug., 1851. Priv., 26 Dec., 1851. Corpl., 1 June, 1852. Sergt., 11 April, 1853. 1st Sergt., 1 June, 1853. Discharged 1 Oct., 1855. 1st Sergt. Co. K, 1st Drag., 1 Oct., 1855. Discharged 1 Oct., 1860. Capt. 1st Cal. Cav., 23 Aug., 1861. Maj., 1 May, 1863. Bvt. Lieut. Col. Vols., 13 March, 1865, for his successful pursuit of and gallantry in the engagement with the Apache Indians. Mustered out 19 Oct., 1866. 2nd Lieut. 8th Cav., 28 July, 1866. 1st Lieut., 6 March, 1867. Capt., 10 Aug., 1869. Retired 20 March, 1879, for disability.

McCLEERY, JAMES. [Born in Ohio. Appointed from Ohio.]
Priv. Co. D, 19th Ohio Vols., 27 April, 1861. 2nd Lieut. 41st Ohio Vols., 26 Aug., 1861. 1st Lieut., 9 Jan., 1862. Capt., 26 May, 1863. Bvt. Maj. Vols., 13 March, 1865, for valuable and constant service during the war. Lieut. Col., 13 March, 1865, for gallant and meritorious service at the Battles of Pittsburg Landing and Stone River, Tenn., and Col. and Brig. Gen. Vols., 3 March, 1865, for gallant and distinguished service in the Battles of Shiloh and Stone River, Tenn.; Chickamauga, Ga.; Mission Ridge, East Tenn., and for markel faithfulness during the war. Mustered out 27 Nov., 1865. Capt. 45th Inf., 28 July, 1866. Unassigned 22 July, 1869. Retired 15 Dec., 1870. Died 5 Nov., 1871. Bvt. Maj., 2 March, 1867, for gallant and meritorious service at the Battle of Mission Ridge, Tenn.

McCLEERY, JOHN B. [Born in Penn. Appointed from Kan.]
Post Chap., 20 May, 1881.

McCLEERY, WM P. [Born in Penn. Appointed from Penn.]
2nd Lieut. 18th Inf., 14 May, 1861. 1st Lieut., 24 Oct., 1861. Capt., 31 Dec., 1864. Resigned 11 July, 1868. Bvt. Capt., 13 Dec., 1862, for gallant and meritorious service at the Battle of Murfreesboro, Tenn.

McCLELLAN, ELY. [Born in Penn. Appointed from Penn.]
1st Lieut. Asst. Surg., 5 Aug., 1861. Bvt. Capt. and Maj., 13 March, 1865, for faithfuland meritorious service during the war. Capt. Asst. Surg., 28 July, 1866. Maj. Surg., 26 June, 1876. Lieut. Col. Surg., 11 Sept., 1891. Died 8 May, 1893.

McCLELLAN, GEORGE B.* [Born in Penn. Appointed from Penn.]
Bvt. 2nd Lieut. Eng., 1 July, 1846. 2nd Lieut., 24 April, 1847. 1st Lieut., 1 July, 1853. Capt. 1st Cav., 3 March, 1855. Resigned 16 Jan., 1857. Bvt. 1st Lieut., 20 Aug., 1847, for gallant and meritorious conduct at Contreras and Churubusco. Bvt. Capt., 13 Sept., 1847, for gallant and meritorious conduct at Chapultepec. Maj. Gen. Ohio Vols., 23 April, 1861. Maj. Gen. U. S. A., 14 May, 1861. Commander-in-Chief of the Army, 1 Nov., 1861, to 11 March, 1862. By resolution of the House of Representatives, 16 July, 1861, it was "*Resolved*, That the thanks of this House be presented to Maj. Gen. George B. McClellan and the officers and soldiers under his command for the series of brilliant and decisive victories which they have recently achieved by their skill and bravery over traitors and rebels in arms on the battlefields of Western Va." Resigned 8 Nov., 1864. Died 29 Oct., 1885.

McCLELLAN, JOHN* [Born in Penn. Appointed from Penn.]
Bvt. 2nd Lieut. Art., 1 July, 1826. 2nd Lieut. 1st Art., 1 July, 1826. Reg. Adj., 21 Oct., 1831, to 1 Dec., 1833. 1st Lieut., 30 Sept., 1833. Resigned 19 Nov., 1836. Capt. Top. Eng., 7 July, 1838. Died 1 Sept., 1854. Bvt. Maj., 20 Aug., 1847, for gallant and meritorious conduct at Contreras and Churubusco. Bvt. Lieut. Col., 13 Sept., 1847, for gallant and meritorious conduct in military operations before the City of Mexico..

McCLELLAN, JOHN.* [Born in Ill. Appointed from Minn.]
2nd Lieut. 5th Art., 17 June, 1867. 1st Lieut. 5 Jan., 1870. Capt., 25 Oct., 1894. Maj. Chf. Ord. Off. Vols., 18 July, 1898, to 12 May, 1899. Graduate of the Artillery School, 1888.

M CLELLAND, GEORGE C.* [Born in Penn. Appointed from Penn.]
Bvt. 2nd Lieut. 3rd Inf., 1 July, 1843. Resigned 30 April, 1846. Corpl. 1st Penn. Vols., 8 Dec., 1846. Discharged 17 March, 1847. 2nd Lieut. of Inf., 16 Feb., 1847; 11th Inf., 9 April, 1847. Cashiered 13 Oct., 1847. Died 26 Oct., 1888.

McCLELLAND, ROBT. [Born in ——. Appointed from N. Y.]
Ensign 6th Inf., 3 Jan., 1812. 2nd Lieut., 4 Oct., 1812. 1st Lieut., 1 May, 1814. Disbanded 15 June, 1815. Reinstated 17 May, 1816, in Corps Art. Disbanded 1 June, 1821.

McCLERMONT, ROBT. [Born in N. Y. Appointed from D. C.]
Sergt. and 1st Sergt. Troop D, 11th N. Y. Cav., 2 Dec., 1861. 2nd Lieut., 20 Aug., 1864. Mustered out 30 Sept., 1865. 2nd Lieut. 4th Cav., 30 Jan., 1866. 1st Lieut., 28 July, 1866. Capt. 41st Inf., 22 Jan., 1867. Unassigned 11 Nov., 1869. Ass'd to 11th Inf., 1 Jan., 1871. Died 23 Dec., 1873.

McCLERNAND, EDWARD J.* [Born in Ill. Appointed at Large.]
2nd Lieut. 2nd Cav., 15 June, 1870. 1st Lieut., 9 May, 1879. Capt., 24 March, 1890. Lieut. Col. A. A. G. Vols., 9 May, 1898, to 16 Aug., 1899. Col. 44th U. S. Vols., 17 Aug., 1899. Bvt. 1st Lieut., 27 Feb., 1890, for gallantry in the pursuit of Indians and in action against them in the Bear Paw Mountains, Mont., 30 Sept., 1877. Medal of Honor for most distinguished gallantry in action against hostile Nez Perce Indians at Bear Paw Mountain, Mont., 30 Sept., 1877, in command of a troop, attacking a band of hostiles and conducting the combat with excellent skill and boldness; while 2nd Lieut. 2nd Cav.

McCLINTOCK, JOHN. [Born in Penn. Appointed from Penn.]
1st Lieut. 14th Inf., 14 May, 1861. Capt., 30 April, 1863. Trans. to 18th Inf., 21 March, 1866. Trans. to 36th Inf., 21 Sept., 1866. Unassigned 19 May, 1869. Mustered out 1 Jan., 1871. Bvt. Capt., 2 July, 1863, for gallant and meritorious service at the Battle of Gettysburg, Penn. Bvt. Maj., 13 March, 1865, for gallant and meritorious service during the war.

McCLINTOCK, JOHN. [Born in Wis. Appointed from N. Y.]
Maj. 203rd N. Y. Vols., 22 July, 1898, to 25 March, 1899. 2nd Lieut. 11th Inf., 22 March, 1899. Trans. to 5th Cav., 15 May, 1899 (to rank from 11 April, 1899). Capt. 46th U. S. Vols., 17 Aug., 1899.

McCLINTOCK, WM. L. [Born in Mass. Appointed from Army.]
Priv. and Sergt. 3rd Art., 1 July, 1812, to 20 May, 1813. 3rd Lieut. 3rd Art., 20 May, 1813. 2nd Lieut., 20 June, 1813. Trans. to Corps Art., 12 May, 1814. 1st Lieut., 29 Sept., 1817. Trans. to 4th Art., 1 June, 1821. Capt., 11 Aug., 1823. Trans. to 3rd Art., 31 Jan., 1827. Maj. 2nd Art., 27 June, 1843. Trans. to 3rd Art., 2 Dec., 1843. Died 29 Oct., 1848. Bvt. Maj., 11 Aug., 1833, for ten years' faithful service in one grade.

McCLOSKEY, MANUS.* [Born in Penn. Appointed form Penn.]
2nd Lieut. 5th Art., 26 April, 1898.

McCLOUD, COLLIN. [Born in ——. Appointed from Ohio.]
2nd Lieut. 26th Inf., 20 May, 1813. Trans. to 19th Inf., 12 May, 1814. Trans. to 3rd Inf., 17 May, 1815. Resigned 31 Dec., 1818.

McCLUNG, CHAS. [Born in Ala. Appointed from Ala.]
2nd Lieut. 13th Inf., 5 May, 1847. Resigned 31 Dec., 1847.

McCLURE, ALBERT N. [Born in Ky. Appointed from Ky.]
2nd Lieut. 14th Inf., 15 Feb., 1899.

McCLURE, CHAS. [Born in Penn. Appointed from Penn.]
Capt. C. S. Vols., 28 April, 1862. Bvt. Maj., Lieut. Col. and Col. Vols., 21 Oct., 1865, for faithful and meritorious service. Capt. C. S. U. S. A., 17 Aug., 1866. Bvt. Maj., 17 Aug., 1866, for faithful service in the Sub. Dept. Maj. P. M., 30 Aug., 1880.

McCLURE, CHARLES.* [Born in Ill. Appointed from Ill.]
2nd Lieut. 18th Inf., 13 June, 1879. 1st Lieut., 21 June, 1887. Capt., 30 Jan., 1895. Maj. J. A. Vols., 17 April, 1899.

McCLURE, CHARLES, Jr. [Born in Iowa. Appointed from Minn.]
2nd Lieut. 1st Inf., 1 June, 1899.

McCLURE, DANIEL.* [Born in Ind. Appointed from Ind.]
Bvt. 2nd Lieut. Mounted Rifles, 1 July, 1849. Resigned 30 Nov., 1850. Maj. and P. M., 23 Oct., 1858. Bvt. Lieut. Col., 13 March, 1865, for faithful and meritorious service during the war. Bvt. Col., 13 March, 1865, for faithful and meritorious service in the Pay Dept. Col. Asst. P. M. G., 28 July, 1866. Retired by operation of law 30 Dec., 1888.

McCLURE, GEORGE W.* [Born in N. Y. Appointed from N. Y.]
Bvt. 2nd Lieut. 5th Inf., 1 July, 1830. Trans. to 1st Drag., 14 Aug., 1833. 2nd Lieut., 31 May, 1834. Died 21 July, 1834.

McCLURE, JAMES.* [Born in Penn. Appointed from Penn.]
Bvt. 2nd Lieut. 1st Inf., 1 July, 1833. 2nd Lieut., 4 Sept., 1836. Died 5 April, 1838.

McCLURE, NATHANIEL F.* [Born in Wis. Appointed from Iowa.]
2nd Lieut. 4th Cav., 12 June, 1887. 1st Lieut. 5th Cav., 6 June, 1894.

McCLURE, SAMUEL V.* [Born in Penn. Appointed from Penn.]
2nd Lieut. 7th Inf., 12 June, 1896. Retired for disability, with rank of 1st Lieut., 16 Sept., 1898.

McCOACH, DAVID. [Born in Penn. Appointed from Penn.]
2nd Lieut. 7th Art., 9 July, 1898. Trans. to 5th Art., 4 April, 1899.

McCOMAS, DAVID H. [Born in Md. Appointed from Mich.]
Priv. and Sergt. Co. E, 8th Mich. Vols., 30 Sept., 1861, to 15 June, 1865. 2nd Lieut. 45th Inf., 7 March, 1867. Unassigned 22 July, 1869. Resigned 26 July, 1870.

McCOMAS, ELISHA W. [Born in Va. Appointed from Va.]
Capt. of Inf., 23 Feb., 1847; 11th Inf., 9 April, 1847. Disbanded 20 July, 1848.

McCONIHE, SAML. [Born in N. H. Appointed from N. Y.]
Capt. 93rd N. Y. Vols., 9 Jan., 1862. Maj., 3 Dec., 1863. Mustered out 15 Feb., 1865. Bvt. Lieut. Col., Col. and Brig. Gen. Vols., 13 March, 1865, for conspicuous gallantry in the Battles of the Wilderness and Spottsylvania, and for gallant and meritorious service during the war. 2nd Lieut. and 1st Lieut. 14th Inf., 23 Feb., 1866. Bvt. Capt., 2 March, 1867, for gallant and meritorious service in the Battle of the Wilderness, Va. Bvt. Maj., 2 March, 1867, for gallant and meritorious service in the Battle of Spottsylvania, Va. Bvt. Lieut. Col., 2 March, 1867, for gallant and meritorious service during the war. Capt. 14th Inf., 25 Feb., 1876. Died 7 Sept., 1897.

McCONNELL, EDWARD. [Born in Ill. Appointed from Ill.]
1st Lieut. 16th Inf., 31 Aug., 1861. Capt., 30 Sept., 1864. Resigned 19 March, 1866. Bvt. Capt., 31 Dec., 1862, for gallant and meritorious service at the Battle of Murfreesboro, Tenn. Bvt. Maj., 1 Sept., 1864, for gallant and meritorious service during the Atlanta campaign and at the Battle of Jonesboro, Ga.

McCONNELL, FRANCIS J. [Born in Conn. Appointed from Del.]
2nd Lieut. 12th Inf., 10 April, 1899.

McCONNELL, JOSEPH. [Born in Mich. Appointed from Army.]
Priv. 18th Inf., 16 Sept. to 4 Nov., 1861. 2nd Lieut. 18th Inf., 30 Oct., 1861. 1st Lieut., 11 Aug., 1862. Died 14 Jan., 1863, of wounds received at Battle of Murfreesboro, Tenn. Bvt. Capt., 31 Dec., 1862, for gallant and meritorious service at the Battle of Murfreesboro, Tenn.

McCONNELL, THOMAS R.* [Born in Ga. Appointed from Ga.]
Bvt. 2nd Lieut. 3rd Inf., 1 July, 1846. 2nd Lieut. 4th Inf., 16 Feb., 1847. 1st Lieut., 8 Oct., 1848. Reg. Adj., 7 May, 1850, to 19 May, 1854. Capt., 3 Feb., 1855. Resigned 11 March, 1856. Bvt. 1st Lieut., 8 Sept., 1847, for gallant and meritorious conduct at Molino del Rey. Bvt. Capt., 13 Sept., 1847, for gallant and meritorious conduct at Chapultepec. Died 20 April, 1861.

McCOOK, ALEXR. McD.* [Born in Ohio. Appointed from Ohio.]
Bvt. 2nd Lieut. 3rd Inf., 1 July, 1852. 2nd Lieut., 30 June, 1854. 1st Lieut., 6 Dec., 1858. Col. 1st Ohio Vols., 16 April, 1861. Capt. 3rd Inf., 14 May, 1861. Bvt. Maj., 21 July, 1861, for gallant and meritorious service in the Battle of Bull Run, Va. Mustered out of Vol. Service 16 Aug., 1861. Brig. Gen. Vols., 3 Sept., 1861. Bvt. Lieut. Col., 3 March, 1862, for gallant and meritorious service in the capture of Nashville, Tenn. Bvt. Col., 7 April, 1862, for gallant and meritorious service in the Battle of Shiloh, Tenn. Maj. Gen. Vols., 17 July, 1862. Bvt. Brig. Gen., 13 March, 1865, for gallant and meritorious service in the Battle of Perryville, Ky. Bvt Maj. Gen., 13 March, 1865, for gallant and meritorious service in the field during the war. Resigned Vol. commission 21 Oct., 1865. Lieut. Col. 26th Inf., 5 March, 1867. Trans. to 10th Inf., 15 March, 1869. Col. A. de C. to Gen. Sherman, 11 June, 1875, to 15 Dec., 1880. Col. 6th Inf., 16 Dec., 1880. Brig. Gen., 11 July, 1890. Maj. Gen., 9 Nov., 1894. Retired by operation of law, 22 April, 1895.

M COOK, EDWARD M. [Born in Ohio. Appointed from Ind.]
2nd Lieut. 1st Cav., 8 May, 1861. 4th Cav., 3 Aug., 1861. 1st Lieut., 17 July, 1862.

Maj. 2nd Ind. Cav., 29 Sept., 1861. Lieut. Col., 11 Feb., 1862. Col., 30 April, 1862. Brig. Gen. Vols., 27 April, 1864. Mustered out of Vol. Service 15 Jan., 1866. Resigned 9 May, 1866. Bvt. 1st Lieut., 7 April, 1862, for gallant and meritorious service at the Battle of Shiloh, Tenn. Bvt. Capt., 8 Oct., 1862, for gallant and meritorious service at the Battle of Perryville, Ky. Bvt. Maj., 20 Sept., 1863, for gallant and meritorious service at the Battle of Chickamauga, Ga. Bvt. Lieut. Col., 27 Jan., 1864, for gallant and meritorious service during the Cav. operations in East Tenn. Bvt. Col., 13 March, 1865, for gallant and meritorious service in the capture of Selma, Ala. Bvt. Brig. Gen., 13 March, 1865, for gallant and meritorious service in the field during the war.

McCOOK, PAUL H. [Born in Penn. Appointed from Penn.]
Priv. Co. D, 1st Penn. Vols., 11 May, 1898, to 16 Sept., 1899. 2nd Lieut. 5th Inf., 9 Sept., 1898. 1st Lieut. 2nd Inf., 10 Oct., 1899.

McCOOL, JOSEPH A. [Born in Penn. Appointed from Penn.]
Priv. Co. D, 25th Penn. Vols., 18 April to 29 July, 1861. 2nd Lieut. 3rd Inf., 26 April, 1861. 1st Lieut., 20 May, 1861. R. Q. M., 1 Dec., 1861, to 3 Oct., 1863. Capt., 3 Oct., 1863. Dismissed 8 Jan., 1864. Died 6 June, 1867.

McCORKLE, HENRY L. [Born in Tenn. Appointed from Tenn.]
2nd Lieut. of Inf. (25th), 1 Aug., 1891. 1st Lieut., 26 April, 1898. Killed in action at El Caney, Cuba., 1 July, 1898.

McCORMICK, CHARLES. [Born in D. C. Appointed from D. C.]
Asst. Surg., 30 Aug., 1836. Maj. Surg., 7 Dec., 1853. Lieut. Col. Asst. Med. Pur., 26 June, 1876. Died 28 April, 1877. Bvt. Lieut. Col., 13 March, 1865, for faithful and meritorious service during the war.

McCORMICK, LOYD S.* [Born in Ohio. Appointed from Ohio.]
2nd Lieut. 10th Cav., 15 June, 1876. Trans. to 7th Cav., 26 June, 1876. 1st Lieut., 30 June, 1878. Reg. Adj., 14 Sept., 1887, to ——. Capt., 17 July, 1895. Graduate of the Infantry and Cavalry School, 1887. R. Q. M., 5 June, 1899.

McCORMICK, THOS. H. [Born in Penn. Appointed from Penn.]
2nd Lieut. 1st Cav., 27 March, 1861. 1st Lieut., 7 May, 1861. 4th Cav., 3 Aug., 1861. Capt., 14 Dec., 1862. Dismissed 25 July, 1865.

McCORMICK, WILLIAM J. [Born in D. C. Appointed from D. C.]
2nd Lieut. 6th Inf., 5 Aug., 1861. Dismissed 26 July, 1862.

McCORNACK, WILLARD H.* [Born in Ill. Appointed from Ill.]
Addl. 2nd Lieut. 9th Cav., 11 June, 1897. 2nd Lieut. 1st Cav., 31 May, 1898. Trans. to 9th Cav., 27 Aug., 1898.

McCOSKRY, CHAS N. [Born in Penn. Appointed from Penn.]
Post Surg., 12 April, 1820. Asst. Surg., 1 June, 1821. Died 16 Nov., 1821.

McCOWN, JOHN P.* [Born in Tenn. Appointed from Tenn.]
2nd Lieut 4th Art., 1 July, 1840. 1st Lieut., 30 Sept., 1843. R. Q. M., 29 March, 1847, to 12 Jan., 1849. Capt., 9 Jan., 1851. Resigned 17 May, 1861. Bvt. Capt., 18 April, 1847, for gallant and meritorious conduct at Cerro Gordo. Died 22 Jan., 1879.

McCOY, FRANK B. [Born in Ga. Appointed from Ga.]
2nd Lieut. 24th Inf., 26 Nov., 1880. Trans. to 3rd Inf., 20 Feb., 1883. 1st Lieut., 1 Feb., 1887. Capt. 2nd Inf., 26 April, 1898. Trans. to 3rd Inf., 15 Nov., 1899. Lieut. Col. 12th Minn. Vols., 7 May, to muster out, 5 Nov., 1898.

McCOY, FRANK R.* [Born in Penn. Appointed from Penn.]
Addl. 2nd Lieut. 8th Cav., 11 June, 1897. 2nd Lieut. 7th Cav., 11 March, 1898. Trans. to 10th Cav., 4 May, 1898.

McCOY, JAMES C. [Born in Penn. Appointed from Ohio.]
1st Lieut. 54th Ohio Vols., 21 Oct., 1861. Capt., 10 March, 1863, to 19 July, 1863. Capt. A. de C. Vols., 11 March, 1863. Maj. A. de C. Vols., 4 July, 1863. Bvt. Lieut. Col. Vols., 13 March, 1865, for meritorious service in the campaigns of Atlanta and Savannah, Ga., and the Carolinas. Mustered out 1 Sept., 1866. 2nd Lieut. 2nd Inf., 26 July, 1866. 1st Lieut., 29 Dec., 1868. Unassigned 17 April, 1869. Ass'd to 4th Art., 15 Dec., 1870. Addl. Col. A. de C. to Gen. Sherman, 11 Aug., 1866, to 8 March, 1869, and with rank of Col., 8 March, 1869, to 29 May, 1875. Bvt. 1st Lieut., 2 March, 1867, for gallant and meritorious service at the Battle of Shiloh, Tenn. Bvt. Capt., 2 March, 1867, for gallant and meritorious service in the Siege of Vicksburg, Miss. Bvt. Maj., 2 March, 1867, for gallant and meritorious service in the Battle of Atlanta, Ga. Bvt. Lieut. Col., 2 March, 1867, for gallant and meritorious service in the Battle of Bentonville, N. C. Died 29 May, 1875.

McCOY, J. ESPY. [Born in Ohio. Appointed from D. C.]
2nd Lieut. 7th Inf., 1 Sept., 1879. 1st Lieut., 15 May, 1889. Died 23 July, 1889.

McCOY, JOHN. [Born in Tenn. Appointed from Tenn.]
Corpl. and 1st Sergt. Co. F, 2nd Tenn. Vols., 23 Sept., 1861, to 1 Dec., 1863. 2nd Lieut. 8th Tenn. Cav., 1 Dec., 1863. Capt., 25 March, 1865. Mustered out 11 Sept., 1865. 1st Lieut. 11th Inf., 22 Jan., 1867. Trans. to 16th Inf., 14 April, 1869. Resigned 31 Aug., 1871. Bvt. Capt., 2 March, 1867, for gallant and meritorious conduct in action at Morristown, Tenn. Bvt. Maj., 2 March, 1867, for gallant asd meritorious conduct at the capt ure of Saltville, Va., 22 Dec., 1864.

McCOY, RALPH. [Born in Mich. Appointed from Mich.]
1st Lieut. Co. M, 35th Mich. Vols., 13 July, 1898. Capt., 1 March to muster out, 31 March, 1899. 2nd Lieut. 7th Inf., 10 April, 1899.

McCOY, THOS. F. [Born in Penn. Appointed from Penn.]
1st Lieut. of Inf., 18 Feb., 1847; 11th Inf., 9 April, 1847. Disbanded 16 Aug., 1848. Bvt. Capt., 20 Aug., 1847, for gallant and meritorious conduct at Contreras and Churubusco. Col. 107th Penn. Vols., 6 Aug., 1862. Bvt. Brig. Gen. Vols., 1 April, 1865, for gallant and meritorious conduct during the war. Mustered out 13 July, 1865.

McCRABB, JOHN W.* [Born in Tenn. Appointed from Tenn.]
Bvt. 2nd Lieut. 4th Inf., 1 July, 1833. 2nd Lieut., 28 Dec., 1835. 1st Lieut., 30 Sept., 1836. A. Q. M., 24 Nov., 1836, to 7 July, 1838. Capt. A. Q. M., 7 July, 1838. Died 6 Nov., 1839.

McCRATE, THOS.* [Born in Maine. Appointed from Maine.]
Bvt. 2nd Lieut. 1st Drag., 1 July, 1836. 2nd Lieut., 31 July, 1836. Dropped 6 May, 1837. Reinstated 1 Aug., 1837. 1st Lieut., 29 Jan., 1839. Died 18 Sept., 1845.

McCRAY, WM. D. [Born in ——. Appointed from Ohio.]
2nd Lieut. Rifles, 3 Feb., 1819. Trans. to 6th Inf., 1 June, 1821. 1st Lieut., 5 Nov., 1821. Resigned 1 June, 1823.

McCREA, TULLY.* [Born in Miss. Appointed from Ohio.]
2nd Lieut. 1st Art., 17 June, 1862. Bvt. 1st Lieut., 17 Sept., 1862, for gallant and meritorious service in the Battle of Antietam, Md. Bvt. Capt., 3 July, 1863, for gallant and meritorious service in the Battle of Gettysburg, Penn. 1st Lieut. 1st Art., 4 Nov., 1863. Bvt. Maj., 20 Feb., 1864, for gallant and meritorious service in the Battle of Olustee, Fla. R Q. M. 1st Art., 20 June, 1866, to 20 Nov., 1866. Capt. 42nd Inf., 28 July, 1866. Unassigned 22 April, 1869. Ass'd to 1st Art., 15 Dec., 1870. Maj. 5th Art., 4 Dec., 1888. Lieut. Col., 8 March, 1898. Col. 6th Art., 15 July, 1900.

McCREEDY, CHAS. [Born in Vt. Appointed from Vt.]
Surg.'s Mate Light Art., 3 Feb., 1819. Died 24 May, 1821.

McCREERY, GEORGE. [Born in N. Y. Appointed from N. Y.]
Asst. Surg., 17 Feb., 1880. Capt. Asst. Surg., 17 Feb., 1885. Maj. Surg., — ——, 1898. Died 23 Aug., 1898, on steamer "Catania."

McCREERY, WM. M., Jr.* [Born in Va. Appointed at Large.]
Bvt. 2nd Lieut. 3rd Art., 1 July, 1860. Dismissed 3 June, 1861.

McCRIMMON, ARIOSTO.* [Born in Ga. Appointed from Ark.]
Addl. 2nd Lieut. 6th Inf., 15 June, 1877. 2nd Lieut., 20 Sept., 1877. Resigned 28 Jan., 1879.

McCUE, WM. K. [Born in Ky. Appointed from Ky.]
Priv. Co. B, 6th Inf., 13 Sept., 1894, to 31 Aug., 1898. 2nd Lieut. 1st Inf., 9 July, 1898. 1st Lieut. 9th Inf., 4 March, 1900.

McCULLOCH, CHAMPE C., Jr. [Born in Tex. Appointed form Tex.]
Asst. Surg., 5 May, 1892. Capt. Asst. Surg., 5 May, 1897.

McCULLOH, JAMES H. [Born in Md. Appointed from Md.]
Garrison Surg., 17 July, 1814. Disbanded 24 April, 1816.

McCULLOUGH, CHARLES C. [Born in Wis. Appointed from Army.]
Priv. and Corpl. Troop A, 7th Cav., 12 Aug., 1893, to 11 Nov., 1896. Priv. Troop A, 6th Cav., 7 Sept. to 17 Nov., 1899. 2nd Lieut. 9th Cav., 1 Oct., 1899.

McDANIEL, MOSBY. [Born in Tenn. Appointed from Tenn.]
2nd Lieut. 8th Inf., 28 Jan., 1820. Resigned 31 Aug., 1820.

McDANIEL, WILBUR A. [Born in ——. Appointed from ——.]
2nd Lieut. of Inf. (unassigned), 1 Oct., 1899.

McDERMOTT, GEORGE. [Born in Ireland . Appointed from Army.]
Priv., Corpl., Sergt. and 1st Sergt. Co. B, 5th Inf., 8 Nov., 1850, to 4 Jan., 1878. 2nd Lieut. 5th Inf., 17 July, 1862. 1st Lieut., 14 July, 1864. Died 21 June, 1878.

McDERMOTT, GEORGE B. [Born in D. C. Appointed from D. C.]
2nd Lieut. 23rd Inf., 19 Oct., 1867. 1st Lieut., 6 Sept., 1873. Dismissed 24 July, 1874.

McDONALD, ALEX. J. [Born in Canada. Appointed from Army.]
Priv., Corpl., Sergt. and 1st Sergt. Batty K, 3rd Art., 9 May, 1856, to 31 Oct., 1862. 2nd Lieut. 5th Art., 22 Oct., 1862. 1st Lieut., 17 Jan., 1866. Dropped 22 July, 1867. Bvt. 1st Lieut., 13 Dec., 1862, for gallant and meritorious service at the Battle of Fredericksburg, Va. Bvt. Capt., 3 May, 1863, for gallant and meritorious service at the Battle of Chancellorsville, Va.

McDONALD, ANGUS W.* [Born in Va. Appointed from Va.]
3rd Lieut. Corps Art., 17 July, 1817. 2nd Lieut. 7th Inf., 13 Feb., 1818. 1st Lieut., 1 April 1818. Resigned 31 Jan., 1819.

McDONALD, BEDNEY F. [Born in Ga. Appointed from Ga.]
Q. M. Sergt. Ga. Vols., 22 June, 1846, to 20 July, 1847. 2nd Lieut. 3rd Art., 22 May, 1847. Resigned 31 Oct., 1849. Bvt. 1st Lieut., 9 Oct., 1847, for gallant and meritorious conduct at the Battle of Huamantla.

McDONALD, DAVID N.* [Born in Tenn. Appointed from Tenn.]
Addl 2nd Lieut. 4th Cav., 15 June, 1877. 2nd Lieut, 17 May, 1878. 1st Lieut., 1 Oct., 1881. Resigned 4 March, 1888.

McDONALD, EBENEZER. [Born in Md. Appointed from Md.]
2nd Lieut. Ord., 26 Dec., 1814. Resigned 30 Nov., 1815.

McDONALD, ISAIAH H.* [Born in Ohio. Appointed from Ohio.]
Priv. Co. A, 134th Ohio Vols., 6 May, to 31 Aug., 1864. Cadet at Mil. Acad., 1 July, 1865. 2nd Lieut 9th Cav., 15 June, 1870. Resigned 1 July, 1873.

McDONALD, JAMES. [Born in Va. Appointed from Ohio.]
Capt. Rifle Reg., 3 May, 1808. Maj., 1 Aug., 1812. Lieut. Col. 1st Rifles, 24 Jan., 1814. Col. 4th Rifles, 17 Sept., 1814. Trans. to 7th Inf., 17 May, 1815. Resigned 30 April, 1817. Bvt. Col., 17 Sept., 1814, for distinguished and meritorious conduct in the sortie from Fort Erie.

McDONALD, J. G. [Born in Ohio. Appointed from Ind.]
3rd Litut. Mounted Rangers, 25 July, 1832. Disbanded 1 Oct., 1833.

McDONALD, JOHN. [Born in Ireland. Appointed from Army.]
Priv. Co. K, 1st Drag., 18 Aug., 1857. Corpl., 12 Feb., 1860. Sergt., 1 Oct., 1860. 1st Sergt., 17 Jan., 1862. Discharged 18 June, 1862. 1st Sergt., Co. K, 1st Cav., 18 June, 1862. 2nd Lieut. 1st Cav., 17 July, 1862. 1st Lieut., 29 Dec., 1863. Capt., 1 July, 1868. Retired 1 July, 1868.

McDONALD, JOHN B.* [Born in Ala. Appointed from Ala.]
Cadet at Mil. Acad., 14 June, 1876. to 2 March, 1877. Reappointed 8 June. 1877. Addl. 2nd Lieut. 5th Inf., 11 June, 1881. 2nd Lieut. 25th Inf., 6 Aug., 1881. Trans. to 10th Cav., 2 March, 1882. 1st Lieut., 15 Jan., 1889. Capt. 3rd Cav., 23 Sept., 1898. Capt. A. A. G., 12 May, 1898, declined. Lieut. Col. 1st Ala. Vols., 14 May, 1898, to muster out, 31 Oct., 1898.

McDONALD, JOHN E. [Born in N. Y. Appointed from N. Y.]
Surg. 79th N. Y Vols., 1 Dec., 1861, to 28 May, 1863. Asst. Surg. U. S. Vols., March, 1863. Surg. Vols., 13 April, 1863. Bvt. Lieut. Col. Vols., 1 June, 1865, for faithful and meritorious service. Mustered out 12 July, 1865. Asst. Surg., 28 Feb., 1866. Died 10 Sept., 1866.

McDONALD, PHILIP W.* [Born in Penn. Appointed from Penn.]
Bvt. 2nd Lieut. 2nd Drag., 1 July, 1841. 2nd Lieut., 8 Oct., 1841. Reg. Adj., 1 April to 27 July, 1846. 1st Lieut., 3 March, 1847. Died 11 Oct., 1851. Bvt. 1st Lieut. 23 Sept., 1846, for gallant and meritorious conduct in the Battle of Monterey, Mex. Bvt. Capt., 20 Aug., 1847, for gallant and meritorious conduct at Contreras and Churubusco. Bvt. Maj., 13 Sept., 1847, for gallant conduct at Chapultepec.

McDONALD, ROBT. [Born in N. Y. Appointed from Army.]
Priv. Co. E, 5th Inf., 21 July, 1856. Corpl. 11 March, 1858. Sergt., 1 Oct., 1859. Discharged 7 June, 1861. Sergt. Co. E, 5th Inf., 7 June, 1861. 1st Sergt., 10 July, 1862. Discharged 21 Feb., 1864. 1st Sergt. Co. E, 5th Inf., 21 Feb., 1864. 2nd Lieut. 5th Inf., 2 July, 1864. 1st Lieut., 28 Sept., 1865. R. Q. M., 18 Nov., 1866, to 10 Aug., 1869. Capt., 20 March, 1879. Bvt. Capt., 27 Feb., 1890, for conspicuous gallantry in leading his command in a successful charge against Indians, strongly posted at Wolf Mountain, Mont., 8 Jan., 1877, declined. Medal if Honor for most distinguished gallantry in leading his command in a successful charge against superior numbers of hostile Indians, strongly posted, in the Battle of Wolf Mountain, Mont., 8 Jan., 1877; while 1st Lieut. 5th Inf. Retired 12 May, 1886.

McDONALD, WM. [Born in Penn. Appointed from Ohio.]
1st Lieut. 26th Inf., 20 May, 1813. Trans. to 19th Inf., 12 May, 1814. Capt., 11 Nov., 1814. Trans. to 3rd Inf., 17 May, 1815. Maj. A. I. G., 29 April, 1816. Reverted to the line as Capt. 3rd Inf., 20 May, 1820, to rank from 11 Nov., 1814. Dismissed 17 Oct., 1820. Bvt. Maj., 25 July, 1814, for gallant conduct at the Battle of Niagara.

McDONOUGH, MICHAEL J.* [Born in Mass. Appointed from Mass.]
2nd Lieut. 7th Art., 15 Feb., 1899. Trans to 2nd Art., 4 April, 1899.

McDOUGALL, CHAS. [Born in Ohio. Appointed from Ind.]
Asst. Surg., 13 July, 1832. Maj. Surg., 7 July, 1838. Bvt. Col., 24 Nov., 1864. Bvt. Brig. Gen., 13 March, 1865, for faithful and meritorious service during the war. Lieut. Col. Asst. Med. Pur., 28 July, 1866. Retired 22 Feb., 1869. Died 25 July, 1885.

McDOUGALL, GEORGE P. [Born in Ind. Appointed from Ind.]
Priv. Co. E, 11th Ind. Vols., 31 Aug., 1861, to 10 Dec., 1863. 2nd Lieut. Vet. Res. Corps, 26 Nov., 1863. Mustered out 7 July, 1867. 2nd Lieut., 42nd Inf., 22 Jan., 1867. Trans. to 6th Inf., 22 April, 1869. Discharged 26 Oct., 1870.

McDOUGALL, THOS. M. [Born in Wis. Appointed from Kan.]
2nd Lieut., 48th U. S. Col. Troops, 18 Feb., 1864. Capt. 5th U. S. Vols., 2 June, 1865. 2nd Lieut. 14th Inf., 10 May, 1866. Mustered out of Vol. Service, 10 Aug., 1866. Trans. to 32nd Inf., 21 Sept., 1866. 1st Lieut., 5 Nov., 1866. Bvt. Capt., 2 March, 1867, for faithful and meritorious service. Trans. to 21st Inf., 19 April, 1869. Unassigned 21 Oct., 1869. Ass'd to 7th Cav., 31 Dec., 1870. Capt., 15 Dec., 1875. Retired for disability 22 July, 1890.

McDOWELL, ANDREW. [Born in N. H. Appointed from Army.]
Priv. and Sergt. Art., May, 1805, to June, 1808. 2nd Lieut. Light Art., 18 June, 1808. 1st Lieut., 20 April, 1809. Capt., 1 April, 1812. Trans. to 1st Art., 1 June, 1821. Resigned 1 Dec., 1822. Died in 1829.

McDOWELL, IRVIN.* [Born in Ohio. Appointed from Ohio.]
Bvt. 2nd Lieut. 1st Art., 1 July, 1838. 2nd Lieut., 7 July, 1838. 1st Lieut., 7 Oct., 1842. Bvt. Capt., 23 Feb., 1847, for gallant and meritorious conduct in the Battle of Buena Vista, Mex. Bvt. Capt. A. A. G., 13 May, 1847. Bvt. Maj. A. A. G., 31 March, 1856. Brig. Gen., 14 May, 1861. Maj. Gen. Vols., 14 March, 1862. Bvt. Maj. Gen., 13 March, 1865, for gallant and meritorious service in the Battle of Cedar Mountain, Va. Mustered out of Vol. Service, 1 Sept., 1866. Maj. Gen. U. S. A., 25 Nov., 1872. Retired by operation of law 15 Oct., 1882. Died 4 May, 1885.

McDUFFEE, FRANKLIN.* [Born in N. H. Appointed from N. H.
Bvt. 2nd Lieut. 4th Art., 1 July, 1832. Died 15 July, 1832.

McELDERRY, HENRY. [Born in Md. Appointed from Md.]
Priv. Co. A, 10th Md. Vols., 19 June, 1863. Hosp. Steward, 6 July, 1863. Discharged 29 Jan., 1864. Med. Cadet, 30 March, 1864, to 30 March, 1865. 1st Lieut. Asst. Surg., 28 Feb., 1866. Capt. Asst. Surg., 28 Feb., 1869. Maj. Surg., 7 Dec., 1884. Died 17 April, 1898.

McELHONE, JAMES F. [Born in Penn. Appointed from Penn.]
1st Lieut. 14th Inf., 14 May, 1861. Capt., 18 June, 1864. Retired 4 Nov., 1865. Died 27 Aug., 1866, of wounds received at Battle of Gaines' Mill, Va., 27 June, 1862. Bvt. Capt., 27 June, 1862, for gallant and meritorious service at the Battle of Gaines' Mill, Va. Bvt. Maj., 13 March, 1865, for gallant and meritorious service during the war. Bvt. Lieut. Col., 13 March, 1865, for gallant and meritorious service during the war.

McELRATH, THOMPSON P. [Born in N. Y. Appointed from N. Y.]
Ensign 9th N. Y. Vols., 4 May to 22 June, 1861. 2nd Lieut. 5th Art., 14 May, 1861. 1st Lieut., 1 March, 1862. R. Q. M., 2 Dec., 1862, to 24 Sept., 1867. Capt., 24 Sept., 1867. Resigned 5 Jan., 1870. Bvt. Capt., 27 June, 1862, for gallant and meritorious service at the Battle of Gaines' Mill, Va. Bvt. Maj., 13 March, 1865, for faithful service.

McELROY, JAMES N. [Born in Va. Appointed from Ohio.]
Cadet at Mil. Acad., 1 July, 1856, to 22 Jan., 1858. Maj. 20th Ohio Vols., 25 Sept., 1861. Lieut. Col., 1 May, 1862. Resigned 7 Jan., 1864. Lieut. Col. 60th Ohio Vols., 6 April, 1864. Resigned 9 Aug., 1864. Maj. J. A. Vols., 26 Sept., 1864. Bvt. Lieut. Col. Vols., 13 March, 1865, for gallant and meritorious service during

the war. Mustered out 1 July, 1866. 2nd Lieut. 2nd Cav., 23 April, 1866. Capt. 8th Cav., 6 March, 1867. Discharged 29 Aug., 1870. Bvt. 1st Lieut., Capt. and Maj., 2 March, 1867, for gallant and meritorious service in the Battle of Spottsylvania, Va. Bvt. Lieut. Col., 2 March, 1867, for gallant and meritorious service during the war. Died 26 Dec., 1870.

McELROY, WM. [Born in Penn. Appointed from Ohio.]
Priv. Co. K, 76th Ohio Vols., 17 Oct., 1861, to 28 Sept., 1862. Capt. 72nd U. S. Col. Inf., 3 Dec., 1864. Trans. to 12th U. S. Col. Art., 31 Oct., 1865. Mustered out 24 April, 1866. 1st Lieut. 39th Inf., 28 July, 1866. Trans. to 25th Inf., 20 April, 1869. Mustered out 1 Jan., 1871.

McELVAIN, JOSEPH.* [Born in Ind. Appointed from Ohio.]
Bvt. 2nd Lieut. 1st Drag., 1 July, 1845. 2nd Lieut., 30 June, 1846. Accidentally killed 12 July, 1847.

McEWEN, JOHN S. [Born in Scotland. Appointed from N. Y.]
2nd Lieut. 4th Art., 17 Aug., 1867. Resigned 15 Dec., 1872. Bvt. 1st Lieut., 17 Aug., 1867, for gallant and meritorious service in the Battle of Spottsylvania, Va. Bvt. Capt., 17 Aug., 1867, for gallant and meritorious service in the Battle of Cold Harbor, Va.

McFALLS, THADDEUS B. [Born in Penn. Appointed from D. C.]
Hosp. Chap. Vols., 23 June, 1862. Mustered out 31 May, 1866. Post Chap., 4 Oct., 1867. Died 22 May, 1873.

McFARLAND, MUNROE.* [Born in Md. Appointed from Md.]
2nd Lieut. 21st Inf., 11 June, 1888. 1st Lieut. 13th Inf., 5 July, 1895. Capt. 18th Inf., 26 March, 1899. Graduate of the Infantry and Cavalry School, 1897.

McFARLAND, WALTER.* [Born in N. J. Appointed from N. Y.]
Bvt. 2nd Lieut. Eng., 1 July, 1860. 2nd Lieut., 1 May, 1861. 1st Lieut., 6 Aug., 1861. Bvt. Capt., 23 Nov., 1861, for gallant and meritorious service during the bombardment at Fort Pickens Fla. Capt. Eng., 3 March, 1863. Bvt. Maj., 11 April, 1865, for able, zealous and efficient service in the operations undertaken against Charleston, S. C., in 1863. Lieut. Col. A. A. G., 2 June, 1865, to 1 Aug., 1865. Maj. Eng., 7 March, 1867. Lieut. Col., 12 March, 1884. Died 22 July, 1888.

McFARLAND, WM. C.* [Born in Ohio. Appointed at Large.]
2nd Lieut. 16th Inf., 14 June, 1872. 1st Lieut., 8 July, 1882. Capt., 2 April, 1892. retired for over thirty years' service 19 May, 1899.

McFERRAN, JOHN C.* [Born in Ky. Appointed from Ky.]
Bvt. 2nd Lieut. 3rd Inf., 1 July, 1843. 2nd Lieut. 7th Inf., 9 April, 1846. Trans. to 3rd Inf., 27 June, 1846. R. Q. M., 1 May, 1852, to 20 Oct., 1855. 1st Lieut., 22 Oct., 1847. Capt. A. Q. M., 20 Aug., 1855. Maj. Q. M., 30 Nov., 1863. Col. Q. M. Vols., 2 Aug., 1864, to 3 June, 1865. Lieut. Col. Dep. Q. M. G., 29 July, 1866. Died 25 April, 1872. Bvt. Lieut. Col., Col. and Brig. Gen., 13 March, 1865, for faithful and meritorious service during the war.

McGARRY, EDWARD. [Born in N. Y. Appointed from N. Y.]
2nd Lieut. of Inf., 1 April, 1847; 10th Inf., 9 April, 1847. 1st Lieut., 13 Sept., 1847. Disbanded 21 Aug., 1848. Maj. 2nd Cal. Cav., 17 Oct., 1861. Lieut. Col., 18 Oct., 1864. Col., 29 Nov., 1864. Bvt. Brig. Gen. Vols., 13 March, 1865, for gallant and meritorious service. Mustered out 31 March, 1866. Lieut. Col. 32d Inf., 28 July, 1866. Died 31 Dec., 1867.

M GAVOCK, JOSEPH, Jr. [Born in Va. Appointed from Va.]
Ensign 12th Inf., 12 March, 1812. 3rd Lieut., 29 March, 1813. 2nd Lieut., 26 June, 1813. 1st Lieut., 24 June, 1814. Trans. to 4th Inf., 17 May, 1815. Capt., 31 May, 1817. Resigned 30 April, 1819.

McGEE, WM. [Born in N. J. Appointed from N. J.]
Musician Co. C, 33rd N. J. Vols., 29 Aug., 1863, to 17 July, 1865. 2nd Lieut. 20th Inf., 3 May, 1867. Dismissed 9 April, 1869.

McGILL, GEORGE M. [Born in Penn. Appointed from Penn.]
Asst. Surg., 16 April, 1862. Died 20 July, 1867. Bvt. Capt., 12 May, 1864, for gallant and meritorious service in action at Meadow Bridge, Va. Bvt. Maj., 13 March, 1865, for faithful and meritorious service during the war. Bvt. Lieut. Col., 28 Sept., 1866, for meritorious and distinguished service at Hart's Island, where cholera prevailed. Bvt. Col., 20 July, 1867, for faithful and meritorious service in the Med. Dep. during the prevalence of cholera near Fort Harker, Kan., from which he died.

McGILL, JAMES. [Born in N. Y. Appointed from Army.]
Priv. and Corpl. 15th Inf., April, 1847, to Aug., 1848. Bvt. 2nd Lieut. and 2nd Lieut. 2nd Inf., 28 June, 1848. Resigned 29 March, 1849.

McGILVRAY, JOHN. [Born in N. Y. Appointed from Army.]
Priv. Co. K, 2nd Art., 20 June, 1853. Corpl., 3 Feb., 1855. Sergt., 1 Nov., 1855. 1st Sergt., 1 May, 1856. Discharged 20 June, 1858. Priv. Co. G, 4th Art., 5 Oct., 1858. Corpl., 1 March, 1862. Sergt., 1 Nov., 1862. Sergt. Maj., 26 Jan., 1863. Bvt. 2nd Lieut. 4th Art., 19 Feb., 1863. 2nd Lieut. 2nd Art., 27 April, 1863. 1st Lieut., 6 May, 1864. Bvt. Capt., 22 Sept., 1864, for gallant and meritorious service in the Battle of Fisher's Hill, Va. R. Q. M. 2nd Art., 20 March, 1877, to 20 Jan., 1881. Retired 16 Oct., 1884.

McGINNESS, JOHN R.* [Born in Ireland. Appointed from Ohio.]
1st Lieut. Ord., 11 June, 1863. Bvt. Capt., 1 March, 1864, for gallant and meritorious service during the Siege of Morris Island, S. C. Bvt. Maj., 13 March, 1865, for gallant and meritorious service during the operations before Charleston, S. C. Capt. Ord., 10 Feb., 1869. Maj., 1 June, 1881. Lieut. Col., 7 July, 1898.

McGINNIS, JAMES T. [Born in Penn. Appointed from Ohio.]
Priv. Co. E, 1st Ohio Vols., 14 April, 1861. Discharged 1 Aug., 1861. Priv. Co. E, 84th Ohio Vols., 26 May, 1862. Sergt., 2 June, 1862. Discharged 20 Sept., 1862. 2nd Lieut. 124th Ohio Vols., 29 Sept., 1862. 1st Lieut., 17 April, 1863. Capt., 4 Jan., 1865. Bvt. Maj. Vols., 13 March, 1865, for gallant and meritorious ser-

vice in the Battles of Chickamauga, Ga., Mission Ridge, Tenn., and Dallas, Ga. Mustered out 9 July, 1865. 2nd Lieut. and 1st Lieut. 13th Inf., 23 Feb., 1866. Bvt. Capt., 2 March, 1867, for gallant and meritorious service in the Battle of Chickamauga, Ga. Bvt. Maj., 2 March, 1867, for gallant and meritorious service in the Battle of Mission Ridge, Tenn. R. Q. M. 13th Inf., 1 July, 1867, to 1 June, 1868. Reg. Adj., 1 June, 1868, to 31 Aug., 1871. Capt., 31 Aug., 1871. Retired 26 March, 1879. Died 3 Jan., 1891.

McGINNISS, ROBT. H.* [Born in Mass. Appointed from Ohio.]
Asst. Surg., 3 March, 1847; 14th Inf., 9 April, 1847. Died 1 Sept., 1847.

McGLACHLIN, EDWARD F., Jr.* [Born in Wis. Appointed from Wis.]
Addl. 2nd Lieut., 3rd Art., 12 June, 1889. 2nd Lieut. 5th Art., 4 Oct., 1889. 1st Lieut. 1st Art., 1 June, 1897. Trans. to 5th Art., 9 July, 1897. Graduate of the Artillery School in 1896.

McGLASSIN, GEORGE. [Born in Penn. Appointed from Penn.]
1st Lieut. 15th Inf., 12 March, 1812. Capt., 15 Aug., 1813. Disbanded 15 June, 1815. Reinstated 2 Dec., 1815, in 6th Inf., Dismissed 14 May, 1818. Bvt. Maj., 11 Sept., 1814, for gallant conduct at the Battle of Plattsburg. Died in 1831.

McGONNIGLE, ANDREW J. [Born in N. Y. Appointed from N. Y.]
Capt. A. Q. M. Vols., 18 March, 1864. Bvt. Maj. and lieut. Col. Vols., 13 March, 1865, for faithful and meritorious service in the Q. M. D. during the war. Capt. A. Q. M. U. S. A., 19 May, 1865. Bvt. Maj., 2 March, 1867, for gallantry in the Battles of Winchester, Fisher's Hill and Cedar Creek, Va. Bvt. Lieut. Col., 2 March, 1867, for gallantry in the Battles of Five Forks, Sailor's Creek and Appomattox C. H., Va. Bvt. Col., 11 Feb., 1869, for meritorious service during the Indian campaign. Maj. Q. M., 13 Feb., 1882. Retired by operation of law 4 March, 1893.

McGOWN, GEORGE. [Born in Ireland. Appointed from Army.]
Priv. Co. C, 2nd Inf., 1 June, 1858. Corpl., 4 March, 1860. 2nd Lieut. 7th Inf., 29 Nov., 1861. 1st Lieut., 4 July, 1863. Capt., 19 Sept., 1864. Bvt. Maj., 13 March, 1865, for faithful and meritorious service. Retired 14 March, 1865. Bvt. Lieut. Col., 15 Nov., 1865, for faithful and meritorious service connected with the muster out and disbanding of the Vol. armies of the U. S.

McGRATH, HUGH J.* [Born in Wis. Appointed from Wis.]
2nd Lieut. 4th Cav., 12 June, 1880. 1st Lieut., 26 May, 1886. Capt., 19 June, 1897. Maj. Eng. Off. Vols., 20 June, 1898. Graduate of the Infantry and Cavalry School, 1887. Died of wounds received in action 7 Nov., 1899, at Manila, Philippine Islands.

McGRATH, JOHN P. [Born in Ireland. Appointed from Mo.]
Addl. P. M. Vols., 19 Feb., 1863. Bvt. Lieut. Col. Vols., 1 Dec., 1865, for faithful service in his department. Mustered out 20 July, 1866. Maj. P. M., 28 July, 1866. Appointment expired 4 March, 1867.

McGRATH, PETER. [Born in Ireland. Appointed from Army.]
Priv., Corpl., Sergt. and 1st Sergt. Co. I, Mounted Rifles, 11 Sept., 1851, to 7 July, 1861. 2nd Lieut. 3rd Cav., 14 May, 1861; 6th Cav., 3 Aug., 1861. 1st Lieut., 24 Oct., 1861. Died 1 May, 1862, of wounds received in Battle of Apache Canon, N. M.

McGREGOR, ROBERT.* [Born in Mich. Appointed from Mich.]
Addl. 2nd Lieut. Eng., 12 June, 1889. 2nd Lieut., 26 Feb., 1891. 1st Lieut., 31 March, 1895. Capt., 29 Sept., 1899.

McGREGOR, THOMAS. [Born in Scotland. Appointed from Army.]
Priv. Co. A, 1st Drag., 8 April, 1858. Corpl., 1 Nov., 1858. Sergt., 1 Feb., 1859. 1st Sergt., 1 Sept., 1860. 2nd Lieut. 1st Cav., 17 July, 1862. 1st Lieut., 10 Sept., 1863. Bvt. Capt., 6 May, 1864, for gallant and meritorious service in the Battle of Todd's Tavern, Va. Reg. Adj., 1 Oct., 1864, to 1 April, 1865. Capt. 1st Cav., 16 Oct., 1866. Maj. 2nd Cav., 19 Dec., 1884. Lieut. Col. 8th Cav., 10 Nov., 1894. Col. 9th Cav., 5 July, 1898. Bvt. Maj., 27 Feb., 1890, for gallant services in action against Indians at the Santa Maria Mountains, Ariz., 6 May, 1875.

McGREW, MILTON L.* [Born in D. C. Appointed from N. J.]
2nd Lieut. 11th Inf., 12 June, 1895. 1st Lieut. of Inf., 1 July, 1898. Ass'd to 16th Inf., 1 Jan., 1899. Trans. to 11th Inf., 17 March, 1900.

McGUGIN, DAVID L. [Born in Penn. Appointed from Penn.]
Maj Surg 15th Inf., 31 March, 1848. Disbanded 16 Aug., 1848.

McGUIRE, JOHN P. [Born in Va. Appointed from Va.]
Mil. Storekeeper Ord., 22 Feb., 1822. Resigned 9 June, 1823.

McGUIRE, ROBERT V. [Born in Va. Appointed from Md.]
Maj. Surg. Mounted Rifles, 12 April, 1820. Dropped 27 Dec., 1820.

McGUIRE, THOMAS H. [Born in N. Y. Appointed from Army.]
Priv., Corpl. and Sergt. Co. B, 18th Inf., 12 Jan., 1883, to 17 March, 1888. 2nd Lieut. 25th Inf., 6 Feb., 1888. 1st Lieut. 14th Inf., 1895. Died 31 July, 1895.

McGUIRE, WM. [Born in Va. Appointed from Va.]
Mil. Storekeeper, 29 Oct., 1817. Died 24 Nov., 1820.

McGUIRE, WOODS. [Born in Penn. Appointed from Penn.]
2nd Lieut. 3rd Inf., 5 Aug., 1861. 1st Lieut., 12 March, 1862. Killed 30 June, 1862, at the Battle of Malvern Hill, Va. Bvt. Capt., 1 July, 1862, for gallant and meritorious service at the Battle of Malvern Hill, Va.

McGUNNEGLE, GEORGE K. [Born in Md. Appointed from Md.]
2nd Lieut. 15th Inf., 1 Oct., 1873. 1st Lieut., 23 Aug., 1877. Reg. Adj., 1 Sept., 1886. Capt., 15 June, 1891. Maj. 3rd Inf., 18 Dec., 1899.

McGUNNEGLE, JAMES. [Born in ——. Appointed from Penn.]
Ensign 5th Inf., 3 Jan., 1812. 2nd Lieut., 12 March, 1812. 1st Lieut., 28 April, 1814. Trans. to Rifle Reg., 17 May, 1815. Capt., 12 July, 1818. Trans. to 6th Inf., 1 June, 1821. Capt. A. D. Q. M. G., 25 Sept., 1818. A. Q. M., 1 June, 1821. Died 27 Aug., 1822.

McILVAIN, JESSE. [Born in Penn. Appointed from Penn.]
Ensign 16th Inf., 15 April, 1814. 3rd Lieut., 15 June, 1814. Disbanded 15 June,

1815. Reinstated in Corps Art., 17 May, 1816. 2nd Lieut., 15 July, 1816. 1st Lieut., 20 April, 1818. Dismissed 23 May, 1820.

McILVAINE, CHAS. P. [Born in N. J. Appointed from D. C.]
Chap. and Prof. at the U. S. Mil. Acad., 28 Jan., 1825. Resigned 31 Dec., 1827.

McILVAINE, FRANCIS E. [Born in Ky. Appointed from N. Y.]
Capt. 19th Inf., 18 Nov., 1861. Resigned 13 June, 1865. Bvt. Maj., 1 Sept., 1864. for gallant and meritorious service during the Atlanta campaign. Bvt. Lieut. Col., 13 March, 1865, for faithful and meritorious service.

McILVAINE, JAMES. [Born in Penn. Appointed from Del.]
Ensign 32nd Inf., 17 May, 1813. 3rd Lieut., 6 Oct., 1813. Trans. to 42nd Inf., 11 Jan., 1814. 2nd Lieut., 19 July, 1814. Disbanded 15 June, 1815. Reinstated in 6th Inf., 2 Dec., 1815. 1st Lieut., 30 April, 1819. Resigned 30 Sept., 1828. Died 23 Oct., 1833.

McINDOE, JAMES F.* [Born in Md. Appointed from Md.]
Addl. 2nd Lieut. Eng., 12 June, 1891. 2nd Lieut., 26 Jan., 1895. 1st Lieut., 31 March, 1896.

McINTIRE, ANDREW. [Born in N. Y. Appointed form Army.]
Priv. and Sergt. 26th Inf., 4 July, 1814, to June, 1815, and Q. M. Sergt. Light Art. to 24 Feb., 1818. 2nd Lieut. Light Art., 13 Feb., 1818. Trans. to 1st Art., 1 June, 1821. 1st Lieut., 1 Dec., 1822. Resigned 1 March, 1826. Died 14 Feb., 1836.

McINTIRE, SAML. B.* [Born in Mass. Appointed from Minn.]
2nd Lieut. 5th Art., 17 June, 1862. Trans. to 2nd Art., 6 Oct., 1862. 1st Lieut., 30 March, 1864. Discharged 1 Oct., 1870. Bvt. 1st Lieut., 30 Aug., 1862, for gallant and meritorious service at the Battle of Bull Run (2nd,) Va. Bvt. Capt., 19 Sept., 1864, for gallant and meritorious service at the Battle of Winchester, Va.

McINTOSH, DONALD. [Born in Canada. Appointed from Ore.]
2nd Lieut. 7th Cav., 17 Aug., 1867. 1st Lieut., 22 March, 1870. Killed in action with Indians in Mont. Ter., 25 June, 1876.

McINTOSH, JAMES McQ.* [Born in Fla. Appointed at Large.]
Bvt. 2nd Lieut. 1st Inf., 1 July, 1849. Trans. to 8th Inf., 11 Feb., 1851. 2nd Lieut., 15 May, 1851. 1st Lieut. 1st Cav., 3 March, 1855. Capt., 16 Jan., 1857. Resigned 7 May, 1861. Graduated and served as "James McIntosh."

McINTOSH, JAMES S. [Born in Ga. Appointed from Ga.]
2nd Lieut. Rifle Reg., 13 Nov., 1812. 1st Lieut., 31 Dec., 1813. Disbanded 15 June, 1815. Reinstated 2 Dec., 1815. Capt., 8 March, 1817. Trans. to Ord., 11 Sept., 1818. Trans. to 4th Inf., 1 June, 1821. Maj. 7th Inf., 21 Sept., 1836. Lieut. Col. 5th Inf., 1 July, 1839. Died 26 Sept., 1847, of wounds received in Battle of Molino del Rey, Mex. Bvt. Maj., 8 March, 1827, for ten years' faithful service in one grade. Bvt. Col., 9 May, 1846, for gallant and distinguished service in the Battles of Palo Alto and Resaca de la Palma.

McINTOSH, JOHN. [Born in Mass Appointed from Army.]
(Changed name to John S. McNaught—which see).

McINTOSH, JOHN. [Born in Scotland. Appointed from Penn.]
Capt. 14th Inf., 14 May, 1861. Resigned 17 Sept., 1862.

McINTOSH, JOHN B. [Born in Fla. Appointed at Large.]
Midshipman U. S. N., 27 April, 1848. Resigned 24 May, 1850. 2nd Lieut. 2nd Cav., 8 June, 1861. 5th Cav., 3 Aug., 1861. 1st Lieut., 27 June, 1862. Bvt. Maj., 5 Aug., 1862, for gallant and meritorious service in the Battle of White Oak Swamp, Va. Col. 3rd Penn. Cav., 15 Nov., 1862. Bvt. Lieut. Col., 3 July, 1863, for gallant and meritorious service in the Battle of Gettysburg, Penn. Capt. 5th Cav., 7 Dec., 1863. Bvt. Col., 1 June, 1864, for gallant and meritorious service in the Battle of Ashland, Va. Brig. Gen., Vols., 21 July, 1864. Bvt. Maj. Gen. Vols., 13 March, 1865, for distinguished gallantry and good management in the Battle of Opequan, Va. Bvt. Brig. Gen., 13 March, 1865, for gallant and meritorious service in the Battle of Winchester, Va. Bvt. Maj. Gen., 13 March, 1865, for gallant and meritorious service in the field during the war. Mustered out of Vol. Service, 30 April, 1866. Lieut. Col. 42nd Inf., 28 July, 1866. Unassigned 15 March, 1869. Retired with rank of Brig. Gen., 30 July, 1870. Died 29 June, 1888.

McINTOSH, JOHN N. [Born in Ga. Appointed from Ga.]
1st Lieut. Light Art., 12 Dec., 1808. Capt., 1 May, 1811. Disbanded 15 June, 1815. Reinstated in 4th Inf., 17 May, 1816. Maj. 8th Inf., 1 March, 1819. Resigned 31 Dec., 1820.

McINTOSH, LEONIDAS. [Born in Fla. Appointed from Ga.]
1st Lieut. Inf., 23 Feb., 1847; Voltigeurs, 9 April, 1847. Disbanded 20 July, 1848.

McINTYRE, AUGUSTINE. [Born in Ireland. Appointed from Ill.]
Priv., Corpl. and Sergt. Co. A, Md. Light Art., 15 Dec., 1861, to 28 Dec., 1862. 2nd Lieut. Md. Light Art., 28 Dec., 1862. Resigned 16 April, 1864. Capt. 114th U. S. Col. Inf., 13 Aug., 1864. Mustered out 2 April, 1867. 2nd Lieut. 16th Inf., 19 Aug., 1867. Trans. to 2nd Inf., 17 April, 1869. Killed 10 Feb., 1877, while in command of detachment acting as a posse to U. S. Marshal.

McINTYRE, DAVID C. [Born in N. Y. Appointed from Iowa.]
Sergt. Co. B, and Sergt. Maj. 1st Iowa Cav., 31 July to 24 Sept., 1861. 1st Lieut. 1st Iowa Cav., 24 Sept., 1861. Capt., 19 April, 1863. Mustered out 15 Feb., 1866. 2nd Lieut 6th Cav., 25 Sept., 1867. Dismissed 9 April, 1869.

McINTYRE, FRANK.* [Born in Ala. Appointed from Ala.]
2nd Lieut. 19th Inf., 1 July, 1886. 1st Lieut. 3rd Inf., 4 July, 1892. Trans. to 19th Inf., 12 Aug., 1892. Capt., 2 March 1899. Honor graduate of the Infantry and Cavalry School, 1889. Reg. Adj., 5 May, 1899.

McINTYRE, JAMES B. [Born in Tenn. Appointed from Texas.]
Bvt. 2nd Lieut. 7th Inf., 1 July, 1853. 2nd Lieut. 1st Cav., 3 March, 1855. 1st Lieut., 16 Jan., 1857. R. Q. M., 15 April 1858 to 3 May, 1861. Capt., 3 May, 1861; 4th Cav., 3 Aug., 1861. Maj. 3rd Cav., 28 July, 1866. Died 10 May, 1867. Bvt. Maj., 10 May, 1863, for galant and meritorious service in the Cav. action

at Franklin, Tenn. Bvt. Lieut. Col., 25 Sept., 1863, for gallant and meritorious service in action near Chickamauga, Ga.

McINTYRE, THOMAS H. R. [Born in Ala. Appointed from Army.]
Cadet Mil. Acad., 17 June, 1891, to 24 Jan., 1895. Priv. and Corpl. Co. E, 5th Inf., 29 March, 1895, to 2 May, 1898. 2nd Lieut. 6th Art., 12 April, 1898. Trans. to 1st Art., 4 April, 1899. Trans. to 6th Art., 2 June, 1899.

McIVER, GEORGE W.* [Born in N. C. Appointed from N. C.]
2nd Lieut. 7th Inf., 13 June, 1882. 1st Lieut., 30 Nov., 1889. Capt., 26 April, 1898.

McKAIN, CHARLES L. [Born in Penn. Appointed from Army.]
Priv., Corpl. and Sergt. Batty B, 4th Art., 12 Nov., 1896, to 14 April, 1899. 2nd Lieut. 16th Inf., 5 April, 1899.

McKAVETT, HENRY.* [Born in N. Y. Appointed from N. Y.]
Bvt. 2nd Lieut. 7th Inf., 1 July, 1834. 2nd Lieut., 26 March, 1835. 1st Lieut., 25 Dec., 1837. Trans. to 8th Inf., 7 July, 1838. Capt., 1 Oct., 1840. Killed 21 Sept., 1846, at the Battle of Monterey, Mex.

McKAY, ÆNEAS. [Born in N. Y. Appointed from N. Y.]
Asst. Dep. Comsy. of Ord., 12 March, 1813. Retained as 1st Lieut. of Ord., 8 Feb., 1815, to rank from 12 March, 1813. Discharged 15 June, 1815. Reinstated as 2nd Lieut. Ord., 2 Dec., 1815, with Bvt. of 1st Lieut., from 12 March, 1813. Trans. to Corps Art., 17 May, 1816. 1st Lieut., 1 Dec., 1816. Trans. to 3rd Art., 1 June, 1821. Capt., 31 Dec., 1822. Capt. A. Q. M., 15 July, 1824. Maj. Q. M., 7 July, 1838. Lieut. Col. Dep. Q. M. G., 21 April, 1846. Died 23 May, 1850. Bvt. Col., 30 May, 1848, for meritorious conduct, particularly in performing his duties in prosecuting war with Mexico.

McKEAN, THOS. J.* [Born in Penn. Appointed from Penn.]
Bvt. 2nd Lieut. 4th Inf., 1 July, 1831. 2nd Lieut., 15 Sept., 1833. Resigned 31 March, 1834. 1st Lieut. and Adj. 1st Penn. Vols., 1 Nov., 1837. Resigned 1 April, 1838. Priv. Co. K, 15th Inf., 12 April, 1847. Sergt. Maj., 10 May, 1847. Discharged 7 Aug., 1848. Addl. P. M. Vols., 1 June, 1861. Brig. Gen. Vols., 21 Nov., 1861. Bvt. Maj. Gen. Vols., 13 March, 1865, for gallant and meritorious service during the war. Mustered out 24 Aug., 1865. Died 19 April, 1870.

McKEE, GEORGE W.* [Born in Ky. Appointed from Ky.]
1st Lieut. Ord., 11 June, 1863. Bvt. Capt. and Maj., 13 March, 1865, for efficient and valuable service during the war. Capt. Ord., 23 June, 1874. Maj., 23 Aug., 1881. Died 30 Nov., 1891.

McKEE, J. COOPER. [Born in Penn. Appointed from Penn.]
1st Lieut. Asst. Surg., 2 Oct., 1858. Capt. Asst. Surg., 2 Oct., 1863. Maj. Surg., 22 Dec., 1864. Bvt. Lieut. Col., 13 March, 1865, for faithful and meritorious service during the war. Lieut. Col. Surg., 17 Nov., 1887. Retired for disability, 19 June, 1891.

McKEE, SAMUEL.* [Born in Mo. Appointed from Utah.]
Bvt. 2nd Lieut. Mounted Rifles, 1 July, 1858. Trans. to 1st Drag., 22 June, 1859. 2nd Lieut., 9 Jan., 1860. 1st Lieut., 7 May, 1861. 1st Cav., 3 Aug., 1861. Reg. Adj., 7 Aug. to 14 Nov., 1861. Capt., 14 Nov., 1861. Died 3 June, 1864, of wounds received in action at Cold Harbor, Va.

McKEE, SAMUEL A. [Born in Penn. Appointed from Penn.]
1st Lieut. 62nd Penn. Vols., 22 July to 17 Nov., 1861. 2nd Lieut. 2nd Inf., 5 Aug., 1861. 1st Lieut., 10 Aug., 1861. Capt., 12 Sept., 1862. Killed 11 April, 1864, by guerillas near Greenwich, Va. Bvt. Maj., 3 May, 1863, for gallant and meritorious service at the Battle of Chancellorsville, Va.

McKEE, WM. R.* [Born in Ky. Appointed from Ky.]
Bvt. 2nd Lieut. 3rd Art., 1 July, 1829. 2nd Lieut., 1 July, 1829. 1st Lieut., 13 Aug., 1836. Resigned 15 Sept., 1836. Col. 2nd Ky. Cav., 9 June, 1846. Killed 23 Feb., 1847, at the Battle of Buena Vista, Mex.

McKEEVER, CHAUNCEY.* [Born in Md. Appointed from Md.]
Bvt. 2nd Lieut. 1st Art., 1 July, 1849. 2nd Lieut. 3rd Art., 27 July, 1850. 1st Lieut., 24 Dec., 1853. Bvt. Capt. A. A. G., 1 July, 1861. Capt. A. A. G., 3 Aug., 1861. Maj. A. A. G., 17 July, 1862. Lieut. Col. A. A. G. (Act 17 July, 1862), 20 Aug., 1862, to 31 Dec., 1862. Bvt. Lieut. Col., 24 Sept., 1864, for meritorious and faithful service during the war. Bvt. Col., 13 March, 1865, for diligent, faithful and meritorious service in the A. G. Dept. during the war. Bvt. Brig. Gen., 13 March, 1865, for faithful and meritorious service during the war. Lieut. Col. A. A. G., 3 March, 1875. Col. A. A. G., 28 Feb., 1887. Retired by operation of law, 31 Aug., 1893.

McKEEVER, SAMUEL. [Born in New Brunswick. Appointed from Mass.]
1st Lieut. 16th Mass. Vols., 2 July, 1861. Mustered out 10 Aug., 1862. Capt. 28th Mass. Vols., 31 Oct., 1862. Mustered out 27 July, 1863. Capt. Vet. Res. Corps, 20 Aug., 1863. Bvt. Maj. and Lieut. Col. Vols., 13 March, 1865, for gallant and meritorious service during the war. Mustered out 17 April, 1866. 2nd Lieut. and 1st Lieut. 16th Inf., 23 Feb., 1866. Bvt. Capt., 2 March, 1867, for gallant and meritorious service during the war. Trans. to 2nd Inf., 17 April, 1869. Capt., 4 March, 1879. Retired for disability, 27 May, 1889.

McKENNA, FRANK B.* [Born in Cal. Appointed from Cal.]
2nd Lieut. 15th Inf., 12 June, 1893. 1st Lieut., 26 April, 1898. Capt. A. A. G. Vols., 13 Aug., 1898, to 12 May, 1899. Capt. 46th U. S. Vols., 17 Aug., 1899.

McKENNEY, LESLIE H. [Born in Canada. Appointed from Ill.]
Capt. of Inf., 23 Feb., 1847; 16th Inf., 9 April, 1847. Maj. 15th Inf., 20 Aug., 1847. Disbanded 7 Aug., 1848.

McKENZIE, KENNETH. [Born in Md. Appointed from Md.]
Capt. 14th Inf., 6 July, 1812. Disbanded 15 June, 1815. Retained 2 Dec., 1815 (in reorganization under Act of 3 March of that year), as 1st Lieut. 4th Inf., with Bvt. of Capt. from 6 July, 1812. Trans. to Corps Art., 17 May, 1816. Died 29 Sept., 1817.

McKENZIE, SAMUEL.* [Born in N. C. Appointed from N. C.]
2nd Lieut. Corps Art., 24 July, 1818. Trans. to 3rd Art., 1 June, 1821. Trans. to 2nd Art., 16 Aug., 1821. 1st Lieut., 20 Feb., 1825. Capt., 8 Feb., 1837. Died 19 Oct., 1847.

McKEON, JAMES. [Born in Ireland. Appointed from N. Y.]
Capt. 3rd Art., 12 March, 1812. Trans. to Corps Art., 12 May, 1814. Disbanded 15 June, 1815. Reinstated in 8th Inf., 17 May, 1816. Rejected by Senate, 15 Jan., 1817. Died 29 March, 1823.

McKIBBEN, JOHN G. [Born in ——. Appointed from N. Y.]
Asst. Surg. Vols., 20 Oct., 1847. Resigned 31 May, 1848.

McKIBBIN, CHAMBERS. [Born in Penn. Appointed from Penn.]
Mil. Storekeeper Q. M. D., 2 Oct., 1837. Relieved 18 July, 1839.

McKIBBIN, CHAMBERS. [Born in Penn. Appointed from Army.]
Priv. Gen. Ser., 22 Sept., 1862. 2nd Lieut. 14th Inf., 22 Sept., 1862. 1st Lieut., 10 June, 1864. Bvt. Capt., 18 Aug., 1864, for gallant service in the Battle of the North Anna River, Va., and during the operations on the Weldon Railroad. Trans. to 32nd Inf., 21 Sept., 1866. Capt. 35th Inf., 28 July, 1866. Trans. to 15th Inf., 12 Aug., 1869. Maj. 25th Inf., 25 April, 1892. Lieut. Col. 21st Inf., 1 May, 1896. Col. 12th Inf., 1 April, 1899. Brig. Gen. Vols., 8 July, 1898, to 12 May, 1899.

McKIBBIN, DAVID B. [Born in Penn. Appointed from Penn.]
Cadet Mil. Acad., 1 July, 1846, to 31 Oct., 1848. 2nd Lieut. 9th Inf., 3 March, 1855. 1st Lieut., 1 March, 1861. Capt. 14th Inf., 14 May, 1861. Col. 158th Penn. Vols., 24 Nov., 1862. Mustered out of Vol. Service, 12 Aug., 1863. Bvt. Maj., 1 Aug., 1864, for gallant service in the Battle of North Anna, Va. Bvt. Lieut. Col., 1 Aug., 1864, for gallant service in the Battle of Bethesda Church, Va. Bvt. Col. and Brig. Gen., 13 March, 1865, for gallant and meritorious service during the war. Bvt. Brig. Gen. Vols., 13 March, 1865, for gallant and meritorious service during the war. Col. 214th Penn. Vols., 5 April, 1865. Mustered out of Vol. Service, 30 April, 1866. Trans. to 32nd Inf., 21 Sept., 1866. Maj. 10th Inf., 15 Sept., 1867. Unassigned 15 March, 1869. Ass'd to 10th Cav., 1 Jan., 1871. Retired 31 May, 1875. Died 8 Nov., 1890.

McKIBBIN, ROBT. P. [Born in Penn. Appointed from Penn.]
2nd Lieut. 4th Inf., 5 Aug., 1861. 1st Lieut., 1 Aug., 1862. Capt., 20 Jan., 1865. Resigned 15 March, 1870. Bvt. Capt., 17 Sept., 1862, for gallant and meritorious service at the Battle of Antietam, Md. Bvt. Maj., 13 March, 1865, for gallant and meritorious service in front of Petersburg, Va. Bvt. Lieut. Col., 13 March, 1865, for gallant and meritorious service during the war. Died 21 July, 1873.

McKIM, JAMES. [Born in Ireland. Appointed from Army.]
Priv., Corpl., Sergt. and 1st Sergt. Co. K, 6th Inf., 7 Feb., 1853, to 9 Nov., 1862. 2nd Lieut. 6th Inf., 18 July, 1862. 1st Lieut., 1 Feb., 1865. Capt. 39th Inf., 28 July, 1866. Resigned 31 May, 1867. Bvt. 1st Lieut., 2 July, 1863, for gallant and meritorious service at the Battle of Gettysburg, Penn. Bvt. Capt., 13 March, 1865, for gallant and meritorious service at the Battle of Gettysburg, Penn.

McKIM, WM. W. [Born in Mass. Appointed from Mass.]
Capt. A. Q. M. Vols., 3 Aug., 1861, to 3 Aug., 1864. Capt. A. Q. M., 2 July, 1864. Col. Q. M. (ass'd), 2 Aug., 1864, to 8 March, 1866. Resigned 8 March, 1866. Bvt. Maj., Lieut. Col. and Col., 13 March, 1865, for faithful and meritorious service during the war.

McKINLEY, JAMES F. [Born in Cal. Appointed from Ohio.]
Priv. Co. I, 8th Ohio Vols., 24 June to 21 Nov., 1898. 2nd Lieut. 6th Cav., 3 Feb., 1899.

McKINNEY, JOHN A.* [Born in Tenn. Appointed from Tenn.]
2nd Lieut. 4th Cav., 12 June, 1871. 1st Lieut., 17 May, 1876. Killed 25 Nov., 1876, in action with Indians in Wyoming.

McKINNON, WILLIAM D. [Born in Mass. Appointed from Cal.]
Chap. 1st Cal. Inf., 7 May, 1898, to 21 Sept., 1899. Chap., 27 Oct., 1899.

McKINSTRY, CHARLES H.* [Born in Cal. Appointed from Cal.]
Addl. 2nd Lieut. Eng., 11 June, 1888. 2nd Lieut., 22 July, 1888. 1st Lieut., 11 Oct., 1892. Capt., 5 July, 1898.

McKINSTRY, JUSTUS.* [Born in N. Y. Appointed from Mich.]
2nd Lieut. 2nd Inf., 1 July, 1838. 1st Lieut., 18 April, 1841. Capt., 12 Jan., 1848. Capt. A. Q. M., 3 March, 1847. Maj. Q. M., 3 Aug., 1861. Brig. Gen. Vols., 2 Sept., 1861, to 17 July, 1862. Dismissed 28 Jan., 1863. Bvt. Maj., 20 Aug., 1847, for gallant and meritorious conduct at Contreras and Churubusco.

McKISSACK, DANIEL R. [Born in N. J. Appointed from Ark.]
2nd Lieut. 12th Inf., 31 May, 1848. Disbanded 25 July, 1848.

McKISSACK, WM. M. D.* [Born in N. J. Appointed from N. J.]
Bvt. 2nd Lieut. 5th Inf., 1 July, 1835. 2nd Lieut., 11 Sept., 1836. 1st Lieut., 1 Oct., 1838. Capt., 29 June, 1846. Capt. A. Q. M., 19 Dec., 1839. Died 27 Jan., 1849.

McKNIGHT, GEORGE B. [Born in Penn. Appointed from Penn.]
Surg. Mate 1st Inf., 17 Feb., 1817. Resigned 1 Aug., 1818. Post Surg., 13 Oct., 1820. Asst. Surg., 1 June, 1821. Resigned 1 July, 1824.

McKNIGHT, JAMES. [Born in Penn. Appointed from Penn.]
Capt. Ringgold Art. Penn. Vols., 16 April to 29 June, 1861. Capt. 5th Art., 14 May, 1861. Resigned 9 March, 1866. Bvt. Maj., 19 Oct., 1864, for gallant and meritorious service at the Battles of Spottsylvania, Cold Harbor, and Cedar Creek, Va. Died 1 June, 1888.

McKOWN, JAMES. [Born in N. Y. Appointed from N. Y.]
2nd Lieut. 10th Inf., 9 April, 1847. 1st Lieut., 19 Nov., 1847. Disbanded 22 Aug., 1848. Maj. 44th N. Y. Vols., 9 Oct., 1861. Resigned 2 Jan., 1862.

McLANDBURGH, HENRY J. [Born in Ohio. Appointed from Ohio.]
Capt. 17th Inf., 5 Aug., 1861. Bvt. Maj., 14 Dec., 1862, for gallant and meritorious service at the Battle of Fredericksburg, Va., where he was killed.

McLANE, GEORGE. [Born in Del. Appointed from Md.]
2nd Lieut. Mounted Rifles, 27 May, 1846. 1st Lieut., 9 Oct., 1847. Capt., 30 Dec., 1856. Killed 13 Oct., 1860, in action with Indians in New Mexico. Bvt. 1st Lieut., 20 Aug., 1847, for gallant and meritorious conduct at Contreras and Churubusco. Bvt. Capt., 13 Sept., 1847, for gallant and meritorious conduct at Chapultepec.

McLANE, ROBT. M.* [Born in Del. Appointed from Del.]
2nd Lieut. 1st Art., 1 July, 1837. 2nd Lieut. Top. Eng., 7 July, 1838. Resigned 1 Nov., 1843.

McLAREN, ADAM N. [Born in Scotland. Appointed from S. C.]
Asst. Surg., 2 March, 1833. Maj. Surg., 30 June, 1839. Died 1 Aug., 1874. Bvt. Lieut. Col., 13 March, 1865, for faithful and meritorious service during the war.

McLAUGHLIN, CLENARD. [Born in Mich. Appointed from Army.]
Priv., Corpl. and Sergt. Co. H, 19th Inf., 16 Sept., 1897, to 16 Nov., 1899. 2nd Lieut. 21st Inf., 1 Oct., 1899.

McLAUGHLIN, NAPOLEON B. [Born in Vt. Appointed from N. Y.]
Priv. Co. F, 2nd Drag., 27 May, 1850. Corpl., 25 May, 1851. Sergt., 7 Oct., 1851. Trans. to Gen. Mounted Service, 31 Aug., 1852. Discharged 1 April, 1855. Sergt. Gen. Mounted Service, 1 April, 1855. Priv., 15 Aug., 1858. Discharged 28 April, 1859. 2nd Lieut. 1st Cav., 27 March, 1861. 1st Lieut., 3 May, 1861. 4th Cav., 3 Aug., 1861. Capt., 17 July, 1862. Col. 1st Mass. Vols., 1 Oct., 1862. Bvt. Maj., 3 May, 1863, for gallant and meritorious service in the Battle of Chancellorsville, Va. Bvt. Lieut. Col., 2 July, 1863, for gallant and meritorious service in the Battle of Gettysburg, Penn. Mustered out of Vol. Service, 28 May, 1864. Col. 57th Mass. Vols., 14 Sept., 1864. Bvt. Brig. Gen. Vols., 30 Sept., 1864, for gallant and distinguished service at Poplar Grove Church, Va. Bvt. Col., 13 March, 1865, for gallant and meritorious service during the assault on Fort Steedman, Va. Bvt. Brig. Gen., 13 March, 1865, for gallant and meritorious service in the field during the war. Mustered out of Vol. Service, 10 Aug., 1865. Maj. 10th Cav., 17 May, 1876. Retired, for over 30 years' service, 26 June, 1882. Died 27 Jan., 1887.

McLAUGHLIN, WM. H.* [Born in Penn. Appointed from Penn.]
2nd Lieut. and 1st Lieut. 17th Inf., 23 June, 1865. Trans. to 26th Inf., 21 Sept., 1866. Capt., 31 July, 1867. Unassigned 19 May, 1869. Ass'd to 18th Inf., 31 Dec., 1870. Maj. 16th Inf., 30 Jan., 1895. Lieut. Col., 23 Jan., 1898. Retired, for over thirty years' service, 4 May, 1899.

McLAWS, LAFAYETTE.* [Born in Ga. Appointed from Ga.]
Bvt. 2nd Lieut. 6th Inf., 1 July, 1842. 2nd Lieut. 7th Inf., 16 March, 1844. 1st Lieut., 16 Feb., 1847. Capt., 24 Aug., 1851. Resigned 23 March, 1861.

McLEAN, EUGENE E.* [Born in D. C. Appointed from Md.]
Bvt. 2nd Lieut. 2nd Inf., 1 July, 1842. 2nd Lieut. 1st Inf., 1 March, 1844. 1st Lieut., 10 June, 1850. Capt. A. Q. M., 29 Aug., 1855. Resigned 25 April, 1861.

McLEAN, HANCOCK T. [Born in Ky. Appointed from Ky.]
1st Lieut. 3rd Cav., 14 May, 1861. 6th Cav., 3 Aug., 1861. Capt., 5 July, 1864. Resigned 14 May, 1868.

McLEAN, NATHL. H.* [Born in Ohio. Appointed at Large.]
Bvt. 2nd Lieut. 7th Inf., 1 July, 1848. 2nd Lieut. 2nd Inf., 29 March, 1849. 1st Lieut., 8 Jan., 1853. Reg. Adj., 24 March, 1855, to 10 Sept., 1857. Bvt. Capt. A. A. G., 11 May, 1861. Capt. A. A. G., 3 Aug., 1861. Maj. A. A. G., 17 July, 1862. Resigned 24 June, 1864. Lieut. Col. A. A. G., 18 March, 1875, to rank from 3 March, 1875. Retired 18 March, 1875, to date from 3 March, 1875. Died 28 June, 1884.

McLEAN, WM. [Born in N. Y. Appointed from N. J.]
2nd Lieut. 2nd Cav., 27 March, 1861. 1st Lieut., 9 May, 1861. 5th Cav., 3 Aug., 1861. Capt., 17 July, 1862. Died 13 April, 1863.

McLELLAN, CURWEN B. [Born in Scotland. Appointed from Army.]
Priv. Co. B, 3rd Inf., 17 Nov., 1849. Corpl., 1 Feb., 1851. Sergt., 1 May, 1851. 1st Sergt., 1 Nov., 1851. Sergt., 7 Nov., 1853. Discharged 17 Nov., 1854. Priv. Co. H, 2nd Cav., 7 Aug., 1856. Sergt., 1 Nov., 1856. Discharged 8 June, 1861. 2nd Lieut. 3rd Cav., 14 May, 1861; 6th Cav., 3 Aug., 1861. Reg. Adj., 1 Oct. to 30 Nov., 1861. Bvt. 1st Lieut., 5 May, 1862, for gallant and meritorious service in the Battle of Williamsburg, Va. 1st Lieut. 6th Cav., 17 July, 1862. Bvt. Capt., 3 July, 1863, for gallant and meritorious service in the Gettysburg campaign. Bvt. Maj., 31 March, 1865, for gallant and meritorious service in the Battle of Dinwiddie C. H., Va. Capt. 6th Cav., 28 July, 1866. Maj. 10th Cav., 30 Dec., 1881. Lieut. Col. of Cav. (3rd), 6 May, 1892. Trans. to 1st Cav., 26 May, 1892. Bvt. Lieut. Col., 27 Feb., 1890, for gallant services in action against Indians near Red River, Ind. Ter., 30 Aug., 1874, and in action against Indians in the San Andreas Mountains, N. M., 7 April, 1880. Retired 7 April, 1893. Died 24 Aug., 1898.

McLEMORE, OWEN K.* [Born in Ala. Appointed from Ala.]
Bvt. 2nd Lieut. 8th Inf., 1 July, 1856. 2nd Lieut. 6th Inf., 16 Sept., 1856. Resigned 8 April, 1861.

McLEOD, ALEXR. [Born in Canada. Appointed from Del.]
Chap. 84th Penn. Vols., 28 Dec., 1861. Resigned 6 Oct., 1862. Hosp. Chap. Vols., 28 July, 1862. Mustered out 26 July, 1865. Chap. Post of Fort Delaware, Del., 1 Sept., 1866, to 30 April, 1867. Post Chap., 3 April, 1867. Died 9 Feb., 1877.

McLEOD, HUGH.* [Born in N. Y. Appointed from Ga.]
Bvt. 2nd Lieut. 3rd Inf., 18 Sept., 1835. Resigned 30 June, 1836. Died 2 Jan., 1862.

McLOUGHLIN, GEORGE H. [Born in Ireland. Appointed from Army.]
Priv. Gen. Ser., 21 Feb., 1849. Corpl., 6 Aug., 1849. Trans. to Co. M, 3rd Art., 14 March, 1850. Sergt. Co. D, 3rd Art, 1 April, 1851. 1st Sergt., 8 Oct., 1851. Discharged 21 Feb., 1854. 1st Sergt. Co. E, 2nd Inf., 12 May, 1854. Sergt., 1 Jan., 1856. 1st Sergt., 11 Oct., 1856. Discharged 12 May, 1859. Priv. Co. E,

2nd Inf., 15 Aug., 1859. 1st Sergt., 1 Dec., 1859. Discharged 4 Oct., 1861. 1st Lieut. 8th Iowa Vols., 4 Oct., 1861. Resigned 20 Nov., 1861. 2nd Lieut. 2nd Inf., 24 Oct., 1861. 1st Lieut., 15 Feb., 1862. R. Q. M., 24 Sept., 1862, to 1 Dec., 1863. Capt., 1 Dec., 1863. Bvt. Maj., 1 Aug., 1864, for gallant service in the Battle of North Anna River, Va., and during the campaign before Richmond, Va. Retired 31 Dec., 1870.

McMAHON, JOHN E.* [Born in N. Y. Appointed from N. Y.]
2nd Lieut. 4th Art., 1 July, 1886. 1st Lieut. 2nd Art., 28 Nov., 1892. Trans. to 4th Art., 16 March, 1895. Graduate of the Artillery School, 1898. Capt. A. A. G. Vols., 12 May, 1898, to 13 June, 1899. Maj. 31st U. S. Vols., 5 July, 1899, to ——.

McMAHON, J. FONTE C. [Born in ——. Appointed from D. C.]
Surg.'s Mate 3rd Inf., 21 Nov., 1817. Post Surg., 23 July, 1819. Asst. Surg., 1 June, 1821. Surg., 5 Aug., 1826. Resigned 30 Oct., 1834. Died 14 April, 1837.

McMAHON, THOS. P. [Born in Ireland. Appointed from Penn.]
3rd Lieut. 16th Inf., 16 April, 1813. 2nd Lieut., 19 May, 1813. 1st Lieut., 1 Jan., 1814. R. Q. M., March, 1814, to June, 1815. Disbanded 15 June, 1815. Retained 17 May, 1816 (in reorganization under Act of 3 March, 1815), as 2nd Lieut. of Ord., with Bvt. of 1st Lieut. from 1 Jan., 1814. Resigned 18 April, 1818.

McMANEMY, SAML. [Born in Penn. Appointed from Penn.]
Mil. Storekeeper Q. M. D., 1 Oct., 1852. Appointment expired 3 March, 1853.

McMANN, JOHN T. [Born in N. Y. Appointed from Mich.]
Corpl. Co. G, 21st Mich. Vols., 2 Aug., 1862, to 12 Aug., 1864. 2nd Lieut. 1st U. S. Vet. Eng., 13 Aug., 1864. 1st Lieut., 22 May, 1865. Mustered out 26 Sept., 1865. 2nd Lieut. 1st Inf., 7 March, 1867. Resigned 7 April, 1869.

McMANUS, GEO. H.* [Born in Iowa. Appointed from Iowa.]
Addl. 2nd Lieut. 5th Art., 12 June, 1893. 2nd Lieut. 3rd Art., 30 June, 1893. 1st Lieut., 2 March, 1899. Graduate of the Artillery School, 1898.

McMANUS, WM. S. [Born in Penn. Appointed from N. Y.]
2nd Lieut. 69th N. Y. State Mil., 20 April, 1861. Mustered out 3 Aug., 1861. Capt. 15th Inf., 5 Aug., 1861. Resigned 13 March, 1865. Bvt. Maj., 1 Sept., 1864, for gallant and meritorious service at the Battle of Mission Ridge, Tenn., and during the Atlanta campaign and the Battle of Jonesboro, Ga.

McMARTIN, JOHN.* [Born in N. Y. Appointed from N. Y.]
2nd Lieut. 25th Inf., 15 June, 1877. 1st Lieut., 30 June, 1883. Dismissed 15 July, 1894.

McMARTIN, PETER.* [Born in N. Y. Appointed from N. Y.]
Bvt. 2nd Lieut. Eng., 1 July, 1825. Resigned 30 Sept., 1826. Died 18 March, 1830.

McMASTER, CHAS. [Born in Ireland. Appointed from Army.]
Priv., Corpl., Sergt. and 1st Sergt. Co. I, 4th Cav., 22 Nov., 1858, to 20 Aug., 1863. 2nd Lieut. 2nd Cav., 10 Aug., 1863. 1st Lieut., 19 Sept., 1864. Died 15 Oct., 1864, of wounds received in the Battle of Front Royal, Va.

McMASTER, GEORGE H.* [Born in S. C. Appointed from S. C.]
Cadet at the Mil. Acad., 16 June, 1887, to 27 Jan., 1888. Reappointed 16 June, 1888. 2nd Lieut. 14th Inf., 11 June, 1892. 1st Lieut., 26 April, 1898.

McMASTER, RICHARD H. [Born in S. C. Appointed from Army.]
Priv. and Corpl. Co. D, 10th Inf., 4 March, 1895, to 6 May, 1898. 2nd Lieut. 6th Art., 12 April, 1898.

McMICHAEL, CLAYTON. [Born in Penn. Appointed from Penn.]
2nd Lieut. 9th Inf., 5 Aug., 1861. 1st Lieut., 5 Aug., 1861. R. Q. M., 1 Jan., 1862, to 1 Sept., 1863. Capt., 4 March, 1864. Resigned 28 Sept., 1865. Bvt. Maj., 2 April, 1865, for gallant and meritorious service at the capture of Petersburg, Va.

McMILLAN, JAMES.* [Born in N. Y. Appointed from N. Y.]
Bvt. 2nd Lieut. 2nd Inf., 1 July, 1856. 2nd Lieut., 30 Sept., 1856. 1st Lieut., 3 May, 1861. Reg. Adj., 1 July to 10 Aug., 1861. 1st Lieut. 12th Inf., 14 May, 1861, declined. Reg. Adj., 1 July, 1861, to 10 Aug., 1861. Capt. 2nd Inf., 10 Aug., 1861. Bvt. Maj., 30 March, 1865, for meritorious and faithful service in the recruitment of the armies of the United States. Unassigned 17 April, 1869. Ass'd to 11th Inf., 15 Feb., 1870. Trans. to 3rd Art., 31 Dec., 1870. Maj. 2nd Art., 2 July, 1877. Retired for disability, 26 June, 1882.

McMILLAN, ROBT. [Born in S. C. Appointed from S. C.]
Surg.'s Mate 5th Inf., 4 Dec., 1819. Disbanded 1 June, 1821. Asst. Surg., 1 July, 1822. Maj. Surg., 3 Sept., 1832. Resigned 1 Dec., 1833. Surg. Vols., 8 June, 1847. Discharged 20 July, 1848.

McMILLAN, ROBERT F. [Born in D. C. Appointed from N. Y.]
Cadet at Mil. Acad., 15 June, 1892, to 19 Jan., 1894. Priv., Corpl., Sergt. and 1st Sergt. Batty K, 2nd Art., 17 June, 1898, to 18 April, 1899. 2nd Lieut. 14th Inf., 10 April, 1899.

McMILLAN, THOS. [Born in Ky. Appointed from Ky.]
Asst. Surg., 19 Aug., 1862. Died 6 April, 1873. Bvt. Capt. and Maj., 13 March, 1865, for faithful and meritorious service during the war. Bvt. Lieut. Col., 13 March, 1867, for meritorious and distinguished service during the outbreak of cholera among a detachment of recruits for the 8th Inf., en route from New York to San Francisco.

McMILLION, MARCUS L. [Born in Ala. Appointed from Ala.]
2nd Lieut. 13th Inf., 19 April, 1847. Resigned 27 April, 1848.

McMINN, WM. H. [Born in Penn. Appointed from Penn.]
Priv. Co. F, 3rd Cal. Vols., 12 Nov., 1861. 1st Sergt., 19 Dec., 1861. Discharged 16 March, 1862. 2nd Lieut. 3rd Cal. Vols., 27 March, 1862. Resigned 20 June, 1863. 1st Lieut. 196th Penn. Vols., 22 July, 1864. Mustered out 17 Nov., 1864. Capt. 213th Penn. Vols., 1 March, 1865. Mustered out 18 Nov., 1865. 2nd Lieut. 8th Inf., 7 March, 1867. 1st Lieut., 17 May, 1877. Retired by operation of law, 29 Oct., 1887.

McMORDIE, FRANCIS. [Born in Ky. Appointed from Ky.]
2nd Lieut. of Inf., 5 March, 1847; 16th Inf., 9 April, 1847. Disbanded 5 Aug., 1848.

McMULLIN, GEORGE O. [Born in Penn. Appointed from Army.]
2nd Lieut. 8th Penn. Cav., 3 Oct., 1861. Resigned 22 Feb., 1862. Sergt. Co. G, 2nd Penn. Cav., 1 April to 6 Dec., 1862. Priv. Co. B, 3rd Cav., 6 Dec., 1862, to 20 March, 1863. 2nd Lieut. 3rd Cav., 19 Feb., 1863. 1st Lieut., 6 Sept., 1865. Capt., 28 July, 1868. Trans. to list of Supernumeraries, 25 Oct., 1870. Mustered out 1 Jan., 1871. Bvt. 1st Lieut., 15 Nov., 1863, for gallant and meritorious service in action near Tuscumbia, Ala. Bvt. Capt., 13 March, 1865, for meritorious service.

McMURDY, E. B. [Born in Ohio. Appointed from Ky.]
1st Lieut. 19th Inf., 14 May, 1861. Dropped 5 April, 1862.

McNAB, JOHN. [Born in Vt. Appointed from Army.]
Priv., Corpl. and Sergt. Co. G, and Sergt. Maj. 2nd Inf., 18 April, 1840, to 11 April, 1844. Priv. and Sergt. Maj. 9th Inf., 1 April to 18 Nov., 1847. 2nd Lieut. 9th Inf., 3 Aug., 1847. Reg. Adj., 1 Jan. to 26 Aug., 1848. Disbanded 26 Aug., 1848. 1st Lieut. 10th Inf., 3 March, 1855. Capt., 25 April, 1861. Dismissed 1 July, 1861.

McNAIR, WM. S.* [Born in Mich. Appointed from Mich.]
Addl. 2nd Lieut. 3rd Art., 12 June, 1890. 2nd Lieut. 5th Art., 15 June, 1891. Trans. to 3rd Art., 12 Aug., 1891. 1st Lieut., 8 March, 1898. Graduate of the Artillery School, 1896.

McNALLY, CHRISTOPHER H. [Born in England. Appointed from Army.]
Priv. Co. D, Mounted Rifles, 21 Dec., 1848. Sergt., 15 March, 1849. 1st Sergt., 26 April, 1849. Discharged 21 Oct., 1853. 1st Sergt. Co. D, Mounted Rifles, 21 Oct., 1853. 2nd Lieut. Mounted Rifles, 23 May, 1855. 1st Lieut., 5 May, 1861; 3rd Cav., 3 Aug., 1861. Bvt. Capt., 25 July, 1861, for gallant and meritorious service in action near Mesilla, Arizona Ter. Capt. 3rd Cav., 28 Sept., 1861. Bvt. Maj., 13 March, 1865, for meritorious service during the war. Col. 3rd U. S. Vols., 31 March, 1865. Mustered out of Vol. Service, 29 Nov., 1865. Retired 24 Dec., 1866, of wounds and injuries in line of duty. Died 14 Feb., 1889.

McNALLY, REGINALD E.* [Born in N. Y. Appointed from Ohio.]
2nd Lieut. 25th Inf., 15 Feb., 1899. Trans. to 3rd Cav., 15 Dec., 1899.

McNALLY, VALENTINE. [Born in Scotland. Appointed from D. C.]
Capt. Ord. Storekeeper, 5 May, 1882. Maj. Ord. Storekeeper, 6 June, 1896.

McNAMARA, THOS.* [Born in Va. Appointed from Va.]
Bvt. 2nd Lieut. 7th Inf., 1 July, 1822. 2nd Lieut. 7th Inf., 1 July, 1822. 1st Lieut., 26 May, 1826. Resigned 30 June, 1830. Died 14 Sept., 1834.

McNAMEE, MICHAEL M. [Born in Wis. Appointed from Army.]
Priv., Corpl., Sergt. and 1st Sergt. Troop G, 7th Cav., 15 Nov., 1882, to 4 March, 1889. 2nd Lieut. 3rd Cav., 11 Feb., 1889. 1st Lieut. 9th Cav., 9 Sept., 1896. Trans. to 7th Cav., 17 Nov., 1899. Graduate of the Infantry and Cavalry School, 1893. Maj. 40th U. S. Vols., 17 Aug., 1899, to ——.

McNAUGHT, JOHN S. [Born in Mass. Appointed from Army.]
(Entered service as John McIntosh.) Priv. Co. G, 1st Batt. 11th Inf., 16 Aug., 1861. Trans. to Co. B, 27 Sept., 1861. Sergt., 12 Oct., 1861. Trans. to Co. C, 15 Feb., 1862. 1st Sergt., 16 Feb., 1862. 2nd Lieut. 11th Inf., 19 Feb., 1863. 1st Lieut., 29 May, 1864. Bvt. Capt., 1 Aug., 1864, for gallant service in the Battle of the Wilderness, Va. Trans. to 20th Inf., 21 Sept., 1866. Capt., 5 Oct., 1867. Retired for disability, 15 Oct., 1887.

McNEIL, CLARENCE H.* [Born in N. Y. Appointed from N. Y.
Addl. 2nd Lieut. 1st Art., 12 June, 1896. 2nd Lieut. 5th Art., 28 April, 1897. 1st Lieut., 2 March, 1899.

McNEIL, JOHN, Jr. [Born in N. H. Appointed from N. H.]
Capt. 11th Inf., 12 March, 1812. Maj., 15 Aug., 1813. Trans. to 5th Inf., 17 May, 1815. Lieut. Col. 1st Inf., 24 Feb., 1818. Trans. to 3rd Inf., 12 Dec., 1820. Col. 1st Inf., 28 April, 1826. Resigned 23 April, 1830. Bvt. Lieut. Col., 5 July, 1814, for distinguished and meritorious service at the Battle of Chippewa. Bvt. Col., 25 July, 1814, for gallant and distinguished conduct at the Battle of Niagara. Bvt. Brig. Gen., 24 July, 1824, for ten years' faithful service in one grade. Died 23 Feb., 1850.

McNEILL, BENJ. P. [Born in N. H. Appointed from Mass.]
2nd Lieut. 3rd Art., 8 March, 1847. 1st Lieut., 4 Dec., 1847. Dismissed 12 Dec., 1851. 2nd Lieut. 3rd Art., 2 March, 1853. Died 12 June, 1853.

McNEILL, EDWIN.* [Born in Ga. Appointed from Conn.]
2nd Lieut. 25th Inf., 14 June, 1878. Trans. to 1st Art., 6 July, 1878. Resigned 20 May, 1880.

McNEILL, HENRY C.* [Born in Miss. Appointed from Texas.]
Bvt. 2nd Lieut. Mounted Rifles, 1 July, 1857. 2nd Lieut., 26 Oct., 1857. Resigned 12 May, 1861.

McNEILL, JOHN W. S. [Born in Mich. Appointed from Mich.]
2nd Lieut. 2nd Drag., 8 June, 1836. Killed by Indians in Florida, 11 Sept., 1837.

McNEILL, WM. G.* [Born in N. C. Appointed from N. Y.]
3rd Lieut. Corps Art., 17 July, 1817. 2nd Lieut., 1 March, 1818. 1st Lieut., 4 Dec., 1819. Trans. to 4th Art., 1 June, 1821. Trans. to 1st Art., 16 Aug., 1821. Bvt. Capt. A. Top. Eng., 27 Jan., 1823. Bvt. Maj. Top. Eng., 28 Jan., 1834. Resigned 23 Nov., 1837. Died 16 Feb., 1853.

McNETT, ANDREW J. [Born in N. Y. Appointed from N. Y.]
Capt. 93rd N. Y. Vols., 11 Oct., 1861. Mustered out 12 June, 1863. Lieut. Col. 141st N. Y. Vols., 13 Feb., 1864. Mustered out 8 June, 1865. Bvt. Brig. Gen. Vols., 28 July, 1866, for distinguished service in the Battles of Resaca, Dallas, Culp's Farm and Peach Tree Creek. Capt. 44th Inf., 28 July, 1866. Bvt. Maj., 2 March, 1867, for gallant and meritorious service in the Battle of Resaca, Ga. Bvt. Lieut. Col., 2 March, 1867, for gallant and meritorious service in the Battle of Peach Tree Creek, Ga. Unassigned 27 May, 1869. Retired with rank of Col., 15 Dec., 1870. Died 8 March, 1895.

McNULTA, DONALD. [Born in Ill. Appointed from Ill.]
2nd Lieut. 24th Inf., 9 July, 1898. 1st Lieut. 23rd Inf., 17 July, 1899.

McNUTT, ALBERT S.* [Born in Ind. Appointed from Ind.]
2nd Lieut. 9th Inf., 11 June, 1881. 1st Lieut., 17 Oct., 1888. Retired for disability, 3 Jan., 1895.

McNUTT, JOHN.* [Born in Ohio. Appointed from Ohio.]
Bvt. 2nd Lieut. Ord., 1 July, 1840. 2nd Lieut., 27 March, 1842. 1st Lieut., 3 March, 1847. Capt., 1 July, 1854. Maj., 12 Sept., 1864. Bvt. Lieut. Col., 13 March, 1865, for faithful service in the Ord. Dept. Bvt. Col., 13 March, 1865, for faithful service in his department during the war. Lieut. Col. Ord., 23 June, 1874. Retired 27 May, 1878. Died 28 March, 1881.

McPARLIN, THOS. A. [Born in Md. Appointed from Md.]
1st Lieut. Asst. Surg., 3 March, 1849. Maj. Surg., 21 May, 1861. Bvt. Lieut. Col., 1 Aug., 1864, for faithful and meritorious service in the field. Col. Medical Director (Act 25 Feb., 1865), 25 Feb., 1865. Bvt. Col., 13 March, 1865, for faithful and meritorious service during the war. Relieved as Col. Medical Director (Act 25 Feb., 1865), 30 June, 1865. Bvt. Brig. Gen., 26 Nov., 1866, for meritorious and distinguished service at New Orleans, where cholera and yellow fever prevailed. Lieut. Col. Asst. Med. Pur., 13 April, 1881. Col. Surg., 16 Sept., 1885. Retired by operation of law, 10 July, 1889. Died 28 Jan., 1897.

McPHAIL, DANIEL H. [Born in Md. Appointed from Md.]
2nd Lieut. 5th Inf., 8 March, 1837. 1st Lieut., 1 March, 1840. Capt., 10 July, 1846. Resigned 30 April, 1849. Bvt. Maj., 20 Aug., 1847, for gallant and meritorious conduct at Contreras and Churubusco, Mex. Addl. P. M. Vols., 1 June, 1861. Bvt. Lieut. Col. Vols., 13 March, 1865, for faithful and meritorious service. Mustered out 1 Jan., 1869. Died 30 Jan., 1884.

McPHAIL, LEONARD C. [Born in Md. Appointed from Md.]
Asst. Surg., 30 Nov., 1834. Maj. Surg., 8 Aug., 1848. Resigned 30 April, 1849. Died 23 March, 1867.

McPHERSON, EDWARD. [Born in Md. Appointed from Md.]
2nd Lieut. 3rd Drag., 9 April, 1847. Reg. Adj., 20 Jan. to 16 March, 1848. Killed in a duel, 16 March, 1848.

McPHERSON, JAMES B.* [Born in Ohio. Appointed from Ohio.]
Bvt. 2nd Lieut. Eng., 1 July, 1853. 2nd Lieut., 18 Dec., 1854. 1st Lieut., 13 Dec., 1858. Capt., 6 Aug., 1861. Lieut. Col. A. A. de C., 12 Nov., 1861. Col. A. A. de C., 1 May, 1862. Brig. Gen. Vols., 15 May, 1862. Maj. Gen. Vols., 8 Oct., 1862. Brig. Gen. U. S. A., 1 Aug., 1863. Killed near Atlanta, Ga., 22 July, 1864.

McQUADE, HUGH. [Born in Ireland. Appointed from Army.]
Priv., Corpl., Sergt. and 1st Sergt. Co. F, Mounted Rifles, 11 Aug., 1851, to 11 June, 1861. 2nd Lieut. 3rd Cav., 14 May, 1861; 6th Cav., 3 Aug., 1861. Capt. 38th N. Y. Vols., 3 June, 1861. Died 26 Dec., 1861, in Confederate prison, of wounds received at the Battle of Bull Run, Va.

McQUESTEN, JAMES F.* [Born in N. H. Appointed from N. H.]
2nd Lieut. 2nd Drag., 6 May, 1861. 2nd Cav., 3 Aug., 1861. 1st Lieut., 13 Aug., 1861. Reg. Adj., 1 Jan., 1862, to 17 Oct., 1863. Capt., 13 Feb., 1864. Killed 19 Sept., 1864, at the Battle of Opequan, Va.

McQUISTON, CHARLES.* [Born in Ind. Appointed from Ind.]
2nd Lieut. 4th Inf., 13 June, 1883. 1st Lieut. 19th Inf., 24 Feb., 1891. Trans. to 15th Inf., 20 July, 1891. Trans. to 1st Inf., 5 Nov., 1891. Trans. to 4th Inf., 8 Dec., 1891. Capt. of Inf., 23 July, 1898. Ass'd to 4th Inf., 1 Jan., 1899.

McQUISTON, HENRY. [Born in Ohio. Appointed from Army.]
Priv. Co. K, 6th Cav., 31 July, 1861. Sergt., 1 Sept., 1861. 2nd Lieut. 6th Cav., 17 July, 1862. Bvt. 1st Lieut., 9 June, 1863, for gallant and meritorious service in the Battle of Beverly Ford, Va. Bvt. Capt., 21 June, 1863, for gallant and meritorious service in action at Upperville, Va. Retired 26 Sept., 1863.

McRAE, ALEXANDER.* [Born in N. C. Appointed from N. C.]
Bvt. 2nd Lieut. Mounted Rifles, 1 July, 1851. 2nd Lieut., 1 July, 1851. 1st Lieut., 26 Jan., 1857. Capt., 10 June, 1861. 3rd Cav., 3 Aug., 1861. Killed 21 Feb., 1862, at the Battle of Val Verde, N. M.

McRAE, JAMES H.* [Born in Ga. Appointed from Ga.]
2nd Lieut. 3rd Inf., 1 July, 1886. 1st Lieut. 14th Inf., 14 Oct., 1892. Trans. to 3rd Inf., 27 Dec., 1892. Capt., 2 March, 1899. Adj., 2 March, 1899.

McREA, JAMES M. [Born in La. Appointed from La.]
Mil. Storekeeper, 8 April, 1851. Resigned 31 July, 1851.

McREE, SAML.* [Born in N. C. Appointed from N. C.]
2nd Lieut. 8th Inf., 1 July, 1820. Trans. to 1st Inf., 1 June, 1821. 1st Lieut., 30 Sept., 1823. Capt., 31 Dec., 1831. Capt. A. Q. M., 7 July, 1838. Maj. Q. M., 8 Nov., 1839. Died 15 July, 1849. Bvt. Lieut. Col.,30 May, 1848, for meritorious conduct while serving in the enemy's country.

McREE, WM.* [Born in N. C. Appointed from N. C.]
2nd Lieut. Eng., 1 July, 1805. 1st Lieut., 30 Oct., 1806. Capt., 23 Feb., 1808. Maj., 31 July, 1812. Lieut. Col., 12 Nov., 1818. Resigned 31 March, 1819. Bvt. Lieut. Col., 25 July, 1814, for gallant conduct at the Battle of Niagara. Bvt. Col. 15 Aug., 1814, for distinguished and meritorious service in defence of Fort Erie, U. C.

McREYNOLDS, ANDREW T. [Born in Ireland. Appointed from Mich.]
Capt. of Inf., 9 March, 1847; 3rd Drag., 9 April, 1847. Disbanded 31 July, 1848. Bvt. Maj., 20 Aug., 1847, for gallant and meritorious conduct at Contreras and Churubusco, Mex. Col. 1st N. Y. Cav., 15 June, 1861. Mustered out 15 June, 1864.

McSHERRY, RICH'D. [Born in Va. Appointed from Va.]
Asst. Surg., 21 Aug., 1838. Resigned 30 April, 1840. Asst. Surg. U. S. N., 22 Nov., 1843. Resigned 17 April, 1851.

McTAGGART, CALVIN P. [Born in Canada. Appointed from Ind.]
Corp. Co. A, 3rd Mich. Vols., 10 June, 1861. 2nd Lieut., 24 Sept., 1862. 1st Lieut., 11 May to 15 Dec., 1863. 1st Lieut. Vet. Res. Corps, 26 Nov., 1863. Mustered out 24 Sept., 1866. 2nd Lieut. 44th Inf., 22 Jan., 1867. Trans. to 17th Inf., 27

May, 1869. 1st Lieut., 4 March, 1873. Died 18 Sept., 1876. Bvt. 1st Lieut., 2 March, 1867, for gallant and meritorious service in the Battle of Fair Oaks, Va.

McVAY, HARLAN E. [Born in Ohio. Appointed from Ohio.]
Asst. Surg., 29 Oct., 1889. Capt. Asst. Surg., 29 Oct., 1894. Died 4 Jan., 1899, in the Philippine Islands.

McVICKAR, JOHN. [Born in —. Appointed from N. Y.]
Chap. Posts of Forts Columbus and Wood, N. Y., 1 Aug., 1844, to 17 Oct., 1862.

McWATTY, ROBERT. [Born in Ireland. Appointed from Penn.]
Post Chap., 4 May, 1882.

MEACHAM, FRANK. [Born in Mass. Appointed from Mass.]
Asst. Surg. 14th Ky. Vols., 30 March, 1862. Mustered out 10 Nov., 1862. Asst. Surg. Vols., 23 April, 1863. Maj. Surg. Vols., 9 July, 1863. Bvt. Lieut. Col. Vols., 9 Aug., 1865, for faithful and meritorious service. Mustered out 10 Aug., 1865. 1st Lieut. Asst. Surg., 14 May, 1867. Capt. Asst. Surg., 21 June, 1867. Maj. Surg., 6 Oct., 1882. Died 9 Oct., 1888.

MEADE, FRANCIS K.* [Born in Va. Appointed from Va.]
2nd Lieut. 21st Inf., 26 April, 1898. 1st Lieut., 2 March, 1899.

MEADE, GEORGE. [Born in Penn. Appointed from Penn.]
Cadet at Mil. Acad., 1 July, 1860, to 21 June, 1862. 2nd Lieut. 6th Pa. Cav., 21 Oct., 1862, to 30 May, 1863. Capt. A. de C. Vols., 22 May, 1863. Bvt. Maj. Vols., 1 Aug., 1864, for faithful and meritorious service in the field. Bvt. Lieut. Col. Vols., 1 April, 1865, for gallant and meritorious service during the recent operations resulting in the fall of Richmond, Va., and the surrender of the insurgent army under Gen. R. E. Lee. Mustered out 1 Sept., 1866. 1st Lieut. 9th Inf., 29 Nov., 1865. Capt. 31st Inf., 28 July, 1866. Trans. to 22nd Inf., 15 May, 1869. Unassigned 25 Oct., 1870. Assd. to 1st Art., 1 Jan., 1871. Resigned 1 Oct., 1874. Bvt. Maj., 2 March, 1867, for gallant and meritorious service at the Battle of Gettysburg, Pa. Bvt. Lieut. Col., 2 March, 1867, for gallant and meritorious service in the campaign ending in the surrender of the Army of Northern Virginia.

MEADE, GEORGE G.* [Born in Spain. Appointed from Penn.]
Bvt. 2nd Lieut. 3rd Art., 1 July, 1835. 2nd Lieut., 31 Dec., 1835. Resigned 26 Oct., 1836. 2nd Lieut. Top. Eng., 19 May, 1842. 1st Lieut., 4 Aug., 1851. Capt., 19 May, 1856. Maj., 18 June, 1862. Trans. to Eng., 3 March, 1863. Brig. Gen. Vols., 31 Aug., 1861. Maj. Gen. Vols., 29 Nov., 1862. Brig. Gen. U. S. A., 3 July, 1863. Maj. Gen. U. S. A., 18 Aug., 1864. Died 6 Nov., 1872. Bvt. 1st Lieut., 23 Sept., 1846, for gallant conduct in the several conflicts at Monterey, Mex. By resolution of 28 Jan., 1864, it was *"Resolved,* By the Senate and House of Representatives of America, in Congress assembled, That the gratitude of the American people and the thanks of their Representatives in Congress are due, and are hereby tendered, to Maj. Gen. George G. Meade and the officers and soldiers of the Army of the Potomac, for the skill and heroic valor which at Gettysburg repulsed, defeated and drove back, broken and despoiled, beyond the Rappahannock, the veteran army of the Rebellion." Died 6 Nov., 1872.

MEADE, HUGH K. [Born in Va. Appointed from Ky.]
3rd Lieut. Corps Art., 23 May, 1814. 2nd Lieut., 16 Sept., 1814. Disbanded 15 June, 1815. Reinstated 17 May, 1816. 1st Lieut., 20 April, 1818. Trans. to 4th Art., 1 June, 1821. Resigned 1 March, 1825.

MEADE, RICHD. K., Jr.* [Born in Va. Appointed from Va.]
Bvt. 2nd Lieut. Eng., 1 July, 1857. 2nd Lieut., 29 July, 1858. Resigned 1 May, 1861.

MEADS, WASH'N. [Born in Penn. Appointed from Penn.]
2nd Lieut. 11th Inf., 9 April, 1847. Died 26 Aug., 1847.

MEAGHER, PATRICK. [Born in Ireland. Appointed from Army.]
Priv., Corpl. and Sergt. Co. C, 5th Inf., 13 Dec., 1856, to 13 Dec., 1861. 2nd Lieut. 13th Inf., 24 Oct., 1861. 1st Lieut., 4 Jan., 1862. Cashiered 4 March, 1867. Bvt. Capt., 4 July, 1863, for gallant and meritorious service during the Siege of Vicksburg, Miss.

MEANS, JOHN W. [Born in Penn. Appointed from Penn.]
2nd Lieut. 8th Inf., 5 Aug., 1861. 1st Lieut., 27 Feb., 1862. Resigned 25 Sept., 1867.

MEARNS, EDGAR A. [Born in N. Y. Appointed from N. Y.]
Asst. Surg., 3 Dec., 1883. Capt. Asst. Surg., 3 Dec., 1888. Maj. Brig. Surg. Vols., 4 June, 1898. Maj. Chief Surg. Vols., 7 Jan., 1899.

MEARNS, ROBERT W.* [Born in Penn. Appointed from Penn.]
2nd Lieut. 20th Inf., 11 June, 1892. 1st Lieut., 26 April, 1898. Graduate of the Infantry and Cavalry School, 1897.

MEARS, FREDK. [Born in N. Y. Appointed from Ill.]
2nd Lieut. 9th Inf., 26 April, 1861. 1st Lieut., 17 May, 1861. Lieut. Col. 1st U. S. Sharpshooters, 1 Oct., 1861. Mustered out of Vol. Service, 30 Nov., 1861. Capt. 9th Inf., 27 Aug., 1863. Bvt. Maj., 13 March, 1865, for faithful and meritorious service during the war. Maj. 25th Inf., 2 April, 1883. Lieut. Col. 4th Inf., 24 April, 1888. Died 2 Jan., 1892.

MEARS, JAMES R. [Born in N. Y. Appointed from Wis.]
Addl. P. M. Vols., 26 Nov., 1862. Mustered out 1 Dec., 1865. Maj. P. M., 13 March, 1867. Retired 3 March, 1875. Died 26 April, 1877.

MEBANE, JOHN A.* [Born in N. C. Appointed from N. C.]
Bvt. 2nd Lieut. 2nd Art., 1 July, 1850. 2nd Lieut., 30 June, 1851. 1st Lieut., 1 Nov., 1853. Died 27 Sept., 1854.

MECHEM, ABEL F. [Born in Md. Appointed from Md.]
Asst. Surg., 11 Oct., 1860. Maj. Surg., 16 June, 1867. Died 14 July, 1871. Bvt. Maj., 13 March, 1865, for faithful and meritorious service during the war.

MECHLING, AUGUSTUS A. [Born in Penn. Appointed from Army.]
Priv. and Sergt. Co. A, 3rd Batt., 18th Inf., 4 Oct., 1861, to 20 July, 1862. 2nd Lieut. 18th Inf., 9 June, 1862. Resigned 24 Dec., 1862. Capt. 211th Pa. Vols., 14 Sept., 1862. Maj., 16 Sept., 1864. Resigned 3 May, 1865. Died 18 Jan., 1876.

MECHLING, WM. T.* [Born in Penn. Appointed from Penn.]
Bvt. 2nd Lieut. 3rd Inf., 1 July, 1848. 2nd Lieut. 8th Inf., 26 June, 1849. 1st Lieut., 23 April, 1855. Dismissed 15 Aug., 1855.

MEDARY, CHAS. S. [Born in Ohio. Appointed from Ohio.]
Served 3 months' Ohio Vols., April to July, 1861. Priv., Sergt. and 1st. Sergt. Co. F, 2nd Batt. 18th Inf., 16 Oct., 1861, to 13 April, 1862. 2nd Lieut. 3rd Art., 19 Feb., 1862. 1st Lieut., 8 Feb., 1864. Resigned 14 Jan., 1865. 2nd Lieut. 3rd Art., 7 March, 1867. 1st Lieut., 31 Oct., 1868. Discharged 15 Sept., 1870.

MEDCALFE, WM. M.* [Born in Md. Appointed from N. Y.]
2nd Lieut. 4th Art., 15 June, 1876. 1st Lieut. of Ord., 18 March, 1881. Died 21 Oct., 1886.

MEEK, JOHN. [Born in —. Appointed from Ohio.]
Ensign 7th Inf., 10 Feb., 1812. 2nd Lieut., 20 Jan., 1813. 1st Lieut., 19 April, 1814. Resigned 30 Sept., 1814. Received by resolution of Congress, 13 Feb., 1835, the testimonial of a sword for being engaged in the defence of Fort Stephenson, Ohio. Mil. Storekeeper Ord., 10 July, 1838. Removed 30 June, 1841.

MEHAFFY, CALVIN D. [Born in Penn. Appointed from Penn.]
2nd Lieut. 1st Inf., 5 Aug., 1861. 1st Lieut., 24 Oct., 1861. Capt., 26 Nov., 1864. Retired 31 Dec., 1870. Died 27 Jan., 1871.

MEHAFFY, FRANKLIN. [Born in Penn. Appointed from Penn.]
1st Lieut. of Inf., 2 March, 1847; 11th Inf., 9 April, 1847. Died 13 June, 1847.

MEIGS, JOHN R.* [Born in D. C. Appointed at Large.]
1st Lieut. Eng., 11 June, 1863. Killed 3 Oct., 1864, by guerrillas near Harrisonburg, Va. Bvt. Capt., 19 Sept., 1864, for gallant and meritorious service at the Battle of the Opequan, Va. Bvt. Maj., 22 Sept., 1864, for gallant and meritorious service at the Battle of Fisher's Hill, Va.

MEIGS, MONTGOMERY C.* [Born in Ga. Appointed from Penn.]
2nd Lieut. 1st Art., 1 July, 1836. Resigned 31 July, 1837. Bvt. 2nd Lieut. Eng., 1 Aug., 1837, to rank from 1 July, 1836. 1st Lieut., 7 July, 1838. Capt., 3 March, 1853. Col. 11th Inf., 14 May, 1861. Brig. Gen. Q. M. Gen., 15 May, 1861. Bvt. Maj. Gen., 5 July, 1864, for distinguished and meritorious service during the present war. Retired, over 62 years of age, 6 Feb., 1882. Died 2 Jan., 1892.

MEINELL, HENRY. [Born in N. Y. Appointed from N. Y.]
2nd Lieut. 3rd Art., 24 Oct., 1861. 1st Lieut., 1 Nov., 1861. Resigned 1 Jan., 1870. Bvt. Capt., 13 Dec., 1862, for gallant and meritorious service at the Battle of Fredericksburg, Va.

MEINHOLD, CHAS. [Born in Prussia. Appointed from Army.]
Priv., Corpl., Sergt. and 1st Sergt. Co. K, and Sergt. Maj. Mtd. Rifles (3rd Cav.), 5 May, 1851, to 1 Jan., 1862. 1st Lieut. and Adj. 5th N. Mex. Vols., 2 Jan., 1862. Trans. to 1st N. Mex. Cav., 31 May, 1862. Resigned 13 Dec., 1862. 2nd Lieut. 3rd Cav., 17 July, 1862. 1st Lieut., 10 Dec., 1863. R. Q. M., 29 July, 1864, to 1 Dec., 1866. Capt., 1 Dec., 1866. Died 14 Dec., 1877. Bvt. 1st Lieut., 1 May, 1863, for gallant and meritorious service in action at Blackwater Bridge, Miss. Bvt. Capt., 22 May, 1863, for gallant and meritorious service in an assault on Vicksburg, Miss.

MELBOURNE, WILBUR F. [Born in Md. Appointed from Army.]
Priv. Co. G, 2nd Drags., 24 April, 1852, to 24 April, 1857. Priv. Co. H, 2nd Drags., 7 Dec., 1860, to 20 June, 1861. 2nd Lieut. 15th Inf., 14 May, 1861. 1st Lieut., 24 Oct., 1861. Resigned 28 Dec., 1864.

MELENDY, PETER, Jr. [Born in N. H. Appointed from N. H.]
3rd Lieut. 11th Inf., 30 March, 1813. 3rd Lieut. 1st Art., 29 June, 1813. 2nd Lieut., 29 June, 1813. Trans. to Corps Art., 12 May, 1814. 1st Lieut., 24 Oct., 1817. Trans. to 1st Art., 1 June, 1821. Died 15 May, 1823.

MELLEN, ALBERT H.* [Born in Mass. Appointed from Mass.]
2nd Lieut. 2nd Art., 17 June, 1874. Died 21 Sept., 1876.

MELLEN, HENRY B. [Born in N. H. Appointed from Cal.]
1st Lieut. 2nd Cal. Cav., 21 Sept., 1861. Capt., 26 Oct., 1861. Maj., 5 June, 1865. Mustered out 21 June, 1866. 2nd Lieut. 6th Cav., 4 May, 1866. 1st Lieut., 22 Jan., 1867. Retired 4 Oct., 1872.

MELLON, CHAS. [Born in Penn. Appointed from Penn.]
3rd Lieut. 1st Art., 17 March, 1814. 2nd Lieut., 1 May, 1814. Trans. to Corps Art., 12 May, 1814. 1st Lieut., 20 April, 1818. Trans. to 2nd Art., 1 June, 1821. Capt., 28 Dec., 1835. Killed 8 Feb., 1837, in action with Indians in Florida. Bvt. Capt., 20 April, 1828, for ten years' faithful service in one grade.

MELOAN, PERRY O. [Born in —. Appointed from Ky.]
Maj. Surg. Rifles, 10 Aug., 1818. Resigned 31 Oct., 1820.

MELVIN, GEORGE W. [Born in Ga. Appointed from Ga.]
2nd Lieut. Light Art., 12 Dec., 1808. 1st Lieut., 17 April, 1810. Capt., 24 Aug., 1812. Disbanded 15 June, 1815. Reinstated 17 May, 1816, in 4th Inf. Resigned 24 Aug., 1820.

MENDELL, GEORGE H.* [Born in Penn. Appointed from Penn.]
Bvt. 2nd Lieut. Top. Eng., 1 July, 1852. 2nd Lieut., 3 March, 1855. 1st Lieut., 1 July, 1856. Capt., 28 Sept., 1861. Trans. to Eng., 3 March, 1863. Bvt. Lieut. Col., 15 Aug., 1864, for gallant and meritorious service during the present campaign before Richmond, Va. Maj. Eng., 15 Aug., 1864. Bvt. Col., 13 March, 1865, for gallant and meritorious service during the war. Lieut. Col. Eng., 30 June, 1879. Col., 16 Sept., 1886. Retired by operation of law, 12 Oct., 1895.

MENDENHALL, CHAS. [Born in Del. Appointed from Del.]
Surg.'s Mate 5th Inf., 10 Aug., 1818. Asst. Surg., 1 June, 1821. Died 15 Oct., 1823.

MENDENHALL, JOHN.* [Born in Ind. Appointed from Ind.]
Bvt. 2nd Lieut. 1st Drag., 1 July, 1851. Trans. to 4th Art., 20 Feb., 1852. 2nd Lieut., 8 Oct., 1853. 1st Lieut., 12 March, 1856. Capt., 3 July, 1861. Bvt. Maj., 7 April, 1862, for gallant and meritorious service in the Battle of Shiloh, Tenn. Maj. J. A. Vols., 17 March, 1863. Bvt. Lieut. Col., 20 Sept., 1863, for gallant and meritorious service in the Battle of Chickamauga, Ga. Lieut. Col. A. I. G., 27

Feb., 1864, to 26 Sept., 1864. Bvt. Col., 13 March, 1865, for gallant and meritorious service during the war. Mustered out of Vol. Service, 23 Oct., 1865. Maj. 1st Art., 10 Jan., 1877. Lieut. Col. 4th Art., 2 Oct., 1883. Col. 2nd Art., 4 Dec., 1888. Died 1 July, 1892.

MENOHER, CHARLES T.* [Born in Penn. Appointed from Penn.]
2nd Lieut. 1st Art., 1 July, 1886. 1st Lieut. 3rd Art., 23 Dec., 1892. Trans. to 6th Art., 8 March, 1898. Graduate of the Artillery School, 1894.

MENZIES, ALEXR. [Born in England. Appointed from Army.]
Priv. and Corpl. Co. E, 10th Inf., 23 Dec., 1857, to 1 July, 1862. Sergt. Maj. 17th Inf., 1 July to 9 Nov., 1862. 2nd Lieut. 17th Inf., 13 Oct., 1862. 1st Lieut., 25 Nov., 1862. Reg. Adj., 1 Jan., 1864, to 18 Aug., 1865. Capt., 18 Aug., 1865. Died 25 Oct., 1865.

MERCER, HUGH W.* [Born in Va. Appointed from Va.]
Bvt. 2nd Lieut. 2nd Art., 1 July, 1828. 2nd Lieut., 1 July, 1828. 1st Lieut., 10 Oct., 1834. Resigned 30 April, 1835. Died 9 June, 1877.

MERCER, JOHN T.* [Born in Ga. Appointed from Ga.]
Bvt. 2nd Lieut. 6th Inf., 1 July, 1854. 2nd Lieut. 1st Drag., 3 March, 1855. 1st Lieut., 8 Jan., 1861. Resigned 26 April, 1861. Killed 19 April, 1864.

MERCER, WM. A. [Born in N. Y. Appointed from Conn.]
2nd Lieut. 8th Inf., 23 Nov., 1880. 1st Lieut., 9 March, 1889. Capt., 7 Aug., 1897. Trans. to 7th Cav., 14 Oct., 1898. Graduate of the Infantry and Cavalry School, 1885.

MERCER, WM. N. [Born in Va. Appointed from Va.]
Hosp. Surg. Mate., 18 May, 1813. Maj. Surg. 22nd Inf., 7 Aug., 1813. Trans. to 38th Inf., 11 April, 1814. Hosp. Surg., 22 Nov., 1814. Disbanded 15 June, 1815. Reinstated as Post Surg., 17 May, 1816. Asst. Surg., 1 June, 1821. Resigned 1 July, 1821.

MERCHANT, ANDERSON. [Born in Va. Appointed from N. Y.]
2nd Lieut. 2nd Art., 8 March, 1847. 1st Lieut., 21 April, 1848. Resigned 2 May, 1861.

MERCHANT, BERT H. [Born in Mich. Appointed from Army.]
Priv. Troops E and K, 1st Cav., 30 Aug., 1893, to 29 May, 1897. 2nd Lieut. 8th Inf., 5 May, 1897. 1st Lieut., 2 March, 1899.

MERCHANT, CHAS. G.* [Born in N. H. Appointed at Large.]
Bvt. 2nd Lieut. 8th Inf., 1 July, 1843. 2nd Lieut., 9 May, 1846. 1st Lieut., 2 Aug., 1848. Died 4 Sept., 1855. Bvt. 1st Lieut., 8 Sept., 1847, for gallant and meritorious conduct at Molino del Rey, Mex. Bvt. Capt., 13 Sept., 1847, for gallant and meritorious conduct at Chapultepec, Mex.

MERCHANT, CHAS. S.* [Born in N. Y. Appointed from N. Y.]
3rd Lieut. 1st Art., 11 March, 1814. 2nd Lieut., 1 May, 1814. Trans. to Corps Art., 12 May, 1814. 1st Lieut., 20 April, 1818. Trans. to 2nd Art., 1 June, 1821. Bvt. Capt., 20 April, 1828, for ten years' faithful service in one grade. Capt. 2nd Art., 17 Nov., 1834. Maj. 3rd Art., 14 Feb., 1849. Lieut. Col., 10 June, 1857. Col. 4th Art., 28 Aug., 1861. Retired 1 Aug., 1863. Bvt. Brig. Gen., 13 March, 1865, for long and faithful service in the army. Died 6 Dec., 1879.

MERCUR, JAMES.* [Born in Penn. Appointed from Penn.]
2nd Lieut. Eng., 18 June, 1866. 1st Lieut., 7 March, 1867. Capt., 9 Dec., 1875. Prof. Mil. Acad., 29 Sept., 1884.

MEREDITH, DAVID M. [Born in Ind. Appointed from Ind.]
1st Lieut. 15th Inf., 14 May, 1861. Capt., 27 May, 1862. Trans. to 33rd Inf., 21 Sept., 1866. Resigned 7 March, 1867. Bvt. Maj., 20 Sept., 1863, for gallant and meritorious service at the Battle of Chickamauga, Ga. Died 4 April, 1867.

MERILLAT, ALFRED C.* [Born in Ohio. Appointed from Ohio.]
Addl. 2nd Lieut. 5th Art., 12 June, 1890. 2nd Lieut., 20 Feb., 1891. Trans. to 8th Cav., 13 May, 1891. 1st Lieut. 3rd Cav., 22 Dec., 1896.

MERKLE, CHRISTOPHER F. [Born in Germany. Appointed from Army.]
Priv., Corpl., Sergt. and 1st Sergt. Co. E, 4th Art., 20 April, 1853, to 29 Oct., 1862. 2nd Lieut. 4th Art., 22 Oct., 1862. 1st Lieut., 11 May, 1864. Resigned 14 July, 1866. Bvt. 1st Lieut., 3 July, 1863, for gallant and meritorious service at the Battle of Gettysburg, Pa. Bvt. Capt., 30 Nov., 1864, for gallant and meritorious service at the Battle of Franklin, Tenn. Died 15 Oct., 1868.

MERRELL, WM. H. [Born in N. Y. Appointed from N. Y.]
Priv. and Corpl. Co. E, 27th N. Y. Vols., 21 May, 1861, to 31 March, 1862. 1st Lieut., 108th N. Y. Vols., 18 Aug., 1862. Capt., 11 March, 1863. Mustered out 28 July, 1863. 1st Lieut. Vet. Res. Corps, 8 Aug., 1863. Capt., 10 Dec., 1863. Mustered out 23 Oct., 1866. 1st Lieut. 42nd Inf., 28 July, 1866. Bvt. Capt., 2 March, 1867, for gallant and meritorious service in the Battle of Bull Run (1st.) Va. Capt. 42nd Inf., 10 Sept., 1868. Unassigned 22 April, 1869. Retired 31 Dec., 1870. Died 20 Feb., 1897.

MERIWETHER, FRANK T. [Born in Ky. Appointed from N. C.]
Asst. Surg., 31 Oct., 1891. Retired for disability 1 Oct., 1895.

MERRIAM, HENRY C. [Born in Maine. Appointed from Maine.]
Capt. 20th Maine Vols., 29 Aug., 1862. Resigned 7 Jan., 1863. Capt. 80th U. S. Col. Troops, 11 March, 1863. Lieut. Col. 85th U. S. Col. Troops, 21 May, 1864. Lieut. Col. 73rd U. S. Col. Troops, 3 June, 1864. Bvt. Col. Vols., 26 March, 1865, for faithful and meritorious service during the campaign against the City of Mobile and its defences. Mustered out 24 Oct., 1865. Maj. 38th Inf., 28 July, 1866. Bvt. Lieut. Col., 2 March, 1867, for gallant and meritorious service in the Battle of Antietam, Md. Bvt. Col., 2 March, 1867, for conspicuous gallantry in the capture of Fort Blakely, Ala. Trans. to 24th Inf., 15 March, 1869. Lieut. Col. 2nd Inf., 10 June, 1876. Col. 7th Inf., 10 July, 1885. Brig. Gen., 30 June, 1897. Medal of Honor for conspicuous gallantry in the assault on Fort Blakely, Ala., 9 April, 1865, voluntarily and successfully leading his regiment over the works in advance of orders, permission being given him at his own request; while serving as Lieut. Col. commanding the 73rd U. S. Col. Troops. Maj. Gen. Vols., 4 May, 1898, to 24 Feb., 1899.

MERRIAM, HENRY M. [Born in Maine. Appointed from Wash.]
2nd Lieut. 3rd Art., 9 July, 1898.

MERRIAM, LEWIS. [Born in Maine. Appointed from Maine.]
Sergt. Co. H, 20th Maine Vols., 5 Aug., 1862. 2nd Lieut. 61st U. S. Col. Troops, 21 March, 1865. Mustered out 30 Dec., 1865. 2nd Lieut. 65th U. S. Col. Troops, 20 Feb., 1866. 1st Lieut., 1 June, 1866. Mustered out 8 Jan., 1867. 2nd Lieut. 4th Inf., 27 July, 1872. 1st Lieut., 27 April, 1880. Retired with rank of Capt., 18 May, 1893.

MERRICK, RICHARD T. [Born in Md. Appointed from Md.]
Capt. Inf., 16 Feb., 1847; 3rd Drag., 9 April, 1847. Disbanded 31 July, 1848. Died 23 June, 1885.

MERRIFIELD, EDWIN R. [Born in N. Y. Appointed from Mich.]
2nd Lieut. Inf., 9 March, 1847; 15th Inf., 9 April, 1847. Resigned 17 Feb., 1848.

MERRIFIELD, JOHN A. [Born in Ky. Appointed from Ky.]
2nd Lieut. Ky. Cav., 22 June, 1846. 2nd Lieut. Inf., 8 March, 1847; 3rd Drag., 9 April, 1847. Died 29 June, 1847.

MERRIHEW, WM. [Born in Mass. Appointed from N. Y.]
2nd Lieut. Inf., 8 March, 1847; 3rd Drag., 9 April, 1847. Disbanded 31 July, 1848.

MERRILL, ABNER H.* [Born in N. Y. Appointed from N. Y.]
2nd Lieut. 1st Art., 18 June, 1866. 1st Lieut., 1 May, 1870. Capt., 14 Aug., 1887. Maj. 3rd Art., 23 Feb., 1899. Graduate of the Artillery School, 1878.

MERRILL, AYRES P. [Born in Mass. Appointed from Mass.]
Surg.'s Mate 8th Inf., 19 March, 1819. Asst. Surg., 1 June, 1821. Resigned 21 Sept., 1823.

MERRILL, DANA T. [Born in Maine. Appointed from Maine.]
Priv. Co. H, 1st Maine Vols., 11 May to 18 Sept., 1898. 2nd Lieut. 12th Inf., 9 Sept., 1898. 1st Lieut. 7th Inf., 15 Nov., 1899.

MERRILL, ELIJAH H.* [Born in N. H. Appointed from N. H.]
Addl. 2nd Lieut. 9th Inf., 14 June, 1878. 2nd Lieut., 28 June, 1878. Resigned 1 June, 1879.

MERRILL, HAMILTON W.* [Born in Va. Appointed from Va.]
2nd Lieut. 2nd Drag., 1 July, 1838. 1st Lieut., 18 Feb., 1840. Capt., 31 March, 1846. Resigned 28 Feb., 1857. Bvt. Maj., 8 Sept., 1847, for gallant and meritorious service at Molino del Rey, Mex.

MERRILL, HENRY.* [Born in Mass. Appointed at Large.]
Bvt. 2nd Lieut. 5th Inf., 1 July, 1845. Accidentally killed 23 Oct., 1845.

MERRILL, JAMES C. [Born in Mass. Appointed from Mass.]
1st Lieut. Asst. Surg., 26 June, 1875. Capt. Asst. Surg., 26 June, 1880. Maj. Surg., 13 March, 1884.

MERRILL, LEWIS.* [Born in Penn. Appointed from Penn.]
Bvt. 2nd Lieut. 1st Drag., 1 July, 1855. 2nd Lieut. 2nd Drag., 13 Dec., 1855. 1st Lieut., 24 April, 1861. 1st Cav., 3 Aug., 1861. Col. 2nd Mo. Cav., 23 Aug., 1861. Capt. 1st Cav., 1 Oct., 1861. Bvt. Maj., 10 Sept., 1862, for gallant and meritorious service against the rebel forces in North Missouri. Bvt. Lieut. Col., 10 Sept., 1863, for gallant and meritorious service in the capture of Litle Rock, Ark. Bvt. Col., 5 March, 1865, for gallant and meritorious service against the rebel forces in Northwest Georgia under the command of the rebel Gen. Wofford, and which terminated in his surrender. Bvt. Brig. Gen. Vols., 13 March, 1865, for gallant and meritorious service during the war. Mustered out of Vol. Service, 14 Dec., 1865. Maj. 7th Cav., 27 Nov., 1868. Retired 21 May, 1886. Reappointed Lieut. Col. of Cav., 21 Jan., 1891, to rank from 9 Jan., 1886. Retired for disability 22 Jan., 1891. Bvt. Brig. Gen., 27 Feb., 1890, for gallant services in action against Indians at Canyon Creek, Mont., 13 Sept., 1877. Died 27 Feb., 1896.

MERRILL, MOSES E.* [Born in Maine. Appointed from Maine.]
Bvt. 2nd Lieut. 5th Inf., 1 July, 1826. 2nd Lieut., 1 July, 1826. 1st Lieut., 4 March, 1833. Capt., 22 June, 1837. Killed 8 Sept., 1847, at the Battle of Molino del Rey, Mex.

MERRILL, SHERMAN M. [Born in N. Y. Appointed from Ga.]
Chap. 177th N. Y. Vols., 21 Nov., 1862, to 23 May, 1863. Post Chap., 27 July, 1882. Retired for disability 6 June, 1894.

MERRILL, THOMAS E.* [Born in Ohio. Appointed from Ky.]
2nd Lieut. 1st Art., 26 April, 1898.

MERRILL, WM. E.* [Born in Wis. Appointed from Va.]
Bvt. 2nd Lieut. Eng., 1 July, 1859. 2nd Lieut., 20 Feb., 1861. 1st Lieut., 6 Aug., 1861. Bvt. Capt., 16 April, 1862, for gallant and meritorious conduct in an engagement with the enemy before Yorktown, Va. Capt. Eng., 3 March, 1863. Bvt. Maj., 19 Sept., 1863, for faithful and meritorious service in the Battle of Chickamauga, Ga. Col. 1st U. S. Vet. Vol. Eng., 30 Aug., 1864. Bvt. Lieut. Col., 13 March, 1865, for faithful and meritorious service in the Battles of Lookout Mountain and Missionary Ridge, Tenn. Bvt. Col., 13 March, 1865, for faithful and meritorious service in the Battles of Resaca and New Hope Church, Ga. Mustered out of Vol. Service, 26 Sept., 1865. Maj. Eng., 7 March, 1867. Lieut. Col., 20 Feb., 1883. Died 14 Dec., 1891.

MERRIMAN, EDWARD M.* [Born in N. Y. Appointed from N. Y.]
2nd Lieut. 1st Art., 17 June, 1867. Mustered out 8 Dec., 1870.

MERRITT, CHAS. W. [Born in Ill. Appointed from Ill.]
2nd Lieut. 9th Cav., 1 Oct., 1873. Dismissed 26 Nov., 1879. Died 12 Dec., 1879.

MERRITT, THOS E. [Born in N. Y. Appointed from Cal.]
Priv. Co. C, 13th N. Y. State Mil., 23 April, 1861. Discharged 6 Aug., 1861. Sergt. Co. H, 53rd N. Y. Vols., 6 Sept., 1861. Discharged 21 March, 1862. Sergt. Co. I, 128th N. Y. Vols., 22 Aug., 1862. 2nd Lieut. 128th N. Y. Vols., 15 June, 1863. Discharged 30 Aug., 1863. Capt. 90th U. S. Col. Troops, 3 Oct., 1863. Mustered out 9 Sept., 1864. Capt. 7th U. S. Vet. Vols., 1 March, 1865. Mustered out 23 April, 1866. 2nd Lieut. 11th Inf., 11 May, 1866. Trans. to 29th Inf., 21 Sept., 1866. 1st Lieut., 2 Nov., 1867. Unassigned 25 April, 1869. Ass'd to 24th Inf., 1 Jan., 1871. Capt., 28 June, 1878. Retired 20 March, 1879.

MERRITT, WESLEY.* [Born in N. Y. Appointed from Ill.]
Bvt. 2nd Lieut. 2nd Drag., 1 July, 1860. 2nd Lieut., 28 Jan., 1861. 1st Lieut., 13 May, 1861. 2nd Cav., 3 Aug., 1861. Reg. Adj., 1 July, 1861, to 1 Jan., 1862. Capt., 5 April, 1862. Brig. Gen. Vols., 29 June, 1863. Bvt. Maj., 1 July, 1863, for gallant and meritorious service in the Battle of Gettysburg, Penn. Bvt. Lieut. Col., 11 May, 1864, for gallant and meritorious service in the Battle of Yellow Tavern, Va. Bvt. Col., 28 May, 1864, for gallant and meritorious service in the Battle of Hawes Shop, Va. Bvt. Maj. Gen. Vols., 19 Oct., 1864, for gallant and meritorious service in the Battles of Winchester and Fisher's Hill, Va. Bvt. Brig. Gen., 13 March, 1865, for gallant and meritorious service in the Battle of Five Forks, Va. Bvt. Maj. Gen., 13 March, 1865, for gallant and meritorious service during the campaign ending with the surrender of the insurgent army of Northern Virginia. Maj. Gen. Vols., 1 April, 1865, for gallant service. Mustered out of Vol. Service, 1 Feb., 1866. Lieut. Col. 9th Cav., 28 July, 1866. Col. 5th Cav., 1 July, 1876. Brig. Gen., 16 April, 1887. Maj. Gen., 25 April, 1895. Retired — June, 1900.

MERRY, WILLIAM T.* [Born in N. Y. Appointed from N. Y.]
2nd Lieut. 23rd Inf., 15 June, 1899.

MESPLIE, TOUSSAINT. [Born in France. Appointed from Idaho.]
Post Chap., 17 Aug., 1872. Dismissed 15 Jan., 1884.

METCALF, RICHARD. [Born in Ireland. Appointed from Army.]
Priv., Corpl. and Sergt. Co. H, 5th Art., 26 July, 1861, to 27 Feb., 1863. Bvt. 2nd Lieut. 5th Art., 27 Feb., 1863. 2nd Lieut., 27 April, 1863. Dismissed 25 July, 1865. Priv. and Sergt. Co. E, 14th Inf. (under name of I. N. Ward), 28 Aug., 1865. Deserted 2 Jan., 1866.

METCALFE, CHAS. [Born in Conn. Appointed from Army.]
Priv. Co. A, and Sergt. Maj. 1st Inf., 16 July, 1869, to 2 Aug., 1872. 2nd Lieut. 1st Inf., 27 July, 1872. Trans. to 17th Inf., 13 Aug., 1872. Resigned 30 Sept., 1874. Died 17 Sept., 1881.

METCALFE, HENRY.* [Born in N. Y. Appointed from Mass.]
2nd Lieut. Ord., 15 June, 1868. 1st Lieut., 23 June, 1874. Capt., 4 March, 1879. Retired for disability 26 Oct., 1893.

METCALFE, JOHN T.* [Born in Miss. Appointed from Miss.]
2nd Lieut. 3rd Art., 1 July, 1838. 2nd Lieut. Ord., 9 July, 1838. Resigned 31 May, 1840.

MEYER, ANTON. [Born in Prussia. Appointed from Army.]
3rd Lieut. 5th N. Y. Mil., 1 May to 1 Aug., 1861. Priv., Sergt. and 1st Sergt. Co. E, 14th Inf., 1 Oct., 1861, to 23 Aug., 1863. 2nd Lieut. 12th Inf., 10 Aug., 1863. 1st Lieut., 28 Oct., 1863. Dismissed 23 Nov., 1864.

MEYER, EDWARD S. [Born in Ohio. Appointed from Ohio.]
Priv. and Sergt.Co. A, 19th Ohio Vols., 20 April to 31 Oct., 1861. 1st Lieut. 19th Ohio Vols., 1 Nov., 1861. Resigned 27 Sept., 1862. Capt. 107th Ohio Vols., 11 Nov., 1862. Resigned 1 Jan., 1865. Maj. 5th U. S. Vet. Vols., 18 Feb., 1865. Bvt. Lieut. Col., Col. and Brig. Gen. Vols., 13 March, 1865, for gallant and meritorious service during the war. Mustered out 20 March, 1866. Capt. 35th Inf., 28 July, 1866. Bvt. Maj., 2 March, 1867, for gallant and meritorious service in the Battle of Shiloh, Tenn. Bvt. Lieut. Col., 2 March, 1867, for gallant and meritorious service in the Battle of Chancellorsville, Va. Unassigned 12 Aug., 1869. Ass'd to 19th Inf., 5 Aug., 1870. Trans. to 9th Cav., 31 Dec., 1870. Retired 24 Aug., 1872, for wounds in line of duty.

MEYER, OREN B.* [Born in Texas. Appointed from Ohio.]
Addl. 2nd Lieut. 1st Cav., 12 June, 1890. 2nd Lieut. 2nd Cav., 18 Sept., 1890. 1st Lieut 3rd Cav., 28 June, 1897.

MEYER, RALPH E. [Born in Ohio. Appointed from Ohio.]
2nd Lieut. 12th Inf., 9 Sept., 1898. Died 11 April, 1899, at sea, *en route* to Philippine Islands.

MEYLER, JAMES J.* [Born in N. J. Appointed from N. J.]
Addl. 2nd Lieut. Eng., 12 June, 1887. 2nd Lieut., 1 Dec., 1887. 1st Lieut., 20 Sept., 1892. Capt., 5 July, 1898.

MICHAELIS, OTHO E. [Born in Germany. Appointed from N. Y.]
Priv. 23rd Reg. N. G. State N. Y., — June, 1863. 2nd Lieut. Sig. Corps. 30 Sept., 1863. 2nd Lieut. Ord., 24 Nov., 1863. 1st Lieut. Ord., 12 Sept., 1864. Bvt. Capt., 13 March, 1865, for faithful and meritorious service. Capt. Ord., 23 June, 1874. Maj., 28 Feb., 1889. Died 1 May, 1890.

MICHIE, DENNIS M.* [Born in N. Y. Appointed from N. Y.]
2nd Lieut. Inf. (17th), 11 June, 1892. 1st.Lieut., 1898. Killed in action at San Juan, Santiago, Cuba, 1 July, 1898.

MICHIE, PETER S.* [Born in,Scotland. Appointed from Ohio.]
1st Lieut. Eng., 11 June, 1863. Bvt. Capt. and Maj., 28 Oct., 1864, for gallant and meritorious service during the campaign of 1864, against Richmond, Va. Bvt. Brig. Gen. Vols., 1 Jan., 1865, for meritorious service in 1864. Bvt. Lieut. Col., 9 April, 1865, for gallant and meritorious service during the campaign terminating at Appomattox, C. H., Va. Lieut. Col. A. I. G., 23 March, 1865, to 6 June, 1865. Capt. Eng., 23 Nov., 1865. Prof. of Natural and Experimental Philosophy, 14 Feb., 1871, at Mil. Acad.

MICHIE, ROBERT E. L.* [Born in Va. Appointed from Va.]
2nd Lieut. 2nd Cav., 14 June, 1885. 1st Lieut. 5th Cav., 14 Jan., 1892. Trans. to 7th Cav., 9 Feb., 1892. Trans. to 2nd Cav., 26 May, 1892. Capt. A. A. G. Vols., 12 May, 1898. Maj. A. A. G. Vols., 4 Oct., 1898, to 13 June, 1899. Maj. A. A. G. Vols., 26 July, 1899. Capt. 10th Cav., 10 Jan., 1900.

MICHLER, FRANCIS.* [Born in N. Y. Appointed from Penn.]
2nd Lieut. 5th Cav., 15 June, 1870. 1st Lieut., 12 Nov., 1876. Capt., 23 May, 1888. Lieut. Col. A. A. G. Vols., 9 May, 1898, to 12 May, 1899. Lieut. Col. 46th U. S. Vols., 17 Aug., 1899 (declined). Bvt. 1st Lieut., 27 Feb., 1890, for

gallant services in actions against Indians at Muchos Canons, Ariz., 25 Sept., 1872, and at the head of Tonto Creek, Ariz., 22 Jan., 1873.

MICHLER, NATHL.* [Born in Penn. Appointed from Penn.]
Bvt. 2nd Lieut. Top. Eng., 1 July, 1848. 2nd Lieut., 7 April, 1854. 1st Lieut., 19 May, 1856. Capt., 9 Sept., 1861. Trans. to Eng., 3 March, 1863. Maj., 22 April, 1864. Bvt. Lieut. Col., 1 Aug., 1864, for faithful and meritorious service in the field. Bvt. Col., 2 April, 1865, for gallant and meritorious service during the Siege of Petersburg, Va. Bvt. Brig. Gen., 2 April, 1865, for gallant and meritorious service during the war. Lieut. Col. Eng., 16 Oct., 1877. Died 17 July, 1881.

MICHLER, WM. H. H. [Born in Penn. Appointed from Penn.]
Asst. Surg., 9 Oct., 1867. Cashiered 19 June, 1871.

MIDDLETON, HENRY.* [Born in S. C. Appointed from S. C.]
2nd Lieut. Eng., 2 March, 1815. Resigned 15 July, 1816.

MIDDLETON, JOHNSON V. D. [Born in D. C. Appointed from D. C.]
1st Lieut. Asst. Surg., 5 Aug., 1861. Bvt. Capt. and Maj., 13 March, 1865, for faithful and meritorious service during the war. Capt. Asst. Surg., 28 July, 1866. Maj. Surg., 26 June, 1876. Lieut. Col. Dep. Surg. Gen., 8 May, 1893. Retired by operation of law, 15 Dec., 1898.

MIDDLETON, PASSMORE. [Born in Penn. Appointed from Penn.]
1st Lieut. Asst. Surg., 15 Feb., 1865. Bvt. Capt., 13 March, 1895, for faithful and meritorious service during the war. Capt., Asst. Surg., 15 Feb., 1868. Maj. Surg., 2 July, 1884. Retired for disability 3 Dec., 1891. Died 14 Feb., 1895.

MILES, DIXON S.* [Born in Md. Appointed from Md.]
Bvt. 2nd Lieut. 4th Inf., 1 July, 1824. 2nd Lieut. 7th Inf., 1 July, 1824. 1st Lieut., 30 April, 1833. Reg. Adj., 31 May, 1830, to 10 Feb., 1836. Capt., 8 June, 1836. Capt. A. Q. M., 16 Jan., 1839, to 30 Sept., 1845. Maj. 5th Inf., 16 Feb., 1847. Lieut. Col. 3rd Inf., 15 April, 1851. Col. 2nd Inf., 19 Jan., 1859. Died 16 Sept., 1862, of wounds received in action at Harper's Ferry, Va. Bvt. Maj., 9 May, 1846, for gallant and distinguished conduct in defence of Fort Brown, Texas. Bvt. Lieut. Col., 23 Sept., 1846, for gallant and meritorious conduct at Monterey, Mex.

MILES, EVAN. [Born in Penn. Appointed from Penn.]
1st Lieut. 12th Inf., 5 Aug., 1861. Q. M. 1st Batt., 5 Aug., 1863, to 19 Nov., 1863. R. Q. M., 19 Nov., 1863, to 20 Jan., 1865. Bvt. Capt., 18 Aug., 1864, for gallant service during the operations in the Weldon Railroad, Va. Capt. 12th Inf., 20 Jan., 1865. Trans. to 21st Inf., 21 Sept., 1866. Maj. 25th Inf., 24 April, 1888. Lieut. Col. 20th Inf., 25 April, 1892. Trans. to 22nd Inf., 11 Sept., 1895. Trans. to 1st Inf., 4 Nov., 1895. Col., 4 May, 1897. Brig. Gen. Vols., 6 Oct., 1898, to 10 Jan., 1899. Retired for disability 19 July, 1899. Bvt. Maj., 27 Feb., 1890, for gallant services in actions against Indians at the Clearwater, Idaho, 11 and 12 July, 1877, and against Indians at the Umatilla Agency, Oregon, 13 July, 1878.

MILES, JOSEPH J. [Born in ——. Appointed from La.]
Capt. 44th Inf., 11 March, 1814. Disbanded 15 June, 1815. Reinstated 17 May, 1816, in 1st Inf. Died 23 July, 1820.

MILES, NELSON A. [Born in Mass. Appointed from Mass.]
Capt. 22nd Mass. Vols., 9 Sept., 1861. Lieut. Col. 61st N. Y. Vols., 31 May, 1862. Col., 30 Sept., 1862. Brig. Gen., 12 May, 1864, for distinguished service during the Battles of the Old Wilderness and Spottsylvania Court House, Va. Bvt. Maj. Gen. Vols., 25 Aug., 1864, for highly meritorious and distinguished conduct throughout the campaign, and particularly for gallantry and valuable service in the Battle of Ream's Station, Va. Maj. Gen. Vols., 21 Oct., 1865. Mustered out 1 Sept., 1866. Col. 40th Inf., 28 July, 1866. Bvt. Brig. Gen., 2 March, 1867, for gallant and meritorious service in the Battle of Chancellorsville, Va. Bvt. Maj. Gen., 2 March, 1867, for gallant and meritorious service in the Battle of Spottsylvania, Va. Trans. to 5th Inf., 15 March, 1869. Brig. Gen., 15 Dec., 1880. Maj. Gen., 5 April, 1890. Medal of Honor for distinguished gallantry in the Battle of Chancellorsville, Va., 3 May, 1863, while holding, with his command, a line of abbattis and rifle pits against a strong force of the enemy until severely wounded; while Col. 61st N. Y. Vols., commanding the line of skirmishers in front of the 1st Div. 2nd Army Corps. Lieut. Gen., 6 June, 1900.

MILES, PERRY L.* [Born in Ohio. Appointed from Ohio.]
2nd Lieut. 14th Inf., 12 June, 1895. 1st Lieut., 1 July, 1898. Capt. A. Q. M. Vols., 10 Oct., 1899.

MILES, SMYTHE M. [Born in S. C. Appointed from Ga.]
Asst. Surg. Vols., 4 Aug., 1847. Disbanded 20 July, 1848.

MILEY, JOHN D.* [Born in Ill. Appointed from Ill.]
Addl. 2nd Lieut. 5th Art., 12 June, 1887. 2nd Lieut. 4th Art., 15 Oct., 1887. Trans. to 5th Art., 12 Nov., 1887. 1st Lieut., 3 Feb., 1894. Trans. to 2nd Art., 4 May, 1898. Maj. A. A. G. Vols., 12 July, 1898. Lieut. Col., I. G. Vols., 8 Sept., 1898. Died at Manila, Philippine Islands, 19 Sept., 1899.

MILHAU, JOHN J. [Born in France. Appointed from N. Y.]
Asst. Surg., 30 April, 1851. Maj. Surg., 16 April, 1862. Resigned 1 Oct., 1876. Bvt. Lieut. Col., 2 Dec., 1864, for gallant service during the Campaign before Richmond. Bvt. Col., 13 March, 1865, for gallant and meritorious service during the war. Bvt. Brig. Gen., 28 Sept., 1866, for meritorious and distinguished service at Hart's Island, N. Y. Harbor, where cholera prevailed.

MILLAR, EDWARD A.* [Born in Ky. Appointed from Ky.]
2nd Lieut. 3rd Art., 13 June, 1882. 1st Lieut. 2nd Art., 7 Jan., 1891. Trans. to 3rd Art., 9 Feb., 1892. Trans to 6th Art., 8 March, 1898. Capt., 2 March, 1899. Graduate of the Artillery School, 1886.

MILLAR, JAMES F. [Born in N. Y. Appointed from Oregon.]
1st Lieut. 14th Inf., 14 May, 1861. Capt., 17 Sept., 1862. Killed by Indians in Ariz., 22 March, 1866. Bvt. Maj., 1 Aug., 1864, for gallant service at the Battle of the Wilderness, etc.

MILLARD, HARRISON. [Born in Mass. Appointed from N. Y.]
1st Lieut. 19th Inf., 14 May, 1861. Resigned 7 Nov., 1863.

MILLER, A. GALBRAITH.* [Born in Penn. Appointed from Wis.]
Bvt. 2nd Lieut. 6th Inf., 1 July, 1848. 2nd Lieut. 1st Inf., 11 April, 1849. 1st Lieut., 1 May, 1852. Capt., 11 Feb., 1856. Resigned 31 Oct., 1857. Col. 1st Md. Cav., 20 Dec., 1861. Resigned 22 May, 1862. Died 21 Oct., 1865.

MILLER, ALBERT S.* [Born in Tenn. Appointed from Tenn.]
Bvt. 2nd Lieut. 7th Inf., 1 July, 1823. 2nd Lieut. 1st Inf., 1 July, 1823. 1st Lieut., 31 May, 1829. Capt., 4 Nov., 1836. Maj. 2nd Inf., 15 March, 1848. Died 7 Sept., 1852. Bvt. Maj., 23 Sept., 1846, for gallant and meritorious conduct at Monterey, Mex.

MILLER, ALEXR. M.* [Born in D. C. Appointed at Large.]
1st Lieut. Eng., 23 June, 1865. Capt., 22 Feb., 1869. Maj., 16 April, 1883. Lieut. Col., 5 July, 1898.

MILLER, ALEXANDER M., Jr.* [Born in N. Y. Appointed from Tenn.]
2nd Lieut. 10th Cav., 12 June, 1896. 1st Lieut. 9th Cav., 7 Nov., 1899.

MILLER, ANDREW T. [Born in Md. Appointed from Army.]
Priv. and Corpl. Co. D and Q. M. Sergt. 6th Cav., 12 July, 1870, to 10 Nov., 1874. 2nd Lieut. 23rd Inf., 31 Oct., 1874. Died 7 March, 1875.

MILLER, BURNET E. [Born in N. Y. Appointed from N. Y.]
1st Lieut. 149th N. Y. Vols., 18 Jan., 1864. Mustered out 12 June, 1865. 2nd Lieut. 8th Inf., 23 Feb., 1866. 1st Lieut., 28 July, 1866. Unassigned 10 Dec., 1869. Discharged 24 Dec., 1870.

MILLER, CHARLES. [Born in Germany. Appointed from the Army.]
Priv. Corpl. Sergt and 1st Sergt. Troop M, 8th Cav., 21 Jan., 1884, to 7 Nov., 1890. 2nd Lieut. 11th Inf., 6 Nov., 1890. 1st Lieut. 16 Inf., 7 Aug., 1897. Capt. 34th U. S. Vols., 5 July, 1899. Graduate of the Infantry and Cavalry School, 1893. Capt. 2nd Inf., 2 Feb., 1900.

MILLER, CHAS. F. [Born in Ohio. Appointed from Army.]
Priv. and Sergt. Maj. 19th Inf., 29 Oct., 1861, to 9 June, 1862. 2nd Lieut. 19th Inf., 1 May, 1862. 1st Lieut., 16 July, 1863. Died 22 Sept., 1863, of wounds received at the Battle of Chickamauga, Ga. Bvt. 1st Lieut., 19 Sept., 1863, for gallant and meritorious service at the Battle of Chickamauga, Ga.

MILLER, CHAS. P. [Born in N. Y. Appointed from Army.]
2nd Lieut. 6th N. Y. Art., 15 April, 1863. Resigned 9 March, 1864. Priv. Co. E, 5th Art., 30 May, 1864. 2nd Lieut. and 1st Lieut. 7th Inf., 20 Oct., 1864. Wholly retired 12 Oct., 1867. Reinstated and placed on retired list 29 Sept., 1868. Dropped 12 Nov., 1884. Died 19 Aug., 1887.

MILLER, CLAUD H.* [Born in Va. Appointed from Va.]
Addl. 2nd Lieut. 18th Inf., 11 June, 1897. 2nd Lieut. 24th Inf., 7 Aug., 1897. 1st Lieut., 2 March, 1899.

MILLER, CROSBY P.* [Born in Vt. Appointed from Vt.]
Corpl. Co. G, 16th Vt. Vols., 4 Sept., 1862. Discharged 12 March, 1863. Cadet at Mil. Acad., 1 July, 1863. 2nd Lieut. 4th Art., 17 June, 1867. 1st Lieut., 1 Dec., 1869. R. Q. M., 31 March to 24 Nov., 1887. Capt. A. Q. M., 21 Nov., 1887. Maj. Q. M., 4 Feb., 1898. Lieut. Col. Chief Q. M. Vols., 9 May, 1898, to 12 July, 1898. Col. Q. M. Vols., 12 July, 1898, to 2 March, 1899. Graduate of the Artillery School, 1874.

MILLER, FREDK. W. [Born in Penn. Appointed from Army.]
Priv. and Sergt. 4th Inf., 28 Aug., 1818, to 13 Aug., 1819. 2nd Lieut. 4th Inf., 13 Aug., 1819. Disbanded 1 June, 1821. Asst. Surg. Vols., 18 Jan., 1847. Resigned 28 July, 1847. Maj. Surg. Vols., 3 March, 1848. Disbanded 21 July, 1848. Died in 1853.

MILLER, GEORGE McC. [Born in N. J. Appointed from Del.]
Asst. Surg. Vols., 6 July, 1863. Bvt. Capt. Vols., 6 Oct., 1865, for faithful and meritorious service. Mustered out 9 Oct., 1865. Asst. Surg., 28 Feb., 1866. Resigned 1 Jan., 1877.

MILLER, HARRY W.* [Born in N. Y. Appointed from N. Y.]
2nd Lieut. 13th Inf., 26 April, 1898. 1st Lieut., 2 March, 1899.

MILLER, HUGH R. [Born in Penn. Appointed from Penn.]
Priv. Co. G, 8th Pa. Vols., 11 May to 12 Sept., 1898. 2nd Lieut. 10th Inf., 9 Sept., 1898. Resigned 9 July, 1899.

MILLER, ISRAEL. [Born in Mass. Appointed from N. Y.]
2nd Lieut. 9th Inf., 3 March, 1855. Drowned 30 Sept., 1856.

MILLER, JAMES. [Born in N. H. Appointed from N. H.]
Maj. 4th Inf., 8 July, 1808. Lieut. Col. 5th Inf., 30 Nov., 1810. Trans. to 6th Inf., 14 Sept., 1812. Col. 21st Inf., 9 March, 1814. Trans. to 5th Inf., 17 May, 1815. Resigned 1 Jan., 1819. Bvt. Col., 9 Aug., 1812, for distinguished service at Brownstown. Bvt. Brig. Gen., 25 July, 1814, for distinguished service at Niagara. Received by resolution of Congress 3 Nov., 1814, the presentation of a gold medal in testimony of the high sense entertained by Congress of his gallantry and good conduct in the several conflicts of Chippewa, Niagara and Fort Erie, U. C. Died 7 July, 1851.

MILLER, JAMES. [Born in Mass. Appointed from Mass.]
Priv. Co. B, 50th Mass. Vols., 11 Sept., 1862. Discharged 24 Aug., 1863. 2nd Lieut. 4th Mass. Cav., 9 Jan., 1864. 1st Lieut., 8 Feb., 1864. Mustered out 14 Nov., 1865. 2nd Lieut. 16th Inf., 23 Feb., 1866. 1st Lieut., 28 July, 1866. Trans. to 2nd Inf., 17 April, 1869. R. Q. M., 1 Jan., 1871, to 20 Aug., 1873. Capt., 7 June, 1879. Maj. 20th Inf., 26 April, 1898.

MILLER, JAMES P. [Born in Tenn. Appointed from Ark.]
2nd Lieut. of Inf., 6 March, 1847; 12th Inf., 9 April, 1847. Resigned 31 March, 1848.

MILLER, JOHN. [Born in —. Appointed from Ohio.]
Lieut. Col. 17th Inf., 12 March, 1812. Col. 19th Inf., 6 July, 1812. Trans. to 17th Inf., 12 May, 1814. Trans. to 3rd Inf., 17 May, 1815. Resigned 10 Feb., 1818. Died 18 March, 1846.

MILLER, JOHN. [Born in N. Y. Appointed from Army.]
Priv. Co. M, 1st Va. Vols., 17 Nov., 1847. Discharged 3 Aug., 1848. Priv. Co. I, 4th Inf., 23 Oct., 1848. Discharged 23 Oct., 1853. Priv. Co. K, 4th Inf., 5 Jan., 1854. Corpl., 1 Feb., 1854. Sergt., 4 Dec., 1855. Discharged 1 Dec., 1858. Sergt. Co. K, 4th Inf., 1 Dec., 1858. 1st Sergt., 1 May, 1860. 2nd Lieut. 4th Inf., 18 July, 1862. Bvt. 1st Lieut., 3 May, 1863, for gallant and meritorious service in the Battle of Chancellorsville, Va. Bvt. Capt., 2 July, 1863, for gallant and meritorious service in the Battle of Gettysburg, Pa. 1st Lieut. 4th Inf., 19 Oct., 1863. Capt., 18 July, 1866. Retired 20 March, 1879.

MILLER, JOHN B. [Born in N. Y. Appointed from Ohio.]
1st Lieut. of Inf., 24 Feb., 1847; 15th Inf., 9 April, 1847. Resigned 31 Dec., 1847. Capt 13th Inf., 14 May, 1861. Wholly retired 3 May, 1864. Died 4 Jan., 1877.

MILLER, JOHN H.* [Born in Penn. Appointed from Penn.]
Bvt. 2nd Lieut. 4th Art., 1 July, 1833. 2nd Lieut., 31 Jan., 1835. 1st Lieut., 17 Dec., 1836. Reg. Adj., 17 Aug., 1838, to 1 Oct., 1846. Capt., 3 March, 1847. Died 12 Sept., 1850. Bvt. Maj., 12 Oct., 1847, for gallant and meritorious conduct in defence of Puebla, Mex.

MILLER, JOHN K.* [Born in Penn. Appointed from Penn.]
2nd Lieut. 8th Inf., 11 June, 1892. 1st Lieut., 26 April, 1898.

MILLER LAWRENCE S.* [Born in Md. Appointed from Vt.]
Addl. 2nd Lieut. 4th Art., 11 June, 1897. 2nd Lieut., 28 Feb., 1898. 1st Lieut., 14 March, 1899. Trans. to 6 Cav., 2 March, 1900.

MILLER, MARCUS P.* [Born in Mass. Appointed from Mass.]
Bvt. 2nd Lieut. 4th Art., 1 July, 1858. 2nd Lieut., 27 Sept., 1859. 1st Lieut., 14 May, 1861. R. Q. M., 14 Feb., 1862, to 1 April, 1862. Reg. Adj., 1 April, 1862, to 11 May, 1864. Bvt. Capt., 1 July, 1862, for gallant and meritorious service in the Battle of Malvern Hill, Va. Capt. 4th Art., 11 May, 1864. Bvt. Maj., 13 March, 1865, for gallant and meritorious service in the Cav. campaign from Winchester to Richmond, Va. Bvt. Lieut. Col., 13 March, 1865, for gallant and meritorious service in the Battle of Dinwiddie Court House, Va. Maj. 5th Art., 14 Sept., 1883. Lieut. Col. 1st Art., 10 Oct., 1894. Col. 3rd Art., 30 April, 1897. Brig. Gen., 15 Feb., 1899. Brig. Gen. Vols., 27 May, 1898, to 23 Feb., 1899. Retired by operation of law 27 March, 1899. Bvt. Col., 27 Feb., 1890, for gallant and meritorious service in action against Indians in the Lava Beds, Cal., 17 April, 1873, and special gallantry and military ability in action against Indians at the Clearwater, Idaho, 11 and 12 July, 1877.

MILLER, MORRIS S.* [Born in N. Y. Appointed from N. Y.]
Bvt. 2nd Lieut. 3rd Art., 1 July, 1834. 2nd Lieut., 28 Dec., 1835. 1st Lieut., 19 Aug., 1837. Capt., 11 May, 1846. Capt. A. Q. M., 13 Sept., 1845. Maj. Q. M., 17 May, 1861. Lieut. Col. Dep. Q. M. G., 29 July, 1866. Died 11 March, 1870. Bvt. Lieut. Col., Col. and Brig. Gen., 13 March, 1865, for faithful and meritorious service in the Q. M. D. during the war.

MILLER, ROBERT. [Born in Tenn. Appointed from Tenn.]
Sergt. Co. E, 4th Tenn. Vols., 15 June, 1863, to 2 Aug., 1865. 1st Lieut. 16th Inf., 28 July, 1866. Resigned 20 Dec., 1867.

MILLER, SAML. H.* [Born in N. Y. Appointed from N. Y.]
Bvt. 2nd Lieut. 3rd Art., 1 July, 1831. 2nd Lieut., 30 June, 1833. Resigned 30 Nov., 1833. Died 4 Jan., 1834.

MILLER, SAMUEL W.* [Born in Penn. Appointed from Penn.]
2nd Lieut. 5th Inf., 13 June, 1879. 1st Lieut., 7 March, 1885. R. Q. M., 30 Sept., 1889. Capt., 26 Jan., 1898. Maj. 46th U. S. Vols., 17 Aug., 1899.

MILLER, SILAS A. [Born in N. Y. Appointed from Army.]
Priv. and Sergt. Co. A, and Sergt. Maj. 2nd Batt. 12th Inf., 17 Aug., 1861, to 23 March, 1863. 2nd Lieut. 12th Inf., 19 Feb., 1863. 1st Lieut., 3 June, 1863. Killed 2 July, 1863, at the Battle of Gettysburg, Pa. Bvt. 1st Lieut., 2 July, 1863, for gallant and meritorious service at the Battle of Gettysburg, Pa.

MILLER, THOS. E.* [Born in Ky. Appointed from Ky.]
Bvt. 2nd Lieut. 3rd Art., 1 July, 1856. 2nd Lieut., 31 Oct., 1856. 1st Lieut., 14 May, 1861. Retired 25 Aug., 1862. Died 13 Nov., 1864.

MILLER, WENTZ C.* [Born in Penn. Appointed from Penn.]
Priv. Sig. Corps, 20 Feb., 1864. Discharged 30 June, 1865. Cadet at Mil. Acad., 1 July, 1865. 2nd Lieut. 4th Cav., 15 June, 1869. 1st Lieut., 29 Sept., 1874. Reg. Adj., 6 May, 1875, to 31 Oct., 1876. Resigned 2 Sept., 1879.

MILLER, WESLEY F. [Born in Penn. Appointed from Minn.]
Priv. Co. E, 1st Minn. Vols., 29 April to 3 Sept., 1861. 2nd Lieut. 7th Inf., 5 Aug., 1861. 1st Lieut., 9 Sept., 1861. Killed 2 July, 1863, at the Battle of Gettysburg, Pa. Bvt. Capt., 2 July, 1863, for gallant and meritorious service at the Battle of Gettysburg, Pa.

MILLER, WM. A. [Born in Ky. Appointed from Ky.]
Priv. Co. F, 8th Ky. Vols., 17 Sept., 1861. 1st Sergt., 28 Feb., 1863. Priv. Co. E, 8th Ky. Vols., 6 Jan., 1864. Discharged 20 March, 1865. 2nd Lieut. 16th Inf., 23 Feb., 1866. Trans. to 25th Inf., 21 Sept., 1866. 1st Lieut., 21 Sept., 1866. Trans. to 18th Inf., 26 April, 1869. Capt., 20 Feb., 1882. Retired for disability 20 Feb., 1891.

MILLER, WM. H.* [Born in Ala. Appointed from Ala.]
2nd Lieut. 1st Cav., 14 June, 1872. R. Q. M., 15 Aug., 1878, to 31 March, 1887. 1st Lieut., 4 March, 1879. Capt. A. Q. M., 4 Sept., 1890. Maj. Chief. Q. M. Vols., 11 Aug., 1898. Bvt. 1st Lieut., 27 Feb., 1890, for gallant service in action against Indians at the Lava Beds, Cal., 17 April, 1873, and gallant and meritorious conduct during the Modoc war.

MILLER, WM. H. [Born in Penn. Appointed from Ill.]
Priv. Co. I, 9th Ind. Vols., 18 April, 1861. Discharged 29 July, 1861. Sergt. Co. E, 48th Ind. Vols., 20 Oct., 1861. 2nd Lieut. 48th Ind. Vols., 10 Jan., 1863. Capt., 14 Nov., 1864. Mustered out 15 July, 1865. 2nd Lieut. 27th Inf., 18 June, 1867. Trans. to 9th Inf., 14 June, 1869. 1st Lieut., 1 July, 1877. Retired 28 June, 1878.

MILLHOFF, CLARENCE B. [Born in Penn. Appointed from Penn.]
Asst. Surg., 30 Jan., 1899.

MILLIS, JOHN.* [Born in Mich. Appointed from Mich.]
2nd Lieut. Eng., 11 June, 1881. 1st Lieut., 15 June, 1882. Capt., 20 Sept., 1892.

MILLS, ALBERT L.* [Born in N. Y. Appointed from N. Y.]
2nd Lieut. 1st Cav., 13 June, 1879. 1st Lieut., 23 Jan., 1889. Capt. 6th Cav., 24 Oct., 1898. Trans. to 1st Cav., 9 Aug., 1899. Capt. A. A. G. Vols., 12 May to 24 Sept., 1898. Superintendent Mil. Acad., with the rank of Col., 22 Aug., 1898.

MILLS, ANSON. [Born in Ind. Appointed from Texas.]
Cadet at Mil. Acad., 1 July, 1855, to 18 Feb., 1857. 1st Lieut. 18th Inf., 14 May, 1861. Bvt. Capt., 31 Dec., 1862, for gallant and meritorious service in the Battle Murfreesboro, Tenn. Capt. 18th Inf., 27 April, 1863. Bvt. Maj., 1 Sept., 1864. for gallant and meritorious service in the Battle of Chickamauga, Ga., and during the Atlanta campaign. Bvt. Lieut. Col., 16 Dec., 1864, for gallant and meritorious service in the Battle of Nashville, Tenn. Trans. to 3rd Cav., 1 Jan., 1871. Maj. 10th Cav., 4 April, 1878. Lieut. Col. 4th Cav., 25 March, 1890. Col. 3rd Cav., 16 Aug., 1892. Brig. Gen., 16 June, 1897. Retired for over thirty years' service, 22 June, 1897.

MILLS, CALVIN J. [Born in N. Y. Appointed from N. Y.]
2nd Lieut. of Inf., 18 March, 1847; 10th Inf., 9 April, 1847. Disbanded 16 Aug., 1848.

MILLS, FRANK H. [Born in Texas. Appointed from N. Y.]
2nd Lieut. 24th Inf., 1 Oct., 1873. 1st Lieut., 20 Aug., 1878. R. Q. M., 1 Nov., 1882, to 18 April, 1887. Retired with the rank of Capt., 4 July, 1892. Died 29 July, 1899.

MILLS, FREDK. D. [Born in Conn. Appointed from Iowa.]
Maj. of Inf., 3 March, 1847; 15th Inf., 9 April, 1847. Killed 20 Aug., 1847, in attack on San Antonio Garita, Mex.

MILLS, JOHN. [Born in Ireland. Appointed from Army.]
Musician 4th Inf., 7 July, 1808, to 1 June, 1815. Priv. Co. B, and Musician Co. A, and Princ. Musician 1st Inf., 14 Oct., 1819, to 7 April, 1865. 2nd Lieut. 1st Inf., 1 April, 1865. Retired 8 June, 1865. Died 21 June, 1867.

MILLS, MADISON. [Born in N. Y. Appointed from N. Y.]
Asst. Surg., 1 April, 1834. Maj. Surg., 16 Feb., 1847. Col. Med. I. G., 1 Dec., 1864, to 31 Oct., 1865. Died 28 April, 1873. Bvt. Lieut. Col. and Col., 29 Nov., 1864, for meritorious service during the campaign and Siege of Vicksburg, Miss. Bvt. Brig. Gen., 13 March, 1865, for faithful and meritorious service during the war.

MILLS, MORRILL M. [Born in Va. Appointed from Va.]
2nd Lieut. 5th Art., 9 July, 1898.

MILLS, SAML. F. [Born in N. Y. Appointed from Army.]
(Served as an enlisted man under the name of Samuel Franklin.) Priv., Corpl. and Sergt. Batty M, 2nd Art., 14 Dec., 1854, to 19 April, 1860. Bvt. 2nd Lieut. 2nd Art., 13 Sept., 1859. 2nd Lieut. 3rd Art., 30 May, 1860. 1st Lieut., 14 May, 1861. Retired 16 Nov., 1861. Died 2 July, 1863.

MILLS, SAMUEL M. [Born in Penn. Appointed from Penn.]
2nd Lieut. and 1st Lieut. 19th Inf., 23 June, 1865. Adj. 2nd Batt., 1 May, 1866, to 21 Sept., 1866. Trans. to 28th Inf., 21 Sept., 1866. Reg. Adj., 30 Nov., 1866, to 31 March, 1869. Trans. to 19th Inf., 31 March, 1869. Reg. Adj., 12 April, 1869, to 10 May, 1870. Trans. to 5th Art., 10 May, 1870. Capt., 18 April, 1883. Maj. 6th Art., 8 March, 1898. Graduate of the Artillery School, 1882.

MILLS, STEPHEN C.* [Born in N. Y. Appointed from Ill.]
Addl. 2nd Lieut. 17th Inf., 15 June, 1877. 2nd Lieut. 12th Inf., 30 June, 1877. 1st Lieut., 28 May, 1884. Capt., 16 Dec., 1894. Maj. I. G., 25 July, 1898. Maj. I. G. Vols., 12 May, 1898, to 28 July, 1898. Bvt. 1st Lieut., 27 Feb., 1890, for gallant services in action against Indians in the San Andreas Mountains, N. M., 7 April, 1880, and in the Los Animas Mountains, N. M., 28 April, 1882.

MILLS, WM. [Born in Mich. Appointed from Army.]
Priv. Co. C, 5th Inf., 28 Oct., 1858. Corpl., 1 March, 1860. Sergt., 1 July, 1861. 1st Sergt., 21 July, 1861. 2nd Lieut. and 1st Lieut. 16th Inf., 19 Feb., 1863. R. Q. M., 12 Oct., 1865, to 13 Feb., 1866. Bvt. Capt., 1 Sept., 1864, for gallant and meritorious service during the Atlanta campaign and in the Battle of Jonesboro, Ga. Capt. 16th Inf., 13 Feb., 1866. Trans. to 2nd Inf., 17 April, 1869. Died 30 Dec., 1890.

MILLS, WM. H. [Born in Maine. Appointed from Mo.]
1st Lieut. 14th Inf., 6 March, 1862. Capt., 23 Dec., 1865. Trans. to 32nd Inf., 21 Sept., 1866. Resigned 12 Dec., 1868. Bvt. Capt., 3 July, 1863, for gallant and meritorious service in the Battles of Cancellorsville and Gettysburg. Bvt. Maj., 9 April, 1865, for meritorious service in the campaign terminating with the surrender of the insurgent army of Northern Virginia.

MILTIMORE, ALONZO E. [Born in Ill. Appointed from Wis.]
Priv. Co. E, 33rd Wis. Vols., 21 Aug., 1862. Discharged 10 Aug., 1863. Priv. 12th Batty Wis. Light Art., 5 Jan., 1864. Discharged 8 Nov., 1864. 2nd Lieut. 1st Wis. Art., 17 Nov., 1864. Mustered out 26 June, 1865. 2nd Lieut. 1st Art., 23 Feb., 1866. 1st Lieut., 28 July, 1866. Capt. A. Q. M., 23 June, 1879. Dismissed 25 Aug., 1890.

MIMMACK, BERNARD P. [Born in England. Appointed from Army.]
Priv. and Sergt. Gen. Ser. and Sergt. Maj. 12th Inf., 15 Jan., 1858, to 20 Sept., 1861. 2nd Lieut. 12th Inf., 16 Sept., 1861. 1st Lieut., 24 Oct., 1861. Reg. Adj., 29 July, 1862, to 30 Jan., 1865. Capt., 3 May, 1865. Trans. to 30th Inf., 21 Sept., 1866. Resigned 29 Oct., 1868. Bvt. Capt., 2 July, 1863, and Maj., 13 March, 1865, for gallant and meritorious service at the Battle of Gettysburg, Pa.

MINER, CHAS. W. [Born in Ohio. Appointed from Ohio.]
Priv. Co. D, 2nd Ohio Vols., 17 April, 1861. Discharged 9 Aug., 1861. Capt. 22nd Ohio Vols., 1 May, 1862. Mustered out 28 Aug., 1865. 2nd Lieut. 19th Inf., 31 March, 1866. Trans. to 28th Inf., 21 Sept., 1866. 1st Lieut., 1 Jan., 1867. Capt.

22nd Inf., 7 March, 1867. Maj. 6th Inf., 29 Dec., 1894. Lieut. Col., 1 July, 1898. Bvt. Maj., 27 Feb., 1890, for gallant services in action against Indians at Spring Creek, Mont., 15 and 16 Oct., 1876. Col. 6th Inf., 15 Dec., 1899.

MINER, CHRISTOPHER C.* [Born in Conn. Appointed from Conn.]
2nd Lieut. 9th Inf., 13 June, 1879. 1st Lieut., 2 Oct., 1887. Dismissed 30 Sept., 1891.

MINIS, PHILIP. [Born in Ga. Appointed from Ga.]
Asst. Surg., 12 April, 1826. Maj. Surg., 1 Dec., 1836. Resigned 21 July, 1837.

MINNIER, FRANCIS P. [Born in Penn. Appointed from Penn.]
Col. 3rd Pa. Vols., 20 April to 29 July, 1861. Capt. 12th Inf., 14 May, 1861. Appointment expired 6 Aug., 1861.

MINOR, CHAS. L. C.* [Born in Va. Appointed from Va.]
Bvt. 2nd Lieut. 5th Inf., 1 July, 1826. 2nd Lieut. 3rd Inf., 1 July, 1826. Died 31 Oct., 1833.

MINOR, COLVILLE J.* [Born in D. C. Appointed from D. C.]
Bvt. 2nd Lieut. 3rd Art., 1 July, 1846. 2nd Lieut., 3 March, 1847. Died 17 Aug., 1847.

MINOR, WM. C. [Born in East Indies. Appointed from N. Y.]
1st Lieut. Asst. Surg., 28 Feb., 1866. Bvt. Capt., 28 Sept., 1866, for meritorious and distinguished service at Fort Columbus, N. Y. Harbor, where cholera prevailed. Capt. Asst. Surg., 30 May, 1869. Retired 15 Dec., 1870.

MINTER, JOSEPH F. [Born in Va. Appointed from Washington Ter.]
2nd Lieut. 2nd Cav., 3 March, 1855. R. Q. M., 1 Oct., 1856, to 31 March, 1861. 1st Lieut., 31 Jan., 1861. Resigned 31 March, 1861. Died 15 Aug., 1885.

MINTON, HENRY H. [Born in N. J. Appointed from Army.]
Sergt. 13th Inf., 29 Jan. to 27 Oct., 1813. Ensign 13th Inf., 27 Oct., 1813. 3rd Lieut., 31 Jan., 1814. 2nd Lieut., 12 Sept., 1814. Disbanded 15 June, 1815. Reinstated 2 Dec., 1815, in Corps Art. 1st Lieut., 26 April, 1818. Died 3 Sept., 1820.

MINUS, JOSIAH C.* [Born in Texas. Appointed from S. C.]
2nd Lieut. 20th Inf., 15 Feb., 1899.

MISHLER, LYMAN.* [Born in Penn. Appointed from Penn.]
Bvt. 2nd Lieut. 7th Inf., 1 July, 1860. 2nd Lieut. 5th Inf., 25 Feb., 1861. 1st Lieut., 14 May, 1861. Killed at the Battle of Val Verde, N. M., 21 Feb., 1862. Bvt. Capt., 21 Feb., 1862, for gallant and meritorious service at the Battle of Val Verde, N. M.

MITCHAM, ORIN B.* [Born in Va. Appointed from Va.]
2nd Lieut. 4th Art., 17 June, 1874. Trans. to Ord. Dept., 23 June, 1879. 1st Lieut., 23 June, 1879. Capt. (14 years' service), 17 June, 1888.

MITCHEL, ORMSBY M.* [Born in Ky. Appointed from Ohio.]
Bvt. 2nd Lieut. 2nd Art., 1 July, 1829. 2nd Lieut., 1 July, 1829. Brig. Gen. Vols., 9 Aug., 1861. Maj. Gen. Vols., 11 April, 1862. Resigned 30 Sept., 1832. Died 30 Oct., 1862.

MITCHEL, ORMSBY M., Jr.* [Born in Ohio. Appointed at Large.]
2nd Lieut. 17th Inf., 23 June, 1865. 1st Lieut., 23 June, 1865. Reg. Adj., 29 Oct., 1865, to 31 Dec., 1866. Trans. to 4th Art., 19 Aug., 1867. Resigned 30 Nov., 1871. Died 27 May, 1875.

MITCHELL, ALEXR. M.* [Born in N. C. Appointed from N. C.]
Bvt. 2nd Lieut. 4th Inf., 1 July, 1835. 2nd Lieut., 16 March, 1836. Resigned 25 March, 1837. Col. 1st Ohio Vols., 23 June, 1846. Mustered out 23 June, 1847. Died 28 Feb., 1861.

MITCHELL, ALFRED. [Born in Del. Appointed from Del.]
2nd Lieut. 1st Inf., 3 March, 1819. 1st Lieut., 1 Dec., 1820. Trans. to 6th Inf., 6 Jan., 1823. Resigned 1 Aug., 1825. Died in 1833.

MITCHELL, AMERICUS.* [Born in Ala. Appointed from Ala.]
2nd Lieut. 5th Inf., 12 June, 1895. 1st Lieut. of Inf., 1 July, 1898. Ass'd to 5th Inf., 1 Jan., 1899.

MITCHELL, ANDREW D. [Born in Penn. Appointed from Penn.]
Post Chaplain, 27 June, 1876. Died 26 March, 1882.

MITCHELL, DAVID D. [Born in Mo. Appointed from Mo.]
2nd Lieut. 15th Inf., 29 Feb., 1876. 1st Lieut., 31 Jan., 1882. Capt., 13 July, 1896. Graduate of the Infantry and Cavalry School 1883. Maj. 1st Ter. Inf., 11 July, 1898. Lieut. Col., 8 Sept., 1898, to muster out 15 Feb., 1899.

MITCHELL EDWARD B. [Born in Ga. Appointed from Army.]
Priv. Batty M, 3rd Art. and Hosp. Corps, 9 Sept., 1896, to 19 Nov., 1899. 2nd Lieut. 24th Inf., 1 Oct., 1899.

MITCHELL, EDWARD L. [Born in N. Y. Appointed from N. Y.]
1st Lieut. 16th Inf., 14 May, 1861. Killed 7 April, 1862, at the Battle of Shiloh, Tenn. Bvt. Capt., 7 April, 1862, for gallant and meritorious service at the Battle of Shiloh, Tenn.

MITCHELL, ENOS G.* [Born in Conn. Appointed from Conn.]
Bvt. 2nd Lieut. 1st Inf., 1 July, 1828. 2nd Lieut., 1 July, 1828. 1st Lieut., 25 Oct., 1835. Capt., 7 July, 1838. Died 10 June, 1839.

MITCHELL, FREDERICK A. [Born in Ohio. Appointed from Army.]
2nd Lieut. 16th Inf., 25 March, 1863. Resigned 17 Aug., 1863.

MITCHELL, GEORGE. [Born in Ireland. Appointed from Conn.]
1st Lieut. 57th N. Y. Vols., 1 Nov., 1862. Mustered out 1 Nov., 1864. Bvt. Maj. Vols., 13 March, 1865, for faithful service. Bvt. Lieut. Col. Vols., 13 March, 1865, for gallant and meritorious service during the war. 1st Lieut. 7th U. S. Vet. Vols., 9 June, 1865. Capt., 27 Sept., 1865. Mustered out 24 April, 1866. 2nd Lieut. 13th Inf., 30 April, 1866. Trans. to 31st Inf., 21 Sept., 1866. 1st Lieut., 10 June, 1868. Unassigned 15 May, 1869. Ass'd to 2nd Art., 15 Dec., 1870. Reg. Adj., 21 May, 1875, to 24 March, 1877. Capt., 22 March, 1885. Graduate of the Artillery School, 1880. Retired for disability with rank of Maj., 8 March, 1898.

MITCHELL, GEORGE E. [Born in Md. Appointed from Md.]
Maj. 3rd Art., 1 May, 1812. Lieut. Col., 3 March, 1813. Trans. to Corps Art., 12 May, 1814. Trans. to 3rd Art., 1 June, 1821. Resigned 1 June, 1821. Bvt. Col., 5 May, 1814, for gallant conduct at the Battle of Oswego. Died 28 June, 1832.

MITCHELL, GEORGE E.* [Born in Mich. Appointed from Mich.]
Addl. 2nd Lieut. 2nd Cav., 11 June, 1897. 2nd Lieut. 7th Cav., 29 June, 1897.

MITCHELL, JAMES. [Born in Ireland. Appointed from Army.]
Priv., Corpl. and Sergt. Troop L and Q. M. Sergt. 7th Cav., 6 Dec., 1867, to 6 Dec., 1872. Priv. and Sergt. Signal Corps, 19 Dec., 1872, to 17 Aug., 1885. 2nd Lieut. Sig. Corps, 15 Aug., 1885. 2nd Lieut. 15th Inf., 4 Feb., 1891, to rank from 15 Aug., 1885. 1st Lieut. 9th Inf., 18 June, 1892. Trans. to 14th Inf., 12 Aug., 1892. Died of wounds received in action at Manila, Philippine Islands, 6 Feb., 1899.

MITCHELL, JAMES B. [Born in N. Y. Appointed from N. Y.]
1st Lieut. 3rd N. Y. Vols., 17 Aug. to 24 July, 1898. 2nd Lieut. 4th Art., 9 July, 1898.

MITCHELL, JAMES E. [Born in Pa. Appointed from Army.]
Priv. and Sergt. Co. H, 2nd Batt. 18th Inf., 14 Feb., 1862, to 21 April, 1863. 2nd Lieut. 18th Inf., 19 Feb., 1863. Died 13 Sept., 1863.

MITCHELL, JOHN. [Born in Ireland. Appointed from Army.]
Priv., Corpl., Sergt. and 1st Sergt. Batty B, 4th Art., 22 June, 1853, to 14 Aug., 1863. 2nd Lieut. 4th Art., 10 Aug., 1863. 1st Lieut., 13 Oct., 1865. Capt. 43rd Inf., 28 July, 1866. Trans. to 1st Inf., 8 April, 1869. Unassigned 7 June, 1869. Died 13 Nov., 1869. Bvt. 1st Lieut., 18 Aug., 1864, for gallant and meritorious service in Battle on the Weldon Railroad, Va. Bvt. Capt., 29 March, 1865, for gallant and meritorious service during the operations against Petersburg, Va.

MITCHELL, JOHN F. B., Jr. [Born in N. Y. Appointed from N. Y.]
2nd Lieut. 7th Inf., 9 July, 1898. Trans. to 12th Inf., 1 Feb., 1899. 1st Lieut., 20 Sept., 1899.

MITCHELL, OSCAR R. [Born in Ohio. Appointed from Ohio.]
2nd Lieut. 15th Inf., 30 Dec., 1847. Disbanded 4 Aug., 1848.

MITCHELL, WARREN H.* [Born in Minn. Appointed from Penn.]
Addl. 2nd Lieut. of Art. (2nd), 12 June, 1894. 2nd Lieut., 14 July, 1894, to rank from 12 June, 1894. Died 26 Nov., 1895.

MITCHELL, WM. [Born in Ireland. Appointed from Army.]
Priv. Co. D, 2nd Inf., 4 Jan., 1855. Corpl., 1 Aug., 1855. Sergt., 3 Jan., 1857. Discharged 7 Nov., 1859. Sergt. Co. D, 2nd Inf., 7 Nov., 1859. 1st Sergt., 4 Oct., 1862. 2nd Lieut. 3rd Inf., 22 April, 1863. Bvt. 1st Lieut., 2 July, 1863, for gallant and meritorious service in the Battle of Gettysburg, Pa. 1st Lieut. 3rd Inf., 10 Nov., 1864. R. Q. M., 1 Aug., 1863, to 11 Aug., 1869. Bvt. Capt., 13 March, 1865, for gallant and meritorious service in the Battle of Gettysburg, Pa. Capt., 31 May, 1883. Retired for disability 24 April, 1886. Died 21 May, 1895.

MITCHELL, WM. G. [Born in Penn. Appointed from Penn.]
Priv. Co. E, 25th Pa. Vols., 18 April, 1861. Trans. to 7th Pa. Vols., 23 April, 1861. Sergt. Maj., 23 April, 1861. 1st Lieut. 7th Pa. Vols., 27 June, 1861. Mustered out 5 Aug., 1861. 1st Lieut. 49th Pa. Vols., 25 Aug., 1861. Maj. A. de C. Vols., 25 June, 1863. Bvt. Lieut. Col. Vols., 1 Aug., 1864, for meritorious and distinguished conduct and for gallantry in action, especially in the Wilderness. Bvt. Col. Vols., 27 Oct., 1864, for gallant and meritorious service in the Battle of Boydton Plank Road, Va. Bvt. Brig. Gen. Vols., 13 March, 1865, for distinguished and most valuable service during the war. Lieut. Col. A. I. G., 1 Aug., 1865, to 11 June, 1866. Mustered out 31 July, 1866. Capt. 37th Inf., 28 July, 1866. Bvt. Maj., 2 March, 1867, for gallant and meritorious service in the Battle of the Wilderness, Va. Bvt. Lieut. Col., 2 March, 1867, for gallant and meritorious service in the Battle of Boydton Road, Va. Bvt. Col., 2 March, 1867, for gallant and meritorious service in the Battle of Spottsylvania, Va., 12 May, 1864. Trans. to 5th Inf., 19 May, 1869. Maj. A. A. G., 1 July, 1881. Died 30 May, 1883.

MITCHELL, WM. W. [Born in Ohio. Appointed from Army.]
Priv. Batty B, 2nd Art., 26 Feb., 1851, to 26 Feb., 1856. Priv., Corpl., Sergt. and 1st Sergt. Batty K and Sergt Maj. and Q. M. Sergt. 4th Art., 24 May, 1856, to 15 July, 1863. Ord. Sergt., 15 July to 11 Nov., 1863. 2nd Lieut. 2nd Inf., 31 Oct., 1863. 1st Lieut., 18 April, 1866. R. Q. M., 1 July, 1864, to 18 April, 1869. Unassigned 17 April, 1869. Discharged 1 Nov., 1870. Bvt. 1st Lieut., 5 May, 1864, for gallant and meritorious service at the Battle of the Wilderness, Va. Bvt. Capt., 24 May, 1864, for gallant and meritorious service at the Battle of North Anna River, Va.

MIX, JOHN. [Born in N. Y. Appointed from Army.]
Priv. Co. F, 2nd Drag., 11 April, 1852. Corpl., 1 Sept, 1854. Sergt., 1 June, 1856. Discharged 11 Feb., 1857. Sergt. Co. F, 2nd Drag., 11 Feb., 1857. 1st Sergt., 14 Oct., 1858. Sergt., 15 June, 1861. 2nd Lieut. 2nd Cav., 14 Aug., 1861. Maj. 3rd N. Y. Cav., 17 Sept., 1861. Lieut. Col., 26 April, 1862. 1st Lieut. 2nd Cav., 17 July, 1862. Resigned from Vol. Service, 27 Dec., 1862. Capt. 2nd Cav., 19 Oct., 1865. Maj. 9th Cav., 25 Jan., 1881. Died 26 Oct., 1881.

MIX, WM. A. [Born in N. Y. Appointed from N. Y.]
2nd Lieut. 6th Inf., 13 Feb., 1818. Disbanded 1 June, 1821. Died 4 April, 1823.

MIZNER, HENRY R. [Born in N. Y. Appointed from Mich.]
Capt. 18th Inf., 14 May, 1861. Col. 14th Mich. Vols., 22 Dec., 1862. Bvt. Maj., 31 Dec., 1862, for gallant and meritorious service in the Battle of Murfreesboro, Tenn. Bvt. Lieut. Col., 1 Sept., 1864, for gallant and meritorious service during Atlanta campaign and in the Battle of Jonesboro, Ga. Bvt. Brig. Gen. Vols., 13 March, 1865, for gallant and meritorious service during the war. Mustered out of Vol. Service, 18 July, 1865. Trans to 36th Inf., 21 Sept., 1866. Maj. 20th Inf., 22 Feb., 1869. Trans. to 12th Inf., 15 March, 1869. Trans. to 8th Inf., 14 May, 1877. Lieut. Col. 10th Inf., 15 Dec., 1880. Col. 17th Inf., 2 Jan., 1888. Retired by operation of law 1 Aug., 1891.

MIZNER, JOHN K.* [Born in N. Y. Appointed from Mich.]
Bvt. 2nd Lieut. 2nd Drag., 1 July, 1856. 2nd Lieut., 28 Feb., 1857. 1st Lieut., 9 May, 1861. 2nd Cav., 3 Aug., 1861. Capt., 12 Nov., 1861. Col. 3rd Mich. Cav., 7 March, 1862. Bvt. Maj., 4 Oct., 1862, for gallant and meritorious service in the Battle of Corinth, Miss. Bvt. Lieut. Col., 12 June, 1863, for gallant and meritorious service in action at Panola, Miss. Bvt. Brig. Gen. Vols., 13 March, 1865, for gallant and meritorious service during the war. Mustered out of Vol. Service, 12 Feb., 1866. Maj. 4th Cav., 26 Jan., 1869. Lieut. Col. 8th Cav., 9 Jan., 1886. Col. 10th Cav., 15 April, 1890. Brig. Gen., 26 May, 1897. Retired, after forty years' service, 7 June, 1897. Died 8 Sept., 1898.

MOALE, EDWARD. [Born in Md. Appointed from Md.]
1st Lieut. 19th Inf., 14 May, 1861. R. Q. M., 22 Aug., 1861, to 20 July, 1862. Capt., 13 Sept., 1864. Bvt. Maj., 2 Dec., 1864, for gallant and distinguished service in the Battle of Spottsylvania, and during the campaign before Richmond, Va. Bvt. Col. Vols., 13 March, 1865, for gallant and meritorious service during the war. Lieut. Col. A. A. G., 21 March, 1865. Bvt. Lieut. Col., 2 April, 1865, for gallant and meritorious service in front of Petersburg, Va. Relieved as Lieut. Col. A. A. G., 1 Aug., 1865. Trans. to 37th Inf., 21 Sept., 1866. Trans. to 3rd Inf., 11 Aug., 1869. Maj. 1st Inf., 1 Feb., 1887. Lieut. Col. 3rd Inf., 4 Dec., 1891. Col. 15th Inf., 4 Feb., 1897.

MOBERLEY, WILL J.* [Born in Ky. Appointed from Ky.]
2nd Lieut. 4th Cav., 18 June, 1866. 1st Lieut., 16 Aug., 1867. Resigned 31 July, 1869.

MOCK, WM.* [Born in N. C. Appointed from N. C.]
Bvt. 2nd Lieut. 3rd Art., 1 July, 1836. 2nd Lieut., 31 Aug., 1836. 1st Lieut., 7 July, 1838. Resigned 30 June, 1841.

MOFFATT, ISAAC F. [Born in Canada. Appointed from Penn.]
Priv. Co. H, 6th Pa. Cav., 12 Oct., 1861. 1st Lieut., 26 Sept., 1864. Capt., 23 March, 1865. Mustered out 7 Aug., 1865. 1st Lieut. 9th Cav., 28 July, 1866. Capt., 16 July, 1869. Died 2 Oct., 1870. Bvt. Capt., 2 March, 1867, for gallant and meritorious service during the war.

MOFFATT, PETER. [Born in Canada. Appointed from Cal.]
1st Lieut. Asst. Surg., 9 Oct., 1867. Capt. Asst. Surg., 9 Oct., 1870. Died 15 June, 1882.

MOFFATT, WM. [Born in N. Y. Appointed from Army.]
Musician Cos. E and H, 17th Inf., 12 Jan., 1871, to 12 Jan., 1876. Musician and Corpl. Co. A, 21st Inf., and Priv. and Corpl. Gen. Service, 2 June to 13 July, 1880. 2nd Lieut. 2nd Inf., 24 June, 1880. Died 25 Jan., 1890.

MOLINARD, ALBERT J. S.* [Born in N. Y. Appointed from N. Y.]
Bvt. 2nd Lieut. 4th Art., 1 July, 1851. 2nd Lieut. 2nd Art., 28 Sept., 1852. 1st Lieut., 20 Feb., 1855. Capt., 12 Nov., 1861. Wholly retired 1 Oct., 1863. Died 14 Sept., 1872.

MOLINARD, JULIAN. [Born in France. Appointed from N. Y.]
Teacher of French at the U. S. Mil. Acad., 19 Nov., 1830. Resigned 12 Sept., 1839. Mil. Storekeeper, Ord. Dept., 3 Feb., 1862. Died 13 Jan., 1863.

MONAHAN, DEANE. [Born in Ireland. Appointed from Army.]
Priv. Co. I, Mtd Rifles, 29 July, 1856. Corpl., 31 Jan., 1860. Discharged 29 May, 1861. Corpl. Co. I, Mtd Rifles, 29 May, 1861. Sergt., 1 Aug., 1861. 1st Sergt., 22 Feb., 1862. Sergt. Maj., 9 Sept., 1862. Discharged 20 Dec., 1862. 2nd Lieut. 3rd Cav., 17 July, 1862. Bvt. 1st Lieut., 15 Nov., 1863, for gallant and meritorious service in action near Tuscumbia, Ala. 1st Lieut. 3rd Cav., 18 May, 1865. Reg. Adj., 29 May, 1867, to 9 July, 1868. Capt., 9 July, 1868. Retired for disability, 26 Nov., 1884.

MONIAC, DAVID.* [Born in Ala. Appointed from Ala.]
Bvt. 2nd Lieut. 6th Inf., 1 July, 1822. Resigned 31 Dec., 1822. Capt. Creek Mtd Vols., 17 Aug., 1836. Maj., 15 Nov., 1836. Killed 31 Nov., 1836, in battle with the Seminole Indians at Wahoo Swamp, Fla. (He was a Creek Indian.)

MONROE, AUGUSTIN G. [Born in Va. Appointed from Va.]
2nd Lieut. 6th Inf., 12 July, 1820. Disbanded 1 June, 1821.

MONROE, FRANCIS LE BARON. [Born in Mass. Appointed from Mass.]
Asst. Surg. Mass. Light Art., 20 April, 1861. Mustered out 3 Aug., 1861. Asst. Surg. 1st Mass. Vols., 2 Sept., 1861. Surg. 15th Mass. Vols., 19 Jan., 1863. Mustered out 28 July, 1864. Asst. Surg., 26 May, 1867. Resigned 31 Dec., 1875.

MONROE, JAMES.* [Born in Va. Appointed from Va.]
3rd Lieut. Corps Art., 2 March, 1815. 2nd Lieut., 2 May, 1817. 1st Lieut., 31 Dec., 1818. Trans. to 4th Art., 1 June, 1821. Resigned 30 Sept., 1832. Bvt. Capt., 31 Dec., 1828, for ten years' faithful service in one grade. Died 7 Sept., 1870.

MONROE, JAMES, Jr. [Born in Va. Appointed from Va.]
2nd Lieut. 6th Inf., 17 Aug., 1837. 1st Lieut., 7 July, 1838. Capt., 9 May, 1846. Resigned 9 May, 1855.

MONROE, THOMAS J. C. [Born in Va. Appointed from Ohio.]
Surg.'s Mate 6th Inf., 12 Sept., 1811. Resigned 20 Jan., 1812. Garrison Surg.'s Mate, 29 April, 1814. Disbanded 15 June, 1815. Post Surg., 29 April, 1816. Asst. Surg., 1 June, 1821. Died 23 Oct., 1839.

MONTIETH, RANDOLPH V. [Born in N. Y. Appointed from Army.]
Entered service under name of Robert McLean. Priv. Cos. L and A, 2nd Art., 11 Feb., 1847, to 11 Feb., 1852. Priv. and Sergt. Co. D, 1st Drag., 21 June, 1852, to 5 July, 1858. Priv., Sergt. and 1st Sergt. Cos. H and C, and Sergt. Maj. 3rd Art., 26 July, 1860, to 18 May, 1864. 2nd Lieut. 2nd Art., 7 April, 1864. 1st Lieut., 7 Feb., 1865. Resigned 21 Nov., 1865. Priv. and Sergt. Co. E, 12th Inf. and Com. Sergt., 7 June, 1869. Dishonorably discharged 10 Aug., 1870.

MONTGOMERY, ALEXR.* [Born in Penn. Appointed from Penn.]
Bvt. 2nd Lieut. 7th Inf., 1 July, 1834. 2nd Lieut., 3 Dec., 1835. 1st Lieut., 7 July, 1838. Capt. A. Q. M., 11 May, 1846. Capt. 7th Inf., 16 Feb., 1847. Vacated

line commission. 16 Feb., 1847. Maj. Q. M., 17 May, 1861. Dismissed 18 July, 1863. Reinstated 14 June, 1864. Lieut. Col. Dep. Q. M. G., 6 June, 1872. Retired 15 Jan., 1874. Died 13 Oct., 1893.

MONTGOMERY, ALEXR. B. [Born in Ga. Appointed from Ga.]
2nd Lieut. 3rd Art., 22 June, 1857. Trans. to 4th Art., 31 Aug., 1857. Resigned 3 March, 1861.

MONTGOMERY, DAVID L. [Born in Penn. Appointed from Penn.]
1st Lieut. 17th Inf., 14 May, 1861. Capt., 28 Nov., 1863. Trans. to 26th Inf., 21 Sept., 1866. Died 10 June, 1868. Bvt. Capt., 27 June, 1862, for gallant and meritorious service at the Battle of Gaines' Mills, Va. Bvt. Maj., 2 July, 1863, for gallant and meritorious service at the Battle of Gettysburg, Penn. Bvt. Lieut. Col., 13 March, 1865, for gallant and meritorious service.

MONTGOMERY, ELIJAH. [Born in Va. Appointed from Ky.]
Ensign 7th Inf., 12 Dec., 1808. 2nd Lieut., 1 Dec., 1809. 1st Lieut., 24 June, 1811. Capt., 1 May, 1814. Disbanded 1 June, 1821. Bvt. Maj., 8 Jan., 1815, for gallant conduct at the Siege of New Orleans.

MONTGOMERY, GEORGE.* [Born in Ireland. Appointed from N. Y.]
Addl. 2nd Lieut. 2nd Art., 12 June, 1890. 2nd Lieut. 3rd Art., 1 April, 1891. Trans. to 2nd Art., 23 May, 1891. 1st Lieut. Ord., 19 June, 1894. Honor graduate of the Artillery School, 1894.

MONTGOMERY, HAMILTON. [Born in Tenn. Appointed from Tenn.]
2nd Lieut. 14th Inf., 29 March, 1848. Resigned 14 June, 1848.

MONTGOMERY, RICHD. R. [Born in N. Y. Appointed from N. Y.]
Maj. J. A. Vols., 30 June, 1865. Trans. to U. S. A., 25 Feb., 1867. Resigned 14 Feb., 1868.

MONTGOMERY, ROBT. H. [Born in Penn. Appointed from Army.]
Priv. Co. C, 2nd Cav., 6 Aug., 1860. Corpl., 1 Jan., 1861. Sergt. Co. C, 5th Cav., 20 Oct., 1861. 1st Sergt., 6 Sept., 1862. 2nd Lieut. 5th Cav., 29 Nov., 1862. Bvt. 1st Lieut., 9 June, 1863, for gallant and meritorious service in the Battle of Beverly Ford, Va. Bvt. Capt., 1 Aug., 1863, for gallant and meritorious service in the Battle of Brandy Station, Va. Dismissed 19 Nov., 1863. Reinstated 2nd Lieut. 5th Cav., 16 Feb., 1865. 1st Lieut., 25 April, 1865. R. Q. M., 3 Aug., 1865, to 31 Dec., 1866. Reg. Adj., 31 Dec., 1866, to 12 July, 1869. Capt., 3 Jan., 1870. Maj. 10th Cav., 8 March, 1891. Retired, over thirty years' service, 8 April, 1892. Bvt. Maj., 27 Feb., 1890, for gallant services in action against Indians at Muchos Canons, Ariz., 25 Sept., 1872, and in a scout made by him through Tonto Basin, Ariz., during the months of Nov. and Dec., 1874.

MONTGOMERY, SAML. H. [Born in Penn. Appointed from Penn.]
Capt. A. Q. M., Vols., 4 Jan., 1847. Dismissed 25 Feb., 1848. Capt. A. Q. M. Vols., 27 June, 1848. Disbanded 15 Oct., 1848. Mil. Storekeeper Q. M. D., 14 March, 1857. Died 15 June, 1864.

MONTGOMERY, THOMAS. [Born in Md. Appointed from Md.]
Capt. 14th Inf., 12 March, 1812. Maj. 19th Inf., 21 Dec., 1814. Disbanded 15 June, 1815. Maj. P. M. Art. Batt., 29 April, 1816. Died 11 Dec., 1816.

MONTGOMERY, THOMAS J.* [Born in Maine. Appointed from Maine.]
Bvt. 2nd Lieut. 8th Inf., 1 July, 1845. 2nd Lieut. 4th Inf., 9 Sept., 1846. 1st Lieut., 26 Dec., 1847. Capt., 27 March, 1854. Died 22 Nov., 1854.

MONTGOMERY, WM. R.* [Born in N. J. Appointed from N. J.]
Bvt. 2nd Lieut. 3rd Inf., 1 July, 1825. 2nd Lieut., 1 July, 1825. 1st Lieut., 31 Aug., 1833. Capt. 8th Inf., 7 July, 1838. Maj. 2nd Inf., 7 Dec., 1852. Dismissed 8 Dec., 1855. Bvt. Maj., 9 May, 1846, for gallant conduct at Palo Alto and Resaca de la Palma. Bvt. Lieut. Col., 8 Sept., 1847, for gallant and meritorious conduct at Molino del Rey, Mex. Col. 1st N. J. Vols., 21 May, 1861. Brig. Gen. Vols., 17 May, 1861. Resigned 4 April, 1864. Died 31 May, 1871.

MOODY, GIDEON C. [Born in N. Y. Appointed from Ind.]
1st Lieut. 9th Ind. Vols., 19 April, 1861. Capt., 26 April, 1861. Mustered out 29 July, 1861. Capt. 19th U. S. Inf., 14 May, 1861. Lieut. Col. 9th Ind. Vols., 5 Sept., 1861. Col., 15 Nov., 1861. Mustered out of Vol. Service, 19 Aug., 1862, and resigned from U. S. A., 16 March, 1864.

MOODY, THOMAS M. [Born in Wis. Appointed from Army.]
Priv., Corpl. and Sergt. Co. D. and Sergt. Maj. 9th Inf., 8 March, 1879, to 26 March, 1888. 2nd Lieut. 22nd Inf., 6 Feb., 1888. 1st Lieut. 20th Inf., 26 April, 1895. Capt. 16th Inf., 2 March, 1899. Graduate of the Infantry and Cavalry School, 1891. Adj., 17 Nov., 1899.

MOOKLAR, WM. T. [Born in Va. Appointed from Va.]
3rd Lieut. Corps Art., 11 Aug., 1814. 2nd Lieut., 14 Nov., 1814. Disbanded 15 June, 1815. 2nd Lieut. Corps Art., 27 Aug., 1819. Disbanded 1 June, 1821.

MOON, ALBERT G. [Born in Va. Appointed from Va.]
2nd Lieut. Inf., 23 Feb., 1847; 14th Inf., 9 April, 1847. Died 17 July, 1847.

MOON, HENRY B.* [Born in N. J. Appointed from Mo.]
2nd Lieut. 20th Inf., 12 June, 1880. 1st Lieut., 31 Aug., 1887. Capt., 31 May, 1895.

MOON, SQUIRE. [Born in N. Y. Appointed from N. Y.]
1st Lieut. Inf., 3 March, 1847; 10th Inf., 9 April, 1847. Disbanded 14 Aug., 1848.

MOONEY, JAMES. [Born in England. Appointed from N. Y.]
Capt. 19th Inf., 12 Nov., 1861. Dismissed 26 Sept., 1865.

MOORE, ALEXANDER. [Born in Ireland. Appointed from Ill.]
Capt., A. de C. Vols., 10 Nov., 1862. Expired by constitutional limitation 4 March, 1863, and revoked 27 April, 1863. Capt. A. de C. Vols., 30 May, 1863. Bvt. Maj. Vols., 6 March, 1865. Bvt. Lieut. Col. Vols., 13 March, 1865, for gallant and distinguished conduct in several campaigns of the Army of the Potomac prior to the Battle of Gettysburg, Penn. Bvt. Col. Vols., 13 March, 1865, for gallant and highly meritorious conduct in the Battle of Gettysburg, Penn. Musterer out of Vol. Service, 26 Sept., 1866. Capt. 38th Inf., 22 Jan., 1867. Bvt. Maj., 2 March, 1867, for gallant and meritorious service in the Battle of Gettys-

burg, Penn. Unassigned 11 Nov., 1869. Ass'd to 3rd Cav., 15 Dec., 1870. Resigned 10 Aug., 1879.

MOORE, BENJAMIN D. [Born in Ky. Appointed from Ill.]
Midshipman U. S. N., 2 Feb., 1829. Resigned 2 Jan., 1833. 1st Lieut. Mtd Rangers, 6 Nov., 1832. 1st Lieut. 1st Drag., 19 Sept., 1833. Capt., 15 June, 1837. Killed 6 Dec., 1846, in the action at San Pasqual, Cal.

MOORE, CHAS. E.* [Born in N. Y. Appointed at Large.]
2nd Lieut. 16th Inf., 23 June, 1865. 1st Lieut., 23 June, 1865. R. Q. M., 5 Aug., 1866, to 14 April, 1869. Trans. to 2nd Inf., 17 April, 1869. Cashiered 18 March, 1872. Died 5 Dec., 1885.

MOORE, DAN. T. [Born in Ala. Appointed from N. Y.]
2nd Lieut. Co. I, 3rd Conn. Vols., 19 Sept., 1898, to muster out, 20 March, 1899. 2nd Lieut. 15th Inf., 10 April, 1899.

MOORE, EDWARD C. [Born in D. C. Appointed from Ill.]
2nd Lieut. 2nd Inf., 27 June, 1856. Died 16 Jan., 1857.

MOORE, FRANCIS. [Born in Scotland. Appointed from La.]
Priv. Co. M, 1st Colo. Cav., 10 Sept., 1861. Sergt., 31 Dec., 1862. Capt. 65th U. S. Col. Troops, 29 Dec., 1863. Bvt. Lieut. Col. Vols., 13 March, 1865, for faithful and meritorious service during the war. Lieut. Col. 65th U. S. Col. Troops, 18 Feb., 1865. Mustered out 21 June, 1865. Maj. 65th U. S. Col. Troops, 21 June, 1865. 2nd Lieut. 9th Cav., 28 July, 1866. Mustered out of Vol. Service 8 Jan., 1867. Reg. Com. 9th Cav., 15 May, 1867, to 15 July, 1870. 1st Lieut. 9th Cav., 12 July, 1867. R. Q. M., 1 Sept., 1870, to 24 Aug., 1872. Capt., 24 Aug., 1872. Maj. 5th Cav., 28 July, 1892. Lieut. Col. 10th Cav., 6 May, 1899.

MOORE FREDK. W.* [Born in Ohio. Appointed from Ohio.]
2nd Lieut. 5th Ohio Vols., 20 April, 1861. 1st Lieut., 14 Sept., 1861. Capt., 9 Jan., 1862. Mustered out 23 July, 1862. Col. 83rd Ohio Vols., 13 Sept., 1862. Bvt. Brig. Gen. Vols., 26 March, 1865, for gallant and meritorious service during the campaign against the City of Mobile and its defences. Mustered out 24 July, 1865. 2nd Lieut. 19th Inf., 23 Feb., 1866. 1st Lieut., 23 Feb., 1866. Resigned 16 April, 1867.

MOORE, GEORGE D.* [Born in Ill. Appointed from Ill.]
2nd Lieut. 18th Inf., 12 June, 1890. 1st Lieut. 23rd Inf., 17 April, 1897. Maj. 5th Mo. Vols., 22 May, 1898, until muster out, 9 Nov., 1898. Capt. 20th Inf., 15 Dec., 1899.

MOORE, HARRY DEW.* [Born in Penn. Appointed from Penn.]
2nd Lieut. 21st Inf., 14 June, 1872. 1st Lieut., 19 July, 1876. Drowned 10 May, 1878.

MOORE, ISAIAH N.* [Born in Penn. Appointed from Penn.]
Bvt. 2nd Lieut. 1st Drag., 1 July, 1851. 2nd Lieut., 21 Feb., 1853. 1st Lieut., 3 March, 1855. Capt., 20 April, 1861. 1st Cav., 3 Aug., 1861. Died 16 Jan., 1862.

MOORE, JAMES J. [Born in Ky. Appointed from Ky.]
2nd Lieut. Inf., 8 March, 1847; 3rd Drag., 9 April, 1847. Disbanded 31 July, 1848. Died 19 Feb., 1850.

MOORE, JAMES M. [Born in Penn. Appointed from Penn.]
Priv. Co. G, 19th Penn. Vols., 18 April, 1861. Mustered out 8 Aug., 1861. 2nd Lieut. 90th Penn. Vols., 21 Feb., 1862. 1st Lieut., 10 March, 1862. Resigned 7 April, 1863. Capt. A. Q. M. Vols., 11 March, 1863. Capt. A. Q. M., U. S. A., 2 July, 1864. Bvt. Maj., 13 March, 1865, for faithful and meritorious service during the war. Bvt. Lieut. Col., 24 Nov., 1865, for faithful and meritorious service. Maj. Q. M., 13 June, 1867. Lieut. Col. Dep. Q. M. G., 2 July, 1883 Col. A. Q. M. G., 14 Jan., 1895.

MOORE, JAMES S.* [Born in Ga. Appointed from Ga.]
Bvt. 2nd Lieut. 5th Inf., 1 July, 1829. Resigned 31 Oct., 1829. Died 25 July, 1869.

MOORE, JAMES T.* [Born in Conn. Appointed from Mich.]
2nd Lieut. 3rd Inf., 11 June, 1892. 1st Lieut., 26 April, 1898.

MOORE, JOHN. [Born in Ind. Appointed from Ind.]
1st Lieut. Asst. Surg., 29 June, 1853. Capt. Asst. Surg., 29 June, 1858. Maj. Surg., 11 June, 1862. Bvt. Lieut. Col., 1 Sept., 1864, for gallant and meritorious service during the Atlanta campaign. Col. Med. Director, 25 Feb., 1865. Bvt. Col., 13 March, 1865, for faithful and meritorious service during the war. Relieved as Col. Med. Director, 30 June, 1865. Lieut. Col. Asst. Med. Pur., 8 Oct., 1883. Brig. Gen., Surg. Gen., 18 Nov., 1886. Retired, by operation of law, 16 Aug., 1890.

MOORE, JOHN C.* [Born in Tenn. Appointed from Tenn.]
Bvt. 2nd Lieut. 4th Art., 1 July, 1849. 2nd Lieut. 2nd Art., 10 Sept., 1850. 1st Lieut., 18 Oct., 1853. Resigned 28 Feb., 1855.

MOORE, JOHN K.* [Born in Ohio. Appointed from Ohio.]
Addl. 2nd Lieut. 7th Inf., 11 June, 1897. 2nd Lieut. 15th Inf., 7 July, 1897. 1st Lieut., 2 March, 1899.

MOORE, MARTIN M. [Born in Penn. Appointed from Penn.]
Capt., Inf., 16 Feb., 1847; 11th Inf., 9 April, 1847. Died 25 July, 1847.

MOORE, MICHAEL. [Born in N. Y. Appointed from Army.]
Musician Capt. Sproull's Co. 13th Inf., 30 April, 1812. Discharged 1 May, 1817. Musician Co. A, 2nd Inf., 4 Feb., 1819. Discharged 4 Feb., 1824. Re-enlisted 20 April, 1824. Discharged 12 Feb., 1829. Out of service 12 May, 1830. Restored to service 11 June, 1830. Discharged 12 Feb., 1834. Musician Co. A, 2nd Inf., 2 Sept., 1834. Prin. Musician 2nd Inf., — Nov., 1834. Discharged 2 Sept., 1837. Re-enlisted 2 Sept., 1837. Discharged 2 Sept., 1840. Sergt. Co. B, Music Boys, 4 May, 1841. Discharged 4 May, 1846. Re-enlisted 4 May, 1846. Discharged 4 May, 1851. Re-enlisted 5 May, 1851. Discharged 5 May, 1856. Re-enlisted 5 May, 1856. Discharged 6 May, 1861. Re-enlisted 6 May, 1861. Discharged 5 Jan., 1864. Re-enlisted 5 Jan., 1864. Discharged 5 Jan., 1869. Re-enlisted 15 Jan., 1869. 2nd Lieut. 9th Inf., 19 Jan., 1869. Unassigned 14 June, 1869. Retired 15 Dec., 1870. Died 3 Aug., 1897.

MOORE, ORLANDO H. [Born in Pa. Appointed from Mich.]
2nd Lieut. 6th Inf., 27 June, 1856. 1st Lieut., 2 March, 1861. 1st Lieut. 19th Inf., 14 May, 1861, declined. Capt. 6th Inf., 26 May, 1861. Lieut. Col. 13th Mich. Vols., 17 Jan., 1862. Resigned Vol. commission 4 July, 1862. Col. 25th Mich. Vols., 22 Sept., 1862. Bvt. Maj., 4 July, 1863, for gallant and meritorious service in action at Tebbs Bend, Ky. Bvt. Lieut. Col., 13 March, 1865, for gallant and meritorious service during the war. Mustered out of Vol. Service, 24 June, 1865. Maj. 6th Inf., 8 June, 1874. Lieut. Col. 17th Inf., 11 April, 1882. Retired for disability 15 Sept., 1884. Died 31 Oct., 1890.

MOORE, SAML. D. J.* [Born in N. C. Appointed from Ala.]
Bvt. 2nd Lieut 6th Inf., 1 July, 1837, declined.

MOORE, SAML. P. [Born in S. C. Appointed from S. C.]
Asst. Surg., 14 March, 1835. Maj. Surg., 30 April, 1848. Resigned 25 Feb., 1861. Died 31 May, 1889.

MOORE, STEPHEN W.* [Born in S. C. Appointed from S. C.]
Bvt. 2nd Lieut. 7th Inf., 1 July, 1827. 2nd Lieut., 1 July, 1827. 1st Lieut., 21 May, 1834. Capt., 7 July, 1838. Resigned 19 April, 1846.

MOORE, THOS. P. [Born in Va. Appointed from Ky.]
2nd Lieut. Ill. Vols., 16 June to 7 Aug., 1832. Lieut. Col. of Inf., 3 March, 1847; 3rd Drag., 9 April, 1847. Disbanded 31 July, 1848. Died 21 July, 1853.

MOORE, THOS. W. C. [Born in N. Y. Appointed from Wis.]
Priv. Co. B, 24th Wis. Vols., 21 Aug., 1862. 2nd Lieut., 16 March, 1863, to 25 June, 1864. Capt. A. de C. Vols., 18 May, 1864. Maj. A. A. G. Vols., 8 March, 1865. Bvt. Maj. Vols., 13 March, 1865, for gallant and meritorious service. Bvt. Lieut. Col. Vols., 13 March, 1865, for gallant and meritorious service during the recent campaign resulting in the surrender of the insurgent army under Gen. R. E. Lee. Mustered out 1 Aug., 1866. 2nd Lieut. 11th Inf., 11 May, 1866. Capt. 40th Inf., 28 July, 1866. Unassigned 20 April, 1869. Discharged 5 Aug., 1870. Bvt. Maj., 2 March, 1867, for gallant and meritorious service at the Battle of Todd's Tavern, Va. Bvt. Lieut. Col., 2 March, 1867, for gallant and meritorious service in the Battle of Cedar Creek, Va. Died 6 Nov., 1881.

MOORE, TREDWELL.* [Born in Ohio. Appointed from Ohio.]
Bvt. 2nd Lieut. 8th Inf., 1 July, 1847. 2nd Lieut. 2nd Inf., 20 Aug., 1847. 1st Lieut., 11 June, 1851. Capt. A. Q. M., 21 May, 1859. Maj. Q. M., 28 July, 1866. Lieut. Col. Dep. Q. M. G., 6 June, 1872. Died 29 May, 1876. Bvt. Maj., 13 March, 1865, for gallant and meritorious service during the war. Bvt. Lieut. Col., 13 March, 1865, for faithful and meritorious service in Nevada, 1861. Bvt. Col., 13 March, 1865, for meritorious service during Morgan's raid into Ohio, in 1863. Bvt. Brig. Gen., 13 March, 1865, for faithful and meritorious service during the war.

MOORE, TREDWELL W. [Born in Nev. Appointed from N. Y.]
2nd Lieut. 22nd Inf., 30 Oct., 1884. 1st Lieut. 9th Inf., 30 Sept., 1891. Trans. to 22nd Inf., 14 March, 1892. Capt. 21st Inf., 16 Jan., 1899. Graduate of the Infantry and Cavalry School, 1887.

MOORE, WM. G. [Born in D. C. Appointed from D. C.]
Priv., Corpl. and Sergt. National Rifle D. C. Vols., 15 April to 15 July, 1861. Maj. A. A. G. Vols., 1 May, 1865, to 15 Nov., 1866. Maj. P. M., 14 Nov., 1866. Resigned 12 April, 1870. Bvt. Lieut. Col. and Col. Vols., 2 Dec., 1865. Bvt. Lieut. Col., 2 March, 1867, for faithful and meritorious service.

MOORHEAD, HENRY C.* [Born in Penn. Appointed from Penn.]
Bvt. 2nd Lieut. 1st Drag., 1 July, 1836. Resigned 30 Sept., 1836. Died 15 April, 1861.

MOORHEAD, WM. J. [Born in Penn. Appointed from Penn.]
1st Lieut. 17th Inf., 14 May, 1861. Capt., 27 June, 1862. Resigned 21 July, 1865. Bvt. Maj., 6 July, 1864, for gallant service during the war, especially at the Battles of Fredericksburg, Va., and Gettysburg, Pa.

MORDECAI, ALFRED.* [Born in N. C. Appointed from N. C.]
Bvt. 2nd Lieut. and 2nd Lieut. Eng., 1 July, 1823. Capt. Ord., 30 May, 1832. Maj., 31 Dec., 1854. Resigned 5 May, 1861. Bvt. Maj., 30 May, 1848, for meritorious conduct, particularly in performance of his duties in the prosecution of the war with Mexico.

MORDECAI, ALFRED.* [Born in Penn. Apopinted at Large.]
Bvt. 2nd Lieut. Top. Eng., 24 June, 1861. 2nd Lieut., 3 Aug., 1861. Trans. to Ord., 23 Oct., 1861. 1st Lieut., 3 March, 1863. Capt., 1 June, 1863. Bvt. Maj., 7 Sept., 1863, for gallant and meritorious service in the Siege of Fort Wagner, S. C. Bvt. Lieut. Col., 13 March, 1865, for distinguished service in the field, and faithful and meritorious service in the Ord. Dept. during the war. Maj. Ord., 23 June, 1874. Lieut. Col., 4 Dec., 1882. Col., 31 Jan., 1891.

MOREHEAD, FRANK C. [Born in Ky. Appointed from Mo.]
2nd Lieut. 5th Cav., 4 Sept., 1867. 1st Lieut., 3 Jan., 1870. Discharged 1 Oct., 1870.

MORELL, GEORGE W.* [Born in N. Y. Appointed from N. Y.]
Bvt. 2nd Lieut. Eng., 1 July, 1835. 2nd Lieut., 31 Oct., 1836. Resigned 30 June, 1837. Brig. Gen. Vols., 9 Aug., 1861. Maj. Gen. Vols., 4 July, 1862. Appointment as Maj. Gen. expired 4 March, 1863. Mustered out 15 Dec., 1864. Died 12 Feb., 1883.

MORFORD, WILLIAM H. [Born in Ohio. Appointed from Army.]
Priv., Corpl. and Sergt. Co. C, 21st Inf., 29 Jan., 1889, to 24 July, 1892. 2nd Lieut. of Inf. (3rd), 4 July, 1892. Dismissed 15 Oct., 1897.

MORGAN, ALGERNON S. M. [Born in Penn. Appointed from Penn.]
2nd Lieut. 12th Penn. Vols., 25 April, 1861. Mustered out 31 July, 1861. Lieut. Col. 63rd Penn. Vols., 1 Aug., 1861. Col., 6 Oct., 1862. Mustered out 18 April, 1863. Ord. Storekeeper, 5 Dec., 1863. Capt. Ord. Storekeeper, 28 July, 1866. Retired 6 June, 1894, for disability.

MORGAN, CHAS. H.* [Born in N. Y. Appointed from N. Y.]
Bvt. 2nd Lieut. 3rd Art., 1 July, 1857. 2nd Lieut. 4th Art., 10 Sept., 1857. 1st Lieut., 1 April, 1861. Capt., 5 Aug., 1862. Lieut. Col. A. I. G., 1 Jan., 1863, to 25 May, 1865. Brig. Gen. Vols., 21 May, 1865. Mustered out Vols., 15 Jan., 1866. Maj., 5 Feb., 1867. Died 20 Dec., 1875. Bvt. Maj., 3 July, 1863, for gallant and meritorious service at the Battle of Gettysburg, Penn. Bvt. Lieut. Col., 14 Oct., 1863, for gallant and meritorious service in action at Bristow Station, Va. Bvt. Col., 12 May, 1864, for gallant and meritorious service at the Battle of Spottsylvania, Va. Bvt. Col. of Vols., 1 Aug., 1864, for distinguished and valuable service and gallantry throughout the campaign, especially at the Wilderness and Spottsylvania, Va. Bvt. Brig. Gen. Vols., 2 Dec., 1864, for gallant and distinguished service as Chief of Staff of 2nd Army Corps during the campaign before Richmond, Va. Bvt. Brig. Gen. U. S. A., 13 March, 1865, for gallant and meritorious service in the field during the war.

MORGAN, EDWIN W.* [Born in Penn. Appointed from Penn.]
2nd Lieut. 2nd Art., 1 July, 1837. 1st Lieut., 7 July, 1838. Resigned 31 May, 1839. Maj. of Inf., 3 March, 1847; 11th Inf., 9 April, 1847. Lieut. Col. 13th Inf., 13 Sept., 1847. Disbanded 31 July, 1848. Died 16 April, 1869.

MORGAN, GEORGE H.* [Born in Canada. Appointed from Minn.]
2nd Lieut. 3rd Cav., 12 June, 1880. 1st Lieut., 26 Nov., 1884. Capt., 15 March, 1896. Bvt. 1st Lieut., 27 Feb., 1890, for gallant services in action against Indians at Big Dry Wash, Ariz., 17 July, 1882, where he was severely wounded. Maj. 28th U. S. Vols., 5 July, 1899, to ——. Medal of Honor for distinguished conduct in action against hostile Apache Indians at the Big Dry Wash, Ariz., 17 July, 1882, by gallantly holding his ground at a critical moment and firing upon the advancing enemy until himself disabled by a shot; while 2nd Lieut. 3rd Cav., and serving as a Vol. with Lieut. West's command of Indian scouts and Troop I, 6th Cav.

MORGAN, GEORGE W. [Born in Penn. Appointed from Ohio.]
Cadet at Mil. Acad., 1 July, 1841, to 27 June, 1843. Col. 2nd Ohio Vols., 23 June, 1846. Col. of Inf., 3 March, 1847. Bvt. Brig. Gen. Vols., 20 Aug., 1847, for gallant and meritorious conduct at the Battles of Contreras and Churubusco, Mex. Discharged 7 Aug., 1848. Brig. Gen. Vols., 12 Nov., 1861. Resigned 8 June, 1863. Bvt. Brig. Gen., 20 Aug., 1847, for gallant and meritorious conduct at Contreras and Churubusco, Mex.

MORGAN, GEORGE W. [Born in Tenn. Appointed from Tenn.]
1st Lieut. of Inf., 5 March, 1847; 14th Inf., 9 April, 1847. Capt., 3 Dec., 1847. Disbanded 25 July, 1848.

MORGAN, HENRY C. [Born in N. Y. Appointed from N. Y.]
1st Lieut. 12th Inf., 14 May, 1861. Capt., 16 June, 1863. Bvt. Maj., 2 July, 1863, for gallant and meritorious service in the Battle of Gettysburg, Penn. Bvt. Lieut. Col., 5 May, 1864, for gallant and meritorious service in the Battle of the Wilderness, Va. Trans. to 30th Inf., 21 Sept., 1866. Retired 17 Feb., 1868.

MORGAN, HENRY S.* [Born in Ga. Appointed from Ga.]
Addl. 2nd Lieut. Eng., 11 June, 1897. 2nd Lieut., ——, 1897. Drowned in Tyler Roads, Ga., 31 Aug., 1898.

MORGAN, JAMES M.* [Born in N. Y. Appointed from N. Y.]
Bvt. 2nd Lieut. 2nd Art., 1 July, 1835. 2nd Lieut., 28 Dec., 1835. 1st Lieut., 31 May, 1837. 1st Lieut. Ord., 9 July, 1838. Capt., 3 March, 1847. Died 20 Sept., 1853.

MORGAN, JAMES N. [Born in Ill. Appointed from Ill.]
2nd Lieut. 22nd Ill. Vols., 25 June, 1861. 1st Lieut., 1 March, 1862. Capt., 13 June, 1862. Mustered out 7 July, 1864. Capt. 144th Ill. Vols., 10 Sept., 1864. Maj., 26 Sept., 1864. Lieut. Col., 18 March, 1865. Mustered out 14 July, 1865. 2nd Lieut. 38th Inf., 28 July, 1866. Bvt. 1st Lieut. and Capt., 2 March, 1867, for gallant and meritorious service in the Battle of Stone River, Tenn. Bvt. Maj., 2 March, 1867, for gallant and meritorious service in the Battle of New Hope Church, Ga. 1st Lieut. 38th Inf., 12 June, 1867. Trans. to 24th Inf., 11 Nov., 1869. Capt., 20 June, 1873. Retired for disability, with rank of Maj., 17 April, 1897.

MORGAN, JOHN M.* [Born in Ohio. Appointed from Ohio.]
2nd Lieut. 8th Cav., 12 June, 1893. 1st Lieut., 2 March, 1899.

MORGAN, JOHN R. [Born in N. C. Appointed from Army.]
Priv., Corpl. and Sergt. 43rd Inf., 12 Oct., 1813. Priv., Corpl. and Sergt. Batty I, Art. Corps, 4 Aug., 1817, to June, 1819. 2nd Lieut. Corps Art., 3 March, 1819. Died 18 June, 1819.

MORGAN, LEWIS. [Born in Penn. Appointed from Penn.]
2nd Lieut. 2nd Art., 12 March, 1812. Trans. to Corps Art., 12 May, 1814. 1st Lieut., 17 Nov., 1814. Resigned 15 July, 1816.

MORGAN, MICHAEL R.* [Born in Nova Scotia. Appointed from La.]
2nd Lieut. 3rd Art., 1 July, 1854. 1st Lieut., 11 Nov., 1856. Capt. 11th Inf., 14 May, 1861, declined. Capt. C. S., 3 Aug., 1861. Lieut. Col. C. S., 8 Nov., 1862. Bvt. Maj., Lieut. Col. and Col., 6 July, 1864, for distinguished service as Chief C. S. of the armies operating in the campaign of 1864 before Richmond, Va. Bvt. Brig. Gen., 9 April, 1865, for gallant and meritorious service during the campaign terminating with the surrender of the insurgent army under Gen. Robert E. Lee. Relieved as Lieut. Col. C. S., 5 June, 1865. Lieut. Col. I. S. Dept., 6 June, 1865. Maj. C. S., 17 Nov., 1865. Relieved as Lieut. Col. I. S. Dept., 29 Dec., 1865. Lieut. Col. Asst. C. G. S., 28 Aug., 1888. Col. Asst. C. G. S., 14 July, 1890. Brig. Gen. C. G. S., 8 Oct, 1894 Retired by operation of law, 18 Jan. 1897.

MORGAN, PHILANDER. [Born in Tenn. Appointed from Army.]
Priv. and 1st Sergt. Co. E, 13th Inf., 20 April, 1847, to 15 April, 1848. 2nd Lieut. 13th Inf., 3 March, 1848. Disbanded 15 July, 1848.

MORGAN, ROBT. C. [Born in N. Y. Appointed from N. Y.]
1st Lieut. of Inf., 1 April, 1847; 10th Inf., 9 April, 1847. R. Q. M., 13 Oct., 1847, to 8 May, 1848. Capt., 8 May, 1848. Disbanded 26 Aug., 1848. Capt. A. Q. M. Vols., 18 June, 1862. Bvt. Maj. and Lieut. Col. Vols., 13 March, 1865, for faithful and meritorious service during the war. Mustered out 1 Oct., 1867. Died 26 Jan., 1884.

MORGAN, WILLOUGHBY. [Born in Va. Appointed from Va.]
Capt. 12th Inf., 25 April, 1812. Maj., 26 June, 1813. Retained 17 May, 1815, as Capt. Rifle Reg. Maj., 8 March, 1817. Lieut. Col., 10 Nov., 1818. Trans. to 6th Inf., 1 June, 1821. Trans. to 5th Inf., 1 Oct., 1821. Trans. to 3rd Inf., 31 Jan., 1829. Col. 1st Inf., 23 April, 1830. Died 4 April, 1832. Retained — May, 1815 (in reorganization under Act of 3 March, 1815), as Capt. Rifles, with Bvt. of Maj. from 26 June, 1813, date of his appointment as Maj. 12th Inf. Bvt. Col., 10 Nov., 1828, for ten years' faithful service in one grade.

MORIARTY, AMBROSE I.* [Born in Conn. Appointed from Conn.]
2nd Lieut. 6th Inf., 12 June, 1887. Resigned 15 Dec., 1887. Reappointed 2nd Lieut. 9th Inf., 21 Dec., 1889. Retired 6 June, 1894.

MORLEY, ROBT. F. [Born in Penn. Appointed from Penn.]
Capt. 17th Inf., 9 Aug., 1861. Resigned 9 Aug., 1862.

MORONEY, PATRICK H. [Born in Ireland. Appointed from Army.]
Priv., Corpl., Sergt. and 1st Sergt. Cos. B, G and C, 10th Inf., 27 Jan., 1855, to May, 1862, and F, 14th Inf., to 10 Aug., 1862. 2nd Lieut. 14th Inf., 27 June, 1862. 1st Lieut., 11 July, 1863. Retired 26 Jan., 1865. Dismissed 8 July, 1875. Bvt. Capt., 13 March, 1865, for gallant and meritorious service during the war.

MORRIS, ARTHUR. [Born in Va. Appointed at Large.]
2nd Lieut. 4th Art., 24 March, 1862. Bvt. 1st Lieut., 30 June, 1862, for gallant and meritorious service in the Battle of White Oak Swamp, Va. Bvt. Capt., 17 Sept., 1862, for gallant and meritorious service in the Battle of Antietam, Md. 1st Lieut. 4th Art., 12 Nov., 1863. Capt., 10 Jan., 1877. Retired for disability, 5 Oct., 1887. Died 26 Sept., 1892.

MORRIS, CHAS.* [Born in Mass. Appointed from Mass.]
2nd Lieut. and 1st Lieut. 19th Inf., 23 June, 1865. Trans. to 37th Inf., 21 Sept., 1866. Reg. Adj., 14 Dec., 1866, to 31 Oct., 1868. Trans. to 5th Inf., 19 May, 1860. R. Q. M., 10 Aug., 1869, to 10 June, 1870. Reg. Adj., 10 June, to 15 Dec., 1870. Trans. to 5th Art., 15 Dec., 1870. Graduate of the Artillery School, 1878. Capt., 6 March, 1882. Maj. 7th Art., 8 March, 1898.

MORRIS, CHAS. F.* [Born in N. Y. Appointed from N. Y.]
Bvt. 2nd Lieut. 8th Inf., 1 July, 1841. 2nd Lieut., 28 Sept., 1841. 1st Lieut., 18 June, 1846. Died 17 Sept., 1847, of wounds received in Battle of Molino del Rey, Mex.

MORRIS, EDWARD R. [Born in Ind. Appointed from Ind.]
Asst. Surg., 17 Sept., 1885. Capt. Asst. Surg., 17 Sept., 1890. Maj. Brig. Surg., 4 June, 1898.

MORRIS, GEORGE N. [Born in Conn. Appointed from N. Y.]
2nd Lieut. Light Art., 13 March, 1813. 1st Lieut., 23 Oct., 1813. Capt., 15 Jan., 1817. Trans. to 3rd Art., 1 June, 1821. Died 2 March, 1825.

MORRIS, GOUVERNEUR. [Born in N. Y. Appointed from N. Y.]
Cadet Mil. Acad., 30 Sept., 1818, to 1 Aug., 1823. 2nd Lieut. 4th Inf., 24 May, 1824. 1st Lieut., 30 April, 1831. Capt., 6 Sept., 1837. Maj. 3rd Inf., 31 Jan., 1850. Lieut. Col. 1st Inf., 31 May, 1857. Retired 9 Sept., 1861. Died 18 Oct., 1868. Bvt. Maj., 9 May, 1845, for gallant and meritorious conduct at Palo Alto and Resaca de la Palma.

MORRIS, LEWIS N.* [Born in N. Y. Appointed from N. Y.]
2nd Lieut. Corps Art., 1 July, 1820. Trans. to 3rd Inf., 24 Aug., 1820. 1st Lieut., 31 Dec., 1825. Capt., 31 Oct., 1833. Killed 21 Sept., 1846, at the Battle of Monterey, Mex. Bvt. Maj., 9 May, 1846, for gallant and distinguished conduct at Palo Alto and Resaca de la Palma..

MORRIS, LEWIS O. [Born in N. Y. Appointed from N. Y.]
2nd Lieut. 1st Art., 8 March, 1847. 1st Lieut., 23 Dec., 1847. Capt., 21 April, 1861. Col. 7th N. Y. Art., 14 Aug., 1862. Killed in action at Cold Harbor, Va., 4 June, 1864.

MORRIS, LEWIS McL. [Born in Del. Appointed from N. J.]
1st Lieut. 4th N. J. Vols., 25 April, 1861. Mustered out 31 July, 1861. 1st Lieut. 6th N. J. Vols., 26 Aug., 1861. Capt., 2 Jan., 1863. Trans. to 8th N. J. Vols., 7 Sept., 1864. Maj., 6 May, 1865. Mustered out 17 July, 1865. 2nd Lieut. 20th Inf., 28 July, 1866. 1st Lieut., 22 Oct., 1867. Died 7 April, 1877. Bvt. 1st Lieut. and Capt., 2 March, 1867, for gallant and meritorious service during the war.

MORRIS, LOUIS T. [Born in Ind. Appointed from Ind.]
1st Lieut. 19th Inf., 14 May, 1861. Bvt. Capt., 1 Sept., 1864, for gallant and meritorious service during the Atlanta campaign. Bvt. Maj., 16 Dec., 1864, for gallant and meritorious service in the Battle of Nashville, Tenn. Capt. 19th Inf., 15 Feb., 1865. Trans. to 28th Inf., 21 Sept., 1866. Trans. to 37th Inf., 30 Nov., 1867. Trans. to 3rd Inf., 11 Aug., 1869. Trans. to 8th Cav., 29 Dec., 1873. Maj. 3rd Cav., 11 April, 1889. Lieut. Col. 1st Cav., 29 June, 1897. Trans. to 4th Cav., 11 Aug., 1897. Retired for disability, 13 July, 1898. Died 7 Jan., 1899.

MORRIS, RICHARD L., Jr. [Born in N. Y. Appointed from N. Y.]
Priv. Co. K, 7th N. Y. State Militia, 26 April, 1861. Discharged 3 June, 1861. 1st Lieut. 18th Inf., 14 May, 1861. Capt., 31 Dec., 1862. Bvt. Maj., 31 Dec., 1862, for gallant and meritorious service in the Battle of Murfreesboro, Tenn. Maj. 5th Inf., 6 Feb., 1882. Died 6 May, 1882.

MORRIS, ROBT. M. [Born in D. C. Appointed from D. C.]
Cadet Mil. Acad., 1 July, 1841, to 17 Jan., 1842. 2nd Lieut. Mounted Rifles, 27 May, 1846. Bvt. 1st Lieut., 20 Aug., 1847, for gallant and meritorious conduct in the Battle of Contreras. Bvt. Capt., 13 Sept., 1847, for gallant and meri-

torious conduct in the Battle of Chapultepec. 1st Lieut. Mounted Rifles, 8 June, 1848. R. Q. M., 5 Oct., 1854, to 1 Feb., 1855. Capt., 14 June, 1858. 3rd Cav., 3 Aug., 1861. Bvt. Maj., 21 Feb., 1862, for gallant and meritorious service in the Battle of Val Verde, N. M. Maj. 6th Cav., 11 March, 1863. Bvt. Lieut. Col., 31 March, 1865, for gallant and meritorious service in the Battle of Dinwiddie Court House, Va. Retired 21 Feb., 1873. Died 7 Dec., 1896.

MORRIS, THOS. A.* [Born in Ky. Appointed from Ind.]
Bvt. 2nd Lieut. 1st Art., 1 July, 1834. 2nd Lieut., 25 Feb., 1835. Resigned 13 April, 1836. Brig. Gen. Ind. Vols., 27 April, 1861. Mustered out 27 July, 1861.

MORRIS, THOMPSON.* [Born in Ohio. Appointed from Ohio.]
2nd Lieut. 2nd Inf., 1 July, 1822. 1st Lieut., 26 May, 1830. Capt., 6 Nov., 1836. Maj. 1st Inf., 12 Jan., 1848. Lieut. Col. 4th Inf., 3 March, 1855. Retired 9 Sept., 1861. Died 13 Feb., 1870. Bvt. Maj., 18 April, 1847, for gallant and meritorious conduct at Cerro Gordo. Bvt. Lieut. Col., 20 Aug., 1847, for gallant and meritorious conduct at Contreras and Churubusco, Mex.

MORRIS, WM. H.* [Born in N. Y. Appointed from N. Y.]
Bvt. 2nd Lieut. 2nd Inf., 1 July, 1851. 2nd Lieut., 3 Dec., 1851. Resigned 28 Feb., 1854. Capt. A. A. G. Vols., 20 Aug., 1861. Resigned 1 Sept., 1862. Col. 6th N. Y. Art., 2 Sept., 1862. Brig. Gen. Vols., 29 Nov., 1862. Bvt. Maj. Gen. Vols., 13 March, 1865, for gallant and meritorious service in the Battle of the Wilderness, Va. Mustered out 24 Aug., 1865.

MORRIS, WM. W.* [Born in N. Y. Appointed from N. Y.]
2nd Lieut. 6th Inf., 1 July, 1820. 1st Lieut., 11 Aug., 1823. Trans. to 4th Art., 30 July, 1824. Capt., 17 Dec., 1836. Maj., 4 Nov., 1853. Lieut. Col., 14 May, 1861. Col. 2nd Art., 1 Nov., 1861. Died 11 Dec., 1865. Bvt. Maj., 27 Jan., 1837, for gallant conduct, etc., in war against Florida Indians. Bvt. Brig. Gen., 9 June, 1862, for faithful and meritorious service. Bvt. Maj. Gen., 10 Dec., 1865, for faithful and meritorious service during the rebellion.

MORRISON, CHAS. C.* [Born in Ohio. Appointed from Ohio.]
2nd Lieut. 6th Cav., 12 June, 1871. 1st Lieut., 27 Jan., 1875. Trans. to Ord., 14 April, 1879. Capt. (14 years' service), 14 June, 1886. Died 13 May, 1894.

MORRISON, EDWIN A. [Born in Ky. Appointed from New Mexico.]
2nd Lieut. 3rd Inf., 18 June, 1855. Dismissed 4 June, 1856.

MORRISON, GUY. [Born in Penn. Appointed from Army.]
Priv. Co. H, and Hosp. Stwd. 13th Inf., 24 Feb., 1864, to 1 June, 1866. 2nd Lieut. 10th Inf., 7 April, 1866. Dropped 21 Aug., 1866.

MORRISON, JAMES C., Jr.* [Born in Ohio. Appointed from Ohio.]
2nd Lieut. 1st Art., 15 June, 1868. Drowned 4 May, 1871.

MORRISON, JASPAR N. [Born in Mo. Appointed from Mo.]
Maj. J. A., 18 Feb., 1896.

MORRISON, JOHN, Jr.* [Born in Iowa. Appointed from Iowa.]
Addl. 2nd Lieut. 2nd Cav., 12 June, 1896. 2nd Lieut. 3rd Cav., 9 Sept., 1896. 1st Lieut. 1st Cav., 13 Dec., 1899. Trans. to 4th Cav., 23 Feb., 1900.

MORRISON, JOHN F.* [Born in N. Y. Appointed from N. Y.]
2nd Lieut. 20th Inf., 11 June, 1881. 1st Lieut. 1st Inf., 27 Nov., 1890. Trans. to 20th Inf., 20 July, 1891. Capt., 26 April, 1898. Honor graduate of the Infantry and Cavalry School, 1885. Capt. A. A. G., 12 May, 1898 (declined). R. Q. M., 16 Nov., 1899.

MORRISON, JOHN T. [Born in N. Y. Appointed from Minn.]
Priv. Co. A, 1st Minn. Vols., 29 April, 1861. Discharged 11 March, 1862. 1st Lieut. 2nd Minn. Cav., 20 Oct., 1863. Mustered out 17 Nov., 1865. 2nd Lieut. 10th Cav., 7 March, 1867. 1st Lieut., 31 July, 1867. R. Q. M., 30 June, 1875, to 31 Aug., 1878. Reg. Adj., 18 Nov., 1881, to 19 Dec., 1882. Capt., 19 Dec., 1882. Retired for disability, 23 Dec., 1887.

MORRISON, PITCAIRN. [Born in N. Y. Appointed from N. Y.]
2nd Lieut. Corps Art., 27 Oct., 1820. Trans. to 4th Art., 1 June, 1821. Trans. to 2nd Art., 16 Aug., 1821. Trans. to 4th Inf., 29 Aug., 1822. 1st Lieut., 26 Aug., 1826. Capt., 13 Sept., 1836. Bvt. Maj., 9 May, 1846, for gallant and meritorious conduct in the Battles of Palo Alto and Resaca de la Palma. Maj. 8th Inf., 26 Sept., 1847. Lieut. Col. 7th Inf., 9 June, 1853. Col. 8th Inf., 6 June, 1861. Retired 20 Oct., 1863. Bvt. Brig. Gen., 13 March, 1865, for long and faithful service in the army. Died 5 Oct., 1887.

MORRISON, THEOPHILUS W. [Born in Ind. Appointed from Ind.]
2nd Lieut. 18th Ind. Vols., 16 Aug., 1861. 1st Lieut., 1 Nov., 1862. Mustered out 27 Feb., 1863. Capt. A. A. G. Vols., 27 Feb., 1863. Resigned 25 Jan., 1865. Lieut. Col. 146th Ind. Vols., 25 April, 1865. Mustered out 31 Aug., 1865. 2nd Lieut. 34th Inf., 28 July, 1866. Trans. to 16th Inf., 14 April, 1869. 1st Lieut., 6 Aug., 1873. Capt., 6 Sept., 1886. Killed in action 1 July, 1898, at San Juan, Santiago, Cuba.

MORRISON, WM. A. [Born in N. Y. Appointed from Army.]
Priv. Co. G, 13th Inf., 18 March to 26 June, 1847. 2nd Lieut. 13th Inf., 9 April, 1847. Resigned 9 Oct., 1847.

MORRISON, WM. L. E.* [Born in Mo. Appointed from Ill.]
Bvt. 2nd Lieut. 2nd Inf., 1 July, 1828. Resigned 16 Oct., 1830.

MORROW, ALBERT P. [Born in Ill. Appointed from Penn.]
Sergt. Co. K, 17th Penn. Vols., 18 April, 1861. Discharged 1 Aug., 1861. Sergt. Co. C, 6th Penn. Cav., 9 Dec., 1861. 1st Sergt. Co. I, 18 Dec., 1861. Sergt. Maj., 1 March, 1862. Discharged 27 March, 1862. 2nd Lieut., 27 March, 1862. 1st Lieut., 20 Nov., 1862. Capt., 8 Feb., 1864. Maj., 10 Feb., 1865. Bvt. Col. Vols., 13 March, 1865, for conspicuous gallantry in action. Lieut. Col. 6th Penn. Cav., 29 March, 1865. Mustered out 7 Aug., 1865. Capt. 7th Cav., 28 July, 1866. Maj. 9th Cav., 6 March, 1867. Lieut. Col. 6th Cav., 17 Dec., 1882. Col. 3rd Cav., 18 Feb., 1891. Retired, for over 30 years' service, 16 Aug., 1892.

MORROW, ALEX. [Born in Maine. Appointed from Maine.]
1st Lieut. 9th Inf., 9 April, 1847. Trans. to 6th Inf., 26 Aug., 1847. Died 7 Jan., 1851. Bvt. Capt., 13 Sept., 1847, for gallant and meritorious conduct at Chapultepec.

MORROW, FRANK J. [Born in Utah. Appointed from Army.]
Priv. and Corpl. Co. G, 16th Inf., 21 Jan., 1892. 1st Lieut. 17th Inf., 26 April, 1898.

MORROW, HENRY A. [Born in Va. Appointed from Mich.]
Priv. Co .C, Watson's Reg. D. C. and Md. Vols., 18 May, 1846. Discharged 30 May, 1847. Col. 24th Mich. Vols., 15 Aug., 1862. Bvt. Brig. Gen., 1 Aug., 1864, for gallant and distinguished service during the campaign before Richmond, Va. Bvt. Maj. Gen. Vols., 13 March, 1865, for distinguished and conspicuous gallantry, and for good conduct before Petersburg, Va. Mustered out 19 July, 1865. Lieut. Col. 36th Inf., 28 July, 1866. Bvt. Col., 2 March, 1867, for gallant and meritorious service in the Battle of Hatcher's Run, Va., 6 Feb., 1865. Trans. to 13th Inf., 15 March, 1869. Col. 21st Inf., 27 April, 1879. Died 31 Jan., 1891.

MORROW, JAY J.* [Born in W. Va. Appointed from Penn.]
Addl. 2nd Lieut. Eng., 12 June, 1891. 2nd Lieut., 3 Feb., 1895. 1st Lieut., 26 May, 1896. Maj. 3rd Vol. Eng., 15 Sept., 1898, to 6 Oct., 1898.

MORROW, JAMES E. [Born in W. Va. Appointed from Nebr.]
Sergt. and 1st Sergt. Co. G, 1st W. Va. Vols., 30 Oct., 1861, to 28 Feb., 1862. 2nd Lieut. 1st W. Va. Vols., 28 Feb., 1862. 1st Lieut., 1 Nov., 1862. Capt., 1 Jan., 1863. Mustered out 26 Nov., 1864. 2nd Lieut. 15th Inf., 18 June, 1867. Cashiered 29 June, 1868.

MORROW, ROB'T. [Born in Tenn. Appointed from Tenn.]
Capt. A. A. G. Vols., 14 Sept., 1863. Maj. A. A. G. Vols., 25 July, 1865. Bvt. Maj. Vols., 13 March, 1865, and Lieut. Col. Vols., 12 April, 1865, for uniform gallantry and good conduct during the war, and Col. Vols., 13 April, 1865, for conspicuous gallantry and good conduct at the capture of Salisbury, N. C. Mustered out 30 Nov., 1866. Maj. P. M., 9 May, 1867. Died 27 Nov., 1873.

MORROW, WM. M. [Born in Mich. Appointed from Army.]
Priv., Corpl. and Sergt. Co. F, 17th Inf., 31 Dec., 1888, to 1 Aug., 1891. 2nd Lieut. 21st Inf., 31 July, 1891. 1st Lieut., 23 April, 1898. Graduate of the Infantry and Cavalry School, 1897.

MORSE, BENJAMIN C.* [Born in Mo. Appointed from Mich.]
2nd Lieut. 23rd Inf., 15 June, 1884. 1st Lieut. 15th Inf., 15 June, 1891. Trans. to 18th Inf., 20 July, 1891. Trans. to 23rd Inf., 22 May, 1894. Capt. of Inf., 1 Nov., 1898. Ass'd to 17th Inf., 1 Jan., 1899.

MORSE, CHAS. E. [Born in England. Appointed from Army.]
Priv. 17th Inf., 8 Jan., 1863. Priv. Co. C, 2nd Batt. 17th Inf., 19 Sept., 1863. Trans. to Co. B, 1st Batt., 20 Feb., 1864. Sergt., 15 May, 1864. Q. M. Sergt. 2nd Batt., 25 May, 1864. 2nd Lieut. and 1st Lieut. 17th Inf., 9 Oct., 1865. Trans. to 26th Inf., 21 Sept., 1866. Capt., 2 Oct., 1868. Unassigned 19 May, 1869. Ass'd to 16th Inf., 1 Jan., 1871. Retired for disability, 26 Nov., 1884.

MORSE, JOSEPH B. [Born in ——. Appointed from ——.]
2nd Lieut. 9th Inf., — ——, 1899. Died 15 Aug., 1899, at Manila, Philippine Islands.

MORTON, ALEXANDER H.* [Born in N. Y. Appointed from N. Y.]
Bvt. 2nd Lieut. 2nd Inf., 1 July, 1821. 2nd Lieut. 7th Inf., 1 July, 1821. 1st Lieut., 31 July, 1824. Resigned 12 July, 1833. Died 24 Oct., 1853.

MORTON, ALEX. L.* [Born in Ky. Appointed from Mo.]
2nd Lieut. 5th Art., 15 June, 1868. 1st Lieut., 22 Nov., 1876. Resigned 31 Oct., 1885.

MORTON, ALFRED. [Born in Maine. Appointed from Cal.]
Sergt. Co. F, 2nd Cal. Cav., 13 Sept., 1861. Com. Sergt., 1 Jan., 1862. Discharged 6 Jan., 1862. 1st Lieut. 2nd Cal. Vols., 26 Jan., 1862. Capt., 14 Feb., 1863. Maj. 7th Cal. Vols., 25 Nov., 1864. Mustered out 17 March, 1866. 2nd Lieut. 9th Inf., 3 March, 1866. R. Q. M., 1 June, 1866, to 20 March, 1879. 1st Lieut., 28 July, 1866. Capt., 20 March, 1879. Retired, by operation of law, 16 Jan., 1898.

MORTON, CHAS.* [Born in Ohio. Appointed from Mo.]
Priv. Co. I, 13th Mo. Vols., 29 July, 1861. Priv. Co. I, 25th Mo. Vols., — Feb., 1862. Priv. Co. H, 1st Mo. Eng., 17 Feb., 1864. Discharged 14 Sept., 1864. Cadet Mil. Acad., 1 July, 1865. 2nd Lieut. 3rd Cav., 15 June, 1869. 1st Lieut., 25 Sept., 1876. Capt., 17 Nov., 1883. Maj. 4th Cav., 23 Sept., 1898. Bvt. 1st Lieut., 27 Feb., 1890, for gallant services in action against Indians in the Tonto Country, Ariz., 5 June, 1871 (declined).

MORTON, CHARLES E. [Born in Nebr. Appointed from Mich.]
Priv., Corpl. and Sergt. Co. B, 19th Inf., 27 Aug., 1894, to 6 Sept., 1898. 2nd Lieut. 22nd Inf., 10 Oct., 1898. 1st Lieut. 16th Inf., 2 Feb., 1900.

MORTON, CHAS. F. [Born in N. Y. Appointed from N. Y.]
Lieut. Asst. Dep. Comsy. of Ord., 26 Dec., 1814. Retained as 2nd Lieut. Ord., 26 Dec., 1814. 1st Lieut., 31 March, 1819. Trans. to 2nd Inf., 1 June, 1821. Capt., 26 May, 1830. Resigned 13 Sept., 1831.

MORTON, CHARLES G.* [Born in Maine. Appointed from Mass.]
2nd Lieut. 6th Inf., 13 June, 1883. 1st Lieut., 1 Feb., 1890. Capt., 7 Aug., 1897. Lieut. Col. 1st Maine Vols., 14 May, 1898, until mustered out 30 Oct., 1898.

MORTON, JAMES ST. C.* [Born in Penn. Appointed from Penn.]
Bvt. 2nd Lieut. Eng., 1 July, 1851. 2nd Lieut., 1 April, 1854. 1st Lieut., 1 July, 1856. Capt., 6 Aug., 1861. Brig. Gen. Vols., 29 Nov., 1862. Mustered out of Vol. Service, 7 Nov., 1863. Maj., 3 July, 1863. Killed 17 June, 1864, at the assault of Petersburg, Va. Bvt. Lieut. Col., 2 Jan., 1863, for gallant and meritorious service at the Battle of Stone River, Tenn. Bvt. Col., 20 Sept., 1863, for gallant and meritorious service at the Battle of Chickamauga, Ga. Bvt. Brig. Gen., 17 June, 1864, for gallant and meritorious service at the assault of Petersburg, Va.

MORTON, JOHN. [Born in N. Y. Appointed from N. Y.]
Capt. Dep. Comsy. of Ord., 11 Se[illegible], 1812. Ret[illegible]ed as Capt. Ord., 11 Sept., 1812. Disbanded 1 June, 1821.

MORTON, KENNETH.* [Born in Mass. Appointed from Mass.]
Addl. 2nd Lieut. 3rd Art., 11 June, 1892. 2nd Lieut., 13 July, 1892. 1st Lieut. Ord., 4 Oct., 1898.

MOSELEY, EDWARD B. [Born in Penn. Appointed from Penn.]
1st Lieut. Asst. Surg., 10 Nov., 1874. Capt. Asst. Surg., 10 Nov., 1879. Maj. Surg., 9 Jan., 1892.

MOSELEY, GEORGE V. H.* [Born in Ill. Appointed from Ill.]
2nd Lieut. 9th Cav., 15 Feb., 1899.

MOSELEY, W. G. [Born in N. C. Appointed from Fla.]
2nd Lieut. 3rd Drag., 12 April, 1847. Disbanded 4 Aug., 1848.

MOSES, ANDREW.* [Born in Tex. Appointed from Tex.]
Addl. 2nd Lieut. 11th Inf., 11 June, 1897. 2nd Lieut. 7th Art., 8 March, 1898. 1st Lieut. 3rd Art., 9 Nov., 1899.

MOSES, GEORGE W.* [Born in Ohio. Appointed from Ohio.]
2nd Lieut. 3rd Cav., 12 June, 1896. 1st Lieut. 4th Cav., 14 Sept., 1899. Maj. Addl. P. M., 3 June, 1898, to 13 May, 1899.

MOSES, ISRAEL. [Born in N. Y. Appointed from N. Y.]
Lieut. Col. 72nd N. Y. Vols., 23 July, 1861. Mustered out 23 Oct., 1862. Surg. U. S. Vols., 4 Oct., 1862. Bvt. Lieut. Col. Vols., 1 June, 1865, for faithful and meritorious service. Mustered out 27 July, 1865. Asst. Surg., 8 Jan., 1847. Resigned 31 May, 1855. Died 4 Oct., 1870.

MOSHER, THEODORE. [Born in Md. Appointed from Army.]
Sergt. Sig. Corps, 8 Aug., 1870. Discharged 8 Aug., 1875. Priv. Sig. Corps, 8 Aug., 1875. Sergt., 10 Aug., 1875. 2nd Lieut. 22nd Inf., 19 April, 1877. Expired by constitutional limitation, 3 Dec., 1877; reappointed 26 Jan., 1878, with rank from 19 April, 1877. 1st Lieut., 22 Sept., 1882. Capt., 29 Dec., 1894. Maj. P. M., 1 Feb., 1899. Lieut. Col. 1st D. C. Vols., 9 Sept. to 20 Nov., 1898. Retired for disability, 2 March, 1899.

MOSS, HENRY N.* [Born in Penn. Appointed from Penn.]
2nd Lieut. 1st Cav., 17 June, 1867. 1st Lieut., 14 Sept., 1869. R. C. S., 9 June to 23 Dec., 1869. R. Q. M., 23 Dec., 1869, to 19 Sept., 1870. Resigned 5 June, 1876.

MOSS, JAMES A.* [Born in La. Appointed from La.]
2nd Lieut. 25th Inf., 12 June, 1894. 1st Lieut. 24th Inf., 26 April, 1898.

MOTT, GERSHAM, Jr. [Born in N. J. Appointed from N. J.]
2nd Lieut. 10th Inf., 23 April, 1847. Disbanded 22 Aug., 1848. Lieut. Col. 5th N. J. Vols., 17 Aug., 1861. Col. 6th N. J. Vols., 7 May, 1862. Brig. Gen. Vols., 7 Sept., 1862. Maj. Gen. Vols., 26 May, 1865. Bvt. Maj. Gen. Vols., 1 Aug., 1864, for distinguished service during the war. Resigned 20 Feb., 1866. Died 29 Nov., 1884.

MOTT, T. BENTLEY.* [Born in Va. Appointed from Va.]
Addl. 2nd Lieut. 1st Art., 1 July, 1886. 2nd Lieut., 7 July, 1886. 1st Lieut. 2nd Art., 23 Dec., 1892. Trans. to 1st Art., 14 Jan., 1893. Trans. to 7th Art., 8 March, 1898. Capt. A. A. G. Vols., 12 May, 1898. Maj. A. A. G. Vols., 10 Nov., 1898, to 13 June, 1899.

MOTT, SEWARD.* [Born in N. Y. Appointed from N. Y.]
Addl. 2nd Lieut. 6th Cav., 1 July, 1886. 2nd Lieut. 10th Cav., 6 July, 1886. Died 4 March, 1887, at San Carlos, Ariz., of wounds received in an assault made upon him by an Indian.

MOTT, THADDEUS P. [Born in N. Y. Appointed from N. Y.]
Capt. 3rd N. Y. Batty, 21 May, 1861. Resigned 8 July, 1862. Capt. 19th U. S. Inf., 29 Oct., 1861. Resigned 30 Jan., 1863. Lieut. Col. 14th N. Y. Cav., 26 Feb., 1863. Col., 10 July, 1863. Discharged 18 Jan., 1864.

MOTT, WALLACE.* [Born in N. Y. Appointed from N. Y.]
2nd Lieut. 8th Inf., 12 June, 1871. 1st Lieut., 26 July, 1880. R. Q. M., 1 March, 1882, to 29 Feb., 1884. Retired for disability, with rank of Capt. 9 March, 1891.

MOTTE, JACOB RHETT. [Born in S. C. Appointed from S. C.]
Asst. Surg., 4 July, 1836. Resigned 14 March, 1845.

MOTZ, JOHN. [Born in Germany. Appointed from Penn.]
1st Lieut. 11th Inf., 9 April, 1847. Capt., 2 Aug., 1847. Disbanded 14 Aug., 1848. Bvt. Maj., 20 Aug., 1847, for gallant and meritorious conduct at Contreras and Churubusco, Mex.

MOULD, WM. E. [Born in Ill. Appointed from Mich.]
2nd Lieut. 16th Inf., 24 July, 1899.

MOULTON, CHAS. W. [Born in Ohio. Appointed from Ohio.]
Capt. A. Q. M. Vols., 26 June, 1861. Capt. A. Q. M. U. S. A., 13 March, 1863. Col. Q. M., 9 Feb. to 4 Oct., 1865. Resigned 4 Oct., 1865. Bvt. Maj., Lieut. Col. and Col., 13 March, 1865, for faithful and meritorious service during the war. Died 24 Jan., 1888.

MOULTON, HARRISON. [Born in N. H. Appointed from Army.]
Priv., Corpl., Sergt. and 1st Sergt. Co. B, 1st Drag. (1st Cav.), 8 Sept., 1857, to 8 Sept., 1862. 2nd Lieut. 1st Cav., 17 July, 1862. 1st Lieut., 13 Oct., 1863. Reg. Adj., 10 Sept., 1865, to 1 June, 1866. Capt., 11 April, 1867. Mustered out 1 Jan., 1871. Bvt. 1st Lieut., 21 June, 1863, for gallant and meritorious service in action at Upperville, Va.

MOUNT, JOHN F. [Born in N. Y. Appointed from N. Y.]
Priv. Albany Burgesses' Corps 25th N. Y. State Militia, 4 May, 1861. Discharged 4 Aug., 1861. 2nd Lieut. 113th N. Y. Vols., 18 Aug., 1862. 1st Lieut. 7th N. Y. Art., 23 Dec., 1863. Capt., 14 Oct., 1864. Maj., 15 March, 1865. Mustered out 1 Aug., 1865. 2nd Lieut. 3rd Art., 23 Feb., 1866. 1st Lieut., 28 July, 1866. Bvt. Capt., 2 March, 1867, for meritorious service during the war. Capt., 3 Dec., 1884. Resigned 30 Nov., 1888.

MOUNT, JOHN M. [Born in Ohio. Appointed from Ohio.]
2nd Lieut. 15th Inf., 3 March, 1848. Disbanded 20 July, 1848.

MOUNTFORD, JOHN. [Born in Mass. Appointed from Mass.]
2nd Lieut. 3rd Art., 24 March, 1812. 1st Lieut., 20 May, 1813. Trans. to Corps Art., 12 May, 1814. Capt., 11 Aug., 1819. Trans. to 2nd Art., 1 June, 1821. Resigned 2 April, 1838. Bvt. Capt., 11 Sept., 1814, for gallant conduct at the Battle of Plattsburg. Bvt. Maj., 11 Aug., 1829, for ten years' faithful service in one grade. Died 22 Oct., 1851.

MOUNTJOY, THOMAS. [Born in ——. Appointed from Ky.]
2nd Lieut. 17th Inf., 12 March, 1812. 1st Lieut., 13 March, 1813. Trans. to 3rd Inf., 17 May, 1815. Trans. to 8th Inf., 1 Jan., 1816. Capt., 15 Jan., 1817. Resigned 25 Sept., 1817.

MOUNTZ, GEORGE W. [Born in ——. Appointed from D. C.]
2nd Lieut. Corps Art., 28 Jan., 1820. Trans. to 4th Inf., 1 June, 1821. 1st Lieut., 1 May, 1824. Dismissed 17 March, 1829.

MOURTON, STANLEY. [Born in N. Y. Appointed from Army.]
Priv., Corpl., Sergt. and 1st Sergt. Co. H, 3rd Inf., 29 June, 1858, to 9 Nov., 1862. 2nd Lieut 3rd Inf., 18 July, 1862. 1st Lieut., 8 Jan., 1864. Dismissed 24 Dec., 1864.

MOUTON, JOHN J. A. A.* [Born in La. Appointed from La.]
Bvt. 2nd Lieut. 7th Inf., 1 July, 1850. Resigned 16 Sept., 1850. Died 8 April, 1864.

MOWER, JOSEPH A. [Born in Vt. Appointed from Conn.]
Priv. and Artif. Co. A, Eng., 29 March, 1847. Discharged 25 July, 1848. 2nd Lieut. 1st Inf., 18 June, 1855. 1st Lieut., 13 March, 1857. Capt., 9 Sept., 1861. Col. 11th Mo. Vols., 3 May, 1862. Brig. Gen. Vols., 29 Nov., 1862. Maj. Gen. Vols., 12 Aug., 1864. Mustered out 1 Feb., 1866. Col. 39th Inf., 28 July, 1866. Trans. to 25th Inf., 15 March, 1869. Died 6 Jan., 1870. Bvt. Maj., 9 May, 1862, for gallant and meritorious service at the Battle of Farmington, Miss. Bvt. Lieut. Col., 19 Sept., 1862, for gallant and meritorious service at the Battle of Iuka, Miss. Bvt. Col., 14 May, 1863, for gallant and meritorious service in the capture of Jackson, Miss. Bvt. Brig. Gen., 13 March, 1865, for gallant and meritorious service at the Battle of Fort de Russy, La. Bvt. Maj. Gen., 13 March, 1865, for gallant and meritorious service at the passage of the Salkehatchie, Ga.

MOWER, THOMAS G. [Born in Mass. Appointed from Mass.]
Surg.'s Mate 9th Inf., 2 Dec., 1812. Maj. Surg. 9th Inf., 30 June, 1814. Trans. to 6th Inf., 17 May, 1815. Retained as Maj. Surg., 1 June, 1821. Died 7 Dec., 1853.

MOWRY, SYLVESTER.* [Born in R. I. Appointed from R. I.]
Bvt. 2nd Lieut. 3rd Art., 1 July, 1852. 2nd Lieut., 6 Sept., 1853. 1st Lieut., 3 March, 1855. Resigned 31 July, 1858. Died 17 Oct., 1871.

MOYLAN, MYLES. [Born in Mass. Appointed from Army.]
Priv. Co. C, 2nd Drag., 8 June, 1857. Corpl., 1 Oct., 1858. Sergt., 1 Oct., 1860. 1st Sergt., 17 May, 1861. Discharged 1 April, 1862. 1st Sergt. Co. C, 2nd Cav., 1 April, 1862. 2nd Lieut. 5th Cav., 19 Feb., 1863. Dismissed 20 Oct., 1863. Priv. Co. A, 4th Mass. Cav., 2 Dec., 1863. Sergt., 26 Dec., 1863. 1st Lieut. 4th Mass. Cav., 25 Jan., 1864. Capt., 1 Dec., 1864. Bvt. Maj. Vols., 9 April, 1865, for gallant and distinguished service during the campaign in Virginia. Mustered out 14 Nov., 1865. Priv. Gen. Mounted Ser., 25 Jan., 1866. Corpl., 10 March, 1866. Priv. 7th Cav., 20 Aug., 1866. Sergt. Maj., 1 Sept., 1866. 1st Lieut. 7th Cav., 28 July, 1866. Capt., 1 March, 1872. Maj. 10th Cav., 8 April, 1892. Bvt. Maj., 27 Feb., 1890, for gallant services in action against Indians at Bear Paw Mountain, Mont., 30 Sept., 1877, where he was severely wounded. Medal of Honor for most distinguished gallantry in action against hostile Nez Perce Indians at Bear Paw Mountain, Mont., 30 Sept., 1877, in leading his command until severely wounded; while Capt. 7th Cav. Retired, over thirty years' service, 15 April, 1893.

MUDD, BENJ'N S. [Born in La. Appointed from La.]
2nd Lieut. 14th Inf., 16 July, 1847. Died 29 Jan., 1848.

MUDGE, ROBT. R.* [Born in Mass. Appointed from Mass.]
Bvt. 2nd Lieut. 3rd Art., 1 July, 1833. 2nd Lieut., 31 Aug., 1835. Killed in action with Indians in Florida, 28 Dec., 1835, at Dade's Massacre.

MUHLENBERG, BENJ. S. [Born in Penn. Appointed from Penn.]
Maj. Surg. Vols., 4 Jan., 1847. Resigned 30 April, 1847.

MUHLENBERG, CHAS. P. [Born in Penn. Appointed from Penn.]
Priv. Co. A, 25th Penn. Vols., 18 April to 25 July, 1861. 1st Lieut. 5th Art., 14 May, 1861. Resigned 7 Feb., 1867. Bvt. Capt., 3 June, 1864, for gallant and meritorious service at the Battle of Cool Arbor, Va. Bvt. Maj., 13 March, 1865, for good conduct and gallant service during the war. Died 9 Jan., 1872.

MUHLENBERG, EDWARD D. [Born in Penn. Appointed from Penn.]
1st Lieut. 4th Art., 22 Oct., 1861. R. Q. M., 13 Aug. to 29 Nov., 1864. Reg. Adj., 29 Nov., 1864, to 5 Jan., 1865. Resigned 8 May, 1866. Died 10 March, 1883.

MUHLENBERG, FRANK P. [Born in Penn. Appointed from Penn.]
Priv. Co. G, 1st Penn. Vols., 20 April to 28 June, 1861. 1st Lieut. 13th Inf., 14 May, 1861. Capt., 4 Jan., 1862. Resigned 5 April, 1866. Bvt. Maj., 21 April, 1865, for faithful and meritorious service connected with the recruitment of the armies of the United States.

MUHLENBERG, JOHN C. [Born in Penn. Appointed from Penn.]
Maj. P. M., 20 March, 1882.

MUHLENBERG, PETER. [Born in Penn. Appointed from Penn.]
1st Lieut. 6th Inf., 12 Dec., 1808. Capt., 1 Oct., 1810. Maj. 31st Inf., 1 May, 1814. Disbanded 15 June, 1815. Reinstated 1 Jan., 1816, as Capt. 4th Inf. Maj. 5th Inf., 24 Feb., 1818. Disbanded 1 June, 1821. Maj. P. M., 2 Feb., 1835. Died 21 Aug., 1844. Retained in 1815 (in reorganization under Act of 3 March, of that year), as Capt. 4th Inf., with Bvt. of Maj., from 1 May, 1814. Died 21 Aug., 1844.

MUHLENBERG, WM. C. [Born in Penn. Appointed from Penn.]
2nd Lieut. 2nd Inf., 14 Dec., 1876. 1st Lieut., 15 March, 1883. Died 10 April, 1888.

MUIR, CHARLES H.* [Born in Mich. Appointed from Mich.]
2nd Lieut. 17th Inf., 14 June, 1885. 1st Lieut. 14th Inf., 9 Jan., 1892. Trans. to 2nd Inf., 9 Feb., 1892. Capt., 2 March, 1899. Honor graduate of the Infantry and Cavalry School, 1895. Maj. 38th U. S. Vols., 17 Aug., 1899, to ——.

MUIR, SAML C. [Born in D. C. Appointed from D. C.]
Surg.'s Mate 1st Inf., 7 April, 1813. Disbanded 15 June, 1815. Reinstated in 8th Inf., 13 Sept., 1815. Hosp. Surg.'s Mate, 31 Oct., 1817. Post Surg., 18 April, 1818. Resigned 1 Aug., 1818. Post Surg., 28 Sept., 1818. Dropped 27 July, 1819. Died 24 Sept., 1832.

MULFORD, LAMBERT L. [Born in N. J. Appointed from N. J.]
2nd Lieut. 2nd N. J. Cav., 28 Aug., 1863. Capt., 1 Sept., 1864. Mustered out 1 Nov., 1865. 2nd Lieut. 3rd Cav., 23 Feb., 1866. 1st Lieut., 24 Dec., 1866. Mustered out 1 Jan., 1871.

MULHALL, STEPHEN J. [Born in N. Y. Appointed from Army.]
Priv. 4th Art., 26 June, 1862. 3rd Class Musician 4th Art., 1 Nov., 1862. Discharged 25 June, 1865. Priv. and Musician Co. I, 42nd Inf., 20 July, 1867. Trans. to 6th Inf., 22 April, 1869. Discharged 23 July, 1869. Priv. Gen. Ser., 7 July, 1875. 2nd Lieut. 14th Inf., 29 Feb., 1876. 1st Lieut., 1 July, 1888. Retired for disability, 17 April, 1891.

MULLAN, JOHN.* [Born in Va. Appointed at Large.]
Bvt. 2nd Lieut. 1st Art., 1 July, 1852. 2nd Lieut. 2nd Art., 10 May, 1853. 1st Lieut., 28 Feb., 1855. Capt., 11 Aug., 1862. Resigned 23 May, 1863.

MULLANY, JAMES R. [Born in Ireland. Appointed from N. Y.]
Maj. 13th Inf., 13 March, 1812. Trans. to 23rd Inf., 26 Aug., 1812. Lieut. Col. 23rd Inf., 3 March, 1813. Disbanded 15 June, 1815. Col. Q. M. Gen., 29 April, 1816. Disbanded 14 April, 1818. Died 15 Aug., 1846.

MULLAY, PATRICK. [Born in Ohio. Appointed from Army.]
Priv., Corpl. and Sergt. Co. F, 4th Inf., 29 Aug., 1894, to 28 Aug., 1897. Priv. and Corpl. Troop B, 6th Cav., 29 Aug., 1897, to 29 April, 1898. 2nd Lieut. 14th Inf., 12 April, 1898. 1st Lieut., 2 March, 1899.

MULLAY, WM. H. [Born in Ohio. Appointed from Army.]
Priv. and Corpl. Troop A, 1st Cav., 11 July, 1891, to 3 Nov., 1893. 2nd Lieut. 21st Inf., 7 Oct., 1893. 1st Lieut., 26 April, 1898.

MULLIGAN, JAMES B. [Born in N. H. Appointed from N. J.]
Capt. A. de C. N. J. Militia, 30 April, 1861, to 31 July, 1861. Capt. 19th Inf., 26 Oct., 1861. Resigned 31 Aug., 1869. Bvt. Maj., 20 Sept., 1863, for gallant and meritorious service at the Battles of Murfreesboro, Tenn., and Chickamauga, Ga. Bvt. Lieut. Col., 1 Sept., 1864, for gallant and meritorious service during the Atlanta campaign and in the Battle of Jonesboro, Ga.

MULLIKEN, DAVID B. [Born in La. Appointed from N. H.]
2nd Lieut. 16th Inf., 9 July, 1898. 1st Lieut. 6th Inf., 2 March, 1899.

MULLIKIN, JAMES R. [Born in N. J. Appointed from Ind.]
Capt. 35th Ind. Vols., 12 Dec., 1861. Mustered out 24 Nov., 1862. Priv. Co. A, 124th Ind. Vols., 8 Oct., 1863. Sergt., 14 Nov., 1863. 1st Lieut., 25th U. S. Col. Troops, 18 March, 1864. 1st Lieut. 97th U. S. Col. Troops, 7 Dec., 1865. Mustered out 6 April, 1866. 2nd Lieut. 4th Inf., 23 Feb., 1866. 1st Lieut., 18 July, 1866. Unassigned 23 March, 1869. Retired 15 Dec., 1870.

MULLINS, GEORGE G. [Born in Ky. Appointed from Ill.]
Chap. 25th Inf., 20 Jan., 1875. Retired for disability, 25 Feb., 1891.

MULLINS, JOHN.* [Born in Tenn. Appointed from Miss.]
Bvt. 2nd Lieut. 7th Inf., 1 July, 1854. 2nd Lieut. 2nd Drag., 3 March, 1855. 1st Lieut., 14 June, 1858. Resigned 24 April, 1861.

MULLINS, MARTIN. Born in Ireland. Appoinfed from Army.]
Priv., Corpl. and Sergt. Co. K, and Sergt. Maj. 5th Inf., 28 Aug., 1851, to 27 Nov., 1861. 2nd Lieut. 5th Inf., 24 Oct., 1861. 1st Lieut., 21 Feb., 1862. Capt., 14 July, 1864. Cashiered 15 May, 1869.

MUMFORD, FERDINAND S.* [Born in N. Y. Appointed from N. Y.]
2nd Lieut. 1st Inf., 1 July 1838. 1st Lieut., 11 June, 1839. Capt., 15 March, 1848. Resigned 31 Aug., 1849. Died 1 Oct., 1872.

MUMFORD, THOS. S.* [[Born in Texas. Appointed at Large.]
2nd Lieut. 9th Cav., 12 June, 1871. Trans. to 13th Inf., 13 June, 1872. 1st Lieut., 8 Jan., 1873. R. Q. M., 1 March, 1882, to 1 Sept., 1886. Retired for disability, with rank of Capt., 24 Feb., 1891.

MUNDAY, BENJAMIN. [Born in Va. Appointed from Va.]
Asst. Surg., 23 May, 1882. Capt. Asst. Surg., 23 May, 1887. Wholly retired 21 Jan., 1899.

MUNN, CURTIS E. [Born in Vt. Appointed from Mass.]
Hosp. Stwd. 1st Mass. Cav., 21 Dec., 1861. Asst. Surg. 27th Mass. Vols., 11 July, 1863. Mustered out 30 Dec., 1864. Maj. Surg. 2nd Mass. Vols., 19 Jan., 1865. Mustered out 14 July, 1865. 1st Lieut. Asst. Surg., 16 Nov., 1868. Capt. Asst. Surg., 2 Dec., 1869. Maj. Surg., 29 March, 1889. Retired by operation of law, 2 Feb., 1900.

MUNN, JOHN G. [Born in Conn. Appointed from Conn.]
Ensign 25th Inf., 12 March, 1812. 2nd Lieut., 13 March, 1813. 1st Lieut., 15 Aug., 1813. Disbanded 15 June, 1815. Reinstated 2 Dec., 1815, as 2nd Lieut. 2nd Inf. 1st Lieut., 17 June, 1816. Resigned 1 Jan., 1817. Retained 1815 (in reorganization under Act of 3 March, of that year) as 2nd Lieut. 2nd Inf., with Bvt. of 1st Lieut. from 15 Aug., 1813.

MUNRO, JAMES N.* [Born in Minn. Appointed from Minn.]
Addl. 2nd Lieut. 1st Cav., 11 June, 1897. 2nd Lieut. 4th Cav., 15 Nov., 1897.

MUNROE, JOHN.* [Born in Scotland. Appointed from N. Y.]
3rd Lieut. 1st Art., 11 March, 1814. 2nd Lieut., 1 May, 1814. Trans. to Corps Art., 12 May, 1814. 1st Lieut., 20 April, 1818. Trans. to 4th Art., 1 June, 1821.

Capt., 2 March, 1825. Maj. 2nd Art., 18 Aug., 1846. Lieut. Col. 4th Art., 11 Nov., 1856. Died 28 April, 1861. Bvt. Maj., 15 Feb., 1838, for faithful and meritorious conduct, &c., during three campaigns against the Florida Indians. Bvt. Lieut. Col., 23 Sept., 1846, for gallant and meritorious conduct at Monterey, Mexico. Bvt. Col., 23 Feb., 1847, for gallant and meritorious conduct at the Battle of Buena Vista, Mex.

MUNSON, EDWARD L. [Born in Conn. Appointed from Conn.]
Asst. Surg., 12 May, 1893. Capt. Asst. Surg., 12 May, 1898.

MUNSON, FRED. L. [Born in Ind. Ter. Appointed from Army.]
Priv., Corpl. and Sergt. Co. A, 6th Inf., 11 Jan.,1893, to 21 June, 1897. 2nd Lieut. 9th Inf., 3 June, 1897. 1st Lieut., 2 March, 1899. Reg. Com., 5 Oct., 1899.

MUNSON, JACOB F. [Born in N. Y. Appointed from N. Y.]
Priv. Co. C, 83rd N. Y. Vols., 14 Sept., 1861. Corpl., 8 May, 1862. Sergt., 11 Nov., 1862. 2nd Lieut. 83rd N. Y. Vols., 21 Oct., 1863. Mustered out 23 June,, 1864. 2nd Lieut. 8th U. S. Vet. Vols., 31 Dec., 1864. Bvt. 1st Lieut. and Capt. Vols., 13 March, 1865, for gallant and meritorious service during the war. Mustered out 15 Feb., 1866. 2nd Lieut. 6th Inf., 11 May, 1866. 1st Lieut. 31 Oct., 1866. Reg. Adj., 1 April, 1867, to 22 April, 1869, and from 29 May, 1869, to 31 Jan., 1875. Capt., 15 Dec., 1880. Retired by operation of law, 19 Nov., 1896.

MUNSON, SAML. [Born in East Indies. Appointed from Maine.]
Sergt. Co. H, 5th Me. Vols., 6 May, 1861. 2nd Lieut., 27 May, 1861. Mustered out 4 Sept., 1861. 2nd Lieut. 9th Inf., 5 Aug., 1861. 1st Lieut., 31 Dec., 1862. R. Q. M., 9 May, 1864, to 7 July, 1865. Capt. Asst. Q. M. Vols., 27 Feb., 1865. Capt. 9th Inf., 28 Sept., 1865. Mustered out Vol. service, 27 June, 1866. Died 2 Oct., 1887.

MUNTON, CHARLES H.* [Born in Mich. Appointed from Mich.]
2nd Lieut. 23rd Inf., 26 April, 1898. 1st Lieut. 12th Inf., 2 March, 1899.

MURAT, CONRAD. [Born in Vt. Appointed from Army.]
Priv. and Corpl. Co. D, 1st Drag., 25 March, 1858, to 25 March, 1863. 2nd Lieut. 5th Cav., 19 July, 1863. Dismissed 27 Aug., 1863.

MURDOCK, DANL. H. [Born in Penn. Appointed from Iowa.]
Priv. Co. D, 3rd Iowa Cav., 30 Aug., 1862. Corpl., 3 Aug., 1864. Discharged 5 Oct., 1864. 2nd Lieut. 122nd U. S. Col. Troops, 5 Oct., 1864. 1st Lieut., 10 Jan., 1865. Mustered out 8 Feb., 1866. 2nd Lieut. 6th Inf., 23 Feb., 1866. 1st Lieut., 28 July, 1866. Capt., 7 Oct., 1874. Accidentally drowned, 6 June, 1886.

MURDOCK, FRANCIS B.* [Born in Conn. Appointed from Conn.]
2nd Lieut. Light Art., 3 Jan., 1812. 1st Lieut., 24 Aug., 1812. Resigned 1 Jan., 1815. 2nd Lieut. 1st Inf., 19 Feb., 1817. Resigned 1 Nov., 1817. Died 2 Sept., 1866.

MURDOCK, GEORGE. [Born in Md. Appointed from Md.]
2nd Lieut. 14th Inf., 15 April, 1812. 1st Lieut., 14 Nov., 1813. Disbanded 15 June, 1815. 3rd Lieut. Corps Art., 15 Nov., 1817. 2nd Lieut. 7th Inf., 13 Feb., 1818. 1st Lieut., 31 Jan., 1819. R. Q. M., 1 Nov., 1818, to 1 June, 1821. Capt., 31 Dec., 1822. Resigned 31 July, 1824.

MURDOCK, JOHN B. [Born in Conn. Appointed from Conn.]
1st Lieut. 25th Inf., 12 March 1812. Capt., 16 April, 1813. Trans. to 6th Inf., 17 May, 1815. Died 5 Sept., 1815. Bvt. Maj., 25 July, 1814, for gallant conduct at the Battle of Niagara.

MURDOCK, JOHN S. [Born in Conn. Appointed from Conn.]
2nd Lieut. 25th Inf., 7 Oct., 1891. 1st Lieut., 26 April, 1898. Graduate of the Infantry and Cavalry School, 1895. Resigned 30 June, 1899.

MURPHY, CHARLES N. [Born in Nev. Appointed from Nev.]
Priv. and Sergt. Troop M, 2nd Cav., 19 May, 1898, to 19 Sep., 1898. 2nd Lieut. 22nd Inf., 9 Sep., 1898. 1st Lieut., 15 Nov., 1899.

MURPHY, DENNIS. [Born in Md. Appointed from Va.]
Mil. Storekeeper Ord. Dept., 7 April, 1858. Dismissed 19 July, 1861.

MURPHY, EDWARD. [Born in N. Y. Appointed from Army.]
Priv. and Sergt. Co. E, 2nd (5th) Cav., 28 Sept., 1860, to 23 March, 1863. 2nd Lieut. 5th Cav., 19 Feb., 1863. 1st Lieut., 7 Dec., 1863. Retired 25 April, 1865. Died 6 Oct., 1871. Bvt. Capt., 6 May, 1864, for gallant and meritorious service at the Battle of Todd's Tavern, Va. Bvt. Maj., 19 Sept., 1864, for gallant and meritorious service at the Battle of Winchester, Va.

MURPHY, EUGENE P.* [Born in N. Y. Appointed at Large.]
2nd Lieut. 2nd Art., 17 June, 1867. 1st Lieut., 1 Jan., 1871. Resigned 1 April, 1872.

MURPHY, JOHN. [Born in Ireland. Appointed from Tenn.]
Priv. and Corpl. Co. G, 1st (4th) Cav., 25 July, 1855, to 2 Aug., 1862. 1st Lieut. Adj. 5th Tenn. Cav., 31 Aug., 1862. Maj., 13 Feb., 1863. Col., 1 July, 1864. Mustered out 19 Jan., 1865. 2nd Lieut. 4th Cav., 20 Dec., 1865. 1st Lieut., 28 July, 1866. R. Q. M., 27 June to 15 Oct., 1868. Resigned 31 July, 1869. Died 26 Feb., 1871.

MURPHY, JOHN. [Born in Ireland. Appointed from Army.]
Priv. Detachment Drag., Mil. Acad., 21 May, 1858. Trans. to Co. D, 5th Art., 26 June, 1861. Sergt., 1 July, 1861. 1st Sergt., 1 Nov., 1862. Discharged 21 May, 1863. Priv. Detachment Cav., Mil. Acad., 4 June, 1863. Trans. to Co. I, 5th Art., 3 Dec., 1863. Sergt., 3 Dec., 1863. 1st Sergt., 1 Aug., 1864. 2nd Lieut. 14th Inf., 16 Aug., 1867. 1st Lieut., 1 Feb., 1876. Capt., 9 Jan., 1892. Maj. P. M., 12 July, 1899. Retired for over forty years' service, 17 July, 1899.

MURPHY, PIERCE A.* [Born in Wyo. Appointed from Wash.]
Addl. 2nd Lieut. 4th Cav., 11 June, 1897. 2nd Lieut. 7th Cav., 5 Aug., 1897.

MURPHY, TRUMAN O.* [Born in Ohio. Appointed from Ohio.]
2nd Lieut. 19th Inf., 12 June, 1891. 1st Lieut. 10th Inf., 7 Sept., 1897. Capt. 19th Inf., 5 Feb., 1900.

MURPHY, WM. L. [Born in Iowa. Appointed from Iowa.]
2nd Lieut. 24th Inf., 26 April, 1898. 1st Lieut., 2 March, 1899. Reg. Com., 12 July, 1899. Capt. 39th U. S. Vols., 17 Aug., 1899, to ——.

MURRAY, ALBERT M.* [Born in N. Y. Appointed from N. Y.]
2nd Lieut. 5th Art., 17 June, 1862. Trans. to 2nd Art., 6 Oct., 1862. 1st Lieut., 30 March, 1864. Died 12 Aug., 1864, while prisoner of war. Bvt. Capt., 16 Sept., 1862, for gallant and meritorious service at the Battle of Antietam, Md. Bvt. Maj., 22 July, 1864, for gallant and meritorious conduct before Atlanta, Ga.

MURRAY, ARTHUR.* [Born in Mo. Appointed from Mo.]
2nd Lieut. 1st Art., 17 June, 1874. 1st Lieut., 14 June, 1878. Capt. A. Q. M., 14 Oct., 1896, declined. Honor graduate of the Artillery School, 1880. Capt. 1st Art., 10 Feb., 1898. Col. 43rd U. S. Vols., 17 Aug., 1899, to ——.

MURRAY, CHAS. D. [Born in Ky. Appointed from Ind.]
Lieut. Col. 20th Ind. Vols., 22 July, 1861. Resigned 23 Nov., 1861. Col. 89th Ind. Vols., 28 Aug., 1862. Mustered out 19 July, 1865. Died 3 Aug., 1873. Capt. 19th Inf., 14 May, 1861. Resigned 27 July, 1861.

MURRAY, CUNLIFFE H.* [Born in S. C.. Apointed from N. Y.]
2nd Lieut. 4th Cav., 15 June, 1877. 1st Lieut., 2 Sept., 1879. Capt., 15 April, 1890. Maj. I. G. Vols., 21 Jan., 1899, to ——.

MURRAY, DOUGLAS A. [Born in England. Appointed from Army.]
Priv., Corpl. and Sergt. Batty F, 1st Art., 23 Nov., 1850, to 23 March, 1855. Priv. Batty F, 1st Art. and Gen. Ser., 7 Oct., 1856, to 10 Oct., 1861. Lieut. Col. 3rd Ohio Cav., 10 Oct., 1861. Resigned 7 June, 1863. 2nd Lieut. 4th Cav., 17 July, 1862. Resigned 18 June, 1863.

MURRAY, EDWARD.* [Born in Md. Appointed from Md.]
Bvt. 2nd Lieut. 2nd Inf., 1 July, 1841. 2nd Lieut., 17 Oct., 1842. 1st Lieut., 22 Aug., 1847. Capt., 8 Jan., 1853. Resigned 3 Feb., 1855. Died 3 July, 1874.

MURRAY, HUGH C. [Born in Mo. Appointed from Ill.]
2nd Lieut. of Inf., 8 March, 1847; 14th Inf., 9 April, 1847. Resigned 31 March, 1848.

MURRAY, JOHN W.* [Born in Penn. Appointed from Penn.]
Bvt. 2nd Lieut. 7th Inf., 1 July, 1830. Killed by being thrown from a horse, 14 Feb., 1831.

MURRAY, PETER.* [Born in Cal. Appointed from Cal.]
2nd Lieut. 3rd Inf., 12 June, 1890. 1st Lieut. 5th Inf., 18 March, 1897. Trans. to 21st Inf., 21 July, 1897. Capt. 18th Inf., 26 Nov., 1899.

MURRAY, ROBT. [Born in Md. Appointed from Md.]
Asst. Surg., 29 June, 1846. Maj. Surg., 23 June, 1860. Bvt. Lieut. Col. and Col., 13 March, 1865, for faithful and meritorious service during the war. Lieut. Col. Asst. Med. Purveyor, 28 July, 1866. Col. Surg., 26 June, 1876. Col. Asst. Surg. Gen., 14 Dec., 1882. Brig. Gen. Surg. Gen., 23 Nov., 1883. Retired by operation of law, 6 Aug., 1886.

MURRAY, THOMAS. [Born in Md. Appointed from Md.]
2nd Lieut. Art., 17 Jan., 1805. 1st Lieut., 11 April, 1807. Capt. 1st Art., 10 Feb., 1813. Trans. to Corps Art., 12 May, 1814. Died — Sept., 1817.

MURRAY, WM. G. [Born in Ireland. Appointed from Penn.]
Sergt. Co. G., 2nd Pa. Vols., 26 Dec., 1846. 2nd Lieut. of Inf., 5 March, 1847; 11th Inf., 9 April, 1847. Disbanded 14 Aug., 1848. Col. 84th Pa. Vols., 28 Dec., 1861. Killed 23 March, 1862, at the Battle of Winchester, Va.

MURRIN, THOS. D. [Born in Ireland. Appointed from W. Va.]
Sergt. Co. D., 10th Ohio Vols., 3 June, 1861, to 16 March, 1862. Capt. 10th W. Va. Vols. 17 March, 1862. Mustered out 18 March, 1865. 2nd Lieut. 12th Inf., 26 April, 1866. Trans. to 30th Inf., 21 Sept., 1866. 1st Lieut., 17 Feb., 1868. R. Q. M., 10 Dec., 1866, to 25 Aug., 1868. Dismissed 25 Aug., 1868.

MURRY, ALEX'R. [Born in Pa. Appointed from Pa.]
Cadet at Mil. Acad., 1 July, 1847, to 10 Jan., 1848. 2nd Lieut. 10th Inf., 3 March, 1855. 1st. Lieut., 19 Jan., 1861. Trans. to 13th Inf., 14 May, 1861. Capt., 24 Oct., 1861. Retired 30 March, 1864.

MUSE, SAML. E. [Born in N. C. Appointed from Ga.]
2nd Lieut. 1st Inf., 1 Aug., 1838. 1st Lieut., 12 Nov., 1839. Resigned 1 March, 1844.

MUSSER, ABRAHAM. [Born in Penn. Appointed from Penn.
2nd Lieut. 3rd Inf., 18 April, 1818. 1st Lieut., 1 June, 1819. R. Q. M., 19 June, 1819, to 1 June, 1821. Dismissed 3 Sept., 1822.

MUSSEY, REUBEN D. [Born in N. H. Appointed from Ohio.]
Capt. 19th Inf., 14 May, 1861. Col. 100th U. S. Col. Troops, 14 June, 1864. Mustered out Vols., 26 Dec., 1865. Resigned 19 Feb., 1866. Bvt. Maj., Lieut. Col., and Col., 13 March, 1865, for gallant and meritorious conduct during the war, and Brig. Gen. Vols., 13 March, 1865, for faithful service in the recruitment and organization of colored troops.

MYER, ALBERT J. [Born in N. Y. Appointed from N. Y.]
Asst. Surg., 18 Sept., 1854. Maj. Chief Sig. Officer, 27 June, 1860. Bvt. Lieut. Col., 27 May 1862, for gallant and meritorious service in the Battle of Hanover C. H., Va. Bvt. Col., 2 July, 1862, for gallant and meritorious service in the Battle of Malvern Hill, Va. Col. Chief Sig. Officer, 3 March, 1863. Appointment of Col. Chief Sig. Officer expired by constitutional limitation, 4 July, 1864, and revoked 21 July, 1864. Bvt. Brig. Gen., 13 March, 1865, for distinguished service in organizing, instructing, and commanding the Sig. Corps of the army, and for its special service on 5 Oct., 1864, the day on which the post and garrison at Allatoona, Ga., and a most valuable depository of provisions there, attacked by the rebel army, were saved by troops brought up by signals just in time to defend it, the messages being sent over the heads of the enemy, and when communication in any other way was impossible. Col. Chief Sig. Officer, 28 July, 1866. Brig. Gen. Chief Sig. Officer, 16 June, 1880. Died 24 Aug., 1880.

MYER, ALBERT L. [Born in N. Y. Appointed from Army.]
Priv. Co. F, 3rd Batt. 11th Inf., 26 Oct., 1865. Trans. to 29th Inf., 21 Sept., 1866. Sergt., 1 Nov., 1866. Q. M. Sergt., 18 Feb., 1867. 2nd Lieut. 29th Inf., 6 Dec., 1867. Trans. to 11th Inf., 25 April, 1869. 1st Lieut., 28 June, 1878. Capt. 8 Dec. 1886. Maj., 2 March, 1899.

**MYER, EDGAR A.** [Born in Tex. Appointed from N. Y.]
2nd Lieut. 11th Inf., 10 April, 1899.

**MYERS, ABRAHAM C.*** [Born in S. C. Appointed from S. C.]
Bvt. 2nd Lieut. 4th Inf., 1 July, 1833. 2nd Lieut., 31 Dec., 1835. 1st Lieut., 6 Sept., 1837. Asst. Q. M., 21 Nov., 1839. Resigned 28 Jan., 1861. Bvt. Maj., 9 May, 1846, for gallant and meritorious conduct at Palo Alto and Resaca de la Palma. Bvt. Lieut. Col., 20 Aug., 1847, for gallant conduct at Churubusco. Died 20 June, 1889.

**MYERS, EDWARD.** [Born in Germany. Appointed from Army.]
Priv., Corpl., Sergt. and 1st Sergt. Co. H, 1st Drags. (1st Cav.), 26 Aug., 1857, to 26 Aug., 1862. 2nd Lieut. 1st Cav., 17 July, 1862. 1st Lieut., 23 Sept., 1863. Capt. 7th Cav., 28 July, 1866. Died 11 July, 1871. Bvt. Capt., 6 May, 1864, for gallant and meritorious service at the Battle of Todd's Tavern, Va. Bvt. Maj., 1 April, 1865, for gallant ard meritorious service at the Battle of Five Forks, Va. Bvt. Lieut. Col., 1 April, 1865, for gallant and meritorious service during the war.

**MYERS, FREDK.*** [Born in Conn. Appointed from Conn.]
Bvt. 2nd Lieut. 5th Inf., 1 July, 1846. 2nd Lieut., 23 Nov., 1846. 1st Lieut. 7 Oct., 1848. R. Q. M., 1 Jan., 1855, to 1 May, 1856. Capt. Asst. Q. M., 29 Aug., 1856. Maj. A. A. de C., 23 May, 1862. Lieut. Col. A. A. de C., 15 July, 1862. Mustered out as A. de C., 31 May, 1866. Maj. Q. M., 12 Aug., 1864. Lieut. Col. Dep. Q. M. Gen., 4 March, 1867. Died 7 July, 1874. Bvt. Lieut. Col. and Brig. Gen., 13 March, 1865, for faithful and meritorious service during the war.

**MYERS, JASPER.*** [Born in Ind. Appointed from Ind.]
2nd Lieut. Ord., 17 June, 1862. 1st Lieut., 3 March, 1863. Capt., 7 March, 1867. Discharged 31 Dec., 1870. Bvt. Capt., 13 March, 1865, for faithful and meritorious service in the Ord. Dept.

**MYERS, JOHN E.*** [Born in N. Y. Appointed from Neb.]
2nd Lieut. 3rd Art., 13 June, 1873. 1st Lieut., 20 Sept., 1880. Died 28 May, 1894.

**MYERS, J. WILL.** [Born in Va. Appointed from W. Va.]
Priv. Co. I, 3rd W. Va. Vols., 10 July 1861, to 20 March, 1863. Sergt. and 1st Sergt. Troop L, 4th W. Va. Cav., 30 Aug., 1863, to 10 March, 1864. Priv. and 1st Sergt. Troop G, 5th W. Va. Cav., 4 April to 14 Aug., 1864. 2nd Lieut. 5th W. Va. Cav., 14 Aug., 1864. Mustered out 9 April, 1866. 2nd Lieut. 10th Cav., 24 Sept., 1867. Cashiered 27 May, 1875.

**MYERS, S. ETTING.** [Born in Md. Appointed from S. C.]
Asst. Surg., 13 July, 1832. Resigned 31 March, 1836.

**MYERS, WM.*** [Born in Penn. Appointed from Penn.]
Bvt. 2nd Lieut. 5th Inf., 1 July, 1852. 2nd Lieut. 4th Inf., 27 March, 1854. 2nd Lieut. 9th Inf., 3 March, 1855. 1st Lieut., 1 May, 1857. Capt. Asst. Q. M., 17 May, 1861. Col. A. A. de C., 14 June, 1862. Bvt. Brig. Gen. Vols., 13 March, 1865, for faithful and meritorious service during the war. Bvt. Maj., Lieut. Col., Col., and Brig. Gen., 13 March, 1865, for faithful and meritorious service during the war. Mustered out as Col. A. A. de C., 31 May, 1866. Lieut. Col. Dep. Q. M. G., 22 Jan., 1881. Retired for disability, 15 March, 1883. Died 11 Nov., 1887.

**MYRICK, JOHN D.** [Born in Maine. Appointed from Maine.]
2nd Lieut. 1st Me. Cav., 2 Nov., 1861. 1st Lieut., 9 Dec., 1862. Capt., 28 Aug., 1863. Bvt. Maj. Vols., 31 March, 1865, for gallant and meritorious service at the Battle of Dinwiddie C. H., Va. Mustered out 1 Aug., 1865. 1st Lieut. 10th Cav., 7 March, 1867. Resigned 17 May, 1872. Bvt. Capt., 7 March, 1867, for gallant and meritorious service in the Battle of Dinwiddie C. H., Va. Died 27 Dec., 1882.

**MYRICK, JOHN R.** [Born in N. J. Appointed from N. Y.]
Priv. Co. B, 13th N. Y. State Militia, 23 April, 1861. Discharged 6 Aug., 1861. 2nd Lieut. and 1st Lieut. 3rd Art., 18 Nov., 1861. Reg. Adj., 10 Oct., 1867, to 1 Dec., 1872. Bvt. Capt., 20 Feb., 1864, for gallant and meritorious service in the Battle of Olustee, Fla. Bvt. Maj., 7 Oct., 1864, for gallant and meritorious service in action on the Newmarket Road, near Richmond, Va. Capt. 38th Inf., 28 July, 1866, declined. Capt. 3rd Art., 1 Dec., 1872. Maj., 12 Feb., 1895. Trans. to 5th Art., 5 Oct., 1896. Lieut. Col. 2nd Art., 16 Oct., 1899.

**NAGLEE, HENRY M.*** [Born in Penn. Appointed from Penn.]
Bvt. 2nd Lieut. 5th Inf., 1 July, 1835. Resigned 31 Dec., 1835. Lieut. Col. 16th Inf., 14 May, 1861. Resigned 10 Jan., 1862. Capt. 1st N. Y. Vols., 15 Aug., 1846. Mustered out 26 Oct., 1848. Lieut. Col. 16th Inf., 14 May, 1861. Resigned 10 Jan., 1862. Brig. Gen. Vols., 4 Feb., 1862. Mustered out 4 April, 1864. Died 5 March 1886.

**NANCE, JOHN T.*** [Born in Ill. Appointed from Ill.]
2nd Lieut. 2nd Cav., 1 July, 1886. 1st Lieut. 6th Cav., 15 Aug., 1892.

**NAPIER, LEROY.*** [Born in Ga. Appointed from Ga.]
Bvt. 2nd Lieut. Drag., 1 July, 1858. 2nd Lieut. 1st Drag., 6 Jan., 1859. Resigned 28 Feb., 1860. Died 16 Aug., 1867.

**NASH, BENJAMIN F.** [Born in N. Y. Appointed from Army.]
Priv., Corpl. and Sergt. Co. F, 3rd Art. and F, 5th Art., 24 Sept., 1859, to 16 Aug., 1863. 2nd Lieut. 5th Art., 10 Aug., 1863. Resigned 13 Dec., 1864.

**NASH, PRESTON G., Jr.** [Born in Ala. Appointed from Fla.]
Post Chaplain, 18 July, 1876. Resigned 14 May, 1878.

**NASH, WM. H.** [Born in Ohio. Appointed from Ohio.]
Capt. C. S Vols., 26 Nov., 1862. Bvt. Maj. Vols., 31 March, 1865, for gallant and distinguished service. Capt. C. S., 17 Nov., 1865. Bvt. Maj., 17 Nov., 1865, for faithful and meritorious service in the Sub. Dept. during the war. Maj. C. S., 14 July, 1890. Lieut. Col. Asst. C. G. Sub., 10 June, 1896. Col. Asst. C. G. S., 4 Feb., 1898. Brig. Gen. C. G. S., 21 April, 1898. Retired, at his own request, 2 May, 1898, being over 62 years of age.

NAUMAN, GEORGE.* [Born in Penn. Appointed from Penn.]
Bvt. 2nd Lieut. 2nd Art., 1 July, 1823. 2nd Lieut. 1st Art., 1 July, 1823. 1st Lieut., 30 May, 1832. Capt., 4 Feb., 1837. Maj. 3rd Art., 24 Dec., 1853. Lieut. Col. 1st Art., 23 July, 1861. Col. 5th Art., 1 Aug., 1863. Died 11 Aug., 1863. Bvt. Maj., 18 April, 1847, for gallant and meritorious conduct at Cerro Gordo. Bvt. Lieut. Col., 20 Aug., 1847, for gallant and meritorious conduct at Contreras and Churubusco.

NAVE, ANDREW H.* [Born in Tenn. Appointed from Tenn.]
2nd Lieut. 7th Cav., 12 June, 1871. 1st Lieut., 25 June, 1876. Capt., 16 Jan., 1884. Retired for disability, 23 Sept., 1885.

NAVE, ORVILLE J. [Born in Ohio. Appointed from Ohio.]
Priv. Co. A, 111th Ill. Vols., 14 Aug., 1862. Discharged 6 June, 1865. Post Chap., 27 July, 1882.

NAYLOR, WM. K. [Born in Ill. Appointed from Minn.]
2nd Lieut. 14th Minn. Vols., 8 May 1898, to 28 July, 1898. 2nd Lieut. 9th Inf., 9 July, 1898. 1st Lieut. 18th Inf., 2 March, 1899. Trans. to 9th Inf., 29 Aug., 1899.

NEAL, HENRY R. [Born in Penn. Appointed from Kansas.]
Corpl. and Sergt. B and A Mounted Rifles, 21 Dec., 1846, to 25 Aug., 1848. 2nd Lieut. 13th Kan. Vols., 9 Aug., 1862. Capt., 20 Sept., 1862. Resigned 2 Dec., 1864. 2nd Lieut. 26th Inf., 22 Jan., 1867. Died 21 Nov., 1867.

NEALE, FIELDING. [Born in England. Appointed from N. Y.]
Capt. 1st N. Y. Eng., 14 Feb., 1862. Resigned 1 Sept., 1862. 1st Lieut. 96th N. Y. Vols., 1 May, 1864. Discharged 23 Nov., 1864. 2nd Lieut. Vet. Res. Corps, 2 May, 1865, to 15 Oct., 1866. 2nd Lieut. 45th Inf., 28 July, 1866. Died 18 Nov., 1866.

NEALL, JOHN M.* [Born in Cal. Appointed from Nev.]
2nd Lieut. 4th Cav., 13 June, 1883. 1st Lieut., 15 April, 1890. Capt., April, 1898. Dismissed 15 July, 1899.

NEALY, OSCAR H. [Born in Ind. Appointed from Army.]
Musician K, 10th Ind. Vols., 22 April to 6 Aug., 1861. Priv. and Corpl. Co. E, 11th Inf., 25 Oct., 1861, to 7 Oct., 1862. Resigned 18 Feb., 1866. Priv. Co. D, 6th Cav. (under name of T. H. McDougall), 7 April to 16 Aug., 1866. Died 22 Jan., 1889. 2nd Lieut. 11th Inf., 25 Sept., 1862. 1st Lieut., 6 Jan., 1864. Resigned 18 Feb., 1866. Bvt. Capt., 13 March, 1865, for gallant and meritorious service at the Battle of Gettysburg, Penn.

NEAR, LOUIS L. [Born in ——. Appointed from Del.]
Surg.'s Mate 2nd Art., 6 July, 1812. Maj. Surg. 4th Rifles, 17 March, 1814. Trans. to Rifles, 17 May, 1815. Discharged 15 June, 1815.

NEARY, WM. C. [Born in Ga. Appointed from Army.]
Priv. and Corpl. Co. E, Batt. Eng., 2 Oct., 1884, to 15 March, 1888. 2nd Lieut. 3rd Inf., 6 Feb., 1888. 1st Lieut. of Inf. (4th), 19 Feb., 1895. Graduate of the Infantry and Cavalry School, 1891. Died of wounds received in action, 9 July, 1898, on hospital ship "Relief."

NEELY, ROBERT. [Born in Md. Appointed from Md.]
Sergt. Co. G, 1st Md. Vols., 27 May, 1861. 2nd Lieut., 1 Feb., 1862. 1st Lieut., 1 May, 1863. Capt., 20 Aug., 1864. Maj., 21 Feb., 1865. Mustered out 2 July, 1865. 2nd Lieut. 41st Inf., 28 July, 1866. 1st Lieut., 20 Sept., 1867. Trans. to 24th Inf., 11 Nov., 1869. Dropped 5 Oct., 1784.

NEES, JOHN. [Born in ——. Appointed from Ill.]
2nd Lieut. Mounted Rangers, 28 July, 1832. Disbanded 1 Oct., 1833.

NEFF, ALBERT J.* [Born in Penn. Appointed from Penn.]
Priv. Co. C, 3rd Pa. Vols., 20 April to 29 July, 1861. 2nd Lieut. 2nd Cav., 18 June, 1866. 1st Lieut., 1 Nov., 1867. Died 5 July, 1868.

NEIDE, HORACE. [Born in Penn. Appointed from Penn.]
2nd Lieut. 2nd Pa. Res. Corps, 1 Aug., 1861. 1st Lieut., 12 Dec., 1861. Capt., 2 April, 1862. Maj., 1 Aug., 1862. Resigned 24 Nov., 1862. Capt. Vet. Res. Corps, 8 June, 1863. Maj., 4 Dec., 1863. Lieut. Col., 20 June 1864. Bvt. Col. Vols., 13 March, 1865, for gallant service in the Batles of Mechanicsville, Gaines' Mill, and Charles City Cross-Roads, Va. Bvt. Brig. Gen. Vols., 13 March, 1865, for gallant service in the Battles of Mechanicsville, Gaines' Mill, and Charles City Cross-Roads, Va., and for faithful and meritorious service during the war. Mustered out 10 Jan., 1867. 1st Lieut. 44th Inf., 28 July, 1866. Bvt. Capt., 2 March, 1867, for gallant and meritorious service in the Battle of Gaines' Mill, Va. Bvt. Maj., 2 March, 1867, for gallant and meritorious service in action at Glendale, Va. Unassigned 27 May, 1869. Ass'd to 4th Inf., 15 Dec., 1870. Capt., 27 April, 1880. Retired, for over thirty years' service, 4 April, 1893.

NEIL, ADRIAN. [Born in ——. Appointed from S. C.]
1st Lieut. 2nd Art., 12 March, 1812. Trans. to Corps Art., 12 May, 1814. Disbanded 15 June, 1815. Reinstated 1 Jan., 1816, in Corps Art. Capt., 1 Dec., 1816. Died 24 Nov., 1817.

NEILL, JAMES P. W. [Born in Penn. Appointed from Penn.]
Ensign 23rd Pa. Vols., 21 April to 27 June, 1861. 1st Lieut. 18th Inf., 14 May, 1861. Reg. Adj., 16 Jan., 1862, to 12 Dec., 1863. Capt., 12 Dec., 1863. Trans. to 36th Inf., 21 Sept., 1866. Trans. to 7th Inf., 19 May, 1869. Unassigned 4 April, 1870. Mustered out 1 Jan., 1871. Bvt. Capt., 20 Sept., 1863, for gallant and meritorious service at the Battle of Chickamauga, Ga.

NEILL, LEWIS.* [Born in Va. Appointed from Va.]
Bvt. 2nd Lieut. Rifles, 1 July, 1843. 2nd Lieut., 15 Dec., 1843; 2nd Drag., 4 April, 1844. Reg. Adj., 27 July, 1846, to 20 Dec., 1847. 1st Lieut., 20 Dec., 1847. Died 13 Jan., 1850. Bvt. 1st Lieut., 25 March, 1847, for gallant and meritorious conduct in the affair at Medelin.

NEILL, THOS. H.* [Born in Penn. Appointed from Penn.]
Bvt. 2nd Lieut. 4th Inf., 1 July, 1847. 2nd Lieut. 5th Inf., 8 Sept., 1847. 1st

Lieut.., 31 July, 1850. Capt., 1 April, 1857. Col. 23rd Penn. Vols., 17 Feb., 1862. Bvt. Maj., 1 July, 1862, for gallant and meritorious service in the Battle of Malvern Hill, Va. Bvt. Lieut. Col., 3 May, 1863, for gallant and meritorious service in the Battle of Chancellorsville, Va. Brig. Gen. Vols., 29 Nov., 1862. Maj. 11th Inf., 26 Aug., 1863. Bvt. Col., 12 May, 1864, for gallant and meritorious service in the Battle of Spottsylvania, Va. Bvt. Brig. Gen., 13 March, 1865, for gallant and meritorious service in the field during the war. Bvt. Maj. Gen. Vols., 13 March, 1865, for gallant and meritorious service during the war., Mustered outof Vol. Service 24 Aug., 1865. Trans. to 20th Inf., 21 Sept., 1866. Lieut. Col. 1st Inf., 22 Feb., 1869. Unassigned 15 March, 1869. Assd'd to 6th Cav., 15 Dec., 1870. Col. 8th Cav., 2 April, 1879. Retired for disability, 2 April, 1883. Died 12 March, 1885.

NEILLY, JOHN. [Born in Ireland. Appointed from N. Y.]
2nd Lieut. 5th Inf., 3 March, 1848. Died 13 March, 1854.

NEILSON, WM. W. [Born in Md. Appointed from Md.]
2nd Lieut. Light Drag., 1 May, 1812. 1st Lieut., 7 June, 1813. Trans. to 4th Inf., 17 May, 1815. Capt., 1 Dec., 1816. Resigned 31 July, 1817.

NELSON, ANDERSON D.* [Born in Ky. Appointed from Ohio.]
Bvt. 2nd Lieut. 6th Inf., 1 July, 1841. 2nd Lieut., 10 Feb., 1842. 1st Lieut., 18 Nov., 1849. Capt. 10th Inf., 3 March, 1855. Maj. 1st Inf., 13 March, 1863. Lieut. Col. A. I. G., 8 Feb. to 1 Aug., 1865. Bvt. Lieut. Col., 13 March, 1865, for faithful and efficient service during the war. Bvt. Col., 13 March, 1865, for faithful and meritorious service during the war. Lieut. Col. 5th Inf., 12 Jan., 1868. Unassigned 15 March. 1869. Ass'd to 12th Inf., 15 Dec., 1870. Retired 7 June, 1879. Died 30 Dec., 1885.

NELSON, ARTHUR. [Born in Md. Appointed from Md.]
Surg.'s Mate 8th Inf., 31 Oct., 1817. Resigned 1 May, 1818. Died 6 Oct., 1841.

NELSON, CHARLES J. [Born in ——. Appointed from ——.]
2nd Lieut. (unassigned), 1 Dec., 1899.

NELSON, HUNTER B.* [Born in Tenn. Appointed from Tenn.]
2nd Lieut. 24th Inf., 12 June, 1893. 1st Lieut., 26 April, 1898.

NELSON, JAMES H. [Born in Mich. Appointed from Mich.]
Addl. P. M., 23 Feb., 1864. Maj. P. M., 17 Jan., 1867. Dismissed 31 Jan., 1881. Died 19 April, 1881.

NELSON, JOSEPH S. [Born in Md. Appointed from Md.]
1st Lieut 14th Inf., 12 March, 1812. Capt. 36th Inf., 30 April, 1813. Disbanded 15 June, 1815. Reinstated as 1st Lieut. of Ord., 3 May, 1816, with Bvt. of Capt., to rank from 30 April, 1813. Capt., 13 Aug., 1819. Trans. to 3rd Inf., 1 June, 1821. Maj. 7th Inf., 1 July, 1839. Bvt. Maj., 13 Aug., 1829, for ten years' faithful service in one grade. Died 27 Feb., 1843.

NELSON, ROBERT. [Born in Ohio. Appointed from Army.]
Priv., Corpl. and Sergt. Co. B, and Q. M. Sergt. 13th Inf., 18 Sept., 1861, to 10 Aug., 1863. 2nd Lieut. 13th Inf., 10 Aug., 1863. Appointment revoked 18 March, 1864.

NELSON, THOMAS N. [Born in ——. Appointed from Va.]
Capt. 10th Inf., 12 March, 1812. Maj. 30th Inf., 19 July, 1814. Trans. to 18th Inf., 24 Jan., 1815. Retained as Capt. 4th Inf., 17 May, 1815, but declined. Retained — May, 1815 (in reorganization under Act of 3 March, 1815), as Capt. 4th Inf., with Bvt. of Maj. from 19 July, 1814.

NELSON, WM. [Born in Ind. Appointed from Army.]
Priv. Co. B, 1st Batt. 13th Inf., 5 Sept., 1861. Sergt., 1 Dec., 1861. 1st Sergt., 1 Jan., 1862. 2nd Lieut. 13th Inf., 31 May, 1862. 1st Lieut., 2 Oct., 1862. Bvt. Capt. 10 Jan., 1863, for gallant and meritorious service in the Battle of Arkansas Post, Ark. Bvt. Maj., 4 July, 1863, for gallant and meritorious service in the siege of Vicksburg, Miss. Q. M. 1st Batt. 13th Inf., 27 March, 1865, to 30 Nov., 1865. Trans. to 22nd Inf., 21 Sept., 1866. Capt., 9 July, 1867. Unassigned 15 May, 1869. Ass'd to 21st Inf., 15 Dec., 1870. Retired 29 May, 1874.

NELSON, WM. H. [Born in Tenn. Appointed from Tenn.]
1st Lieut. 5th Tenn. Cav., 6 Aug., 1863. Capt., 25 June, 1865. Mustered out 14 Aug., 1865. 2nd Lieut. 7th Inf., 18 May, 1866. 1st Lieut., 7 March, 1871. Retired 20 March, 1879.

NESBITT, WM. B. [Born in Ohio. Appointed from Ohio.]
Corpl. Co. D, 12th Ohio Vols., 22 April to 20 June, 1861. Sergt., 21 June, 1861. Sergt. Maj., 28 June, 1861. 2nd Lieut., 16 July, 1862. 1st Lieut. and Adj., 19 Nov., 1862. Mustered out 11 July, 1864. Lieut. Col. 176th Ohio Vols., 23 Sept., 1864. Mustered out 14 June, 1865. 1st Lieut. 40th Inf., 16 May, 1867. Trans. to 25th Inf., 20 April, 1869. Unassigned 6 July, 1869. Discharged 1 Sept., 1870.

NESBITT, WM. F.* [Born in Ohio. Appointed from Ohio.]
2nd Lieut. 6th Inf., 26 April, 1898. 1st Lieut., 2 March, 1899.

NESMITH, CLARENCE E. [Born in N. H. Appointed from N. H.]
Priv. Co. B, 1st Mass. Art., 4 Aug., 1862, to 8 Jan., 1863. Capt. C. S. Vols., 18 May, 1864. Bvt. Maj. Vols., 30 Nov., 1865, for faithful service in the Subsist Dept. 2nd Lieut. 6th Cav., 18 April, 1866. 1st Lieut., 12 Dec., 1866, to 28 Feb., 1870. Capt., 22 May, 1872. Died 20 Sept., 1874.

NESMITH, LOUIS A. [Born in N. H. Appointed from N. H.]
Hosp. Steward U. S. A., 24 Dec., 1863. Discharged 5 Aug., 1865. 2nd Lieut. 6th U. S. Col. Cav., 22 March, 1866. Mustered out 15 April, 1866. 2nd Lieut. 12th Inf., 12 Jan., 1867. 1st Lieut., 26 April, 1873. Retired 28 June, 1878. Died 1 Nov., 1880.

NETTERVILLE, WM. McC. [Born in N. Y. Appointed from Army.]
Priv. and Sergt. Co. C, and Com. Sergt. 12th Inf., 18 Sept., 1861, to 26 June, 1862. 2nd Lieut. 12th Inf., 25 May, 1862. 1st Lieut., 20 Dec., 1862. Capt., 19 Feb., 1866. Trans. to 21st Inf., 21 Sept., 1866. Dropped 2 June, 1876. Bvt. Capt., 5 May, 1864, for gallant and meritorious service at the Battle of the Wilderness, Va.

NEUBER, AUGUST Q. [Born in Germany. Appointed from Army.]
Priv., Corpl., Sergt. and 1st Sergt. Co. H, and Sergt. Maj. 7th Inf., 17 Sept., 1852, to 25 Nov., 1862. 2nd Lieut. 7th Inf., 31 Oct., 1862. Dismissed 26 Dec., 1862.

NEVILL, MORGAN. [Born in Ohio. Appointed from Ohio.]
Maj. P. M., 4 July, 1836. Resigned 18 Oct., 1836. Died 1 March, 1839.

NEVILL, PRESLEY J. [Born in Penn. Appointed from Penn.]
2nd Lieut. 2nd Art., 20 April, 1813. Trans. to Corps Art., 12 May, 1814. 1st Lieut., 19 June, 1817. Resigned 1 July, 1818. Died 1 Dec., 1818.

NEVIN, ROBERT R. [Born in ——. Appointed from ——.]
2nd Lieut. 22nd Inf., — ——, 1898. Resigned 10 Jan., 1899.

NEVINS, JOHN S. [Born in N. J. Appointed from N. J.]
2nd Lieut. 10th Inf., 9 April, 1847. Disbanded 21 Aug., 1848.

NEWBILL, WILLARD D.* [Born in Va. Appointed from Va.]
Addl. 2nd Lieut. 5th Inf., 11 June, 1897. 2nd Lieut. 7th Art., 8 March, 1898. Capt. 34th U. S. Vols., 5 July, 1899, to ——.

NEWBOLD, CHAS. [Born in Penn. Appointed from Penn.]
2nd Lieut. 3rd Cav., 16 Nov., 1861. Trans. to 5th Inf., 20 Aug., 1862. 1st Lieut.[, 26 Aug., 1863. Capt. 19th Inf., 28 July, 1866. Resigned 18 Nov., 1867. Bvt. Capt., 30 Jan., 1863, for gallant and meritoroious service in action with Navajo Indians. Maj. P. M., 22 July, 1899.

NEWBOLD, HENRY L.* [Born in Cal. Appointed from Md.]
2nd Lieut. 7th Art., 26 April, 1898.

NEWBURY, SAML. S. [Born in Ind. Appointed from Mich.]
1st Lieut. 12th Inf., 14 May, 1861. Capt. 21 July, 1862. Killed 19 Aug., 1864, in the Battle on Weldon Railroad, Va. Bvt. Maj. 18 Aug., 1864, for gallant and meritorious service in the Battle on the Weldon Railroad, Va.

NEWBY, EDWARD W. B. [Born in Va. Appointed from Ill.]
Capt. 1st Ill. Vols., 22 May, 1847. Col., 8 June, 1847. Mustered out 16 Oct., 1848. Capt. 1st Cav., 3 March, 1855. 4th Cav., 3 Aug., 1861. Maj. 3rd Cav., 17 July, 1862. Retired 25 Sept., 1863. Died 29 March, 1870.

NEWCOMB, FRANCIS D.* [Born in Mass. Appointed from Mass.]
Bvt. 2nd Lieut. 2nd Inf., 1 July, 1824. 2nd Lieut. 4th Inf., 1 July, 1824. A. Q. M., 7 Oct., 1830, to 30 Sept., 1836. 1st Lieut. ,4 April, 1832. Resigned 30 Sept., 1836. Died 28 Nov., 1872.

NEWCOMB, WARREN P.* [Born in Conn. Appointed from Conn.]
2nd Lieut 5th Art., 13 June, 1882. 1st Lieut., 9 Dec., 1887. Capt., 2 March, 1899. Honor graduate of the Artillery School, 1894.

NEWCOMER, HENRY C.* [Born in Penn. Appointed from Ill.]
2nd Lieut. Eng., 1 July, 1886. 1st Lieut., 23 July, 1888. Capt., 31 July, 1897.

NEWELL, ISAAC.* [Born in Ga. Appointed from Ga.]
2nd Lieut. 22nd Inf., 12 June, 1896. 1st Lieut. of Inf., 21 Sept., 1898. Ass'd to 22nd Inf., 1 Jan., 1899.

NEWELL, JOHN E.* [Born in N. C. Appointed from N. C.]
Bvt. 2nd Lieut. 1st Inf., 1 July, 1823. 2nd Lieut., 7th Inf., 1 July, 1823. 1st Lieut., 10 Nov., 1829. Died 26 March, 1835.

NEWGARDEN, GEORGE J. [Born in Pa. Appointed from Pa.]
Asst. Surg., 4 Nov., 1892. Capt. Ast. Surg., 4 Nov., 1897.

NEWKIRK, EDWARD P. [Born in N. Y. Appointed from N. Y.]
1st Sergt. Co. F, 1st N. Y. Light Art., 19 Sept., 1861. 2nd Lieut., 6 June, 1863. 1st Lieut., 18 April, 1864. Bvt. Capt. Vols., 13 March, 1865, for faithful and meritorious service. Mustered out 23 June, 1865. 2nd Lieut. 4th Art., 23 Feb., 1866. 1st Lieut., 26 July, 1866. Dismissed 13 Aug., 1875. Died 14 June, 1886.

NEWLANDS, WM. L. [Born in Mo. Appointed from Cal.]
Asst. Surg., 26 June, 1875. Resigned 25 Oct., 1878.

NEWLIN, ALFRED S. [Born in Penn. Appointed from Penn.]
Cadet Nav. Acad., 25 Sept., 1860, to 10 June, 1862. 2nd Lieut. 114th Pen. Vols., 28 July, 1862. 1st Lieut., 1 July, 1863. Capt., 26 Feb., 1864. Bvt. Maj. Vols., 9 April, 1865, for gallant and meritorious service during the operations resulting in the fall of Richmond and the surrender of the insurgent army under Gen. R. E. Lee. Mustered out 29 May, 1865. 2nd Lieut. 12th Inf., 23 Feb., 1866. 1st Lieut., 23 Feb., 1866. Trans. to 21st Inf., 21 Sept., 1866. Died 18 Feb., 1867.

NEWLIN, CHAS. S. [Born in Pa. Appointed from Army.]
Priv. Commonwealth Pa. Art., 30 April, 1861. 1st Lieut. 71st Pa. Vols., 1 July, 1861. Capt., 15 Feb., 1862. Resigned 19 July, 1862. Priv. and Sergt. 13th Inf., 2 Feb. to 22 April, 1863. 2nd Lieut. 13th Inf., 22 April, 1863. 1st Lieut., 10 Jan., 1864. Reg. Adj., 12 Nov., 1864, to 10 July, 1866. Trans. to 31st Inf., 21 Sept., 1866. Unassigned 8 May, 1869. Discharged 1 Sept., 1870. Bvt. 1st Lieut., 14 July, 1863, for gallant and meritorious service during the Siege of Vicksburg, Miss. Bvt. Capt., 25 Nov., 1863, for gallant and meritorious service at the Battle of Mission Ridge, Tenn.

NEWMAN, RICHARD. [Born in Va. Appointed from Va.]
2nd Lieut. 7th Inf., 3 March, 1825. Died 18 June, 1825.

NEWMAN, SAMUEL.* [Born in Mass. Appointed from Mass.]
2nd Lieut. Light Art., 12 Dec., 1808. 1st Lieut., 11 June, 1809. Resigned 25 June, 1810.

NEWMAN, THOMAS. [Born in N. Y. Appointed from Army.]
Priv., Corpl. and Sergt. Cos. A and D, Eng. Batt., 28 Nov., 1861, to 1 Dec., 1866. 2nd Lieut. 13th Inf., 1 Dec., 1866. Mustered out 5 Dec., 1870.

NEWMAN, THOS. W. [Born in Maine. Appointed from Iowa.]
Capt. 11th Inf., 5 Aug., 1861. Resigned 1 May, 1863.

NEWMAN, WALTER. [Born in Ind. Appointed from Ind.]
2nd Lieut 7th Inf., 30 Oct., 1861. 1st Lieut., 21 Jan., 1863. Died 1 Jan., 1864.

NEWMAN, WM.* [Born in Tenn. Appointed from Tenn.]
2nd Lieut. 13th Inf., 11 June, 1892. 1st Lieut., 26 April, 1898. Trans. to 1st Inf., 14 March, 1899.

NEWMAN WM. A. [Born in Vt. Appointed from Vt.]
2nd Lieut. 9th Inf., 9 April, 1847. Disbanded 26 Aug., 1848. Mil. Storekeeper, 29 Dec., 1848. Dismissed 2 April, 1856. Bvt. 1st Lieut., 20 Aug., 1847, for gallant and meritorious conduct in the Battles of Contreras and Churubusco. Died 5 March, 1870.

NEWTON, JOHN.* [Born in Va. Appointed from Va.]
2nd Lieut. Eng., 1 July, 1842. 1st Lieut., 16 Oct., 1852. Capt. 1 July, 1856. Maj., 6 Aug., 1861. Brig. Gen. Vols., 23 Sept., 1861. Bvt. Lieut. Col., 17 Sept., 1862, for gallant and meritorious service in the Battle of Antietam, Md. Maj. Gen. Vols., 30 March, 1863. Bvt. Col., 3 July, 1863, for gallant and meritorious service in the Battle of Gettysburg, Penn. Commission as Maj. Gen. Vols., 30 March, 1863, revoked 18 April, 1864. Brig. Gen. Vols., 18 April, 1864. Bvt. Brig. Gen., 13 March, 1865, for gallant and meritorious service in the Battle of Peach Tree Creek, Ga., and in the campaign against Atlanta, Ga. Bvt. Maj. Gen., 13 March, 1865, for gallant and meritorious service in the field during the war. Bvt. Maj. Gen. Vols., 13 March, 1865, for gallant and meritorious service during the war. Lieut. Col. Eng., 28 Dec., 1865. Mustered out of Vol. Service 31 Jan., 1866. Col. Eng., 30 June, 1879. Brig. Gen. Chf. of Eng., 6 March, 1884. Retired for over forty years' service 27 Aug., 1886. Died 1 May, 1895.

NEWTON, JOHN. [Born in N. Y. Appointed from Kan.]
2nd Lieut. 16th Inf., 1 Sept., 1879. 1st Lieut., 20 March, 1885. Capt., 26 April, 1898.

NEWTON, NOAH. [Born in Conn. Appointed from Ohio.]
1st Lieut. Mounted Rifles, 27 May, 1846. Capt., 8 Jan., 1848. Died 30 Aug., 1853.

NEWTON, RICHARD C. [Born in Mass. Appointed from N. J.]
Asst. Surg., 17 Feb., 1880. Capt. Asst. Surg., 17 Feb., 1885. Resigned 22 May, 1889.

NEWTON, ROB'T. [Born in Penn. Appointed from Penn.]
Asst. Surg., 30 Oct., 1846. Died 9 Aug., 1848.

NEWTON, WALKER A. [Born in Va. Appointed from Penn.]
1st Lieut. 40th N. J. Vols., 10 March, 1865. Mustered out 13 July, 1865. 2nd Lieut. 34th Inf., 17 Aug., 1867. Unassigned 12 April, 1869. Dropped 25 July, 1870.

NEWTON, WASHINGTON I. [Born in D. C. Appointed from Va.]
2nd Lieut. 2nd Drag., 1 Aug., 1838. 1st Lieut., 1 April, 1841. Capt., 13 July, 1848. Maj. 2nd Cav., 1 Oct., 1861. Retired 26 Oct., 1861. Died 6 Feb., 1876.

NEWTON, WM. S.* [Born in Va. Appointed from D. C.]
2nd Lieut. Light Art., 24 July, 1818. Trans. to 3rd Art., 1 June, 1821. 1st Lieut., 31 Dec., 1822. Died 16 March, 1837. Bvt. Capt., 31 Dec., 1832, for ten years' faithful service in one grade.

NICHOLAS, CARY. [Born in Va. Appointed from Ky.]
1st Lieut. 7th Inf., 3 May, 1808. Capt., 1 March, 1811. Maj. A. A. G., 25 April, 1813. Maj. 14th Inf., 15 May, 1814. Disbanded 15 June, 1815. Batt. and Dist. P. M., 17 Feb., 1817. Disbanded 1 June, 1821.

NICHOLAS, ROBERT C. [Born in ——. Appointed from Ky.]
Capt. 7th Inf., 3 May, 1808. Maj. 3rd Inf., 3 Sept., 1810. Lieut. Col. 1st Inf., 15 Aug., 1812. Col. 19th Inf., 4 Sept., 1814. Trans. to 8th Inf., 17 May, 1815. Resigned 20 April, 1819.

NICHOLAS, SPEAR. [Born in Va. Appointed from Va.]
2nd Lieut. 11th Inf., 14 April, 1847. Disbanded 17 Aug., 1848.

NICHOLLS, FRANCIS R. T* [Born in La. Appointed from La.]
Bvt. 2nd Lieut. 2nd Art., 1 July, 1855. 2nd Lieut. 3rd Art., 19 Oct., 1855. Resigned 1 Oct., 1856.

NICHOLLS, JAMES W. [Born in D. C. Appointed from Tenn.]
Addl. P. M. Vols., 19 Feb., 1863. Bvt. Lieut. Col. Vols., 13 March, 1865, for faithful and meritorious service during the war. Maj. P. M., 17 Jan., 1867. Resigned 23 July, 1875.

NICHOLLS, JESSE C.* [Born in Ala. Appointed from Ala.]
2nd Lieut. 1st Art., 15 Feb., 1899.

NICHOLLS, JOHN.* [Born in Conn. Appointed from Conn.]
Bvt. 2nd Lieut. 4th Inf., 1 July, 1823. 2nd Lieut. 6th Inf., 1 July, 1823. 1st Lieut., 31 Oct., 1827. Dismissed 6 May, 1835.

NICHOLS, DAVID C. [Born in Md. Appointed from Md.]
3rd Lieut. 3rd Art., 27 April, 1813. 2nd Lieut., 22 July, 1814. Disbanded 15 June, 1815. 3rd Lieut. Corps Art., 19 Feb., 1818. 2nd Lieut., 20 April, 1818. Dismissed 16 Oct., 1818.

NICHOLS, E. DE RUSSY. [Born in Va. Appointed from Kan.]
2nd Lieut. 23rd Inf., 31 Oct., 1874. Died 23 July, 1876

NICHOLS, FREDERIC C. [Born in Canada. Appointed from Mo.]
Capt. 25th Mo. Vols., 20 June, 1861. Maj., 25 April, 1862. Maj. 1st Mo. Eng., 17 Feb., 1864. Mustered out 18 Nov., 1864. Maj. 9th U. S. Vet. Vols., 20 Jan., 1865. Bvt. Lieut. Col. and Col. Vols., 13 March, 1865, for gallant and meritorious service during the war. Mustered out 31 March, 1866. 2nd Lieut. 14th Inf., 22 Jan., 1867. 1st Lieut., 19 Oct., 1868. Unassigned 22 July, 1869. Ass'd to 1st Art., 31 Dec., 1870. Capt., 11 Aug., 1887. Graduate of the Artillery School, 1876. Retired by operation of law. 14 Aug., 1887.

NICHOLS, JOHN H. [Born in N. Y. Appointed from Ill.]
1st Lieut. 81st N. Y. Vols., 21 Dec., 1861, to 1 Feb., 1862. 2nd Lieut. 1st Cav., 14 July, 1862. 1st Lieut., 13 Aug., 1862. R. C. S., 1 Sept., 1863, to 13 April, 1864. Killed 12 June, 1864, in the Battle of Trevilian Station, Va.

NICHOLS, MAURY. [Born in D. C. Appointed from N. Y.]
2nd Lieut. 16th Inf., 21 Nov., 1883. 1st Lieut. 14th Inf., 17 April, 1891. Trans. to

7th Inf., 20 July, 1891. Capt. of Inf., 8 Sept., 1898. Ass'd to 3rd Inf., 1 Jan., 1899.

NICHOLS, ROWLAND S. [Born in Mass. Appointed from Mass.]
Chap. 9th N. Y. Vols., 3 June, 1898, until muster out, 15 Nov., 1898. Post Chap., 27 Nov., 1899.

NICHOLS, THOMAS. [Born in Ireland. Appointed from La.]
2nd Lieut. 14th Inf., 24 March, 1848. Disbanded 20 July, 1848.

NICHOLS, THOS. B.* [Born in Canada. Appointed from N. Y.]
2nd Lieut. 6th Cav., 14 June, 1872. Resigned 30 June, 1876.

NICHOLS, WM. A.* [Born in Penn. Appointed from Penn.]
Bvt. 2nd Lieut. 2nd Art., 1 July, 1838. 2nd Lieut., 7 July, 1838. 1st Lieut., 1 June, 1844. Reg. Adj., 18 Aug., 1846, to 8 Dec., 1847, and 1 Sept., 1848, to 2 Sept., 1852. Bvt. Capt. A. A. G., 29 July, 1852. Bvt. Maj. A. A. G., 7 March, 1861. Lieut. Col. A. A. G., 3 Aug., 1861. Col. A. A. G., 1 June, 1864. Died 8 April, 1869. Bvt. Capt., 23 Sept., 1846, for gallant conduct at Monterey. Bvt. Maj, 8 Sept., 1847, for gallant and meritorious conduct at Molino del Rey. Bvt. Brig. Gen., 24 Sept., 1864, for meritorious and faithful service during the war. Bvt. Maj. Gen., 13 March, 1865, for meritorious and faithful service during the war.

NICHOLS WM. A. [Born in N. M. Appointed from Kan.]
2nd Lieut. 23rd Inf., 7 May, 1877. Expired by constitutional limitation 3 Dec., 1877. Reappointed 2nd Lieut. 23rd Inf., 26 Jan., 1878, with rank from 7 May, 1877. 1st Lieut., 1 March, 1886. Capt., 27 Aug., 1896. Graduate of the Infantry and Cavalry School, 1887.

NICHOLSON, WM. J. [Born in D. C. Appointed from D. C.]
2nd Lieut 7th Cav., 15 Aug., 1876. 1st Lieut., 16 Jan., 1884. Capt., 27 Aug., 1896. Graduate of the Infantry and Cavalry School, 1883. Maj. Chf. Ord. Off. Vols., 18 July, 1898, to 13 March, 1899.

NICKELS, DANIEL. [Born in Md. Appointed from Md.]
2nd Lieut. 1st Art., 13 July, 1848. Resigned 31 Dec., 1851.

NICKERSON, AZOR H. [Born in Ohio. Appointed from Ohio.]
2nd Lieut. 8th Ohio Vols., 17 Aug., 1861. 1st Lieut., 30 April, 1862. Capt., 20 Jan. 1863. Discharged 20 Nov., 1863. Capt. Vet. Res. Corps, 12 Nov., 1863. Bvt. Maj. Vols., 13 March, 1865, for gallant conduct in the Battles of Antietam and Gettysburg. Mustered out of Vet. Res. Corps, 19 April, 1866. 2nd Lieut. and 1st Lieut. 14th Inf., 23 Feb., 1866. Trans. to 23rd Inf., 21 Sept., 1866. Capt. 23rd Inf., 8 July, 1868. Maj. A. A. G., 15 June, 1878. Retired 28 June, 1882. Resigned 15 Nov., 1883.

NICKERSON, JAMES D. [Born in Ill. Appointed from Army.]
Priv. Co. H, 141st Ill. Vols., 20 May, 1864. Discharged 10 Oct., 1864. Priv. Co. H, 9th Ill. Cav., 20 March, 1865. Discharged 31 Oct., 1865. Priv. Co. A, 10th Inf., 13 Sept., 1867. Trans. to Gen. Ser., 1 Dec., 1868. Corpl., 1 April, 1869. Discharged 13 Sept., 1870. Corpl. Gen. Ser., 13 Sept., 1870. Priv., 20 July, 1875. Discharged 13 Sept., 1875. Priv. Gen. Ser., 13 Sept., 1875. Trans. to Co. D, 1st Inf., 14 Sept., 1875. Trans. to Gen. Ser., 15 Sept., 1875. 2nd Lieut. 17th Inf., 15 Oct., 1875. 1st Lieut., 26 June, 1882. Capt., 23 May, 1896. Graduate of Infantry and Cavalry School, 1889. Bvt. 1st Lieut., 27 Feb., 1890, for gallant service in action against Indians at Spring Creek, Mont., 15 and 16 Oct., 1876, declined.

NICKLIN, BENJAMIN P. [Born in Tenn. Appointed from Army.]
Priv., Corpl. and Sergt. Troop I, 1st Cav., 22 Jan., 1895, to 6 July, 1898. 2nd Lieut. 9th Inf., 22 June, 1898. 1st Lieut. 4th Inf., 2 March, 1899.

NICKS JOHN. [Born in N. C. Appointed from N. C.]
Capt. 3rd Inf., 1 July, 1808. Maj. 7th Inf., 9 Oct., 1813. Disbanded 15 June, 1815. Restored as Capt. 8th Inf., 2 Dec., 1815, to rank from 1 July, 1808. Maj. 7th Inf., 1 June, 1816. Lieut. Col., 1 June, 1819. Disbanded 1 June, 1821. Died 8 Jan., 1832.

NICODEMUS, WM. J. L.* [Born in Va. Appointed from Md.]
Bvt. 2nd Lieut. 5th Inf., 1 July, 1858. 2nd Lieut., 19 Jan., 1859. 1st Lieut. 11th Inf., 14 May, 1861. Capt., 24 Oct., 1861. Col. 4th Md. Vols., 11 Oct., 1862. Resigned from Vols., 17 Nov., 1862. Maj. Sig. Corps, 18 Sept., 1863, to rank from 3 March, 1863. Lieut. Col. Sig. Corps, 30 June, 1864, to rank from 3 March, 1863. Dismissed 26 Dec., 1864, and restored to his former rank in 12th Inf. Unassigned 4 June, 1869. Discharged 29 Dec., 1870. Bvt. Maj., 21 Feb., 1862, for gallant and meritorious service at the Battle of Val Verde, N. M. Died 6 Jan., 1879.

NICOLL, WM. H. [Born in N. Y. Appointed from N. Y.]
Surg.'s Mate 6th Inf., 19 Feb., 1817. Post Surg., 28 Jan., 1820. Asst. Surg., 1 June, 1821. Maj. Surg., 28 July, 1830. Died 5 March, 1831.

NICOLL, WM. H. [Born in Ga. Appointed from N. J.]
Ensign 2nd Inf., 6 July, 1812. 2nd Lieut., 6 July, 1812. 1st Lieut., 22 Nov., 1814. Trans. to Corps Art., 17 May, 1814. Resigned 30 May, 1819.

NICOLLS MALCOM H. [Born in La. Appointed from La.]
2nd Lieut. 10th Inf., 3 March, 1855. Resigned 31 Jan., 1856.

NIGH, ELIAS. [Born in Ohio. Appointed from Ohio.]
Capt. A. Q. M. Vols., 5 Aug., 1861. Capt. A. Q .M., 13 March, 1863. Lieut. Col. Q. M. Vols., 1 Jan., 1863, to 27 June, 1864. Resigned 27 June, 1864.

NILES, ALANSON E. [Born in Penn. Appointed from Penn.]
Capt. 1st Penn. Rifles, 21 June, 1861. Maj., 1 March, 1863. Lieut. Col., 15 May, 1863. Resigned 26 March, 1864. Maj. Vet. Res. Corps, 14 April, 1864. Bvt. Lieut. Col. Vols., 13 March, 1865, for gallant and meritorious service during the war. Bvt. Col. Vols., 13 March, 1865, for gallant conduct at Gettysburg. Mustered out 4 Jan., 1867. 2nd Lieut. 42nd Inf., 28 July, 1866. Bvt. Capt., 2 March, 1867, for gallant and meritorious service in the Battle of Gettysburg. Penn. 1st Lieut., 4 Jan., 1867. Unassigned 22 April, 1869. Retired with rank of Capt., 15 Dec., 1870. Died 8 Oct., 1891.

NILES, LOTUS.* [Born in Ill. Appointed from Ill.]
2nd Lieut. 2nd Art., 16 June, 1875. 1st Lieut., 29 Jan., 1882. R. Q. M., 5 May, 1887. Capt., 8 March, 1898. Graduate of the Artillery School, 1880.

NILES, SAML. V. [Born in Md. Appointed from Ill.]
2nd Lieut. of Inf., 8 March, 1847; 16th Inf., 9 April, 1847. Disbanded 7 Aug., 1848. Died 12 Oct., 1887.

NIMMO, WM. A.* [Born in Tenn. Appointed from Tenn.]
Bvt. 2nd Lieut. 4th Art., 1 July, 1849. 2nd Lieut., 30 April, 1850. 1st Lieut., 18 Dec., 1854. Died 12 March, 1856.

NININGER, ALEXR. R. [Born in Penn. Appointed from Minn.]
2nd Lieut. 84th Penn. Vols., 10 March, 1862. 1st Lieut., 6 Aug., 1862. Discharged 2 Jan., 1863. Capt. A. A. G. Vols., 7 June, 1864. Bvt. Maj. and Lieut. Col. Vols., 13 March, 1865, for meritorious service during the war. Mustered out 1 Sept., 1866. Capt. 28th Inf., 7 March, 1867. Unassigned 31 March, 1869. Discharged 1 Oct., 1870.

NISKERN, ALBERT D.* [Born in Ill. Appointed from Mich.]
2nd Lieut. 20th Inf., 1 July, 1886. Resigned 8 June, 1887. 2nd Lieut. 20th Inf., 14 April, 1891. 1st Lieut. 2nd Inf., 8 Aug., 1897. Capt. C. S., 14 March, 1898. Maj. C. S. Vols., 22 July, 1898, to 2 Feb., 1899.

NISSEN, AUGUST C.* [Born in Ohio. Appointed from Ohio.]
Addl. 2nd Lieut. 5th Cav., 12 June, 1895. 2nd Lieut., 17 June, 1895. Trans. to 6th Cav., 30 July, 1895. 1st Lieut., 2 March, 1899.

NIXON, COURTLAND. [Born in Texas. Appointed from N. J.]
2nd Lieut. 1st Inf., 9 July, 1898. 1st Lieut. 2nd Inf., 9 March 1899.

NIXON, JOHN B. [Born in W. Va. Appointed from Ill.]
2nd Lieut. 102nd Ill. Vols., 2 Sept., 1862. 1st Lieut., 20 April, 1863. Capt. 17th U. S. Col. Troops, 3 Dec., 1863. Bvt. Maj. and Lieut. Col. Vols., 13 March, 1865, for faithful and meritorious service during the war. Mustered out 3 Nov., 1866. 1st Lieut. 38th Inf., 12 June, 1867. Trans. to 24th Inf., 11 Nov., 1869. R. Q. M., 1 March, 1871, to 5 Jan., 1877. Capt., 5 Jan., 1877. Retired for disability 26 Nov., 1884. Died 14 July, 1898.

NOBLE, CHAS. H. [Born in Ohio. Appointed from Ind.]
Priv. Co. K, 1st Ind. Cav., 20 June, 1861. Corpl., 24 Feb., 1863. Discharged 19 June, 1864. 2nd Lieut. 16th Inf., 23 Feb., 1866. Trans. to 34th Inf., 21 Sept., 1866. 1st Lieut., 10 Feb., 1867. Trans. to 16th Inf., 14 April, 1869. Capt., 26 Nov., 1884. Maj. 25th Inf., 4 Oct., 1898.

NOBLE, HENRY B.* [Born in N. Y. Appointed from N. Y.]
2nd Lieut. 8th Inf., 6 May, 1861. 1st Lieut., 11 June, 1861. Bvt. Capt., 9 Aug., 1862, for gallant and meritorious service in the Battle of Cedar Mountain, Va. Capt. 8th Inf., 13 Feb., 1866. Retired 18 Feb., 1869. Died 3 April, 1898.

NOBLE, PATRICK.* [Born in S. C. Appointed from S. C.]
Bvt. 2nd Lieut. 1st Drag., 1 July, 1842. 2nd Lieut., 31 Dec., 1843. 1st Lieut., 6 Dec., 1846. Died 27 Dec., 1848.

NOBLE, ROBERT H.* [Born in Md. Appointed from Md.]
2nd Lieut. 1st Inf., 15 June, 1884. 1st Lieut. 15th Inf., 15 June, 1891. Trans. to 1st Inf., 20 July, 1891. Capt. of Inf., 12 Oct., 1898. Ass'd to 3rd Inf., 1 Jan., 1899. Maj. A. A. G. Vols. 20 June, 1898, to 19 March, 1899. Maj. A. A. G. Vols., 5 Sept., 1899.

NOBLE, WILLIAM H. [Born in N. Y. Appointed from Army.]
Priv., Corpl. and Sergt. Co. E, Batt. Eng., 1 Feb., 1893, to 15 Nov., 1899. 2nd Lieut. 13th Inf., 1 Oct., 1899.

NOE, ALLEN T. [Born in Ky. Appointed from Ky.]
Asst. Surg., 3 March, 1847; 16th Inf., 9 April, 1847. Resigned 7 July, 1847.

NOEL, THOS.* [Born in Md. Appointed from Md.]
2nd Lieut. 6th Inf., 1 July, 1820. 1st Lieut., 16 April, 1823. Reg. Adj., 17 July, 1825, to 1 May, 1827. Capt., 1 May, 1827. Maj. 7th Inf., 9 May, 1846. Died 14 Aug., 1848. Bvt. Maj., 25 Dec., 1837, for gallant conduct in the Battle of Kissimme, Fla.

NOELL, THOS. E. [Born in Mo. Appointed from Mo.]
Maj. Mo. State Militia, July, 1861, to April, 1862. Capt. 19th Inf., 6 March, 1862. Resigned 20 Feb., 1865. Died 4 Oct., 1867.

NOGGLE, CHAS. L. [Born in Ill. Appointed from Wis.]
Sergt. Co. G, and Q. M. Sergt. 8th Wis. Vols., 4 Sept. to 16 Dec., 1861. 1st Lieut. Adj. 3rd Wis. Cav., 16 Dec., 1861, to 17 April, 1862. 2nd Lieut. 2nd Inf., 19 Feb., 1862. Cashiered 21 July, 1862. 2nd Lieut. 2nd Inf., 31 Jan., 1863. 1st Lieut., 1 Dec., 1863. Resigned 15 Aug., 1867.

NOLAN, DENNIS E. [Born in N. Y. Appointed from N. Y.]
Addl. 2nd Lieut. 3rd Inf., 12 June, 1896. 2nd Lieut. 1st Inf., 27 Aug., 1896. 1st Lieut. of Inf., 14 Dec., 1898. Ass'd to 1st Inf., 1 Jan., 1899. Trans. to 13th Inf., 14 March, 1899. Maj. 11th U. S. Vol. Cav., 10 Aug., 1899.

NOLAN, NICHOLAS. [Born in Ireland. Appointed from Army.]
Priv. Co. M, 4th Art., 9 Dec., 1852. Corpl., 1 Nov., 1855. Discharged 9 Oct., 1857. Corpl. Co. M, 4th Art., 9 Oct., 1857. Trans. to Priv. Co. K, 2nd Drag., 1 Sept., 1858. Corpl., 1 Dec., 1858. 1st Sergt., 4 Dec., 1859. Sergt., 22 May, 1860. Trans. to Sergt. Co. B, 6th Cav., 5 Sept., 1861. 1st Sergt. 21 Sept., 1861. 2nd Lieut. 6th Cav., 17 July, 1862. Bvt. 1st Lieut., 1 Aug., 1863, for gallant and meritorious service in the Battle of Brandy Station, Va. 1st Lieut. 6th Cav., 5 July, 1864. Bvt. Capt., 31 March, 1865, for gallant and meritorious service in the Battle of Dinwiddie C. H., Va. Capt. 10th Cav., 28 July,, 1866. Maj. 3rd Cav., 19 Dec., 1882. Died 25 Oct., 1883.

NOLAN, JAMES E.* [Born in Wis. Appointed from Wis.]
2nd Lieut. 4th Cav., 1 July, 1886. 1st Lieut. of Cav. (10th), 26 July, 1893. Tran., to 4th Cav., 10 Sept., 1894. Died 5 Dec., 1898.

NOLAND, CHAS. F. M. [Born in Va. Appointed from Va.]
Cadet at Mil. Acad., 1 July, 1823, to 1 Aug., 1825. 1st Lieut. Mounted Rangers, 5 March, 1833. 1st Lieut. 1st Drag., 19 Sept., 1833. Resigned 1 March, 1836.

NOLEN, LEWIS. [Born in Del. Appointed from Del.]
1st Lieut. 2nd Del. Vols., 12 Aug., 1861. Capt., 4 March, 1863. Mustered out 9 Jan., 1865. Capt. 6th U. S. Vet. Vols., 6 Feb., 1865. Mustered out 1 March, 1866. 2nd Lieut. 12th Inf., 4 May, 1866. 1st Lieut., 17 Oct., 1867. Mustered out 1 Jan., 1871. Died 1 Jan., 1887.

NONES, ALBERT S. [Born in Maine. Appointed from Del.]
Sergt. Co. E, and Hosp. Steward 1st Del. Cav., 5 Jan. to 28 Dec., 1864. 1st Lieut. 1st Del. Vols., 6 Jan., 1865. Resigned 20 May, 1865. 2nd Lieut. 8th Inf., 19 April, 1866. Resigned 17 Oct., 1866.

NONES, JEFFERSON H. [Born in Md. Appointed from Del.]
2nd Lieut. 2nd Art., 30 Dec., 1847. 1st Lieut., 10 Sept., 1850. Resigned 12 March, 1856.

NOON, DARBY. [Born in N. Y. Appointed from N. Y.]
Maj. 41st Inf., 1 Aug., 1813. Disbanded 15 June, 1815. Dep. Com. of Purchases, 15 July, 1815. Disbanded 1 June, 1821. Died 9 Sept., 1823.

NORCOM, FREDK.* [Born in N. C. Appointed from N. C.]
Bvt. 2nd Lieut. 4th Inf., 1 July, 1825. 2nd Lieut. 3rd Inf., 1 July, 1825. Trans. to 4th Art., 19 April, 1826. Resigned 31 Aug., 1832. Died 9 Dec., 1865.

NORCROSS, AUGUSTUS W. [Born in Maine. Appointed from Maine.]
Mil. Storekeeper Q. M. D., 13 March, 1863. Resigned 25 Sept., 1865.

NORDSTROM, CHAS. E. [Born in Maine. Appointed from Maine.]
Priv. Co. E, 1st Maine Cav., 26 Aug., 1862. Discharged 28 May, 1865. 2nd Lieut. 10th Cav., 18 June, 1867. 1st Lieut., 1 Sept., 1869. R. Q. M., 1 Dec., 1888, to 20 Aug., 1889. Capt., 20 Aug., 1889. Died 11 Jan., 1898.

NORMAN, TRABER.* [Born in Mo. Appointed from Mo.]
2nd Lieut. 8th Inf., 11 June, 1892. 1st Lieut., 26 April, 1898.

NORMENT, ALFRED A. [Born in N. C. Appointed from N. C.]
2nd Lieut. of Inf., March, 1847; 3rd Drag., 9 April, 1847. Resigned 5 Aug., 1847.

NORMOYLE, JAMES E.* [Born in Mich. Appointed from Ill.]
Addl. 2nd Lieut. 23rd Inf., 12 June, 1889. 2nd Lieut., 22 June, 1889. 1st Lieut. 25th Inf., 6 Jan., 1897. Trans. to 5th Inf., 24 June, 1897. Capt. 20th Inf., 20 Sept., 1899. Trans. to 5th Inf., 24 Oct., 1899. Graduate of the Infantry and Cavalry School, 1895. Reg. Q. M., 8 Nov., 1899.

NORRIS, BASIL. [Born in Md. Appointed from Md.]
1st Lieut. Asst. Surg., 11 Oct., 1852. Maj. Surg., 16 April, 1862. Bvt. Lieut. Col., 13 March, 1865, for meritorious service in the campaign and Siege of Vicksburg, Miss. Bvt. Col., 13 March, 1865, for meritorious service and diligent discharge of duties during the war. Lieut. Col. Surg., 14 Dec., 1882. Col. Surg., 14 Nov., 1888. Retired by operation of law 9 March, 1892. Died 10 Nov., 1895.

NORRIS, CHAS. E.* [Born in Ind. Appointed from Ind.]
Bvt. 2nd Lieut. 2nd Drag., 1 July, 1851. 2nd Lieut., 9 July, 1853. 1st Lieut., 3 March, 1855. R. Q. M., 14 May to 4 Oct., 1860. Capt., 11 May, 1861; 2nd Cav., 3 Aug., 1861. Lieut. Col. 2nd Ind. Cav., 27 Sept., 1861. Resigned from Vols., 11 Feb., 1862. Maj. 1st Cav., 31 Aug., 1866. Dismissed 10 Feb., 1870. Bvt. Maj., 3 July, 1863, for gallant and meritorious service in the Gettysburg campaign. Died 31 Oct., 1875.

NORRIS, HARDMAN P. [Born in Penn. Appointed from Penn.]
2nd Lieut. 1st Art., 5 Aug., 1861. 1st Lieut., 5 Aug., 1861. Dropped 14 Dec., 1865.

NORRIS, WM. F.* [Born in Maine. Appointed from Minn.]
2nd Lieut. 9th Inf., 14 June, 1872. 1st Lieut., 22 June, 1879. Resigned 15 June, 1881.

NORRIS, WM. F. [Born in Penn. Appointed from Penn.]
Asst. Surg., 13 June, 1863. Resigned 20 Oct., 1865. Bvt. Capt., 13 March, 1865, for faithful and meritorious service during the war.

NORTHROP, LUCIUS B. [Born in S. C. Appointed from S. C.]
Bvt. 2nd Lieut. 7th Inf., 1 July, 1831. Trans. to 1st Drag., 14 Aug., 1833. 2nd Lieut., 21 July, 1834. 1st Lieut., 4 July, 1836. Dropped 8 Jan., 1848. Reappointed with former rank, 12 Aug., 1848. Capt., 21 July, 1848. Resigned 8 Jan., 1861.

NORTHRUP, EDWARD B. [Born in N. Y. Appointed from N. Y.]
Priv. and Corpl. Co. B, 44th N. Y. Vols., 8 Aug., 1861, to 26 Oct., 1862. 2nd Lieut. Vet. Res. Corps, 8 Aug., 1863. 1st Lieut., 26 May, 1865. Mustered out 17 Nov., 1866. 2nd Lieut. 44th Inf., 28 July, 1866. Trans. to 17th Inf., 27 May, 1869. 1st Lieut., 1 Jan., 1871. Died 4 March, 1873. Bvt. 1st Lieut., 2 March, 1867, for gallant and meritorious service at the Battle of Malvern Hill, Va.

NORTON, ALLEN H.* [Born in Ohio. Appointed from Ohio.]
Bvt. 2nd Lieut. 1st Inf., 1 July, 1842. 2nd Lieut. 4th Inf., 13 Sept., 1842. 1st Lieut., 12 Oct., 1846. Drowned at sea 27 Nov., 1846.

NORTON, CHAS. C.* [Born in Maine. Appointed from Maine.]
2nd Lieut. 1st Cav., 17 June, 1874. Resigned 4 Sept., 1879.

NORTON, GEORGE D. [Born in Maine. Appointed from Maine.]
Capt. 14th Inf., 14 May, 1861. Dismissed 5 Oct., 1865.

NORTON, HENRY. [Born in N. Y. Appointed from N. Y.]
1st Lieut. 63rd N. Y. Vols., 28 March, 1862. Capt. A. de C. Vols., 20 Aug., 1862. Maj. 6th U. S. Vols., 5 May, 1865. Bvt. Lieut. Col. Vols., 5 May, 1865, for distinguished gallantry at the Battle of Malvern Hill, and meritorious service during the campaign on the Peninsula of Va. Mustered out 10 Oct., 1866. 2nd Lieut. 17th Inf., 28 July, 1866. 1st Lieut. 29 Sept., 1867. Mustered out 1 Jan., 1871. Bvt. 1st Lieut., 2 March, 1867, for gallant and meritorious service at the Battle of Malvern Hill, Va. Bvt. Capt., 2 March, 1867, for gallant and meritorious service at the Battle of Bull Run (2nd), Va.

NORTON, LEMUEL B. [Born in Penn. Appointed from Penn.]
1st Lieut. 10th Pa. Res., 21 July, 1861. Capt., 1 May, 1863. Resigned 27 June, 1863. Capt. Sig. Corps, 3 March, 1863. Bvt. Maj. Vols., 13 March, 1865, for gallant and meritorious service at the Battle of Gettysburg, Penn., and Lieut. Col. Vols., 13 March, 1865, for faithful and meritorious service in the campaign against Richmond, Va. Mustered out 7 May, 1867. 2nd Lieut. 30th Inf., 28 July, 1866. 1st Lieut., 1 Sept., 1868. Unassigned 23 March, 1869. Ass'd to 1st Art., 1 Jan., 1871. Died 23 Dec., 1871. Bvt. 1st Lieut., 2 March, 1867, for gallant and meritorious service at the Battle of Gettysburg, Pa. Bvt. Capt., 2 March, 1867, for gallant and meritorious service during the war. Bvt. Maj., 2 March, 1867, for meritorious service in the Sig. Corps, during the war, especially while Chf. Sig. Off. of the Army of the Potomac, Dept. of Va. and N. C., and Dept. of the Susquehanna.

NORTON, MARTIN. [Born in Ill. Appointed from Ill.]
Com. Sergt. 100th Ill. Vols., 30 Aug., 1862, to 19 March, 1863. Capt. A. A. G. Vols., 29 Feb., 1864. Mustered out 1 July, 1866. 2nd Lieut. 2nd Inf., 24 May, 1866. 1st Lieut., 21 May, 1868. Resigned 1 Oct., 1868. Bvt. 1st Lieut., 2 March, 1867, for gallant and meritorious service in the Battle of Bull Run (2nd), Va. Bvt. Capt., 2 March, 1867, for faithful and meritorious service during the war.

NORTON, SENECA H.* [Born in Pa. Appointed from W. Va.]
2nd Lieut. 2nd Cav., 23 June, 1865. 1st Lieut., 6 March, 1866. Reg. Adj., 1 July, 1866, to 1 May, 1867, and 10 July to 31 July, 1869. Capt., 26 Oct., 1869. Resigned 15 Dec., 1873.

NORTON, THOS. H. [Born in Penn. Appointed from W. Va.]
2nd Lieut. 1st W. Va. Vols., 11 May, 1861. Mustered out 27 Aug., 1861. Capt. 15th Inf., 5 Aug., 1861. Bvt. Maj., 1 Sept., 1864, for gallant and meritorious service in the Battle of Mission Ridge, Tenn., and in the Atlanta campaign and Battle of Jonesboro, Ga. Trans. to 24th Inf., 21 Sept., 1866. Trans. to 11th Inf., 25 April, 1869. Unassigned 17 Dec., 1869. Retired 15 Dec., 1870.

NORTON, WM. A.* [Born in N. Y. Appointed from N. Y.]
Bvt. 2nd Lieut. 4th Art., 1 July, 1831. 2nd Lieut., 1 July, 1831. Resigned 30 Sept., 1833. Died 21 Sept., 1883.

NORVELL, GUY S. [Born in Texas. Appointed from D. C.]
Priv. and Corpl. Troop D, 4th Cav., 2 Aug., 1897, to 27 April, 1899. 2nd Lieut. 8th Cav., 10 April, 1899.

NORVELL, JOHN M. [Born in Mich. Appointed from Mich.]
2nd Lieut. 2nd Mich. Vols., 25 May, 1861. Capt. A. A. G. Vols., 30 Aug., 1861. Maj. A. A. G. Vols., 22 Aug., 1862. Bvt. Lieut. Col. Vols., 9 April, 1865, for meritorious service in the recent campaign terminating with the surrender of the insurgent army under Gen. R. E. Lee. Resigned 21 June, 1865. 1st Lieut. 31st Inf., 28 July, 1866. Bvt. Capt., 2 March, 1867, for gallant and meritorious service in the Battle of Getysburg, Penn. Bvt. Maj., 2 March, 1867, for gallant and meritorious service in the Battle of the Wilderness, Va. Unassigned 15 May, 1869. Ass'd to 12th Inf., 1 Jan., 1871. Reg. Adj., 7 Feb., 1871, to 17 Jan., 1873. Capt., 31 Jan., 1874. Retired for disability 29 Dec., 1890. Died 18 Dec., 1893.

NORVELL, RALPH G. [Born in Tenn. Appointed from Ind.]
Capt. A. Q. M. Vols., 2 Dec., 1846. Maj. of Inf., 3 March, 1847; 16th Inf., 9 April, 1847. Lieut. Col. 10th Inf., 3 Dec., 1847. Disbanded 12 Aug., 1848.

NORVELL, SPENCER. [Born in Penn. Appointed from Mich.]
2nd Lieut. 5th Inf., 20 Oct., 1839. 1st Lieut., 18 May, 1846. Capt., 30 April, 1849. Died 12 Aug., 1850.

NORVELL, STEVENS T. [Born in Mich. Appointed from Army.]
Priv. Co. A, 5th Inf., 23 Jan., 1858. Sergt., 3 Oct., 1858. 1st Sergt., 1 May, 1861. Sergt. 1 Feb., 1862. Discharged 23 Jan. 1863. Sergt. Co. A, 5th Inf., 23 Jan., 1863. Acting 2nd Lieut. 5th Inf., 28 Jan., 1862, to 19 Feb., 1863. 2nd Lieut. army under Gen. R. E. Lee. Resigned 21 June, 1865. 1st Lieut. 31st Inf., 28 1866. Capt., 10 June, 1868. Unassigned 15 May, 1869. Ass'd to 10th Cav., 1 Jan., 1871. Maj. 25 March, 1890. Lieut. Col. 9th Cav., 1 July, 1898. Retired by operation of law 14 Feb., 1899.

NORWOOD, JOHN W. [Born in N. C. Appointed from N. C.]
2nd Lieut. 23rd Inf., 1 Sept., 1899.

NORWOOD, RANDOLPH. [Born in Md. Appointed from Md.]
2nd Lieut. 1st Md. Cav., 30 Oct., 1861. 1st Lieut., 14 Feb., 1863. Capt., 1 Sept., 1863. Mustered out 27 Oct., 1864. 2nd Lieut. 2nd Cav., 23 Feb., 1866. 1st Lieut., 31 Aug., 1866. Reg. Adj., 1 to 19 July, 1876. Capt., 19 July, 1876. Bvt. Maj., 7 Feb., 1890, for gallantry in action against Indians on the Rosebud, Mont., 7 May, 1877, and gallant service in action against Indians at Camas Meadows, Idaho, 20 Aug., 1877. Retired for disability 22 June, 1889.

NOTSON, WM. M. [Born in Penn. Appointed from Penn.]
1st Lieut. Asst. Surg., 16 April, 1862. Bvt. Capt., 3 July, 1863, for gallant and meritorious service in the Battle of Gettysburg, Penn. Bvt. Maj., 13 March, 1865, for faithful and meritorious service during the war. Capt. Asst. Surg., 28 July, 1866. Maj. Surg., 31 Dec., 1876. Died 23 June, 1882.

NOURSE, BENJ. F. [Born in D. C. Appointed from D. C.]
Asst. Surg., 1 Jan., 1836. Died 19 May, 1836.

NOURSE, CHAS. J. [Born in N. Y. Appointed from D. C.]
1st Lieut. 2nd Light Drag., 7 May, 1812. Capt. Asst. Dep. Q. M. G., 7 Aug., 1813. Maj. A. A. G., 14 Sept., 1814. Retained 17 May, 1815, as 1st Lieut. 2nd Inf. Bvt. Maj. A. A. G., 3 May, 1816, to rank from 14 Sept., 1814. Capt. 2nd Inf., 17 June, 1816. Trans. to 2nd Art., 1 June, 1821. A. A. G. of Army, 8 May, 1822, to 7 March, 1825. Resigned 20 Feb., 1827. Bvt. Capt., 15 Aug., 1813, for meritorious service. Died 19 March, 1851.

NOWLAN, HENRY J. [Born in Corfu. Appointed from N. Y.]
1st Lieut. 14th N. Y. Cav., 17 Jan., 1863. Trans. to 18th N. Y. Cav., 12 June, 1865.

Capt., 15 Jan., 1866. Mustered out 31 May, 1866. 2nd Lieut. 7th Cav., 28 July, 1866. 1st Lieut., 3 Dec., 1866. Reg. Com., 1 Nov., 1867, to 15 July, 1870. R. Q. M., 1 March, 1872, to 25 June, 1876. Capt., 25 June, 1876. Bvt. Maj., 27 Feb., 1890, for gallant service in action against Indians at Canyon Creek, Mont., 13 Sept., 1877. Maj. of Cav. (7th), 17 July, 1895. Died 10 Nov., 1898.

NOYES, CHAS. [Born in Mass. Appointed from D. C.]
Asst. Surg., 21 Aug.. 1838. Died 26 July, 1841.

NOYES, CHAS. R.* [Born in Mass. Appointed from Mass.]
2nd Lieut. 9th Inf., 13 June, 1879. 1st Lieut., 28 Aug., 1887. Capt., 26 April, 1898. Reg. Adj., 19 May, 1899.

NOYES, HENRY E.* [Born in Maine. Appointed from Mass.]
Bvt 2nd Lieut. and 2nd Lieut. 2nd Drag., 24 June, 1861; 2nd Cav., 3 Aug., 1861. 1st Lieut. 2nd Cav., 15 Feb., 1862. Bvt. Capt., 1 Aug., 1863, for gallant and meritorious service in the Battle of Brandy Station, Va. Capt. 2nd Cav., 25 Jan., 1865. Bvt. Maj., 2 April, 1865, for gallant and meritorious service in the capture of Selma, Ala. Maj. 4th Cav., 14 June, 1879. Lieut. Col. 5th Cav., 1 July, 1891. Trans. to 2nd Cav., 12 Aug., 1892. Col., 31 May, 1898.

•NOYES, SAMUEL W. [Born in Wyo. Appointed from Cal.]
Sergt. Troops B and C, 1st U. S. Vol. Cav., 4 May, to 15 Sept., 1898. 2nd Lieut. 23rd Inf., 1 June, 1899.

NUGEN, JOHN.* [Born in Ohio. Appointed from Ohio.]
Bvt. 2nd Lieut. 2nd Inf., 1 July, 1852. 2nd Lieut. 4th Inf., 29 Sept., 1853. Died 22 Oct., 1857.

NUGENT, GEORGE A.* [Born in Mich. Appointed from N. D.]
2nd Lieut. 6th Art., 26 April, 1898. Trans. to 4th Art., 18 June, 1898. Capt. 3rd U. S. Vol. Cav., 23 May to 8 Sept., 1898.

NUGENT, ROBT. [Born in Ireland. Appointed from N. Y.]
Lieut. Col. 69th N. Y. Vols., 20 April, 1861. Mustered out 3 Aug., 1861. Capt. 13th Inf., 5 Aug., 1861. Col. 69th N. Y. Vols., 1 Nov., 1861. Bvt. Maj., 27 June, 1862, for gallant and meritorious service in the Battle of Gaines' Mill, Va. Bvt. Lieut. Col., 13 Dec., 1862, for gallant and meritorious service in the Battle of Fredericksburg, Va. Mustered out of Vol. Service 28 Nov., 1863. Col. 69th N. Y. Vols., 30 Oct., 1864. Bvt. Brig. Gen. Vols., 13 March, 1865, for gallant and meritorious service during the war. Bvt. Col., 2 April, 1865, for gallant and meritorious service in front of Petersburg, Va. Mustered out of Vol. Service 30 June, 1865. Maj. 24th Inf., 10 June, 1876. Retired 20 March, 1879.

NUTE, LEVI M.* [Born in N. H. Appointed from N. H.]
2nd Lieut. 6th Inf., 1 July, 1823. 1st Lieut., 7 July, 1826. Capt., 31 July, 1836. Resigned 31 Jan., 1838. Died — July, 1846.

NUTTMAN, LOUIS M.* [Born in N. J. Appointed from N. J.]
2nd Lieut. 21st Inf., 12 June, 1895. 1st Lieut., 14th Inf., 2 July, 1898.

NYE, FRANK E.* [Born in Maine. Appointed from Maine.]
2nd Lieut. 2nd Cav., 15 June, 1869. Resigned 10 April, 1873. Capt. C. S., 4 Oct., 1889. Maj. C. S., 10 June, 1896. Lieut. Col., C. S. Vols., 22 July, 1898. Col. C. S. Vols., 7 Oct., 1898, to 2 March, 1899.

NYE, THOMAS L. [Born in N. Y. Appointed from Army.]
Priv., and 1st Sergt. Co. A, and Sergt. Maj. 2nd Batt. 15th Inf., 16 Sept., 1864, to 19 May, 1866. 2nd Lieut. 15th Inf., 6 April, 1866. Trans. to 24th Inf., 21 Sept., 1866. 1st Lieut., 13 Dec., 1866. Resigned 28 May, 1868.

OAKES, JAMES.* [Born in Penn. Appointed from Penn.]
Bvt. 2nd Lieut. 2nd Drag., 1 July, 1846. Bvt. 1st Lieut., 25 March, 1847, for gallant and meritorious conduct at the affair at Medlin. 2nd Lieut. 2nd Drag., 29 July, 1847. Bvt. Capt., 8 Sept., 1848, for gallant and meritorious conduct in the Battle of Molino del Rey. R. Q. M. 2nd Drag., 30 Oct., 1847, to 15 Aug., 1849. 1st Lieut., 30 June, 1851. Capt. 2nd Cav., 3 March, 1855. Maj. 2nd Cav., 6 April, 1861; 5th Cav., 3 Aug., 1861. Brig. Gen. Vols., 17 May, 1861, declined. Lieut. Col. 4th Cav., 12 Nov., 1861. Bvt. Col. and Brig. Gen., 30 March, 1865, for meritorious and faithful service in the recruitment of the armies of the U. S. Col. 6th Cav., 31 July, 1866. Retired 29 April, 1879.

OAKES, JOHN C.* [Born in N. Y. Appointed from N. Y.]
Addl. 2nd Lieut. Eng., 11 June, 1897. 2nd Lieut., 5 July, 1898. 1st Lieut., 5 July, 1898.

O'BANNON, LAWRENCE W. [Born in S. C. Appointed from S. C.]
2nd Lieut. 3rd Inf., 3 March, 1848. 1st Lieut., 30 Sept., 1855. R. Q. M., 9 Feb., 1856, to 31 March, 1861. Resigned 31 March, 1861. Died 2 June, 1882.

O'BEIRNE, RICHARD F. [Born in Canada. Appointed from Mich.]
1st Lieut 14th Inf., 14 May, 1861. Capt., 25 Oct., 1861. Bvt. Maj., 1 Aug., 1864, for gallant service in the Battle of the North Anna, Va. Bvt. Lieut. Col., 18 Aug., 1864, for gallant service in Battle on the Weldon Railroad, Va. Trans. to 32nd Inf., 21 Sept., 1866. Trans. to 21st Inf., 19 April, 1869. Maj. 24th Inf., 20 March, 1879. Lieut. Col. 15th Inf., 18 April, 1884. Col. 21st Inf., — —, 1890. Died 24 Feb., 1891.

O'BRIEN, ALONZO L.* [Born in Va. Appointed from W. Va.]
2nd Lieut. 2nd Cav., 13 June, 1879. 1st Lieut., 9 Jan., 1886. Died 12 Dec., 1886.

O'BRIEN, JOHN J. [Born in Ireland. Appointed from Army.]
Priv. Co. F, 4th Art., 1 Sept., 1854. Corpl., 1 Dec., 1855. Sergt., 1 Sept., 1856. Priv., 5 June, 1857. Discharged 1 Sept., 1859. Corpl. Co. B, 1st N. Y. Cav., 19 July, 1861. Sergt., 12 Aug., 1861. Trans. to Co. K, 31 Oct., 1862. Trans. to Co. F, 1 Nov., 1862. 1st Sergt. Co. F, 12 Nov., 1862. Discharged 31 March, 1864. 2nd Lieut. 1st N. Y. Cav., 1 April, 1864. Capt., 27 Dec., 1864. Mustered out 27 June, 1865. Priv. Co. F, 1st Batt. 12th Inf., 29 July, 1865. Corpl., 1 Sept., 1865. Sergt., 1 Sept., 1865. 2nd Lieut. 30th Inf., 6 May, 1867. Trans. to 4th Inf., 23 March, 1869. 1st Lieut., 16 March, 1879. Capt., 14 Sept., 1892. Retired for disability, 22 April, 1896.

O'BRIEN, JOHN P. J.* [Born in Penn. Appointed from Penn.]
2nd Lieut. 4th Art., 1 July, 1836. 1st Lieut., 7 July, 1838. Capt. Asst. Q. M., 18 Jan., 1847, to 16 May, 1849. Capt. 4th Art., 16 May, 1849. Died 31 March, 1850. Bvt. Maj., 23 Feb., 1847, for gallant and meritorious conduct at Buena Vista.

O'BRIEN, LUCIUS. [Born in Md. Appointed from Md.]
Asst. Surg., 13 July, 1832. Resigned 31 Dec., 1835. 2nd Lieut. 3rd Inf., 3 Sept., 1837. Trans. to 8th Inf., 7 July, 1838. 1st Lieut., 1 Dec., 1839. Died 7 Jan., 1841.

O'BRIEN, LYSTER M. [Born in Mich. Appointed from Mich.]
2nd Lieut. 27th Mich. Vols., 25 Feb., 1863. 1st Lieut., 8 March, 1864. Capt., 14 Dec., 1864. Bvt. Maj. Vols., 13 March, 1865, for gallant and meritorious service before Petersburg, Va. Mustered out 26 July, 1865. 2nd Lieut. 16th Inf., 11 May, 1866. Trans. to 25th Inf., 21 Sept., 1866. 1st Lieut., 21 Sept., 1867. Unassigned 26 April, 1869. Ass'd to 17th Inf., 15 Dec., 1870. Capt., 22 March, 1879. Maj., 26 April, 1898.

O'BRIEN, MARTIN E. [Born in N. Y. Appointed from Iowa.]
Priv. Co. D. 1st Ark. Cav., 3 June, 1862. 1st Sergt. Co. C, 31 July, 1862. Priv., 1 Oct., 1863. Capt. 2nd Ark. Cav., 12 Oct., 1863. Mustered out 20 Aug., 1865. 2nd Lieut. 2nd Cav., 7 Aug., 1867. 1st Lieut., 3 Dec., 1868. Capt., 1 April, 1880. Died 28 Dec., 1888.

O'BRIEN, MICHAEL. [Born in Ireland. Appointed from Army.]
Priv. Ord. Dept., 11 July, 1859. Artificer, 1 Jan., 1860. Armorer, 1 Nov., 1860. Hosp. Stwd. U. S. A., 16 May, 1862. 2nd Lieut. 1st Art., 18 May, 1864. 1st Lieut., 30 Nov., 1864. Resigned 12 Feb., 1867. 1st Lieut. 1st Art., 15 April, 1867. Mustered out 1 Jan., 1871. 1st Lieut. 4th Art., 1 Sept., 1879, to rank from 15 April, 1867. Retired for disability, 23 Sept., 1885. Died 28 Aug., 1894.

O'BRIEN, MICHAEL J.* [Born in Mass. Appointed from Mass.]
2nd Lieut 13th Inf., 14 June, 1885. 1st Lieut. of Inf. (2nd), 2 Jan., 1892. Trans. to 5th Inf., 9 Feb., 1892. Honor graduate of the Infantry and Cavalry School, 1893. Died 16 Sept., 1898.

O'BRIEN, WM. [Born in D. C. Appointed from N. Y.]
1st Lieut. 18th Inf., 14 May, 1861. Appointment expired 6 Aug., 1861.

OCCLESTON, WM. B. [Born in Mass. Appointed from Army.]
Priv., Corpl. and Sergt. Troop G, 1st Cav., 16 Feb., 1857, to 13 July, 1861. 2nd Lieut. 15th Inf., 14 May, 1861. 1st Lieut., 24 Oct., 1861. Capt., 1 July, 1865. Trans. to 33rd Inf., 21 Sept., 1866. Died 24 Oct., 1867. Bvt. Capt., 7 April, 1862, for gallant and meritorious service at the Battle of Shiloh, Tenn. Bvt. Maj., 31 Dec., 1862, for gallant and meritorious service at the Battle of Murfreesboro,' Tenn.

O'CONNELL, JOHN. [Born in Ireland. Appointed from N. Y.]
Priv. Co. H, 71st N. Y. Vols., 1 May, 1861. Sergt. Maj., 7 July, 1861. 2nd Lieut. 71st N. Y. Vols., 16 June, 1862. 1st Lieut., 5 Aug., 1862. Capt., 16 March, 1864. Mustered out 30 July, 1864. Capt. 5th U. S. Vet. Vols., 11 Feb., 1865. Mustered out 6 June, 1865. 2nd Lieut. 8th Inf., 22 Jan., 1867. 1st Lieut., 15 Dec., 1874. Resigned 8 April, 1885.

O'CONNELL, JOHN D.* [Born in Penn. Appointed from Penn.]
Bvt. 2nd Lieut. 2nd Inf., 1 July, 1852. 2nd Lieut., 31 July 1853. 1st Lieut., 15 Jan., 1857. R. Q. M., 1 May, 1856, to 1 Oct., 1858. Capt. 14th Inf., 14 May, 1861. Maj. 17th Inf., 11 Aug., 1866. Died 16 Sept., 1867. Bvt. Maj., 27 June, 1862, for gallant and meritorious service at the Battle of Gaines' Mills, Va. Bvt. Lieut. Col., 13 Dec., 1862, for gallant and meritorious service at the Battle of Fredericksburg, Va. Bvt. Col., 13 March, 1865, for gallant and meritorious service during the war.

O'CONNELL, JOHN J. [Born in Ireland. Appointed from Army.]
Priv. Co. A, Batt. of Eng., 3 Feb., 1865. Artf., 15 March, 1867. 2nd Lieut. 1st Inf., 28 Oct., 1867. 1st Lieut., 28 June, 1878. Capt., 14 April, 1887. Maj., 2 March, 1899.

O'CONNELL, JOHN J.* [Born in Ohio. Appointed from Ohio.]
2nd Lieut. 21st Inf., 11 June, 1892. 1st Lieut., 26 April, 1898.

O'CONNELL, WM. [Born in Ireland. Appointed from Army.]
Priv. Det. Drag. Mil. Acad., 24 Nov., 1854. Trans. to Co. B, 1st Cav., 9 April, 1855. Sergt., 1 May, 1855. 1st Sergt., 23 July, 1855. Discharged 24 Sept., 1859. 1st Sergt. Co. B, 1st Cav., 24 Sept., 1859. Discharged 21 Aug., 1861. 1st Lieut. 3rd Ill. Cav., 29 Aug., 1861. Discharged 7 Nov., 1861. 2nd Lieut. 4th Cav., 24 Oct., 1861. 1st Lieut., 14 Dec., 1862. Bvt. Capt., 22 May, 1863, for gallant and meritorious service in action at Middleton, Tenn. Bvt. Maj., 2 April, 1865, for gallant and meritorious service in the capture of Selma, Ala. Capt. 4th Cav., 27 Sept., 1866. Retired 2 April, 1879. Died 7 Nov., 1895.

O'CONNOR, CHAS. M.* [Born in Iowa. Appointed from Iowa.]
2nd Lieut. 8th Cav., 13 June, 1873. 1st Lieut., 17 March, 1881. Reg. Adj., 31 March, 1887. Capt., 18 Feb., 1891.

O'CONNOR, EDGAR.* [Born in Ohio. Appointed from Wis.]
Bvt. 2nd Lieut. 7th Inf., 1 July, 1851. 2nd Lieut., 3 March, 1855. R. Q. M., 18 March to 1 May, 1858. Resigned 22 Oct., 1858. Col. 2nd Wis. Vols., 2 Aug., 1861. Killed 28 Aug., 1862, at the Battle of Groveton, Va.

O'CONNOR, JOHN M. [Born in Penn. Appointed from N. Y.]
1st Lieut. 3rd Art., 12 March, 1812. Capt., 13 March, 1813. Trans. to Corps Art., 12 May, 1814. Maj. A. A. G., 20 June, 1814. Disbanded 15 June, 1815. Reinstated as Capt. 4th Inf., 2 Dec., 1815. Trans. to Corps Art., 1 Jan., 1816. Disbanded 1 June, 1821.

O'CONNOR, LAWRENCE L. [Born in Ireland. Appointed from N. Y.]
2nd Lieut. 5th N. Y. Cav., 31 Oct., 1861. 1st Lieut., 10 Dec., 1862. Capt., 8 Aug., 1864. Mustered out 19 July, 1865. 2nd Lieut. 3rd Cav., 23 Feb., 1866. 1st Lieut., 9 Nov., 1866. Mustered out 1 Jan., 1871. Died 26 Sept., 1874.

O'CONNOR, STEPHEN. [Born in N. Y. Appointed from Army.]
Priv. Co. B, 8th Inf., 21 June, 1860. Trans. to Co. E, 22 May, 1863. Corpl., 3 Aug., 1863. Sergt., 1 Nov., 1863. Discharged 8 July, 1864. Sergt. Co. E, 8th Inf., 9 July, 1864. Trans. to Co. C, 17 Sept., 1864. Q. M. Sergt. Co. C, 8th Inf., 21 Sept., 1866. 2nd Lieut. 8th Inf., 28 Dec., 1866. 1st Lieut., 4 Jan., 1869. Unassigned 3 May, 1869. Ass'd to 23rd Inf., 31 Dec., 1870. Dismissed 16 March, 1877. 2nd Lieut. 23rd Inf., 9 June, 1877. Expired by constitutional limitation, 3 Dec., 1877. Reappointed 11 Feb., 1878, to rank from 9 June, 1878. 1st Lieut., 1 April, 1886. Capt., 17 April, 1897. Retired, for over 30 years' service, 19 April, 1900.

O'DONNOGHUE, FLORENCE. [Born in D. C. Appointed from D. C.]
Capt. Med. Storekeeper, 3 Aug., 1867. Died 29 June, 1882.

O'FALLON, JOHN. [Born in ——. Appointed from Ky.]
Ensign 1st Inf., 28 Sept., 1812. 2nd Lieut., 20 Jan., 1813. 1st Lieut. 24th Inf., 15 Aug., 1813. Capt. 2nd Rifles, 17 March, 1814. Trans. to Rifle Reg., 17 May, 1815. Resigned 31 July, 1818.

OFFLEY, ROBT. H. [Born in N. Y. Appointed from N. Y.]
Midshipman U. S. N., 19 Oct., 1850, to 12 June, 1851. 2nd Lieut. 1st Inf., 14 May, 1857. 1st Lieut., 14 May, 1861. Capt., 23 Nov., 1861. Bvt. Maj., 4 July, 1863, for gallant and meritorious service during the Siege of Vicksburg, Miss. Maj. 19th Inf., 6 May, 1879. Lieut. Col. 17th Inf., 15 Sept., 1884. Col. 10th Inf., 9 March, 1891. Died 14 Oct., 1891.

OFFLEY, ROBERT S. [Born in Mich. Appointed from Army.]
Sergt. Sig. Corps, 16 Sept., 1891, to 4 Nov., 1894. 2nd Lieut. 10th Inf., 31 Oct., 1894. 1st Lieut. 7th Inf., 2 May, 1898.

O'FLYNG, PATRICK. [Born in Ireland. Appointed from N. Y.]
Ensign and 3rd Lieut. 9th Inf., 31 July, 1814. 2nd Lieut., 31 July, 1814. Resigned 14 Jan., 1815. 2nd Lieut. 46th Inf., 11 Feb., 1815. Trans. to 4th Inf., 17 May, 1815. Died 1 Nov., 1815. Bvt. 1st Lieut., 17 Sept., 1814, for gallant conduct in sortie from Fort Erie.

OGDEN, CORNELIUS A.* [Born in N. J. Appointed from N. J.]
2nd Lieut. Eng., 1 July, 1819. 1st Lieut., 1 July, 1824. Capt., 15 May, 1835. Maj., 7 Dec., 1838. Died 23 Aug., 1856. Bvt. Capt., 30 June, 1834, for ten years' faithful service in one grade.

OGDEN, EDMUND A.* [Born in N. Y. Appointed from N. Y.]
Bvt. 2nd Lieut. 1st Inf., 1 July, 1831. 2nd Lieut., 1 July, 1831. 1st Lieut., 17 Dec., 1836. Trans. to 8th Inf., 7 July, 1838. Capt. A. Q. M., 7 July, 1838. Capt. 8th Inf., 1 Dec., 1849. Resigned Reg. Com., 18 June, 1846. Died 3 Aug., 1855. Bvt. Maj., 30 May, 1848, for meritorious conduct.

OGDEN, FREDK. C. [Born in N. J. Appointed from R. I.]
2nd Lieut. 1st Cav., 21 Nov., 1861. 1st Lieut., 17 July, 1862. Killed 11 June, 1864, in action at Trevillian Station, Va.

OGDEN, MORGAN L. [Born in Ala. Appointed from D. C.]
Midshipman U. S. N., 19 Sept., 1857, to 23 Sept., 1859. 1st Lieut. 18th Inf., 14 May, 1861. Capt., 12 Aug., 1863. Dismissed 30 June, 1877. Bvt. Capt., 31 Dec., 1862, for gallant and meritorious service at the Battle of Murfreesboro, Tenn. Died 4 Nov., 1888.

OGDEN, RICHD. L. [Born in N. Y. Appointed from Cal.]
1st Lieut. 14th Inf., 14 May, 1861. Capt. A. Q. M., 5 Aug., 1861. Resigned 14 May, 1864.

OGILBY, FRED'K. D. ]Born in N. J. Appointed from N. Y.]
1st Lieut. 15th Inf., 14 May, 1861. Reg. Adj., 1 June, 1863, to 27 June, 1864. Capt., 27 June, 1764. Trans. to 33rd Inf., 21 Sept., 1866. Trans. to 8th Inf., 3 May, 1869. Died 30 May, 1877. Bvt. Capt. and Maj., 31 Dec., 1862, for gallant and meritorious service at the Battle of Murfreesboro, Tenn.

OGILVIE, HENRY. [Born in England. Appointed from Army.]
Priv., Corpl. and Q. M. Sergt. Co. K, 1st Drag. (1st Cav.), 9 Sept., 1857, to 9 Sept., 1862. 2nd Lieut. 1st Cav., 17 July, 1862. 1st Lieut., 9 June, 1863. R. C. S., 4 Nov., 1862, to 1 Sept., 1863. Reg. Adj., 1 Sept. to 13 Oct., 1863. Dropped 13 Oct., 1863.

OGLE, ALEXR.* [Born in Penn. Appointed from Penn.]
Cadet at Naval Acad., 24 Sept., 1864, to 23 Feb., 1865. Cadet at Mil. Acad., 1 Sept., 1868. 2nd Lieut. 17th Inf., 14 June, 1872. 1st Lieut., 28 June, 1878. Died 8 Aug., 1891.

OGLE, ALFRED McC.* [Born in Ohio. Appointed from Ohio.]
2nd Lieut. 19th Inf., 13 June, 1879. Resigned 1 July, 1885.

OGLE, CHAS. H.* [Born in Pa. Appointed from Pa.]
Bvt. 2nd Lieut. 1st Drag., 1 July, 1848. 2nd Lieut., 4 Aug., 1849. 1st Lieut., 20 Jan., 1855. Reg. Adj., 3 March, 1855, to 30 April, 1860. Dismissed 23 April, 1861. Maj. 1st N. Y. Cav., 13 Sept., 1861. Discharged 24 Nov., 1862. Died 7 March, 1863.

O'HARA, JAMES.* [Born in Ireland. Appointed from N. Y.]
2nd Lieut. 3rd Art., 18 June, 1866. 1st Lieut., 26 March, 1867. Capt., 30 Nov., 1888. Graduate of the Artillery School, 1878.

O'HARA, THEODORE. [Born in Ky. Appointed from Ky.]
Capt. A. Q. M. Vols., 26 June, 1846. Disbanded 15 Oct., 1848. Capt. 2nd Cav., 3 March, 1855. Resigned 1 Dec., 1856. Bvt. Maj., 20 Aug., 1847, for gallant and meritorious conduct in the Battles of Contreras and Churubusco, Mex. Died 6 June, 1867.

O'HERN, EDWARD P.* [Born in N. Y. Appointed from N. Y.]
2nd Lieut. 3rd Art., 12 June, 1894. 1st Lieut., 2 March, 1899. 1st Lieut. Ord., 23 Oct., 1899.

OKIE, WM. T. [Born in Penn. Appointed from Penn.]
Asst. Surg., 3 Feb., 1862. Resigned 29 June, 1865.

OLCOTT, EGBERT. [Born in N. Y. Appointed from N. Y.]
Maj. 121st N. Y. Vols., 23 Aug., 1862. Lieut. Col., 10 April, 1863. Col., 18 April, 1865. Bvt. Col. Vols., 19 Oct., 1864, for distinguished gallantry in the Battle of Cedar Creek, Va. Mustered out 25 June, 1865. 2nd Lieut. 11th Inf., 11 May, 1866. Trans. to 29th Inf., 21 Sept., 1866. 1st Lieut., 18 Dec., 1866. Resigned 26 March, 1868.

OLCOTT, EGBERT W. [Born in N. Y. Appointed from N. Y.]
2nd Lieut. 1st Art., 24 Oct., 1861. 1st Lieut., 20 Feb., 1862. Cashiered 17 Feb., 1868. Bvt. Capt., 30 June, 1862, for gallant and meritorious service at the Battle of New Market Cross Roads, Va. Bvt. Maj., 13 March, 1865, for good conduct and gallant service during the war.

OLDHAM, RICHARD. [Born in N. C. Appointed from Ky.]
Served in the Revol. Army. 1st Lieut. 7th Inf., 3 May, 1808. Capt., 1 Dec., 1809. Maj. 17th Inf., 9 April, 1814. Discharged 15 June, 1815. Mil. Storekeeper, 16 March, 1819. Disbanded 1 June, 1821.

OLDS, MARQUIS L. [Born in Ohio. Appointed from Ohio.]
2nd Lieut. 2nd Ohio Vols., 4 Sept., 1847, to 24 July, 1848. 2nd Lieut. 15th Inf., 17 June, 1848. Disbanded 5 Aug., 1848.

OLIVER, LLEWELLYN W.* [Born in Mich. Appointed from Mich.]
2nd Lieut. 2nd Inf., 15 Feb., 1899.

OLIVER, ROBT. S. [Born in Mass. Appointed from Mass.]
2nd Lieut. 5th Mass. Cav., 13 Oct., 1864. Mustered out 31 Oct., 1865. 2nd Lieut. 17th Inf., 23 Feb., 1866. Resigned 27 July, 1866. 2nd Lieut. 8th Cav., 28 July, 1866. 1st Lieut., 7 March, 1867. Reg. Com., 26 Aug., 1867, to 19 Oct., 1869. Resigned 31 Oct., 1869.

OLIVER, WM. G. [Born in Penn. Appointed from Penn.]
Capt. 42nd Inf., 1 Aug., 1813. Disbanded 15 June, 1815. 2nd Lieut. 5th Inf., 12 Nov., 1818. Disbanded 1 June, 1821.

OLMSTEAD, FREEMAN E. [Born in N. Y. Appointed from Mich.]
Corpl. Co. C, 18th Mich. Vols., 7 Aug., 1862. Discharged 22 March, 1864. 2nd Lieut. 12th Tenn. Cav., 23 March, 1864. Resigned 12 May, 1865. 2nd Lieut. 10th Inf., 23 Feb., 1866. 1st Lieut., 28 July, 1866. Retired 28 June, 1878.

OLMSTED, GEORGE T.* [Born in N. J. Appointed from N. J.]
2nd Lieut. and 1st Lieut. 19th Inf., 23 June, 1865. Capt., 18 Nov., 1867. Unassigned 31 March, 1869. Ass'd to 2nd Art., 1 Jan., 1871. Dismissed 24 July, 1874. Capt. U. S. A., 24 July, 1876. Dismissed 22 Oct., 1884.

OLMSTED, JERAULD A.* [Born in N. Y. Appointed from N. Y.]
2nd Lieut. 4th Cav., 15 June, 1870. Trans. to 13th Inf., 13 June, 1872. 1st Lieut., 1 July, 1872. R. Q. M., 1 Aug., 1874, to 1 Sept., 1880. Trans. to 9th Cav., 1 Aug., 1881. R. Q. M., 1 May, 1883, to 14 April, 1884. Capt., 14 April, 1884. Retired for disability, with rank of Maj., 16 Oct., 1898.

OLMSTED, WM. A. [Born in N. Y. Appointed from N. Y.]
Capt. 2nd N. Y. Vols., 14 May, 1861. Lieut. Col., 27 July, 1861. Mustered out 26 May, 1863. Col. 5th N. Y. Vols., 3 Nov., 1864. Bvt. Brig. Gen. Vols., 9 April, 1865, for meritorious service during the campaign terminating with the surrender of the insurgent army under Gen. R. E. Lee. Mustered out 30 June, 1865. 2nd Lieut. 13th Inf., 11 May, 1866. Trans. to 22nd Inf., 21 Sept., 1866. 1st Lieut., 15 Sept., 1867. Resigned 4 May, 1869. Bvt. Capt., 15 Sept., 1867, for gallant and meritorious service at the Battle of Malvern Hill, Va. Bvt. Maj., 15 Sept., 1867, for gallant and meritorious service in the Battle of Fredericksburg, Va. Bvt. Lieut. Col., 15 Sept., 1867, for gallant and meritorious service in the Battle of Hatcher's Run, Va.

O'NEALE, HENRY L. [Born in Ga. Appointed from Ga.]
Ensign 8th Inf., 20 May, 1813. 3rd Lieut., 2 Dec., 1813. 2nd Lieut., 11 July, 1814. Trans. to 7th Inf., 17 May, 1815. Resigned 31 Dec., 1816.

O'NEALE, JOHN H. P. [Born in D. C. Appointed from D. C.]
2nd Lieut. 2nd Drag., 8 June, 1836. 1st Lieut., 1 Oct., 1837. Resigned 30 Nov., 1838.

O'NEIL, JOSEPH P. [Born in N. Y. Appointed from Nebr.]
2nd Lieut. 14th Inf., 4 Feb., 1884. 1st Lieut. 6th Inf., 20 April, 1891. Trans. to 25th Inf., 20 July, 1891. Capt. of Inf., 16 Sept., 1898. Ass'd to 25th Inf., 1 Jan., 1899. Graduate of the Infantry and Cavalry School, 1887. Reg. Adj., 8 Nov., 1899.

OPIE, LEROY. [Born in Va. Appointed from Va.]
2nd Lieut. 5th Inf., 3 May, 1808. 1st Lieut., 10 July, 1809. Capt., 26 June, 1813. Discharged 15 June, 1815. Batt. P. M., 12 April, 1816. Died 30 Oct., 1819.

ORD, EDWARD O. C.* [Born in Md. Appointed from D. C.]
2nd Lieut. 3rd Art., 1 July, 1839. 1st Lieut., 1 July, 1841. Capt., 7 Sept., 1850. Brig. Gen. Vols., 14 Sept., 1861. Maj. 4th Art., 21 Nov., 1861. Bvt. Lieut. Col., 20 Dec., 1861, for gallant and meritorious service in the Batle of Drainesville, Va. Maj. Gen. Vols., 2 May, 1862. Bvt. Col., 19 Sept., 1862, for gallant and meritorious service in the Battle of Iuka, Miss. Bvt. Brig. Gen., 13 March, 1865, for gallant and meritorious service in the Battle of the Hatchie, Miss. Bvt. Maj. Gen., 13 March, 1865, for gallant and meritorious service in the assault on Fort Harrison, Va. Lieut. Col. 1st Art., 11 Dec., 1865. Brig. Gen. U. S. A., 26 July, 1866. Mustered out of Vol. Service, 1 Sept., 1866. Retired, with the rank of Maj. Gen., by Act of Congress, 28 Jan., 1881. Died 22 July, 1883.

ORD, EDWARD O. C., Jr. [Born in Cal. Appointed from Texas.]
Cadet Naval Acad., 18 Sept., 1875, to 20 June, 1876. 2nd Lieut. 22nd Inf., 1 Sept., 1879. 1st Lieut., 2 June, 1889. Capt., 26 April, 1898.

ORD, JAMES C. [Born in Mich. Appointed from Wyo. Ter.]
2nd Lieut. 25th Inf., 1 Oct., 1873. 1st Lieut., 20 March, 1879. Capt., 11 Nov., 1890. Retired for disability, with rank of Maj., 8 June, 1899.

ORD, JULES G. [Born in Mich. Appointed from Army.]
Priv. Co. H, and Q. M. Sergt. 1st Inf., 16 Aug., 1887, to 9 Nov., 1890. 2nd Lieut.

of Inf. (18th), 6 Nov., 1890. 1st Lieut. 6th Inf., 7 Aug., 1897. Killed in action at San Juan, Santiago, Cuba, 1 July, 1898.

ORD, PLACIDUS. [Born in D. C. Appointed from Cal.]
Capt. A. A. G. Vols., 11 June, 1862. Maj. A. A. G. Vols., 11 June, 1862. Bvt. Lieut. Col. Vols., 29 Sept., 1864, for gallant conduct in the campaign of 1864, and Bvt. Col. Vols., 13 March, 1865, for gallant conduct in the field. Mustered out 31 July, 1866. 2nd Lieut. 1st Inf., 11 May, 1866. 1st Lieut., 18 Sept., 1867. Unassigned 8 April, 1869. Ass'd to 19th Inf., 15 Dec., 1870. Died 9 July, 1876. Bvt. 1st Lieut., 2 March, 1867, for gallant and meritorious service in the Siege of Vicksburg, Miss. Bvt. Capt., 2 March, 1867, for gallant and meritorious service in the Siege of Petersburg, Va. Bvt. Maj., 2 March, 1867, for gallant and meritorious service in the Battle of Chapin's Farm, Va.

ORDWAY, GODWIN. [Born in Va. Appointed from D. C.]
2nd Lieut. 3rd Cav., 10 April, 1899.

O'REILLY, LUKE. [Born in Canada. Appointed from Mo.]
2nd Lieut. 33rd Mo. Vols., 17 Dec., 1862. Bvt. Maj. Vols., 13 March, 1865, for meritorious conduct in the Battle of Bayou de Glaze, La. Capt. A. de C. Vols., 12 May, 1865. Mustered out 29 Jan., 1866. 1st Lieut. 39th Inf., 28 July, 1866. Reg. Adj., 7 Jan., 1867, to 1 Oct., 1868. Bvt. Capt., 2 March, 1867, for gallant and meritorious service in the capture of Savannah, Ga. Capt. 39th Inf., 1 Oct., 1868. Unassigned 20 April, 1869. Ass'd to 19th Inf., 1 Jan., 1871. Dismissed 24 Nov., 1879.

O'REILLY, ROBERT M. [Born in Penn. Appointed from Penn.]
Med. Cadet, 7 Jan., 1864, to 8 Jan., 1865, and from 6 Feb., 1865, to 23 Sept., 1865. Asst. Surg., 14 May, 1867. Capt. Asst. Surg., 14 May, 1870. Maj. Surg., 1 Nov., 1886. Lieut. Col. Chief. Surg. Vols., 9 May, 1898, to 12 May, 1899.

O'REILLY, THOS. P. [Born in Ireland. Appointed from N. J.]
Priv. Co. G, 13th N. J. Vols., 25 Aug., 1862. Trans. to Vet. Res. Corps, 7 June, 1863. Discharged 17 Aug., 1864. Capt. 116th U. S. Col. Inf., 18 Aug., 1864. Maj., 6 July, 1865. Bvt. Lieut. Col. and Col. Vols., 13 March, 1865, for gallant and meritorious service during the war. Mustered out 17 Jan., 1867. 2nd Lieut. 22nd Inf., 7 March, 1867. Dismissed 24 July, 1872.

ORLEMAN, LOUIS H. [Born in Germany. Appointed from D. C.]
Priv. Co. C, 103rd N. Y. Vols., 29 Jan., 1862. Discharged 8 May, 1862. 1st Lieut. 119th N. Y. Vols., 11 Aug., 1862. Capt., 3 May, 1863. Mustered out 27 June, 1865. 2nd Lieut. 10th Cav., 20 Sept., 1867. 1st Lieut., 16 Oct., 1874. Retired 20 Nov., 1879.

O'RORKE, PATRICK H.* [Born in Ireland. Appointed from N. Y.]
Bvt. 2nd Lieut. Eng., 24 June, 1861. 2nd Lieut., 24 June, 1861. 1st Lieut., 3 March, 1863. Col. 140th N. Y. Vols., 19 Sept., 1862. Bvt. Capt., 15 March, 1862, for meritorious service with the Port Royal Expeditionary Corps. Bvt. Maj., 13 Dec., 1862, for gallant and meritorious service at the Battle of Fredericksburg, Va. Bvt. Lieut. Col., 1 May, 1863, for gallant and meritorious service at the Battle of Chancellorsville, Va. Bvt. Col., 2 July, 1863, for gallant and meritorious service at the Battle of Gettysburg, Penn., where he was killed, 2 July, 1863.

ORR, JOHN D.* [Born in Ky. Appointed from Ky.]
3rd Lieut. Corps Art., 17 July, 1817. Resigned 1 Dec., 1817. Capt. A. D. Q. M. G., 17 May, 1820. Disbanded 1 June, 1821. Mil. Storekeeper Q. M. Dept., 1 June, 1821. Discharged 31 Dec., 1821. Died 11 May, 1822.

ORR, SOLON.* [Born in Tenn. Appointed from Mo.]
2nd Lieut. 5th Art., 18 June, 1866. Died 16 Sept., 1867.

ORTON, EDWARD P.* [Born in Ark. Appointed from Ark.]
Addl. 2nd Lieut. 9th Cav., 12 June, 1896. 2nd Lieut. 2nd Cav., 2 June, 1897.

ORTON, SAML. H. [Born in N. J. Appointed from N. J.]
Asst. Surg., 22 Nov., 1862. Resigned 15 Dec., 1865. Bvt. Capt. and Maj., 13 March, 1865, for faithful and meritorious service during the war.

OSBORN, ALBERT C. [Born in ——. Appointed from Army.]
Priv., Corpl. and Sergt. Co. E, 18th Inf., 28 Sept., 1894, to 28 Nov., 1899. 2nd Lieut. 20th Inf., 1 Oct., 1899.

OSBORNE, WM. H.* [Born in Penn. Appointed from Penn.]
2nd Lieut. of Cav. (1st), 12 June, 1891. Died 23 Aug., 1898.

OSBORNE, NATHAN W. [Born in Mass. Appointed from Mass.]
Capt. 13th Inf., 14 May, 1861. Bvt. Maj., 4 July, 1863, for gallant and meritorious service in the Siege of Vicksburg, Miss. Maj. 15th Inf., 11 Dec., 1873. Lieut. Col. 6th Inf., 6 Feb., 1882. Col. 5th Inf., 5 Aug., 1888. Died 30 Jan., 1895.

OSGOOD, CHARLES H.* [Born in Mass. Appointed from Mass.]
2nd Lieut. 12th Inf., 13 June, 1883. Died 1 May, 1886.

OSGOOD, EDWARD S. [Born in Maine. Appointed from Maine.]
2nd Lieut. 6th Inf., 24 Oct., 1839. Resigned 31 March, 1841. Died 28 June, 1848.

OSGOOD, HENRY B.* [Born in Maine. Appointed from Maine.]
2nd Lieut. 27th Maine Vols., 30 Sept., 1862. 1st Lieut., 15 Dec., 1862. Mustered out 17 July, 1863. Cadet Mil. Acad., 1 Sept., 1863. 2nd Lieut. 3rd Art., 17 June, 1867. 1st Lieut., 25 April, 1870. Medal of Honor for voluntarily remaining in the service during the invasion of Penn., July, 1863, his term of service having expired; while serving as 1st Lieut. Co. I, 27th Maine Inf., on duty in the defences of Washington. Capt. C. S., 5 Oct., 1889. Maj. C. S., 26 Jan., 1897. Lieut. Col. C. S. Vols., 5 Aug., 1898, to 24 Oct., 1898, and from 20 Dec, 1898, to 2 March, 1899. Graduate of the Artillery School, 1882.

OSGOOD, LEMUEL H. [Born in Mass. Appointed from Army.]
Priv., Corpl. and Q. M. Sergt. Corps Art., 22 Sept., 1812, to May, 1813. 3rd Lieut. 3rd Art., 20 May, 1813. 2nd Lieut., 20 June, 1813. Trans to Corps Art., 12 May, 1814. 1st Lieut., 30 Sept., 1817. Disbanded 1 June, 1821. Mil. Storekeeper, 21 April, 1837. Removed 30 Nov., 1841. Died 8 Sept., 1846.

OSGOOD, WORTH.* [Born in Ohio. Appointed from N. Y.]
2nd Lieut. 2nd Art., 15 June, 1869. Mustered out 1 Jan., 1871.

O'SHEA, JOHN. [Born in Ireland. Appointed from Army.]
Priv. Co. F, 15th Inf., Priv. Hosp. Corps, and Priv. and Corpl. Batty I, 1st Art., 13 Dec., 1884, to 1 Aug., 1891. 2nd Lieut 7th Cav., 31 July, 1891. 1st Lieut. 4th Cav., 5 July, 1898. Graduate of the Infantry and Cavalry School, 1895.

OSMAN, WILLIAM. [Born in Ill. Appointed from Ill.]
2nd Lieut. 16th Inf., 30 Dec., 1847. Disbanded 20 July, 1848.

OSTHEIM, LOUIS.* [Born in Penn. Appointed from Penn.]
2nd Lieut. 3rd Art., 13 June, 1883. 1st Lieut. 2nd Art., 22 May, 1891. Trans to 6th Art., 8 March, 1898. Capt. 1st Art., 15 Oct., 1899. Graduate of the Artillery School, 1890.

OSTRANDER, JAMES S. [Born in N. Y. Appointed from Army.]
Priv. and Sergt. Co. C, 3rd Batt. 18th Inf., 15 Nov., 1861, to 27 March, 1863. 2nd Lieut. 18th Inf., 19 Feb., 1863. 1st Lieut., 1 Dec., 1863. Resigned 30 Sept., 1864.

O'SULLIVAN, MICHAEL. [Born in Ireland. Appointed from Army.]
Priv. and Corpl. Co. E, 3rd Inf., 10 Feb., 1844, to 23 March, 1847. 2nd Lieut., 3rd Inf., 3 March, 1847. Resigned 31 Oct., 1847.

OTEY, VAN RENSALAER. [Born in Va. Appointed from Va.]
2nd Lieut Inf., 23 Feb., 1847; Voltigeurs, 9 April, 1847. Disbanded 15 Aug., 1848.

OTIS, ELMER.* [Born in Mass. Appointed from Ohio.]
Bvt. 2nd Lieut. 1st Inf., 1 July, 1853. 2nd Lieut. 4th Inf., 3 Feb., 1855. 2nd Lieut. 1st Cav., 3 March, 1855. 1st Lieut., 28 Feb., 1856. Capt., 1 May, 1861. 4th Cav., 3 Aug., 1861. Maj. 1st Cav., 9 May, 1864. Bvt. Lieut. Col., 19 Oct., 1864, for industry, zeal and faithful service. Bvt. Col., 15 April, 1865, for faithful and meritorious service during the war. Lieut. Col. 7th Cav., 25 June, 1876. Col. 8th Cav., 2 April, 1883. Retired for disability 7 Feb., 1891. Died 18 Aug., 1897.

OTIS, ELWELL S. [Born in Md. Appointed from N. Y.]
Capt. 140th N. Y. Vols., 13 Sept., 1862. Lieut. Col., 23 Dec., 1863. Mustered out 24 June, 1865. Bvt. Col. Vols., 13 March, 1865, for gallant and meritorious service in the Battle of Spottsylvania, Va. Bvt. Brig. Gen. Vols., 13 March, 1865, for gallant and meritorious service in the Battle of Chappel House, Va. Lieut. Col. 22nd Inf., 28 July, 1866. Bvt. Col., 2 March, 1867, for gallant and meritorious service in the Battle of Spottsylvania, Va. Col. 20th Inf., 8 Feb., 1880. Brig. Gen., 28 Nov., 1893. Maj. Gen. Vols., 4 May, 1898. Bvt. Maj. Gen. U. S. A., 4 Feb., 1899, for military skill and most distinguished services in the Philippine Islands. Maj. Gen., U. S. A, June, 1900.

OTIS GEORGE A. [Born in Mass. Appointed from Mass.]
Maj. Surg. 27th Mass. Vols., 14 Sept., 1861. Discharged 20 July, 1864. Asst. Surg. Vols., 30 June, 1864. Maj. Surg. Vols., 30 Aug., 1864. Bvt. Lieut. Col. Vols., 13 March, 1865, for faithful and meritorious service during the war. Mustered out 4 June, 1866. 1st Lieut. Asst. Surg., 28 Feb., 1866. Capt. Asst. Surg., 28 July, 1866. Bvt. Capt. and Maj., 29 Sept., 1866, for faithful and meritorious service in the Med. Dept. Bvt. Lieut. Col., 29 Sept., 1866, for faithful and meritorious service during the war. Maj. Surg., 17 March, 1880. Died 23 Feb., 1881.

OTIS, HARRISON G.* [Born in N. J. Appointed at Large.]
2nd Lieut. 4th Cav., 17 June, 1874. Trans. to 4th Art., 27 Feb., 1877. Resigned 1 July, 1881.

O'TOOLE, WM. D.* [Born in Mo. Appointed from Mo.]
2nd Lieut. 13th Inf., 23 June, 1865. 1st Lieut., 23 June, 1865. Trans. to 21st Inf., 21 Sept., 1866. Reg. Adj., 28 Dec., 1866, to 16 March, 1867. Unassigned 15 May, 1869. Discharged 23 Aug., 1870.

OTTERSON, JOHN D. [Born in S. C. Appointed from S. C.]
2nd Lieut. Inf., 4 March, 1847; 12th Inf., 9 April, 1847. Died 26 Dec., 1847.

OTWELL, CURTIS W.* [Born in Ohio. Appointed from Kan.]
2nd Lieut. 7th Inf., 26 April, 1898. 1st Lieut., 2 March, 1899.

OURY, WM. H. [Born in Va. Appointed from Neb.]
Capt. 1st Neb. Vols., 10 May, to 5 Sept., 1898. 2nd Lieut. 23rd Inf., 9 July, 1898. 1st Lieut. 12th Inf., 2 March, 1899.

OUTLAW, WM. W. [Born in N. C. Appointed from Army.]
Priv. 39th Inf., 17 Sept., 1814, to — June, 1815. Priv., Corpl. and Sergt. 7th Inf., to 16 Dec., 1819. 2nd Lieut. 7th Inf., 4 Dec., 1819. 1st Lieut., 21 Feb., 1823. Died 26 May, 1826.

OVENSHINE, ALEXANDER T. [Born in Kan. Appointed from Army.]
Priv., Corpl. and Sergt. Co. C, 21st Inf., 1 May, 1894, to 28 Feb., 1897. 2nd Lieut. 17th Inf., 16 Feb., 1897. 1st Lieut. 23rd Inf., 6 Feb., 1899.

OVENSHINE, ENGLEBERT G. [Born in Kan. Appointed from Army.]
Priv., Corpl. and Sergt. Co. C, 23rd Inf., 2 April, 1894, to 21 June, 1898. 2nd Lieut. 16th Inf., 22 June, 1898. 1st Lieut., 2 March, 1899.

OVENSHINE, SAM'L. [Born in Pa. Appointed from Md.]
2nd Lieut. 5th Inf., 5 Aug., 1861. 1st Lieut., 25 Sept., 1861. Reg. Adj., 1 Jan., 1863, to 30 March, 1864. Capt., 30 March, 1864. Maj. 23rd Inf., 10 July, 1885. Lieut. Col. 15th Inf., 31 Jan., 1891. Col. 23rd Inf., 26 April, 1895. Brig. Gen. Vols., 13 Aug. to 5 Sept., 1898, and from 17 April, 1899, to 20 Oct., 1899. Brig. Gen. U. S. A., 19 Oct., 1899. Retired for over thirty years' service, 20 Oct., 1899.

OVERMAN, LEWIS C.* [Born in Pa. Appointed at Large.]
1st Lieut. Eng., 23 June, 1865. Capt., 3 June, 1867. Maj., 26 March, 1883. Resigned 20 Sept., 1892.

OVERTON, CLOUGH.* [Born in Ind. Appointed from Texas.]
2nd Lieut. 4th Cav., 11 June, 1888. 1st Lieut. 1st Cav., 21 Dec., 1895.

OVERTON, GILBERT E. [Born in N. Y. Appointed from N. Y.]
2nd Lieut. 4th N. Y. Cav., 26 Sept., 1861. Mustered out 30 April, 1862. 1st Lieut. and Adj. 12th N. Y. Cav., 25 Oct., 1862. Mustered out 2 March, 1863. 1st

Lieut 12th N. Y. Cav., 21 Sept., 1863. Mustered out 19 July, 1865. 2nd Lieut. 6th Cav., 2 Oct., 1867. 1st Lieut., 22 May, 1872. Reg. Adj., 5 April, 1873, to 3 April, 1874. Bvt. Capt., 27 Feb., 1890, for gallant services in leading a cavalry charge in the action against Indians on McLellan's Creek, Texas, 8 Nov., 1874. Capt., 30 Dec., 1881. Retired for disability 24 Feb., 1891.

OVERTON, GILES B. [Born in Pa. Appointed from Pa.]
Capt. 14th Inf., 14 May, 1861. Resigned 25 July, 1865. Bvt. Maj., 13 March, 1865, for gallant and meritorious service during the war.

OVERTON, WALTER H. [Born in Tenn. Appointed from Tenn.]
1st Lieut. 7th Inf., 3 May, 1808. Capt., 3 Dec., 1810. Maj. 3rd Rifles, 21 Feb., 1814. Trans. to Corps Art., 17 May, 1815. Resigned 31 Oct., 1815. Bvt. Lieut. Col., 23 Dec., 1814, for gallant conduct at Siege of New Orleans, La. Died 4 Jan., 1846.

OVERTON, WINFIELD S.* [Born in N. Y. Appointed from N. Y.]
Addl. 2nd Lieut. 1st Art., 11 June, 1897. 2nd Lieut. 3rd Art., 8 March, 1898. 1st Lieut. 7th Art., 15 March, 1899.

OWEN, FRANK. [Born in Ore. Appointed from Army.]
Priv., Corpl. and Sergt. Co. C, 9th Inf., 7 July, 1882, to 22 Oct., 1886. 2nd Lieut. 8th Inf., 22 Oct., 1886. 1st Lieut. Inf. (14th), 1 March, 1894. Graduate of the Infantry and Cavalry School, 1895. Dismissed 1 March, 1897.

OWEN, PHILIP A. [Born in Tenn. Appointed from Ala.]
2nd Lieut. 9th Inf., 3 March, 1855. 1st Lieut., 1 Aug., 1857. Reg. Adj., 15 July, 1856, to 25 June, 1861. Capt., 25 June, 1861. Resigned 31 Dec., 1873. Died 28 Aug., 1879.

OWEN, RICHARD. [Born in Scotland. Appointed from Ind.]
Capt. of Inf., 12 March, 1847; 16th Inf., 9 April, 1847. Disbanded 7 Aug., 1848. Lieut. Col., 15th Ind. Vols., 14 June, 1861. Col. 60th Ind. Vols., 1 Jan., 1862. Resigned 11 June, 1863. Died 24 March, 1890.

OWEN, WM. McK. [Born in Ind. Appointed from Cal.]
Priv. and Corpl. Co. D, 1st Cal. Vols., 28 Aug., 1861, to 4 Sept., 1863. 2nd Lieut. 6th Cal. Vols., 4 Sept., 1863. 1st Lieut., 2 Sept., 1864. Mustered out 31 Oct., 1865. 2nd Lieut. 14th Inf., 4 May, 1866. Trans. to 32nd Inf., 21 Sept., 1866. 1st Lieut., 21 Sept., 1866. Trans. to 21st Inf., 19 April, 1869. Discharged 1 Oct., 1870.

OWEN, WM. O. [Born in Tenn. Appointed from Va.]
Asst. Surg., 23 May, 1882. Capt. Asst. Surg., 23 May, 1887. Maj. Brig. Surg. Vols., from 4 June, 1898, to 30 June, 1899.

OWENS, WESLEY. [Born in Ohio. Appointed from Ohio.]
2nd Lieut. 2nd Cav., 1 July, 1856. 1st Lieut., 21 March, 1861. 5th Cav., 3 Aug., 1861. Capt., 15 Jan., 1862. Lieut. Col. A. I. G., ass'd, 1 Jan. to 12 Mar., 1863. Col. 8th Ohio Cav., 12 May, 1865. Mustered out of Vol. Service, 30 June, 1865. Died 11 Aug., 1867. Bvt. Maj., 27 May, 1862, for gallant and meritorious service at the Battle of Hanover C. H., Va. Bvt. Lieut. Col., 13 March, 1865, for gallant and meritorious service during the war.

OYSTER, JOSEPH S.* [Born in D. C. Appointed from D. C.]
2nd Lieut. 1st Art., 17 June, 1874. 1st Lieut., 15 May, 1880. R. Q. M., 5 May, 1887, to —. Graduate of the Artillery School, 1886. Retired for disability 17 June, 1897.

PADDOCK, GEORGE H.* [Born in Ill. Appointed from Ill.]
2nd Lieut. 4th Art., 13 June, 1873. 1st Lieut., 19 April, 1877. Trans. to 5th Cav., 12 June, 1884. Capt., 16 Jan., 1889. Graduate of the Artillery School 1880.

PADDOCK, JAMES V. S.* [Born in Ill. Appointed from Ill.]
2nd Lieut. 5th Cav., 15 June, 1877. 1st Lieut., 11 June, 1886. Retired for disability from wounds 17 April, 1891.

PADDOCK, RICHARD B. [Born in Ill. Appointed from Ill.]
2nd Lieut. 13th Inf., 10 Oct., 1883. Trans. to 6th Cav., 26 Feb., 1885. 1st Lieut. 8th Cav., 1 July, 1891. Trans. to 6th Cav., 22 April, 1892. Capt. 4th Cav., 15 July, 1899. Trans. to 6th Cav., 9 Aug., 1899. Graduate of the Infantry and Cavalry School, 1887.

PAGE, CHAS. [Born in Va. Appointed from Va.]
1st Lieut. Asst. Surg., 2 Dec., 1851. Capt. Asst. Surg., 2 Dec., 1856. Maj. Surg., 16 April, 1862. Bvt. Lieut. Col., 13 March, 1865, for faithful and meritorious service during the war. Lieut. Col. Med. Director (Act 25 Feb., 1865), 26 March, 1865, to 30 June, 1865. Lieut. Col. Surg., 30 June, 1882. Col. Asst. Surg. Gen., 17 Nov., 1887. Retired by operation of law 4 Dec., 1893.

PAGE, DANIEL M. [Born in Ohio. Appointed from Ill.]
Priv., Corpl. and Sergt. Co. B, 43rd Ohio Vols., 12 Oct., 1861, to 24 Jan., 1864. 1st Sergt. Co. D, 111th U. S. Col. Inf., 24 Jan., 1864. Sergt. Maj., 29 March, 1864. 2nd Lieut., 3 July, 1865. 1st Lieut., 13 July, 1865. Bvt. Capt. Vols., 30 April, 1865, for faithful and meritorious service during the war. Mustered out 30 April, 1866. 1st Lieut. 38th Inf., 22 July, 1867. Unassigned 11 Nov., 1869. Mustered out Jan., 1871.

PAGE, FRANCIS N.* [Born in Va. Appointed from Va.]
Bvt. 2nd Lieut. 7th Inf., 1 July, 1841. 2nd Lieut., 30 Oct., 1841. 1st Lieut., 22 Aug., 1846. Reg. Adj., 25 Oct., 1845, to 13 May, 1847. Bvt. Capt. A. A. G., 13 May, 1847. Died 25 March, 1860. Bvt. 1st Lieut., 9 May, 1846, for gallant conduct in defense of Fort Brown, Texas. Bvt. Maj., 20 Aug., 1847, for gallant and meritorious conduct at Contreras and Churubusco, Mex.

PAGE, FRANK A. [Born in Vt. Appointed from Vt.]
Priv. Co. H, 4th Vt. Vols., 21 Sept., 1861, to 12 Dec., 1862. 2nd Lieut. Vet. Res. Corps, 3 Dec., 1864. Bvt. 1st Lieut. Vols., 13 March, 1865, for gallant and meritorious services at the Battle of Lee's Mill, Va., and Capt., 13 March, 1865, for gallant and meritorious services during the war. Mustered out 13 Sept., 1866. 2nd Lieut. 44th Inf., 28 July, 1866. Unassigned 27 May, 1869. Ass'd to 10th Inf., 3 Aug., 1870. Retired 29 Sept., 1871. Dismissed 27 May, 1874. Died 12 Oct., 1889.

PAGE, HENRY. [Born in Md. Appointed from Md.]
Asst. Surg., 6 Nov., 1897.

PAGE, JOHN. [Born in Maine. Appointed from Mass.]
2nd Lieut. 8th Inf., 13 Feb., 1818. 1st Lieut., 1 Jan., 1819. Trans. to 4th Inf., 1 June, 1821. Capt. 4th Inf., 30 April, 1830. Died 12 June, 1846, of wounds received in the Battle of Palo Alto. Bvt. Capt., 1 Jan., 1829, for 10 years' faithful service in one grade.

PAGE, JOHN H. [Born in Del. Appointed from Ill.]
Priv. Co. A, 1st Ill. Light Art., 25 Aug. to 24 Oct., 1861. 2nd Lieut. 3rd Inf., 5 Aug., 1861. 1st Lieut., 12 March, 1862. Bvt. Capt., 13 Dec., 1862, for gallant and meritorious service in the Battle of Fredericksburg, Va. Bvt. Maj., 2 July, 1863, for gallant and meritorious service in the Battle of Gettysburg, Pa. Capt. 3rd Inf., 6 May, 1864. Maj. 11th Inf., 12 Sept., 1885. Lieut. Col. 22nd Inf., 24 Feb., 1891. Col. 3rd Inf., 31 May, 1895. Brig. Gen. Vols., 21 Sept. to 30 Nov., 1898.

PAGE, JOHN H., Jr. [Born in La. Appointed at Large.]
2nd Lieut. 3rd Inf., 1 Sept., 1899.

PAGE, POWHATTAN R. [Born in Va. Appointed from Va.]
2nd Lieut. of Inf., 8 March, 1847; 13th Inf., 9 April, 1847. 1st Lieut., 20 Aug., 1847. R. Q. M., 1 Feb. to 15 July, 1848. Disbanded 15 July, 1848.

PAGUE, SAML. S.* [Born in Ohio. Appointed from Ohio.]
2nd Lieut. 15th Inf., 15 June, 1876. 1st Lieut., 27 June, 1884. Dismissed 31 Dec., 1895.

PAIGE, GEORGE H.* [Born in N. H. Appointed at Large.]
Bvt. 2nd Lieut. 6th Inf., 1 July, 1848. 2nd Lieut. 2nd Inf., 10 March, 1849. 1st Lieut., 23 Feb., 1852. R. Q. M., 24 May, 1853, to 1 May, 1856. Capt. A. Q. M., 26 Dec., 1856. Died 18 April, 1859.

PAIGE, TIMOTHY.* [Born in N. H. Appointed from N. H.]
Bvt. 2nd Lieut. 3rd Inf., 1 July, 1824. 2nd Lieut. 1st Inf., 1 July, 1824. Trans. to 4th Inf., 29 Sept., 1827. 1st Lieut., 4 March, 1833. Resigned 16 March, 1836. Died 14 June, 1867.

PAIMBOEUF, LOUIS. [Born in La. Appointed from La.]
Mil. Storekeeper, 19 June, 1837. Removed 31 May, 1841.

PAINE, CHARLES H.* [Born in Vt. Appointed from Md.]
2nd Lieut. 13th Inf., 12 June, 1895. 1st Lieut. of Inf., 1 July, 1898. Ass'd to 13th Inf., 1 Jan., 1899.

PAINE, ELEAZER A.* [Born in Ohio. Appointed from Ohio.]
2nd Lieut. 1st Inf., 1 July, 1839. Resigned 11 Oct., 1840. Col. 9th Ill. Vols., 26 July, 1861. Brig. Gen. Vols., 3 Sept., 1861. Resigned 5 April, 1865. Died 16 Dec., 1882.

PAINE, FERDINAND.* [Born in Maine. Appointed from Maine.]
Bvt. 2nd Lieut. 4th Inf., 1 July, 1848. 2nd Lieut. 2nd Inf., 7 May, 1849. Died 23 June, 1854.

PAINE, WM. [Born in Penn. Appointed from Penn.]
Mil. Storekeeper, 27 July, 1818. Died 26 Sept., 1827.

PAINE, WM. C.* [Born in Mass. Appointed from Mass.]
Bvt. 2nd Lieut. Eng., 1 July, 1858. 2nd Lieut., 20 Oct., 1859. 1st Lieut., 6 Aug., 1861. Capt., 3 March, 1863. Resigned 6 Nov., 1863.

PAINE, WM. H.* [Born in Conn. Appointed from Conn.]
2nd Lieut. 2nd Cav., 12 June, 1894. 1st Lieut. 2 March, 1899.

PALEN, VINCENT. [Born in N. Y. Appointed from Va.]
Hosp. Chaplain Vols., 31 May, 1862. Mustered out 1 Sept., 1867. Post Chaplain U. S. A., 11 Sept., 1867. Retired 1 Dec., 1868. Died 13 Dec., 1884.

PALFREY, CARL F.* [Born in Mass. Appointed from Maine.]
2nd Lieut. 1st Art., 15 June, 1870. Trans. to Eng., 10 June, 1872. 1st Lieut., 2 Sept., 1874. Capt., 26 March, 1883. Retired for over thirty years' service 25 Oct., 1895.

PALFREY, EDWARD A.* [Born in La. Appointed from La.]
Bvt. 2nd Lieut. 7th Inf., 1 July, 1851. 2nd Lieut., 24 Aug., 1851. 1st Lieut., 9 Jan., 1856. Resigned 1 Aug., 1857.

PALFREY, JOHN C.* [Born in Mass. Appointed from Mass.]
Bvt. 2nd Lieut. Eng., 1 July, 1857. 2nd Lieut., 31 Dec., 1857. 1st Lieut., 3 Aug., 1861. Capt., 3 March, 1863. Lieut. Col. A. I. G. Vols., 15 March to 1 Aug., 1865. Resigned 1 May, 1866. Bvt. Maj., 23 Aug., 1864. for meritorious and distinguished service during the Sieges of Forts Gaines and Morgan, Ala. Bvt. Lieut. Col., 26 March, 1865, for gallant and meritorious service at the Siege of Mobile, Ala. Bvt. Col. and Brig. Gen., 26 March, 1865, for gallant and meritorious service during the war.

PALMER, ALFRED M. [Born in Ind. Appointed from Army.]
Priv. Co. I, 5th Art., 22 April, 1867, to 22 April, 1870. Priv., Corpl. and Sergt. Co. M, Sergt. Maj. and Q. M. Sergt. 4th Art., 16 May, 1870, to 7 July, 1880. 2nd Lieut. 24th Inf., 24 June, 1880. 1st Lieut., 29 April, 1886. Capt. A. Q. M., 18 Feb., 1897.

PALMER, ALPHEUS T. [Born in Maine. Appointed from Maine.]
2nd Lieut. of Inf., 23 Feb., 1847; 9th Inf., 9 April, 1847. 1st Lieut., 4 Dec., 1847. Disbanded 26 Aug., 1848. 1st Lieut. 9th Inf., 3 March, 1855. Resigned 16 Oct., 1855. Bvt. 1st Lieut., 20 Aug., 1847, for gallant and meritorious conduct in the Battles of Contreras and Churubusco, Mex. Died 15 Feb., 1890.

PALMER, ANDREW T. [Born in Maine. Appointed from Maine.]
Capt. of Inf., 23 Feb., 1847; 9th Inf., 9 April, 1847. Maj. 14th Inf., 8 Sept., 1847. Resigned 4 Dec., 1847. Died 20 June, 1858.

PALMER, APPLETON D.* [Born in Ohio. Appointed from Ohio.]
2nd Lieut. 12th Inf., 23 June, 1865. 1st Lieut., 23 June, 1865. Trans. to 30th Inf., 21 Sept., 1866. Capt., 29 Oct., 1868. Unassigned 23 March, 1869. Ass'd to 4th Art., 1 Jan., 1871. Resigned 29 April, 1873.

PALMER, CHARLES D.* [Born in Ohio. Appointed from Iowa.]
2nd Lieut. 4th Art., 11 June, 1888. 1st Lieut. 3rd Art., 10 Oct., 1894. Trans. to 6th Art., 8 March, 1898. Capt. A. Q. M. Vols., 28 May to 9 June, 1898. Capt. A. Q. M., 1 March, 1900.

PALMER, EUGENE L. [Born in Mo. Appointed from Mo.]
Priv. 6th Maine Batty, 1 Jan. to 23 Oct., 1862. 2nd Lieut. Vet. Res. Corps, 11 Aug., 1863. Mustered out 20 Nov., 1865. 1st Lieut. 43rd Inf., 28 July, 1866. Dismissed 11 Jan., 1868. Bvt. Capt., 2 March, 1867, for gallant and meritorious conduct at the Battle of Cedar Mountain, Va.

PALMER, FRANK H. [Born in Del. Appointed from Army.]
Priv. Co. M, 7th Pa. Cav., 2 April, 1862, to 23 Aug., 1865. Priv. Co. H, 24th Inf., 25 June, 1866, to 22 Aug., 1867. 2nd Lieut. 36th Inf., 7 Aug., 1867. Resigned 29 Oct., 1867.

PALMER, FREDERICK L.* [Born in Ga. Appointed from Ga.]
2nd Lieut. 21st Inf., 15 June, 1884. 1st Lieut. 2nd Inf., 22 April, 1891. Trans. to 21st Inf., 20 July, 1891. Capt. of Inf., 17 Sept., 1898. Ass'd to 9th Inf., 1 Jan., 1899.

PALMER, GEORGE.* [Born in Wis. Appointed from Wis.]
2nd Lieut. 24th Inf., 15 June, 1876. Trans. to 9th Inf., 28 July, 1876. 1st Lieut., 15 June, 1883. R. Q. M., 1 July, 1887. Capt., 16 Jan., 1898.

PALMER, GEORGE H. [Born in N. Y. Appointed from Ill.]
Bugler Co. G, 1st Ill. Cav., 24 April, 1861. Discharged 9 Oct., 1861. 1st Lieut. 83rd Ill. Vols., 21 Aug., 1862. Capt., 6 March, 1863. Mustered out 26 June, 1865. 2nd Lieut. 27th Inf., 22 Jan., 1867. 1st Lieut., 2 Aug., 1867. Unassigned 14 June, 1869. Ass'd to 16th Inf., 15 Dec., 1870. Capt., 20 March, 1885. Maj. 4th Inf., 11 Jan., 1899. Retired for over thirty years' service 27 Feb., 1899. Medal of Honor for most distinguished gallantry in action at the Battle of Lexington, Mo., 18, 19 and 20 Sept., 1861, volunteering to fight in the trenches, and also leading a charge which resulted in the recapture of a Union hospital, together with the capture of rebel sharpshooters then occupying the same; while serving as bugler, Co. G, 1st Ill. Cav.

PALMER, GUY G. [Born in N. Y. Appointed from Army.]
Priv., Corpl. and Sergt. Cos. I and H, 8th Inf., 20 Sept., 1889, to 27 Nov., 1892. 2nd Lieut. 16th Inf., 19 Nov., 1892. 1st Lieut., 26 April, 1898.

PALMER, INNIS N.* [Born in N. Y. Appointed from N. Y.]
Bvt. 2nd Lieut. Mtd. Rifles, 1 July, 1846. 2nd Lieut., 20 July, 1847. Bvt. 1st Lieut., 20 Aug., 1847, for gallant and meritorious conduct in the Battles of Contreras and Churubusco. Bvt. Capt., 13 Sept., 1847, for gallant conduct at Chapultepec. Reg. Adj. Mtd. Rifles, 1 May, 1850, to 1 July, 1854. 1st Lieut., 27 Jan., 1853. Capt. 2nd Cav., 3 March, 1855. Maj. 2nd Cav., 25 April, 1861; 5th Cav., 3 Aug., 1861. Bvt. Lieut. Col., 21 July, 1861, for gallant and meritorious service in the Battle of Bull Run, Va. Brig. Gen. Vols., 23 Sept., 1861. Lieut. Col. 2nd Cav., 23 Sept., 1863. Bvt. Col. and Brig. Gen., 13 March, 1865, for gallant and meritorious service in the field during the war. Bvt. Maj. Gen. Vols., 13 March, 1865, for long and meritorious service. Mustered out of Vol. Service, 15 Jan., 1866. Col. 2nd Cav., 9 June, 1868. Retired 20 March, 1879.

PALMER, JAMES. [Born in N. Y. Appointed from N. Y.]
3rd Lieut. 29th Inf., 30 April, 1813. 2nd Lieut., 20 Dec., 1813. 1st Lieut., 5 Aug., 1814. Retained as 2nd Lieut. 2nd Inf., 17 May, 1815. Resigned 1 May, 1819. Retained, — May, 1815, as 2nd Lieut. 2nd Inf. (under reorganization made under Act of 3 March, 1815), with Bvt. of 1st Lieut. from 5 Aug., 1814.

PALMER, JOHN McA.* [Born in Ill. Appointed from Ill.]
2nd Lieut. 15th Inf., 11 June, 1892. 1st Lieut., 26 April, 1898.

PALMER, LORING. [Born in Mass. Appointed from Mass.]
2nd Lieut. 9th Inf., 12 March, 1812. 1st Lieut., 26 June, 1813. Capt., 25 July, 1814. Disbanded 15 June, 1815. 2nd Lieut. 3rd Inf., 18 April, 1818. Trans. to Rifles 4 May, 1818. 1st Lieut., 10 Nov., 1818. R. Q. M., — Feb., 1819, to 1 June, 1821. Trans. to 6th Inf., 1 June, 1821. Dismissed 2 Oct., 1822.

PALMER, WATERMAN.* [Born in Va. Appointed from Penn.]
Bvt. 2nd Lieut. 8th Inf., 1 July, 1854. Resigned 11 Oct., 1854. 2nd Lieut. 1st Art., 7 June, 1855. Died 18 Nov., 1855.

PALMER, WM.* [Born in Penn. Appointed from Ind.]
Bvt. 2nd Lieut. Art., 1 July, 1828. 2nd Lieut. 1st Art., 1 July, 1828. 1st Lieut., 6 April, 1835. Died 23 July, 1835.

PALMER, WM. R. [Born in N. J. Appointed from N. J.]
2nd Lieut. Top. Eng., 7 July, 1838. 1st Lieut., 31 May, 1848. Capt., 3 March, 1853. Maj., 9 Sept., 1861. Died 18 June, 1862. Bvt. Lieut. Col., 20 Oct., 1861. Bvt. Col., 5 May, 1862, for gallant and meritorious service at the Battle of Williamsburg, Va.

PALMER, ZALMON C. [Born in Conn. Appointed from Army.]
Priv., Corpl., Sergt. and Sergt. Maj. 11th Inf., 2 June, 1812, to — June, 1815, and Sergt. Maj. 6th Inf., — June, 1815, to 20 June, 1817. 2nd Lieut. 6th Inf., 16 June, 1817. 1st Lieut., 1 March, 1820. Reg. Adj., 1 July, 1820, to 30 April, 1821. Capt., 15 Feb., 1826. Resigned 31 Dec., 1836. Died in 1842.

PARDEE, JULIUS H.* [Born in N. Y. Appointed from N. M.]
2nd Lieut. 25th Inf., 12 June, 1871. Trans. to 23rd Inf., 4 Aug., 1871. 1st Lieut., 16 March, 1877. Resigned 10 April, 1885.

PARDEE, WILLIAM J. [Born in N. Y. Appointed from N. Y.]
2nd Lieut. 18th Inf., 30 Oct., 1884. 1st Lieut. 25th Inf., 4 Dec., 1891. Capt. 2 March, 1899. Graduate of the Infantry and Cavalry School, 1887.

PARK, ROSWELL.* [Born in Conn. Appointed from N. Y.]
Bvt. 2nd Lieut. and 2nd Lieut. Eng., 1 July, 1831. Resigned 30 Sept., 1836. Died 16 July, 1869.

PARKE, JOHN B. [Born in Penn. Appointed from Penn.]
Priv. Co. F, 25th Pa. Vols., 2 May, 1861. Discharged 26 June, 1861. 1st Lieut.

17th Inf., 14 May, 1861. Capt., 14 July, 1864. Bvt. Maj., 1 Aug., 1864, for gallant and meritorious service in the Battle of Spottsylvania, and during the operations before Richmond, Va. Bvt. Lieut. Col., 2 April, 1865, for gallant and meritorious service at Fort Steedman, and in the assault on Fort Sedgwick, Va. Trans. to 26th Inf., 21 Sept., 1866. Trans. to 10th Inf., 19 May, 1869. Maj. 16th Inf., 1 Aug., 1886. Lieut. Col. of Inf. (2nd), 19 June, 1891. Died 29 Dec., 1894.

**PARKE, JOHN G.*** [Born in Penn. Appointed from Penn.]
Bvt. 2nd Lieut. Top. Eng., 1 July, 1849. 2nd Lieut., 18 April, 1854. 1st Lieut., 1 July, 1856. Capt. 13th Inf., 14 May, 1861, declined. Capt. Top. Eng., 9 Sept., 1861. Brig. Gen. Vols., 23 Nov., 1861. Bvt. Lieut. Col., 26 April, 1862, for gallant and meritorious service in the capture of Fort Macon, N. C. Maj. Gen. Vols., 18 July, 1862. Trans. to Eng., 3 March, 1863. Bvt. Col., 12 July, 1863, for gallant and meritorious service in the capture of Jackson, Miss. Maj. Eng., 17 June, 1864. Bvt. Brig. Gen., 13 March, 1865, for gallant and meritorious service in the defence of Knoxville, Tenn. Bvt. Maj. Gen., 13 March, 1865, for gallant and meritorious service in the repulse of Fort Stedman, Va. Mustered out of Vol. Service, 15 Jan., 1866. Lieut. Col. Eng., 4 March, 1879. Col., 17 March, 1884. Retired after forty years' service, 2 July, 1889.

**PARKE, JOHN S., Jr.*** [Born in Tenn. Appointed from Tenn.]
2nd Lieut. 21st Inf., 13 June, 1879. 1st Lieut., 21 Oct., 1886. Capt., 26 April, 1896.

**PARKER, ALLEN.** [Born in Ind. Appointed from Ind.]
2nd Lieut. 25th Inf., 10 April, 1899.

**PARKER, AUSTIN ALLEN.** [Born in Mich. Appointed from Ind.]
2nd Lieut. 24th Inf., 22 July, 1899.

**PARKER, CHAS.** [Born in N. Y. Appointed from Ill.]
Capt. 71st Ill. Vols., 23 July, 1862. Mustered out 29 Oct., 1862. Capt. 17th Ill. Cav., 22 Jan., 1874. Maj., 1 Nov., 1865. Mustered out 23 Nov., 1865. 2nd Lieut. 9th Cav., 28 July, 1866. Bvt. 1st Lieut. and Capt., 2 March, 1867, for gallant and meritorious service in the Battle of Nashville, Tenn. 1st Lieut. 9th Cav., 12 June, 1867. Capt., 16 Jan., 1870. Mustered out 1 Jan., 1871. Reappointed Capt. 9th Cav., 1 May, 1874, with rank from 16 Jan., 1870. Died 12 Dec., 1890.

**PARKER, CHARLES F.*** [Born in Ala. Appointed from Ala.]
2nd Lieut. 2nd Art., 14 June, 1885. 1st Lieut. 1st Art., 1 July, 1892. Trans. to 2nd Art., 14 Jan., 1893. Graduate of the Artillery School 1896.

**PARKER, DAINGERFIELD.** [Born in N. Y. Appointed from D. C.]
2nd Lieut. 3rd Inf., 26 April, 1861. 1st Lieut., 30 May, 1861. Bvt. Maj., 2 July, 1863, for gallant and meritorious service in the Battle of Gettysburg, Pa. Capt. 3rd Inf., 20 Oct., 1863. Maj. 9th Inf., 14 April, 1884. Lieut. Col. 20th Inf., 15 May, 1889. Trans. to 13th Inf., 10 Dec., 1890. Col. 18th Inf., 26 Nov., 1894. Retired by operation of law 23 May, 1896.

**PARKER, DANIEL.** [Born in Mass. Appointed from Mass.]
Brig. Gen., Adj. and I. G., 22 Nov., 1814. P. M. G., 1 June, 1821. Superseded 8 May, 1822. Died 5 April, 1846.

**PARKER, DEXTER W.*** [Born in Conn. Appointed from Conn.]
2nd Lieut. 6th Cav., 15 June, 1870. Resigned 16 July, 1871.

**PARKER, ELY S.** [Born in N. Y. Appointed from N. Y.]
Capt. A. A. G. Vols., 25 May, 1863. Lieut. Col. Mil. Sec. to Gen. Grant, 30 Aug., 1864, to 25 July, 1866. Mustered out 1 July, 1866. 2nd Lieut. 2nd Cav., 22 March, 1866. 1st Lieut., 1 June, 1867. Col. A. de C. to Gen. Grant, 25 July, 1866, to 4 March, 1869. Bvt. Col. Vols., 24 Feb., 1865, for faithful and meritorious service. Bvt. Brig. Gen. Vols., 9 April, 1865, for gallant and meritorious service during the campaign terminating with the surrender of the insurgent army under Gen. Robert E. Lee. Resigned 26 April, 1869. Bvt. 1st Lieut., Capt., Maj., Lieut. Col., Col. and Brig. Gen., 2 March, 1867, for faithful and meritorious service during the war.

**PARKER, FRANCIS H.*** [Born in N. Y. Appointed from N. Y.]
2nd Lieut. 2nd Drag., 24 June, 1861; 2nd Cav., 3 Aug., 1861. Trans. to Ord., 24 Oct., 1861. 1st Lieut., 3 March, 1863. Bvt. Capt., 13 March, 1865, for faithful and meritorious service in the Ord. Dept. Bvt. Maj., 13 March, 1865, for faithful and meritorious service in the Ord. Dept. and in the field. Capt. Ord., 1 Dec., 1865. Maj., 14 April, 1875. Lieut. Col., 3 Jan., 1887. Died 22 Feb., 1897.

**PARKER, FRANCIS LE J.*** [Born in S. C. Appointed from S. C.]
2nd Lieut. 5th Cav., 12 June, 1894. 1st Lieut., 2 March, 1899.

**PARKER, FRANK.*** [Born in S. C. Appointed from S. C.]
2nd Lieut. 15th Inf., 12 June, 1894. Trans. to 5th Cav., 19 Oct., 1894. 1st Lieut., 2 March, 1899.

**PARKER, HENRY W.** [Born in Md. Appointed from Army.]
Priv., Corpl. and Sergt Troop F, 2nd Cav., 31 Aug., 1894, to 30 Aug., 1897. Sergt. Maj. 21st Kan. Vols., 14 May, 1898. 1st Lieut. and Adj., 3 June to 22 Oct., 1898. 1st Lieut. 12th N. Y. Vols., 29 Dec., 1898, to 20 April, 1899. Priv. and Corpl. Troop K, 6th Cav., 12 Aug. to 16 Nov., 1899. 2nd Lieut. 2nd Cav., 1 Oct., 1899.

**PARKER, JAMES.*** [Born in N. J. Appointed from N. J.]
2nd Lieut. 4th Cav., 15 June, 1876. 1st Lieut., 23 July, 1879. Reg. Adj., 1 Jan. to 16 June, 1886. R. Q. M., 1 May, 1887, to 2 Oct., 1888. Capt., 2 Oct., 1888. Maj. 12th N. Y. Vols., 13 May, 1898. Lieut. Col., 1 Oct., 1898, to 20 April, 1899. Lieut. Col. 42nd U. S. Vols., 17 Aug., 1899. Trans. to 45th U. S. Vols., 1 Sept., 1899.

**PARKER, JAMES P.** [Born in Ky. Appointed from Mo.]
Bvt. 2nd Lieut. 4th Inf., 24 June, 1861. Dismissed 16 July, 1861.

**PARKER, JAMES S.*** [Born in D. C. Appointed from D. C.]
Addl. 2nd Lieut. 4th Cav., 12 June, 1895. 2nd Lieut. 10th Cav., 8 Aug., 1895. Trans. to 4th Cav., 1 Feb., 1896. 1st Lieut. 6th Cav., 8 April, 1899.

**PARKER, JOHN D.** [Born in N. Y. Appointed from Mo.]
Post. Chap., 29 July, 1882. Retired by operation of law, 8 Sept., 1895.

**PARKER, JOHN H.*** [Born in Mo. Appointed from Mo.]
2nd Lieut. 13th Inf., 11 June, 1892. 1st Lieut. 25th Inf., 26 April, 1898. Maj. 40th U. S. Vols., 17 Aug., 1899. Trans. to 39th U. S. Vols., 23 Sept., 1899.

PARKER, JOHN R. [Born in S. C. Appointed from S. C.]
2nd Lieut. 2nd Drag., 14 Oct., 1837. Resigned 31 March, 1838.

PARKER, LEOPOLD O. [Born in Mo. Appointed from Va.]
2nd Lieut. 4th U. S. Vols., 14 Jan., 1865. Mustered out 18 June, 1866. 2nd Lieut. 1st Inf., 9 Oct., 1866. Reg. Adj., 25 Sept., 1867, to 20 May, 1868. Trans. to 4th Cav., 16 Sept., 1869. 1st Lieut., 10 Feb., 1870. Reg. Adj., 1 Jan., 1872, to 6 May, 1875. Capt., 12 Nov., 1879. Trans. to 1st Inf., 6 Dec., 1880. Maj. 22nd Inf., 26 April, 1898. Retired for disability 20 Sept., 1899.

PARKER, MONTGOMERY D. [Born in Mass. Appointed from Mass.]
2nd Lieut. 9th Cav., 1 Sept., 1879. 1st Lieut., 22 Nov., 1884. Capt. 7th Cav., 11 Dec., 1896. Trans. to 8th Inf., 14 Oct., 1898 (to rank from 7 Aug., 1897).

PARKER, PERCY.* [Born in Mass. Appointed from La.]
2nd Lieut. 8th Inf., 13 June, 1879. Resigned 8 July, 1882.

PARKER, RICHARD. [Born in Va. Appointed from Va.]
Mil. Storekeeper Ord., 26 Dec., 1838. Resigned 11 May, 1847.

PARKER, RICHARD C. [Born in Penn. Appointed from Penn.]
Sergt. Maj. 5th Penn. Vols., 21 April to 25 June, 1861. 1st Lieut. 12th Inf., 14 May, 1861. Bvt. Capt., 3 May, 1863, for gallant and meritorious service in the Battle of Chancellorsville, Va. Capt. 12th Inf., 31 Dec., 1863. Bvt. Maj., 13 March, 1865, for gallant and meritorious service in the field during the war. Retired 20 May, 1879.

PARKER, ROBT. B.* [Born in N. Y. Appointed at Large.]
2nd Lieut. 4th Inf., 1 July, 1841. Died 13 Sept., 1842.

PARKER, THEOPHILUS.* [Born in N. C. Appointed from N. C.]
2nd Lieut. 8th Inf., 15 June, 1877. Resigned 27 Aug., 1879.

PARKER, THOS. D. [Born in Mass. Appointed from Army.]
Priv., Corpl., Sergt. and 1st Sergt. Co. I, 8th Inf., 6 Jan., 1860, to 30 Oct., 1861. 2nd Lieut. 2nd Inf., 24 Oct., 1861. Killed 27 June, 1862, at Battle of Gaines' Mills, Va. Bvt. 1st Lieut., 27 June, 1862, for gallant and meritorious service at the Battle of Gaines' Mills, Va.

PARKER, WALTER S. [Born in Ind. Appointed from Ind.]
Priv. Co. E, 16th Ind. Vol., 14 May to 23 Oct., 1861. 2nd Lieut. 4th Inf., 24 Oct., 1861 Resigned 7 Dec., 1861. Sergt. 16th Ind. Vols., 21 July, 1862. Killed 20 Aug., 1862, at the Battle of Richmond, Ky.

PARKER, WILLIAM M. [Born in Mass. Appointed from Army.]
Priv. Co. B, 7th Inf. and Co. B, 1st Inf., 9 April, 1898, to 18 Feb., 1899. 2nd Lieut. 1st Inf., 9 Feb., 1899.

PARKHURST, CHAS. D.* [Born in Mass. Appointed from R. I.]
2nd Lieut. 5th Cav., 14 June, 1872. 1st Lieut, 23 Aug., 1878. Trans. to 4th Art., 12 June, 1884. Capt. 2nd Art., 8 March, 1898. Graduate of the Artillery School, 1892.

PARKHURST, JABEZ.* [Born in Vt. Appointed from Vt.]
3rd Lieut. Light Art., 21 July, 1814. Trans. to Corps Art., 17 May, 1815. 2nd Lieut. 30 Aug., 1816. 1st Lieut., 1 July, 1818. Batt. Adj., 1 July, 1818, to 1 June, 1821. Trans. to 4th Art., 1 June, 1821. Died 6 July, 1821.

PARKINSON, DAVID. [Born in Mich. Appointed from Army.]
Priv., Corpl. and Sergt. Co. A, 2nd Batt. 16th Inf., 21 April, 1862, to 21 April, 1865. 2nd Lieut. 16th Inf., 13 April, 1865. 1st Lieut., 13 April, 1865. Trans. to 25th Inf., 21 Sept., 1866. R. Q. M., 15 Dec., 1866, to 22 June, 1868. Capt., 22 June, 1868. Unassigned 26 April, 1869. Discharged 13 Aug., 1870.

PARKINSON, PETER, Jr. [Born in Tenn. Appointed from Tenn.]
2nd Lieut. 1st Cav., 3 March, 1855. Resigned 27 Aug., 1855.

PARKS, EDWIN R. [Born in Mich. Appointed from Mich.]
Priv. and Sergt. 13th Inf., 10 Dec., 1861, to 29 Aug., 1863. 2nd Lieut. 16th Inf., 23 Feb., 1866. 1st Lieut., 20 Dec., 1867. Unassigned 14 April, 1869. Ass'd to 13th Inf., 20 July, 1869. Mustered out 1 Jan., 1871.

PARKS, MARTIN P.* [Born in N. C. Appointed from N. C.]
Bvt. 2nd Lieut. 2nd Art., 1 July, 1826. Resigned 5 April, 1828. Chap. and Prof. at Mil. Acad., 5 Dec., 1840. Resigned 31 Dec., 1846. Died 21 July, 1853.

PARKS, MARTIN P., Jr.* [Born in N. C. Appointed from N. C.]
Bvt. 2nd Lieut. 3rd Inf., 1 July, 1851. 2nd Lieut., 24 July, 1851. Died 5 June, 1852.

PARMERTER, ALMON L.* [Born in N. Y. Appointed from N. Y.]
2nd Lieut. 21st Inf., 14 June, 1885. 1st Lieut. 14th Inf., 16 Jan., 1892. Trans. to 21st Inf., 14 March, 1892. Capt., 2 March, 1899. Honor graduate of the Infantry and Cavalry School, 1893.

PARNELL, WM. R. [Born in Ireland. Appointed from N. Y.]
1st Lieut. 4th N. Y. Cav., 29 Aug., 1861. Capt., 19 Dec., 1862. Maj., 25 May, 1863. Lieut. Col., 28 Jan., 1864. Discharged 15 Dec., 1864. 2nd Lieut. 1st Cav., 23 Feb., 1866. 1st Lieut., 15 Oct., 1866. Bvt. Capt., 2 March, 1867, for gallant and meritorious service in action at Upperville, Va., 21 June, 1863. Bvt. Maj., 2 March, 1867, for gallant and meritorious service during the war. Bvt. Lieut. Col., 26 Sept., 1867, for conspicuous gallantry in charging a large body of Indians, strongly fortified in the Infernal Caverns, Pitt River, Cal., 26 Sept., 1867. Capt. 1st Cav., 29 April, 1879. Retired for wounds in line of duty, 11 Feb., 1887. Bvt. Col., 27 Feb., 1890, for gallant services in action against Indians at White Bird Canon, Idaho, 17 June, 1877. Medal of Honor for most distinguished gallantry in action at White Bird Canyon, Idaho, 17 June. 1877. This officer, then 1st Lieut., 1st Cav., saved the life of a soldier. The troop was retreating through the canyon, pursued by a largely superior force of Indians, and while crossing a marsh a trooper's horse was killed and its rider left in the tule swamp. Lieut. Parnell, with a few men, in the face of a very heavy fire and at imminent peril, returned, extricated the man, and rescued him. The loss in Troop H was 14 killed and 1 wounded out of 54 officers and men taken into action.

PARROTT, RALPH B. [Born in N. Y. Appointed from N. J.]
2nd Lieut. 22nd Inf., 9 July, 1898. 1st Lieut. 15th Inf., 8 June, 1899.

PARROTT, ROBERT P.* [Born in N. H. Appointed from N. H.]
Bvt. 2nd Lieut. 1st Art., 1 July, 1824. 2nd Lieut. 3rd Art., 1 July, 1824. 1st Lieut., 27 Aug., 1831. Resigned 31 Oct., 1836. Capt. Ord., 13 Jan., 1836. Resigned 31 Oct., 1836. Died 24 Dec., 1877.

PARROTT, WM. H. [Born in D. C. Appointed from D. C.]
2nd Lieut. Light Art., 27 Oct., 1820. Resigned 1 June, 1821.

PARRY, EDWARD R. [Born in Penn. Appointed from Minn.]
1st Lieut. 11th Inf., 14 May, 1861. Capt., 14 Oct., 1864. Trans. to 20th Inf., 21 Sept., 1866. Unassigned 18 Sept., 1869. Discharged 1 Aug., 1870. Bvt. Maj., 13 March, 1865, for gallant and meritorious serivce. Died 13 April, 1874.

PARRY, HENRY C. [Born in Penn. Appointed from Penn.]
Asst. Surg. 8th Pa. Vols., 23 April, 1861. Asst. Surg., 26 Aug., 1861, Wholly retired 30 March, 1869. Bvt. Capt. and Maj., 13 March, 1865, for faithful and meritorious service during the war.

PARRY, WM. W. [Born in Penn. Appointed from Penn.]
Priv. Co. D, Ind. Batt. Penn. Mil., 25 June to 8 Aug., 1863. Priv. Capt. Lambert's Co. Cav. Pa. Mil., 12 Aug. to 25 Nov., 1864. 2nd Lieut. 16th Inf., 23 Feb., 1866. Trans. to 34th Inf., 21 Sept., 1866. 1st Lieut., 10 Feb., 1867. Unassigned 14 April, 1869. Ass'd to 13th Inf., 1 Jan., 1871. Died 4 Sept., 1871.

PARSONS, CHAS. C.* [Born in Ohio. Appointed from Ohio.]
2nd Lieut. 4th Art., 24 June, 1861. 1st Lieut., 24 June, 1861. Dismissed 5 Sept., 1864. Reinstated 11 Oct., 1864. Capt., 28 July, 1866. Discharged 31 Dec., 1870. Bvt. Capt., 8 Oct., 1862, for gallant and meritorious service at the Battle of Perryville, Ky. Bvt. Maj., 31 Dec., 1862, for gallant and meritorious service at the Battle of Stone River, Tenn. Bvt. Lieut. Col., 13 March, 1865, for gallant and meritorious service during the war.

PARSONS, ELIAS H. [Born in Mass. Appointed from Ohio.]
Q. M. Sergt. 46th Ohio Vols., 16 Dec., 1861. 2nd Lieut., 12 March, 1863. 1st Lieut., 15 April, 1864. Capt., 8 Sept., 1864. Mustered out 22 July, 1865. 1st Lieut. 12th Inf., 28 July, 1866. Unassigned 19 March, 1869. Discharged 13 Aug., 1870.

PARSONS, FOSTER E. [Born in Mass. Appointed from Army.]
Priv., Sergt., Com. Sergt. and Sergt. Maj. 2nd Batt. 13th Inf., 28 Nov., 1863, to 24 May, 1866. 2nd Lieut. 13th Inf., 6 Dec., 1865. 1st Lieut., 6 Dec., 1865. Trans. to 31st Inf., 21 Sept., 1866. R. Q. M., 31 March, 1867, to 15 May, 1869. Trans. to 22nd Inf., 15 May, 1869. Discharged 19 Dec., 1870.

PARSONS, JAMES K. [Born in Ala. Appointed from Ala.]
1st Lieut. Co. L, 3rd Ala. Vols., 5 Aug., 1898, to 20 March, 1899. 2nd Lieut. 20th Inf., 10 April, 1899.

PARSONS, LANNING.* [Born in Ohio. Appointed from Ohio.]
Addl. 2nd Lieut. 9th Cav., 12 June, 1896. 2nd Lieut. 10th Cav., 1 June, 1897. Trans. to 9th Cav., 11 Aug., 1897.

PARTELLO, JOSEPH K. [Born in D. C. Appointed from Ga.]
2nd Lieut. 5th Inf., 10 April, 1899.

PARTELLO, JOSEPH M. T. [Born in Ohio. Appointed from D. C.]
Priv. Gen. Service, 2 Aug., 1872. Sergt., 2 Dec., 1875. Discharged 2 Aug., 1877. Sergt. Gen. Service, 2 Aug., 1877. Discharged 11 May, 1878. 2nd Lieut. 5th Inf., 1 Sept., 1879. 1st Lieut., 10 July, 1885. Capt., 26 April, 1898.

PARTRIDGE, ALDEN.* [Born in Vt. Appointed from Vt.]
1st Lieut. Eng., 20 Oct., 1806. Capt., 23 July, 1810. Resigned 15 April, 1818. Died 17 Jan., 1854.

PASCHAL, JAMES W. [Born in Ohio. Appointed from Army.]
Priv. and Sergt. Co. B, 13th Inf., 16 Sept., 1861, to 28 Aug., 1863. 2nd Lieut. 13th Inf., 10 Aug., 1863. Resigned 14 May, 1864.

PASCO, WILLIAM D. [Born in Fla. Appointed from Fla.]
2nd Lieut. 18th Inf., 1 July, 1899.

PATCH, ALEXR. M.* [Born in Penn. Appointed from Penn.]
Addl. 2nd Lieut. 8th Cav., 15 June, 1877. 2nd Lieut. 4th Cav., 7 Dec., 1877. 1st Lieut., 5 May, 1880. R. Q. M., 1 Oct., 1880, to 1 May, 1887. Retired for disability with rank of Capt., 9 March, 1891.

PATRICK, MARSENA R.* [Born in N. Y. Appointed from N. Y.]
Bvt 2nd Lieut. 2nd Inf., 1 July, 1835. 2nd Lieut., 31 Oct., 1836. 1st Lieut., 1 March, 1839. Capt., 22 Aug., 1847. Resigned 30 June, 1850. Bvt. Maj., 30 May, 1848, for meritorious conduct while serving in the enemy's country. Brig. and I. G. N. Y. Vols. in U. S. Service, 16 May, 1861, to 9 Feb., 1862. Brig. Gen. Vols., 17 March, 1862. Bvt. Maj. Gen. Vols., 13 March, 1865, for faithful and meritorious service during the war. Died 27 July, 1888.

PATRICK, MASON M.* [Born in W. Va. Appointed from W. Va.]
Addl. 2nd Lieut. Eng., 1 July, 1886. 2nd Lieut., 16 Sept., 1886. 1st Lieut., 2 July, 1889. Capt., 18 May, 1898.

PATRICK, MATTHEW A. [Born in Md. Appointed from Army.]
Sergt. 29th Inf., — April, 1813, to — March, 1814. Ensign 29th Inf., 30 March, 1814. 3rd Lieut., 1 May, 1814. Disbanded 15 June, 1815. 3rd Lieut. Corps Art., 18 Aug., 1817. 2nd Lieut., 23 March, 1818. 1st Lieut., 11 Aug., 1820. Trans. to 1st Art., 1 June, 1821. Capt., 4 Feb., 1833. Died 6 March, 1834.

PATTEN, FRANCIS J.* [Born in Maine. Appointed from Maine.]
Addl. 2nd Lieut. 21st Inf., 15 June, 1877. 2nd Lieut., 17 June, 1877. 1st Lieut., 22 Sept., 1884. Resigned 28 Sept., 1889.

PATTEN, GEORGE.* [Born in S. C. Appointed from S. C.]
Bvt. 2nd Lieut. 3rd Art., 1 July, 1847. 2nd Lieut., 13 Aug., 1847. Resigned 21 July, 1851. Capt. A. A. G. Vols., 11 March, 1863. Resigned 2 July, 1863. 1st Lieut. R. C. S. 3rd N. J. Cav., 10 Feb., 1864. Resigned 15 May, 1865.

PATTEN, GEORGE H.* [Born in Maine. Appointed from Maine.]
2nd Lieut. 22nd Inf., 13 June, 1882. 1st Lieut. 6th Inf., 24 Jan., 1891. Trans. to 22nd Inf., 20 July, 1891. Capt. 14th Inf., 26 April, 1898. Reg. Adj., 1 Aug., 1899.

PATTEN, GEORGE W.* [Born in R. I. Appointed from R. I.]
Bvt. 2nd Lieut. 2nd Inf., 1 July, 1830. 2nd Lieut., 1 July, 1830. 1st Lieut., 13 Feb., 1837. Capt., 18 June, 1846. Bvt. Maj., 18 April, 1847, for gallant and meritorious conduct in the Battle of Cerro Gordo. Maj. 9th Inf., 30 April, 1861. Lieut. Col. 2nd Inf., 7 June, 1862. Retired 17 Feb., 1864. Died 28 April, 1882.

PATTEN, HUDSON T. [Born in S. C. Appointed from N. Y.]
2nd Lieut. 1st Art., 9 July, 1898.

PATTEN, WM. S. [Born in N. Y. Appointed from N. Y.]
2nd Lieut. 18th Inf., 15 Oct., 1875. Capt. A. Q. M., 12 Sept., 1883. Maj. Q. M., 22 Sept., 1896. Col. Q. M. Vols., 12 July, 1898, to 2 March, 1899.

PATTEN WILLIAM T.* [Born in S. C. Appointed at Large.]
2nd Lieut. 13th Inf., 15 Feb., 1899.

PATTERSON, CHAS. E.* [Born in Ind. Appointed from Mo.]
2nd Lieut. 4th Inf., 6 May, 1861. Dismissed 6 June, 1861. Died 8 April, 1862.

PATTERSON, C. STUART, Jr. [Born in Penn. Appointed from Penn.]
2nd Lieut. 7th Art., 9 July, 1898. Trans. to 6th Art., 27 March, 1899.

PATTERSON, FRANCIS E. [Born in Penn. Appointed from Penn.]
2nd Lieut. 1st Art., 24 June, 1847. 1st Lieut., 29 Oct., 1848. Capt. 9th Inf., 3 March, 1855. Resigned 1 May, 1857. Col. 17th Pa. Vols., 25 April, 1861. Mustered out 2 Aug., 1861. Brig. Gen. Vols., 11 April, 1862. Died 22 Nov., 1862.

PATTERSON, GEORGE T. T.* [Born in Ohio. Appointed from Ohio.]
Priv. 22nd Ind. Batt. Ohio Light Art., 6 July, 1863. Discharged 13 July, 1865. Cadet at Mil. Acad., 1 July, 1868. 2nd Lieut. 14th Inf., 14 June, 1872. R. Q. M., 23 April, 1879. 1st Lieut., 15 March, 1883. Capt. of Inf. (14th), 14 Oct., 1892. Died 14 Aug., 1894.

PATTERSON, GEORGE T.* [Born in Neb. Appointed from Neb.]
Addl. 2nd Lieut. 5th Art., 12 June, 1896. 2nd Lieut. 3rd Art., 23 Sept., 1897. 1st Lieut., 2 March, 1899.

PATTERSON, HENRY W. [Born in Pa. Appointed from Pa.]
2nd Lieut. 8th Penn. Res., 24 April to 12 Nov., 1861. 2nd Lieut. 4th Inf., 24 Oct., 1861. 1st Lieut., 28 Dec., 1862. R. Q. M., 3 Jan., 1863, to 21 April, 1866. Capt., 21 April, 1866. Unassigned 19 Feb., 1870. Discharged 1 Nov., 1870. Bvt. Capt., 2 July, 1863, for gallant and meritorious service at the Battle of Gettysburg, Penn.

PATTERSON, JAMES H. [Born in Ind. Appointed from Army.]
Priv., Corpl. and Sergt. Co. A, 2nd and G, 1st Batt. 19th Inf., 23 July, 1862, to 18 May, 1865. 2nd and 1st Lieut. 19th Inf., 23 Jan., 1865. Capt., 19 Sept., 1866. Trans. to 28th Inf., 21 Sept., 1866. Unassigned 31 March, 1869. Ass'd to 25th Inf., 15 Dec., 1870. Died 19 Aug., 1873.

PATTERSON, JOHN H. [Born in N. Y. Appointed from N. Y.]
1st Lieut. 11th Inf., 14 May, 1861. Bvt. Capt., 1 Oct., 1864, for gallant service in the Battle of Chappel House, Va. Trans. to 20th Inf., 21 Sept., 1866. Capt., 28 July, 1866. Maj. 3rd Inf., 19 May, 1891. Lieut. Col. 1st Inf., 21 Jan., 1895. Trans. to 22nd Inf., 4 Nov., 1895. Col. 20th Inf., 28 Sept., 1898. Brig. Gen., 18 Jan., 1899. Brig. Gen. Vols., 21 Sept. to 30 Nov., 1898. Retired, for over thirty years' service, 6 Feb., 1899. Medal of Honor for most distinguished gallantry in action at the Wilderness, Va., 5 May, 1864, under the heavy fire of the advancing enemy, in picking up and carrying several hundred yards, to a place of safety, a wounded officer of his regiment, who was helpless and would otherwise have been burned in the forest; while serving as 1st Lieut. 11th U. S. Inf.

PATTERSON, ROBT. [Born in Ireland. Appointed from Penn.]
Capt., Lieut. Col. and Col. Pa. Mil., 2 Oct., 1812, to 2 April, 1813. 1st Lieut. 22nd Inf., 5 April, 1813. Trans. to 32nd Inf., 27 May, 1813. Capt. Asst. Dep. Q. M. G., 24 June, 1813, to 5 June, 1814. Capt. 32nd Inf., 19 April, 1814. Disbanded 15 June, 1815. Maj. Gen. Vols., 7 July, 1846. Disbanded 20 July, 1848. Maj. Gen. Penn. Vols., 15 April, 1861. Mustered out 27 July, 1861. Died 7 Aug., 1881.

PATTERSON, ROBT. E.* [Born in Penn. Appointed at Large.]
Bvt. 2nd Lieut. 6th Inf., 1 July, 1851. 2nd Lieut., 27 Jan., 1853. 1st Lieut., 16 Sept., 1856. Resigned 1 May, 1857. Addl. P. M. Vols., 1 June, 1861. Col. 115th Pa. Vols., 25 June, 1862. Bvt. Brig. Gen. Vols., 13 March, 1865, for meritorious service during the war. Resigned as Col. Vols., 2 Dec., 1862, and as Addl. P. M., 23 Dec., 1862.

PATTERSON, ROBERT H. [Born in D. C. Appointed from D. C.]
2nd Lieut. 1st Art., 23 Sept., 1867. 1st Lieut., 1 Oct., 1874. Capt., 29 June, 1896. Graduate of the Artillery School, 1871.

PATTERSON, ROSWELL B. [Born in Mo. Appointed from Ill.]
2nd Lieut. 9th Ill. Vols., 10 Aug., 1861. 1st Lieut., 18 Oct., 1862. Mustered out 20 Aug., 1864. 2nd Lieut. 7th Inf., 23 Feb., 1866. Resigned 17 Jan., 1867.

PATTERSON, THOS. C.* [Born in Penn. Appointed from Ohio.]
2nd Lieut. 1st Art., 15 June, 1877. 1st Lieut., 2 Jan., 1881. Retired for disability, 2 Oct., 1894. Died 15 April, 1896.

PATTERSON, WM. J. [Born in Ohio. Appointed from Tenn.]
Sergt. Co. D, 1st Ohio Art., 17 Oct., 1861, to 15 Oct., 1863. 1st Lieut. 1st Tenn. Art., 15 Oct., 1863. Capt., 14 Sept., 1864. Mustered out 1 Aug., 1865. 2nd Lieut. 5th Art., 15 May, 1866. 1st Lieut., 22 July, 1867. Dropped 2 July, 1870.

PATTERSON, WM. W. [Born in N. Y. Appointed from Army.]
Priv. and Sergt. Co. F. 2nd Batt. 12th Inf., 9 Oct., 1861, to 31 March, 1863. 2nd Lieut. 12th Inf., 19 Feb., 1863. 1st Lieut., 2 July, 1863. Resigned 7 May, 1864.

PATTISON, HARRY H.* [Born in Ohio. Appointed from Ind.]
Addl. 2nd Lieut. 3rd Cav., 12 June, 1893. 2nd Lieut., 21 July, 1893. 1st Lieut., 2 March, 1899. Reg. Com., 4 Oct., 1899.

PATTON, ISAAC W. [Born in Va. Appointed from Va.]
2nd Lieut. Inf., 8 March, 1847; 10th Inf., 9 April, 1847. 2nd Lieut. 3rd Art., 13 July, 1848. 1st Lieut., 2 Oct., 1853. Resigned 15 Feb., 1855.

PATTON, ROBERT, Jr. [Born in Va. Appointed from Tenn.]
2nd Lieut. Inf., 5 March, 1847; 12th Inf., 9 April, 1847. Died in 1847, at Vera Cruz, Mex.

PATZKI, JULIUS H. [Born in Prussia. Appointed from Penn.]
Priv. Co. G, 15th N. Y. Art., 13 July, 1863. Asst. Surg. 15th N. Y. Vols., 11 Jan., 1864. Mustered out 22 Aug., 1865. 1st Lieut. Asst. Surg., 11 Nov., 1867. Capt. Asst. Surg., 30 March, 1869. Maj. Surg., 28 Feb., 1889. Retired for disability, 9 Jan., 1892.

PAUL, AUGUSTUS C. [Born in N. Y. Appointed from Mo.]
Capt. Ky. Mtd. Inf., 16 May, 1861. Mustered out 17 Aug., 1861. Capt. 23rd Ky. Vols., 2 Jan., 1862. Capt. A. A. G. Vols., 1 June, 1863. Bvt. Maj. Vols., 13 March, 1865, for gallant and meritorious service in the Battle of the Wilderness, Va. Bvt. Lieut. Col., 13 March, 1865, for gallant and meritorious service in the Battle of Spottsylvania, Va. Mustered out 19 Sept., 1865. 2nd Lieut. 12th Inf., 11 May, 1866, declined. 2nd Lieut. 3rd Cav., 23 Jan., 1869. 1st Lieut., 20 Dec., 1872. Resigned 24 May, 1881.

PAUL, CHAS. R. [Born in Penn. Appointed from N. J.]
Priv. Co. C, 7th N. J. Vols., 28 Aug., 1861. Com. Sergt. 7th N. J. Vols., 27 Nov., 1861. Discharged 15 Aug., 1862. 2nd Lieut. 15th N. J. Vols., 25 Aug., 1862. 1st Lieut., 10 Aug., 1863. Capt., 10 Sept., 1864. Bvt. Maj. Vols., 19 Oct., 1864, for gallantry throughout the campaign before Richmond, Va., and particularly in the engagements at Winchester, Fisher's Hill, and Cedar Creek, in the Valley of the Shendandoah. Bvt. Lieut. Col. Vols., 2 April, 1865, for gallant and meritorious service before Petersburg, Va. Mustered out 11 July, 1865. 2nd Lieut. and 1st Lieut. 16th Inf., 23 Feb., 1866. Trans. to 25th Inf., 21 Sept., 1866. Bvt. Capt., 2 March, 1867, for gallant and meritorious service in the Battle of Petersburg, Va. Trans. to 18th Inf., 26 April, 1869. Capt. 18th Inf., 20 March, 1879. Maj., 26 April, 1898. Lieut. Col. 20th Inf., 29 Jan., 1900.

PAUL, FRANK W. [Born in Italy. Appointed from Penn.]
Priv. Commonwealth Penn. Art., 24 April to 5 Aug., 1861. 1st Lieut. 2nd Penn. Art., 12 Nov., 1861. Bvt. Capt. Vols., 13 March, 1865, for gallant and meritorious service during the war. Mustered out 17 Nov., 1864. 1st Lieut. 24th Inf., 28 July, 1866. Resigned 21 April, 1868. Bvt. Capt., 2 March, 1867, for gallant and meritorious service at Petersburg Mine, Va.

PAUL, GABRIEL R.* [Born in Mo. Appointed from Mo.]
Bvt. 2nd Lieut. 7th Inf., 1 July, 1834. 2nd Lieut., 4 Dec., 1834. 1st Lieut., 26 Oct., 1836. Capt., 19 April, 1846. Bvt. Maj., 13 Sept., 1847, for gallant and meritorious conduct in the Battle of Chapultepec. Maj. 8th Inf., 22 April, 1861. Col. 4th N. Mex. Vols., 9 Dec., 1861. Mustered out 31 May, 1862. Lieut. Col. 8th Inf., 25 April, 1862. Brig. Gen. Vols., 5 Sept., 1862. Expired by constitutional limitation, 4 March, 1863. Brig. Gen. Vols., 18 April, 1863. Col. 14th Inf., 13 Sept., 1864. Retired with rank of Col., 16 Feb., 1865. Bvt. Brig. Gen., 23 Feb., 1865, for gallant and meritorious service in the Battle of Gettysburg, Penn. Retired with rank of Brig. Gen., 28 July, 1866. Mustered out of Vol. Service, 1 Sept., 1866. Died 5 May, 1886.

PAULDING, HOLMES O. [Born in D. C. Appointed from D. C.]
1st Lieut. Asst. Surg., 10 Nov., 1874. Capt. Asst. Surg., 10 Nov., 1879. Died 1 May, 1883.

PAULDING, TATNALL. [Born in N. Y. Appointed from N. Y.]
1st Lieut. 3rd Cav., 14 May, 1861; 6th Cav., 3 Aug., 1861. Capt., 20 Oct., 1864. Resigned 1 July, 1866. Bvt. Capt., 3 July, 1863, for gallant and meritorious service in the Gettysburg campaign. Bvt. Maj. and Lieut. Col., 11 Nov., 1865, for meritorious service during the war.

PAULDING, WM. [Born in N. Y. Appointed from N. Y.]
2nd Lieut. 10th Inf., 1 Oct., 1873. 1st Lieut., 11 April, 1882. Capt., 16 Sept., 1892.

PAULDING, WM. K. [Born in ——. Appointed from Tenn.]
Ensign 24th Inf., 9 Aug., 1813. 3rd Lieut., 15 Oct., 1813. 2nd Lieut., 20 June, 1814. Disbanded 15 June, 1815. Reinstated 17 May, 1816, in 1st Inf. 1st Lieut., 31 May, 1817. Dropped 2 Jan., 1818.

PAULUS, JACOB. [Born in Prussia. Appointed from Penn.]
Priv. Co. K, 5th Penn. Vols., 20 April, 1861. Discharged 24 July, 1861. Sergt. Co. F, 50th Penn. Vols., 10 Aug., 1861. Sergt. Co. F, 50th Penn. Vet. Vols., 31 Dec., 1863. 2nd Lieut. 50th Penn. Vols., 16 April, 1865. Capt., 18 June, 1865. Mustered out 30 July, 1865. 2nd Lieut. 18th Inf., 11 May, 1866. Trans. to 27th Inf., 21 Sept., 1866. 1st Lieut., 17 Jan., 1867. Unassigned 14 June, 1869. Ass'd to 25th Inf., 14 July, 1869. Capt., 19 Aug., 1873. Wholly retired 22 March, 1879. Died 3 April, 1881

PAWLING, JOSEPH H.* [Born in Pa. Appointed from Pa.]
Bvt. 2nd Lieut. 1st Inf., 1 July, 1829. Resigned 30 Nov., 1830. Died 9 July, 1847.

PAXTON, ALEXIS R. [Born in Penn. Appointed from Penn.]
2nd Lieut. 15th Inf., 3 March, 1877. 1st Lieut., 31 Oct., 1884. Capt., 7 Nov., 1896. Graduate of the Infantry and Cavalry School, 1885.

PAXTON, JOSEPH R. [Born in Penn. Appointed from Penn.]
Capt. 15th Inf., 26 Oct., 1861. Resigned 1 July, 1865.

PAXTON, ROBERT G.* [Born in Va. Appointed from Va.]
2nd Lieut. 10th Cav., 12 June, 1887. 1st Lieut. 4th Cav., 30 Aug., 1894. Trans. to 10th Cav., 10 Sept., 1894. Graduate of the Infantry and Cavalry School, 1891. Capt. A. A. G. Vols., 12 May, 1898, to 12 May, 1899.

PAYNE, BROOKE.* [Born in Va. Appointed from Va.]
Addl. 2nd Lieut. 4th Art., 12 June, 1895. 2nd Lieut. 5th Art., 6 June, 1896. 1st Lieut., 2 March, 1899.

PAYNE, DAVID W.* [Born in N. Y. Appointed from N. Y.]
1st Lieut. Eng., 23 June, 1865. Resigned 1 Oct., 1869.

PAYNE, JOHN A. [Born in Ind. Appointed from Ill.]
Priv. Co. A, 12th Ill. Vols., 26 April, 1861. Discharged 31 July, 1861. 1st Lieut. 1st Mo. State Mil. Vols., 13 March, 1862. Capt., 1 Oct., 1862. Mustered out 2 Dec., 1864. Capt., 14th Mo. Cav., 3 Dec., 1864. Maj., 31 July, 1865. Mustered out 1 Nov., 1865. 2nd Lieut. 28th Inf., 6 May, 1867. Trans. to 19th Inf., 31 March, 1869. 1st Lieut., 13 May, 1878. Retired for disability, with rank of Capt., 20 Feb., 1891.

PAYNE, J. SCOTT.* [Born in Va. Appointed from Tenn.]
2nd Lieut. 5th Cav., 18 June, 1866. 1st Lieut., 23 May, 1867. Resigned 12 Sept., 1868. 2nd Lieut. 6th Cav., 3 Feb., 1873. 1st Lieut. 5th Cav., 8 Sept., 1874, with rank from 23 May, 1867. Capt., 4 June, 1875. Bvt. Maj., 27 Feb., 1890, for gallant services in action against Indians at Milk Creek, Colo., 29 and 30 Sept. and 1 Oct., 1879, where he was wounded. Retired for disability, 24 April, 1886. Died 16 Dec., 1895.

PAYNE, MATTHEW M. [Born in Va. Appointed from Va.]
1st Lieut. 20th Inf., 12 March, 1812. Capt., 2 March, 1814. Disbanded 15 June, 1815. Restored 17 May, 1816, in Corps Art. Trans. to 4th Art., 1 June, 1821. Maj. 2nd Art., 27 June, 1836. Lieut. Col. 4th Art., 27 June, 1843. Col. 2nd Art., 11 Nov., 1856. Resigned 23 July, 1861. Bvt. Maj., 2 March, 1824, for ten years' faithful service in one grade. Bvt. Col., 9 May, 1846, for gallant and distinguished service in the Battles of Palo Alto and Resaca de la Palma. Died 1 Aug., 1862.

PAYSON, ALBERT H.* [Born in Mass. Appointed from Mass.]
2nd Lieut. Eng., 15 June, 1868. 1st Lieut., 6 Jan., 1870. Capt. (fourteen years' service), 15 June, 1882. Resigned 1 Dec., 1887.

PEABODY, JOSE K. [Born in Maine. Appointed from N. Y.]
2nd Lieut. 3rd Cav., 27 July, 1872. Resigned 31 May, 1873.

PEACOCK, JOHN. [Born in Penn. Appointed from Penn.]
2nd Lieut. 3rd Inf., 4 Dec., 1818. Disbanded 1 June, 1821.

PEALE, JAMES T. [Born in Penn. Appointed from Penn.]
2nd Lieut. 4th Penn. Cav., 12 March, 1862. Capt., 5 June, 1862. Maj., 9 Sept., 1864. Bvt. Lieut. Col. Vols., 13 March, 1865, for gallant and meritorious service during the war, and particularly in the engagement at Wyatt's Farm. Mustered out 1 July, 1865. 2nd Lieut. 2nd Cav., 23 Feb., 1866. 1st Lieut., 28 July, 1866. Capt., 3 March, 1875. Dismissed 20 Dec., 1880.

PEARCE, EARLE, D'A.* [Born in Ga. Appointed from Ga.]
Addl. 2nd Lieut. 5th Cav., 11 June, 1897. 2nd Lieut. 3rd Cav., 19 Nov., 1897. Trans. to 6th Art., 8 March, 1898. 1st Lieut., 31 March, 1899.

PEARCE, FRED A.* [Born in Ark. Appointed from Ark.]
Addl. 2nd Lieut. 16th Inf., 11 June, 1897. 2nd Lieut. 6th Art., 8 March, 1898. Died 6 June, 1899, at Manila, Philippine Islands.

PEARCE, HENRY S. [Born in Md. Appointed from Army.]
Priv., Corpl. and Sergt. and 1st Sergt. Co. F, 1st Drag., 11 Sept., 1855, to 13 Sept., 1859. Bvt. 2nd Lieut. 1st Drag., 13 Sept., 1859. Resigned 11 March, 1861. Priv. and 1st Sergt. Troop C, 1st Cal. Cav., 7 Sept., 1861, to 7 Sept., 1864. Priv. Co. D, 3rd Batt. and Sergt. Maj. 32nd Inf., 23 Nov., 1865, to 2 Aug., 1867. 2nd Lieut. 2nd Cav., 8 June, 1867. 1st Lieut., 5 July, 1868. Cashiered 3 Dec., 1868.

PEARCE, NICHOLAS B.* [Born in Ky. Appointed from Ky.]
Bvt. 2nd Lieut. 7th Inf., 1 July, 1850. 2nd Lieut., 8 March, 1851. 1st Lieut., 3 March, 1855. Resigned 20 April, 1858.

PEARCE, SAMUEL A., Jr. [Born in R. I. Appointed from R. I.]
Addl. P. M. Vols., 28 May, 1864. Bvt. Lieut. Col. Vols., 20 Sept., 1866, for faithful and meritorious service in the Pay Dept. Mustered out 20 Sept., 1866. Maj. P. M., 9 March, 1867. Resigned 1 Aug., 1869.

PEARCE, THOMAS A.* [Born in N. C. Appointed from Texas.]
Addl. 2nd Lieut. 14th Inf., 12 June, 1895. 2nd Lieut. 7th Inf., 3 Aug., 1895. 1st Lieut. of Inf., 11 Aug., 1898. Ass'd to 7th Inf., 1 Jan., 1899. Trans. to 5th Inf., 20 Sept., 1899.

PEARCE, THOS. H.* [Born in Penn. Appointed from Penn.]
Bvt. 2nd Lieut. 1st Inf., 1 July, 1826. 2nd Lieut. 6th Inf., 1 July, 1826. Resigned 31 March, 1829. Died 21 Nov., 1862.

PEARSON, DANL. C.* [Born in Mass. Appointed from Mass.]
2nd Lieut. 2nd Cav., 15 June, 1870. 1st Lieut., 23 April, 1879. R. Q. M., 8 Sept., 1881, to 1 April, 1887. Capt., 22 June, 1889.

PEARSON, EDWARD P. [Born in Penn. Appointed from Penn.]
Priv. Co. A, 25th Penn. Vols., 18 April, 1861. 1st Lieut and Adj. 75th Penn. Vols., 1 May, 1861. Mustered out 24 June, 1861. 1st Lieut. 17th Inf., 14 May, 1861. Capt., 16 Aug., 1862. Bvt. Maj., 3 May, 1863, for gallant and meritorious service in the Battle of Chancellorsville, Va. Bvt. Lieut. Col., 1 Sept., 1864, for gallant and meritorious service during the Atlanta campaign. Maj. 21st Inf., 19 May, 1881. Lieut. Col. 24th Inf., 19 April, 1886. Col. 10th Inf., 14 Oct., 1891. Brig. Gen. Vols., 12 July to 30 Nov., 1898. Retired for over thirty years' service, 16 May, 1899.

PEARSON, ROBT. H. C. [Born in ——. Appointed from Ky.]
Surg.'s Mate 3rd Inf., 18 July, 1817. Resigned 9 Oct., 1817.

PEARSON, SAMUEL B. [Born in Cal. Appointed from Army.]
Priv., Corpl. and Sergt. Troop I, 1st Cav., 14 April, 1897, to 17 Nov., 1899. 2nd Lieut. 9th Cav., 1 Oct., 1899.

PEARSON, WM. H. [Born in Ohio. Appointed from Ohio.]
Priv. Co. C, 56th Ohio Vols., 7 March, 1865, to 6 March, 1866. Post Chap., 1 April, 1886. Retired for disability 2 March, 1898.

PEASE, WALTER B. [Born in Ohio. Appointed from Ohio.]
Capt. 1st Ohio Vols., 16 April to 28 June, 1861. Capt. 17th Inf., 14 May, 1861. Unassigned 25 April, 1870. Discharged 15 Dec., 1870. Bvt. Maj., 13 March, 1865, for gallant and meritorious service in the Battle of Bethesda Church, Va., in 1864, and subsequent Battles of the Army of the Potomac. Bvt. Lieut. Col., 13 March, 1865, for gallant and meritorious service in the Battle of the Wilderness in 1864, and in subsequent Battles of the Army of the Potomac. Died 6 Nov., 1882.

PEASE, WM. B. [Born in Conn. Appointed from Conn.]
Priv. Co. H, 15th Conn. Vols., 11 Aug., 1862. Discharged 31 Dec., 1862. 2nd Lieut. 8th U. S. Col. Troops, 15 Oct., 1863. 1st Lieut., 3 Dec., 1864. Resigned 18 Sept., 1865. 1st Lieut. 11th Inf., 7 March, 1867. Unassigned 14 April, 1869. Ass'd to 9th Inf., 15 Dec., 1870. Reg. Adj., 4 March to 2 April, 1883. Capt., 2 April, 1883. Retired for disability 15 June, 1887.

PEASE, WM. R.* [Born in N. Y. Appointed from N. Y.]
Bvt. 2nd Lieut 10th Inf., 1 July, 1855. 2nd Lieut. 7th Inf., 16 Oct., 1855. 1st Lieut., 23 March, 1861. Capt., 8 June, 1861. Col. 117th N. Y. Vols., 15 Aug., 1862. Bvt. Maj., 4 May, 1863, for gallant and meritorious service in the Siege of Suffolk, Va. Resigned Vol. commission, 26 Aug., 1863. Bvt. Brig. Gen. Vols., 13 March, 1865, for gallant and meritorious service during the war. Bvt. Lieut. Col., 9 Nov., 1865, for faithful and meritorious service connected with the muster out and disbanding of the Vol. armies of the U. S. Retired for disability 28 Aug., 1863. Died 7 June, 1895.

PEAY, JOHN C. [Born in Ky. Appointed from Ark.]
2nd Lieut. Ark. Mtd. Vols., 7 July, 1846, to 7 June, 1847. 2nd Lieut. 2nd Inf., 3 March, 1848. Disbanded 25 July, 1848.

PECK, FREMONT P.* [Born in N. Y. Appointed from N. Y.]
Addl. 2nd Lieut. 4th Art., 12 June, 1887. 2nd Lieut. 1st Art., 14 Aug., 1887. 1st Lieut. Ord., 9 March, 1891. Killed 19 Feb., 1895, at Sandy Hook Proving Ground, N. J., by the bursting of a Hotchkiss rapid-fire gun.

PECK, HENRY C. [Born in Ohio. Appointed from Army.]
Priv. and Sergt. Co. H, 3rd and G, 1st Batt. 14th Inf., 1 Nov., 1861, to 23 July, 1862, 2nd Lieut. 14th Inf., 30 June, 1862. 1st Lieut., 14 May, 1864. Dismissed 25 Aug., 1865.

PECK, JOHN J.* [Born in N. Y. Appointed from N. Y.]
Bvt. 2nd Lieut. 2nd Art., 1 July, 1843. 2nd Lieut., 16 April, 1846. 1st Lieut., 3 March, 1847. Resigned 31 March, 1853. Bvt. Capt., 20 Aug., 1847, for gallant and meritorious conduct in the Battles of Contreras and Churubusco. Bvt. Maj., 8 Sept., 1847, for gallant and meritorious conduct in the Battle of Molino del Rey. Brig. Gen. Vols., 9 Aug., 1861. Maj. Gen. Vols., 4 July, 1862. Mustered out 24 Aug., 1865. Died 21 April, 1878.

PECK, LAFAYETTE.* [Born in Tenn. Appointed from Tenn.]
Bvt. 2nd Lieut. 8th Inf., 1 July, 1857. 2nd Lieut. 7th Inf., 20 April, 1858. Trans. to 8th Inf., 30 Nov., 1858. 1st Lieut., 13 May, 1861. Resigned 23 Aug., 1861. Died 25 March, 1864.

PECK, ROBERT H.* [Born in Cal. Appointed from Cal.]
2nd Lieut. 10th Inf., 15 Feb., 1899.

PECK, WM. G.* [Born in Conn. Appointed from Conn.]
Bvt. 2nd Lieut. Top. Eng., 1 July, 1844. 2nd Lieut., 31 May, 1848. 1st Lieut., 3 March, 1853. Resigned 2 Oct., 1855.

PECK, WM. W. [Born in Canada. Appointed from Ill.]
2nd Lieut. 8th Inf., 23 May, 1861. Capt. 11th Inf., 14 May, 1861. Died 17 March, 1862.

PEEPLES, SAML. [Born in Ireland. Appointed from Army.]
Priv., Corpl., Sergt. and 1st Sergt. Batty L, 4th and D, 5th Art., 19 June, 1856, to 31 Oct., 1862. 2nd Lieut. 5th Art., 22 Oct., 1862. 1st Lieut., 3 April, 1866. Trans. to 19th Inf., 10 May, 1870. Died 10 Sept., 1870. Bvt. 1st Lieut., 3 July, 1863, for gallant and meritorious service at the Battle of Gettysburg, Penn. Bvt. Capt., 19 Sept., 1864, for gallant and meritorious service in the Battle of Winchester, Va.

PEGRAM, GEORGE H.* [Born in Va. Appointed from Va.]
Bvt. 2nd Lieut. 1st Inf., 1 July, 1833. 2nd Lieut., 11 June, 1836. Reg. Adj., 1 Aug., 1836, to 16 Sept., 1838. 1st Lieut., 1 July, 1838. Capt., 5 Aug., 1840. Resigned 30 April, 1841. Died 9 Sept., 1854.

PEGRAM, JOHN.* [Born in Va. Appointed from Va.]
Bvt. 2nd Lieut. 1st Drag., 1 July, 1854. 2nd Lieut. 2nd Drag., 3 March, 1855. 1st Lieut., 28 Feb., 1857. Reg. Adj., 8 Sept., 1857, to 8 Aug., 1859. Resigned 10 May, 1861. Killed 6 Feb., 1865, in Confederate Service.

PEIRCE, AUSTIN L.* [Born in N. Y. Appointed from N. Y.]
2nd Lieut. 4th Cav., 15 June, 1870. Died 30 Nov., 1870.

PEIRCE, CHAS. H. [Born in Mass. Appointed from Army.]
Priv., Artificer and Sergt. Co. A, Eng., 10 June, 1846, to 26 March, 1849, and from 16 June, 1849, to 29 March, 1861. 2nd Lieut. 2nd Art., 23 March, 1861. 1st Lieut. 14 May, 1861. Capt., 11 June, 1864. Mustered out 31 Dec., 1870.

PIERCE, CONSTANTIUS. [Born in Mass. Appointed from Mass.]
3rd Lieut. Corps Art., 18 April, 1818. 2nd Lieut., 20 April, 1818. 1st Lieut., 14 May, 1861. Capt., 11 June, 1864. Mustered out 31 Dec., 1870.

PEIRCE, GEORGE S. [Born in Ohio. Appointed from Iowa.]
Priv. Co. I, 1st Iowa Vols., 14 May to 20 Aug., 1861. Capt. 19th Inf., 19 Feb., 1862. Trans. to 28th Inf., 21 Sept., 1866. Trans. to 19th Inf., 31 March, 1869. Mustered out 31 Dec., 1870. Bvt. Maj., 20 Sept., 1863, for gallant and meritorious service at the Battle of Chickamauga, Ga. Died 8 Jan., 1877.

PEIRCE, LUTHER H. [Born in Maine. Appointed from Maine.]
Capt. A. Q. M., 18 May, 1864. Lieut. Col. Q. M., 15 June, 1864, to 1 Aug., 1865. Resigned 1 Jan., 1868. Bvt. Maj. and Lieut. Col., 13 March, 1865, for faithful and meritorious service during the war.

PEIRCE, WM. S.* [Born in Vt. Appointed from Vt.]
Addl. 2nd Lieut. 1st Art., 11 June, 1888. 2nd Lieut. 2nd Art., 3 Sept., 1888. 1st Lieut. Ord., 15 Jan., 1892. Capt., 7 July, 1898.

PELHAM, PETER. [Born in N. C. Appointed from Mass.]
2nd Lieut. 21st Inf., 12 March, 1812. 1st Lieut., 16 April, 1813. Capt., 28 Feb., 1814. Trans. to 5th Inf., 17 May, 1815. Disbanded 1 June, 1821. Died 10 July, 1826.

PELOUZE, LOUIS H.* [Born in Penn. Appointed from Penn.]
Bvt. 2nd Lieut. 4th Art., 1 July, 1853. 2nd Lieut., 11 Nov., 1853. 1st Lieut., 1 May, 1856. Reg. Adj., 14 Dec., 1857, to 24 April, 1861. Capt. 15th Inf., 14 May, 1861. Maj. A. A. de C., 3 July, 1862. Lieut. Col. A. A. G., 20 Aug., 1862, to 17 Aug., 1863. Maj. A. A. G., 24 March, 1864. Died 2 June, 1878. Bvt. Lieut. Col., 24 Sept., 1864, for gallant and meritorious service at Cedar Mountain, Va. Bvt. Col., 13 March, 1865, for diligent, faithful and meritorious service in the A. G. Dept. during the war. Bvt. Brig. Gen., 13 March, 1865, for most valuable and meritorious service both in the field and in the A. G. Dept. during the war.

PEMBERTON, JOHN C.* [Born in Pa. Appointed from Pa.]
2nd Lieut. 4th Art., 1 July, 1837. 1st Lieut., 19 March, 1842. Capt., 16 Sept., 1850. Resigned 29 April, 1861. Bvt. Capt., 23 Sept., 1846, for gallant conduct at Monterey. Bvt. Maj., 8 Sept., 1847, for gallant and meritorious conduct at Molino del Rey. Died 13 July, 1881.

PENCE, WM. P.* [Born in Ind. Apointed from Ind.]
2nd Lieut. 5th Art., 12 June, 1894. 1st Lieut., 2 March, 1899.

PENDER, WM. D.* [Born in N. C. Appointed from N. C.]
Bvt. 2nd Lieut. 1st Art., 1 July, 1854. 2nd Lieut. 2nd Art., 16 Aug., 1854. Trans. to 2nd Drag., 3 March, 1855. 1st Lieut., 17 May, 1858. Reg. Adj., 31 Aug., 1860, to 31 Jan., 1861. Resigned 21 March, 1861. Died 18 July, 1863, of wounds received at Battle of Gettysburg, Pa., while in Confederate Service.

PENDLETON, EDMUND. [Born in Va. Appointed from Va.]
2nd Lieut. 3rd Art., 24 Oct., 1861. 1st Lieut., 26 Oct., 1861. Dismissed 14 Oct., 1864. Reinstated 12 Nov., 1867, which was revoked 9 July, 1868.

PENDLETON, EDWIN P.* [Born in R. I. Appointed from R. I.]
2nd Lieut. 23rd Inf., 13 June, 1879. 1st Lieut., 24 Jan., 1889. Capt., 26 April, 1898.

PENDLETON, JOHN B. [Born in Ga. Appointed from N. Y.]
2nd Lieut. 7th Inf., 12 July, 1820. Trans. to 2nd Inf., 1 June, 1821. 1st Lieut., 17 Sept., 1828. Died 2 Feb., 1830.

PENDLETON, NATHANIEL G. [Born in N. Y. Appointed from N. Y.]
3rd Lieut. Corps Art., 22 Nov., 1814. Resigned 1 May, 1816. Died 20 Oct., 1821.

PENDLETON, WM. F. [Born in Va. Appointed from Va.]
Ensign 20th Inf., 5 June, 1812. 3rd Lieut., 30 March, 1813. 2nd Lieut., 16 April, 1813. 1st Lieut., 30 May, 1814. Trans. to 4th Inf., 17 May, 1815. Resigned 31 Dec., 1816.

PENDLETON, WM. N.* [Born in Va. Appointed from Va.]
Bvt. 2nd Lieut. 2nd Art., 1 July, 1830. 2nd Lieut 2nd Art., 1 July, 1830. Trans. to 4th Art., 27 Oct., 1832. Resigned 31 Oct., 1833. Died 15 Jan., 1883.

PENFIELD, WALTER G. [Born in Conn. Appointed from Conn.]
Priv. and 1st Sergt. Batty. C, 1st Conn. Art., 7 May to 19 Oct., 1898. 2nd Lieut. 1st Conn. Art., 21 to 29 Oct., 1898. 2nd Lieut. 1st Inf., 10 April, 1899.

PENN, JULIUS A.* [Born in Ill. Appointed from Ohio.]
2nd Lieut. 13th Inf., 1 July, 1886. 1st Lieut. 2nd Inf., 29 July, 1893. Capt. 7th Inf., 2 March, 1899. Graduate of the Infantry and Cavalry School, 1891. Capt. A. Q. M. Vols., 12 May to 30 Nov., 1898. Maj. 34th U. S. Vols., 5 July, 1899, to —.

PENNEY, CHAS. G. [Born in Ohio. Appointed from Ohio.]
Priv. Co. C, 76th Ohio Vols., 2 Sept., 1862. 2nd Lieut. 51st U. S. Col. Troops, 10 July, 1863. 1st Lieut., 8 Jan., 1864. Capt., 20 March, 1864. Mustered out 10 June, 1866. 2nd Lieut. 38th Inf., 28 July, 1866. Bvt. 1st Lieut., 2 March, 1867, for gallant and meritorious service in the Battle of Vicksburg, Miss. Bvt. Capt., 2 March, 1867, for gallant and meritorious service in the capture of Fort Blakely, Ala. 1st Lieut. 38th Inf., 4 Nov., 1867. Reg. Adj., 4 May, 1867, to 11 Nov., 1869. Unassigned 11 Nov., 1869. Ass'd to 6th Inf., 15 Dec., 1870. R. Q. M., 30 Oct., 1871, to 1 March, 1883. Capt., 26 June, 1883. Maj., 8th Inf., 15 Aug., 1898. Trans. to 2nd Inf., 24 Oct., 1898.

PENNEY, SAML. G. [Born in Penn. Appointed from Penn.]
2nd Lieut. 9th Inf., 1 Nov., 1861. 1st Lieut., 31 Dec., 1862. Wholly retired 10 Nov., 1867. Died 27 Feb., 1869.

PENNINGTON, ALEXR. C. M.* [Born in N. J. Appointed from N. J.]
Bvt. 2nd Lieut. 2nd Art., 1 July, 1860. 2nd Lieut., 1 Feb., 1861. 1st Lieut., 14 May, 1861. Bvt. Capt., 9 June, 1863, for gallant and meritorious service in the Battle of Beverly Ford, Va. Bvt. Maj., 3 July, 1863, for gallant and meritorious service during the Gettysburg campaign. Capt. 2nd Art., 30 March, 1864. Col. 3rd N. J. Cav., 1 Oct., 1864. Bvt. Lieut. Col., 19 Oct., 1864, for gallant and meritorious service in the Battle of Cedar Creek, Va. Bvt. Col., 13 March, 1865, for gallant and meritorious service during the war. Bvt. Brig. Gen. Vols., 15 July, 1865, for faithful and meritorious service. Mustered out of Vol. Service, 1 Aug., 1865. Maj. 4th Art., 8 Nov., 1882. Lieut. Col., 28 Nov., 1892. Col. 2nd Art., 29 Oct., 1896. Brig. Gen., 16 Oct., 1899. Brig. Gen. Vols., 4 May, 1898, to 12 April, 1899. Retired, over forty years' service, 17 Oct., 1899.

PENNINGTON, EDWARD R. [Born in N. J. Appointed from N. J.]
Capt. 12th Inf., 4 Oct., 1861. Resigned 20 Dec., 1862.

PENNOCK, WM. T. [Born in N. H. Appointed from Army.]
Priv. Co. G, 1st Drag., 23 Oct., 1857. Corpl., 15 Oct., 1859. Sergt., 24 June, 1860. 1st Sergt., 6 Aug., 1861. Disharged 23 Oct., 1862. 1st Sergt. Co. G, 1st Cav., 23 Oct., 1862. 2nd Lieut. 1st Cav., 17 July, 1862. 1st Lieut., 1 Sept., 1863. Bvt. Capt., 6 May, 1864, for gallant and meritorious service in the Battle of Todd's Tavern, Va. Retired 1 July, 1865. Died 21 Aug., 1887.

PENNYPACKER, GALUSHA. [Born in Penn. Appointed from Penn.]
Q. M. Sergt. 9th Penn. Vols., 22 April, 1861. Discharged 29 July, 1861. Capt. 97th Penn. Vols., 22 Aug., 1861. Maj., 7 Oct., 1861. Lieut. Col., 3 April, 1864. Col., 15 Aug., 1864. Bvt. Brig. Gen. Vols., 15 Jan., 1865, for gallant service in the capture of Fort Fisher. Brig. Gen. Vols., 18 Feb., 1865. Bvt. Maj. Gen. Vols., 13 March, 1865, for gallant and meritorious service during the war. Resigned 30 April, 1866. Col. 34th Inf., 28 July, 1866. Bvt. Brig. Gen., 2 March, 1867, for gallant and meritorious service in the capture of Fort Fisher, N. C. Bvt. Maj. Gen., 2 March, 1867, for gallant and meritorious service during the war. Trans. to 16th Inf., 15 March, 1869. Retired for disability from wounds, 3 July, 1883. Medal of Honor for bravery in the Battle of Fort Fisher, N. C., where he was severely wounded Jan. 15, 1865, while leading the charge over a traverse and planting the colors of one of his regiments thereon, while serving as Col. 97th Pa. Inf., commanding brigade.

PENROSE, CHAS. B. [Born in Penn. Appointed from Penn.]
Capt. C. S. Vols., 3 Aug., 1861. Bvt. Maj. Vols., 13 March, 1865, for meritorious service during the war. Capt. C. S., U. S. A., 13 May, 1865. Bvt. Maj., 13 May, 1865, for faithful and meritorious service in the Sub. Dept. during the war. Bvt. Lieut. Col., 11 Nov., 1867, for faithful and meritorious service during the war. Maj. C. S., 4 Oct., 1889. Died 18 Sept., 1895.

PENROSE, CHARLES W. [Born in Mich. Appointed from N. Y.]
2nd Lieut. 11th Inf., 30 Oct., 1884. 1st Lieut., 13 April, 1889. Capt., 26 April, 1898. Graduate of the Infantry and Cavalry School, 1891.

PENROSE, JAMES W.* [Born in Mo. Appointed from Mo.]
Bvt. 2nd Lieut. 2nd Inf., 1 July, 1828. 2nd Lieut., 1 July, 1828. 1st Lieut., 3 July, 1836. Capt., 18 June, 1846. Died 1 Jan., 1849. Bvt. Maj., 18 April, 1847, for gallant and meritorious conduct in the Battle of Cerro Gordo.

PENROSE, WM. H. [Born in N. Y. Appointed from Mich.]
2nd Lieut. 3rd Inf., 13 April, 1861. 1st Lieut., 14 May, 1861. Reg. Adj., 1 March to 18 April, 1863. Col. 15th N. J. Vols., 18 April, 1863. Bvt. Capt., 3 May, 1863, for gallant and meritorious service in the Battle of Marye's Heights, Va. Bvt. Maj., 2 July, 1863, for gallant and meritorious service in the Battle of Gettysburg, Pa. Capt. 3rd Inf., 11 Sept., 1863. Bvt. Lieut. Col., 5 May, 1864, for gallant and meritorious service in the Battle of the Wilderness, Va. Bvt. Col., 19 Oct., 1864, for gallant and meritorious service in the Battle of Cedar Creek, Va. Bvt. Brig. Gen. Vols., 19 Oct., 1864, for gallant and meritorious service in the Battle of Middletown, Va. Bvt. Brig. Gen., 9 April, 1865, for gallant and meritorious service in the field during the war. Brig. Gen. Vols., 27 June, 1865. Mustered out of Vol. Service, 15 Jan., 1866. Maj. 12th Inf., 31 May, 1883. Lieut. Col. 16th Inf., 21 Aug., 1888. Col. 20th Inf., 28 Nov., 1893. Trans. to 16th Inf., 15 Sept., 1894. Retired by operation of law, 10 March, 1896.

PENTECOST, JOSEPH. [Born in Penn. Appointed from Mo.]
1st Lieut. Mounted Rangers, 30 July, 1832. Disbanded 1 Oct., 1833.

PENTLAND, CHAS. [Born in Penn. Appointed from Penn.]
Ensign 4th Rifles, 16 Sept., 1814. 3rd Lieut., 19 Sept., 1814. Retained in Rifles, 17 May, 1815. 2nd Lieut., 9 Oct., 1817. 1st Lieut., 31 July, 1818. Reg. Adj., Feb., 1818, to April, 1821. Trans. to 6th Inf., 1 June, 1821. Reg. Adj., 1 June, 1821, to 21 July, 1823. Capt., 21 July, 1823. Dismissed 15 Feb., 1826.

PENTLAND, JOSEPH.* [Born in Penn. Appointed from Penn.]
Bvt. 2nd Lieut. 6th Inf., 1 July, 1821. 2nd Lieut., 1 July, 1821. 1st Lieut., 1 June, 1823. Reg. Adj., 1 Nov., 1823, to 17 July, 1825. Capt., 31 Oct., 1827. Dismissed 22 April, 1830. Died, ———, 1833.

PEPOON, SILAS. [Born in Ohio. Appointed from Ore.]
Corpl. Troop A, 1st Ore. Cav., 27 Nov., 1861. 2nd Lieut., 8 April, 1863. 1st Lieut., 29 Nov., 1865. Mustered out 20 Nov., 1866. 2nd Lieut. 10th Cav., 17 Aug., 1867. 1st Lieut., 17 May, 1872. Died 16 Oct., 1874.

PEPPER, GEORGE W. [Born in Ireland. Appointed from Ohio.]
Capt. 80th Ohio Vols., 7 Jan., 1862. Resigned 13 June, 1862. Chap. 80th Ohio Vols., 3 Dec., 1863. Mustered out 30 Aug., 1865. Chap. 40th Inf., 7 Jan., 1867. Unassigned 5 April, 1869. Ass'd to 10th Cav., 21 Dec., 1870. Discharged 31 Dec., 1870.

PERCEVAL, JAMES G. [Born in Conn. Appointed from Conn.]
Asst. Surg., 4 March, 1824. Resigned 1 Aug., 1824. Died 2 March, 1857.

PERIN, GLOVER. [Born in Ohio. Appointed from Ohio.]
1st Lieut. Asst. Surg., 4 Dec., 1847. Capt. Asst. Surg., 4 Dec., 1852. Maj. Surg., 21 May, 1861. Bvt. Lieut. Col., 13 March, 1865, for faithful and meritorious service during the war. Lieut. Col. Surg., 28 April, 1877. Col. Asst. Surg. Gen., 2 July, 1884. Retired by operation of law, 17 Nov., 1887. Died 15 Dec., 1890.

PERKINS, BENJAMIN R. [Born in Conn. Appointed from Conn.]
1st Lieut. 12th Inf., 14 May, 1861. Capt., 17 July, 1863. Mustered out 1 Jan., 1871. Bvt. Capt., 9 Aug., 1862, for gallant and meritorious service at the Battle of Cedar Mountain, Va. Bvt. Maj., 2 July, 1863, for gallant and meritorious service at the Battle of Gettysburg, Pa. Died 7 Feb., 1871.

PERKINS, DAVID.* [Born in Penn. Appointed from Penn.]
Bvt. 2nd Lieut. Inf., 1 July, 1827. 2nd Lieut. 5th Inf., 1 July, 1827. 1st Lieut. 1st Drag., 4 March, 1833. Capt., 4 Nov., 1833. Resigned 2 Feb., 1839. Died 18 Dec., 1848.

PERKINS, DELAVAN D.* [Born in N. Y. Appointed from N. Y.]
Bvt. 2nd Lieut. 2nd Art., 1 July, 1849. 2nd Lieut. 4th Art., 31 March, 1850. 1st Lieut., 27 May, 1854. Capt., 17 May, 1861. Maj. A. A. de C., 18 Nov., 1861.

Lieut. Col. A. I. G., 20 Aug., 1862, to 11 April, 1863. Maj. A. A. G., 1 June, 1864. Died 6 Jan., 1865.

PERKINS, EDWARD W. [Born in Mich. Appointed from N. Y.]
2nd Lieut. 8th Inf., 9 July, 1898. 1st Lieut. 1st Inf., 14 Aug., 1899.

PERKINS, FREDERICK.* [Born in Maine. Appointed from Maine.]
2nd Lieut. 5th Inf., 13 June, 1883. 1st Lieut. 16th Inf., 24 Feb., 1891. Trans. to 8th Inf., 20 July, 1891. Capt. of Inf., 26 July, 1898. Ass'd to 8th Inf., 1 Jan., 1899.

PERKINS, JOHN N. [Born in Tenn. Appointed from Ala.]
2nd Lieut. Inf., 5 March, 1847; 13th Inf., 9 April, 1847. 1st Lieut., 31 Dec., 1847. Disbanded 15 July, 1848. 1st Lieut. 1st Cav., 3 March, 1855. Cashiered 4 May, 1859.

PERKINS, JOSEPH W. [Born in Tenn. Appointed from Tenn.]
Capt. 14th Inf., 9 April, 1847. Died 22 Oct., 1847.

PERKINS, ROLLIN. [Born in Vt. Appointed from Mass.]
Corpl. Co. K, 6th Mass Vols., 30 Aug., 1862. Discharged 3 June, 1863. Priv. and Corpl. Co. B, 6th Mass. Vols., 7 July, 1864, to 27 Oct., 1864. 1st Lieut. 24th U. S. Col. Troops, 11 April, 1865. Mustered out 30 Sept., 1865. 2nd Lieut. 8th Inf., 23 Feb., 1866. 1st Lieut., 28 July, 1866. Retired 10 June, 1868.

PERKINS, SAM'L. [Born in Conn. Appointed from D. C.]
Ensign 1st Inf., 9 Dec., 1807. 2nd Lieut., 30 Nov., 1808. 1st Lieut., 31 Dec., 1812. Capt. Asst. Dep. Q. M. Gen., 25 April, 1813. Disbanded 15 June, 1815. Mil. Storekeeper, 9 March, 1819. Died 30 Dec., 1837.

PERLEY, HARRY O. [Born in Maine. Appointed from Mich.]
1st Lieut. Asst. Surg., 5 Aug., 1876. Capt. Asst. Surg., 5 Aug., 1881. Maj. Surg., 7 Dec., 1895.

PERRAULT, PAUL H. [Born in Penn. Appointed from Va.]
Maj. Top. Eng., 12 April, 1813. Disbanded 15 June, 1815. Maj. Top. Eng., 17 Feb., 1817. Died 28 Jan., 1834. Bvt. Lieut. Col., 17 Feb., 1827, for ten years' faithful service in one grade.

PERRIN, ABNER M. [Born in S. C. Appointed from N. C.]
2nd Lieut. of Inf., 5 March, 1847; 12th Inf., 9 April, 1847. 1st Lieut., 31 Dec., 1847. Disbanded 25 July, 1848. Killed 12 May, 1864, in Confederate Service.

PERRIN, JAMES M. [Born in S. C. Appointed from S. C.]
2nd Lieut. 12th Inf., 3 March, 1848. Disbanded 25 July, 1848.

PERRINE, HENRY A. [Born in N. J. Appointed from N. J.]
Priv. and Sergt. Co. G, 10th Inf., 3 March, 1847, to 3 March, 1848. 2nd Lieut. 10th Inf., 3 March, 1848. Disbanded 23 Aug., 1848. Capt. 10th N. J. Vols., 12 Oct., 1861. Maj., 24 July, 1864. Discharged 29 March, 1865.

PERRINE, HENRY P.* [Born in N. J. Appointed from N. J.]
2nd Lieut. 6th Cav., 15 June, 1869. 1st Lieut., 20 June, 1872. Capt., 15 Jan., 1884. Retired for disability, 1 July, 1891.

PERRY, ALEXR. J.* [Born in Conn. Appointed from Conn.]
Bvt. 2nd Lieut. 2nd Art., 1 July, 1851. 2nd Lieut., 1 July, 1852. 1st Lieut., 27 Sept., 1854. Capt. A. Q. M., 17 May, 1861. Lieut. Col. Q. M. (Act 17 July, 1862), 20 Aug., 1862, to 15 Jan., 1863. Col. Q. M. (Act 4 July, 1864), 2 Aug., 1864. Bvt. Maj., Lieut. Col. and Col., 13 March, 1865, for faithful and meritorious service during the war. Bvt. Brig. Gen., 13 March, 1865, for faithful and meritorious service in the Q. M. Dept. during the war. Maj. Q. M., 29 July, 1866. Relieved as Col. Q. M. (Act 4 July, 1864), 1 Jan., 1867. Lieut. Col. D. Q. M. G., 3 March, 1875. Col. Asst. Q. M. G., 31 Aug., 1883. Retired by operation of law, 11 Dec., 1892.

PERRY, ALEXANDER W. [Born in D. C. Appointed from N. Y.]
Addl. 2nd Lieut. 1st Inf., 11 June, 1888. 2nd Lieut. 10th Inf., 21 Aug., 1888. Trans. to 9th Cav., 11 Feb., 1889. 1st Lieut. 3rd Cav., 8 June, 1896. Trans. to 9th Cav., 9 July, 1896. Capt. A. Q. M. Vols., 3 June, 1898.

PERRY, CHRISTOPHER R.* [Born in R. I. Appointed from R. I.]
Bvt. 2nd Lieut. 8th Inf., 1 July, 1842. 2nd Lieut. 4th Inf., 29 Nov., 1844. 1st Lieut. 16 Feb., 1847. Died 8 Oct., 1848.

PERRY, DAVID. [Born in Conn. Appointed from N. J.]
2nd Lieut. 1st Cav., 24 March, 1862. 1st Lieut., 27 July, 1862. Capt., 12 Nov., 1864. Bvt. Maj., 1 April, 1865, for gallant and meritorious service in the Battle of Five Forks, Va. Bvt. Lieut. Col., 26 Dec., 1866, for gallantry in an engagement with a large band of Indians on the Owyhee River, Idaho, 26 Dec., 1866. Bvt. Col., 5 April, 1868, or gallantry in an engagement with a large band of Indians on the Malheur River, Ore., 5 April, 1868. Maj. 6th Cav., 29 April, 1879. Lieut. Col. 10th Cav., 20 April, 1891. Col. 9th Cav., 11 Dec., 1896. Retired for disability, 5 July, 1898.

PERRY, DAVID. [Born in Mass. Appointed from Mass.]
2nd Lieut. 9th Inf., 12 March, 1812. 1st Lieut., 30 June, 1813. Capt., 1 Sept., 1814. Trans. to 5th Inf., 17 May, 1815. Resigned 1 April, 1822.

PERRY, FRANK W. [Born in Ohio. Appointed from Army.]
Priv. and Sergt. Maj. 14th Inf., 1 Nov., 1861, to 19 June, 1862. 2nd Lieut. 14th Inf., 9 June, 1862. 1st Lieut., 7 Feb., 1863. Capt., 9 July, 1866. Trans. to 32nd Inf., 21 Sept., 1866. Unassigned 19 April, 1869. Ass'd to 24th Inf., 18 Dec., 1869. Resigned 1 Feb., 1873. Bvt. Capt., 1 Aug., 1864, for gallant service at the Battle of the Wilderness, Va. Bvt. Maj., 18 Aug., 1864, for gallant service at the Battle on the Weldon Railroad, Va. Died 18 June, 1876.

PERRY, HOWARD R.* [Born in Ill. Appointed from Ill.]
Cadet at Mil. Acad., 1 Sept., 1886, to 17 June, 1887. Reappointed 15 June, 1889. 2nd Lieut. 17th Inf., 12 June, 1893. 1st Lieut., 26 April, 1898. Trans. to 7th Inf., 20 Sept., 1899.

PERRY, JOHN ADAMS. [Born in Kan. Appointed from Conn.]
2nd Lieut. 10th Inf., 10 Oct., 1883. 1st Lieut. 8th Inf., 9 March, 1891. Capt. of Inf., 11 Aug., 1898. Ass'd to 13th Inf., 1 Jan., 1899. Capt. A. Q. M. Vols., 3 June, 1898, declined. Graduate of the Infantry and Cavalry School, 1895.

PERRY, JOHN S. [Born in Ohio. Appointed from Ohio.]
Capt. of Inf., 8 March, 1847; 15th Inf., 9 April, 1847. Disbanded 4 Aug., 1848.

PERRY, ROBT. C. [Born in N. Y. Appointed from N. Y.]
Sergt. Co. I, 75th N. Y. Vols., 2 Nov., 1861. 1st Lieut. 111th N. Y. Vols., 20 Aug., 1862. Capt., 1 May, 1863. Mustered out 9 Nov., 1864. Capt. Vet. Res. Corps, 30 Nov., 1864. Bvt. Maj. and Lieut. Col. Vols., 13 March, 1865, for gallant and meritorious service during the war. Mustered out 20 July, 1866. 1st Lieut. 42nd Inf., 22 Jan., 1867. Bvt. Capt., 2 March, 1867, for gallant and meritorious service in the Battle of the Wilderness, Va. Bvt. Maj., 2 March, 1867, for gallant and meritorious service in the Battle of Spottsylvania, Va. Unassigned 22 April, 1869. Retired with rank of Lieut. Col., 31 Dec., 1870. Died 1 Oct., 1884.

PERSHING, JOHN J.* [Born in Mo. Appointed from Mo.]
2nd Lieut. 6th Cav., 1 July, 1886. 1st Lieut. 10th Cav., 20 Oct., 1892. Maj. Chief Ord. Off. Vols., 18 Aug., 1898, to 12 May, 1899. Maj. A. A. G. Vols., 6 June, 1899.

PERSHING, WARD B. [Born in Mo. Appointed from Ill.]
2nd Lieut. 6th Art., 9 July, 1898. Trans. to 4th Cav., 3 April, 1899.

PESHINE, JOHN H. H. [Born in N. J. Appointed from N. J.]
2nd Lieut. 31st U. S. Col. Troops, 14 Dec., 1864. Mustered out 7 Nov., 1865. 2nd Lieut. 13th Inf., 1 Oct., 1873. 1st Lieut., 7 May, 1882. Capt., 5 July, 1895. Graduate of the Artillery School, 1878.

PETERNELL, CHAS. [Born in Germany. Appointed from Ohio.]
2nd Lieut. of Inf., 8 March, 1847; 15th Inf., 9 April, 1847. 1st Lieut., 20 Aug., 1847. Disbanded 4 Aug., 1848. Bvt. Capt., 13 Sept., 1847., for gallant and meritorious conduct at the Battle of Chapultepec.

PETERS, DE WITT C. [Born in N. Y. Appointed from N. Y.]
Asst. Surg., 15 Aug., 1854. Resigned 1 Oct., 1856. Asst. Surg., 23 June, 1860. Maj. Surg., 28 July, 1866. Died 22 April, 1876. Bvt. Maj. and Lieut. Col., 13 March, 1865, for faithful and meritorious service during the war.

PETERS, GEORGE P.* [Born in N. H. Appointed from N. H.]
Ensign 4th Inf., 18 June, 1808. 2nd Lieut., 3 June, 1809. 1st Lieut., 29 Oct., 1811. Reg. P. M., 14 Dec., 1812, to 29 Aug., 1813. Maj. A. I. G., 29 Aug., 1813, to 28 Sept., 1814. Maj. A. A. G., 28 Sept., 1814, to 15 June, 1815. Capt. 4th Inf., 21 Feb., 1814. Trans. to Corps Art., 17 May, 1815. Died 28 Nov., 1819.

PETERSON, HAMILTON C. [Born in Ohio. Appointed from Ill.]
Priv. Co. G, 64th Ill. Vols., 1 March, 1864, to 26 May, 1865. 2nd Lieut. 17th Inf., 23 Feb., 1866. Trans. to 26th Inf., 21 Sept., 1866. 1st Lieut., 7 March, 1827. Unassigned 19 May, 1869. Dismissed 16 April, 1870.

PETERSON, JOHN C. [Born in N. Y. Appointed from N. Y.]
Cadet Mil. Acad., 1 July, 1848, to 23 June, 1849. Capt. 15th Inf., 5 Aug., 1861. Resigned 11 Aug., 1864.

PETERSON, JOHN P. [Born in Sweden. Appointed from Ill.
Priv. Co. D, 15th Inf., 20 Oct., 1862. Discharged 20 Oct., 1865. 2nd Lieut. 23rd Inf., 3 May, 1867. Resigned 19 Feb., 1870.

PETERSON, MATT R.* [Born in N. C. Appointed from N. C.]
2nd Lieut. 10th Inf., 12 June, 1889. Trans. to 13th Inf., 8 June, 1895. Trans. to 6th Inf., 10 Sept., 1895. 1st Lieut. 7th Inf., 27 Aug., 1896. Trans. to 6th Inf., 23 Nov., 1896. Capt. C. S., 3 Oct., 1898. Maj. 161st Ind. Vols., 15 July, 1898. Discharged 29 Nov., 1898. Graduate of the Infantry and Cavalry School, 1895.

PETHERBRIDGE, CHAS. W. [Born in Md. Appointed from Va.]
Post Chap., 23 Oct., 1873. Resigned 24 Oct., 1874.

PETHERBRIDGE, JOHN B. [Born in N. J. Appointed from N. Y.]
Surg. 65th N. Y. Vols., 11 June, 1861, to 28 June, 1864. Asst. Surg. U. S. V., 18 May, 1864. Surg. Vols., 18 March, 1865. Bvt. Lieut. Col. Vols., 1 June, 1865, for faithful and meritorious service. Mustered out 24 June, 1865. Asst. Surg., 28 Feb., 1866. Died 23 Feb., 1867.

PETIGRU, CHAS.* [Born in S. C. Appointed from S. C.]
Bvt. 2nd Lieut. 4th Art., 1 July, 1829. 2nd Lieut., 1 July, 1829. Died 6 Oct., 1835.

PETIGRU, DANIEL. [Born in S. C. Appointed from S. C.]
1st Lieut. of Inf., 2 March, 1847; 3rd Drag., 9 April, 1847. Capt., 23 Dec., 1847. Disbanded 20 July, 1848.

PETRIKIN, REUBEN W.* [Born in Penn. Appointed at Large.]
2nd Lieut. 2nd Art., 23 June, 1865. Trans. to 1st Art., 28 Sept., 1865. 1st Lieut., 1 Feb., 1866. Trans. to Eng., 2 June, 1866. Resigned 1 Feb., 1869. Killed 19 Oct., 1882, by Indians in Mexico.

PETTEE, LEMUEL. [Born in Mass. Appointed from Army.]
Priv. and Sergt. Co. B, 11th Inf., 25 Oct., 1861, to 6 Oct., 1862. 2nd Lieut. 11th Inf., 25 Sept., 1862. 1st Lieut., 26 April, 1864. Trans. to 29th Inf., 21 Sept., 1866. Capt., 2 Nov., 1867. Unassigned 25 April, 1869. Ass'd to 25th Inf., 1 Jan., 1871. Resigned 30 Nov., 1873. Bvt. 1st Lieut., 2 July, 1863, for gallant and meritorious service at the Battle of Gettysburg, Pa. Bvt. Capt., 13 March, 1865, for gallant and meritorious service at the Battle of Gettysburg, Pa.

PETTES, WM. H.* [Born in Vt. Appointed from Vt.]
Bvt. 2nd Lieut. 1st Art., 1 July, 1832. 2nd Lieut., 30 Sept., 1833. Resigned 11 Sept., 1836. Lieut. Col. 50th N. Y. Eng., 18 Sept., 1861. Col., 3 June, 1863. Mustered out 14 June, 1865.

PETTIT, CHAS. H. [Born in D. C. Appointed from D. C.]
2nd Lieut. 2nd Cav., 7 Aug., 1867. Resigned 10 Feb., 1869.

PETTIT, COLVILLE M.* [Born in N. Y. Appointed from N. Y.]
2nd Lieut. 8th Inf., 1 July, 1886. Died 30 Dec., 1890.

PETTIT, JAMES S.* [Born in Ohio. Appointed from Ohio.]
2nd Lieut. 1st Inf., 14 June, 1878. 1st Lieut., 15 Sept., 1882. Capt. 1st Inf., 22 Oct., 1891. Maj. A. A. G. Vols., 12 May, 1898, declined. Col. 4th U. S. Vols., 20 May, 1898, to 8 June, 1899. Col. 31st U. S. Vols., 5 July, 1899.

PETTIT, SILAS W. [Born in Penn. Appointed from Penn.]
1st Lieut. 16th Inf., 14 May, 1861. Rejected by Senate, 5 Aug., 1861. 2nd Lieut.

15th Inf., 20 Feb., 1862. Resigned 14 June, 1862. Capt. 213th Pa. Vols., 1 March, 1865. Mustered out 18 Nov., 1865.

PEW, WM. W. [Born in Penn. Appointed from Penn.]
2nd Lieut. 1st Inf., 5 Oct., 1838. Died 12 June, 1839.

PEYCHAUD, ANATOLE. [Born in La. Appointed from La.]
Capt. 44th Inf., 11 March, 1814. Trans. to 1st. Inf., 17 May, 1815. Resigned 30 March, 1819.

PEYTON, EPHRAIM G.* [Born in Miss. Appointed from Miss.]
2nd Lieut. 6th Inf., 15 Feb., 1899.

PEYTON, JOHN B. [Born in Md. Appointed from Md.]
2nd Lieut. 3rd Inf., 1 Oct., 1838. Dropped 18 Nov., 1840.

PEYTON, JOHN S. [Born in Va. Appointed from Va.]
1st Lieut. 2nd Art., 12 March, 1812. Capt., 15 Dec., 1813. Trans. to Corps Art., 12 May, 1814. Trans. to Light Art., 17 May, 1815. Resigned 1 April, 1816.

PEYTON, RICHARD H.* [Born in Va. Appointed from Va.]
Bvt. 2nd Lieut. 2nd Art., 1 July, 1831. 2nd Lieut., 1 July, 1831. 1st Lieut., 28 June, 1836. Capt. A. Q. M., 7 July, 1838. Died 11 Nov., 1839.

PHELPS, ELBERT. [Born in Vt. Appointed from Vt.]
1st Lieut. 19th Inf., 14 May, 1861. Capt., 16 March, 1864. Resigned 18 March, 1865.

PHELPS, FRED'K. E.* [Born in Ohio. Appointed from Ohio.]
2nd Lieut. 8th Cav., 15 June, 1870. 1st Lieut., 20 March, 1879. Capt., 28 Sept., 1889. Retired for disability, 20 April, 1891.

PHELPS, JOHN E. [Born in Mo. Appointed from Mo.]
2nd Lieut. 3rd Cav., 11 June, 1862. 1st Lieut., 1 Oct., 1863. Col. 2nd Ark. Cav., 18 March, 1864. Mustered out of Vol. Service, 20 Aug., 1865. Resigned 28 Sept., 1865. Bvt. Capt., 13 March, 1865, for gallant and meritorious service during the fall campaign of 1864, in Southwestern Missouri. Bvt. Maj. and Lieut. Col., 13 March, 1865, for gallant and meritorious service during the war, and Brig. Gen. Vols., 13 March, 1865, for gallant and meritorious service during the campaign of 1864 in Southwestern Mo.

PHELPS, JOHN W.* [Born in Vt. Appointed from Vt.]
Bvt. 2nd Lieut. 4th Art., 1 July, 1836. 2nd Lieut., 28 July, 1836. 1st Lieut., 7 July, 1838. Capt., 31 March, 1850. Resigned 2 Nov., 1859. Col. 1st Vt. Vols., 9 May, 1861. Brig. Gen. Vols., 17 May, 1861. Resigned 21 Aug., 1862. Died 2 Feb., 1885.

PHELPS, OLIVER. [Born in Va. Appointed from W. Va.]
Corpl. Co. E, 4th W. Va. Vols., 20 July, 1861. 2nd Lieut. 9th W. Va. Vols., 28 Feb., 1862. 1st Lieut., 2 May, 1862. Capt., 2 Feb., 1864. Trans. to 1st W. Va. Vols., 9 Nov., 1864. Mustered out 21 July, 1865. 2nd Lieut. 19th Inf., 23 Feb., 1866. 1st Lieut., 23 Feb., 1866. Trans. to 37th Inf., 21 Sept., 1866. Trans. to 5th Inf., 19 May, 1869. Unassigned 8 June, 1869. Ass'd to 7th Inf., 1 Jan., 1871. Resigned 7 March, 1871.

PHIFER, CHAS. W. [Born in Tenn. Appointed from Miss.]
2nd Lieut. 2nd Cav., 3 March, 1855. 1st Lieut., 22 Feb., 1861. Resigned 1 April, 1861.

PHILBRICK, JOHN. [Born in Vt. Appointed from Vt.]
3rd Lieut. Corps Art., 18 April, 1818. 2nd Lieut., 20 April, 1818. Trans. to 8th Inf., — May, 1818. 1st Lieut. 8th Inf., 11 April, 1819. Trans. to 7th Inf., 1 June, 1821. Capt., 1 May, 1824. Resigned 30 June, 1828.

PHILBRICK, JOHN H.* [Born in Maine. Appointed from Maine.]
2nd Lieut. 11th Inf., 15 June, 1877. 1st Lieut., 24 April, 1886. Reg. Adj., 1 Dec., 1889, to 24 July, 1890. Died 24 July, 1890.

PHILLIPS, ASHER. [Born in ——. Appointed from Ohio.]
Ensign 19th Inf., 12 March, 1812. 2nd Lieut., 20 May, 1813. Trans. to 17th Inf., 12 May, 1814. Trans. to 3rd Inf., 17 May, 1815. 1st Lieut., 17 May, 1816. Reg. P. M., 26 Aug., 1815, to 1 June, 1821. Maj. P. M., 26 Aug., 1815. Resigned 17 Jan., 1834. Died 20 May, 1843.

PHILLIPS, CHAS. B.* [Born in Mass. Appointed from Mass.]
1st Lieut. Eng., 13 June, 1864. Bvt. Capt., 9 April, 1865, for faithful and meritorious service during the recent operations resulting in the fall of Richmond, Va., and the surrender of the insurgent army under Gen. Robert E. Lee. Capt. Eng., 7 March, 1867. Died 14 June, 1881.

PHILLIPS, CHARLES L.* [Born in Ill. Appointed from Maine.]
Addl. 2nd Lieut. 4th Art., 11 June, 1881. 2nd Lieut., 1 July, 1881. 1st Lieut., 31 Dec., 1887. Capt., 2 March, 1899. Graduate of the Artillery School, 1890.

PHILLIPS, EDWIN D.* [Born in N. Y. Appointed from Mich.]
Bvt. 2nd Lieut. 1st Inf., 1 July, 1852. 2nd Lieut., 1 June, 1853. 1st Lieut., 31 Oct., 1856. Reg. Adj., 1 Aug., 1860, to 14 May, 1861. Capt., 14 May, 1861. Died 26 Nov., 1864.

PHILLIPS, ELIAS.* [Born in N. J. Appointed from N. J.]
2nd Lieut. 4th Inf., 1 July, 1823. 1st Lieut., 30 March, 1831. Resigned 31 Jan., 1836. Died 11 Sept., 1856.

PHILLIPS, ERVIN L. [Born in N. Y. Appointed from N. Y.]
2nd Lieut. 6th Cav., 1 Aug., 1891. 1st Lieut. 3rd Cav., 9 July, 1898. Graduate of the Infantry and Cavalry School, 1895.

PHILLIPS, HENRY J. [Born in England. Appointed from N. Y.]
Maj. Surg. 53rd N. Y. Vols., 17 Oct., 1861. Mustered out 12 March, 1862. Maj. Surg. 102nd N. Y. Vols., 19 May, 1862. Resigned 28 May, 1862. 1st Lieut. Asst. Surg., 30 March, 1861. Capt. Asst. Surg., 28 Oct., 1866. Died 10 Oct., 1879.

PHILLIPS, JOHN L. [Born in N. C. Appointed from N. C.]
Asst. Surg., 3 Dec., 1883. Capt. Asst. Surg., 3 Dec., 1888. Maj. Brig. Surg. Vols., 4 June, 1898. Maj. Chief. Surg. Vols., 30 Jan., 1899, to 30 April, 1899.

PHILLIPS, JOHN W. [Born in S. C. Appointed from S. C.]
2nd Lieut. Ord., 2 Dec., 1815. 1st Lieut., 4 Aug., 1819. Trans. to 4th Art., 1 June, 1821. Trans. to 3rd Art., 3 Oct., 1821. Resigned 31 May, 1829.

PHILLIPS, JOHN W. L. [Born in N. Y. Appointed from Army.]
Priv., Corpl. and Sergt. Troop A, 7th Cav., 6 Feb., 1891, to 11 Nov., 1894. 2nd Lieut. 11th Inf., 31 Oct., 1894. 1st Lieut., 26 April, 1898.

PHILLIPS, JOSEPH A.* [Born in N. J. Appointed from N. J.]
2nd Lieut. 7th Inf., 1 July, 1823. 1st Lieut., 30 June, 1828. Reg. Adj., 16 May, 1825, to 31 May, 1830. Capt., 4 May, 1835. Trans. to 8th Inf., 7 July, 1838. Resigned 30 Sept., 1840. Died 4 Jan., 1846.

PHILLIPS, WILLIAM A.* [Born in Texas. Appointed from Tenn.]
2nd Lieut. 22nd Inf., 12 June, 1889. 1st Lieut. 2nd Inf., 27 Aug., 1896. Capt. 10th Inf., 15 July, 1899.

PHIPPS, FRANK H.* [Born in Mass. Appointed from Penn.]
1st Lieut. Ord., 11 June, 1863. Bvt. Capt., 13 March, 1865, for faithful and meritorious service in the Ord. Dept. Capt. Ord., 23 June, 1874. Maj., 4 Dec., 1882. Lieut. Col., 7 July, 1898.

PHISTER, NAT. P.* [Born in Ky. Appointed from Ky.]
Addl. 2nd Lieut. 1st Inf., 14 June, 1878. 2nd Lieut., 28 June, 1878. 1st Lieut., 14 Dec., 1883. Capt. 1st Inf., 4 Nov., 1896. Graduate of the Infantry and Cavalry School, 1893.

PHISTERER, FRED'K. [Born in Germany. Appointed from Army.]
Priv., Corpl. and Sergt. Batty A, 3rd Art., 6 Dec., 1855, to 6 Dec., 1860. Priv. and Sergt. Maj. 18th Inf., 31 July to 4 Nov., 1861. 2nd Lieut. 18th Inf., 30 Oct., 1861. 1st Lieut., 27 Feb., 1862. Reg. Adj., 11 Nov., 1864, to 15 Feb., 1866. Capt., 15 Feb., 1866. Trans. to 36th Inf., 21 Sept., 1866. Trans. to 7th Inf., 19 May, 1869. Unassigned 7 Jan., 1870. Discharged 4 Aug., 1870. Bvt. Capt., 14 May, 1864, for gallant and meritorious service at the Battles of Mission Ridge, Tenn., and Resaca, Ga.

PHISTERER, FREDERICK W. [Born in Ohio. Appointed from N. Y.]
2nd Lieut. 1st Art., 9 July, 1898.

PIATT, BENJ. McC. [Born in Ky. Appointed from Kan.]
Capt. A. A. G. Vols., 16 May, 1862. Bvt. Maj. Vols., 2 March, 1865. Maj. A. A. G. Vols., 13 March, 1865. Mustered out 25 Nov., 1865. 2nd Lieut. 44th Inf., 2 July, 1867. Bvt. 1st Lieut., 2 July, 1867, for gallant and meritorious service in the Battle of Chancellorsville, Va. Bvt. Capt., 2 July, 1867, for gallant and meritorious service in the Battle of Gettysburg, Pa. Unassigned 27 May, 1869. Retired 37 Dec., 1870. Died 17 April, 1885.

PIATT, JOHN H. [Born in Conn. Appointed from Ohio.]
1st Lieut. 1st Batt. 1st Ohio Cav., 11 Oct., 1861. Mustered out 13 June, 1862. Capt. A. A. de C., 11 July, 1862. Bvt. Maj. Vols., 13 March, 1865, for gallant and meritorious service. Mustered out 1 Sept., 1866. Capt. 31st Inf., 28 July, 1866. Resigned 13 May, 1869.

PIATT, WM. [Born in N. J. Appointed from N. J.]
2nd Lieut. 11th Inf., 2 March, 1799. Retained 16 Feb., 1801, in 3rd Inf. Trans. to 2nd Inf., 15 April, 1802. 1st Lieut., 16 June, 1804. Capt., 17 Feb., 1809. Col. Q. M. G., 23 June, 1813, to 30 June, 1814. Maj. 34th Inf., 9 March, 1814. Disbanded 15 June, 1815. Maj. P. M., 20 May, 1830. Died 16 Aug., 1834. Bvt. Lieut. Col., 23 Dec., 1814, for gallant conduct at the Siege of New Orleans.

PICHEVIN, ANTHONY. [Born in France. Appointed from Army.]
Priv. and Corpl. 2nd Art. and Sergt. and Q. M. Sergt. Corps Art., 7 Dec., 1812, to 1 Oct., 1818. 2nd Lieut. Corps Art., 13 Aug., 1819. Trans. to 1st Art., 1 June, 1821. Resigned 1 April, 1822. Died in 1838.

PICKELL, JOHN.* [Born in Penn. Appointed from N. Y.]
Bvt. 2nd Lieut. 4th Art., 1 July, 1822. 2nd Lieut., 1 July, 1822. 1st Lieut., 28 May, 1831. Reg. Adj., 15 Oct., 1836, to 5 Aug., 1838. Resigned 5 Aug., 1838. Col. 13th N. Y. Vols., 19 Aug., 1861. Resigned 4 March, 1862. Died 23 Jan., 1865.

PICKERING, ABNER.* [Born in Ind. Appointed from Ind.]
2nd Lieut. 2nd Inf., 14 June, 1878. 1st Lieut., 27 Feb., 1887. Capt., 8 Aug., 1897.

PICKERING, JAMES N.* [Born in Ohio. Appointed from Ark.]
Addl. 2nd Lieut. 10th Inf., 12 June, 1896. 2nd Lieut. 1st Inf., 24 Oct., 1896. 1st Lieut. of Inf., 15 Dec., 1898. Ass'd to 1st Inf., 1 Jan., 1899.

PICKETT, EUGENE. [Born in Mass. Appointed from N. Y.]
Sergt. Co. A, 83rd N. Y. Vols., 27 May, 1861. 1st Sergt., 25 July, 1861. 2nd Lieut., 6 Aug., 1861. 1st Lieut., 23 Feb., 1862. Resigned 31 Dec., 1862. Capt. Vet. Res. Corps., 18 March, 1864. Bvt. Maj. and Lieut. Col. Vols., for distinguished gallantry at the Battles of 2nd Bull Run, Va., and Antietam, Md. Mustered out 22 Aug., 1867. 2nd Lieut. 12th Inf., 9 Aug., 1867. Unassigned 9 April, 1869. Ass'd to 22nd Inf., 3 Aug., 1870. Discharged 31 Dec., 1870. Died 10 Oct., 1884.

PICKETT, GEORGE B. [Born in Ill. Appointed from Ky.]
Priv. Co. A, 37th Ill. Vols., 27 May, 1862, to 6 March, 1863. Priv. Co. H, 132nd Ill. Vols., 8 July to 17 Oct., 1864. 2nd Lieut. 16th Inf., 20 July, 1866. Trans. to 34th Inf., 21 Sept., 1866. Trans. to 16th Inf., 12 April, 1869. 1st Lieut., 24 Sept., 1871. Resigned 6 Aug., 1873.

PICKETT, GEORGE E.* [Born in Va. Appointed from Ill.]
Bvt. 2nd Lieut. 8th Inf., 1 July, 1846. 2nd Lieut. 2nd Inf., 3 March, 1847. Trans. to 7th Inf., 13 July, 1847. Trans. to 8th Inf., 18 July, 1847. 1st Lieut., 28 June, 1849. Capt. 9th Inf., 3 March, 1855. Resigned 25 June, 1861. Bvt. 1st Lieut., 20 Aug., 1847, for gallant and meritorious conduct at Contreras and Churubusco. Bvt. Capt., 13 Sept., 1847, for gallant conduct at Chapultepec. Died 30 July, 1875.

PICKETT, JAMES C. [Born in —. Appointed from Ohio.]
3rd Lieut. 2nd Art., 4 Aug., 1813. 2nd Lieut., 19 April, 1814. Trans. to Corps Art., 12 May, 1814. Disbanded 15 June, 1815. Capt. Asst. Dep. Q. M. G., 16 June, 1818. Disbanded 1 June, 1821. Died 10 July, 1872.

PICTON, JOHN M. W.* [Born in N. J. Appointed from N. Y.]
Bvt. 2nd Lieut. 2nd Art., 1 July, 1824. 2nd Lieut., 1 July, 1824. Resigned 1 March, 1832. Died 28 Oct., 1859.

PICTON, THOS. [Born in Wales. Appointed from N. J.]
Chap. Mil. Acad., 23 July, 1818. Resigned 1 Jan., 1825. Died 6 Feb., 1861.

PIERCE, BENJAMIN K. [Born in N. H. Appointed from N. H.]
1st Lieut. 3rd Art., 12 March, 1812. Capt., 1 Oct., 1813. Trans. to Corps Art., 12 May, 1814. Trans. to 4th Art., 1 June, 1821. Maj. 1st Art., 11 June, 1836. Lieut. Col. 1st Art., 19 March, 1842. Died 1 April, 1850. Bvt. Maj., 1 Oct., 1823, for ten years' faithful service in one grade. Bvt. Lieut. Col., 21 Aug., 1836, for distinguished service in the affair at Fort Drane.

PIERCE, CHARLES C. [Born in N. J. Appointed from Ill.]
Chap. 9th Cav., 12 Dec., 1882. Resigned 30 June, 1884. Appointed Post. Chap., 12 May, 1888.

PIERCE, FRANCIS E. [Born in N. Y. Appointed from N. Y.]
Capt. 108th N. Y. Vols., 18 Aug., 1862. Maj., 17 Sept., 1862. Lieut. Col., 2 March, 1863. Bvt. Brig Gen. Vols., 13 March, 1865, for gallant and meritorious service during the war. Mustered out 28 May, 1865. Col. 8th U. S. Vet. Vols., 15 June, 1865. Mustered out 22 March, 1866. 2nd Lieut. 1st Inf., 8 May, 1866. 1st Lieut., 9 Sept., 1867. R. Q. M., 20 Sept., 1874. Capt., 8 Jan., 1880. Died 4 Nov., 1886.

PIERCE, FRANKLIN. [Born in N. H. Appointed from N. H.]
Col. of Inf., 16 Feb., 1847. Brig. Gen., 3 March, 1847. Resigned 20 March, 1848. President of the U. S., 4 March, 1853, to 4 March, 1857. Died 8 Oct., 1869.

PIERCE, HENRY H. [Born in Mass. Appointed from Mass.]
1st Sergt. Co. A, 4th Conn. Vols., 22 May, 1861. 2nd Lieut. 1st Conn. Art., 6 Nov., 1861. 1st Lieut., 1 March, 1862. Capt., 9 Feb., 1863. Bvt. Maj. Vols., 13 March, 1865, for conspicuous gallantry. Maj. 1st Conn. Art., 24 May, 1865. Mustered out 25 Sept., 1865. 2nd Lieut. 1st Inf., 16 Oct., 1867. Bvt. 1st Lieut., 16 Oct., 1867, for gallant and meritorious service in the Battle of Petersburg Mine, Va. Bvt. Capt., 16 Oct., 1867, for gallant and meritorious service in action at Graveyard Bend. Unassigned 8 April, 1869. Ass'd to 21st Inf., 3 Aug., 1870. 1st Lieut., 19 May, 1874. Reg. Adj., 1 Oct., 1880, to 14 Oct., 1882. Died 17 July, 1883.

PIERCE, JACOB R. [Born in Ky. Apointed from Miss.]
2nd Lieut. 24th Inf., 18 Dec., 1871. 1st Lieut., 28 June, 1878. Dismissed 11 March, 1885.

PIERCE, JOHN S. [Born in N. H. Appointed from N. H.]
3rd Lieut., 3rd Art., 5 April, 1814. 2nd Lieut., 1 May, 1814. Trans. to Corps Art., 12 May, 1814. 1st Lieut., 20 April, 1818. Trans. to 2nd Art., 1 June, 1821. Trans. to 1st Art., 16 Aug., 1821. Resigned 1 Feb., 1823. Died in 1825.

PIERCE, PALMER E.* [Born in Ill. Appointed from Iowa.]
2nd Lieut. 9th Inf., 12 June, 1891. Trans. to 6th Inf., 16 July, 1891. 1st Lieut. 13th Inf., 23 March, 1898.

PIERCE, THOS. P. [Born in N. H. Appointed from N. H.]
2nd Lieut. of Inf., 10 March, 1847; 9th Inf., 9 April, 1847. 1st Lieut., 9 Oct., 1847. Resigned 16 March, 1848. Bvt. 1st Lieut., 20 Aug., 1847, for gallant and meritorious conduct in the Battles of Contreras and Churubusco, Mex. Col. 2nd N. H. Vols., 30 April, 1861. Resigned 4 June, 1861. Died 14 Oct., 1887.

PIERSON, WM. H. [Born in N. J. Appointed from N. J.]
Surg. Mate 1st Inf., 4 Aug., 1814. Disbanded 15 June, 1815. Reinstated 17 May, 1816, in Rifle Reg. Post Surg., 14 Nov., 1818. Died 12 Nov., 1820.

PIKE, ALBERT F. [Born in Mass. Appointed from Mass.]
2nd Lieut. 5th Art., 21 July, 1866. Trans. to 3rd Inf., 23 Oct., 1866. 1st Lieut., 9 July, 1868. Died 21 May, 1875.

PIKE, HORACE L. [Born in Maine. Appointed from Maine.]
2nd Lieut. 1st Art., 19 Feb., 1862. 1st Lieut., 1 Aug., 1863. Dismissed 14 Oct., 1864. Reinstated 26 Jan., 1867. Retired 21 Feb., 1867. Died 25 March, 1875.

PIKE, JAMES. [Born in Ohio. Appointed from Ohio.]
Corpl. Co. A, 4th Ohio. Cav., 20 Nov., 1861, to 1 April, 1865. 2nd Lieut. 1st Cav., 31 March, 1866. 1st Lieut., 27 Sept., 1867. Died 14 Oct., 1867.

PILCHARD, SEWELL N. [Born in Md. Appointed from Del.]
Post. Chap., 24 April, 1896.

PILCHER, JAMES E. [Born in Mich. Appointed from N. Y.]
Asst. Surg., 3 Dec., 1883. Capt. Asst. Surg., 3 Dec., 1888. Maj. Brig. Surg., 4 June, 1898, to 22 March, 1899.

PINDER, JOSEPH W. [Born in Ga. Appointed from Ga.]
Asst. Com. of Purchases, 26 Nov., 1813. Disbanded 1 June, 1821. Died 23 March, 1865.

PINDER, JOSEPH W. [Born in Ga. Appointed from Ga.]
2nd Lieut. 8th Cav., 15 Aug., 1876. Resigned 1 June, 1883.

PINKHAM, EDWARD W. [Born in Mass. Appointed from Mass.]
Asst. Surg., 12 Dec., 1898.

PINKNEY, NINIAN. [Born in Md. Appointed from Md.]
1st Lieut. 9th Inf., 8 Jan., 1799. Reg. P. M., 4 March, 1799. Discharged 15 June, 1800. 1st Lieut. 1st Inf., 16 Feb., 1801. Capt., 9 Dec., 1807. Maj. 5th Inf., 20 Jan., 1813. Col. I. G., 1 Dec., 1813. Lieut. Col. 22nd Inf., 15 April, 1814. Trans. to 2nd Inf., 17 May, 1815. Col. 6th Inf., 13 May, 1820. Trans. to 3rd Inf., 1 June, 1821. Died 16 Dec., 1825.

PIPER, ALEXANDER.* [Born in Penn. Appointed from Penn.]
Bvt. 2nd Lieut. 3rd Art., 1 July, 1851. 2nd Lieut., 12 Dec., 1851. 1st Lieut., 31 Jan., 1855. Capt. 18th Inf., 14 May, 1861, declined. Capt. 3rd Art., 14 May, 1861. Bvt. Maj., 30 Aug., 1862, for gallant and meritorious service during the campaign in Northern Virginia. Col. 10th N. Y. Art., 7 Jan., 1863. Bvt. Lieut. Col., 15 June, 1864, for gallant and meritorious service in the Siege of Petersburg, Va. Mustered out of Vol. Service, 6 July, 1865. Maj. 4th Art., 20 Dec., 1875. Lieut. Col. 1st Art., 8 Nov., 1882. Trans. to 3rd Art., 10 Nov., 1882. Trans. to 1st Art., 25 Jan., 1884. Col. 5th Art., 10 Aug., 1887. Retired after forty years' service, 1 July, 1891.

PIPER, ALEXANDER R.* [Born in N. Y. Appointed from Idaho.]
2nd Lieut. 8th Inf., 12 June, 1889. Trans. to 2nd Inf., 5 June, 1891. 1st Lieut. 15th Inf., 16 July, 1896. Capt. C. S. Vols., 12 May, 1898, to 12 July, 1899. Retired with rank of Capt. for disability, 11 July, 1899.

PIPER, JAMES W. [Born in Penn. Appointed from Penn.]
Priv. Co. A, 3rd Batt. D. C. Vols., 15 April to 20 June, 1861. 1st Lieut. 5th Art., 14 May, 1861. Capt., 28 July, 1866. Died 30 Oct., 1876. Bvt. Capt., 26 June, 1862, for gallant and meritorious service at the Battle of Mechanicsville, Va.

PIPES, HENRY A.* [Born in La. Appointed from La.]
2nd Lieut. 8th Inf., 11 June, 1892. Retired for disability 6 Sept., 1895. Died 22 March, 1897.

PITCHER, JOHN.* [Born in Texas. Appointed at Large.]
2nd Lieut. 9th Inf., 15 June, 1876. Trans. to 1st Cav., 28 July, 1876. 1st Lieut., 27 Nov., 1882. Reg. Adj., 27 Nov., 1882, to 30 Nov., 1885. Capt., 22 July, 1892.

PITCHER, MATTHEW S. [Born in N. Y. Appointed from N. Y.]
Capt. 10th Inf., 9 April, 1847. Maj. 11th Inf., 13 Sept., 1847. Disbanded 14 Aug., 1848. Capt. 10th Inf., 3 March, 1855. Died 17 Sept., 1858.

PITCHER, THOS. G.* [Born in Ind. Appointed from Ind.]
Bvt. 2nd Lieut. 5th Inf., 1 July, 1845. 2nd Lieut. 8th Inf., 21 Sept., 1846. Bvt. 1st Lieut., 20 Aug., 1847, for gallant and meritorious conduct in the Battles of Contreras and Churubusco. 1st Lieut., 8th Inf., 26 June, 1849. R. Q. M., 2 Oct., 1848, to 1 July, 1849. Reg. Adj., 1 July, 1849, to 1 July, 1854. R. Q. M., 1 July, 1854, to 5 March, 1857. Capt., 19 Oct., 1858. Bvt. Maj., 9 Aug., 1862, for gallant and meritorious service in the Battle of Cedar Mountain, Va. Brig. Gen. Vols., 29 Nov., 1862. Maj. 16th Inf., 19 Sept., 1863. Bvt. Lieut. Col. and Col., 13 March, 1865, for gallant and meritorious service during the war. Bvt. Brig. Gen., 13 March, 1865, for gallant and meritorious service in the field during the war. Mustered out of Vol. Service, 30 April, 1866. Col. 44th Inf., 28 July, 1866. Unassigned 15 March, 1869. Ass'd to 1st Inf., 15 Dec., 1870. Retired 28 June, 1878. Died 19 Oct., 1895.

PITCHER, WM. L. [Born in Texas. Appointed from D. C.]
Cadet at Naval Acad., 30 June, 1868, to 7 Oct., 1870. 2nd Lieut. 10th Cav., 18 Dec., 1871. Trans. to 8th Inf., 13 June, 1872. 1st Lieut., 1 March, 1882. Capt. 8th Inf., 9 March, 1891. Maj. 4th Inf., 20 Oct., 1899. Trans. to 8th Inf., 28 Oct., 1899.

PITCHER, ZINA. [Born in N. Y. Appointed from N. Y.]
Asst. Surg., 8 May, 1822. Maj. Surg., 13 July, 1832. Resigned 31 Dec., 1836. Asst. Surg., 2 Feb., 1839. Resigned 31 Aug., 1839. Died 5 April, 1872.

PITKIN, LUCIUS.* [Born in Vt. Appointed from Vt.]
2nd Lieut. 2nd Art., 1 July, 1838. 1st Lieut., 4 Jan., 1842. Resigned 1 June, 1844. Died 12 Oct., 1867.

PITMAN, JOHN.* [Born in R. I. Appointed from Tenn.]
Priv. Co. G, 1st R. I. Vols., 18 July, 1861. Discharged 2 Aug., 1861. Priv. Co. D, 10th R. I. Vols., 26 May, 1862. Discharged 30 Aug., 1862. Sergt. Maj. 11th R. I. Vols., 22 Sept., 1862. 2nd Lieut., 14 April, 1863. Mustered out 13 July, 1863. Cadet Mil. Acad., 29 Sept., 1863. 2nd Lieut. Ord., 17 June, 1867. 1st Lieut., 23 June, 1874. Capt., 27 May, 1878. Maj., 2 Sept., 1894.

PITMAN, JOSEPH S. [Born in N. H. Appointed from R. I.]
Capt. of Inf., 16 Feb., 1847; 9th Inf., 9 April, 1847. Maj. 14th Inf., 8 Sept., 1847. Discharged 21 July, 1848. Lieut. Col. 1st R. I. Vols., 2 May, 1861. Mustered out 2 Aug., 1861. Died 15 Sept., 1883.

PLATT, EDWARD R.* [Born in Vt. Appointed from Vt.]
Bvt. 2nd Lieut. 3rd Art., 1 July, 1849. 2nd Lieut. 2nd Art., 8 July, 1850. 1st Lieut., 8 Oct., 1853. Capt., 15 May, 1861. Bvt. Maj., 21 July, 1861, for gallant and meritorious service in the Battle of Bull Run, Va. Lieut. Col. A. I. G. (Act 17 July, 1862), 4 Sept., 1862. Bvt. Lieut. Col., 13 Dec., 1862, for gallant and meritorious service in the Battle of Fredericksburg, Va. Relieved as Lieut. Col. A. I. G. (Act 17 July, 1862), 1 Nov., 1863. Maj. J. A. Vols., 2 Nov., 1863. Mustered out of Vol. Service, 28 July, 1865. Maj. A. A. G., 6 March, 1873. Died 17 June, 1884.

PLATT, RICHARD. [Born in N. Y. Appointed from N. Y.]
Batt. P. M., 20 Nov., 1817. Resigned 25 Nov., 1820. Died 3 March, 1830.

PLEASANTS, CHAS. I. [Born in Penn. Appointed from Penn.]
Sergt. 11th Pa. Vols., 23 April to 15 July, 1861. 1st Lieut. 11th Inf., 14 May, 1861. Killed 5 May, 1864, in the Battle of the Wilderness, Va. Bvt. Capt., 5 May, 1864, for gallant and meritorious service at the Battle of the Wilderness, Va.

PLEASONTON, ALFRED.* [Born in D. C. Appointed from D. C.]
Bvt. 2nd Lieut. 1st Drag., 1 July, 1844. 2nd Lieut. 2nd Drag., 3 Nov., 1845. 1st Lieut., 30 Sept., 1849. Reg. Adj., 1 July, 1854, to 3 March, 1855. Capt., 3 March, 1855. 2nd Cav., 3 Aug., 1861. Maj., 15 Feb., 1862. Brig. Gen. Vols., 16 July, 1862. Maj. Gen. Vols., 22 June, 1863. Mustered out Vols., 15 Jan., 1866. Resigned 1 Jan., 1868. Bvt. 1st Lieut., 9 May, 1846, for gallant and meritorious conduct at Palo Alto and Resaca de la Palma. Bvt. Lieut. Col., 17 Sept., 1862, for gallant and meritorious service at Antietam, Md. Bvt. Col., 2 July, 1863, for gallant and meritorious service at Gettysburg, Pa. Bvt. Brig. Gen., 13 March, 1865, for gallant and meritorious service in the campaign against the rebel Gen. Price, in Mo. Bvt. Maj. Gen., 13 March, 1865, for gallant and meritorious service in the field during the war. Maj. retired 3 Oct., 1888, to rank from 19 Oct., 1888 (Act 19 Oct., 1888). Died 17 Feb., 1897.

PLEASONTON, AUGUSTUS. [Born in Penn. Appointed from Penn.]
2nd Lieut. 1st Drag., 26 April, 1861. 1st Lieut., 14 May, 1861; 1st Cav., 3 Aug., 1861. Wholly retired 13 Aug., 1862.

PLEASONTON, AUGUSTUS J.* [Born in D. C. Appointed from D. C.]
Bvt. 2nd Lieut. 6th Inf., 1 July, 1826. 2nd Lieut. 3rd Art., 1 July, 1826. Trans. to 1st Art., 24 Oct., 1826. Resigned 30 June, 1830.

PLUMMER, AUGUSTUS H.* [Born in Ohio. Appointed from Pa.]
Bvt. 2nd Lieut. 6th Inf., 1 July, 1853. 2nd Lieut. 7th Inf., 3 March, 1855. 1st Lieut., 2 Jan., 1858. Capt. 19th Inf., 14 May, 1861. Trans. to 37th Inf., 21 Sept., 1866. Died 18 Nov., 1866.

PLUMMER, EDWARD H. [Born in Md. Appointed from Md.]
2nd Lieut. 10th Inf., 15 June, 1877. 1st Lieut., 29 Nov., 1884. R. Q. M., 7 May, 1888, to — May, 1892. Capt., 26 April, 1898. Lieut. Col. 35th U. S. Vols., 5 July, 1899.

PLUMMER, HENRY V. [Born in Md. Appointed from Md.]
Chap. 9th Cav., 1 July, 1884. Died 10 Nov., 1894.

PLUMMER, JOHN H. [Born in —. Appointed from Tenn.]
Dep. Com. of Purchases, 4 June, 1812. Disbanded 1 June, 1821.

PLUMMER, JOSEPH B.* [Born in Mass. Appointed from Mass.]
2nd Lieut. 1st Inf., 1 July, 1841. 1st Lieut., 15 March, 1848. R. Q. M., 1 Jan., 1848, to 1 March, 1852. Capt., 1 May, 1852. Maj. 8th Inf., 25 April, 1862. Col. 11th Mo. Vols., 25 Sept., 1861. Brig. Gen. Vols., 22 Oct., 1861. Died 9 Aug., 1862.

PLUMMER, SAML. M.* [Born in Maine. Appointed from Maine.]
Bvt. 2nd Lieut. 1st Inf., 1 July, 1835. 2nd Lieut., 14 Nov., 1836. 1st Lieut., 7 July, 1838. Reg. Adj., 16 Sept., 1838, to 19 Oct., 1839. Capt. A. Q. M., 22 Nov., 1839, to 18 June, 1846. Capt. 1st Inf., 1 May, 1841. Died 17 Oct., 1851.

PLUMMER, SATTERLEE C.* [Born in Wis. Appointed at Large.]
2nd and 1st Lieut. 17th Inf., 23 June, 1865. Trans. to 26th Inf., 21 Sept., 1866. Reg. Adj., 17 July, 1867, to 1 May, 1868. Capt., 10 June, 1868. Unassigned 19 May, 1869. Ass'd to 7th Cav., 9 Aug., 1869. Discharged 15 Dec., 1870. 2nd Lieut. 4th Inf., 19 May, 1876. Dismissed 1 July, 1877. 2nd Lieut. 15th Inf., 20 Jan., 1880. Died 14 Nov., 1881.

PLYMPTOM, JOSEPH C. [Born in Mass. Appointed from Mass.]
2nd Lieut. 4th Inf., 3 Jan., 1812. 1st Lieut., 31 July, 1813. Trans. to 5th Inf., 17 May, 1815. Capt., 1 June, 1821. Maj. 2nd Inf., 22 Sept., 1840. Lieut. Col. 7th Inf., 9 Sept., 1846. Col. 1st Inf., 9 June, 1853. Died 5 June, 1860. Bvt. Maj., 1 June, 1831, for ten years' faithful service in one grade. Bvt. Col., 18 April, 1847, for gallant and meritorious conduct in the Battle of Cerro Gordo, Mex.

PLYMPTON, PETER W. L.* [Born in Mo. Appointed at Large.]
Bvt. 2nd Lieut. 7th Inf., 1 July, 1847. 2nd Lieut., 13 Sept., 1847. 1st Lieut., 3 March, 1855. Capt., 26 Feb., 1861. Maj. 17th Inf., 3 Dec., 1863. Died 10 Aug., 1866. Bvt. Maj., 21 Feb., 1862, for gallant and meritorious service at the Battle of Val Verde, N. M. Bvt. Lieut. Col., 15 April, 1862, for gallant and meritorious service at the Battle of Peralta, N. M.

POE, ORLANDO M.* [Born in Ohio. Appointed from Ohio.]
Bvt. 2nd Lieut. Top. Eng., 1 July, 1856. 2nd Lieut., 7 Oct., 1856. 1st Lieut., 1 July, 1860. Col. 2nd Mich. Vols., 16 Sept., 1861. Discharged 16 Feb., 1863. Brig. Gen. Vols., 29 Nov., 1862. Capt. Eng., 3 March, 1863. Appointment of Brig. Gen. Vols., expired by constitutional limitation, 4 March, 1863. Bvt. Maj., 6 July, 1864, for gallant service in the Siege of Knoxville. Bvt. Lieut. Col., 1 Sept., 1864, for gallant service in the capture of Atlanta. Bvt. Col., 21 Dec., 1864, for gallant service in the capture of Savannah. Bvt. Brig. Gen., 13 March, 1865, for gallant and meritorious service in the campaign terminating with the surrender of the insurgent army under Gen. J. E. Johnston. Maj. Eng., 7 March, 1867. Col. A. de C. to the Gen., 1 Jan., 1873. Lieut. Col., 30 June, 1882. Col., 23 July, 1888. Died 2 Oct., 1895.

POHLMAN, HENRY C. [Born in Ill. Appointed from Army.]
Priv., Sergt. and 1st Sergt. Co. C, 2nd Batt. 18th Inf., 28 Aug., 1861, to 17 Aug., 1863. 2nd Lieut. 18th Inf., 10 Aug., 1863. Died 27 Nov., 1863, while prisoner of war.

POILLON, RICHARD H.* [Born in N. Y. Appointed from N. Y.]
2nd Lieut. 23rd Inf., 12 June, 1871. Resigned 1 Aug., 1874.

POINDEXTER, JEFFERSON D. [Born in Va. Appointed from Va.]
Cadet Mil. Acad., 1 July, 1883, to 16 Jan., 1884. Asst. Surg., 11 March, 1887. Capt. Asst. Surg., 11 March, 1892.

POIST, WM. [Born in —. Appointed from Penn.]
2nd Lieut. Corps Art., 13 Aug., 1819. Resigned 15 June, 1820.

POLAND, JOHN S.* [Born in Ind. Appointed from Ind.]
2nd Lieut. 2nd Inf., 6 May, 1861. 1st Lieut., 6 June, 1861. R. Q. M., 10 Aug., 1861, to 27 June, 1862. Capt., 27 June, 1862. Bvt. Maj., 13 Dec., 1862, for gallant and meritorious service in the Battle of Antietam and Shepardstown Ford, Md., and Fredericksburg, Va. Bvt. Lieut. Col., 3 May, 1863, for gallant and meritorious service in the Battle of Chancellorsville, Va. Unassigned 17 April, 1869. Ass'd to 6th Inf., 14 July, 1869. Maj. 18th Inf., 15 Dec., 1880. Lieut. Col. 21st Inf., 1 March, 1886. Col. of Inf. (17th), 1 Aug., 1891. Brig. Gen. Vols., 6 May, 1898. Died 8 Aug., 1898.

POLAND, MARTIN L.* [Born in Vt. Appointed from Vt.]
2nd Lieut. Ord., 13 June, 1864. 1st Lieut., 15 Dec., 1867. Capt., 23 June, 1874. Died 20 Aug., 1878. Bvt. 1st Lieut. and Capt., 14 Dec., 1865, for faithful and meritorious service.

POLHEMUS, ADRIAN S. [Born in N. Y. Appointed from N. Y.]
Asst. Surg., 3 Dec., 1883. Capt. Asst. Surg., 3 Dec., 1888. Maj. Brig. Surg. Vols., 4 June, 1898, to 30 Nov., 1898.

POLK, EDWARD. [Born in Md. Appointed from D. C.]
3rd Lieut. Corps Art., 13 Feb., 1818. 2nd Lieut., 2 April, 1818. Resigned 31 July, 1819. 2nd Lieut. Rifles, 12 July, 1820. Dismissed 6 Oct., 1820. Died 22 Sept., 1822.

POLK, LEONIDAS.* [Born in N. C. Appointed from N. C.]
Bvt. 2nd Lieut. Art., 1 July, 1827. Resigned 1 Dec., 1827. Died 14 June, 1864.

POLK, MARSHALL T.* [Born in N. C. Appointed at Large.]
Bvt. 2nd Lieut. 2nd Inf., 1 July, 1852. 2nd Lieut., 8 Jan., 1853. Resigned 10 April, 1856. Died 29 Feb., 1884.

**POLK, WM. H.** [Born in Tenn. Appointed from Tenn.]
Maj. 3rd Drag., 31 Aug., 1847. Disbanded 20 July, 1848. Died 16 Dec., 1862.

**POLLOCK, EDWIN.** [Born in Penn. Appointed from Penn.]
Priv. Co. F, 25th Pa. Vols., 2 May to 28 July, 1861. 2nd Lieut. 9th Inf., 5 Aug., 1861. 1st Lieut., 31 Dec., 1862. R. Q. M., 1 Sept., 1863, to 20 April, 1864. Capt., 20 April, 1864. Retired 2 Feb., 1885. Died 24 Feb., 1885.

**POLLOCK, OTIS W.** [Born in Penn. Appointed from Penn.]
1st Lieut. 63rd Ohio Vols., 10 Oct., 1861. Capt., 30 June, 1862. Mustered out 8 July, 1865. 2nd Lieut. and 1st Lieut. 14th Inf., 23 Feb., 1866. Trans. to 23rd Inf., 21 Sept., 1866. Reg. Adj., 7 Dec., 1869, to 22 Jan., 1873. Capt., 22 Jan., 1873. Maj. 24th Inf., 27 Aug., 1896. Retired by operation of law 7 Aug., 1897.

**POLLOCK, ROBT.** [Born in Penn. Appointed from Cal.]
Sergt. Co. H, 1st Va. Vols., 6 Jan., 1847. 2nd Lieut., 6 May, 1847. Mustered out 31 July, 1848. Maj. 3rd Cal. Vols., 4 Sept., 1861. Lieut. Col., 12 Dec., 1861. Col., 29 March, 1863. Mustered out 14 Nov., 1864. Lieut. Col. 2nd Cal. Vols., 7 Jan., 1865. Bvt. Col. Vols., 13 March, 1865, for faithful and meritorious service. Mustered out 23 June, 1866. 1st Lieut. 32nd Inf., 28 July, 1866. Trans. to 21st Inf., 19 April, 1869. Capt., 19 Feb., 1873. Retired by operation of law 17 Sept., 1883. Bvt. Maj., 27 Feb., 1890, for marked bravery and gallant service in action against Indians at the Clearwater, Idaho, 11 and 12 July, 1877.

**POLLOCK, WM. K.** [Born in Penn. Appointed from Penn.]
2nd Lieut. 1st Art., 6 March, 1862. Died 4 Aug., 1863.

**POMEROY, CHAS. C.** [Born in Penn. Appointed from Ohio.]
Capt. 11th Inf., 14 May, 1861. Trans. to 20th Inf., 21 Sept., 1866. Resigned 5 Oct., 1867. Bvt. Maj., 22 June, 1865, for faithful and meritorious service in the recruitment of the armies of the U. S. Bvt. Lieut. Col., 13 Nov., 1865, for faithful and meritorious service in connection with the mustering out of service and disbanding of the Vol. Army of the U. S.

**POMEROY, GEORGE.** [Born in N. Y. Appointed from N. Y.]
Addl. P. M. Vols., 2 Oct., 1862. Bvt. Lieut. Col. Vols., 16 April, 1865, for faithful service in the Pay Dept. Maj. P. M., 28 July, 1866. Died 1 Jan., 1869.

**POMEROY, R. C.** [Born in Vt. Appointed from S. C.]
2nd Lieut. Ord., 26 Dec., 1814. 1st Lieut., 1 Sept., 1818. Trans. to 3rd Inf., 1 June, 1821. Dismissed 11 Aug., 1823.

**POMROY, GEORGE K.** [Born in Mass. Appointed from Mass.]
Priv. Cos. H and B, 13th Mass. Vols., 1 Aug., 1861, to 8 Oct., 1862. 2nd Lieut. 3rd Inf., 17 July, 1862. 1st Lieut., 20 Oct., 1863. Resigned 21 March, 1865.

**POND, GEORGE B.** [Born in N. C. Appointed from N. C.]
2nd Lieut. 3rd Inf., 9 Sept., 1898.

**POND, GEORGE E.*** [Born in Conn. Appointed from Conn.]
Priv. Co. K, 21st Conn. Vols., 9 Dec., 1863. Discharged 7 June, 1865. Cadet at Mil. Acad., 1 July, 1868. 2nd Lieut. 8th Cav., 14 June, 1872. 1st Lieut., 18 Jan., 1881. Capt. A. Q. M., 23 Oct., 1883. Maj. Q. M., 11 Feb., 1897. Lieut. Col. Chief Q. M. Vols., 9 May, 1898. Col. Q. M. Vols., 3 Feb. to 12 May, 1899.

**POND, RICHARD H.** [Born in N. Y. Appointed from Army.]
Priv. and Sergt. Co. D, 12th Inf., 11 Nov., 1861, to 26 June, 1862. 2nd Lieut. 12th Inf., 25 May, 1862. 1st Lieut., 7 Feb., 1863. Capt., 5 April, 1866. Resigned 1 Feb., 1873. Bvt. Capt., 1 Aug., 1834, for gallant service in the Battle of Bethesda Church, and during the campaign before Richmond. Bvt. Maj., 9 April, 1865, for gallant and meritorious service during the campaign terminating with the surrender of Gen. Lee. Died 16 Sept., 1886.

**POOLE, BENJN.*** [Born in Maine. Appointed from Maine.]
Bvt. 2nd Lieut. 3rd Art., 1 July, 1830. 2nd Lieut., 1 July, 1830. 1st Lieut., 31 Aug., 1836. Died 9 Nov., 1839.

**POOLE, DE WITT C.** [Born in N. Y. Appointed from Wis.]
1st Lieut. 1st Wis. Vols., 17 May, 1861. Mustered out 21 Aug., 1861. Lieut. Col., 12th Wis. Vols., 31 Oct., 1861. Resigned 3 July, 1863. Lieut. Col. Vet. Res. Corps, 15 Nov., 1863. Resigned 10 Feb., 1866. Capt. 25th Inf., 22 Jan., 1867. Unassigned 26 April, 1869. Ass'd to 22nd Inf., 25 Oct., 1870. Maj. P. M., 5 July, 1882. Retired by operation of law, 28 Sept., 1892.

**POOLE, WM. L.** [Born in ——. Appointed from S. C.]
Mil. Storekeeper Ord., 4 April, 1834. Resigned 7 Nov., 1842.

**POOLER, ROBT. W.*** [Born in England. Appointed from Ga.]
Bvt. 2nd Lieut. Eng., 4 March, 1815. 2nd Lieut., 1 Oct., 1817. Resigned 14 Aug., 1818. Died 25 Dec., 1853.

**POOLEY, JAMES H.** [Born in England. Appointed from N. Y.]
Asst. Surg., 5 Aug., 1861. Resigned 27 April, 1863. Died 3 June, 1890.

**POORE, BENJAMIN A.*** [Born in Ala. Appointed from Mass.]
2nd Lieut. 12th Inf., 1 July, 1886. 1st Lieut. 10th Inf., 16 Sept., 1892. Trans. to 6th Inf., 28 Sept., 1892. Capt., 2 March, 1899. Graduate of the Infantry and Cavalry School, 1893. Reg. Adj., 10 March, 1899.

**POPE, BENJN. F.** [Born in N. Y. Appointed from N. Y.]
Asst. Surg. 10th N. Y. Art., 18 July, 1864. Mustered out 19 July, 1865. 1st Lieut. Asst. Surg., 14 May, 1867. Capt. Asst. Surg., 13 May, 1869. Maj. Surg., 16 Sept., 1885. Lieut. Col. Dep. Surg. Gen., 21 Dec., 1898. Lieut. Col. Chief Surg. Vols., 9 May to 31 Oct., 1898.

**POPE, CURREN.*** [Born in Ky. Appointed from Ky.]
Bvt. 2nd Lieut. 2nd Art., 1 July, 1834. Resigned 31 Dec., 1834. Col. 15th Ky. Vols., 3 Dec., 1861. Died 5 Nov., 1862, of wounds received 8 Oct., 1862, at the Battle of Perryville, Ky.

**POPE, DOUGLASS.** [Born in Ill. Appointed from Mo.]
Cap. A. A. de C. Vols., 30 June, 1862. Bvt. Maj. Vols., 13 March, 1865, for distinguished service in the campaign of the army of Virginia in the Dept. of the N. W. and in the Mil. Div. of Mo. Mustered out 1 Oct., 1866. 1st Lieut. 37th Inf., 28 July, 1866. R. Q. M., 27 April, 1867, to 31 Dec., 1868. Unassigned 19

May, 1869. Ass'd to 13th Inf., 1 Jan., 1871. Resigned 10 Oct., 1871. Bvt. Capt., 2 March, 1867, for gallant and meritorious service at the Battle of Groveton, Va. Bvt. Maj., 2 March, 1867, for gallant and meritorious service during the war. Died 7 Feb., 1880.

POPE, FRANCIS H.* [Born in Kan. Appointed from Mo.]
Addl. 2nd Lieut. 2nd Cav., 11 June, 1897. 2nd Lieut., 19 June, 1897.

POPE, HENRY C. [Born in Ky. Appointed from Ky.]
Capt. Mounted Rifles, 27 May, 1846. Resigned 31 Dec., 1847. Killed in a duel in May, 1848.

POPE, JAMES W.* [Born in Ky. Appointed from Ind.]
2nd Lieut. 5th Inf., 15 June, 1868. 1st Lieut., 20 March, 1879. Capt. A. Q. M., 20 Feb., 1885. Maj. Q. M., 11 June, 1897. Lieut. Col. Chief Q. M. Vols., 9 May, 1898, to 2 Sept., 1899.

POPE, JOHN.* [Born in Ky. Appointed from Ill.]
Bvt. 2nd Lieut. Top. Eng., 1 July, 1842. 2nd Lieut., 9 May, 1846. Bvt. 1st Lieut., 23 Sept., 1846, for gallant and meritorious conduct in the several conflicts at Monterey, Mex. Bvt. Capt., 23 Feb., 1847, for gallant and meritorious conduct in the Battle of Buena Vista, Mex. 1st Lieut. Top. Eng., 3 March, 1853. Capt., 1 July, 1856. Brig. Gen. Vols., 17 May, 1861. Maj. Gen. Vols., 21 March, 1862. Brig. Gen. U. S. A., 14 July, 1862. Bvt. Maj. Gen., 13 March, 1865, for gallant and meritorious service at the capture of Island No. 10. Mustered out of Vol. Service, 1 Sept., 1866. Maj. Gen., 26 Oct., 1882. Retired 16 March, 1866. Died 23 Sept., 1892.

POPE, JOHN Jr.* [Born in Ill. Appointed from Ill.]
2nd Lieut. 26th Inf., 15 June, 1868. Unassigned 19 May, 1869. Ass'd to 1st. Art., 14 July, 1869. 1st Lieut., 22 Nov., 1877. Graduate of the Artillery School, 1874. Retired for disability with rank of Capt., 10 Feb., 1898.

PORTER, ALEXANDER S. [Born in Md. Appointed from Md.]
Asst. Surg., 26 Oct., 1893. Retired for disability, with rank of Capt., 8 June, 1899.

PORTER, ANDREW. [Born in Penn. Appointed from Penn.]
Cadet at Mil. Acad., 1 July, 1836, to 4 Jan., 1837. 1st Lieut. Mounted Rifles, 27 May, 1846. Capt., 15 May, 1847. Col. 16th Inf., 14 May, 1861. Brig. Gen. Vols., 17 May, 1861. Resigned 20 April, 1864. Bvt. Maj., 20 Aug., 1847, for gallant and meritorious conduct at Contreras and Churubusco. Bvt. Lieut. Col., 13 Sept., 1847, for gallant and meritorious conduct at Chapultepec, Mex. Mustered out Vols., 4 April, 1864. Died 4 Jan., 1872.

PORTER, A. PARKER.* [Born in Penn. Appointed from Penn.]
2nd Lieut. 2nd Cav., 1 July, 1856. 1st Lieut., 20 March, 1861; 5th Cav., 3 Aug., 1861. R. Q. M., 1 April to 3 Aug., 1861. Capt. C. S., 3 Aug., 1861. Lieut. Col. C. S. Vols., 20 Aug., 1862, to 3 July, 1865. Died 15 Aug., 1866. Bvt. Maj., 13 March, 1865, for faithful and meritorious service during the war.

PORTER, CHAS. [Born in Ireland. Appointed from Army.]
Priv. Co. E, 5th Inf., 26 April, 1858. Corpl., 15 Jan., 1863. Q. M. Sergt. 5th Inf., 17 April, 1863. Discharged 26 April, 1863. Q. M. Sergt. 5th Inf., 26 April, 1863. 2nd Lieut. 5th Inf., 31 Oct., 1863. 1st Lieut., 20 Feb., 1865. Trans. to 8th Inf., 18 Jan., 1870. Capt., 1 Aug., 1872. Maj. 5th Inf., 10 March, 1896. Lieut. Col. 22nd Inf., 28 Sept., 1898. Bvt. Maj., 27 Feb., 1890, for gallant services in actions against Indians in Arizona, Aug., 15, 1876; Oct. 4, 1876, and Jan. 7, 1878; and in action against Indians in Arizona, 3 April, 1878. Retired for disability, 23 Dec., 1898.

PORTER, DAVID E. [Born in D. C. Appointed at Large.]
2nd Lieut. 1st Art., 24 Oct., 1861. 1st Lieut., 13 July, 1862. Dropped 28 Feb., 1866. Reinstated 23 May, 1866. Trans. to 28th Inf., 6 Oct., 1866. Resigned 20 Aug., 1867. Bvt. Capt., 9 April, 1865, for meritorious service in campaign against the rebel army in Northern Virginia, commencing in front of Petersburg, 29 March, 1865, and ending 9 April, 1865.

PORTER, DAVID M.* [Born in Tenn. Appointed from Tenn.]
Bvt. 2nd Lieut. and 2nd Lieut. 4th Inf., 1 July, 1821. Trans. to 6th Inf., 1 July, 1821. Resigned 21 July, 1823. Died in 1866.

PORTER, DAVID R.* [Born in Penn. Appointed from Penn.]
2nd Lieut. 4th Cav., 23 June, 1865. 1st Lieut., 8 March, 1866. Died 28 Nov., 1866.

PORTER, DAVID ST. LEON. [Born in N. H. Appointed from La.]
2nd Lieut. 14th Inf., 22 May, 1847. Died 30 June, 1847.

PORTER, DAVID W. [Born in N. Y. Appointed from Ore.]
1st Lieut. 1st Ore. Cav., 1 Feb., 1862, to 11 Jan., 1863. Capt. A. Q. M. Vols., 21 Nov., 1862. Mustered out 4 Jan., 1866. Capt. A Q. M., 18 Jan., 1867. Died 15 Oct., 1871.

PORTER, FITZ JOHN.* [Born in N. H. Appointed at Large.]
Bvt. 2nd Lieut. 4th Art., 1 July, 1845. 2nd Lieut., 18 June, 1846. 1st Lieut., 29 May, 1847. Bvt. Capt. A. A. G., 27 June, 1856. Col. 15th Inf., 14 May, 1861. Brig. Gen. Vols., 17 May, 1861. Maj. Gen. Vols., 4 July, 1862. Cashiered 21 Jan., 1863. Bvt. Capt., 8 Sept., 1847, for gallant and meritorious conduct at Molino del Rey. Bvt. Maj., 13 Sept., 1847, for gallant and meritorious service at Chapultepec. Bvt. Brig. Gen., 27 June, 1862, for gallant and meritorious conduct at Chickahominy, Va. Restored to duty as Col. of Inf., 5 Aug., 1886, to rank from 14 May, 1861. (Act 1 July, 1886.) Retired 7 Aug., 1886.

PORTER, GEORGE L. [Born in N. H. Appointed from Penn.]
Asst. Surg., 17 July, 1862. Resigned 16 July, 1868. Bvt. Capt. and Maj., 13 March, 1865, for faithful and meritorious service during the war.

PORTER, GILES.* [Born in N. Y. Appointed from N. Y.]
2nd Lieut. Corps Art., 24 July, 1818. Trans. to 1st Art., 1 June, 1821. 1st Lieut., 1 Feb., 1823. Capt., 30 Sept., 1833. Maj. 4th Art., 16 Feb., 1847. Retired 3

Sept., 1861. Died 31 May, 1878. Bvt. Capt., 1 Feb., 1833, for ten years' faithful service in one grade.

PORTER, HORACE.* [Born in Pa. Appointed from Pa.]
Bvt. 2nd Lieut. Ord., 1 July, 1860. 2nd Lieut., 22 April, 1861. 1st Lieut., 7 June, 1861. Capt., 3 March, 1863. Lieut. Col. A. de C. to Lieut. Gen. Grant, 4 April, 1864, to 25 July, 1866, and Col. A. de C. to Gen. Grant, 25 July, 1866, to 4 March, 1869. Col. A. de C. to Gen. Sherman, 8 March, 1869. Maj., 7 March, 1867, to 1 Jan., 1873. Resigned 31 Dec., 1873. Bvt. Capt., 11 April, 1862, for gallant and meritorious service at the Siege of Fort Pulaski, Ga. Bvt. Maj., 6 May, 1864, for gallant and meritorious service at the Battle of the Wilderness, Va. Bvt. Lieut. Col., 16 Aug., 1864, for gallant and meritorious service in the action of New Market Heights, Va. Bvt. Col., 13 March, 1865, for gallant and meritorious service during the war. Bvt. Brig. Gen., 13 March, 1865, for gallant and meritorious service in the field during the war.

PORTER, JAMES E.* [Born in Maine. Appointed from Maine.]
2nd Lieut. 7th Cav., 15 June, 1869. 1st Lieut., 1 March, 1872. Killed 25 June, 1876, in action with Indians in Montana Ter.

PORTER, JEREMIAH. [Born in Mass. Appointed from Texas.]
Chap. 1st Ill. Light Art., 5 March, 1862. Mustered out 31 July, 1865. Post Chap., 2 July, 1870. Retired 30 June, 1882. Died 25 July, 1893.

PORTER, JOHN B. Born in Conn. Appointed from Conn.]
Asst. Surg., 1 Dec., 1833. Maj. Surg., 4 Oct., 1846. Retired 27 Aug., 1862. Died 15 June, 1869.

PORTER, JOHN M.* [Born in Ala. Appointed from Ala.]
2nd Lieut. 3rd Cav., 13 June, 1879. 1st Lieut., 26 June, 1882. Dropped 30 Nov., 1883.

PORTER, JOSEPH Y. [Born in Fla. Appointed from Fla.]
1st Lieut. Asst. Surg., 26 June, 1875. Capt. Asst. Surg., 25 June, 1880. Resigned 29 Aug., 1889.

PORTER, MOSES. [Born in Mass. Appointed from Mass.]
Served in Revolutionary Army. Lieut. Art., 29 Sept., 1789. Capt., 4 Nov., 1791. Maj. 1st Art. and Eng., 26 May, 1800. Retained in Art., 1 April, 1802. Col. Light Art., 12 March, 1812. Trans. to 1st Art., 1 June 1821. Died 14 April, 1822. Bvt. Brig. Gen., 10 Sept., 1813, for distinguished service in the campaign of 1813.

PORTER, ROBT. H. [Born in Pa. Appointed from Pa.]
1st Lieut. 14th Inf., 26 Oct., 1861. Capt., 4 Nov., 1865. Retired 24 May, 1867. Died 22 April, 1869. Bvt. Maj., 4 Nov., 1865, for faithful and meritorious service.

PORTER, SAML. A. [Born in Ohio. Appointed from Ill.]
Priv. Co. B, 33rd Ill. Vols., 20 Aug., 1861. Discharged 4 April, 1862. 2nd Lieut. 104th Ill. Vols., 27 Aug., 1862. 1st Lieut., 8 March, 1863. Capt., 3 Oct., 1863. Mustered out 24 Aug., 1864. 1st Lieut. Vet. Res. Corps, 22 Aug., 1864. Capt., 29 Aug., 1864. Mustered out 6 Oct., 1864. Col. 123rd U. S. Col. Troops, 13 Oct., 1864. Bvt. Brig. Gen. Vols., 13 March, 1865, for gallant and meritorious service during the war. Mustered out 16 Oct., 1865. 2nd Lieut. 14th Inf., 11 May, 1866, and 2nd Lieut. 44th Inf., 28 July, 1866. 1st Lieut., 20 March, 1867. Reg. Adj., 13 July, 1868, to 27 May, 1869. Trans. to 17th Inf., 27 May, 1869. R. Q. M., 27 May, 1869, to 15 Dec., 1870. Bvt. Capt., 20 March, 1867, for gallant and meritorious service in the Battle of Chickamauga, Ga. Bvt. Maj., 20 March, 1867, for faithful and meritorious service during the war. Retired with rank of Capt., 15 Dec., 1870. Died 21 April, 1880.

PORTER, THEODORE H. [Born in D. C. Appointed from Penn.]
Cadet at Mil. Acad., 1 July, 1835, to 22 Jan., 1836. 2nd Lieut. 4th Inf., 1 July, 1839. Killed in action in Mex., 9 April, 1846.

PORTER, WM. L. [Born in India. Appointed from Ky.]
Priv. and Sergt. Co. B, 20th Ohio Vols., 18 April to 26 July, 1861. Priv. Co. B, 24th Ohio Vols., 26 July, 1861, to 15 Oct., 1862. 1st Lieut. 56th Ohio Vols., 10 Nov., 1862. Discharged 10 Nov., 1864. Capt. A. A. G. Vols., 13 March, 1865. Bvt. Maj. Vols., 13 March, 1865, for faithful and meritorious service during the war. Mustered out 1 Oct., 1866. 2nd Lieut. 5th Cav., 9 Aug., 1867. Died 23 April, 1868.

POST, JAMES C.* [Born in N. Y. Appointed from N. Y.]
2nd Lieut. 5th Art., 23 June, 1865. Trans. to Eng., 1 May, 1866. 1st Lieut., 1 May, 1866. Capt., 10 Oct., 1871. Maj., 16 Sept., 1886. Died 6 Jan., 1896.

POSTLETHWAITE, GABRIEL L. [Born in Ky. Appointed from Ky.]
Capt. 13th Inf., 5 Aug., 1861. Resigned 18 June, 1862. Died in 1877.

POSTLETHWAITE, WM. M. [Born in ——. Appointed from ——.]
Chap. and Prof. at Mil. Acad. from 18 Feb., 1893. Died 10 Jan., 1896.

POSTLEY, CLARENCE A.* [Born in N. Y. Appointed from Col.]
2nd Lieut. 3rd Art., 15 June, 1870. 1st Lieut., 20 March, 1879. Resigned 31 Jan., 1883.

POSTLEY, THOMAS. [Born in N. Y. Appointed from N. Y.]
Capt. of Inf., 18 March, 1847; 10th Inf., 9 April, 1847. Killed by a soldier 8 May, 1848.

POTTER, ASHTON H. [Born in ——. Appointed from ——.]
2nd Lieut. of Cav. (unassigned), 1 Dec., 1899.

POTTER, CARROLL H. [Born in R. I. Appointed from Mass.]
Cadet at Mil. Acad., 1 July, 1855, to 15 Jan., 1857. Capt. A. A. G. Vols., 21 Oct., 1861. Maj. A. A. G. Vols., 25 Feb., 1865. Bvt. Brig. Gen. Vols., 13 March, 1865, for meritorious service during the war. Col. 6th U. S. Vols., 27 March, 1865. Mustered out 10 Oct., 1866. 1st Lieut. 18th Inf., 28 July, 1866. Reg. Adj., 1 Jan., 1867, to 20 March, 1879. Capt., 20 March, 1879. Maj. 14th Inf., 26 April, 1898.

POTTER, CHARLES L.* [Born in Me. Appointed from Me.]
2nd Lieut. 5th Cav., 1 July, 1886. Trans. to Eng., 2 Feb., 1887. 1st Lieut., 12

Aug., 1890. Capt., 5 July, 1898. Lieut. Col. Chief. Eng. Vols., 22 June, 1898, to 2 Sept., 1899.

POTTER, HORATIO, Jr. [Born in N. Y. Appointed from N. Y.]
2nd Lieut. 7th N. Y. Art., 20 Dec., 1862. 1st Lieut., 1 April, 1864. Capt., 12 Jan., 1865. Bvt. Maj. Vols., 2 April, 1865, for gallant and meritorious conduct before Petersburg, Va. Mustered out 3 July, 1865. 2nd Lieut. 17th Inf., 18 April, 1866. 1st Lieut., 13 Sept., 1867. Reg. Adj., 15 Dec., 1870, to 25 July, 1874. Died 25 July, 1874.

POTTER, IRWIN W. [Born in Wis. Appointed from Wis.]
1st Lieut. 15th Inf., 11 Sept., 1861. Capt., 6 April, 1865. Died 28 Feb., 1869. Bvt. Capt., 1 Sept., 1864, for gallant and meritorious service during the Atlanta campaign.

POTTER, JAMES B. M. [Born in R. I. Appointed from R. I.]
Addl. P. M., 1 June, 1861. Maj. P. M., 15 July, 1864. Bvt. Lieut. Col., 13 March, 1865, for faithful and meritorious service during the war. Lieut. Col. Dep. P. M. G., 17 March, 1882. Retired, by operation of law, 1 Oct., 1882.

POTTER, JAMES D. [Born in N. Y. Appointed from N. Y.]
2nd Lieut. 1st N. Y. Vols., 28 Nov., 1847, to March, 1848. 2nd Lieut. 3rd Drag., 3 March, 1848. Disbanded 31 July, 1848. Maj. 38th N. Y. Vols., 8 June, 1861. Lieut. Col., 23 Dec., 1862. Resigned 25 Jan., 1863. Died 24 Oct., 1888.

POTTER, JAMES G. [Born in Penn. Appointed from Wis.]
2nd Lieut. 2nd Cav., 19 Feb., 1862. 1st Lieut., 25 Nov., 1862. Resigned 27 April, 1863.

POTTER, JOSEPH A. [Born in N. Y. Appointed from Mich.]
1st Lieut. 15th Inf., 27 Sept., 1861. Capt. A. Q. M., 27 Sept., 1861. Col. Q. M. (Act 4 July, 1864), 24 Sept., 1864. Bvt. Maj., Lieut. Col., Col. and Brig. Gen., 13 March, 1865, for faithful and meritorious service during the war. Relieved as Col. Q. M. (Act 4 July, 1864), 1 Jan., 1867. Maj. Q. M., 18 Jan., 1867. Retired 21 April, 1879. Died 1 April, 1888.

POTTER, JOSEPH A. [Born in Ohio. Appointed from Ind.]
Musician Cos. K and B, 60th Ind. Vols., 21 Nov., 1861, to 21 March, 1865. Post Chap., 26 Feb., 1885.

POTTER, JOSEPH H.* [Born in N. H. Appointed from N. H.]
Bvt. 2nd Lieut. 1st Inf., 1 July, 1843. 2nd Lieut. 7th Inf., 21 Oct., 1845. Bvt. 1st Lieut., 23 Sept., 1846, for gallant and meritorious conduct in the Battle of Monterey. 1st Lieut. 7th Inf., 30 Oct., 1847. Reg. Adj., 16 Nov., 1853, to 9 Jan., 1856. Capt., 9 Jan., 1856. Col. 12th N. H. Vols., 22 Sept., 1862. Bvt. Lieut. Col., 13 Dec., 1862, for galant and meritorious service in the Battle of Fredericksburg, Va. Bvt. Col., 3 May, 1863, for gallant and meritorious service in the Battle of Chancellorsville, Va. Maj. 19th Inf., 4 July, 1863. Bvt. Brig. Gen., 13 March, 1865, for gallant and meritorious service in the campaign terminating with the surrender of the insurgent army under Gen. R. E. Lee. Brig. Gen. Vols., 1 May, 1865. Mustered out of Vol. Service, 15 Jan., 1866. Lieut. Col. 30th Inf., 28 July, 1866. Trans. to 4th Inf., 15 March, 1869. Col. 24th Inf., 11 Dec., 1873. Brig. Gen., 1 April, 1886. Retired, by operation of law, 12 Oct. 1886. Died 1 Dec., 1892.

POTTER, REUBEN M. [Born in N. J. Appointed from Texas.]
Mil. Storekeeper, Q. M. D., 23 March, 1848. Capt., 28 July, 1866. Retired 30 June, 1882. Died 18 March, 1890.

POTTER, WOODBURNE. [Born in Penn. Appointed from Penn.]
2nd Lieut. 7th Inf., 16 Aug., 1837. Resigned 31 Aug., 1839.

POTTS, ELIAS K. [Born in D. C. Appointed from D. C.]
2nd Lieut. 7th Inf., 14 May, 1857. Died 23 April, 1859.

POTTS, RAMSEY D. [Born in D. C. Appointed from D. C.]
2nd Lieut 3rd Art., 7 March, 1867. 1st Lieut., 2 Nov., 1869. Capt., 13 July, 1892. Graduate of the Artillery School, 1870.

POTTS, RICHARD. [Born in Md. Appointed from Md.]
Asst. Surg., 16 Sept., 1853. Resigned 7 May, 1861.

POUSSIN, WM. TELL. [Born in France. Appointed from France.]
Capt. Asst. Top. Eng., 6 March, 1817. Maj. Top. Eng., 15 Jan., 1829. Resigned 31 July, 1832. Bvt. Maj., 6 March, 1827, for ten years' faithful service in one grade. Died in Nov., 1876.

POWELL, ALBERT M.* [Born in Md. Appointed from Md.]
Bvt. 2nd Lieut. 8th Inf., 1 July, 1860. 2nd Lieut. 10th Inf., 10 Sept., 1860. 1st Lieut. 13th Inf., 14 May, 1861. Capt., 24 Oct., 1861. Lieut. Col. 1st Mo. Light Art., 21 Oct., 1862. Mustered out Vols., 1 Aug., 1865. Trans. to 31st Inf., 21 Sept., 1866. Died 10 June, 1868. Bvt. Maj., 4 Oct., 1862, for gallant and meritorious service at the Battle of Corinth, Miss. Bvt. Lieut. Col., 4 July, 1863, for gallant and meritorious service during the Siege of Vicksburg, Miss.

POWELL, CHAS. F.* [Born in Ill. Appointed from S. C.]
Priv. and Corpl. Co. B, and Sergt. Maj. 5th Wis. Vols., 10 May, 1861, to 28 Sept., 1863. Cadet at Mil. Acad., 1 July, 1863. 2nd Lieut. Eng., 17 June, 1867. 1st Lieut., 23 April, 1869. Capt. (fourteen years' service), 17 June, 1881. Maj., 26 Jan., 1895.

POWELL, GARSTON. [Born in Md. Appointed from D. C.]
2nd Lieut. 1st Inf., 13 Feb., 1818. 1st Lieut., 1 July, 1818. R. Q. M., 5 Oct., 1820, to 1 June, 1821. Capt., 1 May, 1822. Resigned 31 Dec., 1824.

POWELL, HIRAM McL.* [Born in Ala. Appointed from Ala.]
2nd Lieut. 2nd Inf., 12 June, 1890. 1st Lieut. 1st Inf., 6 Feb., 1897. Capt. 11th Inf., 19 Oct., 1899.

POWELL, JAMES. [Born in Md. Appointed from Army.]
Priv. Co. H, 11th Inf., 11 Feb., 1848. Discharged 15 Aug., 1848. Priv. Co. I, 1st Drag., 26 March, 1851. Discharged 26 March, 1856. Priv. Co. I, 1st Cav., 17 Nov., 1856. Corpl., 3 April, 1857. Sergt., 1 Sept., 1858. 1st Sergt., 28 April,

1860. 2nd Lieut. 18th Inf., 14 May, 1861. 1st Lieut., 24 Oct., 1861. Bvt. Capt., 20 Sept., 1863, for gallant and meritorious service in the Battle of Chickamauga. Ga. Bvt. Maj., 1 Sept., 1864, for gallant and meritorious service during the Atlanta campaign, and in the Battle of Jonesboro, Ga. Capt. 18th Inf., 9 Sept., 1864. Trans. to 27th Inf., 21 Sept., 1866. Bvt. Lieut. Col., 2 Aug., 1867, for gallant conduct in the fight with the Indians near Fort Philip Kearney, D. T., 2 Aug., 1867. Retired 8 Jan., 1868.

POWELL, JAMES E. [Born in England. Appointed from Maine.]
Priv. and Sergt. Co. E, 9th Inf., 4 Aug., 1847, to 28 Aug., 1848. 2nd Lieut. 1st Inf., 7 June, 1855. 1st Lieut., 8 Dec., 1856. Capt., 11 June, 1861. Maj. 25th Mo. Vols., 24 March, 1862. Killed at Battle of Shiloh, Tenn., 6 April, 1862. Bvt. Maj., 7 April, 1862, for gallant and meritorious service at the Battle of Shiloh, Tenn.

POWELL, JAMES W. [Born in Ohio. Appointed from Ohio.]
Priv. Co. A, 13th Ohio Vols., 22 April, 1861. Discharged 18 Aug., 1861. 1st Lieut. 1st Ohio Vols., 24 Aug., 1861. Resigned 17 June, 1862. Capt. 10th U. S. Col. Troops, 30 Nov., 1863. Mustered out 17 May, 1866. 2nd Lieut. 15th Inf., 28 March, 1866. Trans. to 33rd Inf., 21 Sept., 1866. 1st Lieut., 7 March, 1867. Trans. to 8th Inf., 3 May, 1869. Capt., 3 July, 1883. Died 23 May, 1884.

POWELL, JAMES W., Jr. [Born in N. Y. Appointed from N. Y.]
Priv. Co. B, 7th N. Y. State Militia, 21 April, 1861. Discharged 3 June, 1861. 1st Lieut. 71st N. Y. Vols., 20 June, 1861. 1st Lieut. Vet. Res. Corps, 22 May, 1863. Capt., 28 Oct., 1863. Bvt. Maj. and Lieut. Col. Vols., 13 March, 1865, for gallant and meritorious service during the war. Mustered out 3 June, 1866. Capt. 42nd Inf., 28 July, 1866. Trans. to 6th Inf., 22 April, 1869. Maj., 1 Aug., 1891. Trans. to 21st Inf., 16 April, 1892. Lieut. Col. 15th Inf., 26 April, 1895. Col. 17th Inf., 16 Jan., 1899. Retired, over thirty years' service, 8 Sept., 1899.

POWELL, JOSEPH S. [Born in D. C. Appointed from Army.]
Priv. Sig. Corps, 1 April, 1873. Corpl., 1 Aug., 1875. Sergt., 23 July, 1876. Discharged 31 March, 1878. Sergt. Sig. Corps, 1 April, 1878. Discharged 12 Nov., 1879. 2nd Lieut. Sig. Corps, 1 Nov., 1879. Died 14 March, 1887.

POWELL, JUNIUS L. [Born in Va. Appointed from Md.]
1st Lieut. Asst. Surg., 6 June, 1878. Capt. Asst. Surg., 6 June, 1883. Maj. Surg., 1 Oct., 1897.

POWELL, PHILIP P. [Born in Va. Appointed from Army.]
Priv., Corpl. and Sergt. Co. D, 6th Cav., 27 Oct., 1875, to 24 July, 1880. 2nd Lieut. 9th Cav., 24 June, 1880. 1st Lieut., 12 Jan., 1886. Capt., 13 Jan., 1897.

POWELL, RICHARD. [Born in Ireland. Appointed from N. Y.]
Asst. Surg. 88th N. Y. Vols., 28 Sept., 1861. Surg., 11 Nov., 1863. Mustered out 21 Nov., 1864. Asst. Surg., 14 May, 1867. Died 23 May, 1872.

POWELL, R. J. [Born in N. C. Appointed from N. C.]
2nd Lieut. 2nd Inf., 1 Dec., 1839. Resigned 12 Jan., 1841. Died 18 Aug., 1883.

POWELL, WM. H. [Born in D. C. Appointed from D. C.]
Priv. 4th Batt. D. C. Militia, 17 April, 1861. Discharged 17 July, 1861. 2nd Lieut. 4th Inf., 24 Oct., 1861. Reg. Adj., 1 March, 1862, to 29 Jan., 1863. 1st Lieut., 16 Sept., 1862. Bvt. Capt., 17 Sept., 1862, for gallant and meritorious service in the Battle of Antietam, Md. Capt. 4th Inf., 2 Feb., 1865. Bvt. Maj., 2 April, 1865, for gallant and meritorious service in front of Petersburg, Va. Maj. 22nd Inf., 5 Aug., 1888. Lieut. Col. 11th Inf., 4 May, 1892. Col. 9th Inf., 27 June, 1897. Retired, over thirty years' service, 25 April, 1899.

POWER, JOHN. [Born in Ireland. Appointed from Army.]
Priv., Corpl., Sergt. and 1st Sergt. Co. I, 1st Inf., 19 Aug., 1858, to 24 Oct., 1861. 2nd Lieut. 16th Inf., 24 Oct., 1861. 1st Lieut., 15 Feb., 1862. Capt., 11 Feb., 1865. Trans. to 34th Inf., 21 Sept., 1866. Trans. to 16th Inf., 14 April, 1869. Resigned 12 Sept., 1869. Bvt. Capt. and Maj., 31 Dec., 1862, for gallant and meritorious service at the Battle of Murfreesboro, Tenn.

POWERS, CLINTON J.* [Born in Ohio. Appointed from Ohio.]
2nd Lieut. 4th Cav., 23 June, 1865. 1st Lieut., 21 April, 1866. Capt., 10 June, 1870. Died 21 April, 1872.

POWERS, ROBERT B.* [Born in Ky. Appointed from Ky.]
Addl. 2nd Lieut. 10th Cav., 12 June, 1896. 2nd Lieut. 7th Cav., 13 June, 1897.

POWERS, STEPHEN. [Born in Maine. Appointed from N. Y.]
1st Lieut. 10th Inf., 9 April, 1847. Disbanded 16 Aug., 1848.

POWERS, THOMAS J., Jr. [Born in Penn. Appointed from Penn.]
2nd Lieut. 25th Inf., 9 July, 1898. 1st Lieut. 20th Inf., 8 Sept., 1899.

PRATT, EDWARD B. [Born in Va. Appointed from Mich.]
2nd Lieut. 23rd Inf., 12 Dec., 1872. 1st Lieut., 25 June, 1878. Capt., 15 Jan., 1891. Maj., 19 July, 1899. Lieut. Col. 46th U. S. Vols., 17 Aug., 1899.

PRATT, HENRY C.* [Born in Mass. Appointed from Mass.]
2nd Lieut. 2nd Art., 1 July, 1837. 1st Lieut., 11 Dec., 1838. Reg. Adj., 11 Jan. to 21 April, 1848. Bvt. Capt., 19 Oct., 1847, for gallant and meritorious conduct in the affair at Atlixco, Mex. Capt. 2nd Art., 21 April, 1848. Maj. P. M., 14 June, 1861. Bvt. Lieut. Col., 13 March, 1865, for faithful and meritorious service during the war. Retired 19 June, 1879. Died 14 Feb., 1884.

PRATT, HENRY C. [Born in N. Y. Appointed from N. Y.]
2nd Lieut. 38th N. Y. Vols., 11 Jan., 1862. 1st Lieut., 30 July, 1862. Capt., 21 Nov., 1862. Mustered out 22 June, 1863. 1st Lieut. 13th N. Y. Art., 20 Nov., 1863. Capt., 12 Dec., 1864. Mustered out 24 Aug., 1865. 2nd Lieut. 13th Inf., 11 May, 1866. Bvt. 1st Lieut., 2 March, 1867, for gallant and meritorious service in the Battle of Blackburn's Ford, Va. Bvt. Capt., 2 March, 1867, for gallant and meritorious service in the Battle of Fair Oaks, Va. 1st Lieut. 13th Inf., 1 July, 1867. Reg. Adj., 1 Sept., 1871, to 10 June, 1876. Capt., 10 June, 1876. Died 1 March, 1887.

PRATT, JAMES. [Born in Mass. Appointed from Mass.]
Ensign 21st Inf., 12 March, 1812. 2nd Lieut., 13 March, 1813. 1st Lieut., 7 March,

1814. Capt., 30 Sept., 1814. Trans. to 5th Inf., 17 May, 1815. Died 9 Jan., 1821.

PRATT, JAMES. [Born in Maine. Appointed from N. Y.]
Priv. Co. B, 127th Ill. Vols., 21 Aug., 1862. Sergt., 6 Sept., 1862. Discharged 3 Nov., 1862. 1st Lieut. 87th U. S. Col. Troops, 16 Oct., 1863. Capt., 1 Dec., 1864. Bvt. Maj. Vols., 13 March, 1865, for faithful and meritorious service during the war. Capt. 84th U. S. Col. Troops, 31 Aug., 1865. Mustered out 14 March, 1866. 2nd Lieut. 41st Inf., 28 July, 1866. 1st Lieut., 12 Dec., 1867. Unassigned 11 Nov., 1869. Ass'd to 25th Inf., 1 Jan., 1871. Died 6 Aug., 1881.

PRATT, JAMES P. [Born in Ind. Appointed from Army.]
Priv. and Sergt. 19th Inf., 28 Oct., 1861, to 19 March, 1862. 2nd Lieut. 11th Inf., 19 Feb., 1862. 1st Lieut., 10 May, 1862. Killed 29 May, 1864, at Battle of Bethesda Church, Va. Bvt. Capt., 29 May, 1864, for gallant and meritorious service at the Battle of Bethesda Church, Va.

PRATT, JOHN T.* [Born in Ky. Appointed from Ky.]
Priv. Ky. Vols. in 1813. Cadet at Mil. Acad., 20 Sept., 1814. 2nd Lieut. 1st Inf., 24 July, 1818. Resigned 1 June, 1819. Died 29 Nov., 1883.

PRATT, RICH. H. [Born in N. Y. Appointed from Ind.]
Corpl. Co. A, 9th Ind. Vols., 20 April, 1861. Discharged 29 July, 1861. Sergt. Co. A, 2nd Ind. Cav., 18 Sept., 1861. 1st Lieut. 11th Ind. Cav., 20 April, 1864. Capt., 1 Sept., 1864. Mustered out 29 May, 1865. 2nd Lieut. 10th Cav., 7 March, 1867. Bvt. 1st Lieut. and Capt., 7 March, 1867, for gallant and meritorious service during the war. 1st Lieut. 10th Cav., 31 July, 1867. Capt., 17 Feb., 1883. Maj. 5th Cav., 28 July, 1892. Lieut. Col. 10th Cav., 6 May, 1899.

PRATT, SEDGWICK.* [Born in D. C. Appointed at Large.]
2nd Lieut. 4th N. Y. Art., 11 Jan., 1863. Mustered out 3 Sept., 1863. Cadet at Mil. Acad., 9 Sept., 1863. 2nd Lieut. 3rd Art., 17 June, 1867. 1st Lieut., 21 Sept., 1871. R. Q. M., 1 Nov., 1877, to 1 May, 1880, and 20 May, 1884, to 1 March, 1887. Capt., 10 Oct., 1894. Graduate of the Artillery School, 1882.

PRENTICE, SARTELL. [Born in N. Y. Appointed from N. Y.]
1st Lieut. 12th Inf., 14 May, 1861. Capt., 10 May, 1864. Resigned 3 May, 1865. Bvt. Maj., 1 Aug., 1864, for gallant service at the Battle of the Wilderness, and during the campaign before Richmond, Va.

PRENTISS, GEORGE H.* [Born in Vt. Appointed from Vt.]
Bvt. 2nd Lieut. Inf., 1 July, 1827. Resigned 29 Jan., 1828. Died 3 Sept., 1833.

PRENTISS, HENRY E.* [Born in Maine. Appointed from Maine.]
Bvt. 2nd Lieut. 2nd Art., 1 July, 1831. 2nd Lieut., 1 July, 1831. Resigned 10 Sept., 1835. Died 2 July, 1873.

PRENTISS, JAMES H.* [Born in Mass. Appointed from Ind.]
Bvt. 2nd Lieut. 1st Art., 1 July, 1830. 2nd Lieut., 1 July, 1830. 1st Lieut., 29 Feb., 1836. Bvt. Capt. A. A. G., 24 May, 1839, to 18 June, 1846. Capt. 1st Art., 18 June, 1846. Died 22 Sept., 1848.

PRESCOTT, JONATHAN.* [Born in Mass. Appointed from Mass.]
Bvt. 2nd Lieut. 2nd Art., 1 July, 1821. 2nd Lieut. 1st Art., 1 July, 1821. 1st Lieut., 31 March, 1827. Resigned 30 Sept., 1833. Died 12 Aug., 1837.

PRESCOTT, WM. H. [Born in Mass. Appointed from N. H.]
2nd Lieut. 2nd N. H. Vols., 5 June to 7 Aug., 1861. Capt. 16th Inf., 5 Aug., 1861. Resigned 15 Oct., 1864.

PRESTON, ALBERT W. [Born in N. Y. Appointed from N. Y.]
1st Sergt. Co. F, 13th N. Y. Vols., 14 May, 1861. 1st Lieut. 25th N. Y. Vols., 22 Nov., 1861. Capt., 1 Jan., 1862. Mustered out 22 Sept., 1862. Capt. Vet. Res. Corps, 8 June, 1863. Bvt. Maj. Vols., 13 March, 1865, for gallant and meritorious service in the various actions in the Peninsula, from Hanover C. H. to Malvern Hill, and also in the Battle of Antietam, Md. Mustered out 30 Sept., 1867. 2nd Lieut. 8th Cav., 10 Sept., 1867. Bvt. 1st Lieut., 10 Sept., 1867, for gallant and meritorious service in the Battle of Gaines' Mills, Va. Bvt. Capt., 10 Sept., 1867, for gallant and meritorious service in the Battle of Malvern Hill, Va. 1st Lieut. 8th Cav., 1 March, 1870. Retired, with rank of Col., 15 Dec., 1870. Died 13 Sept., 1883.

PRESTON, GUY H.* [Born in Mass. Appointed from Mass.]
Addl. 2nd Lieut. 1st Cav., 11 June, 1888. 2nd Lieut. 9th Cav., 16 July, 1888. 1st Lieut. 4th Cav., 25 Feb., 1896. Trans. to 9th Cav., 14 March, 1896. Maj. 41st U. S. Vols., 17 Aug., 1899, to ——.

PRESTON, JOHN F., Jr.* [Born in Md. Appointed from Md.]
2nd Lieut. 16th Inf., 12 June, 1894. 1st Lieut., 26 April, 1898.

PREVOST, GRAYSON M. [Born in Penn. Appointed from Penn.]
Asst. Surg., 31 Dec., 1845. Resigned 7 June, 1848.

PREVOST, MAURICE. [Born in West Indies. Appointed from La.]
Asst. Com. of Purchases, 4 May, 1813. Disbanded 1 June, 1821.

PRICE, BUTLER D. [Born in Penn. Appointed from Penn.]
2nd Lieut. 2nd Penn. Cav., 6 Dec., 1861. 1st Lieut., 2 Feb., 1863. Mustered out 5 Jan., 1865. Reg. Adj., 1 Sept., 1881, to 17 Sept., 1886. 2nd Lieut. 4th Inf., 11 May, 1866. 1st Lieut., 25 Nov., 1873. Capt., 17 Sept., 1886. Maj., 2 March, 1899.

PRICE, CURTIS E. [Born in Ohio. Appointed from Ill.]
Asst. Surg. 12th Tenn. Cav., 11 May, 1864. Maj. Surg. 12th Tenn. Cav., 10 March, 1865. Bvt. Lieut. Col. Vols., 13 March, 1865, for valuable and meritorious service during the war, and more especially for gallant conduct in the Battle of Nashville, Tenn. Mustered out 7 Oct., 1865. 1st Lieut. Asst. Surg., 26 June, 1875. Capt. Asst. Surg., 26 June, 1880. Maj. Surg., 8 May, 1893. Died 9 Nov., 1896.

PRICE, DAVID.* [Born in Wales. Appointed from Iowa.]
Addl. 2nd Lieut. 1st Art., 15 June, 1877. 2nd Lieut. 2nd Art., 7 June, 1878. Trans. to 1st Art., 14 June, 1878. 1st Lieut., 1 July, 1885. Capt., 2 March, 1899. Maj. 3rd Va. Vols., 1 June to 5 Nov., 1898. Graduate of the Art. Sch., 1882. Reg. Q. M., 24 April, 1899.

PRICE, EDWARD B. [Born in Md. Appointed from Ill.]
Maj. Surg. Vols., 7 July, 1846. Asst. Surg. U. S. A., 3 March, 1847; 14th Inf., 9 April, 1847. Disbanded 26 July, 1848.

PRICE, FREDERICK S. L. [Born in Ga. Appointed from Ga.]
2nd Lieut. 6th Inf., 9 July, 1898.

PRICE, GEORGE F. [Born in N. Y. Appointed from Cal.]
1st Lieut. 2nd Cal. Cav., 3 Sept., 1861. Capt., 14 Nov., 1861. 2nd Lieut. 5th Cav., 23 Feb., 1866. Mustered out of Vol. Service, 9 July, 1866. 1st Lieut. 5th Cav., 31 July, 1866. R. Q. M., 1 May to 29 Aug., 1872. Capt., 29 Aug., 1872. Died 23 May, 1888.

PRICE, HARRISON J. [Born in W. Va. Appointed from Ohio.]
2nd Lieut. 24th Inf., 7 Oct., 1891. 1st Lieut. 2nd Inf., 26 April, 1898. Graduate of the Infantry and Cavalry School, 1897.

PRICE, HOWARD C. [Born in Penn. Appointed from Penn.]
1st Lieut. and Adj. 6th Penn. Vols., 5 May to 17 Oct., 1898. 2nd Lieut. 5th Inf., 10 April, 1899.

PRICE, JOHN T. [Born in Mo. Appointed from Mo.]
2nd Lieut. 5th Inf., 1 May, 1861. 1st Lieut., 8 Aug., 1861. Lieut. Col. 1st Mo. Cav., 4 Dec., 1862. Resigned from Vol. Service, 2 Oct., 1863. Capt., 26 Aug., 1863. Resigned 14 May, 1864.

PRICE, PHILIP M.* [Born in Penn. Appointed from Penn.]
2nd Lieut. 2nd Art., 15 June, 1869. Trans. to Eng., 10 June, 1872. 1st Lieut., 30 Sept., 1873. Capt., 10 Jan., 1883. Died 4 Oct., 1894.

PRICE, ROBERT N.* [Born in Penn. Appointed from Penn.]
2nd Lieut. 10th Cav., 15 June, 1870. Resigned 27 April, 1872. Died 5 April, 1889.

PRICE, WM. H.* [Born in Penn. Appointed from Penn.]
Bvt. 2nd Lieut. 1st Inf., 1 July, 1834. Resigned 31 Aug., 1836.

PRICE, WM. R. [Born in Ohio. Appointed from Ohio.]
2nd Lieut. 3rd Penn. Cav., 15 Jan., 1862. 1st Lieut., 7 Sept., 1862. Capt., 1 May, 1863. Maj. A. A. G. Vols., 5 Aug., 1864. Bvt. Lieut. Col. Vols., 23 Jan., 1865, for industry, zeal, and faithful service during the recent campaign before Richmond Va. Bvt. Col. Vols., 13 March, 1865, for gallant and meritorious service. Bvt. Brig. Gen. Vols., 13 March, 1865, for faithful and meritorious service during the war. Maj. 8th Cav., 28 July, 1866. Mustered out of Vol. Service, 1 Sept., 1866. Bvt. Lieut. Col., 2 March, 1867, for gallant and meritorious service in the Battle of Five Forks, Va. Bvt. Col., 10 Dec., 1868, for gallant and meritorious service in an engagement with Indians in the vicinity of Walker's Springs, in the Aquarious range in Arizona, on 10 Dec. and 13 Dec., 1868. Lieut. Col. 6th Cav., 2 April, 1879. Died 30 Dec., 1881.

PRIME, FRED'K. E.* [Born in Italy. Appointed from N. Y.]
Bvt. 2nd Lieut. Eng., 1 July, 1850. 2nd Lieut., 13 Sept., 1853. 1st Lieut., 1 July, 1856. Capt., 6 Aug., 1861. Bvt. Maj., 4 Oct., 1862, for gallant and meritorious service in the Battle of Corinth, Miss. Maj. Eng., 1 June, 1863. Bvt. Lieut. Col., 4 July, 1863, for gallant and meritorious service during the Siege of Vicksburg, Miss. Brig. Gen. Vols., 4 Aug., 1863 (declined). Bvt. Col., 13 March, 1865, for gallant and meritorious service during the war. Bvt. Brig. Gen., 13 March, 1865, for gallant and meritorious service during the war. Retired 5 Sept., 1871.

PRIME, NATHANIEL. [Born in N. Y. Appointed from N. Y.]
1st Lieut. 17th Inf., 14 May, 1861. R. Q. M., 2 Nov., 1861, to 9 Aug., 1862. Capt., 9 Aug., 1862. Bvt. Maj., 1 Aug., 1864, for gallant service in the Battle of Spottsylvania. Bvt. Lieut. Col., 1 Aug., 1864, for gallant service in the Battle of the Wilderness. Trans. to 26th Inf., 21 Sept., 1866. Trans. to 10th Inf., 19 May, 1869. Retired 20 March, 1879. Died 8 July, 1885.

PRINCE, HENRY.* [Born in Maine. Appointed from Maine.]
Bvt. 2nd Lieut. 4th Inf., 18 Sept., 1835. 2nd Lieut., 11 June, 1836. 1st Lieut., 7 July, 1838. Reg. Adj., 21 Nov., 1846, to 26 Sept., 1847. Bvt. Capt., 20 Aug., 1847, for gallant and meritorious conduct in the Battles of Contreras and Churubusco, Mex. Bvt. Maj., 8 Sept., 1847, for gallant and meritorious conduct in the Battle of Molino del Rey. Capt. 4th Inf., 26 Sept., 1847. Maj. P. M., 23 May, 1855. Brig. Gen. Vols., 28 April, 1862. Bvt. Lieut. Col., 9 Aug., 1862, for gallant and meritorious service in the Battle of Cedar Mountain, Va. Bvt. Col., 13 March, 1865, for faithful and meritorious service during the war. Bvt. Brig. Gen., 13 March, 1865, for gallant and meritorious service in the field during the war. Mustered out of Vol. Service, 30 April, 1866. Lieut. Col. D. P. M. Gen., 3 March, 1877. Retired 31 Dec., 1879. Died 19 Aug., 1892.

PRINCE, JOSEPH P. [Born in S. C. Appointed from S. C.]
3rd Lieut. 2nd Art., 12 April, 1813. 2nd Lieut., 16 April, 1813. Trans. to Corps Art., 12 May, 1814. Disbanded 15 June, 1815. Reinstated 2 Dec., 1815. 1st Lieut., 13 May, 1817. Dismissed 20 Oct., 1818.

PRINCE, LEONARD M.* [Born in Ill. Appointed from Ill.]
2nd Lieut. 2nd Inf., 11 June, 1892. Died 1 Nov., 1895.

PRINCE, OLIVER H. [Born in Ga. Appointed from Ga.]
2nd Lieut. of Inf., 10 March, 1847; 13th Inf., 9 April, 1847. Resigned 20 Aug., 1847.

PRINCE, WM. [Born in N. Y. Appointed from N. Y.]
1st Lieut. 159th N. Y. Vols., 1 Jan., 1864. 2nd Lieut. Ord., 29 Jan., 1864. Mustered out Vol. Service, 30 June, 1864. Bvt. 1st Lieut. and Capt., 31 March, 1865, for gallant and distinguished service. 1st Lieut. Ord., 6 April, 1866. Capt., 23 June, 1874. Died 18 Dec., 1880.

PRINCE, WM. E. [Born in Mass. Appointed from Mass.]
2nd Lieut. 1st Inf., 1 Aug., 1838. 1st Lieut., 8 Nov., 1839. Bvt. Capt., 16 March, 1848, for gallant and meritorious conduct in the Battle of Santa Cruz de Rosales, Mex. Capt. 1st Inf., 31 Aug., 1849. Maj. 3rd Inf., 23 Nov., 1861. Retired 30 March, 1864. Bvt. Lieut. Col., 13 March, 1865, for faithful and meritorious service during the war. Died 21 Jan., 1892.

PRIOLEAU, GEORGE W. [Born in S. C. Appointed from Ohio.]
Chap. 9th Cav., 25 April, 1895.

PRITCHARD, GEORGE B., Jr.* [Born in Ga. Appointed from Ga.]
Addl. 2nd Lieut. 9th Cav., 12 June, 1895. 2nd Lieut., 21 Dec., 1895. 1st Lieut., 8 May, 1899.

PROCTER, JOHN R., Jr. [Born in Ky. Appointed from Ky.]
2nd Lieut. 5th Art., 9 July, 1898.

PROCTER, ROBERT G.* [Born in Ky. Appointed from Ky.]
2nd Lieut. 5th Art., 1 July, 1886. Retired 15 June, 1891. Died 10 May, 1894.

PROCTOR, JOSEPH L. [Born in Mass. Appointed from Mass.]
1st Lieut. 18th Inf., 14 May, 1861. Capt., 15 Jan., 1863. Trans. to 36th Inf., 21 Sept., 1866. Unassigned 19 May, 1869. Discharged 13 Oct., 1870. Bvt. Capt., 31 Dec., 1862, for gallant and meritorious service at the Battle of Murfreesboro, Tenn.

PULIZZI, VENERANDO. [Born in D. C. Appointed from D. C.]
2nd Lieut. 2nd Art., 30 June, 1855. Resigned 21 Sept., 1855. 1st Lieut. 11th Inf., 14 May, 1861. Resigned 9 Sept., 1861.

PULLMAN, JOHN W.* [Born in Mich. Appointed from Wash.]
2nd Lieut. 8th Cav., 15 June, 1869. 1st Lieut., 15 Jan., 1873. Capt. A. Q. M., 27 Feb., 1884. Maj. Q. M., 18 Feb., 1897. Lieut. Col. Q. M. Vols., 10 Aug., 1888, to 2 March, 1899.

PULFORD, JOHN. [Born in N. Y. Appointed from Mich.]
1st Lieut. 5th Mich. Vols., 28 Aug., 1861. Capt., 15 May, 1862. Maj., 1 Jan., 1863. Lieut. Col., 3 May, 1863. Col., 12 July, 1864. Bvt. Brig. Gen. Vols., 13 March, 1865, for good conduct and meritorious service during the war. Mustered out 5 July, 1865. 2nd Lieut. and 1st Lieut. 19th Inf., 23 Feb., 1866. Trans. to 37th Inf., 21 Sept., 1866. Unassigned 19 May, 1869. Retired, with rank of Col., 15 Dec., 1870. Died 11 July, 1896.

PURCELL, EDWARD. [Born in Va. Appointed from Va.]
Hosp. Surg.'s Mate, 2 May, 1813. Post Surg., 18 April, 1818. Maj. Surg. 5th Inf., 21 July, 1818. Retained as Maj. Surg., 1 June, 1821. Died 11 Jan., 1825.

PURCELL, JOHN H. [Born in Ireland. Appointed from Army.]
Priv. and Corpl. Cos. B and K, 2nd Inf., 11 Dec., 1852, to 11 Dec., 1857. Priv., Artif., Armorer and Master Armorer Ord. Dept., 3 Aug., 1860, to 14 July, 1862. 2nd Lieut. 1st Inf., 14 July, 1862. 1st Lieut., 26 Nov., 1864. Unassigned 8 April, 1869. Ass'd to 21st Inf., 25 Oct., 1869. Discharged 2 Dec., 1870.

PURDY, CLARENCE N.* [Born in Ind. Appointed from Ind.]
Addl. 2nd Lieut. 2nd Inf., 12 June, 1896. 2nd Lieut. 6th Inf., 27 Aug., 1896. 1st Lieut. of Inf., 5 Oct., 1898. Ass'd to 6th Inf., 1 Jan., 1899.

PURDY, SAML., Jr. [Born in N. Y. Appointed from Cal.]
2nd Lieut. 1st Wash. Ter. Vols., 1 April, 1862. 1st Lieut., 31 March, 1863. Mustered out 3 April, 1865. 2nd Lieut. 14th Inf., 7 March, 1867. Resigned 26 Nov., 1869.

PURINGTON, GEORGE A. [Born in Ohio. Appointed from Ohio.]
1st Sergt. 19th Ohio Vols., 22 April, 1861. Discharged 31 Aug., 1861. Capt. 2nd Ohio Cav., 27 Aug., 1861. Maj., 10 Sept., 1861. Lieut. Col., 10 July, 1863. Mustered out 1 Nov., 1864. Capt. 9th Cav., 28 July, 1866. Bvt. Maj., 2 March, 1867, for gallant and meritorious service in the Battle of the Wilderness, Va. Bvt. Lieut. Col., 2 March, 1867, for gallant and meritorious service in the Battle of Winchester, Va. Bvt. Col., 2 March, 1867, for gallant and meritorious service in the Battle of Cedar Creek, Va. Maj. 3rd Cav., 25 Oct., 1883. Lieut. Col. of Cav. (3rd), 20 Oct., 1892. Retired for disability, 17 July, 1895.

PURSSELL, BENJAMIN M. [Born in Ohio. Appointed from Army.]
Priv. and Sergt. Sig. Corps, 13 May, 1873, to 14 Oct., 1883. 2nd Lieut. Sig. Corps, 13 Oct., 1883. 2nd Lieut. 4th Inf., 4 Feb., 1891. 1st Lieut. 20th Inf., 17 April, 1891. Trans. to 19th Inf., 20 July, 1891. Capt. of Inf., 22 Aug., 1898. Ass'd to 10th Inf., 1 Jan., 1899.

PURVIANCE, SAMUEL A. [Born in Penn. Appointed from Penn.]
Priv. Troop G, 6th Cav., 25 May to 4 Sept., 1898. 2nd Lieut. 4th Cav., 10 April, 1899.

PURVIANCE, WM. E. [Born in Ind. Appointed from Ill.]
Asst. Surg., 9 March, 1892. Capt. Asst. Surg., 9 March, 1897.

PUTNAM, ALFRED B.* [Born in Mass. Appointed from Mass.]
2nd Lieut. 7th Art., 15 Feb., 1899. Trans. to 3rd Art., 4 April, 1899.

PUTNAM, AT LEE W. [Born in Mass. Appointed from Conn.]
2nd Lieut. 7th Inf., 26 April, 1861. 1st Lieut., 16 May, 1861. Capt. A. Q. M., 3 Aug., 1861. Died 2 May, 1863.

PUTNAM, GEO. I.* [Born in N. H. Appointed from N. H.]
2nd Lieut. 16th Inf., 14 June, 1885. Resigned 3 Nov., 1889.

PUTNAM, HALDEMAND S.* [Born in N. H. Appointed from N. H.]
Bvt. 2nd Lieut. Top. Eng., 1 July, 1857. 2nd Lieut., 1 April, 1861. 1st Lieut., 3 Aug., 1861. Capt. Eng., 3 March, 1863. Col. 7th N. H. Vols., 14 Dec., 1861. Bvt. Maj., 21 July, 1861, for gallant and meritorious service in the Manassas Campaign. Bvt. Lieut. Col., 10 July, 1863, for gallant and meritorious service at the descent upon Morris Island, S. C. Bvt. Col., 18 July, 1863, for gallant service at the assault of Fort Wagner, S. C., where he was killed.

PUTNAM, HENRY R. [Born in Maine. Appointed from Minn.]
Capt. 1st Minn. Vols., 26 April to 8 Aug., 1861. Capt. 12th Inf., 5 Aug., 1861. Maj. A. de C. Vols., 7 Oct., 1864. Mustered out of Vol. Service, 20 July, 1865. Trans. to 21st Inf., 21 Sept., 1866. Discharged 23 Nov., 1870. Bvt. Maj., 13 March, 1865, for gallant and meritorious service during the riots in N. Y. City, in July, 1863. Died 12 Feb., 1872.

PUTNAM, ISRAEL. [Born in N. Y. Appointed from N. Y.]
2nd Lieut. 14th Inf., 10 April, 1899. Trans. to 6th Inf., 6 June, 1899.

PUTNAM, JAMES E. [Born in Maine. Appointed from Army.]
Priv., Sergt. and 1st Sergt. Co. F, 2nd Batt. 12th Inf., 25 Sept., 1861, to 14 Aug., 1863. 2nd Lieut. 12th Inf., 10 Aug., 1863. 1st Lieut., 19 Dec., 1863. Reg. Adj., 30 Jan., 1865, to 18 Aug., 1866. Capt., 22 Feb., 1869. Resigned 31 March, 1873. Bvt. Capt., 5 May, 1864, for gallant and meritorious service at the Battle of the Wilderness, Va.

PYLE, GEORGE W.* [Born in Ohio. Appointed at Large.]
2nd Lieut. 3rd Cav., 15 June, 1868. Died 29 Dec., 1868.

PYNE, CHAS. M. [Born in N. J. Appointed from D. C.]
Corpl. Co. A, 3rd Batt. D. C. Vols., 15 April, 1861. Discharged 15 July, 1861. 2nd Lieut. 6th Inf., 5 Aug., 1861. Bvt. 1st Lieut., 30 Aug., 1862, for gallant and meritorious service in the Battle of Bull Run (2nd), Va. 1st Lieut. 6th Inf., 8 Aug., 1863. Bvt. Capt., 23 Jan., 1865. Capt. 42nd Inf., 28 July, 1866. Unassigned 22 April, 1869. Retired 15 Dec., 1870. Died 4 Feb., 1892.

QUACKENBOS, MANGLE M. [Born in N. Y. Appointed from N. Y.]
1st Lieut. 41st Inf., 1 Aug., 1813. Capt., 7 Jan., 1814. Trans. to 8th Inf., 17 May, 1815. Resigned 15 March, 1816. Mil. Storekeeper, 9 March, 1819. Disbanded 1 June, 1821. Died — 1837.

QUARLES, AUGUSTUS. [Born in Mass. Appointed from Wis.]
Capt. of Inf., 16 March, 1847; 15th Inf., 9 April, 1847. Killed 20 Aug., 1847, at the Battle of Churubusco, Mex.

QUATTLEBAUM, PAUL J.* [Born in S. C. Appointed from S. C.]
Bvt. 2nd Lieut. 3rd Inf., 1 July, 1857. 2nd Lieut. 9th Inf., 1 Aug., 1857. Resigned 29 June, 1861. Died 4 Jan., 1883.

QUAY, ANDREW G. C.* [Born in Penn. Appointed from Penn.]
Addl. 2nd Lieut. 8th Cav., 11 June, 1888. 2nd Lieut. 5th Cav., 21 Aug., 1888. 1st Lieut. 3rd Cav., 5 April, 1896. Capt. A. Q. M., 16 June, 1897. Maj. Q. M. Vols., 11 Aug., 1898. Resigned 31 Aug., 1899.

QUENTIN, JULIUS E. [Born in Germany. Appointed from N. Y.]
Capt. 103rd N. Y. Vols., 6 March, 1862. Discharged 19 Jan., 1863. Capt. 103rd N. Y. Vols., 30 Aug., 1863. Mustered out 15 March, 1865. 1st Lieut. Vet. Res. Corps, 15 March, 1865. Mustered out 7 Jan., 1867. 2nd Lieut. 45th Inf., 28 July, 1866. 1st Lieut., 1 March, 1867. Trans. to 14th Inf., 22 July, 1869. Capt., 15 June, 1887. Retired for disability, 15 June, 1888. Died 14 June, 1890.

QUIMBY, H. BAXTER. [Born in N. H. Appointed from N. H.]
1st Sergt. Co. H, 9th N. H. Vols., 11 Aug., 1862. 2nd Lieut. 9th N. H. Vols., 22 Nov., 1862. 1st Lieut., 15 Feb., 1864. Mustered out 10 June, 1865. 2nd Lieut. 108th U. S. Col. Troops, 20 Sept., 1865. Mustered out 21 March, 1866. 2nd Lieut. 39th Inf., 28 July, 1866. 1st Lieut., 31 July, 1867. R. Q. M., 1 Feb., 1868, to 20 April, 1869. Trans. to 25th Inf., 20 April, 1869. R. Q. M., 25 April, 1869, to 3 Sept., 1878. Capt., 31 Dec., 1880. Died 19 Feb., 1883.

QUIMBY, THOS. R. [Born in Maine. Appointed from Maine.]
2nd Lieut. 7th Inf., 1 Aug., 1845. Resigned 21 Oct., 1845.

QUIMBY, WM. M. [Born in Maine. Appointed from Maine.]
Capt. 1st Maine Vols., 3 May, 1861. Mustered out 5 Aug., 1861. Capt. 12th Inf., 5 Aug., 1861. Retired 20 Jan., 1865. Died 11 April, 1876. Bvt. Maj., 9 Aug., 1862, for gallant and meritorious service at the Battle of Cedar Mountain, Va.

QUINAN, PASCAL A. [Born in Ky. Appointed from Md.]
Asst. Surg., 15 Aug., 1855. Resigned 7 July, 1862.

QUINAN, WM. R.* [Born in Md. Appointed from Md.]
2nd Lieut. 4th Art., 15 June, 1870. 1st Lieut., 12 May, 1873. Resigned 11 Nov., 1881.

QUINBY, DE HART G. [Born in R. I. Appointed from N. Y.]
Cadet at Naval Acad., 20 July, 1865, to 21 June, 1866. 2nd Lieut. 5th Inf., 1 Nov., 1866. Died 10 March, 1873.

QUINBY, IRA. [Born in N. Y. Appointed from Col.]
1st Sergt. Co. D, 2nd Colo. Vols., 5 Sept., 1861. 2nd Lieut., 5 June, 1862. 1st Lieut., 7 May, 1864. Mustered out 18 Nov., 1865. 2nd Lieut. 15th Inf., 23 Feb., 1866. 1st Lieut., 28 March, 1866. Trans. to 24th Inf., 21 Sept., 1866. R. Q. M., 1 March, 1867, to 25 April, 1869. Trans. to 11th Inf., 25 April, 1869. R. Q. M., 25 April, 1869, to 3 Sept., 1878. Capt., 21 Dec., 1880. Maj. 1st Inf., 30 June, 1898. Retired by operation of law, 13 March, 1899.

QUINBY, ISAAC F.* [Born in N. J. Appointed from N. J.]
Bvt. 2nd Lieut. 2nd Art., 1 July, 1843. 2nd Lieut. 3rd Art., 20 Dec., 1845. 1st Lieut., 3 March, 1847. R. Q. M., 24 Oct., 1848, to 10 Oct., 1850. Reg. Adj., 10 Oct., 1850, to 1 Nov., 1851. Resigned 16 March, 1852. Col. 13th N. Y. Vols., 14 May, 1861. Resigned 4 Aug., 1861. Brig. Gen. Vols., 17 March, 1862. Resigned 31 Dec., 1863.

QUINN, JAMES B.* [Born in Ohio. Appointed from Ohio.]
2nd Lieut. Eng., 18 June, 1866. 1st Lieut., 7 March, 1867. Capt., 4 March, 1879. Maj., 22 July, 1888.

QUINN, THOS. F. [Born in Ireland. Appointed from Army.]
Music Boy Gen. Ser., 14 April, 1853. Musician Co. C, 2nd Art., 25 Feb., 1854. Discharged 13 April, 1858. Priv. Gen. Ser., 3 Feb., 1859. Priv. Band 4th Inf., 29 Nov., 1860. Drum Maj. 4th Inf., 1 Dec., 1861. Prin. Musician, 30 June, 1862. Sergt. Maj. 4th Inf., 21 July, 1863. 2nd Lieut. 4th Inf., 31 Oct., 1863. 1st Lieut., 2 Feb., 1865. Bvt. Capt., 2 April, 1865, for gallant and meritorious service in front of Petersburg, Va. Capt. 4th Inf., 10 Jan., 1876. Retired, after forty years' service, 3 Feb., 1894.

QUITMAN, JOHN A. [Born in N. Y. Appointed from Miss.]
Brig. Gen. Vols., 1 July, 1846. Maj. Gen., 14 April, 1847. Disbanded 20 July, 1848. Bvt. Maj. Gen. U. S. A., 23 Sept., 1846, for gallant and meritorious conduct in the Battle of Monterey, Mex. Received by resolution of Congress, 2 March, 1847, the testimonial of a sword "in testimony of the high sense entertained by Congress of his gallantry and good conduct in storming Monterey." Died 17 July, 1858.

QUINTON, WM. [Born in Ireland. Appointed from Ill.]
Sergt. Co. C, 19th Ill. Vols., 17 June, 1861. 2nd Lieut. 19th Ill. Vols., 2 Nov., 1861. 1st Lieut., 1 March, 1863. 2nd Lieut. Sig. Corps, 3 March, 1863. Mustered out 1 May, 1866. 1st Lieut. 33rd Inf., 12 June, 1867. Ass'd to 7th Inf., 3 May, 1870. Capt., 18 April, 1884. Trans. to 25th Inf., 16 Sept., 1898. Maj. 14th Inf., 16 Sept., 1898.

QUINTON, WILLIAM W. [Born in Ill. Appointed from N. Y.]
Asst. Surg., 26 Oct., 1893. Capt. Asst. Surg., 26 Oct., 1898.

QUIRK, PAUL. [Born in Ireland. Appointed from Army.]
Priv. Co. F, 2nd Drag., 15 April, 1852. Discharged 15 April, 1857. Priv. Co. F, 2nd Drag., 16 April, 1857. Corpl., 1 Jan., 1858. Sergt., 1 Dec., 1858. Discharged 17 Feb., 1862. 1st Sergt. Co. F, 2nd Cav., 17 Feb., 1862. 2nd Lieut. 2nd Cav., 17 July, 1862. Bvt. 1st Lieut., 17 Sept., 1862, for gallant and meritorious service during the Maryland campaign. Bvt. Capt., 9 June, 1863, for gallant and meritorious service in the Battle of Beverly Ford, Va. 1st Lieut. 2nd Cav., 13 Feb., 1864. Retired 5 Jan., 1865. Bvt. Maj., 13 March, 1865, for gallant and meritorious service during the war. Retired, with rank of Capt. Mounted, 28 July, 1866. Died 9 Nov., 1897.

RABB, JAMES D.* [Born in Ind. Appointed from Ky.]
1st Lieut. Eng., 11 June, 1863. Died 26 Aug., 1863.

RADCLIFF, HERMAN G. [Born in N. Y. Appointed from N. Y.]
1st Lieut. 18th Inf., 14 May, 1861. Died 22 March, 1863.

RADETZKI, GUSTAVE H. [Born in Russia. Appointed from Texas.]
Priv. and Sergt. Co. L, 3rd Mass. Cav., 15 June to 15 Oct., 1862. 2nd Lieut. 2nd Tex. Cav., 8 Dec., 1862. 1st Lieut., 7 Dec., 1863. Trans. to 1st Tex. Cav., 10 Sept., 1864. Capt., 26 Sept., 1864. Mustered out 31 Oct., 1865. 2nd Lieut. 28th Inf., 28 July, 1866. 1st Lieut., 8 Aug., 1868. Unassigned 31 March, 1869. Ass'd to 9th Cav., 1 Jan., 1871. Dismissed 15 Oct., 1872. Reinstated 6 Jan., 1873. Dismissed 19 Nov., 1873.

RADFORD, RICHARD C. W.* [Born in Va. Appointed from Va.]
Bvt. 2nd Lieut. 1st Drag., 1 July, 1845. 2nd Lieut. 2nd Drag., 18 May, 1846. Trans. to 1st Drag., 9 July, 1846. 1st Lieut., 24 Oct., 1848. Capt., 4 Sept., 1855. Resigned 30 Nov., 1856. Died 2 Nov., 1885.

RADZIMINSKI, CHAS. [Born in Poland. Appointed from La.]
2nd Lieut. of Inf., 8 March, 1847; 3rd Drag., 9 April, 1847. R. Q. M., 15 June to 13 Oct., 1847. Reg. Adj., 16 March to 31 July, 1848. Disbanded 31 July, 1848. 1st Lieut. 2nd Cav., 30 June, 1855. Died 18 Aug., 1858.

RAFFERTY, OGDEN. [Born in N. J. Appointed from N. J.]
Asst. Surg., 26 March, 1888. Capt. Asst. Surg., 26 March, 1893. Maj. Brig. Surg. Vols., 4 June to 30 Nov., 1898. Maj. Surg. 27th U. S. Vols., 5 July, 1899.

RAFFERTY, THOS. [Born in Ireland. Appointed from N. Y.]
Capt. 71st N. Y. Vols., 7 July, 1861. Maj., 1 Aug., 1862. Lieut. Col., 10 Feb., 1864. Mustered out 30 July, 1864. 2nd Lieut. 12th Inf., 11 May, 1866. Resigned 10 Sept., 1866. Died 21 Feb., 1888.

RAFFERTY, WM. A.* [Born in N. J. Appointed at Large.]
2nd Lieut. 6th Cav., 23 June, 1865. 1st Lieut., 1 May, 1866. Reg. Adj., 12 Dec., 1866, to 14 May, 1868. Capt., 14 May, 1868. Maj. 2nd Cav., 20 Nov., 1889. Lieut. Col., 31 May, 1898. Col. 5th Cav., 18 Oct., 1899. Bvt. Maj., 27 Feb., 1890, for gallant services in actions against Indians on the Little Wichita River, Tex., 5 Oct., 1870, and in the Hatchet Mountains, New Mex., 28 April, 1882.

RAFFERTY, WILLIAM C.* [Born in Ind. Appointed from Ill.]
2nd Lieut. 1st Art., 12 June, 1880. 1st Lieut., 11 Aug., 1887. Capt., 2 March, 1899. Graduate of the Artillery School, 1884.

RAGAN, ABRAM B. [Born in Ga. Appointed from Ga.]
Addl. P. M., 29 March, 1848. Disbanded 1 July, 1849. P. M., 15 March, 1857. Resigned 30 June, 1861.

RAGAN, DANIEL. [Born in Va. Appointed from Va.]
Mil. Storekeeper Ord., 11 Aug., 1837. Died 4 Dec., 1845.

RAGAN, ZACHARIAH. [Born in Penn. Appointed from Penn.]
Chap. 25th Ohio Vols., 26 July, 1861, to 6 Jan., 1863. Hosp. Chap. Vols., 9 Dec., 1862. Mustered out 20 Nov., 1865. Capt. Post Chap., 28 March, 1868. Died 27 Nov., 1875.

RAGUET, LLEWELLYN. [Born in Ohio. Appointed from Ohio.]
2nd Lieut. Mounted Rifles, 27 May, 1846. Resigned 29 May, 1847.

RAIBOURN, WILLIAM A. [Born in Ind. Appointed from Army.]
Priv., Corpl. and Sergt. Batty F, 3rd Art., 16 May, 1891, to 4 Oct., 1894. 2nd Lieut. 4th Inf., 31 Oct., 1894. 1st Lieut. 10th Inf., 26 April, 1898.

RAILEY, JOHN C. [Born in Ky. Appointed from Ky.]
2nd Lieut. 16th Inf., 27 June, 1848. Disbanded 20 July, 1848.

RAINS, GABRIEL J.* [Born in N. C. Appointed from N. C.]
Bvt. 2nd and 2nd Lieut. 7th Inf., 1 July, 1827. 1st Lieut., 28 Jan., 1834. Capt., 25 Dec., 1837. Maj. 4th Inf., 9 March, 1851. Lieut. Col. 5th Inf., 5 June, 1860. Resigned 31 July, 1861. Bvt. Maj., 28 April, 1840, for gallant and meritorious conduct in action with Seminole Indians, near Fort King, Fla. Died 6 Aug., 1881.

RAINS, GEORGE W.* [Born in N. C. Appointed from Ala.]
2nd Lieut. Eng., 1 July, 1842. Trans. to 4th Art., 7 July, 1843. 1st Lieut., 3 March, 1847. Capt., 14 Feb., 1856. Resigned 31 Oct., 1856. Bvt. Capt., 20 Aug., 1847, for gallant and meritorious conduct at Contreras and Churubusco, Mex. Bvt. Maj., 13 Sept., 1847, for gallant conduct at Chapultepec, Mex.

RAINS, SEVIER M.* [Born in Mich. Appointed from Ga.]
2nd Lieut. 1st Cav., 15 June, 1876. Killed 3 July, 1877, in action with Indians in Idaho, at Craig's Mountain.

RALLINS, SAM'L. [Born in Va. Appointed from Va.]
2nd Lieut. 7th Inf., 27 Oct., 1820. Disbanded 1 June, 1821.

RAMSAY, CHARLES R. [Born in Md. Appointed from Md.]
Priv. Co. A, 5th Md. Vols., 14 May to 19 Aug., 1898. 2nd Lieut. 21st Inf., 9 July, 1898. 1st Lieut., 10th Inf., 16 Sept., 1899.

RAMSAY, DOUGLAS. [Born in D. C. Appointed from D. C.]
2nd Lieut. 1st Art., 7 June, 1855. 1st Lieut., 25 Feb., 1861. Killed 21 July, 1861, at the Battle of Bull Run, Va.

RAMSAY, GEORGE D.* [Born in Va. Appointed from D. C.]
2nd Lieut. Corps Art., 1 July, 1820. Trans. to 1st Art., 1 June, 1821. 1st Lieut., 1 March, 1826. Reg. Adj., 1 Dec., 1833, to 25 Feb., 1835. Capt. Ord., 25 Feb., 1835. Bvt. Maj., 23 Sept., 1846, for gallant and meritorious conduct in the several conflicts at Monterey. Maj. Ord., 22 April, 1861. Lieut. Col., 3 Aug., 1861. Col., 1 June, 1863. Brig. Gen. Chief of Ord., 15 Sept., 1863. Retired 12 Sept., 1864. Bvt. Maj. Gen., 13 March, 1865, for long and faithful service in the army. Died 23 May, 1882.

RAMSAY, GEORGE D., Jr.* [Born in D. C. Appointed from D. C.]
2nd Lieut. 1st Art., 11 June, 1863. Trans. to Ord., 6 Nov., 1863. 1st Lieut., 6 Nov., 1863. Capt., 23 June, 1874. Died 5 July, 1878. Bvt. Capt., 13 March, 1865, for meritorious service in the Ord. Dept. during the war.

RAMSAY, JOSEPH G. [Born in Penn. Appointed at Large.]
2nd Lieut. 2nd Art., 5 Aug., 1861. 1st Lieut., 12 Nov., 1861. Reg. Adj., 4 Nov., 1863, to 17 Nov., 1864. Capt. A. A. G. Vols., 17 Nov., 1864. Bvt. Capt., 13 March, 1865, for gallant and meritorious service during the war. Mustered out of Vol. Service, 3 Aug., 1865. R. Q. M., 23 June, 1866, to 5 Feb., 1867. Capt. 2nd Art., 5 Feb., 1867. Maj. 3rd Art., 30 Sept., 1891. Trans. to 5th Art., 7 Oct., 1896. Lieut. Col. 7th Art., 8 March, 1898. Died 13 Feb., 1899.

RAMSEUR, DAVID P. [Born in N. C. Appointed from N. C.]
Asst. Surg., 15 Oct., 1860. Dismissed 17 Aug., 1861.

RAMSEUR, STEPHEN D.* [Born in N. C. Appointed from N. C.]
Bvt. 2nd Lieut. 3rd Art., 1 July, 1860. 2nd Lieut. 4th Art., 1 Feb., 1861. Resigned 6 April, 1861. Died 20 Oct., 1864.

RAMSEY, ALBERT C. [Born in Penn. Appointed from Penn.]
Col. of Inf., 3 March, 1847; 11th Inf., 9 April, 1847. Disbanded 14 Aug., 1848. Died 9 March, 1869.

RAMSEY, FRANK DEW.* [Born in N. Y. Appointed from N. Y.]
2nd Lieut. 9th Inf., 14 June, 1885. 1st Lieut. 2nd Inf., 25 Jan., 1892. Trans. to 14th Inf., 9 Feb., 1892. Trans. to 9th Inf., 12 Aug., 1892. Capt., 2 March, 1899.

RAMSEY, HENRY K. [Born in Penn. Appointed from Penn.]
2nd Lieut. of Inf., 3 March, 1847; 16th Inf., 9 April, 1847. 1st Lieut., 14 June, 1847. Disbanded 5 Aug., 1848. Died 9 Sept., 1855.

RAMSEY, SAM'L. [Born in Ohio. Appointed from Ohio.]
2nd Lieut. 15th Inf., 3 March, 1848. Disbanded 4 Aug., 1848.

RAMSEY, THOS. [Born in Penn. Appointed from Ohio.]
2nd Lieut. 1st Rifles, 27 Jan., 1809. 1st Lieut., 31 July, 1810. Capt. 1st Rifles, 30 Nov., 1812. Disbanded 15 June, 1815. Reinstated 2 Dec., 1815, in Rifle Reg. Died 6 Aug., 1818.

RAMSEY, WM. R. [Born in Penn. Appointed from Penn.]
Asst. Surg., 5 Aug., 1861. Resigned 9 June, 1868. Bvt. Capt. and Maj., 13 March, 1865, for faithful and meritorious service during the war.

RAND, IRVING W. [Born in N. H. Appointed from N. H.]
Asst. Surg., 6 Nov., 1895.

RAND, LEWIS H.* [Born in N. J. Appointed from N. J.]
2nd Lieut. Eng., 15 Feb., 1899.

RANDAL, HORACE.* [Born in Tenn. Appointed from Tex.]
Bvt. 2nd Lieut. 8th Inf., 1 July, 1854. 2nd Lieut. 1st Drag., 3 March, 1855. Resigned 27 Feb., 1861. Died 30 April, 1864.

RANDALL, BURTON. [Born in Md. Appointed from Md.]
Asst. Surg., 24 Oct., 1832. Maj. Surg., 7 July, 1838. Bvt. Lieut. Col., 13 March, 1865, for faithful and meritorious service during the war. Retired 17 Oct., 1868. Died 8 Feb., 1886.

RANDALL, DANIEL. [Born in Md. Appointed from D. C.]
Asst. Dist. P. M., 8 June, 1814. Disbanded 15 June, 1815. Maj. P. M. 1st Inf., 21 July, 1818. Lieut. Col. Dep. P. M. G., 3 March, 1847. Died 17 Dec., 1851.

RANDALL, EDWARD L. [Born in Penn. Appointed from Penn.]
Corpl. Co. E, 33rd Pa. Vol. Militia, 24 June, 1863. Discharged 31 July, 1863. 2nd Lieut. 1st U. S. Col. Troops, 29 Jan., 1864. 1st Lieut., 13 Oct., 1864. Mustered out 29 Sept., 1865. 2nd Lieut. 5th Inf., 23 Feb., 1866. 1st Lieut., 31 Oct., 1866. Capt., 27 June, 1884. Retired for disability, with rank of Maj., 17 Sept., 1898.

RANDALL, GEORGE M. [Born in Ohio. Appointed from Penn.]
Priv. Co. A, 4th Penn. Vols., 20 April, 1861. Discharged 25 July, 1861. 2nd Lieut. 4th Inf., 24 Oct., 1861. Bvt. Capt., 17 Sept., 1862, for gallant and meritorious service in the Battle of Antietam, Md. 1st Lieut. 4th Inf., 6 Nov., 1862. Maj. 14th N. Y. Art., 16 Aug., 1864. Bvt. Lieut. Col. and Col. Vols., 26 March, 1865, for gallantry in the attack on Fort Stedman, Va. Bvt. Maj., 2 April, 1865, for gallant and meritorious service in front of Petersburg, Va. Lieut. Col. 14th N. Y. Art., 1 June, 1865. Mustered out of Vol. Service, 26 Aug., 1865. Capt. 4th Inf., 23 Sept., 1865. Unassigned 23 March, 1869. Ass'd to 23rd Inf., 1 Jan., 1871. Maj. 4th Inf., 15 Jan., 1891. Lieut. Col. 8th Inf., 1 March, 1894. Col. 17th Inf., 8 Aug., 1898. Trans. to 8th Inf., 16 Sept., 1898. Brig. Gen. Vols., 4 May, 1898, to 12 April, 1899. Bvt. Lieut. Col., 27 Feb., 1890, for gallant services in action against Indians at Turret Mountain, Ariz., 27 March, 1873, and at Diamond Butte, Ariz., 22 April, 1873. Bvt. Col., 27 Feb., 1890, for gallant services in action against Indians near Pinal, Ariz., 8 March, 1874, and distinguished services during the campaign against Indians in Ariz., in 1874. Brig. Gen. Vols., 1900.

RANDALL, JOHN N. [Born in N. H. Appointed from Ill.]
Asst. Surg., 9 Oct., 1867. Resigned 17 Oct., 1868.

RANDALL, LEONARD. [Born in N. C. Appointed from Tex.]
Asst. Surg., 3 March, 1847; 12th Inf., 9 April, 1847. Resigned 3 Aug., 1847.

RANDALL, RICHARD. [Born in Md.. Appointed from Md.]
Surg.'s Mate 2nd Inf., 10 Aug., 1818. Trans. to 4th Inf., 28 Sept., 1818. Post Surg., 12 Oct., 1820. Asst. Surg., 1 June, 1821. Resigned 15 Aug., 1821.

RANDALL, THOS. [Born in Md. Appointed from Md.]
2nd Lieut. 14th Inf., 12 March, 1812. 1st Lieut., 13 March, 1813. Capt., 1 Dec., 1814. Trans. to Corps Art., as 1st Lieut., 17 May, 1815. Resigned 15 June, 1817. Retained in the reorganization of 1815, under the Act of 3 March, 1815, as 1st Lieut. of Art., with Bvt. of Capt. from 1 Dec., 1814.

RANDLETT, JAMES F. [Born in N. H. Appointed from N. H.]
Capt. 3rd N. H. Vols., 23 Aug., 1861. Maj., 6 April, 1864. Lieut. Col., 15 Oct., 1864. Mustered out 20 July, 1865. Capt. 39th Inf., 6 June, 1867. Unassigned 20 April, 1869. Ass'd to 8th Cav., 15 Dec., 1870. Maj. 9th Cav., 5 July, 1886. Lieut. Col., 14 Oct., 1896. Retired by operation of law, 8 Dec., 1896.

RANDOL, ALANSON M.* [Born in N. Y. Appointed from N. Y.]
Bvt. 2nd Lieut. 4th Art., 1 July, 1860. Trans. to Ord., 9 Oct., 1860. Trans. to 3rd Art., 14 Jan., 1861. 2nd Lieut. 1st Art., 22 Nov., 1860. 1st Lieut., 14 May, 1861. Bvt. Capt., 30 June, 1862, for gallant and meritorious service in action at Newmarket, Va. Capt. 1st Art., 11 Oct., 1862. Bvt. Maj., 3 July, 1863, for gallant and meritorious service in the Battle of Gettysburg, Penn. Col. 2nd N. Y. Cav., 23 Dec., 1864. Bvt. Lieut. Col., 13 March, 1865, for gallant and meritorious service in the Battle of Five Forks, Va. Bvt. Col., 13 March, 1865, for gallant and meritorious service during the war. Mustered out of Vol. Service, 23 June, 1865. Bvt. Brig. Gen. Vols., 24 June, 1865, for meritorious service during the war. Maj. 3rd Art., 19 April, 1882. Trans. to 1st Art., 5 May, 1882. Died 7 May, 1887.

RANDOLPH, BENJN. H.* [Born in R. I. Appointed from R. I.]
2nd Lieut. 3rd Art., 15 June, 1876. 1st Lieut., 23 April, 1879. Capt., 8 March, 1898. Graduate of the Artillery School, 1875.

RANDOLPH, EDWARD B. [Born in Va. Appointed from Va.]
Ensign 20th Inf., 15 May, 1812. 2nd Lieut., 14 Aug., 1813. 1st Lieut., 31 Dec., 1814. Trans. to 4th Inf., 17 May, 1815. Reg. P. M., 28 March, 1816, to 31 Oct., 1817. Resigned 31 Oct., 1817. Bvt. 1st Lieut., 25 July, 1814, for gallant conduct at the Battle of Niagara, U. C.

RANDOLPH, JOHN A. [Born in Tenn. Appointed from Tex.]
Chap. 3rd Miss. Vols., 6 Sept., 1898, to 17 March, 1899. Chap., 6 March, 1899.

RANDOLPH, JOHN B. [Born in D. C. Appointed from D. C.]
Priv. Co. A. 3rd Batt. D. C. Vols., 15 April to 15 July, 1861. 2nd Lieut. 5th Inf., 5 Aug., 1861. 1st Lieut., 26 Oct., 1861. Resigned 30 April, 1863.

RANDOLPH, JOHN F. [Born in Va. Appointed from La.]
1st Lieut. Asst. Surg., 24 Dec., 1855. Capt. Asst. Surg., 24 Dec., 1859. Maj. Surg., 27 Aug., 1862. Col. Med. Director (Act 25 Feb., 1865), 25 Feb., 1865. Bvt. Lieut. Col., 13 March, 1865, for faithful and meritorious service during the war. Relieved as Col. Med. Director (Act 25 Feb., 1865), 30 June, 1865. Died 14 May, 1880.

RANDOLPH, MURRAY W. [Born in D. C. Appointed from Ga.]
2nd Lieut. 4th Inf., 30 June, 1855. Appointment cancelled, 17 May, 1856.

RANDOLPH, PHILIP G. [Born in Va. Appointed from Va.]
Asst. Surg., 8 Oct., 1824. Resigned 1 May, 1829.

RANDOLPH, THOMAS B.* [Born in Va. Appointed from Va.]
2nd Lieut. Light Art., 3 Jan., 1812. 1st Lieut., 20 Jan., 1813. Capt. 20th Inf., 5 April, 1813. Resigned 6 Feb., 1815. Lieut. Col. 1st Va. Vols., 7 Jan., 1847. Mustered out 20 July, 1848. Died 12 Nov., 1867.

RANDOLPH, WALLACE F. [Born in Penn. Appointed from Penn.]
Priv. Co. F. 17th Penn. Vols., 18 April to 28 June, 1861. 2nd Lieut. 5th Art., 14 May, 1861. 1st Lieut., 1 March, 1862. Bvt. Capt., 14 June, 1863, for gallant and meritorious service in the defence of Winchester, Va. Bvt. Maj., 13 March, 1865, for good conduct and gallant service during the war. Capt. 5th Art., 28 July, 1866. Maj. 3rd Art., 25 April, 1888. Lieut. Col., 8 March, 1898. Col. 1st Art., 17 Oct., 1899.

RANKIN, JAMES L.* [Born in Penn. Appointed from Penn.]
2nd Lieut. 3rd Art., 1 July, 1839. 1st Lieut., 1 April, 1840. Accidentally killed 20 Dec., 1845.

RANKIN, WM. G. [Born in Penn. Appointed from Wash. Ter.]
Capt. 13th Inf., 14 May, 1861. Trans. to 31st Inf., 21 Sept., 1866. Unassigned 15 May, 1869. Ass'd to 13th Inf., 14 July, 1869. Discharged 31 Dec., 1870. Bvt. Maj. and Lieut. Col., 13 March, 1865, for faithful service during the war.

RANSOM, DUNBAR R. [Born in N. C. Appointed from Vt.]
Cadet at Mil. Acad., 1 July, 1847, to 30 Sept., 1850. 2nd Lieut. 3rd Art., 7 June, 1855. 1st Lieut., 31 Dec., 1856. Capt., 1 Nov., 1861. Dismissed 20 Oct., 1872. Bvt. Maj., 13 Dec., 1862, for gallant and meritorious service at the Battle of Fredericksburg, Va. Bvt. Lieut. Col., 3 July, 1863, for gallant and meritorious service at the Battle of Gettysburg, Penn. Bvt. Col., 25 Aug., 1864, for gallant and meritorious service in action at Kearneysville, Va. Appointed Capt. U. S. A., 3 Jan., 1895 (Act 1 Aug., 1894). Retired 14 Jan., 1895. Died 11 July, 1897.

RANSOM, HYATT C.* [Born in N. Y. Appointed from N. Y.]
2nd Lieut. Mounted Rifles, 1 July, 1851. 1st Lieut., 30 Dec., 1856. Capt. A. Q. M., 15 Oct., 1859. Lieut. Col. Q. M. Vols., 10 Nov., 1863, to 3 July, 1865. Maj. Q. M., 28 July, 1866. Lieut. Col. Dep. Q. M. G., 6 June, 1862. Died 16 March, 1874. Bvt. Maj. and Lieut. Col., 13 March, 1865, for faithful and meritorious service during the war.

RANSOM, OWEN. [Born in Conn. Appointed from Conn.]
Cornet 1st Light Drag., 14 Sept., 1812. 2nd Lieut., 1 Dec., 1812. 1st Lieut. 26th Inf., 19 April, 1814. Trans. to 2nd Inf., 17 May, 1815. Reg. P. M., 16 Oct., 1815,

to 9 July, 1816. Capt., 25 Jan., 1823. Died 3 July, 1836. Bvt. Maj., 25 Jan., 1833, for ten years' faithful service in one grade.

RANSOM, OWEN P.* [Born in Conn. Appointed from Conn.]
2nd Lieut. 2nd Drag., 1 July, 1838. 1st Lieut., 18 Feb., 1840. Dismissed 3 Nov., 1845. Col. 1st Ohio Cav., 17 Aug., 1861. Resigned 11 Jan., 1862. Died 10 Jan., 1880.

RANSOM, ROB'T.* [Born in N. C. Appointed from N. C.]
Bvt. 2nd Lieut. 1st Drag., 1 July, 1850. 2nd Lieut., 9 Oct., 1851. 1st Lieut. 1st Cav., 3 March, 1855. Reg. Adj., 25 May, 1855, to 17 Feb., 1857. Capt., 31 Jan., 1861. Resigned 24 May 1861.

RANSOM, TRUEMAN B. [Born in Vt. Appointed from Vt.]
Maj. of Inf., 16 Feb., 1847; Col., 16 March, 1847; 9th Inf., 9 April, 1847. Killed 13 Sept., 1847, at the Battle of Chapultepec, Mex.

RAPHALL, ALFRED M. [Born in England Appointed from N. Y.]
2nd Lieut. 40th N. Y. Vols., 14 June, 1861. 1st Lieut. Adj., 27 June, 1861. Mustered out 24 Jan., 1862. 1st Lieut. 40th N. Y. Vols., 19 Jan., 1862. Capt., 4 Feb., 1864. Mustered out 24 July, 1864. 1st Lieut. Vet. Res. Corps, 3 Oct., 1864. Bvt. Capt. Vols., 13 March, 1865, for gallant service in the Battle of Gettysburg, Penn. Bvt. Maj. Vols., 13 March, 1865, for highly meritorious service while in the field and on detached duty with Gen. Sickles in South America. Mustered out 30 June, 1866. 2nd Lieut. 43rd Inf., 22 Jan., 1867. Bvt. 1st Lieut., 2 March, 1867, for gallant and meritorious service in the Battle of Gettysburg, Penn. Unassigned 8 April, 1869. Ass'd to 11th Inf., 3 Aug., 1870. 1st Lieut., 30 Dec., 1871. Retired from loss of right arm and disability, 24 Aug., 1886.

RASH, OTWAY W. [Born in Ky. Appointed from Ky.]
Asst. Surg., 23 July, 1898. Resigned 1 Dec., 1898. Reappointed Asst. Surg., 14 June, 1899.

RATHBONE, HENRY R. [Born in N. Y. Appointed from N. Y.]
Capt. 12th Inf., 14 May, 1861. Maj. A. A. G. Vols., 11 March, 1865. Resigned from Vols., 8 July, 1867. Maj. 5th Inf., 22 Feb., 1869. Unassigned 15 March, 1869. Discharged 31 Dec., 1870. Bvt. Maj. 1 Aug., 1864, for gallant and meritorious service in the Battles of the campaign from the Rapidan to Petersburg. Bvt. Lieut. Col., 13 March, 1865, for meritorious service in the office of the Provost Marshal of the U. S. Bvt. Col., 13 March, 1865, for faithful and meritorious service connected with the organizetion of the Vol. armies of the U. S. during the war.

RATHBONE, JARED L.* [Born in N. Y. Appointed at Large.]
2nd Lieut. 12th Inf., 23 June, 1865. 1st Lieut., 23 June, 1865. Trans. to 1st Art., 5 March, 1869. Resigned 28 June, 1872.

RATHBONE, JOEL H. [Born in N. Y. Appointed from N. Y.]
2nd Lieut. Marine Corps, 25 Oct., 1858. 1st Lieut 26 June, 1861. Resigned 16 Jan., 1862. Capt. 12th Inf., 17 Feb., 1862. Resigned 24 Dec., 1864. Died in 1865.

RAULSTON, GEORGE F. [Born in N. Y. Appointed from N. Y.]
2nd Lieut. 24th N. Y. Cav., 28 Dec., 1863. 1st Lieut., 22 July, 1864. Capt., 30 Nov., 1864. Mustered out 26 June, 1865. 2nd Lieut. 10th Cav., 28 July, 1866. 1st Lieut., 31 July, 1867. Mustered out 28 Dec., 1870. Bvt. 1st Lieut. and Capt., 2 March, 1867, for gallant and meritorious service in the Battle on the Weldon Railroad, Va.

RAWLES, JACOB B.* [Born in Mich. Appointed from Mich.]
2nd Lieut. 3rd Art., 6 May, 1861. 1st Lieut. 5th Art., 14 May, 1861. R. Q. M., 10 May, 1861, to 2 Dec., 1862. Bvt. Capt., 8 July, 1863, for gallant and meritorious service in the Siege of Port Hudson, La. Bvt. Maj., 9 April, 1865, for gallant and meritorious service during the campaign terminating with the surrender of the insurgent forces under Gen. R. E. Lee. Capt. 5th Art., 28 July, 1866. Maj. 4th Art., 10 Aug., 1887. Lieut. Col. 1st Art, 30 April, 1897. Col. 3rd Art., 23 Feb., 1899.

RAWLINS, JOHN A. [Born in Ill. Appointed from Ill.]
Capt. A. A. G. Vols., 30 Aug., 1861. Maj. A. A. G. Vols., 14 May, 1862. Lieut. Col. A. A. G. Vols., 1 Nov., 1862, to 30 Aug., 1863. Brig. Gen. Vols., 11 Aug., 1863. Brig. Gen. Chf. of Staff U. S. A., 3 March, 1865. Bvt. Maj. Gen. Vols., 24 Feb., 1865, for faithful and meritorious service. Resigned 12 March, 1869. Bvt. Maj. Gen., 9 April, 1865, for gallant and meritorious service during the campaign terminating with the surrender of the insurgent army under Gen. Lee. Sec. of War, 11 March, 1869, till he died, 6 Sept., 1869.

RAWN, CHAS. C. [Born in Penn. Appointed from Penn.]
Priv. Co. F, 25th Penn. Vols., 2 May, 1861. Discharged 26 July, 1861. 2nd Lieut. 7th Inf., 5 Aug., 1861. 1st Lieut., 9 July, 1862. Capt., 4 Nov., 1863. Maj. 24th Inf., 18 April, 1884. Died 6 Oct., 1887.

RAWOLLE, WM. C. [Born in Prussia. Appointed from N. Y.]
2nd Lieut. 2nd N. Y. Art., 26 Oct., 1861. 1st Lieut. 2nd N. Y. Art., 4 March, 1862. Capt. A. A. de C., 21 June, 1862. Bvt. Maj. Vols., 13 March, 1865, for gallant and meritorious service in the Army of the Potomac from Aug., 1862, to Jan., 1863, including the Battles of Second Bull Run, South Mountain, Antietam, Warrenton, Sulphur Spring and Fredericksburg. Bvt. Lieut. Col. Vols., 13 March, 1865, for service in the West, including the Cav. campaign in East Tenn., and expeditions into Northern Miss., and for gallant, daring and good conduct in the Battle of Brice's Cross Roads, Miss. Resigned 11 Aug., 1865. 2nd Lieut. 2nd Cav., 6 June, 1868. 1st Lieut., 26 April, 1869. R. Q. M., 15 July, 1870, to 15 Sept., 1874. Reg. Adj., 31 March, 1878. Capt., 20 Dec., 1880. Died 10 June, 1895.

RAWSON, WM.* [Born in Ill. Appointed from Mo.]
2nd Lieut. 2nd Cav., 15 June, 1869. Died 1 Sept., 1869

RAY, JAMES B. [Born in ——. Appointed from ——.]
2nd Lieut. 7th Inf., — ——, 1899. Resigned 9 March, 1899.

RAY, P. HENRY. [Born in Wis. Appointed from Wis.]
Priv. Co. K, 2nd Wis. Vols., 7 May, 1861. Corpl., 2 Sept., 1861. Trans. to Co. A; 1st Wis. Heavy Art., 9 Dec., 1861. Sergt., 1 Sept., 1862. 1st Sergt., 15 April, 1863. 2nd Lieut. 1st Wis. Heavy Art., 13 July, 1863. Capt., 13 Sept., 1864. Mus-

tered out 30 May, 1865. Capt. 6th U. S. Vet. Vols., 14 Aug., 1865. Mustered out 12 April, 1866. 2nd Lieut. 33rd Inf., 7 March, 1867. Trans. to 8th Inf., 3 May, 1869. 1st Lieut., 31 Dec., 1875. Capt., 27 May, 1889. Maj., 2 March, 1899. Col. 3rd U. S. Vols., 20 May, 1898, to 2 May, 1899.

RAYMOND, CHAS. W.* [Born in Conn. Appointed from N. Y.]
1st Lieut. Eng., 23 June, 1865. Capt., 21 March, 1867. Maj. 20 Feb., 1883. Lieut. Col., 18 May, 1898.

RAYMOND, HENRY I. [Born in Ind. Appointed from Ind.]
Asst. Surg., 22 Oct., 1881. Resigned 1 Sept., 1883. Reappointed Asst. Surg., 12 Jan., 1885. Capt. Asst. Surg., 12 Jan., 1890.

RAYMOND, JOHN C.* [Born in N. Y. Appointed from Penn.]
Addl. 2nd Lieut. 3rd Cav., 11 June, 1897. 2nd Lieut. 6th Cav., 31 May, 1898.

RAYMOND, ROBERT R* [Born in N. Y. Appointed from N. Y.]
Addl. 2nd Lieut. Eng., 12 June, 1893. 2nd Lieut., 25 Oct., 1895. 1st Lieut., 5 July, 1898.

RAYMOND, THOMAS U. [Born in Ind. Appointed from Ind.]
Asst. Surg., 6 June, 1890. Capt. Asst. Surg., 6 June, 1895. Maj. Surg. 40th U. S. Vols., 17 Aug., 1899.

RAYNER, JAMES O. [Born in England. Appointed from Wash. Ter.]
Chap. Post of Fort Stellacoom, Wash. Ter., 28 May, 1864, to 4 June, 1867. Post Chap., 3 April, 1867. Retired by operation of law 19 Feb., 1887. Died 18 June, 1888.

RAYNOLDS, WM. F.* [Born in Ohio. Appointed from Ohio.]
Bvt. 2nd Lieut. 5th Inf., 1 July, 1843. Trans. to Top. Eng., 20 July, 1843. 2nd Lieut., 3 March, 1847. 1st Lieut., 3 March, 1853. Capt. 1 July, 1857. Col. A. A. de C., 31 March, 1862. Maj. Eng., 3 March, 1863. Bvt. Lieut. Col. and Col., 13 March, 1865. for faithful and meritorious service during the war. Bvt. Brig. Gen., 13 March, 1865, for meritorious service in the field during the war. Mustered out as Col. A. A. de C., 31 May, 1866. Lieut. Col. Eng., 7 March, 1867. Col., 2 Jan., 1881. Retired by operation of law, 17 March, 1884. Died 19 Oct., 1894.

REA, CHAS. H.* [Born in Pa. Appointed from Ill.]
2nd Lieut. 7th Cav., 15 June, 1869. Resigned 14 Sept., 1870.

READ, ALVAN C.* [Born in Tenn. Appointed from La.]
2nd Lieut. 13th Inf., 26 April, 1898. 1st Lieut., 2 March, 1899.

READ, EDWIN W. H [Born in Ohio. Appointed from Ind.]
2nd Lieut. 8th Inf., 27 June, 1856. 1st Lieut., 3 May, 1861. Capt., 26 Oct., 1861. Resigned 29 May, 1873. Bvt. Maj., 2 July, 1863, for gallant and meritorious service at the Battle of Gettysburg, Penn. Died 11 Nov., 1875.

READ, GEORGE B. [Born in Ind. Ter. Appointed from Md.]
2nd Lieut. 19th Inf., 1 Oct., 1873. 1st Lieut., 24 Feb., 1882. Resigned 15 June, 1882.

READ GEORGE W.* [Born in Iowa. Appointed from Iowa.]
2nd Lieut. 16th Inf., 13 June, 1883. Trans. to 5th Cav., 13 Sept., 1883. 1st Lieut. 8th Cav., 18 March, 1891. Trans. to 5th Cav., 27 April, 1891. Capt. 9th Cav., 29 March, 1899. Reg. Adj., 1 Dec., 1899.

READ, JOHN G. [Born in Mass. Appointed from Iowa.]
Capt. 12th Inf., 14 May, 1861. Killed 30 Aug., 1862, at the Battle of Bull Run, Va. Bvt. Maj., 30 Aug., 1862, for gallant and meritorious service at the Battle of Bull Run (2nd), Va.

READ, OGDEN B. [Born in Vt. Appointed from Vt.]
Priv. Co. D, 10th Vt. Vols., 4 Aug., 1862. Corpl., 26 Dec., 1862. Discharged 2 April, 1864. Capt. 39th U. S. Col. Troops, 5 Apri, 1864. Bvt. Maj. Vols., 13 March, 1865, for gallant and meritorious service. Mustered out 4 Dec., 1865. 2nd Lieut. and 1st Lieut. 11th Inf., 23 Feb., 1866. Trans. to 29th Inf., 21 Sept., 1866. Reg. Adj. 18 Dec., 1866. to 25 April, 1869. Trans. to 11th Inf., 25 April, 1869. Reg. Adj., 23 Jan., 1871, to 18 Sept., 1874. Capt., 28 June, 1878. Died 13 April, 1889.

READ, ROBT. D., Jr.* [Born in Tenn. Appointed from Tenn.]
2nd Lieut. 10th Cav., 15 June, 1877. 1st Lieut., 14 Jan., 1884. Capt., 26 July, 1893. Graduate of the Infantry and Cavalry School, 1885.

READ, THOS. M. [Born in R. I. Appointed from R. I.]
1st Lieut. 25th Inf., 12 March, 1812. R. Q. M., July, 1812, to April., 1813. Capt., 16 April, 1813. Disbanded 15 June, 1815. Reinstated in 6th Inf., 2 Dec., 1815. Died 25 Dec., 1819.

READ, WM.* [Born in Del. Appointed from Del.]
Bvt. 2nd Lieut. 6th Inf., 1 July, 1844. 2nd Lieut. 5th Inf., 18 May, 1846. 1st Lieut., 9 Dec., 1847. Resigned 31 July, 1850. Died 29 April, 1884.

READ, WM. M. [Born in Penn. Appointed from Penn.]
1st Lieut. 3rd Art., 6 July, 1812. Trans. to 2nd Art., — March, 1813. Trans. to Corps Art., 12 May, 1814. Capt., 28 Sept., 1817. Disbanded 1 June, 1821. Died 6 Feb., 1835.

READE, HARRY. [Born in Mass. Appointed from Mass.]
2nd Lieut. 25th Inf., 4 March, 1872. 1st Lieut., 11 April, 1878. Capt., 1 April, 1888. Wholly retired 11 Nov., 1890.

READE, PHILIP. [Born in Mass. Appointed from Mass.]
Cadet Mil. Acad., 1 July, 1864, to 14 Jan., 1865, and from 20 June, 1865, to 23 Jan., 1867. 2nd Lieut. 3rd Inf., 13 May, 1867. 1st Lieut., 8 Dec., 1878. Capt., 13 Nov., 1889. Maj. 8th Inf., 31 March, 1899. Trans. to 4th Inf., 28 Oct., 1899. Maj. I. G. Vols., 12 May, 1898. Lieut. Col. I. G. Vols., 21 Dec., 1898.

REAMS, JAMES D. [Born in Ky. Appointed from Army.]
2nd and 1st Class Priv. and Corpl. Cos. C and D, Batt. Eng., 18 Feb., 1897, to 13 April, 1899. 2nd Lieut. 1st Inf., 5 April, 1899.

REAP, FRANK P.* [Born in Penn. Appointed from Penn.]
2nd Lieut. 10th Cav., 14 June, 1872. Resigned 18 Nov., 1874.

REBER, SAMUEL.* [Born in Mo. Appointed from Mo.]
2nd Lieut. 4th Cav., 1 July, 1886. 1st Lieut. 9th Cav., 28 July, 1892. 1st Lieut.

Sig. Corps, 27 Jan., 1894. Maj A. A. G. Vols., 12 May to 4 June, 1898. Maj. Chf. Sig. Off. Vols., 20 May, 1898. Lieut. Col. Chf. Sig. Off. Vols., 18 July, 1898. to 17 April, 1899. Capt. Sig. Off. Vols., 17 April, 1899.

RECTOR, WHARTON. [Born in Va. Appointed from Ark.]
2nd Lieut. Rifles, 12 July, 1820. Resigned 20 Nov., 1821. Maj. P. M., 15 Aug., 1836. Died 8 Feb., 1842.

REDMOND, NICHOLAS. [Born in Ireland. Appointed from Army.]
Priv., Corpl., Sergt. and 1st Sergt. Batty M, 4th Art., 19 March, 1849, to 13 Aug., 1861, and Ord. Sergt. to 10 Aug., 1863. 2nd Lieut. 4th Art., 10 Aug., 1863. 1st Lieut., 31 Aug., 1864. Retired 7 Dec., 1867. Died 21 May, 1878. Bvt. 1st Lieut., 20 Sept., 1863, for gallant and meritorious service at the Battle of Chickamauga, Ga. Bvt., Capt., 13 March, 1865, for good conduct and gallant service during the war.

REED, HARVEY D. [Born in N. Y. Appointed from Army.]
2nd Class Priv. Co. E, Batt. Eng., 1 June, 1876. 1st Class Priv., 1 Oct., 1876. Corpl., 8 Jan., 1879. 2nd Lieut. 25th Inf., 14 Aug., 1879. 1st Lieut., 17 Aug., 1886. Resigned 30 June, 1890.

REED, HENRY A.* [Born in N. Y. Appointed from Wis.]
Sergt. Co. I, 24th Wis. Vols., 14 Aug., 1862. 1st Sergt., 1 May, 1864. 1st Lieut. 24th Wis. Vols., 19 Feb., 1865. Mustered out 10 June, 1865. Cadet Mil. Acad., 1 Sept., 1866. 2nd Lieut. 2nd Art., 15 June, 1870. 1st Lieut., 21 May, 1875. Capt. 5th Art., 8 March, 1898. Graduate of the Artillery School, 1874.

REED, HORATIO B. [Born in N. Y. Appointed from N. Y.]
2nd Lieut. 5th Art., 14 May, 1861. 1st Lieut., 19 Sept., 1863. Lieut. Col. 22nd N. Y. Cav., 26 Nov., 1864. Col., 14 April, 1865. Mustered out of Vol. Service, 1 Aug., 1865. Reg. Adj., 1 Dec., 1867, to 8 May, 1870. Resigned 8 May, 1870. Bvt. 1st Lieut., 21 July, 1861, for gallant and meritorious service at the Battle of Bull Run, Va. Bvt. Capt., 1 July, 1862, for gallant and meritorious service during the Peninsular campaign in Va. Bvt. Maj., 14 Oct., 1863, for gallant and meritorious service at the Battle of Bristow Station, Va. Bvt. Lieut. Col., 13 March, 1865, for gallant and meritorious service during the war. Died 7 March, 1888..

REED, HUGH T.* [Born in Ind. Appointed from Ind.]
2nd Lieut. 1st Inf., 13 June, 1873. 1st Lieut., 1 July, 1879. Retired for disability 23 April, 1889.

REED, JAMES. [Born in Penn. Appointed from Penn.]
2nd Lieut. Art., 17 Jan., 1805. 1st Lieut., 31 Dec., 1806. Capt., 1st Art., 12 March, 1812. Trans. to Corps Art., 12 May, 1814. Died 11 Aug., 1819.

REED, JAMES G.* [Born in Pa. Appointed from Pa.]
Bvt. 2nd Lieut. 7th Inf., 1 July, 1834. 2nd Lieut., 4 May, 1835. Resigned 30 June, 1837. Died 23 Feb., 1856.

REED, SARDINE P.* [Born in Ohio. Appointed from Ohio.]
Bvt. 2nd Lieut. 3rd Inf., 1 July, 1858. 2nd Lieut. 10th Inf., 10 Sept., 1858. Died 5 Feb., 1859.

REED, THOS. B. [Born in Penn. Appointed from Penn.]
Sergt. Co. D, 5th Penn. Res. Corps, 5 June, 1861. 1st Sergt., 20 Jan., 1862. 1st Lieut. 5th Pa. Vet. Res. Corps, 5 March, 1863. Mustered out 11 June, 1864. Capt. 205th Pa. Vols., 3 Sept., 1864. Bvt. Capt. Vols., 13 March, 1865, for gallant conduct in the Battle of Gettysburg, Penn. Bvt. Lieut. Col. Vols., 1 June, 1865, for faithful and meritorious service during the war. Mustered out 2 June, 1865. 2nd Lieut. 29th Inf., 22 July, 1867. Unassigned 25 April, 1869. Ass'd to 9th Cav., 14 July, 1869. Trans. to 24th Inf., 3 Feb., 1870. Retired 14 Nov., 1871.

REED, WALTER. [Born in Va. Appointed from Va.]
1st Lieut. Asst. Surg., 26 June, 1875. Capt. Asst. Surg., 26 June, 1880. Maj. Surg., 4 Dec., 1893.

REED, WM. I. [Born in Mass. Appointed from Cal.]
1st Lieut. and R. Q. M. 6th Cal. Vols., 14 March, 1863. Mustered out 31 Oct., 1865. 2nd Lieut. 5th Inf., 23 Feb., 1866. 1st Lieut., 28 July, 1866. Unassigned 19 May, 1869. Ass'd to 7th Inf., 1 Jan., 1871. Capt., 23 Feb., 1883. Retired for disability 23 April, 1889.

REED, WILLIAM L. [Born in N. J. Appointed from Army.]
Cadet Mil. Acad., 21 June, 1893, to 26 June, 1897. 2nd Lieut 8th N. Y. Vols., 18 May to 30 Nov., 1898. Priv. and Actg. Steward Hosp. Corps, 28 Nov., 1898, to 1 May, 1899. 2nd Lieut. 1st Inf., 5 April, 1899.

REEDER, HOWARD. [Born in Penn. Appointed from Penn.]
2nd Lieut. 1st Inf., 24 Oct., 1861. Resigned 23 July, 1862.

REEDER, RUSSELL P. [Born in Ohio. Appointed from Ohio.]
Capt. and Adj. 1st Ohio Vols., 6 May to 25 Oct., 1898. 2nd Lieut. 1st Inf., 10 April, 1899.

REEDY, WM. J. [Born in Del. Appointed from Del.]
1st Lieut. 1st Del. Cav., 20 Jan., 1863. Mustered out 19 June, 1865. 2nd Lieut. 13th Inf., 23 Feb., 1866. 1st Lieut., 19 June, 1866. Trans. to 22nd Inf., 21 Sept., 1866. Resigned 10 March, 1877.

REES, JOSEPH H. [Born in N. Y. Appointed from N. Y.]
2nd Lieut. 3rd Art., 12 March, 1812. 1st Lieut., 13 March, 1813. Trans. to Corps Art., 12 May, 1814. Capt. Dep. Com. of Ord., 16 Feb., 1814. Retained as Capt. Ord., 8 Feb., 1815. Died in 1821.

REES, HARRY L. [Born in Ore. Appointed from Ore.]
Maj. P. M., 3 March, 1899.

REES, RICH'D. [Born in Wales. Appointed from Ill.]
Priv. Co. F, 16th Ill. Vols., 24 May, 1861, to 13 April, 1862. 2nd Lieut. 21st Mo. Vols., 14 April, 1862. 1st Lieut., 4 Aug., 1862. Capt., 1 Feb., 1866. Bvt. Capt. Vols., 26 March, 1865, for faithful and meritorious service during the campaign against the city of Mobile, Ala., and its defences. Mustered out, 19 April, 1866. 2nd Lieut. 6th Inf., 24 Aug., 1867. Mustered out 23 Dec., 1870.

REES, ROBERT I. [Born in ——. Appointed from Army.]
Corpl. Batt. Eng., 7 May, 1897, to 24 Nov., 1899. 2nd Lieut. 3rd Inf., 1 Oct., 1899.

REES, THOMAS H.* [Born in Mich. Appointed from Mich.]
Addl. 2nd Lieut. Eng., 1 July, 1886. 2nd Lieut., 31 Dec., 1886. 1st Lieut., 1 April, 1890. Capt., 5 July, 1898.

REESE, AQUILA A. [Born in Md. Appointed from Md.]
Capt. Post Chap., 3 April, 1867. Retired 2 March, 1877. Died 7 March, 1878.

REESE, AQUILA A., Jr. [Born in Md. Appointed from Md.]
Priv. Co. A, 47th N. Y. State Militia, 27 May, to 1 Sept., 1862. 2nd Lieut. 3rd Md. Vols., 6 Dec., 1862. Resigned 20 Feb., 1863. Priv. Baltimore Light Art., 21 July, 1863, to 27 Feb., 1865. 2nd Lieut. 91st N. Y. Vols., 27 Feb., 1865. Mustered out 3 July, 1865. 2nd Lieut. 8th Cav., 9 Sept., 1867. Resigned 3 Nov., 1868.

REESE, CHAUNCEY B.* [Born in N. Y. Appointed from N. Y.]
Bvt. 2nd Lieut. Eng., 1 July, 1859. 2nd Lieut., 20 Feb., 1861. 1st Lieut., 6 Aug., 1861. Capt., 3 March, 1863. Lieut. Col. A. I. G., 3 June to 1 Aug., 1865. Maj. Eng., 7 March, 1867. Died 22 Sept., 1870. Bvt. Maj., Lieut. Col. and Col., 21 Dec., 1864, for gallant and distinguished service during the campaign through Ga., and ending in the capture of Savannah, Ga. Bvt. Brig. Gen., 13 March, 1865, for faithful and meritorious service during the campaigns in Ga. and the Carolinas.

REESE, HENRY B. [Born in Ohio. Appointed from Ohio.]
Addl. P. M., 1 June, 1861. Bvt. Lieut. Col. Vols., 13 March, 1865, for faithful and meritorious service during the war. Maj. P. M., 17 Jan., 1867. Retired at his own request, having served over twenty years, 3 July, 1888 (Act 5 July, 1884).

REESE, JOHN C. [Born in S. C. Appointed from Army.]
Priv. Co. F, 13th Inf., 10 June to 8 Sept., 1847. 2nd Lieut. 13th Inf., 28 Aug., 1847. Resigned 30 Dec., 1847.

REESE, WM. I.* [Born in Ky. Appointed from Ky.]
2nd Lieut. 6th Cav., 15 June, 1869. 1st Lieut., 12 June, 1872. Died 20 June, 1872.

REEVE, EARNEST M. [Born in Tenn. Appointed from Army.]
Priv., Corpl. and Sergt. Troop A, 6th Cav., 19 Aug., 1896, to 15 April, 1899. 2nd Lieut. 15th Inf., 5 April, 1899.

REEVE, HORACE M.* [Born in Tenn. Appointed from Tenn.]
2nd Lieut. 3rd Inf., 11 June, 1892. 1st Lieut., 26 April, 1898.

REEVE, ISAAC V. D.* [Born in N. Y. Appointed from N. Y.]
Bvt. 2nd Lieut. 4th Inf., 1 July, 1835. 2nd Lieut., 2 May, 1836. 1st Lieut. 8th Inf., 7 July, 1838. Capt., 18 June, 1846. Bvt. Maj., 20 Aug., 1847, for gallant and meritorious conduct in the Battles of Contreras and Churubusco. Bvt. Lieut. Col., 8 Sept., 1847, for gallant and meritorious conduct in the Battle of Molino del Rey. Maj. 1st Inf., 14 May, 1861. Lieut. Col. 13th Inf., 16 Sept., 1862. Col., 14 Oct., 1864. Bvt. Brig. Gen., 13 March, 1865, for faithful and meritorious service during the war. Unassigned 15 March, 1869. Retired 1 Jan., 1871. Died 31 Dec., 1890.

REEVES, IRA L. [Born in Mo. Appointed from Army.]
Priv., Corpl. and Sergt. Co. B, 4th Inf., 11 Dec., 1893, to 10 May, 1897. 2nd Lieut. 17th Inf., 19 April, 1897. 1st Lieut., 2 March, 1899. Trans. to 4th Inf., 31 Aug., 1899.

REEVES, ISAAC S. K.* [Born in S. C. Appointed from S. C.]
2nd Lieut. 1st Art., 1 July, 1838. 1st Lieut., 21 June, 1839. Capt., 1 April, 1850. Died 22 Feb., 1851.

REEVES, JAMES H.* [Born in Ala. Appointed from Ala.]
2nd Lieut. 4th Cav., 11 June, 1892. Trans. to 6th Cav., 24 June, 1897. 1st Lieut. 2nd Cav., 10 Nov., 1898. Graduate of the Infantry and Cavalry School, 1897.

REEVES, NATHAN L. [Born in ——. Appointed from Ohio.]
Ensign 27th Inf., 20 May, 1813. Trans. to 19th Inf., 12 May, 1814. 3rd Lieut., 6 July, 1814. 2nd Lieut., 1 Nov., 1814. Disbanded 15 June, 1815. 2nd Lieut. Rifle Reg., 19 Sept., 1818. Dismissed 11 March, 1819.

REEVES, THOS. H. [Born in N. C. Appointed from Tenn.]
Priv. Co. D, 4th Tenn. Vols., 15 Nov., 1861. 1st Lieut., 19 Feb., 1863. Capt., 29 May, 1863. Maj., 10 Aug., 1864. Lieut. Col., 5 June, 1865. Mustered out 2 Aug., 1865. Capt. 39th Inf., 28 July, 1866. Bvt. Maj. and Lieut. Col., 2 March, 1867, for faithful and meritorious service duringe the war. Retired 5 June, 1868.

REGAN, JAMES. [Born in N. Y. Appointed from Army.]
Musician Co. H, 2nd Inf., 1 June, 1858. Discharged 1 June, 1863. Musician Co. B, Music Boys' Gen. Ser., 8 March, 1864. Sergt., 1 Nov., 1864. 2nd Lieut. 18th Inf., 1 Dec., 1866. 1st Lieut., 12 Aug., 1867. Unassigned 26 April, 1869. Ass'd to 9th Inf., 15 Dec., 1870. R. Q. M., 22 June, 1879. Capt., 15 June, 1887. Maj., 2 March, 1899.

REICHMANN, CARL. [Born in Germany. Appointed from Army.]
Priv., Corpl., Sergt. and 1st Sergt. C. I, 20th Inf., 6 Dec., 1881, to 6 Aug., 1884. 2nd Lieut. 24th Inf., 4 Aug., 1884. 1st Lieut. 7th Inf., 19 June, 1891. Trans. to 9th Inf., 20 July, 1891. Capt. Inf., 13 Dec., 1898. Ass'd to 17th Inf., 1 Jan., 1899. Graduate of the Infantry and Cavalry School, 1889. Capt. A. A. G., Vols., 12 May to 13 Dec., 1898.

REID, CHAS. M.* [Born in Conn. Appointed from Conn.]
2nd Lieut. 19th Inf., 23 June, 1865. 1st Lieut., 23 June, 1865. Died 8 Dec., 1865.

REID, J. CHESTER.* [Born in N. Y. Appointed from N. Y.]
Bvt. 2nd Lieut. 5th Inf., 1 July, 1833. 2nd Lieut., 1 April, 1836. 1st Lieut., 7 July, 1838. Died 17 Nov., 1845.

REID, JAMES R.* [Born in N. Y. Appointed from N. Y.]
2nd Lieut. 10th Inf., 11 June, 1863. 1st Lieut., 1 Jan., 1864. Capt., 10 June, 1865. Resigned 14 March, 1866.

REID, JOHN. [Born in ——. Appointed from Tenn.]
Ensign 1st Inf., 21 April, 1806. 2nd Lieut., 9 Dec., 1807. Resigned 31 Jan., 1809. Capt. 44th Inf., 15 July, 1814. Trans. to 1st Inf., 17 May, 1815. Died 18 Jan., 1816. Bvt. Maj., 23 Dec., 1814, for gallant conduct at the Siege of New Orleans.

REILLY, BERNARD, Jr. [Born in Penn. Appointed from Penn.]
Priv. Co. H, 25th Pa. Vols., 18 April, to 18 July, 1861. 2nd Lieut. 2nd Pa. Cav., 18 Nov., 1861. 1st Lieut. 1 July, 1863. Resigned 21 April, 1864. 2nd Lieut. 5th Cav., 4 May, 1868. 1st Lieut., 1 March, 1870. Resigned 4 June, 1878.

REILLY, HENRY J. [Born in Ireland. Appointed from Army.]
Priv. Co. B, 5th Art., 22 Sept., 1864. Corpl., 1 Nov., 1865. Sergt., 15 March, 1866. 2nd Lieut. 5th Art., 1 Dec., 1866. 1st Lieut., 18 Sept., 1868. Capt., 3 Jan., 1894. Graduate of the Artillery School, 1876.

REILLY, JAMES W.* [Born in Penn. Appointed from Penn.]
1st Lieut Ord., 11 June, 1863. Dismissed 15 Aug., 1865. Reinstated 24 April, 1866. Bvt. Capt., 13 March, 1865, for faithful and meritorious service in the campaign of Nov. and Dec., 1864, including the Battles of Franklin and Nashville. Capt. Ord., 23 June, 1874. Maj., 9 May, 1885. Lieut. Col., 7 April, 1899.

REILLY, TERRENCE. [Born in Scotland. Appointed from Army.]
Priv., Corpl., Sergt. and 1st Sergt. Batty M, 2nd Art., 12 Dec., 1857, to 12 Dec., 1862. Bvt. 2nd Lieut. 2nd Art., 19 Feb., 1863. 2nd Lieut. 4th Art., 19 March, 1863. 1st Lieut., 18 July, 1864. Cashiered 21 Dec., 1865. Bvt. Capt. and Maj., 13 March, 1865, for gallant and meritorious service during the war.

REILY, CLAJON. [Born in ——. Appointed from D. C.]
Surg.'s Mate 5th Inf., 22 March, 1813. Trans. to 8th Inf., 17 May, 1815. Hosp. Surg.'s Mate, 31 Oct., 1817. Died 25 Feb., 1818.

REILY, JOHN T. [Born in D. C. Appointed from Neb.]
Asst. Surg., 16 April, 1862. Died 5 May, 1864.

REILY, THOS. A. [Born in Penn. Appointel from Penn.]
Priv. and Corpl. Co. H, 195th Pa. Vols., 24 July to 4 Nov., 1864. 2nd Lieut. 5th Inf., 7 March, 1867. Mustered out 16 Dec., 1870.

REILY, WM. VAN W. [Born in D. C. Appointed from D. C.]
2nd Lieut. 10th Cav., 15 Oct., 1875. Trans. to 7th Cav., 26 Jan., 1876. Killed June, 1876, in action with Indians at the Little Big Horn River. Mont.

REISINGER, PAUL.* [Born in Penn. Appointed from
Addl. 2nd Lieut. 4th Cav., 12 June, 1896. 2nd Lieut. 10th Cav., 26 Aug., 1896. signed 1 June, 1899.

REMAK, STANISLAUS.* [Born in Pa. Appointed from Pa.]
2nd Lieut. 5th Art., 17 June, 1867. 1st Lieut, 1 Jan., 1871. Resigned 1 Sept., 1871.

REMINGTON, PHILIP H.* [Born in Conn. Appointed from Ill.]
2nd Lieut. 8th Inf., 24 June, 1861. 1st Lieut., 23 Aug., 1861. Reg. Adj., 21 April, 1863, to 18 Oct., 1864, and from 2 Feb., 1865, to 31 Jan., 1866. Capt., 28 July, 1866. Unassigned 3 May, 1869. Ass'd to 19th Inf., 28 Dec., 1869. Retired for disability 20 Feb., 1891. Died 17 Dec., 1891.

RENALDO, HERMAN O. [Born in Germany. Appointed from Army.]
Priv., Corpl., Sergt. and 1st Sergt. Co. I, 6th Inf., 28 March, 1856, to 21 Dec., 1861. 2nd Lieut. 9th Inf., 24 Oct., 1861. Resigned 20 June, 1863.

RENDLEBROCK, JOSEPH. [Born in Prussia. Appointed from Army.]
Priv. Co. A, Mounted Rifles, 22 May 1851. Corpl., 1 June, 1852. Sergt., 1 March, 1853. 1st Sergt., 12 Oct., 1854. Discharged 22 May, 1856. Private Co. G, 1st Cav., 16 Aug., 1856. Corpl., 23 Aug., 1856. Sergt., 1 Nov., 1856. 1st Sergt., 17 March, 1860. Discharged 13 July, 1861. 1st Sergt. Co. G, 1st Cav., 13 July, 1861. 2nd Lieut. 4th Cav., 29 Nov., 1862. Bvt. 1st Lieut., 10 May, 1863, for gallant and meritorious service in the Cav. action at Franklin, Tenn. Bvt. Capt., 4 Oct., 1863, for gallant and meritorious service in action at McMinnville, Tenn. 1st Lieut. 4th Cav., 15 Dec., 1863. R. Q. M., 20 Aug., 1866, to 13 Aug., 1867. Bvt. Maj., 2 April, 1865, for gallant and meritorious service in the capture of Selma, Ala. Capt. 4th Cav., 13 Aug., 1867. Retired 23 July, 1879. Died 13 March, 1889.

RENICK, ROBT. M.* [Born in Ohio. Appointed from Va.]
Bvt. 2nd Lieut. 4th Art., 1 July, 1835. Resigned 30 April, 1836. Died 10 Jan., 1875.

RENO, JESSE L.* [Born in Va. Appointed from Pa.]
Bvt. 2nd Lieut. Ord., 1 July, 1836. 2nd Lieut., 3 March, 1847. 1st Lieut., 3 March, 1853. Capt., 1 July, 1860. Brig. Gen. Vols., 12 Nov., 1861. Maj. Gen. Vols., 18 July, 1862. Killed at the Battle of South Mountain, Md., 14 Sept., 1862. Bvt. 1st Lieut., 18 April, 1847, for gallant and meritorious conduct at Cerro Gordo. Bvt. Capt., 13 Sept., 1847, for gallant and meritorious conduct at Chapultepec.

RENO, MARCUS A.* [Born in Ill. Appointed from Ill.]
Bvt. 2nd Lieut. 1st Drag., 1 July, 1857. 2nd Lieut., 14 June, 1858. 1st Lieut., 25 April, 1861. 1st Cav., 3 Aug., 1861. Capt., 12 Nov., 1861. Bvt. Maj., 17 March, 1863, for gallant and meritorious service in action at Kelly's Ford, Va. Bvt. Lieut. Col., 19 Oct. 1864, for gallant and meritorious service in the Battle of Cedar Creek, Va. Col. 12th Penn. Cav., 1 Jan. 1865. Bvt. Col., 13 March, 1865, for gallant and meritorious service during the war. Bvt. Brig. Gen. Vols., 13 March, 1865, for meritorious service during the war. Mustered out of Vol. Service 20 July 1865, Maj. 7th Cav., 26 Dec., 1868. Dismissed 1 April, 1880. Died 30 March, 1889.

RETHERS, HARRY F. [Born in Cal. Appointed from Army.]
Priv., Corpl. and Sergt. Co. A, 1st Inf., 7 June, 1893, to 9 April, 1896. 2nd Lieut. 9th Inf., 23 March, 1896. 1st Lieut. of Inf., 8 Sept., 1898. Ass'd to 2nd Inf., 1 Jan., 1899. Trans. to 9th Inf., 23 Feb., 1899.

REXFORD, WM. H. [Born in Mich. Appointed from Mich.]
1st Lieut. 24th Mich. Vols., 13 Aug., 1862. Capt., 20 Dec., 1862. Discharged 1 Nov., 1863. Ord. Storekeeper, 16 May, 1865. Capt. Ord. Storekeeper, 28 July, 1866. Maj. P. M. at National Armory 6 Dec., 1889. Retired for disability 3 Nov., 1898.

REYBURN, ROB'T. [Born in Scotland. Appointed from D. C.]
Asst. Surg. Vols., 4 June, 1863. Surg. Vols., 13 June, 1863. Bvt. Lieut. Col. Vols., 13 March, 1865, for faithful and efficient service. Mustered out 3 June, 1867. Asst. Surg., 14 May, 1867. Resigned 24 June, 1867.

REYNOLDS, ALEXANDER W.* [Born in Va. Appointed from Va.]
2nd Lieut. 1st Inf., 1 July, 1838. 1st Lieut., 11 June, 1839. Reg. Adj., 19 Oct., 1839, to 1 March, 1840. Capt. A. Q. M., 5 Aug., 1847. Dismissed 8 Oct., 1855. Reinstated 29 March, 1858, with former date of rank. Dropped 4 Oct., 1861. Died 26 May, 1876.

REYNOLDS, ALFRED * [Born in Penn. Appointed from N. J.]
2nd Lieut. 20th Inf., 17 June, 1874. 1st Lieut., 1 June, 1880. Capt., 24 Feb., 1891. Maj. 22nd Inf., 20 Sept., 1899.

REYNOLDS, BAINBRIDGE.* [Born in N. Y. Appointed from Ind.]
2nd Lieut. 3rd Cav., 13 June, 1873. Reg. Adj., 21 Aug., 1879, to 1 Sept., 1883. R. Q. M., 1 Sept., 1883, to 22 Nov., 1884. 1st Lieut., 21 Aug., 1879. Capt., 17 Jan., 1881. Resigned 1 Feb., 1891.

REYNOLDS, CHAS. [Born in England. Appointed from Kan.]
Chap. 2nd Kan. Cav., 9 Jan., 1862. Mustered out 31 Dec., 1864. Chap. Post of Fort Riley, Kan., 1 Sept., 1864, to 29 April, 1867. Post Chap., 3 April, 1867. Retired 30 June, 1882. Died 28 Dec., 1885.

REYNOLDS, CHAS. A. [Born in Md. Appointed from Md.]
Priv. Co. F, D. C. and Md. Batt. Vols., 23 July, 1847. Discharged 6 Feb., 1848. 2nd Lieut. 9th Inf., 3 March, 1855. 1st Lieut., 20 Feb., 1861. Capt. A. Q. M., 18 Nov., 1861. Lieut. Col. Q. M., 1 Nov., 1862, to 22 April, 1863. Bvt. Maj. and Lieut. Col., 13 March, 1865, for gallant and meritorious service during the war. Maj. Q. M., 3 March, 1875. Lieut. Col. D. Q. M. G., 9 April, 1885. Retired, for over thirty years' service, 11 Nov., 1887. Died 2 March, 1896.

REYNOLDS, FRANCIS. [Born in N. Y. Appointed from Army.]
Priv., Corpl. and 1st Sergt. Batty. C, 1st Art., 5 Aug., 1854, to 30 Nov., 1862. 2nd Lieut. 1st Art., 22 Oct., 1862. Cashiered 20 March, 1864. Reinstated 2 Aug., 1864. Dismissed 30 Dec., 1865.

REYNOLDS, FRANK. [Born in Ireland. Appointed from N. Y.]
Maj. Surg. 88th N. Y. Vols., 26 Sept., 1861. Asst. Surg. U. S. Vols., 7 Aug., 1863. Resigned 22 Sept., 1864. Bvt. Lieut. Col. Vols., 13 March, 1865, for faithful and meritorious service. Maj. Surg. 2nd U. S. Vet. Vols., 23 March, 1865. Mustered out 18 March, 1866. 1st Lieut. Asst. Surg., 16 Nov., 1868. Capt., 29 Dec., 1868. Retired 28 June, 1878. Died 4 March, 1887.

REYNOLDS, FRANK A.* [Born in Va. Appointed from N. Mex.]
Bvt. 2nd Lieut. 2nd Drag., 24 June, 1861. Dismissed 16 July, 1861. Died 19 July, 1875.

REYNOLDS, FREDERICK P. [Born in N. Y. Appointed from N. Y.]
Asst. Surg., 5 May, 1892. Capt. Asst. Surg., 5 May, 1897.

REYNOLDS, JOHN C. [Born in Md. Appointed from Penn.]
Asst. Surg., 1 May, 1835. Resigned 25 July, 1838. Maj. Surg. Vols., 17 Dec., 1846. Disbanded 8 Aug., 1848.

REYNOLDS, JOHN E. [Born in Maine. Appointed from Maine.]
1st Lieut. and Adj. 2nd Me. Vols., 28 May, 1861, to 5 March, 1862. Capt. 17th Inf., 19 Feb., 1862. Resigned 26 Jan., 1864.

REYNOLDS, JOHN F.* [Born in Penn. Appointed from Penn.]
Bvt. 2nd Lieut. 3rd Art., 1 July, 1841. 2nd Lieut., 23 Oct., 1841. 1st Lieut., 18 June, 1846. R. Q. M., 25 Oct., 1850, to 1 March, 1852. Capt., 3 March, 1855. Lieut. Col. 14th Inf., 14 May, 1861. Col. 5th Inf., 1 June, 1863. Brig. Gen. Vols., 20 Aug., 1861. Maj. Gen. Vols., 29 Nov., 1862. Killed at Battle of Gettysburg, Pa., 1 July, 1863. Bvt. Capt., 23 Sept., 1846, for gallant and meritorious conduct at Monterey. Bvt. Maj., 23 Feb., 1847, for gallant and meritorious conduct at Buena Vista.

REYNOLDS, JOSEPH J.* [Born in Ky. Appointed from Ind.]
Bvt. 2nd Lieut. 4th Art., 1 July, 1843. 2nd Lieut. 3rd Art., 11 May, 1846. 1st Lieut., 3 March, 1847. Resigned 28 Feb., 1857. Col. 10th Ind. Vols., 25 April, 1861. Brig. Gen. Vols., 17 May, 1861. Resigned 23 Jan., 1862. Brig. Gen. Vols., 17 Sept., 1862, for meritorious service in W. Va. Maj. Gen. Vols., 29 Nov., 1862. Mustered out of Vol. Service, 1 Sept., 1866. Col. 26th Inf., 28 July, 1866. Bvt. Brig. Gen., 2 March, 1867, for gallant and meritorious service in the Battle of Chickamauga, Ga. Bvt. Maj. Gen., 2 March, 1867, for gallant and meritorious service in the Battle of Missionary Ridge. Unassigned 15 March, 1869. Ass'd to 25th Inf., 8 Jan., 1870. Trans. to 3rd Cav., 15 Dec., 1870. Retired 25 June, 1877. Died 25 Feb., 1899.

REYNOLDS, ROBT. B. [Born in Tenn. Appointed from Tenn.]
Capt. A. Q. M., 26 June, 1846. Maj. P. M., 3 March, 1847. Resigned 23 June, 1861.

REYNOLDS, SAML. H.* [Born in Va. Appointed from Va.]
Bvt. 2nd Lieut. 1st Inf., 1 July, 1849. 2nd Lieut., 17 Oct., 1851. 1st Lieut., 8 Dec., 1855. Resigned 28 July, 1861. Died — 1867.

REYNOLDS, WM.* [Born in Del. Appointed from Del.]
2nd Lieut. 1st Inf., 1 July, 1823. 1st Lieut., 1 May, 1829. Resigned 1 Aug., 1830. Died 30 Aug., 1830.

REYNOLDS, WM. B. [Born in Ill. Appointed from Ill.]
Cadet Mil. Acad., 1 July, 1841, to 20 Jan., 1842. 2nd Lieut. 16th Inf., 30 Dec., 1847. Disbanded 7 Aug., 1848. 2nd Lieut. 6th Inf., 29 May, 1855. Dismissed 9 May, 1856.

REYNOLDS, WM. B.* [Born in Wash. Ter. Appointed at Large.]
2nd Lieut. 14th Inf., 13 June, 1879. 1st Lieut., 10 June, 1890. Capt., 13 Aug., 1894. Graduate of the Infantry and Cavalry School, 1891.

REYNOLDS, WM. F., Jr.* [Born in Ind. Appointed from Ind.]
2nd Lieut. 1st Art., 17 June, 1867. 1st Lieut., 4 May, 1871. Died 22 Nov., 1877.

RHEA, JAMES C.* [Born in Iowa. Appointed from Texas.]
2nd Lieut., 15 Feb., 1899.

RHEA, WM.* [Born in Va. Appointed from Tenn.]
Bvt. 2nd Lieut. 6th Inf., 1 July, 1845. 2nd Lieut. 3rd Inf., 21 Sept., 1846. Died 7 Jan., 1847.

RHEEM, EDWARD B. [Born in Penn. Appointed from Penn.]
Priv. Co. A, 7th Penn. Res. Corps, 8 July, 1861. Discharged 16 June, 1864. 2nd Lieut. 32nd Inf., 30 Oct., 1867. Trans. to 21st Inf., 19 April, 1869. Unassigned 19 Aug., 1869. Ass'd to 21st Inf., 29 Jan., 1870. 1st Lieut., 8 July, 1874. Capt., 24 April, 1886. Died 14 Nov., 1890.

RHETT, THOS. G.* [Born in S. C. Appointed from S. C.]
Bvt. 2nd Lieut. Ord., 1 July, 1845. 2nd Lieut. Mounted Rifles, 27 May, 1846. 1st

Lieut., 18 April, 1847. Capt., 16 Sept., 1853. Maj. P. M., 7 April, 1858. Resigned 1 April, 1861. Bvt. Capt., 12 Oct., 1847, for gallant and meritorious conduct in defence of Puebla. Died 28 July, 1878.

RHETT, THOS. S.* [Born in S. C. Appointed at Large.]
Bvt. 2nd Lieut. 4th Art., 1 July, 1848. 2nd Lieut. 2nd Art., 15 April, 1849. 1st Lieut., 10 May, 1853. Resigned 20 Feb., 1855.

RHEY, JAMES W. [Born in Penn. Appointed from Penn.]
2nd Lieut. 11th Inf., 21 Aug., 1847. Resigned 14 June, 1848.

RHOADS, LEVI. [Born in N. H. Appointed from Ohio.]
1st Lieut. of Inf., 8 March, 1847; 15th Inf., 9 April, 1847. Died 4 July, 1847, of wounds received in action at San Juan, Mex., 11 June, 1847.

RHODES, CHARLES D.* [Born in Ohio. Appointed from Ohio.]
Addl. 2nd Lieut. 7th Cav., 12 June, 1889. 2nd Lieut. 6th Cav., 19 Aug., 1889. 1st Lieut. 7th Cav., 8 Dec., 1896. Trans. to 6th Cav., 3 March, 1897. Capt. A. A. G. Vols., 3 June, 1898, to 7 April, 1899.

RIBBEL, CHAS. H.* [Born in N. Y. Appointed from N. Y.]
2nd Lieut. 20th Inf., 12 June, 1871. Resigned 31 Dec., 1874.

RIBLETT, JACOB R.* [Born in Ill. Appointed from Ill.]
2nd Lieut. 5th Inf., 14 June, 1872. Resigned 1 May, 1873.

RICE, EDMUND. [Born in Mass. Appointed from Mass.]
Capt. 19th Mass. Vols., 28 Aug., 1861. Maj., 1 Oct., 1862. Lieut. Col., 27 July, 1864. Mustered out 30 June, 1865. 1st Lieut. 40th Inf., 28 July, 1866. Bvt. Capt., 2 March, 1867, for gallant and meritorious service in the Battle of Antietam, Md. Bvt. Maj., 2 March, 1867, for gallant and meritorious service in the Battle of Gettysburg, Penn. Bvt. Lieut. Col., 2 March, 1867, for gallant and meritorious service in the Battle of the Wilderness, Va. Unassigned 20 April, 1869. Ass'd to 5th Inf., 1 Jan., 1871. Reg. Adj., 5 July, 1879. Capt., 10 March, 1883. Maj. 3rd Inf., 11 Aug., 1898. Medal of Honor for conspicuous bravery in leading his regiment in the countercharge against Pickett's division, himself falling severely wounded within the enemy's lines, in the Battle of Gettysburg, Penn., 3 July, 1863; while serving as Maj. 19th Mass. Inf. Lieut. Col. I. G. Vols., 9 May, 1898. Col. 6th Mass. Vols., 7 Aug., 1898, to 21 Jan., 1899. Col. 26th U. S. Vols., 5 July, 1899.

RICE, FRANK R. [Born in Mich. Appointed from Mich.]
Priv. Co. A, 1st Mich. Vols., 1 May, 1861. Discharged 7 Aug., 1861. Sergt. Co. F, 1st Mich. Vols., 1 Sept., 1861. 1st Sergt., 1 July, 1862. 2nd Lieut. 1st Mich. Vols., 30 Aug., 1862. 1st Lieut., 1 Nov., 1862. Mustered out 2 July, 1863. 2nd Lieut. Vet. Res. Corps, 27 June, 1863. 1st Lieut., 28 Oct., 1863. Mustered out 21 Nov., 1866. 2nd Lieut. 44th Inf., 28 July, 1866. Bvt. 1st Lieut. and Capt., 2 March, 1867, for gallant and meritorious service in the Battle of Fredericksburg, Va. 1st Lieut. 44th Inf., 5 June, 1867. R. Q. M., 15 Jan., 1867, to 27 May, 1869. Unassigned 27 May, 1869. Retired 15 Dec., 1870.

RICE, FRANK S.* [Born in Ohio. Appointed from Ohio.]
2nd Lieut. 1st Art., 17 June, 1874. 1st Lieut., 1 July, 1879. Honor graduate of the Artillery School, 1876. Retired for disability, 20 Feb., 1891. Maj. 1st Cal. Vol. Art., 9 May, 1898, to 21 Sept., 1899.

RICE, HENRY F. [Born in Maine. Appointed from Army.]
Priv., Corpl. and Sergt. Co. B, 17th Inf., 2 May, 1862, to 14 Nov., 1863. 2nd Lieut. 17th Inf., 31 Oct., 1863. 1st Lieut., 26 Jan., 1864. Resigned 14 May, 1864.

RICE, JAMES H. [Born in Mass. Appointed from Mass.]
1st Lieut. 19th Mass. Vols., 28 Aug., 1861. Capt., 7 Sept., 1862. Mustered out 30 June, 1863. Capt. Vet. Res. Corps, 24 June, 1863. Bvt. Maj. and Lieut. Col. Vols., 13 March, 1865, for faithful and meritorious service during the war. Mustered out 31 March, 1867. 2nd Lieut. 44th Inf., 22 Jan., 1867. Bvt. 1st Lieut., 2 March, 1867, for gallantry in action in front of Richmond, Va., 25 June, 1862. Bvt. Capt., 2 March, 1867, for meritorious service during the war. Trans. to 17th Inf., 27 May, 1869. 1st Lieut., 31 Dec., 1872. Retired 23 Dec., 1873.

RICE, JOHN H.* [Born in Mo. Appointed from Mo.]
2nd Lieut. 3rd Cav., 12 June, 1893. 1st Lieut Ord., 21 Nov. 1898.

RICE, JOHN W. [Born in S. C. Appointed from Ala.]
Capt. of Inf., 5 March, 1847; 13th Inf., 9 April, 1847. Resigned 31 Jan., 1848.

RICE, OLIN F.* [Born in Ga. Appointed from Ky.]
2nd Lieut. 9th Inf., 6 May, 1861. Trans. to 6th Inf., 25 May, 1861. Dismissed 6 June, 1861.

RICE, OSMOND E. [Born in Miss. Appointed from Army.]
Priv., Corpl., Sergt. and 1st Sergt. Co. H, 7th Inf., 8 May, 1855, to 17 Sept., 1862. 2nd Lieut. 7th Inf., 18 July, 1862. Appointment revoked, 1 Jan., 1863.

RICE, SEDGWICK. [Born in Minn. Appointed from Minn.]
2nd Lieut. 2nd Inf., 10 Oct., 1883. Trans. to 7th Cav., 10 June, 1886. 1st Lieut. 2nd Cav., 5 May, 1892. Trans. to 7th Cav., 26 May, 1892. Maj. 48th U. S. Vols., 9 Sept., 1899.

RICE, WM. F. [Born in Mass. Appointed from Ky.]
Priv. Co. G, 1st Mass. Vols., 23 May, 1861. Discharged 15 Aug., 1861. 1st Sergt. Co. F, 19th Mass. Vols., 16 Aug., 1861. Priv., 16 Oct., 1862. Sergt. Co. E, 19th Mass. Vols., 1 May, 1863. 2nd Lieut. 19th Mass. Vols., 13 Nov., 1863. 1st Lieut., 15 Nov., 1863. Capt. 17 Aug., 1864. Mustered out 4 Oct., 1864. 1st Lieut., N. Y. Cav., 30 Dec., 1864. Mustered out 30 June, 1865. 2nd Lieut. 23rd Inf., 28 July, 1866. 1st Lieut., 8 July, 1868. R. Q. M., 6 Sept., 1873, to 5 June, 1884. Killed by fall from railroad car 5 June, 1884.

RICH, LUCIUS L.* [Born in Mo. Appointed from Mo.]
Bvt. 2nd Lieut. 5th Inf., 1 July, 1853. 2nd Lieut., 3 March, 1855. 1st Lieut., 19 Jan., 1859. Resigned 13 May, 1861. Died 9 Aug., 1862.

RICH, THOS. H. [Born in Penn. Appointed from D. C.]
Priv. Co. G, 14th Me. Vols. and Sergt. Sig. Corps, 6 Jan., 1862, to 6 Jan., 1865. 2nd Lieut. 32nd Inf., 22 Jan., 1867. Resigned 19 March, 1869.

RICHARD, CHARLES. [Born in N. Y. Appointed from N. Y.]
1st Lieut. Asst. Surg., 3 June, 1979. Capt. Asst. Surg., 3 June, 1884. Maj. Surg., 15 Nov., 1897.

RICHARDS, GEORGE C.* [Born in N. Y. Appointed from N. Y.]
Bvt. 2nd Lieut. 2nd Art., 1 July, 1823. 2nd Lieut. 4th Art., 1 July, 1823. Died 22 Nov., 1825.

RICHARDS, GEORGE S., Jr. [Born in Va. Appointed from N. Y.]
Priv. Co. E, 3rd N. Y. Vols., 17 May, 1898. 1st Lieut. Co. L, 201st N. Y. Vols., 20 Aug. to 3 April, 1899. 2nd Lieut. 6th Inf., 10 April, 1899.

RICHARDS, JAMES R., Jr.* [Born in Va. Appointed from Va.]
Addl. 2nd Lieut. 9th Cav., 14 June, 1878. 2nd Lieut., 28 June, 1878. Trans. to 4th Cav., 5 Sept., 1878. 1st Lieut., 28 Dec., 1882. Reg. Adj., 24 March, 1883, to 31 Dec., 1885. Capt., 22 April, 1891. Retired for disability 25 Feb., 1896.

RICHARDS, MELZAR C.* [Born in Mich. Appointed from N. Y.]
2nd Lieut. 2nd Art., 11 June, 1881. 1st Lieut., 20 Nov., 1887. Retired for disability, 15 June, 1891.

RICHARDS, WALTER P. [Born in N. C. Appointed from N. C.]
Capt. of Inf., 5 March, 1847; 12th Inf., 9 April, 1847. Died 27 June, 1847.

RICHARDS, WILLIAM E. [Born in Miss. Appointed from Miss.]
Asst. Surg., 26 Oct., 1896.

RICHARDS, WM. V. [Born in Ireland. Appointed from Mich.]
1st Lieut. 1st Mich. Lancers, 1 Nov., 1861. Mustered out 20 March, 1862. 1st Lieut. 17th Mich. Vols., 2 July, 1862. Capt., 4 Aug., 1864. Bvt. Maj. Vols., 2 Dec., 1864, for gallant service during the war. Mustered out 3 June, 1865. 2nd Lieut. 11th Inf., 11 May, 1866. Bvt. 1st Lieut., 2 March, 1867, for gallant and meritorious service in the Battle of South Mountain, Md. Bvt. Capt., 2 March, 1867, for gallant and meritorious service in the Battle of Spottsylvania, Va. 1st Lieut. 11th Inf., 19 June, 1868. R. Q. M., 12 Aug., 1868, to 14 April, 1869. Trans. to 16th Inf., 14 April, 1869. R. Q. M., 14 April, 1869, to 1 Aug., 1874. Reg. Adj., 1 Aug., 1874, to 30 June, 1880. R. Q. M., 1 July, 1880, to 28 June, 1885. Capt., 28 June, 1885. Maj. 7th Inf., 6 Feb., 1899. Lieut. Col. A. A. G. Vols., 3 June, 1898.

RICHARDSON, ASA.* [Born in Vt. Appointed from Vt.]
2nd Lieut. 6th Inf., 1 July, 1823. 1st Lieut., 1 May, 1827. Resigned 18 April, 1835.

RICHARDSON, ISRAEL B.* [Born in Vt. Appointed from Vt.]
Bvt. 2nd Lieut. 3rd Inf., 1 July, 1841. 2nd Lieut., 30 Sept., 1841. 1st Lieut., 21 Sept., 1846. Capt., 5 March, 1851. Resigned 30 Sept., 1855. Bvt. Capt., 20 Aug., 1847, for gallant and meritorious conduct at Contreras and Churubusco, Mex. Bvt. Maj., 13 Sept., 1847, for gallant and meritorious conduct at Chapultepec, Mex. Col. 2nd Mich. Vols., 25 May, 1861. Brig. Gen. Vols., 17 May, 1861. Maj. Gen. Vols., 4 July, 1862. Died 3 Nov., 1862, of wounds received 17 Sept., 1862, at the Battle of Antietam, Md.

RICHARDSON, JAMES P. [Born in Mass. Appointed from Mass.]
Capt. 3rd Mass. Militia, 23 April, 1861. Mustered out 22 July, 1861. Capt. 38th Mass. Vols., 18 Aug., 1862. Maj., 4 Dec., 1862. Lieut. Col., 5 Aug., 1863. Mustered out 30 June, 1865. 2nd Lieut. 17th Inf., 11 May, 1866. Trans. to 26th Inf., 21 Sept., 1866. 1st Lieut., 31 July, 1867. R. Q. M., 1 June, 1868, to 1 March, 1869. Unassigned 19 May, 1869. Discharged 23 Aug., 1870.

RICHARDSON, LORRAIN T.* [Born in Wis. Appointed from Wis.]
2nd Lieut. 20th Inf., 12 June, 1895. 1st Lieut. of Inf., 1 July, 1898. Ass'd to 20th Inf., 1 Jan., 1899.

RICHARDSON, ROB'T D. [Born in Va. Appointed from Ohio.]
Capt. Dep. Com. of Ord., 5 Aug., 1813. Retained as Capt. Ord., 8 Feb., 1815. Trans. to 7th Inf., 1 June, 1821. Trans. to 1st Inf., 24 Sept., 1821. Resigned 1 June, 1822.

RICHARDSON, WILDS P.* [Born in Texas. Appointed from Texas.]
2nd Lieut. 8th Inf., 15 June, 1884. 1st Lieut., 16 Dec., 1889. Capt., 26 April, 1898.

RICHE, CHARLES S.* [Born in Penn. Appointed from Penn.]
Addl. 2nd Lieut. Eng., 1 July, 1886. 2nd Lieut., 12 Oct., 1886. 1st Lieut., 5 Oct., 1889. Capt., 5 July, 1898. Col. 1st Vol. Inf., 20 May to 28 Oct., 1898.

RICHY, JOHN A.* [Born in Ohio. Appointed from Ohio.]
Bvt. 2nd Lieut. 4th Inf., 1 July, 1845. 2nd Lieut. 5th Inf., 29 June, 1846. Murdered by Mexicans, 13 Jan., 1847, while bearer of dispatches.

RICHMOND, EPHRAIM T. C.* [Born in Md. Appointed from Md.]
2nd Lieut. 2nd Art., 17 June, 1867. 1st Lieut., 1 April, 1872. Capt., 30 Sept., 1891. Col. 41st U. S. Vols., 17 Aug., 1899. Graduate of the Artillery School, 1884.

RICKETTS, JAMES B.* [Born in N. Y. Appointed from N. Y.]
2nd Lieut. 1st Art., 1 July, 1839. 1st Lieut., 21 April, 1846. R. Q. M., 15 June, 1849, to 3 Aug., 1852. Capt., 3 Aug., 1852. Bvt. Lieut. Col., 21 July, 1861, for gallant and meritorious service in the Battle of Bull Run, Va. Brig. Gen. Vols., 21 July, 1861, for gallant and meritorious conduct in the Battle of Bull Run, Va. Maj. 1st Art., 1 June, 1863. Bvt. Col., 3 June, 1864, for gallant and meritorious service in the Battle of Cold Harbor, Va. Bvt. Maj. Gen. Vols., 1 Aug., 1864, for gallant conduct during the war, and particularly in the Battles of the campaign under Gen. Grant, the Monocacy under Gen. Wallace, and Opequan, Fisher's Hill, and Cedar Creek, in the Shenandoah campaign under Gen. Sheridan. Bvt. Brig. Gen., 13 March, 1865, for gallant and meritorious service in the Battle of Cedar Creek, Va. Bvt. Maj. Gen., 13 March, 1865, for gallant and meritorious service in the field during the war. Mustered out of Vol. Service 30 April, 1866. Lieut. Col. 21st Inf., 28 July, 1866, declined. Retired with rank of Maj. Gen., 3 Jan., 1867. Died 22 Sept., 1887.

RIDDICK, RICHARD H. [Born in N. C. Appointed from N. C.]
2nd Lieut. 1st Cav., 27 March, 1855. 1st Lieut., 2 Dec., 1860. Resigned 9 May, 1861. Died 27 June, 1862.

RIDDLE, DAVID. [Born in Penn. Appointed from Penn.]
2nd Lieut. 15th Inf., 9 April, 1812. 1st Lieut., 13 March, 1813. Trans. to 8th Inf., 17 May, 1815. Capt., 3 Dec., 1816. Died 9 July, 1820. Bvt. Capt., 25 July, 1814, for gallant conduct in the Battle of Niagara. Bvt. Maj., 17 Sept., 1814, for gallant conduct in the sortie from Fort Erie, U. C.

RIDDLE, SAML. [Born in Penn. Appointed from Army.]
Priv. and Sergt. 2nd Light Drag., 20 May, 1812, to June, 1813. Cornet 1st Light Drag., 20 May, 1813. 3rd Lieut. 15th Inf., 17 March, 1814. 2nd Lieut., 21 Sept., 1814. Disbanded 15 June, 1815. Reinstated 2 Dec., 1815, in 8th Inf. 1st Lieut., 13 Aug., 1817. Capt., 11 April, 1819. Disbanded 1 June, 1821. Bvt. 2nd Lieut., 17 Sept., 1814, for gallant conduct in the Sortie from Fort Erie, U. C.. Died 4 Aug., 1823.

RIDENOUR, EDGAR.* [Born in Ohio. Appointed from Ind.]
2nd Lieut. 16th Inf., 26 April, 1898. 1st Lieut., 2 March, 1899.

RIDGELY, AQUILA T. [Born in Md. Appointed from Md.]
Asst. Surg., 30 June, 1851. Resigned 23 June, 1861.

RIDGELY, CHAS. G.* [Born in Del. Appointed from Del.]
Bvt. 2nd Lieut. 1st Inf., 1 July, 1826. Resigned 22 Feb., 1827. Died 15 June, 1844.

RIDGELY, FRANK. [Born in Md. Appointed from Mo.]
2nd Lieut. 6th Inf., 5 Aug., 1861. Resigned 22 Aug., 1862.

RIDGELY, HENDERSON. [Born in Md. Appointed from Mo.]
2nd Lieut. 4th Inf., 19 May, 1841. 1st Lieut., 21 Sept., 1846. Killed 24 Nov., 1847, in action at Pass Gualaxara, Mex.

RIDGELY, RANDOLPH.* [Born in Md. Appointed from Md.]
2nd Lieut. 3rd Art., 1 July, 1837. 1st Lieut., 17 July, 1838. Reg. Adj., 8 March, 1838, to 1 May, 1841. Bvt. Capt. A. A. G., 7 July, 1846. Accidentally killed 27 Oct., 1846. Bvt. Capt., 9 May, 1846, for gallant and distinguished conduct at Palo Alto and Resaca de la Palma, Tex.

RIDGELY, SAML. C.* [Born in Md. Appointed from Md.]
Bvt. 2nd Lieut. 4th Art., 1 July, 1831. 2nd Lieut., 1 July, 1831. 1st Lieut., 16 Sept., 1836. Capt., 16 Feb., 1847. Died 6 July, 1859. Bvt. Maj., 20 Aug., 1847, for gallant and meritorious conduct at Contreras and Churubusco, Mex.

RIDGELY, SAML. H.* [Born in Md. Appointed from Md.]
Bvt. 2nd Lieut. 1st Inf., 1 July, 1826. Died 3 April, 1827.

RIDGELY, THOS. H. [Born in Fla. Appointed from Penn.]
Asst. Surg. 3rd Penn. Cav., 28 Dec., 1861, to 15 Sept., 1862. Asst. Surg., 16 Sept., 1862. Resigned 15 Feb., 1866.

RIDGELY, THOMAS P. [Born in Md. Appointed from Md.]
2nd Lieut. Corps Art., 13 Aug., 1819. Trans. to 2nd Art., 1 June, 1821. Resigned 31 Dec., 1830. 2nd Lieut. 2nd Art., 29 May, 1835. 1st Lieut., 31 Dec., 1836. Capt., 18 June, 1846. Died 6 Dec., 1847.

RIDGWAY, THOMAS.* [Born in N. Y. Appointed from N. Y.]
2nd Lieut. 5th Art., 13 June, 1883. 1st Lieut. 4th Art., 12 Feb., 1891. Trans. to 5th Art., 23 May, 1891. Trans. to 6th Art., 8 March, 1898. Trans. to 5th Art., 29 April, 1898. Capt., 18 March, 1899. Graduate of the Artillery School, 1896. Reg. Adj., 12 May, 1899.

RIELL, JOHN A. [Born in N. Y. Appointed from N. Y.]
2nd Lieut. 8th Inf., 7 July, 1838. 1st Lieut., 8 Jan., 1841. Died 22 June, 1841.

RIFE, JOSEPH B. [Born in Penn. Appointed from Penn.]
2nd Lieut. 6th Inf., 5 Aug., 1861. 1st Lieut., 9 Sept., 1861. Capt., 7 Nov., 1865. Resigned 1 March, 1872. Bvt. Capt., 17 Sept., 1862, for gallant and meritorious service at the Battle of Antietam, Md. Accidentally killed 29 Jan., 1889.

RIFENBERICK, RICHARD P., Jr. [Born in Ohio. Appointed from Ohio.]
Cadet Mil. Acad., 17 June, 1891, to 16 Jan., 1892. 2nd Lieut. 16th Inf., 10 April, 1899.

RIGAIL, LOUIS A. [Born in N. Y. Appointed from N. Y.]
3rd Lieut. Ord., 18 April, 1818. 2nd Lieut., 4 Aug., 1819. Trans. to 3rd Art., 1 June, 1821. 1st Lieut., 17 Feb., 1827. Resigned 11 Sept., 1828.

RIGAL, WM. F.* [Born in N. Y. Appointed from N. Y.]
3rd Lieut. Ord., 2 March, 1815. 2nd Lieut., 17 May, 1816. Dropped 1 Jan., 1818.

RIGG, EDWIN A. [Born in Pa. Appointed from Cal.]
Capt. 1st Cal. Vols., 24 Aug., 1861. Maj., 5 Sept., 1861. Lieut. Col., 28 April, 1862. Col., 4 Dec., 1862. Mustered out 30 Sept., 1864. Lieut. Col. 1st Cal. Vet. Vols., 24 March, 1865. Mustered out 9 Oct., 1866. 1st Lieut. 38th Inf., 22 Jan., 1867. Unassigned 11 Nov., 1869. Ass'd to 25th Inf., 6 April, 1870. Mustered out 1 Jan., 1871.

RIGGS, JOEL.* [Born in Ala. Appointed from Ala.]
Bvt. 2nd Lieut. 1st Inf., 1 July, 1833. Resigned 9 Oct., 1833. Died 13 Nov., 1865.

RILEY, BENNETT. [Born in Md. Appointed from Md.]
Ensign Rifles, 19 Jan., 1813. 3rd Lieut., 12 March, 1813. 2nd Lieut., 15 April, 1814. 1st Lieut., 31 March, 1817. Reg. Adj., Dec., 1816, to July, 1817. Capt., 6 Aug., 1818. Trans. to 5th Inf., 1 June, 1821. Trans. to 6th Inf., 3 Oct., 1821. Maj. 4th Inf., 26 Sept., 1837. Lieut. Col. 2nd Inf., 1 Dec., 1839. Col. 1st Inf., 31 Jan., 1850. Died 9 June, 1853. Bvt. Maj., 6 Aug., 1828, for ten years' faithful service in one grade. Bvt. Col., 2 June, 1840, for bravery, good conduct, etc., at the Battle of Chokachatta, Fla., etc. Bvt. Brig. Gen., 18 April, 1837, for gallant and meritorious conduct at the Battle of Cerro Gordo. Bvt. Maj. Gen., 20 Aug., 1847, for gallant conduct at Contreras, Mex.

RILEY, EDWARD B. D.* [Born in Indian Ter. Appointed at Large.]
Bvt. 2nd Lieut. 6th Inf., 1 July, 1860. 2nd Lieut. 4th Inf., 31 Jan., 1861. Resigned 13 June, 1861.

RILEY, JAMES. [Born in Md. Appointed from Penn.]
Priv. Commonwealth of Pa. Art., 21 May to 5 Aug., 1861. Priv. Anderson Troop Pa. Cav., 30 Nov., 1861, to 26 March, 1862. 2nd Lieut. 37th Inf., 7 March, 1867. Dismissed 9 June, 1868. 2nd Lieut. 32nd Inf., 18 Jan., 1869. Trans. to 21st Inf., 19 April, 1869. Mustered out 1 Jan., 1871.

RILEY, THOS. F. [Born in Fla. Appointed from Army.]
Priv. Ord., 1 July, 1863. 1st Class Priv. Ord., 1 Nov., 1865. 2nd Lieut. 12th Inf., 23 March, 1866. Trans. to 21st Inf., 21 Sept., 1866. 1st Lieut., 29 Oct., 1867. Unassigned 19 April, 1869. Ass'd to 21st Inf., 16 Aug., 1869. Capt., 28 June, 1878. Dismissed 15 Aug., 1880.

RING, FRANKLIN M. [Born in N. Y. Appointed from Army.]
2nd Lieut. 60th Ill. Vols., 26 April, 1862. Resigned 23 June, 1862. Priv. Co. M, 2nd Art., 24 Sept., 1862, to 8 June, 1865. 2nd Lieut. 2nd Art., 26 May, 1865. 1st Lieut., 28 March, 1866. Mustered out 1 Jan., 1871.

RINGGOLD, GEORGE H.* [Born in Md. Appointed from Md.]
Bvt. 2nd Lieut. 6th Inf., 1 July, 1833. 2nd Lieut., 15 Aug., 1836. Resigned 31 May, 1837. Addl. P. M., 4 Aug., 1846. Maj P. M. U. S. A., 21 July, 1847. Lieut. Col. Dep. P. M. Gen., 28 May, 1862. Died 4 April, 1864.

RINGGOLD, SAML.* [Born in D. C. Appointed from Md.]
2nd Lieut. Corps Art., 24 July, 1818. Trans. to 2nd Art., 1 June, 1821. Trans. to 3rd Art., 16 Aug., 1821. 1st Lieut., 8 May, 1822. Capt. 3rd Art., 31 Aug., 1836. Died 11 May, 1846, of wounds received in the Battle of Palo Alto, Mex. Bvt. Capt., 8 May, 1832, for ten years' faithful service in one grade. Bvt. Maj., 15 Feb., 1838, for meritorious conduct, and activity and efficiency in war against the Florida Indians.

RINGGOLD, THOS. L.* [Born in Va. Appointed from D. C.]
2nd Lieut. 4th Art., 1 July, 1838. Trans. to Ord., 1 July, 1840. 1st Lieut., 3 March, 1847. Capt., 1 July, 1853. Died 11 May, 1854.

RINNER PETER. [Born in N. Y. Appointed form Army.]
Priv. Co. B, 7th Inf., 10 Oct., 1850, to 10 Oct., 1855. Priv., Corpl., Sergt. and 1st Sergt. Cos. G and C, 2nd Drag., 21 Nov., 1855, to 21 Nov., 1860, and in Co. K, 2nd Drag. (2nd Cav.), 19 Dec., 1860, to 23 Sept., 1862. 2nd Lieut. 2nd Cav., 17 July, 1862. Cashiered 13 Feb., 1864.

RIPLEY, ELEAZER W. [Born in N. H. Appointed from Mass.]
Lieut. Col. 21st Inf., 12 March, 1812. Col., 12 March, 1813. Presented by Resolution of Congress, 3 Nov., 1814, with a gold medal, with suitable emblems and devices in testimony of the high sense entertained by Congress of his gallantry and good conduct in the several conflicts of Chippewa, Niagara and Erie, U. C. Brig. Gen., 15 April, 1814. Resigned 1 Feb., 1820. Bvt. Maj. Gen., 25 June, 1814, for gallant conduct at the Battle of Niagara. Died 2 March, 1839.

RIPLEY, FITZ H. [Born in Ala. Appointed from Ala.]
2nd Lieut. of Inf., 8 March, 1847; 13th Inf., 9 April, 1847. 1st Lieut., 30 July, 1847. Resigned 29 Feb., 1848.

RIPLEY, HENRY A. [Born in Mich. Appointed from Mich.]
2nd Lieut. 35th Mich. Vols., 18 July, 1898. 1st Lieut., 1 Feb. to 31 March, 1899. 2nd Lieut. 22nd Inf., 1 June, 1899.

RIPLEY, HENRY L. [Born in Mass. Appointed from Army.]
2nd Class Priv. Co. E, Batt. Eng., 1 April, 1876. 1st Class Priv., 1 May, 1876. Corpl., 17 June, 1877. 2nd Lieut. 24th Inf., 28 June, 1879. 1st Lieut., 26 Nov., 1884. Trans. to 3rd Cav., 23 Feb., 1887. Capt., 8 Aug., 1895. Honor graduate of the Infantry and Cavalry School, 1885-

RIPLEY, HOMER J. [Born in Penn. Appointed from Army.]
Priv. and Sergt. Co. B. and Com. Sergt. 2nd Batt. 14th Inf., 27 Aug., 1862, to 8 July, 1865. 2nd Lieut. 14th Inf., 30 June, 1865. 1st Lieut., 30 June, 1865. Trans. to 32nd Inf., 21 Sept., 1866. Reg. Adj., 31 Jan. to 15 July, 1867. Capt., 15 Sept., 1867. Unassigned 19 April, 1869. Discharged 31 Dec., 1870.

RIPLEY, JAMES W.* [Born in Conn. Appointed from Conn.]
2nd Lieut. Corps Art., 1 June, 1814. 1st Lieut., 20 April, 1818. Batt. Q. M., 28 Dec., 1816, to 1 June, 1821. Trans. to 4th Art., 1 June, 1821. Capt., 1 Aug., 1825. Capt. Ord., 30 May, 1832. Maj., 7 July, 1838. Lieut. Col., 31 Dec., 1854. Col. Chief of Ord., 3 April, 1861. Brig. Gen. Chief of Ord., 3 Aug., 1861. Retired 15 Sept., 1863. Died 15 March, 1870. Bvt. Lieut. Col., 30 May, 1848, for meritorious conduct, particularly in performing his duty in the prosecution of war with Mexico. Bvt. Brig. Gen., 2 July, 1861. Bvt. Maj. Gen., 13 March, 1865, for long and faithful service in the army.

RIPLEY, ROSWELL S.* [Born in Ohio. Appointed from N. Y.]
Bvt. 2nd Lieut. 3rd Art., 1 July, 1843. 2nd Lieut. 2nd Art., 26 March, 1846. 1st Lieut., 3 March, 1847. Resigned 2 March, 1853. Bvt. Capt., 18 April, 1847, for gallant and meritorious conduct in the Battle of Cerro Gordo, Mex. Bvt. Maj., 13 Sept., 1847, for gallant and meritorious conduct in the Battle of Chapultepec, Mex. Died 29 March, 1887.

RISLEY, DOUGLAS G. [Born in N. Y. Appointed from Ind.]
Sergt. Co. C, 9th Ind. Vols., 19 April, 1861. Discharged 29 July, 1861. Capt. 9th Ind. Vols., 5 Sept., 1861. Mustered out 30 May, 1863. Capt. 9th U. S. Col. Troops, 27 Nov., 1863. Mustered out 15 May, 1865. 2nd Lieut. 42nd Inf., 28 July, 1866. Unassigned 22 April, 1869. Retired with rank of Capt., 31 Dec., 1870. Died 18 Nov., 1882.

RITCHIE, ROBERT R. [Born in Va. Appointed from Va.]
Maj. Surg. of Inf., 27 March, 1847; 12th Inf., 9 April, 1847. Disbanded 25 July, 1848.

RITTENHOUSE, BENJ'N. F. [Born in Penn. Appointed from D. C.]
2nd Lieut. 5th Art., 14 May, 1861. 1st Lieut., 13 July, 1862. Bvt. Capt., 1 Aug., 1864, for gallant service in the Battle of Bethesda Church, and during the campaign before Richmond, Va. Bvt. Maj., 13 March, 1865, for good conduct and gallant service during the war. Capt. 20th Inf., 28 July, 1866, declined. Capt. 5th Art., 5 Jan., 1870. Graduate of the Artillery School, 1869. Retired for wounds 7 Oct., 1874.

RITTENHOUSE, HENRY N. [Born in Penn. Appointed from Penn.]
Med. Storekeeper, 13 Aug., 1862. Resigned 13 Feb., 1865.

RITNER, I. NEWTON. [Born in Pa. Appointed from Pa.]
Sergt. Co. I, 49th Pa. Vols., 24 Oct., 1861. 2nd Lieut. 49th Pa. Vols., 28 Aug., 1862.

1st Lieut., 18 Nov., 1862, until mustered out 19 Nov., 1863. Bvt. Capt., 13 March, 1865, for faithful and meritorious services during the war. Post Chap., 20 July, 1891. Retired for disability 20 Dec., 1898.

RITNER, JOSEPH.* [Born in Penn. Appointed from Penn.]
Bvt. 2nd Lieut. 4th Inf., 1 July, 1830. 2nd Lieut., 1 July, 1830. Died 18 Feb., 1834.

RITNER, JOSEPH M. [Born in Conn. Appointed from Ind.]
1st Lieut. 11th Inf., 14 May, 1861. Dismissed 16 July, 1864. Died 9 Sept., 1883.

RITTER, JOHN F.* [Born in Penn. Appointed from Penn.]
2nd Lieut. 5th Inf., 1 July, 1856. 1st Lieut., 27 March, 1861. Trans. to 15th Inf., 14 May, 1861. Capt., 24 Oct., 1861. Col. 1st Mo. Cav., 9 Aug., 1862. Resigned from Vol. Service, 5 Dec., 1864. Trans. to 33rd Inf., 21 Sept., 1866. Trans. to 8th Inf., 3 May, 1869. Died 1 Aug., 1872. Bvt. Maj., 28 March, 1862, for gallant and meritorious service at the Battle of Apache Canon, N. M. Bvt. Lieut. Col., 10 Sept., 1863, for gallant and meritorious service at the capture of Little Rock, Ark.

RITZIUS, HENRY P. [Born in Prussia. Appointed from Penn.]
Priv. Co. A, 5th N. Y. State Militia, 1 May, 1861. Discharged 7 Aug., 1861. 1st Sergt. Co. G, 52nd N. Y. Vols., 17 Sept., 1861. Discharged 23 Aug., 1862. 1st Lieut. 52nd N. Y. Vols., 23 Aug., 1862. Capt., 23 Oct., 1863. Mustered out 2 Aug., 1864. Maj. 52nd N. Y. Vols., 8 Dec., 1864. Mustered out 1 July, 1865. 1st Lieut. 7th U. S. Vet. Vols., 22 Aug., 1865. Mustered out 30 April, 1866. 2nd Lieut. 39th Inf., 23 Oct., 1867. Trans. to 25th Inf., 20 April, 1869. 1st Lieut., 3 March, 1875. R. Q. M., 1 Jan., 1878. Capt., 1 Sept., 1887. Retired for disability, with rank of Maj., 2 March, 1899.

RIVERS, TYREE R.* [Born in Miss. Appointed from Tenn.]
2nd Lieut. 3rd Cav., 13 June, 1883. 1st Lieut., 17 Jan., 1889. Capt. 4th Cav., 16 Oct., 1898.

RIVERS, WM. C.* [Born in Tenn. Appointed from Tenn.]
2nd Lieut 1st Cav., 12 June, 1887. 1st Lieut., 3rd Cav., 18 Aug., 1894. Trans. to 1st Cav., 7 Nov., 1895.

RIVERS, WM. M. [Born in S. C. Appointed from S. C.]
Surg.'s Mate 1st Inf., 10 Aug., 1818. Resigned 15 Feb., 1821.

RIVES, WM. F. [Born in Va. Appointed from Va.]
2nd Lieut. 13th Inf., 8 June, 1847. Disbanded 15 July, 1848.

RIVES, WRIGHT.* [Born in D. C. Appointed from D. C.]
2nd Lieut. 6th Inf., 6 May, 1861. 1st Lieut., 17 May, 1861. Capt. A. A. de C. Vols., 4 June, 1862. Capt. 6th Inf., 23 Feb., 1864. Bvt. Maj. and Lieut. Col., 13 March, 1865, for gallant and meritorious service during the advance on Corinth and at the Siege of Vicksburg, Miss. Unassigned 22 April, 1869. Retired 31 Dec., 1870.

ROACH, GEORGE H. [Born in N. Y. Appointed from N. Y.]
Priv. Co. F, 26th Ill. Vols., 27 Feb., 1864. Discharged 20 July, 1865. 2nd Lieut. 17th Inf., 1 Oct., 1873. 1st Lieut., 28 June, 1878. Capt., 4 Feb., 1893.

ROACH, HAMPTON M. [Born in Ill. Appointed from the Army.]
Priv., Corpl., Sergt. and 1st Sergt. Co. F, 5th Cav., 15 May, 1876, to 5 Julyy, 1883. 2nd Lieut. 1st Inf., 3 July, 1883. Retired for disability, 18 May, 1894. Medal of Honor for gallantry in action against hostile Ute Indians at Milk Creek, Col., Sept. 29 to Oct. 5, 18.9, in building breastworks under fire and keeping the command supplied with water three consecutive nights, while exposed to the fire of ambushed Indians at close range, while serving as Corpl. Troop F, 5th Cav.

ROACH, ISAAC, Jr. [Born in Penn. Appointed from Penn.]
2nd Lieut. 2nd Art., 2 July, 1812. Capt. 23rd Inf., 13 April, 1813. Trans. to Corps Art., 17 May, 1815. Trans. to 2nd Art., 1 June, 1821. Resigned 1 April, 1824. Bvt. Maj., 13 April, 1823, for ten years' faithful service in one grade. Died 29 Dec., 1848.

ROACH, LEON L. [Born in N. Y. Appointed from Ohio.]
2nd Lieut. 19th Inf., 10 April, 1899.

ROANE, JAMES H. [Born in N. C. Appointed from N. C.]
Ensign 10th Inf., 12 March, 1812. 3rd Lieut., 24 March, 1813. 2nd Lieut., 15 Aug., 1813. 1st Lieut., 23 Sept., 1814. Discharged 15 June, 1815. 2nd Lieut. 7th Inf., 19 Feb., 1817. Resigned 18 Oct., 1817.

ROANE, JUNIUS B. [Born in Va. Appointed from Va.]
2nd Lieut. 4th Art., 14 May, 1857. Died 10 Feb., 1859.

ROBBINS, HAYWOOD. [Born in N. C. Appointed from the Army.]
Priv., Corpl. and Sergt. Batty L, 5th Art., 13 July, 1897, to 15 Nov., 1899. 2nd Lieut. 15th Inf., 1 Oct., 1899.

ROBBINS, KENELM.* [Born in Mass. Appointed from Mass.]
2nd Lieut. 5th Cav., 11 June, 1863. 1st Lieut., 12 June, 1864. Reg. Adj., 31 July to 31 Dec., 1866. R. C. S., 31 Dec., 1866, to 22 Jan., 1867. Capt. 43rd Inf., 22 Jan., 1867. Unassigned 8 April, 1869. Died 28 Feb., 1870. Bvt. 1st Lieut., 1 Aug., 1863, for gallant and meritorious service at the Battle of Brandy Station, Va. Bvt. Capt., 19 Sept., 1864, for gallant and meritorious service at the Battle of Winchester, Va.

ROBBINS, SAMUEL M. [Born in N. Y. Appointed from Colo.]
Capt. 1st Colo. Cav., 30 Nov., 1861. Mustered out 26 Oct., 1865. 1st Lieut. 7th Cav., 28 July, 1866. Capt., 27 Nov., 1868. Resigned 1 March, 1872. Died 25 Sept., 1878.

ROBE, CHAS. F. [Born in N. Y. Appointed from Mich.]
1st Lieut. 147th N. Y. Vols., 11 Sept., 1862. Capt., 10 Nov., 1863. Mustered out 11 March, 1864. Capt. Vet. Res. Corps, 5 March, 1864. Mustered out 7 Sept., 1866. 1st Lieut. 29th Inf., 28 July, 1866. Unassigned 25 April, 1869. Ass'd to 25th Inf., 31 Jan., 1870. Capt., 25 Jan., 1872. Maj. 14th Inf., 5 July, 1895. Lieut. Col. 17th Inf., 16 Sept., 1898.

ROBERDEAU, ISAAC. [Born in Penn. Appointed from Penn.]
Maj. Top. Eng., 29 April, 1813. Disbanded 15 June, 1815. Reinstated 13 May, 1816. Died 15 Jan., 1829. Bvt. Lieut. Col., 29 April, 1823, for ten years' faithful service in one grade.

ROBERT, HENRY M.* [Born in S. C. Appointed from Ohio.]
Bvt. 2nd Lieut. Eng., 1 July, 1857. 2nd Lieut., 13 Dec., 1858. 1st Lieut., 3 Aug., 1861. Capt., 3 March, 1863. Maj., 7 March, 1867. Lieut. Col., 10 Jan., 1883. Col., 3 Feb., 1895.

ROBERTS, BENJ'N. K. [Born in Tenn. Appointed from Conn.]
2nd Lieut. 7th Iowa Cav., 25 July, 1863. Capt. A. A. G. Vols., 12 Nov., 1864. Bvt. Maj. Vols., 13 March, 1865, for faithful and meritorious service during the war. Mustered out 1 July, 1866. 2nd Lieut. 5th Art., 18 April, 1866. 1st Lieut., 7 Feb., 1867. Capt., 25 April, 1888. Maj. 2nd Art., 17 Oct., 1899.

ROBERTS, BENJ'N. S.* [Born in Vt. Appointed from Vt.]
Bvt. 2nd Lieut. 1st Drag., 1 July, 1835. 2nd Lieut., 31 May, 1836. 1st Lieut., 31 July, 1837. Resigned 28 Jan., 1839. 1st Lieut. Mounted Rifles, 27 May, 1846. Capt., 16 Feb., 1847. Maj., 13 May, 1861; 3rd Cav., 3 Aug., 1861. Brig. Gen. Vols., 16 June, 1862. Mustered out of Vol. Service., 15 Jan., 1866. Lieut. Col. 3rd Cav., 28 July, 1866. Retired 15 Dec., 1870. Died 29 Jan., 1875. Bvt. Maj., 13 Sept., 1847, for gallant and meritorious conduct at Chapultepec. Bvt. Lieut. Col., 24 Nov., 1847, for gallant and meritorious conduct at Matamoras, and the Pass of Gualaxara, Mex. Bvt. Col., 21 Feb., 1862, for gallant and meritorious service at Val Verde, N. M. Bvt. Brig. Gen., 13 March, 1865, for gallant and meritorious service at Cedar Mountain, Va., and Maj. Gen. Vols., 13 March, 1865, for gallant and meritorious service in the Battle of Cedar Mountain, Va., 9 Aug., 1862, and in Battle of Manassas, Va., 29 and 30 Aug., 1862. Died 29 Jan., 1875.

ROBERTS, CHAS. D.* [Born in Dak. Appointed from Wyo.]
Addl. 2nd Lieut. 17th Inf., 11 June, 1897. 2nd Lieut. 21 Inf., 27 June, 1897. Trans. to 17th Inf., 31 Aug., 1897. 1st Lieut., 2 March, 1899. Capt. 35th U. S. Vols., 5 July, 1899, to —. Medal of Honor for distinguished bravery in Battle El Caney, Cuba, in assisting in rescuing wounded from in front of the lines under heavy fire of the enemy, 1 July, 1898.

ROBERTS, CYRUS S. [Born in Conn. Appointed from Conn.]
Priv. Co. A, 22nd N. Y. State Militia, 28 May, 1862. Priv. Co. A, 150th N. Y. Vols., 6 Sept., 1862. Sergt. Maj., 150th N. Y. Vols., 11 Oct., 1862. 2nd Lieut. 150th N. Y. Vols., 13 Feb., 1863. 1st Lieut., 1 Jan., 1865. Bvt. Capt. Vols., 13 March, 1865, for gallant and meritorious service. Bvt. Maj. Vols., 13 March, 1865, for gallant and meritorious service during the campaign in W. Va. and the Shenandoah Valley. Mustered out 8 June, 1865. Capt. A. de C. Vols., 22 June, 1865. Mustered out 7 Dec., 1865. 2nd Lieut. 17th Inf., 11 May, 1866. Bvt. 1st Lieut., 2 March, 1867, for gallant and meritorious service in the Battle of Winchester, Va., 19 Sept., 1864. Bvt. Capt., 2 March, 1867, for gallant and meritorious service at the Battle of Fisher's Hill, Va., 22 Sept., 1864. 1st Lieut. 17th Inf., 18 Sept., 1867. Capt., 28 June, 1878. Capt. A. J. A., 3 June, 1885, to 11 April, 1886. Maj., 26 April, 1898. Lieut. Col. 13th Inf., 14 Aug., 1899.

ROBERTS, ERASTUS. [Born in Mass. Appointed from Army.]
Cadet Mil. Acad., 3 Dec., 1807, to 15 April, 1809. Priv., Corpl., Sergt. and Q. M. Sergt. 6th Inf., 1 June, 1812, to March, 1814. Ensign 6th Inf., 11 March, 1814. 3rd Lieut., 1 May, 1814. 2nd Lieut., 2 June, 1814. Disbanded 15 June, 1815. Reinstated 17 May, 1816, in Corps Art. Died 2 May, 1817.

ROBERTS, HARRIS L.* [Born in D. C. Appointed from D. C.]
2nd Lieut 4th Inf., 12 June, 1880. Trans. to 19th Inf., 22 March, 1881. 1st Lieut. 21st Inf., 14 Nov., 1890. Trans. to 19th Inf., 20 July, 1891. Capt., 26 April, 1898.

ROBERTS, H. B. [Born in Ky. Appointed from Mo.]
3rd Lieut. Mounted Rangers, 6 Nov., 1832. Disbanded 1 Oct., 1833.

ROBERTS, HUGH A.* [Born in Ga. Appointed from Ga.]
2nd Lieut. 8th Cav., 15 Feb., 1899.

ROBERTS, JOSEPH.* [Born in Del. Appointed from Del.]
Bvt. 2nd Lieut. 4th Art., 1 July, 1835. 2nd Lieut., 10 June, 1836. 1st Lieut., 7 July, 1838. Capt., 20 Aug., 1848. Maj., 3 Sept., 1861. Col. 3rd Penn. Art., 19 March, 1863. Lieut. Col. 4th Art., 11 Aug., 1863. Bvt. Col., 13 March, 1865, for faithful and meritorious service during the war. Bvt. Brig. Gen., 13 March, 1865, for meritorious and distinguished service during the war. Bvt. Brig. Gen. Vols., 9 April, 1865, for meritorious and distinguished service during the war. Mustered out of Vol. Service, 13 Nov., 1865. Col. 4th Art., 10 Jan., 1877. Retired 2 July, 1877. Died 18 Oct., 1898.

ROBERTS, THADDEUS. [Born in N. Y. Appointed from Army.]
Priv. Gen. Ser., 19 July, 1858, to 1 March, 1862. 1st Lieut. 148th N. Y. Vols., 14 Sept., 1862. Capt., 9 Feb., 1865 Resigned 15 May, 1865. Priv. and Artif. Co. B, Batt. Eng., 29 Aug., 1865, to 24 March, 1867. 2nd Lieut. 23rd Inf., 8 Feb., 1867. Mustered out 31 Dec., 1870.

ROBERTS, THOMAS A.* [Born in Ill. Appointed from Ill.]
Addl. 2nd Lieut. 1st Cav., 11 June, 1897. 2nd Lieut. 10th Cav., 26 Feb., 1898.

ROBERTS, WM. [Born in Ga. Appointed from Ga.]
Asst. Surg., 31 Dec., 1845. Died 13 Oct., 1847, of wounds received at Battle of Molino del Rey, Mexico.

ROBERTSON, BEVERLY H.* [Born in Va. Appointed from Va.]
Bvt. 2nd Lieut. 2nd Drag., 1 July, 1849. 2nd Lieut., 25 July, 1850. 1st Lieut., 3 March, 1855. Reg. Adj., 26 Aug., 1860, to 3 March, 1861. Capt., 3 March, 1861. Dismissed 8 Aug., 1861.

ROBERTSON, CLAUDE S. [Born in Scotland. Appointed from Army.]
Priv., Corpl., Sergt. and 1st Sergt. Co. H, 10th Inf., 1 May, 1856, to 23 Nov., 1861. 2nd Lieut. 10th Inf., 24 Oct., 1861. 1st Lieut., 12 June, 1863. R. Q. M., 20 June, 1863, to 6 Dec., 1864. Capt., 13 Sept., 1864. Resigned 10 June, 1865.

ROBERTSON, EDGAR B.* [Born in Mass. Appointed from Mass.]
2nd Lieut. 9th Inf., 17 June, 1874. 1st Lieut., 15 June, 1881. Reg. Adj., 15 June, 1883, to 1 July, 1887. Capt., 15 June, 1891. Trans. to 16th Inf., 29 Aug., 1899. Trans. to 20th Inf., 23 Oct., 1899. Maj. Q. M. Vols., 3 June, 1898, to 5 Feb., 1900. Maj. 15th Inf., 12 Jan., 1900.

ROBERTSON, F. J. [Born in Tenn. Appointed from Tenn.]
Asst. Surg. 3rd Drag., 9 April, 1847. Disbanded 31 July, 1848.

ROBERTSON, JAMES M. [Born in N. H. Appointed from Army.]
Entered service as James M. Robinson.) Priv. Co. F, 2nd Art., 8 Dec., 1838. Corpl., 1 July, 1839. Priv., 20 May, 1842. Discharged 2 Nov., 1843. Priv. and Artif. Co. H, 2nd Art., 2 Nov., 1843. Priv., 1 Aug., 1846. Artif., 1 Dec., 1846. Q. M. Sergt. 2nd Art., 7 March, 1847. Bvt. 2nd Lieut. 2nd Art., 28 June, 1848. 2nd Lieut., 28 June, 1848. 1st Lieut., 28 Sept., 1852. Capt., 14 May, 1861. Bvt. Maj., 27 June, 1862, for gallant and meritorious service in the Batle of Gaines' Mill, Va. Bvt. Lieut. Col., 3 July, 1863, for gallant and meritorious service in the Getysburg campaingn. Bvt. Col., 31 May, 1864, for gallant and meritorious service in the Battle of Cold Harbor, Va. Bvt. Brig. Gen., 13 March, 1865, for distinguished service while Chf of Horse Art. attached to the Army of the Potomac during the campaign from May to Aug., 1864, including the Battles of the Wilderness, Cold Harbor, Hawes Shop and Trevillian Station, Va. Maj. 2nd Art., 17 June, 1874. Trans. to 3rd Art., 1 Feb., 1875. Retired 20 March, 1879. Died 21 Jan., 1891.

ROBERTSON, JOEFFREY. [Born in ——. Appointed from Tenn.]
2nd Lieut. 7th Inf., 12 Dec., 1808. 1st Lieut., 30 Nov., 1810. Capt. 7th Inf., 21 Feb., 1814. Died 31 Aug., 1817.

ROBERTSON, JOHN. [Born in Del. Appointed from Del.]
Asst. Surg., 15 June, 1840. Died 20 May, 1842.

ROBERTSON, JOHN. [Born in Canada. Appointed from Army.]
Priv., Corpl. and Sergt. Troop C, 2nd Cav., 27 Aug., 1894, to 25 April, 1898. 2nd Lieut. 6th Inf., 12 April, 1898. 1st Lieut., 2 March, 1899.

ROBERTSON, REUBEN L. [Born in Va. Appointed from Va.]
Asst. Surg., 3 Dec., 1883. Capt. Asst. Surg., 3 Dec., 1888. Resigned 3 July, 1895.

ROBERTSON, SAMUEL C.* [Born in Va. Appointed from Tenn.]
2nd Lieut. 1st Cav., 13 June, 1879. 1st Lieut., 16 Jan., 1889. Resigned 30 June, 1893.

ROBERTSON, WM.* [Born in Tenn. Appointed from Tenn.]
Bvt. 2nd Lieut. 2nd Drag., 1 July, 1840. 2nd Lieut., 1 Feb., 1841. Resigned 10 July, 1843. Died 17 Feb., 1870.

ROBESON, WM. L. [Born in ——. Appointed from N. C.]
Ensign 3rd Inf., 31 Oct., 1812. 3rd Lieut., 12 March, 1813. 2nd Lieut., 9 Oct., 1813. 1st Lieut., 2 May, 1814. Reg. P. M., June, 1814, to June, 1815. Disbanded 15 June, 1815. Reinstated 17 May, 1816, in Corps Art. Capt. A. D. Q. M. G., 30 Aug., 1816. Resigned 11 Sept., 1818.

ROBESON, WM. P. [Born in N. J. Appointed from N. J.]
1st Lieut. 3rd N. J. Vols., 28 May, 1861. Capt., 13 Aug., 1862. Resigned 12 Jan., 1864. Maj. 3rd N. J. Cav., 14 Jan., 1864. Lieut. Col., 6 Dec., 1864. Bvt. Col. and Brig. Gen. Vols., 13 March, 1865, for distinguished and meritorious service. Mustered out 1 Aug., 1865. Capt. 7th Cav., 28 July, 1866. Resigned 8 June, 1867. Died 15 Sept., 1881.

ROBICHON, HECTOR A.* [Born in Canada. Appointed from N. Y.]
2nd Lieut. 13th Inf., 15 Feb., 1899.

ROBINETT, CHAS. [Born in Russia. Appointed from N. Y.]
Priv. Co. G, 14th Maine Vols., 25 June, 1862, to 1 Nov., 1863. 2nd Lieut. 76th U. S. Col. Inf., 22 Jan., 1864. 1st Lieut., 19 Feb., 1865. Capt., 3 Oct., 1865. Mustered out 31 Dec., 1865. Capt. 51st U. S. Col. Inf., 29 Jan., 1866. Mustered out 16 June, 1866. 2nd Lieut. 11th Inf., 20 July, 1866. Trans. to 20th Inf., 21 Sept., 1866. 1st Lieut. 5 Oct., 1867. Mustered out 1 Jan., 1871. Died 1 July, 1884.

ROBINETT, HENRY C. [Born in Va. Appointed from Del.]
2nd Lieut. 1st Inf., 5 Aug., 1861. 1st Lieut., 23 Nov., 1861. Capt. A. de C. Vols., 25 March, 1864. Discharged from Vols., 8 May, 1865. Dismissed 29 Dec., 1865. Reinstated 24 April, 1866. Capt., 28 July, 1866. Died 22 April, 1868. Bvt. Capt., 4 Oct., 1862, for gallant and meritorious service at the Batle of Corinth, Miss. Bvt. Maj., 4 July, 1863, for gallant and meritorious service during the Siege of Vicksburg, Miss., and Bvt. Maj. Vols., 9 April, 1865, for meritorious service in the campaign against the rebel army of Northern Va., commencing in front of Petersburg, 29 March, and ending 9 April, 1865.

ROBINS, ERNEST S.* [Born in Ind. Appointed from Ind.]
2nd Lieut. 3rd Cav., 15 June, 1884. 1st Lieut. of Cav. (9th), 21 April, 1891. Trans. to 3rd Cav., 27 April, 1891. Died 18 Aug., 1894.

ROBINS, RICHARD. [Born in Mass. Appointed from Army.]
Priv and Corpl. Co. D, 11th Inf., 10 Oct., 1861, to 8 Oct., 1862. 2nd Lieut. 11th Inf., 27 June, 1862. 1st Lieut., 25 July, 1863. Capt. 39th Inf., 22 Jan., 1867. Resigned 20 July, 1868. Bvt. 1st Lieut., 2 July, 1863, for gallant and meritorious service at the Battle of Gettysburg Pa. Bvt. Capt., 13 March, 1865, for gallant and meritorious service at the Battle of Gettysburg, Penn.

ROBINSON, AUGUSTUS G.* [Born in Maine. Appointed from Maine.]
Bvt. 2nd Lieut. 4th Art., 1 July, 1857. 2nd Lieut. 3rd Art., 12 Oct., 1858. 1st Lieut., 14 May, 1861. Capt. A. Q. M., 19 Feb., 1863. Bvt. Maj., 13 March, 1865, for faithful and meritorious service during the war. Maj. Q. M., 4 March, 1879. Lieut. Col. Dep. Q. M. G., 10 July, 1890. Col. A. Q. M. G., 22 Sept., 1896. Retired by President, being over 62 years of age, 15 Oct., 1897. Died 1 Oct., 1898.

ROBINSON, DANIEL. [Born in Ireland. Appointed from Army.]
Priv. Co C, 7th Inf., 26 Sept., 1849. Corpl., 27 Dec., 1852. Discharged 5 Sept., 1854. Corpl. Co. C, 7th Inf., 5 Sept., 1854. Sergt., 21 Feb., 1856 Discharged 22 July, 1859. Sergt. Co. C, 7th Inf., 22 July, 1859. 1st Sergt., 1 April, 1862. Ord. Sergt. U. S. A., 11 March, 1863. 2nd Lieut. 7th Inf., 10 Aug., 1863. 1st Lieut., 8 May, 1864. Dismissed 3 May, 1865. Priv. Co. G, 2nd Batt. 16th Inf., 23 June, 1865. Sergt., 1 July, 1865. Q. M. Sergt., 5 Oct., 1865. 2nd Lieut. 7th Inf., 28 May, 1886. 1st Lieut., 1 March, 1872. Capt., 16 Dec., 1888. Retired for over forty years' service, 30 Nov., 1889.

ROBINSON, EDWARD W. [Born in Wis. Appointed from Wash.]
Cadet at Mil. Acad., 15 June, 1896, to 31 May, 1897. Priv. Troop B, 2nd Cav., 7 May, 1898, to 23 Jan., 1899. 2nd Lieut. 23rd Inf., 10 April, 1899. Capt. 35th U. S. Vols., 5 July, 1899.

ROBINSON, EUSTACE.* [Born in Va. Appointed from Va.]
Bvt. 2nd Lieut. 4th Inf., 1 July, 1834. Resigned 11 June, 1835. Died 7 Dec., 1859.

ROBINSON, FAYETTE. [Born in Va. Appointed from Va.]
2nd Lieut. 1st Drag., 25 Jan., 1837. 1st Lieut., 3 Feb., 1839. Resigned 3 Dec., 1841.

ROBINSON, FRANK U. [Born in N. Y. Appointed from N. Y.]
2nd Lieut. 41st U. S. Col. Troops, 1 Oct., 1864. Mustered out 10 Dec., 1865. 2nd Lieut. 125th U. S. Col. Troops, 26 April, 1866. Mustered out 20 Dec., 1867. 2nd Lieut. 19th Inf., 13 March, 1868. Unassigned 31 March, 1869. Ass'd to 2nd Cav., 14 July, 1869. 1st Lieut., 31 March, 1878. Capt., 28 Dec., 1888.

ROBINSON, FREDERICK. [Born in Ireland. Appointed from Army.]
Priv. Co. A, 4th Art., 19 Sept., 1849. Discharged 19 Sept., 1854. Priv. Detachment Drag at Mil. Acad., 18 Aug., 1858. Trans. to Co. D, 5th Art., — May, 1861. Corpl., 1 July, 1861. Sergt., 1 Dec., 1861. Discharged 30 Oct., 1862. 2nd Lieut. 5th Art., 30 Oct., 1862. Bvt. 1st Lieut., 3 June, 1864, for gallant and meritorious service in the Battle of Cold Harbor, Va. Bvt. Capt., 19 Oct., 1864, for gallant and meritorious service in the Battle of Cedar Creek, Va. 1st Lieut. 5th Art., 28 July, 1866. Died 1 Nov., 1882.

ROBINSON, GEORGE. [Born in N. Y. Appointed from N.Y.]
2nd Lieut. 123rd N. Y. Vols., 4 Sept., 1862. 1st Lieut., 11 Nov., 1863. Bvt. Capt. Vols., 13 March, 1865, for gallant and meritorious service during the campaign in Georgia and the Carolinas. Mustered out 8 June, 1865. Post Chap., 1 March, 1877.

ROBINSON, GEORGE F. [Born in Maine. Appointed from Maine.]
Priv. Co. B, 8th Maine Vols., 15 Aug., 1863, to 19 May, 1865. Maj. P. M., 23 June, 1879. Retired by operation of law, 13 Aug., 1896.

ROBINSON, GEORGE T. [Born in Penn. Appointed from Md.]
2nd Lieut. 56th Penn. Vols., 7 Nov., 1862. Discharged 15 Aug., 1863. 1st Lieut. 11th Kan. Cav., 7 July, 1864. Maj. 14th Mo. Cav., 17 July, 1865. Mustered out 26 Oct., 1865. Capt. 10th Cav., 28 July, 1866. Cashiered 15 April, 1875.

ROBINSON, HENRY E.* [Born in Penn. Appointed from Penn.]
2nd Lieut. 4th Inf., 12 June, 1871. 1st Lieut., 20 March, 1879. R. Q. M., 1 Nov., 1883, to 1 Nov., 1887. Capt., 4 April, 1893.

ROBINSON, JAMES M. [Born in N. H. Appointed from N. H.]
(Changed name to James M. Robertson—which see.)

ROBINSON, JAMES W.* [Born in Va. Appointed from Mo.]
Bvt. 2nd Lieut. 1st Art., 1 July, 1852. 2nd Lieut., 31 March, 1853. 1st Lieut., 3 May, 1855. Resigned 15 May, 1861.

ROBINSON, JOHN C. [Born in N. Y. Appointed from N. Y.]
Cadet Mil. Acad., 1 July, 1835, to 14 March, 1838. 2nd Lieut. 5th Inf., 27 Oct., 1839. 1st Lieut., 18 June, 1846. R. Q. M., 28 March to 1 Sept., 1847, and 27 Jan., 1849, to 12 Aug., 1850. Capt., 12 Aug., 1850. Col. 1st Mich. Vols., 1 Sept., 1861. Maj. 2nd Inf., 20 Feb., 1862. Brig. Gen. Vols., 28 April, 1862. Bvt. Lieut. Col., 1 July, 1863, for gallant and meritorious service in the Battle of Gettysburg, Penn. Bvt. Col., 5 March, 1864, for gallant and meritorious service in the Battle of the Wilderness, Va. Bvt. Maj. Gen. Vols., 27 June, 1864, for gallant and meritorious service in the field. Bvt. Brig. Gen., 13 March, 1865, for gallant and meritorious service in the Battle of Spottsylvania, Va. Bvt. Maj. Gen., 13 March, 1865, for gallant and meritorious service in the field during the war. Col. 43rd Inf., 28 July, 1866. Mustered out of Vol. Service 1 Sept., 1866. Retired with rank of Maj. Gen., 6 May, 1869. Died 18 Feb., 1897.

ROBINSON, JOSE A. A. [Born in N. Y. Appointed from Mass.]
2nd Lieut. 36th U. S. Col. Inf., 23 July, 1864. 1st Lieut., 24 Oct., 1864. Mustered out 28 Oct., 1866. 2nd Lieut. 17th Inf., 25 Oct., 1867. Unassigned 27 May, 1869. Ass'd to 1st Art., 14 July, 1869. Cashiered 15 April, 1870. 2nd Lieut. 24th Inf., 9 March, 1871. Resigned 27 July, 1871.

ROBINSON, LEVI H. [Born in Vt. Appointed from Vt.]
Sergt. Co. F, 10th Vt. Vols., 16 July, 1862, to 17 Feb., 1865. 2nd Lieut. 119th U. S. Col. Inf., 18 Feb., 1865. Mustered out 27 April, 1866 2nd Lieut. 14th Inf., 19 April, 1866. 1st Lieut., 11 Aug., 1866. Killed 9 Feb., 1874, by Indians in Wyo., near Laramie Peak.

ROBINSON, OLIVER O. G. [Born in Penn. Appointed from Army.]
Capt. 3rd Penn. Cav., 17 Aug., 1861. Maj., 11 Dec., 1862. Discharged 24 Aug., 1864. Priv. and Sergt. Co. C, 1st Cav., 7 Dec., 1864, to 30 March, 1865. 2nd Lieut. 2nd Cav., 12 March, 1865. 1st Lieut., 12 March, 1865. Capt., 9 June, 1868. Trans. to list of supernumeraries, 10 Aug., 1870. Discharged 1 Nov., 1870.

ROBINSON, SAML. Q. [Born in Mass. Appointed from Mass.]
1st Lieut. Asst. Surg., 9 Jan., 1877. Capt. Asst. Surg., 9 Jan., 1882. Maj. Surg., 2 May, 1896. Died 6 Nov., 1899.

ROBINSON, SCOTT H. [Born in Ky. Appointed from Ky.]
Sergt. Co. C, 6th Ky. Cav., 23 Dec., 1861. 1st Lieut., 8 May, 1862. Capt., 31 Jan., 1863. Mustered out 23 Dec., 1864. 2nd Lieut. 3rd Cav., 7 March, 1867. 1st Lieut., 28 Dec., 1868. Died 26 Jan., 1870.

ROBINSON, SOLOMON S. [Born in Ohio. Appointed from Ohio.]
1st Sergt. Co. A, 2nd Ohio Vols., 29 May, 1846, to 21 June, 1847. Capt. 22nd Ohio Vols., 20 April, 1861. Mustered out 19 Aug., 1861. Capt. 16th Inf., 14 May, 1861. Resigned 4 Jan., 1865. Bvt. Maj., 1 Sept., 1864, for gallant and meritorious service during the campaign at Atlanta, Ga.

ROBINSON, THOS. B. [Born at Sea. Appointed from Army.]
Priv. Co. B, 2nd Batt. 12th Inf., 30 April, 1862. Corpl., 1 July, 1862. Q. M. Sergt. 2nd Batt. 12th Inf., 1 Dec., 1862. Discharged 30 April, 1865. Q. M. Sergt. 1st

Batt. 12th Inf., 1 May, 1865. Trans. to 2nd Batt., 20 Dec., 1865. 2nd Lieut. 8th Inf., 16 June, 1866. 1st Lieut., 6 Aug., 1867. Unassigned 3 May, 1869. Ass'd to 19th Inf., 1 Sept., 1869. Capt., 24 Nov., 1879. Retired for disability, 24 March, 1888.

ROBINSON, WILLIAM G.* [Born in Canada. Appointed from N. C.]
Bvt. 2nd Lieut. 7th Inf., 1 July, 1858. 2nd Lieut. 2nd Inf., 18 April, 1859. Resigned 17 May, 1861.

ROBINSON, WM. W., Jr.* [Born in Ohio. Appointed from Wis.]
Priv. Co. E, 7th Wis. Vols., 17 March, 1865. Discharged 3 July, 1865. Cadet at Mil. Acad., 1 July, 1865. 2nd Lieut. 3rd Cav., 15 June, 1869. Trans. to 7th Cav., 26 June, 1876. 1st Lieut., 14 Aug., 1876. R. Q. M., 7 Nov., 1883, to 7 Nov., 1887. Capt. A. Q. M., 1 June, 1891.

ROBINSON, WIRT.* [Born in Va. Appointed from Va.]
2nd Lieut. 4th Art., 12 June, 1887. 1st Lieut., 1 Aug., 1893. Capt. A. Q. M. Vols 20 June, 1898, to 12 April, 1899.

ROBY, GEORGE W. [Born in Md. Appointed from Md.]
Capt. C. S. Vols., 18 Aug., 1864. Bvt. Maj. Vols., 15 Jan., 1866, for faithful services in the Sub. Dept. Mustered out 27 Jan., 1866. 2nd Lieut. 1st Inf., 26 Sept., 1866. Dismissed 15 June, 1871.

ROCHE, EDWARD A.* [Born in R. I. Appointed from R. I.]
Addl. 2nd Lieut. 21st Inf., 11 June, 1897. 2nd Lieut. 15th Inf., 15 Nov., 1897. 1st Lieut., 2 March, 1899.

ROCHE, JAMES R. [Born in Md. Appointed from D. C.]
Maj. P. M., 3 March, 1875. Retired, on his own request, being over sixty-two years of age, 31 Oct., 1893. Died 1 Dec., 1895.

ROCHESTER, WM. B. [Born in N. Y. Appointed from N. Y.]
Addl. P. M., 1 June, 1861. Bvt. Lieut. Col. Vols., 13 March, 1865, for faithful and meritorious service during the war. Maj. P. M., 17 Jan., 1867. Brig. Gen. P. M. G., 17 Feb., 1882. Retired by operation of law, 15 Feb., 1890.

ROCHFORD, HENRY. [Born in Ireland. Appointed from Army.]
Priv. and Corpl. Co. I, 4th Art., 7 Oct., 1856, to 7 Oct., 1861. Priv., Sergt. and 1st Sergt. Co. E, 11th Inf., 25 Oct., 1861, to 23 March, 1863. 2nd Lieut. 11th Inf., 19 Feb., 1863. Killed 2 July, 1863, at Battle of Gettysburg, Penn.

ROCKEFELLER, CHAS. M. [Born in N. Y. Appointed from N. Y.]
Priv. Co. E, 7th N. Y. State Mil., 26 April, 1861. Discharged 3 June, 1861. Priv. Co. C, 8th N. Y. State Mil., 3 June, 1861. Discharged 2 Aug., 1861. 1st Lieut. 178th N. Y. Vols., 17 Oct., 1863. Mustered out 20 April, 1866. 2nd Lieut. 9th Inf., 3 Sept., 1867. 1st Lieut., 11 March, 1878. Graduate of the Infantry and Cavalry School, 1883. Capt. 9th Inf., 15 Aug., 1889. Maj. 6th Inf., 16 March, 1899. Medal of Honor for most distinguished gallantry in action at Fort Blakely, Ala., 9 April, 1865, in volunteering and reconnoitering the work alone, under a heavy fire from the enemy, and obtaining valuable information, which with a few followers, advancing beyond the line exposed to the fire of both attack and defence: while serving as 1st Lieut 178th N. Y. Vols. Missing since — April, 1899, while officer of the day on outpost duty near Manila, P. I.

ROCKENBACH, SAMUEL D. [Born in Va. Appointed from Mo.]
2nd Lieut. 10th Cav., 1 Aug., 1891. 1st Lieut. 9th Cav., 31 July, 1898. Trans. to 10th Cav., 5 Oct., 1898.

ROCKWELL, ALMON F. [Born in N. Y. Appointed from N. Y.]
1st Lieut. A. de C. Vols., 26 Oct., 1861, to 17 Sept., 1863 (Act 3 March, 1879). Capt. A. A. G., 15 Sept., 1863. Maj. A. A. G. Vols., 23 Feb., 1865. Bvt. Lieut. Col. Vols., 13 March, 1865, for efficient and meritorious service. Capt. A. Q. M., 18 Jan., 1867. Bvt. Maj. and Lieut. Col., 2 March, 1867, for gallant and meritorious service during the war. Mustered out of Vol. service, 1 April, 1867. Col. and Superintendent Public Buildings, 1 April, 1881, to 1 June, 1885. Maj. Q. M., 22 Jan., 1885. Lieut. Col. Dep. Q. M. G., 14 Jan., 1895. Retired, over thirty years' service, 11 Feb., 1897.

ROCKWELL, CHAS. F.* [Born in Vt. Appointed from Vt.]
1st Lieut. Ord., 11 June, 1863. Died 13 Nov., 1868. Bvt. Capt., 13 March, 1865, for meritorious service in the Ord. Dept.

ROCKWELL, CHAS. H.* [Born in Ohio. Appointed from Ohio.]
2nd Lieut. 5th Cav., 15 June, 1869. 1st Lieut., 29 Aug., 1872. Capt., 24 April, 1886. Died 21 Aug., 1888.

ROCKWELL, JAMES, Jr.* [Born in N. Y. Appointed from N. Y.]
2nd Lieut. 1st Cav., 15 June, 1870. Reg. Adj., 1 Feb., 1872, to 31 Aug., 1874. Trans. to Ord., 1 Nov., 1874. 1st Lieut., 1 Nov., 1874. Capt., 4 Dec., 1882. Lieut. Col. Chief Ord. Officer Vols., 18 July, 1898, to 12 May, 1899.

RODENBOUGH, THEOPHILUS F. [Born in Penn. Appointed from Penn.]
2nd Lieut. 2nd Drag., 27 March, 1861. 1st Lieut., 14 May, 1861. 2nd Cav., 3 Aug., 1861. Capt., 17 July, 1862. Bvt. Maj., 19 Sept., 1864, for gallant and meritorious service in the Battles of Trevillian Station and Opequan, Va. Bvt. Lieut. Col., 13 March, 1865, for gallant and meritorious service during the war. Bvt. Col., 13 March, 1865, for gallant and meritorious service in the Battle of Todd's Tavern, Va. Bvt. Brig. Gen., 13 March, 1865, for gallant and meritorious service in the Battle of Cold Harbor, Va. Bvt. Brig. Gen. Vols., 13 April, 1865, for gallant and meritorious service during the war. Col. 18th Penn. Cav., 29 April, 1865. Mustered out of Vol. Service, 31 Oct., 1865. Maj. 42nd Inf., 28 July, 1866. Unassigned 15 March, 1869. Retired with rank of Col., 15 Dec., 1870. Medal of Honor for distinguished gallantry in action at Trevillian Station, Va., 11 June, 1864, where he was severely wounded while handling his regiment with skill and valor; while serving as Capt. 2nd U. S. Cav., commanding regiment.

RODER, JOHN W. [Born in Mo. Appointed from Army.]
Priv. Co. H, 2nd Art., 30 March, 1855. Corpl., 1 March, 1856. Sergt., 20 May, 1858. 1st Sergt., 1 June, 1858. Discharged 1 Feb., 1860. 1st Sergt. Co. H, 2nd Art., 1 Feb., 1860. Bvt. 2nd Lieut. 2nd Art., 22 Oct., 1862. 2nd Lieut. 4th Art., 13 Dec., 1862. 1st Lieut., 11 July, 1864. Bvt. Capt., 27 Oct., 1864, for

distinguished service in the Battle of Boydton Plank Road, Va. Reg. Adj. 4th Art., 7 March, 1865, to 25 Aug., 1879. Bvt. Maj., 6 April, 1865, for gallant and meritorious service in the Battle of Sailor's Creek, Va. Capt. 17th Inf., 28 July, 1866, declined. Capt. 4th Art., 25 Aug., 1879. Died 14 Aug., 1889.

RODGERS, ALEXR.* [Born in N. J. Appointed at Large.]
2nd Lieut. 4th Cav., 16 June, 1875. 1st Lieut., 6 July, 1879. R. Q. M., 1 Feb. to 1 Oct., 1880. Capt., 11 Feb., 1887. Maj. 6th Cav., 14 Sept., 1899. Maj. I. G. Vols., 12 May to 13 July, 1898. Lieut. Col. 3rd Conn. Vols., 3 July to 20 March, 1899.

RODGERS, ALEXR. P.* [Born in N. Y. Appointed at Large.]
Bvt. 2nd Lieut. 4th Inf., 1 July, 1846. 2nd Lieut., 12 Oct., 1846. Killed at the Battle of Chapultepec, Mex., 13 Sept., 1847.

RODGERS, CALBRAITH P. [Born in Md. Appointed from Md.]
2nd Lieut. 5th Cav., 19 Nov., 1866. 1st Lieut., 15 Aug., 1867. Capt., 29 July, 1876. Killed 23 Aug., 1878, by lightning.

RODGERS, JOHN F. [Born in Conn. Appointed from N. Y.]
Mil. Storekeeper Q. M. D., 21 July, 1862. Capt., 28 July, 1866. Retired, by operation of law, 13 Jan., 1895. Died 25 Aug., 1899.

RODGERS, JOHN I.* [Born in Penn. Appointed from Penn.]
2nd Lieut. 2nd Art., 6 May, 1861. 1st Lieut., 14 May, 1861. Capt., 11 June, 1864. Maj. 1st Art., 2 Oct., 1883. Lieut. Col. 2nd Art., 25 Oct., 1894. Col. 5th Art., 1 June, 1897. Brig. Gen. Vols., 4 May to 31 Oct., 1898.

RODMAN, JOHN B.* [Born in Penn. Appointed at Large.]
2nd Lieut. 20th Inf., 15 June, 1868. Reg. Adj., 4 Nov., 1873, to 22 Oct., 1886. 1st Lieut., 4 Aug., 1875. Capt., 15 Oct., 1887. Maj., 2 March, 1899. Maj. Chief Ord. Officer Vols., 18 July, 1898, to 12 May, 1899.

RODMAN, SAMUEL, Jr.* [Born in Mass. Appointed from Mass.]
Addl. 2nd Lieut. 5th Art., 13 June, 1882. 2nd Lieut. 1st Art., 30 June, 1882. 1st Lieut of Art. (2nd), 31 Jan., 1891. Resigned 23 Sept., 1892.

RODMAN, THOS. J.* [Born in Ind. Appointed from Ind.]
Bvt. 2nd Lieut. and 2nd Lieut. Ord., 1 July, 1841. 1st Lieut., 3 March, 1847. Capt., 1 July, 1855. Maj., 1 June, 1863. Lieut. Col., 7 March, 1867. Died 7 June, 1871. Bvt. Lieut. Col., Col. and Brig. Gen., 13 March, 1865, for faithful, meritorious and distinguished service in the Ord. Dept.

RODNEY, GEORGE B. [Born in Del. Appointed from Del.]
Priv. Commonwealth Art. Penn. Vols., 24 April, 1861. Discharged 5 Aug., 1861. 2nd Lieut. and 1st Lieut. 4th Art., 5 Aug., 1861. Bvt. Capt., 31 Dec., 1862, for gallant and meritorious service in the Battle of Stone River, Tenn. Bvt. Maj., 26 Sept., 1863, for gallant and meritorious service in the Battle of Chickamauga, Ga. Capt. 4th Art., 4 March, 1869. Maj., 28 Nov., 1892. Lieut. Col., 13 Feb., 1899. Graduate of the Artillery School, 1869.

RODNEY, GEORGE C.* [Born in Del. Appointed from Del.]
2nd Lieut. 3rd Art., 1 July, 1837. 1st Lieut., 9 July, 1838. Died 5 Nov., 1839.

ROE, CHAS. F. [Born in N. Y. Appointed from N. Y.]
Priv. Co. C, 9th N. Y. Vols., 4 May, 1861. Corpl., 1 Sept., 1861. Discharged 20 May, 1863. 1st Lieut. 3rd U. S. Col. Troops, 11 Aug., 1863. Mustered out 31 Oct., 1865. 2nd Lieut. 26th Inf., 28 July, 1866. 1st Lieut., 10 June, 1868. Unassigned 19 May, 1869. Ass'd to 11th Inf., 15 Dec., 1870. Capt., 24 April, 1886. Retired for disability 29 Dec., 1890.

ROE, CHAS. F.* , [Born in N. Y. Appointed from N. Y.]
2nd Lieut. 1st Cav., 15 June, 1868. Trans. to 2nd Cav., 29 Oct., 1870. Mustered out 28 Dec., 1870. 2nd Lieut. 2nd Cav., 9 Dec., 1871. Reg. Adj., 2 Nov., 1876, to 31 March, 1878, and 20 Dec., 1880, to 1 May, 1886. Resigned 31 Jan., 1888.

ROE, FAYETTE W.* [Born in Va. Appointed from Va.]
2nd Lieut. 24th Inf., 12 June, 1871. Trans. to 3rd Inf., 4 Aug., 1871. 1st Lieut., 15 March, 1883. Reg. Adj., 26 March, 1885, to 24 May, 1888. .Capt., 4 July, 1892. Lieut. Col. J. A. Vols., 9 May to 15 Sept., 1898. Retired, for over thirty years' service, 13 Dec., 1898.

ROE, WM. J., Jr.,* [Born in N. Y. Appointed from N. Y.]
2nd Lieut. 5th Art., 17 June, 1867. Resigned 29 March, 1869.

ROEMER, PAUL. [Born in Germany. Appointed from Army.]
Priv. Gen. Service, 23 Aug., 1858. Corpl., 24 Sept., 1859. Sergt., 10 Aug., 1860. Trans. to Co. C, 5th Art., 20 Oct., 1861. 1st Sergt., 1 Feb., 1862. Discharged 10 Aug., 1863. Priv. 10 Aug., 1863. 1st Sergt. Co. C, 5th Art., 21 July, 1864. 2nd Lieut. 5th Art., 8 April, 1865. 1st Lieut., 13 Aug., 1866. Capt., 10 Aug., 1887. Graduate of the Artillery School, 1875. Retired, for over thirty years' service, 1 Oct., 1898.

ROESSLER, SOLOMON W.* [Born in Ill. Appointed from Ill.]
2nd Lieut. Eng., 15 June, 1877. 1st Lieut., 13 Dec., 1880. Capt., 1 Dec., 1887. Maj., 5 July, 1898.

ROGERS, ALFRED H.* [Born in La. Appointed at Large.]
2nd Lieut. 15th Inf., 14 June, 1872. Trans. to 8th Cav., 12 Dec., 1872. Retired 28 June, 1878. Died 30 April, 1879.

ROGERS, BENJ'N. H. [Born in R. I. Appointed from R. I.]
Priv. Co. F, 1st R. I. Vols., 2 May, 1861. Discharged 1 Aug., 1861. Corpl. Co. F, 1st R. I. Art., 7 Oct., 1861. Sergt., 29 May, 1862. Trans. to 1st R. I. Cav., 22 Nov., 1862. Discharged 10 Oct., 1864. 2nd Lieut. 12th Inf., 16 March, 1866. Trans. to 21st Inf., 21 Sept., 1866. 1st Lieut., 18 Feb., 1867. Unassigned 9 July, 1870. Ass'd to 13th Inf., 1 Jan., 1871. Capt., 18 Feb., 1874. Maj. 8th Inf., 4 May, 1897. Retired, for over thirty years' service, 6 Oct., 1897.

ROGERS, CHAS. G.* [Born in N. C. Appointed from Va.]
Bvt. 2nd Lieut. 2nd Drag., 1 July, 1854. Resigned 1 Feb., 1855. Died 24 Feb., 1888.

ROGERS, DANIEL G.* [Born in Penn. Appointed from Penn.]
Bvt. 2nd Lieut. 2nd Drag., 1 July, 1840. 2nd Lieut., 23 June, 1841. 1st Lieut., 16 Feb., 1847. Died 21 July, 1848.

ROGERS, EARL M. [Born in Penn. Appointed from Wis.]
Priv. and 1st Sergt. Co. I, 6th Wis. Vols., 16 July to 13 Dec., 1861. 2nd Lieut. 6th Wis. Vols., 13 Dec., 1861. 1st Lieut., 16 Aug., 1863. Capt., 20 Dec., 1864. Bvt. Capt. Vols., 13 March, 1865, for gallant and meritorious service at the Battle of the Wilderness, Va., and Maj. Vols., 13 March, 1865, for gallant and meritorious service in front of Petersburg, Va. Mustered out 10 March, 1865. 2nd Lieut. 3rd Inf., 7 March, 1867. Resigned 26 March, 1868.

ROGERS, HARRY L. [Born in D. C. Appointed from Mich.]
Maj. P. M., 2 May, 1898.

ROGERS, JAMES S.* [Born in Penn. Appointed from Col.]
2nd Lieut. 20th Inf., 12 June, 1880. 1st Lieut., 25 Aug., 1887. R. Q. M., 1 Sept., 1887. Capt., 26 April, 1895.

ROGERS, JASON.* [Born in N. Y. Appointed from N. Y.]
Bvt. 2nd and 2nd Lieut. 2nd Inf., 1 July, 1821. Trans. to 6th Inf., 1 July, 1821. 1st Lieut., 21 July, 1823. Reg. Adj., 14 July, 1827, to 30 Aug., 1828. Capt., 30 Aug., 1828. Resigned 31 July, 1836. Lieut. Col. 1st Ky. Vols., 17 May, 1846. Mustered out 17 May, 1847. Died — May, 1848.

ROGERS, JOHN. [Born in R. I. Appointed from R. I.]
Mil. Storekeeper, 9 March, 1819. Disbanded 1 June, 1821.

ROGERS, J. SUMNER. [Born in Maine. Appointed from Maine.]
Priv. Co. A, 2nd Maine Vols., 28 May, 1861, to 9 June, 1863. 2nd Lieut. 31st Maine Vols., 4 Oct., 1864. Capt., 18 Oct., 1864. Bvt. Maj. Vols., 13 March, 1865, for meritorious service during the war. 2nd Lieut. 1st Inf., 1 Oct., 1867. Resigned 3 Oct., 1877.

ROGERS, ROBERT M.* [Born in Penn. Appointed from Ga.]
Priv. Co. A, 3rd W. Va. Cav., 19 Oct., 1861. 2nd Lieut. 5th W. Va. Vols., 8 April, 1862. 1st Lieut. 73rd Ohio Vols., 20 Nov., 1862. Mustered out 5 Nov., 1863. Cadet at Mil. Acad., 29 Sept., 1863. 2nd Lieut. 2nd Art., 17 June, 1867. 1st Lieut., 13 April, 1870. Capt., 29 May, 1891. Graduate of the Artillery School, 1876.

ROGERS, THOMAS S. [Born in ——. Appointed from Ga.]
Ensign 3rd Inf., 29 June, 1813. 3rd Lieut., 15 Aug., 1813. 2nd Lieut., 15 April, 1814. Disbanded 15 June, 1815. Reinstated 2 Dec., 1815, as 2nd Lieut. 8th Inf., with Bvt. of 1st Lieut., from 20 July, 1814. Trans. to 1st Inf., 30 March, 1816. Reg. Adj., 2 Nov., 1816, to 20 June, 1818. R. Q. M., 20 June, 1818, to 1 Aug., 1818. 1st Lieut., 31 Oct., 1816. Capt. Asst. Dep. Q. M. G., 16 June, 1818. Died 27 Sept., 1819.

ROGERS, WILLIAM C.* [Born in N. Y. Appointed from N. Y.]
2nd Lieut. 7th Inf., 12 June, 1893. 1st Lieut., 26 April, 1898.

ROGERS, WM. E.* [Born in Penn. Appointed from Ga.]
Priv. Independent Co. Pa. Vols., — July, 1863. Cadet at Mil. Acad., 1 Sept., 1863. 2nd Lieut. Eng., 17 June, 1867. Resigned 1 Sept., 1869.

ROGERS, WM. P. [Born in Md. Appointed from Md.]
Corpl. Co. H, 7th Md. Vols., 21 Aug., 1862. Discharged 4 May, 1865. 2nd Lieut. 44th Inf., 28 July, 1866. Trans. to 17th Inf., 27 May, 1869. 1st Lieut., 3 Oct., 1872. Reg. Adj., 25 July, 1874, to 23 Dec., 1884. Capt., 23 Dec., 1884. Maj. 20th Inf., 15 Dec., 1898.

ROGERS, WM. W. [Born in Penn. Appointed from Penn.]
Priv. Co. B, 3rd Penn. Cav., 23 July, 1861. 2nd Lieut. 3rd Penn. Cav., 31 Dec., 1861. 1st Lieut., 1 Aug., 1862. Capt., 1 May, 1863. Capt. Vet. Res. Corps, 6 Feb., 1864. Bvt. Maj. Vols., 13 March, 1865, for gallant and meritorious service. Bvt. Lieut. Col. Vols., 13 March, 1865, for gallant conduct in the field. Mustered out 13 Jan., 1867. 1st Lieut. 45th Inf., 28 July, 1866. Bvt. Capt., 2 March, 1867, for gallant and meritorious service in the Battle of Gettysburg, Pa. Trans. to 14th Inf., 22 July, 1869. Trans. to 9th Inf., 22 May, 1871. Capt., 27 March, 1879. Retired for disability 15 Aug., 1889. Died 14 Dec., 1890.

ROLAND, JOHN F.* [Born in Penn. Appointed from Penn.]
Bvt. 2nd Lieut. 2nd Art., 1 July, 1836. 2nd Lieut., 4 July, 1836. 1st Lieut., 7 July, 1838. Capt., 3 March, 1847. Died 28 Sept., 1852. Bvt. Capt., 9 May, 1846, for gallant and meritorious conduct in the Battles of Palo Alto and Resaca de la Palma, Mex. Bvt. Maj., 23 Sept., 1846, for gallant and meritorious conduct in the Battle of Monterey, Mex.

ROLLINS, JAMES H.* [Born in Mo. Appointed from Mo.]
Bvt. 2nd Lieut. 4th Art., 17 June, 1862. 2nd Lieut. 2nd Art., 24 July, 1862. Trans. to Ord., 27 April, 1863. 1st Lieut., 27 April, 1863. Bvt. Capt., 13 March, 1865, for faithful and meritorious service in the Ord. Dept. Capt. Ord., 5 July, 1867. Retired for disability 15 March, 1883. Died 5 Feb., 1898.

ROMAN, RICH'D. [Born in Ill. Appointed from Army.]
Priv. and Corpl. Co. A, and Com. Sergt. 13th Inf., 18 Dec., 1862, to 23 Nov., 1863. 2nd Lieut. 13th Inf., 31 Oct., 1863. 1st Lieut., 9 April, 1864. Resigned 24 Dec., 1864.

ROMAYNE, JAMES T. B. [Born in N. Y. Appointed from N. Y.]
Capt. 3rd Art., 2 July, 1812. Trans. to Corps Art., 12 May, 1814. Maj. A. I. G., 11 Feb. to 15 June, 1815. Died 17 Sept., 1818.

ROMEYN, CHARLES A.* [Born in Ind. Ter. Appointed at Large.]
2nd Lieut. 10th Cav., 15 Feb., 1899.

ROMEYN, HENRY. [Born in N. Y. Appointed from Mich.]
Corpl. Co. G, 105th Ill. Vols., 15 Aug., 1862. Priv., — ——, 1862. Sergt., 1 March, 1863. Capt. 14th U. S. Col. Trops, 15 Nov., 1863. Bvt. Maj. Vols., 13 March, 1865, for gallant and meritorious conduct in the Battle of Nashville, Tenn. Mustered out 26 March, 1866. 1st Lieut. 37th Inf., 22 Jan., 1867. Bvt. Capt., 2 March, 1867, for gallant and meritorious service in the Battle of Nashville, Tenn. Unassigned 19 May, 1869. Ass'd to 5th Inf., 14 Aug., 1869. Capt., 10 July, 1885. Retired, by operation of law, 1 June, 1897. Bvt. Maj., 27 Feb., 1890, for gallant services in action against Indians at their village in Bear Paw

Mountain, Mont., 30 Sept., 1877, where he was severely wounded. Medal of Honor for most distinguished gallantry in action against hostile Nez Perce Indians at Bear Paw Mountain, Mont., 30 Sept., 1877, in leading his command into close range of the enemy, there maintaining his position, and vigorously prosecuting the fight until he was severely wounded; while 1st Lieut. 5th Inf.

RONAYNE, JAMES. [Born in Ireland. Appointed from Army.]
Priv., Corpl. and Sergt. Co. F, and Sergt. Maj. 10th Inf., 6 Oct., 1887, to 23 Nov., 1892. 2nd Lieut. 19th Inf., 19 Nov., 1892. 1st Lieut., 26 April, 1898.

ROOT, CHESTER. [Born in Mass. Appointed from N. Y.]
2nd Lieut. 3rd Art., 25 April, 1812. Reg. P. M., 30 Oct., 1812, to 12 May, 1814. 1st Lieut., 13 March, 1813. Trans. to Corps Art., 12 May, 1814. Capt., 5 March, 1819. Disbanded 1 June, 1821. Bvt. Capt., 11 Sept., 1814, for gallant and duct at the Battle of Plattsburg.

ROOT, DEWITT N.* [Born in N. Y. Appointed from N. Y.]
Bvt. 2nd Lieut. 3rd Art., 1 July, 1851. Died 4 Aug., 1851.

ROOT, EDWIN A.* [Born in Ind. Appointed from Ind.]
2nd Lieut. 22nd Inf., 13 June, 1883. 1st Lieut. 19th Inf., 20 Feb., 1891. Capt. of Inf., 1 July, 1898. Ass'd to 10th Inf., 1 Jan., 1899. Maj. Eng., Vols., 16 July, 1898, to 12 May, 1899.

ROOT, WM. [Born in N. Y. Appointed from N. Y.]
2nd Lieut. 5th Inf., 8 March, 1837. 1st Lieut., 3 April, 1839. Resigned 18 May, 1846.

ROPER, JAMES W., Jr. [Born in Penn. Appointed from Penn.]
Asst. Surg., 13 July, 1832. Died 23 March, 1834.

ROPES, JAMES M. [Born in N. Y. Appointed from N. J.]
1st Lieut. 2nd Cal. Cav., 13 Sept., 1861. Capt., 31 Jan., 1863. Bvt. Maj. Vols., 13 March, 1865, for faithful and meritorious service during the war. Mustered out 1 Feb., 1866. 2nd Lieut. 8th Cav., 18 June, 1867. 1st Lieut., 28 Dec., 1868. Capt., 9 Oct., 1882. Retired for disability 20 Feb., 1891. Died 4 June, 1897.

ROSE, EDWIN.* [Born in N. Y. Appointed from N. Y.]
Bvt. 2nd Lieut. 3rd Art., 1 July, 1830. 2nd Lieut., 1 July, 1830. 1st Lieut., 31 Aug., 1836. Resigned 30 June, 1837. Col. 81st N. Y. Vols., 28 Jan., 1862. Resigned 7 July, 1862. Died 13 Jan., 1864.

ROSE, GEORGE S. [Born in Canada. Appointed from Mass.]
Asst. Surg. Vols., 24 Sept., 1863. Bvt. Capt. Vols., 25 Oct., 1865, for faithful and meritorious service. Mustered out 31 Oct., 1865. Asst. Surg., 14 May, 1867. Capt. Asst. Surg., 14 May, 1872. Died 26 Nov., 1876.

ROSE, GEORGE W.* [Born in N. Y. Appointed from N. Y.]
Bvt. 2nd Lieut. Top. Eng., 1 July, 1852. 2nd Lieut., 3 March, 1855. Resigned 7 Oct., 1856. Died 19 May, 1870.

ROSE, HUGH F. [Born in Va. Appointed from Va.]
Hosp. Surg.'s Mate, 21 May, 1814. Resigned 1 May, 1816.

ROSE, ROBERT W. [Born in Va. Appointed from Army.]
Priv. Artf., Corpl. and Sergt. Co. C, 16th Inf., 10 Sept., 1883, to 3 March, 1889. 2nd Lieut. 5th Inf., 11 Feb., 1889. 1st Lieut. 17th Inf., 1 Jan., 1896. Capt. 21st Inf., 14 May, 1899. Graduate of the Infantry and Cavalry School, 1893.

ROSE, THOS. E. [Born in Penn. Appointed from Penn.]
Priv. Co. I, 12th Penn. Vols., 25 April, 1861. Discharged 5 Aug., 1861. Capt. 77th Penn. Vols., 28 Oct., 1861. Col., 1 Feb., 1863. Bvt. Brig. Gen. Vols., 22 July, 1865, for gallant and meritorious service. Mustered out 6 Dec., 1865. Capt. 11th Inf., 28 July, 1866. Bvt. Maj., 2 March, 1867, for gallant and meritorious service in the Battle of Liberty Gap, Tenn. Bvt. Lieut. Col., 2 March, 1867, for gallant and meritorious service in the Battle of Chickamauga, Ga. Unassigned 14 April, 1869. Ass'd to 16th Inf., 15 Feb., 1870. Maj. 18th Inf., 2 April, 1892. Retired, by operation of law, 12 March, 1894.

ROSE, WM.* [Born in N. Y. Appointed from N. Y.]
Bvt. 2nd Lieut. 2nd Art., 1 July, 1822. 2nd Lieut. 4th Art., 1 July, 1822. Died 22 Nov., 1825.

ROSECRANTZ, MORTIMER.* [Born in N. Y. Appointed from Mich.]
Bvt. 2nd Lieut. 5th Inf., 1 July, 1841. 2nd Lieut., 8 June, 1845. 1st Lieut., 10 July, 1846. Died 7 Oct., 1848. Bvt. Capt., 20 Aug., 1847, for gallant and meritorious conduct in the Battles of Contreras and Churubusco, Mex.

ROSECRANZ, WM. S.* [Born in Ohio. Appointed from Ohio.]
Bvt. 2nd Lieut. Eng., 1 July, 1842. 2nd Lieut., 3 April, 1843. 1st Lieut., 3 March, 1853. Resigned 1 April, 1854. Vol. A. de C. and Col. Eng. Ohio Vols., 23 April to 12 June, 1861. Brig. Gen., 10 May, 1861. Maj. Gen. Vols., 21 March, 1862. By resolution of 3 March, 1863, it was resolved, "That the thanks of Congress be and they are hereby presented to Maj. Gen. Wm. S. Rosecranz, and through him to the officers and men under his command, for their distinguished gallantry and good conduct, at the Battle of Murfreesboro, Tenn., where they achieved a signal victory for our arms." Mustered out Vols., 15 Jan., 1866. Resigned 28 March, 1867. Bvt. Maj. Gen., 13 March, 1865, for gallant and distinguished service at the Battle of Stone River, Tenn.

ROSENBAUM, OTHO B.* [Born in Va. Appointed from Va.]
2nd Lieut. 7th Inf., 12 June, 1894. 1st Lieut., 26 April, 1898.

ROSENCRANTZ, FREDERIK. [Born in Sweden. Appointed from N. Y.]
1st Lieut. 20th N. Y. Vols., 21 Oct., 1862. Mustered out 1 June, 1863. Capt. A. A. G. Vols., 7 June, 1864. Bvt. Maj. Vols., 1 Aug., 1864, for faithful and meritorious service in the field. Bvt. Lieut. Col. Vols., 9 April, 1865, for gallant and meritorious service during the operations resulting in the fall of Richmond, Va., and the surrender of the insurgent army under Gen. R. E. Lee. Mustered out 11 Nov., 1865. 2nd Lieut. 16th Inf., 11 May, 1866. Trans. to 34th Inf., 21 Sept., 1866. Trans. to 16th Inf., 14 April, 1869. 1st Lieut., 31 Aug., 1871. Died 7 Dec., 1879.

ROSENQUEST, J. WESLEY. [Born in N. Y. Appointed from Army.]
Served as Priv., Corpl. and Sergt. Co. G, 1st Art. and Gen. Ser., under name of Wm. G. Foster, 14 Jan., 1871, to 19 Aug., 1876. 2nd Lieut. 4th Cav., 15 Aug., 1876. Dropped 7 Dec., 1877.

ROSS, ANDREW. [Born in Canada. Appointed from Army.]
Sergt. 7th Inf., 1 Nov., 1809, to — May, 1813. 3rd Lieut. 7th Inf., 2 May, 1813. 2nd Lieut., 21 Feb., 1814. 1st Lieut., 9 June, 1814. Resigned 30 April, 1817. Died 11 Dec., 1836.

ROSS, ANDREW. [Born in Pa. Appointed from Pa.]
2nd Lieut. Inf., 5 March, 1847; 11th Inf., 9 April, 1847. Died at sea, in May, 1847.

ROSS, EDWARD. [Born in N. Y. Appointed from Wash. Ter.]
Cadet at Mil. Acad., 1 July, 1854, to 2 Feb., 1855. 2nd Lieut. 7th Inf., 26 April, 1861. 1st Lieut., 23 May, 1861. Died 23 July, 1862.

ROSS, EDWARD C.* [Born in Penn. Appointed from Penn.]
Bvt. 2nd and 2nd Lieut. 4th Art., 1 July, 1821. 1st Lieut., 27 Nov., 1826. Resigned 31 July, 1839. Died 16 May, 1851.

ROSS, FRANCIS H.* [Born in Ind. Appointed from Ind.]
2nd Lieut. 16th Inf., 23 June, 1865. 1st Lieut., 23 June, 1865. Trans. to 25th Inf., 21 Sept., 1866. Capt., 21 Nov., 1868. Unassigned 26 April, 1869. Discharged 1 Nov., 1870.

ROSS, JOHN M. [Born in Ohio. Appointed from N. Y.]
2nd Lieut. 38th U. S. Col. Troops, 3 March, 1865. 1st Lieut., 17 Jan., 1867. Mustered out 21 March, 1867. 2nd Lieut. 21st Inf., 7 March, 1867. 1st Lieut., 15 Oct., 1871. Reg. Adj., 7 Aug., 1879, to 30 Sept., 1880. R. Q. M., 30 Sept., 1880, to 10 March, 1884. Died 10 March, 1884.

ROSS, REUBEN R.* [Born in Tenn. Appointed from Tenn.]
Bvt. 2nd Lieut. 1st Inf., 1 July, 1853. Resigned 24 Jan., 1854. Died 16 Dec., 1864.

ROSS, RICHARD H.* [Born in Md. Appointed from Md.]
Bvt. 2nd Lieut. 7th Inf., 1 July, 1830. 2nd Lieut., 1 July, 1830. 1st Lieut., 1 June, 1835. Capt., 26 Nov., 1841. Died 24 Aug., 1851. Bvt. Maj., 23 Sept., 1846, for gallant and meritorious conduct in the Battle of Monterey. Bvt. Lieut. Col., 20 Aug., 1847, for gallant and meritorious conduct in the Battle of Contreras, Mex.

ROSS, RICHARD W. [Born in Ind. Appointed from Iowa.]
Corpl. and Sergt. Co. E, 4th Iowa Vols., 8 Aug., 1861, to 12 March, 1863. 2nd Lieut. 4th Iowa Vols., 12 March, 1863. Resigned 29 Sept., 1864. 2nd Lieut. 6th Inf., 23 Feb., 1866. 1st Lieut., 28 July, 1866. Retired 31 Dec., 1870. Died 12 Aug., 1876.

ROSS, ROB'T. [Born in La. Appointed from La.]
2nd Lieut. 7th Inf., 27 Oct., 1820. Resigned 1 March, 1822.

ROSS, SAML. [Born in N. Y. Appointed from Iowa.]
Priv. Co. A, 8th Inf., 14 Dec., 1837. Corpl., 14 Feb., 1838. Sergt., 24 June, 1839. Discharged 13 Dec., 1840. Priv. Co. B, 2nd Art., 6 March, 1841. Corpl., 9 Dec., 1841. Sergt., 1 April, 1842. 1st Sergt., 1 Aug., 1843. Discharged 6 March, 1846. Priv. Co. H, 15th Inf., 7 Nov., 1846. Corpl. Gen. Rec. Service, 1 Dec., 1846. 1st Sergt. Co. H, 15th Inf., 27 April, 1847. Bvt. 2nd Lieut. 3rd Inf., 28 June, 1848. Resigned 30 May, 1849. Capt. 14th Inf., 14 May, 1861. Col. 20th Conn. Vols., 8 Sept., 1862. Bvt. Maj., 3 May, 1863, for gallant and meritorious service in the Battle of Chancellorsville, Va. Bvt. Lieut. Col., 13 Dec., 1864, for gallant and meritorious service during the Atlanta and Savannah campaigns. Bvt. Col., 13 March, 1865, for gallantry and ability as Brigade Commander in the Savannah campaign. Bvt. Brig. Gen. Vols., 13 April, 1865, for gallant and meritorious service in the campaign against Atlanta. Mustered out of Vol. Service, 13 June, 1865. Trans. to 23rd Inf., 21 Sept., 1866. Maj. 28th Inf., 8 July, 1868. Unassigned 15 March, 1869. Mustered out 1 Jan., 1871. 2nd Lieut. 7th Inf., 5 Feb., 1872. Retired with rank of Brig. Gen., 20 May, 1872, to date from 1 Jan., 1871. Retired with rank of Col., 3 March, 1875. Drowned 11 July, 1880.

ROSS, TENNEY. [Born in N. H. Appointed from D. C.]
2nd Lieut. 3rd Inf., 9 July, 1898. 1st Lieut., 2 March, 1899.

ROSS, WM. J. [Born in Scotland. Appointed from Conn.]
Corpl. Co. A, 18th Conn. Vols., 23 July, 1862, to 26 Jan., 1864. Capt. 29th Conn. Vols., 3 Feb., 1864. Maj., 12 May, 1865. Mustered out 24 April, 1865. 2nd Lieut. 32nd Inf., 5 May, 1868. Trans. to 21st Inf., 19 April, 1869. Resigned 18 Oct., 1875.

ROSSANDER, CHAS. A. [Born in Sweden. Appointed from N. Y.]
1st Lieut. 3rd R. I. Art., 5 Jan., 1862. Resigned 7 Feb., 1863. 2nd Lieut. 6th Cav., 5 June, 1867. Died 17 Sept., 1867.

ROSSELL, NATHAN B. [Born in N. J. Appointed from N. J.]
2nd Lieut. 5th Inf., 1 Aug., 1838. 1st Lieut., 3 Nov., 1840. Capt., 8 Sept., 1847. Maj. 3rd Inf., 25 Sept., 1861. Bvt. Maj., 8 Sept., 1847, for gallant and meritorious conduct at Molino del Rey, Mex. Bvt. Lieut. Col., 27 June, 1862, for gallant and meritorious service at the Battle of Gaines' Mills, Va., where he was killed.

ROSSELL, WM. H. [Born in N. J. Appointed from N. J.]
2nd Lieut. 10th Inf., 3 March, 1855. 1st Lieut., 29 Dec., 1860. Capt., 7 Dec., 1861. Bvt. Maj., 21 Feb., 1862, for gallant and meritorious service in the Battle of Val Verde, N. M. Retired 28 Nov., 1863. Died 20 July, 1885.

ROSSELL, WM. T.* [Born in Ala. Appointed from N. J.]
2nd Lieut. Eng., 13 June, 1873. 1st Lieut., 12 Sept., 1877. Capt., 17 March, 1884. Maj., 6 Jan., 1896.

ROSSON, ROLAND L. [Born in Va. Appointed from Va.]
1st Lieut. Asst. Surg., 26 June, 1875. Dismissed 22 March, 1879.

ROTHERMEL, JAMES A. [Born in Pa. Appointed from Pa.]
Priv. Cos. B and E, 15th Pa. Cav., 22 Aug., 1862, to 10 Oct., 1863. 2nd Lieut. 19th Pa. Cav., 13 Oct., 1863. Resigned 20 July, 1864. 2nd Lieut. 8th Cav., 18 June, 1867. Died 15 Feb., 1868.

ROUDIEZ, LEON S. [Born in France. Appointed from Army.]
Priv., Corpl., Sergt and 1st Sergt. Co. H, 16th Inf., 26 Jan., 1879, to 6 Aug., 1884. 2nd Lieut. 15th Inf., 4 Aug., 1884. 1st Lieut. 6th Inf., 1 Aug., 1891. Trans. to 1st Inf., 6 Oct., 1891. Capt. of Inf., 20 Dec., 1898. Ass'd to 25th Inf., 1 Jan., 1899. Maj. Q. M. Vols., 16 July, 1898.

ROUMFORT, AUGUSTUS L.* [Born in Pa. Appointed from Pa.]
2nd Lieut. Marines, 15 April, 1817. Resigned 18 Aug., 1818. Mil. Storekeeper, 19 Dec., 1834. Resigned 14 April, 1841. Died 2 Aug., 1878.

ROUNDY, WM. C. [Born in Mass. Appointed from Army.]
Priv. Co. G, 6th Mass. Vols., 22 April to 2 Aug., 1861. Priv. Co. H, 26th Mass. Vols., 13 Sept., 1861, to 13 Sept., 1865. Priv., Corpl. and Sergt. Co. G, 32nd and G, 21st Inf., 9 July, 1867, to 28 June, 1870. Priv., Sergt. and 1st Sergt. Co. O, 21st Inf., 10 Feb., 1871, to 22 Jan., 1874. 2nd Lieut. 8th Inf., 1 Oct., 1873. Cashiered 2 May, 1877.

ROUSSEAU, DAVID Q. [Born in Ky. Appointed from Ky.]
Corpl. Co. E, 1st Ky. Vols., 17 May, 1846. Sergt., 4 April, 1847. Discharged 17 May, 1847. 1st Lieut. 5th Ky Vols., 9 Sept., 1861. Resigned 20 Oct., 1862. 2nd Lieut. 5th Inf., 7 March, 1867. 1st Lieut., 20 March, 1879. Wholly retired 17 Nov., 1879.

ROUSSEAU, GEORGE L. [Born in Ky. Appointed from Ky.]
2nd Lieut. 20th Inf., 10 March, 1875. 1st Lieut., 18 Dec., 1880. Dismissed 4 June, 1881. Died 22 Sept., 1882.

ROUSSEAU, GUSTAVE S.* [Born in La. Appointed from La.]
Bvt. 2nd Lieut. 6th Inf., 1 July, 1828. 2nd Lieut., 1 July, 1828. Resigned 30 April, 1833. Capt. 2nd La. Vols., 12 May, 1846. Mustered out 8 Aug., 1846. Died 29 Jan., 1879.

ROUSSEAU, JOHN C. [Born in Penn. Appointed from Army.]
Priv. and Sergt. Co. C, and Q. M. Sergt. 6th Cav., 18 Oct., 1861, to 23 Sept., 1862. 2nd Lieut. 6th Cav., 17 July, 1862. Resigned 13 Jan., 1863.

ROUSSEAU, LOVELL H. [Born in Ky. Appointed from Ky.]
Capt. 2nd Ind. Vols., 22 June, 1846. Mustered out 23 June, 1847. Col. 3rd Ky. Vols., 9 Sept., 1861. Brig. Gen. Vols., 1 Oct., 1861. Maj. Gen. Vols., 8 Oct., 1862. Resigned 30 Nov., 1865. Brig. Gen., 28 March, 1867. Died 7 Jan., 1869. Bvt. Maj. Gen., 28 March, 1867, for gallant and meritorious service during the war.

ROUSSEAU, RICH'D. H. [Born in Ky. Appointed from Ky.]
2nd Lieut. 1st Cav., 3 May, 1867. Resigned 14 Feb., 1868. Died 8 June, 1881.

ROWAN, ANDREW S.* [Born in Va. Appointed from W. Va.]
2nd Lieut. 15th Inf., 11 June, 1881. 1st Lieut. 9th Inf., 28 Nov., 1890. Trans. to 19th Inf., 20 July, 1891. Capt., 26 April, 1898. Lieut. Col. 6th U. S. Vols., 31 May, 1898, to 15 March, 1899.

ROWAN, HAMILTON.* [Born in Ind. Appointed at Large.]
2nd Lieut. 6th Inf., 15 June, 1876. Trans. to 2nd Art., 9 Jan., 1877. 1st Lieut., 28 March, 1885. Capt. 1st Art., 23 Feb., 1899. Graduate of the Artillery School 1882. R. Q. M., 24 April, 1899.

ROWE, CHAS. H. [Born in Conn. Appointed from Conn.]
Asst. Surg. 18th Conn. Vols., 3 Sept., 1864. Mustered out 27 June, 1865. Asst. Surg., 28 Feb., 1866. Died 4 Sept., 1867.

ROWE, THEODORE F. [Born in N. H. Appointed from N. H.]
Capt. of Inf., 23 Feb., 1847; 9th Inf., 9 April, 1847. Disbanded 26 Aug., 1848. Bvt. Maj., for gallant and meritorious conduct in defence of Puebla, Mex., from 13 Sept. to 12 Oct., 1847. Died 20 April, 1868.

ROWELL, CHAS. W.* [Born in N. Y. Appointed from N. Y.]
2nd Lieut. 2nd Inf., 17 June, 1874. Reg. Adj., 14 May, 1878, to 8 March, 1887. 1st Lieut., 26 Sept., 1881. Capt. of Inf. (2nd), 29 May, 1896. Killed in action at Santiago, Cuba, 10 July, 1898.

ROWELL, FRANK W. [Born in Idaho. Appointed from Mont.]
2nd Lieut. 2nd Inf., 9 Sept., 1898.

ROWELL, MELVIN W.* [Born in Maine. Appointed from Mass.]
2nd Lieut. 10th Cav., 12 June, 1890. 1st Lieut. 5th Cav., 2 March, 1897.

ROWLEY, GEORGE A. [Born in Vt. Appointed from Mo.]
Capt. 3rd Mo. Res. Corps, 8 May to 18 Aug., 1861. 2nd Lieut. 2nd Inf., 12 May, 1862. Cashiered 21 July, 1862. 2nd Lieut. 2nd Inf., 31 Jan., 1863. 1st Lieut., 11 April, 1864. Resigned 28 Feb., 1866. Bvt. Capt., 13 March, 1865, for gallant and meritorious service at the Battle of Gettysburg, Pa.

ROY, JAMES P.* [Born in England. Appointed from Va.]
Bvt. 2nd Lieut. 8th Inf., 1 July, 1849. 2nd Lieut. 2nd Inf., 31 Aug., 1850. 1st Lieut., 3 March, 1855. Capt., 14 May, 1861. Maj. 6th Inf., 16 Feb., 1865. Lieut. Col. 15th Inf., 8 June, 1874. Died 24 Oct., 1874.

ROYALL, WM. B. [Born in Va. Appointed from Mo.]
1st Lieut. Co. D, 2nd Mo. Mounted Vols. (one year), 31 July, 1846. Retained 14 Aug., 1847, as 1st Lieut. Adj. Santa Fe Batt. Mustered out 20 Oct., 1848. 1st Lieut. 2nd Cav., 3 March, 1855. Capt. 2nd Cav., 21 March, 1861; 5th Cav., 3 Aug., 1861. Bvt. Maj., 27 May, 1862, for gallant and meritorious service in the Battle of Hanover C. H., Va. Bvt. Lieut. Col., 13 June, 1862, for gallant and meritorious service in the Cav. action at Old Church, Va. Maj. 5th Cav., 7 Dec., 1863. Bvt. Col., 13 March, 1865, for arduous and faithful service in the recruitment of the armies of the U. S. Lieut. Col. 3rd Cav., 2 Dec., 1875. Col. 4th Cav., 1 Nov., 1882. Retired for disability 19 Oct., 1887. Bvt. Brig. Gen., 27 Feb., 1890, for gallant services in action against Indians on Rosebud Creek, Mont., 17 June, 1876. Died 13 Dec., 1895.

ROYDEN, HERBERT N.* [Born in Conn. Appointed from Conn.]
2nd Lieut. 23rd Inf., 12 June, 1891. 1st Lieut., 26 April, 1898.

ROYS, ELBRIDGE G. [Born in Ohio. Appointed from Army.]
Priv., Corpl. and Sergt. Troop B, 1st Cav. (4th), 2 Dec., 1856, to 17 Sept., 1862. 2nd Lieut. 4th Cav., 17 July, 1862. 1st Lieut., 1 Dec., 1863. Killed 2 April, 1865, in action near Selma, Ala.

ROYS, RUFUS A.* [Born in N. H. Appointed from N. H.]
Bvt. 2nd Lieut. Eng., 1 July, 1848. Died 30 July, 1850.

ROYSTER, THOS. J.* [Born in Tenn. Appointed from La.]
Bvt. 2nd Lieut. 6th Inf., 1 July, 1830. Died 5 Sept., 1832.

RUBOTTOM, E. HOLLAND. [Born in Ind. Appointed from Cal.]
2nd Lieut. 9th Cav., 1 June, 1899.

RUCKER, DANIEL H. [Born in N. J. Appointed from Mich.]
2nd Lieut. 1st Drag., 13 Oct., 1837. 1st Lieut., 8 Oct., 1844. Capt., 7 Feb., 1847. Bvt. Maj., 23 Feb., 1847, for gallant and meritorious conduct in the Battle of Buena Vista. Trans. to Capt. A. Q. M., 23 Aug., 1849. Maj. 6th Cav., 14 May, 1861, declined. Maj. Q. M., 3 Aug., 1861. Col. A. A. de C., 28 Sept., 1861. Brig. Gen. Vols., 23 May, 1863. Bvt. Lieut. Col., Col. and Brig. Gen., 5 July, 1864, for diligent and faithful service during the war. Bvt. Maj. Gen., 13 March, 1865, for faithful and meritorious service during the war. Bvt. Maj. Gen. Vols., 13 March, 1865, for faithful and meritorious service during the war. Col. A. Q. M. G., 28 July, 1866. Mustered out of Vol. Service, 1 Sept., 1866. Brig. Gen. Q. M. G., 13 Feb., 1882. Retired for over forty years' service, 23 Feb., 1882.

RUCKER, FRANCIS D. [Born in Mich. Appointed from Mich.]
2nd Lieut. 11th Inf., 1 Sept., 1879. Trans. to 2nd Cav., 18 April, 1881. 1st Lieut., 31 Jan., 1888. Died 18 Jan., 1893.

RUCKER, JOHN A. [Born in Mich. Appointed from Mich.]
Cadet Mil. Acad., 1 July, 1868, to 30 June, 1870. 2nd Lieut. 6th Cav., 27 July, 1872. Drowned 11 July, 1878.

RUCKER, LOUIS H. [Born in Ill. Appointed from Ill.]
Sergt. Co. G, 8th Ill. Cav., 14 Sept., 1861. Priv., ———. Sergt., 1 Feb., 1862. 1st Sergt., 12 Feb., 1862. Discharged 29 Feb., 1864. 2nd Lieut. 8th Ill. Cav., 9 Feb., 1864. 1st Lieut., 14 Dec., 1864. Mustered out 21 April, 1865. 2nd Lieut. 9th Cav., 28 July, 1866. 1st Lieut., 21 July, 1867. R. Q. M., 25 Aug., 1872, to 20 March, 1879. Capt., 20 March, 1879. Maj. 4th Cav., 13 Jan., 1897.

RUCKER, LOUIS S. D., Jr. [Born in Mich. Appointed from Mich.]
2nd Lieut. 15th Inf., 9 July, 1898. Trans. to 16th Inf., 23 Oct., 1899.

RUCKER, WM. A. [Born in Mich. Appointed from Mich.]
Capt. C. S. Vols., 30 Aug., 1862. Addl. P. M., 26 Nov., 1862. Maj. P. M., 16 April, 1866. Bvt. Lieut. Col. Vols., 13 March, 1865, for faithful and meritorious service during the war. Lieut. Col. Dep. P. M. G., 1 Oct., 1882. Col. A. P. M. G., 30 Dec., 1888. Died 22 Jan., 1893.

RUCKMAN, JOHN W. [Born in Ill. Appointed from Ill.]
2nd Lieut. 5th Art., 13 June, 1883. 1st Lieut. 1st Art., 20 Feb., 1891. Trans. to 7th Art., 8 March, 1898. Capt. 2nd Art., 28 Aug., 1899. Graduate of the Artillery School, 1888.

RUFF, CHAS. F.* [Born in Penn. Appointed from Penn.]
2nd Lieut. 1st Drag., 1 July, 1838. Resigned 31 Dec., 1842. Lieut. Col. 1st Mo. Mounted Vols., 18 June, 1846. Resigned 17 Sept., 1846. Capt. Mounted Rifles, 7 July, 1846. Bvt. Maj., 1 Aug., 1847, for gallant and meritorious conduct in the affair at San Juan de los Llanos, Mex. Maj. Mounted Rifles, 30 Dec., 1856. Lieut. Col., 10 June, 1861; 3rd Cav., 3 Aug., 1861. Retired 30 March, 1864. Bvt. Col. and Bvt. Brig. Gen., 13 March, 1865, for faithful and meritorious service in recruiting the armies of the United States. Died 1 Oct., 1885.

RUFFIN, ROBERT R. [[Born in Va. Appointed from N. C.]
1st Lieut. 2nd Art., 12 March, 1812. Reg. P. M., Dec., 1812, to — May, 1814. Trans. to Corps Art., 12 May, 1814. Capt., 20 March, 1818. Resigned 31 Dec., 1818. Died 5 Aug., 1830.

RUFFNER, ERNEST H.* [Born in Ky. Appointed from Va.]
2nd Lieut. Eng., 17 June, 1867. 1st Lieut., 17 June, 1867. Capt., 31 Oct., 1879. Maj., 2 July, 1889.

RUGER, THOS. H.* [Born in N. Y. Appointed from Wis.]
Bvt. 2nd Lieut. Eng., 1 July, 1854. Resigned 1 April, 1855. Lieut. Col. 3rd Wis. Vols., 29 June, 1861. Col., 1 Sept., 1861. Brig. Gen. Vols., 29 Nov., 1862. Bvt. Maj. Gen. Vols., 30 Nov., 1864, for gallant and meritorious service in the Battle of Franklin, Tenn. Mustered out 1 Sept., 1866. Col. 33rd Inf., 28 July, 1866. Bvt. Brig. Gen., 2 March, 1867, for gallant and meritorious service in the Battle of Gettysburg, Pa. Trans. to 18th Inf., 15 March, 1869. Brig. Gen., 19 March, 1886. Maj. Gen., 8 Feb., 1895. Retired by operation of law 2 April, 1897.

RUGG, SYLVANUS T. [Born in Mass. Appointed from Army.]
Priv., Corpl., Sergt. and 1st Sergt. Batty G, 2nd Art., 22 Dec., 1857, to 19 Dec., 1862. Bvt. 2nd Lieut. 2nd Art., 22 Oct., 1862. 2nd Lieut. 4th Art., 22 Oct., 1862. Dismissed 22 July, 1864.

RUGGLES, COLDEN L. H.* [Born in N. Y. Appointed from N. Y.]
Addl. 2nd Lieut. 1st Art., 12 June, 1890. 2nd Lieut. 3rd Art., 7 Jan., 1891. 1st Lieut. Ord., 8 Dec., 1893. Capt., 29 April, 1899. Maj. Chief Ord. Officer Vols., 22 Aug., 1898, declined.

RUGGLES, DANIEL.* [Born in Mass. Appointed from Mass.]
Bvt. 2nd Lieut. 5th Inf., 1 July, 1833. 2nd Lieut., 18 Feb., 1836. 1st Lieut., 7 July, 1838. Capt., 18 June, 1846. Resigned 7 May, 1861. Bvt. Maj., 20 Aug., 1847, for gallant and meritorious conduct at Contreras and Churubusco, Mex. Bvt. Lieut. Col., 13 Sept., 1847, for gallant and meritorious conduct at Chapultepec, Mex.

RUGGLES, GEORGE D.* [Born in N. Y. Appointed from N. Y.]
Bvt. 2nd Lieut. 1st Inf., 1 July, 1855. 2nd Lieut. 2nd Inf., 1 July, 1855. Reg. Adj., 10 Sept., 1857, to 1 July, 1861. 1st Lieut., 2 May, 1861. 1st Lieut. 12th Inf., 14 May, 1861, declined. Bvt. Capt. A. A. G., 1 July, 1861. Capt. A. A. G., 3 Aug., 1861. Col. A. A. de C., 28 June, 1862. Maj. A. A. G., 17 July, 1862. Bvt. Lieut. Col. and Col., 13 March, 1865, for gallant and meritorious service during the war. Bvt. Brig. Gen., 13 March, 1865, for gallant and meritorious service during the campaign terminating with the surrender of the insurgent army of Northern

Virginia. Bvt. Brig. Gen. Vols., 9 April, 1865, for gallant and meritorious service during the recent operations resulting in the fall of Richmond, Va., and the surrender of the insurgent army under Gen. Robert E. Lee. Mustered out as Col. A. A. de C., 31 May, 1866. Lieut. Col. A. A. G., 15 June, 1880. Col. A. A. G., 7 June, 1889. Brig. Gen. A. G., 6 Nov., 1893. Retired by operation of law 11 Sept., 1897.

RUGGLES, JAMES P. [Born in Mass. Appointed from Army.]
Priv., Corpl. and Sergt. Troop H. 2nd Drag. (2nd Cav.), 3 April, 1860, to 3 April, 1865. 2nd Lieut. 5th Cav., 3 May, 1865. 1st Lieut., 17 Feb., 1866. Cashiered 15 Aug., 1867. Reinstated 31 Dec., 1867. Cashiered 9 June, 1868.

RUHLEN, GEORGE.* [Born in Germany. Appointed from Ohio.]
2nd Lieut. 17th Inf., 14 June, 1872. 1st Lieut., 18 Sept., 1876. R. Q. M., 27 Aug., 1878, to 1 July, 1879. Reg. Adj., 1 July, 1889, to —. Capt. A. Q. M., 14 Aug., 1890. Maj. Chief Q. M. Vols., 3 June, 1898. Lieut. Col. Q. M. Vols., 10 Aug., 1898, to 2 March, 1899.

RUMBOUGH, DAVID J. [Born in Va. Appointed from Va.]
2nd Lieut. 3rd Art., 12 June, 1880. 1st Lieut., 30 Nov., 1888. Capt., 2 March, 1899. Graduate of the Artillery School, 1884.

RUNCIE, JAMES E.* [Born in Iowa. Appointed from Ohio.]
2nd Lieut. 5th Cav., 13 June, 1879. Trans. to 1st Art., 11 Aug., 1879. 1st Lieut., 25 Nov., 1886. Retired for disability 22 March, 1894. Maj. 1st Ohio Cav., 9 May to 25 Oct., 1898.

RUNDELL, CHAS H.* [Born in N. Y. Appointed from N. Y.]
Bvt. 2nd Lieut. 3rd Inf., 1 July, 1852. 2nd Lieut. 4th Inf., 5 Aug., 1853. 1st Lieut., 31 Jan., 1861. Dismissed 6 June, 1861.

RUNKLE, BENJ'N. P. [Born in Ohio. Appointed from Ohio.]
Capt. 13th Ohio Vols., 22 April, 1861. Maj., 8 Nov., 1861. Mustered out 18 Aug., 1862. Col. 45th Ohio Vols., 19 Aug., 1862. Mustered out 21 July, 1864. Lieut. Col. Vet. Res. Corps, 22 Aug., 1864. Bvt. Col., Brig. Gen. and Maj. Gen. Vols., 9 Nov., 1865, for meritorious service. Mustered out 5 Oct., 1866. Maj. 45th Inf., 28 July, 1866. Bvt. Lieut. Col., 2 March, 1867, for gallant and meritorious service in the Battle of Shiloh, Tenn. Bvt. Col., 2 March, 1867, for gallant and meritorious service during the war. Unassigned 15 March, 1869. Retired 15 Dec., 1870. Dismissed 16 Jan., 1873. Reinstated 4 Aug., 1877. Dropped 12 Nov., 1884. Restored to list of retired officers 27 June, 1887, and to be borne on the rolls as never having been legally separated from the Army.

RUPP, JOSEPH D.* [Born in Mass. Appointed from Mass.]
2nd Lieut. Light Art., 1 July, 1819. Trans. to 4th Art., 1 June, 1821. Died 17 Dec., 1821.

RUSH, RICHARD H.* [Born in England. Appointed at Large.]
Bvt. 2nd Lieut. 2nd Art., 1 July, 1846. 2nd Lieut., 3 March, 1847. 1st Lieut., 6 Dec., 1847. Resigned 1 July, 1854. Col. 6th Pa. Cav., 27 July, 1861. Resigned 1 July, 1864.

RUSS, CHARLES P.* [Born in N. Y. Appointed from N. Y.]
2nd Lieut. 11th Inf., 11 June, 1888. 1st Lieut. 18th Inf., 12 May, 1895. Trans. to 23rd Inf., 8 June, 1895. Trans. to 11th Inf., 5 Nov., 1896. Reg. Adj., 22 July, 1898. Died at San Juan, Porto Rico, 13 Feb., 1899.

RUSSEL, EDGAR.* [Born in Mo. Appointed from Mo.]
2nd Lieut. 3rd Art., 12 June, 1887. 1st Lieut. 5th Art., 2 Nov., 1893. Trans. to 6th Art., 8 March, 1898. Capt. Sig. Corps Vols., 20 June, 1898, to —.

RUSSELL, ALBERT J.* [Born in Ohio. Appointed from Conn.]
2nd Lieut. 10th Cav., 15 June, 1876. Trans. to 7th Cav., 26 June, 1876. 1st Lieut., 30 Nov., 1881. Retired for disability with rank of Capt. 23 May, 1896.

RUSSELL, ANDREW H.* [Born in Mass. Appointed from Mass.]
2nd Lieut. 3rd Cav., 12 June, 1871. 1st Lieut. of Ord., 21 April, 1876. Capt. (fourteen years' service), 12 June, 1885. Maj. Chief Ord. Officer Vols., 18 July to 30 Nov., 1898.

RUSSELL, CHARLES E.* [Born in Texas. Appointed from Texas.]
Addl. 2nd Lieut. 18th Inf., 12 June, 1896. 2nd Lieut. 7th Inf., 27 Aug., 1896. 1st Lieut. of Inf., 13 Dec., 1898. Ass'd to 8th Inf., 1 Jan., 1899.

RUSSELL, CHAS. P. [Born in Penn. Appointed from N. Y.]
Asst. Surg., 4 Sept., 1862. Resigned 3 Sept., 1863.

RUSSELL, CHAS. S. [Born in Mass. Appointed from Ind.]
Capt. 11th Inf., 14 May, 1861. Lieut. Col. U. S. Col. Inf., 1 May, 1864. Col. 28th U. S. Col. Inf., 27 Aug., 1864. Mustered out of Vol. Service, 8 Nov., 1865. Trans. to 20th Inf., 21 Sept., 1866. Died 2 Nov., 1866. Bvt. Maj., 17 Sept., 1862, for gallant and meritorious service at the Battle of Antietam, Md. Bvt. Lieut. Col., 3 May, 1863, for gallant and meritorious service at the Battle of Chancellorsville, Va. Bvt. Col., 30 July, 1864, for gallant and meritorious service in action that succeeded the explosion of the Petersburg mine, Va. Bvt. Brig. Gen. Vols., 30 July, 1864, for distinguished service in the assault on Cemetery Hill, Va.

RUSSELL, DAVID A.* [Born in N. Y. Appointed from N. Y.]
Bvt. 2nd Lieut. 1st Inf., 1 July, 1845. 2nd Lieut. 4th Inf., 21 Sept., 1846. 1st Lieut., 1 Jan., 1848. Capt., 22 June, 1854. Maj. 8th Inf., 9 Aug., 1862. Col. 7th Mass. Vols., 18 Feb., 1862. Brig. Gen. Vols., 29 Nov., 1862. Killed in the Battle of Opequan, Va., 19 Sept., 1864. Bvt. 1st Lieut., 15 Aug., 1847, for gallant and meritorious conduct at Paso Ovejas, National Bridge, and Cerro Gordo, Mex. Bvt. Lieut. Col., 1 July, 1862, for gallant and meritorious service in the Peninsula campaign. Bvt. Col., 1 July, 1863, for gallant and meritorious service at the Battle of Gettysburg, Pa. Bvt. Brig. Gen., 6 May, 1864, for gallant and meritorious service at the Battle of the Wilderness, Va. Bvt. Maj. Gen., 9 Sept., 1864, for gallant and meritorious service at the Battle of Opequan, Va., where killed.

RUSSELL, EDMUND.* [Born in Penn. Appointed from Penn.]
Bvt. 2nd Lieut. 2nd Inf., 1 July, 1846. 2nd Lieut. 4th Inf., 16 Feb., 1847. 1st Lieut., 31 Jan., 1850. Killed 24 March, 1853, in action with Indians in Cal. Bvt.

1st Lieut., 8 Sept., 1847, for gallant and meritorious conduct in the Battle of Molino del Rey, Mex.

RUSSELL, EDMUND K. [Born in N. Y. Appointed from N. Y.]
Cadet Mil. Acad., 1 July, 1858, to 22 June, 1861. 2nd Lieut. 67th N. Y. Vols., 24 June, 1861. 1st Lieut., 14 April, 1862. Capt., 3 May, 1863. Bvt. Maj. Vols., 2 Dec., 1864, for faithful and meritorious service in the line of his duty. Maj. 65th N. Y. Vols., 24 June, 1865. Mustered out 17 July, 1865. 2nd Lieut. 1st Art., 11 May, 1866. 1st Lieut., 21 Feb., 1867. Graduate of the Artillery School, 1874. Capt., 9 July, 1884. Retired for disability with rank of Maj., 8 March, 1898.

RUSSELL, FRANCIS L. D. [Born in Mass. Appointed from Mass.]
Served as Priv. in Co. K, 5th N. Y. Vols., 9 May to 1 Nov., 1861, under name of John H. Conway. 2nd Lieut. 1st Art., 21 Oct., 1861. 1st Lieut., 5 Aug., 1862. Died 11 May, 1864.

RUSSELL, FRANCIS S. K. [Born in N. Y. Appointed from Mich.]
Cadet Mil. Acad., 1 July, 1841, to 4 July, 1843. 2nd Lieut. Mounted Rifles, 27 May, 1846. 1st Lieut., 15 March, 1848. Dismissed 24 May, 1852. Bvt. 1st Lieut., 13 Sept., 1847, for gallant and meritorious conduct in the Battle of Chapultepec, Mex. Died 31 Jan., 1857.

RUSSELL, FRANK W.* [Born in N. H. Appointed from N. H.]
2nd Lieut. 6th Cav., 15 June, 1868. Resigned 10 June, 1872.

RUSSELL, FREDERICK F. [Born in N. Y. Appointed from N. Y.]
Asst. Surg., 12 Dec., 1898.

RUSSELL, GEORGE B. [Born in Mass. Appointed from Mass.]
2nd Lieut. 38th Mass. Vols., 20 Aug., 1862. 1st Lieut., 1 Jan., 1863. Capt., 5 April, 1863. 1st Lieut. Vet. Res. Corps, 25 Aug., 1864. Capt., 15 Sept., 1864. Bvt. Maj. Vols., 13 March, 1865, for meritorious service. Bvt. Lieut. Col. Vols., 13 March, 1865, for gallant and meritorious conduct during the Siege of Port Hudson, La. Mustered out 1 Sept., 1866. Capt. 44th Inf., 28 July, 1866. Bvt. Maj., 2 March, 1867, for gallant and meritorious conduct in the assault on Port Hudson, La. Unassigned 27 May, 1869. Ass'd to 7th Inf., 7 April, 1870. Trans. to 9th Inf., 30 April, 1870. Maj. 5th Inf., 22 April, 1892. Lieut. Col. 14th Inf., 10 March, 1896. Retired for disability, 25 March, 1898.

RUSSELL, GERALD. [Born in Ireland. Appointed from Army.]
Priv. Co. F, Mounted Rifles, 21 July, 1851. Corpl., 15 Feb., 1856. Discharged 21 July, 1856. Priv. Co. D, Mounted Rifles, 25 Jan., 1857. Corpl., 10 May, 1858. Sergt., 1 May, 1860. 1st Sergt., 16 Oct., 1860. Discharged 25 Jan., 1862. 1st Sergt. Co. D, 3rd Cav., 25 Jan., 1862. Discharged 15 Sept., 1862. 2nd Lieut. 3rd Cav., 17 July, 1862. Bvt. 1st Lieut., 4 July, 1863, for gallant and meritorious service in the Siege of Vicksburg, Miss. 1st Lieut. 3rd Cav., 4 Aug., 1864. Capt., 14 Nov., 1867. Maj. 5th Cav., 29 Oct., 1888. Retired for disability, 17 Dec., 1890.

RUSSELL, HIRAM. [Born in N. Y. Appointed from N. Y.]
Cadet at Mil. Acad., 1 July, 1845, to 31 Oct., 1846. 2nd Lieut. of Inf., 3 March, 1847; 10th Inf., 9 April, 1847. 1st Lieut., 21 Jan., 1848. Disbanded 24 Aug., 1848.

RUSSELL, JAMES W. [Born in N. Y. Appointed from N. Y.]
Asst. Surg., 22 June, 1839. Resigned 1 March, 1853.

RUSSELL, JOHN B. F.* [Born in Mass. Appointed from Mass.]
2nd Lieut. Light Art., 24 July, 1818. Trans. to 5th Inf., 1 June, 1821. 1st Lieut., 1 Nov., 1821. Capt. A. Q. M., 14 March, 1828, to 13 Oct., 1830. Capt. 5th Inf., 23 April, 1830. Resigned 22 June, 1837. Died 3 Jan., 1861.

RUSSELL, JOSEPH P. [Born in Vt. Appointed from Vt.]
Surg.'s Mate 4th Inf., 25 May, 1814. Trans. to 5th Inf., 17 May, 1815. Post Surg., 10 Aug., 1818. Maj. Surg. 8th Inf., 28 Jan., 1820. Asst. Surg., 1 June, 1821. Died 19 Sept., 1849.

RUSSELL, ROBERT M.* [Born in Tenn. Appointed from Tenn.]
Bvt. 2nd Lieut. 5th Inf., 1 July, 1848. 2nd Lieut. 2nd Inf., 1 Jan., 1849. Resigned 31 Aug., 1850.

RUSSELL, SAML. A. [Born in N. Y. Appointed from N. Y.]
2nd Lieut. 7th Inf., 5 Aug., 1861. 1st Lieut., 5 Aug., 1861. Capt. A. de C. Vols., 4 May to 28 Aug., 1863. Capt., 28 Aug., 1863. Discharged 1 Jan., 1871. Bvt. Maj., 22 April, 1865 for meritorious service during the war.

RUSSELL, SAMUEL L. [Born in N. Y. Appointed from N. Y.]
2nd Lieut. 2nd Inf., 13 Aug., 1819. 1st Lieut., 31 Dec., 1827. Capt., 28 June, 1836. Killed by Indians in Florida, 28 Feb., 1839.

RUSSELL, THOMAS. [Born in Mass. Appointed from Mass.]
Hosp. Surg.'s Mate, 21 July, 1814. Post Surg., 18 April, 1818. Died 24 Aug., 1819.

RUSSELL, WM., Jr. [Born in N. Y. Appointed from Va.]
1st Lieut. R. Q. M. 18th N. Y. Vols., 21 Sept., 1861, to 22 April, 1863. Maj. A. A. G. Vols., 15 April, 1863. Bvt. Lieut. Col. Vols., 13 March, 1865, for meritorious service during the war. Mustered out 10 Feb., 1866. 2nd Lieut. 4th Cav., 25 Oct., 1867. Died 15 May, 1870, of wounds received in action with Indians in Texas. Bvt. 1st Lieut., 25 Oct., 1867, for gallant and meritorious service in the Battle of Antietam, Md. Bvt. Capt., 25 Oct., 1867, for gallant and meritorious service in the Battle of Gettysburg, Penn. Bvt. Maj., 25 Oct., 1867, for gallant and meritorious service in the Battle of Petersburg, Va.

RUST, ARMISTEAD T. M.* [Born in Va. Appointed from Va.]
2nd Lieut. 1st Drag., 1 July, 1842. Resigned 31 March, 1845.

RUTHERFORD, ALLEN. [Born in N. Y. Appointed from N. Y.]
Capt. 83rd N. Y. Vols., 27 May, 1861. Maj., 7 Jan., 1862. Lieut. Col., 1 Oct., 1862. Resigned 25 Nov., 1862. Lieut. Col. Vet. Res. Corps, 4 Dec., 1863. Bvt. Lieut. Col. and Col. Vols., 13 March, 1865, for faithful service during the war. Mustered out 9 Jan., 1867. 1st Lieut. 44th Inf., 28 July, 1866. Capt., 20 March, 1867. Unassigned 25 May, 1869. Resigned 1 May, 1870. Bvt. Capt. and Maj., 2 March, 1867, for gallant and meritorious service in the Battle of Bull Run (2nd), Va.

RUTHERFORD, ROBERT G. [Born in N. Y. Appointed from N. Y.]
2nd Lieut. 83rd N. Y. Vols., 19 Nov., 1861. 1st Lieut., 7 Jan., 1862. Capt., 1 Nov., 1862. Mustered out 26 Feb., 1863. Capt. Vet. Res. Corps, 11 Sept., 1863. Bvt. Maj. and Lieut. Col. Vols., 13 March, 1865, for gallant and meritorious service in the Battle of Rappahannock Station, Va., and for meritorious service during the war. Mustered out 30 April, 1867. 2nd Lieut. 45th Inf., 7 March, 1867. Bvt. 1st Lieut., 7 March, 1867, for gallant and meritorious service in the Battle of Rappahannock Station, Va. Bvt. Capt., 7 March, 1867, for gallant and meritorious service during the war. Unassigned 22 July, 1869. Ass'd to 12th Inf., 3 Aug., 1870. 1st Lieut., 24 May, 1873. Retired 28 June, 1878.

RUTHERFORD, ROBERT G., Jr. [Born in ——. Appointed from ——.]
2nd Lieut. of Inf. (unassigned), 1 Dec., 1899.

RUTHERFORD, SAML. McP.* [Born in Penn. Appointed from Penn.]
2nd Lieut. 8th Cav., 11 June, 1892. Trans. to 4th Cav., 31 Aug., 1892. 1st Lieut., 2 March, 1899.

RUTHERS, GEORGE W. [Born in W. Va. Appointed from Army.]
Priv. and Corpl. Co. F, 16th Inf., 24 April, 1880, to 6 Aug., 1884. 2nd Lieut. 8th Inf., 4 Aug., 1884. 1st Lieut. 8th Inf., 10 July, 1891. Capt. of Inf., 15 Dec., 1898. Ass'd to 24th Inf., 1 Jan., 1899. Graduate of the Infantry and Cavalry School, 1893. Maj. Chief C. S. Vols., 16 July, 1898, to 13 May, 1899. Maj. C. S. Vols., 8 July, 1899, to ——.

RUTLEDGE, ARTHUR M.* [Born in Tenn. Appointed from Tenn.]
2nd Lieut. 1st Art., 1 July, 1837. Resigned 31 Aug., 1838. Died 17 June, 1876.

RUTLEDGE, BENJAMIN H. [Born in S. C. Appointed from S. C.]
3rd Lieut. Corps Art., 12 Dec., 1814. Resigned 20 April, 1817. Died in Sept., 1835.

RUTLEDGE, HUGH R. [Born in S. C. Appointed from S. C.]
Asst. Surg. Vols., 10 Sept., 1847. Disbanded 12 July, 1848.

RYAN, DENIS. [Born in Ireland. Appointed from N. Y.]
Priv., Corpl., Sergt. and 1st Sergt. Troop I, 6th Cav., 14 Jan., 1870, to 14 Jan., 1875. 2nd Lieut. 22nd Inf., 6 Nov., 1876. Resigned 8 Jan., 1877.

RYAN, EDMUND T. [Born in N. Y. Appointed from Army.]
Musician Gen. Ser., 1 Dec., 1856, to 1 Dec., 1864, and Priv. Gen. Ser., 3 July, 1865, to 10 March, 1868. 2nd Lieut. 15th Inf., 20 Nov., 1867. Cashiered 15 Jan., 1873.

RYAN, GEORGE.* [Born in Mass. Appointed from Conn.]
Bvt. 2nd Lieut. 6th Inf., 1 July, 1857. 2nd Lieut. 1st Inf., 31 Oct., 1857. Trans. to 7th Inf., 24 June, 1858. 1st Lieut., 22 April, 1861. Reg. Adj., 1 Sept., 1861, to 9 July, 1862. Capt., 9 July, 1862. Col. 140th N. Y. Vols., 29 Aug., 1863. Killed at the Battle of Laurel Hill, Va., 8 May, 1864.

RYAN, JAMES A.* [Born in Conn. Appointed from Conn.]
2nd Lieut. 10th Cav., 12 June, 1890. 1st Lieut. 9th Cav., 3 Feb., 1897.

RYAN, JOHN P.* [Born in N. Y. Appointed from N. Y.]
Addl. 2nd Lieut. 3rd Cav., 11 June, 1888. 2nd Lieut. 4th Cav., 2 Oct., 1888. Trans. to 3rd Cav., 30 Nov., 1888. 1st Lieut. 6th Cav., 20 May, 1896. Honor graduate of the Infantry and Cavalry School, 1895.

RYAN, STEPHEN V. R.* [Born in Conn. Appointed from N. Y.]
Bvt. 2nd Lieut. 1st Art., 1 July, 1825. 2nd Lieut., 1 July, 1825. Resigned 31 March, 1833. Died in 1840.

RYER, BENJN. F. [Born in N. Y. Appointed from N. Y.]
1st Lieut. 20th N. Y. Batty, 29 Dec., 1862. Capt., 12 Sept., 1863. Mustered out 31 July, 1865. 2nd Lieut. 2nd Art., 23 Feb., 1866. 1st Lieut., 28 July, 1866. Cashiered 13 April, 1870.

RYER, WASH'N. M. [Born in N. Y. Appointed from N. Y.]
Asst. Surg., 13 Dec., 1847. Resigned 8 Dec., 1849.

RYLAND, KIRTLEY. [Born in Mo. Appointed from Mo.]
Asst. Surg., 28 April, 1859. Died 22 Sept., 1861.

RYTHER, DWIGHT W. [Born in N. Y. Appointed from Army.]
Cadet Mil. Acad., 16 June, 1887, to 15 Jan., 1889. Priv. and Corpl. Co. C, and Q. M. Sergt. 6th Inf., 5 Oct., 1892, to 10 Nov., 1895. 2nd Lieut. 2nd Inf., 6 Nov., 1895. Trans. to 6th Inf., 2 Dec., 1895. 1st Lieut. of Inf., 11 Aug., 1898. Ass'd to 4th Inf., 1 Jan., 1899. Trans. to 6th Inf., 19 June, 1899.

RZIHA, JOHN. [Born in Poland. Appointed from Iowa.]
Changed name to John Laube de Laubenfels,—which see.

SABIN, ALBERT. [Born in Vt. Appointed from Vt.]
2nd Lieut. 1st Inf., 19 Feb., 1862. 1st Lieut., 1 Aug., 1863. Died 29 Sept., 1863.

SACHS, HENRY. [Born in Germany. Appointed from Army.]
Priv., Corpl., Sergt. and 1st Sergt. Troop K, 2nd Drag., 1 Oct., 1857, to 24 Oct., 1861. 2nd Lieut. 3rd Cav., 24 Oct., 1861. 1st Lieut., 17 July, 1862. R. Q. M., 15 Oct., 1863, to 1 June, 1864. Resigned 25 Jan., 1865.

SACKET, DELOS B.* [Born in N. Y. Appointed from N. Y.]
Bvt. 2nd Lieut. 2nd Drag., 1 July, 1845. Bvt. 1st Lieut., 9 May, 1846, for gallant and meritorious conduct in the Battles of Palo Alto and Resaca de la Palma. 2nd Lieut. 1st Drag., 30 June, 1846. 1st Lieut., 27 Dec., 1848. Capt. 1st Cav., 3 March, 1855. Maj. 1st Cav., 31 Jan., 1861. Lieut. Col. 2nd Cav., 3 May, 1861; 5th Cav., 3 Aug., 1861. Col. I. G., 1 Oct., 1861. Bvt. Brig. Gen., 13 March, 1865, for gallant and meritorious service in the field during the war. Bvt. Maj. Gen., 13 March, 1865, for faithful and meritorious service during the war. Brig. Gen. I. G., 2 Jan., 1881. Died 8 March, 1885.

SACKETT, DANIEL. [Born in N. Y. Appointed from N. Y.]
1st Lieut. 41st Inf., 11 Nov., 1813. Disbanded 15 June, 1815. Reinstated 2 Dec., 1815, in 4th Inf. Dropped 4 Sept., 1816.

SACKETT, JOHN H. [Born in N. Y. Appointed from N. Y.]
Surg.'s Mate, 25 March, 1812. Hosp. Surg.'s Mate, 22 March, 1813. Retained 15 June, 1815, as Garrison Surg.'s Mate. Post Surg., 24 April, 1816, to rank from 22 March, 1813. Disbanded 1 June, 1821. Died 15 June, 1822.

SACRISTI, LOUIS J. [Born in Del. Appointed from Penn.]
2nd Lieut. 116th Penn. Vols., 1 Sept., 1862. 1st Lieut., 1 March, 1863. Capt., 22 Sept., 1864. Bvt. Maj. Vols., 13 March, 1865, for gallant and meritorious conduct during the war. Mustered out 3 June, 1865. Capt. 6th U. S. Vet. Vols., 29 July, 1865. Mustered out 8 April, 1866. 2nd Lieut. 20th Inf., 18 June, 1867. Mustered out 1 Jan., 1871.

SAFFARANS, GEORGE C.* [Born in Tenn. Appointed from Ky.]
2nd Lieut. 6th Inf., 12 June, 1891. 1st Lieut. 25th Inf., 10 March, 1898. Trans. to 10th Inf., 18 April, 1898. Maj. 3rd Ky. Vols., 21 May, 1898, until muster out, 16 May, 1899.

SAFFOLD, MARION B.* [Born in Ala. Appointed from Ala.]
2nd Lieut. 13th Inf., 13 June, 1879. 1st Lieut., 16 Dec., 1889. R. Q. M., 16 Dec., 1889, to 1893. Capt., 26 April, 1898. Killed in action at Cavite Viego, Luzon, P. I., 8 Oct., 1899.

SAFFORD, ROBT. E.* [Born in Ohio. Appointed from Ohio.]
2nd Lieut. 10th Cav., 15 June, 1877. Died 19 July, 1879.

SAGE, CORWIN. [Born in Ohio. Appointed from Ohio.]
2nd Lieut. 17th Inf., 26 Nov., 1880. Dropped 14 Feb., 1886.

SAGE, GEORGE E. [Born in N. Y. Appointed from Ill.]
Cadet at Naval Acad., 27 Sept., 1864, to 26 June, 1865. 2nd Lieut. 19th Inf., 30 Sept., 1868. Unassigned 13 March, 1869. Ass'd to 5th Art., 14 July, 1869. Graduate of the Artillery School, 1871. Capt. 6th Art., 8 March, 1898.

SAGE, WM. H.* [Born in N. Y. Appointed from N. Y.]
2nd Lieut. 5th Inf., 13 June, 1882. 1st Lieut. 23rd Inf., 15 Jan., 1891. Capt. 14th Inf., 26 April, 1898. Trans. to 23rd Inf., 19 Nov., 1898.

SAGE, WM. N. [Born in N. Y. Appointed from N. Y.]
1st Lieut. 137th N. Y. Vols., 3 Sept., 1862. Capt., 4 Dec., 1863. Mustered out 9 June, 1865. 2nd Lieut. 39th U. S. Col. Troops, 21 Aug., 1865. 1st Lieut., 9 Nov., 1865. Mustered out 4 Dec., 1865. 2nd Lieut. and 1st Lieut. 11th Inf., 23 Feb., 1866. Trans. to 29th Inf., 21 Sept., 1866. Trans. to 11th Inf., 25 April, 1869. Capt., 7 June, 1879. Retired for disability, 19 Sept., 1890.

SAILER, ISAAC D. [Born in Penn. Appointed from Penn.]
Priv. Commonwealth Art. Penn. Vols., 24 April to 21 June, 1861. 1st Lieut. 15th Inf., 14 May, 1861. Capt., 3 Jan., 1862. Dismissed 17 Dec., 1863.

SALTZMAN, CHARLES McK.* [Born in Iowa. Appointed from Iowa.]
Addl. 2nd Lieut. 5th Cav., 12 June, 1896. 2nd Lieut. 1st Cav., 27 Aug., 1896. 1st Lieut. 9th Cav., 13 Dec., 1899.

SAMPLE, WM. R.* [Born in Tenn. Appointed from Ark.]
Addl. 2nd Lieut. 14th Inf., 11 June, 1888. 2nd Lieut., 1 July, 1888. 1st Lieut. 13th Inf., 1 Oct., 1895. Capt. 3rd Inf., 1 April, 1899. Capt. A. A. G. Vols., 20 May, 1898, to 7 April, 1899.

SAMUELS, JOSEPH. [Born in Va. Appointed from Va.]
2nd Lieut. of Inf., 23 Feb., 1847: 11th Inf., 9 April, 1847. 1st Lieut., 2 Aug., 1847. Died 9 Dec., 1847.

SANBORN, WASHN. I. [Born in Maine. Appointed from Wash. Ter.]
2nd Lieut. 1st Wash. Ter. Vols., 3 Oct., 1862. Capt. A. A. G. Vols., 1 Feb., 1865. Mustered out 1 Oct., 1866. 2nd Lieut. 13th Inf., 11 May, 1866. 1st Lieut. 13th Inf., 10 Feb., 1869. Unassigned 20 July, 1869. Ass'd to 25th Inf., 31 Dec., 1870. Capt., 4 Dec., 1884. Retired for disability, with rank of Maj., 1 Nov., 1898.

SANBOURNE, MATTSON C. [Born in Maine. Appointed from Army.]
Priv. Co. A, 1st Maine Art., 18 Dec., 1861, to 15 Nov., 1862. 2nd Lieut. 20th Maine Vols., 16 Nov., 1862. 1st Lieut., 3 July, 1864. Bvt. Capt. Vols., 6 July, 1864, for gallant and distinguished service at the Battle of Bethesda Church, and during the campaign before Richmond, Va. Resigned 2 June, 1865. Priv. and Sergt. Co. A, 15th Inf., 30 Sept., 1865, to 5 Sept., 1866. 2nd Lieut. 7th Inf., 25 May, 1866. 1st Lieut., 11 Oct., 1871. Died 12 Jan., 1873. Bvt. 1st Lieut. and Capt., 2 March, 1867, for gallant and meritorious service during the war.

SANDERS, JOHN.* [Born in Ky. Appointed from Fla.]
Bvt. 2nd Lieut. Eng., 1 July, 1834. 2nd Lieut., 30 Sept., 1836. 1st Lieut., 7 July, 1838. Capt., 7 Dec., 1838. Died 29 July, 1858. Bvt. Maj., 23 Sept., 1846, for gallant and meritorious conduct at Monterey, Mex.

SANDERS, WM. P.* [Born in Ky. Appointed from Miss.]
Bvt. 2nd Lieut. 1st Drag., 1 July, 1856. 2nd Lieut. 2nd Drag., 27 May, 1857. 1st Lieut., 10 May, 1861. Capt. 3rd Cav., 14 May, 1861; 6th Cav., 3 Aug., 1861. Col. 5th Ky. Cav., 4 March, 1863. Brig. Gen. Vols., 18 Oct., 1863. Died 19 Nov., 1863, of wounds received in battle before Knoxville, Tenn.

SANDERS, WM. W. [Born in Penn. Appointed from Penn.]
2nd Lieut. 6th Inf., 23 June, 1860. 1st Lieut., 9 May, 1861. Reg. Adj., 1 Dec., 1861, to 27 June, 1862. Capt., 27 June, 1862. Bvt. Maj., 2 Dec., 1864, for faithful and meritorious service in the field. Col. 2nd Penn. Cav., 26 March, 1865. Bvt. Lieut Col., 2 April, 1865, for gallant and meritorious service in front of Petersburg, Va. Bvt. Col., 9 April, 1865, for gallant and meritorious service in the campaign terminating with the surrender of the insurgent army under Gen. R. E. Lee. Mustered out of Vol. Service, 13 July, 1865. Lieut. Col. 1st U. S. Vet. Vols., 4 Aug., 1865. Mustered out of Vol. Service, 1 March, 1866. Maj. 8th Inf., 15 Dec., 1880. Died 26 Jan., 1883.

SANDERSON, GEORGE K. [Born in Penn. Appointed from Army.]
Priv. 15th Inf., 24 Oct., 1861. 2nd Lieut. 15th Inf., 31 Oct., 1861. Bvt. 1st Lieut., 7 April, 1862, for gallant and meritorious service in the Battle of Shiloh, Tenn. 1st Lieut. 15th Inf., 9 Nov., 1862. Bvt. Capt., 1 Sept., 1864, for gallant and meritorious service during the Atlanta campaign. R. Q. M. 15th Inf., 6 April, 1865, to 28 March, 1866. Capt. 15th Inf., 28 March, 1866. Trans. to 33rd Inf., 21 Sept., 1866. Unassigned 3 May, 1869. Ass'd to 11th Inf., 18 Dec., 1869. Maj. of Inf. (18th), 19 March, 1891. Retired, for over thirty years' service, 2 April, 1892. Died 2 Feb., 1893.

SANDERSON, JAMES A.* [Born in Ohio. Appointed from Ohio.]
2nd Lieut. 1st Art., 17 June, 1862. Died 10 April, 1864, of wounds received in Battle of Pleasant Hill, La.

SANDERSON, JAMES S. [Born in Mass. Appointed from Army.]
Priv., Sergt. and 1st Sergt. Co. B. and Sergt. Maj. 7th Inf., 7 March, 1825, to 1 March, 1838. 2nd Lieut. 7th Inf., 1 March, 1838. Killed 19 May, 1840, in action with Indians in Florida.

SANDERSON, JOHN P. [Born in Penn. Appointed from Penn.]
Lieut. Col. 15th Inf., 14 May, 1861. Col. 13th Inf., 4 July, 1863. Died 14 Oct., 1864.

SANDERSON, WINSLOW F. [Born in N. Y. Appointed from Ohio.]
Capt. Mounted Rifles, 27 May, 1846. Maj., 8 Jan., 1848. Died 16 Sept., 1853. Bvt. Maj., 20 Aug., 1847, for gallant and meritorious conduct at Contreras and Churubusco, Mex.

SANDS, ABRAHAM L.* [Born in N. Y. Appointed from Conn.]
2nd Lieut. Art., 18 Feb., 1809. 1st Lieut. 1st Art., 10 Feb., 1813. Trans. to Corps Art., 12 May, 1814. Capt., 17 Sept., 1818. Trans. to 4th Art., 1 June, 1821. Resigned 1 Nov., 1823. Died 25 Dec., 1840.

SANDS, GEORGE H.* [Born in D. C. Appointed from D. C.]
2nd Lieut. 6th Cav., 12 June, 1880. 1st Lieut., 19 Oct., 1887. Capt., 3 Dec., 1897. Maj. Eng. Off. Vols., 19 May, 1898, to 24 April, 1899.

SANDS, JAMES H. [Born in Ind. Appointed from Ind.]
1st Lieut. 6th Ind. Cav., 5 Aug., 1862. Capt., 18 Aug., 1862. Mustered out 17 June, 1865. 2nd Lieut. 6th Cav., 24 Sept., 1867. 1st Lieut., 1 Dec., 1869. Reg. Adj., 3 April, 1874, to 30 Sept., 1876. Retired 30 Nov., 1879.

SANDS, RICHARD M. [Born in Md. Appointed from Md.]
Ensign 38th Inf., 20 May, 1813. 3rd Lieut., 22 April, 1814. 2nd Lieut., 9 July, 1814. Disbanded 15 June, 1815. Reinstated 2 Dec., 1815, in 4th Inf. R. Q. M., 16 Oct., 1815, to 31 Aug., 1816. 1st Lieut., 12 March, 1817. Capt., 30 April, 1819. Died 13 Sept., 1836. Bvt. Maj., 30 April, 1829, for ten years' faithful service in one grade.

SANFORD, GEORGE B. [Born in Conn. Appointed from Conn.]
2nd Lieut. 1st Drag., 26 April, 1861. 1st Lieut. 1st Drag., 30 July, 1861. 1st Cav., 3 Aug., 1861. Capt., 1 Oct., 1862. Bvt. Maj., 19 Oct., 1864, for gallant and meritorious service in the Battle of Cedar Creek, Va. Bvt. Lieut. Col., 13 March, 1865, for gallant and meritorious service during the war. Maj. 1st Cav., 25 June, 1876. Lieut. Col. 9th Cav., 20 Aug., 1889. Col. 6th Cav., 22 July, 1892. Retired, for over thirty years' service, 28 July, 1892.

SANFORD, GEORGE P. [Born in Conn. Appointed from Army.]
Priv., Sergt. and 1st Sergt. Co. F, 13th Inf., 8 Nov., 1861, to 2 April, 1863. 2nd Lieut. 13th Inf., 19 Feb., 1863. Dismissed 10 Nov., 1863. Reinstated 13 June, 1864, with rank of 1st Lieut. from 13 Nov., 1863. Dismissed 7 Dec., 1864.

SANFORD, JAMES C.* [Born in N. Y. Appointed from N. Y.]
2nd Lieut. Eng., 15 June, 1884. 1st Lieut., 12 Oct., 1886. Capt., 13 Aug., 1895.

SANFORD, JOHN B. [Born in N. Y. Appointed from Vt.]
2nd Lieut. 24th Inf., 10 April, 1899.

SANFORD, JOHN T. [Born in Va. Appointed from La.]
2nd Lieut. of Inf., 11 March, 1847; 14th Inf., 9 April, 1847. 1st Lieut., 23 May, 1848. Disbanded 25 July, 1848.

SANGER, JOSEPH P. [Born in Mich. Appointed from Mich.]
2nd Lieut. 1st Mich. Vols., 1 May, 1861. Mustered out 7 Aug., 1861. 2nd Lieut. 1st Art., 5 Aug., 1861. 1st Lieut., 26 Oct., 1861. Bvt. Capt., 28 May, 1864, for gallant and meritorious service in action at Bermuda Hundred, Va. Bvt. Maj., 13 March, 1865, for gallant and meritorious service in the Battle of Deep Bottom, Va., 16 Aug., 1864. Reg. Adj. 1st Art., 31 Jan., 1866, to 13 Feb., 1868. Capt. 7th Cav., 28 July, 1866, declined. Capt. 1st Art., 7 Feb., 1875. Maj. I. G., 12 Feb., 1889. Lieut. Col. and Mil. Sec. to Lieut. Gen. J. M. Schofield, commanding Army, 1895. Lieut. Col. I. G., 7 July, 1898. Honor graduate of the Artillery School, 1869. Lieut. Col. I. G. Vols., 9 May, 1898. Brig. Gen. Vols., 27 May, 1898, to 12 June, 1899. Director census of Cuba and Porto Rico, 1899.

SANGER, LOUIS H. [Born in Maine. Appointed from Army.]
Priv. Co. C, 1st Batt. 17th Inf., 19 Sept., 1861. Corpl., 1 July, 1862. Sergt., 18 July, 1862. 2nd Lieut. 17th Inf., 19 July, 1862. 1st Lieut., 9 Aug., 1862. Bvt. Capt., 2 July, 1863, and Bvt. Maj., 13 March, 1865, for gallant and meritorious service in the Battle of Gettysburg, Penn. Capt. 17th Inf., 21 July, 1865. Dismissed 24 July, 1872. Reinstated 6 Jan., 1873. Died 23 Dec., 1884.

SANGSTER, THOMAS. [Born in Va. Appointed from D. C.]
Capt. 12th Inf., 30 April, 1812. Trans. to 4th Inf., 17 May, 1815. Resigned 10 May, 1816.

SANNO, JAMES M. J.* [Born in N. J. Appointed from N. J.]
2nd Lieut. 7th Inf., 11 June, 1863. 1st Lieut., 3 Dec., 1863. Reg. Adj., 5 Sept., 1864, to 19 May, 1869, and from 1 Sept., 1869, to 15 May, 1871. Capt. 28th Inf., 28 July, 1866, declined. Capt. 7th Inf., 15 May, 1871. Maj. 3rd Inf., 12 May, 1895. Lieut. Col. 4th Inf., 11 Aug., 1898. Bvt. Maj., 27 Feb., 1890, for gallant services in action against Indians at the Big Hole, Mont., 9 Aug., 1877. Col. 18th Inf., 18 Dec., 1899.

SARGENT, ALDEN.* [Born in Maine. Appointed from Maine.]
Bvt. 2nd Lieut. 6th Inf., 1 July, 1850. 2nd Lieut., 15 April, 1851. 1st Lieut. 9th Inf., 3 March, 1855. Resigned 7 June, 1856. Died 20 Oct., 1873.

SARGENT, FREDERIC H. [Born in Ill. Appointed from Army.]
Priv. and Corpl. Co. G, 7th Inf., 21 Jan., 1886, to 7 March, 1889. 2nd Lieut. 7th Inf., 11 Feb., 1889. 1st Lieut. 8th Inf., 10 March, 1896. Capt., 19 May, 1899. Graduate of the Infantry and Cavalry School, 1893. Reg. Adj., 1 July, 1899.

SARGENT, HENRY A. [Born in N. H. Appointed from Mass.]
2nd Lieut. 2nd Inf., 18 June, 1855. Resigned 30 Sept., 1856.

SARGENT, HERBERT H.* [Born in Ill. Appointed from Ill.]
2nd Lieut. 2nd Cav., 13 June, 1883. 1st Lieut., 19 June, 1890. Capt., 2 March, 1899. Maj. A. A. G. Vols., 12 May, 1898, declined. Col. 5th Vol. Inf., 20 May, 1898, to 31 May, 1899. Lieut. Col. 29th U. S. Vols., 5 July, 1899.

SARGENT, JAMES H. [Born in Mass. Appointed from Mass.]
Garrison Surg.'s Mate, 6 March, 1806. Disbanded 1 June, 1815. Reinstated 15 June, 1815. Post Surg., 24 April, 1816. Asst. Surg., 1 June, 1821. Resigned 22 Aug., 1846.

SARRATT, EDWIN O.* [Born in S. C. Appointed from S. C.]
Addl. 2nd Lieut. 3rd Art., 11 June, 1897. 2nd Lieut., 10 Feb., 1898. 1st Lieut. 6th Art., 2 March, 1899.

SARSON, HORACE B. [Born in England. Appointed from Army.]
Priv. Co. H, 3rd Batt. 16th Inf., 6 Sept., 1864. Sergt. Maj., 1 Jan., 1866. 2nd Lieut. 16th Inf., 16 Nov., 1866. Trans. to 2nd Inf., 17 April, 1869. 1st Lieut., 16 Aug., 1876. R. Q. M., 15 June, 1889, to ——. Capt. of Inf. (2nd), 30 Dec., 1890. Retired for disability, 27 Aug., 1896. Died 22 June, 1897.

SARTLE, WM. J.* [Born in Vt. Appointed from Vt.]
2nd Lieut. 15th Inf., 17 June, 1867. Reg. Adj., 26 Nov., 1867, to 27 Jan., 1873. 1st Lieut., 14 May, 1868. Died 27 Jan., 1873.

SATER, WILLIAM A.* [Born in Ohio. Appointed from Kans.]
2nd Lieut. of Inf. (13th), 12 June, 1894. 1st Lieut., ——, 1898. Killed in action, at San Juan, Santiago, Cuba, 1 July, 1898.

SATTERLEE, CHAS. B.* [Born in Penn. Appointed from Penn.]
2nd Lieut. 3rd Art., 15 June, 1876. 1st Lieut., 31 Jan., 1883. R. Q. M., 1 March to 1 May, 1887. Reg. Adj., 1 May, 1887, to ——. Capt. 6th Art., 8 March, 1898. Graduate of the Artillery School, 1880. Died at Honolulu, Hawaiian Islands, 10 July, 1899.

SATTERLEE, RICHD. S. [Born in N. Y. Appointed from Mich.]
Asst. Surg., 25 Feb., 1822. Maj. Surg., 13 July, 1832. Bvt. Lieut. Col., Col. and Brig. Gen., 2 Sept., 1864, for diligent care and attention in procuring proper army supplies as Med. Purveyor, and for economy and fidelity in the disbursement of large sums of money. Lieut. Col. Chief Med. Purveyor, 28 July, 1866. Retired 22 Feb., 1869. Died 10 Nov., 1880.

SAUNDERS, CYRUS. [Born in Va. Appointed from Va.]
Ensign 2nd Inf., 15 April, 1814. 3rd Lieut., 1 May, 1814. 2nd Lieut., 14 July, 1814. Trans. to 3rd Inf., 17 May, 1815. Resigned 31 Oct., 1816.

SAUNDERS, FRANKLIN.* [Born in N. C. Appointed from N. C.]
Bvt. 2nd Lieut. 2nd Drag., 1 July, 1837. 2nd Lieut., 11 Sept., 1837. Resigned 30 June, 1838. Capt. 1st Ky. Vols., 30 May, 1846. Mustered out 17 May, 1847. Died 4 Feb., 1856.

SAUNDERS, HENRY. [Born in Va. Appointed from Va.]
3rd Lieut. 20th Inf., 4 April, 1813. Trans. to 2nd Inf., 22 Jan., 1814. 2nd Lieut., 7 Sept., 1813. 1st Lieut., 14 July, 1814. R. Q. M., May, 1814, to June, 1815. Disbanded 15 June, 1815. Reinstated 2 Dec., 1815, in 1st Inf. Trans. to 1st Art., 1 June, 1821. Capt., 4 Nov., 1823. Resigned 31 Aug., 1844. Bvt. Maj., 4 Nov., 1833, for ten years' faithful service in one grade. Died 20 Feb., 1876.

SAUNDERS, JOHN S.* [Born in Va. Appointed from Va.]
Bvt. 2nd Lieut. 2nd Art., 1 July, 1858. Trans. to Ord., 1 Sept., 1858. 2nd Lieut., 1 Feb., 1861. Resigned 22 April, 1861.

SAUNDERS, RAIMEY G.* [Born in Va. Appointed from Va.]
Ensign 2nd Inf., 20 March, 1814. 3rd Lieut., 1 May, 1814. 2nd Lieut., 14 July, 1814. Trans. to 3rd Inf., 17 May, 1815. Resigned 15 July, 1816.

SAUNDERS, THOS. M. [Born in Va. Appointed from Va.]
2nd Lieut. 3rd Art., 27 June, 1856. 1st Lieut., 12 Oct., 1858. Capt., 21 Nov., 1861. Died 20 Jan., 1864.

SAUNDERS, WM. H. [Born in Va. Appointed from Va.]
2nd Lieut. 2nd Drag., 1 Aug., 1838. 1st Lieut., 23 June, 1841. Reg. Adj., 10 to 25 April, 1849. Capt., 25 April, 1849. Resigned 30 June, 1851. Died 6 July, 1857.

SAVAGE, EGBERT. B. [Born in N. Y. Appointed from N. Y.]
1st Lieut. 115th N. Y. Vols., 26 Aug., 1862. Capt., 1 Nov., 1862. Mustered out 30 Aug., 1865. 2nd Lieut. and 1st Lieut. 15th Inf., 23 Feb., 1866. Trans. to 33rd Inf., 21 Sept., 1866. Trans. to 8th Inf., 3 May, 1869. Capt., 30 May, 1877. Maj., 26 April, 1898. Lieut. Col. 14th Inf., 14 May, 1899. Retired, for over thirty years' service, 14 Aug., 1899.

SAVAGE, FRANK M.* [Born in Ala. Appointed from Ala.]
Addl. 2nd Lieut. 5th Inf., 11 June, 1897. 2nd Lieut. 15th Inf., 6 Oct., 1897. 1st Lieut. 14th Inf., 2 March, 1899. Reg. Com., 23 Sept., 1899.

SAVAGE, JOHN. [Born in Penn. Appointed from Penn.]
Capt. 3rd Cav., 14 May, 1861; 6th Cav., 3 Aug., 1861. Resigned 23 Dec., 1862.

SAVAGE, JOHN H. [Born in Tenn. Appointed from Tenn.]
Maj. of Inf., 3 March, 1847; 14th Inf., 9 April, 1847. Lieut. Col. 11th Inf., 8 Sept., 1847. Disbanded 14 Aug., 1848.

SAVAGE, RICHD. H.* [Born in N. Y. Appointed from Cal.]
Bvt. 2nd Lieut. Eng., 15 June, 1868. Discharged 31 Dec., 1870. Maj. 2nd U. S. Vol. Eng., 1898, to 20 May, 1899. Capt. 27th U. S. Vols., 5 July, 1899. Discharged 21 Dec., 1899.

SAVILLE, MATHEW E.* [Born in Mo. Appointed from Mo.]
2nd Lieut. 22nd Inf., 12 June, 1893. Trans. to 13th Inf., 13 Sept., 1893. Trans. to 10th Inf., 8 June, 1895. 1st Lieut., 26 April, 1898.

SAWTELLE, CHAS. G.* [Born in Maine. Appointed from Maine.]
Bvt. 2nd Lieut. 2nd Inf., 1 July, 1854. 2nd Lieut. 6th Inf., 3 March, 1855. 1st Lieut., 5 June, 1860. R. Q. M., 15 Feb., 1857, to 19 June, 1861. Capt. A. Q. M., 17 May, 1861. Lieut. Col. Q. M., 20 Aug. to 4 Oct., 1862. Lieut. Col. Q. M., 12 Nov., 1862, to 15 Feb., 1864. Lieut. Col. Q. M., 27 May, 1864. Bvt. Maj., Lieut. Col. and Col., 13 March, 1865, for faithful and meritorious service during the

war. Bvt. Brig. Gen., 13 March, 1865, for faithful and meritorious service in the Q. M. Dept. during the war. Relieved as Lieut. Col. Q. M., 24 May, 1865. Col. Q. M., 25 May, 1865, to 1 Jan., 1867. Maj. Q. M., 18 Jan., 1867. Lieut. Col. D. Q. M. G., 24 Jan., 1881. Col. A. Q. M. G., 12 Sept., 1894. Brig. Gen. Q. M. G., 19 Aug., 1896. Retired, after forty years' service, 16 Feb., 1897.

SAWTELLE, CHARLES G., Jr.* [Born in Cal. Appointed from Maine.]
Addl. 2nd Lieut. 7th Cav., 12 June, 1893. 2nd Lieut. 2nd Cav., 14 Aug., 1893. 1st Lieut., 2 March, 1899. Capt. A. Q. M. Vols., 3 June, 1898.

SAWYER, FREDERICK A. [Born in Vt. Appointed from Vt.]
Ensign 11th Inf., 12 March, 1812. 2nd Lieut., 26 June, 1813. 1st Lieut., 12 Dec., 1813. Trans. to 6th Inf., 17 May, 1815. Resigned 30 June, 1819. Died 28 April, 1831.

SAWYER, J. ESTCOURT. [Born in D. C. Appointed from N. J.]
2nd Lieut. 5th Art., 11 Nov., 1867. 1st Lieut., 10 Nov., 1874. Capt. A. Q. M., 1 Dec., 1893. Maj. Q. M. Vols., 12 May, 1898. Graduate of the Artillery School, 1871.

SAWYER, NATHAN D. A. [Born in Mass. Appointed from Mass.]
Corpl. and Sergt. Co. A, 2nd Mass. Vols., 25 May, 1861, to 10 Aug., 1862. 2nd Lieut. 2nd Mass. Vols., 10 Aug., 1862. 1st Lieut., 2 Jan., 1863. Capt., 1 Nov., 1863. Mustered out 15 May, 1865. Capt. Mil. Storekeeper Q. M. D., 28 July, 1866. Cashiered 30 Nov., 1872.

SAWYER, ROSSWELL M. [Born in N. Y. Appointed from Wis.]
1st Lieut. 1st Wis. Vols., 8 Oct., 1861. Capt. A. A. G. Vols., 6 March, 1862. Maj. A. A. G. Vols., 4 July, 1863. Lieut. Col. A. A. G., 25 March, 1864, to 1 Aug., 1865. Bvt. Col. Vols., 13 March, 1865, for meritorious service in the campaigns of Atlanta, Savannah, and the Carolinas. Mustered out 25 Oct., 1866. Capt. 25th Inf., 28 July, 1866. Died 26 Dec., 1866.

SAXTON, ALBERT E.* [Born in Cal. Appointed from Nev.]
Addl. 2nd Lieut. 8th Cav., 12 June, 1894. 2nd Lieut., 25 Aug., 1894. 1st Lieut., 2 March, 1899.

SAXTON, ISAAC A. [Born in Mich. Appointed from Mich.]
2nd Lieut. 4th Inf., 9 Sept., 1898.

SAXTON, MIRAND W. [Born in Mass. Appointed from Mass.]
Cadet Mil. Acad., 1 July, 1861, to 13 Feb., 1863. 2nd Lieut. 33rd U. S. Col. Inf., 19 Nov., 1863. Capt. 128th U. S. Col. Inf., 28 March, 1865. Mustered out 29 Jan., 1867. 2nd Lieut. 38th Inf., 22 Jan., 1867. Trans. to 24th Inf., 11 Nov., 1869. 1st Lieut., 27 May, 1871. Resigned 20 Aug., 1878.

SAXTON, RUFUS.* [Born in Mass. Appointed from Mass.]
Bvt. 2nd Lieut. 3rd Art., 1 July, 1849. 2nd Lieut. 4th Art., 12 Sept., 1850. 1st Lieut., 2 March, 1855. Capt. A. Q. M., 13 May, 1861. Brig. Gen. Vols., 15 April, 1862. Bvt. Maj. Gen. Vols., 12 Jan., 1865. Bvt. Maj., Lieut. Col. and Col., 13 March, 1865, for faithful and meritorious service during the war. Bvt. Brig. Gen., 9 April, 1865, for faithful and meritorious service during the war. Mustered out of Vol. Service, 15 Jan., 1866. Maj. Q. M., 29 July, 1866. Lieut. Col Dep. Q. M. G., 6 June, 1872. Col. A. Q. M. G., 10 March, 1882. Retired by operation of law, 19 Oct., 1888. Medal of Honor for distinguished gallantry and good conduct in the defence of Harper's Ferry, Va., from 26 to 30 May, 1862; while serving as Brig. Gen. of Vols.

SAYER, EDMUND S., Jr. [Born in ——. Appointed from ——.]
2nd Lieut. of Inf., 1 Dec., 1899 (unassigned).

SAYRE, FERRAND.* [Born in Mo. Appointed from Mo.]
2nd Lieut. 8th Cav., 15 June, 1884. 1st Lieut. 5th Cav., 17 April, 1891. Trans. to 8th Cav., 27 April, 1891. Capt., 6 May, 1899.

SCALES, WALLACE B.* [Born in Tex. Appointed from Tex.]
2nd Lieut. 15th Inf., 26 April, 1898. Trans. to 6th Cav., 26 Sept., 1898.

SCALLAN, JAMES. [Born in Va. Appointed from Va.]
3rd Lieut. Light Art., 15 April, 1814. 2nd Lieut. Corps Art., 19 May, 1814. Resigned 28 July, 1815. 2nd Lieut. 1st Inf., 31 Oct., 1816. 1st Lieut., 31 Jan., 1818. Capt., 23 July, 1820. Resigned 31 Jan., 1821.

SCAMMON, ELIAKIM P.* [Born in Maine. Appointed from Maine.]
2nd Lieut. 4th Art., 1 July, 1837. 2nd Lieut. Top. Eng., 7 July, 1838. 1st Lieut., 21 Sept., 1846. Capt., 3 March, 1853. Dismissed 4 June, 1856. Col. 23rd Ohio Vols., 27 June, 1861. Brig. Gen. Vols., 15 Oct., 1862. Mustered out 24 Aug., 1865.

SCANTLAND, JAMES M. [Born in Va. Appointed from Tenn.]
Capt. of Inf., 22 March, 1847; 14th Inf., 9 April, 1837. Disbanded 20 July, 1848. Bvt. Maj., 13 Sept., 1847, for gallant and meritorious conduct at Chapultepec. Died 22 July, 1848.

SCANTLING, JOHN C. [Born in Ind. Appointed from Ind.]
Corpl. Co. K, 9th Ind. Vols., 20 April, 1861. Discharged 29 July, 1861. Priv. Co. A, 2nd Batt. 17th Inf., 1 Jan., 1862. 1st Sergt., 25 July, 1862. Discharged 31 Dec., 1864. Capt. 157th Ind. Vols., 3 April, 1865. Maj. 155th Ind. Vols., 20 April, 1865. Mustered out 4 Aug., 1865. 2nd Lieut. 15th Inf., 11 May, 1866. Trans. to 33rd Inf., 21 Sept., 1866. 1st Lieut., 1 July, 1868. Unassigned 3 May, 1869. Ass'd to 2nd Art., 1 Jan., 1871. Capt., 2 May, 1887. Maj., 13 Feb., 1899. Graduate of the Artillery School, 1875.

SCARRIT, JEREMIAH M.* [Born in N. H. Appointed from Ill.]
2nd Lieut. 6th Inf., 1 July, 1838. 2nd Lieut. Eng., 7 July, 1838. 1st Lieut., 1 July, 1839. Capt., 3 March, 1853. Died 22 June, 1854. Bvt. Capt., 23 Sept., 1846, for gallant and meritorious conduct at Monterey.

SCHAEFFER, CHAS. M.* [Born in Penn. Appointed from Ill.]
2nd Lieut. 15th Inf., 14 June, 1878. Trans. to 9th Cav., 12 June, 1879. Resigned 31 July, 1883.

SCHAFF, MORRIS.* [Born in Ohio. Appointed from Ohio.]
2nd Lieut. Ord., 17 June, 1862. 1st Lieut., 3 March, 1863. Capt., 7 March, 1867.

Resigned 31 Dec., 1871. Bvt. Capt., 6 May, 1864, for gallant and meritorious service at the Battle of the Wilderness, Va.

SCHAFFER, FRANCIS B. [Born in Md. Appointed from Cal.]
2nd Lieut. 3rd Art., 7 June, 1855. Resigned 6 Feb., 1856.

SCHALL, WM. P. [Born in Penn. Appointed from Penn.]
Priv. Co. D, 51st Penn. Vols., 29 Oct., 1861, to 24 Jan., 1865. 2nd Lieut. 15th Inf., 23 Feb., 1866. 1st Lieut., 23 April, 1867. Resigned 14 May, 1868. Priv. Co. D, 21st Inf., 24 Oct., 1871, to 24 Oct., 1876. Priv. Co. I, 21st Inf., 12 March, 1884, to 11 March, 1889.

SCHAURTE, FREDERICK W. [Born in Prussia. Appointed from Army.]
Priv., Corpl. and 1st Sergt. Co. G, 2nd Inf., 13 Nov., 1854, to 21 Oct., 1861. Mustered out 10 Aug., 1862. 2nd Lieut. 2nd Cav., 11 June, 1862. 1st Lieut., 27 April, 1863. Lieut. Col. 2nd Ind. Home Guards, 27 Dec., 1862. Mustered out of Vol. Service, 31 May, 1865. Capt. 2nd Cav., 31 Aug., 1866. Resigned 7 May, 1867. Bvt. Capt., Maj. and Lieut. Col., 13 March, 1865, for gallant and meritorious service during the war.

SCHELL, HENRY S. [Born in Penn. Appointed from Penn.]
Asst. Surg., 5 Aug., 1861. Resigned 10 July, 1869. Bvt. Capt. and Maj., 13 March, 1865, for faithful and meritorious service during the war. Bvt. Lieut. Col., 28 Sept., 1866, for meritorious and distinguished service at Tybee Island, and Savannah, Ga., where cholera prevailed. Died 15 March, 1890.

SCHENCK, ALEXR. D.* [Born in Ohio. Appointed from Ala.]
Priv. Co. F, 1st Ohio Vols., 17 April, 1861. Discharged 16 Aug., 1861. Sergt. Co. B, 2nd Ohio Vols., 31 Aug., 1861. Discharged 18 Sept., 1863. Cadet Mil. Acad., 29 Sept., 1863. 2nd Lieut. 2nd Art., 17 June, 1867. 1st Lieut., 27 Jan., 1873. Capt., 8 March, 1894. Graduate of the Artillery School, 1869, 1886.

SCHENCK, BARD P.* [Born in Md. Appointed from N. Y.]
Addl. 2nd Lieut. 7th Inf., 12 June, 1887. 2nd Lieut. 12th Inf., 1 Sept., 1887. 1st Lieut. of Inf. (9th), 3 Jan., 1895. Wholly retired 10 July, 1896. Died 10 March, 1900.

SCHENCK, EDWIN.* [Born in N. Y. Appointed from N. Y.]
Bvt. 2nd Lieut. Art., 1 July, 1827. Resigned 30 Sept., 1828. Died 2 July, 1848.

SCHENCK, PETER V. [Born in N. J. Appointed from N. J.]
Asst. Surg., 28 May, 1861. Resigned 1 Jan., 1867. Bvt. Capt. and Maj., 13 March, 1865, for faithful and meritorious service during the war. Died 11 March, 1885.

SCHENCK, WILLIAM T. [Born in Md. Appointed from Army.]
Priv., Corpl. and Sergt. Troop I, 1st Cav., 25 Nov., 1891, to 1 Nov., 1894. 2nd Lieut. 10th Inf., 31 Oct., 1894. 1st Lieut. 25th Inf., 30 June, 1898. Killed in action, Philippine Islands, — Jan., 1900.

SCHENOFSKY, JULES C. A. [Born in Belgium. Appointed from Mo.]
Capt. A. A. de C., 11 June, 1862. Resigned 22 May, 1865. Capt. 9th U. S. Vet. Vols., 29 May, 1865. Mustered out 20 April, 1866. 2nd Lieut. 7th Inf., 11 May, 1866. Trans. to 5th Cav., 30 March, 1867. 1st Lieut., 12 Sept., 1868. Discharged 1 Oct., 1870.

SCHERER, LOUIS C.* [Born in Minn. Appointed from Minn.]
2nd Lieut. 5th Cav., 12 June, 1891. 1st Lieut. 4th Cav., 21 Nov., 1897. Capt. A. A. G. Vols., 12 May, 1898, to 7 March, 1899. Capt. 27th U. S. Vols., 5 July, 1899.

SCHIFFLER, JOHN K. [Born in Bavaria. Appointed from Army.]
Priv., Sergt. and 1st Sergt. Co. B, and Sergt. Maj. 16th Inf., 25 July, 1861, to 10 June, 1863. 2nd Lieut. 16th Inf., 1 June, 1863. 1st Lieut., 19 Oct., 1863. Cashiered 18 June, 1864.

SCHINDEL, JEREMIAH P. [Born in Penn. Appointed from Penn.]
1st Sergt. Co. A, 104th Penn. Vols., 6 Sept., 1861. Discharged 4 Nov., 1861. 2nd Lieut. 6th Inf., 24 Oct., 1861. Bvt. 1st Lieut., 30 Aug., 1862, for gallant and meritorious service in the Battle of Bull Run (2nd), Va. Bvt. Capt., 2 July, 1863, for gallant and meritorious service in the Battle of Gettysburg, Penn. 1st Lieut. 6th Inf., 8 Feb., 1864. R. Q. M., 1 July, 1865, to 1 Aug., 1866. Capt., 25 Feb., 1868. Died 9 Nov., 1894.

SCHINDEL, LOUIS P. [Born in Dak. Appointed from Penn.]
2nd Lieut. 6th Inf., 9 Sept., 1898.

SCHINDEL, S. J. BAYARD.* [Born in N. J. Appointed from Penn.]
Addl. 2nd Lieut. 3rd Art., 12 June, 1893. 2nd Lieut., 2 Nov., 1893. Trans. to 16th Inf., 25 Feb., 1895 (to rank from 12 June, 1894). Trans. to 6th Inf., 12 April, 1895. 1st Lieut., 26 April, 1898. Reg. Com., 10 March, 1899.

SCHLEY, THOMAS F. [Born in Md. Appointed from Army.]
Priv., 1st Cl. Priv., Corpl., Sergt. and 1st Cl. Sergt. Sig. Corps, 18 Jan., 1884, to 1 Aug., 1891. 2nd Lieut. 23rd Inf., 31 July, 1891. 1st Lieut., 26 April, 1898. Graduate of the Infantry and Cavalry School, 1897.

SCHMIDT, CLAUDIUS. [Born in Denmark. Appointed from Mass.]
1st Lieut. 18th Inf., 14 May, 1861. Resigned 30 June, 1862.

SCHMUCK, JACOB. [Born in Germany. Appointed from Army.]
Sergt. 2nd Art., 13 April, 1812, to Feb., 1814. 3rd Lieut. 2nd Art., 10 Feb., 1814. 2nd Lieut., 1 May, 1814. Trans. to Corps Art., 12 May, 1814. 1st Lieut., 20 April, 1818. Trans. to 4th Art., 1 June, 1821. Capt., 11 April, 1825. Died 10 April, 1835. Bvt. 1st Lieut., 25 July, 1814, for gallant conduct at the Battle of Niagara. Bvt. Capt., 25 July, 1824, for ten years' faithful service in one grade.

SCHOEFFEL, FRANCIS H.* [Born in N. Y. Appointed from N. Y.]
2nd Lieut. 17th Inf., 12 June, 1891. Trans. to 9th Inf., 10 June, 1892. 1st Lieut. 5th Inf., 16 Sept., 1897. Trans. to 9th Inf., 23 Nov., 1897.

SCHOEFFEL, JOHN B. [Born in N. Y. Appointed from Army.]
Priv. Co. —, 9th Inf., 26 Jan., 1894, to 25 Sept., 1897. Priv. and Corpl. Co. B, 9th Inf., 16 Dec., 1897, to 6 July, 1898. 2nd Lieut. 3rd Inf., 22 June, 1898. Trans. to 9th Inf., 27 Aug., 1898. 1st Lieut., 2 March, 1899.

SCHOFIELD, CHAS. B.* [Born in Ill. Appointed from Ill.]
2nd Lieut. 2nd Cav., 15 June, 1870. 1st Lieut., 14 June, 1879. Reg. Adj., 1 May, 1886, to 17 Jan., 1889. Capt., 19 June, 1890.

SCHOFIELD, GEORGE W. [Born in N. Y. Appointed from Mo.]
1st Lieut. 1st Mo. Art., 5 Oct., 1861. Capt., 1 Sept., 1862. Lieut. Col. 2nd Mo. Art., 9 March, 1864. Bvt. Col. Vols. and Bvt. Brig. Gen. Vols., 26 Jan., 1865, for gallant and meritorious service during the campaign in Georgia and Tennessee. Mustered out 20 Nov., 1865. Maj. 41st Inf., 28 July, 1866. Bvt. Lieut. Col., 2 March, 1867, for gallant and meritorious service in the Battle of Champion Hill, Miss. Bvt. Col., 2 March, 1867, for gallant and meritorious service in the Siege of Vicksburg, Miss. Unassigned 15 March, 1869. Ass'd to 10th Cav., 15 Dec., 1870. Lieut. Col. 6th Cav., 30 Dec., 1881. Died 17 Dec., 1882.

SCHOFIELD, JOHN M.* [Born in N. Y. Appointed from Ill.]
Bvt. 2nd Lieut. 2nd Art., 1 July, 1853. 2nd Lieut. 1st Art., 31 Aug., 1853. 1st Lieut., 3 March, 1855. Maj. 1st Mo. Vols., 26 April, 1861. Capt. 1st Art., 14 May, 1861. Capt. 11th Inf., 14 May, 1861, declined. Maj. 1st Mo. Art., 26 June, 1861. Brig. Gen. Vols., 21 Nov., 1861. Maj. Gen. Vols., 29 Nov., 1862. Expired by constitutional limitation, 4 March, 1863. Brig. Gen. Vols., 4 March, 1863. Maj. Gen. Vols., 12 May, 1863, to rank from 29 Nov., 1862. Brig. Gen. U. S. A., 30 Nov., 1864. Bvt. Maj. Gen., 13 March, 1865, for gallant and meritorious service in the Battle of Franklin, Tenn. Mustered out of Vol. Service, 1 Sept., 1866. Maj. Gen. U. S. A., 4 March, 1869. Lieut. Gen., 5 Feb., 1895. Retired by operation of law, 29 Sept., 1895. Medal of Honor for conspicuous gallantry at the Battle of Wilson's Creek, Mo., 10 Aug., 1861, where he led a regiment in a successful charge against the enemy; while Capt. 1st U. S. Art., Maj. 1st Missouri Inf., and acting Adj. Gen., Army of the West.

SCHOFIELD, RICHMOND McA. [Born in Va. Appointed from N. Y.]
2nd Lieut. 4th Cav., 11 Feb., 1889. 1st Lieut. 5th Cav., 14 Oct., 1896. Reg. Com., 27 May, 1899.

SCHONBORN, LOUIS. [Born in Prussia. Appointed from D. C.]
Priv., Corpl. and Sergt. Co. K, 2nd Art., and Gen. Ser., 3 May, 1854, to 1 April, 1863. 2nd Lieut. 3rd Inf., 19 Oct., 1867. Dismissed 15 Sept., 1871.

SCHOOLEY, DAVID. [Born in Penn. Appointed from Penn.]
Capt. 2nd Penn. Art., 26 Aug., 1862. Maj., 18 May, 1865. Mustered out 29 Jan., 1866. Capt. 40th Inf., 28 July, 1866. Trans. to 25th Inf., 20 April, 1869. Retired by operation of law, 1 April, 1888.

SCHOONOVER, RODOLPHUS. [Born in Penn. Appointed from Ind.]
1st Lieut. of Inf., 8 March, 1847; 3rd Drag., 9 April, 1847. Disbanded 31 July, 1848.

SCHOONOVER, WM. [Born in Penn. Appointed from Penn.]
2nd Lieut. 11th Inf., 30 Dec., 1847. Disbanded 17 Aug., 1848. Priv. Co. C. 176th Penn. Vols., 3 Nov., 1862. Maj., 28 Nov., 1862. Mustered out 19 Aug., 1863.

SCHREINER, EDWARD R. [Born in Penn. Appointed from Penn.]
Asst. Surg., 23 July, 1898.

SCHREINER, HERMAN. [Born in Penn. Appointed from Penn.]
Capt. C. S. Vols., 30 Aug., 1862. Bvt. Maj. Vols., 13 March, 1865, for meritorious service in his department during the war. 2nd Lieut. 11th Inf., 24 Feb., 1866. Bvt. Lieut. Col. Vols., 15 May, 1866, for long, faithful and zealous service. Mustered out of Vol. Service, 31 May, 1866. Trans. to 20th Inf., 21 Sept., 1866. 1st Lieut., 1 Nov., 1866. Unassigned 22 May, 1869. Ass'd to 9th Cav., 31 Dec., 1870. Capt., 9 Dec., 1871. Retired 20 March, 1879.

SCHREYER, GUSTAVUS. [Born in Germany. Appointed from Kan.]
Sergt. Co. A, 1st Mo. Cav., 20 Sept., 1862. Capt., 23 May, 1863. Mustered out 1 Sept., 1865. 2nd Lieut. 6th Cav., 23 Feb., 1866. 1st Lieut., 28 July, 1866. Discharged 1 Dec., 1870.

SCHRIVER, EDMUND.* [Born in Penn. Appointed from Penn.]
Bvt. 2nd Lieut. 2nd Art., 1 July, 1833. 2nd Lieut., 31 July, 1834. 1st Lieut., 1 Nov., 1836. Bvt. Capt. A. A. G., 7 July, 1838. Capt. 2nd Art., 17 Aug., 1842. Vacated commission of Capt. 2nd Art., 18 June, 1846. Resigned 31 July, 1846. Lieut. Col. 11th Inf., 14 May, 1861. Col A. A. de C., 18 May, 1862. Col. I. G., 13 March, 1863. Bvt. Brig. Gen., 1 Aug., 1864, for faithful and meritorious service in the field. Bvt. Maj. Gen., 13 March, 1865, for meritorious and distinguished service during the war. Retired, for over sixty-two years of age, 4 Jan., 1881. Died 10 Feb., 1899.

SCHROEDER, HENRY A.* [Born in Wis. Appointed from Wis.]
2nd Lieut. 4th Art., 12 June, 1880. Resigned 1 Oct., 1885.

SCHROEDER, HENRY B.* [Born in Md. Appointed from Md.]
Bvt. 2nd Lieut. 3rd Inf., 1 July, 1844. 2nd Lieut., 18 June, 1846. 1st Lieut., 4 Dec., 1847. Capt., 31 May, 1857. Resigned 30 May, 1861. Bvt. 1st Lieut., 20 Aug., 1847, for gallant and meritorious conduct at Contreras and Churubusco.

SCHUE, EUGENE D. [Born in Ky. Appointed from N. Y.]
Asst. Surg., 17 Feb., 1880. Died 1 Oct., 1882.

SCHULER, JOHN J.* [Born in Penn. Appointed from Penn.]
Bvt. 2nd Lieut. 2nd Art., 1 July, 1822. 2nd Lieut., 1st Art., 1 July, 1822. Resigned 30 April, 1828.

SCHULL, HERMAN W.* [Born in England. Appointed from S. Dak.]
2nd Lieut. 6th Art., 15 Feb., 1899. Trans. to 2nd Art., 4 April, 1899.

SCHULTZ, JOHN N. [Born in N. J. Appointed from Ind.]
Chap. 38th Inf., 28 July, 1866. Trans. to 24th Inf., 11 Nov., 1869. Resigned 23 July, 1875.

SCHULTZE, THILO. [Born in Prussia. Appointed from Mo.]
Priv. Co. K, 12th and Sergt. Co. H, 15th Mo. Vols., 13 Feb., 1863, to 13 March, 1865. 1st Lieut. 15th Mo. Vols., 13 March, 1865. Mustered out 25 Dec., 1865. 2nd Lieut. 14th Inf., 21 May, 1866. 1st Lieut., 24 May, 1867. R. Q. M., 19 April to 1 Oct., 1867. Reg. Adj., 1 Oct., 1867, to 30 April, 1869. Unassigned 22 July, 1869. Ass'd to 18th Inf., 3 May, 1870. Died 5 Oct., 1874.

SCHULZ, EDWARD H.* [Born in W. Va. Appointed from W. Va]. Addl. 2nd Lieut. Eng., 12 June, 1895. 2nd Lieut., 26 May, 1896. 1st Lieut., 5 July, 1898.

SCHUMM, HERMAN C.* [Born in Wis. Appointed from Wis.] Addl. 2nd Lieut. 3rd Art., 12 June, 1887. 2nd Lieut. 2nd Art., 20 Nov., 1887. 1st Lieut., 8 March, 1894. Graduate of the Artillery School, 1894.

SCHUREMAN, JAMES W.* [Born in N. J. Appointed from N. J.] Bvt. 2nd Lieut. 7th Inf., 1 July, 1842. 2nd Lieut. 2nd Inf., 25 Jan., 1844. 1st Lieut., 12 Jan., 1848. Died 30 Jan., 1852. Bvt. 1st Lieut., 20 Aug., 1847, for gallant and meritorious conduct at Contreras and Churubusco.

SCHUYLER, PHILIP, Jr. [Born in N. Y. Appointed from N. Y.] 1st Lieut. 14th Inf., 14 May, 1861. Reg. Adj., 5 Nov., 1861, to 11 July, 1862. Capt., 11 July, 1862. Resigned 30 June, 1865. Bvt. Maj., 9 April, 1865, for gallant and meritorious service during the campaign terminating with the surrender of Gen. Lee.

SCHUYLER, WALTER S.* [Born in N. Y. Appointed from N. Y.] 2nd Lieut. 5th Cav., 15 June, 1870. 1st Lieut., 20 July, 1876. Capt., 21 April, 1887. Maj. 2nd Cav., 18 Oct., 1899. Maj. A. A. G. Vols., 12 May, 1898, to 8 July, 1898. Col. 203rd N. Y. Vols., 9 July, 1898, to 25 March, 1899. Col. 46th U. S. Vols., 17 Aug., 1899. Bvt. 1st Lieut., 27 Feb., 1890, for gallant services in actions against Indians at Muchos Canons, Ariz., 25 Sept., 1872; on Lost River, Ariz., 26 June, 1873; at Salt River, Ariz., 28 April, 1874, and in the Red Rock Country, Ariz., 14 May, 1874. Bvt. Capt., 27 Feb., 1890, for gallantry in action against Indians in the Big Horn Mountains, Mont., 25 Nov., 1876.

SCHWAN, THEODORE. [Born in Germany. Appointed from Army.] Priv. Co. K, 10th Inf., 12 June, 1857. Corpl., 4 March, 1860. Sergt., 1 Sept., 1860. 1st Sergt., 1 April, 1861. Discharged 1 June, 1862. 1st Sergt., Co. K, 10th Inf., 1 June, 1862. Q. M. Sergt. 10th Inf., 12 April, 1863. 2nd Lieut. 10th Inf., 31 Oct., 1863. 1st Lieut., 9 April, 1864. R. Q. M., 6 Dec., 1864, to 14 March, 1866. Bvt. Capt., 1 Oct., 1864, for gallant service in the Battle of Chappel House, Va. Capt. 10th Inf., 14 March, 1866. Bvt. Maj., 2 March, 1867, for gallant and meritorious service during the war. Unassigned 19 May, 1869. Ass'd to 11th Inf., 13 Dec., 1869. Maj. A. A. G., 6 July, 1886. Lieut. Col. A. A. G., 19 Feb., 1895. Col. A. A. G., 18 May, 1898. Brig. Gen. Vols., 4 May, 1898, to 14 April, 1899 Brig. Gen. Vols., 14 April, 1899. Medal of Honor for most distinguished gallantry in action at Peebles' Farm, Va., 1 Oct., 1864, while in command of his regiment, which was on the picket line, and falling back before a superior force of the enemy, at the imminent risk of his own life, in dragging a wounded and helpless officer of his regiment to the rear, thus saving him from death or capture; while serving as 1st Lieut. 10th Inf.

SCHWARTZ, JOHN A. [Born in N. Y. Appointed from Ind.] 2nd Lieut. 6th Md. Vols., 2 Aug., 1862. 1st Lieut., 2 Sept., 1862. Resigned 24 Sept., 1864. 1st Lieut. Vet. Res. Corps, 28 Sept., 1864. Resigned 22 Feb., 1866. 2nd Lieut. 10th Inf., 23 Feb., 1866. Dismissed 30 Jan., 1867.

SCHWATKA, FREDK.* [Born in Ill. Appointed from Ore.] 2nd Lieut. 3rd Cav., 12 June, 1871. 1st Lieut., 20 March, 1879. Resigned 31 Jan., 1885.

SCHWENK, SAML. K. [Born in Penn. Appointed from Penn.] 1st Lieut. 50th Penn. Vols., 9 Sept., 1861. Capt., 1 Nov., 1862. Mustered out 12 Oct., 1864. Maj. 50th Penn. Vet. Vols., 28 Feb., 1865. Bvt. Lieut. Col., 25 March, 1865, for constant gallantry before Petersburg, and in the assault on Fort Steedman, Va. Lieut. Col. 50th Pa. Vet. Vols., 18 May, 1865. Bvt. Col. and Brig. Gen. Vols., 24 July, 1865, for meritorious service during the war. Mustered out 30 July, 1865. Capt. 9th U. S. Vet. Vols., 25 Oct., 1865. Mustered out 25 April, 1866. 1st Lieut. 41st Inf., 28 July, 1866. Reg. Adj., 15 June to 16 Dec., 1867. Bvt. Capt., 2 March, 1867, for gallant and meritorious service in the Battle of Spottsylvania, Va. Bvt. Maj., 2 March, 1867, for gallant and meritorious service in the Battle of Ny River, Va. Bvt. Lieut. Col., 2 March, 1867, for gallant and meritorious service in the Battle of Cold Harbor, Va. Capt. 41st Inf., 16 Dec., 1867. Unassigned 11 Nov., 1869. Ass'd to 8th Cav., 1 Jan., 1871. Retired 17 May, 1876.

SCOTT, ALBERT B.* [Born in Tex. Appointed from Md.] 2nd Lieut. 13th Inf., 12 June, 1880. 1st Lieut. 6th Inf., 12 Nov., 1890. Trans. to 13th Inf., 20 July, 1891. Capt., 26 April, 1898.

SCOTT, ALEXR. [Born in Md. Appointed from Ga.] Capt. of Inf., 8 March, 1847; 13th Inf., 9 April, 1847. Resigned 30 July, 1847.

SCOTT, DAVID I. [Born in England. Appointed from Army.] Priv. Co. K, 7th N. Y. State Militia, 16 June to 20 July, 1863. Priv. and Sergt. Co. G, 14th Inf.,27 Aug., 1863, to 19 July, 1864. 2nd Lieut. 10th Inf., 18 May, 1864. 1st Lieut., 3 Feb., 1865. Resigned 26 March, 1868. Bvt. 1st Lieut., 19 May, 1864, for gallant and meritorious service at the Battle of Spottsylvania, Va. Died 10 Feb., 1879.

SCOTT, DAVID P. [Born in Pa. Appointed from Army.] Priv. and Sergt. Co. F, 11th Inf., 27 Jan., 1864, to 27 Jan., 1867. 2nd Lieut. 11th Inf., 3 Jan., 1867. Trans. to 16th Inf., 14 April, 1869. Mustered out 1 Jan., 1871.

SCOTT, DAVID W. [Born in Va. Appointed from Ind.] 1st Lieut. of Inf., 10 March, 1847; 16th Inf., 9 April, 1847. Disbanded 20 July, 1848.

SCOTT, DOUGLAS M. [Born in Mass. Appointed from Penn.] 2nd Lieut. 4th Cav., 19 June, 1867. Trans. to 1st Inf., 16 Sept., 1869. 1st Lieut., 28 June, 1878. Capt., 20 Feb., 1884. Capt. C. S., 10 Dec., 1888. Retired for disability, with rank of Maj., 10 June, 1896.

SCOTT, EBEN G. [Born in Penn. Appointed from Penn.] 1st Lieut. 5th Art., 14 May, 1861. Resigned 27 April, 1863.

SCOTT, ERNEST D.* [Born in Canada. Appointed from Nebr.] 2nd Lieut. 6th Art., 26 April, 1898. Capt. 37th U. S. Vols., 5 July, 1899.

SCOTT, GEORGE E. [Born in N. Y. Appointed from Wis.]
1st Sergt. Co. G, 1st Wis. Vols., 17 May to 21 Aug., 1861. 1st Lieut. 1st Wis. Vols., 8 Oct., 1861. Mustered out 24 May, 1863. 1st Lieut. Vet. Res. Corps, 8 Aug., 1863. Capt., 29 Dec., 1863. Maj., 11 Feb., 1865. Bvt. Lieut. Col. Vols., 13 March, 1865, for faithful and meritorious service in the recruitment of the armies of the U. S. Mustered out 1 Nov., 1866. Capt. 24th Inf., 28 July, 1866. Died 16 July, 1868. Bvt. Maj., 2 March, 1867, for gallant and meritorious service in the action of Lawrenceburg, Ky.

SCOTT, GEORGE L.* [Born in Ore. Appointed from Ore.]
2nd Lieut. 6th Cav., 16 June, 1875. 1st Lieut., 29 May, 1881. Capt., 1 July, 1891.

SCOTT, GUY T. [Born in W. Va. Appointed from W. Va.]
2nd Lieut. 3rd Art., 9 July, 1898.

SCOTT, HARRY E. [Born in N. Y. Appointed from N. Y.]
Priv. Co. F, 22nd N. Y. Cav., 12 April to 1 Aug., 1865. 2nd Lieut. 6th Cav., 30 Nov., 1866. 1st Lieut., 8 June, 1867. Resigned 11 Sept., 1869.

SCOTT, HENRY L.* [Born in N. C. Appointed from N. C.]
Bvt. 2nd Lieut. 4th Inf., 1 July, 1833. 2nd Lieut., 31 Jan., 1836. 1st Lieut., 1 March, 1838. Reg. Adj., 30 Nov., 1838, to 1 April, 1840. Capt., 16 Feb., 1847. Lieut. Col. A. de C., to Lieut. Gen. Scott, 7 March, 1855, to 14 May, 1861. Col. I. G., 14 May, 1861. Retired 30 Oct., 1861. Resigned 31 Oct., 1862. Bvt. Maj., 20 Aug., 1847, for gallant and meritorious conduct at Contreras and Churubusco. Bvt. Lieut. Col., 13 Sept., 1847, for gallant and meritorious conduct at Chapultepec. Died 6 Jan., 1886.

SCOTT, HUGH L.* [Born in Ky. Appointed from N. J.]
2nd Lieut. 9th Cav., 15 June, 1876. Trans. to 7th Cav., 26 June, 1876. 1st Lieut., 28 June, 1878. Capt., 24 Jan., 1895. Maj. A. A. G. Vols., 12 May, 1898 Lieut. Col. A. A. G. Vols., 17 Aug., 1899.

SCOTT, JAMES R. [Born in Penn. Appointed from Penn.]
2nd Lieut. 7th Inf., 25 Oct., 1839. 1st Lieut., 15 July, 1845. Died 30 Oct., 1847.

SCOTT, JOHN. [Born in Scotland. Appointed from Ill.]
Corpl. Co. H, 25th Ill. Vols., 27 July, 1861. 2nd Lieut. 25th Ill. Vols., 23 Feb., 1863. 1st Lieut., 4 April, 1863. Capt., 1 March, 1864. Bvt. Maj. Vols., 13 March, 1865, for faithful and meritorious service. Mustered out 21 Sept., 1865. 2nd Lieut. 30th Inf., 7 March, 1867. R. Q. M., 1 Jan., 1869, to 23 March, 1869. Trans. to 4th Inf., 23 March, 1869. R. Q. M., 1 March, 1876. 1st Lieut., 1 March, 1876. Died 10 Nov., 1886.

SCOTT, JOHN B.* [Born in Conn. Appointed from Conn.]
Bvt. 2nd Lieut. 4th Art., 1 July, 1821. 2nd Lieut., 1 July, 1821. 1st Lieut., 31 July, 1827. Capt., 25 June, 1841. Maj. 3rd Art., 10 June, 1857. Died 22 Nov., 1860. Bvt. Maj., 9 May, 1846, for gallant conduct at Palo Alto and Resaca de la Palma.

SCOTT, JOHN F.* [Born in N. Y. Appointed from N. Y.]
Bvt. 2nd Lieut. 1st Art., 1 July, 1821. 2nd Lieut. 3rd Art., 1 July, 1821. Resigned 10 Oct., 1825. Died 7 Aug., 1837.

SCOTT, JOHN M.* [Born in Ky. Appointed from Ky.]
Bvt. 2nd Lieut. 1st Inf., 1 July, 1835. 2nd Lieut., 30 Nov., 1836. 1st Lieut., 7 July, 1838. Capt., 18 June, 1846. Died 26 Oct., 1850. Bvt. Maj., 23 Sept., 1846, for gallant and meritorious conduct at Monterey, Mex.

SCOTT, JOHN W.* [Born in Ohio. Appointed from Ohio.]
Bvt. 2nd Lieut. 2nd Inf., 1 July, 1835. Resigned 15 March, 1836. Died 5 Jan., 1859.

SCOTT, LUTHER. [Born in Penn. Appointed from Penn.]
1st Lieut. 2nd Art., 24 March, 1812. Trans. to Corps Art., 12 May, 1814. Capt., 24 May, 1817. Died 7 April, 1819. Bvt. Capt., 20 Feb., 1815, for distinguished and meritorious service.

SCOTT, MARTIN. [Born in Vt. Appointed from Vt.]
2nd Lieut. 26th Inf., 21 April, 1814. 1st Lieut., 20 May, 1814. Disbanded 15 June, 1815. 2nd Lieut. Rifle Reg., 18 April, 1818. 1st Lieut., 2 Nov., 1819. Trans. to 5th Inf., 1 June, 1821. Capt., 16 Aug., 1828. Maj. 5th Inf., 29 June, 1846. Killed 8 Sept., 1847, in Battle of Molino del Rey, Mex. Bvt. Maj., 9 May, 1846, for gallant conduct at Palo Alto and Resaca de la Palma. Bvt. Lieut. Col., 23 Sept., 1846, for gallant and meritorious conduct in the several conflicts at Monterey.

SCOTT, MOSES.* [Born in N. J. Apointed from N. J.]
Bvt. 2nd Lieut. 5th Inf., 1 July, 1831. 2nd Lieut., 1 Oct., 1833. Resigned 31 Aug., 1835. Died in 1858.

SCOTT, RICHARD W. [Born in Va. Appointed from Va.]
Ensign 35th Inf., 31 March, 1813. 3rd Lieut., 3 March, 1814. 2nd Lieut., 1 Oct., 1814. Trans. to 7th Inf., 17 May, 1815. 1st Lieut., 30 April, 1817. Killed 30 Nov., 1817, by Indians in Florida.

SCOTT, ROBT. J.* [Born in Va. Appointed from Md.]
3rd Lieut. Corps Art., 2 March, 1815. 2nd Lieut., 15 June, 1817. Resigned 4 Nov., 1818. Died 4 May, 1834.

SCOTT, ROBERT N. [Born in Tenn. Appointed from Cal.]
2nd Lieut. 4th Inf., 21 Feb., 1857. 1st Lieut., 14 May, 1861. Reg. Adj., 1 July to 25 Sept., 1861. Capt., 25 Sept., 1861. Bvt. Maj., 27 June, 1862, for gallant and meritorious service in the Battle of Gaines' Mills, Va. Maj. A. A. G. Vols., 28 Sept., 1864. Bvt. Lieut. Col., 13 March, 1865, for meritorious service in connection with the organization of the Vol. army of the U. S. Lieut. Col. A. A. G., 5 July, 1865, to 1 Aug., 1865. Mustered out of Vol. Service, 1 Jan., 1867. Unassigned 23 March, 1869. Ass'd to 16th Inf., 29 Jan., 1870. Trans. to 3rd Art., 31 Dec., 1870. Maj., 20 March, 1879. Lieut. Col., 22 March, 1885. Died 5 March, 1887.

SCOTT, SAML. C. [Born in Va. Appointed from La.]
2nd Lieut. 14th Inf., 30 Dec., 1847. Disbanded 26 July, 1848.

SCOTT, SAML. D. [Born in Penn. Appointed from Penn.]
Asst. Surg. of Inf., 23 Feb., 1847; 11th Inf., 9 April, 1847. Resigned 14 Feb., 1848.

SCOTT, WALTER S. [Born in Ark. Appointed from Cal.]
2nd Lieut. 25th Inf., 31 Oct., 1874. 1st Lieut., 22 March, 1879. Capt. 25th Inf., 24 Feb., 1891. Maj. 4th Inf., 8 Sept., 1899.

SCOTT, WM. H. [Born in Va. Appointed from Miss.]
2nd Lieut. of Inf., 8 March, 1847; 11th Inf., 9 April, 1847. Trans. to 4th Inf., 14 March, 1848. 1st Lieut., 1 Aug., 1852. Resigned 7 July, 1853. Bvt. 1st Lieut., 20 Aug., 1847, for gallant and meritorious conduct at Contreras and Churubusco, Mex.

SCOTT, WILLIAM H. [Born in Penn. Appointed from Ill.]
Post Chap., 19 Feb., 1884. Retired for disability, 9 Sept., 1897.

SCOTT, WILLIAM S.* [Born in Texas. Appointed from Texas.]
2nd Lieut. 1st Cav., 12 June, 1880. 1st Lieut. 7th Cav., 15 Jan., 1891. Trans. to 1st Cav., 27 Feb., 1891. Capt., 2 March, 1899. Capt. A. A. G. Vols., 28 May, 1898. Maj. A. A. G. Vols., 17 Sept., 1898, to 12 May, 1899. Lieut. Col. 44th U. S. Vols., 17 Aug., 1899. Graduate of the Infantry and Cavalry School, 1887.

SCOTT, WINFIELD. [Born in Va. Appointed from Va.]
Capt. Light Art., 3 May, 1808. Lieut. Col. 2nd Art., 6 July, 1812. Col., 12 March, 1813. Brig. Gen., 9 March, 1814. Maj. Gen., 25 June, 1841. Commander-in-Chief of the Army, 5 July, 1841, to 1 Nov., 1861. Retired 1 Nov., 1861. Died 29 May, 1866. Bvt. Maj. Gen., 25 July, 1814, for distinguished service in the Battles of Chippewa, Niagara, etc. Bvt. Lieut. Gen., 29 March, 1847, for eminent service in the war with Mex., the day on which the U. S. forces under his command captured Vera Cruz, and the Castle of San Juan d'Ulloa. Presented with a gold medal under resolution of Congress, 3 Nov., 1814, with suitable emblems and devices, in testimony of the high sense entertained by Congress of his distinguished services in the successive conflicts of Chippewa and Niagara, and of his uniform gallantry and good conduct in sustaining the reputation of the arms of the U. S. The following resolution of Congress is of 9 March, 1848: "That the thanks of Congress be, and they are hereby, presented to Maj. Gen. Winfield Scott, Commander-in-Chief of the Army in Mex., and through him to the officers and men of the Regular and Vol. Corps under him, for their uniform gallantry and good conduct conspiciously displayed at the siege and capture of the city of Vera Cruz and Castle of San Juan d'Ulloa, 29 March, 1847, for the successive Battles of "Section 2. That the President of the U. S. be, and is hereby, requested to cause Cerro Gordo, 19 and 20 April, and the victories achieved in front of the City of Mexico, 8, 11, 12 and 13 Sept., and the Capture of the Metropolis, 14 Sept., 1847, in which the Mexican troops, greatly superior in numbers, and with every advantage of position, were in every conflict signally defeated by the American arms. "Section 2. That the President of the U. S. be, and is hereby, requested to cause to be struck a gold medal with devices emblematical of the series of brilliant victories achieved by the Army, and presented to Maj. Gen. Winfield Scott, as a testimony of the high sense entertained by Congress of his valor, skill and judicious conduct in the memorable campaign of 1847."

SCOTT, WINFIELD. [Born in Mich. Appointed from Nev.]
Capt. 126th N. Y. Vols., 22 Aug., 1862, to 23 Sept., 1864. Post Chap., 27 July, 1882. Retired for disability, 26 March, 1898.

SCOUTEN, ABRAHAM. [Born in N. Y. Appointed from N. Y.]
2nd Lieut. 10th Inf., 22 May, 1847. Disbanded 15 Aug., 1848.

SCREVEN, RICHD. B.* [Born in S. C. Appointed from S. C.]
Bvt. 2nd Lieut. 2nd Inf., 1 July, 1829. 2nd Lieut., 1 July, 1829. Trans. to 4th Inf., 18 Aug., 1831. 1st Lieut., 31 Jan., 1836. Capt. 8th Inf., 7 July, 1838. Died 15 May, 1851. Bvt. Maj., 23 Sept., 1846, for gallant and meritorious conduct at Monterey. Bvt. Lieut. Col., 8 Sept., 1847, for gallant and meritorious conduct at Molino del Rey, Mex.

SCRIVEN, GEORGE P.* [Born in Penn. Appointed from Ill.]
2nd Lieut. 8th Inf., 14 June, 1878. Trans. to 3rd Art., 13 June, 1879. 1st Lieut., 6th April, 1885. 1st Lieut. Sig. Corps, 18 Dec., 1890. Capt. (fourteen years' service), 14 June, 1892. Maj. Chf. Sig. Off. Vols., 20 May, 1898, to 17 April, 1899. Maj. Sig. Off. Vols., 17 April, 1899.

SCULL, EDWARD. [Born in Penn. Appointed from Ind.]
Surg. Ind. Vols., 1811 to 1812. Surg. 19th Inf., 8 April, 1814. Trans. to 22nd Inf., 21 May, 1814. Trans. to 1st Inf., 17 May, 1815. Died 28 Nov., 1815.

SCULLY, JAMES W. [Born in Ireland. Appointed from Tenn.]
Priv. Co. K, 1st Art., 20 Sept., 1856. Corpl., 21 Sept., 1858. Sergt., 2 Jan., 1860. Discharged 20 Sept., 1861. 1st Lieut. R. Q. M. 10th Tenn. Vols., 14 July, 1862. Lieut. Col. 10th Tenn. Vols., 21 Aug., 1863. Col., 6 June, 1864. Mustered out 25 May, 1865. Capt. A. Q. M. Vols., 25 Sept., 1865. Capt. A. Q. M., U. S. A., 27 Sept., 1865, Bvt. Maj., 27 Sept., 1865, for gallant and meritorious service in the Battle of Mill Springs, Ky. Bvt. Lieut. Col., 27 Sept., 1865, for gallant and meritorious service in the Battle of Shiloh, Tenn. Bvt. Col., 27 Sept., 1865, for gallant and meritorious service in the Battle of Nashville, Tenn. Maj. Q. M., 25 Jan., 1883. Lieut. Col. D. Q. M. G., 12 Sept., 1894. Col. A. Q. M. G., 4 Feb., 1898.

SEARIGHT, JOSEPH D.* [Born in Md. Appointed from Pa.]
Bvt. 2nd Lieut. 4th Inf., 1 July, 1826. 2nd Lieut. 6th Inf., 1 July, 1826. 1st Lieut., 18 April, 1835. Capt., 25 Dec., 1837. Resigned 7 Nov., 1845. Died 22 Jan., 1885.

SEARLE, FREDK.* [Born in England. Appointed from Mass.]
Bvt. 2nd Lieut. 1st Art., 1 July, 1823. 2nd Lieut. 4th Art., 1 July, 1823. 1st Lieut., 20 Aug., 1831. Capt. A. Q. M., 7 July, 1838. Died 19 July, 1853. Bvt. Maj., 25 Nov., 1839, for gallant and good conduct in the war against the Florida Indians.

SEARLE, ZETUS S.* [Born in N. J. Appointed from N.Y.]
Bvt. 2nd Lieut. 8th Inf., 1 July, 1850. Resigned 31 Oct., 1850. Died 2 April, 1876.

SEARS, CLAUDIUS W.* [Born in Mass. Appointed from N. Y.]
2nd Lieut. 8th Inf., 1 July, 1841. Resigned 10 Oct., 1842.

SEARS, CLINTON B.* [Born in N. Y. Appointed from Va.]
Priv. Co. G, 95th Ohio Vols., 24 July, 1862. Corpl., 19 Aug., 1862. Discharged 20 Sept., 1863. Cadet at Mil. Acad., 16 Sep., 1863. 2nd Lieut. Eng., 17 June, 1867. 1st Lieut., 17 June, 1867. Capt., 9 April, 1880. Maj., 20 Sept., 1892.

SEARS, HENRY B.* [Born in Mass. Appointed from Mass.]
Bvt. 2nd Lieut. 2nd Art., 1 July, 1846. 2nd Lieut., 3 March, 1847. 1st Lieut., 27 Oct., 1847. Resigned 30 June, 1849. Bvt. 1st Lieut., 15 Aug., 1847, for gallant and meritorious conduct in several affairs with Guerrilleros at Paso Ovejas, National Bridge, and Cerro Gordo, Mex. Died 12 Feb., 1880.

SEATON, AUGUSTINE F.* [Born in D. C. Appointed from D. C.]
Bvt. 2nd Lieut. 7th Inf., 1 July, 1833. 2nd Lieut., 28 Sept., 1834. Died 18 Nov., 1835.

SEATON, WM. [Born in D. C. Apointed from D. C.]
2nd Lieut. 1st Inf., 13 Feb., 1818. 1st Lieut., 1 Jan., 1819. Dropped 26 July, 1819.

SEAWELL, WASHINGTON.* [Born in Va. Appointed from Va.]
Bvt. 2nd Lieut. 7th Inf., 1 July, 1825. 2nd Lieut., 1 July, 1825. 1st Lieut. 1st Drag., 4 March, 1833, declined. 1st Lieut. 7th Inf., 12 July, 1833. Capt., 31 July, 1836. Bvt. Maj., 18 July, 1841, for meritorious and sucessful service in the war against the Florida Indians. Maj. 2nd Inf., 3 March, 1847. Lieut. Col. 8th Inf., 23 Feb., 1852. Col. 6th Inf., 17 Oct., 1860. Retired 20 Feb., 1862. Bvt. Brig. Gen., 13 March, 1865, for long and faithful service in the Army. Died 8 Jan., 1888.

SEAWELL, WM. H. [Born in Va. Appointed from Tenn.]
2nd Lieut. of Inf., 22 March, 1847; 14th Inf., 9 April, 1847. R. Q. M., 8 Aug., 1847, to 29 July, 1848. 1st Lieut., 21 Dec., 1847. Disbanded 29 July, 1848. Died 29 May, 1875.

SEAY, SAMUEL, Jr.* [Born in Tenn. Appointed from Tenn.]
2nd Lieut. 21st Inf., 12 June, 1887. 1st Lieut. 14th Inf., 13 Aug., 1894. Capt. 23rd Inf., 2 March, 1899. Capt. A. A. G. Vols., 12 May to 30 Nov., 1898.

SEBREE, LEROY E. [Born in Ill. Appointed from Ill.]
Priv. Sig. Corps, 29 Feb., 1872. Sergt., 8 Feb., 1873. Re-enlisted 28 Feb., 1877. Discharged 3 Nov., 1878. 2nd Lieut. Sig. Corps, 1 Nov., 1878. Died 29 Jan., 1888.

SEDDON, JOHN. [Born in Va. Appointed from Va.]
2nd Lieut. of Inf., 8 March, 1847; 11th Inf., 9 April, 1847. Resigned 13 May, 1847.

SEDGWICK, JOHN.* [Born in Conn. Appointed from Conn.]
2nd Lieut. 2nd Art., 1 July, 1837. 1st Lieut., 19 April, 1839. Capt., 26 Jan., 1849. Maj. 1st Cav., 8 March, 1855. Lieut. Col. 2nd Cav., 16 March, 1861. Col. 1st Cav., 25 April, 1861; 4th Cav., 3 Aug., 1861. Brig. Gen. Vols., 31 Aug., 1861. Maj. Gen. Vols., 4 July, 1862. Killed 9 May, 1864, at the Battle of Spottsylvania, Va. Bvt. Capt., 20 Aug., 1847, for gallant and meritorious conduct at Contreras and Churubusco. Bvt. Maj., 13 Sept., 1847, for gallant and meritorious conduct at Chapultepec.

SEELEY, ERWIN. [Born in Penn. Appointed from Army.]
Priv. and Sergt. Maj. 4th Art., 1 Sept., 1863, to 8 Sept., 1864. 2nd Lieut. 4th Art., 30 Aug., 1864. 1st Lieut., 3 July, 1866. Cashiered 22 Aug., 1870.

SEELEY, FRANCIS W. [Born in Ohio. Appointed from Army.]
Priv., Corpl., Sergt. and 1st Sergt. Batty E, 3rd Art., 15 Feb., 1855, to 26 Feb., 1861. Bvt. 2nd Lieut. 3rd Art., 19 Sept., 1860. 2nd Lieut. 4th Art., 4 Feb., 1861. 1st Lieut., 14 May, 1861. R. Q. M., 1 Oct., 1863, to 11 July, 1864. Capt., 11 July, 1864. Resigned 31 Aug., 1864.

SEHON, JOHN L. [Born in Ga. Appointed from Ga.]
2nd Lieut. 4th Inf., 10 Oct., 1883. 1st Lieut. 11th Inf., 12 March, 1891. Trans. to 20th Inf., 20 July, 1891. Capt. A. A. G. Vols., 12 May to 15 Nov., 1898. Graduate of the Infantry and Cavalry School, 1889. Retired for disability with rank of Capt., 15 Aug., 1898.

SELDEN, GEORGE DE V. [Born in Penn. Appointed from Army.]
2nd Lieut. 150th Pa. Vols., 4 Sept., 1862, to 2 April, 1863. Priv. Gen. Mounted Ser. 6 April, 1863. 2nd Lieut. 2nd Cav., 6 April, 1863. Died 17 Sept., 1863, of wounds received at the Battle of Gettysburg, Pa.

SELDEN, HENRY R.* [Born in Vt. Appointed from Vt.]
Bvt. 2nd Lieut. 1st Inf., 1 July, 1843. 2nd Lieut. 5th Inf., 25 March, 1846. 1st Lieut., 8 Sept., 1847. Reg. Adj., 1 May to 18 Oct., 1855. Capt., 18 Oct., 1855. Maj. 13th Inf., 1 July, 1863. Col. 1st N. Mex. Vols., 25 April, 1864. Died 2 Feb., 1865.

SELDEN, JOSEPH. [Born in Va. Appointed from Va.]
Capt. 2nd Light Drag., 12 March, 1812. Maj. 3rd Rifles, 21 Feb., 1814. Retained 17 May, 1815, as Capt. Rifle Reg., with Bvt. of Maj. from 21 Feb., 1814. Trans. to Corps Art., 7 Jan., 1820. Resigned 13 May, 1820. Bvt. Maj., 21 Feb., 1814, for meritorious service. Bvt. Lieut. Col., 1 May, 1815, for distinguished service.

SELDEN, JOSEPH. [Born in Va. Appointed from Va.]
2nd Lieut. 8th Inf., 7 July, 1838. 1st Lieut., 7 Sept., 1841. Capt., 1 Jan., 1848. Resigned 27 April, 1861. Bvt. Capt., 20 Aug., 1847, for gallant and meritorious conduct at Contreras and Churubusco. Bvt. Maj., 13 Sept., 1847, for gallant and meritorious conduct at Chapultepec, Mex.

SELLERS, EDWIN E. [Born in Penn. Appointed from Penn.]
2nd Lieut. 10th Inf., 24 Oct., 1861. Bvt. 1st Lieut., 3 May, 1863, for gallant and meritorious service in the Battle of Chancellorsville, Va. 1st Lieut. 10th Inf., 1 June, 1863. Bvt. Capt., 2 July, 1863, for gallant and meritorious service in

the Battle of Gettysburg, Penn. Capt. 10th Inf., 17 Feb., 1864. Bvt. Maj., 13 March, 1865, for gallant and meritorious service during the war. Died 8 April, 1884.

SELLMER, CHAS. [Born in Germany. Appointed from Maine.]
Priv. Co. D, 1st Art., 8 Nov., 1854. Corpl., 8 Dec., 1856. Sergt., 1 Sept., 1857. Discharged 8 Sept., 1859. Sergt. Co. D, 1st Art., 8 Sept., 1859. 1st Sergt., 20 Aug., 1861. Discharged 30 June, 1863. 1st Lieut. 11th Maine Vols., 1 July, 1863. Capt., 17 July, 1864. Bvt. Maj. Vols., 2 April, 1865, for conspicuous gallantry in the assault on Fort Gregg, Va. Bvt. Lieut. Col. Vols., 13 March, 1865, for gallant and meritorious service during the war. Mustered out 9 Feb., 1866. 2nd Lieut. 2nd Inf., 2 Sept., 1867. Bvt. 1st Lieut., 2 Sept., 1867, for gallant and meritorious service in the capture of Fort Gregg, Va. Bvt. Capt., 2 Sept., 1867, for gallant and meritorious service in the Battle of Appomattox C. H., Va. Unassigned 17 April, 1869. Ass'd to 3rd Art., 14 July, 1869. 1st Lieut., 2 July, 1877. Graduate of the Artillery School, 1872. Retired for over thirty years' service, 31 July, 1891.

SELLS, DAVID M. [Born in Iowa. Appointed from Iowa.]
Corpl. Co. D, 2nd Iowa Vols., 27 May to 27 Aug., 1861. 2nd Lieut. U. S. Marine Corps, 25 Nov., 1861. Resigned 17 July, 1863. Lieut. Col. 107th U. S. Col. Inf., 24 July, 1864. Bvt. Col. Vols., 13 March, 1865, for faithful service. Mustered out 22 Nov., 1866. Capt. 41st Inf., 28 July, 1866. Unassigned 1 Sept., 1969. Discharged 31 Dec., 1870.

SEMIG, BERNARD G. [Born in Hungary. Appointed from Cal.]
Priv. Co. H, 9th N. Y. Vols., 4 May, 1861, to 1 April, 1863. Hosp. Stwd., 20 May, 1863. Discharged 27 June, 1864. Med. Cadet, 2 July, 1864, to 5 April, 1865. 1st Lieut. Asst. Surg., 10 Nov., 1874. Capt. Asst. Surg., 10 Nov., 1879. Died 1 Aug., 1883.

SEMPLE, JAMES Y. [Born in Pa. Appointed from Army.]
Sergt. and 1st Sergt. Co. B, 6th Ohio Vols., 20 April to 11 Oct., 1861. Priv. 15th Inf., 11 Oct. to 4 Nov., 1861. 2nd Lieut. 15th Inf., 30 Oct., 1861. 1st Lieut., 24 June, 1862. Reg. Adj., 14 Aug. to 29 Dec., 1865. Capt., 29 Dec., 1865. Died 11 May, 1867. Bvt. Capt., 31 Dec., 1862, for gallant and meritorious service at the Battle of Murfreesboro, Tenn.

SEMPLE, JOSEPH E. [Born in Penn. Appointed from N. Y.]
Asst. Surg. U. S. N., 22 Sept., 1854. Resigned 1 May, 1860. Asst. Surg., 5 Aug., 1861. Died 27 Aug., 1872. Bvt Capt. and Maj., 13 March, 1865, for faithful and meritorious service during the war.

SENTER, GERMAN. [Born in Mass. Appointed from Mass.]
Surg.'s Mate 3rd Art., 14 April, 1812. Maj. Surg. 29th Inf., 9 July, 1814. Disbanded 15 June, 1815. Reinstated as Post Surg., 17 May, 1816. Dismissed 2 Oct., 1820.

SERGEANT, WM. [Born in Penn. Appointed from Penn.
Capt. 12th Inf., 14 May, 1861. Col. 210th Penn. Vols., 24 Sept., 1864. Died 11 April, 1865, of wounds received in action at Gravelly Run, Va., 31 March, 1865.

SETON, HENRY. [Born in N. Y. Apointed from N. Y.]
Capt. 54th N. Y. Vols., 16 April, 1864. Mustered out 14 April, 1866. 2nd Lieut. 4th Inf., 11 May, 1866. 1st Lieut., 17 May, 1872. Capt., 3 Jan., 1885. Maj. 12th Inf., 23 Dec., 1898. Retired for over thirty years' service, 10 Oct., 1899.

SETTLE, DOUGLAS.* [Born in N. C. Appointed from N. C.]
2nd Lieut. 10th Inf., 12 June, 1891. 1st Lieut., 26 April, 1898, Capt. A. A. G. Vols., 12 May to 31 Dec., 1898.

SEVER, WM. J. [Born in Mass. Appointed from Mass.]
3rd Lieut. 1st Art., 1 Aug., 1813. 2nd Lieut., 31 Dec., 1813. Trans. to Corps Art., 12 May, 1814. Resigned 1 Dec., 1815. Died 15 Sept., 1835.

SEVIER, ROBT.* [Born in Tenn. Appointed from Tenn.]
Bvt. 2nd Lieut. 6th Inf., 1 July, 1828. 2nd Lieut., 1 July, 1828. 1st Lieut., 10 Aug., 1836. Reg. Adj., 1 Aug., 1836, to 31 Oct., 1837. Resigned 31 Oct., 1837. Died 16 May, 1879.

SEWARD, AUGUSTUS H.* [Born in N. Y. Appointed at Large.]
Bvt. 2nd Lieut. 8th Inf., 1 July, 1847. 2nd Lieut. 5th Inf., 13 Sept., 1847. 1st Lieut., 30 April, 1853. Capt., 19 Jan., 1859. Maj. P. M., 27 March, 1861. Died 11 Sept., 1876. Bvt. Lieut. Col., 13 March, 1865, for faithful and meritorious service during the war. Bvt. Col., 13 March, 1865, for faithful and meritorious service in the Pay Dept. during the war.

SEWARD, DUDLEY. [Born in N. Y. Appointed from Ohio.]
Sergt. Co. G, 19th Ohio Vols., 22 April to 31 Aug., 1861. Capt. 2nd Ohio Cav., 19 Sept., 1861. Maj., 18 Sept., 1862. Lieut. Col., 1 May, 1865. Mustered out 11 Sept., 1865. Capt. 8th Cav., 28 July, 1866. Mustered out 28 Dec., 1870. Bvt. Maj., 2 March, 1867, for gallant and meritorious service in action at Monticello, Ky., 9 June, 1863. Died 24 May, 1882.

SEWELL, JOHN S.* [Born in Tenn. Appointed from Ky.]
Addl. 2nd Lieut. Eng., 12 June, 1891. 2nd Lieut., 18 Sept., 1894. 1st Lieut., 25 Oct., 1895. Maj. 1st Vol. Eng., 31 May, 1898, to 25 Jan., 1899.

SEWELL, ROBERT. Born in N. J. Appointed from N. J.]
2nd Lieut. 7th Cav., 7 June, 1892. 1st Lieut. 1st Cav., 24 Oct., 1898. Capt. A. Q. M., 1 Sept., 1899. Capt. A. A. G. Vols., 12 May, 1898, to 24 Aug., 1899. Capt. 41st U. S. Vols., 17 Aug. to 1 Sept., 1899

SEYBURN, JOHN R [Born in Maine. Appointed from Maine.]
Priv., Corpl. and Sergt. Co. A, 18th Inf., 23 June, 1887, to 7 Nov., 1890. 2nd Lieut. 24th Inf., 6 Nov., 1890. 1st Lieut.8th Inf., 7 Aug., 1897. Graduate of the Infantry and Cavalry School, 1895.

SEYBURN, STEPHEN Y. [Born in Maine. Appointed from La.]
2nd Lieut. 10th Inf., 15 Oct., 1875. 1st Lieut., 17 March, 1883. Capt. 10th Inf., 19 May, 1893. Maj. I. G. Vols., 12 May, 1898. Col. 202nd N. Y. Vols., 1 Aug., 1898. Resigned 15 July, 1899.

SEYMOUR, THOS. H. [Born in Conn. Appointed from Conn.]
Maj. of Inf., 16 March, 1847; 9th Inf., 9 April, 1847. Lieut. Col 12th Inf., 12 Aug., 1847. Disbanded 25 July, 1848. Bvt. Col., 13 Sept., 1847, for gallant and meritorious conduct in the Batle of Chapultepec, Mex. Died 3 Sept., 1868.

SEYMOUR, THOS. H. [Born in Conn. Appointed from Conn.]
2nd Lieut. 25th Inf., 6 July, 1812. 1st Lieut., 20 June, 1813. Capt., 25 July, 1814. Trans. to 6th Inf., 17 May, 1815. Dismissed 7 June, 1815.

SEYMOUR, TRUMAN.* [Born in Vt. Appointed from Vt.]
Bvt. 2nd Lieut. 1st Art., 1 July, 1846. 2nd Lieut., 3 March, 1847. Bvt. 1st Lieut., 18 April, 1847, for gallant and meritorious conduct in the Battle of Cerro Gordo. Bvt. Capt., 20 Aug., 1847, for gallant and meritorious conduct in the Battles of Contreras and Churubusco. 1st Lieut. 1st Art., 26 Aug., 1847. Capt., 22 Nov., 1860. Bvt. Maj., 14 April, 1861, for gallant and meritorious service during the defence of Fort Sumter, S. C. Trans. to 5th Art., 14 May, 1861. Brig. Gen. Vols., 28 April, 1862. Bvt. Lieut. Col., 14 Sept., 1862, for gallant and meritorious service in the Battle of South Mountain, Md. Bvt. Col., 17 Sept., 1862, for gallant and meritorious service in the Battle of Antietam, Md. Bvt. Brig. Gen., 13 March, 1865, for gallant and meritorious service in the capture of Petersburg, Va. Bvt. Maj. Gen., 13 March, 1865, for gallant and meritorious service in the field during the war. Bvt. Maj. Gen. Vols., 13 March, 1865, for ability and energy in handling his division, and for gallantry and valuable service in action. Mustered out of Vol. Service, 24 Aug., 1865. Maj. 5th Art., 13 Aug., 1866. Retired 1 Nov., 1876. Died 30 Oct., 1891.

SHAAFF, ARTHUR. [Born in D. C. Appointed from Ga.]
2nd Lieut. 4th Inf., 30 June, 1855. Resigned 10 July, 1861.

SHAAFF, JOHN T.* [Born in D. C. Appointed from D. C.]
Bvt. 2nd Lieut. 6th Inf., 1 July, 1851. 2nd Lieut., 9 June, 1853. Trans. to 2nd Cav., 3 March, 1855. 1st Lieut., 1 May, 1856. Resigned 22 Feb., 1861. Died 2 July, 1877.

SHACKELFORD, GEORGE T. [Born in Va. Appointed from Va.]
Priv. and Corpl. Gen. Ser., 19 Feb., 1847, to 28 Jan., 1848. 2nd Lieut. 6th Inf., 30 Dec., 1847. Died 28 Sept., 1848.

SHACKELFORD, MUSCOE L.* [Born in Va. Appointed from Va.]
Bvt. 2nd Lieut. 2nd Art., 1 July, 1836. 2nd Lieut., 31 July, 1836. 1st Lieut., 7 July, 1838. Died 12 Oct., 1847, of wounds received in the Battle of Molino del Rey, Mex.

SHADE, WM. G. [Born in Md. Appointed from Md.]
Ensign 14th Inf., 18 March, 1813. 3rd Lieut., 1 Oct., 1813. Reg. Adj., Nov., 1813, to June, 1815. 2nd Lieut., 31 Aug., 1814. Disbanded 15 June, 1815. Reinstated 2 Dec., 1815, in Corps Art. Resigned 1 April, 1816. 2nd Lieut. Rifle Reg., 22 May, 1817. 1st Lieut., 15 Feb., 1818. Resigned 10 Nov., 1818.

SHAFFER, PEARL M. [Born in Iowa. Appointed from Iowa.]
2nd Lieut 13th Inf., 9 July, 1898. 1st Lieut, 2 March, 1899.

SHAFTER, WM. R. [Born in Mich. Appointed from Mich.]
1st Lieut. 7th Mich. Vols., 22 Aug., 1861. Discharged 22 Aug., 1862. Maj. 19th Mich. Vols., 5 Sept., 1862. Lieut. Col., 5 June, 1863. Col. 17th U. S. Col. Troops, 19 April, 1864. Bvt. Brig. Gen. Vols., 13 March, 1865, for gallant and meritorious service during the war. Mustered out 2 Nov., 1866. Lieut. Col. 41st Inf., 28 July, 1866. Bvt. Col., 2 March, 1867, for gallant and meritorious service in the Battle of Gettysburg, Pa. Unassigned 15 March, 1869. Ass'd to 24th Inf., 14 April, 1869. Col. 1st Inf., 4 March, 1879. Brig. Gen., 3 May, 1897. Maj. Gen. Vols., 4 May, 1898. Retired by operation of law, 16 Oct., 1899. Medal of Honor for most distinguished gallantry in the Battle of Fair Oaks, Va., 31 May, 1862; while serving as 1st Lieut. Co. I, 7th Mich. Inf., in command of pioneers; voluntarily taking an active part in that battle, and remaining on the field, although wounded, until the close of the engagement.

SHALER, CHAS.* [Born in Penn. Appointed from Fla.]
Sergt. Co. I, 12th Penn. Vols., 25 April, 1861. Discharged 5 Aug., 1861. Cadet Mil. Acad., 1 Sept., 1863. 2nd Lieut. 5th Art., 17 June, 1867. Trans. to Ord., 5 July, 1867. 1st Lieut., 23 June, 1874. Capt., 4 March, 1879. Maj., 22 Feb., 1897. Lieut Col. Chf. Ord. Off. Vols., 18 July, 1898, declined.

SHANKS, DAVID C.* [Born in Va. Appointed from Va.]
2nd Lieut. 18th Inf., 15 June, 1884. 1st Lieut., 22 June, 1890. Capt., 26 April, 1898. Maj. 2nd Va. Vols., 1 June to 16 Dec., 1898.

SHANNON, SAML. [Born in Penn. Appointed from Army.]
Sergt. 36th Inf., 19 March to July, 1814. Ensign 14th Inf., 27 July, 1814. 3rd Lieut., 5 Aug., 1814. Disbanded 15 June, 1815. 2nd Lieut. Rifle Reg., 10 Sept., 1818. 1st Lieut., 23 Feb., 1820. Trans. to 6th Inf., 1 June, 1821. Trans. to 1st Inf., 6 Jan., 1823. Capt., 28 July, 1831. Died 4 Sept., 1836. Bvt. Capt., 23 Feb., 1830, for ten years' faithful service in one grade.

SHANNON, WM. C. [Born in N. H. Appointed from Maine.]
1st Lieut. Asst. Surg., 26 June, 1875. Capt. Asst. Surg., 26 June, 1880. Maj. Surg., 18 April, 1895. Retired for disability, 23 April, 1898.

SHARON, GEORGE B. [Born in Nev. Appointed from Nev.]
2nd Lieut. 25th Inf., 1 June, 1899.

SHARP, ALEX'R. [Born in Penn. Appointed from Mo.]
Maj. P. M., 26 Jan., 1877. Retired by operation of law, 29 July, 1889.

SHARP, BERNARD. [Born in Tenn. Appointed from Army.]
Priv., Corpl. and Sergt. Batty L, 3rd Art., 18 June, 1895, to 24 May, 1899. 2nd Lieut. 3rd Inf., 5 April, 1899.

SHARP, FRED. DENT. [Born in Mo. Appointed from D. C.]
2nd Lieut. 20th Inf., 14 Dec., 1876. 1st Lieut., 19 Sept., 1884. Capt., 12 March, 1894. Retired for disability 30 June, 1898.

SHARP, THOS. [Born in Penn. Appointed from Penn.]
Priv. Co. A, 7th Penn. Res. Vet. Corps, 21 April, 1861. Discharged 18 Nov., 1861.

Capt. 65th U. S. Col. Troops, 29 Dec., 1863. Mustered out 15 Aug., 1865. 2nd Lieut. 41st Inf., 28 July, 1866. 1st Lieut., 14 Feb., 1868. Unassigned 11 Nov., 1869. Ass'd to 1st Inf., 1 Jan., 1871. Trans. to 17th Inf., 23 April, 1878. Capt., 26 Nov., 1884. Retired for disability, with rank of Maj., 1 Nov., 1898.

SHARPE, ALFRED C. [Born in Ohio. Appointed from Iowa.]
Cadet Mil. Acad., 1 July, 1872, to 29 June, 1875. 2nd Lieut. 10th Cav., 21 June, 1876. Trans. to 22nd Inf., 28 July, 1876. 1st Lieut., 30 June, 1881. Capt., 1 Feb., 1893. Maj. A. A. G. Vols., 12 May, 1898, to 17 April, 1899. Maj. I. G. Vols., 17 April, 1899. Bvt. 1st Lieut., 27 Feb., 1890, for gallant services in action against Indians at Spring Creek, Mont., 15 and 16 Oct., 1876.

SHARPE, EDWIN. [Born in N. C. Appointed from N. C.]
2nd Lieut. 2nd Art., 12 March, 1812. 1st Lieut., 16 June, 1813. Trans. to Corps Art., 12 May, 1814. Resigned 1 March, 1818.

SHARPE, HENRY G.* [Born in N. Y. Appointed from N. Y.]
2nd Lieut. 4th Inf., 12 June, 1880. Resigned 1 June, 1882. Appointed Capt. C. S., 13 Nov., 1884. Maj. C. S., 11 Nov., 1895. Lieut. Col. Asst. Com. Gen., 11 May, 1898. Col. C. S. Vols., 1 Oct. to 9 Nov., 1898, and from 2 Feb. to 2 March, 1899.

SHATTUCK, AMOS B.* [Born in N. H. Appointed from N. H.]
2nd Lieut. 6th Inf., 1 July, 1886. 1st Lieut. 25th Inf., 19 Oct., 1892. Capt., 2 March, 1899.

SHAWMBURG, JAMES W. [Born in La. Appointed from La.]
2nd Lieut. Mounted Rangers, 28 March, 1833. 2nd Lieut. 1st Drag., 19 Sept., 1833. 1st Lieut., 1 March, 1836. Resigned 31 July, 1836. Reinstated 29 July, 1844. Dropped 24 March, 1845.

SHAW, FREDERICK B. [Born in Penn. Appointed from Army.]
Priv. and Corpl. C. A, 21st Inf., 9 Nov., 1892, to 5 April, 1896. 2nd Lieut. 5th Inf., 23 March, 1896. 1st Lieut. of Inf., 22 Aug., 1898. Ass'd to 19th Inf., 1 Jan., 1899.

SHAW, GEORGE W.* [Born in Ohio. Appointed from Ohio.]
Bvt. 2nd Lieut. 1st Inf., 1 July, 1835. Resigned 31 Oct., 1836. Died 18 Sept., 1854.

SHAW, HENRY A. [Born in Mass. Appointed from Mass.]
Asst. Surg., 31 Oct., 1891. Capt. Asst. Surg., 31 Oct., 1896.

SHAW, JAMES W. [Born in Ind. Appointed from Ohio.]
Priv. Co. K, 11th Ohio Vols., 24 April to 17 Aug., 1861. 1st Lieut. 8th Ohio Cav., 23 Sept., 1861. Capt., 1 Sept., 1863. Maj., 12 May, 1864. Mustered out 30 July, 1865. 2nd Lieut. 19th Inf., 11 May, 1866. Trans. to 28th Inf., 21 Sept., 1866. 1st Lieut., 31 Oct., 1867. Dismissed 28 Dec., 1868.

SHAW, JOHN A. [Born in Penn. Appointed from Penn.]
Ensign 1st Inf., 22 April, 1809. 2nd Lieut., 26 Aug., 1812. 1st Lieut., 21 Feb., 1814. Disbanded 15 June, 1815. Reinstated 17 May, 1816, in Light Art. Died 8 Aug., 1819.

SHAW, JOHN J. [Born in N. Y. Appointed from Army.]
Priv., Corpl., Sergt. and 1st Sergt. Co. C, 6th Inf., 24 June, 1875, to 7 July, 1880. 2nd Lieut. 6th Inf., 24 June, 1880. Dropped 9 May, 1887.

SHAW, JOSEPH B. [Born in Penn. Appointed from Penn.]
2nd Lieut. 4th Inf., 12 Nov., 1818. 1st Lieut., 3 Feb., 1822. Died 31 March, 1831.

SHAW, RICHD. G. [Born in R. I. Appointed from R. I.]
Capt. 3rd R. I. Art., 7 Sept., 1861. Mustered out 13 Jan., 1864. Maj. 11th U. S. Col. Art., 31 Jan., 1864. Mustered out 2 Oct., 1865. 2nd Lieut. 1st Art., 27 March, 1866. 1st Lieut., 28 July, 1866. Bvt. Capt., 2 March, 1867, for gallant and meritorious service on Morris Island, S. C. Capt., 20 Sept., 1883. Graduate of the Artillery School, 1873. Retired by operation of law, 29 June, 1-896. Died 30 April, 1898.

SHAW, SAMUEL. [Born in Vt. Appointed from Vt.]
Hosp. Surg., 6 April, 1813. Disbanded 15 June, 1815. Reinstated 13 Sept., 1815. Post Surg., 18 April, 1818. Resigned 31 Dec., 1818. Died 9 July, 1834.

SHAYLER, EPHRAIM. [Born in Mass. Appointed from Conn.]
Ensign 25th Inf., 12 March, 1812. 2nd Lieut., 13 March, 1813. 1st Lieut., 15 Aug., 1813. Reg. Adj., March to Aug., 1814. Trans. to 6th Inf., 17 May, 1815. Reg. Adj., 4 April, 1816, to 30 April, 1819. Capt., 30 April, 1819. Resigned 1 May, 1827.

SHEA, STEPHEN. [Born in ——. Appointed from Penn.]
Ensign 1st Inf., 11 March, 1814. 3rd Lieut., 19 April, 1814. 2nd Lieut., 31 May, 1814. Disbanded 15 June, 1815. 2nd Lieut. Rifles, 28 Jan., 1820. Disbanded 1 June, 1821.

SHEA, THOS. [Born in Ind. Appointed from Ind.]
1st Lieut. 22nd Ind. Vols., 15 Aug., 1861. Capt., 10 Jan., 1862. Maj., 10 Dec., 1862. Lieut. Col., 20 May, 1865. Col. 9 June, 1865. Mustered out 24 July, 1865. 1st Lieut. 44th Inf., 22 Jan., 1867. Bvt. Capt. and Maj., 2 March, 1867, for gallant and meritorious service in action at Rome, Ga. Bvt. Lieut. Col., 2 March, 1867, for gallant and meritorious service in the Battle of Peach Tree Creek, Ga. Bvt. Col., 2 March, 1867, for gallant and meritorious service during the war. Capt. 44th Inf., 5 June, 1867. Trans. to 17th Inf., 27 May, 1869. Retired with rank of Lieut. Col., 15 Dec., 1870.

SHEETZ, JOSIAH A. [Born in Penn. Appointed from Ill.]
2nd Lieut. 8th Ill. Vols., 25 April, 1861. 1st Lieut., 25 July, 1861. Capt., 22 Feb., 1862. Maj., 6 June, 1863. Lieut. Col., 28 Aug., 1863. Col., 25 Nov., 1864. Bvt. Brig. Gen. Vols., 26 March, 1865, for faithful and meritorious service during the campaign against the city of Mobile, Ala., and its defences. Resigned 9 Feb., 1866. Priv., Corpl. and 1st Sergt. Co. F, 1st Inf., 30 April, 1866, to 8 May, 1867. 1st Lieut. 30th Inf., 7 March, 1867. Trans. to 4th Inf., 23 March, 1869. Cashiered 9 Dec., 1875. Bvt. Capt., 7 March, 1867, for gallant and meritorious service in the Battle of Vicksburg, Miss. Bvt. Maj., 7 March, 1867, for gallant and meritorious service in the capture of Mobile, Ala.

SHEIBNER, EUGENE W. [Born in Germany. Appointed from Army.]
Priv., Corpl., Sergt. and 1st Sergt. Batty E, 1st Art., 20 Aug., 1866, to 15 Nov.,

1861. 1st Lieut. 7th N. Y. Batty, 1 Jan., 1862. Resigned 25 June, 1862. 2nd Lieut. 3rd Penn. Art., 11 Nov., 1862. Capt., 27 March, 1863. Dismissed 10 Aug., 1864. Priv., Sergt. and 1st Sergt. Cos. B and D, 15th Inf., 1 Sept., 1864, to 8 July, 1865. 2nd Lieut. 15th Inf., 30 June, 1865. 1st Lieut., 30 June, 1865. Trans. to 33rd Inf., 21 Sept., 1866. Capt., 11 Oct., 1868. Unassigned 3 May, 1869. Discharged 13 Aug., 1870.

SHEILDS, WM. [Born in Maine. Appointed from Maine.]
Sergt. Co. D. 4th Maine Vols., 15 June, 1861. 2nd Lieut., 1 March, 1862. 1st Lieut., 21 Oct., 1862. Resigned 7 Sept., 1863. 1st Lieut. Vet. Res. Corps, 28 Aug., 1863. Capt., 25 March, 1865. Mustered out 4 Dec., 1866. 2nd Lieut. 44th Inf., 28 July, 1866. 1st Lieut., 15 Jan., 1867. Unassigned 27 May, 1869. Mustered out 1 Jan., 1871. Bvt. Capt., 2 March, 1867, for gallant and meritorious service at the Battle of Fredericksburg, Va.

SHELBY, ISAAC O. [Born in Ind. Appointed from Ill.]
Priv. Co. B, 25th Iowa Vols., 21 Aug., 1862. Discharged 31 May, 1865. 2nd Lieut., 34th Inf., 25 July, 1867. Trans. to 16th Inf., 14 April, 1869. 1st Lieut., 1 July, 1879. Died 9 Aug., 1883.

SHELDON, ALEX'R. E. [Born in N. Y. Appointed from N. Y.]
2nd Lieut. 4th Inf., 5 Aug., 1861. 1st Lieut., 30 June, 1862. Capt., 25 Aug., 1864. Resigned 21 April, 1866. Bvt. Capt., 3 May, 1863, for gallant and meritorious service at the Battle of Chancellorsville, Va. Bvt. Maj., 2 April, 1865, for gallant and meritorious service at the capture of Petersburg, Va.

SHELDON, GEORGE W. [Born in Vt. Appointed from Vt.]
Priv., Corpl. and 1st Sergt. Batty I, 4th Art., 15 Sept., 1856, to 15 Sept., 1861. 1st Lieut. 7th Vt. Vols., 12 Feb., 1862. Reg. Adj., 9 Dec., 1862. Mustered out 8 Dec., 1865. 2nd Lieut. 4th Art., 11 May, 1866. 1st Lieut., 28 July, 1866. Dismissed 24 Jan., 1873.

SHELDON, H. LAWRENCE. [Born in Conn. Appointed from Conn.]
Asst. Surg. U. S. N., 17 April, 1856. Resigned 5 July, 1861. Asst. Surg., 26 July, 1861. Resigned 1 July, 1866. Bvt. Capt. and Maj., 13 March, 1865, for faithful and meritorious service during the war.

SHELDON, RAYMOND. [Born in N. J. Appointed from N. J.]
2nd Lieut. 2nd Inf., 9 July, 1898. 1st Lieut. 22nd Inf., 1 April, 1899.

SHELL, HENRY. [Born in Penn. Appointed from Penn.]
Ensign 6th Inf., 3 May, 1808. 2nd Lieut., 1 Sept., 1809. 1st Lieut., 9 March, 1811. Capt., 21 March, 1814. Trans. to 2nd Inf., 17 May, 1815. Disbanded 1 June, 1821. Died 25 Feb., 1839.

SHELLABARGER, JACOB H. [Born in Penn. Appointed from Ohio.]
2nd Lieut. 7th Cav., 12 Aug., 1867. 1st Lieut., 1 March, 1869. Dismissed 18 Sept., 1869.

SHELTON, EDWIN H.* [Born in Conn. Appointed from Conn.]
2nd Lieut. 1st Cav., 15 June, 1870. 1st Lieut., 30 March, 1877. Died 13 Jan., 1880.

SHELTON, GEORGE H.* [Born in Conn. Appointed from Conn.]
2nd Lieut. 11th Inf., 12 June, 1896. 1st Lieut. of Inf., 18 Sept., 1898. Ass'd to 11th Inf., 1 Jan., 1899.

SHEPARD, CHAS. H. [Born in N. Y. Appointed from N. Y.]
Priv. Co. G, and Com. Sergt. 7th N. Y. Cav., 26 Aug., 1862, to 12 May, 1863. 2nd Lieut. 7th N. Y. Cav., 12 May, 1863. 1st Lieut., 5 June, 1865. Mustered out 29 Nov., 1865. 2nd Lieut. 9th Inf., 23 Feb., 1866. 1st Lieut., 28 July, 1866. Resigned 15 Sept., 1871.

SHEPHEARD, JOHN J. [Born in Md. Appointed from Cal.]
2nd Lieut. 2nd Cal. Vols., 7 March, 1862. 1st Lieut., 27 March, 1863. Mustered out 27 March, 1866. 2nd Lieut. 32nd Inf., 28 July, 1866. R. Q. M., 1 May, 1867, to 12 May, 1869. 1st Lieut., 5 Nov., 1867. Unassigned 19 April, 1869. Ass'd to 12th Inf., 16 Aug., 1869. Mustered out 1 Jan., 1871.

SHEPHERD, CHAS. M. [Born in Ill. Appointed from Ill.]
Priv. Co. G, 11th Mo. Vols., 29 April to 31 Oct., 1864. Cadet at Naval Acad., 3 Dec., 1864, to 15 June, 1867. 2nd Lieut. 3rd Inf., 7 Aug., 1867. Mustered out 1 Jan., 1871.

SHEPHERD, JOHN B. [Born in Va. Appointed from Ky.]
Maj. 1st Ky. Vols., 30 May, 1846. Mustered out 17 May, 1847. 2nd Lieut. 7th Inf., 1 Aug., 1838. Resigned 17 Sept., 1839.

SHEPHERD, OLIVER L.* [Born in N. Y. Appointed from N. Y.]
Bvt. 2nd Lieut. 4th Inf., 1 July, 1840. 2nd Lieut. 3rd Inf., 2 Oct., 1840. 1st Lieut., 3 Nov., 1845. Bvt. Capt., 20 Aug., 1847, for gallant and meritorious conduct in the Battles of Contreras and Churubusco. Bvt. Maj., 13 Sept., 1847, for gallant and meritorious conduct in the Battle of Chapultepec. Capt. 3rd Inf., 1 Dec., 1847. Lieut. Col. 18th Inf., 14 May, 1861. Bvt. Col., 17 May, 1862, for gallant and meritorious service in the Siege of Corinth, Miss. Col. 15th Inf., 21 Jan., 1863. Bvt. Brig. Gen., 13 March, 1865, for gallant and meritorious service in the Battle of Stone River, Tenn. Retired 15 Dec., 1870. Died 15 April, 1894.

SHEPHERD, THOMAS D. [Born in Ill. Appointed from Ill.]
Priv., Corpl. and Sergt. Co. K, 70th Ill. Vols., 9 June to 23 Oct., 1862. Priv. Co. K, 9th Ind. Cav., 26 April, 1864, to 15 June, 1865. 2nd Lieut. 11th Inf., 5 March, 1866. 1st Lieut., 22 Jan., 1867. Resigned 19 June, 1868.

SHEPPARD, AUGUSTUS L. [Born in D. C. Appointed from D. C.]
Priv. and Sergt. Washington Co., Florida War, 1 June to 31 Dec., 1836. 2nd Lieut. 8th Inf., 7 July, 1838. 1st Lieut., 23 June, 1841. Capt., 23 Feb., 1847. Died 22 Jan., 1849.

SHEPPERD, SAMUEL T.* [Born in D. C. Appointed from N. C.]
Bvt. 2nd Lieut. 2nd Inf., 1 July, 1854. 2nd Lieut. 2nd Drag., 3 March, 1855. Died 27 June, 1855.

SHERBURNE, JOHN P. [Born in N. H. Appointed from N. H.]
Cadet at Mil. Acad., 1 July, 1849, to 31 Jan., 1853. 2nd Lieut. 1st Inf., 27 June, 1856. 1st Lieut., 8 April, 1861. Capt. 19th Inf., 24 Oct., 1861. Maj. A. A. G., 17 July, 1862. Col. 11th N. Y. Cav., 8 March, 1864. Resigned from Vols., 15

March, 1865. Mustered out 28 Dec., 1870. Bvt. Lieut. Col. and Col., 13 March, 1865, for faithful and meritorious service during the war.

SHERIDAN, ANDREW. [Born in Penn. Appointed from N. J.]
2nd Lieut. 3rd Inf., 23 March, 1861. 1st Lieut., 14 May, 1861. Capt., 9 Feb., 1863. Unassigned 11 Aug., 1869. Ass'd to 24th Inf., 1 Jan., 1871. Resigned 5 Jan., 1877. Bvt. Maj., 2 July, 1863, for gallant and meritorious service at the Battle of Gettysburg, Penn.

SHERIDAN, MICHAEL V. [Born in Ohio. Appointed from Ohio.]
1st Lieut. 2nd Mo. Vols., 7 Sept., 1863. Capt. A. A. de C. Vols., 18 May, 1864. Bvt. Maj. Vols., 13 March, 1865, for gallant and meritorious service. 2nd Lieut. 5th Cav., 23 Feb., 1866. Capt. 7th Cav., 28 July, 1866. Mustered out of Vol. Service, 1 Aug., 1866. Bvt. Maj., 2 March, 1867, for gallant and meritorious service in the Battle of the Opequan. Bvt. Lieut. Col., 2 March, 1867, for gallant and meritorious service in the Battle of Fisher's Hill, Va. Lieut. Col. A. de C. to the Lieut. Gen., 1 Aug., 1870. Lieut. Col. Mil. Secy. to the Lieut. Gen., 9 April, 1878, to 1 June, 1888. Col. A. de C. to Gen. Sheridan 1 June to 5 Aug., 1888. Maj. A. A. G., 7 June, 1883. Lieut. Col. A. A. G., 9 July, 1892. Col. A. A. G., 25 Jan., 1897. Brig. Gen. Vols., 27 May, 1898, to 12 May, 1899.

SHERIDAN, PHILIP H.* [Born in Ohio. Appointed from Ohio.]
Bvt. 2nd Lieut. 1st Inf., 1 July, 1853. 2nd Lieut. 4th Inf., 22 Nov., 1854. 1st Lieut., 1 March, 1861. Capt. 13th Inf., 14 May, 1861. Col. 2nd Mich. Cav., 25 May, 1862. Brig. Gen. Vols., 1 July, 1862. Maj. Gen. Vols., 31 Dec., 1862. Brig. Gen. U. S. A., 20 Sept., 1864. Maj. Gen. U. S. A., 8 Nov., 1864, for the personal gallantry, military skill, and just confidence in the courage and patriotism of his troops, displayed by him on 19 Oct., at Cedar Run, whereby, under the blessing of Providence, his routed army was reorganized, a great national disaster averted, and a brilliant victory achieved over the rebels for the third time in pitched battle within thirty days. The thanks of Congress were tendered to Maj. Gen. Philip H. Sheridan and to the officers and soldiers under his command, by joint resolution approved 9 Feb., 1865, for the gallantry, military skill, and courage displayed in the brilliant series of victories achieved by them in the Valley of the Shenandoah, and especially for their services at Cedar Run on the 19th day of Oct., 1864, which retrieved the fortunes of the day and thus averted a great disaster. Lieut. Gen., 4 March, 1869. Gen., 1 June, 1888. Com.-in-Chf. of the Army, 1 Nov., 1883, to 5 Aug., 1888. Died 5 Aug., 1888.

SHERMAN, DUNCAN. [Born in N. Y. Appointed from N. Y.]
2nd Lieut. 1st Cav., 22 Jan., 1867. 1st Lieut., 2 Aug., 1869. Resigned 31 July, 1873.

SHERMAN, HORACE P. [Born in Mass. Appointed from Ohio.]
Hosp. Steward 7th Mass. Vols., 15 June, 1861, to 8 Aug., 1862. Hosp. Steward 18th Mass., Vols., 28 Nov., 1862, to 2 Sept., 1864. 2nd Lieut. 35th Inf., 8 June, 1867. Trans. to 15th Inf., 12 Aug., 1869. 1st Lieut., 1 Feb., 1873. Died 6 Oct., 1877.

SHERMAN, JAMES L.* [Born in D. C. Appointed from Ala.]
2nd and 1st Lieut. 19th Inf., 23 June, 1865. Trans. to 28th Inf., 21 Sept., 1866. Trans. to 1st Art., 6 Oct., 1866. R. Q. M., 28 Dec., 1866, to 18 Jan., 1869. Died 15 May, 1880.

SHERMAN, THOS. W.* [Born in R. I. Appointed from R. I.]
2nd Lieut. 3rd Art., 1 July, 1836. 1st Lieut., 14 March, 1838. Capt., 28 May, 1846. Bvt. Maj., 23 Feb., 1847, for gallant and meritorious conduct in the Battle of Buena Vista. Maj. 3rd Art., 27 April, 1861. Lieut. Col. 5th Art., 14 May, 1861. Brig. Gen. Vols., 17 May, 1861. Col. 3rd Art., 1 June, 1863. Bvt. Brig. Gen., 13 March, 1865, for gallant and meritorious service in the capture of Port Hudson, La. Bvt. Maj. Gen., 13 March, 1865, for gallant and meritorious service during the war. Bvt. Maj. Gen. Vols., 13 March, 1865, for gallant and meritorious service during the war. Mustered out of Vol. Service, 30 April, 1866. Retired with rank of Maj. Gen., 31 Dec., 1870. Died 16 March, 1879.

SHERMAN, WILLIAM T.* [Born in Ohio. Appointed from Ohio.]
2nd Lieut. 3rd Art., 1 July, 1840. 1st Lieut., 30 Nov., 1841. Bvt. Capt., 30 May, 1848, for gallant and meritorious service in Cal., during the war with Mexico. Capt. C. S., 27 Sept., 1850. Resigned 6 Sept., 1853. Col. 13th Inf., 14 May, 1861. Brig. Gen. Vols., 17 May, 1861. Maj. Gen. Vols., 1 May, 1862. Brig. Gen. U. S. A., 4 July, 1863. The thanks of Congress and of the people of the U. S., tendered to Maj. Gen. W. T. Sherman and the officers and soldiers of the Army of the Tenn., by joint resolution approved 19 Feb., 1864, for their gallant and arduous service in marching to the relief of the Army of the Cumberland, and for their gallantry and heroism in the Battle of Chattanooga, which contributed in a great degree to the success of our arms in that glorious victory. Appointed Maj. Gen. U. S. A., 12 Aug., 1864, for gallant and distinguished service as commander of the Mississippi Division in the conduct of the campaign in Ga. The thanks of the people and of Congress of the U. S., tendered to Maj. Gen. W. T. Sherman and the officers and soldiers of his command, by joint resolution approved 10 Jan., 1865, for their gallantry and good conduct in their late campaign from Chattanooga to Atlanta, and the triumphal march thence through Ga. to Savannah, terminating in the capture and occupation of that city. Lieut. Gen., 25 July, 1866. Gen., 4 March, 1869. Retired by operation of law, 8 Feb., 1884. Died 14 Feb., 1891.

SHERWOOD, GEORGE P. [Born in Maine. Appointed from Maine.]
Capt. 5th Maine Vols., 24 June, 1861. Resigned 18 Jan., 1863. Capt. Vet. Res. Corps, 3 July, 1863. Bvt. Maj. Vols., 13 March, 1865, for gallant and meritorious service at the First Battle of Bull Run, Va. Mustered out 12 April, 1867. 1st Lieut. 42nd Inf., 22 Jan., 1867. Trans. to 6th Inf., 22 April, 1869. Wholly retired 25 Oct., 1870.

SHERWOOD, WALTER.* [Born in N. J. Appointed from N. J.]
2nd Lieut. 7th Inf., 1 July, 1837. Killed 28 Dec., 1840, in action with Indians in Florida.

SHERWOOD, WM. L. [Born in N. Y. Appointed from N. Y.]
2nd Lieut. 21st Inf., 3 Sept., 1867. 1st Lieut., 22 July, 1872. Died 14 April, 1873, of wounds received from Modoc Indians in Oregon, while receiving a flag of truce.

SHIELDS, DAVID H. [Born in Penn. Appointed from Penn.]
Post Chap., 16 Aug., 1897.

SHIELDS, GEORGE H., Jr. [Born in Mo. Appointed from Mo.]
Corpl. Batty A, Mo. Light Art., 4 May to 20 Sept., 1898. 2nd Lieut. 12th Inf., 9 Sept., 1898.

SHIELDS, HAMILTON L.* [Born in Va. Appointed from Va.]
Bvt. 2nd Lieut. 2nd Art., 1 July, 1846. 2nd Lieut. 3rd Art., 3 March, 1847. 1st Lieut., 22 Sept. , 1847. Resigned 17 March, 1854. Bvt. 1st Lieut., 20 Aug., 1847, for gallant and meritorious conduct at Contreras and Churubusco. Bvt. Capt., 8 Sept., 1847, for gallant and meritorious conduct at Molino del Rey, Mexico.

SHIELDS, MEED B. [Born in ——. Appointed from Ill.]
3rd Lieut. Mounted Rangers, 1 July, 1832. Disbanded 1 Oct., 1833.

SHIELDS, THOS. [Born in Miss. Appointed from La.]
1st Lieut. of Inf., 5 March, 1847; 14th Inf., 9 April, 1847. R. Q. M., 17 July, to 8 Aug., 1847. Capt., 21 Oct., 1847. Disbanded 25 July, 1848.

SHILLOCK, PAUL. [Born in Minn. Appointed from Minn.]
Cadet Mil. Acad., 1 July, 1882, to 24 June, 1884. Asst. Surg., 31 Jan., 1888. Capt. Asst. Surg., 31 Jan., 1893. Maj. Brig. Surg. Vols., 4 June, to 30 Nov., 1898.

SHIMER, IRA A. [Born in Penn. Appointed from Penn.]
Asst. Surg., 23 July, 1898.

SHINN, JOHN B.* [Born in N. J. Appointed from Ohio.]
Bvt. 2nd Lieut. 3rd Art., 1 July, 1856. 2nd Lieut., 1 Sept., 1856. 1st Lieut., 30 May, 1860. Capt., 20 Jan., 1864. Discharged 27 Dec., 1870. Bvt. Maj., 13 March, 1865, for arduous and meritorious service in successfully bringing his battery across the Yuma and Gila deserts, and for faithful service in New Mexico.

SHIPLEY, ALEX. N. [Born in Penn. Appointed from Army.]
Priv., Corpl. and Sergt. Co. E, and Q. M. Sergt. 1st Inf., 13 April, 1848, to 1 June, 1857. Bvt. 2nd Lieut. 5th Inf., 1 June, 1857. 2nd Lieut. 3rd Inf., 1 June, 1857. 1st Lieut., 13 May, 1861. Capt. A. Q. M., 24 March, 1862. Lieut. Col. Q. M. Vols., 15 March to 6 July, 1865. Resigned 6 July, 1865. Bvt. Maj. and Lieut. Col., 13 March, 1865, for faithful and meritorious service during the war.

SHIPMAN, HERBERT.
Chap. on duty at Mil. Acad. since 25 April, 1898.

SHIPMAN, WM. W. [Born in N. J. Appointed from Army.]
Priv., Corpl. and Sergt. Co. K, 12th Inf., 7 April, 1873, to 1 Nov., 1875. 2nd Lieut. 11th Inf., 15 Oct., 1875. Resigned 10 Aug., 1876.

SHIPP, ARTHUR M. [Born in Va. Appointed from Va.]
2nd Lieut. 20th Inf., 10 April, 1899.

SHIPP, EDMUND. [Born in Ky. Appointed from Ky.]
Ensign 17th Inf., 8 May, 1812. 2nd Lieut., 13 March, 1813. 1st Lieut., 17 March, 1814. Capt., 26 May, 1814. Trans. to Rifle Reg., 17 May, 1815. Died 22 April, 1817. Received by resolution of Congress of 13 Feb., 1835, by his oldest male representative the testimonial of a sword, for being engaged in the defence of Fort Stephenson, Ohio.

SHIPP, WM. E.* [Born in N. C. Appointed from N. C.]
2nd Lieut. 10th Cav., 13 June, 1883. 1st Lieut., 25 Dec., 1889. Killed in action 1 July, 1898, at San Juan, Santiago, Cuba.

SHIPTON, JAMES A.* [Born in Ohio. Appointed from Ohio.]
Addl. 2nd Lieut. 4th Art., 11 June, 1892. 2nd Lieut. 1st Art., 8 Dec., 1892. 1st Lieut., 2 March, 1899. Capt. 41st U. S. Vols., 17 Aug. to 2 Nov., 1899. Maj. 47th U. S. Vols., 26 Oct., 1899.

SHIRAS ALEXANDER E.* [Born in Penn. Appointed from N. J.]
Bvt. 2nd Lieut. 4th Art., 1 July, 1833. 2nd Lieut., 6 Oct., 1835. 1st Lieut., 31 May, 1837. Capt., 3 March, 1847. Capt. C. S., 3 March, 1847.Maj., 1 May, 1861. Col. A. C. G. S., 9 Feb., 1863. Brig. Gen. C. G. S., 23 June, 1874. Died 14 April, 1875. Bvt. Brig. Gen., 17 Sept., 1864, for meritorious and distinguished service in the Sub. Dept., and in supplying the armies during the war. Bvt. Maj. Gen., 13 March, 1865, for faithful, meritorious and distinguished service in the Sub. Dept. during the war.

SHOEMAKER, FRANK L.* [Born in Penn. Appointed from Penn.]
2nd Lieut. 4th Cav., 15 June, 1868. 1st Lieut., 1 May, 1873. Capt., 1 Nov., 1881. Resigned 30 June, 1883.

SHOEMAKER, WM. R. [Born in Penn. Appointed from Ill.]
Ord. Storekeeper, 3 Aug., 1841. Capt. Ord. Storekeeper, 28 July, 1866. Retired 30 June, 1882. Died 16 Sept., 1886.

SHOFNER, JAMES C.* [Born in Tenn. Appointed from Tenn.]
2nd Lieut. 21st Inf., 15 June, 1877. Resigned 1 June, 1881.

SHOLLENBERGER, JOHN H.* [Born in Pa. Appointed from Pa.]
2nd Lieut. 10th Inf., 13 June, 1883. 1st Lieut., 23 Aug., 1888. Capt., 26 April, 1898. R. Q. M., 27 Sept., 18[illegible]

SHOMO, JOSEPH. [Born in Va. Appointed from Va.]
Ensign 12th Inf., 12 March, 1812. 3rd Lieut., 29 March, 1813. 2nd Lieut., 24 March, 1814. Trans. to 4th Inf., 17 May, 1815. 1st Lieut., 31 Dec., 1816. Capt., 1 March, 1819. Resigned 31 Dec., 1820.

SHORB, J. CAMPBELL. [Born in Penn. Appointed from Penn.]
Asst. Surg., 11 Oct., 1860. Resigned 3 Sept., 1864. Died 1 Oct., 1889.

SHORKLEY, GEORGE. [Born in N. Y. Appointed from Penn.]
1st Lieut. 51st Pa. Vols., 16 Nov., 1861. Capt., 22 April, 1864. Bvt. Maj. Vols., 30 July, 1864, for gallant and distinguished service in the operations before Petersburg, Va. Bvt. Lieut. Col. Vols., 25 March, 1865, for gallant and meritorious service at Fort Stedman, Va. Bvt. Col. Vols., 9 April, 1865, for long faithful and valued service. Mustered out 27 July, 1865. 2nd and 1st Lieut. 15th Inf., 23 Feb., 1866. Bvt. Capt., 2 March, 1867, for gallant and meritorious service in the Battle of Antietam, Md. Bvt. Maj., 2 March, 1867, for gallant and meritorious service in the engagement at Fort Steadman, Va. Capt. 15th Inf., 13 Oct., 1867. Retired for disability 23 Sept., 1885.

SHORT, DANIEL M. [Born in Del. Appointed from Texas.]
1st Lieut. 12th Inf., 2 June, 1847. Disbanded 25 July, 1848.

SHORT, WALTER C. [Born in Ohio. Appointed from Ohio.]
2nd Lieut. 6th Cav., 7 Oct., 1891. 1st Lieut. 10th Cav., 23 Sept., 1898. Capt. A. A. G. Vols., 12 May, 1898, declined. Maj. 35th U. S. Vols., 5 July, 1899.

SHORTELLE, JAMES E. [Born in Penn. Appointed from Penn.]
Cadet at Mil. Acad., 1 July, 1866, to 12 June, 1871. 2nd Lieut. 11th Inf., 12 June, 1871. Died 5 Aug., 1871.

SHOUP, FRANCIS A.* [Born in Ind. Appointed fgrom Ind.]
Bvt. 2nd Lieut. 1st Art., 1 July, 1855. 2nd Lieut., 6 Dec., 1855. Resigned 10 Jan., 1860.

SHOVER, WM. H.* [Born in Ohio. Appointed from Ohio.]
2nd Lieut. 3rd Art., 1 July, 1838. 1st Lieut., 1 March, 1839. Capt. A. Q. M., 18 Jan. to 22 March, 1847. Capt. 3rd Art., 22 March, 1847. Died 7 Sept., 1850. Bvt. Capt., 23 Sept., 1846, for gallant conduct at Monterey. Bvt. Maj., 23 Feb., 1847, for gallant and meritorious conduct at Buena Vista, Mexico.

SHUFELDT, ROBT. W. [Born in N. Y. Appointed from D. C.]
1st Lieut. Asst. Surg., 5 Aug., 1876. Capt. Asst. Surg., 5 Aug., 1881. Retired for disability 25 Feb., 1891.

SHULZE, JOHN A. [Born in Penn. Appointed from Penn.]
2nd Lieut. 1st Cav., 5 Aug., 1861. 1st Lieut., 26 Oct., 1861. Resigned 24 Feb., 1862.

SHUNK, FRANCIS J.* [Born in Penn. Appointed at Large.]
Bvt. 2nd Lieut. Ord., 1 July, 1853. 2nd Lieut., 8 June, 1854. 1st Lieut., 1 July, 1856. Capt., 3 March, 1863. Maj., 7 March, 1867. Died 15 Dec., 1867. Bvt. Maj., 13 March, 1865, for faithful and meritorious service in the Ord. Dept.

SHUNK, FRANCIS R.* [Born in Penn. Appointed from Penn.]
Addl. 2nd Lieut. Eng., 12 June, 1887. 2nd Lieut., 22 Oct., 1887. 1st Lieut., 22 Feb., 1891. Capt., 5 July, 1898.

SHUNK, WM. A.* [Born in Ind. Appointed from Ind.]
2nd Lieut. 8th Cav., 13 June, 1879. 1st Lieut., 23 July, 1885. Capt., 5 Oct., 1892. Maj. Eng. Off. Vols., 19 May, 1898, to 31 March, 1899. Maj. 34th U. S. Vols., 5 July, 1899. Honor graduate of the Infantry and Cavalry School, 1887.

SHURLY, EDMUND R. P. [Born in England. Appointed from Ill.]
1st Lieut. 26th N. Y. Vols., 21 May, 1861. Capt., 7 Aug., 1861. Mustered out 25 April, 1863. Capt. Vet. Res. Corps., 28 Aug., 1863. Bvt. Maj. Vols., 13 March, 1865, for gallant and meritorious service at the Battle of Fredericksburg, Va., 13 Dec., 1862. Bvt. Lieut. Col. Vols., 13 March, 1865, for gallant and meritorious service during the war. Mustered out 7 Oct., 1865. 2nd Lieut. 18th Inf., 11 May, 1866. Trans. to 27th Inf., 21 Sept., 1866. Resigned 12 Feb., 1867. 2nd Lieut. 27th Inf., 15 March, 1867. Bvt. 1st Lieut., 15 March, 1867, for gallant and meritorious service in the Battle of Fredericksburg, Va. Bvt. Capt., 15 March, 1867, for gallant and meritorious service during the war. 1st Lieut. 27th Inf., 29 Sept., 1868. Retired 2 Dec., 1868. Bvt. Maj., 27 Feb., 1890, for gallant service in the successful defence of a government supply train against a large force of Indians, near Goose Creek, Dak., 4 Nov., 1877, where he was severely wounded.

SHUTTLEWORTH, EDWARD A. [Born in Mass. Appointed from Vt.]
2nd Lieut. 11th Inf., 1 Aug., 1891. 1st Lieut., 26 April, 1898. Graduate of the Infantry and Cavalry School, 1895.

SIBERT, WILLIAM L.* [Born in Ala. Appointed from Ala.]
2nd Lieut. Eng., 15 June, 1884. 1st Lieut., 7 April, 1888. Capt., 31 March, 1896.

SIBLEY, CALEB C.* [Born in Mass. Appointed from Mass.]
Bvt. 2nd Lieut. 5th Inf., 1 July, 1829. 2nd Lieut., 1 July, 1829. 1st Lieut., 31 Oct., 1836. Reg. Adj., 4 Aug., 1838, to 22 Sept., 1840. Capt., 22 Sept., 1840. Maj. 3rd Inf., 19 Jan., 1859. Lieut. Col. 9th Inf., 9 Oct., 1861. Col. 16th Inf., 20 April, 1864. Retired 22 Feb., 1869. Died 19 Feb., 1875. Bvt. Brig. Gen., 13 March, 1865, for faithful and meritorious service during the war. Died 19 Feb., 1875.

SIBLEY, EBENEZER S.* [Born in Ohio. Appointed from Mich.]
Bvt. 2nd Lieut. Art., 1 July, 1827. 2nd Lieut. 1st Art., 1 July, 1827. 1st Lieut., 6 March, 1834. Capt., 31 Aug., 1814. Capt. A. Q. M., 7 July, 1838. Maj. Q. M., 22 Dec., 1856. Lieut. Col. Dep. Q. M. G., 3 Aug., 1861. Resigned 15 April, 1864. Bvt. Maj., 23 Feb., 1847, for gallant and meritorious conduct at Buena Vista. Bvt. Lieut. Col., 6 May, 1861, and Col., 12 June, 1861. Died 14 Aug., 1884.

SIBLEY, FREDK. W.* [Born in Texas. Appointed from Ga.]
2nd Lieut. 2nd Cav., 17 June, 1874. 1st Lieut., 20 Oct., 1881. Reg. Adj., 17 Jan., 1889, to 7 March, 1893. Capt., 7 March, 1893. Reg. Adj., 14 March, 1899. Bvt. 1st Lieut., 27 Feb., 1890, for gallant service in action against Indians on the Little Big Horn River, Mont., 7 July, 1876.

SIBLEY, HENRY H.* [Born in La. Appointed from La.]
2nd Lieut. 2nd Drag., 1 July, 1838. 1st Lieut., 8 March, 1840. Reg. Adj., 1 Jan., 1841, to 16 April, 1842, and 17 Sept., 1842, to 1 April, 1846. Capt., 16 Feb., 1847. Maj. 1st Drag., 13 May, 1861. Resigned 13 May, 1861. Bvt. Maj., 25 March, 1847, for gallant and meritorious conduct at Medelin, near Vera Cruz, N. M. Died 23 Aug., 1886.

SIBLEY, ROBT. H. [Born in La. Appointed from La.]
Asst. Surg., 17 Oct., 1827. Resigned 15 July, 1829. Died in April, 1853.

SICKEL, HORATIO G., Jr.* [Born in Pa. Appointed from Pa.]
2nd Lieut. 14th Inf., 15 June, 1876. Trans. to 7th Cav., 28 July, 1876. 1st Lieut., 17 Dec., 1882. Capt., 23 May, 1896. Reg. Adj., 5 June, 1899.

SICKLES, DANIEL E. [Born in N. Y. Appointed from N.Y.]
Col. 70th N. Y. Vols., 29 June, 1861. Brig. Gen. Vols., 3 Sept., 1861. Maj. Gen. Vols., 29 Nov., 1862. Col. 42nd Inf., 28 July, 1866. Bvt. Brig. Gen., 2 March, 1867, for gallant and meritorious service in the Battle of Fredericksburg, Va. Bvt. Maj. Gen., 2 March, 1867, for gallant and meritoriou service in the Battle of Gettysburg, Penn. Mustered out of Vol. Service 1 Jan., 1868. Retired with rank of Maj. Gen., 14 April, 1869. Medal of Honor for most distinguished gal-

lantry in action at Gettysburg, Pa., 2 July, 1863, displayed on the field both before and after the loss of his leg; while serving as Maj. Gen. of Vols., commanding the 3rd Army Corps.

SICKLES, ETHAN C.* [Born in N. Y. Appointed from N. Y.]
2nd Lieut. Light Art., 1 July, 1819. Trans. to 4th Art., 1 June, 1821. Died 12 Oct., 1823.

SIDELL, WM. H.* [Born in N. Y. Appointed from N. Y.]
Bvt. 2nd Lieut. 1st Art., 1 July, 1833. Resigned 1 Oct., 1833. Maj. 15th Inf., 14 May, 1861. Lieut. Col. 10th Inf., 6 May, 1864. Unassigned 15 May, 1869. Retired 15 Dec., 1870. Died 1 July, 1873. Bvt. Col., 13 March, 1865, for meritorious and faithful service in the recruiting of the armies of the U. S. Bvt. Brig. Gen., 13 March, 1865, for faithful and efficient service during the war.

SIEVERT, HERMAN A. [Born in Ohio. Appointed from Army.]
Priv., Corpl. and Sergt. Cos. K and D, 11th Inf., 11 Dec., 1888, to 10 Dec., 1893. Priv. and Corpl. Co. G, 12th Inf., 22 Dec., 1893, to 6 April, 1896. 2nd Lieut. 9th Cav., 23 March, 1896. 1st Lieut. 4th Cav., 1 July, 1899.

SIGERFOOS, EDWARD. [Born in Ohio. Appointed from Ohio.]
2nd Lieut. 5th Inf., 1 Aug., 1891. 1st Lieut., 26 April, 1898. Honor graduate of the Infantry and Cavalry School, 1895.

SIGWORTH, JOHN M. [Born in Penn. Appointed from Army.]
Priv. and Corpl. Batty L, 1st Art., 6 Jan., 1886, to 7 March, 1889. 2nd Lieut. 10th Inf., 11 Feb., 1889. 1st Lieut. 9th Inf., 15 April, 1896. Capt., 2 June, 1899. Graduate of the Infantry and Cavalry School, 1893.

SILL, HENRY G.* [Born in Conn. Appointed from Conn.]
Bvt 2nd Lieut. 1st Art., 1 July, 1832. 2nd Lieut., 1 July, 1832. Died 1 Dec., 1835.

SILL, JOSHUA W.* — Born in Ohio. Appointed from Ohio.]
Bvt. 2nd Lieut. Ord., 1 July, 1853. 2nd Lieut., 11 May, 1854. 1st Lieut., 1 July, 1856. Resigned 25 Jan., 1861. Col. 33rd Ohio Inf., 27 Aug., 1861. Brig. Gen. Vols., 16 July, 1862. Killed 31 Dec., 1862, at the Battle of Stone River, Tenn.

SILLIMAN, HENRY R. [Born in Penn. Appointed from Penn.]
1st Lieut. Asst. Surg., 28 May, 1861. Bvt. Capt. and Maj., 13 March, 1865, for faithful and meritorious service during the war. Capt. Asst. Surg., 28 May, 1866. Retired 9 May, 1867. Died 1 Jan., 1883

SILLS, WILLIAM G.* [Born in Ala. Appointed from N. C.]
Addl. 2nd Lieut. 2nd Cav., 12 June, 1895. 2nd Lieut., 14 June, 1895. 1st Lieut. 8th Cav., 2 March, 1899.

SILVA, VALENTINE M. C. [Born in N. Y. Appointed from Army.]
Priv. and Corpl. Co. K, 9th N. Y. Vols., 9 Aug., 1861, to 18 Sept., 1862. Hosp. Steward, 18 Sept., 1862, to 10 Oct., 1865. 2nd Lieut. 12th Inf., 2 Oct., 1865. 1st Lieut., 2 Oct., 1865. Trans. to 21st Inf., 21 Sept., 1866. Capt., 22 July, 1872. Resigned 19 May, 1874.

SILVEY, WM.* [Born in Ohio. Appointed from Ohio.]
Bvt. 2nd Lieut. 3rd Art., 1 July, 1849. 2nd Lieut. 1st Art., 6 Nov., 1849. 1st Lieut., 31 Oct., 1853. Reg. Adj., 1 July, 1857, to 14 May, 1861. Capt., 14 May, 1861. Maj. 5th Art., 7 Feb., 1875. Retired 1 May, 1875. Died 23 Oct., 1875. Bvt. Maj., 30 March, 1865, for meritorious and faithful service in the recruitment of the armies of the U. S. Bvt. Lieut. Col., 13 Nov., 1865, for faithful and meritorious service in connection with the mustering out of service and disbanding of the Vol. armies of the U. S.

SIMKINS, JOHN C. [Born in S. C. Appointed from S. C.]
1st Lieut. of Inf., 22 March, 1847; 12th Inf., 9 April, 1847. Disbanded 25 July, 1848. Bvt. Capt., 20 Aug., 1847, for gallant and meritorious conduct at Contreras and Churubuscco, Mexico.

SIMMONS, BENJAMIN T.* [Born in N. C. Appointed from N. C.]
2nd Lieut. 16th Inf., 12 June, 1895. 1st Lieut. of Inf., 26 July, 1898. Ass'd to 16th Inf., 1 Jan., 1899.

SIMMONS, CHAS. [Born in Maine. Appointed from Maine.]
2nd Lieut. of Inf., 18 March, 1847; 9th Inf., 9 April, 1847. 1st Lieut., 23 Feb., 1848. R. Q. M., 1 April to 26 Aug., 1848. Disbanded 26 Aug., 1848.

SIMMONS, GEORGE W. [Born in Ala. Appointed from Army.]
Priv. Co. F, 13th Inf., 22 May, 1847, to 12 May, 1848. 2nd Lieut. 13th Inf., 29 March, 1848. Resigned 15 July, 1848.

SIMMONS, JAMES W. [Born in ——. Appointed from Texas.]
Mil. Storekeeper, 2 Aug., 1850. Resigned 30 April, 1851.

SIMMONS, SENECA G.* [Born in Vt. Appointed from Vt.]
Bvt. 2nd Lieut. 7th Inf., 1 July, 1834. 2nd Lieut., 31 Dec., 1834. 1st Lieut., 19 Jan., 1837. Capt., 16 Feb., 1847. Maj. 4th Inf., 9 Sept., 1861. Col. 5th Penn. Res., 21 June, 1861. Killed at Battle of White Oak Swamp, Va., 30 June, 1862.

SIMON, CHAS. [Born in Germany. Appointed from Army.]
Priv., Corpl., Sergt. and 1st Sergt. Batty K, 3rd and F, 5th Art., 1 Aug., 1853, to 31 Oct., 1862. 2nd Lieut. 5th Art., 22 Oct., 1862. 1st Lieut., 9 March, 1866. Died 7 March, 1867. Bvt. 1st Lieut., 13 Dec., 1862, for gallant and meritorious service at the Battle of Fredericksburg, Va. Bvt. Capt., 3 June, 1864, for gallant and meritorious service at the Battle of Cold Harbor, Va.

SIMON, LOUIS S. [Born in ——. Appointed from D. C.]
Sword Master Mil. Acad., 5 Oct., 1826. Resigned 30 Nov., 1831.

SIMONDS, GEORGE S.* [Born in Iowa. Appointed from Iowa.]
2nd Lieut. 22nd Inf., 15 Feb., 1899.

SIMONDS, JONAS. [Born in ——. Appointed from Penn.]
Capt. in Revolutionary Army. Col. 6th Inf., 6 July, 1808. Disbanded 15 June, 1815. A. C. S., — April, 1816. Died 14 July, 1816.

SIMONDS, LAWRENCE B. [Born in N. Y. Appointed from Army.]
Priv. and Corpl. Co. E, 21st Inf., 30 Aug., 1893, to 3 Nov., 1895. 2nd Lieut. 8th Inf., 31 Oct., 1895. 1st Lieut. of Inf., 11 Aug., 1898. Ass'd to 8th Inf., 1 Jan., 1899. Capt. A. J. A., 18 May, 1899.

SIMONS, HENRY M. [Born in S. C. Appointed from S. C.]
3rd Lieut. Corps Art., 23 May, 1814. 2nd Lieut., 16 Sept., 1814. Disbanded 15 June, 1815. Reinstated 17 May, 1816. 1st Lieut., 20 April, 1818. Died 23 Aug., 1820.

SIMONS, JAMES. [Born in S. C. Appointed from S. C.]
Asst. Surg., 11 July, 1839. Capt. Asst. Surg., 11 Feb., 1847. Dismissed 15 Jan., 1856. Reappointed 24 Oct., 1856, to rank from 11 July, 1839. Appointed Maj. Surg., 11 March, 1859, to rank from 29 Aug., 1856. Bvt. Lieut. Col. and Col., 13 March, 1865, for faithful and meritorious service during the war. Lieut. Col. Surg., 26 June, 1876. Retired by operation of Law, 30 June, 1882. Died 11 Nov., 1885.

SIMONS, JAMES. [Born in Penn. Appointed from Army.]
Priv., Corpl., Sergt. and 1st Sergt. Batty K, 4th Art., 16 Nov., 1850, to 16 Nov., 1856, and F, 4th Art., 16 Dec., 1856, to 29 June, 1861. 2nd Lieut. 18th Inf., 14 May, 1861. R. Q. M., 26 July to 5 Oct., 1861. 1st Lieut., 24 Oct., 1861. Died 14 Jan., 1863, of wounds received at the Battle of Murfreesboro, Tenn. Bvt. Capt., 31 Dec., 1862, for gallant and meritorious service at the Battle of Murfreesboro, Tenn.

SIMONS, JOHN. [Born in England. Appointed from Army.]
Priv. and Corpl. Co. H, and Sergt. Maj. 4th Inf., 10 Sept., 1859, to 8 Dec., 1862. 2nd Lieut. 4th Inf., 29 Nov., 1862. 1st Lieut., 9 Nov., 1863. Reg. Adj., 29 Jan., 1863, to 1 Jan., 1865. Dismissed 11 Feb., 1865.

SIMONS, WILLIAM H. [Born in S. C. Appointed from S. C.]
2nd Lieut. 6th Inf., 7 Oct., 1891. 1st Lieut., 26 April, 1898. Graduate of the Infantry and Cavalry School, 1895.

SIMONSON, JAMES.* [Born in N. Y. Appointed from N. Y.]
3rd Lieut. Ord., 2 March, 1815. 2nd Lieut., 27 May, 1817. 1st Lieut., 10 Oct., 1819. Trans. to 1st Art., 1 June, 1821. Dropped 30 Nov., 1833. Died 7 Aug., 1839.

SIMONSON, JOHN S. [Born in Penn. Appointed from Ind.]
3rd Sergt., Capt. H. F. Knapp's Co. N. Y. Militia, 1 May, 1814. Discharged 8 Nov., 1814. Capt. Mounted Rifles, 27 May, 1846. Bvt. Maj., 13 Sept., 1847, for gallant and meritorious conduct in the Battle of Chapultepec. Maj., Mounted Rifles, 16 Sept., 1853. Col., 13 May, 1861. Retired 28 Sept., 1861. Bvt. Brig. Gen., 13 March, 1865, for long and faithful service in the army. Died 5 Dec., 1881.

SIMONTON, EDWARD. [Born in Maine. Appointed from Maine.]
1st Sergt. Co. G, 20th Maine Vols., 29 Aug., 1862. 2nd Lieut., 13 Jan., 1863. Resigned 3 March, 1863. 2nd Lieut. 1st U. S. Col. Inf., 27 July, 1863. 1st Lieut., 25 July, 1864. Capt., 28 May, 1865. Bvt. Maj. and Lieut. Col. Vols., 13 March, 1865, for gallant conduct before Petersburg, Va., and for general good conduct and meritorious service. Mustered out 29 Sept., 1865. 2nd Lieut. 4th Inf., 23 Feb., 1866. 1st Lieut., 21 April, 1866. Unassigned 28 March, 1870. Discharged 20 Sept., 1870. Bvt. Capt., 2 March, 1867, for gallant and meritorious service in the Battle of Petersburg, Va.

SIMONTON, ISAAC P.* [Born in Ohio. Appointed from Ohio.]
Bvt. 2nd Lieut. 2nd Inf., 1 July, 1827. 2nd Lieut., 1 July, 1827. 1st Lieut. 1st Drag., 4 March, 1833. Capt., 4 July, 1836. Died 21 Feb., 1842.

SIMPSON, GEORGE B. [Born in N. Y. Apponted from Ore.]
Addl. P. M. Vols., 26 Nov., 1862. Resigned 2 May, 1864. Maj. P. M., 6 March, 1867. Died 4 Oct., 1867.

SIMPSON, GEORGE W. [Born in Md. Appointed from Md.]
Post Chap., 1 Feb., 1876. Retired for disability 25 Feb., 1891.

SIMPSON, JAMES F. [Born in Mass. Appointed from Conn.]
2nd Lieut. 14th Conn. Vols., 20 Aug., 1862. 1st Lieut., 4 Feb., 1863. Capt., 20 Oct., 1863. Discharged 14 Nov., 1864. Capt. 2nd U. S. Vet. Vols., 16 Feb., 1865. Mustered out 26 March, 1866. 2nd Lieut. 40th Inf., 17 Aug., 1867. Bvt. 1st Lieut., 17 Aug. 1867, for gallant and meritorious service in the Battle of the Wilderness, Va. Bvt. Capt., 17 Aug., 1867, for gallant and meritorious service in the Battle of Ream's Station, Va. Trans. to 25th Inf., 20 April, 1869. Trans. to 3rd Cav., 15 March, 1871. 1st Lieut., 14 Dec., 1877. R. Q. M., 24 July, 1879, to 1 Sept., 1883. Capt., 26 Nov., 1884. Retired for disability, 25 Nov., 1887. Died 29 June, 1899.

SIMPSON, JAMES H.* [Born in N. J. Appointed from N. J.]
Bvt. 2nd Lieut. 3rd Art., 1 July, 1832. 2nd Lieut., 30 Nov., 1833. 1st Lieut., 30 April, 1837. 1st Lieut. Top. Eng., 7 July, 1838. Capt., 3 March, 1853. Maj., 6 Aug., 1861. Col., 4th N. J. Vols., 12 Aug., 1861. Resigned Vol. commission, 24 Aug., 1862. Trans. to Eng., 3 March, 1863. Lieut. Col., 1 June, 1863. Bvt. Col., 13 March, 1865, for meritorious service during the war. Bvt. Brig. Gen., 13 March, 1865, for faithful and meritorious service during the war. Col. Eng., 7 March, 1867. Retired 31 March, 1880. Died 2 March, 1883.

SIMPSON, JOHN. [Born in Ohio. Appointed from Ohio.]
Priv. Co. A., 5th Ohio Cav., 27 Sept., 1862. Mustered out 28 May, 1865. 2nd Lieut. 4th Art., 17 Aug., 1867. 1st Lieut., 28 March, 1873. R. Q. M., 1 May, 1873, to 30 July, 1875. Capt. Asst. Q. M., 17 July, 1875. Maj. Q. M., 20 April, 1892. Lieut. Col. D. Q. M. G., 11 June, 1897. Graduate of the Artillery School, 1873.

SIMPSON, JOSIAH. [Born in N. J. Appointed from Penn.]
Asst. Surg., 11 July, 1837. Maj. Surg., 12 Aug., 1855. Died 3 March, 1874. Bvt. Lieut. Col. and Col., 13 March, 1865, for faithful and meritorious service during the war.

SIMPSON, MARCUS D. L.* [Born in N. Y. Appointed from N. Y.]
Bvt. 2nd Lieut. 2nd Art., 1 July, 1846. 2nd Lieut., 3 March, 1847. Bvt. 1st Lieut., 20 Aug., 1847, for gallant and meritorious conduct in the Battles of Contreras and Churubusco. Bvt. Capt., 13 Sept., 1847, for gallant and meritorious conduct in the Battle of Chapultepec. 1st Lieut. 2nd Art., 27 Oct., 1847. R. Q. M., 8 March, 1848, to 26 March, 1855. Capt. C. S., 26 March, 1855. Maj. C. S., 1 July, 1861. Lieut. Col., A. C. G. S., 9 Feb., 1863. Bvt. Col. Brig. Gen. and Maj. Gen., 13 March, 1865, for meritorious service during the war. Col. A. C. G. S., 23 June, 1874. Retired by operation of law, 28 Aug., 1888.

SIMPSON, RICHD. F. [Born in Va. Appointed from Va.]
Asst. Surg., 1 Aug., 1840. Maj. Surg., 23 June, 1860. Died 4 July, 1861.

SIMPSON, WENDELL L.* [Born in N. Y. Appointed from Mich.]
2nd Lieut. 3rd Cav., 15 June, 1884. Trans. to 24th Inf., 4 Jan., 1887. 1st Lieut. 20th Inf., 20 April, 1891. Trans. to 9th Inf., 20 July, 1891. Capt. of Inf., 17 Sept., 1898. Ass'd to 6th Inf., 1 Jan., 1899.

SIMPSON, WM. A.* [Born in N. Y. Appointed from N. Y.]
2nd Lieut. 2nd Art., 16 June, 1875. 1st Lieut., 8 Nov., 1882. Capt. 7th Art., 8 March, 1898. Maj. A. A. G., 8 July, 1898. Maj. A. A. G. Vols., 20 May to 19 Sept., 1898. Graduate of the Artillery School, in 1882.

SIMPSON, WM. S. [Born in ——. Appointed from ——.]
2nd Lieut. 10th Inf., 1898. Resigned 13 Oct., 1898.

SIMS, JOHN L. [Born in S. C. Appointed from Ala.]
2nd Lieut. 13th Inf., 24 April, 1847. Disbanded 15 July, 1848.

SIMS, WM. H.* [Born in Ga. Appointed from Ga.]
Bvt. 2nd Lieut. 6th Inf., 1 July, 1826. Resigned 28 March, 1827. Died in Sept., 1847.

SIMSON, THOS. W. [Born in N. Y. Appointed from Army.]
Priv. and Corpl. Troop I, 1st Cav. (4th Cav.), 19 Oct., 1858, to 27 March, 1863. 2nd Lieut. 6th Cav., 27 Feb., 1863. 1st Lieut., 3 Feb., 1865. Retired 22 Feb., 1865. Died 26 Oct., 1865.

SINCLAIR, JAMES B. [Born in N. Y. Appointed from N. Y.]
2nd Lieut. 79th N. Y. Vols., 27 May, 1861. Mustered out 29 Oct., 1861. 1st Lieut. 14th Inf., 26 Oct., 1861. Bvt. Capt., 1 Aug., 1864, for gallant service in the Battle of Spottsylvania, Va. Bvt. Maj., 1 Oct., 1864, for gallant service in the Battle of Chappel House, Va. Bvt. Lieut. Col. and Col., 13 March, 1865, for gallant and meritorious service during the war. R. Q. M., 23 Aug. to 11 Dec., 1864. Capt. 14th Inf., 25 July, 1865. Trans. to 23rd Inf., 21 Sept., 1866. Mustered out Jan.1, 1871. 2nd Lieut. 16th Inf., 9 March, 1871. Retired with rank of 1st Lieut., 3 March, 1875, and with rank of Capt., 21 June, 1876. Died 5 April, 1885.

SINCLAIR, WM.* [Born in Ohio. Appointed from Ohio.]
Bvt. 2nd Lieut. 2nd Art., 1 July, 1857. 2nd Lieut., 3d Art., 31 July, 1858. 1st Lieut., 30 April, 1861. Bvt. Capt., 4 May, 1862, for gallant and meritorious service in the Siege of Yorktown, Va. Col. 6th Pa. Res. Corps, 27 June, 1862. Bvt. Maj., 13 Dec., 1862, for gallant and meritorious service in the Battle of Fredericksburg, Va. Mustered out of Vol. Service 6 June, 1863. Lieut Col. A. I. G., 12 Oct., 1863, to 3 July, 1865. Capt. 3rd Art., 11 Dec., 1865. Maj. 2nd Art., 6 April, 1885. Lieut. Col. 5th Art., 6 June, 1896. Col. 7 Art., 8 March, 1898. Brig. Gen., 8 Feb., 1899. Retired after forty years' service, 13 Feb., 1899.

SINCLAIR, WM. S. [Born in Texas. Appointed from Texas.]
2nd Lieut. 14th Inf., 1 July, 1899.

SING, CHAS. B.* [Born in N. Y. Appointed from N. Y.]
Bvt. 2nd Lieut. 4th Art., 1 July, 1836. 2nd Lieut., 1 July, 1836. Resigned 31 Aug., 1837. Died 28 Feb., 1878.

SINGLETON, GEORGE W. [Born in Ky. Appointed from Ky.]
1st Lieut. Inf., 3 March, 1847; 16th Inf., 9 April, 1847. Capt., 20 Aug., 1847. Disbanded 7 Aug., 1848.

SIRMYER, EDGAR A.* [Born in Mich. Appointed from Mich.]
Add'l 2nd Lieut. 6th Cav., 11 June, 1897. 2nd Lieut. 3d Cav., 8 March, 1898. Capt. 33rd U. S. Vols., 5 July, 1899. Maj., 12 Nov., 1899.

SITGREAVES, JOHN S. [Born in N. C. Appointed from S. C.]
Capt. Inf., 2 March, 1847; 3rd Drag., 9 April, 1847. Disbanded 31 July, 1848.

SITGREAVES, LORENZO.* [Born in Pa. Appointed from Pa.]
Bvt. 2nd Lieut. 1st Art., 1 July, 1832. 2nd Lieut., 30 Sept., 1833. Resigned 31 Aug., 1836. 2nd Lieut. Top. Eng., 7 July, 1838. 1st Lieut., 18 July, 1840. Bvt. Capt., 23 Feb., 1847, for gallant and meritorious conduct in the Battle of Buena Vista Capt. Top. Eng., 3 March, 1853. Maj., 6 Aug., 1861. Trans. to Eng., 3 March, 1863. Lieut. Col., 22 April, 1864. Retired 10 July, 1866. Died 14 May, 1888.

SIVITER, FRANCIS P.* [Born in Pa. Appointed from Pa.]
2nd Lieut. 12th Inf., 12 June, 1895. 1st Lieut. Inf., 1 July, 1898. Ass'd to 18th Inf., 1 Jan., 1899. Trans. to 11th Inf., 13 May, 1899. Capt. 41st U. S. Vols., 17 Aug., 1899.

SKELTON, JOHN F. [Born in N. Y. Appointed from Iowa.]
Sergt. Co. D, 17th Iowa Vols., 26 March, 1862. 1st Lieut., 12 Feb., 1863. Capt., 1 Sept., 1864, to 25 Feb., 1865. Capt. C. S. Vols., 23 Jan., 1865. Bvt. Maj. Vols., 13 March, 1865, for faithful service. Mustered out 22 Sept., 1866. 1st Lieut. 45th Inf., 17 May, 1867. Dismissed 29 June, 1868.

SKENE, ALEX'R. GRANT. [Born in Canada. Appointed from Army.]
(Served under the name of Alexr. Grant—which see.)

SKERRETT, DELAMERE.* [Born in Ohio. Appointed from N. Y.]
Add'l 2nd Lieut. 2nd Art., 12 June, 1889. 2nd Lieut. 1st Art., 30 Sept., 1889. Trans. to 5th Art., 27 Oct., 1893. 1st Lieut. 3rd Art., 30 Sept., 1897. Graduate of the Artillery School, 1896.

SKINNER, JOHN O. [Born in Md. Appointed from Md.]
2nd Lieut. 5th Inf., 1 July, 1820. Disbanded 1 June, 1821. Died in 1822.

SKINNER, GEORGE A. [Born in Iowa. Apointed from Minn.]
Asst. Surg., 26 Oct., 1896.

SKINNER, JOHN O. [Born in Md. Appointed from N. Y.]
1st Lieut. Asst. Surg., 10 Nov., 1874. Capt. Asst. Surg., 10 Nov., 1879. Maj. Surg., 9 March, 1892. Retired for disability 26 Oct., 1893.

SKINNER, PRESCOTT M. [Born in Conn. Appointed from Mich.]
Sergt. Co. B., 20th Mich. Vols., 16 Aug., 1862. 1st Sergt., 15 Oct., 1862. 1st Lieut., 30 June, 1864. Mustered out 30 May, 1865. 2nd Lieut. 18th Inf., 23 Feb., 1866. 1st Lieut., 23 Feb., 1866. Resigned 24 Oct., 1867.

SKINNER, RICHARD. [Born in Ill. Appointed from Ill.]
2nd Lieut 10th Inf., 23 Sept., 1862. 1st Lieut., 16 Oct., 1863. Died 23 June, 1864.

of wounds received in action near Petersburg, Va. Bvt. Capt., 19 June, 1864, for gallant and meritorious service in action in front of Petersburg, Va.

**SLADE, CHAS. E.** [Born in Pa. Appointed from Pa.]
Priv. and Corpl. Co. D, 90th, and D, 11th Pa. Vols., 3 March, 1862, to 2 March, 1865. 2nd Lieut. 15th Inf., 12 Oct., 1868. Resigned 31 Aug., 1873.

**SLADE, JAMES B.** [Born in N. C. Appointed from La.]
Maj. Surg. Inf., 3 March, 1847; 15th Inf., 9 April, 1847. Died 30 Nov., 1847.

**SLADE, WM. H.** [Born in Ill. Appointed from Ill.]
2nd Lieut. Inf., 23 Feb., 1847; 16th Inf., 9 April, 1847. 1st Lieut., 6 Nov., 1847. Disbanded 31 July, 1848.

**SLADEN, FRED W.*** [Born in Mass. Appointed from Neb.]
2nd Lieut. 14th Inf., 12 June, 1890. 1st Lieut., 4th Inf., 10 Feb., 1897. Capt., 8th Inf., 20 Oct., 1899.

**SLADEN, JOS. A.** [Born in England. Appointed from Mass.]
Priv. Co. A., 33rd Mass. Vols., 6 Aug., 1862. Corpl., 9 Aug., 1862. Priv., 1 Aug., 1863. 2nd Lieut. 14th U. S. Col. Troops, 1 Jan., 1865. Bvt. 1st Lieut. Vols., 13 March, 1865, for gallant and meritorious conduct during the Atlanta and Carolina campaigns. 1st Lieut. 14th U. S. Col. Troops, 24 Oct., 1865. Mustered out 26 March, 1866. 2nd Lieut. 17th Inf., 27 March, 1866. Trans. to 26th Inf., 21 Sept., 1866. Bvt. 1st Lieut. and Capt., 2 March, 1867, for gallant and meritorious service in the Battle of Jonesboro, Ga. 1st Lieut. 26th Inf., 17 July, 1867. Unassigned 19 May, 1869. Ass'd to 14th Inf., 15 Dec., 1870. R. Q. M., 25 July, 1887, to 15 June, 1888. Capt., 15 June, 1888. Medal of Honor for most distinguished gallantry in the Battle of Resaca, Ga., 14 May, 1864, while private Co. A, 33rd Mass. Inf.,; in voluntarily engaging in action at a critical juncture, and by the coolness and courage of his example inspiring the panic-stricken troops to repel the fierce assaults of the enemy. Retired 8 April, 1889, for loss of right leg from injury in line of duty.

**SLAKER, ADAM.*** [Born in Ill. Appointed from Ill.]
Addl. 2nd Lieut. 5th Art., 15 June, 1877. 2nd Lieut. 1st Art., 13 Oct., 1877. 1st Lieut., 30 June, 1882. Capt. 6th Art., 8 March, 1898. Graduate of the Artillery School, 1884-1892.

**SLAUGHTER, JAMES E.** [Born in Va. Appointed from Va.]
2nd Lieut. Inf., 5 March, 1847; Voltigeurs, 9 April, 1847. 2nd Lieut. 1st Art., 27 June, 1848. 1st Lieut., 3 Aug., 1852. Dismissed 14 May, 1861.

**SLAUGHTER, LEE.** [Born in Md. Appointed from Army.]
Priv., Corpl. and Sergt. 14th and 4th Inf., 6 Sept., 1813, to — April, 1818. 2nd Lieut. 4th Inf., 18 April, 1818. 1st Lieut., 30 April, 1819. R. Q. M., 10 Oct., 1819, to 1 June, 1821. Resigned 1 Jan., 1823. Died in 1842.

**SLAUGHTER, WM. A.*** [Born in Ky. Appointed from Ind.]
Bvt. 2nd Lieut. 2nd Inf., 1 July, 1848. 2nd Lieut. 4th Inf., 6 Nov., 1848. 1st Lieut., 22 June, 1854. Killed 4 Dec., 1855, in action with Indians in Washington Ter.

**SLAVENS, THOMAS H.*** [Born in Ind. Appointed from Mo.]
2nd Lieut. 4th Cav., 12 June, 1887. 1st Lieut. 6th Cav., 15 April, 1894. Trans. to 4th Cav., 14 March, 1896. Capt. A. Q. M., 13 Nov., 1899. Honor graduate of the Infantry and Cavalry School, 1893. Maj. 3d Mo. Vols., 21 May to 7 Nov., 1898.

**SLEMMER, ADAM J.*** [Born in Pa. Appointed from Pa.]
Bvt. 2nd Lieut. 1st Art., 1 July, 1850. 2nd Lieut., 22 Feb., 1851. 1st Lieut., 30 April, 1854. Maj. 16th Inf., 14 May, 1861. Brig. Gen. Vols., 29 Nov., 1862. Mustered out Vols. 24 Aug., 1865. Lieut. Col. 4th Inf., 8 Feb., 1864. Died 7 Oct., 1868. Bvt. Lieut. Col., 31 Dec., 1862, for gallant and meritorious service at the Battle of Murfreesboro, Tenn. Bvt. Col. and Brig. Gen., 13 March, for gallant and meritorious service during the war.

**SLIDELL, WM. J.** [Born in La. Appointed from R. I.]
1st Lieut. 16th Inf., 14 May, 1861. Capt., 19 Nov., 1861. Resigned 19 Oct., 1865. Bvt. Maj., 25 Nov., 1863, for gallant and meritorious service at the Battles of Murfreesboro and Mission Ridge, Tenn.

**SLOAN, BENJN. F., Jr.*** [Born in S. C. Appointed from S. C.]
Bvt. 2nd Lieut. 2nd Drag., 1 July, 1860. Resigned 2 March, 1861.

**SLOAN, CHARLES.** [Born in Md. Appointed from Md.]
Surg. Mate 8th Inf., 28 Jan., 1820. Asst. Surg., 1 June, 1821. Died 4 Nov., 1821.

**SLOAN, HENRY C.** [Born in Wis. Appointed from Wis.]
Priv. Cos. D and C, 5th Wis. Vols., 7 Dec., 1863, to 25 July, 1864. 2nd Lieut. 4th Inf., 23 Feb., 1866. 1st Lieut., 28 July, 1866. Discharged 1 Dec., 1870.

**SLOAN, P. ELMENDORF.*** [Born in N. Y. Appointed at Large.]
2nd Lieut. and 1st Lieut. 19th Inf., 23 June, 1865. Resigned 13 Jan., 1868.

**SLOAN, WM. H.** [Born in N. J. Appointed from N. J.]
Sergt. Co. A., 15th N. J. Vols., 25 Aug., 1862, to 3 Jan., 1863. Priv. Co. A, N. J. Militia, 3 to 13 July, 1863. 2d Lieut. 31st U. S. Col. Inf., 18 Feb., 1865. 1st Lieut., 6 July, 1865. Mustered out 7 Nov., 1865. 2nd Lieut. 11th Inf., 5 June, 1867. Unass'd 27 March, 1869. Ass'd to 12th Inf., 14 July, 1869. Resigned 30 Nov., 1869.

**SLOAN, WM. J.** [Born in Pa. Appointed from Pa.]
Asst. Surg., 12 July, 1837. Capt. Asst. Surg., 11 Feb., 1847. Maj. Surg., 20 Dec., 1855. Col. Med. Director, 25 Feb., 1865. Bvt. Lieut. Col. and Col., 13 March, 1865, for faithful and meritorious service during the war. Relieved as Col. Med. Insp., 30 June, 1865. Bvt. Brig. Gen., 28 Sept., 1866, for meritorious and distinguished service at several military posts in N. Y. Harbor, where cholera prevailed. Lieut. Col. Surg., 26 June, 1876. Col. Surg., 28 Sept., 1877. Died 17 March, 1880.

**SLOCUM, HENRY W.*** [Born in N. Y. Appointed from N. Y.]
2nd Lieut. 1st Art., 1 July, 1852. 1st Lieut., 3 March, 1855. Resigned 31 Oct., 1856. Col. 27th N. Y. Vols., 21 May, 1861. Brig. Gen. Vols., 9 Aug., 1861. Maj. Gen. Vols., 4 July, 1862. Resigned 28 Sept., 1865.

**SLOCUM, HERBERT J.** [Born in Ohio. Appointed from Ill.]
Cadet at Mil. Acad., 1 July, 1872, to 22 June, 1876. 2nd Lieut. 25th Inf., 21 June,

1876. Trans. to 7th Cav., 28 July, 1876. 1st Lieut., 22 Sept., 1883. Capt., 26 Aug., 1896. Graduate of the Infantry and Cavalry School, 1883. Bvt. 1st Lieut., 27 Feb., 1890, for galant services in action against Indians at Canon Creek, Mont., 13 Sept., 1877 Maj. I. G. Vols., 12 May, 1898, to 12 May, 1899.

SLOCUM, JOHN S. [Born in R. I. Appointed from R. I.]
1st Lieut. Inf., 18 Feb., 1847; 9th Inf., 9 April, 1847. Capt., 25 Sept., 1847. Disbanded 26 Aug., 1848. Bvt. Capt., 20 Aug., 1847, for gallant and meritorious conduct at Contreras and Churubusco, Mex. Col. 2nd R. I. Vols., 5 June, 1861. Killed 21 July, 1861, at the Battle of Bull Run, Va.

SLOCUM, STEPHEN L'H. [Born in Ohio. Appointed from N. Y.]
2nd Lieut. 18th Inf., 1 Sept., 1879. Trans. to 8th Cav., 1 June, 1883. 1st Lieut., 28 Sept., 1889. Capt., 2 March, 1899. Graduate of the Infantry and Cavalry School, 1883.

SLOO, JOHN R.* .. [Born in Ky. Appointed from Ohio.]
3rd Lieut. Corps. Art., 2 March, 1815. 2nd Lieut., 20 April, 1817. Resigned 30 April, 1818. Died in 1837.

SMALL, JOHN F. [Born in Tenn. Appointed from Army.]
Priv., Corpl. and Sergt. Troop H, 1st Cav., 6 Nov., 1861. to — May, 1864. 2nd Lieut. 1st Cav., 18 May, 1864. 1st Lieut., 29 Aug., 1864. Died 22 Feb., 1869. Bvt. 1st Lieut., 31 May, 1864, for gallant and meritorious service at the Battle of Cold Harbor. Va. Bvt. Capt., 8 Sept., 1867, for gallantry in charging a band of Indians, killing and capturing more of the enemy than he had men, on Silver Lake, Ore., 8 Sept., 1867.

SMALL, MICHAEL P.* [Born in Pa. Appointed from Pa.]
Bvt. 2nd Lieut. 3rd Art., 1 July, 1855. 2nd Lieut. 2nd Art., 21 Sept., 1855. 1st Lieut., 27 April, 1861. R. Q. M., 10 July to 3 Aug., 1861. Capt. C. S., 3 Aug., 1861. Lieut. Col. C. S. (Act 17 July, 1862), 14 Aug., 1863. Bvt. Col. Vols., 1 Jan., 1865, for distinguished and meritorious service in the campaign of 1863-1864. Bvt. Maj., 13 March, 1865, for meritorious service in the Sub. Dept. during the war. Bvt. Lieut. Col., 13 March, 1865, for meritorious service in his department during the war. Bvt. Col., 13 March, 1865, for meritorious service in the Sub. Dept. during the war. Bvt. Brig. Gen., 9 April, 1865, for faithful and meritorious service in his department during the war. Relieved as Lieut. Col. C. S. (Act 17 July, 1862), 25 May, 1865. Col. C. S., 25 May, 1865, to 29 Dec., 1865. Maj. C. S., 23 June, 1874. Lieut Col. Asst. C. G. S., 4 Oct., 1889. Died 1 Aug., 1892.

SMALLEY, HENRY A.* [Born in Vt. Appointed from Vt.]
Bvt. 2nd Lieut. 1st Art., 1 July, 1854. 2nd Lieut. 2nd Art., 2 Oct., 1854. 1st Lieut., 25 April, 1861. Col. 5th Vt. Vols., 16 Sept., 1861. Resigned from Vol. Service, 10 Sept., 1862. Capt. 2nd Art., 1 Aug., 1863. Resigned 8 March, 1865. Died 13 May, 1888.

SMALLWOOD, JENIFER H.* [Born in Fla. Appointed from N. J.]
2nd Lieut. 2nd Cav., 15 June, 1869. Trans. to 9th Inf., 17 March, 1873. Resigned 18 Dec., 1873.

SMART, CHAS. [Born in Scotland. Appointed from N. Y.]
Asst. Surg. 63rd N. Y. Vols., 5 Nov., 1862. Mustered out 15 April, 1864. 1st Lieut. Asst. Surg., 30 March, 1864. Bvt. Capt., 2 Dec., 1864, for meritorious service in the field during the campign before Richmond, Va. Capt. Asst. Surg., 28 July, 1866. Maj. Surg., 30 June, 1882. Lieut. Col. Dep. Surg. Gen., 3 May, 1897.

SMEAD, ABNER.* [Born in Ga. Appointed from Ga.]
Bvt. 2nd Lieut. 4th Art., 1 July, 1854. 2nd Lieut. 1st Art., 4 Nov., 1854. 1st Lieut., 22 Nov., 1860. Dropped 11 April, 1861.

SMEAD, A. D. BACHE. [Born in Penn. Appointed from Penn.]
2nd Lieut. 3rd Cav., 21 Feb., 1868. 1st Lieut., 5 May, 1871. Reg. Adj., 18 May, 1878, to 1 March, 1879. Resigned 29 Feb., 1880.

SMEAD, JOHN R.* [Born in N. Y. Appointed at Large.]
2nd Lieut. 2nd Art., 1 July, 1854. 1st Lieut., 3 March, 1857. Capt. Co. A, 3rd Batt. D. C. Vols., 15 April to 15 July, 1861. Capt. 5th Art., 14 May, 1861. Killed 30 Aug., 1862, at the Battle of Bull Run, Va.

SMEAD, RAPHAEL C.* [Born in N. H. Appointed from N. Y.]
Bvt. 2nd Lieut. 4th Art., 1 July, 1825. 2nd Lieut., 1 July, 1825. 1st Lieut., 30 Sept., 1832. Capt., 13 Oct., 1845. Died 20 Aug., 1848.

SMEDBERG, CHAS. G. [Born in N. Y. Appointed from Army.]
Priv. and Sergt. Co. H, 14th Inf., 1 May to 1 Aug., 1862. 2nd Lieut. 14th Inf., 30 June, 1862. Died 1 June, 1863.

SMEDBERG, WM. R. [Born in N. Y. Appointed from Mo.]
Priv. Co. A, 3rd Batt. D. C. Vols., 15 April, 1861. Discharged 4 July, 1861. 1st Lieut. 14th Inf., 14 May, 1861. Capt., 25 Oct., 1861. Bvt. Maj., 2 July, 1863, for gallant and meritorious service in the Battle of Gettysburg, Penn. Bvt. Lieut. Col., 5 May, 1864, for gallant and meritorious service in the Battle of the Wilderness, Va. Capt. 45th Inf., 22 Jan., 1867, declined. Unassigned 22 July, 1869. Retired with rank of Capt. Mounted, 15 Dec., 1870.

SMEDBERG, WM. R., Jr.* [Born in Cal. Appointed from Cal.]
2nd Lieut. 4th Cav., 12 June, 1893. 1st Lieut., 2 March, 1899.

SMILEY, SAMUEL E.* [Born in Ind. Appointed from N. J.]
2nd Lieut. 8th Inf., 14 June, 1885. 1st Lieut. 15th Inf., 25 April, 1892. Capt., 2 March, 1899.

SMITH, ABIEL L.* [Born in Mo. Appointed from Mo.]
Addl. 2nd Lieut. 19th Inf., 14 June, 1878. 2nd Lieut., 28 June, 1878. Trans. to 4th Cav., 3 Feb., 1879. 1st Lieut., 30 June, 1883. Capt., 6 May, 1892. Capt. C. S., 28 June, 1892. Maj. C. S., 11 March, 1898. Lieut. Col. C. S. Vols., 22 July, 1898, to 2 March, 1899. Bvt. Capt., 27 Feb., 1890, for gallant services in the campaign against Geronimo's band of Indians in Sonora, Mex., from July to Sept., 1886.

SMITH, ALBERT J. [Born in Va. Appointed from Va.]
Maj. P. M., 1 June, 1849. Dismissed 20 June, 1861. Died 28 March, 1871.

SMITH, ALFRED T.* [Born in Mo. Appointed from Ill.]
Bvt. 2nd Lieut. 4th Inf., 1 July, 1860. 2nd Lieut. 8th Inf., 17 Oct., 1860. 1st Lieut., 14 May, 1861. Bvt. Capt., 1 July, 1862, for gallant and meritorious service during the Peninsula campaign. Capt. 8th Inf., 19 Sept., 1863. Bvt. Maj. and Lieut. Col., 13 March, 1865, for gallant and meritorious service during the war. Col. 156th Ill. Vols., 4 April, 1865. Mustered out of Vol. Service, 20 Sept., 1865. Maj. 7th Inf., 3 July, 1883. Lieut. Col. 8th Inf., 16 Dec., 1888. Col. 13th Inf., 1 March, 1894. Retired over thirty years' service 16 June, 1899.

SMITH, ALFRED T. [Born in D. C. Appointed from Army.]
Priv., Corpl. and Sergt. Co. H, 6th Inf., 1 Sept., 1894, to 23 May, 1897. 2nd Lieut. 12th Inf., 3 May, 1897. 1st Lieut., 2 March, 1899.

SMITH, ALGERNON E. [Born in N. Y. Appointed from N. Y.]
2nd Lieut. 117th N. Y. Vols., 20 Aug., 1862. 1st Lieut., 25 April, 1864. Capt., 12 Oct., 1864. Bvt. Maj. Vols., 13 March, 1865, for gallant and meritorious service at the storming of Fort Fisher, N. C. Mustered out 15 May, 1865. 2nd Lieut. 7th Cav., 9 Aug., 1867. 1st Lieut., 5 Dec., 1868. R. Q. M., 31 March to 7 July, 1869. Killed 25 June, 1876, in action with Indians in Mont. Bvt. 1st Lieut., 9 Aug., 1867, for gallant and meritorious service in the Battle of Drury's Farm. Bvt. Capt., 9 Aug., 1867, for gallant and meritorious service in the capture of Fort Fisher, N. C.

SMITH, ALLEN. [Born in Fla. Appointed from Penn.]
Cadet Naval Acad., 8 July, 1863, to 3 April, 1866. 2nd Lieut. 1st Inf., 18 July, 1866. 1st Lieut., 22 April, 1868. Reg. Adj., 21 April, 1869, to 16 March, 1880. R. Q. M., 16 March to 1 May, 1880. Capt., 21 May, 1880. Trans. to 4th Cav., 6 Dec., 1880. Maj. 1st Cav., 21 Nov., 1897.

SMITH, ALLEN, Jr. [Born in S. D. Appointed from Wash.]
Corpl. Co. I, 1st Wash. Vols., 25 April, 1898, to 26 April, 1899. 2nd Lieut. 9th Inf., 10 April, 1899.

SMITH, ALLEN M. [Born in N. Y. Appointed from N. Y.]
Asst. Surg., 6 June, 1890. Capt. Asst. Surg., 6 June, 1895. Maj. Surg. 41st U. S. Vols., 17 Aug., 1899, to —.

SMITH, ANDREW H. [Born in N. Y. Appointed from N. Y.]
Asst. Surg. 43rd N. Y. Vols., 31 Dec., 1861. Surg. 94th N. Y. Vols., 11 May to 5 Sept., 1862. Asst. Surg., 17 July, 1862. Resigned 24 April, 1868. Bvt. Capt. and Bvt. Maj., 13 March, 1865, for faithful and meritorious service during the war.

SMITH, ANDREW J.* [Born in Pa. Appointed from Pa.]
2nd Lieut. 1st Drag., 1 July, 1838. 1st Lieut., 4 March, 1845. Capt., 16 Feb., 1847. Maj., 13 May, 1861. 1st Cav., 3 Aug., 1861. Col. 2nd Cal. Cav., 2 Oct., 1861. Resigned from Vol. Service, 3 Nov., 1861. Brig. Gen. Vols., 17 March, 1862. Maj. Gen. Vols., 12 May, 1864. Mustered out of Vol. Service, 15 Jan., 1866. Lieut. Col. 5th Cav., 9 May, 1864. Col. 7th Cav., 28 July, 1866. Resigned 6 May, 1869. Bvt. Col., 10 April, 1864, for gallant and meritorious service in the Battle of Pleasant Hill, La. Bvt. Brig. Gen., 13 March, 1865, for gallant and meritorious service at the Battle of Tupelo, Miss. Bvt. Maj. Gen., 13 March, 1865, for gallant and meritorious service at the Battle of Nashville, Tenn. Col. of Cav., 5 Jan., 1889 (Act of 24 Dec., 1888). Retired 22 Jan., 1889. Died 30 Jan., 1897.

SMITH, ANDREW K. [Born in Conn. Appointed from Conn.]
1st Lieut. Asst. Surg., 26 July, 1853. Capt. Asst. Surg., 26 July, 1858. Maj. Surg., 11 June, 1862. Bvt. Lieut. Col., 13 March, 1865, for faithful and meritorious service during the war. Lieut. Col. Surg., 2 July, 1884. Col. Surg., 10 July, 1889. Retired by operation of law 9 Feb., 1890. Died 14 Aug., 1899.

SMITH, A. SIDNEY. [Born in Mo. Appointed from Ky.]
Priv. and Sergt. Co. I, 5th Ky. Vols., 9 Sept., 1861, to 1 Feb., 1862. 2nd Lieut. 5th Ky. Vols., 1 Feb., 1862. 1st Lieut., 1 March, 1863. Resigned 25 March, 1864. 2nd Lieut. 37th Inf., 18 June, 1867. Trans. to 3rd Cav., 30 July, 1868. Resigned 31 Jan., 1871.

SMITH, BENJ'N. F.* [Born in N. J. Appointed from N. J.]
Bvt. 2nd Lieut. 1st Inf., 1 July, 1853. 2nd Lieut. 6th Inf., 3 March, 1855. 1st Lieut., 24 Dec., 1856. Capt., 14 May, 1861. Col. 1st Ohio Vols., 12 Oct., 1861. Discharged 2 June, 1862. Col. 126th Ohio Vols., 10 Sept., 1862. Mustered out of Vol. Service, 25 June, 1865. Maj. 27th Inf., 28 July, 1866. Died 22 June, 1868. Bvt. Maj., 7 April, 1862, for gallant and meritorious service at the Battle of Shiloh, Tenn. Bvt. Lieut. Col., 2 April, 1865, for gallant and meritorious service in front of Petersburg, Va.

SMITH, C. LAMSON. [Born in Tenn. Appointed from Army.]
Priv. Co. E, 5th Art., 24 Dec., 1862, to 25 June, 1863. 2nd Lieut. 9th Inf., 11 June, 1863. Resigned 14 May, 1864. Died — Aug., 1866.

SMITH, CALEB. [Born in Va. Appointed from Va.]
2nd Lieut. 2nd Art., 21 June, 1848. Trans. to 2nd Inf., 24 April, 1849. 1st Lieut., 30 Jan., 1852. Resigned 3 May, 1861. Died 22 Dec., 1874.

SMITH, CHARLES, Jr. [Born in Va. Appointed from the Army.]
Priv., Corpl., Sergt. and 1st Sergt. Co. H, 3rd Art., 15 May, 1880, to 14 Aug., 1882. 2nd Lieut. 8th Inf., 26 July, 1882. Died 30 Nov., 1883.

SMITH, CHAS. C. [Born in Ind. Appointed from Ind.]
Capt. 10th Ind. Vols., 22 April, 1861, to 26 May, 1861. Capt. 13th Inf., 14 May, 1861. Resigned 5 Nov., 1864.

SMITH, CHARLES C.* [Born in Ohio. Appointed from N. Y.]
2nd Lieut. 22nd Inf., 12 June, 1894. Trans. to 20th Inf., 11 Aug., 1894. 1st Lieut., 2 April, 1898.

SMITH, CHAS. F.* [Born in Pa. Appointed from Pa.]
Bvt. 2nd Lieut. 2nd Art., 1 July, 1825. 2nd Lieut., 1 July, 1825. 1st Lieut., 30 May, 1832. Capt., 7 July, 1838. Maj. 1st Art., 25 Nov., 1854. Lieut. Col. 10th Inf., 3 March, 1855. Col. 3rd Inf., 9 Sept., 1861. Brig. Gen. Vols., 31 Aug., 1861. Maj. Gen. Vols., 21 March, 1862. Died 25 April, 1862. Bvt. Maj., 9 May, 1846, for gallant and distinguished conduct at Palo Alto and Resaca de la Palma, Mex. Bvt.

Lieut. Col., 23 Sept., 1846, for gallant conduct at Monterey, Mex. Bvt. Col., 20 Aug., 1847, for gallant and meritorious conduct at Contreras and Churubusco, Mex.

SMITH, CHAS. G.* [Born in Conn. Appointed from Conn.]
2nd Lieut. 3rd Art., 1 July, 1822. Died 25 Sept., 1827.

SMITH, CHAS. H. [Born in Maine. Appointed from Maine.]
Capt. 1st Maine Cav., 19 Oct., 1861. Maj., 16 Feb., 1863. Lieut. Col., 1 March, 1863. Col., 18 June, 1863. Bvt. Brig. Gen. Vols., 1 Aug., 1864, for distinguished conduct in the engagement at St. Mary's Church, Va. Bvt. Maj. Gen. Vols., 13 March, 1865, for highly distinguished and meritorious service. Mustered out 11 Aug., 1865. Col. 28th Inf., 28 July, 1866. Bvt. Brig. Gen., 2 March, 1867, for gallant and meritorious service in the Battle of Sailor's Creek, Va. Bvt. Maj. Gen., 2 March, 1867, for gallant and meritorious service during the war. Trans. to 19th Inf., 15 March, 1869. Retired by operation of law 1 Nov., 1891. Medal of Honor for distinguished gallantry at the action of St. Mary's Church, Va., 24 June, 1864, in remaining upon the field and retaining the command of his regiment until the close of the fight, although severely wounded; while serving as Col. 1st Maine Cav.

SMITH, CHAS. H. [Born in Va. Appointed from Va.]
Asst. Surg., 13 Dec., 1847. Resigned 25 April, 1861. Died 23 March, 1879.

SMITH, CHAS. H. [Born in Va. Appointed from Va.]
Batt. P. M., 24 Nov., 1819. Maj. P. M., 1 June, 1821. Resigned 31 May, 1849.

SMITH, CHARLES M. [Born in —. Appointed from —.]
2nd Lieut. 18th Inf., —, 1899. Died of wounds received in action at Iloilo, Panay, P. I., 22 Nov., 1899.

SMITH, CHAS. P.* [Born in Pa. Appointed from Pa.]
2nd Lieut. and 1st Lieut. 17th Inf., 23 June, 1865. Trans. to 35th Inf., 21 Sept., 1866. Reg. Adj., 1 Feb., 1867, to 30 Jan., 1869. Capt., 30 Jan., 1869. Unassigned 12 Aug., 1869. Discharged 1 Dec., 1870.

SMITH, CHAS. S.* [Born in Vt. Appointed from Ill.]
2nd Lieut. 4th Art., 18 June, 1866. 1st Lieut., 28 July, 1866. Trans. to Ord., 1 Nov., 1874. Capt., 2 Aug., 1879. Maj., 22 Feb., 1897. Lieut. Col. Chief Ord. Officer Vols., 18 July, 1898, declined.

SMITH, CLARENCE B. [Born in S. C. Appointed from S. C.]
1st Lieut. 1st S. C. Vols., 20 May to 10 Nov., 1898, when mustered out. 2nd Lieut. 8th Inf., 10 April, 1899.

SMITH, CLARKE S.* [Born in Ill. Appointed from Ill.]
Addl. 2nd Lieut. Eng., 26 April, 1898. 2nd Lieut., 5 July, 1898.

SMITH, CONSTANTINE. [Born in Ireland. Appointed from N. Y.]
Trans. from Marine Corps to 2nd Art., 20 Nov., 1830, with rank of 2nd Lieut. from 27 Aug., 1825. 1st Lieut., 30 May, 1832. Killed 28 Dec., 1835, by Indians in Fla.

SMITH, CORNELIUS C. [Born in Ariz. Appointed from Army.]
Priv., Corpl., Sergt. and 1st Sergt. Troop K, 6th Cav., 9 April, 1890, to 22 Nov., 1892. 2nd Lieut. 2nd Cav., 19 Nov., 1892. 1st Lieut., 2 March, 1899. Medal of Honor for gallantry in action against hostile Sioux Indians on the north bank of the White River, near the mouth of Little Grass Creek, S. Dak., 1 Jan., 1891, with four men of his troop driving a superior force of the enemy and holding his position against their repeated efforts to recapture it, and subsequently pursuing them a great distance; while serving as 1st Sergt. Troop K, 6th Cav.

SMITH, EDMUND D.* [Born in Conn. Appinted from Conn.]
2nd Lieut. 19th Inf., 13 June, 1879. 1st Lieut., 3 Dec., 1889. Capt., 3 Jan., 1895.

SMITH, EDMUND K.* [Born in Fla. Appointed from Fla.]
Bvt. 2nd Lieut. 5th Inf., 1 July, 1845. 2nd Lieut. 7th Inf., 22 Aug., 1846. 1st Lieut., 9 March, 1851. Capt. 2nd Cav., 3 March, 1855. Maj., 31 Jan., 1861. Resigned 6 April, 1861. Bvt. 1st Lieut., 18 April, 1847, for gallant and meritorious conduct at Cerro Gordo, N. M. Bvt. Capt., 20 Aug., 1847, for gallant and meritorious conduct at Contreras, Mex.

SMITH, EDMUND L. [Born in Pa. Appointed from Pa.]
Capt. 19th Inf., 14 May, 1861. Resigned 23 July, 1867. Bvt. Maj., 20 Sept., 1863, for gallant and meritorious service at the Battle of Chickamauga, Ga.

SMITH, EDWARD J. [Born in Pa. Apointed from Colo.]
Priv. Co. H, 20th Pa. Res., 30 April, 1861, to 6 Aug., 1861. Priv. Co. G, 23rd Pa. Vols., 31 Dec., 1861, to 10 Dec., 1862. 1st Lieut. 157th Pa. Vols., 3 Jan., 1863. Mustered out 27 Feb., 1863. 1st Sergt. Co. H, 186th Pa. Vols., 1 April, 1864. 2nd Lieut., 13 May, 1864. Mustered out 14 Aug., 1865. 2nd Lieut. 22nd Inf., 7 Aug., 1867. Resigned 30 Sept., 1868.

SMITH, EDWARD S. [Born in England. Appointed from N. Y.]
1st Sergt. 4th N. Y. Batty, 4 Sept., 1861. 2nd Lieut., 4 June, 1862. 1st Lieut., 4 April, 1863. Trans. to 15th N. Y. Batty, 4 Dec., 1863. Bvt. Capt. Vols., 9 April, 1865, for conspicuous gallantry, judgment and precision in action during the campaign terminating with the surrender of the insurgent army under Gen. R. E. Lee. Mustered out 2 July, 1862. 2nd Lieut. 4th Art., 1 June, 1865. 1st Lieut., 14 July, 1866. Mustered out 8 Dec., 1870. Bvt. 1st Lieut. and Capt., 1 June, 1865, for gallant and meritorious service.

SMITH, EDWARD W. [Born in Vt. Appointed from Ill.]
1st Lieut. 15th Inf., 14 May, 1861. Maj. A. A. G. Vols., 30 Oct., 1862. Capt. 15th Inf., 17 Feb., 1863. Lieut. Col. A. A. G. (Act 17 July, 1862), 1 July, 1863. Bvt. Maj., 18 July, 1863, for gallant and meritorious service in the assault on Fort Wagner, S. C. Bvt. Col. Vols., 1 Jan., 1865, for meritorious service in the campaigns of 1863 and 1864. Bvt. Brig. Gen. Vols., 13 March, 1865, for faithful and meritorious service during the war. Bvt. Lieut. Col., 2 April, 1865, for gallant and meritorious service in front of Petersburg, Va. Relieved as Lieut. Col., A. A. G., 1 Aug., 1865. Mustered out of Vol. Service, 20 July, 1866. Trans. to 24th Inf., 21 Sept., 1866. Unassigned 25 April, 1869. Ass'd to 18th Inf., 4 March, 1870. Maj. 22nd Inf., 20 Feb., 1882. Died 21 May, 1883.

SMITH, E. KIRBY.* [Born in Conn. Appointed from Fla.]
Bvt. 2nd Lieut. 2nd Inf., 1 July, 1826. 2nd Lieut. 5th Inf., 1 July, 1826. 1st Lieut.,

4 March, 1833. Dismissed 6 Oct., 1830. Reinstated 26 April, 1832. Capt., 7 July, 1838. Died 11 Sept., 1847, of wounds received in the Battle of Molino del Rey, Mex.

SMITH, ERNESTE V.* [Born in Mo. Appointed from Mo.]
2nd Lieut. 3rd Inf., 1 July, 1886. 1st Lieut. 4th Inf., 18 May, 1893. Capt., 2 March, 1899. Graduate of the Infantry and Cavalry School 1889.

SMITH, EZRA.* [Born in Mass. Appointed from Vt.]
2nd Lieut. Art., 1 March, 1811. 1st Lieut., 11 May, 1813. Trans to Corps Art., 12 May, 1814. Capt. A. Dep. Q. M. G., 19 April, 1813. Disbanded 15 June, 1815. Died 17 Dec., 1867.

SMITH, FINE W.* [Born in Ky. Appointed from Ky.]
2nd Lieut. 12th Inf., 12 June, 1895. 1st Lieut., 11 July, 1898.

SMITH, FRANCIS. [Born in Va. Appointed from Ky.]
Ensign 2nd Rifles, 17 March, 1814. Disbanded 15 June, 1815. 2nd Lieut. Rifles, 13 Feb., 1818. 1st Lieut., 6 Aug., 1818. Resigned 15 Dec., 1818.

SMITH, FRANCIS G. [Born in —. Appointed from —.]
2nd Lieut. 14th Inf., ——, 1896. Resigned 1 Nov., 1896.

SMITH, FRANCIS H.* [Born in Va. Appointed from Va.]
Bvt. 2nd Lieut. 1st Art., 1 July, 1833. 2nd Lieut., 30 Nov., 1833. Resigned 1 May, 1836. Died 21 March, 1890.

SMITH, FRANK G. [Born in Pa. Appointed from Ohio.]
2nd Lieut. and 1st Lieut. 4th Art., 5 Aug., 1861. Bvt. Capt., 31 Dec., 1862, for gallant and meritorious service in the Battle of Stone River, Tenn. Bvt. Maj., 20 Sept., 1863, for gallant and meritorious service in the Battle of Chickamauga, Ga. Capt. 4th Art., 5 Feb., 1867. Maj. 2nd Art., 28 Aug., 1891. Lieut. Col. 6th Art., 8 March, 1898.

SMITH, FREDERICK A.* [Born in Mass. Appointed from Mass.]
Bvt. 2nd Lieut. Eng., 1 July, 1833., 2nd Lieut., 21 Jan., 1835. Capt., 7 July, 1838. Died 16 Oct., 1852.

SMITH, FRED'K. A.* [Born in N. Y. Appointed from N. Y.]
2nd Lieut. 12th Inf., 13 June, 1873. 1st Lieut., 28 June, 1878. Reg. Adj., 17 Nov., 1878, to 31 March, 1887. Capt. 12th Inf., 29 Dec., 1890 . Maj. 1st Inf., 20 June, 1899. Maj. Chf. C. S. Vols., 16 July, 1898, to 13 June, 1899.

SMITH, FRED. E.* [Born in Ill. Appointed from Ill.]
2nd Lieut. 13th Inf., 15 June, 1876. Resigned 20 Sept., 1877.

SMITH, FRED'K. W. [Born in Mass. Appointed from Mass.]
Priv Co. A, 8th Mass. Militia, 30 April to 1 Aug., 1861. Sergt. Co. A, 23rd Mass. Vols., 28 Sept., 1861, to 12 Nov., 1863. 2nd Lieut. 1st U. S. Col. Cav., 13 Nov., 1863 1st Lieut., 1 Nov., 1865. Mustered out 4 Feb., 1866. 2nd Lieut. 9th Cav., 28 July, 1866. 1st Lieut., 12 July, 1867. Died 22 Dec., 1869. Bvt. 1st Lieut. and Capt., 2 March, 1867, for gallant and meritorious service in the operations before Petersburg, Va.

SMITH, GEORGE B. [Born in England. Appointed from Navy.]
Priv., Corpl., Sergt. and 1st Sergt. Co. E, 4th Inf., 21 Sept., 1857, to 21 Sept., 1862. Surg. Stewd. U. S. N. to Oct., 1863. 2nd Lieut. 4th Inf., 19 Feb., 1863. Dismissed 26 Sept., 1864.

SMITH, GEORGE G. [Born in Mich. Appointed from Md.]
Mate U. S. N., 27 Jan., 1865. Actg. Eng., 3 May, 1865. Discharged 14 Aug., 1865. 2nd Lieut. 23d Inf., 1 Oct., 1873. Died 13 Feb., 1875.

SMITH, GEORGE R.* [Born in N. Y. Appointed from N. Y.]
Cadet at Mil. Acad., 1 July to 10 Dec., 1870. Reappointed 1 July, 1871. 2nd Lieut. 12th Inf., 16 June, 1875. 1st Lieut., 11 Jan., 1881. Maj. P. M., 5 July, 1882.

SMITH, GEORGE W. [Born in Pa. Appointed from Pa.]
2nd Lieut. Batty B, Knapp's Batt. Pa. Art., 23 May, 1864. Mustered out 3 Sept., 1864. 1st Lieut. 5th Pa. Art., 8 Sept. 1864. Capt., 10 May, 1865. Mustered out 30 June, 1865. 2nd Lieut. 17th Inf., 11 May, 1866. Trans. to 26th Inf., 21 Sept., 1866. 1st Lieut., 4 Nov., 1867. R. Q. M., 1 March, 1867, to 1 June, 1868. Unassigned 19 May, 1869. Discharged 15 Dec., 1870.

SMITH, GEORGE W. [Born in Va. Appointed from Kan.]
Capt. 18th Inf., 5 Aug., 1861. Bvt. Maj., 20 Sept., 1863, for gallant and meritorious service in the Battle of Chickamauga, Ga. Bvt. Lieut. Col., 1 Sept., 1864, for gallant and meritorious service during the Atlanta campaign and in the Battle of Jonesboro, Ga. Resigned 15 May, 1866. 2nd Lieut. 9th Cav., 6 Aug., 1873. Killed 19 Aug., 1881, by Apache Indians.

SMITH, GEORGE W. [Born in Vt. Appointed from Army.]
Priv., Corpl. and Sergt. Co. E, 17th Inf., 10 May to 9 Nov., 1862. 2nd Lieut. 17th Inf., 13 Oct., 1862. 1st Lieut., 11 Dec., 1862. R. Q. M., 15 June, 1864, to 19 Oct., 1865. Capt., 19 Oct., 1865. Trans. to 35th Inf., 21 Sept., 1866. Unassigned 25 June, 1869. Resigned 31 Dec., 1869. Bvt. Capt., 2 July, 1863, for gallant and meritorious service at the Battle of Gettysburg, Pa. Bvt. Maj., 10 May, 1864, for gallant and meritorious service at the Battle of Spottsylvania, Va.

SMITH, GERARD D. [Born in N. Y. Appointed from N. Y.]
2nd Lieut. 6th Inf., 3 Jan., 1812. 1st Lieut., 31 Oct., 1812. Reg. Adj., — May, 1813, to — May, 1814. Capt., 30 June, 1814. Trans. to 2nd Inf., 17 May, 1815. Trans. to 6th Inf., 22 March, 1819. Resigned 30 April, 1819. Bvt. Maj., 25 July, 1814, for gallant conduct at the Battle of Niagara. Died 15 March, 1835.

SMITH, GILBERT C. [Born in N. Y. Appointed from Cal.]
1st Sergt. Co. D. 5th Cal. Vols., 17 Sept., 1861. Discharged 27 Dec., 1861. 2nd Lieut. 5th Cal. Vols., 27 Dec., 1861. Discharged 24 July, 1864. Capt. A. Q. M. Vols., 18 May, 1864. 2nd Lieut. 9th Inf., 12 May, 1866. Mustered out of Vol. Service, 3 Nov., 1866. Capt. A. Q. M., 18 Jan., 1867. 1st Lieut. 9th Inf., 10 Sept., 1867 to 14 Feb., 1868. Maj. Q. M., 9 April, 1885. Lieut. Col. Dept. Q. M. Gen., 21 Aug., 1895. Col. Q. M. Vols., 12 July, 1898. Died 13 July, 1899.

SMITH, GUSTAVUS W.* [Born in Ky. Appointed from Ky.]
Bvt. 2nd Lieut. Eng., 1 July, 1842. 2nd Lieut., 1 Jan., 1845. 1st Lieut., 3 March, 1853. Resigned 18 Dec., 1854. Bvt. 1st Lieut., 18 April, 1847, for gallant and

meritorious conduct at Cerro Gordo. Bvt. Capt., 20 Aug., 1847, for gallant and meritorious conduct at Contreras, Mexico.

SMITH, GUY H. B.* [Born in Mich. Appointed from Md.]
2nd Lieut. 4th Inf., 12 June, 1891. 1st Lieut. 26 April, 1898. Honor graduate of the Infantry and Cavalry School, 1897.

SMITH, HAMILTON A.* [Born in Fla. Appointed from Ga.]
2nd Lieut. 3rd Inf., 12 June, 1893. 1st Lieut., 26 April, 1898.

SMITH, HAROLD B. [Born in ——. Appointed from Pa.]
2nd Lieut. 13th Inf., 9 July, 1898. Resigned 26 Jan., 1899.

SMITH, HARRY A.* [Born in Kan. Appointed from Kan.]
2nd Lieut. 1st Inf., 12 June, 1891. 1st Lieut. 5th Inf., 5 March, 1898. Maj. 21st Kan. Vols., 14 May to 10 Dec., 1898.

SMITH, HARRY E.* [Born in Maine. Appointed from Minn.]
2nd Lieut. 1st Art., 12 June, 1895. 1st Lieut., 2 March, 1899.

SMITH, HARRY M. [Born in Pa. Appointed from Army.]
Priv. 3 months' Ohio Vols., May to Aug., 1861. Priv. and Sergt. Maj. 19th Inf., 6 May, 1862, to 6 May, 1865. 2nd Lieut. 19th Inf., 9 Feb., 1865. 1st Lieut., 9 Feb., 1865. Trans. to 28th Inf., 21 Sept., 1866. Capt., 1 Nov., 1866. Unassigned 31 March, 1869. Ass'd to 21st Inf., 5 July, 1870. Died 23 April, 1877.

SMITH, HENRY.* [Born in N. Y. Appointed from N. Y.]
3rd Lieut. Corps Art., 2 March, 1815. 2nd Lieut. 2nd Inf., 17 June, 1816. R. Q. M., 9 Dec., 1819, to 1 June, 1821. A. Q. M., 25 Oct., 1822, to 10 July, 1823. 1st Lieut., 8 Jan., 1823. Trans. to 6th Inf., 30 July, 1823. Capt., 7 July, 1826. Resigned 16 Nov., 1836. Maj. Q. M. Vols., 3 March, 1847. Died 24 July, 1847.

SMITH, HENRY E. [Born in N. Y. Appointed from N. Y.]
Color Sergt. 71st N. Y. Vols., 20 April to 21 June, 1861. 1st Lieut. 12th Inf., 14 May, 1861. Capt., 31 Aug., 1863. Trans. to 21st Inf., 21 Sept., 1866. Discharged 31 Dec., 1870. Bvt. Capt., 27 June, 1862, for gallant and meritorious service at the Battle of Gaines' Mill, Va. Bvt. Maj., 2 July, 1863, for gallant and meritorious service at the Battle of Gettysburg, Pa.

SMITH, HENRY L.* [Born in Maine. Appointed from Maine.]
2nd Lieut. Eng., 1 July, 1839. 1st Lieut., 25 April, 1846. Capt., 1 July, 1853. Died 13 Sept., 1853.

SMITH, HENRY W. [Born in N. Y. Appointed from Mich.]
Capt. A. A. G. Vols., 19 Sept., 1861. Bvt. Maj. and Lieut. Col. Vols., 13 March, 1865, for faithful and meritorious service during the war. Mustered out 1 Sept., 1867. 2nd Lieut. 3rd Cav., 9 Aug., 1867. Died 8 March, 1869. Bvt. 1st Lieut., Capt. and Maj., 9 Aug., 1867, for gallant and meritorious conduct during the war.

SMITH, HENRY WALWORTH. [Born in Conn. Appointed from Mass.]
2nd Lieut. 4th Mass. Cav., 27 Jan., 1864. 1st Lieut., 15 Dec., 1864. Capt., 20 June, 1865. Mustered out 14 Nov., 1865. 2nd Lieut. 7th Cav., 17 Aug., 1867. 1st Lieut., 18 Sept., 1869. Dropped 9 Jan., 1871.

SMITH, HORACE.* [Born in N. Y. Appointed from N. Y.]
Bvt. 2nd Lieut. 1st Art., 1 July, 1825. 2nd Lieut. 2nd Art., 1 July, 1825. Died 8 Jan., 1828.

SMITH, ISAAC W. [Born in Va. Appointed from Va.]
2nd Lieut. of Inf., 8 March, 1847; Voltigeurs, 9 April, 1847. Disbanded 31 Aug., 1848.

SMITH, JACOB H. [Born in Ohio. Appointed from Ill.]
1st Lieut. 2nd Ky. Vols., 5 June, 1861. Capt., 28 Jan., 1862. Capt. Vet. Res. Corps, 25 June, 1863. Mustered out 21 Oct., 1865. Capt. 13th Inf., 7 March, 1867. Bvt. Maj., 7 March, 1867, for gallant conduct in the Battle of Shiloh, Tenn., 6 April, 1862. Uuassigned 25 May, 1869. Maj. J. A., 25 May, 1869. Appointment revoked 10 Dec., 1869. Ass'd to 19th Inf., 15 Dec., 1870. Maj. 2nd Inf., 26 Nov., 1894. Lieut. Col. 12th Inf., 30 June, 1898. Col. 17th Inf., 20 Oct., 1899.

SMITH, J. ALLEN.* [Born in Pa. Appointed from Pa.]
(Changed name to J. A. S. Izard—which see.)

SMITH, JAMES. [Born in S.C. Appointed from S. C.]
Ensign 3rd Inf., 27 March, 1812. 2nd Lieut., 19 Nov., 1812. 1st Lieut., 15 April, 1814. Disbanded 15 June, 1815. Reinstated 17 May, 1816, as 2nd Lieut. 1st Inf. Retained 17 May, 1816 (in reorganization under Act of 3 March, 1815), as 2nd Lieut. 1st Inf., with Bvt. of 1st Lieut. from 15 April, 1814. 1st Lieut., 10 June, 1816. Resigned 1 Jan., 1819.

SMITH, JAMES. [Born in Ohio. Appointed from Army.]
Priv., Corpl. and Sergt. Batty L. 3rd Art., 9 Feb., 1860, to 19 Nov., 1863. 2nd Lieut. 3rd Art., 31 Oct., 1863. Dropped 12 Jan. 1866.

SMITH, JAMES A.* [Born in Tenn. Appointed at Large.]
Bvt. 2nd Lieut. 6th Inf., 1 July, 1853. 2nd Lieut., 3 March, 1855. 1st Lieut., 2 Dec., 1859. Resigned 9 May, 1861.

SMITH, JAMES MADISON. [Born in Va. Appointed from Miss.]
2nd Lieut. 3rd Inf., 31 July, 1838. 1st Lieut., 2 Oct., 1840. Capt., 21 Sept., 1846. Died 4 Dec., 1847.

SMITH, JAMES M. [Born in Ky. Appointed from Ky.]
2nd Lieut. of Inf., 5 March, 1847; 16th Inf., 9 April, 1847. Dismissed 4 Sept., 1847.

SMITH, JAMES M. [Born in Mass. Appointed from Mass.]
2nd Lieut. 29th U. S. Col. Troops, 8 Dec., 1864. Mustered out 6 Nov., 1865. 2nd Lieut. 19th Inf., 23 Feb., 1866. Trans. to 28th Inf., 21 Sept., 1866. 1st Lieut., 30 Nov., 1866. Unassigned 31 March, 1869. Retired 31 Dec., 1870. Died 25 April, 1893.

SMITH, JARED A.* [Born in Maine. Appointed from Maine.]
2nd Lieut. Eng., 17 June, 1862. Bvt. 1st Lieut., 9 Aug., 1862, for gallant and meritorious service in the Battle of Cedar Mountain, Va. 1st Lieut. Eng., 3 March, 1863. Capt., 25 June, 1864. Bvt. Maj., 13 March, 1865, for gallant and meritorious service during the war of the rebellion. Maj. Eng., 13 Jan., 1874. Lieut. Col., 7 April, 1888. Col., 5 Feb., 1897.

SMITH, JOHN. [Born in Pa. Appointed from Pa.]
2nd Lieut. Corps Art., 13 Aug., 1819. Trans. to 3rd Art., 1 June, 1821. Died 31 Aug., 1824.

SMITH, JOHN E. [Born in Pa. Appointed from Ill.]
Col. 45th Ill. Vols., 23 July, 1861. Brig. Gen. Vols., 29 Nov., 1862. Bvt. Maj. Gen. Vols., 12 Jan., 1865, for faithful and efficient service and for gallantry in action. Mustered out 30 April, 1866. Col. 27th Inf., 28 July, 1866. Bvt. Brig. Gen., 2 March, 1867, for gallant and meritorious service in the Siege of Vicksburg, Miss. Bvt. Maj. Gen., 2 March, 1867, for gallant and meritorious service in action at Savannah, Ga., — Dec., 1864. Unassigned 15 March, 1869. Ass'd to 15th Inf., 15 Dec., 1870. Trans. to 14th Inf., 20 Dec., 1870. Retired, over sixty-two years of age, 19 May, 1881. Died 29 Jan., 1897.

SMITH, JOHN F. [Born in Conn. Appointed from D. C].
Sergt. Co. A, and Sergt. Maj. 71st Pa. Vols., 21 May to 1 July, 1861. 1st Lieut. 71st Pa. Vols., 1 July, 1861. Discharged 8 March, 1863. 1st Lieut. Vet. Res. Corps, 8 June, 1863. Mustered out 21 Nov., 1866. 2nd Lieut. 11th Inf., 28 July, 1866. Trans. to 16th Inf., 14 April, 1869. Mustered out 1 Jan., 1871. Died 28 Dec., 1874.

SMITH, JOHN H. [Born in England. Appointed from Army.]
Priv. Co. L, 2nd Art., 27 Jan., 1854. Corpl., 1 Sept., 1854. Sergt., 1 Jan., 1855. Priv., 1 Oct., 1856. Corpl., 1 Aug., 1857. Sergt., 1 Dec., 1857. Discharged 27 Jan., 1859. Sergt., Co. L, 2nd Art., 22 Feb., 1859. 2nd Lieut. 2nd Art., 10 Aug., 1863. 1st Lieut., 13 June, 1864. Bvt. Capt., 13 March, 1865, for gallant and faithful service during the war. Retired 31 Dec., 1870. Died 8 Sept., 1885.

SMITH, JOHN LIND. [Born in S. C. Appointed from N. Y.].
2nd Lieut. Eng., 16 Oct., 1813. 1st Lieut., 1 Oct., 1817. Capt., 29 Aug., 1820. Maj., 7 July, 1838. Died 13 Oct., 1858. Bvt. Maj., 29 Aug., 1830, for ten years' faithful service in one grade. Bvt. Lieut. Col., 18 April, 1847, for gallant and meritorious conduct at the Battle of Cerro Gordo. Bvt. Col., 20 Aug., 1847, for gallant and meritorious conduct at the Battles of Contreras and Churubusco, Mexico.

SMITH, JOHN W. A.* [Born in Maine. Appointed from Maine.]
Bvt. 2nd Lieut. 2nd Art., 1 July, 1824. 2nd Lieut. 1st Art., 1 July, 1824. Dismissed 12 Feb., 1828. Died 29 June, 1835.

SMITH, JOHN W. [Born in Conn. Appointed from Mo.]
Addl. P. M. Vols., 30 June, 1862. Bvt. Lieut. Col. Vols., 6 Feb., 1866, for faithful and zealous service in the Pay Dept. Maj. P. M., 17 Jan., 1867. Resigned 13 May, 1870

SMITH, JOSEPH B.* [Born in D. C. Appointed from D. C.]
Bvt. 2nd Lieut. 4th Art., 1 July, 1829. 2nd Lieut., 1 July, 1829. Resigned 31 May, 1832. Capt. A. A. G. Vols., 3 Aug., 1861. Bvt. Maj. Vols., 13 March, 1865, for gallant and meritorious service during the war. Mustered out 11 Nov., 1865.

SMITH, JOSEPH L. [Born in Conn. Appointed from Conn.]
Maj. 25th Inf., 12 March, 1812. Lieut. Col. 24th Inf., 12 March, 1813. Trans. to 25th Inf., 12 Sept., 1814. Trans. to 5th Inf., 17 May, 1815. Col. 3rd Inf., 10 Feb., 1818. Disbanded 1 June, 1821.

SMITH, JOSEPH L. K.* [Born in N. Y. Appointed at Large.]
Bvt. 2nd Lieut. Top. Eng., 1 July, 1857. 2nd Lieut., 9 Dec., 1857. 1st Lieut., 3 Aug., 1861. Col. 43rd Ohio Vols., 28 Sept., 1861. Bvt. Capt., 25 Aug., 1861, for gallant and meritorious service in the Shenandoah Valley, Va. Bvt. Maj., 7 April, 1862, for gallant and meritorious service at the capture of Island No. 10, in the Mississippi River. Bvt. Lieut. Col., 28 May, 1862, for gallant and meritorious service at the Siege of Corinth, Miss., where he repulsed a rebel sortie. Bvt. Col., 4 Oct., 1862, for gallant and meritorious service at the Battle of Corinth, Miss., where he was mortally wounded and died 12 Oct., 1862.

SMITH, JOSEPH P.* [Born in N. H. Appointed from N. H.]
Bvt. 2nd Lieut. 5th Inf., 1 July, 1844. 2nd Lieut., 18 June, 1846. Killed 13 Sept., 1847, in the storming of Chapultepec, Mex.

SMITH, JOSEPH P. [Born in N. Y. Appointed from Ind.]
Capt. of Inf., 2 March, 1847; 16th Inf., 9 April, 1847. Disbanded 31 July, 1848.

SMITH, JOSEPH R. [Born in N. Y. Appointed from N. Y.]
1st Lieut. Asst. Surg., 15 Dec., 1854. Capt. Asst. Surg., 15 Dec., 1859. Maj. Surg 11 June, 1865. Captured and paroled by the Insurgents, April, 1861. Act. Surg Gen., Aug., 1862. Lieut. Col. Med. Director, 25 Feb., 1865. Bvt. Lieut. Col., 13 March, 1865, for superior ability and excellent management of the affairs of his department. Relieved as Lieut. Col. Med. Director, 30 June, 1865. Bvt. Col., 22 Nov., 1866, for meritorious service and devotion to the sick during the prevalence of the cholera at Little Rock, Ark. Lieut. Col. Surg., 9 Jan., 1885. Col. Surg., 9 Feb., 1890. Retired by operation of law, 18 April, 1895.

SMITH JOSEPH R.* [Born in N. Y. Appointed from N. Y.]
2nd Lieut. 2nd Inf., 1 July, 1823. 1st Lieut., 22 March, 1832. Reg. Adj., 17 Sept., 1835, to 26 April, 1838. Capt., 26 April, 1838. Maj. 7th Inf., 11 June, 1851. Retired 25 Sept., 1861. Died 3 Sept., 1868. Bvt. Maj., 18 April, 1847, for gallant and meritorious conduct at Cerro Gordo. Bvt. Lieut. Col., 20 Aug., 1847, for gallant and meritorious conduct at Contreras and Churubusco. Bvt. Col., 9 April, 1865, for meritorious service during the war. Bvt. Brig. Gen., 13 March, 1865, for long and faithful service.

SMITH, JOSEPH S. [Born in Va. Appointed from D. C.]
Asst. Surg., 28 May, 1861. Died 8 Sept., 1867. Bvt. Capt. and Maj., 13 March, 1865, for faithful and meritorious service during the war.

SMITH, LARKIN.* [Born in Va. Appointed from Va.]
Bvt. 2nd Lieut. 3rd Inf., 1 July, 1835. 2nd Lieut., 31 Oct., 1836. 1st Lieut. 8th Inf., 7 July, 1838. Reg. Adj., 1 Sept., 1845, to 18 Feb., 1846. Capt., 21 July, 1846. Resigned 13 May, 1861. Bvt. Maj., 20 Aug., 1847, for gallant and meritorious conduct at Contreras and Churubusco, Mex. Died 3 Dec., 1884.

SMITH, LEMUEL. [Born in N. J. Appointed from Army.]
Priv., Sergt. and 1st Sergt. Batty I, 5th Art., 5 Oct., 1861, to 5 Nov., 1863. 2nd Lieut. 5th Art., 31 Oct., 1863. 1st Lieut., 28 July, 1866. Died 1 Jan., 1867. Bvt.

1st Lieut., 1 Sept., 1864, for gallant and meritorious service during the Atlanta campaign.

SMITH, LESLIE. [Born in Ireland. Appointed from Mich.]
Priv. Gen. Ser., 27 July, 1849. Corpl., 1 Sept., 1850. Sergt., 1 Oct., 1851. Discharged 27 July, 1854. 2nd Lieut. 1st Inf., 30 April, 1861. 1st Lieut., 11 June, 1861. Capt., 6 April, 1862. Bvt. Maj., 13 March, 1865, for faithful and meritorious service during the war. Maj. 2nd Inf., 21 May, 1880. Lieut. Col. 20th Inf., 8 Oct., 1885. Retired by operation of law, 15 May, 1889.

SMITH, LEWIS. [Born in Ireland. Appointed from Army.]
Priv. Co. G, 3rd Art., 1 July, 1851. Corpl., — ——. Sergt., 15 March, 1854. Sergt. Maj. 3rd Art., 1 April, 1856. Discharged 1 May, 1856. Sergt. Maj. 3rd Art., 1 May, 1856. Discharged 1 May, 1861. Sergt. Maj. 3rd Art., 1 May, 1861. 2nd Lieut. 3rd Art., 22 Oct., 1862. 1st Lieut., 30 Dec., 1864. R. Q. M., 27 Oct., 1862, to 1 Feb., 1873. Capt., 10 April, 1879. Graduate of the Artillery School, 1875. Maj 4th Art., 30 April, 1897. Retired, after forty years' service, 10 Feb., 1898.

SMITH, LOUIS P. [Born in D. C. Appointed from D. C.]
Asst. Surg., 9 Nov., 1896.

SMITH, MARTIN L.* [Born in N. Y. Appointed from N. Y.]
Bvt. 2nd Lieut. Eng., 1 July, 1842. 2nd Lieut., 1 Nov., 1843. 1st Lieut., 3 March, 1853. Capt., 1 July, 1856. Resigned 1 April, 1861. Bvt. 1st Lieut., 30 May, 1848, for meritorious conduct while serving in the enemy's country. Died 29 July, 1866.

SMITH, MATHEW C.* [Born in Ala. Appointed from Ala.]
2nd Lieut. 2nd Cav., 12 June, 1893. 1st Lieut., 2 March, 1899.

SMITH, MELANCHTON.* [Born in Ala. Appointed from Ala.]
Bvt. 2nd Lieut. 8th Inf., 1 July, 1851. 2nd Lieut., 7 Dec., 1852. Resigned 9 Nov., 1854. Died 1 Nov., 1881.

SMITH, MORTON F.* [Born in Colo. Appointed from Mich.]
2nd Lieut. 20th Inf., 12 June, 1895. 1st Lieut. of Inf., 1 July, 1898. Ass'd to 20th Inf., 1 Jan., 1899.

SMITH, NATHANIEL. [Born in ——. Appointed from Tenn.]
Lieut. of Tenn. Vols., 1812-13. 1st Lieut. 39th Inf., 29 July, 1813. Disbanded 15 June, 1815. Reinstated 2 Dec., 1815, in 1st Inf. Resigned 10 June, 1816. Col. 1st E. Tenn. Vols., 9 July, 1836. Resigned 13 Jan., 1837.

SMITH, OSKALOOSA M. [Born in Ind. Appointed from Ind.]
Musician Co. I, 13th Ind. Vols., 1 Dec., 1861. Q. M. Sergt., 19 June, 1864. Discharged 30 Nov., 1864. 1st Lieut. 155th Ind. Vols., 25 April, 1865. Mustered out 4 Aug., 1865. 2nd Lieut. 31st Inf., 18 June, 1867. Trans. to 22nd Inf., 15 May, 1869. 1st Lieut., 28 June, 1876. R. Q. M., 25 June, 1879, to 1 Oct., 1881. Reg. Adj., 1 Oct., 1881, to 22 May, 1884. Capt. C. S., 14 Aug., 1890. Maj. C. S., 15 Nov., 1897. Lieut. Col. C. S. Vols., 22 July, 1898, to 2 March, 1899. Bvt. Capt., 27 Feb., 1890, for gallant services in action against Indians at Spring Creek, Mont., 15 and 16 Oct., 1876.

SMITH, PERSIFOR F. [Born in Pa. Appointed from La.]
Col. La. Vols., 2 Feb., 1836. Mustered out 13 May, 1836. Brig. Gen. La. Vols., 15 May, 1846. Col. Mounted Rifles 27 May, 1846. Brig. Gen., 30 Dec., 1856. Died 17 May, 1858. Bvt. Brig. Gen., 23 Sept., 1846, for gallant and meritorious conduct at Monterey. Bvt. Maj. Gen., 20 Aug., 1847, for gallant and meritorious conduct at Contreras and Churubusco, Mex.

SMITH, REUBEN. [Born in Minn. Appointed from Minn.]
2nd Lieut. Co. G, 14th Minn. Vols., 8 May to 18 Nov., 1898. 2nd Lieut. 9th Inf., 10 April, 1899.

SMITH, RICHARD H. [Born in Tenn. Appointed from Tenn.]
2nd Lieut. 14th Inf., 30 Dec., 1847. 2nd Lieut. 3rd Art., 21 June, 1848. 1st Lieut., 6 Sept., 1853. Lost at sea, 24 Dec., 1853.

SMITH, RICHARD S.* [Born in Pa. Appointed from Pa.]
Bvt. 2nd Lieut. 2nd Inf., 1 July, 1834. Resigned 19 Oct., 1836. 2nd Lieut. 7th Inf., 31 Dec., 1840. 1st Lieut., 19 April, 1846. Trans. to 4th Art., 31 Aug., 1848. Resigned 13 Jan., 1856. Maj. 12th Inf., 14 May, 1861. Resigned 30 May, 1863. Died 23 Jan., 1877.

SMITH, RICHMOND. [Born in Pa. Appointed from Wis.]
2nd Lieut. 12th Inf., 1 July, 1899.

SMITH, ROBT. B. [Born in N. Y. Appointed from N. J.]
1st Lieut. 11th Inf., 14 May, 1861. R. Q. M., 18 Sept., 1861, to 15 April, 1862. Resigned 1 Jan., 1866. Bvt. Capt., 1 Oct., 1864, for gallant service at the Battle of Chappel House, Va.

SMITH, ROBT. E. [Born in Mo. Appointed from Mo.]
Priv. Co. M, 9th Mo. Cav., 1 Aug., 1863. Discharged 17 June, 1865. 1st Lieut. Asst. Surg., 26 June, 1875. Resigned 1 April, 1880.

SMITH, ROBT. P.* [Born in Miss. Appointed from Miss.]
Bvt. 2nd Lieut. 2nd Art., 1 July, 1832. 2nd Lieut., 1 July, 1832. 1st Lieut., 30 Sept., 1836. Resigned 31 Dec., 1836. Died 4 Oct., 1847.

SMITH, ROBT. S. [Born in Ohio. Appointed from Ohio.]
2nd Lieut. 2nd Drag., 4 May, 1861. 1st Lieut., 6 June, 1861; 2nd Cav., 3 Aug., 1861. Capt., 27 April, 1863. Resigned 25 Jan., 1865.

SMITH, RODNEY. [Born in Vt. Appointed from Ky.]
Maj. P. M., 23 Feb., 1864. Lieut. Col. D. P. M. G., 24 Jan., 1881. Col. Asst. P. M. G., 8 Dec., 1886. Retired by operation of law, 3 Jan., 1893.

SMITH, SAMUEL. [Born in ——. Appointed from Ill.]
1st Lieut. Mounted Rangers, 29 June, 1832. Resigned 5 March, 1833.

SMITH, SAML. B. [Born in Pa. Appointed from Pa.]
Post Surg., 12 Nov., 1816. Asst. Surg., 1 June, 1821. Died 28 Nov., 1834.

SMITH, SAMUEL P. [Born in N. Y. Appointed from Cal.]
Capt. 2nd Cal. Cav., 27 Sept., 1861. Maj., 9 May, 1865. Mustered out 20 June, 1866. Capt. 8th Cav., 28 July, 1866. Discharged 13 Oct., 1870.

SMITH, SAMUEL STANHOPE.* [Born in Del. Appointed from Del.]
2nd Lieut. Corps Art., 24 July, 1818. 1st Lieut., 30 Nov., 1820. Trans. to 1st Art., 1 June, 1821. Trans. to 3rd Art., 16 Aug., 1821. Died 10 Sept., 1828.

SMITH, SEBREE.* [Born in Mo. Appointed from Kan.]
2nd Lieut. 6th Cav., 15 June, 1870. 1st Lieut., 4 Oct., 1872. R. Q. M., 17 May, 1873, to 4 April, 1874. Trans. to 2nd Art., 6 Feb., 1877. R. Q. M., 20 Jan., 1881, to 5 May, 1887. Capt. 3rd Art., 8 March, 1898. Graduate of the Artillery School, 1880.

SMITH, SIDNEY. [Born in Va. Appointed from Va.]
2nd Lieut. 4th Inf., 1 July, 1839. 1st Lieut., 9 May, 1846. Died 16 Sept., 1847, of wounds received in the capture of the City of Mexico.

SMITH, SIMEON. [Born in N. Y. Appointed from Minn.]
Maj. 2nd Minn. Vols., 23 July, 1861. Resigned 6 Sept., 1861. Maj. P. M., 29 Aug., 1861. Bvt. Lieut. Col., 13 March, 1865, for faithful and meritorious service during the war. Retired 10 June, 1879. Died 28 Dec., 1884.

SMITH, THEODORE. [Born in Germany. Appointed from Army.]
Priv. Gen. Ser., 31 Oct., 1867. Trans. to Sig. Corps, 8 Sept., 1868. Corpl., 1 May, 1870. Sergt., 1 July, 1870. Discharged 31 Oct., 1870. Sergt. Sig. Corps, 15 Nov., 1870. 2nd Lieut. 15th Inf., 1 Oct., 1873. 1st Lieut., 6 Oct., 1877. Died 27 June, 1884.

SMITH, THOS. A. [Born in Va. Appointed from Ga.]
2nd Lieut. Art., 15 Dec., 1803. 1st Lieut., 31 Dec., 1805. Capt. Rifles, 3 May, 1808. Lieut. Col., 31 July, 1810. Col. Rifles, 6 July, 1812. Brig. Gen., 24 Jan., 1814. Retained 17 May, 1815, as Col. Rifle Reg. Resigned 10 Nov., 1818. Retained 17 May, 1815 (in reorganization under Act of 3 March, 1815), as Col. Rifle Reg., with Bvt. of Brig. Gen. from 24 Jan., 1814. Died — Dec., 1818.

SMITH, THOS. C. H. [Born in Mass. Appointed from Ohio.]
Lieut. Col. 1st Ohio Cav., 5 Sept., 1861. Discharged 27 April, 1863. Brig. Gen. Vols., 29 Nov., 1862. Mustered out 15 Jan., 1866. Maj. P. M., 17 April, 1878. Retired by operation of law, 24 March, 1883. Died 8 April, 1897.

SMITH, THOS. F. [Born in Va. Appointed from Ky.]
2nd Lieut. 8th Inf., 30 June, 1855. Resigned 1 April, 1858.

SMITH, THOS. F. [Born in Va. Appointed from Ky.]
Ensign 1st Rifles, 2 July, 1813. 3rd Lieut., 20 Nov., 1813. 2nd Lieut., 11 May, 1814. Disbanded 15 June, 1815. Reinstated 2 Dec., 1815, in Rifle Reg. 1st Lieut., 22 April, 1817. Capt., 25 April, 1819. Trans. to 1st Inf., 1 June, 1821. Resigned 30 Oct., 1837. Bvt. Maj., 25 April, 1829, for ten years' faithful service in one grade. Died ——, 1844.

SMITH, THOMAS L.* [Born in Ind. Appointed from Ind.]
2nd Lieut. 17th Inf., 12 June, 1893. 1st Lieut., 26 April, 1898. Reg. Com., 5 Aug., 1899.

SMITH, THOS. M. K. [Born from Pa. Appointed from Army.]
Priv. Co. B, 1st Batt. 17th Inf., 31 March, 1864. Corpl., 1 May, 1864. Sergt., 15 May, 1864. 2nd Lieut. and 1st Lieut. 17th Inf., 2 July, 1864. Trans. to 26th Inf., 21 Sept., 1866. Capt., 7 March, 1867. Unassigned 19 May, 1869. Ass'd to 23rd Inf., 15 Dec., 1870. Maj. 1st Inf., 11 Oct., 1894. Lieut. Col. 10th Inf., 30 June, 1898. Retired, for over thirty years' service, 14 May, 1899.

SMITH, VERRES N. [Born in Ky. Appointed from Kan.]
Capt. 19th Inf., 14 May, 1861. Resigned 16 July, 1863.

SMITH, WALTER. [Born in N. Y. Appointed from N. Y.]
Ensign 29th Inf., 30 Sept., 1813. 3rd Lieut., 7 Nov., 1813. 2nd Lieut., 12 March, 1814. Trans. to Light Art., 17 May, 1815. 1st Lieut., 5 June, 1819. Reg. Adj., — Jan. to 1 June, 1821. Trans. to 1st Art., 1 June, 1821. Capt., 31 May, 1832. Resigned 30 Sept., 1833.

SMITH, WM. [Born in Vt. Appointed from Minn.]
Addl. P. M., 29 Aug., 1861. Bvt. Lieut. Col. Vols., 13 March, 1865, for faithful and meritorious service during the war. Mustered out 20 July, 1866. Maj. P. M., 17 Jan., 1867. Lieut. Col. D. P. M. G., 6 Sept., 1888. Brig. Gen. P. M. G., 10 March, 1890. Retired by operation of law, 26 March, 1895.

SMITH, WM.* [Born in N. Y. Appointed from N. Y.]
(Changed name to Wm. D. Fraser—which see.)

SMITH, WM. D.* [Born in Ga. Appointed from Ga.]
Bvt. 2nd Lieut. 2nd Drag., 1 July, 1846. 2nd Lieut., 18 Aug., 1847. 1st Lieut., 8 Aug., 1851. Capt., 4 June, 1858. Resigned 28 Jan., 1861. Died 4 Oct., 1862.

SMITH, WM. F.* [Born in Vt. Appointed from Vt.]
Bvt. 2nd Lieut. Top. Eng., 1 July, 1845. 2nd Lieut., 14 July, 1849. 1st Lieut., 3 March, 1853. Capt., 1 July, 1859. Maj. Eng., 3 March, 1863. Col. 3rd Vt. Vols., 16 July, 1861. Brig. Gen. Vols., 13 Aug., 1861. Maj. Gen. Vols., 4 July, 1862, which appointment expired 4 March, 1863. Maj. Gen. Vols., 9 March, 1864. Resigned from Vol. Service, 4 Nov., 1865. Resigned 21 March, 1867. Bvt. Lieut. Col., 28 June, 1862, for gallant and meritorious service at the Battle of White Oak Swamp, Va. Bvt. Col., 17 Sept., 1862, for gallant and meritorious service at Antietam, Md. Bvt. Brig. Gen., 13 March, 1865, for gallant and meritorious service at the Battle of Chattanooga, Tenn. Bvt. Maj. Gen., 13 March, 1865, for gallant and meritorious service in the field during the war. Appointed Maj. of Eng., 1 March, 1889, to rank from 27 Feb., 1889 (Act of 27 Feb. 1889). Retired 1 March, 1889.

SMITH, WM. F. [Born in Ireland. Appointed from R. I.]
Asst. Surg. 2nd R. I. Vols., 24 March, 1864. Surg., 18 March, 1865. Mustered out 13 July, 1865. Asst. Surg., 28 Feb., 1866. Resigned 5 Jan., 1870.

SMITH, WM. F.* [Born in N. Y. Appointed from N. Y.]
2nd Lieut. 5th Cav., 15 June, 1869. Declined 3 July, 1869.

SMITH, WM. H.* [Born in Mo. Appointed from Mo.]
2nd Lieut. 10th Cav., 13 June, 1883. 1st Lieut., 25 March, 1890. Honor graduate of the Infantry and Cavalry School, 1897. Killed in action 1 July, 1898, at San Juan, Santiago, Cuba.

SMITH, WILLIAM O. [Born in Ariz. Appointed from Mo.]
2nd Lieut. 7th Inf., 1 Sept., 1899.
SMITH, WM. P. [Born in Pa. Appointed from Pa.]
2nd Lieut. Corps Art., 28 Jan., 1820. Resigned 1 March, 1820.
SMITH, WM. P.* [Born in Va. Appointed from Va.]
Bvt. 2nd Lieut. Top. Eng., 1 July, 1857. Resigned 2 April, 1861.
SMITH, WILLIAM R.* [Born in Tenn. Appointed from Tenn.]
Addl. 2nd Lieut. 1st Art., 11 June, 1892. 2nd Lieut., 23 Sept., 1892. 1st Lieut., 2 March, 1899. 1st Lieut. of Ord., 29 Sept., 1899, declined.
SMITH, WM. S. [Born in N. Y. Appointed from N. Y.]
Maj. P. M., 22 March, 1824. Resigned 1 July, 1824.
SMITH, WM. S.* [Born in Ohio. Appointed from Ohio.]
Bvt. 2nd Lieut. 3rd Art., 1 July, 1853. 2nd Lieut. 2nd Art., 9 July, 1853. Resigned 19 June, 1854. Col. 13th Ohio Vols., 26 June, 1861. Brig. Gen. Vols., 15 April, 1862. Resigned 15 July, 1864.
SMITH, WM. S.* [Born in N. Y. Appointed from N. Y.
2nd Lieut. 1st Art., 1 July, 1839. 1st Lieut., 18 June, 1846. Died 6 Nov., 1849.
SMITH, WM. T. [Born at Sea. Appointed from Maine.]
2nd Lieut. 13th Maine Vols., 31 Dec., 1861. 1st Lieut., 10 July, 1862. Resigned 13 Feb., 1864. Priv. and Artf. Co. D, Batt. Engs., 12 Dec., 1864, to 28 April, 1866. 2nd Lieut. 9th Inf., 23 Feb., 1866. Died 31 July, 1866.
SMITH, WRIGHT. [Born in N. Y. Appointed from Del.]
2nd Lieut. 6th Art., 9 July, 1898.
SMITHER, HENRY C.* [Born in Ind. Ter. Appointed from Colo.]
Addl. 2nd Lieut. 8th Cav., 11 June, 1897. 2nd Lieut. 1st Cav., 11 Dec., 1897.
SMITHER, ROBT. G. [Born in Ind. Appointed from Ind.]
Priv. Co. I, 26th Ind. Vols., 31 Aug., 1861. Discharged 5 Nov., 1862. 1st Sergt. Co. H, 7th Ind. Cav., 9 Aug., 1863. 2nd Lieut. 7th Ind. Cav., 30 Sept., 1864. 1st Lieut. 7 March, 1865. Mustered out 18 Feb., 1866. 1st Lieut. 10th Cav., 12 June, 1867. Reg. Adj., 25 Jan., 1877, to 18 Nov., 1881. Capt., 18 Nov., 1881. Retired for disability from wound, 10 May, 1888.
SMOKE, SAMUEL A.* [Born in Fla. Appointed from Fla.]
Addl. 2nd Lieut. 6th Inf., 12 June, 1887. 2nd Lieut. 18th Inf., 30 Sept., 1887. 1st Lieut. 19th Inf., 3 Jan., 1895. Capt. 5th Inf., 2 March, 1899. Capt. A. Q. M. Vols., 20 June, 1898, to 13 June, 1899. Graduate of the Inf. and Cav. Sch., 1891.
SMOOT, WM. S. [Born in Va. Appointed from Md.]
1st Lieut. 1st Md. Vols., 23 Dec., 1863, to 1 July, 1864. 2nd Lieut. Ord., 29 Jan., 1864. 1st Lieut., 7 March, 1867. Discharged 31 Dec., 1870. Bvt. 1st Lieut., 13 March, 1865, for faithful and meritorious service in the Ord. Dept. Died 18 Feb., 1886.
SMYSER, JACOB H.* [Born in Pa. Appointed from Pa.]
2nd Lieut. 3rd Art., 6 May, 1861. 1st Lieut. 5th Art., 14 May, 1861. Trans. to Ord., 27 April, 1863. Capt., 7 March, 1867. Resigned 10 Feb., 1869. Bvt. Capt., 13 March, 1865, for faithful and meritorious service in the Ord. Dept. Died 6 May, 1885.
SMYTH, HAROLD. [Born in Va. Appointed from Va.]
1st Lieut. 3rd Art., 14 April, 1812. Trans. to Corps Art., 12 May, 1814. Resigned 2 May, 1816. Bvt. Capt., 11 Sept., 1814, for gallant conduct at the Battle of Plattsburg.
SMYTH, JOHN L. [Born in Ireland. Appointed from Army.]
Priv., Corpl., Sergt. and 1st Sergt. Co. K, 10th Inf., 3 June, 1857, to 17 Aug., 1863. 2nd Lieut. 10th Inf., 10 Aug., 1863. 1st Lieut., 28 Jan., 1864. Capt., 7 Nov., 1865. Unassigned 19 May, 1869. Ass'd to 23rd Inf., 14 July, 1869. Died 22 Jan., 1873. Bvt. 1st Lieut., 2 July, 1863, for gallant and meritorious service at the Battle of Gettysburg, Pa. Bvt. Capt., 30 July, 1864, for gallant and meritorious service in action in front of Petersburg, Va.
SMYTH, WM. H. [Born in Maine. Appointed from Kan.]
Priv. Co. A, 5th Kans. Cav., 16 July to 14 Nov., 1861. 1st Lieut. 16th Inf., 26 Oct., 1861. Capt., 26 Dec., 1864. Unassigned 17 April, 1869. Resigned 10 May, 1869. Bvt. Capt. and Maj., 19 Sept., 1863, for gallant and meritorious service at the Battle of Chickamauga, Ga.
SMYTH, WM. H. [Born in N. Y. Appointed from N. Y.]
Maj. P. M., 20 Sept., 1882. Resigned 9 Jan., 1885.
SMYTHE, JAMES H. [Born in Md. Appointed from Md.]
2nd Lieut. of Inf., 7 March, 1847; Voltigeurs, 9 April, 1847. Resigned 23 June, 1848.
SNEED, ARCHIBALD H. [Born in N. C. Appointed from N. C.]
1st Lieut. Light Drag., 12 March, 1812. Reg. P. M., 12 Jan., 1813. District P. M., 5 June, 1814. Disbanded 15 June, 1815. Batt. P. M., 29 April, 1816. Resigned 18 April, 1817.
SNELLING, JAMES G. S.* [Born in Minn. Appointed from Ohio.]
Bvt. 2nd Lieut. 8th Inf., 1 July, 1845. 2nd Lieut., 21 July, 1846. 1st Lieut., 22 Jan., 1849. Capt. 10th Inf., 3 March, 1855. Died 25 Aug., 1855. Bvt. 1st Lieut., 20 Aug., 1847, for gallant and meritorious conduct at Contreras and Churubusco, Mex. Bvt. Capt., 8 Sept., 1847, for gallant and meritorious conduct at Molino del Rey, Mex.
SNELLING, JOSIAH. [Born in Mass. Appointed from Mass.]
1st Lieut. 4th Inf., 3 May, 1808. Capt., 12 June, 1809. Maj. A. I. G., 25 April, 1813. Lieut. Col. 4th Rifles, 21 Feb., 1814. Col. I. G., 12 April, 1814. Retained 17 May, 1815, as Lieut. Col. 6th Inf. Col. 5th Inf., 1 June, 1819. Died 20 Aug., 1828. Bvt. Maj., for gallant conduct at the Battle of Brownstown, 9 Aug., 1812.
SNIFFEN, CULVER C. [Born in N. Y. Appointed from N. Y.]
Maj. P. M., 3 March, 1877. Lieut. Col. D. P. M. G, 31 March, 1899.
SNODGRASS, JAMES C. [Born in Pa. Appointed from Pa.]
2nd Lieut. 2nd Drag., 26 April, 1861. Resigned 13 June, 1861.

SNOW, CHAS. L. [Born in N. Y. Appointed from N. Y.]
Cadet at Mil. Acad., 1 July, 1864, to 2 July, 1868. 2nd Lieut. 24th Inf., 13 July, 1868. Trans. to 11th Inf., 25 April, 1869. Dismissed 29 Aug., 1871.

SNOW, WILLIAM J.* [Born in N. Y. Appointed from N. J.]
Addl. 2nd Lieut. 1st Art., 12 June, 1890. 2nd Lieut., 1 July, 1891. 1st Lieut. 7th Art., 8 March, 1898. Graduate of the Artillery School, 1898.

SNOWDEN, ISAAC W. [Born in Pa. Appointed from Pa.]
Surg.'s Mate 7th Inf., 19 Feb., 1817. Resigned 8 Oct., 1818.

SNOWDEN, JONATHAN. [Born in N. J. Appointed from N. J.]
Capt. in the levies of 1791. Mil. Storekeeper, 5 May, 1808. Died 25 Dec., 1824.

SNYDER, ANTES.* [Born in Pa. Appointed from Pa.]
Bvt. 2nd Lieut. 2nd Inf., 1 July, 1829. Resigned 25 Sept., 1830. Died 18 Dec., 1861.

SNYDER, CHAS. [Born in Pa. Appointed from Pa.]
2nd Lieut. 8th Inf., 5 Aug., 1861. 1st Lieut., 21 June, 1864. Reg. Adj., 1 Nov., 1864, to 2 Feb., 1865. Capt., 6 Aug., 1867. Unassigned 3 May, 1869. Discharged 20 Dec., 1870. Bvt. 1st Lieut., 9 Aug., 1862, for gallant and meritorious service at the Battle of Cedar Mountain, Va. Bvt. Capt., 30 July, 1864, for gallant and meritorious service in action in front of Petersburg, Va.

SNYDER, FREDERIC A. [Born in Ill. Appointed from Ill.]
2nd Lieut. of Inf., 8 March, 1847; 16th Inf., 9 April, 1847. Disbanded 5 Aug., 1848.

SNYDER, GEORGE D. [Born in Pa. Appointed from Md.]
Ensign 5th Inf., 30 April, 1812. 2nd Lieut., 1 Sept., 1812. 1st Lieut., 25 June, 1814. Disbanded 15 June, 1815. Reinstated 17 May, 1816, as 2nd Lieut. Corps Art. 1st Lieut., 30 Aug., 1816. Resigned 31 Oct., 1819. 2nd Lieut. Rifle Reg., 13 Oct., 1820. Disbanded 1 June, 1821. Retained — May, 1816 (in reorganization under Act of 3 March, 1815), as 2nd Lieut. of Art., with Bvt. of 1st Lieut. from 1 June, 1814.

SNYDER, GEORGE W.* [Born in N. Y. Appointed from N. Y.]
Bvt. 2nd Lieut. Eng., 1 July, 1856. 2nd Lieut., 23 Aug., 1856. 1st Lieut., 1 July, 1860. Died 17 Nov., 1861. Bvt. Capt., 14 April, 1861, for gallant and meritorious service in defence of Fort Sumter, S. C. Bvt. Maj., 21 July, 1861, for gallant and meritorious service in the Manassas campaign.

SNYDER, HENRY D. [Born in Pa. Appointed from Pa.]
Asst. Surg., 6 June, 1890. Capt. Asst. Surg., 6 June, 1895. Maj. Surg. 43rd U. S. Vols., 17 Aug., 1899.

SNYDER, JAMES A. [Born in D. C. Appointed from Va.]
2nd Lieut. 3rd Inf., 5 Aug., 1861. Bvt. 1st Lieut., 3 May, 1863, for gallant and meritorious service in the Battle of Chancellorsville, Va. Bvt. Capt., 2 July, 1863, for gallant and meritorious service in the Battle of Gettysburg, Pa. 1st Lieut. 3rd Inf., 3 Oct., 1863. Reg. Adj., 1 Jan., 1866, to 6 Aug., 1866. Capt., 31 Dec., 1867. Retired for disability, 13 Nov., 1889. Died in 1900.

SNYDER, LOUIS T. [Born in Pa. Appointed from Pa.]
Priv. Co. H, 25th Pa. Vols., 18 April to 25 July, 1861. 1st Lieut. 19th Inf., 14 May, 1861. Wholly retired 28 Dec., 1863. Died 31 Jan., 1890.

SNYDER, SIMON. [Born in Pa. Appointed from Pa.]
2nd Lieut. 5th Inf., 26 April, 1861. 1st Lieut., 25 June, 1861. Capt., 1 July, 1863. Maj. 11th Inf., 10 March, 1883. Trans. to 5th Inf., 17 May, 1883. Lieut. Col. 10th Inf., 2 Jan., 1888. Col. 19th Inf., 16 Sept., 1892. Brig. Gen. Vols., 4 May, 1898, to 12 May, 1899. Bvt. Maj., 27 Feb., 1890, for gallant services in action against Indians at Bear Paw Mountain, Mont., 30 Sept., 1877.

SOKALSKI, GEORGE O.* [Born in N. Y. Appointed from N. Y.]
2nd Lieut. 2nd Drag., 6 May, 1861; 2nd Cav., 3 Aug., 1861. 1st Lieut., 1 Oct., 1861. Lieut. Col. A. I. G. Vols., 12 May, 1864, to 6 Feb., 1865. Capt., 19 Sept., 1864. Dismissed 10 July, 1866. Reinstated 26 Oct., 1866. Died 12 Feb., 1867.

SOLEY, JAMES R.* [Born in Mass. Appointed from Mass.]
Bvt. 2nd Lieut. 4th Art., 1 July, 1837. 2nd Lieut., 31 Aug., 1837. 1st Lieut., 20 July, 1842. Died 31 Oct., 1845.

SOLOMON, OWEN F.* [Born in Ga. Appointed from Ga.]
Bvt. 2nd Lieut. 2nd Art., 1 July, 1853. 2nd Lieut. 4th Art., 25 Nov., 1853. 1st Lieut., 31 Oct., 1856. Died 27 Sept., 1859.

SOMERBY, RUFUS. [Born in Ky. Appointed from Ky.]
Priv. Co. A, 9th Ky. Vols., 10 May, 1862. 1st Lieut., 10 May, 1862. Capt., 1 Aug., 1862. Resigned 10 June, 1863. Priv. Co. K, and Sergt. Maj. 11th Ky. Cav., 27 Nov., 1863, to 25 March, 1864. 2nd Lieut. 11th Ky. Cav., 25 March, 1864. Mustered out 6 July, 1865. Priv., Corpl. and 1st Sergt. Co. I, and Sergt. Maj. 1st Cav., 9 Oct., 1865, to 22 Oct., 1867. 2nd Lieut. 8th Cav., 18 June, 1867. 1st Lieut., 7 Sept., 1869. Resigned 1 March, 1870. Bvt. 1st Lieut., 30 Aug., 1868, for gallant conduct in engagements with the Apache Indians between 30 Aug., 1868, and 12 Sept., 1868. Bvt. Capt., 7 Oct., 1868, for gallant and efficient service in action with the Apache Indians between 7 and 23 Oct., 1868. Priv., Corpl., Sergt. and 1st Sergt. Batty E, 5th Art., 3 March, 1870, to 1 July, 1874. Priv., Corpl. and Sergt. Co. B, 1st Cav., 4 Dec., 1874, to 3 Dec., 1879. Priv. and Corpl. Batty B, 4th Art., 13 Dec., 1879. Trans. to Troop E, 6th Cav., 16 March, 1881. Sergt. 1 Aug., 1881. Died 27 Dec., 1882.

SOMMER, HENRY. [Born in Germany. Appointed from Army.]
Priv. Co. E, 7th Inf., 7 Dec., 1857, to 15 March, 1860. Priv. Co. E, and Sergt. Maj. 2nd Inf., 25 July, 1860, to 27 March, 1863. 2nd Lieut. 2nd Inf., 19 Feb., 1863. 1st Lieut., 16 Feb., 1865. Resigned 21 May, 1868. Bvt. 1st Lieut., 5 May, 1864, for gallant and meritorious service at the Battle of the Wilderness, Va. Bvt. Capt., 12 May, 1864, for gallant and meritorious service at the Battle of Spottsylvania C. H., Va.

SOPER, SYLVESTER. [Born in N. Y. Appointed from N. Y.]
Capt. 5th Cal. Vols., 18 Sept., 1861. Resigned 9 June, 1862. Priv. Co. B, 11th Vt. Vols., 25 Sept., 1862. Sergt. Maj., 28 Dec., 1862. Discharged 2 Feb., 1864. 1st Lieut. 26th Col. Inf., 3 Feb., 1864. Capt., 10 Feb., 1865. Mustered out 28 Aug., 1865. 2nd Lieut. 40th Inf., 22 Jan., 1867. Died 4 Jan., 1869.

SORLEY, LEWIS S.* [Born in England. Appointed from Tex.]
2nd Lieut. 16th Inf., 12 June, 1891. 1st Lieut., 26 April, 1898.

SORREL, FRANCIS. [Born in Ga. Appointed from Ga.]
Asst. Surg., 29 June, 1849. Resigned 27 June, 1856.

SOUDERS, JACOB A. [Born in Ohio. Appointed from Ohio.]
1st Lieut. 8th Ohio Cav., 12 Sept., 1861. Capt., 26 June, 1862. Maj., 11 May, 1864. Resigned 29 May, 1865. 2nd Lieut. 38th Inf., 17 May, 1867. Resigned 10 April, 1869. Bvt. 1st Lieut., 17 May, 1867, for gallant and meritorious service in the Battle of Fort Sanders, Tenn. Bvt. Capt., 17 May, 1867, for gallant and meritorious service in the Battle of Winchester, Va.

SOULE, FRANK, Jr.* [Born in Miss. Appointed from Cal.]
2nd Lieut. Ord., 18 June, 1866. Resigned 27 Aug., 1870.

SOUTHERLAND, SAMUEL U.* [Born in N. C. Appointed from N. C.]
2nd Lieut. 4th Art., 1 July, 1823. Resigned 15 July, 1824. Died in 1836.

SOUTHGATE, ROB'T. [Born in Va. Appointed from Va.]
Asst. Surg., 30 Aug., 1836. Resigned 31 May, 1853. Asst. Surg., 22 Feb., 1854. Resigned 31 March, 1856. Died in 1864.

SOUTHWORTH, SAMUEL D. [Born in Mich. Appointed from Army.]
Priv. Mich. Vols., May, 1861, to Jan., 1863. Priv., Corpl. and Sergt. Batty B, 5th Art., 4 Jan., 1863, to 23 July, 1864. 2nd Lieut. 2nd Art., 30 June, 1864. Killed 19 Oct., 1864, at the Battle of Cedar Creek, Va.

SPALDING, CHAS. H. [Born in Ga. Appointed from N. Y.]
Cadet at Mil. Acad., 1 July, 1824, to 2 Jan., 1826. 1st Lieut. 2nd Drag., 11 June, 1836. Resigned 15 Dec., 1837.

SPALDING, GEORGE S. [Born in Ohio. Appointed from Ohio.]
Priv. and Sergt. 27th Ohio Vols., 13 Aug., 1861, to 3 March, 1863. 2nd Lieut. 27th Ohio Vols., 3 March, 1863. Resigned 1 April, 1864. 2nd Lieut. 33rd Inf., 28 July, 1866. 1st Lieut., 28 July, 1866. Unassigned 3 May, 1869. Discharged 1 Oct., 1870. Bvt. Capt., 2 March, 1867, for faithful and meritorious service.

SPALDING JOHN L. [Born in Conn. Appointed from Conn.]
Sergt. Maj. 1st Conn. Vols., 23 April to 31 July, 1861. Capt. 18th Mass. Vols., 24 Aug., 1861. Discharged 23 Oct., 1863. 1st Lieut. Adj. 29th Conn. Vols., 29 Jan., 1864. Mustered out 24 Oct., 1865. 2nd Lieut. 1st Inf., 6 April, 1866. 1st Lieut., 1 Aug., 1866. Dismissed 9 Sept., 1867. Reinstated 13 Dec., 1867. Unassigned 8 April, 1869. Mustered out 1 Jan., 1871.

SPANGLER, JOHN W. [Born in Ky. Appointed from Army.]
Priv. and 1st Sergt. Troop H, 2nd Cav., 11 July, 1855, to 8 June, 1861. 2nd Lieut. 3rd Cav., 14 May, 1861; 6th Cav., 3 Aug., 1861. 1st Lieut., 24 Oct., 1861. Reg. Adj., 1 July to 1 Oct., 1861. R. Q. M., 1 Oct., 1861, to 1 Feb., 1863, and 5 Nov., 1865, to 28 July, 1866. Capt., 28 July, 1866. Died 17 Sept., 1867. Bvt. Capt., 3 July, 1863, for gallant and meritorious service in the Gettysburg campaign.

SPARROW, SOLOMON E.* [Born in Mass. Appointed from Mass.]
2nd Lieut. 21st Inf., 14 June, 1878. 1st Lieut., 1 April, 1885. Capt., 25 March, 1898.

SPAULDING, EDWARD J. [Born in N. Y. Appointed from Army.]
Priv. Co. I, 2nd Drag., 22 Jan., 1857. Corpl., 26 Sept., 1857. Sergt., 29 Aug., 1860. Q. M. Sergt. 2nd Cav., 27 Oct., 1861. Discharged 1 Dec., 1861. Q. M. Sergt. 2nd Cav., 1 Dec., 1861. 2nd Lieut. 2nd Cav., 17 July, 1862. Reg. Com., 1 Oct., 1862, to 12 Feb., 1867. 1st Lieut., 9 June, 1863. Bvt. Capt., 9 June, 1863, for gallant and meritorious service in the Battle of Beverly Ford, Va. Capt. 2nd Cav., 12 Feb., 1867. Maj. 4th Cav., 9 Jan., 1886. Accidentally killed 10 Dec., 1888.

SPAULDING, OLIVER L., Jr. [Born in Mich. Appointed from Mich.]
2nd Lieut. 3rd Art., 9 July, 1898.

SPEED, CHAS. [Born in England. Appointed from Army.]
Priv., Corpl., Sergt. and 1st Sergt. Co. H, 3rd Inf., 3 April, 1855, to 24 Oct., 1861. 2nd Lieut. 5th Inf., 24 Oct., 1861. 1st Lieut., 1 June, 1862. Dismissed 29 Jan., 1867.

SPEER, CALVIN T. [Born in Mass. Appointed from Army.]
1st Lieut. 4th N. J. Vols., 13 Aug., 1861. Resigned 9 Sept., 1862. 1st Lieut. 5th U. S. Col. Inf., 25 Aug., 1863. Capt., 21 Dec., 1863. Dismissed 21 Aug., 1864. Priv. Co. H, 2nd Inf., 25 June to 27 July, 1867. 2nd Lieut. 8th Inf., 27 July, 1867. Unassigned 3 May, 1869. Ass'd to 11th Inf., 1 Jan., 1871. Dismissed 16 Jan., 1874. Died 30 Aug., 1883.

SPENCE, ROBERT E. L.* [Born in Ga. Appointed from Ga.]
2nd Lieut. 16th Inf., 12 June, 1893. 1st Lieut., 26 April, 1898. Maj. 3rd Ga. Vols., 9 Aug., 1898. Lieut. Col., 25 Oct., 1898, to 22 April, 1899. Maj. 32nd U. S. Vols., 5 July, 1899.

SPENCE, ROBT. T. [Born in Md. Appointed from Md.]
Asst. Surg. 9th Inf., 22 July, 1847. Disbanded 26 Aug., 1848.

SPENCER, ABNER F. [Born in N. Y. Appointed from N. Y.]
1st Lieut. 29th Inf., 30 April, 1813. Capt., 14 March, 1814. Trans. to 2nd Inf., 17 May, 1815. Resigned 17 June, 1816.

SPENCER, DAVID B. [Born in Va. Appointed from Va.]
Mil. Storekeeper, 8 March, 1837. Resigned 17 Oct., 1837.

SPENCER, EUGENE J.* [Born in Mo. Appointed from Mo.]
2nd Lieut. 4th Cav., 13 June, 1882. Trans. to Eng., 7 June, 1883. 1st Lieut., 19 March, 1884. Resigned 12 Aug., 1890.

SPENCER, GEORGE C. [Born in Va. Appointed from Ind.]
2nd Lieut. 1st Inf., 13 Feb., 1818. 1st Lieut., 1 Oct., 1818. Capt., 1 June, 1822. Resigned 31 Dec., 1831.

SPENCER, GEORGE K. [Born in Pa. Appointed from Iowa.]
Priv Co. B, 2nd Iowa Vols., 27 May, 1861. 1st Lieut. 35th Iowa Vols., 18 Sept., 1862. Capt., 22 Nov., 1863. Mustered out 10 Aug., 1865. 2nd Lieut. 19th Inf., 17 Aug., 1867. 1st Lieut., 28 June, 1878. Retired for disability with rank of Capt., 20 Feb., 1891.

SPENCER, JAMES H. [Born in Mass. Appointed from Mass.]
Priv. Co. K, 6th Mass. Vols., 16 April, 1861. Discharged 2 Aug., 1861. Sergt. Co. F, 20th Mass. Vols., 23 Aug., 1861. 1st Lieut. 20th Mass. Vols., 23 Nov., 1863. Capt., 6 July, 1864. Mustered out 16 July, 1865. 2nd Lieut. and 1st Lieut. 12th Inf., 23 Feb., 1866. Trans. to 30th Inf., 21 Sept., 1866. Trans. to 4th Inf., 23 March, 1869. Capt., 20 March, 1879. Bvt. Capt., 27 Feb., 1890, for gallant services in action against Indians near Fort Steele, Wyo., 22 March, 1869. Retired for wound and injury 3 Jan., 1885.

SPENCER, JAMES M.* [Born in N. W. Ter. Appointed from Ind.]
3rd Lieut. Corps Art., 17 July, 1817. 2nd Lieut., 28 Sept., 1817. 1st Lieut., 26 June, 1819. Trans. to 2nd Art., 1 June, 1821. Trans. to 2nd Art., 16 June, 1821. Died 16 Aug., 1829.

SPENCER, JOEL. [Born in S. C. Appointed from S. C.]
Ensign 3rd Rifles, 17 March, 1814. 3rd Lieut., 1 May, 1814. Trans. to 8th Inf., 17 Dec., 1814. Disbanded 15 June, 1815. Capt. A. D. Q. M. G., 18 April, 1818. Resigned 30 Nov., 1819.

SPENCER, PHILIP D. [Born in N. Y. Appointed from N. Y.]
Midshipman U. S. N., 1 Dec., 1810. 2nd Lieut 3rd Art, 22 May, 1812. 1st Lieut., 13 May, 1813. A. D. P. M. G., 30 Dec., 1813. Trans. to Corps Art., 12 May, 1814. Maj. A. I. G., 15 Sept., 1814, to 17 May, 1815. Died 5 May, 1817.

SPENCER, S. F. [Born in Va. Appointed from Va.]
2nd Lieut. Rifles, 12 July, 1820. Dismissed 21 July, 1820.

SPENCER, THEODORE M. [Born in Vt. Appointed from Army.]
Priv. and Corpl. Co. H, 2nd Drag. (2nd Cav.), 7 Jan., 1859, to 22 July, 1862, and Hosp. Stwd. to March, 1863. 2nd Lieut. 2nd Cav., 19 Feb., 1863. Dismissed 5 Dec., 1863.

SPENCER, THOS. [Born in Mass. Appointed from N. Y.]
Maj. Surg. 10th Inf., 5 May, 1847. Disbanded 16 Aug., 1848. Died 30 May, 1857.

SPENCER, THOS. J. [Born in Mich. Appointed from Mich.]
Priv. Co. A, 1st Mich. Light Art., 28 May, 1861. 2nd Lieut. 1st Ala. Cav., 21 Aug., 1862. Mustered out 16 Sept., 1865. 2nd Lieut. 10th Cav., 28 July, 1866. Bvt. 1st Lieut. and Capt., 2 March, 1867, for gallant and meritorious service in the Battle of Atlanta, Ga. 1st Lieut. 10th Cav., 1 June, 1867. Dismissed 24 April, 1875. 1st Lieut. 10th Cav., 3 May, 1877, with rank from 1 June, 1867. Capt., 20 March, 1879. Dismissed 18 Nov., 1881.

SPENCER, WM. C. [Born in Md. Appointed from Md.]
2nd Lieut. 2nd Inf., 18 June, 1855. 1st Lieut., 30 April, 1861. Capt. 17th Inf., 14 May, 1861. Resigned 11 Dec., 1862. Appointed Capt. of Inf., 29 July, 1892 (Act of 28 July, 1892). Retired 30 July, 1892.

SPENCER, WM. C. [Born in N. Y. Appointed from N. Y.]
1st Lieut. Asst. Surg., 28 May, 1861. Bvt. Capt., Maj. and Lieut. Col., 13 March, 1865, for faithful and meritorious service during the war. Capt. Asst. Surg., 28 May, 1866. Maj. Surg., 28 July, 1866. Died 22 March, 1888.

SPENCER, WM. G. [Born in N. Y. Appointed from N. Y.]
1st Lieut. Asst. Surg., 26 June, 1875. Capt. Asst. Surg., 26 June, 1880. Retired for disability, 6 June, 1894. Died 26 March, 1896.

SPENCER, WM. V. [Born in Va. Appointed from Oregon.]
Capt. 1st Wash. Ter. Vols., 17 Sept., 1862. Resigned 9 March, 1865. 1st Lieut. 13th Inf., 22 Jan., 1867. Resigned 19 Jan., 1872.

SPERING, CHAS. F. [Born in Pa. Appointed from Pa.]
2nd Lieut. Corps Art., 13 Aug., 1819. Resigned 30 Sept., 1820.

SPILMAN, BALDWIN D.* [Born in Va. Appointed at Large.]
Addl. 2nd Lieut. 7th Cav., 14 June, 1878. 2nd Lieut., 28 June, 1878. Resigned 1 Sept., 1887.

SPINKS, MARCELLUS G.* [Born in Miss. Appointed from Miss.]
2nd Lieut. 5th Art., 26 April, 1898.

SPOONER, EDMUND D. [Born in Ind. Appointed from Ohio.]
Sergt. Co. G, 5th Ohio Vols., 20 April to 4 July, 1861. 2nd Lieut. 5th Art., 14 May, 1861. 1st Lieut., 2 July, 1863. Resigned 26 Jan., 1865.

SPOOR, CHAS. H. E.* [Born in N. Y. Appointed from N. Y.]
Bvt. 2nd Lieut. 4th Inf., 1 July, 1836. 2nd Lieut., 30 Sept., 1836. Died 26 Jan., 1838.

SPOTTS, SAMUEL. [Born in Pa. Appointed from Del.]
2nd Lieut. 1st Art., 10 Feb., 1812. Trans. to Corps Art., 12 May, 1814. 1st Lieut., 22 May, 1814. Trans. to 4th Art., 1 June, 1821. Capt., 8 May, 1822. Trans. to 4th Art., 31 Jan., 1827. Resigned 15 May, 1829. Bvt. Capt., 8 Jan., 1815, for distinguished and meritorious service in the battle at New Orleans, La., and for his uniform gallant conduct in the Army. Died 11 July, 1853.

SPRAGUE, CHAS. J. [Born in Maine. Appointed from Cal.]
Cadet at Mil. Acad., 1 July to 8 Dec., 1838, and from 1 Sept., 1839, to 3 Feb., 1840. 1st Lieut. Inf., 24 March, 1847. 1st Lieut., 9th Inf., 9 April, 1847. Reg. Adj., — June to 21 Sept., 1847. Capt., 9 Oct., 1847. Bvt. Capt., 20 Aug., 1847, for gallant and meritorious conduct in the Battles of Contreras and Churubusco, Mex. Disbanded 26 Aug., 1848. Addl. P. M., 17 Aug., 1861. Bvt. Lieut. Col. Vols., 13 March, 1865, for faithful and meritorious service during the war. Maj. P. M. U. S. A., 17 Jan., 1867. Retired by operation of law, 12 April, 1887. Died 3 May, 1896.

SPRAGUE, HAVILAH M. [Born in Conn. Appointed from Conn.]
Asst. Surg., 28 May, 1861. Resigned 5 May, 1865. Died 30 May, 1874.

SPRAGUE, JOHN T. [Born in Mass. Appointed from Mass.]
2nd Lieut. Marine Corps, 17 Oct., 1834. Resigned 3 July, 1837. 2nd Lieut. 5th Inf., 3 July, 1837. Trans. to 8th Inf., 7 July, 1838. 1st Lieut., 1 May, 1839. Reg. Adj., 12 Dec., 1839, to 1 Sept., 1842, and 1 Nov., 1843, to 1 Sept., 1845. Capt., 21 Sept., 1846. Maj. 1st Inf., 14 May, 1861. Lieut. Col. 11th Inf., 13 March, 1863. Col. 7th Inf., 12 June, 1865. Unassigned 15 March, 1869. Retired 15 Dec., 1870.

Died 6 Sept., 1878. Bvt. Capt., 15 March, 1842, for meritorious and successful conduct in the war against the Florida Indians. Bvt. Maj., 30 May, 1848, for meritorious conduct.

SPRAGUE, LAWRENCE. [Born in Mass. Appointed from Maine.]
Asst. Surg., 22 June, 1825. Died 7 Aug., 1853.

SPRAGUE, WELLINGTON G. [Born in Ohio. Appointed from Wis.]
Priv. Co. A, 1st Wis. Heavy Art., 31 March, 1862. Corpl., 6 July, 1863. Discharged 26 Sept., 1863. Capt. 1st U. S. Col. Troops, 7 Oct., 1863. Bvt. Maj. and Lieut. Col. Vols., 13 March, 1865, for gallant conduct before Petersburg, Va., and for general good conduct and meritorious service. Mustered out 29 Sept., 1865. 2nd Lieut. 16th Inf., 3 April, 1866. Trans. to 34th Inf., 21 Sept., 1866. Unassigned 14 April, 1869. Retired with rank of Capt., 21 May, 1870.

SPRINGER, ANTON, Jr.* [Born in France. Appointed from N. Y.]
Addl. 2nd Lieut. 21st Inf., 12 June, 1895. 2nd Lieut., 5 July, 1895. 1st Lieut. of Inf., 6 Aug., 1898. Ass'd to 21st Inf., 1 Jan., 1899.

SPRINGER, FRANCIS. [Born in Pa. Appointed from Ill.]
Chap. 10th Ill. Cav., 30 Sept., 1861. Resigned 10 April, 1863. Chap. 1st Ark. Vols., 11 April, 1863. Resigned 18 Jan., 1864. Chap., Ft. Smith, Ark., 26 Dec., 1863, to 13 May, 1867. Post Chap., 3 April, 1867. Resigned 23 Aug., 1867.

SPRINGER, RUTER W. [Born in Ill. Appointed from Ill.]
Post Chap., 6 June, 1894.

SPRINGETT, HOWARD A.* [Born in Ohio. Appointed from Ohio.]
2nd Lieut. 4th Art., 15 June, 1877. Resigned 18 Oct., 1884.

SPROLE, HENRY W.* [Born in N. Y. Appointed from N. Y.]
Cadet at Naval Acad., 29 Sept. to 12 Oct., 1863. Cadet at Mil. Acad., 17 Oct., 1865. 2nd Lieut. 8th Cav., 15 June, 1869. 1st Lieut., 29 March, 1873. Capt., 23 July, 1885. Maj. 5th Cav., 6 May, 1899. Trans. to 8th Cav., 23 May, 1899. Bvt. Capt., 27 Feb., 1890, for gallant services in the pursuit of Indians on the Washita River, Tex., 14 and 15 Oct., 1874, and in the action against Indians on Muster Creek, Tex., 29 Nov., 1874.

SPROLE, SAML. M. [Born in Pa. Appointed from N. Y.]
2nd Lieut. 4th Inf., 4 May, 1861. 1st Lieut., 14 May, 1861. Capt., 1 Aug., 1862. Resigned 14 July, 1863.

SPROLE, WM. T. [Born in ——. Appointed from D. C.]
Chap and Prof. of Ethics at Mil. Acad., 2 March, 1847; superceded 16 Aug., 1856.

SPROUL, JOHN. [Born in N. Y. Appointed from N. Y.]
Capt. 13th Inf., 12 March, 1812. Maj., 25 July, 1814. Retained 17 May, 1815, as Capt. 2nd Inf. Resigned 1 May, 1819. Retained — May, 1815, as Capt. 2nd Inf. (in reorganization under Act of 3 March, 1815), with Bvt. of Maj. from 25 July, 1814.

SPURGIN, DAVID G. [Born in Ohio. Appointed from Army.]
Cadet at Mil. Acad., 14 June, 1885, to 25 June, 1888. Priv. and Corpl. Co. C, 21st Inf., 11 Jan., 1892, to 1 Nov., 1894. 2nd Lieut. 21st Inf., 31 Oct., 1894. 1st Lieut., 26 April, 1898.

SPURGIN, WM. F. [Born in Ky. Appointed from Ind.]
Cadet Mil. Acad., 1 July, 1858, to 12 March, 1861. 1st Lieut. 54th Ind. Vols., 19 June, 1862. Mustered out 26 Sept., 1863. Capt. 15th U. S. Col. Troops, 9 April, 1864. Capt. 100th U. S. Col. Troops, 9 June, 1864. Bvt. Maj. Vols., 13 March, 1865, for special gallantry at Johnsonville, in Nov., 1864, and at Nashville, Tenn., 16 Dec., 1864, and for faithful and meritorious service in the Bureau of R., F., and A. L. Mustered out 26 Dec., 1865. 1st Lieut. 38th Inf., 28 July, 1866. Bvt. Capt., 2 March, 1867, for gallant and meritorious service in action at Johnsonville, Tenn. Bvt. Maj., 2 March, 1867, for gallant and meritorious service in the Battle of Nashville, Tenn. R. Q. M. 38th Inf., 29 March, 1867, to 11 Nov., 1869. Trans. to 24th Inf., 11 Nov., 1869. Unassigned 14 April, 1870. Ass'd to 21st Inf., 1 Jan., 1871. R. Q. M., 8 July, 1874, to 2 June, 1876. Capt., 2 June, 1876. Maj. 23rd Inf., 2 Dec., 1897. Lieut. Col. 16th Inf., 4 May, 1899.

SQUIER, GEORGE O.* [Born in Mich. Appointed from Mich.]
2nd Lieut. 3rd Art., 12 June, 1887. 1st Lieut., 30 June, 1893. 1st Lieut. Sig. Corps, 23 Feb., 1899. Lieut. Col. Sig. Off. Vols., 18 July, 1898, to 7 Dec., 1898. Capt. Sig Off. Vols., 17 April, 1899, to ——.

SQUIERS, HERBERT G. [Born in Canada. Appointed from Minn.]
2nd Lieut. 1st Inf., 12 Oct., 1877. Expired by constitutional limitation 3 Dec., 1877. Reappointed 26 Jan., 1878, with rank from 12 Oct., 1877. Trans. to 7th Cav., 31 Aug., 1880. 1st Lieut. of Cav. (1st), 17 Dec., 1890. Trans. to 7th Cav., 27 Feb., 1891. Resigned 28 Nov., 1891.

STACEY, CROMWELL. [Born in Nev. Appointed from Army.]
Priv., Corpl. and Sergt. Co. C, 21st Inf., 16 May, 1895, to 14 July, 1898. 2nd Lieut. 19th Inf., 22 June, 1898. 1st Lieut., 2 March, 1899.

STACEY, MAY H. [Born in Pa. Appointed from Pa.]
1st Lieut. 12th Inf., 14 May, 1861. Adj. 1st Batt., 20 Aug., 1862, to 24 Feb., 1863. Q. M. 3rd Batt., 24 Feb., 1863, to 11 Feb., 1864. Q. M. 1st Batt. 11 Feb., 1864, to 19 Aug., 1864. Bvt. Capt., 18 Aug., 1864, for gallant service during the operations on the Weldon Railroad, Va. Capt. 12th Inf., 19 Aug., 1864. Bvt. Maj., 9 April, 1865, for gallant and meritorious service during the campaign terminating with the surrender of the insurgent army under Gen. R. E. Lee. Bvt. Lieut. Col., 9 April, 1865, for gallant and effective service in the engagements on the Weldon Railroad, Va., on the 18, 19 and 21 Aug., 1864. Died 12 Feb., 1886.

STACEY, SAML. S. [Born in Maine. Appointed from N. H.]
Priv., Sergt. and Sergt. Maj. Corps Art., 5 Feb., 1813, to 29 May, 1815. 2nd Lieut. 5th Inf., 22 July, 1817. Resigned 4 Aug., 1821. Addl. P. M., 3 March, 1847. Disbanded 4 March, 1849.

STACY, LUCIAN.* [Born in Maine. Appointed from Maine.]
2nd Lieut. of Inf. (20th), 12 June, 1896. Died 4 Sept., 1898.

STAFFORD, JOSEPH S. [Born in Pa. Appointed from N. J.]
Priv. Co. D, 4th N. J. Militia, 24 April to 31 July, 1861. Priv. and Sergt. Co. B, 3rd

Pa. Art., 20 Jan., 1862, to 21 Dec., 1864. 2nd Lieut. 3rd Pa. Art., 21 Dec., 1864. Mustered out 11 July, 1865. 1st Lieut. 13th Inf., 28 July, 1866. Unassigned 10 Aug., 1869. Ass'd to 20th Inf., 1 Jan., 1871. Died 27 July, 1875.

STAFFORD, JOHN. [Born in Ill. Appointed from Army.]
Priv., Corpl. and Sergt. Co. K, 1st Cav., 2 June, 1876, to 2 May, 1882. 2nd Lieut. 8th Inf., 27 March, 1882. 1st Lieut., 27 May, 1889. Capt., 26 April, 1898. R. Q. M., 30 April, 1899. Graduate of the Infantry and Cavalry School, 1887.

STAFFORD, STEPHEN R. [Born in N. Y. Appointed from N. Y.]
Priv. Co. G, 13th N. Y. Vols., 2 May, 1861. Trans. to Co. C, 3rd N. Y. Cav., 2 May, 1861. Discharged 18 Sept., 1861. 2nd Lieut. 8th N. Y. Art., 22 Aug., 1862. 1st Lieut., 22 Feb., 1864. Capt., 10 Jan., 1865. Bvt. Maj. Vols., 13 March, 1865, for faithful and meritorious service during the war. Mustered out 5 June, 1865. 2nd Lieut. 38th Inf., 21 May, 1867. Unassigned 11 Nov., 1869. Ass'd to 15th Inf., 5 March, 1870. 1st Lieut., 15 Jan., 1873. R. Q. M., 1 Jan., 1875, to 1 Jan., 1881. Capt., 31 Jan., 1882. Retired for disability, with rank of Maj., 1 July, 1898.

STAFFORD, WM. R. [Born in Md. Appointed from Ohio.]
2nd Lieut. of Inf., 22 Feb., 1847; 15th Inf., 9 April, 1847. 1st Lieut., 4 July, 1847. Disbanded 31 July, 1848.

STALL, GEORGE W. [Born in Germany. Appointed from Ohio.]
Ensign 19th Inf., 12 March, 1812. 2nd Lieut., 6 April, 1813. Trans. to 17th Inf., 12 May, 1814. 1st Lieut., 1 Oct., 1814. Disbanded 15 June, 1815. 2nd Lieut. 3rd Inf., 4 Sept., 1817. Died 6 Feb., 1819.

STAMBAUGH, CHAS. B. [Born in Ohio. Appointed from Ohio.]
Priv. Co. H, 11th Ohio Cav., 8 March, 1864, to 2 May, 1866. 2nd Lieut. 2nd Cav., 7 March, 1867. 1st Lieut., 5 July, 1868. Killed 4 May, 1870, in Indian affair in Wyoming.

STAMPER, WILLSON Y. [Born in N. Y. Appointed from N. Y.]
2nd Lieut. 21st Inf., 21 Nov., 1883. 1st Lieut., 7 Aug., 1890. Capt. 8th Inf., 26 April, 1898. Graduate of the Infantry and Cavalry School, 1887.

STANHOPE, PHILIP W. [Born in R. I. Appointed from Ohio.]
Capt. 12th Inf., 14 May, 1861. Bvt. Maj., 18 Aug., 1864, for gallant and meritorious service during the operation on the Weldon Railroad, Va. Bvt. Lieut. Col., 2 Oct., 1864, for gallant and meritorious service in action at Saltville, Va. Mustered out 1 Jan., 1871. Maj. of Inf., 27 May, 1879, to rank from 10 Dec., 1873 (Act of 3 March, 1879). Retired 27 May, 1879. Died 24 June, 1895.

STANIFORD, THOMAS. [Born in Conn. Appointed from Vt.]
Ensign 11th Inf., 12 Oct., 1812. 2nd Lieut., 26 June, 1813. 1st Lieut., 1 Sept., 1814. Asst. Dep. P. M. G., 26 Aug., 1813, to 17 May, 1815. Trans. to 6th Inf., 17 May, 1815. Reg. Adj., 30 April, 1819, to 30 June, 1820. Capt., 1 March, 1820. Trans. to 2nd Inf., 1 June, 1821. Trans. to 8th Inf., 31 July, 1838. Maj. 4th Inf., 1 Dec., 1839. Trans. to 5th Inf., 22 Oct., 1845. Lieut. Col. 8th Inf., 29 June, 1846. Col. 3rd Inf. 23 Feb., 1852. Died 3 Feb., 1855. Bvt. Maj., 1 March, 1830, for ten years' faithful service in one grade. Bvt. Lieut. Col., 9 May, 1846, for gallant conduct in the Battles of Palo Alto and Resaca de la Palma. Bvt. Col., 23 Sept., 1846, for gallant and meritorious conduct at Monterey, Mex.

STANLEY, DAVID S.* [Born in Ohio. Appointed from Ohio.]
Bvt. 2nd Lieut. 2nd Drag., 1 July, 1852. 2nd Lieut., 6 Sept., 1853. 2nd Lieut. 1st Cav., 3 March, 1855. 1st Lieut., 27 March, 1855. Capt., 16 March, 1861. 4th Cav., 3 Aug., 1861. Brig. Gen. Vols., 28 Sept., 1861. Bvt. Lieut. Col., 31 Dec., 1862, for gallant and meritorious service in the Battle of Stone River, Tenn. Maj. Gen. Vols., 29 Nov., 1862. Maj. 5th Cav., 1 Dec., 1863. Bvt. Col., 15 May, 1864, for gallant and meritorious service in the Battle of Resaca, Ga. Bvt. Brig. Gen., 13 March, 1865, for gallant and meritorious service in the Battle of Ruff's Station, Ga. Bvt. Maj. Gen., 13 March, 1865, for gallant and meritorious service in the Battle of Franklin, Tenn. Mustered out of Vol. Service, 1 Feb., 1866. Col. 22nd Inf., 28 July, 1866. Brig. Gen., 24 March, 1884. Retired by operation of law, 1 June, 1892. Medal of Honor for distinguished bravery in the Battle of Franklin. Tenn., 30 Nov., 1864, where he was severely wounded; while serving as Maj. Gen. of Vols., commanding 4th Army Corps.

STANLEY, DAVID S.* [Born in Dakota. Appointed from D. C.]
2nd Lieut. 22nd Inf., 12 June, 1895. 1st Lieut. of Inf., 23 July, 1898. Ass'd to 22nd Inf., 1 Jan., 1899.

STANLEY, WM. [Born in N. Y. Appointed from Army.]
Priv., Corpl. and Sergt. Co. K, and Sergt. Maj. 10th Inf., 28 June, 1855, to 7 Nov., 1863. 2nd Lieut. 10th Inf., 31 Oct., 1863. 1st Lieut., 11 June, 1864. Reg. Adj., 8 Nov., 1863, to 22 Jan., 1867. Capt., 22 Jan., 1867. Unassigned 19 May, 1869. Ass'd to 20th Inf., 14 July, 1870. Dismissed 25 Aug., 1874. Bvt. 1st Lieut., 19 May, 1864, for gallant and meritorious service at the Battle of Spottsylvania, Va. Bvt. Capt., 3 June, 1864, for gallant and meritorious service at the Battle of Cold Harbor, Va.

STANSBURY, HOWARD. [Born in N. Y. Appointed from N. Y.]
1st Lieut. Top. Eng., 7 July, 1838. Capt., 18 July, 1840. Maj., 6 Aug., 1861. Retired 28 Sept., 1861. Died 17 April, 1863.

STANSBURY, HOWARD E. [Born in D. C. Appointed from Minn.]
Priv. Co. A, 1st Minn. Vols., 29 April to 1 July, 1861. 1st Lieut. 19th Inf., 14 May, 1861. Capt., 25 Nov., 1863. Trans. to 28th Inf., 21 Sept., 1866. Trans. to 19th Inf., 31 March, 1869. Dismissed 18 March, 1878. Bvt. Capt., 1 Sept., 1864, for gallant and meritorious service during the Atlanta campaign. Bvt. Maj., 16 Dec., 1864, for gallant and meritorious service at the Battles of Franklin and Nashville, Tenn.

STANSBURY, SMITH.* [Born in La. Appointed from Md.]
Bvt. 2nd Lieut. Ord., 1 July, 1841. Resigned 31 May, 1844. Died 25 April, 1864.

STANTON, ALEX'R. H. [Born in Ohio. Appointed from Ohio.]
Capt. 16th Inf., 14 May, 1861. Cashiered 26 Dec., 1864. Capt. 8th U. S. Vet. Vols., 12 July, 1865. Mustered out 23 April, 1866. 2nd Lieut. 1st Cav., 4 May, 1866.

1st Lieut., 1 July, 1868. Died 2 Jan., 1870. Bvt. Capt., 5 April, 1868, for gallantry in an engagement with a large band of Indians on Malheur River, Ore., 5 April, 1868.

STANTON, HENRY. [Born in Vt. Appointed from Vt.]
3rd Lieut. Light Art., 29 June, 1813. 2nd Lieut., 7 March, 1814. Capt. A. D. Q. M. G., 12 July, 1813, to 26 May, 1814. Resigned 1 Dec., 1817. Capt. A. D. Q. M. G., 13 Feb., 1818. Maj. Dep. Q. M. G., 13 May, 1820. Retained as Maj. Q. M., 1 June, 1821. Col. A. Q. M. G., 7 July, 1838. Died 1 Aug., 1856. Bvt. Lieut. Col., 13 May, 1830, for ten years' faithful service in one grade. Bvt. Brig. Gen., 1 Jan., 1847, for meritorious conduct, particularly in performing his duties in prosecuting the war with Mexico.

STANTON, HENRY W.* [Born in N. Y. Appointed at Large.]
Bvt. 2nd Lieut 1st Drag., 1 July, 1842. 2nd Lieut., 8 Oct., 1844. 1st Lieut., 7 Feb., 1847. Reg. Adj., 17 Aug., 1846, to 1 Jan., 1851. Capt., 25 July, 1854. Killed 20 Jan., 1855, in action with Indians in New Mexico.

STANTON, THADDEUS H. [Born in Ind. Appointed from Iowa.]
Priv. Co. A, 3rd Batt. D. C. Vols., 15 April, 1861. Discharged 15 July, 1861. Capt. 19th Iowa Vols., 18 Aug., 1862. Discharged 18 Dec., 1862. Addl. P. M., 3 Oct., 1862. Bvt. Lieut. Col., 13 March, 1865, for faithful and meritorious service during the war. Maj. P. M. U. S. A., 17 Jan., 1867. Lieut. Col. Dep. P. M. G., 15 March, 1890. Col. Asst. P. M. G., 22 Jan., 1893. Brig. Gen. P. M. G., 27 March, 1895. Bvt. Lieut. Col., 27 Feb., 1890, for gallant services in action against Indians under Crazy Horse, on the Powder River, Mont., 17 March, 1876.

STANTON, WM. [Born in N. Y. Appointed from Mich.]
Priv. Co. G, 43rd Ohio Vols., 3 Sept., 1862. Corpl., 7 Sept., 1862. Sergt., 4 Oct., 1862. Discharged 11 March, 1863. 2nd Lieut. 2nd Art., 3 Sept., 1867. 1st Lieut., 16 Nov., 1874. Trans. to 6th Cav., 9 Feb., 1877. Capt., 21 May, 1886. Maj. 8th Cav., 9 June, 1899. Graduate of the Artillery School, 1871.

STANTON, WM. S.* [Born in N. Y. Appointed from N. Y.]
1st Lieut. Eng., 23 June, 1865. Capt., 14 Feb., 1871. Maj., 19 March, 1884.

STANWOOD, FRANK. [Born in Maine. Appointed from Mass.]
2nd Lieut. 3rd Cav., 5 Aug., 1861. 1st Lieut., 21 Feb., 1862. R. Q. M., 12 July, 1862, to 15 Jan., 1863. Capt., 28 July, 1866. Died 20 Dec., 1872. Bvt. Capt., 13 March, 1865, for coolness, energy, and skill in battle. Bvt. Maj. and Lieut. Col., 1 Aug., 1865, for faithful and meritorious service during the war.

STAPLES, WRIGHT. [Born in England. Appointed from Army.]
Priv. 4th Cav., 11 June to 15 July, 1862. 2nd Lieut. 11th Inf., 30 June, 1862. 1st Lieut., 4 Nov., 1863. Bvt. Capt., 5 May, 1864, for gallant and meritorious service in the Battle of the Wilderness, Va., where he was killed, 5 May, 1864.

STARBIRD, ALFRED A. [Born in Maine. Appointed from Maine.]
Sergt. Co. D, 1st Maine Vols., 13 May to 24 July, 1898. 2nd Lieut. 6th Art., 9 July, 1898.

STARK, ALEXANDER N. [Born in Va. Appointed from Va.]
Asst. Surg., 12 May, 1893. Capt. Asst. Surg., 12 May, 1898.

STARKE, EDWIN. [Born in Va. Appointed from Va.]
Mil. Storekeeper, — ——, 1813. Disbanded 1 June, 1821.

STARR, AUGUSTUS W. [Born in Ohio. Appointed from Cal.]
2nd Lieut. 2nd Cal. Cav., 13 Sept., 1861. 1st Lieut., 23 July, 1862. Capt., 1 Feb., 1863. Bvt. Maj. Vols., 13 March, 1865, for faithful and meritorious service. Mustered out 27 June, 1866. 2nd Lieut. 8th Cav., 28 July, 1866. 1st Lieut., 10 June, 1867. R. Q. M., 7 Sept. to 9 Nov., 1869. Capt., 9 Nov., 1869. Discharged 1 Dec., 1870.

STARR, CHAS. G.* [Born in Ill. Appointed from Ill.]
Addl. 2nd Lieut. 1st Inf., 14 June, 1878. 2nd Lieut., 28 June, 1878. 1st Lieut., 20 Sept., 1883. R. Q. M., 5 Aug., 1888, to ——. Capt. 1st Inf., 6 April, 1895. Maj. I. G. Vols., 13 Aug., 1898, to 6 Sept., 1899. Lieut. Col. 11th U. S. Vol. Cav, 12 Aug., 1899, to ——.

STARR, IRWIN M. [Born in N. Y. Appointed from N. Y.]
Priv. and Sergt. Troop A, 3rd N. Y. Cav., 17 July to 19 May, 1864. 2nd Lieut. 3rd N. Y. Cav., 19 May, 1864. Capt., 8 Jan., 1865. Trans. to 7th N. Y. Cav., 21 July, 1865. Bvt. Maj. Vols., 13 March, 1865, for gallant and meritorious service during the war. Mustered out 29 Nov., 1865. 2nd Lieut. 9th Cav., 24 July, 1867. 1st Lieut., 1 Dec., 1869. Died 19 April, 1875.

STARR, SAML. H. [Born in N. Y. Appointed from Army.]
Priv., Corpl. and Sergt. Co. G, 4th Art., 27 Oct., 1822, to 26 Oct., 1837. Priv. Co. A, Batt. Eng., 23 June, 1846. Corpl., — —— ——. Sergt., 1 Nov., 1846. Bvt. 2nd Lieut. 2nd Drag., 28 June, 1848. 2nd Lieut., 13 July, 1848. 1st Lieut., 10 Nov., 1851. Capt., 14 June, 1858. Col. 5th N. J. Vols., 24 Aug., 1861. Bvt. Maj., 4 May, 1862, for gallant and meritorious service in the Battle of Williamsburg, Va. Resigned commission of Col. 5th N. J. Vols., 20 Oct., 1862. Maj. 6th Cav., 25 April, 1863. Bvt. Lieut. Col., 21 June, 1863, for gallant and meritorious service in action at Upperville, Va. Bvt. Col., 2 July, 1863, for gallant and meritorious service in the Gettysburg campaign. Retired with rank of Col., 15 Dec., 1870. Died 23 Nov., 1891.

STARRING, WM. S.* [Born in N. Y. Appointed from Ill.]
2nd Lieut. 18th Inf., 23 June, 1865. 1st Lieut., 23 June, 1865. Trans. to 36th Inf., 21 Sept., 1866. Reg. Adj., 1 March, 1867, to 19 May, 1869. Trans. to 7th Inf., 19 May, 1869. Reg. Adj., 19 May, 1869, to 23 Aug., 1869. Trans. to 2nd Art., 1 Jan., 1871. Trans. to Ord., 1 Nov., 1874. 1st Lieut., 1 Nov., 1874. Capt., 29 May, 1879. Died 12 Feb., 1889.

STEARNS, CHAS. W. [Born in Mass. Appointed from Mass.]
Asst. Surg., 16 Aug., 1841. Disbanded 23 Sept., 1842. Surg. 3rd N. Y. Vols., 13 Oct., 1861. Resigned 14 May, 1863. Died 8 Sept., 1887.

STEARNS, MICHAEL A. [Born in Va. Appointed from Army.]
1st Lieut. and Adj. 65th N. Y. Vols., 11 June, 1861. Resigned 6 Feb., 1862. Capt.

12th N. Y. Cav., 12 Feb., 1863. Mustered out 23 June, 1863. Capt. 25th N. Y. Cav., 18 Oct., 1864. Resigned 10 Jan., 1865. Priv. 18th U. S. Inf., 18 Jan. to 13 April, 1865. 2nd Lieut. 18th Inf., 13 April, 1865. 1st Lieut., 13 April, 1865. Trans. to 27th Inf., 21 Sept., 1866. Resigned 31 Jan., 1867.

STEBBINS, EDWARD N. [Born in N. Y. Appointed from Pa.]
Mil. Storekeeper Ord. Dept., 10 June, 1861. Resigned 10 Oct., 1865.

STEDMAN, CLARENCE A.* [Born in Mass. Appointed from Pa.]
2nd Lieut. 9th Cav., 15 June, 1870. 1st Lieut., 19 April, 1875. R. Q. M., 24 June, 1879, to 17 March, 1880. Reg. Adj., 18 March, 1880, to 8 Jan., 1885. Capt., 3 July, 1885. Maj. 10th Cav., 8 April, 1899.

STEEDMAN, RICHD. R. [Born in Pa. Appointed from Mass.]
2nd Lieut. 16th Inf., 1 Feb., 1876. 1st Lieut., 20 Dec., 1883. Capt. 11th Inf., 26 April, 1898. (For the advancement of this officer to present position see Act 24 Feb., 1899.)

STEEL, ARCHIBALD. [Born in Va. Appointed from Pa.]
Mil. Storekeeper, 28 April, 1816. Disbanded 1 June, 1821. Died 29 Oct., 1822.

STEEL, GEORGE H. [Born in Ill. Appointed from Army.]
Priv. and Corpl. Co. D, 5th Inf., 1 Sept., 1894, to 28 March, 1897. 2nd Lieut. 19th Inf., 2 March, 1897. 1st Lieut., 26 April, 1899. Resigned 30 June, 1899.

STEELE, CHARLES L.* [Born in Miss. Appointed from Tenn.]
2nd Lieut. 18th Inf., 13 June, 1879. 1st Lieut., 6 Oct., 1887. Capt., 12 May, 1895.

STEELE, FREDK.* [Born in N. Y. Appointed from N. Y.]
Bvt. 2nd Lieut. 2nd Inf., 1 July, 1843. 2nd Lieut., 15 March, 1846. 1st Lieut., 6 June, 1848. Reg. Adj., 6 Sept., 1849, to 5 Feb., 1855. Capt., 5 Feb., 1855. Maj. 11th Inf., 14 May, 1861. Lieut. Col. 3rd Inf., 26 Aug., 1863. Col. 8th Iowa Vols., 23 Sept., 1861. Brig. Gen. Vols., 29 Jan., 1862. Maj. Gen. Vols., 29 Nov., 1862. Mustered out of Vol. Service, 1 Jan., 1867. Col. 20th Inf., 28 July, 1866. Died 12 Jan., 1868. Bvt. 1st Lieut., 20 Aug., 1847, for gallant and meritorious conduct at Contreras. Bvt. Capt., 13 Sept., 1847, for gallant and meritorious conduct at Chapultepec. Bvt. Col., 4 July, 1863, for gallant and meritorious service in the campaign resulting in the capture of Vicksburg, Miss. Bvt. Brig. Gen., 13 March, 1865, for gallant and meritorious service in the capture of Little Rock, Ark. Bvt. Maj. Gen., 13 March, 1865, for gallant and meritorious service during the war.

STEELE, GEORGE G. [Born in Va. Appointed from Pa.]
Capt. 16th Inf., 12 March, 1812. Maj. 30th Inf., 4 Sept., 1814. Disbanded 15 June, 1815. Retained 17 May, 1816 (in reorganization under Act of 3 March, 1815), as Capt. 2nd Inf., with Bvt. of Maj. from 4 Sept., 1814. Resigned 1 Nov., 1817.

STEELE, GEORGE W. [Born in Ind. Appointed from Ind.]
1st Lieut. 12th Ind. Vols., 20 July, 1861. Mustered out 19 May, 1862. 1st Lieut. 101st Ind. Vols., 2 Sept., 1862. Capt., 6 Sept., 1862. Maj., 27 Jan., 1863. Lieut. Col., 31 May, 1863. Mustered out 24 June, 1865. 2nd and 1st Lieut. 14th Inf., 23 Feb., 1866. R. Q. M., 6 March, 1868, to 1 Jan., 1873. Resigned 1 Feb., 1876.

STEELE, HARRY L. [Born in Ark. Appointed from Army.]
Priv. and Corpl Batty A, 5th Art., 27 Aug., 1895, to 6 July, 1898. 2nd Lieut. 7th Art., 22 June, 1898.

STEELE, HORACE B. [Born in Ohio. Appointed from Army.]
Priv. Co. —, 86th Ohio Vols., 13 July, 1863. Discharged 8 Aug., 1863. 1st Lieut. and Adj. 129th Ohio Vols., 10 Aug., 1863. Discharged 10 March, 1864. Priv. Co. —, 6th Cav., 14 Feb., 1877. Trans. to Gen. Ser., 24 July, 1877. 2nd Lieut. 12th Inf., 28 June, 1879. Trans. to 19th Inf., 1 Dec., 1879. Dropped 5 May, 1880.

STEELE, JAMES W. [Born in Ill. Appointed from Kan.]
Priv. Co. H, 38th Ind. Inf., 18 Sept., 1861, to 25 May, 1863. 2nd Lieut. 83rd U. S. Col. Inf., 17 March, 1864. 1st Lieut. Adj., 17 Dec., 1864. Resigned 24 Feb., 1865. 2nd Lieut. 38th Inf., 19 Aug., 1867. Trans. to 24th Inf., 11 Nov., 1869. Resigned 23 May, 1870.

STEELE, JOHN. [Born in N. H. Appointed from N. H.]
2nd Lieut. 1st N. H. Cav., 20 April, 1864. 1st Lieut., 10 March, 1865. Mustered out 15 July, 1865. 2nd Lieut. 2nd Cav., 7 March, 1867. Resigned 14 Feb., 1868.

STEELE, MATTHEW F.* [Born in Ala. Appointed from Ala.]
2nd Lieut. 8th Cav., 13 June, 1883. 1st Lieut. 4th Cav., 9 March, 1891. Trans. to 8th Cav., 27 April, 1891. Capt. 6th Cav., 2 March, 1899. Adj., 26 April, 1899. Maj. 30th U. S. Vols., 5 July, 1899, to ——.

STEELE, RICHARD. [Born in N. Y. Appointed from La.]
2nd Lieut. of Inf., 5 March, 1847; 14th Inf., 9 April, 1847. 1st Lieut., 1 Oct., 1847. Disbanded 26 July, 1848.

STEELE, WM.* [Born in N. Y. Appointed from N. Y.]
Bvt. 2nd Lieut. 2nd Drag., 1 July, 1840. 2nd Lieut., 2 Feb., 1841. 1st Lieut., 9 May, 1846. Reg. Adj., 20 Dec., 1847, to 10 April.1849. Capt., 10 Nov., 1851. Resigned 30 May, 1861. Bvt. Capt., 20 Aug., 1847, for gallant and meritorious conduct at Contreras and Churubusco, Mex. Died 12 Jan., 1885.

STEELHAMMER, CHAS. [Born in Sweden. Appointed from Army.]
Priv. Co. B, 83rd N. Y. Vols., 27 May, 1861. Hosp. Stwd., U. S. A., 12 May, 1862. 2nd Lieut. and 1st Lieut. 17th Inf., 2 Sept., 1864. Trans. to 35th Inf., 21 Sept., 1866. Capt., 1 Nov., 1866. Trans. to 15th Inf., 12 Aug., 1869. Retired for disability, 31 Oct., 1884.

STEEN, ALEXR. E. [Born in Mo. Appointed from Mo.]
2nd Lieut. of Inf., 6 March, 1847; 12th Inf., 9 April, 1847. Disbanded 25 July, 1848. 2nd Lieut. 3rd Inf., 30 June, 1852. 1st Lieut., 28 Sept., 1857. Resigned 10 May, 1861. Bvt. 1st Lieut., 20 Aug., 1847, for gallant and meritorious conduct at Contreras and Churubusco, Mex. Died 27 Nov., 1862.

STEEN, ENOCH. [Born in Ky. Appointed from Mo.]
2nd Lieut. Mounted Rangers, 26 July, 1832. 2nd Lieut. 1st Drag., 19 Sept., 1833. 1st Lieut., 5 March, 1836. Capt., 31 Dec., 1840. Bvt. Maj., 23 Feb., 1847, for gallant and meritorious conduct in the Battle of Buena Vista. Maj. 2nd Drag.,

15 July, 1853. Trans. to 1st Drag., 23 Oct., 1855. 1st Cav., 3 Aug., 1861. Lieut. Col. 2nd Cav., 28 Sept., 1861. Retired 23 Sept., 1863. Died 22 Jan., 1880.

STEER, SAMUEL L. [Born in Va. Appointed from Pa.]
Asst. Surg., 12 Dec., 1898.

STEEVER, EDGAR Z.* [Born in Pa. Appointed from Pa.]
2nd Lieut. 3rd Cav., 12 June, 1871. 1st Lieut., 18 May, 1878. Reg. Adj., 1 Sept., 1883, to 4 March, 1885. Capt., 18 Jan., 1886. (Served as Capt. under letter of promotion issued during recess, from 4 March, 1885, to 2 July, 1886.) Maj. 3rd Cav., 8 May, 1899.

STEINBERGER, JUSTUS. [Born in Pa. Appointed from Wash. Ter.]
Capt. A. A. G. Vols., 28 Sept., 1861. Resigned 10 Oct., 1861. Col. 1st Wash. Ter. Vols., 19 Oct., 1861. Mustered out 18 March, 1865. Maj. P. M., 8 Nov., 1866. Died 13 Oct., 1870.

STEINECKE, HENRY. [Born in Pa. Appointed from Pa.]
Asst. Surg., 8 May, 1826. Maj. Surg., 31 Dec., 1836. Died 20 Dec., 1855.

STEINER, HENRY H. [Born in Md. Appointed from Pa.]
Asst Surg., 22 June, 1839. Resigned 31 Jan., 1852.

STEINER, JOSEPHUS M. [Born in Md. Appointed from Ohio.]
Asst. Surg., 16 Feb., 1847. Dropped 9 May, 1856. Died 20 May, 1873.

STEINMETZ, WM. R. [Born in Germany. Appointed from Pa.]
Priv. Gen. Ser., 3 May, 1860. Hosp. Stwd., 23 Jan., 1861. Discharged 16 March, 1865. 1st Lieut. Asst. Surg., 16 Nov., 1868. Capt. Asst. Surg., 16 Nov., 1871. Retired for disability, 26 Feb., 1891.

STELGES, CLAUS. [Born in Germany. Appointed from Army.]
Priv. and Corpl. Batty I, 4th Art., 22 June, 1854, to 22 June, 1859. Priv., Corpl. and 1st Sergt. Batty D, 4th Art., 8 Aug., 1859, to 8 Nov., 1863. 2nd Lieut. 4th Art., 31 Oct., 1863. Dismissed 2 Sept., 1864. Sergt. Troop I, 2nd Cal. Cav., 13 Jan., 1865. Mustered out 9 June, 1866.

STEMBEL, JAMES McB. [Born in Ohio. Appointed from N. Y.]
Cadet at Naval Acad., 26 Sept., 1862, to 18 March, 1865. 2nd Lieut. 27th Inf., 19 Oct., 1867. Trans. to 9th Inf., 14 June, 1869. 1st Lieut., 27 March, 1879. R. Q. M., 28 Nov., 1886, to 1 July, 1887. Reg. Adj., 1 July, 1887, to 4 Nov., 1890. Retired for disability, with rank of Capt., 4 Nov., 1890.

STEPHEN, ROBT. D. [Born in Va. Appointed from Va.]
2nd Lieut. 3rd Inf., 30 Dec., 1839. Resigned 20 Feb., 1842.

STEPHENS, CHAS. [Born in Va. Appointed from Ga.]
Ensign 3rd Inf., 29 June, 1813. 3rd Lieut., 4 Aug., 1813. 2nd Lieut., 15 April, 1814. 1st Lieut., 20 July, 1814. Disbanded 15 June, 1815. Reinstated 2 Dec., 1815, as 2nd Lieut. in 8th Inf. 1st Lieut., 3 Dec., 1816. Dropped 12 Sept., 1817. Retained — Dec., 1815 (in reorganization under Act of 3 March, 1815), as 2nd Lieut. 8th Inf., with Bvt. of 1st Lieut.from 20 July, 1814. Died 23 Jan., 1849.

STEPHENS, John E.* [Born in Tenn. Appointed from Tenn.]
2nd Lieut. 7th Art., 26 April, 1898.

STEPHENS, JOHN F. [Born in Ireland. Appointed from Army.]
Priv., Corpl. and Sergt. Cos. I and B, 11th Inf., 1 Feb., 1887, to 27 Feb., 1893. 2nd Lieut. 10th Inf., 28 Jan., 1893. 1st Lieut., 26 April, 1898. Graduate of the Infantry and Cavalry School, 1897.

STEPHENSON, JAMES R.* [Born in Va. Appointed from Va.]
2nd Lieut. 7th Inf., 1 July, 1822. 1st Lieut., 4 Oct., 1825. Capt., 31 Dec., 1834. Died 26 Nov., 1841.

STEPHENSON, JOHN M. [Born in Pa. Appointed from Pa.]
2nd Lieut. 4th Art., 24 Oct., 1861. 1st Lieut., 1 July, 1863. Cashiered 3 July, 1866. Reinstated 18 Sept., 1866. Trans. to 17th Inf., 19 Aug., 1867. Resigned 1 Nov., 1867. Died 27 April, 1870.

STEPHENSON, THOMAS T.* [Born in D. C. Appointed from D. C.]
2nd Lieut. Corps Art., 21 July, 1814. Trans. to Ord., 1 Jan., 1816. 1st Lieut. 30 June, 1818. Died 4 Aug., 1819.

STEPHENSON, WM. [Born in England. Appointed from Army.]
Priv. Co. C, 1st Batt. 13th Inf., 16 Nov., 1864. Corpl., 1 March, 1865. Sergt., 20 Feb., 1866. Sergt. Maj. 13th Inf., 1 Dec., 1866. 2nd Lieut. 27th Inf., 8 June, 1867. 1st Lieut., 2 Dec., 1868. Unassigned 14 June, 1869. Ass'd to 8th Cav., 1 Jan., 1871. Retired 23 April, 1879. Died 22 April, 1898.

STEPHENSON,, WM. [Born in Maine. Appointed from Maine.]
Asst. Surg., 3 Dec., 1883. Capt. Asst. Surg., 3 Dec., 1888. Maj. Brig. Surg. Vols., 4 June, 1898, to 30 April, 1899.

STEPTOE, EDWARD J.* [Born in Va. Appointed from Va.]
2nd Lieut. 3rd Art., 1 July, 1837. 1st Lieut., 9 July, 1838. Capt., 3 March, 1847. Maj. 9th Inf., 3 March, 1855. Lieut. Col. 10th Inf., 9 Sept., 1861. Resigned 1 Nov., 1861. Bvt. Maj., 18 April, 1847, for gallant and meritorious conduct at Cerro Gordo. Bvt. Lieut. Col., 13th Sept., 1847, for gallant and meritorious conduct at Chapultepec.

STERLING, GEORGE A.* [Born in Conn. Appointed from Conn.]
Bvt. 2nd Lieut. 7th Inf., 1 July, 1829. 2nd Lieut., 1 July, 1829. Resigned 31 Dec., 1831.

STERLING, WM. H. [Born in Pa. Appointed from Pa.]
Cadet at Mil. Acad., 1 July to 15 Oct., 1849. 2nd Lieut. 1st Inf., 18 May, 1861. 1st Lieut. 28 July, 1861. Reg. Adj., 1 Sept., 1861, to 2 July, 1863. Capt., 2 July, 1863. Discharged 1 Oct., 1870.

STERNBERG, GEORGE M. [Born in N. Y. Appointed from N. Y.]
1st Lieut. Asst. Surg., 28 May, 1861. Bvt. Capt. and Maj., 13 March, 1865, for faithful and meritorious service during the war. Capt. Asst. Surg., 28 May, 1866. Maj. Surg., 1 Dec., 1875. Lieut. Col. Surg., 2 Jan., 1891. Brig. Gen. Surg. Gen., 30 May, 1893.

STERNBURG, SIGISMUND. [Born in Prussia. Appointed from D. C.]
1st Lieut. 175th N. Y. Vols., 26 Sept., 1862. Resigned 13 Feb., 1864. Capt. 7th N. Y. Vols., 22 Oct., 1864. Mustered out 4 Aug., 1865. 1st Lieut 82nd U. S. Col. Inf., 10 Sept., 1865. Capt., 30 June, 1866. Mustered out 10 Sept., 1866. 2nd Lieut. 27th Inf., 7 March, 1867. Killed 1 Aug., 1867, in action with Indians in Mon. Ter.

STERUE, WM. [Born in Mass. Appointed from Mass.]
Surg.'s Mate 40th Inf., 11 March, 1814. Trans. to 6th Inf., 17 May, 1815. Post Surg., 26 Oct., 1818. Disbanded 1 June, 1821.

STERRETT, ESSEX.* [Born in Md. Appointed from Md.]
Bvt. 2nd Lieut. Art., 1 July, 1827. Resigned 21 June, 1828. Died 6 July, 1835.

STETSON, FREDERIC T.* [Born in Minn. Appointed from N. Y.]
2nd Lieut. 4th Inf., 11 June, 1892. 1st Lieut. 3rd Inf., 26 April, 1898.

STETSON, PRINCE R. [Born in N. Y. Appointed from N. Y.]
1st Lieut. 6th N. Y. Militia. 19 April to 24 June, 1861. 1st Lieut. 15th Inf., 14 May, 1861. Reg. Adj., 12 Oct., 1861, to 9 Feb., 1863. Capt., 22 Dec., 1862. Resigned 21 Dec., 1864.

STEUART, ADAM D. [Born in Va. Appointed from Va.]
Maj. P. W., 14 Jan., 1833. Lieut. Col. Dep. P. M. G., 20 July, 1854. Resigned 1 Feb., 1855. Maj. P. M., 31 May, 1861. Died 17 Oct., 1867. Bvt. Lieut. Col., 30 May, 1848, for meritorious conduct while serving in the enemy's country. Bvt. Lieut. Col., 13 March, 1865, for faithful and meritorious service during the war.

STEUART, ALEXANDER H. [Born in Mass. Appointed from Conn.]
2nd Lieut. 1st Inf., 14 Oct., 1837. 1st Lieut., 11 July, 1838. Resigned 1 March, 1839.

STEUART, GEORGE H.* [Born in Md. Appointed at Large.]
Bvt. 2nd Lieut. 2nd Drag., 1 July, 1848. 2nd Lieut., 11 Nov., 1849. 1st Lieut. 1st Cav., 3 March, 1855. Capt., 20 Dec., 1855. Resigned 22 April, 1861.

STEVENS, CHARLES J.* [Born in N. Y. Appointed from N. Y.]
2nd Lieut. 9th Cav., 13 June, 1882. 1st Lieut., 16 July, 1888. Capt. 2nd Cav., 1 July, 1898. Maj. 39th U. S. Vols., 17 Aug., 1899, declined. Graduate of the Infantry School and Cavalry School, 1897.

STEVENS, EDWARD G.* [Born in Mass. Appointed from Mas.]
2nd Lieut. 5th Cav., 15 June, 1870. Resigned 1 Dec., 1871.

STEVENS, GEORGE.* [Born in Vt. Appointed from Vt.]
Bvt. 2nd Lieut. Rifles, 1 July, 1843. 2nd Lieut. 2nd Drag., 31 Aug., 1843. Drowned 18 May, 1846.

STEVENS, GUSTAVE W. S.* [Born in Va. Appointed from La.]
Addl. 2nd Lieut. 4th Art., 1 July, 1886. 2nd Lieut. 5th Art., 18 July, 1886. 1st Lieut. 1st Art., 23 Dec., 1892. Trans. to 6th Art., 8 March, 1898. Graduate of the Artillery School, 1890. Capt. Sig. Corps Vols., 20 May, 1898. Maj., 18 July, 1898, to 17 Aug., 1899. Capt. Vol. Sig. Corps, 17 April, 1898.

STEVENS, HENNEL. [Born in Pa. Appointed frm Conn.]
Med. Storekeeper, 13 Aug., 1862. Resigned 14 March, 1866.

STEVENS, ISAAC I.* [Born in Mass. Appointed from Mass.]
2nd Lieut. Eng., 1 July, 1839. 1st Lieut., 1 July, 1840. Resigned 16 March, 1863. Bvt. Capt., 20 Aug., 1847, for gallant and meritorious conduct at Contreras and Churubusco. Bvt. Maj., 13 Sept., 1847, for gallant and meritorious conduct at Chapultepec, Mex. Col. 79th N. Y. Vols., 30 July, 1861. Brig. Gen. Vols., 28 Sept., 1861. Maj. Gen. Vols., 4 July, 1862. Killed 1 Sept., 1862, at the Battle of Chantilly, Va.

STEVENS, JUSTIN E. [Born in Mass. Appointed from Mass.]
Maj. Surg. of Inf., 3 March, 1847; 9th Inf., 9 April, 1847. Disbanded 26 Aug., 1848.

STEVENS, PHINEAS. [Born in Vt. Appointed from N. Y..
1st Lieut. 49th N. Y. Vols., 30 Aug., 1861. Resigned 29 April, 1862. Capt. 112th N. Y. Vols., 11 Sept., 1862. Resigned 11 Jan., 1864. Capt. 1st U. S. Vet. Vols., 15 Feb., 1865. Mustered out 15 Feb., 1866. 2nd Lieut. and 1st Lieut. 17 Inf., 23 Feb., 1866. Trans. to 35th Inf., 21 Sept., 1866. Unassigned 12 June, 1869. Discharged 30 Aug., 1870. Bvt. Capt., 2 March, 1867, for gallant and meritorious service during the war.

STEVENS, RAYMOND R. [Born in Pa. Appointed from D. C.]
Cadet at Naval Acad., 29 Nov., 1879, to 14 June, 1882. 2nd Lieut. 23rd Inf., 30 Oct., 1884. Ist. Lieut. 20th Inf., 14 Oct., 1891. Trans. to 23rd Inf., 5 Nov., 1891. Capt. 16th Inf., 6 Feb., 1899. Trans. to 23rd Inf., 28 Oct., 1899.

STEVENS, RICHD. H. [Born in ——. Appointed from Mo.]
Asst. Surg. Vols., 22 July, 1846. Disbanded 25 Aug., 1846.

STEVENS, ROBT. R.* [Born in Texas. Appointed from Miss.]
2nd Lieut. 6th Inf., 15 June, 1877. 1st Lieut., 16 Jan., 1884. Capt. A. Q. M., 20 Feb., 1894.

STEVENS, WALTER H.* [Born in N. Y. Appointed from N. Y.]
Bvt. 2nd Lieut. Eng., 1 July, 1848. 2nd Lieut., 28 May, 1853. 1st Lieut., 1 July, 1855. Dismissed 2 May, 1861. Died 12 Nov., 1867.

STEVENSON, CARTER L.* [Born in Va. Appointed from Va.]
2nd Lieut., 5th Inf., 1 July, 1838. 1st Lieut., 22 Sept., 1840. Capt., 30 June, 1847. Dismissed 25 June, 1861.

STEVENSON, HENRY. [Born in Va. Appointed from Va.]
Surg.'s Mate 6th Inf., 13 Nov., 1818. Disbanded 1 June, 1821. Asst. Surg., 16 July, 1821. Resigned 31 Aug., 1833.

STEVENSON, JAMES. [Born in Va. Appointed from Va.]
Hosp. Surg.'s Mate, 27 May, 1812. Died 1 Sept., 1817.

STEVENSON, JOHN D. [Born in Va. Appointed from Mo.]
Capt. Mo. Mounted Vols., 27 June, 1846, to 24 June, 1847. Col. 7th Mo. Inf., 1

June, 1861. Brig. Gen. Vols., 29 Nov., 1862. Resigned 22 April, 1864. Brig. Gen. Vols., 7 Aug., 1864, to rank from 29 Nov., 1862. Bvt. Maj. Gen. Vols., 13 March, 1865, for meritorious service during the war. Mustered out 15 Jan., 1866. Col. 30th Inf., 28 July, 1866. Unassigned 15 March, 1869. Ass'd to 25th Inf., 31 Dec., 1870. Discharged 31 Dec., 1870. Bvt. Brig. Gen., 2 March, 1867, for gallant and meritorious service at the Battle of Champion Hill, Miss.

STEVENSON, JONATHAN D. [Born in N. Y. Appointed from N. Y.]
Com. Sergt., 102nd N. Y. Vols., 15 Oct., 1861. Discharged 28 April, 1862. Priv. Troop M, 25th N. Y. Cav., 25 Aug., 1864. Discharged 19 Oct., 1864. 1st Lieut. 25th N. Y. Cav., 20 Oct., 1864. Mustered out 27 June, 1865. 2nd Lieut. 8th Cav., 28 July, 1866. 1st Lieut., 26 Aug., 1867. Capt., 20 March, 1879. Died 9 Oct., 1882.

STEVENSON, MATTHEW R.* [Born in N. Y. Appointed from N. Y.]
Bvt. 2nd Lieut. 1st Inf., 1 July, 1846. Capt. 2nd N. Y. Vols., 1 July, 1846. Mustered out Vols., 26 Oct., 1848. 2nd Lieut. 7th Inf., 16 Feb., 1847. 1st Lieut. 24 Aug., 1851. Dismissed 20 Sept., 1856. Reinstated 14 June, 1858, as Capt 7th Inf., from 2 Jan., 1858. Died 2 Jan., 1863.

STEVENSON, WM. W. [Born in Pa. Appointed from N. Y.]
1st Lieut. 18th Inf., 14 May, 1861. Died 27 Feb., 1862.

STEVER, MITCHELL. [Born in Pa. Appointed from Pa.]
2nd Lieut. 11th Inf., 9 April, 1847. Resigned 17 June, 1848.

STEWARD, JAMES. [Born in ——. Appointed from ——.]
2nd Lieut. 4th Inf., 19 Feb., 1817. Resigned 25 April, 1817.

STEWARD, THEOPHILUS G. [Born in N. J. Appointed from D. C.]
Chap. 25th Inf., 20 July, 1891.

STEWART, ABRAHAM. [Born in Mass. Appointed from Mass.]
Garrison Surg.'s Mate, 6 March, 1806. Resigned 24 Feb., 1815. Reinstated 15 June, 1815. Resigned 20 March, 1816.

STEWART, ALEXANDER. [Born in Md. Appointed from Md.]
Maj. 26th Inf., 25 March, 1813. Trans. to 5th Inf., 10 Oct., 1814. Disbanded 15 June, 1815. 2nd Lieut. Corps Art., 4 Dec., 1819. Trans. to 3rd Art., 1 June, 1821. Resigned 1 June, 1822.

STEWART, CECIL.* [Born in Va. Appointed from Cal.]
2nd Lieut. 3rd Cav., 1 July, 1886. 1st Lieut. 4th Cav., 26 July, 1892.

STEWART, CHAS. S.* [Born at Sea. Appointed from N. J.]
2nd Lieut. Eng., 1 July, 1846. 1st Lieut., 1 July, 1853. Capt., 1 July, 1860. Maj., 3 March, 1863. Bvt. Lieut. Col., 25 Feb., 1865, for long, faithful and efficient service. Bvt. Col., 13 March, 1865, for gallant and meritorious service during the war, declined. Lieut. Col. Eng., 7 March, 1867. Col., 30 June, 1882. Retired after forty years' service, 16 Sept., 1886.

STEWART, GEORGE E. [Born in N. S. Wales. Appointed from Army.]
Priv. Batty A, 5th Art., 5 Oct., 1896, to 28 Feb., 1899, and from 2 March to 14 April, 1899. 2nd Lieut. 19th Inf., 5 April, 1899.

STEWART, HENRY R.* [Born in Md. Appointed from D. C.]
2nd Lieut. 1st Inf. 1 July, 1823. Resigned 14 July, 1828.

STEWART, ISAAC S. [Born in Ind. Appointed from Ind.]
Addl. P. M. Vols., 26 Nov., 1862. Bvt. Lieut. Col. Vols., 1 Jan., 1866, for faithful service in the Pay Dept. Mustered out 10 April, 1867. Maj. P. M., 18 Oct., 1867. Resigned 31 July, 1870.

STEWART, JAMES. [Born in Scotland. Appointed from Army.]
Priv. Co. B, 4th Art., 29 Oct., 1851. Corpl., 1 Oct., 1853. Sergt., 1 Jan., 1855. 1st Sergt., 6 Oct., 1855. Discharged29 Aug., 1856. 1st Sergt. Co. B, 4th Art., 29 Aug., 1856. Discharged 1 July, 1861. 1st Sergt. Co. B, 4th Art., 1 July, 1861. 2nd Lieut. 4th Art., 15 Nov., 1861. 1st Lieut., 3 July, 1863. Bvt. Capt., 1 Aug., 1864, for gallant and meritorious service in the Battle of Spottsylvania C. H., and during the campaign before Richmond, Va. Bvt. Maj., 18 Aug., 1864, for gallant and meritorious service in the Battle on the Weldon Railroad, Va. Capt. 18th Inf., 28 July, 1866. Retired 20 March, 1879, for wound and injury.

STEWART, JAMES H. [Born in N. Y. Appointed from Nev.]
1st Lieut. 2nd Cal. Vols., 6 Sept., 1861. Capt., 22 Oct., 1864. Mustered out 2 July, 1866. 2nd Lieut. 15th Inf., 23 Feb., 1866. 1st Lieut., 23 Feb., 1866. Capt., 17 Sept., 1867. Dismissed 25 Aug., 1877.

STEWART, JOHN. [Born in Ky. Appointed from Army.]
Priv. 39th Inf., 20 July, 1814, to June, 1815, and Sergt. 7th Inf., June, 1815, to Aug., 1819. 2nd Lieut. 7th Inf., 13 Aug., 1819. 1st Lieut., 6 Oct., 1822. Capt., 30 June, 1828. Died 8 Dec., 1838.

STEWART, JOSEPH.* [Born in Ky. Appointed from Ky.]
Bvt. 2nd Lieut. 1st Art., 1 July, 1842. 2nd Lieut. 3rd Art., 27 June, 1843. 1st Lieut., 17 Oct., 1846. Capt., 3 Jan., 1856. Maj. 4th Art., 11 Dec., 1865. Lieut. Col. 3rd Art., 18 July, 1879. Retired 25 Aug., 1879, for thirty years' service.

STEWART, MERCH B.* [Born in Va. Appointed from N. Y.]
Addl. 2nd Lieut. 11th Inf., 12 June, 1896. 2nd Lieut. 8th Inf., 27 Aug., 1896. 1st Lieut. of Inf., 12 Oct., 1898. Ass'd to 8th Inf., 1 Jan., 1899. Reg. Com., 30 April, 1899.

STEWART, REID T.* [Born in Pa. Appointed from Pa.]
2nd Lieut. 5th Cav., 12 June, 1871. Killed 27 Aug., 1872, by Indians in Arizona.

STEWART, WALTER E. Jr. [Born in N. J. Appointed from N. J.]
2nd Lieut. 3rd Inf., 10 April, 1899.

STEWART, WM. [Born in Bahama Islands. Appointed from Md.]
Hosp. Surg.'s Mate, 30 March, 1814. Post Surg., 18 April, 1818. Asst. Surg., 1 June, 1821. Died 23 Sept., 1823.

STEWART, WM F. [Born in R. I. Appointed from R. I.]
2nd Lieut. 4th Art., 1 Dec., 1866. 1st Lieut., 19 Nov., 1869. Capt., 14 Aug., 1889. Graduate of the Artillery School, 1871. Bvt. Capt., 27 Feb., 1890, for gallant service in action against Indians at Clearwater, Idaho, 11 and 12 July, 1877.

STEWART, WILLIAM F., Jr. [Born in Cal. Appointed from Va.]
2nd Lieut. 1st Art., 9 July, 1898.

STEWART, WM. J. [Born in Pa. Appointed from Ohio.]
1st Lieut. 16th Inf., 14 May, 1861. R. Q. M., 10 Aug., 1861, to 21 Nov., 1862. Capt., 5 May, 1863. Cashiered 16 Feb., 1865.

STICKLE, HORTON W.* [Born in Iowa. Appointed from Iowa.]
2nd Lieut. Eng., 15 Feb., 1899.

STICKNEY, AMOS.* [Born in Mo. Appointed from N. Y.]
1st Lieut. Eng., 13 June, 1864. Bvt. Capt., 21 Dec., 1864, for zeal and efficiency in the discharge of his duties with the army of the Tennessee during the campaign in Ga. in 1864. Bvt. Maj., 13 March, 1865, for faithful and meritorious service druing the campaign through Ga. and the Carolinas. Capt. Eng., 7 March, 1867. Maj., 2 Jan., 1881. Lieut. Col., 18 May, 1893.

STICKNEY, CLIFFORD. [Born in R. I. Appointed from Ill.]
2nd Lieut. 72nd Ill. Vols., 21 Aug., 1862. 1st Lieut. Sig. Corps, 3 March, 1863. Maj. A. A. G. Vols., 7 Aug., 1865. Bvt. Capt. Vols., 9 April, 1865, for gallant and meritorious service during the campaign terminating with the surrender of the insurgent army under Gen. R. E. Lee. Mustered out 5 Oct., 1866. 1st Lieut. 20th Inf., 28 July, 1866. Died 3 Oct., 1867. Bvt. Capt., 2 March, 1867, for gallant and meritorious service in the capture of Atlanta, Ga., 22 July, 1864.

STICKNEY, JAMES W. H. [Born in Maine. Appointed from N. J.]
Capt. 3rd N. J. Vols., 28 May, 1861. Maj., 13 Sept., 1862. Resigned 25 June, 1863. Maj. Vet. Res. Corps, 15 Oct., 1863. Mustered out 15 Dec., 1866. 1st Lieut., 42nd Inf., 28 July, 1866. Appointment expired 4 March, 1867.

STILES, DANIEL F. [Born in Mass. Appointed from D. C.]
Q. M. Sergt. 1st D. C. Vols., 6 Aug., 1861. Com. Sergt., 20 Sept., 1861. 2nd Lieut. 1st D. C. Vols., 1 Dec., 1862 Trans to 2nd D. C. Vols., 28 Feb., 1865. 1st Lieut., 21 March, 1865. Mustered out 12 Sept., 1865. 2nd Lieut. 26th Inf., 22 Jan., 1867. Trans. to 10th Inf., 19 May, 1869. 1st Lieut., 2 Nov., 1876. Capt., 6 March, 1888. Retired for over thirty years' service, 19 May, 1893.

STILES, HENRY R. [Born in Conn. Appointed from Conn.]
Asst. Surg., 4 Nov., 1892. Capt. Asst. Surg., 4 Nov., 1897.

STILLE, LOUIS R. [Born in Md. Appointed from Pa.]
2nd Lieut. 3rd Pa. Cav., 9 Sept., 1862. 1st Lieut., 1 May, 1863. Capt., 2 May, 1864. Bvt. Maj. Vols., 9 April, 1865, for gallant and meritorious service during the operations resulting in the fall of Richmond, Va., and the surrender of the insurgent army under Gen. R. E. Lee. Capt. 5th Pa. Cav., 8 May, 1865. Mustered out 7 Aug., 1865. 2nd Lieut. 14th Inf., 16 March, 1866. Trans. to 23rd Inf., 21 Sept., 1866. 1st Lieut., 4 Oct., 1866. Capt., 20 March, 1879. Died 15 July, 1890.

STILLWELL, WM. S.* [Born in N. Y. Appointed from Mass.]
Bvt. 2nd Lieut. 3rd Inf., 1 July, 1827. 2nd Lieut., 1 July, 1827. Resigned 31 March, 1833. Died — ——, 1837.

STIMPSON, FRANK E. [Born in Mass. Appointed from Army.]
Priv., Corpl., Sergt. and 1st Sergt. Co. B, 2nd Batt. 17th Inf., 31 July, 1862, to 20 March, 1863. 2nd Lieut. 17th Inf., 17 March, 1863. 1st Lieut., 25 May, 1863. Died 28 May, 1864, of wounds received at the Battle of Laurel Hill, Va. Bvt. Capt., 5 May, 1864, for gallant and meritorious service at the Battle of the Wilderness, Va.

STITH, DONALD C.* [Born in Turkey. Appointed from Md.]
Bvt. 2nd Lieut. 5th Inf., 1 July, 1850. 2nd Lieut., 30 April, 1853. 1st Lieut., 18 Oct., 1855. Capt., 8 Aug., 1861. Dismissed 25 Sept., 1861.

STIVERS, CHAS. B.* [Born in Ky. Appointed from Ky.]
2nd Lieut. 7th Inf., 1 July, 1856. 1st Lieut., 20 April, 1861. R. Q. M., 1 April, 1860, to 9 Sept., 1861. Capt. 7th Inf., 9 Sept., 1861. Dismissed 14 July, 1863. Reinstated 11 Aug., 1863. Retired 30 Dec., 1864. Dropped 1 March, 1891.

STIVERS, CHAS. P.* [Born in La. Appointed from Ohio.]
2nd Lieut. 9th Inf., 13 June, 1879. 1st Lieut., 30 Aug., 1887. Resigned 17 Oct., 1888.

STIVERS, EDWIN J. [Born in Ohio. Appointed from Ill.]
Fifer Co. K, 89th Ill. Vols., 7 Aug., 1852. Fife Maj., 4 Sept., 1862. Sergt. Maj., 15 Jan., 1863. Priv. Co. K, 29 Nov., 1863. Discharged 1 Dec., 1863. 2nd Lieut. 17th U. S. Col. Troops, 2 Dec., 1863. 1st Lieut., 5 Feb., 1864. Capt., 2 Aug., 1865. Mustered out 3 Nov., 1866. 2nd Lieut. 40th Inf., 28 July, 1866. Bvt. 1st Lieut., 2 March, 1867, for gallant and meritorious service in the Battle of Nashville, Tenn. 1st Lieut. 40th Inf., 15 Sept., 1868. Trans. to 25th Inf., 20 April, 1869. Capt., 19 Feb., 1883. Retired for disability 24 Feb., 1891.

STOCKHAM, EDWARD V.* [Born in N. J. Appointed from N. J.]
Addl. 2nd Lieut. 17th Inf., 12 June, 1889. 2nd Lieut., 22 June, 1889. Resigned 30 Sept., 1889.

STOCKLE, GEORGE E.* [Born in Nev. Appointed from Nev.]
2nd Lieut. 25th Inf., 11 June, 1888. Trans. to 10th Cav., 11 Feb., 1889. 1st Lieut. 8th Cav., 31 May, 1896. Reg. Com., 29 April, 1899.

STOCKLY, PAUL D [Born in Ohio. Appointed from N. Y.]
2nd Lieut. 21st Inf., 22 Aug., 1899.

STOCKTON, EDWARD D.* [Born in Ky. Appointed from Ky.]
Bvt. 2nd Lieut. 7th Inf., 1 July, 1849. 2nd Lieut. 1st Inf., 31 Aug., 1849. 1st Lieut., 2 March, 1853. Died 13 March, 1857.

STOCKTON, GEORGE. [Born in Va. Appointed from Ky.]
Capt. 28th Inf., 20 May, 1813. Trans. to 3rd Inf., 17 May, 1815. Resigned 1 May, 1816.

STOCKTON, HOWARD. [Born in Pa. Appointed from R. I.]
Capt. A. A. de C., 9 June, 1862. Resigned 7 Feb., 1863. 1st Lieut. 3rd R. I. Cav., 22 March to 21 July, 1864. 2nd Lieut. Ord., 23 May, 1864. 1st Lieut., 13 May, 1867. Resigned 1 Aug., 1871. Bvt. 1st Lieut. and Capt., 14 Sept., 1866, for meritorious service.

STOCKTON, PHILIP.* [Born in N. J. Appointed from N. J.]
Bvt. 2nd Lieut. 8th Inf., 1 July, 1852. 2nd Lieut., 11 Oct., 1853. Trans. to 1st Cav., 3 March, 1855. 1st Lieut., 1 Oct., 1855. Resigned 27 Feb., 1861. Died 25 March, 1879.

STOCKTON, RICHD. G.* [Born in Ky. Appointed from Ky.]
Bvt. 2nd Lieut. 1st Drag., 1 July, 1836. 2nd Lieut., 4 July, 1836. Resigned 30 April, 1837. 2nd Lieut. 1st Drag., 13 May, 1837. Resigned 30 April, 1838. Brig. Gen. Mo. State Militia, 24 Oct., 1862. Resigned 8 Jan., 1863. Died 14 June, 1874.

STOCKTON, ROBT. F. [Born in N. J. Appointed from N. J.]
2nd Lieut. 5th Cav., 23 Feb., 1866. 1st Lieut., 31 Oct., 1866. Resigned 14 Feb., 1868.

STOCKTON, SAML. W. [Born in N. J. Appointed from N. J.]
2nd Lieut. 1st Cav., 4 May, 1861. 1st Lieut., 24 May, 1861; 4th Cav., 3 Aug., 1861. Capt. A. de C. Vols., 8 Nov., 1862. Discharged from Vol. Service, 15 Aug., 1863. Capt. 4th Cav., 14 March, 1865. Resigned 27 Sept., 1866. Bvt. Capt., 18 June, 1864, for gallant and meritorious service during the expedition of Gen. Hunter against Lynchburg, Va. Bvt. Maj. and Lieut. Col., 13 March, 1865, for gallant and meritorious service during the war.

STOCKTON, THOMAS. [Born in Del. Appointed from Del.]
Capt. 3rd Art., 10 Sept. 1812. Trans. to 42nd Inf., 3 Oct., 1813. Maj., 15 April, 1814. Retained 17 May, 1815. (in reorganization under Act. of 3 March, 1815), as Capt. 6th Inf., with Bvt. of Maj., from 15 April, 1814. Trans. to Corps Art., 17 May, 1816. Trans. to 3rd Art., 1 June, 1821. Resigned 6 July, 1825. Died 2 March, 1846.

STOCKTON, THOS.* [Born in Del. Appointed from Del.]
Bvt. 2nd Lieut. 5th Inf., 1 July, 1831. 2nd Lieut., 1 July, 1835. Resigned 31 Oct., 1836. Died 25 May, 1860.

STOCKTON, THOS. B. W.* [Born in N. Y. Appointed from N. Y.]
Bvt. 2nd Lieut. 1st Inf., 1 July, 1827. 2nd Lieut., 1 July, 1827. 1st Lieut., 4 March, 1833. A. Q. M., 11 July, 1832, to 31 Dec., 1835. Resigned 30 Nov., 1836. Col. 1st Mich. Vols., 9 Dec., 1847. Mustered out 9 July, 1848. Col. 16th Mich. Vols. 8 Sept., 1861. Resigned 18 May, 1863.

STOCKTON, WM. T.* [Born in Pa. Appointed from Pa.]
Bvt. 2nd Lieut. 2nd Art., 1 July, 1834. 2nd Lieut., 1 Dec., 1834. Resigned 31 March, 1836. Died 4 March, 1869.

STODDARD, ASA A. [Born in Conn. Appointed from Conn.]
2nd Lieut of Inf., 23 Feb., 1847; 9th Inf., 9 April, 1847. 1st Lieut., 8 Sept., 1847. Disbanded 26 Aug., 1848. Bvt. 1st Lieut., 13 Sept., 1847, for gallant and meritorious conduct at Chapultepec.

STODDARD, JOHN. [Born in N. H. Appointed from Army.]
Priv., Corpl., Sergt. and 1st Sergt. Troops D and I, 2nd (5th) Cav., 1 Nov., 1858, to 20 March, 1863. 2nd Lieut. 5th Cav., 19 Feb., 1863. Resigned 25 May, 1863.

STODDARD, JOHN S.* [Born in N. Y. Appointed from N. Y.]
Bvt. 2nd Lieut. 5th Inf., 1 July, 1830, declined. Died 3 June, 1862.

STODTER, CHARLES E.* [Born in Pa. Appointed from Ohio.]
2nd Lieut. 9th Cav., 12 June, 1896. 1st Lieut., 7th Cav., 18 Oct., 1899. Trans. to 9th Cav., 17 Nov., 1899.

STOGSDALL, RALPH R.* [Born in Ind. Appointed from Ind.]
2nd Lieut. 4th Inf., 12 June, 1894. 1st Lieut. 10th Inf., 26 April, 1898. Trans. to 3rd Inf., 28 Dec., 1899.

STOKES, JAMES H.* [Born in Md. Appointed from Md.]
Capt. Chicago Board of Trade Batty Ill. Vols., 31 July, 1862. Capt. A. A. G. Vols., 22 Aug., 1864. Lieut. Col. Q. M., 10 Feb. to 22 Aug., 1864. Brig. Gen. Vols., 20 July, 1865. Mustered out 24 Aug., 1865. Bvt. 2nd Lieut. 2nd Art., 1 July, 1835. Trans. to 4th Art., 14 Aug., 1835. 2nd Lieut., 11 June, 1836. 1st Lieut., 7 July, 1838. Capt. A. Q. M., 21 May, 1839. Resigned 30 Sept., 1843.

STOKES, MARCUS B.* [Born in S. C. Appointed from S. C.]
2nd Lieut. 10th Inf., 11 June, 1892. 1st Lieut., 26 April, 1898. Maj. 1st S. C. Vols., 12 May to 10 Nov., 1898.

STOKES, WM. A. [Born in Pa. Appointed from Pa.]
Maj. 18th Inf., 7 Sept., 1861. Appointment revoked 12 March, 1862.

STOLBRAND, VASA E. [Born in Ill. Appointed from S. C.]
2nd Lieut. 13th Inf., 1 Sept., 1879. Resigned 10 March, 1885.

STOLL, ANDREW. [Born in N. J. Appointed from Army.]
Priv. and Corpl. Batty G. 4th Art., 21 Oct., 1850. to 21 Oct., 1855. Priv., Corpl., Sergt. and 1st Sergt. Troops K, 1st and F, 6th Cav., 1 May, 1856. to 5 Nov., 1861. 2nd Lieut. 6th Cav., 1 Nov., 1861. 1st Lieut., 19 Nov., 1863. Died 28 Sept., 1864, while prisoner of war.

STOLL, WALTER R.* [Born in N. J. Appointed from N. J.]
Addl. 2nd Lieut. 9th Inf., 11 June, 1881. 2nd Lieut., 15 June, 1881. Resigned 1 June, 1885.

STOMMEL, JULIUS. [Born in Germany. Appointed from D. C.]
Priv., Co. A, 41st N. Y. Vols., 6 June, 1861. 2nd Lieut., 7 June, 1863. 1st Lieut., 20 Nov., 1863. Capt., 10 Sept., 1864, to 8 Dec., 1864. 1st Lieut. Vet. Res. Corps, 3 Dec., 1864. Mustered out 30 June, 1866. 2nd Lieut. 43rd Inf., 28 July, 1866. Trans. to 1st Inf., 8 April, 1869. Unasigned 7 June, 1869. Ass'd to 8th Inf., 3 Aug., 1870. Mustered out 27 Dec., 1870.

STONE, CHARLES B., Jr. [Born in Cal. Appointed from Cal.]
Priv. 7th Cal. Vols., 5 May to 8 Oct., 1898. 2nd Lieut. 16th Inf., 10 April, 1899.

STONE, CHAS. P.* [Born in Mass. Appointed from Mass.]
Bvt. 2nd Lieut. Ord., 1 July, 1845. 2nd Lieut., 3 March, 1847. 1st Lieut., 26 Feb., 1853. Resigned 17 Nov., 1856. Col. I. G. and Commander D. C. Vols., 16 April, to 23 July, 1861. Brig. Gen. Vols., 17 May, 1861. Mustered out of Vol. Service, 14 April, 1864. Col. 14th Inf., 14 May, 1861. Resigned 13 Sept., 1864. Bvt. 1st Lieut., 8 Sept., 1847, for gallant and meritorious conduct at Molino del Rey. Bvt.

Capt., 13 Sept., 1847, for gallant and meritorious conduct at Chapultepec. Died 24 Jan., 1887.

**STONE, DAVID L.*** [Born in Miss. Appointed from Miss.]
2nd Lieut. 22nd Inf., 26 April, 1898. 1st Lieut., 2 March, 1899.

**STONE, EBENEZER W.** [Born in Mass. Appointed from Mass.]
Capt. 1st Mass. Vols., 24 May, 1861. Mustered out 25 May, 1864. Lieut. Col. 61st Mass. Vols., 28 Feb., 1865 Bvt. Col. Vols., 9 April, 1865, for gallant and meritorious service during the campaign resulting in the fall of Richmod, Va., and the surrender of the insurgent army under Gen. R. E. Lee. Mustered out 16 July, 1865. 2nd Lieut. 12th Inf., 11 May, 1866. Trans. to 21st Inf., 21 Sept., 1866. Bvt. 1st Lieut. and Capt., 2 March, 1867, for gallant and meritorious service at the Battle of Williamsburg, Va. Bvt. Maj., 2 March, 1867, for gallant and meritorious service at the Battle of Chancellorsville, Va. Bvt. Lieut. Col., 2 March, 1867, for gallant and meritorious service at the Battle of Gettysburg, Pa. 1st Lieut. 21st Inf., 26 March, 1868. Unassigned 19 April, 1869. Assd, to 21st Inf., 15 Dec., 1870. Capt., 11 Nov., 1879. Retired for disability with rank of Maj., 26 April, 1898.

**STONE, EDWARD R.** [Born in Mass. Appointed from Mass.]
Priv., Corpl. and Sergt. Co. K, 12th Inf., 3 June, 1898, to 17 June, 1899. 2nd Lieut. 4th Inf., 1 May, 1899.

**STONE, HENRY L.** [Born in Mass. Appointed from Mass.]
Priv. and Corpl. Co. H, 23rd Mass. Vols., 28 Sept., 1861, to 27 May, 1863. 1st Lieut. 35th U. S. Col. Inf., 27 May, 1863. Capt. 103rd U. S. Col. Inf., 19 April, 1865. Mustered out 15 April, 1866. 1st Lieut., 41st Inf., 28 July, 1866. Unasigend 11 Nov., 1869. Died 25 May, 1870.

**STONE, HIRAM.** [Born in Conn. Appointed from Kan.]
Chap. Post of Fort Leavenworth, Kan., 26 Sept., 1859, to 30 April, 1867. Post Chap. 3 April, 1867. Resigned 31 Jan., 1876.

**STONE, JOHN, Jr.** [Born in Va. Appointed from Va.]
Mil. Storekeeper, 7 Jan., 1818. Resigned 3 April, 1818. 2nd Lieut. 1st Inf., 18 April, 1818. R. Q. M., 1 Aug. to 25 Oct., 1818. Died 10 Nov., 1818.

**STONE, JOHN H.** [Born in Md. Appointed from D. C.]
Asst. Surg., 6 Nov., 1895.

**STONE, LYMAN H.** [Born in Vt. Appoited from Vt.]
Asst. Surg., 13 Dec., 1847. Maj. Surg., 21 May, 1861. Dismissed 16 Sept., 1862.

**STONE, RODERIC.*** [Born in Maine. Appointed from Minn.]
Bvt. 2nd Lieut. 1st Inf., 1 July, 1859. 2nd Lieut. 5th Inf., 22 Aug., 1859. 1st Lieut. 14th Inf., 14 May, 1861. Capt., 24 Oct., 1861. Died 3 March, 1862, of wounds received at the Battle of Val Verde, N. M. Bvt. Maj., 21 Feb., 1862, for gallant and meritorious service at the Battle of Val Verde, N. M.

**STONE, VALENTINE H.** [Born in Ky. Appointed from Ind.]
1st Lieut. 5th Art., 14 May, 1861. Capt., 28 July, 1866. Died 24 Sept., 1867. Bvt. Capt., 23 Jan., 1865. Bvt. Maj., 13 March, 1865, for gallant and meritorious service during the war.

**STONE, WM.** [Born in Maine. Appointed from Mass.]
Priv., Corpl. and Sergt. Co. C, 19th Mass. Vols., 28 Aug., 1861, to 1 Jan., 1863. 2nd Lieut. 19th Mass. Vols., 1 Jan., 1863. 1st Lieut., 1 May, 1863. 2nd Lieut. Vet. Res. Corps, 20 Aug., 1863. 1st Lieut., 28 Oct., 1863. Capt., 25 March, 1865. Bvt. Maj. Vols., 4 Oct., 1865, for meritorious service in connection with the recruitment of the armies of the U. S. Mustered out 4 Jan., 1867. 1st Lieut. 45th Inf., 28 July, 1866. Unassigned 22 July, 1869. Discharged 21 Dec., 1870.

**STONE, WILLIAM P.*** [Born in Ark. Appointed from Ark.]
2nd Lieut. 2nd Art., 13 June, 1883. 1st Lieut 5th Art., 20 Feb., 1891. Trans. to 4th Art., 23 May, 1891. Trans. to 7th Art., 8 March, 1898. Capt., 20 April, 1899. Graduate of the Artillery School, 1886.

**STONEMAN, GEORGE.*** [Born in N. Y. Appointed from N. Y.]
Bvt 2nd Lieut. 1st Drag., 1 July, 1846. 2nd Lieut., 12 July, 1847. 1st Lieut., 25 July, 1854. Reg. Adj., 22 Oct., 1854, to 3 March, 1855. Capt. 2nd Cav., 3 March, 1855. Maj. 1st Cav., 9 May, 1861. 4th Cav., 3 Aug., 1861. Brig. Gen. Vols., 13 Aug., 1861. Maj. Gen. Vols., 29 Nov., 1862. Bvt. Col., 18 Dec., 1862, for gallant and meritorious service in the Battle of Fredericksburg, Va. Lieut. Col. 3rd Cav., 30 March, 1864. Bvt. Brig. Gen., 13 March, 1865, for gallant and meritorious service in the capture of Charlotte, N. C. Bvt. Maj. Gen., 13 March, 1865, for gallant and meritorious service in the field during the war. Col. 21st Inf., 28 July, 1866. Mustered out of Vol. Service, 1 Sept., 1866. Retired 16 Aug., 1874. Resigned 15 Sept., 1882. Appointed Col. of Inf., 9 Feb., 1891 (Act 15 Dec., 1890), Retired 24 Feb., 1891. Died 5 Sept., 1894.

**ST. ONGE, SAML. E.** [Born in N. Y. Appointed from Army.]
(His proper name was Samuel E. St. Onge Chapleau.) Priv. and Com. Sergt. 16th Inf., 26 Oct., 1861, to 9 Aug., 1862. 2nd lieut. 16th Inf., 7 April, 1862. 1st Lieut., 9 Nov., 1862. R. Q. M., 22 Aug., 1864, to 14 Aug., 1865. Capt., 14 Aug., 1865. Unassigned 17 April, 1869. Discharged 31 Dec., 1870. Bvt. Capt., 31 Dec., 1862, for gallant and meritorious service at the Battle of Murfreesboro, Tenn. Bvt. Maj., 1 Sept., 1864, for gallant and meritorious service during the Atlanta campaign and at the Battle of Jonesboro, Ga.

**STORER, WM. H.*** [Born in Maine. Appointed from N. Y.]
Bvt. 2nd Lieut. 1st Inf., 1 July, 1832. 2nd Lieut., 30 June, 1835. 1st Lieut., 17 Oct., 1837. Resigned 15 Nov., 1839. Died 21 Aug., 1878.

**STORROW, SAM'L. A.** [Born in Va. Appointed from D. C.]
Asst. Surg., 5 Aug., 1861. Maj. Surg., 26 June, 1876. Died 12 July, 1879. Bvt. Capt. and Maj., 13 March, 1865, for faithful and meritorious service during the war.

**STORROW, SAM'L. A.** [Born in N. H. Appointed from Mass.]
J. A., 9 July, 1816. Resigned 5 Feb., 1820.

**STORY, HORACE C.** [Born in Mass. Appointed from Mass.]
2nd Lieut. Eng., 11 March, 1814. 1st Lieut., 15 April, 1818. Died 28 July, 1823. Bvt. 1st Lieut., 17 Sept., 1814, for gallant conduct in the defence of Fort Erie.

STORY, HENRY C.* [Born in La. Appointed from La.]
Bvt. 2nd Lieut. 7th Inf., 1 July, 1842. 2nd Lieut., 31 Dec., 1842. Resigned 30 Nov., 1844. Died 9 Feb., 1868.

STORY, JOHN P.* [Born in Wis. Appointed from Wis.]
2nd Lieut. and 1st Lieut. 16th Inf., 23 June, 1865. Trans. to 34th Inf., 21 Sept., 1866. Unassigned 14 April, 1869. Ass'd to 2nd Art., 15 Dec., 1870. Trans. to 4th Art., 1 Jan., 1871. Capt., 14 Sept., 1883. Maj. 7th Art., 8 March, 1898.

STOTSENBURG, JOHN M.* [Born in Ind. Appointed from Ind.]
2nd Lieut. 6th Cav., 11 June, 1881. 1st Lieut., 19 Aug., 1889. Capt., 14 Dec., 1898. Graduate of the Infantry and Cavalry School, 1897. Maj. 1st Neb. Vols., 9 May, 1898. Killed in action at Quinqua, Philippine Islands, 23 April, 1899.

STOTLER, VICTOR E.* [Born in Conn. Appointed from Conn.]
2nd Lieut. 10th Inf., 13 June, 1882. 1st Lieut., 6 March, 1888. Retired for disability with rank of Capt., 26 April, 1898.

STOUCH, GEORGE W. H. [Born in Pa. Appointed from Army.]
Priv. Co. B, 1st Batt. 11th Inf., 30 Nov., 1861. Corpl., 8 April, 1862. Sergt. Maj. 11th Inf., 1 May, 1863. Discharged 27 Feb., 1864. Sergt. Maj. 11th Inf., 27 Feb., 1864. 2nd Lieut. 3rd Inf., 18 May, 1864. 1st Lieut., 31 Dec., 1864. Capt., 14 April, 1884. Maj. 20th Inf., 30 Aug., 1898. Maj. Chf. Com. Vols., 9 June to 30 Aug., 1898. Retired for disability 15 Dec., 1898.

STOUGH, JACOB L. [Born in Pa. Appointed from Army.]
Priv. and Sergt. 12th Inf., 1 Feb., 1862, to 1 Nov., 1863. 2nd Lieut. 12th Inf., 31 Oct., 1863. 1st Lieut., 10 May, 1864. Dismissed 11 Feb., 1865.

STOUGHTON, EDWIN H.* [Born in Vt. Appointed from Vt.]
Bvt. 2nd Lieut. 4th Inf., 1 July, 1859. 2nd Lieut. 6th Inf., 5 Sept., 1859. Resigned 4 March, 1861. Col. 4th Vt. Vols., 21 Sept., 1861. Brig. Gen. Vols., 5 Nov., 1862. Appointment expired 4 March, 1863. Died 25 Dec., 1868.

STOUT, CHAS. M. [Born in Pa. Appointed from Ill.]
2nd Lieut. 11th Inf., 29 March, 1848. Disbanded 16 Aug., 1848.

STOUT, HARRY H.* [Born in Ariz. Appointed from Pa.]
2nd Lieut. 6th Cav., 12 June, 1895. 1st Lieut. of Ord., 21 Nov., 1898.

STRAAT, JOHN N., Jr. [Born in Mo. Appointed from Mo.]
2nd Lieut. 25th Inf., 9 July, 1898. 1st Lieut., 12 July, 1899.

STRANG, EDWARD J. [Born in N. Y. Appointed from N. Y.]
1st Lieut. 15th N. Y. Vols., 17 June, 1861. Discharged 14 April, 1863. Capt. A. Q. M. Vols., 13 April, 1863. Bvt. Lieut. Col. Vols., 13 March, 1865, for long and faithful service during the war. Capt. A. Q. M. U. S. A., 18 Jan., 1867. Bvt. Maj. 2 March, 1867, for faithful and meritorious service in his department during the war. Bvt. Lieut. Col., 2 March, 1867, for faithful and meritorious service during the war. Retired by operation of law, 9 July, 1884. Died 20 June, 1891.

STRAUB, OSCAR I.* [Born in Pa. Appointed from Pa.]
Addl. 2nd Lieut. 1st Art., 12 June, 1887. 2nd Lieut., 11 Aug., 1887. 1st Lieut. 5th Art., 3 Jan., 1894. Graduate of the Artillery School, 1892.

STRAUB, PAUL F. [Born in Germany. Appointed from Iowa.]
Asst. Surg., 4 Nov., 1892. Capt. Asst. Surg., 4 Nov., 1897. Maj. Surg. 36th U. S. Vols., 5 July, 1899.

STREET, HARLOW L. [Born in Ill. Appointed from Cal.]
Corpl. Troop E, 2nd Cal. Cav., 20 Sept., 1861. 2nd Lieut., 31 Jan., 1863. 1st Lieut., 9 March, 1864. Capt., 9 May, 1865. Mustered out 18 May, 1866. 2nd Lieut. 1st Cav., 22 Jan., 1867. 1st Lieut., 22 Feb., 1869. Mustered out 1 Jan., 1871.

STREET, NATH'L H.* [Born in N. C. Appointed from N. C.]
Bvt. 2nd Lieut. 4th Inf., 1 July, 1825. 2nd Lieut. 6th Inf., 1 July, 1825. Resigned 1 Sept., 1826. Died 6 July, 1876.

STREET, WASH'N P.* [Born in Ill. Appointed from Iowa.]
Bvt. 2nd Lieut. 5th Inf., 1 July, 1847. 2nd Lieut. 8th Inf., 10 Sept., 1847. 1st Lieut., 4 Aug., 1849. Died 13 Sept., 1852.

STRETCH, JOHN F.* [Born in Ind. Appointed from Ind.]
2nd Lieut. 10th Inf., 18 June, 1866. Reg. Adj., 1 May, 1867, to 19 May, 1869. 1st Lieut., 26 March, 1868. Reg. Adj., 12 July, 1869, to 13 Dec., 1871, and from 1 June, 1879, to 6 Dec., 1884. Capt., 6 Dec., 1884. Maj 8th Inf., 1 Nov., 1898.

STRIBLING, FRANCIS. [Born in Va. Appointed from Va.]
Ensign Rifle Reg., 3 May, 1808. 2nd Lieut., 1 July, 1809. 1st Lieut Light Art., 1 March, 1811. Capt., 1 Nov., 1813. Resigned 1 May, 1816.

STRICKLAND, LYMAN S. [Born in Maine. Appointed from Maine.]
1st Lieut. 16th Inf., 14 May, 1861. Capt., 5 May, 1864. Resigned 2 April, 1866. Bvt. Maj., 1 Sept., 1864, for gallant and meritorious service during the Atlanta campaign and at the Battle of Jonesboro, Ga.

STRITZINGER, FREDERICK G., Jr.* [Born in Pa. Appointed from Pa.]
2nd Lieut 23rd Inf., 12 June, 1894. 1st Lieut., 26 April, 1898.

STRODE, EDWARD C. [Born in Ill. Appointed from Ill.]
Asst. Surg., 11 July, 1862. Resigned 24 Dec., 1864.

STRONG, BYRON F. [Born in N. Y. Appointed from N. Y.]
Priv. Co. B, 24th N. Y. Vols., 17 May, 1861, to 29 May, 1863. 2nd Lieut. 20th U. S. Col. Inf., 18 Dec., 1863. 1st Lieut., 3 Aug., 1864. Mustered out 7 Oct., 1865. 2nd Lieut. 10th U. S. Col. Art., 19 Dec., 1865. Mustered out 22 Feb., 1867. 2nd Lieut. 41st Inf., 7 March, 1867. Dismissed 31 May, 1869.

STRONG, ERASTUS B. [Born in Ark. Appointed from Ark.]
Bvt. 2nd Lieut. 7th Inf., 1 July, 1844. 2nd Lieut. 5th Inf., 18 May, 1846. Killed 8 Sept., 1847, at the Battle of Molino del Rey, Mexico

STRONG, FREDERICK S.* [Born in Mich. Appointed from Mich.]
2nd Lieut. 4th Art., 12 June, 1880. 1st Lieut., 6 May, 1887. Capt., 2 March, 1899. Graduate of the Artillery School, 1884. Maj. A. A. G. Vols., 12 May, 1898, to 31 March, 1899. Reg. Adj., 2 March, 1899.

STRONG, GEORGE C.* [Born in Vt. Appointed from Mass.]
Bvt. 2nd Lieut. Ord., 1 July, 1857. 2nd Lieut., 31 July, 1859. 1st Lieut., 25 Jan., 1861. Capt., 3 March, 1863. Maj. A. A. G. Vols., 1 Oct., 1861, which expired

17 July, 1862. Brig. Gen. Vols., 29 Nov., 1862. Maj. Gen. Vols., 18 July, 1863. Died 30 July, 1863, of wounds received in action at Fort Wagner, S. C.

STRONG, JASPER.* [Born in Vt. Appointed from Vt.]
2nd Lieut. 8th Inf., 1 July, 1819. Trans. to 1st Inf., 1 June, 1821. 1st Lieut., 1 Jan., 1823. Resigned 25 Dec., 1823. Died 6 Nov., 1865.

STRONG, JOSEPH.* [Born in Pa. Appointed from Pa.]
2nd Lieut. Corps Art., 24 July, 1818. Trans. to 2nd Art., 1 June, 1821. Trans. to 4th Art., 16 Aug., 1821. 1st Lieut., 1 July, 1822. Trans. to 2nd Art., 31 Dec., 1824. Resigned 31 May, 1826. Died — ——, 1857.

STRONG, NORTON. [Born in Mich. Appointed from Mich.]
Asst. Surg., 16 June, 1880. Capt. Asst. Surg., 16 June, 1885. Retired for disability with rank of Maj., 23 Aug., 1898.

STRONG, RICH'D P. [Born in N. Y. Appointed from N. Y.]
Priv. Co. H, 71st N. Y. State Militia, 20 April, 1861. Discharged 30 July, 1861. 2nd Lieut. 139th N. Y. Vols., 9 Sept., 1862. 1st Lieut. Sig. Corps, 3 March, 1863. Bvt. Capt. and Maj. Vols., 13 March, 1865, for faithful and meritorious service. Mustered out 19 April, 1866. 2nd Lieut 7th Inf., 23 Feb., 1866, and 1st Lieut., 1 May, 1866. Bvt. Capt., 2 March, 1867, for gallant and meritorious service in the capture of Fort Blakely, Ala. Unassigned 19 May, 1869. Ass'd to 25th Inf., 14 July, 1869. Trans. to 4th Art., 20 Sept., 1869. Capt., 25 Jan., 1889. Graduate of the Artillery School, 1872. Maj. Chf. Sig. Off. Vols., 20 May, 1898. Lieut. Col. Chf. Sig. Off. Vols., 18 July, 1898, to 12 May, 1899.

STRONG, RICHARD P. [Born in Va. Appointed from Md.]
Asst. Surg., 23 July, 1898.

STROTHER, JOHN. [Born in Va. Appointed from Va.]
3rd Lieut. 1st Inf., 29 March, 1813. 2nd Lieut., 20 Nov., 1813. Discharged 15 June, 1815. Reinstated 2 Dec., 1815, in 6th Inf. Dropped 4 Sept., 1816.

STROTHER, LEWIS H. [Born in Va. Appointed from Va.]
2nd Lieut. 1st Inf., 1 Sept., 1879. 1st Lieut., 23 Sept., 1885. R. Q. M., 18 Aug., 1880, to 11 March, 1882, and 11 May, 1887, to 5 Aug., 1888. Reg. Adj., 20 March, 1889, to ——. Capt., 26 April, 1898. Trans. to 22nd Inf., 23 Jan., 1899. Maj. Eng. Vols., 17 May, 1898, to 12 May, 1899. Lieut. Col. 32nd U. S. Vols., 5 July, 1899. Graduate of the Infantry and Cavalry School, 1885.

STUART, ALEX'R P.* [Born in Tenn. Appointed from Tenn.]
2nd Lieut. 3rd Art., 1 July, 1842. Resigned 31 May, 1845.

STUART, EDWIN R.* [Born in W. Va. Appointed from W. Va.]
Addl. 2nd Lieut. Eng., 12 June, 1896. 2nd Lieut., 31 July, 1897. 1st Lieut., 5 July, 1898.

STUART, GEORGE. [Born in Conn. Appointed from Conn.]
1st Lieut. 13th Inf., 14 May, 1861. Died 12 July, 1863.

STUART, GEORGE W.* [Born in Iowa. Appointed from Iowa.]
2nd Lieut. 7th Inf., 15 Feb., 1899.

STUART, JAMES.* [Born in S. C. Appointed from S. C.]
Bvt. 2nd Lieut. Mounted Rifles, 1 July, 1846. 2nd Lieut., 9 Oct., 1847. Died 18 June, 1851, of wounds received in action with Indians in Oregon. Bvt. 1st Lieut., 20 Aug., 1847, for gallant and meritorious conduct at Contreras and Churubusco. Bvt. Capt., 13 Sept., 1847, for gallant and meritorious conduct at Chapultepec.

STUART, JAMES D. [Born in Ky. Appointed from Ky.]
Asst. Surg. 16th Inf., 11 May, 1847. Resigned 6 Nov., 1847.

STUART, JAMES E. B.* [Born in Va. Appointed from Va.]
Bvt. 2nd Lieut. Mounted Rifles, 1 July, 1854. 2nd Lieut., 31 Oct., 1854. Trans. to 1st Cav., 3 March, 1855. 1st Lieut., 20 Dec., 1855. R. Q. M., 5 July, 1855, to 31 May, 1857. Capt., 22 April, 1861. Resigned 14 May, 1861. Died 12 May, 1864, of wounds received in Confederate service.

STUART, RICE L. [Born in ——. Appointed from Ky.]
Ensign 17th Inf., 17 March, 1814. 3rd Lieut., 15 July, 1814. Trans. to Corps Art., 17 May, 1815. Resigned 16 June, 1816.

STUART, SAM'L D. [Born in Ohio. Appointed from Ohio.]
1st Lieut. 2nd Ohio Vols., 6 June, 1846. Mustered out 22 June, 1847. 2nd Lieut. 15th Inf., 4 Aug., 1847. Resigned 21 Dec., 1847.

STUART, SIDNEY E.* [Born in Pa. Appointed from Mass.]
2nd Lieut. 1st Art., 12 June, 1880. 1st Lieut. Ord., 6 Aug., 1885. Capt. (fourteen years' service), 12 June, 1894. Honor graduate of the Artillery School, 1884 Killed at Dupont Powder Works, 29 April, 1899.

STUBBS, JAMES R.* [Born in Ohio. Appointed from Ohio.]
Bvt. 2nd Lieut. Light Art., 11 Dec., 1815. Resigned 15 Nov., 1817. Capt. A. Dep. Q. M. G., 30 Nov., 1819. Disbanded 1 June, 1821. Died 4 Aug., 1832.

STURGEON, JAMES G. [Born in Pa. Appointed from Pa.]
Mil. Storekeeper Ord., 27 May, 1846. Died 19 June, 1847.

STURGEON, SHELDON.* [Born in N. Y. Appointed from N. Y.]
2nd Lieut. 1st Inf., 6 May, 1861. 1st Lieut., 24 June, 1861. Capt., 25 April, 1862. Bvt. Maj. and Lieut. Col., 13 March, 1865, for gallant and meritorious service during the war. Col. 1st N. O. Vols., 25 April, 1865. Mustered out of Vol. Service, 15 Aug., 1865. Trans. to 6th Cav., 1 Jan., 1871. Retired 17 May, 1876. Died 22 July, 1892.

STURGIS, JAMES G.* [Born in N. M. Appointed at Large.]
2nd Lieut. 7th Cav., 16 June, 1875. Killed 25 June, 1876, in action with Indians at Little Big Horn River, Mont.

STURGIS, SAML. D.* [Born in Pa. Appointed at Large.]
Bvt. 2nd Lieut. 2nd Drag., 1 July, 1846. 2nd Lieut. 1st Drag., 16 Feb., 1847. R. Q. M., 1 April, 1851, to 1 March, 1852. 1st Lieut., 15 July, 1853. Capt. 1st Cav., 3 March, 1855. Maj. 1st Cav., 3 May, 1861; 4th Cav., 3 Aug., 1861. Bvt. Lieut. Col., 10 Aug., 1861, for gallant and meritorious service in the Battle of Wilson's Creek, Mo. Brig. Gen. Vols., 10 Aug., 1861. Bvt. Col., 29 Aug., 1862, for gallant and meritorious service in the Battle of Second Bull Run, Va. Lieut. Col. 6th Cav., 27 Oct., 1863. Bvt. Brig. Gen., 13 March, 1865, for gallant and meritorious service

in the Battle of South Mountain, Va. Bvt. Maj. Gen., 13 March, 1865, for gallant and meritorious service in the Battle of Fredericksburg, Va. Mustered out of Vol. Service, 24 Aug., 1865. Col. 7th Cav., 6 May, 1869. Retired by operation of law, 11 June, 1886. Died 28 Sept., 1889.

STURGIS, SAMUEL D.* [Born in Mo. Appointed from Dak.]
2nd Lieut. 1st Art., 15 June, 1884. 1st Lieut. 4th Art., 1 July, 1891. Trans to 6th Art., 8 March, 1898. Maj. A. A. G. Vols., 12 May, 1898.

SCTURGUS, ROB'T. , [Born in ——. Appointed from Ky.]
Ensign 2nd Inf., 28 Sept., 1812. 2nd Lieut., 1 Nov., 1812. 1st Lieut., 9 March, 1814. Trans. to 3rd Inf., 17 May, 1815. Resigned 10 Feb., 1818.

STURTEVANT, GIRARD.* [Born in N. Y. Appointed from N. Y.]
2nd Lieut. 25th Inf., 12 June, 1895. 1st Lieut. of Inf., 30 July, 1898. Ass'd to 23rd Inf., 1 Jan., 1899.

STYER, CHAS. [Born in Pa. Appointed from Pa.]
Asst. Surg. 45th Pa. Vols., 1 Aug., 1862. Surg. 99th Pa. Vols., 16 Jan., 1863. Dismissed 1 May, 1863. Asst. Surg., 9 Oct., 1867. Resigned 30 June, 1878.

STYER, HENRY D.* [Born in Pa. Appointed from Pa.]
2nd Lieut. 21st Inf., 15 June, 1884. 1st Lieut. 22nd Inf., 19 May, 1891. Trans. to 13th Inf., 20 July, 1891. Capt. of Inf., 4 Oct., 1898. Ass'd to 13th Inf., 1 Jan., 1899. R. Q. M., 2 Aug., 1899.

STYLES, JOSIAH S. [Born in New Brunswick. Appointed from Wis.]
Sergt. Co. D, and Sergt. Maj. 32nd Wis. Vols., 25 Sept., 1862, to 15 Jan., 1864. 2nd Lieut. 32nd Wis. Vols., 15 Jan., 1864. 1st Lieut. and Adj., 14 Sept., 1864. Mustered out 12 June, 1865. 2nd Lieut. 19th Inf., 23 Feb., 1866. Trans. to 28th Inf., 21 Sept., 1866. 1st Lieut., 1 Nov., 1866. R. Q. M., 1 Jan., 1867, to 31 May, 1869. Unassigned 31 March, 1869. Mustered out 1 Jan., 1871.

SUCKLEY, GEORGE. [Born in N. Y. Appointed from N. Y.]
Asst. Surg., 2 Dec., 1853. Resigned 3 Oct., 1856. Surg. U. S. Vols., 3 Aug., 1861. Bvt. Lieut. Col. and Col. Vols., 15 Aug., 1865, for faithful and meritorious service. Resigned 22 April, 1865. Died 30 July, 1869.

SUDLER, THOS. E* [Born in Md. Appointed from Md.]
3rd Lieut. Ord., 1 July, 1820. Trans. to 3rd Art., 1 June, 1821, with rank of 2nd Lieut. from 1 July, 1820. Trans. to 1st Art., 16 Aug., 1821. Resigned 16 Nov., 1821. Died 31 Dec., 1860.

SUGGETT, GEORGE W. [Born in Ky. Appointed from Ky.]
2nd Lieut. 1st Drag., 25 Jan., 1837. Died 8 Aug., 1837.

SULLIVAN, GEORGE R.* [Born in Mass. Appointed from Mass.]
(Changed name to George R. J. Bowdoin—which see.)

SULLIVAN, JAMES B. [Born in Va. Appointed from Va.]
Asst. Surg., 5 May, 1829. Resigned 31 Dec., 1835.

SULLIVAN, JOHN [Born in Ireland. Appointed from Army.]
Priv. Co. G, 14th N. H. Vols., 8 Dec., 1863, to 8 July, 1865. Priv. Co. H, 4th Art., 9 March, 1866, to 27 March, 1867. 2nd Lieut. 37th Inf., 22 Jan., 1867. Trans. to 3rd Inf., 11 Aug., 1869. Mustered out 1 Jan., 1871. Died 4 Sept., 1882.

SULLIVAN, THOMAS C.* [Born in Ohio. Appointed from Ohio.]
2nd Lieut. 1st Art., 1 July, 1856. 1st Lieut., 27 April, 1861. Capt. 18th Inf., 14 May, 1861, declined. Capt., C. S., 3 Aug., 1861. Lieut. Col. C. S. 20 Aug., 1862, to 27 Jan., 1863. Bvt. Maj. and Lieut. Col., 13 March, 1865, for faithful and meritorious service during the war. Lieut. Col. C. S., 21 March, 1865, to 1 Aug., 1865. Maj. C. S., 14 April, 1875. Lieut. Col. A. C. G. S., 14 July, 1890. Col. A. C. G. S., 27 Dec., 1892. Brig. Gen. C. G. S., 18 Jan., 1897. Retired by operation of law., 14 Nov., 1897.

SULLIVAN, THOS. W. [Born in Ireland. Appointed from Army.]
Priv., Corpl. and Sergt. Troop C, 1st Cav., 10 March, 1857, to 1 Sept., 1861. 1st Lieut. 3rd Ill., Cav., 1 Oct., 1861, to 2 May, 1862. 2nd Lieut. 4th Cav., 24 March, 1862. Reg. Adj., 13 Aug., 1863, to 6 Feb., 1865. 1st Lieut., 5 Nov., 1863. Retired 6 Feb., 1865. Dismissed 19 June, 1865. Died 7 Oct., 1871.

SULLIVAN, WADE. [Born in Va. Appointed from Va.]
Asst. Surg., 21 Nov., 1836. Died 15 May, 1838.

SULLY, ALFRED.* [Born in Pa. Appointed from Pa.]
2nd Lieut. 2nd Inf., 1 July, 1841. 1st Lieut., 11 March, 1847. R. Q. M., 9 Oct., 1848, to 23 Feb., 1852. Capt., 23 Feb., 1852. Col. 1st Minn. Vols., 4 March, 1862. Maj. 8th Inf., 15 March, 1862. Bvt. Lieut. Col., 1 June, 1862, for gallant and meritorious service in the Battle of Fair Oaks, Va. Bvt. Col., 1 July, 1862, for gallant and meritorious service in the Battle of Malvern Hill, Va. Brig. Gen. Vols., 26 Sept., 1862. Bvt. Maj. Gen. Vols., 8 March, 1865. Bvt. Brig. Gen., 13 March, 1865, for gallant and meritorious service in the campaign against the Indians in the Northwest, and in the Battle of White Stone Hill, Dak. Mustered out of Vol. Service, 30 April, 1866. Lieut. Col., 3rd Inf., 28 July, 1866. Unassigned 15 March, 1869. Ass'd to 19th Inf., 15 Dec., 1870. Col. 21st Inf., 10 Dec., 1873. Died 27 April, 1879.

SUMMERALL, CHARLES P.* [Born in Fla. Appointed from Fla.]
2nd Lieut. 1st Inf., 11 June., 1892. Trans. to 5th Art., 6 March, 1893. 1st Lieut., 2 March, 1899.

SUMMERHAYES, JOHN W. [Born in N. Y. Appointed from N. Y.]
Priv. Co. I, 20th Mass. Vols., 9 Sept., 1861. Corpl., 1 Nov., 1861. Sergt., — ——, . Sergt. Maj. 20th Mass. Vols., 1 Jan., 1863. 2nd Lieut 20th Mass. Vols., 14 March, 1863. 1st Lieut., 8 Sept., 1863. Capt., 10 Oct., 1863. Bvt. Maj. Vols., 9 April, 1865, for meritorious service in the campaign terminating with the surrender of the insurgent army under Gen. R. E. Lee. Mustered out 6 June, 1865. 2nd Lieut. 33rd Inf., 22 Jan., 1867. Bvt. 1st Lieut., 2 March, 1867, for gallant and meritorious service in the Battle of Ball's Bluff, Va. Bvt. Capt., 2 March, 1867, for gallant and meritorious service in the Battle of Cold Harbor, Va. Trans. to 8th Inf., 3 May, 1869. 1st Lieut., 15 Dec., 1874. Reg. Adj., 1 Jan. to 19 May, 1886. R. Q. M., 20 May, 1886, to 9 March, 1889. Capt. A. Q. M., 25 Feb., 1889. Maj. Q. M., 11 Nov., 1898. Maj. Chf. Q. M. Vols., 12 May, 1898, to 2 Dec., 1898.

SUMMERLIN, GEORGE T.* [Born in La. Appointed from La.]
Addl. 2nd Lieut. 6th Cav., 12 June, 1896. 2nd Lieut. 8th Cav., 5 Jan., 1897. Capt. 32nd U. S. Vols., 5 July, 1899.

SUMMERS, JOHN E. [Born in Va. Appointed from Va.]
1st Lieut. Asst. Surg., 13 Dec., 1847. Capt. Asst. Surg., 13 Dec., 1852. Maj. Surg., 21 May, 1861. Lieut. Col. Med. Inspector, 27 Feb., 1863. Bvt. Lieut. Col. 13 March, 1865, for faithful and meritorious service during the war, declined. Mustered out as Lieut. Col. Med. Inspector, 31 Oct., 1865. Lieut. Col. Surg., 17 March, 1880. Col. Surg., 9 Jan., 1885. Retired by operation of law, 24 Jan., 1886.

SUMMERS, RICHARD. [Born in Prussia. Appointed from Army.]
Priv. and Sergt. Co. F, 11th N. Y. Cav., 25 April, 1862, to 24 April, 1865. Priv., Sergt. and 1st Sergt. Co. I, Q. M. Sergt. and Sergt. Maj. 27th Inf., 5 Sept., 1866, to 19 Aug., 1868. 2nd Lieut. 27th Inf., 2 March, 1868. Trans .to 9th Inf., 14 June, 1869. Died 18 Oct., 1870.

SUMNER, EDWIN V. [Born in Mass. Appointed from N. Y.]
2nd Lieut. 2nd Inf., 3 March, 1819. 1st Lieut., 25 Jan., 1823. Capt. 1st Drag., 4 March, 1833. Maj 2nd Drag., 30 June, 1846. Lieut. Col. 1st Drag., 13 July, 1848. Col. 1st Cav., 3 March, 1855. Brig. Gen., 16 March, 1861. Maj. Gen. Vols., 4 July, 1862. Died 21 March, 1863. Bvt. Lieut. Col., 18 April, 1847, for gallant and meritorious conduct at Cerro Gordo. Bvt. Col.,8 Sept.,1847, for gallant and meritorious conduct at Molino del Rey. Bvt. Maj. Gen., 31 March, 1862, for gallant and meritorious conduct in the Battle of Fair Oaks, Va. Died 21 March, 1863.

SUMNER, EDWIN V. [Born in Pa. Appointed from N. Y.]
2nd Lieut. 1st Cav., 5 Aug., 1861. 1st Lieut 12 Nov., 1861. Maj. A. A. de C. Vols., 19 May, 1863. Discharged from Vol. Service, 15 Aug., 1863. Capt. 1st Cav., 23 Sept., 1863. Bvt. Maj., 6 May, 1864, for gallant and meritorious service in the Battle of Todd's Tavern, Va. Col. 1st N. Y. Mounted Rifles, 8 Sept., 1864. Bvt. Lieut. Col., 13 March, 1865, for gallant and meritorious service during the war. Bvt. Brig. Gen. Vols., 28 March, 1865, for gallant and meritorious service in the field. Mustered out of Vol. Service, 29 Nov., 1865. Maj. 5th Cav., 4 March, 1879. Lieut. Col. 8th Cav., 15 April, 1890. Col. 7th Cav., 10 Nov., 1894. Brig. Gen., 27 March, 1899. Brig. Gen. Vols., 27 May, 1898, to 24 Feb., 1899. Retired for over thirty years' service, 30 March, 1899.

SUMNER, SAMUEL S. [Born in Pa. Appointed from N. Y.]
2nd Lieut. 2nd Cav., 11 June, 1861; 5th Cav., 3 Aug., 1861. Bvt. 1st Lieut., 1 June, 1862, for gallant and meritorious service in the Battle of Fair Oaks, Va. 1st Lieut. 5th Cav., 17 July, 1862. Capt. A. de C. Vols., 20 Aug., 1862. Bvt. Capt., 17 Sept., 1862, for gallant and meritorious service in the Battle of Antietam, Md. Discharged from Vol. Service, 15 Aug., 1863. Capt. 5th Cav., 30 March, 1864. Bvt. Maj., 13 March, 1865, for gallant and meritorious conduct during the campaign against Vicksburg, Miss. Maj. 8th Cav., 2 April, 1879. Lieut. Col. 6th Cav., 18 Feb.,, 1891. Col. 23 May, 1896. Brig. Gen. Vols., 4 May, 1898. Maj. Gen. Vols., 7 Sept., 1898, to 15 April, 1899. Bvt. Lieut. Col., 27 Feb., 1890, for gallant services in action against Indians at Summit Springs, Colo., 11 July, 1869.

SUMTER, WM.* [Born in S. C. Appointed from S. C.]
2nd Lieut. Light Art., 3 Jan., 1812. 1st Lieut., 27 May, 1813. Disbanded 15 June, 1815. Reinstated 17 May, 1816, in 1st Inf. Capt., 31 May, 1817. Resigned 1 July, 1818. Died in 1826.

SUNDERLAND, JAMES W. [Born in N. Y. Appointed from Pa.]
Priv. Co. K, 19th Pa. Vols., 27 April to 9 Aug., 1861. 1st Sergt. Co. H, 72nd Pa. Vols., 10 Aug., 1861. Sergt. Maj., 1 May, 1862. 2nd Lieut., 8 July, 1862. 1st Lieut., 1 Jan., 1863. 1st Lieut. Vet. Res. Corps, 11 Sept., 1863. Capt., 26 May, 1865. Mustered out 30 Dec., 1867. 2nd Lieut. 24th Inf., 5 Oct., 1867. Trans. to 11th Inf., 25 April, 1869. Dropped 7 Nov., 1870.

SUPLEE, EDWIN M.* [Born in Pa. Appointed from Iowa.]
Addl. 2nd Lieut. 2nd Cav., 11 June, 1888. 2nd Lieut., 24 July, 1888. 1st Lieut. 3rd Cav., 15 March, 1896. Graduate of the Infantry and Cavalry School, 1891.

SUTER, ALEXANDER F. [Born in D. C. Appointed from D. C.]
Asst. Surg., 27 March, 1835. Died 17 Dec., 1847.

SUTER, CHAS. R.* [Born in N. Y. Appointed at Large.]
2nd Lieut. Eng., 17 June, 1862. 1st Lieut., 3 March, 1863. Bvt. Capt., 18 July, 1863, for gallant and meritorious service during the siege of Morris Island, S. C. Capt. Eng., 17 June, 1864. Bvt. Maj., 13 March, 1865, for faithful and meritorious service during the war. Maj. Eng., 10 Oct., 1871. Lieut. Col., 10 Jan., 1887. Col., 12 Oct., 1895.

SUTER, WM. N. [Born in Va. Appointed from Va.]
Asst. Surg., 16 May, 1887.

SUTHERLAND, CHAS. [Born in Pa. Appointed from Pa.]
1st Lieut. Asst. Surg., 5 Aug., 1852. Capt. Asst. Surg., 5 Aug., 1857. Maj. Surg., 16 April, 1862. Bvt. Lieut. Col., 13 March, 1865, for faithful and meritorious service during the war. Bvt. Col., 13 March, 1865, for meritorious service and diligent discharge of duties during the war. Lieut. Col. Asst. Med. Purveyor, 28 July, 1866. Col. Surg., 26 June, 1876. Brig. Gen. Surg. Gen., 23 Dec., 1890. Retired by operation of law, 29 May, 1893. Died 10 May, 1895.

SUTHERLAND, JOSEPH H. [Born in Pa. Appointed from W. Va.]
Post Chap., 4 April, 1898.

SUTHERLAND, ROB'T. [Born in N. Y. Appointed from N. Y.]
1st Lieut. 18th Inf., 5 Aug., 1861. Resigned 31 Jan., 1864.

SUTHERLAND, WM. A. [Born in Ohio. Appointed from Ohio.]
Priv. Co. C. 2nd Ohio Vols., 17 April to 31 July, 1861. 2nd Lieut. 19th Ohio Vols., 1 Jan., 1862. 1st Lieut., 10 Dec., 1862, to 9 May, 1864. Capt. A. A. G. Vols., 18 March, 1864. Maj. A. A. G. Vols., 19 Aug., 1865. Mustered out 8 Dec., 1865. 2nd Lieut. and 1st Lieut. 17th Inf., 23 Feb., 1866. Resigned 1 Sept., 1867.

SUTORIUS, ALEXANDER. [Born in Switzerland. Appointed from Army.]
Priv. Band, Chief Bugler, Q. M. Sergt. and Sergt. Maj. Mounted Rifles (3d Cav.),

15 Sept., 1854, to 30 April, 1863. 2nd Lieut. 3rd Cav., 22 April, 1863. Reg. Adj., 1 Oct., 1863, to 29 May, 1867. Reg. Com., 29 May to 3 Oct., 1867. R. Q. M., 3 Oct., 1867, to 1 Dec., 1868. 1st Lieut., 9 Oct., 1865. Capt., 6 May, 1869. Dismissed 25 Sept., 1876. Bvt. 1st Lieut., 15 Nov., 1863, for gallant and meritorious service in action near Tuscumbia, Ala.

SUTTON, ALBERT G. [Born in N. J. Appointed from Ohio.]
1st Lieut. Inf., 8 March, 1847; 15th Inf., 9 April, 1847. Capt., 23 May, 1848. Disbanded 3 Aug., 1848. Bvt. Capt., 13 Sept., 1847, for gallant and meritorious conduct at Chapultepec, Mex.

SUTTON, ANTHONY S. [Born in N. Y. Appointed from Army.]
Priv. Co. B, Mounted Rifles and Sergt. Co. C, 15th Inf., 13 Jan., 1846, to 28 June, 1848. Bvt. 2nd Lieut. 7th Inf., 28 June, 1848. 2nd Lieut., 17 Sept., 1849. Resigned 8 March, 1851. 2nd Lieut. 8th Ohio Vols., 24 June, 1861. Resigned 22 Feb., 1862.

SWAIM, DAVID G. [Born in Ohio. Appointed from Ohio.]
2nd Lieut. 65th Ohio Vols., 4 Oct., 1861. 1st Lieut., 4 Nov., 1861. Mustered out 17 June, 1862. Capt. A. A. G. Vols., 16 May, 1862. Maj. A. A. G. Vols., 7 Feb., 1865. Bvt. Lieut. Col. and Col. Vols., 13 March, 1865, for faithful and meritorious service during the war. 2nd Lieut. 34th Inf., 28 July, 1866. Mustered out as Maj. A. A. G. Vols., 15 Sept., 1866. Bvt. 1st Lieut., Capt. and Maj., 2 March, 1867, for gallant and meritorious service during the war. Unass'd 14 April, 1869. Maj. J. A., 9 Dec., 1869. Brig. Gen. J. A. G., 18 Feb., 1881. Retired by direction of the President, being over sixty-two years of age, 22 Dec., 1894. Died 17 Aug., 1897.

SWAIN, HUGH.* [Born in Texas. Appointed from Texas.]
2nd Lieut. 23rd Inf., 12 June, 1890. Resigned 1 Dec., 1893.

SWAIN, JAMES B. [Born in N. Y. Appointed from N. Y.]
2nd Lieut. 1st Cav., 1 Nov., 1861. 1st Lieut., 24 Feb., 1862. Col. 11th N. Y. Cav., 30 April, 1862. Discharged 12 Feb., 1864, from Vol. and Reg. Service.

SWAINE, PETER T.* [Born in N. Y. Appointed from N. Y.]
Bvt. 2nd Lieut. 1st Inf., 1 July, 1852. 2nd Lieut., 31 Dec., 1852. 2nd Lieut. 10th Inf., 3 March, 1855. 1st Lieut., 8 Aug., 1855. R. Q. M., 7 Dec., 1855, to 30 April, 1860. Capt. 15th Inf., 14 May, 1861. Bvt. Maj., 7 April, 1862, for gallant and meritorious service in the Battle of Shiloh, Tenn. Col. 99th Ohio Vols., 4 Sept., 1862. Bvt. Lieut. Col., 31 Dec., 1862, for gallant and meritorious service in the Battle of Murfreesboro, Tenn. Mustered out of Vol. Service 31 Dec., 1864. Bvt. Col., 13 March, 1865, for faithful and meritorious service during the war. Maj. 16th Inf., 29 Dec., 1865. Trans. to 25th Inf., 21 Sept., 1866. Trans. to 2nd Inf., 15 March, 1869. Lieut. Col., 15th Inf., 24 Oct., 1874. Col. 22nd Inf., 18 April, 1884. Retired by operation of law, 21 Jan., 1895.

SWAINE, WM. M.* [Born in Utah. Appointed from N. Mex.]
2nd Lieut. 22nd Inf., 1 July, 1886. 1st Lieut., 3rd Inf., 29 Nov., 1892. Trans. to 22nd Inf., 27 Dec., 1892. Capt. 22nd Inf., 2 March, 1899. Trans. to 1st Inf., 5 May, 1899.

SWAN, ROB'T. [Born in Md. Appointed from Md.]
2nd Lieut. Inf., 23 Feb., 1847; Voltigeurs, 9 April, 1847. Disbanded 31 Aug., 1848.

SWAN, WM. W. [Born in Mass. Appointed from Mass.]
1st Lieut. 17th Inf., 14 May, 1861. Capt., 20 April, 1864. Trans. to 35th Inf., 21 Sept., 1866. Resigned 1 Nov., 1866. Bvt. Maj., 1 Aug., 1864, for gallant services at the Battle of the Wilderness, and during the campaign before Richmond, Va. Bvt Lieut. Col., 1 April, 1865, for gallant and meritorious service at Five Forks, Va.

SWARTWOUT, HENRY.* [Born in N. Y. Appointed from N. Y.]
Bvt. 2nd Lieut., 3rd Inf., 1 July, 1832. 2nd Lieut., 31 March, 1834. 1st Lieut., 7 July, 1838. Capt., 31 Jan., 1842. Trans. to 2nd Art., 15 May, 1844. Died 1 July, 1852.

SWARTWOUT, HENRY A. [Born in La. Appointed from N. Y.]
Capt. 5th N. Y. Vols., 9 May to 29 July, 1861. 1st Lieut. 17th Inf., 14 May, 1861. Reg. Adj., 4 Nov., 1862, to 1 Sept., 1863. Capt., 26 May, 1864. Died 8 Oct., 1867. Bvt. Maj., 1 Aug., 1864, for gallant service at the Battles of Spottsylvania and North Anna, and during the campaign before Richmond, Va.

SWARTWOUT, ROB'T. [Born in N. Y. Appointed from N. Y.]
Col. N. Y. Militia, in 1812-13. Brig. Gen. Q. M. G., 21 March, 1813. Disbanded 5 June, 1816. Died 9 July, 1848.

SWAYNE, WAGER. [Born in Ohio. Appointed from Ohio.]
Maj. 43rd Ohio Vols., 31 Aug., 1861. Lieut. Col., 14 Dec., 1861. Col., 18 Oct., 1862. Brig. Gen. Vols., 8 March, 1865 Maj. Gen. Vols., 20 June, 1865. Col. 45th Inf., 28 July, 1866. Bvt. Brig. Gen., 2 March, 1867, for gallant and meritorious service in the action of Rivers Bridge, S. C. Bvt. Maj. Gen., 2 March, 1867, for gallant and meritorious service during the war. Mustered out of Vol. Service, 1 Sept., 1867. Unass'd, 15 March, 1869. Retired 1 July, 1870, for loss of right leg from wound. Medal of Honor for conspicuous gallantry in leading his regiment in a charge on the enemy in the Battle of Corinth, Miss., 4 Oct., 1862; while serving as Lieut. Col. 43rd Ohio Vol. Inf., commanding regiment.

SWEARINGEN, JOSEPH V.* [Born in Md. Appointed from Md.]
Bvt. 2d Lieut. 1st Inf., 1 July, 1824. 2nd Lieut. 6th Inf., 1 July, 1824. 1st Lieut., 12 May, 1829. Capt., 31 July, 1827. Killed 25 Dec., 1837, in battle with Indians at Okeechobee, Fla.

SWEATMAN, ROB'T. [Born in England. Appointed from Army.]
Priv., Corpl., Sergt. and 1st Sergt. Co. E, 2nd (5th) Cav., 7 June, 1858, to 12 Sept., 1862. 2nd Lieut. 5th Cav., 17 July, 1862. 1st Lieut., 25 Sept., 1863. Capt., 4 Nov., 1867. Cashiered 3 Jan., 1870. Bvt. 1st Lieut., 3 July, 1863, for gallant and meritorious service in the Gettysburg campaign. Bvt. Capt., 10 May, 1864, for gallant and meritorious service in action at Beaver Dam, Va.

SWEENEY, HENRY. [Born in Ireland. Appointed from Ark.]
Priv. Co. H, 2nd Drag., 11 Sept., 1854. Bugler, — June, 1855. Priv., 8 Sept., 1857.

Corpl., 1 Feb., 1859. Hosp. Steward, 20 Jan., 1859. Discharged 15 July, 1859. Hosp. Steward, 15 July, 1859. Discharged 8 Oct., 1863. Capt. 60th U. S. Col. Troops, 15 Oct., 1863. Bvt. Maj. Vols., 13 March, 1865, for long and faithful service. 2nd Lieut. 15th Inf., 18 June, 1867. Mustered out of Vol. Service, 11 Aug., 1867. 1st Lieut. 15th Inf., 27 July, 1868. Unass'd, 12 Aug., 1869. Ass'd to 4th Cav., 31 Dec., 1870. Capt., 2 April, 1879. Retired for disability 24 April, 1886.

SWEENEY, WALTER C. [Born in W. Va. Appointed from W. Va.]
Priv. and Corpl. 1st W. Va. Vols., 7 May, 1898, to 4 Jan., 1899. 2nd Lieut., 5 Jan. to 4 Feb., 1899. 2nd Lieut. 24th Inf., 1 June, 1899.

SWEENEY, THOS. W. [Born in Ireland. Appointed from N. Y.]
2nd Lieut. Co. A, 2nd N. Y. Vols., 23 Nov., 1846. 2nd Lieut. 2nd Inf., 3 March, 1848. 1st Lieut., 11 June, 1851. Capt., 19 Jan., 1861. Brig. Gen. Mo. Vols., 20 May, 1861. Mustered out 14 Aug., 1861. Col. 52nd Ill. Vols., 21 Jan., 1862. Brig. Gen. Vols., 29 Nov., 1862. Maj. 16th Inf., 20 Oct., 1863. Mustered out of Vol. Service, 24 Aug., 1865. Dismissed 29 Dec., 1865. Reinstated 8 Nov., 1866. Unass'd 15 March, 1869. Retired with rank of Brig. Gen., 11 May, 1870. Died 10 April, 1892.

SWEET, JOHN E. [Born in N. Y. Appointed from Ind.]
2nd Lieut. 20th Ind. Vols., 22 July, 1861. 1st Lieut., 1 July, 1862. Mustered out 8 Oct., 1864. Lieut. Col. 151st Ind. Vols., 4 March, 1865. Mustered out 19 Sept., 1865. 2nd Lieut. 12th Inf., 11 May, 1866. Trans. to 30th Inf., 21 Sept., 1866. Resigned 25 Jan., 1867. Died 13 Feb., 1875.

SWEET, JOHN J.* [Born in Ill. Appointed from Ill.]
Bvt. 2nd Lieut. 2nd Cav., 1 July, 1860. 2nd Lieut., 31 Jan., 1861. 1st Lieut., 16 April, 1861; 5th Cav., 3 Aug., 1861. Killed 27 June, 1862, at the Battle of Gaines' Mills, Va.

SWEET, JOSHUA. [Born in N. Y. Appointed from Miss.]
Chaplain post of Fort Ridgeley, Minn., 2 Nov., 1854, to 7 May, 1867. Post Chap., 3 April, 1867. Resigned 30 June, 1867.

SWEET, OWEN J. [Born in Conn. Appointed from N. Y.]
2nd Lieut. 137th N. Y. Vols., 6 Sept., 1862. 1st Lieut., 19 March, 1863. Capt., 12 March, 1864. Mustered out 9 June, 1865. 2nd Lieut. 40th Inf., 27 May, 1867. Trans. to 25th Inf., 20 Sept., 1869. 1st Lieut., 19 Aug., 1873. Capt., 19 Oct., 1886. Maj. 23rd Inf., 2 March, 1899.

SWEET, WM. [Born in Vt. Appointed from Vt.]
2nd Lieut. 1st Inf., 5 Aug., 1861. Capt. 17th Inf., 26 Oct., 1861. Died 11 Oct., 1864.

SWEET, WM. E. [Born in Ohio. Appointed from D. C.]
Priv. Co. B, 23rd Ohio Vols., 2 June, 1861. Sergt. Maj., 1 Oct., 1862. 2nd Lieut., 2 July, 1864. 1st Lieut., 15 July, 1864. Capt., 9 Oct., 1864. Bvt. Maj. Vols., 13 March, 1865, for gallant and meritorious service in the Battle of Winchester, Va. Resigned 13 March, 1865. 1st Lieut. 38th Inf., 22 Jan., 1867. Trans. to 24th Inf., 11 Nov., 1869. Discharged 25 Oct., 1870. Bvt. Capt., 2 March, 1867, for gallant and meritorious service in the Battle of Berryville, Va. Bvt. Maj., 2 March, 1867, for gallant and meritorious service in the Battle of Winchester, Va.

SWEEZEY, CLAUDE B.* [Born in Ind. Appointed from Kan.]
2nd Lieut. 8th Cav., 11 June, 1892. 1st Lieut., 14 Dec., 1898.

SWEITZER, NELSON B.* [Born in Pa. Appointed from Pa.]
Bvt. 2nd Lieut. 2nd Drag., 1 July, 1853. 2nd Lieut. 1st Drag., 25 July, 1854. 2nd Lieut. 2nd Cav., 3 March, 1855, declined. 1st Lieut. 1st Drag., 4 Sept., 1855. Capt., 7 May, 1861. 1st Cav., 3 Aug., 1861. Capt. 16th Inf., 14 May, 1861, declined. Lieut. Col. A. A. de C., 28 Sept., 1861. Bvt. Maj., 1 July, 1862, for gallant and meritorious service during the Peninsular Campaign in Va. Relieved as Lieut. Col. A. A. de C., 31 March, 1863. Bvt. Lieut., Col., 19 March, 1864, for gallant and meritorious service in the Battle of Winchester, Va. Col. 16th N. Y. Cav., 12 Nov., 1864. Bvt. Col., 13 March, 1865, for distinguished gallantry in the Battles of Yellow Tavern and Meadow Bridge, Va. Bvt. Brig. Gen., 13 March, 1865, for gallant and meritorious service during the war. Bvt. Brig. Gen. Vols., 13 March, 1865, for meritorious and distinguished service. Col. 3rd N. Y. Prov. Cav., 23 June, 1865. Mustered out of Vol. Service, 21 Sept., 1865. Maj. 2nd Cav., 28 July, 1866. Lieut. Col. 8th Cav., 25 June, 1877. Col. 2nd Cav., 9 Jan., 1886. Retired for over thirty years' service 29 Oct., 1888. Died 7 March 1898.

SWETT, MOSES. [Born in N. H. Appointed from N. H.]
2nd Lieut. 16th Inf., 8 Jan., 1799. Discharged 15 June, 1800. 1st Lieut. 2nd Art. and Eng., 16 Feb., 1801. Trans. to Art., 1 April, 1802. Capt., 30 June, 1807. 1st Art., — March, 1812. Trans. to Corps Art., 12 May, 1814. Disbanded 15 June, 1815. Reinstated in Corps Art., 2 Dec., 1815. Died 14 Sept., 1819. Bvt. Maj., 30 June, 1817, for ten years' faithful service in one grade.

SWETT, NATH'L F. [Born in Maine. Appointed from Maine.]
2nd Lieut. of Inf., 23 Feb., 1847; 9th Inf., 9 April, 1847. Resigned 4 Dec., 1847. 2nd Lieut. 9th Inf., 17 Dec., 1847. Disbanded 19 Aug., 1848. 1st Lieut. 13th Inf., 14 May, 1861. Died 25 April, 1862.

SWIFT, ALEX'R J.* [Born in N. C. Appointed from N. C.]
Bvt. 2nd Lieut. Eng., 1 July, 1830. 1st Lieut., 31 Oct., 1836. Capt., 7 July, 1838. Died 24 April, 1847.

SWIFT, EBENEZER. [Born in Mass. Appointed from Ohio.]
1st Lieut. Asst. Surg., 30 Aug., 1847. Capt. Asst. Surg., 30 Aug., 1852. Maj. Surg 21 May, 1861. Lieut. Col. Med. Director (Act 25 Feb., 1865), 25 Feb., 1865. Bv Lieut. Col. and Col., 13 March, 1865, for faithful and meritorious service during th war. Col. Med. Director (Act 25 Feb., 1865), ——, to 30 June, 1865. Bvt. Brig. Gen., 20 July, 1867, for meritorious service voluntarily rendered during the prevalence of cholera at Fort Harker, Kan. Lieut. Col. Asst. Med. Purveyor, 31 Dec., 1876. Retired 8 Oct., 1883. Died 24 Dec., 1885.

SWIFT, EBEN.* [Born in Texas. Appointed at Large.]
2nd Lieut. 14th Inf., 15 June, 1876. Trans. to 5th Cav., 28 July, 1876. Reg. Adj., 4 June, 1878, to 9 March, 1887. 1st Lieut., 13 Oct., 1884. Capt., 11 Dec., 1893. Maj.

7th Ill. Vols., 18 May, 1898. Lieut. Col., 9th Ill. Vols., 7 July, 1898. Col. 4th Ill. Vols., 18 Nov., 1898, to 2nd May, 1899. Maj. Porto Rican Batt., 1 Dec., 1899, to ——.

SWIFT, EUGENE L. [Born in Pa. Appointed from N. Y.]
Asst. Surg., 12 Aug., 1887. Capt. Asst. Surg., 12 Aug., 1892. Maj. Brig. Surg. Vols., 4 June, 1898, to 10 Feb., 1899. Maj. Surg. 35th U. S. Vols., 11 Nov., 1899, to ——.

SWIFT, FOSTER. [Born in Mass. Appointed from Mass.]
Garrison Surg.'s Mate, 18 Feb., 1814. Post Surg., 24 April, 1816. Asst. Surg., 1 June, 1821. Died 18 Aug., 1835.

SWIFT, HENRY. [Born in Pa. Appointed from Dak.]
Post Chap., 21 Jan., 1887.

SWIFT, JAMES A. [Born in Md. Appointed from Army.]
Sergt. Sig. Corps, 30 Oct., 1878. Discharged 31 Oct., 1878. 2nd Lieut. Sig. Corps, 1 Nov., 1878. 2nd Lieut. of Cav. (7th), 4 Feb., 1891, to rank from 1 Nov., 1878. 1st Lieut. of Cav. (1st), 7 Feb., 1891. Trans. to 9th Cav., 27 April, 1891. Died 9 Jan., 1896.

SWIFT, JOSEPH G.* [Born in Mass. Appointed from Mass.]
2nd Lieut. Eng., 12 Oct., 1802. 1st Lieut., 11 June, 1805. Capt., 30 Oct., 1806. Maj. 23 Feb., 1808. Lieut. Col., 6 July, 1812. Col. Chf. Eng., 31 July, 1812. Resigned 12 Nov., 1818. Bvt. Brig. Gen., 19 Feb., 1814, for meritorious service. Died 23 July, 1865.

SWIFT, JOSEPH G.* [Born in N. Y. Appointed at Large.]
2nd Lieut. 5th Art., 18 June, 1866. 1st Lieut., 1 Oct., 1867. Died 2 March, 1871.

SWIFT, WM. H. [Born in Mass. Appointed from Mass.]
2nd Lieut. Corps Art., 1 July, 1819. Trans. to 1st Art., 1 June, 1821. 1st Lieut., 5 Aug., 1824. Bvt. Capt. Asst. Top. Eng., 1 Aug., 1832. Capt. Top. Eng., 7 July, 1838. Resigned 31 July, 1849. Died 7 April, 1879.

SWIGERT, SAML. M.* [Born in Ky. Appointed from Ky.]
2nd Lieut. 2nd Cav., 15 June, 1868. 1st Lieut., 26 Oct., 1869. Capt., 20 Oct., 1881. Maj. 3rd Cav., 30 June, 1898.

SWITZER, JOHN S.* [Born in Pa. Appointed from Pa.]
2nd Lieut. 4th Inf., 12 June, 1891. 1st Lieut., 26 April, 1898. Graduate of the Infantry and Cavalry School, 1895.

SWORDS, THOS.* [Born in N. Y. Appointed from N. Y.]
Bvt. 2nd Lieut. 4th Inf., 1 July, 1829. 2nd Lieut., 1 July, 1829. 1st Lieut. 1st Drag., 4 March, 1833. Capt., 3 March, 1837. Capt. A. Q. M., 7 July, 1838. Maj. Q. M., 21 April, 1846. Bvt. Lieut. Col., 30 May, 1848, for meritorious conduct while serving in the enemy's country. Lieut. Col. Dep. Q. M. G., 1 Aug., 1856. Col. A. Q. M. G., 3 Aug., 1861. Bvt. Brig. Gen. and Maj. Gen., 13 March, 1865, for faithful and efficient service in the Q. M. Dept. during the war. Retired 22 Feb., 1869. Died 20 March, 1886.

SYBERG, ARNOLD. [Born in Germany. Appointed from Pa.]
Capt. of Inf., 16 Feb., 1847; 11th Inf., 9 April, 1847. Disbanded 15 Aug., 1848.

SYDENHAM, ALVIN H.* [Born in Iowa. Appointed from Neb.]
2nd Lieut. 8th Cav., 12 June, 1889. Trans. to 5th Art., 13 May, 1891, to rank from 12 June, 1890. Died 10 Sept., 1893.

SYKES, GEORGE.* [Born in Md. Appointed from Md.]
Bvt. 2nd Lieut. 3rd Inf., 1 July, 1842. 2nd Lieut., 31 Dec., 1843. 1st Lieut., 21 Sept., 1846. Bvt. Capt., 18 April, 1847, for gallant and merieorious conduct in the Battle of Cerro Gordo, Mexico. Capt. 3rd Inf., 30 Sept., 1855. Maj. 14th Inf., 14 May, 1861. Brig. Gen. Vols., 28 Sept., 1861. Bvt. Col., 27 June, 1862, for gallant and meritorious service in the Battle of Gaines' Mill, Va. Maj. Gen. Vols., 29 Nov., 1862. Lieut. Col. 5th Inf., 16 Oct., 1863. Bvt. Brig. Gen., 13 March, 1865, for gallant and meritorious service in the Battle of Gettysburg, Pa. Bvt. Maj. Gen., 13 March, 1865, for gallant and meritorious service in the field during the war. Mustered out of Vol. Service, 15 Jan., 1866. Col. 20th Inf., 12 Jan., 1868. Died 8 Feb., 1880.

SYLVESTER, JOSEPH H. [Born in Maine. Appointed from Maine.]
Sergt. Co. B, 2nd Maine Vols., 28 May, 1861, to 9 June, 1863. 2nd Lieut. Vet. Res. Corps, 3 Feb., 1864. 1st Lieut., 30 Jan., 1865. Mustered out 20 Nov., 1865. 1st Lieut. 44th Inf., 28 July, 1866. Unassigned 27 May, 1869. Discharged 31 Dec., 1870.

SYMINGTON, JOHN.* [Born in Md. Appointed from Md.]
3rd Lieut. Ord., 2 March, 1815. 2nd Lieut., 8 April, 1818. 1st Lieut., 17 May, 1820. Trans. to 4th Art., 1 June, 1821. Trans. to 1st Art., 16 Aug., 1821. Capt. Ord., 30 May, 1832. Maj. 27 March, 1842. Col., 3 Aug., 1861. Retired 1 June, 1863. Died 4 April, 1864. Bvt. Capt., 17 May, 1830, for ten years' faithful service in one grade.

SYMMES, JOHN C.* [Born in Ky. Appointed from Ohio.]
2nd Lieut. 4th Art., 1 July, 1847. Trans. to Ord., 24 April, 1849. 1st Lieut., 1 July, 1853. Capt. 10th Inf., 3 March, 1855, declined. Capt. Ord., 1 July, 1861. Retired 1 Nov., 1861. Died 16 March, 1895.

SYMMONDS, CHARLES J.* [Born in Mich. Appointed from Wis.]
2nd Lieut. 18th Inf., 12 June, 1890. Trans. to 7th Cav., 7 March, 1891. 1st Lieut. 9th Cav., 29 June, 1897. Trans. to 7th Cav., 1 Oct., 1897. Capt. A. Q. M. Vols., 26 Nov. to 26 Dec., 1898.

MONDS, HENRY C.* [Born in Mass. Apponted from Mass.]
Bvt. 2nd Lieut. 1st Art., 1 July, 1853. 2nd Lieut. 2nd Art., 18 Oct., 1853. 1st Lieut., 31 Jan., 1856. Capt. C. S., 16 May, 1861. Maj., 9 Feb., 1863. Resigned 17 Nov., 1865. Bvt. Lieut. Col. and Col., 13 March, 1865, for faithful and meritorious ser- during the war.

SYMONS, THOS. W.* [Born in N. Y. Appointed from Mich.]
2nd Lieut. Eng., 17 June, 1874. 1st Lieut., 2 May, 1878. Capt., 2 June, 1884. Maj., 31 March, 1896.

TABER, HENRY S.* [Born in N. Y. Appointed from N. Y.]
2nd Lieut. Eng., 13 June, 1873. 1st Lieut., 29 Jan., 1877. Capt., 3 July, 1883. Died 12 April, 1894.

TAGGARD, FRANK W. [Born in Mass. Appointed from Mass.]
2nd Lieut. 1st Mass. Art., 5 July, 1861. 1st Lieut., 24 Jan., 1862. Capt. A. A. G. Vols., 11 March, 1863. Maj. A. A. G. Vols., 23 Feb., 1865. Bvt. Lieut. Col. Vols., 13 March, 1865, for efficient and meritorious service. Mustered out 18 July, 1867. 1st Lieut. 41st Inf., 9 May, 1867. Trans. to 24th Inf., 11 Nov., 1869. Mustered out 1 Jan., 1871.

TAGGART, DAVID. [Born in Pa. Appointed from Pa.]
Maj P. M., 30 May, 1861. Resignned 11 Sept., 1873. Bvt. Lieut. Col., 13 March, 1865, for faithful and meritorious service during the war. Died 30 June, 1888.

TAGGART, ELMORE F.* [Born in Ohio. Appointed from Ohio.]
2nd Lieut. 6th Inf., 13 June, 1883. 1st Lieut. 4th Inf., 20 Feb., 1891. Trans. to 6th Inf., 20 July, 1891. Capt. of Inf., 1 July, 1898. Ass'd to 6th Inf., 1 Jan., 1899. Capt. C. S. Vols., 12 May, 1898. Maj. Chf. C. S., 28 Oct., 1898, to 10 June, 1899. Maj. 28th U. S. Vols., 5 July, 1899, to ——.

TALBOT, THEODORE. [Born in D. C. Appointed from Ky.]
Sergt. Maj. Cal. Batt. Vols., 23 July, 1846. 1st Lieut. Adj., 8 Aug., 1846. Discharged 6 Feb., 1847. 2nd Lieut. 1st Art., 22 May, 1847. 1st Lieut., 22 Sept., 1848. Bvt. Capt. A. A. G., 16 March, 1861. Bvt. Maj. A. A. G., 3 July, 1861. Maj. A. A. G., 3 Aug., 1861. Died 22 April, 1862.

TALBOTT, JAMES M. [Born in Ind. Appointed from Ind.]
Maj. of Inf., 3 March, 1847; 16th Inf., 9 April, 1847. Died 15 June, 1848.

TALCOTT, ANDREW.* [Born in Conn. Appointed from Conn.]
Bvt. 2nd Lieut. Eng., 24 July, 1818. 2nd Lieut., 14 Aug., 1818. 1st Lieut., 1 Oct., 1820. Capt., 22 Dec., 1830. Resigned 21 Sept., 1836. Bvt. Capt., 1 Oct., 1830, for ten years' faithful service in one grade. Died 22 April, 1883.

TALCOTT, GEORGE. [Born in Conn. Appointed from N. Y.]
2nd Lieut. 25th Inf., 10 July, 1813. 1st Lieut., 14 March, 1814. Capt. Ord., 5 Aug., 1813. Trans. to 2nd Art., 1 June, 1821. Lieut. Col. Ord., 30 May, 1832. Col. Chf. of Ord., 25 March, 1848. Dismissed 10 July, 1851. Bvt. Maj., 5 Aug., 1823, for ten years' faithful service in one grade. Bvt. Brig. Gen., 30 May, 1848, for meritorious conduct, particularly in performing his duties in prosecuting the war with Mexico. Died 25 April, 1862.

TALCOTT, GEORGE H.* [Born in N. Y. Appointed from N. Y.]
Bvt. 2nd Lieut. 3rd Art., 1 July, 1831. 2nd Lieut., 30 June, 1833. 1st Lieut., 15 Sept., 1836. 1st Lieut. Ord., 9 July, 1838. Capt., 3 March, 1847. Maj. Voltigeurs, April, 1847. Died 8 June, 1854. Bvt. 1st Lieut., 31 Dec., 1835, for gallant conduct in the war against the Florida Indians. Bvt. Maj. and Lieut. Col., 8 Sept., 1847, for gallant and meritorious conduct in the Battle of Molino del Rey, Mexico.

TALCOTT, WM. A. [Born in ——. Appointed from ——.]
2nd Lieut. 7th Inf., — ——, 1898. Died 1 Sept., 1898.

TALIAFERRO, HENRY L. [Born in Ky. Appointed from Ky.]
2nd Lieut. 5th Art., 14 May, 1861. Resigned 29 Dec., 1862.

TALIAFERRO, LAURENCE. [Born in Va. Appointed from Va.]
Ensign 1st Inf., 2 July, 1813. 2nd Lieut., 14 Aug., 1813. 1st Lieut., 30 June, 1814. Trans. to 3rd Inf., 17 May, 1815. Resigned 1 April, 1819. Mil. Storekeeper Q. M. Dept., 14 March, 1857. Retired 27 Aug., 1863. Died 20 Jan., 1871.

TALIAFERRO, WM. B. [Born in Va. Appointed from Va.]
Capt. of Inf., 23 Feb., 1847; 11th Inf., 9 April, 1847. Maj. 9th Inf., 12 Aug., 1847. Disbanded 26 Aug., 1848.

TALLMADGE, CHAS. B. [Born in N. Y. Appointed from N. Y.]
Asst Dist. P. M., 15 Nov., 1814. Disbanded 15 June, 1815. Maj. P. M. Light Art., 27 March, 1818. Retained as Maj. P. M., 1 June, 1821. Died 31 Dec., 1832.

TALLMADGE, GRIER.* [Born in N. Y. Appointed from N. Y.]
Bvt. 2nd Lieut. 1st Art., 1 July, 1848. 2nd Lieut. 4th Art., 20 May, 1849. 1st Lieut., 4 Nov., 1853. Capt. A. Q. M., 17 May, 1861. Died 11 Oct., 1862.

TANFIELD, JAMES W. [Born in England. Appointed from Cal.]
Priv. and Sergt. Co. K, and Sergt. Maj. 1st Cal. Cav., 28 March, 1863, to 19 July, 1865. 1st Lieut. Adj. N. M. Cav., 20 July, 1865. Mustered out 7 Oct., 1866. 1st Lieut. Batt. N. M. Cav., 8 Oct., 1866. Mustered out 9 Oct., 1867. 2nd Lieut. 4th Inf., 24 Aug., 1867. Trans. to 17th Inf., 24 Aug., 1868. Unassigned 27 May, 1869. Ass'd to 23rd Inf., 14 July, 1869. Resigned 5 Jan., 1870.

TANNATT, THOS. R.* [Born in N. Y. Appointed from Mass.]
Bvt. 2nd Lieut. 3rd Art., 1 July, 1858. 2nd Lieut. 4th Art., 6 July, 1859. 1st Lieut., 14 May, 1861. Capt., 11 Aug., 1863. Col. 16th Mass. Vols., 14 July, 1862. Trans. to 1st Mass. Art., 28 Dec., 1862. Resigned from Vols., 15 July, 1864, and from U. S. Army, 18 July, 1864.

TANNER, EARLE W. [Born in N. Y. Appointed from D. C.]
2nd Lieut. 1st Art., 9 July, 1898. Trans. to 17th Inf., 4 April, 1899, to rank from 23 March, 1899. Capt. 35th U. S. Vols., 5 July, 1899, to ——.

TANNYHILL, WM. S. [Born in Md. Appointed from Ohio.]
1st Lieut. of Inf., 8 March, 1847; 15th Inf., 9 April, 1847. Capt., 20 Aug., 1847. Resigned 6 May, 1848.

TAPLIN, CHAS. [Born in N. Y. Appointed from Mo.]
1st Lieut. of Inf., 5 March, 1847; 12th Inf., 9 April, 1847. Capt., 31 March, 1848. Resigned 23 May, 1848. Bvt. Capt., 20 Aug., 1847, for gallant and meritorious conduct in the Battles of Contreras and Churubusco, Mexico.

TAPPAN, SAM'L. [Born in N. Y. Appointed from N. Y.]
Ensign 23rd Inf., 1 May, 1812. 2nd Lieut. 20 June, 1813. 1st Lieut., 14 June, 1814. Trans. to 6th Inf., 17 May, 1815. Dismissed 30 Jan., 1816.

TAPPEN, ALEX'R H.* Born in Ohio. Appointed from Ohio.]
Bvt. 2nd Lieut. 5th Inf., 1 July, 1835. 2nd Lieut. 31 July, 1836. Resigned 31 July, 1838. Died in 1852.

TARDY, JOHN A.* [Born in N. Y. Appointed from N. Y.]
Bvt. 2nd Lieut. Eng., 1 July, 1860. 2nd Lieut., 2 May, 1861. 1st Lieut., 6 Aug., 1861. Capt., 3 March, 1863. Maj., 7 March, 1867. Died 3 June, 1867. Bvt. Maj., 13 March, 1865, for gallant and meritorious service during the war.

TARLTON, ELISHA W. [Born in Ky. Appointed from Ky.]
2nd Lieut. 3rd Cav., 5 Aug., 1861. 1st Lieut., 5 Aug., 1861. Capt., 27 Oct., 1863. Trans. to Supernumerary list, 26 Sept., 1870. Discharged 25 Oct., 1870. Bvt. Maj., 15 Nov., 1863, for gallant and meritorious service in action at Tuscumbia, Ala.

TARRANT, JOHN. [Born in S. C. Appointed from S. C.]
Ensign 3rd Inf., 3 Jan., 1812. 2nd Lieut., 12 March, 1812. 1st Lieut., 15 April, 1814. Trans. to 1st Inf., 17 May, 1815. Resigned 1 March, 1818.

TASSIN, AUGUSTUS G. [Born in France. Appointed from Ind.]
1st Lieut. 35th Ind. Vols., 9 Oct., 1861. Capt., 17 June, 1863. Lieut. Col., 9 Aug., 1864. Col., 4 March, 1865. Mustered out 30 Sept., 1865. Capt. 12th Inf., 28 July, 1866. Bvt. Maj., 2 March, 1867, for gallant and meritorious service in the Battle of Mission Ridge, Tenn. Bvt. Lieut. Col., 2 March, 1867, for gallant and meritorious service in the capture of Atlanta, Ga. Bvt. Col., 2 March, 1867, for gallant and meritorious service in the Battle of Nashville, Tenn. Discharged 1 Dec., 1870. Priv. Sig. Corps. 18 June, 1872. 2nd Lieut. 12th Inf., 19 March, 1873. 1st Lieut., 28 June, 1878. Capt., 23 April, 1890. Died 19 Oct., 1893.

TATE, DANIEL L.* [Born in Ky. Appointed from Ky.]
2nd Lieut. 1st Cav., 12 June, 1880. 1st Lieut. 3rd Cav., 31 Jan., 1891. Capt., 2 March, 1899.

TATE, ROBERT B. A. [Born in Md. Appointed from Md.]
2nd Lieut. 4th Inf., 3 March, 1819. Resigned 4 May, 1822.

TATHAM, WM. [Born in England. Appointed from Va.]
Mil. Storekeeper, 7 June, 1817. Resigned 31 Dec., 1817. Accidentally killed 22 Feb., 1819.

TAYLER, GEORGE. [Born in Ohio. Appointed from Ohio.]
2nd Lieut. 10th Cav., 20 Sept., 1867. Resigned 1 Jan., 1871.

TAYLOR, ALEX'R H. M. [Born in England. Appointed from N. Y.]
Priv. Co. B, 83rd N. Y. Vols., 30 Nov., 1861. Sergt. General Service, 10 Sept., 1862. Discharged 30 April, 1863. 2nd Lieut. 17th Inf., 16 March, 1866. 1st Lieut., 1 Sept., 1867. Discharged 1 Dec., 1870. Hosp. Steward U. S. A., 24 May, 1872. 2nd Lieut. 19th Inf., 1 Oct., 1873. 1st Lieut., 24 Nov., 1879. Capt., 4 May, 1892. Retired for disability, 7 June, 1894.

TAYLOR, ALFRED B. [Born in D. C. Appointed from Army.]
Priv. Co. H, 22nd N. Y. State Militia, 28 May, 1862. Discharged 5 Sept., 1862. Priv. Co. K, 5th Cav., 29 June, 1863. 2nd Lieut. 5th Cav., 31 Oct., 1863. 1st Lieut., 12 Sept., 1864. Bvt. Capt., 9 April, 1865, for gallant and meritorious conduct during the campaign terminating with the surrender of the insurgent army under Gen. R. E. Lee. R. Q. M. 5th Cav., 31 Dec., 1866, to 22 June, 1869. Capt., 22 June, 1869. Retired 1 May, 1879.

TAYLOR, ALGERNON S. [Born in Va. Appointed from Va.]
2nd Lieut. 5th Inf., 1 Aug., 1838. 2nd Lieut. Marine Corps, 21 Feb., 1839. 1st Lieut., 3 March, 1847. Capt., 17 July, 1857. Bvt. Capt., 27 March, 1847, for gallant and meritorious conduct at bombardment and capture of Vera Cruz, and at capture of Tuspan, Mexico. Dismissed 6 May, 1861.

TAYLOR, ARCHIBALD. [Born in Va. Appointed from Va.]
Asst. Surg., 4 Feb., 1852. Resigned 31 Oct., 1856.

TAYLOR, ARTHUR W. [Born in N. Y. Appointed from N. Y.]
Asst. Surg., 16 June, 1880. Capt. Asst. Surg., 16 June, 1885. Retired for disability, 5 Feb., 1892.

TAYLOR, ASHER C. [Born in N. Y. Appointed from Wis.]
Corpl. Co. D, 3rd Wis. Vols., 25 April, 1861. Sergt., 1 Dec., 1862. Sergt. Maj., 12 April, 1863. Discharged 21 Dec., 1863. Sergt. Maj. 3rd Wis. Vet. Vols., 21 Dec., 1863. 1st Lieut. 3rd Wis. Vet. Vols., 29 Oct., 1864. Reg. Adj., 1 April to 18 July, 1865. Mustered out 18 July, 1865. 2nd Lieut. 15th Inf., 16 Oct., 1867. 1st Lieut., 25 Aug., 1868. Unassigned 12 Aug., 1869. Ass'd to 2nd Art., 31 Dec., 1870. Capt., 20 Jan., 1889. Graduate of the Artillery School, 1876.

TAYLOR, BENJN., Jr. [Born in Conn. Appointed from Conn.]
Priv., Corpl. and 1st Sergt. Co. A. 1st Conn. Art., 22 May, 1861, to 1 March, 1862. 2nd Lieut. 1st Conn. Art., 1 March to 23 April, 1862. 2nd Lieut. 5th Inf., 19 Feb., 1862. 1st Lieut., 1 Dec., 1863. Resigned 28 Sept., 1865.

TAYLOR, BLAIR D. [Born in Va. Appointed from Va.]
1st Lieut. Asst. Surg., 26 June, 1875. Capt. Asst. Surg., 26 June, 1880. Maj. Surg., 31 May, 1893.

TAYLOR, CHAS. W.* [Born in N. Y. Appointed from N. Y.]
2nd Lieut. 9th Cav., 13 June, 1879. 1st Lieut., 7 May, 1884. R. Q. M., 12 Feb., 1885, to 1 March, 1889. Capt., 28 July, 1892. Bvt. 1st Lieut., 27 Feb., 1890, for gallant service in action against Indians in the San Andreas Mountains, N. M., 7 April, 1880.

TAYLOR, DANL. M.* [Born in D. C. Appointed at Large.]
2nd Lieut. 1st Art., 15 June, 1869. Trans. to Ord., 1 Nov., 1874. 1st Lieut., 1 Nov., 1874. Capt., 1 June, 1881. Maj., 7 July, 1898.

TAYLOR, DAVID. [Born in Ohio. Appointed from Ohio.]
Addl. P. M. Vols., 1 June, 1861. Bvt. Lieut. Col. Vols., 13 March, 1865, for faithful and meritorious service during the war. Mustered out 1 Feb., 1869. Maj. P. M., 3 Feb., 1869. Died 21 Feb., 1878.

TAYLOR, DAVID B. [Born in Scotland. Appointed from Army.]
Priv. Co. A. Batt. Eng., 23 Nov., 1860. Artificer, 1 July, 1861. Trans. to Co. D, 1 July, 1862. Corpl., 12 July, 1862. Sergt., 1 May, 1863. Discharged 11 July, 1864. Sergt. Co. D, Batt. Eng., 11 July, 1864. 1st Sergt. Co. C, 4 Sept., 1864. 2nd Lieut. 24th Inf., 7 March, 1867. Trans. to 11th Inf., 25 April, 1869. 1st Lieut., 29 Oct., 1873. Retired 24 Aug., 1886. Died 12 Dec., 1886.

TAYLOR, EDWARD.* [Born in Ill. Appointed from Idaho.]
2nd Lieut. 12th Inf., 12 June, 1893. 1st Lieut., 26 April, 1898. Died 26 Dec., 1899, at Bautista, P. I.

TAYLOR, F. BEERS. [Born in N. Y. Appointed from N. Y.]
2nd Lieut. 25th Inf., 5 Sept., 1867. Trans. to 18th Inf., 26 April, 1869. Trans. to 9th Cav., 18 Sept., 1875. 1st Lieut., 25 Feb., 1876. Capt., 15 June, 1888. Retired for disability, 22 April, 1891. Died 10 Aug., 1897.

TAYLOR, FRANCIS.* [Born in Va. Appointed from Va.]
Bvt. 2nd Lieut. 4th Art., 1 July, 1825. 2nd Lieut. 1st Art., 1 July, 1825. 1st Lieut., 31 Jan., 1833. Capt., 7 July, 1838. Maj., 3 March, 1855. Died 12 Oct., 1858. Bvt. Maj., 18 April, 1847, for gallant and meritorious conduct at Cerro Gordo. Bvt. Lieut. Col., 20 Aug., 1847, for gallant and meritorious conduct at Churubusco, Mexico.

TAYLOR, FRANCK E. [Born in D. C. Appointed from D. C.]
2nd Lieut. and 1st Lieut. 1st Art., 5 Aug., 1861. Bvt. Capt., 8 July, 1863, for gallant and meritorious service in the capture of Port Hudson, La. Bvt. Maj., 19 Sept., 1864, for gallant and meritorious service in the Battle of Winchester, Va. Capt. 1st Art., 1 Feb., 1866. Died 25 Nov., 1886.

TAYLOR, FRANK. [Born in France. Appointed from Iowa.]
Priv. General Service, 24 Oct., 1860. Sergt., 19 Dec., 1862. Discharged 1 April, 1863. 2nd Lieut. 2nd Inf., 29 Oct., 1867. Unassigned 17 April, 1869. Ass'd to 14th Inf., 31 July, 1869. 1st Lieut., 25 Feb., 1876. Capt., 23 March, 1892.

TAYLOR, GEORGE. [Born in Md. Appointed from Md.]
Asst. Surg., 1 April, 1856. Maj. Surg., 27 Aug., 1862. Died 5 Aug., 1867. Bvt. Lieut. Col., 13 March, 1865, for faithful and meritorious service during the war.

TAYLOR, GEORGE.* [Born in Ga. Appointed from Ga.]
2nd Lieut. 3rd Art., 1 July, 1837. 1st Lieut., 7 July, 1838. Capt., 16 Feb., 1847. Drowned 24 Dec., 1853. Bvt. Capt., 1 March, 1842, for gallant and meritorious service in the war against the Florida Indians. Bvt. Maj., 9 Oct., 1847, for gallant and meritorious conduct in the Battle of Huamantla, Mexico.

TAYLOR, GEORGE. [Born in Ohio. Appointed from Ohio.]
2nd Lieut. 10th Cav., 20 Sept., 1867. Resigned 1 Jan., 1871.

TAYLOR, GEORGE McM. [Born in Ohio. Appointed from Ohio.]
Priv. Co. F, 79th and Co. I, 73rd Ohio Vols., 12 May, 1863, to 20 July, 1865. 2nd Lieut. 14th Inf., 20 July, 1866. Trans. to 23rd Inf., 21 Sept., 1866. 1st Lieut., 16 Dec., 1867. Dismissed 25 April, 1877.

TAYLOR, GEORGE W. [Born in N. J. Appointed from N. J.]
Midshipman U. S. N., 1 Nov., 1827, to 19 Dec., 1831. 1st Lieut. of Inf., 8 March, 1847; 10th Inf., 9 April, 1847. Capt., 13 Sept., 1847. Disbanded 23 Aug., 1848. Col. 3rd N. J. Vols., 4 June, 1861. Brig. Gen. Vols., 9 May, 1862. Died 31 Aug., 1862, of wounds received 27 Aug., 1862, in action at Cub Run, Va.

TAYLOR, HARRY.* [Born in N. H. Appointed from N. H.]
2nd Lieut. Eng., 15 June, 1884. 1st Lieut., 1 Dec., 1887. Capt., 6 Jan., 1896.

TAYLOR, HENRY. [Born in Mass. Appointed from Mass.]
Ensign 34th Inf., 30 April, 1813. 3rd Lieut., 1 Nov., 1813. 2nd Lieut., 31 May, 1814. Disbanded 1 June, 1815. 2nd Lieut. 6th Inf., 17 Feb., 1817. 1st Lieut., 1 March, 1820. Died 5 Nov., 1821.

TAYLOR, HUGH K. [Born in Ky. Appointed from Army.]
Priv. Co. C, 12th Inf., Priv., Corpl., Sergt. and 1st Sergt. Battys M and O, 4th Art., 27 Sept., 1897, to 15 Nov., 1899. 2nd Lieut. 6th Inf., 1 Oct., 1899.

TAYLOR, JAMES D., Jr. [Born in Florida. Appointed from Florida.]
2nd Lieut. 20th Inf., 9 July, 1898. 1st Lieut. 24th Inf., 25 April, 1899.

TAYLOR, JAMES H.* [Born in N. Y. Appointed from N. Y.]
Bvt. 2nd Lieut. 3rd Inf., 1 July, 1830. 2nd Lieut., 31 Oct., 1833. Drowned 17 Oct., 1835.

TAYLOR, JOHN G. [Born in Ky. Appointed from Ky.]
Cadet at Mil. Acad., 1 July, 1845, to 27 June, 1848. 2nd Lieut. 8th Inf., 7 June, 1855. 1st Lieut., 31 Dec., 1860. Resigned 7 June, 1861. Killed 30 June at Battle of White Oak Swamp, Va.

TAYLOR, JOHN McL. [Born in D. C. Appointed from Ky.]
2nd Lieut. 3rd Art., 3 March, 1848. 1st Lieut., 30 June, 1851. Capt. C. S., 11 May, 1861. Maj., 9 Feb., 1863. Died 21 Nov., 1875. Bvt. Lieut. Col., 13 March, 1865, for faithful and meritorious service during the war. Bvt. Col., 13 March, 1865, for faithful and meritorious service in his Dept. during the war.

TAYLOR, JOHN R. M.* [Born in D. C. Appointed from D. C.]
2nd Lieut. 7th Inf., 12 June, 1889. 1st Lieut. 23rd Inf., 27 Aug., 1896. Capt. 14th Inf., 17 July, 1899. Graduate of the Infantry and Cavalry School, 1897.

TAYLOR, JOSEPH H.* [Born in Ky. Appointed from Md.]
Bvt. 2nd Lieut. 1st Cav., 1 July, 1856. 2nd Lieut., 16 Jan., 1857. 1st Lieut., 22 April, 1861. Capt. 6th Cav., 14 May, 1861. Bvt. Maj., 1 June, 1862, for gallant and meritorious service in the Battle of Fair Oaks, Va. Lieut. Col. A. A. G. (Act 17 July, 1862), 20 Aug., 1862. Bvt. Lieut. Col., 17 Sept., 1862, for gallant and meritorious service in the Battle of Antietam, Md. Bvt. Col. Vols., 3 March, 1865, Maj. A. A. G., 30 March, 1866. Relieved as Lieut. Col. A. A. G. (Act 17 July, 1862), 11 June, 1866. Bvt. Col., 13 Aug., 1866, for faithful and meritorious service during the war. Died 13 March, 1885.

TAYLOR, JOSEPH P. [Born in Ky. Appointed from Ky.]
3rd Lieut. 28th Inf., 20 May, 1813. 2nd Lieut., 1 Aug., 1813. 1st Lieut., 5 July, 1814. Disbanded 15 June, 1815. Reinstated 17 May, 1816, as 2nd Lieut. Corps Art. 1st Lieut., 24 Nov., 1817. Trans. to 3rd Art., 1 June, 1821. Capt., 6 July, 1825. Capt C. S., 10 March, 1829. Maj. C. S., 7 July, 1838. Lieut. Col. A. C. G. S., 30 Nov., 1841. Col. C. G. S., 29 Sept., 1861. Brig. Gen. C. G. S., 9 Feb., 1863. Died 29 June, 1864. Retained — May, 1816 (in reorganization under the Act of 3 March, 1815), as 2nd Lieut. Art., with Bvt. of 1st Lieut. from 15 July, 1814 (date of appointment as 1st Lieut. 28th Inf.) Bvt. Col., 30 May, 1848, for meritorious conduct, particularly in performing his duties in prosecuting the war with Mexico.

TAYLOR, LEWIS. [Born in Pa. Appointed from Pa.]
Asst. Surg., 3 March, 1857. Maj. Surg., 14 Aug., 1863. Died 6 Jan., 1868. Bvt. Lieut. Col., 13 March, 1865, for faithful and meritorious service during the war.

TAYLOR, MARCUS E. [Born in Miss. Appointed from Miss.]
1st Lieut. Asst. Surg., 26 June, 1875. Capt. Asst. Surg., 26 June, 1880. Died 25 Jan., 1896.

TAYLOR, MORSE K. [Born in N. Y. Appointed from Iowa.]
Maj. Surg. 26th Ill. Vols., 29 Aug., 1861. Discharged 15 Aug., 1862. Maj. Surg. Vols., 8 Aug., 1862. Bvt. Lieut. Col. Vols., 7 Oct., 1865, for faithful and meritorious service. Mustered out 12 Oct., 1865. Capt. Asst. Surg., 14 May, 1867. Maj. Surg., 30 June, 1882. Retired by operation of law, 14 May, 1887. Died 20 Oct., 1889.

TAYLOR, OLIVER H. P.* [Born in R. I. Appointed from R. I.]
Bvt. 2nd Lieut. 1st Drag., 1 July, 1846. 2nd Lieut., 16 Feb., 1847. 1st Lieut., 21 Feb., 1853. Killed 17 March, 1858, in action with Indians in Utah. Bvt. 1st Lieut., 4 Feb., 1847, for gallant and meritorious conduct at Embudo and Taos, Mexico. Bvt. Capt., 16 March, 1848, for gallant and meritorious conduct at Santa Cruz de Rosales.

TAYLOR, RODNEY M. [Born in N. Y. Appointed from N. Y.]
Capt. 12th N. Y. Cav., 13 Dec., 1862. Maj., 5 Jan., 1864. Bvt. Lieut. Col. and Col., 13 March, 1865, for faithful and meritorious service. Mustered out 19 July, 1865. 1st Lieut. 12th Inf., 28 July, 1866. Unassigned 16 Aug., 1869. Ass'd to 20th Inf., 1 Jan., 1871. Capt., 22 Oct., 1876. Retired by operation of law, 19 Sept., 1884.

TAYLOR, SIDNEY W. [Born in D. C. Appointed from N. Y.]
2nd Lieut. 4th Art., 3 Sept., 1867. 1st Lieut., 26 April, 1873. Capt., 28 Nov., 1892. Graduate of the Artillery School. 1871. Bvt. Capt., 27 Feb., 1890, for gallant and meritorious conduct in action against Indians during the Modoc war of 1873.

TAYLOR, WM. [Born in ——. Appointed from S. C.]
1st Lieut. 5th Inf., 14 May, 1799. Retained — Feb., 1801, in 3rd Inf., declined. Capt. 18th Inf., 12 March, 1812. Trans. to 3rd Inf., 17 May, 1815. Trans. to 4th Inf., 2 Dec., 1815. Resigned 12 March, 1817.

TAYLOR, WM. F. [Born in Va. Appointed from Va.]
Ensign 12th Inf., 28 June, 1814. R. Q. M., Aug., 1814, to June, 1815. 3rd Lieut., 28 Nov., 1814. Disbanded 15 June, 1815. 2nd Lieut. 4th Inf., 18 Aug., 1817. 1st Lieut., 24 Feb., 1818. Dismissed 23 July, 1818.

TAYLOR, WM. H. H. [Born in Ohio. Appointed from Ohio.]
1st Lieut. 18th Inf., 14 May, 1861. Capt., 11 Aug., 1862. Resigned 12 Dec., 1863.

TAYLOR, WALTER L.* [Born in Ga. Appointed from Ga.]
Addl. 2nd Lieut. 16th Inf., 12 June, 1887. 2nd Lieut. 20th Inf., 31 Aug., 1887. 1st Lieut. 22nd Inf., 29 Dec., 1894. Died 18 Sept., 1898.

TAYLOR, WM. W. [Born in N. Y. Appointed from Ind.]
1st Lieut. Mounted Rifles, 27 May, 1846. Capt., 19 Aug., 1848. Resigned 31 Oct., 1848.

TAYLOR, WOODBURY M. [Born in Vt. Appointed from Ill.]
2nd Lieut. 8th Ill. Cav., 18 Sept., 1861. 1st Lieut., 10 Sept., 1862. Capt., 12 Dec., 1863, to 13 April, 1864. Capt. C. S. Vols., 18 March, 1864. Bvt. Maj. Vols. 13 March, 1865, for meritorious service in his Dept. during the war. Mustered out 21 Feb., 1866. Capt. 10th Cav., 22 Jan., 1867. Resigned 29 May, 1867.

TAYLOR, ZACHARY. [Born in Va. Appointed from Ky.]
1st Lieut. 7th Inf., 3 May, 1808. Capt., 30 Nov., 1810. Maj. 26th Inf., 15 May, 1814. Retained 17 May, 1815, as Capt. 7th Inf., but declined. Reinstated as Maj. 3rd Inf., 17 May, 1816. Lieut. Col. 4th Inf., 20 April, 1819. Trans. to 8th Inf., 13 Aug., 1819. Trans. to 1st Inf., 1 June, 1821. Trans. to 7th Inf., 16 Aug., 1821. Trans. to 1st Inf., 1 Jan., 1822. Col., 4 April, 1832. Trans. to 6th Inf., 7 July, 1843. Bvt. Maj., 5 Sept., 1812, for gallant conduct in the defence of Fort Harrison. Bvt. Brig. Gen., 25 Dec., 1837, for distinguished service in the Battle of Okeechobee with Semiuole Indians. Bvt. Maj. Gen., 28 May, 1846, for gallant conduct and distinguished service at Palo Alto and Resaca de la Palma, on 8 and 9 May, 1846. Maj. Gen., 29 June, 1846. Tendered the thanks of Congress, 16 July, 1846, "for the fortitude, skill, enterprise and courage which have distinguished the recent operations on the Rio Grande, with the presentation of a gold medal with appropriate devices and inscriptions thereon, in the name of the Republic, as a tribute to his good conduct, valor and generosity to the vanquished." By resolution of 2 March, 1847: "for the fortitude, skill, enterprise and courage which distinguished the late brilliant military operations at Monterey," and with the presentation of a gold medal, "emblematical of this splendid achievement, as a testimony of the high sense entertained by Congress of his judicious and distinguished conduct on that memorable occasion," and by resolution of 9 May, 1848, "for himself and the troops under his command for their valor, skill and gallant conduct conspicuously displayed on the 22nd and 23rd of Feb. last, in the Battle of Buena Vista, in defeating a Mexican army of more than four times their number, consisting of chosen troops under their favorite commander, Gen. Santa Anna, with the presentation of a gold medal emblematical of this splendid achievement, as a testimony of the high sense entertained by Congress of his judicious and distinguished conduct on that memorable occasion." Resigned 31 Jan., 1849. President of the U. S. from 4 March, 1849, until he died, 9 July, 1850.

TAYLOR, ZACHARY. [Born in Md. Appointed from La.]
2nd Lieut. 2nd Cav., 22 Jan., 1867. 1st Lieut., 9 June, 1868. Resigned 3 July, 1869.

TAYMAN, CHARLES E. [Born in Pa. Appointed from Army.]
Cadet at Mil. Acad., 1 July, 1880, to 10 Jan., 1881. Priv., Corpl. and Sergt. Co. K, 1st Inf., 22 Oct., 1884, to 22 March, 1888. 2nd Lieut. 24th Inf., 6 Feb., 1888. 1st Lieut. 10th Inf., 30 April, 1895. Trans. to 24th Inf., 16 May, 1895. Capt. 1st Inf., 2 March, 1899. Graduate of the Infantry and Cavalry School, 1893. Capt. A. Q. M. Vols., 26 Nov., 1898, to 8 June, 1899.

TEAR, C. C.* [Born in Ill. Appointed from Ill.]
2nd Lieut. 25th Inf., 13 June, 1883. Resigned 1 Jan., 1888.

TEAR, WALLACE. [Born in Ohio. Appointed from Ill.]
Sergt. Co. K, 96th Ill. Vols., 4 Aug., 1862. 1st Lieut. 14th U. S. Col. Troops, 15 Nov., 1863. Mustered out 26 March, 1866. 2nd Lieut. 40th Inf., 9 Aug., 1867. Trans. to 25th Inf., 20 April, 1869. 1st Lieut., 30 Nov., 1873. Resigned 30 June, 1883.

TEBBETS, CLINTON H.* [Born in Ark. Appointed from Ark.]
2nd Lieut. 4th Cav., 15 June, 1870. Resigned 1 Sept., 1872.

TEBBETTS, HARRY H.* [Born in N. H. Appointed from Mass.]
Addl. 2nd Lieut. 12th Inf., 12 June, 1896. 2nd Lieut. 10th Inf., 11 Nov., 1896. 1st Lieut of Inf., 23 Dec., 1898. Ass'd to 1st Inf., 1 Jan., 1899.

TELLFORD, JOHN G. [Born in Ohio. Appointed from Ohio.]
1st Lieut. 44th Ohio Vols., 9 Oct., 1861, to 12 April, 1864. Capt. A. A. G. Vols., 29 Feb., 1864. Mustered out 10 July, 1866. 2nd Lieut. 13th Inf., 21 March, 1866. Trans. to 31st Inf., 21 Sept., 1866. 1st Lieut., 1 Nov., 1867. Unassigned 15 May, 1869. Ass'd to 2nd Art., 15 Dec., 1870. Died 10 Feb., 1873. Bvt. 1st Lieut., 2 March, 1867, for gallant and meritorious service in the Battle of Lewisburg, Va., 23 May, 1862. Bvt. Capt., 2 March, 1867, for gallant and meritorious service in the action at Cumberland Gap, in 1863.

TEMPLE, ROBT. E.* [Born in Vt. Appointed from Vt.]
Bvt. 2nd Lieut. 3rd Art., 1 July, 1828. 2nd Lieut., 1 July, 1828. 1st Lieut. 22 June, 1836. 1st Lieut. Ord., 9 July, 1838. Resigned 15 Nov., 1839. Col. of Inf., 3 March, 1847; 10th Inf., 9 April, 1847. Disbanded 26 Aug., 1848. Died 20 July, 1854.

TEMPLE, WM J. [Born in N. Y. Appointed from N. Y.]
Capt. 17th Inf., 5 Aug., 1861. Killed 1 May, 1863, at Battle of Chancellorsville, Va. Bvt. Maj., 3 May, 1863, for gallant and meritorious service at the Battle of Chancellorsville, Va.

TEMPLEMAN, GEORGE.* [Born in Mass. Appointed from D. C.]
2nd Lieut. Light Art., 3 Jan., 1812. Resigned 1 Nov., 1812. 1st Lieut. 26th Inf., 21 April, 1814. Capt., 15 Nov., 1814. Disbanded 15 June, 1815. 2nd Lieut. 1st Inf., 17 March, 1819. Dropped 27 Dec., 1820. Died 1 Feb., 1852.

TEMPLETON, GEORGE M. [Born in Pa. Appointed from Pa.]
Corpl. Co. D, 129th Pa. Vols., 23 Aug., 1862, to 24 Feb., 1864. Capt. 32nd U. S. Inf. Col. Inf., 4 March, 1864. Mustered out 22 Aug., 1865. 2nd Lieut. 18th Inf., 23 Feb., 1866. 1st Lieut., 23 Feb., 1866. Trans. to 27th Inf., 21 Sept., 1866. Capt., 19 Oct., 1867. Unassigned 14 June, 1869. Died 4 May, 1870.

TEMPLETON, LEWIS W. [Born in Ind. Appointed from Ohio.]
2nd Lieut. of Inf., 8 March, 1847; 15th Inf., 9 April, 1847. Resgined 5 June, 1848.

TEN BROECK, ALEX'R P. [Born in N. Y. Appointed from Army.]
Priv., Corpl. and Sergt. Co. G, 3rd Inf., 10 June, 1841, to 26 Jan., 1848. 2nd Lieut. 10th Inf., 30 Dec., 1847. Disbanded 14 Aug., 1848.

TEN BROECK, PETER G. S. [Born in Maine. Appointed from N. Y.]
Asst. Surg., 13 Dec., 1847. Maj. Surg., 21 May, 1861. Died 19 Dec., 1867. Bvt. Lieut. Col., 13 March, 1865, for faithful and meritorious service during the war.

TEN EYCK, BENJAMIN L. [Born in N. Y. Appointed from N. Y.]
Asst. Surg., 7 June, 1889. Capt. Asst. Surg., 7 June 1894.

TEN EYCK, BENJAMIN L. [Born in N. Y. Appointed from N. Y.]
Corpl. Co. H, 12th Wis. Vols., 16 Oct., 1861, to 21 March, 1862. Capt. 18th Inf., 19 Feb., 1862. Unassigned 26 April, 1869. Mustered out 1 Jan., 1871. Bvt. Maj., 13 March, 1865, for gallant and meritorious service during the war. Mustered out. 1 Jan., 1871 (Act 15 July, 1870). Appointed Capt. of Inf., 28 Feb., 1891 (Act of 29 Sept., 1890, as amended by Act of 24 Feb., 1891).

TERRANT, C. [Born in ——. Appointed from Ky.]
Chap., 10 Dec., 1814. Died 17 Feb., 1816.

TERRELL, CHAS. M. [Born in Ind. Appointed from Ky.]
Addl. P. M., 30 June, 1862. Bvt. Lieut. Col. Vols., 15 Aug., 1865, for faithful and meritorious service. Maj. P. M. U. S. A., 17 Jan., 1867. Lieut. Col. and Dep. P. M. G., 30 Dec., 1888. Col. A. P. M. G., 6 Jan., 1893. Retired by operation of law, 24 Feb., 1896.

TERRETT, BURDETT A. [Born in Va. Appointed from Va.]
3rd Lieut. Mounted Rangers, 10 July, 1833. 2nd Lieut. 1st Drag., 7 Nov., 1833. 1st Lieut., 31 March, 1836. Capt. A. Q. M., 7 July, 1838, to 8 Jan., 1841. Capt. 1st Drag., 21 Feb., 1842. Accidentally killed 17 March, 1845.

TERRETT, COLVILLE P. [Born in D. C. Appointed from Army.]
2nd Class Priv. Sig. Corps, 13 July, 1878. 1st Class Priv., 16 July, 1879. Discharged 16 Oct., 1879. 2nd Lieut. 8th Inf., 1 Sept., 1879. 1st Lieut., 2 July, 1886. Capt., 27 Aug., 1896.

TERRETT, JOHN C. [Born in Va. Appointed from Va.]
2nd Lieut. 1st Inf., 16 Nov., 1839. 1st Lieut., 18 June, 1846. Killed in Battle of Monterey, Mex., 21 Sept., 1846.

TERRETT, WASHINGTON. [Born in Va. Appointed from Va.]
2nd Lieut. of Inf., 4 March, 1847; Voltigeurs, 9 April, 1847. R. Q. M., 17 May, to 10 Aug., 1847. Reg. Adj., 24 Oct., 1847, to 31 Aug., 1848. Disbanded 31 Aug., 1848.

TERRILL, WM. R.* [Born in Va. Appointed from Va.]
Bvt. 2nd Lieut. 3rd Art., 1 July, 1853. 2nd Lieut. 4th Art., 4 Nov., 1853. 1st Lieut., 31 March, 1856. Capt. 5th Art., 14 May, 1861. Brig. Gen. Vols., 9 Sept., 1862. Killed 8 Oct., 1862, at the Battle of Perryville, Ky.

TERRY, ALFRED H. [Born in Conn. Appointed from Conn.]
Col. 2nd Conn. Vols., 7 May, 1861. Mustered out 7 Aug., 1861. Col. 7th Conn. Vols., 17 Sept., 1861. Brig. Gen. Vols., 25 April, 1862. Bvt. Maj. Gen. Vols., 26 Aug., 1864, for meritorious and distinguished service during the war. Nominated for, and confirmed as Brig. Gen. U. S. A., 15 Jan., 1865, for distinguished service during the war, and for gallantry and generalship in the capture of Fort Fisher, N.

C. Provisionally appointed Maj. Gen. Vols., 15 Jan., 1865. Commissioned Maj. Gen. Vols., 20 April, 1865, to rank from 15 Jan., 1865, for gallant service in the capture of Fort Fisher. The thanks of Congress tendered, 24 Jan., 1865, "To Bvt. Maj. Gen. Alfred H. Terry, and to the officers and soldiers under his command, for the unsurpassed gallantry and skill exhibited by them in the attack upon Fort Fisher, and the brilliant and decisive victory by which that important work has been captured from the rebel forces, and placed in the possession, and under the authority of the U. S., and for their long and faithful service, and unwavering devotion to the cause of the country, in the midst of the greatest difficulties and dangers." Bvt. Maj. Gen., 13 March, 1865, for gallant and meritorious service in the capture of Wilmington, N. C. Mustered out of Vol. Service 1 Sept., 1866. Maj. Gen., 3 March, 1886. Retired for disability, 5 April, 1888. Died 16 Dec., 1890.

TESSON, LOUIS S. [Born in Mo. Appointed from Mo.]
1st Lieut. Asst. Surg., 26 June, 1875. Capt. Asst. Surg., 26 June, 1880. Maj. Surg., 26 Sept., 1895.

TEVIS, WASHINGTON C.* [Born in Pa. Appointed at Large.]
Bvt. 2nd Lieut. Mounted Rifles, 1 July, 1849. Resigned 12 May, 1850. Lieut. Col. 4th Del. Vols., 18 Aug., 1862. Mustered out 25 Sept., 1863. Lieut. Col. 3rd Md. Cav., 26 Sept., 1863. Col., 23 Dec., 1863. Bvt. Brig. Gen. Vols., 13 March, 1865, for gallant and meritorious service during the war. Discharged 20 July, 1864. (Served in Vols. under name of C. Carrol Tevis.)

TEXTER, THEODORE. [Born in Germany. Appointed from Army.]
Priv., Corpl., Sergt. and 1st Sergt. Troop A, Mounted Rifles (3rd Cav.), 10 July, 1855, to 16 Dec., 1862. 2nd Lieut. 3rd Cav., 17 July, 1862. Appointment revoked 1 Jan., 1863.

THATCHER, AMOS R. [Born in Pa. Appointed from Pa.]
2nd Lieut. 8th Inf., 13 Aug., 1819. Disbanded 1 June, 1821. Died 18 July, 1825.

THATCHER, HORACE K. [Born in Ind. Appointed from Ohio.]
1st Lieut. and Adj. 2nd Ohio Vols., 17 April to 21 June, 1861. Capt. 14th Inf., 14 May, 1861. Dismissed 23 Dec., 1865. Bvt. Maj., 1 Aug., 1864, for gallant service at the Battles of North Anna, Bethesda Church, &c. Priv. and Sergt. Troops A and D, and Sergt. Maj. 3rd Cav., 23 March, 1868, to 22 July, 1869. Died — ——, 1877.

THAYER, ARTHUR.* [Born in Ind. Appointed from Ind.]
2nd Lieut. 3rd Cav., 1 July, 1886. 1st Lieut. 4th Cav., 2 July, 1892. Trans. to 3rd Cav., 5 Dec., 1892.

THAYER, EPHRAIM M. [Born in Mass. Appointed from Ohio.]
2nd Lieut. 2nd Drag., 29 Dec., 1839. Died 16 Sept., 1841.

THAYER, RUSSELL.* [Born in Pa. Appointed from Pa.]
2nd Lieut. 11th Inf., 17 June, 1874. Resigned 30 Sept., 1874.

THAYER, SYLVANUS.* [Born in Mass. Appointed from Mass.]
2nd Lieut. Eng., 23 Feb., 1808. 1st Lieut., 1 July, 1812. Capt. Dep. Com. of Ord., 22 Sept., 1812. Capt. Eng., 13 Oct., 1813. Maj., 24 May, 1828. Lieut. Col., 7 July, 1838. Col., 3 March, 1863. Retired 1 June, 1863. Died 7 Sept., 1872. Bvt. Maj., 20 Feb., 1815, for distinguished and meritorious service at Norfolk, Va. Bvt. Lieut. Col., 3 March, 1823, for distinguished and meritorious service. Bvt. Col., 3 March, 1833, for ten years' faithful service in one grade. Bvt. Brig. Gen., 13 March, 1865, for long and faithful service.

THEAKER, HUGH A. Born in Ohio. Appointed from Ohio.]
1st Lieut. 16th Inf., 14 May, 1861. Bvt. Capt., 25 Nov., 1863, for gallant and meritorious service in the Battle of Mission Ridge, Tenn. Capt. 16th Inf., 28 July, 1864. Trans. to 34th Inf., 21 Sept., 1866. Trans. to 16th Inf., 14 April, 1869. Maj. 15th Inf., 6 Sept., 1886. Lieut. Col. 14th Inf., 10 July, 1891. Col. 16th Inf., 10 March, 1896. Retired for over thirty years' service 11 Aug., 1898.

THELLER, EDWARD R. [Born in Vt. Appointed from Cal.]
Capt. 2nd Cal. Vols., 25 Oct., 1861. Bvt. Maj. Vols., 13 March, 1865, for faithful and meritorious service. Mustered out 10 May, 1866. 2nd Lieut. 9th Inf., 7 March, 1867. Trans. to 21st Inf., 30 Aug., 1869. 1st Lieut., 31 Aug., 1871. Killed 17 June, 1877, in action with Indians in Idaho.

THIBAULT, JEAN PIERRE. [Born in ——. Appointed from La.]
Lieut. and Maj. La. Vols., 28 Dec., 1812, to Nov., 1813. 1st Lieut. 44th Inf., 11 March, 1814. Trans. to 1st Inf., 17 May, 1815. Resigned 16 May, 1816.

THIBAULT, FRED'K W. [Born in Germany. Appointed from N. Y.]
2nd Lieut. 7th N. Y. Vols., 23 April, 1861. 1st Lieut., 11 July, 1861. Capt., 28 Sept., 1862. Mustered out 8 May, 1863. Capt. Vet. Res. Corps, 15 Oct., 1863. Bvt. Maj. Vols., 19 July 1865, for gallant and meritorious service during the war Mustered out 29 June, 1867. 2nd Lieut. 6th Inf., 22 Jan., 1867. 1st Lieut., 25 Feb., 1868. Capt., 6 June, 1886. Died 7 Aug., 1897.

THIEMAN, AUGUST. [Born in Germany. Appointed from Army]
Priv., Corpl. and Sergt. Co. E, 9th Inf., 20 Dec., 1856, to 20 Nov., 1861. Priv., Sergt. and 1st Sergt. Co. B, 12th Inf., 26 Dec., 1861, to 23 Nov., 1862. 2nd Lieut. 12th Inf., 6 Nov., 1862. 1st Lieut., 10 April, 1863. Capt. 33rd Inf., 28 July, 1866, which appointment expired 4 March, 1867, and returned to 1st Lieut. 12th Inf. Wholly retired 17 Oct., 1867. Bvt. Capt., 1 Aug., 1864, for gallant service at the Battle of Spottsylvania, Va. Bvt. Maj., 18 Aug., 1864, for gallant service at the Battle on the Weldon Railroad, Va. Priv. Co. G, 15th Inf., 5 Sept., 1870, to 4 May 1872. Priv. and Sergt. Co. E, 10th Inf., 28 Jan., 1875, to 1 May, 1876. Priv. Co. D, 2nd Cav., 5 July, 1881, to 12 June, 1882.

THIES, FRED'K. [Born in Germany. Appointed from Army.]
Priv. 19th Inf., 12 March, 1866. Corpl., 1 May, 1866. Sergt., 7 June, 1866. Trans. to Co. C, 37th Inf., 21 Sept., 1866. Priv., 13 Jan., 1867. Sergt., 16 Jan., 1867. 1st Sergt., 7 Feb., 1867. Sergt. Maj. 37th Inf., 1 Dec., 1868. Discharged 12 March, 1869. Sergt. Maj. 37th Inf., 12 March, 1869. Discharged 30 Dec., 1869. Priv. General Service, 12 Jan., 1870. Discharged 8 June, 1870. Priv. Co. M, 7th Cav., 7 July, 1870. Corpl., 8 Aug., 1870. 1st Sergt., 1 Nov., 1870. 2nd Lieut. 3rd Inf.,

1 Oct., 1873. 1st Lieut., 14 April, 1884. R. Q. M., 16 April, 1885, to 20 Jan., 1888. Died 20 Jan., 1888.

THOBURN, STEPHEN B. [Born in Ohio. Appointed from Ky.]
Priv. Co. D, and Sergt. Maj. 56th Ohio Vols., 11 Nov., 1861, to 4 Feb., 1865. 2nd Lieut. 56th Ohio Vols., 4 Feb., 1865. Mustered out 25 April, 1866. 2nd Lieut. 23rd Inf., 4 Oct., 1867. Died 2 July, 1871.

THOM, GEORGE.* [Born in N. H. Appointed from N. H.]
Bvt. 2nd Lieut. Top. Eng., 1 July, 1839. 2nd Lieut., 18 July, 1840. 1st Lieut., 26 Sept., 1849. Capt., 1 July, 1853. Maj., 9 Sept., 1861. Col. A. A. de C., 16 Nov., 1861. Trans. to Eng., 3 March, 1863. Bvt. Lieut. Col., 13 March, 1865, for meritorious service during the war. Bvt. Col. and Brig. Gen., 13 March, 1865, for faithful and meritorious service during the war. Mustered out as Col. A. A. de C., 31 May, 1866. Lieut. Col. Eng., 10 July, 1866. Col., 31 March, 1880. Retired for over forty years' service, 20 Feb., 1883. Died 29 June, 1891.

THOM, JOSEPH P. [Born in Va. Appointed from Va.]
2nd Lieut. 11th Inf., 13 May, 1847. Disbanded 14 Aug., 1848.

THOM, REUBEN T. [Born in Va. Appointed from Ala.]
2nd Lieut. 13th Inf., 3 Aug., 1847. Disbanded 15 July, 1848.

THOMAS, ALEXANDER. [Born in N. Y. Appointed from Army.]
Priv., Corpl. and Sergt. Batty G, 4th Art., 4 Sept., 1880, to 5 July, 1883. 2nd Lieut. 9th Inf., 3 July, 1883. Resigned 31 March, 1884.

THOMAS, BRYAN M.* [Born in Ga. Appointed from Ga.]
Bvt. 2nd Lieut. 8th Inf., 1 July, 1858. 2nd Lieut. 5th Inf., 19 Jan., 1859. Resigned 6 April, 1861.

THOMAS, CHAS. [Born in Pa. Appointed from Pa.]
3rd Lieut. Ord., 13 Aug., 1819. 2nd Lieut. 4th Art., 1 June, 1821. Trans. to 3rd Art., 16 Aug., 1821. Trans. to 7th Inf., 16 Oct., 1822. 1st Lieut., 1 March, 1824. Capt., 30 April, 1833. Maj. Q. M., 7 July, 1838. Lieut. Col. Dep. Q. M. G., 23 May, 1850. Col A. Q. M. G., 1 Aug., 1856. Retired 29 July, 1866. Died 1 Feb., 1878. Bvt. Lieut. Col., 30 May, 1848, for meritorious conduct while serving in the enemy's country. Bvt. Brig. Gen., 5 July, 1864, for faithful and meritorious service during the war. Bvt. Maj. Gen., 13 March, 1865, for faithful, meritorious and distinguished service in the Q. M. Dept. during the war.

THOMAS, CHAS. W.* [Born in Maine. Appointed at Large.]
Bvt. 2nd Lieut. 5th Inf., 1 July, 1855. 2nd Lieut. 1st Inf., 7 Aug., 1855. R. Q. M., 1 June, 1858, to 31 March, 1860. 1st Lieut., 15 March, 1861. Capt. A. Q. M., 14 June, 1861. Lieut. Col. Q. M., 20 Aug., 1862, to 3 Aug., 1863. Maj. Q. M., 3 Oct., 1864, to 10 Dec., 1866. Resigned 31 May, 1872. Bvt. Maj. and Lieut. Col., March, 1865, for faithful and meritorious service during the war.

THOMAS, DANIEL G. [Born in Pa. Appointed from Pa.]
Mil. Storekeeper Q. M. D., 15 Aug., 1861. Capt. Mil. Storekeeper Q. M. D., 28 July, 1866. Died 8 Nov., 1870.

THOMAS, EARL D.* [Born in Ill. Appointed from Ill.]
Priv. Co. H. 8th Ill. Cav., 1 April, 1862. Corpl., 6 Aug., 1863. Re-enlisted 1 Jan., 1864. Sergt. Maj. 8th Ill. Cav., 4 April, 1864. Discharged 18 April, 1865. Cadet Mil. Acad., 1 July, 1855. 2nd Lieut. 5th Cav., 15 June, 1869. 1st Lieut., 1 March, 1872. Capt., 1 April, 1885. Maj. 8th Cav., 14 Feb., 1899. Trans. to 5th Cav., 23 May, 1899. Maj. I. G. Vols., 12 May, 1898, to 7 March, 1899. Bvt. Capt., 27 Feb., 1890, for gallant service in action against Indians at the Caves, Ariz., 28 Dec., 1872, and distinguished service in the campaign against Indians in Ariz. in April, 1874.

THOMAS, EVAN. [Born in D. C. Appointed from D. C.]
2nd Lieut. 4th Art., 9 April, 1861. 1st Lieut., 14 May, 1861. Capt., 31 Aug., 1864. Killed 26 April, 1873, in Cal., in action with Modoc Indians. Bvt. Capt., 13 Dec., 1862, for gallant and meritorious service at the Battle of Fredericksburg, Va. Bvt. Maj., 3 July, 1863, for gallant and meritorious service at the Battle of Gettysburg, Pa.

THOMAS, FRANCIS J.* [Born in Va. Appointed from Md.]
Bvt. 2nd Lieut. 3rd Art., 1 July, 1844. 2nd Lieut. 2nd Art., 18 June, 1846. Trans. to 3rd Art., 19 Oct., 1846. 1st Lieut., 22 March, 1847. Resigned 30 June, 1852. Killed 21 July, 1861, in Confederate service.

THOMAS, FREDERICK.* [Born in Vt. Appointed from Vt.]
2nd Lieut. Marines, 1 July, 1825. Trans. to 7th Inf., 10 June, 1826, to rank as 2nd Lieut. from 2 July, 1825. 2nd Lieut. 7th Inf., 1 July, 1825. Drowned 27 May, 1831.

THOMAS, GEORGE C.* [Born in N. J. Appointed from N. J.]
Bvt. 2nd Lieut. 4th Art., 1 July, 1836. 2nd Lieut., 15 Aug., 1836. 1st Lieut., 6 Aug., 1838. Resigned 31 Jan., 1842. Died 2 Dec., 1882.

THOMAS, GEORGE H.* [Born in Va. Appointed from Va.]
2nd Lieut. 3rd Art., 1 July, 1840. 1st Lieut., 30 April, 1844. Capt., 24 Dec., 1853. Maj. 2nd Cav., 12 May, 1855. Lieut. Col., 25 April, 1861. Col., 3 May, 1861. 5th Cav., 3 Aug., 1861. Brig. Gen. Vols., 3 Aug., 1861. Maj. Gen. Vols., 25 April, 1862. Brig. Gen. U. S. A., 27 Oct., 1863. Maj. Gen. U. S. A., 15 Dec., 1864. Bvt. 1st Lieut., 6 Nov., 1841, for gallant and good conduct in the war against the Florida Indians. Bvt. Capt., 23 Sept., 1846, for gallant conduct at Monterey, Mexico. Bvt. Maj., 23 Feb., 1847, for gallant and meritorious conduct in the Battle of Beuna Vista. Tendered the thanks of Congress by resolution of 3 March, 1865: "That the thanks of Congress are due, and are hereby tendered to Maj. Gen. Geo. H. Thomas, and the officers and soldiers under his command, for their skill and dauntless courage by which the rebel army under Gen. Hood was signally defeated and driven from the State of Tenn." Died 28 March, 1870.

THOMAS, HENRY G. [Born in Maine. Appointed from Maine.]
Capt. 5th Maine Vols., 24 June, 1861. Discharged 26 Aug., 1861. Capt. 11th Inf., 5 Aug., 1861. Col. 79th U. S. Col Troops, 20 March, 1863. Discharged 11 July, 1863. Col. 19th U. S. Col. Troops, 16 Jan., 1864. Bvt. Maj., 12 May, 1864, for

gallant and meritorious service in the Battle of Spottsylvania, Va. Bvt. Lieut. Col., 30 July, 1864, for gallant and meritorious service in front of Petersburg, Va. Brig Gen. Vols., 30 Nov., 1864. Discharged as Col. 19th U. S. Col. Troops, 8 Dec., 1864. Bvt. Col. and Brig. Gen., 13 March, 1865, for gallant and meritorious service during the war. Bvt. Maj. Gen. Vols., 13 March, 1865, for gallant and meritorious service during the war. Mustered out as Brig. Gen. Vols., 15 Jan., 1866. Trans. to 20th Inf., 21 Sept., 1866. Maj. 41st Inf., 28 July, 1866, declined. Maj. 4th Inf., 22 Oct., 1876. Trans. to Pay Dept., 23 May, 1878. Retired for over thirty years' service, 2 July, 1891. Died 23 Jan., 1897.

THOMAS, JOHN A.* [Born in Tenn. Appointed from Tenn.]
Bvt. 2nd Lieut. 3rd Art., 1 July, 1833. 2nd Lieut., 1 Dec., 1835. 1st Lieut., 30 June, 1837. Capt., 19 Nov., 1843. Resigned 28 May, 1846. Died 26 March, 1858.

THOMAS, JOHN M. [Born in ——. Appointed from D. C.]
Asst. Surg., 1 Dec., 1833. Died 28 Dec., 1834.

THOMAS, JOHN R., Jr. [Born in Ill. Appointed from Ill.]
1st Lieut. 1st U. S. Vol. Cav., 14 May to 15 Sept., 1898. 2nd Lieut. 17th Inf., 10 April, 1899.

THOMAS, JOHN W. [Born in Vt. Appointed from Vt.]
Priv. Co. F, 1st U. S. S. S., 11 Sept., 1861, to 9 Nov., 1862. Priv. and Sergt. Co. F, and Sergt. Maj. 9th Vt. Vols., 21 July, 1863, to 11 April, 1865. 2nd Lieut. 9th Vt. Vols., 11 April, 1865. 1st Lieut., 31 Aug., 1865. Mustered out 1 Dec., 1865. 2nd Lieut. 3rd Inf., 23 Feb., 1866. 1st Lieut., 28 July, 1866. Discharged 31 Dec., 1870.

THOMAS, LORENZO.* [Born in Del. Appointed from Del.]
2nd Lieut. 4th Inf., 1 July, 1823. 1st Lieut., 17 March, 1829. Reg. Adj., 1 March, 1828, to 15 Feb., 1831. Capt., 23 Sept., 1836. A. Q. M., 3 Sept., 1836, to 7 July, 1838. Bvt. Maj. A. A. G., 7 July, 1838. Maj. 4th Inf., 1 Jan., 1848. Lieut. Col. A. A. G., 15 July, 1852. Col. A. G., 7 March, 1861. Brig. A. G., 3 Aug., 1861 Retired 22 Feb., 1869. Died 2 March, 1875. Bvt. Lieut. Col., 23 Sept., 1846, for gallant and meritorious conduct at Monterey. Bvt. Brig. Gen., 7 May, 1861. Bvt. Maj. Gen., 13 March, 1865, for faithful and meritorious service during the war.

THOMAS, LORENZO, Jr. [Born in Del. Appointed from D. C.]
2nd Lieut. 1st Art., 24 April, 1861. 1st Lieut., 14 May, 1861. Reg. Adj., 28 May to 4 Nov., 1863. Capt., 4 Nov., 1863. Resigned 1 Feb., 1866. Bvt. Maj., 13 March, 1865, for gallant and meritorious service during the war.

THOMAS, MARTIN. [Born in Pa. Appointed from Pa.]
Ensign 16th Inf., 8 April, 1814. 3rd Lieut., 1 May, 1814. 2nd Lieut., 17 Dec., 1814. Discharged 17 May, 1815. 3rd Lieut. Ord., 5 March, 1817. 2nd Lieut., 31 March, 1819. Trans. to 2nd Art., 1 June, 1821. 1st Lieut., 27 Oct., 1828. Dismissed 31 Jan., 1831.

THOMAS, PHILIP K. [Born in Mich. Appointed from Kan.]
2nd Lieut. 3rd Cav., 24 Oct., 1861. 1st Lieut., 17 July, 1862. Cashiered 4 April, 1866. Reinstated 29 June, 1866. Capt., 28 July, 1866. Cashiered 16 Dec., 1867. Bvt. Capt., 4 July, 1863, for gallant and meritorious service during the Siege of Vicksburg, Miss. Died 19 April, 1879.

THOMAS, PIERRE. [Born in France. Appointed from France.]
Sword Master Mil. Acad., 1 March, 1814. Resigned 12 Dec., 1825.

THOMAS, ROBT. B.* [Born in Ky. Appointed from Miss.]
Bvt. 2nd Lieut. 2nd Art., 1 July, 1852. 2nd Lieut., 28 Sept., 1852. 1st Lieut., 25 Nov., 1854. Resigned 31 Jan., 1856.

THOMAS, TURBY F. [Born in ——. Appointed from Tenn.]
Capt. in Miss. Vols., 1812-13. 3rd Lieut. 7th Inf., 29 June, 1813. 2nd Lieut., 9 July, 1813. Trans. to 2nd Inf., 22 Jan., 1814. 1st Lieut., 30 June, 1814. Trans. to 3rd Inf., 17 May, 1815. R. Q. M., 9 June, 1816, to 31 Oct., 1818. Resigned 31 Oct., 1818.

THOMAS, WM. [Born in N. Y. Appointed from N. Y.]
Hosp. Surg.'s Mate, 7 July, 1809. Hosp. Surg., 18 Feb., 1814. Discharged 15 June, 1815. Reinstated 13 Sept., 1815, as Surg. Rifle Reg. Resigned 15 Nov., 1816.

THOMASSON, NELSON. [Born in Ky. Appointed from Ill.]
Priv. Sturgis Rifles Ill. Vols., 12 Sept. to 18 Nov., 1861. 2nd Lieut. 5th Inf., 31 Oct., 1861. 1st Lieut., 1 July, 1863. R. Q. M., 1 May, 1865, to 18 Nov., 1866. Capt., 7 Jan., 1867. Unassigned 19 May, 1869. Discharged 28 Dec., 1870.

THOMPSON, ABNER B. [Born in Mass. Appointed from Maine.]
Lieut. Col. of Inf., 16 Feb., 1847; 9th Inf., 9 April, 1847. Resigned 16 July, 1847.

THOMPSON, AI B. [Born in N. H. Appointed from N. H.]
2nd Lieut., 2nd N. H. Vols., 3 June, 1861. Mustered out 7 Aug., 1861. Capt. 18th Inf., 5 Aug., 1861. Bvt. Maj., 31 Dec., 1862, for gallant and meritorious service in the Battle of Murfreesboro, Tenn. Retired 6 May, 1864. Died 12 Sept., 1890.

THOMPSON, ALEX'R R.* [Born in N. Y. Appointed from N. Y.]
1st Lieut. 6th Inf., 3 Jan., 1812. Capt., 1 May, 1814. Trans. to 2nd Inf., 17 May, 1815. Maj. 6th Inf., 4 April, 1832. Lieut. Col., 6 Sept., 1837. Killed 25 Dec., 1837, in action with Indians in Florida. Bvt. Maj., 1 May, 1824, for ten years' faithful service in one grade.

THOMPSON, ARTHUR W. [Born in Ireland. Appointed from Maine.]
Priv., Corpl. and Sergt. Batty D, 1st Art., 9 Nov., 1854, to 9 Sept., 1863. Ord. Sergt., 9 Sept., 1863, to 5 May, 1865. 2nd Lieut., 16th Inf., 13 April, 1865. 1st Lieut., 13 April, 1865. Died 13 July, 1865.

THOMPSON, CHAS. B. [Born in Pa. Appointed from Pa.]
2nd Lieut. 5th Inf., 9 Jan., 1877. 1st Lieut., 14 March, 1882. R. Q. M., 14 Oct., 1885, to 30 Sept., 1889. Capt., A. Q. M., 2 Nov., 1891. Maj. Q. M. Vols., 17 Oct., 1898.

THOMPSON, EDMUND F. [Born in Mass. Appointed from Army.]
Priv. 18th Inf., 2 Nov., 1864. Sergt. Maj. 18th Inf., 1 April, 1865. 2nd Lieut. and 1st Lieut. 18th Inf., 14 Dec., 1865. Trans. to 27th Inf., 21 Sept., 1866. Capt., 5 March, 1867. Unassigned 14 June, 1869. Ass'd to 12th Inf., 15 Dec., 1870. Died 16 Dec., 1880.

**THOMPSON, EDWARD W.** [Born in Maine. Appointed from Maine.]
Capt. 5th Maine Vols., 24 June, 1861. Resigned 8 Sept., 1861. Capt., 1st Maine Batty, 18 Dec., 1861. Resigned 19 Dec., 1862. Capt. 12th Maine Vols., 4 March, 1865. 2nd Lieut. 19th Inf., 7 March, 1867. Resigned 21 April, 1868.

**THOMPSON, FRANCIS B.** [Born in England. Appointed from Ill.]
Asst. Surg. Vols., 29 March, 1848. Disbanded 25 July, 1848. Surg. 56th Ill. Vols., 27 Feb., 1862. Resigned 27 Nov., 1862.

**THOMPSON, HENRY A.*** [Born in Md. Appointed from Md.]
2nd Lieut. Corps Art., 1 July, 1819. Trans. to 4th Art., 1 June, 1821. Reg. Adj., 1 Oct., 1822, to 31 Aug., 1836. 1st Lieut., 31 Dec., 1822. Capt., 31 Aug., 1836. Resigned 15 Oct., 1836. Bvt. Capt., 31 Dec., 1832, for ten years' faithful service in one grade. Died 12 March, 1880.

**THOMPSON, JAMES K.*** [Born in Iowa. Appointed from Iowa.]
2nd Lieut. 23rd Inf., 15 June, 1884. 1st Lieut., 27 April, 1891. Capt. of Inf., 28 Sept., 1898. Ass'd to 15th Inf., 1 Jan., 1899. Capt. A. A. G. Vols., 12 March, 1898, to 3 March, 1899.

**THOMPSON, J. MILTON.** [Born in N. H. Appointed from N. H.]
Priv. Co. E, 7th N. H. Vols., 7 Nov., 1861. 1st Lieut. 33rd U. S. Col. Troops, 27 Jan., 1863. Capt., 7 Nov., 1863. Mustered out 31 Jan., 1866. 2nd Lieut. 38th Inf., 28 July, 1866. Bvt. 1st Lieut., 2 March, 1867, for gallant and meritorious service at James Island, S. C. 1st Lieut. 38th Inf., 4 Nov., 1867. Trans. to 24th Inf., 11 Nov., 1869. Capt., 23 Dec., 1878. Maj., 26 April, 1898. Lieut. Col. 14th Inf., 19 Oct., 1899. Col. 42nd U. S. Vols., 17 Aug., 1899.

**THOMPSON, JAMES.** [Born in N. Y. Appointed from Army.]
Priv., Corpl., Sergt. and 1st Sergt., Batty G, 4th Art., 29 June, 1853, to 29 Oct., 1862. 2nd Lieut. 4th Art., 22 Oct., 1862. 1st Lieut., 29 May, 1864. Trans. to 37th Inf., 25 Feb., 1867. Capt., 25 Feb., 1867. Unassigned 19 May, 1869. Ass'd to 23rd Inf., 1 Jan., 1871. Resigned 1 Sept., 1873. Bvt. 1st Lieut., 30 Jan., 1863, for gallant and meritorious service at the Siege of Suffolk, Va. Bvt. Capt., 13 March, 1865, for gallant and meritorions service during the war.

**THOMPSON, JAMES.*** [Born in N. Y. Appointed from N. Y.]
Bvt. 2nd Lieut. 2nd Art., 1 July, 1851. 2nd Lieut., 1 July, 1852. 1st Lieut., 16 Aug., 1854. Capt., 14 June, 1861. Bvt. Maj., 30 June, 1862, for gallant and meritorious service in the Battle of Glendale, Va. Bvt Lieut. Col., 13 March, 1865, for gallant and meritorious service in the Battle of Chickamauga, Ga. Retired 6 May, 1869. Died 14 Feb., 1880.

**THOMPSON, JAMES L.** [Born in Mich. Appointed from Mich.]
2nd Lieut. 10th Inf., 27 June, 1856. Resigned 7 Aug., 1859.

**THOMPSON, JAMES L.*** [Born in Tenn. Appointed from Tenn.]
Bvt. 2nd Lieut. 5th Inf., 1 July, 1828. 2nd Lieut., 1 July, 1828. 1st Lieut., 31 Oct., 1836. Capt., 1 March, 1840. Resigned 18 May, 1846. Drowned 21 June, 1851.

**THOMPSON, JAMES S.*** [Born in Md. Appointed from Md.]
(Changed name to H. St. James Linden—which see.)

**THOMPSON, JAMES W.** [Born in N. H. Appointed from Maine.]
Capt of Inf., 23 Feb., 1847; 9th Inf., 9 April, 1847. Died 25 Sept., 1847.

**THOMPSON, JOHN A.** [Born in Ohio. Appointed from Va.]
2nd Lieut. 1st Drag., 25 June, 1855. Trans. to 1st Cav., 29 Aug., 1855. 1st Lieut., 31 Jan., 1861. Capt., 14 May, 1861; 4th Cav., 3 Aug., 1861.. Maj. 7th Cav., 25 Aug., 1867. Murdered 14 Nov., 1867, by desperadoes in Texas. Bvt. Maj., 26 June, 1863, for gallant and meritorious service at the Battle of Hoover's Gap, Tenn.

**THOMPSON, JOHN A.** [Born in Mass. Appointed from Mo.]
Capt. 18th Inf., 26 Oct., 1861. Died 30 June, 1863, of wounds received in action at Hoover's Gap, Tenn.

**THOMPSON, JOHN C.*** [Born in Md. Appointed from Md.]
2nd Lieut. 3rd Cav., 18 June, 1866. 1st Lieut., 28 July, 1868. R. Q. M., 1 Dec., 1868, to 1 Oct., 1874. Reg. Adj., 1 March, 1879, to 10 Aug., 1879. Capt., 10 Aug., 1879. Died 31 Aug., 1889.

**THOMPSON, JOHN P.** [Born in N. H. Appointed from N. H.]
Priv. Co. I, 1st R. I. Cav., 28 Oct., 1861. Priv. 1st R. I. Vet. Vols., 2 Jan., 1864. 2nd Lieut. 1st N. H. Cav., 23 April, 1864. Mustered out 15 July, 1865. 2nd Lieut. 3rd Inf., 23 Feb., 1866. 1st Lieut., 24 July, 1867. Capt., 20 April, 1886. Retired for disability, 18 May, 1893.

**THOMPSON, JOHN T.*** [Born in Ky. Appointed from Ky.]
2nd Lieut. 2nd Art., 13 June, 1882. 1st Lieut., 20 Jan., 1889. Trans. to Ord., 15 Dec., 1890. Capt. (fourteen years' service), 15 June, 1898. Graduate of the Artillery School, 1890. Lieut. Col. Chf. Ord. Off. Vols., 18 July, 1898, to 12 May, 1899.

**THOMPSON, JOHN W.** [Born in Md. Appointed from Md.]
2nd Lieut. 14th Inf., 12 March, 1812. 1st Lieut., 26 June, 1813. Disbanded 15 June, 1815. Retained as 2nd Lieut. Ord., 17 May, 1815. 1st Lieut., 21 May, 1817. Trans. to 2nd Art., 1 June, 1821. Resigned 1 Jan., 1825. Retained — May, 1815 (in reorganization under act of that year), as 2nd Lieut. Ord., with Bvt. of 1st Lieut. from 26 June, 1813.

**THOMPSON, LEWIS.** [Born in Pa. Appointed from Maine.]
2nd Lieut. 2nd Cav., 19 Feb., 1862. 1st Lieut., 28 Oct., 1862. Capt., 28 July, 1866. Died 19 July, 1876. Bvt. Capt., 21 June, 1863, for gallant and meritorious service in action at Upperville, Va. Bvt. Maj., 25 Sept., 1865, for meritorious service during the war.

**THOMPSON, OSCEOLA A.** [Born in Maine. Appointed from R. I.]
Sergt. Co. E, 3rd R. I. Art., 21 Aug., 1861. 2nd Lieut., 8 July, 1862. 1st Lieut., 21 Jan., 1863. Capt., 26 April, 1864. Mustered out 5 Oct., 1864. 2nd Lieut. 13th Inf., 17 March, 1866. 1st Lieut., 4 March, 1867. Died 8 Jan., 1873.

THOMPSON, PHILIP R.* [Born in Ga. Appointed from Ga.]
Bvt. 2nd Lieut. 1st Drag., 1 July, 1835. 2nd Lieut., 26 May, 1836. 1st Lieut., 30 June, 1837. Reg. Adj., 1 Jan., 1839, to 1 Dec., 1841. Capt., 30 June, 1846. Dismissed 4 Sept., 1855. Bvt. Maj., 28 Feb., 1847, for gallant and meritorious conduct at the Battle of Sacramento, Mex.

THOMPSON, RICHARD E.* [Born in Maine. Appointed from R. I.]
2nd Lieut. 6th Inf., 15 June, 1868. 1st Lieut., 30 March, 1880. Reg. Adj., 30 March, 1880, to 10 April,, 1882. Capt. Sig. Corps, 20 Dec., 1890. Maj., 1 Dec., 1899. Maj. Chf. Sig. Off. Vols., 20 May, 1898. Lieut. Col. Chf. Sig. Off. Vols., 18 July, 1898, to 17 April, 1899. Maj. Sig. Off. Vols., 17 April, 1899, to 1 Dec., 1899.

THOMPSON, SAM'L K. [Born in Ohio. Appointed from Kan.]
Priv. Co. F, 5th Kan. Cav., 12 July, 1861, to 26 Aug., 1863. 2nd Lieut. 54th U. S. Col. Inf., 27 Aug., 1863. 1st Lieut., 15 Nov., 1864. Bvt. Capt. and Maj. Vols., 13 March, 1865, for faithful and meritorious service during the war. Mustered out 27 Aug., 1866. 2nd Lieut. 39th Inf., 16 Oct., 1867. Trans. to 25th Inf., 20 April, 1869. Cashiered 10 Aug., 1874. 2nd Lieut. 25th Inf., 19 May, 1876. Dismissed 4 June, 1877. Died 7 July, 1880.

THOMPSON, THOS. W. [Born in S. C. Appointed from S. C.]
2nd Lieut. 2nd Inf., 12 Nov., 1838. Trans. to 2nd Drag., 14 Dec., 1838. Resigned 30 April, 1839.

THOMPSON, W. BEVERHOUT.* [Born in N. Y. Appointed from N. Y.]
Bvt. 2nd Lieut. 5th Inf., 1 July, 1824. 2nd Lieut., 1 July, 1824. 1st Lieut., 30 Sept., 1828. Resigned 31 Dec., 1830. Died in 1867.

THOMPSON, WM. [Born in Md. Appointed from Army.]
Sergt. 14th Inf., 10 May, 1812, to March, 1813. Ensign 14th Inf., 13 March, 1813. 3rd Lieut., 12 May, 1813. 2nd Lieut., 5 Aug., 1814. Discharged 15 June, 1815. 2nd Lieut. Rifles, 27 Oct., 1820. Disbanded 1 June, 1821. Died 8 Aug., 1844.

THOMPSON, WM. [Born in Pa. Appointed from Iowa.]
Capt. 1st Iowa Cav., 31 July, 1861. Maj., 18 May, 1863. Col., 20 June, 1864. Bvt. Brig. Gen., 13 March, 1865, for gallant and meritorious service. Mustered out 15 March, 1866. Capt. 7th Cav., 28 July, 1866. Bvt. Maj., 2 March, 1867, for gallant and meritorious service in action at Prairie Grove. Bvt. Lieut. Col., 2 March, 1867, for gallant and meritorious service in action at Bayou Metoe, Ark. Retired 15 Dec., 1875. Died 7 Oct., 1897.

THOMPSON, WM. A. [Born in Md. Appointed from Md.]
Priv. Co. G, 1st Md. Vols., 18 Aug., 1862. Q. M. S. 1st Md. Vols., 6 Dec., 1864. Discharged 3 June, 1865. 2nd Lieut. 4th Cav., 18 June, 1867. 1st Lieut., 31 July, 1869. Reg. Adj., 1 Sept., 1877, to 1 March, 1878. Capt., 23 July, 1879. Maj. 2nd Cav., 19 June, 1897. Retired for over thirty years' service, 7 Nov., 1898. Bvt. Capt., 27 Feb., 1890, for gallant services in actions against Indians in the canon near Red River, Tex., 27 and 28 Sept., 1874, and at Las Lagunas Quatro, Tex., 5 Nov., 1874.

THOMSON, WM. [Born in Pa. Appointed from Pa.]
Asst. Surg., 5 Aug., 1861. Resigned 28 Feb., 1866. Bvt. Capt. and Maj., 13 March, 1865, for faithful and meritorious service during the war.

THORINGTON, MONROE P.* [Born in Iowa. Appointed from Iowa.]
2nd Lieut. 5th Inf., 15 June, 1877. Died 10 Sept., 1878.

THORN, HERMANN. [Born in N. Y. Appointed from N. Y.]
2nd Lieut. 2nd Inf., 15 Oct., 1846. Trans. to 3rd Drag., 9 April, 1847. 1st Lieut., 16 July, 1847. Disbanded 31 July, 1848, and reverted to his appointment in 2nd Inf. 1st Lieut. 2nd Inf., 1 Jan., 1849. Drowned 16 Oct., 1849. Bvt. 1st Lieut., 20 Aug., 1847, for gallant and meritorious conduct at the Battles of Contreras and Churubusco, and Capt., 8 Sept., 1847, for gallant and meritorious conduct in the Battle of Molino del Rey, Mex.

THORNBURG, THOS. T.* [Born in Tenn. Appointed from Tenn.]
Priv. Co. A and Sergt. Maj. 6th Tenn. Vols., 20 April, 1862, to 1 Sept., 1863. Cadet Mil. Acad., 1 Sept., 1863. 2nd Lieut. 2nd Art., 17 June, 1867. 1st Lieut., 21 April, 1870. Maj. P. M., 26 April, 1875. Trans. to 4th Inf., 23 May, 1878. Killed 29 Sept., 1879, in action with Indians in Colo.

THORNE, GEORGE E. [Born in Ind. Appointed from Ind.]
2nd Lieut. 22nd Inf., 9 Sept., 1898.

THORNE, PLATT M. [Born in N. Y. Appointed from N. Y.]
Capt. 150th N. Y. Vols., 10 Oct., 1862. Lieut. Col. A. D. C., 26 May to 1 Aug., 1865. Bvt. Maj. Vols., 13 March, 1865, for faithful and meritorious service during the war, and Lieut. Col., 13 March, 1865, for faithful and meritorious service. Mustered out 8 June, 1865. 2nd Lieut. 13th Inf., 23 Feb., 1866, and 1st Lieut., 5 April, 1866. Trans. to 31st Inf., 21 Sept., 1866. Trans. to 22nd Inf., 15 May, 1869. Reg. Q. M., 1 July, 1872, to 4 March, 1879. Capt., 4 March, 1879. Retired for disability, 17 March, 1896. Died 16 March, 1897.

THORNTON, ARTHUR W. [Born in N. Y. Appointed from N. Y.]
Ensign Rifles, 3 May, 1808. 2nd Lieut., 1 July, 1809. Trans. to Light Art., 1 March, 1811. 1st Lieut., 1 March, 1811. Capt., 20 Jan., 1813. Resigned 1 Jan., 1817. 2nd Lieut. 4th Inf., 30 Nov., 1819. 1st Lieut., 25 April, 1823. Capt., 28 Nov., 1835. Died 2 Nov., 1836. Bvt. Capt., 25 April, 1833, for ten years' faithful service in one grade.

THORNTON, JOHN R. [Born in Pa. Appointed from Ohio.]
2nd Lieut. Corps Art., 13 Aug., 1819. Resigned 15 June, 1820.

THORNTON, SETH B. [Born in Va. Appointed from Ala.]
2nd Lieut. 2nd Drag., 8 Jan., 1836. 1st Lieut., 16 Nov., 1837. Capt., 1 Feb., 1841. Killed in a skirmish in Mex., 18 Aug., 1847.

THORNTON, WM. A.* [Born in N. Y. Appointed from N. Y.]
Bvt. 2nd Lieut. 1st Art., 1 July, 1825. 2nd Lieut. 4th Art., 1 July, 1825. 1st Lieut., 31 Jan., 1835. Capt. Ord., 7 July, 1838. Maj., 28 May, 1861. Lieut. Col., 3

March, 1863. Col., 15 Sept., 1863. Died 6 April, 1866. Bvt. Maj., 30 May, 1848, for meritorious conduct. Bvt. Brig. Gen., 13 March, 1865, for faithful and meritorious service in the Ord. Dept.

THORP, FRANK. [Born in Maine. Appointed from Maine.]
2nd Lieut. 28th Maine Vol., 14 Oct., 1862. Mustered out 31 Aug., 1863. 2nd Lieut. 1st Maine Light Art., 30 Dec., 1863. Mustered out 21 June, 1865. 2nd Lieut. 5th Art., 11 May, 1866. 1st Lieut., 6 June, 1867. R. Q. M., 22 Nov., 1876, to 15 April, 1887. Capt., 24 April, 1891. Graduate of the Artillery School, 1875.

THORP, WESLEY C. [Born in Ohio. Appointed from Ohio.]
Capt. 13th Inf., 14 May, 1861. Trans. to 22nd Inf., 21 Sept., 1866. Resigned 9 July, 1867.

THRELKELD, HANSFORD L.* [Born in Ky. Appointed from Ky.]
2nd Lieut. 13th Inf., 11 June, 1892. 1st Lieut., 26 April, 1898.

THROCKMORTON, CHAS. B. [Born in Va. Appointed from Md.]
2nd Lieut. 4th Art., 16 March, 1861. 1st Lieut., 14 May, 1861. Capt., 18 July, 1864. Bvt. Maj., 13 March, 1865, for gallant and meritorious conduct during the war. Maj. 2nd Art., 1 Dec., 1883. Retired for over thirty years' service, 8 March, 1894.

THRUSTON, CHAS. M.* [Born in Ky. Appointed from D. C.]
2nd Lieut. Corps Art., 21 July, 1814. 1st Lieut., 20 April, 1818. Trans. to 3rd Art., 1 June, 1821. Reg. Adj., 1 June, 1821, to 17 Feb., 1827. Capt., 17 Feb., 1827. Resigned 31 Aug., 1836. Brig. Gen. Vols., 7 Sept., 1861. Resigned 17 April, 1862. Died 18 Feb., 1873.

THRUSTON, WM. S. [Born in Conn. Appointed from Md.]
Capt. 18th Inf., 14 May, 1861. Resigned 12 Aug., 1863. Drowned 10 June, 1864.

THURSTON, GEORGE A. [Born in N. Y. Appointed from Nev.]
1st Lieut. 1st Nev. Vols., 10 April, 1864. Capt., 28 June, 1864. Mustered out 15 Dec., 1865. 2nd Lieut. 4th Cav., 7 March, 1867. 1st Lieut., 15 Feb., 1868. Trans. to 3rd Art., 13 Jan., 1874. Capt., 10 Dec., 1889. Died 13 July, 1892.

THURSTON, JOHN. [Born in N. H. Appointed from N. H.]
Asst. Surg., 23 Dec., 1824. Resigned 1 May, 1833. Died 10 Dec., 1835.

THURSTON, WALTER A.* [Born in Ala. Appointed from Ala.]
2nd Lieut. 16th Inf., 13 June, 1879. 1st Lieut., 26 Nov., 1884. Capt., 26 April, 1898. Lieut. Col. 2nd Ala. Vols., 27 May to 31 Oct., 1898.

THYNG, GEORGE P. [Born in N. H. Appointed from N. H.]
2nd Lieut. 1st N. H. Art., 17 Sept., 1863. 1st Lieut., 9 Feb., 1864. Capt., 18 Oct., 1864. Mustered out 11 Sept., 1865. 2nd Lieut. 1st Art., 23 Feb., 1866. 1st Lieut., 1 May, 1866. Trans. to 9th Inf., 3 April, 1869. Unassigned 14 June, 1869. Discharged 10 Sept., 1870.

TIBBATTS, JOHN W. [Born in Ky. Appointed from Ky.]
Col. of Inf., 3 March, 1847; 16th Inf., 9 April, 1847. Disbanded 10 Aug., 1848. Died 5 July, 1852.

TIBBATTS, JOHN W. [Born in Ky. Appointed from Ky.]
1st Lieut. 13th Inf., 14 May, 1861. Resigned 15 April, 1863.

TIBBATTS, STEPHEN T.* [Born in Ky. Appointed from Ky.]
Bvt. 2nd Lieut. 2nd Inf., 1 July, 1835. Trans. to 4th Inf., 1 Jan., 1836. 2nd Lieut., 7 Aug., 1836. 1st Lieut., 1 Nov., 1838. Died 29 Dec., 1838.

TIDBALL, JOHN C.* [Born in Va. Appointed from Ohio.]
Bvt. 2nd Lieut. 3rd Art., 1 July, 1848. 2nd Lieut. 2nd Art., 14 Feb., 1849. 1st Lieut., 31 March, 1853. Capt., 14 May, 1861. Capt. 12th Inf., 14 May, 1861, declined. Bvt Maj., 27 June, 1862, for gallant and meritorious service in the Battle of Gaines' Mills, Va. Bvt. Lieut. Col., 17 Sept., 1862, for gallant and meritorious service in the Battle of Antietam, Md. Col. 4th N. Y. Art., 28 Aug., 1863. Bvt. Brig. Gen. Vols., 1 Aug., 1864, for gallant and distinguished service in the Battles of tthe Potomac, Spottsylvania C. H., and during the operations in front of Petersburg, Va. Bvt. Col., 13 March, 1865, for gallant and meritorious service during the rebel attack on Fort Steedman, Va. Bvt. Brig. Gen., 13 March, 1865, for gallant and meritorious service in the field during the war. Bvt. Maj. Gen., 2 April, 1865, for gallant and meritorious service at Forts Steedman and Sedgwick, Va. Mustered out of Vol. Service, 26 Sept., 1865. Maj. 2nd Art., 5 Feb., 1867. Lieut. Col. 3rd Art., 30 June, 1882. Trans. to 1st Art., 10 Nov., 1882. Trans. to 3rd Art., 25 Jan., 1884. Col. A de C. to Gen. Sherman, 1 Jan., 1881, to 8 Feb., 1884. Col. 1st Art., 22 March, 1885. Retired by operation of law, 25 Jan., 1889.

TIDBALL, JOSEPH L.* [Born in Pa. Appointed from Ohio.]
Bvt. 2nd Lieut. 4th Inf., 1 July, 1849. 2nd Lieut. 6th Inf., 31 March, 1850. 1st Lieut., 10th Inf., 3 March, 1855. Capt., 25 Aug., 1855. Retired 1 Nov., 1861.

TIERNON, JOHN L. [Born in Ind. Appointed from Mo.]
2nd Lieut. 3rd Art., 19 Feb., 1862. 1st Lieut., 20 Jan., 1864. Capt., 2 July, 1877. Maj. 1st Art., 1 Sept., 1896. Graduate of the Artillery School, 1869.

TIFFANY, GEORGE S. [Born in N. Y. Appointed from D. C.]
2nd Lieut. 12th Inf., 10 April, 1899.

TIFFANY, HARRY. [Born in Md. Appointed from Army.]
Priv. Co. B. 4th Cav., 9 Aug., 1869. Corpl., 24 Dec., 1871. Sergt., 1 Feb., 1872. Sergt. Maj., 20 Feb., 1872. Discharged 9 Aug., 1874. Priv. Co. H, 3rd Inf., 1 Jan., 1875. Corpl., 16 March, 1875. 2nd Lieut. 11th Inf., 15 Aug., 1876. Dropped 11 Feb., 1879.

TIFFANY, WM. H. [Born in D. C Appointed from Mon. Ter.]
Eng. Cadet at U. S. N., 1 Oct., 1871, to 24 Oct., 1872. 2nd Lieut. 10th Cav., 10 March, 1875. Resigned 27 Jan., 1876.

TILDEN, BRYANT P., Jr.* [Born in Mass. Appointed from Mass.]
2nd Lieut. 2nd Inf., 1 July, 1840. 1st Lieut., 16 Feb., 1847. Resigned 6 June, 1848. Died 27 Dec., 1849.

TILDEN, HARVEY. [Born in Ohio. Appointed from Ohio.]
Capt. 16th Inf., 14 May, 1861. Dropped 15 Feb., 1862.

TILDEN, THOS. B. [Born in ——. Appointed from Md.]
2nd Lieut. Corps Art., 28 Jan., 1820. Disbanded 1 June, 1821.

TILFORD, JAMES D. [Born in N. Dakota. Appointed from N. Y.]
Priv. Troop C, N. Y. Vol. Cav., 23 July to 25 Nov., 1898. 2nd Lieut. 1st Cav., 10 April, 1899.

TILFORD, JOSEPH G.* [Born in Ky. Appointed from Ky.]
Bvt. 2nd Lieut. Mounted Rifles, 1 July, 1851. 2nd Lieut., 27 Jan., 1853. 1st Lieut., 14 June, 1858. Capt., 31 July, 1861. 3rd Cav., 3 Aug., 1861. Bvt. Maj., 21 Feb., 1862, for gallant and meritorious service in the Battle of Val Verde, N. Mex. Bvt. Lieut. Col., 13 March, 1865, for faithful and meritorious service during the war. Maj. 7th Cav., 14 Nov., 1867. Lieut. Col., 22 Sept., 1883. Col. 9th Cav., 11 April, 1889. Retired after forty years' service, 1 July, 1891.

TILGHMAN, LLOYD.* [Born in Md. Appointed from Md.]
Bvt. 2nd Lieut. 1st Drag., 1 July, 1836. 2nd Lieut., 4 July, 1836. Resigned 30 Sept., 1836 Capt. Md. and D. C. Art., 14 Aug., 1847. Mustered out 13 July, 1848. Killed 16 May, 1863, while in Confederate service.

TILGHMAN, RICHD. C.* [Born in Md. Appointed from Md.]
Bvt. 2nd Lieut. 1st Art., 1 July, 1828. 2nd Lieut., 1 July, 1828. 1st Lieut., 23 Oct., 1834. Reg. Adj., 1 June to 3 Nov., 1835. Resigned 31 March, 1836. Died 14 March, 1879.

TILGHMAN, TENCH.* [Born in Md. Appointed from Md.]
Bvt. 2nd Lieut. 4th Art., 1 July, 1832. Resigned 30 Nov., 1833. Died 22 Dec., 1874.

TILLINGHAST, NICHOLAS.* [Born in Mass. Appointed from Mass.]
2nd Lieut. 7th Inf., 1 July, 1824. 1st Lieut., 30 June, 1830. Capt., 1 June, 1835. Resigned 31 July, 1836. Died 9 April, 1856.

TILLINGHAST, OTIS H.* [Born in N. Y. Appointed from N. Y.]
Bvt. 2nd Lieut. 3rd Art., 1 July, 1847. 2nd Lieut. 1st Art., 20 Aug., 1847. 1st Lieut., 22 Feb., 1851. R. Q. M., 18 June, 1856, to 5 June, 1860. Capt. Asst. Q. M., 13 May, 1861. Died 23 July, 1861, of wounds received in the Battle of Bull Run, Va.

TILLMAN, BENJAMIN J. [Born in S. C. Appointed from S. C.]
2nd Lieut. 7th Inf., 9 July, 1898. 1st Lieut., 2 March, 1899.

TILLMAN, SAML. E.* [Born in Tenn. Appointed at Large.]
2nd Lieut. 4th Art., 15 June, 1869. Trans. to Eng., 10 June, 1872. 1st Lieut., 10 June, 1872. Prof. Mil. Acad., 21 Dec., 1880.

TILLOTSON, EPHRAIM. [Born in N. Y. Appointed from Tenn.]
Priv., Corpl. and Sergt. Batty G, 3rd N. Y. Art., 23 March, 1864, to 12 June, 1865. 2nd Lieut. 122nd U. S. Col. Inf., 10 Aug., 1865. Mustered out 8 Feb., 1866. 2nd Lieut. 27th Inf., 6 May, 1867. 1st Lieut., 11 Nov., 1868. Unassigned 14 June, 1869. Discharged 31 Dec., 1870.

TILLSON, JOHN. [Born in Ill. Appointed from Ill.]
Capt. 10th Ill Vols., 29 April, 1861. Maj., 27 May, 1861. Mustered out 29 July, 1861. Lieut. Col. 10th Ill. Vols., 9 Sept., 1861. Col., 17 July, 1862. Bvt. Brig. Gen. Vols., 10 March, 1865. Mustered out 4 July, 1865. Capt. 19th Inf., 26 Oct., 1861. Resigned 29 Jan., 1866. Bvt. Maj. and Lieut. Col., 13 March, 1865, for gallant and meritorious service during the war.

TILLSON, JOHN C. F.* [Born in N. Y. Appointed from N. Y.]
Addl. 2nd Lieut. 5th Inf., 14 June, 1878. 2nd Lieut., 21 June, 1878. 1st Lieut., 24 March, 1883. Reg. Adj., 29 Oct., 1889 to ——. Capt., 14th Inf., 18 March, 1897.

TILTON, HENRY R. [Born in N. J. Appointed from N. J.]
1st Lieut. Asst. Surg., 26 Aug., 1861. Bvt. Capt. and Maj., 13 March, 1865, for faithful and meritorious service during the war. Capt. Asst. Surg., 28 July, 1866. Maj. and Surg., 26 June, 1876. Lieut. Col. Dep. Surg. Gen., 12 Aug., 1893. Medal of Honor for distinguished gallantry in action against Indians at Bear Paw Mountain, Mont., 30 Sept., 1877, where he fearlessly exposed his life and displayed great gallantry in rescuing and protecting the wounded men; while serving as Maj. and Surg.

TILTON, JAMES. [Born in Del. Appointed from Ind.]
1st Lieut. of Inf., 5 March, 1847; Voltigeurs, 9 April, 1847. Disbanded 3 Aug., 1848. Died 24 Nov. 1878.

TILTON, PALMER. [Born in Mass. Appointed from Mass.]
2nd Lieut 20th Inf., 15 Oct., 1875. 1st Lieut., 22 Jan., 1881. Retired for disability, 17 April, 1891.

TILTON, THOS. B. [Born in N. Y. Appointed from Ohio.]
2nd Lieut. of Inf., 22 March, 1847; 15th Inf., 9 April, 1847. Reg. Adj., 28 Oct., 1847, to 7 Aug., 1848. 1st Lieut., 6 May, 1848. Disbanded 7 Aug., 1848.

TIMBERLAKE, EDWARD J., Jr.* [Born in Tenn. Appointed from Tenn.]
Addl. 2nd Lieut. 2nd Art., 12 June, 1893. 2nd Lieut., 1 July, 1893. 1st Lieut., 2 March, 1899. Graduate of the Artillery School, 1898.

TIMONY, EDWARD McB. [Born in La. Appointed from Iowa.]
1st Lieut. 15th Inf., 14 May, 1861. Capt., 11 June, 1864. Resigned 6 April, 1865.

TINGLE, CHAS. A.* [Born in Ohio. Appointed from Ohio.]
2nd Lieut. 2nd Art., 16 June, 1875. Resigned 1 June, 1882.

TINGLEY, WM. H. [Born in Pa. Appointed from Pa.]
Asst. Surg., 24 March, 1851. Resigned 2 Dec., 1851. Died 19 July, 1865.

TIPPIN, ANDREW H. [Born in Pa. Appointed from Pa.]
2nd Lieut. of Inf., 5 March, 1847; 11th Inf., 9 April, 1847. 1st Lieut., 6 Dec., 1847. Disbanded 15 Aug., 1848. Bvt. 1st Lieut., 20 Aug., 1847, for gallant and meritorious conduct in the Battles of Contreras and Churubusco. Maj. 20th Pa. Vols., 30 April to 6 Aug., 1861. Col. 68th Pa. Vols., 1 Sept., 1862. Mustered out 9 June, 1865. Died — Feb., 1870.

TIPTON, JACOB. [Born in ——. Appointed from Tenn.]
Ensign 1st Rifles, 31 Dec., 1812. 3rd Lieut., 12 March, 1813. 2nd Lieut., 1 Jan., 1814. 1st Lieut., 7 Nov., 1814. Disbanded 15 June, 1815. Retained 17 May, 1816, (in reorganization under Act of 3 March, 1815), as 2nd Lieut. 7th Inf., with Bvt. of 1st Lieut., from 7 Nov., 1814 (date of appointment as 1st Lieut. Rifles). 1st Lieut., 5 July, 1816. Capt., 1 June, 1817. Dropped 31 Jan., 1818.

TIPTON, JOHN.* [Born in Ind. Appointed from Ind.]
2nd Lieut. 3rd Art., 1 July, 1856. 1st Lieut., 31 Dec., 1859. Died 17 May, 1861.

TIPTON, SPEAR S. [Born in Ind. Appointed from Ind.]
Capt. 1st Ind. Vols., 14 to 18 June, 1846. 1st Lieut. Mounted Rifles, 27 May, 1846. Died 20 July, 1847.

TISDALL, WM. N. [Born in Pa. Appointed from Pa.]
2nd Lieut. 1st Inf., 24 Oct., 1861. 1st Lieut., 2 July, 1863. R. Q. M., 8 May, 1865, to 13 Jan., 1869. Capt., 13 June, 1869. Unassigned 8 April, 1869. Ass'd to 1st Inf., 1 Jan., 1871. Retired by operation of law, 6 April, 1895. Died 18 Nov., 1899.

TITUS, PLATT S. [Born in N. Y. Appointed from Mich.]
2nd Lieut. of Inf., 9 March, 1847; 15th Inf., 9 April, 1847. Disbanded 6 Aug., 1848. Bvt. 1st Lieut., 13 Sept., 1847, for gallant and meritorious conduct in the Battle of Chapultepec. 1st Lieut. 10th Mich. Vols., 6 Feb., 1862. Capt., 29 April, 1863. Mustered out 1 April, 1865.

TOBEY, THOS. F. [Born in R. I. Appointed from Army.]
Sergt. Co. D, 10th R. I. Vols., 26 May, 1862. Discharged 6 Aug., 1862. Capt. 7th R. I. Vols., 4 Sept., 1862. Maj., 7 Jan., 1863. Mustered out 9 Feb., 1864. Priv. Co. F, 2nd Batt. 14th Inf., 27 Feb., 1865. Sergt., 1 March, 1865. 2nd Lieut., 14th Inf., 3 May, 1865, and 1st Lieut., 6 May, 1865. Reg. Adj., 16 Jan., 1866, to 30 Sept., 1867. Capt., 23 Nov., 1874. Retired for disability, 9 Jan., 1892.

TOBEY, WM. C. [Born in N. Y. Appointed from Pa.]
2nd Lieut. 4th Inf., 3 March, 1848. Resigned 31 July, 1848.

TODD, ALBERT.* [Born in R. I. Appointed from Kan.]
2nd Lieut. 1st Art., 15 June, 1877. 1st Lieut., 19 April, 1882. Capt. 6th Art., 8 March, 1898. R. Q. M., 1 Sept., 1899. Honor graduate of the Artillery School, 1886.

TODD, CHARLES C. [Born in Tex. Appointed from Tex.]
2nd Lieut. 3rd Inf., 9 July, 1898. 1st Lieut. 20th Inf., 2 March, 1899.

TODD, HENRY D., Jr.* [Born in N. Y. Appointed from Pa.]
Addl. 2nd Lieut., 3rd Art., 12 June, 1890. 2nd Lieut. 5th Art., 8 Jan., 1891. Trans. to 3rd Art., 23 May, 1891. 1st Lieut. 1st Art., 10 Feb., 1898. Trans. to 7th Art., 8 March, 1898.

TODD, JOHN B. S.* [Born in Ky. Appointed from Ill.]
2nd Lieut. 6th Inf., 1 July, 1837. 1st Lieut., 25 Dec., 1837. Capt., 22 Nov., 1843. Resigned 16 Sept., 1856. Brig. Gen. Vols., 19 Sept., 1861. Appointment expired, 17 July, 1862. Died 5 Jan., 1872.

TODD, JOHN H. [Born in Ky. Appointed from Ky.]
Cadet Mil. Acad., 1 Sept., 1862, to 25 July, 1864. 2nd Lieut. 18th Inf., 22 Aug., 1867. 1st Lieut., 20 March, 1879. Died 18 Nov., 1883.

TODD, JOHN W.* [Born in Ky. Appointed from Ky.]
Bvt. 2nd Lieut. Ord., 1 July, 1852. 2nd Lieut., 20 Sept., 1853. 1st Lieut., 1 July, 1855. Capt., 14 Sept., 1862. Maj., 7 March, 1867. Died 10 May, 1878.

TODD, WM. A. [Born in Pa. Appointed from Pa.]
2nd Lieut. 11th Inf., 30 Dec., 1847. Resigned 30 June, 1848. 1st Lieut. 71st Pa. Vols., 21 May, 1861. Discharged 17 Oct., 1862.

TODSON, GEORGE P. [Born in La. Appointed from La.]
Asst. Surg., 20 Jan., 1824. Dismissed 25 March, 1826.

TOFFEY, JOHN J., Jr. [Born in N. J. Appointed from N. J.]
2nd Lieut. 16th Inf. 9 July, 1898. 1st Lieut. 4th Inf., 2 March, 1899.

TOLL, ISAAC DeG. [Born in N. Y. Appointed from Mich.]
Capt. of Inf., 2 March, 1847; 15th Inf., 9 April, 1847. Resigned 4 Dec., 1847.

TOLLES, CORNELIUS W. [Born in N. J. Appointed from N. J.]
Capt. A. A. G. N. J. Militia, 3 to 31 July, 1861. 1st Lieut. 13th Inf., 14 May, 1861. Capt., 7 Oct., 1864. Lieut. Col. Q. M., 20 Aug., 1862, to 7 Nov., 1864. Died 8 Nov., 1864, of wounds received in action at Winchester, Va. Bvt. Maj., 19 Sept., 1864, for gallant and meritorious service at the Battle of Winchester, Va.

TOLMAN, THOS. M.* [Born in Maine. Appointed from Maine.]
2nd Lieut. 6th Cav., 23 June, 1865. 1st Lieut, 25 Jan., 1866. Capt., 18 Nov., 1867. Trans. to 1st Inf., 1 Jan., 1871. Died 14 Dec., 1883.

TOLSON, WM. [Born in Md. Appointed from Md.]
2nd Lieut. 3rd Inf., 12 July, 1820. Resigned 1 Dec., 1821.

TOMKINS, JAMES S. [Born in Ill. Appointed from Army.]
Priv. Co. G, 1st Batt. 12th Inf., 27 Jan., 1865. Corpl., 1 March, 1865. 2nd Lieut. and 1st Lieut. 12th Inf., 26 May, 1865. Trans. to 30th Inf., 21 Sept., 1866. Reg. Adj., 9 Feb., 1867, to 30 July, 1868. Capt., 30 July, 1868. Unassigned 23 March, 1869. Ass'd to 25th Inf., 31 Dec., 1870. Retired 20 March, 1879.

TOMPKINS, CHARLES H. [Born in Va. Appointed from N. Y.]
Cadet at Mil. Acad., 1 July, 1847, to 23 June, 1849. Priv. Co. F, 1st Drag., 21 Jan., 1856. Corpl., 17 Oct., 1856. Sergt., 1 Oct., 1859. Discharged 10 Jan., 1861. 2nd Lieut. 2nd Cav., 23 March, 1861. 1st Lieut., 30 April, 1861. 5th Cav., 3 Aug., 1861. R. Q. M., 28 Aug., 1861, to 13 Nov., 1861. Capt. A. Q. M., 13 Nov., 1861. Col. 1st Vt. Cav., 24 April, 1862. Resigned Vol. Commission, 9 Sept., 1862. Bvt. Maj., 13 March, 1865, for gallant conduct at Fairfax C. H., Va., 31 May, 1861. Bvt. Lieut. Col., 13 March, 1865, for meritorious service in the campaigns of Gens. Banks and McDowell, in 1862 and 1863. Bvt. Col., 13 March, 1865, for meritorious service in the Q. M. D. in 1863, 1864, 1865. Bvt. Brig. Gen., 13 March, 1865, for faithful and meritorious service during the war. Lieut. Col. Q. M., 1 July, 1865, to 11 June, 1866. Col. Q. M. (Act 4 July, 1864), 13 June, 1866. Lieut.

Col. Dep. Q. M. G, 29 July, 1866. Relieved as Col. Q. M. (Act 4 July, 1864), 1 Jan., 1867. Col. A. Q. M. G., 24 Jan., 1881. Retired by operation of law, 12 Sept., 1894. Medal of Honor for distinguished gallantry in action at Fairfax, C. H., Va., June, 1 1861; while serving as 1st Lieut. 2nd U. S. Cav.

TOMPKINS, CHRISTOPHER Q.* [Born in Va. Appointed from Va.]
Bvt. 2nd Lieut. 3rd Art., 1 July, 1836. 2nd Lieut., 31 Aug., 1836. 1st Lieut., 7 July, 1838. Capt., 18 June, 1846. Resigned 22 Sept., 1847. Died 28 May, 1877.

TOMPKINS, DANIEL D.* [Born in N. Y. Appointed from N. Y.]
3rd Lieut. Ord., 1 July, 1820. Trans. to 2nd Art., 1 June, 1821, to rank as 2nd Lieut. from 1 July, 1820. Trans. to 1st Art., 16 Aug., 1821. 1st Lieut., 1 March, 1825. Capt., 31 Dec., 1835. Capt. A. Q. M., 7 July, 1838. Maj. Q. M., 22 July, 1842. Lieut. Col. Dep. Q. M. G., 16 Sept., 1851. Col. A. Q. M. G., 22 Dec., 1856. Died 26 Feb., 1863. Bvt. Maj., 11 Sept., 1836, for gallant and meritorious conduct in war against Florida Indians. Bvt. Lieut. Col., 30 May, 1848, for meritorious conduct in the war with Mex.

TOMPKINS, FRANK. [Born in D. C. Appointed from N. Y.]
2nd Lieut. 8th Cav., 1 Aug., 1891. Trans. to 7th Cav., 24 Oct., 1891. 1st Lieut. 2nd Cav., 13 July, 1898. Graduate of the Infantry and Cavalry School, 1897.

TOMPKINS, SELAH R. H. [Born in D. C. Appointed from Ill.]
2nd Lieut. 7th Inf., 30 Oct., 1884. Trans. to 7th Cav., 12 March, 1886. 1st Lieut., 8 April, 1892. Reg. Com., 1 July, 1899.

TOMPKINS, WM. W [Born in N. Y. Appointed from N. Y.]
2nd Lieut. 3rd Art., 24 Oct., 1861. 1st Lieut., 1 Nov., 1861. Resigned 25 April, 1870.

TOMPKINS, WM. W. [Born in N. Y. Appointed from N. Y.]
Capt. 2nd Drag., 8 June, 1836. Resigned 31 Dec., 1838. Capt. of Inf., 23 Feb., 1847; 10th Inf., 9 April, 1847. Disbanded 24 Aug., 1848. Died 7 Feb., 1882.

TONE, WM. T. W. [Born in N. Y. Appointed from N. Y.]
2nd Lieut. Light Art., 12 July, 1820. Trans. to 1st Art., 1 June, 1821. Resigned 31 Dec., 1826. Died 10 Oct., 1828.

TORBERT, ALFRED T. A.* [Born in Del. Appointed from Del.]
Bvt. 2nd Lieut. 2nd Inf., 1 July, 1855. 2nd Lieut. 5th Inf., 19 July, 1855. 1st Lieut., 25 Feb., 1861. Capt. A. Q. M., 3 Aug. to 25 Sept., 1861. Capt. 5th Inf., 25 Sept., 1861. Col. 1st N. J. Vols., 16 Sept., 1861. Brig. Gen. Vols., 25 Nov., 1862. Mustered out of Vol. Service, 15 Jan., 1866. Resigned 31 Oct., 1866. Bvt. Maj., 4 July, 1863, for gallant and meritorious service at the Battle of Gettysburg, Pa. Bvt. Lieut. Col., 28 May, 1864, for gallant and meritorious service at the Battle of Hawes' Shop, Va. Bvt. Col., 19 Sept., 1864, for gallant and meritorious service at the Battle of Winchester, Va. Bvt. Brig. Gen., 13 March, 1865, for gallant and meritorious service at the Battle of Cedar Creek, Va. Bvt. Maj. Gen., 13 March, 1865, for gallant and meritorious service in the field during the war. Drowned at sea, 29 Aug., 1880.

TORBETT, FELIX H. [Born in Tenn. Appointed from Army.]
Priv., Corpl. and Sergt. Co. H, 2nd Inf., 11 Dec., 1859, to 10 June, 1863. 2nd Lieut. 16th Inf., 19 Feb., 1863. 1st Lieut., 5 May, 1863. Capt., 19 March, 1866. Trans. to 25th Inf., 21 Sept., 1866. Trans. to 18th Inf., 26 April, 1869. Mustered out 1 Jan., 1871. Bvt. Capt. and Maj., 1 Sept., 1864, for gallant and meritorious service during the Atlanta campaign, and at the Battle of Jonesboro, Ga. Died 6 Sept., 1876.

TORBETT, HENRY W. [Born in Pa. Appointed from Pa.]
2nd Lieut. 78th Pa. Vols., 4 Oct., 1861. 1st Lieut., 30 Nov., 1862. Capt., 3 Dec., 1864. Lieut. Col., 26 March, 1865. Mustered out 11 Sept., 1865. 2nd Lieut. 29th Inf., 7 March, 1867. Trans. to 11th Inf., 25 April, 1869. Died 8 June, 1871.

TORNEY, GEORGE H. [Born in Md. Appointed from Md.]
1st Lieut. Asst. Surg., 26 June, 1875. Capt. Asst. Surg., 26 June, 1880. Maj. Surg., 6 June, 1894.

TORRENCE, ALBERT. [Born in ——. Appointed from N. C.]
Mil. Storekeeper, 1 April, 1841. Disbanded 1 Oct., 1842.

TORRENCE, SAMUEL.* [Born in Pa. Appointed from Ohio.]
Bvt. 2nd Lieut. 4th Inf., 1 July, 1828. 2nd Lieut., 1 July, 1828. Died 1 Sept., 1832.

TORREY, JOHN. [Born in N. Y. Appointed from N. Y.]
Asst. Surg., 5 Aug., 1824. Resigned 31 Aug., 1828. Died 10 March, 1873.

TORREY, ROBT. A. [Born in N. Y. Appointed from Ill.]
2nd Lieut. 13th Inf., 19 Feb., 1862. 1st Lieut., 18 June, 1862. R. Q. M., 1 March, 1865, to 19 June, 1866. Capt., 19 June, 1866. Resigned 7 May, 1882.

TORREY, WM. G.* [Born in N. Y. Appointed from N. Y.]
Bvt. 2nd Lieut. 1st Drag., 1 July, 1840. 2nd Lieut. 2nd Drag., 1 April, 1841. Dropped 16 July, 1844. Died 23 Jan., 1847.

TORREY, ZERAH W.* [Born in Mass. Appointed from Mass.]
2nd Lieut. 6th Inf., 12 June, 1880. 1st Lieut., 6 June 1886. Capt. 6th Inf., 19 Nov., 1896. R. Q. M., 1 Feb., 1890.

TOTTEN, CHAS. A. L.* [Born in Conn. Appointed from Conn.]
2nd Lieut. 4th Art., 13 June, 1873. 1st Lieut., 1 Nov., 1874. Resigned 1 Aug., 1893.

TOTTEN, EDWARD H.* [Born in D. C. Appointed at Large.]
2nd Lieut. 16th Inf., 23 June, 1865. 1st Lieut., 23 June, 1865. Trans. to 34th Inf., 21 Sept., 1866. Reg. Adj., 10 Feb., 1867, to 14 Feb., 1868. Unassigned 14 April, 1869. Ass'd to 13th Inf., 14 July, 1869. Trans. to 1st Art., 1 Jan., 1871. R. Q. M., 1 Sept., 1874, to 1 March, 1875. Reg. Adj., 1 March, 1875, to 30 July, 1877. Accidentally killed 14 June, 1878.

TOTTEN, JAMES.* [Born in Pa. Appointed from Va.]
Bvt. 2nd Lieut. 2nd Art., 1 July, 1841. 2nd Lieut., 17 Aug., 1842. 1st Lieut., 3 March, 1847. Capt., 20 Oct., 1855. Maj. A. I. G., 12 Nov., 1861. Maj. 1st Mo. Art., 19 Aug., 1861. Lieut. Col., 1 Sept., 1861. Brig. Gen. Mo. State Mil., 20 Feb., 1862, to 15 June, 1865. Lieut. Col. A. I. G., 13 June, 1867. Dismissed 22 July, 1870. Bvt. Maj., 17 June, 1861, for gallant and meritorious service in action at Booneville, Mo. Bvt. Lieut. Col., 10 Aug., 1861, for gallant and meritorious

service at the Battle of Wilson's Creek, Mo. Bvt. Col., 13 March, 1865, for gallant and meritorious service during the Siege of Mobile, Ala. Bvt. Brig. Gen., 13 March, 1865, for gallant and meritorious service in the field during the war. Died 2 Oct., 1871.

TOTTEN, JOHN R.* [Born in Fla. Appointed from Neb.]
2nd Lieut. 1st Inf., 14 June, 1878. Trans. to 4th Art., 23 June, 1879. 1st Lieut., 2 Jan., 1886. Resigned 1 April, 1891.

TOTTEN, JOSEPH G.* [Born in Conn. Appointed from Conn.]
2nd Lieut. Eng., 1 July, 1805. Resigned 31 March, 1806. 2nd Lieut. Eng., 23 Feb., 1808. 1st Lieut., 23 July, 1810. Capt., 31 July, 1812. Maj., 12 Nov., 1818. Lieut. Col., 24 May, 1828. Col. Chief Eng., 7 Dec., 1838. Brig. Gen. Chief of Eng., 3 March, 1863. Died 22 April, 1864. Bvt. Maj., 6 June, 1813, for meritorious service. Bvt. Lieut. Col., 11 Sept., 1814, for gallant conduct at the Battle of Plattsburg. Bvt. Col., 11 Sept., 1824, for ten years' faithful service in one grade. Bvt. Brig. Gen., 29 March, 1847, for gallant and meritorious conduct at the Siege of Vera Cruz. Bvt. Maj. Gen., 21 April, 1864, for long, faithful and eminent service.

TOTTEN, JOSEPH S. [Born in R. I. Appointed from D. C.]
Cadet Mil. Acad., 1 July, 1843, to 1 Sept., 1845. 2nd Lieut. 2nd Art., 8 March, 1847. 1st Lieut., 21 April, 1848. Died 10 May, 1853.

TOUEY, TIMOTHY A.* [Born in N. Y. Appointed from N. Y.]
2nd Lieut. 6th Cav., 16 June, 1875. 1st Lieut., 3 June, 1880. Died 28 Sept., 1887.

TOURTELLOTTE, JOHN E. [Born in Conn. Appointed from Minn.]
Priv. Co. H, 4th Minn. Vols., 30 Sept., 1861. Capt. 4th Minn. Vols., 13 Dec., 1861. Lieut. Col., 1 Sept., 1862. Col., 5 Oct., 1864. Bvt. Brig. Gen., 13 March, 1865, for gallant and meritorious service Mustered out of Vol. Service, 21 June, 1865. Capt. 28th Inf., 28 July, 1866. Bvt. Maj., 2 March, 1867, for gallant and meritorious service in the Siege of Vicksburg, Miss. Bvt. Lieut. Col., 2 March, 1867, for gallant and meritorious service in the Battle of Allatoona, Ga. Bvt. Col., 2 March, 1867, for gallant and meritorious service in the Battle of Bentonville, N. C. Unassigned 31 March, 1869. Ass'd tc 7th Cav., 15 Dec., 1870. Col. A. de C. to Gen. Sherman, 1 Jan., 1871, to 8 Feb., 1884. Maj., 22 Sept., 1883. Retired for disability, 20 March, 1885. Died 22 July, 1891.

TOWAR, ALBERT S. [Born in Canada. Appointed from Mich.]
Maj. P. M., 3 March, 1875. Lieut. Col. Dep. P. M. G., 1 Feb., 1899.

TOWER, ZEALOUS B.* [Born in Mass. Appointed from Mass.]
2nd Lieut. Eng., 1 July, 1841. Bvt. 1st Lieut., 18 April, 1847, for gallant and meritorious conduct in the Battle of Cerro Gordo. 1st Lieut. Eng., 24 April, 1847. Bvt. Capt., 20 Aug., 1847, for gallant and meritorious service in the Battles of Contreras and Churubusco, Mex. Bvt. Maj., 13 Sept., 1847, for gallant and meritorious service in the Battle of Chapultepec. Capt. Eng., 1 July, 1855. Maj., 6 Aug., 1861. Bvt. Lieut. Col., 22 Nov., 1861, for gallant and meritorious service during the defence of Fort Pickens, Fla. Brig. Gen. Vols., 23 Nov., 1861. Bvt. Col., 9 Aug., 1862, for gallant and meritorious service in the Battle of Cedar Mountain, Va. Bvt. Brig. Gen., 13 March, 1865, for gallant and meritorious service in the Battle of Groveton, Va. Bvt. Maj. Gen., 13 March, 1865, for gallant and meritorious service in the field during the war. Bvt. Maj. Gen. Vols., 12 June, 1865, for gallant and meritorious service during the war. Lieut. Col. Eng., 11 Nov., 1865. Mustered out of Vol. Service, 15 Jan., 1866. Col. Eng., 13 Jan., 1874. Retired, after forty years' service, 10 Jan., 1883.

TOWERS, JOHN A.* [Born in S. C. Appointed from S. C.]
2nd Lieut. 1st Art., 1 July, 1886. 1st Lieut. 2nd Art., 29 Sept., 1892. Died 23 March, 1893.

TOWLE, GEORGE F. [Born in N. H. Appointed from N. H.]
1st Lieut. 4th N. H. Vols., 18 Sept., 1861. Capt., 13 Feb., 1862. Maj., 3 Feb., 1865. Lieut. Col. A. I. G., 22 April, 1865, to 1 Aug., 1865. Mustered out 23 Aug., 1865. 2nd Lieut. and 1st Lieut. 19th Inf., 23 Feb., 1866. Trans. to 28th Inf., 21 Sept., 1866. Bvt. Capt., 2 March, 1867, for galant and meritorious service at Fort Wagner, S. C. Bvt. Maj., 2 March, 1867, for gallant and meritorious service at Russell's Mill. Bvt. Lieut. Col., 2 March, 1867, for gallant and meritorious service in the capture of Fort Fisher, N. C. Trans. to 19th Inf., 31 March, 1869. Capt., 18 March, 1878. Retired, over thirty years' service, 4 June, 1892.

TOWLER, REGINALD H. [Born in N. Y. Appointed from Oregon.]
Maj. P. M., 3 March, 1875. Died 8 Aug., 1880.

TOWN, FRANCIS L. [Born in N. H. Appointed from Pa.]
1st Lieut. Asst. Surg., 28 May, 1861. Bvt. Capt. and Maj., 13 March, 1865, for faithful and meritorious service. Bvt. Lieut. Col., 13 March, 1865, for faithful and meritorious service during the war. Capt. Asst. Surg., 28 May, 1866. Maj. Surg., 20 Oct., 1866. Lieut. Col. Surg., 10 July, 1889. Col. Asst. Surg. Gen., 28 June, 1894. Retired, over thirty years' service, 10 Oct., 1896.

TOWN, FRANKLIN E. [Born in Mass. Appointed from N. Y.]
2nd Lieut. 42nd N. Y. Vols., 22 June, 1861. 1st Lieut., 12 Nov., 1862, to 22 Jan., 1864. Capt. Sig. Corps, 3 March, 1863. Resigned 29 Nov., 1864. Capt. 4th U. S. Vet. Vols., 31 Dec., 1864. Mustered out 2 April, 1866. 2nd Lieut. 11th Inf., 7 March, 1867. Trans. to 16th Inf., 12 April, 1869. Unassigned 15 April, 1869. Ass'd to 16th Inf., 3 Aug., 1870. Discharged 19 Sept., 1870. Bvt. 1st Lieut., 7 March, 1867, for gallant and meritorious service in the Battle of Boydton Plank Road, Va.

TOWNSEND, ALFRED. [Born in Pa. Appointed from Army.]
Priv. Co. H, 9th Pa. Res., 24 May, 1861, to 9 Nov., 1862. Priv. General Service, 10 Nov., 1862. 2nd Lieut. 18th Inf., 10 Nov., 1862. 1st Lieut., 30 May, 1863. Bvt. Capt., 20 Sept., 1863, for gallant and meritorious service in the Battle of Chickamauga, Ga. Retired 1 Feb., 1865. Retired with rank of Capt., 28 July, 1866. Died 26 Sept., 1891.

TOWNSEND, CURTIS McD.* [Born in N. Y. Appointed from N. Y.]
Addl. 2nd Lieut. Eng., 13 June, 1879. 2nd Lieut., 30 June, 1879. 1st Lieut., 15 June, 1883. Capt., 5 Oct., 1889.

TOWNSEND, DAVID S. [Born in Mass. Appointed from Mass.]
1st Lieut. 9th Inf., 6 July, 1812. Capt., 13 May, 1813. Maj. A. A. G., 27 July, 1814. Disbanded 15 June, 1815. Batt. P. M., 29 April, 1816. Retained as Maj. P. M., 1 June, 1821. Died 28 Jan., 1853.

TOWNSEND, EDWARD D.* [Born in Mass. Appointed from Mass.]
2nd Lieut. 2nd Art., 1 July, 1837. Reg. Adj., 7 July, 1838, to 18 Aug., 1846. 1st Lieut., 16 Sept., 1838. Bvt. Capt. A. A. G., 8 Aug., 1846. Capt. 2nd Art., 21 April, 1848. Vacated commission of Capt. 2nd Art., 21 April, 1848. Bvt. Maj. A. A. G., 15 July, 1852. Lieut. Col. A. A. G., 7 March, 1861. Col. A. A. G., 3 Aug., 1861. Bvt. Brig. Gen., 24 Sept., 1864, for meritorious and faithful service during the war. Bvt. Maj. Gen., 13 March, 1865, for faithful, meritorious and distinguished service in the Adj. Gen.'s Dept. during the war. Brig. Gen., Adj. Gen., 22 Feb., 1869. Retired 15 June, 1880. Died 10 May, 1893.

TOWNSEND, EDWIN F.* [Born in N. Y. Appointed from Wis.]
Bvt. 2nd Lieut. 3rd Art., 1 July, 1854. 2nd Lieut., 31 Jan., 1855. Resigned 11 March, 1856. 1st Lieut. 14th Inf., 14 May, 1861. Reg. Adj., 8 July, 1861, to 27 Aug., 1861. Capt. 16th Inf., 14 May, 1861. Bvt. Maj. 7 April, 1862, for gallant and meritorious service in the Battle of Shiloh, Tenn. Bvt. Lieut. Col., 13 March, 1865, for continued and faithful service in the Ord. Dept. Trans. to 25th Inf., 21 Sept., 1866. Maj. 27th Inf., 22 June, 1868. Trans. to 9th Inf., 15 March, 1869. Lieut. Col. 11th Inf., 20 March, 1879. Col. 12th Inf., 13 Oct., 1886. Retired, at his own request, over sixty-two years of age, 1 Oct., 1895.

TOWNSEND, EUGENE H. [Born N. Y. Appointed from Army.]
Priv. Co. F, 21st Iowa Vols., 9 Sept., 1862, to 4 April, 1863. Priv., Corpl., Sergt. and 1st Sergt. Co. D, 13th Inf., 3 Feb., 1864, to 23 May, 1866. 2nd Lieut. 13th Inf., 7 April, 1866. 1st Lieut., 30 June, 1867. Resigned 1 July, 1872.

TOWNSEND, FREDERICK. [Born in N. Y. Appointed from N. Y.]
Col. 3rd N. Y. Vols., 10 May to 12 June, 1861. Maj. 18th Inf., 14 May, 1861. Lieut. Col. 9th Inf., 20 April, 1864. Resigned 26 March, 1868. Bvt. Lieut. Col., 31 Dec., 1862, for gallant and meritorious service at the Battle of Murfreesboro, Tenn. Bvt. Col., 30 March, 1865, for meritorious and faithful service in the recruitment of the armies of the United States. Bvt. Brig. Gen., 30 March, 1865, for faithful and meritorious service during the war.

TOWNSEND, GROSVENOR L. [Born in N. Y. Appointed from N. Y.]
Capt. 201st N. Y. Vols., 22 July, 1898, until 3 April, 1899. 2nd Lieut. 1st Inf., 10 April, 1899.

TOWNSEND, JOEL C.* [Born in N. H. Appointed from N. H.]
Bvt. 2nd Lieut. 3rd Art., 1 July, 1826. Died 1 Oct., 1826.

TOWNSEND, THOS. G.* [Born in D. C. Appointed at Large.]
2nd Lieut. 6th Inf., 12 June, 1871. 1st Lieut., 15 Dec., 1880. Capt., 20 April, 1891. Retired for disability, 27 Aug., 1896.

TOWNSLEY, CLARENCE P. [Born in N. Y. Appointed from Iowa.]
Addl. 2nd Lieut. 4th Art., 11 June, 1881. 2nd Lieut. 21 Oct., 1881. 1st Lieut., 16 Jan., 1888. Capt., 2 March, 1899. Graduate of the Artillery School, 1884. Maj. Chief Ord. Off. Vols., 27 July, 1898, to 12 May, 1899. R. Q. M., 19 April, 1899.

TOWSLEY, CHARLES D.* [Born in Wis. Appointed from Wis.]
2nd Lieut. 2nd Inf., 14 June, 1885. Retired for disability, 20 Feb., 1891.

TOWSON, NATHAN. [Born in Md. Appointed from Md.]
Capt. 2nd Art., 12 March, 1812. Trans. to Corps Art., 12 May, 1814. Trans. to Light Art., 17 May, 1815. P. M. G., 28 Aug., 1819. Col. 2nd Art., 1 June, 1821, which was negatived by Senate 22 May, 1822, and was reappointed Col. P. M. G., 8 May, 1822. Died 20 July, 1854. Bvt. Maj., 8 Oct., 1812, for capturing the Brig "Caledonia" under the guns of Fort Erie. Bvt. Lieut. Col., 5 July, 1814, for gallant and distinguished conduct in the Battle of Chippewa. Bvt. Lieut. Col., 15 Aug., 1814, for gallant conduct in the assault upon Fort Erie. Bvt. Brig. Gen., 30 June, 1834. Bvt. Maj. Gen., 30 May, 1848, for meritorious conduct in the war with Mexico.

TRACY, ALBERT. [Born in N. Y. Appointed from Maine.]
1st Lieut. Inf., 24 Feb., 1847. 1st Lieut. 9th Inf., 9 April, 1847. Bvt. Capt., 13 Sept., 1847, for gallant and meritorious conduct in the Battle of Chapultepec. Capt. 9th Inf., 23 Feb., 1848. Disbanded 26 Aug., 1848. Capt. 10th Inf., 3 March, 1855. Col. A. A. de C., 31 March, 1862. Maj. 15th Inf., 1 June, 1863. Discharged as Col. A. A. de C., 25 Nov., 1863. Bvt. Lieut. Col., 13 March, 1865, for meritorious service during the campaign of 1862, under Gen. Fremont, in Virginia. Bvt. Col., 13 March, 1865, for faithful and meritorious service during the war. Retired 4 Nov., 1865. Died 3 June, 1893.

TRACY, CHESTER F. [Born in N. Y. Appointed from N. Y.]
2nd Lieut. Corps Art., 4 Dec., 1819. Disbanded 1 June, 1821.

TRACY, FREDERICK A. [Born in N. Y. Appointed from N. Y.]
2nd Lieut. 12th Inf., 24 Oct., 1861. 1st Lieut., 21 July, 1862. Died 3 June, 1863.

TRACY, GEORGE H. [Born in Mass. Appointed from Conn.]
1st Lieut. 15th Inf., 14 May, 1861. Capt., 11 Aug., 1864. Died 17 Sept., 1867. Bvt. Maj., 13 Dec., 1864, for gallant and meritorious service during the Atlanta and Savannah campaigns.

TRACY, JOSEPH P.* [Born in D. C. Appointed from Pa.]
Addl. 2nd Lieut. 1st Art., 12 June, 1896. 2nd Lieut. 5th Art., 30 April, 1897. 1st Lieut., 2 March, 1899.

TRACY, THOS. G. [Born in Mass. Appointed from Cal.]
Cadet at Mil. Acad., 1 July, 1862, to 19 Feb., 1864. Priv. Co. F, 165th N. Y. Vols., 7 April, 1864. 1st Lieut., 25 Nov., 1864. Mustered out 1 Sept., 1865. 2nd Lieut. 9th Inf., 7 March, 1867. Mustered out 28 Dec., 1870.

TRAPIER, JAMES H.* [Born in S. C. Appointed from S. C.]
2nd Lieut. 1st Art., 1 July, 1838. 2nd Lieut. Eng., 7 July, 1838. 1st Lieut., 1 July, 1839. Resigned 28 Feb., 1848. Died 2 Jan., 1866.

TRASK, IRA W. [Born in Maine. Appointed from Ill.]
2nd Lieut. 9th Cav., 18 June, 1867. 1st Lieut., 1 Jan., 1868. Discharged 31 Dec.,

1870. Bvt. 1st Lieut., 18 June, 1867, for gallantry at the Battle of Mechanicsville, Va., 9 June, 1862. Bvt. Capt., 18 June, 1867, for gallantry at the Battle of Gettysburg, Pa.

TRASK, THOS. S. [Born in Mo. Appointed from Ohio.]
2nd Lieut. 15th Inf., 29 March, 1848. Disbanded 4 Aug., 1848.

TRASK, THOS. S.* [Born in Vt. Appointed from Vt.]
Bvt. 2nd Lieut. Inf., 1 July, 1827. 2nd Lieut. 2nd Inf., 1 July, 1827. Died 1 Aug., 1828.

TRAUB, PETER E.* [Born in N. Y. Appointed from N. Y.]
2nd Lieut. 1st Cav., 1 July, 1886. 1st Lieut. 5th Cav., 12 Dec., 1892. Trans. to 1st Cav., 27 Dec., 1892.

TRAVIS, CHAS. E. [Born in Ala. Appointed from Texas.]
Capt. 2nd Cav., 3 March, 1855. Dismissed 1 May, 1856. Died in 1860.

TRAVIS, JOHN N. [Born in Ohio. Appointed from Ohio.]
Priv. and Corpl. Co. A, 8th Ohio Vols., 26 April, 1861, to 7 Nov., 1862. 2nd Lieut. 8th Ohio Vols., 7 Nov., 1862. Mustered out 13 July, 1864. 2nd Lieut. 2nd U. S. Vet. Vols., 20 Feb., 1865. 1st Lieut., 26 Sept., 1865. Mustered out 16 March, 1866. 2nd Lieut. 14th Inf., 22 Jan., 1867. Resigned 11 Aug., 1868. Bvt. 1st Lieut., 2 March, 1867, for gallant and meritorious service at the Battle of Gettysburg, Pa.

TRAVIS, PIERCE M. B.* [Born in Ala. Appointed from Mo.]
2nd Lieut. 11th Inf., 12 June, 1880. 1st Lieut., 24 Aug., 1886. Reg. Adj., 1891, to 1895. Capt., 30 April, 1897.

TREACY, EDWARD. [Born in Ireland. Appointed from Army.]
Priv., Corpl. and Sergt. Co. F, Mounted Rifles, 16 Sept., 1851, to 16 June, 1855. 2nd Lieut. Mounted Rifles, 23 May, 1855. 1st Lieut., 10 May, 1861; 3rd Cav., 3 Aug., 1861. Capt., 5 Nov., 1861. Died 15 Feb., 1864.

TREADWELL, THOS. J.* [Born in N. H. Appointed from N. H.]
Bvt. 2nd Lieut. Ord., 1 July, 1854. 2nd Lieut., 17 Nov., 1856. 1st Lieut., 1 July, 1860. Capt., 3 March, 1863. Bvt. Maj. and Lieut. Col., 13 March, 1865, for faithful and meritorious service during the war. Maj. Ord., 7 March, 1867. Lieut. Col., 27 May, 1878. Died 2 Aug., 1879.

TREADWELL, WM. [Born in ——. Appointed from Fla.]
Asst. Surg., 25 Aug., 1847. Died 24 Oct., 1847.

TREAT, CHARLES G.* [Born in Maine. Appointed from Wis.]
2nd Lieut. 5th Art., 13 June, 1882. 1st Lieut., 15 April, 1889. Capt. 7th Art., 2 March, 1899. Graduate of the Artillery School, 1888. Reg. Adj., 16 May, 1899. Capt. A. A. G. Vols., 12 May, 1898. Maj. A. A. G. Vols., 10 Jan. to 12 May, 1899.

TREE, ARTHUR D. [Born in Pa. Appointed from Pa.]
Priv., Corpl. and Sergt. Co. F, 1st Drag., 3 Aug., 1835, to 3 Aug., 1838. Priv. and Sergt. 1st Drag., 30 Dec., 1841, to 3 Nov., 1842, and Sergt. Maj. 2nd Drag., 3 Nov., 1842, to 30 Dec., 1846. 2nd Lieut. 2nd Drag., 20 May, 1847. R. Q. M., 12 July to 1 Nov., 1847. 1st Lieut., 11 Oct., 1851. Reg. Adj., 20 June to 23 Sept., 1849. R. Q. M., 23 Sept., 1849, to 9 Sept., 1853. Died 2 Feb., 1857. Bvt. 1st Lieut., 20 Aug., 1847, for gallant and meritorious conduct at Contreras and Churubusco, Mex.

TREMAINE, WM. S. [Born in Prince Edward's Island. Appointed from N. Y.]
Asst. Surg. 24th Mass. Vols., 7 Aug., 1863. Mustered out 12 April, 1864. Maj. Surg. 31st U. S. Col. Troops, 2 May, 1864. Resigned 9 Sept., 1864. Asst. Surg. Vols., 1 Sept., 1864. Mustered out 4 June, 1866. 1st Lieut. Asst. Surg., 28 Feb., 1866. Capt. Asst. Surg., 16 Sept., 1866. Maj. Surg., 30 June, 1882. Retired for disability, 27 Feb., 1891. Died 9 Jan., 1898.

TREMOR, EUSTACE.* [Born in N. Y. Appointed from Vt.]
2nd Lieut. 4th Inf., 1 July, 1822. 1st Lieut., 29 Nov., 1826. Capt. 1st Drag., 4 March, 1833. Maj., 30 June, 1846. Died 16 Feb., 1847.

TRESCOT, GEORGE.* [Born in S. C. Appointed from S. C.]
2nd Lieut. Eng., 16 Oct., 1813. 1st Lieut., 9 Feb., 1815. Resigned 31 March, 1819. Bvt. 1st Lieut., 11 Sept., 1814, for gallant conduct at the Battle of Plattsburg, N. Y. Died 12 May, 1827.

TREVITT, JOHN.* [Born in N. H. Appointed from Ohio.]
Bvt. 2nd Lieut. 2nd Inf., 1 July, 1844. 2nd Lieut. 3rd Inf., 18 May, 1846. 1st Lieut., 1 Dec., 1847. Capt., 31 Dec., 1856. Resigned 17 April, 1861.

TREVITT, JOHN. [Born in N. H. Appointed from N. H.]
Garrison Surg.'s Mate, 8 April, 1814. Post Surg., 18 April, 1814. Retained as Surg.'s Mate, 17 May, 1815. Asst. Surg., 1 June, 1821. Died 18 Aug., 1821.

TREVOR, JOHN. [Born in N. Y. Appointed from Army.]
Priv., Corpl. Sergt. and 1st Sergt. General Service, and Batty C, 5th Art., 12 Oct., 1858, to 1 June, 1864. 2nd Lieut. 5th Cav., 18 May, 1864. 1st Lieut., 19 Sept., 1864. Died 29 Sept., 1864, of wounds received in Battle near Winchester, Va.

TRIMBLE, ARMON. [Born in Md. Appointed from N. J.]
Priv. Co. B, 3rd N. J. Vols., 25 May, 1861, to 24 March, 1862. 2nd Lieut. 3rd Cav., 19 Feb., 1862. Appointment revoked 7 Feb., 1863. 1st Lieut. 28th U. S. Col. Inf., 3 Sept., 1864. Mustered out 8 Nov., 1865.

TRIMBLE, ISAAC R.* [Born in Va. Appointed from Ky.]
Bvt. 2nd Lieut. 3rd Art., 1 July, 1822. 2nd Lieut. 1st Art., 1 July, 1822. Resigned 31 May, 1832. Died 2 Jan., 1888.

TRIMBLE, JAMES. [Born in ——. Appointed from Pa.]
Surg.'s Mate 2nd Art., 6 July, 1812. Hosp. Surg.'s Mate, 17 July, 1814. Resigned 1 Sept., 1816.

TRIMBLE, JOEL G. [Born in Pa. Appointed from Army.]
Priv. Co. E, 1st Drag., 5 Feb., 1855. Corpl., 27 March, 1856. Sergt., 30 Jan., 1857. Priv., 10 Dec., 1857. Discharged 5 Feb., 1860. Priv. Co. A, 2nd Drag., 16 June, 1860. Corpl. Co. A, 2nd Cav., 1 April, 1862. Sergt., 1 Jan., 1863. 2nd Lieut. 1st Cav., 19 Feb., 1863. 1st Lieut., 3 June, 1864. Bvt. Capt., 11 June, 1864, for gallant and meritorious service in the Battle of Trevillian Station, Va. Reg. Adj. 1st Cav., 1 July, 1864, to 1 Oct., 1864. Bvt. Maj., 13 March, 1865, for gallantry in

the Battles of Trevillian Station and Cedar Creek, Va. R. Q. M. 1st Cav., 19 April, 1866, to 5 July, 1866. Capt. 9th Cav., 28 July, 1866, declined. Reg. Com. 1st Cav., 25 April, 1867, to 26 Dec., 1868. Capt., 26 Dec., 1868. Retired 21 Aug., 1879.

TRIMBLE, WM. A. [Born in Ky. Appointed from Ohio.]
Maj. 26th Inf., 18 March, 1813. Trans. to 19th Inf., 12 May, 1814. Lieut. Col. 1st Inf., 30 Nov., 1814. Trans. to 8th Inf., 17 May, 1815. Resigned 1 March, 1819. Bvt. Lieut. Col., 17 Sept., 1814, for gallant conduct in defence of Fort Erie. Died 13 Dec., 1821.

TRIPLER, CHAS. S. [Born in Mich. Appointed from Army.]
2nd Lieut. 12th Inf., 24 Nov., 1865. 1st Lieut., 24 Nov., 1865. Capt., 22 Jan., 1867. Resigned 1 Sept., 1873.

TRIPLER, CHAS. S. [Born in N. Y. Appointed from N. Y.]
Asst. Surg., 30 Oct., 1830. Maj. Surg., 7 July, 1838. Died 20 Oct., 1866. Bvt. Col., 29 Nov., 1864, and Bvt. Brig. Gen., 13 March, 1865, for faithful and meritorious service during the war.

TRIPLETT, JOSHUA B. [Born in Va. Appointed from Va.]
2nd Lieut. Corps Art., 27 Oct., 1820. Trans. to 4th Inf., 1 June, 1821. 1st Lieut., 31 May, 1825. Dismissed 26 Aug., 1826.

TRIPP, FREDERIC A.* [Born in Mich. Appointed from N. Y.]
2nd Lieut. 1st Inf., 12 June, 1887. Died 29 Sept., 1893.

TRIPPE, PERCY E.* [Born in Ga. Appointed from Ga.]
2nd Lieut. 10th Cav., 12 June, 1880. 1st Lieut., 17 Jan., 1888. Capt., 11 March, 1898. Reg. Adj., 30 April, 1899. Graduate of the Infantry and Cavalry School, 1887.

TROLINGER, ANDREW M. [Born in Tenn. Appointed from Tenn.]
2nd Lieut. 10th Tenn. Vols., 7 July, 1862. 1st Lieut., 1 July, 1864. Mustered out 23 June, 1865. 2nd Lieut. 12th Inf., 23 Feb., 1866. 1st Lieut., 28 July, 1866. Unassigned 9 April, 1869. Discharged 1 Oct., 1870.

TROTT, CLEMENT A.* [Born in Wis. Appointed from Wis.]
2nd Lieut. 7th Inf., 15 Feb., 1899.

TROTTER, ALDEN. [Born in ——. Appointed from ——.]
2nd Lieut. of Inf., 1 Dec., 1899. (Unassigned.)

TROTTER, FRED'K E. [Born in N. Y. Appointed from N. Y.]
Priv. Co. G, 7th N. Y. Militia, 26 April to 3 June, 1861. Capt. 102nd N. Y. Vols., 18 Dec., 1861. Maj., 16 July, 1862. Mustered out 18 March, 1863. Capt. Vet. Res. Corps, 18 June, 1863. Maj., 15 Oct., 1863. Lieut. Col., 30 March, 1864. Bvt. Col. and Brig. Gen. Vols., 13 March, 1865, for gallant and meritorious service during the war. Mustered out 11 Oct., 1866. Capt. 45th Inf., 28 July, 1866. Bvt. Maj. and Lieut. Col., 2 March, 1867, for faithful and meritorious service during the war. Trans. to 14th Inf., 22 July, 1869. Maj. 24th Inf., — ——, 1892. Died 28 June, 1892.

TROUSDALE, WM. [Born in N. C. Appointed from Tenn.]
Col. 2nd Tenn. Mounted Vols., 14 June, 1836, to 8 Jan., 1837. Col. of Inf., 3 March, 1847; 14th Inf., 9 April, 1847. Disbanded 29 July, 1848. Bvt. Brig. Gen., 13 Sept., 1847, for gallant and meritorious conduct at the Battle of Chapultepec, Mex. Died 27 March, 1872.

TROUT, HARRY G.* [Born in Pa. Appointed from Pa.]
2nd Lieut. 9th Cav., 1 July, 1886. 1st Lieut. 2nd Cav., 7 March, 1893.

TROUT, JOHN F. [Born in Pa. Appointed from Pa.]
Priv. Co. A, 10th Pa. Vols., 24 April to 31 July, 1861. 1st Sergt. Co. B, 45th Pa. Vols., 2 Sept., 1861. Capt., 4 Sept., 1862. Maj., 27 Dec., 1864. Mustered out 17 July, 1865. 2nd Lieut. 9th Inf., 15 May, 1866. 1st Lieut., 10 Nov., 1867. Dismissed 2 Jan., 1869. 1st Lieut. of Inf., 25 March, 1870, with rank from 10 Nov., 1867. Unassigned 25 March, 1870. Ass'd to 23rd Inf., 31 Dec., 1870. Retired for disability, 15 March, 1883.

TROWBRIDGE, CHAS. F. [Born in Mich. Appointed from Mich.]
Sergt. Maj. 3rd Mich. Vols., 24 April to 1 July, 1861. 1st Lieut. 16th Inf., 14 May, 1861. Capt., 13 Jan., 1863. Trans. to 2nd Inf., 17 April, 1867. Died 9 Feb., 1878. Bvt. Capt., 4 July, 1862, for gallant and meritorious service during the Peninsula campaign in Virginia. Bvt. Maj., 1 Sept., 1864, for gallant and meritorious service in the Battle of Kelly's Ford, Va., and during the Atlanta campaign.

TROWBRIDGE, JOSEPH M. [Born in N. Y. Appointed from Ohio.]
Cadet at Mil. Acad., 1 July, 1841, to 18 July, 1843. Capt. 16th Inf., 14 May, 1861. Resigned 14 May, 1864.

TROWBRIDGE, WM. P.* [Born in Mich. Appointed from Mich.]
Bvt. 2nd Lieut. Eng., 1 July, 1848. 2nd Lieut., 30 Nov., 1849. 1st Lieut., 18 Dec., 1854. Resigned 1 Dec., 1856.

TROXEL, THOS. G. [Born in Pa. Appointed from Iowa.]
Priv. Co. E, 25th Iowa Vols., 21 Aug., 1862. 1st Sergt., — ——, 1862. Discharged 6 June, 1865. 2nd Lieut. 17th Inf., 23 Feb., 1866. 1st Lieut., 6 July, 1867. R. Q. M., 20 Oct., 1872, to 28 June, 1878. Capt., 28 June, 1878. Retired for disability, 22 June, 1889.

TRUBY, ALBERT E. [Born in N. Y. Appointed from N. Y.]
Asst. Surg., 23 July, 1898.

TRUBY, WILLARD F. [Born in N. Y. Appointed from Pa.]
Asst. Surg., 12 Dec., 1898.

TRUE, THEODORE E. [Born in Ill. Appointed from Ill.]
Corpl. Co. B, 7th Ill. Vols., 25 April to 25 July, 1861. Sergt. Co. D, 41st Ill. Vols., 30 July, 1861. 2nd Lieut. 41st Ill. Vols., 15 Feb., 1862. Capt. 6th U. S. Col. Art., 28 Nov., 1863. Resigned 14 Nov., 1864. 2nd Lieut. 4th Inf., 24 July, 1866. Reg. Adj., 26 Feb., 1876. 1st Lieut., 26 Feb., 1876. Capt. A. Q. M., 22 Oct., 1889. Maj. Q. M., 13 Nov., 1898. Maj. Q. M. Vols., 12 July to 25 Nov., 1898. Lieut. Col. Q. M., 26 Nov., 1898, to 2 March, 1899.

TRUEX, WM. S. [Born in N. J. Appointed from Army.]
Cadet at Mil. Acad., 1 July, 1837, to 4 July, 1838. Priv. and 1st Sergt. Co. G, and

Sergt. Maj. 10th Inf., 12 March, 1847, to 8 Feb., 1848. 2nd Lieut. 10th Inf., 30 Dec., 1847. Disbanded 23 Aug., 1848. Maj. 5th N. J. Vols., 24 Aug., 1861. Lieut. Col. 10th N. J. Vols., 7 March, 1862. Col. 14th N. J. Vols., 23 Aug., 1862. Bvt. Brig. Gen. Vols., 2 April, 1865, for gallant and meritorious service before Petersburg, Va. Mustered out 18 June, 1865. Died 5 Sept., 1889.

TRUITT, CHAS. M.* [Born in Ky. Appointed from Kansas.]
2nd Lieut. 21st Inf., 13 June, 1879. 1st Lieut., 24 April, 1886. Capt., 26 April, 1898. Reg. Adj., 15 March, 1899. Capt. A. A. G. Vols., 12 May to 2 Sept., 1898.

TRUMAN, CHAS. L. [Born in N. Y. Appointed from N. Y.]
1st Lieut. 18th Inf., 6 March, 1862. Killed 20 Sept., 1863. at Battle of Chickamauga, Ga. Bvt. Capt., 19 Sept., 1863, for gallant and meritorious service at the Battle of Chickamauga, Ga.

TSCHAPPAT, WM. H.* [Born in Ohio. Appointed from Ohio.]
Addl. 2nd Lieut. 5th Art., 12 June, 1896. 2nd Lieut., 27 Aug., 1896. 1st Lieut. Ord., 4 Oct., 1898.

TUBBS, JOHN L. [Born in Tenn. Appointed from Army.]
Priv. and Corpl. Co. C, 12th Inf., 8 April to 6 Dec., 1847. Bvt. 2nd Lieut. 6th Inf., 28 June, 1848. 2nd Lieut., 18 Nov., 1849. Resigned 6 May, 1851.

TUCKER, HENRY. [Born in Pa. Appointed from Pa.]
1st Lieut. 6th Cav., 5 Aug., 1861. R. C. S., 26 Oct., 1862, to 6 Aug., 1865, and 3 Nov., 1865, to 28 July, 1866. Capt., 28 July, 1866. Died 20 Oct., 1866. Bvt. Capt., 3 July, 1863, for gallant and meritorious service in the Gettysburg campaign. Bvt. Maj., 13 March, 1865, for gallant and meritorious conduct.

TUCKER, JOHN. [Born in Maine. Appointed from Maine.]
2nd Lieut. 1st Inf., 4 Dec., 1819. Died 10 Oct., 1821.

TUCKER, STEPHEN S. [Born in Vt. Appointed from Ark.]
Capt. Mounted Rifles, 27 May, 1846. Resigned 30 June, 1851. Bvt. Maj., 13 Sept., 1847, for gallant and meritorious conduct in the Battle of Chapultepec, Mex.

TUCKER, WM. F. [Born in Mass. Appointed from Ill.]
Maj. P. M., 20 March, 1882.

TUFTS, DANFORTH H.* [Born in N. Y. Appointed from Vt.]
Bvt. 2nd Lieut. 1st Art., 1 July, 1826. 2nd Lieut. 4th Art., 1 July, 1826. 1st Lieut., 10 June, 1836. Died 4 Oct., 1840.

TUFTS, JOHN M.* [Born in N. Y. Appointed from N. Y.]
2nd Lieut. Corps Art., 1 July, 1820. Trans. to 3rd Inf., 1 June, 1821. Trans. to 2nd Art., 25 July, 1821. Trans. to 3rd Art., 16 Aug., 1821. Resigned 1 Nov., 1822. Died 25 March, 1888.

TULL, JOSEPH L. [Born in Pa. Appointed from Del.]
2nd Lieut. 26th U. S. Col. Inf., 15 Nov., 1864. Mustered out 28 Aug., 1865. 2nd Lieut. 82nd U. S. Col. Inf., 26 Nov., 1865. Mustered out 15 June, 1866. 2nd Lieut. 15th Inf., 19 April, 1866. Trans. to 33rd Inf., 21 Sept., 1866. Dismissed 9 June, 1868.

TULLY, REDMOND. [Born in Ireland. Appointed from Army.]
Priv., Corpl., Sergt. and 1st Sergt. Batty K, 1st Art., 12 June, 1855, to 11 Dec., 1861. 2nd Lieut. 1st Art., 15 Nov., 1861. 1st Lieut., 1 June, 1863. Trans. to 12th Inf., 5 March, 1869. Mustered out 1 Jan., 1871. Bvt. Capt., 7 Oct., 1864, for gallant and meritorious service in action on the Darbytown Road, near Richmond, Va. Appointed 1st Lieut. Inf., 22 March, 1881, (Act of Congress 3 March, 1881). Ass'd to 25th Inf., 5 April, 1881. Retired for disability, 17 April, 1891. Died 10 Sept., 1895.

TULLY, WM. K. [Born in N. Y. Appointed from Fla.]
Post Chap., 23 April, 1887. Resigned 17 Nov., 1893.

TUPES, HERSCHEL.* [Born in Ohio. Appointed from Ohio.]
2nd Lieut. 15th Inf., 12 June, 1896. 1st Lieut. of Inf., 17 Sept., 1898. Ass'd to 1st Inf., 1 Jan., 1899.

TUPPER, THOS. [Born in Md. Appointed from Army.]
Priv., Corpl. and Q. M. Sergt. 11th Inf., 15 April to Aug., 1813. Ensign 11th Inf., 23 Aug., 1813. 3rd Lieut., 19 Nov., 1813. 2nd Lieut., 2 May, 1814. Trans. to 6th Inf., 17 May, 1815. Capt. A. D. Q. M. G., 15 Nov., 1816. Dismissed 31 Dec., 1818.

TUPPER, TULLIUS C. [Born in Ohio. Appointed from Army.]
Priv. Co. E, 6th Cav., 19 July, 1861. 1st Sergt., 1 Oct., 1861. Sergt. Maj. 6th Cav., 12 May, 1862. 2nd Lieut. 6th Cav., 17 July, 1862. Bvt. 1st Lieut., 3 July, 1863, for gallant and meritorious service in the Battle of Gettysburg, Pa. 1st Lieut. 6th Cav., 28 Sept., 1864. Reg. Adj., 25 Oct., 1863, to 11 Nov., 1864. Bvt. Capt. and Maj., 13 March, 1865, for gallant and meritorious service during the war. Capt. 6th Cav., 17 Sept., 1867. Maj., 19 Oct., 1887. Bvt. Lieut. Col., 27 Feb., 1890. for gallant services in successfully leading a cavalry charge against Indians, in the action on Red River, Tex., 30 Aug., 1874, and gallant services in action against Indians at the Las Animas Mountains, N. M., 28 April, 1882. Retired 25 July, 1893. Died 1 Sept., 1898.

TURMAN, REUBEN S. [Born in Miss. Appointed from Miss.]
Cadet at Mil. Acad., 17 June, 1890, to 20 Jan., 1891, and from 17 June, 1891, to 9 May, 1893. Priv. and Corpl. Co. G, 16th Inf., 27 May, 1893, to 7 April, 1896. 2nd Lieut. 6th Inf., 23 March, 1896. Died 4 July, 1898.

TURNBULL, CHAS. N.* [Born in D. C. Appointed at Large.]
Bvt. 2nd Lieut. Top. Eng., 1 July, 1854. 2nd Lieut., 30 April, 1856. 1st Lieut., 1 July, 1859. Capt., 14 July, 1862. Trans. to Corps Eng., 3 March, 1863. Resigned 31 Dec., 1865. Bvt. Maj., 1 Aug., 1864, for gallant and meritorious service in the campaign before Richmond, Va. Bvt. Lieut. Col. and Col., 13 March, 1865, for gallant and meritorious conduct during the Rebellion.

TURNBULL, JOHN G. [Born in D. C. Appointed at Large.]
2nd Lieut. and 1st Lieut. 3rd Art., 5 Aug., 1861. Bvt. Capt., 3 May, 1863, for gallant and meritorious service in the Battle of Chancellorsville, Va. Bvt. Maj., 3 July, 1863, for gallant and meritorious service in the Battle of Gettysburg, Pa.

Capt. 3rd Art., 20 April, 1870. Maj. of Art. (5th), 10 Oct., 1894. Trans. to 1st Art., 22 Dec., 1894. Retired for disability, 27 Aug., 1896. Died 8 May, 1898.

TURNBULL, WM.* [Born in Md. Appointed from Md.]
2nd Lieut. Corps Art., 1 July, 1819. Trans. to 4th Art., 1 June, 1821. 1st Lieut., 15 Jan., 1823. Bvt. Capt. Asst. Top. Eng., 20 Aug., 1831. Capt. Top. Eng., 23 Nov., 1837. Maj., 7 July, 1838. Died 9 Dec., 1857. Bvt. Lieut. Col., 20 Aug., 1847, for gallant and meritorious conduct at Contreras and Churubusco, Mex. Bvt. Col., 13 Sept., 1847, for gallant and meritorious conduct at Chapultepec, Mex.

TURNER, DANIEL.* [Born in N. C. Appointed from N. C.]
2nd Lieut. Corps Art., 21 July, 1814. Disbanded 15 June, 1815. Died 21 July, 1860.

TURNER, EDWARD P. [Born in Pa. Appointed from Pa.]
Priv. Troop H, 5th Cav., 3 Oct., 1870, to 10 May, 1871. 2nd Lieut. 10th Cav., 18 Dec., 1871. Resigned 25 June, 1878.

TURNER, GEORGE F. [Born in Mass. Appointed from Mass.]
Asst. Surg., 23 July, 1833. Maj. Surg., 1 Jan., 1840. Died 17 Oct., 1854.

TURNER, GEORGE L.* [Born in Maine. Appointed from Maine.]
2nd Lieut. 18th Inf., 17 June, 1874. 1st Lieut., 16 Jan., 1884. Reg. Adj., 8 Sept., 1886. Dismissed 20 Nov., 1890.

TURNER, G. SOULARD. [Born in Mo. Appointed from Mo.]
2nd Lieut. 8th Inf., 9 July, 1898. 1st Lieut. 10th Inf., 2 March, 1899.

TURNER, GEORGE W.* [Born in Va. Appointed from Va.]
Bvt. 2nd Lieut. 1st Art., 1 July, 1831. 2nd Lieut., 1 July, 1831. Resigned 30 June, 1836. Killed 17 Oct., 1859, by Brown's raid in Va.

TURNER, HENRY S.* [Born in Va. Appointed from Va.]
Bvt. 2nd Lieut. 1st Drag., 1 July, 1834. 2nd Lieut., 15 Aug., 1835. Reg. Adj., 1 June, 1836, to 17 Nov., 1838, and 1 Dec., 1841, to 17 June, 1846. 1st Lieut., 3 March, 1837. Bvt. Capt. A. A. G., 17 Nov., 1838, to 16 April, 1839. Capt. 1st Drag., 21 April, 1846. Resigned 21 July, 1848. Bvt. Maj., 6 Dec., 1846, for gallant and meritorious conduct in the Battles of San Pasqual, San Gabriel, and Plains of Mesa, Cal. Died 16 Dec., 1881.

TURNER, JOHN W.* [Born in N. Y. Appointed from Ill.]
Bvt. 2nd Lieut. 3rd Art., 1 July, 1855. 2nd Lieut. 1st Art., 18 Nov., 1855. 1st Lieut., 21 April, 1861. Capt. C. S., 3 Aug., 1861. Col. A. A. de C., 3 May, 1862. Brig. Gen. Vols., 7 Sept., 1863. Mustered out Vols., 1 Sept., 1866. Resigned 4 Sept., 1871. Bvt. Maj., 6 Sept., 1863, for gallant and meritorious service at the Siege of Fort Wagner, S. C. Bvt. Lieut. Col., 30 July, 1864, for gallant and meritorious service in action which followed the explosion of the Petersburg Mine, Va. Bvt. Col., 13 March, 1865, for gallant and meritorious service at the capture of Fort Gregg, Va. Bvt. Brig. Gen., 13 March, 1865, for gallant and meritorious service during the war. Bvt. Maj. Gen., 13 March, 1865, for gallant and meritorious service in the field during the war; and Maj. Gen. Vols., 1 Oct., 1864, for gallant and meritorious service in the campaign of 1864.

TURNER, REUBEN B.* [Born in N. Y. Appointed from N. Y.]
2nd Lieut. 6th Inf., 11 June, 1881. 1st Lieut., 25 Jan., 1889. Capt., 12 Jan., 1897.

TURNER, THEOPHILUS H. [Born in N. J. Appointed from N. J.]
Asst. Surg. Vols., 23 Aug., 1864. Bvt. Capt. Vols., 1 Oct., 1865, for faithful and meritorious service. Mustered out 9 Aug., 1865. Asst. Surg., 28 Feb., 1866. Died 27 July, 1869.

TURNER, THOS. E. [Born in Pa. Appointed from Cal.]
2nd Lieut. 2nd Art., 20 May, 1857. Trans. to 4th Inf., 17 March, 1858. 1st Lieut., 14 May, 1861. Capt., 25 Nov., 1861. Died 1 Aug., 1862. Bvt. Maj., 27 June, 1862, for gallant and meritorious service at the Battle of Gaines' Mills, Va.

TURNER, TILMAN. [Born in ——. Appointed from Ga.]
Ensign 3rd Inf., 27 March, 1812. 2nd Lieut., 4 Aug., 1813. 1st Lieut., 1 May, 1814. Trans. to 1st Inf., 17 May, 1815. Died 22 May, 1815.

TURNER, WM. [Born in Md. Appointed from Md.]
2nd Lieut. 4th Inf., 17 Sept., 1818. Dismissed 19 Feb., 1821.

TURNER, WM. [Born in R. I. Appointed from R. I.]
Garrison Surg.'s Mate, 29 Sept., 1812. Post Surg., 24 April, 1816. Asst. Surg., 1 June, 1821. Died 26 Sept., 1837.

TURNER, WM. J. [Born in R. I. Appointed from Pa.]
Priv. Co. H, 5th Cav., 3 Oct., 1870. Discharged 26 June, 1871. 2nd Lieut. 2nd Inf., 1 Oct., 1873. 1st Lieut., 8 May, 1881. Capt. 2nd Inf., 22 Jan., 1892.

TURNEY, DANIEL. [Born in Ky. Appointed from Ohio.]
Surg.'s Mate 19th Inf., 31 Dec., 1812. Maj. Surg. 2nd Rifles, 21 Feb., 1814. Disbanded 15 June, 1815. Asst. Surg. Vols., 7 July, 1846. Maj. Surg., 13 July, 1847. Disbanded 26 Oct., 1848.

TURNLEY, PARMENAS T.* [Born in Tenn. Appointed from Tenn.]
Bvt. 2nd Lieut. 2nd Inf., 1 July, 1846. 2nd Lieut. 1st Inf., 31 Oct., 1846. R. Q. M., 1 March to 1 July, 1852. 1st Lieut., 10 June, 1850. Capt. A. Q. M., 2 March, 1855. Retired 17 Sept., 1863. Resigned 31 Dec., 1865.

TURNOCK, EDWIN. [Born in England. Appointed from Ind.]
Corpl. Co. B, 15th Ind. Vols., 14 June, 1861. 2nd Lieut., 21 Sept., 1862. Mustered out 25 June, 1864. Priv. Co. I, 12th Ind. Cav., 11 Nov., 1864. 1st Lieut. 23 May, 1865. Capt., 20 Oct., 1865. Mustered out 10 Nov., 1865. 2nd Lieut. 17th Inf., 16 Oct., 1867. Unassigned 27 May, 1869. Ass'd to 20th Inf., 14 July, 1869. Resigned 20 June, 1872.

TURPIN, BEVERLY. [Born in ——. Appointed from Ky.]
2nd Lieut. Light Drag., 12 March, 1812. 1st Lieut., 6 July, 1812. Disbanded 15 June, 1815. Reinstated 2 Dec., 1815, as 2nd Lieut. 4th Inf. Resigned 31 Oct., 1816. Retained ——, 1815 (in reorganization under Act of 3 March of that year), as 2nd Lieut. 4th Inf., with Bvt. of 1st Lieut. from 6 July, 1812.

TURRILL, HENRY S. [Born in Conn. Appointed from N. Y.]
Asst. Surg., 17th Conn. Vols., 13 Feb., 1864. Mustered out 19 July, 1865. 1st Lieut.

Asst. Surg., 26 June, 1875. Capt. Asst. Surg., 26 June, 1880. Maj. Surg., 7 April, 1893. Lieut. Col. Chf. Surg. Vols., 7 Nov., 1898, to 28 Feb., 1899.

TURTELOT, AUGUSTUS C. [Born in N. Y. Appointed from N. Y.]
Asst. Surg., 21 June, 1836. Died 8 Dec., 1837.

TURTLE, THOS. [Born in Ireland. Appointed from Mass.]
2nd Lieut. Eng., 17 June, 1867. 1st Lieut., 13 Aug., 1867. Capt., 2 Jan., 1881. Maj., 18 May, 1893. Died 18 Sept., 1894.

TUTHERLY, HERBERT E.* [Born in N. H. Appointed from N. H.]
2nd Lieut. 1st Cav., 14 June, 1872. 1st Lieut., 4 April, 1879. Capt., 17 Dec., 1890.

TUTTLE, EDMUND B. [Born in N. Y. Appointed from Ill.]
Hosp. Chap. Vols., 23 June, 1862. Mustered out 20 Nov., 1865. Post Chap., 20 Sept., 1867. Died 30 April, 1881.

TUTTLE, STEPHEN.* [Born in N. J. Appointed from N. J.]
Bvt. 2nd Lieut. Eng., 1 July, 1820. 2nd Lieut., 29 Aug., 1820. 1st Lieut., 24 May, 1828. Died 21 Jan., 1835.

TWEEDALE, JOHN. [Born in Pa. Appointed from Pa.]
Priv. Co. B, 160th Pa. Vols., and Co. I, 15th Pa. Cav., 22 Aug., 1862, to 28 Feb., 1865. Maj. Asst. Chf. of Record and Pension Office, 2 March, 1899.

TWIGGS, DAVID E. [Born in Ga. Appointed from Ga.]
Capt. 8th Inf., 12 March, 1812. Maj. 28th Inf., 21 Sept., 1814. Disbanded 15 June, 1815. Reinstated 2 Dec., 1815, as Capt. 7th Inf. Maj. 1st Inf., 14 May, 1825. Lieut. Col. 4th Inf., 15 July, 1831. Col. 2nd Drag., 8 June, 1836. Brig. Gen., 30 June, 1846. Dismissed 1 March, 1861. Retained 2 Dec., 1815 (in reorganization under Act of 3 March, 1815), as Capt. 7th Inf., with Bvt. of Maj. from 21 Sept., 1814 (date of his appointment as Maj. 28th Inf.) Bvt. Maj. Gen., 23 Sept., 1846, for gallant and meritorious conduct in several conflicts at Monterey, Mex. Received by Resolution of Congress, of 2 March, 1847, the presentation of a sword "in testimony of the high sense entertained by Congress of his gallantry and good conduct in storming Monterey." Died 15 July, 1862.

TWINING, WM. J.* [Born in Ind. Appointed from Ind.]
1st Lieut. Eng., 11 June, 1863. Capt. A. A. de C. Vols., 30 June, 1864. Bvt. Capt., 16 Dec., 1864, for gallant and meritorious service in action during the Siege of Nashville, Tenn. Bvt. Maj. and Lieut. Col. Vols., 26 Jan., 1865, for gallant and meritorious service during the campaign in Georgia and Tennessee. Bvt. Maj., 13 March, 1865, for gallant and meritorious service during the war. Resigned Vol. commission, 30 Aug., 1865. Capt. Eng., 28 Dec., 1865. Maj., 16 Oct., 1877. Died 5 May, 1882.

TWISS, THOS. S.* [Born in N. Y. Appointed from Vt.]
Bvt. 2nd Lieut. Eng., 1 July, 1826. Resigned 30 June, 1829.

TYLER, AUGUSTUS C.* [Born in Conn. Appointed from Tenn.]
2nd Lieut. 4th Cav., 13 June, 1873. Resigned 1 July, 1878.

TYLER, CHAS. H.* [Born in Va. Appointed at Large.]
Bvt. 2nd Lieut. 2nd Drag., 1 July, 1848. 2nd Lieut., 25 April, 1849. 1st Lieut., 6 Sept., 1853. Capt., 28 Jan., 1861. Dismissed 6 June, 1861. Died 17 March, 1882.

TYLER, CHAS. R.* [Born in Ky. Appointed from Ky.]
2nd Lieut. 16th Inf., 17 June, 1874. 1st Lieut., 9 Aug., 1883. Capt. 19th Inf., 6 April, 1898.

TYLER, DANIEL.* [Born in Conn. Appointed from Conn.]
2nd Lieut. Light Art., 1 July, 1819. Trans. to 1st Art., 1 June, 1821. Trans. to 1st Art., 12 June, 1821. 1st Lieut., 6 May, 1824. Resigned 31 May, 1834. Col. 1st Conn. Vols., 23 April, 1861. Brig. Gen. Conn. Vols., 10 May, 1861. Mustered out 11 Aug., 1861. Brig. Gen. Vols., 13 March, 1862. Resigned 6 April, 1864. Died 30 Nov., 1882.

TYLER, EDWIN. [Born in Conn. Appointed from Conn.]
1st Lieut. Dep. Com. of Ord., 12 March, 1813. Capt. Dep. Com. of Ord., 5 Aug., 1813. Retained as Capt. Ord., 8 Feb., 1815. Dismissed 13 Aug., 1819.

TYLER, GEORGE L. [Born in Md. Appointed from Md.]
2nd Lieut. 7th Md. Vols., 20 Sept., 1862. 1st Lieut., 22 Jan., 1863. Resigned 3 Nov., 1864. Bvt. Capt. Vols., 13 March, 1865, for gallant and meritorious service in the Battle of the Wilderness, Va. Capt. 36th Inf., 28 July, 1866. Unassigned 19 May, 1869. Ass'd to 2nd Cav., 15 Dec., 1870. Died 20 Oct., 1881.

TYLER, JOHN. [Born in Mich. Appointed from Mich.]
Priv. Co. A, 1st Mich. Vols., 1 May, 1861. Discharged 7 Aug., 1861. 1st Lieut. 17th Mich. Vols., 19 July, 1862. Capt., 2 Feb., 1863. Resigned 8 May, 1864. Capt. Vet. Res. Corps, 3 May, 1864. Bvt. Maj. Vols., 13 March, 1865, for gallant and meritorious conduct in the Battle of Campbell's Station, Tenn. Mustered out 30 Jan., 1867. 1st Lieut. 43rd Inf., 28 July, 1866. Bvt. Capt., 2 March, 1867, for gallant and meritorious service in the Battle of South Mountain, Md. Bvt. Maj., 2 March, 1867, for gallant and meritorious service in the attack on Campbell's Station, Tenn. Trans. to 1st Inf., 8 April, 1869. R. Q. M., 18 May, 1869, to 1 Feb., 1874. Retired 29 May, 1874. Died 3 Aug., 1889.

TYLER, JOHN, Jr. [Born in Va. Appointed from Va.]
Capt. of Inf., 6 March, 1847; 13th Inf., 9 April, 1847. Resigned 28 May, 1847.

TYLER, JOHN W. [Born in Va. Appointed from D. C.]
Maj. Surg., 3 March, 1847; Voltigeurs, 9 April, 1847. Disbanded 25 Aug., 1848.

TYLER, RICH'D W. [Born in Mich. Appointed from Mich.]
Sergt. Co. K, 1st U. S. S. S., 26 Dec., 1861. 1st Sergt., 23 March, 1861. 2nd Lieut. 1st U. S. S. S., 25 May, 1864. 1st Lieut., 4 Aug., 1864. Resigned 9 Nov., 1864. 2nd Lieut. Vet. Res. Corps, 25 Oct., 1864. Bvt. 1st Lieut. and Capt. Vols., 13 March, 1865, for gallant and meritorious service during the war. Mustered out 15 Oct., 1866. 1st Lieut. 44th Inf., 28 July, 1866. Bvt. Capt., 2 March, 1867, for gallant and meritorious service in the Battle of Deep Bottom, Va. Unassigned 27 May, 1869. Retired, with rank of Capt., 15 Dec., 1870, for loss of left arm from wound.

TYLER, ROB'T. O.* [Born in N. Y. Appointed from Conn.]
Bvt. 2nd Lieut. 2nd Art., 1 July, 1853. 2nd Lieut. 3rd Art., 24 Dec., 1853. 1st

Lieut., 1 Sept., 1856. Capt. A. Q. M., 17 May, 1861. Col. 1st Conn. Art., 29 Aug., 1861. Brig. Gen. Vols., 29 Nov., 1862. Mustered out Vols., 15 Jan., 1866. Lieut. Col. Dep. Q. M. G., 29 July, 1866. Died 1 Dec., 1874. Bvt. Maj., 13 Dec., 1862, for gallant and meritorious service at the Battle of Fredericksburg, Va. Bvt. Lieut. Col., 2 July, 1863, for gallant and meritorious service at the Battle of Gettysburg. Bvt. Col., 17 May, 1864, for gallant and meritorious service at the Battle of Spottsylvania, Va. Bvt. Brig. Gen., 13 March, 1865, for gallant and meritorious service at the Battle of Cold Harbor, Va. Bvt. Maj. Gen., 13 March, 1865, for gallant and meritorious service in the field during the war, and Maj. Gen. Vols., 1 Aug., 1864, for gallantry at the Battle of Cold Harbor, Va.

TYLER, WM. H.* [Born in Va. Appointed from Va.]
Bvt. 2nd Lieut. 5th Inf., 1 July, 1846. 2nd Lieut. 7th Inf., 16 Feb., 1847. 1st Lieut., 24 Aug., 1851. Died 24 Oct., 1853. Bvt. 1st Lieut., 20 Aug., 1847, for gallant and meritorious conduct in the Battles of Contreras and Churubusco, Mex.

TYLER, WM. W. [Born in N. Y. Appointed from N. Y.]
Priv. Co. E, 94th N. Y. Vols., 14 Oct., 1861. Sergt., ——. Discharged 19 May, 1862. 1st Lieut. 94th N. Y. Vols., 20 May, 1862. Capt., 2 March, 1863. Mustered out 17 March, 1863. 1st Lieut. Vet. Res. Corps, 6 June, 1863. Capt., 10 Dec., 1863. 2nd Lieut. 9th Cav., 13 Aug., 1867. Mustered out of Vol. Service, 30 Sept., 1867. 1st Lieut. 9th Cav., 9 Dec., 1871. Trans. to 13th Inf., 1 Aug., 1881 (to rank in Inf. from 1 July, 1872). Retired for disability, with rank of Capt., 24 Feb., 1891.

TYSON, LAURENCE D.* [Born in N. C. Appointed from N. C.]
2nd Lieut. 9th Inf., 13 June, 1883. 1st Lieut. 15th Aug., 1889. Resigned 15 April, 1896.

TYSON, J. WASHINGTON. [Born in Pa. Appointed from Pa.]
Com. Gen. of Purchases, 11 Oct., 1841. Rejected by Senate, 22 April, 1842.

ULINE, WILLIS.* [Born in Mo. Appointed from Ind.]
2nd Lieut. 12th Inf., 12 June, 1890. 1st Lieut. 11th Inf., 30 April, 1897. Trans. to 12th Inf., 21 March, 1898. Graduate of the Infantry and Cavalry School, 1897. Capt. 15th Inf., 18 Dec., 1899.

ULIO, JAMES. [Born in Ireland. Appointed from Army.]
Priv. Co. I, 9th Inf., 29 May, 1859. 1st Sergt., 1 July, 1855. Sergt., 8 Feb., 1856. 1st Sergt., 3 Nov., 1857. Discharged 31 May, 1860. 1st Sergt. Co. I, 9th Inf., 7 Nov., 1860. Discharged 28 Oct., 1862. 2nd Lieut. 6th Cal. Vols., 29 Oct., 1862. 1st Lieut., 20 Feb., 1863. Capt., 6 Aug., 1864. Bvt. Maj. Vols., 13 March, 1865, for faithful and meritorious service. Mustered out 25 Oct., 1865. Priv. Co. F, 3rd Batt. 16th Inf., 9 Feb., 1866. 1st Sergt., 21 Feb., 1866. 2nd Lieut. 16th Inf., 25 April, 1866. Reg. Adj., 25 Sept., 1868, to 17 April, 1869. Trans. to 2nd Inf., 17 April, 1869. 1st Lieut., 21 Sept., 1871. Capt., 20 March, 1885. Retired by operation of law, 29 May, 1896.

UMBSTAETTER, CHAS. L.* [Born in Ohio. Appointed at Large.]
2nd Lieut. 3rd Inf., 18 June, 1866. 1st Lieut., 13 May, 1868. Mustered out 1 Jan., 1871.

UNDERHILL, FRED'K A.* [Born in N. Y. Appointed from N. Y.]
2nd Lieut. Eng., 1 July, 1819. Resigned 1 Nov., 1823. Died 21 July, 1829.

UNDERWOOD, CHAS. N. [Born in Ky. Appointed from Army.]
Priv. and Sergt. Co. D, and Band Mounted Rifles, 17 July, 1846, to 1 Aug., 1848. Bvt. 2nd Lieut. 1st Inf., 28 June, 1848. 2nd Lieut., 28 June, 1848. 1st Lieut., 17 Oct., 1851. Died 7 Aug., 1855.

UNDERWOOD, EDMUND. [Born in Pa. Appointed from Pa.]
2nd Lieut. 4th Inf., 3 March, 1848. 1st Lieut., 24 March, 1853. Capt., 11 March, 1856. Maj. 18th Inf., 14 May, 1861. Retired 27 Feb., 1862. Died 5 Sept., 1863.

UPDEGRAFF, JOSEPH. [Born in Va. Appointed from Va.]
Priv. Batty E, 3rd Art., and Corpl. and Sergt. Co. H, 5th Inf., 9 March, 1846, to 28 June, 1848. Bvt. 2nd Lieut. 5th Inf., 28 June, 1848. 2nd Lieut., 7 Oct., 1848. 1st Lieut., 31 Dec., 1854. Capt., 25 Feb., 1861. Maj. 9th Inf., 1 Dec., 1863. Died 19 June, 1866.

UPHAM, FRANK K. [Born in Maine. Appointed from Cal.]
2nd Lieut. 7th Cal. Vols., 1 Nov., 1864. Mustered out 26 April, 1866. 2nd Lieut. 1st Cav., 7 March, 1867. 1st Lieut., 27 Aug., 1869. R. Q. M., 3 Sept., 1876, to 15 Aug., 1878. Reg. Adj., 7 Sept., 1879, to 1 Nov., 1882. Capt., 1 Nov., 1882. Retired for disability, 4 Feb., 1892. Died 17 Oct., 1899.

UPHAM, JOHN J.* [Born in Del. Appointed from Wis.]
Bvt. 2nd Lieut. 9th Inf., 1 July, 1859. 2nd Lieut. 6th Inf., 2 Dec., 1859. 1st Lieut., 4 May, 1861. Reg. Adj., 1 July, 1871, to 9 Sept., 1861. Capt., 9 Sept., 1861. Bvt. Maj., 2 July, 1863, for gallant and meritorious service in the Battle of Gettysburg, Pa. Trans. to 6th Cav., 1 Jan., 1871. Maj. 5th Cav., 1 Aug., 1874. Lieut. Col. 3rd Cav., 29 Oct., 1888. Col. of Cav. (8th), 14 Jan., 1892. Retired, for over thirty years' service, 30 Jan., 1892. Died 21 Oct., 1898.

UPHAM, WM. H.* [Born in Mass. Appointed at Large.]
Priv. Co. F, 2nd Wis. Vols., 23 April, 1861, to 5 May, 1862. Cadet at Mil. Acad., 1 July, 1862. 2nd Lieut. 5th Art., 18 June, 1866. Trans. to 4th Art., 23 Oct., 1866. 1st Lieut., 4 March, 1869. Resigned 18 Nov., 1869.

UPMAN, DIEDRICK. [Born in Germany. Appointed from Wis.]
1st Lieut. of Inf., 6 March, 1847; 15th Inf., 9 April, 1847. Capt., 6 May, 1848. Disbanded 4 Aug., 1848.

UPTON, EMORY.* [Born in N. Y. Appointed from N. Y.]
2nd Lieut. 4th Art., 6 May, 1861. 1st Lieut. 5th Art., 14 May, 1861. Col. 121st N. Y. Vols., 23 Oct., 1862. Bvt. Maj., 8 Nov., 1863, for gallant and meritorious service in the Battle of Rappahannock Station, Va. Bvt. Lieut. Col., 10 May, 1864, for gallant and meritorious service in the Battle of Spottsylvania, Va. Brig. Gen. Vols., 12 May, 1864, for gallant and distinguished service in the eight days' Battles in the Old Wilderness and at Spottsylvania C. H., Va. Bvt. Col., 19 Sept., 1864, for gallant and meritorious service in the Battle of Winchester,

Va. Bvt. Maj. Gen. Vols., 19 Oct., 1864, for gallant and meritorious service in the Battle of Winchester, Va. Capt. 5th Art., 22 Feb., 1865. Bvt. Brig. Gen., 13 March, 1865, for gallant and meritorious service in the Battle and capture of Selma, Ala. Bvt. Maj. Gen., 13 March, 1865, for gallant and meritorious service in the field during the war. Mustered out of Vol. Service, 30 April, 1866. Lieut. Col. 25th Inf., 28 July, 1866. Trans. to 18th Inf., 15 March, 1869. Unassigned 1 July, 1870. Ass'd to 1st Art., 15 Dec., 1870. Trans. to 4th Art., 16 March, 1877. Col. 4th Art., 1 July, 1880. Died 15 March, 1881.

UPTON, LA ROY S.* [Born in Mich. Appointed from Mich.]
2nd Lieut. 21st Inf., 12 June, 1891. 1st Lieut. 2nd Inf., 1 Feb., 1898.

URBAN, GUSTAVUS. [Born in Prussia. Appointed from Army.]
Priv., Corpl. and Sergt. Co. B and Q. M. Sergt. 2nd Cav., 18 July, 1855, to 16 Sept., 1861. Capt. A. A. G. Vols., 16 Sept., 1861. Resigned 30 Jan., 1863. 2nd Lieut. 5th Cav., 17 July, 1862. 1st Lieut., 17 July, 1862. Capt., 28 July, 1866. Died 11 Jan., 1871. Bvt. Capt., 9 June, 1863, for gallant and meritorious service at the Battle of Beverly Ford, Va. Bvt. Maj., 28 July, 1864, for gallant and meritorious service at the Battle of Deep Bottom, Va.

URMSTON, THOS. D. [Born in Conn. Appointed from Army.]
Priv., Corpl. and Sergt. Co. F, 12th Inf., 13 Nov., 1861, to 1 July, 1862. 2nd Lieut. 12th Inf., 25 May, 1862. 1st Lieut., 6 Feb., 1863. Killed 1 Oct., 1864, in Battle at Chappel House, Va. Bvt. Capt., 1 Oct., 1864, for gallant and meritorious service at the Battle of Chappel House, Va.

URY, ASBURY.* [Born in Tenn. Appointed from Tenn.]
Bvt. 3rd Lieut. Mounted Rangers, 1 July, 1832. Trans. to 1st Drag., as Bvt. 2nd Lieut., 14 Aug., 1833, to rank from 1 July, 1832. 2nd Lieut., 30 June, 1835. 1st Lieut., 3 March, 1837. Died 13 April, 1838.

USHER, FRANCIS M. C. [Born in Ky. Appointed from Ky.]
Asst. Surg., 12 Dec., 1898.

VAIL, JEFFERSON.* [Born in France. Appointed from Md.]
Bvt. 2nd and 2nd Lieut. 1st Inf., 1 July, 1821. 1st Lieut., 14 May, 1825. Capt., 11 July, 1833. Died 25 Oct., 1835.

VALEAU, MING. [Born in N. Y. Appointed from N. Y.]
Cadet at Mil. Acad., 10 Aug., 1814, to 8 Nov., 1817. 2nd Lieut. 3rd Inf., 13 Aug., 1819. Disbanded 1 June, 1821. Died 7 July, 1822.

VALENTINE, WATTS C. [Born in Nebr. Appointed from Nebr.]
2nd Lieut. 19th Inf., 9 July, 1898. 1st Lieut., 2 March, 1899.

VALENTINE, WILLIAM S.* [Born in N. Y. Appointed from Tex.]
Addl. 2nd Lieut. 10th Cav., 11 June, 1897. 2nd Lieut. 5th Cav., 21 Nov., 1897.

VALLE, LOUIS.* [Born in Mo. Appointed from Mo.]
2nd Lieut. Art., 13 June, 1808, declined.

VALOIS, GUSTAVUS. [Born in Prussia. Appointed from Army.]
Sergt. Co. C, 4th Md. Vols., 12 April, 1862. 1st Sergt. Co. E, 3rd Md. Vols., 1 Jan., 1863. Q. M. Sergt. 3rd Md. Vols., 26 Jan., 1864. 1st Lieut. 3rd Md. Vols., 27 April, 1864. Capt., 9 May, 1865. Mustered out 29 May, 1865. Priv. Co. I. 5th Cav., 11 Dec., 1865. Corpl., 1 Sept., 1866. Sergt., 12 July, 1867. 2nd Lieut. 9th Cav., 18 July, 1868. 1st Lieut., 25 Aug., 1872. R. Q. M., 18 March to 31 Dec., 1880. Capt., 22 Nov., 1884. Retired for disability, 11 Feb., 1887. Died 20 Dec., 1892.

VAN ALEN, CHAS. [Born in N. Y. Appointed from N. Y.]
2nd Lieut. of Inf., 16 March, 1847; 10th Inf., 9 April, 1847. Disbanded 23 Aug., 1848.

VAN ANTWERP, VERPLANCK. [Born in N. Y. Appointed from Iowa.]
Maj. A. A. de C., 29 Jan., 1862. Discharged 21 March, 1862. Maj. A. A. de C., 19 April, 1862. Bvt. Brig. Gen. Vols., 13 Feb., 1862. Mustered out 1 July, 1866. Capt. Mil. Storekeeper Q. M. Dept., 28 July, 1866. Died 2 Dec., 1875.

VAN BOKKELEN, WM. K.* [Born in N. Y. Appointed from N. Y.]
Bvt. 2nd Lieut. 7th Inf., 1 July, 1843. 2nd Lieut. 3rd Inf., 26 Nov., 1845. Trans. to 7th Inf., 27 June, 1846. R. Q. M., 17 Jan., 1848, to 20 Sept., 1850. 1st Lieut., 16 July, 1850. Capt. A. Q. M., 28 July, 1853. Cashiered 8 May, 1861. Bvt. 1st Lieut., 20 Aug., 1847, for gallant and meritorious conduct in the Battles of Contreras and Churubusco, Mex.

VAN BUREN, ABRAHAM.* [Born in N. Y. Appointed from N. Y.]
Bvt. 2nd Lieut. 2nd Inf., 1 July, 1827. 2nd Lieut., 1 July, 1827. 1st Lieut. 1st Drag., 4 March, 1833. Capt., 4 July, 1836. Resigned 3 March, 1837. Maj. P. M., 26 June, 1846. Resigned, 1 June, 1854. Bvt. Lieut. Col., 20 Aug., 1847, for gallant and meritorious conduct at Contreras and Churubusco, Mex.

VAN BUREN, DANIEL T.* [Born in N. Y. Appointed from N. Y.]
2nd Lieut. 2nd Art., 1 July, 1847. 1st Lieut., 14 Feb., 1849. Resigned 31 March, 1855. Capt. 20th N. Y. Militia, 4 May, 1861. Maj. A. A. G. Vols., 3 Aug., 1861. Col. A. A. de C. Vols., 1 June, 1862. Bvt. Brig. Gen. Vols., 13 March, 1865, for faithful and meritorious service during the war. Mustered out 20 March, 1866.

VAN BUREN, MICHAEL E. [Born in Md. Appointed from Mich.]
1st Lieut. Mounted Rifles, 27 May, 1846. Capt., 9 Oct., 1847. Died 20 July, 1854, of wounds received 11 July, 1854, in action with Indians near San Diego, Tex. Bvt. Capt., 20 Aug., 1847, for gallant and meritorious conduct at Contreras and Churubusco, Mex.

VAN BUREN, PETER B. [Born in N. Y. Appointed from N. Y.]
Capt. 29th Inf., 30 April, 1813. Trans. to 2nd Inf., 17 May, 1815. Resigned 10 Jan., 1816.

VAN BUREN, WM. H. [Born in Pa. Appointed from Pa.]
Asst. Surg., 15 June, 1840. Resigned 31 Dec., 1845. Died 25 March, 1883.

VAN CAMP, CORNELIUS.* [Born in Pa. Appointed from Pa.]
Bvt. 2nd Lieut. 1st Cav., 1 July, 1855. 2nd Lieut. 2nd Cav., 1 July, 1855. Killed 1 Oct., 1858, in action with Indians in Texas.

VANCE, CAPERS D.* [Born in Ark. Appointed from Ark.]
Addl. 2nd Lieut. 21st Inf., 11 June, 1888. 2nd Lieut., 16th Inf., 1 Oct., 1888. Died 12 Feb., 1893.

VANCE, DUNCAN M. [Born in Ohio. Appointed from Ohio.]
1st Lieut. 11th Inf., 14 May, 1861. Bvt. Capt., 3 July, 1862, for gallant and meritorious service during the Peninsula campaign. Bvt. Maj., 2 July, 1863, for gallant and meritorious service in the Battle of Gettysburg, Pa. Capt. 11th Inf., 6 Jan., 1864. Trans. to 16th Inf., 14 April, 1869. Maj. 13th Inf., 28 June, 1885. Died 27 Feb., 1887.

VANCE, JOSEPH C.* [Born in Ohio. Appointed from Ohio.]
Bvt. 2nd Lieut. 2nd Art., 1 July, 1832. 2nd Lieut., 31 Dec., 1833. Resigned 31 Oct., 1835. Died 9 Sept., 1840.

VANCE, RICHARD. [Born in Ky. Appointed from Ky.]
Hosp. Steward 26th Ky. Vols., 1 Oct., 1861. 2nd Lieut. 26th Ky. Vols., 22 June, 1862. 1st Lieut., 31 Jan., 1863. Mustered out 10 July, 1865. 2nd Lieut. 19th Inf., 23 Feb., 1866. Trans. to 28th Inf., 21 Sept., 1866. 1st Lieut., 19 Sept., 1866. Trans. to 19th Inf., 31 March, 1869. Capt., 19 June, 1879. Retired for over thirty years' service 30 Nov., 1892.

VANCE, SAML. B. H. [Born in Pa. Appointed from Pa.]
1st Lieut. 3rd Drag., 9 April, 1847. Disbanded 31 July, 1848.

VANCE, ZEBULON B. [Born in N. C. Appointed from N. C.]
2nd Lieut. 19th Inf., 7 Jan., 1884. 1st Lieut. 22nd Inf., 18 April, 1891. Trans. to 11th Inf., 20 July, 1891. Capt. of Inf., 8 Sept., 1898. Ass'd to 10th Inf., 1 Jan., 1899. Trans. to 11th Inf., 6 April, 1899. Graduate of the Infantry and Cavalry School, 1887.

VAN CLEVE, HORATIO P.* [Born in N. J. Appointed from N. J.]
Col. 2nd Minn. Vols., 22 July, 1861. Brig. Gen. Vols., 21 March, 1862. Bvt. Maj. Gen. Vols., 13 March, 1865, for gallant and meritorious service during the war. Mustered out 24 Aug., 1865. Bvt. 2nd Lieut. 5th Inf., 1 July, 1831. 2nd Lieut., 31 Dec., 1834. Resigned 11 Sept., 1836. 2nd Lieut. of Inf., 19 June, 1890 (Act 11 June, 1890). Retired 1 July, 1890. Died April 24, 1891.

VAN DEMAN, RALPH H. [Born in Ohio. Appointed from Ohio.]
2nd Lieut. 21st Inf., 1 Aug., 1891. 1st Lieut., 26 April, 1898. Graduate of the Infantry and Cavalry School, 1895.

VANDERBILT, GEORGE W.* [Born in N. Y. Appointed from N. Y.]
Bvt. 2nd Lieut. 9th Inf., 1 July, 1860. 2nd Lieut. 10th Inf., 27 Feb., 1861. 1st Lieut., 14 June, 1861. Capt. A. A. de C., 17 April, 1862. Capt., 19 Sept., 1863. Died 1 Jan., 1864.

VANDERSLICE, JOSEPH H. [Born in Pa. Appointed from Army.]
Priv. Co. A, Batt. Eng., 30 Jan. 1851. Artificer, 1 Jan., 1853. Corp., 1 July, 1855. Discharged 30 Nov., 1855. Corpl. Co. A, Batt. Eng., 30 Nov., 1855. Sergt., 1 Oct., 1856. Discharged 30 Nov., 1860. Sergt. Co. A Batt. Eng., 30 Nov., 1860. 2nd Lieut., 14th Inf., 14 May, 1861. 1st Lieut., 24 Oct., 1861. Bvt. Capt., 17 Sept., 1862, for gallant and meritorious service in the Battle of Antietam, Md. Cashiered 10 May, 1865. Reinstated 27 Dec., 1865. Capt. 14th Inf., 22 March, 1866. Retired 23 April, 1879, for disability. Died 27 Feb., 1894.

VAN DERVEER, JOHN S.* [Born in N. J. Appointed from N. J.]
Bvt. 2nd Lieut. 6th Inf., 1 July, 1830. 2nd Lieut. 1st Drag., 4 March, 1833. 1st Lieut., 15 Aug., 1835. Capt., 3 Feb., 1839. Resigned 31 Dec., 1840. Died 4 June, 1879.

VAN DEURSEN, CHARLES A. [Born in N. J. Appointed from N. J.]
Priv. Co. G, 1st N. J. Vols., 28 May to 29 Aug., 1861. 1st Lieut. 15th U. S. Inf., 5 Aug., 1861. Resigned 24 June, 1862. Sergt. Co. K, 50th Ohio Vols., 24 Aug., 1862. 2nd Lieut., 1 July, 1863. Trans. to 183rd Ohio Vols., May, 1865. Bvt. 1st Lieut. Vols., 13 March, 1865, for gallant and meritorious service during the war. Mustered out 17 July, 1865. 2nd Lieut. 6th Inf., 7 March, 1867. Cashiered 15 Aug., 1867.

VAN DEUSEN, GEORGE W.* [Born in Mass. Appointed from Mass.]
2nd Lieut. 4th Cav., 12 June, 1880. Trans. to 1st Art., 31 Jan., 1884. 1st Lieut., 9 Aug., 1889. Capt. 7th Art., 2 March, 1899. Graduate of the Artillery School, 1892.

VAN DE VENTER, CHRISTOPHER.* [Born in N. Y. Appointed from N. Y.]
2nd Lieut. Art., 9 Jan., 1809. 1st Lieut. 1st Art., 12 March, 1812. Trans. to Corps Art., 12 May, 1814. (Maj. Dep. Q. M. G., 26 March, 1813, to 15 June, 1815.) Maj. A. A. G., 11 Jan., 1815, to 17 May, 1815. Maj. D. Q. M. G., 24 April, 1816, to rank from 26 March, 1813. Resigned 30 Aug., 1816. Died 22 April, 1838.

VAN DE VENTER, EUGENE. [Born in N. Y. Appointed from N. Y.]
Cadet Mil. Acad., 1 July, 1831, to 13 Jan., 1832. Capt. 15th Inf., 9 April, 1847. Maj. 13th Inf., 22 Dec., 1847. Disbanded 15 July, 1848.

VAN DE VENTER, MICHAEL F.* [Born in N. Y. Appointed from N. Y.]
3rd Lieut. Corps Art., 2 March, 1815. Disbanded 15 June, 1815. 2nd Lieut. 2nd Inf., 22 July, 1817. Died 27 Aug., 1821.

VANDE WIELE, JOHN B. [Born in N. Y. Appointed from N. Y.]
Corpl. Co. E, 8th N. Y. State Militia, 25 April, 1861. Discharged 2 Aug., 1861. 1st Lieut. 4th N. Y. Heavy Art., 1 Nov., 1861. Capt., 29 Sept., 1862. Mustered out 1 Feb., 1865. Bvt. Maj. Vols., 13 March, 1865, for gallant and meritorious service during the war. 1st Lieut. 1st U. S. Vet. Vols., 20 May, 1865. Capt. 8th U. S. Vet. Vols., 24 Aug., 1865. Mustered out 28 April, 1866. Capt. 10th Cav., 22 Jan., 1867. Bvt. Maj., 2 March, 1867, for gallant and meritorious service in the Battle of Ream's Station, Va. Retired 20 March, 1879. Died 9 Nov., 1889.

VAN DORN, EARL.* [Born in Miss. Appointed from Miss.]
Bvt. 2nd Lieut. 7th Inf., 1 July, 1842. 2nd Lieut., 30 Nov., 1844. 1st Lieut., 3 March, 1847. Capt. 2nd Cav., 3 March, 1855. Maj., 28 June, 1860. Resigned 31 Jan., 1861. Bvt. Capt., 18 April, 1847, for gallant and meritorious conduct at Cerro Gordo, Mex. Bvt. Maj., 20 Aug., 1847, for gallant and meritorious conduct at Contreras and Churubusco, Mex. Murdered 8 May, 1863.

VAN DUYNE, FREDERICK W.* [Born in N. J. Appointed from N. J.]
2nd Lieut. 24th Inf., 15 Feb., 1899.

VAN DUZER, CHAS. F. [Born in N. Y. Appointed from Army.]
Priv. Gen. Ser., 20 to 30 Sept., 1861. 2nd Lieut. 12th Inf., 25 Sept., 1861. Killed 27

June, 1862, at the Battle of Gaines' Mills, Va. Bvt. 1st Lieut., 27 June, 1862, for gallant and meritorious service at the Battle of Gaines' Mills, Va.

VAN HORN, JAMES J.* [Born in Ohio. Appointed from Ohio.]
Bvt. 2nd Lieut. 1st Inf., 1 July, 1858. 2nd Lieut. 8th Inf., 19 July, 1858. 1st Lieut., 14 May, 1861. Capt., 19 Feb., 1862. Bvt. Maj., 4 June, 1864, for gallant and meritorious service in the Battle of Cold Harbor, Va. Maj. 13th Inf., 7 June, 1879. Lieut. Col. 25th Inf., 28 June, 1885. Col. of Inf. (8th), 20 April, 1891. Died 30 Aug., 1898.

VAN HORN, ROBT. O. [Born in Ariz. Appointed from the Army.]
Priv., Copl., Sergt. and Q. M. Sergt. Co. C., 12th Inf., 15 Aug., 1897, to 26 Aug., 1898. 2nd Lieut. 17th Inf., 9 July, 1898. 1st Lieut., 2 March, 1899.

VAN HORNE, JEFFERSON.* [Born in Pa. Appointed from Ohio.]
Bvt. 2nd Lieut. 3rd Inf., 1 July, 1827. 2nd Lieut., 1 July, 1827. 1st Lieut., 1 April, 1836. Capt., 1 Dec., 1840. Died 28 Sept., 1857. Bvt. Maj., 20 Aug., 1847, for gallant and meritorious conduct at Contreras and Churubusco, Mex.

VAN HORNE, THOS. B. [Born in Ohio. Appointed from Wis.]
Chap. 13th Ohio Vols., 10 July, 1862. Mustered out 26 June, 1864. Chap. Post of Chattanooga, Tenn., 14 Oct., 1864, to 29 April, 1867. Post Chap., 3 April, 1867. Resigned 2 Aug., 1869. Post Chap., 2 July, 1870. Retired, over sixty-two years of age, 26 Feb., 1885. Died 5 April, 1895.

VAN HORNE, WM. McC. [Born in Ohio. Appointed from Ohio.]
Priv. Co. E, 2nd Ohio Vols., 14 Aug., 1861. Discharged 10 Oct., 1864. Recruiting 2nd Lieut. 184th Ohio Vols., 4 Jan., 1865. Capt. 195th Ohio Vols., 17 March, 1865. Mustered out 18 Dec., 1865. 2nd Lieut. and 1st Lieut. 17th Inf., 23 Feb., 1866. Reg. Adj., 1 Feb., 1869, to 15 Dec., 1870. R. Q. M., 15 Dec., 1870, to 24 July, 1872. Capt., 31 Dec., 1872. Maj. 22d Inf., 23 May, 1896. Lieut. Col. 18th Inf., 1 Nov., 1898.

VAN KLEEK, LAWRENCE L. [Born in N. Y. Appointed from N. Y.]
Mil. Storekeeper Ord., 15 Aug., 1836. Removed 30 Nov., 1841.

VAN LIEU, FRED'K. [Born in N. J. Appointed frim N. J.]
2nd Lieut. 6th Inf., 1 Aug., 1838. Died 31 Dec., 1839.

VAN LIEW, FREDERICK T.* [Born in N. Y. Appointed from N. Y.]
Addl. 2nd Lieut. 16th Inf., 11 June, 1881. 2nd Lieut. 2nd Inf., 26 Sept., 1881. 1st Lieut. 11th Inf., 29 Dec., 1890. Trans. to 2nd Inf., 20 July, 1891. Capt. 26 April, 1898. Dismissed 20 Nov., 1899.

VAN NESS, DAVID. [Born in N. Y. Appointed from N. Y.]
2nd Lieut. Corps Art., 3 March, 1819. Trans. to 1st Art., 1 June, 1821. 1st Lieut., 4 Nov., 1823. Capt., 23 Oct., 1834. Maj. 3rd Art., 29 Oct., 1848. Died 14 Feb., 1849. Bvt. Capt., 4 Nov., 1835, for ten years' faithful service in one grade.

VAN NESS, EUGENE. [Born in N. Y. Appointed from N. Y.]
Addl. P. M., 12 July, 1838. Maj. P. M., 18 Dec., 1839. Lieut. Col. Dep. P. M. G., 1 Feb., 1855. Died 28 May, 1862.

VAN NESS, WM. [Born in N. Y. Appointed from N. Y.]
2nd Lieut. 2nd Inf., 30 Nov., 1819. Resigned 29 March, 1820.

VAN NESS, WM. P. [Born in N. Y. Appointed from Mich.]
2nd Lieut. 1st Art., 20 Sept., 1867. 1st Lieut., 1 Sept., 1874. Capt., 1 July, 1892. Graduate of the Artillery School, 1871.

VAN ORSDALE, JOHN T.* [Born in N. Y. Appointed from N. Y.]
2nd Lieut. 7th Inf., 14 June, 1872. 1st Lieut., 20 Aug., 1877. R. Q. M., 1 June, 1885, to 13 June, 1889. Capt., 30 Nov., 1889. Maj., 1 April, 1899. Bvt. 1st Lieut., 27 Feb., 1890, for gallant services in action against Indians at the Big Hole, Montana, 9 Aug., 1877.

VAN REED, WM. E. [Born in Pa. Appointed from Pa.]
Corpl. Co. H, 5th Pa. Vols., 20 April, 1861. 2nd Lieut. 5th Art., 14 May, 1861. 1st Lieut., 2 July, 1863. Bvt. Capt., 18 Aug., 1864, for gallat service during the operations on the Weldon Railroad. Capt. 5th Art., 1 March, 1875. Retired 9 Dec., 1887. Died 8 Aug., 1896.

VAN RENSSELAER, COURTLANDT. [Born in N. J. Appointed from N. Y.]
1st Lieut. 13th Inf., 14 May, 1861. Reg. Adj., 1 Sept., 1861, to 18 June, 1862. Capt., 18 June, 1862. Died 7 Oct., 1864.

VAN RENSSELAER, HENRY.* [Born in N. Y. Appointed from N. Y.]
Bvt. 2nd Lieut. 5th Inf., 1 July, 1831. Resigned 27 Jan., 1832. Col. A. A. de C., 5 Aug., 1861. Discharged 1 Nov., 1861. Col. I. G., 12 Nov., 1861. Died 23 March, 1864.

VAN RENSSELAER, STEPHEN. [Born in N. Y. Appointed from N. Y.]
1st Lieut. 12th Inf., 14 May, 1861. Capt., 20 Dec., 1862. Resigned 9 Sept., 1863.

VANSANT, JOHN. [Born in Va. Appointed from Va.]
Asst. Surg. U. S. N., 1 May, 1855. Passed Asst. Surg., 4 May, 1860. Resigned 22 June, 1860. Asst. Surg., 23 June, 1860. Maj. Surg., 28 July, 1866. Resigned 1 May, 1867. Bvt. Maj. and Lieut. Col., 13 March, 1865, for faithful and meritorious service during the war.

VAN SHAICK, LOUIS J. [Born in N. Y. Appointed from N. Y.]
Cadet at Mil. Acad., 15 June, 1896, to 3 May, 1897, and again from 18 June, 1897, to 28 Jan., 1899. 2nd Lieut. 4th Inf., 10 April, 1899.

VAN VALZAH, DAVID D. [Born in Ill. Appointed from Pa.]
1st Lieut. 12th Inf., 14 May, 1861. Bvt. Capt., 1 Aug., 1864, for gallant service in the Battle of the Wilderness, during the campaign before Richmond, Va. Capt. 12th Inf., 10 Aug., 1864. Trans. to 30th Inf., 21 Sept., 1866. Unassigned 23 March, 1869. Ass'd to 25th Inf., 1 Jan., 1871. Maj. 20th Inf., 19 Oct., 1886. Lieut. Col., 24th Inf., 14 Oct., 1891. Col. 18th Inf., 23 May, 1896. Retired for over thirty years' service, 20 June, 1899.

VAN VLIET, FRED'K. [Born in N. Y. Appointed from N. Y.]
2nd Lieut. 3rd Cav., 5 Aug., 1861. Reg. Adj., 12 July, 1862, to 9 Jan., 1863. 1st Lieut., 17 July, 1862. Bvt. Capt., 1 Aug., 1864, for gallant and meritorious service in the battles of the campaign from the Rapidan to Petersburg. Bvt. Maj., 8 April,

1865, for gallant and meritorious service during the Siege of Mobile, Ala. Bvt. Lieut. Col., 30 Sept., 1865, for meritorious service during the war. Capt. 3rd Cav., 28 July, 1866. Maj. 10th Cav., 26 June, 1882. Died 8 March, 1891.

VAN VLIET, ROBT. C. [Born in Kan. Appointed from N. J.]
Cadet at Mil. Acad., 1 July, 1875, to 29 Dec., 1875. 2nd Lieut. 10th Inf., 14 Dec., 1876. 1st Lieut., 7 May, 1884. Reg. Adj., 1 Jan., 1885, to 31 Dec., 1888. Capt., 8 March, 1898.

VAN VLIET, STEWART.* [Born in N. Y. Appointed from N. Y.]
2nd Lieut. 3rd Art., 1 July, 1840. 1st Lieut., 19 Nov., 1843. R. Q. M., 28 March, 1847, to 4 June, 1847. Capt. A. Q. M., 4 June, 1847. Capt. 3rd Art., 24 Dec., 1853. Vacated commission of Capt. 3rd Art., 24 Dec., 1853. Maj. Q. M., 3 Aug., 1861. Brig. Gen. Vols., 23 Sept., 1861. Expired by constitutional limitation, 17 July, 1862. Bvt. Lieut. Col., Col. and Brig. Gen., 28 Oct., 1864, for faithful and meritorious service during the war. Bvt. Maj. Gen., 13 March, 1865, for faithful and distinguished service in the Q. M. D. during the war. Brig. Gen. Vols., 13 March, 1865. Bvt. Maj. Gen. Vols., 13 March, 1865, for faithful and meritorious service during the war. Lieut. Col. Dep. Q. M. G., 29 July, 1866. Mustered out of Vol. Service, 1 Sept., 1866. Col. A. Q. M. G., 6 June, 1872. Retired 22 Jan., 1881, over thirty-two years' service.

VAN VOAST, JAMES.* [Born in N. Y. Appointed from N. Y.]
Bvt. 2nd Lieut. 3rd Art., 1 July, 1852. 2nd Lieut., 22 Aug., 1853. 1st Lieut. 9th Inf., 3 March, 1855. R. Q. M., 4 July, 1855, to 11 June, 1858. Capt., 1 March, 1861. Maj. 18th Inf., 29 Dec., 1863. Lieut. Col. 16th Inf., 16 Aug., 1871. Col. 9th Inf., 20 Feb., 1882. Retired for disability 2 April, 1883.

VAN WINKLE, PETER G., Jr. [Born in N. J. Appointed from N. Y.]
Priv. Co. G, 2nd N. J. Vols., 1 May to 31 July, 1861. Capt. 2nd N. J. Cav., 15 Aug., 1863. Dismissed 14 Aug., 1865. 2nd Lieut. 3rd Cav., 26 July, 1866. Cashiered 15 Aug., 1867.

VAN WYCK, GEORGE P. [Born in N. Y. Appointed from N. Y.]
Chap. 56th N. Y. Vols., 8 April, 1863. Mustered out 17 Oct., 1865. Post Chap., 7 Aug., 1867. Retired 1 Aug., 1879. Died 5 Aug., 1899.

VARNEY, ALMON L. [Born in Maine. Appointed from Maine.]
1st Lieut. 13th Maine Vols., 9 Dec., 1861. Capt., 22 Nov., 1862. Mustered out 6 Jan., 1865. 2nd Lieut. Ord., 15 Feb., 1865. 1st Lieut., 23 June, 1874. Capt., 29 Oct., 1874. Maj., 30 Nov., 1891.

VARNUM, CHAS. A.* [Born in N. Y. Appointed from Fla.]
2nd Lieut. 7th Cav., 14 June, 1872. 1st Lieut., 25 June, 1876. R. Q. M., 14 Nov., 1876, to 31 Oct., 1879. Capt., 22 July, 1890. Medal of Honor for most distinguished gallantry in action at White Clay Creek, South Dakota, Dec. 30, 1890; this officer was in command of Troop B and part of Troop E, 7th U. S. Cav., the regiment then retiring by detachments before a superior force of hostile Indians. While executing an order to withdraw, Capt. Varnum saw that a continuance of the movement would result in exposure of another troop of his regiment to being cut off and surrounded. Disregarding orders to retire, he placed himself in front of his men, led a charge upon the advancing Indians, regained a commanding position that had just been vacated, and thus insured the safe withdrawal of both detachments without further loss.

VASHON, GEORGE. [Born in Md. Appointed from Va.]
1st Lieut. 10th Inf., 12 March, 1812. Reg. Adj., April to Nov., 1813. Capt., 29 Nov., 1813. Trans. to 7th Inf., 17 May, 1815. Resigned 31 Dec., 1819. Died 31 Dec., 1835.

VATTMAN, EDWARD J. [Born in Prussia. Appointed from Ohio.]
Post Chap., 6 Dec., 1890.

VAUGHAN, JOHN C. [Born in S. C. Appointed from Pa.]
Mil. Storekeeper Ord. Dept., 7 Aug., 1861. Resigned 3 Oct., 1863.

VAUX, WM. [Born in England. Appointed from D. C.]
Chap. Post of Fort Laramie, Neb., 29 Sept., 1849, to 1 July, 1862. Hosp. Chap. Vols., 6 Aug., 1864. Mustered out 29 April, 1867. Post Chap., 26 March, 1867. Retired, over sixty-two years of age, 8 June, 1880. Died 22 July, 1882.

VEDDER, NICHOLAS. [Born in N. Y. Appointed from Ill.]
Addl. P. M., 5 Sept., 1861. Bvt. Lieut. Col. Vols., 13 March, 1865, for faithful and meritorious service during the war. Maj. P. M., 17 Jan., 1867. Retired by operation of law, 2 Sept., 1882. Died 15 April, 1892.

VEDDER, SIMON C. [Born in N. Y. Appointed from N. Y.]
1st Lieut. 16th N. Y. Vols., 15 May, 1861. Mustered out 13 Sept., 1862. Capt. C. S. Vols., 22 July, 1864. Bvt. Maj. Vols., 3 June, 1865, for meritorious service. Mustered out June 14, 1865. 2nd Lieut. 28th Inf., 7 March, 1867. Bvt. 1st Lieut., 7 March, 1867 for gallant and meritorious service in the Battle of Gaines' Mills, Va. Trans. to 19th Inf., 31 March, 1869. 1st Lieut., 18 March, 1878. R. Q. M., 24 Feb., 1882, to 31 March, 1887. Retired for disability, with rank of Capt., 20 Feb., 1891. Died 5 Dec., 1892.

VEECH, DAVID H. [Born in Pa. Appointed from Pa.]
1st Lieut. 5th Art., 14 May, 1861. Resigned 16 June, 1863. Capt. C. S. Vols., 11 Nov., 1863. Resigned 6 Jan., 1865. Died 2 May, 1874.

VEIL, CHAS. H. [Born in Pa. Appointed from Army.]
Priv. Co. G, 9th Pa. Res., 29 July, 1861, to 31 Dec., 1863. Priv. Gen. Mounted Ser., 1 Jan. to 22 April, 1864. 2nd Lieut. 1st Cav., 7 April, 1864. 1st Lieut., 1 July, 1864. Mustered out 1 Jan., 1871. Bvt. 1st Lieut., 6 May, 1864, for gallant and meritorious service at the Battle of Todd's Tavern, Va. Bvt. Capt., 1 April, 1865, for gallant and meritorious service at the Battle of Five Forks, Va. Bvt. Maj., 1 April, 1865, for gallant and meritorious service at the Battle of Five Forks, Va.

VEITENHEIMER, CARL. [Born in Germany. Appointed from Pa.]
Bugler Co. K, 74th Pa. Vols., 5 Aug., 1861. 2nd Lieut., 24 Dec., 1862. 1st Lieut., 1 Jan., 1864. Capt., 7 July, 1864. Lieut. Col., 2 May, 1865. Mustered out 29 Aug., 1865. 2nd Lieut. 4th Inf., 23 April, 1866. 1st Lieut., 16 Nov., 1866. Died 25 Nov., 1873.

VERMANN, OTTO. [Born in Germany. Appointed from Mo.]
Corpl., Sergt. and 1st Sergt. Batty. B. 2nd Art., 19 Nov., 1851 to 17 Sept., 1861. 2nd Lieut. 1st N. Y. Eng., 3 Oct., 1861. 1st Lieut., 8 Dec., 1862. Resigned 22 July, 1863. Priv. Co. D, 44th Mo. Vols., 30 Aug., 1864. 2nd Lieut., 3 Sept., 1864. 1st Lieut., 4 Feb. 1865. Mustered out 11 July, 1865. 2nd Lieut. 13th Inf., 23 Feb., 1866. Died July 28, 1866.

VERNAY, JAMES D. [Born in Ill. Appointed from Ill.]
Priv. Co. B, 11th Ill. Vols., 31 Oct., 1861. 2nd Lieut., 16 May, 1862. Bvt. Maj. Vols., 13 March, 1865, for gallant conduct at the Battle of Vicksburg, Miss. Resigned 9 July, 1864. 2nd Lieut. 17th Inf., 28 April, 1866. Trans. to 35th Inf., 21 Sept., 1866. 1st Lieut., 12 July, 1867. Dismissed 18 April, 1870. Bvt. Capt., 12 July, 1867, for gallant and meritorious service during the war.

VERNON, CHAS. F. [Born in Ky. Appointed from Ky.]
2nd Lieut. Inf., 4 March, 1847; Voltigeurs, 9 April, 1847. Resigned 20 Dec., 1847.

VERNON, GEORGE R. [Born in N. Y. Appointed from Army.]
Priv. Co. F, 6th N. Y. State Mil., 26 April to 3 June, 1861. Priv. and Sergt. Co. F, 14th Inf., 29 Sept., 1862, to 25 March, 1863. 2nd Lieut. 14th Inf., 27 Feb., 1863. 1st Lieut., 18 June. 1864. Capt., 24 May, 1867. Unass'd, 22 July, 1869. Mustered out 1 Jan., 1871. Bvt. Capt., 27 Oct., 1864. for gallant and meritorious service in the Battles of Poplar Spring Church and Hatcher's Run, Va.

VERNOU, CHAS. A. [Born in Pa. Appointed from Pa.]
2nd Lieut. 3rd Pa. Cav., 18 April, 1862. Mustered out 8 July, 1862. 2nd Lieut. 3rd Pa. Cav., 9 May, 1863. Mustered out 24 Aug., 1864. 1st Lieut. 6th Pa. Cav., 19 Feb., 1865. Capt., 22 March, 1865. Mustered out 7 Aug., 1865. 2nd Lieut. 4th Cav., 7 March, 1867. 1st Lieut., 13 Jan., 1868. Trans. to 19th Inf., 10 July, 1873. Capt., 18 Dec., 1886. Maj. 17th Inf., 2 March, 1899. Retired, over thirty years' service, 8 June, 1899.

VERPLANCK, ABRAM G. [Born in N. Y. Appointed from N. Y.]
2nd Lieut. 11th N. Y. Vols., 5 Oct., 1861. 1st Lieut. 65th N. Y. Vols., 1 April, 1862. Discharged 11 Sept., 1864. 1st Lieut. 14th N. Y. Art., 12 Sept., 1864. Bvt. Capt. Vols., 13 March, 1865, for faithful and meritorious service during the Georgia and Carolina campaigns. Mustered out 26 Aug., 1865. 2nd Lieut 3rd Art., 23 Feb., 1866. 1st Lieut., 13 Aug., 1866. Bvt. Capt., 2 March, 1867, for gallant and meritorious service during the campaign of Atlanta, Ga. Bvt. Maj., 2 March, 1867, for gallant and meritorious service during Maj. Gen. Sherman's campaigns in Georgia and South and North Carolina. Dismissed 23 Feb., 1880. Died 9 March, 1880.

VESTAL, SAMUEL C. [Born in Ind. Appointed from the Army.]
Priv., Corpl. and Sergt. Co. E, 7th Inf., 14 Aug., 1895, to 29 April, 1898. 2nd Lieut. 7th Art., 12 April, 1898.

VESTAL, SOLOMON P.* [Born in N. C. Appointed from Ind.]
2nd Lieut. 5th Cav., 11 June, 1888. 1st Lieut., 7th Cav., 17 July, 1895.

VIALL, GEORGE E. [Born in N. Y. Appointed from Army.]
Priv., Corpl., Sergt. and 1st Sergt. Co. H. 11th, and Co. D, 20th Inf., 5 Sept., 1863, to 11 April, 1867. 2nd Lieut. 20th Inf., 28 Dec., 1866. 1st Lieut., 1 Nov., 1867. Died 26 Oct., 1868.

VICARS, THOMAS A. [Born in Canada. Appointed from the Army.]
Priv., Corpl. and Q. M. Sergt. Co. A, 21st Inf., 19 Sept., 1892, to 4 April, 1899. 2nd Lieut. 21st Inf., 5 April, 1899.

VICKERY, RICHARD S. [Born in Ireland. Appointed from Mich.]
Priv. Co. F, 2nd Mich. Vols., 17 May, 1861. Discharged 23 Oct., 1862. Asst. Surg., 2nd Mich. Vols., 23 Oct., 1862. Mustered out 11 March, 1865. 1st Lieut. Asst. Surg., 14 May, 1867. Capt. Asst. Surg., 28 Dec., 1867. Maj. Surg., 8 Oct., 1883. Retired by operation of law, 7 Dec., 1895.

VIDMER, GEORGE.* [Born in Ala. Appointed from Ala.]
2nd Lieut. 10th Inf., 12 June, 1894. Trans. to 10th Cav., 31 Oct., 1894. 1st Lieut., 2 March, 1899.

VIELE, CHAS. D. [Born in N. Y. Appointed from N. Y.]
2nd Lieut., 1st Inf., 24 Oct., 1861. 1st Lieut., 6 April, 1862. Bvt. Capt., 4 July, 1863, for gallant and meritorious service during the Siege of Vicksburg, Miss. Capt. 1st. Inf., 22 April, 1868. Unass'd 8 April, 1869. Ass'd to 10th Cav., 1 Jan., 1871. Maj. 1st Cav., 20 Aug., 1889. Lieut. Col., 21 Nov., 1897. Col. 4th Cav., 14 Sept., 1899.

VIELE, EGBERT L.* [Born in N. Y. Appointed from N. Y.]
Bvt. 2nd Lieut. 2nd Inf., 1 July, 1847. 2nd Lieut. 1st Inf., 8 Sept., 1847. 1st Lieut., 26 Oct., 1850. Resigned 1 June, 1853. Capt. Eng., 7th N. Y. State Militia, 19 to 30 April, 1861. Brig. Gen. Vols., 17 Aug., 1861. Resigned 20 Oct., 1863.

VILLARD, HIPPOLITE H.* [Born in D. C. Appointed from D. C.]
Ensign 1st Inf., 1 March, 1811. 2nd Lieut., 1 March, 1811. 1st Lieut., 20 Jan., 1813. Capt., 14 July, 1814. Trans. to Corps Art., 17 May, 1815. Resigned 13 May, 1816. Died 6 July, 1824.

VILLEPIGUE, JOHN B.* [Born in S. C. Appointed from S. C.]
Bvt. 2nd Lieut. 2nd Drag., 1 July, 1854. 2nd Lieut., 3 March, 1855. 1st Lieut., 27 May, 1857. Resigned 31 March, 1861. Died 9 Nov., 1862.

VINAL, WM. H. [Born in Ohio. Appointed from Ohio.]
Musician 17th Ind. Batty Ohio Light Art., 28 July, 1862. Corpl., 1 Sept., 1863. Priv., 25 July, 1865. Discharged 16 Aug., 1865. 2nd Lieut. 11th Inf., 23 Feb., 1866. 1st Lieut., 4 Oct., 1866. Trans. to 16th Inf., 14 April, 1869. Reg. Adj., 1 July, 1880, to 11 April, 1883. Capt., 11 April, 1883. Retired for disability, 14 April, 1887.

VINCENT, ALBERT O. [Born in Ohio. Appointed from Ohio.]
2nd Lieut. 2nd Art., 24 Oct., 1861. 1st Lieut., 11 Aug., 1862. Bvt. Capt., 17 Sept., 1862. for gallant and meritorious service in the Battle of Antietam, Md. Bvt. Maj., 3 July, 1863. for gallant and meritorious service in the Battle of Gettysburg, Pa. Maj. 4th Ark. Cav., 23 April, 1864. Mustered out of Vol. Ser., 1 Nov., 1865. Bvt. Lieut. Col., 13 Nov., 1865, for faithful and meritorious service in connection with

the mustering out of service and disbanding the Vol. army of the U. S. Capt. 38th Inf., 28 July, 1866, declined. Retired 15 Dec., 1870. Died 9 Dec., 1882.

VINCENT, BENJ'N. [Born in Pa. Appointed from Pa.]
2nd Lieut. 7th Inf., 18 April, 1818. Resigned 31 Aug., 1819.

VINCENT, FREDK. R. [Born in Prince Edward's Island. Appointed from Mo.]
Priv. and Sergt. Troop F, 11th and 2nd Mo. State Militia (Cav.), 24 March, 1862, to 6 Sept., 1863. 1st Lieut. 2nd Mo. State Militia (Cav.), 6 Sept., 1863. Capt., 11 Dec., 1863. Mustered out, 29 March, 1865. 2nd Lieut. 9th Cav., 18 June, 1867. 1st Lieut., 16 July, 1869. Died 20 April, 1872, of wounds received in action with Indians in Texas.

VINCENT, THOS. M.* [Born in Ohio. Appointed from Ohio.]
Bvt. 2nd Lieut. 2nd Art., 1 July, 1853. 2nd Lieut., 8 Oct., 1853. 1st Lieut., 20 Oct., 1855. R. Q. M., 1 June to 1 July, 1861. Capt. 18th Inf., 14 May, 1861, declined. Bvt. Capt. A. A. G., 3 July, 1861. Capt. A. A. G., 3 Aug., 1861. Maj. A. A. G., 17 July, 1862. Capt. 2nd Art., 25 July, 1863. Resigned commission of Capt. 2nd Art., 11 June, 1864. Bvt. Lieut. Col. and Col., 24 Sept., 1864. Bvt. Brig. Gen., 13 March, 1865, for meritorious and faithful service during the war. Lieut. Col. A. A. G., 1 July, 1881. Col. A. A. Gen., 2 Aug., 1890. Retired by operation of law, 15 Nov., 1896

VINING, BENJAMIN C.* [Born in Del. Appointed from Del.]
3rd Lieut. Ord., 24 July, 1818. 2nd Lieut., 13 Aug., 1819. Trans. to 1st Art., 1 June, 1821. Died 8 April, 1822.

VINSON, WEBSTER. [Born in D. C. Appointed from Va.]
Maj. P. M., 3 April, 1899.

VINTON, DAVID H.* [Born in R. I. Appointed from R. I.]
Bvt. 2nd Lieut. 1st Art., 1 July, 1822. 2nd Lieut. 4th Art., 1 July, 1822. Trans. to 6th Inf., 19 March, 1823. 1st Lieut., 7 April, 1825. Trans. 3rd Art., 24 March, 1826. A. Q. M., 19 Oct., 1836, to 7 July, 1838. Capt., 7 July, 1838. Capt. A. Q. M., 7 July, 1838. Maj. Q. M., 3 March, 1847. Lieut. Col. D. Q. M. G., 3 Aug., 1861. Col. Q. M., 2 Aug., 1864, to 29 July, 1866. Col. A. Q. M. G., 29 July, 1866. Retired 29 July, 1866. Died 21 Feb., 1873. Bvt. Col. Brig. Gen. and Maj. Gen., 13 March, 1865, for faithful and meritorious service during the war.

VINTON, FRANCIS.* [Born in R. I. Appointed from R. I.]
Bvt. 2nd Lieut. 3rd Art., 1 July, 1830. 2nd Lieut., 1 July, 1830. Resigned 31 Aug., 1836. Died 29 Sept., 1872.

VINTON, FRANCIS L.* [Born in Maine. Appointed at Large.]
2nd Lieut. 1st Cav., 1 July, 1856. Resigned 30 Sept., 1856. Capt. 16th Inf., 5 Aug., 1861. Col. 43rd N. Y. Vols., 31 Oct., 1861. Brig. Gen. Vols., 19 Sept., 1862. Appt. as Brig. Gen. exp'd, 4 March, 1863. Brig. Gen. Vols., 13 March, 1863. Resigned from Vol. Ser. and U. S. A., 5 May, 1863. Died 6 Oct., 1879.

VINTON, JOHN R.* [Born in R. I. Appointed from R. I.]
3rd Lieut. Corps Art., 17 July, 1817. 2nd Lieut., 31 Oct., 1817. 1st Lieut., 30 Sept., 1819. Trans. to 4th Art., 1 June, 1821. Trans. to 3rd Art., 5 Dec., 1821. Capt., 28 Dec., 1835. Killed 22 March, 1847, at the Siege of Vera Cruz, Mex. Bvt. Capt., 30 Sept., 1829, for ten years' faithful service in one grade. Bvt. Maj., 23 Sept., 1846, for gallant conduct at Monterey.

VIVEN, JOHN L. [Born in N. Y. Appointed from New Mexico.]
Priv. Co. D, 1st Cal. Cav., 6 Sept., 1861. Sergt., 13 Sept., 1861. Priv., 18 Aug., 1862. 2nd Lieut. 1st N. Mex. Cav., 16 March, 1864. 1st Lieut., 25 March, 1865. Mustered out 19 April, 1866. 2nd Lieut. 12th Inf., 23 Feb., 1866. 1st Lieut., 5 April, 1866. Bvt. Capt., 2 March, 1867, for faithful and meritorious service during the war. R. Q. M. 12th Inf., 1 March, 1869, to 28 Feb., 1871. Capt. 12th Inf., 31 March, 1873. Died 9 Jan., 1896.

VOGDES, ANTHONY W. [Born in N. Y. Appointed from N. Y.]
2nd Lieut. 100th N. Y. Vols., 13 Aug., 1863. 1st Lieut., 19 March, 1864. Mustered out 28 Aug., 1865. 2nd Lieut. 4th Inf., 26 April, 1866. 1st Lieut., 15 May, 1867. Trans. to 5th Art., 22 May, 1875. R. Q. M., 15 April, 1887, to 1 Oct., 1889. Capt., 1 Oct., 1889. Graduate of the Artillery School, 1882.

VOGDES, CHAS. B.* [Born in Fla. Appointed from Md.]
2nd Lieut. 1st Inf., 12 June, 1880. 1st Lieut., 20 March, 1889. Capt., 26 April, 1898.

VOGDES, ISRAEL.* [Born in Pa. Appointed from Pa.]
2nd Lieut. 1st Art., 1 July, 1837. 1st Lieut., 9 July, 1838. Capt., 20 Aug., 1847. Maj., 14 May, 1861. Brig. Gen. Vols., 29 Nov., 1862. Lieut. Col. 5th Art., 1 June, 1863. Col. 1st Art., 1 Aug., 1863. Bvt. Brig. Gen., 9 April, 1865, for gallant and meritorious service in the field during the war. Mustered out of Vol. Ser., 15 Jan., 1866. Retired, on his own request, aften forty years' service, 2 Jan., 1881. Died 7 Dec., 1889.

VOLKMAR, WALTER S. [Born in Pa. Appointed from Army.]
Priv. Sig. Corps, 10 Aug., 1896, to 7 July, 1898. 2nd Lieut. 4th Art., 23 June, 1898. 2nd Lieut. Vol. Sig. Corps, 20 May to 7 July, 1898. 1st Lieut. Signal Corps, 7 July, 1899, declined.

VOLKMAR, WM. J.* [Born in Pa. Appointed from Pa.]
Sergt. Co. D, 33rd Pa. Vols., 19 June, 1863. Discharged 4 Aug., 1863. Cadet Mil. Acad., 1 July, 1864. 2nd Lieut. 5th Cav., 15 June, 1868. 1st Lieut., 19 March, 1870. Capt., 2 April, 1879. Lieut. Col. A. de C. to Lieut. Gen. Sheridan, 6 June, 1881, to 28 March, 1885. Maj. A. A. G., 27 March, 1885. Lieut. Col. A. A. G., 6 Nov., 1893. Col. A. A. G., 26 Feb., 1898. Retired for disability, 28 April, 1900.

VOLLUM, EDWARD P. [Born in N. Y. Appointed from N. Y.]
1st Lieut. Asst. Surg., 31 May, 1853. Capt. Asst. Surg., 31 May, 1858. Maj. and Surg., 12 May, 1862. Lieut. Col. Med. Inspector, 11 June, 1862. Bvt. Lieut. Col., 13 March, 1865, for faithful and meritorious service during the war. Relieved as Lieut. Col. Med. Inspector, 31 Oct., 1865. Lieut. Col. Surg., 30 Jan., 1883. Col. Surg., 23 April, 1889. Col. Chf. Med. Purveyor, 28 Aug., 1890. Retired by operation of law, 11 Sept., 1891.

VON BLUCHER, GUSTAV. [Born in Denmark. Appointed from W. Va.]
2nd Lieut. 1st Batt. N. Y. Light Art., 2 Sept., 1862. 1st Lieut., 31 Dec., 1862. Capt.

31st N. Y. Batty, 17 Jan., 1864. Mustered out, 31 Oct., 1864. 1st Lieut. 16th Inf., 22 Jan., 1867. Unass'd. 17 April, 1869. Ass'd to 9th Inf., 6 April, 1870. Discharged 1 Oct., 1870. 2nd Lieut. 22nd Inf., 21 Aug., 1872. Resigned 5 June, 1875. Bvt. Capt., 2 March, 1867, for gallant and meritorious service at the Battle of Chancellorsville, Va. Bvt. Maj., 2 March, 1867, for gallant and meritorious service in the Battle of Gettysburg, Pa.

VON HERRMANN, CHAS J. [Born in Prussia. Appointed from Conn.]
Maj. A. A. de C., 5 Nov., 1861. Bvt. Lieut. Col., 9 April, 1865, for coolness, gallantry and valuable service during the campaign terminating with the surrender of the insurgent army under Gen. R. E. Lee. Mustered out 12 March, 1866. Capt. 33rd Inf., 28 July, 1866. Bvt. Maj., 2 March, 1867, for gallant and meritorious service in the Siege of Port Hudson, La. Unassigned 3 May, 1869. Ass'd to 4th Inf., 19 Feb., 1870. Retired by operation of law, 17 Sept., 1886. Died 16 March, 1889.

VON LUETTWITZ, ADOLPHUS H. [Born in Prussia. Appointed from Kan.]
Priv. Co. E. 54th N. Y. Vols., 1 Jan., 1862. Discharged 18 June, 1862. 2nd Lieut. 54th N. Y. Vols., 18 June, 1862. 1st Lieut. 1 Sept., 1862. Capt., 1 Nov., 1862. Mustered out 18 Sept., 1865. 2nd Lieut. 3rd Cav., 30 Aug., 1867. 1st Lieut., 26 Jan., 1870. Cashiered 8 July, 1870. Reinstated as 1st Lieut. 3rd Cav., 8 Sept., 1874, with former date and rank from 26 Jan., 1870. Retired 5 May, 1879. Died 29 March, 1889.

VON MICHALOWSKI, THEOPH. B. [Born in Prussia. Appointed from Army.]
Priv. Cos. C and G. 2nd Inf. and Sergt. Maj. 11th Inf., 16 April, 1860, to 28 Oct., 1861. 2nd Lieut. 1st Art., 28 Oct., 1861. 1st Lieut., 28 May, 1863. Resigned 28 Aug., 1867. Bvt. 1st Lieut., 17 Sept., 1862, for gallant and meritorious service at the Battle of Antietam, Md. Bvt. Capt., 24 June, 1864, for gallant and meritorious service in action near St. Mary's Church, Va.

VON SCHIRACH, FRED'K C. [Born in Prussia. Appointed from Mo.]
Musician Band and Co. A, 54th N. Y. Vols., 14 Oct., 1861. Discharged 1 March, 1862. 2nd Lieut. 54th N. Y. Vols., 1 March, 1862. 1st Lieut., 1 Jan., 1863. Mustered out 27 May, 1863. 1st Lieut. Vet. Res. Corps, 26 May, 1863. Bvt. Maj. Vols., 13 March, 1865, for gallant and meritorious service during the war. Capt. Vet. Res. Corps, 25 March, 1865. Mustered out 6 Jan., 1867. 1st Lieut. 43rd Inf., 28 July, 1866. Bvt. Capt., 2 March, 1867, for gallant and meritorious service in the Battle of Bull Run (2nd), Va. Unassigned 7 April, 1869. Retired with rank of Capt., 15 Dec., 1870.

VON SCHRADER, ALEX'R. [Born in Germany. Appointed from Ohio.]
Lieut. Col. 74th Ohio Vols., 10 Dec., 1861. Resigned 10 April, 1865. Lieut. Col. A. I. G., 28 Jan., 1863, to 1 Aug., 1865. Maj. A. A. G. Vols., 1 Feb., 1865. Bvt. Col. Vols., 13 March, 1865, for faithful and meritorious service during the war. Brig. Gen. Vols., 13 March, 1865, for gallant and meritorious service during the Battles of Stone River, Tenn., and Chickamauga, Ga., and during the Atlanta campaign, particularly for the Battle of Jonesboro, Ga. Mustered out 1 April, 1867. 2nd Lieut. 11th Inf., 28 July, 1866. Maj. 39th Inf., 28 July, 1866. Died 6 Aug., 1867. Bvt. Lieut. Col., 2 March, 1867, for gallant and meritorious service at the Batttle of Stone River, Tenn. Bvt. Col., 2 March, 1867, for gallant and meri-service at the Battle of Jonesboro, Ga. ,

VON SCHRADER, FRED'K. [Born in Ill. Appointed from Mich.]
2nd Lieut. 12th Inf., 1 Oct., 1873. 1st Lieut. 17 Nov., 1878. R. Q. M., 1 April, 1887, to ——. Capt. A. Q. M., 24 April, 1893. Maj. Q. M. Vols., 12 May, 1898.

VOORHIES, GORDON.* [Born in Ky. Appointed from Ky.]
2nd Lieut. of Inf. (25th), 12 June, 1891. Trans. to 4th Cav., 25 Aug., 1892, with rank from 24 Aug., 1892. Resigned 15 Nov., 1897.

VORIS, SAM'L P. [Born in Ohio. Appointed from Ill.]
Corpl. Co. E, 38th Ill. Vols., 21 Aug., 1861. Capt., 8 July, 1862. Mustered out 1 Sept., 1866. 2nd Lieut. 17th Inf., 11 May, 1866. Died 21 Sept., 1867. Bvt. 1st Lieut., 2 March, 1867, for gallant and meritorious service in the Battle of Stone River, Tenn. Bvt. Capt., 2 March, 1867, for gallant and meritorious service in the Battle of Chickamauga, Ga. Bvt. Maj., 2 March, 1867, for gallant and meritorious service at the Battle of Mission Ridge, Tenn.

VOSE, JOSIAH H. [Born in Mass. Appointed from Mass.]
Capt. 21st Inf., 9 April, 1812. Maj. 21st Inf., 4 Aug., 1814. Retained 17 May, 1815, as Capt. 5th Inf., with Bvt. of Maj. from 4 Aug., 1814. Maj. 8th Inf., 31 Dec., 1820. Retained as Capt. 4th Inf., 1 June, 1821. Trans. to 3rd Inf., 4 June, 1821. Trans. to 6th Inf., 26 June, 1821. Maj. 5th Inf., 1 Jan., 1822, to rank from 31 Dec., 1820. Lieut. Col. 3rd Inf., 23 April, 1830. Col. 4th Inf., 31 Jan., 1842. Died 15 July, 1845.

VOSE, JOSIAH, H., Jr. [Born in Mass. Appointed from N. Y.]
2nd Lieut 3rd Inf., 2 Dec., 1837. 1st Lieut., 18 Dec., 1839. Died 20 June, 1841.

VOSE, WM. P.* [Born in Maine. Appointed from Maine.]
2nd Lieut. 2nd Art., 13 June, 1864. 1st Lieut., 8 March, 1865. Bvt. Capt., 29 March, 1865, for gallant and meritorious service in the Siege of Petersburg, Va. Capt., 2 Oct., 1883. Maj. 6th Art., 8 March, 1898.

VROOM, PETER D. [Born in N. J. Appointed from N. J.]
1st Lieut. and Adj. 1st N. J. Vols., 28 Aug., 1862. Resigned 19 Sept., 1863. Maj. 2nd N. J. Cav., 25 Sept., 1863. Bvt. Lieut. Col. and Col. Vols., 13 March, 1865, for gallant and meritorious service during the war. Mustered out 24 Oct., 1865. 2nd Lieut. 3rd Cav., 23 Feb., 1866. 1st Lieut., 28 July, 1866. Reg. Com., 1 Dec., 1866, to 28 May, 1867. Reg. Adj., 28 Dec., 1868, to 15 May, 1871. Capt., 17 May, 1876. Maj. I. G., 10 Dec., 1888. Lieut. Col. I. G., 2 Jan., 1895. Col. I. G., 19 Dec., 1899.

WADDELL, JAMES F. [Born in N. C. Appointed from N. C.]
2nd Lieut. of Inf., 8 March, 1847; 12th Inf., 9 April, 1847. 1st Lieut., 31 March, 1848. Disbanded 25 July, 1848.

WADDELL, PEMBERTON. [Born in Pa. Appointed from Pa.]
Cadet Mil. Acad., 1 July, 1828, to 14 July, 1831. Capt. of Inf., 2 March, 1847; 11th Inf., 9 April, 1847. Died 25 Sept., 1847.

WADDY, JOHN R. [Born in Va. Appointed from Va.]
2nd Lieut. 4th Art., 21 Feb., 1857. 1st Lieut., 4 Feb., 1861. Resigned 26 July, 1861.

WADE, HENRY P. [Born in Ohio. Appointed from Ohio.]
1st Lieut. 5th U. S. Col. Cav., 20 May, 1864. Capt., 16 Nov., 1864. Resigned 10 March, 1866. Capt. U. S. Col. Cav., 10 March, 1866. Bvt. Maj. and Lieut. Col. Vols., 13 March, 1865, for faithful and meritorious service. Mustered out 15 April, 1866. 2nd Lieut. 5th Cav., 4 May, 1866. Capt. 8th Cav., 7 March, 1867. Resigned 10 Aug., 1869. Bvt. 1st Lieut., Capt. and Maj., 2 March, 1867, for gallant and meritorious service in action at Saltville, Va.

WADE, JAMES F. [Born in Ohio. Appointed from Ohio.]
1st Lieut. 3rd Cav., 14 May, 1861; 6th Cav., 3 Aug., 1861. Bvt. Capt., 9 June, 1863, for gallant and meritorious service in the Battle of Beverly Ford, Va. Lieut. Col. 6th U. S. Col. Cav., 1 May, 1864. Col. 6th U. S. Col. Cav., 19 Sept., 1864. Bvt. Maj., 19 Dec., 1864, for gallant and meritorious service in the action at Marion, E. Tenn. Bvt. Brig. Gen., 13 Feb., 1865, for gallant service in the campaign in Southwestern Va. Bvt. Lieut. Col. and Col., 13 March, 1865, for gallant and meritorious service during the war. Mustered out of Vol. Service, 15 April, 1866. Capt. 6th Cav., 1 May, 1866. Maj. 9th Cav., 28 July, 1866. Lieut. Col. 10th Cav., 20 March, 1879. Col. 5th Cav., 21 April, 1887. Brig. Gen., 26 May, 1897. Maj. Gen. Vols., 4 May, 1898, to 12 June, 1899.

WADE, JOHN P.* [Born in Ohio. Appointed from Ohio.]
Addl. 2nd Lieut. 5th Cav., 12 June, 1896. 2nd Lieut. 2nd Cav., 6 Nov., 1896. Trans. to 5th Cav., 8 Jan., 1897.

WADE, RICHARD D. A. [Born in N. Y. Appointed from N. Y.]
2nd Lieut. Corps Art., 27 Oct., 1820. Trans. to 7th Inf., 1 June, 1821. Trans. to 3rd Art., 16 Oct., 1822. 1st Lieut., 10 Sept., 1828. Capt., 26 Dec., 1840. Died 13 Feb., 1850. Bvt. Maj., 6 Nov., 1841, for gallant and successful service in the war against the Florida Indians. Bvt. Lieut. Col., 8 Sept., 1847, for gallant and meritorious conduct at the Battle of El Molino del Rey.

WADE, ROBT. B.* [Born in Ga. Appointed at Large.]
2nd Lieut. 17th Inf., 23 June, 1865. 1st Lieut 23 June, 1865. Capt., 29 Sept., 1867. Unassigned 27 March, 1869. Discharged 31 Dec., 1870. Died 8 Jan., 1884.

WADE, WM. [Born in N. J. Appointed from Pa.]
1st Lieut. Asst. Dep. Com. of Ord., 12 March, 1813. Capt., 9 Feb., 1815. Trans. to 4th Art., 1 June, 1821. Trans. to Ord. 30 May, 1832, but declined and left the service. Bvt. Maj., 9 Feb., 1825, for ten years' faithful service in one grade. Died 24 Jan., 1875.

WADSWORTH, DECIUS. [Born in ——. Appointed from Conn.]
Capt. Art. and Eng., 2 June, 1794. Resigned 19 July, 1796. Capt. Art. and Eng., 1 June, 1798. Maj. 2nd Art. and Eng., 9 Jan., 1800. Retained 15 April, 1802, as Maj. Art. Maj. Eng., 8 July, 1802. Resigned 10 Feb., 1805. Col. C. G. of Ord., 2 July, 1812. Retained as Col. and Chf. of Ord., 17 May, 1815. Disbanded 1 June, 1821. Died 8 Nov., 1821.

WAGER, BARNET.* [Born in N. Y. Appointed from Miss.]
2nd Lieut. 2nd Art., 17 June, 1867. 1st Lieut., 25 March, 1873. R. Q. M., 28 April, 1875, to 20 March, 1877. Died 9 Aug., 1883.

WAGER, PHILIP. [Born in Va. Appointed from Va.]
Ensign 12th Inf., 12 March, 1812. 3rd Lieut., 29 March, 1813. 2nd Lieut., 17 March, 1814. Trans. to 4th Inf., 17 May, 1815. R. Q. M., 1 Sept., 1816, to 21 May, 1817. 1st Lieut., 1 Dec., 1816. Capt., 8 May, 1818. Died 28 Nov., 1835. Bvt. Maj., 8 May, 1828, for ten years' faithful service in one grade.

WAGGAMAN, GEORGE G.* [Born in Va. Appointed from D. C.]
Bvt. 2nd Lieut. 1st Art., 1 July, 1835. 2nd Lieut., 31 March, 1836. 1st Lieut., 15 Feb., 1838. Capt. C. S., 2 Dec., 1841. Resigned 10 May, 1861. Bvt. Maj., 23 Sept., 1846, for gallant and meritorious conduct at Palo Alto and Resaca de la Palma, Texas. Died 9 Sept., 1884.

WAGLEY, WM. C. [Born in Ky. Appointed from Ky.]
2nd Lieut. 3rd Drag., 9 April, 1847. Disbanded 31 July, 1848.

WAGNER, ARTHUR L.* [Born in Ill. Appointed from Ill.]
2nd Lieut. 6th Inf., 16 June, 1875. 1st Lieut., 18 Oct., 1882. Capt., 2 April, 1892. Maj. A. A. G., 17 Nov., 1896. Lieut. Col. A. A. G., 26 Feb., 1898.

WAGNER, CLINTON. [Born in Md. Appointed from Md.]
Asst. Surg., 11 Oct., 1860. Maj. Surg., 28 July, 1866. Resigned 25 March, 1869. Bvt. Maj. and Lieut. Col., 13 March, 1865, for faithful and meritorious service during the war.

WAGNER, HENRY. [Born in Germany. Appointed from Army.]
Priv. General Service, 14 April, 1856. Corpl., 30 May, 1857. Sergt., 1 Nov., 1857. Priv., 21 March, 1860. Discharged 14 Feb., 1861. Priv. General Service, 14 Feb., 1861. Priv. Co. G, 1st Inf., — Nov., 1861. Trans. to Co. F, 3rd Inf., 6 Feb., 1862. Sergt., 1 March, 1862. Trans. to Com. Sergt. 1st Batt. 11th Inf., 14 July, 1862. Q. M. Sergt. 11th Inf., 4 Sept., 1862. 2nd Lieut. 11th Inf., 19 Feb., 1863. 1st Lieut., 5 May, 1864. Bvt. Capt., 2 April, 1865, for gallant and meritorious service in front of Petersburg, Va. Trans. to 29th Inf., 21 Sept., 1866. R. Q. M., 6 Dec., 1866, to 27 Jan., 1869. Capt., 27 Jan., 1869. Unassigned 25 April, 1869. Ass'd to 1st Cav., 31 Dec., 1870. Maj. 5th Cav., 17 Dec., 1890. Lieut. Col. 4th Cav., 13 July, 1898. Retired by direction of the President, being over sixty-two years of age, 1 July, 1899.

WAGNER, HENRY S. [Born in Pa. Appointed from Pa.]
2nd Lieut. 8th Inf., 9 July, 1898. 1st Lieut. 14th Inf., 30 Aug., 1899.

WAGNER, JACOB. [Born in Pa. Appointed from Pa.]
Priv. Co. H, and Q. M. Sergt. 48th Pa. Vols., 19 Sept., 1861, to 22 Dec., 1862. 1st Lieut. R. Q. M. 48th Pa. Vols., 22 Dec., 1862. Maj., 21 June, 1865. Mustered out 17 July, 1865. 1st Lieut. 29th Inf., 28 July, 1866. Unassigned 25 April, 1869. Ass'd to 10th Inf., 14 July, 1869. Discharged 9 Dec., 1870.

WAGNER, JEAN P. [Born in Belgium. Appointed from Army.]
Priv., Corpl. and Sergt. Co. G, 8th Inf., 7 Jan., 1851, to 7 Jan., 1856. Priv. and

Corpl. Co. K, 2nd Inf., 3 May, 1856, to 3 May, 1861. Priv. and 1st Sergt. Co. C, 12th Inf., 20 May, 1861, to 19 April, 1863. 2nd Lieut. 12th Inf., 10 March, 1863. 1st Lieut., 17 July, 1863. Died 16 May, 1864, of wounds received at the Battle of the Wilderness, Va. Bvt. Capt., 5 May, 1864, for gallant and meritorious service at the Battle of the Wilderness, Va.

WAGNER, ORLANDO G.* [Born in Pa. Appointed from Pa.]
Bvt. 2nd Lieut. Top. Eng., 1 July, 1859. 2nd Lieut., 14 May, 1861. 1st Lieut., 3 Aug., 1861. Died 21 April, 1862, of wounds received before Yorktown, Va. Bvt. Capt., 10 Sept., 1861, for gallant and meritorious service in the campaign in Western Va. Bvt. Maj., 17 April, 1862, for gallant and meritorious service at the Siege of Yorktown, Va., where he was mortally wounded while reconnoitering the enemy's works.

WAGNER, JOSEPH J. [Born in Ohio. Appointed from Army.]
Priv. and 1st Sergt. Co. B, 19th Inf., 10 Sept. to 29 Nov., 1861. 2nd Lieut. 19th Inf., 20 Nov., 1861. 1st Lieut., 30 Sept., 1862. R. Q. M., 26 Dec., 1864, to 13 June, 1865. Capt., 13 June, 1865. Died 12 Sept., 1866. Bvt. Capt., 1 Sept., 1864, for gallant and meritorious service during the Atlanta campaign. Bvt. Maj., 13 June, 1865, for meritorious service in the Battle before Atlanta, Ga.

WAHL, LUTZ.* [Born in Wis. Appointed from Wis.]
2nd Lieut. 5th Inf., 12 June, 1891. 1st Lieut 21st Inf., 25 March, 1898.

WAINWRIGHT, GEORGE.* [Born in Mass. Appointed from Mass.]
Bvt. 2nd Lieut. 8th Inf., 1 July, 1844. 2nd Lieut., 18 June, 1846. Died 2 Aug., 1848.

WAINWRIGHT, ROB'T A.* [Born in Mass. Appointed from Mass.]
Bvt. 2nd Lieut. 5th Inf., 1 July, 1835. 2nd Lieut. 4th Art., 22 Oct., 1836. 2nd Lieut. Ord., 9 July, 1838. 1st Lieut., 27 March, 1842. Capt., 3 March, 1853. Maj., 3 Aug., 1861. Lieut. Col., 15 Sept., 1863. Died 22 Dec., 1866. Bvt. Col., 13 March, 1865, for faithful service in the Ord. Dept.

WAINWRIGHT, ROB'T P. P.* [Born in Pa. Appointed from N. Y.]
Cadet at Mil. Acad., 1 July, 1870, to 10 Dec., 1870. Reappointed 1 July, 1871. 2nd Lieut 1st Cav., 16 June, 1875. 1st Lieut., 12 June, 1880. Capt., 4 Feb., 1892. Adj., 29 May, 1899. Bvt. 1st Lieut., 27 Feb., 1890, for gallant service in action against Indians at the Umatilla Agency, Ore., 13 July, 1878.

WAINWRIGHT, SAM'L A. [Born in Mass. Appointed from D. C.]
Capt. 13th Inf., 14 May, 1861. Trans. to 31st Inf., 21 Sept., 1866. Trans. to 22nd Inf., 15 May, 1869. Maj. 16th Inf., 1 July, 1872. Dismissed 23 Aug., 1878.

WAINWRIGHT, WM. A [Born in N. H. Appointed from Ind.]
Corpl. Co. I, 6th Ind. Vols., 23 April to 2 Aug., 1861. Priv. Musician 8th Ind. Cav., 29 Aug., 1861, to 13 Jan., 1862. Sergt. Co. D, 75th Ind. Vols., 15 July, 1862. 1st Lieut. R. Q. M., 29 Sept., 1862. Capt. A. Q. M. Vols., 5 Dec., 1863, to 25 March, 1867. Capt. A. Q. M., 18 Jan., 1867. Discharged 9 Sept., 1870.

WAITE, CARLOS A. [Born in N. Y. Appointed from N. Y.]
2nd Lieut. 2nd Inf., 28 Jan., 1820. 1st Lieut., 1 May, 1828. Capt., 3 July, 1836. (Capt. A. Q. M., 7 July, 1838, to 8 May, 1845.) Maj. 8th Inf., 16 Feb., 1847. Lieut. Col. 5th Inf., 10 Nov., 1851. Col. 1st Inf., 5 June, 1860. Retired 8 Feb., 1864. Died 7 May, 1866. Bvt. Lieut. Col., 20 Aug., 1847, for gallant and meritorious conduct at Contreras and Churubusco. Bvt. Col., 8 Sept., 1847, for gallant and meritorious conduct at Molino del Rey. Bvt. Brig. Gen., 13 March, 1865, for long and faithful service in the army.

WAITE, EDWARD D. [Born in N. Y. Appointed from N. Y.]
2nd Lieut. 9th Inf., 12 Nov., 1861. 1st Lieut., 9 March, 1863. Reg. Adj., 1 May, 1864, to 1 July, 1865. Lost at sea, 30 July, 1865.

WAITE, HENRY DE H.* [Born in N. Y. Appointed from Ohio.]
2nd Lieut. 2nd Inf., 13 June, 1879. Trans. to 5th Cav., 4 Sept., 1879. 1st Lieut., 4 June, 1888. Graduate of the Artillery School, 1886-1888. Retired 6 June, 1894. Capt. Troop E, 1st Ohio Vol. Cav., 9 May to 22 Oct., 1898.

WAITE, JAMES M. [Born in N. Y. Appointed from N. Y.]
Cadet at Mil. Acad., 1 July, 1861, to 25 March, 1862. 1st Sergt. 22nd N. Y. Batty, 28 Oct., 1862, to 14 Jan., 1863. 2nd Lieut. 5th N. Y. Art., 15 Jan., 1863. Mustered out 30 June, 1863. Priv. 1st N. Y. Light Art., 3 Sept., 1864, to 15 May, 1865. 2nd Lieut. 8th N. Y. Art., 15 May, 1865. Trans. to 4th N. Y. Art., 4 June, 1865. Mustered out 12 June, 1865. 2nd Lieut 4th Art., 23 Feb., 1866. 1st Lieut., 28 July, 1866. Trans. to 25th Inf., 20 Sept., 1869. Dismissed 2 March, 1870.

WAKEMAN, WM. J. [Born in Conn. Appointed from Conn.]
Asst. Surg., 23 May, 1882. Capt. Asst. Surg., 23 May, 1887. Maj. Brig. Surg. Vols., 4 June, 1898, to 30 April, 1899.

WALBACH, JOHN DE B. [Born in Germany. Appointed from Pa.]
Lieut Light Drag., 8 Jan., 1799. Trans. to 2nd Art. and Eng., 16 Feb., 1801. Retained in Reg. of Art., 1 April, 1802. Capt., 31 Jan., 1806. Trans. to Corps Art., 12 May, 1814. A. D. Q. M. G., 3 April, 1812. Maj. A. A. G., 27 June, 1813. Col. A. G., 6 Aug., 1813, to 15 June, 1815. Retained as Capt. Corps Art., 17 May, 1815. Maj. Corps Art., 25 April, 1818. Trans. to 1st Art., 1 June, 1821. Lieut. Col., 30 May, 1832. Col. 4th Art., 19 March, 1842. Died 10 June, 1857. Bvt. Maj., 11 Nov., 1813, for gallant conduct at the Battles of Crysler's Farm and Lawrence, U. C. Bvt. Lieut. Col., 1 May, 1815, for meritorious service. Bvt. Col., 1 May, 1825, for ten years' faithful service in one grade. Bvt. Brig. Gen., 11 Nov., 1823, for meritorious service.

WALBACH, LOUIS A. DE B.* [Born in N. H. Appointed from N. H.]
Bvt. 2nd Lieut. 1st Art., 1 July, 1834. 2nd Lieut., 1 Oct., 1835. 1st Lieut., 19 May, 1837. Trans. to Ord., 15 Aug., 1838, to rank as 2nd Lieut. from 1 Oct., 1835. 1st Lieut., 16 Nov., 1839. Capt., 25 March, 1848. Died 26 June, 1853.

WALBORN, R. FRANK. [Born in Pa. Appointed from Army.]
Priv. and Corpl. Co. G, 6th Pa. Res., 29 May, 1861, to 24 Dec., 1862. 2nd Lieut. 214th Pa. Vols., 25 March, 1865. Mustered out 21 March, 1866. Priv. Troop L, 6th Cav., 25 July to 11 Dec., 1866. 2nd Lieut. 31st Inf., 28 July, 1866. Died 23 Nov., 1868.

WALBRIDGE, GEORGE R. [Born in N. Y. Appointed from Wis.]
1st Lieut. 8th Wis. Vols., 21 Jan., 1862. Discharged 15 Dec., 1862. 1st Lieut Vet. Res. Corps, 8 Aug., 1863. Capt., 20 June, 1864. Mustered out 12 May, 1867. 2nd Lieut 6th Inf., 7 March, 1867. Resigned 14 May, 1868.

WALBRIDGE, TRUMAN K.* [Born in N. Y. Appointed from N. Y.]
Bvt. 2nd Lieut. 4th Art., 1 July, 1848. 2nd Lieut., 16 May, 1849. 1st Lieut., 8 Oct., 1853. Died 16 Nov., 1856.

WALCOTT, DANIEL W. [Born in R. I. Appointed from Army.]
Priv., Corpl., Sergt. and 1st Sergt. Troops K and H, 1st Cav., 27 Nov., 1861, to 30 March, 1865. 2nd Lieut 1st Cav., 12 March, 1865. 1st Lieut., 1 Aug., 1866. Resigned 27 Aug., 1869.

WALCOTT, WM. H. [Born in Mass. Appointed from R. I.]
Priv. Tompkins' Batty R. I. Light Art., 2 May to 1 June, 1861. Sergt. Co. A, 1st R. I. Light Art., 6 June, 1861. Discharged 24 Aug., 1861. 1st Lieut. 17th Inf., 14 May, 1861. Bvt. Capt., 3 May, 1863. Bvt. Maj., 2 July, 1863, for gallant and meritorious service in the Battle of Gettysburg, Pa. Capt. 17th Inf., 14 Feb., 1864. Retired 7 Jan., 1865. Bvt. Lieut. Col. and Col., 13 March, 1865, for gallant and meritorious service during the war.

WALCUTT, CHAS. C. [Born in Ohio. Appointed from Ohio.]
Maj. 46th Ohio Vols., 1 Oct., 1861. Lieut Col., 30 Jan., 1862. Brig. Gen. Vols., 30 July, 1864. Bvt. Maj. Gen. Vols., 13 March, 1865, for special gallantry at the Battle of Griswoldville, Ga. Mustered out 15 Jan., 1866. Lieut. Col. 10th Cav., 28 July, 1866. Resigned 1 Dec., 1866.

WALCUTT, CHARLES C., Jr.* [Born in Ohio. Appointed from Ohio.]
2nd Lieut. 8th Cav., 1 July, 1886. 1st Lieut. 3rd Cav., 16 Aug., 1892. Trans. to 8th Cav., 5 Dec., 1892. Graduate of the Infantry and Cavalry School, 1893. Capt. A. Q. M. Vols., 12 May, 1898, to 18 Sept., 1899. Maj. 44th U. S. Vols., 17 Aug., 1899, to ——.

WALDO, RHINELANDER. [Born in N. Y. Appointed from N. Y.]
2nd Lieut. 17th Inf., 10 April, 1899.

WALDRON, ALBERT E.* [Born in Iowa. Appointed from Ill.]
2nd Lieut. 1st Art., 15 Feb., 1899.

WALDRON, WM. H. [Born in W. Va. Appointed from W. Va.]
Q. M. Sergt. and 1st Sergt. Co. E, W. Va. Vols., 30 June, 1898, to 10 April, 1899. 2nd Lieut. 9th Inf., 10 April, 1899.

WALES, JOHN P. [Born in Del. Appointed from Del.]
Capt. 17th Inf., 14 May, 1861. Resigned 10 March, 1865. Bvt. Maj., 18 Aug., 1864, for gallant service during the operations on the Weldon Railroad, Va.

WALES, PHILIP G. [Born in Pa. Appointed from D. C.]
Asst. Surg., 7 Feb., 1884. Resigned 5 Nov., 1886. Reappointed 7 June, 1889. Capt. Asst. Surg., 7 June, 1894. Maj. Brig. Surg. Vols., 4 June, 1898, to 26 April, 1899. Maj. Surg. 39th U. S. Vols., 17 Aug., 1899, to ——.

WALKE, WILLOUGHBY.* [Born in Va. Appointed from Va.]
2nd Lieut. 2nd Art., 13 June, 1883. 1st Lieut 5th Art., 24 April, 1891. Trans. to 7th Art., 8 March, 1898. Capt. 2nd Art., 28 Aug., 1899. Graduate of the Artillery School, 1888.

WALKER, BENJAMIN.* [Born in Vt. Appointed from N. H.]
3rd Lieut. Ord., 1 July, 1819. 2nd Lieut., 31 Dec., 1819. Trans. to 1st Art., 1 June, 1821. Trans. to 3rd Inf., 3 Oct., 1821. 1st Lieut., 13 Oct., 1823. Capt., 31 Aug., 1833. Maj. P. M., 17 Dec., 1839. Died 28 May, 1858.

WALKER, CHAS. J.* [Born in Ky. Appointed from Ky.]
Bvt. 2nd Lieut. 2nd Drag., 1 July, 1857. 2nd Lieut., 14 June, 1858. 1st Lieut., 11 May, 1861. 2nd Cav., 3 Aug., 1861. Capt., 15 Feb., 1862. Col. 10th Ky. Cav., 12 Dec., 1862. Resigned from Vols., 1 Sept., 1863. Resigned 25 July, 1865. Bvt. Maj., 15 April, 1865, for faithful and meritorious service. Died 4 March, 1879.

WALKER, EDGAR S.* [Born in Mo. Appointed from Mo.]
2nd Lieut. 17th Inf., 13 June, 1883. 1st Lieut. 25th Inf., 24 Feb., 1891. Trans. to 8th Inf., 20 July, 1891. Capt. of Inf., 10 July, 1898. Ass'd to 8th Inf., 1 Jan., 1899.

WALKER, FERGUS. [Born in Ireland. Appointed from N. Y.]
Priv. and Q. M. Sergt. 38th N. Y. Vols., 3 June to 15 June, 1861. 2nd Lieut. 38th N. Y. Vols., 6 Aug., 1861. 1st Lieut., 2 May, 1862. Capt., 24 April, 1863. Mustered out 22 June, 1863. Capt. Vet. Res. Corps, 1 Oct., 1863. Mustered out 20 July, 1866. Capt. 43rd Inf., 28 July, 1866. Bvt. Maj., 2 March, 1867, for gallant and meritorious service in the Battle of Chancellorsville, Va. Trans. to 1st Inf., 8 April, 1869. Died 15 Sept., 1882.

WALKER, FREEMAN V. [Born in Ga. Appointed from Ga.]
Asst. Surg., 27 July, 1886. Capt. Asst. Surg., 27 July, 1891. Wholly retired, 4 Dec., 1895.

WALKER, GEORGE B.* [Born in Ind. Appointed from Ind.]
2nd Lieut. 6th Inf., 14 June, 1872. 1st Lieut., 15 Dec., 1880. Capt., 1 Aug., 1891.

WALKER, GEORGE W. [Born in Ohio. Appointed from Iowa.]
2nd Lieut 9th Inf., 19 Feb., 1862. 1st Lieut., 25 July, 1863. Capt., 7 Feb., 1867. Died 10 Sept., 1867.

WALKER, HENRY H.* [Born in Va. Appointed from Va.]
Bvt. 2nd Lieut. 3rd Inf., 1 July, 1853. 2nd Lieut. 6th Inf., 3 March, 1855. 1st Lieut., 1 May, 1857. Resigned 3 May, 1861.

WALKER, HENRY P.* [Born in N. Y. Appointed from N. Y.]
2nd Lieut. 17th Inf., 17 June, 1874. 1st Lieut. 27 Aug., 1878. Died 11 Sept., 1880.

WALKER, JAMES H. [Born in Tenn. Appointed from Ark.]
Capt. A. Q. M. Vols., 4 Aug., 1846. Resigned 9 Sept. 1847. Capt. Voltigeurs, 9 Sept., 1847. Disbanded 31 Aug., 1848.

WALKER, JOHN D. [Born in N. H. Appointed from N. H.]
Asst. Surg., 3 March, 1847; 9th Inf., 9 April, 1847. Resigned 26 June, 1847. Died 4 Sept., 1858.

WALKER, JOHN G. [Born in Mo. Appointed from Mo.]
1st Lieut. Mounted Rifles, 27 May, 1846. Capt., 30 June, 1851. Resigned 31 July, 1861. Bvt. Capt., 1 Aug., 1847, for gallant and meritorious conduct at San Juan de los Llanos, Mexico.

WALKER, JOHN H. [Born in N. Y. Appointed from N. Y.]
Priv. Co. D, 13th N. Y. State Militia, 23 April, 1861. Discharged 20 June, 1861. 1st Lieut. 14th Inf., 14 May, 1861. Bvt. Capt., 27 June, 1862, for gallant and meritorious service at the Battle of Gaines' Mills, Va. Bvt. Maj., 17 Sept., 1862, for gallant and meritorious service in the Battle of Antietam, Md. Adj. 2nd Batt. 14th Inf., — Feb., 1865, to 6 May, 1865. Capt., 6 May, 1865. Trans. to 23rd Inf., 21 Sept., 1866. Retired 27 March, 1869. Died 11 June, 1891.

WILKER, JOHN P.* [Born in Ohio. Appointed from Ohio.]
2nd Lieut. 13th Inf., 18 June, 1866. Trans. to 22nd Inf., 21 Sept., 1866. Reg. Adj., 12 May, 1867, to 31 Jan., 1868. 1st Lieut., 5 Jan., 1869. Unassigned 15 May, 1869. Ass'd to 3rd Cav., 31 Dec., 1870. Capt., 30 Nov., 1879. Retired for disability 17 Nov., 1883.

WALKER, JOHN S. [Born in Va. Appointed from Army.]
Priv., Corpl. and Sergt. Co. D, 1st Drag. (1st Cav.), 23 June, 1858, to 17 July, 1862. 2nd Lieut. 1st Cav., 17 July, 1862. 1st Lieut., 12 Feb., 1864. Reg. Com., 13 April to 14 Aug., 1864. Killed 15 Aug., 1864, in action near Harper's Ferry, Va.

WALKER, JOHN S. [Born in Maine. Appointed from Maine.]
Addl. P. M. Vols., 23 Feb., 1864, to 5 April, 1867. Bvt. Lieut. Col. Vols., 15 June, 1866, for faithful and meritorious conduct. Maj. P. M., 17 Jan., 1867. Lost at sea, 27 Jan., 1873.

WALKER, JOSEPH. [Born in Bermuda. Appointed from Ill.]
Asst. Surg., 21 Aug., 1838. Resigned 2 April, 1849.

WALKER, KENZIE W.* [Born in Texas. Appointed from Texas.]
Addl. 2nd Lieut. 9th Cav., 12 June, 1893. 2nd Lieut., 30 June, 1893. 1st Lieut., 2 March, 1899.

WALKER, KIRBY.* [Born in Ohio. Appointed from Ohio.]
2nd Lieut. 3rd Cav., 11 June, 1892. 1st Lieut. 6th Cav., 14 Dec., 1898. Trans. to 4th Cav., 6 Feb., 1899.

WALKER, LEICESTER. [Born in Ohio. Appointed from Ohio.]
2nd Lieut. 2nd Cav., 8 May, 1861; 5th Cav., 3 Aug., 1861. 1st Lieut., 15 Jan., 1862. Capt., 2 Nov., 1863. Discharged 30 Dec., 1870. Bvt. Capt., 9 June, 1863, for gallant and meritorious service at the Battle of Beverly Ford, Va. Bvt. Maj., 11 May, 1864, for gallant and meritorious service at the Battle of Yellow Tavern, Va.

WALKER, LEVERETT H.* [Born in Pa. Appointed from Ill.]
2nd Lieut. 15th Inf., 12 June, 1871. 1st Lieut., 2 Nov., 1875. Trans. to 4th Art., 12 Aug., 1882. Capt., 8 March, 1898. Graduate of the Artillery School, 1888.

WALKER, LUCIUS M.*. [Born in Tenn. Appointed at Large.]
Bvt. 2nd Lieut. 2nd Drag., 1 July, 1850. 2nd Lieut., 8 Aug., 1851. Resigned 31 March, 1852. Died 19 Sept., 1863

WALKER, MARK. [Born in Pa. Appointed from Ind.]
Priv., Sergt. and 1st Sergt. Co. D, 15th Ind. Vols., 14 June, 1861, to 1 Jan., 1863. 2nd Lieut. 15th Ind. Vols., 1 Jan., 1863. Mustered out 25 June, 1864. Capt., 214th Pa. Vols., 30 March, 1865. Bvt. Maj. Vols., 13 March, 1865, for gallant and meritorious service during the war. Mustered out 22 Jan., 1866. 2nd Lieut. 19th Inf., 23 Feb., 1866. 1st Lieut., 23 Feb., 1866. Dismissed 13 May, 1878. Bvt. Capt., 2 March, 1867, for good conduct throughout the war. Died 1 Jan., 1884.

WALKER, MERIWETHER.* [Born in Va. Appointed from Va.]
Addl. 2nd Lieut. Eng., 12 June, 1893. 2nd Lieut., 12 Oct., 1895. 1st Lieut., 5 July, 1898.

WALKER, MOSES B. [Born in Ohio. Appointed from Ohio.]
Capt. 12th Inf., 23 Aug., 1861. Col. 31st Ohio Vols., 27 Sept., 1861. Bvt. Maj. and Lieut. Col., 13 March, 1865, for gallant and meritorious service during the war. Bvt. Brig. Gen. Vols., 27 March, 1865, for gallant and meritorious conduct during the war. Mustered out of Vol. Service, 20 July, 1865. Retired 19 Feb., 1866. Retired with rank of Col., 28 July, 1866. Died 17 Dec., 1895.

WALKER, PHILIP E. M. [Born in Va. Appointed from Va.]
2nd Lieut. 16th Inf., 9 July, 1898. 1st Lieut. 3rd Inf., 2 March, 1899.

WALKER, ROBT. C. [Born in Pa. Appointed from Pa.]
Capt. C. S. Vols., 31 Oct., 1861. Addl. P. M. Vols., 29 Nov., 1862. Mustered out 15 Nov., 1865. Maj. P. M., 4 May, 1866. Resigned 3 Sept., 1874. Reappointed 19 June, 1878, and retired 22 June, 1878. Died 5 June, 1894.

WALKER, SAM'L. [Born in Pa. Appointed from Pa.]
Priv. Co. H, 13th Pa. Vols., 25 April, 1861. Discharged 6 Aug., 1861. Priv. Co. F, 155th Pa. Vols., 22 Aug., 1862. Sergt., 22 Aug., 1862. 2nd Lieut. Vet. Res. Corps, 20 Feb., 1864. Bvt. 1st Lieut. and Capt. Vols., 13 March, 1865, for gallant and meritorious service during the war. Mustered out 27 Aug., 1868. 2nd Lieut. 45th Inf., 16 Sept., 1868. Unassigned 22 July, 1869. Retired 31 Dec., 1870. Died 4 July, 1896.

WALKER, SAM'L H. [Born in Md. Appointed from Texas.]
Capt. Texas Mounted Rangers, 11 April, 1846. Lieut. Col., 24 June, 1846. Mustered out 2 Oct., 1846. Capt. Mounted Rifles, 27 May, 1846. Killed 9 Oct., 1847, in action at Huamantla, Mexico.

WALKER, THOS. W.* [Born in Ind. Appointed from Ind.]
2nd Lieut. 3rd Inf., 1 July, 1856. 1st Lieut., 11 April, 1861. Capt., 20 May, 1851. Bvt. Maj., 27 June, 1862, for gallant and meritorious service in the Battle of Gaines' Mills, Va. Retired 11 Sept., 1863. Died 9 Dec., 1890.

WALKER, WM. [Born in Ala. Appointed from Ala.]
2nd Lieut. 3rd Drag., 5 March, 1847. 1st Lieut., 23 Dec., 1847. Disbanded 31 July, 1848.

WALKER, WM. H. T.* [Born in Ga. Appointed from Ga.]
Bvt. 2nd Lieut. 6th Inf., 1 July, 1837. 2nd Lieut., 31 July, 1837. 1st Lieut., 1 Feb., 1838. Resigned 31 Oct., 1838. Reappointed 18 Nov., 1840, with former date of

rank. Capt. 6th Inf., 7 Nov., 1845. Maj. 10th Inf., 3 March, 1855. Resigned 22 Dec., 1860. Bvt. 1st Lieut., 25 Dec., 1837, for gallant and good conduct in the war against the Florida Indians. Bvt. Maj., 20 Aug., 1847, for gallant and meritorious conduct in the Battles of Contreras and Churubusco. Bvt. Lieut. Col., 8 Sept., 1847, for gallant and meritorious conduct in the Battle of Molino del Rey, Mexico.

WALKER, WM. S. [Born in Pa. Appointed from Miss.]
1st Lieut. of Inf., 27 Feb., 1847; Voltigeurs 9 April, 1847. Reg. Adj., 1 May to 15 June, 1847. Disbanded 31 Aug.,1848. Capt. 1st Cav., 3 March, 1855. Resigned 1 May, 1861. Bvt. Capt., 13 Sept., 1847, for gallant and meritorious conduct at the Battle of Chapultepec, Mexico.

WALKLEY, CHARLES S. [Born in England. Appointed from Ohio.]
Musician Cos. F and C, 58th Pa. Vols. and Priv. 51st Co. 2 Batt. Vet. Res. Corps, 20 Sept., 1861, to 19 Sept., 1865. Post Chap., 2 April, 1897.

WALL, ASA. [Born in Va. Appointed from Va.]
Asst. Surg., 29 Aug., 1856. Resigned 11 May, 1861.

WALL, RICHD. [Born in Ireland. Appointed from Army.]
Priv., Corpl., Sergt. and 1st Sergt. Co. C, Mounted Rifles, 1 Dec., 1855, to 15 Sept., 1862. 2nd Lieut. 3rd Cav., 17 July, 1862. 1st Lieut., 15 Feb., 1864. Capt., 24 Dec., 1866. Died 28 July, 1868. Bvt. 1st Lieut., 15 Nov., 1863, for gallant and meritorious service in action near Tuscumbia, Ala.

WALL, WM.* [Born in Pa. Appointed from Pa.]
Bvt. 2nd Lieut. 3rd Art., 1 July, 1832. 2nd Lieut., 30 Sept., 1833. 1st Lieut., 16 March, 1837. (Capt. A. Q. M., 19 Jan., 1841, to 18 June, 1846.) Capt. 3rd Art., 27 June, 1843. Died 13 Aug., 1847.

WALLACE, DAVID.* [Born in Ohio. Appointed from Ohio.]
Bvt. 2nd Lieut. 2nd Art., 1 July, 1821. 2nd Lieut., 2nd Art., 1 July, 1821. Resigned 1 June, 1822. Died 4 Sept., 1859.

WALLACE, EDWARD T. [Born in Ind. Appointed from Ind.]
Priv. Ind. Vols., Oct., 1847, to July, 1848. Capt. 11th Ind. Vols., 25 April, 1861. Mustered out 4 Aug., 1861. Capt. 11th Ind. Vols., 31 Aug., 1861. Resigned 9 Sept., 1863. Capt. Vet. Res. Corps. 8 Dec., 1863. Mustered out 3 Sept., 1866. 2nd Lieut. 24th Inf., 22 Jan., 1867. 1st Lieut., 7 Feb., 1868. Unassigned 25 April, 1869. Mustered out 1 Jan., 1871. Died 30 Dec., 1885.

WALLACE, ELMER J. [Born in Dak. Appointed from S. D.]
2nd Lieut. 1st Art., 9 July, 1898.

WALLACE, GEORGE D.* [Born in S. C. Appointed from S. C.]
2nd Lieut 7th Cav., 14 June, 1872. 1st Lieut., 25 June, 1876. Reg. Adj., 25 June, 1876, to 6 June, 1877. Capt., 23 Sept., 1885. Killed 29 Dec., 1890, in action with Indians at the crossing of Wounded Knee Creek, S. D.

WALLACE, GEORGE H. [Born in Canada. Appointed from Army.]
1st Lieut. Adj. 123rd N. Y. Vols., 4 Sept., 1862. Capt., 11 Nov., 1863. Resigned 11 Jan., 1864. Priv. 3rd Inf., 9 Jan. to 16 April, 1864. 2nd Lieut. 3rd Inf., 7 April, 1864. 1st Lieut., 24 Dec., 1864. Resigned 7 May, 1867.

WALLACE, GEORGE W. [Born in Pa. Appointed from Pa.]
2nd Lieut 1st Inf., 1 July, 1839. 1st Lieut., 1 March, 1844. Capt., 10 June, 1850. Maj. 6th Inf., 10 Jan., 1862. Lieut. Col. 12th Inf., 15 March, 1866. Retired 15 Dec., 1870. Died 12 Oct., 1888.

WALLACE, GEORGE W. [Born in Kan. Appointed from Col.]
2nd Lieut. 9th Inf., 10 April, 1899.

WALLACE, HAMILTON S. [Born in D. C. Appointed from D. C.]
Addl. P. M. Vols., 24 Oct., 1898, to 12 Sept., 1899. Maj. P. M., 9 Sept., 1899.

WALLACE, IRWIN M. [Born in Ky. Appointed from Pa.]
1st Lieut. 18th Inf., 26 Oct., 1861. Died 19 Feb., 1862.

WALLACE, JOHN P. [Born in Ala. Appointed from Ala.]
2nd Lieut. of Inf., 5 March, 1847; 13th Inf., 9 April, 1847. Resigned 24 Sept., 1847.

WALLACE, JOSEPH. [Born in Md. Appointed from N. Y.]
Hosp. Surg.'s Mate, 15 July, 1813. Post Surg., 18 April, 1818. Asst. Surg., 1 June, 1821. Resigned 30 Aug., 1827.

WALLACE, JOSEPH C. [Born in Pa. Appointed from Pa.]
2nd Lieut. 3rd Drag., 16 Feb., 1847. Resigned 23 Aug., 1847.

WALLACE, ROBERT B.* [Born in Ill. Appointed from Mont.]
2nd Lieut. 2nd Cav., 12 June, 1890. 1st Lieut., 4 Jan., 1897. Lieut. Col. 1st Mont. Vols., 9 May, 1898, to 10 July, 1899. Col. 37th U. S. Vols., 5 July, 1899, to ——.

WALLACE, SAM'L B. [Born in Pa. Appointed from Army.]
Priv., Corpl., Sergt. and 1st Sergt. Co. B, 1st Inf., 3 Dec., 1859, to 22 Aug., 1863. 2nd Lieut. 1st Inf., 10 Aug., 1863. 1st Lieut., 28 July, 1866. Died 27 Aug., 1867.

WALLACE, THOS. S. [Born in Kan. Appointed from N. Y.]
1st Lieut. 4th N. Y. Art., 20 May, 1865. Mustered out 26 Sept., 1865. 2nd Lieut. 3rd Inf., 27 April, 1866. 1st Lieut., 31 Dec., 1867. Died 8 Dec., 1878.

WALLACE, WM. [Born in Ind. Appointed from Ind.]
2nd Lieut. 7th Inf., 7 Oct., 1891. 1st Lieut., 26 April, 1898. Graduate of the Infantry and Cavalry School, 1895.

WALLACE, WM. B.* [Born in Pa. Appointed from N. J.]
2nd Lieut 1st Art., 1 July, 1836. Resigned 30 Sept., 1836. Died 9 Nov., 1841.

WALLACE, WM. M. [Born in Wis. Appointed from N. Y.]
1st Lieut. 13th N. Y. Art., 29 March, 1864. Mustered out 6 May, 1864. 2nd Lieut. 8th Inf., 2 Oct., 1866. 1st Lieut., 25 Sept., 1867. Unassigned 3 May, 1869. Ass'd to 6th Cav., 15 Dec., 1870. Capt., 17 May, 1876. Maj. 2nd Cav., 10 Nov., 1894. Lieut. Col., 18 Oct., 1899.

WALLACE, WM. S. [Born in Pa. Appointed from Ill.]
Maj. P. M., 15 May, 1861. Retired 7 March 1866. Died 22 May, 1867.

WALLACH, ROBERT R. [Born in D. C. Appointed from D. C.]
2nd Lieut. 7th Art., 9 July, 1898. Trans. to 3rd Cav., 29 March, 1899.

WALLEN, HENRY D.* [Born in Ga. Appointed from Florida.]
Bvt. 2nd Lieut., 3rd Inf., 1 July, 1840. 2nd Lieut. 4th Inf., 4 Oct., 1840. 1st Lieut., 9 Sept., 1846. Reg. Adj., 1 Feb., 1849, to 31 Jan., 1850. Capt., 31 Jan., 1850.

Maj. 7th Inf., 25 Nov., 1861. Bvt. Lieut. Col. and Col., 23 Feb., 1865, for meritorious service rendered by him in N. M. during the war. Bvt. Brig. Gen., 13 March, 1865, for faithful and meritorious service during the war. Lieut. Col. 14th Inf., 30 July, 1865. Unassigned 15 March, 1869. Ass'd to 8th Inf., 15 Dec., 1870. Col. 2nd Inf., 19 Feb., 1873. Retired 18 Feb., 1874. Died 2 Dec., 1886.

WALLEN, HENRY D., Jr.* [Born in Mo. Appointed at Large.]
2nd Lieut. 3rd Art., 17 June, 1867. Unassigned 13 May, 1869. Ass'd to 21st Inf., 3 Aug., 1870. Discharged 1 Sept., 1870. Died 23 Dec., 1889.

WALLER, HENRY.* [Born in Ky. Appointed from Ky.]
Bvt. 2nd Lieut. 2nd Art., 1 July, 1833. Resigned 9 Oct., 1833.

WALLINGFORD, DAVID W. [Born in Vt. Appointed from Kan.]
Corpl. Co. C, 2nd Kans. Vols., 20 June to 24 Aug., 1861. 2nd Lieut. 15th Kans. Cav., 29 Aug., 1863. Discharged 28 April, 1865. 2nd Lieut. 7th Cav., 28 July, 1866. 1st Lieut., 8 June, 1867. Dismissed 10 May, 1870.

WALMSLEY, ROBERT McG. [Born in N. Y. Appointed from N. Y.]
Surg.'s Mate 29th Inf., 1 July, 1813. Trans. to 7th Inf., 17 May, 1815. Post Surg., 10 Aug., 1818. Maj. Surg. 8th Inf., 13 May, 1820. Discharged 1 June, 1821.

WALRADT, WM. L. [Born in N. Y. Appointed from N. Y.]
Capt. of Inf., 3 March, 1847; 10th Inf., 9 April, 1847. Disbanded 14 Aug., 1848.

WALSH, EDWARD. [Born in Ireland. Appointed from Army.]
Priv., Corpl. and Sergt. Co. D, and Sergt. Maj. 5th Inf., 23 Aug., 1854, to 10 Aug., 1863. 2nd Lieut. 5th Inf., 10 Aug., 1863. Resigned 2 Feb., 1865.

WALSH, JAMES W. [Born in Ireland. Appointed from Md.]
Priv., Corpl., Sergt. and 1st Sergt. Co. G, Mounted Rifles, 19 Dec., 1850, to 19 Oct., 1860. Capt. 3rd Pa. Cav., 1 Jan., 1862. Maj., 4 Dec., 1863. Lieut. Col., 31 Oct., 1864. Trans. to 5th Pa. Cav., 8 May, 1865. Bvt. Col. Vols., 9 April, 1865, for gallant and meritorious service during the operations resulting in the fall of Richmon, Va., and the surrender of the insurgent army under Gen. R. E. Lee. Mustered out 7 Aug., 1865. 2nd Lient. 5th Cav., 4 May, 1866. Capt. 10th Cav., 28 July, 1866. Died 3 March, 1873.

WALSH, ROBERT D.* [Born in Cal. Appointed from Cal.]
2nd Lieut. 22nd Inf., 13 June, 1883. Trans. to 4th Cav., 13 Sept., 1883. Bvt. 1st Lieut., 27 Feb., 1890, for gallant service in action against Indians in the Patagonia Mountains, Mex., 6 June, 1886. 1st Lieut. 5th Cav., 16 March, 1891. Trans. to 4th Cav., 27 April, 1891. Capt. 9th Cav., 2 March, 1899. Maj. 35th U. S. Vols., 5 July, 1899, to ——.

WALSH, SAML. A. [Born in N. Y: Appoinnted from N. Y.]
Post Surg., 9 Aug., 1813. Discharged 15 June, 1815. Reinstated 17 May, 1816. Resigned 1 Oct., 1820.

WALSHE, JOHN C. [Born in England. Appointed from Army.]
Priv., Sergt. and 1st Sergt. Co. I, 19th Inf., 20 Dec., 1869, to 20 Dec., 1874. Priv. and Sergt. Sig. Corps, 15 Jan., 1875, to 27 April, 1883. 2nd Lieut. Sig. Corps, 27 April, 1883. 2nd Lieut 10th Cav., 4 Feb., 1891, to rank from 27 April, 1883. Retired for disability, with the rank of 1st Lieut., 24 Feb., 1891.

WALTER, ISAAC N. [Born in N. Y. Appointed from Ohio.]
Sergt. Co. F, 2nd Ohio Vols., 17 April to 31 July, 1861. Priv. Co. C, 5th Ohio Vols., 6 Sept., 1861. 2nd Lieut. 47th Ohio Vols., 11 Jan., 1862. 1st Lieut., 25 Feb., 1863. Mustered out 22 June, 1864. 2nd Lieut. 6th Cav., 24 April, 1867. 1st Lieut., 18 Nov., 1867. Retired 31 Dec., 1870. Died 31 March, 1889.

WALTERS, WM [Born in England. Appointed from N. Y.]
Mil. Storekeeper Ord. Dept., 16 Sept., 1862. Died 27 June, 1864.

WALTON, EDWARD S. [Born in La. Appointed from Army.]
Priv. and Corpl. Co. F, 15th Inf., 31 Aug., 1894, to 12 May, 1897. 2nd Lieut. 18th Inf., 19 April, 1897. 1st Lieut., 2 March, 1899.

WALTON, JOHN M. [Born in Pa. Appointed from Pa.]
2nd Lieut. 4th Cav., 24 Oct., 1867. 1st Lieut., 1 Jan., 1871. R. Q. M., 25 March, 1870, to 20 April, 1872. Retired 28 June, 1878.

WALTON, ROMULUS F.* [Born in Ala. Appointed from Ala.]
2nd Lieut. 10th Inf., 26 April, 1898 1st Lieut., 2 March, 1899. Reg. Com., 1 June, 1899

WALTZ, MILLARD F.* [Born in Md. Appointed from Md.]
Addl. 2nd Lieut. 12th Inf., 14 June, 1878. 2nd Lieut., 28 June, 1878. 1st Lieut., 15 Oct., 1884 Capt., 9 Jan., 1896.

WANDS, ALEX'R H. [Born in N. Y. Appointed from N. Y.]
1st Lieut. 18th N. Y. Vols., 17 May, 1861. Resigned 18 July, 1862. 1st Lieut. Vet. Res. Corps, 1 July, 1863. Capt., 26 July, 1864 Bvt. Maj. Vols., 13 March, 1865, for gallant and meritorious service, and Lieut. Col. Vols., for faithful and meritorious service. Mustered out 15 March, 1866. 2nd Lieut. 18th Inf., 16 March, 1866. 1st Lieut., 28 July, 1866. Trans. to 36th Inf., 21 Sept., 1866. R. Q. M., 1 March, 1867, to 1 June, 1868. Unassigned 19 May, 1869. Discharged 31 Aug., 1870.

WANLESS, JOHN A. [Born in S. C. Appointed from Kan.]
Corpl. and Sergt. Co. C, 2nd Kan. Cav., 3 Dec, 1861, to 17 Sept., 1863. Capt. 15th Kan. Cav., 17 Sept., 1863. Dismissed 27 April, 1865. 2nd Lieut. 2nd Cav., 23 Feb., 1866. 1st Lieut., 28 July, 1866. Mustered out 1 Jan., 1871.

WANN, WM. L., Jr. [Born in Ohio. Appointed from Ohio.]
Priv. 136th Pa. Vols., 14 Aug., 1862, to 19 May, 1863. Priv. Co. D, 162nd Ohio Vols., 20 May to 4 Sept., 1864. Musician Co. F, and Prin. Musician 184th Ohio Vols., 19 Feb. to 20 Sept., 1865. 2nd Lieut. 13th Inf., 2 July, 1867. Mustered out 19 Dec., 1870.

WANSBORO, THOMAS A. [Born in ——. Apointed from——.]
2nd Lieut. 7th Inf., — ——, 1898. Killed in action, 1 July, 1898, at El Caney, Santiago, Cuba.

WARD, CHAS. [Born in N. H. Appointed from Md.]
3rd Lieut. Ord., 17 May, 1816. 2nd Lieut., 1 Oct., 1818. Trans. to 4th Art.,

1 June, 1821. 1st Lieut., 20 July, 1822. Capt., 27 June, 1836. Resigned 31 Aug., 1836. Bvt. Capt., 20 July, 1832, for ten years' faithful service in one grade. Died 21 April, 1850.

WARD, CHAS. R.* [Born in Pa. Appointed from Pa.]
2nd Lieut. 10th Cav., 12 June, 1871. 1st Lieut., 17 May, 1876. Dismissed 17 Jan., 1888.

WARD, DELOS A. [Born in N. Y. Appointed from Wis.]
Priv., Co. I, 1st Wis. Vols., 17 May to 21 Aug., 1861. Com. Sergt. 14th Wis. Vols., 30 Jan., 1862. 2nd Lieut., 18 April, 1862. Capt., 27 Feb., 1863. Resigned 22 July, 1863. Capt. 65th U. S. Col. Inf., 25 Jan., 1864. Trans. to 55th U. S. Col. Inf., 12 July, 1865. Mustered out 21 Jan., 1866. Capt. 39th Inf., 28 July, 1866. Trans. to 25th Inf., 20 April, 1869. Mustered out 1 Jan., 1871.

WARD, EDWARD W. [Born in Ky. Appointed from Ky.]
1st Lieut. Ky. Scouts, 26 Dec., 1861. Capt., 24 March, 1863. Trans. to 3rd Ky. Cav., 27 July, 1863. Mustered out 15 July, 1865. 2nd Lieut. 5th Cav., 22 July, 1867. 1st Lieut., 25 April, 1869. Capt., 23 Aug., 1878. Retired 1 May, 1879.

WARD, FRED'K K.* [Born in Ohio. Appointed from Ohio.]
2nd Lieut. 1st Cav., 15 June, 1870. 1st Lieut., 11 Nov., 1875. Reg. Adj., 1 Dec., 1885, to 30 Sept., 1886. Capt., 11 Feb., 1887. Maj. 10th Cav., 11 July, 1899. Trans. to 1st Cav., 2 Aug., 1899.

WARD, GEORGE S. L. [Born in Pa. Appointed from Pa.]
2nd Lieut. 3rd Pa. Cav., 16 May, 1863. 1st Lieut., 5 Oct., 1864. Capt., 31 Oct., 1864. Mustered out 7 Aug., 1865. 2nd Lieut. 13th Inf., 11 May, 1866. Trans. to 31st Inf., 21 Sept., 1866. Trans. to 22nd Inf., 15 May, 1869. 1st Lieut., 1 July, 1872. Capt., 24 April, 1883. Retired for disability, 18 April, 1891.

WARD, GEORGE W.* [Born in Mass. Appointed from Mass.]
Bvt. 2nd Lieut. 2nd Art., 1 July, 1832. 2nd Lieut., 1 July, 1832. 1st Lieut., 11 Sept., 1836. Resigned 31 Dec., 1836. Died 13 Oct., 1851.

WARD, HENRY C. [Born in Mass. Appointed from Mass.]
Priv. Co. D, 15th Mass. Vols., 31 July, 1861. Sergt. Maj. 15th Mass. Vols., 1 Nov., 1862. 2nd Lieut. 15th Mass. Vols., 9 April, 1863. Mustered out 4 Sept., 1863. 1st Lieut. 57th Mass. Vols., 9 March, 1864. Capt., 24 Oct., 1864. Mustered out 30 July, 1865. 2nd Lieut. and 1st Lieut. 11th Inf., 23 Feb., 1866. Bvt. Capt., 2 March, 1867, for gallant and meritorious service in action at Fort Steedman, Va., 24 March, 1865. Trans. to 16th Inf., 14 April, 1869. R. Q. M., 1 March, 1875 to 8 Feb., 1880. Capt., 8 Feb., 1880. Maj. 16th Inf., 26 April, 1898. Maj. I. G. Vols., 12 May, 1898, declined.

WARD, ISAAC M. [Born in Ky. Appointed from Army.]
Priv., Corpl., Sergt. and 1st Sergt. Troop A, 1st Cav. and 6th Cav., 26 Jan., 1857, to 29 Oct., 1861. 2nd Lieut. 6th Cav., 26 Oct., 1861. 1st Lieut., 20 Oct., 1862. Killed 9 June, 1863, at Battle of Beverly Ford, Va.

WARD, JAMES. [Born in Md. Appointed from Md.]
3rd Lieut. 38th Inf., 20 May, 1813. Capt., A. D. Q. M. G., 31 Aug., 1813. Disbanded 15 June, 1815. Mil. Storekeeper, 12 Aug., 1817. Disbanded 1 June, 1821.

WARD, JAMES N.* [Born in Ky. Appointed from Ga.]
Bvt. 2nd Lieut. 6th Inf., 1 July, 1845. 2nd Lieut. 3rd Inf., 21 Sept., 1846. 1st Lieut., 5 March, 1851. Capt., 28 Sept., 1857. Died 6 Dec., 1858. Bvt. 1st Lieut., 18 April, 1847, for gallant and meritorious conduct at Cerro Gordo.

WARD, MATTHEW H. [Born in N. Y. Appointed from N. Y.]
1st Lieut. R. Q. M. 9th Mich. Cav., 5 Nov., 1862. Discharged 30 Nov., 1864. 2nd Lieut. 2nd Art., 7 Nov., 1866. Died 3 July, 1867.

WARD, PHILIP R. [Born in N. Y. Appointed from N. Y.]
Cadet at Mil. Acad., 15 June, 1893, to 26 Jan., 1897. 2nd Lieut. 7th Art., 20 April, 1898.

WARD, ROBERT J. [Born in Ireland. Appointed from Army.]
Priv., Corpl. and Sergt. Troop D, 1st Drag., 7 Oct., 1857, to 7 Oct., 1862. Priv. Mounted Service, 23 Dec., 1862, to 8 June, 1863. 2nd Lieut. 1st Cav., 1 June, 1863. 1st Lieut., 12 June, 1864. Cashiered 1 Aug., 1866. Bvt. 1st Lieut., 6 May, 1864, for gallant and meritorious service at the Batle of Todd's Tavern, Va. Bvt. Capt., 12 June, 1864, for gallant and meritorious service at the Battle of Trevillian Station, Va.

WARD, THOS.* [Born in N. Y. Appointed from N. Y.]
2nd Lieut. 1st Art., 11 June, 1863. Bvt. 1st Lieut., 3 June, 1864, for gallant and meritorious service in the Battle of Cold Harbor, Va. 1st Lieut. 1st Art., 18 July, 1864. Bvt. Capt., 13 March, 1865, for gallant and meritorious service during the war. Capt. 1st Art., 1 Nov., 1876. Maj. A. A. G., 28 June, 1884. Lieut. Col. A. A. G., 31 Aug., 1893. Col. A. A. G., 11 Sept., 1897.

WARDEN, JAMES K. [Born in N. Y. Appointed from N. Y.]
1st Sergt. Co. A, 75th N. Y. Vols., 26 Nov., 1861. 2nd Lieut., 15 Aug., 1862. 1st Lieut., 17 Nov., 1863, to 25 Aug., 1864. 2nd Lieut. Vet. Res. Corps, 22 Aug., 1864. 1st Lieut., 21 Feb., 1865. Mustered out 8 Oct., 1866. 1st Lieut. 45th Inf., 28 July, 1866. Reg. Adj., 25 March, 1867, to 22 July, 1869. Trans. to 14th Inf., 22 July, 1869. Drowned 15 Dec., 1869.

WARDWELL, HENRY.* [Born in R. I. Appointed from N. Y.]
Bvt. 2nd Lieut. 7th Inf., 1 July, 1840. 2nd Lieut. 8th Inf., 28 Sept., 1840. Died 21 July, 1841.

WARE, ISAAC P. [Born in Maine. Appointed from Maine.]
Asst. Surg., 5 May, 1892. Capt. Asst. Surg., 5 May, 1897. Wholly retired 29 Sept., 1899.

WARFIELD, CLAUDIUS. [Born in Md. Appointed from Md.]
Asst. Surg., 14 May, 1867. Resigned 15 Jan., 1868.

WARFIELD, ELDRED D. [Born in Md. Appointed from Md.]
Capt. Co. D, 5th Md. Vols., 14 May to 22 Oct., 1898. 2nd Lieut. 11th Inf., 10 April, 1899.

WARFIELD, WM. H.* [Born in Md. Appointed from Md.]
Bvt. 2nd Lieut. 3rd Inf., 1 July, 1829. Resigned 12 Oct., 1832. Died 26 March, 1857.

WARING, JOHN K. [Born in N. Y. Appointed from N. Y.]
2nd Lieut. 2nd Inf., 8 May, 1867. 1st Lieut., 27 April, 1879. Capt. 2nd Inf., 17 April, 1891. Retired for disability, with rank of Maj., 15 Nov., 1899.

WARNER, CHAS. N.* [Born in Pa. Appointed from Pa.]
Bvt. 2nd Lieut. 2nd Art., 17 June, 1862. 2nd Lieut. 4th Art., 5 Aug., 1862. 1st Lieut., 11 May, 1864. Mustered out 1 Jan., 1871. Bvt. 1st Lieut., 3 July, 1863, for gallant and meritorious service at the Battle of Gettysburg, Pa. Bvt. Capt., 2 April, 1865, for gallant and meritorious service at the capture of Selma, Ala.

WARNER, EDWARD R.* [Born in Pa. Appointed from Pa.]
Bvt. 2nd Lieut. 1st Art., 1 July, 1857. 2nd Lieut. 3rd Art., 3 Dec., 1858. 1st Lieut., 14 May, 1861. R. Q. M., 27 Sept., 1861, to 27 Oct., 1862. Lieut. Col. 1st N. Y. Art., 1 Nov., 1862. Bvt. Capt., 3 July, 1863, for meritorious service in the Battle of Gettysburg, Pa. Bvt. Col. Vols., 1 Aug., 1864, for gallant and distinguished service in the Battle of Gettysburg, and in the operations in front of Petersburg. Bvt. Maj., 13 March, 1865, for gallant and meritorious service during the Siege of Petersburg, Va. Bvt. Lieut. Col., 13 March, 1865, for good conduct and gallant service during the war. Bvt. Brig. Gen. Vols., 9 April, 1865, for faithful and meritorious service during the operations resulting in the fall of Richmond, Va., and the surrender of the insurgent army under Gen. R. E. Lee. Mustered out of Vol. Service, 21 June, 1865. Capt. 3rd Art., 28 July, 1866. Maj. 1st Art., 7 May, 1887. Retired, for over thirty years' service, 11 Aug., 1887.

WARNER, JAMES M.* [Born in Vt. Appointed from Vt.]
Bvt. 2nd Lieut. 10th Inf., 1 July, 1860. 2nd Lieut. 8th Inf., 28 Feb., 1861. 1st Lieut., 30 May, 1861. Col. 11th Vt. Vols., 1 Sept., 1862. Brig. Gen. Vols., 8 May, 1865. Mustered out of Vol. Service, 15 Jan., 1866. Capt. 8th Inf., 8 Oct., 1864. Resigned 13 Feb., 1866. Bvt. Maj., Lieut. Col. and Col., 13 March, 1865, for gallant and meritorious service during the war. Bvt. Brig. Gen., 9 April, 1865, for gallant and meritorious service in the field during the war.

WARNER, THOS. [Born in N. Y. Appointed from N. Y.]
Chap. and Prof. Mil. Acad., 1 Jan., 1828. Resigned 1 Sept., 1838. Died 1848.

WARNER, WM. H.* [Born in N. Y. Appointed from N. Y.]
2nd Lieut. 1st Art., 1 July, 1836. 2nd Lieut. Top. Eng., 7 July, 1838. 1st Lieut., 1 Sept., 1841. Killed 26 Sept., 1849, by Indians in the Sierra Nevada. Bvt. Capt., 6 Dec., 1846, for gallant and meritorious service in Cal.

WARREN, GOUVERNEUR K.* [Born in N. Y. Appointed from N. Y.]
Bvt. 2nd Lieut. Top. Eng., 1 July, 1850. 2nd Lieut., 1 Sept., 1854. 1st Lieut., 1 July, 1856. Capt. 17th Inf., 14 May, 1861, declined. Lieut. Col. 5th N. Y. Vols., 14 May, 1861. Capt. Top. Eng., 9 Sept., 1861. Col. 5th N. Y. Vols., 11 Sept., 1861. Bvt. Lieut. Col., 27 June, 1862, for gallant and meritorious service in the Battle of Gaines' Mills, Va. Discharged from Vol. Service, 26 Sept., 1862. Brig. Gen. Vols., 26 Sept., 1862, for distinguished conduct in the Battle of Gaines' Mills. Trans. to Eng., 3 March, 1863. Bvt. Col., 4 July, 1863, for gallant and meritorious service in the Battle of Gettysburg, Pa. Maj. Gen. Vols., 3 May, 1863. Maj. Eng., 25 June, 1864. Bvt. Brig. Gen., 13 March, 1865, for gallant and meritorious service in the Battle of Bristow Station, Va. Bvt. Maj. Gen., 13 March, 1865, for gallant and meritorious service in the field during the war. Resigned commission of Maj. Gen. Vols., 27 May, 1865. Lieut. Col. Eng., 4 March, 1879. Died 8 Aug., 1882.

WARREN, JAMES G.* [Born in N. Y. Appointed from N. Y.]
Addl. 2nd Lieut. Eng., 11 June, 1881. 2nd Lieut., 5 April, 1882. 1st Lieut., 26 March, 1883. Capt., 12 April, 1894.

WARREN, LUCIUS H. [Born in Mass. Appointed from Mass.]
2nd Lieut. 32nd Mass. Vols., 11 Aug., 1862. 1st Lieut., 14 Dec., 1862. Maj. 38th U. S. Col. Vols., 9 April, 1864. Lieut. Col., 12 April, 1866. Bvt. Lieut. Col. and Brig. Gen. Vols., 13 March, 1865, for gallant and meritorious service during the war. Mustered out 25 Jan., 1867. 1st Lieut., 39th Inf., 28 July, 1866. Capt., 31 July, 1867. Unassigned 20 April, 1869. Discharged 15 Oct., 1870. Bvt. Maj. and Lieut. Col., 31 July, 1867, for gallant and meritorious service in the Siege of Petersburg, Va.

WARREN, LYMAN H. [Born in N. H. Appointed from Army.]
Priv., Corpl. and Sergt. Co. D, 17th Inf., 16 Sept., 1861, to 9 Nov., 1862. 2nd Lieut. 17th Inf., 13 Oct., 1862. 1st Lieut., 14 Dec., 1862. Capt., 25 Oct., 1865. Died 18 Sept., 1867. Bvt. Capt., 2 July, 1863, for gallant and meritorious service at the Battle of Gettysburg, Pa.

WARREN, ROBT. P. [Born in N. Y. Appointed from N. Y.]
Priv. Co. F, 7th N. Y. State Militia, 25 May to 5 Sept., 1862. 2nd Lieut. 146th N. Y. Vols., 14 Aug., 1863. 1st Lieut., 20 Nov., 1863. Capt., 1 April, 1865. Bvt. Capt. Vols., 13 March, 1865, for gallant and meritorious service at the Battle of Chappel House, Va., and Bvt. Maj. Vols., 1 April, 1865, for gallant service at the Battle of Five Forks, Va. Mustered out 16 July, 1865. 2nd Lieut. 24th Inf., 22 Jan., 1867. 1st Lieut. 28 May, 1868. Unassigned 25 April, 1869. Ass'd to 14th Inf., 15 Dec., 1870. Died 23 Jan., 1876.

WARRENS, CHAS. H. [Born in Prussia. Appointed from Mo.]
1st Lieut. 4th Mo. Vols., 20 May, 1861. Mustered out 1 Aug., 1861. Capt. 5th Mo. Cav., 1 Feb., 1862. Maj., 7 July, 1862. Mustered out 16 Oct., 1862. Capt. 29th Mo. Vols., 18 Oct., 1862. Mustered out 13 June, 1863. Capt. Vet. Res. Corps, 5 Sept., 1863. 2nd Lieut. 18th Inf., 11 May, 1866. Trans. to 27th Inf., 21 Sept., 1866. Mustered out of Vet. Res. Corps, 25 Oct., 1866. 1st Lieut. 27th Inf., 7 Jan., 1867. R. Q. M., 1 July, 1867, to 14 June, 1869. Trans. to 9th Inf., 14 June, 1869. Trans. to 14th Inf., 22 May, 1871. R. Q. M., 1 Jan., 1873, to 30 June, 1878. Capt., 2 April, 1883. Retired at his own request, sixty-two years of age, 29 Sept., 1891.

WARRINGTON, LEWIS. [Born in D. C. Appointed from D. C.]
2nd Lieut. 4th Cav., 18 June, 1867. 1st Lieut., 31 July, 1869. Died 4 Jan., 1879.

WARWICK, OLIVER B. [Born in Ala. Appointed from Ala.]
Cadet at Mil. Acad., 1 Sept., 1868, to 6 Feb., 1873. 2nd Lieut. 18th Inf., 1 Oct., 1873. 1st Lieut., 20 Feb., 1882. Capt. 18th Inf., 30 Nov., 1892. Killed in action at Passi, Central Panay, Philippine Islands, 26 Nov., 1899.

WASH, RICHARD. [Born in S. C. Appointed from S. C.]
2nd Lieut. 7th Inf., 18 April, 1818. 1st Lieut., 30 June, 1820. Capt., 24 Sept., 1824. Died 4 Oct., 1825.

WASHBURN, SAM'L. [Born in Vt. Appointed from Army.]
Corpl and Sergt. Light Art., Oct., 1809, to May, 1813. 3rd Lieut. Light Art., 20 May, 1813. 2nd Lieut., 13 Dec., 1813. 1st Lieut., 15 Jan., 1817. R. Q. M., Oct., 1816, to Jan., 1820. Trans. to 4th Art., 1 June, 1821. Died 23 Aug., 1821.

WASHINGTON, EDWARD C. [Born in Va. Appointed from Tex.]
Capt. 13th Inf., 14 May, 1861. Died 20 May, 1863, of wounds received in action before Vicksburg, Miss. Bvt. Maj., 20 May, 1863, for gallant and meritorious service in action before Vicksburg, Miss.

WASHINGTON, GEORGE A.* [Born in Va. Appointed from D. C.]
3rd Lieut. Corps Art., 2 March, 1815. 2nd Lieut., 13 May, 1817. Died 9 Dec., 1817.

WASHINGTON, JOHN M.* [Born in Va. Appointed from Va.]
3rd Lieut. Corps Art., 17 July, 1817. 2nd Lieut., 20 March, 1818. 1st Lieut., 23 May, 1820. Trans. to 4th Art., 1 June, 1821. Capt., 30 May, 1832. (Capt. A. Q. M., 7 July, 1838, to 11 April, 1839). Maj. 3rd Art., 16 Feb., 1847. Drowned 24 Dec., 1853. Bvt. Capt., 23 May, 1830, for ten years' faithful service in one grade. Bvt. Lieut. Col., 23 Feb., 1847, for gallant and meritorious conduct in the Battle of Buena Vista, Mex.

WASHINGTON, READE M. [Born in Pa. Appointed from Pa.]
Cadet at Mil. Acad., 1 July, 1865, to 29 Jan., 1867. 2nd Lieut. 9th Cav., 24 June, 1869. 1st Lieut., 30 Sept., 1874. Dismissed 25 Feb., 1876.

WASHINGTON, THORNTON A.* [Born in Va. Appointed from Va.]
Bvt. 2nd Lieut. 6th Inf., 1 July, 1849. 2nd Lieut. 1st Inf., 26 June, 1850. 1st Lieut., 8 Dec., 1855. Reg. Adj., 31 Oct., 1857, to 31 May, 1860. R. Q. M., 31 May, 1860, to 8 April, 1861. Resigned 8 April, 1861.

WASHINGTON, WM. T. [Born in Va. Appointed from D. C.]
Cadet at Mil. Acad., 24 June, 1819, to 19 Aug., 1823. Bvt. 2nd Lieut. 4th Art., 19 Aug., 1823. 2nd Lieut., 19 Aug., 1823. Dropped 1 May, 1825.

WASSELL, WILLIAM H.* [Born in Pa. Appointed from Pa.]
Addl. 2nd Lieut. 9th Inf., 12 June, 1887. 2nd Lieut., 28 Aug., 1887. Resigned 31 Jan., 1888. Appointed 2nd Lieut. 22nd Inf., 8 Oct., 1891. 1st Lieut., 26 April, 1898.

WASSON, JAMES R.* [Born in Ohio. Appointed from Iowa.]
Priv. Cos. B and C, 34th Iowa Vols., 26 Jan., 1864. Discharged 15 Aug., 1865. Cadet at Mil. Acad., 1 July, 1867. 2nd Lieut. 4th Cav., 12 June, 1871. Resigned 1 July, 1872. Maj. P. M., 14 Sept., 1876. Dismissed 3 July, 1883.

WATERBURY, WM. M. [Born in N. Y. Appointed from N. Y.]
2nd Lieut. 4th N. Y. Art., 4 Jan., 1862. 1st Lieut., 6 Jan., 1863. Mustered out 3 Jan., 1865. 1st Lieut. 19th Inf., 28 July, 1866. Unassigned 31 March, 1869. Ass'd to 13th Inf., 14 July, 1869. Capt., 18 Oct., 1871. Retired for disability with rank of Maj., 5 July, 1895.

WATERHOUSE, ANDREW O. [Born in Ky. Appointed from Ky.]
2nd Lieut. 6th Inf., 13 Aug., 1819. Resigned 15 June, 1820.

WATERHOUSE, BENJ'N. [Born in Mass. Appointed from Mass.]
Hosp. Surg., 29 June, 1813. Post Surg., 18 April, 1818. Disbanded 1 June, 1821. Died 2 Oct., 1846.

WATERHOUSE, SAMUEL M. [Born in Ohio. Appointed from N. Y.]
Asst. Surg., 23 July, 1898.

WATERMAN, C. DOUGLAS.* [Born in Pa. Appointed from Pa.]
1st Lieut. Eng., 13 June, 1864. Died 28 Sept., 1864.

WATERMAN, HENRY E.* [Born in Minn. Appointed from Minn.]
2nd Lieut. Eng., 13 June, 1883. 1st Lieut., 20 April, 1886. Capt., 10 May, 1895. Died 26 Oct., 1898.

WATERMAN, HENRY S. [Born in Conn. Appointed from Conn.]
2nd Lieut. 3rd Art., 5 Aug., 1861. 1st Lieut., 5 Aug., 1861. Dismissed 25 June, 1863.

WATERMAN, JOHN C.* [Born in Mich. Appointed from Mich.]
2nd Lieut. 7th Cav., 11 June, 1881. 1st Lieut. 8th Cav., 20 Feb., 1891. Capt. 7th Cav., 2 March, 1899. Graduate of the Infantry and Cavalry School, 1895.

WATERS, BASIL N. [Born in Md. Appointed from Army.]
Priv. Sig. Corps, 24 July, 1873. 2nd Lieut. 15th Inf., 15 Oct., 1875. Reg. Adj., 25 Aug., 1877, to 3 Nov., 1879. Resigned 18 Oct., 1880.

WATERS, CHAS. O. [Born in N. Y. Appointed from Iowa.]
Asst. Surg. of Inf., 3 March, 1847; 15th Inf., 9 April, 1847. Resigned 10 June, 1847.

WATERS, JAMES H.* [Born in Wis. Appointed from Wis.]
2nd Lieut. 20th Inf., 11 June, 1881. Resigned 18 Jan., 1888.

WATERS, GEORGE W.* [Born in Mass. Appointed from Mass.]
2nd Lieut. 6th Inf., 1 July, 1823. 1st Lieut., 15 Feb., 1826. Capt., 4 March, 1833. Resigned 30 April, 1837. Died 14 March, 1846.

WATERS, JOSEPH G. [Born in Ky. Appointed from Ill.]
Priv. Co. A, 84th Ill. Vols., 1 Sept., 1862. 1st Lieut., 24 April, 1863. Mustered out 8 June, 1865. 2nd Lieut. 15th Inf., 23 Feb., 1866. Trans. to 33rd Inf., 21 Sept., 1866. 1st Lieut., 1 Nov., 1866. Wholly retired 28 July, 1869. Bvt. Capt., 2 March, 1867, for gallant conduct at the Battle of Franklin, Tenn., 30 Nov., 1864.

WATERS, WM. E. [Born in D. C. Appointed from D. C.]
Asst. Surg. D. C. Militia, 13 May, to 3 Aug., 1861. Maj. Surg. Vols., 3 Aug., 1861. 1st Lieut. Asst. Surg., 16 April, 1862. Vacated commission of Surg. Vols., 5 Aug., 1862. Bvt. Capt. and Maj., 13 March, 1865, for faithful and meritorious service during the war. Capt. Asst. Surg., 6 June, 1866. Maj. Surg., 10 Jan., 1879. Lieut. Col. Dep. Surg. Gen., 1 Oct., 1895. Retired by operation of law, 15 Nov., 1897.

WATKINS, BENJAMIN H. [Born in Ky. Appointed from Ky.]
2nd Lieut. 2nd Inf., 9 July, 1898. 1st Lieut. 15th Inf., 30 June, 1899.

WATKINS, LOUIS D. [Born in Florida. Appointed from D. C.]
Priv. Co. A, 3rd Batt. D. C. Vols., 15 April, 1861. 1st Lieut. 14th Inf., 14 May, 1861. Trans. to 5th Cav., 22 June, 1861. Capt., 17 July, 1862. Col. 6th Ky. Cav., 1 Feb., 1863. Brig. Gen. Vols., 25 Sept., 1865. Mustered out Vols., 1 Sept., 1866. Lieut. Col. 20th Inf., 28 July, 1866. Died 29 March, 1868. Bvt. Maj. 8 Jan., 1863, for gallant and meritorious service in the expedition to East Tenn. under Brig. Gen. Carter, U. S. Vols. Bvt. Lieut. Col., 5 March, 1863, for gallant and meritorious service at the Battle of Thompson's Station, Tenn. Bvt. Col. 24 June, 1864, for gallant and meritorious service at the Battle of Lafayette, Ga. Bvt. Brig. Gen., 13 March, 1865, for gallant and meritorious conduct in defence of Resaca, Ga.

WATKINS, ROBERT B. [Born in Va. Appointed from Army.]
Cadet Mil. Acad., 1 July, 1870, to 28 June, 1873. Priv. and Sergt. Sig. Corps, 3 Oct., 1873, to 29 April, 1883. 2nd Lieut. Sig. Corps, 26 April, 1883. 2nd Lieut. 1st Cav., 4 Feb., 1891 (to rank from 26 April, 1883). 1st Lieut. 6th Cav., 24 Feb., 1891. Trans. to 9th Cav., 27 April, 1891. Retired for disability, 27 Aug., 1896.

WATKINS, TOBIAS. [Born in Md. Appointed from Md.]
Maj. Surg. 38th Inf., 20 May, 1813. Hosp. Surg., 30 March, 1814. Provisionally retained 15 June, 1815. Asst. Surg. Gen., 18 April, 1818. Disbanded 1 June, 1821. Died 14 Nov., 1855.

WATKINS, THOMAS J. [Born in Ohio. Appointed from Army.]
Priv., Corpl., Sergt. and 1st Sergt. Batty C, 3rd Art., 30 Dec., 1881, to 15 March, 1888. 2nd Lieut. 11th Inf., 6 Feb., 1888. Dropped 27 Feb., 1891.

WATKYNS, ALFRED. [Born in N. Y. Appointed from N. Y.]
Asst. Surg., 11 June, 1823. Resigned 1 Feb., 1824.

WATMOUGH, JOHN G. [Born in Del. Appointed from Pa.]
3rd Lieut. 2nd Art., 22 Sept., 1813. 2nd Lieut., 19 April, 1814. Trans. to Corps Art., 12 May, 1814. Resigned 1 Oct., 1816. Bvt. 1st Lieut., 15 Aug., 1814, for gallant conduct in defence of Fort Erie. Died 27 Nov., 1861.

WATROUS, JEROME A. [Born in N. Y. Appointed from Ark.]
Priv. Co. E, and Sergt. Maj. 6th Wis. Vols., 16 July, 1861, to 18 Oct., 1864. 1st Lieut. and Adj., 19 Oct., 1864, to 15 May, 1865. Maj. P. M., 15 June, 1898.

WATSON, BENJAMIN. [Born in R. I. Appointed from R. I.]
2nd Lieut. 25th Inf., 12 March, 1812. 1st Lieut., 13 March, 1813. Reg. Adj., Jan., to Aug., 1813. Capt., 15 Aug., 1813. Trans. to 6th Inf., 17 May, 1815. Trans. to 3rd Inf., 1 June, 1821. Died 4 Oct., 1827. Bvt. Maj., 25 July, 1814, for gallant conduct at the Battle of Niagara.

WATSON, CHAS. B. [Born in Maine. Appointed from Ind.]
Cadet Mil. Acad., 1 July, 1851, to 7 March, 1854. 2nd Lieut. 2nd Inf., 21 Feb., 1857. 1st Lieut. 14th Inf., 14 May, 1861. Capt., 24 Oct., 1861. Died 30 April, 1863.

WATSON, EDWARD H. [Born in Pa. Appointed from Pa.]
Asst. Surg., 11 Aug., 1853. Lost at Sea in Sept., 1853.

WATSON, FRANK B.* [Born in Va. Appointed from N. J.]
Addl. 2nd Lieut. 19th Inf., 12 June, 1895. 2nd Lieut., 5 July, 1895. 1st Lieut. of Inf., 7 Aug., 1898. Ass'd to 19th Inf., 1 Jan., 1899.

WATSON, GEORGE.* [Born in Maine. Appointed from Maine.]
Bvt. 2nd Lieut. 1st Art., 1 July, 1832. 2nd Lieut., 31 May, 1833. 1st Lieut., 30 Sept., 1836. Resigned 31 Oct., 1838. Died 22 March, 1868.

WATSON, JAMES T. [Born in Cal. Appointed at Large.]
Priv. and Corpl. Troop E, 7th Cav., 14 Feb., 1898, to 16 June, 1899. 2nd Lieut. 2nd Inf., 1 June, 1899.

WATSON, JAMES W.* [Born in Miss. Appointed from Miss.]
2nd Lieut. 10th Cav., 12 June, 1880., 1st Lieut., 23 Dec., 1887. Capt., 11 Jan., 1898. Bvt. Capt., 7 March, 1890, for gallant services in action against Indians near Salt River, Arizona, 7 March, 1890.

WATSON, JOHN L. [Born in Va. Appointed from Va.]
2nd Lieut. Mounted Rangers, 5 March, 1833. 2nd Lieut. 1st Drag., 19 Sept., 1833. Resigned 30 June, 1835. Died 21 Nov., 1835.

WATSON, MALBONE F.* [Born in N. Y. Appointed from N. Y.]
2nd Lieut. 1st Cav., 6 May, 1861. 1st Lieut. 5th Art., 14 May, 1861. Bvt. Capt., 27 June, 1862, for gallant and meritorious service in the Battle of Gaines' Mills, Va. Bvt. Maj., 2 July, 1863, for gallant and meritorious service in the Battle of Gettysburg, Pa. Capt. 5th Art., 9 March, 1866. Retired with rank of Capt. Mounted, 18 Sept., 1868. Died 9 Dec., 1891.

WATSON, PERRIN. [Born in Tenn. Appointed from Tenn.]
2nd Lieut. of Inf., 5 March, 1847; 14th Inf., 9 April, 1847. Died 3 Jan., 1848.

WATT, JOHN. [Born in Scotland. Appointed from D. C.]
1st Lieut. 16th Inf., 9 Sept., 1861. Appointment revoked, 3 Feb., 1862. Priv. and Corpl. Batty B, 13th N. Y. Art., 12 Aug., 1863, to 20 May, 1865. 2nd Lieut. 38th U. S. Col. Inf., 20 May, 1865. 1st Lieut., 17 Jan., 1866. Mustered out 25 Jan., 1867.

WATTERSON, HENRY, Jr. [Born in D. C. Appointed from Ky.]
Priv. and Corpl. Co. K, 1st Ky. Inf., 13 May, 1898, to 24 Feb., 1899. 2nd Lieut. 10th Inf., 1 June, 1899.

WATTS, ARTHUR P. [Born in Tex. Appointed from Tex.]
2nd Lieut. 4th Inf., 1 July, 1899. Trans. to 23rd Inf., 9 Oct., 1899.

WATTS, CHAS. H.* [Born in N. Y. Appointed from N. Y.]
2nd Lieut. 5th Cav., 14 June, 1872. 1st Lieut., 2 April, 1879. Capt., 8 March, 1891.

WATTS, GEORGE. [Born in N. Y. Appointed from N.Y.]
3rd Lieut. Light Drag., 18 March, 1813. 2nd Lieut., 1 Aug., 1813. Trans. to 1st Inf., 17 May, 1815. Resigned 15 Jan., 1816. Bvt. 1st Lieut., 5 July, 1814, for gallant conduct at the Battle of Chippewa.

WATTS, GEORGE O.* [Born in Ky. Appointed from Ky.]
Bvt. 2nd Lieut. Mounted Rifles, 24 June, 1861. Resigned 10 Aug., 1861.

WATTS, WM. M. [Born in Pa. Appointed from Pa.]
2nd Lieut. 3rd Cav., 19 Feb., 1862. 1st Lieut., 11 March, 1863. Resigned 27 July, 1863. Priv. Troop I, 7th Pa. Cav., 27 Feb., 1864. 1st Lieut. and Adj., 15 May, 1865. Mustered out 23 Aug., 1865.

WAUGH, ALEX'R. [Born in D. C. Appointed from Va.]
2nd Lieut. 1st Inf., 1 July, 1839. Resigned 31 May, 1842.

WAY, HENRY N.* [Born in Ill. Appointed from Ill.]
2nd Lieut. 4th Inf., 15 Feb., 1899.

WAYMAN, SAM'L P.* [Born in Ky. Appointed from Ky.]
2nd Lieut. 24th Inf., 15 June, 1877. Died 16 Dec., 1879.

WAYMIRE, JAMES A. [Born in Mo. Appointed from Ore.]
Priv. Troop B, 1st Ore. Cav., 16 Dec., 1861. 2nd Lieut., 23 April, 1863. Resigned 29 Nov., 1864. 2nd Lieut. 1st Cav., 22 Jan., 1867. 1st Lieut., 8 April, 1869. Resigned 2 Aug., 1869.

WAYNE, HENRY C.* [Born in Ga. Appointed from Ga.]
2nd Lieut. 4th Art., 1 July, 1838. Trans. to 1st Art., 12 July, 1838. 1st Lieut., 16 May, 1842. Capt. A. Q. M., 11 May, 1846. Resigned 31 Dec., 1860. Bvt. Maj., 20 Aug., 1847, for gallant and meritorious conduct at Contreras and Churubusco. Died 15 March, 1883.

WAYNE, RICH'D. [Born in Ga. Appointed from Ga.]
Asst. Surg., 13 July, 1832. Resigned 31 Jan., 1834.

WEAVER, ERASMUS M., Jr.* [Born in Ind. Appointed from Ind.]
2nd Lieut. 2nd Art., 16 June, 1875. 1st Lieut., 2 Oct., 1883. Capt. 1st Art., 14 May, 1898. Capt. A. A. G. Vols., 12 May, 1898, declined. Lieut. Col. 5th Mass. Vols., 1 July, 1898, to 31 March, 1899. Honor graduate of the Artillery School, 1888.

WEAVER, FRANCIS H. [Born in Pa. Appointed from Pa.]
Priv. Co. C, 53rd Pa. Vols., 10 Oct., 1861. Trans. to Vet. Res. Corps, 20 Jan., 1864. Discharged 17 Oct., 1864. Priv. Co. K. 44th Inf., 1 Aug. to 30 Nov., 1868. Chap. 10th Cav., 16 June, 1880. Retired for disability, 16 Aug., 1897.

WEAVER, HANSON E. [Born in Pa. Appointed from D. C.]
2nd Lieut. 8th Inf., 25 June, 1861. 1st Lieut., 27 Feb., 1862. Resigned 9 Jan., 1866.

WEAVER, STANTON. [Born in Ohio. Appointed from Ohio.]
Priv. Co. C, 3rd and 10th Kan. Vols., 30 July, 1861, to 27 May, 1862. Sergt. Co. G, 104th Ohio Vols., 30 Aug., 1862. 2nd Lieut., 31 Jan., 1863. 1st Lieut., 17 Aug., 1863. Mustered out 15 Jan., 1864. Capt. 62nd U. S. Col. Inf., 18 Feb., 1865. Bvt. Maj. and Lieut. Col. Vols., 13 March, 1865, for meritorious service. Mustered out 31 March, 1866. 2nd Lieut. 11th Inf., 25 April, 1866. Trans. to 20th Inf., 21 Sept., 1866. 1st Lieut., 6 Dec., 1866. Discharged 15 Dec., 1870.

WEBB, ALEXANDER S.* [Born in N. Y. Appointed from N. Y.]
Bvt. 2nd Lieut. 4th Art., 1 July, 1855. 2nd Lieut. 2nd Art., 20 Oct., 1855. 1st Lieut., 28 April, 1861. Capt. 11th Inf., 14 May, 1861. Maj. 1st R. I. Light Art., 14 Sept., 1861. Lieut. Col. A. I. G., 20 Aug., 1862, to 28 June, 1863. Brig. Gen. Vols., 23 June, 1863. Mustered out of Vol. Service, 15 Jan., 1866. Lieut. Col. 44th Inf., 28 July, 1866. Trans. to 5th Inf., 15 March, 1869. Unassigned 24 March, 1869. Discharged 5 Dec., 1870. Bvt. Maj., 3 July, 1863, for gallant and meritorious service at the Battle of Gettysburg, Pa. Bvt. Lieut. Col., 11 Oct., 1863, for gallant and meritorious service at the Battle of Bristow Station, Va. Bvt. Col., 12 May, 1864, for gallant and meritorious service at the Battle of Spottsylvania, Va. Bvt. Brig. Gen., 13 March, 1865, for gallant and meritorious service in the campaign terminating with the surrender of Gen. Lee. Bvt. Maj. Gen., 13 March, 1865, for gallant and meritorious service during the war.

WEBB, CHAS. A. [Born in Vt. Appointed from Vt.]
1st Lieut. 1st Vt. Vols., 9 May, 1861. Mustered out 15 Aug., 1861. Capt. 13th Inf., 5 Aug., 1861. Bvt. Maj., 4 July, 1863, for gallant and meritorious service in the Siege of Vicksburg, Miss. Trans. to 22nd Inf., 21 Sept., 1866. Maj. 16th Inf., 4 March, 1879. Died 31 Jan., 1882.

WEBB, EDWARD. [Born in N. Y. Appointed from N. Y.]
Ensign 6th Inf., 3 May, 1808. 2nd Lieut., 2 Feb., 1809. 1st Lieut., 1 Oct., 1810. Capt., 21 Feb., 1814. Disbanded 15 June, 1815. 2nd Lieut. 8th Inf., 3 Feb., 1819. 1st Lieut., 31 July, 1819. Trans. to 4th Inf., 1 June, 1821. Resigned 31 Oct., 1826.

WEBB, GEORGE.* [Born in Md. Appointed from Md.]
2nd Lieut. Corps Art., 24 July, 1818. Trans. to 1st Art., 1 June, 1821. 1st Lieut., 15 May, 1823. Died 20 April, 1832.

WEBB, GEORGE W. [Born in Md. Appointed from Army.]
Priv. and Artf. Co. H, 33rd Inf.; Priv., Corpl. and Sergt. Co., B, 8th Inf., and Com. Sergt., 12 Dec., 1866, to 16 May, 1876. Sergt. and 1st Sergt. Co. B, 8th Inf., 27 May, 1876, to 7 July, 1880. 2nd Lieut. 25th Inf., 24 June, 1880. 1st Lieut., 1 April, 1888. Resigned 31 Jan., 1889.

WEBB, HENRY L. [Born in N. Y. Appointed from Ill.]
Capt. 2nd Ill. Vols., 3 June, 1846. Resigned 13 Nov., 1846. Lieut. Col. of Inf.,

3 March, 1847; 16th Inf., 9 April, 1847. Col. 9th Inf., 23 May, 1848. Disbanded 8 Aug., 1848.

WEBB, JAMES W. [Born in N. Y. Appointed from N. Y.]
2nd Lieut. Corps Art., 13 Aug., 1819. Trans. to 2nd Art., 1 June, 1821. Trans. to 3rd Inf., 25 July, 1821. 1st Lieut., 11 Aug., 1823. Reg. Adj., 19 Dec., 1826, to 19 Feb., 1827. Resigned 23 Sept., 1827. Died 7 June, 1884.

WEBB, NATHL. S. [Born in Conn. Appointed from Conn.]
Capt. of Inf., 16 March, 1847; 9th Inf., 9 April, 1847. Disbanded 26 Aug., 1848. Capt. 10th Inf., 3 March, 1855. Resigned 20 July, 1856. Bvt. Maj., 13 Sept., 1847, for gallant and meritorious conduct at the Battle of Chapultepec.

WEBB, ROBT. W. [Born in Asia. Appointed from N. Y.]
Priv. Cos. K and B, 147th N. Y. Vols., 21 Aug., 1862, to 29 Feb., 1864. 2nd Lieut. 32nd U. S. Col. Inf., 3 March, 1864. Mustered out 22 Aug., 1865. 2nd Lieut. 40th Inf., 7 March, 1867. Trans. to 41st Inf., 27 Nov., 1867. Trans. to 24th Inf., 11 Nov., 1869. Resigned 31 May, 1870. Bvt. 1st Lieut., 7 March, 1867, for gallant and meritorious service during the war.

WEBB, STEPHEN H. [Born in N. Y. Appointed from Vt.]
Ensign 30th Inf., 30 April, 1813. 3rd Lieut., 23 June, 1814. Disbanded 15 June, 1815. 1st Lieut. 8th Inf., 13 Feb., 1818. Capt., 9 July, 1820. Trans. to 1st Inf., 1 June, 1821. Trans. to 3rd Inf., 14 Dec., 1831. Resigned 31 Aug., 1833. Mil. Storekeeper, 11 Nov., 1834. Disbanded 1 Oct., 1842. Capt. A. Q. M. Vols., 26 June, 1846. Disbanded 30 June, 1847. Capt. C. S. Vols., 5 Aug., 1861. Discharged 6 Sept., 1864. Died — Feb., 1873.

WEBB, WATSON. [Born in N. Y. Appointed from N. Y.]
2nd Lieut. 3rd Art., 26 April, 1861. 1st Lieut., 14 May, 1861. Reg. Adj., 22 Jan., 1862, to 18 Oct., 1866. Capt., 18 Oct., 1866. Resigned 20 April, 1870. Died 3 Dec., 1876.

WEBB, WM. A.* [Born in Maine. Appointed from Maine.]
Bvt. 2nd Lieut. 4th Inf., 1 July, 1853. 2nd Lieut. 5th Inf., 31 Dec., 1854. 1st Lieut., 1 April, 1857. Capt. 16th Inf., 14 May, 1861. Col. 42nd Ill. Vols., 22 July, 1861. Died 24 Dec., 1861.

WEBB, WILLIAM R. [Born in N. Y. Appointed from N. Y.]
2nd Lieut. 16th Inf., 9 July, 1898. Died 9 March, 1899.

WEBB, WM. W. [Born in N. Y. Appointed from D. C.]
Priv. Co. A, 3rd Batt. D. C. Vols., 15 April to 18 May, 1861. 2nd Lieut. 1st Cav., 17 May, 1861. 4th Cav., 3 Aug., 1861. 1st Lieut., 17 July, 1862. Capt., 28 July, 1866. Resigned 1 May, 1873. Bvt. Maj., 2 March, 1867, for gallant and meritorious service in the Atlanta campaign.

WEBBER, CHAS. H. [Born in D. C. Appointed from Mass.]
2nd Lieut. 1st Art., 29 May, 1855. 1st Lieut., 22 Nov., 1860. Capt., 25 Oct., 1861. Dismissed 11 Oct., 1862.

WEBBER, EDWIN H. [Born in Pa. Appointed from Pa.]
2nd Lieut. 20th Inf., 24 Nov., 1880. 1st Lieut., 15 Oct., 1887. Graduate of the Infantry and Cavalry School, 1883. Retired for disability, 7 Dec., 1896.

WEBBER, HENRY A. [Born in Mass. Appointed from Mass.]
Asst. Surg., 6 Nov., 1897.

WEBBER, JOHN A.* [Born in Mass. Appointed from Mass.]
Bvt. 2nd Lieut. Light Art., 11 Dec., 1815. 2nd Lieut., 30 Sept., 1816. 1st Lieut., 31 Oct., 1819. Trans. to 3rd Art., 1 June, 1821. Trans. to 2nd Art., 16 Aug., 1821. Resigned 20 Feb., 1825. Mil. Storekeeper Ord., 12 Oct., 1837. Died 6 May, 1855.

WEBER, JULIUS H. [Born in Mo. Appointed from Army.]
Priv. and Sergt. Sig. Corps, 16 April, 1874, to 12 July, 1884. 2nd Lieut. Sig. Corps, 1 July, 1884. 2nd Lieut. 8th Inf., 4 Feb., 1891 (to rank from 1 July, 1884). Retired for disability 20 Feb., 1891.

WEBSTER, AMOS. [Born in Mass. Appointed from D. C.]
Corpl. Co. D, 1st Mass. Vols., 24 May, 1861. 2nd Lieut., 8 May, 1862. 1st Lieut., 1 Oct., 1862. Mustered out 30 June, 1864. Capt. A. Q. M. Vols., 1 Oct., 1864. Bvt. Maj. Vols., 9 April, 1865, for meritorious service in the campaign against the rebel army of Northern Va., commencing in front of Petersburg, Va., 29 March, and ending 9 April, 1865, and Lieut. Col. Vols., 9 April, 1865, for faithful and meritorious service. Mustered out 1 Oct., 1867. 2nd Lieut. 5th Cav., 7 March, 1867. 1st Lieut., 9 June, 1868. Resigned 15 April, 1869. Bvt. 1st Lieut., Capt. and Maj., 7 March, 1867, for faithful and meritorious service during the war.

WEBSTER, EDMUND K.* [Born in La. Appointed from Pa.]
2nd Lieut. 2nd Inf., 17 June, 1874. 1st Lieut., 26 Sept., 1881. Capt. 2nd Inf., 26 July, 1893.

WEBSTER, FRANK D.* [Born in Mo. Appointed from Mo.]
2nd Lieut. 25th Inf., 12 June, 1891. Trans. to 6th Inf., 3 Oct., 1891. 1st Lieut. 20th Inf., 7 Dec., 1896. Capt. 18th Inf., 8 Sept., 1899. Graduate of the Infantry and Cavalry School, 1897. Trans. to 20th Inf., 6 Dec., 1899.

WEBSTER, GEORGE O.* [Born in Conn. Appointed from Conn.]
2nd Lieut. 4th Inf., 18 June, 1866. Reg. Adj., 15 Nov., 1867, to 6 May, 1875. 1st Lieut., 25 Nov., 1873. Capt., 5 Aug., 1888. Maj. 4th Inf., —— 1899. Retired ——, 1899. Died 10 Oct., 1899.

WEBSTER, HORACE.* [Born in Vt. Appointed from Vt.]
2nd Lieut. 3rd Inf., 24 July, 1818. 1st Lieut., 5 April, 1820. Resigned 31 Dec., 1825. Died 12 July, 1871.

WEBSTER, ISAAC T.* [Born in N. Y. Appointed from Nebr.]
2nd Lieut. 3rd Art., 18 June, 1866. Trans. to 1st Art., 28 Sept., 1866. 1st Lieut., 1 Jan., 1871. Died 7 July, 1886.

WEBSTER, JOHN G. [Born in England. Appointed from Army.]
Priv. Troop K, and Sergt. Maj. 1st (4th) Cav., 31 Aug., 1858, to 19 March, 1863. 2nd Lieut. 4th Cav., 19 Feb., 1863. 1st Lieut., 14 March, 1865. Died 8 March, 1866. Bvt. 1st Lieut., 16 Dec., 1864, for gallant and meritorious service in pursuit

of rebel forces under Gen. Hood. Bvt. Capt., 2 April, 1865, for gallant and meritorious service at the capture of Selma, Ala. Bvt. Maj., 2 April, 1865, for gallantry during pursuit of Hood after the Battle of Nashville, and in the charge of his regiment against the earth-works at Selma, Ala.

WEBSTER, JOHN McA.* [Born in Ohio. Appointed from Ohio.]
2nd Lieut. 197th Ohio Vols., 20 April, 1865. Mustered out 31 July, 1865. Cadet at Mil. Acad., 1 Sept., 1866. 2nd Lieut. 22nd Inf., 12 June, 1871. 1st Lieut., 4 March, 1879. Reg. Adj., 22 May to 1 Sept., 1884. R. Q. M., 1 Sept., 1884, to 22 May, 1888. Capt., 18 April, 1891. Retired, for over thirty years' service, 20 Dec., 1898.

WEBSTER, JOSEPH D. [Born in N. H. Appointed from Mass.]
2nd Lieut. Top. Eng., 7 July, 1838. 1st Lieut., 14 July, 1849. Capt., 3 March, 1853. Resigned 7 April, 1854. Maj. Addl. P. M. Vols., 1 June, 1861. Col. 1st Ill. Light Art., 1 Feb., 1862. Brig. Gen. Vols., 29 Nov., 1862. Bvt. Maj. Gen. Vols., 13 March, 1865, for faithful aad meritorious service during tht war. Resigned 6 Nov., 1865. Died 12 March, 1876.

WEBSTER, LUCIEN B.* [Born in Vt. Appointed from Vt.]
Bvt. 2nd Lieut. 3rd Art., 1 July, 1823. 2nd Lieut. 1st Art., 1 July, 1823. 1st Lieut., 30 May, 1832. Capt., 30 Sept., 1836. Maj. 4th Art., 3 Aug., 1852. Died 4 Nov., 1853. Bvt. Maj., 23 Sept., 1846, for gallant and meritorious conduct at Monterey. Bvt. Lieut. Col., 23 Feb., 1847, for gallant and meritorious conduct at Buena Vista.

WEBSTER, WARREN. [Born in N. H. Appointed from Mass.]
1st Lieut. Asst. Surg., 23 June, 1860. Bvt. Capt., 3 May, 1863, for gallant and meritorious service in the Battle of Chancellorsville, Va. Bvt. Maj., 13 March, 1865, for faithful and meritorious service during the war. Capt. Asst. Surg., 23 June, 1865. Maj. Surg., 28 July, 1866. Bvt. Lieut. Col., 28 Sept., 1866, for meritorious and distinguished service at Hart's Island and David's Island, N. Y., where cholera prevailed. Retired for disability, 28 Feb., 1889. Died 13 Jan., 1896.

WEDEMEYER WM. G. [Born in Germany. Appointed from Army.]
Priv. Co. —, 1st Batt. 16th Inf., 16 Nov., 1861. Sergt., 4 Dec., 1861. Sergt. Co. H, 19 May, 1862. Sergt. Maj. 1st Batt. 16th Inf., 2 Aug., 1862. 2nd Lieut. 16th Inf., 13 Aug., 1862. 1st Lieut., 14 Feb., 1863. Bvt. Capt., 20 Sept., 1863, for gallant and meritorious service in the Battle of Chickamauga, Ga. Capt. 16th Inf., 16 Nov., 1865. Trans. to 34th Inf., 21 Sept., 1866. Trans. to 16th Inf., 14 April, 1869. Retired for disability, with rank of Maj., 24 Feb., 1891.

WEED, STEPHEN H.* [Born in N. Y. Appointed from N. Y.]
Bvt. 2nd Lieut. 2nd Art., 1 July, 1854. 2nd Lieut. 4th Art., 18 Dec., 1854. 1st Lieut., 16 Nov., 1856. Capt. 5th Art., 14 May, 1861. Brig. Gen. Vols., 6 June, 1863. Killed at the Battle of Gettysburg, Pa., 2 July, 1863.

WEEDEN, JOHN H.* [Born in R. I. Appointed from R. I.]
2nd Lieut. Eng., 18 June, 1866. 1st Lieut., 7 March, 1867. Died 29 Jan., 1877.

WEEDS, JAMES F. [Born in England. Appointed from Ohio.]
Asst. Surg., 28 May, 1861. Maj. Surg., 27 Oct., 1868. Died 1 Oct., 1875. Bvt. Capt. and Maj., 13 March, 1865, for faithful and meritorious service during the war.

WEEKS, CHARLES W. [Born in Iowa. Appointed from Nebr.]
Priv. and Sergt. Co. F, 2nd Nebr. Vols., 9 May to 24 Oct., 1898. 2nd Lieut. 16th Inf., 1 June, 1899.

WEEKS, EDWIN B. [Born in N. Y. Appointed from Cal.]
2nd Lieut. 5th Inf., 30 Oct., 1884. Died 11 May, 1890.

WEEKS, GEORGE H.* [Born in N. H. Appointed from Maine.]
Bvt. 2nd Lieut. 1st Art., 1 July, 1857. 2nd Lieut. 4th Art., 10 Feb., 1859. 1st Lieut., 14 May, 1861. R. Q. M., 24 Aug., 1861, to 30 Dec., 1861. Reg. Adj., 30 Dec., 1861, to 1 April, 1862. Capt. A. Q. M., 24 March, 1862. Bvt. Maj. and Lieut. Col., 13 March, 1865, for faithful and meritorious service in the Q. M. D. during the war. Maj. Q. M., 29 May, 1876. Lieut. Col. D. Q. M. G., 19 Oct., 1888. Col. A. Q. M. G., 16 May, 1895. Brig. Gen. Q. M. G., 16 Feb., 1897. Retired by operation of law, 3 Feb., 1898.

WEEKS, GEORGE McD.* [Born in Mo. Appointed from Army.]
Addl. 2nd Lieut. 15th Inf., 11 June, 1892. 2nd Lieut., 18 June, 1892. 1st Lieut., 26 April, 1898. Graduate of the Infantry and Cavalry School, 1897.

WEEKS, HARRISON S.* [Born in Mich. Appointed from Mich.]
2nd Lieut. 8th Cav., 15 June, 1868. 1st Lieut., 28 Dec., 1871. Capt., 4 April, 1885. Retired for disability, 28 Sept., 1889. Died 20 Jan., 1892.

WEEKS, MARION M. [Born in Wash. Appointed from D. C.
2nd Lieut. 21st Inf., 9 Sept., 1898. 1st Lieut. 11th Inf., 2 Oct., 1899.

WEIGEL, WILLIAM.* [Born in N. J. Appointed from N. J.]
2nd Lieut. 11th Inf., 12 June, 1887. 1st Lieut. 22nd Inf., 6 June, 1894. Trans. to 11th Inf., 22 June, 1894. Capt., 2 March, 1899. Capt. A. Q. M. Vols., 26 Nov., 1898, to 16 June, 1899. R. Q. M., 12 May, 1899.

WEIGHTMAN, RICH'D. [Born in D. C. Appointed from D. C.]
Post Surg., 21 Aug., 1818. Asst. Surg., 1 June, 1821. Died 30 Oct., 1841.

WEILANDT, DANIEL H. [Born in Germany. Appointed from Army.]
Priv. and Corpl. Co. I, and Sergt. Maj. 6th Inf., 6 Sept., 1860, to 19 Oct., 1865. 2nd Lieut. 6th Inf., 9 Oct., 1865. 1st Lieut., 7 Nov., 1865. R. Q. M., 20 Nov., 1866, to 8 Feb., 1867. Dropped 9 Feb., 1867.

WEINBERG, JEROME J. [Born in Mo. Appointed from Army.]
Priv. and Sergt. Sig. Corps, 3 July, 1873, to 9 March, 1878. Priv. Troops B and A, 3rd Cav. and Hosp. Stwd., 30 Sept., 1878, to 6 Oct., 1884. 2nd Lieut. 13th Inf., 4 Aug., 1884. Died 23 Aug., 1886.

WEIR, GULIAN V. [Born in N. Y. Appointed at Large.]
Priv. Co. B, 7th N. Y. State Militia, 26 April, 1861. Discharged 3 June, 1861. 2nd Lieut. 5th Art., 14 May, 1861. Bvt. 1st Lieut., 1 July, 1862, for gallant and meritorious service during the Peninsula campaign in Va. 1st Lieut. 5th Art.,

8 Oct., 1862. Bvt. Capt., 13 Dec., 1862, for gallant and meritorious service in the Battle of Fredericksburg, Va. Capt. 39th Inf., 28 July, 1866, declined. Reg. Adj. 5th Art., 1 April, 1867, to 1 Dec., 1867. Capt. 5th Art., 10 Nov., 1874. Died 18 July, 1886.

WEIR, JAMES W. [Born in Pa. Appointed from Pa.]
1st Lieut. 14th Inf., 26 Oct., 1861. Capt., 14 Aug., 1865. Unassigned 22 July, 1869. Dismissed 25 Nov., 1869. Bvt. Capt., 18 Aug., 1864, for gallant service at the Battle on the Weldon Railroad, Va.

WEIR, JOHN H. [Born in Pa. Appointed from Pa.]
Asst. Surg. of Inf., 3 March, 1847; 11th Inf., 9 April, 1847. Disbanded 14 Aug., 1848.

WEIR, ROBT. F. [Born in N. Y. Appointed from N. Y.]
Asst. Surg., 5 Aug., 1861. Resigned 1 March, 1865.

WEIR, ROBERT W. [Born in N. Y. Appointed from N. Y.]
Teacher Mil. Acad., 8 May, 1834. Prof. Mil. Acad., 8 Aug., 1846. Retired with pay of Col., 25 July, 1876. Died 1 May, 1889.

WELLS, BRIANT H.* [Born in Utah. Appointed from Utah.]
2nd Lieut. 3rd Mich. Cav., 13 Oct., 1861. 1st Lieut., 19 June, 1862. Capt., 1 Nov., 1862. Maj., 18 Jan., 1865. Lieut. Col., 6 Nov., 1865. Mustered out 12 Feb., 1866. 1st Lieut. 7th Cav., 28 July, 1866. R. C. S., 24 Feb., 1867, to 31 July, 1867. Capt. 31 July, 1867. Died 9 Dec., 1876. Bvt. Maj., 31 July, 1867, for gallant and meritorious service in the Battle of Farmington, Tenn. Bvt. Lieut. Col., 31 July, 1867, for gallant and meritorious service in the engagement with Gen. Forrest near Ripley, Miss., 1 Dec., 1863.

WEIR, WM. B.* [Born in N. Y. Appointed at Large.]
2nd Lieut. 5th Art., 15 June, 1870. 1st Lieut. of Ord., 1 Nov., 1874. Killed 20 Oct., 1879, by Indians in Colo.

WEIRMAN, EUGENE H. [Born in Md. Appointed from Army.]
Priv. Batty G, 3rd Art., 21 July, 1865, to 19 Aug., 1866. 2nd Lieut. 5th Art., 21 July, 1866. Trans. to 4th Art., 23 Oct., 1866. 1st Lieut., 4 April, 1869. Resigned 1 Dec., 1869.

WEISEL, DANIEL. [Born in Md. Appointed from Md.]
1st Lieut. Asst. Surg., 9 Oct., 1867. Capt. Asst. Surg., 9 Oct., 1870. Died 30 Oct., 1888.

WEITZEL, GODFREY.* [Born in Ohio. Appointed from Ohio.]
Bvt. 2nd Lieut. Eng., 1 July, 1855. 2nd Lieut., 27 July, 1856. 1st Lieut., 1 July, 1860. Brig. Gen. Vols., 29 Aug., 1862. Bvt. Maj., 27 Oct., 1862, for gallant and meritorious service in the Battle of Thibodeaux, La. Capt. Eng., 3 March, 1863. Bvt. Lieut. Col., 8 July, 1863, for gallant and meritorious service in the capture of Fort Hudson, La. Bvt. Maj. Gen. Vols., 26 Aug., 1864, for meritorious and distinguished service during the war. Bvt. Col., 29 Sept., 1864, for gallant and meritorious service in the capture of Fort Harrison, Va. Maj. Gen. Vols., 17 Nov., 1864. Bvt. Brig. Gen., 13 March, 1865, for gallant and meritorious service in the campaign terminating with the surrender of the insurgent army under Gen. Robt. E. Lee. Bvt. Maj. Gen., 13 March, 1865, for gallant and meritorious service in the field during the war. Mustered out of Vol. Service, 1 March, 1866. Maj. Eng., 8 Aug., 1866. Lieut. Col., 23 June, 1882. Died 19 March, 1884.

WELBORN, IRA C.* [Born in Miss. Appointed from Miss.]
2nd Lieut. 9th Inf., 26 April, 1898. 1st Lieut., 2 March, 1899. Medal of Honor for distinguished bravery in battle, Santiago, Cuba, voluntarily leaving his shelter and rushing under fire to the aid of a private of his company, who was wounded, 2 July, 1898.

WELBORN, LUTHER S.* [Born in Ind. Appointed from Ind.]
2nd Lieut. 5th Cav., 13 June, 1879. 1st Lieut., 21 April, 1887. Retired for disability, 17 April, 1891.

WELCH, ALLEN T. [Born in Va. Appointed from Mich.]
2nd Lieut. 15th Inf., 17 June, 1848. Disbanded 20 July, 1848.

WELCH, DAVID T. [Born in Conn. Appointed from Conn.]
1st Lieut. 37th Inf., 30 April, 1813. Reg. P. M., 6 Oct., 1813, to July, 1814. Capt., 20 June, 1814. Disbanded 15 June, 1815. Reinstated 1 Jan., 1816, as 1st Lieut. Ord., with Bvt. of Capt. from 20 June, 1814. Trans. to 3rd Art., 1 June, 1821. Capt., 1 Dec., 1822. Trans. to 3rd Art., 23 Aug., 1823. Died 30 Aug., 1825.

WELCH, HUGH P. [Born in Conn. Appointed from Conn.]
2nd Lieut. Corps Art., 27 Oct., 1820. Trans. to 4th Art., 1 June, 1821. Trans. to 1st Art., 16 Aug., 1821. Resigned 30 April, 1826.

WELCH, LOUIS D.* [Born in Conn. Appointed from Conn.]
Bvt. 2nd Lieut. 3rd Art., 1 July, 1845. 2nd Lieut., 27 Oct., 1846. 1st Lieut., 8 Sept., 1847. Died 24 March, 1848.

WELCH, LYMAN M.* [Born in Cal. Appointed from Cal.]
Addl. 2nd Lieut. 24th Inf., 11 June, 1897. 2nd Lieut. 20th Inf., 8 March, 1898. 1st Lieut., 2 March, 1899.

WELCKER, GEORGE L.* [Born in Tenn. Appointed from Tenn.]
Bvt. 2nd Lieut. Eng., 1 July, 1836. 1st Lieut., 7 July, 1838. Capt., 25 April, 1846. Died 24 May, 1848.

WELCKER, WM. T.* [Born in Tenn. Appointed from Tenn.]
Bvt. 2nd Lieut. Ord., 1 July, 1851. 2nd Lieut., 26 June, 1853. 1st Lieut., 1 July, 1855. Dismissed 22 July, 1861.

WELD, CHAS. T. [Born in Conn. Appointed from Conn.]
Priv. Co. A, 1st Conn. Vols., 24 May to 25 June, 1861. 1st Lieut. 17th Inf., 14 May, 1861. Died 14 May, 1863, of wounds received at the Battle of Chancellorsville, Va. Bvt. Capt., 3 May, 1863, for gallant and meritorious service at the Battle of Chancellorsville, Va.

WELD, THOS. B. J.* [Born in Maine. Appointed from Maine.]
Bvt. 2nd Lieut. 1st Art., 1 July, 1845. 2nd Lieut. 2nd Art., 16 Feb., 1847. 1st Lieut., 19 Oct., 1847. Died 10 Oct., 1850.

WELDY, SETH. [Born in Ohio. Appointed from Army.]
Priv. and Sergt. Co. C, 2nd Batt. 18th Inf., 7 Aug., 1861, to 26 June, 1862. 2nd Lieut. 1st Inf., 12 May, 1862. 1st Lieut., 28 May, 1864. Capt. 23rd Inf., 28 July, 1866. Resigned 16 Dec., 1867. Bvt. 1st Lieut., 4 July, 1863, for gallant and meritorious service during the Siege of Vicksburg, Miss.

WEIR, WILLIAM B.* [Born in N. Y. Appointed at Large.]
2nd Lieut. 5th Art., 15 June, 1870. 1st Lieut. of Ord., 1 Nov., 1874. Killed by Ute Indians, near White River Agency, Colo., 20 Oct., 1879.

WELLBORN, JOHN C. [Born in Ga. Appointed from Ala.]
Cadet Mil. Acad., 1 July, 1842, to 20 Jan., 1843. 2nd Lieut. of Inf., 8 March, 1847; 13th Inf., 9 April, 1847. Disbanded 15 July, 1848.

WELLES, ROB'T G. [Born in Conn. Appointed from Conn.]
2nd Lieut. 10th Inf., 5 Aug., 1861. 1st Lieut., 13 Sept., 1862. Capt., 28 Nov., 1863. Resigned 29 Dec., 1865.

WELLS, ALMOND B. [Born in N. Y. Appointed from Nev.]
1st Lieut. 1st Batt. Nev. Cav., 13 July, 1863. Capt., 1 May, 1864. Mustered out 18 Nov., 1865. 2nd Lieut. 8th Cav., 28 July, 1866. 1st Lieut., 31 July, 1867. Capt., 23 May, 1870. Maj. 4th Cav., 1 July, 1891. Trans. to 8th Cav., 8 July, 1891. Lieut. Col. 9th Cav., 14 Feb., 1899.

WELLS, BRIANT H.* [Born in Utah. Appointed from Utah.]
2nd Lieut. 2nd Inf., 12 June, 1894. 1st Lieut. 18th Inf., 26 April, 1898. Reg. Com., 24 May, 1899.

WELLS, DAN'L T. [Born in Vt. Appointed from Mich.]
2nd Lieut. 1st Mich. Cav., 16 Dec., 1861. 1st Lieut., 5 July, 1862. Capt., 30 Dec., 1862. Mustered out 23 June, 1863. 2nd Lieut. 8th Inf., 19 Feb., 1863. Bvt. 1st Lieut., 29 Sept., 1864, for gallant and meritorious service in the assault on Fort Harrison, Va. Bvt. Capt., 2 April, 1865, for gallant and meritorious service in front of Petersburg, Va. Bvt. Maj., 2 April, 1865, for gallant conduct in the capture of Fort Harrison, Va., and succeeding engagements at that place. 1st Lieut. 8th Inf., 13 Feb., 1866. Reg. Adj., 21 Nov., 1866, to 1 March, 1868. Capt., 15 Dec., 1874. Retired for disability, with rank of Maj., 7 Aug., 1897. Died 27 Nov., 1899.

WELLS, ELIJAH R. [Born in N. Y. Appointed from Army.]
Priv. Co. H, 2nd Drag., 8 April, 1858. Corpl., 1 April, 1861. Sergt., 1 June, 1861. 1st Sergt., 22 July, 1862. 2nd Lieut. 2nd Cav., 17 July, 1862. Bvt. 1st Lieut., 9 June, 1863, for gallant and meritorious service in the Battle of Beverly Ford, Va. 1st Lieut. 2nd Cav., 25 Nov., 1863. Bvt. Capt., 19 Oct., 1864, for gallant and meritorious service in the Battle of Cedar Creek, Va. Bvt. Maj., 13 March, 1865, for gallant and meritorious service during the war. Capt. 9th Cav., 28 July, 1866, declined. Capt. 2nd Cav., 7 May, 1867. Retired 23 April, 1879. Died 21 March, 1891.

WELLS, EUGENE. [Born in Mo. Appointed from Mo.]
1st Lieut. 12th Inf., 14 May, 1861. Capt., 9 Sept., 1863. Trans. to 30th Inf., 21 Sept., 1866. Unassigned 23 March, 1869. Ass'd to 4th Inf., 10 April, 1869. Discharged 27 Oct., 1870. 2nd Lieut. 1st Art., 6 July, 1875. Dismissed 13 Oct., 1877.

WELLS, FRANK L.* [Born in Ind. Appointed from Ind.]
2nd Lieut. 11th Inf., 12 June, 1894. 1st Lieut., 26 April, 1898.

WELLS, GEORGE E. [Born in Mass. Appointed from Mass.]
3rd Lieut. Light Art., 3 May, 1813. 2nd Lieut., 2 Oct., 1813. 1st Lieut., 30 Sept., 1816. Disbanded 1 June, 1821.

WELLS, GEORGE M. [Born in Ind. Appointed from Ind.]
Asst. Surg., 4 May, 1891. Capt. Asst. Surg., 4 May, 1896.

WELLS, HENRY F. [Born in N. Y. Appointed from R. I.]
2nd Lieut. 4th Inf., 15 Aug., 1876. Resigned 1 Dec., 1877.

WELLS, JAMES M.* [Born in Md. Appointed from D. C.]
Bvt. 2nd Lieut. 7th Inf., 1 July, 1835. 2nd Lieut., 31 Aug., 1836. 1st Lieut., 9 Dec., 1838. Resigned 31 May, 1839. Maj. Tex. Rifles, 13 June to 24 Aug., 1846. Capt. of Inf., 13 March, 1847; 12th Inf., 9 April, 1847. Disbanded 25 July, 1848. Died ——, 1853.

WELLS, JOHN B. [Born in Md. Appointed from Ga.]
Asst. Surg., 1 Feb., 1834. Maj. Surg., 24 Oct., 1846. Died 24 July, 1853.

WELLS, JOHN C. [Born in Va. Appointed from Va.]
2nd Lieut. 4th Inf., 19 Feb., 1817. 1st Lieut., 30 May, 1817. Dismissed 23 July, 1818.

WELLS, RICHARD. [Born in Md. Appointed from Md.]
2nd Lieut. Rifles, 27 Oct., 1820. Trans. to 6th Inf., 1 June, 1821. Resigned 1 Dec., 1821.

WELLS, RUSH S. [Born in N. M. Appointed from S. D.]
1st Lieut. Troop C, 3rd U. S. Vol. Cav., 18 May to 24 July, 1898. 2nd Lieut. 2nd Art., 9 July, 1898. Trans. to 8th Cav., 29 March, 1899.

WELLS, WM.* [Born in Mass. Appointed from Mass.]
3rd Lieut. Light Art., 21 July, 1814. 2nd Lieut., 10 Oct., 1814. 1st Lieut., 28 Aug., 1819. R. Q. M., — Jan., 1820, to 1 June, 1821. Trans. to 2nd Art., 1 June, 1821. Resigned 1 Dec., 1834. Bvt. Capt., 28 Aug., 1829, for ten years' faithful service in one grade. Died 19 Dec., 1851.

WELLS, WM. W.* [Born in Ind. Appointed from Ind.]
Bvt. 2nd Lieut. 3rd Art., 1 July, 1821. 2nd Lieut. 4th Art., 1 July, 1821. 1st Lieut., 11 April, 1825. Resigned 31 July, 1831. Died 8 Sept., 1832.

WELSH, BLANTON C.* [Born in Pa. Appointed from Pa.]
2nd Lieut. 15th Inf., 13 June, 1882. 1st Lieut. 1st Inf., 13 Feb., 1891. Trans. to 15th Inf., 20 July, 1891. Retired for disability, 27 Nov., 1894.

WELSH, CHAS. B. [Born in Pa. Appointed from Pa.]
Asst. Surg., 1 Dec., 1833. Died 2 Aug., 1834.

WELSH, THOS. [Born in Pa. Appointed from Pa.]
Priv. Co. E, 2nd Ky. Vols., 9 June, 1846. Discharged 10 June, 1847. 2nd Lieut.

11th Inf., 30 Dec., 1847. Disbanded 16 Aug., 1848. Capt. 2nd Pa. Vols., 20 April, 1861. Lieut. Col., 20 April, 1861. Mustered out 26 July, 1861. Col. 45th Pa. Vols., 21 Oct., 1861. Brig. Gen. Vols., 29 Nov., 1862. Appointment expired 4 March, 1863. Brig. Gen. Vols., 13 March, 1863. Died 14 Aug., 1863.

WELSH, WM. [Born in Pa. Appointed from Ohio.]
Priv., Corpl. and 1st Sergt. Co. A, 4th Ohio Vols., 15 April, 1861, to 5 June, 1862. 2nd Lieut., 5 June, 1862. 1st Lieut., 14 Dec., 1862. Capt. 19th U. S. Col. Inf., 19 March, 1864. Maj., 13 May, 1865. Lieut. Col., 11 July, 1866. Bvt. Col. Vols., 13 March, 1865, for gallant and efficient service during the war. Brig. Gen. Vols., 13 March, 1865, for gallant conduct during the war and especially in the defence of the picket line at Bermuda Hundred, Va. Mustered out 15 Jan., 1867. Capt. 40th Inf., 22 Jan., 1867. Trans. to 25th Inf., 20 April, 1869. Mustered out 1 Jan., 1871. Bvt. Maj., 2 March, 1867, for gallant and meritorious service in the Battle of Fredericksburg, Va. Bvt. Lieut. Col., 2 March, 1867, for gallant and meritorious service in the Battle of Gettysburg, Pa.

WELSH, WM. E.* [Born in Pa. Appointed from Pa.]
2nd Lieut. 8th Inf., 12 June, 1894. 1st Lieut. 10th Inf., 26 April, 1898.

WELTON, HENRY S. [Born in Conn. Appointed from Va.]
Capt. 4th W. Va. Vols., 7 June to 31 Aug., 1861. Capt. 19th Inf., 5 Aug., 1861. Resigned 25 Nov., 1863.

WENCKEBACH, ENNO F. [Born in Germany. Appointed from Army.]
1st Lieut. and Adj. 4th N. Y. Cav., 23 April, 1862. Dropped 13 Aug., 1862. 1st Lieut. 4th N. Y. Cav., 3 Feb., 1863. Mustered out 20 Nov., 1864. Priv. and Sergt. 13th U. S. Inf., 7 March to 11 July, 1865. 2nd Lieut. 13th Inf., 22 June, 1865. 1st Lieut., 22 June, 1865. Trans. to 22nd Inf., 21 Sept., 1866. Capt., 15 Sept., 1867. Unassigned 15 May, 1869. Mustered out 1 Jan., 1871. 2nd Lieut. 6th Inf., 18 March, 1881. Resigned 31 July, 1881. Died — Jan., 1882.

WENDELL, ABRAHAM.* [Born in N. Y. Appointed from N. Y.]
3rd Lieut. Corps Art., 2 March, 1815. 2nd Lieut. 3rd Inf., 5 March, 1817. Died 17 Oct., 1817.

WENIE, THOS. M. [Born in N. Y. Appointed from Del.]
1st Lieut. 2nd Del. Vols., 12 June, 1861. Capt., 23 April, 1862. Mustered out 14 Sept., 1864. Capt. 1st Del. Vet. Vols., 26 Oct., 1864. Mustered out 12 July, 1865. Capt. 4th U. S. Vet. Vols., 23 Aug., 1865. Mustered out 23 March, 1866. 2nd Lieut. 28th Inf., 7 March, 1867. Trans. to 19th Inf., 31 March, 1869. 1st Lieut., 9 July, 1876. Died 11 Oct., 1882.

WERNINGER, ALSTORPHIUS, Jr. [Born in Va. Appointed from W. Va.]
Sergt. and 1st Sergt. Co. B, and Sergt. Maj. 6th W. Va. Cav., 25 June, 1861, to 25 March, 1865. 2nd Lieut. 6th W. Va. Cav., 25 March, 1865. 1st Lieut., 21 April, 1865. Mustered out 22 May, 1866. 2nd Lieut. 3rd Cav., 23 Feb., 1866. Trans. to 2nd Inf., 28 Sept., 1866. 1st Lieut., 15 Aug., 1867. Unassigned 17 April, 1869. Discharged 1 Nov., 1870.

WESCOTT, GEORGE C. [Born in N. J. Appointed from N. J.]
2nd Lieut. 2nd Inf., 1 Aug., 1838. 1st Lieut., 15 March, 1846. R. Q. M., 15 April, 1847, to 17 Oct., 1848. Capt., 7 May, 1849. Died 8 Jan., 1853. Bvt. Capt., 13 Sept., 1847, for gallant and meritorious conduct in the Battle of Chapultepec.

WESCOTT, ROBERT H. [Born in Wis. Appointed from Wis.]
2nd Lieut. 2nd Inf., 10 April, 1899.

WESENDORF, MAX. [Born in Prussia. Appointed from D. C.]
1st Lieut. Wash. Ter. Vols., 7 April, 1862. Mustered out 12 May, 1865. 2nd Lieut. 24th Inf., 22 Jan., 1867. 1st Lieut., 21 April, 1868. Unassigned 25 April, 1869. Ass'd to 1st Cav., 1 Jan., 1871. Capt., 12 June, 1880. Retired for disability, 9 March, 1891.

WESSELLS, HENRY W.* [Born in Conn. Appointed from Conn.]
Bvt. 2nd Lieut. 2nd Inf., 1 July, 1833. 2nd Lieut., 28 June, 1836. 1st Lieut., 7 July, 1838. Capt., 16 Feb., 1847. Bvt. Maj., 20 Aug., 1847, for gallant and meritorious conduct in the Battles of Contreras and Churubusco, Mex. Maj. 6th Inf., 6 June, 1861. Col. 8th Kan. Vols., 29 Sept., 1861. Resigned Vol. commission, 7 Feb., 1862. Brig. Gen. Vols., 25 April, 1862. Bvt. Lieut. Col., 31 May, 1862, for gallant and meritorious service in the Battle of Fair Oaks, Va. Bvt. Col., 20 April, 1864, for gallant and meritorious service during the rebel attack on Plymouth, N. C. Lieut. Col. 18th Inf., 16 Feb., 1865. Bvt. Brig. Gen., 13 March, 1865, for gallant and meritorious service during the war. Mustered out of Vol. Service, 15 Jan., 1866. Unassigned 15 March, 1869. Retired 1 Jan., 1871. Died 12 Jan., 1889.

WESSELLS, HENRY W., Jr. [Born in N. Y. Appointed from Army.]
Cadet at Naval Acad., 20 Sept., 1862, to 12 Nov., 1864. Priv. Co. K, 7th Inf., 1 March, 1865. Sergt., 14 March, 1865. Trans. to Co. D, 29 May, 1865. 2nd Lieut. and 1st Lieut. 7th Inf., 21 July, 1865. Trans. to 3rd Cav., 31 Dec., 1870. Capt., 20 Dec., 1872. Maj., 16 Aug., 1892. Lieut. Col., 8 May, 1899.

WESSELLS, MORRIS C. [Born in N. J. Appointed from Mo.]
2nd Lieut. 24th Inf., 18 Dec., 1871. 1st Lieut., 15 May, 1877. Capt., 22 Dec., 1887. Resigned 4 Dec., 1895.

WEST, BARRINGTON K.* [Born in Ky. Appointed from Ky.]
2nd Lieut. 6th Cav., 13 June, 1882. 1st Lieut. 9th Cav., 20 Feb., 1891. Trans. to 6th Cav., 27 April, 1891. Capt. C. S., 4 Feb., 1898. Maj. C. S. Vols., 5 Aug., 1898, to 2 March, 1899.

WEST, EDWARD W. [Born in Mass. Appointed from Army.]
Priv. Co. F, 7th N. Y. Militia, 26 April to 28 May, 1861. 2nd Lieut. 4th R. I. Vols., 30 Oct., 1861. 1st Lieut., 20 Nov., 1861. Resigned 11 Aug., 1863 (he was appointed Lieut. Col. 33rd N. J. Vols., but was not mustered in). Bvt. Col. and Brig. Gen. Vols., 13 March, 1865, for gallant and meritorious service during the war. Priv. and Sergt. Co. F, 14th Inf., 29 Aug., 1863, to 7 Oct., 1863. 2nd Lieut. 1st Art., 3 Oct., 1863. Resigned 18 March, 1864.

WEST, FRANK.* [Born in N. Y. Appointed from N. Y.]
2nd Lieut. 6th Cav., 14 June, 1872. 1st Lieut., 17 May, 1876. Capt., 19 Oct., 1887. Bvt. 1st Lieut., 27 Feb., 1890, for gallant services in action against Indians on the Washita River, Tex., 9, 10 and 11 Sept., 1874. Medal of Honor for distinguished conduct in action against hostile Apache Indians at the Big Dry Wash, Ariz., 17 July, 1882, in rallying his command and leading it to the advance against the fortified position of the enemy; while serving as 1st Lieut. 6th Cav., commanding Troop I, and a detachment of Indian scouts.

WEST, HENRY T. [Born in Pa. Appointed from Wis.]
2nd Lieut. 2nd Art., 9 July, 1898. Resigned 1 May, 1899.

WEST, JAMES.* [Born in Md. Appointed from Md.]
Bvt. 2nd Lieut. 7th Inf., 1 July, 1830. 2nd Lieut., 1 July, 1830. Died 28 Sept., 1834.

WEST, PARKER W.* [Born in Cal. Appointed from La.]
Addl. 2nd Lieut. 3rd Cav., 11 June, 1881. 2nd Lieut., 26 June, 1881. 1st Lieut., 25 Nov., 1887. Capt. 8th Cav., 31 May, 1898. Trans. to 5th Cav., 3 May, 1899. Capt. C. S. Vols., 12 May, 1898, declined. Maj. Chief C. S., 26 Nov., 1898, to 17 April, 1899. Maj. I. G. Vols., 17 April, 1899.

WEST, RICHARD, Jr. [Born in Md. Appointed from Md.]
2nd Lieut. 1st Drag., 25 Jan., 1837. 2nd Lieut., 29 Jan., 1839. Died 19 July, 1844.

WEST, ROB'T M. [Born in N. J. Appointed from Pa.]
Priv. Co. F, Mounted Rifles, 12 April, 1856, to 5 Feb., 1861. Capt. 1st Pa. Light Art., 25 July, 1861. Maj., 13 Sept., 1861. Col., 28 July, 1862. Trans. to 5th Pa. Cav., 29 April, 1864. Bvt. Brig. Gen. Vols., 1 April, 1865, for gallant and meritorious conduct at the Battle of Five Forks, Va. Mustered out 7 Aug., 1865. Capt. 7th Cav., 28 July, 1866. Resigned 1 March, 1869. Bvt. Maj., 2 March, 1867, for gallant and meritorious service in action at Charles City C. H., Va., 13 Dec., 1863. Bvt. Lieut. Col., 2 March, 1867, for gallant and meritorious service in the Battle of New Market Heights, Va. Bvt. Col., 2 March, 1867, for gallant and meritorious service in the Battle of Five Forks, Va. Died 3 Sept., 1869.

WEST, WM. [Born in Ireland. Appointed from Army.]
Priv., Corpl. and Sergt. Co. H, 3rd Inf., 6 July, 1857, to 29 Oct., 1861. 2nd Lieut. 2nd Inf., 24 Oct., 1861. 1st Lieut., 27 Aug., 1862. Capt., 16 Feb., 1865. Cashiered 15 Aug., 1867. Bvt. Capt., 1 Aug., 1864, for gallant service at the Battle of Spottsylvania, and during the campaign before Richmond.

WESTERN, CHAS. B. [Born in N. Y. Appointed from N. Y.]
Priv. Co. C, 8th N. Y. Militia, 29 May to 10 Sept., 1862. Sergt. Co. K, 156th N. Y. Vols., 15 Sept., 1862. 1st Lieut. 156th N. Y. Vols., 11 Feb., 1864. Capt., 18 Oct., 1864. Mustered out 23 Oct., 1865. 2nd Lieut. and 1st Lieut. 14th Inf., 23 Feb., 1866. Capt., 23 April, 1879. Died 10 June, 1890.

WESTMORE, STEPHEN M.* [Born in S. C. Appointed from S. C.]
Entered Mil. Acad. under the name of Stephen W. Moore. Bvt. 2nd Lieut. and 2nd Lieut. 7th Inf., 1 July, 1827. 1st Lieut., 31 May, 1834. Reg. Adj., 10 Feb., 1836, to 7 July, 1838. Capt., 7 July, 1838. Resigned 19 April, 1846.

WESTNEDGE, RICHARD B. [Born in ——. Appointed from Iowa.]
Asst. Surg., 12 Dec., 1898. Died 10 June, 1899, at Manila, P. I.

WESTON, CHAS. [Born in Maine. Appointed from Ill.]
Mil. Storekeeper Ord. Dept., 27 Nov., 1861. Resigned 16 Sept., 1862.

WESTON, JOHN F. [Born in Ky. Appointed from Ky.]
1st Lieut. 4th Ky. Cav., 24 Dec., 1861. Capt., 9 Feb., 1863. Maj., 1 Nov., 1864. Mustered out 21 Aug., 1865. 2nd Lieut. 7th Cav., 9 Aug., 1867. 1st Lieut., 27 Nov., 1868. R. Q. M., 1 Jan., 1871, to 29 Feb., 1872. Capt. C. S., 24 Nov., 1875. Graduate of the Artillery School, 1875. Maj. C. S., 1 Aug., 1892. Lieut. Col. A. C. G. S., 15 Nov., 1897. Col. A. C. G. S., 30 April, 1898. Brig. Gen. Vols., 21 Sept., 1898, to 24 March, 1899. Medal of Honor for gallantry at Wetumpka, Ala., 13 April, 1865; while serving as Maj. 4th Ky. Cav.

WETHERILL, ALEX'R M. [Born in Pa. Appointed from Pa.]
2nd Lieut. 6th Inf., 9 May, 1867. 1st Lieut., 28 April, 1875. R. Q. M., 1 March, 1887, to 3 Jan., 1890. Capt., 3 Jan., 1890. Killed in action 1 July, 1898, at San Juan, Santiago, Cuba.

WETHERILL, ALEXANDER M. [Born in Dak. Appointed from R. I.]
2nd Lieut. 6th Inf., 9 Sept., 1898.

WETHERILL, HENRY E. [Born in Mass. Appointed from Pa.]
Asst. Surg., 23 July, 1898.

WETMORE, ALPHONSO. [Born in N. Y. Appointed from N. Y.]
Ensign 23rd Inf., 14 April, 1812. 2nd Lieut., 26 June, 1813. 1st Lieut., 9 July, 1814. Trans. to 6th Inf., 17 May, 1815. Capt., 25 Dec., 1819. Reg. P. M., 14 Oct., 1815, to 1 June, 1821. Retained as Maj. P. M., 1 June, 1821, to rank from 14 Oct., 1815. Resigned 1 May, 1833. Died 13 June, 1849.

WETMORE, LEONIDAS. [Born in N. Y. Appointed from Mo.]
2nd Lieut. 6th Inf., 31 Dec., 1839. 1st Lieut., 9 May, 1846. R. Q. M., 17 Dec., 1847, to 30 June, 1848. Died 18 Nov., 1849. Bvt. Capt., 8 Sept., 1847, for gallant and meritorious conduct in the Battle of El Molino del Rey.

WETMORE, OLIVER, Jr. [Born in N. J. Appointed from N. Y.]
1st Lieut. 5th N. Y. Vols., 9 May, 1861. Capt., 8 Sept., 1861. Resigned 20 June, 1862. Capt. Marine Art. N. Y. Vols., 30 Dec., 1862. Mustered out 31 March, 1863. Maj. 13th N. Y. Art., 12 Sept., 1863. Mustered out 18 July, 1865. 1st Lieut. 19th Inf., 28 July, 1866. Resigned 31 Dec., 1872.

WETMORE, SAML. W.* [Born in Mass. Appointed from Mass.]
2nd Lieut. Corps Art., 21 July, 1814. Resigned 16 July, 1816. Died 9 Feb., 1819.

WETMORE, WM. B.* [Born in N. Y. Appointed at Large.]
2nd Lieut. 6th Cav., 14 June, 1872. Resigned 1 Dec., 1876.

WEVER, BENJAMIN S.* [Born in N. Y. Appointed from N. Y.]
2nd Lieut. 1st Inf., 12 June, 1880. 1st Lieut., 14 April, 1887. Dropped 10 Sept., 1891.

WHAM, JOSEPH W. [Born in Ill. Appointed from Ill.]
Priv. Co. G, 21st Ill. Vols., 10 June, 1861. Sergt., 1 Nov., 1864. Discharged 27 July, 1865. 1st Lieut. 21st Ill. Vols., 28 July, 1865. Mustered out 16 Dec., 1865. 2nd Lieut. 35th Inf., 22 May, 1867. Unassigned 20 May, 1869. Discharged 1 Jan., 1871. Maj. P. M., 3 March, 1877.

WHARTENBY, RICH'D. [Born in Pa. Appointed from Pa.]
1st Lieut. 5th Inf., 3 May, 1808. Capt., 3 May, 1810. Maj. 40th Inf., 1 May, 1814. Retained 17 May, 1815, as Capt. 7th Inf., with Bvt. of Maj. from 1 May, 1814. Maj. 1st Inf., 30 May, 1817. Died 14 May, 1825.

WHARTON, CLIFTON. [Born in Pa. Appointed from D. C.]
2nd Lieut. Light Art., 28 Oct., 1818. Trans. to 1st Art., 1 June, 1821. Trans. to 3rd Art., 16 Aug., 1821. 1st Lieut., 6 July, 1825. Trans. to 6th Inf., 24 March, 1826. Capt. A. Q. M., 19 May, 1826, to 6 Oct., 1830. Capt. 6th Inf., 22 April, 1830. Trans. to 1st Drag., 4 March, 1833. Maj., 4 July, 1836. Lieut. Col. 1st Drag., 30 June, 1846. Died 13 July, 1847.

WHARTON, HENRY C.* [Born in Ark. Appointed from Neb.]
2nd Lieut. Eng., 17 June, 1862. 1st Lieut., 3 March, 1863. Capt., 11 Nov., 1865. Lieut. Col. U. S. Vet. Vols. Eng., 27 Aug., 1864. Mustered out of Vol. Service, 10 March, 1865. Resigned 6 Jan., 1870. Bvt. Capt., 5 Dec., 1864, for meritorious service in his Dept., in the Dept. of the Cumberland. Died 8 April, 1870.

WHARTON, HENRY W. [Born in D. C. Appointed from Ala.]
2nd Lieut. 6th Inf., 31 Oct., 1837. 1st Lieut., 11 Aug., 1838. Capt., 16 Feb., 1847. Maj. 9th Inf., 9 Sept., 1861. Col. 2nd Del. Vols., 13 July, 1861. Resigned from Vol. Service 6 Oct., 1862. Retired 1 Dec., 1863. Died 23 March, 1868.

WHARTON, JESSE B. [Born in Md. Appointed from Md.]
2nd Lieut. 7th Inf., 30 June, 1855. Resigned 31 Aug., 1859. Died 1 April, 1862.

WHARTON, JOHN S. [Born in N. Y. Appointed from N. Y.]
1st Lieut. 14th Inf., 14 May, 1861. Bvt. Capt., 30 Aug., 1862, for gallant and meritorious service in the Battle of Bull Run (2nd), Va. Capt. 14th Inf., 30 June, 1865. Unassigned 22 July, 1869. Ass'd to 19th Inf., 15 Dec., 1870. Retired for disability, 18 Dec., 1886. Died 15 Oct., 1896.

WHARTON, WM. L. [Born in D. C. Appointed from D. C.]
Asst. Surg., 1 Sept., 1828. Maj. Surg., 22 July, 1837. Died 4 Oct., 1846.

WHATLEY, WILSON. [Born in S. C. Appointed from S. C.]
Ensign 18th Inf., 29 June, 1813. 3rd Lieut., 11 Sept., 1813. 2nd Lieut., 31 March, 1814. Resigned 15 July, 1814. 3rd Lieut. Corps Art., 4 Sept., 1817. 2nd Lieut. 8th Inf., 13 Feb., 1818. 1st Lieut., 24 Dec., 1818. Resigned 1 Jan., 1820.

WHEATON, CHAS. [Born in R. I. Appointed from R. I.]
1st Lieut. 2nd Mass. Vols., 25 May, 1861. Capt. C. S. Vols., 17 July, 1862. Bvt. Maj. Vols., 13 March, 1865, for meritorious service in his Dept. during the war. Lieut. Col. C. S. (Act 17 July, 1862), 9 June, 1865, to 8 Jan., 1866. Bvt. Lieut. Col. and Col. Vols., 1 Dec., 1865, for faithful and meritorious service in the Sub. Dept. Mustered out 31 May, 1866. Capt. 33rd Inf., 17 July, 1867. Unassigned 3 May, 1869. Ass'd to 23rd Inf., 1 Jan., 1871. Retired for disability, 22 June, 1889.

WHEATON, FRANCIS L. [Born in R. I. Appointed from R. I.]
Asst. Surg., 3 March, 1847; 9th Inf., 9 April, 1847. Disbanded 26 Aug., 1848. Surg. 2nd R. I. Vols., 5 June, 1861. Discharged 12 Sept., 1862.

WHEATON, FRANK. [Born in R. I. Appointed from R. I.]
1st Lieut. 1st Cav., 3 March, 1855. Capt., 1 March, 1861. 4th Cav., 3 Aug., 1861. Lieut. Col. 2nd R. I. Vols., 10 July, 1861. Col., 21 July, 1861. Brig. Gen. Vols., 29 Nov., 1862. Maj. 2nd Cav., 5 Nov., 1863. Bvt. Lieut. Col., 5 May, 1864, for gallant and meritorious service in the Battle of the Wilderness, Va. Bvt. Col., 19 Oct., 1864, for gallant and meritorious service in the Battle of Cedar Creek, Va. Bvt. Maj. Gen. Vols., 19 Oct., 1864, for gallant and meritorious service in the Battles of Opequan, Fisher's Hill, and Middletown, Va. Bvt. Brig. Gen., 13 March, 1865, for gallant and meritorious service in the capture of Petersburg, Va. Bvt. Maj. Gen., 13 March, 1865, for gallant and meritorious service in the field during the war. Mustered out of Vol. Service, 30 April, 1866. Lieut. Col. 39th Inf., 28 July, 1866. Trans. to 21st Inf., 15 March, 1869. Col. 2nd Inf., 15 Dec., 1874. Brig. Gen., 18 April, 1892. Maj. Gen., 2 April, 1897. Retired by operation of law, 8 May, 1897.

WHEATON, HENRY. [Born in N. Y. Appointed from N. Y.]
J. A., 6 Aug., 1814. Discharged 9 May, 1816. Died 11 March, 1848.

WHEATON, LOYD. [Born in Mich. Appointed from Ill.]
1st Sergt. Co. E, 8th Ill. Vols., 20 April, 1861. 1st Lieut., 25 July, 1861. Capt., 25 March, 1862. Maj., 28 Aug., 1863. Lieut. Col., 25 Nov., 1864. Bvt. Col. Vols., 26 March, 1865, for faithful and meritorious service during the campaign against the City of Mobile and its defences. Mustered out 4 May, 1866. Capt. 34th Inf., 28 July, 1866. Bvt. Maj., 2 March, 1867, for gallant and meritorious service in the Siege of Vicksburg, Miss. Bvt. Lieut. Col., 2 March, 1867, for gallant and meritorious service in the assault on Fort Blakely, Ala. Unassigned 14 April, 1869. Ass'd to 20th Inf., 1 Sept., 1869. Maj., 14 Oct., 1891. Lieut. Col. 22nd Inf., 31 May, 1895. Trans. to 20th Inf., 11 Sept., 1895. Trans. to 2nd Inf., 30 Dec., 1898. Col. 20th Inf., 6 Feb., 1899. Brig. Gen. Vols., 27 May, 1898, to 15 April, 1899, when reappointed same date, to ——. Medal of Honor for distinguished gallantry in the assault on Fort Blakely, Ala., 9 April, 1865, leading the right wing of his regiment, springing through an embrasure against a strong fire of artillery and musketry, the first to enter the enemy's works; while serving as Lieut. Col. 8th Ill. Inf.

WHEATON, WALTER V. [Born in N. Y. Appointed from R. I.]
Hosp. Surg., 28 March, 1813. Disbanded 15 June, 1815. Reinstated 3 May, 1816, as Post Surg. Maj. Surg. 2nd Inf., 4 Sept., 1816. Retained as Maj. Surg., 1 June, 1821, to rank from 4 Sept., 1816. Died 23 April, 1860.

WHEDBEE, THOS. M.* [Born in N. C. Appointed from N. C.]
Bvt. 2nd Lieut. 3rd Art., 1 July, 1846. Trans. to Ord., 12 Sept., 1846. 2nd Lieut., 3 March, 1847. Died 28 March, 1849.

WHEEDEN, JOHN J. [Born in N. C. Appointed from N. C.]
2nd Lieut. of Inf., 25 March, 1847; 12th Inf., 9 April, 1847. Died 4 Jan., 1848.

WHEELAN, JAMES N. [Born in Pa. Appointed from N. Y.]
1st Sergt. Co. A, 1st N. Y. Mounted Rifles, 18 July, 1861. 2nd Lieut. 1st N. Y. Mounted Rifles, 7 Jan., 1862. Capt., 7 Feb., 1862. Maj., 13 Aug., 1862. Bvt. Col. Vols., 13 March, 1865, for gallant and meritorious service during the war. Lieut. Col. 1st N. Y. Mounted Rifles, 17 Aug., 1865. Mustered out 29 Nov., 1865. 2nd Lieut. 2nd Cav., 23 Feb., 1866. 1st Lieut., 28 July, 1866. Capt., 15 Dec., 1873. Maj. 8th Cav., 7 March, 1893. Lieut. Col. 7th Cav., 9 June, 1899. Bvt. Maj., 27 Feb., 1890, for gallant services in action against Indians on the Rosebud, Mont., 7 May, 1877.

WHEELER, CHARLES B. [Born in Ill. Appointed from Minn.]
* 2nd Lieut. 5th Art., 12 June, 1887. 1st Lieut. Ord., 15 Dec., 1890. Capt., 7 July, 1898.

WHEELER, DANIEL D. [Born in Vt. Appointed from Vt.]
2nd Lieut. 4th Vt. Vols., 21 Sept., 1861. 1st Lieut., 21 April, 1862. Capt. A. A. G. Vols., 30 June, 1864. Bvt. Maj. Vols., 29 Sept., 1864, for gallant and meritorious service in the campaign of 1864. Maj. A. A. G. Vols., 27 Dec., 1864. Lieut. Col. A. A. G. Vols., 26 May, 1865, to 11 June, 1866. Bvt. Col. Vols., 1 Dec., 1865, for faithful and meritorious service. Mustered out 19 Oct., 1866. 2nd Lieut. 1st Art., 11 May, 1866. 1st Lieut., 12 Feb., 1867. Bvt. Capt., 2 March, 1867, for gallant and meritorious service in the Battles of Salem Heights and Cold Harbor, Va. Capt. A. Q. M., 2 July, 1879. Maj. Q. M., 6 Sept., 1893. Lieut. Col. Dep. Q. M. G., 11 Nov., 1898. Graduate of the Artillery School, 1873. Lieut. Col. Chief Q. M. Vols., 9 May, 1898, to 10 Nov., 1898. Col. Q. M. Vols., 3 Sept., 1898, to 2 March, 1899. Medal of Honor for distinguished bravery in the Battle of Salem Heights, Va., 3 May, 1863; while serving as 1st Lieut. 4th Vt. Inf., and A. de C. to Brig. Gen. W. T. H. Brooks.

WHEELER, DAVID P.* [Born in Ohio. Appointed from Ohio.]
2nd Lieut. 23rd Inf., 26 April, 1898. 1st Lieut. 22nd Inf., 2 March, 1899.

WHEELER, EDWARD D.* [Born in Ohio. Appointed from Ohio.]
2nd Lieut. 1st Art., 13 June, 1864. 1st Lieut., 4 Sept., 1865. Wholly retired 6 July, 1878. Died 12 Oct., 1883.

WHEELER, ELBERT.* [Born in Mass. Appointed from Mass.]
2nd Lieut. 1st Art., 16 June, 1875. Resigned 12 June, 1877.

WHEELER, FRED.* [Born in Wis. Appointed from Wis.]
Addl. 2nd Lieut. 4th Cav., 14 June, 1878. 2nd Lieut., 28 June, 1878. 1st Lieut., 1 Nov., 1881. Capt., 9 March, 1891.

WHEELER, GEORGE M.* [Born in Mass. Appointed from Colo.]
2nd Lieut. Eng., 18 June, 1866. 1st Lieut., 7 March, 1867. Capt., 4 March, 1879. Retired for disability, 15 June, 1888. Appointed Maj. on the retired list, 2 Oct., 1890, to rank from 23 July, 1888 (Act of 27 Sept., 1890).

WHEELER, HARRIS A. [Born in Maine. Appointed from Maine.]
2nd Lieut. 25th Inf., 4 March, 1872. Resigned 31 Dec., 1873.

WHEELER, HOMER W. [Born in Vt. Appointed from Kan.]
2nd Lieut. 5th Cav., 15 Oct., 1875. Graduate of the Infantry and Cavalry School, 1883. 1st Lieut., 13 Oct., 1884. Capt., 7 April, 1893.

WHEELER, JAMES.* [Born in N. Y. Appointed from N. Y.]
Bvt. 2nd Lieut. 2nd Drag., 1 July, 1855. 2nd Lieut. 1st Drag., 8 Sept., 1855. 1st Lieut., 20 April, 1861. 1st Cav., 3 Aug., 1861. Capt., 7 Sept., 1861. Cashiered 20 May, 1862. Died 7 Dec., 1879.

WHEELER, JOSEPH.* [Born in Ga. Appointed from N. Y.]
Bvt. 2nd Lieut. 1st Drag., 1 July, 1859. Trans. to Mounted Rifles, 21 June, 1860. 2nd Lieut., 1 Sept., 1860. Resigned 22 April, 1861. Brig. and Maj. Gen. Vols., 1898-9; Brig. Gen. U. S. A., 1900.

WHEELER, JOSEPH, Jr.* [Born in Ala. Appointed from Ala.]
Addl. 2nd Lieut. 4th Art., 12 June, 1895. 2nd Lieut. 5th Art., 21 Dec., 1895. Trans. to 2nd Art., 30 Jan., 1896. Trans. to 4th Art., 29 June, 1896. 1st Lieut., 2 March, 1899. Maj. Chf. Ord. Off. Vols., 18 Aug., 1898, to 31 March, 1899. Maj. 34th U. S. Vols., 5 July, 1899.

WHEELER, JUNIUS B.* [Born in N. C. Appointed from Army.]
Priv. Co. I, 12th Inf., 15 May to 14 Dec., 1847; 2nd Lieut. 11th Inf., 9 Sept., 1847. Disbanded 14 Aug., 1848. Cadet Mil. Acad., 1 July, 1851. Bvt. 2nd Lieut. 2nd Cav., 1 July, 1855. 2nd Lieut., 21 Aug., 1855. Trans. to Top. Eng., 27 June, 1856. 1st Lieut., 1 July, 1860. Capt. Eng., 3 March, 1863. Bvt. Maj., 30 April, 1864, for gallant and meritorious service at the Battle of Jenkins' Ferry, Ark. Bvt. Lieut. Col. and Col., 13 March, 1865, for gallant and meritorious service during the war. Maj. Eng., 10 July, 1866. Prof. of Civil and Mil. Engineering, 16 Sept., 1871. Retired with pay of Col., for over thirty years' service, 29 Sept., 1884. Died 15 July, 1886.

WHEELER, MARK. [Born in Kan. Appointed from Kan.]
2nd Lieut. 4th Inf., 9 July, 1898. 1st Lieut., 2 March, 1899.

WHEELER, MORTIMER M. [Born in La. Appointed from Ill.]
2nd Lieut. 5th Iowa Cav., 22 Sept., 1861. 1st Lieut., 26 Dec., 1861. Capt., 8 Dec., 1862. Resigned 3 June, 1863. Ensign U. S. N., 23 Jan., 1864, to 2 Feb., 1867. 2nd Lieut. 8th Cav., 28 July, 1866. 1st Lieut., 26 Aug., 1867. R. C. S., 19 Oct., 1869, to 15 July, 1870. Discharged 30 Oct., 1870.

WHEELER, OTIS.* Born in N. H. Appointed from N. H.]
2nd Lieut. 3rd Inf., 1 July, 1821. 1st Lieut., 28 April, 1826. Capt., 31 Oct., 1835. Resigned 29 Feb., 1844. Died 1 June, 1872.

WHEELER, WM. B.* [Born in N. Y. Appointed from Iowa.]
2nd Lieut. 18th Inf., 12 June, 1871. 1st Lieut., 6 Feb., 1882. Capt., 20 Feb., 1891. Maj., 8 Sept., 1899.

WHEELER, WM. H.* [Born in Ohio. Appointed from Wis.]
2nd Lieut. 11th Inf., 17 June, 1874. 1st Lieut., 9 Oct., 1885. Retired for disability, with rank of Capt., 25 Feb., 1891.

WHEELER, WM. H. [Born in N. Y. Appointed from Army.]
Priv., Corpl. and Sergt. Co. A, Eng. Batt., 5 March, 1853, to 17 Dec., 1862. 2nd Lieut. 19th Inf., 29 Nov., 1862. Resigned 11 May, 1863.

WHEELOCK, JOHN. [Born in ——. Appointed from Ky.]
2nd Lieut. 8th Inf., 13 Feb., 1818. 1st Lieut., 19 March, 1819. Trans. to 7th Inf., 1 June, 1821. Died 21 Feb., 1823.

WHEELOCK, JOSEPH H.* [Born in Mass. Appointed from Mass.]
Bvt. 2nd Lieut. 3rd Art., 1 July, 1850. 2nd Lieut. 4th Art., 27 Sept., 1850. 1st Lieut., 13 Jan., 1856. Resigned 31 March, 1857. Col. 7th Mass. Vols., 20 Nov., 1861. Resigned 31 Jan., 1862. Died — April, 1862.

WHEELOCK, THOMPSON B.* [Born in Mass. Appointed from Mass.]
Bvt. 2nd Lieut. and 2nd Lieut. 4th Art., 1 July, 1822. Trans. to 3rd Art., 18 Feb., 1823. Trans. to 2nd Art., 22 July, 1826. Resigned 30 June, 1829. 1st Lieut. 1st Drag., 19 Sept., 1833. Died 15 June, 1836.

WHEELRIGHT, WASHINGTON.* [Born in Mass. Appointed from Mass.]
Bvt. 2nd Lieut. 1st Art., 1 July, 1821. 2nd Lieut., 1 July, 1821. 1st Lieut., 20 April, 1832. Col. Chief of Ord. Ill. Vols., 9 May to 11 Oct., 1832. Resigned 31 May, 1833. Died 31 Oct., 1871.

WHERRY, WM. M. [Born in Mo. Appointed from Mo.]
1st Lieut. 3rd Mo. Vols., 8 May, 1861. Mustered out 18 Aug., 1861. 1st Lieut. 13th Inf., 26 Oct., 1861. Maj. A. de C. Vols., 12 May, 1864. Bvt. Capt., 1 Sept., 1864, for gallant and meritorious service during the Atlanta campaign. Bvt. Maj., 16 Dec., 1864, for gallant and meritorious service in the Battles of Franklin and Nashville, Tenn. Bvt. Lieut. Col. and Col., 13 March, 1865, for gallant and meritorious service during the war. Bvt. Col. Vols., 13 March, 1865, for gallant and meritorious service during the campaign in Georgia and Tennessee. Bvt. Brig. Gen. Vols., 13 March, 1865, for gallant and meritorious service. Mustered out of Vol. Service, 9 Feb., 1866. Capt. 13th Inf., 5 April, 1866. Trans. to 31st Inf., 21 Sept., 1866. Unassigned 15 May, 1869. Ass'd to 6th Inf., 15 Feb., 1870. Maj. 21st Inf., 20 April, 1891. Trans. to 6th Inf., 16 April, 1892. Lieut. Col. 2nd Inf., 20 Dec., 1894. Col. 17th Inf., 30 Aug., 1898. Brig. Gen., 7 Jan., 1899. Brig. Gen. Vols., 21 Sept. to 30 Nov., 1898. Retired, for over thirty years' service, 18 Jan., 1899. Medal of Honor for distinguished gallantry in the Battle of Wilson's Creek, Mo., 10 Aug., 1861; displaying conspicuous coolness and heroism in rallying troops that were recoiling under a most destructive fire; while 1st Lieut. 3rd U. S. Res. Corps, Mo. Inf., and A. de C. to Gen. Lyon.

WHIPPLE, AMIEL W.* [Born in Mass. Appointed from Mass.]
2nd Lieut. 1st Art., 1 July, 1831. Trans. to Top. Eng., 28 Sept., 1841. 1st Lieut., 24 April, 1851. Capt., 1 July, 1855. Maj., 9 Sept., 1861. Trans. to Eng., 3 March, 1863. Brig. Gen. Vols., 14 April, 1862. Maj. Gen. Vols., 6 May, 1863. Died 7 May, 1863, of wounds received at the Battle of Chancellorsville, Va. Bvt. Lieut. Col., 21 July, 1861, for gallant and meritorious service in the Manassas campaign. Bvt. Col., 13 Dec., 1862, for gallant and meritorious service in the Battle of Fredericksburg, Va. Bvt. Brig. Gen., 4 May, 1863, for gallant and meritorious service at the Battle of Chancellorsville, where he was mortally wounded. Bvt. Maj. Gen., 7 May, 1863, for gallant and meritorious service during the war.

WHIPPLE, CHARLES H. [Born in N. Y. Appointed from Minn.]
Maj. P. M., 18 Feb., 1881.

WHIPPLE, CHARLES H., Jr. [Born in Minn. Appointed from Minn.]
2nd Lieut. 1st Art., 9 July, 1898.

WHIPPLE, CHAS. W.* [Born in N. H. Appointed at Large.]
2nd Lieut. 3rd Art., 15 June, 1868. Trans to Ord., 19 July, 1875. 1st Lieut., 19 July, 1875. Capt. (fourteen years' service), 9 May, 1885. Graduate of the Artillery School, 1874. Lieut. Col. I. G. Vols., 22 June, 1898, to 15 March, 1899.

WHIPPLE, HERBERT S.* [Born in Pa. Appointed from Wis.]
2nd Lieut. 10th Cav., 14 June, 1885. 1st Lieut. 9th Cav., 27 March, 1892. Trans. to 7th Cav., 12 April, 1892. Lieut. Col. 2nd Ky. Inf., 17 May to 31 Oct., 1898.

WHIPPLE, JOSEPH H.* [Born in Mass. Appointed from Mass.]
Bvt. 2nd Lieut. 5th Inf., 1 July, 1835. 2nd Lieut., 31 Oct., 1836. 1st Lieut., 1 Nov., 1838. Capt., 29 June, 1846. Died 30 June, 1847.

WHIPPLE, STEPHEN G. [Born in Vt. Appointed from Cal.]
Lieut. Col. 1st Batt. Cal. Vols., 22 June, 1863. Bvt. Col. Vols., 13 March, 1865, for faithful and meritorious service. Mustered out 14 Jan., 1865. Capt. 32nd Inf., 22 Jan., 1867. Unassigned 19 April, 1869. Ass'd to 1st Cav., 15 Dec., 1870. Retired for disability, 31 Oct., 1884. Bvt. Maj., 27 Feb., 1890, for gallant services in action against Indians at the Clearwater, Idaho, 11 and 12 July, 1877. Died 21 Oct., 1895.

WHIPPLE, THOS. J. [Born in N. H. Appointed from N. H.]
1st Lieut. 9th Inf., 9 April, 1847. Reg. Adj., 20 April to 15 June, 1847. Resigned 23 Feb., 1848. Lieut. Col. 1st N. H. Vols., 29 April to 9 Aug., 1861. Col. 4th N. H. Vols., 18 Sept., 1861. Discharged 18 March, 1862. Died 21 Dec., 1889.

WHIPPLE, WM. D.* [Born in N. Y. Appointed from N. Y.]
Bvt. 2nd Lieut. 3rd Inf., 1 July, 1851. 2nd Lieut., 9 Sept., 1851. 1st Lieut., 31 Dec., 1856. Bvt. Capt. A. A. G., 11 May, 1861. Capt. A. A. G., 3 Aug., 1861. Lieut. Col. A. A. de C., 10 Feb., 1862. Maj. A. A. G., 17 July, 1862. Brig. Gen. Vols., 17 July, 1863. Appointment expired 4 July, 1864. Brig. Gen. Vols., 6 Sept., 1864. Bvt. Lieut. Col., Col. and Brig. Gen., 13 March, 1865, for gallant and meritorious service in the Atlanta campaign, and in the Battles before Nashville, Tenn. Bvt. Maj. Gen., 13 March, 1865, for gallant and meritorious service in the field during the war. Mustered out of Vol. Service, 15 Jan., 1866. Col. A. de C. to the Gen., 1 Jan., 1873. Lieut. Col. A. A. G., 3 March, 1875. Col. A. A. G., 28 Feb., 1887. Retired by operation of law, 2 Aug., 1890.

WHISTLER, GARLAND N. [Born in N. Y. Appointed from N. Y.]
2nd Lieut. 5th Art., 9 Oct., 1867. 1st Lieut., 7 Oct., 1874. Capt. 1st Art., 8 March, 1898. Trans. to 5th Art., 7 May, 1898. Graduate of the Artillery School, 1870.

WHISTLER, GEORGE W.* [Born in Ind. Appointed from Ky.]
2nd Lieut. Corps Art., 1 July, 1819. Trans. to 1st Art., 1 June, 1821. Trans. to 2nd Art., 16 Aug., 1821. 1st Lieut., 16 Aug., 1829. Resigned 31 Dec., 1833. Died 7 April, 1849.

WHISTLER, JACOB. [Born in Ireland. Appointed from Pa.]
Ensign 16th Inf., 9 April, 1812. 1st Lieut., 1 Aug., 1813. Disbanded 15 June, 1815. Reinstated 2 Dec., 1815, in 1st Inf. Dropped 15 Aug., 1816. Mil. Storekeeper, 5 March, 1817. Removed 13 Aug., 1817.

WHISTLER, JOSEPH N. G.* [Born in Wis. Appointed at Large.]
Bvt. 2nd Lieut. 8th Inf., 1 July, 1846. 2nd Lieut. 3rd Inf., 7 Jan., 1847. Bvt. 1st Lieut., 20 Aug., 1847, for gallant and meritorious service in the Battles of Contreras and Churubusco, Mex. 1st Lieut. 3rd Inf., 6 June, 1852. Capt., 14 May, 1861. Col. 2nd N. Y. Art., 6 May, 1863. Bvt. Maj., 24 May, 1864, for gallant and meritorious service in the Battle of North Anna, Va. Bvt. Lieut. Col., 19 June, 1864, for gallant and meritorious service in front of Petersburg, Va. Maj. 13th Inf., 31 Dec., 1864. Bvt. Col., 13 March, 1865, for gallant and meritorious service during the war. Bvt. Brig. Gen. Vols., 13 March, 1865, for gallant and meritorious service during the war. Mustered out of Vol. Service, 12 Sept., 1865. Trans. to 31st Inf., 21 Sept., 1866. Trans. to 22nd Inf., 15 March, 1869. Lieut. Col. 5th Inf., 18 Feb., 1874. Col. 15th Inf., 31 May, 1883. Retired by operation of law, 19 Oct., 1886. Died 20 April, 1899.

WHISTLER, WM. [Born in Md. Appointed from N. W. Ter.]
2nd Lieut. 1st Inf., 8 June, 1801. 1st Lieut., 4 March, 1807. Capt., 31 Dec., 1812. Trans. to 3rd Inf., 17 May, 1815. Maj. 2nd Inf., 28 April, 1826. Lieut. Col. 7th Inf., 21 July, 1834. Col. 4th Inf., 15 July, 1845. Retired 9 Oct., 1861. Died 4 Dec., 1863. Bvt. Maj., 31 Dec., 1822, for ten years' faithful service in one grade.

WHITACRE, CHAS. [Born in Ohio. Appointed from Army.]
Priv. and Corpl. Co. G, 2nd Batt. 18th Inf., 27 April to 29 Dec., 1862. 2nd Lieut. 18th Inf., 19 Nov., 1862. 1st Lieut., 17 June, 1863. Dismissed 1 Dec., 1863.

WHITALL, JOHN A. [Born in D. C. Appointed from D. C.]
2nd Lieut. 5th Inf., 1 Aug., 1838. 1st Lieut., 8 June, 1845. Capt., 11 Sept., 1847. Maj. P. M., 8 Aug., 1861. Died 31 March, 1866. Bvt. Capt., 9 May, 1846, for gallant and meritorious conduct at Palo Alto and Resaca de la Palma. Bvt. Lieut. Col., 13 March, 1865, for faithful and meritorious service during the war.

WHITALL, SAM'L R. [Born in Mich. Appointed from D. C.]
Cadet at Naval Acad., 24 Sept., 1861, to 1 July, 1862. 2nd Lieut. 2nd N. Y. Art., 5 May, 1864. Discharged 23 Sept., 1864. 2nd Lieut. 11th Inf., 7 March, 1867. Trans. to 16th Inf., 14 April, 1869. 1st Lieut., 4 March, 1879. Capt., 14 April, 1887. Maj., 2 March 1899.

WHITCOMB, SAM'L N. [Born in Vt. Appointed from Ind.]
Priv. Co. H, 16th Inf., 20 March to 17 June, 1847. 2nd Lieut. 16th Inf., 22 May, 1847. Disbanded 31 July, 1848. Priv. Co. B, 44th Ill. Vols., 13 Sept., 1861. Mustered out 15 Sept., 1864.

WHITE, ALVIN G. [Born in Mass. Appointed from Nebr.]
Chap. Post of Fort Kearny, Nebr., 2 March, 1866, to 6 May, 1867. Post Chap., 3 April, 1867. Dismissed 17 Oct., 1868.

WHITE, CHAS. B. [Born in N. Y. Appointed from N. Y.]
1st Lieut. Asst. Surg., 28 May, 1861. Bvt. Capt. and Maj., 13 March, 1865, for faithful and meritorious service during the war. Capt. Asst. Surg., 28 May, 1866. Maj. Surg., 1 Oct., 1875. Died 10 Aug., 1881.

WHITE, CHESTER B. [Born in Va. Appointed from Mo.]
Mil. Storekeeper Q. M. D., 30 March, 1857. Died 12 Jan., 1858.

WHITE, DAVID. [Born in Tenn. Appointed from Ill.]
Priv. Co. I, 107th Ill. Vols., 2 Aug., 1862. Discharged 10 March, 1864. Chap. 107th Ill. Vols., 10 March, 1864. Mustered out 21 June, 1865. Chap. Post of Fort Reno, Dak., 15 May, 1866, to 17 June, 1867. Post Chap., 3 April, 1867. Retired by operation of law, 30 June, 1882.

WHITE, EDWARD. [Born in Mass. Appointed from Mass.]
2nd Lieut. 25th Inf., 12 March, 1812. 1st Lieut., 16 April, 1813. Capt., 14 March, 1814. Trans. to 6th Inf., 17 May, 1815. Resigned 31 Oct., 1815.

WHITE, EDWARD B.* [Born in S. C. Appointed from S. C.]
Bvt. 2nd Lieut. 1st Art., 1 July, 1826. 2nd Lieut. 3rd Art., 1 July, 1826. 1st Lieut., 1 Dec., 1835. Resigned 13 Aug., 1836.

WHITE, GEORGE P.* [Born in Minn. Appointed from Iowa.]
2nd Lieut. 3rd Cav., 12 June, 1891. 1st Lieut., 9th Cav., 19 Nov., 1897. Graduate of the Infantry and Cavalry School, 1897.

WHITE, GEORGE Q. [Born in Mass. Appointed from Ill.]
Priv. Co. B, 1st Ill. Light Art., 16 July, 1861. Discharged 18 Jan., 1862. Capt. A. Q. M. Vols., 12 May, 1862. Bvt. Maj. Vols., 26 April, 1866, for faithful service in the Q. M. D. Vacated 20 July, 1867. Capt. 44th Inf., 2 July, 1867. Bvt. Maj., 2 July, 1867, for meritorious service during the rebellion. Unassigned 27 May, 1869. Retired 15 Dec., 1870. Died 28 March, 1897.

WHITE, HERBERT A.* [Born in Iowa. Appointed from Iowa.]
2nd Lieut. 6th Cav., 12 June, 1895. 1st Lieut., 2 March, 1899.

WHITE, JAMES L.* [Born in Fla. Appointed from Fla.]
Bvt. 2nd Lieut. 2nd Art., 1 July, 1853. 2nd Lieut. 3rd Art., 24 Dec., 1853. 1st Lieut., 11 Nov., 1856. Resigned 3 March, 1861.

WHITE, JOHN C. [Born in N. Y. Appointed from Army.]
Priv. Co. A, 17th Pa. Vols., 18 April, 1861. Discharged 2 Aug., 1861. Priv. Co. B, 1st Batt. 11th Inf., 8 May, 1863. Corpl., 23 Oct., 1863. Sergt., 1 Jan., 1864. 2nd Lieut. 10th Inf., 18 May, 1864. Bvt. 1st Lieut., 18 June, 1864, for gallant and meritorious service in front of Petersburg, Va. Bvt. Capt., 19 Aug., 1864, for

gallant and meritorious service in the Battle on the Weldon Railroad, Va. 1st Lieut. 10th Inf., 13 Sept., 1864. Unassigned 19 May, 1869. Ass'd to 1st Art., 31 Dec., 1870. Capt., 18 July, 1879. Graduate of the Artillery School, 1872. Retired for disability, 20 Sept., 1883.

WHITE, JOHN G. S. [Born in Mass. Appointed from Mass.]
Corpl. and Sergt. Co. D, 1st Mass. Vols., 24 May, 1861. to 8 March, 1864. 2nd Lieut. 5th Mass. Cav., 19 March, 1864. 1st Lieut., 19 March, 1865. Mustered out 31 Oct., 1865. 2nd Lieut. 15th Inf., 23 Feb., 1866. 1st Lieut., 2 April, 1866. Trans. to 33rd Inf., 21 Sept., 1866. Unassigned 3 May, 1869. Discharged 30 Nov., 1870.

WHITE, JOHN V.* [Born in Miss. Appointed from Miss.]
Addl. 2nd Lieut. 4th Art., 15 June, 1877. 2nd Lieut. 1st Art., 22 Nov., 1877. 1st Lieut., 20 Sept., 1883. Capt. 7th Art., 8 March, 1898. Honor graduate of the Artillery School, 1882.

WHITE, JOSEPH A. [Born in Ga. Appointed from Ga.]
1st Lieut. of Inf., 13 March, 1847; 13th Inf., 9 April, 1847. Capt., 31 Jan., 1848. Disbanded 15 July, 1848.

WHITE, MOSES J.* [Born in Miss. Appointed from Miss.]
Bvt. 2nd Lieut. Ord., 1 July, 1858. Resigned 7 Feb., 1861. Died 29 Jan., 1864.

WHITE, RICH'D M.* [Born in S. C. Appointed from S. C.]
3rd Lieut. Light Art., 11 Dec., 1815. 2nd Lieut., 1 Dec., 1817. Resigned 31 Aug., 1820. Died 19 Jan., 1849.

WHITE, ROB'T H. [Born in Va. Appointed from Pa.]
1st Lieut. Asst. Surg., 14 May, 1867. Capt. Asst. Surg., 14 May, 1870. Maj. Surg., 14 May, 1887. Retired, for over thirty years' service, 6 July, 1898. Resigned 31 Aug., 1899.

WHITE, ULYSSES G.* [Born in Ohio. Appointed from Ohio.]
2nd Lieut. 4th Cav., 12 June, 1871. Resigned 31 July, 1873. Civil Eng. U. S. N., 22 Jan., 1877.

WHITE, WHARTON. [Born in Pa. Appointed from Pa.]
2nd Lieut. 20th Inf., 7 March, 1867. 1st Lieut., 1 Feb., 1869. Unassigned 7 May, 1869. Discharged 1 Dec., 1870.

WHITE, WM. J. H. [Born in D. C. Appointed from D. C.]
Asst. Surg., 12 March, 1850. Maj. Surg., 16 April, 1862. Killed 17 Sept., 1862, at the Battle of Antietam, Md.

WHITEHEAD, FRED'K F. [Born in N. Y. Appointed from Mo.]
1st Lieut. 7th Mo. Vols., 21 Aug., 1861. Discharged 20 May, 1863. Capt. A. A. G. Vols., 1 May, 1863. Bvt. Maj. Vols., 13 March, 1865, for faithful and meritorious service during the campaign in Georgia and the Carolinas. Mustered out of Vol. Service, 19 Sept., 1865. 1st Lieut. 18th Inf., 28 July, 1866. Bvt. Capt., 2 March, 1867, for gallant and meritorious service in the Battle of Champion Hill, Miss. Bvt. Maj., 2 March, 1867, for gallant and meritorious service in the Siege of Vicksburg, Miss. Capt. C. S., 14 April, 1875. Died 13 Oct., 1888.

WHITEHEAD, HENRY C.* [Born in Tex. Appointed from Tex.]
Addl. 2nd Lieut. 7th Cav., 12 June, 1896. 2nd Lieut. 10th Cav., 3 Feb., 1897.

WHITEHEAD, NATHANIEL J.* [Born in N. J. Appointed from N. J.]
2nd Lieut. 4th Inf., 13 June, 1879. Resigned 1 Jan., 1883.

WHITEHEAD, WM. E. [Born in N. J. Appointed from N. J.]
1st Lieut. Asst. Surg., 13 April, 1863. Bvt. Capt., 13 March, 1865, for faithful and meritorious service during the war. Capt. Asst. Surg., 28 July, 1866. Died 15 Jan., 1882.

WHITEHORNE, SAM'L.* [Born in R. I. Appointed from R. I.]
Bvt. 2nd Lieut. 5th Inf., 1 July, 1836. 2nd Lieut., 31 Oct., 1836. 1st Lieut., 1 Jan., 1839. Died 2 Nov., 1840.

WHITELEY, ROB'T H. K.* [Born in Md. Appointed from Del.]
Bvt. 2nd Lieut. 2nd Art., 1 July, 1830. 2nd Lieut., 1 July, 1830. 1st Lieut., 28 Dec., 1835. Bvt. Capt., 19 July, 1836, for gallant conduct in the war against the Florida Indians. 1st Lieut. Ord., 9 July, 1838. Capt., 27 March, 1842. Maj., 3 Aug., 1861. Lieut. Col., 1 June, 1863. Bvt. Col. and Brig. Gen., 13 March, 1865, for meritorious service in the Ord. Dept. Col. Ord., 6 April, 1866. Retired 14 April, 1875. Died 9 June, 1896.

WHITFIELD, ROBERT. [Born in Ga. Appointed from Ga.]
Priv. and Sergt. Co. I, 3rd U. S. Vols., 26 June, 1898, to 31 Jan., 1899. 2nd Lieut., 1 Feb. to 2 May, 1899. 2nd Lieut. 22nd Inf., 5 Oct., 1899.

WHITING, CHAS. J.* [Born in Mass. Appointed from Maine.]
Bvt. 2nd Lieut. 2nd Art., 1 July, 1835. 2nd Lieut., 10 Sept., 1835. Resigned 31 May, 1836. Capt. 2nd Cav., 3 March, 1855; 5th Cav., 3 Aug., 1861. Maj. 2nd Cav., 17 July, 1862. Dismissed 5 Nov., 1863. Restored 2 Aug., 1866, as Maj. 3rd Cav., to rank from 17 July, 1862. Lieut. Col. 6th Cav., 6 May, 1869. Trans. to list of Supernumeraries, 15 Dec., 1870. Mustered out 1 Jan., 1871. Died 8 Jan., 1890.

WHITING, DANL. P.* [Born in N. Y. Appointed from N. Y.]
Bvt. 2nd Lieut. 7th Inf., 1 July, 1832. 2nd Lieut., 15 Dec., 1833. 1st Lieut., 8 June, 1836. Capt., 18 April, 1845. Bvt. Maj., 18 April, 1847, for gallant and meritorious conduct in the Battle of Cerro Gordo. Maj. 10th Inf., 20 Dec., 1860. Lieut. Col. 6th Inf., 15 Feb., 1862. Retired 4 Nov., 1863. Died 2 Aug., 1892.

WHITING, FABIUS. [Born in Mass. Appointed from Mass.]
2nd Lieut. Art., 10 Feb., 1812. 1st Lieut., 20 June, 1813. Trans. to Corps Art., 12 May, 1814. Capt., 10 Sept., 1819. Trans. to 1st Art., 1 June, 1821. Died 16 May, 1842. Bvt. Maj., 10 Sept., 1829, for ten years' faithful service in one grade.

WHITING, HENRY. [Born in Mass. Appointed from Mass.]
Cornet Light Drag., 20 Oct., 1808. 2nd Lieut., 15 Sept., 1809. 1st Lieut., 20 Aug., 1811. Trans. to 5th Inf., 17 May, 1815. Capt., 8 March, 1817. Trans. to 1st Art., 1 June, 1821. Maj. Q. M., 23 Feb., 1835. Lieut. Col. Dep. Q. M. G., 7 July, 1838. Col. A. Q. M. G., 21 April, 1846. Died 16 Sept., 1851. Bvt. Capt.,

17 March, 1814, for meritorious service. Bvt. Maj., 17 March, 1824, for ten years' faithful service. Bvt. Lieut. Col., 30 June, 1834, for faithful and meritorious service. Bvt. Brig. Gen., 23 Feb., 1847, for gallant and meritorious conduct at the Battle of Buena Vista, Mex.

WHITING, HENRY.* [Born in N. Y. Appointed from N. Y.]
2nd Lieut. 23rd Inf., 1 May, 1812. 1st Lieut., 20 June, 1813. Capt., 1 Sept., 1814. Trans. to 2nd Inf., 17 May, 1815. Disbanded 1 June, 1821.

WHITING, HENRY.* [Born in N. Y. Appointed from N. Y.]
2nd Lieut. 5th Inf., 1 July, 1840. Resigned 25 March, 1846. Col. 2nd Vt. Vols., 25 June, 1861. Resigned 14 Feb., 1863. Died 23 June, 1887.

WHITING, HENRY M.* [Born in Mass. Appointed at Large.]
Bvt. 2nd Lieut. 4th Art., 1 July, 1842. 2nd Lieut., 20 July, 1842. 1st Lieut., 3 March, 1847. Died 8 Oct., 1853. Bvt. 1st Lieut., 23 Feb., 1847, for gallant and meritorious conduct in the Battle of Buena Vista, Mex.

WHITING, LEONARD J. [Born in Maine. Appointed from Maine.]
Corpl. and Sergt. Batty B and C, 1st R. I. Art., 25 Aug., 1861, to 25 May, 1862. 1st Lieut. R. I. Cav., 1 Nov., 1862. 2nd Lieut. Vet. Res. Corps, 22 Dec., 1863. 1st Lieut., 5 Aug., 1864. Capt., 10 May, 1865. Mustered out 19 Nov., 1866. 2nd Lieut. 45th Inf., 28 July, 1866. 1st Lieut., 29 June, 1868. Unassigned 22 July, 1869. Retired 15 Dec., 1870. Died 10 Nov., 1876. Bvt. 1st Lieut., 2 March, 1867, for gallant and meritorious service in the Peninsula campaign. Bvt. Capt., 2 March, 1867, for gallant and merit orious service during the war.

WHITING, LEVI. [Born in Mass. Appointed from Mass.]
2nd Lieut. Art., 10 Feb., 1812. Trans. to Corps Art., 12 May, 1814. 1st Lieut., 14 June, 1814. Trans. to 4th Art., 1 June, 1821. Capt., 21 May, 1822. Maj. 1st Art., 19 March, 1842. Lieut. Col., 1 April, 1850. Died 3 Aug., 1852. Bvt. Maj., 21 May, 1832, for ten years' faithful service in one grade.

WHITING, WM. H. C.* [Born in Miss. Appointed at Large.]
2nd Lieut. Eng., 1 July, 1845. 1st Lieut., 16 March, 1853. Capt., 13 Dec., 1858. Resigned 20 Feb., 1861. Died 10 March, 1865.

WHITMAN, FRANK H.* [Born in Kan. Appointed from Kan.]
Addl. 2nd Lieut. 7th Inf., 12 June, 1896. 2nd Lieut. 2nd Inf., 16 July, 1896. 1st Lieut. of Inf., 4 Oct., 1898. Ass'd to 2nd Inf., 1 Jan., 1899. Maj. 20th Kan. Vols., 10 May, 1898, to 28 Oct., 1899.

WHITMAN, JOHN. [Born in Mass. Appointed from Mass.]
2nd Lieut. 8th Inf., 13 Feb., 1818. Dismissed 30 May, 1819.

WHITMAN, ROYAL E. [Born in Maine. Appointed from Maine.]
Sergt. Maj. 23rd Maine Vols., 10 Sept., 1862. Capt. 23rd Maine Vols., 1 March, 1863. Mustered out 15 July, 1863. Maj. 30th Maine Vols., 29 Dec., 1863. Lieut. Col., 1 Sept., 1864. Col., 14 Aug., 1865. Mustered out 20 Aug., 1865 2nd Lieut. 3rd Cav., 2 July, 1867. Bvt. 1st Lieut., 2 July, 1867, for gallantry in the Battle of Sabine Cross Roads, La. 1st Lieut. 3rd Cav., 12 Aug., 1869. Retired 20 March, 1879.

WHITMAN, WALTER M.* [Born in N. Y. Appointed from N. Y.]
2nd Lieut. 2nd Inf., 12 June, 1891. Trans. to 1st Cav., 3 May, 1893. 1st Lieut., 2 March, 1899. Reg. Com., 24 May, 1899.

WHITNEY, FOLLIOT A. [Born in D. C. Appointed from D. C.]
2nd Lieut. 1st Md. Cav., 25 April, 1862. Mustered out 7 April, 1863. 2nd Lieut. Vet. Res. Corps, 6 June, 1863. Bvt. 1st Lieut., Capt. and Maj. Vols., 13 March, 1865, for gallant and meritorious service. Mustered out 18 June, 1866. 2nd Lieut. 8th Inf., 15 May, 1866. 1st Lieut., 21 Nov., 1866. R. Q. M., 17 May, 1877, to 19 Sept., 1878. Reg. Adj., 4 July, 1879, to 6 Feb., 1882. Capt., 6 Feb., 1882. Maj. 6th Inf., 1 July, 1898.

WHITNEY, HARRY E. [Born in Iowa. Appointed from Iowa.]
2nd Lieut. 1st Inf., 9 July, 1898. 1st Lieut. ——, 1899. Died at Cienfuegos, Cuba, 13 May, 1899.

WHITNEY, HENRY H.* [Born in Pa. Appointed from Pa.]
Addl. 2nd Lieut. 4th Art., 11 June, 1892. 2nd Lieut., 28 Nov., 1892. 1st Lieut., 2 March, 1899. Capt. A. A. G. Vols., 12 May, 1898, to 12 May, 1899.

WHITNEY, JOHN. [Born in Mass. Appointed from Ohio.]
Sergt. Co. D, 2nd Ohio Vols., 17 April, to 9 Aug., 1861. 2nd Lieut. 3rd Inf., 5 Aug., 1861. 1st Lieut., 11 Feb., 1863. Bvt. Maj. and Lieut. Col. Vols., 13 March, 1865, for gallant and meritorious service during the war. Resigned 25 April, 1865. Capt. 8th U. S. Vet. Vols., 21 Aug., 1865. Mustered out 27 April, 1866. 2nd Lieut. 15th Inf., 11 May, 1866. Trans. to 24th Inf., 21 Sept., 1866. 1st Lieut., 1 March, 1867. Trans. to 11th Inf., 25 April, 1869. Capt., 9 Oct., 1885. Retired for disability, 24 April, 1886. Died 15 May, 1891.

WHITNEY, STEPHEN. [Born in Conn. Appointed from Conn.]
2nd and 1st Lieut. 4th Art., 5 Aug., 1861. Resigned 12 Nov., 1863.

WHITRIDGE, WM. C. [Born in R. I. Appointed from Conn.]
Mil. Storekeeper Ord. Dept., 16 Dec., 1851. Resigned 15 Feb., 1853.

WHITSIDE, SAML. M. [Born in Canada. Appointed from Army.]
Priv. Gen. Mounted Ser., 10 Nov., 1858. Trans. to 6th Cav., 27 July, 1861. Sergt. Maj., 1 Aug., 1861. 2nd Lieut. 6th Cav., 1 Nov., 1861. 1st Lieut., 25 Jan., 1864. Bvt. Capt. and Maj., 13 March, 1865, for faithful and meritorious service. Capt. 6th Cav., 20 Oct., 1866. Maj. 7th Cav., 20 March, 1885. Lieut. Col. 3rd Cav., 17 July, 1895. Trans. to 5th Cav., 15 Oct., 1895. Col. 10th Cav., 16 Oct., 1898.

WHITSIDE, WARREN W. [Born in Canada. Appointed from Tenn.]
2nd Lieut. 10th Cav., 10 April, 1899.

WHITTELSEY, CHAS. H. [Born in Conn. Appointed from N. Y.]
2nd Lieut. 1st Conn. Art., 12 March, 1862. 1st Lieut., 18 June, 1862. Capt. A. A. G. Vols., 15 May, 1863. Maj. A. A. G. Vols., 26 May, 1865. Bvt. Maj. Vols., 19 Oct., 1864, for faithful and meritorious service in the field during the campaigns before Richmond, and in the Shenandoah Valley, Va. Bvt. Lieut. Col. Vols., 2 April, 1865, for gallant and meritorious service in the battles before Petersburg,

Va. Bvt. Col. Vols., 9 April, 1865, for gallant and meritorious service during the campaign terminating with the surrender of the insurgent army under Gen. Robert E. Lee. Bvt. Brig. Gen. Vols., 13 March, 1865, for gallant and meritorious service during the war. Mustered out 1 Sept., 1866. Capt. 30th Inf., 28 July, 1866. Unassigned 23 March, 1869. Ass'd to 13th Inf., 1 Sept., 1869. Died 18 Oct., 1871. Bvt. Maj., 2 March, 1867, for gallant and meritorious service in the Battle of Petersburg, Va., 2 April, 1865.

WHITTEMORE, EDWARD W. [Born in Mass. Appointed from Mass.]
2nd Lieut. 17th Inf., 24 Oct., 1861. 1st Lieut., 10 May, 1862. Capt., 10 March, 1865. Bvt. Maj., 13 March, 1865, for faithful and meritorious service. Trans. to 35th Inf., 21 Sept., 1866. Trans. to 15th Inf., 12 Aug., 1869. Maj. 10th Inf., 17 Feb., 1889. Lieut. Col. 12th Inf., 14 Oct., 1892. Retired, for over thirty years' service, 7 March, 1893.

WHITTEMORE, JAMES M.* [Born in Mass. Appointed from Mass.]
Bvt. 2nd Lieut. 2nd Art., 1 July, 1860. 2nd Lieut. 3rd Art., 27 Sept., 1860. Trans. to Ord., 5 May, 1861. 1st Lieut., 1 July, 1861. Capt., 3 March, 1863. Bvt. Maj., 13 March, 1865, for meritorious service in the Ord. Dept. during the war. Maj. Ord., 23 June, 1874. Lieut. Col., 2 Aug., 1879. Col., 3 Jan., 1887.

WHITTEN, EDWIN A. [Born in Maine. Appointed from Maine.]
2nd Lieut. of Inf., 10 March, 1847; 9th Inf., 9 April, 1847. Resigned 3 Aug., 1847.

WHITTEN, JAMES H. [Born in Ind. Appointed from Ind.]
Musician Co. H, 2nd Batt. 11th Inf., 28 July, 1862, to 28 July, 1865. 2nd Lieut. 5th Inf., 17 July, 1867. Resigned 31 May, 1877.

WHITTEN, JOHN W. [Born in Ind. Appointed from Army.]
Corpl. and Sergt. Co. C, 2nd, and F, 1st Batt., and Sergt. Maj. 11th Inf., 8 March, 1862, to 15 June, 1864. 2nd Lieut. 2nd Inf., 18 May, 1864. 1st Lieut., 28 July, 1866. Reg. Adj., 30 Nov., 1864, to 17 April, 1869. Unassigned 17 April, 1869. Discharged 1 Nov., 1870.

WHITTIER, CHAS. A. [Born in Maine. Appointed from Mass.]
2nd Lieut. 20th Mass. Vols., 8 Aug., 1861. 1st Lieut., 1 Jan., 1862. Capt., 1 April, 1863. Lieut. Col. A. A. G. Vols., 31 Jan. to 1 Aug., 1865. Bvt. Lieut. Col. Vols., 19 Oct., 1864, for faithful and meritorious service in the field during the campaign before Richmond, Va. Bvt. Col. and Brig. Gen. Vols., 9 April, 1865, for highly valuable and meritorious service during the campaign terminating with the surrender of the insurgent army under Gen. Robert E. Lee. Mustered out 30 Nov., 1866. Capt. 32nd Inf., 28 July, 1866. Unassigned 19 April, 1869. Ass'd to 19th Inf., 15 Feb., 1870. Discharged 3 Aug., 1870.

WHITTINGHAM, EDWARD T. [Born in N. Y. Appointed from N. J.]
Asst. Surg., 16 April, 1862. Resigned 12 Nov., 1863. Died 26 Oct., 1886.

WHITTLESEY, CHAS.* [Born in Conn. Appointed from Ohio.]
Bvt. 2nd Lieut. 6th Inf., 1 July, 1831. Trans. to 5th Inf., 20 Oct., 1831. Resigned 30 Sept., 1832. Col. 20th Ohio Inf., 16 Aug., 1861. Resigned 19 April, 1862. Died 18 Oct., 1886.

WHITTLESEY, JOSEPH H.* [Born in N. Y. Appointed from N. Y.]
Bvt. 2nd Lieut. 6th Inf., 1 July, 1831. Trans. to 5th Inf., 20 Oct. 1831. Resigned 30 Sept., 1832. Col. 20th Ohio Inf., 16 Aug., 1861. Resigned 19 April, 1862. Died 18 Oct., 1886.

WHITWORTH, PEGRAM.* [Born in La. Appointed from La.]
2nd Lieut. 18th Inf., 12 June, 1894. 1st Lieut., 26 April, 1898.

WHOLLEY, JOHN H.* [Born in Mass. Appointed from Mass.]
2nd Lieut. 4th Inf., 12 June, 1890. 1st Lieut. 24th Inf., 3 March, 1897. Col. 1st Wash. Vols., 13 May, 1898, to 1 Nov., 1899. Col. 41st U. S. Vols., 17 Aug., 1899.

WHYTE, FRED'K. [Born in England. Appointed from D. C.]
Artficer Ord. Dept. U. S. A., 1 Aug., 1843. Discharged 31 Aug., 1845. Ord. Storekeeper, 9 Oct., 1865. Capt. Ord. Storekeeper, 28 July, 1866. Retired 30 June, 1882. Died 5 Aug., 1895.

WIATT, EDWIN. [Born in Tenn. Appointed from Tenn.]
(Appointed under name of Edwin Wyatt.) Surg. Rifle Reg., 17 Feb., 1817. Resigned 16 April, 1818.

WICKHAM, FRANK D. [Born in Mo. Appointed from Mo.]
Priv., Corpl., Sergt. and 1st Sergt. Troop K, 8th Cav., 25 Jan., 1894, to 24 April, 1897. Priv. Co. C, 2nd Mo. Vols., 12 May, 1898. 1st Lieut. Co. I, 4th Mo. Vols., 16 May to 8 July, 1898. 2nd Lieut. 16th Inf., 27 June, 1898. 1st Lieut. 18th Inf., 2 March, 1899.

WICKHAM, ROB'T C. [Born in Va. Appointed from Va.]
Asst. Surg., 16 Feb., 1847. Died 13 May, 1847.

WICKLIFFE, CHAS.* [Born in Ky. Appointed from Ky.]
2nd Lieut. 1st Drag., 1 July, 1839. Dropped 12 April, 1842. Capt. of Inf., 5 March, 1847; 16th Inf., 9 April, 1847. Maj. 14th Inf., 12 Feb., 1848. Disbanded 22 July, 1848. Died 27 April, 1862.

WICKLIFFE, NATH'L. [Born in Ky. Appointed from Ky.]
2nd Lieut. 9th Inf., 30 June, 1855. 1st Lieut., 15 March, 1861. Resigned 17 May, 1861.

WICKLIFFE, WM. N. [Born in Ky. Appointed from Ky.]
2nd Lieut. 6th Inf., 20 Sept., 1819. 1st Lieut., 27 Aug., 1822. Capt., 15 Feb., 1826. Resigned 31 July, 1837.

WIEGENSTEIN, HENRY. [Born in ——. Appointed from ——.]
2nd Lieut. of Inf., 1 Oct., 1899. (Unassigned.)

WIETING, ORLANDO L.* [Born in Pa. Appointed from Pa.]
Priv. Batty F, Pa. Light Art., 4 June, 1864, to 9 June, 1865. Cadet at Mil. Acad., 17 Oct., 1865. 2nd Lieut. 3rd Cav., 15 June, 1870. Resigned 29 Dec., 1870. 2nd Lieut. 23rd Inf., 30 July, 1872. 1st Lieut., 25 April, 1877. Capt., 15 July, 1890. Retired for disability, 21 Oct., 1891. Died 4 Feb., 1893.

WIGGIN, AUGUSTUS W. [Born in N. H. Appointed from N. H.]
Med. Cadet, 17 June, 1864, to 15 March, 1865. Asst. Surg. 5th U. S. Col. Art., 15 June, 1865. Bvt. Capt. and Maj. Vols., 13 March, 1865, for faithful and meritorious service. Mustered out 20 May, 1866. Asst. Surg., 16 Nov., 1868. Died 7 March, 1875.

WIGHTMAN, LEONARD. [Born in N. Y. Appointed from Mich.]
Priv. and Corpl. Co. E, 1st Mich. Light Art., 21 Nov., 1861, to 10 Dec., 1862. 2nd Lieut. 1st Mich. Light Art., 10 Dec., 1862. 1st Lieut., 25 April, 1864. Bvt. Capt. Vols., 30 June, 1865, for meritorious service. Mustered out 30 July, 1865. 2nd Lieut. 3rd Cav., 29 May, 1867. 1st Lieut., 3 Jan., 1869. Discharged 23 Sept., 1870.

WIGMORE, HUBERT L.* [Born in Cal. Appointed from Cal.]
2nd Lieut. 5th Cav., 15 Feb., 1899.

WIKOFF, CHAS. A. [Born in Pa. Appointed from Pa.]
Priv. Co. H, 1st Pa. Vols., 20 April to 25 June, 1861. 1st Lieut. 15th Inf., 14 May, 1861. Bvt. Capt., 7 April, 1862, for gallant and meritorious service in the Battle of Shiloh, Tenn. Bvt. Maj., 25 Nov., 1863, for gallant and meritorious service in the Battles of Chickamauga, Ga., and Mission Ridge, Tenn. Capt. 15th Inf., 15 Aug., 1864. Trans. to 24th Inf., 21 Sept., 1866. Trans. to 11th Inf., 25 April, 1869. Maj. 14th Inf., 8 Dec., 1886. Lieut. Col. of Inf. (19th), 1 Nov., 1891. Col. 22nd Inf., 28 Jan., 1897. Killed in action at San Juan, Santiago, Cuba, 1 July, 1898.

WILBAR, JOSEPH Q. [Born in Va. Appointed from Tenn.]
2nd Lieut. 14th Inf., 9 Sept., 1847. Disbanded 24 July, 1848.

WILBUR, HARRY F. [Born in Pa. Appointed from Pa.]
2nd Lieut. 5th Art., 9 July, 1898.

WILCOX, CADMUS M.* [Born in N. C. Appointed from Tenn.]
Bvt. 2nd Lieut. 4th Inf., 1 July, 1846. 2nd Lieut. 7th Inf., 16 Feb., 1847. 1st Lieut., 24 Aug., 1851. Capt., 20 Dec., 1860. Resigned 8 June, 1861. Bvt. 1st Lieut., 13 Sept., 1847, for gallant and meritorious conduct at Chapultepec, Mex.

WILCOX, DE LAFAYETTE. [Born in Conn. Appointed from Army.]
Ensign 25th Inf., 16 Nov., 1813. 2nd Lieut., 14 March, 1814. 1st Lieut., 2 Oct., 1814. Trans. to 6th Inf., 17 May, 1815. Trans. to 5th Inf., 1 June, 1821. Died 3 Jan., 1842. Bvt. Maj., 1 April, 1832, for ten years' faithful service in one grade.

WILCOX, E. NORVILLE. [Born in Mass. Appointed from Army.]
2nd Lieut. 18th Inf., 19 Feb., 1863. 1st Lieut., 20 Sept., 1863. Capt., 22 Jan., 1867. Unassigned 26 April, 1869. Mustered out 1 Jan., 1871. Bvt. Capt., 1 Sept., 1864, for gallant and meritorious service at the Battle of Murfreesboro, Tenn., and in the Atlanta campaign and Battle of Jonesboro, Ga.

WILCOX, FRANK A.* [Born in Mass. Appointed from Mass.]
2nd Lieut. 1st Inf., 11 June, 1892. 1st Lieut., 26 April, 1898.

WILCOX, JAMES H. G.* [Born in Ky. Appointed from Ky.]
Cadet at Mil. Acad., 1 Sept., 1875. Resigned 30 May, 1876. Reinstated 1 Sept., 1876. 2nd Lieut. 7th Cav., 12 June, 1880. Dismissed 5 July, 1887.

WILCOX, JEREMIAH C. [Born in Ohio. Appointed from Neb.]
2nd Lieut. 6th Cav., 23 Feb., 1866. 1st Lieut., 28 July, 1866. Resigned 1 Dec., 1869.

WILCOX, JOHN A. [Born in D. C. Appointed from D. C.]
2nd Lieut. 1st Cav., 28 March, 1861. 1st Lieut., 14 May, 1861. 4th Cav., 3 Aug., 1861. Capt., 1 Dec., 1863. Maj. 8th Cav., 20 March, 1879. Lieut. Col. 1st Cav., 7 Feb., 1891. Trans. to 3rd Cav., 26 May, 1892. Retired by operation of law, 20 Oct., 1892.

WILCOX, JOHN R.* [Born in Vt. Appointed from Ohio.]
2nd Lieut. 5th Inf., 1 July, 1822. Resigned 31 July, 1824. Died 3 Oct., 1839.

WILCOX, TIMOTHY E. [Born in N. Y. Appointed from N. Y.]
Asst. Surg. 6th N. Y. Heavy Art., 4 Jan., 1865. Discharged 11 May, 1865. Asst. Surg. Vols., 25 April, 1865. Mustered out 4 June, 1866. 1st Lieut. Asst. Surg., 14 May, 1867. Resigned 1 July, 1868. 1st Lieut. Asst. Surg., 10 Nov., 1874. Capt. Asst. Surg., 10 Nov., 1879. Maj. Surg., 24 Feb., 1891. Lieut. Col. Chf. Surg. Vols., 7 Nov., 1898, to 12 May, 1899.

WILD, FREDERICK S. [Born in N. Y. Appointed from Army.]
Priv., Corpl. and Sergt. Co. B, 17th Inf., 21 Feb., 1887, to 30 Jan., 1890. 2nd Lieut. 17th Inf., 17 Dec., 1889. 1st Lieut. 6th Inf., 12 Jan., 1897. Trans. to 12th Inf., 7 May, 1897. Capt. 13th Inf., 8 Oct., 1899. Graduate of the Infantry and Cavalry School, 1893.

WILDER, CALEB. [Born in N. H. Appointed from N. Y.]
Capt. of Inf., 31 March, 1847; 10th Inf., 9 April, 1847. Disbanded 15 Aug., 1848.

WILDER, WILBER E.* [Born in Mich. Appointed from Mich.]
2nd Lieut. 4th Cav., 15 June, 1877. 1st Lieut., 12 Nov., 1879. Bvt. Capt., 27 Feb., 1890, for gallant services in action against Indians, inclusive of the rescue, while under heavy fire, of an enlisted man who was severely wounded, at Horseshoe Canon, N. Mex., 23 April, 1882. Capt., 25 Feb., 1891. Medal of Honor for most distinguished gallantry in action against hostile Indians at Horseshoe Canon, N. Mex., 23 April, 1882, in assisting to rescue, under heavy fire, Priv. Edward Leonard, who was wounded; while serving as 1st Lieut. 4th Cav. Lieut. Col. A. A. G. Vols., 9 May, 1898, declined. Col. 14th N. Y. Vols., 6 May to 27 Oct., 1898. Lieut. Col. 43rd U. S. Vols., 17 Aug., 1899, to ——.

WILDER, WM. T.* [Born in N. C. Appointed from N. C.]
Cadet at Mil. Acad., 1 Sept., 1883, to 16 Jan., 1884. Reappointed 15 June, 1884. 2nd Lieut. 19th Inf., 11 June, 1888. 1st Lieut. 25th Inf., 5 July, 1895. Capt. 11th Inf., 31 March, 1899. Maj. 2nd N. C. Vols., from 17 May to 25 Nov., 1898.

WILDRICK, ABRAM C.* [Born in N. J. Appointed from N. J.]
Bvt. 2nd Lieut. 3rd Art., 1 July, 1857. 2nd Lieut., 5 Oct., 1857. 1st Lieut., 27 April, 1861. Capt., 8 Feb., 1864. Col. 39th N. J. Vols., 11 Oct., 1864. Bvt. Maj.,

13 March, 1865, for gallant and meritorious service during the Siege of Petersburg, Va. Bvt. Lieut. Col., 13 March, 1865, for gallant and meritorious service during the war. Bvt. Brig. Gen. Vols., 2 April, 1865, for gallant and meritorious service in front of Petersburg, Va. Mustered out of Vol. Service, 17 June, 1865. Maj. 5th Art., 3 Nov., 1882. Lieut. Col. of Art. (1st), 1 July, 1892. Retired for disability, 1894. Died 16 Nov., 1894.

WILDS, DAVID G. [Born in S. C. Appointed from Ga.]
2nd Lieut. of Inf., 10 March, 1847; 13th Inf., 9 April, 1847. Resigned 18 April, 1848.

WILEY, JAMES W. [Born in N. Y. Appointed from Ohio.]
2nd Lieut. of Inf., 22 March, 1847; 15th Inf., 9 April, 1847. 1st Lieut., 4 Dec., 1847. Dismissed 22 May, 1848. Bvt. 1st Lieut., 20 Aug., 1847, for gallant and meritorious conduct in the Battles of Contreras and Churubusco, Mex.

WILEY, MOSES. [Born in Ala. Appointed from Tenn.]
Priv. Troop C, 1st N. Y. Cav., 19 July, 1861, to 12 March, 1863. 2nd Lieut. 1st East Tenn. Cav., 22 May, 1863. Capt., 9 Nov., 1863. Mustered out 10 June, 1865. 2nd Lieut. 6th Cav., 23 Feb., 1866. 1st Lieut., 28 July, 1866. R. Q. M., 25 Nov., 1867, to 6 May, 1869. Resigned 6 May, 1869.

WILEY, WM. Y. [Born in Pa. Appointed from Ind.]
Mil. Storekeeper Ord. Dept., 10 March, 1863. Capt., 28 July, 1866. Discharged 1 Oct., 1870.

WILHELM, THOS. [Born in Pa. Appointed from Pa.]
Capt. 6th Pa. Rifles, 23 April, 1861. Mustered out 26 July, 1861. Capt. 2nd Pa. Heavy Art., 19 Dec., 1861. Maj., 25 Nov., 1862. Col. 2nd Prov. Pa. Heavy Art., 20 April, 1864, to 26 Aug., 1864. Maj. 2nd Pa. Heavy Art., 26 Aug., 1864. Mustered out 11 July, 1865. Capt. 7th U. S. Vet. Vols., 19 July, 1865. Mustered out 24 April, 1866. 2nd Lieut. 8th Inf., 11 May, 1866. 1st Lieut., 14 Aug., 1866. Bvt. Capt., 2 March, 1867, for gallant and meritorious service in the Battle of the Wilderness, Va. Bvt. Maj., 2 March, 1867, for gallant and meritorious service in the Battle of Cold Harbor, Va. Reg. Adj. 8th Inf., 1 March, 1868, to 7 June, 1879. Capt., 7 June, 1879. Maj. 21st Inf., 26 April, 1898. Retired, for over thirty years' service, 16 March, 1899.

WILHELM, WM. H.* [Born in Pa. Appointed from Pa.]
2nd Lieut. 10th Inf., 11 June, 1888. 1st Lieut. 14th Inf., 31 July, 1895. Capt. 21st Inf., 31 March, 1899.

WILHELMI, LOUIS. [Born in Prussia. Appointed from Pa.]
Cadet Mil. Acad., 1 Jan., 1872, to 29 Dec., 1873. 2nd Lieut. 1st Inf., 15 Oct., 1875. 1st Lieut., 16 March, 1880. Reg. Adj., 16 March, 1880, to 19 April, 1886. Died 19 April, 1886.

WILHIGHT, THOMAS C. [Born in N. C. Appointed from N. C.]
2nd Lieut. 18th Inf., 12 March, 1812. 1st Lieut., 26 June, 1813. Disbanded 15 June, 1815. 2nd Lieut. 7th Inf., 18 April, 1818. 1st Lieut., 25 Sept., 1819. Disbanded 1 June, 1821.

WILKESON, BAYARD. [Born in N. Y. Appointed from N. Y.]
2nd Lieut. 4th Art., 22 Oct., 1861. 1st Lieut., 14 Aug., 1862. Killed 1 July, 1863, at the Battle of Gettysburg, Pa. Bvt. Capt., 1 July, 1863, for gallantry and skill at the Battle of the Deserted House, Va. Bvt. Maj., 1 July, 1863, for gallant and meritorious service at the Battle of Fredericksburg, Va. Bvt. Lieut. Col., 1 July, 1863, for gallant and meritorious service at the Battle of Gettysburg, Pa.

WILKESON, FRANK. [Born in N. Y. Appointed from Army.]
Priv. 11th N. Y. Batty, 26 March to 21 June, 1864. Priv. Batty K, 4th U. S. Art., 25 to 30 June, 1864. 2nd Lieut. 4th Art., 30 June, 1864. Resigned 14 March, 1866. Bvt. 1st Lieut. and Capt., 13 March, 1865, for faithful and meritorious service.

WILKIN, ALEX'R. [Born in N. Y. Appointed from N. Y.]
Capt. of Inf., 23 Feb., 1847; 10th Inf., 9 April, 1847. Resigned 6 March, 1848. Capt. 1st Minn. Vols., 29 April, 1861. Mustered out 18 Sept., 1861. Capt. 17th U. S. Inf., 5 Aug., 1861. Maj. 2nd Minn. Vols., 18 Sept., 1861. Lieut. Col., 31 March, 1862. Col. 9th Minn. Vols., 24 Aug., 1862. Killed 14 July, 1864, at the Battle of Tupelo, Miss.

WILKINS, CHAS. [Born in Mass. Appointed from Mass.]
Mil. Storekeeper Ord. Dept., 3 Feb., 1862. Died 18 Jan., 1865.

WILKINS, CHAS. [Born in N. H. Appointed from N. H.]
2nd Lieut. 1st Inf., 19 Feb., 1862. Died 20 June, 1863, of wounds received in action before Vicksburg, Miss. Bvt. Capt., 20 June, 1863, for gallant and meritorious service in action in front of Vicksburg, Miss.

WILKINS, GEORGE S. [Born in Pa. Appointed from Pa.]
3rd Lieut. 22nd Inf., 29 July, 1813. 2nd Lieut., 3 May, 1814. Trans. to Corps Art., 17 May, 1815. 1st Lieut., 20 April, 1818. Trans. to 2nd Art., 1 June, 1821. Trans. to 3rd Art., 16 Aug., 1821. Dismissed 26 Feb., 1827.

WILKINS, HARRY E.* [Born in Ill. Appointed from Iowa.]
2nd Lieut. 2nd Inf., 12 June, 1887. 1st Lieut. 6th Inf., 23 March, 1894. Trans. to 2nd Inf., 3 Aug., 1896. Capt. 10th Inf., 2 March, 1899. Maj. Chief C. S. Vols., 20 June, 1898, to 17 April, 1899. Capt. C. S. Vols., 17 April, 1899, to 12 June, 1899.

WILKINS, HENRY. [Born in Pa. Appointed from Pa.]
2nd Lieut. 5th Inf., 18 April, 1818. Disbanded 1 June, 1821.

WILKINS, JOHN D.* [Born in N. Y. Appointed from Pa.]
Bvt. 2nd Lieut. 4th Inf., 1 July, 1846. 2nd Lieut. 3rd Inf., 31 Dec., 1846. Bvt. 1st Lieut., 20 Aug., 1847, for gallant and meritorious conduct in the Battles of Contreras and Churubusco, Mex. 1st Lieut. 3rd Inf., 10 Nov., 1851. Reg. Adj., 19 Jan., 1856, to 1 May, 1860. Capt., 17 April, 1861. Bvt. Maj., 1 July, 1862, for gallant and meritorious service in the Battle of Malvern Hill, Va. Bvt. Lieut. Col., 3 May, 1863, for gallant and meritorious service in the Battles of Fredericksburg and Chancellorsville, Va. Maj. 15th Inf., 6 May, 1864. Trans. to 33rd Inf., 21 Sept., 1866. Trans. to 8th Inf., 15 March, 1869. Lieut. Col., 19

Feb., 1873. Col. 5th Inf., 22 June, 1882. Retired by operation of law, 1 Aug., 1886.

WILKINS, JOHN H. [Born in Pa. Appointed from Pa.]
2nd Lieut. Light Art., 30 March, 1813. 1st Lieut., 3 Dec., 1813. Capt., 28 Aug., 1819. Trans. to 2nd Inf., 1 June, 1821. Resigned 31 Dec., 1827. Died ——, 1840.

WILKINS, SAM'L A. [Born in N. C. Appointed from N. C.]
2nd Lieut. 12th Inf., 3 March, 1848. Disbanded 25 July, 1848.

WILKINS, WM. D. [Born in Pa. Appointed from Mich.]
2nd Lieut. of Inf., 2 March, 1847; 15th Inf., 9 April, 1847. 1st Lieut., 20 Aug., 1847. R. Q. M., 12 Jan. to 7 Aug., 1848. Disbanded 7 Aug., 1848. Bvt. 1st Lieut., for gallant and meritorious conduct in several affairs with guerillas at Paso Ovejas, National Bridge, and Cerro Gordo, on 10, 12 and 15 Aug., 1847. Brig. Gen. Mich. Vols., 24 April to July, 1861. Capt. A. A. G. Vols., 27 Aug., 1861. Bvt. Maj. and Lieut. Col. Vols., 13 March, 1865, for gallant and meritorious service during the war. Resigned 29 Aug., 1863. Died 31 March, 1882.

WILKINSON, FRED'K.* [Born in N. Y. Appointed from N. Y.]
Bvt. 2nd Lieut. 4th Inf., 1 July, 1831. 2nd Lieut., 18 Feb., 1834. Resigned 31 Dec., 1835. Died 22 March, 1841.

WILKINSON, JOAB. [Born in N. Y. Appointed from Ill.]
1st Lieut. 16th Inf., 19 April, 1847. Resigned 13 May, 1848. Capt. 12th Inf., 5 Aug., 1861. Dismissed 6 Feb., 1863. Died 9 Nov., 1887.

WILKINSON, JOHN F. [Born in Tex. Appointed from Army.]
Priv., Corpl. and Sergt. Troop D, 4th Cav., 24 Aug., 1894, to 23 Aug., 1897. 2nd Lieut. 15th Inf., 23 June, 1898. 1st Lieut., 2 March, 1899.

WILKINSON, JOHN W.* [Born in Mo. Appointed from Mont. Ter.]
2nd Lieut. 8th Cav., 14 June, 1872. Trans. to 7th Cav., 26 June, 1876. 1st Lieut., 9 Dec., 1876. Reg. Adj., 30 Nov., 1881, to 14 Aug., 1886. Capt., ——, 1892. Died 22 March, 1892.

WILKINSON, MELVILLE C. [Born in N. Y. Appointed from N. Y.]
1st Lieut. 123rd N. Y. Vols., 16 May, 1861. Resigned 7 Nov., 1861. 1st Lieut. 107th N. Y. Vols., 24 July, 1862. Capt., 9 Aug., 1862. Resigned 26 Jan., 1863. 1st Lieut. Vet. Res. Corps, 13 Aug., 1863. Capt., 10 Dec., 1863. Mustered out 30 June, 1866. 2nd Lieut. 42nd Inf., 28 July, 1866. Bvt. 1st Lieut., 2 March, 1867, for gallant and meritorious service in the Battle of Antietam, Md. Bvt. Capt., 2 March, 1867, for gallant and meritorious service during the war. Trans. to 6th Inf., 22 April, 1869. Unassigned 28 June, 1869. Ass'd to 3rd Inf., 3 Aug., 1870. 1st Lieut., 1 Jan., 1871. Capt., 24 April, 1886. Bvt. Maj., 27 Feb., 1890, for gallant services in actions against Indians, at the Clearwater, Idaho, 11 and 12 July, 1877, and at Kamiah, Idaho, 13 July, 1877. Killed in action with Indians at Bear Island, Leech Lake, Minn., 5 Oct., 1898.

WILKINSON, NATHANIEL G. [Born in Ga. Appointed from Ga.]
3rd Lieut. 2nd Art., 20 April, 1814. Trans. to Corps Art., 12 May, 1814. 2nd Lieut., 22 July, 1814. 1st Lieut., 20 April, 1818. Trans. to 7th Inf., 31 Jan., 1821. Capt., 31 July, 1824. Resigned 1 June, 1835.

WILKINSON, THEOPHILUS F. J.* [Born in Ala. Appointed from Ala.]
Bvt. 2nd Lieut. 2nd Art., 1 July, 1832. 2nd Lieut., 30 April, 1834. Resigned 28 Feb., 1835. Died 4 Aug., 1840.

WILLARD, GEORGE L. [Born in N. Y. Appointed from Army.]
Priv. and Sergt. Co. B, 15th Inf., 13 April, 1847, to 19 July, 1848. Bvt. 2nd Lieut. 8th Inf., 28 June, 1848. 2nd Lieut., 2 Aug., 1848. 1st Lieut., 31 Dec., 1853. Capt., 27 April, 1861. Maj. 19th Inf., 19 Feb., 1862. Col. 125th N. Y. Vols., 27 Aug., 1862. Killed at the Battle of Getysburg, Pa., 2 July, 1863. Bvt. Lieut. Col., 4 July, 1862, for gallant and meritorious service during the Peninsula campaign in Va. Bvt. Col., 2 July, 1863, for gallant and meritorious service at the Battle of Gettysburg, Pa.

WILLARD, JOHN P. [Born in N. Y. Appointed from Wis.]
1st Lieut. 31st Wis. Vols., 21 Dec., 1862, to 11 April, 1863. Capt. A. de C. Vols., 11 March, 1863. Bvt. Maj. Vols., 3 June, 1865, for faithful service. Bvt. Lieut. Col. and Col. Vols., 3 June, 1865, for gallant and meritorious service during the Atlanta campaign and at the Battle of Nashville, Tenn. 2nd Lieut. and 1st Lieut. 17th Inf., 23 Feb., 1866. Mustered out Vols., 10 July, 1866. Trans. to 26th Inf., 21 Sept., 1866. Bvt. Capt., 2 March, 1867, for gallant and meritorious service in the Batle of Chattanooga, Tenn. Bvt. Maj., 2 March, 1867, for gallant and meritorious service in the capture of Atlanta, Ga. Bvt. Lieut. Col., 2 March, 1867, for gallant and meritorious service in the Battle of Nashville, Tenn. Unassigned 19 May, 1869. Ass'd to 15th Inf., 15 Dec., 1870. R. Q. M., 1 Oct., 1871, to 31 March, 1874. Capt. 15th Inf., 31 March, 1874. Maj. P. M., 3 March, 1875. Died 1 Sept., 1891.

WILLARD, JOSEPH H.* [Born in Ill. Appointed from Ill.]
Bvt. 2nd Lieut. Eng., 15 June, 1868. 2nd Lieut., 23 April, 1869. 1st Lieut., 11 July, 1871. Capt. (fourteen years' service), 15 June, 1882. Maj., 13 Aug., 1895.

WILLARD, SIMON.* [Born in Mass. Appointed from Mas.]
3rd Lieut. Ord., 2 March, 1815. Resigned 1 May, 1816. Died 24 Aug., 1874.

WILLARD, WELLS. [Born in Mass. Appointed from Mass.]
1st Lieut. 21st Mass. Vols., 5 Aug., 1861. Capt., 34th Mass. Vols., 2 Oct., 1862. Mustered out 16 June, 1865. 2nd Lieut. 19th Inf., 11 May, 1866. Trans. to 37th Inf., 21 Sept., 1866. Bvt. 1st Lieut., 2 March, 1867, for gallant and meritorious service at the Battle of Chantilly, Va. Bvt. Capt., 2 March, 1867, for gallant and meritorious service in the Battle of Newmarket, Va. 1st Lieut. 37th Inf., 5 Nov., 1868. Unassigned 11 Aug., 1869. Ass'd to 5th Art., 31 Dec., 1870. Capt. C. S., 24 May, 1882. Maj. C. S., 18 Sept., 1895. Lieut. Col. A. C. G. S., 30 April, 1898. Graduate of the Artillery School, 1880. Retired by operation of law, 9 Sept., 1898.

WILLARD, WM. T. [Born in Vt. Appointed from Vt.]
3rd Lieut. 26th Inf., 21 April, 1814. 2nd Lieut., 1 Oct., 1814. Disbanded 15 June, 1815. Reinstated in Corps Art., 2 Dec., 1815. 1st Lieut., 20 April, 1818. Trans. to 1st Art., 1 June, 1821. Trans. to 4th Art., 26 Oct., 1824. Trans. to 1st Art., 31 Jan., 1825. Trans. to 4th Art., 20 Sept., 1825. Resigned 31 Dec., 1827.

WILLCOX, CHARLES. [Born in Pa. Appointed from N. Y.]
Asst. Surg., 29 Oct., 1889. Capt. Asst. Surg., 29 Oct., 1894.

WILLCOX, CORNELIUS DEW.* [Born in Switzerland. Appointed from Ga.]
2nd Lieut. 2nd Art.,14 June, 1885. 1st Lieut., 30 Sept., 1891. Trans. to 7th Art., 8 March, 1898. Graduate of the Artillery School, 1892. Capt. A. A. G. Vols., 12 May, 1898, to 7 April, 1899.

WILLCOX, E. FARNSWORTH.* [Born in Mich. Appointed at Large.]
Addl. 2nd Lieut. 12th Inf., 14 June, 1878. 2nd Lieut., 28 June, 1878. Trans. to 6th Cav., 13 Feb., 1882. 1st Lieut., 21 May, 1886. Capt., 6 Feb., 1897.

WILLCOX, FRANCIS W.* [Born in Tenn. Appointed from Tenn.]
2nd Lieut. 4th Art., 12 June, 1889. Resigned 15 Sept., 1891.

WILLCOX, ORLANDO B.* [Born in Mich. Appointed from Mich.]
2nd Lieut. 4th Art., 1 July, 1847. 1st Lieut., 30 April, 1850. Resigned 10 Sept., 1857. Col. 1st Mich. Vols., 1 May, 1861. Brig. Gen. Vols., 21 July, 1861. Bvt. Maj. Gen. Vols., 1 Aug., 1864, for distinguished and gallant service in the several actions since crossing the Rapidan. Mustered out 15 Jan., 1866. Col. 29th Inf., 28 July, 1866. Bvt. Brig. Gen., 2 March, 1867, for gallant and meritorious service in the Battle of Spottsylvania C. H., Va. Bvt. Maj. Gen., 2 March, 1867, for gallant and meritorious service in the capture of Petersburg, Va. Trans. to 12th Inf., 15 March, 1869. Brig. Gen., 13 Oct., 1886. Medal of Honor for most distinguished gallantry in the Battle of Bull Run, Va., 21 July, 1861, where he voluntarily led repeated charges of the 1st Mich. Inf. and the 11th N. Y. Inf., until he was wounded and taken prisoner; while Col. 1st Mich. Inf. commanding brigade. Retired by operation of law, 16 April, 1887.

WILLEY, THOS. M.* [Born in Conn. Appointed from Conn.]
2nd Lieut. 6th Inf., 15 June, 1868. Resigned 30 Nov., 1875.

WILLIAMS, ALEX'R B. [Born in D. C. Appointed from D. C.]
2nd Lieut. 3rd Cav., 22 July, 1867. Resigned 25 Sept., 1867.

WILLIAMS, ALEX'R E.* [Born in N. C. Appointed from N. C.]
2nd Lieut. 2nd Inf., 26 April, 1898. 1st Lieut., 2 March, 1899.

WILLIAMS, ANDREW E.* [Born in S. C. Appointed from Tex.]
2nd Lieut. 3rd Cav., 12 June, 1893. 1st Lieut., 2 March, 1899.

WILLIAMS, ALEX'R J.* [Born in Pa. Appointed from Pa.]
2nd Lieut. Eng., 1 March, 1811. 1st Lieut., 1 July, 1812. Capt. 2nd Art., 17 March, 1813. Trans. to Corps Art., 12 May, 1814. Killed 15 Aug., 1814, in the defence of Fort Erie, U. C.

WILLIAMS, ARTHUR. [Born in Pa. Appointed from Ky.]
2nd Lieut. 3rd Inf., 31 Oct., 1874. 1st Lieut., 26 March, 1885. Capt., 18 May, 1893. Graduate of the Infantry and Cavalry School, 1883.

WILLIAMS, AUGUSTUS H. D. [Born in Pa. Appointed from Army.]
1st Lieut. 11th Pa. Cav., 6 Sept., 1861. Mustered out 7 Sept., 1864. Priv. and Corpl. Troop E, 5th Cav., 6 Oct., 1864, to 29 March, 1865. 2nd Lieut. 5th Cav., 12 March, 1865. 1st Lieut., 31 Jan., 1866. Retired 20 July, 1868. Died 12 May, 1876. Bvt. 1st Lieut. and Capt., 2 April, 1865, for gallant and meritorious service at the capture of Petersburg, Va.

WILLIAMS, CHAS. A.* [Born in Va. Appointed from Mo.]
2nd Lieut. 21st Inf., 17 June. 1874. Bvt. 1st Lieut., 27 Feb., 1890, for gallant services in action against Indians at the Clearwater, Idaho, 11 July, 1877, where he was severely wounded. 1st Lieut., 11 Nov., 1879. R. Q. M., 25 March, 1884, to ——. Capt., 14 Nov., 1890. Maj. 17th Inf., 8 June, 1899.

WILLIAMS, CHAS. W.* [Born in Ky. Appointed from Ky.]
2nd Lieut. 18th Inf., 16 June, 1875. Capt. A. Q. M., 30 June, 1879. Maj. Q. M., 4 March, 1893. Lieut. Col. Dep. Q. M. G., 1898. Died 11 Nov., 1898.

WILLIAMS, CLARENCE C.* [Born in Ga. Appointed from Ga.]
2nd Lieut. 4th Art., 12 June, 1894. Trans. to 6th Art., 8 March, 1898. 1st Lieut. Ord., 4 Oct., 1898. Graduate of the Artillery School, 1898.

WILLIAMS, CONSTANT. [Born in Pa. Appointed from Army.]
Priv. Co. B, 31st and 82nd Pa. Vols., 23 July, 1861. Sergt., 25 Dec., 1861. Priv., 20 June, 1862. Discharged 11 Sept., 1862. Priv. Gen. Ser., 20 Feb., 1863. 2nd Lieut. 7th Inf., 29 June, 1863. 1st Lieut., 1 Jan., 1864. Capt., 10 May, 1873. Maj. 7th Inf., 28 Jan., 1897. Trans. to 17th Inf., 23 Feb., 1897. Trans. to 19th Inf., 21 Oct., 1898. Lieut. Col. 15th Inf., 16 Jan., 1899. Bvt. Maj., 27 Feb., 1890, for gallant services in action against Indians at the Big Hole, Mont., 9 Aug., 1877, where he was twice wounded.

WILLIAMS, DENNIS H. [Born in Ohio. Appointed from Ohio.]
1st Lieut. 43rd Ohio Vols., 21 Dec., 1861. Capt., 1 Feb., 1863. Lieut. Col. 185th Ohio Vols., 23 Feb., 1865. Mustered out 26 Sept., 1865. Capt. A. A. G. Vols., 17 Dec., 1864. Bvt. Maj. and Lieut. Col. Vols., 13 March, 1865, for uniform gallantry and meritorious conduct during the war. Mustered out 3 Oct., 1866. 1st Lieut. 41st Inf., 22 Jan., 1867. Resigned 14 Feb., 1868.

WILLIAMS, EDWARD R.* [Born in Conn. Appointed from Conn.]
Bvt. 2nd Lieut. 1st Inf., 1 July, 1829. 2nd Lieut., 1 July, 1829. Resigned 30 June, 1835.

WILLIAMS, EPHRAIM. [Born in Mass. Appointed from Mass.]
Priv. Co. C, 27th Mass. Vols., 27 Aug., 1862. Priv. Co. C, 27th Mass. Vet. Vols., 1 Jan., 1864. 2nd Lieut. 1st U. S. Vols., 18 April, 1864. 1st Lieut., 9 July, 1864. Mustered out 10 May, 1866. 2nd Lieut. 5th Inf., 23 Feb., 1866. 1st Lieut., 28 July, 1866. Bvt. Capt., 23 Sept., 1867, for coolness, gallantry and good conduct in action with Cheyenne Indians near Pawnee Forks, Kan., 23 Sept., 1867. Retired 3 April, 1869.

WILLIAMS, EZEKIEL J. [Born in Ga. Appointed from Ga.]
2nd Lieut. 5th Inf., 9 July, 1898. 1st Lieut., 2 March, 1899.

WILLIAMS, GEORGE. [Born in Iowa. Appointed from Ill.]
2nd Lieut. 4th Art., 9 July, 1898. Trans. to 2nd Art., 27 Dec., 1898. Trans. to 8th Cav., 29 March, 1899.

WILLIAMS, GEORGE. [Born in Ohio. Appointed from Ore.]
2nd Lieut. 4th Inf., 14 April, 1862. Bvt. Capt., 2 July, 1863, for gallant and meritorious service in the Battle of Gettysburg, Pa. 1st Lieut. 4th Inf., 14 July, 1863. Retired 11 Nov., 1863.

WILLIAMS, GEORGE A.* [Born in N. Y. Appointed from N. Y.]
Bvt. 2nd Lieut. 1st Inf., 1 July, 1852. 2nd Lieut., 2 March, 1853. 1st Lieut., 11 Feb., 1856. Capt., 14 May, 1861. Bvt. Maj., 4 Oct., 1862, for gallant and meritorious service in the Battle of Corinth, Miss. Bvt. Lieut. Col., 4 July, 1863, for gallant and meritorious service during the Siege of Vicksburg, Miss. Maj. 6th Inf., 15 March, 1866. Trans. to 20th Inf., 15 March, 1869. Retired 15 Dec., 1870. Died 2 April, 1889.

WILLIAMS, GEORGE A. [Born in Va. Appointed from Va.]
Asst. Surg., 21 Aug., 1838. Resigned 31 Dec., 1840.

WILLIAMS, HARRY C. [Born in Miss. Appointed from Miss.]
2nd Lieut. 15th Inf., 5 Oct., 1899.

WILLIAMS, HENRY R. [Born in N. Y. Appointed from N. Y.]
Priv. Co. D, 84th N. Y. Vols., 18 May, 1861. Corpl., 1 Nov., 1861. 2nd Lieut. 84th N. Y. Vols., 1 Oct., 1862. Mustered out 25 April, 1864. Priv. Gen. Ser., 16 June, 1864. 2nd Lieut. Vet. Res. Corps, 5 Jan., 1865. Bvt. 1st Lieut. Vols., 7 Nov., 1865, for gallant and meritorious service. Mustered out 17 Jan., 1867. 2nd Lieut. 45th Inf., 28 July, 1866. 1st Lieut., 12 Dec., 1868. Unassigned 22 July, 1869. Retired 15 Dec., 1870.

WILLIAMS, HERBERT O.* [Born in Miss. Appointed from Miss.]
2nd Lieut. 11th Inf., 12 June, 1891. 1st Lieut., 26 April, 1898. Trans. to 21st Inf., 23 Oct., 1899. Honor graduate of the Infantry and Cavalry School, 1897. Lieut. Col. 1st Miss. Vols., 23 May to 20 Dec., 1898.

WILLIAMS, JAMES C. D. [Born in Mich. Appointed from Mich.]
2nd Lieut. 3rd Drag., 9 March, 1847. 1st Lieut., 8 Jan., 1848. Disbanded 31 July, 1848.

WILLIAMS, JAMES M.* [Born in Ala. Appointed from Ala.]
2nd leut. 1st Art., 12 June, 1894. Trans. to 7th Art., 19 April, 1898. 1st Lieut., 2 March, 1899.

WILLIAMS, JAMES M. [Born in N. Y. Appointed from Kan.]
Capt. 5th Kan. Cav., 12 July, 1861. Lieut. Col. 79th U. S. Col. Inf., 13 Jan., 1863. Col., 2 May, 1863. Bvt. Brig. Gen. Vols., 13 Feb., 1865. Mustered out 1 Oct., 1865. Capt. 8th Cav., 28 July, 1866. Resigned 29 March, 1873. Bvt. Maj., 9 July, 1867, for conspicuous gallantry displayed in engagements with Indians on the Verde, Ariz., 16 and 17 April, and Yavapai Valley, Ariz., 14 June, 1867, and near Music Mountain, Ariz., 9 July, 1867. Capt. of Cav., 7 Jan., 1891 (Act 29 Sept., 1890). Retired 12 Jan., 1891.

WILLIAMS, JAMES S.* [Born in Ga. Appointed from Ga.]
Bvt. 2nd Lieut. 6th Inf., 1 July, 1831. 2nd Lieut., 31 May, 1834. 1st Lieut., 30 April, 1837. Resigned 6 Sept., 1837. Died 7 Sept., 1871.

WILLIAMS, JOHN. [Born in Ireland. Appointed from Army.]
Priv., Corpl., Sergt. and 1st Sergt. Co. G, Mounted Rifles, 25 April, 1851, to 30 June, 1855. 2nd Lieut. 1st Drag., 18 June, 1855. Murdered by a soldier, 30 June, 1855.

WILLIAMS, JOHN. [Born in England. Appointed from Army.]
Priv. and 1st Sergt. Co. C, 15th Inf., 12 Sept., 1861, to 9 June, 1863. 2nd Lieut. 15th Inf., 1 June, 1863. 1st Lieut., 23 July, 1864. Trans. to 24th Inf., 21 Sept., 1866. Capt., 5 Oct., 1867. Unassigned 25 April, 1869. Ass'd to 25th Inf., 1 Jan., 1871. Wholly retired 25 Jan., 1872. Bvt. 1st Lieut., 20 Sept., 1863, for gallant and meritorious service at the Battle of Chickamauga, Ga. Bvt. Capt., 1 Sept., 1864, for gallant and meritorious service during the Atlanta campaign. Died 14 Oct., 1886.

WILLIAMS, JOHN B.* [Born in Mich. Appointed from Mich.]
2nd Lieut. 3rd Inf., 6 May, 1861. 1st Lieut., 6 June, 1861. Dismissed 11 Feb., 1863.

WILLIAMS, JOHN R.* [Born in N. Y. Appointed from N. Y.]
2nd Lieut. 3rd Art., 15 June, 1876. 1st Lieut., 15 March, 1881. Capt. 7th Art., 8 March, 1898. Honor graduate of the Artillery School, 1886.

WILLIAMS, JOHN W. [Born in D. C. Appointed from D. C.]
1st Lieut. Asst. Surg., 11 July, 1862. Bvt. Capt., 18 Aug., 1863, for gallant and meritorious service in action at Berryville, Va. Bvt. Maj., 13 March, 1865, for faithful and meritorious service during the war. Capt. Asst. Surg., 28 July, 1866. Maj. Surg., 8 Nov., 1877. Died 15 April, 1889.

WILLIAMS, LAWRENCE A.* [Born in D. C. Appointed at Large.]
Bvt. 2nd Lieut. 7th Inf., 1 July, 1852. 2nd Lieut. 4th Inf., 22 June, 1854. Trans. to 10th Inf., 3 March, 1855. 1st Lieut., 20 July, 1856. Capt., 1 July, 1861. Maj. 6th Cav., 7 Sept., 1861. Dismissed 11 March, 1863. Died 21 June, 1879.

WILLIAMS, MATTHEW J.* [Born in Ga. Appointed from Ga.]
(Graduated as M. R. T. Harrison.) Bvt. 2nd Lieut. 1st Art., 1 July, 1825. 2nd Lieut. 4th Art., 1 July, 1825. Trans. to 3rd Inf., 19 April, 1826. Resigned 31 Oct., 1827. Died 21 June, 1873.

WILLIAMS, RICH'D A.* [Born in Pa. Appointed from Pa.]
2nd Lieut. 8th Cav., 15 June, 1870. 1st Lieut., 17 May, 1876. Capt., 24 April, 1886. Died 20 June, 1890.

WILLIAMS, ROB'T.* [Born in Va. Appointed from Va.]
Bvt. 2nd Lieut. 1st Drag., 1 July, 1851. 2nd Lieut., 15 July, 1853. 1st Lieut., 7 June, 1855. Bvt. Capt. A. A. G., 11 May, 1861. Capt. A. A. G., 3 Aug., 1861. Col. 1st Mass. Cav., 7 Oct., 1861. Maj. A. A. G., 17 July, 1862. Resigned Vol. commission, 1 Oct., 1862. Bvt. Lieut. Col., 24 Sept., 1864, for meritorious and

faithful service during the war. Bvt. Col. and Brig. Gen., 13 March, 1865, for diligent, faithful and meritorious service in the A. G. Dept. during the war. Lieut. Col. A. A. G., 22 Feb., 1869. Col. A. A. G., 1 July, 1881. Brig. Gen., Adj. Gen., 5 July, 1892. Retired by operation of law, 5 Nov., 1893.

WILLIAMS, ROBERT C. [Born in D. C. Appointed from D. C.]
Cadet Mil. Acad., 15 June, 1884, to 16 Jan., 1885. 2nd Lieut. 1st Cav., 7 Oct., 1891. 1st Lieut. 7th Cav., 2 Aug., 1898. Trans. to 1st Cav., 3 Oct., 1898. Graduate of the Infantry and Cavalry School, 1895.

WILLIAMS, ROBERT C.* [Born in Ohio. Appointed from Ohio.]
2nd Lieut. 15th Inf., 1 July, 1886. 1st Lieut. 2nd Inf., 18 May, 1893. Trans. to 15th Inf., 13 Dec., 1893. Retired for disability, with rank of Capt., 2 March, 1899.

WILLIAMS, SETH.* [Born in Maine. Appointed from Maine.]
Bvt. 2nd Lieut. 2nd Art., 1 July, 1842. 2nd Lieut. 1st Art., 31 Aug., 1844. 1st Lieut., 3 March, 1847. Bvt. Capt. A. A. G., 16 Aug., 1853. Bvt. Maj. A. A. G., 11 May, 1861. Maj. A. A. G., 3 Aug., 1861. Lieut. Col. A. A. G., 17 July, 1862. Brig. Gen. Vols., 23 Sept., 1861. Died 23 March, 1866. Bvt. Capt., 18 April, 1847, for gallant and meritorious conduct at Cerro Gordo. Bvt. Col., 3 July, 1863, for gallant and meritorious service at Gettysburg, Pa. Bvt. Brig. Gen., 13 March, 1865, for gallant and meritorious service in the campaign terminating in Gen. Lee's surrender. Bvt. Maj. Gen., 13 March, 1865, for gallant and meritorious service in the field during the war.

WILLIAMS, SOLOMON.* [Born in N. C. Appointed from N. C.]
Bvt. 2nd Lieut. 2nd Drag., 1 July, 1858. 2nd Lieut., 9 March, 1859. Resigned 3 May, 1861. Killed 9 June, 1863, in Confederate service.

WILLIAMS, THOS.* [Born in N. Y. Appointed from Mich.]
2nd Lieut. 4th Art., 1 July, 1837. 1st Lieut., 5 Oct., 1840. Capt., 12 Sept., 1850. Maj. 5th Art., 14 May, 1861. Brig. Gen. Vols., 28 Sept., 1861. Killed at the Battle of Baton Rouge, La., 5 Aug., 1862. Bvt. Capt., 20 Aug., 1847, for gallant and meritorious conduct at Contreras and Churubusco. Bvt. Maj., 13 Sept., 1847, for gallant and meritorious conduct at Chapultepec, Mex.

WILLIAMS, THOS., Jr. [Born in Pa. Appointed from Pa.]
1st Lieut. 5th Art., 14 May, 1861. Resigned 25 Oct., 1866. Bvt. Capt., 30 Aug., 1862, for gallant and meritorious service at the Battle of Manassas, Va. Bvt. Maj., 13 March, 1865, for meritorious service during the war.

WILLIAMS, THOS. C. [Born in Va. Appointed from Mo.]
Capt. 19th Inf., 19 Aug., 1861. Died 27 Dec., 1869. Bvt. Maj., 7 April, 1862, for gallant and meritorious service in the Battle of Shiloh, Tenn. Bvt. Lieut. Col., 15 Aug., 1864, for gallant and meritorious service at the Battles of Chickamauga and Mission Ridge, and in the expedition under Gen. L. H. Rousseau.

WILIAMS, THOS. G.* [Born in Va. Appointed at Large.]
Bvt. 2nd Lieut. 2nd Inf. 1 July, 1849. 2nd Lieut. 1st Inf., 10 June, 1850. 1st Lieut., 7 Aug., 1855. Resigned 15 March, 1861. Died 22 Jan., 1885.

WILLIAMS, THOS. H. [Born in Md. Appointed from Md.]
Asst. Surg., 2 March, 1849. Resigned 1 June, 1861.

WILLIAMS, WM. [Born in Pa. Appointed from Pa.]
Maj. 14th Inf., 14 May, 1861. Resigned 8 June, 1863.

WILLIAMS, WM. [Born in Pa. Appointed from Pa.]
Hosp. Surg.'s Mate, 1 Aug., 1813. Disbanded 14 April, 1818. Died 25 Jan., 1831.

WILLIAMS, WM. G.* [Born in S. C. Appointed from S. C.]
2nd Lieut. 7th Inf., 1 July, 1824. 1st Lieut., 30 April, 1833. Bvt. Capt. Top. Eng., 28 Jan., 1834. Capt. Top. Eng., 7 July, 1838. Killed 21 Sept., 1846, at the Battle of Monterey, Mexico.

WILLIAMS, WM. H. [Born in Mo. Appointed from N. C.]
2nd Lieut. 12th Inf., 9 July, 1898. 1st Lieut., — ——, 1899. Died 25 Nov., 1899.

WILLIAMS, WM. M. [Born in Ohio. Appointed from Ohio.]
Priv. Co. G, 45th Ohio Vols., 31 July, 1862. Q. M. Sergt., 1 Dec., 1862. 2nd Lieut. 45th Ohio Vols., 12 June, 1863. 1st Lieut., 2 April, 1864. Capt., 18 Feb., 1865. Bvt. Maj. Vols., 13 March, 1865, for gallant and meritorious service in the pursuit of the rebel guerilla Morgan through Ind. and Ohio. Mustered out 12 June, 1865. 2nd Lieut. 28th Inf., 13 Nov., 1867. Trans. to 19th Inf., 31 March, 1869. 1st Lieut., 27 Nov., 1878. Retired for disability, with rank of Capt., 27 Aug., 1896.

WILLIAMS, WM. N. [Born in Ireland. Appointed from Ind.]
1st Sergt. Co. A, 6th Ind. Vols, 19 April, 1861. Discharged 2 Aug., 1861. Sergt. Maj. 6th Ind. Vols., 20 Sept., 1861. 2nd Lieut. 6th Ind. Vols., 30 March, 1862. 1st Lieut., 29 May, 1862. Mustered out 3 May, 1864. 1st Lieut. Vet. Res. Corps, 23 April, 1864. Resigned 30 June, 1864. 2nd Lieut. 3rd Inf., 18 June, 1867. Retired 28 June, 1878.

WILLIAMS, WM. O. [Born in N. Y. Appointed from Va.]
2nd Lieut. 2nd Cav., 23 March, 1861. 1st Lieut., 25 April, 1861. Resigned 10 June, 1861. Executed as a spy at Franklin, Tenn., 9 June, 1863, while in Confederate service.

WILLIAMS, WM. W. [Born in Ala. Appointed from Army.]
Priv., Corpl. and Sergt. Batty A, 2nd Art., 20 April, 1859, to 10 Jan., 1863. Bvt. 2nd Lieut. 2nd Art., 29 Nov., 1862. 2nd Lieut. 5th Art., 29 Dec., 1862. Killed 5 July, 1863, in action near Boonsboro, Md.

WILLIAMS, WOLVERT E.* [Born in N. Y. Appointed from N. Y.]
3rd Lieut. Ord., 2 Dec., 1815. 2nd Lieut., 30 June, 1818. Trans. to 2nd Art., 1 June, 1821. 1st Lieut., 1 April, 1824. Dismissed 10 May, 1826. Died — ——, 1837.

WILLIAMSON, ANDREW J.* [Born in Va. Appointed from Ohio.]
Bvt. 2nd Lieut. 4th Inf., 1 July, 1842. 2nd Lieut. 3rd Inf., 29 Feb., 1844. 1st Lieut., 16 Feb., 1847. Resigned 9 Sept., 1851.

WILLIAMSON, GEO. McK.* [Born in Pa. Appointed from Pa.]
Addl. 2nd Lieut. 6th Cav., 12 June, 1887. 2nd Lieut., 28 Sept., 1887. 1st Lieut. 8th Cav., 3 Jan., 1895. Capt. A. Q. M., 21 July, 1899. Capt. A. Q. M. Vols., 28 May, 1898, to 23 July, 1899.

WILLIAMSON, JOHN.* [Born in N. J. Appointed from N. J.]
Bvt. 2nd Lieut. 4th Art., 1 July, 1826. 2nd Lieut. 1st Art., 1 July, 1826. 1st Lieut., 30 Sept., 1833. Trans. to Ord., 9 July, 1838. Capt., 22 May, 1840. Died 23 Dec., 1849.

WILLIAMSON, LLEWELLYN P. [Born in Ky. Appointed from Mo.]
Asst. Surg., 12 Dec., 1898.

WILLIAMSON, ROBT. S.* [Born in N. Y. Appointed from N. J.]
Bvt. 2nd Lieut. Top. Eng., 1 July, 1848. 2nd Lieut., 26 Oct., 1853. 1st Lieut., 20 April, 1856. Capt., 6 Aug., 1861. Bvt. Maj., 14 March, 1862, for gallant and meritorious service in action at Newbern, N. C. Bvt. Lieut. Col., 26 April, 1862, for gallant and meritorious service in the Siege of Fort Macon, N. C. Trans. to Eng., 3 March, 1863. Maj., 7 May, 1863. Lieut. Col., 22 Feb., 1869. Retired 23 June, 1882. Died 10 Nov., 1882.

WILLIAMSON, SAM'L C. [Born in Ohio. Appointed from Army.]
Priv. Co. G, 19th Ohio Vols., 27 April to 31 Aug., 1861. Priv. and Sergt. Co. D, 18th Inf., 21 Oct., 1861, to 21 April, 1863. 2nd Lieut. 18th Inf., 19 Feb., 1863. 1st Lieut., 13 Nov., 1863. Retired 24 Jan., 1864. Capt. 42nd Inf., 22 Jan., 1867. Trans. to 6th Inf., 22 April, 1869. Unassigned 21 June, 1869. Mustered out 1 Jan., 1871.

WILLIAMSON, THOS. T. [Born in ——. Appointed from Ala.]
2nd Lieut. 4th Inf., 24 March, 1818. 1st Lieut., 8 Jan., 1819. Disbanded 1 June, 1821.

WILLIARD, HARRY O.* [Born in Ohio. Appointed from Mont.]
Addl. 2nd Lieut. 10th Cav., 12 June, 1896. 2nd Lieut. 7th Cav., 30 Sept., 1896. Trans. to 10th Cav., 16 Feb., 1897.

WILLIS, LEWIS B. [Born in Va. Appointed from Va.]
1st Lieut. 12th Inf., 12 March, 1812. Reg. P. M., 24 June, 1812, to Jan., 1814. Capt., 31 Jan., 1814. Disbanded 15 June, 1815. Reinstated 2 Dec., 1815, as 1st Lieut. 8th Inf., with Bvt. of Capt. from 31 Jan., 1814. Capt., 1 June, 1816. Disbanded 1 June, 1821.

WILLIS, PERRIN. [Born in Va. Appointed from Va.]
Ensign 2nd Inf., 28 April, 1809. 2nd Lieut., 13 Feb., 1810. 1st Lieut., 1 Nov., 1812. Capt., 20 June, 1814. Disbanded 15 June, 1815. Maj. A. A. G., 3 April, 1817. Disbanded 1 June, 1821. Died 12 Feb., 1822.

WILLISTON, EDWARD B. [Born in Vt. Appointed from Cal.]
2nd Lieut. 2nd Art., 5 Aug., 1861. 1st Lieut., 27 Sept., 1861. Bvt. Capt., 3 May, 1863, for gallant and meritorious service in action at Salem Heights, Va. Bvt. Maj., 3 July, 1863, for gallant and meritorious service in the Gettysburg campaign. Bvt. Lieut. Col., 19 Sept., 1864, for gallant and meritorious service in the Battle of Winchester, Va. Capt. 2nd Art., 8 March, 1865. Bvt. Col., 13 March, 1865, for gallant and meritorious service during the war. Maj. 3rd Art., 22 March, 1885. Lieut. Col., 12 Feb., 1895. Col. 6th Art., 8 March, 1898. Brig. Gen. Vols. from 4 May, 1898, to 12 June, 1899. Medal of Honor for distinguished gallantry in the action at Trevillian Station, Va., 12 June, 1864; while serving as 1st Lieut. 2nd Art.

WILLS, DAVID. [Born in Pa. Appointed from D. C.]
Post Chap., 3 June, 1879. Retired by operation of law, 7 Jan., 1886.

WILLS, JOHN H.* [Born in Va. Appointed from Mo.]
Addl. 2nd Lieut. 22nd Inf., 11 June, 1881. 2nd Lieut., 30 June, 1881. 1st Lieut. of Inf. (12th), 29 Dec., 1890. Trans. to 22nd Inf., 20 July, 1891. Died 16 Feb., 1896.

WILLS, VAN LEER. [Born in Tenn. Appointed from Tenn.]
2nd Lieut. 12th Inf., 10 Oct., 1898.

WILSON, ALFRED D. [Born in N. J. Appointed from N. Y.]
Asst. Surg. 3rd N. Y. Art., 17 May, 1863. Surg., 18 June, 1864. Mustered out 15 July, 1865. Asst. Surg., 14 May, 1867. Died 30 Nov., 1875.

WILSON, ALFRED McC. [Born in Pa. Appointed from Pa.]
2nd Lieut. 20th Inf., 1 June, 1899.

WILSON, BENJ'N. B. [Born in Pa. Appointed from Pa.]
Asst. Surg. U. S. Vols., 2 Jan., 1863. Surg. Vols., 26 March, 1863. Bvt. Lieut. Col. Vols., 24 Oct., 1865, for faithful and meritorious service. Mustered out 30 Nov., 1865. Asst. Surg., 14 May, 1867. Resigned 9 July, 1867.

WILSON, CHAS. I. [Born in D. C. Appointed from D. C.]
1st Lieut. Asst. Surg., 28 May, 1861. Bvt. Capt., 13 March, 1865, for meritorious and distinguished service in the Battles of Todd's Tavern and Yellow Tavern, Va. Bvt. Maj., 13 March, 1865, for highly meritorious and distinguished service in his department in twelve engagements in the Shenandoah Valley, Va. Capt. Asst. Surg., 31 May, 1866. Resigned 1 Jan., 1867. Capt. 16th Inf., 22 Jan., 1867. Bvt. Maj., 2 March, 1867, for meritorious service in the Battle of Todd's Tavern, Va. Unassigned 17 April, 1869. Discharged 31 Dec., 1870. Maj. P. M., 3 March, 1875. Lieut. Col. Dep. P M. G., 10 June, 1898. Col. A. P. M. G., 12 July, 1899.

WILSON, CLARENDON J. L.* [Born in Va. Appointed from Va.]
Bvt. 2nd Lieut. 1st Drag., 1 July, 1846. 2nd Lieut., 6 Dec., 1846. 1st Lieut. 4 Aug., 1849. Died 21 Feb., 1853. Bvt. 1st Lieut., 4 Feb., 1847, for gallant and meritorious conduct in the conflicts at Embudo and Taos, N. M.

WILSON, DAVID. [Born in Pa. Appointed from D. C.]
Post Chap., 16 June, 1880. Retired by operation of law, 30 March, 1890.

WILSON, DAVID B. [Born in Pa. Appointed from Pa.]
1st Lieut. 131st Pa. Vols., 18 Aug., 1862. Mustered out 23 May, 1863. 1st Lieut. 1st U. S. Vet. Vols., 4 Aug., 1864. Mustered out 29 Sept., 1865. 2nd Lieut. 40th Inf., 28 July, 1866. Reg. Adj., 13 July, 1868, to 15 Sept., 1868. Trans. to 25th Inf., 20 April, 1869. 1st Lieut., 20 Dec., 1871. Reg. Adj., 1 Jan., 1876, to 16 July, 1886. Capt., 16 July, 1886. Maj., 2 March, 1899.

WILSON, DAVID R. [Born in D. C. Appointed from Ill.]
Priv. Batty A. Chicago Light Art., 17 April to 16 July, 1861. 1st Lieut. 16th Inf., 14 May, 1861. Dismissed 14 Feb., 1863.

WILSON, EUGENE T.* [Born in Ohio. Appointed from Ohio.]
Addl. 2nd Lieut. 5th Art., 11 June, 1888. 2nd Lieut. 1st Art., 4 Dec., 1888. 1st Lieut. 3rd Art., 12 Feb., 1895. Capt. Sig. Corps Vols., 20 May to 4 Oct., 1898. Maj. C. S. Vols., 24 Sept., 1898. Lieut. Col. C. S. Vols., 24 Oct., 1898, to 2 March, 1899.

WILSON, EVERT R. [Born in Ind. Appointed from Army.]
Priv., Corpl. and Sergt. Battys G and I, 7th Art., 19 July, 1897, to 16 Nov., 1899. 2nd Lieut. 10th Inf., 1 Oct., 1899.

WILSON, FRANCIS H. [Born in Pa. Appointed from Pa]
2nd Lieut. 5th Inf., 14 Nov., 1861. 1st Lieut., 17 July, 1862. Trans. to 3rd Cav., 20 Aug., 1862. R. C. S., Oct., 1862, to 15 Jan., 1863. Capt., 9 Nov., 1866. Discharged 25 Oct., 1870. Bvt. Capt., 15 Nov., 1863, for gallant and meritorious service in action near Tuscumbia, Ala.

WILSON, GEORGE.* [Born in Ohio. Appointed from Ohio.]
Bvt. 2nd Lieut. 1st Inf., 1 July, 1830. 2nd Lieut., 1 July, 1830. 1st Lieut., 30 Nov., 1836. Resigned 31 Dec., 1837. Died 3 March, 1880.

WILSON, GEORGE S. [Born in Ind. Appointed from Ind.]
Corpl., Co. C, 17th Ind. Vols., 31 May, 1861. Sergt., 9 Dec., 1861. 2nd Lieut., 17th Ind. Vols., 1 March, 1864. 1st Lieut., 3 June, 1864. Mustered out 8 Aug., 1865. 2nd Lieut. 12th Inf., 2 July, 1867. Reg. Adj., 12 June, 1873, to 20 Feb., 1875. 1st Lieut., 28 Dec., 1876. Capt., 12 Feb., 1886. Maj. A. A. G., 6 Nov., 1893. Died 12 Jan., 1897

WILSON, HENRY. [Born in Pa. Appointed from Pa.]
Ensign 32nd Inf., 17 May, 1813. 2nd Lieut., 9 April, 1814. Disbanded 15 June, 1815. Reinstated in 4th Inf., 2 Dec., 1815. 1st Lieut. 31 Dec., 1816. Reg. Adj., 7 Sept., 1816, to 20 April, 1819. Capt., 20 April, 1819. Maj. 3rd Inf., 1 Nov., 1828. Lieut. Col. 1st Inf., 14 June, 1842. Col. 7th Inf., 11 June, 1851. Resigned 25 Feb., 1861. Bvt. Maj., 20 April, 1829, for ten years' faithful service in one grade. Bvt. Col., 23 Sept., 1846, for gallant and meritorious conduct in several conflicts at Monterey, Mexico. Died 21 Feb., 1872.

WILSON, HENRY H. [Born in Mass. Appointed from Mass.]
Cadet at Naval Acad., 24 Sept., 1862, to 12 Sept., 1863. 1st Lieut. 31st U. S. Col. Inf., 14 May, 1864. Capt. 104th U. S. Col. Inf., 6 April, 1865. Lieut. Col., 1 July, 1865. Mustered out 5 Feb., 1866. 2d Lieut. 6th Cav., 9 April, 1866. Died 24 Dec., 1866.

WILSON, HORATIO A.* [Born in N. Y. Appointed from N. Y.]
Bvt. 2nd Lieut. 2nd Art., 1 July, 1824. 2nd Lieut. 4th Art., 1 July, 1824. 1st Lieut., 30 May, 1832. Resigned 31 Jan., 1835. Died 17 Jan., 1850.

WILSON, JAMES E.* [Born in D. C. Appointed from D. C.]
2nd Lieut. 5th Art., 17 June, 1862. Trans. to 2nd Art., 6 Oct., 1862. 1st Lieut., 1 Oct., 1863. R. Q. M., 10 Dec., 1863, to 2 April, 1866. Capt. 38th Inf., 28 July, 1866, declined. Capt. 2nd Art., 24 July, 1874. Died 20 Nov., 1887.

WILSON, JAMES E. [Born in N. Y. Appointed from Army.]
Priv., Artif., Corpl. and Sergt. Co. A, Batt. Eng., 3 Oct., 1852, to 11 Sept., 1862, and Priv. and Sergt. Co. E, Batt. Eng., 19 Jan. to 19 April, 1863. Bvt. 2nd Lieut. 1st Art., 11 March, 1863. 2nd Lieut. 5th Art., 27 April, 1863. 1st Lieut., 28 July, 1866. Wholly retired 24 March, 1869. Bvt. 1st Lieut., 1 July, 1864, for gallant and meritorious service in action in front of Petersburg, Va. Died 27 July, 1870.

WILSON, JAMES E. [Born in Ireland. Appointed from Army.]
Priv., Corpl. and Sergt. Cos. C and D, Eng. Batt., and Priv. and Corpl. General Service, 23 Aug., 1873, to 23 April, 1882. 2nd Lieut. 5th Inf., 27 March, 1882. 1st Lieut. of Inf. (11th), 29 Dec., 1890. Trans. to 5th Inf., 20 July, 1891. Retired for disability, 18 April, 1895. Resigned 6 Jan., 1896.

WILSON, JAMES H.* [Born in Tenn. Appointed from Tenn.]
Bvt. 2nd Lieut. 1st Inf., 1 July, 1850. Resigned 1 Sept., 1851.

WILSON, JAMES H.* [Born in Ill. Appointed from Ill.]
Bvt. 2nd Lieut. Top. Eng., 1 July, 1860. 2nd Lieut., 10 June, 1861. 1st Lieut., 9 Sept., 1861. Trans. to Eng., 3 March, 1863. Capt., 7 May, 1863. Lieut. Col. A. I. G., 8 Nov., 1862, to 17 Nov., 1863. Brig. Gen. Vols., 30 Oct., 1863. Maj. Gen. Vols., 6 May, 1865. Mustered out of Vol. Service 8 Jan., 1866. Lieut. Col. 35th Inf., 28 July, 1866. Unassigned 3 March, 1869. Discharged 31 Dec., 1870. Bvt. Maj., 11 April, 1862, for gallant and meritorious service at the capture of Fort Pulaski, Ga. Bvt. Lieut. Col., 24 Nov., 1864, for gallant and meritorious service at the Battle of Chattanooga, Tenn. Bvt. Col., 5 May, 1864, for gallant and meritorious service at the Battle of the Wilderness, Va. Bvt. Brig. Gen., 13 March, 1865, for gallant and meritorious service at the Battle of Nashville, Tenn. Bvt. Maj. Gen., 13 March, 1865, for gallant and meritorious service in the capture of Selma, Ala.

WILSON, JAMES L.* [Born in Va. Appointed from W. Va.]
Priv. and Bugler Co. K, 2nd W. Va. Vols., 1 Dec., 1862. Discharged 4 Dec., 1865. Cadet at Mil. Acad., 1 July, 1870. 2nd Lieut. 4th Art., 17 June, 1874. 1st Lieut., 1 Jan., 1880. Capt. 6th Art., 8 March, 1898. Graduate of the Artillery School, 1896. Maj. Chf. Q. M. Vols., 20 June, 1898, to ——.

WILSON, JAMES S. [Born in N. Y. Appointed from Ill.]
Sergt. Co. I, 42nd Ill. Vols., 1 Aug., 1861, to 19 Sept., 1864. 2nd Lieut. 19th Inf., 23 Feb., 1866. 1st Lieut., 1 April, 1867. Unassigned 19 April, 1869. Discharged 23 Oct., 1870.

WILSON, JAMES S. [Born in Cal. Appointed from Md.]
Asst. Surg., 16 Dec., 1893.

WILSON, JOHN. [Born in England. Appointed from S. C.]
Maj. Top. Eng., 29 April, 1816. Resigned 15 Sept., 1816.

WILSON, JOHN. [Born in N. Y. Appointed from N. Y.]
1st Lieut. 46th Inf., 21 April, 1814. Resigned 5 Dec., 1814. 2nd Lieut. Ord., 26 Dec., 1814. 1st Lieut., 1 Sept., 1818. Dismissed 17 March, 1820.

WILSON, JOHN D. [Born in Md. Appointed from Army.]
Priv. Batty C, 1st Art., 20 May, 1854, to 20 May, 1859. Priv., Corpl., Sergt. and

1st Sergt. Batty H, 1st Art., 11 Aug., 1860, to 17 Nov., 1863. 2nd Lieut. 1st Art., 31 Oct., 1863. Dismissed 12 Aug., 1864. Priv., Corpl. and Sergt. Troop C, 3rd Cav., 10 Dec., 1864, to 10 Dec., 1867.

WILSON, JOHN M.* [Born in D. C. Appointed from Wash. Ter.]
Bvt. 2nd Lieut. 1st Art., 1 July, 1860. Trans. to Ord., 9 Oct., 1860. Trans. to 1st Art., 14 Jan., 1861. 2nd Lieut. 2nd Art., 28 Jan., 1861. 1st Lieut., 14 May, 1861. Bvt. Capt., 27 June, 1862, for gallant and meritorious service in the Battle of Gaines' Mills, Va. Bvt. Maj., 1 July, 1862, for gallant and meritorious service in the Battle of Malvern Hill, Va. Trans. to Top. Eng., 24 July, 1862. Trans. to Eng., 3 March, 1863. Capt., 1 June, 1863. Lieut. Col. A. I. G. (Act of 17 July, 1862,), 26 May, 1864, to 1 Aug., 1865. Bvt. Col. Vols., 26 March, 1865, for faithful and meritorious service during the campaign against the city of Mobile and its defences. Bvt. Lieut. Col., 8 April, 1865, for gallant and meritorious service in the capture of Spanish Fort, Mobile Harbor, Ala. Bvt. Col., 8 April, 1865, for gallant and meritorious service at Spanish Fort and Fort Blakely, Ala. Maj. Eng., 3 June, 1867. Medal of Honor for most distinguished gallantry in action at Malvern Hill, Va., 6 Aug., 1862, in remaining on duty while suffering from an acute illness and very weak, and participating with distinguished gallantry in the action of that date; while 1st Lieut. Corps of Eng., serving with Battys B and L, 2nd U. S. Art. Lieut. Col. Eng., 17 March, 1884. Col. superintendent public buildings and grounds, 1 June, 1885, to 17 Aug., 1889. Superintendent Mil. Acad., with rank of Col., 17 Aug., 1889, to ——. Col., 31 March, 1895. Brig. Gen. Chf. of Eng., 1 Feb., 1897.

WILSON, JOSEPH K. [Born in Ohio. Appointed from Army.]
Priv., Corpl. and Sergt. Cos. A and B, and Sergt. Maj. and Q. M. Sergt. 8th Inf., 9 July, 1844, to 7 Sept., 1853. Ord. Sergt., 7 Sept., 1853, to 9 June, 1854. Sergt. Maj. 8th Inf., 15 Dec., 1855, to 7 May, 1863. 2nd Lieut. 8th Inf., 7 May, 1863. 1st Lieut., 19 July, 1866. R. Q. M., 10 March, 1868, to 19 Sept., 1869. Died 19 Sept., 1869. Bvt. 1st Lieut., 30 July, 1864, for gallant and meritorious service in an assault on Petersburg, Va.

WILSON, LEWIS. [Born in Ohio. Appointed from Ohio.]
Col. 2nd Ohio Vols., 17 April, 1861. Resigned 20 June, 1861. Capt. 19th Inf., 14 May, 1861. Resigned 28 July, 1864.

WILSON, LOUIS D. [Born in N. C. Appointed from N. C.]
Capt. N. C. Vols., 5 Jan., 1847. Col. of Inf., 3 March, 1847; 12th Inf., 9 April, 1847. Died 12 Aug., 1847.

WILSON, PETER. [Born in ——. Appointed from D. C.]
2nd Lieut. Corps Art., 13 Aug., 1819. Disbanded 1 June, 1821.

WILSON, RICHARD. [Born in Malta. Appointed from Army.]
Priv., Corpl., Sergt. and 1st Sergt. Batty C, 4th Art., 28 June, 1852, to 28 June, 1857. Priv., Corpl., Sergt. and 1st Sergt. General Service, and Batty C, 4th Art., 22 Jan., 1858, to 16 Jan., 1862, and Ord. Sergt., 16 Jan., 1862, to 10 Aug., 1863. 2nd Lieut. 3rd Art., 10 Aug., 1863. 1st Lieut., 11 Dec., 1865. Dropped 2 April, 1868. Bvt. 1st Lieut., 1 June, 1864, for gallant and meritorious service in action at Ashland, Va. Bvt. Capt., 23 Sept., 1864, for gallant and meritorious service in action in front of Petersburg, Va. Priv. and 1st Sergt. Batty K, 4th Art., 9 June, 1869, to 9 June, 1874.

WILSON, RICHARD H.* [Born in Mich. Appointed from Mich.]
2nd Lieut. 8th Inf., 15 June, 1877. 1st Lieut., 1 Jan., 1886. Capt., 31 July, 1894.

WILSON, ROBERT. [Born in Pa. Appointed from S. C.]
Mil. Storekeeper Ord., 9 Sept., 1814. Disbanded 1 June, 1821.

WILSON, ROBERT P. [Born in Va. Appointed from Va.]
1st Lieut. 17th Inf., 26 Oct., 1861. Capt., 7 Jan., 1865. Trans. to 26th Inf., 21 Sept., 1866. Trans. to 10th Inf., 19 May, 1869. Died 24 March, 1878, from injuries received 22 March, 1878, by accidental explosion of gun. Bvt. Capt., 2 July, 1863, and Bvt. Maj., 13 March, 1865, for gallant and meritorious service at the Battle of Gettysburg, Pa.

WILSON, ROBERT P. [Born in Pa. Appointed from Army.]
1st Lieut. and Adj. 3rd Pa. Cav., 24 Jan., 1862. Mustered out 2 Oct., 1862. Priv. 12th Inf., 7 April to 3 June, 1863. 2nd Lieut. 5th Cav., 1 June, 1863. 1st Lieut., 8 May, 1864. Capt., 12 June, 1869. Resigned 29 July, 1876. Bvt. 1st Lieut., 1 Aug., 1863, for gallant and meritorious service at the Battle of Brandy Station, Va. Bvt. Capt., 10 May, 1864, for gallant and meritorious service in action at Beaver Dam, Va.

WILSON, THOS.* [Born in D. C. Appointed from D. C.]
Bvt. 2nd Lieut. 6th Inf., 1 July, 1853. 2nd Lieut. 5th Inf., 26 Oct., 1854. 1st Lieut., 1 April, 1857. Capt. C. S., 25 Oct., 1861. Lieut. Col. C. S. (Act 17 July, 1862), 26 Dec., 1863. Bvt. Col. Vols., 1 Aug., 1864, for faithful and meritorious service in the field. Bvt. Brig. Gen. Vols., 13 March, 1865, for faithful and meritorious service during the war. Bvt Maj., Lieut. Col., Col. and Brig. Gen., 13 March, 1865, for faithful and meritorious service during the war. Relieved as Lieut. Col. C. S. (Act 17 July, 1862), 1 Aug., 1865. Maj. C. S., 20 May, 1882. Lieut. Col. A. C. G. S., 1 Aug., 1892. Col. A. C. G. S., 1 June, 1896. Retired by operation of law, 10 June, 1896.

WILSON, THOMAS H. [Born in Va. Appointed from Army.]
Priv., Corpl. and Sergt. Co. K, 4th Cav., 24 Sept., 1878, to 18 Aug., 1882. 2nd Lieut. 2nd Inf., 26 July, 1882. 1st Lieut. 5th Inf., 20 Feb., 1891. Trans. to 2nd Inf., 20 July, 1891. Capt of Inf., 1 July, 1898. Ass'd to 2nd Inf., 1 Jan., 1899.

WILSON, WALTER M. [Born in Mo. Appointed from Mass.]
2nd Lieut. 1st Cav., 26 April, 1861. 1st Lieut., 14 May, 1861. 4th Cav., 3 Aug., 1861. R. Q. M., 5 March to 30 Nov., 1862. Capt., 9 May, 1864. Resigned 21 April, 1866. Died 27 May, 1873.

WILSON, WASH'N L. [Born in N. Y. Appointed from Ark.]
1st Lieut. of Inf., 6 March, 1847; 12th Inf., 9 April, 1847. Resigned 22 Dec., 1847.

WILSON, WM. [Born in Md. Appointed from Md.]
Lieut 1st Art. and Eng., 17 July, 1794. Resigned 24 Sept., 1799. Lieut. 2nd Art.

and Eng., 16 Feb., 1801. Trans. to Reg. Art., 1 June, 1802. Capt., 3 May, 1808. Trans. to Corps Art., 12 May, 1814. Trans. to 3rd Art., 1 June, 1821 Maj. 4th Art., 8 May, 1822. Died 15 Sept., 1825. Bvt. Maj., 3 May, 1818, for ten years' faithful service in one grade.

WILSON, WM. H. [Born in Texas. Appointed from Mo.]
Asst. Surg., 26 Oct., 1893. Capt. Asst. Surg., 26 Oct., 1898.

WILSON, WM. J. [Born in Ireland. Appointed from Mo.]
Asst. Surg. 13th Ohio Cav., 6 May, 1865. Mustered out 10 Aug., 1865. 1st Lieut. Asst. Surg., 9 Oct., 1867. Capt. Asst. Surg., 5 July, 1870. Died 2 May, 1886.

WILSON, WM. P. [Born in Pa. Appointed from Pa.]
1st Lieut. 148th Pa. Vols., 1 Sept., 1862. Capt., 15 Nov., 1863. Capt. A. de C. Vols., 23 Jan., 1865. Bvt. Maj. Vols., 2 Dec., 1864, for gallant service during the campaign before Richmond, Va., and Lieut. Col. Vols., 13 March, 1865, for service throughout the war. Mustered out 10 July, 1866. Capt. 21st Inf., 28 July, 1866. Unassigned 19 April, 1869. Discharged 23 Oct., 1870. Bvt. Maj., 2 March, 1867, for gallant and meritorious service in the Battle of the Wilderness, Va. Died 5 Aug., 1886.

WINANS, EDWIN B., Jr.* [Born in Mich. Appointed from Mich.]
2nd Lieut. 5th Cav., 12 June, 1891. 1st Lieut. 4th Cav., 30 April, 1898. Maj. 34th Mich. Vols., 25 May to 26 Nov., 1898.

WINANS, FRAZEY M. [Born in N. J. Appointed from Mich.]
Capt. of Inf., 2 March, 1847; 15th Inf., 9 April, 1847. Resigned 6 May, 1848. Bvt. Maj., 15 Aug., 1847, for gallant and meritorious conduct in several affairs with Guerilleros at Paso Ovejas, National Bridge, and Cerro Gordo, Mexico. Lieut. Col. 7th Mich. Vols., 19 June, 1861. Resigned 21 May, 1862.

WINCHESTER, HIRAM F. [Born in Md. Appointed from Md.]
1st Lieut. 1st Md. Cav., 8 March, 1864. Mustered out 28 June, 1865. 2nd Lieut. 10th Cav., 31 Aug., 1867, declined. 2nd Lieut. 6th Cav., 27 Sept., 1867. Reg. Adj., 1 Sept., 1870, to 5 April, 1873. 1st Lieut., 1 Jan., 1871. Died 29 May, 1881.

WINDER, CHAS. S.* [Born in Md. Appointed from Md.]
Bvt. 2nd Lieut. 4th Art., 1 July, 1850. 2nd Lieut., 3rd Art., 21 July, 1851. 1st Lieut., 5 April, 1854. Reg. Adj., 4 April, 1854, to 3 March, 1855. Capt., 9th Inf., 3 March, 1855. Resigned 1 April, 1861. Died 9 Aug., 1862.

WINDER, EDWARD S. [Born in Md. Appointed from Md.]
Capt. 2nd Drag., 8 June, 1836. Died 7 March, 1840.

WINDER, JAMES M. [Born in Md. Appointed from Md.]
2nd Lieut. of Inf., 23 Feb., 1847; Voltigeurs, 9 April, 1847. Died 6 Sept., 1847, of wounds received in action at the National Bridge, Mexico.

WINDER, JOHN H.* [Born in Md. Appointed from Md.]
2nd Lieut. Corps Art., 1 July, 1820. Trans. to Rifles, 23 Oct., 1820. Trans. to 4th Art., 1 June, 1821. Resigned 31 Aug., 1823. 2nd Lieut. 1st Art., 2 April, 1827. 1st Lieut. 30 Nov., 1833. Reg. Adj., 23 May, 1838, to 20 Jan., 1840. Capt., 7 Oct., 1842. Maj. 3rd Art., 22 Nov., 1860. Resigned 27 April, 1861. Bvt. Maj., 20 Aug., 1847, for gallant and meritorious conduct at Contreras and Churubusco. Bvt. Lieut. Col., 14 Sept., 1847, for gallant conduct on entering the City of Mexico. Died 7 Feb., 1865.

WINDER, RIDER H. [Born in Md. Appointed from Md.]
Maj. J. A., 9 July, 1814. Disbanded 15 July, 1815. Restored 3 May, 1816. Resigned 23 July, 1818.

WINDER, WM. A. [Born in Md. Appointed from Md.]
2nd Lieut. 3rd Art., 24 March, 1848. 1st Lieut., 22 Aug., 1853. Capt., 14 May, 1861. Resigned 18 Oct., 1866.

WINDLE, LUCIUS S. [Born in Ohio. Appointed from Ohio.]
Priv. Co. A, 3rd Ohio Vols., 24 April to 15 Aug., 1861. Priv., Sergt. and 1st Sergt. Co. D, 46th Ohio Vols., 16 Oct., 1861, to 14 June, 1862. 2nd Lieut. 113th Ohio Vols., 13 Aug., 1862. 1st Lieut., 21 April, 1863. Capt., 25 June, 1864. Mustered out 6 July, 1865. 2nd Lieut. 19th Inf., 7 March, 1867. Died 8 Feb., 1870. Bvt. 1st Lieut., 7 March, 1867, for gallant and meritorious service in the Battle of Jonesboro, Ga.

WINEBRENER, JOHN A. [Born in Pa. Appointed from Army.]
Priv. Ord., 14 to 17 Nov., 1863. 2nd Lieut. 3rd Inf., 14 Nov., 1863. Trans. to Ord., 24 Nov., 1863. 1st Lieut., 1 Dec., 1865. Resigned 13 May, 1867.

WING, THEODORE W. [Born in Ky. Appointed from Ky.]
Cadet Mil. Acad., 1 July, 1862, to 26 June, 1863. 1st Lieut. Adj. 3rd Ky. Vols., 2 Oct., 1863. Mustered out 29 Dec., 1864. 2nd Lieut. 4th Cav., 27 May, 1867. Died 26 Sept., 1867.

WINGARD, CHAS. W. [Born in Pa. Appointed from Pa.]
Maj. 137th Pa. Vols., 25 Aug., 1862. Lieut. Col. 137th Pa. Vols., 15 March, 1863. Mustered out 1 June, 1863. Addl. P. M., 10 May, 1864. Bvt. Lieut. Col. Vols., 15 June, 1866, for faithful and meritorious conduct. Maj. P. M. U. S. A., 17 Jan., 1867. Died 30 Aug., 1882.

WINGATE, BENJ'N. [Born in Ind. Appointed from Army.]
Priv., Corpl. and Sergt. Co. G, Mounted Rifles, 13 Aug., 1846, to 4 July, 1848. 2nd Lieut. 5th Inf., 14 June, 1848. 1st Lieut., 26 Oct., 1854 Capt., 22 Aug., 1859. Died 1 June, 1862, of wounds received in the Battle of Val Verde, N. M. Bvt. Maj., 21 Feb., 1862, for gallant and meritorious service at the Battle of Val Verde, N. M.

WINN, FRANK L.* [Born in Ky. Appointed from Ky.]
2nd Lieut. 1st Inf., 1 July, 1886. 1st Lieut. 12th Inf., 28 April, 1893. Capt., 2 March, 1899. Reg. Adj., 2 March, 1899.

WINN, JOHN S.* [Born in Ky. Appointed from Ky.]
2nd Lieut. 2nd Cav., 11 June, 1888. 1st Lieut. 1st Cav., 14 June, 1895. Trans. to 2nd Cav., 7 Nov., 1895.

WINNE, CHAS. K. [Born in N. Y. Appointed from N. Y.]
1st Lieut. Asst. Surg., 5 Aug., 1861. Resigned 15 Oct., 1873. Bvt. Capt. and Maj., 13 March, 1865, for faithful and meritorious service during the war. Capt. Asst. Surg., 28 July, 1866. Bvt. Lieut. Col., 28 Sept., 1866, for meritorious and dis-

tinguished service at Tybee Island, Ga., where cholera prevailed. Resigned 15 Oct., 1873. 1st Lieut. Asst. Surg., 10 Nov., 1874. Capt. Asst. Surg., 10 Nov., 1879. Maj. Surg., 22 Feb., 1891.

WINSHIP, OSCAR F.* [Born in N. Y. Appointed from N. Y.]
2nd Lieut. 2nd Drag., 1 July, 1840. 1st Lieut., 13 Sept., 1844. Capt., 30 June, 1851. Bvt. Capt. A. A. G., 7 July, 1846. Bvt. Maj. A. A. G., 26 Dec., 1847. Died 13 Dec., 1855. Bvt. Capt., 9 May, 1846, for gallant and meritorious conduct at Palo Alto and Resaca de la Palma. Bvt. Maj., 20 Aug., 1847, for gallant conduct at Churubusco.

WINSLOW, E. EVELETH.* [Born in D. C. Appointed from Mass.]
Addl. 2nd Lieut. Eng., 12 June, 1889. 2nd Lieut., 2 July, 1889. 1st Lieut., 12 April, 1894. Capt., 5 July, 1898.

WINSLOW, GORDON. [Born in N. Y. Appointed fromN. Y.]
2nd Lieut. 5th N. Y. Vols., 30 Aug., 1862. 1st Lieut., 29 Oct., 1862. Mustered out 14 May, 1863. 1st Lieut. 5th N. Y. Vet. Vols., 19 Oct., 1863. Dismissed 8 Feb., 1864. Private Co. B, 5th N. Y. Vet. Vols., 21 March, 1864. Capt. 5th N. Y. Vet. Vols., 28 July, 1864. Bvt. Maj. Vols., 1 April, 1865, for gallant and meritorious service during the war. Mustered out 21 Aug., 1865. 2nd Lieut. 15th Inf., 3 March, 1866. Trans. to 33rd Inf., 21 Sept., 1866. 1st Lieut., 17 Jan., 1867. Trans. to 8th Inf., 3 May, 1869. Capt., 23 May, 1884. Retired for disability, 27 May, 1889. Died 22 Oct., 1896.

WINSLOW, REUBEN C. [Born in Pa. Appointed from Pa.]
Priv. Co. G, 42nd Pa. Vols., 29 May to 29 Aug., 1861. 2nd Lieut. 5th Cav., 5 Aug., 1861. Trans. to 17th Inf., 21 Sept., 1861. 1st Lieut., 24 Oct., 1861. Died 10 May, 1862.

WINSTON, DONALD.* [Born in Va. Appointed from Va.]
Addl. 2nd Lieut. 10th Inf., 14 June, 1878. 2nd Lieut., 28 June, 1878. Died 26 Oct., 1882.

WINSTON, EDWARD T.* [Born in Tenn. Appointed from Tenn.]
2nd Lieut. 14th Inf., 12 June, 1889. 1st Lieut. 19th Inf., 27 Aug., 1896. Capt. 5th Inf., 11 July, 1899. Trans. to 19th Inf., 11 Aug., 1899. Graduate of the Infantry and Cavalry School, 1893.

WINSTON, THOMAS M. [Born in Ky. Appointed from Ky.]
Cadet Mil. Acad., 1 July, 1842, to 4 July, 1844. 2nd Lieut. 16th Inf., 25 May, 1847. Disbanded 30 July, 1848. Maj. P. M., 5 April, 1860. Resigned 30 Sept., 1866. Bvt. Lieut. Col., 13 March, 1865, for faithful and meritorious service during the war.

WINSTON, THOMAS W.* [Born in Ill. Appointed from Ill.]
Addl. 2nd Lieut. 4th Art., 12 June, 1890. 2nd Lieut. 5th Art., 12 Feb., 1891. 1st Lieut. 1st Art., 10 Feb., 1898.

WINSTON, WM. O. [Born in Va. Appointed from Miss.]
1st Lieut. 24th Inf., 13 March, 1812. Reg. Adj., Nov., 1812, to Aug., 1813. Capt., 15 Aug., 1813. Disbanded 15 June, 1815. J. A., 29 April, 1816. Disbanded 14 April, 1818.

WINT, THEODORE J. [Born in Pa. Appointed from Army.]
Priv. Co. F, 6th Pa. Cav., 12 Oct., 1861. Corpl., — —, 1863. Sergt., 1 Oct., 1863. 1st Lieut. 6th Pa. Cav., 1 July, 1864. Mustred out 30 Sept., 1864. Priv. General Mounted Service, 20 Feb., 1865. 2nd Lieut. 4th Cav., 24 Nov., 1865. 1st Lieut., 9 May, 1866. Reg. Adj., 26 Aug., 1868, to 31 Dec., 1871. Capt., 21 April, 1872. Maj. 10th Cav., 6 May, 1892. Lieut. Col. 6th Cav., 8 April, 1899.

WINTER, FRANCIS A. [Born in La. Appointed from Mo.]
Asst. Surg., 9 March, 1892. Capt. Asst. Surg., 9 March, 1897. Maj. Surg. 37th U. S. Vols., 5 July, 1899.

WINTERS JAMES H. [Born in Ohio. Appointed from Cal.]
2nd Lieut. 23rd Inf., 1 Oct., 1873. Dismissed 23 Aug., 1875.

WINTERS, WILLIAM H. [Born in Ohio. Appointed from Army.]
Priv. Co. A, 6th Ohio Vols., 20 April, 1861. 1st Lieut. 27th Ohio Vols., 2 Aug., 1861. Capt., 1 July, 1862. Resigned 22 Oct., 1862. Priv. Co. I, 1st Cav., 18 Sept., 1864. Corpl., 1 Oct., 1864. Sergt., 15 Nov., 1864. 1st Sergt., 16 Nov., 1864. 2nd Lieut. 1st Cav., 12 March, 1865. 1st Lieut., 8 Aug., 1866. R. Q. M., 11 Nov., 1875, to 25 June, 1876. Capt., 25 June, 1876. Died 12 June, 1880.

WINTERS, WILLIAM H. [Born in Cal. Appointed from Army.]
Priv. Troop D, 4th Cav., 24 Aug., 1894, to 13 June, 1895. Priv. and Acting Steward Hosp. Corps, 14 June, 1895, to 20 Dec., 1898. Priv. and Corpl. Troop B, 6th Cav., 10 March to 16 Nov., 1899. 2nd Lieut. 3rd Cav., 1 Oct., 1899.

WINTHROP, FRED'K. [Born in N. Y. Appointed from N. Y.]
Priv. Co. F, 71st N. Y. Militia, 20 April, to 30 July, 1861. Capt. 12th Inf., 26 Oct., 1861. Col. 5th N. Y. Vols., 6 Aug., 1864. Bvt. Brig. Gen. Vols., 1 Aug., 1864, for brave and constant service in the battles and marches of the campaigns. Bvt. Maj. Gen. Vols., 1 April, 1865, at the Battle of Five Forks, Va. Killed 1 April, 1865, in the Battle of Five Forks, Va.

WINTHROP, WM. [Born in Conn. Appointed from N. Y.]
Priv. Co. F, 7th N. Y. State Militia, 26 April, 1861. Mustered out 3 June, 1861. 1st Lieut. 1st U. S. Sharp Shooters, 1 Oct., 1861. Capt., 22 Sept., 1862. Mustered out 16 Sept., 1864. Maj. J. A. Vols., 19 Sept., 1864. Bvt. Lieut. Col. Vols., 13 March, 1865, for faithful and meritorious service in his Dept. in the field. Bvt. Col. Vols., 13 March, 1865, for faithful and meritorious service in the field, and in the Bureau of Mil. Justice. J. A. U. S. A., 25 Feb., 1867. Lieut. Col. Dep. J. A. G., 5 July, 1884. Col. A. J. A. G., 3 Jan., 1895. Retired by operation of law, 3 Aug., 1895. Died 8 April, 1899.

WIRTZ, HORACE R. [Born in Pa. Appointed from Pa.]
Asst. Surg., 5 Dec., 1846. Maj. Surg., 16 April, 1862. Died 24 Jan., 1874. Bvt. Lieut. Col., 13 March, 1865, for faithful and meritorious service during the war.

WISE, HUGH D.* [Born in Va. Appointed from N. Y.]
2nd Lieut. 9th Inf., 12 June, 1894. 1st Lieut., 26 April, 1898. Capt. A. A. G. Vols., 12 Sept., 1898, to 12 May, 1899. Maj. 47th U. S. Vols., 17 Aug., 1899.

**WISE, WM. W.** [Born in Pa. Appointed from Pa.]
Capt. 15th Inf., 14 May, 1861. Died 3 Jan., 1863, of wounds received in the Battle of Murfreesboro, Tenn. Bvt. Maj., 7 April, 1862, for gallant and meritorious service at the Battle of Shiloh, Tenn. Bvt. Lieut. Col., 31 Dec., 1862, for gallant and meritorious service at the Battle of Murfreesboro, Tenn.

**WISHART, ALEX'R.** [Born in Pa. Appointed from Pa.]
Midshipman U. S. N., 2 Oct., 1850, to 22 March, 1851. Capt., 8th Pa. Vet. Res. Corps., 22 June, 1861 Resigned 10 Sept., 1862. 2nd Lieut. 27th Inf., 22 Jan., 1867. Bvt. 1st Lieut., 2 March, 1867, for gallant and meritorious service in the Battle of Gaines' Mills, Va. Bvt. Capt., 2 March, 1867, for gallant and meritorious service during the war. 1st Lieut. 27th Inf., 19 Oct., 1867. Unassigned 14 June, 1869. Ass'd to 20th Inf., 15 Dec., 1870. Dismissed 22 Jan., 1881.

**WISSER, JOHN P.*** [Born in Mo. Appointed from Mo.]
2nd Lieut. 1st Art., 17 June, 1874. 1st Lieut., 13 Jan., 1880. Capt. 7th Art., 8 March, 1898. Graduate of the Artillery School, 1878.

**WISTER, FRANCIS.** [Born in Pa. Appointed from Pa.]
Capt. 12th Inf., 5 Aug., 1861. Col. 215th Pa. Vols., 21 April, 1865. Mustered out of Vols., 28 Aug., 1865. Resigned 5 April, 1866. Bvt. Maj., 3 May, 1863, for gallant and meritorious service at the Battle of Chancellorsville, Va. Bvt. Lieut. Col., 2 July, 1863, for gallant and meritorious service at the Battle of Gettysburg, Pa.

**WITCHER, JOHN S.** [Born in Va. Appointed from W. Va.]
1st Lieut. 3rd W. Va. Cav., 13 Dec., 1862. Capt., 8 Sept., 1863. Maj., 23 May, 1864. Lieut. Col., 6 May, 1865. Bvt. Brig. Gen., 13 March to 30 June, 1865. Maj. P. M., 30 Aug., 1880. Retired for disability, 8 Sept., 1899.

**WITHERELL, CHAS. T.** [Born in Maine. Appointed from Maine.]
Sergt. Co. K, 6th Maine Vols., 7 May, 1861. 2nd Lieut. 6th Maine Vols., 10 March, 1862. 1st Lieut., 12 Feb., 1863. Capt., 13 Aug., 1863. Capt. 1st Maine Vet. Vols., 21 Aug., 1864. Bvt. Maj. Vols., 19 Oct., 1864, for gallant conduct during the whole campaign before Richmond, and especially in the Battles of Winchester, Fisher's Hill, and Cedar Creek, Va. Mustered out 28 June, 1865. 1st Lieut. 28th Inf., 28 July, 1866. Bvt. Capt., 2 March, 1867, for gallant and meritorious service in the Battle of Marye's Height, Va. Bvt. Maj., 2 March, 1867, for gallant and meritorious service in the Battle of Rappahannock Station, Va. Trans. to 19th Inf., 31 March, 1869. Capt., 20 March, 1879. Retired for over thirty years' service, 6 April, 1898.

**WITHERELL, JAMES B.** [Born in Mich. Appointed from Mich.]
2nd Lieut. 2nd Cav., 3 March, 1855. 1st Lieut., 28 June, 1860. Drowned 20 March, 1861.

**WITHERS, JOHN.*** [Born in Tenn. Appointed from Miss.]
Bvt. 2nd Lieut. 5th Inf., 1 July, 1849. 2nd Lieut. 4th Inf., 31 Jan., 1850. 1st Lieut., 31 July, 1854. R. Q. M., 30 Sept., 1853, to 10 Sept., 1856. Bvt. Capt. A. A. G., 27 June, 1856. Resigned 1 March, 1861.

**WITHERS, JONES M.*** [Born in Ala. Appointed from Ala.]
Bvt 2nd Lieut. 1st Drag., 1 July, 1835. Resigned 5 Dec., 1835. Lieut. Col. of Inf., 3 March, 1847; 13th Inf., 9 April, 1847. Col. 9th Inf., 13 Sept., 1847. Resigned 23 May, 1848. Died 13 March, 1890.

**WITHERSPOON, JOHN J.** [Born in Ky. Appointed from Ala.]
2nd Lieut. 13th Inf., 9 Sept., 1847. Died 22 Oct., 1847.

**WITTENMYER, EDMUND.*** [Born in Ohio. Appointed from Ohio.]
Addl. 2nd Lieut. 9th Inf., 12 June, 1887. 2nd Lieut., 15 June, 1887. 1st Lieut. 15th Inf., 27 Nov., 1894. Capt. 10th Inf., 2 March, 1899. Trans. to 15th Inf., 3 July, 1899. Graduate of the Infantry and Cavalry School, 1895. Reg. Adj., 18 July, 1899.

**WITTER, HENRY F.*** [Born in Pa. Appointed from Pa.]
Bvt. 2nd Lieut. 5th Inf., 1 July, 1851. 2nd Lieut., 13 March, 1854. Resigned 20 May, 1855. Died 9 Aug., 1856.

**WITTICH, WILLIS.*** [Born in Ohio. Appointed from Ohio.]
2nd Lieut. 21st Inf., 17 June, 1874. 1st Lieut., 7 Aug., 1879. Reg. Adj., 10 July, 1888. Capt., 18 July, 1890. Maj., 14 May, 1899.

**WOART, JOHN.** [Born in Mass. Appointed from Pa.]
Hosp. Chap. Vols., 22 March, 1865. Mustered out 2 June, 1866. Chap. Post Fort Union, N. M., 2 June, 1866, to 9 May, 1867. Post Chap., 3 April, 1867. Retired by operation of law, 30 June, 1882. Died 24 Nov., 1893.

**WOFFORD, JOHN.** [Born in Tenn. Appointed from Ga.]
Capt. of Inf., 20 March, 1847; 13th Inf., 9 April, 1847. Resigned 20 Aug., 1847.

**WOLCOTT, ALEX.** [Born in Conn. Appointed from Conn.]
Garrison Surg.'s Mate, 25 March, 1812. Post Surg., 24 April, 1816. Resigned 1 April, 1817.

**WOLCOTT, CHRISTOPHER C.*** [Born in Ohio. Appointed at Large.]
2nd Lieut. 3rd Art., 17 June, 1867. 1st Lieut., 1 May, 1873. Resigned 1 Nov., 1881.

**WOLCOTT, ERASTUS B.** [Born in N. Y. Appointed from N. Y.]
Asst. Surg., 1 Jan., 1836. Resigned 15 April, 1839.

**WOLCOTT, SOLOMON.** [Born in Conn. Appointed from Del.]
Garrison Surg.'s Mate, 8 April, 1814. Post Surg. 29 April, 1816. Resigned 15 Nov., 1816.

**WOLF, LOUIS C.*** [Born in Wis. Appointed from Wis.]
Addl. 2nd Lieut. Eng., 11 June, 1897. 2nd Lieut., 28 June, 1898. 1st Lieut., 26 Oct., 1898.

**WOLF, PAUL A.*** [Born in Ill. Appointed from Ill.]
2nd Lieut. 3rd Inf., 12 June, 1890. 1st Lieut. 4th Inf., 10 April, 1897. Graduate of the Infantry and Cavalry School, 1897. Reg. Com., 1 May, 1899.

**WOLF, SILAS A.*** [Born in Pa. Apointed from Pa.]
Addl. 2nd Lieut. 4th Inf., 14 June, 1878. 2nd Lieut., 28 June, 1878. 1st Lieut., 5 Aug., 1888. Capt., 19 Feb., 1895. Graduate of the Infantry and Cavalry School, 1885.

WOLFE, EDWIN P. [Born in Iowa. Appointed from N. Y.]
Asst. Surg., 12 Dec., 1898.

WOLFE, NATHANIEL. [Born in Ky. Appointed from Ky.]
Sergt. Maj. 28th Ky. Vols., 3 Jan., 1862. 1st Lieut. 28th Ky. Vols., 30 April, 1862. Mustered out 5 March, 1864. 2nd Lieut. 34th Inf., 22 Jan., 1867. Unassigned 14 April, 1869. Ass'd to 2nd Art., 14 July, 1869. 1st Lieut., 28 April, 1875. Died 4 Nov., 1886.

WOLFE, ORRIN R. [Born in Ky. Appointed from Army.]
Cadt Mil. Acad., 1 Sept., 1889, to 17 Jan., 1890. Priv. and Corpl. Cos. I and H, 14th Inf., 28 May, 1890, to 4 Feb., 1893. 2nd Lieut. 22nd Inf., 19 Nov., 1892. 1st Lieut., 26 April, 1898. Graduate of the Infantry and Cavalry School, 1897.

WOLFE, WM. V. [Born in Ky. Appointed from Ky.]
1st Lieut. 15th Ky. Vols., 14 Dec., 1861. Mustered out 9 Dec., 1862. 2nd Lieut. 35th Inf., 7 March, 1867. Unassigned 12 Aug., 1869. Ass'd to 2nd Inf., 29 April, 1870. 1st Lieut., 4 March, 1879. Died 8 May, 1881.

WOLLSTONECRAFT, CHARLES. [Birn in England. Appointed from Pa.]
Lieut. Art. and Eng., 4 June, 1798; Art., 1 June, 1802. Capt., 15 March, 1805. Trans. to Corps Art., 12 May, 1814. Died 28 Sept., 1817. Bvt. Maj., 15 March, 1815, for ten years' faithful service in one grade.

WOLVERTON, WM. D. [Born in N. J. Appointed from N. J.]
1st Lieut. Asst. Surg., 5 Aug., 1861. Bvt. Capt., Maj. and Lieut. Col., 13 March, 1865, for faithful and meritorious service during the war. Capt. Asst. Surg., 28 July, 1866. Maj. Surg., 26 June, 1876. Lieut. Col. Asst. Med. Pur., 9 March, 1892. Retired by operation of law, 21 Dec., 1898.

WOOD, ABRAM E.* [Born in Iowa. Appointed from Iowa.]
Corpl. Co. F, 13th Iowa Vols., 4 Oct., 1861. Sergt., 10 April, 1862. Re-enlisted Jan., 1864. 1st Sergt., 24 Dec., 1864. 2nd Lieut. 13th Iowa Vols., 1 July, 1865. Mustered out 21 July, 1865. Cadet at Mil. Acad., 1 July, 1868. 2nd Lieut. 4th Cav., 14 June, 1872. 1st Lieut., 25 Nov., 1876. R. Q. M., 6 July, 1879, to 1 Feb., 1880. Capt., 30 June, 1883. Died 14 April, 1894.

WOOD, ALLEN. [Born in Pa. Appointed from Ark.]
Capt. of Inf., 6 March, 1847; 12th Inf., 9 April, 1847. Disbanded 25 July, 1848. Bvt. Maj., 20 Aug., 1847, for gallant and meritorious conduct in the Battles of Contreras and Churubusco, Mex.

WOOD, BRADFORD R., Jr. [Born in N. Y. Appointed from N. Y.]
1st Lieut. 44th N. Y. Vols., 30 Aug., 1861. Capt., 7 Feb., 1864. Bvt. Maj. Vols., 13 March, 1865, for gallant and meritorious service during the war. Mustered out 13 Oct., 1864. 2nd Lieut. 22nd Inf., 28 July, 1866. Resigned 1 Jan., 1868. Bvt. 1st Lieut., 2 March, 1867, for gallant and meritorious service in the Battle of Spottsylvania, Va. Bvt. Capt., 2 March, 1867, for gallant and meritorious service at the Battle of Poplar Grove Churc, Va.

WOOD, CHAS. E. S.* [Born in Pa. Appointed at Large.]
2nd Lieut. 21st Inf., 17 June, 1874. 1st Lieut., 28 June, 1878. Resigned 22 Sept., 1884.

WOOD, CHAS. O. [Born in Ind. Appointed from Ind.]
2nd Lieut. 9th Inf., 26 April, 1861. 1st Lieut., 14 May, 1861. Capt., 30 May, 1863. Lieut. Col. 8th Cal. Vols., 1 Feb., 1865. Mustered out of Vols., 24 Oct., 1865. Unassigned 30 April, 1870. Discharged 13 Aug., 1870. Bvt. Maj., 13 March, 1865, for faithful and meritorious service. Bvt. Col. Vols., 13 March, 1865, for faithful and meritorious service.

WOOD, DAVID L. [Born in Conn. Appointed from Ohio.]
Capt. 18th Inf., 14 May, 1861. Wholly retired 11 Sept., 1863.

WOOD, EDWARD E.* [Born in Pa. Appointed from Pa.]
Com. Sergt. Co. C, 17th Pa. Cav., 8 Sept., 1862. 1st Sergt., 5 April, 1864. 1st Lieut. 17th Pa. Cav., 22 July, 1864. Mustered out 7 Aug., 1865. Cadet at Mil. Acad., 1 July, 1866. 2nd Lieut. 8th Cav., 15 June, 1870. 1st Lieut., 31 July, 1873. Capt., 20 Jan., 1886. Prof. Mil. Acad., 1 Oct., 1892.

WOOD, ELEAZER D.* [Born in N. Y. Appointed from N. Y.]
2nd Lieut. Eng., 30 Oct., 1806. 1st Lieut., 23 Feb., 1808. Capt., 1 July, 1812. Killed 17 Sept., 1814, in the Sortie from Fort Erie, U. C. Bvt. Maj., 6 May, 1813, for distinguished service in defence of Fort Meigs. Bvt. Lieut. Col., 25 July, 1814, for gallant conduct in the Battle of Niagara.

WOOD, EPHRAIM M. [Born in Ohio. Appointed from Ohio.]
Capt. 15th Inf., 14 May, 1861. Resigned 17 Feb., 1863.

WOOD, FRANCIS C. [Born in Vt. Appointed from Army.]
Priv., Corpl. and Sergt. Co. K, and Sergt. Maj. 1st (4th) Cav., 30 May, 1860, to 18 May, 1863. 2nd Lieut. 4th Cav., 12 May, 1863. Died 22 May, 1863, of wounds received in action at Middletown, Tenn.

WOOD, GEORGE K. [Born in N. J. Appointed from N. Y.]
Asst. Surg., 29 June, 1849. Resigned 1 Jan., 1861. Died 9 April, 1873.

WOOD, GEORGE W. [Born in Maine. Appointed from Maine.]
2nd Lieut. 18th Inf., 23 Feb., 1866. 1st Lieut., 21 Dec., 1866. Unassigned 15 April, 1870. Mustered out 1 Jan., 1871.

WOOD, GEORGE W. F. [Born in Pa. Appointed from Pa.]
2nd Lieut. 1st Inf., 1 Aug., 1838. 1st Lieut., 16 Nov., 1839. Reg. Adj., 1 March, 1840, to 31 July, 1843. Capt. A. Q. M., 3 March, 1847. Died 8 Nov., 1854. Bvt. Maj., 20 Aug., 1847, for gallant and meritorious conduct at Contreras and Churubusco, Mex.

WOOD, HENRY C. [Born in Maine. Appointed from Maine.]
2nd Lieut. 1st Inf., 27 June, 1856. 1st Lieut., 10 May, 1861. 1st Lieut., 11th Inf., 14 May, 1861. Capt., 24 Oct., 1861. Maj. A. A. G., 24 June, 1864. Bvt. Lieut. Col., 13 March, 1865, for gallant and meritorious service in the Battle of Wilson's Creek, Mo., 10 Aug., 1861. Bvt. Col., 13 March, 1865, for diligent, faithful and meritorious service in the A. G. Dept. during the war. Lieut. Col. A. A. G., 28 Feb., 1887. Col. A. A. G., 6 Nov., 1893. Retired by operation of law, 26 May, 1896. Medal of Honor for distinguished gallantry in the Battle

of Wilson's Creek, Mo., 10 Aug., 1861, where he was wounded; while serving as 1st Lieut., 11th U. S. Inf., commanding a detachment of recruits.

WOOD, INGHAM.* [Born in Pa. Appointed from Pa.]
Bvt. 2nd Lieut. 1st Inf., 1 July, 1831. 2nd Lieut., 30 Sept., 1833. Resigned 17 Dec., 1836. Died 13 Oct., 1837.

WOOD, JOHN. [Born in N. Y. Appointed from N. Y.]
Ensign 6th Inf., 29 July, 1813. 3rd Lieut., 17 Jan., 1814. 2nd Lieut., 1 May, 1814. Trans. to 2nd Inf., 17 May, 1815. 1st Lieut., 1 Jan., 1817. Resigned 31 Dec., 1819.

WOOD, JOHN D. [Born in Va. Appointed from Ill.]
Maj. Ill. Vols. (Black Hawk war), 16 June to 17 Aug., 1832. Maj. of Inf., 3 March, 1847; 14th Inf., 9 April, 1847. Resigned 12 Feb., 1848.

WOOD, JOSEPH H. [Born in N. Y. Appointed from Army.]
Priv. 2nd Cav., 24 Feb., 1863. 2nd Lieut. 6th Cav., 25 Feb., 1863. Maj. 15th N. Y. Cav., 16 Sept., 1863. Lieut. Col. 2nd N. Y. Mounted Rifles, 15 April, 1865. Mustered out Vols. 10 Aug., 1865. 1st Lieut., 20 Oct., 1864. Resigned 7 May, 1867. Bvt. 1st Lieut., 3 July, 1863, for gallant and meritorious service at the Battle of Gettysburg, Pa. Bvt. Capt., 28 July, 1864, for gallant and meritorious service in the campaign against the Sioux Indians.

WOOD, LAFAYETTE.* [Born in N. H. Appointed from Mass.]
Bvt. 2nd Lieut. 8th Inf., 1 July, 1843. 2nd Lieut., 31 Dec., 1845. 1st Lieut., 1 Jan., 1848. Capt., 19 July, 1858. Died 19 Oct., 1858. Bvt. 1st Lieut., 23 Sept., 1846, for gallant and meritorious conduct at Monterey. Bvt. Capt., 20 Aug., 1847, for gallant and meritorious conduct at Contreras and Churubusco, Mex.

WOOD, LEONARD. [Born in N. H. Appointed from Mass.]
Asst. Surg., 5 Jan., 1886. Capt. Asst. Surg., 5 Jan., 1891. Col. 1st U. S. Vols. Cav., 8 May, 1898. Brig. Gen. Vols., 8 July, 1898. Maj. Gen. Vols., 7 Dec., 1898, to 13 April, 1899. Brig. Gen. Vols., 13 April, 1899.

WOOD, MARSHALL W. [Born in N. Y. Appointed from N. Y.]
Priv. Co. E, 186th N. Y. Vols., 5 Sept., 1864. Discharged 15 June, 1865. Hosp. Stwd., 15 July, 1870. Discharged 12 Feb., 1875. 1st Lieut. Asst. Surg., 26 June, 1875. Capt. Asst. Surg., 26 June, 1880. Maj. Surg., 28 June, 1894.

WOOD, OLIVER E.* [Born in Conn. Appointed from Va.]
Priv. Co. B, 1st Conn. Cav., 29 July, 1862. Discharged 9 Sept., 1863. Cadet at Mil. Acad., 16 Sept., 1863. 2nd Lieut. 5th Art., 17 June, 1867. 1st Lieut., 11 June, 1870. Capt., 27 Aug., 1896. Lieut. Col. Chf. C. S. Vols., 9 May, 1898, to 17 April, 1899. Maj. C. S. Vols., 17 April, 1899. Graduate of the Artillery School, 1869, 1888.

WOOD, PALMER G. [Born in N. Y. Appointed from Cal.]
2nd Lieut. 7th Cal. Vols., 28 Oct., 1864. 1st Lieut., 7 Dec., 1865. Mustered out 26 April, 1866. 2nd Lieut. 5th Inf., 23 Feb., 1866. 1st Lieut., 7 Jan., 1867. Unassigned 19 May, 1869. Ass'd to 12th Inf., 14 July, 1869. Resigned 24 May, 1873. 2nd Lieut. 12th Inf., 1 March, 1877. 1st Lieut., 16 Oct., 1882. Capt., 11 Dec., 1893. Maj. 41st U. S. Vols., 17 Aug., 1899.

WOOD, PALMER G., Jr. [Born in Cal. Appointed from Cal.]
2nd Lieut. 12th Inf., 1 Sept., 1899.

WOOD, ROBT. C. [Born in R. I. Appointed from R. I.]
Asst. Surg., 28 May, 1825. Maj. Surg., 4 July, 1836. Col. Asst. Surg. Gen., 14 June, 1862, to 31 Oct., 1865. Died 28 March, 1869. Bvt. Lieut. Col., Col. and Brig. Gen., 13 March, 1865, for gallant and meritorious service during the war.

WOOD, ROBT. C., Jr. [Born in Minn. Appointed from La.]
Cadet at Mil. Acad., 1 July, 1850, to 15 Aug., 1853. 2nd Lieut. 2nd Cav., 3 March, 1855. Resigned 1 Jan., 1858.

WOOD, THOMAS J.* [Born in Ky. Appointed from Ky.]
Bvt. 2nd Lieut. Top. Eng., 1 July, 1845. Trans. to 2nd Drag., 19 Oct., 1846. 2nd Lieut., 2 Dec., 1846. Bvt. 1st Lieut., 23 Feb., 1847, for gallant and meritorious conduct in the Battles of Buena Vista. Reg. Adj., 23 Sept., 1849, to 1 July, 1854. 1st Lieut. 2nd Drag., 30 June, 1851. Capt. 1st Cav., 3 March, 1855. Maj., 16 March, 1861. Lieut. Col., 9 May, 1861; 4th Cav., 3 Aug., 1861. Brig. Gen. Vols., 11 Oct., 1861. Col. 2nd Cav., 12 Nov., 1861. Maj. Gen. Vols., 27 Jan., 1865. Bvt. Brig. Gen., 13 March, 1865, for gallant and meritorious service in the Battle of Chickamauga, Ga. Bvt. Maj. Gen., 13 March, 1865, for gallant and meritorious service in the Battle of Nashville, Tenn. Mustered out of Vol. Service, 1 Sept., 1866. Retired with rank of Maj. Gen., 9 June, 1868, and with rank of Brig. Gen., 3 March, 1875.

WOOD, WALWORTH W. [Born in Kan. Appointed from D. C.]
Priv. Co. E, 50th Pa. Vols., 23 Feb. to 12 Sept., 1864. 2nd Lieut. 1st Inf., 15 Oct., 1867. Unassigned 8 April, 1869. Ass'd to 20th Inf., 6 April, 1870. 1st Lieut., 25 Aug., 1874. Died 4 Aug., 1875.

WOOD, WM. H.* [Born in Mass. Appointed from Mass.]
Bvt. 2nd Lieut. 7th Inf., 1 July, 1845. 2nd Lieut. 3rd Inf., 21 Sept., 1846. 1st Lieut., 9 Sept., 1851. Reg. Adj., 1 May, 1860, to 11 April, 1861. Capt., 11 April, 1861. Maj. 17th Inf., 14 May, 1861. Lieut. Col. 1st Inf., 3 Dec., 1863. Bvt. Col., 13 March, 1865, for faithful and meritorious service during the war, declined. Col. 17th Inf., 22 Feb., 1869. Unassigned 15 March, 1869. Ass'd to 11th Inf., 15 Dec., 1870. Retired for over thirty years' service, 26 June, 1882. Died 1 Jan., 1887.

WOOD, WM. M. [Born in Kan. Appointed from Army.]
Cadet Mil. Acad., 16 June, 1887, to 25 June, 1888. Priv., Corpl. and Sergt. Co. E, and Sergt. Maj. 3rd Inf., 18 Dec., 1888, to 1 Aug., 1891. 2nd Lieut. of Inf. (12th), 31 July, 1891.

WOOD, WM. T.* [Born in Ill. Appointed from Ill.]
Adj. 2nd Lieut. 4th Inf., 15 June, 1877. 2nd Lieut. 18th Inf., 30 June, 1877. 1st Lieut., 15 Oct., 1886. R. Q. M., 21 June, 1887, to 22 Dec., 1888, and 22 June, 1890. Capt., 6 June, 1894.

WOOD, WM. W. [Born in Pa. Appointed from Pa.]
2nd Lieut. 32nd Inf., 15 May, 1867. Trans. to 21st Inf., 19 April, 1869. Unassigned 19 Aug., 1869. Ass'd to 13th Inf., 26 April, 1870. Resigned 1 May, 1872.

WOOD, WINTHROP S.* [Born in D. C. Appointed from Maine.]
Addl. 2nd Lieut. 2nd Cav., 12 June, 1889. 2nd Lieut. 10th Cav., 20 Aug., 1889. 1st Lieut. 9th Cav., 11 Dec., 1896. Capt. A. Q. M., 28 Nov., 1898. Honor graduate of the Infantry and Cavalry School, 1895.

WOODBRIDGE, FRANCIS.* [Born in Vt. Appointed from Vt.]
2nd Lieut. 2nd Art., 1 July, 1837. 1st Lieut., 9 July, 1838. R. Q. M., 8 Oct. to 6 Dec., 1847. Capt., 6 Dec., 1847. Died 20 Oct., 1855. Bvt. Capt., 20 Aug., 1847, for gallant and meritorious conduct in the Battles of Contreras and Churubusco, Mex. Bvt. Maj., 8 Sept., 1847, for gallant and meritorious conduct in the Battle of Molino del Rey, Mex.

WOODBRIDGE, FRANCIS. [Born in Mich. Appointed from Pa.]
Priv. Gen Ser., 11 May, 1869. Discharged 11 May, 1874. Priv. Gen. Ser., 11 May, 1874. Discharged 1 July, 1874. 2nd Lieut. 7th Inf., 1 Feb., 1876. 1st Lieut. 23 Feb., 1883. Retired for disability, 20 Feb., 1891. Died 22 April, 1891.

WOODBRIDGE, GEORGE.* [Born in Mass. Appointed from Mass.]
Bvt. 2nd Lieut. 1st Art., 1 July, 1826. 2nd Lieut. 3rd Art., 1 July, 1826. Resigned 30 June, 1829. Died 14 Feb., 1878.

WOODBURY, DANIEL P.* [Born in N. H. Appointed from N. H.]
2nd Lieut. 3rd Art., 1 July, 1836 Trans to Eng., 1 July, 1837, with rank of Bvt. 2nd Lieut. from 1 July, 1836. 1st Lieut., 7 July, 1838. Capt., 3 March, 1853. Maj., 6 Aug., 1861. Lieut. Col. A. A. de C., 28 Sept., 1861. Brig. Gen. Vols., 19 March, 1862. Lieut. Col., 1 June, 1863. Died 15 Aug., 1864. Bvt. Col., 1 July, 1862, for gallant and meritorious service during the Virginia Peninsular campaign. Bvt. Brig. Gen., 13 Dec., 1862, for gallant and meritorious service at the Battle of Fredericksburg, Va. Bvt. Maj. Gen., 15 Aug., 1864, for gallant and meritorious service during the war.

WOODBURY, PHINEAS. [Born in Vt. Appointed from Vt.]
Surg.'s Mate 25th Inf., 6 July, 1812. Maj. Surg., 30 March, 1814. Trans. to 8th Inf., 17 May, 1815. Died in Feb., 1818.

WOODBURY, THOS. C.* [Born in Ky. Appointed at Large.]
2nd Lieut. 16th Inf., 14 June, 1872. 1st Lieut., 9 March, 1880. R. Q. M., 1 Aug., 1889. Capt. 16th Inf., 29 Dec., 1890. Maj. 19th Inf., 8 July, 1899.

WOODHOUSE, LEVI. [Born in Conn. Appointed from Conn.]
2nd Lieut. of Inf., 16 March, 1847; 9th Inf., 9 April, 1847. 1st Lieut., 16 March, 1848. Disbanded 26 Aug., 1848. Bvt. 1st Lieut., 13 Sept., 1847, for gallant and meritorious conduct in the Battle of Chapultepec, Mex. Col. 4th Conn. Vols., 23 May, 1861. Resigned 31 Aug., 1861.

WOODHULL, ALFRED A. [Born in N. J. Appointed from Kan.]
1st Lieut. Asst. Surg., 19 Sept., 1861. Bvt. Capt., Maj. and Lieut. Col., 13 March, 1865, for faithful and meritorious service during the war. Capt. Asst. Surg., 28 July, 1866. Maj. Surg., 1 Oct., 1876. Lieut. Col. Dep. Surg. Gen., 16 May, 1894.

WOODMAN, STEPHEN. [Born in Maine. Appointed from Maine.]
2nd Lieut. 33rd Inf., 30 April, 1813. 1st Lieut., 31 May, 1814. Disbanded 15 June, 1815. Capt. of Inf., 23 Feb., 1847; 9th Inf., 9 April, 1847. Resigned 9 Oct., 1847.

WOODROW, HOWARD C. [Born in Ohio. Appointed from Ohio.]
Sergt. Co. H, 13th Ohio Vols., 21 June, 1861, to July, 1861. 1st Lieut. 17th Inf., 14 May, 1861. Capt., 8 Dec., 1863. Lieut. Col. 2nd La. Cav., 1 April, 1864. Mustered out Vols., 7 Sept., 1864. Resigned 19 Oct., 1865.

WOODRUFF, ALDEN M. [Born in Ark. Appointed from Ark.]
2nd Lieut. of Inf., 6 March, 1847; 12th Inf., 9 April, 1847. Disbanded 25 July, 1848.

WOODRUFF, CARLE A. [Born in N. Y. Appointed at Large.]
2nd Lieut. 2nd Art., 22 Oct., 1861. 1st Lieut., 24 July, 1862. Bvt. Capt., 3 July, 1863, for gallant and meritorious service in the Battle of Gettysburg, Pa. Bvt. Maj., 11 June, 1864, for gallant and meritorious service in the Battle of Trevillian Station, Va. Bvt. Lieut. Col., 13 March, 1865, for good conduct and gallant service during the war. Capt. 12th Inf., 28 July, 1866, declined. Capt. 2nd Art., 6 May, 1869. Maj. 8 March, 1894. Lieut. Col. 7th Art., 13 Feb., 1899. Medal of Honor for distinguished gallantry in action at Newby's Cross Roads, Va., 24 July, 1863; while serving as 1st Lieut., 2nd U. S. Art., commanding a section of horse Batty M, same Reg.

WOODRUFF, CHAS. A.* [Born in Vt. Appointed from Vt.]
Priv. Co. A, 10th Vt. Vols., 5 Jan., 1862. Corpl., 19 May, 1863. Discharged 18 Aug., 1865. Cadet at Mil. Acad., 1 July, 1867. 2nd Lieut. 7th Inf., 12 June, 1871. 1st Lieut., 9 Aug., 1877. Capt. C. S., 28 March, 1878. Maj. C. S., 27 Dec., 1892. Liuet. Col. A. C. G., 4 Feb., 1898. Col. A. C. G., 11 May, 1898. Bvt. Capt., 27 Feb., 1890, for gallant services in action against Ird ans at the Big Hole, Mont., 9 Aug., 1877, where he was three times wounded.

WOODRUFF, CHAS. E. [Born in N. Y. Appointed from N. Y.]
2nd Lieut. 2nd Inf., 8 March, 1837. 1st Lieut., 27 Nov., 1839. Died 17 April, 1841.

WOODRUFF, CHARLES E. [Born in Pa. Appointed from Pa.]
Asst. Surg., 14 April, 1887. Capt. Asst. Surg., 14 April, 1892. Maj. Brig. Surg. Vols., 4 June, 1898, to 22 Feb., 1899.

WOODRUFF, DICKINSON. [Born in N. J. Appointed from N. J.]
Lieut. Col. Batt. N. J. Vols., 4 Sept., 1847, to 20 July, 1848. Capt. 9th Inf., 3 March, 1855. Maj. 12th Inf., 30 May, 1863. Trans. to 21st Inf., 21 Sept., 1866. Lieut. Col. 9th Inf., 26 March, 1868. Unassigned 15 March, 1869. Retired 15 Dec., 1870. Died 11 Aug., 1896.

WOODRUFF, EDWARD C. [Born in N. Y. Appointed from N. J.]
Drum Maj. 2nd N. J. Vols., 2 May, 1861. Hosp. Stwd. 2nd N. J. Vols., — —, —. Discharged 31 July, 1861. 1st Lieut. 5th N. Y. Cav., 31 Oct., 1861. Mustered out 6 April, 1862. 2nd Lieut. 7th Inf., 24 March, 1862. Reg. Adj., 1 Jan., 1863, to 5 Sept., 1864. Bvt. 1st Lieut., 2 July, 1863, for gallant and meritorious service in the Battle of Gettysburg, Pa. 1st Lieut. 7th Inf., 10 Sept., 1863. Capt., 30 Dec., 1864. Bvt. Maj., 13 March, 1865, for gallant and meritorious service in the Battle of Gettysburg, Pa. Unassigned 19 May, 1869. Ass'd to 12th Inf., 14 July, 1869. Maj. 5th Inf., 2 Jan., 1888. Lieut. Col. 11th Inf. 22 April, 1892. Retired for over thirty years' service, 4 May, 1892.

WOODRUFF, EUGENE A.* [Born in Conn. Appointed from Iowa.]
2nd Lieut. Eng., 18 June, 1866. 1st Lieut., 7 March, 1867. Died 30 Sept., 1873.

WOODRUFF, EZRA. [Born in Ky. Appointed from Ky.]
Hosp. Stwd. 15th Ky. Vols., 3 Dec., 1861. Asst. Surg. 15th Ky. Vols., 7 March, 1863. Mustered out 18 Nov., 1863. 1st Lieut. Asst. Surg., 16 Nov., 1868. Capt. Asst. Surg., 7 March, 1871. Maj. Surg., 23 April, 1889.

WOODRUFF, GEORGE A.* [Born in Mich. Appointed from Mich.]
2nd Lieut. and 1st Lieut. 1st Art., 24 June, 1861. Died 4 July, 1863, of wounds received at the Battle of Gettysburg, Pa.

WOODRUFF, HARRY A. [Born in Ind. Appointed from N. Y.]
2nd Lieut. 13th Inf., 10 April, 1899. Trans. to 17th Inf., 8 June, 1899.

WOODRUFF, ISRAEL C.* [Born in N. J. Appointed from N. J.]
Bvt. 2nd Lieut. 3rd Art., 1 July, 1836. 2nd Lieut., 31 Aug., 1836. 2nd Lieut. Top. Eng., 7 July, 1838. 1st Lieut., 31 March, 1842. Capt., 3 March, 1853. Maj., 6 Aug., 1861. Trans. to Eng., 3 March, 1863. Lieut. Col., 15 Aug., 1864. Col., 22 Feb., 1869. Died 10 Dec., 1878. Bvt. Col., 13 March, 1865, for faithful and meritorious service in the Eng. Dept. during the war. Bvt. Brig. Gen., 13 March, 1865, for meritorious service during the war.

WOODRUFF, JAMES A.* [Born in Mont. Appointed from Vt.]
2nd Lieut. Eng., 15 Feb., 1899.

WOODRUFF, JOSEPH. [Born in Ga. Appointed from Ga.]
Capt. 3rd Inf., 12 Dec., 1808. Maj., 21 Feb., 1814. Discharged 15 June, 1815. Batt. P. M., 29 April, 1816. Retained as Maj. P. M., 1 June, 1821, to rank from 29 April, 1816. Resigned 31 May, 1822.

WOODRUFF, THOS. M.* [Born in N. Y. Appointed at Large.]
2nd Lieut. 5th Inf., 12 June, 1871. 1st Lieut., 5 July, 1879. Capt. 5th Inf., 9 March, 1891. Died 11 July, 1899, at Santiago, Cuba.

WOODS, BENJ'N W. [Born in Md. Appointed from Ky.]
Asst. Surg., 21 Aug., 1838. Disbanded 23 Sept., 1842.

WOODS, CHAS. R.* [Born in Ohio. Appointed from Ohio.]
Bvt 2nd Lieut. 1st Inf., 1 July, 1852. 2nd Lieut., 31 July, 1852. 2nd Lieut. 9th Inf., 3 March, 1855. 1st Lieut., 16 Oct., 1855. Capt., 1 April, 1861. Col. 76th Ohio Vols., 13 Oct., 1861. Bvt. Lieut. Col., 4 July, 1863, for gallant and meritorious service in the capture of Vicksburg, Miss. Brig. Gen. Vols., 4 Aug., 1863 Bvt. Col., 24 Nov., 1863, for gallant and meritorious conduct in the Battle of Chattanooga, Tenn. Maj. 18th Inf., 20 April, 1864. Bvt. Maj. Gen. Vols., 22 Nov., 1864, for long and continued service and for special gallantry at Griswoldville, Ga. Bvt. Brig. Gen., 13 March, 1865, for gallant and meritorious service in the Battles before Atlanta, Ga. Bvt. Maj. Gen., 13 March, 1865, for gallant and meritorious service in the Battle of Bentonville, N. C. Mustered out of Vol. Service, 1 Sept., 1866. Trans. to 27th Inf., 21 Sept., 1866. Lieut. Col. 33rd Inf., 28 July, 1866. Unassigned 15 March, 1869. Ass'd to 5th Inf., 24 March, 1869. Col. 2nd Inf., 18 Feb., 1874. Retired 15 Dec., 1874. Died 26 Feb., 1885.

WOODS, JAMES S.* [Born in Pa. Appointed from Pa.]
Bvt. 2nd Lieut. 4th Inf., 1 July, 1844. 2nd Lieut. 2nd Inf., 18 June, 1846. Killed 21 Sept., 1846, in the Battle of Monterey, Mex. Bvt. 1st Lieut., 9 May, 1846, for gallant conduct in the Battles of Palo Alto and Reseca de la Palma.

WOODS, JOSEPH J.* [Born in Ohio. Appointed from Ohio.]
2nd Lieut. 1st Art., 1 July, 1847. 1st Lieut., 29 Oct., 1848. Resigned 31 Oct., 1853. Col. 12th Iowa Vols., 25 Nov., 1861. Mustered out 22 Nov., 1864. Died 27 Sept., 1889.

WOODS, SAM'L.* [Born in Ind. Appointed from Ind.]
2nd Lieut. 6th Inf., 1 July, 1837. 1st Lieut., 25 Dec., 1837. Capt., 27 Feb., 1843. Maj. 15th Inf., 9 April, 1847, to 7 Aug., 1848. Bvt. Maj. and Lieut. Col., 13 Sept., 1847, for gallant and meritorious conduct in the Battle of Chapultepec. Maj. P. M., 24 Dec., 1856. Bvt. Lieut. Col., 13 March, 1865, for faithful and meritorious service during the war. Lieut. Col. Dep. P. M. G., 7 June, 1879. Col. A. P. M. G., 8 June, 1880. Retired for over forty years' service, 24 Jan., 1881. Died 22 Sept., 1887.

WOODSON, ALBERT E. [Born in Ky. Appointed from Idaho.]
Priv. Co. E, 1st Wash. Vols., 27 May, 1862. Hosp. Stwd. 1st Wash. Vols., 31 Aug., 1862. 2nd Lieut. 1st Wash. Vols., 14 April, 1863. Mustered out 25 March, 1865. 1st Lieut. 36th Inf., 5 Aug., 1867. Unassigned 19 May, 1869. Ass'd to 5th Cav., 15 Dec., 1870. Capt., 1 July, 1876. Maj. 9th Cav., 14 Oct., 1896.

WOODSON, GEORGE T. [Born in Va. Appointed from Mo.]
Priv. Co. A. 3rd Batt. D. C. Vols., 15 April, to 20 June, 1861. Capt. 16th Inf., 14 May, 1861. Dismissed 13 Jan., 1863.

WOODSON, ROBERT S. [Born in Va. Appointed from Ala.]
Cadet Mil. Acad., 1 Sept., 1884, to 16 Jan., 1885. Asst. Surg., 5 May, 1892. Capt. Asst. Surg., 5 May, 1897.

WOODWARD, AMOS. [Born in Md. Appointed from Md.]
2nd Lieut 14th Inf., 4 June, 1812. 1st Lieut., 13 May, 1813. Disbanded 15 June, 1815. 3rd Lieut. Ord., 13 Aug., 1819. 2nd Lieut., 17 May, 1820. Trans. to 3rd Inf., 1 June, 1821. Resigned 1 Nov., 1821.

WOODWARD, CHAS. G.* [Born in Md. Appointed from Md.]
Addl. 2nd Lieut. 4th Art., 15 June, 1877. 2nd Lieut. 3rd Art., 2 July, 1877. 1st Lieut., 3 Dec., 1884. Capt. 4th Art., 13 Feb., 1899. Trans. to 6th Art., 21 April, 1899. Graduate of the Artillery School, 1882. Reg. Adj., 14 Aug., 1899.

WOODWARD, GEORGE A. [Born in Pa. Appointed from Pa.]
Capt. 2nd Pa. Res. Vet. Corps, 27 May, 1861. Maj., 2 April, 1862. Lieut. Col., 20 Feb., 1863. Mustered out, 29 Aug., 1863. Maj. Vet. Res. Corps, 24 Aug., 1863. Lieut. Col., 25 Sept., 1863. Col., 4 Dec., 1863. Mustered out 20 July, 1866. Lieut. Col. 45th Inf., 28 July, 1866. Bvt. Col., 2 March, 1867, for gallant and meritorious service in the Battle of Gettysburg, Pa. Trans. to 14th Inf., 15 March, 1869. Col. 15th Inf., 10 Jan., 1876. Retired 20 March, 1879, for disability from wound.

WOODWARD, JOHN E.* [Born in Vt. Appointed from Vt.]
2nd Lieut. 16th Inf., 11 June, 1892. 1st Lieut., 26 April, 1898. Reg. Com., 31 May, 1899.

WOODWARD, JOSEPH J. [Born in Pa. Appointed from Pa.]
1st Lieut. Asst. Surg., 5 Aug., 1861. Bvt. Capt., Maj. and Lieut. Col., 13 March, 1865, for faithful and meritorious service during the war. Capt. Asst. Surg., 28 July, 1866. Maj. Surg., 26 June, 1876. Died 17 Aug., 1884.

WOODWARD, SAML. L. [Born in N. J. Appointed from Ky.]
Priv. Co. G, 6th Ill. Cav., 1 Feb., 1862. 2nd Lieut. 6th Ill. Cav., 1 Nov., 1862. 1st Lieut., 16 March, 1863. Capt. A. A. G. Vols., 21 July, 1863. Maj. A. A. G. Vols., 11 Feb., 1865. Mustered out 19 Sept., 1865. 2nd Lieut. 10th Cav., 18 June, 1867. Reg. Adj., 1 Oct., 1867, to 1 Oct., 1876, and from 24 Sept., 1883, to 30 Sept., 1887. 1st Lieut., 11 Dec., 1867. Bvt. Capt., 11 Dec., 1867, for gallant and meritorious service during the raid through Miss. in April, 1863. Bvt. Maj., 11 Dec., 1867, for gallantry during the fight at Egypt Station, Miss., 28 Dec., 1864. Capt., 5 Oct., 1887.

WOODWARD, SOLOMON E. [Born in Mass. Appointed from Vt.]
1st Leiut. 15th Inf., 5 Aug., 1861. Capt., 13 March, 1865. Trans. to 24th Inf., 21 Sept., 1866. Resigned 30 Sept., 1866. Bvt. Capt., 31 Dec., 1862, for gallant and meritorious service at the Battle of Murfreesboro, Tenn. Bvt. Maj., 1 Sept., 1864, for gallant and meritorious service during the Atlanta campaign.

WOOL, JOHN E. [Born in N.Y. Appointed from N. Y.]
Capt. 13th Inf., 14 April, 1812. Maj. 29th Inf., 13 April, 1813. Trans. to 6th Inf., 17 May, 1815. Col. I. G., 29 April, 1816, to 25 June, 1841. Lieut. Col. 6th Inf., 10 Feb., 1818. Brig. Gen., 25 June, 1841. Maj. Gen., 16 May, 1862. Retired 1 Aug., 1863. Bvt. Lieut. Col., 11 Sept., 1814, for gallant conduct at the Batle of Platsburg. Bvt. Brig. Gen., 29 April, 1826, for ten years' faithful service in one grade. Bvt. Maj. Gen., 23 Feb., 1847, for gallant and meritorious conduct in the Battle of Buena Vista, Mex. By resolution of Congress of 15 Jan., 1854, it was resolved: "That the thanks of Congress are due, and are hereby tendered, to Bvt. Maj. Gen. John E. Wool, for his distinguished service in the war with Mex., and especially for the skill, enterprise and courage which distinguished his conduct at the Battle of Buena Vista that the President be requested to cause a sword with suitable devices to be presented to Gen. Wool, as a testimony of the high sense entertained by Congress of his gallant and judicious conduct on that memorable occasion." Died 10 Nov., 1869.

WOOLEY, FREDERICK.* [Born in N. C. Appointed from N. C.]
2nd Lieut. 10th Inf., 14 June, 1878. 1st Lieut., 16 Feb., 1885. Resigned 1 Jan., 1897.

WOOLFOLK, AUSTIN C. [Born in Mo. Appointed from Ill.]
Capt. A. Q. M. Vols., 19 Feb., 1862. Capt. A. Q. M., 5 Dec., 1863 Resigned 1 May, 1886. Bvt. Maj., 13 March, 1865, for faithful and meritorious service during the war. Died 15 Feb., 1880.

WOOLFORD, JAMES H. [Born in Md. Appointed from Md.]
1st Lieut. of Inf., 24 Feb., 1847; Voltigeurs, 9 April, 1847. Resigned 31 Dec., 1847. Died 15 May, 1888.

WOOLLEY, ABRAM R. [Born in N. J. Appointed from N. J.]
Capt. Dep. Com. Ord., 4 Dec., 1812. Maj. Ord., 9 Feb., 1815. Trans. to 7th Inf., 1 June, 1821. Trans. to 6th Inf., 11 March, 1823. Lieut. Col. 6th Inf., 16 Dec., 1826. Dismissed 1 May, 1829. Bvt. Lieut. Col., 9 Feb., 1825, for ten years' faithful service in one grade.

WOOSTER, CHAS. F.* [Born in N. Y. Appointed from N. Y.]
2nd Lieut. 4th Art., 1 July, 1837. 1st Lieut., 10 June, 1842. Capt., 27 Sept., 1850. Died 14 Feb., 1856. Bvt. Capt., 28 Feb., 1847, for gallant and meritorious conduct at Sacramento, near Chihuahua, Mex.

WOOTEN, WM. P.* [Born in N. C. Appointed from N. C.]
Addl. 2nd Lieut. Eng., 26 April, 1898. 2nd Lieut., 5 July, 1898.

WORDEN, CHAS A.* [Born in N. Y. Appointed from N. Y.]
2nd Lieut. 7th Inf., 14 June, 1872. 1st Lieut., 20 March, 1879. Reg. Adj., 1 Oct., 1885, to 1 Sept., 1889. 1st Lieut., 20 March, 1879. Capt. of Inf. (7th), 10 July, 1891. Died 21 Sept., 1898.

WORDEN, JOHN L., Jr. [Born in D. C. Appointed from N. Y.]
Cadet Mil. Acad., 1 July, 1862, to 1 April, 1864. 2nd Lieut., 13th N. Y. Art., 27 July, 1864. Trans. to 6th N. Y. Art., 27 June, 1865. Capt. A. A. G. Vols., 21 July, 1865. Mustered out 10 Nov., 1865. 2nd Lieut. 1st Inf., 25 April, 1866. 1st Lieut., 1 Jan., 1867. Died 4 May, 1873.

WORKIZER, JOHN G.* [Born in Mo. Appointed from Mo.]
Addl. 2nd Lieut. 2nd Inf., 11 June, 1897. 2nd Lieut. 19th Inf., 8 March, 1898. Trans. to 2nd Inf., 1 Dec., 1898. 1st Lieut., 2 March, 1899.

WORRELL, EDWARD. [Born in Del. Appointed from Del.]
Asst. Surg., 24 Feb., 1832. Disbanded 23 Sept., 1842. Died 25 March, 1877.

WORRILOW, ULYSSES G. [Born in Pa. Appointed from Army.]
Priv. and Corpl. Co. D, 13th Inf., 12 March, 1889, to 1 Nov., 1894. 2nd Lieut. 20th Inf., 31 Oct., 1894. 1st Lieut., 26 April, 1898.

WORTH, HENRY A. F.* [Born in Va. Appointed at Large.]
Bvt. 2nd Lieut. 8th Inf., 1 July, 1859. 2nd Lieut. 6th Inf., 5 June, 1860. 1st Lieut., 7 May, 1861. Capt., 27 June, 1862. Resigned 14 July, 1863.

WORTH, JOSEPH S.* [Born in Mass. Appointed from N. Y.]
Bvt. 2nd Lieut. 3rd Inf., 1 July, 1825. 2nd Lieut. 6th Inf., 1 July, 1825. 1st Lieut., 22 April, 1830. Capt., 31 July, 1837. Trans. to 8th Inf., 7 July, 1838. Died 21 July, 1846.

WORTH, WM. J. [Born in N. Y. Appointed from N. Y.]
1st Lieut. 23rd Inf., 19 March, 1813. Capt., 19 Aug., 1814. Trans. to 2nd Inf., 17 May, 1815. Trans. to 1st Art., 1 June, 1821. Maj. Ord., 30 May, 1832. Col. 8th Inf., 7 July, 1838. Bvt. Capt., 5 July, 1814, for gallant and distinguished conduct at the Battle of Chippewa. Bvt. Maj., 25 July, 1814, for gallantry and good conduct at the Battle of Niagara. Bvt. Lieut. Col., 25 July, 1824, for ten years' faithful service in the grade of Bvt. Maj. Bvt. Brig. Gen., 1 March, 1842, for gallant and highly distinguished service in the war against the Florida Indians. Bvt. Maj. Gen., 23 Sept., 1846, for gallant and meritorious conduct at Monterey, Mex. Presented with a sword by resolution of Congress, 2 March, 1847, in testimony of the high sense entertained of his gallantry and good conduct in the storming of Monterey, Mex. Died 7 May, 1849.

WORTH, WM. S. [Born in N. Y. Appointed from N. Y.]
2nd Lieut. 8th Inf., 26 April, 1861. 1st Lieut., 7 June, 1861. Reg. Adj., 25 Sept., 1861, to 13 April, 1862. Bvt. Capt., 1 Aug., 1864, for gallant and distinguished service in the assault on the enemy's lines before Petersburg, and in the operations in the campaign against Richmond, Va. Bvt. Maj., 9 April, 1865, for gallant and meritorious service during the campaign terminating with the surrender of the insurgent army under Gen. R. E. Lee. Capt. 8th Inf., 14 Jan., 1866. Maj. 2nd Inf., 9 March, 1891. Lieut. Col. 13th Inf., 26 Nov., 1894. Col. 16th Inf., 11 Aug., 1898. Brig. Gen., 20 Oct., 1898. Brig. Gen. Vols., 12 July to 30 Oct., 1898. Retired, over thirty years' service, 9 Nov., 1898.

WORTHINGTON, JAMES C. [Born in Md. Appointed from Md.]
1st Lieut. Asst. Surg., 26 June, 1875. Capt. Asst. Surg., 26 June, 1880. Maj. Surg., 31 May, 1893. Died 11 Aug., 1896.

WORTHINGTON, THOS.* [Born in Ohio. Appointed from Ohio.]
Bvt. 2nd Lieut. Art., 1 July, 1827. Resigned 8 Nov., 1828. 1st Lieut. and Adj. 2nd Ohio Vols., 23 June to 31 Oct., 1846. Lieut. Col. 46th Ohio Vols., 23 Oct., 1861. Col., 30 Jan., 1862. Resigned 21 Nov., 1862. Died 23 Feb., 1884.

WOTHERSPOON, ALEX. S. [Born in N. Y. Appointed from N. Y.]
Asst. Surg., 11 Nov., 1843. Died 4 May, 1854.

WOTHERSPOON, WM. W. [Born in D. C. Appointed from D. C.]
2nd Lieut. 12th Inf., 1 Oct., 1873. 1st Lieut., 20 March, 1879. R. Q. M., 1 July, 1879. Capt., 28 April, 1893.

WRAGG, SAM'L.* [Born in S. C. Appointed from S. C.]
Bvt. 2nd Lieut. 4th Inf., 1 July, 1822. 2nd Lieut. 1st Inf., 1 July, 1822. Trans. to 1st Inf., 23 Dec., 1822. Reg. Adj., 17 Sept., 1823, to 1 Aug., 1825. Died 27 Nov., 1838.

WREN, WM. C. [Born in Minn. Appointed from N. Y.]
Cadet at Mil. Acad., 1 July, 1880, to 15 Feb., 1882. 2nd Lieut. 10th Inf., 30 Oct., 1884. 1st Lieut. 17th Inf., 8 Aug., 1891. Capt. of Inf., 23 Dec., 1898. Ass'd to 7th Inf., 25 Dec., 1898. Trans. to 17th Inf., 11 Jan., 1899. Graduate of the Infantry and Cavalry School, 1891.

WRIGHT, AARON M.* [Born in N. H. Appointed from N. H.]
Bvt. 2nd Lieut. 3rd Inf., 1 July, 1822. 2nd Lieut., 1 July, 1822. Dismissed 31 March, 1826.

WRIGHT, ABEL W. [Born in Conn. Appointed from Wis.]
2nd Lieut. of Inf., 6 March, 1847; 15th Inf., 9 April, 1847. Disbanded 4 Aug., 1848.

WRIGHT, ALLEN G. [Born in ——. Appointed from ——.]
2nd Lieut. 14th Inf., — ——, 1898. Resigned 31 Dec., 1898.

WRIGHT, ALPHA. [Born in Vt. Appointed from Neb.]
Chap. 25th Mo. Vols., 25 April, 1863. Trans. to 1st Mo. Eng., 17 Feb., 1864. Discharged 20 April, 1864. Chap. 6th Mo. Cav., 20 April, 1864. Mustered out 6 March, 1865. Chap. 2nd U. S. Vols., 7 March, 1865. Mustered out 11 Dec., 1865. Chap. Post of Fort Laramie, 11 Dec., 1865, to 18 May, 1867. Post Chap., 3 April, 1867. Retired 3 Oct., 1879. Died 30 Nov., 1888.

WRIGHT, ANDREW C. [Born in Ill. Appointed from Army.]
Priv., Corpl. and Sergt. Batty C, 5th Art., 8 Sept., 1896, to 15 Nov., 1899. 2nd Lieut. 12th Inf., 1 Oct., 1899.

WRIGHT, BENJN. H.* [Born in N. Y. Appointed from N. Y.]
2nd Lieut. 2nd Inf., 1 July, 1822. Resigned 1 June, 1823. Died 13 May, 1881.

WRIGHT, CLINTON. [Born in Md. Appointed from Md.]
Cornet 1st Light Drag., 19 Jan., 1813. 3rd Lieut., 29 April, 1813. 2nd Lieut. 2nd Light Drag., 19 April, 1814. Trans. to 4th Inf., 17 May, 1815. Maj. A. A. G., 29 April, 1816. Drowned 24 Feb., 1818.

WRIGHT, CRAFTS J.* [Born in N. Y. Appointed from Ohio.]
Bvt. 2nd Lieut. Inf., 1 July, 1828. Resigned 8 Nov., 1828. Col. 13th Mo. Vols., 13 Aug., 1861. Resignation changed to 22nd Ohio Vols., 29 May, 1862. Resigned 16 Sept., 1862. Died 23 July, 1883.

WRIGHT, EDMUND S.* [Born in Ga. Appointed from Ky.]
2nd Lieut. 9th Cav., 1 July, 1886. 1st Lieut. 1st Cav., 30 June, 1893.

WRIGHT, EDWARD. [Born in Mass. Appointed from Ill.]
Maj. 1st Ill. Cav., 7 Sept., 1861. Mustered out 14 July, 1862. Maj. A. D. C. Vols., 8 Nov., 1862. Discharged 15 Aug., 1863. Maj. P. M., 23 Feb., 1864. Resigned 1 Oct., 1873. Bvt. Lieut. Col., 13 March, 1865, for faithful and meritorious service

during the war. Bvt. Col., 13 March, 1865, for gallant service at James' Island, S. C. Died 24 Dec., 1873.

WRIGHT, EDWARD H. [Born in N. J. Appointed from N. J.]
Maj. 3rd Cav., 14 May, 1861. 6th Cav., 3 Aug., 1861. Lieut. Col A. de C. to Lieut. Gen. Scott, 1 June, 1861, to 19 Aug., 1861. Col. A. A. de C., 19 Aug., 1861. Discharged as A. A. de C., 1 Nov., 1861. Col. A. A. de C., 15 Jan., 1862. Discharged as A. A. de C., 31 March, 1863. Resigned 25 April, 1863.

WRIGHT, EDWARD M.* [Born in Ind. Appointed from Ind.]
2nd Lieut. Ord., 18 June, 1866. 1st Lieut., 23 June, 1874. Capt., 25 March, 1876. Died 24 April, 1880.

WRIGHT, GEORGE.* [Born in Vt. Appointed from Vt.]
2nd Lieut. 3rd Inf., 1 July, 1822. 1st Lieut., 23 Sept., 1827. Reg. Adj., 1 Feb., 1831, to 30 Oct., 1836. Capt., 30 Oct., 1836. Trans. to 8th Inf., 7 July, 1838. Maj. 4th Inf., 1 Jan., 1848. Lieut. Col., 3 Feb., 1855. Col. 9th Inf., 3 March, 1855. Brig. Gen. Vols., 28 Sept., 1861. Drowned 30 July, 1865. Bvt. Maj., 15 March, 1842, for meritorious conduct, zeal, energy and perseverance in the war against the Florida Indians. Bvt. Lieut. Col., 20 Aug., 1847, for gallant and meritorious conduct at Contreras and Churubusco, Mex. Bvt. Col., 8 Sept., 1847, for gallant and meritorious conduct at Molino del Rey. Bvt. Brig. Gen., 19 Dec., 1864, for long, faithful and meritorious service.

WRIGHT, GEORGE. [Born in Pa. Appointed from Army.]
Hosp. Stwd., 10 June, 1861, to 23 Aug., 1862. Med. Storekeeper, 13 Aug., 1862. Resigned 1 Jan., 1866. Capt. Med. Storekeeper, 28 July, 1866. Died 19 May, 1872.

WRIGHT, GEORGE B. [Born in Ohio. Appointed from Ohio.]
Mil. Storekeeper Ord., 24 Nov., 1863. Resigned 31 March, 1864.

WRIGHT, GEORGE H. [Born in Canada. Appointed from Wis.]
Priv. Co. B, 1st Wis. Cav., 15 Sept., 1861. Discharged 30 Dec., 1862. 1st Lieut. 39th Wis. Vols., 3 June, 1864. Mustered out 22 Sept., 1864. 2nd Lieut. 7th Inf., 7 March, 1867. 1st Lieut., 12 Jan., 1873. Died 4 March, 1881.

WRIGHT, GEORGE M. [Born in Mass. Appointed from Mass.]
2nd Lieut. 3rd Art., 19 Feb., 1862. 1st Lieut., 24 July, 1862. Dismissed 30 Dec., 1864.

WRIGHT, HENRY H. [Born in D. C. Appointed from D. C.]
2nd Lieut. 9th Cav., 12 Dec., 1872. 1st Lieut., 18 March, 1880. Capt., 12 Dec., 1890. Bvt. 1st Lieut., 27 Feb., 1890, for gallant services in actions against Indians in the Florida Mountains, N. M., 24 Jan., 1877; in the Sacramento Mountains, N. M., 29 July, 1878; and in the Miembres Mountains, N. M., 29 May, 1879.

WRIGHT, HORATIO G.* [Born in Conn. Appointed from Conn.]
2nd Lieut. Eng., 1 July, 1841. 1st Lieut., 28 Feb., 1848. Capt., 1 July, 1855. Maj. 13th Inf., 14 May, 1861, declined. Maj. Eng., 6 Aug., 1861. Brig. Gen. Vols., 14 Sept., 1861. Maj. Gen. Vols., 18 July, 1862. Rejected by the Senate, 12 March, 1863, and revoked 24 March, 1863. Brig. Gen. Vols., 24 March, 1863. Bvt. Lieut. Col., 8 Nov., 1863, for gallant and meritorious service in the Battle of Rappahannock Station, Va. Bvt. Col., 12 May, 1864, for gallant and meritorious service in the Battle of Spottsylvania, Va. Maj. Gen. Vols., 12 May, 1864. Bvt. Brig. Gen., 13 March, 1865, for gallant and meritorious service in the Battle of Cold Harbor, Va. Bvt. Maj. Gen., 13 March, 1865, for gallant and meritorious service in the capture of Petersburg, Va. Lieut. Col. Eng., 23 Nov., 1865. Mustered out of Vol. Service, 1 Sept., 1866. Col. Eng., 4 March, 1879. Brig. Gen. Chief of Eng., 30 June, 1879. Retired by operation of law, 6 March, 1884. Died 2 July, 1899.

WRIGHT, IRWIN B. [Born in Ind. Appointed from Ind.]
Priv. Co. B, 20th Ohio Vols., 14 May to 1 June, 1861. 2nd Lieut. 11th Inf., 19 Feb., 1862. 1st Lieut., 15 Dec., 1862. Trans. to 20th Inf., 21 Sept., 1866. Resigned 1 Nov., 1866. Bvt. Capt., 2 July, 1863, for gallant and meritorious at the Battle of Gettysburg, Pa.

WRIGHT, JAMES.* [Born in Canada. Appointed from N. Y.]
Bvt. 2nd Lieut. Mounted Rifles, 1 July, 1854. 2nd Lieut., 3 March, 1855. Died 26 Oct., 1857.

WRIGHT, JAMES H.* [Born in Ga. Appointed from S. C.]
Bvt. 2nd Lieut. 6th Inf., 1 July, 1829. Died 21 Sept, 1830.

WRIGHT, JOHN.* [Born in Vt. Appointed from Vt.]
2nd Lieut. Eng., 30 March, 1814. Resigned 23 July, 1818. Died 10 Sept., 1860.

WRIGHT, JOHN W. [Born in Mo. Appointed from D. C.]
1st Lieut. 5th U. S. Vols., 9 June, 1898. Capt., 9 Feb. to 31 May, 1899. 2nd Lieut. 5th Inf., 10 April, 1899.

WRIGHT, JOSEPH J. B. [Born in Pa. Appointed from Pa.]
Asst. Surg., 25 Oct., 1833. Maj. Surg., 26 March, 1844. Col. and Surg., 26 June, 1876. Retired 31 Dec., 1876. Died 14 May, 1878. Bvt. Col., 23 Nov., 1865. Bvt. Brig. Gen., 13 March, 1865, for faithful and meritorious service during the war.

WRIGHT, JOSEPH P. [Born in Pa. Appointed from Pa.]
1st Lieut. Asst. Surg., 28 May, 1861. Bvt. Capt., Maj. and Lieut. Col., 13 March, 1865, for faithful and meritorious service during the war. Capt. Asst. Surg., 28 May, 1866. Maj. Surg., 28 July, 1866. Lieut. Col. Surg., 23 April, 1889. Col. Asst. Surg. Gen., 16 May, 1894.

WRIGHT, MOSES H.* [Born in Tenn. Appointed from Tenn.]
Bvt. 2nd Lieut. Ord., 1 July, 1859. 2nd Lieut., 3 April, 1861. Resigned 30 May, 1861. Died 8 Jan., 1886.

WRIGHT, ROBERT. [Born in Md. Appointed from Md.]
Cadet at Mil. Acad., 9 June, 1814, to 4 June, 1818. 2nd Lieut. Corps Art., 13 Aug., 1819. Disbanded 1 June, 1821. Died 21 April, 1884.

WRIGHT, THOMAS. [Born in Pa. Appointed from Pa.]
Ensign 22nd Inf., 9 April, 1812. 2nd Lieut., 16 April, 1813. 1st Lieut., 17 March, 1814. Reg. P. M., 8 Dec., 1812, to June, 1815. Trans. to 8th Inf., 17 May, 1815. Capt., 25 Sept., 1817. Retained 1 June, 1821, as Maj. P. M., to rank from 22 June, 1815. Died 9 Nov., 1834.

WRIGHT, THOS.* [Born in Ga. Appointed from Ga.]
Bvt. 2nd Lieut. 7th Inf., 1 July, 1849. 2nd Lieut. 2nd Inf., 16 Oct., 1849. 1st Lieut., 5 Feb., 1855. Died 12 Oct., 1857.

WRIGHT, THOS. F. [Born in Mo. Appointed from Cal.]
1st Lieut. R. Q. M. 2nd Cal. Cav., 2 Oct., 1861. Resigned 31 Jan., 1863. Maj. 6th Cal. Cav., 1 Feb., 1863. Maj. 2nd Cal. Vols., 3 Oct., 1864. Lieut. Col., 23 Nov., 1864. Col., 6 Jan., 1865. Bvt. Brig. Gen. Vols., 13 March, 1865, for faithful and meritorious service. Mustered out 16 April, 1866. 1st Lieut. 32nd Inf., 28 July, 1866. R. Q. M., 15 July, 1867, to 12 May, 1869. Unassigned 12 May, 1869. Ass'd to 12th Inf., 31 Jan., 1870. Reg. Adj., 8 March to 8 June, 1870. Killed 26 April, 1872, by Modoc Indians in Oregon.

WRIGHT, THOS. J.* [Born in Pa. Appointed at Large.]
Bvt. 2nd Lieut. 2nd Drag., 1 July, 1854. 2nd Lieut., 3 March, 1855. 1st Lieut., 28 Feb., 1857. Reg. Adj., 12 June, 1855, to 30 April, 1857. Died 30 April, 1857.

WRIGHT, THOS. S. [Born in Mass. Appointed from Army.]
Priv. and Sergt. Co. H, 14th Inf., 21 Aug., 1861, to 27 June, 1862. 2nd Lieut. 14th Inf., 9 June, 1862. Cashiered 21 July, 1862.

WRIGHT, WALTER K.* [Born in N. Y. Appointed from N. Y.]
2nd Lieut. 16th Inf., 13 June, 1883. 1st Lieut., 1 Oct., 1888. Capt. 7th Inf., 26 April, 1898. Maj. C. S. Vols., 7 June, 1898, to 12 May, 1899.

WRIGHT, WM. [Born in Md. Appointed from Md.]
Cadet at Mil. Acad., 4 Feb., 1816, to 5 Aug., 1817. Lieut. Marine Corps, 28 Jan., 1818, to 8 May, 1818. 3rd Lieut. Corps Art., 18 April, 1818. 2nd Lieut., 20 April, 1818. 1st Lieut., 23 Aug., 1820. Trans. to 4th Art., 1 June, 1821. Resigned 31 Dec., 1822.

WRIGHT, WM. D. [Born in Ga. Appointed from Army.]
Priv. and Sergt. Sig. Corps, 19 April, 1872, to 20 March, 1882. 2nd Lieut. Sig. Corps, 27 Jan., 1882. Dropped 28 April, 1890.

WRIGHT, WM. H.* [Born in N. C. Appointed from N. C.]
2nd Lieut. 1st Art., 1 July, 1838. 2nd Lieut. Eng., 7 July, 1838. 1st Lieut., 7 Dec., 1838. Died 29 Dec., 1845.

WRIGHT, WM. M. [Born in N. J. Appointed from N. J.]
Cadet at Mil. Acad., 1 July, 1882, to 11 Jan., 1883. 2nd Lieut. 2nd Inf., 19 Jan., 1885. 1st Lieut. 5th Inf., 17 Dec., 1891. Trans. to 2nd Inf., 9 Feb., 1892. Capt., 2 March, 1899. Graduate of the Infantry and Cavalry School, 1891. Capt. A. A. G. Vols., 20 May, 1898, to 12 May, 1899.

WRIGHT, WM. O. [Born in Ill. Appointed from Ill.]
Priv. Co. A, 31st Mich. Vols., 8 May to 28 Sept., 1898. 2nd Lieut. 19th Inf., 9 Sept., 1898.

WYATT, EDWIN. [Born in Tenn. Appointed from Tenn.]
(See Wiatt, Edwin.)

WYATT, WALTER S.* [Born in Ohio. Appointed from Ohio.]
Priv. Batty L, 4th N. Y. Art., 21 Sept., 1864, to 5 June, 1865. Cadet at Mil. Acad., 1 July, 1867. 2nd Lieut. 3rd Cav., 12 June, 1871. Trans. to 9th Inf., 8 May, 1872. 1st Lieut., 22 June, 1879. Resigned 28 Aug., 1887.

WYCHE, OSCAR D. [Born in Va. Appointed from Tex.]
2nd Lieut. of Inf., 15 March, 1847; 12th Inf., 9 April, 1847. 1st Lieut., 16 July, 1847. Reg. Adj., 1 Jan. to 25 July, 1848. Disbanded 25 July, 1848.

WYETH, MARLBOROUGH C. [Born in R. I. Appointed from N. J.]
Asst. Surg., 18 Feb., 1881. Capt. Asst. Surg., 18 Feb., 1886. Maj. Surg., 8 June, 1899. Maj. Brig. Surg. Vols., 4 June, 1898, to 22 Feb., 1899.

WYGANT, HENRY.* [Born in N. Y. Appointed from Ark.]
2nd Lieut. 24th Inf., 14 June, 1872. 1st Lieut., 28 June, 1878. Capt., 15 May, 1888. Maj., 2 March, 1899.

WYGANT, HENRY S. [Born in Tex. Appointed from Ky.]
2nd Lieut. 3rd Inf., 9 July, 1898. 1st Lieut. 14th Inf., 2 March, 1899. Trans. to 3rd Inf., 11 Oct., 1899.

WYLLIE, ROBERT E. [Born in E. Ind. Appointed from Army.]
Priv. Band 3rd Art., 20 Aug., 1895, to 6 Oct., 1896. Priv. Band 1st Art., 7 Oct., 1896, to 7 May, 1898. Priv. Batty L, 7th Art., 8 May to 6 July, 1898. 2nd Lieut. 1st Art., 22 June, 1898.

WYMAN, ASA N. [Born in Maine. Appointed from Maine.]
2nd Lieut. 9th Inf., 29 March, 1848. Disbanded 20 July, 1848.

WYMAN, POWELL T.* [Born in Mass. Appointed from Mass.]
Bvt. 2nd Lieut. 3rd Art., 1 July, 1850. 2nd Lieut. 1st Art., 16 Sept., 1850. 1st Lieut., 24 Dec., 1853. Reg. Adj., 4 Nov., 1854, to 25 May, 1857. Resigned 13 July, 1860. Col. 16th Mass. Vols., 5 Aug., 1861. Killed 30 June, 1862, at the Battle of Glendale, Va.

WYNNE, ROBT. B. [Born in Tenn. Appointed from Tenn.]
2nd Lieut. 14th Inf., 30 Dec., 1847. Disbanded 25 July, 1848.

WYNNE, THOS. [Born in Ireland. Appointed from Army.]
Priv., Corpl., Sergt. and 1st Sergt. Co. E, 7th Inf., 27 Sept., 1850, to 1 May, 1860. Priv., Sergt. and 1st Sergt. Co. C, 10th Inf., 26 May, 1860, to 9 Nov., 1863. Ord. Sergt., 9 Nov., 1863, to 23 Dec., 1864. 2nd Lieut. 7th Inf., 23 Dec., 1864. 1st Lieut., 30 Dec., 1864. Cashiered 3 April, 1866.

WYSE, FRANCIS O.* [Born in Md. Appointed from Md.]
Bvt. 2nd Lieut. 3rd Art., 1 July, 1837. 2nd Lieut., 31 July, 1837. 1st Lieut., 31 July, 1838. Capt., 3 March, 1847. Bvt. Maj., 12 July, 1847, for gallant and meritorious conduct in the affair with the enemy at Calabosa River, Mex. Maj. 4th Art., 14 May, 1861. Lieut. Col., 1 Nov., 1861. Resigned 25 July, 1863. Lieut. Col. 4th Art., 19 Feb., 1879 (Act 15 Feb., 1879). Retired 28 Feb., 1879. Died 21 Jan., 1893.

YANCEY, JEREMIAH. [Born in Va. Appointed from Va.]
Ensign 5th Inf., 12 Dec., 1808. Resigned 20 Oct., 1809. 3rd Lieut. Corps Art., 18 Aug., 1817. 2nd Lieut., 13 Feb., 1818. R. Q. M., Aug., 1819, to 31 March, 1820. Trans. to 4th Inf., 1 June, 1821. Capt., 31 May, 1825. Died 9 Jan., 1829.

YANCEY, JOEL. [Born in Va. Appointed from Va.]
2nd Lieut. 8th Inf., 27 Oct., 1820. Disbanded 1 June, 1821.

YANCEY, LEWIS. [Born in Va. Appointed from N. C.]
2nd Lieut. 10th Inf., 23 March, 1813. 1st Lieut., 24 March, 1814. Disbanded 15 June, 1815. Reinstated 17 May, 1816, in 4th Inf. Resigned 31 Dec., 1816.

YARD, BENJ'N. [Born in N. J. Appointed from N. J.]
2nd Lieut. of Inf., 22 March, 1847; 10th Inf., 9 April, 1847. Died 21 Oct., 1847.

YARD, JOHN E. [Born in Pa. Appointed from Cal.]
2nd Lieut. 9th Inf., 12 Nov., 1861. 1st Lieut., 30 May, 1863. Capt., 28 July, 1866. Maj. 10th Cav., 7 March, 1867. Unassigned 15 Dec., 1870. Ass'd to 20th Inf., 31 Dec., 1870. Lieut. Col. 24th Inf., 4 March, 1879. Col. 18th Inf., 19 April, 1886. Died 17 Feb., 1889.

YARD, JOSEPH A. [Born in N. J. Appointed from N. J.]
Capt. of Inf., 25 March, 1847; 10th Inf., 9 April, 1847. Disbanded 21 Aug., 1848.

YATES, ARTHUR W. [Born in Wis. Appointed from Wis.]
2nd Lieut. 9th Inf., 1 Aug., 1891. 1st Lieut., 26 April, 1898. Graduate of the Infantry and Cavalry School, 1895.

YATES, GEORGE W. [Born in N. Y. Appointed from N. Y.]
Q. M. Sergt. 4th Mich. Vols., 20 June, 1861. 1st Lieut., 26 Sept., 1862. Mustered out 28 June, 1864. 1st Lieut. 45th Mo. Vols., 24 Aug., 1864. Capt. 13th Mo. Cav., 22 Sept., 1864. Bvt. Maj. Vols., 13 March, 1865, for gallant and meritorious service during the war; and Lieut. Col. Vols., 13 March, 1865, for conspicuous gallantry at Fredericksburg and Beverly Ford, Va., and at Gettysburg, Pa. Mustered out 11 Jan., 1866. 2nd Lieut. 2nd Cav., 26 March, 1866. R. Q. M., 12 May to 28 Oct., 1867. Capt. 7th Cav., 12 June, 1867. Killed 25 June, 1876, in action with Indians in Mont. Ter.

YATES, HALSEY E.* [Born in Neb. Appointed from Neb.]
2nd Lieut. 5th Inf., 15 Feb., 1899.

YATES, THEODORE. [Born in Mo. Appointed from Mo.]
Capt. 1st Mo. Vols., 25 April, 1861. Capt. 13th Inf., 5 Aug., 1861. Bvt. Maj., 4 July, 1863, for gallant and meritorious service in the Siege of Vicksburg, Miss. Trans. to 31st Inf., 21 Sept., 1866. Retired, with rank of Col., 1 Nov., 1867. Died 15 Jan., 1899.

YATES, WILLIAM.* [Born in S. C. Appointed from Ga.]
2nd Lieut. 1st Cav., 12 June, 1893; 1st Lieut, 2 March, 1899.

YEAGER, HIRAM B. [Born in Pa. Appointed from Pa.]
2nd Lieut. 3rd Drag., 29 March, 1848. Disbanded 31 July, 1848. 2nd Lieut. 99th Pa. Vols., 18 Jan., 1862. Resigned 2 April, 1862. Capt. 68th Pa. Vols., 2 Sept., 1862. Resigned 7 Jan., 1863.

YEATMAN, RICHD. T.* [Born in Ohio. Appointed from Ohio.]
2nd Lieut. 14th Inf., 14 June, 1872. 1st Lieut., 15 March, 1883. R. Q. M., 30 June, 1886, to 25 July, 1887. Reg. Adj., 25 July, 1887, to 1891. Capt., 28 March, 1892.

YEATON, FRANKLIN.* [Born in New Brunswick. Appointed at Large.]
2nd Lieut. 3rd Cav., 15 June, 1869. Reg. Com., 1 Feb. to 15 July, 1870. Retired as Capt., 14 Nov., 1871. Died 17 Aug., 1872.

YEATON, HOPLEY. [Born in N. H. Appointed from N. H.]
2nd Lieut. Art., 6 March, 1806. 1st Lieut., 31 July, 1808. Capt. Asst. Dep. Q. M. G., 28 April, 1813. Capt. 1st Art., 20 May, 1813. Trans. to Corps Art., 12 May, 1814. Disbanded 15 June, 1815. Reinstated 1 Jan., 1816. Dismissed 12 Dec., 1818.

YECKLEY, JONATHAN A. [Born in N. Y. Appointed from N. Y.]
Priv. Co. D, 126th N. Y. Vols., 7 Aug., 1862. Discharged 25 Aug., 1863. 2nd Lieut. Vet. Res. Corps, 30 Jan., 1865. Mustered out 31 March, 1867. 2nd Lieut. 44th Inf., 22 Jan., 1867. Unassigned 27 May, 1869. Ass'd to 20th Inf., 14 July, 1869. 1st Lieut., 15 Jan., 1873. Retired 28 June, 1878.

YOEMANS, AUGUSTUS A. [Born in Canada. Appointed at Large.]
1st Lieut. Asst. Surg., 14 May, 1867. Capt. Asst. Surg., 14 May, 1870. Died 19 May, 1880.

YOAKUM, HENDERSON K.* [Born in Tenn. Appointed from Tenn.]
Bvt. 2nd Lieut. 3rd Art., 1 July, 1832. Resigned 31 March, 1833. 1st Lieut. 1st Tex. Mounted Rifles, 6 June, 1846. Mustered out 2 Oct., 1846. Died 29 Nov., 1856.

YONGE, WM. P. [Born in Ga. Appointed from Ga.]
2nd Lieut. Light Art., 12 Aug., 1820. Resigned 27 Oct., 1820.

YORK, JOSEPH S. [Born in N. Y. Appointed from N. Y.]
1st Lieut. 5th N. Y. Vols., 9 May to 11 Sept., 1861. Capt. 15th Inf., 29 Aug., 1861. Died 23 April, 1867. Bvt. Maj., 31 Dec., 1862, for gallant and meritorious service at the Battles of Shiloh and Murfreesboro, Tenn.

YORKE, LOUIS E. [Born in N. J. Appointed from N. J.]
Capt. 13th Inf., 5 Aug., 1861. Lieut. Col. A. I. G. Vols., 20 Sept., 1864, to 1 Aug., 1865. Resigned 21 Nov., 1865. Bvt. Maj., 4 July, 1863, for gallant and meritorious service during the Siege of Vicksburg, Miss; and Brig. Gen. Vols., 13 March, 1865, for meritorious service during the war.

YOUNG, ANDREW H. [Born in N. H. Appointed from N. H.]
1st Lieut. R. Q. M. 7th N. H. Vols., 22 Oct., 1861. Capt. A. Q. M. Vols., 26 Nov., 1862, to 1 July, 1864. Addl. P. M. Vols., 28 May, 1864, to 20 July, 1866. Bvt. Lieut. Col. Vols., 13 March, 1865, for faithful and meritorious services during the war. Capt. A. Q. M. U. S. A., 13 Nov., 1884. Died 10 Dec., 1890.

YOUNG, CHARLES.* [Born in Ky. Appointed from Ohio.]
Addl. 2nd Lieut. 10th Cav., 31 Aug., 1889. Trans. to 25th Inf., 4 Oct., 1889. 2nd Lieut., 4 Oct., 1889. Trans. to 9th Cav., 31 Oct., 1889. 1st Lieut. 7th Cav., 22 Dec., 1896. Trans. to 9th Cav., 1 Oct., 1896. Maj. 9th Ohio (Col.) Vols., 14 May, 1898, to 28 Jan., 1899.

YOUNG, DANIEL J. [Born in Pa. Appointed from W. Va.]
Ord. Storekeeper, 26 Dec., 1865. Capt. Ord. Storekeeper, 28 July, 1866. Retired 11 Dec., 1888. Died 30 Sept., 1893.

YOUNG, EDWARD C. [Born in ——. Appointed from ——.]
2nd Lieut. 18th Inf., — June, 1887. Resigned 30 Sept., 1887.

YOUNG, FRANK F. [Born in Pa. Appointed from Pa.]
Priv. Co. B, 11th Pa. Res., 29 July, 1861, to 6 Nov., 1862. 2nd Lieut. 67th Pa. Vols., 10 Dec., 1862. Mustered out 16 Jan., 1865. 2nd Lieut. 5th Inf., 22 Jan., 1867. Retired 24 Nov., 1868. Died 8 May, 1869.

YOUNG, GEORGE S. [Born in Va. Appointed from W. Va.]
2nd Lieut. 7th Inf., 20 Jan., 1875. 1st Lieut., 31 March, 1882. Capt., 12 May, 1895.

YOUNG, HOWARD G. [Born in N. Y. Appointed from Pa.]
Priv. Troop I, 1st U. S. Vol. Cav., 19 May, 1898, to 24 Aug., 1898. 2nd Lieut. 3rd U. S. Vol. Inf., 25 Aug., 1898. 1st Lieut. Co. E, 22 March to 4 May, 1899. 2nd Lieut. 6th Inf., 1 May, 1899.

YOUNG, HUGH. [Born in ——. Appointed from Tenn.]
Capt. Asst. Top. Eng., 19 Feb., 1817. Died 3 Jan., 1822.

YOUNG, JAMES. [Born in Pa. Appointed from Pa.]
Ensign 6th Inf., 13 Jan., 1813. 3rd Lieut., 12 March, 1813. 2nd Lieut., 21 Feb., 1814. 1st Lieut., 30 June, 1814. Trans. to 2nd Inf., 17 May, 1815. Capt., 31 Dec., 1827. Died 26 May, 1830. Bvt. Capt., 30 June, 1824, for ten years' faithful service in one grade.

YOUNG, JAMES S., Jr. [Born in Pa. Appointed from Pa.]
Priv. Co. D, 10th Pa. Vols., 28 June, 1898, to 12 Feb., 1899.

YOUNG, JOHN H. [Born in Ohio. Appointed from Ind.]
Capt. A. Q. M. Vols., 9 March, 1847. Disbanded 15 Oct., 1848. Capt. 13th Inf., 14 May, 1861. Trans. to 33rd Inf., 21 Sept., 1866. Wholly retired 1 Nov., 1866. Bvt. Maj., 20 Sept., 1863, for gallant and meritorious service at the Battle of Chickamauga, Ga. Died 23 Sept., 1868.

YOUNG, JOSEPH A. [Born in Mo. Appointed from Mo.]
Priv., Corpl. and Sergt. Co. B, 32nd Mo. Vols., 8 Dec., 1862, to 30 June, 1865. 2nd Lieut. 15th Inf., 1 May, 1866. 1st Lieut., 11 May, 1867. Dismissed 27 July, 1868.

YOUNG, MALCOLM. [Born in Ohio. Appointed from Army.]
Priv., Corpl. and Sergt. Troop G, 4th Cav., 31 Aug., 1895, to 6 July, 1898. 2nd Lieut. 2nd Art., 22 June, 1898.

YOUNG, NATH'L. [Born in Pa. Appointed from Pa.]
Ensign 16th Inf., 19 Aug., 1813. 3rd Lieut., 8 March, 1814. 2nd Lieut., 2 June, 1814. Trans. to 8th Inf., 17 May, 1815. Reg. Adj., Oct., 1815, to Nov., 1816. 1st Lieut., 26 June, 1817. Capt., 1 Jan., 1819. Trans. to 7th Inf., 1 June, 1821. Maj. 3rd Inf., 25 Dec., 1837. Resigned 1 Oct., 1838. Bvt. Maj., 1 Jan., 1829, for ten years' faithful service in one grade.

YOUNG, ROB'T H. [Born in Ky. Appointed from Ky.]
Priv. Co. F, 9th Ky. Cav., 12 Aug., 1862. Corpl., 1 Sept., 1862. Sergt., 1 Jan., 1863. Discharged 11 Sept., 1863. Capt. 54th Ky. Mounted Inf., 30 Sept., 1864. Mustered out 1 Sept., 1865. 2nd Lieut. 30th Inf., 7 March, 1867. Trans. to 4th Inf., 23 March, 1869. 1st Lieut., 28 June, 1878. Retired for disability, 20 Feb., 1891.

YOUNG, RICHARD W.* [Born in Utah. Appointed from Utah.]
Addl. 2nd Lieut. 3rd Art., 13 June, 1882. 2nd Lieut. 5th Art., 26 June, 1882. Resigned 12 April, 1889.

YOUNG, SAML. B. M. [Born in Pa. Appointed from Pa.]
Priv. Co. K, 12th Pa. Vols., 25 April, to 5 Aug., 1861. Capt. 4th Pa. Cav., 6 Sept., 1861. Maj., 20 Sept., 1862. Lieut. Col., 1 Oct., 1864. Col., 29 Dec., 1864. Bvt. Brig. Gen. Vols., 9 April, 1865, for gallant and meritorious service during the campaign terminating with the surrender of the insurgent army under Gen. R. E. Lee. Mustered out 1 July, 1865. 2nd Lieut., 12th Inf., 11 May, 1866. Capt. 8th Cav., 28 July, 1866. Bvt. Maj., 2 March, 1867, for gallant and meritorious service in action at Sulphur Springs, Va. Bvt. Lieut. Col., 2 March, 1867, for gallant and meritorious service in action at Amelia Spring, Va. Bvt. Col., 2 March, 1867, for gallant and meritorious service in the Battle of Sailor's Creek, Va. Maj. 3rd Cav., 2 April, 1883. Lieut. Col. 4th Cav., 16 Aug., 1892. Col. 3rd Cav., 19 June, 1897. Brig. Gen. Vols., 4 May, 1898. Maj. Gen. Vols., 8 July, 1898, to 13 April, 1899. Brig. Gen. Vols., 13 April, 1899. Brig. Gen. U. S. A., — ——, 1900.

YOUNG, WILLARD.* [Born in Utah. Appointed from Utah.]
2nd Lieut. Eng., 16 June, 1875. 1st Lieut., 31 Oct., 1879. Capt., 12 Oct., 1886. Resigned 22 Feb., 1891.

YOUNG, WM. C.* [Born in Ohio. Appointed from N. Y.]
Bvt. 2nd Lieut. 2nd Art., 1 July, 1822. 2nd Lieut. 3rd Art., 1 July, 1822. Resigned 31 May, 1826.

YOUNGS, WHITE. [Born in N. Y. Appointed from N. Y.]
Capt. 15th Inf., 12 March, 1812. Trans. to 8th Inf., 17 May, 1815. Resigned 8 March, 1819. Bvt. Maj., 11 Sept., 1814, for gallant conduct in the defence of Plattsburg, N. Y. Died 8 Dec., 1822.

YULE, EDGAR H. [Born in ——. Appointed from ——.]
2nd Lieut. of Inf. (unassigned), 1 Dec., 1899.

ZALINSKI, EDMUND L. [Born in Poland. Appointed from N. Y.]
2nd Lieut. 2nd N. Y. Art., 23 Feb., 1865. Mustered out 29 Sept., 1865. 2nd Lieut. 5th Art., 23 Feb., 1866. 1st Lieut., 1 Jan., 1867. Graduate of the Artillery School, 1880. Capt. 5th Art., 9 Dec., 1887. Retired for disability, 3 Feb., 1894.

ZALINSKI, MOSES G. [Born in N. Y. Appointed from Army.]
Priv., Corpl. and Sergt. Batty G. and H, 1st Art., 21 Oct., 1885, to 3 March, 1889. 2nd Lieut. Ind. Art., 12 March, 1812. 1st Lieut., 13 March, 1813. Trans. to 2nd Art., 16 March, 1895. Capt. A. Q. M., 9 March, 1898. Graduate of the Artillery School, 1894.

ZANTZINGER, RICHARD A. [Born in Pa. Appointed from N. J.]
2nd Lieut. 2nd Art., 12 March, 1812. 1st Lieut., 13 March, 1813. Trans. to Corps Art., 12 May, 1814. Capt., 12 Dec., 1818. Trans. to 2nd Art., 1 June, 1821. Died 4 Jan., 1842. Bvt. Capt., 15 Aug., 1814, for gallant conduct in the defence of Fort Erie. Bvt. Maj., 15 Aug., 1824, for ten years' faithful service in one grade.

ZEIGLER, GEORGE H. [Born in Pa. Appointed from Pa.]
Priv. Co. F, 4th Pa. Cav., 16 May to 27 July, 1861. 1st Sergt. Co. B, 2nd Pa. Res., 29 Oct., 1861, to 5 Feb., 1863. 2nd Lieut. Vet. Res. Corps, 15 Nov., 1863. Mustered out 23 Oct., 1866. 1st Lieut. 43rd Inf., 28 July, 1866. Unassigned 8 April, 1869. Mustered out 1 Jan., 1871.

ZINN, GEORGE A.* [Born in Pa. Appointed from Pa.]
2nd Lieut. Eng., 13 June, 1883. 1st Lieut., 2 June, 1884. Capt., 3 Feb., 1895.

ZOELLER, CHRISTIAN E. [Born in Germany. Appointed from N. J.]
Teacher Drawing, Mil. Acad., 1 Sept., 1808. Resigned 30 April, 1810. Reappointed 1 July, 1812. Resigned 5 Jan., 1819.

ZOELLER, VICTOR. [Born in Germany. Appointed from N. Y.]
Med. Storekeeper, 13 Aug., 1862. Resigned 6 April, 1863.

## COMMANDERS IN CHIEF OF THE ARMIES OF THE UNITED STATES SINCE THE INAUGURATION OF THE FIRST PRESIDENT IN 1789.

| Names. | Term of Service. | | Rank. |
|---|---|---|---|
| | From | To | |
| JOSIAH HARMAR | Sept., 1789, | March, 1791, | Lieut. Colonel Infantry. |
| ARTHUR ST. CLAIR | March 4, 1791, | March 5, 1792, | Major General. |
| ANTHONY WAYNE | March 5, 1792, | December 15, 1796, | Major General. |
| JAMES WILKINSON | December 15, 1796, | July 3, 1798, | Brigadier General. |
| GEORGE WASHINGTON | July 3, 1798, | December 14, 1799, | Lieut. General and General. |
| JAMES WILKINSON | June 15, 1800, | January 27, 1812, | Brigadier General. |
| HENRY DEARBORN | January 27, 1812, | June 15, 1815, | Major General. |
| JACOB BROWN | June 15, 1815, | February 24, 1828, | Major General. |
| ALEXANDER MACOMB | May 24, 1828, | June 25, 1841, | Major General. |
| WINFIELD SCOTT | June 25, 1841, | November 1, 1861, | Major General. |
| GEORGE B. McCLELLAN | November 1, 1861, | March 11, 1862, | Major General. |
| HENRY W. HALLECK | July 11, 1862, | March 12, 1864, | Major General. |
| ULYSSES S. GRANT | March 12, 1864, | March 4, 1869, | Lieut. General and General. |
| WILLIAM T. SHERMAN | March 4, 1869, | November 1, 1883, | General. |
| PHILIP SHERIDAN | November 1, 1883, | August 5, 1888, | General. |
| JOHN M. SCHOFIELD | August 5, 1888, | September 29, 1895, | Lieut. General. |
| NELSON A. MILES | September 29, 1895, | . . . . . . . . . . | Lieut. General. |

# LIST

OF

# OFFICERS OF VOLUNTEERS

IN THE

# SERVICE OF THE UNITED STATES.

JUNE 1, 1900.

---

ORGANIZED UNDER THE ACT OF MARCH 2, 1899.

AN ACT for increasing the efficiency of the Army of the United States, and for other purposes.

*Be it enacted by the Senate and House of Representatives of the United States of America in Congress assembled,* * * *

SEC. 12. That to meet the present exigencies of the military service the President is hereby authorized to maintain the Regular Army at a strength of not exceeding sixty-five thousand enlisted men, to be distributed amongst the several branches of the service, including the Signal Corps, according to the needs of each, and raise a force of not more than thirty-five thousand volunteers to be recruited as he may determine from the country at large, or from the localities where their services are needed, without restriction as to citizenship or educational qualifications, and to organize the same into not more than twenty-seven regiments organized as are infantry regiments of war strength in the Regular Army, and three regiments to be composed of men of special qualifications in horsemanship and markmanship, to be organized as cavalry for service mounted or dismounted: *Provided,* That each regiment shall have one surgeon, with the rank of major; two assistant surgeons, one of whom shall have the rank of captain and one that of first lieutenant, and three hospital stewards: *Provided further,* That such increased regular and volunteer force shall continue in service only during the necessity therefor, and not later than July first, nineteen hundred and one.

All enlistments for the volunteer force herein authorized shall be for the term of two years and four months unless sooner discharged.

SEC 13. That the President shall have power to continue in service or to appoint, by and with the advice and consent of the Senate, brigadier generals of volunteers, who, including the brigadier generals of the Regular Army, shall not exceed one for every four thousand enlisted men actually in service, and major generals of volunteers, who, including the major generals of the Regular Army, shall not exceed one for every twelve thousand enlisted men: *Provided,* That Regular Army officers continued or appointed as general officers or as field or staff officers of volunteers, under the provisions of this act, shall not vacate their Regular Army commissions: *And provided further,* That no general officers appointed under the provisions of this section shall be continued in service as such beyond July first, nineteen hundred and one. * * *

SEC. 14. That the President is hereby authorized to continue in service, or to appoint by and with the advice and consent of the Senate, officers of the volunteer staff as follows:

Three assistant adjutant generals with the rank of lieutenant colonel, and six assistant adjutant generals with the rank of major.

Three inspectors general with the rank of lieutenant colonel, and six inspectors general with the rank of major.

Five judge advocates with the rank of major.

Thirty quartermasters with the rank of major, and forty assistant quartermasters with the rank of captain.

Six commissaries of subsistence with the rank of major, and twelve assistant commissaries of subsistence with the rank of captain.

Thirty-four surgeons with the rank of major.

Thirty additional paymasters with the rank of major.

Four signal officers with the rank of major, nine signal officers with the rank of captain, nine signal officers with the rank of first lieutenant, and nine signal officers with the rank of second lieutenant.

*Provided,* That for each Regular Army officer of a staff corps or department who may be retained in or appointed to a higher volunteer rank in said staff corps or department than that actually held by him in the regular establishment, there may be appointed one officer of volunteers of the lowest grade mentioned in this section for such staff corps or department, but no appointment shall be made which will increase the total number of officers, regular and volunteer, serving in any grade, above the number authorized by this act: *And provided also,* That all the volunteer staff officers herein authorized to be appointed or retained in the service shall be honorably discharged on July first, nineteen hundred and one, or sooner if their services are no longer required: *And provided further,* That the officers herein authorized shall be appointed by the President, by and with the advice and consent of the Senate.

SEC. 15. That the officers and enlisted men of the Volunteer Army shall be mustered out of the military service of the United States and discharged as provided in the act of April twenty-second, eighteen hundred and ninety-eight: *Provided,* That enlisted men of volunteers who desire to remain in the military service, either in the Regular Army or the temporary force authorized by this act, may, if found qualified therefor, be transferred to and enlisted in such batteries, troops, or companies as may be below the maximum authorized strength, and when so transferred and enlisted shall be credited on their new enlistment with the periods of service rendered by them, respectively, as volunteers: *And provided further,* That the President is authorized to enlist temporarily in service for absolutely necessary purposes in the Philippine Islands volunteers, officers and men, individually or by organization, now in those islands and about to be discharged, provided their retention shall not extend beyond the time necessary to replace them by troops authorized to be maintained under the provisions of this act and not beyond a period of six months: *Provided, also,* That each and every provision of this act shall continue in force until July first, nineteen hundred and one; and on and after that date all the general, staff, and line officers appointed to the Army under this act shall be discharged. * * *

[Approved, March 2, 1899.]

## NOTES AND EXPLANATIONS.

**Officers are credited with actual service in the permanent establishment from date of acceptance, except in the case of graduates of the Military Academy, whose services commence from date of admission to the Academy.**

**Officers are credited with actual service in the volunteers from date of muster into the service of the United States during the Civil War, and from date of enrollment during the Spanish-American War, or from date of acceptance in the cases where service was rendered under a commission by the President of the United States.**

**NOTE.—The word (Regular) following an officer's name denotes that he belongs to the permanent establishment, and his record is to be found in the Alphabetical List.**

# LIST
OF
# OFFICERS OF VOLUNTEERS
IN THE
## SERVICE OF THE UNITED STATES.
## JUNE 1, 1900.

---

COMMANDER-IN-CHIEF,
WILLIAM McKINLEY,
*President.*

SECRETARY OF WAR,
ELIHU ROOT.

ASSISTANT SECRETARY OF WAR,
GEORGE D. MEIKELJOHN.

---

### GENERAL OFFICERS.

#### *Major Generals.*

SHAFTER, WM. R. (Regular), Maj. Gen., 4 May, 1898.
OTIS, ELWELL S. (Regular), Capt. 140th N. Y. Inf., 13 Sept., 1862. Lieut. Col., 23 Dec., 1863. Mustered out 24 Jan., 1865. Bvt. Brig. Gen., 13 March, 1865. Maj. Gen., 4 May, 1898.
MACARTHUR, ARTHUR (Regular), 1st Lieut. Adj. 24th Wis. Inf., 4 Aug., 1862. Maj., 25 Jan., 1864. Bvt. Col., 13 March, 1865. Lieut. Col. 24 Wis. Inf., 18 May, 1865. Mustered out 10 June, 1865. Brig. Gen., 27 May, 1898. Maj. Gen., 13 August, 1898.
WOOD, LEONARD (Regular), Col. U. S. Cav., 8 May, 1898. Maj. Gen., 5 Dec., 1899.
BATES, JOHN C. (Regular), Maj. Gen., 2 Jan., 1900.

#### *Brigadier Generals.*

LEE, FITZHUGH, Maj. Gen., 4 May, 1898. Discharged 12 April, 1899. Brig. Gen., 12 April, 1899.
WHEELER JOSEPH (Regular), Maj. Gen., 4 May, 1898. Discharged 12 April, 1899. Brig. Gen. 12 April, 1899.
WILSON, JAMES H. (Regular), Maj. Gen., 4 May, 1898. Discharged 12 April, 1899. Brig. Gen., 12 April, 1899.
CHAFFEE, ADNA R. (Regular), Brig. Gen., 4 May, 1898; Maj. Gen., 8 July, 1898; Brig. Gen., 13 April, 1899.
DAVIS, GEORGE W. (Regular), Brig. Gen., 4 May, 1898.
SCHWAN, THEODORE (Regular), Brig. Gen., 4 May, 1898.
HALL, ROBERT H. (Regular), Brig. Gen., 15 April, 1899.
WHEATON, LOYD (Regular), Brig. Gen., 15 April, 1899. Bvt. Maj. Gen., 19 June, 1899.
GRANT, FREDERICK D., Brig. Gen., 27 May, 1898. Discharged 15 April, 1899. Reappointed 15 April, 1899. Brig. Gen., 15 April, 1899.
HUGHES, ROBERT P. (Regular), Brig. Gen., 3 June, 1898.
SMITH, JAMES F., Col. 1st Cal. Inf., 27 April, 1898. Discharged 24 April, 1899. Brig. Gen., 24 April, 1899.

FUNSTON, FREDERICK, Col. 20th Kans., Inf., 13 May, 1898. Discharged 4 May, 1899. Brig. Gen., 1 May, 1899.
KOBBE, William A. (Regular), Brig. Gen., 5 Dec., 1899.
BELL, J. FRANKLIN (Regular), Brig. Gen., 5 Dec., 1899.
RANDALL, GEORGE M. (Regular), Brig. Gen., 20 Jan., 1900.
BELL, JAMES M. (Regular), Brig. Gen., 20 Jan., 1900.
SMITH, JACOB H. (Regular), Brig. Gen., 1 June, 1900.
HARE, LUTHER R. (Regular), Brig. Gen., 1 June, 1900.

*Assistant Adjutants General.*

(With rank of Lieutenant Colonel.)

RICHARDS, WILLIAM V. (Regular), Lieut. Col. A. A G., 3 June, 1898.
SCOTT, HUGH L. (Regular), Lieut. Col. A. A. G., 17 Aug., 1899.
STURGIS, SAMUEL D. (Regular), Lieut. Col. A. A. G., 24 Jan., 1900.

(With rank of Major.)

PERSHING, JOHN J. (Regular), Maj. A. A. G., 6 June, 1899.
MICHIE, ROBERT E. L. (Regular), Maj. A. A. G., 26 July, 1899.
HICKEY, JAMES B. (Regular), Maj. A. A. G., 5 Sept., 1899.
GREBLE, EDWIN ST. J. (Regular), Maj. A. A. G., 5 Sept., 1899.
NOBLE, ROBERT H. (Regular), Maj. A. A. G., 5 Sept., 1899.
ALVORD, BENJAMIN (Regular), Maj. A. A. G., 18 Oct., 1899.

*Inspectors General.*

(With rank of Lieutenant Colonel.)

MAUS, MARION P. (Regular), Lieut. Col. Insp. Gen., 9 May, 1898.
READE, PHILIP (Regular), Lieut. Col. Insp. Gen., 21 Dec., 1898.
HARRISON, RUSSELL B., Lieut. Col., 24 Jan., 1900.

(With rank of Major.)

ROLFE, ROBERT H., Maj. Insp. Gen., 7 Jan., 1899.
MURRAY, CUNLIFFE H. (Regular), Maj. Insp. Gen., 21 Jan., 1899.
SHARPE, ALFRED C. (Regular), Maj. Insp. Gen., 17 April, 1899.
WEST, PARKER W. (Regular), Maj. Insp. Gen., 17 April, 1899.
BEACH, WILLIAM D. (Regular), Maj. Insp. Gen., 6 Sept., 1899.
BROWN, ROBERT A. (Regular), Maj. Insp. Gen., 30 Sept., 1899.

*Judge Advocates.*

(With rank of Major.)

DUDLEY, EDGAR S. (Regular), Maj. J. A., 7 April, 1899.
McCLURE, CHARLES (Regular), Maj. J. A., 17 April, 1899.
CARBAUGH, HARVEY C. (Regular), Maj. J. A., 17 April, 1899.
HULL, JOHN A., Lieut. Col. J. A., 9 May, 1898. Discharged 17 April, 1899. Maj. J. A., 17 April, 1899.
DUNN, GEORGE M., Maj. 1st U. S. Cav., 9 May, 1898. Mustered out 15 Sept., 1898. Maj. J. A., 17 April, 1899.

*Quartermasters.*

(With rank of Major.)

JONES, SAMUEL R. (Regular), Maj. Q. M., 12 May, 1898.
SAWYER, J. ESTCOURT (Regular), Maj. Q. M., 12 May, 1898.
VON SCHRADER, FREDERICK (Regular), Maj. Q. M., 12 May, 1898.
LONG, OSCAR F. (Regular), Lieut. Col. Q. M. (Act 7 July, 1898), 10 Aug., 1898, to 2 March, 1899.
MARTIN, MEDAD C. (Regular), Lieut. Col. Q. M. (Act 7 July, 1898), 10 Aug., 1898, to 2 March, 1899.
CRUSE, THOMAS (Regular), Maj. Q. M., 12 May, 1898.
HODGSON, FREDERICK G. (Regular), Lieut. Col. Q. M. (Act 7 July, 1898), 10 Aug., 1898, to 2 March, 1899.
LADD, EUGENE F. (Regular), Maj. Q. M., 12 May, 1898.
CARSON, JOHN M., Jr. (Regular), Maj. Chf. Q. M., 17 May, 1898.
HUTCHINS, MORRIS C., Priv. Co. D, 2nd Ky. Inf., 11 June, 1861, to 19 Dec., 1861. 2nd Lieut. 16th Ky. Inf., 7 Jan., 1862. 1st Lieut., 2 Sept., 1862. Capt., 5 Nov., 1864. Mustered out 15 July, 1865. Maj. Chf. Q. M., 4 June, 1898.
WILSON, JAMES L. (Regular), Maj. Chf. Q. M., 20 June, 1898.
BELLINGER, JOHN B. (Regular), Maj. Q. M., 16 July, 1898.
ROUDIEZ, LEON S. (Regular), Maj. Q. M., 16 July, 1898.
MILLER, WILLIAM H. (Regular), Maj. Q. M., 11 Aug., 1898.
THOMPSON, CHARLES B. (Regular), Maj. Q. M., 17 Oct., 1898.
DEVOL, CARROLL A. (Regular), Maj. Q. M., 17 Oct., 1898.
BROOKS, JOHN C. W. (Regular), Maj. Q. M., 12 Nov., 1898.
BINGHAM, GONZALEZ S. (Regular), Maj. Chf. Q. M., 26 Nov., 1898.
SCHREINER, FRANCIS M., Capt. A. Q. M., 12 May, 1898. Maj. Q. M. (Act 7 July, 1898), 14 July, 1898, to 25 Nov., 1898. Maj. Q. M., 26 Nov., 1898.
YOUNG, HALDIMAND P., Capt. A. Q. M., 12 May, 1898. Maj. Chf. Q. M., 26 Nov., 1898.
BAKER, CHAUNCEY B. (Regular), Maj. Chf. Q. M., 7 Jan., 1899.
WHITE, WILLIAM J., Priv. Co. B, 78th Ohio Inf., 10 Dec., 1861, to 18 Sept., 1863. Sergt. Maj. 5th U. S. Col. Heavy Art, 18 Sept. to 10 Dec., 1863. 2nd Lieut. 5th U. S. Col. Art., 10 Dec., 1863. 1st Lieut., 2 Feb., 1864. Capt., 21 March, 1864. Bvt. Maj., 13 March, 1865. Mustered out 20 May, 1866. Lieut. Col. 3rd Ohio Inf., 11 May, 1898. Maj. Chf. Q. M., 7 Jan., 1899.

ALESHIRE, JAMES B. (Regular), Maj. Q. M., 1 April, 1899.
CREAGER, NOBLE H., Priv. Co. E, 7th Md. Inf., 15 Aug., 1862. to 24 Jan., 1865. 1st Lieut. 7th Md. Inf., 25 Jan., 1865. Mustered out 31 May, 1865. Maj. Q. M., 20 May, 1898. Lieut. Col. Q. M., 26 Nov., 1898. Discharged 17 April, 1899. Maj. Q. M., 1 April, 1899.
FRENCH, JOHN T., Jr. (Regular), Maj. Q. M., 6 July, 1899.
KNIGHT, JOHN T. (Regular), Maj Q. M., 6 July, 1899.
CARTWRIGHT, GEORGE S. (Regular), Maj. Q. M., 11 July, 1899.
BICKHAM, ABRAHAM S., Capt. A. Q. M., 12 May, 1898. Maj. Q. M., 10 Nov., 1899.
STEVENS, ROBERT R. (Regular), Maj. Q. M., 11 Jan., 1900.
LITTELL, ISAAC W. (Regular), Maj. Q. M., 15 Feb., 1900.

*Assistant Quartermasters.*
(With the rank of Captain.)

PARSONS, ELIAS H., Priv. Co. F, and Q. M. Sergt. 46th Ohio Inf., 16 Dec., 1861, to 11 March, 1863. 2nd Lieut. 46th Ohio Inf., 12 March, 1863. 1st Lieut., 15 April, 1864. Capt. 8 Sept., 1864. Mustered out 22 July, 1865. Capt. A. Q. M., 12 May, 1898.
BAILEY, GEORGE G., Capt. A. Q. M., 12 May, 1898.
McDOWELL, EDWARD C., Capt. A. Q. M., 12 May, 1898.
AUGUR, CHARLES M., Capt. A. Q. M., 12 May, 1898.
KING, CYRIL W., Capt. A. Q. M., 27 May, 1898.
WILLIAMS, LEWIS V., Capt. A. Q. M., 27 May, 1898.
PATTON, JONATHAN N., 2nd Lieut. 36th Ohio Inf., 22 Aug., 1861. 1st Lieut. and Adj., 1 Sept., 1862. Discharged 16 Nov., 1864. Capt. A. Q. M. 28 May, 1898.
SWOBE, THOMAS, Corpl. Co. E, 12th Mich. Inf., 19 Dec., 1861, to 7 Jan., 1865. 2nd Lieut. 12th Mich Inf., 7 Jan., 1865. 1st Lieut., 13 April, 1865. Mustered out, 15 Feb., 1866. Capt. A. Q. M., 28 May, 1898.
KIMBALL, AMOS W., 1st Lieut. Q. M. 7th Cal. Inf., 5 May, 1898. Discharged, —. Capt. A. Q. M., 28 May, 1898.
WALTON, MOSES, Jr., Capt. A. Q. M., 28 May, 1898.
BROWN, ROBERT L., Capt. A. Q. M., 28 May, 1898.
PERRY, ALEXANDER W. (Regular), Capt. A. Q. M., 3 June, 1898.
SAWTELLE, CHARLES G., Jr. (Regular), Capt. A. Q. M., 3 June, 1898.
ALLEN, WALTER (Regular), Capt. A. Q. M., 3 June, 1898.
FENTON, CLIFTON L., Capt. A. Q. M., 8 June, 1898.
LAFITTE, JACQUES DE L. (Regular), Capt. A. Q. M., 10 June, 1898.
EKIN, WILLIAM M., Capt. A. Q. M., 13 June, 1898.
HAM, SAMUEL V. (Regular), Capt. A. Q. M., 20 June, 1898.
COULLING, WILLIAM M., Capt. A. Q. M., 20 June, 1898.
SULZER, RAYMOND, Priv. and Corp. Co. C, 3rd N. J. Inf., 27 April, 1898, to 7 July, 1898. Capt. A. Q. M., 23 June, 1898.
BRADLEY, JOHN J. (Regular), Capt. A. Q. M., 16 July, 1898.
COLQUHOUN, WILLIAM C. R., Capt. A. Q. M., 16 July, 1898.
BAKER, CHARLES T., Capt. A. Q. M., 16 July, 1898.
CHAMBERLIN, HARRY B., Q. M. Sergt. 1st Vt. Inf., 11 May, 1898, to 31 July, 1898. Capt. A. Q. M., 16 July, 1898. *NN*
DOWNS, THOMAS, Priv. Co. K, 54th Ind. Inf., 10 June, 1862, to 16 Sept., 1862. Priv. and Corpl. Co. K, 16th Ind. Inf., and Co. K, 13th Ind. Cav., 2 Oct., 1862, to 1 Oct., 1865. Capt. A. Q. M., 16 July, 1898.
SCOTT, WILLIAM S., Capt. A. Q. M., 16 July, 1898.
McHARG, JOHN W., Capt. A. Q. M., 16 July, 1898.
GOODALE, GEORGE L., Corpl. Co. B, 43rd Mass. Inf., 11 Oct., 1862, to 30 July, 1863. Capt. A. Q. M., 16 July, 1898.
McMILLIN, MARION M., Priv. Batty A, 1st Conn. Art., 4 May, 1898, to 23 July, 1898. Capt. A. Q. M., 16 July, 1898.
BARKER, WALTER B., Capt. A. Q. M., 16 July, 1898.
BAKER, JESSE M., Priv. Co. H, 6th Pa. Inf., 8 May, 1898, to 12 July, 1898. Capt. A. Q. M., 23 July, 1898.
DARE, JEREMIAH Z., Capt. A. Q. M., 11 Aug., 1898. Maj. Q. M. (Act 7 July, 1898), 3 Sept., 1898, to 2 March, 1899.
MICHAEL, JAMES S., Capt. A. Q. M., 1 Oct., 1898.
HAAN, WILLIAM G. (Regular), Capt. A. Q. M., 17 Oct., 1898.
BLUNT, J. Y. MASON (Regular), Capt. A. Q. M., 26 Nov., 1898.
HAY, WILLIAM H. (Regular), Capt. A. Q. M., 26 Nov., 1898.
SYMMONDS, CHARLES J. (Regular), Capt. A. Q. M., 26 Nov., 1898.
HORTON, WILLIAM E., 1st Lieut. and Adj. 1st D. C., Inf., 11 May, 1898. Discharged 3 June, 1898. Capt. A. A. G., 12 May, 1898. Discharged 7 April, 1899. Capt. A. Q. M., 1 April, 1899.
GARRARD, LOUIS F., Jr., 1st Lieut. 3rd Ga. Inf., 25 June, 1898. Capt., 27 Oct., 1898. Mustered out 22 April, 1899. Capt. A. Q. M., 1 April, 1899.
CANNON, WILLIAM C., 1st Class Sergt. Sig. Corps, 22 June, 1898, to 14 July, 1898. 2nd Lieut. Sig. Off., 7 July,, 1898. Vacated 22 April, 1898. Capt. A. Q. M., 1 April, 1899.
BATCHELDER, NATHAN P., Capt. A. Q. M., 1 April, 1899.
FREDENDALL, IRA L., Capt. A. Q. M., 10 April, 1899.
MAY, HENRY J., Capt. 2nd Ohio Inf., 25 April, 1898. Discharged 11 July, 1898. Maj. Addl. P. M., 21 June, 1898. Discharged 13 June, 1899. Capt. A. Q. M., 14 June, 1899.
PETTUS, HARRY L., Capt. A. Q. M., 14 June, 1899.
McCAULL, PATRICK H., Capt. C. S., 11 Aug., 1898. Discharged 12 June, 1899. Capt. A. Q. M., 21 June, 1899.
ORR, SYLVANUS G., 1st Lieut. Q. M. 3rd Ga. Inf., 27 June, 1898. Mustered out 22 April, 1899. Capt. A. Q. M., 7 July, 1899.
IRWIN, GEORGE LER. (Regular), Capt. A. Q. M., 13 July, 1899.

ARNOLD, DANIEL W., Priv. Co. B, 134th Ill. Inf., 14 May, 1864, to 25 Oct., 1864. Maj. Addl. P. M., 17 May, 1898. Discharged 13 June, 1899. Capt. A. Q. M., 17 July, 1899.
BAKER, LAURANCE C., Capt. A. Q. M., 9 June, 1898. Discharged 30 June, 1899. Capt. A. Q. M., 25 July, 1899.
POVEY, GEORGE W., 2nd Lieut. 2nd Ore. Inf., 27 April, 1898. Mustered out 7 Aug., 1899. Capt. A. Q. M., 28 Aug., 1899.
JOHNSON, BENJAMIN, Capt. A. Q. M., 12 May, 1898. Discharged 12 June, 1899. Capt. A. Q. M., 28 Aug., 1899.
MILES, PERRY L. (Regular), Capt. A. Q. M., 10 Oct., 1899.
BUTT, ARCHIBALD W., Capt. A. Q. M., 2 Jan., 1900.
GILLEM, ALVAN C., Capt. 1 Tenn. Inf., 19 May, 1898. Maj., 21 Aug., 1898. Mustered out 23 Nov., 1899. Capt. A Q. M., 24 March, 1900.
LAMOREUX, THOMAS B. (Regular), Capt. A. Q. M., 18 April, 1900.
GIBBON, JOHN, Jr., Capt. A. Q. M., 18 April, 1900.
HAMPTON, KENSEY J., Capt. A. Q. M., 9 May, 1900.
DAVISON, PETER W. (Regular), Capt. A. Q. M., 12 May, 1900.

*Commissaries of Subsistence.*
(With rank of Major.)

GALLAGHER, HUGH J. (Regular), Lieut. Col. C. S. (Act 7 July, 1898), 9 Sept., 1898, to 2 March, 1899.
MERCER, CARROLL, Maj. Chf. C. S., 7 Jan., 1899.
WOOD, OLIVER E. (Regular), Maj. C. S., 17 April, 1899.
DAVIS, GEORGE B. (Regular), Maj. C. S., 17 April, 1899.
RUTHERS, GEORGE W. (Regular), Maj. C. S., 8 July, 1899.
PETERSON, MATT R. (Regular), Maj. C. S., 15 Feb., 1900.

*Assistant Commissaries of Subsistence.*
(With rank of Captain.)

FENTON, EBEN B., Priv. Unassigned 5th Conn. Inf., 12 Aug., 1862, to 23 Sept., 1863. 2nd Lieut. 20th Conn. Inf., 24 Sept., 1863. Discharged 17 Oct., 1864. Capt. C. S., 12 May, 1898.
HACKER, THEODORE B., Capt. C. S., 12 May, 1898.
BOOTES, SAMUEL B., Capt. C. S., 12 May, 1898.
MILLIKEN, SETH M., Capt. C. S., 17 May, 1898.
DEMING, PETER C., Capt. C. S., 17 May, 1898.
POMROY, FREDERIC H., Capt. C. S., 8 June, 1898.
READ, JAMES C., Capt. C. S., 16 July, 1898.
RYAN, THOMAS F., Capt. C. S., 16 July, 1898.
STREET, HARLOW L., Corpl. Co. E. 2nd Cal. Cav., 20 Sept., 1861, to 31 Jan., 1863. 2nd Lieut. 2nd Cal. Cav., 31 Jan., 1863. 1st Lieut., 9 March, 1864. Capt., 9 May, 1865. Mustered out 18 May, 1866. Capt. C. S., 3 Aug., 1898.
MOTHERSILL, PHILIP, 1st Sergt. Co. I, 1st Mich. Eng. and Mech., 6 Dec., 1861, to 21 April, 1862. Sergt. and 1st Sergt. Co. A, 5th Mich. Cav., 26 Aug., 1862, to 1 March, 1864. 2nd Lieut. 5th Mich. Cav., 1 March, 1864. 1st Lieut., 12 Nov., 1864. Capt., 21 Feb., 1865. Bvt. Maj., 13 March, 1865. Mustered out 22 June, 1865. Maj. Chf. C. S., 28 May, 1898. Discharged 17 April, 1899. Capt. Asst. C. S., 17 April, 1899.
INGALLS, RALPH, 2nd Lieut. 5th Mo. Inf., 4 May, 1898. Mustered out 9 Nov., 1898. 1st Lieut. 44th U. S. Inf., 17 Aug., 1899. Discharged 10 Nov., 1899. Capt. Asst. C. S., 2 Jan., 1900.
LAWTON, FRANK H. (Regular), Capt. Asst. C. S., 12 March, 1900.
FRANKLIN, THOMAS (Regular), Capt. Asst. C. S., 28 April, 1900.
COLE, HENRY G., Capt. Asst. C. S., 15 May, 1900.

*Surgeons.*
(With rank of Major.)

HYSELL, JAMES H., Asst. Surg. 9th W. Va. Inf., 28 Feb., 1862. Surg. 1st W. Va. Vet. Inf., 9 Nov., 1864. Mustered out 21 July, 1865. Maj. Chf. Surg., 20 May, 1898.
CARDWELL, HERBERT W., Capt. Asst. Surg. 2nd Ore. Inf., 8 May, 1898. Mustered out, 25 May, 1898. Maj. Chf. Surg., 20 May, 1898.
HOYT, HENRY F., Maj. Chf. Surg., 20 May, 1898.
EDIE, GUY L. (Regular), Maj. Brig. Surg., 4 June, 1898.
CROSBY, WILLIAM D. (Regular), Maj. Brig. Surg., 4 June, 1898.
IVES, FRANCIS J. (Regular), Maj. Brig. Surg., 4 June, 1898.
KENDALL, WILLIAM P. (Regular), Maj. Brig. Surg., 4 June, 1898.
HARRIS, HENRY S. T. (Regular), Maj. Brig. Surg., 4 June, 1898.
ARMSTRONG, SAMUEL T., Maj. Brig. Surg., 4 June, 1898.
POTTER, SAMUEL O. L., Priv. and Corpl. Cos. I and K, 13th N. Y. Cav., 24 Nov., 1863, to 13 Feb., 1865. Maj. Brig. Surg., 4 June, 1898.
PENROSE, GEORGE H., Maj. Brig. Surg., 16 June, 1898.
DE NIEDEMAN, WILLIAM F., Capt. Asst. Surg. 22 Kans. Inf., 17 May, 1898. Discharged 15 July, 1898. Maj. Brig. Surg., 8 July, 1898.
SHIELS, GEORGE F., Maj. Brig. Surg., 8 July, 1898.
CARR, LAWRENCE C., Maj. Brig. Surg., 8 July, 1898.
DAVIS, JOHN G., Priv. Co. E, 81st Ind. Inf., 22 Aug., 1862, to 23 Nov., 1863. Maj. Surg. 7th U. S. Inf., 13 June, 1898. Vacated 11 Aug., 1898. Maj. Brig. Surg., 11 Aug., 1898.
BROWN, IRA C., Maj. Brig. Surg., 11 Aug., 1898.
TURNBULL, WILFRID, Maj. Brig. Surg., 15 Sept., 1898.
BALCH, LEWIS, Maj. Surg. 2nd N. Y. Inf., 2 May, 1898. Mustered out 2 Nov., 1898. Maj. Brig. Surg., 10 Oct., 1898.

WINN, WILLIAM B., Maj. Brig. Surg., 13 Oct., 1898.
MATTHEWS, WILLARD S. H., Maj. Surg. 51st Iowa Inf., 24 April, 1898. Vacated 14 Nov., 1898. Maj. Brig. Surg., 24 Oct., 1898.
ECHEVERRIA, RAFAEL F., Maj. Brig. Surg., 15 Nov., 1898.
THOMASON, HENRY D., Maj. Surg. 33rd Mich. Inf., 27 July, 1898. Discharged 9 Dec., 1898. Maj. Brig. Surg., 28 Nov., 1898.
LAINE, DAMASO T., Maj. Brig. Surg., 14 Dec., 1898.
DUCKER, ORLANDO, Maj. Brig. Surg., 21 Jan., 1899.
COMBE, FREDERICK J., Maj. Brig. Surg., 30 Jan., 1899.
MEACHAM, FRANKLIN A., Maj. Surg. 2nd U. S. Eng., 16 June, 1898. Maj. Surg., 5 April, 1899.
KEAN, JEFFERSON R. (Regular), Maj. Surg., 17 April, 1899.
DRAKE, CHARLES M., Maj. Surg., 5 July, 1899.
KEEFER, FRANK R. (Regular), Maj. Surg., 1 Oct., 1899.
FISHER, HENRY C. (Regular), Maj. Surg., 1 Oct., 1899.
EWING, CHARLES B. (Regular), Maj. Surg., 1 Nov., 1899.
BANISTER, WILLIAM B. (Regular), Maj. Surg., 11 Nov., 1899.
TITUS, FRANK H., Maj. Surg., 4 Jan., 1900.
SWIFT, EUGENE L. (Regular), Maj. Brig. Surg., 4 June, 1898. Discharged 10 Feb., 1899. Maj. Surg. 35th U. S. Inf., 11 Nov., 1899. Maj. Surg., 24 Jan., 1900.

*Additional Paymasters.*

(With rank of Major.)

GAMBRILL, WILLIAM G., Maj. Addl. P. M., 12 May, 1898.
HOWELL, SEYMOUR, 2nd Lieut. 6th Mich. Inf. (Sub. 1st Mich. Heavy Art.), 19 Aug., 1861. 1st Lieut., 3 May, 1862. Capt., 15 Sept., 1863. Maj., 31 Aug., 1864. Mustered out 20 Aug., 1865. Maj. Addl. P. M., 17 May, 1898.
LORD, HERBERT M., Maj. Addl. P. M., 17 May, 1898.
HOLLOWAY, GEORGE T., Maj. Addl. P. M., 19 May, 1898.
ROCHESTER, WILLIAM B., Jr., Maj. Addl. P. M., 17 May, 1898.
DOWNEY, GEORGE F., Maj. Addl. P. M., 17 May, 1898.
RAY, BEECHER B., Maj. Addl. P. M., 17 May, 1898.
SMITH, ROBERT S., Maj. Addl. P. M., 17 May, 1898.
KELEHER, TIMOTHY D., Maj. Addl. P. M., 17 May, 1898.
SCHOFIELD, WILLIAM B., Maj. Addl. P. M., 19 May, 1898.
HOUSTON, JAMES B., Maj. Addl. P. M., 27 May, 1898.
CANBY, JAMES, Maj. Addl. P. M., 28 May, 1898.
DAWES, JAMES W., Maj. Addl. P. M., 28 May, 1898.
BECKER, OTTO, Priv. Co. F, 23rd Mo. Inf., 22 Nov., 1861, to 31 May, 1862. Maj. Addl. P. M., 28 May, 1898.
PICKETT, GEORGE E., Maj. Addl. P. M., 28 May, 1898.
MONAGHAN, WILLIAM, Priv. Corpl. Co. F, 104th Ohio Inf., 30 Aug., 1862, to 13 June, 1865. Maj. Addl. P. M., 3 June, 1898.
CURRY, MANLY B., Maj. Addl. P. M., 3 June, 1898.
WILKINS, JOSEPH S., Maj. Addl. P. M., 3 June, 1898.
COFFIN, EUGENE, Priv. Co. G, 23rd Ohio Inf., 1 June, 1863, to 31 Aug., 1863. Priv. and 2nd Class Mus. Band, 1st Brig. 2nd Div. Dept. W. Va., 31 Aug., 1863, to 7 July, 1865. Maj. Addl. P. M., 8 June, 1898.
VARNEY, THADDEUS P., Maj. Addl. P. M., 13 June, 1898.
LYNCH, JOHN R., Maj. Addl. P. M., 21 June, 1898.
STERNBERG, THEODORE, 1st Lieut. and Q. M. 121st N. Y. Inf., 23 Aug., 1862. Mustered out 25 June, 1865. Maj. Addl. P. M., 16 July, 1898.
GOODMAN, THOMAS C., Maj. Addl. P. M., 16 July, 1898.
SANDERS, JUNIUS G., Corpl., Sergt. and 1st Sergt. Co. F, 4th Ohio Inf., 4 May, 1861, to 21 June, 1864. Maj. Addl. P. M., 16 July, 1898.
GRAHAM, WILLIAM R., Maj. Addl. P. M., 16 July, 1898.
STANTON, CHARLES E., Maj. Addl. P. M., 3 Aug., 1898.
ARTHUR, GEORGE G., Maj. Addl. P. M., 11 Aug., 1898.
STEVENS, PIERRE C., Maj. Addl. P. M., 9 Sept., 1898.
SLAUGHTER, BRADNER D., 2nd Lieut. 2nd U. S. Inf., 2 Feb., 1899. Discharged 14 March, 1899. Maj. Addl. P. M., 11 March, 1899.
BELKNAP, HUGH R., Maj. Addl. P. M., 11 March, 1899.

*Signal Officers.*

(With rank of Major.)

SCRIVEN, GEORGE P. (Regular), Maj. Sig. Off., 17 April, 1899.
GLASSFORD, WILLIAM A. (Regular), Maj. Sig. Off., 17 April, 1899.
MAXFIELD, JOSEPH E. (Regular), Maj. Sig. Off., 17 April, 1899.
GREENE, FRANK (Regular), Maj. Sig. Off., 6 Dec., 1899.

(With rank of Captain.)

RUSSEL, EDGAR (Regular), Capt. Sig. Off., 20 June, 1898.
REBER, SAMUEL (Regular), Capt. Sig. Off., 17 April, 1899.
STEVENS, GUSTAVE W. S. (Regular), Capt. Sig. Off., 17 April, 1899.
IVES, EDWARD B. (Regular), Capt. Sig. Off., 17 April, 1899.
SQUIER, GEORGE O. (Regular), Capt. Sig. Off., 17 April, 1899.
FECHET, EUGENE O., Sergt. and 1st Sergt. Art. Co. 2nd Mich. Cav. (Batty B, 1st Mich. Light Art.), 26 Nov., 1861, to 10 April, 1864. Maj. Sig. Off., 20 May, 1898. Discharged 17 April, 1899. Capt. Sig. Off., 17 April, 1899.
MONTGOMERY, BENJAMIN F., Capt. Sig. Off., 20 May, 1898. Lieut. Col. Chf. Sig. Off., 1 Aug., 1898. Discharged 17 April, 1899. Capt. Sig. Off., 17 April, 1899.
HEPBURN, CHARLES B., Capt. Sig. Off., 2 June, 1898. Discharged 17 April, 1899. 2nd Lieut. Sig. Off., 17 April, 1899. Capt. Sig. Off., 26 April, 1899.

CARR, DANIEL J., Capt. Sig. Off., 20 May, 1898. Discharged 17 April, 1899. 1st Lieut. Sig. Off., 17 April, 1899. Capt. Sig. Off., 2 June, 1899.

(With rank of First Lieutenant.)

HARTMANN, CARL F., Capt. Sig. Off., 20 May, 1898. Discharged 17 April, 1899. 1st Lieut. Sig. Off., 17 April, 1899.
WILDMAN, LEONARD D., 1st Lieut. Sig. Off., 20 May, 1898. Capt. Sig. Off., 13 Jan., 1899. Discharged 17 April, 1899. 1st Lieut. Sig. Off., 17 April, 1899.
RYAN, JOHN J., 1st Lieut. Sig. Off., 20 May, 1898. Capt. Sig. Off., 18 July, 1898. Discharged 17 April, 1899. 1st Lieut. Sig. Off., 17 April, 1899.
LYMAN, FRANK E., Jr., Capt. Sig. Off., 20 May, 1898. Discharged 17 April, 1899. 1st Lieut. Sig. Off., 17 April, 1899.
TALBOTT, WILLIAM M., 2nd Lieut. Sig. Off., 20 May, 1898. 1st Lieut. Sig. Off., 26 April, 1899.
BURNELL, GEORGE C., 2nd Lieut. Sig. Off., 20 May, 1898. 1st Lieut. Sig. Off., 1 Aug., 1898. Discharged 17 April, 1899. 2nd Lieut. Sig. Off., 17 April, 1899. 1st Lieut. Sig. Off., 26 April, 1899.
CLARKE, WALTER L., 2nd Lieut. Sig. Off., 20 May, 1898. 1st Lieut. Sig. Off., 13 Jan., 1899. Discharged 17 April, 1899. 2nd Lieut. Sig. Off., 17 April, 1899. 1st Lieut. Sig. Off., 15 May, 1899.
LENOIR, BASIL O., 2nd Lieut. Sig. Off., 20 May, 1898. 1st Lieut. Sig. Off., 2 June, 1899.
BAILEY, WILLIAM O., 2nd Lieut. Sig. Off., 20 May, 1898. 1st Lieut. Sig. Off., 13 Jan., 1899. Discharged 26 April, 1899. 2nd Lieut. Sig. Off., 26 April, 1899. 1st Lieut. Sig. Off., 16 Aug., 1899.

(With rank of Second Lieutenant.)

STAMFORD, HENRY W., 2nd Lieut. Sig. Off., 2 June, 1898.
JONES, FREDERICK M., 2nd Lieut. Sig. Off., 2 June, 1898.
WALLACE, CHARLES S., 2nd Lieut. Sig. Off., 7 July, 1898.
GIBBS, GEORGE S., Jr., Priv. and Q. M. Sergt. Co. C, 51st Iowa Inf., and 1st Class Sergt. Sig. Corps, 3 May, 1898, to 30 Jan., 1899. 2nd Lieut. Sig. Off., 13 Jan., 1899.
CLIFTON, ALFRED T., Priv., Sergt. and 1st Class Sergt. Sig. Corps, 15 June, 1898, to 24 March, 1899. 2nd Lieut. Sig. Off., 15 March, 1899.
CUNNINGHAM, MACK K., Priv. Co. B, 1st Idaho Inf., and Priv., Sergt. and 1st Class Sergt. Sig. Corps, 9 May, 1898, to 21 March, 1899. 2nd Lieut. Sig. Off., 15 March, 1899.
ROGAN, CHARLES B., Jr., 2nd Lieut. Sig. Off., 20 May, 1898. 1st Lieut. Sig. Off., 7 July, 1898. Discharged 17 April, 1899. 2nd Lieut. Sig. Off., 17 April, 1899.
MITCHELL, WILLIAM, Priv. Co. M, 1st Wis. Inf., 1 May, 1898, to 7 June, 1898. 2nd Lieut. Sig. Off., 20 May, 1898. 1st Lieut. Sig. Off., 21 Jan., 1899. Discharged 17 April, 1899. 2nd Lieut. Sig. Off., 17 April, 1899.
SHEPHERD, VICTOR, 2nd Lieut. Sig. Off., 20 May 1898. 1st Lieut. Sig. Off., 1 Aug., 1898. Discharged 17 April, 1899. 2nd Lieut. Sig. Off., 17 April, 1899.
RICKARD, RICHARD O., 1st Lieut. Sig. Off., 20 May, 1898. Capt. Sig. Off., 3 Aug., 1898. Discharged 26 April, 1899. 2nd Lieut. Sig. Off., 26 April, 1899.
COLT, WILLIAM W., 2nd Lieut. Sig. Off., 20 May, 1898. 1st Lieut. Sig. Off., 13 Jan., 1899. Discharged 15 May, 1899. 2nd Lieut. Sig. Off., 15 May, 1899.
DAVIES, WILLIAM E., 2nd Lieut. Sig. Off., 20 May, 1898. 1st Lieut. Sig. Off., 13 Jan., 1899. Discharged 15 May, 1899. 2nd Lieut. Sig. Off., 15 May, 1899.
DUFFY, CHARLES M., 1st Lieut. Sig. Off., 20 June, 1898. Discharged 15 May, 1899. 2nd Lieut. Sig. Off., 15 May, 1899.
YURGENSEN, NIELS P., 2nd Lieut. Sig. Off., 16 Aug., 1899.
KENNEDY, JOHN, 2nd Lieut. Sig. Off., 7 May, 1900.

## 11TH CAVALRY U. S. VOLUNTEERS.

*Colonel.*

LOCKETT, JAMES (Regular), Col. 11th U. S. Cav., 10 Aug., 1899.

*Lieutenant Colonel.*

STARR, CHARLES G. (Regular), Lieut. Col. 11th U. S. Cav., 12 Aug., 1899.

*Majors.*

CARSON, THOMAS G. (Regular), Maj. 11th U. S. Cav., 10 Aug., 1899.
NOLAN, DENNIS E. (Regular), Maj. 11th U. S. Cav., 10 Aug., 1899.
SIME, HUGH T., Maj. 1st Cal. Inf., 27 April, 1898. Discharged 11 Aug., 1899. Maj. 11th U. S. Cav., 10 Aug., 1899.

*Surgeon with rank of Major.*

GHISELIN, ALEXANDER D., Capt. Asst. Surg. 11th U. S. Cav., 10 Aug., 1899. Maj. Surg., 14 March, 1900.

*Assistant Surgeons with rank of Captain.*

BEASLEY, SHADWORTH O., 1st Lieut. Asst. Surg. 11th U. S. Cav., 10 Aug., 1899. Capt. Asst. Surg., 14 March, 1900.

*With rank of First Lieutenant.*

STUART, STANLEY MacC., 1st Lieut. Asst. Surg. 11th U. S. Cav., 16 March, 1900.

*Captains.*

YOUNG, EVAN E., Adj., 12 Aug., 1899. 2nd Lieut. 1st S. Dak. Inf., 25 April, 1898. 1st Lieut. and Adj., 13 April, 1899. Discharged 10 Aug., 1899. Capt. 11th U. S. Cav., 10 Aug., 1899.

DAVIDSON, JOSEPH T., 1st Lieut. and Adj. 51st Iowa Inf., 26 April, 1898. Capt. and Adj., 11 Oct., 1898. Discharged 11 Aug., 1899. Capt. 11th U. S. Cav., 10 Aug., 1899.
GLASGOW, EDWARD L., 1st Lieut. 2nd Kans. Inf., 10 May, 1898. Capt., 4 March, 1899. Discharged 11 Aug., 1899. Capt. 11th U. S. Cav., 10 Aug., 1899.
ARNDT, ALVIN, Q. M., 12 Aug., 1899. Capt. 11th U. S. Cav., 10 Aug., 1899.
KING, EDWARD L. (Regular), Capt. 11th U. S. Cav., 11 Aug., 1899.
STURGES, EDWARD A., Capt. 1st Wash. Inf., 30 April, 1898. Discharged 11 Aug., 1899. Capt. 11th U. S. Cav., 11 Aug., 1899.
HAZARD, RUSSELL T., 2nd Lieut. 1st Wash. Inf., 30 April, 1898. Discharged 11 Aug., 1899. Capt. 11th U. S. Cav., 11 Aug., 1899.
GREEN, FRANK E., 1st Lieut. 1st Mont. Inf., 1 May, 1898. Capt., 9 May, 1898. Discharged 24 Aug., 1899.
AGNEW, ERNEST H., 2nd Lieut. 20th Kans. Inf., 2 May, 1898. 1st Lieut.. 23 July, 1898. Discharged 11 Aug., 1899.
GREEN, WILLIAM A., 1st Lieut. 20th Kans. Inf., 12 May, 1898. Discharged 11 Aug., 1899. Capt. 11th U. S. Cav.. 11 Aug., 1899.
YARSON, SAMUEL G., 1st Sergt. Co. C, 1st S. Dak. Inf., 25 April, 1898, to 13 May, 1898. 2nd Lieut. 1st S. Dak. Inf., 14 May, 1898. 1st Lieut., 9 May, 1899. Discharged 10 Aug., 1899. Capt. 11th U. S. Cav., 11 Aug., 1899.
ENGLAND, LLOYD (Regular), Capt. 11th U. S. Cav., 12 Aug., 1899.
ROSS, JAMES O., 2nd Lieut. 51st Iowa Inf., 26 April, 1898. 1st Lieut., 8 Oct., 1898. Discharged 11 Aug., 1899. 1st Lieut. 11th U. S. Cav., 11 Aug., 1899. Capt., 12 Aug., 1899.
KIPP, WILLIAM J., 1st Lieut. 1st Idaho Inf., 3 May, 1898. Capt. 11th U. S. Cav., 12 Aug., 1899.

*First Lieutenants.*

WINTERBURN, GEORGE W., Com., 12 Aug., 1899. Priv. and Q. M. Sergt. 20th Kans. Inf., 22 March, 1898. Discharged 28 July, 1899. Priv. 11th U. S. Cav., 29 July, 1899, to 11 Aug., 1899. 1st Lieut. 11th U. S. Cav., 10 Aug., 1899.
GUSTIN, MORROW C., 1st Lieut. 1st Wash. Inf., 25 April, 1898. 1st Lieut. 11th U. S. Cav., 11 Aug., 1899.
TROWBRIDGE, CHARLES R., 2nd Lieut. 13th Minn. Inf., 29 April, 1898. 1st Lieut. 11th U. S. Cav., 11 Aug., 1899.
GIGNOUX, FREDERICK E., 1st Lieut. 1st Troop Nev. Cav., 14 May, 1898. Discharged 11 Aug., 1899. 1st Lieut. 11th U. S. Cav., 11 Aug., 1899.
COTCHETT, WALTER V., Sergt. and 1st Sergt. Co. G, 1st Wash. Inf., 30 April, 1898, to 19 April, 1899. 2nd Lieut. 1st Wash. Inf., 20 April, 1899. 1st Lieut. 11th U. S. Cav., 11 Aug., 1899.
ENSLOW, RAYMOND S., Sergt. and 1st Sergt. Co. K, 20th Kans. Inf., 13 May, 1898. Discharged 28 July, 1899. Pvt. 11th U. S. Cav., 29 July, 1899, to 11 Aug., 1899. 1st Lieut. 11th U. S. Cav., 11 Aug., 1899.
HILL, HOLLY V., Sergt. Co. H, 1st Wash. Inf., 1 May, 1898, to 11 Aug., 1899. 1st Lieut. 11th U. S. Cav., 11 Aug., 1899.
PARKS, FRED H., Priv. and Sergt. Co. F, 1st S. Dak. Inf., 25 April, 1898, to 2 Aug., 1899. Priv. 11th U. S. Cav., 3 Aug. to 11 Aug., 1899. 1st Lieut. 11th U. S. Cav., 11 Aug., 1899.
MORRIS, JOSEPH W., Priv., Corpl., Sergt., Q. M. Sergt. and 1st Sergt. Co. A, 20th Kans. Inf., 7 May to 30 July, 1899. Pvt. 11th U. S. Cav., 1 Aug. to 11 Aug., 1899. 1st Lieut. 11th U. S. Cav., 11 Aug., 1899.
CHEATHAM, LINDZY E., 1st Lieut. 11th U. S. Cav., 11 Aug., 1899.
LINCOLN, FRANCIS H., Sergt. Co. A, 51st Iowa Inf., 26 April, 1898, to 11 Aug., 1899. 1st Lieut. 11th U. S. Cav., 11 Aug., 1899.
WRAY, GEORGE M., Priv. 11th U. S. Cav., 4 Aug. to 11 Aug., 1899. 1st Lieut. 11th U. S. Cav., 11 Aug., 1899.
HAZZARD, OLIVER P. M., Priv. and Corpl. Co. M, 1st Wash. Inf., 20 June, 1898, to 11 Aug., 1899. 1st Lieut. 11th U. S. Cav., 11 Aug., 1899.
WINNA, CHARLES C., 1st Sergt. Co. C, 1st Tenn. Inf., 23 May, 1898, to 25 July, 1899. Sergt. Co. C, 37th U. S. Inf., 26 July, to 10 Aug., 1899. 2nd Lieut. 1st Tenn. Inf., 15 Aug., 1899. Discharged 5 Sept., 1899. 1st Lieut. 11th U. S. Cav., 12 Aug., 1899.
FOERSTER, LEWIS, 2nd Lieut. 11th U. S. Cav., 11 Aug., 1899. 1st Lieut., 12 Aug., 1899.
BURRITT, CHARLES H., Priv. and 1st Sergt. Co. C, 1st Wyo. Inf., 25 April, 1898, to 28 July, 1899. Priv. 11th U. S. Cav., 1 Aug., to 11 Aug., 1899. 2nd Lieut. 11th U. S. Cav., 11 Aug., 1899. 1st Lieut., 5 Sept., 1899.

*Second Lieutenants.*

CURRY, GEORGE, Capt. 1st U. S. Cav., 7 May, 1898. Mustered out 15 Sept., 1898. 2nd Lieut. 11th U. S. Cav., 11 Aug., 1899.
WEST, EMORY S., Priv. Co. G, 1st S. Dak. Inf., 15 May, 1898. 2nd Lieut. 11th U. S. Cav., 11 Aug., 1899.
HOLTMAN, JOHN, 2nd Lieut. 11th U. S. Cav., 11 Aug., 1899.
McKELVEY, ALEXANDER C., 2nd Lieut. 11th U. S. Cav., 11 Aug., 1899.
KIRKMAN, HUGH, Sergt. Co. G, 1st Terr. Inf., 12 July, 1898, to 11 Feb., 1899.
CUTTS, LEO M., Priv. Co. E, 13th Minn. Inf., 29 April, 1898, to 9 Aug., 1899. 2nd Lieut. 11th U. S. Cav., 11 Aug., 1899.
WHITE, HENRY C., Jr., Sergt. Co. B, 1st Ohio Cav., 26 April, to 22 Oct., 1898. 2nd Lieut. 11th U. S. Cav., 12 Aug., 1899.
RETHORST, OTTO W., Priv., Corpl. and Sergt. Co. H, 20th Kans. Inf., 9 May, 1898. Discharged 5 Aug., 1899. Priv. 11th U. S. Cav., 10 Aug., to 5 Sept., 1899. 2nd Lieut. 11th U. S. Cav., 12 Aug., 1899.
SUTHERLAND, GEORGE, Priv., Sergt. and 1st Sergt. Troop M, 11th U. S. Cav., 5 Sept., 1899, to 15 May, 1900. 2nd Lieut. 11th U. S. Cav., 27 April, 1900.
LUTHI, EDWARD S., Priv., Sergt. and 1st Sergt. Troop C, 11th U. S. Cav., 8 Aug., 1899, to 15 May, 1900. 2nd Lieut. 11th U. S. Cav., 27 April, 1900.

## 26TH U. S. VOLUNTEER INFANTRY.

*Colonel.*

RICE, EDMUND (Regular), Col., 5 July, 1899.

*Lieutenant Colonel.*

DICKMAN, JOSEPH T. (Regular), Lieut. Col., 13 Sept., 1899.

*Majors.*

ANDERSON, EDWARD D. (Regular), Maj., 5 July, 1899.
COOK, FRANK A. (Regular), Maj. 5 July, 1899.
HENRY, GUY V., Jr. (Regular), Maj., 13 Sept., 1899.

*Surgeon with rank of Major.*

MASON, CHARLES F. (Regular), Maj. Surg., 5 July, 1899.

*Assistant Surgeons with rank of Captain.*

WASHBURN, FREDERIC A., Jr., Asst Surg. 6th Mass. Inf., 5 May, 1898. Mustered out 21 Jan., 1899. Capt. Asst. Surg. 26th U. S. Inf., 5 July, 1899.

*With rank of First Lieutenant.*

GRISWOLD, RICHARD S., Asst. Surg. 1st Conn. Inf., 4 May, 1898. Mustered out 31 Oct., 1898. 1st Lieut. Asst. Surg. 26th U. S. Inf., 5 July, 1899.

*Captains.*

BARKER, ALVIN A., Maj. 1st R. I. Inf., 30 April, 1898. Mustered out 30 March, 1899. Capt. 26th U. S. Inf., 5 July, 1899.
McDONALD, FRED, Capt. 5th Mass. Inf., 23 June, 1898. Mustered out 31 March, 1899. Capt. 26th U. S. Inf., 5 July, 1899.
GREIG, ALEXANDER, Jr., Capt. 6th Mass. Inf., 12 May, 1898. Mustered out 21 Jan., 1899. Capt. 26th U. S. Inf., 5 July, 1899.
PENDLETON, HARRIS, Adj., 7 Dec., 1899. 1st Sergt. Co. I, 3rd Conn. Inf., 30 June, to 28 July, 1898. 2nd Lieut. 3rd Conn. Inf., 29 July, 1898. 1st Lieut., 15 Oct., 1898. Mustered out 20 March, 1899. Capt., 26th U. S. Inf., 5 July, 1899.
BORDMAN, JOHN, Jr., Capt. 1st Mass. Heavy Art., 26 April, 1898. Mustered out 14 Nov., 1898. Capt. 26th U. S. Inf., 5 July, 1899.
MEEKS, WILLIAM F., Q. M., 1 Dec., 1899. Capt. 71st N. Y. Inf., 2 May, 1898. Mustered out 15 Nov., 1898. Capt. 26th U. S. Inf., 5 July, 1899.
TALBOT, THOMAS, 2nd Lieut. 6th Mass. Inf., 9 July, 1898. Mustered out 21 Jan., 1899. Capt. 26th U. S. Inf., 5 July, 1899.
BROWNELL, CORNELIUS M., Capt. 1st Vt. Inf., 4 May, 1898. Mustered out 7 Nov., 1898. Capt. 26th U. S. Inf., 5 July, 1899.
WHIPPLE, REUBEN A., Priv. Co. B, 8th Mass. Inf., 16 July, 1864, to 10 Nov., 1864. Maj. 2nd Mass. Inf., 3 May, 1898. Mustered out 3 Nov., 1898. Capt. 26th U. S. Inf., 5 July, 1899.
HICKEY, JOHN, Maj. 1st Conn. Inf., 4 May, 1898. Mustered out 31 Oct., 1898. Capt. 26th U. S. Inf., 5 July, 1899.
TUTHERLY, WILLIAM, Maj. 1st N. H. Inf., 12 May, 1898. Mustered out 31 Oct., 1898. Capt. 26th U. S. Inf., 5 July, 1899.
HUBBARD, GEORGE O., 1st Lieut. 1st Maine Inf., 11 May, 1898. Mustered out 30 Oct., 1898. Capt. 26th U. S. Inf., 5 July, 1899.
PECK, FRANK H., Priv. Co. F and Sergt. Maj. 9th N. Y. Inf., 21 May, to 2 June, 1898. 2nd Lieut. N. Y. Inf., 3 June, 1898. Capt., 23 July, 1898. Mustered out 15 Nov., 1898. Capt. 26th U. S. Inf., 5 July, 1899.
CONNELL, WILLIAM M., 1st Lieut. 12th N. Y. Inf., 2 May, 1898. Capt., 13 Nov., 1898. Mustered out 20 April, 1899. 1st Lieut. 26th U. S. Inf., 5 July, 1899. Capt., 13 Sept., 1899.

*First Lieutenants.*

CROCKETT, HENRY G., Capt. 1st Maine Heavy Art., 2 May, 1898. Mustered out 31 March, 1899. 1st Lieut. 26th U. S. Inf., 5 July, 1899.
CLARE, JAMES P., Drum. Co. E, Prin. and 1st Prin. Musician 19th Mass. Inf., 28 Aug., 1861, to 30 June, 1865. Capt. 5th Mass. Inf., 24 June, 1898. Mustered out 31 March, 1899. 1st Lieut. 26th U. S. Inf., 5 July, 1899.
GOODALE, JAMES R., Sergt. and Sergt. Maj. 1st N. Y. Inf., 2 May, to 17 July, 1898. 2nd Lieut. 1st N. Y. Inf., 18 July, 1898. Mustered out 17 March, 1899. 1st Lieut. 12th N. Y. Inf., 27 March, 1899. Mustered out 20 April, 1899. 1st Lieut. 26th U. S. Inf., 5 July, 1899.
AVERY, SOLOMON, Jr., 1st Lieut. and Adj. 203rd N. Y. Inf., 11 July, 1898. Capt., 2 Feb., 1899. Mustered out 25 March, 1899. 1st Lieut. 26th U. S. Inf., 5 July, 1899.
FALES, HENRY M., Capt. 3rd N. Y. Inf., 1 May, 1898. Mustered out 7 Dec., 1898. 1st Lieut. 26th U. S. Inf., 5 July, 1899.
HASBROUCK, ALFRED, 1st Sergt. Co. C, 201st N. Y. Inf., 7 July, to 25 Sept., 1898. 2nd Lieut. 201st N. Y. Inf., 26 Sept., 1898. 1st Lieut., 3 Jan., 1899. Mustered out 3 April, 1899. 1st Lieut. 26th U. S. Inf., 5 July, 1899.
MOYNIHAN, DANIEL J., 2nd Lieut. 2nd Mass. Inf., 3 May, 1898. Mustered out 3 Nov., 1898. 1st Lieut. 26th U. S. Inf., 5 July, 1899.
PLUMMER, WILLIAM H., 2nd Lieut. 2nd Mass. Inf., 3 May, 1898. Mustered out 3 Nov., 1898. 1st Lieut. 26th U. S. Inf., 5 July, 1899.

SULLIVAN, WILLIAM, Capt. 1st N. H. Inf., 11 May, 1898. Mustered out 31 Oct., 1898. 1st Lieut. 26th U. S. Inf., 5 July, 1899.

GOLDERMAN, PHILIP S., Sergt. Co. I, and Color Sergt. 203rd N. Y. Inf., 11 July, to 27 Oct., 1898. 2nd Lieut. 203rd N. Y. Inf., 28 Oct., 1898. Mustered out 25 March, 1899. 1st Lieut. 26th U. S. Inf., 5 July, 1899.

RICE, GEORGE D., Chap. 6th Mass. Inf., 4 Oct., 1898. Mustered out 21 Jan., 1899. 1st Lieut. 26th U. S. Inf., 5 July, 1899.

MASON, ALFRED M., 1st Sergt. Co. B, 1st Vt. Inf., 5 May, to 15 Aug., 1898. 2nd Lieut. 1st Vt. Inf., 16 Aug., 1898. Mustered out 5 Nov., 1898. 1st Lieut. 26th U. S. Inf., 5 July, 1899.

EDWARDS, FRANK E., Com., 1 Aug., 1899 Pvt. Co. A, 6th Mass. Inf., 27 June, to 18 Dec., 1898. 2nd Lieut. 6th Mass. Inf., 19 Dec., 1898. Mustered out 21 Jan., 1899. 1st Lieut. 26th U. S. Inf., 5 July, 1899.

FORTESCUE, GRANVILLE R., Corpl. Troop E, 1st U. S. Cav., 5 May, to 15 Sept., 1898. 1st Lieut. 26th U. S. Inf., 5 July, 1899.

ELLIOTT, DUNCAN, 1st Lieut. 26th U. S. Inf., 5 July, 1898.

COMSTOCK, HARRY E., 1st Lieut. 3rd Conn. Inf., 22 June, 1898. Mustered out 20 March, 1899. 2nd Lieut. 26th U. S. Inf., 5 July, 1899. 1st Lieut., 13 Sept., 1899.

*Second Lieutenants.*

GRANT, HOMER B., Sergt. Co. G, 5th Mass. Inf., 25 June, 1898, to 7 July, 1898. 2nd Lieut. 5th Mass. Inf., 8 July, 1898. 1st Lieut., 3 March, 1899. Mustered out 31 March, 1899. 2nd Lieut. 26th U. S. Inf., 5 July, 1899.

OLIN, HILDEN, 2nd Lieut. 71st N. Y. Inf., 2 May, 1898. Mustered out 15 Nov., 1898. 2nd Lieut. 26th U. S. Inf., 5 July, 1899.

WAGNER, MAX, 2nd Lieut. Sig. Off., 2 June, 1898. Discharged 5 Dec., 1898. 2nd Lieut. 26th U. S. Inf., 5 July, 1899.

WORTHINGTON, SANFORD E., 2nd Lieut. 1st Vt. Inf., 18 May, 1898. Mustered out 2 Nov., 1898. 2nd Lieut. 26th U. S. Inf., 5 July, 1899.

BALL, GARRISON, 1st Sergt. Co. —, 201st N. Y. Inf., 8 July, 1898, to 31 Oct., 1898. 2nd Lieut. 201st N. Y. Inf., 1 Nov., 1898. Mustered out 3 April, 1899. 2nd Lieut. 26th U. S. Inf., 5 July, 1899.

COUGHLAN, TIMOTHY M., Priv. and 1st Sergt. Co. A, 201st N. Y. Inf., 11 July, 1898, to 12 Nov., 1898. 2nd Lieut. 201st N. Y. Inf., 13 Nov., 1898. Mustered out 3 April, 1899. 2nd Lieut. 26th U. S. Inf., 5 July, 1899.

JEUNET, ERNEST A., Sergt. Sig. Corps, 6 July, 1898, to 29 April, 1899. 2nd Lieut. 26th U. S. Inf., 5 July, 1899.

RYAN, JOHN T., Sergt. and 1st Sergt. Cos. A and G, 202nd N. Y. Inf., 9 July, 1898, to 15 April, 1899. 2nd Lieut. 26th U. S. Inf., 5 July, 1899.

FERNALD, ROY L., 2nd Lieut. 26th U. S. Inf., 5 July, 1899.

SILLMAN, ROBERT H., 2nd Lieut. 26th U. S. Inf., 5 July, 1899.

MacGREGOR, GEORGE R. D., Q. M. Sergt. Co. G, and Sergt. Maj. 1st R. I. Inf., 28 April, 1898, to 8 Dec., 1898. 2nd Lieut. 1st R. I. Inf., 9 Dec., 1898. Mustered out 30 March, 1899. Priv. and Sergt. Maj. 26th U. S. Inf., 20 July, 1899, to 17 Sept., 1899. 2nd Lieut. 26th U. S. Inf., 13 Sept., 1899.

GARITY, GEORGE, Priv. and Com. Sergt. 26th U. S. Inf., 24 July, 1899, to 25 Sept., 1899. 2nd Lieut. 26th U. S. Inf., 25 Sept., 1899.

## 27TH U. S. VOLUNTEER INFANTRY.

*Colonel.*

CUMMINS, ALBERT S. (Regular), Lieut. Col. 27th U. S. Inf., 5 July, 1899. Col., 4 Feb., 1900.

*Lieutenant Colonel.*

BYRAM, GEORGE L. (Regular), Maj. 27th U. S. Inf., 5 July, 1899. Lieut. Col., 4 Feb., 1900.

*Majors.*

CASSATT, EDWARD B. (Regular), Capt. A. A. G., 12 May, 1898. Discharged 12 May, 1899. Maj. 27th U. S. Inf., 5 July, 1899.

HUNT, CLYDE D. V., Capt. A. Q. M., 3 June, 1898. Discharged 12 July, 1899. Maj. 27th U. S. Inf., 5 July, 1899.

SCHERER, LOUIS C. (Regular), Capt. A. A. G., 12 May, 1898. Discharged 7 March, 1899. Capt. 27th U. S. Inf., 5 July, 1899. Maj., 4 Feb., 1900.

*Surgeon with rank of Major.*

RAFFERTY, OGDEN (Regular), Maj. Brig. Surg., 4 June, 1898. Discharged 30 Nov., 1898. Maj. Surg. 27th U. S. Inf., 5 July, 1899.

*Assistant Surgeons with rank of Captain.*

BOWEN, WILLIAM, Maj. Surg. 3rd Tenn. Inf., 5 May, 1898. Mustered out 31 Jan., 1899. Capt. Asst. Surg. 27th U. S. Inf., 5 July, 1899.

*With rank of First Lieutenant.*

GRAVES, LEONARD K., 1st Lieut. Asst. Surg. 201st N. Y. Inf., 27 June, 1898. Mustered out 3 April, 1899. 1st Lieut. Asst. Surg. 27th U. S. Inf., 5 July, 1899.

*Captains.*

**JUDSON, WILLIAM F.**, Capt. 12th N. Y. Inf., 2 May, 1898. Mustered out 20 April, 1899. Capt. 27th U. S. Inf., 5 July, 1899.
**CASTEEL, DELPHEY T. E.**, Col. 2nd W. Va. Inf., 25 May, 1898. Mustered out 10 April, 1899. Capt. 27th U. S. Inf., 5 July, 1899.
**ATKINSON, HOWARD**, Maj. 2nd W. Va. Inf., 25 May, 1898. Mustered out 10 April, 1899. Capt. 27th U. S. Inf., 5 July, 1899.
**SLOAN, ALBERT B.**, Capt. 6th Mo. Inf., 11 July, 1898. Mustered out 10 May, 1899. Capt. 27th U. S. Inf., 5 July, 1899.
**GRACIE, WILLIAM B.**, Capt. 1st N. Y. Inf., 2 May, 1898. Mustered out 20 Feb., 1899. Capt. 27th U. S. Inf., 5 July, 1899.
**CURREY, EASTMAN G.**, Q. M., 16 July, 1899. 1st Lieut. and Adj. 2nd Tenn. Inf., 3 May, 1898. Mustered out 8 Feb., 1899. Capt. 27th U. S. Inf., 5 July, 1899.
**STURGES, DEXTER**, Priv. Co. B, 3rd N. Y. Inf., 1 May, 1898, to 29 July, 1898. 1st Lieut. 203rd N. Y. Inf., 30 July, 1898. Mustered out 25 March, 1899. 1st Lieut. 27th U. S. Inf., 5 July, 1899. Capt. 5 July, 1899.
**BRANDLE, GEORGE W.**, Capt. 7th Ohio Inf., 25 April, 1898. Mustered out 6 Nov., 1898. Capt. 27th U. S. Inf., 5 July, 1899.
**GRAHAM, FRANK L.**, Capt. 1st D. C. Inf., 15 May, 1898. Mustered out 20 Nov., 1898. Capt. 27th U. S. Inf., 5 July, 1899.
**BECHT, CHARLES**, Capt. 1st Ohio Inf., 25 April, 1898. Mustered out 25 Oct., 1898. Capt. 27th U. S. Inf., 5 July, 1899.
**TAYLOR, THEODORE B.**, 2nd Lieut. 8th N. Y. Inf., 2 May, 1898. 1st Lieut., 6 July, 1898. Trans. to 12th N. Y. Inf., 1 Nov., 1898. Capt., 11 Jan., 1899. Mustered out 20 April, 1899. 1st Lieut. 27th U. S. Inf., 5 July, 1899. Capt., 21 Oct., 1899.
**GAUJOT, JULIEN E.**, Capt. 2nd W Va. Inf., 26 May, 1898. Mustered out 10 April, 1899. 1st Lieut. 27th U. S. Inf., 5 July, 1899. Capt., 2 Nov., 1899.
**FAUNTLEROY, JAMES D.**, 1st Lieut. 3rd U. S. Eng., 7 July, 1898. Capt., 24 Jan., 1899. Mustered out 17 May, 1899. 1st Lieut. 27th U. S. Inf., 5 July, 1899. Capt., 1 Dec., 1899.
**COLLETT, ZAN F.**, Capt. 1st W. Va. Inf., 27 April, 1898. Mustered out 4 Feb., 1899. 1st Lieut. 27th U. S. Inf., 5 July, 1899. Capt., 4 Feb., 1900.

*First Lieutenants.*

**KENNEDY, JOHN J.**, Capt. 69th N. Y. Inf., 2 May, 1898. Mustered out 31 Jan., 1899. 1st Lieut. 27th U. S. Inf., 5 July, 1899.
**HARTSHORN, EDWIN S.**, 1st Lieut. 201st N. Y. Inf., 6 July, 1898. Capt., 3 Jan., 1899. Mustered out 3 April, 1899. 1st Lieut. 27th U. S. Inf., 5 July, 1899.
**HANNAH, JAMES G.**, 1st Lieut. 203rd N. Y. Inf., 11 July, 1898. Mustered out 25 March, 1899. 1st Lieut. 27th U. S. Inf., 5 July, 1899.
**RODNEY, GEORGE B.**, 2nd Lieut. 1st Del. Inf., 18 May, 1898. Mustered out 19 Dec., 1898. 1st Lieut. 27th U. S. Inf., 5 July, 1899.
**WEED, OSCAR D.**, Capt. 9th N. Y. Inf., 2 May, 1898. Mustered out 15 Nov., 1898. 1st Lieut. 27th U. S. Inf., 5 July, 1899.
**GRIFFITHS, JOSEPH H.**, Com., 11 July, 1899. 1st Lieut. 1st D. C. Inf., 15 May, 1898. Mustered out 20 Nov., 1898. 1st Lieut. 27th U. S. Inf., 5 July, 1899.
**O'FLAHERTY, EDWARD**, 1st Lieut. 27th U. S. Inf., 5 July, 1899.
**GRIFFIN, FRANCIS W.**, Corpl. and Sergt. Co. —, 3rd U. S. Eng., 21 July, 1898, to 1 Sept., 1898. 2nd Lieut. 3rd U. S. Eng., 26 Aug., 1898. 1st Lieut., 15 April, 1899. Mustered out 17 May, 1899. 2nd Lieut. 27th U. S. Inf., 5 July, 1899. 1st Lieut. 5 Sept., 1899.
**PLUMMER, FREDERICK H.**, 1st Sergt. Co. K, 4th Va. Inf., 25 April, 1898, to 5 Oct., 1898. 2nd Lieut. 4th Va. Inf., 6 Oct., 1898. Mustered out 27 April, 1899. 2nd Lieut. 27th U. S. Inf., 5 July, 1899. 1st Lieut., 8 Sept., 1899.
**KNOX, ROBERT S.**, 2nd Lieut. 3rd Va. Inf., 23 April, 1898. Mustered out 5 Nov., 1898. 2nd Lieut. 27th U. S. Inf., 5 July, 1899. 1st Lieut., 12 Sept., 1899.
**SHAW, GEORGE C.**, 1st Lieut. 1st D. C. Inf., 16 May, 1898. Mustered out 20 Nov., 1898. Priv. 27th U. S. Inf., 12 July, 1899, to 19 July, 1899. 2nd Lieut. 27th U. S. Inf., 5 July, 1899. 1st Lieut., 12 Sept., 1899.
**MUNFORD, LOUIE ST. CLAIR**, 2nd Lieut. 2nd Ala. Inf., 24 May, 1898. Mustered out 31 Oct., 1898. 2nd Lieut. 27th U. S. Inf., 5 July, 1899. 1st Lieut., 21 Oct., 1899.
**FAULKNER, ALBERT U.**, Priv. Troop C, N. Y. Cav., 11 June, 1898, to 25 Nov., 1898. 2nd Lieut. 27th U. S. Inf., 5 July, 1899. 1st Lieut., 2 Nov., 1899.
**CASSELS, JOHN C.**, Priv. and Sergt. Co. K, 3rd Pa. Inf., 20 July, 1898, to 8 Oct., 1898. 2nd Lieut. 27th U. S. Inf., 5 July, 1899. 1st Lieut., 1 Dec., 1899.
**BREWER, RICHARD H.**, 2nd Lieut. 27th U. S. Inf., 5 July, 1899. 1st Lieut., 4 Feb., 1900.
**VERNON, GEORGE A.**, Priv. Co. C, 3rd Neb. Inf., 17 June, 1898, to 27 Sept., 1898. 2nd Lieut. 27th U. S. Inf., 5 July, 1899. 1st Lieut., 31 March, 1900.

*Second Lieutenants.*

**OLIVER, JOHN**, 2nd Lieut. 27th U. S. Inf., 5 July, 1899.
**HYMAN, DANIEL**, 2nd Lieut. 27th U. S Inf., 5 July, 1899.
**KNOX, THOMAS MACALLISTER**, Priv. and Sergt. Co. D, 27th U. S. Inf., 21 July, 1899, to 15 Aug., 1899. 2nd Lieut. 27th U. S. Inf., 12 Aug., 1899.
**WARD, MATTHEW T. E.**, Sergt. and 1st Sergt. Co. C, 27th U. S. Inf., 12 July, 1899, to 6 Sept., 1899. 2nd Lieut. 27th U. S. Inf., 5 Sept., 1899.
**McCOY, ARTHUR L.**, 1st Sergt. Co. H, 7th Ohio Inf., 25 April, 1898, to 6 Nov., 1898. 1st Sergt. Co. B, 27th U. S. Inf., 22 July, 1899, to 13 Sept., 1899. 2nd Lieut. 27th U. S. Inf., 13 Sept., 1899.
**LACOUR, JOSEPH W.**, Hosp. Steward 27th U. S. Inf., 18 July, 1899, to 17 Sept., 1899. 2nd Lieut. 27th U. S. Inf., 14 Sept., 1899.

HENNESSY, FREDERICK B., Priv. and Corpl. Co. A, 1st R. I. Inf., 29 April, 1898, to 30 March, 1899. 1st Sergt. Co. D, 27th U. S. Inf., 15 July, 1899, to 17 Sept., 1899. 2nd Lieut. 27th U. S. Inf., 14 Sept., 1899.
RAYMOND, WILLIAM H., Sergt. and 1st Sergt. Co. C, 27th U. S. Inf., 13 July, 1899, to 27 Nov., 1899. 2nd Lieut. 27th U. S. Inf., 27 Nov., 1899.
PERKINS, ALVIN S., Priv. Co. G, 6th U. S. Inf., 6 July, 1898, to 15 March, 1899. Sergt. Co. E, 27th U. S. Inf., 11 July, 1899, to 27 Nov., 1899. 2nd Lieut. 27th U. S. Inf., 27 Nov., 1899.
CRUSAN, CLYDE B., Priv. Co. K, 14th Pa. Inf., 14 June, 1898, to 28 Feb., 1899. Q. M. Sergt. Co. C, Batt. and Reg. Sergt. Maj. 27th U. S. Inf., 15 July, 1899, to 12 Feb., 1900. 2nd Lieut. 27th U. S. Inf., 29 Jan., 1900.
CARPENTER, CHARLES E., Sergt. Co. D, 27th U. S. Inf., 5 Aug., 1899, to 2 April, 1900. 2nd Lieut. 27th U. S. Inf., 12 March, 1900.

## 28TH U. S. VOLUNTEER INFANTRY.

### *Colonel.*

BIRKHIMER, WILLIAM E. (Regular), Col. 28th U. S. Inf., 5 July, 1899.

### *Lieutenant Colonel.*

LEONARD, ROBERT W., Priv. Co. B, 7th N. Y. State Militia, 26 April, 1861, to 3 June, 1861, and from 19 June, 1862, to 5 Sept., 1862. 1st Lieut. and Adj. 162nd N. Y. Inf., 15 Sept., 1862. Maj., 1 Sept., 1863. Discharged 5 Feb., 1864. Bvt. Lieut. Col., 13 March, 1865. Col. 12th N. Y. Inf., 2 May, 1898. Mustered out 20 April, 1899. Lieut. Col. 28th U. S. Inf., 5 July, 1899.

### *Majors.*

MORGAN, GEORGE H. (Regular), Maj. 28th U. S. Inf., 5 July, 1899.
TAGGART, ELMORE F. (Regular), Maj. 28th U. S. Inf., 5 July, 1899.
PORTER, JOHN B., Col. 2nd Pa. Inf., 28 April, 1898. Mustered out 15 Nov., 1898. Maj. 28th U. S. Inf., 5 July, 1899.

### *Surgeon with rank of Major.*

CHALMERS, THOMAS C., 1st Lieut. Asst. Surg. 12th N. Y. Inf., 6 May, 1898. Capt. Asst. Surg., 7 Oct., 1898. Maj. Surg., 1 Nov., 1898. Mustered out 20 April, 1899. Maj. Surg. 28th U. S. Inf., 5 July, 1899.

### *Assistant Surgeons with rank of Captain.*

DE KRAFFT, SAMUEL C., Capt. Asst. Surg. 1st Md. Inf., 28 April, 1898. Mustered out 28 Feb., 1899. Capt. Asst. Surg. 28th U. S. Inf., 5 July, 1899.

### *With rank of First Lieutenant.*

PEED, GEORGE P., Capt. Asst. Surg. 4th Va. Inf., 5 May, 1898. Mustered out 27 April, 1899. 1st Lieut. Asst. Surg. 28th U. S. Inf., 5 July, 1899.

### *Captains.*

HOWLAND, CHARLES R. (Regular), Capt. 28th U. S. Inf., 5 July, 1899.
CARSON, ADAM C., Capt. 4th U. S. Inf., 22 June, 1898. Mustered out 8 June, 1899. Capt. 28th U. S. Inf., 5 July, 1899
BICKHAM, CHARLES G., Corpl. Co. G, 3rd Ohio Inf., 26 April, 1898, to ——. Capt. 9th U. S. Inf., 19 July, 1898. Mustered out 25 May, 1899. Capt. 28th U. S. Inf., 5 July, 1899.
CRENSHAW, FRANK F., 2nd Lieut. 3rd U. S. Inf., 17 June, 1898. 1st Lieut., 12 Aug., 1898. Mustered out 2 May, 1899. Capt. 28th U. S. Inf., 5 July, 1899.
VREDENBURGH, PETER, Capt. 3rd N. J. Inf., 27 April, 1898. Mustered out 11 Feb., 1899. Capt. 28th U. S. Inf., 5 July, 1899.
CRAWFORD, SAMUEL D., Maj. 15th Pa. Inf., 27 April, 1898. Mustered out 31 Jan., 1899. Capt. 28th U. S. Inf., 5 July, 1899.
FRIES, CLAUDE S., Capt. 4th N. J. Inf., 7 July, 1898. Mustered out 6 April, 1899. Capt. 28th U. S. Inf., 5 July, 1899.
BIEGLER, GEORGE W., Capt. 159th Ind. Inf., 26 April, 1898. Mustered out 23 Nov., 1898. Capt. 28th U. S. Inf., 5 July, 1899.
DUNN, JOHN H., Capt. 9th Mass. Inf., 4 May, 1898. Mustered out 26 Nov., 1898. Capt. 28th U. S. Inf., 5 July, 1899.
CAMPBELL, CHARLES S., Adj., 17 July, 1899. 1st Lieut. and Adj. 2nd Pa. Inf., 28 April, 1898. Mustered out 15 Nov., 1898. Capt. 28th U. S. Inf., 5 July, 1898.
KING, WILLIAM C., Maj. 12th Pa. Inf., 27 April, 1898. Mustered out 29 Oct., 1898. Capt. 28th U. S. Inf., 5 July, 1899.
COUCH, EDWARD H. D., Capt. 5th Ill. Inf., 26 April, 1898. Mustered out 16 Oct., 1898. Capt. 28th U. S. Inf., 5 July, 1899.
PRICE, SAMUEL A., Maj. 6th Pa. Inf., 28 April, 1898. Mustered out 17 Oct., 1898. Capt. 28th U. S. Inf., 5 July, 1899.
CROASMUN, JOHN D., Capt. 16th Pa. Inf., 15 July, 1898. Mustered out 28 Dec., 1898. Capt. 28th U. S. Inf., 5 July, 1899.

*First Lieutenants.*

TEAGARDEN, JOHN P., Capt. C. S., 4 June, 1898. Discharged 30 June, 1899. 1st Lieut. 28th U. S. Inf., 5 July, 1899.
EASTON, ALPHA T., Capt. 14th Pa. Inf., 27 April, 1898. Mustered out 28 Feb., 1899. 1st Lieut. 28th U. S. Inf., 5 July, 1899.
BOICE, CHARLES H., 1st Lieut. 1st N. Y. Inf., 1 May, 1898. Mustered out 25 Feb., 1899. 1st Lieut. 28th U. S. Inf., 5 July, 1899.
BARBER, CHARLES W., 2nd Lieut. 4th N. J. Inf., 7 July, 1898. 1st Lieut., 27 Sept., 1898. Capt., 3 March, 1899. Mustered out 6 April, 1899. 1st Lieut. 28th U. S. Inf., 5 July, 1899.
WALDRON, LEONARD T., Com., 14 Aug., 1899. Capt. 202nd N. Y. Inf., 25 July, 1898. Mustered out 15 April, 1899. 1st Lieut. 28th U. S. Inf., 5 July, 1899.
BEATTY, CHARLES L., Capt. 10th U. S. Inf., 21 June, 1898. Mustered out 8 March, 1899. 1st Lieut. 28th U. S. Inf., 5 July, 1899.
DUNN, JOHN M., 1st Lieut. and Adj. 1st Del. Inf., 28 April, 1898. Mustered out 16 Nov., 1898. 1st Lieut. 28th U. S. Inf., 5 July, 1899.
WILLITS, SAMUEL, Capt. 4th Pa. Inf., 28 April, 1898. Mustered out 16 Nov., 1898. 1st Lieut. 28th U. S. Inf., 5 July, 1899.
STAYER, EDGAR S., 2nd Lieut. 5th Pa. Inf., 27 April, 1898. Mustered out 7 Nov., 1898. 1st Lieut. 28th U. S. Inf., 5 July, 1899.
WOOTTEN, BRADLEY J., 1st Lieut. 2nd N. C. Inf., 17 May, 1898. Mustered out 25 Nov., 1898. 1st Lieut. 28th U. S. Inf., 5 July, 1899.
ALLEN, CHARLES C., 1st Lieut. 1st Pa. Inf., 28 April, 1898. Mustered out 26 Oct., 1898. 1st Lieut. 28th U. S. Inf., 5 July, 1899.
TERRELL, HENRY S., 2nd Lieut. Batty C, 1st Conn. Heavy Art., 7 May, 1898. 1st Lieut., 19 Oct., 1898. Mustered out 29 Oct., 1898. 1st Lieut. 28th U. S. Inf., 5 July, 1899.
GEINTY, DANIEL H., 1st Lieut. and Adj. N. H. Inf., 10 May, 1898. Mustered out 31 Oct., 1898. 1st Lieut. 28th U. S. Inf., 5 July, 1899.
WOOD, GEORGE H., Sergt. Co. G, 3rd Ohio Inf., 26 April, 1898, to 15 May, 1898. 2nd Lieut. 3rd Ohio Inf., 10 May, 1898. Mustered out 26 Oct., 1898. 1st Lieut. 28th U. S. Inf., 5 July, 1899.
NEILSON, FREDERICK B., Priv. Philadelphia City Cav., 28 April, 1898, to 21 Nov., 1898. 1st Lieut. 28th U. S. Inf., 5 July, 1899.
PORTER, HARRY A., 1st Class Priv. Co. E, 1st U. S. Eng., 25 June, 1898, to 25 Jan., 1899. 1st Lieut. 28th U. S. Inf., 5 July, 1899.

*Second Lieutenants.*

LYONS, WILLIAM H., Capt. 1st W. Va., Inf., 26 April, 1898. Maj., 23 May, 1898. Mustered out 4 Feb., 1899. 2nd Lieut. 28th U. S. Inf., 5 July, 1899.
CLARK, LEWIS M., 1st Lieut. 16th Pa. Inf., 27 April, 1898. Mustered out 28 Dec., 1898. 2nd Lieut. 28th U. S. Inf., 5 July, 1899.
HANSBURY, ROBERT S., 2nd Lieut. 10th U. S. Inf., 29 June, 1898. Mustered out 8 March, 1899. 2nd Lieut. 28th U. S. Inf., 5 July, 1899.
RUSSELL, ROBERT D., 2nd Lieut. 12th N. Y. Inf., 21 Nov., 1898. 1st Lieut., 1 Feb., 1899. Mustered out 20 April, 1899. 2nd Lieut. 28th U. S. Inf., 5 July, 1899.
MITCHELL, RALPH M. Sergt. Co. K, 4th N. J. Inf., 7 July, 1898, to 5 Dec., 1898. 2nd Lieut. 4th N. J. Inf., 6 Dec., 1898. Mustered out 6 April, 1899. 2nd Lieut. 28th U. S. Inf., 5 July, 1899.
WILSON, JOSEPH C., 2nd Lieut. 28th U. S. Inf., 5 July, 1899.
YOUNG, HUGH C., Priv. Co. K, 5th Pa. Inf., 14 July, 1898, to 9 Nov., 1898. 2nd Lieut. 28th U. S. Inf., 5 July, 1899.
DANNER, JAMES D., Priv. Co. A, 8th Pa. Inf., 28 April, 1898, to 7 March, 1899. 2nd Lieut. 28th U. S. Inf., 5 July, 1899.
NEWHALL, GEORGE T., Priv. Light Batty A, Pa. Art., 27 April, 1898, to 19 Nov., 1898. 2nd Lieut. 28th U. S. Inf., 5 July, 1899.
MABSON, MARION B., 2nd Lieut. 28th U. S. Inf., 5 July, 1899.
JONES, C. RODMAN, Priv. Co. D, 1st Pa. Inf., 28 April, 1898, to 26 Oct., 1898. 2nd Lieut. 28th U. S. Inf., 5 July, 1899.
TURNER, FREDERICK G., 1st Lieut. 12th N. Y. Inf., 2 May, 1898. Capt., 26 Oct., 1898. Discharged 16 Dec., 1898. Priv. and Sergt. Maj. 28th U. S. Inf., 12 Sept., 1899, to 16 Oct., 1899. 2nd Lieut. 28th U. S. Inf., 13 Oct., 1899.

## 29TH U. S. VOLUNTEER INFANTRY.

*Colonel.*

HARDIN, EDWARD E. (Regular), Col. 29th U. S. Inf., 5 July, 1899.

*Lieutenant Colonel.*

SARGENT, HERBERT H. (Regular), Lieut. Col. 29th U. S. Inf., 5 July, 1899.

*Majors.*

HAWTHORNE, HARRY L. (Regular), Maj. 29th U. S. Inf., 5 July, 1899.
JOHNSON, EVAN M., Jr. (Regular), Maj. 29th U. S. Inf., 5 July, 1899.
CASE, DAVID B., Col. 4th Pa. Inf., 28 April, 1898. Mustered out 16 Nov., 1898. Maj. 29th U. S. Inf., 5 July, 1899.

*Surgeon with rank of Major.*

ANDERSON, CHARLES L. G., Maj. Surg. 29th U. S. Inf., 5 July, 1899.

*Assistant Surgeons with rank of Captain.*

MINOR, JAMES C., Surg. 1st Ark. Inf., 7 May, 1898. Mustered out 25 Oct., 1898. Capt. Asst. Surg. 29th U. S. Inf., 5 July, 1899.

*With rank of First Lieutenant.*

SANFORD, JOSEPH L., 1st Lieut. Asst. Surg. 29th U. S. Inf., 15 Aug., 1899.

*Captains.*

PURINTON, HOLMAN G., Priv. Co. B, 29th Maine Inf., 1 Feb., 1865, to 2 Feb., 1866. Maj. 2nd Ill. Inf., 26 April, 1898. Mustered out 26 April, 1899. Capt. 29th U. S. Inf., 5 July, 1899.
LIDDELL, JAMES M., Maj. 5th U. S. Inf., 22 June, 1898. Mustered out 31 May, 1899. Capt. 29th U. S. Inf., 5 July, 1899.
PAUL, WILLIAM A., 1st Lieut. Batty A, 1st Maine Heavy Art., 2 May, 1898. Mustered out 31 March, 1899. Capt. 29th U. S. Inf., 5 July, 1899.
STERN, PHILIP H., 1st Lieut. 5th U. S. Inf., 13 July, 1898. Capt., 3 Feb., 1899. Mustered out 31 May, 1899. Capt. 29th U. S. Inf., 5 July, 1899.
FAULKNER, WILLIAM S., 2nd Lieut. 3rd Va. Inf., 20 April, 1898. Capt., 27 May, 1898. Discharged 21 Oct., 1898. Capt. 6th Va. Inf., 22 Oct., 1898. Mustered out 28 Jan., 1899. Capt. 29th U. S. Inf., 5 July, 1899.
McGHEE, CHARLES G., Capt. 3rd Miss. Inf., 5 July, 1898. Mustered out 15 March, 1899. Capt. 29th U. S. Inf., 5 July, 1899.
LOVELL, GEORGE E., Capt. 1st Fla. Inf., 18 May, 1898. Mustered out 27 Jan., 1899. Capt. 29th U. S. Inf., 5 July, 1899.
SHIELDS, DEVEREUX, Lieut. Col. 2nd Miss. Inf., 24 April, 1898. Mustered out 20 Dec., 1898. Capt. 29th U. S. Inf., 5 July, 1899.
KENAN, OWEN T., Maj. 1st Ga. Inf., 2 May, 1898. Mustered out 18 Nov., 1898. Capt. 7th U. S. Inf., 21 Jan., 1899. Mustered out 28 Feb., 1899. Capt. 29th U. S. Inf., 5 July, 1899.
WILLCOXON, CLEVELAND, Capt. 2nd Ga. Inf., 29 April, 1898. Mustered out 30 Nov., 1898. Capt. 29th U. S. Inf., 5 July, 1899.
GRANT, JOSEPH H., 1st Lieut. and Adj. 1st S. C. Inf., 4 May, 1898. Mustered out 10 Nov., 1898. Capt. 29th U. S. Inf., 5 July, 1899.
WILLIAMS, ALBERT S., Sergt. Co. C, 2nd Ala. Inf., 6 May, 1898, to 13 Oct., 1898. Capt. 29th U. S. Inf., 5 July, 1899.
WHITMAN, FRANK S., Priv. Co. G, 71st N. Y. Inf., 2 May, 1898, to 15 Nov., 1898. Capt. 29th U. S. Inf., 5 July, 1899.
RASH, JAMES R., 2nd Lieut. 3rd Ky. Inf., 7 May, 1898. Mustered out 16 May, 1899. 1st Lieut. 29th U. S. Inf., 5 July, 1899. Capt., 29 July, 1899.

*First Lieutenants.*

HILL, EDWARD, Capt. 1st N. C. Inf., 27 April, 1898. Mustered out 22 April, 1899. 1st Lieut. 29th U. S. Inf., 5 July, 1899.
LONGSTREET, JAMES, Jr., 2nd Lieut. Batty A, Ga. Art., 7 May, 1898. Mustered out 17 Oct., 1898. 1st Lieut. 9th U. S. Inf., 28 Nov., 1898. Mustered out 25 May, 1899. 1st Lieut. 29th U. S. Inf., 5 July, 1899.
FUQUA, STEPHEN O., Capt. 2nd U. S. Inf., 8 July, 1898. Mustered out 22 June, 1899. 1st Lieut. 29th U. S. Inf., 5 July, 1899.
UNDERWOOD, THOMAS H., Capt. 5th U. S. Inf., 13 July, 1898. Mustered out 31 May, 1899. 1st Lieut. 29th U. S. Inf., 5 July, 1899.
WHEATLEY, WALTER K., Capt. 3rd U. S. Inf., 22 June, 1898. Maj., 17 March, 1899. Mustered out 2 May, 1899. 1st Lieut. 29th U. S. Inf., 5 July, 1899.
KIMBROUGH, JAMES M., Jr., 1st Lieut. 3rd Ga. Inf., 29 June, 1898. Capt., 11 Feb., 1899. Mustered out 22 April, 1899. 1st Lieut. 29th U. S. Inf., 5 July, 1899.
CLARK, WILLIAM P., 2nd Lieut. 3rd Ga. Inf., 30 June, 1898. 1st Lieut. 19 Oct., 1898. Mustered out 22 April, 1899. 1st Lieut. 29th U. S. Inf., 5 July, 1899.
BLOUNT, JAMES H., Jr., 2nd Lieut. 3rd U. S. Inf., 5 July, 1898. 1st Lieut., 14 Nov., 1898. Mustered out 2 May, 1899. 1st Lieut. 29th U. S. Inf., 5 July, 1899.
ARNOLD, ROBERT J., Capt. 3rd Tenn. Inf., 25 April, 1898. Mustered out 31 Jan., 1899. 1st Lieut. 29th U. S. Inf., 5 July, 1899.
SCREWS, WILLIAM P., 2nd Lieut. 3rd Ala. Inf., 24 June, 1898. Mustered out 20 March, 1899. 1st Lieut. 29th U. S. Inf., 5 July, 1899.
ALMAND, EDWARD H., Maj. 2nd Ga. Inf., 28 April, 1898. Mustered out 30 Nov., 1898. 1st Lieut. 29th U. S. Inf., 5 July, 1899.
WINSHIP, BLANTON, Capt. 1st Ga. Inf., 2 May, 1898. Mustered out 18 Nov., 1898. 1st Lieut. 29th U. S. Inf., 5 July, 1899.
CARSON, LAWRENCE S., Capt. 1st S. C. Inf., 5 May, 1898. Mustered out 10 Nov., 1898. 1st Lieut. 29th U. S. Inf., 5 July, 1899.
WILSON, MADISON H., 1st Sergt. Co. K, 1st Fla. Inf., 24 May, 1898, to 7 Aug., 1898. 2nd Lieut. 1st Fla. Inf., 8 Aug., 1898. Mustered out 3 Dec., 1898. 1st Lieut. 29th U. S. Inf., 5 July, 1899.
GRINSTEAD, ROBERT E., 1st Sergt. Cos. I and D, 2nd Ky. Inf., 3 May, 1898, to 31 Oct., 1898. 1st Lieut. 29th U. S. Inf., 5 July, 1899.
WELLS, WILLIAM S., Jr., 2nd Lieut. 3rd Ala. Inf., 30 April, 1898. 1st Lieut., 17 June, 1898. Mustered out 20 March, 1899. 2nd Lieut. 29th U. S. Inf., 5 July, 1899. 1st Lieut., 29 July, 1899.

*Second Lieutenants.*

ELMORE, VINCENT M., Jr., 1st Lieut. 2nd Ala. Inf., 2 May, 1898. Mustered out 31 Oct., 1898. 2nd Lieut. 3rd Ala. Inf., 31 Oct., 1898. Mustered out 20 March, 1899. 2nd Lieut. 29th U. S. Inf., 5 July, 1899.

MOORMAN, THOMAS S., Jr., 1st Lieut. 2nd S. C. Inf., 6 Aug., 1898. Mustered out 19 April, 1899. 2nd Lieut. 29th U. S. Inf., 5 July, 1899.
HOLLEY, GEORGE M., 2nd Class Priv., Sergt. and 1st Sergt. Co. H, 3rd U. S. Eng., 25 July, 1898, to 30 Oct., 1898. 2nd Lieut. 3rd U. S. Eng., 20 Oct., 1898. Mustered out 17 May, 1899. 2nd Lieut. 29th U. S. Inf., 5 July, 1899.
PATTERSON, ROBERT O., Corpl. and Sergt. Co. F, 1st N. C. Inf., 27 April, 1898, to 23 Nov., 1898. 2nd Lieut. 1st N. C. Inf., 24 Nov., 1898. Mustered out 22 April, 1899. 2nd Lieut. 29th U. S. Inf., 5 July, 1899.
MILLER, JOHN J., Priv., Sergt. and 1st Sergt. Co. I, 3rd Ga. Inf., 7 July, 1898, to 9 March, 1899. 2nd Lieut. 3rd Ga. Inf., 10 March, 1899. Mustered out 22 April, 1899. 2nd Lieut. 29th U. S. Inf., 5 July, 1899.
HOLLINGSWORTH, MILTON H., Sergt. Co. —, and Q. M. Sergt. 4th Tenn. Inf., 24 June, 1898, to 6 May, 1899. 2nd Lieut. 29th U. S. Inf., 5 July, 1899.
PIKE, ROWLAND S., 2nd Lieut. 29th U. S. Inf., 5 July, 1899.
PERKINS, EDWARD O., 2nd Lieut. 29th U. S. Inf., 5 July, 1899.
PENDLETON, CHARLES M., Corpl. Co. H, 71st N. Y. Inf., 29 April, 1898, to 15 Nov., 1898. 2nd Lieut. 29th U. S. Inf., 9 Sept., 1899.
FARWELL, JUDGE L., Priv., Sergt. Co. A, and Sergt. Maj. 4th Mo. Inf., 27 April, 1898, to 10 Feb., 1899. 2nd Lieut. 29th U. S. Inf., 18 Sept., 1899.
HOLMES, CALVIN F., Priv. and Corpl. Co. A, 2nd Ga. Inf., 3 May, 1898, to 30 Nov., 1898. Priv. Co. G, and Sergt. Maj. 29th U. S. Inf., 24 July, 1899, to 20 Sept., 1899. 2nd Lieut. 29th U. S. Inf., 18 Sept., 1899.
RENZIEHAUSEN, WILLIAM B., Priv., Sergt. and 1st Sergt. Co. A, 29th U. S. Inf., 13 July, 1899, to 21 Sept., 1899. 2nd Lieut. 29th U. S. Inf., 18 Sept., 1899.

## 30TH U. S. VOLUNTEER INFANTRY.

*Colonel.*

GARDENER, CORNELIUS (Regular), Col. 30th U. S. Inf., 5 July, 1899.

*Lieutenant Colonel.*

CAMPBELL, JAMES R., Col. 9th Ill. Inf., 28 June, 1898. Mustered out 20 May, 1899. Lieut. Col. 30th U. S. Inf., 5 July, 1899.

*Majors.*

LOVERING, LEONARD A. (Regular), Maj. 30th U. S. Inf., 5 July, 1899.
STEELE, MATTHEW F. (Regular), Maj. 30th U. S. Inf., 5 July, 1899.
HARTIGAN, THOMAS L., Maj. 30th U. S. Inf., 5 July, 1899.

*Surgeon with rank of Major.*

McDILL, JOHN R., 1st Lieut. Asst. Surg. 1st Wis. Inf., 28 April, 1898. Maj. Brig. Surg., 4 June, 1898. Discharged 30 June, 1899. Maj. Surg. 30th U. S. Inf., 5 July, 1899.

*Assistant Surgeons with rank of Captain.*

ERWIN, JAMES J., 1st Lieut. Asst. Surg. 10th Ohio Inf., 29 June, 1898. Mustered out 23 March, 1899. Capt. Asst. Surg. 30th U. S. Inf., 5 July, 1899.

*With rank of First Lieutenant.*

EBER, ALBERT H., 1st Lieut. Asst. Surg. 35th Mich. Inf., 27 Jan., 1899. Mustered out 31 March, 1899. 1st Lieut. Asst. Surg. 30th U. S. Inf., 5 July, 1899.

*Captains.*

BURR, KENNETH M., Capt. 160th Ind. Inf., 26 April, 1898. Mustered out 25 April, 1899. Capt. 30th U. S. Inf., 5 July, 1899.
NEWBERRY, CHARLES P., Capt. 4th U. S. Inf., 10 June, 1898. Mustered out 8 June, 1899. Capt. 30th U. S. Inf., 5 July, 1899.
SCRANTON, GILMORE G., 2nd Lieut. 34th Mich. Inf., 26 April, 1898. Mustered out 1 Aug., 1898. Capt. 35th Mich. Inf., 2 Aug., 1898. Mustered out 31 March, 1899. Capt. 30th U. S. Inf., 5 July, 1899.
WEBB, MERRELL E., Maj. 33rd Mich. Inf., 26 April, 1898. Mustered out 31 Dec., 1898. Capt. 30th U. S. Inf., 5 July, 1899.
BURTON, FRANK H., Q. M., 18 Sept., 1899. Maj. 33rd Mich. Inf., 26 April, 1898. Mustered out 31 Dec., 1898. Capt. 30th U. S. Inf., 5 July, 1899.
LATIMER, FRANK W., Capt. 6th Ill. Inf., 26 April, 1898. Mustered out 25 Nov., 1898. Capt. 30th U. S. Inf., 5 July, 1899.
SMITH E. ROSS, Capt. 159th Ind. Inf., 26 April, 1898. Mustered out 23 Nov., 1898. Capt. 30th U. S. Inf., 5 July, 1899.
NEWBERRY, FRANK D., Priv. Co. K, 5th N. Y. Inf., 28 June, 1861, to 14 May, 1863. Capt. 32nd Mich. Inf., 26 April, 1898. Mustered out 5 Nov., 1898. Capt. 30th U. S. Inf., 5 July, 1899.
FITZGERALD, EDWIN H., Maj. 157th Ind. Inf., 26 April, 1898. Mustered out 1 Nov., 1898. Capt. 30th U. S. Inf., 5 July, 1899.
REESE, CHARLES E., Adj., 4 Aug., 1899. Capt. 157th Ind. Inf., 26 April, 1898. Mustered out 1 Nov., 1898. Capt. 30th U. S. Inf., 5 July, 1899.
CONNOLLY, GEORGE F., 1st Lieut. 7th Ill. Inf., 26 April, 1898. Mustered out 20 Oct., 1898. Capt. 30th U. S. Inf., 5 July, 1899.

MILLER, EDWARD Y., Capt. 5th Ill. Inf., 25 April, 1898. Mustered out 16 Oct., 1898. Capt. 30th U. S. Inf., 5 July, 1899.
KERRICK, HARRISON S., Priv. and Corpl. Co. G, 2nd Ill. Inf., 18 June, 1898, to 7 Nov., 1898. 2nd Lieut. 2nd Ill. Inf., 8 Nov., 1898. Mustered out 26 April, 1899. Capt. 30th U. S. Inf., 5 July, 1899.
PORTERFIELD, JOSEPH W., Capt. 9th Ill. Inf., 28 June, 1898. Mustered out 20 May, 1899. 1st Lieut. 30th U. S. Inf., 5 July, 1899. Capt. 22 Aug., 1899.

*First Lieutenants.*

BUCKINGHAM, FRANK D., Capt. 35th Mich. Inf., 6 June, 1898. Mustered out 31 March, 1899. 1st Lieut. 30th U. S. Inf., 5 July, 1899.
McCABE, ALBERT E., Capt. 35th Mich. Inf., 6 June, 1898. Mustered out 31 March, 1899. 1st Lieut. 30th U. S. Inf., 5 July, 1899.
BARROWS, FREDERICK J., 1st Lieut. 15th Minn. Inf., 2 July, 1898. Capt., 17 Aug., 1898. Mustered out 27 March, 1899. 1st Lieut. 30th U. S. Inf., 5 July, 1899.
TOMPKINS, EDMOND R., Sergt. Maj. 2nd S. C. Inf., 15 July, 1898, to 9 Sept., 1898. 1st Lieut. 2nd S. C. Inf., 10 Sept., 1898. Mustered out 19 April, 1899. 1st Lieut. 30th U. S. Inf., 5 July, 1899.
CORBETT, WALTER P., 2nd Lieut. 1st Ga. Inf., 5 May, 1898. 1st Lieut., 29 Aug., 1898. Mustered out 18 Nov., 1898. 1st Lieut. 30th U. S. Inf., 5 July, 1899.
McBRIDE, JOHN, Jr., 2nd Lieut. 32nd Mich. Inf., 26 April, 1898. Mustered out 9 Nov., 1898. 1st Lieut. 30th U. S. Inf., 5 July, 1899.
TARLTON, CHARLES S., Capt. 158th Ind. Inf., 26 April, 1898. Mustered out 4 Nov., 1898. 1st Lieut. 30th U. S. Inf., 5 July, 1899.
ANDRES, EDWARD H., Capt. 32nd Mich. Inf., 26 April, 1898. Mustered out 31 Oct., 1898. 1st Lieut. 30th U. S. Inf., 5 July, 1899.
FOLEY, JOHN J., 2nd Lieut. 2nd Wis. Inf., 28 April, 1898. Mustered out 20 Oct., 1898. 1st Lieut. 30th U. S. Inf., 5 July, 1899.
BLASLAND, HARRY D., Capt. 5th Ill. Inf., 25 April, 1898. Mustered out 16 Oct., 1898. 1st Lieut. 30th U. S. Inf., 5 July, 1899.
PECKENPAUGH, VIRDEN C., 2nd Lieut. 5th Ill. Inf., 25 April, 1898. 1st Lieut., 18 Aug., 1898. Mustered out 16 Oct., 1898. 1st Lieut. 30th U. S. Inf., 5 July, 1899.
WHITSON, KAOLIN L., Sergt. and 1st Sergt. Co. A, 1st Md. Inf., 4 May, 1898, to 28 Feb., 1899. 1st Lieut. 30th U. S. Inf., 5 July, 1899.
WELLS, DANIEL, Priv. Co. E, 1st N. Y. Inf., 26 July, 1898, to 21 Feb., 1899. 1st Lieut. 30th U. S. Inf., 5 July, 1899.
McMILLAN, ALBERT C., Priv. Troop B, 1st U. S. Cav., 23 May, 1898, to 24 Oct., 1898. 1st Lieut. 30th U. S. Inf., 5 July, 1899.
CHADWICK, HARRY R., Mus. and Batt. Sergt. Maj. 1st Ohio Inf., 26 April, 1898, to 25 Oct., 1898. 1st Lieut. 30th U. S. Inf., 5 July, 1899.
ABBOTT, JOHN W. C., 1st Sergt. Co. F, 3rd Neb. Inf., 27 May, 1898, to 11 Oct., 1898. 2nd Lieut. 3rd Neb. Inf., 12 Oct., 1898. Mustered out 11 May, 1899. 2nd Lieut. 30th U. S. Inf., 5 July, 1899. 1st Lieut., 20 Oct., 1899.

*Second Lieutenants.*

GARBER, GUILFORD S., 1st Lieut. 159th Ind. Inf., 26 April, 1898. Mustered out 23 Nov., 1898. 2nd Lieut. 30th U. S. Inf., 5 July, 1899.
ERRINGTON, CHARLES H., 1st Lieut. 1st Ill. Inf., 26 April, 1898. Mustered out 17 Nov., 1898. 2nd Lieut. 30th U. S. Inf., 5 July, 1899.
BOYLE, GUY A., 1st Lieut. and Adj. 158th Ind. Inf., 26 April, 1898. Mustered out 4 Nov., 1898. 2nd Lieut. 30th U. S. Inf., 5 July, 1899.
PACK, WILIAM F., 2nd Lieut. 33rd Mich. Inf., 16 May, 1898. Mustered out 1 Nov., 1898. 2nd Lieut. 30th U. S. Inf., 5 July, 1899.
BEAR, CHARLES U., 1st Lieut. 1st Ill. Cav., 26 April, 1898. Mustered out 11 Oct., 1898. 2nd Lieut. 30th U. S. Inf., 5 July, 1899.
ELLISON, FRANCIS J., Sergt. Maj. 202nd N. Y. Inf., 14 July, 1898, to 6 Nov., 1898. 2nd Lieut. 202nd N. Y. Inf., 8 Nov., 1898. Mustered out 15 April, 1899. 2nd Lieut. 30th U. S. Inf., 5 July, 1899.
COCHNOWER, GEORGE W., Priv. Co. E, 1st Ill. Inf., 26 April, 1898, to 17 Nov., 1898. 2nd Lieut. 30th U. S. Inf., 5 July, 1899.
RALSTON, FRANCIS W., Jr., Priv., Sergt., Corpl. and 1st Sergt. Batty A, Pa. Light Art., 27 April, 1898, to 19 Nov., 1898. 2nd Lieut. 30th U. S. Inf., 5 July, 1899.
BRADFORD, A. HOLT, Priv. and Corpl. Co. H, 6th Ill. Inf., 26 April, 1898, to 25 Nov., 1898. 2nd Lieut. 30th U. S. Inf., 5 July, 1899.
GULICK, ROBERT H., Corpl. Co. B, 1st Ohio Inf., 26 April, 1898, to 25 Oct., 1898. 2nd Lieut. 30th U. S. Inf., 5 July, 1899.
BROOKS, ROBERT E., 1st Lieut. 2nd Ill. Inf., 26 April, 1898. Capt., 8 Nov., 1898 Mustered out 26 April, 1899. Priv., Sergt. and 1st Sergt Co. E, 30th U. S. Inf., 17 July, 1899, to 17 Sept., 1899. 2nd Lieut. 30th U. S. Inf., 16 Sept., 1899.
CAMPBELL, JOHN, 1st Class Priv. and Sergt. Co. I, 3rd U. S. Eng., 6 Aug., 1898, to 17 May, 1899. Priv. and 1st Sergt. Co. M, 30th U. S. Inf., 25 July, 1899, to 15 Jan., 1900. 2nd Lieut. 30th U. S. Inf., 11 Dec., 1899.

## 31st U. S. VOLUNTEER INFANTRY.

*Colonel.*

PETTIT, JAMES S. (Regular), Col. 31st U. S. Inf., 5 July, 1899.

*Lieutenant Colonel.*

BRETT, LLOYD M. (Regular), Lieut. Col., 31 May, 1900.

*Majors.*

LIGGETT, HUNTER (Regular), Maj. 31st U. S. Inf., 5 July, 1899.
McMAHON, JOHN E. (Regular), Maj. 31st U. S. Inf., 5 July, 1899.
STIVERS, CHARLES P., Priv. Co. E, 2nd Wis. Inf., 28 April, 1898, to 16 June, 1898. Priv., Sergt. and 1st Sergt. Troop E, 1st Ohio Cav., 17 June, 1898, to 23 Oct., 1898. Capt. 31st U. S Inf., 5 July, 1899. Maj., 31 May, 1900.

*Surgeon with rank of Major.*

HENRY, JOSEPH N., Maj. Surg. 4th U. S. Inf., 31 May, 1898. Mustered out 8 June, 1899. Maj. Surg. 31st U. S. Inf., 5 July, 1899.

*Assistant Surgeons with rank of Captain.*

HAINES, ABRAM L., 1st Lieut. Asst. Surg. 203rd N. Y. Inf., 5 July, 1898. Maj. Surg., 10 Dec., 1898. Mustered out 25 March, 1899. Capt. Asst. Surg. 31st U. S. Inf., 5 July, 1899.

*With rank of First Lieutenant.*

PORTER, RALPH S., 1st Lieut. Asst. Surg. 2nd Ill. Inf., 7 July, 1898. Mustered out 26 April, 1899. 1st Lieut. Asst. Surg. 31st U. S. Inf., 5 July, 1899.

*Captains.*

BURCHFIELD, JAMES L., Capt. 3rd Ky. Inf., 27 April, 1898. Mustered out 16 May, 1899. Capt. 31st U. S. Inf., 5 July, 1899.
SHARPLEY, ARTHUR G., Q. M., 23 Aug., 1899. 1st Lieut. 3rd Ky. Inf., 7 May, 1898. Mustered out 16 May, 1899. Capt. 31st U. S. Inf., 5 July, 1899.
PHILIP, JOHN VAN NESS, Adj. 13 July, 1899. 1st Lieut. and Adj. 4th U. S. Inf., 31 May, 1898. Mustered out 8 June, 1899. Capt. 31st U. S. Inf., 5 July, 1899.
WAGNER, JOHN A., Capt. 2nd N. C. Inf., 24 May, 1898. Mustered out 7 Nov., 1898. Capt. 1st N. C. Inf., 15 Nov., 1898. Mustered out 22 April, 1899. 1st Lieut. 29th U. S. Inf. (declined), 5 July, 1899. Capt. 31st U. S. Inf., 5 July, 1899.
WHITE, WILLIAM J., Capt. 2nd Ohio Inf., 25 April, 1898. Mustered out 10 Feb., 1899. Capt. 31st U. S. Inf., 5 July, 1899.
BENNETT, LUCIUS C., Capt. 2nd Ohio Inf., 25 April, 1898. Mustered out 10 Feb., 1899. Capt. 31st U. S. Inf., 5 July, 1899.
GALLEHER, PAUL C., Capt. 1st Ky. Inf., 13 May, 1898. Mustered out 24 Feb., 1899. Capt. 31st U. S. Inf., 5 July, 1899.
REYNOLDS, CHARLES A., Capt. 10th Ohio Inf., 23 June, 1898. Mustered out 23 March, 1899. Capt. 31st U. S. Inf., 5 July, 1899.
GILLENWATER, WILLIAM H., Capt. 6th U. S. Inf., 29 June, 1898. Mustered out 15 March, 1899. Capt. 31st U S. Inf., 5 July, 1899.
GILMER, ELLISON L., 1st Lieut. 2nd N. C. Inf., 30 April, 1898. Mustered out 12 Nov., 1898. Capt. 31st U. S. Inf., 5 July, 1899.
SCOFIELD, WILLIAM M., Capt. 1st Ohio Cav., 25 April, 1898. Mustered out 22 Oct., 1898. Capt. 31st U. S. Inf., 5 July, 1899.
CABELL, WILLIAM E., Sergt. Maj. 2nd Ky. Inf., 12 March, 1898, to 9 July, 1898. 1st Lieut. and Adj. 2nd Ky. Inf., 10 July, 1898. Mustered out 31 Oct., 1898. Capt. 31st U. S. Inf., 5 July, 1899.
PAYNE, ROBERT C., 2nd Lieut. 3rd Ky. Inf., 27 April, 1898. Mustered out 16 May, 1899. 1st Lieut. 31st U. S. Inf., 5 July, 1899. Capt., 30 Aug., 1899.
STARK, BENJAMIN, Jr., 1st Lieut. 4th U. S. Inf., 31 May, 1898. Mustered out 8 June, 1899. 1st Lieut 31st U. S. Inf., 5 July, 1899. Capt., 31 May, 1900.

*First Lieutenants.*

BROWNING, KENT, 2nd Lieut. 4th U. S. Inf., 10 June, 1898. Mustered out 8 June, 1899. 1st Lieut. 31st U. S. Inf., 5 July, 1899.
PRESTON, HUGH C., Capt. 4th U. S. Inf., 29 June, 1898. Mustered out 8 June, 1899. 1st Lieut. 31st U. S. Inf., 5 July, 1899.
BALENTINE, ARTHUR T., 1st Lieut. 2nd U. S. Eng., 1 July, 1898. Mustered out 16 May, 1899. 1st Lieut. 31st U. S. Inf., 5 July, 1899.
REED, WILLIAM O., 1st Lieut. 1st Ky. Inf., 13 May, 1898. Mustered out 24 Feb., 1899, 1st Lieut. 31st U. S. Inf., 5 July, 1899.
THOMAS, CHARLES O., Jr., Capt. 8th U. S. Inf., 13 July, 1898. Mustered out 6 March, 1899. 1st Lieut. 31st U. S. Inf., 5 July, 1899.
WILHOIT, MARION B., Priv. Co. G, 4th Ky. Inf., 10 July, 1898, to 27 July, 1898. 1st Lieut. 4th Ky. Inf., 28 July, 1898. Mustered out 12 Feb., 1899. 1st Lieut. 31st U. S. Inf., 5 July, 1899.
LOWRY, FRANK S., Capt. 7th Ohio Inf., 25 April, 1898. Mustered out 6 Nov., 1898. 1st Lieut. 31st U. S. Inf., 5 July, 1899.
CASTLE, WILLIAM A., Capt. 7th Ohio Inf., 25 April, 1898. Mustered out 5 Nov., 1898. 1st Lieut. 31st U. S. Inf., 5 July, 1899.
FONNER, JOHN B., 1st Lieut. 157th Ind. Inf., 26 April, 1898. Mustered out 1 Nov., 1898. 1st Lieut. 31st U. S. Inf., 5 July, 1899.
THOMPSON, ALBERT C., Jr., 1st Lieut. Sig. Off., 20 May, 1898. Discharged 5 Dec., 1898. 1st Lieut. 31st U. S. Inf., 5 July, 1899.
HAWKINS, PERCY H., Capt. 1st Ohio Inf., 25 April, 1898. Mustered out 25 Oct., 1898. 1st Lieut. 31st U. S. Inf., 5 July, 1899.
RICHMOND, CHARLES F., Priv. Co. E, 4th Ill. Inf., 28 June, 1898, to 2 May, 1899. 1st Lieut. 31st U. S. Inf., 5 July, 1899.
CHAMBERLIN, DE WITT W., 1st Lieut. 31st U. S. Inf., 5 July, 1899.

MONROE, WILLIAM H., Capt. 4th U. S. Inf., 17 June, 1898. Mustered out 8 June, 1899. 2nd Lieut. 31st U. S. Inf., 5 July, 1899. 1st Lieut., 30 Aug., 1899.
LINDSEY, WATSON, Capt. 1st Ky. Inf., 13 May, 1898. Mustered out 24 Feb., 1899. 2nd Lieut. 31st U. S. Inf., 5 July, 1899. 1st Lieut. 20 Nov., 1899.
TWYMAN, WILFORD, 2nd Lieut. 1st Ky. Inf., 13 May, 1898. Mustered out 24 Feb., 1899. 2nd Lieut. 31st U. S. Inf., 5 July, 1899. 1st Lieut., 31 May, 1900.

*Second Lieutenants.*

GIBBINS, HENRY, 1st Lieut. 3rd Tenn. Inf., 25 April, 1898. Mustered out 31 Jan., 1899. 2nd Lieut. 31st U. S. Inf., 5 July, 1899.
MITCHELL, HARRY D., 2nd Lieut. 3rd Ohio Inf., 2 June, 1898. 1st Lieut., 1 Sept., 1898. Mustered out 26 Oct., 1898. 2nd Lieut 31st U. S. Inf., 5 July, 1899.
SNYDER, DAVID A., Musician Co. I; Sergt. and 1st Sergt. Co. M, and Batt. Sergt. Maj. 1st Ohio Inf., 25 April, 1898, to 25 Oct., 1898. 2nd Lieut. 31st U. S. Inf., 5 July, 1899.
EULASS, WILLIAM B., Priv. Co. A, 1st Ohio Inf., 25 April, 1898, to 25 Oct., 1898. 2nd Lieut. 31st U. S. Inf., 5 July, 1899.
STEVENS, ALBERT H., 2nd Lieut. 31st U. S. Inf., 5 July, 1899.
DEITSCH, ANSWELL E., Corpl. Co. M, 10th Ohio Inf., 1 July, 1898, to 23 March, 1899. 2nd Lieut. 31st U. S. Inf., 5 July, 1899.
BOWMAN, WALTER O., Corpl. Co. K, 160th Ind. Inf., 26 April, 1898, to 25 April, 1899. 2nd Lieut. 31st U. S. Inf., 5 July, 1899.
SPURR, JOHN P., 1st Sergt. Co. F, 1st Tenn. Inf., 18 June, 1898, to 6 May, 1899. 2nd Lieut. 31st U. S. Inf., 5 July, 1899.
WILSON, JENNINGS B., Sergt. Maj. 4th U. S. Inf., 7 June, 1898, to 21 Sept., 1898. 2nd Lieut. 4th U. S. Inf., 15 Sept., 1898. Mustered out 8 June, 1899. Priv. and Sergt. Maj. 31st U. S. Inf., 11 July, 1899, to 8 Sept., 1899. 2nd Lieut. 31st U. S. Inf., 30 Aug., 1899.
CORWINE, RICHARD M., Priv., Sergt. and 1st Sergt. Co. A, and Sergt. Maj. 4th U. S. Inf., 28 May, 1898, to 30 April, 1899. 2nd Lieut. 4th U. S. Inf., 1 May, 1899. Mustered out 8 June, 1899. Q. M. Sergt. 31st U. S. Inf., 25 July, 1899, to 25 Oct., 1899. 2nd Lieut. 31st U. S. Inf., 25 Oct., 1899.
DANFORTH, CHARLES H., Priv., Sergt. and 1st Sergt. Co. H, and Sergt. Maj. 4th U. S. Inf., 5 June, 1898, to 22 Jan., 1899. 2nd Lieut. 4th U. S. Inf., 8 Dec., 1898. Batt. and Reg. Sergt. Maj., 31st U. S. Inf., 29 July, 1899, to 28 Dec., 1899. 2nd Lieut. 31st U. S. Inf., 28 Nov., 1899.

## 32ND U. S. VOLUNTEER INFANTRY.

*Colonel.*

CRAIG, LOUIS A. (Regular), Col. 32nd U. S. Inf., 5 July, 1899.

*Lieutenant Colonel.*

STROTHER, LEWIS H. (Regular), Lieut. Col. 32nd U. S. Inf., 5 July, 1899.

*Majors.*

SPENCE, ROBERT E. L. (Regular), Maj. 32nd U. S. Inf., 5 July, 1899.
HENRY, MORTON J., Maj. 32nd U. S. Inf., 5 July, 1899.
CABELL, CHARLES ELLET, Capt. C. S., 28 May, 1898. Discharged 14 Nov., 1898. Maj. 6th Va. Inf., 25 Oct., 1898. Mustered out 28 Jan., 1899. Maj. 32nd U. S. Inf., 5 July, 1899.

*Surgeon with rank of Major.*

HEREFORD, JOHN R., Maj. Surg. 1st Mo. Inf., 28 June, 1898. Mustered out 31 Oct., 1898. Capt. Asst. Surg. 32nd U. S. Inf., 5 July, 1899. Maj. Surg., 4 Dec., 1899.

*Assistant Surgeons with rank of Captain.*

COOK, WILLIAM H., Capt. 6th Cal. Inf., 29 April, 1898. Mustered out 15 Dec., 1898. Lieut. Asst. Surg. 32nd U. S. Inf., 5 July, 1899. Capt. Asst. Surg., 4 Dec., 1899.

*With rank of First Lieutenant.*

DUDLEY, FRANK W., 1st Lieut. Asst. Surg. 8th Cal. Inf., 22 June, 1898. Maj. Surg., 19 July, 1898. Mustered out 6 Feb., 1899. 1st Lieut. Asst. Surg. 32nd U. S. Inf., 13 Dec., 1899.

*Captains.*

SUMMERLIN, GEORGE T. (Regular), Adj., 19 July, 1899. Capt. 32nd U. S. Inf., 5 July, 1899.
GRINSTEAD, JOHN P., Sergt. Co. E, 9th Ky. Inf., 26 Nov., 1861, to 17 Aug., 1862. 2nd Lieut. 9th Ky. Inf., 18 Aug., 1862. 1st Lieut., 10 Jan., 1863. Capt., 21 Sept., 1864. Mustered out 15 Dec., 1864. Capt. 21st Kans. Inf., 2 May, 1898. Mustered out 10 Dec., 1898. Capt. 32nd U. S. Inf., 5 July, 1899.
GOLDMAN, JOHN H., Capt. 6th Mo. Inf., 2 July, 1898. Mustered out 10 May, 1899. Capt. 32nd U. S. Inf., 5 July, 1899.
PEED, HENRY A., Priv. Co. G, 132nd Ind. Inf., 18 May, 1864, to 7 Sept., 1864. Priv. and Sergt. Co. E, and Sergt. Maj. 148th Ind. Inf., 16 Feb., 1865, to 5 Sept., 1865. Capt. 4th Mo. Inf., 27 April, 1898. Mustered out 10 Feb., 1899. Capt. 32nd U. S. Inf., 5 July, 1899.

SEVIER, GRANVILLE, Capt. 2nd Penn. Inf., 24 May, 1898. Mustered out 8 Feb., 1899. Capt. 32nd U. S. Inf., 5 July, 1899.
COMFORT, CHARLES D., Lieut. Col. 7th U. S. Inf., 13 June, 1898. Mustered out 28 Feb., 1899. Capt. 32nd U. S. Inf., 5 July, 1899.
BRANDT, AMOS W., Capt. 7th U. S. Inf., 28 June, 1898. Mustered out 28 Feb., 1899. Capt. 32nd U. S. Inf., 5 July, 1899.
RUMBOLD, FRANK M., Capt. Light Batty A, Mo. Art., 26 April, 1898. Mustered out 30 Nov., 1898. Capt. 32nd U. S. Inf., 5 July, 1899.
ECKERS, FRANK W., 1st Lieut. 50th Iowa Inf., 26 April, 1898. Capt., 15 May, 1898. Mustered out 30 Nov., 1898. Capt. 32nd U. S. Inf., 5 July, 1899.
HAYSON, THOMAS R., 1st Lieut. 21st Kans. Inf., 5 May, 1898. Capt., 27 Aug., 1898. Mustered out 10 Dec., 1898. Capt. 32nd U. S. Inf., 5 July, 1899.
GRIFFITH, EDWIN J., Capt. 3rd Mo. Inf., 4 May, 1898. Mustered out 7 Nov., 1898. Capt. 32nd U. S. Inf., 5 July, 1899.
CRAVENS, LANIER, Q. M., 7 Nov., 1899. 1st Lieut. 3rd Mo. Inf., 4 May, 1898. Mustered out 7 Nov., 1898. Capt. 32nd U. S. Inf., 5 July, 1899.
CULVER, JACOB H., Capt. 3rd U. S. Cav., 14 May, 1898. Mustered out 8 Sept., 1898. Capt. 32nd U. S. Inf., 5 July, 1899.
COLLINS, HARRY J., Priv. and Corpl. Co. I, 1st Colo. Inf., 1 May, 1898, to 7 July, 1899. Priv. and Corpl. Co. B, and Com. Sergt. 36th U. S. Inf., 10 July, 1899, to 26 Sept., 1899. Capt. 32nd U. S. Inf., 5 July, 1899.

*First Lieutenants.*

RALSTON, GEORGE S., 1st Lieut. 3rd Neb. Inf., 27 May, 1898. Mustered out 11 May, 1899. 1st Lieut. 32nd U. S. Inf., 5 July, 1899.
MORROW, HENRY M., 2nd Lieut. 3rd Neb. Inf., 27 May, 1898. 1st Lieut., 5 Jan., 1899. Mustered out 11 May, 1899. 1st Lieut. 32nd U. S. Inf., 5 July, 1899.
HIXSON, JAMES C., Com., 8 Nov., 1899. 1st Lieut. 5th U. S. Inf., 8 June, 1898. Capt., 13 July, 1898. Mustered out 31 May, 1899. 1st Lieut. 32nd U. S. Inf., 5 July, 1899.
SMITH, CHARLES C., 1st Lieut. 161st Ind. Inf., 24 June, 1898. Mustered out 30 April, 1899. 1st Lieut. 32nd U. S. Inf., 5 July, 1899.
GILLESPIE, GRANT, 1st Lieut. 6th Mo. Inf., 6 July, 1898. Mustered out 10 May, 1899. 1st Lieut. 32nd U. S. Inf., 5 July, 1899.
WILLIAMS-FOOTE, AMBROSE C. G., 1st Lieut. 8th U. S. Inf., 8 June, 1898. Mustered out 6 March, 1899. 1st Lieut. 32nd U. S. Inf., 5 July, 1899.
CALDWELL, GEORGE H., 1st Sergt. Co. H, 161st Ind. Inf., 27 June, 1898, to 5 Sept., 1898. 2nd Lieut. 161st Ind. Inf., 10 Sept., 1898. Mustered out 30 April, 1899. 1st Lieut. 32nd U. S. Inf., 5 July, 1899.
SHOOK, JOHN M., 2nd Lieut. 21st Kans. Inf., 13 May, 1898. Mustered out 10 Dec., 1898. 1st Lieut. 32nd U. S. Inf., 5 July, 1899.
WHITSETT, GEORGE P., Capt. 5th Mo. Inf., 4 May, 1898. Mustered out 9 Nov., 1898. 1st Lieut. 32nd U. S. Inf., 5 July, 1899.
MAPES, WILLIAM S., Maj. 2nd Neb. Inf., 29 April, 1898. Mustered out 24 Oct., 1898. 1st Lieut. 32nd U. S. Inf., 5 July, 1899.
SCHAEFFER, ARTHUR B., 1st Lieut. 22nd Kans. Inf., 13 May, 1898. Mustered out 9 Nov., 1898. 1st Lieut. 32nd U. S. Inf., 5 July, 1899.
WEAVER, WILLIAM S., 1st Lieut. 2nd Kans. Inf., 14 May, 1898. Mustered out 3 Nov., 1898. 1st Lieut. 32nd U. S. Inf., 5 July, 1899.
LONG, JAMES L., Capt. 1st Ark. Inf., 13 May, 1898. Mustered out 25 Oct., 1898. 1st Lieut. 32nd U. S. Inf., 5 July, 1899.
CRAWFORD, ROBERT T., Priv., Corpl. and Sergt. Co. E, 49th Iowa Inf., 26 April, 1898, to 13 May, 1899. 1st Lieut. 32nd U. S. Inf., 5 July, 1899.
DENSMORE, GEORGE A., 1st Lieut. 32nd U. S. Inf., 5 July, 1899.
GOODRICH, GEORGE E., 1st Lieut. 161st Ind. Inf., 24 June, 1898. Mustered out 30 April, 1899. 2nd Lieut. 32nd U. S. Inf., 5 July, 1899. 1st Lieut., 25 Oct., 1899.

*Second Lieutenants.*

WADE, BENJAMIN R., 2nd Lieut. 2nd Mo. Inf., 28 April, 1898. 1st Lieut., 21 Feb., 1899. Mustered out 27 Feb., 1899. 2nd Lieut. 32nd U. S. Inf., 5 July, 1899.
MILLER, ARCHIE, 1st Lieut. 6th Mo. Inf., 4 Aug., 1898. Mustered out 10 May, 1899. 2nd Lieut. 32nd U. S. Inf., 5 July, 1899.
CLOPTON, WILLIAM H., Jr., Sergt. Co. C, 1st Mo. Inf., 4 May, 1898, to 11 Aug., 1898. 2nd Lieut. 6th Mo. Inf., 12 Aug., 1898. 1st Lieut. and Adj., 9 Dec., 1898. Mustered out 10 May, 1899. 2nd Lieut. 32nd U. S. Inf., 5 July, 1899.
CRAWFORD, GEORGE R., 1st Lieut. 22nd Kans., Inf., 2 May, 1898. Mustered out 3 Nov., 1898. 2nd Lieut. 32nd U. S. Inf., 5 July, 1899.
WILSON, CHARLES H., Capt. 2nd Neb., Inf., 27 April, 1898. Mustered out 24 Oct., 1898. 2nd Lieut. 32nd U. S. Inf., 5 July, 1899.
MOWRY, PHILIP, 2nd Lieut. 32nd U. S. Inf., 5 July, 1899.
ARMITAGE, GEORGE H., Sergt. Co. A, 50th Iowa Inf., 26 April, 1898, to 30 Nov., 1898. 2nd Lieut. 32nd U. S. Inf., 5 July, 1899.
MORISON, CHARLES R. W., Priv. Co. A, 5th Md. Inf., 25 April, 1898, to 22 Oct., 1898. 2nd Lieut. 32nd U. S. Inf., 5 July, 1899.
LOVE, HENRY K., Priv. and Corpl. Troop D, 1st U. S. Cav., 4 May, 1898, to 15 Sept., 1898. 2nd Lieut. 32nd U. S. Inf., 5 July, 1899.
BALLARD, ROY T., 2nd Lieut. 32nd U. S. Inf., 5 July, 1899.
SCHACK, HENRY E., Priv. and Sergt. Maj. 32nd U. S. Inf., 24 July, 1899, to 22 Sept., 1899. 2nd Lieut. 32nd U. S. Inf., 22 Sept., 1899.
WERNER, FRANK, Priv. Co. D, 5th Mo. Inf., 27 June, 1898, to 2 Oct., 1898. Priv. and Sergt. Co. G, and Batt. and Regl. Sergt. Maj. 32nd U. S. Inf., 27 July, 1899, to 16 Jan., 1900. 2nd Lieut. 32nd U S. Inf., 4 Dec., 1899.

## 33RD U. S. VOLUNTEER INFANTRY.

*Colonel.*

HARE, LUTHER R. (Regular), Col. 33rd U. S. Inf., 5 July, 1899.

*Lieutenant Colonel.*

CRONIN, MARCUS D. (Regular), Lieut. Col. 2 Dec., 1899.

*Majors.*

MARCH, PEYTON C. (Regular), Maj. 33rd U. S. Inf., 5 July, 1899.
SIRMYER, EDGAR A. (Regular), Maj. 33rd U. S. Inf., 12 Nov., 1899.
ASHBURN, THOMAS Q. (Regular), Capt. 33rd U. S. Inf., 5 July, 1899. Maj., 2 Dec., 1899.

*Surgeon with rank of Major.*

LIEBERMAN, B. ALBERT, 2nd Lieut. 3rd Mo. Inf., 27 April, 1898. Discharged 18 July, 1898. Asst. Surg. 6th Mo. Inf., 19 July, 1898. Maj. Surg., 1 Jan., 1899. Mustered out 10 May, 1899. Maj. Surg. 33rd U. S. Inf., 5 July, 1899.

*Assistant Surgeons with rank of Captain.*

HADRA, FREDERICK, Maj. Surg. 1st Texas Cav., 9 May, 1898. Mustered out 14 Nov., 1898. Capt. Asst. Surg. 33rd U. S. Inf., 5 July, 1899.

*With rank of First Lieutenant.*

GREENEWALT, JOHN C., 1st Lieut. Asst. Surg. 5th U. S. Inf., 22 April, 1899. Mustered out 31 May, 1899. 1st Lieut. Asst. Surg. 33rd U. S. Iuf., 5 July, 1899.

*Captains.*

SHIELDS, EDMUND G., Capt. 3rd Texas Inf., 29 April, 1898. Mustered out 16 Feb., 1899. Capt. 33rd U. S. Inf., 5 July, 1899.
JENKINSON, HENRY L., Capt. 8th U. S. Inf., 10 June, 1898. Mustered out 6 March, 1899. 1st Lieut. 28th U. S. Inf., 5 July, 1899. Vacated 30 July, 1899. Capt. 33rd U. S. Inf., 5 July, 1899.
VAN WAY, CHARLES W., Capt. 21st Kans. Inf., 4 May, 1898. Mustered out 10 Dec., 1898. Capt. 33rd U. S. Inf., 5 July, 1899.
BUTLER, JAMES S., Capt. 2nd Miss. Inf., 22 May, 1898. Mustered out 20 Dec., 1898. Capt. 33rd U. S. Inf., 5 July, 1899.
DAVIS, EDWARD, 2nd Lieut. 1st Ill. Inf., 26 April, 1898. Mustered out 17 Nov., 1898. Capt. 33rd U. S. Inf., 5 July, 1899.
HULEN, JOHN A., Q. M., 31 Jan. 1900. Maj. 1st Texas Cav., 28 April, 1898. Lieut. Col., 2 June, 1898. Mustered out 14 Nov., 1898. Capt. 33rd U. S. Inf., 5 July, 1899.
GREEN, JOHN F., Capt. 1st Texas Cav., 28 April, 1898. Mustered out 14 Nov., 1898. Capt. 33rd U. S. Inf., 5 July, 1899.
BURROUGHS, JAMES M., Adj. 1st Lieut. 1st Texas Cav., 28 April, 1898. Mustered out 14 Nov., 1898. Capt. 33rd U. S. Inf., 5 July, 1899.
FOWLER, GODFREY R., Capt. 2nd Texas Inf., 3 May, 1898. Mustered out 9 Nov., 1898. Capt. 33rd U. S. Inf., 5 July, 1899.
DAVIES, ARTHUR L. B., 1st Lieut. 2nd U. S. Cav., 1 May, 1898. Capt., 17 July, 1898. Mustered out 24 Oct., 1898. Capt. 33rd U. S. Inf., 5 July, 1899.
ELLIS, RICHARD T., 2nd Lieut. 4th U. S. Inf., 10 June, 1898. 1st Lieut., 1 May, 1899. Mustered out 8 June, 1899. 1st Lieut. 33rd U. S. Inf., 5 July, 1899. Capt., 12 Sept., 1899.
SCHULTZ, THEODORE, Capt. 6th Mo. Inf., 14 July, 1898. Mustered out 10 May, 1899. 1st Lieut. 33rd U. S. Inf., 5 July, 1899. Capt., 13 Sept., 1899.
CUNNINGHAM, WILLIAM S., 1st Lieut. 4th Texas Inf., 29 June, 1898. Mustered out 10 March, 1899. 1st Lieut. 33rd U. S. Inf., 5 July, 1899. Capt., 12 Nov., 1899.
RUCKER, LINDSEY P., 1st Lieut. 4th Texas Inf., 28 June, 1898. Mustered out 7 March, 1899. 1st Lieut. 33rd U. S. Inf., 5 July, 1899. Capt., 2 Dec., 1899.

*First Lieutenants.*

COFFEY, EDGAR N., Capt. 1st Miss. Inf., 10 May, 1898. Mustered out 20 Dec., 1898. 1st Lieut. 33rd U. S. Inf., 5 July, 1899.
POWER, CARROLL, 1st Lieut. 2nd Ky. Inf., 6 May, 1898. Mustered out 31 Oct., 1898. 1st Lieut. 33rd U. S. Inf., 5 July, 1899.
WARD, JOHN W., 1st Lieut. 1st Ark. Inf., 11 May, 1898. Mustered out 25 Oct., 1898. 1st Lieut. 33rd U. S. Inf., 5 July, 1899.
JEFFERS, SOLOMON L., Capt. 1st Ark. Inf., 14 May, 1898. Mustered out 25 Oct., 1898. 1st Lieut. 33rd U. S. Inf., 5 July, 1899.
HALL, JESSE L., Capt. 1st U. S. Inf., 21 June, 1898. Mustered out 28 Oct., 1898. 1st Lieut. 33rd U. S. Inf., 5 July, 1899.
TOMPKINS, FRANK D., 1st Lieut. 1st U. S. Inf., 21 June, 1898. Mustered out 28 Oct., 1898. 1st Lieut. 33rd U. S. Inf., 5 July, 1899.
CAMPBELL, TILMAN, 1st Sergt. Co. A, and Sergt. Maj. 2nd Ark. Inf., 25 April, 1898 to 20 Jan., 1899. 2nd Lieut. 2nd Ark. Inf., 24 Jan., 1899. Mustered out 25 Feb., 1899. 1st Lieut. 33rd U. S. Inf., 5 July, 1899.
LOWE, WILLIAM L., Priv. and Corpl. Co. G, 1st D. C. Inf., 12 May, 1898, to 22 Oct., 1898. 1st Lieut. 33rd U. S. Inf., 5 July, 1899.

FEBIGER, GEORGE LEA, Com., 20 Sept., 1899. 1st Lieut. 9th U. S. Inf., 17 June, 1898. Capt., 10 Jan., 1899. Mustered out 25 May, 1899. 2nd Lieut. 33rd U. S. Inf., 5 July, 1899. 1st Lieut. 24 Aug., 1899.
CASE, FRANK L., 2nd Lieut. 6th U. S. Inf., 29 June, 1898. 1st Lieut., 7 Jan., 1899. Mustered out 15 March, 1899. 2nd Lieut. 33rd U. S. Inf., 5 July, 1899. 1st Lieut., 12 Sept., 1899.
EDMUNDSON, EARLE, Capt. 1st Terr. Inf., 10 July, 1898. Mustered out 13 Feb., 1899. Sergt. Co. H, 33rd U. S. Inf., 9 Aug., 1899, to 4 Sept., 1899. 2nd Lieut. 33rd U. S. Inf., 5 July, 1899. 1st Lieut., 13 Sept., 1899.
SHERBURNE, THOMAS L., 2nd Lieut. 1st La. Inf., 1 May, 1898. Mustered out 3 Oct., 1898. 2nd Lieut. 33rd U. S. Inf., 5 July, 1899. 1st Lieut., 13 Sept., 1899.
LIPOP, JOHN, J., Sergt. Maj. 5th U. S. Inf., 18 June, 1898, to 16 Feb., 1899. 2nd Lieut. 5th U. S. Inf., 3 Feb., 1899. Mustered out 31 May, 1899. 2nd Lieut. 33rd U. S. Inf., 5 July, 1899. 1st Lieut., 31 Oct., 1899.
HEALEY, JOHN W., 1st Lieut. 6th Va. Inf., 29 Oct., 1898. Mustered out 28 Jan., 1899. 2nd Lieut. 33rd U. S. Inf., 5 July, 1899. 1st Lieut., 12 Nov., 1899.
WILLARD, CHARLES L., Priv., Corpl. and Q. M. Sergt. Co. A, 1st Texas Inf., 4 May, 1898, to 18 April, 1899. 2nd Lieut. 33rd U. S. Inf., 5 July, 1899. 1st Lieut., 2 Dec., 1899.
PICKEL, ARTHUR N., Corpl. Co. C, 3rd Tenn. Inf., 25 April, 1898, to 31 Jan., 1899. 2nd Lieut. 33rd U. S. Inf., 5 July, 1899. 1st Lieut., 10 April, 1900.

*Second Lieutenants.*

McKENNEY, HENRY J., 2nd Lieut. 33rd U. S. Inf., 5 July, 1899.
McCLELLAND, DONALD C., Priv. and Corpl. Co. E, 71st N. Y. Inf., 2 May, 1898, to 15 Nov., 1898. 2nd Lieut. 33rd U. S. Inf., 5 July, 1899.
WILLIAMS, HUGH, Sergt. Co. C, 2nd La. Inf., 2 May, 1898, to 18 April, 1899. 2nd Lieut. 33rd U. S. Inf., 5 July, 1899.
CORDILL, RICHARD P., Priv. Cos. C and L, 2nd La. Inf., 28 May, 1898, to 18 April, 1899. 2nd Lieut. 33rd U. S. Inf., 5 July, 1899.
TRUE, WILLIAM M., Priv. Light Batty A, Mo. Art., 14 June, 1898, to 30 Nov., 1898. 2nd Lieut. 33rd U. S. Inf., 24 Aug., 1899.
GODDARD, WALLACE W., Priv. and Sergt. Cos. I and G, and Sergt. Maj. 4th Ky. Inf., 27 June, 1898, to 12 Feb., 1899. Sergt. Maj. 33rd U. S. Inf., 31 July, 1899, to 12 Sept., 1899. 2nd Lieut. 33rd U. S. Inf., 12 Sept., 1899.
JACKSON, JOHN A., 1st Sergt. Co. G, 1st Texas Inf., 2 May, 1898, to 8 Sept., 1898. 2nd Lieut. 1st Texas Inf., 9 Sept., 1898. Mustered out 15 April, 1899. 1st Sergt. Co. I, 33rd U. S. Inf., 12 Aug., 1899, to 13 Sept., 1899. 2nd Lieut. 33rd U. S. Inf., 13 Sept., 1899.
FLEMISTER, JOHN M., Priv., Sergt. and 1st Sergt. Cos. D and M, 4th Texas Inf., 28 June, 1898, to 7 March, 1899. Q. M. Sergt., 33rd U. S. Inf., 15 July, 1899, to 13 Sept., 1899. 2nd Lieut. 33rd U. S. Inf., 14 Sept., 1899.
BUJAC, ÉTIENNE DE P., Capt. 1st U. S. Inf., 21 June, 1898. Mustered out 28 Oct., 1898. Batt. Sergt. Maj. and Sergt. Maj. 3rd U. S. Inf., 9 Aug., 1899, to 25 Nov., 1899. 2nd Lieut. 33rd U. S. Inf., 25 Nov., 1899.
COE, FREDERICK E., Priv. and Sergt. Co. I, 33rd U. S. Inf., 8 Aug., 1899, to 25 Nov., 1899. 2nd Lieut. 33rd U. S. Inf., 25 Nov., 1899.
SCOTT, WALTER J., Priv. and Corpl. Co. M, 3rd Texas Inf., 29 April, 1898, to 16 Feb., 1899. Priv., Sergt. and 1st Sergt. Co. C, 33rd U. S. Inf., 31 July, 1899, to 3 Feb., 1900. 2nd Lieut. 33rd U. S. Inf., 11 Jan., 1900.
HUMPHRY, LAMAR G., 1st Sergt. Co. D, 1st Ark. Inf., 5 May, 1898, to 20 Aug., 1898. 2nd Lieut. 1st Ark. Inf., 21 Aug., 1898. Mustered out 25 Oct., 1898. Sergt. Co. B, 33rd U. S. Inf., 25 July, 1899, to ——, 1900. 2nd Lieut. 33rd U. S. Inf., 22 May, 1900.

## 34TH U. S. VOLUNTEER INFANTRY.

*Colonel.*

KENNON, LYMAN W. V. (Regular), Col. 34th U. S. Inf., 5 July, 1899.

*Lieutenant Colonel.*

HOWZE, ROBERT L. (Regular), Lieut. Col. 34th U. S. Inf., 5 July, 1899.

*Majors.*

SHUNK, WILLIAM A. (Regular), Maj. 34th U. S. Inf., 5 July, 1899.
PENN, JULIUS A. (Regular), Maj. 34th U. S. Inf., 5 July, 1899.
WHEELER, JOSEPH, Jr. (Regular), Maj. 34th U. S. Inf., 5 July, 1899.

*Surgeon with rank of Major.*

SHELLENBERGER, JAMES E., Mus. Co. B, 94th Ohio Inf., 23 Aug., 1862, to 5 June, 1865. Maj. Surg. 3rd Ohio Inf., 11 May, 1898. Mustered out 26 Oct., 1898. Maj. Surg. 34th U. S. Inf., 5 July, 1899.

*Assistant Surgeons with rank of Captain.*

FOXWORTHY, FRANK W., Capt. Asst. Surg. 160th Ind. Inf., 26 April, 1898. Mustered out 25 April, 1899. Capt. Asst. Surg. 34th U. S. Inf., 5 July, 1899.

*With rank of First Lieutenant.*

EDMONSTON, RAPHAEL A., 1st Lieut. Asst. Surg. 34th U. S. Inf., 8 Feb., 1900.

*Captains.*

MILLER, CHARLES (Regular), Capt. 34th U. S. Inf., 5 July, 1899.
NEWBILL, WILLARD D. (Regular), Adj., 28 July, 1899. Capt. 34th U. S. Inf., 5 July, 1899.
MORGAN, ALFRED S., Capt. 13th Minn. Inf., 29 April, 1898. Mustered out 3 Oct., 1899. Capt. 34th U. S. Inf., 5 July, 1899.
CARR, CLARK M., Maj. Addl. P. M., 20 June, 1898. Discharged 13 June, 1899. Capt. 34th U. S. Inf., 5 July, 1899.
FRENCH, FRANK L., 1st Lieut. 3rd Wis. Inf., 28 April, 1898. Capt., 13 Oct., 1898. Mustered out 12 Jan., 1899. Capt. 34th U. S. Inf., 5 July, 1899.
ROLLIS, CHRISTOPHER J., Capt. 4th Wis. Inf., 30 June, 1898. Mustered out 28 Feb., 1899. Capt. 34th U. S. Inf., 5 July, 1899.
RUSSELL, FRANK G., Capt. 1st Terr. Inf., 27 June, 1898. Maj., 13 Sept., 1898. Mustered out 15 Feb., 1899. Capt. 34th U. S. Inf., 5 July, 1899.
GOEDECKE, FREDERICK, Capt. and Adj. 50th Iowa Inf., 26 April, 1898. Mustered out 30 Nov., 1898. Capt. 34th U. S. Inf., 5 July, 1899.
GREEN, CHARLES A., Q. M., 24 Aug., 1899. 1st Lieut. 2nd Wis. Inf., 28 April, 1898. Capt., 12 May, 1898. Mustered out 15 Nov., 1898. Capt. 34th U. S. Inf., 5 July, 1899.
SULLIVAN, FRANK A., 1st Lieut. 1st Wis. Inf., 3 May, 1898. Mustered out 12 Nov., 1898. Capt. 34th U. S. Inf., 5 July, 1899.
CALVERLEY., ROBERT, Capt. 2nd U. S. Cav., 25 April, 1898. Maj., 17 July, 1898. Mustered out 24 Oct., 1898. Capt. 34th U. S. Inf., 5 July, 1899.
DAME, WILLIAM E., 1st Sergt. Co. E, 1st U. S. Cav., 6 May, 1898, to 10 Aug., 1898. 2nd Lieut. 1st U. S. Cav., 11 Aug., 1898. Mustered out 15 Sept., 1898. Capt. 34th U. S. Inf., 5 July, 1899.
RICE, CUSHMAN A., 1st Lieut. 15th Minn. Inf., 2 July, 1898. Mustered out 27 March, 1899. 1st Lieut. 34th U. S. Inf., 5 July, 1899. Capt., 8 Sept., 1899.
GIBSON, GEORGE E., 1st Sergt. Co. G, 14th Minn. Inf., 28 April, 1898, to 23 June, 1898. Capt. 15th Minn. Inf., 2 July, 1898. Mustered out 27 March, 1899. 1st Lieut. 34th U. S. Inf., 5 July, 1899. Capt., 24 Sept., 1899.

*First Lieutenants.*

NEWTON, HARRY W., Capt. 3rd Wis. Inf., 28 April, 1898. Mustered out 9 Jan., 1899. 1st Lieut. 34th U. S. Inf., 5 July, 1899.
BARNES, HARRY C., Capt. 1st Terr. Inf., 24 June, 1898. Mustered out 13 Feb., 1899. 1st Lieut. 34th U. S. Inf., 5 July, 1899.
HEATON, WILSON G., Capt. 50th Iowa Inf., 26 April, 1898. Mustered out 30 Nov., 1898. 1st Lieut. 34th U. S. Inf., 5 July, 1899.
DECKER, STEWART McC., Capt. 14th Minn. Inf. 26 April, 1898. Mustered out 18 Nov., 1898. 1st Lieut. 34th U. S. Inf., 5 July, 1899.
DEITRICK, LEONARD L., 1st Lieut. 2nd U. S. Cav., 1 May, 1898. Mustered out 24 Oct., 1898. 1st Lieut. 34th U. S. Inf., 5 July, 1899.
BRACKEN, EDWIN J., 2nd Lieut. 1st Wis. Inf., 28 April, 1898. Mustered out 19 Oct., 1898. 1st Lieut. 34th U. S. Inf., 5 July, 1899.
COLEMAN, SHERRARD, 2nd Lieut. 1st U. S. Cav., 6 May, 1898. 1st Lieut., 7 Sept., 1898. Mustered out 15 Sept., 1898. 1st Lieut. 34th U. S. Inf., 5 July, 1899.
DAY, RICHARD C., Com., 11 Aug., 1899. 2nd Lieut. 1st U. S. Cav., 14 May, 1898. Capt., 11 Aug., 1898. Mustered out 15 Sept., 1898. 1st Lieut. 34th U. S. Inf., 5 July, 1899.
MATSON, JOSEPH, Sergt. Co. M, 50th Iowa Inf., 26 April, 1898, to 30 Nov., 1898. 1st Lieut. 34th U. S. Inf., 5 July, 1899.
MONTGOMERY, GRENVILLE D., Priv. Batty A, Pa. Light Art., 15 June, 1898, to 23 July, 1898. 1st Lieut. 34th U. S. Inf., 5 July, 1899.
GREEN, JOHN V., Priv. Co. M, 2nd Wis. Inf., 28 April, 1898, to 9 Nov., 1898. 1st Lieut. 34th U. S. Inf., 5 July, 1899.
HAUSSERMANN, JOHN W., 2nd Lieut. 20th Kans. Inf., 5 May, 1898. 1st Lieut., 4 March, 1899. Discharged 27 Aug., 1899. 1st Lieut. 34th U. S. Inf., 3 Aug., 1899.
DORRINGTON, LAFAYETTE A., 1st Lieut. 2nd Neb. Inf., 27 April, 1898. Mustered out 24 Oct., 1898. 2nd Lieut. 2nd U. S. Inf., 25 Oct., 1898. Mustered out 22 June, 1899. 2nd Lieut. 34th U. S. Inf., 5 July, 1899. 1st Lieut., 8 Sept., 1899.
McALLISTER, SAMUEL D., 1st Sergt. Troop A, 1st Tenn. Inf., 25 April, 1898, to 29 June, 1898. 2nd Lieut. 4th Tenn. Inf., 13 July, 1898. Mustered out 6 May, 1899. 2nd Lieut. 34th U. S. Inf., 5 July, 1899. 1st Lieut., 24 Sept., 1899.
DUNCAN, ARTHUR G., Priv. Troop C, 1st U. S. Cav., 28 May, 1898, to 15 Sept., 1898. 2nd Lieut. 34th U. S. Inf., 5 July, 1899. 1st Lieut., 15 Nov., 1899.
CORLISS, ROBERT C., 2nd Lieut. 34th U. S. Inf., 5 July, 1899. 1st Lieut., 30 April, 1900.

*Second Lieutenants.*

HIRST, CHARLES P., Sergt. Co. G, 1st Cal. Inf., 27 April, 1898, to 7 Sept., 1899. 2nd Lieut. 34th U. S. Inf., 5 July, 1899.
LANSING, CLEVELAND C., Priv., Corpl. and Sergt. Co. M. 4th Va. Inf., 25 April, 1898, to 27 April, 1899. 2nd Lieut. 34th U. S. Inf., 5 July, 1899.
DUNN, JOHN T., 2nd Lieut. 34th U. S. Inf., 5 July, 1899.
SHAW, THOMAS J., 2nd Lieut. 34th U. S. Inf., 5 July, 1899.
VERDI, DENNY, 2nd Lieut. 34th U. S. Inf., 5 July, 1899.
LYLES, DE WITT C., Priv. Co. M, 5th Md. Inf., 28 April, 1898, to 22 Oct., 1898. 2nd Lieut. 34th U. S. Inf., 5 July, 1899.
NEFF, JOHN H., 2nd Lieut. 34th U. S. Inf., 5 July, 1899.
RITTENHOUSE, BASIL N., Priv. Co. L, 27th U. S. Inf., 11 Aug., 1899, to 18 Aug., 1899. 2nd Lieut. 34th U. S. Inf., 5 July, 1899.
PETERSON, HARRY G., Sergt. Maj. 3rd Ohio Inf., 26 April, 1898, to 31 Aug., 1898. 2nd Lieut. 3rd Ohio Inf., 1 Sept., 1898. Mustered out 26 Oct., 1898. 1st Sergt. Co. D,

34th U. S. Inf., 7 Aug., 1899, to 12 Sept., 1899. 2nd Lieut. 34th U. S. Inf., 9 Sept., 1899.
NICHOLS, ODE C., 1st Lieut. 1st U. S. Cav., 14 May, 1898. Mustered out 15 Sept., 1898. Priv., Sergt. and 1st Sergt. Co. C, and Batt. and Reg. Sergt. Maj. 34th U. S. Inf., 15 Aug., 1899, to 3 Feb., 1900. 2nd Lieut. 34th U. S. Inf., 10 Jan., 1900.
JERNIGAN, FRANK A., Hosp. Steward 34th U. S. Inf., 19 July, 1899, to 26 Feb., 1900. 2nd Lieut. 34th U. S. Inf., 7 Feb., 1900.

## 35TH U. S. VOLUNTEER INFANTRY.

*Colonel.*

PLUMMER, EDWARD H. (Regular), Col., 16 Dec., 1899.

*Lieutenant Colonel.*

WALSH, ROBERT D. (Regular), Lieut. Col., 16 Dec., 1899.

*Majors.*

SHORT, WALTER C. (Regular), Maj. 35th U. S. Inf., 5 July, 1899.
LAWS, ALBERT (Regular), Maj. 35th U. S. Inf., 5 July, 1899.
GEARY, WILLIAM L. (Regular), Mus. Band 28th Pa. Inf., 17 July, 1861. Discharged 10 Sept. 1862. Capt. 2nd U. S. Eng., 13 July, 1898. Mustered out 16 May, 1899. Capt. 35th U. S. Inf., 5 July, 1899. Maj., 16 Dec., 1899.

*Surgeon with rank of Major.*

GRANDY, LUTHER B., Maj. Surg. 3rd Ga. Inf., 27 June, 1898. Mustered out 22 April, 1899. Capt. Asst. Surg. 35th U. S. Inf., 5 July, 1899. Maj. Surg., 14 Feb., 1900.

*Assistant Surgeons with rank of Captain.*

METZGER, JOHN A., 1st Lieut. Asst. Surg. 35th U. S. Inf., 5 July, 1899. Capt. Asst. Surg., 14 Feb., 1900.

*With rank of First Lieutenant.*

CARLING, JOHN, 1st Lieut. Asst. Surg. 35th U. S. Inf., 16 Feb., 1900.

*Captains.*

DARRAH, THOMAS W. (Regular), Adj., 17 July, 1899. Capt. 35th U. S. Inf., 5 July, 1899.
ROBERTS, CHARLES D. (Regular), Capt. 35th U. S. Inf., 5 July, 1899.
PRESCOTT, AUSTIN F., Capt. 2nd Ore. Inf., 26 April, 1898. Mustered out 25 July, 1899. Capt. 35th U. S. Inf., 5 July, 1899.
CROWNE, EUGENE P., 1st Lieut. and Adj. 2nd Ore. Inf., 30 April, 1898. Mustered out 26 July, 1899. Capt. 35th U. S. Inf., 5 July, 1899.
BRAZEE, ALBERT J., 2nd Lieut. 2nd Ore. Inf., 2 May, 1898. 1st Lieut., 12 May, 1898. Mustered out 26 July, 1899. Capt. 35th U. S. Inf., 5 July, 1899.
TANNER, EARLE W. (Regular), Capt. 35th U. S. Inf., 5 July, 1899.
ALDRICH, JAMES H., Capt. 9th U. S. Inf., 29 June, 1898. Mustered out 25 May, 1899. Capt. 35th U. S. Inf., 5 July, 1899.
SCHREIBER, WILLIAM G., Lieut. Col. 7th Cal. Inf., 5 May, 1898. Mustered out 2 Dec., 1898. Capt. 35th U. S. Inf., 5 July, 1899.
HALPIN, ARTHUR F., 2nd Lieut. 7th Cal. Inf., 5 May, 1898. Mustered out 2 Dec., 1898. Capt. 35th U. S. Inf., 5 July, 1899.
MATTHEWS, HARRY T., Capt. 7th Cal. Inf., 9 May, 1898. Mustered out 2 Dec., 1898. Capt. 35th U. S. Inf., 5 July, 1899.
ROBINSON, EDWARD W. (Regular), Capt. 35th U. S. Inf., 5 July, 1899.
BECKER, GEORGE L., 1st Lieut. 15th Minn. Inf., 2 July, 1898. Mustered out 27 March, 1899. 1st Lieut. 35th U. S. Inf., 5 July, 1899. Capt., 22 Sept. 1899.
RUGGLES, JAMES A., 1st Lieut. 3rd Ill. Inf., 26 April, 1898. Mustered out 16 Jan., 1899. 1st Lieut. 35th U. S. Inf., 5 July, 1899. Capt., 16 Dec., 1899.
COOTES, HARRY N., Priv., Sergt. and 1st Sergt. Co. L, 4th U. S. Inf., 7 June, 1898, to 3 Oct., 1898. 2nd Lieut. 4th U. S. Inf., 1 Oct., 1898. Mustered out 8 June, 1899. 1st Lieut. 35th U. S. Inf., 5 July, 1899. Capt., 21 Feb., 1900.

*First Lieutenants.*

LEWIS, JOHN H., Capt. 7th U. S. Inf., 20 June, 1898. Mustered out 28 Feb., 1899. 1st Lieut. 35th U. S. Inf., 5 July, 1899.
HUGHES, JOHN L., 2nd Lieut. 6th Cal. Inf., 30 April, 1898. Capt., 4 Nov., 1898. Mustered out 15 Dec., 1898. 1st Lieut. 35th U. S. Inf., 5 July, 1899.
McMANUS, JAMES M., 2nd Lieut. 50th Iowa Inf., 26 April, 1898. Mustered out 30 Nov., 1898. 1st Lieut. 35th U. S. Inf., 5 July, 1899.
STEELE, THEOPHILUS B., 1st Sergt. Co. E, 202nd N. Y. Inf., 17 July, 1898, to 3 Oct., 1898. 2nd Lieut. 202nd N. Y. Inf., 4 Oct., 1898. Mustered out 15 April, 1899. 1st Lieut. 35th U. S. Inf., 5 July, 1899.
VORIS, ALVIN C., Priv. and Corpl. Co. E, 4th Ill. Inf., 26 April, 1898, to 21 Dec., 1898. 2nd Lieut. 4th Ill. Inf., 23 Dec., 1898. Mustered out 2 May, 1899. 1st Lieut. 35th U. S. Inf., 5 July, 1899.
BAKER, LEONARD T., Sergt. and 1st Sergt. Co. H, 1st Texas Inf., 1 May, 1898, to 30 Jan., 1899. 2nd Lieut. 1st Texas Inf., 31 Jan., 1899. Mustered out 18 April, 1899. 1st Lieut. 35th U. S. Inf., 5 July, 1899.

THOMAS, BISSELL, 1st Lieut. 35th U. S. Inf., 5 July, 1899.
HARDING, JACK E., Corpl. Co. C, Ind. Batt. Wash. Inf., 27 June, 1898, to 26 Oct., 1898. 1st Lieut. 35th U. S. Inf., 5 July, 1899.
FLINT, GROVER, 1st Lieut. 35th U. S. Inf., 5 July, 1899.
GODSON, WILLIAM F., 1st Lieut. 35th U. S. Inf., 5 July, 1899.
FISK, ASA F., Mus. Co. L, and Priv. and Sergt. Band 1st Mont. Inf., 5 May, 1898, to 1 June, 1899. 1st Lieut. 35th U. S. Inf., 5 July, 1899.
VANDER VOORT, PERRY W., 1st Lieut. 35th U. S. Inf., 5 July, 1899.
COLLINS, ROBERT W., 1st Lieut. 3rd U. S. Inf., 13 July, 1898. Mustered out 2 May, 1899. 2nd Lieut. 35th U. S. Inf., 5 July, 1899. 1st Lieut., 22 Sept., 1899.
ELLIOTT, CLARK R., 2nd Lieut. 15th Minn. Inf., 2 July, 1898. Mustered out 27 March, 1899. 2nd Lieut. 35th U. S. Inf., 5 July, 1899. 1st Lieut., 16 Dec., 1899.
KIMBALL, GORDON N., 2nd Lieut. 1st Utah Cav., 9 May, 1898. Mustered out 23 Dec., 1898. 2nd Lieut. 35th U. S. Inf., 5 July, 1899. 1st Lieut., 21 Feb., 1900.
CHAPPELEAR, LOUIS S., 1st Lieut. 7th Cal. Inf., 5 May, 1898. Mustered out 2 Dec., 1898. 2nd Lieut. 35th U. S. Inf., 5 July, 1899. 1st Lieut., 26 April, 1900.

*Second Lieutenants.*

ENGLISH, SAMUEL M., Priv. Co. A, 1st Cal. Heavy Art., 15 June, 1898, to 7 July, 1898. 2nd Lieut. 8th Cal. Inf., 9 July, 1898. Mustered out 31 Jan., 1899. 2nd Lieut. 35th U. S. Inf., 5 July, 1899.
HARD, CARL B., Corpl. Troop I, 2nd U. S. Cav., 3 May, 1898, to 10 Oct., 1898. 2nd Lieut. 35th U. S. Inf., 5 July, 1899.
DEGEN, JOHN A., Sergt. Co. F, 1st Maine Inf., 2 May, 1898, to 8 Nov., 1898. 1st Lieut. 35th U. S. Inf., 5 July, 1899.
LEFORT, ALLAN, 2nd Lieut. 35th U. S. Inf., 5 July, 1899.
KOSSMAN, BENJAMIN, 2nd Lieut. 35th U. S. Inf., 5 July, 1899.
McCARTHY, JOHN F., Corpl. and Sergt. Co. F, and Q. M. Sergt. 2nd U. S. Inf., 30 May, 1898, to 22 June, 1899. 2nd Lieut. 35th U. S. Inf., 5 July, 1899.
TREMAINE, WILLIAM C., 2nd Lieut. 35th U. S. Inf., 5 July, 1899.
HASSON, JOHN P., Corpl. Co. G, 1st Wash. Inf., 26 April, 1898, to 17 Aug., 1898. 2nd Lieut. 35th U. S. Inf., 5 July, 1899.
DUVAL, ROGER, Priv. and Com. Sergt. 35th U. S. Inf., 28 July, 1899, to 24 Sept., 1899. 2nd Lieut. 35th U. S. Inf., 23 Sept., 1899.
OTIS, FRANK I., Priv., Corpl. and Sergt. Co. A, 35th U. S. Inf., 13 July, 1899, to 9 March, 1900. 2nd Lieut. 35th U. S. Inf., 25 Jan., 1900.
SMITH, SELWYN D., Priv., Corpl. and Sergt. Co. C, 35th U. S. Inf., 7 Aug., 1899, to 2 April, 1900. 2nd Lieut. 35th U. S. Inf., 16 March, 1900.
STRONG, DONALD W., Sergt. Co. K, 7th Cal. Inf., 5 May, 1898, to 2 Dec., 1898. Priv., Corpl. and Sergt. Co. A, 35th U. S. Inf., 14 Sept., 1899, to ——, 1900. 2nd Lieut. 35th U. S. Inf., 31 May, 1900.

## 36TH U. S. VOLUNTEER INFANTRY.

*Colonel.*

GROVE, WILLIAM R., Capt. 1st Colo. Inf., 1 May, 1898. Maj., 27 Sept., 1898. Discharged 11 July, 1899. Lieut. Col. 36th U. S. Inf., 5 July, 1899. Col., 24 Dec., 1899.

*Lieutenant Colonel.*

LUHN, WILLIAM L., 1st Lieut. and Adj. 1st Wash. Inf., 30 April, 1898. Discharged 12 July, 1899. Maj. 36th U. S. Inf., 5 July, 1899. Lieut. Col., 24 Dec., 1899.

*Majors.*

BISHOP, WILLIAM H., Capt. 20th Kans. Inf., 2 May, 1898. Maj., 9 May, 1899. Discharged 12 July, 1899. Maj. 36th U. S. Inf., 5 July, 1899.
BRADEN, JOHN Q. A., Priv. Co. L, 1st S. Dak. Inf., 8 May, 1898, to 16 May, 1898. 1st Lieut. 1st S. Dak. Inf., 17 May, 1898. Discharged 11 July, 1899. Maj. 36th U. S. Inf., 5 July, 1899.
ABERNETHY, ROBERT S. (Regular), Capt. 36th U. S. Inf., 5 July, 1899. Maj., 24 Dec., 1899.

*Surgeon with rank of Major.*

STRAUB, PAUL F. (Regular), Maj. Surg. 36th U. S. Inf., 5 July, 1899.

*Assistant Surgeons with rank of Captain.*

MATHEWS, GEORGE W., Capt. Asst. Surg. 36th U. S. Inf., 5 July, 1899.

*With rank of First Lieutenant.*

BREWER, ISAAC W., 1st Lieut. Asst. Surg. 36th U. S. Inf., 5 July, 1899.

*Captains.*

ICKIS, WARREN H., Capt. 51st Iowa Inf., 26 April, 1898. Discharged 14 July, 1899. Capt. 36th U. S. Inf., 5 July, 1899.
STONE, CARL L., 2nd Lieut. 13th Minn. Inf., 29 April, 1898. Discharged 12 July 1899. Capt. 36th U. S. Inf., 5 July, 1899.
FRY, EDGAR A., 1st Lieut. 20th Kans. Inf., 30 April, 1898. Capt., 22 July, 1899. Discharged 30 July, 1899. Capt. 36th U. S. Inf., 5 July, 1899.

BOOTH, EWING E., Adj., 15 Jan., 1900. Capt. 1st Colo. Inf., 1 May, 1898. Discharged 14 July, 1899. Capt. 36th U. S. Inf., 5 July, 1899.
MEAD, CHARLES W., 1st Lieut. 1st Mont. Inf., 1 May, 1898. Discharged 12 July, 1899. Capt. 36th U. S. Inf., 5 July, 1899.
CRAIG, DANIEL F., 1st Lieut. 20th Kans. Inf., 2 May, 1898. Capt., 9 May, 1899. Discharged 12 July, 1899. Capt. 36th U. S. Inf., 5 July, 1899.
HEGEMAN, HARRY A., Capt. 1st S. Dak. Inf., 4 May, 1898. Discharged 12 July, 1899. Capt. 36th U. S. Inf., 5 July, 1899.
STEERE, HENRY, Q. M., 19 Jan., 1900. Capt. 1st Cal. Heavy Art., 8 May, 1898. Discharged 12 July, 1899. Capt. 36th U. S. Inf., 5 July, 1899.
DODGE, FREDERICK R., Sergt. Maj. 20th Kans. Inf., 13 May, 1898, to 23 Sept., 1898. 2nd Lieut. 20th Kans. Inf., 24 Sept., 1898. Discharged 11 July, 1899. Capt. 36th U. S. Inf., 5 July, 1899.
BELL, HARRY, Capt. 36th U. S. Inf., 5 Juy, 1899.
FITZHUGH, SMITH K., Priv. and Corpl. Co. B, 1st Wash. Inf., 30 April, 1898, to 12 July, 1899. Capt. 36th U. S. Inf., 5 July, 1899.
POINT, WILL H., 1st Lieut. 51st Iowa Inf., 26 April, 1898. Discharged 14 July, 1899. 1st Lieut. 36th U. S. Inf., 5 July, 1899. Capt., 26 July, 1899.
O'KEEFE, CORNEALIAUS F., 1st Lieut. 1st Colo. Inf., 1 May, 1898. Discharged 12 July, 1899. 1st Lieut. 36th U. S. Inf., 5 July, 1899. Capt., 31 Oct., 1899.
CHEEVER, LOREN E., 2nd Lieut. 1st Wyo. Inf., 7 May, 1898. 1st Lieut., 16 May, 1899. Discharged 12 July, 1899. 1st Lieut. 36th U. S. Inf., 5 July, 1899. Capt., 24 Dec., 1899.

*First Lieutenants.*

SMITH, FRED E., Q. M. Sergt. Co. D, and Sergt. Maj. 1st N. Dak. Inf., 27 April, 1898, to 23 Feb., 1899. 2nd Lieut. 1st N. Dak. Inf., 24 Feb., 1899. Discharged 12 July, 1899. 1st Lieut. 36th U. S. Inf., 5 July, 1899.
LEAR, BEN., Jr., 1st Sergt. Co. C, 1st Colo. Inf., 1 May, 1898, to 31 March, 1899. 2nd Lieut. 1st Colo. Inf., 1 April, 1899. Discharged 11 July, 1899. 1st Lieut. 36th U. S. Inf., 5 July, 1899.
COREY, MILO C., 1st Sergt. Co. A, 1st Wash. Inf., 28 April, 1898, to 7 June, 1899. 2nd Lieut. 1st Wash. Inf., 8 June, 1899. Discharged 12 July, 1899. 1st Lieut. 36th U. S. Inf., 5 July, 1899.
McGEE, OSCAR A., Sergt. Co. B, 1st Wash. Inf., 30 April, 1898, to 23 July, 1899. 1st Lieut. 36th U. S. Inf., 5 July, 1899.
BACH, CHRISTIAN A., Sergt. Co. D, 13th Minn. Inf., 29 April, 1898, to 13 July, 1899. 1st Lieut. 36th U. S. Inf., 5 July, 1899.
DAVIDSON, ALEXANDER H., 1st Lieut. 36th U. S. Inf., 5 July, 1899.
GOEHR, ALEXANDER, Com., 13 July, 1899. 1st Lieut. 36th U. S. Inf., 5 July, 1899.
WIDDIFIELD, SAMUEL W., Priv. and Corpl. Co. L, 1st Cal. Inf., 27 April, 1898, to 20 July, 1899. 1st Lieut. 36th U. S. Inf., 5 July, 1899.
FERGUSON, ARTHUR M., Corpl. and Sergt. Co. E, 20th Kans. Inf., 2 May, 1898, to 14 July, 1899. 1st Lieut. 36th U. S. Inf., 5 July, 1899.
HARPER, WINFIELD, 1st Lieut. 36th U. S. Inf., 5 July, 1899.
CROCKETT, THOMAS B., Priv. and Corpl. Co. B, 1st Wash. Inf., 30 April, 1898, to 13 July, 1899. 1st Lieut. 36th U. S. Inf., 5 July, 1899.
TREADWELL, ROSCOE, Sergt. Co. H, 1st Idaho Inf., 2 May, 1898, to 14 July, 1899. 1st Lieut. 36th U. S. Inf., 5 July, 1899.
READ, WILLIAM C., 1st Lieut. 36th U. S. Inf., 3 Aug., 1899.
BOWMAN, GEORGE T., Capt. 65th N. Y. Inf., 1 May, 1898. Discharged 19 Nov., 1898. 2nd Lieut. 36th U. S. Inf., 5 July, 1899. 1st Lieut., 24 Dec., 1899.
McGOWAN, EDWARD, 1st Lieut. 2nd Miss. Inf., 4 May, 1898. Discharged 20 Dec., 1898. 2nd Lieut. 36th U. S. Inf., 5 July, 1899. 1st Lieut., 7 Feb., 1900.
GWYNNE, WILLIAM F., Priv. and Corpl. Co. B, 2nd Miss. Inf., 9 July, 1898, to 20 Dec., 1898. 2nd Lieut. 36th U. S. Inf., 5 July, 1899. 1st Lieut., 25 May, 1900.

*Second Lieutenants.*

GRAHAM, WILLIAM B., Sergt. Co. L, 8th Ohio Inf., 25 April, 1898, to 21 Nov., 1898. 2nd Lieut. 36th U. S. Inf., 5 July, 1899.
MANN, EDWIN E., Sergt. and Q. M. Sergt. Co. K, 1st S. Dak. Inf., 4 May, 1898 to 2 July, 1899. 2nd Lieut. 36th U. S. Inf., 5 July, 1899.
PETTY, JAMES M., Corpl. Co. G, 1st D. C. Inf., 12 May, 1898, to 20 Nov., 1898. 2nd Lieut. 36th U. S. Inf., 5 July, 1899.
PEDLAR, LYLE H., Priv., Sergt. and 1st Sergt. Batty C, 1st Cal. Heavy Art., 7 May, 1898, to 3 Feb., 1899. 2nd Lieut. 36th U. S. Inf., 5 July, 1899.
McNARNEY, FRANK T., 2nd Lieut. 36th U. S. Inf., 5 July, 1899.
ODEN, GEORGE J., Priv. and Sergt. Co. A, and Batt. and Reg. Sergt. Maj. 36th U. S. Inf., 8 July, 1899, to 4 March, 1900. 2nd Lieut. 36th U. S. Inf., 12 Feb., 1900.
HUNTSMAN, JOHN A., Priv. and Corpl. Co. H, 20th Kans. Inf., 29 April, 1898, to 30 June, 1899. Priv. and Sergt. Co. E, 36th U. S. Inf., 1 July, 1899, to 4 March, 1900. 2nd Lieut. 36th U. S. Inf., 12 Feb., 1900.
COSTELLO, ISRAEL F., Priv. and Corpl. Co. H, 1st Wash. Inf., 2 May, 1898, to 6 July, 1899. Priv., Sergt. and 1st Sergt. Co. K, 36th U. S. Inf., 10 July, 1899, to 4 March, 1900. 2nd Lieut. 36th U. S. Inf., 12 Feb., 1900.
CRAIG, JOHN M., Sergt. and Q. M. Sergt. Co. E, 20th Kans. Inf., 2 May, 1898, to 30 June, 1899. Priv. and Sergt. Co. L, and Batt. Sergt. Maj. 36th U. S. Inf., 1 July, to 4 March, 1900. 2nd Lieut. 36th U. S. Inf., 12 Feb., 1900.
YOUNG, GEORGE F., Sergt. Co. I, 1st Mont. Inf., 28 April, 1898, to 6 July, 1899. Priv., Batt. Sergt. Maj. and Q. M. Sergt. 36th U. S. Inf., 13 July, 1899, to 4 March, 1900. 2nd Lieut. 36th U. S. Inf., 12 Feb., 1900.

## 37TH U. S. VOLUNTEER INFANTRY.

*Colonel.*

CHEATHAM, B. FRANK, Maj. 1st Tenn. Inf., 23 May, 1898. Discharged 22 Aug., 1899. Maj. 37th U. S. Inf., 5 July, 1899. Col., 13 March, 1900.

*Lieutenant Colonel.*

HAMER, THOMAS R., Capt. 1st Idaho Inf., 28 April, 1898. Lieut. Col., 5 March, 1899. Discharged 10 July, 1899. Lieut. Col. 37th U. S. Inf., 5 July, 1899.

*Majors.*

BOYD, CHARLES T. (Regular), Maj. 37th U. S. Inf., 5 July, 1899.
ORWIG, HENRY B., Capt. 20th Kans. Inf., 29 April, 1898. Discharged 12 July, 1899. Maj. 37th U. S. Inf., 5 July, 1899.
KOEHLER, BENJAMIN M. (Regular), Capt. 37th U. S. Inf., 5 July, 1899. Maj., 10 April, 1900.

*Surgeon with rank of Major.*

WINTER, FRANCIS A. (Regular), Maj. Surg. 37th U. S. Inf., 5 July, 1899.

*Assistant Surgeons with rank of Captain.*

ANDERSON, THOMAS B., Capt. Asst. Surg. 37th U. S. Inf., 5 July, 1899.

*With rank of First Lieutenant.*

SINKS, EDWARD D., 1st Lieut. Asst. Surg. 37th U. S. Inf., 5 July, 1899.

*Captains.*

VAN LEER, SAM, Capt. 1st Tenn. Inf., 25 April, 1898. Discharged 15 July, 1899. Capt. 37th U. S. Inf., 5 July, 1899.
FOSTER, LEO F., 1st Lieut. 1st S. Dak. Inf., 25 April, 1898. Discharged 12 July, 1899. Capt. 37th U. S. Inf., 5 July, 1899.
MYERS, H. U. B., 1st Lieut. 1st Tenn. Inf., 26 April, 1898. Capt., 5 May, 1898. Discharged 17 July, 1899. Capt. 37th U. S. Inf., 5 July, 1899.
LYLE, DAVID E. W. (Regular), Adj., 10 Aug., 1899. Capt. 37th U. S. Inf., 5 July, 1899.
SCOTT, ERNEST D. (Regular), Capt. 37th U. S. Inf., 5 July, 1899.
CLARK, CHARLES N., 1st Lieut. 13th Minn. Inf., 29 April, 1898. Discharged 4 Aug., 1899. Capt. 37th U. S. Inf., 5 July, 1899.
MORAN, JOHN E., Capt. 1st Mont. Inf., 1 May, 1898. Discharged 16 Aug., 1899. Capt. 37th U. S. Inf., 5 July, 1899.
HANNA, WILLIAM B., Sergt. Co. L, 1st Mont. Inf., 5 May, 1898, to 10 May, 1898. 1st Lieut. Batt. Adj. 1st Mont. Inf., 11 May, 1898. Discharged 13 July, 1899. Capt. 37th U. S. Inf., 5 July, 1899.
RICHMOND, HENRY R., Capt. 1st Tenn. Inf., 23 May, 1898. Discharged 29 July, 1899. Capt. 37th U. S. Inf., 5 July, 1899.
GIVENS, NICK K., Capt. 1st Tenn. Inf., 26 May, 1898. Discharged 15 July, 1899. Capt. 37th U. S. Inf., 5 July, 1899.
HUTCHINGS, HENRY A., Capt. 37th U. S. Inf., 5 July, 1899.
FLAHERTY, MICHAEL, Capt. 37th U. S. Inf., 5 July, 1899.
ERICKSON, ALBERT J., Q. M., 10 Aug., 1899. Corpl., Sergt. and 1st Sergt. Co. G, 1st Mont. Inf., 28 April, 1898, to 12 July, 1899. Priv. (unassigned) 36th U. S. Inf., 13 July, 1899. 1st Lieut. 36th U. S. Inf., 5 July, 1899. Capt. 37th U. S. Inf., 3 Aug., 1899.
SLEEPER, CHARLES H., 1st Lieut. 1st Colo. Inf., 1 May, 1898. Discharged 14 July, 1899. 1st Lieut. 37th U. S. Inf., 5 July, 1899. Capt., 10 April, 1900.

*First Lieutenants.*

RAGSDALE, ROBERT O., 2nd Lieut. 1st Tenn. Inf., 25 April, 1898. 1st Lieut. 15 Oct., 1898. Discharged 16 July, 1899. 1st Lieut. 37th U. S. Inf., 5 July, 1899.
McLESTER, CHARLES M., 2nd Lieut. 1st Tenn. Inf., 25 April, 1898. Discharged 17 July, 1899. 1st Lieut., 5 July, 1899.
BRIGHT, ALBERT J., 1st Lieut. 1st Tenn. Inf., 23 May, 1898. Discharged 15 July, 1899. 1st Lieut. 37th U. S. Inf., 5 July, 1899.
PATTON, JOHN C., 1st Lieut. 1st Tenn. Inf., 24 May, 1898. Discharged 29 July, 1899. 1st Lieut. 37th U. S. Inf., 5 July, 1899.
CHAPMAN, GRANVILLE L., 1st Lieut. 1st Tenn. Inf., 26 May, 1898. Discharged 29 July, 1899. 1st Lieut. 37th U. S. Inf., 5 July, 1899.
MURPHY, ERNEST VAN D., Priv., Corpl., Sergt. and 1st Sergt. Cos. C and B, 1st Mont. Inf., 1 May, 1898, to 3 Jan., 1899. 2nd Lieut. 1st Mont. Inf., 4 Jan., 1899. Discharged 11 July, 1899. 1st Lieut. 37th U. S. Inf., 5 July, 1899.
VAUGHAN, WILLIAM T., Corpl. Co. B, 1st Tenn. Inf., 25 April, 1898, to 11 June, 1899. 2nd Lieut. 1st Tenn. Inf., 12 June, 1899. Discharged 15 July, 1899. 1st Lieut. 37th U. S. Inf., 5 July, 1899.
BALCH, EDWARD T., 1st Lieut. 37th U. S. Inf., 5 July, 1899.
LOWENBERG, JESSE G., 1st Lieut. 37th U. S. Inf., 5 July, 1899.
CLARK, RUFUS B., Com., 10 Aug., 1899. Priv. and Corpl. Co. C, and Q. M. Sergt. 1st Wash. Inf., 30 April, 1898, to 27 July, 1899. Priv. Co. I, 37th U. S. Inf., 28 July, 1899, to 4 Aug., 1899. 1st Lieut. 37th U. S. Inf., 5 July, 1899.

AUSWALD, FRANK, Corpl. and Sergt. Co. B, 20th Kans. Inf., 9 May, 1898, to 22 July, 1899. Priv. Co. F, 37th U. S. Inf., 24 July, 1899, to 4 Aug., 1899. 1st Lieut. 37th U. S. Inf., 5 July, 1899.
YOUNG, JOHN S. E., 1st Lieut. 37th U. S. Inf., 5 July, 1899.
KEITHLEY, IRA, Corpl., Sergt. and 1st Sergt. Co. D, 20th Kans. Inf., 11 May, 1898, to 25 July, 1899. Priv. Co. I, 37th U. S. Inf., 28 July, 1899, to 4 Aug., 1899. 1st Lieut. 37th U. S. Inf., 5 July, 1899.
PILCHER, WINSTON, 2nd Lieut. 1st Tenn. Inf., 19 May, 1898. 1st Lieut., 12 June, 1899. Discharged 29 July, 1899. 2nd Lieut. 37th U. S. Inf., 5 July, 1899. 1st Lieut., 9 Jan., 1900.
McINTYRE, SAMUEL B., Capt. 3rd Tenn. Inf., 28 April, 1898. Discharged 31 Jan., 1899. 2nd Lieut. 37th U. S. Inf., 5 July, 1899. 1st Lieut., 10 April, 1900.
BASKETTE, ALVIN K., 1st Sergt. Co. F, 1st Tenn. Inf., 25 April, 1898, to 25 Oct., 1898. 2nd Lieut. 1st Tenn. Inf., 26 Oct., 1898. Discharged 17 July, 1899. 2nd Lieut. 37th U. S. Inf., 5 July, 1899. 1st Lieut., 25 May, 1900.

*Second Lieutenants.*

PECK, THOMAS F., 1st Lieut. 6th U. S. Inf., 29 June, 1898. Discharged 15 March, 1899. 2nd Lieut. 37th U. S. Inf., 5 July, 1899.
FULLER, JOHN T., 1st Lieut. 6th U. S. Inf., 29 June, 1898. Discharged 15 March, 1899. 2nd Lieut. 37th U. S. Inf., 5 July, 1899.
BASKETTE, REUBEN V., Capt. 8th U. S. Inf., 5 July, 1898. Discharged 6 March, 1899. 2nd Lieut. 37th U. S. Inf., 5 July, 1899.
MILES, YILLIAM G., Capt. 158th Ind. Inf., 26 April, 1898. Discharged 4 Nov., 1898. 2nd Lieut. 37th U. S. Inf., 5 July, 1899.
SHEARER, ROBERT M., Capt. 2nd Ky. Inf., 6 May, 1898. Discharged 31 Oct., 1898. 2nd Lieut. 37th U. S. Inf., 5 July, 1899.
CASS, LEWIS W., Priv. and Corpl. Co. M, 2nd Mo. Inf., and Corpl. Cos. D and C, 6th U. S. Inf., 4 May, 1898, to 15 March, 1899. 2nd Lieut. 37th U. S. Inf., 5 July, 1899.
AIKEN, WILLIAM B., Priv. Co. H, 3rd Tenn. Inf., and Priv. and Sergt. Co. F, 6th U. S. Inf., 29 July, 1898, to 15 March, 1899. 2nd Lieut. 37th U. S. Inf., 5 July, 1899.
O'BRIEN, HARRY J., Corpl. and Sergt. Co. M, 3rd Ill. Inf., 26 April, 1898, to 17 Jan., 1899. 2nd Lieut. 37th U. S. Inf., 5 July, 1899.
STORCK, JOHN, Priv. and Sergt. Maj. 37th U. S. Inf., 29 July, 1899, to 20 Jan., 1900. 2nd Lieut. 37th U. S. Inf., 5 Dec., 1899.
WALKER, RICHARD W., Priv., Corpl. and Sergt. Cos. A and L, 1st Tenn. Inf., 30 May, 1898, to 8 July, 1899. Priv. and Sergt. Co. A, and Batt. Sergt. Maj. 37th U. S. Inf., 9 July, 1899, to 5 Feb., 1900. 2nd Lieut. 37th U. S. Inf., 11 Jan., 1900.
GUNN, THOMAS W., Priv., Sergt. and 1st Sergt. Co. K, 37th U. S. Inf., 28 July, 1899, to 18 May, 1900. 2nd Lieut. 37th U. S. Inf., 27 April, 1900.

## 38TH U. S. VOLUNTEER INFANTRY.

*Colonel.*

ANDERSON, GEORGE S. (Regular), Col. 38th U. S. Inf., 17 Aug., 1899.

*Lieutenant Colonel.*

CRANE, CHARLES J. (Regular), Lieut. Col. 38th U. S. Inf., 17 Aug., 1899.

*Majors.*

MUIR, CHARLES H. (Regular), Maj. 38th U. S. Inf., 17 Aug., 1899.
HOLBROOK, WILLARD A. (Regular), Maj. 38th U. S. Inf., 17 Aug., 1899.
GOODIER, LEWIS E., Capt. 1st N. Y. Inf., 2 May, 1898. Maj. 203rd N. Y. Inf., 20 July, 1898. Lieut. Col., 2 Feb., 1899. Mustered out 25 March, 1899. Maj. 38th U. S. Inf., 17 Aug., 1899.

*Surgeon with rank of Major.*

GLENNAN, JAMES D. (Regular), Maj. Surg. 38th U. S. Inf., 17 Aug., 1899.

*Assistant Surgeons with rank of Captain.*

DEWEY, FREDERICK S., Capt. Asst. Surg. 38th U. S. Inf., 17 Aug., 1899.

*With rank of First Lieutenant.*

HICKS, GEORGE L., Jr., Asst. Surg. 1st Md. Inf., 7 Nov., 1898. Mustered out 28 Feb., 1899. 1st Lieut. Asst. Surg. 38th U. S. Inf., 17 Aug., 1899.

*Captains.*

ALLEN, DAVID F., Corpl. Co. E, 10th Ind. Inf., 25 April, 1861, to 6 Aug., 1861. Priv Co. C, and Sergt. Maj. 10th Ind. Inf., 1 Feb., 1862, to 28 Oct., 1862. 2nd Lieut 10th Ind. Inf., 28 Oct., 1862. Mustered out 19 Sept., 1864. Capt. 158th Ind. Inf. 26 April, 1898. Mustered out 4 Nov., 1898. Capt. 38th U. S. Inf., 17 Aug., 1899
NICHOLS, ROSS A., 1st Lieut. 40th Iowa Inf., 26 April, 1898. Capt., 6 Jan., 1899. Mus Capt. 38th U. S. Inf., 17 Aug., 1899.
MOORE, JOHN W., 1st Lieut. 1st Texas Inf., 25 April, 1898. Capt., 6 Jan., 1899. Mustered out 18 April, 1899. Capt. 38th U. S. Inf., 17 Aug., 1899.

READ, BEVERLY A., Adj., 1 Oct., 1899. Capt. A. A. G., 12 May, 1898. Discharged 12 May, 1899. Capt. 38th U. S. Inf., 17 Aug., 1899.

JORDAN, JOHN L., Capt. 4th Penn. Inf., 18 June, 1898. Mustered out 6 May, 1899. Capt. 38th U. S. Inf., 17 Aug., 1899.

NOLAN, ROBERT M., Capt. 9th U. S. Inf., 29 June, 1898. Mustered out 25 May, 1899. Capt. 38th U. S. Inf., 17 Aug., 1899.

FLEISCHHAUER, YILLIAM G., Q. M., 1 Oct., 1899. Capt. 35th Mich. Inf., 9 June, 1898. Mustered out 31 March, 1899. Capt. 38th U. S. Inf., 17 Aug., 1899.

GRINSTEAD, CLARENCE L., Capt. 1st Ky. Inf., 13 May, 1898. Mustered out 24 Feb., 1899. Capt. 38th U. S. Inf., 17 Aug., 1899.

COLLIER, WILLIAM H., 1st Lieut. 2nd Ky. Inf., 9 May, 1898. Resigned 7 July, 1898. Maj. 4th Ky. Inf., 8 July, 1898. Mustered out 12 Feb., 1899. Capt. 38th U. S. Inf., 17 Aug., 1899.

POWELL, JOHN S., Capt. 3rd Ga. Inf., 6 Aug., 1898. Mustered out 22 April, 1899. Capt. 38th U. S. Inf., 17 Aug., 1899.

VAIDEN, WILLIAM J., Capt. 2nd Ala. Inf., 24 May, 1898. Mustered out 31 Oct., 1898. 2nd Lieut. 3rd Ala. Inf., 10 Jan., 1899. Mustered out 20 March, 1899. Capt. 38th U. S. Inf., 17 Aug., 1899.

WEBER, JOHN E., 1st Lieut. Batty A, Mo. Light Art., 4 May, 1898. Mustered out 30 Nov., 1898. Capt. 38th U. S. Inf., 17 Aug., 1899.

SAWYER, CLAUDE E., Capt. 1st S. C. Inf., 7 May, 1898. Mustered out 10 Nov., 1898. Capt. 38th U. S. Inf., 17 Aug., 1899.

PAVEY, NEIL P., Capt. 1st Ill. Inf., 26 April, 1898. Mustered out 2 May, 1899. 1st Lieut. 38th U. S. Inf., 17 Aug., 1899 Capt., 1 Dec., 1899.

*First Lieutenants.*

DOANE, WILLIAM G., 1st Lieut. 3rd Neb. Inf., 27 May, 1898. Mustered out 11 May, 1899. 1st Lieut. 38th U. S. Inf., 17 Aug., 1899.

MORRIS, JOHN E., Capt. 2nd U. S. Inf., 8 July, 1898. Mustered out 22 June, 1899. 1st Lieut. 38th U. S. Inf., 17 Aug., 1899.

COVINGTON, WILLIAM A., 1st Lieut. 4th Tenn. Inf., 18 June, 1898. Mustered out 6 May, 1899. 1st Lieut. 38th U. S. Inf., 17 Aug., 1899.

HOWARD, LOUIE D., 2nd Lieut. 6th Mo. Inf., 10 July, 1898. Mustered out 10 May, 1899. 1st Lieut. 38th U. S. Inf., 17 Aug., 1899.

STEVENS, HENRY V., Capt. 3rd Tenn. Inf., 25 April, 1898. Mustered out 31 Jan., 1899. 1st Lieut. 38th U. S. Inf., 17 Aug., 1899.

KRAEMER, JOSEPH L., 1st Lieut. 35th Mich. Inf., 5 July, 1898. Mustered out 31 March, 1899. 1st Lieut. 38th U. S. Inf., 17 Aug., 1899.

BROWN, ANDREW J., Jr., 2nd Lieut. 6th U. S. Inf., 29 June, 1898. 1st Lieut., 7 Jan., 1899. Mustered out 15 March, 1899. 1st Lieut. 38th U. S. Inf., 17 Aug., 1899.

BLANCHARD, REUBEN D., 2nd Lieut. 4th Wis. Inf., 30 June, 1898. Mustered out 28 Feb., 1899. 1st Lieut. 38th U. S. Inf., 17 Aug., 1899.

WOODS, ROBERT F., Sergt. Co. A, Ind. Batt. 2nd S. C. Inf., 5 May, 1898, to 25 Aug., 1898. 1st Lieut. 2nd S. C. Inf., 26 Aug., 1898. Mustered out 19 April, 1899. 1st Lieut. 38th U. S. Inf., 17 Aug., 1899

MORRISON, IRA I., Com., 29 Jan., 1900. 1st Lieut. 1st Terr. Inf., 17 July, 1898. Mustered out 13 Feb., 1899. 1st Lieut. 38th U. S. Inf., 17 Aug., 1899.

THOMPSON, FRED A., Capt. 3rd Mo. Inf., 27 April, 1898. Mustered out 7 Nov., 1898. 1st Lieut. 38th U. S. Inf., 17 Aug., 1899.

KELLY, AMZI B., Capt. 2nd Texas Inf., 3 May, 1898. Mustered out 9 Nov., 1898. 1st Lieut. 38th U. S. Inf., 17 Aug., 1899.

KREBS, FRANK S., 2nd Lieut. 1st Mo. Inf., 4 May, 1898. Mustered out 31 Oct., 1898. 1st Lieut. 38th U. S. Inf., 17 Aug. 1899.

JACOBS, DOUGLAS H., Priv. 1st Troop Philadelphia City Cav., 11 June, 1898, to 21 Nov., 1898. 1st Lieut. 38th U. S. Inf., 17 Aug., 1899.

SEIGLE, THADDEUS B., 1st Lieut. 38th U. S. Inf., 17 Aug., 1899.

JOHNSON, DANIEL R., 1st Lieut. N. C. Inf., 27 April, 1898. Mustered out 22 April, 1899. 2nd Lieut. 38th U. S. Inf., 17 Aug., 1899. 1st Lieut., 1 Dec., 1899.

*Second Lieutenants.*

ABBOTT, ELISHA G., 1st Lieut. 3rd Texas Inf., 29 April, 1898. Mustered out 16 Feb., 1899. 2nd Lieut. 38th U. S. Inf., 17 Aug., 1899.

THORNTON, WILLIAM O., 1st Lieut. 3rd Ga. Inf., 6 Aug., 1898. Mustered out 22 April, 1899. 2nd Lieut. 38th U. S. Inf., 17 Aug., 1899.

HUDSON, WALTER C., 2nd Lieut. 1st Ark. Inf., 4 May, 1898. Mustered out 25 Oct., 1898. 2nd Lieut. 38th U. S. Inf., 17 Aug., 1899.

BURY, FRED, Priv. Co. A, 31st Mich. Inf., 26 April, 1898, to 17 May, 1899. 2nd Lieut. 38th U. S. Inf., 17 Aug., 1899.

MAXWELL, JOHN R., Hosp. Steward 5th U. S. Inf., 9 June, 1898, to 31 May, 1899. 2nd Lieut. 38th U. S. Inf., 17 Aug., 1899.

HUSMAN, FREDERICK C., Priv. Co. D, 1st Mo. Inf., 13 May, 1898, to 31 Oct., 1898. 2nd Lieut. 38th U. S. Inf., 17 Aug., 1899.

SHARTLE, SAMUEL G., Priv. and Corpl. Co. C, 8th Pa. Inf., 10 May, 1898, to 7 March, 1899. 2nd Lieut. 38th U. S. Inf., 17 Aug., 1899.

WEINHEIMER, CHARLES J., Priv., Sergt. and Q. M. Sergt. Co. C, 4th U. S. Inf., 2 June, 1898, to 7 Oct., 1898. Priv., Sergt. and 1st Sergt. Co. L, 27th U. S. Inf., 27 July, 1899, to 5 Sept., 1899. 2nd Lieut. 38th U. S. Inf., 17 Aug., 1899.

ALLEN, ALBERT C., Priv. and Sergt. Batty C, Utah Light Art., 1 July, 1898, to 17 Nov., 1898. 2nd Lieut. 38th U. S. Inf., 17 Aug., 1899.

MENDEL, DANIEL G., 2nd Lieut. 38th U. S. Inf., 17 Aug., 1899.

ELLIS, ROWLAND B., Sergt. Co. L, 1st Cal. Inf., 27 April, 1898, to 21 Sept., 1899. 2nd Lieut. 38th U. S. Inf., 17 Aug., 1899.

WOUDE, ALBERT J., Capt. 10th U. S. Inf., 21 June, 1898. Mustered out 8 March, 1899. Priv. and Com. Sergt. 38th U. S. Inf., 16 Sept., 1899, to 15 Jan., 1900. 2nd Lieut. 38th U. S. Inf., 6 Dec., 1899.

### 39TH U. S. VOLUNTEER INFANTRY.

*Colonel.*

BULLARD, ROBERT L. (Regular), Col. 39th U. S. Inf., 17 Aug., 1899.

*Lieutenant Colonel.*

CROWDER, ENOCH H. (Regular), Lieut. Col. 39th U. S. Inf., 17 Aug., 1899.

*Majors.*

LANGHORNE, GEORGE T. (Regular), Maj. 39th U. S. Inf., 17 Aug., 1899.
PARKER, JOHN H. (Regular), Trans. to 39th U. S. Inf., 23 Sept., 1899.
MULFORD, HARRY B., Capt. 2nd Neb. Inf., 27 April, 1898. Maj. 1st Neb. Inf., 10 May, 1898. Col., 28 April, 1899. Mustered out 23 Aug., 1899. Maj. 39th U. S. Inf., 17 Aug., 1899.

*Surgeon with rank of Major.*

WALES, PHILIP G. (Regular), Maj. Surg. 39th U. S. Inf., 17 Aug., 1899.

*Assistant Surgeons with rank of Captain.*

NORMAN, SEATON, Maj. Surg. 3rd U. S. Inf., 8 June, 1898. Mustered out 2 May, 1899. Capt. Asst. Surg. 39th U. S. Inf., 17 Aug., 1899.

*With rank of First Lieutenant.*

BEESON, EDWARD G., Priv. Co. F, 49th Iowa Inf., 21 June, 1898, to 30 Sept., 1898. 1st Lieut. Asst. Surg. 49th Iowa Inf., 14 Feb., 1899. Mustered out 13 May, 1899. 1st Lieut. Asst. Surg. 39th U. S. Inf., 17 Aug., 1899.

*Captains.*

MURPHY, WILLIAM L. (Regular), Capt. 39th U. S. Inf., 17 Aug., 1899.
TAYLOR, WALLACE C., Capt. 1st Neb. Inf., 27 April, 1898. Maj., 28 April, 1899. Mustered out 23 Aug., 1899. Capt. 39th U. S. Inf., 17 Aug., 1899.
HILTON, CHARLES H., Jr., 1st Lieut. 1st Colo. Inf., 1 May, 1898. Capt., 1 April, 1899. Mustered out 8 Sept., 1899. 2nd Lieut. 39th U. S. Inf., 17 Aug., 1899.
GAINES, NOEL, Adj., 19 Oct., 1899. Capt. 3rd Ky. Inf., 20 May, 1898. Mustered out 16 May, 1899. Capt. 39th U. S. Inf., 17 Aug., 1899.
MACMANUS, AUGUSTUS F. W., Capt. 1st Texas Inf., 1 May, 1898. Mustered out 15 April, 1899. Capt. 39th U. S. Inf., 17 Aug., 1899.
RICHARDSON, MACK, Capt. 6th Mo. Inf., 6 July, 1898. Mustered out 10 May, 1899. Capt. 39th U. S. Inf., 17 Aug., 1899.
THORNBURN, JOHN L., Capt. 35th Mich. Inf., 7 June, 1898. Mustered out 31 March, 1899. Capt. 39th U. S. Inf., 17 Aug., 1899.
CAUGHEY, JOSEPH B., Maj. 3rd Ill. Inf., 26 April, 1898. Mustered out 24 Jan., 1899. Capt. 39th U. S. Inf., 17 Aug., 1899.
GREEN, GEORGE W., Capt. 8th U. S. Inf., 7 July, 1898. Mustered out 6 March, 1899. Capt 39th U. S. Inf., 17 Aug., 1899.
KREGER, EDWARD A., Capt. 52nd Iowa Inf., 26 April, 1898. Mustered out 30 Oct., 1898. 1st Lieut. 39th U. S. Inf., 17 Aug., 1899. Capt., 17 Aug., 1899.
HARDEMAN, THOMAS Q. M., 21 Oct., 1899. 1st Lieut. 1st Ala. Inf., 1 May, 1898. Mustered out 31 Oct., 1898. Capt. 39th U. S. Inf., 17 Aug., 1899.
BURT, ANDREW J., 2nd Lieut. 2nd U. S. Cav., 14 May, 1898. 1st Lieut., 17 July, 1898. Mustered out 24 Oct., 1898. Capt. 39th U. S. Inf., 17 Aug., 1899.
LONG, FRANK S., Capt. 6th Iowa Batty, 24 June, 1898. Mustered out 5 Sept., 1898. Capt 39th U. S. Inf., 17 Aug., 1899.
BAKER, HIRAM C., Capt. 4th Texas Inf., 28 June, 1898. Mustered out 10 March, 1899. 1st Lieut. 39th U. S. Inf., 17 Aug., 1899. Capt., 13 Oct., 1899.

*First Lieutenants.*

MALONEY, FRANK, 1st Lieut. 6th U. S. Inf., 29 June, 1898. Capt., 7 Jan., 1899. Mustered out 15 March, 1899. 1st Lieut. 39th U. S. Inf., 17 Aug., 1899.
TRENT, GRANT T., 2nd Lieut. 6th U. S. Inf., 29 June, 1898. 1st Lieut., 13 Oct., 1898. Mustered out 15 March, 1899. 1st Lieut. 39th U. S. Inf., 17 Aug., 1899.
CROMWELL, ELLIS, Capt. 2nd Miss. Inf., 26 April, 1898. Mustered out 20 Dec., 1898. 1st Lieut. 39th U. S. Inf., 17 Aug., 1899.
WELSH, ROBERT S., Capt. 34th Mich. Inf., 26 April, 1898. Mustered out 21 Nov., 1898. 1st Lieut. 39th U. S. Inf., 17 Aug., 1899.
COXE, ALEXANDER B., 1st Lieut. Q. M. 14th Minn. Inf., 29 April, 1898. Mustered out 18 Nov., 1898. 1st Lieut. 39th U. S. Inf., 17 Aug., 1899.
SMITH, PERRIN L., 1st Lieut. 12th Minn. Inf., 29 April, 1898. Capt., 19 July, 1898. Mustered out 5 Nov., 1898. 1st Lieut. 39th U. S. Inf., 17 Aug., 1899.
COBB, THOMAS M., Jr., 1st Lieut. and Adj. 5th Mo. Inf., 4 May, 1898. Mustered out 9 Nov., 1898. 1st Lieut. 39th U. S. Inf., 17 Aug., 1899.

MERKLIN, ALBERT J., 2nd Lieut. 1st Mo. Inf., 4 May, 1898. 1st Lieut., 11 July, 1898. Mustered out 31 Oct., 1898. 1st Lieut. 39th U. S. Inf., 17 Aug., 1899.
COURTNEY, HARRY E., 2nd Lieut. 1st Ark. Inf., 15 May, 1898. Mustered out 25 Oct., 1898. 1st Lieut. 39th U. S. Inf., 17 Aug., 1899.
BOYER, FREDERICK, 2nd Lieut. 1st Ill. Cav., 10 May, 1898. Mustered out 11 Oct., 1898. 1st Lieut. 39th U. S. Inf., 17 Aug., 1899.
APPLE, GEORGE M., Sergt. and 1st Sergt. Co. I, 2nd U. S. Eng., 17 June, 1898, to 7 May, 1899. 2nd Lieut. 2nd U. S. Eng., 8 May, 1899. Mustered out 16 May, 1899. 1st Lieut. 39th U. S. Inf., 17 Aug., 1899.
LAWSON, LAURIN L., Priv. Cos. D and B. 1st Wash Inf., 30 April, 1898, to 16 Oct., 1899. 1st Lieut. 39th U. S. Inf., 17 Aug., 1899.
BANE, HOWARD K., Priv. and Sergt. 1st Troop Nev. Cav., 17 May, 1898, to 6 Nov., 1899. 1st Lieut. 39th U. S. Inf., 17 Aug., 1899.
PETITE, ALBERT M., Sergt. Co. H, 2nd U. S. Eng., 27 June, 1898, to 15 April, 1899. 1st Lieut. 39th U. S. Inf., 17 Aug., 1899.
LEE, GEORGE M., 1st Lieut. 39th U. S. Inf., 17 Aug., 1899.
ORTON, ARTHUR W., 1st Lieut. 5th U. S. Inf., 13 July, 1898. Mustered out 31 May, 1899. 2nd Lieut. 39th U. S. Inf., 17 Aug., 1899. 1st Lieut., 13 Oct., 1899.

*Second Lieutenants.*

WHITE, EDWARD H., 1st Lieut. 7th Ill. Inf., 26 April, 1898. Mustered out 20 Oct., 1898. 2nd Lieut. 39th U. S. Inf., 17 Aug., 1899.
MOHR, W. FRANK, Priv. Governor's Troop, Pa. Cav., 13 June, 1898, to 21 Nov., 1898. 2nd Lieut. 39th U. S. Inf., 17 Aug., 1899.
WILLIAMS, GIDEON H., Sergt. Co. H, 6th U. S. Inf., 18 July, 1898, to 15 March, 1899. 2nd Lieut. 39th U. S. Inf., 17 Aug., 1899.
WOOD, CHARLES R., Priv. and Corpl. Co. L, 158th Ind. Inf., 17 June, 1898, to 4 Nov., 1898. 2nd Lieut. 39th U. S. Inf., 17 Aug., 1899.
FRANK, CHARLES S., 2nd Lieut. 39th U. S. Inf., 17 Aug., 1899.
BURNETT, FRANK C., Priv. Co. D, 51st Iowa Inf. and Priv. and Corpl. Sig. Corps, 15 June, 1898, to 10 Oct., 1899. 2nd Lieut. 39th U. S. Inf., 17 Aug., 1899.
BOWDLE, CHARLES W., 1st Sergt. Co. K, 3rd Ohio Inf., 2 June, 1898, to 26 Oct., 1898. 2nd Lieut. 39th U. S. Inf., 17 Aug., 1899.
SHELTON, NATHAN J., 2nd Lieut. 39th U. S. Inf., 17 Aug., 1899.
COVELL, MARCUS, Q. M. Sergt. 39th U. S. Inf., 15 Sept., 1899, to 12 Oct., 1899. 2nd Lieut. 39th U. S. Inf., 13 Oct., 1899.
POLK, FRANK M., Priv. and Corpl. Co. C, 39th U. S. Inf., 23 Sept., 1899, to 27 March, 1900. 2nd Lieut. 39th U. S. Inf., 5 March, 1900.
CASEY, HENRY R., 2nd Lieut. 3rd Ala. Inf., 28 June, 1898. Mustered out 20 March, 1899. Batt. Sergt. Maj. 39th U. S. Inf., 14 Sept., 1899, to 15 May, 1900. 2nd Lieut. 39th U. S. Inf., 27 April, 1900.
GAVETT, ELMER B., Corpl. Co. E, 32nd Mich. Inf., 26 April, 1898, to 27 Oct., 1898. Priv. and Q. M. Sergt. Co. H, 39th U. S. Inf., 28 Aug., 1899, to ——, 1900. 2nd Lieut. 39th U. S. Inf., 25 May, 1900.

## 40TH U. S. VOLUNTEER INFANTRY.

*Colonel.*

GODWIN, EDWARD A. (Regular), Col. 40th U. S. Inf., 17 Aug., 1899.

*Lieutenant Colonel.*

BYRNE, BERNARD A. (Regular), Lieut. Col. 40th U. S. Inf., 17 Aug., 1899.

*Majors.*

CRAIGHILL, WILLIAM E. (Regular), Maj. 40th U. S. Inf., 17 Aug., 1899.
McNAMEE, MICHAEL M. (Regular), Maj. 40th U. S. Inf., 17 Aug., 1899.
CASE, JAMES F., Capt. 2nd Ore. Inf., 30 April, 1898. Bvt. Maj., 17 May, 1899. Mustered out 7 Aug., 1899. 1st Lieut. 45th U. S. Inf., 17 Aug., 1899 (declined). Maj. 40th U. S. Inf., 17 Aug., 1899.

*Surgeon with rank of Major.*

RAYMOND, THOMAS U. (Regular), Maj. Surg. 40th U. S. Inf., 17 May, 1899.

*Assistant Surgeons with rank of Captain.*

ROMIG, EDWARD A., Capt. Asst. Surg. 40th U. S. Inf., 17 Aug., 1899.

*With rank of First Lieutenant.*

BURCHARD, EASTON, Asst. Surg. 5th Mo. Inf., 4 May, 1898. Mustered out 9 Nov., 1898. 1st Lieut. Asst. Surg. 40th U. S. Inf., 17 Aug., 1899.

*Captains.*

MILLAR, THOMAS, Capt. 1st Wyo. Inf., 25 April, 1898. Mustered out 23 Sept., 1899. Capt. 40th U. S. Inf., 17 Aug., 1899.
MARPLE, CHARLES H., Capt. 3rd Neb. Inf., 27 May, 1898. Mustered out 11 May, 1899. Capt. 40th U. S. Inf., 17 Aug., 1899.
ELLIOTT, WALTER B., 1st Lieut. 6th Mo. Inf., 5 July, 1898. Mustered out 10 May, 1899. Capt. 40th U. S. Inf., 17 Aug., 1899.

LILIENTHAL, ALBERT W., Adj., 1 Dec., 1899. Capt. 7th U. S. Inf., 22 June, 1898. Mustered out 28 Feb., 1899. Capt. 40th U. S. Inf., 17 Aug., 1899.
MAYES, JAMES J., Capt. 7th U. S Inf., 25 June, 1898. Mustered out 28 Feb., 1899. Capt. 40th U. S. Inf., 17 Aug., 1899.
FRANCE, JAMES C., 1st Lieut. 50th Iowa Inf., 26 April, 1898. Mustered out 30 Nov., 1898. Capt. 40th U. S. Inf., 17 Aug., 1899.
KENDRICK, WILLIAM J., Maj. 2nd Ga. Inf., 28 April, 1898. Mustered out 30 Nov., 1898. Capt. 40th U. S. Inf., 17 Aug., 1899.
McGIRR, THOMAS L., Capt. 6th Ill. Inf., 26 April, 1898. Mustered out 25 Nov., 1898. Capt. 40th U. S. Inf., 17 Aug., 1899.
LAMBDIN, WILLIAM McK., Capt. 2nd Texas Inf., 28 April, 1898. Mustered out 9 Nov., 1898. Capt. 40th U. S. Inf., 17 Aug., 1899.
GREEN, JOHN WESLEY, 1 Lieut. 1st U. S. Cav., 7 May, 1898. Mustered out 15 Sept., 1898. Capt. 40th U. S. Inf., 17 Aug., 1899.
KELLY, LUTHER S., Capt. 7th U. S. Inf., 14 Nov., 1898. Mustered out 28 Feb., 1899. Capt. 40th U. S. Inf., 17 Aug., 1899.
SMITH, PAUL, Capt. 40th U. S. Inf., 17 Aug., 1899.
WATSON, WILLIAM J., 1st Lieut. 20th Kans. Inf., 29 April, 1898. Capt., 23 March, 1899. Mustered out 28 Oct., 1899. 1st Lieut. 40th U. S. Inf., 17 Aug., 1899. Capt., 11 Nov., 1899.
BARTON, EUGENE E., Q. M., 2 March, 1900. Capt. 4th Ill Inf., 26 April, 1888. Mustered out 2 May, 1899. 1st Lieut. 40th U. S. Inf., 17 Aug., 1899. Capt., 13 Dec., 1899.

*First Lieutenants.*

PULIS, CHARLES C., 2nd Lieut. 3rd Neb. Inf., 3 June, 1898. Mustered out 11 May, 1899. Priv., Sergt. and 1st Sergt. Co. L, 32 U. S. Inf., 24 July to 25 Sept., 1899. 1st Lieut. 40th U. S. Inf., 17 Aug., 1899.
POURILE, JAMES R., 1st Lieut. 6th Mo. Inf., 9 July, 1898. Mustered out 10 May, 1899. 1st Lieut. 40th U. S. Inf., 17 Aug., 1899.
DODGE, DAVID M., Com., 20 Sept., 1899. Prin. Mus. 2 Mo. Inf., 27 April to 15 May, 1898. 2nd Lieut. 2nd Mo. Inf., 16 May, 1898. 1st Lieut., 5 Nov., 1898. Mustered out, 3 March, 1899. 1st Lieut. 40th U. S. Inf., 17 Aug., 1899.
CRAWFORD, WILLIAM P., Capt. 2nd S. C. Inf., 20 July, 1898. Mustered out 19 April, 1899. 1st Lieut. 40th U. S. Inf., 17 Aug., 1899.
CROTTY, JOHN, 1st Lieut. and Q. M. 4 Texas Inf., 20 June, 1898. Mustered out 10 March, 1899. 1st Lieut. 40th U. S. Terr. Inf., 17 Aug., 1899.
CRAVENS, RICHARD K., 1st Lieut. Terr. Inf., 10 July, 1898. Mustered out 13 Feb., 1899. 1st Lieut. 40th U. S. Inf., 17 Aug., 1899.
McDOWELL, QUINCY E., Capt. 159th Ind., 26 April, 1898. Mustered out 23 Nov., 1898. 1st Lieut. 40th U. S. Inf., 17 Aug., 1899.
WHEELER, JAMES M., 1st Lieut. 1st Terr. Inf., 18 July, 1898. Capt., 14 Jan., 1899. Mustered out 13 Feb., 1899. 1st Lieut. 40th U. S. Inf., 17 Aug., 1899.
BOWIE, HAMILTON, 2nd Lieut. 1st Ala. Inf., 1 May, 1898. Mustered out 31 Oct., 1898. 1st Lieut. 40th U. S. Inf., 17 Aug., 1899.
SAYRE, HAL, Jr., 2nd Lieut. 1st U. S. Cav., 17 May, 1898. Mustered out 15 Sept., 1898. 1st Lieut. 40th U. S. Inf., 17 Aug., 1899.
MASTELLER, KENNETH C., 1st Sergt. Co. G, 6th Cal. Inf., 29 April to 2 Sept., 1898. 2nd Lieut. 6th Cal. Inf., 3 Sept., 1898. Mustered out 15 Dec., 1898. 1st Lieut. 40th U. S. Inf., 17 Aug., 1899.
FLETCHER, HENRY P., Priv. Troop K, 1st U. S. Cav., 21 May to 11 Nov., 1898. 1st Lieut. 40th U. S. Inf., 17 Aug., 1899.
RYAN, THOMAS, 1st Lieut. 40th U. S. Inf., 17 Aug., 1899.
FITZPATRICK, YILLIAM C., 1st Lieut. 4th Tex. Inf., 28 June, 1898. Mustered out 10 March, 1899. 2nd Lieut. 40th U. S. Inf., 17 Aug., 1899. 1st Lieut., 11 Nov., 1899.
MITCHELL, CULLEN C., 1st Lieut. 3rd Miss. Inf., 15 July, 1898. Mustered out 15 March, 1899. 2nd Lieut. 40th U. S. Inf., 17 Aug., 1899. 1st Lieut., 13 Dec., 1899.
UTTERBACK, WILLIAM E., 1st Lieut. 1st Miss. Inf., 27 April, 1898. Mustered out 20 Dec., 1898. 2nd Lieut. 40th U. S. Inf., 17 Aug., 1899. 1st Lieut., 23 Feb., 1900.

*Second Lieutenants.*

KELSO, JOHN M., Jr., 2nd Lieut. 1st Ark. Inf., 14 May, 1898. Mustered out 25 Oct., 1898. 2nd Lieut. 40th U. S. Inf., 17 Aug., 1899.
MITCHELL, BURTON J., Priv. Co. I and Q. M. Sergt. 20 Kans. Inf., 14 June, 1898, to 22 March, 1899. 2nd Lieut. 20th Kans. Inf., 23 March, 1899. 1st Lieut., 10 Aug., 1899. Mustered out 28 Oct., 1899. 2nd Lieut. 40th U. S. Inf., 17 Aug., 1899.
RIGHTER, JOSEPH C., Jr., Priv. Co. G, 12th Pa. Inf., 27 April to 29 Oct., 1898. 2nd Lieut. 40th U. S. Inf., 17 Aug., 1899.
MITCHELL, ROBERT B., Sergt. Co. C, 22nd Kans. Inf., 4 May to 3 Nov., 1898. 2nd Lieut. 40th U. S. Inf., 17 Aug., 1899.
BUGBEE, FRED W., Priv. Troop A, 1st U. S. Cav., 2 May to 5 Oct., 1898. 2nd Lieut. 40th U. S. Inf., 17 Aug., 1899.
CARTMELL, NATHANIEL M., Jr., Priv. 1st U. S. Cav., 21 May to 15 Sept., 1898. 2nd Lieut. 40th U. S. Inf., 17 Aug., 1899.
PATERSON, EDMUND T., 2nd Lieut. 40th U. S. Inf., 17 Aug., 1899.
WHITTHORNE, WILLIAM J., Jr., Priv. and Corpl. Troop B, 11th U. S. Cav., 2 Sept., 1899, to 7 Feb., 1900. 2nt Lieut. 40th U. S. Inf., 13 Dec., 1899.
WINSTON, WILLIAM, Jr., 1st Lieut. 2nd Texas Inf., 28 April, 1898. Mustered out 9 Nov., 1898. Priv., Sergt. and 1st Sergt. Co. L, 40th U. S. Inf., 20 Oct., 1899, to 28 April, 1900. 2nd Lieut. 40th U. S. Inf., 20 March, 1900.
CAFFEY, LOCHLIN W., Corpl. and Sergt. Co. A, 2nd Ga. Inf., 30 April to 30 Nov., 1898. Priv., Sergt. and 1st Sergt. Co. B, 40th U. S. Inf., 2 Sept., 1899, to 17 May, 1900. 2nd Lieut. 40th U. S. Inf., 20 March, 1900.

ROBINSON, OLIVER P., Corpl., Sergt. and 1st Sergt. Co. C, 4th Ill. Inf., 26 April, 1898, to 2 May, 1899. Priv., Sergt. and 1st Sergt. Co. F, 40th U. S. Inf., 14 Sept., to ——, 1900. 2nd Lieut. 40th U. S. Inf., 27 April, 1900
ELLIS, TOM B., Priv. and Corpl. Co. D, 1st Ga. Inf., 2 May to 18 Nov., 1898. Priv., Corpl., Sergt. and 1st Sergt. Cos. B and H, 40th U. S. Inf., 12 Sept., 1899, to ——, 1900. 2nd Lieut. 40th U. S. Inf., 27 April, 1900.

## 41st U. S. VOLUNTEER INFANTRY.

### *Colonel.*

RICHMOND, EPHRAIM T. C. (Regular), Col. 41st U. S. Inf., 17 Aug., 1899.

### *Lieutenant Colonel.*

MALLORY, JOHN S. (Regular), Lieut. Col. 41st U. S. Inf., 17 Aug., 1899.

### *Majors.*

WOOD, PALMER G. (Regular), Maj. 41st U. S. Inf., 17 Aug., 1899.
PRESTON, GUY H. (Regular), Maj. 41st U. S. Inf., 17 Aug., 1899.
WHOLLEY, JOHN H. (Regular), Maj. 41st U. S. Inf., 17 Aug., 1899.

### *Surgeon with rank of Major.*

SMITH, ALLEN M. (Regular), Maj. Surg. 41st U. S. Inf., 17 Aug., 1899.

### *Assistant Surgeons with rank of Captain.*

MARSHALL, THOMAS R., Capt. Asst. Surg. 41st U. S. Inf., 17 Aug., 1899.

### *With rank of First Lieutenant.*

BARRETT, EDWARD J., 1st Lieut. Asst. Surg. 2nd U. S. Eng., 13 July, 1898. Maj. Surg., 8 May, 1899. Mustered out 16 May, 1899. 1st Lieut. Asst. Surg. 41st U. S. Inf., 17 Aug., 1899.

### *Captains.*

SIVITER, FRANCIS P. (Regular), Capt. 41st U. S. Inf., 17 Aug., 1899.
MOWER, CARL K., Q. M., 27 Sept., 1899. Capt. Com. Sub., 8 June, 1898. Discharged 10 June, 1899. Capt. 41st U. S. Inf., 17 Aug., 1899.
FANNING, RICHARD J., Capt. A. Q. M., 28 May, 1898. Discharged 1 May, 1899. Capt. 41st U. S. Inf., 17 Aug., 1899.
WADSWORTH, CHARLES W., Capt. 6th U. S. Inf., 29 June, 1898. Mustered out 15 March, 1899. Capt. 41st U. S. Inf., 17 Aug., 1899.
MARTIN, JAMES H., Priv. Co. D, 10th Pa. Inf., 21 June to 9 Aug., 1898. 1st Lieut., 2nd W. Va. Inf., 10 Aug., 1898. Mustered out 10 April, 1899. Capt. 41st U. S. Inf., 17 Aug., 1899.
NETTLES, CLARENCE S., Q. M. Sergt. Co. A, 2nd S. C. Inf., 5 May to 8 Aug., 1898. Capt. 10th U. S. Inf., 9 Aug., 1898. Mustered out 9 March, 1899. 1st Liuet. 41st U. S. Inf., 17 Aug., 1899. Capt., 17 Aug., 1899.
HEGARTY, JOHN C., 2nd Lieut. 9th N. Y. Inf., 2 May, 1898. 1st Lieut., 4 Aug., 1898. Mustered out 15 Nov., 1898. Capt. 41st U. S. Inf., 17 Aug., 1899.
DAVIDSON, FRED L., Capt. 1st Ohio Inf., 26 April, 1898. Capt. 41st U. S. Inf., 17 Aug., 1899.
CLARK, JAMES, Capt. 7th Ill. Inf., 26 April, 1898. Mustered out 20 Oct., 1898. Capt. 41st U. S. Inf., 17 Aug., 1899.
STANDIFORD, WILLIAM R., Capt. 2nd W. Va. Inf., 25 May, 1898. Mustered out 10 April, 1899. 1st Lieut. 41st U. S. Inf., 17 Aug., 1899. Capt., 1 Sept., 1899.
GREENOUGH, ERNEST A., Capt. 2nd N. Y. Inf., 2 May, 1898. Mustered out 28 Oct., 1898. 1st Lieut. 12th N. Y. Inf., 8 Dec., 1898. Mustered out 20 April, 1899. 1st Lieut. 41st U. S. Inf., 17 Aug., 1899. Capt., 28 Oct., 1899.
RUTTENCUTTER, BRADY G., 2nd Lieut. 1st W. Va. Inf., 27 April, 1898. 1st Lieut., 3 June, 1898. Mustered out 4 Feb., 1899. 1st Lieut. 41st U. S. Inf., 17 Aug., 1899. Capt., 2 Nov., 1899.
FOREMAN, ALBERT Y., 2nd Lieut. 1st Del. Inf., 7 May, 1898. Mustered out 19 Dec., 1898. 1st Lieut. 41st U. S. Inf., 17 Aug., 1899. Capt., 18 Nov., 1899.
BOSTON, JOHN H., Jr., 1st Lieut. 2nd Ga. Inf., 29 April, 1898. Mustered out 30 Nov., 1898. 1st Lieut. 41st U. S. Inf., 17 Aug., 1899. Capt., 31 May, 1900.

### *First Lieutenants.*

McINTOSH, CLARENCE A., 1st Lieut. 6th Ill Inf., 26 April, 1898. Mustered out 25 Nov., 1898. 1st Lieut. 41st U. S. Inf., 17 Aug., 1899.
CHRISTEY, ARTHUR B., Capt. 65th N. Y. Inf., 1 May, 1898. Mustered out 19 Nov., 1898. 1st Lieut. 41st U. S. Inf., 17 Aug., 1899.
BOISEAU, LOUIS T., 2nd Lieut. 1st D. C. Inf., 13 May, 1898. 1st Lieut., 12 Sept., 1898. Mustered out 20 Nov., 1898. 1st Lieut. 41st U. S. Inf., 17 Aug., 1899.
JOHNSTON, JOHN S., 2nd Lieut. 157th Ind. Inf., 26 April, 1898. Mustered out 1 Nov., 1898. 1st Lieut. 41st U. S. Inf., 17 Aug., 1899.
JAGMETTY, JOSHUA, 1st Sergt. Co. F, 4th N. J. Inf., 12 July to 9 Nov., 1898. 2nd Lieut. 4th N. J. Inf., 10 Nov., 1898. Mustered out 6 April, 1899. 1st Lieut. 41st U. S. Inf., 17 Aug., 1899.
KOCH, FREDERICK, 1st Lieut. 41st U. S. Inf., 17 Aug., 1899.

KENNEDY, JOHN, Com., 24 Oct., 1899. 1st Lieut. 41st U. S. Inf., 17 Aug., 1899.
GOODALE, WILLIAM M., 1st Lieut. 41st U. S. Inf., 17 Aug., 1899.
HARVEY, WALTER, Priv. and Corpl. Co. L, 7th Ohio Inf., 25 April to 6 Nov., 1898. 1st Lieut. 41st U. S. Inf., 17 Aug., 1899.
HEMPHILL, JOHN E., 1st Lieut. 41st U. S. Inf., 17 Aug., 1899.
CUMINGS, CHARLES A., Priv. and Artf. Co. E, 15th Pa. Inf., 27 April, 1898, to 31 Jan., 1899. 1st Lieut. 41st U. S. Inf., 17 Aug., 1899.
BUTLER, LAWRENCE P., Priv. and Sergt. Co. I, 4th Mo. Inf., 24 May to 15 July, 1898. 1st Lieut. 3rd U. S. Eng., 7 July, 1898. Mustered out 17 May, 1899. 2nd Lieut. 41st U. S. Inf., 17 Aug., 1899. 1st Lieut., 1 Sept., 1899.
GLOVER, FRANK Y., Corpl. Co. L, 1st Texas Inf., 3 May to 26 July, 1898. 2nd Lieut. 3rd Ala. Inf., 8 Aug., 1898. Mustered out 20 March, 1899. 2nd Lieut. 41st U. S. Inf., 17 Aug., 1899. 1st Lieut., 28 Oct., 1899.
MILLER, FRANK J., 1st Lieut. 3rd N. Y. Inf., 1 May, 1898. Mustered out 30 Nov., 1898. 2nd Lieut. 41st U. S. Inf., 17 Aug., 1899. 1st Lieut., 2 Nov., 1899.
NOWLEN, EDWIN J., 2nd Lieut. 2nd Pa. Inf., 28 April, 1898. Mustered out 15 Nov., 1898. 2nd Lieut. 41st U. S. Inf., 17 Aug., 1899. 1st Lieut., 18 Nov., 1899.
TOWSON, BENJAMIN L., 2nd Lieut. 6th U. S. Inf., 7 Jan., 1899. Mustered out 15 March, 1899. 2nd Lieut. 41st U. S. Inf., 17 Aug., 1899. 1st Lieut., 31 May, 1900.

*Second Lieutenants.*

BEALL, RUSSELL, Priv. and Corpl. Co. A, 18th Pa. Inf., 27 April to 12 Oct., 1898. 2nd Lieut. 41st U. S. Inf., 17 Aug., 1899.
BAILEY, GEORGE F., Sergt. Co. F, 1st Vt. Inf., 10 May to 26 Oct., 1898. 2nd Lieut 41st U. S. Inf., 17 Aug., 1899.
TAYLOR, WILLIAM R., Priv. 1st U. S. Cav., 4 June to 12 Oct., 1898. 2nd Lieut. 41st U. S. Inf., 17 Aug., 1899.
SEOANE, CONSUELO A., 2nd Lieut. 41st U. S. Inf., 17 Aug., 1899.
LANDERS, HOWARD LEE, 2nd Lieut. 41st U. S. Inf., 17 Aug., 1899.
MITCHELL, HENRY T., Priv., Corpl. and Sergt. Co. E, 14th N. Y. Inf., 14 May to 1 Nov., 1898. 2nd Lieut. 41st U. S. Inf., 17 Aug., 1899.
CLAXTON, HORACE N., Priv. Co. D, 1st Pa. Inf., 1 Aug. to 26 Oct., 1898. Priv. Co. F, 28th U. S. Inf., 7 Aug. to 6 Sept., 1899. 2nd Lieut 41st U. S. Inf., 17 Aug., 1899.
CALDWELL, RALPH C., Priv. and Sergt. Co. H, 41st U. S. Inf., 14 Sept. to 22 Oct., 1899. 2nd Lieut. 41st U. S. Inf., 21 Oct., 1899.
SIMMONS, HARVEY J., Corpl. and Sergt. Co. A, 2nd W. Va. Inf., 23 June to 31 Oct., 1898. 2nd Lieut. 2nd W. Va. Inf., 1 Nov., 1898. Mustered out 10 April, 1899. Priv. and Sergt. Co. E, 41st U. S. Inf., 18 Sept. to 14 Nov., 1899. 2nd Lieut. 41st U. S. Inf., 13 Nov., 1899.
REEDER, ODUS J., Priv., Sergt. and 1st Sergt. Cos. A and D, 41st U. S. Inf., 25 Sept. to 14 Nov., 1899. 2nd Lieut. 41st. U. S. Inf., 13 Nov., 1899.
WESSELL, HENRY, Priv. and Batt. Sergt. Maj. 41st U. S. Inf., 6 Oct. to 19 Nov., 1899. 2nd Lieut. 41st U. S. Inf., 18 Nov., 1899.

## 42ND U. S. VOLUNTEER INFANTRY.

*Colonel.*

THOMPSON, J. MILTON (Regular), Col. 42nd U. S. Inf., 17 Aug., 1899.

*Lieutenant Colonel.*

BEACOM, JOHN H. (Regular), Lieut. Col. 45th U. S. Inf., 17 Aug., 1899. Trans. to 42nd U. S. Inf., 1 Sept., 1899.

*Majors.*

BROWN, WILLIAM C. (Regular), Maj. 45th U. S. Inf., 17 Aug., 1899. Trans. to 42nd U. S. Inf., 14 Sept., 1899.
CAREY, EDWARD G. (Regular), Maj. 42nd U. S. Inf., 17 Aug., 1899.
PRIME, JOHN R., Priv. Co. K, 27th Iowa Inf., 20 Feb. to — July, 1864. Priv. Co. K, 12th Iowa Inf., 9 July to 20 Jan., 1866. Maj. 42nd U. S. Inf., 17 Aug., 1899.

*Surgeon with rank of Major.*

McCAW, YALTER D. (Regular), Maj. Surg. 42nd U. S. Inf., 17 Aug., 1899.

*Assistant Surgeons with rank of Captain.*

BELL, WILLIAM D., Maj. Surg. 71st N. Y. Inf., 2 May, 1898. Mustered out 15 Nov., 1898. Capt. Asst. Surg. 42nd U. S. Inf., 17 Aug., 1899.

*With rank of First Lieutenant.*

GRIFFITH, LEWIE A., 1st Lieut. Asst. Surg. 2nd S. C. Inf., 27 June, 1898. Mustered out 19 April, 1899. 1st Lieut. 40th U. S. Inf., 17 Aug., 1899, declined. 1st Lieut. Asst. Surg. 42nd U. S. Inf., 17 Aug., 1899.

*Captains.*

BJORNSTAD, ALFRED W., 1st Lieut. 13th Minn. Inf., 29 April, 1898. Capt., 16 May, 1898. Mustered out 3 Oct., 1899. Capt. 42nd U. S. Inf., 17 Aug., 1899.
CATLIN, GEORGE DE G. (Regular), Capt. 42nd U. S. Inf., 17 Aug., 1899.

BURNS, CHARLES S., Priv. Co. C, 79th N. Y. Inf., 27 May to 11 Dec., 1861. 1st Sergt. Co. E, 76th Pa. Inf., 18 Oct., 1864, to 18 July, 1865. Maj. 12th N. Y. Inf., 2 May, 1898. Mustered out 20 April, 1899. Capt. 42nd U. S. Inf., 17 Aug., 1899.
HENDERSON, DUNCAN, Capt. 31st Mich. Inf., 26 April, 1898. Mustered out 17 March, 1899. Capt. 42nd U. S. Inf., 17 Aug., 1899.
KAUTZMAN, WORTHINGTON, Maj. 2nd Ohio Inf., 25 April, 1898. Mustered out 10 Feb., 1899. Capt. 42nd U. S. Inf., 17 Aug., 1899.
DU BOIS, EDMUND, Capt. 4th N. J. Inf., 30 June, 1898. Maj., 2 March, 1899. Mustered out 6 April, 1899. Capt. 42nd U. S. Inf., 17 Aug., 1899.
LANG, LOUIS M., Adj., 17 Aug., 1899. Capt. 202nd N. Y. Inf., 9 July, 1898. Mustered out 15 April, 1899. Capt. 42nd U. S. Inf., 17 Aug., 1899.
RILEY, PETER T., Capt. 8th Cal. Inf., 24 June, 1898. Mustered out 31 Jan., 1899. Capt. 42nd U. S. Inf., 17 Aug., 1899.
KECK, FRANK, Capt. 71st N. Y. Inf., 2 May, 1898. Maj., 31 May, 1898. Mustered out 15 Nov., 1898. Capt. 42nd U. S. Inf., 17 Aug., 1899.
HILL, JAMES E., Maj. 9th Ill. Inf., 19 Nov., 1898. Mustered out 20 May, 1899. Capt. 42nd U. S. Inf., 17 Aug., 1899.
SHALLENBERGER, JAMES M., 1st Lieut. 1st Ohio Cav., 25 April, 1898. Mustered out 23 Oct., 1898. 1st Lieut. 47th U. S. Inf., 17 Aug., 1899, declined. Capt. 42nd U. S. Inf., 17 Aug., 1899.
CUNNINGHAM, JOSEPH V., Capt. 16th Pa. Inf., 5 July, 1898. Mustered out 28 Dec., 1898. Capt. 42nd U. S. Inf., 17 Aug., 1899.
HERMAN, FRED J., Q. M., 14 Oct., 1899. Capt. 1st Ohio Cav., 5 May, 1898. Mustered out 24 Oct., 1898. Capt. 42nd U. S. Inf., 17 Aug., 1899.
STOPFORD, FRED W., Capt. 8 Mass. Inf., 28 April, 1898. Mustered out 28 April, 1899. 1st Lieut. 42nd U. S. Inf., 17 Aug., 1899. Capt., 24 Oct., 1899.

*First Lieutenants.*

McFEELY, HENRY F., 1st Lieut. 42nd U. S. Inf., 17 Aug., 1899.
April, 1899. 1st Lieut. 42nd U. S. Inf., 17 Aug., 1899.
BEALE, CHARLES T., 2nd Lieut. 2nd W. Va. Inf., 26 May, 1898. Mustered out 10 April, 1899. 1st Lieut. 42nd U. S. Inf., 17 Aug., 1899.
McANDREWS, JOSEPH R., 2nd Lieut. 2nd U. S. Eng., 28 June, 1898. 1st Lieut., 13 July, 1898. Mustered out 16 May, 1899. 1st Lieut. 42nd U. S. Inf., 17 Aug., 1899.
WHITE, GEORGE H., 1st Lieut. 35th Mich. Inf., 6 June, 1898. Mustered out 31 March, 1899. 1st Lieut. 42nd U. S. Inf., 17 Aug., 1899.
McCOOL, HARRY C., 2nd Lieut. 3rd U. S. Inf., 13 July, 1898. 1st Lieut., 28 Nov., 1898. Mustered out 2 May, 1899. 1st Lieut. 42nd U. S. Inf., 17 Aug., 1899.
LITTLE, JAMES H., 2nd Lieut. 69th N. Y. Inf., 2 May, 1898. 1st Lieut., 30 Nov., 1898. Mustered out 31 Jan., 1899. 1st Lieut. 42nd U. S. Inf., 17 Aug., 1899.
POILLON, ARTHUR, 2nd Lieut. 201st N. Y. Inf., 7 July, 1898. 1st Lieut., 13 Nov., 1898. Mustered out 3 April, 1899. 1st Lieut. 42nd U. S. Inf., 17 Aug., 1899.
SPILLER, ROBERT K., 2nd Lieut. 2nd Va. Inf., 13 May, 1898. 1st Lieut., 22 Oct., 1898. Mustered out 17 Dec., 1898. 1st Lieut. 42nd U. S. Inf., 17 Aug., 1899.
MOLINARD, WILLIAM R., 1st Lieut. 1st U. S. Eng., 21 June, 1898. Mustered out 25 Jan., 1899. 1st Lieut. 42nd U. S. Inf., 17 Aug., 1899.
REISER, THEODORE C., Capt. 1st N. J. Inf., 2 May, 1898. Mustered out 4 Nov., 1898. 1st Lieut. 42nd U. S. Inf., 17 Aug., 1899.
ROESSING, CHARLES H., Capt. 18th Pa. Inf., 27 April, 1898. Mustered out 22 Oct., 1898. 1st Lieut. 42nd U. S. Inf., 17 Aug., 1899.
JOHNSON, WALTER H., Sergt. Co. F, 13th Minn. Inf., 29 April, 1898, to 23 July, 1899. 2nd Lieut. 13 Minn. Inf., 25 July, 1899. 1st Lieut., 10 Aug., 1899. Mustered out 3 Oct., 1899. 1st Lieut. 42nd U. S. Inf., 17 Aug., 1899.
HARGIS, ROBERT B., Sergt. Co. —, 1st Florida Inf., 1 May to 22 Nov., 1898. 2nd Lieut. 1st Florida Inf., 22 Nov., 1898. Mustered out 3 Dec., 1898. 1st Lieut. 42nd U. S. Inf., 17 Aug., 1899.
POWERS, PHILIP, Com., 27 Sept., 1899. 1st Lieut. 42nd U. S. Inf., 17 Aug., 1899.
LOMAX, FRANCIS H., Priv. and Corpl. Co. D, 71st N. Y. Inf., 2 May to 15 Nov., 1898. 1st Lieut. 42nd U. S. Inf., 17 Aug., 1899.
WEBSTER, HORACE, 2nd Lieut. 3rd N. Y. Inf., 1 May, 1898. Resigned 10 Nov., 1898. 2nd Lieut 203rd N. Y. Inf., 11 Nov., 1898. Mustered out 25 March, 1899. 2nd Lieut. 42nd U. S. Inf., 17 Aug., 1899. 1st Lieut., 24 Oct., 1899.

*Second Lieutenants.*

WILLIAMS, R. HOWARD, Sergt. and Q. M. Sergt. Co. B, 4th N. J. Inf., 2 July to 8 Nov., 1898. 2nd Lieut. 4th N. J. Inf., 9 Nov., 1898. Mustered out 6 April, 1899. 2nd Lieut. 42nd U. S. Inf., 17 Aug., 1899.
HACKETT, EDWARD F., Jr., Priv. Co. A, 1st N. Y. Inf., 2 May, 1898, to 20 Feb., 1899. 2nd Lieut. 12th N. Y. Inf., 21 Feb., 1899. Mustered out 20 April, 1899. 2nd Lieut. 42nd U. S. Inf., 17 Aug., 1899.
KECK, MORRIS M., Sergt. Co. D, 9th Pa. Inf., 27 April to 14 Sept., 1898. 2nd Lieut. 9 Pa. Inf., 15 Sept., 1898. Mustered out 29 Oct., 1898. 2nd Lieut. 42nd U. S. Inf., 17 Aug., 1899.
WARFIELD, AUGUSTUS B., Priv. and Corpl. Co. K, 202nd N. Y. Inf., 30 July, 1898, to 15 April, 1899. 2nd Lieut. 42nd U. S. Inf., 17 Aug., 1899.
JUDD, BRUCE N., 2nd Lieut. 42nd U. S. Inf., 17 Aug., 1899.
ABBOTT, JAMES E., Priv. and Sergt. U. S. Sig. Corps, 7 July to 29 Nov., 1898. 2nd Lieut 42nd U. S. Inf., 17 Aug., 1899.
NOVAK, MARTIN, 2nd Lieut. 42nd U. S. Inf., 17 Aug., 1899.
JACKSON, FRANKLIN P., Corpl. Co. E, 2nd N. Y. Inf., 2 May to 31 Oct., 1898. 2nd Lieut 42nd U. S. Inf., 17 Aug., 1899.
KITTS, WILLIAM P., Priv. and Corpl. Co. D, 22nd N. Y. Inf., 2 May to 23 Nov., 1898. 2nd Lieut. 42nd U. S. Inf., 17 Aug., 1899.
CALDWELL, ROBERT A., 2nd Lieut. 42nd U. S. Inf., 17 Aug., 1899.

HAMNER, WALKER W., Priv. Co. D, 2nd U. S. Inf., 23 April to 18 July, 1898. 2nd Lieut. 2nd U. S. Inf., 8 July, 1898. 1st Lieut., 30 Sept., 1898. Mustered out 22 June, 1899. Priv. Co. K, and Sergt. Maj. 42nd U. S. Inf., 26 Aug. to 20 Nov., 1899. 2nd Lieut. 42nd U. S. Inf., 20 Nov., 1899.

CARL, THOMAS, 1st Lieut. 10th U. S. Inf., 17 June, 1898. Mustered out 8 March, 1899. Priv. Q. M. Sergt. and 1st Sergt. Co. A, 42nd U. S. Inf., 16 Oct., 1899, to ——, 1900. 2nd Lieut. 42nd U. S. Inf., 9 May, 1900.

## 43RD U. S. VOLUNTEER INFANTRY.

### *Colonel.*

MURRAY, ARTHUR (Regular), Col. 43rd U. S. Inf., 17 Aug., 1899.

### *Lieutenant Colonel.*

WILDER, WILBER E. (Regular), Lieut. Col. 43rd U. S. Inf., 17 Aug., 1899.

### *Majors.*

ALLEN, HENRY T. (Regular), Maj. 43rd U. S. Inf., 17 Aug., 1899.
ANDREWS, LINCOLN C. (Regular), Maj. 43rd U. S. Inf., 17 Aug., 1899.
GILMORE, JOHN C., Jr. (Regular), Maj. 43rd U. S. Inf., 17 Aug., 1899.

### *Surgeon with rank of Major.*

SNYDER, HENRY D. (Regular), Maj. 43rd U. S. Inf., 17 Aug., 1899.

### *Assistant Surgeons with rank of Captain.*

WEBB, WALTER D., 1st Lieut. Asst. Surg. 1st U. S. Eng., 29 June, 1898. Mustered out 25 Jan., 1899. Capt. Asst. Surg. 43rd U. S. Inf., 17 Aug., 1899.

### *With rank of First Lieutenant.*

WELCH, DUDLEY W., 1st Lieut. Asst. Surg. 43rd U. S. Inf., 17 Aug., 1899.

### *Captains.*

BEAVERS, WILLIAM R., 1st Lieut. 1st N. C. Inf., 27 April, 1898. Capt., 24 Nov., 1898. Mustered out 22 April, 1899. Capt. 43rd U. S. Inf., 17 Aug., 1899.

TILTON, ERNEST R., Adj., 25 Oct., 1899. Capt. 12th N. Y. Inf., 2 May, 1898. Mustered out 20 April, 1899. Capt. 43rd U. S. Inf., 17 Aug., 1899.

PRESTON, WILLIAM B., 1st Lieut. 4th U. S. Inf., 5 July, 1898. Mustered out 8 June, 1899. Capt. 43rd U. S. Inf., 17 Aug., 1899.

POLK, LUCIUS E., 1st Lieut. 4th Tenn. Inf., 18 June, 1898. Mustered out 6 May, 1899. Capt. 43rd U. S. Inf., 17 Aug., 1899.

DEY, HARRY M., 1st Lieut. 4th N. J. Inf., 30 June, 1898. Capt., 30 Nov., 1898. Mustered out 6 April, 1899. 1st Lieut. 43rd U. S. Inf., 17 Aug., 1899. Capt., 17 Aug., 1899.

HANSON, LINWOOD E., Capt. 5th Mass. Inf., 25 June, 1898. Maj., 7 Jan., 1899. Mustered out 31 March, 1899. Capt. 43rd U. S. Inf., 17 Aug., 1899.

SPELLMAN, MICHAEL J., Maj. 69th N. Y. Inf., 2 May, 1898. Mustered out 31 Jan., 1899. Capt. 43rd U. S. Inf., 17 Aug., 1899.

COOKE, JOHN, Capt. Batty C. Cal. Heavy Art., 7 May, 1898. Mustered out 3 Feb., 1899. Capt. 43rd U. S. Inf., 17 Aug., 1899.

DUNCAN, GEORGE O., Capt. 6th Cal. Inf., 28 April, 1898. Mustered out 15 Dec., 1898. Capt. 43rd U. S. Inf., 17 Aug., 1899.

ELLIOTT, WILLIAM, Q. M., 14 Nov., 1899. Capt. 8th Cal. Inf., 24 June, 1898. Mustered out 31 Jan., 1899. Capt. 43rd U. S. Inf., 17 Aug., 1899.

PRESCOTT, FRANK C., Maj. 7th Cal. Inf., 5 May, 1898. Mustered out 2 Dec., 1898. Capt. 43rd U. S. Inf., 17 Aug., 1899.

GOLDSBOROUGH, WASHINGTON L., Capt. 71st N. Y. Inf., 2 May, 1898. Mustered out 15 Nov., 1898. Capt. 43rd U. S. Inf., 17 Aug., 1899.

FAIR, JOHN S., 1st Lieut. and Adj. 5th Pa. Inf., 27 April, 1898. Mustered out 7 Nov., 1898. Capt. 43rd U. S. Inf., 17 Aug., 1899.

DOW, WILLIAM C., Capt. 8th Mass. Inf., 28 April, 1898. Mustered out 28 April, 1899. 1st Lieut. 43rd U. S. Inf., 17 Aug., 1899. Capt., 8 Nov., 1899.

### *First Lieutenants.*

POWER, EDWARD O., 2nd Lieut. 12th N. Y. Inf., 2 May, 1898. 1st Lieut., 27 Oct., 1898. Mustered out 20 April, 1899. 1st Lieut. 43rd U. S. Inf., 17 Aug., 1899.

STEWART, HENRY J., Capt. 3rd Ga. Inf., 25 June, 1898. Mustered out 22 April, 1899. 1st Lieut. 43rd U. S. Inf., 17 Aug., 1899.

GASSER, LORENZO D., Capt. 2nd Ohio Inf., 25 April, 1898. Mustered out 10 Feb., 1899. 1st Lieut. 43rd U. S. Inf., 17 Aug., 1899.

LE MASURIER, ROBERT, Capt. 3rd Va. Inf., 23 April, 1898. Mustered out, 21 Oct., 1898. Capt. 6th Va. Inf., 22 Oct., 1898. Mustered out 28 Jan., 1899. Capt. 43rd U. S. Inf., 17 Aug., 1899.

DUTTON, JAMES W., 2nd Lieut. Batty C, Maine Heavy Art., 29 June, 1898. Mustered out 31 March, 1899. 1st Lieut. 43rd U. S. Inf., 17 Aug., 1899.

MORRIS, MICHAEL E., Capt. 9th Mass. Inf., 4 May, 1898. Mustered out 26 Nov., 1898. 1st Lieut. 43rd U. S. Inf., 17 Aug., 1899.

CONROW, WILLIAM S., 1st Lieut. 22nd N. Y. Inf., 9 May, 1898. Mustered out 23 Nov., 1898. 1st Lieut. 43rd U. S. Inf., 17 Aug., 1899.
DONNELLY, EDWARD T., Capt. 8th N. Y. Inf., 2 May, 1898. Mustered out 3 Nov., 1898. 1st Lieut. 43rd U. S. Inf., 17 Aug., 1899.
PHILLIPS, ALBERT E., Capt. 1st La. Inf., 1 May, 1898. Mustered out 3 Oct., 1898. 1st Lieut. 43rd U. S. Inf., 17 Aug., 1899.
JONES, DELBERT R., 1st Lieut. 1st Conn. Inf., 22 June, 1898. Mustered out 31 Oct., 1898. 1st Lieut. 43rd U. S. Inf., 17 Aug., 1899.
CILLEY, JONATHAN, 1st Lieut. 43rd U. S. Inf., 17 Aug., 1899.
SEAMAN, CLAUDIUS M., 1st Sergt. Co. E, 4th Pa. Inf., 28 April to 16 Nov., 1898. 1st Lieut. 43rd U. S. Inf., 17 Aug., 1899.
SWEENEY, JOSEPH T., Sergt. Co. —, 69th N. Y. Inf., 2 May to 30 Nov., 1898. 2 Lieut. 69th N. Y. Inf., 1 Dec., 1898. Mustered out 31 Jan., 1899. 2nd Lieut. 43rd U. S. Inf., 17 Aug., 1899. 1st Lieut., 26 Oct., 1899.
THAYER, HENRY A., 2nd Lieut. 6th Mass. Inf., 6 May, 1898. Mustered out 21 Jan., 1899. 2nd Lieut. 43rd U. S. Inf., 17 Aug., 1899. 1st Lieut., 8 Nov., 1899.
SWANN, HAROLD S., Q. M. Sergt. Co. A, 4th N. J. Inf., 2 July, 1898, to 23 Feb., 1899. 2nd Lieut. 4th N. J. Inf., 24 Feb., 1899. Mustered out 6 April, 1899. Priv. and Sergt. Co. K, and Batt. Sergt. Maj. 27th U. S. Inf., 24 July to 26th Aug., 1899. 2nd Lieut. 43rd U. S. Inf., 17 Aug., 1899. 1st Lieut., 30 Nov., 1899.
AVERY, MORTON L., Priv. Co. G, 12th Pa. Inf., 27 April to 29 Oct., 1898. 2nd Lieut. 43rd U. S. Inf., 17 Aug., 1899. 1st Lieut., 11 May, 1900.

*Second Lieutenants.*

STERRETT, ROBERT, Priv. and Corpl. U. S. Sig. Corps, 21 June to 15 Sept., 1898. 2nd Lieut. 43rd U. S. Inf., 17 Aug., 1899.
BURT, WILLIAM H., Corpl. Co. M, 1st Vt. Inf., 4 May to 7 Nov., 1898. 2nd Lieut 43rd U. S. Inf., 17 Aug., 1899.
PRICE, WALTER S., Corpl. and Sergt. Co. K, 2nd Pa. Inf., 28 April to 15 Nov., 1898. 2nd Lieut. 43rd U. S. Inf., 17 Aug., 1899.
ANDREWS, CHARLES F., Priv. Co. M, 8th N. Y. Inf., 16 June to 3 Nov., 1898. 2nd Lieut. 43rd U. S. Inf., 17 Aug., 1899.
MILLS, FRED. W., Jr., 2nd Lieut. 43rd U. S. Inf., 17 Aug., 1899.
WILSON, WILLIAM H., Priv. and Corpl. Co. C, 22nd N. Y. Inf., 9 May to 23 Nov., 1898. 2nd Lieut. 43rd U. S. Inf., 17 Aug., 1899.
JOHNSTON, GORDON, Priv. Co. M, 2nd Miss. Inf., and Troop M, 1st U. S. Cav., 8 June to 15 Sept., 1898. 2nd Lieut. 43rd U. S. Inf., 17 Aug., 1899.
LEAF, LOUIS H., Priv. Co. G, 6th Pa. Inf., 3 May to 17 Oct., 1898. 2nd Lieut. 43rd U. S. Inf., 17 Aug., 1899.
ESTES, CHARLES C., Capt. 8th U. S. Inf., 17 June, 1898. Mustered out 6 March, 1899. Priv. Co. G, 43rd U. S. Inf., 2 Nov. to 14 Nov., 1899. 2nd Lieut. 43rd U. S. Inf., 13 Nov., 1899.
ELMER, JAMES L., Sergt. Co. I and Q. M. Sergt. 1st Vt. Inf., 8 May to 7 Nov., 1898. Priv. Co. D, 43rd U. S. Inf., 20 Sept. to 14 Nov., 1899. 2nd Lieut. 43rd U. S. Inf., 13 Nov., 1899.
TRUDEN, JOHN N., Priv. and 1st Sergt. Co. A, 43rd U. S. Inf., 8 Sept. to 30 Nov., 1899. 2nd Lieut. 43rd U. S. Inf., 30 Nov., 1899.

## 44TH U. S. VOLUNTEER INFANTRY.

*Colonel.*

McCLERNAND, EDWARD J. (Regular), Col. 44th U. S. Inf., 17 Aug., 1899.

*Lieutenant Colonel.*

SCOTT, YILLIAM S. (Regular), Maj. A. A. G., 17 Sept., 1898. Discharged 12 May, 1899. Lieut. Col. 44th U. S. Inf., 17 Aug., 1899.

*Majors.*

HALE, HARRY C. (Regular), Maj. 44th U. S. Inf., 17 Aug., 1899.
WALCUTT, CHARLES C., Jr. Regular), Maj. 44th U. S. Inf., 17 Aug., 1899.
McCOY, HENRY B., Lieut. Col. 1st Colo. Inf., 1 May, 1898. Col., 27 Sept., 1898. Mustered out 8 Sept., 1899. Maj. 44th U. S. Inf., 17 Aug., 1899.

*Surgeon with rank of Major.*

LIPPITT, WILLIAM F., Jr. (Regular), Maj. Surg. 44th U. S. Inf., 17 Aug., 1899.

*Assistant Surgeons with rank of Captain.*

FURBUSH, CHARLES L., Capt. Asst. Surg. 44th U. S. Inf., 17 Aug., 1899.

*With rank of First Lieutenant.*

JACKSON, THOMAS T., 1st Lieut. Asst. Surg. 2nd Texas Inf., 8 May, 1898. Mustered out 1 Nov., 1898. 1st Lieut. Asst. Surg. 1st Texas Inf., 2 Nov., 1898. Mustered out 18 April, 1899. 1st Lieut. Asst. Surg. 44th U. S. Inf., 17 Aug., 1899.

*Captains.*

ANDERSON, JAMES L., Capt. 161st Ind. Inf., 21 June, 1898. Mustered out 30 April, 1899. Capt. 44th U. S. Inf., 17 Aug., 1899.

LEE, GEORGE D., Capt. 1st Ky. Inf., 13 May, 1898. Mustered out 24 Feb., 1899. Capt. 44th U. S. Inf., 17 Aug., 1899.
LEONARD, THOMAS, Capt. 15th Minn. Inf., 2 July, 1898. Mustered out 27 March, 1899. Capt. 44th U. S. Inf., 17 Aug., 1899.
CROSSFIELD, AMASA S., Capt. 15th Minn. Inf., 2 July, 1898. Mustered out 27 March, 1899. Capt. 44th U. S. Inf., 17 Aug., 1899.
WELLER, DANA R., Maj. 7th Cal. Inf., 5 May, 1898. Mustered out 2 Dec., 1898. Capt. 44th U. S. Inf., 17 Aug., 1898.
STUART, EDWARD A., Adj., 29 Sept., 1899. Maj. 2nd Texas Inf., 4 May, 1898. Mustered out 9 Nov., 1898. Capt. 44th U. S. Inf., 17 Aug., 1899.
CURTIS, FRANK R., Capt. 8th N. Y. Inf., 2 May, 1898. Mustered out 3 Nov., 1898. Capt. 44th U. S. Inf., 17 Aug., 1899.
MALLEY, JAMES L., Capt. 7th Ill. Inf., 26 April, 1898. Mustered out 20 Oct., 1898. Capt. 44th U. S. Inf., 17 Aug., 1899.
SAMUELS, SAMUEL C., Q. M., 29 Sept., 1899. Priv., Sergt. and 1st Sergt. Co. M, 5th U. S. Inf., 23 July, 1898, to 6 March, 1899. 2nd Lieut. 5th U. S. Inf., 9 Feb., 1899. Mustered out 31 May, 1899. Capt. 44th U. S. Inf., 17 Aug., 1899.
BISSELL, EUGENE V. N., Priv. Co. L, 71st N. Y. Inf., 2 May to 15 Nov., 1898. Capt. 44th U. S. Inf., 17 Aug., 1899.
KETCHAM, JOHN L., Jr., Sergt. Co. D, 158th Ind. Inf., 26 April to 4 Nov., 1898. Capt. 44th U. S. Inf., 17 Aug., 1899.
WIGGINS, JAMES K., Priv., Corpl., Sergt. and Q. M. Sergt. Troop H, 1st Ill. Cav., 26 April to 11 Oct., 1898. Capt. 44th U. S. Inf., 17 Aug., 1899.
SMITH, KIRWIN TAYLOR, Capt. 44th U. S. Inf., 17 Aug., 1899.
RAYSOR, MARION C., 1st Lieut. 1st Texas Inf., 27 April, 1898. Mustered out 18 April, 1899. 1st Lieut. 44th U. S. Inf., 17 Aug., 1899. Capt., 30 Nov., 1899.

*First Lieutenants.*

BUCHANAN, RICHARD W., 2nd Lieut. 161st Ind. Inf., 24 June, 1898. Capt., 9 March, 1899. Mustered out 30 April, 1899. 1st Lieut. 44th U. S. Inf., 17 Aug., 1899.
LEVENS, LEWIS H., 1st Lieut. 2nd Mo. Inf., 27 April, 1898. Mustered out 1 March, 1899. 1st Lieut. 44th U. S. Inf., 17 Aug., 1899.
YOUNG, FREDERICK S., Capt. 3rd Texas Inf., 28 April, 1898. Mustered out 24 Feb., 1899. 1st Lieut. 44th U. S. Inf., 17 Aug., 1899.
WHITE, WILLIAM J., 1st Lieut. and Adj. 1st W. Va. Inf., 26 April, 1898. Mustered out 4 Feb., 1899. 1st Lieut. 44th U. S. Inf., 17 Aug., 1899.
MOULD, STEPHEN H., 1st Lieut. 203rd N. Y. Inf., 6 July, 1898. Mustered out 25 March 1899. 1st Lieut. 44th U. S. Inf., 17 Aug., 1899.
GOING, RICHARD B., 1st Lieut. 1st Ala. Inf., 30 April, 1898. Mustered out 31 Oct., 1898. 1st Lieut. 44th U. S. Inf., 17 Aug., 1899.
PARKER, CLYDE B., Capt. 22nd Kans. Inf., 3 May, 1898. Mustered out 3 Nov., 1898. 1st Lieut. 44th U. S. Inf., 17 Aug., 1899.
WILSON, FRED L., Capt. 2nd Ky. Inf., 3 May, 1898. Mustered out 31 Oct., 1898. 1st Lieut. 44th U. S. Inf., 17 Aug., 1899.
PERRY, ORVILLE R., 1st Lieut. 2nd Neb. Inf., 27 April, 1898. Mustered out 24 Oct., 1898. 1st Lieut. 44th U. S. Inf., 17 Aug., 1899.
EVANS, HERBERT L., Priv. and Corpl. Co. F, 6th Ohio Inf., 26 April to 15 Dec., 1898. 1st Lieut. 44th U. S. Inf., 17 Aug., 1899.
HEYBURN, JOHN B., Priv. Co. L, 1st Wash. Inf., 27 June, 1898, to 1 Nov., 1899. 1st Lieut. 44th U. S. Inf., 17 Aug., 1899.
BARRY, MICHAEL H., Com., 19 Sept., 1899. 1st Lieut. 44th U. S. Inf., 17 Aug., 1899.
LYNCH, FRANK E., Priv. Co. D, 2nd Ala. Inf., 2 May to 31 Oct., 1898. 1st Lieut. 44th U. S. Inf., 17 Aug., 1899.
LEVACK, THEODORE, 2nd Lieut. 2nd Ark. Inf., 25 April, 1898. Mustered out 25 Feb., 1899. Priv., Sergt. and 1st Sergt. Cos. D and K, 33rd U. S. Inf., 31 July to 22 Aug., 1899. 2nd Lieut. 44th U. S. Inf., 17 Aug., 1899. 1st Lieut., 10 Nov., 1899.
HALL, BENJAMIN R., 2nd Lieut. 3rd Ill. Inf., 26 April, 1898. Mustered out 20 Jan., 1899. 2nd Lieut. 44th U. S. Inf., 17 Aug., 1899. 1st Lieut., 29 Nov., 1899.
KOONTZ, HOWARD M., 1st Lieut. 21st Kans. Inf., 7 May, 1898. Mustered out 10 Dec., 1898. 2nd Lieut. 44th U. S. Inf., 17 Aug., 1899. 1st Lieut., 30 Nov., 1899.

*Second Lieutenants.*

CADDEN, ARTHUR J., 2nd Lieut. 22nd Kans. Inf., 4 May, 1898. Mustered out 3 Nov., 1898. 2nd Lieut. 44th U. S. Inf., 17 Aug., 1899.
DENGLER, FREDERICK L., 1st Lieut. 1st Ark. Inf., 4 May, 1898. Mustered out 25 Oct., 1898. 2nd Lieut. 44th U. S. Inf., 17 Aug., 1899.
HAYCRAFT, WILLIAM A., Sergt. Cos. M and G, 4th Ky. Inf., 28 June to 29 Nov., 1898. 2nd Lieut. 4th Ky. Inf., 30 Nov., 1898. Mustered out 12 Feb., 1899. 2nd Lieut. 44th U. S. Inf., 17 Aug., 1899.
SUTHERLAND, RICHARD H., Priv. and Corpl. Batty A, Ill. Light Art., 30 April to 25 Nov., 1898. Priv. and Corpl. Co. M, 30th U. S. Inf., 24 July to 31 Aug., 1899. 2nd Lieut. 44th U. S. Inf., 17 Aug., 1899.
PARSONS, WILLIAM E., Priv. Co. H, 157th Ind. Inf., 26 April to 1 Nov., 1898. 2nd Lieut. 44th U. S. Inf., 17 Aug., 1899.
CUSICK, ALTON B., Sergt. and 1st Sergt. Co. A, 10th Ohio Inf., 25 June, 1898, to 23 March, 1899. 2nd Lieut. 44th U. S. Inf., 17 Aug., 1899.
SCHLACHTER, GUSTAV F., Sergt. Co. — 3rd Pa. Inf., 28 April to 22 Oct., 1898. 2nd Lieut. 44th U. S. Inf., 17 Aug., 1899.
BLAIR, WILLIAM S., Priv. Co. M, 50th Iowa Inf., 14 May to 30 Nov., 1898. 2nd Lieut. 44th U. S. Inf., 17 Aug., 1899.
THOMAS, LEO L., Priv. and Corpl. Co. M, 35th Mich. Inf., 5 July, 1898, to 31 March, 1899. 2nd Lieut. 44th U. S. Inf., 17 Aug., 1899.

BENNETT, GEORGE, Priv. and Sergt. Maj., 44th U. S. Inf., 10 Sept. to 12 Nov., 1899. 2nd Lieut. 44th U. S. Inf., 10 Nov., 1899.
VAN HOUTEN, WALTER E., Priv. and Q. M. Sergt. 44th U. S. Inf., 27 April, 1899, to 23 Jan., 1900. 2nd Lieut. 44th U. S. Inf., 30 Nov., 1899.
STRANGE, PLINY R., Corpl. and Sergt. Co. M, 6th Mo. Inf., 16 July, 1898, to 8 March, 1899. 2nd Lieut. 6th Mo. Inf., 10 March, 1899. Mustered out 10 May, 1899. Priv., Sergt. and 1st Sergt. Co. F, 44th U. S. Inf., 8 Sept., 1899, to 2 Feb., 1900. 2nd Lieut. 44th U. S. Inf., 18 Dec., 1899.

## 45TH U. S. VOLUNTEER INFANTRY.

*Colonel.*

DORST, JOSEPH H. (Regular), Col. 45th U. S. Inf., 17 Aug., 1899.

*Lieutenant Colonel.*

PARKER, JAMES (Regular), Lieut. Col. 42nd U. S. Inf., 17 Aug., 1899. Trans. to 45th U. S. Inf., 1 Sept., 1899.

*Majors.*

FREDERICK, DANIEL A. (Regular), Maj. 45th U. S. Inf., 17 Aug., 1899.
COLE, EDWIN T. (Regular), Maj. 45th U. S. Inf., 17 Aug., 1899.
BIRKHAEUSER, THEODORE K., Maj. 4th Wis. Inf., 6 July, 1898. Mustered out 28 Feb., 1899. Maj. 45th U. S. Inf., 17 Aug., 1899.

*Surgeon with rank of Major.*

IRELAND, MERRITTE W. (Regular), Maj. Surg. 45th U. S. Inf., 17 Aug., 1899.

*Assistant Surgeons with rank of Captain.*

ARTAUD, FRANK E., Maj. Surg. 1st La. Inf., 1 May, 1898. Mustered out 3 Oct., 1898. Capt. Asst. Surg. 45th U. S. Inf., 17 Aug., 1899.

*With rank of First Lieutenant.*

BERLIN, WILLIAM C., 1st Lieut. Asst. Surg. 45th U. S. Inf., 17 Oct., 1899.

*Captains.*

COGSWELL, ADELBERT W., Capt. 1st N. Dak. Inf., 27 April, 1898. Mustered out 25 Sept., 1899. Capt. 45th U. S. Inf., 17 Aug., 1899.
WORRICK, ELMER O., Capt. 2nd Ore. Inf., 28 April, 1898. Mustered out 7 Aug., 1899. Capt. 45th U. S. Inf., 17 Aug., 1899.
WILLIS, PERCY, Maj. 2nd Ore. Inf., 30 April, 1898. Mustered out 7 Aug., 1899. Capt. 45th U. S. Inf., 17 Aug., 1899.
LEE, ORISON P., Capt. 160th Ind. Inf., 26 April, 1898. Mustered out 25 April, 1899. Capt. 45th U. S. Inf., 17 Aug., 1899.
SIMPSON, NATHAN F., Q. M., 21 Oct., 1899. Capt. 35th Mich. Inf., 6 June, 1898. Mustered out 31 March, 1899. Capt. 45th U. S. Inf., 17 Aug., 1899.
HAND, DANIEL W., Maj. 15th Minn. Inf., 2 July, 1898. Mustered out 27 March, 1899. Capt. 45th U. S. Inf., 17 Aug., 1899.
ROGERS, THOMAS J., Capt. 1st Wis. Inf., 28 April, 1898. Mustered out 7 Dec., 1898. Capt. 45th U. S. Inf., 17 Aug., 1899.
PATRICK, BENJAMIN F., Adj., 26 Sept., 1899. 1st Lieut. 1st Ill. Inf., 26 April, 1898. Mustered out 17 Nov., 1898. Capt. 45th U. S. Inf., 17 Aug., 1899.
MONTFORT, EUGENE C., 1st Lieut. 14th Minn. Inf., 29 April, 1898. Capt., 12 July, 1898. Mustered out 18 Nov., 1898. Capt. 45th U. S. Inf., 17 Aug., 1899.
STEINHAUSER, ALBERT, Capt. 12th Minn. Inf., 29 April, 1898. Mustered out 5 Nov., 1898. Capt. 45th U. S. Inf., 17 Aug., 1899.
CAPPS, W. LEE, Capt. and Q. M. 5th Ill. Inf., 25 April, 1898. Mustered out 16 Oct., 1898. Capt. 45th U. S. Inf., 17 Aug., 1899.
RICKEMAN, GEORGE W., 2nd Lieut. 1st Wis. Inf., 28 April, 1898. Mustered out 19 Oct., 1898. Capt. 45th U. S. Inf., 17 Aug., 1899.
ROSS, JAMES, Capt. Ind. Batt. Wash. Inf., 21 June, 1898. Mustered out 21 Oct., 1898. Capt. 45th U. S. Inf., 17 Aug., 1899.
LOYE, JOHN N., Sergt. and Batt. Sergt. Maj. 13th Minn. Inf., 29 April to 3 Oct., 1898. Capt. 45th U. S. Inf., 17 Aug., 1899.

*First Lieutenants.*

BROWN, WILLIAM, 1st Lieut. Batt. Adj. 1st Mont. Inf., 27 April, 1898. Mustered out 17 Oct., 1899. 1st Lieut. 45th U. S. Inf., 17 Aug., 1899.
FLYNN, WILLARD M., Capt. 49th Iowa Inf., 26 April, 1898. Mustered out 13 May, 1899. 1st Lieut. 45th U. S. Inf., 17 Aug., 1899.
OWENS, TEMPLE H., 2nd Lieut. 161st Ind. Inf., 24 June, 1898. Mustered out 30 April, 1899. 1st Lieut. 45th U. S. Inf., 17 Aug., 1899.
HILGARD, MILOSH R., 1st Sergt. Co. D. 4th Ill. Inf., 26 April to 4 Aug., 1898. 2nd Lieut. 4th Ill. Inf., 4 Aug., 1898. Mustered out 2 May, 1899. 1st Lieut. 45th U. S. Inf., 17 Aug., 1899.
EDWARDS, WILLIAM A., 1st Lieut. 15th Minn. Inf., 2 July, 1898. Mustered out 27 March, 1899. 1st Lieut. 45th U. S. Inf., 17 Aug., 1899.

TIBBITTS, ARTHUR S., 2nd Lieut. 2nd Wis. Inf., 28 April, 1898. Mustered out 17 Nov., 1898. 1st Lieut. 45th U. S. Inf., 17 Aug., 1899.
BLAKER, ALLAN G., 2nd Lieut. 12th Minn. Inf., 29 April, 1898. Mustered out 5 Nov., 1898. 1st Lieut. 45th U. S. Inf., 17 Aug., 1899.
MORRISON, FRED W., Capt. 32nd Mich. Inf., 26 April, 1898. Mustered out 25 Oct., 1898. 1st Lieut. 45th U. S. Inf., 17 Aug., 1899.
COOK, FREDERICK P., 1st Lieut. 1st Wis. Inf., 28 April, 1898. Mustered out 19 Oct., 1898. 1st Lieut. 45th U. S. Inf., 17 Aug., 1899.
CASTLE, ALFRED L., 1st Lieut. 5th Ill. Inf., 25 April, 1898. Mustered out 16 Oct., 1898. 1st Lieut. 45th U. S. Inf., 17 Aug., 1899.
TYNER, GEORGE P., Capt. 1st Ill. Cav., 26 April, 1898. Mustered out 11 Oct., 1898. 1st Lieut. 45th U. S. Inf., 17 Aug., 1899.
McCORMICK, DAVID L., Com., 1 May, 1900. 2nd Lieut. 159th Ind. Inf., 19 June, 1898. Mustered out 23 Nov., 1898. 1st Lieut. 45th U. S. Inf., 17 Aug., 1899.
KUMPE, GEORGE E., Sergt. Co. A, 1st Mont. Inf., 1 May, 1898, to 23 March, 1899. 2nd Lieut. 1st Mont. Inf., 24 March, 1899. 1st Lieut., 2 Aug., 1899. Mustered out 17 Oct., 1899. 1st Lieut. 45th U. S. Inf., 17 Aug., 1899.
RYAN, LEWIS S., Priv. and Corpl. Co. H, and Q. M. Sergt. 1st Neb. Inf., 3 May, 1898, to 4 May, 1899. 2nd Lieut. 1st Neb. Inf., 5 May, 1899. Mustered out 23 Aug., 1899. 1st Lieut. 45th U. S. Inf., 17 Aug., 1899.
WATSON, JAMES D., 1st Lieut. 45th U. S. Inf., 17 Aug., 1899.
LAWRENCE, CHARLES G., 1st Lieut. 45th U. S. Inf., 17 Aug., 1899.

*Second Lieutenants.*

TAYLOR, ROY L., 1st Lieut. 35th Mich. Inf., 14 June, 1898. Mustered out 31 March, 1899. 2nd Lieut. 45th U. S. Inf., 17 Aug., 1899.
MacKINLAY, WILLIAM E. W., Priv. Co. C, 3rd Ill. Inf. and Priv., Corpl. and Sergt. 4th Co. U. S. Sig. Corps, 26 April, 1898, to 25 March, 1899. 2nd Lieut. 45th U. S. Inf., 17 Aug., 1899.
HOWARD, CHARLES E. N., 2nd Lieut. 45th U. S. Inf., 17 Aug., 1899.
LONG, EDWIN C., Corpl. Co. H, 10th Pa. Inf., 27 April, 1898, to 3 March, 1899. 2nd Lieut. 45th U. S. Inf., 17 Aug., 1899.
MENDER, MICHAEL J., 2nd Lieut. 45th U. S. Inf., 17 Aug., 1899.
MUMFORD, EDGAR W., Priv. Co. C, 1st Ill. Inf. and 1st Class Priv. U. S. Sig. Corps, 26 April, 1898, to 16 Jan., 1899. 2nd Lieut. 45th U. S. Inf., 17 Aug., 1899.
SHUMAN, JOHN B., Sergt. Co. M, and Q. M. Sergt. 3rd Wis. Inf., 28 April, 1898, to 11 Jan., 1899. 2nd Lieut. 45th U. S. Inf., 17 Aug., 1899.
BARBER, EDWARD P., Priv. Co. B and Sergt. Maj. 8th Ohio Inf., 26 April to 21 Nov., 1898. 2nd Lieut. 45th U. S. Inf., 17 Aug., 1899.
KELLOND, FREDERIC G., Priv. and Corpl. Co. E, 1st Ky. Inf., 13 May, 1898, to 24 Feb., 1899. 2nd Lieut. 45th U. S. Inf., 17 Aug., 1899.
ODELL, ALBERT S., Sergt. Maj. 3rd Batt. 3rd U. S. Eng., 7 July, 1898, to 17 May, 1899. 2nd Lieut. 45th U. S. Inf., 17 Aug., 1899.
MOBLEY, GRIER P., 2nd Lieut. 45th U. S. Inf., 17 Aug., 1899.
SWEITZER, CHARLES McG., Priv., Corpl. and Sergt. Co. B, 145th U. S. Inf., 13 Sept., 1900, to 4 Feb., 1900. 2nd Lieut. 45th U. S. Inf., 19 Jan., 1900.

## 46TH U. S. VOLUNTEER INFANTRY.

*Colonel.*

SCHUYLER, WALTER S, (Regular), Col. 46th U. S. Inf., 17 Aug., 1899.

*Lieutenant Colonel.*

PRATT, EDWARD B. (Regular), Lieut. Col. 46th U. S. Inf., 17 Aug., 1898.

*Majors.*

MILLER, SAMUEL W. (Regular), Maj. 46th U. S. Inf., 17 Aug., 1898.
JOHNSTON, WILLIAM H. (Regular), Maj. 46th U. S. Inf., 17 Aug., 1899.
BROOKE, WILLIAM (Regular), Maj. 46th U. S. Inf., 17 Aug., 1899.

*Surgeon with rank of Major.*

COGSWELL, WILLIAM, Maj. Surg. 8th Miss. Inf., 28 April, 1898. Mustered out 28 April, 1899. Maj. Surg. 46th U. S. Inf., 17 Aug., 1899.

*Assistant Surgeons with rank of Captain.*

LEE, HENRY H., Maj. Surg. 1st Vt. Inf., 3 May, 1898. Discharged 16 Aug., 1898. Maj. Brig. Surg., 11 Aug., 1898. Discharged 22 March, 1899. Capt. Asst. Surg. 46th U. S. Inf., 17 Aug., 1899.

*With rank of First Lieutenant.*

ANDREWS, ROBERT W., 1st Lieut. Asst. Surg. 46th U. S. Inf., 17 Aug., 1899.

*Captains.*

McKENNA, FRANK B. (Regular), Capt. 46th U. S. Inf., 17 Aug., 1899.
McCLINTOCK, JOHN (Regular), Adj., 1 Oct., 1899. Capt. 46th U. S. Inf., 17 Aug., 1899.
GLIDDEN, JOSEPH W. (Regular), Capt. 46th U. S. Inf., 17 Aug., 1899.

MAIR, THOMAS L., Capt. 2nd Ill. Inf., 26 April, 1898. Mustered out 26 April, 1899. Capt. 46th U. S. Inf., 17 Aug., 1899.
PATSTONE, LEWIS, Capt. 1st R. I. Inf., 5 May, 1898. Mustered out 30 March, 1899. Capt. 46th U. S. Inf., 17 Aug., 1899.
CONNER, DAVID, Capt. 3rd Conn. Inf., 28 June, 1898. Mustered out 20 March, 1899. Capt. 46th U. S. Inf., 17 Aug., 1899.
REANEY, ROBERT J., Capt. 2nd Pa. Inf., 28 April, 1898. Mustered out 15 Nov., 1898. Capt. 46th U. S. Inf., 17 Aug., 1899.
O'CONNOR, SAMUEL S., Capt. 9th N. Y. Inf., 2 May, 1898. Mustered out 15 Nov., 1898. Capt. 46th U. S. Inf., 17 Aug., 1899.
HARDIN, JOSEPH S., Capt. 1st S. C. Inf., 4 May, 1898. Mustered out 10 Nov., 1898. Capt. 46th U. S. Inf., 17 Aug., 1899.
McCONNELL, GEORGE T., Capt. Batty A, 1st Ohio Light Art., 26 April, 1898. Mustered out 23 Oct., 1898. Capt. 46th U. S. Inf., 17 Aug., 1899.
BAKER, ISAIAH H., Capt. 1st Maine Inf., 2 May, 1898. Mustered out 27 Oct., 1898. Capt. 46th U. S. Inf., 17 Aug., 1899.
COMMISKEY, ARCHIBALD F., Priv. Troop C, N. Y. Cav., 2 May to 25 Nov., 1898. Capt. 46th U. S. Inf., 17 Aug., 1899.
BAKER, JOHN H., Sergt. Co. G, 1st Wis. Inf., 28 April to 27 Oct., 1898. Capt. 46th U. S. Inf., 17 Aug., 1899.
SHEEN, HENRY H., Capt. 4th Va. Inf., 25 April, 1898. Mustered out 27 April, 1899. 1st Lieut. 46th U. S. Inf., 17 Aug., 1899. Capt., 10 April, 1900.

*First Lieutenants.*

WONSON, CHARLES F., 1st Lieut. and Q. M. 8th Mass. Inf., 28 April, 1898. Mustered out 28 April, 1899. 1st Lieut. 46th U. S. Inf., 17 Aug., 1899.
WOOD, CHARLES D., 1st Lieut. and Adj. 9th U. S. Inf., 17 June, 1898. Capt., 28 Nov., 1898. Mustered out 25 May, 1899. 1st Lieut. 46th U. S. Inf., 17 Aug., 1899.
HOPKINS, FRANK E., Com., 1 Oct., 1899. 1st Lieut. and Q. M. 1st R. I. Inf., 10 May, 1898. Mustered out 30 March, 1899. 1st Lieut. 46th U. S. Inf., 17 Aug., 1899.
MURPHY, TERENCE E., Capt. 2nd N. J. Inf., 2 May, 1898. Mustered out 17 Nov., 1898. 1st Lieut. 4th N. J. Inf., 10 Jan., 1899. Mustered out 6 April, 1899. 1st Lieut. 46th U. S. Inf., 17 Aug., 1899.
AUSTIN, FRED T., 1st Lieut. and Adj. 5th Mass. Inf., 25 June, 1898. Mustered out 31 March, 1899. 1st Lieut. 46th U. S. Inf., 17 Aug., 1899.
CONSTABLE, JOHN G., Batt. Sergt. Maj. 1st Md. Inf., 25 April to 5 July, 1898. 2nd Lieut. 1st Md. Inf., 6 July, 1898. Mustered out 28 Feb., 1899. 1st Lieut. 46th U. S. Inf., 17 Aug., 1899.
WEBB, JAMES B., 1st Lieut. 65th N. Y. Inf., 1 May, 1898. Mustered out 19 Nov., 1898. 1st Lieut. 46th U. S. Inf., 17 Aug., 1899.
HERRINGSHAW, WILLIAM F., 2nd Lieut. 5th Ohio Inf., 26 April, 1898. Mustered out 5 Nov., 1898. 1st Lieut. 46th U. S. Inf., 17 Aug., 1899.
PHILBROOK, EDWARD E., 2nd Lieut. 1st Maine Inf., 2 May, 1898. Mustered out 25 Oct., 1898. 1st Lieut. 46th U. S. Inf., 17 Aug., 1899.
ELY, HARRY A., Priv., Corpl., Sergt. and 1st Sergt. Cos. C and I, 4th N. J. Inf., 2 July, 1898, to 2 March, 1899. 2nd Lieut. 4th N. J. Inf., 3 March, 1899. Mustered out 6 April, 1899. 1st Lieut. 46th U. S. Inf., 17 Aug., 1899.
BUTTRICK, CONANT S., 1st Lieut. 46th U. S. Inf., 17 Aug., 1898.
BATCHELDER, WALLACE N., Priv. Troop K, 1st U. S. Cav., 11 July to 15 Sept., 1898. 1st Lieut. 46th U. S. Inf., 17 Aug., 1899.
SWEET, PHILIP K., Priv., Corpl. and Sergt. 1st U. S. Cav., 5 May to 6 Oct., 1898. 1st Lieut. 46th U. S. Inf., 17 Aug., 1899.
THUN, LEOPOLD, 1st Lieut. 46th U. S. Inf., 17 Aug., 1899.
LUKENS, BENJAMIN P., Priv. and Corpl. Co. A, 1st Ohio Inf., 26 April to 25 Oct., 1898. 1st Lieut. 46th U. S. Inf., 17 Aug., 1899.
KAVANAGH, RICHARD B., Sergt. Co. I, 7th Ill. Inf., 26 April to 9 July, 1898. 2nd Lieut. 7th Ill. Inf., 10 July, 1898. Mustered out 20 Oct., 1898. 2nd Lieut. 46th U. U. S. Inf., 17 Aug., 1899. 1st Lieut., 10 April, 1900.

*Second Lieutenants.*

ROSS, MOSES R., Priv. and Sergt. Co. I, 5th Pa. Inf., 5 July to 7 Nov., 1898. 2nd Lieut. 46th U. S. Inf., 17 Aug., 1899.
LEISENRING, FRANK S., Priv. Co. C, 8th Pa. Inf., 7 May, 1898, to 7 March, 1899. 2nd Lieut. 46th U. S. Inf., 17 Aug., 1899.
AUSTIN, WILLIAM A., 2nd Lieut. 46th U. S. Inf., 17 Aug., 1899.
JOHNSTON, JAMES H., Sergt. Co. E, 1st N. H. Inf., 7 May to 31 Oct., 1898. 2nd Lieut. 46th U. S. Inf., 17 Aug., 1899.
WEST, SOLOMON B., Priv. Co. E, and Sergt. Maj. 1st N. H. Inf., 7 May to 31 Oct., 1898. 2nd Lieut. 46th U. S. Inf., 17 Aug., 1899.
POWERS, EDWARD D., Corpl. Batty A, 1st Mass. Heavy Art., 26 April to 14 Nov., 1898. 2nd Lieut. 46th U. S. Inf., 17 Aug., 1899.
EARL, GEORGE W., Jr., Priv. and Corpl. Co. G, 6th Pa. Inf., 4 May to 17 Oct., 1898. Priv. Co. H, 28th U. S. Inf., 4 Aug. to 28 Aug., 1899. 2nd Lieut. 46th U. S. Inf., 17 Aug., 1899.
GRUENER, THEODORE, Priv. and Corpl. Co. K, 1st Conn. Inf., 4 May to 31 Oct., 1898. 2nd Lieut. 46th U. S. Inf., 17 Aug., 1899.
McELGIN, HUGH J. B., Priv. Co. H, 14th N. Y. Inf., 2 May to 1 Nov., 1898. 2nd Lieut. 46th U. S. Inf., 17 Aug., 1899.
PIERCE, CARLOS W., Q. M. Sergt. Co. L, 1st Vt. Inf., 6 May to 31 Oct., 1898. 2nd Lieut. 46th U. S. Inf., 17 Aug., 1899.
HOPSON, SIDNEY H., 2nd Lieut. 46th U. S. Inf., 16 Sept., 1899.
CLENDENIN, WILLIAM H., Corpl. Co. M, 8th Mass. Inf., 5 May, 1898, to 3 Feb., 1899. 2nd Lieut. 8th Mass. Inf., 4 Feb., 1899. Mustered out 28 April, 1899. Priv. and 1st Sergt. Co. K, and Sergt. Maj. 46th U. S. Inf., 17 Sept., 1899, to 26 May, 1900. 2nd Lieut. 46th U. S. Inf., 8 May, 1900.

## 47TH U. S. VOLUNTEER INFANTRY.

*Colonel.*

HOWE, WALTER (Regular), Col. 47th U. S. Inf., 17 Aug., 1899.

*Lieutenant Colonel.*

EDWARDS, CLARENCE R. (Regular), Lieut. Col. 47th U. S. Inf., 17 Aug., 1899.

*Majors.*

WISE, HUGH D. (Regular), Maj. 47th U. S. Inf., 17 Aug., 1899.
ANDERSON, KELLER, Col. 2nd Tenn. Inf., 25 April, 1898. Mustered out 8 Feb., 1899. Maj. 47th U. S. Inf., 17 Aug., 1899.
SHIPTON, JAMES A. (Regular), Maj. 47th U. S. Inf., 26 Oct., 1899.

*Surgeon with rank of Major.*

CLARKE, JOSEPH T. (Regular), Maj. Surg. 47th U. S. Inf., 17 Aug., 1899.

*Assistant Surgeons with rank of Captain.*

ROBINS, ROBERT P., 1st Lieut. Asst. Surg. 2nd Pa. Inf., 28 April, 1898. Mustered out 15 Nov., 1898. Capt. Asst. Surg. 47th U. S. Inf., 17 Aug., 1899.

*With rank of First Lieutenant.*

GALBRAITH, CHARLES M., 1st Lieut. Asst. Surg. 4th Ill. Inf., 26 April, 1898. Mustered out 2 May, 1899. 1st Lieut. Asst. Surg. 47th U. S. Inf., 17 Aug., 1899.

*Captains.*

GORDON, CHARLES H., 2nd Lieut. Sig. Officer., 20 May, 1898. 1st Lieut., 21 Jan., 1899. Discharged 26 Sept., 1899. Capt. 47th U. S. Inf., 17 Aug., 1899.
HUSTON, ROBERT B., Capt. 1st U. S. Cav., 4 May, 1898. Mustered out 15 Sept., 1898. Maj. Addl. P. M., 27 Sept., 1898. Discharged 13 June, 1899. Capt. 47th U. S. Inf., 17 Aug., 1899.
McLAIN, CHARLES C., Capt. 14th Pa. Inf., 27 April, 1898. Mustered out 28 Feb., 1899. Capt. 47th U. S. Inf., 17 Aug., 1899.
BENTLEY, GEORGE H., 1st Lieut. 2nd Va. Inf., 23 April, 1898. Mustered out 21 Oct., 1898. Capt. 6th Va. Inf., 22 Oct., 1898. Mustered out 28 Jan., 1899. Capt. 47th U. S. Inf., 17 Aug., 1899.
HART, AUGUSTUS C., 1st Lieut. 1st Fla. Inf., 25 April, 1898. Mustered out 27 Jan., 1899. Capt. 47th U. S. Inf., 17 Aug., 1899.
BETTS, ARLINGTON U., Maj. 10th Ohio Inf., 1 July, 1898. Mustered out 23 March, 1899. Capt. 47th U. S. Inf., 17 Aug., 1899.
SIMONS, LESTER H., 2nd Lieut. 16th Pa. Inf., 27 April, 1898. Mustered out 28 Dec., 1898. Capt. 47th U. S. Inf., 17 Aug., 1899.
LIVINGSTON, JOHN G., 1st Lieut. 1st U. S. Eng., 21 June, 1898. Capt., 14 Dec., 1898. Mustered out 25 Jan., 1899. Capt. 47th U. S. Inf., 17 Aug., 1899.
WALSH, HARRY, Capt. 1st D. C. Inf., 11 May, 1898. Mustered out 20 Nov., 1898. Capt. 47th U. S. Inf., 17 Aug., 1899.
FIELD, JOHN M., Q. M., 24 Sept., 1899. 1st Lieut. and Q. M. 1st D. C. Inf., 11 May, 1898. Mustered out 20 Nov., 1898. Capt. 47th U. S. Inf., 17 Aug., 1899.
TERRY, EDWARD W., Capt. 1st La. Inf., 1 May, 1898. Mustered out 3 Oct., 1898. Capt. 47th U. S. Inf., 17 Aug., 1899.
BISHOP, OSCAR, 1st Lieut. 3rd Ky. Inf., 27 April, 1898. Mustered out 16 May, 1899. 1st Lieut. 47th U. S. Inf., 17 Aug., 1899. Capt., 30 Oct., 1899.
GARWOOD, JESSE S., 2nd Lieut. 2nd Ill. Inf., 26 April, 1898. Mustered out 26 April, 1899. 1st Lieut. 47th U. S. Inf., 17 Aug., 1899. Capt., 1 Nov., 1899.
GULICK, JOHN W., 1st Lieut. 1st N. C. Inf., 27 April, 1898. Mustered out 22 April, 1899. 1st Lieut. 47th U. S. Inf., 17 Aug., 1899. Capt., 9 Nov., 1899.

*First Lieutenants.*

GODDARD, LEONARD S., 1st Lieut. 4th Tenn. Inf., 18 June, 1898. Mustered out 6 May, 1899. 1st Lieut. 47th U. S. Inf., 17 Aug., 1899.
CAMPBELL, THOMAS R. J., 2nd Lieut. Sig. Off., 20 May, 1898. 1st Lieut., 13 Jan., 1899. Discharged 12 April, 1899. 1st Lieut. 47th U. S. Inf., 17 Aug., 1899.
RIGGS, SAMUEL, Capt. 1st Md. Inf., 25 April, 1898. Mustered out 28 Feb., 1899. 1st Lieut. 47th U. S. Inf., 17 Aug., 1899.
DYER, LORENZO D., Capt. 3rd N. J. Inf., 27 April, 1898. Mustered out 11 Feb., 1899. 1st Lieut. 47th U. S. Inf., 17 Aug., 1899.
CHRISTIE, A. LARUE, Capt. 4th N. J. Inf., 30 June, 1898. Mustered out 6 April, 1899. 1st Lieut. 47th U. S. Inf., 17 Aug., 1899.
COLE, CASPER W., 1st Lieut. 202nd N. Y. Inf., 15 July, 1898. Mustered out 15 April, 1899. Priv. and Sergt. 26th U. S. Inf., 4 Aug. to 29 Aug., 1899. 1st Lieut. 47th U. S. Inf., 17 Aug., 1899.
BISHOP, WILLIAM T., 1st Sergt. Co. C, 3rd N. J. Inf., 27 April to 7 Aug., 1898. Capt. 8th U. S. Inf., 27 July, 1898. Mustered out 6 March, 1899. 1st Lieut. 47th U. S. Inf., 17 Aug., 1899.
YOST, PHILIP, 1st Lieut. 8th Ohio Inf., 26 April, 1898. Capt. 5 Sept., 1898. Mustered out 21 Nov., 1898. 1st Lieut. 47th U. S. Inf., 17 Aug., 1899.
ENGLAND, GEORGE W., Capt. 1st D. C. Inf., 12 May, 1898. Mustered out 20 Nov., 1898. 1st Lieut. 47th U. S. Inf., 17 Aug., 1899.

MEEKINS, EDWARD N., 2nd Lieut. 1st D. C. Inf., 16 May, 1898. Mustered out 20 Nov., 1898. 1st Lieut. 47th U. S. Inf., 17 Aug., 1899.
GRAY, HARRY T., 2nd Lieut. 2nd Mass. Inf., 3 May, 1898. Mustered out 3 Nov., 1898. 1st Lieut. 47th U. S. Inf., 17 Aug., 1899.
STEDJE, JENS E., 1st Lieut. 47th U. S. Inf., 17 Aug., 1899.
PITCAIRN, HUGH H., Priv. Co. G, 12th Pa. Inf., 7 May to 29 Oct., 1898. 1st Lieut. 47th U. S. Inf., 17 Aug., 1899.
MURPHY, THOMAS P., 2nd Lieut. 13th Pa. Inf., 27 April, 1898. Mustered out 11 March, 1899. 2nd Lieut. 47th U. S. Inf., 17 Aug., 1899. 1st Lieut., 30 Oct., 1899.
MORROW, CHARLES H., 2nd Lieut. 1st Ky. Inf., 25 May, 1898. 1st Lieut., 3 Nov., 1898. 2nd Lieut. 47th U. S. Inf., 17 Aug., 1899. 1st Lieut., 1 Nov., 1899.
GARRISON, HARVEY, 2nd Lieut. 22nd N. Y. Inf., 9 May, 1898. Mustered out 23 Nov., 1898. 2nd Lieut. 47th U. S. Inf., 17 Aug., 1899. 1st Lieut., 9 Nov., 1899.

*Second Lieutenants.*

HARRISON, WILLIAM R., 2nd Lieut. 1st D. C. Inf., 10 May, 1898. Mustered out 20 Nov., 1898. 2nd Lieut. 47th U. S. Inf., 17 Aug., 1899.
LANHAM, CHARLES L., 1st Lieut. 1st D. C. Inf., 17 May, 1898. Mustered out 20 Nov., 1898. 2nd Lieut. 47th U. S. Inf., 17 Aug., 1899.
SLACK, WALTER T., 2nd Lieut. 2nd Ky. Inf., 6 May, 1898. Mustered out 31 Oct., 1898. 2nd Lieut. 47th U. S. Inf., 17 Aug., 1899.
HARRISON, PAUL W., Sergt. and 1st Sergt. Co. H, 3rd Ga. Inf., 13 July to 29 Oct., 1898. 2nd Lieut. 3rd Ga. Inf., 30 Oct., 1898. Mustered out 22 April, 1899. 2nd Lieut. 47th U. S. Inf., 17 Aug., 1899.
SMYSER, RUDOLPH E., Priv. Co. A, 8th Pa. Inf., 10 June, 1898, to 7 March, 1899. 2nd Lieut. 47th U. S. Inf., 17 Aug., 1899.
EGLE, HENRY F., Priv. Co. C, 15th Pa. Inf., 27 April, 1898, to 27 Jan., 1899. 2nd Lieut. 47th U. S. Inf., 17 Aug., 1899.
PURINGTON, GEORGE A., 2nd Lieut. 2nd U. S. Eng., 28 June, 1898. 1st Lieut., 24 April,
BRIGGS. ALLAN L., 2nd Lieut. 47th U. S. Inf., 17 Aug., 1899.
DENT, JOSEPH H., Priv. and Sergt. Co. F, and Batt. Sergt. Maj. 47th U. S. Inf., 14 Sept. to 2 Nov., 1899. 2nd Lieut. 47th U. S. Inf., 30 Oct., 1899.
PURINGTON, GEORGE A., 2nd Lieut. 2nd U. S. Eng., 28 June, 1899. 1st Lieut., 24 April, 1899. Mustered out 16 May, 1899. Priv., Sergt. and 1st Sergt. Co. C, 47th U. S. Inf., 12 Sept. to 2 Nov., 1899. 2nd Lieut. 47th U. S. Inf., 1 Nov., 1899.
DISQUE, BRICE P., Priv., Sergt. and 1st Sergt. Co. E, 47th U. S. Inf., 13 Sept. to 12 Nov., 1899. 2nd Lieut. 47th U. S. Inf., 13 Nov., 1899.
BRITT, STARKEY Y., Priv. and Batt. Sergt. Maj. 47th U. S. Inf., 4 Oct., 1899, to ——, 1900. 2nd Lieut. 47th U. S. Inf., 23 May, 1900.

## 48TH U. S. VOLUNTEER INFANTRY.

*Colonel.*

DUVALL, WILLIAM P. (Regular), Col. 48th U. S. Inf., 9 Sept., 1899.

*Lieutenant Colonel.*

JONES, THADDEUS W. (Regular), Lieut. Col. 48th U. S. Inf., 9 Sept., 1899.

*Majors.*

RICE, SEDGWICK (Regular), Maj. 48th U. S. Inf., 9 Sept., 1899.
DADE, ALEXANDER L. (Regular), Maj. 48th U. S. Inf., 9 Sept., 1899.
HOWARD, JOHN (Regular), Maj. 48th U. S. Inf., 9 Sept., 1899.

*Surgeon with rank of Major.*

KIEFFER, CHARLES F. (Regular), Maj. Surg. 48th U. S. Inf., 9 Sept., 1899.

*Assistant Surgeons with rank of Captain.*

GRUBE, HOWARD A., Capt. Asst. Surg. 35th Mich. Inf., 15 June, 1898. Maj. Surg., 11 Jan., 1899. Mustered out 31 March, 1899. Capt. Asst. Surg. 48th U. S. Inf., 9 Sept., 1899.

*With rank of First Lieutenant.*

PURNELL, WILLIAM W., 1st Lieut. Asst. Surg. 8th U. S. Inf., 25 June, 1898. Mustered out 6 March, 1899. 1st Lieut. Asst. Surg. 48th U. S. Inf., 9 Sept., 1899.

*Captains.*

HAMLIN, JAMES E., Capt. 3rd N. C. Inf., 27 April, 1898. Mustered out 8 Feb., 1899. Capt. 48th U. S. Inf., 9 Sept., 1899.
DENISON, LEON W., Capt. 8th Ill. Inf., 28 June, 1898. Mustered out 3 April, 1899. Capt. 48th U. S. Inf., 9 Sept., 1899.
RUDD, ROBERT R., Capt. 9th Ohio Batt. Inf., 26 April, 1898. Mustered out 28 Jan., 1899. Capt. 48th U. S. Inf., 9 Sept., 1899.
SMITH, JAMES W., 1st Lieut. 9th Ohio Batt. Inf., 26 April, 1898. Mustered out 28 Jan., 1899. Capt. 48th U. S. Inf., 9 Sept., 1899.
JACKSON, WILLIAM H., 1st Lieut. 6th Mass. Inf., 6 May, 1898. Mustered out 21 Jan., 1899. Capt. 48th U. S. Inf., 9 Sept., 1899.

BRIGHT, AARON D., Adj., 27 Oct., 1899. 2nd Lieut. 2nd Tenn. Inf., 23 May, 1898. Mustered out 8 Feb., 1899. 1st Lieut. 48th U. S. Inf., 9 Sept., 1899. Capt., 9 Sept., 1899.
GRANT, THOMAS, 2nd Lieut. 10th U. S. Inf., 21 July, 1898. 1st Lieut., 26 July, 1898. Mustered out 8 March, 1899. Capt. 48th U. S. Inf., 9 Sept., 1899.
RICHARDSON, ALEXANDER V., 1st Lieut. 9th U. S. Inf., 24 Oct., 1898. Mustered out 25 May, 1899. Capt. 48th U. S. Inf., 9 Sept., 1899.
HANKINS, WILLIAM A., Capt. 6th Va. Inf., 28 June, 1898. Mustered out 26 Jan., 1899. Capt. 48th U. S. Inf., 9 Sept., 1899.
OLIVER, JOHN J., Priv., Sergt. and 1st Sergt. Co. G, 10th U. S. Inf., 5 July to 24 Aug., 1898. 2nd Lieut. 10th U. S. Inf., 20 Aug., 1898. Mustered out 8 March, 1899. Capt. 48th U. S. Inf., 9 Sept., 1899.
STARR, STEPHEN, 2nd Lieut. 9th U. S. Inf., 28 Nov., 1898. Mustered out 25 May, 1899. Capt. 48th U. S. Inf., 9 Sept., 1899.
BROWN, WILLIAM H., 2nd Lieut. 7th U. S. Inf., 7 Jan., 1899. Mustered out 28 Feb., 1899. Capt. 48th U. S. Inf., 9 Sept., 1899.
BUCK, JOHN, 2nd Lieut. 7th U. S. Inf., 7 Jan., 1899. Mustered out 28 Feb., 1899. Capt. 48th U. S. U. S. Inf., 9 Sept., 1899.
THOMASON, HUGH, 1st Lieut. 48th U. S. Inf., 9 Sept., 1899. Capt., 1 May, 1900.

*First Lieutenants.*

GATCHELL, WALTER G., 1st Lieut. 1st R. I. Inf., 7 May, 1898. Capt., 29 Sept., 1898. Mustered out 30 March, 1899. 1st Lieut. 48th U. S. Inf., 9 Sept., 1899.
WHITE, JERRY M., 1st Lieut. 23rd Kans. Inf., 2 July, 1898. Mustered out 10 April, 1899. 1st Lieut. 48th U. S. Inf., 9 Sept., 1899.
CALDWELL, CHARLES C., 1st Lieut. 9th Ohio Batt. Inf., 25 April, 1898. Mustered out 28 Jan., 1899. 1st Lieut. 48th U. S. Inf., 9 Sept., 1899.
BROWN, JOHN W., 2nd Lieut. 9th U. S. Inf., 24 Oct., 1898. Mustered out 25 May, 1899. 1st Lieut. 48th U. S. Inf., 9 Sept., 1899.
SMITH, JACOB C., 2nd Lieut. 9th U. S. Inf., 24 Oct., 1898. Mustered out 25 May, 1899. 1st Lieut. 48th U. S. Inf., 9 Sept., 1899.
POWELL, JAMES F., 2nd Lieut. 1st Ind. Inf., 29 June, 1898. Mustered out 20 Jan., 1899. 1st Lieut. 48th U. S. Inf., 9 Sept., 1899.
ANDERSON, JOHN H., 1st Lieut. 10th U. S. Inf., 2 Aug., 1898. Mustered out 8 March, 1899. 1st Lieut. 48th U. S. Inf., 9 Sept., 1899.
McCOWN, PETER, 2nd Lieut. 7th U. S. Inf., 7 Jan., 1899. Mustered out 28 Feb., 1899. 1st Lieut. 48th U. S. Inf., 9 Sept., 1899.
PARKER, HAMMOND J., Priv., Sergt. and 1st Sergt. Co. A, 10th U. S. Inf., 7 July, 1898, to 8 March, 1899. 1st Lieut. 48th U. S. Inf., 9 Sept., 1899.
SMITH, LEWIS M., 1st Lieut. 48th U. S. Inf., 9 Sept., 1899.
ALLEN, WILLIAM H., 1st Lieut. 48th U. S. Inf., 9 Sept., 1899.
CHEEK, FRANK W., Priv. Co. K, 32nd Mich. Inf., 26 April, 1898. Mustered out 9 Nov., 1898. 1st Lieut. 48th U. S. Inf., 9 Sept., 1899.
WEBBER, GEORGE, Com., 28 Sept., 1899. 1st Lieut. 48th U. S. Inf., 9 Sept., 1899.
CABANNE, ARTHUR L., Corpl. Co. C, 1st Mo. Inf., 4 May, 1898. Mustered out 31 Oct., 1898. 1st Lieut. 48th U. S. Inf., 26 Oct., 1899.
COLEMAN, JAMES B., 1st Lieut. 7th U. S. Inf., 26 July, 1898. Mustered out 28 Feb., 1899. 2nd Lieut. 48th U. S. Inf., 9 Sept., 1899. 1st Lieut., 13 Dec., 1899.
SMITH, FREDERICK McC., Priv. and Sergt. Maj. 38th U. S. Inf., 25 Aug., 1899, to ——, 1900. 1st Lieut. 48th U. S. Inf., 24 May, 1900.

*Second Lieutenants.*

RICE, JOHN K., 1st Lieut. 6th Va. Inf., 20 July, 1898. Mustered out 26 Jan., 1899. 2nd Lieut. 48th U. S. Inf., 9 Sept., 1899.
BALLARD, WILSON, Priv., Corpl. and Sergt. Co. B, 9th Ohio Batt. Inf., 4 May to 31 July, 1898. 2nd Lieut. 9th Ohio Batt. Inf., 1 Aug., 1898. Mustered out 28 Jan., 1899. 2nd Lieut. 48th U. S. Inf., 9 Sept., 1899.
MOORE, JOSEPH, 1st Lieut. 8th U. S. Inf., 19 July, 1898. Mustered out 6 March, 1899. 2nd Lieut. 48th U. S. Inf., 9 Sept., 1899.
JEFFERS, DAVID B., 2nd Lieut. 10th U. S. Inf., 21 Jan., 1899. Mustered out 8 March, 1899. 2nd Lieut. 48th U. S. Inf., 9 Sept., 1899.
WASHINGTON, LINCOLN, 2nd Lieut. 48th U. S. Inf., 9 Sept., 1899.
GREEN, WALTER, 2nd Lieut. 48th U. S. Inf., 9 Sept., 1899.
ANDREWS, JOSEPH C., Priv. Co. L, 6th Mass. Inf., 15 June, 1898, to 21 Jan., 1899. 2nd Lieut. 48th U. S. Inf., 9 Sept., 1899.
CHISHOLM, FRANK R., Priv. Co. L, 6th Mass. Inf., 6 May, 1898, to 21 Jan., 1899. 2nd Lieut. 48th U. S. Inf., 9 Sept., 1899.
MARION, GREEN F., Sergt. and 1st Sergt. Co. G, 3rd Ala. Inf., 27 June, 1898, to 20 March, 1899. 2nd Lieut. 48th U. S. Inf., 9 Sept., 1899.
TURNER, CHARLES B., 2nd Lieut. 48th U. S. Inf., 9 Sept., 1899.
TAYLOR, GEORGE W., Priv. and Q. M. Sergt. Co. B, and Q. M. Sergt. 3rd N. C. Inf., 27 April, 1898, to 8 Feb., 1899. 2nd Lieut. 48th U. S. Inf., 9 Sept., 1899
GEE, HERBERT E., Priv. and Sergt. Co. M, and Sergt Maj. 8th U. S. Inf., 3 Aug., 1898, to 6 March, 1899. Priv. Co. D and Sergt. Maj. 48th U. S. Inf., 27 Sept., 1899, to 4 Feb., 1900. 2nd Lieut. 48th U. S. Inf., 20 Dec., 1899.

## 49th U. S. VOLUNTEER INFANTRY.

*Colonel.*

BECK, WILLIAM H. (Regular), Col. 49th U. S. Inf., 9 Sept., 1899. Inf., 9 Sept., 1899.

*Lieutenant Colonel.*

DUCAT, ARTHUR C. (Regular), Lieut. Col. 49th U. S. Inf., 9 Sept., 1899.

*Majors.*

JOHNSON, CARTER P. (Regular), Maj. 49th U. S. Inf., 9 Sept., 1899.
HINDS, ERNEST (Regular), Maj. 49th U. S. Inf., 9 Sept., 1899.

*Surgeon with rank of Major.*

BURNS, ROBERT, Surg. 1st N. H. Inf., 7 May, 1898. Discharged 11 Oct., 1898. Maj. Brig. Surg., 4 Oct., 1898. Discharged 12 May, 1899. Capt. Asst. Surg. 49th U. S. Inf., 9 Sept., 1899. Maj. Surg., 20 May, 1900.

*Assistant Surgeons with rank of Captain.*

WARMSLEY, WILLIAM C., 1st Lieut. Asst. Surg. 49th U. S. Inf., 9 Sept., 1899. Capt. Asst. Surg., 24 May, 1900.

*Captains.*

GAGE, ROBERT, Adj., 9 Oct., 1899. Capt. 3rd Ala. Inf., 3 June, 1898. Mustered out 20 March, 1899. Capt. 49th U. S. Inf., 9 Sept., 1899.
HAWKINS, WILLIAM M., Capt. 23rd Kans. Inf., 30 June, 1898. Mustered out 10 April, 1899. Capt. 49th U. S. Inf., 9 Sept., 1899.
BASS, EMMANUEL D., 2nd Lieut. 9th Ohio Batt. Inf., 14 May, 1898. 1st Lieut., 19 Aug., 1898. Mustered out 28 Jan., 1899. Capt. 49th U. S. Inf., 9 Sept., 1899.
CRUMBLY, FLOYD H., 1st Lieut. 10th U. S. Inf., 21 July, 1898. Mustered out 8 March, 1899. Capt. 49th U. S. Inf., 9 Sept., 1899.
BAKER, EDWARD L., Jr., 1st Lieut. 10th U. S. Inf., 2 Aug., 1898. Mustered out 8 March, 1899. Capt. 49th U. S. Inf., 9 Sept., 1899.
PROCTOR, JOHN C., 1st Lieut. 8th U. S. Inf., 29 July, 1898. Mustered out 6 March, 1899. Capt. 49th U. S. Inf., 9 Sept., 1899.
WOODS, ROBERT G., 2nd Lieut. 9th U. S. Inf., 24 Oct., 1898. Mustered out 25 May, 1899. Capt. 49th U. S. Inf., 9 Sept., 1899.
CAMPBELL, THOMAS, 1st Lieut. 7th U. S. Inf., 26 July, 1898. Mustered out 28 Feb., 1899. Capt. 49th U. S. Inf., 9 Sept., 1899.
STEWARD, FRANK R., Priv., Corpl., Sergt. and 1st Sergt. Cos. M and A, 8th U. S. Inf., 12 Aug., 1898, to 27 Jan., 1899. 2nd Lieut. 8th U. S. Inf., 10 Jan., 1899. Mustered out 6 March, 1899. Capt. 49th U. S. Inf., 9 Sept., 1899.
JEFFERSON, CHARLES W., Capt. 49th U. S. Inf., 9 Sept., 1899.
STAFF, WILLIAM R., Capt. 49th U. S. Inf., 9 Sept., 1899.
EDWARDS, WILLIAM D., Capt. 49th U. S. Inf., 9 Sept., 1899.
SMITH, GILBERT C., Q. M., 20 Sept., 1899. Capt. 49th U. S. Inf., 9 Sept., 1899.
BLUNT, HAMILTON H., 1st Lieut. 9th U. S. Inf., 19 July, 1898. Mustered out 25 May, 1899. 1st Lieut. 49th U. S. Inf., 9 Sept., 1899. Capt., 7 Nov., 1899.

*First Lieutenants.*

GILMER, DAVID J., 1st Lieut. 3rd N. C. Inf., 23 June, 1898. Capt., 3 Dec., 1898. Mustered out 4 Feb., 1899. 1st Lieut. 49th U. S. Inf., 9 Sept., 1899.
BUTLER, WILLIAM H., 1st Lieut. 7th U. S. Inf., 13 July, 1898. Mustered out 28 Feb., 1899. 1st Lieut. 49th U. S. Inf., 9 Sept., 1899.
JORDAN, LEON H., 1st Lieut. 7th U. S. Inf., 26 July, 1898. Mustered out 28 Feb., 1899. 1st Lieut. 49th U. S. Inf., 9 Sept., 1899.
BUTLER, THOMAS C., 2nd Lieut. 9th U. S. Inf., 24 Oct., 1898. Mustered out 25 May, 1899. 1st Lieut. 49th U. S. Inf., 9 Sept., 1899.
THOMAS, JAMES H., 1st Lieut. 1st Ind. Inf., 28 June, 1898. Mustered out 20 Jan., 1899. 1st Lieut. 49th U. S. Inf., 9 Sept., 1899.
RUSSELL, MACON, 2nd Lieut. 8th U. S. Inf., 29 July, 1898. Mustered out 6 March, 1899. 1st Lieut. 49th U. S. Inf., 9 Sept., 1899.
PRITCHARD, WILLIAM D., 2nd Lieut. 10th U. S. Inf., 10 Jan., 1899. Mustered out 8 March, 1899. 1st Lieut. 49th U. S. Inf., 9 Sept., 1899.
SPURLOCK, CHARLES, 1st Lieut. 49th U. S. Inf., 9 Sept., 1899.
PERRY, CHARLES, 1st Lieut. 49th U. S. Inf., 9 Sept., 1899.
MOLONY, ISAAC W., Priv. Troop H, 1st Ohio Cav., 5 May to 24 Oct., 1898. 1st Lieut. 49th U. S. Inf., 9 Sept., 1899.
TILLMAN, LAFAYETTE A., Priv. and Q. M. Sergt. Co. K, 7th U. S. Inf., 5 July, 1898, to 28 Feb., 1899. 1st Lieut. 49th U. S. Inf., 9 Sept., 1899.
DOBLER, FRED, Com., 9 Sept., 1899. 1st Lieut. 49th U. S. Inf., 9 Sept., 1899.
MADEN, EBBERT W., 1st Lieut. 49th U. S. Inf., 9 Sept., 1899.
BLAKEMAN, ROBERT, Priv. and 1st Sergt. Co. H, 8th Ill. Inf., 21 July, 1898, to 3 April, 1899. 1st Lieut. 49th U. S. Inf., 9 Sept., 1899.
BLANEY, WILLIAM, Priv. and Sergt. 10th U. S. Inf., 1 July to 29 July, 1898. 2nd Lieut. 10th U. S. Inf., 26 July, 1898. Mustered out 8 March, 1899. 2nd Lieut. 49th U. S. Inf., 9 Sept., 1899. 1st Lieut., 7 Nov., 1899.

*Second Lieutenants.*

RAY, ALFRED M., 1st Lieut. 10th U. S. Inf., 2 Aug., 1898. Mustered out 8 March, 1899. 2nd Lieut 49th U. S. Inf., 9 Sept., 1899.
MCBRYAR, WILLIAM, 2nd Lieut. 8th U. S. Inf., 29 July, 1898. 1st Lieut., 7 Sept., 1898. Mustered out 6 March, 1899. 2nd Lieut. 49th U. S. Inf., 9 Sept., 1899.
HUFFMAN, WYATT, 2nd Lieut. 8th U. S. Inf., 29 July, 1898. Mustered out 6 March, 1899. 2nd Lieut. 49th U. S. Inf., 9 Sept., 1899.
PEREA, BEVERLY, 2nd Lieut. 7th U. S. Inf., 16 Sept., 1898. 1st Lieut., 7 Jan., 1899. Mustered out 28 Feb., 1899. 2nd Lieut. 49th U. S. Inf., 9 Sept., 1899.
PAYNE, GEORGE E., 1st Sergt. Co. F, 23 Kans. Inf., 16 July to 14 Dec., 1898. 2nd Lieut. 23 Kans. Inf., 15 Dec., 1898. Mustered out 10 April, 1899. 2nd Lieut. 49th U. S. Inf., 9 Sept., 1899.
GOUGH, ROBERT L., 2nd Lieut. 49th U. S. Inf., 9 Sept., 1899.
HAYES, LEANDER W., Q. M. Sergt. and 1st Sergt. Co. A, 3rd N. C. Inf., 27 April, 1898, to 2 Feb., 1899. 2nd Lieut. 49th U. S. Inf., 9 Sept., 1899.
WHEATON, HORACE F., Priv. Co. L, 6th Mass. Inf., 6 May, 1898, to 21 Jan., 1899. 2nd Lieut. 49th U. S. Inf., 9 Sept., 1899.
WALLS, HENRY F., 1st Lieut. 49th U. S. Inf., 9 Sept., 1899.
CAMPBELL, GUILFORD E., Priv. and Sergt. Co. E, 8th Ill. Inf., 28 June, 1898, to 16 March, 1899. 2nd Lieut. 49th U. S. Inf., 9 Sept., 1899.
DICKERSON, JAMES M., Priv. and Sergt. Maj. 49th U. S. Inf., 12 Oct. to 10 Nov., 1899. 2nd Lieut. 49th U. S. Inf., 10 Nov., 1899.

## PORTO RICO REGIMENT, U. S. VOLUNTEER INFANTRY.

*Lieutenant Colonel.*

BUCHANAN, JAMES A. (Regular), Lieut. Col. Porto Rico Regt. Inf., 19 Feb., 1900.

*Majors.*

SWIFT, EBEN (Regular), Maj. Porto Rico Batt. Inf., 1 Dec., 1899.
ALMY, WILLIAM E. (Regular), Maj. Porto Rico Reg. Inf., 1 March, 1900.

*Assistant Surgeons with rank of Captain.*

LUGO-VINA, JOSE, Capt. and Asst. Surg. Porto Rico Reg. Inf., 1 March, 1900.

*With rank of First Lieutenant.*

MORET, GUSTAVE, 1st Lieut. and Asst. Surg. Porto Rico Reg. Inf., 30 March, 1900.

*Captains.*

MAGINNIS, THOMAS F. (Regular), Capt. Porto Rico Batt. Inf., 13 May, 1899.
LATROBE, OSMAN, Capt. 4th U. S. Inf., 31 May, 1898. Maj., 8 Dec., 1898. Discharged 17 May, 1899. Capt. Porto Rico Batt. Inf., 13 May, 1899.
PAGE, FRED M., Capt. A. A. G., 3 June, 1898. Discharged 12 May, 1899. Capt. Porto Rico Batt. Inf., 13 May, 1899.
RAYMOND, ALLEN D., Capt. 1st U. S. Eng., 7 June, 1898. Mustered out 25 Jan., 1899. 1st Lieut. Porto Rico Batt. Inf., 12 July, 1899. Capt., 7 Dec., 1899.
CARTER, JESSE McI. (Regular), Capt. Porto Rico Reg. Inf., 1 March, 1900.
BRIAND, CHRISTIAN, 1st Lieut. and Q. M. 5th U. S. Inf., 31 May, 1898. Mustered out 31 May, 1899. 1st Lieut. Porto Rico Batt. Inf., 26 June, 1899. Capt. Porto Rico Reg. Inf., 1 March, 1900.
ORD, JAMES T., 1st Lieut. 9th U. S. Inf., 10 Jan., 1899. Discharged 19 May, 1899. 1st Lieut. Porto Rico Batt. Inf., 13 May, 1899. Capt. Porto Rico Reg. Inf., 1 March, 1900.
BUTLER, WILLIAM P., Maj. 1st Ill. Cav., 26 April, 1898. Mustered out 11 Oct., 1898. Capt. Porto Rico Regt. Inf., 1 March, 1900.

*First Lieutenants.*

HAMILTON, CHARLES H., 1st Lieut. and Adj. 3rd U. S. Eng., 22 June, 1898. Mustered out 17 May, 1899. 1st Lieut. Porto Rico Batt. Inf., 20 June, 1899
TOWNSHEND, ORVAL P., Capt. 9th Ill. Inf., 28 June, 1898. Mustered out 20 May, 1899. 1st Lieut. Porto Rico Reg. Inf., 1 March, 1900.
COOPER, HARRY L., 1st Sergt. Co. C, 1st Pa. Inf., 28 April to 4 July, 1898. 2nd Lieut. 1st Pa. Inf., 5 July, 1898. Mustered out 26 Oct., 1898. 2nd Lieut. Porto Rico Batt. Inf., 2 Aug., 1899. 1st Lieut. Porto Rico Reg. Inf., 1 March, 1900.
BENNETT, LOUIS E., Maj. 4th Ill. Inf., 26 April, 1898. Mustered out 2 May, 1899. 1st Lieut. Porto Rico Reg. Inf., 1 March, 1900.
BESSELL, WILLIAM W., 2nd Lieut. Porto Rico Batt. Inf., 3 Nov., 1899. 1st Lieut. Porto Rico Reg. Inf., 1 March, 1900.
WYKE, JACOB E., 2nd Lieut. Porto Rico Batt. Inf., 28 Nov., 1899. 1st Lieut. Porto Rico Reg. Inf., 1 March, 1900.
SEAMAN, A. OWEN, 1st Sergt. Co. K, 4th Ill. Inf., 19 May, 1898, to 15 Feb., 1899. 2nd Lieut. 4th Ill. Inf., 16 Feb., 1899. 1st Lieut., 14 March, 1899. Mustered out 2 May, 1899. 1st Lieut. Porto Rico Reg. Inf., 1 March, 1900.
STEGER, JOHN O., 1st Lieut. Porto Rico Reg. Inf., 1 March, 1900.
LOCKE, MORRIS E., 1st Lieut. Porto Rico Reg. Inf., 1 March, 1900.
BALLARD, WILLIAM W., Jr., 1st Lieut. Porto Rico Reg. Inf., 1 March, 1900.

*Second Lieutenants.*

NADAL, BLAS, Priv. and Sergt. Co. A, Porto Rico Batt. Inf., 3 April to 13 Aug., 1899. 2nd Lieut. Porto Rico Batt. Inf., 14 Aug., 1899.
MARTIN, WALTER F., Priv. Batty A, Mo. Light Art., 14 June to 21 July, 1898. 2nd Lieut. 6th Mo. Inf., 28 July, 1898. 1st Lieut., 14 March, 1899. Mustered out 10 May, 1899. 2nd Lieut. Porto Rico Reg. Inf., 1 March, 1900.
SWIFT, EBEN, Jr., 2nd Lieut. 7th Ill. Inf., 18 May, 1898. Mustered out 20 Oct., 1898. 2nd Lieut. Porto Rico Reg. Inf., 1 March, 1900.
KERNEY, CHARLES B., Sergt. Batty A, Mo. Art., 26 April to 30 Nov., 1898. 2nd Lieut. Porto Rico Reg. Inf., 1 March, 1900.
WUTTKE, PAUL, Priv. and 1st Sergt. Co. A, Porto Rico Batt. Inf., 17 May, 1899, to 23 March, 1900. 2nd Lieut. Porto Rico Reg. Inf., 1 March, 1900.
HAWES, FREDERICK W., Priv. Troop M, 1st U. S. Cav., 8 July to 15 Sept., 1898. 2nd Lieut. Porto Rico Reg. Inf., 1 March, 1900.
HAMILL, TERENCE, 2nd Lieut. Porto Rico Reg. Inf., 1 March, 1900.
OAKES, JEAN S., Corpl. and Sergt. Co. F, 201st N. Y. Inf., 18 July, 1898, to 26 Feb., 1899. 2nd Lieut. Porto Rico Reg. Inf., 1 March, 1900.

NOTE.—Two battalions of Porto Rico troops were organized under authority given March 10, 1899, and February 9, 1900, respectively, the first being designated "The Porto Rico Battation." Upon the organization of the second battalion, the two battalions were designated "Porto Rico Regiment, U. S. Volunteer Infantry."

## SQUADRON PHILIPPINE CAVALRY.

*Majors.*

BATSON, MATTHEW A. (Regular), Maj. Sq. Philippine Cav., 3 April, 1900.

*Assistant Surgeon with rank of Captain.*

SIMPSON, MAXWELL S., Capt. Asst. Surg. Sq. Philippine Cav., 3 April, 1900.

*Captains.*

CASTNER, JOSEPH C. (Regular), Capt. Sq. Philippine Cav., 3 April, 1900.
GEIGER, WILLIAM C. (Regular), Capt. Sq. Philippine Cav., 3 April, 1900.
MUNRO, JAMES N. (Regular), Capt. Sq. Philippine Cav., 3 April, 1900.
CAMERON, FRANCIS H., Jr., Capt. 10th U. S. Inf., 20 Aug., 1898. Mustered out 8 March, 1899. 1st Lieut. 35th U. S. Inf., 5 July, 1899. Vacated 26 April, 1900. Capt. Sq. Philippine Cav., 3 April, 1900.

*First Lieutenants.*

BIDDLE, DAVID H., 2nd Lieut. 36th U. S. Inf., 5 July, 1899. Vacated 30 April, 1900. 1st Lieut. Sq. Philippine Cav., 3 April, 1900.
QUINLAN, DENNIS P., Priv. and Sergt. Maj., 11th U. S. Cav., 22 Aug. to 5 Sept., 1899. 2nd Lieut. 11th U. S. Cav., 12 Aug., 1899. Vacated 24 April, 1900. 1st Lieut. Sq. Philippine Cav., 3 April, 1900.
CONWAY, JAMES, 1st Lieut. Sq. Philippine Cav., 3 April, 1900.
CULVER, CLARENCE C., 1st Lieut. Sq. Philippine Cav., 3 April, 1900.

## CASUALTIES IN THE VOLUNTEER FORCE.

*Appointments declined* (119).

Adams, Henry H., Jr., of New York, First Lieutenant, Forty-second Infantry, September 1, 1899.
Archibald, Samuel S., of Virginia, Second Lieutenant, Tewnty-seventh Infantry, July 19, 1899.
Armfield, Joseph F., of North Carolina, Major, Forty-sixth Infantry, August 26, 1899.
Austin, Elmore T., of New York, Captain, Forty-second Infantry, August 23, 1899.
Ayres, Charles G., Captain, Tenth U. S. Cavalry, Major, Twenty-ninth Infantry, July 12, 1899.
Barrows, Cornelius, of Rhode Island, First Lieutenant, Forty-eighth Infantry, September 19, 1899.
Barthman, Henry C., of New York, Captain, Forty-fourth Infantry, September 1, 1899.
Beck, Howard L., of New York, First Lieutenant, Forty-sixth Infantry, September 2, 1899.
Bell, J. Franklin, Captain, Seventh U. S. Cavalry, Lieutenant-Colonel, Thirty-second Infantry, July 11, 1899.
Bell, John A., of West Virginia, First Lieutenant, Forty-eighth Infantry, October 25, 1899.
Bigelow, John, Jr., Captain, Tenth U. S. Cavalry, Lieutenant-Colonel, Forty-seventh Infantry, August 18, 1899.
Black, Allen, of Virginia, First Lieutenant, Assistant Surgeon, Twenty-eighth Infantry, July 12, 1899.
Blocksom, Augustus P., Captain, Sixth U. S. Cavalry, Major, Twenty-seventh Infantry, July 11, 1899.
Bossieux, Cyrus G., of Virginia, First Lieutenant, Twenty-eighth Infantry, July 27, 1899.
Bowen, Ellsworth G., of Illinois, First Lieutenant, Thirtieth Infantry, July 13, 1899.
Boyd, John E., of South Carolina, First Lieutenant, Assistant Surgeon, Twenty-sixth Infantry, July 11, 1899.
Bradbury, Arthur W., of California, First Lieutenant, Thirty-fifth Infantry.

Brooks, Edward C., First Lieutenant, Sixth U. S. Cavalry, Major, Forty-sixth Infantry, September 18, 1899.
Broussard, Edwin S., of Louisiana, Second Lieutenant, Thirty-third Infantry, July 17, 1899.
Brumm, Fred E., of Idaho, Captain, Forty-fourth Infantry, October 5, 1899.
Butler, Charles L., of South Dakota, Second Lieutenant, Forty-third Infantry, September 8, 1899.
Butler, Mighetto B., of New York, Captain Forty-sixth Infantry, August 30, 1899.
Case, James F., of Oregon, First Lieutenant, Forty-fifth Infantry, August 28, 1899.
Chapin, Frank M., of New York, First Lieutenant, Twenty-sixth Infantry, August 26, 1899.
Chapin, William H., of New York, Captain, Forty-fourth Infantry, September 11, 1899.
Clark, Winslow, of Massachusetts, Second Lieutenant, Eleventh Cavalry, August 23, 1899.
Clarke, Walton W., of Georgia, Second Lieutenant, Thirty-third Infantry, July 22, 1899.
Coffin, William H., Captain, Fifth U. S. Artillery, Major, Twenty-sixth Infantry, July 11, 1899.
Colt, Alonzo B., of Ohio, Captain, Forty-second Infantry, September 26, 1899.
Coward, Jacob M., of New Jersey, Captain, Forty-seventh Infantry, September 11, 1899.
Cowley, Frederic W., of Michigan, First Lieutenant, Thirty-eighth Infantry, August 28, 1899.
Coxe, William L., of Nevada, Captain, Forty-fourth Infantry, September 20, 1899.
Croft, James M., of Montana, Captain, Thirty-seventh Infantry, August 3, 1899.
Croscup, Homer C., of New York, First Lieutenant, Forty-second Infantry, September 4, 1899.
Davis, Charles E., of Maine, Captain, Twenty-sixth Infantry, July 20, 1899.
Davis, Willis C., of Georgia, First Lieutenant, Twenty-ninth Infantry, July 16, 1899.
Dows, William G., of Iowa, Major, Forty-fifth Infantry, August 28, 1899.
Duboce, Victor D., of California, Major, Forty-fourth Infantry, September 13, 1899.
Dyer, Alexander B., Captain, Sixth U. S. Artillery, Major, Thirty-second Infantry, August 3, 1899.
Egell, Henry L., of Washington, Captain, Eleventh Cavalry, August 24, 1899.
Elliott, Charles D., of West Virginia, Major, Forty-seventh Infantry, September 12, 1899.
Everett, Vernon L., of Kansas, First Lieutenant, Fortieth Infantry, August 23, 1899.
Ewing, Alec. A., of Pennsylvania, Second Lieutenant, Forty-first Infantry, September 12, 1899.
Feland, Logan, of Kentucky, First Lieutenant, Thirty-first Infantry, July 14, 1899.
Ferguson, Ursil A., of New York, Second Lieutenant, Twenty-sixth Infantry, July 16, 1899.
Fisher, Lee D., of Missouri, Second Lieutenant, Thirty-second Infantry, August 11, 1899.
Forbes, Edwin A., of California, Captain, Thirty-eighth Infantry, September 14, 1899.
Foreman, Milton J., of Illinois, Captain, Thirtieth Infantry, July 15, 1899.
Frost, Alfred S., Captain, Twenty-second U. S. Infantry, Major, Thirty-ninth Infantry, October 23, 1899.
Gaither, Charles D., of Maryland, Captain, Twenty-seventh Infantry, August 14, 1899.
Gihon, Edward J., of Massachusetts, Captain, Twenty-sixth Infantry, July 27, 1899.
Grant, Charles S., of Iowa, Captain, Assistant Surgeon, Forty-ninth Infantry, September 14, 1899.
Graham, Frank O., of Pennsylvania, Second Lieutenant, Twenty-eighth Infantry, July 18, 1899.
Granger, Ross P., of Michigan, First Lieutenant, Thirtieth Infantry, July 28, 1899.
Graves, Benjamin A., of Virginia, Captain, Forty-ninth Infantry, September 14, 1899.
Griffin, William E., of New Mexico, Second Lieutenant, Eleventh Cavalry, August 22, 1899.
Griffith, Lewie A., of South Carolina, First Lieutenant, Fortieth Infantry, August 24, 1899.
Hager, James F., of Tennessee, Captain, Eleventh Cavalry, August 24, 1899.
Hake, Charles F., Jr., of Ohio, Captain, Forty-fourth Infantry September 14, 1899.
Hamilton, Louis McL., of New York, First Lieutenant, Forty-first Infantry, October 24, 1899.
Hepburn, James H., of Pennsylvania, Captain, Assistant Surgeon, Twenty-seventh Infantry, July 11, 1899.
Howard, Charles A., of South Dakota, Captain, Forty-first Infantry, September 28, 1899.
Howland, Eben W., of Wisconsin, First Lieutenant, Forty-fifth Infantry, September 10, 1899.
Hume, Frank M., of Maine, Captain, Twenty-sixth Infantry, July 26, 1899.
Humphrey, William B., of Iowa, Captain, Thirty-ninth Infantry, August 26, 1899.
Kalmback, William B., of Michigan, Captain, Thirty-ninth Infantry, August 26, 1899.
Kennedy, James S., of Pennsylvania, First Lieutenant, Assistant Surgeon, Thirty-third Infantry, July, 18, 1899.
Kennedy, Samuel W., of Ohio, Captain, Thirty-first Infantry, July 19, 1899.
Kennett, Alfred Q., of Missouri, Captain, Thirty-second Infantry, July 13, 1899.
Kirkland, Charles P., of Connecticut, First Lieutenant, Forty-eighth Infantry, September 19, 1899.
Laird, Richard D., of Pennsylvania, First Lieutenant, Twenty-eighth Infantry, August 18, 1899.
Leepere, Matthew, of Texas, First Lieutenant, Assistant Surgeon, Thirty-third Infantry, July 14, 1899.
Lehman, Herman, Sergeant, Fourth U. S. Cavalry, First Lieutenant, Eleventh Cavalry, August 24, 1899.
Logan, Guy E., of Iowa, Captain, Eleventh Cavalry, August 18, 1899.
Manning, Guy E., of Ohio, First Lieutenant, Thirty-first Infantry, July 16, 1899.
Marden, Walter A., of Wisconsin, Captain, Forty-fifth Infantry, September 18, 1899.
McCaughrin, Silas J., of South Carolina, First Lieutenant, Thirty-eighth Infantry, August 23, 1899.
McKittrick, William H., of California, Captain, Forty-sixth Infantry, October 11, 1899.
McClelland, Paul D. M., of South Dakota, First Lieutenant, Thirty-ninth Infantry, October 19, 1899.
Menzies, Winston, of Indiana, First Lieutenant, Thirty-ninth Infantry, September 2, 1899.
Michler, Francis, Captain, Fifth U. S. Cavalry, Lieutenant Colonel, Forty-sixth Infantry, August 19, 1899.

Mobley, Fred, of South Carolina, First Lieutenant, Thirty-ninth Infantry, September 2, 1899.
Myer, Albert J., of New York City, Captain, Forty-third Infantry, August 31, 1899.
Neill, Hugh, of Arkansas, Second Lieutenant, Thirty-sixth Infantry, July 28, 1899.
Nurzy, Walter F., of New York, First Lieutenant, Forty-first Infantry, September 7, 1899.
O'Leary, Arthur, of Montana, First Lieutenant, Thirty-seventh Infantry, August 1, 1899.
Packard, Philo F., of Massachusetts, First Lieutenant, Forty-sixth Infantry, September 11, 1899.
Parker, Roy S., of Iowa, First Lieutenant, Forty-fourth Infantry, October 30, 1899.
Parker, William E., of Louisiana, Captain, Assistant Surgeon, Thirty-third Infantry, July 11, 1899.
Parks, John H., of Iowa, Second Lieutenant, Thirty-ninth Infantry, September 5, 1899.
Peabody, Jacob C. R., of Massachusetts, Captain, Twenty-sixth Infantry, July, 20, 1899.
Porter, Daniel P., Jr., of Mississippi, Captain, Thirty-eighth Infantry, August 31, 1899.
Pulver, Theodore S., of New York, First Lieutenant, Twenty-seventh Infantry, July 17, 1899.
Robinson, Charles H., of Virginia, First Lieutenant, Forty-ninth Infantry, September 14, 1899.
Rogers, Arthur C., of Ohio, Captain, Forty-seventh Infantry, August 24, 1899.
Sague, John K., of New York, Captain, Forty-seventh Infantry, August 30, 1899.
Shallenberger, James M., of Ohio, First Lieutenant, Forty-seventh Infantry, August 23, 1899.
Smith, Emery T., Sergeant, Fourteenth U. S. Infantry, Second Lieutenant, Thirty-sixth Infantry, July 28, 1899.
Smith, Lauran F., of Maryland, Captain, Forty-eighth Infantry, October 4, 1899.
Stearns, Daniel A., of Wisconsin, Captain, Thirty-ninth Infantry, September 11, 1899.
Stevens, Charles J., Captain, Second U. S. Cavalry, Major, Thirty-ninth Infantry, October 10, 1899.
Strong, Putnam B., of New York, Major, Forty-second Infantry, September 4, 1899.
Styer, Louis S., of Washington, First Lieutenant, Eleventh Cavalry, August 26 1899.
Turley, Linn, of Arkansas, First Lieutenant, Thirty-ninth Infantry, August 29, 1899.
Wagner, John A., of North Carolina, First Lieutenant, Twenty-ninth Infantry, July 16, 1899.
Ward, Francis G., of New York, Major, Thirty-third Infantry, July 25, 1899.
Webb, Pleasant, of Virginia, Captain, Forty-eighth Infantry, September 14, 1899.
Weber, Ernest O., of Nebraska, First Lieutenant, Fortieth Infantry, September 12, 1899.
Weisenburger, John J., of Washington, Lieutenant Colonel, Eleventh Cavalry, August 24, 1899.
Welch, Frank B. W., of Maine, First Lieutenant, Forty-seventh Infantry, August 31, 1899.
Whitthorne, William J., of Tennessee, Captain, Fortieth Infantry, December 2, 1899.
Wild, Thaddeus, of Wisconsin, First Lieutenant, Thirty-fourth Infantry, July 22, 1899.
Wiley, Ariosto A., of Alabama, Major, Forty-first Infantry, September 22, 1899.
Willrich, George, of Texas, First Lieutenant, Thirty-third Infantry, July 24, 1899.
Wilson, Frederic C., of Massachusetts, Second Lieutenant, Forty-ninth Infantry, September 22, 1899.
Wilson, Melville A., of Florida, Second Lieutenant, Thirty-third Infantry, August 15, 1899.
Wolcott, Henry, of Rhode Island, Captain, Forty-sixth Infantry, August 22, 1899.
Wood, Charles S., of Pennsylvania, Captain, Twenty-eighth Infantry, July, 22, 1899.
Woodruff, Fred E., of Iowa, Second Lieutenant, Thirty-ninth Infantry, November 10, 1899.

*Commissions vacated by new appointment* (25).

Barry, Thomas H., Lieutenant Colonel, Assistant Adjutant General, U. S. Army, his commission as Lieutenant Colonel Assistant Adjutant General, U. S. Volunteers, January, 10, 1900.
Bates, John C., Major General, his commission as Brigadier General, January 10, 1900.
Bell, J. Franklin, Brigadier General, his commission as Colonel Thirty-sixth Infantry, December 24, 1899.
Bell, James M., Brigadier General, his commission as Colonel Twenty-seventh Infantry, February 4, 1900.
Brainard, David L., Major, Commissary of Subsistence, U. S. Army, his commission as Major, Chief Commissary of Subsistence Volunteers, February 12, 1900.
Brooke, William, Major, Forty-sixth Infantry, his commission as Captain, Thirty-fifth Infantry, September 22, 1900.
Carey, Edward C., Major, Forty-second Infantry, his commission as Captain, Thirty-fourth Infantry, September 23, 1899.
Duvall, William P., Colonel, Forty-eighth Infantry, his commission as Lieutenant Colonel, Twenty-sixth Infantry, September 13, 1899.
Erickson, Albert J., Captain, Thirty-seventh Infantry, his commission as First Lieutenant, Thirty-sixth Infantry, August 5, 1899.
Heyl, Charles H., Lieutenant Colonel, Inspector General, U. S. Army, his commission as Lieutenant Colonel, Inspector General, U. S. Volunteers, December 19, 1899.
Kobbe, William A., Brigadier General, his commission as Colonel Thirty-fifth Infantry, December 16, 1899.
Landstreet, John, Jr., his commission as Captain, Assistant Quartermaster, September 18, 1899.
Langhorne, George T., Major, Thirty-ninth Infantry, his commission as Captain, Twenty-seventh Infantry, November 2, 1899.
Ludlow, William, Brigadier General, U. S. Army, his commission as Brigadier General, U. S. Volunteers, January 29, 1900.
Newbold, Charles, Major, Paymaster, U. S. Army, his commission as Major, Additional Paymaster, U. S. Volunteers, July 24, 1899.
Ruhlen, George, Major, Quartermaster, U. S. Army, his commission as Major, Quartermaster, U. S. Volunteers, January 6, 1900.

Sewell, Robert, Captain, Forty-first Infantry, his commission as Captain, Assistant Adjutant General, August 24, 1899.
Sewell, Robert, Captain, Assistant Quartermaster, U. S. Army, his commission as Captain, Forty-first Infantry, September 1, 1899.
Shipton, James A., Major, Forty-seventh Infantry, his commission as Captain, Forty-first Infantry, November 2, 1899.
Swift, Eugene L., Major, Surgeon, his commission as Major, Surgeon Thirty-fifth Infantry, February 14, 1900.
Thompson, Richard E., Major, Signal Corps, U. S. Army, his commission as Major, Signal Officer, U. S. Volunteers, December 1, 1899.
Wallace, Hamilton S., Major, Paymaster, U. S. Army, his commission as Major, Additional Paymaster, U. S. Volunteers, September 12, 1899.
Williamson, George McK., Captain, Assistant Quartermaster, U. S. Army, his commission as Captain, Assistant Quartermaster, U. S. Volunteers, July 23, 1899.
Wood, Leonard, Major General, his commission as Brigadier General, December 13, 1899.
Young, Samuel B. M., Brigadier General, U. S. Army, his commission as Brigadier General, U. S. Volunteers, January 10, 1900.

*Killed in action* (6).

Davis, Julian L., Second Lieutenant, Thirty-sixth Infantry, November 11, 1899, near Bamban, P. I.
Evens, John H., First Lieutenant, Forty-third Infantry, May 11, 1900, near Matagiano, Samar, P. I.
Howard, Guy, Major, Chief Quartermaster, October 22, 1899, at Rio Grande River, P. I.
Lawton, Henry W., Major General, December 19, 1899, at San Mateo, Luzon, P. I.
Logan, John A., Major Thirty-third Infantry, November 12, 1899, near San Jacinto, P. I.
Tilley, George H., Captain, Signal Officer, May 27, 1899, at Escalante, Negros, P. I.

*Died from wounds received in action* (2).

French, Charles, Captain, Thirty-sixth Infantry, October 31, 1899, near Florida, Blanco, P. I.
Galleher, John B., First Lieutenant, Fortieth Infantry, February 23, 1900, at Libmanan, Nueva Caceres, P. I.

*Died* (17).

Armstrong, Frank C., Major, Surgeon, Thirty-second Infantry, December 4, 1899, at Manila, P. I.
Brereton, John J., Lieutenant Colonel, Thirty-third Infantry, December 2, 1899, at Santo Thomas, Luzon, P. I.
Bowman, Daniel T., First Lieutenant, Thirty-seventh Infantry, January 9, 1900, at Los Banos, P. I.
Clendenin, Paul, Major, Brigade Surgeon, July 4, 1899, at Santiago, Cuba.
Heatwole, Joseph H., Major, Chief Commissary of Subsistence, July 6, 1899, at Santiago, Cuba.
Jackson, George L., Second Lieutenant, Forty-seventh Infantry, May 21, 1900, at Manila, P. I.
Langworthy, Samuel R., Captain, Thirty-fifth Infantry, February 21, 1900, at Balinag, Bulucan, P. I.
Luna, Maximiliano, First Lieutenant, Thirty-fourth Infantry, November 18, 1899, near San Nicholas, P. I.
McLaughlin, James B., Second Lieutenant, Signal Officer, July 6, 1899, at Santiago, Cuba.
McNabb, Lewis W., Captain, Forty-ninth Infantry, November 7, 1899, at Jefferson Barracks, Mo.
Miley, John D., Lieutenant Colonel, Inspector General, September 19, 1899, at Manila, P. I.
Toncray, James P., First Lieutenant, Thirty-sixth Infantry, February 7, 1900, at Manila, P. I.
Wallace, Robert B., Colonel Thirty-seventh Infantry, March 13, 1900, at Fort Huachuca, A. T.
Waugh, John R., Second Lieutenant, Thirty-ninth Infantry, February 27, 1900, at Calamba, Luzon, P. I.
Weber, Louis P., Second Lieutenant, Forty-second Infantry, March 9, 1900, at ——, P. I.
White, Grant A., First Lieutenant, Thirty-third Infantry, April 10, 1900, at Augaki, P. I.
Wing, Eugene G., Second Lieutenant, Thirty-sixth Infantry, January 24, 1900, at Manila, P. I.

*Honorably discharged* (423).

Adams, James B., Captain, Thirty-first Infantry, August 30, 1899.
Allen, James, Colonel, Signal Officer, May 12, 1899.
Allison, Charles J., Major, Engineer Officer, April 1, 1899.
Allison, James N., Lieutenant Colonel, Chief Commissary of Subsistence, April 12, 1899.
Allison, William B., Jr., Captain Assistant Adjutant General, May 12, 1899.
Almy, William E., Major, Assistant Adjutant General, April 5, 1899.
Ames, Azel, Major, Brigade Surgeon, June 30, 1899.
Anderson, Davis C., Second Lieutenant, Fortieth Infantry, February 3, 1900.
Anderson, Lomax S., First Lieutenant, Assistant Surgeon, Twenty-ninth Infantry, August 14, 1899.
Anderson, James P., Second Lieutenant, Signal Officer, May 12, 1899.
Anderson, Thomas M., Major General, June 12, 1899.
Anderson, William H., Captain, Assistant Commissary of Subsistence, November 15, 1899.
Archinard, John J., Major, Brigade Surgeon, March 22, 1899.
Arnold, Abraham K., Brigadier General, May 12, 1899.
Arrasmith, James M., Major, Chief Commissary of Subsistence, June, 13, 1899.

Arrick, Clifford, Major, Additional Paymaster, May 13, 1899.
Avery, Joseph W., Second Lieutenant, Twenty-ninth Infantry, August 29, 1899.
Babcock, Sherrill, Captain, Assistant Adjutant General, March 7, 1899.
Bach, Edmund W., Major, Chief Commissary of Subsistence, April 12, 1899.
Bailey, Frank H., First Lieutenant, Signal Officer, October 31, 1899.
Baird, Samuel, Captain, Assistant Quartermaster, April 2, 1899.
Baker, George L., Jr., Captain, Forty-first Infantry, May 31, 1900.
Baldridge, James C., Captain, Commissary of Subsistence, June 5, 1899.
Baldwin, Frank D., Lieutenant Colonel, Inspector General, May 12, 1899.
Baldwin, Henry C., Second Lieutenant, Signal Officer, May 12, 1899.
Baldwin, Wm. H., Lieutenant Colonel, Chief Commissary of Subsistence, March, 7, 1899.
Ballard, Charles L., Second Lieutenant, Eleventh Cavalry, May 10, 1900.
Barrett, Edwin F., Captain, Assistant Quartermaster, April 12, 1899.
Bartlett, George T., Major, Chief Commissary of Subsistence, June 13, 1899.
Bawsel, Edward E., Second Lieutenant, Signal Officer, April 12, 1899.
Beckham, Robert H., Captain, Commissary of Subsistence, May 12, 1899.
Belford, Samuel W., Captain, Thirty-third Infantry, September 13, 1899.
Bell, Joseph L., First Lieutenant, Assistant Surgeon, Thirty-fourth Infantry, February 5, 1900.
Bement, Robert B. C., Major, Engineer Officer, March 20, 1899.
Benham, Henry H., Major, Chief Ordnance Officer, May 3, 1899.
Benson, Harry C., Major, Inspector General, May 12, 1899.
Berry, Lucien G., Captain, Assistant Adjutant General, May 31, 1899.
Biddle, John, Lieutenant Colonel, Chief Engineer Officer, May 12, 1899.
Bigelow, Edward A., Major, Additional Paymaster, May 13, 1899.
Bird, Charles, Colonel, Quartermaster, May 13, 1899.
Birnie, Rogers, Lieutenant Colonel, Chief Ordnance Officer, April 10, 1899.
Bishop, Harry L., Captain, Forty-first Infantry, November 18, 1899.
Black, John D., Major, Chief Commissary of Subsistence, May 12, 1899.
Black, William J., Major, Additional Paymaster, March 7, 1899.
Black, William M., Lieutenant Colonel, Chief Engineer Officer, June 13, 1899.
Bliss, Tasker H., Lieutenant Colonel, Chief Commissary of Subsistence, June 13, 1899.
Bloom, Jacob E., Captain, Assistant Adjutant General, May 12, 1899.
Borden, William C., Major, Brigade Surgeon, March 31, 1899.
Borup, Henry D., Lieutenant Colonel, Chief Ordnance Officer, March 16, 1899.
Bourns, Frank S., Major, Brigade Surgeon, September 30, 1899.
Boynton, Henry V., Brigadier General, April 12, 1899.
Bradley, Alfred E., Major, Brigade Surgeon, November 10, 1899.
Bradley, Thomas G., First Lieutenant, Twenty-seventh Infantry, September 12, 1899.
Brady, Jasper E., Jr., Captain, Signal Officer, March 2, 1899.
Brewster, Andre W., Captain, Assistant Quartermaster, May 12, 1899.
Brice, Stewart M., Captain, Commissary of Subsistence, March 11, 1899.
Bridgman, Samuel N., Captain, Commissary of Subsistence, May 12, 1899.
Bristol, George W., Captain, Forty-seventh Infantry, November 9, 1899.
Brookes, Albert S., Captain, Commissary of Subsistence, March 7, 1899.
Brown, Alfred V., First Lieutenant, Forty-fourth Infantry, November 29, 1899.
Brown, Harrison B., First Lieutenant, Forty-eighth Infantry, December 13, 1899.
Bryant, William S., Major, Brigade Surgeon, May 12, 1899.
Bunn, George B., Major, Brigade Surgeon, May 12, 1899.
Butler, Edwin R., Captain, Assistant Quartermaster, January 1, 1900.
Butler, Matthew C., Jr., Major, Chief Ordnance Officer, May 12, 1899.
Butler, Matthew C., Major General, April 15, 1899.
Byrne, John J., Second Lieutenant, Twenty-sixth Infantry, September 23, 1899.
Cabell, Julian M., Major, Brigade Surgeon, October 1, 1899.
Calhoun, James E., Captain, Commissary of Subsistence, April 24, 1899.
Campbell, James A., Captain, Assistant Quartermaster, May 12, 1899.
Carpenter, Gilbert S., Brigadier General, June 12, 1899.
Carpenter, Louis H., Brigadier General June 12, 1899.
Caziarc, Louis V., Major, Assistant Adjutant General, May 12, 1899.
Cecil, George R., Lieutenant Colonel, Assistant Adjutant General, June 13, 1899.
Chamberlain, John L., Major, Chief Ordnance Officer, April 12, 1899.
Chance, William W., Captain, Signal Officer, July 13, 1899.
Chandler, Charles De F., First Lieutenant, Signal Officer, April 26, 1899.
Cheever, Benjamin H., Major, Inspector General, April 7, 1899.
Clark, Winfield M., Major, Additional Paymaster, May 13, 1899.
Clarke, John B., Captain, Commissary of Subsistence, May 31, 1899.
Clayton, Frederick A., Captain, Forty-eighth Infantry, April 30, 1900.
Cleland, Jonas M., Major, Additional Paymaster, May 13, 1899.
Cloman, Sydney A., Captain, Assistant Quartermaster, September 7, 1899.
Clous, John W., Brigadier General, March 24, 1899.
Cocke, Joe B., Second Lieutenant, Thirty-seventh Infantry, November 28, 1899.
Coiner, Beverly W., Major, Additional Paymaster, May 13, 1899.
Cole Frederick W., Captain, Assistant Quartermaster, June 21, 1899.
Cole, Nelson, Brigadier General, March 8, 1899.
Colvin, James A., Captain, Assistant Adjutant General, April 12, 1899.
Comba, Richard, Brigadier General, April 15, 1899.
Conrad, Holmes, Jr., Second Lieutenant, Twenty-ninth Infantry, September 18, 1899.
Cosby, Arthur F., Captain, Assistant Adjutant General, April 7, 1899.
Coudert, C. Dupont, Captain, Assistant Commissary of Subsistence, November 25, 1899
Cowden, William J., Major, Additional Pawmaster, March 7, 1899.
Cowin, William B., Captain, Commissary of Subsistence, May 12, 1899.
Cummings, Thomas A., Major, Additional Paymaster, May 13, 1899.
Daggett, Byron B., Second Lieutenant, Signal Officer, June, 2, 1899.
Dallam, Philip, Major, Additional Paymaster, June 13, 1899.
Darnell, Carl, Second Lieutenant, Signal Officer, June 12, 1899.

Davenny, Wilson I., Captain, Commissary of Subsistence, March 28, 1899.
Davenport, William T., Second Lieutenant, Signal Officer, June 20, 1899.
Davis, Edward, Major, Assistant Adjutant General, April 15, 1899.
Davis, John M. K., Major, Inspector General, March 7, 1899.
Davison, Lorenzo P., Major, Porto Rico Battalion of Infantry, December 1, 1899.
Dean, James T., Major, Chief Ordnance Officer, May 12, 1899.
de la Calle, Ezequiel, Major, Brigade Surgeon, June 30, 1899.
Demeritt, John, Major, Additional Paymaster, April 7, 1899.
Derby, George McC., Lieutenant Colonel, Chief Engineer Officer, May 12, 1899.
De Shon, George D., Major, Surgeon, Eleventh Cavalry, March 14, 1899.
Devine, Patrick H., Second Lieutenant, Forty-seventh Infantry, June 1, 1900.
Dillion, Lewis W., Second Lieutenant, Thirty-ninth Infantry, April 15, 1900.
Dillon, Albert J., Second Lieutenant, Twenty-ninth Infantry, September 18, 1899.
D'Isay, Isaac, Captain, Commissary of Subsistence, May 12, 1899.
Dodge, Don A., Captain, Commissary of Subsistence, April 12, 1899.
Dolz, William, Major, Brigade Surgeon, April 5, 1899.
Donaldson, Frank, First Lieutenant, Assistant Surgeon, Forty-fifth Infantry, October 17, 1899.
Douglas, Henry T., Brigadier General, May 12, 1899.
Doyon, Moses R., Major, Additional Paymaster, June 13, 1899.
Dravo, Edward E., Lieutenant Colonel, Chief Commissary of Subsistence, March 7, 1899.
Du Barry, Joseph N., Jr., Captain, Commissary of Subsistence, April 12, 1899.
Dunn, William F., Captain, Commissary of Subsistence, April 12, 1899.
Dutton, Salmon F., Captain, Commissary of Subsistence, June 19, 1899.
Dwight, William B., Major, Additional Paymaster, May 27, 1899.
Edgerly, Winfield S., Lieutenant Colonel, Inspector General, April 12, 1899.
Edmunds, Frank H., Major, Chief Ordnance Officer, May 12, 1899.
Edson, John J., Jr., Major, Additional Paymaster, March 7, 1899.
Egan, Peter R., Major, Brigade Surgeon, March 22, 1899.
Ernst, Oswald H., Brigadier General, June 12, 1899.
Evans, John G., Major, Inspector General, June 13, 1899.
Evans, Joseph F., Captain, Assistant Commissary of Subsistence, September 2, 1899.
Ewers, Ezra P., Brigadier General, April 20, 1899.
Falk, Otto H., Major, Chief Quartermaster, June 20, 1899.
Fay, George H., Major, Additional Paymaster, June 13, 1899.
Fenton, Charles W., Captain, Assistant Adjutant General, May 12, 1899.
Fishback, George W., Major, Additional Paymaster, February 15, 1900.
Fitzgerald, Henry C., Major, Additional Paymaster, June 30, 1899.
Fitzhugh, Robert H., Major, Chief Commissary of Subsistence, October 31, 1899.
Fogler, John W., Major, Additional Paymaster, June 30, 1899.
Foote, Newton J., Major, Additional Paymaster, March 7, 1899.
Ford, Francis C., Major, Brigade Surgeon, May 12, 1899.
Forrest, Charles M., Captain, Assistant Quartermaster, May 12, 1899.
Forsyth, Lewis H., First Lieutenant, Forty-third Infantry, October 26, 1899.
Frank, Royal T., Brigadier General, May 12, 1899.
Gandy, Charles M., Major, Chief Surgeon, March 22, 1899.
Garnett, Evylyn S., Major, Chief Commissary of Subsistence, March 7, 1899.
Geishbush, Charles J., First Lieutenant, Thirty-fourth Infantry, August 2, 1899.
Gilmore, John C., Brigadier General, June, 12, 1899.
Gilmore, Tiffin, Captain, Forty-third Infantry, November 8, 1899.
Girard, Alfred C., Lieutenant Colonel, Chief Surgeon, April 12, 1899.
Goff, Charles J., Captain, Assistant Quartermaster, May 31, 1899.
Golden, Charles E., Captain, Commissary of Subsistence, May 12, 1899.
Gonzales, Ambrose E., Captain, Assistant Quartermaster, May 12, 1899.
Gordon, Frank, First Lieutenant, Forty-third Infantry, November 30, 1899.
Gordon, Hugh H., Major, Engineer Officer, April 30, 1899.
Gordon, William W., Brigadier General, March 24, 1899.
Grant, James C., Captain, Commissary of Subsistence, April 12, 1899.
Grant, Hiram L., Major, Additional Paymaster, June 13, 1899.
Gregg, David McM., Second Lieutenant, Twenty-seventh Infantry, August 12, 1899.
Grierson, Charles H., Lieutenant Colonel, Chief Commissary of Subsistence, March 17, 1899.
Griscom, Lloyd C., Captain, Assistant Quartermaster, April 20, 1899.
Groff, George S., Major, Brigade Surgeon, June 30, 1899.
Guessaz, Oscar C., Captain, Assistant Quartermaster, May 31, 1899.
Guild, George B., Major, Additional Paymaster, June 13, 1899.
Guthrie, Orlando F., Captain, Forty-fourth Infantry, November 30, 1899.
Gyger, George R., Captain, Signal Officer, June 30, 1899.
Haisch, John J., First Lieutenant, Thirty-sixth Infantry, May 25, 1900.
Hale, Irving, Brigadier General, October 1, 1899.
Hale, William B., Captain, Commissary of Subsistence, June 5, 1899.
Hamilton, Harry W., Captain, Forty-second Infantry, October 24, 1899.
Hammond, Frank M., Major, Additional Paymaster, May 13, 1899.
Hancock, William F., Captain, Assistant Adjutant General, April 14, 1899.
Handy, Joseph B., Captain, Assistant Commissary of Subsistence, October 31, 1899.
Harman, John A., Major, Chief Ordnance Officer, May 5, 1899.
Harrison, Edward B., Captain, Assistant Quartermaster, June 12, 1899.
Hartzell, Ralph, Major, Additional Paymaster, June 13, 1899.
Harvey, Samuel S. Major, Additional Paymaster, June 30, 1899.
Hasbrouck, Henry C., Brigadier General, June 12, 1899.
Havens, Benjamin F., Major, Additional Paymaster, June 30, 1899.
Haverstick, Washington, Major, Additional Paymaster, May 13, 1899.
Hay, Samuel W., Major, Chief Commissary of Subsistence, April 6, 1899.
Hayes, Webb C., Lieutenant Colonel, Thirty-first Infantry, May 31, 1900.
Hays, Samuel D. C., Major, Additional Paymaster, June 13, 1899.
Hecker, Frank J., Colonel, Quartermaster, May 1, 1899.

Heg, Elmer E., Major, Brigade Surgeon, May 12, 1899.
Hellings, Martin L., Captain, Signal Officer, April 1, 1899.
Henry, Guy V., Major General, June 12, 1899.
Henry, Morton J., Captain, Assistant Commissary of Subsistence, August 24, 1899.
Higgins, Ambrose, First Lieutenant, Signal Officer, August 15, 1899.
Higgins, James A., Second Lieutenant, Signal Officer, May 12, 1899.
Hill, Frederick A., Lieutenant Colonel, Judge Advocate, June 24, 1899.
Hirsch, Gustav, Second Lieutenant, Signal Officer, June 15, 1899.
Hogan, Daniel, Captain, Assistant Commissary of Subsistence, July 5, 1899.
Holden, Giles H., Captain, Assistant Quartermaster, April 4, 1899.
Hopkins, George H., Major, Assistant Adjutant General, August 31, 1899.
Hosmer, James R., Captain, Assistant Quartermaster, May 12, 1899.
Houston, Samuel S., Captain, Forty-seventh Infantry, October 30, 1899.
Hoyle, Eli D., Major, Chief Ordnance Officer, May 12, 1899.
Hubbell, Henry W., Major, Forty-seventh Infantry, October 26, 1899.
Humphrey, Charles F., Brigadeier General, June 12, 1899.
Hunter, Randall R., Major, Brigade Surgeon, June 30, 1899.
Hurlbut, Edwin H., Captain, Commissary of Subsistence, May 12, 1899.
Hutcheson, Grote, Captain, Assistant Adjutant General, April 13, 1899.
Hutchins, Edward R., Captain, Assistant Commissary of Subsistence, April 22, 1900.
Ingalls, Ralph, First Lieutenant, Forty-fourth Infantry, November 10, 1899.
Jackson, Charles W., Captain, Forty-first Infantry, October 28, 1899.
Jacobs, Joshua W., Lieutenant Colonel, Chief Quartermaster, May 12, 1899.
James, William A., Second Lieutenant, Thirty-second Infantry, September 15, 1899.
Jarvie, William, Jr., First Lieutenant, Signal Officer, April 17, 1899.
Jarvis, Nathan S., Major, Brigade Surgeon, April 12, 1899.
Jeffery, John B., Captain, Assistant Quartermaster, July 13, 1899.
Jenkins, James F., Captain, Commissary of Subsistence, April 12, 1899.
Jenkins, William D., Major, Engineer Officer, April 12, 1899.
Jones, Arthur R., Second Lieutenant, Forty-fifth Infantry, December 10, 1899.
Jones, Francis B., Lieutenant Colonel, Chief Quartermaster, May 13, 1899.
Jones, Fred T., Major, Additional Paymaster, April 7, 1899.
Keene, James D., Second Lieutenant, Eleventh Cavalry, March 7, 1900.
Keifer, J. Warren, Major General, May 12, 1899.
Kelly, Edward E., Second Lieutenant, Signal Officer, September 2, 1899.
Kenner, James B., Major, Additional Paymaster, June 30, 1899.
Kenyon, Brewster C., Major, Additional Paymaster, May 13, 1899.
Kernachan, William J., Major, Brigade Surgeon, April 30, 1899.
Kline, Jacob, Brigadier General, March 15, 1899.
Kilbourne, Charles E., Jr., First Lieutenant, Signal Officer, September 2, 1899.
King, Charles, Brigadier General, August 2, 1899.
Kinnison, Henry L., Captain, Assistant Quartermaster, May 12, 1900.
Knapp, Louis, Major, Additional Paymaster, June 13, 1899.
Kneedler, William L., Major Brigade Surgeon, June 30, 1899.
Kramer, Simon P., Major, Brigade Surgeon, October 31, 1899.
Krause, John C., Major, Additional Paymaster, March 7, 1899.
Krauthoff, Charles R., Captain, Assistant Commissary of Subsistence, March 11, 1900.
Kress, John A., Lieutenant Colonel, Chief Ordnance Officer, May 12, 1899.
Kuhn, Joseph E., Major, Engineer Officer, April 12, 1899.
Landstreet, John, Jr., Captain, Commissary of Subsistence, June 12, 1899.
Landstreet, John, Jr., Captain, Assistant Commissary of Subsistence, December 31, 1899.
Lang, Merrill W., Major, Additional Paymaster, March 7, 1899.
Lansing, Horace C., Second Lieutenant, Signal Officer, June 20, 1899.
Lawrence, George E., Captain, Signal Officer, September 2, 1899.
Le Crone, James W., Second Lieutenant, Fortieth Infantry, November 17, 1899.
Leigh, Frederick T., Captain, Signal Officer, April 17, 1899.
Lincoln, James R., Brigadier General, March 15, 1899.
Lincoln, Winslow S., Captain, Commissary of Subsistence, June 1, 1899.
Lino, Paul B., Captain, Thirty-eighth Infantry, December 1, 1899.
Lissack, Ormond M., Major, Chief Ordnance Officer, May 12, 1899.
Loffhagen, Edward H., Captain, Thirty-third Infantry, September 12, 1899.
Logan, Glen H., Major, Additional Paymaster, June 30, 1899.
Logan, James A., Jr., Captain, Assistant Commissary of Subsistence, May 15, 1900.
Longstreet, Robert L., Major, Chief Commissary of Subsistence, June 10, 1899.
Lord, Frank H., Captain, Commissary of Subsistence, June 13, 1899.
Lord, Frederic C., Major, Additional Paymaster, May 13 1899.
Loveland, William M., Captain, Commissary of Subsistence, May 12, 1899.
Lucas, Eugene W. Van C., Major, Engineer Officer, March 2, 1899.
Lydig, Philip M., Captain, Assistant Commissary of Subsistence, July 15, 1899.
Macdonald, Godfrey H., Major, Chief Ordnance Officer, May 12, 1899.
MacNaughton, Peter D., Major, Brigade Surgeon, May 12, 1899.
Macumber, John L., Major, Brigade Surgeon, May 12, 1899.
Marsh, Charles B., Major, Additional Paymaster, June 13, 1899.
Marshall, Martin M., Captain, Commissary of Subsistence, April 12, 1899.
Martin, Charles H., Captain, Signal Officer, May 12, 1899.
Martin, Charles H., Captain, Assistant Quartermaster, June 13, 1899.
Maus, Louis M., Lieutenant Colonel, Chief Surgeon, April 21, 1899.
May, Henry B., Major, Additional Paymaster, June 30, 1899.
McAlexander, Ulysses G., Captain, Assistant Quartermaster, May 12, 1899.
McCallum, George B., Captain, Commissary of Subsistence, April 6, 1899.
McClellan, John, Major, Chief Ordnance Officer, May 12, 1899.
McDonald, Charles G., First Lieutenant, Twenty-seventh Infantry, September 12, 1899.
McGrath, Hugh J., Major, Engineer Officer, May 12, 1899.
McKee, William J., Brigadier General, March 15, 1899.

McKenna, Elmore A., Major, Signal Officer, September 2, 1899.
McKenna, Patrick J., First Lieutenant, Assistant Surgeon, Thirty-fourth Infantry, September 8, 1899.
McKibbin, Chambers, Brigadier General, May 12, 1899.
McKittrick, William, Captain, Assistant Adjutant General, May 12, 1899.
McLeary, James H., Major, Inspector General, April 7, 1899.
Mearns, Edgar A., Major, Chief Surgeon, March 22, 1899.
Meek, William M., First Lieutenant, Thirty-first Infantry, November 20, 1899.
Mendoza, Ramon G., Captain, Assistant Adjutant General, May 12, 1899.
Messer, Nathaniel T., Captain, Commissary of Subsistence, April 5, 1899.
Michler, Francis, Lieutenant Colonel, Assistant Adjutant General, May 12, 1899.
Mitchell, Hiram E., Captain, Assistant Quartermaster, June 12, 1899.
Montgomery, Robert B., Second Lieutenant, Signal Officer, June 30, 1899.
Moody, James M., Major, Chief Commissary of Subsistence, May 12, 1899.
Morrow, Albert P., First Lieutenant, Thirty-third Infantry, August 24, 1899.
Morton, Joseph B., Captain, Assistant Adjutant General, April 12, 1899.
Morris, Edward R., Major, Brigade Surgeon, December 31, 1899.
Moses, George W., Major, Additional Paymaster, May 13, 1899.
Mott, T. Bentley, Major, Assistant Adjutant General, June 13, 1899.
Mullikin, James C., Major, Chief Commissary of Subsistence, May 12, 1899.
Neal, Charles W., Captain, Commissary of Subsistence, May 12, 1899.
Nesmith, Otto A., Captain, Signal Officer, May 13, 1899.
Nicholson, William J., Major, Chief Ordnance Officer, March 13, 1899.
Oates, William C., Brigadier General, March 10, 1899.
Opdycke, Henry G., First Lieutenant, Signal Officer, June 13, 1899.
O'Reilly, Robert M., Lieutenant Colonel, Chief Surgeon, May 12, 1899.
Otis, Harrison G., Brigadier General, July 2, 1899.
Ovenshine, Samuel, Brigadier General, October 20, 1899.
Owen, William O., Major, Brigade Surgeon, June 30, 1899.
Page, Henry, Major, Chief Commissary of Subsistence, May 31, 1899.
Palmer, Charles D., Captain, Assistant Quartermaster, March 1, 1900.
Paxton, Robert G., Captain, Assistant Adjutant General, May 12, 1899.
Payson, Francis L., Captain, Assistant Quartermaster, March 22, 1900.
Peabody, Jacob C. R., Captain, Assistant Quartermaster, May 17, 1899.
Penney, Charles G., Lieutenant Colonel, Chief Quartermaster, March 15, 1899.
Pennington, Alexander C. M., Brigadier General, April 12, 1899.
Perkins, Philip J., Captain, Signal Officer, July 13, 1899.
Pettijohn, Orson, Captain, Commissary of Subsistence, April 12, 1899.
Phelps, Walter L., Captain, Assistant Quartermaster, May 12, 1899.
Phillips, Charles A., First Lieutenant, Thirty-second Infantry, October 25, 1899.
Phillips, John L., Major, Chief Surgeon, April 30, 1899.
Pierce, Josiah, Jr., Major, Engineer Officer, June 1, 1899.
Pierson, Charles O., Second Lieutenant, Signal Officer, April 30, 1900.
Pilcher, James E., Major, Brigade Surgeon, March 22, 1899.
Piper, Alexander R., Captain, Assistant Commissary of Subsistence, July 12, 1899.
Pond, George E., Lieutenant Colonel, Chief Quartermaster, May 12, 1899.
Pope, James W., Lieutenant Colonel, Chief Quartermaster, September 2, 1899.
Potter, Charles L., Lieutenant Colonel, Chief Engineer Officer, September 2, 1899.
Purdy, William A., Major, Additional Paymaster, June 13, 1899.
Quay, Andrew G. C., Major, Chief Quartermaster, June 30, 1899.
Randall, George M., Brigadier General, April 12, 1899.
Randall, Walter F., Captain, Twenty-seventh Infantry, October 21, 1899.
Ranke, William F., Captain, Thirty-ninth Infantry, October 13, 1899.
Raymond, Henry I., Major, Brigade Surgeon, January 18, 1900.
Reeve, Charles McC., Brigadier General, April, 27, 1899.
Rhodes, Charles D., Captain, Assistant Adjutant General, April 7, 1899.
Ribbel, Charles H., Lieutenant Colonel, Judge Advocate, June 13, 1899.
Rix, Fred N., Major, Additional Paymaster, March 7, 1899.
Robertson, Edgar B., Major, Quartermaster, February 5, 1900.
Robinson, Wirt, Captain, Assistant Quartermaster, April 12, 1899.
Rodman, John B., Major, Chief Ordnance Officer, May 12, 1899.
Rockwell, James, Jr., Lieutenant Colonel, Chief Ordnance Officer, May 12, 1899.
Root, Edwin A., Major, Engineer Officer, May 12, 1899.
Rudd, Alson J., First Lieutenant, Signal Officer, July 22, 1899.
Russell, John L., First Lieutenant, Thirty-seventh Infantry, May 25, 1900.
Ryan, John F., Captain, Thirtieth Infantry, August 22, 1899.
Ryan, William J., Captain, Commissary of Subsistence, March 7, 1899.
Sample, William R., Captain, Assistant Adjutant General, April 7, 1899.
Sands, George H., Major, Engineer Officer, April, 24, 1899.
Sanger, Joseph P., Brigadier General, June 12, 1899.
Savage, Richard H., Captain, Twenty-seventh Infantry, December 1, 1899.
Saxton, Samuel S., Captain, Assistant Adjutant General, May 12, 1899.
Schuelke, Julius A., Major, Surgeon, Thirty-fith Infantry, November 11, 1899.
Sears, John M., Major, Additional Paymaster, August 15, 1899.
Sewell, William J., Jr., First Lieutenant, Twenty-ninth Infantry, September 5, 1899.
Shea, Charles C., Second Lieutenant, Signal Officer, May 12, 1899.
Shakespeare, Edward O., Major, Brigade Surgeon, June 30, 1899.
Sheridan, Michael V., Brigadier General, May 12, 1899.
Sherman, George D., Major, Additional Paymaster, June 13, 1899.
Sheary, Michael F., Major, Additional Paymaster, October 31, 1899.
Simpson, James A., Second Lieutenant, Thirty-first Infantry, October 25, 1899.
Slocum, Herbert J., Major Inspector General, May 12, 1899.
Smith, Stephen O., Càptain, Forty-seventh Infantry, November 1, 1899.
Smith, Frederick A., Major, Chief Commissary of Subsistence, June 13, 1899.
Smoke, Samuel A., Captain, Assistant Quartermaster, June 13, 1899.

Snyder, Simon, Brigadier General, May 12, 1899.
Stephenson, William, Major, Brigade Surgeon, April 30, 1899.
Stewart, George C., Major, Additional Paymaster, March 7, 1899.
Strong, Frederick S., Major, Assistant Adjutant General, March 31, 1899.
Strong, Putnam B., Major, Assistant Adjutant General, August 29, 1899.
Strong, Richard P., Lieutenant Colonel, Chief Signal Officer, May 12, 1899.
Strong, Wilson B., First Lieutenant, Thirty-third Infantry, October 31, 1899.
Stroup, Henry, First Lieutenant, Thirty-third Infantry, September 13, 1899.
Stuart, James E. B., Captain, Commissary of Subsistence, June 13, 1899.
Sumner, Samuel S., Major General, April 15, 1899.
Swigart, Harry A., Second Lieutenant, Signal Officer, June 30, 1899.
Tate, Frank P., First Lieutenant, Signal Officer, April 12, 1899.
Tayman, Charles E., Captain, Assistant Quartermaster, June 8, 1899.
Teagarden, John P., Captain, Commissary of Subsistence, June 30, 1899.
Thomas, Earl D., Major, Inspector General, March 7, 1899.
Thomas, William B., Captain, Forty-sixth Infantry, April 10, 1900.
Thompson, Arthur, Captain, Assistant Quartermaster, May 31, 1899.
Thompson, Alvar G., Captain, Signal Officer, May 31, 1899.
Thompson, Henry T., Captain, Twenty-ninth Infantry, July, 29 1899.
Thompson, James K., Captain, Assistant Adjutant General, March 3, 1899.
Thompson, John T., Lieutenant Colonel, Chief Ordnance Officer, May 12, 1899.
Thompson, Richard W., Jr., Captain, Commissary of Subsistence, April 12, 1899.
Thorn, Solomon F., Major, Chief Commissary of Subsistence, June 13, 1899.
Thrift, William H., Major, Additional Paymaster, June 13, 1899.
Townsend, John H., Major, Additional Paymaster, June 13, 1899.
Townsend, Rufus M., Major, Chief Commissary of Subsistence, May 12, 1899.
Townsley, Clarence P., Major, Chief Ordnance Officer, May 12, 1899.
Treat, Charles G., Major, Assistant Adjutant General, May 12, 1899.
Tucker, William A., Captain, Commissary of Subsistence, May 5, 1899.
Twombly, Henry H., Major, Additional Paymaster, March 7, 1899.
Tyler, S. Heth, Major, Additional Paymaster, June 30, 1899.
Van Voorhis, Daniel, Captain, Assistant Commissary of Subsistence, October 31, 1899.
Varnedoe, James O., Major, Chief Commissary of Subsistence, May 12, 1899.
Vaughan, Victor C., Major, Chief Surgeon, June 30, 1899.
Vickers, John H., Jr., Second Lieutenant, Thirty-ninth Infantry, April 15, 1900.
Voorhies, Gordon, Captain, Assistant Adjutant General, March 7, 1899.
Wade, James F., Major General, June 12, 1899.
Wakeman, William J., Major, Brigade Surgeon, April 30, 1899.
Walton, Clifford S., Major, Additional Paymaster, June 13, 1899.
Warner, George W., Second Lieutenant Twenty-eighth Infantry, October 13, 1899.
Waties, James R., Brigadier General, March 24, 1899.
Weigel, William, Captain, Assistant Quartermaster, June 16, 1899.
Weiser, Charles, Captain, Commissary of Subsistence, June 12, 1899.
Weiss, Webster C., Major, Additional Paymaster, June 13, 1899.
Weston, John F., Brigadier General, March 24, 1899.
Whitehead, Troup, Second Lieutenant, Forty-sixth Infantry, September 16, 1899.
Whipple, Charles W., Lieutenant Colonel, Inspector General, March 15, 1899.
Whitney, Henry H., Captain, Assistant Adjutant General, May 12, 1899.
Wilcox, Timothy E., Lieutenant Colonel, Chief Surgeon, May 12, 1899.
Wiley, John A., Brigadier General, March 15, 1899.
Wilkins, Harry E., Captain, Commissary of Subsistence, June 12, 1899.
Wilcox, Cornelius De W., Captain, Assistant Adjutant General, April 7, 1899
Williams, William P., Major, Chief Commissary of Subsistence, March 10, 1899.
Williams, William P., Captain, Assistant Quartermaster, May 12, 1899.
Williard, Joseph E., Captain, Assistant Quartermaster, April 2, 1899.
Willis, Edward, Captain, Assistant Quartermaster, April 12, 1899.
Williston, Edward B., Brigadier General, June 12, 1899.
Wilson, David B., Major, Chief Commissary of Subsistence, May 12, 1899.
Wilson, Eugene T., Major, Chief Commissary of Subsistence, June 13, 1899.
Wing, Charles M., Captain, Fortieth Infantry, November 11, 1899.
Wright, John N., First Lieutenant, Thirtieth Infantry, October 20, 1899.
Wright, Walter K., Major, Chief Commissary of Subsistence, May 12, 1899.
Wright, William M., Captain, Assistant Adjutant General, May 12, 1899.
Wrigley, Charles M., Captain, Assistant Quartermaster, May 12, 1899.
Wood, Joseph D., First Lieutenant, Signal Officer, June 30, 1899.
Woodbury, Charles L., Major, Engineer Officer, May 20, 1899.
Woodring, Frank W., Captain, Assistant Quartermaster, August 5, 1899.
Wooten, Julien P., Captain, Signal Officer, May 31, 1899.
Worthington, Chester B., Captain, Assistant Quartermaster, August 14, 1899.
Wyman, William C., Captain Thirty-fourth Infantry, September 8, 1899.
Yancey, Asbery W., Captain, Signal Officer, April 26, 1899.
Young, Harold, Captain, Assistant Quartermaster, April 12, 1899.

*Discharged* (1).

Evins, Thomas E., Major, Surg. Forty-ninth Infantry, May 24, 1900.

*Dismissed* (5).

Bailey, Clayton J., First Lieutenant, Twenty-seventh Infantry, March 31, 1900.
Cramer, Robert B., First Lieutenant, Thirty-fourth Infantry, April 30, 1900.
Gregg, Robert C., First Lieutenant, Forty-ninth Infantry, March 31, 1900.
Johnson, Edward B., Second Lieutenant, Forty-ninth Infantry, May 31, 1900.
Kirkman, George W., Major, Forty-ninth Infantry, March 31, 1900.

# ADDENDA

## APPOINTMENTS, PROMOTIONS AND CASUALTIES, BETWEEN JUNE 1 AND JUNE 20, 1900.

### APPOINTMENTS.

*General Officers.*

Brigadier General Loyd Wheaton to be Major General, June 18, 1900.
Lieutenant Colonel Thomas H. Barry, Assistant Adjutant General, U. S. Army, to be Brigadier General, June 18, 1900.

*Medical Department.*

Captain John S. Kulp, Assistant Surgeon, U. S. Army, to be Surgeon of Volunteers, with the rank of Major, June 11, 1900.
Captain Frederick P. Reynolds, Assistant Surgeon, U. S. Army, to be Surgeon of Volunteers, with the rank of Major, June 16, 1900.

*Subsistence Department.*

First Lieutenant John E. Woodward, 16th Infantry, U. S. Army, to be Asistant Commissary of Subsistence of Volunteers, with the rank of Captain, June 15, 1900.

*Signal Officers.*

*To be Signal Officers, with the rank of first lieutenant.*

Second Lieutenant Charles B. Rogan, Signal Officer, June 8, 1900.
Second Lieutenant William Mitchell, Signal Officer, June 8, 1900.
Second Lieutenant Henry W. Stamford, Signal Officer, June 8, 1900.
Second Lieutenant Frederick M. Jones, Signal Officer, June 8, 1900.
Second Lieutenant Victor Shepherd, Signal Officer, June 8, 1900.
Second Lieutenant William E. Davies, Signal Officer, June 8, 1900.
Second Lieutenant Richard O. Rickard, Signal Officer, June 8, 1900.
Second Lieutenant Charles S. Wallace, Signal Officer, June 8, 1900.
Second Lieutenant George S. Gibbs, Jr., Signal Officer, June 8, 1900.
Second Lieutenant Mack K. Cunningham, Signal Officer, June 8, 1900.

*To be Signal Officers, with the rank of second lieutenant.*

First-class Sergeant John T. Sayles, Signal Corps, U. S. Army, June 8, 1900.
First-class Sergeant Charles O. Hastings, Signal Corps, U. S. Army, June 8, 1900.
First-class Sergeant Burt E. Grabo, Signal Corps, U. S. Army, June 8, 1900.
First-class Sergeant Magnus Nordquist, Signal Corps, U. S. Army, June 8, 1900.
First-class Sergeant Otto B. Grim, Signal Corps, U. S. Army, June 8, 1900.
First-class Sergeant Charles E. Booth, Signal Corps, U. S. Army, June 8, 1900.
First-class Sergeant Henry S. Hathaway, Signal Corps, U. S. Army, June 8, 1900.
First-class Sergeant Peter Bartsch, Signal Corps, U. S. Army, June 8, 1900.
First-class Sergeant Rush P. Wheat, Signal Corps, U. S. Army, June 8, 1900.
First-class Sergeant Clifton R. Berry, Signal Corps, U. S. Army, June 8, 1900.

*33rd Regiment of Infantry.*

Sergeant Major Albert E. Gebert, to be Second Lieutenant, June 9, 1900.

*34th Regiment of Infantry.*

H. Brookman Wilkinson, of Alabama, to be Assistant Surgeon, with the rank of First Lieutenant, June 8, 1900.
Corporal John H. Ruff, Company H, to be Second Lieutenant, June 2, 1900.

*45th Regiment of Infantry.*

Sergeant Major Oscar Danielson, to be Second Lieutenant, June 9, 1900.

*49th Regiment of Infantry.*

Joseph H. Carroll, of Ohio, to be Assistant Surgeon, with the rank of First Lieutenant, June 4, 1900.
Sergeant Major John R. Blackburn, to be Second Lieutenant, June 15, 1900.

*Squadron Philippine Cavalry.*

First Sergeant Boss Reese, Company D, 29th Regiment of Infantry, to be Second Lieutenant, June 15, 1900.
Sergeant Edward B. Howell, Company A, 29th Regiment of Infantry, to be Second Lieutenant, June 15, 1900.

PROMOTIONS.

*11th Regiment of Cavalry.*

First Lieutenant George W. Winterburn, to be Captain, June 7, 1900.
Second Lieutenant George Curry, to be First Lieutenant, June 7, 1900.

*32nd Regiment of Infantry.*

Second Lieutenant Benjamin R. Wade, to be First Lieutenant, June 6, 1900.

*33rd Regiment of Infantry.*

Lieutenant Colonel Marcus D. Cronin, to be Colonel, June 9, 1900.
Major Peyton C. March, to be Lieutenant Colonel, June 9, 1900.
Captain Edmund G. Shields, to be Major, June 9, 1900.
First Lieutenant Edgar N. Coffey, to be Captain, June 9, 1900.
Second Lieutenant Henry J. McKenney, to be First Lieutenant, June 9, 1900.

*43rd Regiment of Infantry.*

Second Lieutenant Robert Sterrett, to be First Lieutenant, June 13, 1900.

*45th Regiment of Infantry.*

First Lieutenant William Brown, to be Captain, June 10, 1900.
Second Lieutenant Roy I. Taylor, to be First Lieutenant, June 10, 1900.

*49th Regiment of Infantry.*

Captain Robert Gage, to be Major, June 15, 1900.

CASUALTIES.

*Commissions vacated by new appointment.*

Major General Elwell S. Otis, U. S. Army, his commission as Major General, U. S. Volunteers, June 16, 1900.
Brigadier General Luther R. Hare, his commission as Colonel 33rd Infantry, June 9, 1900.
Brigadier General Joseph Wheeler, U. S. Army, his commission as Brigadier General, U. S. Volunteers, June 18, 1900.
Major General Loyd Wheaton, his commission as Brigadier General, June 20, 1900.

*Commissions expired by constitutional limitation.*

Lloyd England, his commission as Captain, 11th Cavalry, June 7, 1900.
Michael J. Mender, his commission as Second Lieutenant, 45th Infantry, June 7, 1900.

*Honorably Discharged.*

Major Frank R. Keefer, Surgeon, June 15, 1900.
Major George F. Shiels, Surgeon, June 10, 1900.
First Lieutenant William S. Weaver, 32nd Infantry, June 6, 1900.

*Died.*

First Lieutenant Jonathan Cilley, 43rd Infantry, June 13, 1900, at Manila, P. I.
First Lieutenant Raphael A. Edmondston, Assistant Surgeon, 34th Infantry, June 2, 1900, at Manila, P. I.
Captain Orison P. Lee, 45th Infantry, drowned, June 10, 1900, off coast at Albay, P. I.

*Dismissed.*

Captain Peter C. Deming, Assistant Commissary of Subsistence, June 12, 1900.

# GENERAL OFFICERS

OF THE

# REVOLUTION

# GENERAL OFFICERS

OF THE

# CONTINENTAL ARMY OF THE REVOLUTION.

---

ALEXANDER, WM. [Born in N. Y. Appointed from N. J.]
Brig. Gen., 1 March, 1776. Maj. Gen., 19 Feb., 1777. Died 15 Jan., 1783.

ARMSTRONG, JOHN. [Born in Ireland. Appointed from Penn.]
Brig. Gen., 1 March, 1776. Died 9 March, 1795.

ARNOLD, BENEDICT. [Born in Conn. Appointed from Conn.]
Brig. Gen., 10 Jan., 1776. Maj. Gen., 17 Feb., 1777. Deserted to the enemy, 25 Sept., 1780. Died 14 June, 1801.

CADWALADER, JOHN. [Born in Penn. Appointed from Penn.]
Brig. Gen., 21 Feb., 1777. Died 10 Feb., 1786.

CLINTON, GEORGE. [Born in N. Y. Appointed from N. Y.]
Brig. Gen., 25 March, 1777. Died 20 April, 1812.

CLINTON, JAMES. [Born in N. Y. Appointed from N. Y.]
Brig. Gen., 9 Aug., 1776. Died 22 Dec., 1812.

CONWAY, THOMAS. [Born in Ireland. Appointed from France.]
Brig. Gen., 13 May, 1777. Maj. Gen., 13 Dec., 1777. Died about 1800.

DAYTON, ELIAS. [Born in N. J. Appointed from N. J.]
Brig. Gen., 7 Jan., 1783. Died 17 July, 1807.

DE BORRE, PRUD'HOMME. [Born in France. Appointed from France.]
Brig. Gen., 1 Dec., 1776. Resigned 14 Dec., 1777. Died ———.

DE COUDRAY, PHILIP. [Born in France. Appointed from ———.]
Maj. Gen. I. G. of Ord., 11 Aug., 1777. Drowned 17 Sept., 1777.

DE FERMOY, MATTHIAS A. R. [Born in France. Appointed from ———.]
Brig. Gen., 5 Nov., 1776. Resigned — Jan., 1778. Died ———.

DE HAAS, JOHN P. [Born in Holland. Appointed from Penn.]
Brig. Gen., 21 Feb., 1777. Died ———, 1794.

DE KALB, JOHN. [Born in Bavaria. Appointed from ———.]
Maj. Gen., 15 Sept., 1777. Died 19 Aug., 1780, of wounds received at Camden.

DE ROUERIE, ARMAND T. [Born in France. Appointed from ———.]
Brig. Gen., 26 March, 1783. Died ———, 1791.

DE WOEDTKE, FREDK. WM. [Born in Prussia. Appointed from ———.]
Brig. Gen., 16 March, 1776. Died — July, 1776.

DUPORTAIL, LOUIS L. B. [Born in France. Appointed from ———.]
Brig. Gen., 17 Nov., 1777. Maj. Gen., 16 Nov., 1781. Died ———, 1793.

FRYE, JOSEPH. [Born in Mass. Appointed from Mass.]
Brig. Gen., 10 Jan., 1776. Resigned 23 April, 1776. Died ———, 1794.

GADSDEN, CHRISTOPHER. [Born in S. C. Appointed from S. C.]
Brig. Gen., 16 Sept., 1776. Died 28 Aug., 1805.

GATES, HORATIO. [Born in England. Appointed from Va.]
Brig. Gen. Adj. Gen., 15 June, 1775. Maj. Gen., 16 May, 1776. Died 10 April, 1806.

GIST, MORDECAI. [Born in Md. Appointed from Md.]
Brig. Gen., 9 Jan., 1779. Died 9 July, 1792.

GLOVER, JOHN. [Born in Mass. Appointed from Mass.]
Brig. Gen., 21 Feb., 1777. Died 30 Jan., 1797.

GREATON, JOHN. [Born in Mass. Appointed from Mass.]
Brig. Gen., 7 Jan., 1783. Died — Feb., 1784.

GREENE, NATHANIEL. [Born in R. I. Appointed from R. I.]
Brig. Gen., 22 June, 1775. Maj. Gen., 9 Aug., 1776. Died 19 June, 1786.

HAND, EDWARD. [Born in Ireland. Appointed from Penn.]
Brig. Gen., 1 April, 1777. Died 3 Sept., 1802.

HEATH, WM. [Born in Mass. Appointed from Mass.]
Brig. Gen., 22 June, 1775. Maj. Gen., 9 Aug., 1776. Died 24 Jan., 1814.

HOGAN, JAMES. [Born in ———. Appointed from N. C.]
Brig. Gen., 9 Jan., 1779. Died ———.

HOWE, ROBERT. [Born in England. Appointed from N. C.]
Brig. Gen., 1 March, 1776. Maj. Gen., 20 Oct., 1777. Died — Jan., 1787.

HUGER, ISAAC. [Born in S. C. Appointed from S. C.]
Brig. Gen., 9 Jan., 1779. Died — Nov., 1789.

HUNTINGDON, JEDEDIAH. [Born in Conn. Appointed from Conn.]
Brig. Gen., 12 May, 1777. Died 25 Sept., 1818.

IRVINE, WM. [Born in Ireland. Appointed from Penn.]
Brig. Gen., 12 May, 1779. Died 29 July, 1804.

KNOX, HENRY. [Born in Mass. Appointed from Mass.]
Brig. Gen., 27 Dec., 1776. Maj. Gen., 22 March, 1782. Died 25 Oct., 1806.

LAFAYETTE, MARIE P. J. G. DE M. [Born in France. Appointed from France.]
Maj. Gen., 31 July, 1777. Died 20 May, 1834.

LEARNED, EBENEZER. [Born in Mass. Appointed from Mass.]
Brig. Gen., 2 April, 1777. Resigned 24 March, 1778. Died 1 April, 1801.

LEE, CHARLES. [Born in England. Appointed from Va.]
Maj. Gen., 7 June, 1775. Dismissed 10 Jan., 1780. Died 2 Oct., 1782.

LEWIS, ANDREW. [Born in Ireland. Appointed from Va.]
Brig. Gen., 1 March, 1776. Resigned 15 April, 1777. Died ———, 1780.

LINCOLN, BENJAMIN. [Born in Mass. Appointed from Mass.]
Brig. Gen., 19 Feb., 1777. Died 9 May, 1810.

MARION, FRANCIS. [Born in S. C. Appointed from S. C.]
Brig. Gen. State Troops, — Aug., 1780. Died 27 Feb., 1795.

MAXWELL, WM. [Born in Ireland. Appointed from N. J.]
Brig. Gen., 23 Oct., 1776. Resigned 25 July, 1780. Died 12 Nov., 1798.

McDOUGALL, ALEXANDER. [Born in Scotland. Appointed from N. Y.]
Brig. Gen., 9 Aug., 1776. Maj. Gen., 20 Oct., 1777. Died 8 June, 1786.

McINTOSH, LACHLAN. [Born in Scotland. Appointed from Ga.]
Brig. Gen., 16 Sept., 1776. Died 20 Feb., 1806.

MERCER, HUGH. [Born in Scotland. Appointed from Va.]
Brig. Gen., 5 June, 1776. Died 11 Jan., 1777, of wounds received at the Battle of Princeton.

MIFFLIN, THOMAS. [Born in Penn. Appointed from Penn.]
Brig. Gen., 16 May, 1776. Maj. Gen., 19 Feb., 1777. Resigned 25 Feb., 1779. Died 21 Jan., 1800.

MONTGOMERY, RICHARD. [Born in Ireland. Appointed from N. Y.]
Brig. Gen., 22 June, 1775. Maj. Gen., 9 Dec., 1775. Killed 31 Dec., 1775, in the assault on Quebec.

MOORE, JAMES. [Born in ———. Appointed from N. C.]
Brig. Gen., 1 March, 1776. Died ———, 1776.

MORGAN, DANIEL. [Born in N. J. Appointed from Va.]
Brig. Gen., 13 Oct., 1780. Died 6 July, 1802.

MOULTRIE, WM. [Born in S. C. Appointed from S. C.]
Brig. Gen., 16 Sept., 1776. Maj. Gen., 15 Oct., 1782. Died 27 Sept., 1805.

MUHLENBERG, JOHN PETER G. [Born in Penn. Appointed from Va.]
Brig. Gen., 21 Feb., 1777. Died 1 Oct., 1807.

NASH, FRANCIS. [Born in Va. Appointed from N. C.]
Brig. Gen., 5 Feb., 1777. Died 17 Oct., 1777, of wounds received at the Battle of Germantown.

NIXON, JOHN. [Born in Mass. Appointed from Mass.]
Brig. Gen., 9 Aug., 1776. Resigned 12 Sept., 1780. Died 24 March, 1815.

PARSONS, SAML. H. [Born in Conn. Appointed from Conn.]
Brig. Gen., 9 Aug., 1776. Maj. Gen., 23 Oct., 1780. Drowned 17 Nov., 1789.

PATTERSON, JOHN. [Born in Conn. Appointed from Mass.]
Brig. Gen., 21 Feb., 1777. Died 19 July, 1808.

PICKENS, ANDREW. [Born in Penn. Appointed from S. C.]
Brig. Gen. of State Troops. Died 17 Aug., 1817.

POMEROY, SETH. [Born in Mass. Appointed from Mass.]
Brig. Gen., 22 June, 1775. Resigned — July, 1775. Died — Feb., 1777.

POOR, ENOCH. [Born in Mass. Appointed from N. H.]
Brig. Gen., 21 Feb., 1777. Died 8 Sept., 1780.

PULASKI, CASIMIR. [Born in Poland. Appointed from ———.]
Brig. Gen., 15 Sept., 1777. Died 11 Oct., 1777, of wounds received at the Siege of Savannah.

PUTNAM, ISRAEL. [Born in Mass. Appointed from Conn.]
Maj. Gen., 19 June, 1775. Died 19 May, 1790.

PUTNAM, RUFUS. [Born in Mass. Appointed from Mass.]
Brig. Gen., 7 Jan., 1783. Died 1 May, 1824.

REED, JAMES. [Born in Mass. Appointed from N. H.]
Brig. Gen., 9 Aug., 1776. Died 13 Feb., 1807.

REED, JOSEPH. [Born in N. J. Appointed from Penn.]
Brig. Gen. Adj. Gen., 12 May, 1777. Died 5 March, 1785.

SCHUYLER, PHILIP. [Born in N. Y. Appointed from N. Y.]
Maj. Gen., 19 June, 1795. Resigned 19 April, 1779. Died 18 Nov., 1804.

SCOTT, CHARLES. [Born in Va. Appointed from Va.]
Brig. Gen., 1 April, 1777. Died 22 Oct., 1820.

SMALLWOOD, WM. [Born in Md. Appointed from Md.]
Brig. Gen., 23 Oct., 1776. Maj. Gen., 15 Sept., 1780. Died 14 Feb., 1792.

SPENCER, JOSEPH. [Born in Conn. Appointed from Conn.]
Brig. Gen., 22 June, 1775. Maj. Gen., 9 Aug., 1776. Died 13 Jan., 1789.

STARK, JOHN. [Born in N. H. Appointed from N. H.]
Brig. Gen., 5 Oct., 1777. Died 8 May, 1822.

STEUBEN, FREDERICK W. A. [Born in Prussia. Appointed from ———.]
Maj. Gen., 20 March, 1778. Died 28 Nov., 1794.

ST. CLAIR, ARTHUR. [Born in Scotland. Appointed from Penn.]
Brig. Gen., 9 Aug., 1776. Maj. Gen., 19 Feb., 1777. Died 31 Aug., 1818.

STEPHEN, ADAM. [Born in ———. Appointed from Va.]
Brig. Gen., 4 Sept., 1776. Maj. Gen., 19 Feb., 1777. Died ———.

SULLIVAN, JOHN. [Born in N. H. Appointed from N. H.]
Brig. Gen., 22 June, 1775. Maj. Gen., 9 Aug., 1776. Resigned 30 Nov., 1779. Died 23 Jan., 1795.

SUMNER, JETHRO. [Born in Va. Appoinetd from N. C.]
Brig. Gen., 9 Jan., 1779. Died ———.

SUMTER, THOMAS. [Born in Va. Appointed from S. C.]
Brig. Gen. State Troops, — July, 1780. Died 1 June, 1832.

THOMAS, JOHN. [Born in Mass. Appointed from Mass.]
Brig. Gen., 22 June, 1775. Maj. Gen., 6 March, 1776. Died 30 May, 1776.

THOMPSON, WM. [Born in Ireland. Appointed from Penn.]
Brig. Gen., 1 March, 1776. Died 4 Sept., 1781.

VARNUM, JAMES M. [Born in Mass. Appointed from R. I.]
Brig. Gen., 21 Feb., 1777. Resigned 5 March, 1779. Died 17 Jan., 1789.

WARD, ARTEMUS. [Born in Mass. Appointed from Mass.]
Maj. Gen., 17 June, 1775. Resigned 23 April, 1776. Died 27 Oct., 1800.

WARREN, JOSEPH. [Born in Mass. Appointed from Mass.]
Maj. Gen. State Troops, 14 June, 1775. Killed 17 June, 1775, at the Battle of Bunker Hill.

WASHINGTON, GEORGE. [Born in Va. Appointed from Va.]
Gen. and Commander-in-Chief, 15 June, 1775. Died 14 Dec., 1799.

WAYNE, ANTHONY. [Born in Penn. Appointed from Penn.]
Brig. Gen., 21 Feb., 1777. Died 15 Dec., 1796.

WEEDON, GEORGE. [Born in Va. Appointed from Va.]
Brig. Gen., 21 Feb., 1777. Died ———.

WHITCOMB, JOHN. [Born in Mass. Appoinetd from Mass.]
Brig. Gen., 5 June, 1776. Died ———, 1812.

WILLIAMS, OTHO H. [Born in Md. Appointed from Md.]
Brig. Gen., 9 May, 1782. Died 16 July, 1794.

WOODFORD, WM. [Born in Va. Appointed from Va.]
Brig. Gen., 21 Feb., 1777. Died 13 Nov., 1780.

WOOSTER, DAVID. [Born in Conn. Appointed from Conn.]
Brig. Gen., 22 June, 1775. Died 2 May, 1777, of wounds received at the Battle of Richfield.

# GENERAL OFFICERS

OF THE

# Line and Staff of the Regular Establishment.

# GENERAL OFFICERS

OF THE

# LINE OF THE REGULAR ESTABLISHMENT.

---

[For details see Individual Records.]

ANDERSON, ROBERT, Brig. Gen., 15 May, 1861.
ANDERSON, THOMAS M., Brig. Gen., 31 March, 1899.
ARMSTRONG, JOHN, Brig. Gen., 6 July, 1812.
ATKINSON, HENRY, Brig. Gen., 13 May, 1820.
AUGUR, C. C., Brig. Gen., 4 March, 1869.
BISSELL, DANIEL, Brig. Gen., 9 March, 1814.
BLISS, ZENAS R., Brig. Gen., 25 April, 1865; Maj. Gen., 6 June, 1900.
BLOOMFIELD, JOSEPH, Brig. Gen., 27 March, 1812.
BOYD, J. P., Brig. Gen., 26 Aug., 1812.
BROOKE, JOHN R., Brig. Gen., 6 April, 1888; Maj. Gen., 6 June, 1900.
BROOKS, JOHN, Brig. Gen., 11 April, 1792.
BROWN, JACOB, Brig. Gen., 19 July, 1813; Maj. Gen., 24 Jan., 1814.
BURKE, DANIEL W., Brig. Gen., 20 Oct., 1899.
CADWALADER, GEORGE, Brig. Gen., 3 March, 1847.
CANBY, E. R. S., Brig. Gen., 28 July, 1866.
CARPENTER, G. S., Brig. Gen., 5 Dec., 1899.
CARPENTER, L. H., Brig. Gen., 18 Oct., 1899.
CARR, EUGENE A., Brig. Gen., 19 July, 1892.
CARLTON, C. H., Brig. Gen., 29 June, 1897.
CASS, LEWIS, Brig. Gen., 12 March, 1813.
CHANDLER, JOHN, Brig. Gen., 8 July, 1812.
COOKE, P. ST. GEORGE, Brig. Gen., 12 Nov., 1861.
COPPINGER, JOHN J., Brig. Gen., 25 April, 1895.
COVINGTON, LEONARD, Brig. Gen., 1 Aug., 1813.
CROOK, GEORGE, Brig. Gen., 29 Oct., 1873; Maj. Gen., 6 April, 1888.
DAVIE, A. W., Brig. Gen., 19 July, 1798.
DEARBORN, HENRY, Maj. Gen., 27 March, 1812.
FLOURNOY, THOMAS, Brig. Gen., 18 June, 1812.
FRANK, ROYAL T., Brig. Gen., 17 Oct., 1899.
FREMONT, JOHN C., Maj. Gen., 14 May, 1861.
FORSYTH, J. W., Brig. Gen., 9 Nov., 1894; Maj. Gen., 13 May, 1897.
GAINES, E. P., Brig. Gen., 9 March, 1814.
GANSEVOORT, PETER, Brig. Gen., 15 Feb., 1809.
GIBBON, JOHN, Brig. Gen., 10 July, 1885.
GRAHAM, W. M., Brig. Gen., 26 May, 1897.
GRANT, U. S., Maj. Gen., 4 July, 1863; Lieut. Gen., 2 March, 1864; Gen., 25 July, 1866.
GRIERSON, B. H., Brig. Gen., 5 April, 1890.
HALLECK, H. W., Maj. Gen., 19 Aug., 1861.
HAMPTON, WADE, Maj. Gen., 2 March, 1813.
HANCOCK, W. S., Brig. Gen., 12 Aug., 1864; Maj. Gen., 26 July, 1866.
HAND, EDWARD, Maj. Gen., 19 July, 1798.
HARNEY, W. S., Brig. Gen., 14 June, 1858.
HARRISON, W. H., Brig. Gen., 22 Aug., 1812; Maj. Gen., 2 March, 1813.
HAWKINS, H. S., Brig. Gen., 28 Sept., 1898.
HENRY, G. V., Brig. Gen., 11 Oct., 1898.
HOOKER, JOSEPH, Brig. Gen., 20 Sept., 1862.
HOPPING, E. D., Brig. Gen., 3 March, 1847.
HOWARD, BENJ., Brig. Gen., 12 March, 1813.
HOWARD, O. O., Brig. Gen., 12 Dec., 1864; Maj. Gen., 19 March, 1886.
HALL, WM., Brig. Gen., 8 April, 1812.
HUNTINGTON, E., Brig. Gen., 19 July, 1798.
IZARD, GEORGE, Brig. Gen., 12 March, 1813; Maj. Gen., 24 Jan., 1814.
JACKSON, ANDREW, Brig. Gen., 19 April, 1814; Maj. Gen., 1 May, 1814.
KAUTZ, A. V., Brig. Gen., 20 April, 1891.
KEARNEY, S. W., Brig. Gen., 30 June, 1846.

KELLOGG, E. R., Brig. Gen., 5 Dec., 1899.
KENT, J. F., Brig. Gen., 4 Oct., 1898.
LEE, HENRY, Maj. Gen., 19 July, 1798.
LEWIS, MORGAN, Maj. Gen., 2 March, 1813.
LUDLOW, WM., Brig. Gen., 1900.
MACKENZIE, R. S., Brig. Gen., 26 Oct., 1882.
MACOMB, ALEX'R, Brig. Gen., 24 Jan., 1814; Maj. Gen., 24 May, 1828.
MANSFIELD, J. K. F., Brig. Gen., 6 May, 1861.
MACARTHUR, ARTHUR, Brig. Gen., 1900.
McARTHUR, DUNCAN, Brig. Gen., 12 March, 1813.
McCLELLAN, G. B., Maj. Gen., 14 May, 1861.
McCOOK, A. McD., Brig. Gen., 11 July, 1890; Maj. Gen., 9 Nov., 1894.
McDOWELL, IRWIN, Brig. Gen., 14 May, 1861; Maj. Gen., 25 Nov., 1872.
McPHERSON, J. B., Brig. Gen., 1 Aug., 1863.
MEADE, GEORGE G., 3 July, 1863; Maj. Gen., 18 Aug., 1864.
MERRIAM, H. C., Brig. Gen., 30 June, 1897.
MERRITT, WESLEY, Brig. Gen., 16 April, 1887; Maj. Gen., 25 April, 1895.
MILES, N. A., Brig. Gen., 15 Dec., 1880; Maj. Gen., 5 April, 1890; Lieut. Gen., 6 June, 1900.
MILLS, ANSON, Brig. Gen., 19 June, 1897.
MIZNER, J. K., Brig. Gen., 1 June, 1897.
ORD, E. O. C., Brig. Gen., 26 July, 1866; Maj. Gen., 28 Jan., 1881.
OTIS, E. S., Brig. Gen., 28 Nov., 1893; Maj. Gen., 13 June, 1900.
OVENSHINE, SAM'L, Brig. Gen., 19 Oct., 1899.
PARKER, THOS., Brig. Gen., 12 March, 1813.
PATTERSON, J. H., Brig. Gen., 18 Jan., 1899.
PENNINGTON, A. C. M., Brig. Gen., 17 Oct., 1899.
PILLOW, G. J., Maj. Gen., 13 April, 1847.
PINCKNEY, C. C., Maj. Gen., 19 July, 1798.
PINCKNEY, THOS., Maj. Gen., 27 March, 1812.
POPE, JOHN, Brig. Gen., 14 July, 1862; Maj. Gen., 26 Oct., 1882.
POSEY, THOS., Brig. Gen., 14 Feb., 1793.
POTTER, J. H., Brig. Gen., 1 April, 1886.
PUTNAM, RUFUS, Brig. Gen., 4 May, 1792.
QUITMAN, J. A., Maj. Gen., 14 April, 1847.
RICKETTS, J. B., Maj. Gen., 3 Jan., 1867.
RIPLEY, E. W., Brig. Gen., 15 April, 1814.
ROBINSON, J. C., Maj. Gen., 6 May, 1869.
ROSECRANS, W. S., Brig. Gen., 16 May, 1861.
ROSS, SAMUEL, Brig. Gen., 1 Jan., 1871.
ROUSSEAU, L. H., Brig. Gen., 28 March, 1867.
RUGER, T. H., Brig. Gen., 19 March, 1886; Maj. Gen., 8 Feb., 1895.
SCOTT, WINFIELD, Brig. Gen., 9 March, 1814; Maj. Gen., 25 June, 1841; Bvt. Lieut. Gen., —.
SCHOFIELD, JNO. M., Brig. Gen., 30 Nov., 1864; Maj. Gen., 4 March, 1869; Lieut. Gen., 5 Feb., 1895.
SEVIER, JNO., Brig. Gen., 19 July, 1798.
SHAFTER, WM. R., Brig. Gen., 3 May, 1897.
SHERIDAN, P. H., Brig. Gen., 20 Sept., 1864; Maj. Gen., 8 Nov., 1864; Lieut. Gen., 4 March, 1869; Gen., 1 June, 1888.
SHERMAN, W. T., Brig. Gen., 4 July, 1863; Maj. Gen., 12 Aug., 1864; Lieut. Gen., 25 July, 1866; Gen., 4 March, 1869.
SHERMAN, T. W., Maj. Gen., 31 Dec., 1870.
SICKLES, D. E., Maj. Gen., 14 April, 1869.
SMITH, P. F., Brig. Gen., 30 Dec., 1856.
SMITH, T. A., Brig. Gen., 24 Jan., 1814.
STANLEY, D. S., Brig. Gen., 24 March, 1884.
SUMNER, E. V., Brig. Gen., 16 March, 1861.
SUMNER, E. V., Jr., Brig. Gen., 27 March, 1899.
SWEENEY, T. W., Brig. Gen., 11 May, 1870.
TAYLOR, ZACHARY, Brig. Gen., 25 Dec., 1837; Maj. Gen., 29 June, 1846.
TERRY, A. H., Brig. Gen., 15 Jan., 1865; Maj. Gen., 3 March, 1886.
WADE, JAS. F., Brig. Gen., 26 May, 1897.
WASHINGTON, GEORGE, Lieut. Gen., 3 July, 1798.
WASHINGTON, W. A., Brig. Gen., 19 July, 1798.
WAYNE, ANTHONY, Maj. Gen., 5 March, 1792.
WHEATON, FRANK, Brig. Gen., 18 April, 1892; Maj. Gen., 15 April, 1897.
WHITE, A. W., Brig. Gen., 19 July, 1798.
WILKINSON, JAMES, Brig. Gen., 5 March, 1792; Maj. Gen., 2 March, 1813.
WILCOX, O. B., Brig. Gen., 13 Oct., 1886.
WILLIAMS, W. R., Brig. Gen., 9 July, 1813.
WINCHESTER, JAMES, Brig. Gen., 27 March, 1812.
WINDER, W. H., Brig. Gen., 12 March, 1813.
WOOL, JOHN E., Brig. Gen., 16 May, 1862.
WORTH, W. S., Brig. Gen., 1 Nov., 1898.

# GENERAL OFFICERS

OF THE

# STAFF OF THE REGULAR ESTABLISHMENT.

[For details see Individual Records.]

AINSWORTH, F. C., Brig. Gen., 2 March, 1899; in Ch. of Records.
ALVORD, BENJAMIN, Brig. Gen., 22 July, 1876; P. M. G.
BAIRD, ABSOLAM, Brig. Gen., 8 June, 1880; I. G.
BARNES, JOS. K., Brig. Gen., 22 Aug., 1864; Surg. Gen.
BATCHELDER, R. N., Brig. Gen., 11 July, 1890; Q. M. G.
BELL, WM. H., Brig. Gen., 14 Nov., 1897; C. G. S.
BENET, S. V., Brig. Gen., 23 June, 1874; Ch. of Ord.
BRECK, SAM'L, Brig. Gen., 11 Sept., 1897; A. G.
BRECKINRIDGE, J. C., Brig. Gen., 30 Jan., 1889; I. G.
BRICE, B. W., Brig. Gen., 28 July, 1866; P. M. G.
BROWN, N. W., Brig. Gen., 8 June, 1880; Surg. Gen.
BUFFINGTON, A. R., Brig. Gen., 5 April, 1899; Ch. of Ord.
CASEY, T. L., Brig. Gen., 6 July, 1888; Ch. of Eng.
CORBIN, H. C., Brig. Gen., 25 Feb., 1898; A. G.; Maj. Gen., 6 June, 1900.
CRAIGHILL, W. P., Brig. Gen., 10 May, 1895; Ch. of Eng.
CRANE, C. H., Brig. Gen., 3 July, 1882; Surg. Gen.
CUSHING, S. T., Brig. Gen., 4 Feb., 1898; C. G. S.
DAVIS, N. H., Brig. Gen., 11 March, 1885; I. G.
DELAFIELD, RICHARD, Brig. Gen., 22 April, 1864; Ch. of Eng.
DRUM, R. C., Brig. Gen., 15 June, 1880; A. G.
DUANE, J. C., Brig. Gen., 11 Oct., 1886; Ch. of Eng.
DU BARRY, BEEKMAN, Brig. Gen., 10 July, 1890; C. G. S.
DUNN, W. McK., Brig. Gen., 1 Dec., 1875; J. A. G.
DYER, A. B., Brig. Gen., 12 Sept., 1864; Ch. of Ord.
EAGAN, C. P., Brig. Gen., 3 May, 1898; C. G. S.
EATON, A. B., Brig. Gen., 29 June, 1864; C. G. S.
FLAGLER, D. W., Brig. Gen., 23 Jan., 1891; Ch. of Ord.
FRY, J. B., Brig. Gen., 21 April, 1864; Provost Mar. Gen.
GREELEY, A. W., Brig. Gen., 3 March, 1887; Ch. Sig. Off.
HAMILTON, ALEX'R, Maj. Gen., 19 July, 1798; I. G.
HAMMOND, W. A., Brig. Gen., 25 April, 1862; Surg. Gen.
HAWKINS, J. P., Brig. Gen., 22 Dec., 1892; C. G. S.
HAZEN, W. B., Brig. Gen., 15 Dec., 1880; Ch. Sig. Off.
HOLABIRD, S. B., Brig. Gen., 1 July, 1883; Q. M. G.
HOLT, JOSEPH, Brig. Gen., 22 June, 1864; J. A. G.
HUMPHREYS, A. A., Brig. Gen., 8 Aug., 1866; Ch. of Eng.
INGALLS, RUFUS, Brig. Gen., 23 Feb., 1882; Q. M. G.
JESUP, T. S., Brig. Gen., 8 May, 1818; Q. M. G.
JOHNSTON, J. E., Brig. Gen., 28 June, 1860; Q. M. G.
JONES, ROGER, Brig. Gen., 20 Aug., 1888; I. G.
KELTON, J. C., Brig. Gen., 7 June, 1889; A. G.
LIEBER, G. NORMAN, Brig. Gen., 3 Jan., 1895; J. A. G.
LEWIS, MORGAN, Brig. Gen., 3 April, 1812; Q. M. G.
LUDINGTON, M. I., Brig. Gen., 3 Feb., 1898; Q. M. G.
MACFEELY, R., Brig. Gen., 14 April, 1875; C. G. S.
MARCY, R. B., Brig. Gen., 12 Dec., 1878; I. G.
MEIGS, M. C., Brig. Gen., 15 May, 1861; Q. M. G.
MOORE, JOHN, Brig. Gen., 18 Nov., 1886; Surg. Gen.
MORGAN, M. R., Brig. Gen., 8 Oct., 1894; C. G. S.
MURRAY, ROBERT, Brig. Gen., 23 Nov., 1883; Surg. Gen.
MYER, ALBERT J., Brig. Gen., 16 June, 1880; Ch. Sig. Off.
NASH, W. H., Brig. Gen., 30 April, 1898; C. G. S.
NEWTON, JOHN, Brig. Gen., 6 March, 1884; Ch. of Eng.
NORTH, WM., Brig. Gen., 19 July, 1798; A. G.

PARKER, DANIEL, Brig. Gen., 22 Nov., 1814; A. G. and I. G.
PIKE, ZEBULON M., Brig. Gen., 12 March, 1813; A. G. and I. G.
RAMSAY, G. D., Brig. Gen., 15 Sept., 1863; Ch. of Ord.
RAWLINS, J. A., Brig. Gen., 3 March, 1865; Ch. of Staff.
RIPLEY, J. W., Brig. Gen., 3 Oct., 1861; Ch. of Ord.
ROCHESTER, W. B., Brig. Gen., 17 Feb., 1882; P. M. G.
RUCKER, D. H., Brig. Gen., 13 Feb., 1882; Q. M. G.
RUGGLES, G. D., Brig. Gen., 6 Nov., 1893; A. G.
SACKETT, D. B., Brig. Gen., 2 Jan., 1881; I. G.
SAWTELLE, C. G., Brig. Gen., 19 Aug., 1896; Q. M. G.
SHIRES, A. E., Brig. Gen., 23 June, 1874; C. G. S.
SMITH, WM., Brig. Gen., 10 March, 1890; P. M. G.
SMYTH, ALEX'R, Brig. Gen., 6 July, 1812; I. G.
STANTON, T. H., Brig. Gen., 27 March, 1895; P. M. G.
STERNBERG, G. M., Brig. Gen., 30 May, 1893; Surg. Gen.
SULLIVAN, T. C., Brig. Gen., 26 Jan., 1897; C. G. S.
SUTHERLAND, CHAS., Brig. Gen., 23 Dec., 1890; Surg. Gen.
SWAIM, D. G., Brig. Gen., J. A. G., 18 Feb., 1881.
SWARTWOUT, ROBERT, Brig. Gen., 21 March, 1813; Q. M. G
THOMAS, LORENZO, Brig. Gen., 3 Aug., 1861; A. G.
TOWNSEND, E. D., Brig. Gen., 22 Feb., 1869; A. G.
WEEKS, G. W., Brig. Gen., 16 Feb., 1897; Q. M. G.
WILLIAMS, ROBERT, Brig. Gen., 5 July, 1892; A. G.
WILSON, J. M., Brig. Gen., 1 Feb., 1897; Ch. of Eng.
WRIGHT, H. G., Brig. Gen., 30 June, 1879; Ch. of Eng

# APPOINTMENTS

MADE BY THE

# President in the Volunteer Service.

---

**1861-65.**

# A LIST OF APPOINTMENTS

MADE BY THE

# PRESIDENT IN THE VOLUNTEER SERVICE

## DURING THE CIVIL WAR—1861-65.

---

Abbott, Asa T., 2nd Lieut. Sig. Corps, 3 March, 1863. Mustered out 29 Aug., 1865.
Abbott, Isaac C., Capt. A. Q. M., 8 July, 1863. Mustered out 10 Aug., 1865.
Abbott, John C., 2nd Lieut. Sig. Corps, 3 March, 1863. Mustered out 11 Sept., 1865.
Abel, William H., Capt. A. A. G., 11 March, 1863. Resigned 4 Feb., 1865.
Abercrombie, John J., Brig. Gen., 31 Aug., 1861. Mustered out 24 June, 1864.
Aborn, James, Capt. A. Q. M., 26 Nov., 1862. Resigned 21 May, 1863.
Acheson, John W., Capt. A. A. G., 29 Feb., 1864. Mustered out 19 Sept., 1865.
Adair, John D., Capt. C. S., 30 Aug., 1862. Mustered out 9 Oct., 1865.
Adair, Samuel L., Hosp. Chap., 13 June, 1862. Discharged 7 July, 1864.
Adams, Daniel M., Maj. P. M., 19 Feb., 1863. Mustered out 31 Aug., 1866.
Adams, Edward P., 2nd Lieut. Sig. Corps, 3 March, 1863. Resigned 6 July, 1865.
Adams, Frank, Capt. A. A. G., 20 Oct., 1864. Mustered out 1 Aug., 1865.
Adams, George M., Capt. C. S., 17 Aug., 1861. P. M., 28 May, 1864. Resigned 19 May, 1865.
Adams, Henry J., Capt. C. S., 23 Jan., 1865. Mustered out 23 Sept., 1865.
Adams, Henry J., Maj. P. M., 5 Sept., 1861. Dismissed 22 Aug., 1864.
Adams, John Q., Asst. Surg., 27 Feb., 1863. Mustered out 9 Oct., 1865.
Adams, John Q., 2nd Lieut. Sig. Corps, 3 March, 1863. Mustered out 1 Sept., 1865.
Adams, Myron, Jr., 2nd Lieut. Sig. Corps, 3 March, 1863. Resigned 1 Aug., 1865.
Adams, Moses S., Capt. C. S., 5 Sept., 1862. Resigned 10 Jan., 1865.
Adams, Oscar, Maj. P. M., 18 March, 1864. Mustered out 15 Nov., 1865.
Adams, Robert, Jr., Capt. A. A. G., 18 May, 1864. Mustered out 4 Jan., 1866.
Adams, Samuel E., Maj. P. M., 26 Nov., 1862. Mustered out 15 Jan., 1866.
Adams, Samuel R., Capt. A. A. G., 7 April, 1865. Mustered out 18 Sept., 1865.
Adrian, C., Capt. A. Q. M., 29 Nov., 1862. Appointment expired 4 March, 1863.
Agnew, D. Hayes, Maj. Surg., 4 Oct., 1862. Resigned 7 April, 1863.
Aiken, Dwi. A., Capt. C. S., 26 Nov., 1862. Resigned 12 March, 1865.
Ainsworth, Fred. S., Maj. Surg., 7 Nov., 1862. Mustered out 27 July, 1865.
Alberger, Morris H., Capt. A. Q. M., 17 Nov., 1864. Mustered out 31 May, 1866.
Albert, Anselme, Col. Addl. A. de C., 31 March, 1862. Resigned 8 June, 1864.
Alden, A. Sidney, Capt. A. A. G., 7 April, 1864. Maj., 21 Feb., 1865. Mustered out 30 April, 1866.
*Alden, George E., Capt. A. Q. M., 12 March, 1863.
Alden, John P., Capt. C. S., 2 July, 1863. Discharged 20 March, 1865.
Aldrich, Edwin J., Capt. C. S., 18 May, 1864. Mustered out 19 Dec., 1865.
Alexander, Barton S., Lieut. Col. Addl. A. de C., 28 Sept., 1861. Mustered out 31 May, 1866.
Alexander, Demas M., Capt. C. S., 30 July, 1863. Mustered out 21 Aug., 1866.
Alexander, Fredk. W., Capt. C. S., 28 Feb., 1865. Mustered out 10 Jan., 1866.
Alexander, James B., Capt. C. S., 23 Sept., 1861. Vacated appointment 6 Dec., 1861.
Alexander, Joshua H., Capt., A. Q. M., 26 Nov., 1862. Appointment cancelled.
Allen, Abner J., Capt. A. Q. M., 30 June, 1862. Resigned 3 June, 1864.
Allen, Charles, Capt. C. S., 19 Feb., 1863. Died 9 Sept., 1863.
Allen, Charles L., Maj. Surg., 23 June, 1862. Resigned 5 Aug., 1864.
Allen, Charles J. F., Maj. P. M., 16 July, 1862. Mustered out 15 Nov., 1865.
Allen, Chas. S., Capt. C. S., 7 Dec., 1864. Mustered out 26 June, 1865.
Allen, Daniel P., Capt. C. S., 21 April, 1862. Mustered out 9 Oct., 1865.
Allen, Edward S., Capt. A. Q. M., 5 Dec., 1863. Mustered out 19 Nov., 1866.
Allen, George T., Maj. Surg., 4 April, 1862; Lieut. Col. Med. Insp., 14 June, 1862. Mustered out 31 Oct., 1865.
Allen, John T., Capt. A. Q. M., 26 Nov., 1862. Mustered out 19 July, 1865.
Allen, Norman M., Maj. P. M., 19 Feb., 1863. Resigned 27 April, 1863.
Allen, Robert, Col. Addl. A. de C., 19 Feb., 1862; Brig. Gen., 23 May, 1863. Mustered out 1 Sept., 1866.
Allen, Wm., Maj. P. M., 1 June, 1861. Resigned 4 Oct., 1865.
Allen, Wm. H. H., Maj. P. M., 22 Sept., 1863. Mustered out 1 Dec., 1865.
Allen, Wm. T., Capt. C. S., 10 Aug., 1864. Mustered out 11 May, 1866.
Alley, John H., Capt. C. S., 21 April, 1864. Mustered out 24 June, 1865.
Allin, Thomas, Capt. C. S., 19 Feb., 1862. Resigned 31 May, 1864.

Allison, John, Maj. P. M., 1 Nov., 1861. Mustered out 31 July, 1865.
Allison, Thomas S., Maj. P. M., 1 June, 1861. Appointed P. M., U. S. A., April, 1867.
Almstadt, Henry, Maj. P. M., 19 Feb., 1863. Resigned 1 May, 1865.
Almy, George C., Capt. C. S., 30 June, 1864. Mustered out 12 June, 1866.
Alton, Davis, Maj. P. M., 19 Feb., 1863. Resigned 1 May, 1865.
Alvord, Benjamin, Brig. Gen., 15 April, 1862. Resigned 8 Aug., 1865.
Ambrose, Mordecai J. W., Hosp. Chap., 28 Sept., 1863. Appointment revoked 14 July, 1864.
Amee, Josiah L. C., Capt. A. Q. M., 18 March, 1864. Mustered out 30 March, 1866.
Ames, Adelbert, Brig. Gen., 20 May, 1863. Mustered out 30 April, 1866.
Ames, Almon S., Hosp. Chap., 24 Feb., 1865. Mustered out 21 Aug., 1865.
Ames, George, Capt. C. S., 26 Nov., 1862. Mustered out 30 March, 1866.
Ames, Franklin, Maj. P. M., 28 May, 1864. Mustered out 30 April, 1866.
Ammen, Jacob, Brig. Gen., 16 July, 1862. Resigned 4 Jan., 1865.
Ammen, Wm. P., Capt. A. A. G., 11 March, 1863. Resigned 19 May, 1865.
Amory, Charles B., Capt. A. A. G., 18 May, 1864. Resigned 9 May, 1865.
Amsden, Frederick J., 2nd Lieut. Sig. Corps, 3 March, 1863. Mustered out 25 Nov., 1865.
Anderson, Finley, Capt. A. A. G., 7 Oct., 1864; Maj., 6 June, 1865. Mustered out 19 June, 1866.
Anderson, George W., Jr., Capt. A. Q. M., 26 Nov., 1862. Mustered out 31 Oct., 1865.
Anderson, John C., Capt. Addl. A. de C., 24 May, 1862. Resigned 13 June, 1863.
Anderson, John F., Maj. A. de C., 9 June, 1863. Resigned 27 March, 1865.
Anderson, Joseph, Hosp. Chap., 2 Feb., 1863. Mustered out 4 Aug., 1865.
Anderson, Thomas J., Capt. A. A. G., 27 Feb., 1863; Maj., 25 May, 1863. Resigned 28 March, 1865.
Anderson, Wm. P., Capt. A. A. G., 15 Sept., 1862. Resigned 18 March, 1864.
Andres, Hiram, Capt. C. S., 27 Aug., 1864. Mustered out 10 Aug., 1865.
Andrews, Christopher C., Brig. Gen., 5 Jan., 1864. Mustered out 15 Jan., 1866.
Andrews, Edward W., Capt. A. A. G., 20 April, 1864. Mustered out 29 Oct., 1864.
X Andrews, George L., Brig. Gen., 10 Nov., 1862. Mustered out 24 Aug., 1865.
Andrews, Henry P., Maj. P. M., 1 June, 1861. Resigned 22 Aug., 1863.
Andrews, Wm. S., 1st Lieut. Sig. Corps, 3 March, 1863. Resigned 21 July, 1864.
Antisel, Thos., Maj. Surg., 2 Oct., 1861. Mustered out 7 Oct., 1865.
Applegate, Joseph W., Asst. Surg., 19 Feb., 1863; Surg., 26 Jan., 1865. Mustered out, 1 Nov., 1867.
Applegate, Lewis, Asst. Surg., 9 Sept., 1864. Mustered out 9 Oct., 1865.
Armsby, James H., Asst. Surg., 24 Jan., 1865. Mustered out 18 Jan., 1866.
Armstrong, George A., Capt. A. Q. M., 18 May, 1864. Mustered out 13 March, 1866.
Armstrong, Wm. B., Capt. A. Q. M., 26 Nov., 1862. Mustered out 16 Aug., 1867.
Arnold, Lewis G., Brig. Gen., 24 Jan., 1862. Appointment cancelled 8 Feb., 1864.
Arnold, Richard, Brig. Gen., 29 Nov., 1862. Mustered out 24 Aug., 1865.
Arrowsmith, George, Capt. A. A. G., 19 Aug., 1862. Resigned 6 Nov., 1862.
Artand, Theodore, Asst. Surg., 4 Dec., 1863; Maj. Surg., 13 Jan., 1865. Mustered out 15 July, 1865.
Arthur, John W., Hosp. Chap., 22 April, 1863. Appointment revoked 13 Aug., 1864.
Arthur, Walter C., Capt. C. S., 7 June, 1864. Mustered out 10 Sept., 1866.
Artsman, Gus., Capt. A. Q. M., 13 Sept., 1864. Mustered out 4 Aug., 1866.
Asboth, Alexander, Brig. Gen., 21 March, 1862. Mustered out 24 Aug., 1865.
Ash, Franklin P., Capt. C. S., 19 Aug., 1862. Dismissed 16 May, 1863.
Ashmerad, Albert S., Capt. A. Q. M., 5 Aug., 1863. Mustered out 11 Nov., 1865.
Ashwander, Joseph, Hosp. Chaplain 1 Dec., 1862. Mustered out 24 Aug., 1865.
Asmunsen, Charles W., Maj. A. A. G., 9 Sept., 1864. Mustered out 10 July 18[illegible].
Aspinwall, Nath'l P., Capt. A. Q. M., 11 March, 1863. Resigned 28 Nov., 1864.
Asson, William T., Maj. P. M., 28 May, 1864. Mustered out 15 Jan., 1866.
Atchison, Charles B., Capt. Addl. A. de C., 11 July, 1862. Mustered out 1 Sept., 1866.
Atkinson, George S., Capt. A. Q. M., 3 Aug., 1864. Resigned 25 March, 1865.
Atkinson, Hoffman, Capt. A. A. G., 28 May, 1862. Resigned 15 April, 1863.
Atkinson, John R., Maj. P. M., 30 June, 1862. Resigned 2 May, 1864.
Atwell, Joseph D., Maj. P. M., 28 May, 1864. Mustered out 1 June, 1867.
Atwood, Alfred T., Capt. A. Q. M., 26 Nov., 1862. Mustered out 3 June, 1865.
Atwood, George E., Capt. A. Q. M., 21 Jan., 1865. Mustered out 27 Jan., 1866.
Atwood, William, Capt. A. A. G., 2 March, 1865. Mustered out 31 Oct., 1866.
Auchmuty, Rich'd T., Capt. A. A. G., 3 Oct., 1861. Resigned 16 Aug., 1862. Capt. A. A. G., 27 Feb., 1863; Maj., 7 June, 1864. Resigned 2 June, 1865.
Audenried, Joseph C., Capt. A. de C., 29 Aug., 1862. Mustered out 15 Aug., 1863. Capt. A. de C., 27 Oct., 1863.
Augur, Christopher C., Brig. Gen., 12 Nov., 1861; Maj. Gen., 9 Aug., 1862. Mustered out 1 Sept., 1866.
Austin, Adoniram, Capt. A. Q. M., 7 April, 1864. Resigned 18 May, 1865.
Austin, Albert S., Capt. C. S., 17 July, 1862. Dismissed 1 April, 1864.
Austin, John M., Maj. P. M., 21 Oct., 1862. Mustered out 30 April, 1866.
Averell, William W., Brig. Gen., 26 Sept., 1862. Resigned 18 May, 1865.
Avery, William L., Capt. A. de C., 6 Nov., 1863; Maj., 15 March, 1865. Mustered out, 15 Aug., 1865.
Avis, Samuel, Capt. A. Q. M., 2 July, 1864. Mustered out 7 Oct., 1865.
Ayres, Henry, 1st Lieut. Sig. Corps, 3 March, 1863. Mustered out 1 May, 1866.
Ayres, Romeyn B., Brig. Gen., 29 Nov., 1862. Mustered out 30 April, 1866.
Ayres, S. C., Asst. Surg., 19 May, 1865. Mustered out 3 Jan., 1866.
Azpel, T. F., Maj. Surg., 7 Oct., 1861. Mustered out 23 Oct., 1865.
Babbitt, William M., Maj. P. M., 27 Feb., 1863. Resigned 26 Oct., 1863.
Babcock, Charles P., Maj. P. M., 19 Feb., 1863. Appointment revoked, 25 Aug., 1863.
Babcock, Paul, Jr., Capt. Sig. Corps, 3 March, 1863. Resigned 30 April, 1864.
Baber, Richard P. L., Maj. P. M., 12 Sept., 1861. Mustered out 15 Nov., 1865.
Bache, Thomas H., Maj. Surg., 4 Sept., 1861. Mustered out 20 Sept., 1865.
Bachtell, Samuel, Capt. Sig. Corps, 3 March, 1863. Mustered out 20 June, 1866.

Backx, Augustus, Capt. Addl. A. de C., 1 May, 1862. Appointment revoked 9 June, 1864.
Bacon, Francis, Maj. Surg., 8 Aug., 1862. Resigned 25 Aug., 1864.
Bacon, Theodore C., Capt. A. A. G., 9 Sept., 1862. Resigned 5 Feb., 1864.
Bacon, Winchel D., Maj. P. M., 21 April, 1863. Resigned 14 July, 1863.
Badeau, Adam, Capt. Addl. A. de C., 29 April, 1862. Mustered out 1 July, 1866.
Badger, Norman, Hosp. Chaplain., 30 June, 1864. Mustered out 23 Sept., 1865.
Bagg, Sylvester, Capt. A. Q. M., 25 Oct., 1862. Mustered out 22 Nov., 1865.
Bailey, E. Stillman, Maj. P. M., 19 Feb., 1863. Mustered out 30 April, 1866.
Bailey, George W., Lieut. Sig. Corps, 3 March, 1863. Resigned 21 June, 1865.
Bailey, Joseph, Brig. Gen., 10 Nov., 1864. Resigned 7 July, 1865.
Bailey, Marcellus, Capt. A. A. G., 29 Feb., 1864. Resigned 8 Dec., 1864.
Bailhache, Morgan H., Capt. A. A. G., 11 March, 1863. Mustered out 25 Nov., 1865.
Bailhache, Wm. H., Capt. A. Q. M., 28 Sept., 1861. Resigned 5 June, 1866.
Baily, Wm., Maj. P. M., 28 May, 1864. Mustered out 31 July, 1865.
Bainbridge, Edmond C., Maj. A. de C., 3 Sept., 1864. Mustered out 1 July, 1866.
Bainbridge, Wm. P., Capt., A. de C., 3 Sept., 1864. Mustered out 9 Feb., 1866.
Baird, Absalom, Brig. Gen., 28 April, 1862. Mustered out 1 Sept., 1866.
Baird, Chambers, Maj. P. M., 17 Aug., 1863. Mustered out 1 July, 1866.
Baird, Edward C., Capt. A. A. G., 19 Sept., 1861. Maj., 18 Sept., 1863. Resigned 25 Feb., 1865.
Baird, Samuel, Capt. A. Q. M., 29 Feb., 1864. Mustered out 5 Oct., 1866.
Baird, Zebulon, Capt. Addl. A. de C., 30 May, 1862. Resigned 30 Aug., 1864.
Baker, Asa D., Capt. C. S., 18 Nov., 1862. Resigned 12 March, 1865.
Baker, Calvin, Capt. A. Q. M., 4 July, 1863. Mustered out 31 July, 1865.
Baker, D. Ira, Maj. P. M., 24 Feb., 1865. Mustered out 31 July, 1865.
Baker, George W., Capt. C. S., 20 Nov., 1862. Mustered out 18 Jan., 1866.
Baker, John P., Capt. A. de C., 20 Aug., 1862. Appointment revoked, 14 Feb., 1863.
Baker, Lafayette C., Brig. Gen., 26 April, 1865. Mustered out 15 Jan., 1866.
Balch, Frank S., Capt. A. Q. M., 13 Feb., 1865. Mustered out 31 July, 1865.
Baldwin, Burr, Hosp. Chap., 23 June, 1862. Discharged 10 Feb., 1863.
Baldwin, George E., Capt. C. S., 14 April, 1862. Maj. P. M., 30 June, 1862. Resigned 9 April, 1865.
Baldwin, George W., Capt. A. A. G., 9 June, 1862. Resigned 18 April, 1863.
Baldwin, Harvey, Jr., Maj. A. A. G., 24 March, 1863. Resigned 18 Feb., 1864.
Ball, Flamen, Capt. Addl. A. de C., 9 June, 1862. Resigned 2 July, 1865.
Ball, Gideon J., Maj. P. M., 1 June, 1861. Resigned 24 Dec., 1863.
Ball, James H., Capt. A. Q. M., 10 Aug., 1864. Resigned 9 Jan., 1865.
Ball, Levi C., Maj. P. M., 19 Feb., 1863. Mustered out 1 Aug., 1865.
Ball, W. T. W., Capt. C. S., 1 Nov., 1862. Resigned 30 Sept., 1864.
Ballard, Irving T., Maj. P. M., 26 Nov., 1862. Mustered out 15 Nov., 1865.
Ballard, Orville W., Maj. P. M., 26 Nov., 1862. Mustered out 20 July, 1866.
Balloch, George W., Capt. C. S., 21 July, 1862. Mustered out 1 Sept., 1868.
Balloch, James, Hosp. Chap., 17 Nov., 1864. Mustered out 26 July, 1865.
Ballou, Sylvester A., Capt. C. S., 2 March, 1864. Mustered out 20 April, 1866.
Banburg, Thos. M., Capt. C. S., 20 Feb., 1865. Mustered out 31 July, 1865.
Bancker, Girard, Capt. A. Q. M., 3 July, 1863. Appointment revoked, 7 July, 1864.
Banckerd, Josiah, Capt. A. A. G., 14 Feb., 1865. Mustered out 10 Aug., 1865.
Banes, Chas. H. Capt. A. A. G., 15 May, 1863. Resigned 12 Sept., 1864.
Banks, Nathaniel P., Maj. Gen., 16 May, 1861. Mustered out 24 Aug., 1865.
Banks, William A., Asst. Surg., 14 May, 1863. Mustered out 27 July, 1865.
Banning, William L., Capt. C. S., 24 Aug., 1861. Resigned 16 July, 1863.
Bannister, Dwight, Maj. P. M., 1 June, 1861. Appointed P. M., U. S. A., 3 March, 1868.
Bantley, John, Hosp. Chap., 21 April, 1864. Mustered out 20 Nov., 1865.
Barber, Merritt, Capt. A. A. G., 31 Dec., 1864. Mustered out 19 Sept., 1865.
Barber, Oliver, Capt. C. S., 11 June, 1862. Resigned 11 Aug., 1864.
Barbour, Ira C., Capt. A. Q. M., 29 Feb., 1864. Resigned 19 May, 1865.
Barker, John A. G., Maj. P. M., 2 July, 1864. Mustered out 31 July, 1865.
Barker, Nathan, Capt. A. Q. M., 5 Aug., 1861. Mustered out 20 Sept., 1865.
Barker, William W., Capt. C. S., 30 June, 1864. Resigned 10 June, 1865.
Barlow, Edward E., Capt. A. A. G., 27 Oct., 1862. Resigned 30 July, 1863.
Barlow, Francis C., Brig. Gen., 19 Sept., 1862. Maj. Gen., 25 May, 1865. Resigned 16 Nov., 1865.
Barlow, William H., Capt. A. Q. M., 9 Feb., 1865. Mustered out 3 Nov., 1866.
Barnaby, James, Capt. C. S., 26 Nov., 1862. Died 4 March, 1864.
Barnard, Charles, Capt. A. Q. M., 2 July, 1864. Mustered out 20 Aug., 1868.
Barnard, John G., Brig. Gen., 23 Sept., 1861. Mustered out 15 Jan., 1866.
Barnard, Phineas P., Capt. A. Q. M., 13 May, 1863. Mustered out 6 Dec., 1865.
Barnes, Darwin H., Capt. A. Q. M., 31 Jan., 1865. Mustered out 28 July, 1865.
Barnes, James, Brig. Gen., 29 Nov., 1862. Mustered out 15 Jan., 1866.
Barnes, John W., Capt. A. A. G., 25 Nov., 1863. Maj., 15 July, 1864. Mustered out 4 Jan., 1866.
Barnes, Norman S., Asst. Surg., 9 Oct., 1863. Maj. Surg., 19 Jan., 1864. Mustered out 15 Nov., 1865.
Barnes, Robert C., Capt. A. Q. M., 26 Nov., 1862. Resigned 8 Feb., 1864.
Barnes, Stuart, Capt. A. Q. M., 7 Feb., 1865. Mustered out 1 July, 1866.
Barney, Lewis T., Capt. A. A. G., 29 Feb., 1864. Resigned 21 June, 1864.
Barney, William C., Maj. P. M., 22 Aug., 1861. Rejected by the Senate, 11 March, 1862.
Barnhart, Levant W., Capt. A. A. G., 22 May, 1865. Mustered out 20 March, 1866.
Barnum, Henry A., Brig. Gen., 31 May, 1865. Resigned 9 Jan., 1866.
Barr, Thomas J., Capt. A. Q. M., 19 July, 1862. Resigned 7 July, 1864.
Barr, William, Capt. C. S., 28 April, 1863. Died 17 Dec., 1864.
Barrett, Addison, Capt. C. S., 21 Dec., 1864. Mustered out 8 Dec., 1866.
Barrett, Clarence T., Capt. A. de C., 27 May, 1864. Mustered out 11 Sept., 1865.
Barrett, Curtis S., Capt. A. Q. M., 5 Dec., 1863. Mustered out 20 Oct., 1866.
Barrett, William F., 2nd Lieut. Sig. Corps, 3 March, 1863. Mustered out 12 Aug., 1865.

Barringer, Augustus V., Capt. A. Q. M., 5 Aug., 1861. Resigned 19 May, 1865.
Barry, A. Constantine, Hosp. Chap., 10 Feb., 1865. Mustered out 1 Aug., 1865.
Barry, William F., Brig. Gen., 20 Aug., 1861. Mustered out 15 Jan., 1866.
Barstow, Simon F., Capt. Addl. A. de C., 18 March, 1862. Maj. A. A. G., 15 July, 1862. Mustered out 31 July, 1866.
Barstow, Wilson, Capt. Addl. A. de C., 20 June, 1862. Mustered out 31 May, 1866.
Barth, Charles G., Capt. C. S., 18 May, 1864. Mustered out 10 Aug., 1865.
Bartholf, John H., Asst. Surg., 12 Jan., 1865. Mustered out 9 Oct., 1865.
Bartlett, Joseph J., Brig. Gen., 4 Oct., 1862. Appointment expired 4 March, 1863. Brig. Gen., 30 March, 1863. Mustered out 15 Jan., 1866.
Bartlett, Wm. C., Capt. A. de C., 19 March, 1864. Vacated appointment 17 Nov., 1864.
Bartlett, Wm. F., Brig. Gen., 20 June, 1864. Mustered out 18 July, 1866.
Barton, Chas. C., Capt. Addl. A. de C., 26 April, 1862. Mustered out 21 Feb., 1866.
Barton, David, Capt. A. Q. M., 26 Nov., 1862. Resigned 5 Aug., 1864.
Bascom, Gustavus M., Capt. A. A. G., 20 Aug., 1861. Maj., 7 Oct., 1862. Mustered out 1 July, 1866.
Bassett, George T., Capt. C. S., 9 March, 1865. Mustered out 15 July, 1866.
Batchelder, George A., Maj. P. M., 7 March, 1865. Mustered out 5 Oct., 1866.
Batchelder, Richard N., Capt. A. Q. M., 3 Aug., 1861. Capt. A. Q. M., U. S. A., 16 Feb., 1865.
Bates, Caleb, Maj. A. de C., 11 March, 1863. Mustered out 22 Nov., 1865.
Bates, Edward F., Asst. Surg., 7 Jan., 1863. Maj. Surg., 8 Oct., 1863. Died 6 March, 1864.
Batly, John H., Capt. A. Q. M., 19 Sept., 1864. Mustered out 7 Oct., 1865.
Bauduy, Jerome K., Asst. Surg., 6 July, 1863. Resigned 12 Dec., 1863.
Bauer, Adolph Ernest, Capt. Addl. A. de C., 2 June, 1862. Resigned 17 Aug., 1862.
Baxter, Algernon S., Capt. A. Q. M., 23 Nov., 1861. Resigned 27 April, 1862.
Baxter, Henry, Brig. Gen., 12 March, 1863. Mustered out 24 Aug., 1865.
Baxter, Jedediah H., Maj. Surg., 4 April, 1862. Vacated commission 30 July, 1867.
Baxter, John P. G., Maj. Surg., 24 Dec., 1861. Mustered out 23 Oct., 1865.
Bayard, George D., Brig. Gen., 28 April, 1862. Killed 14 Dec., 1862, at Battle of Fredericksburg, Va.
Bayles, Mason, Capt. C. S., 23 Feb., 1864. Mustered out 4 Aug., 1865.
Bayley, Wm. C., Capt. A. Q. M., 26 Nov., 1862. Appointment revoked 13 March, 1863.
Bayne, John H., Maj. Surg., 28 July, 1863. Mustered out 1 Sept., 1867.
Beach, Chandler B., Capt. A. Q. M., 21 Feb., 1865. Mustered out 18 Jan., 1866.
Beach, George W., Capt. C. S., 26 Nov., 1862. Mustered out 5 Aug., 1866.
Beaham, Thomas G., Maj. A. de C., 6 Nov., 1863. Resigned 12 Sept, 1864.
Beal, George L., Brig. Gen., 30 Nov., 1864. Mustered out 15 Jan., 1866.
Bean, Eli B., Capt. A. Q. M., 20 Feb., 1864. Mustered out 30 Oct., 1865.
Bean, Henry D., Capt. A. A. G., 9 Feb., 1865. Mustered out 19 Sept., 1865.
Bean, Sylvanus B., Capt. A. Q. M., 26 Nov., 1862. Mustered out 19 May, 1866.
Bear, Richard McA., Hosp. Chap., 20 June, 1862. Mustered out 11 July, 1865.
Beardslee, Fred'k E., Capt. A. Q. M., 19 Nov., 1862. Resigned 8 Sept., 1864. 2nd Lieut. Sig. Corps, 3 March, 1863. Mustered out 12 Aug., 1865.
Beardsley, Sam'l R., Capt. A. A. G., 28 Sept., 1863. Died 28 Dec., 1863.
Beatty, John, Brig. Gen., 29 Nov., 1862. Resigned 28 Jan., 1864.
Beatty, Samuel, Brig. Gen., 29 Nov., 1862. Mustered out 15 Jan., 1866.
Beatty, Samuel M., Hosp. Chap., 17 April, 1863. Mustered out 12 July, 1865.
Beaumont, Eugene B., Capt. A. de C., 13 May, 1863. Maj. A. A. G., 20 Oct., 1864. Mustered out 19 March, 1866.
Beaznell, John W., Capt. A. Q. M., 11 Nov., 1861. Maj. P. M., 26 Nov., 1862. Mustered out 1 Nov., 1865.
Becker, Edwin C., Capt. A. Q. M., 14 April, 1862. Mustered out 27 Nov., 1865.
Beckwith, Amos, Col. Addl. A. de C., 1 Jan., 1862. Mustered out 31 May, 1866.
Beckwith, Edw'd G., Col. Addl. A. de C., 5 July, 1862. Mustered out 31 May, 1866.
Bedford, Wimer, Capt. A. A. G., 11 March, 1863. Resigned 18 Feb., 1865.
Beebe, Gaylord D., Maj. Surg., 24 Dec., 1861. Resigned 9 March, 1863.
Beecher, Edwin, Maj. P. M., 26 Nov., 1862. Mustered out 1 March, 1869.
Beecher, Rob't E., Capt. A. A. G., 30 June, 1864. Mustered out 19 Sept., 1865.
Beeler, Abraham, Maj. P. M., 18 March, 1864. Died 28 Oct., 1864, of wound received in an attack at Randolph, Tenn.
Belcher, John H., Capt. A. Q. M., 14 Oct., 1864. Vacated commission 2 Aug., 1866.
Belger, James, Col. Addl. A. de C., 11 July, 1862. Out of service 30 Nov., 1863.
Belknap, Wm. W., Brig. Gen., 30 July, 1864. Mustered out 24 Aug., 1865.
Bell, Joseph M., Maj. A. A. G., 7 Nov., 1863. Resigned 18 Jan., 1865.
Bell, Joseph McC., Capt. A. A. G., 24 July, 1862. Mustered out 9 Sept., 1866.
Bell, Luther V., Maj. Surg., 3 Aug., 1861. Died 11 Feb., 1862.
Bell, Molyneux, Capt. C. S., 18 Sept., 1862. Mustered out 4 Aug., 1865.
Bell, Sam'l, Jr., Maj. P. M., 26 Nov., 1862. Mustered out 20 July, 1866.
Bellanger, James B., Asst. Surg., 14 May, 1863. Maj. Surg., 29 June, 1863. Died 6 Oct., 1864.
Beman, Edgar C., Capt. C. S., 14 Nov., 1861. Mustered out 1 Sept., 1868.
Benedict, Abel C., Asst. Surg., 19 Feb., 1863. Maj. Surg., 16 Sept., 1863. Mustered out 15 July, 1865.
Benedict, Chas. O., Maj. P. M., 30 June, 1864. Mustered out 1 Nov., 1865.
Benedict, James, Capt. C. S., 9 Sept., 1862. Mustered out 21 Feb., 1866.
Benedict, Le Grand, Capt. A. A. G., 22 Sept., 1862. Resigned 23 Jan., 1865.
Benham, Henry W., Brig. Gen., 13 Aug., 1861. Mustered out 15 Jan., 1866.
Benham, Spencer C., Capt. C. S., 31 Oct., 1861. Mustered out 9 Oct., 1865.
Benkard, James, Capt. Addl. A. de C., 16 June, 1862. Resigned 29 April, 1864.
Benner, Dan'l J., Maj. A. de C., 13 March, 1863. Mustered out 17 June, 1865.
Benner, Henry L., Maj. P. M., 1 June, 1861. Died 26 April, 1862.
Benner, Milton, 2nd Lieut. Sig. Corps, 3 March, 1863. 1st Lieut., 3 March, 1863. Appointment as 1st Lieut. expired 4 July, 1864, and declined appointment as 2nd Lieut.
Bennett, Ebenezer J., Capt. C. S., 12 Oct., 1864. Mustered out 10 Sept., 1866.
Bennett, Joseph F., Capt. A. A. G., 15 May, 1863. Mustered out 21 Feb., 1863.
Bennett, Wm. C., Asst. Surg., 4 June, 1863. Maj. Surg., 4 Dec., 1863. Resigned 9 Nov., 1864.

Benson, Fred'k S., 2nd Lieut. Sig. Corps, 3 March, 1863. Mustered out 17 Aug., 1865.
Benson, Harvey W., 2nd and 1st Lieut. Sig. Corps, 3 March, 1863. Appointment as 1st Lieut. expired 4 July, 1864. Mustered out 12 Aug., 1865.
Bentel, Christian G., Hosp. Chap., 15 July, 1863. Resigned 3 Dec., 1863.
Bentley, Edwin, Maj. Surg., 4 Sept., 1861. Mustered out 4 June, 1866.
Benton, Wm. P., Brig. Gen., 28 April, 1862. Mustered out 4 July, 1865.
Berier, Francis E., Capt. C. S., 14 Nov., 1861. Mustered out 15 Nov., 1866.
Bernay, Chas. L., Maj. P. M., 11 March, 1863. Mustered out 1 Dec., 1865.
Berridge, Leeds K., Hosp. Chap., 11 July, 1862. Mustered out 12 Aug., 1864.
Berry, Hiram G., Brig. Gen., 17 March, 1862. Maj. Gen., 29 Nov., 1862. Killed 2 May, 1863, at Battle of Chancellorsville, Va.
Bertolette, John D., Capt. A. A. G., 25 Sept., 1862. Mustered out 2 Feb., 1866.
Bertram, Joseph H. M. Maj. P. M., 26 Nov., 1862. Resigned 27 July, 1863.
Bestow, Marcus P., Capt. A. A. G., 23 Dec., 1862. Maj., 26 June, 1865. Mustered out 1 Sept., 1866.
Beust, Bernard, Maj. Surg., 4 April, 1862. Resigned 26 May, 1864.
Bevans, Henry L., Maj. P. M., 17 July, 1862. Resigned 20 Jan., 1864.
Bibber, Andrew H., Capt. A. A. G.,18 March, 1865. Mustered out 18 Sept., 1865.
Bickford, Nathan B. E., Capt. C. S., 25 March, 1864. Mustered out 24 June, 1865.
Biddle, Henry J., Capt. A. A. G., 3 Aug., 1861. Died 20 July, 1862, of wounds received at Battle of New Market X Roads, Va.
Biddle, James C., Maj. Addl. A. de C., 8 July, 1862. Mustered out 7 Oct., 1865.
Biddle, Wm. F., Capt. Addl. A. de C., 31 Jan., 1862. Resigned 1 April, 1863.
Bidwell, Daniel D., Brig. Gen., 11 Aug., 1864. Killed 19 Oct., 1864, at the Battle of Cedar Creek, Va.
Bielaski, Alex., Capt. Addl. A. de C., 10 Aug., 1861. Killed 7 Nov., 1861, at Battle of Belmont, Mo.
Bier, Philip G., Capt. A. A. G., 29 Feb., 1864. Died 19 Oct., 1864, of wounds received at Battle of Cedar Creek, Va.
Bierce, Lucius V., Maj. A. A. G., 5 May, 1863. Mustered out 11 Nov., 1865.
Biglow, Sam'l L., Maj. Surg., 4 April, 1862. Resigned 6 Nov., 1862.
Billingsley, Amos S., Hosp. Chap., 13 Feb., 1865. Mustered out 26 July, 1865.
Bilyew, Aaron P., Capt. C. S., 24 Sept., 1862. Resigned 2 July, 1865.
Bingham, Henry H., Maj. J. A., 20 Sept., 1864. Mustered out 2 July, 1866.
Bingham, John A., Maj. J. A., 12 Jan., 1864. Resigned 3 Aug., 1864.
Binmore, Henry, Capt. A. A. G., 19 Feb., 1862. Dismissed 27 Nov., 1863.
Binney, Amos, Maj. P. M., 5 Aug., 1861. Mustered out 26 Dec., 1865.
Bird, Wellington, Capt. C. S., 18 May, 1864. Resigned 30 Aug., 1864.
Birdsall, Sam'l. Asst. Surg., 31 March, 1865. Mustered out 27 Nov., 1865.
Birge, Henry W., Brig. Gen., 19 Sept., 1863. Resigned 18 Oct., 1865.
Birney, David B., Brig. Gen., 3 Feb., 1862. Maj. Gen., 23 May, 1863. Died 18 Oct., 1864.
Birney, Fitzhugh, Capt. A. A. G., 1 Aug., 1862. Maj., 15 Sept., 1863. Died 17 June, 1864, of wounds received at the Battle of Cold Harbor, Va.
Birney, Wm., Brig. Gen., 22 May, 1863. Mustered out 24 Aug., 1865.
Biscaccianti, Allessandro, Capt. A. Q. M., 7 April, 1864. Mustered out 28 June, 1864.
Bishop, Dan'l E., Maj. P. M., 26 Nov., 1862. Resigned 12 May, 1865.
Black, Sam'l, Capt. A. Q. M., 30 June. 1862. Discharged 25 Jan., 1864.
Blackman, George C., Maj. Surg., 14 Sept., 1861. Resigned 31 July, 1862.
Blackman, Hudson B., Capt. A. Q. M., 29 Feb., 1864. Mustered out 3 Nov., 1866.
Blackwell, Shubarl M., Capt. C. S., 2 March, 1864. Mustered out 31 Aug., 1865.
Blair, Frank P., Jr., Brig. Gen., 7 Aug., 1862. Maj. Gen., 29 Nov., 1862. Resigned 1 Nov., 1865.
Blair, George T., Maj. P. M., 3 March, 1865. Mustered out 31 July, 1865.
Blair, John M., Capt. C. S., 14 April, 1862. Mustered out 7 April, 1866.
Blake, Chas. M., Hosp. Chap., 4 June, 1862. Resigned 21 July, 1863. Hosp. Chap., 26 Sept., 1864. Discharged 10 May, 1865.
Blake, E. Sanford, Capt. C. S., 19 Feb., 1863. Resigned 6 Oct., 1863.
Blake, Evans, Capt. C. S., 9 March, 1865. Mustered out 4 Aug., 1866.
Blake, Wm. E., Capt. A. de C., 4 Sept., 1862. Mustered out 10 July, 1866.
Blakely, Cyrene H., Capt. C. S., 18 May, 1864. Mustered out 9 Oct., 1865.
Blanchard, Ozias, Capt. A. Q. M., 29 Feb., 1864. Mustered out 10 Aug., 1865.
Blanchard, C. D., Capt. A. Q. M., 28 Aug., 1861. Discharged 9 May, 1863.
Blaney, J. V. Z., Maj. Surg., 3 Aug., 1861. Mustered out 7 Oct., 1865.
Blenker, Louis, Brig. Gen., 9 Aug., 1861. Discharged 31 March, 1863.
Blinn, John P., Capt. A. A. G., 24 March, 1863. Died 14 July, 1863, of wounds received at Battle of Gettysburg, Penn.
Bliss, Alex'r, Capt. A. Q. M., 3 Feb., 1862. A. Q. M., U. S. A., 13 March, 1863.
Bliss, D. Willard, Maj. Surg., 21 Sept., 1861. Mustered out 8 Dec., 1865.
Bliss, Fred'k E., Capt. C. S., 9 June, 1862. Resigned 21 Nov., 1863.
Bliss, Zenos E., Maj. Surg., 12 Sept., 1862. Mustered out 2 Feb., 1866.
Bliven, Chas. E., Capt. A. Q. M., 23 Oct., 1864. Mustered out 31 May, 1866.
Blockl, Anton, Capt. A. A. G., 11 March, 1863. Resigned 6 Dec., 1864.
Blodget, John J., Capt. A. A. G., 7 Sept., 1862. Resigned 12 Nov., 1863.
Blodgett, Gains M., Hosp. Chap., 15 July, 1862. Mustered out 26 July, 1865.
Blodgett, Gardner S., Capt. A. Q. M., 3 Aug., 1861. Capt. A. Q. M., U. S. A., 2 July, 1864.
Blodgett, Wells H., Maj. J. A., 10 March, 1863. Appointment expired 24 June, 1863.
Blood, Henry B., Capt. A. Q. M., 15 Oct., 1862. Mustered out 9 Nov., 1865.
Blunt, Asa P., Capt. A. Q. M., 29 Feb., 1864. Appointed Capt. A. Q. M., U. S. A., 28 March, 1867.
Blunt, James G., Brig. Gen., 8 April, 1862. Maj. Gen., 29 Nov., 1862. Mustered out 29 July, 1865.
Blythe, Joseph W., Hosp. Chap., 16 July, 1862. Mustered out 4 Aug., 1865.
Bobbs, J. S., Maj. Surg., 3 Aug., 1861. Mustered out 5 Aug., 1865.
Bockee, Jacob, Maj. Surg., 4 April, 1862. Mustered out 1 March, 1866.
Boggess, Henry H., Capt. A. Q. M., 3 Aug., 1861. Mustered out 15 June, 1865.
Bohlen, Henry, Brig. Gen., 28 April, 1862. Killed 22 Aug., 1862, in action at Freeman's Ford, Va.

Bohn, Herman, Capt. A. Q. M., 8 March, 1863. Mustered out 11 Dec., 1865.
Bokum, Herman, Hosp. Chap., 26 Nov., 1862. Mustered out 26 July, 1865.
Bolles, John A., Capt. Addl. A. de C., 30 Jan., 1862. Maj., 20 June, 1862. Resigned 17 July, 1865. Maj. J. A., 3 Sept., 1862. Resigned 18 July, 1863.
Bond, Frank S., Maj. A. de C., 11 March, 1863. Resigned 18 Nov., 1864.
Bond, John W., Capt. C. S., 26 Nov., 1862. Mustered out 15 June, 1866.
Bonebrake, George H., Capt. C. S., 24 March, 1865. Mustered out 11 Oct., 1865.
Bonsall, Henry W., Capt. C. S., 26 Nov., 1862. Resigned 1 Jan., 1865.
Bonsall, Samuel N., Capt. A. Q. M., 26 Nov., 1862. Died 19 July, 1865.
Bontecou, Reed B., Maj. Surg., 14 Sept., 1861. Mustered out 4 June, 1866.
Boone, Wm. M., Capt. A. A. G., 17 July, 1862. Mustered out 26 Oct., 1865.
Booth, Chas A., Capt. A. A. G., 20 June, 1863. Mustered out 10 Feb., 1866.
Booth, Thos. R., Capt. C. S., 22 July, 1864. Mustered out 1 Dec., 1865.
Bosbyshell, Wm., Capt. A. Q. M., 26 Nov., 1862. Resigned 10 Aug., 1863.
Botts, Randolph, Capt. A. Q. M., 17 July, 1862. Mustered out 22 Nov., 1865.
Bottsford, James L., Capt. A. A. G., 27 Oct., 1862. Resigned 25 Feb., 1865.
Boucher, James H., Maj. Surg., 4 April, 1862. Mustered out 10 Jan., 1866.
Boughner, James V., Maj. P. M., 28 May, 1864. Resigned 5 Feb., 1865.
Bournonville, Augustus C., Maj. Surg., 7 Nov., 1862. Resigned 23 March, 1863.
Bowdish, Isaac B., Capt. C. S., 29 Aug., 1861. Died 11 April, 1863.
Bowen, Chas. J., Hosp. Chap., 31 May, 1862. Mustered out 10 June, 1865.
Bowen, James, Brig. Gen., 11 Oct., 1862. Resigned 27 July, 1864.
Bowen, Jesse, Maj. P. M., 14 March, 1863. Mustered out 1 March, 1869.
Bowen, John J., Capt. A. Q. M., 30 June, 1862. Mustered out 28 July, 1865.
Bowers, Henry W., Capt. A. A. G., 14 April, 1862. Mustered out 30 June, 1865.
Bowers, Theodore S., Capt. A. de C., 1 Nov., 1862. Maj. J. A., 19 Feb., 1863. Capt. A. Q. M., U. S. A., 29 July, 1864.
Bowles, Theodore C., Capt. A. Q. M., 14 April, 1862. Mustered out 25 March, 1866.
Bowman, Henry, Capt. A. Q. M., 29 Feb., 1864. Mustered out 15 Aug., 1886.
Bowman, John A., Hosp. Chap., 31 May, 1862. Mustered out 21 Aug., 1865.
Bowman, Nathan P., Maj. P. M., 28 May, 1864. Resigned 18 Feb., 1865.
Boyer, Edward, Maj. P. M., 1 June, 1861. Died 28 Feb., 1862.
Boyd Edward B., Capt. A. Q. M., 12 Jan., 1865. Mustered out 5 June, 1866.
Boyd, Joseph F., Capt. A. Q. M., 7 Oct., 1861. Appointment expired 4 March, 1863. Capt. A. Q. M., 4 March, 1863. Mustered out 13 March, 1866.
Boyd, Parker D., Capt. C. S., 9 Feb., 1863. Resigned 5 Nov., 1864.
Boyden, Augustus H., Maj. P. M., 20 Nov., 1862. Resigned 26 May, 1865.
Boyle, Francis E., Hosp. Chap., 13 June, 1862. Mustered out 26 July, 1865.
Boyle, Jeremiah T., Brig. Gen., 9 Nov., 1861. Resigned 26 Jan., 1864.
Boyle, John, Capt. A. A. G., 16 May, 1862. Resigned 20 Aug., 1862.
Boyle, John Rit., Capt. A. Q. M., 25 July, 1864. Mustered out 20 March, 1866.
Braden, David, Capt. A. A. G., 24 March, 1862. Vacated commission 10 May, 1863.
Braden, Robt. L., Asst. Surg., 19 Feb., 1863. Discharged 22 Oct., 1863.
Bradford, John E., 2nd Lieut. Sig. Corps, 3 March, 1863. Mustered out 12 Aug., 1865.
Bradford, J. Thayer, Maj. Surg., 4 April, 1862. Discharged 19 Feb., 1863.
Bradley, George W., Capt. A. Q. M., 26 Nov., 1862. Capt. A. Q. M., U. S. A., 4 Nov., 1865.
Bradley, Jerome, Capt. A. Q. M., 19 Feb., 1863. Resigned 9 Jan., 1865.
Bradley, John, Asst. Surg., 27 March, 1863. Maj. Surg., 13 June, 1863. Mustered out 7 Oct., 1865.
Bradley, James W., Capt. A. Q. M., 2 March, 1865. Mustered out 15 Aug., 1865.
Bradley, Luther P., Brig. Gen., 30 July, 1864. Resigned 30 June, 1865.
Bradley, Thos. H., Capt. A. A. G., 6 June, 1863. Maj., 1 May, 1865. Mustered out 1 Sept., 1866.
Bradshaw, Albert M., Capt. A. Q. M., 8 July, 1863. Mustered out 20 Sept., 1865.
Bradshaw, James M., Capt. A. Q. M., 20 June, 1861. Mustered out 31 July, 1865.
Bragg, Edward S., Brig. Gen., 25 June, 1864. Mustered out 9 Oct., 1865.
Bragg, Henry M., Capt. A. de C., 17 Aug., 1863. Mustered out 3 Nov., 1865.
Brakeman, Nelson L., Hosp. Chap., 29 Feb., 1864. Mustered out 4 Aug., 1865.
Brand, Joseph C., Capt. C. S., 2 March, 1864. Discharged 30 May, 1864. Capt. A. Q. M., 7 Sept., 1864. Mustered out 26 June, 1865.
Brannan, John M., Brig. Gen., 28 Sept., 1861. Mustered out 31 May, 1866.
Brastow, George O., Maj. P. M., 5 Aug., 1862. Resigned 7 March, 1863.
Brauns, Frederick W., Hosp. Chap., 13 June, 1862. Mustered out 26 July, 1865.
Brayman, Mason, Brig. Gen., 24 Sept., 1862. Mustered out 24 Aug., 1865.
Breck, Sam'l, Maj. Addl. A. de C., 23 May, 1862. Vacated commission 17 July, 1862.
Breckenridge, Marcus P., Capt. C. S., 2 Sept., 1862. Mustered out 10 Jan., 1866.
Breed, Bowman B., Maj. Surg., 4 Oct., 1862. Mustered out 5 Aug., 1865.
Breed, Wm. M., Maj. Surg., 7 Nov., 1862. Resigned 7 April, 1863.
Brent, Sam'l J., 2nd Lieut. Sig. Corps, 3 March, 1863. Mustered out 24 Aug., 1865.
Brevoort, Henry W., Maj. A. A. G., 22 Aug., 1862. Resigned 21 May, 1863.
Brewer, Anson L., Maj. P. M., 19 Feb., 1863. Drowned 2 Feb., 1866.
Brewer, John W., Asst. Surg., 4 Oct., 1862. Resigned 26 Nov., 1862.
Brewster, Chas., Capt. C. S., 26 Nov., 1862. Appointment expired 4 March, 1863. Capt. C. S., 2 March, 1864. Mustered out 15 July, 1865.
Brewster, Cyrus, Hosp. Chap., 28 July, 1864. Mustered out 26 July, 1865.
Bricker, John R., Capt. C. S., 18 May, 1864. Mustered out 9 Oct., 1865.
Bridges, Chas., Capt. A. Q. M., 10 Feb., 1865. Mustered out 4 Aug., 1865.
Bridges, Edwin T., Capt. C. S., 17 March, 1863. Mustered out 31 July, 1866.
Bridges, Leverett L., Capt. C. S., 30 June, 1864. Mustered out 5 Aug., 1865.
Bridgman, Frank, Maj. P. M., 5 Sept., 1861. Mustered out 1 Jan., 1869.
Bridgdon, J. W., Maj. P. M., 26 Nov., 1862. Mustered out 1 Nov., 1865.
Briggs, Ephraim A., 2nd Lieut. Sig. Corps, 3 March, 1863. Mustered out 12 Aug., 1865.
Briggs, Henry S., Brig. Gen., 17 July, 1862. Mustered out 4 Dec., 1865.
Brigham, Elisha D., Capt. C. S., 30 Sept., 1861. Capt. C. S., U. S. A., 9 Feb., 1863.

Brigham, Henry O., Maj. P. M., 1 June, 1861. Resigned 30 Sept., 1864.
Brigham, John L., Capt. C. S., 25 Oct., 1864. Mustered out 9 Oct., 1865.
Bright, Marshall H., Capt. C. S., 25 Oct., 1861. Mustered out 19 Dec., 1865.
Brightly, Chas. H., Maj. Addl. A. de C., 17 June, 1862. Appointment revoked, 7 Feb., 1863.
Brinkerhoff, Roeliff, Capt. A. Q. M., 4 Nov., 1861. Mustered out 30 Sept., 1866.
Brinton, Daniel G., Maj. Surg., 9 Feb., 1863. Mustered out 5 Aug., 1865.
Brinton, John H., Maj. Surg., 3 Aug., 1861. Resigned 9 March, 1865.
Brinton, Nathan S., Maj. P. M., 1 June, 1861. Mustered out 1 Oct., 1865.
Brisbane, Chas. F., Asst. Surg., 24 Oct., 1863. Mustered out 27 July, 1865.
Brisbin, James S., Brig. Gen., 1 May, 1865. Mustered out 15 Jan., 1866.
Briscoe, James C., Maj. A. de C., 3 Sept., 1864. Vacated appointment, 3 Dec., 1864.
Broach, John H., Capt. A. A. G., 7 June, 1864. Resigned 3 July, 1865.
Broadhead, Josiah A., Capt. A. Q. M., 14 April, 1862. Maj. P. M., 26 Nov., 1862. Mustered out 1 April, 1869.
Brodie, Paul, 1st Lieut. Sig. Corps, 3 March, 1863. Mustered out 4 Sept., 1865.
Brodie, Wm., Maj. Surg., 3 Aug., 1861. Rejected by Senate, 3 Feb., 1862.
Bromett, Michael, Capt. A. Q. M., 18 May, 1864. Resigned 26 September, 1864.
Bronson, John O., Maj. Surg., 7 Nov., 1862. Mustered out 11 Nov., 1865.
Brooke, Edmond H., Maj. P. M., 1 April, 1865. Vacated commission 17 Jan., 1867.
Brooke, H. Jones, Capt. C. S., 20 Aug., 1861. Resigned 16 July, 1863.
Brooke, Hunter, Capt. Addl. A. de C., 3 April, 1862. Mustered out 1 Sept., 1866.
Brooke, John R., Brig. Gen., 12 May, 1864. Resigned 1 Feb., 1866.
Brookfield, Edward V., Capt. C. S., 20 April, 1864. Mustered out 9 Oct., 1865.
Brooks, James C., Capt. A. Q. M., 1 May, 1862. Mustered out 20 March, 1866.
Brooks, James, Capt. C. S., 1 Jan., 1863. Mustered out 19 Dec., 1865.
Brooks, Lowell M., Capt. A. Q. M., 29 Feb., 1864. Died 5 Oct., 1864.
Brooks, Thos. B., Maj. A. de C., 17 Aug., 1863. Resigned 6 Oct., 1864.
Brooks, Wm. T. H., Brig. Gen., 28 Sept., 1861. Maj. Gen., 10 June, 1863. Appointment as Maj. Gen. revoked, 18 April, 1864. Resigned 14 July, 1864.
Brotherline, John H., Maj. P. M., 4 March, 1863. Resigned 23 Feb., 1865.
Brower, Dan'l R., Asst. Surg., 18 May, 1864. Mustered out 3 Nov., 1865.
Brown, Chas. P., Capt. A. A. G., 28 Sept., 1864. Mustered out 19 Dec., 1865.
Brown, Dyer D. S., Maj. P. M., 19 Feb., 1863. Resigned 7 Dec., 1864.
Brown, Edward A., Capt. C. S., 28 May, 1864. Mustered out 9 Oct., 1865.
Brown, Edward O., Capt. Addl. A. de C., 30 April, 1862. Mustered out 6 Sept., 1865. Maj. A. de C., 4 May, 1863, which was revoked 23 March, 1865.
Brown, Egbert B., Brig. Gen., 29 Nov., 1862. Resigned 10 Nov., 1865.
Brown, Fayette, Maj. P. M., 1 June, 1861. Resigned 14 May, 1862.
Brown, Fredk. T., Hosp. Chap., 1 July, 1862. Discharged 24 Jan., 1863.
Brown, Hubert S., Capt. A. A. G., 3 Feb., 1865. Mustered out 1 Sept., 1866.
Brown, Hugh G., Capt. A. de C., 28 Aug., 1863. Mustered out 10 July, 1866.
Brown, James A., Hosp. Chap., 27 June, 1862. Resigned 20 Aug., 1864.
Brown, James H., Hosp. Chap., 12 Nov., 1863. Mustered out 15 July, 1865.
Brown, John H., Capt. A. Q. M., 18 May, 1864. Mustered out 27 Jan., 1866.
Brown, John M., Capt. A. A. G., 23 June, 1863. Resigned 10 May, 1864.
Brown, John T., Asst. Surg., 6 July, 1864. Mustered out 15 Nov., 1865.
Brown, Joseph M., Capt. A. Q. M., 29 Feb., 1864. Mustered out 17 July, 1867.
Brown, Joseph W., 2nd Lieut. Sig. Corps, 3 March, 1863. Mustered out 19 Dec., 1865.
Brown, Morris B., Maj. P. M., 23 Jan., 1865. Mustered out 31 July, 1865.
Brown, Moses C., Capt. A. A. G., 10 March, 1863. Dismissed 23 Sept., 1863.
Brown, Orlando, Capt. A. Q. M., 13 Oct., 1863. Vacated commission 19 June, 1865.
Brown, Rich'd B., Asst. Surg., 9 Feb., 1865. Mustered out 27 Jan., 1866.
Brown, Rob't B., Asst. Surg., 5 July, 1864. Mustered out 1 Nov., 1866.
Brown, Rufus K., Maj. Surg., 30 Sept., 1861. Resigned 10 Dec., 1862.
Brown, Simon B., Capt. A. Q. M., 21 Sept., 1861. Mustered out 20 March, 1866.
Brown, S. Lockwood, Capt. A. Q. M., 31 Oct., 1861. Mustered out 1 April, 1867.
Brown, Wm. H., Capt., A. Q. M., 20 Oct., 1862. Mustered out 25 Aug., 1865.
Brown, Wm. W., Capt. C. S., 19 July, 1862. Resigned 17 Nov., 1864.
Brown, Wm. Y., Hosp. Chap., 31 May, 1862. Mustered out 18 Sept., 1865.
Browne, Chas. C., Maj. P. M., 20 April, 1864. Resigned 25 April, 1865.
Browne, George, Maj. P. M., 26 Nov., 186 . Mustered out 15 Nov., 1865.
Bromwell, Seymour, Capt. C. S., 28 Oct., 1862. Resigned 15 Oct., 1864.
Browning, George T., Capt. A. Q. M., 29 Nov., 1862. Mustered out 5 Oct., 1866.
Browning, Rob't L., Capt. A. Q. M., 26 Nov., 1862. Resigned 27 April, 1863.
Brownson, Edward B., Capt. Addl. A. de C., 2 June, 1862. Died 25 Aug., 1864, of wounds received in action before Petersburg, Va.
Brownson, Harry, Capt. A. Q. M., 29 Feb., 1864. Mustered out 30 Oct., 1865.
Brownson, Henry F., Capt. A. A. G., 3 April, 1863. Resigned 2 July, 1865.
Brua, John P., Maj. P. M., 1 June, 1861. P. M. U. S. A., 23 Feb., 1864.
Bruch, Sam'l, Capt. A. Q. M., 8 Aug., 1862. Died 31 March, 1865.
Bruehl, James, Hosp. Chap., 28 July, 1862. Appointment expired 4 March, 1863. Hosp. Chap., 22 April, 1863. Discharged 20 May, 1863.
Brumley, John D., Maj. Surg., 19 Feb., 1863. Mustered out 13 March, 1866.
Bruner, Franklin S., Capt. A. Q. M., 25 Feb., 1865. Mustered out 24 Aug., 1865.
Bruyn, Wilson, 1st Lieut. Sig. Corps., 3 March, 1863. Mustered out 16 Aug., 1865.
Bryan, James, Maj. Surg., 2 Nov., 1861. Discharged 5 March, 1865.
Bryan, Orlando M., Maj. Surg., 4 Sept., 1861. Mustered out 7 Oct., 1865.
Bryant, Henry, Maj. Surg., 3 Aug., 1861. Resigned 16 July, 1863.
Bryan, Rob't E., Capt. C. S., 3 Feb., 1862. Mustered out 18 Aug., 1865.
Buchanan, David C., Capt. C. S., 6 Feb., 1865. Resigned 8 June, 1865.
Buchanan, Evan M., Capt. C. S., 24 March, 1862. Killed near Charlestown, Va., 30 Sept., 1864, by guerillas.
Buchanan, Rob't C., Brig. Gen., 29 Nov., 1862. Appointment expired 4 March, 1863.

Buck, Ephraim W., Asst. Surg., 21 July, 1864. Mustered out 15 Aug., 1865.
Buck, Francis N., Capt. C. S., 3 Aug., 1861. Resigned 11 June, 1864.
Buck, Harman A., Asst. Surg., 2 Feb., 1865. Mustered out 5 Aug., 1865.
Buck, Horatio B., Asst. Surg., 7 Jan., 1863. Mustered out 9 Oct., 1865.
Buck, Isaac N., Capt. A. Q. M., 29 Feb., 1864. Mustered out 20 Sept., 1865.
Buckingham, Catherimes P., Brig. Gen., 16 July, 1862. Resigned 11 Feb., 1863.
Buckland, Ralph P., Brig. Gen., 29 Nov., 1862. Resigned 6 Jan., 1865.
Bucklin, Benj. F., Capt. C. S., 26 Nov., 1862. Mustered out 3 Aug., 1865.
Buckman, Edwin D., Asst. Surg., 24 Oct., 1863. Resigned 26 June, 1865.
Buckmaster, Henry, Maj. Surg., 28 June, 1862. Resigned 1 Feb., 1865.
Budlong, Syria M., Capt. A. A. G., 7 Oct., 1864. Appointment revoked 25 March, 1865.
Buell, Don Carlos, Brig. Gen., 17 May, 1861. Maj. Gen., 21 March, 1862. Mustered out 23 May, 1864.
Buford, John, Brig. Gen., 27 July, 1862. Maj. Gen., 1 July, 1863. Died 16 Dec., 1863.
Buford, Louis M., Maj. A. de C., 11 March, 1863. Resigned 17 Dec., 1864.
Buford, Napoleon B., Brig. Gen., 15 April, 1862. Maj. Gen., 29 Nov., 1862. Appointment expired 4 March, 1863. Mustered out 24 Aug., 1865.
Bugh, Jacob, Maj. P. M., 3 March, 1865. Mustered out 31 July, 1865.
Bulkley, Chas. S., Capt. A. Q. M., 15 Jan., 1863. Appointment expired 4 March, 1863. Capt. A. Q. M., 4 March, 1863. Resigned 7 Sept., 1864.
Bull, Hiram C., Maj. P. M., 30 June, 1862. Resigned 11 Aug., 1865.
Bullard, John L., Capt. C. S., 29 Nov., 1862. Mustered out 31 Dec., 1865.
Bullock, Dyer D., Capt. A. Q. M., 30 June, 1864. Mustered out 31 May, 1866.
Bundy, Martin L., Maj. P. M., 31 Aug., 1861. Mustered out 15 April, 1866.
Bundy, Philo, Maj. P. M., 4 July, 1864. Mustered out 1 Nov., 1865.
Bunker, Dumont, Capt. C. S., 20 Jan., 1865. Mustered out 18 Aug., 1865.
Buntin, Toussaint C., Capt. A. Q. M., 11 June, 1862. Mustered out 14 June, 1865.
Burbank, Jacob E., Maj. P. M., 19 Feb., 1863. Appointed Maj. P. M., U. S. A., 17 Jan., 1867.
Burbridge, Stephen G., Brig. Gen., 9 June, 1863. Resigned 1 Dec., 1865.
Burch, Bushrod, Maj. A. de C., 3 Sept., 1862. Appointment expired 7 Nov., 1862.
Burchard, Sam'l D., Capt. A. Q. M., 24 Jan., 1865. Mustered out 13 Oct., 1865.
Burdett, Michael, Hosp. Chap., 30 June, 1864. Mustered out 4 Aug., 1865.
Burdette, John S., Capt. C. S., 19 Feb., 1862. Resigned, 5 June, 1865.
Bureau, Leonard P., Capt. C. S., 18 May, 1864. Mustered out 10 Jan., 1866.
Burger, Wm. L. M., Capt. A. A. G., 30 June, 1862. Maj., 28 Feb., 1865. Mustered out 12 March, 1866.
Burke, Francis N., Maj. Surg., 4 Sept., 1861. Mustered out 4 Sept., 1865.
Burleigh, Henry M., Capt. A. A. G., 9 June, 1862. Mustered out 19 Sept., 1865.
Burnett, Henry L., Maj. J. A., 10 Aug., 1863. Mustered out 1 Dec., 1865.
Burnham, George P., Capt. C. S., 28 Nov., 1862. Resigned 11 Aug., 1864.
Burnham, George S., Capt. A. Q. M., 18 May, 1864. Mustered out 10 Aug., 1865.
Burnham, Hiram, Brig. Gen., 26 April, 1864. Killed 30 Sept., 1864, in action at Chapin's Bluff, Va
Burns, George W., Maj. P. M., 30 June, 1862. Resigned 18 March, 1864.
Burns, Wm. W., Brig. Gen., 28 Sept., 1861. Resigned 20 March, 1863.
Burnside, Ambrose E., Brig. Gen., 6 Aug., 1861. Maj. Gen., 18 March, 1862. Resigned 15 April, 1865.
Burnside, James O. P., Capt. C. S., 29 Nov., 1862. Resigned 20 Nov., 1863.
Burr, Arthur G., Capt. A. Q. M., 26 Nov., 1862. Appointment expired 4 March, 1863. Reappointed 4 March, 1863. Mustered out 31 Oct., 1865.
Burr, George, Maj. Surg., 11 Oct., 1861. Mustered out 20 June, 1865.
Burr, Hudson, Capt. A. A. G., 25 May, 1863. Resigned 3 Sept., 1864.
Burr, Raymond, Capt. A. Q. M., 14 July, 1862. Mustered out 3 Nov., 1866.
Burrill, Truman H., Capt. C. S., 30 June, 1864. Mustered out 28 Feb., 1866.
Burritt, Henry Le W., Asst. Surg., 2 Sept., 1863. Maj. Surg., 18 May, 1864. Mustered out 27 July, 1865.
Burroughs, George T., Capt. C. S., 19 Feb., 1863. Resigned 22 June, 1865.
Burroughs, Edwin B., Capt. A. Q. M., 31 Jan., 1865. Mustered out 20 April, 1866.
Burt, Andrew S., Capt. Addl. A. de C., 3 May, 1862. Capt. U. S. A., 30 May, 1863.
Burt, John B., Capt. C. S., 7 Nov., 1862. Appointment expired 4 March, 1863. Maj. A. de C., 25 April, 1863. Appointment revoked 7 Jan., 1865.
Burt, Thos. M., Maj. P. M., 5 Sept., 1861. Resigned 5 April, 1865.
Burtnette, D. Henry, Maj. Addl. A. de C., 22 April, 1862. Dismissed 19 Oct., 1862.
Burton, Benj., Capt. A. Q. M., 5 Dec., 1863. Mustered out 31 March, 1866.
Burton, George W., Capt. C. S., 17 July, 1862. Maj. A. A. G., 21 April, 1864. Resigned 7 March, 1865.
Bussey, Cyrus, Brig. Gen., 5 Jan., 1864. Mustered out 24 Aug., 1865.
Busteed, Richard, Brig. Gen., 7 Aug., 1862. Appointment expired 4 March, 1863.
Butler, Andrew J., Capt. C. S., 1 Nov., 1861. Rejected by Senate, 6 Feb., 1862.
Butler, Benj. F., Maj. Gen., 16 May, 1861. Resigned 30 Nov., 1865.
Butler, John G., Hosp. Chap., 31 May, 1862. Mustered out 21 Aug., 1865.
Butler, John S., Capt. A. A. G., 5 Dec., 1863. Mustered out 14 June, 1865.
Butler, Speed, Col. Addl. A. de C., 30 June, 1862. Resigned 22 Aug., 1864.
Butterfield, Daniel, Brig. Gen., 7 Sept., 1861. Maj. Gen., 29 Nov., 1862. Mustered out 24 Aug., 1865.
Butterfield, George W., Capt. A. A. G., 18 March, 1865. Resigned 3 July, 1865.
Butterfield, Wm., Capt. C. S., 5 Aug., 1861. Resigned 3 Dec., 1864.
Buttrick, Edward K., Capt. A. A. G., 25 Jan., 1865. Mustered out 31 Oct., 1865.
Butze, Frank C., Capt. A. Q. M., 18 May, 1864. Mustered out 20 Sept., 1865.
Byrne, Chas. C., Capt. C. S., 28 May, 1864. Resigned 15 March, 1865.
Cadle, Cornelius, Jr., Capt. A. A. G., 1 May, 1863. Maj., 3 April, 1865. Mustered out 1 Sept., 1866.
Cadwalader, George, Maj. Gen., 25 April, 1862. Resigned 5 July, 1865.
Cadwalader, Geo. B., Capt. A. Q. M., 8 July, 1863. Mustered out 10 Sept., 1866.
Cadwell, Jay, Capt. A. Q. M., 19 Feb., 1863. Discharged, 27 Oct., 1863.
Caldwell, George H., Capt. A. A. G., 29 July, 1862. Mustered out 20 March, 1866.
Caldwell, John C., Brig. Gen., 28 April, 1862. Mustered out 15 Jan., 1866.
Caldwell, Wm. M., Maj. P. M., 16 July, 1862. Resigned 13 June, 1864.

Calhoun, George W., Maj. P. M., 28 May, 1864. Appointment cancelled 10 Oct., 1864.
Callender, Nath'l, Hosp. Chap., 14 July, 1862. Mustered out 20 Nov., 1865.
Cambern, S. Monte, Capt. A. A. G., 3 Feb., 1865. Mustered out 19 Sept., 1865.
Camblos, Henry S., Capt. A. Q. M., 30 June, 1862. Resigned 22 Sept., 1863.
Came, Mark R., Capt. C. S., 19 Feb., 1862. Mustered out 8 July, 1865.
Cameron, Robert A., Brig. Gen., 11 Aug., 1863. Resigned 22 June, 1865.
Camp, Erskine M., Capt. A. Q. M., 19 May, 1863. Mustered out 31 July, 1866.
Camp, Jacob A., Maj. P. M., 1 June, 1861. Mustered out 8 Nov., 1865.
Camp, Norman H., 1st Lieut. Sig. Corps, 3 March, 1863. Resigned 5 June, 1865.
Camp, Norman W., Hosp. Chap., 29 May, 1863. Mustered out 21 Aug., 1865.
Camp, William F., Maj. P. M., 5 Aug., 1861. Resigned 24 July, 1862.
Campbell, Archibald B., Maj. Surg., 3 Aug., 1861. Mustered out 28 Nov., 1865.
Campbell, Benjamin B., Capt. A. A. G., 21 July, 1864. Mustered out 12 Jan., 1866.
Campbell, Charles F. H., Maj. Surg., 8 Nov., 1861. Mustered out 29 June, 1865.
Campbell, Charles H., Capt. A. A. G., 1 June, 1865. Mustered out 11 May, 1866.
Campbell, Charles T., Brig. Gen., 13 March, 1863. Mustered out 15 Jan., 1866.
Campbell, Charles W., Maj. P. M., 5 Aug., 1861. Mustered out 15 Jan., 1866.
Campbell, George W., Capt. C. S., 9 Sept., 1861. Mustered out 10 Sept., 1866.
Campbell, James, Capt. A. Q. M., 22 June, 1863. Mustered out 10 Sept., 1866.
Campbell, James R., Capt. A. A. G., 14 Feb., 1865. Mustered out 19 Sept., 1865.
Campbell, John A., Maj. A. A. G., 27 Oct., 1862. Mustered out 1 Sept., 1866.
Campbell, John B., Capt. A. Q. M., 7 May, 1864. Mustered out 20 June, 1866.
Campbell, John C., Maj. J. A., 29 Feb., 1864. Mustered out 10 Feb., 1866.
Campbell, Joseph B., Capt. Addl. A. de C., 16 May, 1862. Mustered out 10 July, 1865.
Campbell, Robert G., Capt. A. Q. M., 30 June, 1862. Resigned 10 July, 1865.
Campbell, Wm. B., Brig. Gen., 30 June, 1862. Resigned 26 Jan., 1863.
Canby, Edward R. S., Brig. Gen., 31 March, 1862. Maj. Gen., 7 May, 1864. Mustered out 1 Sept., 1866.
Canby, James P., Maj. P. M., 28 May, 1864.
Candee, George W., Maj. P. M., 23 Feb., 1864. Mustered out 5 Jan., 1866.
Candler, Wm. L., Capt. A. de C., 10 Nov., 1862. Resigned 12 May, 1863.
Candy, Charles, Capt. A. A. G., 21 Sept., 1861. Resigned 3 Dec., 1861.
Cannon, John R., Capt. A. Q. M., 9 June, 1862. Resigned 6 Nov., 1862.
Cannon, Le Grand B., Maj. Addl. A. de C., 28 Aug., 1861. Col., 1 Feb., 1862. Resigned 11 June, 1862.
Cantine, Wm. W., Capt. C. S., 17 July, 1862. Mustered out 9 Oct., 1865.
Cantwell, Jacob Y., Asst. Surg., 5 Dec., 1863. Maj. Surg., 18 May, 1864. Mustered out 23 Sept., 1865.
Capron, Adin B., 1st Lieut. Sig. Corps, 3 March, 1863. Mustered out 1 Sept., 1865.
Capron, Thadeus H., Capt. A. Q. M., 1 June, 1865. Mustered out 31 Oct., 1865.
Carleton, Alfred L., Capt. C. S., 11 March, 1863. Mustered out 11 Nov., 1865.
Carleton, Charles A., Capt. A. A. G., 15 July, 1864. Maj., 15 Jan., 1865. Mustered out 19 Dec., 1865.
Carleton, James H., Brig. Gen., 28 April, 1862. Mustered out 30 April, 1866.
Carlin, Wm. P., Brig. Gen., 29 Nov., 1862. Mustered out 24 Aug., 1865.
Carlisle, Thomas J., Capt. A. Q. M., 26 Nov., 1862. Mustered out 19 May, 1866.
Carnahan, Thomas L., Maj. P. M., 19 Feb., 1863. Mustered out 20 July, 1866.
Carncross, Septimus, Capt. A. de C., 17 Sept., 1862. Capt. A. A. G., 4 Sept., 1863. Maj., 20 April, 1864. Resigned 21 March, 1865.
Carner, Andrew Y., Capt. A. Q. M., 7 April, 1864. Mustered out 8 Nov., 1865.
Carney, George J., Capt. A. Q. M., 29 Feb., 1864. Resigned 6 July, 1865.
Carnochan, Warren H., Capt. A. Q. M., 25 Feb., 1865. Mustered out 28 July, 1865.
Carothers, Andrew E., Asst. Surg., 11 Jan., 1864. Mustered out 18 Jan., 1866.
Carpenter, C. C., Capt. C. S., 24 March, 1862. Mustered out 14 July, 1865.
Carpenter, George F., Maj. P. M., 19 Feb., 1863. Mustered out 1 Nov., 1865.
Carpenter, George N., Capt. C. S., 18 May, 1864. Mustered out 21 June, 1865.
Carpenter, George W., Capt. A. Q. M., 29 Sept., 1864. Dismissed 12 May, 1865.
Carpenter, James W., Maj. P. M., 1 June, 1861. Resigned 1 June, 1865.
Carpenter, John T., Maj. Surg., 4 Sept., 1861. Resigned 15 May, 1864.
Carpenter, Preston, 2nd Lieut. Sig. Corps, 3 March, 1863. Mustered out 12 Aug., 1865.
Carpenter, Samuel T., Hosp. Chap., 10 Jan., 1863. Died 26 Dec., 1864.
Carper, Leo, Capt. A. A. G., 7 April, 1864. Resigned 31 May, 1865.
Carr, Bryon O., Capt. A. Q. M., 29 Sept., 1862. Mustered out 28 July, 1865.
Carr, Eugene A., Brig. Gen., 7 March, 1862. Mustered out 15 Jan., 1866.
Carr, Horace M., Hosp. Chap., 27 Nov., 1863. Mustered out 4 Aug., 1865.
Carr, Joseph B., Brig. Gen., 7 Sept., 1862. Appointment expired 4 March, 1863. Brig. Gen., 30 March, 1863. Mustered out 24 Aug., 1865.
Carrington, Henry B., Brig. Gen., 29 Nov., 1862. Mustered out 24 Aug., 1865.
Carrinque, Thos. H., 1st Lieut. Sig. Corps, 3 March, 1863. Mustered out 21 Aug., 1865.
Carroll, Sam'l S., Brig. Gen., 12 May, 1864. Mustered out 15 Jan., 1866.
Carroll, Wm., Asst. Surg., 14 May, 1863. Mustered out 8 Dec., 1866.
Carruth, Wm. W., Capt. A. A. G., 4 Sept., 1863. Resigned 22 Dec., 1863.
Carson, John L., Capt. C. S., 11 March, 1863. Mustered out 1 July, 1865.
Carter, Buell C., Capt. A. Q. M., 29 Feb., 1864. Mustered out 10 June, 1866.
Carter, Elbert V., Maj. P. M., 30 June, 1864. Mustered out 15 Nov., 1865.
Carter, John C., Asst. Surg., 30 March, 1864. Mustered out 10 Aug., 1865.
Carter, Richard, Capt. A. Q. M., 18 May, 1864. Mustered out 27 Nov., 1865.
Carter, Sam'l P., Brig. Gen., 1 May, 1862. Mustered out 15 Jan., 1866.
Carter, Solon A., Capt. A. A. G., 15 July, 1864. Resigned 3 July, 1865.
Carver, Henry L., Capt. A. Q. M., 29 Feb., 1864. Mustered out 13 March, 1866.
Carver, Thos. G., Hosp. Chap., 31 July, 1862. Mustered out 10 June, 1865.
Carpenter, Seymour D., Asst. Surg., 19 Feb., 1863. Maj. Surg., 13 April, 1863. Mustered out 31 July, 1865.
Case, Daniel L., Maj. P. M., 18 March, 1864. Resigned 7 Dec., 1864.
Case, Rufus K., Capt. A. Q. M., 23 Nov., 1864. Mustered out 31 May, 1866.
Case, Theodore S., Capt. A. Q. M., 9 June, 1862. Resigned 18 March, 1865.

Casey, Isaac C., Capt. Addl. A. de C., 4 June, 1862. Mustered out 2 Feb., 1866.
Casey, Silas, Brig. Gen., 31 Aug., 1861. Maj. Gen., 31 May, 1862. Mustered out 24 Aug., 1865.
Caslow, John F., Capt. A. Q. M., 3 Aug., 1861. Mustered out 18 Aug., 1865.
Castle, George T., Capt. C. S., 26 Nov., 1862. Mustered out 18 Aug., 1865.
Catlin, Thos. G., Maj. Surg., 4 April, 1862. Resigned 7 April, 1863.
Catterson, Robt. F., Brig. Gen., 31 May, 1865. Mustered out 15 Jan., 1866.
Caughey, Miles W., Capt. C. S., 18 May, 1864. Resigned 28 June, 1864.
Cavade, Fred'k F., Capt. A. A. G., 14 July, 1862. Resigned 25 July, 1862.
Chadbourne, Benj'n L., Capt. C. S., 2 March, 1864. Mustered out 1 Sept., 1865.
Chadwick, Peter R., Capt. A. A. G., 23 Dec., 1862. Resigned 2 April, 1864.
Chalfant, John E., Capt. C. S., 30 June, 1863. Mustered out 10 Aug., 1865.
Chellenor, Thos., Capt. C. S., 19 Feb., 1863. Mustered out 19 July, 1865.
Chamberlain, Cyrus N., Asst. Surg., 27 March, 1863. Maj. Surg., 13 April, 1863. Mustered out 7 Oct., 1865.
Chamberlain, Hiram S., Capt. A. Q. M., 18 May, 1864. Mustered out 26 Oct., 1865.
Chamberlain, Jacob S., Hosp. Chap., 29 Nov., 1864. Mustered out 4 Aug., 1865.
Chamberlain, Joshua L., Brig. Gen., 18 June, 1864. Mustered out 15 Jan., 1866.
Chamberlain, Wm. D., Capt. C. S., 7 April, 1864. Mustered out 9 Oct., 1865.
Chamberlain, Lot, Maj. P. M., 28 May, 1864. Resigned 30 Nov., 1864.
Chambers, Alex., Brig. Gen., 11 Aug., 1863. Rejected by Senate, 6 April, 1864.
Chambers, Wm. M., Maj. Surg., 4 Oct., 1861. Resigned 12 May, 1865.
Champlin, Edward P., Capt. A. Q. M., 30 June, 1864. Resigned 19 May, 1865.
Champlin, Stephen G., Brig. Gen., 29 Nov., 1862. Died 26 Jan., 1864.
Champlin, Thos. A. P., Capt. C. S., 14 April, 1862. Resigned 22 Oct., 1864.
Chandler, George W., Capt. C. S., 20 April, 1864. Mustered out 27 Dec., 1866.
Chandler, Robt., Capt. A. A. G., 28 Aug., 1861. Mustered out 1 Sept., 1866.
Channing, Wm. H., Hosp. Chap., 8 Nov., 1862. Resigned 19 July, 1865.
Chapel, Artemus, Maj. Surg., 1 May, 1862. Mustered out 1 Oct., 1865.
Chapin, Andrew B., Asst. Surg., 12 Sept., 1862. Resigned 20 Aug., 1864.
Chapin, Edward P., Brig. Gen., 27 June, 1863. Killed 27 May, 1864, in action at Port Hudson, La.
Chapin, Lebens C., Asst. Surg., 29 Oct., 1864. Mustered out 22 Aug., 1865.
Chapin, Marshall P., Capt. C. S., 4 Sept., 1863. Mustered out 3 Aug., 1865.
Chapman, Chandler B., Maj. Surg., 9 Oct., 1861. Resigned 24 March, 1862.
Chapman, Edward D., Capt. A. Q. M., 3 Aug., 1861. Mustered out 30 March, 1866.
Chapman, George H., Brig. Gen., 21 July, 1864. Mustered out 7 Jan., 1866.
Chapman, Wm. H., Hosp. Chap., 4 July, 1862. Resigned 1 Oct., 1863.
Charlat, C. S., Maj. A. A. G., 8 March, 1864. Mustered out 10 July, 1866.
Chase, Champion S., Maj. P. M., 26 Nov., 1862. Appointment expired 4 March, 1863. Maj. P. M., 8 May, 1863. Mustered out 15 Jan., 1866.
Chase, Dudley, Hosp. Chap., 7 April, 1864. Mustered out 21 Aug., 1865.
Chase, Elmore Y., Asst. Surg., 11 Sept., 1862. Maj. Surg., 27 May, 1863. Mustered out 11 May, 1866.
Chase, Jackson H., Capt. C. S., 26 Nov., 1862. Resigned 15 Feb., 1865.
Chase, Joseph H., Capt. A. A. G., 29 Feb., 1864. Mustered out 26 May, 1865.
Cheney, Rufus, Maj. P. M., 5 Sept., 1861. Discharged 12 Aug., 1863.
Chester, George M., Capt. A. Q. M., 12 Oct., 1863. Rejected by Senate, 23 Feb., 1864. Reappointed 30 June, 1864. Resigned 7 Nov., 1864.
Chetlain, Augustus L., Brig. Gen., 18 Dec., 1863. Mustered out 15 Jan., 1866.
Chetwood, Bradbury C., Maj. A. de C., 20 Aug., 1862. Resigned 16 April, 1863.
Chevalier, Arthur H., Capt. C. S., 18 May, 1864. Mustered out 2 Feb., 1866.
Childs, Sam'l D., Capt. A. Q. M., 24 Jan., 1865. Mustered out 30 July, 1866.
Chipman, Norton P., Col. Addl. A. de C., 17 April, 1862. Mustered out 30 Nov., 1865.
Chittenden, Chas. B., Capt. A. Q. M., 10 July, 1863. Mustered out 11 May, 1866.
Cholwell, Jacob., Capt. C. S., 21 April, 1864. Resigned 4 Aug., 1864.
Christensen, Chas., Capt. A. de C., 12 May, 1865. Mustered out 12 Jan., 1866.
Christensen, Christian T., Maj. A. de C., 13 Sept., 1862. Maj. A. A. G., 11 March, 1863. Resigned 22 July, 1865.
Christian, James, Capt. C. S., 5 Sept., 1862. Mustered out 10 Aug., 1864.
Christian, Robt. A., Maj. Surg., 5 Nov., 1861. Mustered out 24 June, 1865.
Christiancy, Henry C., Capt. A. de C., 5 April, 1865. Mustered out 20 Jan., 1866.
Chrysler, Morgan H., Brig. Gen., 11 Nov., 1865. Mustered out 15 Jan., 1866.
Church, Truman K., Capt. A. Q. M., 26 Nov., 1862. Mustered out 15 Aug., 1865.
Church, Wm. C., Capt. C. S., 4 Oct., 1862. Resigned 18 June, 1863.
Church, Wm. E., Capt. A. A. G., 29 March, 1865. Mustered out 23 Oct., 1865.
Church, Wm. H., Maj. Surg., 3 Aug., 1861. Resigned 26 Oct., 1863.
Churchill, James O., Capt. A. Q. M., 30 June, 1864. Mustered out 15 Sept., 1866.
Churchman, Henry S., Maj. Surg., 4 Oct., 1862. Mustered out 14 July, 1865.
Cilley, Clinton A., Capt. A. A. G., 15 July, 1864. Maj., 21 March, 1865. Mustered out 1 Sept., 1866.
Cilley, John K., Capt. A. Q. M., 7 April, 1864. Mustered out 8 Jan., 1866.
Cist, Henry M., Capt. A. A. G., 20 April, 1864. Maj., 13 March, 1865. Mustered out 4 Jan., 1866.
Clapp, Channing, Capt. A. A. G., 8 May, 1863. Resigned 21 June, 1865.
Clapp, Wm. H., Capt. A. A. G., 15 May, 1863. Mustered out 5 Dec., 1865.
Clark, Augustus M., Asst. Surg., 11 Sept., 1862. Maj. Surg., 4 Dec., 1862. Mustered out 6 July, 1865.
Clark, Chas. A., Capt. A. A. G., 18 May, 1864. Resigned 26 Oct., 1864.
Clark, Cyrus C., Maj. P. M., 27 Feb., 1863. Mustered out 1 Nov., 1865.
Clark, Elijah A., Asst. Surg., 18 May, 1864. Maj. Surg., 30 June, 1864. Dismissed 28 April, 1865.
Clark, Ezra W., Capt. A. A. G., 29 Feb., 1864. Mustered out 30 Oct., 1865.
Clark, Fred'k L., Capt. A. Q. M., 18 May, 1864. Mustered out 28 July, 1865.
Clark, George F., Capt. A. Q. M., 24 March, 1862. Mustered out 8 Feb., 1866.
Clark, Gilbert S., Capt. C. S., 24 June, 1863. Mustered out 26 Oct., 1865.
Clark, Isaiah R., Capt. C. S., 10 Nov., 1863. Resigned 31 March, 1865.
Clark, James C., Capt. A. A. G., 12 May, 1862. Resigned 3 Dec., 1862.
Clark, James T., Capt. A. Q. M., 2 Dec., 1863. Mustered out 30 April, 1866.

Clark, John. Capt. C. S., 7 Sept., 1861. Resigned 26 Aug., 1864.
Clark, John S., Col. Addl. A. de C., 18 Nov., 1861. Resigned 16 Aug., 1865.
Clark, John W., Capt. A. Q. M., 7 April, 1864. Resigned 6 Dec., 1864.
Clark, J. Warren, Capt. A. Q. M., 26 Nov., 1862. Resigned 21 May, 1864.
Clark, Rauslure W., Capt. A. Q. M., 11 June, 1862. Mustered out 26 Oct., 1865.
Clark, Thos. W., Hosp. Chap., 30 June, 1864. Mustered out 31 Oct., 1865.
Clark, Wm. J., 2nd Lieut. Sig. Corps, 14 Feb., 1865. Resigned 31 May, 1865.
Clark, Wm. T., Capt. A. A. G., 6 March, 1862. Maj., 24 Nov., 1862. Brig. Gen., 31 May, 1865. Mustered out 1 Feb., 1866.
Clarke, Alpheus E., Capt. C. S., 26 Sept., 1862. Mustered out 19 Dec., 1865.
Clarke, Chas. F., Capt. A. A. G., 12 June, 1862. Died 10 Dec., 1862.
Clarke, George J., 1st Lieut. Sig. Corps, 3 March, 1863. Mustered out 12 Aug., 1865.
Clarke, Haswell C., Capt. A. de C., 9 Nov., 1863. Mustered out 22 Nov., 1865.
Clarke, Henry F., Col. Addl. A. de C., 28 Sept., 1861. Mustered out 31 May, 1866.
Clarke, Robt. D., Maj. P. M., 12 Aug., 1863. Appointed Maj. P. M., U. S. A., 17 Jan., 1867.
Clarke, Sidney, Capt. A. A. G., 9 Feb., 1863. Resigned 20 Feb., 1865.
Clarke, Temple, Capt. A. A. G., 7 April, 1862. Resigned 22 July, 1863.
Clarke, Wm. H., Capt. A. A. G., 9 Sept., 1862. Maj., 15 Sept., 1863. Resigned 30 Sept., 1865.
Clarke, Wm. Penn, Maj. P. M., 22 Jan., 1863. Mustered out 20 April, 1866.
Clarke, Wm. T., Capt. A. A. G., 3 Feb., 1865. Mustered out 19 Oct., 1865.
Clary, Robert E., Col. Addl. A. de C., 5 July, 1862. Mustered out 31 May, 1866.
Clay, Cassius M., Maj. Gen., 11 April, 1862. Resigned 11 March, 1863.
Clay, Henry, Capt. A. A. G., 15 Oct., 1861. Died 5 June, 1862.
Clayton, Powell, Brig. Gen., 1 Aug., 1864. Mustered out 24 Aug., 1865.
Cleary, Peter J. A., Asst. Surg., 4 Oct., 1862. Maj. Surg., 13 April, 1863. Mustered out 10 Aug., 1865.
Cleavland, Guy K., Maj. P. M., 19 Feb., 1863. Mustered out 1 Dec., 1865.
Clemens, Fred'k W., Capt. C. S., 3 Aug., 1863. Mustered out 6 Dec., 1865.
Clemens, Gilbert H., Capt. A. Q. M., 29 Feb., 1864. Mustered out 1 Jan., 1866.
Clemens, Oliver M., Capt. C. S., 20 May, 1863. Mustered out 18 Aug., 1865.
Clemens, Wm. W., 2nd Lieut. Sig. Corps, 3 March, 1863. Mustered out 12 Aug., 1865.
Clements, Alex. H., Capt. C. S., 30 Aug., 1862. Mustered out 23 Sept., 1865.
Clements, John T., Capt. C. S., 2 March, 1865. Mustered out 31 July, 1865.
Clements, Joseph C., Capt. A. Q. M., 13 Nov., 1862. Mustered out 8 Feb., 1866.
Clendenin, George, Jr., Capt. A. A. G., 11 March, 1863. Maj. 24 Dec., 1864. Mustered out 19 Sept., 1865.
Clendenin, Wm., Maj. Surg., 5 Aug., 1861. Mustered out 5 Aug., 1865.
Clinton, Henry P., Capt. C. S., 20 Nov., 1862. Mustered out 31 May, 1866.
Cloak, Burkitt, Maj. Surg., 9 June, 1862. Mustered out 22 Nov., 1865.
Clow, James Beach, Capt. C. S., 3 Aug., 1861. Resigned 1 Jan., 1865.
Clowry, R. C., Capt. A. Q. M., 27 Oct., 1863. Mustered out 31 May, 1866.
Clubb, Henry S., Capt. A. Q. M. 11 June, 1862. Mustered out 7 April, 1866.
Clum, Henry R., Capt. Sig. Corps 3 March, 1863. Mustered out 4 Sept., 1865.
Cluseret, Gustave Paul, Col. Addl. A. de C., 10 March, 1862. Brig. Gen., 14 Oct., 1862. Resigned 2 March, 1863.
Clyde, Eugene, 2nd Lieut. Sig. Corps, 3 March, 1863. Dismissed 8 March, 1865.
Clymer, Meredith, Maj. Surg., 25 Dec., 1861. Mustered out 7 Oct., 1865.
Coale, John H., Capt. C. S., 30 Aug., 1862. Mustered out 26 June, 1865.
Coale, R. W., Asst. Surg., 18 Jan., 1865. Mustered out 4 June, 1866.
Coale, Wm. E., Capt. C. S., 3 Aug., 1861. Resigned 18 Feb., 1865.
Cobb, Stephen A., Capt. C. S., 18 May, 1864. Mustered out 23 Sept., 1865.
Coburn, Joseph L., Capt. C. S., 22 July, 1864. Mustered out 22 Nov., 1865.
Cochran, Milton B., Asst. Surg., 18 May, 1864. Maj. Surg., 25 Nov., 1864. Mustered out 11 Nov., 1865.
Cochran, Wm. H. D., Capt. A Q. M., 27 Feb., 1863. Mustered out 15 June, 1866.
Cochrane, John, Brig. Gen., 17 July, 1862. Resigned 25 Feb., 1863.
Cocke, John S., Maj. P. M., 30 June, 1862. Resigned 14 June, 1865.
Coffin, Edward W., Capt. C. S., 24 March, 1862. Mustered out 13 Dec., 1865.
Coffin, Oliver S., Capt. A. Q. M., 24 Sept., 1862. Mustered out 11 Dec., 1865.
Cofran, La Roy, Capt. A. Q. M., 18 March, 1864. Appointment revoked 12 Jan., 1865.
Coggswell, Mason F., Asst. Surg., 18 May, 1864. Maj. Surg., 3 Jan., 1865. Died 21 Jan., 1865.
Cohen, Andrew J., Capt. A. A. G., 4 Aug., 1862. Mustered out 28 June, 1865.
Colburn, Albert V., Lieut. Col. Addl. A. de C., 28 Sept., 1861. Died 17 June, 1863.
Colburn, Nathan P., Maj. P. M., 27 Feb., 1863. Resigned 16 Jan., 1864.
Colburn, Webster J., Capt. A. Q. M., 19 Sept., 1864. Mustered out 5 June, 1866.
Cole, David, Capt. C. S., 18 May, 1864. Resigned 3 Feb., 1865.
Cole, Elijah T., Maj. P. M., 28 May, 1864. Resigned 27 May, 1865.
Cole, Seth P., Capt. C. S., 11 March, 1863. Resigned 17 June, 1863.
Cole, Wm. L., Maj. P. M., 26 Nov., 1862. Rejected by Senate 27 Feb., 1863.
Colman, Wm. D., Capt. A. Q. M., 21 Aug., 1861. Discharged 12 Nov., 1861. Capt. A. A. G., 11 June, 1862. Killed 6 Oct., 1862, at Battle of Corinth, Miss.
Collins, James, Asst. Surg., 10 Feb., 1864. Maj. Surg., 7 Feb., 1865. Mustered out 19 July, 1865.
Collins, Robt. M., Capt. C. S., 14 Oct., 1863. Mustered out 17 June, 1865.
Collins, Thos. H., Capt. C. S., 11 June, 1862. Resigned 31 May, 1863.
Colt, Thos. G., Capt. A. A. G., 12 Dec., 1864. Mustered out 28 June, 1865.
Colton, John B., Capt. A. Q. M., 26 Nov., 1862. Resigned 17 Nov., 1863.
Colton, John J., Maj. P. M., 24 Feb., 1865. Mustered out 31 July, 1865.
Colvin, Hervey A., Capt. A. A. G., 28 March, 1865. Mustered out 21 Feb., 1866.
Colvin, John D., 2nd Lieut. Sig. Corps, 14 Feb., 1865. Mustered out 21 Aug., 1865.
Comfort, Aaron J., Asst. Surg., 18 Feb., 1864. Mustered out 3 Nov., 1865.
Comley, Rich'd N., Capt. C. S., 3 Aug., 1861. Resigned 9 June, 1865.
Comstock, Alden H., Capt. A. Q. M., 8 Sept., 1864. Mustered out 31 May, 1866.
Comstock, H. N., Capt. C. S., 2 March, 1864. Mustered out 9 Oct., 1865.
Comstock, Isaac N., Capt. C. S., 2 March, 1864. Mustered out 11 July, 1865.
Comstock, James B., Capt. A. A. G., 14 Feb., 1865. Mustered out 14 Dec., 1865.
Conant, Horace A., Capt. A. Q. M., 12 May, 1862. Died 5 Aug., 1862.

Conant, Roger, Capt. C. S., 1 Feb., 1865. Resigned 24 May, 1865.
Congdon, George B., Maj. P. M., 14 May, 1863. Mustered out 19 Oct., 1865.
Conklin, James T., Capt. A. Q. M., 31 July, 1863. Mustered out 8 Nov., 1865.
Conn, Alex'r, Capt. A. Q. M., 27 April, 1863. Mustered out 13 July, 1866.
Connelly, James H., 2nd Lieut. Sig. Corps, 3 March, 1863. Mustered out 20 June, 1866.
Conner, Wm. H., Capt. A. A. G., 14 July, 1862. Resigned 24 Dec., 1862.
Connor, Patrick E., Brig. Gen., 30 March, 1863. Mustered out 30 April, 1866.
Connor, Selden, Brig. Gen., 11 June, 1864. Mustered out 7 April, 1866.
Conover, Wm. A., Asst. Surg., 4 Oct., 1862. Maj. Surg., 8 May, 1863. Mustered out 13 March, 1866.
Conrad, Joseph S., Lieut. Col. Addl. A. de C., 5 May, 1862. Discharged 21 Jan., 1864.
Conrad, Wm. C., Capt. C. S., 30 June, 1863. Resigned 16 Jan., 1864.
Constable, Nathaniel S., Capt. A. Q. M., 23 Sept., 1862. Mustered out 4 Aug., 1865.
Convers, Edward S., Capt. C. S., 16 July, 1862. Mustered out 9 Oct., 1865.
Cook, James A., Capt. C. S., 2 July, 1863. Discharged 8 Sept., 1864.
Cook, John, Brig. Gen., 21 March, 1862. Mustered out 24 Aug., 1865.
Cook, Martin K., Capt. A. de C., 13 March, 1863. Mustered out 10 June, 1865.
Cook, Milton J., Capt. C. S., 21 Feb., 1865. Mustered out 15 June, 1865.
Cooke, Henry P., Capt. A. A. G., 7 Oct., 186[illegible]. Resigned 1 May, 1865.
Cooke, Hosmer A., Capt. A. Q. M., 21 July, 1863. Mustered out 19 Oct., 1865.
Cooke, Isaac N., Maj. P. M., 1 June, 1861. Dismissed 26 Dec., 1863.
Cooley, E. E., Capt. C. S., 13 Sept., 1864. Mustered out 23 Oct., 1865.
Coon, John, Maj. P. M., 1 June, 1861. Resigned 9 March, 1865.
Cooney, George W., Capt. C. S., 26 Nov., 1862. Resigned 1 May, 1865.
Cooney, John M., Capt. A. A. G., 23 Oct., 1862. Resigned 26 Jan., 1864.
Coonley, Benjamin, Capt. A. Q. M., 3 Dec., 1864. Mustered out 23 Oct., 1865.
Cooper, James, Brig. Gen., 17 May, 1861. Died 28 March, 1863.
Cooper, John E. S., Capt. C. S., 2 Feb., 1865. Mustered out 13 Dec., 1865
Cooper, Joseph A., Brig. Gen., 30 July, 1864. Mustered out 15 Jan., 1866.
Cope, Emmor B., Capt. A. de C., 20 April, 1864. Maj., 9 Feb., 1865. Mustered out 26 June, 1865.
Copeland, Frederick A., Capt. A. A. G., 30 June, 1864. Mustered out 19 Sept., 1865.
Copeland, Joseph T., Brig. Gen., 29 Nov., 1862. Resigned 8 Nov., 1865.
Copeland, Robert M., Maj. A. A. G., 27 Nov., 1861. Resigned 1 Aug., 1862.
Copp, Turton J., Capt. C. S., 2 March, 1864. Mustered out 9 Oct., 1865.
Corcoran, Michael, Brig. Gen., 21 July, 1861. Died 22 Dec., 1863.
Corkhill, George B., Capt. C. S., 3 Feb., 1862. Maj. P. M., 27 Sept., 1864. Mustered out 18 Aug., 1865.
Corkhill, Wm. H., Hosp. Chap., 31 Jan., 1863. Resigned 21 March, 1865.
Cornell, Dudley E., Capt. C. S., 9 Feb., 1865. Mustered out 20 July, 1865.
Corning, Edward, Capt. A. Q. M., 24 March, 1862. Resigned 12 June, 1865.
Cornyn, John W., Capt. C. S., 23 April, 1863. Mustered out 14 July, 1865.
Corse, John M., Brig. Gen., 11 Aug., 1863. Mustered out 30 April, 1866.
Corson, Richard R., Capt. A. A. G., 12 May, 1862. Capt. A. Q. M., 17 July, 1862. Mustered out 7 Oct., 1865.
Corts, George P., Capt. A. A. G., 8 May, 1863. Mustered out 22 June, 1865.
Corwine, Richard M., Maj. Addl. A. de C., 31 March, 1862. Resigned 27 July, 1863.
Coryell, Ingham, Capt. A. Q. M., 22 Aug., 1861. Resigned 11 Aug., 1865.
Cosper, Elias, Maj. P. M., 18 Nov., 1863. Resigned 29 May, 1865.
Cottman, John A., Capt. C. S., 7 April, 1864. Mustered out 15 Sept., 1866.
Cottrell, Charles A., Capt. A. Q. M., 3 March, 1865. Mustered out 28 July, 1865.
Couch, Darius N., Brig. Gen., 17 May, 1861. Maj. Gen., 4 July, 1862. Resigned 26 May, 1865.
Coulter, John F., Capt. A. Q. M., 28 July, 1863. Dismissed 18 March, 1864.
Coulter, Will A., Capt. A. A. G., 27 Feb., 1865. Mustered out 25 Nov., 1865.
Courtwright, Geo. S., Asst. Surg., 15 Aug., 1863. Mustered out 10 Aug., 1865.
Coverdale, Robert L., Capt. A. Q. M., 19 Sept., 1864. Mustered out 13 March, 1866.
Cowan, B. Rush, Maj. P. M., 1 June, 1861. Mustered out 18 Jan., 1866.
Cowan, Calvert W., Capt. A. A. G., 30 June, 1862. Resigned 20 June, 1863.
Cowan, John F., Hosp. Chap., 23 June, 1862. Died 29 Sept., 1862.
Cowdin, Robert, Brig. Gen., 26 Sept., 1862. Appointment expired 4 March, 1863.
Cowdrey, Frank H., Capt. A. A. G., 20 April, 1864. Mustered out 19 Sept., 1865.
Cowgill, Clayton A., Maj. Surg., 4 Oct., 1862. Mustered out 10 Jan., 1866.
Cowie, Wm. P., Capt. C. S., 10 Sept., 1862. Mustered out 20 March, 1866.
Cox, Abraham L., Maj. Surg., 4 April, 1862. Died 28 July, 1864.
Cox, Christopher C., Maj. Surg., 7 Oct., 1861. Resigned 31 Dec., 1864.
Cox, Jacob D., Brig. Gen., 17 May, 1861. Maj. Gen., 6 Oct., 1862. Appointment as Maj. Gen. expired 4 March, 1863. Maj. Gen., 7 Dec., 1864. Resigned 1 Jan., 1866.
Cox, John C., Capt. C. S., 5 Aug., 1861. Resigned 27 June, 1864.
Cox, Roland, Capt. A. A. G., 19 Sept., 1863. Resigned 6 Jan., 1865.
Cox, Theodore, Capt. A. A. G., 2 July, 1864. Maj., 6 Feb., 1865. Mustered out 22 Nov., 1865.
Cox, Thos. J., Capt. A. Q. M., 11 June, 1862. Died 17 Sept., 1866.
Coxe, John R., Capt. C. S., 28 Aug., 1862. Mustered out 11 July, 1865.
Coyle, Wm. H., Maj. J. A., 18 May, 1865. Mustered out 31 May, 1866.
Craft, David L., 2nd Lieut. Sig. Corps, 3 March, 1863. Mustered out 4 Sept., 1865.
Craft, Elijah R., Capt. A. A. G., 25 Aug., 1864. Resigned 23 Oct., 1865.
Craig, Allen A., Maj. P. M., 23 Feb., 1864. Resigned 5 April, 1865.
Craig, James, Brig. Gen., 21 March, 1862. Resigned 5 May, 1863.
Craig, James G., Capt. C. S., 9 May, 1863. Resigned 14 July, 1865.
Craig, John, Capt. A. Q. M., 30 May, 1863. Appointed Mil. Storekeeper U. S. A., 31 Jan., 1865.
Craig, John N., Capt. A. A. G., 3 Oct., 1862. Mustered out 19 May, 1866.
Craig, John R., Capt. A. Q. M., 25 Nov., 1862. Mustered out 7 Oct., 1865.
Craig, Sam'l R., Capt. A. Q. M., 30 Oct., 1862. Mustered out 11 Nov., 1865.
Craigie, David J., Capt. A. A. G., 2 July, 1864. Mustered out 19 Sept., 1865.
Crain, Fred'k, Capt. A. Q. M., 18 May, 1864. Mustered out 8 Feb., 1866.

Cram, Thos. J., Col. Addl. A. de C., 25 Sept., 1861. Vacated commission 23 Nov., 1865.
Cramer, James L., Maj. P. M., 19 Feb., 1863. Mustered out 15 Feb., 1866.
Cramer, Michael J., Hosp. Chap., 30 June, 1864. Mustered out 29 June, 1865.
Crandal, Fred'k M., Capt. A. A. G., 2 Oct., 1862. Vacated commission, 8 Aug., 1863.
Crandall, Warren D., Maj. A. A. G., 5 Nov., 1862. Resigned 6 Dec., 1864.
Crandall, W. H. H., Capt. A. Q. M., 14 July, 1862. Discharged 17 April, 1863.
Crandon, T. Franklin P., Capt. A. Q. M., 6 Feb., 1865. Mustered out 10 July, 1866.
Crane, Francis W., Maj. P. M., 1 June, 1861. Mustered out 15 Nov., 1865.
Crane, James B., Hosp. Chap., 20 Aug., 1862. Appointment expired 4 March, 1863. Reappointed 22 April, 1863. Mustered out 26 July, 1865.
Crane, John C., Capt. A. Q. M., 11 June, 1862. Mustered out 31 Jan., 1867.
Crane, Joseph G., Capt. C. S., 28 June, 1861. Appointed Capt. C. S., U. S. A., 25 April, 1865.
Crane, Walter, Maj. P. M., 11 March, 1863. Mustered out 1 Dec., 1865.
Cranford, Henry L., Capt. C. S., 19 Feb., 1863. Mustered out 6 July, 1865.
Crapo, Angelo, Capt. C. S., 7 April, 1864. Mustered out 26 June, 1865.
Craven, John J., Maj. Surg., 4 Sept., 1861. Mustered out 27 Jan., 1866.
Cravens, John O., Capt. A. A. G., 27 Feb., 1863. Maj. 15 May, 1863. Resigned 26 June, 1865.
Cravens, John R., Maj. P. M., 30 June, 1862. Mustered out 15 Jan., 1866.
Crawford, Chas., Maj. P. M., 23 Feb., 1864. Mustered out 1 Nov., 1866.
Crawford, Frank J., Capt. C. S., 20 Nov., 1862. Mustered out 21 June, 1865.
Crawford, J. Agnew, Hosp. Chap., 5 Aug., 1863. Mustered out 21 Aug., 1865.
Crawford, John T., Maj. Surg., 2 Oct., 1861. Died 7 June, 1862.
Crawford, LeRoy, Capt. A. Q. M., 30 March, 1864. Resigned 25 Feb., 1865.
Crawford, Medoren, Capt. A. Q. M., 28 April, 1862. Resigned 16 April, 1864.
Crawford, Robert P., Capt. A. A. G., 4 Sept., 1863. Resigned 1 May, 1865.
Crawford, Sam'l W., Brig. Gen., 25 April, 1862. Mustered out 15 Jan., 1866.
Crever, Benj. H., Hosp. Chap., 24 July, 1862. Mustered out 10 Aug., 1865.
Crispell, Abraham, Maj. Surg., 4 April, 1862. Resigned 31 May, 1865.
Crist, La Tour M., Capt. A. Q. M., 3 March, 1865. Mustered out 15 Aug., 1865.
Crittenden, Thos. L., Brig. Gen., 27 Sept., 1861. Maj. Gen., 17 July, 1862. Resigned 13 Dec., 1864.
Crittenden, Thos. T., Brig. Gen., 28 April, 1862. Resigned 5 May, 1863.
Crocker, Marcellus M., Brig. Gen., 29 Nov., 1862. Died 26 Aug., 1865.
Crockett, John R., Capt. A. Q. M., 30 June, 1862. Resigned 5 Sept., 1862.
Crombergar, Thos. S., Capt. C. S., 2 Aug., 1862. Mustered out 8 July, 1865.
Crook, George, Brig. Gen., 7 Sept., 1862. Maj. Gen., 21 Oct., 1864. Mustered out 15 Jan., 1866.
Crosby, Alpheus B., Maj. Surg., 5 Sept., 1861. Resigned 30 June, 1862.
Crosby, John Schuyler, Capt. A. de C., 3 June, 1863. Mustered out 1 Aug., 1866.
Crosby, Stephen M. Maj. P. M., 26 Nov., 1862. Mustered out 15 Jan., 1866.
Crosby, Thos. R., Maj. Surg., 11 Sept., 1862. Mustered out 27 July, 1865.
Cross, Chas. F., 1st Lieut. Sig. Corps, 3 March, 1863. Mustered out 15 Sept., 1865.
Cross, Daniel K., Capt. A. de C., 6 Nov., 1863. Resigned 30 April, 1864.
Croswell, Micah S., Capt. C. S., 27 March, 1863. Mustered out 4 Aug., 1866.
Crouch, Christopher J., Hosp. Chap., 23 Feb., 1864. Mustered out 26 July, 1865.
Crowell, John, Jr., Capt. A. A. G., 1 May, 1863. Resigned 6 May, 1865.
Crowell, John H., Capt. A. Q. M., 7 April, 1864. Mustered out 20 April, 1866.
Croxton, John T., Brig. Gen., 30 July, 1864. Resigned 26 Dec., 1865.
Croxton, Lafayette J., Capt. A. Q. M., 19 Feb., 1863. Resigned 5 June, 1865.
Cruft, Chas., Brig. Gen., 16 July, 1862. Mustered out 24 Aug., 1865.
Crumbacker, David, Maj. P. M., 6 Feb., 1865. Died 17 March, 1865.
Cruttenden, Joel D., Capt. A. Q. M., 19 Feb., 1862. Mustered out 3 Nov., 1866.
Culbertson, Howard, Maj. Surg., 7 Nov., 1862. Mustered out 7 Oct., 1865.
Culbertson, John C., Maj. P. M., 26 Nov., 1862. Resigned 8 Aug., 1863.
Cullum, George W., Col. A. A. de C., 6 Aug., 1861. Brig. Gen., 1 Nov., 1861. Mustered out 1 Sept., 1866.
Culver, J. O., Maj. P. M., 5 Aug., 1861. Mustered out 3 Nov., 1865.
Cumback, Will, Maj. P. M., 1 June, 1861. Mustered out 10 July, 1865.
Cummings, Alex. M., Capt. A. Q. M., 18 April, 1863. Mustered out 31 May, 1866.
Cummings, Finley O., Capt. A. A. G., 31 July, 1865. Mustered out 18 Sept., 1865.
Cummings, George W., Capt. C. S., 16 Nov., 1861. Resigned 14 May, 1862.
Cummings, J. Frank, Capt. C. S., 28 Jan., 1865. Mustered out 15 June, 1865.
Currey, James H., Asst. Surg., 27 March, 1863. Maj. Surg., 2 Sept., 1863. Mustered out 7 Oct., 1862.
Currie, Leonard D. H., Capt. A. A. G., 30 Sept., 1861. Resigned 26 July, 1862.
Currie, Wm., Capt. A. Q. M., 30 June, 1864. Mustered out 7 April, 1866.
Curry, James, Capt. C. S., 25 July, 1862. Mustered out 13 March, 1867.
Cursh, Waldemar, Capt. C. S., 21 April, 1864. Mustered out 18 Aug., 1865.
Curtice, Chas. E., Maj. P. M., 19 Feb., 1863. Resigned 18 Feb., 1865.
Curtis, Albert A., Capt. A. Q. M., 26 Nov., 1862. Resigned 21 April, 1864.
Curtis, David W., Capt. A. Q. M., 1 March, 1865. Mustered out 28 July, 1865.
Curtis, Henry, Jr., Capt. A. A. G., 17 July, 1862. Resigned 10 Feb., 1865.
Curtis, Henry Z., Capt. A. Q. M., 3 Aug., 1861. Capt. A. A. G., 26 Nov., 1861. Maj., 28 April, 1862. Killed 5 Oct., 1863, in action at Baxter's Springs, Kansas.
Curtis, Joseph B., Capt. A. A. G., 9 June, 1862. Resigned 27 Aug., 1862.
Curtis, Josiah, Maj. Surg., 4 Sept., 1861. Mustered out 31 Oct., 1865.
Curtis, N. Martin, Brig. Gen., 15 Jan., 1865. Mustered out 15 Jan., 1866.
Curtis, Rob't G., Capt. A. A. G., 20 April, 1864. Resigned 15 June, 1865.
Curtis, Sam'l R., Brig. Gen., 17 May, 1861. Maj. Gen., 21 March, 1862. Mustered out, 30 April, 1866.
Curtis, Wm. B., Capt. A. A. G., 1 Oct., 1862. Resigned 3 Sept., 1864.
Cusack, John, Capt. C. S., 1 Aug., 1863. Mustered out 31 May, 1866.
Cushing, George W., Capt. A. Q. M., 24 July, 1863. Mustered out 15 July, 1867.
Curtis, Walter, Capt. A. Q. M., 27 Nov., 1862. Resigned 21 Jan., 1864.
Custer, George A., Capt. Addl. A. de C., 5 June, 1862. Discharged 31 March, 1863. Brig. Gen., 29 June, 1863. Maj. Gen., 15 April, 1865. Mustered out 1 Feb., 1866.

Cutler, Alex. K., Capt. A. Q. M., 10 Aug., 1864. Mustered out 20 Sept., 1865.
Cutler, Benj. C., Capt. A. A. G., 6 Aug., 1862. Mustered out 20 Jan., 1866.
Cutler, Horace D. B., Capt. A. A. G., 21 Jan., 1865. Mustered out 25 Nov., 1865.
Cutler, Lysander, Brig. Gen., 29 Nov., 1862. Resigned 30 June, 1865.
Cutter, Ammie, Capt. A. Q. M., 18 March, 1864. Mustered out 30 March, 1866.
Cutting, James D. W., Capt. Addl. A. de C., 23 May, 1862. Resigned 8 Dec., 1864.
Cutting, Marquis F., Capt. A. Q. M., 13 Feb., 1865. Mustered out 28 July, 1865.
Cutting, Walter. Capt. Addl. A. de C., 9 July, 1862. Maj. A. de C., 29 Feb., 1864. Mustered out 1 July, 1866.
Cutting, Wm., Capt. A. Q. M., 16 Nov., 1861. Maj. A. de C., 22 July, 1862. Resigned 8 May, 1865.
Cutts, Joseph B., Asst. Surg., 30 June, 1864. Maj. Surg., 18 March, 1865. Mustered out 12 Oct., 1865.
Cutts, Rich'd D., Col. Addl. A. de C., 29 Nov., 1861. Resigned 1 June, 1865.
Dade, Francis T., Asst. Surg., 11 Sept., 1862. Resigned 14 Oct., 1863.
Dahlgren, Ulric, Capt. Addl. A. de C., 29 May, 1862. Killed 4 March, 1864, in action near King and Queen's Court House, Va.
Dailey, Edward D., Maj. Surg., 4 April, 1862. Discharged 15 Oct., 1863.
Daily, Marven A., Capt. C. S., 19 Feb., 1863. Mustered out 20 April, 1866.
Daily, Wm. M., Hosp. Chap., 9 May, 1863. Mustered out 4 Aug., 1865.
Dale, Edward, Capt. C. S., 20 April, 1864. Mustered out 27 Jan., 1866.
Dale, John A., Maj. P. M., 28 May, 1864. Appointment revoked 5 Sept., 1864.
Dallam Francis A., Capt. A. A. G., 24 March, 1862. Resigned 23 Dec., 1862.
Dalrymple, Aaron P., Maj., Surg., 9 June, 1862. Mustered out 2 Feb., 1866.
Dalton, Edward B., Asst. Surg., 11 March, 1863. Maj. Surg., 26 March, 1863. Resigned 12 May, 1865.
Dalton, Henry R., Capt. A. A. G., 28 May, 1862. Maj. 30 June, 1864. Resigned 25 Nov., 1864.
Dalton, John C., Jr., Maj. Surg., 3 Aug., 1861. Resigned 5 March, 1864.
Dana, Amasa E., Capt. A. A. G., 20 April, 1864. Maj., 12 Nov., 1864. Resigned 25 May, 1865.
Dana, Chas. A., Maj. A. A. G., 1 June, 1863. Appointment expired 4 July, 1864.
Dana, Gustavus S., Capt. Sig. Corps, 3 March, 1863. Resigned 21 Sept., 1864.
Dana, Milton, Capt. A. Q. M., 16 Feb., 1865. Mustered out 19 May, 1866.
Dana, Nap'l J. T., Brig. Gen., 3 Feb., 1862. Maj. Gen., 29 Nov., 1862. Resigned 27 May, 1865.
Dangler, David A., Capt. A. Q. M., 3 Nov., 1862. Resigned 30 May, 1863.
Daniels, Milton J., Capt. C. S. 23 Feb., 1865. Mustered out 13 Dec., 1865.
Daniels, Waldo C., Asst. Surg., 9 Sept., 1863. Maj. Surg., 30 June, 1864. Mustered out 5 Aug., 1865.
Daniels, Wm. H., Capt. A. Q. M., 16 July, 1862. Mustered out 10 Sept., 1866.
Daniels, Wm. V., Hosp. Chap., 14 July, 1862. Mustered out 21 Aug., 1865.
Darling, Henry A., Capt. C. S., 15 Sept., 1863. Mustered out 23 June, 1866.
Darr, Francis, Capt. C. S., 3 Aug., 1861. Resigned 31 July, 1864.
Darrach, Barton, Maj. Surg., 4 Oct., 1862. Died 19 July, 1863.
Darrow, Chas. Capt. A. Q. M., 26 Nov., 1862. Mustered out 31 May, 1866.
Darst, Wm. P., Capt. C. S., 6 March, 1862. Discharged 14 Feb., 1863.
Daum, Philip, Col. Addl. A. de C., 26 May, 1862. Dismissed 7 April, 1863.
David, James I. Capt. A. Q. M., 11 June, 1862. Vacated commission 15 May, 1863.
David, Thomas B. A., Capt. A. Q. M., 17 July, 1862. Resigned 20 Jan., 1864.
Davidson, John W., Brig. Gen., 3 Feb., 1862. Mustered out 15 Jan., 1866.
Davies, Chas F., Maj. P. M., 5 Aug., 1861. Died 3 Dec., 1865.
Davies, Henry E., Brig. Gen., 16 Sept., 1863. Maj. Gen., 4 May, 1865. Resigned 1 Jan., 1866.
Davies, Richard E., Capt. C. S., 23 Nov., 1861. Mustered out 26 Oct., 1865.
Davies, Thos. A., Brig. Gen., 7 March, 1862. Mustered out 24 Aug., 1865.
Davis, Alex'r H., Capt. A. A. G., 11 March, 1863. Resigned 18 Jan., 1864.
Davis, Andrew J., Capt. A. A. G., 4 Sept., 1863. Resigned 8 June, 1864.
Davis, Chas. H., Capt. C. S., 21 April, 1864. Mustered out 9 Oct., 1865.
Davis, Chas. L., Capt. Sig. Corps, 3 March, 1863. Mustered out 18 Aug., 1865.
Davis, Chas. W., Capt. A. Q. M., 23 March, 1865. Mustered out 19 Sept., 1865.
Davis, Edmund J., Brig. Gen., 10 Nov., 1864. Mustered out 24 Aug., 1865.
Davis, Edward M., Capt. A. Q. M., 3 Aug., 1861. Resigned 7 July, 1862.
Davis, George F., Capt. A. Q. M., 1 May, 1863. Resigned 31 July, 1863.
Davis, George W., Capt. A. Q. M., 22 May, 1865. Mustered out 20 April, 1866.
Davis, Henry W., Asst. Surg., 18 May, 1864. Maj. Surg., 30 Aug., 1864. Mustered out 27 July, 1865.
Davis, Horatio N., Capt. C. S., 19 Feb., 1863. Mustered out 2 Feb., 1866.
Davis, James, Capt. C. S., 5 Sept., 1862. Discharged 2 Dec., 1863.
Davis, James W., Capt. C. S., 2 March, 1864. Mustered out 9 Oct., 1865.
Davis, Jefferson C., Brig. Gen., 18 Dec., 1861. Mustered out 11 Sept., 1866.
Davis, John S., Capt. C. S., 1 May, 1862. Resigned 11 Aug., 1862.
Davis, John S., Jr., Capt. A. Q. M., 19 Feb., 1863. Mustered out 20 July, 1865.
Davis, Joseph S., Maj. P. M., 3 March, 1865 Mustered out 31 July, 1865.
Davis, Murray, Capt. A. A. G., 17 Aug., 1864. Maj. 15 Feb., 1865. Mustered out 1 Oct., 1866.
Davis, Phineas A., Capt. A. A. G., 16 Sept., 1863. Maj. 21 March, 1865. Mustered out 19 May, 1866.
Davis, Robt. S., Capt. A. de C., 1 Oct., 1862. Maj. A. A. G., 9 Nov., 1863. Mustered out 26 Oct., 1865.
Davis, Sam'l B., Maj. Surg., 19 Feb., 1863. Mustered out 7 Oct., 1865.
Davison, Henry H., Capt. C. S., 21 April, 1864. Mustered out 15 Aug., 1865.
Day, D. C., Asst. Surg., 11 Oct., 1864. Mustered out 18 Jan., 1866.
Day, Denning W. H., Capt. A. Q. M., 7 April, 1864 Mustered out 2 Feb., 1866.
Day, Robert, Hosp. Chap., 13 Aug., 1863. Mustered out 27 Dec., 1866.
Dayton, Lewis M., Capt. A. de C., 11 March, 1863. Maj. A. A. G. 12 Jan., 1865. Mustered out 1 Sept., 1866.
Dean, Austin S., Capt. Addl. A. de C., 1 April, 1862. Died 19 July, 1863.
Dean, Daniel W., Maj. P. M., 11 March, 1863. Mustered out 31 July, 1865.
Deane, Chas. H., Capt. A. Q. M., 5 Dec., 1863. Rejected by Senate 23 Feb., 1864. Capt. A. Q. M., 2 July, 1864. Mustered out 30 April 1866.
Deane, Wm. W., Capt. A. A. G., 29 Feb., 1864. Mustered out 1 Nov., 1866.
Deaton, Enoch F., Capt. C. S. 26 Nov., 1862. Mustered out 5 Aug., 1865.

De Costa, George W., Maj. P. M., 21 April, 1864. Mustered out 15 Feb., 1866.
De Gress, Jacob C., Maj. A. de C., 12 May, 1865. Mustered out 1 Sept., 1866.
De Hanne, J. Victor, Asst. Surg., 21 Dec., 1864 Asst. Surg., U. S. A., 14 March, 1867.
De Hauteville, Frederic S. G., Capt. A. A. G., 30 June, 1862. Resigned 24 Feb., 1863.
Deitzler, George W., Brig. Gen., 29 Nov., 1862. Resigned 27 Aug., 1863.
De Lamatar, Jacob J., Asst. Surg., 7 Jan., 1863. Maj. Surg., 9 July, 1863. Mustered out 1 Nov., 1867.
Delaney, Alfred, Asst. Surg., 26 Jan., 1864. Mustered out 10 Jan., 1866.
Delaney, Patrick K., Capt. A. Q. M., 23 July, 1864. Mustered out 20 Sept., 1865.
Delay, James W., Capt. C. S., 24 Oct., 1864. Mustered out 11 July, 1865.
Del Vechio, James R., Capt. A. Q. M., 8 Oct., 1862 Mustered out 31 May, 1866.
De Motte, Mark L., Capt. A. Q. M., 14 April, 1862. Resigned 12 Jan., 1864.
Denig, Edward C., Capt. A. A. G., 23 Dec., 1862. Resigned 12 Dec., 1864.
Dennett, Thos. S., Capt. A. Q. M., 30 June, 1862. Discharged 18 July, 1863.
Dennicke, Ernest A., 1st Lieut. Sig. Corps, 3 March, 1863. Mustered out 20 Dec., 1865.
Dennis, Edgar W., Capt. Addl. A. de C., 11 July, 1862. Maj. J. A., U. S. A., 19 Jan., 1865.
Dennis, Elias S., Brig. Gen., 29 Nov., 1862. Mustered out 24 Aug., 1865.
Dennis, John B., Maj. P. M., 25 Jan., 1865. Mustered out 31 July, 1865.
Dennison, Chas. W., Hosp. Chap., 31 July, 1862. Dropped 23 Jan., 1863.
Denniston, Joseph F., Capt. C. S., 7 April, 1864. Mustered out 1 Jan., 1867.
Denny, Alfred, Capt. A. Q. M., 12 June, 1863. Resigned 3 June, 1864.
De Nordendorf, Czaky S., Capt. Addl. A. de C., 31 March, 1862. Resigned 11 Oct., 1862.
Dent, Fred'k T., Brig. Gen., 5 April, 1865. Mustered out 30 April, 1866.
Denver, James W., Brig. Gen., 14 Aug., 1861. Resigned 5 March, 1863.
Derby, George, Asst. Surg., 18 May, 1864. Maj. Surg., 30 June, 1864. Mustered out 18 Jan., 1866.
Derby, Nelson R., Maj. Surg., 3 Aug., 1861. Mustered out 27 July, 1865.
De Russy, Gustavus A., Brig. Gen., 23 May, 1863. Mustered out 15 Jan., 1866.
Des Anges, Robt., Maj. A. A. G., 7 April, 1864. Mustered out 20 Jan., 1866.
De Trobriand, Philip R., Brig. Gen., 5 Jan., 1864. Mustered out 15 Jan., 1866.
Detshy, Edward, Maj. Addl. A. de C., 16 June, 1862. Mustered out 14 Dec., 1865.
Devan, Thos. T., Hosp. Chap., 13 June, 1862. Discharged 23 Feb., 1864.
Devans, Chas., Brig. Gen., 15 April, 1862. Mustered out 2 June, 1866.
Devereux, Charles B., Capt. C. S., 20 May, 1863. Mustered out 7 April, 1866.
De Villarceau, Achille M. B., Capt. Addl. A de C., 23 Nov., 1861. Resigned 13 Dec., 1862.
Devin, Thos. C., Brig. Gen., 19 Oct., 1864. Mustered out 15 Jan., 1866.
Dewey, Arch. S., Capt. A. Q. M., 1 Nov., 1862. Resigned 30 June, 1865.
Dewey, Israel O., Maj. P. M., 28 May, 1864. Mustered out 1 Dec., 1865.
Dewey, Joel A., Brig. Gen., 13 Dec., 1865. Mustered out 31 Jan., 1866.
Dewing, Thos. S., Hosp. Chap., 23 Jan., 1865. Mustered out 26 July, 1865.
De Witt, Francis, Capt. C. S., 26 Nov., 1862. Mustered out 8 Feb., 1866.
De Witt, Wm. R., Asst. Surg., 7 Aug., 1863. Maj. Surg., 15 Aug., 1863. Mustered out 1 Nov., 1867.
De Wolf, David O., Capt. A. Q. M., 8 July, 1863. Mustered out 4 Aug., 1865.
Dexter, John B., Capt. A. Q. M., 29 Feb., 1864. Mustered out 5 June, 1866.
Dickey, Cyrus E., Capt. A. A. G., 1 May, 1863. Died 13 April, 1864, of wounds received at Battle of Sabina X Roads, La.
Dickey, Jesse C., Maj. P. M., 26 Nov., 1862. Mustered out 30 April, 1866.
Dickey, Wm. B., Capt. A. Q. M., 18 May, 1864. Mustered out 28 July, 1865.
Dickinson, Chas. H., Capt. A. Q. M., 18 March, 1864. Mustered out 27 Jan., 1866.
Dickinson, Joseph, Capt. A. A. G., 22 Aug., 1861. Maj. 22 Aug., 1862. Resigned 26 Jan., 1864.
Dickinson, Wm., Maj. Surg., 4 April, 1862. Resigned 7 Jan., 1865.
Dickson, David T., Maj. P. M., 3 Oct., 1863. Mustered out 15 April, 1866.
Dickson, J. Bates, Capt. A. A. G. 1 May, 1862. Mustered out 24 June, 1865.
Dietrich, Chas. J., Capt. C. S., 19 Feb., 1863. Resigned 28 Aug., 1865.
Dietrich, Chas. W., Capt. A. A. G., 17 Oct., 1862. Resigned 1 Aug., 1863.
Dike, Edward G., Capt. A. A. G., 24 Dec., 1864. Mustered out 29 Sept., 1865.
Dillingham, Chas., Capt. C. S., 1 Nov., 1862. Appointment expired 4 March, 1863.
Dillingham, Lucius A., 2nd Lieut. Sig. Corps, 3 March, 1863. Mustered out 11 Aug., 1865.
Dimond, Wm. H., Capt. A. A. G., 3 March, 1865. Resigned 8 July, 1865.
Diven, Alex., Maj. P. M., 26 Nov., 1862. Resigned 31 Jan., 1865.
Diven, Alex. S., Capt. A. A. G., 13 May, 1863. Resigned 5 April, 1865.
Diven, Eugene, Capt. A. A. G., 26 Sept., 1864. Resigned 5 April, 1865.
Dix, Chas. T., Maj. Addl. A. de C., 20 June, 1862. Resigned 15 March, 1865.
Dix, John A., Maj. Gen., 16 May, 1861. Resigned 30 Nov., 1865.
Dixon, Francis B., Maj. P. M., 23 Feb., 1864. Discharged 6 Sept., 1864.
Dixon, Henry T., Maj. P. M., 1 June, 1861. Mustered out 31 July, 1865.
Doan, George P., Capt. A. Q. M., 27 Sept., 1862. Mustered out 7 March, 1866.
Dobyns, George H., Capt. A. Q. M. 29 Feb., 1864. Mustered out 8 Jan., 1866.
Dock, Joseph, Capt. A. Q. M., 22 June, 1861. Resigned 1 Oct., 1861.
Dod, Chas. H., Capt. A. A. G., 20 April, 1864. Died 26 Aug., 1864.
Dodd, Edward, Asst. Surg., 4 Oct., 1862. Resigned 13 Oct., 1863.
Doddridge, John M., Maj. P. M., 26 Nov., 1862. Mustered out 15 Feb., 1866.
Dodds, Joseph L., Capt. A. Q. M., 3 Aug., 1861. Died 18 Aug., 1862.
Dodge, Chas., Maj. P. M., 30 June, 1862. Mustered out 31 July, 1865.
Dodge, Chas. C., Brig. Gen., 29 Nov., 1862. Resigned 12 June, 1863.
Dodge, George S., Capt. A. Q. M., 12 May, 1862. Mustered out 7 March, 1866.
Dodge, Grenville M., Brig. Gen., 31 March, 1862. Maj. Gen., 7 June, 1864. Resigned 30 May, 1866.
Dodge, John V., Hosp. Chap., 31 May, 1862. Mustered out 26 June, 1865.
Dodge, Nathaniel S., Capt. A. Q. M., 1 June, 1863. Resigned 21 July, 1865.
Dodge, Richard V., Hosp. Chap. 31 May, 1862. Discharged 26 Feb., 1863.
Dodge, Robert P. W., Maj. P. M. 8 Aug., 1861. Mustered out 20 July, 1866.
Dodge, Wm. S., Capt. C. S., 26 Nov., 1862. Resigned 10 July, 1863. Capt. C. S. 21 April, 1864. Mustered out 15 July, 1865.

Doehn, Rudolph, Hosp. Chap., 11 June, 1862. Resigned 17 Jan., 1864.
Doherty, Wm. H., Capt. A. Q. M., 2 July, 1864. Mustered out 6 Dec., 1865.
Dohrman, Francis A., Capt. C. S., 20 Nov., 1863. Mustered out 20 July, 1865.
Dole, Wm. R., Capt. Addl. A. de C., 18 March, 1862. Discharged 18 July, 1863.
Dolman, John H., Maj. P. M., 14 Aug., 1863. Mustered out 20 July, 1866.
Donaldson, Wm., Capt. C. S., 3 Aug., 1861. Resigned 28 April, 1862.
Donnell, Edward P., Capt. C. S., 19 Feb., 1862. Discharged 11 March, 1863.
Doolittle, Chas. C., Brig. Gen., 27 Jan., 1865. Mustered out 30 Nov., 1865.
Doolittle, Henry J., Capt. Addl. A. de C., 19 April, 1862. Died 10 Aug., 1862.
D'Orleans, Louis Philippe, Capt. Addl. A. de C., 24 Sept., 1861. Resigned 15 July, 1862.
D'Orleans, Robt., Capt., Addl. A. de C., 24 Sept., 1861. Resigned 15 July, 1862.
Dorman, Orloff M., Maj. P. M., 17 July, 1862. Mustered out 15 Feb., 1866.
Dorr, James C., Maj. Surg., 11 June, 1862. Resigned 4 May, 1864.
Dorran, Wm. M., Asst. Surg., 20 Sept., 1864. Mustered out 19 Oct., 1865.
Dorsey George W. E., Capt. C. S., 18 May, 1864. Mustered out 3 Aug., 1865.
Dorsheimer, Wm., Maj. Addl. A. de C., 4 Sept., 1861. Discharged 1 Nov., 1861.
Doty, Chas., Capt. C. S., 26 Nov., 1862. Appointment expired 4 March, 1863. Reappointed 25 May, 1863. Mustered out 13 March, 1866.
Doubleday, Abner, Brig. Gen., 3 Feb., 1862. Maj. Gen., 29 Nov., 1862. Mustered out 24 Aug., 1865.
Dougherty, Alex. N., Maj. Surg., 30 Sept., 1861. Mustered out 20 Oct., 1865.
Doughty, John H., Asst. Surg., 7 Aug., 1863. Mustered out 11 Nov., 1865.
Douglass, Harvey F., Capt. A. Q. M., 7 March, 1864. Mustered out 20 Sept., 1865.
Douglass, John C., Capt. A. A. G., 23 June, 1863. Maj., 31 May, 1865. Mustered out 19 Sept., 1865.
Douglass, Levi H., Capt. C. S., 2 March, 1864. Mustered out 31 May, 1866.
Douglass, Wm. H., Capt. C. S., 5 Aug., 1861. Mustered out 24 June, 1865.
Dow, Neal, Brig. Gen., 28 April, 1862. Resigned 30 Nov., 1864.
Dowlin, James P., Asst. Surg., 11 Oct., 1864. Mustered out 22 Nov., 1865.
Downing, Wm. R., Capt. A. Q. M., 11 Sept., 1861. Discharged 24 May, 1864.
Doyle, John A., Capt. C. S., 24 March, 1862. Mustered out 27 Nov., 1865.
Drake, George B., Capt. Addl. A. de C., 22 May, 1862. Maj. A. A. G., 11 March, 1863. Resigned 23 March, 1865.
Drake, Nelson S., Asst. Surg., 18 May, 1864. Mustered out 12 Oct., 1865.
Drennan, John P., Capt. A. Q. M., 29 Feb., 1864. Mustered out 22 Nov., 1865.
Drew, Cyrus K., Capt. A. Q. M., 30 June, 1864. Mustered out 20 March, 1866.
Drew, Joseph W., Maj. P. M., 23 Feb., 1864. Mustered out 1 Feb., 1869.
Drew, Sam'l S., Maj. P. M., 30 June, 1864. Resigned 15 April, 1865.
Driver, Joseph M., Hosp. Chap., 4 June, 1862. Discharged 25 July, 1864.
Driver, Wm. R., Capt. A. A. G., 20 April, 1864. Maj., 17 Nov., 1864. Mustered out 19 Sept., 1865.
Drouillard, James P., Capt. Addl. A. de C., 23 May, 1862. Resigned 1 Feb., 1865.
Drum, James S., Capt. C. S., 17 July, 1862. Died 19 April, 1863.
Drumm, Thos. C., Hosp. Chap., 30 June, 1864. Mustered out 7 Oct., 1865.
Drummond, James, Hosp. Chap., 15 Dec., 1864. Mustered out 4 Aug., 1865.
Du Bois, John V., Col. Addl. A. de C., 19 Feb., 1862. Mustered out 9 Feb., 1866.
Ducachet, Henry W., Asst. Surg., 7 Aug., 1863. Maj. Surg., 15 Aug., 1863. Died 11 Oct., 1865.
Dudley, George B., Maj. P. M., 23 Feb., 1864. Mustered out 23 Sept., 1865.
Dudley, Thomas R., Capt. A. Q. M., 29 Sept., 1863. Mustered out 20 Sept., 1865.
Duff, James B., 2nd Lieut. Sig. Corps., 3 March, 1863. Resigned 6 April, 1865.
Duffee, Washington J., Maj. Surg., 2 Nov., 1861. Discharged 4 April, 1863.
Duffie, Alfred N., Brig. Gen., 23 June, 1863. Mustered out 24 Aug., 1865.
Dugger, Jefferson L., Capt. A. A. G., 11 March, 1863. Died 16 July, 1863.
Dulon, Arnold, Capt. A. de C., 1 Nov., 1862. Discharged 15 Aug., 1863.
Dumont, Ebenezer, Brig. Gen., 3 Sept., 1861. Resigned 28 Feb., 1863.
Dumreicher, Conrad C., Asst. Surg., 11 Sept., 1862. Maj. Surg., 27 May, 1863. Mustered out 27 July, 1865.
Dunan, Sylvester H., Capt. A. Q. M., 27 Feb., 1863. Resigned 20 Feb., 1865.
Dunbar, Gilbert E., Capt. A. Q. M., 5 July, 1863. Mustered out 22 Nov., 1865.
Dunglison, Thos. R., Asst. Surg., 3 Dec., 1864. Mustered out 4 June, 1866.
Dunham, Albert B., Capt. A. Q. M., 18 May, 1864. Resigned 11 March, 1865.
Dunham, Robt. T., Capt. A. A. G., 14 July, 1862. Dishonorably discharged 18 Aug., 1865.
Dunka, Nicolai, Capt. Addl. A. de C., 31 March, 1862. Killed 8 June, 1862, at Battle of Cross Keys, Va.
Dunlap, James, Capt. A. Q. M., 8 Aug., 1861. Resigned 11 June, 1864.
Dunn, Wm. M. K., Jr., Capt. A. A. G., 9 April, 1865. Mustered out 3 May, 1866.
Dunning, Edward, Hosp. Chap., 23 June, 1862. Mustered out 17 Aug., 1865.
Dunton, Augustus T., Capt. A. Q. M., 26 Feb., 1863. Mustered out 12 Oct., 1865.
Du Puy, Horatio A., Capt. A. Q. M., 30 July, 1863. Mustered out 7 May, 1866.
Durbin, Green, Capt. A. Q. M., 30 June, 1862. Mustered out 5 Oct., 1866.
Durham, Benjamin, Asst. Surg., 18 May, 1864. Maj. Surg., 30 Aug., 1864. Mustered out 21 Feb., 1866.
Duryee, Abram, Brig. Gen., 31 Aug., 1861. Resigned 5 Jan., 1863.
Duryee, Wm. B. C., Capt. A. A. G., 11 June, 1862. Resigned 24 Dec., 1863.
Dustan, Chas. W., Capt. Addl. A. de C., 17 April, 1862. Capt. A. A. G., 16 May, 1862. Resigned 18 Feb., 1865.
Dutton, Carlos, Capt. A. Q. M., 9 June, 1862. Resigned 3 June, 1864.
Duval, Isaac H., Brig. Gen., 24 Sept., 1864. Mustered out 15 Jan., 1866.
Duvall, Robert E., 2nd Lieut. Sig. Corps. 3 March, 1863. Mustered out 12 Aug., 1865.
Dwight, Charles C., Capt. A. A. G., 11 June, 1862. Resigned 6 Nov., 1862.
Dwight, George, Maj. P. M., 30 June, 1862. Appointment revoked 6 Dec., 1862.
Dwight, Howard, Capt. A. A. G., 10 Nov., 1862. Killed 4 May, 1863, by guerillas, near Opelousas, La.
Dwight, Theodore T., Capt. A. Q. M., 26 Nov., 1862. Mustered out 8 Nov., 1865.
Dwight, William, Brig. Gen., 29 Nov., 1862. Mustered out 15 Jan., 1866.
D'Wolf, James F., Capt. C. S., 16 Nov., 1861. Resigned 3 Dec., 1864.
Dye, P. Edwin, Maj. P. M., 23 Feb., 1864. Mustered out 1 Dec., 1865.
Dyer, Clarence H., Capt. A. A. G., 25 Sept., 1861. Maj., 2 Aug., 1865. Mustered out 10 Feb., 1866.

Dyer, Douglas H., Capt. A. Q. M., 24 Aug., 1864. Mustered out 8 Jan., 1866.
Dyer, George R., Capt. A. Q. M., 31 Oct., 1861. Resigned 19 May, 1865.
Dyer, George W., Maj. P. M., 19 Feb., 1863. Mustered out 1 Feb., 1869.
Earle, Edward S., Capt. C. S., 9 Sept., 1861. Discharged 1 April, 1863.
Earle, Francis S., Maj. A. A. G., 10 Sept., 1862. Resigned 18 May, 1863.
Earle, James D., Capt. C. S., 10 Sept., 1862. Mustered out 10 Jan., 1866.
Earnest, Cyrus A., Maj. A. de C., 22 June, 1865. Mustered out 10 Feb., 1866.
Earnest, Wm. D., Capt. A. Q. M., 26 Nov., 1862. Dismissed 25 March, 1865.
Earnshaw, John, Capt. A. A. G., 30 June, 1862. Resigned 25 Nov., 1862.
Earnshaw, Wm., Hosp. Chap., 22 April, 1863. Mustered out 1 Sept., 1867.
Eaton, Alonzo, Capt. A. Q. M., 30 June, 1864. Mustered out 30 Oct., 1865.
Eaton, Daniel L., Maj. P. M., 29 Nov., 1862. Mustered out 1 Nov., 1866.
Eaton, Joseph H., Maj. P. M., 1 June, 1861. Maj. P. M., U. S. A., 21 April, 1864.
Eaton, Lucien, Maj. J. A., 2 July, 1864. Mustered out 17 Aug., 1865.
Eaton, Stephen M., Capt. Sig. Corps, 3 March, 1863. Mustered out 20 June, 1866.
Eayre, Thos. W., Capt. A. A. G., 20 Oct., 1862. Killed 12 May, 1864, at Battle of Spottsylvania C. H., Va.
Eckert, Thos. T., Maj. Addl. A. de C., 7 April, 1862. Also appointed Capt. A. Q. M., 17 July, 1862. Resigned 28 Feb., 1867.
Eddy, Augustus, Hosp. Chap., 4 July, 1862. Mustered out 20 Nov., 1865.
Eddy, Ellery W., Maj. P. M., 30 June, 1862. Lost at sea 30 July, 1865.
Eddy, George W., Capt. C. S., 2 March, 1864. Mustered out 6 Dec., 1865.
Edgar, George P., Capt. Addl. A. de C., 10 July, 1862. Resigned 29 April, 1864.
Edmonds, James E., Maj. A. A. G., 30 June, 1865. Mustered out 8 Dec., 1865.
Edwards, Abraham, Capt. A. Q. M., 5 July, 1862. Mustered out 15 July, 1865.
Edwards, Arthur, Capt. A. Q. M., 19 Feb., 1863. Mustered out 13 March, 1866.
Edwards, Henry, Hosp. Chap., 13 Nov., 1862. Discharged 6 March, 1863.
Edwards, James G., Capt. C. S., 30 June, 1862. Mustered out 12 June, 1865.
Edwards, John, Brig. Gen., 26 Sept., 1864. Mustered out 15 Jan., 1866.
Edwards, Ninian W., Capt. C. S., 8 Aug., 1861. Resigned 22 June, 1865.
Edwards, Oliver, Brig. Gen., 19 May, 1865. Mustered out 15 Jan., 1866.
Edwards, Rufus R., Capt. C. S., 2 July, 1864. Mustered out 28 July, 1866.
Edwards, Thos. C., Capt. A. Q. M., 18 Sept., 1861. Died 28 Jan., 1862.
Egan, Costney L., Hosp. Chap., 28 July, 1864. Mustered out 15 July, 1865.
Egan, Thos. W., Brig. Gen., 3 Sept., 1864. Mustered out 15 Jan., 1866.
Egbert, Augustus R., Maj. Surg., 5 Nov., 1861. Mustered out 7 Oct., 1865.
Eggers, Herman, Hosp. Chap., 2 Dec., 1863. Mustered out 15 July, 1865.
Ehrman, Francis H., Capt. C. S., 25 Sept., 1862. Mustered out 15 July, 1865.
Ekin, James A., Capt. A. Q. M., 7 Aug., 1861. Capt. A. Q. M., U. S. A., 13 March, 1863.
Eldrige, Shaler W., Maj. P. M., 11 March, 1863. Resigned 10 March, 1864.
Ellet, Alfred W., Lieut. Col. Addl. A. de C., 28 April, 1862. Brig. Gen., 1 Nov., 1862. Resigned 31 Dec., 1864.
Ellet, Charles, Col. Addl. A. de C., 28 April, 1862. Died 21 June, 1862, of wounds received in naval engagement before Memphis, Tenn.
Elliot, Stephen F., Maj. Surg., 21 April, 1862. Resigned 10 Dec., 1863.
Elliot, Washington L., Brig. Gen., 11 June, 1862. Mustered out 1 March, 1866.
Elliot, Wm., Capt. A. Q. M., 18 May, 1864. Mustered out 10 Aug., 1865.
Elliott, Alban V., Maj. P. M., 1 June, 1861. Mustered out 15 July, 1866.
Elliott, J. Thomas, Capt. C. S., 10 Sept., 1862. Mustered out 22 Nov., 1865.
Elliott, Jesse W., Maj. P. M., 8 March, 1865. Mustered out 29 July, 1865.
Elliott, John W., Hosp. Chap., 8 Nov., 1862. Discharged 15 Sept., 1863.
Elliott, Thos. H., Capt. A. A. G., 29 July, 1862. Killed 20 July, 1864, in action at Peach Tree Creek, Ga.
Elliott, Washington G., Asst. Surg., 21 Dec., 1864. Mustered out 18 Jan., 1866.
Elliott, Wm. St. G., Asst. Surg., 28 Oct., 1864. Mustered out 30 May, 1865.
Ellis, James M., Capt. C. S., 14 Nov., 1861. Resigned 21 July, 1864.
Ellis, John H., Maj. P. M., 30 June, 1864. Mustered out 20 July, 1866.
Ellis, Wm. I., Capt. C. S., 10 Sept., 1862. Resigned 17 March, 1865.
Ellison, John A., Capt. A. Q. M., 27 May, 1863. Mustered out 11 Nov., 1865.
Ellmaker, Nathaniel, Capt. C. S., 19 Sept., 1861. Resigned 20 Feb., 1863.
Ellsworth, Charles C., Maj. P. M., 10 March, 1863. Resigned 8 May, 1865.
Ellsworth, Darius F., Capt. A. Q. M., 30 June, 1864. Mustered out 20 Sept., 1865.
Ellsworth, Pinckney W., Maj. Surg., 3 Aug., 1861. Resigned 1 Nov., 1861.
Ellsworth, Timothy E., Capt. Addl. A. de C., 11 April, 1862. Mustered out 14 Sept., 1865.
Ellsworth, Wm. L., Capt. A. Q. M., 19 Feb., 1863. Mustered out 14 Aug., 1863.
Elston, Isaac C., Jr., Lieut. Col. Addl. A. de C., 9 July, 1862. Resigned 8 June, 1863.
Elwell, John J., Capt. A. Q. M., 3 Aug., 1861. Mustered out 13 March, 1866.
Ely, Alfred B., Capt. A. A. G., 28 April, 1862. Resigned 27 Jan., 1863.
Ely, George, Capt. A. Q. M., 12 May, 1862. Resigned 1 March, 1864.
Ely, George B., Maj. P. M., 19 Feb., 1863. Mustered out 20 July, 1866.
Ely, Isaac M., Hosp. Chap., 26 July, 1864. Mustered out 20 Nov., 1865.
Ely, J. Sykes, Asst. Surg., 20 April, 1864. Mustered out 9 Oct., 1865.
Ely, Wm. S., Asst. Surg., 2 Sept., 1863. Maj. Surg., 20 Jan., 1865. Mustered out 7 Oct., 1865.
Embler, Andrew H., Maj. A. de C., 21 March, 1865. Mustered out 5 Dec., 1865.
Emery, Chas. F., Capt. A. Q. M., 5 Dec., 1863. Mustered out 20 Sept., 1865.
Emery, Frank C., Capt. C. S., 9 March, 1863. Mustered out 3 Aug., 1865.
Emery, Fred'k W., Capt. A. A. G., 13 March, 1863. Maj. 6 Feb., 1865. Mustered out 10 Aug., 1865.
Emery, S. Hopkins, Hosp. Chap., 10 Jan., 1863. Mustered out 24 June, 1865.
Emmerson, Edward M., Capt. C. S., 8 May, 1863. Appointment revoked 4 Feb., 1864.
Emmerson, Warren C., Maj. P. M., 23 Feb., 1864. Mustered out 1 Nov., 1866.
Emmett, Rob't, Capt. A. Q. M., 5 July, 1864. Mustered out 28 July, 1865.
Emmons, Wm. H. H., Capt. A. A. G., 18 May, 1864. Mustered out 1 Aug., 1865.
Emory, George F., Maj. P. M., 5 Sept., 1861. Resigned 23 July, 1864.
Emory, Wm. H., Brig. Gen., 17 March, 1862. Maj. Gen., 25 Sept., 1865. Mustered out 15 Jan., 1866.

England, Thos. Y., Capt. C. S., 19 Feb., 1863. Resigned 2 Dec., 1864.
Engle, Max Paul, Capt. A. Q. M., 31 Oct., 1861. Died — Sept., 1862.
Eno, Frank V. L., Capt. A. A. G., 31 March, 1862. Maj. 8 Feb., 1865. Mustered out 19 Sept., 1865.
Ernst, Franklin, Capt. A. Q. M., 9 June, 1862. Mustered out 19 July, 1865.
Ernst, John F., Capt. A. Q. M., 29 Feb., 1864. Mustered out 20 Sept., 1865.
Erritt, Russell, Maj. P. M., 5 Sept., 1861. Mustered out 11 May, 1866.
Este, George P., Brig. Gen., 26 June, 1865. Resigned 4 Dec., 1865.
Este, Wm. M., Maj. A. de C., 11 March, 1863. Resigned 1 April, 1865.
Estes, Lewellyn G., Capt. A. A. G., 4 Sept., 1863. Maj. 2 Feb., 1865. Mustered out 29 Sept., 1865.
Etting, Frank M., Maj. P. M., 5 Sept., 1861. Maj. P. M., U. S. A., 1 April, 1867.
Eustis, Chas. L., Maj. P. M., 26 Nov., 1862. Resigned 13 Feb., 1862.
Eustis, Henry L., Brig. Gen., 12 Sept., 1863. Resigned 27 June, 1864.
Evans, George, Capt. C. S., 11 June, 1862. Mustered out 15 July, 1865.
Evans, Griffith O., Capt. A. Q. M., 28 Feb., 1865. Mustered out 28 July, 1865.
Evans, Martin, Maj. P. M., 18 March, 1864. Mustered out 1 Dec., 1865.
Everett, Sam'l W., Maj. Surg., 14 Sept., 1861. Killed 6 April, 1862, at Battle of Shiloh, Tenn.
Everett, Thornly S., Capt. A. A. G., 5 Aug., 1861. Resigned 1 April, 1862.
Eversman, Henry, Asst. Surg., 13 Oct., 1863. Maj. Surg., 30 March, 1864. Mustered out 12 July, 1865.
Everts, Louis H., Capt. A. A. G., 1 June, 1863. Mustered out 19 Sept., 1865.
Ewing, Chas., Brig. Gen., 8 March, 1865. Mustered out 1 Dec., 1865.
Ewing, Evarts S., Capt. C. S., 31 Jan., 1865. Mustered out 9 Oct., 1865.
Ewing, Hugh, Brig. Gen., 29 Nov., 1862. Mustered out 15 Jan., 1866.
Ewing, Thos., Jr., Brig. Gen., 13 March, 1863. Resigned 23 Feb., 1865.
Eysenbach, Lewis, Hosp. Chap., 29 Dec., 1864. Mustered out 26 July, 1865.
Fahnestock, Edward G., Maj. P. M., 14 Aug., 1863. Resigned 5 March, 1864.
Fahy, John, Capt. A. Q. M., 7 April, 1864. Mustered out 20 Sept., 1865.
Fairchild, Lucius, Brig. Gen., 19 Oct., 1863. Resigned 2 Nov., 1863.
Farmer, Thos., Maj. P. M., 26 Nov., 1862. Resigned 4 March, 1864.
Farnsworth, Evan J., Brig. Gen., 29 June, 1863. Killed 3 July, 1863, at Battle of Gettysburg, Pa.
Farnsworth, H. J., Capt. A. Q. M., 8 July, 1864. Mustered out 17 July, 1867.
Farnsworth, John F., Brig. Gen., 29 Nov., 1862. Resigned 4 March, 1863.
Farnsworth, John G., Capt. A. Q. M., 14 April, 1862. Mustered out 23 Oct., 1865.
Farnsworth, Simon D., Maj. P. M., 26 Nov., 1862. Resigned 26 April, 1864.
Farnum, Edwin J., Capt. A. Q. M., 21 April, 1864. Mustered out 19 May, 1866.
Farr, Edward P., Capt. A. Q. M., 6 March, 1865. Mustered out 19 May, 1866.
Farrar, Henry W., Capt. A. de C., 7 June, 1864. Mustered out 1 Aug., 1865.
Farrington, Seth C., Maj. J. A., 3 Sept., 1864. Mustered out 31 May, 1866.
Farris, James H., Maj. Surg., 30 Oct., 1861. Resigned 20 June, 1862.
Farrish, James A., Maj. P. M., 26 Nov., 1862. Mustered out 15 Jan., 1866.
Fasses, Julius, Capt. Addl. A. de C., 1 May, 1862. Mustered out 8 Dec., 1865.
Fast, Orlando J., Capt. A. A. G., 3 Feb., 1865. Mustered out 19 Sept., 1865.
Fearey, Thos. H., 2nd Lieut. S'g. Corps, 3 March, 1863. Mustered out 11 Aug., 1865.
Fearing, George R., Capt. Addl. A. de C., 4 April, 1862. Resigned 1 Feb., 1864.
Fegan, Joseph D., Capt. A. A. G., 3 Feb., 1865. Mustered out 19 Sept., 1865.
Felt, Wm. N., Capt. C. S., 19 Feb., 1863. Mustered out 10 Sept., 1866.
Fenno, Jeremiah, Maj. P. M., 26 Nov., 1862. Mustered out 30 April, 1866.
Ferguson, Adam, Capt. C. S., 28 Feb., 1865. Resigned 8 June, 1865.
Ferguson, Sam'l B., Capt. A. A. G., 17 April, 1863. Mustered out 29 Jan., 1866.
Ferree, James I., Hosp. Chap., 14 July, 1862. Mustered out 13 March, 1866.
Ferrero, Edward, Brig. Gen., 10 Sept., 1862. Appointment expired 4 March, 1863. Brig. Gen., 6 May, 1863. Mustered out 24 Aug., 1865.
Ferris, John W., Capt. A. Q. M., 1 March, 1865. Mustered out 28 July, 1865.
Ferry, John H., Capt. A. Q. M., 14 April, 1862. Resigned 27 May, 1865.
Ferry, Orris S., Brig. Gen., 17 March, 1862. Resigned 15 June, 1865.
Ferry, Wm. M., Capt. C. S., 30 June, 1862. Resigned 24 April, 1865.
Fessenden, Francis, Brig. Gen., 10 May, 1864. Maj. Gen., 9 Nov., 1865. Mustered out 1 Sept., 1866.
Fessenden, James D., Col. Addl. A. de C., 16 July, 1862. Brig. Gen., 8 Aug., 1864. Mustered out 16 Jan., 1866.
Fessenden, Wm., Maj. P. M., 1 June, 1861. Dismissed 5 Nov., 1863.
Fetzer, John, Asst. Surg., 5 July, 1864. Resigned 7 Dec., 1864.
Fiala, John T., Col. Addl. A. de C., 31 March, 1862. Resigned 8 June, 1864.
Fick, Henry W., Capt. C. S., 7 July, 1864. Mustered out 9 Oct., 1865.
Field, John, Capt. A. Q. M., 19 Feb., 1863. Mustered out 18 Oct., 1864.
Fifield, Benjamin F., Capt. C. S., 14 April, 1862. Discharged 20 Nov., 1863.
Figyelmesy, Philip, Col. Addl. A. de C., 31 March, 1862. Resigned 20 Dec., 1864.
Filer, Philip, Maj. P. M., 14 Sept., 1864. Mustered out 1 Dec., 1865.
Fillebrown, Henry C., Capt. A. A. G., 13 Nov., 1862. Mustered out 19 Sept., 1865.
Fillmore, John S., Maj. P. M., 26 Aug., 1861. Appointment expired 1 July, 1862. Maj. P. M., 8 Nov., 1862. Died 25 Dec., 1864.
Finkelmeier, John P., Capt. A. A. G., 26 Nov., 1861. Discharged 3 Sept., 1862. Capt. A. A. G., 11 March, 1863. Mustered out 19 Sept., 1865.
Finkler, Wm., Capt. A. Q. M., 11 June, 1862. Resigned 6 May, 1865.
Finley, Henry H., Capt. C. S., 18 May, 1864. Mustered out 8 July, 1865.
Finley, James A., Capt. A. Q. M., 26 Nov., 1862. Died 7 Sept., 1864.
Finney, Chas. G., Capt. A. Q. M., 26 Nov., 1862. Mustered out 23 Oct., 1865.
Fish, Benj. E., Capt. A. Q. M., 8 March, 1865. Mustered out 28 July 1865.
Fish, John D., Capt. A. A. G., 20 April, 1864. Killed 12 May, 1864, in action at Spottsylvania C. H., Va.
Fisher, Adam, Capt. A. Q. M., 19 Feb., 1863. Mustered out 13 March, 1866.
Fisher, Benj. F., Maj. Sig. Corps, 3 March, 1863. Col., 3 Dec., 1864. Appointment expired 28 July, 1866.
Fisher, George A., 1st Lieut. Sig. Corps, 3 March, 1863. Mustered out 6 Oct., 1865.
Fisher, Henry M., Asst. Surg., 19 Feb., 1863. Died 12 March, 1863.
Fisher, James C., Maj. Surg., 4 April, 1862. Mustered out 9 Jan., 1865.
Fisher, Theodore B., Capt. A. Q. M., 28 Feb., 1865. Mustered out 28 July, 1865.

Fisher, Wm., Capt. Addl. A. de C., 11 April, 1862. Resigned 15 June, 1864.
Fisk, Alex'r P., Capt. A. A. G., 7 March, 1862. Mustered out 22 Nov., 1865.
Fisk, Archie C., Capt. A. A. G., 23 June, 1863. Mustered out 20 July, 1865.
Fisk, Clinton B., Brig. Gen., 24 Nov., 1862. Mustered out 1 Sept., 1866.
Fisk, James L., Capt. A. Q. M., 29 May, 1862. Resigned 12 June, 1865.
Fiske, George A., Jr., Capt. A. A. G., 18 May, 1864. Maj. P. M., 30 June, 1864. Resigned 26 Aug., 1864.
Fitch, Butler, Maj. P. M., 12 Dec., 1864. Mustered out 31 July, 1865.
Fitch, Chauncey W., Hosp. Chap., 26 Oct., 1863. Mustered out 20 Nov., 1865.
Fitch, Enoch P., Capt. A. Q. M., 3 Aug., 1861. Died 31 May, 1864.
Fitch, Henry S., Capt. A. Q. M., 3 Aug., 1861. Resigned 11 Jan., 1865.
Fitch, Horace B., Capt. A. de C., 27 Dec., 1864. Mustered out 22 Nov., 1865.
Fitch, James R., Capt. C. S. 26 Nov., 1862. Mustered out 18 Jan., 1866.
Fitch, Julian R., 2nd Lieut. Sig. Corps, 3 March, 1863. Mustered out 25 Nov., 1865.
Fitch, Thomas D., Capt. A. Q. M., 24 March, 1862. Mustered out 23 Oct., 1865.
Fithian, Joel A., Maj. P. M., 28 Feb., 1864. Mustered out 12 Oct., 1865.
Fitts, James G., Capt. C. S., 24 March, 1862. Mustered out 9 Oct., 1865.
Fitzgerald, Edward, Capt. A. Q. M., 30 June, 1864. Mustered out 7 Oct., 1865.
Fitzgibbon, James, Hosp. Chap., 18 March, 1864. Mustered out 17 Aug., 1865.
Fitzpatrick, James W., Maj. Surg., 7 Jan., 1863. Resigned 11 Oct., 1863.
Flagg, Algernon S., Capt. A. Q. M. 18 May, 1864. Mustered out 10 June, 1866.
Flagg, George A., Capt. A. Q. M 10 Sept., 1861. Mustered out 19 May, 1866.
Flagg, Henry F., Maj. P. M., 26 Nov., 1862. Died 23 May, 1864.
Flagg, Newton, Capt. A. Q. M., 3 Feb., 1862. Mustered out 7 Oct., 1865.
Flagg, Othello J., Capt. C. S., 26 Nov., 1862. Mustered out 1 Jan., 1867.
Flanigan, Patrick, Capt. A. Q. M., 2 July, 1863. Mustered out 5 June, 1866.
Fleming, John E., Capt. A. Q. M., 30 June, 1864. Mustered out 13 March, 1866.
Flemming, Wm. M., Maj. P. M., 26 Nov., 1862. Mustered out 1 March 1866.
Fletcher, Arthur W., Maj. P. M., 1 June, 1861. Dismissed 27 Aug., 1863.
Fletcher, Frank H., Maj. P. M., 2 July, 1864. Mustered out 31 March, 1866.
Fletcher, Robt., Asst. Surg., 13 Oct., 1863. Maj. Surg., 20 Nov., 1863. Mustered out 31 Aug., 1867.
Flook, Henry R., 2nd Lieut. Sig. Corps, 3 March, 1863. Mustered out, 24 Aug., 1865.
Flye, Edwin, Maj. P. M., 27 Feb., 1863. Resigned 13 June, 1864.
Flynt, George E., Capt. A. A. G., 31 Aug., 1861. Maj., 11 June, 1862. Died 18 Dec., 1863.
Fobes Edward A., Capt. C. S., 9 June, 1862. Died 9 Feb., 1865.
Foley, John, Capt. C. S., 1 Nov., 1862. Resigned 25 June, 1863.
Foley, John P., Capt. A. A. G., 31 July, 1862. Dismissed 2 Feb., 1863.
Folsom, Chas. W., Capt. A. Q. M., 13 March, 1865. Mustered out 31 Aug., 1868.
Folsom, Ezekiel, Hosp. Chap., 4 June, 1862. Mustered out 21 Aug., 1865.
Folsom, George P., Maj. P. M., 1 June, 1861. Dismissed 1 Aug., 1864.
Foote, Augustus R. S., Capt. A. A. G. 22 March, 1865. Mustered out 12 Jan., 1866.
Foote, Henry, Maj. P. M., 1 June, 1861. Resigned 27 July, 1863.
Foote, Horatio, Hosp. Chap., 4 June, 1862. Mustered out 12 July, 1865.
Forbes, Wm. H., Capt. C. S., 9 Nov., 1862. Mustered out 31 July, 1865.
Forbes, Wm. S., Maj. Surg., 7 Nov., 1862. Resigned 20 Nov., 1863.
Forbes, Wm. T., Capt. A. A. G., 17 Nov., 1864. Maj., 2 Feb., 1865. Mustered out 19 Sept., 1865.
Force, Manning F., Brig. Gen., 11 Aug., 1863. Mustered out 15 Jan., 1866.
Ford, Chas., Capt. C. S., 19 Feb., 1863. Resigned 9 Oct., 1863.
Ford, Chas. W., Capt. A. Q. M., 21 Jan., 1865. Mustered out 20 Sept., 1865.
Ford, Edward L., Capt. A. de C., 24 Aug., 1864. Resigned 13 Dec., 1864.
Ford, Frank C., Capt. C. S., 7 Nov., 1862. Mustered out 27 Jan., 1866.
Ford, George E., Capt. A. de C., 2 Feb., 1865. Mustered out 12 Jan., 1866.
Ford, George W., Capt. A. Q. M., 14 April, 1862. Resigned 3 June, 1864.
Ford, Hobart, Capt. A. de C., 21 April, 1865. Mustered out 10 Feb., 1866.
Ford, Joseph T., Capt. A. Q. M., 11 June, 1862. Resigned 19 Jan., 1863.
Forrest, D. P., Maj. P. M., 23 Feb., 1864. Resigned 2 May, 1864.
Forsha, Stiles E., Capt. C. S., 20 Nov 1862. Appointment expired 4 March, 1863.
Forsyth, James W., Maj. A. A. G., 7 April, 1864. Brig. Gen., 19 May, 1865. Mustered out 15 Jan., 1866.
Forsyth, Lewis Cass, Capt. A. Q. M., 11 June, 1862. Mustered out 3 Nov., 1866.
Fort, Greenbury L., Capt. A. Q. M., 24 March, 1862. Mustered out 20 March, 1866.
Foster, Benj'n B., Maj. A. A. G., 7 Oct., 1862. Resigned 24 Sept., 1864.
Foster, Chas W., Capt. A. A. G., 19 Sept., 1861. Maj., 24 Aug., 1863. Capt. A. Q. M., U. S. A., 4 Nov., 1865.
Foster, John G., Brig. Gen., 23 Oct., 1861. Maj. Gen., 18 July, 1862. Mustered out 1 Sept., 1866.
Foster, Robt. S., Brig. Gen., 12 June, 1863. Resigned 25 Sept., 1865.
Foster, Thos., Jr., Capt. C. S., 28 Oct., 1861. Discharged 15 March, 1865.
Fouke, Chas., Capt. C. S., 10 March, 1863. Mustered out 19 Dec., 1865.
Fowler, David E., Capt. C. S. 19 Feb., 1863. Mustered out 30 June, 1865.
Fowler, Wm., Capt. A. A. G., 22 Feb., 1865. Mustered out 31 Oct., 1866.
Fox, Francis W., Capt. A. A. G., 9 June, 1862. Resigned 31 July, 1865.
Fox, Philip L., Capt. A. Q. M., 26 Nov., 1862. Resigned 27 Aug., 1864.
Foye, John W., Maj. Surg., 26 March, 1863. Mustered out 7 Oct., 1865.
Frankel, Jacob, Hosp. Chap., 10 Sept., 1862. Appointment expired 4 March, 1863. Reappointed 22 April, 1863. Mustered out 1 July, 1865.
Franklin, Edward C., Maj. Surg., 30 Sept., 1861. Resigned 5 Aug., 1863.
Franklin, George M., Capt. A. A. G., 10 July, 1863. Resigned 29 Oct., 1864.
Franklin, Wm. B., Brig. Gen., 17 May, 1861. Maj. Gen., 4 July, 1862. Resigned 10 Nov., 1865.
Frazer, Corwin B., Asst. Surg., 5 July, 1864. Mustered out 9 Oct., 1865.
Frazer, Robt. F., Maj. P. M., 23 April, 1863. Died 5 Sept., 1863.
Fredberg, Alfred, Maj. A. A. G., 31 Dec., 1864. Mustered out 12 Jan., 1866.
Fredericks, James P., Capt. C. S. 7 Sept., 1861. Discharged 28 May, 1862.
Freeman, Adam M., Maj. P. M., 1 June, 1861. Cashiered 26 May, 1865.
Freeman, Alex., Maj. P. M., 19 Feb., 1863. Mustered out 6 June, 1864.

Freeman, Edwin, Asst. Surg., 7 Nov., 1862. Resigned 14 April, 1864.
Freeman, Henry C., Capt. Addl. A. de C., 6 June, 1862. Resigned 18 Dec., 1863.
Freeman, Joseph A., Asst. Surg., 7 Dec., 1863. Died 29 Dec., 1864.
Freeman, Lyman N., Hosp. Chap., 28 Nov., 1862. Resigned 26 Feb., 1863.
Freeman, Sylvanus D., Maj. Surg., 4 Oct., 1862. Mustered out 7 Oct., 1865.
Freer, Joseph W., Maj. Surg., 3 Aug., 1861. Resigned 2 Oct., 1861.
Freese, Jacob R., Capt. A. A. G., 24 Aug., 1861. Resigned 31 Dec., 1863.
French, George F., Asst. Surg., 4 June, 1863. Maj. Surg., 13 June, 1863. Resigned 5 June, 1865.
French, Mansfield, Hosp. Chap., 10 July, 1862. Mustered out 4 Aug., 1865.
French, W. H., Capt. C. S., 19 Feb., 1863. Resigned 28 Sept., 1864.
French, Wm. H., Brig. Gen., 28 Sept., 1861. Maj. Gen., 29 Nov., 1862. Mustered out 6 May, 1864.
Frink, Chas. S., Asst. Surg., 4 Oct., 1862. Maj. Surg., 30 March, 1864. Mustered out 31 July, 1865.
Frizell, John H., Asst. Surg., 9 Jan., 1865. Mustered out 5 Aug., 1865.
Frothingham, John B., Lieut. Col. Addl. A. de C., 16 July, 1862. Resigned 2 March, 1863.
Fry, James B., Col. A. A. de C., 14 Nov., 1861. Col. Pro. Mar. Gen., 17 March, 1863. Brig. Gen. Pro. Mar. Gen., 21 April, 1864. Commission expired by law 27 Aug., 1866.
Fry, John, Capt. C. S., 31 Oct., 1861. Mustered out 2 Feb., 1866.
Fry, Speed S., Brig. Gen., 21 March, 1862. Mustered out 24 Aug., 1865.
Fry, Thos. W., Maj. Surg., 17 Jan., 1862. Mustered out 30 Nov., 1865.
Fry, Thos. W. G., Capt. C. S., 7 Oct., 1862. Appointment expired 4 March, 1863. Reappointed 21 March, 1863. Mustered out 5 Aug., 1865.
Fry, Thos. W., Jr., Capt. A. Q. M., 11 March, 1863. Mustered out 31 May, 1866.
Fuller, Chas. E., Capt. A. Q. M., 3 Aug., 1861. Resigned 18 Nov., 1864.
Fuller, Francis, Capt. A. Q. M., 21 April, 1863. Resigned 26 July, 1864.
Fuller, James E., Capt. A. Q. M., 8 Dec., 1864. Resigned 6 July, 1865.
Fuller, James G., Capt. C. S., 27 Nov., 1861. Discharged 6 Sept., 1862.
Fuller, John W., Brig. Gen., 5 Jan., 1864. Resigned 15 Aug., 1865.
Fuller, Stephen E., Asst. Surg., 4 June, 1863. Maj. Surg., 13 June, 1863. Mustered out 5 Nov., 1865.
Fuller, Wm. G., Maj. P. M., 26 Nov., 1862. Resigned 1 April, 1865.
Fullerton, Joseph S., Maj. A. A. G., 11 March, 1863. Mustered out 10 Sept., 1866.
Fullerton, Wm. G., Maj. P. M., 26 Nov., 1862. Resigned 1 April, 1865.
Furey, John V., Capt. A. Q. M., 7 April, 1864. Capt. A. Q. M., U. S. A., 18 Jan., 1867.
Furness, Wm. E., Maj. J. A., 22 Feb., 1865. Mustered out 7 Oct., 1865.
Gage, Alfred, Capt. C. S., 11 March, 1863. Mustered out 13 March, 1866.
Gage, Rodney, Hosp. Chap., 6 Aug., 1862. Appointment expired 4 March, 1863. Reappointed 22 April, 1863. Mustered out 2 June, 1865.
Gaines, Theophilus, Maj. J. A., 1 Nov., 1862. Mustered out 31 May, 1866.
Galbraith, Wm. J., 1st Lieut. Sig. Corps, 3 March, 1863. Resigned 26 April, 1864.
Gale, Josiah, Maj. P. M., 26 Nov., 1862. Rejected by Senate 11 March, 1863.
Gale, Rollin C., Capt. A. A. G., 25 Aug., 1862. Mustered out 19 Sept., 1865.
Gallagher, Chas. H., Capt. A. Q. M., 19 Aug., 1862. Mustered out 31 May, 1866.
Galt, James, Capt. A. Q. M., 28 Nov., 1862. Mustered out 6 June, 1865.
Gamage, Sam'l, Capt. C. S., 7 Sept., 1861. Resigned 6 Nov., 1862.
Gamble, Wm., Brig. Gen., 25 Sept., 1865. Mustered out 13 March, 1866.
Gantt, Thos. T., Col. Addl. A. de C., 26 Aug., 1861. Resigned 5 July, 1862.
Garber, Michael C., Capt. A. Q. M., 31 Oct., 1861. Mustered out 31 July, 1866.
Garcelon, Chas. A., Capt. A. Q. M., 30 June, 1864. Mustered out 11 May, 1866.
Gardner, Chas. T., Capt. A. A. G., 6 March, 1862. Maj., 22 June, 1865. Mustered out 19 Sept., 1865
Gardner, George W., Capt. C. S., 19 Feb., 1863. Resigned 18 Jan., 1864.
Gardner, Nathan R., Capt. C. S., 28 Feb., 1865. Mustered out 3 Aug., 1865.
Gardner, Rob't S., Capt. A. Q. M., 18 June, 1862. Mustered out 13 March, 1866.
Gardner, Thos. H., Maj. P. M., 28 May, 1864. Mustered out 1 Sept., 1868.
Garfield, Chas. S., Capt. C. S., 28 July, 1863. Mustered out 27 Jan., 1866.
Garfield, George, Capt. C. S., 30 Jan., 1865. Mustered out 11 May, 1866.
Garfield, James A., Brig. Gen., 11 Jan., 1862. Maj. Gen., 19 Sept., 1863. Resigned 5 Dec., 1863.
Garoutte, A. M., Capt. A. Q. M., 30 June, 1864. Discharged 14 Aug., 1866.
Garrard, Kenner, Brig. Gen., 23 July, 1863. Mustered out 24 Aug., 1865.
Garrard, Theophilus T., Brig. Gen., 29 Nov., 1862. Mustered out 4 April, 1864.
Garrett, Chas. F., Capt. A. Q. M., 25 April, 1862. Resigned 3 June, 1864.
Garrettson, Chas., Capt. A. Q. M., 11 June, 1862. Mustered out 5 March, 1864.
Garrison, Amos F., Capt. C. S., 7 Aug., 1861. Mustered out 10 Jan., 1866.
Garvens, Herman, Capt. A. Q. M., 3 July, 1863. Mustered out 27 Nov., 1865.
Garwood, John T., Capt. C. S., 28 May, 1864. Mustered out 19 Dec., 1865.
Gaster, Wm., Capt. A. Q. M., 14 April, 1862. Dismissed 31 Aug., 1864.
Gates, Horace P., Capt. A. A. G., 25 May, 1863. Resigned 19 Dec., 1863.
Gatzmer, Henry S., Maj. P. M., 1 June, 1861. Dismissed 16 Sept., 1862.
Gaubert, Chas. H., Capt. A. Q. M., 24 March, 1862. Mustered out 8 July, 1865.
Gawthrop, Henry, Capt. A. A. G., 14 Feb., 1865. Mustered out 29 Jan., 1866.
Gay, Norman, Maj. Surg., 24 Dec., 1861. Mustered out 27 July, 1865.
Gaylord, George S., Capt. C. S., 9 Feb., 1863. Mustered out 9 Aug., 1865.
Gaylord, Noah M., Hosp. Chap., 10 Jan., 1863. Mustered out 1 July, 1865.
Gear, Alonzo S., Capt. A. Q. M., 7 April, 1864. Mustered out 27 April, 1866.
Geary, John W., Brig. Gen., 25 April, 1862. Mustered out 15 Jan., 1866.
George, Paul R., Capt. A. Q. M., 12 Sept., 1861. Rejected by Senate 20 March, 1862.
George, Wm. G., Capt. A. A. G., 30 Nov., 1861. Resigned 9 Aug., 1862.
Gerard, John C., Capt. A. Q. M., 15 Feb., 1865. Mustered out 10 June, 1866.
Gere, John A., Hosp. Chap., 20 Aug., 1864. Mustered out 26 July, 1865.
Gerker, Fred'k, Capt. C. S., 30 Aug., 1862. Mustered out 9 Oct., 1865.
Gerrish, Hiram F., Capt. A. Q. M., 1 May, 1865. Mustered out 8 Feb., 1866.
Getty, George W., Col. Addl. A. de C., 28 Sept., 1861. Brig. Gen., 25 Sept., 1862. Mustered out 9 Oct., 1866.

Gibbon, John, Brig. Gen., 2 May, 1862. Maj. Gen., 11 June, 1864. Mustered out 15 Jan., 1866.
Gibbons, Thomas P., Maj. Surg., 7 Nov., 1862. Discharged 26 Aug., 1863.
Gibbs, Alfred, Brig. Gen., 19 Oct., 1864. Mustered out 1 Feb., 1866.
Gibbs, Ira B., Capt. C. S., 31 Oct., 1861. Resigned 7 Aug., 1862.
Gibson, Hiram D., Capt. C. S., 5 Oct., 1864. Mustered out 13 Dec., 1865.
Gibson, Moses S., Maj. P. M., 30 June, 1862. Discharged 17 Dec., 1862.
Gibson, Samuel F., Capt. A. Q. M., 23 Nov., 1864. Resigned 8 May, 1865.
Gibson, Wm. R., Maj. P. M., 1 June, 1861. Maj. P. M., U. S. A., 17 Jan., 1867.
Giebner, Jason T., Capt. C. S., 20 April, 1864. Resigned 18 Jan., 1865.
Giesy, Emanuel, Capt. A. Q. M., 5 Dec., 1863. Resigned 6 July, 1865.
Gifford, Edmund, Maj. P. M., 19 Feb., 1863. Mustered out 15 Nov., 1865.
Gilbert, Aaron P., Capt. A. A. G., 28 April, 1864. Resigned 15 Nov., 1864.
Gilbert, Calvin, Capt. C. S., 2 March, 1864. Mustered out 26 Oct., 1865.
Gilbert, Charles C., Brig. Gen., 9 Sept., 1862. Appointment expired 4 March, 1863.
Gilbert, George, Capt. C. S., 28 Feb., 1865. Resigned 10 June, 1865.
Gilbert, James I., Brig. Gen., 9 Feb., 1865. Mustered out 24 Aug., 1865.
Gilbert, Rufus H., Maj. Surg., 3 Aug., 1861. Mustered out 20 July, 1865.
Gilbraith, Erasmus C., Capt. A. Q. M., 23 Jan., 1865. Mustered out 28 July, 1865.
Gilbreth, Fred'k W., Capt. A. de C., 18 May, 1864. Mustered out 8 June, 1866.
Gilder, William H., Capt. A. A. G., 7 Oct., 1864. Mustered out 19 Sept., 1865.
Gile, David H., Capt. A. de C., 18 April, 1863. Resigned 1 Nov., 1864.
Gill, Henry Z., Asst. Surg., 5 Dec., 1863. Maj. Surg., 30 June, 1864. Mustered out 5 Aug., 1865.
Gill, Richard T., Capt. A. Q. M., 13 March, 1863. Resigned 1 Aug., 1863.
Gillem, Alvan C., Brig. Gen., 17 Aug., 1863. Maj. Gen., 3 Nov., 1865. Mustered out 1 Sept., 1866.
Gillespie, Archibald H., Maj. Addl. A. de C., 20 March, 1862. Dismissed 4 June, 1863.
Gillespie, Wm. C. B., Capt. C. S., 6 Sept., 1864. Mustered out 14 July, 1865.
Gillette, James, Capt. C. S., 10 Sept., 1862. Mustered out 27 Dec., 1866.
Gillfillian, Charles D., Maj. P. M., 26 Nov., 1862. Appointment revoked 25 Aug., 1863.
Gillmore, Quincey A., Brig. Gen., 28 April, 1862. Maj. Gen., 10 July, 1863. Resigned 5 Dec., 1865.
Gillum, Henry H., Capt. A. Q. M., 22 Aug., 1864. Rejected by Senate, 10 March, 1865. Reappointed 11 March, 1865. Mustered out 11 Oct., 1865.
Gilmore, James R., Capt. A. Q. M., 3 Nov., 1864. Mustered out 3 Nov., 1866.
Gilmour, Harry L., Capt. C. S., 2 March, 1865. Mustered out 31 July, 1865.
Gilpin, Joseph B., Capt. C. S., 14 April, 1862. Mustered out 13 March, 1866.
Glatfelter, N. M., Asst. Surg., 20 April, 1864. Mustered out 16 Jan., 1867.
Glavis, George O., Hosp. Chap., 13 March, 1863. Dismissed 13 Dec., 1866.
Gleason, James, Capt. A. Q. M., 7 April, 1863. Mustered out 7 May, 1867.
Glenn, George E., Maj. P. M., 24 Nov., 1862. Maj. P. M., U. S. A., 17 Jan., 1867.
Glennon, Patrick, Asst. Surg., 18 May, 1864. Mustered out 1 Nov., 1867.
Glover, Samuel C., Capt. C. S., 7 June, 1864. Mustered out 18 Jan., 1866.
Gobrecht, Wm. H., Maj. Surg., 19 Feb., 1863. Mustered out 7 Oct., 1865.
Goddard, Calvin, Maj. A. de C., 14 Nov., 1862. Maj. A. A. G., 4 March, 1863. Resigned 27 Nov., 1863.
Goddard, Henry S., Maj. P. M., 28 May, 1864. Mustered out 1 Nov., 1865.
Goddard, Paul B., Maj. Surg., 4 Oct., 1862. Discharged 8 April, 1865.
Goddard, Robert H. I., Capt. A. de C., 11 March, 1863. Resigned 3 July, 1865.
Godfrey, John S., Capt. A. Q. M., 10 Sept., 1861. Mustered out 6 June, 1865.
Goff, Henry C., Capt. A. Q. M., 27 Feb., 1863. Died 6 Sept., 1863.
Goff, Willis C., Capt. A. Q. M., 19 Feb., 1863. Resigned 10 Jan., 1865.
Goldie, Wm., Capt. A. Q. M., 30 June, 1862. Mustered out 20 Nov., 1865.
Goldsborough, Jacob L. Capt. A. Q. M., 18 May, 1864. Resigned 19 May, 1865.
Goldsmith, Middleton, Maj. Surg., 30 Oct., 1861. Mustered out 18 Jan., 1866.
Goldthwaite, Joseph A., Capt. C. S., 22 April, 1863. Resigned 15 Aug., 1865.
Gonsalves, Manuel J., Hosp. Chap., 6 Aug., 1862. Discharged 15 Sept., 1863. Reappointed 17 Oct., 1863. Mustered out 4 Aug., 1865.
Goodfellow, Thomas M., Hosp. Chap., 23 March, 1864. Mustered out 19 June, 1865.
Gooding, Edward L., Capt. C. S., 22 Aug., 1863. Resigned 15 June, 1865.
Goodloe, Wm. C., Capt. A. A. G., 1 June, 1863. Resigned 31 Jan., 1864.
Goodman, Chas., Capt. A. Q. M., 12 May, 1862. Mustered out 19 Oct., 1865.
Goodman, Henry E., Asst. Surg., 26 Feb., 1864. Maj. Surg., 18 May, 1864. Mustered out 3 Nov., 1865.
Goodrich, Earl S., Capt. Addl. A. de C., 1 April, 1862. Resigned 21 Nov., 1862.
Goodrich, Edwin R., Capt. C. S., 31 Oct., 1861. Resigned 7 Jan., 1865.
Goodrich, Hiram P., Capt. A. Q. M., 5 Aug., 1861. Mustered out 12 Oct., 1865.
Goodrich, Horace B., Capt. C. S., 7 June, 1864. Died 14 June, 1865.
Goodridge, Moses H., Capt. A. Q. M., 26 Nov., 1862. Mustered out 22 Sept., 1866.
Goodwin, Hollister E., Capt. A. Q. M., 19 Feb., 1863. Mustered out 30 March, 1866.
Goodwin, Robt. M., Capt. A. A. G., 26 Sept., 1864. Resigned 11 May, 1865.
Gordon, Dan'l D. T., Capt. A. Q. M., 19 Feb., 1863. Mustered out 7 Oct., 1865.
Gordon, George H., Brig. Gen., 9 June, 1862. Mustered out 24 Aug., 1865.
Gordon, Wm. A., Capt. A. A. G., 14 July, 1862. Maj., 3 Sept., 1864. Mustered out 20 Jan., 1866.
Gordon, Wm. A., Asst. Surg., 25 Nov., 1864. Mustered out 22 Nov., 1865.
Gorman, James W., Capt. A. A. G., 26 Aug., 1862. Died 19 Feb., 1863.
Gorman, Willis A., Brig. Gen., 7 Sept., 1861. Mustered out 4 May, 1864.
Gorton, Cyrus L., Capt. A. Q. M., 18 May, 1864. Mustered out 7 Oct., 1865.
Goslin, Alex., Capt. A. Q. M., 1 March, 1865. Dismissed 8 April, 1867.
Goss, George G., Hosp. Chap., 4 June, 1862. Mustered out 26 July, 1865.
Gotthelf, Bernhard H., Hosp. Chap., 16 Feb., 1863. Mustered out 21 Aug., 1865
Gould, Chas. A., Capt. A. A. G., 14 Sept., 1863. Mustered out 12 March, 1866.
Gould, David, Maj. P. M., 26 Nov., 1862. Appointment expired 4 March, 1863.
Gould, James R., Capt. Addl. A. de C., 14 July, 1862. Resigned 6 Aug., 1864.
Gould, John, Capt. C. S., 26 Nov., 1862. Mustered out 9 Oct., 1865.
Gould, John P., Maj. P. M., 26 Nov., 1862. Appointment revoked 25 Aug., 1863.

**Gould, Wm. P.**, Maj. P. M., 1 June, 1861. Mustered out 1 July, 1867.
**Goulding, Chas. N.**, Capt. A. Q. M., 4 Sept., 1861. Resigned 16 Sept., 1864.
**Gourand, George E.**, Capt. A. de C., 3 June, 1863. Resigned 14 Oct., 1865.
**Graham, Chas. K.**, Brig. Gen., 29 Nov., 1862. Mustered out 24 Aug., 1865.
**Graham, James**, Capt. A. A. G., 20 Oct., 1864. Mustered out 19 Sept., 1865.
**Graham, Lawrence P.**, Brig. Gen., 31 Aug., 1861. Mustered out 24 Aug., 1865.
**Graham, Richardson**, Hosp. Chap., 19 Aug., 1862. Mustered out 26 July, 1865.
**Graham, Robt.**, Capt. C. S., 11 June, 1862. Mustered out 15 July, 1865.
**Grandin, Wm.**, Capt. C. S., 30 Sept., 1861. Rejected by Senate 3 Feb., 1862.
**Granger, Brownell**, Capt. C. S., 19 Feb., 1862. Mustered out 8 Dec., 1865.
**Granger, Gordon**, Brig. Gen., 26 March, 1862. Maj. Gen., 17 Sept., 1862. Mustered out 15 Jan, 1866.
**Granger, Robert S.**, Brig. Gen., 20 Oct., 1862. Mustered out 24 Aug., 1865.
**Grant, Gabriel**, Maj. Surg., 9 Oct., 1861. Resigned 13 Jan., 1865.
**Grant, Lewis A.**, Brig. Gen., 27 April, 1864. Mustered out 24 Aug., 1865.
**Grant, Ulysses S.**, Brig. Gen., 17 May, 1861. Maj. Gen., 16 Feb., 1862. Maj. Gen. U. S. A., 4 July, 1863.
**Gratiot, Edward H.**, Maj. P. M., 19 Feb., 1863. Mustered out 1 March, 1866.
**Gratz, Edward**, Maj. P. M., 7 May, 1863. Resigned 10 July, 1863.
**Graves, Chas. H.**, Capt. A. A. G., 29 Feb., 1864. Maj., 15 Jan., 1865. Mustered out 1 Sept., 1866.
**Graves, Edward P.**, Capt. A. Q. M., 7 April, 1864. Mustered out 20 April, 1866.
**Graves, Emmons E.**, Maj. A. de C., 27 Dec., 1864. Mustered out 1 Feb., 1866.
**Graves, George E.**, Capt. C. S., 1 Nov., 1862. Resigned 26 May, 1863.
**Graves, Orison**, Capt. C. S., 19 Feb., 1863. Dismissed 2 June, 1863.
**Gray, John C.**, Maj. J. A., 25 July, 1864. Resigned 14 July, 1865.
**Gray, John D.**, Capt. C. S., 25 Jan., 1865. Mustered out 6 Dec., 1865.
**Gray, John F. S.**, Capt. A. A. G., 13 May, 1863. Resigned 5 May, 1865.
**Gray, Thomas**, Capt. C. S., 31 Oct., 1861. Mustered out 31 May, 1866.
**Green, John**, Capt. A. A. G., 11 March, 1863. Mustered out 15 Aug., 1866.
**Green, John M.**, Hosp. Chap., 2 Aug., 1862. Appointment expired 4 March, 1863. Reappointed 22 April, 1863. Mustered out 15 July, 1865.
**Green, John P.**, Capt. A. A. G., 18 Sept., 1862. Resigned 10 Jan., 1865.
**Green, Joseph A.**, Capt. A. Q. M., 19 Feb., 1863. Mustered out 30 Oct., 1865.
**Green, Marvin J.**, Capt. C. S., 31 Oct., 1861. Discharged 6 Sept., 1862.
**Green, Nicholas St. J.**, Maj. P. M., 31 Aug., 1863. Resigned 19 May, 1865.
**Green, Thomas H.**, Capt. Addl. A. de C., 14 May, 1862. Killed 9 Aug., 1862, at Battle of Cedar Mountain, Va.
**Green, Wm. D.**, Maj. A. A. G., 21 April, 1863. Mustered out 19 Sept., 1865.
**Green, Wm. M.**, Capt. C. S., 17 Aug., 1861. Mustered out 27 Nov., 1865.
**Greenarvault, Theodore D.**, Maj. P. M., 26 Nov., 1862. Mustered out 15 Nov., 1865.
**Greene, Chas. T.**, Capt. A. A. G., 4 Sept., 1863. Mustered out 19 Sept., 1865.
**Greene, Elias M.**, Capt. A. Q. M., 3 Oct., 1862. Mustered out 28 July, 1865.
**Greene, Francis**, Asst. Surg., 19 Feb., 1863. Maj. Surg., 10 Nov., 1863. Mustered out 7 Oct., 1865.
**Greene, George S.**, Brig. Gen., 28 April, 1862. Mustered out 30 April, 1866.
**Greene, Jacob L.**, Capt. A. A. G., 21 Sept., 1863. Maj., 11 July, 1865. Mustered out 20 March, 1866.
**Greene, Sam'l C.**, Capt. C. S., 5 Aug., 1862. Mustered out 25 Aug., 1865.
**Greenwood, Theodore E.**, Capt. Addl. A. de C., 16 May, 1862. Died 27 Sept., 1862.
**Gregg, David McM.**, Brig. Gen., 29 Nov., 1862. Resigned 3 Feb., 1865.
**Gregg, John C.**, Hosp. Chap., 18 March, 1864. Mustered out 21 Aug., 1865.
**Gregory, Almon**, Hosp. Chap., 22 April, 1863. Dismissed 27 Oct., 1864.
**Gregory, Asa**, Capt. C. S., 20 Nov., 1862. Mustered out 26 April, 1866.
**Gregory, Benjamin**, Maj. P. M., 18 Sept., 1863. Resigned 9 July, 1864.
**Gregory, J. Shaw**, Capt. A. A. G., 28 Sept., 1861. Resigned 26 Aug., 1862.
**Gregson, John**, Capt. A. Q. M., 29 Feb., 1864. Dismissed 29 Dec., 1864.
**Gresham, Walter Q.**, Brig. Gen., 11 Aug., 1863. Mustered out 30 April, 1866.
**Gribben, David**, Maj. P. M., 20 Oct., 1864. Mustered out 1 June, 1869.
**Grier, James S.**, Capt. Addl. A. de C., 21 June, 1862. Mustered out 21 Feb., 1866.
**Grierson, Benjamin H.**, Brig. Gen., 3 June, 1863. Maj. Gen., 27 May, 1865. Mustered out 30 April, 1866.
**Grierson, John C.**, Capt. A. Q. M., 11 Feb., 1865. Mustered out 9 July, 1868.
**Griest, Elwood**, Capt. C. S., 27 Aug., 1864. Mustered out 11 May, 1866.
**Griffin, Chas.**, Brig. Gen., 9 June, 1862. Maj. Gen., 2 April, 1865. Mustered out 15 Jan., 1866.
**Griffin, Elihu**, Maj. P. M., 13 Nov., 1862. Resigned 6 Feb., 1865.
**Griffin, Simon G.**, Brig. Gen., 12 May, 1864. Mustered out 24 Aug., 1865.
**Griffing, Thos. S.**, Capt. A. A. G., 6 March, 1862. Resigned 6 Nov., 1862.
**Griffith, Albert F.**, Hosp. Chap., 7 Feb., 1865. Mustered out 21 Aug., 1865.
**Griffiths, James J.**, Capt. A. de C., 25 April, 1863. Died 10 July, 1863, of wounds received at Battle of Gettysburg, Pa.
**Grimes, Edward B.**, Capt. A. Q. M., 20 Sept., 1862. Capt. A. Q. M., U. S. A., 26 May, 1865.
**Grimes, Washington M.**, Hosp. Chap., 29 Feb., 1864. Mustered out 24 June, 1865.
**Grinstead, Wm.**, Asst. Surg., 27 Feb., 1863. Maj. Surg., 2 Sept., 1863. Mustered out 18 Aug., 1865.
**Grisson, Samuel**, Maj. P. M., 20 April, 1864. Mustered out 1 Nov., 1865.
**Griswold, Elisha**, Asst. Surg., 30 June, 1864. Maj. Surg., 6 Jan., 1865. Mustered out 15 March, 1867.
**Griswold, Theodore**, Capt. A. Q. M., 26 Nov., 1862. Resigned 20 June, 1863.
**Grose, Wm.**, Brig. Gen., 30 July, 1864. Resigned 31 Dec., 1865.
**Gross, Ferdinand H.**, Maj. Surg., 17 Oct., 1861. Mustered out 31 Oct., 1865.
**Gross, Samuel W.**, Maj. Surg., 3 Aug., 1861. Mustered out 24 July, 1865.
**Gross, Wm. L.**, Capt. A. Q. M., 27 Oct., 1863. Mustered out 1 July, 1866.
**Grout, Henry C.**, Maj. P. M., 22 July, 1863. Mustered out 1 Nov., 1865.
**Grove, J. H.**, Maj. Surg., 4 Oct., 1861. Mustered out 19 Oct., 1865.
**Grover, Cuvier**, Brig. Gen., 14 April, 1862. Mustered out 24 Aug., 1865.
**Grover, James A.**, Capt. A. A. G., 11 March, 1863. Resigned 7 June, 1865.
**Grover, Marshall**, Maj. P. M., 17 June, 1863. Mustered out 15 April, 1866.
**Grube, Franklin**, Asst. Surg., 11 March, 1863. Mustered out 3 Nov., 1865.
**Gruwe, Joseph**, Capt. Addl. A. de C., 1 May, 1862. Appointment revoked 9 June, 1864.
**Gubby, James**, Hosp. Chap., 1 April, 1863. Mustered out 11 July, 1865.

Guindon, Eugene W., Maj. A. de C., 7 May, 1863. Mustered out 11 Nov., 1865.
Gunckel, Michael S., Maj. P. M., 23 Feb., 1864. Mustered out 1 Dec., 1865.
Hackelman, Pleasant A., Brig. Gen., 28 April, 1862. Killed 3 Oct., 1862, at Battle of Corinth, Miss.
Hade, Emanuel, Capt. A. Q. M., 29 Feb., 1864. Mustered out 13 Dec., 1865.
Haggerty, Peter, Maj. A. de C., 9 Nov., 1863. Resigned 20 Nov., 1864.
Haggerty, Rob't A., Maj. P. M., 19 Feb., 1863. Mustered out 1 Nov., 1865.
Haight, Edward, Capt. Addl. A. de C., 11 July, 1862. Vacated commission 16 June, 1864.
Haim, Augustus, Maj. Addl. A. de C., 11 April, 1862. Dismissed 19 March, 1863.
Haines, Thos. J., Col. Addl. A. de C., 1 May, 1862. Mustered out 31 May, 1866.
Hakes, Dwight W., Capt. C. S., 9 March, 1865. Mustered out 17 June, 1865.
Haldeman, Cyrus S., Capt. A. A. G., 1 May, 1862. Mustered out 12 Jan., 1866.
Hale, Chas. H., Capt. Addl. A. de C., 25 June, 1862. Resigned 28 April, 1865.
Hale, Henry A., Capt. A. A. G., 30 June, 1864. Mustered out 11 Nov., 1865.
Hale, Hiram F., Maj. P. M., 18 March, 1864. Mustered out 15 Nov., 1865.
Hale, John M., Capt. A. Q. M., 18 Nov., 1861. Resigned 2 Sept., 1862.
Hale, Morton F., Capt. C. S., 26 Nov., 1862. Mustered out 31 May, 1866.
Hall, Chandler, Capt. A. Q. M., 3 Aug., 1861. Resigned 12 Jan., 1865.
Hall, Charles, Capt. C. S., 27 Aug., 1863. Died 14 Nov., 1863.
Hall, Daniel, Capt. Addl. A. de C., 7 June, 1862. Resigned 21 Nov., 1863.
Hall, Daniel K., Capt. C. S., 21 April, 1864. Mustered out 3 Aug., 1865.
Hall, Daniel K., Capt. C. S., 18 May, 1864. Resigned 10 July, 1865.
Hall, George W., Capt. A. Q. M., 19 Dec., 1864. Mustered out 28 July, 1865.
Hall, James S., Capt. Sig. Corps, 3 March, 1863. Retired 9 March, 1865. Mustered out 30 Nov., 1865.
Hall, James S., Capt. A. Q. M., 17 July, 1862. Resigned 22 May, 1863.
Hall, John, Capt. C. S., 3 Aug., 1861. Resigned 15 July, 1864.
Hall, Lowell, Capt. C. S., 3 March, 1865. Mustered out 31 July, 1865.
Hall, Monroe, Maj. P. M., 13 Feb., 1865. Mustered out 31 July, 1865.
Hall, Peter P. G., Maj. P. M., 6 Nov., 1863. Mustered out 15 Nav., 1865.
Hall, Theron E., Capt. A. Q. M., 22 July, 1862. Resigned 5 Dec., 1864.
Hall, Wm. M., Maj. J. A., 1 March, 1865. Resigned 28 May, 1867.
Halleck, Andrew J., Maj. P. M., 29 Nov., 1862. Appointment revoked 16 May, 1863.
Hallett, Joseph L., 2nd Lieut. and 1st Lieut. Sig. Corps., 3 March, 1863. Appointment as 1st Lieut. expired 4 July, 1864. Resigned 8 Aug., 1864.
Halpine, Chas. G., Maj. A. A. G., 5 Sept., 1861. Resigned 31 July, 1864.
Halsey, Thos. H., Maj. P. M., 1 June, 1861. Maj. P. M., U. S. A., 17 Jan., 1867.
Halstead, George B., Capt. A. A. G., 6 March, 1862. Mustered out 12 March, 1866.
Halsted, Edward L., 2nd Lieut. Sig. Corps, 3 March, 1863. Resigned 3 Jan., 1865.
Halsted, Eminel P., Capt. A. A. G., 14 April, 1862. Resigned 28 June, 1865.
Halsted, Richard F., Capt. A. de C., 25 April, 1863. Mustered out 10 July, 1866.
Hamblin, Joseph E., Brig. Gen., 19 May, 1865. Mustered out 15 Jan., 1866.
Hamer, Rob't W., Capt. C. S., 9 Aug., 1862. Resigned 4 June, 1864.
Hamill, Sam'l R., Capt. A. Q. M., 27 Feb., 1863. Mustered out 1 March, 1868.
Hamilton, Alexander, Jr., Maj. Addl. A. de C., 28 Aug., 1861. Declined 11 Dec., 1861.
Hamilton, Andrew J., Brig. Gen., 14 Nov., 1862. Appointment expired 4 March, 1863. Brig. Gen., 18 Sept., 1863. Resigned 19 June, 1865.
Hamilton, Chas. S., Brig. Gen., 17 May, 1861. Maj. Gen., 19 Sept., 1862. Resigned 13 April, 1863.
Hamilton, Frank H., Maj. Surg., 3 Aug., 1861. Lieut. Col. Med. Insp., 9 Feb., 1863. Resigned 29 Aug., 1863.
Hamilton, Sam'l M., Maj. Surg., 4 April, 1862. Resigned 19 Sept., 1863.
Hamilton, Schuyler, Col. Addl. A. de C., 7 Aug., 1861. Discharged 1 Nov., 1861. Brig. Gen., 12 Nov., 1861. Maj. Gen., 17 Sept., 1862. Resigned 27 Feb., 1863.
Hamlin, Augustus C., Maj. Surg., 4 April, 1862. Lieut. Col. Med. Ins., 9 Feb., 1863. Mustered out 31 Oct., 1865.
Hamlin, Chas., Maj. A. A. G., 27 April, 1863. Mustered out 14 Sept., 1865.
Hamlin, Cyrus, Capt. Addl. A. de C., 3 April, 1862. Vacated commission 2 March, 1863. Brig. Gen., 13 Dec., 1864. Mustered out 15 Jan., 1866.
Hammer, Adam, Maj. Surg., 14 June, 1862. Resigned 31 Jan., 1865.
Hammond, Barnabas B., Maj. P. M., 24 July, 1863. Mustered out 1 Dec., 1865.
Hammond, John H., Capt. A. A. G., 20 Nov., 1861. Maj., 9 June, 1862. Mustered out 23 Aug., 1865.
Hammond, J. Pinckney, Hosp. Chap., 20 June, 1862. Mustered out 26 July, 1865.
Hampton, George S., Capt. A. A. G., 27 Feb., 1863. Resigned 25 April, 1865.
Hance, Sylvanus B., Capt. A. A. G., 23 Nov., 1861. Resigned 7 July, 1862.
Hancock, Fred'k, Capt. A. Q. M., 18 May, 1864. Mustered out 11 May, 1866.
Hancock, John, Capt. A. A. G., 3 Feb., 1862. Maj., 31 March, 1863. Mustered out 1 Sept., 1866.
Hancock, Winfield S., Brig. Gen., 23 Sept., 1861. Maj. Gen., 29 Nov., 1862. Maj. Gen. U. S. A., 26 July, 1866.
Hand, D. W., Maj. Surg., 30 Sept., 1861. Mustered out 13 Dec., 1865.
Hank, George W., Maj. P. M., 19 Sept., 1863. Resigned 23 Feb., 1865.
Hanley, Lawrence, Capt. A. A. G., 3 Oct., 1862. Resigned 25 April, 1864.
Hanna, Benj. J. F., Capt. A. Q. M., 26 Nov., 1862. Mustered out 8 Jan., 1866.
Hanna, Valentine C., Maj. P. M., 15 Aug., 1861. Mustered out 20 July, 1866.
Hannan, Dennis B., Maj. Surg., 7 Jan., 1863. Mustered out 27 July, 1865.
Hanson, Hunn, Capt. A. de C., 21 Feb., 1865. Mustered out 17 Aug., 1865.
Hapgood, Lyman S., Maj. P. M., 1 June, 1861. Mustered out 1 Dec., 1865.
Harbert, Sam'l C., Maj. P. M., 19 Feb., 1863. Mustered out 1 Nov., 1865.
Hardie, James A., Lieut. Col. Addl. A. de C., 28 Sept., 1861. Brig. Gen., 29 Nov., 1862. Appointment as Brig. Gen. revoked 22 Jan., 1863. Vacated appointment as A. de C., 24 March, 1864.
Hardin, Martin D., Brig. Gen., 2 July, 1864. Mustered out 15 Jan., 1866.
Harding, Abner C., Brig. Gen., 13 March, 1863. Resigned 3 June, 1863.
Harding, Edward, Capt. C. S., 21 Aug., 1861. Discharged 12 Nov., 1861. Capt. C. S., 28 April, 1863. Resigned 13 May, 1865.
Harker, Chas. G., Brig. Gen., 20 Sept., 1863. Killed 27 Jan., 1864, at the Battle of Kenesaw, Ga.
Harkey, Simeon W., Hosp. Chap., 17 Jan., 1865. Mustered out 4 Aug., 1865.
Harlan, Edwin, Capt. C. S., 25 Jan., 1865. Mustered out 9 Oct., 1865.

Harlan, Emory B., Capt. A. A. G., 12 Nov., 1864. Mustered out 1 Sept., 1866.
Harlan, John H., Capt. A. Q. M., 6 Sept., 1864. Appointment revoked 25 March, 1865.
Harland, Edward, Brig. Gen., 29 Nov., 1862. Resigned 22 June, 1865.
Harlow, Lewis D., Asst. Surg., 7 Nov., 1862. Maj. Surg., 8 May, 1863. Mustered out 10 Aug., 1865.
Harned, Sanford, Capt. A. Q. M., 30 June, 1864. Mustered out 20 March, 1866.
Harper, Albert M., Capt. A. A. G., 17 Aug., 1864. Mustered out 27 June, 1865.
Harper, James, Maj. P. M., 26 Nov., 1862. Resigned 16 Sept., 1864.
Harral, Wm. W., Capt. A. A. G., 21 July, 1863. Appointment revoked 15 June, 1864.
Harrington, Edward J., Capt. A. A. G., 7 March, 1865. Mustered out 4 Aug., 1866.
Harrington, George D., Capt. C. S., 2 May, 1862. Mustered out 21 Aug., 1866.
Harris, James, Capt. C. S., 15 Feb., 1865. Mustered out 3 Aug., 1865.
Harris, Joseph, Maj. P. M., 23 Feb., 1864. Mustered out 1 Dec., 1865.
Harris, Rob't, Capt. C. S., 26 Nov., 1862. Resigned 20 June, 1863.
Harris, Thos. H., Capt. A. A. G., 17 July, 1862. Mustered out 1 Aug., 1865.
Harris, Thos. M., Brig. Gen., 29 March, 1865. Mustered out 30 April, 1866.
Harris, Wm. F., Capt. A. Q. M., 20 Sept., 1861. Resigned 13 Aug., 1864.
Harrison, George W., Capt. A. Q. M., 14 Nov., 1861. Mustered out 18 Jan., 1866.
Harrison, John T., Asst. Surg., 3 Dec., 1864. Mustered out 9 Oct., 1865.
Harrow, Wm., Brig. Gen., 29 Nov., 1862. Resigned 20 April, 1865.
Hart, Daniel S., Capt. C. S., 1 Nov., 1862. Mustered out 8 Feb., 1866.
Hart, Isaac W., Capt. A. Q. M., 10 March, 1863. Mustered out 13 March, 1866.
Hart, Michael G., Maj. P. M., 23 Feb., 1864. Resigned 20 May, 1865.
Hart, Orson H., Capt. A. A. G., 16 May, 1862. Mustered out 31 Oct., 1866.
Hart, Ralph S., Maj. P. M., 26 Nov., 1862. Resigned 4 June, 1863.
Hart, Rob't S., Capt. A. Q. M., 31 March, 1863. Mustered out 19 May, 1866.
Hart, Sam'l, Asst. Surg., 11 March, 1863. Maj. Surg., 19 Jan., 1864. Mustered out 10 Aug., 1865.
Hart, Wm. B., Capt. A. A. G., 1 Feb., 1865. Mustered out 19 Sept., 1865.
Hartley, John, Capt. C. S., 27 Jan., 1865. Mustered out 12 July, 1865.
Hartranft, John F., Brig. Gen., 12 May, 1864. Mustered out 15 Jan., 1866.
Hartshorn, Dana W., Maj. Surg., 4 Sept., 1861. Resigned 8 Jan., 1864.
Hartsuff, George L., Brig. Gen., 15 April, 1862. Maj. Gen., 29 Nov., 1862. Mustered out 24 Aug., 1865.
Hartz, Wilson T., Capt. A. A. G., 23 Oct., 1862. Mustered out 1 Sept., 1867.
Harvey, Fred'k, Capt. A. A. G., 3 Sept., 1861. Rejected by Senate 11 March, 1862.
Harvey, Isaac J., Capt. Sig. Corps, 3 March, 1863. Retired 15 Feb., 1864. Mustered out 30 Nov., 1865.
Harvey, Jonathan S., Capt. A. Q. M., 7 April, 1864. Mustered out 6 June, 1865.
Harvey, Philip, Asst. Surg., 23 April, 1863. Maj. Surg., 29 June, 1863. Mustered out 25 Aug., 1865.
Harvey, Wm. A., Asst. Surg., 30 June, 1864. Mustered out 22 Aug., 1865.
Hascall, Laurens H., Capt. C. S., 21 Jan., 1865. Mustered out 12 June, 1865.
Hascall, Milo S., Brig. Gen., 25 April, 1862. Resigned 27 Oct., 1864.
Haskell, Hiram W., Capt. C. S., 2 March, 1864. Appointment cancelled 13 Oct., 1864.
Haskell, John G., Capt. A. Q. M., 11 June, 1862. Mustered out 22 Nov., 1865.
Haskell, Joseph T., Capt. C. S., 19 Feb., 1863. Mustered out 8 Dec., 1866.
Haskell, Leonidas, Maj. Addl. A. de C., 16 June, 1862. Resigned 4 June, 1864.
Haskin, Joseph A., Lieut. Col. Addl. A. de C., 26 June, 1862. Brig. Gen., 5 Aug., 1864. Mustered out 30 April, 1866.
Haskin, Wm. E., Maj. P. M., 1 June, 1861. Resigned 28 Sept., 1864.
Hatch, Edward, Brig. Gen., 27 April, 1864. Mustered out 15 Jan., 1866.
Hatch, John P., Brig. Gen., 28 Sept., 1861. Mustered out 15 Jan., 1866.
Hatch, Reuben B., Capt. A. Q. M., 3 Aug., 1861. Mustered out 28 July, 1865.
Hatchitt, James G., Maj. Surg., 4 April, 1862. Mustered out 8 Dec., 1865.
Hatfield, Townsend L., 1st Lieut. Sig. Corps, 3 March, 1863. Resigned 17 June, 1865.
Hathaway, John L., Capt. C. S., 4 Sept., 1861. Mustered out 26 Oct., 1865.
Hathorn, Robt., Maj. P. M., 26 Nov., 1862. Appointment expired 4 March, 1863.
Hatton, Ezra C., Capt. A. A. G., 8 June, 1865. Mustered out 19 Oct., 1865.
Hatton, W. H. D., Hosp. Chap., 19 Jan., 1863. Mustered out 23 Dec., 1864.
Haupt, Herman, Col. Addl. A. de C., 27 April, 1862. Brig. Gen., 5 Sept., 1862. Declined.
Havelock, Chas. F., Col. Addl. A. de C., 23 Nov., 1861. Resigned 31 July, 1863.
Haven, S. R., Maj. Surg., 3 Aug., 1861. Resigned 9 March, 1863.
Havens, Franklin, Jr., Capt. Addl. A. de C., 15 April, 1862. Resigned 11 May, 1865.
Haviland, Thos. P., Maj. P. M., 23 Sept., 1864. Mustered out 30 April, 1866.
Hawes, Granville P., Capt. C. S., 26 Nov., 1862. Resigned 23 Nov., 1864.
Hawes, Marcus M., Capt. A. Q. M., 17 July, 1862. Resigned 25 Feb., 1865.
Hawkes, Henry F., Capt. C. S., 21 Nov., 1862. Mustered out 8 Dec., 1865.
Hawkins, John P., Brig. Gen., 13 April, 1863. Mustered out 1 Feb., 1866.
Hawley, Joseph R., Brig. Gen., 13 Sept., 1864. Mustered out 15 Jan., 1866.
Hawley, Seth C., Capt. A. Q. M., 7 July, 1863. Resigned 1 June, 1864.
Hawley, Wm. A., Capt. A. Q. M., 31 Oct., 1861. Died 24 Dec., 1863.
Hawley, Z. K., Hosp. Chap., 2 Feb., 1863. Mustered out 23 Sept., 1865.
Hawthorne, Leroy R., Capt. C. S., 7 April, 1864. Mustered out 27 Jan., 1866.
Hay, Campbell, Jr., Capt. A. Q. M., 21 April, 1864. Mustered out 22 Nov., 1866.
Hay, John, Maj. A. A. G., 12 Jan., 1864. Mustered out 8 April, 1867.
Hay, John S., Capt. A. Q. M., 28 March, 1865. Mustered out 6 July, 1865.
Hayes, Hiram, Capt. A. Q. M., 26 Nov., 1862. Mustered out 20 Sept., 1865.
Hayes, Isaac I., Maj. Surg., 4 April, 1862. Resigned 3 July, 1865.
Hayes, Job J., Capt. C. S., 4 Sept., 1863. Mustered out 15 July, 1865.
Hayes, Joseph, Brig. Gen., 12 May, 1864. Mustered out 24 Aug., 1865.
Hayes, Richard E., Capt. C. S., 20 April, 1864. Resigned 21 July, 1865.
Hayes, Rutherford B., Brig. Gen., 19 Oct., 1864. Resigned 8 June, 1865.
Hayes, William, Maj. Surg., 9 Nov., 1861. Mustered out 27 July, 1865.
Haymond, Lee, Capt. C. S., 30 June, 1864. Mustered out 10 July, 1865.
Hayner, Henry Z., Maj. Addl. A. de C., 1 Nov., 1861. Mustered out 6 Sept., 1865.
Haynes, Charles F., Asst. Surg., 19 Feb.,

1863. Maj. Surg., 31 March, 1865. Mustered out 19 July, 1865.
Haynes, Silas B. A., Maj. P. M., 30 June, 1862. Mustered out 15 April, 1866.
Haynes, Timothy, Maj. Surg., 7 Oct., 1861. Resigned 6 Nov., 1862.
Haynie, Isham N., Brig. Gen., 29 Nov., 1862. Appointment expired 4 March, 1863.
Hays, Alexander, Brig. Gen., 29 Sept., 1862. Killed 5 May, 1864, at Battle of Wilderness, Va.
Hays, Frank L., Maj. P. M., 7 April, 1864. Resigned 14 Jan., 1865.
Hays, John, Capt. A. Q. M., 26 Nov., 1862. Mustered out 13 Oct., 1865.
Hays, Joseph C., Capt. A. Q. M., 18 May, 1864. Resigned 6 March, 1865.
Hays, William, Lieut. Col. Addl. A. de C., 28 Sept., 1861. Brig. Gen., 29 Nov., 1862. Mustered out 15 Jan., 1866.
Hayden, Augustine F., Capt. A. A. G., 20 March, 1864. Mustered out 1 Dec., 1866.
Hayward, Joseph W., Asst. Surg., 5 July, 1864. Mustered out 22 Nov., 1865.
Haywood, Rufus, Maj. P. M., 23 Feb., 1864. Mustered out 1 Dec., 1865.
Hazelton, John F., Capt. A. Q. M., 27 Feb., 1863. Mustered out 11 Nov., 1865.
Hazelton, Moses K., Maj. P. M., 1 June, 1861. Died 3 Aug., 1863.
Hazen, William B., Brig. Gen., 29 Nov., 1862. Maj. Gen., 13 Dec., 1864. Mustered out 15 Jan., 1866.
Headington, Emmet, Capt. C. S., 6 March, 1865. Mustered out 31 July, 1865.
Healy, Jesse, Capt. A. Q. M., 26 Nov., 1862. Mustered out 28 July, 1865.
Heany, Daniel, Capt. A. Q. M., 11 June, 1862. Mustered out 28 July, 1865.
Heap, David P., Maj. P. M., 26 Nov., 1862. Mustered out 15 Nov., 1865.
Heard, J. Theodore, Maj. Surg., 1 May, 1862. Mustered out 23 Oct., 1865.
Heath, Erastus, Capt. C. S., 30 Sept., 1862. Died 5 July, 1863.
Heaton, Grove L., Capt. A. Q. M., 29 Feb., 1864. Mustered out 27 Jan., 1866.
Heaton, Jacob, Capt. C. S., 17 Aug., 1861. Resigned 26 May, 1864.
Hebard, Daniel, Capt. A. A. G., 3 Feb., 1862. Died 7 Aug., 1862.
Heckman, Charles A., Brig. Gen., 29 Nov., 1862. Resigned 25 May, 1865.
Heintz, Carl, Capt. Addl. A. de C., 10 June, 1862. Mustered out 20 Dec., 1864.
Heintzelman, Samuel P., Brig. Gen., 17 May, 1861. Maj. Gen., 5 May, 1862. Mustered out 24 Aug., 1865.
Heiskell, Otho W., Capt. C. S., 19 Feb., 1862. Mustered out 20 March, 1866.
Heisley, Charles W., Hosp. Chap., 1 Aug., 1863. Resigned 25 June, 1864.
Heistand, Peter, Capt. A. Q. M., 19 Feb., 1862. Mustered out 31 May, 1866.
Heister, Frank M., Maj. Surg., 24 Dec., 1861. Died 9 April, 1864.
Hemenway, Edward, Capt. A. A. G., 19 Sept., 1864. Mustered out 4 Jan., 1866.
Hemphill, James, Capt. A. Q. M., 31 Oct., 1861. Resigned 3 March, 1862.
Hempstead, Charles H., Capt. C. S., 14 July, 1862. Mustered out 21 June, 1865.
Hempstead, Charles S., Maj. P. M., 5 Aug., 1861. Resigned 17 Sept., 1863.
Henderson, James D., Capt. A. Q. M., 19 Jan., 1865. Mustered out 28 July, 1865.
Henderson, Samuel D., Capt. C. S., 19 Feb., 1863. Mustered out 22 Aug., 1865.
Hendricks, Abram W., Maj. P. M., 5 Aug., 1861. Mustered out 1 Dec., 1865.
Henries, Henry C., Hosp. Chap., 31 May, 1862. Died 29 March, 1865.
Henry, Charles A., Capt. A. Q. M., 27 Feb., 1863. Mustered out 19 Oct., 1865.
Henry, Edwin, Capt. C. S., 16 Nov., 1863. Mustered out 15 Aug., 1865.
Henry, Miles S., Maj. P. M., 26 Nov., 1862. Resigned 19 May, 1865.
Henry, Samuel B., Capt. A. Q. M., 3 Aug., 1861. Resigned 1 Oct., 1861. Maj. P. M., 30 June, 1862. Resigned 16 Sept., 1863.
Henry, Thomas C., Asst. Surg., 30 June, 1864. Maj. Surg., 23 Feb., 1865. Mustered out 25 Aug., 1865.
Henshaw, John C., Capt. A. A. G., 7 Aug., 1862. Maj. J. A., 29 Feb., 1864. Discharged 30 Sept., 1864.
Hentig, Fred'k G., Capt. C. S., 7 Nov., 1862. Mustered out 22 Aug., 1865.
Herbert, Charles H., Capt. C. S., 29 Nov., 1862. Resigned 24 Feb., 1865.
Herbert, Freeland D., Maj. P. M., 7 April, 1864. Mustered out 1 Nov., 1865.
Herbert, Jacob, Maj. P. M., 26 Nov., 1862. Mustered out 31 July, 1865.
Herbert, Jasper K., Capt. A. A. G., 28 Nov., 1862. Resigned 11 Feb., 1865.
Herbert, John E., Maj. Surg., 9 Feb., 1863. Mustered out 5 Aug., 1865.
Herr, John, Capt. A. Q. M., 18 May, 1864. Mustered out 28 June, 1865.
Herrick, John S., Maj. P. M., 25 July, 1863. Mustered out 15 Nov., 1865.
Herrick, S. L., Maj. Surg., 4 Sept., 1861. Resigned 17 Aug., 1862.
Herrick, Wm. W., Maj. P. M., 26 Nov., 1862. Mustered out 15 Nov., 1865.
Herron, Francis J., Brig. Gen., 16 July, 1862. Maj. Gen., 29 Nov., 1862. Resigned 7 June, 1865.
Hervey, Oscar P., Capt. A. A. G., 12 June, 1863. Resigned 16 Sept., 1864.
Herzog, Charles, 2nd and 1st Lieut. Sig. Corps, 3 March, 1863. Appointment as 1st Lieut. expired 4 July, 1864. Mustered out 15 Aug., 1865.
Hewey, Andrew C., Maj. P. M., 19 Feb., 1863. Mustered out 10 Aug., 1865.
Hewitt, Benj. L., Maj. P. M., 18 March, 1864. Mustered out 1 Nov., 1865.
Hewitt, Henry S., Maj. Surg., 3 Aug., 1861. Mustered out 7 Oct., 1865.
Hewitt, Ira L., Maj. P. M., 5 Sept., 1861. Died 20 Oct., 1862.
Heys, John, Asst. Surg., 25 Nov., 1864. Appointment revoked 16 Dec., 1864.
Hibbard, George B., Capt. A. Q. M., 11 Nov., 1862. Mustered out 8 Jan., 1866.
Hibberts, Joseph, Jr., Capt. A. A. G., 12 May, 1862. Mustered out 9 June, 1865.
Hickox, Volney, Capt. Addl. A. de C., 29 Jan., 1862. Discharged 21 March, 1862. Reappointed 14 April, 1862. Discharged 1 Jan., 1864.
Hickox, Willard S., Maj. P. M., 23 Feb., 1864. Resigned 6 May, 1864.
Hicks, George A., Capt. A. A. G., 16 Nov., 1861. Mustered out 22 Nov., 1865.
Hicks, John A., Hosp. Chap., 3 Feb., 1865. Mustered out 4 Aug., 1865.
Hillhouse, Thos., Maj. A. A. G., 6 March, 1862. Resigned 1 Jan., 1863.
Hiester, Chas. E., Capt. C. S., 7 Nov., 1862. Mustered out 10 Aug., 1865.
Higly, Mortimer A., Capt. C. S., 26 Nov., 1862. Appointment expired 4 March, 1863.
Hildreth, Joseph S., Maj. Surg., 9 Feb., 1863. Mustered out 10 Dec., 1865.
Hill, Henry, Hosp. Chap., 12 April, 1863. Mustered out 2 Dec., 1865.
Hill, Moses A., Capt. C. S., 23 July, 1862. Mustered out 26 June, 1865.
Hill, Varnum H., Capt. A. Q. M., 29 Feb., 1864. Mustered out 13 Dec., 1865.
Hill, Wm. H., Capt. A. A. G., 14 Oct., 1862. Resigned 18 March, 1864.
Hill, Wm. H., 1st Lieut. Capt. Sig. Corps, 3 March, 1863. Appointment as Capt. expired 4 July, 1864. Resigned 24 Jan., 1865.

Hillhouse, John, Capt. A. A. G., 11 Sept., 1861. Resigned 6 Nov., 1861.
Hills, Miron C., Capt. C. S., 3 Oct., 1864. Resigned 11 April, 1865.
Hillyer, Wm. S., Col. Addl. A. de C., 3 May, 1862. Resigned 15 May, 1863.
Hinckley, Ferdinand. Maj. P. M., 19 Feb., 1863. Resigned 25 Aug., 1864.
Hinks, Edward W., Brig. Gen., 29 Nov., 1862. Resigned 30 June, 1865.
Hinsdill, Chas. B., Capt. C. S., 16 Aug., 1861. Mustered out 7 July, 1865.
Hipple, Sam'l, Capt. A. Q. M., 29 Nov., 1862. Resigned 8 July, 1865.
Hitchcock, Ethan A., Maj. Gen., 10 Feb., 1862. Mustered out 1 Oct., 1867.
Hitchcock, Henry, Maj. A. A. G., 4 Oct., 1864. Mustered out 23 June, 1865.
Hixon, Foster A., Maj. P. M., 28 May, 1864. Mustered out 1 July, 1867.
Hobson, Edward H., Brig. Gen., 29 Nov., 1862. Mustered out 24 Aug., 1865.
Hodgdon, Henry C., Capt. C. S., 17 Sept., 1862. Resigned 25 April, 1865.
Hodge, John L., Maj. P. M., 1 June, 1861. Appointed Maj. P. M., U. S. A., 17 Jan., 1867.
Hodge, Justin, Capt. A. Q. M., 5 Aug., 1861. Mustered out 13 Oct., 1866.
Hodgen, John S., Maj. Surg., 24 Dec., 1861. Resigned 23 Feb., 1864.
Hodges, Horace J., Capt. A. Q. M., 26 Nov., 1862. Drowned 19 April, 1864.
Hoelcke, Wm., Capt. Addl. A. de C., 19 Aug., 1861. Mustered out 12 March, 1866.
Hoeppner, Arnold, Capt. Addl. A. de C., 19 Aug., 1861. Resigned 1 Feb., 1864.
Hoff, Alex. H., Maj. Surg., 3 Aug., 1861. Mustered out 1 March, 1866.
Hoff, John J., Capt. C. S., 26 Nov., 1862. Mustered out 1 Nov., 1866.
Hoffman, Ernest T., Maj. Addl. A. de C., 31 May, 1862. Mustered out 5 July, 1866.
Hoffman, Henry B., Maj. P. M., 23 Feb., 1864. Resigned 27 April, 1865.
Hoffman, Joel E., Capt. A. A. G., 21 July, 1863. Resigned 19 May, 1864.
Hoffman, Southard, Capt. A. A. G., 14 Nov., 1861. Maj., 22 Aug., 1862. Resigned 11 July, 1865.
Hoffman, Wickham, Capt. A. A. G., 6 March, 1862. Maj., 26 Aug., 1863. Mustered out 8 June, 1866.
Hogan, Edward K., Asst. Surg., 13 Oct., 1864. Mustered out 27 Nov., 1865.
Hogan, Michael K., Asst. Surg., 2 Sept., 1863. Maj. Surg., 9 Sept., 1863. Mustered out 1 Nov., 1867.
Hoge, Holmes, Capt. A. Q. M., 13 March, 1863. Mustered out 7 Oct., 1865.
Hogeboom, George W., Asst. Surg., 11 Sept., 1862. Maj. Surg., 9 July, 1865. Mustered out 7 Oct., 1865.
Hogendobler, Israel C., Asst. Surg., 7 Sept., 1864. Mustered out 8 Dec., 1865.
Holabird, Lucius H., Capt. A. Q. M., 19 Feb., 1863. Resigned 15 March, 1865.
Holabird, Samuel B., Maj. Addl. A. de C., 2 July, 1862. Col. Addl. A. de C., 11 July, 1862. Mustered out 31 May, 1866.
Holbrook, Andrew J., 2nd Lieut. Sig. Corps, 3 March, 1863. Resigned 19 Aug., 1864.
Holbrook, James C., Maj. P. M., 26 Nov., 1862. Mustered out 15 Nov., 1865.
Holden, Wm., Capt. A. Q. M., 11 June, 1862. Mustered out 20 April, 1866.
Holland, John E., 2nd and 1st Lieuts. Sig. Corps, 3 March, 1863. Appointment 1st Lieut. expired 4 July, 1864, but declined 2nd Lieut.
Holliday, Samuel V., Maj. P. M., 23 Feb., 1864. Mustered out 1 Dec., 1865.
Hollingshead, Mark, Maj. P. M., 23 Feb., 1864. Mustered out 30 April, 1866.
Hollopeter, John L., 1st Lieut. Sig. Corps, 3 March, 1863. Mustered out 1 May, 1866.
Holloway, George A., Capt. A. A. G., 11 March, 1863. Resigned 27 Dec., 1864.
Holloway, Henry C., Capt. C. S., 18 Nov., 1862. Resigned 28 Nov., 1864.
Holloway, Wm., Maj. P. M., 19 Feb., 1863. Mustered out 15 Nov., 1865.
Hollowbush, Jacob R., Capt. A. Q. M., 10 Sept., 1861. Resigned 26 April, 1864.
Holman, Oliver, Maj. P. M., 5 Sept., 1861. Mustered out 1 Dec., 1865.
Holman, Silas A., Asst. Surg., 2 Sept., 1863. Maj. Surg., 9 Sept., 1863. Mustered out 10 Jan., 1866.
Holman, Wm., Hosp. Chap., 31 May, 1862. Mustered out 20 Nov., 1865.
Holmes, Calvin, Maj. P. M., 26 Nov., 1862. Mustered out 1 July, 1869. The last Officer of Vols. who was mustered out of service.
Holmes, Daniel, Maj. Surg., 28 April, 1862. Resigned 10 Sept., 1862.
Holmes, Robt., Capt. C. S., 14 April, 1862. Resigned 9 June, 1865.
Holmes, Robert, Capt. C. S., 30 June, 1864. Mustered out 30 Oct., 1865.
Holmes, Wm. W., Maj. Surg., 4 April, 1862. Discharged 22 Oct., 1863.
Holstein, Chas. L., Capt. A. A. G., 22 Aug., 1862. Resigned 6 Nov., 1862.
Holston, John G. F., Maj. Surg., 3 Aug., 1861. Resigned 6 May, 1864.
Holt, Asa, Jr., Maj. P. M., 30 June, 1862. Resigned 8 Dec., 1865.
Holt, Chas. W., Capt. A. Q. M., 24 Jan., 1865. Mustered out 13 March, 1866.
Holy, Wenzel, Capt. C. S., 29 Aug., 1862. Mustered out 31 Aug., 1866.
Hood, Chas. H., Asst. Surg., 7 Nov., 1863. Maj. Surg., 25 Nov., 1864. Mustered out 10 Aug., 1865.
Hood, Thos. B., Asst. Surg., 5 Dec., 1863. Maj. Surg., 30 June, 1864. Mustered out 13 Oct., 1866.
Hooker, George H., Maj. A. A. G., 21 Nov., 1864. Mustered out 12 Jan., 1866.
Hooker, George W., Capt. A. A. G., 1 Aug., 1864. Mustered out 4 Jan., 1866.
Hooker, Joseph, Brig. Gen., 17 May, 1861. Maj. Gen., 5 May, 1862. Mustered out 1 Sept., 1866.
Hooper, Edw. H. C., Maj. P. M., 14 July, 1862. Mustered out 16 April, 1866.
Hooper, Edward W., Capt. Addl. A. de C., 17 June, 1862. Resigned 19 May, 1865.
Hooper, William B., Capt. C. S., 13 March, 1863. Mustered out 13 July, 1866.
Hoopes, John J., Capt. A. Q. M., 18 May, 1864. Mustered out 6 June, 1865.
Hoopes, Maris, Maj. P. M., 4 Sept., 1861. Resigned 7 March, 1863.
Hoover, John S., Capt. A. de C., 29 Feb., 1864. Maj., 17 Feb., 1865. Mustered out 6 Sept., 1865.
Hoover, John W., Hosp. Chap., 7 July, 1862. Mustered out 4 Aug., 1865.
Hopkins, Chas., Capt. A. Q. M., 6 Aug., 1861. Mustered out 8 Jan., 1866.
Hopkins, Henry, Hosp. Chap., 31 May, 1862. Resigned 25 May, 1864.
Hopkins, John F., Capt. C. S., 31 Oct., 1861. Resigned 30 Sept., 1861.
Hopkins, John W., Capt. C. S., 7 March, 1865. Mustered out 8 Dec., 1865.
Hopkins, Nelson J., Capt. A. Q. M., 29 Feb., 1864. Died 15 July, 1865.
Hopkins, Orlando J., Capt. C. S., 17 July, 1862. Mustered out 31 May, 1866.
Hopkins, Woolsey R., Capt. A. Q. M., 5 Aug., 1861. Mustered out 31 May, 1866.
Hopkinson, Joseph, Maj. Surg., 4 Oct., 1862. Died 11 July, 1865.
Hopper, John C., Capt. Addl. A. de C., 31 March, 1862. Resigned 11 June, 1864.
Hornor, Caleb W., Asst. Surg., 7 Nov., 1862. Maj. Surg., 13 April, 1863. Mustered out 15 Nov., 1866.
Horton, Chas. P., Capt. A. A. G., 17 July,

1862. Capt. A. de C., 24 Aug., 1863. Mustered out 6 Sept., 1865.
Horton, Daniel W., Capt. C. S., 6 Oct., 1862. Died 14 Feb., 1863.
Horton, Dexter, Capt. C. S., 18 May, 1864. Mustered out 14 July, 1865.
Hosack, Wm. H., Capt. C. S., 23 Oct., 1862. Mustered out 10 Jan., 1866.
Hoskin, John, Capt. Addl. A. de C., 29 Nov., 1861. Resigned 15 March, 1862.
Hoskins, Sam'l W., Capt. A. Q. M., 19 Feb., 1863. Mustered out 8 Dec., 1865.
Hoskinson, Thos. J., Capt. C. S., 26 Aug., 1864. Mustered out 7 July, 1865.
Hosmer, Addison A., Maj. J. A., 24 Nov., 1863. Mustered out 28 Nov., 1865.
Hosmer, James R., Capt. A. Q. M., 12 May, 1863. Resigned 13 Dec., 1864.
Hotaling, John R., Maj. A. de C., 29 Feb., 1864. Resigned 10 Feb., 1865.
Hough, John, Capt. A. A. G., 15 May, 1863. Maj., 2 July, 1864. Mustered out 25 Nov., 1865.
Houghton, Chester W., Capt. C. S., 15 Feb., 1865. Mustered out 9 Oct., 1865.
Houston, David C., Maj. Addl. A. de C., 16 May, 1862. Mustered out 31 May, 1866.
Hovey, Levin P., Brig. Gen., 28 April, 1862. Resigned 7 Oct., 1865.
Hovey, Bleeker L., Asst. Surg., 9 Sept., 1864. Maj. Surg., 19 May, 1865. Mustered out 10 Aug., 1865.
Hovey, Chas. E., Brig. Gen., 5 Sept., 1862. Appointment expired 4 March, 1863.
How, Woodbury S., Capt. A. Q. M., 23 Feb., 1864. Mustered out 10 June, 1866.
Howard, Chas. H., Maj. A. de C., 25 April, 1863. Resigned 5 April, 1865.
Howard, George W., Capt. A. A. G., 8 Feb., 1865. Mustered out 1 Sept., 1866.
Howard, Jacob M., Capt. A. de C., 4 May, 1863. Capt. A. A. G., 18 March, 1864. Maj., 29 March, 1865. Mustered out 19 Sept., 1865.
Howard, John B., Capt. A. Q. M., 30 June, 1862. Mustered out 30 July, 1867.
Howard, John E., Capt. C. S., 26 Nov., 1862. Mustered out 22 Aug., 1865.
Howard, John R., Capt. Addl. A. de C., 19 Sept., 1861. Discharged 1 Nov., 1861. Reappointed 31 March, 1862. Resigned 1 Feb., 1865.
Howard, Joshua, Maj. P. M., 1 June, 1861. Mustered out 31 July, 1865.
Howard, Lous J., Capt. A. de C., 11 March, 1863. Discharged 10 Aug., 1863.
Howard, Ocran H., Capt. Sig. Corps, 3 March, 1863. Mustered out 20 June, 1866.
Howard, Oliver O., Brig. Gen., 3 Sept., 1861. Maj. Gen., 29 Nov., 1862. Mustered out 1 Jan., 1869.
Howe, Albion P., Brig. Gen., 11 June, 1862. Mustered out 15 Jan., 1866.
Howe, Chas. E., Capt. A. A. G., 28 March, 1865. Mustered out 13 Sept., 1866.
Howe, Frank E., Capt. A. Q. M., 11 June, 1862. Resigned 3 June, 1864.
Howe, Wm. R., Capt. A. A. G., 12 June, 1863. Resigned 23 Dec., 1864.
Howell, Rich'd S., Capt. A. A. G., 11 March, 1863. Resigned 9 Nov., 1863.
Howell, Robert H., Maj. P. M., 18 March, 1864. Mustered out 1 Nov., 1865.
*Howell, Wm. T., Capt. A. Q. M., 5 Aug., 1863. Capt. A. Q. M., U. S. A., 26 Oct., 1865
Howgate, Henry W, 1st Lieut. Sig. Corps, 3 March, 1863. Mustered out 20 June, 1866.
Howland, Henry, Capt. A. Q. M., 9 June, 1862. Mustered out 19 Jan., 1867.
Howland, John W., Capt. A. Q. M., 30 Sept., 1862. Appointment expired 4 March, 1863.
Howland, Joseph, Capt. A. A. G., 16 Sept., 1861. Vacated commission 7 March, 1862.
Howland, Livingston, Capt. A. A. G., 30 June, 1864. Mustered out 19 Sept., 1865.
Hoy, Wm. E., Maj. P. M., 5 Sept., 1861. Resigned 19 Jan., 1864.
Hoyt, Albert H., Maj. P. M., 26 Nov., 1862. Mustered out 20 July, 1866.
Hoyt, Chas. F., Capt. C. S., 19 Feb., 1863. Mustered out 31 May, 1866.
Hoyt, Chas. H., Capt. A. Q. M., 12 May, 1862. Appointed Capt. A. Q. M., U. S. A., 22 March, 1867.
Hoyt, Chas. J., Maj. P. M., 19 Sept., 1862. Rejected by Senate 27 Feb., 1863. Reappointed 29 Sept., 1863. Resigned 28 April, 1864.
Hoyt, James T., Capt. A. Q. M., 17 Nov., 1863. Appointed Capt. A. Q. M., U. S. A., 18 Jan., 1867.
Hoyt, Stephen, Capt. C. S., 16 Sept., 1861. Resigned 26 May, 1864.
Hoyt, Thos. J., Capt. A. A. G., 3 Oct., 1861. Resigned 6 Nov., 1862.
Hubbard, George H., Maj. Surg., 30 Sept., 1861. Mustered out 7 Oct., 1865.
Hubbard, John B., Capt. A. A. G., 27 Oct., 1862. Died 27 May, 1863.
Hubbard, Wm. C., Hosp. Chap., 11 May, 1863. Appointment expired 4 July, 1864.
Hubbell, Augustus, Capt. C. S., 23 March, 1865. Mustered out 4 Aug., 1865.
Huber, J. F., Capt. C. S., 25 Oct., 1861. Mustered out 12 Oct., 1865.
Huber, John F., Asst. Surg., 7 Nov., 1863. Maj. Surg., 9 Feb., 1865. Mustered out 4 June, 1866.
Hudson, Edward McK., Lieut. Col. Addl. A. de C., 28 Sept., 1861. Discharged 31 March, 1863.
Hudson, Peter T., Capt. A. de C., 11 March, 1863. Mustered out 31 May, 1866.
Hudson, Robt. N., Col. Addl. A. de C., 31 March, 1862. Resigned 26 Aug., 1863.
Hughes, Daniel W., Capt. Addl. A. de C., 15 May, 1862. Mustered out 31 May, 1866.
Hughes, Joseph R., Capt. C. S., 18 May, 1863. Mustered out 31 May, 1866.
Hulbert, Wm. L., Capt. A. de C., 21 April, 1865. Mustered out 19 May, 1866.
Huling, Lewis J., Capt. C. S., 31 Oct., 1861. Resigned 3 June, 1863.
Hull, Alex., Capt. A. Q. M., 29 Feb., 1864. Mustered out 23 Oct., 1865.
Hull, Walter C., Capt. A. de C., 19 May, 1863. Discharged 15 Aug., 1863.
Humes, Wm. H., Capt. A. Q. M., 29 Feb., 1864. Resigned 24 March, 1865.
Humphrey, Otis M., Asst. Surg., 7 Aug., 1863. Maj. Surg., 4 Dec., 1863. Mustered out 5 Aug., 1865.
Humphreys, Andrew A., Col. Addl. A. de C., 5 March, 1862. Brig. Gen., 28 April, 1862. Maj. Gen., 8 July, 1863. Mustered out 1 Sept., 1866.
Humphreys, Henry H., Maj. A. de C., 5 April, 1865. Mustered out 10 Nov., 1865.
Humphreys, Lewis, Lieut. Col. Med. Insp., 30 June, 1865. Mustered out 31 Oct., 1865.
Hundhausen, Rob't, Maj. P. M., 30 June, 1864. Resigned 4 Aug., 1865.
Hungerford, Arthur L., Capt. C. S., 20 Nov., 1862. Resigned 5 Sept., 1864.
Hunn, Horace H., Maj. P. M., 23 Feb., 1864. Mustered out 7 April, 1866.
Hunt, Henry J., Col. Addl. A. de C., 28 Sept., 1861. Brig. Gen., 15 Sept., 1862. Mustered out 30 April, 1866.
Hunt, John W., Maj. Surg., 12 May, 1862. Discharged 9 Dec., 1862.
Hunt, Leavitt, Maj. A. de C., 20 Aug., 1862. Resigned 25 July, 1863.
Hunt, Lewis C., Brig. Gen., 24 Dec., 1862. Mustered out 15 Jan., 1866.
Hunt, Rob't G., Maj. P. M., 27 Feb., 1863. Mustered out 15 Nov., 1865.
Hunt, Sanford B., Maj. Surg., 19 Feb., 1863. Mustered out 5 Aug., 1865.

Hunt, Thomas B., Capt. A. Q. M., 26 Nov., 1862. Appointed Capt. A. Q. M., U. S. A., 18 Jan., 1867.
Hunter, David, Brig. Gen., 17 May, 1861. Maj. Gen., 13 Aug., 1861. Mustered out 15 Jan., 1866.
Hunter, Hiram A., Hosp. Chap., 28 Sept., 1864. Mustered out 12 Oct., 1865.
Hunter, Wm. A., Capt. A. Q. M., 19 Feb., 1863. Cashiered 1 May, 1865.
Huntington, John M., Capt. A. Q. M., 30 Aug., 1861. Discharged 20 May, 1864.
Hurd, Chas. H., Capt. A. A. G., 22 May, 1863. Mustered out 19 Sept., 1865.
Hurlbut, Lewis, Hosp. Chap., 15 July, 1862. Discharged 10 Sept., 1862.
Hurlbut, Stephen A., Brig. Gen., 17 May, 1861. Maj. Gen., 17 Sept., 1862. Mustered out 20 June, 1865.
Hurlbut, Walter C., Capt. A. Q. M., 31 July, 1863. Resigned 6 May, 1864.
Hurtt, Francis W., Capt. A. Q. M., 31 Oct., 1861. Dismissed 17 June, 1864.
Husted, Gilbert M., Capt. A. Q. M., 28 July, 1863. Resigned 15 March, 1865.
Hutchings, Wm. V., Capt. A. Q. M., 26 Nov., 1862. Resigned 29 May, 1865.
Hutchins, Horace A., Maj. P. M., 1 June, 1861. Mustered out 1 Nov., 1865.
Hutchins, Rob't A., Capt. A. A. G., 7 Sept., 1862. Mustered out 19 Sept., 1865.
Hutchins, Uriel H., Maj. P. M., 26 Nov., 1862. Mustered out 20 July, 1866.
Hutchinson, Buell E., Capt. C. S., 5 Aug., 1861. Resigned 30 April, 1864.
Hutton, Chas. G., Capt. A. de C., 11 March, 1863. Dismissed 28 Sept., 1863. Capt. A. de C., 30 Oct., 1863. Resigned 25 April, 1865.
Hyden, Jesse A., Hosp. Chap., 6 Oct., 1863. Resigned 27 July, 1865.
Hyndshaw, James B., Hosp. Chap., 15 July, 1862. Mustered out 26 July, 1865.
Hynes, John R., Capt. A. Q. M., 20 Sept., 1864. Mustered out 1 May, 1867.
Ihrie, George P., Col. Addl. A. de C., 7 May, 1862. Discharged 18 Aug., 1863.
Ingalls, Rufus, Lieut. Col. Addl. A. de C., 28 Sept., 1861. Brig. Gen., 23 May, 1863. Mustered out 1 Sept., 1866.
Ingledew, Lumley, Capt. C. S., 2 March, 1864. Mustered out 19 July, 1865.
Insley, Martin H., Capt. A. Q. M., 6 Aug., 1861. Capt. A. Q. M., U. S. A., 13 March, 1863.
Ireland, Oscar B., 2nd Lieut. Sig. Corps, 3 March, 1863. Mustered out 12 Aug., 1865.
Irvin, Chas. H., Capt. A. Q. M., 31 July, 1863. Mustered out 6 March, 1867.
Irvine, John A., Capt. C. S., 7 Nov., 1862. Died 1 March, 1865.
Irwin, Richard B., Capt. Addl. A. de C., 22 Aug., 1861. Resigned 19 Sept., 1864.
Irwin, Wm. R., Capt. C. S., 28 April, 1863. Mustered out 13 March, 1866.
Isaac, Montifiore, Capt. A. Q. M., 13 Sept., 1862. Resigned 6 July, 1863.
Isenstein, George, Capt. A. Q. M., 15 Sept., 1864. Mustered out 13 March, 1866.
Ives, Brayton, Capt. A. A. G., 28 April, 1862. Resigned 5 Aug., 1863.
Ives, Noah P., Capt. C. S., 21 April, 1864. Mustered out 15 Aug., 1865.
Ives, Simeon P., Hosp. Chap., 9 Aug., 1862. Appointment expired 14 March, 1863. Reappointed 22 April, 1863. Mustered out 4 Aug., 1865.
Jackson, Amos M., 2nd and 1st Lieut. Sig. Corps, 3 March, 1863. Appointment as 1st Lieut. expired 4 July, 1864. Mustered out 1 Sept., 1865.
Jackson, Conrad F., Brig. Gen., 17 July, 1862. Killed 13 Dec., 1862, at Battle of Fredericksburg, Va.
Jackson, Eliphalet W., Hosp. Chap., 12 July, 1862. Mustered out 28 June, 1865.
Jackson, James S., Brig. Gen., 16 July, 1862. Killed 8 Oct., 1862, at Battle of Perryville, Ky.
Jackson, John H., Capt. A. Q. M., 25 July, 1864. Mustered out 19 May, 1866.
Jackson, Joseph C., Capt. A. de C., 20 Aug., 1862. Appointment revoked 14 Feb., 1863.
Jackson, Nath'l J., Brig. Gen., 24 Sept., 1862. Mustered out 24 Aug., 1865.
Jackson, Oswald, Capt. A. de C., 20 Aug., 1862. Maj. 23 June, 1863. Discharged 10 Aug., 1863.
Jackson, Richard H., Brig. Gen., 19 May, 1865. Mustered out 1 Feb., 1866.
Jackson, Rob't M. S., Maj. Surg., 19 Feb., 1863. Died 18 Jan., 1865.
Jackson, Wm. W., Capt. C. S., 24 March, 1862. Resigned 14 July, 1865.
Jacobi, John C., Hosp. Chap., 18 March, 1864. Mustered out 15 Nov., 1866.
Jacobs, Ferris, Maj. Surg., 4 April, 1862. Resigned 22 Dec., 1862.
Jacobs, George P., Capt. C. S., 19 Feb., 1863. Mustered out 14 July, 1865.
Jacobs, Jesse E., Capt. A. A. G., 17 July, 1862. Mustered out 1 Sept., 1866.
Jacobson, Thorwald, Capt. C. S., 20 Nov., 1862. Died 3 Jan., 1864.
James, De Witt C., Maj. P. M., 6 March, 1865. Mustered out 29 July, 1865.
James, Horace, Capt. A. Q. M., 18 Feb., 1864. Mustered out 8 Jan., 1866.
James, John H., Capt. A. Q. M., 25 July, 1864. Mustered out 19 May, 1866.
James, Reuben R., Capt. C. S., 30 June, 1864. Mustered out 12 July, 1865.
James, Wm. L., Capt. A. Q. M., 26 Nov., 1862. Mustered out 31 July, 1866.
Jameson, Chas. D., Brig. Gen., 3 Sept., 1861. Died 6 Nov., 1862.
Jameson, John, Maj. P. M., 30 June, 1862. Resigned 27 July, 1863.
Jameson, Wm. H., Maj. P. M., 26 Nov., 1862. Mustered out 20 July, 1866.
Janes, Henry, Maj. Surg., 26 March, 1863. Mustered out 4 Jan., 1866.
Janes, Henry W., Capt. A. Q. M., 31 July, 1863. Capt. A. Q. M., U. S. A., 30 Oct., 1863.
Jay, Wm., Capt. Addl. A. de C., 28 Aug., 1861. Resigned 29 May, 1865.
Jayne, Henry, Capt. A. de C., 25 March, 1864. Resigned 9 Jan., 1865.
Jeffers, Stephen, Capt. C. S., 2 March, 1864. Mustered out 10 Jan., 1866.
Jeffries, Noah L., Capt. A. A. G., 26 March, 1862. Maj., 12 Aug., 1863. Resigned 30 Nov., 1863.
Jenkins, Francis K., Capt. C. S., 22 Feb., 1865. Mustered out 14 July, 1865.
Jenkins, Joseph M., Asst. Surg., 9 Jan., 1865. Mustered out 4 June, 1866.
Jenney, Wm. L. B., Capt. Addl. A. de C., 19 Aug., 1861. Mustered out 19 May, 1866.
Jennings, John R., Capt. A. Q. M., 5 Dec., 1863. Mustered out 10 Sept., 1866.
Jennings, Eli F., Maj. P. M., 21 April, 1864. Resigned 18 June, 1864. Capt. C. S., 30 June, 1864. Resigned 11 April, 1865.
Jerome, Aaron B., 1st Lieut. Sig. Corps, 3 March, 1863. Resigned 20 Sept., 1864.
Jerome, John A., Hosp. Chap., 20 June, 1862. Mustered out 26 July, 1865.
Jessop, S. S., Asst. Surg., 20 Sept., 1864. Mustered out 27 Nov., 1865.
Jewett, John E., Capt. Addl. A. de C., 19 May, 1862. Resigned 29 Oct., 1864.
Jewett, Pliny A., Maj. Surg., 7 Nov., 1862. Mustered out 4 Jan., 1866.
Joel, Ephraim M., Capt. A. Q. M., 21 April, 1863. Mustered out 8 Jan., 1866.
Johnes, George W., Capt. A. Q. M., 18 July, 1862. Mustered out 20 Sept., 1865.
Johnson, Albert E. H., Maj. A. A. G., 2 Dec., 1865. Mustered out 1 Sept., 1867.

Johnson, Andrew, Brig. Gen., 4 March, 1862. Resigned 3 March, 1865.
Johnson, Chauncey P. E., Maj. P. M., 1 June, 1861. Mustered out 26 Oct., 1866.
Johnson, George K., Lieut. Col. and Med. Insp., 9 Dec., 1863. Resigned 1 Oct., 1865.
Johnson, Granville E., Capt. A. de C., 20 Aug., 1862. Maj., 24 Aug., 1863. Mustered out 14 Sept., 1864.
Johnson, Henry L., Capt. A. A. G., 4 Sept., 1863. Resigned 17 April, 1865.
Johnson, Henry N., Capt. A. Q. M., 26 Aug., 1864. Resigned 14 Jan., 1865.
Johnson, Henry W., Capt. A. Q. M., 1 June, 1865. Mustered out 5 June, 1866.
Johnson, James, Capt. A. A. G., 29 Feb., 1864. Mustered out 1 Sept., 1866.
Johnson, James G., Capt. A. Q. M., 3 July, 1862. Dismissed 19 June, 1865.
Johnson, James W., Maj. P. M., 26 Nov., 1862. Discharged 4 May, 1864.
Johnson, Jasper, Capt. C. S., 19 Feb., 1863. Mustered out 14 July, 1865.
Johnson, Jasper H., Capt. C. S., 22 Oct., 1862. Mustered out 8 Dec., 1865.
Johnson, John D., Asst. Surg., 19 Feb., 1863. Mustered out 20 July, 1865.
Johnson, John E., Capt. A. Q. M., 15 Feb., 1865. Mustered out 20 Sept., 1865.
Johnson, Louis E., Maj. P. M., 1 June, 1861. Resigned 9 July, 1864.
Johnson, Parrish B., Capt. A. Q. M., 17 Nov., 1863. Mustered out 4 Jan., 1866.
Johnson, Rich'd P., Capt. A. Q. M., 30 June, 1862. Mustered out 25 June, 1865.
Johnson, Rich'd W., Brig. Gen., 11 Oct., 1861. Mustered out 15 Jan., 1866.
Johnson, Rufus H., Maj. Surg., 24 Dec., 1861. Resigned 8 Jan., 1863.
Johnson, Thos. W., Asst. Surg., 17 April, 1865. Mustered out 14 Dec., 1865.
Johnson, Wm. F., Capt. C. S., 21 Dec., 1864. Mustered out 22 Aug., 1867.
Johnson, Wm. H., Capt. A. Q. M., 18 Nov., 1862. Resigned 6 March, 1865.
Johnson, Wm. T., Hosp Chap., 23 March, 1864. Mustered out 24 June, 1865.
Johnston, George H., Capt. A. A. G., 21 April, 1862. Resigned 31 Oct., 1864.
Johnston, Thos. P., Capt. A. Q. M., 19 Feb., 1863. Mustered out 13 Nov., 1867.
Johnston, Wm. H., Maj. P. M., 5 Sept., 1861. Mustered out 20 July, 1866.
Joline, Chas. O., Capt. A. A. G., 14 April, 1862. Resigned 6 Nov., 1862. Maj. A. de C., 24 Nov., 1862. Mustered out 4 Jan., 1866.
Jonas, Edward, Capt. A. de C., 2 Feb., 1865. Mustered out 12 Jan., 1866.
Jones, Amos B., Col. Addl. A. de C., 31 May, 1862. Dismissed 8 May, 1865.
Jones, Chas. C., Maj. P. M., 28 May, 1864. Mustered out 5 Aug., 1865.
Jones, Chas. S., Maj. P. M., 1 June, 1861. Mustered out 1 June, 1867.
Jones, Chas. W., Maj. Surg., 10 Oct., 1861. Mustered out 10 Aug., 1865.
Jones, Daniel D., Capt. A. Q. M., 17 July, 1862. Resigned 3 Feb., 1864.
Jones, David O., Hosp. Chap., 30 June, 1864. Mustered out 4 Aug., 1865.
Jones, Edwin S., Capt. C. S., 19 Feb., 1863. Mustered out 2 Feb., 1866.
Jones, Frank J., Capt. A. de C., 11 March, 1863. Resigned 28 April, 1864.
Jones, George E., Capt. C. S., 2 March, 1864. Mustered out 27 Nov., 1865.
Jones, Henry L., Capt. A. Q. M., 27 Feb., 1863. Resigned 15 March, 1865.
Jones, James E., Capt. A. Q. M., 23 Feb., 1864. Mustered out 19 May, 1866.
Jones, Jules M., Maj. P. M., 8 Aug., 1864. Resigned 12 May, 1865.
Jones, Merritt B., Capt. A. Q. M., 26 Jan., 1865. Mustered out 28 July, 1865.
Jones, Nathan S., Capt. C. S., 28 May, 1864. Resigned 20 Sept., 1864.
Jones, Patrick H., Brig. Gen., 6 Dec., 1864. Resigned 17 June, 1865.
Jones, Solomon, Capt. C. S., 20 May, 1863. Appointment revoked 19 Feb., 1864.
Jones, Stephen E., Capt. Addl. A. de C., 9 July, 1862. Resigned 13 March, 1865.
Jones, William M., Capt. C. S., 21 April, 1864. Mustered out 1 Dec., 1865.
Jones, William C., Maj. P. M., 10 Sept., 1862. Mustered out 15 Nov., 1865.
Jones, William M., Capt. C. S., 21 April, 1864. Mustered out 8 Feb., 1866.
Jones, William P., Maj. Addl. A. de C., 10 Sept., 1861. Resigned 29 Dec., 1862.
Jordan, Francis, Maj. P. M., 1 June, 1861. Resigned 12 Jan., 1864.
Jordan, Gilmore, Capt. C. S., 11 June, 1862. Mustered out 8 July, 1865.
Jordan, John, Capt. C. S., 12 May, 1862. Resigned 22 Aug., 1862.
Joy, Edmund L., Maj. J. A., 15 Sept., 1864. Resigned 7 May, 1865.
Judah, Henry M., Brig. Gen., 21 March, 1862. Mustered out 24 Aug., 1865.
Judd, Edwin D., Maj. P. M., 1 June, 1861. Mustered out 20 July, 1866.
Judson, John A., Capt. A. A. G., 3 Feb., 1862. Mustered out 19 Sept., 1865.
Judson, Oliver A., Maj. Surg., 5 Oct., 1861. Resigned 17 Nov., 1865.
Judson, Philo P., Capt. C. S., 20 April, 1864. Resigned 7 May, 1865.
Justice, Joseph, Capt. A. Q. M., 12 May, 1862. Maj. P. M., 26 Nov., 1862. Resigned 8 Feb., 1865.
Kames, Joshua, Maj. P. M., 11 March, 1863. Resigned 4 Nov., 1863.
Kane, Thomas L., Brig. Gen., 7 Sept., 1862. Resigned 7 Nov., 1863.
Kane, William J., Capt. C. S., 28 Aug., 1861. Capt. A. Q. M., 15 Oct., 1861. Vacated appointment Capt. A. Q. M., 25 July, 1862. Resigned 23 Dec., 1862.
Kappner, Franz, Maj. Addl. A. de C., 14 June, 1862. Mustered out 4 Nov., 1864.
Karsner, Charles, Hosp. Chap., 23 Feb., 1864. Discharged 27 April, 1864.
Kautz, August V., Brig. Gen., 7 May, 1864. Mustered out 15 Jan., 1866.
Kayser, John, Capt. C. S., 2 July, 1863. Resigned 31 May, 1865.
Kearny, Philip, Brig. Gen., 17 May, 1861. Maj. Gen., 4 July, 1862. Killed 1 Sept., 1862, in Battle of Chantilly, Va.
Keatly, John, Maj. P. M., 26 Nov., 1862. Mustered out 1 Dec., 1865.
Keefer, Henry G., Asst. Surg., 30 June, 1864. Mustered out 27 Jan., 1866.
Keeler, Birney B., Maj. J. A., 26 June, 1865. Mustered out 31 May, 1866.
Keenon, John G., Maj. Surg., 9 Oct., 1861. Died 12 Aug., 1864.
Keffer, Fred'k A., Asst. Surg., 4 Oct., 1862. Maj. Surg., 8 May, 1863. Mustered out 15 July, 1865.
Kelly, Daniel J., Capt. Addl. A. de C., 9 April, 1862. Mustered out 20 Aug., 1865.
Keim, William H., Brig. Gen., 20 Dec., 1861. Died 18 May, 1862.
Keith, Abijah, Capt. C. S., 3 Aug., 1861. Resigned 5 Aug., 1862.
Keith, Chas. C. T., 1st Lieut. Sig. Corps, 3 March, 1863. Resigned 13 April, 1864.
Keith, Henry, Capt. A. A. G., 20 Oct., 1862. Resigned 19 Jan., 1863.
Keith, Sidney, Maj. P. M., 29 March, 1865. Mustered out 29 July, 1865.
Keller, Augustus R., Capt. A. Q. M., 30 July, 1864. Mustered out 4 Aug., 1865.
Kelley, Benj'n F., Brig. Gen., 17 May, 1861. Resigned 1 June, 1865.
Kelley, Benj'n F., Jr., Capt. A. Q. M., 18 March, 1864. Mustered out 13 March, 1866.

Kelley, Thomas B., 2nd Lieut. Sig. Corps, 3 March, 1863. Mustered out 1 Sept., 1865.
Kellogg, Charles C., Capt. C. S., 19 Feb., 1863. Mustered out 10 Aug., 1865.
Kellogg, George D., Capt. A. A. G., 12 Aug., 1861. Discharged 12 Nov., 1861. Capt. A. A. G., 15 Nov., 1861. Resigned 3 June, 1862.
Kellogg, George M., Maj. Surg., 28 April, 1862. Mustered out 15 Aug., 1865.
Kellogg, Rowland C., Capt. C. S., 28 May, 1864. Mustered out 3 Aug., 1865.
Kellogg, Sanford C., Capt. A. de C., 11 March, 1863. Mustered out 10 July, 1866.
Kellogg, Wm. H., Capt. C. S., 8 Dec., 1864. Mustered out 9 Oct., 1865.
Kelly, Chas. V., Hosp. Chap., 23 Jan., 1865. Mustered out 31 Aug., 1865.
Kelly, Frederick, Maj. P. M., 20 April, 1864. Mustered out 15 Jan., 1866.
Kelly, John L., Capt. A. Q. M., 8 July, 1863. Mustered out 11 Nov., 1865.
Kelton, John C., Col. Addl. A. de C., 10 April, 1862. Mustered out 31 May, 1866.
Kemble, Edward C., Maj. P. M., 30 June, 1862. Mustered out 3 April, 1866.
Kemble, George S., Maj. Surg., 30 Sept., 1861. Mustered out 19 Oct., 1865.
Kemble, Wm. H., Maj. P. M., 26 Nov., 1862. Appointment revoked 25 Aug., 1863.
Kemper, Andrew C., Capt. A. A. G., 16 Nov., 1861. Appointment expired 17 July, 1862. Capt. A. A. G., 1 Sept., 1862. Resigned 25 July, 1865.
Kenderline, Robert S., Asst. Surg., 7 Jan., 1863. Maj. Surg., 13 April, 1863. Mustered out 12 Oct., 1865.
Kendrick, Albert S., Capt. A. A. G., 27 Feb., 1865. Mustered out 7 April, 1866.
Kendrick, John M., Capt. A. A. G., 19 Feb., 1862. Resigned 30 Sept., 1862.
Kenly, John R., Brig. Gen., 22 Aug., 1862. Mustered out 24 Aug., 1865.
Kenly, William L., Capt. C. S., 19 Aug., 1863. Mustered out 5 Aug., 1865.
Kennedy, Robert P., Capt. A. A. G., 7 Oct., 1862. Maj., 16 Nov., 1864. Resigned 8 April, 1865.
Kennedy, William K., Capt. A. Q. M., 11 June, 1862. Mustered out 11 July, 1865.
Kenney, Dennis, Jr., Capt. C. S., 26 Nov., 1862. Mustered out 11 July, 1865.
Kennon, Wilson S., Maj. P. M., 19 Feb., 1863. Mustered out 19 Dec., 1865.
Kent, Rudolphus, Capt. C. S., 3 Aug., 1861. Mustered out 31 Aug., 1865.
Keogh, Miles W., Capt. Addl. A. de C., 9 April, 1862. Maj. A. de C., 7 April, 1864. Mustered out 1 Sept., 1866.
Kerbey, Joseph A., 2nd Lieut. Sig. Corps, 3 March, 1863. Resigned 9 June, 1865.
Kerlin, Oscar B., Capt. C. S., 7 April, 1864. Mustered out 31 May, 1866.
Kerns, Wm. F., Capt. A. Q. M., 29 Feb., 1864. Mustered out 13 Dec., 1865.
Kerr, Thos. J., Capt. A. Q. M., 5 Aug., 1863. Mustered out 8 Feb., 1866.
Kesley, Wm., Capt. A. A. G., 16 May, 1862. Resigned 29 Sept., 1863.
Ketcham, Henry S., Capt. C. S., 18 May, 1864. Resigned 9 April, 1865.
Ketcham, John H., Brig. Gen., 1 April, 1865. Resigned 2 Dec., 1865.
Ketchum, Edgar, 2nd Lieut. Sig. Corps, 3 March, 1863. Mustered out 12 Aug., 1865.
Ketchum, Isaac S., Hosp. Chap., 23 June, 1862. Died 14 June, 1863.
Ketchum, Wm. S., Brig. Gen., 3 Feb., 1862. Mustered out 30 April, 1866.
Key, John J., Maj. Addl. A. de C., 5 March, 1862. Discharged 27 Sept., 1862.
Key, Thos. M., Col. Addl. A. de C., 19 Aug., 1861. Discharged 31 March, 1863.
Keyes, Edward L., Capt. A. de C., 23 June, 1863. Discharged 10 Aug., 1863.
Keyes, Erasmus D., Brig. Gen., 17 May, 1861. Maj. Gen., 5 May, 1862. Resigned 6 May, 1864.
Keyser, Wm. A., Capt. Addl. A. de C., 18 April, 1862. Resigned 29 Nov., 1864.
Kibler, Chas. H., Capt. A. A. G., 28 Sept., 1863. Resigned 1 Aug., 1864.
Kidder, Winslow L., Capt. A. A. G., 26 July, 1862. Resigned 25 Sept., 1863.
Kirman, Jomes L., Brig. Gen., 1 Aug., 1863. Resigned 3 Feb., 1864.
Kilgore, Damon Y., Capt. A. Q. M., 30 July, 1863. Mustered out 25 Aug., 1865.
Kilpatrick, Judson, Lieut. Col. Addl. A. de C., 29 Jan., 1862. Discharged 21 March, 1862. Brig. Gen., 13 June, 1863. Maj. Gen., 18 June, 1865. Resigned 1 Jan., 1866.
Kimball, Amos S., Capt. A. Q. M., 7 April, 1864. Appointed Capt. A. Q. M., U. S. A., 19 Nov., 1866.
Kimball, Gilman, Maj. Surg., 2 Oct., 1861. Resigned 28 April, 1862.
Kimball, James P., Capt. A. A. G., 14 April, 1862. Resigned 9 Dec., 1863.
Kimball, John, Hosp. Chap., 30 Nov., 1864. Mustered out 26 July, 1865.
Kimball, Milton S., Capt. A. A. G., 23 Dec., 1862. Resigned 1 Sept., 1863.
Kimball, Nathan, Brig. Gen., 15 April, 1862. Mustered out 24 Aug., 1865.
Kimball, Wm. C., Capt. C. S., 2 March, 1864. Resigned 8 Dec., 1864.
Kimball, Wm. M., Capt. A. Q. M., 27 March, 1863. Mustered out 18 Feb., 1866.
King, Adam E., Capt. A. A. G., 11 March, 1863. Maj., 15 July, 1864. Mustered out 31 Oct., 1866.
King, Fred'k C., Capt. C. S., 26 Sept., 1864. Mustered out 9 Oct., 1865.
King, Henry H., Capt. A. A. G., 20 Oct., 1862. Resigned 10 Dec., 1862.
King, Henry L., Maj. P. M., 1 June, 1861. Mustered out 1 Nov., 1865.
King, Horatio C., Capt. A. Q. M., 19 Aug., 1862. Resigned 19 May, 1865.
King, James, Maj. Surg., 5 Aug., 1861. Resigned 6 Nov., 1862.
King, John, Capt. C. S., 3 Aug., 1861. Mustered out 27 Dec., 1866.
King, John C., Capt. C. S., 21 Jan., 1865. Mustered out 28 June, 1865.
King, John H., Brig. Gen., 29 Nov., 1862. Mustered out 15 Jan., 1866.
King, John N., Capt. C. S., 3 Feb., 1862. Mustered out 7 July, 1865.
King, John W., Maj. P. M., 23 Feb., 1864. Resigned 17 Jan., 1865.
King, Nathan G., Capt. C. S., 14 April, 1862. Maj. P. M., 23 Feb., 1864. Mustered out 15 Nov., 1865.
King, Rufus, Brig. Gen., 17 May, 1861. Resigned 20 Oct., 1863.
King, Rufus, Capt. C. S., 2 March, 1864. Mustered out 21 Feb., 1866.
Kingsbury, Alonzo, Capt. A. Q. M., 7 April, 1864. Mustered out 26 June, 1865.
Kingsbury, Chas., Capt. A. A. G., 19 Sept., 1861. Resigned 2 March, 1865.
Kingsbury, Chas. P., Col. Addl. A. de C., 28 Sept., 1861. Appointment expired 17 July, 1862.
Kingsley, Henry W., Capt. C. S., 23 Jan., 1865. Mustered out 10 Aug., 1865.
Kinne, C. Mason, Capt. A. A. G., 1 Feb., 1865. Mustered out 11 July, 1865.
Kinney, Coates, Maj. P. M., 1 June, 1861. Mustered out 15 Nov., 1865.
Kinsman, Josiah B., Lieut. Col. Addl. A. de C., 24 June, 1862. Mustered out 20 July, 1866.
Kinsman, Oliver D., Capt. A. A. G., 31 Aug., 1864. Mustered out 1 Oct., 1866.
Kinsman, Wm. H., Capt. A. A. G., 17 July, 1862. Resigned 17 Sept., 1862.
Kinzie, Arthur M., Capt. A. de C., 8 Nov., 1862. Discharged 15 Aug., 1863.

Kinzie, John H., Maj. P. M., 1 June, 1861. Died 22 June, 1865.
Kip, Lawrence, Maj. A. de C., 20 Aug., 1862. Discharged 15 Aug., 1863.
Kipp, Chas. J., Asst. Surg., 14 May, 1863. Maj. Surg., 30 March, 1864. Mustered out 1 Nov., 1867.
Kirby, Edmund, Brig. Gen., 23 May, 1863. Died 28 May, 1863, of wounds received at Battle of Chancellorsville, Va.
Kirk, Ezra B., Capt. A. Q. M., 5 Dec., 1863. Capt. A. Q. M., U. S. A., 28 July, 1866.
Kirk, Edward N., Brig. Gen., 29 Nov., 1862. Died 29 July, 1863.
Kirke, Henry M., Asst. Surg., 7 Nov., 1863. Mustered out 9 Oct., 1865.
Kirker, James B., Capt. A. Q. M., 20 Oct., 1862. Resigned 17 June, 1863.
Kirkland, Joseph, Capt. Addl. A. de C., 26 Aug., 1861. Maj. A. de C., 20 Aug., 1862. Resigned as Capt., 7 Jan., 1863. Appointment as Maj. A. de C. revoked 14 Feb., 1863.
Kirkpatrick, Thos., Hosp. Chap., 5 Sept., 1864. Mustered out 26 July, 1865.
Kise, Reuben C., Capt. A. A. G., 21 June, 1862. Resigned 16 March, 1864.
Kitchen, Joseph C., Capt. A. Q. M., 24 March, 1865. Mustered out 18 Jan., 1866.
Kitchen, Sam'l, Asst. Surg., 8 Jan., 1864. Mustered out 10 Jan., 1866.
Kittoe, Edward D., Asst. Surg., 7 Nov., 1862. Maj. Surg., 4 Dec., 1862. Lieut. Col. Med. Insp., U. S. A., 30 March, 1864. Mustered out 31 Oct., 1865.
Kittredge, Wm. T., Capt. A. A. G., 30 June, 1864. Mustered out 5 Dec., 1865.
Klein, John S., Maj. P. M., 20 April, 1864. Mustered out 23 Oct., 1865.
Kley, Herman, Capt. C. S., 5 Sept., 1864. Mustered out 30 March, 1866.
Klinck, John G., Capt. A. Q. M., 3 Aug., 1861. Mustered out 28 July, 1865.
Knapp, Nathan M., Maj. P. M., 19 Feb., 1863. Mustered out 15 Jan., 1866.
Kneeland, Sam'l, Asst. Surg., 2 Sept., 1863. Maj. Surg., 9 Sept., 1863. Mustered out 21 Feb., 1866.
Knefler, Fred'k, Capt. A. A. G., 21 Oct., 1861. Maj., 16 May, 1862. Resigned 8 Sept., 1862.
Kniffin, George C., Capt. C. S., 20 Aug., 1861. Mustered out 19 July, 1865.
Knight, Isaac D., Asst. Surg., 19 Jan., 1864. Maj. Surg., 30 June, 1864. Mustered out 10 Nov., 1865.
Knight, James G., Capt. C. S., 10 Sept., 1862. Resigned 11 Nov., 1864.
Knight, J. Lee, Capt. A. Q. M., 21 Jan., 1865. Mustered out 28 July, 1865.
Knight, John H., Capt. A. A. G., 20 Aug., 1861. Capt. 18th Inf., 19 Feb., 1862.
Knipe, Joseph F., Brig. Gen., 29 Nov., 1862. Mustered out 24 Aug., 1865.
Knowles, Edwin, Capt. C. S., 30 Aug., 1862. Resigned 17 Oct., 1863.
Knowles, Henry P., Capt. C. S., 21 Sept., 1864. Mustered out 7 July, 1865.
Knowles, John A., Capt. C. S., 18 March, 1864. Mustered out 9 Oct., 1865.
Knox, George G., Capt. A. de C., 11 March, 1863. Resigned 17 Dec., 1864.
Knox, John C., Maj. J. A., 7 Sept., 1862. Mustered out 31 May, 1866.
Knox, Joseph B., 1st Lieut. Sig. Corps, 3 March, 1863. Mustered out 21 Aug., 1865.
Koerner, Gustavus, Col. Addl. A. de C., 28 Sept., 1861. Discharged 1 Nov., 1861.
Kossack, Wm., Capt. Addl. A. de C., 19 Aug., 1861. Mustered out 10 July, 1866.
Kountz, W. J., Capt. A. Q. M., 16 Nov., 1861. Resigned 2 April, 1862. Capt. A. Q. M., 26 Nov., 1862. Appointment revoked 18 May, 1863.

Krebbs, Wm. H. W., Capt. Addl. A. de C., 3 May, 1862. Mustered out 6 Sept., 1865.
Kretchmar, Godfrey A., Asst. Surg., 3 Oct., 1864. Mustered out 5 Oct., 1866.
Kryzonowski, Wlademier, Brig. Gen., 29 Nov., 1862. Appointment expired 4 March, 1863.
Kuhn, Wm. E., Capt. A. A. G., 12 Nov., 1864. Resigned 21 June, 1865.
Kyle, Wm., Capt. Addl. A. de C., 29 Jan., 1862. Discharged 21 March, 1862.
Lacey, Henry A., Capt. A. Q. M., 14 April, 1862. Mustered out 13 March, 1866.
Lacey, John F., Capt. A. A. G., 30 June, 1864. Mustered out 19 Sept., 1865.
Lacey, Rob't S., Capt. A. Q. M., 30 June, 1864. Mustered out 1 July, 1866.
Lackey, Alex'r H., Hosp. Chap., 18 March, 1864. Dismissed 2 June, 1865.
Lackey, Rob't M., Asst. Surg., 11 Oct., 1864. Mustered out 26 Nov., 1865.
Lacy, Henry B., Capt. A. Q. M., 16 Sept., 1862. Mustered out 6 Dec., 1865.
Ladd, Francis D., Hosp. Chap., 14 June, 1862. Died 10 July, 1862.
Ladd, George P., Capt. A. Q. M., 18 May, 1864. Mustered out 21 Aug., 1866.
Ladd, Jonathan, Maj. P. M., 1 June, 1861. Dismissed 5 July, 1865.
Ladd, John J., Maj. P. M., 2 July, 1864. Mustered out 1 Nov., 1865.
Ladew, Oliver, Capt. A. Q. M., 10 Sept., 1861. Resigned 15 Nov., 1861.
Lagon, Clarke B., Col. Addl. A. de C., 3 May, 1862. Resigned 12 Dec., 1863.
Laing, James M., Asst. Surg., 19 Feb., 1863. Maj. Surg., 30 March, 1864. Mustered out 15 June, 1865.
Lake, James, Maj. Addl. A. de C., 11 April, 1862. Resigned 16 July, 1862.
Lamb, Rob't M., Capt. A. Q. M., 3 Aug., 1861. Resigned 6 Nov., 1862.
Lamb, Samuel T., Capt. A. Q. M., 26 Nov., 1862. Mustered out 28 July, 1865.
Lamb, Wm. S., Maj. P. M., 19 Feb., 1863. Mustered out 15 Nov., 1865.
Lamdin, J. Harrison, Capt. A. A. G., 18 May, 1864. Mustered out 19 Sept., 1865.
Lambert, Louis J., Capt. A. A. G., 29 Jan., 1862. Mustered out 12 June, 1866.
Lambert, Wm. H., Capt. A. Q. M., 21 April, 1863. Mustered out 13 March, 1866.
Lamoreau, Daniel R., Capt. C. S., 8 Nov., 1864. Mustered out 10 Jan., 1866.
LaMotte, William A., Capt. A. A. G., 9 Nov., 1863. Mustred out 1 Sept., 1866.
Lanahan, John, Hosp. Chap., 24 July, 1862. Mustered out 26 July, 1865.
Lander, Fred'k W., Brig. Gen., 17 May, 1861. Died 2 March, 1862.
Lander, Wm. W., Capt. C. S., 17 Feb., 1865. Mustered out 3 Aug., 1865.
Lane, James H., Brig. Gen., 18 Dec., 1861. Appointment cancelled 21 March, 1862.
Lane, Gilbert, Hosp. Chap., 16 July, 1864. Mustered out 26 July, 1865.
Langdon, Chas. S., Capt. C. S., 26 Nov., 1862. Mustered out 30 April, 1866.
Langdon, John P., Capt. C. S., 30 June, 1863. Mustered out 7 July, 1866.
Lapham, Wm. B., Capt. A. Q. M., 21 Feb., 1865. Mustered out 30 Oct., 1865.
Laporte, Sam'l McK., Capt. A. Q. M., 19 Feb., 1862. Mustered out 6 June, 1865.
Lappin, Sam'l, Capt. A. Q. M., 26 Nov., 1862. Mustered out 20 Sept., 1865.
Larimore, James W., Hosp. Chap., 20 March, 1865. Mustered out 15 July, 1865.
Larned, Chas. T., Maj. P. M., 1 June, 1861. Vacated commission 30 Aug., 1861.
Larned, D. R., Capt. A. A. G., 13 March, 1863. Resigned 1 June, 1865.
Larned, William, Maj. P. M., 5 Sept., 1861. Died 24 July, 1864.
Latham, Obadiah B., Maj. P. M., 26 Nov., 1862. Resigned 15 March, 1865.

Latshaw, Henry J., Capt. A. Q. M., 9 June, 1862. Cashiered 16 Nov., 1863.
Latshaw, James H., Capt. C. S., 1 Nov., 1864. Died 17 Feb., 1865.
Latta, James W., Capt. A. A. G., 20 April, 1864. Mustered out 20 Jan., 1866.
Lauffer, Sam'l B., Capt. A. Q. M., 14 Aug., 1863. Mustered out 30 April, 1866.
Laughlin, Matthew M., Capt. C. S., 26 Nov., 1862. Mustered out 31 May, 1866.
Laughton, David H., Capt. C. S., 13 Feb., 1865. Resigned 8 June, 1865.
Lauman, Jacob G., Brig. Gen., 21 March, 1862. Mustered out 24 Aug., 1865.
Laurant, Clement G., Capt. A. A. G., 15 May, 1863. Mustered out 16 Feb., 1866.
Law, Sam'l A., Maj. P. M., 30 June, 1862. Appointment revoked 26 Nov., 1862.
Lawler, Michael K., Brig. Gen., 29 Nov., 1862. Mustered out 15 Jan., 1866.
Lawrence, Abram B., Capt. A. Q. M., 29 Feb., 1864. Mustered out 13 March, 1866.
Lawrence, Center H., Capt. A. A. G., 7 Oct., 1862. Resigned 22 June, 1865.
Lawrence, Edward Z., Capt. C. S., 31 Jan., 1865. Mustered out 26 Oct., 1865.
Lawrence, George P., Maj. P. M., 24 July, 1863. Resigned 3 May, 1864.
Lawrence, Henry C., Capt. A. Q. M., 7 April, 1864. Mustered out 8 June, 1866.
Lawrence, Hoel K., Maj. P. M., 30 June, 1862. Cashiered 15 July, 1864.
Lawrence, James V., Capt. C. S., 14 Oct., 1863. Mustered out 15 June, 1865.
Lawrence, Warren W. H., Capt. A. A. G., 14 April, 1862. Resigned 29 Sept., 1862.
Lawrence, Wm. H., Maj. A. de C., 10 Nov., 1862. Mustered out 10 July, 1866.
Lawton, John W., Asst. Surg., 7 Jan., 1863. Maj. Surg., 29 June, 1863. Mustered out 11 Oct., 1866.
Lawyer, Joseph A., Maj. P. M., 1 June, 1861. Mustered out 30 June, 1866.
Lea, James H., Maj. P. M., 23 Feb., 1864. Resigned 11 May, 1864.
Leach, Wm. B., Capt. A. A. G., 16 May, 1862. Resigned 11 Feb., 1864.
Leakin, George A., Hosp. Chap., 14 June, 1862. Mustered out 26 July, 1865.
Leale, Chas. A., Asst. Surg., 8 April, 1865. Mustered out 20 Jan., 1866.
Lebo, Wm. B., Capt. C. S., 31 Oct., 1861. Resigned 5 April, 1864.
Le Conte, John L., Maj. Surg., 9 June, 1862. Lieut. Col. Med. Ins., 29 Aug., 1863. Mustered out 31 Oct., 1865.
Ledlie, James H., Brig. Gen., 24 Dec., 1862. Appointment expired 4 March, 1863. Brig. Gen., 27 Oct., 1863. Resigned 23 Jan., 1865.
Ledlie, Joseph H., Asst. Surg., 18 May, 1864. Maj. Surg., 8 April, 1865. Mustered out 7 Oct., 1865.
Le Duc, Wm. G., Capt. A. Q. M., 14 April, 1862. Resigned 1 Aug., 1865.
Lee, Albert L., Brig. Gen., 29 Nov., 1862. Resigned 4 May, 1865.
Lee, Benj. F., Capt. C. S., 10 Sept., 1862. Resigned 19 Jan., 1863.
Lee, Bradley D., Capt. C. S., 2 March, 1864. Mustered out 9 Oct., 1865.
Lee, George, Capt. A. A. G., 11 March, 1863. Maj., 19 May, 1865. Mustered out 31 Oct., 1866.
Lee, George W., Capt. A. Q. M., 31 Oct., 1861. Mustered out 31 May, 1866.
Lee, James G. C., Capt. A. Q. M., 26 Nov., 1862. Capt. A. Q. M., U. S. A., 2 July, 1864.
Lee, Rob't M., Maj. P. M., 28 July, 1862. Died 21 Sept., 1863.
Leech, John L., Capt. C. S., 26 Nov., 1862. Resigned 6 March, 1865.
Leefe, John G., Capt. A. A. G., 15 June, 1865. Mustered out 22 Nov., 1865.
Leet, George K., Capt. A. A. G., 3 Oct., 1863. Maj., 25 Feb., 1865. Maj. A. A. G., U. S. A., 23 March, 1866.
Leete, James M., Asst. Surg., 9 Oct., 1863. Maj. Surg., 19 Jan., 1864. Mustered out 5 Aug., 1865.
Lefferts, Skidmore E., Capt. A. Q. M., 11 Feb., 1862. Resigned 7 July, 1862.
Leffingwell, Christopher W., Capt. A. Q. M., 10 Sept., 1861. Mustered out 6 Dec., 1865.
Leggett, Mortimer D., Brig. Gen., 29 Nov., 1862. Maj. Gen., 21 Aug., 1865. Resigned 28 Sept., 1865.
Leggett, Wells W., Capt. A. de C., 16 Aug., 1864. Mustered out 11 July,, 1865.
Legler, Henry T., Asst. Surg., 27 March, 1863. Mustered out 4 June, 1866.
Leiby, Chas. K., Capt. C. S., 19 Feb., 1863. Mustered out 4 Jan., 1866.
Leland, George S., Capt. C. S., 1 Sept., 1862. Mustered out 2 Feb., 1866.
Leland, Wm. W., Capt. C. S., 16 Nov., 1861. Discharged 24 June, 1862.
Lelong, Alex., Asst. Surg., 30 Nov., 1864. Mustered out 20 April, 1866.
Lentz, David H., Capt. A. Q. M., 18 May, 1864. Mustered out 5 June, 1866.
Leonard, Chas. H., Capt. A. A. G., 15 May, 1863. Mustered out 12 Jan., 1866.
Leonard, Chauncey, Hosp. Chap., 27 July, 1864. Mustered out 7 Oct., 1865.
Leonard, J. A., Capt. C. S., 2 March, 1864. Mustered out 9 Oct., 1865.
Leonard, Joseph H., Hosp. Chap., 10 Feb., 1865. Mustered out 11 July, 1865.
Leonard, Wm., 2nd Lieut. Sig. Corps, 3 March, 1863. Appointment cancelled 10 Nov., 1864.
Leonard, Wm. G., Hosp. Chap., 7 May, 1864. Mustered out 4 Aug., 1865.
Le Roy, Rob't, Capt. A. A. G., 9 Sept., 1862. Appointment expired 4 March, 1863. Capt. A. A. G., 8 June, 1863. Died 5 March, 1865.
Leski, Wladislas, Capt. Addl. A. de C., 1 May, 1862. Resigned 23 April, 1864.
Letcher, Wm., Capt. C. S., 16 Feb., 1865. Resigned 8 June, 1865.
Levering, John, Capt. A. Q. M., 3 Aug., 1861. Maj. A. A. G., 7 May, 1863. Mustered out 4 Jan., 1866.
Levis, Rich'd J., Asst. Surg., 7 Jan., 1863. Resigned 14 Oct., 1863.
Levy, Benj. J., Capt. C. S., 11 March, 1865. Mustered out 29 June, 1865.
Levy, Cheme M., Capt. A. Q. M., 26 Nov., 1862. Cashiered 9 Oct., 1863.
Lewis, John B., Maj. Surg., 4 April, 1862. Mustered out 7 Oct., 1865.
Lewis, John V., Capt. A. Q. M., 13 Sept., 1862. Confirmed to rank from 26 Nov., 1862. Resigned 25 March, 1865.
Lewis, Joseph D., Capt. C. S., 25 Nov., 1864. Mustered out 30 March, 1866.
Lewis, Micajah G., Capt. A. A. G., 21 July, 1863. Mustered out 19 Sept., 1865.
Lewis, Wm. M., Capt. Addl. A. de C., 30 May, 1862. Mustered out 24 Sept., 1864.
Lidell, John A., Maj. Surg., 3 Aug., 1861. Mustered out 24 June, 1865.
Liebnau, Joseph H., Capt. A. A. G., 6 March, 1862. Resigned 11 Sept., 1863.
Lightburn, Joseph A. J., Brig. Gen., 14 March, 1863. Resigned 22 June, 1865.
Lilley, Wm., Capt. A. Q. M., 16 Oct., 1861. Rejected by Senate 3 Feb., 1862.
Lilly, Henry M., Asst. Surg., 28 March, 1865. Mustered out 13 March, 1867.
Lincoln, C. D., Capt. A. Q. M., 26 Nov., 1862. Appointment expired 4 March, 1863.
Lincoln, Rob't, Capt. C. S., 11 March, 1865. Resigned 12 May, 1865.
Lincoln, Rob't T., Capt. A. A. G., 11 Feb., 1865. Resigned 10 June, 1865.

Link, Rolls C., Capt. A. Q. M., 30 June, 1864. Appointment revoked 8 Sept., 1864.
Linnard, James M., Capt. A. A. G., 27 July, 1864. Resigned 7 June, 1865.
Little, John E., Capt. A. Q. M., 12 Aug., 1863. Resigned 7 March, 1864.
Little, Samuel J., Capt. C. S., 23 Sept., 1861. Mustered out 10 Jan., 1866.
Littleboy, Wm., Capt. C. S., 7 June, 1864. Mustered out 15 June, 1865.
Littlefield, Chas. R., Maj. P. M., 1 Sept., 1863. Mustered out 30 April, 1866.
Littleton, Henry A., Capt. C. S., 12 Aug., 1862. Resigned 29 July, 1863.
Livezey, John C., Capt. C. S., 2 March, 1864. Resigned 14 June, 1865.
Livingston, Lewis, Capt. Addl. A. de C., 3 July, 1862. Resigned 8 March, 1864.
Livsey, Joseph H., Capt. A. A. G., 5 May, 1863. Mustered out 23 Oct., 1865.
Lloyd, Alex. M., Capt. C. S., 7 Sept., 1861. Resigned 5 Feb., 1862.
Lloyd, Alfred J., Capt. A. Q. M., 7 April, 1864. Mustered out 28 July, 1865.
Lloyd, Fred'k, Asst. Surg., 15 Aug., 1863. Maj. Surg., 14 Nov., 1863. Mustered out 23 Sept., 1865.
Locke, Eric, Maj. P. M., 5 Aug., 1861. Resigned 9 June, 1864.
Locke, Fred'k T., Capt. A. A. G., 2 Sept., 1861. Mustered out 19 Sept., 1865.
Locke, Henry W., Capt. C. S., 18 May, 1864. Mustered out 27 Nov., 1865.
Locke, Richard B., Capt. A. Q. M., 17 July, 1863. Discharged 19 Nov., 1864.
Lockerby, Abner P., Capt. A. Q. M., 7 Feb., 1865. Mustered out 28 July, 1865.
Lockwood, George, Capt. A. Q. M., 18 May, 1864. Mustered out 13 July, 1866.
Lockwood, Henry C., Capt. Addl. A. de C., 31 March, 1862. Mustered out 4 Jan., 1866.
Lockwood, Henry H., Brig. Gen., 8 Aug., 1861. Mustered out 24 Aug., 1865.
Lockwood, John B., Maj. P. M., 21 Feb., 1863. Resigned 5 Aug., 1865.
Loewenthal, Herman, Asst. Surg., 20 April, 1864. Mustered out 24 Aug., 1865.
Lofland, Gordon, Capt. A. A. G., 22 April, 1863. Mustered out 19 Sept., 1865.
Lofland, James R., Maj. P. M., 19 Feb., 1863. Mustered out 15 Jan., 1867.
Logan, John A., Brig. Gen., 21 March, 1862. Maj. Gen., 29 Nov., 1862. Resigned 17 Aug., 1865.
Loman, William G., Maj. Surg., 30 Sept., 1861. Resigned 11 July, 1862.
Long, Andrew K., Jr., Maj. A. A. G., 4 Sept., 1865. Mustered out 31 Jan., 1867.
Long, Christian, Maj. P. M., 19 Feb., 1863. Resigned 21 April, 1863.
Long, Eli, Brig. Gen., 18 Aug., 1864. Mustered out 15 Jan., 1866.
Long, John, Hosp. Chap., 6 Aug., 1862. Mustered out 26 July, 1865.
Long, Wm. H., Capt. A. A. G., 16 Oct., 1862. Maj., 6 Sept., 1864. Mustered out 19 Sept., 1865.
Loomis, M. D. M., Capt. A. Q. M., 5 Aug., 1861. Died 24 Oct., 1862.
Lord, Henry E., Capt. C. S., 7 Nov., 1862. Mustered out 7 July, 1866.
Lord, James H., Capt. A. de C., 22 June, 1865. Mustered out 25 Aug., 1865.
Lord, Thos., Jr., Capt. A. de C., 20 Oct., 1862. Mustered out 31 Oct., 1865.
Loring, Chas. G., Capt. A. Q. M., 3 Feb., 1862. Mustered out 10 Aug., 1865.
Loring, John K., Capt. C. S., 28 May, 1864. Mustered out 28 June, 1865.
Loring, Park H., Asst. Surg., 9 Feb., 1865. Died 16 March, 1865.
Lott, George G., Capt. Addl. A. de C., 2 July, 1862. Mustered out 31 May, 1866.
Loudon, Thomas J., Capt. A. A. G., 21 July, 1863. Drowned 28 Sept., 1863.
Loughead, Joseph P., Capt. C. S., 19 Feb., 1863. Mustered out 13 Dec., 1865.
Lounsberry, Stephen, Maj. P. M., 23 Feb., 1864. Resigned 8 June, 1865.
Lovelace, Chauncey F., Capt. C. S., 7 May, 1864. Mustered out 10 Jan., 1866.
Lovell, Julius, Capt. A. A. G., 24 March, 1862. Mustered out 10 Feb., 1866.
Low, James P., Capt. A. Q. M., 26 Nov., 1862. Mustered out 17 July, 1867.
Lowe, Nath'l, Jr., Capt. A. Q. M., 18 May, 1864. Mustered out 2 Feb., 1866.
Lowe, Uriah S., Capt. A. Q. M., 29 Feb., 1864. Resigned 30 Dec., 1864.
Lowell, Charles R., Brig. Gen., 19 Oct., 1864. Died 20 Oct., 1864, of wounds received in action at Middletown, Va.
Lowrie, James A., Capt. A. A. G., 7 Oct., 1861. Maj. 13 May, 1863. Resigned 12 Oct., 1864.
Lowry, Fielding, Capt. A. Q. M., 18 June, 1861. Resigned 30 June, 1865.
Lowry, John A., Maj. P. M., 5 Sept., 1861. Died 15 April, 1863.
Lowry, Robert, Hosp. Chap., 1 July, 1862. Mustered out 1 Aug., 1866.
Lozier, John H., Hosp. Chap., 2 Feb., 1865. Mustered out 21 Aug., 1865.
Lucas, Josiah M., Capt. C. S., 22 Aug., 1861. Mustered out 26 June, 1865.
Lucas, Thomas J., Brig. Gen., 10 Nov., 1864. Mustered out 15 Jan., 1866.
Ludden, Mandeville T., Capt. C. S., 24 Feb., 1865. Resigned 4 June, 1865.
Luddington, Marshall I., Capt. A. Q. M., 20 Oct., 1862. Maj. Q. M., U. S. A., 18 Jan., 1867.
Ludlow, Edwin, Capt. A. Q. M., 4 April, 1862. Resigned 3 June, 1864.
Ludlow, Jacob R., Maj. Surg., 19 Feb., 1863. Mustered out 10 Nov., 1865.
Ludlow, Wm. H., Maj. Addl. A. de C., 18 Nov., 1861. Mustered out 20 July, 1866.
Ludwick, James B., Capt. Sig. Corps, 3 March, 1863. Mustered out 20 Jan., 1966.
Lunt, Samuel H., Capt. A. Q. M., 26 Nov., 1862. Died 28 July, 1865.
Lupton, James, Maj. P. M., 23 Feb., 1864. Mustered out 30 April, 1866.
Lupton, William C., Maj. P. M., 8 Aug., 1863. Mustered out 31 March, 1866.
Lusby, Robert, Capt. A. A. G., 21 July, 1864. Died 20 Feb., 1865.
Lusk, William T., Capt. A. A. G., 26 June, 1863. Resigned 17 Sept., 1863.
Luther, Henry E., Capt. A. Q. M., 27 Feb., 1865. Mustered out 4 Aug., 1865.
Lyden, Patrick H., Capt. C. S., 2 March, 1865. Mustered out 26 June, 1865.
Lydig, Philip M., Capt. Addl. A. de C., 9 Jan., 1862. Maj. A. A. G., 18 March, 1864. Resigned 25 April, 1865.
Lyman, Charles W., Capt. A. Q. M., 3 Feb., 1862. Resigned 23 March, 1865.
Lyman, George H., Maj. Surg., 3 Aug., 1861. Lieut. Col. Med. Ins., U. S. A., 11 June, 1862. Mustered out 20 Nov., 1865.
Lynch, John A., Capt. A. Q. M., 26 Nov., 1862. Mustered out 20 Sept., 1865.
Lynch, Stafford G., Capt. A. Q. M., 27 Oct., 1863. Mustered out 31 May, 1866.
Lynde, Richard D., Asst. Surg., 19 Feb., 1863. Maj. Surg., 2 Sept., 1863. Mustered out 18 Jan., 1866.
Lynn, Charles F., Capt. C. S., 7 March, 1865. Mustered out 14 Aug., 1865.
Lyon, A. McD., Maj. P. M., 1 June, 1861. Resigned 1 June, 1865.
Lyon, Farnham, Capt. A. Q. M., 18 May, 1864. Mustered out 20 March, 1866.
Lyon, George G., Capt. Addl. A. de C., 2 June, 1862. Maj A. de C., 24 Oct., 1862. Discharged 15 Aug., 1863.
Lyon, Isaac S., 1st Lieut. Sig. Corps, 3 March, 1863. Mustered out 25 Nov., 1865.

Lyon, Lafayette A., Maj. P. M., 1 June, 1861. Resigned 1 June, 1865.
Lyon, Nathaniel, Brig. Gen., 17 May, 1861. Killed 10 Aug., 1861, Battle of Wilson's Creek, Mo.
Lytle, William H., Brig. Gen., 29 Nov., 1862. Died 20 Sept., 1863, of wounds received at the Battle of Chickamauga, Ga.
MacArthur, Chas. L., Capt. A. Q. M., 13 Oct., 1862. Resigned 26 May, 1863.
Mack, Oscar A., Maj. A. de C., 11 March, 1863. Vacated commission 19 June, 1866.
Mackay, Andrew J., Capt. A. Q. M., 7 Oct., 1861. Mustered out 6 Dec., 1865.
Mackenzie, Ranald S., Brig. Gen., 19 Oct., 1864. Mustered out 15 Jan., 1866.
Macomb, John N., Lieut. Col. A. de C., 28 Sept., 1861. Col. Addl. A. de C., 15 May, 1862. Mustered out 31 May, 1866.
Madden, Samuel W., Hosp. Chap., 3 Dec., 1864. Mustered out 21 Aug., 1865.
Mahler, Jacob, Capt. A. Q. M., 21 July, 1862. Resigned 29 June, 1865.
Mahnken, Henry, Capt. A. A. G., 18 May, 1864. Mustered out 15 Sept., 1866.
Maitland, John B., Capt. A. A. G., 23 July, 1864. Resigned 1 July, 1865.
Majer, Adolph, Asst. Surg., 4 Oct., 1862. Maj. Surg., 19 Feb., 1863. Dismissed 6 May, 1864.
Male, Wm. H., Capt. A. de C., 10 June, 1865. Mustered out 2 Feb., 1866.
Mallaby, Theodore, Jr., 2nd Lieut. Sig. Corps, 3 March, 1863. Mustered out 1 Feb., 1866.
Mallam, Chas. E., Capt. A. A. G., 25 Nov., 1864. Mustered out 19 Sept., 1865.
Mallett, Edward J., Maj. P. M., 12 Aug., 1863. Resigned 30 Dec., 1864.
Malloch, Edward C., Asst. Surg., 30 June, 1864. Mustered out 9 Oct., 1865.
Mallory, Wm. L., Capt. C. S., 9 Sept., 1861. Resigned 11 Nov., 1864.
Malone, Benj., Maj. P. M., 10 March, 1863. Mustered out 31 July, 1865.
Maltby, Jasper A., Brig. Gen., 4 Aug., 1863. Mustered out 15 Jan., 1866.
Manchester, Joseph S., Capt. C. S., 25 June, 1864. Mustered out 4 Aug., 1865.
Mandeville, Myron H., Capt. A. Q. M., 18 Nov., 1862. Mustered out 13 March, 1866.
Manly, Uri, Capt. A. Q. M., 26 Nov., 1862. Died 11 Nov., 1864.
Mann, James, Maj. P. M., 30 June, 1862. Mustered out 15 Jan., 1866.
Mann, James C., Capt. A. Q. M., 29 Feb., 1864. Mustered out 8 Dec., 1866.
Mann, Wesley S., Maj. P. M., 16 July, 1862. Resigned 27 April, 1863.
Manning, Stephen H., Capt. A. Q. M., 26 Nov., 1862. Mustered out 5 Oct., 1866.
Mansfield, Joseph K. F., Maj. Gen., 18 July, 1862. Died 18 Sept., 1862, of wounds received at Battle of Antietam, Md.
Manson, Mahlon D., Brig. Gen., 24 March, 1862. Resigned 21 Dec., 1864.
Maple, Chas. H., Capt. C. S., 11 March, 1863. Mustered out 18 Aug., 1865.
Marcy, Randolph B., Brig. Gen., 23 Sept., 1861. Expired by Constitutional limitation 17 July, 1862. Brig. Gen., 13 Sept., 1862, to rank 23 Sept., 1861. Expired by Constitutional limitation 4 March, 1863.
Mark, Cyrus K., Capt. A. Q. M., 17 Nov., 1862. Resigned 15 March, 1865.
Markoe, John, Capt. Addl. A. de C., 23 May, 1862. Resigned 4 Oct., 1862.
Marrener, Edward, Maj. A. A. G., 23 Oct., 1864. Resigned 5 June, 1865.
Marrow, Isaac H., Capt. Addl. A. de C., 18 March, 1862. Resigned 9 May, 1863.
Marsh, Nathan F., Asst. Surg., 13 Oct., 1863. Maj. Surg., 19 Jan., 1864. Mustered out 7 Oct., 1865.
Marshall, George S., Capt. A. A. G., 24 Oct., 1862. Discharged 6 Oct., 1863.
Marshall, George W., Capt. A. Q. M., 8 May, 1864. Mustered out 17 July, 1867.
Marshall, James, Hosp. Chap., 23 June., 1862. Mustered out 7 April, 1866.
Marshall, John E., Capt. A. A. G., 11 March, 1863. Mustered out 11 Nov., 1865.
Marshall, Louis H., Col. Addl. A. de C., 30 June, 1862. Mustered out 28 July, 1865.
Marshall, William L., Maj. A. A. G., 27 May, 1863. Mustered out 19 Sept., 1865.
Marston, Frank W., Maj. Sig. Corps, 3 March, 1863. Resigned 10 Feb., 1865.
Marston, George, Maj. P. M., 1 June, 1861. Mustered out 7 May, 1867.
Marston, Gilman, Brig. Gen., 29 Nov., 1862. Resigned 20 April, 1865.
Marston, Simon R., Maj. P. M., 26 Nov., 1862. Mustered out 30 June, 1866.
Marthell, Emil, Capt. C. S., 19 Feb., 1863. Mustered out 31 July, 1865.
Martin, Benj'n L., Maj. P. M., 15 Sept., 1863. Mustered out 1 Dec., 1865.
Martin, Henry A., Maj. Surg., 4 Oct., 1862. Resigned 5 Nov., 1864.
Martin, James R., Capt. A. Q. M., 18 May, 1864. Appointment cancelled 22 Nov., 1864.
Martin, Malachi, Capt. A. Q. M., 1 May, 1862. Mustered out 13 March, 1866.
Martin, Morgan L., Maj. P. M., 17 Aug., 1861. Resigned 28 April, 1865.
Martin, Oramel, Maj. Surg., 3 Aug., 1861. Resigned 23 July, 1862.
Martin, Wm. J., Maj. P. M., 5 Sept., 1861. Mustered out 20 July, 1866.
Martin, Wm. P., Capt. C. S., 30 Aug., 1862. Mustered out 27 Dec., 1866.
Martindale, Edward, Capt. C. S., 19 Sept., 1861. Resigned 2 May, 1864.
Martindale, Francis E., Asst. Surg., 17 Feb., 1865. Mustered out 4 Jan., 1866.
Martindale, John H., Brig. Gen., 9 Aug., 1861. Resigned 13 Sept., 1864.
Marvin, Azor S., Capt. A. A. G., 29 Oct., 1862. Resigned 18 Jan., 1865.
Marvin, Selden E., Maj. P. M., 27 Aug., 1863. Resigned 27 Dec., 1864.
Mason, Addison G., Capt. A. de C., 25 April, 1863. Discharged 2 May, 1865.
Mason, Albert, Capt. A. Q. M., 7 April, 1864. Mustered out 30 Oct., 1865.
Mason, Eddy D., Capt. A. A. G., 30 Sept., 1862. Mustered out 1 Sept., 1866.
Mason, F. H., Capt. A. de C., 18 June, 1863. Discharged 15 Aug., 1863.
Mason, George W., Capt. A. Q. M., 30 June, 1864. Mustered out 6 Dec., 1865.
Mason, Isaac N., Capt. A. Q. M., 17 July, 1862. Mustered out 31 May, 1866.
Mason, John S., Brig. Gen., 29 Nov., 1862. Mustered out 30 April, 1866.
Mason, Julian O., Maj. P. M., 5 Sept., 1861. Resigned 1 Aug., 1864.
Mason, Wm. P., Capt. Addl. A. de C., 13 Nov., 1861. Discharged 31 March, 1863.
Massett, Benj. W. C., Maj. P. M., 26 Nov., 1862. Died 15 July, 1863.
Massey, George V., Capt. A. A. G., 13 Nov., 1863. Resigned 1 Sept., 1864.
Masters, Hibbert B., Capt. C. S., 10 Sept., 1862. Mustered out 25 Aug., 1865.
Mather, Wm. L., Hosp. Chap., 22 April, 1863. Mustered out 8 July, 1865.
Matteson, Henry C., Capt. A. Q. M., 2 May, 1863. Resigned 13 May, 1864.
Matthews, Howard, Maj. P. M., 1 June, 1861. Discharged 17 Dec., 1862.
Matthews, Oliver, Capt. A. A. G., 11 March, 1863. Mustered out 26 Oct., 1865.
Matthewson, Harley P., Asst. Surg., 7 Jan., 1863. Maj. Surg., 28 March, 1865. Mustered out 7 Oct., 1865.
Matthies, Chas. L., Brig. Gen., 29 Nov., 1862. Resigned 16 May, 1864.
Maupin, Algernon T., Capt. A. Q. M., 26 Nov., 1862. Mustered out 11 Nov., 1864.

**Maxwell**, Hugh W., Capt. C. S., 24 Nov., 1862. Resigned 9 March, 1863.
**May**, George, Capt. C. S., 30 June, 1864. Dismissed 21 April, 1865.
**May**, Henry C., Asst. Surg., 20 April, 1865. Mustered out 11 Oct., 1865.
**Mayall**, Sam'l, Capt. A. Q. M., 11 June, 1862. Resigned 29 July, 1864.
**Mayborn**, Joseph H., Maj. P. M., 19 Feb., 1863. Mustered out 1 Dec., 1865.
**Mayell**, Henry, 2nd Lieut. Sig. Corps, 3 March, 1863. Mustered out 1 May, 1866.
**Mayer**, Brantz, Maj. P. M., 19 Feb., 1863. P. M. U. S. A., 17 Jan., 1867.
**Mayhew**, Nathan, Capt. C. S., 26 Nov., 1862. Resigned 19 Aug., 1864.
**Maylert**, Asa P., Maj. Surg., 4 Sept., 1861. Resigned 5 Jan., 1864.
**Mayo**, Chas., Maj. Surg., 19 Feb., 1863. Resigned 8 Sept., 1863.
**McAllister**, Rich'd, Capt. C. S., 3 Aug., 1861. Resigned 1 June, 1864.
**McAllister**, Wm. H., Maj. P. M., 19 Feb., 1863. Mustered out 15 Jan., 1866.
**McArthur**, John, Brig. Gen., 21 March, 1862. Mustered out 24 Aug., 1865.
**McBlair**, John H., Maj. P. M., 1 June, 1861. Mustered out 1 Nov., 1865.
**McCall**, George A., Brig. Gen., 17 May, 1861. Resigned 31 March, 1863.
**McCall**, Samuel B., Capt. C. S., 11 March, 1865. Mustered out 31 July, 1865.
**McCall**, Thos. C., Capt. A. Q. M., 18 March, 1864. Mustered out 27 Nov., 1865.
**McCallum**, Daniel C., Col. Addl. A. de C., 11 Feb., 1862. Mustered out 31 July, 1866.
**McCammon**, Wm. W., Capt. A. A. G., 3 Feb., 1865. Mustered out 2 Feb., 1866.
**McCann**, T. K., Capt. A. Q. M., 15 July, 1863. Resigned 26 June, 1865.
**McCarthy**, Patrick F., Hosp. Chap., 2 Oct., 1863. Mustered out 21 Aug., 1865.
**McCoy**, Robert B., Maj. Surg., 4 Sept., 1861. Mustered out 20 July, 1865.
**McClellan**, Arthur, Capt. Addl. A. de C., 26 Aug., 1861. Maj. A. de C., 7 March, 1865. Mustered out 13 July, 1865.
**McClellan**, Carswell, Capt. A. A. G., 1 Oct., 1862. Discharged 16 Nov., 1864.
**McClellan**, John J., Capt. A. Q. M., 18 May, 1864. Mustered out 19 May, 1866.
**McClernand**, John A., Brig. Gen., 17 May, 1861. Maj. Gen., 21 March, 1862. Resigned 30 Nov., 1864.
**McClintock**, Ebenezer, Asst. Surg., 30 June, 1864. Mustered out 27 July, 1865.
**McClintock**, John S., Capt. C. S., 24 Oct., 1864. Mustered out 19 May, 1866.
**McClosky**, Francis K., 2nd Lieut. Sig. Corps, 3 March, 1863. Mustered out 29 Aug., 1865.
**McCloughry**, R. W., Maj. P. M., 20 April, 1864. Mustered out 12 Oct., 1865.
**McCluer**, Benj'n, Asst. Surg., 4 Feb., 1864. Maj. Surg., 30 Sept., 1864. Mustered out 27 Feb., 1866.
**McClung**, David W., Capt. A. Q. M., 19 Feb., 1862. Mustered out 8 Nov., 1865.
**McClure**, Alex. K., Maj. A. A. G., 5 Sept., 1862. Resigned 27 Feb., 1863.
**McClure**, Chas., Capt. C. S., 28 April, 1862. Capt. C. S., U. S. A., 17 Aug., 1866.
**McClure**, James R., Capt. Addl. A. de C., 29 Jan., 1862. Discharged 21 March, 1862.
**McClure**, John W., Capt. A. Q. M., 21 Oct., 1862. Mustered out 20 June, 1865.
**McClure**, Wm. J., Capt. C. S., 12 May, 1862. Resigned 19 March, 1863.
**McClurg**, Alex. C., Capt. A. A. G., 29 Feb., 1864. Mustered out 19 Sept., 1865.
**McClurg**, John R., Maj. Surg., 4 Oct., 1862. Mustered out 7 Oct., 1865.
**McConnell**, Benton, Maj. P. M., 19 Feb., 1863. Mustered out 1 Nov., 1865.
**McConnell**, George M., Maj. P. M., 20 April, 1864. Mustered out 31 July, 1865.
**McCook**, Alex. McD., Brig. Gen., 3 Sept., 1861. Maj. Gen., 17 July, 1862. Resigned 21 Oct., 1865.
**McCook**, Daniel, Capt. A. A. G., 9 Nov., 1861. Resigned 10 Oct., 1862. Brig. Gen., 16 July, 1864. Died 17 July, 1864, of wounds received in the Battle of Kennesaw Mountain.
**McCook**, Edward M., Brig. Gen., 27 April, 1864. Mustered out 15 Jan., 1866.
**McCook**, John J., Capt. A. de C., 18 June, 1863. Resigned 13 Oct., 1864.
**McCook**, Rob't L., Brig. Gen., 21 March, 1862. Died 6 Aug., 1862, of wounds received by guerillas while en route to Decherd, Tenn.
**McCormick**, Reuben A., Capt. A. Q. M., 29 Feb., 1864. Mustered out 13 March, 1866.
**McCoy**, Andrew J., Capt. C. S., 20 May, 1863. Mustered out 3 Aug., 1865.
**McCoy**, James C., Capt. A. de C., 11 March, 1863. Maj., 4 July, 1863. Mustered out 1 Sept., 1866.
**McCoy**, Joseph S., Capt. A. A. G., 6 March, 1862. Resigned 25 July, 1862.
**McCracken**, Marcus W., Capt. C. S., 20 May, 1863. Died 4 Aug., 1864.
**McCreary**, Wm. G., Capt. Sig. Corps, 3 March, 1863. Mustered out 30 Aug., 1865.
**McCullough**, Peter, Capt. C. S., 9 Sept., 1864. Mustered out 9 Oct., 1865.
**McCullough**, Wm. P., Capt. A. Q. M., 9 March, 1865. Mustered out 28 July, 1865.
**McCune**, Rob't, Hosp. Chap., 23 June, 1862. Mustered out 21 Aug., 1865.
**McCurdy**, John, Asst. Surg., 8 Jan., 1864. Resigned 10 Feb., 1865.
**McDermid**, John J., Capt. A. Q. M., 18 May, 1864. Mustered out 21 Aug., 1866.
**McDermont**, Clarke, Maj. Surg., 14 April, 1862. Mustered out 30 Dec., 1865.
**McDermott**, Wm. J., Asst. Surg., 26 Oct., 1864. Mustered out 21 Oct., 1865.
**McDill**, Thos. H., Capt. A. Q. M., 27 Feb., 1863. Resigned 2 July, 1863.
**McDonald**, Chas., Capt. A. A. G., 23 Dec., 1862. Resigned 18 Aug., 1863.
**McDonald**, Isaiah B., Capt. C. S., 14 April, 1862. Resigned 27 June, 1864.
**McDonald**, James, Capt. C. S., 26 Nov., 1862. Mustered out 2 Feb., 1866.
**McDonald**, John E., Asst. Surg., 27 March, 1863. Maj. Surg., 13 April, 1863. Mustered out 12 July, 1865.
**McDonald**, Wm. O., Asst. Surg., 14 May, 1863. Maj. Surg., 15 Sept., 1864. Resigned 21 June, 1865.
**McDonnell**, Edward, Maj. Surg., 21 June, 1862. Mustered out 27 July, 1865.
**McDougall**, Wm., Capt. C. S., 3 Aug., 1861. Resigned 4 Feb., 1863.
**McDowell**, Henry Clay, Capt. A. A. G., 19 Nov., 1861. Resigned 27 Aug., 1862.
**McDowell**, Irvin, Maj. Gen., 14 March, 1862. Mustered out 1 Sept., 1866.
**McDowell**, Malcolm, Maj. P. M., 1 June, 1861. Resigned 25 Feb., 1865.
**McDowell**, Wm. P., Maj. A. A. G., 11 March, 1863. Resigned 9 Dec., 1863.
**McElroy**, Frank G., Capt. A. Q. M., 2 July, 1864. Mustered out 26 Oct., 1865.
**McElroy**, James N., Maj. J. A., 26 Sept., 1864. Mustered out 1 March, 1866.
**McEntee**, Chas. S., Capt. A. Q. M., 29 Feb., 1864. Mustered out 31 Oct., 1865.
**McFalls**, Thaddeus B., Hosp. Chap., 23 June, 1862. Mustered out 15 Jan., 1866.
**McFarland**, Henry, Maj. P. M., 26 Nov., 1862. Mustered out 15 Jan., 1866.
**McFarland**, James H., Hosp. Chap., 4 June, 1862. Died 23 March, 1863.
**McFarland**, John D., Capt. A. A. G., 27 Nov., 1862. Resigned 26 Oct., 1864.
**McGinnis**, George F., Brig. Gen., 29 Nov., 1862. Mustered out 24 Aug., 1865.

McGirr, John E., Asst. Surg., 29 Nov., 1864. Mustered out 4 Jan., 1866.
McGlynn, Edward, Hosp. Chap., 22 April, 1863. Mustered out 21 Aug., 1865.
McGonnigle, Andrew J., Capt. A. Q. M., 18 March, 1864. Capt. A. Q. M., U. S. A., 19 May, 1865.
McGowan, Robert, Asst. Surg., 9 Sept., 1863. Mustered out 3 Nov., 1865.
McGowan, Theodore, Capt. A. A. G., 14 July, 1862. Mustered out 1 July, 1866.
McGrane, Peter, Hosp. Chap., 9 Oct., 1862. Appointment expired 4 March, 1863. Reappointed 22 April, 1863. Mustered out 26 July, 1865.
McGrath, John P., Maj. P. M., 19 Feb., 1863. Mustered out 20 July, 1866.
McGrath, Matthew F., Hosp. Chap., 13 June, 1862. Resigned 1 Oct., 1863.
McGraw, Theodore A., Asst. Surg., 30 March, 1864. Resigned 12 June, 1865.
McGregor, John P., Maj. P. M., 26 Nov., 1862. Appointment expired 4 March, 1863.
McGrew, John S., Asst. Surg., 26 July, 1864. Maj. Surg., 20 Jan., 1865. Mustered out 3 Nov., 1865.
McHarg, John, Capt. A. Q. M., 5 Aug., 1861. Mustered out 15 June, 1865.
McHenry, Samuel L., Capt. A. A. G., 1 June, 1863. Mustered out 1 Sept., 1866.
McIlvaine, Isaac, Hosp. Chap., 11 July, 1862. Mustered out 14 July, 1865.
McIntire, James, Maj. P. M., 30 June, 1864. Resigned 29 May, 1865.
McIntire, Samuel B., Capt. C. S., 5 Oct., 1864. Mustered out 10 Aug., 1865.
McIntire, William N., Maj. P. M., 26 Nov., 1862. Resigned 8 Dec., 1865.
McIntosh, Alexander, Capt. A. Q. M., 29 Feb., 1864. Mustered out 20 April, 1866.
McIntosh, John B., Brig. Gen., 21 July, 1864. Mustered out 30 April, 1866.
McKay, James H., Capt. A. Q. M., 14 April 1862. Resigned 31 Dec., 1863.
McKean, Allen, Maj. P. M., 23 Feb., 1864. Resigned 3 June, 1865.
McKean, Edwin R., Capt. C. S., 30 Aug., 1862. Resigned 13 May, 1864.
McKean, Thomas J., Maj. P. M., 1 June, 1861. Brig. Gen., 21 Nov., 1861. Mustered out 24 Aug., 1865.
McKee, D. D., Hosp. Chap., 22 April, 1863. Resigned 14 June, 1865.
McKee, Hugh L., Capt. C. S., 4 May, 1863. Resigned 29 June, 1865.
McKeen, Nineveh S., Capt. C. S., 26 Jan., 1865. Mustered out 18 Aug., 1865.
McKelvey, Samuel, Capt. C. S., 3 Aug., 1861. Mustered out 30 June, 1865.
McKenney, Thomas J., Maj. Addl. A. de C., 17 April, 1862. Mustered out 10 Aug., 1865.
McKenney, James E., Maj. P. M., 23 Feb., 1864. Resigned 8 June, 1865.
McKenzie, Alexander, Capt. A. Q. M., 27 Jan., 1865. Mustered out 15 Aug., 1865.
McKenzie, J. M., Capt. C. S., 31 Oct., 1861. Mustered out 31 Aug., 1865.
McKeon, Matthew J., Maj. P. M., 28 May, 1864. Mustered out 15 Nov., 1865.
McKibben, Thomas, Maj. P. M., 5 Aug., 1861. Resigned 31 July, 1862.
McKibbin, David J., Maj. Surg., 21 Oct., 1861. Mustered out 28 June, 1865.
McKibbin, Gilbert H., Capt. A. A. G., 6 Oct., 1862. Mustered out 19 Sept., 1865.
McKibbin, Joseph C., Col. Addl. A. de C., 29 Nov., 1861. Resigned 29 Jan., 1864.
McKim, John W., Capt. A. Q. M., 30 Oct., 1863. Mustered out 7 May, 1867.
McKim, Philip, Hosp. Chap., 19 Oct., 1863. Mustered out 21 Aug., 1865.
McKim, William W., Capt. A. Q. M., 3 Aug., 1861. Capt. A. Q. M., U. S. A., 2 July, 1864.
McKinney, Albert, Maj. P. M., 28 May, 1864. Mustered out 1 Dec., 1865.
McKinney, David, Capt. A. Q. M., 5 March, 1865. Mustered out 7 Oct., 1865.
McKinney, David L., Capt. A. Q. M., 26 Nov., 1862. Died 18 Feb., 1864.
McKinney, Edward P., Capt. C. S., 18 May, 1864. Mustered out 8 July, 1865.
McKinstry, Justus, Brig. Gen., 2 Sept., 1861. Appointment expired 17 July, 1862.
McKnight, Robert P., Capt. A. A. G., 11 March, 1863. Resigned 25 Feb., 1864.
McKusick, Jonathan E., Capt. A. Q. M., 19 Feb., 1863. Mustered out 27 June, 1866.
McLean, Nath'l C., Brig. Gen., 29 Nov., 1862. Resigned 20 April, 1865.
McLean, William A., Capt. C. S., 18 May, 1864. Mustered out 14 July, 1865.
McLellan, Hayden, Maj. P. M., 25 April, 1865. Mustered out 15 Feb., 1866.
McLelland, Wm. E., Capt. C. S., 19 Feb., 1863. Resigned 18 March, 1864.
McLeod, Alexander, Hosp. Chap., 28 July, 1862. Mustered out 26 July, 1865.
McLyman, Wm. H., Capt. C. S., 6 Oct., 1862. Mustered out 22 Aug., 1865.
McMahan, Abraham, Asst. Surg., 18 May, 1864. Maj. Surg., 30 Aug., 1864. Mustered out 12 Oct., 1865.
McMahon, Martin T., Capt. Addl. A. de C., 25 Oct., 1861. Maj. A. de C., 29 Oct., 1862. Appointment as Maj. A. de C. revoked 14 Feb., 1863. Mustered out 21 Feb., 1866.
McMartin, Thos., Maj. Surg., 8 Aug., 1862. Discharged 10 Feb., 1863.
McMasters, Starling Y., Hosp. Chap., 16 July, 1862. Resigned 25 March, 1863.
McMichael, John, Capt. C. S., 18 Nov., 1862. Cashiered 6 Jan., 1864.
McMichael, Wm., Capt. A. A. G., 15 Aug., 1861. Maj., 16 Aug., 1862. Mustered out 20 March, 1866.
McMillan, Chas., Maj. Surg., 3 Aug., 1861. Mustered out 7 Oct., 1865.
McMillan, James W., Brig. Gen., 29 Nov., 1862. Resigned 15 May, 1865.
McMillan, Lucien, Capt. C. S., 25 Feb., 1865. Mustered out 15 June, 1865.
McMonagle, John H., Hosp. Chap., 17 Feb., 1864. Mustered out 21 Aug., 1865.
McMurdy, Rob't, Hosp. Chap., 11 June, 1862. Mustered out 7 Oct., 1865.
McMurray, John, Capt. C. S., 5 Aug., 1862. Mustered out 11 April, 1866.
McNeal, Francis A., Hosp. Chap., 18 July, 1862. Mustered out 4 Aug., 1865.
McNeal, John, Brig. Gen., 29 Nov., 1862. Resigned 12 April, 1865.
McNulty, James M., Maj. Surg., 19 Feb., 1863. Resigned 5 Feb., 1865.
McNulty, John, Maj. Surg., 2 Oct., 1861. Mustered out 27 July, 1865.
McNutt, Joseph G., Capt. A. Q. M., 18 May, 1864. Mustered out 24 June, 1865.
McPhail, Daniel H., Maj. P. M., 1 June, 1861. Mustered out 1 Jan., 1869.
McPherson, James B., Lieut. Col. Addl. A. de C., 12 Nov., 1861. Col., 1 May, 1862. Brig. Gen., 15 May, 1862. Maj. Gen., 8 Oct., 1862. Killed 22 July, 1864, near Atlanta, Ga.
McPherson, M. L., Capt. C. S., 6 March, 1862. Resigned 12 June, 1865.
McQuade, John F., Capt. A. de C., 20 Aug., 1862. Appointment revoked 14 Feb., 1863.
McQuilkin, Rob't, Capt. C. S., 28 May, 1864. Resigned 3 June, 1865.
McRuer, Daniel, Maj. Surg., 3 Aug., 1861. Resigned 2 Sept., 1862.
McVean, John J., Capt. A. A. G., 13 Aug., 1864. Resigned 9 June, 1865.
McVickar, Brockholst M., Maj. Surg., 4 April, 1862. Resigned 14 May, 1862.
Meacham, Frank, Asst. Surg., 23 April,

1863. Maj. Surg., 9 July, 1863. Mustered out 10 Aug., 1865.
Meacham, Thos. G., Asst. Surg., 7 Feb., 1865. Mustered out 5 Aug., 1865.
Meade, George, Capt. A. de C., 22 May, 1863. Mustered out 1 Sept., 1866.
Meade, George B., Brig. Gen., 31 Aug., 1861. Maj. Gen., 29 Nov., 1862. Maj. Gen. U. S. A., 18 Aug., 1864.
Meade, George U., Capt. A. Q. M., 19 Feb., 1863. Mustered out 27 Nov., 1865.
Meagher, Thos. Francis, Brig. Gen., 3 Feb., 1862. Resigned 15 May, 1865.
Meeker, Edwin I., Capt. Sig. Corps, 3 March, 1863. Mustered out 25 Nov., 1865.
Means, James, Hosp. Chap., 13 June, 1862. Died 6 April, 1863.
Mears, George W., Capt. C. S., 10 Sept., 1862. Resigned 19 Dec., 1863.
Mears, James R., Maj. P. M., 26 Nov., 1862. Mustered out 1 Dec., 1865.
Mears, Rob't, Capt. C. S., 26 Nov., 1862. Resigned 9 March, 1863.
Meatyard, Thos. C., Capt. A. A. G., 30 March, 1863. Mustered out 13 Oct., 1865.
Meech, Wm. W., Hosp. Chap., 15 July, 1862. Mustered out 4 Aug., 1865.
Meek, John B., Hosp. Chap., 18 Aug., 1862. Discharged 26 Dec., 1862.
Meeker, Daniel, Maj. Surg., 2 Oct., 1861. Mustered out 15 Aug., 1865.
Meigs, Sam'l E., Capt. A. Q. M., 14 Nov., 1861. Resigned 31 March, 1863.
Meline, James F., Maj. Addl. A. de C., 30 June, 1862. Mustered out 8 Sept., 1866.
Melton, Rich'd H., Capt. C. S., 2 March, 1864. Resigned 24 Dec., 1864.
Melville, George S., Capt. A. de C., 11 May, 1864. Mustered out 20 July, 1865.
Melvin, Thayer, Capt. A. A. G., 14 July, 1862. Mustered out 3 Nov., 1865.
Mendenhall, John, Maj. J. A., 17 March, 1863. Mustered out 23 Oct., 1865.
Mendenhall, Washington B., Maj. P. M., 26 Nov., 1862. Mustered out 15 Jan., 1866.
Meneely, Clinton H., Maj. Addl. A. de C., 11 April, 1862. Mustered out 31 May, 1866.
Meredith, Aaron A., Capt. C. S., 11 June, 1862. Mustered out 9 Oct., 1865.
Meredith, Solomon, Brig. Gen., 6 Oct., 1862. Mustered out 24 Aug., 1865.
Meredith, Stephen, Capt. C. S., 2 Feb., 1865. Resigned 24 May, 1865.
Meredith, Sullivan A., Brig. Gen., 29 Nov., 1862. Mustered out 24 Aug., 1865.
Merion, Nathaniel, Capt. C. S., 5 Aug., 1861. Resigned 14 May, 1862.
Merrell, Henry B., Capt. C. S., 21 March, 1863. Mustered out 9 Oct., 1865.
Merriam, Joseph W., Asst. Surg., 7 Jan., 1863. Mustered out 27 July, 1865.
Merrill, Elias, Maj. P. M., 29 Nov., 1862. Resigned 27 Oct., 1864.
Merrill, George, Capt. A. A. G., 21 April, 1862. Resigned 25 Sept., 1862.
Merrill, Jesse, Capt. Sig. Corps, 3 March, 1863. Mustered out 3 Oct., 1865.
Merritt, Abraham C., 2nd Lieut. Sig. Corps, 3 March, 1863. Resigned 20 Feb., 1865.
Merritt, Charles M., Capt. A. Q. M., 18 May, 1864. Mustered out 20 Sept., 1865.
Merritt, Edwin A., Capt. C. S., 18 May, 1864. Resigned 27 Dec., 1864.
Merritt, Nehemiah, Capt. Addl. A. de C., 13 May, 1862. Mustered out 10 Aug., 1865.
Merritt, Wesley, Brig. Gen., 29 June, 1863. Maj. Gen., 1 April, 1865. Mustered out 1 Feb., 1866.
Merritt, William H., Col. Addl. A. de C., 29 Jan., 1862. Discharged 21 March, 1862.
Mervine, Catherinus B., Capt. A. A. G., 15 July, 1862. Died 17 Aug., 1864.
Merwin, James B., Hosp. Chap., 13 June, 1862. Mustered out 21 Aug., 1865.
Meserve, John L., Jr., Capt. C. S., 23 Feb., 1865. Mustered out 8 Dec., 1865.
Messenger, Daniel, Capt. A. Q. M., 16 Nov., 1861. Resigned 17 June, 1865.
Messinger, Charles H., 2nd Lieut. Sig. Corps, 3 March, 1863. Mustered out 25 Nov., 1865.
Metcalfe, Joseph H., Capt. A. A. G., 14 Sept., 1863. Resigned 6 March, 1865.
Metcalf, Lyne S., Capt. A. Q. M., 14 April, 1862. Mustered out 4 Jan., 1866.
Meyers, Ernest J., Capt. A. A. G., 18 March, 1865. Mustered out 19 Oct., 1865.
Meysenberg, Theodore A., Maj. A. A. G., 14 April, 1862. Resigned 19 Dec., 1864.
Michaelis, Otho E., 2nd Lieut. Sig. Corps, 30 Sept., 1863. Vacated commission 10 Dec., 1863.
Mighells, Henry R., Capt. A. A. G., 14 April, 1862. Resigned 15 Oct., 1864.
Miles, John C., Asst. Surg., 11 Oct., 1864. Mustered out 19 Oct., 1865.
Miles, Nelson A., Brig. Gen., 12 May, 1864. Maj. Gen., 21 Oct., 1865. Mustered out 1 Sept., 1866.
Millener, Wm. S., Asst. Surg., 30 June, 1864. Mustered out 27 April, 1866.
Miller, Charles H., Capt. A. A. G., 20 April, 1864. Mustered out 19 Sept., 1865.
Miller, Daniel B., Capt. C. S., 12 Dec., 1864. Mustered out 22 Nov., 1865.
Miller, George M., Capt. A. A. G., 8 Aug., 1862. Resigned 6 Nov., 1862.
Miller, George McC., Asst. Surg., 6 July, 1863. Mustered out 9 Oct., 1865.
Miller, Heman, Capt. A. Q. M., 26 Nov., 1862. Mustered out 28 July, 1865.
Miller, James F., Capt. A. A. G., 7 Aug., 1862. Resigned 16 July, 1864.
Miller, John F., Brig. Gen., 5 Jan., 1864. Resigned 25 Sept., 1865.
Miller, Joseph W., Capt. A. A. G., 9 Oct., 1863. Mustered out 1 April, 1866.
Miller, Josiah, Maj. P. M., 28 July, 1863. Resigned 17 May, 1864.
Miller, Oscar O., Capt. A. A. G., 22 May, 1863. Killed 2 Sept., 1864, at the Battle of Jonesboro, Ga.
Miller, Stephen, Brig. Gen., 26 Oct., 1863. Resigned 18 Jan., 1864.
Miller, Stephen C., Capt. C. S., 2 March, 1864. Mustered out 9 Oct., 1865.
Miller, Theodore, Capt. A. A. G., 30 June, 1862. Resigned 25 Oct., 1862.
Miller, Wm. D. W., Capt. A. de C., 25 June, 1863. Resigned 24 Dec., 1864.
Mills, Arthur H., Capt. A. Q. M., 9 Nov., 1862. Mustered out 10 July, 1866.
Mills, Charles C., Capt. A. A. G., 25 July, 1864. Killed 31 March, 1865, in battle at Hatcher's Run, Va.
Mills, Erastus W., Asst. Surg., 2 July, 1864. Mustered out 8 July, 1865.
Mills, John H. W., Capt. C. S., 19 Feb., 1863. Mustered out 14 July, 1865.
Milroy, Robert H., Brig. Gen., 3 Sept., 1861. Maj. Gen., 29 Nov., 1862. Resigned 26 July, 1865.
Minor, Oscar, Capt. A. A. G., 23 Dec., 1862. Resigned 20 Oct., 1864.
Minor, Phineas R., Capt. C. S., 30 June, 1864. Mustered out 9 Oct., 1865.
Mintzer, St. John W., Asst. Surg., 7 Jan., 1863. Maj. Surg., 29 June, 1863. Mustered out 17 May, 1867.
Mitchel, Edward W., Capt. A. Q. M., 9 June, 1862. Resigned 6 Dec., 1862.
Mitchel, Fred'k A., Capt. A. de C., 3 Sept., 1862. Appointment expired 7 Nov., 1862.
Mitchel, Ormsby M., Brig. Gen., 9 Aug., 1861. Maj. Gen., 11 April, 1862. Died 30 Oct., 1862.
Mitchell, George A., Maj. P. M., 5 Aug., 1861. Mustered out 7 May, 1867.
Mitchell, John G., Brig. Gen., 12 Jan., 1865. Resigned 3 July, 1865.
Mitchell, Lewis B., Capt. A. de C., 17 Feb., 1865. Mustered out 6 Sept., 1865.

Mitchell, Robert B., Brig. Gen., 8 April, 1862. Mustered out 15 Jan., 1866.
Mitchell, Robert W., Capt. A. de C., 25 April, 1863. Appointment vacated 12 March, 1864.
Mitchell, Wm. G., Maj. A. de C., 25 June, 1863. Mustered out 31 July, 1866.
Moe, Seth B., Capt. A. A. G., 26 Aug., 1862. Maj., 30 June, 1864. Mustered out 1 Sept., 1866.
Moer, Samuel H., Capt. A. Q. M., 16 Nov., 1861. Died 28 July, 1865.
Moffatt, Edward S., 2nd. Lieut. Sig. Corps, 3 March, 1863. Mustered out 11 Aug., 1865.
Mong, John C., Capt. C. S., 26 Nov., 1862. Resigned 9 March, 1863.
Monroe, George, Capt. A. A. G., 30 Sept., 1864. Resigned 26 June, 1865.
Monroe, John H., Capt. A. A. G., 23 June, 1863. Resigned 6 Jan., 1865.
Monroe, Thos. H., Hosp. Chap., 21 April, 1864. Mustered out 11 July, 1865.
Monroe, Thos. H. W., Hosp. Chap., 30 Aug., 1862. Appointment expired 4 March, 1863.
Monteith, George, Capt. A. de C., 20 Aug., 1862. Appointment revoked 14 Feb., 1863.
Montgomery, James E., Capt. A. A. G., 21 Oct., 1861. Maj., 1 Aug., 1864. Mustered out 10 July, 1866.
Montgomery, Rich'd R., Maj. J. A., 30 June, 1865. Resigned 14 Feb., 1868.
Montgomery, Thos. J., Capt. C. S., 2 July, 1864. Resigned 7 May, 1865.
Montgomery, Wm. R., Brig. Gen., 17 May, 1861. Resigned 4 April, 1864.
Moonlight, Thos., Capt. A. A. G., 14 April, 1862. Resigned 20 Sept., 1862.
Moore, Alex'r, Capt. A. de C., 10 Nov., 1862. Appointment expired 4 March, 1863. Capt. A. de C., 30 May, 1863. Mustered out 25 Sept., 1866.
Moore, Ambrose Y., Hosp. Chap., 6 Aug., 1862. Mustered out 10 June, 1865.
Moore, Chas. S., Maj. P. M., 18 March, 1864. Mustered out 1 Dec., 1865.
Moore, Edward B., Capt. C. S., 28 May, 1864. Mustered out 31 July, 1865.
Moore, E. Lewis, Capt. A. A. G., 27 Oct., 1864. Mustered out 19 Sept., 1865.
Moore, Edwin L., Maj. P. M., 26 Nov., 1862. Mustered out 1 Feb., 1869.
Moore, Festus H., Capt. C. S., 15 Aug., 1861. Resigned 30 June, 1865.
Moore, H. Miles, Capt. C. S., 7 July, 1864. Resigned 20 Feb., 1865.
Moore, James M., Capt. A. A. Q. M., 11 March, 1863. Capt. A. Q. M., U. S. A., 2 July, 1864.
Moore, John H., Capt. A. Q. M., 28 April, 1862. Died 11 Nov., 1865.
Moore, Joseph, Jr., Maj. P. M., 5 Dec., 1863. Resigned 10 Jan., 1865.
Moore, Joseph L., Capt. C. S., 23 March, 1865. Mustered out 11 Oct., 1865.
Moore, Lazarus L., Capt. A. Q. M., 16 Aug., 1862. Mustered out 15 Nov., 1866.
Moore, Thos. W. C., Capt. A. de C., 18 May, 1864. Maj. A. A. G., 8 March, 1865. Mustered out 1 Aug., 1866.
Moore, Wm. G., Maj. A. A. G., 1 May, 1865. Appointed Maj. P. M., U. S. A., 14 Nov., 1866.
Morell, George W., Brig. Gen., 9 Aug., 1861. Maj. Gen., 4 July, 1862. Appointment as Maj. Gen. expired 4 March, 1863. Mustered out 15 Dec., 1864.
Morey, Benj. F., Capt. A. A. G., 26 Aug., 1864. Mustered out 19 Sept., 1865.
Morford, Wm. E., Capt. A. Q. M., 10 Sept., 1861. Mustered out 10 Sept., 1866.
Morgan, Chas. H., Brig. Gen., 21 March, 1865. Mustered out 15 Jan., 1866.
Morgan, Chas. W., Capt. Addl. A. de C., 14 May, 1862. Mustered out 8 Dec., 1865.
Morgan, Christopher A., Col. Addl. A. de C., 30 June, 1862. Died 20 Jan., 1866.
Morgan, Edwin D., Maj. Gen., 28 Sept., 1861. Resigned 1 Jan., 1863.
Morgan, George W., Brig. Gen., 12 Nov., 1861. Resigned 8 June, 1863.
Morgan, James D., Brig. Gen., 17 July, 1862. Mustered out 24 Aug., 1865.
Morgan, Rob't C., Capt. A. Q. M., 18 June, 1862. Mustered out 1 Oct., 1867.
Morgan, Sam'l M., Capt. A. A. G., 29 Feb., 1864. Resigned 1 April, 1865.
Morgan, Wm. H., Capt. A. A. G., 22 Aug., 1862. Maj. 8 May, 1863. Mustered out 8 Dec., 1865.
Morlan, Jonah, Capt. A. Q. M., 5 Dec., 1863. Resigned 5 June, 1865.
Morledge, John R., Capt. C. S., 12 Nov., 1862. Resigned 1 Aug., 1864.
Morong Edward P., Asst. Surg., 9 Oct., 1863. Maj. Surg., 4 Dec., 1863. Mustered out 3 March, 1866.
Morrell, John A. L., Maj. P. M., 4 Sept., 1861. Mustered out 30 April, 1866.
Morrill, Edmund N., Capt. C. S., 9 Aug., 1862. Mustered out 26 Oct., 1865.
Morrill, Stephen S., Hosp. Chap., 5 June, 1862. Resigned 13 March, 1865.
Morris, Arthur B., Capt. A. Q. M., 26 Nov., 1862. Appointment expired 4 March, 1863.
Morris, John, Capt. A. Q. M., 23 May, 1862. Discharged 22 Sept., 1863.
Morris, John A., Capt. A. Q. M., 16 March, 1863. Resigned 12 March, 1865.
Morris, Wm. G., Capt. A. Q. M., 12 May, 1862. Mustered out 8 Feb., 1866.
Morris, Wm. H., Capt. A. A. G., 20 Aug., 1861. Resigned 1 Sept., 1862. Brig. Gen., 29 Nov., 1862. Mustered out 24 Aug., 1865.
Morrison, James W., Capt. C. S., 4 July, 1864. Resigned 7 May, 1865.
Morrison, John T., Capt. A. Q. M., 18 May, 1864. Resigned 11 March, 1865.
Morrison, Joseph B., Asst. Surg., 19 Feb., 1863. Maj. Surg., 29 June, 1863. Mustered out 2 Feb., 1866.
Morrison, Theophilus W., Capt. A. A. G., 27 Feb., 1863. Resigned 25 Jan., 1865.
Morrow, Rob't, Capt. A. A. G., 14 Sept., 1863. Maj., 25 July, 1865. Mustered out 30 Nov., 1866.
Morse, Augustus, Capt. A. Q. M., 14 July, 1862. Resigned 10 June, 1863.
Morse, Chas. F., Capt. C. S., 30 Aug., 1862. Resigned 10 May, 1865.
Morse, Edmund A., Capt. A. Q. M., 1 Nov., 1862. Mustered out 20 Sept., 1865.
Morse, Edwin C., Maj. P. M., 1 June, 1861. Mustered out 1 Nov., 1865.
Morton, Chas. A., Capt. C. S., 10 Sept., 1862. Resigned 14 June, 1865.
Morton, James St. Clair, Brig. Gen., 29 Nov., 1862. Mustered out 7 Nov., 1863.
Morton, Prince G. D., Capt. A. Q. M., 11 June, 1862. Dismissed 10 March, 1865.
Moseley, Nath'l R., Maj. Surg., 17 Oct., 1861. Mustered out 23 Sept., 1865.
Moseley, Wm. W., Capt. A. de C., 7 May, 1863. Mustered out 13 Oct., 1865.
Moses, Isaac, Capt. A. A. G., 25 Sept., 1861. Maj., 27 Aug., 1862. Resigned 6 July, 1864.
Moses, Israel, Maj. Surg., 4 Oct., 1862. Mustered out 27 July, 1865.
Moss, William, Asst. Surg., 4 Oct., 1862. Maj. Surg., 4 Dec., 1862. Resigned 19 Sept., 1863.
Motley, Thomas L., Maj. A. A. G., 25 Nov., 1864. Mustered out 1 Sept., 1866.
Mott, Alexander B., Maj. Surg., 7 Nov., 1862. Mustered out 27 July, 1865.
Mott, Amos B., Capt. C. S., 14 April, 1862. Resigned 20 Feb., 1865.

Mott, Fred'k, Capt. A. A. G., 3 Feb., 1865. Resigned 8 July, 1865.
Mott, Gersham, Brig. Gen., 7 Sept., 1862. Resigned 20 Feb., 1866.
Mott, John O., Maj. P. M., 20 April, 1864. Mustered out 9 June, 1865.
Mott, John W., Capt. C. S., 30 June, 1862. Mustered out 10 Jan., 1866.
Moulton, Charles W., Capt. A. Q. M., 26 June, 1861. Capt. A. Q. M., U. S. A., 13 March, 1863.
Mower, George H., Capt. A. Q. M., 2 Feb., 1865. Mustered out 28 July, 1865.
Mower, Joseph A., Brig. Gen., 29 Nov., 1862. Maj. Gen., 12 Aug., 1864. Mustered out 1 Feb., 1866.
Moxley, Marcellus K., Asst. Surg., 19 Feb., 1863. Mustered out 9 Oct., 1865.
Muhleman, Jacob R., Capt. A. A. G., 23 Dec., 1862. Maj. 4 Sept., 1863. Mustered out 7 June, 1865.
Mulford, Sylvanus S., Asst. Surg., 4 Oct., 1862. Maj. Surg., 4 Dec., 1862. Resigned 18 July, 1865.
Muller, Edward, Capt. C. S., 2 July, 1863. Mustered out 22 Dec., 1865.
Mullin, Loudon, Capt. A. Q. M., 19 Feb., 1863. Mustered out 28 July, 1865.
Munder, Charles, Capt. A. A. G., 24 Aug., 1861. Maj. 16 Aug., 1862. Mustered out 15 Sept., 1866.
Munson, Samuel, Capt. A. Q. M., 27 Feb., 1865. Mustered out 27 June, 1866.
Munther, Frederick R., Capt. Addl. A. de C., 18 March, 1862. Mustered out 1 Aug., 1865.
Murfey, William A., Capt. C. S., 14 April, 1862. Mustered out 9 Oct., 1865.
Murphy, George W., Capt. C. S., 2 July, 1864. Mustered out 10 Jan., 1866.
Murphy, J. G., Asst. Surg., 25 Nov., 1864. Mustered out 9 Oct., 1865.
Murphy, Patrick J. R., Hosp. Chap., 27 Feb., 1865. Mustered out 21 Aug., 1865.
Murphy, William R., Capt. C. S., 10 Sept., 1862. Mustered out 31 Aug., 1865.
Murray, John, Capt. A. A. G., 27 Aug., 1861. Rejected by Senate 11 March, 1862.
Mursick, George A., Asst. Surg., 9 Oct., 1863. Mustered out 27 July, 1865.
Muscott, John M., Maj. P. M., 20 April, 1864. Mustered out 1 Nov., 1865.
Musser, John H., Capt. C. S., 30 Aug., 1862. Mustered out 13 March, 1866.
Musser, Robert M., Capt. C. S., 3 Aug., 1861. Mustered out 31 May, 1866.
Mussey, William H., Maj. Surg., 10 Oct., 1861. Lieut. Col. Med. Insp., 14 June, 1862. Resigned 1 Jan., 1864.
Muzzey, Loring W., Capt. C. S., 21 March, 1864. Mustered out 13 Oct., 1865.
Myers, Frederick, Maj. Addl. A. de C., 23 May, 1862. Lieut. Col., 15 July, 1862. Mustered out 31 May, 1866.
Myers, Lorenzo D., Capt. A. Q. M., 9 June, 1862. Resigned 2 Dec., 1864.
Myers, William, Col. Addl. A. de C., 14 June, 1862. Mustered out 31 May, 1866.
Nagle, James, Brig. Gen., 10 Sept., 1862. Appointment expired 4 March, 1863. Brig. Gen., 13 March, 1863. Resigned 9 May, 1863.
Nagler, Henry M., Brig. Gen., 4 Feb., 1862. Mustered out 4 April, 1864.
Nash, Chas. W., Capt. A. Q. M., 5 April, 1865. Mustered out 27 June, 1866.
Nash, Wm. H., Capt. C. S., 26 Nov., 1862. Capt. C. S., U. S. A., 17 Nov., 1865.
Nassau, Wm. W., Maj. Surg., 4 April, 1862. Resigned 23 Jan., 1863.
Neale, Wm. L., Capt. A. Q. M., 18 May, 1864. Mustered out 28 July, 1865.
Negley, James S., Brig. Gen., 1 Oct., 1861. Maj. Gen., 29 Nov., 1862. Resigned 19 Jan., 1865.
Neill, Edward D., Hosp. Chap., 26 July, 1862. Resigned 4 Jan., 1864.
Neill, Edward M., Capt. A. A. G., 6 March, 1862. Maj., 11 March, 1863. Resigned 22 Oct., 1864.
Neill, John, Maj. Surg., 11 Sept., 1862. Mustered out 5 July, 1865.
Neill, Thos. H., Brig. Gen., 29 Nov., 1862. Mustered out 24 Aug., 1865.
Nelson, George C., Capt. C. S., 28 Oct., 1862. Mustered out 9 Oct., 1865.
Nelson, James H., Maj. P. M., 23 Feb., 1864. Maj. P. M., U. S. A., 17 Jan., 1867.
Nelson, Wm. F., Hosp. Chap., 8 Aug., 1862. Mustered out 11 July, 1865.
Nelson, Wm., Brig. Gen., 16 Sept., 1861. Maj. Gen., 17 July, 1862. Died 29 Sept., 1862.
Nesmith, Arthur S., Capt. A. Q. M., 22 July, 1863. Mustered out 6 July, 1865.
Nesmith, Clarence E., Capt. C. S., 18 May, 1864. Mustered out 8 Dec., 1865.
Nevin, Alfred, Hosp. Chap., 19 Nov., 1863. Mustered out 15 July, 1865.
Nevin, Wilberforce, Capt. A. A. G., 22 May, 1863. Resigned 20 Jan., 1865.
Newcomer, Chas., Maj. P. M., 26 Nov., 1862. Mustered out 19 Oct., 1865.
Newell, James J., Capt. A. Q. M., 5 Aug., 1861. Resigned 1 Nov., 1862.
Newell, John W., Maj. P. M., 5 Sept., 1861. Mustered out 1 June, 1867.
Newhall, Fred'k C., Maj. A. de C., 3 May, 1864. Resigned 26 June, 1865.
Newport, Reese M., Capt. A. Q. M., 26 Nov., 1862. Resigned 7 Feb., 1866.
Newsham, Thos. J., Capt. A. A. G., 3 Oct., 1861. Resigned 14 April, 1862.
Newson, Thos. M., Capt. C. S., 26 Nov., 1862. Mustered out 9 Oct., 1865.
Newton, George B., Capt. C. S., 29 June, 1862. Mustered out 31 July, 1866.
Newton, John, Brig. Gen., 23 Sept., 1861. Maj. Gen., 30 March, 1863. Appointment as Maj. Gen. revoked 18 April, 1864. Mustered out 31 Jan., 1866.
Niccolls, Rob't, Maj. Surg., 24 Oct., 1861. Mustered out 5 Aug., 1865.
Nicholds, Alphonso N., Maj. P. M., 26 Nov., 1862. Resigned 9 Jan., 1865.
Nicholls, James W., Maj. P. M., 19 Feb., 1863. Maj. P. M., U. S. A., 17 Jan., 1867.
Nichols, George W., Capt. Addl. A. de C., 26 April, 1862. Mustered out 23 Oct., 1865.
Nichols, Wm. A., Capt. C. S., 17 Sept., 1863. Mustered out 4 Aug., 1865.
Nicols, Wm. H., Maj. P. M., 26 Nov., 1862. Mustered out 15 Feb., 1866.
Nickerson, Frank S., Brig. Gen., 29 Nov., 1862. Resigned 13 May, 1865.
Nicodemus, Wm. J. L., Lieut. Col. Sig. Corps, 3 March, 1863. Mustered out 23 Aug., 1865.
Nigh, Elias, Capt. A. Q. M., 5 Aug., 1861. Capt. A. Q. M., U. S. A., 13 March, 1863.
Niles, Peter H., 1st Lieut. Sig. Corps, 3 March, 1863. Mustered out 12 Aug., 1865.
Nims, Henry G., Maj. P. M., 28 May, 1864. Mustered out 1 July, 1867.
Ninninger, Alex. R., Capt. A. A. G., 7 June, 1864. Mustered out 1 Sept., 1866.
Nisson, Lawrence I. I., Capt. A. Q. M., 25 June, 1864. Mustered out 27 Nov., 1865.
Noble, Henry T., Capt. A. Q. M., 8 July, 1863. Mustered out 5 Oct., 1866.
Noble, Leander C., Capt. A. Q. M., 19 Aug., 1862. Resigned 15 Dec., 1864.
Noble, Wm. F. P., Hosp. Chap., 21 April, 1864. Mustered out 14 July, 1865.
Noble, Wm. A., Capt. C. S., 18 May, 1864. Mustered out 12 Oct., 1865.
Noblett, Francis W., Capt. A. A. G., 17 Dec., 1864. Resigned 9 June, 1865.
Norcross, Fred'k M., Capt. A. Q. M., 29 Feb., 1864. Mustered out 13 March, 1866.

Norcross, Nicholas W., Maj. P. M., 26 Nov., 1862. Mustered out 24 April, 1866.
Nordendorf, Craky Sauer de, Capt. Addl. A. de C., 31 March, 1862. Mustered out 30 June, 1862. Capt. Addl. A. de C., 3 July, 1862. Resigned 11 Oct., 1862.
Norris, Benj. W., Maj. P. M., 2 Feb., 1865. Mustered out 31 July, 1865.
Norris, George, Capt. A. Q. M., 26 Nov., 1862. Resigned 23 Nov., 1864.
Norris, Wm. B., Maj. P. M., 26 Nov., 1862. Died 22 March, 1864.
Norris, Wm. E., Maj. P. M., 29 Nov., 1862. Resigned 9 March, 1865.
North, Frank, Maj. P. M., 25 Jan., 1865. Mustered out 31 July, 1866.
Northrup, Nehemiah B., Hosp. Chap., 13 June, 1862. Mustered out 21 Aug., 1865.
Norton, Addison S., Maj. Addl. A. de C., 1 May, 1862. Resigned 15 Oct., 1865.
Norton, Alfred, Capt. C. S., 27 Feb., 1863. Mustered out 31 Dec., 1865.
Norton, Chas. B., Capt. A. Q. M., 11 June, 1862. Resigned 26 Jan., 1863.
Norton, Emory E., Capt. C. S., 27 Feb., 1863. Resigned 7 Jan., 1864.
Norton, George A., Capt. A. Q. M., 25 Sept., 1863. Mustered out 8 Nov., 1865.
Norton, Henry, Capt. A. de C., 20 Aug., 1862. Vacated appointment 5 May, 1865.
Norton, John C., Asst. Surg., 9 Sept., 1863 Maj. Surg., 30 June, 1864. Mustered out 13 Dec., 1865.
Norton, Joshua, Capt. A. Q. M., 1 Nov., 1862. Resigned 6 March, 1865.
Norton, Lemuel B., Capt. Sig. Corps, 3 March, 1863. Mustered out 7 May, 1867.
Norton, Martin, Capt. A. A. G., 29 Feb., 1864. Mustered out 1 July, 1866.
Norvell, Freeman, Capt. A. A. G., 8 May, 1863. Resigned 10 May, 1864.
Norvell, John M., Capt. A. A. G., 30 Aug., 1861. Maj., 22 Aug., 1862. Resigned 21 June, 1865.
Noteware, James H., Maj. P. M., 25 Jan., 1865. Mustered out 31 July, 1865.
Nott, Joel B., Capt. C. S., 31 Oct., 1862. Mustered out 7 May, 1865.
Noyes, Edward H., Capt. C. S., 18 May, 1864. Mustered out 26 June, 1865.
Noyes, Frank G., Capt. C. S., 26 Nov., 1862. Mustered out 9 Oct., 1865.
Noyes, George F., Capt. C. S., 21 April, 1862. Resigned 22 March, 1864.
Nunes, Joseph A., Maj. P. M., 1 June, 1861. Mustered out 15 Nov., 1865.
Noble, Benj'n S., Capt. C. S., 28 July, 1862. Resigned 2 Sept., 1862.
Oakley, Frank W., Capt. A. Q. M., 13 April, 1863. Mustered out 10 Aug., 1865.
Oakley, Thos. B., Maj. P. M., 4 Sept., 1861. Mustered out 12 Jan., 1866.
O'Brien, Thos., Capt. A. Q. M., 31 Oct., 1861. Died 25 Oct., 1863.
O'Connell, Patrick A., Asst. Surg., 4 June 1863. Maj. Surg., 13 June, 1863. Mustered out 27 July, 1865.
Odlin, James H., Capt. A. A. G., 9 June, 1862. Resigned 23 Nov., 1864.
O'Donnell, Wm., Capt. Addl. A. de C., 29 Jan., 1862. Discharged 21 March, 1862.
Ogden, Thomson P., Capt. A. A. G., 12 Dec., 1864. Resigned 7 June, 1865.
Oglesbee, Nathan H., Capt. C. S., 2 March, 1864. Mustered out 9 Oct., 1865.
Oglesby, Rich'd J., Brig. Gen., 21 March, 1862. Maj. Gen., 29 Nov., 1862. Resigned 26 May, 1864.
O'Hara, Daniel, Capt. A. Q. M., 9 Sept., 1862. Appointment revoked 22 Jan., 1863.
O'Hare, Thomas, Capt. C. S., 17 Sept., 1864. Mustered out 15 Aug., 1865.
O'Keefe, Joseph, Capt. Addl. A. de C., 24 April, 1862. Resigned 29 Nov., 1864.
Oldershaw, Percival P., Capt. A. A. G., 26 Aug., 1862. Resigned 6 Nov., 1863.
Olin, Rollin C., Capt. A. A. G., 11 March, 1863. Mustered out 20 Jan., 1866.
O'Leary, Chas., Maj. Surg., 3 Aug., 1861. Mustered out 22 Nov., 1865.
Oliver, George H., Maj. Surg., 21 Sept., 1861. Resigned 31 Dec., 1864.
Oliver, John M., Brig. Gen., 12 Jan., 1865. Mustered out 24 Aug., 1865.
Olmstead, Edmund B., Hosp. Chap., 18 March, 1865. Mustered out 4 Aug., 1865.
Olmstead, Samuel G., Hosp. Chap., 4 June, 1862. Mustered out 10 Aug., 1865.
Olmsted, Franklin W., Hosp. Chap., 25 April, 1863. Mustered out 26 July, 1865.
Onderdonk, John R., 2nd Lieut. Sig. Corps, 3 March, 1863. Mustered out 12 Aug., 1865.
Opdyke, Emerson, Brig. Gen., 26 July, 1865. Resigned 1 Jan., 1866.
Ord, Edward O. C., Brig. Gen., 14 Sept., 1861. Maj. Gen., 2 May, 1862. Mustered out 1 Sept., 1866.
Ord, Placidus, Capt. A. A. G., 11 Nov., 1861. Maj., 11 June, 1862. Mustered out 31 July, 1866.
O'Reilly, Luke, Capt. A. de C., 12 May, 1865. Mustered out 29 Jan., 1866.
Orme, George R., Capt. A. Q. M., 18 May, 1864. Mustered out 30 Nov., 1866.
Orme, Wm. W., Brig. Gen., 29 Nov., 1862. Resigned 26 April, 1864.
Ormsley, D'Crump, Hosp. Chap., 22 April, 1863. Mustered out 4 Aug., 1865.
Orr, James L., Capt. C. S., 2 July, 1863. Mustered out 14 July, 1865.
Orr, Sumner E., 2nd Lieut. Sig. Corps, 3 March, 1863. Mustered out 12 Aug., 1865.
Osborn, Eugene A., Maj. P. M., 26 Nov., 1862. Mustered out 30 April, 1866.
Osborn, Thos. O., Brig. Gen., 1 May, 1865. Resigned 28 Sept., 1865.
Osgood, Thos. K., Maj. P. M., 26 Nov., 1862. Died 9 June, 1865.
Osterhous, Peter J., Brig. Gen., 9 June, 1862. Maj. Gen., 23 July, 1864. Mustered out 15 Jan., 1866.
Otis, Ephraim A., Capt. A. A. G., 11 June, 1862. Resigned 23 Nov., 1864.
Otis, George A., Asst. Surg., 30 June, 1864. Maj. Surg., 30 Aug., 1864. Mustered out 4 June, 1866.
Otterson, Wm. C., Maj. Surg., 24 Dec., 1861. Resigned 25 May, 1864.
Overton, George A. J., Capt. C. S., 2 March, 1864. Mustered out 15 July, 1865.
Owen, E. Griffith, Capt. A. Q. M., 5 Aug., 1861. Discharged 3 May, 1862.
Owen, Francis B., Capt. C. S., 24 March, 1862. Mustered out 6 Dec., 1865.
Owen, Fred'k W., Capt. C. S., 27 Feb., 1863. Resigned 18 Nov., 1864.
Owen, Joshua, Maj. Surg., 3 Aug., 1861. Mustered out 27 July, 1865.
Owen, Joshua T., Brig. Gen., 29 Nov., 1862. Appointment expired 4 March, 1863. Brig. Gen., 30 March, 1863. Mustered out 18 July, 1864.
Owen, Rich'd B., Capt. A. Q. M., 30 June, 1862. Mustered out 3 Nov., 1866.
Owen, William H., Capt. A. Q. M., 31 Oct., 1861. Mustered out 19 June, 1865.
Owens, John P., Capt. A. Q. M., 30 Jan., 1865. Mustered out 20 Sept., 1865.
Owings, Nicholas H., Capt. C. S., 15 Aug., 1863. Resigned 14 July, 1865.
Paddock, Joseph W., Capt. A. A. G., 14 April, 1862. Maj., 26 May, 1863. Resigned 25 July, 1863.
Paddock, Wm. H., Hosp. Chap., 5 July, 1862. Discharged 28 March, 1863. Hosp. Chap., 19 June, 1863. Mustered out 7 May, 1867.
Page, Calvin G., Asst. Surg., 8 Aug., 1862. Resigned 28 Aug., 1862.

Page, Henry, Capt. A. Q. M., 26 Nov., 1862. Mustered out 17 July, 1867.
Paige, James A., Hosp. Chap., 4 June, 1862. Mustered out 20 Nov., 1865.
Paine, Albert, Hosp. Chap., 13 June, 1862. Resigned 28 Aug., 1862.
Paine, Chas. J., Brig. Gen., 4 July, 1863. Mustered out 15 Jan., 1866.
Paine, Eleazer A., Brig. Gen., 3 Sept., 1861. Resigned 5 April, 1865.
Paine, Halbert E., Brig. Gen., 13 March, 1863. Resigned 15 May, 1865.
Paine, Jed C., Capt. Sig. Corps, 3 March, 1863. Mustered out 21 Aug., 1865.
Paine, Phelps, Capt. A. A. G., 11 March, 1863. Resigned 11 Jan., 1865.
Paine, Wm. H., Capt. Addl. A. de C., 28 April, 1862. Mustered out 5 Aug., 1865.
Painter, Wm., Capt. A. Q. M., 31 Oct., 1861. Maj. Addl. A. de C., 16 June, 1862. Resigned 14 Sept., 1864.
Palen, Vincent, Hosp. Chap., 31 May, 1862. Mustered out 1 Sept., 1867.
Palmer, David W., Capt. A. A. G., 18 May, 1864. Mustered out 13 June, 1865.
Palmer, Gideon S., Maj. Surg., 2 Oct., 1861. Mustered out 12 Oct., 1865.
Palmer, Gideon W., Maj. P. M., 19 Feb., 1863. Resigned 23 Dec., 1864.
Palmer, Henry, Maj. Surg., 4 April, 1862. Mustered out 7 Oct., 1865.
Palmer, Innis N., Brig. Gen., 23 Sept., 1861. Mustered out 15 Jan., 1866.
Palmer, John J., Capt. C. S., 17 Aug., 1863. Mustered out 19 May, 1866.
Palmer, John M., Brig. Gen., 20 Dec., 1861. Maj. Gen., 29 Nov., 1862. Mustered out 1 Sept., 1866.
Palmer, John M., Capt. C. S., 19 Feb., 1862. Discharged 28 March, 1863.
Palmer, Junius M., Capt. C. S., 17 Feb., 1865. Mustered out 31 Dec., 1865.
Palmer, Thomas, Capt. A. Q. M., 8 July, 1863. Mustered out 30 April, 1866.
Palmer, Wm. L., Capt. C. S., 14 July, 1862. Mustered out 27 Jan., 1866.
Palmer, Wm. R., Capt. C. S., 19 Aug., 1863. Resigned 29 March, 1865.
Pancoast, George L., Maj. Surg., 12 Oct., 1861. Mustered out 7 Oct., 1865.
Pangborn, Zabina K., Maj. P. M., 5 Sept., 1861. Rejected by Senate 11 March, 1862.
Pannes, John B., Capt. A. de C., 23 March, 1865. Mustered out 12 Oct., 1865.
Parke, John G., Brig. Gen., 23 Nov., 1861. Maj. Gen., 18 July, 1862. Mustered out 10 Jan., 1866.
Parker, Dexter F., Capt. A. Q. M., 3 Aug., 1861. Resigned 15 July, 1862.
Parker, Edward G., Capt. A. A. G., 7 Nov., 1862. Resigned 21 Jan., 1864.
Parker, Ely S., Capt. A. A. G., 25 May, 1863. Mustered out 1 July, 1866.
Parker, George B., Asst. Surg., 4 Aug., 1863. Maj. Surg., 30 June, 1864. Mustered out 3 Nov., 1865.
Parker, Gilbert L., Capt. A. Q. M., 28 March, 1863. Mustered out 30 June, 1866.
Parker, Isaac B., Capt. A. de C., 25 June, 1863. Mustered out 20 Jan., 1866.
Parkhurst, Wm. H., Capt. C. S., 2 March, 1864. Mustered out 31 May, 1866.
Parkinson, Edward T., Capt. A. A. G., 7 July, 1863. Mustered out 19 Sept., 1865.
Parks, James H., Hosp. Chap., 5 July, 1862. Resigned 30 Nov., 1864.
Parks, John, Capt. A. Q. M., 7 April, 1864. Mustered out 13 March, 1866.
Parks, Marvin A., Capt. C. S., 10 Sept., 1862. Dismissed 9 Feb., 1865.
Parrott, Marcus J., Capt. A. A. G., 3 Aug., 1861. Resigned 22 Aug., 1862.
Parsons, Chas., Capt. A. Q. M., 10 Sept., 1862. Resigned 5 July, 1864.
Parsons, Enos B., Capt. A. A. G., 29 Feb., 1864. Maj., 24 Dec., 1864. Mustered out 29 Jan., 1866.
Parsons, John, Capt. A. Q. M., 7 April, 1864. Mustered out 13 March, 1866.
Parsons, John, Asst. Surg., 26 Jan., 1865. Mustered out 27 July, 1865.
Parsons, John E., Capt. A. A. G., 30 June, 1864. Resigned 30 Jan., 1865.
Parsons, Lewis B., Capt. A. Q. M., 31 Oct., 1861. Col. Addl. A. de C., 19 Feb., 1862. Brig. Gen., 11 May, 1865. Mustered out 30 April, 1866.
Parsons, Theron E., Capt. A. A. G., 16 Nov., 1864. Resigned 31 May, 1865.
Partridge, Sylvester B., 1st Lieut. Sig. Corps, 3 March, 1863. Resigned 30 May, 1865.
Patrick, Marsena R., Brig. Gen., 17 March, 1862. Resigned 12 June, 1865.
Patrick, Wm. K., Maj. P. M., 28 May, 1864 Mustered out 15 Nov., 1865.
Pettee, George E., Asst. Surg., 4 Oct., 1862. Dropped 14 Oct., 1862.
Patten, George, Capt. A. A. G., 11 March, 1863. Resigned 2 July, 1863.
Patten, Henry D., Capt. A. Q. M., 26 Nov., 1862. Dismissed 12 Sept., 1864.
Patten, Wm., Maj. P. M., 1 June, 1861. Mustered out 15 Nov., 1865.
Patterson, Francis E., Brig. Gen., 11 April, 1862. Died 22 Nov., 1862.
Patterson, Horace S., Capt. A. Q. M., 30 June, 1864. Mustered out 28 July, 1865.
Patterson, John J., Maj. P. M., 19 Sept., 1861. Resigned 31 March, 1862.
Patterson, Rob't E., Maj. P. M., 1 June, 1861. Resigned 23 Dec., 1862.
Patterson, Theodore F., 2nd Lieut. and 1st Lieut. Sig. Corps, 3 March, 1863. Appointment as 1st Lieut. expired 4 July, 1864, and declined to serve as 2nd Lieut.
Patterson, Rob't, Capt. C. S., 18 May, 1864. Mustered out 9 Oct., 1865.
Paul, Augustus C., Capt. A. A. G., 1 June, 1863. Mustered out 19 Sept., 1865.
Paul, Gabriel R., Brig. Gen., 5 Sept., 1862. Expired by Constitutional limitation 4 March, 1863. Brig. Gen., 18 April, 1863. Mustered out 1 Sept., 1866.
Paul, James R., Capt. C. S., 31 Oct., 1861. Resigned 19 Jan., 1865.
Paulding, Edmund E., Maj. P. M., 1 June, 1861. Cashiered 9 July, 1866.
Paxon, John L., Capt. C. S., 18 May, 1864. Mustered out 11 Jan., 1867.
Payne, James G., Capt. A. Q. M., 7 April, 1864. Mustered out 17 July, 1867.
Payson, Ira F., Capt. A. Q. M., 29 Feb., 1864. Died 30 July, 1864.
Peabody, David G., Capt. C. S., 30 July, 1863. Mustered out 9 Oct., 1865.
Peabody, James H., Asst. Surg., 7 Jan., 1863. Maj. Surg., 15 Aug., 1863. Mustered out 18 Aug., 1865.
Peal, J. Burd, Maj. Surg., 30 Oct., 1861. Resigned 27 April, 1863.
Pearce, Enoch, Asst. Surg., 2 Sept., 1863. Maj. Surg., 9 Sept., 1863. Discharged 23 March, 1864.
Pearce, John B., Capt. C. S., 2 June, 1863. Mustered out 14 July, 1865.
Pearce, Sam'l A., Jr., Maj. P. M., 28 May, 1864. Mustered out 20 Sept., 1866.
Pearman, John W., Capt. A. Q. M., 18 May, 1864. Mustered out 31 July, 1866.
Pearsons, Wm. B. C., Maj. P. M., 28 May, 1864. Mustered out 1 Nov., 1865.
Pease, Chas. E., Capt. A. A. G., 25 May, 1863. Resigned 20 April, 1865.
Pease, Roger W., Asst. Surg., 2 Oct., 1863. Maj. Surg., 30 March, 1864. Mustered out 7 Oct., 1865.
Peay, J. Speed, Capt. A. A. G., 15 July, 1862. Resigned 2 May, 1863.
Peck, Chas. H., Capt. A. Q. M., 18 March, 1864. Resigned 29 March, 1865.
Peck, John J., Brig. Gen., 9 Aug., 1861. Maj. Gen., 4 July, 1862. Mustered out 24 Aug., 1865.

Peck, Sandford C., Capt. C. S., 26 Nov., 1862. Mustered out 18 Jan., 1866.
Peirce, Luther H., Capt. A. Q. M., 16 Nov., 1861. Capt. A. Q. M., U. S. A., 18 May, 1864.
Pell, Duncan A., Capt. Addl. A. de C., 4 April 1862. Resigned 19 May, 1865.
Pell, John H., Capt. A. A. G., 25 May, 1863. Resigned 28 March, 1865.
Pelouze, Louis H., Maj. Addl. A. de C., 3 July, 1862. Maj. A. A. G., U. S. A., 24 March, 1864.
Pendergast, Henry A., Maj. P. M., 13 Nov., 1862. Died 9 March, 1863.
Pendleton, E. Boyd, Maj. Surg., 4 April, 1862. Resigned 10 June, 1862.
Pendleton, Philip, Maj. P. M., 1 June, 1861. Dismissed 13 Aug., 1864.
Penney, Richard, Capt. A. Q. M., 29 Feb., 1864. Mustered out 20 March, 1866.
Pennypacker, Galusha, Brig. Gen., 18 Feb., 1865. Resigned 30 April, 1866.
Penrose, Chas. B., Capt. C. S., 3 Aug., 1861. Capt. C. S., U. S. A., 13 May, 1865.
Penrose, Wm. H., Brig. Gen., 27 June, 1865. Mustered out 15 Jan., 1866.
Perce, Legrand W., Capt. A. Q. M., 10 March, 1863. Mustered out 7 Aug., 1865.
Perkins, Benj'n W., Capt. A. Q. M., 12 Aug., 1861. Discharged 20 Feb., 1862.
Perkins, Delavan D., Maj. Addl. A. de C., 18 Nov., 1861. Maj. A. A. G., U. S. A., 1 June, 1864.
Perkins, Francis W., Capt. A. Q. M., 9 June, 1862. Mustered out 20 Sept., 1865.
Perkins, Henry W., Capt. A. A. G., 23 Dec., 1862. Mustered out 12 Jan., 1866.
Perkins, Jabez, Asst. Surg., 9 Sept., 1863. Maj. Surg., 27 Oct., 1863. Mustered out 23 Oct., 1865.
Perkins, Simon, Jr., Capt. A. Q. M., 3 Feb., 1862. Resigned 12 July, 1864.
Perkins, Tarrant A., Maj. Surg., 4 Sept., 1861. Resigned 24 March, 1862.
Perley, Thos. F., Maj. Surg., 23 Oct., 1861. Col. Med. Insp., 1 July, 1862. Resigned 10 Aug., 1863. Maj. Surg., 10 Aug., 1863. Mustered out 27 July, 1865.
Perry, Leonard B., Capt. A. A. G., 28 March, 1865. Mustered out 12 Oct., 1865.
Persing, Henry W., Capt. A. Q. M., 3 July, 1863. Mustered out 13 March, 1866.
Petard, F. C. M., Asst. Surg., 23 Sept., 1864. Mustered out 9 Oct., 1865.
Petherbridge, John B., Asst. Surg., 18 May, 1864. Maj. Surg., 18 March, 1865. Mustered out 24 June, 1865.
Pettigrew, Sam'l, Hosp. Chap., 23 June, 1862. Mustered out 21 Aug., 1865.
Pettinos, James W., Asst. Surg., 14 May, 1863. Maj. Surg., 27 May, 1863. Dismissed 22 Aug., 1864.
Peugnet, Ernest, Capt. A. Q. M., 16 March, 1863. Mustered out 26 Oct., 1865.
Phelps, Abner J., Capt. A. Q. M., 20 March, 1863. Mustered out 20 Sept., 1865.
Phelps, Alonzo J., Maj. Surg., 4 April, 1862. Mustered out 4 Jan., 1866.
Phelps, Edward E., Maj. Surg., 4 Feb., 1862. Mustered out 27 June, 1865.
Phelps, George, Maj. P. M., 5 Aug., 1861. Mustered out 1 Dec., 1865.
Phelps, John S., Brig. Gen., 19 July, 1862. Appointment expired 4 March, 1863.
Phelps, John W., Brig. Gen., 17 May, 1861. Resigned 21 Aug., 1862.
Phelps, Justus M., Maj. P. M., 27 Feb., 1863. Mustered out 15 Feb., 1866.
Phelps, Vincent, Capt. A. Q. M., 31 Oct., 1861. Resigned 10 March, 1865.
Phelps, Wm., Maj. P. M., 11 March, 1863. Mustered out 31 July, 1865.
Philips, Wm., Hosp. Chap., 19 July, 1864. Mustered out 26 July, 1865.
Philips, Wm. A., Capt. Addl. A. de C., 29 Jan., 1862. Discharged 21 March, 1862.
Phillips, Benj'n F., Hosp. Chap., 10 Jan., 1863. Mustered out 14 July, 1865.
*Phillips, James, Asst. Surg., 11 Sept., 1862. Asst. Surg., U. S. A., 22 Nov., 1862.
Phillips, John E., Capt. A. A. G., 11 June, 1862. Resigned 5 Aug., 1864.
Phillips, John H., Maj. Surg., 9 Feb., 1863. Mustered out 30 Nov., 1865.
Phinney, James H., Maj. P. M., 1 June, 1861. Mustered out 5 Oct., 1866.
Piatt, Abraham S., Brig. Gen., 28 April, 1862. Resigned 17 Feb., 1863.
Piatt, Benj'n M., Capt. A. A. G., 16 May, 1862. Maj., 2 March, 1865. Mustered out 22 Nov., 1865.
Piatt, Donn, Capt. A. A. G., 28 June, 1861. Maj., 4 Nov., 1862. Resigned 2 July, 1864.
Piatt, John H., Capt. Addl. A. de C., 11 July, 1862. Mustered out 1 Sept., 1866.
Pick, Augustus T., Asst. Surg., 18 May, 1864. Mustered out 27 Jan., 1866.
Picot, Mitchel H., Asst. Surg., 7 Nov., 1862. Resigned 17 April, 1863.
Pierce, Byron R., Brig. Gen., 7 June, 1864. Mustered out 24 Aug., 1865.
Pierce, Chas. P., Capt. A. A. G., 1 May, 1862. Resigned 12 Sept., 1862.
Pierce, Gilbert A., Capt. A. Q. M., 3 Aug., 1861. Mustered out 7 Oct., 1865.
Pierce, James O., Maj. A. A. G., 8 May, 1863. Mustered out 22 Nov., 1865.
Pierson, Henry L., Jr., Capt. A. A. G., 1 Nov., 1862. Resigned 24 June, 1864.
Pierson, Henry R., Capt. A. Q. M., 18 May, 1864. Mustered out 20 Sept., 1865.
Pigman, Wm. A., 2nd Lieut. Sig. Corps, 3 March, 1863. Mustered out 1 Feb., 1866.
Pile, Wm. A., Brig. Gen., 26 Dec., 1863. Mustered out 24 Aug., 1865.
Pilson, John, Lieut. Col. Addl. A. de C., 31 March, 1862. Resigned 8 June, 1864.
Pinckard, Wm. G., Capt. A. Q. M., 30 June, 1862. Died 16 Feb., 1864.
Pineo, Peter, Maj. Surg., 3 Aug., 1861. Lieut. Col. Med. Insp., 9 Feb., 1863. Mustered out 31 Oct., 1865.
Pinkham, A. Judson, Capt. C. S., 3 Oct., 1864. Mustered out 13 July, 1866.
Pinckney, Joseph C., Capt. C. S., 11 March, 1863. Mustered out 21 Feb., 1866.
Pinner, M., Capt. A. Q. M., 10 Sept., 1861. Resigned 15 Aug., 1862.
Pitcher, Thomas G., Brig. Gen., 29 Nov., 1862. Mustered out 30 April, 1866.
Pitkin, Edward P., Capt. A. Q. M., 2 July, 1863. Died 5 Oct., 1864.
Pitkin, Perley P., Capt. A. Q. M., 19 Feb., 1862. Resigned 7 Nov., 1864.
Pittman, Samuel E., Capt. A. A. G., 22 May, 1863. Resigned Sept., 1864.
Pittman, Wm., Capt. A. A. G., 3 Feb., 1865. Resigned 5 Aug., 1865.
Pitzer, John A., Maj. P. M., 2 July, 1864. Mustered out 15 Nov., 1865.
Plato, Nelson, Capt. A. Q. M., 30 June, 1862. Mustered out 31 Aug., 1866.
Platt, Edward R., Maj. J. A., 2 Nov., 1863. Mustered out 28 July, 1865.
Platt, Obadiah H., Maj. P. M., 1 June, 1861. Dismissed 21 June, 1862.
Platt, Sam'l K., Capt. A. Q. M., 19 Feb., 1863. Mustered out 11 Nov., 1864.
Pleasanton, Alfred, Brig. Gen., 16 July, 1862. Maj. Gen., 22 June, 1863. Mustered out 15 Jan., 1866.
Plumb, Ralph, Capt. A. Q. M., 31 Oct., 1861. Mustered out 11 Nov., 1865.
Plummer, Joseph B., Brig. Gen., 22 Oct., 1861. Died 9 Aug., 1862.
Poe, Orlando M., Brig. Gen., 29 Nov., 1862. Appointment expired 4 March, 1863.
Polk, Burr H., Capt. A. A. G., 11 March, 1863. Maj., 20 April, 1864. Mustered out 21 Feb., 1866.
Pollard, Philip, Capt. C. S., 20 Oct., 1862. Mustered out 30 June, 1865.

Pomeroy, George, Maj. P. M., 2 Oct., 1862. Maj. P. M., U. S. A., 28 July, 1866.
Pomeroy, John M., Maj. P. M., 14 Aug., 1861. Resigned 1 May, 1863.
Pool, Joseph, Capt. A. Q. M., 3 Oct., 1863. Maj. P. M., 8 Sept., 1864. Mustered out 15 Dec., 1865.
Poole, Horace, Capt. A. A. G., 29 Feb., 1864. Resigned 9 June, 1865.
Pooley, Thos. R., Asst. Surg., 18 May, 1864. Mustered out 15 June, 1865.
Poore, Leander A., Capt. A. Q. M., 20 April, 1864. Mustered out 19 May, 1866.
Pope, Chas. H., Capt. C. S., 21 Feb., 1863. Mustered out 26 June, 1865.
Pope, Douglas, Capt. Addl. A. de C., 30 June, 1862. Mustered out 1 Oct., 1866.
Pope, John, Brig. Gen., 17 May, 1861. Maj. Gen., 21 March, 1862. Mustered out 1 Sept., 1866.
Pope, Joseph P., Capt. C. S., 27 Feb., 1863. Mustered out 1 Dec., 1865.
Pope, Nathaniel, Capt. C. S., 28 July, 1862. Mustered out 1 March, 1866.
Pope, Wm. S., Maj. P. M., 30 June, 1862. Mustered out 15 Feb., 1866.
Porter, Andrew, Brig. Gen., 17 May, 1861. Mustered out 4 April, 1864.
Porter, Benj. F., Capt. A. Q. M., 12 May, 1862. Mustered out 20 Sept., 1865.
Porter, Burr, Maj. Addl. A. de C., 2 June, 1862. Discharged 9 Sept., 1862.
Porter, Byron, Capt. A. A. G., 7 Aug., 1862. Mustered out 1 Sept., 1866.
Porter, David W., Capt. A. Q. M., 21 Nov., 1862. Mustered out 4 Jan., 1866.
Porter, Edmund J., Maj. P. M., 30 June, 1862. Mustered out 31 July, 1865.
Porter, Frank G., Asst. Surg., 18 May, 1864. Maj. Surg., 30 Sept., 1864. Mustered out 3 Nov., 1865.
Porter, Fitz John, Brig. Gen., 17 May, 1861. Maj. Gen., 4 July, 1862. Cashiered 21 Jan., 1863.
Porter, Harry, Capt. A. Q. M., 14 April, 1862. Resigned 7 Feb., 1864.
Porter, John H., Asst. Surg., 25 Nov., 1864. Mustered out 10 Jan., 1866.
Porter, Reuben G., Capt. C. S., 16 July, 1862. Mustred out 15 July, 1865.
Porter, Wm. V., Maj. P. M., 23 Feb., 1864. Mustered out 1 Nov., 1865.
Porter, Wm. L., Capt. A. A. G., 13 March, 1865. Mustered out 1 Oct., 1866.
Potter, Carroll H., Capt. A. A. G., 21 Oct., 1861. Maj. 25 Feb., 1865. Vacated commission 27 March, 1865.
Potter, Edward E., Capt. C. S., 3 Feb., 1862. Vacated commission 1 Oct., 1862. Brig. Gen., 29 Nov., 1862. Resigned 24 July, 1865.
Potter, James B. M., Maj. P. M., 1 June, 1861. Maj. P. M., U. S. A., 15 July, 1864.
Potter, James N., Capt. A. de C., 25 April, 1863. Capt. C. S., 2 March, 1864. Resigned 1 Feb., 1865.
Potter, Joseph H., Brig. Gen., 1 May, 1865. Mustered out 15 Jan., 1866.
Potter, Orson O., Capt. A. Q. M., 19 Feb., 1863. Mustered out 18 Jan., 1866.
Potter, Rob't B., Brig. Gen., 13 March, 1863. Maj. Gen., 29 Sept., 1865. Mustered out 15 Jan., 1866.
Potter, Samuel S., Hosp. Chap., 15 July, 1864. Mustered out 15 July, 1865.
Potter, Wm. J., Hosp. Chap., 30 Sept., 1863. Resigned 10 May, 1864.
Potts, Benj'n F., Brig. Gen., 12 Jan., 1865. Mustered out 15 Jan., 1866.
Potts, Jesse N., Capt. C. S., 18 Nov., 1864. Mustered out 13 June, 1865.
Pound, John, Capt. A. A. G., 16 Nov., 1861. Resigned 15 Aug., 1862.
Powell, Cuthbert H., Hosp. Chap., 11 June, 1862. Discharged 20 Aug., 1863.
Powell, Wm. H., Brig. Gen., 19 Oct., 1864. Resigned 5 Jan., 1865.
Power, John, Capt. A. Q. M., 18 March, 1864. Mustered out 20 April, 1866.
Powers, Chas. J., Capt. A. A. G., 6 Nov., 1861. Resigned 9 Oct., 1862.
Powers, Edward M., Asst. Surg., 18 May, 1864. Maj. Surg., 10 March, 1865. Mustered out 7 Oct., 1865.
Powers, Joseph T., Capt. A. Q. M., 28 Sept., 1864. Mustered out 1 Oct., 1867.
Pratt, Calvin E., Brig. Gen., 10 Sept., 1862. Resigned 25 April, 1863.
Pratt, James H., Capt. A. Q. M., 19 Feb., 1863. Mustered out 8 Jan., 1866.
Pratt, John, Capt. A. A. G., 29 Oct., 1862. Mustered out 19 Dec., 1865.
Pratt, Wm., Capt. A. A. G., 24 June, 1863. Resigned 2 April, 1864.
Pratt, Wm. B., Capt. A. de C., 8 Aug., 1864. Mustered out 6 Sept., 1865.
Prentice, Wm. P., Capt. A. A. G., 26 Nov., 1861. Maj., 2 Sept., 1862. Resigned 23 Dec., 1862.
Prentiss, Benj'n M., Brig. Gen., 17 May, 1861. Maj. Gen., 29 Nov., 1862. Resigned 23 Oct., 1863.
Prescott, Albert B., Asst. Surg., 5 July, 1864. Mustered out 25 Aug., 1865.
Prescott, Oliver S., Hosp. Chap., 14 July, 1862. Resigned 29 Sept., 1862.
Preston, Edward V., Maj. P. M., 19 Feb., 1863. Mustered out 31 July, 1865.
Preston, Simon M., Capt. A. A. G., 5 Aug., 1861. Dismissed 23 Sept., 1862.
Prevost, Chas. M., Capt. A. A. G., 1 May, 1862. Resigned 16 Aug., 1862.
Price, Josiah F., Maj. P. M., 19 Feb., 1863. Mustered out 15 Nov., 1865.
Price, Thos. L., Brig. Gen., 21 Sept., 1861. Appointment expired 17 July, 1862.
Price, Wm. R., Maj. A. A. G., 5 Aug., 1864. Mustered out 1 Sept., 1866.
Prime, Mark, Capt. A. Q. M., 19 Feb., 1862. Discharged 2 July, 1863.
Prince, David, Maj. Surg., 3 Aug., 1861. Resigned 22 Sept., 1862.
Prince, Henry, Brig. Gen., 28 April, 1862. Mustered out 30 April, 1866.
Prince, James P., Asst. Surg., 27 Dec., 1864. Maj. Surg., 3 May, 1865. Mustered out 27 Jan., 1866.
Proudfit, Alex'r, Hosp. Chap., 15 Sept., 1862. Mustered out 21 Aug., 1865.
Proudfit, John, Hosp. Chap., 20 June, 1862. Mustered out 21 Aug., 1865.
Puffer, Alfred F., Capt. A. de C., 1 Oct., 1862. Resigned 18 March, 1865.
Pulsifer, Josiah D., Maj. P. M., 23 Feb., 1864. Mustered out 1 Nov., 1865.
Pumphrey, Isaac N., Maj. P. M., 19 Aug., 1861. Died 26 Aug., 1863.
Purdy, E. James, Hosp. Chap., 25 Nov., 1862. Mustered out 15 July, 1865.
Purdy, E. Sparrow, Capt. A. A. G., 19 Sept., 1861. (Maj. A. de C., 20 Aug., 1862. Resigned as A. de C., 6 Nov., 1862.) Resigned 12 April, 1865.
Purington, Dillwyn V., Capt. A. Q. M., 19 Feb., 1865. Mustered out 8 Jan., 1866.
Purnell, Thos. F., Capt. A. Q. M., 8 May, 1863. Mustered out 20 March, 1866.
Purviance, Campbell E., Capt. C. S., 30 June, 1864. Mustered out 10 Aug., 1865.
Putnam, George A., Maj. P. M., 17 Nov., 1863. Resigned 10 May, 1865.
Putnam, Henry R., Maj. A. de C., 7 Oct., 1864. Mustered out 20 July, 1865.
Quay, Elliott S., Capt. A. A. G., 21 May, 1862. Resigned 10 Oct., 1862.
Queen, Columbus J., Capt. C. S., 10 Sept., 1862. Mustered out 4 Aug., 1865.
Quick, Lavington, Maj. Surg., 24 Dec., 1861. Mustered out 27 July, 1865.
Quidor, John E., Maj. Surg., 3 Aug., 1861. Dismissed 30 Nov., 1863.
Quinby, Isaac F., Brig. Gen., 17 March, 1862. Resigned 31 Dec., 1863.

Quinton, Wm., 2nd Lieut. Sig. Corps, 3 March, 1863. Mustered out 1 May, 1866.
Radcliffe, Sam'l J., Asst. Surg., 1 Feb., 1864. Maj. Surg., 19 May, 1865. Mustered out 7 Oct., 1865.
Ragan, Zachariah, Hosp. Chap., 9 Dec., 1862. Mustered out 20 Nov., 1865.
Ramsay, Joseph G., Capt. A. A. G., 17 Nov., 1864. Mustered out 3 Aug., 1865.
Ramsay, Silas, Maj. Addl. A. de C., 12 June, 1862. Mustered out 20 April, 1866.
Ramsdell, Zopher D., Capt. C. S., 30 June, 1864. Mustered out 15 June, 1865.
Ramsey, J. C., Capt. C. S., 12 May, 1862. Resigned 15 Nov., 1864.
Ramsey, Rob't H., Capt. A. A. G., 5 Dec., 1863. Maj., 27 Jan., 1865. Mustered out 8 June, 1866.
Rand, Arnold A., Capt. A. A. G., 3 June, 1863. Resigned 12 Jan., 1864.
Randall, Augustus C., Capt. C. S., 28 May, 1864. Dismissed 3 May, 1865.
Randall, C. L., Asst. Surg., 19 May, 1865. Mustered out 11 Oct., 1865.
Randall, Wm. H. F., Capt. A. A. G., 18 July, 1862. Resigned 19 July, 1865.
Rankin, John W., Capt. A. Q. M., 3 Aug., 1861. Resigned 1 April, 1862.
Rankin, Wm. A., Capt. A. Q. M., 30 July, 1863. Mustered out 13 March, 1866.
Ranney, Henry C., Capt. A. A. G., 10 Oct., 1862. Resigned 1 June, 1863.
Ransom, Albert F., Capt. C. S., 2 March, 1864. Mustered out 26 June, 1865.
Ransom, Edward P., Capt. C. S., 25 Sept., 1862. Mustered out 31 Jan., 1866.
Ransom, Thos. E. G., Brig. Gen., 29 Nov., 1862. Died 29 Oct., 1864.
Rapelge, John T., Capt. A. Q. M., 6 Oct., 1862. Mustered out 23 Oct., 1865.
Rasin, Hanson, Capt. A. Q. M., 17 June, 1863. Mustered out 23 Oct., 1865.
Rathbone, Henry R., Maj. A. A. G., 11 March, 1865. Resigned 8 July, 1867.
Rathbone, Wm. R., Capt. C. S., 29 Nov., 1862. Resigned 6 Aug., 1864.
Rauch, John H., Maj. Surg., 3 Aug., 1861. Mustered out 14 July, 1865.
Raum, Green B., Brig. Gen., 15 Feb., 1865. Resigned 6 May, 1865.
Rawlins, John A., Capt. A. A. G., 30 Aug., 1861. Maj., 14 May, 1862. Brig. Gen., 11 Aug., 1863. Brig. Gen., Chief of Staff of the Gen.-in-Chief, U. S. A., 3 March, 1865.
Rawolle, Wm. C., Capt. Addl. A. de C., 21 June, 1862. Resigned 11 Aug., 1865.
Rawson, Chas. H., Maj. Surg., 19 Feb., 1862. Resigned 22 Aug., 1862.
Rawson, Thos. R., Hosp. Chap., 16 Aug., 1864. Mustered out 31 Oct., 1865.
Raymond, Carrington H., Maj. A. A. G., 23 June, 1862. Resigned 1 Feb., 1865.
Raymond, Chas. A., Hosp. Chap., 30 June, 1864. Mustered out 13 Oct., 1866.
Raymond, Edward A., Capt. Addl. A. de C., 30 Oct., 1861. Resigned 8 Aug., 1862.
Raymond, Rossiter W., Capt. Addl. A. de C., 31 March, 1862. Resigned 6 April, 1864.
Raymond, Wm. G., Hosp. Chap., 25 July, 1862. Discharged 13 April, 1863.
Raynolds, Wm. F., Col. Addl. A. de C., 31 March, 1862. Mustered out 31 May, 1866.
Read, Joseph C., Capt. C. S., 22 July, 1862. Mustered out 13 March, 1866.
Read, Louis W., Asst. Surg., 23 June, 1863. Maj. Surg., 29 June, 1863. Mustered out 18 Jan., 1866.
Read, Theodore, Capt. A. A. G., 24 Oct., 1861. Maj., 25 July, 1864. Killed 6 April, 1865, in action at High Bridge, Va.
Reber, Chas. T., Asst. Surg., 26 Sept., 1864. Maj. Surg., 19 May, 1865. Mustered out 2 Feb., 1866.
Rector, Pierson, Asst. Surg., 29 Nov., 1864. Mustered out 4 June, 1866.
Redington, Edward D., Maj. P. M., 23 Feb., 1864. Mustered out 1 Dec., 1865.
Reed, Thos. B., Maj. Surg., 4 April, 1862. Mustered out 24 June, 1865.
Reese, Henry B., Maj. P. M., 1 June, 1861. Maj. P. M., U. S. A., 17 Jan., 1867.
Reese, John J., Maj. Surg., 7 Nov., 1862. Resigned 20 March, 1864.
Reese, Wm. W., Hosp. Chap., 29 July, 1862. Resigned 15 Feb., 1864.
Reeve, Nathan, Capt. A. A. G., 21 Oct., 1861. Rejected by Senate 26 April, 1862.
Reger, John W., Hosp. Chap., 29 Feb., 1864. Mustered out 17 Aug., 1865.
Reichenbach, E. Chas., Capt. A. Q. M., 1 June, 1863. Mustered out 13 July, 1866.
Reid, Elihu D., Capt. C. S., 10 Sept., 1862. Resigned 9 March, 1864.
Reid, Hugh T., Brig. Gen., 13 March, 1863. Resigned 4 April, 1864.
Reilly, James W., Brig. Gen., 30 July, 1864. Resigned 20 April, 1865.
Reilly, James, Asst. Surg., 8 Dec., 1864. Mustered out 5 Aug., 1865.
Remick, David, Capt. C. S., 5 Aug., 1861. Resigned 31 March, 1862. Capt. C. S., 10 Sept., 1862. Mustered out 14 July, 1865.
Remington, John E., Capt. A. Q. M., 13 Oct., 1863. Mustered out 13 March, 1866.
Reno, Benj. F., Capt. A. Q. M., 17 Nov., 1862. Resigned 15 March, 1865.
Reno, James M., Capt. A. Q. M., 19 Sept., 1864. Mustered out 20 Sept., 1865.
Reno, Jesse L., Brig. Gen., 12 Nov., 1861. Maj. Gen., 18 July, 1862. Killed 14 Sept., 1862, at Battle of South Mountain, Md.
Restieaux, Edward B. W., Capt. A. Q. M., 19 Feb., 1863. Mustered out 26 March, 1867. Revere, Joseph W., Brig. Gen., 25 Oct., 1862. Resigned 10 Aug., 1863.
Rex, George, Maj. Surg., 24 Dec., 1861. Mustered out 28 June, 1865.
Reyburn, Rob't, Asst. Surg., 4 June, 1863. Maj. Surg., 13 June, 1863. Mustered out 3 June, 1867.
Reymer, Michael D., 2nd Lieut. Sig. Corps, 3 March, 1863. Mustered out 16 Aug., 1865.
Reynolds, Chas. H., Capt. A. Q. M., 12 Dec., 1864. Mustered out 8 Jan., 1866.
Reynolds, Ethan S., Maj. P. M., 4 Sept., 1863. Resigned 29 May, 1865.
Reynolds, Frank, Asst. Surg., 7 Aug., 1863. Resigned 22 Sept., 1864.
Reynolds, John F., Brig. Gen., 20 Aug., 1861. Maj. Gen., 29 Nov., 1862. Killed 1 July, 1863, at Battle of Gettysburg, Pa.
Reynolds, Joseph J., Brig. Gen., 17 May, 1861. Resigned 23 Jan., 1862. Brig. Gen., 17 Sept., 1862. Maj. Gen., 29 Nov., 1862. Mustered out 1 Sept., 1866.
Reynolds, Sam'l M., Maj. P. M., 11 March, 1863. Mustered out 31 March, 1866.
Reynolds, Stephen R., Capt. A. A. G., 23 June, 1863. Died 30 July, 1864, of wounds received in Battle at Cold Harbor, Va.
Rhoades, Chas. D., Capt. A. A. G., 9 Feb., 1865. Resigned 9 June, 1865.
Rhoades, Lawrence, Capt. C. S., 2 July, 1864. Mustered out 22 Aug., 1865.
Rhodes, Dudley W., Maj. P. M., 21 April, 1863. Mustered out 15 Nov., 1865.
Rice, Alex'r A., Capt. A. A. G., 11 March, 1863. Resigned 18 March, 1864.
Rice, Americus V., Brig. Gen., 31 May, 1865. Mustered out 15 Jan., 1866.
Rice, Elliott W., Brig. Gen., 20 June, 1864. Mustered out 24 Aug., 1865.
Rice, James C., Brig. Gen., 17 Aug., 1863. Killed 10 May, 1864, in Battle at Laurel Hill, Va.
Rice, James M., Capt. Addl. A. de C., 30 Jan., 1862. Discharged 21 March, 1862. Capt. A. A. G., 5 April, 1862. Mustered out 23 Aug., 1865.

Rice, Lewis C., Asst. Surg., 7 Jan., 1863. Maj. Surg., 15 Aug., 1863. Mustered out 7 Oct., 1865.
Rice, Nathan P., Asst. Surg., 7 Aug., 1863. Maj. Surg., 2 Sept., 1863. Mustered out 27 July, 1865.
Rice, Sam'l A., Brig. Gen., 4 Aug., 1863. Died 6 July, 1864, of wounds received in Battle at Jenkins' Ferry, Ark.
Richards, Alonzo V., 2nd Lieut. Sig. Corps, 14 Feb., 1865. Mustered out 25 Nov., 1865.
Richards, Benj. W., Capt. Addl. A. de C., 12 April, 1862. Resigned 10 March, 1865.
Richards, Edward S., Capt. A. A. G., 6 Sept., 1864. Mustered out 25 Nov., 1865.
Richardson, Israel B., Brig. Gen., 17 May, 1861. Maj. Gen., 4 July, 1862. Died 3 Nov., 1862, of wounds received at Battle of Antietam, Md.
Richardson, Nathaniel A., Capt. C. S., 25 March, 1864. Mustered out 30 April, 1866.
Richardson, Orla C., Capt. C. S., 2 March, 1865. Mustered out 20 July, 1865.
Richardson, Wm., Maj. P. M., 1 June, 1861. Resigned 30 Sept., 1864.
Riche, George I., Maj. P. M., 26 Nov., 1862. Mustered out 15 Nov., 1865.
Richmond, James C., Hosp. Chap., 2 June, 1862. Discharged 28 May, 1863.
Richmond, Lewis, Capt. A. A. G., 13 Sept., 1861. Maj., 28 April, 1862. Resigned 21 April, 1865.
Ricketts, James B., Brig. Gen., 21 July, 1861. Mustered out 30 April, 1866.
Riddle, Wm., Maj. A. de C., 25 April, 1863. Resigned 7 Dec., 1864.
Rider, James H., Capt. A. A. G., 1 Feb., 1865. Mustered out 22 Nov., 1865.
Riggin, John, Jr., Col. Addl. A. de C., 3 May, 1862. Resigned 14 Oct., 1863.
Ringwalt, Sam'l, Capt. A. Q. M., 22 Aug., 1861. Resigned 6 Nov., 1862.
Risley, Arthur, Maj. P. M., 26 Nov., 1862. Appointment expired 4 March, 1863.
Ritchie, John, Maj. Addl. A. de C., 29 Jan., 1862. Discharged 21 March, 1862.
Ritchie, Montgomery, Capt. C. S., 3 Feb., 1862. Resigned 2 Sept., 1862.
Ritter, Wm. H., Maj. P. M., 5 Sept., 1861. Resigned 6 July, 1863.
Rives, Henry E., Capt. C. S., 9 March, 1865. Mustered out 11 Oct., 1865.
Rives, Wright, Capt. A. A. de C., 4 June, 1862. Capt. 6th U. S. Inf., 23 Feb., 1864.
Roberts, Benj'n K., Capt. A. A. G., 12 Nov., 1864. Mustered out 1 July, 1866.
Roberts, Benj'n S., Brig. Gen., 16 July, 1862. Mustered out 15 Jan., 1866.
Roberts, Chas., 2nd Lieut. Sig. Corps, 3 March, 1863. Mustered out 21 Aug., 1865.
Roberts, Chas. S., Asst. Surg., 3 March, 1865. Mustered out 27 July, 1865.
Roberts, Cyrus S., Capt. A. de C., 22 June, 1865. Mustered out 7 Dec., 1865.
Roberts, Henry C., Asst. Surg., 2 Sept., 1863. Discharged 18 July, 1864.
Roberts, Nathan B., 2nd Lieut. Sig. Corps, 3 March, 1863. Resigned 14 June, 1865.
Robertson, Walter S., Capt. A. Q. M., 18 March, 1864. Dismissed 30 June, 1864.
Robie, Fred'k, Maj. P. M., 1 June, 1861. Mustered out 20 July, 1866.
Robinett, Henry C., Capt. A. de C., 25 March, 1864. Discharged 8 May, 1865.
Robins, Chas. M., Capt. C. S., 10 Sept., 1862. Mustered out 25 Aug., 1865.
Robinson, Albert D., Maj. P. M., 26 Nov., 1862. Mustered out 1 Feb., 1869.
Robinson, Alex'r H., Capt. C. S., 16 July, 1862. Mustered out 15 July, 1865.
Robinson, Chas. D., Capt A. Q. M., 4 Sept., 1861. Resigned 21 April, 1864.
Robinson, Chas. E., Capt. C. S., 14 Nov., 1862. Mustered out 2 Aug., 1865.
Robinson, Edward, Jr., Capt. A. A. G., 30 Sept., 1863. Resigned 28 May, 1864.
Robinson, Edward J., Capt. C. S., 30 June, 1864. Mustered out 10 Sept., 1866.
Robinson, George T., Capt. A. de C., 7 Nov., 1862. Discharged 15 Aug., 1863.
Robinson, H. L., Capt. A. Q. M., 6 May, 1862. Mustered out 2 Oct., 1866.
Robinson, J., Capt. A. Q. M., 26 Nov., 1862. Appointment revoked 12 March, 1863.
Robinson, James D., Maj. Surg., 5 Aug., 1861. Resigned 13 Feb., 1863.
Robinson, James M., Capt. A. Q. M., 17 July, 1862. Resigned 15 March, 1865.
Robinson, James S., Brig. Gen., 12 Jan., 1865. Mustered out 31 Aug., 1865.
Robinson, John C., Brig. Gen., 28 April, 1862. Mustered out 1 Sept., 1866.
Robinson, John M., Asst. Surg., 11 Sept., 1862. Maj. Surg., 19 Feb., 1863. Dismissed 6 Jan., 1865. Maj. Surg., 12 June, 1865. Mustered out 31 July, 1865.
Robinson, Joseph W., Capt. C. S., 30 June, 1862. Died 7 April, 1863.
Roby, George W., Capt. C. S., 18 Aug., 1864. Mustered out 27 Jan., 1866.
Rochester, Montgomery, Capt. A. A. G., 13 April, 1862. Mustered out 14 June, 1865.
Rochester, Wm. B., Maj. P. M., 1 June, 1861. Maj. P. M., U. S. A., 17 Jan., 1867.
Rockwell, Almon F., Capt. A. A. G., 15 Sept., 1863. Maj., 23 Feb., 1865. Mustered out 1 April, 1867.
Rockwell, Chas. H., Capt. A. Q. M., 29 Nov., 1862. Resigned 9 May, 1865.
Rockwood, Shepard S., Capt. C. S., 26 Nov., 1862. Mustered out 9 Oct., 1865.
Rodgers, Harris G., Maj. P. M., 22 Oct., 1862. Mustered out 31 March, 1866.
Rodgers, Hiram C., Capt. A. A. G., 30 June, 1862. Maj., 6 Aug., 1862. Resigned 30 Jan., 1865.
Rodman, Isaac P., Brig. Gen., 28 April, 1862. Died 30 Sept., 1862, of wounds received at Battle of Antietam, Md.
Roe, Edward P., Hosp. Chap., 29 Feb., 1864. Resigned 11 Oct., 1865.
Roebling, Wash'n A., Maj. A. de C., 20 April, 1864. Resigned 21 Jan., 1865.
Rogers, Andrew D., Maj. P. M., 26 Nov., 1862. Resigned 8 Oct., 1863.
Rogers, Henry C., Capt. A. Q. M., 26 Nov., 1862. Resigned 12 July, 1864.
Rogers, Isaac, Capt. C. S., 10 Sept., 1863. Appointment revoked 1 June, 1864.
Rogers, James K., Asst. Surg., 15 Aug., 1863. Maj. Surg., 19 Jan., 1864. Mustered out 11 Nov., 1865.
Rogers, Sam'l N., 2nd Lieut. Sig. Corps, 3 March, 1863. Mustered out 11 Sept., 1865.
Roney, Sam'l B., Capt. A. Q. M., 8 July, 1863. Mustered out 13 Dec., 1865.
Rood, Anson, Capt. A. Q. M., 9 Feb., 1865. Mustered out 20 Sept., 1865.
Rood, Tyler P., Capt. A. Q. M., 10 May, 1864. Resigned 9 April, 1865.
Roome, Wm. P., Capt. A. A. G., 27 Feb., 1863. Resigned 18 Jan., 1865.
Roots, Logan H., Capt. C. S., 28 May, 1864. Mustered out 31 May, 1866.
Roper, George S., Capt. C. S., 9 Sept., 1861. Mustered out 27 Jan., 1866.
Roper, John L., Capt. C. S., 20 April, 1864. Resigned 5 Feb., 1865.
Rose, George S., Capt. A. A. G., 3 Aug., 1861. Resigned 3 March, 1862.
Rose, George S., Asst. Surg., 24 Sept., 1863. Mustered out 31 Oct., 1865.
Rose, Lorin L., Capt. C. S., 26 Nov., 1862. Resigned 26 June, 1865.
Rosecrans, Wm. S., Maj. Gen., 21 March, 1862. Mustered out 15 Jan., 1866.
Rosekrans, Isaac A., Capt. C. S., 2 March, 1864. Mustered out 10 Sept., 1866.

Rosenberg, Jacob A., Hosp. Chap., 18 Jan., 1865. Mustered out 4 Aug., 1865.
Rosencrantz, Fredrik, Capt. A. A. G., 7 June, 1864. Mustered out 11 Nov., 1865.
Rosenthal, Leo, Capt. C. S., 7 April, 1864. Died 11 Sept., 1865.
Roskoton, Robert, Maj. Surg., 12 Oct., 1861. Resigned 25 Aug., 1862.
Ross, James R., Maj. A. de C., 21 April, 1864. Mustered out 10 Aug., 1865.
Ross, Leonard F., Brig. Gen., 25 April, 1862. Resigned 22 July, 1863.
Ross, Orlando H., Capt. A. de C., 11 March, 1863. Resigned 7 Sept., 1864.
Round, George C., 2nd Lieut. Sig. Corps, 3 March, 1863. Mustered out 12 Aug., 1865.
Rouse, J. Hill, Hosp. Chap., 2 July, 1862. Mustered out 4 Aug., 1865.
Rousseau, Lovell H., Brig. Gen., 1 Oct., 1861. Maj. Gen., 8 Oct., 1862. Resigned 30 Nov., 1865.
Routt, John L., Capt. A. Q. M., 28 July, 1863. Mustered out 20 Sept., 1865.
Rowe, Chas. H., Hosp. Chap., 15 Aug., 1864. Mustered out 20 Nov., 1865.
Rowell, A. Judson, Capt. C. S., 19 Feb., 1862. Resigned 22 April, 1862.
Rowell, Eliphalet, Maj. P. M., 23 Feb., 1864. Resigned 19 May, 1865.
Rowley, Thos. A., Brig. Gen., 29 Nov., 1862. Resigned 29 Dec., 1864.
Rowley, Wm. R., Capt. Addl. A. de C., 26 Feb., 1862. Maj. A. de C., 1 Nov., 1862. Resigned 30 Aug., 1864.
Royer, Harrison A., Capt. A. Q. M., 11 March, 1865. Mustered out 31 Aug., 1868.
Rucker, Dan'l H., Col. Addl. A. de C., 28 Sept., 1861. Brig. Gen., 23 May, 1863. Mustered out 1 Sept., 1866.
Rucker, Wm. A., Maj. P. M., 26 Nov., 1862. Maj. P. M., U. S. A., 16 April, 1866.
Rucker, Wm. M., Capt. C. S., 30 Aug., 1862. Resigned 4 Dec., 1862.
Randolph, Joseph, Capt. C. S., 28 May, 1864. Mustered out 18 Jan., 1866.
Ruger, Francis H., Capt. A. Q. M., 27 May, 1863. Died 28 June, 1865.
Ruger, Thos. H., Brig. Gen., 29 Nov., 1862. Mustered out 1 Sept., 1866.
Ruger, Wm., Capt. A. A. G., 23 June, 1863. Mustered out 22 Nov., 1865.
Ruggles, D. Colden, Maj. P. M., 30 June, 1862. Died 10 Feb.,1865.
Ruggles, George D., Col. Addl. A. de C., 28 June, 1862. Mustered out 31 May, 1866.
Ruggles, Horace M., Maj. P. M., 26 Nov., 1862. Resigned 7 Jan., 1864.
Ruggles, Levi, Capt. C. S., 11 March, 1863. Mustered out 20 March, 1866.
Rumsey, Will, Capt. A. A. G., 12 Sept., 1863. Maj., 9 Sept., 1864. Mustered out, 19 Sept., 1865.
Rundle, Sam'l E., Capt. A. Q. M., 19 Feb., 1863. Mustered out 8 Dec., 1865.
Runyon, Alex. N., Capt. A. Q. M., 17 Nov., 1863. Mustered out 15 Dec., 1864.
Rusch, Nicholas J., Capt. A. Q. M., 27 Sept., 1862. Died 22 Sept., 1864.
Rush, David G., Asst. Surg., 30 Jan., 1865. Mustered out 8 July, 1866.
Rushby, Thos. P., 1st Lieut. Sig. Corps, 3 March, 1863. Mustered out 12 Aug., 1865.
Rusling, James F., Capt. A. Q. M., 11 June, 1862. Mustered out 17 Sept., 1867.
Russ, Chas. E., Capt. A. Q. M., 14 July, 1862. Resigned 29 May, 1865.
Russell, Avery P., Capt. Addl. A. de C., 29 Jan., 1862. Discharged 21 March, 1862.
Russell, David A., Brig. Gen., 29 Nov., 1862. Killed 19 Sept., 1864, in the Battle of Opequan, Va.
Russell, Edmund H., 1st Lieut. Sig. Corps, 3 March, 1863. Appointment as Capt. expired 4 July, 1864. Capt., 14 Feb., 1865. Mustered out 12 Aug., 1865.
Russell, Harry, Capt. A. de C., 10 Oct., 1862. Resigned 7 July,, 1863.
Russell, Ira, Maj. Surg., 4 April, 1862. Resigned 29 June, 1865.
Russell, John K., Capt. A. Q. M., 24 March, 1862. Mustered out 20 April, 1866.
Russell, Sam'l A., Capt. A. de C., 4 May, 1863. Vacated commission 28 Aug., 1863.
Russell, Warren, Capt. A. Q. M., 26 Nov., 1862. Discharged 12 March, 1864.
Russell, Wm., Jr., Maj. A. A. G., 15 April, 1863. Mustered out 10 Feb., 1866.
Russell, Wm. C., Capt. A. A. G., 28 April, 1862. Killed 20 Sept., 1863, at Battle of Chickamauga, Ga.
Rutherford, Friend S., Capt. C. S., 30 June, 1862. Resigned 2 Sept., 1862. Brig. Gen., 27 June, 1864. Died 20 June, 1864.
Rutherford, George V., Capt. A. Q. M., 2 April, 1863. Mustered out 10 Nov., 1866.
Rutherford, John P., Capt. A. Q. M., 3 Aug., 1861. Mustered out 12 June, 1866.
Rutherford, Reuben C., Capt. C. S., 26 Nov., 1862. Capt. A. Q. M., 20 Dec., 1864. Mustered out 17 July, 1867.
Rynerson, Wm. L., Capt. A. Q. M., 30 June, 1864. Mustered out 3 Nov., 1866.
Saal, Gerhard, Asst. Surg., 9 Sept., 1863. Mustered out 27 July, 1865.
Sabin, Chas. V. H., Capt. A. Q. M., 29 Feb., 1864. Mustered out 20 June, 1865.
Sabin, John A., Maj. P. M., 29 July, 1862. Mustered out 1 May, 1866.
Safford, Sam'l A., Maj. P. M., 1 June, 1861. Mustered out 15 Jan., 1866.
Sage, Orin H., Hosp. Chap., 16 Feb., 1865. Mustered out 24 June, 1865.
Saint, Daniel, Capt. C. S., 3 Aug., 1861. Discharged 7 Aug., 1862.
Salisbury, Albert G., Maj. P. M., 28 May, 1864. Mustered out 21 Oct., 1867.
Salisbury, Javan B., Capt. C. S., 31 Oct., 1861. Resigned 7 Nov., 1864.
Sallade, Andrew M., Maj. P. M., 1 June, 1861. Dropped 13 Aug., 1862.
Salade, Jacob, Maj. P. M., 19 Feb., 1863. Mustered out 15 Feb., 1866.
Solomon, Fred'k, Brig. Gen., 16 June, 1862. Mustered out 24 Aug., 1865.
Salter, Francis, Maj. Surg., 7 Nov., 1862. Mustered out 23 Sept., 1865.
Sample, James P., Capt. A. A. G., 30 June, 1862. Maj., 13 Sept., 1864. Mustered out 20 March, 1866.
Sample, Thos. J., Capt. C. S., 1 Nov., 1861. Discharged 5 June, 1862.
Sampson, Chas. M., Capt. A. Q. M., 27 Feb., 1863. Mustered out 23 Oct., 1865.
Sampson, Jacob P., 1st Lieut. Sig. Corps, 3 March, 1863. Mustered out 12 Aug., 1865.
Sanborn, John B., Brig. Gen., 4 Aug., 1863. Mustered out 30 April, 1866.
Sanborn, Wash'n I., Capt. A. A. G., 1 Feb., 1865. Mustered out 1 Oct., 1866.
Sanders, Wm. P., Brig. Gen., 18 Oct., 1863. Died 19 Nov., 1863, of wounds received in action before Knoxville, Tenn.
Sanderson, James M., Capt. C. S., 7 Sept., 1861. Maj. Addl. A. de C., 15 July, 1862. Mustered out 15 Aug., 1865.
Sanford, Edward S., Col. Addl. A. de C., 26 Feb., 1862. Resigned 8 April, 1867.
Sanford, George P., Maj. P. M., 19 Sept., 1864. Mustered out 1 July, 1866.
Sanford, Isaac, Maj. P. M., 11 March, 1863. Died 19 March, 1864.
Sanford, James, Capt. C. S., 19 Feb., 1863. Discharged 23 Jan., 1864.
Sanger, Eugene F., Maj. Surg., 10 Nov., 1861. Mustered out 10 Aug., 1865.
Sappington, Mark T., Capt. A. Q. M., 5 Dec., 1863. Dismissed 23 March, 1865.
Sappington, Nicholas J., Capt. C. S., 7 Sept., 1861. Mustered out 26 March, 1866.
Sargent, Chas. S., Capt. A. de C., 15 March, 1865. Mustered out 26 Aug., 1865.

Sargent, M. Wheeler, Capt. C. S., 26 Nov., 1862. Appointment expired 4 March, 1863. Maj. P. M., 13 March, 1863. Resigned 12 Nov., 1863.
Saunders, Chas. R., Maj. P. M., 5 Sept., 1861. Rejected by Senate 11 March, 1862.
Saunders, Edwin D., Capt. A. A. G., 23 Dec., 1862. Killed 2 June, 1864, in Battle at Dallas, Ga.
Saunders, Thos. J., Maj. P. M., 23 Feb., 1864. Mustered out 16 April, 1866.
Saunders, Wm. P., Capt. C. S., 19 Aug., 1863. Died 27 Nov., 1864.
Sauvinet, Chas. S., Capt. A. Q. M., 6 March, 1865. Mustered out 28 July, 1865.
Savage, James W., Lieut. Col. Addl. A. de C., 31 March, 1862. Discharged 14 Dec., 1863.
Sawyer, Frank O., Capt. A. Q. M., 30 June, 1864. Mustered out 31 May, 1866.
Sawyer, James, Capt. C. S., 9 Feb., 1865. Mustered out 27 Nov., 1865.
Sawyer, Nath'l C., Maj. P. M., 21 July, 1863. Mustered out 20 July, 1866.
Sawyer, Roswell M., Capt. A. A. G., 6 March, 1862. Maj. 4 July, 1863. Mustered out 25 Oct., 1866.
Saxton, Rufus, Brig. Gen., 15 April, 1866. Mustered out 15 Jan., 1866.
Saxton, Sam'l W., Capt. Addl. A. de C., 30 April, 1862. Mustered out 20 July, 1866.
Saxton, Valentine, Capt. A. Q. M., 12 Dec., 1864. Mustered out 28 July, 1865.
Saylor, Benj'n, Capt. C. S., 20 April, 1864. Mustered out 10 Aug., 1865.
Sayre, James M., Capt. C. S., 26 Nov., 1862. Resigned 12 March, 1865.
Scammon, Chas. T., Maj. A. de C., 7 June, 1864. Mustered out 8 Feb., 1865.
Scammon, Eliakim P., Brig. Gen., 15 Oct., 1862. Mustered out 24 Aug., 1865.
Scates, Walter B., Maj. A. A. G., 30 June, 1862. Mustered out 4 Jan., 1866.
Schaumburg, James W., Maj. P. M., 5 Sept., 1861. Rejected by Senate 11 March, 1862.
Scheffler, Wm., Capt. Addl. A. de C., 16 Nov., 1861. Mustered out 26 May, 1865.
Schemmelfinnig, Alex'r, Brig. Gen., 29 Nov., 1862. Died 7 Sept., 1865.
Schenck, Egbert T. S., Capt. C. S., 7 Sept., 1861. Mustered out 1 Oct., 1867.
Schenck, Gerrett, Capt. C. S., 21 April, 1864. Died 5 Dec., 1865.
Schenck, James W., Capt. A. Q. M., 8 July, 1863. Mustered out 27 Nov., 1865.
Schenck, Rob't C., Brig. Gen., 17 May, 1861. Maj. Gen., 30 Aug., 1862. Resigned 5 Dec., 1863.
Schenk, John, Capt. A. Q. M., 29 Feb., 1864. Mustered out 7 Oct., 1865.
Schenofsky, Jules C. A., Capt. Addl. A. de C., 11 June, 1862. Resigned 22 May, 1865.
Schlaefflin, Henry A., Asst. Surg., 14 May, 1863. Maj. Surg., 27 May, 1863. Resigned 16 Aug., 1864.
Schlater, Wm. H., Capt. A. A. G., 21 Oct., 1861. Resigned 15 Aug., 1862.
Schmidt, Chas. D., Capt. A. Q. M., 10 Sept., 1861. Resigned 12 Aug., 1864.
Schmitt, Carl, Capt. A. A. G., 11 Oct., 1862. Resigned 5 Aug., 1864.
Schoeff, Albin, Brig. Gen., 30 Sept., 1861. Mustered out 15 Jan., 1866.
Schofield, James, Hosp. Chap., 19 Oct., 1863. Mustered out 21 Aug., 1865.
Schofield, John M., Brig. Gen., 21 Nov., 1861. Maj. Gen., 29 Nov., 1862. Appointment expired by Constitutional limitation 4 March, 1863. Brig. Gen., 4 March, 1863. Maj. Gen., 12 May, 1863, to rank from 29 Nov., 1862. Mustered out 1 Sept., 1866.
Scholefield, Chas. M., Maj. P. M., 10 March, 1863. Mustered out 1 Nov., 1865.

52

Schopp, Philip T., Capt. A. A. G., 16 May, 1862. Resigned 13 Sept., 1862.
Schreiner, Herman, Capt. C. S., 30 Aug., 1862. Mustered out 31 May, 1866.
Schriver, Edmund, Col. Addl. A. de C., 18 May, 1862. Col. I. G., U. S. A., 13 March, 1863.
Schroer, Augustus F., Lieut. Col. Addl. A. de C., 31 March, 1862. Mustered out 4 May, 1864.
Schultz, Solomon S., Asst. Surg., 7 Aug., 1863. Maj. Surg., 30 March, 1864. Resigned 28 March, 1865.
Schultze, John S., Capt. A. de C., 25 April, 1863. Maj. A. A. G., 23 June, 1863. Mustered out 22 Nov., 1865.
Schurz, Carl, Brig. Gen., 15 April, 1862. Maj. Gen., 14 March, 1863. Resigned 6 May, 1865.
Schuyler, Montgomery, Hosp. Chap., 23 June, 1862. Resigned 24 Aug., 1863.
Scofield, Hiram, Capt. A. A. G., 9 June, 1862. Appointment vacated 5 May, 1863.
Scofield, James K., Capt. C. S., 3 Aug., 1861. Mustered out 8 July, 1865.
Scofield, Smith O., Capt. A. Q. M., 18 May, 1864. Resigned 3 Feb., 1865.
Scott, David W., Capt. A. Q. M., 30 June, 1864. Mustered out 13 March, 1866.
Scott, Henry B., Capt. A. A. G., 17 July, 1862. Resigned 6 March, 1865.
Scott, James B., Capt. C. S., 2 March, 1864. Dishonorably mustered out 10 Sept., 1866.
Scott, James W., Capt. A. Q. M., 20 Aug., 1861. Resigned 4 Nov., 1861.
Scott, Jesse E., Capt. A. Q. M., 29 Feb., 1864. Mustered out 4 Jan., 1866.
Scott, John N., Maj. P. M., 23 Feb., 1864. Mustered out 15 Nov., 1865.
Scott, Rob't K., Brig. Gen., 12 Jan., 1865. Resigned 6 July, 1868.
Scott, Rob't N., Maj. A. A. G., 28 Sept., 1864. Mustered out 1 Jan., 1867.
Scott, W. H., Maj. P. M., 5 Aug., 1861. Mustered out 1 Sept., 1868.
Scovel, Henry W., Maj. P. M., 27 Feb., 1863. Mustered out 15 April, 1866.
Scovil, Nelson R., Maj. P. M., 26 Nov., 1862. Resigned 11 Feb., 1863.
Scudder, Frank H., Capt. C. S., 24 Oct., 1864. Mustered out 25 Aug., 1865.
Scull, Gideon, Capt. C. S., 3 Aug., 1861. Mustered out 31 May, 1866.
Scully, James W., Capt. A. Q. M., 25 Sept., 1865. Capt. A. Q. M., U. S. A., 27 Sept., 1865.
Seabury, Rob't S., Capt. A. A. G., 12 Sept., 1863. Died 8 May, 1864, of wounds received at Battle of Wilderness, Va.
Seabury, Thos. S., 1st Lieut. Sig. Corps, 3 March, 1863. Resigned 25 Jan., 1864.
Sealy, Israel R., Capt. A. A. G., 12 Aug., 1864. Resigned 7 Feb., 1865.
Seaton, Algernon S., Capt. C. S., 6 March, 1865. Mustered out 19 July, 1865.
Seaverns, Joel, Asst. Surg., 4 Dec., 1863. Maj. Surg., 30 March, 1864. Mustered out 7 Oct., 1865.
Sedgwick, John, Brig. Gen., 31 Aug., 1861. Maj. Gen., 4 July, 1862. Killed 9 May, 1864, at Battle of Spottsylvania C. H., Va.
Sedgwick, Wm. D., Capt. A. A. G., 16 Sept., 1861. Maj., 7 Aug., 1862. Died 27 Sept., 1862, of wounds received at the Battle of Antietam, Md.
See, George C., Capt. C. S., 26 Nov., 1862. Mustered out 15 Jan., 1866.
Seeley, Aaron, Capt. Addl. A. de C., 21 June, 1862. Resigned 29 Dec., 1862.
Seely, Franklin A., Capt. A. Q. M., 26 Nov., 1862. Mustered out 17 July, 1867.
Seelye, Edgar, Capt. A. Q. M., 18 May, 1864. Mustered out 21 Feb., 1866.
Seip, Albert N., 2nd Lieut. Sig. Corps, 3

March, 1863. Mustered out 12 Aug., 1865.
Selfridge, Robert O., Capt. A. A. G., 28 April, 1862. Maj., 14 July, 1862. Resigned 21 Feb., 1865.
Sellers, Alfred J., Capt. A. Q. M., 2 July, 1864. Mustered out 31 Oct., 1865.
Sells, Elijah, Maj. P. M., 9 March, 1863. Resigned 16 May, 1863.
Semple, Alex'r C., Capt. A. A. G., 29 Sept., 1862. Resigned 18 March, 1864.
Semple, Alex'r W., Capt. A. Q. M., 19 Feb., 1863. Resigned 11 April, 1864.
Severance, Martin J., Capt. A. Q. M., 26 Nov., 1862. Appointment expired 4 March, 1863.
Sewall, Fred'k D., Capt. A. A. G., 19 Sept., 1861. Resigned 24 June, 1862.
Seward, Sam'l S., Capt. Addl. A. de C., 16 June, 1862. Maj. A. de C., 28 Aug., 1863. Mustered out 31 Oct., 1865.
Seward, Wm. H., Jr., Brig. Gen., 13 Sept., 1864. Resigned 1 June, 1865.
Seward, Wm. T., Capt. C. S., 13 Sept., 1864 Resigned 14 July, 1865.
Seymour, Chas., Hosp. Chap., 16 Aug., 1862. Resigned 10 Sept., 1863.
Seymour, Fred'k, Maj. Surg., 24 Dec., 1861. Dismissed 19 Feb., 1864.
Seymour, Truman, Brig. Gen., 28 April, 1862. Mustered out 24 Aug., 1865.
Seymour, Wm. R., Capt. C. S., 2 March, 1864. Mustered out 26 Oct., 1865.
Shackelford, James M., Brig. Gen., 2 Jan., 1863. Resigned 18 Jan., 1864.
Shaffer, John W., Capt. A. Q. M., 3 Aug., 1861. Col. Addl. A. de C., 30 Jan., 1862. Resigned 26 Aug., 1864.
Shaler, Alex'r, Brig. Gen., 26 May, 1863. Mustered out 24 Aug., 1865.
Shallenberger, George A., Capt. A. Q. M., 26 Nov., 1862. Mustered out 8 Nov., 1865.
Shannon, Rich'd C., Capt. A. A. G., 2 Oct., 1862. Mustered out 10 Feb., 1866.
Sharp, Jacob, Maj. P. M., 26 Nov., 1862. Resigned 16 April, 1863.
Sharpe, Alex'r B., Capt. Addl. A. de C., 16 June, 1862. Resigned 27 Dec., 1862. Capt. A. de C., 28 Aug., 1863. Resigned 28 Jan., 1865.
Shattuck, Chas. S., Capt. C. S., 23 Feb., 1865. Mustered out 8 July, 1865.
Shaw, Ferdinand, Capt. C. S., 28 Jan., 1865. Mustered out 31 March, 1866.
Shaw, George S., Capt. Addl. A. de C., 9 July, 1862. Mustered out 10 July, 1866.
Shaw, Joel K., Capt. A. Q. M., 11 March, 1863. Mustered out 6 June, 1865.
Shaw, John J., Capt. C. S., 28 July, 1863. Resigned 24 Feb., 1864.
Shedd, Jerome J., Capt. C. S., 2 Feb., 1865. Resigned 16 July, 1865.
Sheets, Levi D., Asst. Surg., 1 Feb., 1864. Mustered out 9 Oct., 1865.
Sheldon, Alvanus W., Capt. C. S., 13 Oct., 1864. Mustered out 20 March, 1866.
Sheldon, Andrew F., Asst. Surg., 4 Oct., 1862. Maj. Surg., 13 April, 1863. Mustered out 18 Aug., 1865.
Sheldon, John A., Capt. C. S., 28 June, 1864. Resigned 5 Feb., 1865.
Sheldon, Lemuel F., Capt. A. Q. M., 27 Oct., 1863. Resigned 3 Nov., 1864.
Shelley, Rich'd L., Capt. Addl. A. de C., 30 Jan., 1862. Discharged 21 March, 1862. Capt. Addl. A. de C., 17 May, 1862. Discharged 18 Aug., 1862.
Shelly, Mortimer, Capt. C. S., 26 Nov., 1862. Appointment revoked 28 April, 1863.
Shelton, Eugene A., Capt. C. S., 19 Feb., 1863. Resigned 14 July, 1865.
Shelton, Orville C., Hosp. Chap., 15 Dec., 1864. Mustered out 23 Sept., 1865.
Shepard, Isaac F., Brig. Gen., 27 Oct., 1863. Appointment expired 4 July, 1864.
Shepard, Jeremiah M., Capt. C. S., 3 March, 1865. Mustered out 10 Aug., 1865.
Shepard, Andrew C., Capt. C. S., 2 July, 1863. Resigned 10 May, 1865.
Shepherd, Levin W., Capt. A. Q. M., 3 Oct., 1862. Mustered out 7 Oct., 1865.
Shepherd, Wm. D., Capt. C. S., 18 May, 1864. Mustered out 9 Oct., 1865.
Shepley, George F., Brig. Gen., 18 July, 1862. Resigned 1 July, 1865.
Sherfy, Wm. H., 1st Lieut. Sig. Corps, 3 March, 1863. Mustered out 1 Sept., 1865.
Sheridan, James B., Maj. P. M., 27 Oct., 1862. Mustered out 15 Feb., 1866.
Sheridan, John, Capt. A. Q. M., 3 July, 1863. Died 30 Aug., 1864.
Sheridan, Michael V., Capt. A. de C., 18 May, 1864. Mustered out 1 Aug., 1866.
Sheridan, Philip H., Brig. Gen., 1 July, 1862. Maj. Gen., 31 Dec., 1862. Maj. Gen., U. S. A., 8 Nov., 1864.
Sherman, Francis T., Brig. Gen., 21 July, 1865. Mustered out 15 Jan., 1866.
Sherman, Hoyt, Maj. P. M., 5 Sept., 1861. Resigned 9 April, 1864.
Sherman, Judson W., Capt. C. S., 7 Sept., 1861. Resigned 9 Nov., 1861.
Sherman, Socrates N., Maj. Surg., 19 Feb., 1863. Mustered out 7 Oct., 1865.
Sherman, Thos. W., Brig. Gen., 17 May, 1861. Mustered out 30 April, 1866.
Sherman, Wm. C. H., Maj. P. M., 10 Sept., 1861. Resigned 27 April, 1865.
Sherman, Wm. T., Brig. Gen., 17 May, 1861. Maj. Gen., 1 May, 1862. Maj. Gen., U. S. A., 12 Aug., 1864.
Sherman, Wm. W., Maj. P. M., 1 June, 1861. Dismissed 4 Jan., 1864.
Sherwood, Thos. H., Asst. Surg., 30 June, 1864. Mustered out 9 Oct., 1865.
Shields, Chas., Capt. A. Q. M., 11 June, 1862. Resigned 1 July, 1862.
Shields, James, Brig. Gen., 19 Aug., 1861. Resigned 28 March, 1863.
Shimmel, August, Capt. A. Q. M., 19 Feb., 1862. Discharged 22 April, 1865.
Shinn, James G., Hosp. Chap., 17 Sept., 1864. Mustered out 26 July, 1865.
Shipman, Azariah B., Maj. Surg., 4 April, 1862. Discharged 23 Feb., 1863.
Shippen, Edward, Maj. Surg., 12 Sept., 1862. Mustered out 11 July, 1865.
Shiras, Alex., Hosp. Chap., 19 Oct., 1863. Mustered out 26 July, 1865.
Shreve, Albert P., Maj. P. M., 23 Feb., 1864. Mustered out 30 Sept., 1867.
Shriber, Chas. H. R., Lieut. Col. Addl. A. de C., 19 May, 1862. Dismissed 4 Aug., 1862.
Shrigley, James, Hosp. Chap., 19 Jan., 1863. Mustered out 26 July, 1865.
Shuart, Wm. D., Maj. P. M., 28 May, 1864. Mustered out 1 Nov., 1865.
Shubert, Prosper, Capt. A. Q. M., 30 June, 1864. Resigned 19 May, 1865.
Shumard, George G., Maj. Surg., 5 Aug., 1861. Resigned 11 March, 1865.
Sibley, Henry H., Brig. Gen., 29 Sept., 1862. Appointment expired 4 March, 1863. Brig. Gen., 20 March, 1863. Mustered out 30 April, 1866.
Sibley, Henry R., Capt. C. S., 30 May, 1863. Mustered out 13 Dec., 1865.
Sickles, Daniel E., Brig. Gen., 3 Sept., 1861. Maj. Gen., 29 Nov., 1862. Mustered out 1 Jan., 1868.
Siebert, Louis, Capt. A. A. G., 22 May, 1863. Resigned 29 Feb., 1865.
Sigel, Franz, Brig. Gen., 17 May, 1861. Maj. Gen., 21 March, 1862. Resigned 4 May, 1865.
Sigmund, Albert M., Asst. Surg., 14 Nov., 1863. Resigned 20 April, 1865.
Sill, Edward E., Capt. A. A. G., 31 May, 1865. Mustered out 18 Sept., 1865.
Sill, Joshua W., Brig. Gen., 16 July, 1862. Killed 31 Dec., 1862, at Battle of Murfreesboro, Tenn.

Sim, Thos., Maj. Surg., 3 Aug., 1861. Mustered out 3 March, 1866.
Simmons, Sam'l, Capt. C. S., 29 Aug., 1861. Resigned 31 Jan., 1864.
Simpson, Anthony C., Capt. C. S., 28 Feb., 1865. Resigned 1 May, 1865.
Simpson, Chas. H., Maj. P. M., 11 March, 1863. Resigned 5 Aug., 1863.
Simpson, George B., Maj. P. M., 26 Nov., 1862. Resigned 2 May, 1864.
Simpson, Theodore W., Hosp. Chap., 7 July, 1862. Mustered out 31 May, 1866.
Sinclair, Wm. H., Capt. A. A. G., 5 Nov., 1862. Maj., 8 May, 1863. Mustered out 1 Sept., 1866.
Singleton, Wm. T., Capt. C. S., 7 June, 1864. Mustered out 3 Aug., 1865.
Sinton, Thos. R., Capt. C. S., 23 Sept., 1861. Resigned 10 Oct., 1862.
Sizer, Wm. S., 2nd Lieut. Sig. Corps, 3 March, 1863. Resigned 29 June, 1864.
Skelton, John F., Capt. C. S., 23 Jan., 1865. Mustered out 22 Sept., 1866.
Skinner, Clark, Hosp. Chap., 11 July, 1862. Discharged 4 Oct., 1862.
Skinner, Holly, Capt. A. Q. M., 5 Dec., 1863. Mustered out 16 Jan., 1867.
Skinner, Ralston, Maj. J. A., 19 Nov., 1862. Resigned 20 March, 1865.
Slack, James R., Brig. Gen., 10 Nov., 1864. Mustered out 15 Jan., 1866.
Slaght, James C., Capt. A. Q. M., 2 Sept., 1861. Resigned 6 May, 1865.
Slaughter, Wm. B., Capt. C. S., 28 April, 1862. Resigned 18 Nov., 1863.
Slagle, Jacob F., Maj. J. A., 12 June, 1865. Resigned 19 July, 1865.
Slavan, John H., Maj. P. M., 30 June, 1864. Appointment cancelled 10 Oct., 1864.
Sleeper, Hiram S., Maj. P. M., 19 Feb., 1863. Resigned 23 Nov., 1864.
Slemmer, Adam J., Brig. Gen., 29 Nov., 1862. Mustered out 24 Aug., 1865.
Slipper, Joseph A., Capt. A. A. G., 9 Sept., 1862. Mustered out 19 Sept., 1865.
Sloan, Isaac O., Hosp. Chap., 4 June, 1862. Appointment revoked 9 Sept., 1862. Hosp. Chap., 3 Dec., 1864. Mustered out 4 Aug., 1865.
Slocum, Henry W., Brig. Gen., 9 Aug., 1861. Maj. Gen., 4 July, 1862. Resigned 28 Sept., 1865.
Slocum, Joseph J., Capt. C. S., 19 Feb., 1862. Mustered out 7 July, 1866.
Sloo, Albert G., Capt. Addl. A. de C., 24 May, 1862. Resigned 23 June, 1863.
Slosson, John S., Capt. Addl. A. de C., 17 May, 1862. Resigned 10 Nov., 1864.
Slough, John P., Brig. Gen., 25 Aug., 1862. Mustered out 24 Aug., 1865.
Smiley, Wm. A., Maj. P. M., 17 Feb., 1865. Mustered out 31 July, 1865.
Smith, Andrew J., Brig. Gen., 17 March, 1862. Maj. Gen., 12 May, 1864. Mustered out 15 Jan., 1866.
Smith, Andrew J., Maj. A. A. G., 7 June, 1865. Mustered out 21 Feb., 1866.
Smith, A. Patterson, Capt. A. Q. M., 7 April, 1864. Mustered out 20 Sept., 1865.
Smith, Arden R., Capt. C. S., 20 Sept., 1862. Mustered out 13 July 1865.
Smith, Benj. F., Capt. A. A. G., 21 April, 1862. Resigned 5 Sept., 1862. Capt. A. A. G., 10 Oct., 1862. Mustered out 22 Nov., 1865.
Smith, Chas. F., Brig. Gen., 31 Aug., 1861. Maj. Gen., 21 March, 1862. Died 25 April, 1862.
Smith, Chas. K., Jr., Capt. A. Q. M., 12 May, 1862. Mustered out 26 Oct., 1866.
Smith, David H., Capt. A. Q. M., 26 Nov., 1862. Died 11 April, 1864.
Smith, David L., Capt. C. S., 19 Feb., 1862. Mustered out 13 March, 1866.
Smith, David P., Maj. Surg., 24 Dec., 1861. Mustered out 18 Aug., 1865.
Smith, De Witt C., Maj. P. M., 23 Feb., 1864. Died 28 Oct., 1864, from wounds received in an attack at Randolph, Tenn.
Smith, Edwin M., Capt. A. A. G., 28 May, 1862. Killed 1 June, 1862, at the Battle of Fair Oaks, Va.
Smith, Edward W., Maj. A. A. G., 30 Oct., 1862. Mustered out 20 July, 1866.
Smith, Edwin J., Capt. A. Q. M., 29 Feb., 1864. Mustered out 30 June, 1866.
Smith, Egbert T., Maj. P. M., 23 Feb., 1864. Resigned 9 July, 1864.
Smith, Francis M., Maj. P. M., 30 June, 1864. Mustered out 15 Nov., 1865.
Smith, George H., Capt. A. Q. M., 17 July, 1862. Resigned 1 Nov., 1864.
Smith, George H., Capt. C. S., 1 Oct., 1862. Discharged 23 March, 1864.
Smith, George N., Capt. A. Q. M., 4 Sept., 1861. Resigned 3 June, 1862. Maj. P. M., 26 Nov., 1862. Resigned 3 June, 1865.
Smith, George R., Maj. P. M., 23 July, 1863. Appointment revoked 5 Sept., 1863.
Smith, Gilbert C., Capt. A. Q. M., 18 May, 1864. Mustered out 3 Nov., 1866.
Smith, Giles A., Brig. Gen., 4 Aug., 1863. Maj. Gen., 24 Nov., 1865. Mustered out 1 Feb., 1866.
Smith, Green Clay, Brig. Gen., 11 June, 1862. Resigned 1 Dec., 1863.
Smith, Gustavus A., Brig. Gen., 19 Sept., 1862. Appointment expired 4 March, 1863.
Smith, Harvey A., Capt. C. S., 25 April, 1862. Died 13 Dec., 1862.
Smith, Henry W., Capt. A. A. G., 19 Sept., 1861. Mustered out 1 Sept., 1867.
Smith, Hiram, Capt. A. Q. M., 3 Feb., 1862. Mustered out 6 July, 1865.
Smith, Horatio M., Capt. A. Q. M., 5 Dec., 1863. Mustered out 13 March, 1866.
Smith, James Tuttle, Hosp. Chap., 4 Dec., 1862. Resigned 26 June, 1865.
Smith, John C., Hosp. Chap., 31 May, 1862. Mustered out 26 July, 1865.
Smith, J. Condith, Capt. A. Q. M., 1 April, 1862. Resigned 30 June, 1864.
Smith, J. C. P., Capt. A. A. G., 2 Oct., 1861. Resigned 14 Dec., 1861.
Smith, John E., Brig. Gen., 29 Nov., 1862. Mustered out 30 April, 1866.
Smith, John Wheeler, Maj. P. M., 30 June, 1862. Maj. P. M., U. S. A., 17 Jan., 1867.
Smith, Joseph Brice, Capt. A. A. G., 3 Aug., 1861. Mustered out 11 Nov., 1865.
Smith, Joseph S., Capt. C. S., 14 Nov., 1861. Mustered out 11 July, 1865.
Smith, Levi N., Capt. C. S., 30 June, 1863. Mustered out 30 April, 1866.
Smith, L. Ward, Hosp. Chap., 24 Nov., 1862. Died 23 Dec., 1863.
Smith, Marquis L., Capt. A. Q. M., 19 Aug., 1863. Resigned 1 June, 1864.
Smith, Morgan L., Brig. Gen., 16 July, 1862. Resigned 12 July, 1865.
Smith, Robert, Maj. P. M., 19 Feb., 1863. Mustered out 1 Nov., 1865.
Smith, Robert, Maj. P. M., 1 June, 1861. Resigned 9 April, 1865.
Smith, Rob't K., Maj. Surg., 10 Nov., 1861. Mustered out 27 July, 1865.
Smith, Thos. C., Capt. C. S., 20 April, 1864. Mustered out 20 July, 1865.
Smith, Thos. C. H., Brig. Gen., 29 Nov., 1862. Mustered out 15 Jan., 1866.
Smith, Thos. K., Brig. Gen., 11 Aug., 1863. Mustered out 15 Jan., 1866.
Smith, Thornton, Capt. A. Q. M., 3 Aug., 1861. Resigned 11 June, 1864.
Smith, Timothy D., Capt. A. Q. M., 21 June, 1862. Resigned 27 March, 1865.
Smith, William, Maj. P. M., 29 Aug., 1861. Mustered out 20 July, 1866.
Smith, Wm. C., Hosp. Chap., 22 April, 1863. Mustered out 19 June, 1865.
Smith, Wm. F., Brig. Gen., 13 Aug., 1861.

Maj. Gen., 4 July, 1862. Appointment as Maj. Gen. expired 4 March, 1863. Maj. Gen., 9 March, 1864. Resigned 4 Nov., 1865.
Smith, Wm. M., Maj. P. M., 23 Feb., 1864. Resigned 1 June, 1865.
Smith, Wm. S., Brig. Gen., 15 April, 1862. Resigned 15 July, 1864.
Smith, Wm. W., Capt. Addl. A. de C., 9 Dec., 1861. Appointment vacated 27 Nov., 1865.
Smyth, Thos. A., Brig. Gen., 1 Oct., 1864. Died 9 April, 1865, of wounds received in action near Farmville, Va.
Smythe, Rob't, Maj. P. M., 21 Nov., 1861. Mustered out 20 July, 1866.
Snelling, Fred'k G., Maj. Surg., 4 April, 1862. Resigned 11 June, 1864.
Snow, Sam'l W., Capt. A. A. G., 3 Feb., 1865. Mustered out 5 Dec., 1865.
Snyder, Henry, Hosp. Chap., 11 July, 1862. Mustered out 21 Aug., 1865.
Snyder, Henry W., Maj. P. M., 23 Feb., 1864. Died 18 April, 1866.
Snyder, Theophilus, Maj. P. M., 20 Jan., 1865. Mustered out 31 July, 1865.
Snyder, Wm. R., Maj. P. M., 21 April, 1864. Mustered out 30 April, 1866.
Sommer, Fred'k, Capt. A. de C., 7 June, 1864. Mustered out 3 March, 1865.
Spackman, Henry S., Hosp. Chap., 15 Nov., 1862. Mustered out 23 Oct., 1865.
Spangler, Bazil L., Capt. A. Q. M., 8 July, 1863. Mustered out 28 June, 1865.
Spear, Chas. Hosp. Chap., 23 June, 1862. Apointment revoked 11 Dec., 1862.
Spear, Edward, Jr., Maj. P. M., 21 Oct., 1864. Mustered out 1 Dec., 1865.
Spear, Henry S., Capt. Addl. A. de C., 26 April, 1862. Resigned 4 Aug., 1862.
Spear, Percy B., Capt. C. S., 30 Nov., 1861. Mustered out 22 Nov., 1865.
Spears, James G., Brig. Gen., 5 March, 1862. Dismissed 30 Aug., 1864.
Speed, Fred'k, Capt. A. A. G., 22 Aug., 1862. Mustered out 1 Sept., 1866.
Speed, John, Capt. A. A. G., 11 March, 1863. Maj. P. M., 22 March, 1865. Resigned 19 May, 1865.
Speed, Philip, Maj. P. M., 11 Sept., 1861. Resigned 23 Dec., 1862.
Speer, Alex. M., Asst. Surg., 19 Feb., 1863. Maj. Surg., 13 June, 1863. Mustered out 7 Oct., 1865.
Speer, John S., 2nd Lieut. Sig. Corps. 3 March, 1863. Mustered out 12 Aug., 1865.
Spencer, George E., Capt. A. A G., 24 Oct., 1862. Resigned 11 Sept., 1863.
Spencer, Joseph H., Capt. Sig. Corps. 3 March, 1863. Maj. 7 Oct., 1865. Mustered out 12 Oct., 1865.
Spencer, Sam'l A., Capt. A. A. G., 13 July, 1865. Mustered out 20 Jan., 1866.
Spencer, T. Rush. Maj. Surg., 5 Aug., 1861. Mustered out 19 July, 1865.
Sperry, Anson, Maj. P. M., 19 Feb., 1863. Mustered out 1 Dec., 1865.
Spicer, John, Capt. C. S., 10 Sept., 1861. Dismissed 13 Aug., 1862.
Spicer, Simeon, Capt. A. Q. M., 18 May, 1864. Mustered out 20 Sept., 1865.
Spillman, G. F., Capt. C. S. 12 May, 1862. Mustered out 19 July, 1865.
Spinola, Francis B., Brig. Gen., 1 Oct., 1862. Resigned 8 June, 1865.
Spooner, John A., Hosp. Chap., 8 Aug., 1862. Appointment expired 4 March 1863. Hosp. Chap., 22 April, 1863. Resigned 8 Feb., 1864.
Sprague, Chas. J., Maj. P. M., 17 Aug., 1861. Maj. P. M., U. S. A., 17 Jan., 1867.
Sprague, John W., Brig. Gen., 30 July, 1864. Mustered out 1 Sept., 1866.
Spraul, Chas., Capt. Addl. A. de C., 31 May, 1862. Mustered out 30 April, 1866.
Springstead, Jacob, Capt. A. Q. M., 10 Sept., 1861. Resigned 9 March, 1863.
Sprinkle, Wm. B., Capt. C. S., 8 March, 1865. Resigned 19 June, 1865.
Spruance, Enoch, Capt. A. Q. M., 30 June, 1864. Resigned 19 May, 1865.
Stackpole, Joseph L., Capt. C. S., 30 Aug., 1862. Maj. J. A., 11 July, 1863. Resigned 30 March, 1865.
Stager, Anson, Capt. A. Q. M., 11 Nov., 1861. Col. Addl. A. de C., 7 April, 1862. Mustered out 1 Sept., 1866.
Stahel, Julius H., Brig. Gen., 12 Nov., 1861. Maj. Gen., 14 March, 1863. Resigned 8 Feb., 1865.
Stahl, Daniel, Asst. Surg., 20 Sept., 1864. Maj. Surg., 13 Jan., 1865. Mustered out 13 Oct., 1865.
St. Albe, Gustavus, Capt. Addl. A. de C., 21 April, 1862. Mustered out 6 Sept., 1865.
Stanage, James O., Capt. C. S., 2 July, 1863. Resigned 11 Feb., 1865.
Stanford, Rob't L., Maj. Surg., 4 Sept., 1861. Resigned 18 Feb., 1865.
Stanley, David S., Brig. Gen., 28 Sept., 1861. Maj. Gen., 29 Nov., 1862. Mustered out 1 Feb., 1866.
Stannard, George J., Brig. Gen., 11 March, 1863. Resigned 28 June, 1866.
Stanton, Byron, Asst. Surg., 9 Feb., 1865. Mustered out 22 Aug., 1865.
Stanton, David, Maj. Surg., 7 Nov., 1862. Mustered out 10 Jan., 1866.
Stanton, Thaddeus H., Maj. P. M, 3 Oct., 1862. Maj. P. M., U. S. A., 17 Jan., 1867.
Staples, Robert G., Capt. A. Q. M., 6 Nov., 1863. Mustered out 31 May, 1866.
Staples, Sam'l C., Maj. P. M., 15 Sept., 1862. Mustered out 20 July, 1866.
Stark, Cyrus, Capt. C. S., 18 May, 1864. Resigned 16 April, 1865.
Starks, Jonathan J., Capt. C. S., 14 May, 1863. Resigned 5 Sept., 1863.
Starkweather, Fred'k T., Capt. A. Q. M., 19 Feb., 1863. Resigned 20 Nov., 1865.
Starkweather, John C., Brig. Gen., 17 July, 1863. Resigned 11 May, 1865.
Starling, Lyne, Capt. A. A. G., 10 Oct., 1861. Maj., 13 Aug., 1862. Resigned 20 Jan., 1864.
Starr, Sydney S., Capt. A. Q. M., 29 Feb., 1864. Mustered out 12 Oct., 1865.
Stealy, George I., Capt. A. Q. M., 3 Aug., 1861. Resigned 19 May, 1864.
Stearns, Geo. L., Maj. A. A. G., 13 June, 1863. Discharged 30 May, 1864.
Stearns, Henry P., Maj. Surg., 21 Sept., 1861. Mustered out 25 Aug., 1865.
Stearns, Joseph E., Capt. A. A. G., 26 Aug., 1862. Resigned 21 Feb., 1863.
Stedman, Hollis, Capt. C. S., 27 Jan., 1865. Mustered out 11 May, 1866.
Steedman, James B., Brig. Gen., 17 July, 1862. Maj. Gen., 20 April, 1864. Resigned 18 Aug., 1866.
Steele, Fred'k. Brig. Gen., 29 Jan., 1862. Maj. Gen., 29 Nov., 1862. Mustered out 1 March, 1867.
Steele, George R., Capt. A. de C., 18 April, 1863. Mustered out 22 Nov., 1865.
Steele, Hiram R., Capt. C. S., 18 May, 1864. Mustered out 4 Jan., 1866.
Steele, John W., Maj. A. de C., 27 Oct., 1864. Mustered out 20 Jan., 1866.
Steele, Sam'l R., Capt. C. S., 19 Feb., 1862. Mustered out 14 June, 1865.
Steger, James H., Capt. A. A. G., 4 Sept., 1863. Mustered out 10 Feb., 1866.
Steinberger, Justus, Capt. A. A. G., 28 Sept., 1861. Resigned 10 Oct., 1861.
Stephan, Joseph A., Hosp. Chap., 18 May, 1863. Mustered out 15 July, 1865.
Stephens, Chas. B., Capt. A. Q. M. 31 Jan., 1865. Mustered out 20 Sept., 1865.
Sterling, Levi, Maj. P. M., 23 Feb., 1864. Resigned 19 May, 1865.

Steuart, Wm. H., Maj. P. M., 28 May, 1864. Mustered out 15 Jan., 1866.
Stevens, Fenton F., Maj. P. M., 23 Feb., 1864. Mustered out 7 May, 1867.
Stevens, Hazzard, Capt. A. A. G., 16 Oct., 1861. Maj., 13 Oct., 1864. Mustered out 19 Sept., 1865.
Stevens, Henry, Hosp. Chap., 13 April, 1863. Mustered out 11 July, 1865.
Stevens, Hiram, Capt. A. A. G., 3 Aug., 1861. Died 9 June, 1863.
Stevens, Isaac I., Brig. Gen., 28 Sept., 1861. Maj. Gen., 18 July, 1862. Killed 1 Sept., 1862, at Battle of Chantilly, Va.
Stevens, Rob't J., Maj. P. M., 18 March, 1864. Resigned 29 May, 1865.
Stevenson, Columbus S., Maj. P. M., 1 June, 1861. Mustered out 23 Sept., 1865.
Stevenson, John D., Brig. Gen., 29 Nov., 1862. Mustered out 15 Jan., 1866.
Stevenson, Richard, Capt. A. Q. M., 7 Oct., 1861. Died 5 Oct., 1862.
Stevenson, Thos. G., Brig. Gen., 14 March, 1863. Killed 10 May, 1864, at Battle of Spottsylvania C. H., Va.
Stewart, Andrew, Capt. A. A. G., 1 Sept., 1862. Mustered out 2 Feb., 1866.
Stewart, Chas., Capt. A. A. G., 11 Sept., 1861. Dismissed 10 Feb., 1862.
Stewart, Chas., Capt. C. S., 2 July, 1864. Mustered out 9 Oct., 1865.
Stewart, Fred'k V., Capt. A. Q. M., 9 June, 1862. Discharged 18 July, 1863.
Stewart, Isaac I., Hosp. Chap., 10 Jan., 1863. Died 15 Aug., 1864.
Stewart, Isaac S., Maj. P. M., 26 Nov., 1862. Mustered out 10 April, 1867.
Stewart, John, Capt. A. Q. M., 19 Feb., 1863. Mustered out 8 Jan., 1866.
Stewart, Wm. D., Maj. Surg., 3 Aug., 1861. Mustered out 3 Aug., 1865.
Stewart, Wm. H., Capt. C. S., 26 Nov., 1862. Resigned 26 Oct., 1863.
Stickney, Clifford., 1st Lieut. Sig. Corps, 3 March, 1863. Maj. A. A. G., 7 Aug., 1865. Mustered out 5 Oct., 1866.
Stickney, Robert C., Capt. C. S., 24 March, 1862. Discharged 20 Nov., 1862.
Stiles, Richard C., Maj. Surg., 11 Sept., 1862. Resigned 16 Jan., 1864.
Stilson, Sherwood H., Capt. A. A. G., 11 March, 1865. Mustered out 22 Nov., 1865.
Stinson, Daniel, Capt. A. Q. M., 3 Aug., 1861. Mustered out 31 May, 1866.
Stinson, Henry M., Capt. A. de C., 25 April, 1863. Died 22 Feb., 1866.
Stipp, George W., Maj. Surg., 21 Sept., 1861. Lieut. Col. Med. Insp., 12 March, 1863. Mustered out 31 Oct., 1865.
Stocker, Anthony E., Maj. Surg., 3 Aug., 1861. Mustered out 15 Sept., 1865.
Stockton, Howard, Capt. Addl. A. de C., 9 June, 1862. Resigned 7 Feb., 1863.
Stockton, J. Addison, Capt. C. S., 21 April, 1864. Cashiered 25 July, 1865.
Stockton, Sam'l W., Capt. A. de C., 8 Nov., 1862. Discharged 15 Aug., 1863.
Stockwell, A. Jerome, Capt. A. Q. M., 21 Jan., 1865. Mustered out 12 Oct., 1865.
Stoddard, Chas. B., Capt. A. Q. M., 11 March, 1865. Mustered out 14 Aug., 1865.
Stoddard, Wm., Capt. A. Q. M., 12 May, 1862. Dismissed 30 May, 1864.
Stokes, James H., Capt. A. A. G., 22 Aug., 1864. Brig. Gen., 20 July, 1865. Mustered out 24 Aug., 1865.
Stolbrand, Carlos J., Brig. Gen., 18 Feb., 1865. Mustered out 15 Jan., 1866.
Stoms, Willard P., Maj. P. M., 11 March, 1863. Mustered out 1 Dec., 1865.
Stone, Brinton, Asst. Surg., 18 May, 1864. Mustered out 11 April, 1866.
Stone, Chas. P., Brig. Gen., 17 May, 1861. Mustered out 4 April, 1864.
Stone, Henry, Capt. A. A. G., 4 April, 1863. Resigned 19 Jan., 1865.
Stone, James, Capt. C. S., 26 Nov., 1862. Mustered out 12 July, 1865.
Stone, Joseph C., Capt. A. A. G., 27 Feb., 1863. Resigned 14 July, 1865.
Stone, Lincoln R., Asst. Surg., 24 Oct., 1863. Maj. Surg., 4 Dec., 1863. Mustered out 7 Oct., 1865.
Stone, Milton J., Maj. P. M., 1 June, 1861. Mustered out 31 July, 1865.
Stoneman, George, Brig. Gen., 13 Aug., 1861. Maj. Gen., 29 Nov., 1862. Mustered out 1 Sept., 1866.
Stoughton, Edwin H., Brig. Gen., 5 Nov., 1862. Appointment expired 4 March, 1863.
Stover, David B., Capt. A. Q. M., 19 Feb., 1863. Mustered out 7 April, 1866.
Stowe, Fred'k W., Capt. A. A. G., 27 Feb., 1863. Resigned 1 Aug., 1864.
Straat, John N., Capt. C. S., 10 Sept., 1862. Resigned 19 May, 1863.
Strang, Edward J., Capt. A. Q. M., 13 April, 1863. Capt. A. Q. M., U. S. A., 18 Jan., 1867.
Strawbridge, James D., Maj. Surg., 4 Sept., 1861. Mustered out 27 July, 1865.
Strew, Wm. W., Maj. Surg., 4 Sept., 1861. Resigned 6 Nov., 1862.
Strickle, Abraham E., Capt. C. S., 2 March, 1862. Died 9 July, 1863.
Strong, George C., Maj. A. A. G., 1 Oct., 1861. Appointment expired 17 July, 1862. Brig. Gen., 29 Nov., 1862. Maj. Gen., 18 July, 1863. Died 30 July, 1863, of wounds received in the assault on Fort Wagner, S. C.
Strong, John A., Capt. C. S., 6 July, 1864. Resigned 8 July, 1865.
Strong, Marcellus G. V., Capt. A. A. G., 1 May, 1862. Mustered out 4 May, 1864.
Strong, Nelson Z., Capt. C. S., 25 Feb., 1865. Mustered out 10 Jan., 1867.
Strong, Richard P., 1st Lieut. Sig. Corps, 3 March, 1863. Mustered out 19 April, 1866.
Strong, Wm. K., Brig. Gen., 28 Sept., 1861. Resigned 20 Oct., 1863.
Strother, David H., Capt. A. A. G., 6 March, 1862. Appointment vacated 1 June, 1862.
Strowbridge, Eli, Hosp. Chap., 16 July, 1862. Discharged 19 Nov., 1862.
Stryker, Wm. S., Maj. P. M., 19 Feb., 1863. Resigned 30 June, 1866.
Stryker, Wm. S., 1st Lieut. Sig. Corps, 3 March, 1863. Mustered out 29 Aug., 1865.
Stuart, David, Brig. Gen., 29 Nov., 1862. Rejected by Senate 11 March, 1863.
Stuart, Lyman Y., Capt. C. S., 10 Sept., 1862. Mustered out 16 June, 1865.
Stubb, George E., Asst. Surg., 9 Jan., 1865. Mustered out 18 Jan., 1866.
Stubbs, Joseph D., Capt. A. Q. M., 6 Nov., 1862. Mustered out 17 July, 1867.
Study, James M., Asst. Surg., 13 Oct., 1863. Maj. Surg., 10 Feb., 1865. Mustered out 11 Nov., 1865.
Stumbaugh, Fred'k S., Brig. Gen., 29 Nov., 1862. Appointment revoked 22 Jan., 1863.
Sturdevant, Sam'l H., Capt. C. S., 3 Aug., 1861. Mustered out 26 June, 1865.
Sturgeon, David B., Asst. Surg., 11 Sept., 1862. Maj. Surg., 27 May, 1863. Resigned 3 April, 1864.
Sturgis, Henry B., Capt. Addl. A. de C., 21 June, 1862. Resigned 14 June, 1865.
Sturgis, Samuel D., Brig. Gen., 10 Aug., 1861. Mustered out 24 Aug., 1865.
Suckley, George, Maj. Surg., 3 Aug., 1861. Resigned 22 April, 1865.
Sullivan, Henry V., Maj. P. M., 5 Sept., 1861. Resigned 8 Feb., 1865.
Sullivan, James, Capt. C. S., 21 July, 1862. Resigned 10 May, 1865.

Sullivan, Jeremiah C., Brig. Gen., 28 April, 1862. Resigned 11 May, 1865.
Sullivan, John H., Asst. Surg., 6 July, 1863. Dismissed 12 Aug., 1863.
Sully, Alfred, Brig. Gen., 26 Sept., 1862. Mustered out 30 April, 1866.
Summers, Moses, Capt. A. Q. M., 18 May, 1864. Mustered out 20 Sept., 1865.
Sumner, Chas. A., Capt. A. Q. M., 26 Nov., 1862. Resigned 30 March, 1864.
Sumner, Edwin V., Maj. Gen., 4 July, 1862. Died 21 March, 1863.
Sumner, Edwin V., Maj. A. de C., 19 May, 1863. Discharged 15 Aug., 1863.
Sumner, Sam'l S., Capt. A. de C., 20 Aug., 1862. Discharged 15 Aug., 1863.
Sutherland, Wm. A., Capt. A. A. G., 18 March, 1864. Maj., 19 Aug., 1865. Mustered out 8 Dec., 1865.
Sutton, George L., Asst. Surg., 4 Oct., 1862. Maj. Surg., 13 April, 1863. Mustered out 31 Oct., 1865.
Suydam, Chas. C., Capt. A. A. G., 6 March, 1862. Resigned 31 Dec., 1863.
Suydam, Simon P., Capt. A. Q. M., 26 Nov., 1862. Mustered out 18 Jan., 1866.
Swaim, David G., Capt. A. A. G., 16 May, 1862. Maj., 7 Feb., 1865. Mustered out 15 Sept., 1866.
Swain, James A., Capt. A. Q. M., 5 Aug., 1861. Mustered out 8 Jan., 1866.
Swain, Julius M., 2nd Lieut. Sig. Corps, 3 March, 1863. Resigned 14 June, 1865.
Swallow, Benj'n, Hosp. Chap., 12 Oct., 1864. Mustered out 4 Aug., 1865.
Swartwout, George H., Capt. C. S., 11 March, 1863. Discharged 30 Oct., 1863.
Swartzwelder, Adam C., Asst. Surg., 27 Feb., 1863. Maj. Surg., 9 July, 1863. Mustered out 1 Nov., 1867.
Swasey, Chas. E., Asst. Surg., 7 Nov., 1862. Maj. Surg., 15 Aug., 1863. Mustered out 19 Oct., 1865.
Swasey, Wm. F., Capt. A. Q. M., 26 Nov., 1862. Mustered out 13 March, 1866.
Swayne, Wager, Brig. Gen., 8 March, 1865. Maj. Gen., 20 June, 1865. Mustered out 1 Sept., 1867.
Swearingen, Thos. B., Capt. A. A. G., 8 Aug., 1862. Mustered out 11 Oct., 1865.
Sweeney, Thos. W., Brig. Gen., 29 Nov., 1862. Mustered out 24 Aug., 1865.
Sweet, Orlando P., Asst. Surg., 20 Jan., 1865. Mustered out 27 Nov., 1865.
Sweitzer, Nelson B., Lieut. Col. Addl. A. de C., 28 Sept., 1861. Discharged 31 March, 1863.
Swetland, Silas A., Capt. C. S., 13 March, 1863. Cashiered 17 Feb., 1865.
Swift, Henry A., Capt. A. Q. M., 26 Nov., 1862. Appointment expired 4 March, 1863.
Swift, Henry M., Capt. C. S., 14 April, 1862 Resigned 26 May, 1864.
Swift, Lucien, Capt. A. Q. M., 28 July, 1863. Resigned 2 Oct., 1863.
Swigart, D. W., Capt. A. Q. M., 31 Oct., 1861. Resigned 28 Oct., 1864.
Swope, Rufus C., Capt. A. Q. M., 26 Nov., 1862. Mustered out 4 Aug., 1866.
Sykes, George, Brig. Gen., 28 Sept., 1861. Maj. Gen., 29 Nov., 1862. Mustered out 15 Jan., 1866.
Sympson, Alex., Capt. A. Q. M., 31 Oct., 1861. Resigned 1 April, 1864.
Szabad, Emeric, Capt. Addl. A. de C., 16 June, 1862. Mustered out 7 Oct., 1865.
Taft, Henry S., Capt. Sig. Corps, 3 March, 1863. Resigned 20 Aug., 1864.
Taggard, Frank W., Capt. A. A. G., 11 March, 1863. Maj., 23 Feb., 1865. Mustered out 18 July, 1867.
Taggart, Grantham J., Capt. C. S., 3 Aug., 1861. Resigned 8 Aug., 1864.
Taggart, Sam'l L., Capt. A. A. G., 4 Sept., 1863. Mustered out 7 Oct., 1865.
Talbot, Benj'n F., Capt. C. S., 7 Nov., 1862. Mustered out 15 July, 1865.
Talbot, Wm. K., Hosp. Chap., 22 April, 1863. Mustered out 15 July, 1865.
Tallman, James H., Capt. A. Q. M., 24 March, 1862. Dismissed 20 Feb., 1866.
Tannatt, George F., Capt. Addl. A. de C., 5 July, 1862. Died 15 Aug., 1862, of wounds received at Battle of Cedar Mountain, Va.
Tappan, Benj'n, Asst. Surg., 3 Dec., 1864. Killed 22 March, 1866, by Indians in Arizona.
Tarbell, Doctor, Capt. C. S., 26 Nov., 1862. Mustered out 27 July, 1865.
Tarkington, Wm. C., Capt. C. S., 3 Aug., 1861. Resigned 11 Sept., 1863.
Tarr, Fred'k C., Capt. A. A. G., 29 Sept., 1862. Maj. P. M., 23 Feb., 1864. Mustered out 1 Nov., 1865.
Tauszky, Rudolph, Asst. Surg., 24 Sept., 1863. Mustered out 27 July, 1865.
Taylor, Alfred K., 2nd Lieut. Sig. Corps, 1 March, 1863. Mustered out 1 May, 1866.
Taylor, David, Maj. P. M., 1 June, 1861. Mustered out 1 Feb., 1869.
Taylor, Edward P., Capt. A. Q. M., 8 March, 1865. Mustered out 8 Dec., 1865.
Taylor, George W., Brig. Gen., 9 May, 1862. Died 31 Aug., 1862, of wounds received in action at Cub Run, Va.
Taylor, Jeremiah G., Capt. A. de C., 6 Nov., 1863. Resigned 6 Aug., 1864.
Taylor, John H., Maj. Surg., 2 Oct., 1861. Mustered out 25 Aug., 1865.
Taylor, John W., Capt. A. Q. M., 22 June, 1861. Resigned 12 Sept., 1863.
Taylor, Lester L., Capt. A. de C., 24 Aug., 1864. Mustered out 12 Jan., 1866.
Taylor, Morse K., Maj. Surg., 8 Aug., 1862. Mustered out 12 Oct., 1865.
Taylor, Peter A., Capt. Sig. Corps, 3 March, 1863. Mustered out 4 Sept., 1865.
Taylor, Robert R., Asst. Surg., 7 Nov., 1862. Maj. Surg., 13 April, 1863. Mustered out 20 March, 1866.
Taylor, Sam'l W., Capt. A. de C., 21 April, 1864. Mustered out 10 July, 1866.
Taylor, Stuart M., Capt. A. A. G., 23 Dec., 1862. Mustered out 31 Oct., 1865.
Taylor, Wilson, Brig. Gen., 7 Sept., 1862. Resigned 19 Jan., 1863.
Taylor, Woodbury M., Capt. C. S., 18 March, 1864. Mustered out 21 Feb., 1866.
Teall, Wm. W., Capt. C. S., 4 Oct., 1862. Resigned 1 Feb., 1864.
Teed, John L., Asst. Surg., 12 June, 1863. Maj. Surg., 29 June, 1863. Mustered out 7 Oct., 1865.
Telford, John G., Capt. A. A. G., 29 Feb., 1864. Mustered out 10 July, 1866.
Templin, Samuel V., Capt. C. S., 2 Feb., 1865. Mustered out 7 June, 1865.
Ten Eyck, Anthony, Maj. P. M., 1 June, 1861. Mustered out 23 Sept., 1865.
Tenny, Horace A., Maj. P. M., 14 July, 1862. Resigned 11 June, 1864.
Terrell, Chas. M., Maj. P. M., 30 June, 1862. Maj. P. M., U. S. A., 17 Jan., 1867.
Terrell, Wm. G., Maj. P. M., 31 Aug., 1861. Mustered out 1 Dec., 1865.
Terrill, Wm. R., Brig. Gen., 9 Sept., 1862. Killed 8 Oct., 1862, at Battle of Perryville, Ky.
Terry, Adrian, Capt. A. A. G., 17 Oct., 1862. Maj., 16 Jan., 1865. Mustered out 11 May, 1866.
Terry, Alfred H., Brig. Gen., 25 April, 1862. Maj. Gen., 15 Jan., 1865. Mustered out 1 Sept., 1866.
Terry, Henry D., Brig. Gen., 17 July, 1862. Resigned 7 Feb., 1865.
Terry, Josiah M., Capt. C. S., 26 Nov., 1862. Resigned 10 Jan., 1865.
Teter, Isaac P., Hosp. Chap., 27 Aug., 1864. Mustered out 23 Sept., 1865.

Thayer, Amos M., 1st Lieut. Sig. Corps, 3 March, 1863. Mustered out 1 Aug., 1865.
Thayer, Homer L., Capt. A. Q. M., 7 April, 1864. Mustered out 26 Feb., 1867.
Thayer, John M., Brig. Gen., 4 Oct., 1862. Appointment expired 4 March, 1863. Brig. Gen., 13 March, 1863. Resigned 19 July, 1865.
Thayer, Nathan, Maj. P. M., 26 Nov., 1862. Mustered out 1 Dec., 1865.
Thayer, Sam'l W., Asst. Surg., 4 Nov., 1864. Mustered out 27 July, 1865.
Tholan, Wm., Capt. A. A. G., 13 March, 1863. Discharged 10 March, 1864.
Thom, George, Col. Addl. A. de C., 16 Nov., 1861. Mustered out 31 May, 1866.
Thomas, Arthur G., Hosp. Chap., 30 July, 1862. Mustered out 26 July, 1865.
Thomas, Augustus L., Capt. A. Q. M., 31 Oct., 1862. Resigned 3 Oct., 1865.
Thomas, Chauncey B., Hosp. Chap., 6 June, 1862. Mustered out 13 July, 1866.
Thomas, Chester, Capt. A. Q. M., 9 Feb., 1863. Resigned 3 June, 1864.
Thomas, Chester, Jr., Capt. C. S., 19 Feb., 1863. Resigned 9 Feb., 1865.
Thomas, Edmond J., Capt. A. Q. M., 7 April, 1864. Resigned 6 July, 1865.
Thomas, George H., Brig. Gen., 17 Aug., 1861. Maj. Gen., 25 April, 1862. Maj. Gen. U. S. A., 15 Dec., 1864.
Thomas, Hanson A., Capt. A. Q. M., 16 March, 1863. Resigned 12 Jan., 1864.
Thomas, Henry G., Brig. Gen., 30 Nov., 1864. Mustered out 15 Jan., 1866.
Thomas, Horace H., Capt. A. A. G., 12 Nov., 1863. Mustered out 20 May, 1865.
Thomas, Stephen, Brig. Gen., 1 Feb., 1865. Mustered out 24 Aug., 1865.
Thomas, Thos. S., Hosp. Chap., 11 July, 1862. Mustered out 30 June, 1865.
Thomas, Webster, Capt. C. S., 28 Feb., 1865. Mustered out 19 July, 1865.
Thomas, Wm. C., Capt. C. S., 21 April, 1864. Resigned 10 May, 1865.
Thomas, Wm. R., Capt. A. A. G., 18 May, 1864. Resigned 12 May, 1865.
Thompson, Ambrose, Capt. A. Q. M., 22 Aug., 1861. Lieut. Col. Addl. A. de C., 19 May, 1862. Resigned 26 Aug., 1863.
Thompson, Bradley M., Maj. P. M., 2 July, 1864. Mustered out 1 Dec., 1865.
Thompson, Chas. H., Capt. C. S., 29 July, 1863. Mustered out 18 Aug., 1865.
Thompson, Chas R., Capt. A. de C., 14 Nov., 1862. Appointment vacated 17 Aug., 1863.
Thompson, George F., Capt. C. S., 10 Sept., 1862. Mustered out 15 June, 1866.
Thompson, James, Capt. A. Q. M., 18 May, 1864. Mustered out 20 Sept., 1865.
Thompson, James H., Asst. Surg., 2 Nov., 1863. Maj. Surg., 4 Dec., 1863. Mustered out 16 Sept., 1865.
Thompson, J. Harry, Maj. Surg., 2 Nov., 1861. Mustered out 18 April, 1862.
Thompson, John R., Capt. C. S., 2 Nov., 1863. Mustered out 27 Jan., 1866.
Thompson, Richard W., Jr., Capt. C. S., 20 Aug., 1861. Mustered out 9 Oct., 1865.
Thompson, Thos., Capt. A. A. G., 2 June, 1863. Mustered out 5 Dec., 1865.
Thompson, Wm., Capt. A. Q. M., 26 Nov., 1862. Capt. C. S., 19 Feb., 1863. Mustered out 4 Aug., 1865.
Thompson, Wm. C., Maj. Surg., 3 Aug., 1861. Resigned 19 Sept., 1862.
Thompson, Wm. D., Maj. P. M., 23 Feb., 1864. Mustered out 1 Nov., 1865.
Thompson, Wm. S., Asst. Surg., 11 Sept., 1862. Maj. Surg., 26 March, 1863. Mustered out 24 June, 1865.
Thoms, Rob't S., Capt. A. de C., 25 April, 1863. Resigned 5 Jan., 1865.
Thorndike, George L., Capt. C. S., 9 Sept., 1861. Resigned 24 March, 1863.
Thorndike, James E., Capt. Addl. A. de C., 17 June, 1862. Resigned 5 June, 1865.
Thorne, Wm. H., Maj. Surg., 4 April, 1862. Mustered out 7 Oct., 1865.
Thornton, James J., Capt. A. Q. M., 19 Feb., 1863. Resigned 12 Sept., 1864.
Thornton, Jesse, Capt. C. S., 6 March, 1862. Mustered out 8 July, 1865.
Thornton, Wm. A., Maj. P. M., 28 Jan., 1865. Mustered out 31 July, 1865.
Thorpe, James C., Asst. Surg., 25 Nov., 1864. Resigned 17 April, 1865.
Thorpe, James H., Capt. C. S., 30 Sept., 1862. Resigned 17 Feb., 1864.
Thrall, Henry, Capt. A. A. G., 20 Aug., 1861. Died 18 Sept., 1863.
Threlkeld, Wm., Asst. Surg., 23 April, 1863. Maj. Surg., 9 July, 1863. Mustered out 25 Aug., 1865.
Thrush, John, Hosp. Chap., 7 July, 1862. Discharged 10 Feb., 1863. Hosp. Chap., 21 March, 1865. Resigned 22 May, 1865.
Thruston, Chas. M., Brig. Gen., 7 Sept., 1861. Resigned 17 April, 1862.
Thruston, Dickinson P., Capt. A. de C., 11 March, 1863. Resigned 1 May, 1865.
Thruston, Gates P., Maj. A. A. G., 4 Sept., 1863. Mustered out 19 Dec., 1865.
Thurm, Ernst W., Maj. Surg., 19 Feb., 1863. Mustered out 10 Aug., 1865.
Thurston, A. Henry, Maj. Surg., 5 Oct., 1861. Mustered out 27 July, 1865.
Thurston, James S., Maj. P. M., 11 Aug., 1863. Mustered out 28 July, 1866.
Thustin, Luther T., Maj. P. M., 11 Sept., 1861. Mustered out 30 April, 1866.
Tibbitts, John A., Capt. C. S., 28 May, 1864. Mustered out 31 July, 1865.
Tibbitts, Wm. B., Brig. Gen., 18 Oct., 1865. Mustered out 15 Jan., 1866.
Tichenor, George C., Maj. A. de C., 2 Feb., 1865. Mustered out 4 Jan., 1866.
Tighe, John H., Capt. A. Q. M., 12 May, 1862. Mustered out 15 June, 1866.
Tilden, Josiah, Maj. P. M., 27 May, 1863. Mustered out 15 April, 1866.
Tillapaugh, James M., Capt. C. S., 9 Sept., 1861. Resigned 15 Aug., 1862.
Tilley, Edward M., Capt. A. Q. M., 9 June, 1862. Resigned 13 April, 1864.
Tillman, Wm., Maj. P. M., 5 Sept., 1861. Mustered out 15 Jan., 1866.
Tillson, Davis, Brig. Gen., 29 Nov., 1862. Mustered out 1 Dec., 1866.
Tilton, Allen P., Capt. A. Q. M., 23 July, 1863. Resigned 15 Oct., 1863.
Tilton, Jeremiah C., Capt. C. S., 3 Aug., 1861. Resigned 22 Aug., 1862.
Tinney, Henry C., Capt. A. A. G., 22 May, 1863. Resigned 12 Dec., 1864.
Tittman, Edward, Capt. C. S., 26 Nov., 1862. Mustered out 15 Aug., 1865.
Todd, John B. S., Brig. Gen., 19 Sept., 1861. Appointment expired 17 July, 1862.
Todd, Lockwood M., Capt. C. S., 25 March, 1864. Mustered out 15 July, 1865.
Todhunter, Lewis, Capt. A. Q. M., 30 June, 1864. Mustered out 20 Sept., 1865.
Tolford, David W., Hosp. Chap., 17 Sept., 1862. Mustered out 4 Aug., 1865.
Toll, Chas. H., Capt. C. S., 3 Oct., 1862. Mustered out 23 Jan., 1866.
Tomlinson, De Witt C., Capt. C. S., 10 Aug., 1863. Mustered out 8 July, 1865.
Tompkins, Logan, Maj. A. de C., 13 Sept., 1864. Mustered out 10 Aug., 1865.
Torbet, Alfred T. A., Brig. Gen., 29 Nov., 1862. Mustered out 15 Jan., 1866.
Tower, Zealous B., Brig. Gen., 23 Nov., 1861. Mustered out 15 Jan., 1866.
Town, Franklin E., Capt. Sig. Corps, 3 March, 1863. Resigned 29 Nov., 1864.
Townes, Rob't R., Capt. A. A. G., 1 May, 1862. Maj., 23 April, 1863. Resigned 28 Feb., 1865.

Townsend, Israel, Maj. P. M., 1 June, 1861. Discharged 5 Jan., 1863.
Townshend, N. S., Lieut. Col. Med. Insp., 11 March, 1863. Mustered out 31 Oct., 1865.
Tracy, Albert, Col. Addl. A. de C., 31 March, 1862. Mustered out 23 Nov., 1863.
Tracy, Henry C., Capt. A. Q. M., 1 March, 1865. Mustered out 28 July, 1865.
Tracy, Wm. G., Capt. A. de C., 7 May, 1863. Mustered out 13 Oct., 1865.
Tracy, Wm. O., Asst. Surg., 7 Dec., 1863. Died 15 March, 1864.
Tracy, Wm. R., Capt. C. S., 30 June, 1864. Mustered out 8 June, 1866.
Train, Chas. R., Capt. A. A. G., 4 Sept., 1862. Resigned 6 Nov., 1862.
Treadway, Joseph D., Capt. A. Q. M., 12 Nov., 1864. Mustered out 20 March, 1866.
Treanor, Bernard S., Capt. C. S., 27 Feb., 1863. Dismissed 6 May, 1864.
Treanor, John, Jr., Asst. Surg., 11 March, 1863. Maj. Surg., 13 Oct., 1863. Mustered out 27 Nov., 1865.
Treat, Richard B., Capt. C. S., 26 Aug., 1862. Mustered out 23 Sept., 1865.
Tremaine, Fred'k L., Capt. A. A. G., 11 Nov., 1863. Resigned 24 Dec., 1864.
Tremaine, Henry E., Maj. A. de C., 25 April, 1863. Mustered out 20 April, 1866.
Tremaine, Wm. S., Asst. Surg., 1 Sept., 1864. Mustered out 4 June, 1866.
Trewhitt, Daniel C., Capt. A. A. G., 30 June, 1862. Resigned 28 Dec., 1863.
Trott, Chas. H., Capt. A. A. G., 3 Feb., 1865. Mustered out 19 Sept., 1865.
Truax, Edmund A., Maj. P. M., 26 Nov., 1862. Mustered out 1 Nov., 1865.
True, Jabez, Maj. P. M., 1 June, 1861. Resigned 3 July, 1863.
Truesdell, George, Maj. P. M., 10 Aug., 1863. Mustered out 1 Feb., 1869.
Trull, Wash'n B., Asst. Surg., 6 July, 1863. Mustered out 8 Dec., 1865.
Trumbull, George I., Capt. C. S., 2 March, 1864. Mustered out 21 Aug., 1866.
Trumbull, James L., Capt. A. Q. M., 21 Nov., 1863. Mustered out 31 May, 1866.
Tubbs, Wm. H., Capt. C. S., 28 Jan., 1865. Mustered out 11 May, 1866.
Tucker, Albert M., Capt. A. Q. M., 15 Aug., 1863. Mustered out 8 Dec., 1865.
Tucker, Nath'l A., Maj. P. M., 13 June, 1864. Mustered out 1 Feb., 1869.
Tuckerman, Sam'l C., 2nd Lieut. Sig. Corps, 3 March, 1863. Mustered out 12 Aug., 1865.
Turchin, John B., Brig. Gen., 17 July, 1862. Resigned 4 Oct., 1864.
Tureman, James F., Maj. P. M., 21 April, 1864. Died 28 Oct., 1864.
Turner, James B., Capt. A. A. G., 23 Dec., 1862. Killed 5 May, 1864, at Battle of Wilderness, Va.
Turner, John W., Col. Addl. A. de C., 3 May, 1862. Brig. Gen., 7 Sept., 1863. Mustered out 1 Sept., 1866.
Turner, Levi C., Maj. J. A., 31 July, 1862. Died 13 March, 1867.
Turner, Theophilus H., Asst. Surg., 23 Aug., 1864. Mustered out 9 Oct., 1865.
Turner, Thomas, Asst. Surg., 6 April, 1865. Mustered out 8 Dec., 1865.
Turner, Wm. B., Capt. C. S., 30 June, 1864. Mustered out 3 Aug., 1865.
Turner, Wm. C., Capt. A. A. G., 15 July, 1862. Resigned 31 Dec., 1862.
Turney, Owen T., Maj. P. M., 14 Aug., 1863. Mustered out 1 Jan., 1869.
Turney, Sam'l D., Asst. Surg., 19 Feb., 1863. Maj. Surg., 26 March, 1863. Mustered out 3 Nov., 1865.
Tuttle, Edmund B., Hosp. Chap., 23 June, 1862. Mustered out 20 Nov., 1865.
Tuttle, James M., Brig. Gen., 9 June, 1862. Resigned 14 June, 1864.
Tuttle, Joseph, Capt. A. Q. M., 8 July, 1864. Mustered out 13 Oct., 1866.
Twining, Edward H., Capt. A. de C., 3 Sept., 1864. Mustered out 23 Oct., 1865.
Twining, Wm. J., Capt. A. de C., 30 June, 1864. Resigned 30 Aug., 1865.
Twitchell, George B., Maj. Surg., 7 Jan., 1863. Discharged 15 Oct., 1863.
Tyler, Chas. R., Capt. A. Q. M., 10 Sept., 1861. Mustered out 5 June, 1866.
Tyler, Daniel, Brig. Gen., 13 March, 1862. Resigned 6 April, 1864.
Tyler, Erastus B., Brig. Gen., 14 May, 1862. Mustered out 24 Aug., 1865.
Tyler, Rob't O., Brig. Gen., 29 Nov., 1862. Mustered out 15 Jan., 1866.
Tyler, Wm. H., Capt. C. S., 26 Nov., 1862. Resigned 14 May, 1864.
Tyndale, Hector, Brig. Gen., 29 Nov., 1862. Resigned 26 Aug., 1864.
Ulffers, Herman A., Capt. A. A. G., 18 March, 1864. Mustered out 10 July, 1866.
Ullman, Daniel, Brig. Gen., 13 Jan., 1863. Mustered out 24 Aug., 1865.
Underwood, Adin B., Brig. Gen., 6 Nov., 1863. Mustered out 24 Aug., 1865.
Underwood, Cornelius S., Maj. P. M., 28 May, 1864. Mustered out 20 July, 1866.
Upham, Calvin H., Capt. C. S., 2 March, 1864. Mustered out 21 June, 1865.
Upton, Emory, Brig. Gen., 12 May, 1864. Mustered out 30 April, 1866.
Urban, Gustavus, Capt. A. A. G., 16 Sept., 1861. Resigned 30 Jan., 1863.
Ure, Walter, Asst. Surg., 23 Sept., 1864. Mustered out 15 Aug., 1865.
Urquhart, Sam'l A., Capt. C. S., 10 Sept., 1862. Mustered out 7 July, 1865.
Usher, Roland G., Maj. P. M., 1 June, 1861. Mustered out 15 Feb., 1866.
Utler, Frank A., Asst. Surg., 19 May, 1865. Mustered out 10 Jan., 1866.
Vahey, John, Hosp. Chap., 1 Nov., 1863. Resigned 30 June, 1864.
Valentine, Alonzo B., Capt. C. S., 2 March, 1864. Mustered out 28 June, 1865.
Valentines, Edward, Capt. Addl. A. de C., 24 May, 1862. Dismissed 5 Sept., 1862.
Vallance, Wm. H., Capt. A. Q. M., 10 June, 1862. Dismissed 16 Nov., 1864.
Van Allen, James H., Brig. Gen., 15 April, 1862. Resigned 14 July, 1863.
Van Alstyne, Pierre, Maj. P. M., 30 June, 1864. Mustered out 1 Dec., 1865.
Van Antwerp, D. D., Hosp. Chap., 10 Nov., 1863. Mustered out 26 Oct., 1865.
Van Antwerps, Verplanck, Maj. Addl. A. de C., 29 Jan., 1862. Discharged 21 March, 1862. Maj. Addl. A. de C., 19 April, 1862. Mustered out 1 July, 1866.
Van Brimer, Joshua, Capt. C. S., 7 June, 1865. Mustered out 14 July, 1865.
Van Buren, Dan'l T., Maj. A. A. G., 3 Aug., 1861. Col. Addl. A. de C., 1 June, 1862. Mustered out 20 March, 1866.
Van Buren, James L., Maj. Addl. A. de C., 7 July, 1862. Mustered out 31 March, 1866.
Van Burkalow, James T., Hosp. Chap., 4 Aug., 1862. Mustered out 10 June, 1865.
Vance, A. Frank, Maj. P. M. 30 Jan., 1865. Mustered out 31 July, 1865.
Vance, George C., Capt. A. Q. M., 19 Feb., 1863. Mustered out 20 Sept., 1865.
Van Cleef, Augustus, Asst. Surg., 4 Feb., 1864. Resigned 6 April, 1865.
Van Cleve, Horatio P., Brig. Gen., 21 March, 1862. Mustered out 24 Aug., 1865.
Vanderbilt, George W., Capt. Addl. A. de C., 17 April, 1862. Vacated commission 19 Sept., 1863.
Vandergrift, Chas. C. V., Capt. A. Q. M., 11 March, 1865. Mustered out 28 July, 1865.
Vanderkieft, Bernard A., Asst. Surg., 11 March, 1863. Maj. Surg., 26 March, 1863. Mustered out 15 Nov., 1865.

Vanderveer, Ferdinand, Brig. Gen., 4 Oct., 1864. Resigned 15 June, 1865.
Vandeventer, James, Capt. C. S., 27 Sept., 1862. Mustered out 27 July, 1865.
Vandever, Wm., Brig. Gen., 29 Nov., 1862. Mustered out 24 Aug., 1865.
Van Duyn, Augustus C., Asst. Surg., 4 Oct., 1862. Maj. Surg., 4 Dec., 1863. Mustered out 7 Oct., 1865.
Van Duyn, John, Asst. Surg., 3 March, 1865. Mustered out 1 Nov., 1865.
Van Duzer, John C., Capt. A. Q. M., 27 Oct., 1863. Mustered out 5 June, 1866.
Van Dyke, Augustus M., Capt. A. A. G., 25 July, 1864. Mustered out 19 Sept., 1865.
Van Horn, Daniel W., Capt. Addl. A. de C., 22 April, 1862. Mustered out 15 April, 1866.
Van Lear, John, Capt. C. S., 20 April, 1864. Mustered out 31 July, 1866.
Van Ness, Wm. W., Capt. A. Q. M., 19 Feb., 1862. Mustered out 13 March, 1866.
Van Patten, James S., Capt. A. Q. M., 18 May, 1864. Mustered out 3 Nov., 1865.
Van Renssalaer, Henry, Col. Addl. A. de C., 5 Aug., 1861. Discharged 1 Nov., 1861.
Vansantwoord, Cornelius, Hosp. Chap., 2 Feb., 1863. Mustered out 15 July, 1865.
Van Slyke, Napoleon B., Capt. A. Q. M., 1 Oct., 1862. Mustered out 28 July, 1865.
Vansyckle, Reuben, Hosp. Chap., 23 June, 1862. Discharged 19 Sept., 1862.
Van Valkenburg, Eli, Maj. P. M., 19 Feb., 1863. Mustered out 15 Feb., 1866.
Van Volkenburg, Barthol'w J., Capt. A. Q. M., 18 May, 1864. Mustered out 15 Aug., 1865.
Van Vliet, Leonard S., Capt. A. Q. M., 12 May, 1862. Mustered out 30 March, 1866.
Van Vliet, Stewart, Brig. Gen., 23 Sept., 1861. Expired by Constitutional limitation 17 July, 1862. Brig. Gen., 13 March, 1865. Lieut. Col. D. Q. M. Gen., 29 July, 1866. Mustered out 1 Sept., 1866.
Van Vliet, Wm. A., Capt. A. Q. M., 15 Aug., 1861. Mustered out 28 July, 1865.
Van Vorhes, Andrew J., Capt. A. Q. M., 19 Feb., 1863. Resigned 25 March, 1865.
Van Wyck, Chas. H., Brig. Gen., 27 Sept., 1865. Mustered out 15 Jan., 1866.
Varian, Wm., Maj. Surg., 4 Sept., 1861. Mustered out 5 Aug., 1865.
Varnum, Atkinson C., Maj. P. M., 28 May, 1864. Mustered out 1 Nov., 1865.
Varnum, George W., Maj. Surg., 9 Feb., 1863. Resigned 28 Aug., 1863.
Vaughan, Champion, Maj. Addl. A. de C., 29 Jan., 1862. Discharged 21 March, 1862. Maj. Addl. A. de C., 11 April, 1862. Mustered out 7 Oct., 1865.
Vaughn, Roswell C., Capt. C. S., 2 July, 1864. Mustered out 31 Oct., 1865.
Vaux, Wm., Hosp. Chap., 6 Aug., 1864. Mustered out 28 April, 1867.
Veatch, James C., Brig. Gen., 28 April, 1862. Mustered out 24 Aug., 1865.
Vedder, Nicholas, Maj. P. M., 5 Sept., 1862. Maj. P. M., U. S. A., 17 Jan., 1867.
Vedder, Simon C., Capt. C. S., 22 July, 1864. Mustered out 14 June, 1865.
Veech, David H., Capt. C. S., 11 Nov., 1863. Resigned 6 Jan., 1865.
Vernam, John R., Maj. P. M., 3 March, 1865. Mustered out 31 July, 1865.
Vial, John G., Capt. A. Q. M., 18 May, 1864. Mustered out 11 Nov., 1865.
Vidal, Theodore C., 1st Lieut. Sig. Corps, 3 March, 1863. Mustered out 21 Aug., 1865.
Viele, Egbert L., Brig. Gen., 17 Aug., 1861. Resigned 20 Oct., 1863.
Vincent, Strong, Brig. Gen., 3 July, 1863. Died 7 July, 1863, of wounds received at Battle of Gettysburg, Pa.
Vinton, Francis L., Brig. Gen., 19 Sept., 1862. Appointment expired 4 March, 1863. Brig. Gen., 13 March, 1863. Resigned 5 May, 1863.
Vinton, Robert S., Hosp. Chap., 13 June, 1862. Mustered out 20 Nov., 1865.
Vogdes, Israel, Brig. Gen., 29 Nov., 1862. Mustered out 15 Jan., 1866.
Voges, Theodore, Capt. A. Q. M., 23 April, 1863. Mustered out 15 Aug., 1865.
Vogelson, Wm. M., Capt. C. S., 18 Nov., 1862. Mustered out 21 Feb., 1866.
Von Cederstrom, Jacob, Capt. Addl. A. de C., 31 March, 1862. Resigned 9 Jan., 1864.
Von Doehn, Wm., Capt. A. A. G., 16 Nov., 1861. Resigned 5 June, 1865.
Von Eickstedt, Gustavus, Capt. Addl. A. de C., 16 Nov., 1861. Mustered out 16 Aug., 1865.
Von Francois, Udo, Capt. A. A. G., 30 June, 1862. Died 8 Dec., 1862.
Von Guttenberg, Otto, Maj. A. A. G., 2 Oct., 1862. Appointment revoked 31 Dec., 1862.
Von Hammerstein, Herbert, Maj. Addl. A. de C., 20 Sept., 1861. Discharged 31 March, 1863.
Von Herman, Chas. J., Maj. Addl. A. de C., 5 Nov., 1861. Mustered out 12 March, 1866.
Von Poblotski, Hugo, Capt. Addl. A. de C., 16 May, 1862. Discharged 3 Sept., 1862.
Von Radowitz, Paul, Lieut. Col. Addl. A. de C., 30 Sept., 1861. Mustered out 12 July, 1865.
Von Schrader, Alex'r, Maj. A. A. G., 1 Feb., 1865. Appointment vacated 28 July, 1866.
Von Steinwehr, Adolph, Brig. Gen., 12 Oct., 1861. Resigned 3 July, 1865.
Von Vegesack, Ernest, Maj. Addl. A. de C., 28 Oct., 1861. Resigned 29 April, 1862. Maj. Addl. A. de C., 8 May, 1862. Resigned 3 Aug., 1863.
Voorhies, Zachariah, Maj. P. M., 23 Feb., 1864. Mustered out 15 Jan., 1866.
Voris, Archibald C., Capt. C. S., 16 July, 1862. Resigned 11 May, 1865.
Voss, Herman H., Capt. C. S., 30 Aug., 1862. Mustered out 31 Oct., 1865.
Vrooman, Wellington, Maj. P. M., 22 April, 1863. Mustered out 1 Feb., 1869.
Wade, Melanchton S., Brig. Gen., 1 Oct., 1861. Resigned 18 March, 1862.
Wade, Randall P., Capt. A. Q. M., 17 July, 1862. Resigned 1 Feb., 1864.
Wadleigh, Gilbert, Maj. P. M., 30 July, 1864. Mustered out 1 Nov., 1865.
Wadsworth, Craig W., Capt. Addl. A. de C., 23 May, 1862. Resigned 16 July, 1864.
Wadsworth, Elisha L., Capt. A. Q. M., 18 March, 1864. Mustered out 20 Sept., 1865.
Wadsworth, James S., Brig. Gen., 9 Nov., 1864. Killed 6 May, 1864, at Battle of Wilderness, Va.
Wadsworth, James W., Capt. A. de C., 24 Jan., 1865. Mustered out 26 June, 1865.
Wager, David C., Capt. A. A. G., 11 March, 1863. Maj., 9 March, 1865. Mustered out 1 Dec., 1866.
Waggener, R. J., Capt. A. A. G., 8 Oct., 1861. Killed 28 May, 1864, in action near Dallas, Ga.
Wagner, Chas. B., Capt. A. Q. M., 31 Oct., 1861. Mustered out 1 Jan., 1867.
Wagner, George D., Brig. Gen., 29 Nov., 1862. Mustered out 24 Aug., 1865.
Wainwright, Daniel W., Maj. Surg., 9 June, 1862. Died 30 July, 1863.
Wainwright, Wm. A., Capt. A. Q. M., 5 Dec., 1863. Capt. A. Q. M., U. S. A., 18 Jan., 1867.
Wait, Sheridan, Capt. A. A. G., 21 April, 1862. Maj., 8 May, 1863. Resigned 10 July, 1863.
Waker, Joseph M., Capt. C. S., 18 May, 1864. Resigned 5 June, 1865.

Walbridge, Chas. E., Capt. A. Q. M., 29 Feb., 1864. Mustered out 7 Oct., 1865.
Walbridge, Frank E., Capt. A. Q. M., 9 June, 1862. Died 6 April, 1863.
Walcott, Edward, Maj. P. M., 7 Oct., 1863. Mustered out 9 June, 1865.
Walcutt, Chas. C., Brig. Gen., 30 July, 1864. Mustered out 15 Jan., 1866.
Wald, Paul, Hosp. Chap., 18 March, 1864. Resigned 8 April, 1865.
Walden, John F., Maj. P. M., 18 March, 1864. Mustered out 20 July, 1866.
Waldron, George W., Capt. C. S., 18 May, 1864. Mustered out 9 Oct., 1865.
Waldron, Sam'l W., Capt. A. A. G., 14 July, 1862. Resigned 30 July, 1863.
Walker, Albert, Capt. C. S., 26 Nov., 1862. Mustered out 15 June, 1865.
Walker, Alvin, Maj. P. M., 10 Sept., 1861. Resigned 29 May, 1865.
Walker, Benj'n P., Capt. C. S., 7 Sept., 1861. Resigned 6 Feb., 1865.
Walker, Chas. M., Capt. C. S., 20 Jan., 1865. Mustered out 15 Aug., 1865.
Walker, Duncan S., Capt. A. A. G., 27 Feb., 1863. Maj., 27 July, 1864. Resigned 12 May, 1865.
Walker, Francis A., Capt. A. A. G., 14 Sept., 1861. Maj., 11 Aug., 1862. Resigned 9 Jan., 1865.
Walker, James B., Capt. A. A. G., 29 Sept., 1863. Discharged 14 April, 1865.
Walker, James E., Maj. P. M., 26 Nov., 1862. Resigned 24 Feb., 1864.
Walker, Jesse W., Maj. A. A. G., 19 Sept., 1864. Mustered out 19 Oct., 1865.
Walker, John S., Maj. P. M., 23 Feb., 1864. Maj. P. M., U. S. A., 17 Jan., 1867.
Walker, John W., Maj. P. M., 26 Nov., 1862. Mustered out 15 Nov., 1865.
Walker, Rob't C., Capt. C. S., 31 Oct., 1861. Maj. P. M., 26 Nov., 1862. Mustered out 15 Nov., 1865.
Walker, Stephen A., Maj. P. M., 1 Nov., 1862. Mustered out 15 Feb., 1866.
Wallace, George, Capt. A. Q. M., 14 July, 1862. Resigned 13 Feb., 1864.
Wallace, John M., Maj. P. M., 5 Aug., 1861. Resigned 22 July, 1862.
Wallace, John W., Maj. P. M., 18 Aug., 1863. Resigned 6 July, 1865.
Wallace, Lewis, Brig. Gen., 3 Sept., 1861. Maj. Gen., 21 March, 1862. Resigned 30 Nov., 1865.
Wallace, Wm., 2nd Lieut. Sig. Corps, 14 Feb., 1865. Mustered out 12 Aug., 1865.
Wallace, Wm. H. L., Brig. Gen., 21 March, 1862. Died 10 April, 1862, of wounds received at Battle of Shiloh, Tenn.
Waller, Royal H., Maj. P. M., 26 Feb., 1863. Resigned 13 Oct., 1863.
Walley, Henshaw B., Maj. P. M., 26 Nov., 1862. Resigned 11 June, 1864.
Warberg, Adolf C., Maj. Addl. A. de C., 24 April, 1862. Discharged 31 March, 1863.
Ward, John, Asst. Surg., 26 Jan., 1865. Mustered out 27 Jan., 1866.
Ward, John H. H., Brig. Gen., 4 Oct., 1862. Mustered out 18 July, 1864.
Ward, Sam'l B., Asst. Surg., 20 April, 1864. Mustered out 7 Oct., 1865.
Ward, Wm. T., Brig. Gen., 18 Sept., 1861. Mustered out 24 Aug., 1865.
Wardner, Horace, Maj. Surg., 4 April, 1862. Mustered out 7 Oct., 1865.
Warwell, Edward H., 2nd Lieut. Sig. Corps, 3 March, 1863. Mustered out 9 Aug., 1865.
Wardwell, Ernest H., Capt. A. Q. M., 11 March, 1865. Mustered out 28 July, 1865.
Wardwell, Newton M., Capt. C. S., 7 April, 1864. Mustered out 13 Dec., 1865.
Ware, Addison, Jr., Capt. A. A. G., 29 Feb., 1864. Maj., 31 May, 1865. Mustered out 12 March, 1866.
Ware, Wm., 1st Lieut. Sig. Corps, 3 March, 1863. Mustered out 1 Sept., 1865.
Warenner, Richard O., Maj. P. M., 5 Aug., 1861. Mustered out 17 Dec., 1862.
Warfield, Lemuel A., Capt. C. S., 5 Aug., 1861. Died 28 Oct., 1862.
Warfield, Wm., Capt. C. S., 31 Oct., 1861. Resigned 30 Dec., 1861.
Warner, Francis B., Maj. P. M., 26 Nov., 1862. Mustered out 16 April, 1866.
Warner, James M., Brig. Gen., 8 May, 1865. Mustered out 15 Jan., 1866.
Warner, Vespasian, Capt. C. S., 10 Feb., 1865. Mustered out 13 July, 1866.
Warren, Edgar W., Capt. C. S., 31 Oct., 1862. Mustered out 5 Aug., 1865.
Warren, Fitz Henry, Brig. Gen., 16 July, 1862. Mustered out 24 Aug., 1865.
Warren, George F., Capt. A. Q. M., 30 July, 1862. Resigned 15 March, 1865.
Warren, Gouverneur K., Brig. Gen., 26 Sept., 1862. Maj. Gen., 3 May, 1863. Resigned 27 May, 1865.
Warren, Joseph H. H., Maj. Surg., 14 Sept., 1861. Resigned 22 May, 1862.
Warren, Wm. A., Capt. A. Q. M., 21 April, 1862. Mustered out 20 Sept., 1865.
Warren, Wm. F., 1st Lieut. Sig. Corps, 3 March, 1863. Resigned 29 May, 1865.
Washburne, Cadwallader C., Brig. Gen., 16 July, 1862. Maj. Gen., 29 Nov., 1862. Resigned 25 May, 1865.
Wasson, Wm. R., Capt. C. S., 14 Sept., 1863. Mustered out 13 Aug., 1864.
Waters, Wm. E., Maj. Surg., 3 Aug., 1861. Maj. Surg., U. S. A., 16 April, 1862.
Watson, Erwen C., Capt. A. A. G., 8 Oct., 1864. Resigned 5 April, 1865.
Watkins, Louis D., Brig. Gen., 25 Sept., 1865. Mustered out 1 Sept., 1866.
Watson, Alex'r T., Maj. Surg., 4 April, 1862. Mustered out 27 Nov., 1865.
Watson, Benj'n F., Maj. P. M., 5 Sept., 1861. Resigned 14 Sept., 1864.
Watson, Chas. T., Capt. A. Q. M., 20 Aug., 1864. Mustered out 17 July, 1867.
Watson, Wm., Asst. Surg., 7 Nov., 1862. Maj. Surg., 2 Sept., 1863. Mustered out 7 Oct., 1865.
Watts, Joshua H., Maj. P. M., 30 June, 1862. Mustered out 1 June, 1869.
Way, George B., Maj. P. M., 1 June, 1861. Dismissed 7 June, 1864.
Way, Walter R., Asst. Surg., 3 Dec., 1864. Mustered out 18 Aug., 1865.
Webb, Alex'r S., Brig. Gen., 23 June, 1863. Mustered out 15 Jan., 1866.
Webb, Ezra, Maj. P. M., 30 June, 1862. Discharged 17 Dec., 1862.
Webb, Moses F., Maj. P. M., 5 Aug., 1861. Dismissed 11 Sept., 1865.
Webb, Rob't S., Maj. P. M., 5 Sept., 1861. Mustered out 1 July, 1867.
Webb, Stephen H., Capt. C. S., 5 Aug., 1861. Discharged 6 Sept., 1864.
Webber, Alfred B., Capt. C. S., 19 Feb., 1863. Resigned 30 June, 1865.
Webebr, Jonathan R., Capt. C. S., 2 July, 1864. Mustered out 14 July, 1865.
Webber, Jules C., Capt. A. de C., 7 June, 1864. Mustered out 27 March, 1865.
Weber, George R., Capt. C. S., 22 June, 1863. Resigned 10 June, 1865.
Weber, Max., Brig. Gen., 28 April, 1862, Resigned 13 May, 1865.
Weber, Thos. E., 2nd Lieut. Sig. Corps, 3 March, 1863. Mustered out 21 Aug., 1865.
Webster, Alonzo, Hosp. Chap., 3 Aug., 1864. Mustered out 7 Oct., 1865.
Webster, Amos, Capt. A. Q. M., 1 Oct., 1864. Mustered out 1 Oct., 1867.
Webster, Chas. D., Capt. A. Q. M., 1 Oct., 1864. Mustered out 13 March, 1866.
Webster, George P., Capt. A. Q. M., 12 May, 1862. Mustered out 20 Oct., 1866.
Webster, John R., Capt. A. Q. M., 30 June, 1864. Mustered out 10 Aug., 1865.
Webster, Joseph D., Maj. P. M., 1 June, 1861. Appointment vacated 1 Feb., 1862.

Brig. Gen., 29 Nov., 1862. Resigned 6 Nov., 1865.
Webster, Ralph C., Capt. A. Q. M., 30 Sept., 1861. Mustered out 3 Nov., 1866.
Weed, Stephen H., Brig. Gen., 6 June, 1863. Killed 2 July, 1863, at Battle of Gettysburg, Pa.
Weed, Theodore J., Maj. Addl. A. de C., 29 Jan., 1862. Discharged 21 March, 1862. Maj. Addl. A. de C., 31 March, 1862. Mustered out 6 Sept., 1865.
Weeks, Benj'n F., Capt. C. S., 21 April, 1864. Mustered out 4 Aug., 1865.
Weeks, George D., Capt. A. Q. M., 15 June, 1865. Mustered out 23 Oct., 1865.
Weeks, George R., Maj. Surg., 19 Feb., 1863. Mustered out 7 Oct., 1865.
Weihl, Chas., 2nd Lieut. Sig. Corps, 3 March, 1863. Mustered out 12 Aug., 1865.
Weir, George H., Capt. C. S., 30 June, 1863. Appointment expired 4 July, 1864. Capt. C. S., 30 July, 1864. Resigned 9 June, 1865.
Weir, Henry C., Capt. A. A. G., 12 May, 1862. Maj., 2 Feb., 1865. Resigned 19 May, 1865.
Weitzel, Godfrey, Brig. Gen., 29 Aug., 1862. Maj. Gen., 17 Nov., 1864. Mustered out 1 March, 1866.
Weitzel, Lewis, Capt. A. de C., 27 Dec., 1864. Mustered out 1 Feb., 1866.
Welch, Benj'n, Col. Addl. A. de C., 11 July, 1862. Died 13 April, 1863.
Welch, Deming N., Capt. A. Q. M., 30 June, 1862. Mustered out 21 Feb., 1866.
Weldon, James, Capt. A. Q. M., 26 Nov., 1862. Dismissed 5 Nov., 1863.
Welles, Thos. G., Capt. A. de C., 17 Feb., 1865. Mustered out 19 May, 1866.
Welles, Thos. R., Capt. C. S., 28 May, 1864. Mustered out 28 Feb., 1866.
Welles, Benj'n W., Capt. C. S., 9 March, 1865. Mustered out 17 Aug., 1865.
Wells, Chas. B., Capt. C. S., 20 Nov., 1862. Resigned 14 July, 1865.
Wells, Ebenezer T., Capt. A. A. G., 29 Feb., 1864. Mustered out 7 June, 1865.
Wells, George W., Capt. A. Q. M., 26 Nov., 1862. Mustered out 31 May, 1866.
Wells, J. Howard, Capt. C. S., 19 Feb., 1862. Resigned 19 May, 1865.
Wells, Levi, Capt. C. S., 18 May, 1864. Mustered out 10 Aug., 1865.
Wells, Wm., Brig. Gen., 19 May, 1865. Mustered out 15 Jan., 1866.
Welsh, Thos., Brig. Gen., 13 March, 1863. Died 14 Aug., 1863.
Wendell, Wm. H., Capt. A. Q. M., 25 June, 1864. Mustered out 8 Nov., 1865.
Wendt, Chas. E., Capt. C. S., 14 July, 1862. Resigned 31 Dec., 1863.
Wentworth, Thos. E., Capt. C. S., 7 June, 1864. Mustered out 25 Aug., 1865.
Wessells, Henry W., Brig. Gen., 25 April, 1862. Mustered out 15 Jan., 1866.
Wesson, Wm. D., Capt. C. S., 16 July, 1862. Resigned 15 Sept., 1864.
West, Benj'n L., Capt. C. S., 19 Feb., 1863. Dismissed 20 Dec., 1863.
West, Clement L., Capt. A. Q. M., 31 Oct., 1861. Resigned 21 Jan., 1863.
West, Joseph R., Brig. Gen., 25 Oct., 1862. Mustered out 4 Jan., 1866.
West, Nath'l, Hosp. Chap., 31 May, 1862. Died 7 Sept., 1864.
Westbrook, Royal L., Capt. A. Q. M., 17 Nov., 1863. Mustered out 18 Jan., 1866.
Wetherbee, George C., Capt. C. S., 19 Aug., 1863. Mustered out 26 June, 1865.
Wetherell, Hiram B., Capt. A. Q. M., 27 Nov., 1861. Resigned 27 April, 1863.
Wetherell, Rob't W., Capt. A. Q. M., 29 Feb., 1864. Mustered out 6 June, 1865.
Wetherill, Horace R., Capt. C. S., 9 Sept., 1861. Resigned 16 July, 1863.
Wetmore, Henry S., Capt. A. A. G., 17 Sept., 1862. Resigned 31 Oct., 1862.
Wever, Frank M., Capt. A. Q. M., 28 May, 1864. Mustered out 28 July, 1865.
Wevill, Rich'd H., Maj. Surg., 24 Dec., 1861. Resigned 16 July, 1863.
Wheaton, Chas., Jr., Capt. C. S., 17 July, 1862. Mustered out 31 May, 1866.
Wheaton, Frank, Brig. Gen., 29 Nov., 1862. Mustered out 30 April, 1866.
Wheeler, Dan'l D., Capt. A. A. G., 30 June, 1864. Maj. 27 Dec., 1864. Mustered out 19 Oct., 1866.
Wheeler, George A., Asst. Surg., 4 Oct., 1862. Maj. Surg., 30 March, 1864. Mustered out 27 July, 1865.
Wheeler, Horatio N., Capt. A. A. G., 7 June, 1864. Mustered out 19 Sept., 1865.
Wheeler, John P., Maj. P. M., 26 Nov., 1862. Resigned 27 July, 1863.
Wheeler, Phineas A., Capt. A. Q. M., 28 May, 1864. Mustered out 4 Nov., 1865.
Wheeler, Underhill H., Capt. A. Q. M., 15 April, 1863. Mustered out 20 March, 1866.
Wheeler, Wm. A., Capt. C. S., 14 Oct., 1863. Mustered out 10 Aug., 1865.
Wheeler, Wm. D., Maj. P. M., 18 March, 1864. Mustered out 1 Nov., 1865.
Wherry, Wm. M., Maj. A. de C., 12 May, 1864. Mustered out 9 Feb., 1866.
Whetsel, Henry B., Capt. A. Q. M., 5 Dec., 1863. Mustered out 19 May, 1866.
Whipple, Amiel W., Brig. Gen., 14 April, 1862. Maj. Gen., 3 May, 1863. Died 7 May, 1863, of wounds received at Battle of Chancellorsville, Va.
Whipple, Henry C., Capt. A. A. G., 19 Sept., 1863. Resigned 26 April, 1865.
Whipple, John, Capt. A. Q. M., 30 Sept., 1862. Mustered out 19 May, 1866.
Whipple, Wm. D., Brig. Gen., 17 July, 1863. Expired by Constitutional limitation 4 July, 1864. Brig. Gen., 17 July, 1864, to rank from 17 July, 1863. Mustered out 15 Jan., 1866.
Whitaker, Walter C., Brig. Gen., 25 June, 1863. Mustered out 24 Aug., 1865.
Whitcomb, John R., Capt. A. Q. M., 30 June, 1864. Mustered out 10 June, 1866.
Whitcomb, Wm. C., Hosp. Chap., 5 July, 1862. Died 28 Oct., 1864.
White, Carlos L., Capt. A. A. G., 18 May, 1864. Died 21 Aug., 1864.
White, Chas. B., Asst. Surg., 24 Oct., 1863. Maj. Surg., 30 March, 1864. Mustered out 27 Jan., 1866.
White, Frank J., Maj. A. A. G., 15 March, 1863. Appointment vacated 30 June, 1865.
White, George Q., Capt. A. Q. M., 12 May, 1862. Resigned 11 March, 1865.
White, Henry K., Asst. Surg., 3 March, 1865. Mustered out 9 Oct., 1865.
White, J. A., Asst. Surg., 7 Aug., 1863. Mustered out 22 Nov., 1865.
White, James, Hosp. Chap., 10 Jan., 1863. Mustered out 14 July, 1865.
White, Julius, Brig. Gen., 9 June, 1862. Resigned 19 Nov., 1864.
White, Wm. H., Maj. Surg., 4 April, 1862. Discharged 26 Sept., 1863.
White, Wm. W., Maj. P. M., 26 Nov., 1862. Mustered out 31 July, 1865.
Whitehead, Asa A., Capt. A. Q. M., 19 Feb., 1863. Discharged 21 May, 1864.
Whitehead, Fred'k F., Capt. A. A. G., 2 May, 1863. Mustered out 19 Sept., 1865.
Whitehead, G. Irvine, Maj. J. A., 11 March, 1863. Mustered out 10 Aug., 1863.
Whitehead, Otis C., Maj. P. M., 26 Nov., 1862. Died 8 Nov., 1863.
Whitehill, James, Maj. P. M., 23 Feb., 1864. Resigned 3 June, 1865.
Whitehill, James C., Maj. Surg., 7 Nov., 1862. Mustered out 10 Sept., 1865.
Whiting, De Garmo J., Capt. A. Q. M., 26 Nov., 1862. Died 24 June, 1864.

Whiting, Rich'd H., Maj. P. M., 26 Nov., 1862. Mustered out 15 April, 1866.
Whitman, Edmund B., Capt. A. Q. M., 18 July, 1862. Mustered out 20 Aug., 1868.
Whitney, Edward J., Asst. Surg., 7 Nov., 1862. Maj. Surg., 13 April, 1863. Mustered out 3 Nov., 1865.
Whitney, Edward L., Capt. C. S., 20 Nov., 1862. Dismissed 10 June, 1865.
Whitney, Henry C., Maj. P. M., 6 Aug., 1861. Resigned 13 March, 1865.
Whitney, Joseph C., Capt. A. Q. M., 23 Feb., 1865. Mustered out 27 Nov., 1865.
Whitney, Leonard, Capt. A. Q. M., 26 Nov., 1862. Mustered out 31 May, 1866.
Whittemore, Chas. B., Capt. A. Q. M., 18 May, 1864. Mustered out 30 Oct., 1865.
Whittemore, George A., Capt. A. Q. M., 18 May, 1864. Mustered out 8 Dec., 1865.
Whitten, Wm. S., Capt. A. A. G., 25 May, 1863. Resigned 28 Feb., 1865.
Whittier, Chas. A., Maj. A. de C., 25 April, 1863. Maj. A. A. G., 7 March, 1865. Mustered out 30 Nov., 1866.
Whittingham, James, Capt. A. Q. M., 30 June, 1864. Mustered out 10 Aug., 1865.
Whittlesey, Chas. H., Capt. A. A. G., 15 May, 1863. Maj., 26 May, 1865. Mustered out 1 Sept., 1866.
Whittlesey, Eliphalet, Capt. A. A. G., 25 Aug., 1862. Maj., 11 March, 1863. Resigned 3 June, 1863. Maj. J. A., 1 Sept., 1864. Appointment vacated 14 June, 1865.
Whittlesey, Henry M., Capt. A. Q. M., 31 Oct., 1861. Mustered out 17 July, 1867.
Whittlesey, John E., Capt. C. S., 18 May, 1864. Resigned 14 Feb., 1865.
Whytal, Thos. G., Capt. A. Q. M., 13 Nov., 1863. Mustered out 5 Oct., 1867.
Wicker, Frank N., 2nd Lieut. and 1st Lieut. Sig. Corps, 3 March, 1863. Appointment as 1st Lieut. expired 4 July, 1864. Mustered out 22 Aug., 1865.
Wickersham, Chas. J., Capt. A. A. G., 25 Aug., 1864. Mustered out 25 Jan., 1867.
Wickersham, Morris D., Capt. A. Q. M., 7 April, 1864. Mustered out 22 Sept., 1866.
Wickizer, John H., Capt. A. Q. M., 4 Nov., 1862. Mustered out 28 July, 1865.
Wiegel, Wm. H., Capt. A. A. G., 17 Sept., 1863. Maj., 2 Feb., 1865. Mustered out 1 Feb., 1868.
Wiget, Bernardin F., Hosp. Chap., 9 Oct., 1862. Mustered out 20 Nov., 1865.
Wiggin, Isaac B., Capt. C. S., 30 June, 1863. Mustered out 31 Dec., 1865.
Wiggins, John C., 1st Lieut. Sig. Corps, 3 March, 1863. Mustered out 21 Jan., 1866.
Wilcox, Aaron M., Capt. C. S., 20 April, 1864. Mustered out 9 Oct., 1865.
Wilcox, Nath'l G., Maj. P. M., 5 Aug., 1861. Resigned 21 Feb., 1863.
Wilcox, Timothy E., Asst. Surg., 25 April, 1865. Mustered out 4 June, 1866.
Wilcox, Wm. H., Capt. A. de C., 25 April, 1863. Dropped 30 Sept., 1863.
Wild, Edward A., Brig. Gen., 24 April, 1863. Mustered out 15 Jan., 1866.
Wilder, Abraham M., Asst. Surg., 11 March, 1863. Maj. Surg., 29 June, 1863. Mustered out 18 Aug., 1865.
Wilder, A. C., Capt. C. S., 7 Aug., 1861. Resigned 22 Aug., 1862.
Wilder, Chas. B., Capt. A. Q. M., 19 Feb., 1863. Mustered out 30 March, 1866.
Wiley, Dan'l D., Capt. C. S., 28 Aug., 1862. Mustered out 26 Oct., 1866.
Wiley, George W., Capt. C. S., 2 Nov., 1861. Resigned 24 Dec., 1862.
Wiley, Wm. M., Maj. P. M., 7 Sept., 1861. Mustered out 15 March, 1866.
Wilkins, Wm. D., Capt. A. A. G., 27 Aug., 1861. Resigned 29 Aug., 1863.
Wilkinson, Ross, Maj. A. de C., 15 March, 1865. Mustered out 12 Oct., 1865.
Willans, John, Capt. A. A. G., 22 May, 1863. Mustered out 10 July, 1866.
Willard, Edwin D., Capt. C. S., 1 May, 1862. Died 31 Oct., 1863.
Willard, John P., Capt. A. de C., 11 March, 1863. Mustered out 10 July, 1866.
Willard, Joseph C., Capt. Addl. A. de C., 3 April, 1862. Maj., 15 July, 1862. Resigned 1 March, 1864.
Willard, Lot S., Maj. A. de C., 18 April, 1863. Resigned 9 Aug., 1864.
Willard, Nathan, Capt. C. S., 30 June, 1864. Mustered out 21 Jan., 1865.
Willcox, Orlando B., Brig. Gen., 28 Sept., 1861. Maj. Gen., 29 Nov., 1862. Mustered out 1 Feb., 1866.
Willett, Thos., Hosp. Chap., 20 May, 1863. Resigned 9 Jan., 1864.
Willey, George F. W., Capt. A. Q. M., 29 Feb., 1864. Mustered out 7 Oct., 1865.
Williams, Alex'r B., Maj. P. M., 5 Sept., 1861. Mustered out 31 July, 1865.
Williams, Alpheus S., Brig. Gen., 17 May, 1861. Mustered out 15 Jan., 1866.
Williams, Augustus P., Asst. Surg., 19 Jan., 1864. Mustered out 10 Jan., 1866.
Williams, Beverly D., Capt. A. de C., 11 March, 1863. Mustered out 11 Nov., 1865.
Williams, Chas. A., Hosp. Chap., 23 June, 1862. Mustered out 21 Aug., 1865.
Williams, David, Asst. Surg., 3 May, 1865. Mustered out 3 Nov., 1865.
Williams, David H., Brig. Gen., 29 Nov., 1862. Appointment expired 4 March, 1863.
Williams, Dennis H., Capt. A. A. G., 17 Dec., 1864. Mustered out 3 Oct., 1866.
Williams, Edward P., Capt. C. S., 1 June, 1863. Resigned 19 May, 1864.
Williams, Greenbury W., Maj. P. M., 19 Feb., 1863. Mustered out 1 Dec., 1865.
Williams, Henry B., Capt. C. S., 9 June, 1862. Resigned 4 Oct., 1862.
Williams, Henry E., Asst. Surg., 7 Aug., 1864. Mustered out 27 July, 1865.
Williams, Henry L., Maj. P. M., 30 June, 1864. Mustered out 15 Nov., 1865.
Williams, Isaac P., Capt. A. Q. M., 26 Nov., 1862. Mustered out 6 June, 1865.
Williams, James C., Capt. A. de C., 3 Sept., 1862. Died 29 Oct., 1862.
Williams, J. Benson, Capt. A. Q. M., 29 Nov., 1862. Appointment expired 4 March, 1863.
Williams, John D., Capt. C. S., 18 Sept., 1861. Mustered out 3 Jan., 1866.
Williams, John W., Capt. A. A. G., 14 April, 1862. Resigned 30 July, 1863.
Williams, Nelson G., Brig. Gen., 29 Nov., 1862. Rejected by Senate 9 March, 1863.
Williams, Seth, Brig. Gen., 23 Sept., 1861. Died 23 March, 1866.
Williams, Thos., Brig. Gen., 28 Sept., 1861. Killed 5 Aug., 1862, at Battle of Baton Rouge, La.
Williams, Thos. E., Maj. P. M., 23 Feb., 1864. Resigned 31 May, 1864.
Williams, Wm., Maj. P. M., 30 June, 1864. Mustered out 13 Oct., 1865.
Williams, Wm. G., Hosp. Chap., 24 Sept., 1864. Mustered out 15 July, 1865.
Williamson, David J., Capt. A. Q. M., 15 Dec., 1865. Mustered out 13 July, 1866.
Williamson, James A., Brig. Gen., 13 Jan., 1865. Mustered out 24 Aug., 1865.
Willich, August, Brig. Gen., 17 July, 1862. Mustered out 15 Jan., 1866.
Willis, Jesse E., Capt. A. Q. M., 7 April, 1864. Mustered out 18 Jan., 1866.
Willis, Joshua G., Capt. C. S., 23 May, 1862. Resigned 10 Oct., 1862.
Wills, Andrew W., Maj. P. M., 5 Dec., 1863. Mustered out 31 Dec., 1867.
Wilson, Alex'r M., Capt. C. S., 28 May, 1864. Mustered out 8 July, 1865.
Wilson, Benj'n B., Maj. Surg., 26 March, 1863. Mustered out 30 Nov., 1865.
Wilson, Bluford, Capt. A. A. G., 6 May, 1863. Resigned 19 July, 1865.

Wilson, Chas. F., Maj. P. M., 23 Feb., 1864. Mustered out 20 July, 1866.
Wilson, Edwin C., Capt. A. Q. M., 16 Aug., 1861. Mustered out 18 Jan., 1866.
Wilson, Fred'k H., Capt. A. A. G., 2 Feb., 1865. Maj., 31 May, 1865. Mustered out 20 April, 1866.
Wilson, Henry C., Capt. C. S., 8 Aug., 1863. Resigned 26 May, 1864.
Wilson, James, Capt. A. Q. M., 26 Nov., 1862. Mustered out 6 Dec., 1865.
Wilson, James H., Brig. Gen., 30 Oct., 1863. Maj. Gen., 6 May, 1865. Mustered out 8 Jan., 1866.
Wilson, James M., Capt. A. A. G., 1 Oct., 1861. Killed 5 May, 1862, at Battle of Williamsburg, Va.
Wilson, James M., Maj. P. M., 14 June, 1862. Mustered out 20 July, 1866.
Wilson, James S., Capt. A. A. G., 1 June, 1863. Mustered out 15 June, 1865.
Wilson, John, Asst. Surg., 11 Sept., 1862. Maj. Surg., 4 Dec., 1862. Lieut. Col. Med. Insp., 10 Aug., 1863. Mustered out 31 Oct., 1865.
Wilson, John L., Maj. P. M., 21 Feb., 1863. Resigned 4 March, 1865.
Wilson, Joseph F., Capt. C. S., 26 Nov., 1862. Resigned 24 Jan., 1865.
Wilson, Joseph H., Capt. A. Q. M., 30 June, 1864. Mustered out 13 March, 1866.
Wilson, Rob't L., Maj. P. M., 5 Aug., 1861. Mustered out 15 Nov., 1865.
Wilson, Rob't P., Capt. A. A. G., 11 March, 1863. Discharged 18 Feb., 1864.
Wilson, Thos. J., Maj. P. M., 26 Nov., 1862. Mustered out 30 June, 1866.
Wilson, Thos. P., Capt. A. Q. M., 7 April, 1864. Mustered out 21 Aug., 1866.
Wilson, Wm., Hosp. Chap., 17 Nov., 1863. Resigned 29 Jan., 1864.
Wilson, Wm., Capt. C. S., 31 Oct., 1861. Drowned 15 April, 1862.
Wilson, Wm. P., Capt. A. de C., 23 Jan., 1865. Mustered out 10 July, 1866.
Wilson, Wm. W., Capt. C. S., 22 April, 1863. Mustered out 12 Oct., 1865.
Wiltbank, Wm. W., Capt. C. S., 22 April, 1863. Mustered out 12 Oct., 1865.
Winchester, Benj'n F., Capt. C. S., 17 July, 1862. Dismissed 9 April, 1865.
Winchester, Benj'n F., Capt. C. S., 26 Nov., 1862. Mustered out 26 July, 1865.
Winchester, Warren W., Hosp. Chap., 5 June, 1862. Mustered out 11 Nov., 1865.
Wines, Fred'k H., Hosp. Chap., 14 June, 1862. Resigned 20 Aug., 1864.
Wing, Chas. T., Capt. A. Q. M., 31 Oct., 1861. Mustered out 27 Jan., 1866.
Wing, Joseph K., Capt. A. Q. M., 12 May, 1862. Mustered out 10 Aug., 1865.
Wingard, Chas. W., Maj. P. M., 10 May, 1864. Maj. P. M., U. S. A., 17 Jan., 1867.
Winslow, Fred'k S., Capt. A. Q. M., 19 Feb., 1862. Resigned 3 June, 1864.
Winslow, George C., Capt. A. Q. M., 10 Aug., 1863. Mustered out 20 April, 1866.
Winslow, John B., Capt. A. Q. M., 14 April, 1862. Mustered out 8 Jan., 1866.
Winters, Gilbert E., Capt. C. S., 11 March, 1863. Mustered out 18 Aug., 1865.
Wise, George D., Capt. A. Q. M., 28 Sept., 1861. Mustered out 1 Oct., 1867.
Wiseman, Theodore, Capt. A. A. G., 27 Feb., 1863. Mustered out 19 Sept., 1865.
Wistar, Isaac J., Brig. Gen., 29 Nov., 1862. Resigned 15 Sept., 1864.
Witherill, Orlando S., Maj. P. M., 31 Aug., 1861. Mustered out 15 Nov., 1865.
Woart, John, Hosp. Chap., 22 March, 1865. Mustered out 2 June, 1866.
Wolcott, Francis E., Maj. J. A., 17 Dec., 1864. Mustered out 30 Sept., 1866.
Wolf, Fred'k, Asst. Surg., 11 Jan., 1864. Maj. Surg., 12 Jan., 1865. Mustered out 15 June, 1865.
Wolfley, Wm. I., Asst. Surg., 18 May, 1864. Maj. Surg., 18 May, 1864. Mustered out 18 July, 1865.
Wood, Chas. S., Asst. Surg., 2 Sept., 1863. Maj. Surg., 9 Sept., 1863. Mustered out 7 Oct., 1865.
Wood, George H., Capt. C. S., 16 Nov., 1861. Mustered out 11 July, 1865.
Wood, Horatio D., Capt. C. S., 21 Jan., 1865. Mustered out 9 Oct., 1865.
Wood, James D., Capt. A. A. G., 11 March, 1863. Mustered out 26 May, 1865.
Wood, John P., Capt. A. A. G., 16 May, 1863. Died 6 March, 1864.
Wood, Thos. J., Brig. Gen., 11 Oct., 1861. Maj. Gen., 27 Jan., 1865. Mustered out 1 Sept., 1866.
Wood, Wm. J., Maj. P. M., 27 Feb., 1863. Mustered out 10 Aug., 1865.
Woodall, James T., Capt. A. Q. M., 20 Feb., 1865. Mustered out 26 Oct., 1866.
Woodbury, Daniel P., Lieut. Col. Addl. A. de C., 28 Sept., 1861. Brig. Gen., 19 March, 1862. Died 15 Aug., 1864.
Woodhull, Maxwell V. L., Capt. A. de C., 11 March, 1863. Maj. A. A. G., 30 June, 1864. Mustered out 31 May, 1866.
Woodman, Chas. W., Maj. P. M., 26 Nov., 1862. Appointment revoked 4 May, 1863.
Woodruff, Henry D., Capt. C. S., 5 Aug., 1861. Mustered out 31 May, 1866.
Woods, Chas. R., Brig. Gen., 4 Aug., 1863. Mustered out 1 Sept., 1866.
Woods, Isaac C., Capt. C. S., 9 Sept., 1861. Resigned 30 Nov., 1861.
Woods, John L., Capt. A. Q. M., 13 Oct., 1862. Mustered out 13 March, 1867.
Woods, Wm. B., Brig. Gen., 31 May, 1865. Mustered out 17 Feb., 1866.
Woods, Wm. M., Capt. A. Q. M., 18 May, 1864. Mustered out 8 Nov., 1865.
Woods, Wm. S., Asst. Surg., 26 Jan., 1864. Maj. Surg., 24 Jan., 1865. Mustered out 8 Feb., 1866.
Woods, W. W., Hosp. Chap., 2 Feb., 1864. Died 29 Oct., 1864.
Woodson, Wm. C., Maj. P. M., 28 May, 1864. Mustered out 15 Nov., 1865.
Woodward, John H., Capt. C. S., 3 Aug., 1861. Resigned 5 June, 1865.
Woodward, Sam'l L., Capt. A. A. G., 21 July, 1863. Maj., 11 Feb., 1865. Mustered out 19 Sept., 1865.
Woodworth, Milton C., Asst. Surg., 8 Jan., 1864. Maj. Surg., 25 Nov., 1864. Resigned 31 March, 1865.
Woolfolk, Austin C., Capt. A. Q. M., 19 Feb., 1862. Capt. A. Q. M., U. S. A., 5 Dec., 1863.
Wooster, Mark H., Capt. C. S., 7 May, 1864. Resigned 29 June, 1864. Capt. C. S., 1 May, 1865. Resigned 8 July, 1865.
Worden, John L., Capt. A. A. G., 21 July, 1865. Mustered out 10 Nov., 1865.
Work, Frank, Capt. A. Q. M., 9 June, 1862. Resigned 11 Jan., 1864.
Worms, Chas., Capt. A. Q. M., 19 Feb., 1863. Resigned 11 March, 1865.
Worrall, Peter, Capt. C. S., 18 May, 1864. Resigned 18 May, 1865.
Worrall, Thos. A., Maj. Surg., 24 Dec., 1861. Resigned 13 Jan., 1865.
Worth, Titus T., Maj. P. M., 19 Sept., 1861. Resigned 1 Oct., 1861.
Wray, James T., Capt. A. Q. M., 3 April, 1863. Mustered out 31 Dec., 1865.
Wright, Edward, Maj. A. de C., 8 Nov., 1862. Discharged 15 Aug., 1863.
Wright, Edward, Capt. A. Q. M., 26 Nov., 1862. Appointment expired 4 March, 1863.
Wright, Edward, Capt. C. S., 20 March, 1863. Died 14 July, 1864.
Wright, Edward H., Col. Addl. A. de C., 19

Aug., 1861. Discharged 1 Nov., 1861. Col. Addl. A. de C., 15 Jan., 1862. Discharged 31 March, 1863.

Wright, George, Brig. Gen., 28 Sept., 1861. Lost at sea 30 July 1865.

Wright, Horatio G., Brig. Gen., 14 Sept., 1861. Maj. Gen., 18 July, 1862. Rejected by the Senate 12 March, 1863, and revoked 24 March, 1863. Brig. Gen., 24 March, 1863. Maj. Gen., 12 May, 1864. Mustered out 1 Sept., 1866.

Wright, James H., Capt. A. de C., 17 Nov., 1863. Mustered out 20 June, 1865.

Wright, John A., Capt. A. A. G., 18 May, 1864. Mustered out 21 Feb., 1866.

Wright, John F., Hosp. Chap., 6 June, 1862. Mustered out 4 Aug., 1865.

Wright, John M., Capt. A. A. G., 25 Sept., 1861. Maj., 30 June, 1862. Resigned 16 Jan., 1864.

Wright, Samuel, Capt. A. A. G., 4 June, 1863. Mustered out 19 Sept., 1865.

Wright, Sam'l I., Capt. A. Q. M., 27 Feb., 1863. Mustered out 17 July, 1867.

Wright, Tappan, Capt. A. A. G., 23 Aug., 1861. Rejected by Senate 11 March, 1862.

Wright, Truman G., Maj. P. M., 5 Sept., 1861. Resigned 31 March, 1862.

Wright, Wm. J., Hosp. Chap., 15 Sept., 1864. Mustered out 10 Aug., 1865.

Wuerpel, Edmund, Capt. A. Q. M., 18 Aug., 1862. Resigned 19 May, 1865.

Wyman, Edward F., Capt. C. S., 20 April, 1866. Mustered out 30 May, 1866

Wyncoop, Alfred, Maj. Surg., 11 Sept., 1862. Mustered out 23 Dec., 1865.

Wythes, Joseph H., Asst. Surg., 11 Sept., 1862. Maj. Surg., 4 Dec., 1862. Resigned 26 Oct., 1863.

Wythes, W. W., Asst. Surg., 19 Feb., 1863 Resigned 19 Oct., 1864.

Yard, Thos. W., Maj. P. M., 1 June, 1861 Resigned 18 March, 1864.

Yardley, Strickland, Capt. A. Q. M., 3 July, 1863. Resigned 11 March, 1865.

Yarnall, Norris L., Maj. P. M., 18 March, 1864. Resigned 8 March, 1865.

Yoder, Chas. T., Maj. P. M., 11 March, 1865. Mustered out 29 July, 1865.

Yohn, James C., Maj. P. M., 5 Sept., 1861. Discharged 17 Dec., 1862.

Young, Andrew H., Capt. A. Q. M., 26 Nov., 1862. Maj. P. M., 28 May, 1864. Mustered out 20 July, 1866.

Young, Berry S., Maj. P. M., 21 April, 1864 Resigned 24 Feb., 1865.

Young, George F., 2nd Lieut. Sig. Corps, 14 Feb., 1865. Mustered out 12 Aug., 1865.

Young, James H., Maj. P. M., 18 May, 1864. Mustered out 20 Nov., 1865.

Young, Joseph B., Capt. C. S., 2 March, 1864. Resigned 26 May, 1864. Maj. P. M., 7 June, 1864. Resigned 6 July, 1865.

Young, Stephen B., Capt. C. S., 25 Oct., 1862. Rejected by Senate 11 March, 1863.

Young, Wm. F., Capt. C. S., 27 Feb., 1863. Resigned 31 Dec., 1863.

Youngman, John C., Capt. A. A. G., 25 July, 1864. Mustered out 19 Sept., 1865.

Zagonyi, Chas., Col. Addl. A. de C., 31 March, 1862. Resigned 4 June, 1864.

Zook, Sam'l K., Brig. Gen., 29 Nov., 1862. Killed 2 July, 1863, at Battle of Gettysburg, Pa.

# DATES OF CERTAIN WARS, CAMPAIGNS, EXPEDITIONS, EVENTS, ETC.

| | |
|---|---|
| 1775-1783 | War of the Revolution, April 19, 1775, to April 11, 1783. |
| 1782-1787 | Wyoming Valley disturbances, Pennsylvania. |
| 1786-1787 | Shay's rebellion. Massachusetts. |
| 1790-1795 | War with Northwest Indians, Miamis, Wyandots, Delawares, Pottawattamies, Shawnees, Chippewas, and Ottawas, September, 1790, to August, 1795. |
| 1791-1794 | Whiskey Insurrection in Pennsylvania. |
| 1798-1800 | War with France, July 9, 1798, to September 30, 1800. |
| 1799 | Fries' Insurrection in Pennsylvania, Spring of 1799. |
| 1801-1805 | War with Tripoli, June, 10, 1801, to June, 4, 1805. |
| 1806 | Burr Conspiracy. |
| 1806 | Sabine Expedition, Louisiana. |
| 1807 | Naval affair in Chesapeake Bay, July 9 to August 5, 1807. |
| 1808 | Embargo troubles, Lake Champlain, 1808. |
| 1811-1813 | War with Northwest Indians, November, 1811, to October, 1813. |
| 1812-1815 | War with Great Britain, June 18, 1812, to February 17, 1815. |
| 1812 | Florida or Seminole War, August 15 to Oct., 1812. |
| 1813 | Peoria Indian War, Illinois, September 19 to October 21, 1813. |
| 1813-1814 | Creek Indian War, Alabama. |
| 1817-1818 | Seminole or Florida War, November 20, 1817, to October 31, 1818. |
| 1819 | Yellowstone Expedition, July 4 to September, 1819. |
| 1823 | Campaign against Blackfeet and Arickaree Indians, Upper Missouri River. |
| 1827 | Winnebago Expedition, Wisconsin (no fighting), June to September, 1827, also called La Fevre Indian War. |
| 1831 | Sac and Fox Indian troubles in Illinois. |
| 1832 | Black Hawk War, April 26 to September 21, 1832. |
| 1832-1833 | Nullification troubles in South Carolina, November, 1832, to February, 1833. |
| 1833-1839 | Cherokee disturbances and removal. |
| 1834 | Pawnee Expedition, Indian Territory, June to September, 1834. |
| 1835-1836 | Toledo War, Ohio and Michigan boundary dispute. |
| 1835-1842 | Seminole or Florida War, November 1, 1835, to August 14, 1842. |
| 1836-1837 | Creek disturbances in Alabama, May 5, 1836, to September 30, 1837. |
| 1836-1837 | Southwestern Frontier, Louisiana, Arkansas, and Texas (Sabine disturbances), no fighting, April, 1836, to June, 1837. |
| 1837 | Osage Indian troubles in Missouri. |
| 1838 | Heatherly Indian disturbances on Missouri and Iowa line. |
| 1838 | Mormon disturbances in Missouri. |
| 1838-1839 | New York, Aroostook, and Canada (Patriot War), Frontier disturbances (no fighting). |
| 1846-1847 | Doniphan's Expedition from Santa Fe, New Mexico, to Chihuahua, Mexico, November, 1846, to February, 1847. |
| 1846-1848 | Mexican War, April 24, 1846, to May 30, 1848. |
| 1846-1848 | New Mexico Expedition, June 30, 1846, to February 13, 1848. |
| 1848 | Cayuse War, Oregon, Oregon Volunteers. |
| 1849-1861 | Navajo troubles, New Mexico. |
| 1849-1861 | Continuous disturbances with Comanche, Cheyenne, Lipan, and Kickapoo Indians in Texas. |
| 1850 | Pitt River Expedition, California, April 28 to September 13, 1850. |
| 1851-1852 | Yuma Expedition, California, December, 1851, to April, 1852. |
| 1851-1853 | Utah Indian disturbance. |
| 1851-1856 | Rogue River, Yakima, Klikitat, Klamath, and Salmon River Indian Wars in Oregon and Washington. |
| 1855 | Winnas Expedition against Snake Indians, Oregon, May, 1824, to September 8, 1855. |
| 1855-1856 | Sioux Expedition, Nebraska Territory, April 3, 1855, to July 27, 1856. |
| 1855 | Yakima Expedition, Washington Territory, October 11 to November 24, 1855. |
| 1855-1856 | Cheyenne and Arapahoe troubles. |
| 1855-1858 | Seminole or Florida War, December 20, 1855, to May 8, 1858. |
| 1856-1858 | Kansas Border troubles. |
| 1857 | Gila Expedition, New Mexico, April 16 to September 16, 1857. |
| 1857 | Sioux Indian troubles in Minnesota and Iowa, March and April, 1857. |
| 1857 | Mountain Meadow Massacre, Utah, September 11, 1857. |
| 1857-1858 | Utah Expedition. |
| 1858 | Expedition against Northern Indians, Washington Territory, July 17 to October 17, 1858. |

| | |
|---|---|
| 1858 | Puget Sound Expedition, Washington Territory, August 10 to September 23, 1858. |
| 1858 | Spokane, Cœur d'Alene and Paloos Indian troubles in Washington Territory. |
| 1858 | Navajo Expedition, New Mexico, September 9 to December 25, 1858. |
| 1858-1859 | Wichita Expedition, Indian Territory, September 11, 1858, to December, 1859. |
| 1859 | Colorado River Expedition, California, February 11 to April 28, 1859. |
| 1859 | Pecos Expedition, Texas, April 16 to August 17, 1859. |
| 1859 | Antelope Hills Expedition, Texas, June 10 to September 23, 1859. |
| 1859 | Bear River Expedition, Utah, June 12 to October 18, 1859. |
| 1859 | San Juan Imbroglio, Washington Territory. 1859. |
| 1859 | John Brown Raid, Virginia, November and December, 1859. |
| 1859-1860 | Cortina troubles on Texas and Mexican border. |
| 1860 | Pah-Ute Expedition, California, April 12 to July 9, 1860. |
| 1860 | Kiowa and Comanche Expedition, Indian Territory, May 8 to October 11, 1860. |
| 1860 | Carson Valley Expedition, Utah, May 14 to July 15, 1860. |
| 1860 | Attack on and murder of emigrants by Bannock Indians at Salmon Fork, Snake River, Idaho, September 13, 1860. |
| 1860-1861 | Navajo Expedition, New Mexico, September 12, 1860, to February 24, 1861. |
| 1861-1890 | Apache Indian War and troubles in Arizona and New Mexico. |
| 1861-1866 | War of the Rebellion, April 19, 1861, to August 20, 1866. Actual hostilities, however, commenced upon the firing on Fort Sumter, April 12, 1861, and ceased by the surrender of the Confederate forces under General Kirby Smith, May 26, 1865. |
| 1862 | Indian Massacres at New Ulm and vicinity, Minnesota, August 17 to 23, 1862. |
| 1862-1867 | Sioux Indian War in Minnesota and Dakota. |
| 1863-1869 | War against the Cheyenne, Arapaho, Kiowa, and Comanche Indians in Kansas, Nebraska, Colorado, and Indian Territory. |
| 1865-1868 | Indian War in Southern Oregon and Idaho, and Northern California and Nevada. |
| 1865-1866 | Fenian Raid, New York and Canada Border disturbances. |
| 1867-1881 | Campaign against Lipan, Kiowa, Kickapoo, and Comanche Indians and Mexican Border disturbances. |
| 1868-1869 | Canadian River Expedition, New Mexico, November 5, 1868, to February 13, 1869. |
| 1871 | Yellowstone Expedition, August 28 to October 25, 1871. |
| 1871 | Fenian troubles, Dakota and Manitoba Frontier, September and October, 1871. |
| 1872 | Yellowstone Expedition, Dakota, July 26 to October 15, 1872. |
| 1872-1873 | Modoc Campaign, November 28, 1872, to June 1, 1873. |
| 1873 | Yellowstone Expedition, Dakota, June 4 to October 4, 1873. |
| 1874-1875 | Campaign against Kiowa, Cheyenne, and Comanche Indians in Indian Territory, August 1, 1874, to February 16, 1875. |
| 1874 | Sioux Expedition, Wyoming and Nebraska, February 13 to August 19, 1874. |
| 1874 | Black Hills Expedition, Dakota, June 20 to August 30, 1874. |
| 1874 | Big Horn Expedition, Wyoming, August 13 to October 10, 1874. |
| 1875 | Expedition against Indians in Eastern Nevada, September 7 to 27, 1875. |
| 1876 | Sioux Expedition, Dakota, May 17 to September 26, 1876. |
| 1876 | Powder River Expedition, Wyoming, November 1 to December 31, 1876. |
| 1876-1877 | Big Horn and Yellowstone Expeditions, Wyoming and Montana, February 17, 1876, to June 13, 1877. |
| 1876-1879 | War with Northern Cheyenne and Sioux Indians in Indian Territory, Kansas, Wyoming, Dakota, Nebraska, and Montana. |
| 1877 | Labor strikes in Pennsylvania and Maryland, July to October, 1877. |
| 1877 | Nez Perce Campaign, June 14 to October 5, 1877. |
| 1878 | Bannock and Piute Campaign, May 30 to September 4, 1878. |
| 1878 | Ute Expedition, Colorado, April 3 to September 9, 1878. |
| 1879 | Snake or Sheepeater Indian troubles, Idaho, August to October, 1879. |
| 1879-1894 | Disturbances of settlers in Indian and Oklahoma Territories, "Oklahoma Boomers," and the Cherokee Strip disturbances. |
| 1879-1880 | Ute Indian Campaign in Colorado and Utah, September 21, 1879, to November 8, 1880. |
| 1885 | Chinese Miner and Labor troubles in Wyoming, September and October, 1885. |
| 1890-1891 | Sioux Indian disturbances in South Dakota, November, 1890, to January, 1891. |
| 1891-1893 | Garza troubles, Texas and Mexican Border disturbances, "Tin Horn War." |
| 1892 | Miner disturbances in Idaho, July to November, 1892. |
| 1892-1896 | Troubles with renegade Apache Indians, under Kidd and Massai, in Arizona and Mexican Border. |
| 1894 | "Industrial Army," "Commonwealers," "Coxeyites," and Labor disturbances. |
| 1894 | Railroad, Pullman, and Labor strikes extending from Illinois to Pacific coast, June to August, 1894. |
| 1895 | Bannock Indian troubles, July and August, 1895. |
| 1898-1899 | War with Spain, April 21, 1898, to April 11, 1899. Actual hostilities ceased August 13, 1898. |
| 1898 | Chippewa Indian disturbances at Leech Lake, Minn., October, 1898. |
| 1899 | Insurrection in Philippine Islands, February 4, 1899, to ——. |
| 1899 | Miner disturbances in Idaho, April 29 to October 20, 1899. |
| 1900 | War of Allied Powers with China. |

# INDEX OF NAMES

## CONTAINED ON PAGES 1 TO 150 INCLUSIVE,

Preceding the Alphabetical List.

A.

H.

Q.



R.

S.

## T.

## Y.



## Z.